Ounces	9x12 envelope, 9x12 SASE number of pages	9x12 SASE (for return trips) number of pages	First Class Postage	Third Class Postage	Postage from U.S. to Canada
under 2	. . .	1 to 2	$ .35*	$ .45	$ .40*
2	1 to 4	3 to 8	.45	.45	.52
3	5 to 10	9 to 12	.65	.65	.74
4	11 to 16	13 to 19	.85	.85	.96
5	17 to 21	20 to 25	1.05	1.00	1.18
6	22 to 27	26 to 30	1.25	1.00	1.40
7	28 to 32	31 to 35	1.45	1.10	1.62
8	33 to 38	36 to 41	1.65	1.10	1.84
9	39 to 44	42 to 46	1.85	1.20	2.06
10	45 to 49	47 to 52	2.05	1.20	2.28
11	50 to 55	53 to 57	2.25	1.30	2.50

*This cost includes an assessment for oversized mail that is light in weight.

1989 Writer's Market

Distributed in Canada by Prentice-Hall of
Canada Ltd., 1870 Birchmount Road,
Scarborough, Ontario M1P 2J7 and in
Australia by Ruth Walls Books Pty. Ltd.,
Private Bag. No. 19, P.O. Alexandria, New
South Wales 2015.

Managing Editor, Market Books Department:
Constance J. Achabal

Library of Congress Catalog Number
31-20772
International Standard Serial Number
0084-2729
International Standard Book Number
0-89879-330-0

Information in U.S. Postage by the Page
chart supplied by Carolyn Hardesty;
Canadian Postage by the Page by Barbara
Murrin

Cover illustration by A.I.R. Studio

1989
Writer's Market

Where & How
To Sell What You Write

Editor: Glenda Tennant Neff

Assistant Editor: Robin Gee

Cincinnati, Ohio

The Writing Profession

The Markets

Contents

Contents

Services & Opportunities

The Writing Profession

From the Editors

Welcome to the 60th edition of *Writer's Market*.

Over the years, many things have changed in the publishing industry, and *Writer's Market* has grown and changed along with it. One of our earliest editions in 1937 was 6x9 with 243 pages of market listings for writers. In the 1942 edition, good payment was 1½-2¢ per word, and short-short articles were 3,000 words long.

By 1956, average payment was about $175 for a full-length article, but *Better Homes and Gardens* was paying up to $1,500, a good rate even today.

In 1964, *Writer's Market* was up to 623 pages and average pay for a full-length article was up to $200-300. *Playboy* was leading the pack by offering $3,000 for a 4,000-word article. By 1976, our 47th edition, average pay was about $400-500, and length for a short article was down to 2,000 words.

With the 1989 edition, *Writer's Market* features more than 1,000 pages of markets. Good payment is now up to $1 a word, and short-shorts are down to 800-1,000 words.

You can see how freelance writing has changed in many ways over the years, but some things have held true for all of our 60 editions. Success in writing requires "knowledge of techniques" and a "brain full of ideas," Editor Kirk Polking wrote in the 1964 edition. "Last, you should know where to submit your material," she continued. "That is the purpose of this new edition of *Writer's Market*, a book which we hope will be as integral a part of your career as your other tools . . ."

With the 1989 edition, we echo that hope.

The newest edition

In preparing the 1989 edition, we contacted writers, editors and publishers about changes in the industry and obtained information on submission policies and manuscript needs from more than 4,000 markets.

In addition, the 1989 *Writer's Market* features:

• Upfront articles on marketing your manuscripts more effectively and making your work more salable.

• Close-up interviews with 15 writers, editors and agents who share their experience, advice and insights on the writing profession.

• More than 600 new markets and hundreds of changes in existing markets, including 275 editor changes, 160 address changes, and 30 publication name changes since our 1988 edition. We've also added a section of listings that came in after the original sections were compiled.

• Updated sample queries for a magazine article and a book manuscript in the revised Business of Writing section.

• Section-by-section lists to give you additional information about markets with changing or no freelance needs.

Your use of Writer's Market

Whether you're working on your first byline or your 101st, *Writer's Market* can make the process of selling your work easier. Experienced writers use it for the most complete information on current freelance opportunities. Students and part-time writers use it to find markets that buy their type of writing, and beginners trying to break in find it indispensable for details on approaching editors and submitting manuscripts.

You'll find markets for book publishers and book packagers, consumer and trade publications, as well as scriptwriting, gag writing, greeting cards and syndicates. The section introductions contain helpful information on trends, industry practices, related sections and methods for submitting your material. In addition, the Services and Opportunities section contains information about author's agents and contests.

We hope you understand that between the time this edition goes to press and the time you read it, some details in the market listings may change. We make additions, corrections and changes in the listings until the book is sent to the printer, but often publishers go out of business; editors find other jobs; and publications change their needs, payment or submission policies. Listings for new markets and changes in others can be found throughout the year in *Writer's Digest*, the monthly magazine for freelance writers.

As editors, we appreciate readers who send us information they discover about new market opportunities. And we want to know if you have complaints about nonpayment or lack of response from any market we've listed. In addition, we're always interested in hearing how you use *Writer's Market* and how we can make it a more useful tool for you as a writer. Always enclose a self-addressed, stamped envelope if you expect a reply.

Best wishes for success,

Glenda Tennant Neff

Robin L. Gee

Using Writer's Market

If you've studied the Table of Contents, you've already found several sections that interest you. Before you plunge into the listings that follow, take time to read this section. It will help you make full use of the individual market listings and will explain the symbols and abbreviations used throughout the book.

Specific symbols and abbreviations are explained in the table on page 5. The most important abbreviation is SASE—self-addressed, stamped envelope. *Always* enclose one when you send unsolicited queries or manuscripts to editors, publishers or agents. This requirement is not included in the individual market listings because it's a "given" that you must follow if you expect to receive a reply.

Review the following sample listing and the explanation section that accompanies it.

contact names (3)

size of market (4)

emphasis and
readership (6)

rights purchased (7)

submission
requirements (8)

reporting time (9)

types of nonfiction
needed (12)

word length (15)

payment rates (16)

photo requirements,
rates and policies (18)

column/department
needs,
rates and policies (19)

inside information
from the editor (20)

(1) ‡TELECOMMUNICATIONS EQUIPMENT RETAILER, The Professional Journal for the High-Tech Merchandiser, Box C-5400, Scottsdale AZ 85261. **(2)** (602)483-0014. **(3)** Managing Editor: Christopher Geoffrey McPherson. **(4)** 20% freelance written. **(5) (6)** Monthly trade journal on retailing of telecommunications equipment. "Although ours is a specialized field, we want information on telecommunications to be informative, fun—but most of all accessible to our readers." Estab. 1988. Circ. 40,000. **(7)** Pays 30 days after publication. Byline given. Buys all rights. **(8)** Submit seasonal/holiday material 3 months in advance. Simultaneous submissions OK. Query for electronic submissions. Computer printout submissions OK. **(9)** Reports in 2 weeks. **(10)** Free sample copy and writer's guidelines.
(11)Nonfiction: (12) Book excerpts, general interest, interview/profile, new product, technical. "No first person, cutesy or nontechnical material." **(13)** Buys 15-20 mss/year. **(14)** Query with published clips. **(15)** Length: 1,500-4,000 words. **(16)** Pays $50-200 for assigned articles; $50-150 for unsolicited articles. **(17)** Sometimes pays expenses of writers on assignment.
Photos: (18) State availability of photos with submission. Reviews contact sheets, transparencies and b&w and color prints. Offers no additional payment for photos accepted with ms. Model releases and identification of subjects required. Buys one-time rights.
Columns/Departments: (19) Down the Line (in-the-future telecommunciations trends), 1,000-1,200 words; Dossier (company or personality profile), 2,000-2,500 words; Making the Sale (sales techniques, tips, do's and dont's), 2,000-2,500 words. Buys 10-15 mss/year. Query. Length: 1,000-2,500 words. Pays $25-100.
Tips: (20) "The telecommunications industry is not—perhaps—the most glamorous world, but *TER* aims to make it interesting and informative. We want interesting articles on product trends, telecommunications companies and how-to stories on the business of retailing telecommunications products. Be precise, clear and concise in your query. Be a good writer and we will use you again and again. You don't have to be a published writer to work for us: just good."

(1) One or more symbols (*, ‡,□) may precede the name and address of the publication or market; check the key on page 5 for their meanings. (This double dagger signifies a new listing.)

(2) A phone number in a listing does not mean the market accepts phone queries. Make a phone query only when your story's timeliness would be lost by following the usual procedures. As a rule, don't call unless you have been invited to do so.

(3) In most listings, names of contact persons are given in the first paragraph or under the bold subheadings. Address your query or submission to a specific name when possible. If the name is not easily recognizable by gender, use the full name (e.g., Dear Dale Smith:). If no contact name is given, consult a sample copy. As a last resort, you can address your query to "Articles editor" or what is appropriate. For more information, read Approaching Markets in the Business of Writing.

(4) A market's general openness to writers is indicated by the percentage of freelance material used or by the percentage of published manuscripts from new, unagented writers.

(5) Since most publications are copyrighted, the information is only given in this spot when the publication is not copyrighted. For information on copyrighting your own work, see Rights and the Writer in the Business of Writing.

(6) A description of the market provides the focus and audience. Established dates are listed only if 1987 or later. The date a market was established can help you evaluate its stability. New markets may be open to freelancers, but they can also be riskier. Circulation figures listed are the total of subscriptions plus off-the-shelf sales.

(7) General business policies give information about rights purchased and time of payment. For more information on types of rights for sale, see Rights and the Writer in the Business of Writing.

(8) Submission requirements include how far in advance to submit seasonal material and whether or not previously published and photocopied material will be considered. Send manuscripts or queries to one market at a time unless it indicates simultaneous submissions are OK. If you send your manuscript to more than one market at a time, always mention in your cover letter that it is a simultaneous submission. Computer printouts and electronic submissions are mentioned only if the market accepts them. See Tools of the Trade in the Business of Writing for more information.

(9) Reporting times indicate how soon a market will respond to your query or manuscript, but times listed are approximate. Quarterly publications, book publishers, literary magazines and all new listings may be slower to respond. Wait four weeks beyond the stated reporting time before you send a polite inquiry.

(10) If you're interested in writing for a particular market, request the writer's guidelines and/ or a sample copy if the market indicates availability. "Writer's guidelines for SASE" means that a business-size envelope (#10) with one First Class stamp will be adequate. You should request a sample copy if you are unable to find the publication at a newsstand or library. A sample copy or book catalog is often available for a 9x12 self-addressed envelope with a specified number of stamps or International Reply Coupons. Most publishers will send, at no extra charge, writer's guidelines with sample copies if you request them.

(11) Subheads in bold (Nonfiction, Photos, etc.) guide you to requirements for those types of materials.

(12) The specific material desired (and often material *not* desired) is listed. Follow the guidelines. Do not send fiction to a publication that only uses nonfiction; do not send a children's book manuscript to a publisher of men's adventure novels.

(13) The number of manuscripts purchased per issue or per year will give you an idea of how easy or difficult it may be to sell your work to a particular market. With new listings, these figures may change dramatically depending on the submissions they receive or changes in policy.

(14) If the market wants to see queries, that's what you should send. The same goes for outlines and sample chapters, etc. Don't send a complete manuscript unless the listing indicates it's acceptable.

(15) Editors know the length of most material they buy; follow their range of words or pages. If your manuscript is longer or shorter (by a wide margin) than the stated requirements, find another market.

(16) Payment ranges tell you what the market usually paid at the time *Writer's Market* was published.

(17) Whether a market sometimes or usually pays expenses of writers on assignment is listed. No mention is made when a market does *not* pay expenses.

(18-19) Needs, rates and policies for specified material.

(20) Helpful suggestions are listed under the subhead Tips in many listings. They describe the best way to submit manuscripts or give special insight into needs and preferences of the market.

Key to Symbols and Abbreviations

‡ New listing in all sections
* Subsidy publisher in Book Publishers section
□ Cable TV market in Scriptwriting section
ms-manuscript; **mss**-manuscripts
b&w-black and white (photo)
SASE-self-addressed, stamped envelope
SAE-self-addressed envelope
IRC-International Reply Coupon, for use on reply mail in Canada and foreign markets.

Important Listing Information

● Listings are based on editorial questionnaires and interviews. They are *not* advertisements; publishers do not pay for their listings. The markets are *not* endorsed by *Writer's Market* editors.
● All listings have been verified before publication of this book. If a listing has not changed from last year, then the editor told us the market's needs have not changed and the previous listing continues to accurately reflect its policies. We require documentation in our files for each listing and never run a listing without its editorial office's approval.
● *Writer's Market* reserves the right to exclude any listing.
● When looking for a specific market, check the index. A market may not be listed for one of these reasons.
1. It doesn't solicit freelance material.
2. It doesn't pay for material.
3. It has gone out of business.
4. It has failed to verify or update its listing for the 1989 edition.
5. It was in the middle of being sold at press time, and rather than disclose premature details, we chose not to list it.
6. It hasn't answered *Writer's Market* inquiries satisfactorily. (To the best of our ability, and with our readers' help, we try to screen out fraudulent listings.)
7. It buys few manuscripts, thereby constituting a very small market for freelancers.
● See the index of additional markets at the end of each major section for specific information on individual markets not listed.

Making Your Manuscripts More Salable

by Glenda Tennant Neff

Editors, agents and professional readers list a variety of reasons for rejecting manuscripts. The most common are colorless writing or poorly handled research, and many manuscripts may be good but just not quite publishable or marketable. Most of the time writers receive only flat "it doesn't meet our needs at this time" rejection slips with their returned manuscripts, giving no reasons for the rejections.

When writers receive rejection slips, some immediately send the work out to another publisher, magazine or agent. Others agonize over possible revisions they can make; some quit submitting the manuscript at that point and forget about trying for publication. For a few writers, creative self-expression of their ideas may be enough, but most want to see their work in print. "Art and commerce do sometimes go hand in hand," says author Raymond Carver[1]. "When I first got something accepted, it gave my life a validation that it didn't otherwise have. It was very important to me."

While you're "creating art," editors, copy editors and writers say you also can improve your manuscript in ways that help sell it. We've collected some of the most basic ways here, along with tips on revising your work. Before you send a unsolicited manuscript or assigned article, be sure it meets the following criteria.

The structure test

Whether you're working on fiction or nonfiction, be sure you've chosen the best form for your writing. If your assignment is a 2,000-word magazine article, but you have enough information to write a book, you'll have to condense or better yet, narrow the material to one aspect that is suitable for an article. Likewise, don't try to stretch a small amount of information over a longer format. "If you find yourself trying to keep a gossamer thread of plot, stretched over too many pages, from snapping in your face, then reconsider your story," freelance copy editor and proofreader Ann Finlayson advises fiction writers. "Maybe it needs a subplot or two. Maybe it needs cutting to 5,000 words." Whatever your choice of forms, be sure that it's the best one for the content.

As the second part of the structure test, be sure that the theme is carried throughout your work. Does *everything* in the story or article contribute to that unity? Approach the manuscript from a reader's point of view, eliminating any digressions and material that, however interesting, do not directly contribute to your nonfiction or advance the plot of your fiction. In *Beyond Style: Mastering the Finer Points of Writing* (Writer's Digest Books), author Gary Provost advises writers to place this sign over their desks: "A STORY IS NOT EVERYTHING THAT HAPPENED. IT'S EVERY IMPORTANT THING THAT HAPPENED. AN ARTICLE IS NOT EVERYTHING THAT'S TRUE. IT'S EVERY IMPORTANT THING THAT'S TRUE."

Good writers also learn to eliminate slow starts. Sometimes it's in a nonfiction article, and the writer backs in to what should be the lead paragraph with unnecessary introductory sentences. Other times a fiction writer will include several pages of background material on the characters and the setting before beginning with the story. "Typical is the prologue to a thriller that starts with Character X en route to a meeting or a mysterious assignment," says Ann Finlayson. "With the reader seeing things through X's eyes, the author introduces X's background, his lifestyle, his ambitions, his outlook on life, his family, his friends, and just as the reader has begun to be mildly interested in X, he is murdered. End of X. The reader has wasted all that effort and is in no mood to start chapter one, with all the weary labor of getting acquainted to do over again."

The message in publishing is plain: Make things happen from the beginning of your manuscript. No one will wade through several pages to see if it gets better or more interesting; you must make it that way from page one. If you are disappointed that some of your prose will be discarded, remember the comment of an expensive hairdresser when his client complained about the small amount of hair he trimmed for the price: "It's not the amount I take away that matters. It's what is left when I'm done."

The readability test

Editors, agents and freelance manuscript readers see hundreds, perhaps thousands, of manuscripts each year. Some are assigned, but many are unsolicited, also known as over-the-transom or slush pile submissions. Again and again editors emphasize that only "original" material will attract their interest. As a writer, you may think it's nearly impossible to develop an article idea that hasn't been covered in some way or write a short story with characters who have problems not dealt with before.

Before you give up, thinking that an "original" manuscript is beyond your reach, approach it from a different view. Don't insist on making the manuscript original in every aspect, but concentrate on making it unique. Work on a new slant for your article, add fresh information, and come up with a great lead paragraph to introduce it. In fiction, make your characters and the situation believable and interesting. Writer Adele Glimm says: "I try to invent a situation which reflects the reader's problems and concerns but is much more intriguing than the reader's life is likely to be. What will surprise readers, entrance them, make them curious, make them react strongly? I search for the meeting point between myself and the reader."

An editor or an agent, like any reader, won't bother to finish a manuscript that is wordy ("in spite of the fact that" written instead of "since") or redundant (current trend, exact opposites, major breakthrough). Go through your manuscript carefully to replace generalizations with specific images; you want to avoid simply *telling* your audience what you can *show* them. Also, be sure to take out cliches. The weather may be hot as blazes in your story, but you can find some other way to write it.

In fiction, writer James N. Frey advises you to put your characters' actions through the *Would He Really* test[2]. Readers must be able to believe, or at least have some previous indication, that the character would do what you're having him do. "If you don't make your people real, you stand small chance of ever being published," Ann Finlayson says. That involves removing cliched characters or giving them more dimensions. In rejected stories, she says often "people are either immensely rich or desperately poor, in which case they are cold and haughty or earnest and hard-working, respectively. Grandparents are invariably dear decrepit old ladies and gentlemen, retired and probably speaking in a hillbilly dialect. Villains are always perfectly mindless."

Finlayson counsels writers to be careful observers and chroniclers of people. "In slush stories, characters never seem to have facial expressions, and yet in real life you take much more careful note of a familiar person's expression than at his features or build," she says. Too many writers "don't seem to pay much attention to what human beings really do: what their natural reactions should be to such-and-such an event, how they are likely to behave under certain circumstances, how they live, what they are apt to think of certain other kinds of people, the jobs available to them, and so on."

The style test

Every writer has others whose work he admires. If imitation is the most sincere form of flattery, then it's not unusual for us to imitate other writers in the same way Little Leaguers regularly practice mannerisms of the big leaguers they admire. As baseball players grow in experience, however, they learn to do what works best for them instead of what worked best for their idols. It's the same in writing. There's nothing wrong with admiring and learning from other writers, but you should work to remove any obvious imitations from your manuscript and let your own voice develop. After imitating others for years, author Ray Bradbury says, "I finally figured out that if you are going to step on a live mine, make it your own. Be blown up, as it were, by your own delights and despairs.³"

In evaluating the style of your manuscript, it's also important to consider the focus and the tone of the work. If it's fiction, do the qualities you started with carry throughout the manuscript? A story with a cynical tone throughout but an unexpectedly idealistic ending will leave readers perplexed. That's not to say that your characters can't change, and with that change cause a change in tone, but you must give the reader some reason for it.

If it's nonfiction, do the focus and tone of the article match the audience you're targeting? Editors are often very specific about the tone of articles they publish—whether it's serious or chatty—and they demand that manuscripts are focused on the subject they assigned and written to address concerns and interests of their readers. One topic can be approached many different ways. For instance, a feminist magazine and a religious magazine may both have articles about abortion, but the focus and tone will be entirely different. Don't underestimate this in affecting acceptance or rejection of your manuscript. "If the article is properly focused, I have a hard time turning it away even if there are other flaws," says *Rider* magazine Editor Tash Matsuoka.

The research test

Whether you're working on fiction or nonfiction, your research must also be credible to anyone considering your work. Insufficient or incorrect data in nonfiction, as well as inappropriate clothing or dialogue in fiction, will be spotted, and editors almost always take it as a sign of sloppy work habits. It's not necessary to know everything you need for a nonfiction article before you accept an assignment, but you must be willing to do the necessary research before you start writing. Freelance writer Debra Kent says in a Bloomington (Ind.) *Sunday Times-Herald* interview: "With every assignment, I get a new education." You'll find that producing a good manuscript often requires that kind of thorough research. If you have questions or are unsure about some aspect of your story or article, the reader probably will be too, so don't be afraid to ask questions.

A tougher thing to spot in your manuscript is overuse of research. It's possible to give readers so many facts, figures and details that your work becomes textbook-like. Some writers are so eager to use all the information they've gathered "that they submit a bibliography on the first page and then rub the reader's nose in it on every page they write," Ann Finlayson says. She cautions writers to "do so much research that you take it for granted: You don't go out of your way to include something, but you don't avoid mentioning it either." Keep in mind Gary Provost's advice too, and make your article, story or book every *important thing*, not *everything* your research included.

The revisions test

Some writers claim never to revise manuscripts; they pull the final page out of the typewriter or off the computer printer and send the manuscript immediately. While this may work for some, it's rare that a manuscript cannot be improved by revision. Many writers even like to let a manuscript sit for a day or two before they begin to revise; the time away allows them to approach it more like an editor reading it for the first time. Poet Pat Parker says, "I see it simply as a task that must be done, like tuning up a car. With servicing, it runs better." Although revising may not be as satisfying as the initial writing, rewritten portions can make the difference between an adequate manuscript and a good manuscript, a sale or a rejection. "The first draft is a surge of emotion," says writer Suzanne Hartman. "Revising is approaching creation with respect and, one hopes, grace."

After you've submitted the manuscript, you may still have to make revisions to suit a publication's or editor's style. There's nothing wrong with discussing changes or giving an editor reasons you think a passage shouldn't be altered. You shouldn't completely reject proposed revisions, however. As a freelance writer, you must be prepared to cope with styles that differ from publication to publication and editor to editor. You may be your own boss in some ways, but when it comes to writing and revising you have "as many bosses as there are projects," according to freelancer Mary Alice Kellogg[4].

As a final note, be sure you are pleased with your work. A manuscript can meet dozens of criteria, but if it doesn't please you, then you won't want to send it out with your name on it. "As I grow more experienced and learn whose judgment to trust, I believe my instincts more and more," says Suzanne Hartman. "If my work in progress moves me, I trust it."

[1] Excerpted from "Raymond Carver, After the Fire, Into the Fire," by Michael Schumacher, in *Writer's Yearbook '88*.
[2] Excerpted from "How to Create Damn Good Characters," by James N. Frey in *Writer's Yearbook '88*.
[3] Excerpted from "Run Fast, Stand Still," by Ray Bradbury in *Writer's Yearbook '88*.
[4] Excerpted from "It's an okay life, being a hired gun," by Mary Alice Kellogg in *Quill*, February 1988.

How to Sell and Re-sell Your Writing

by Duane Newcomb

There are two kinds of article writers. The first one comes up with an idea, puts together an article from that idea and sends the article to a number of magazines. For every article he sells this way, he receives ten or more rejections.

The second type of writer begins by studying one magazine at a time to discover who its readers are, what subjects it publishes and how it puts its articles together. Then he asks, "What can I give this magazine that will meet its editorial needs?" As the second writer begins to understand each magazine, he is often able to sell as much as 90% of what he writes.

This is possible because most magazines try to reach a readership that falls within a certain age group, makes a certain amount of income and has a particular lifestyle. This allows them to provide advertisers with a very specific demographic target. To keep and increase this audience, an individual magazine prints articles that fit that particular magazine's editorial policy and appeal to that publication's target audience.

Demographics of an audience

Popular Science says it is the "What's New magazine" attracting an audience that is fairly young, trendy, and on the edge, with an interest in the latest and the newest.

Popular Mechanics, although in the same field, says their audience is the "New Achiever," an upscale, action-oriented male.

Every article that goes into each of these magazines must fit that magazine's format and help enhance the reader's perceived lifestyle. For *Popular Science* this means articles about the newest developments. For *Popular Mechanics* it means concentrating on articles of interest to action-oriented upscale men.

Since magazines look at the world differently, each approaches articles in similar categories from a different point of view. If you intend to sell to magazines like these, you must become aware of these differences then tailor the article specifically to the magazine you want to write for.

Remembering that *Popular Science* is the "what's new" magazine, let's look at a few articles from the recreational category.
● "Flip Flash, Auto Focus from Kodak"
● "Sneakers that Think: Computerized Sneakers that Give You Data on How Far, How Long You've Walked and More"
● "Wind Tunnel-Tuned Tennis Racket"

What's the common denominator here? All are brand new and different recreational products.

To sell to this market, you would look for unusual and different new products. Possibilities might be "a solar cell equipped tent" or a "backpack with a built-in walkie-talkie," or something similar.

Duane Newcomb *is the founder of Sierra Writing Camp, a summer camp for writers in California's Sierra Nevada Mountains. He has sold more than 5,000 articles and 23 books, three of which have been Book Of the Month Club books. His articles have appeared in* Family Circle, Field and Stream, Better Homes and Gardens *and many other magazines.*

In the *Popular Mechanics'* recreational category you find the following titles:
- "Barrels of Money: You'll Find Beauty, Quality, and Tradition in These Shotguns"
- "Commemorative Firearms: They Can Bring a Sizable Return on Your Investment"
- "The Toys of Summer: PM Gathered Eleven Motorized Beach Toys for a Wet 'n' Wild Showdown at Disney World."

All of these are articles of interest to an upscale male. Notice they are overviews of expensive items. In many articles there is a focus on collecting or investing.

Now, using this common denominator, project some possible article ideas for *Popular Mechanics*. How about upscale tents? Roughing it in style? Items that let you hit the trail with class? Or upscale safaris for the man who's done everything?

As you can see, though *Popular Science* and *Popular Mechanics* are similar, their approach is as different as night and day.

Fitting your ideas to the market

For every article idea there are dozens or maybe even hundreds of potential markets. The problem is that most of us as writers don't know how to find these markets and when we do, we don't understand how to slant the idea to the individual magazine.

Over the years in Sierra Writing Camp classes, we have developed a very simple but effective procedure using *Writer's Market* that will help you find a number of markets for every idea. Here's how it works.

Step 1: Start with the idea. If I begin with the subject of the gold country and gold panning, I ask myself who would be interested? The answer: general readers, recreational vehicle owners, outdoorsmen, adventurers, women who like the outdoors, campers, teenagers, children and retirees.

Step 2: Go through the table of contents of *Writer's Market*. Keeping your audiences from Step 1 in mind, ask yourself which magazine categories might be interested in your article idea? Here is a list from *Writer's Market* I felt might work with my gold country idea.

Associations	Men's
Automotive	Regional
General Interest	Retirement
Health and Fitness	Science
Hobby and Craft	Sports
In-Flight	Travel
Juvenile	Women's

Don't cross off any group automatically because within a particular category or group of magazines you will find a lot of individual variation.

The standard automotive magazines, *Autoweek* and *Car and Driver*, are technically automotive-oriented and wouldn't be interested in the gold country piece. But *Four Wheeler* sometimes takes articles about off-the-road activities, and that's what gold panning can be. *Friends Magazine*, published for Chevrolet owners, sometimes buys travel and travel-related pieces. The gold country would be an interesting destination for a Chevrolet family, and gold panning could well be a family-oriented activity.

Step 3: List all possibilities. Include the category even if there is an outside chance that one magazine within that category might be interested in your article idea. At first glance, the women's group doesn't seem to offer any possibility. But they take so many things that this group is worth exploring.

Step 4: Read the description of the individual magazines under each section. Ask yourself which ones might be interested in your idea and make a list of them.

Step 5: Send for the magazines you are unfamiliar with. In the Sierra Writing Camp classes we simply mail a post card which states "please send me a sample copy of your magazine plus a guide to writers if available." If the magazine asks in *Writer's Market* that you include postage or an envelope, do that.

Besides this, keep looking for new markets or markets you might have missed. To find these, I regularly go through the market announcements in *Writer's Digest* to see if I can turn up new publications. I also thumb through the magazines on the newsstands to look for possibilities. I even go through the magazines at the dentist's office. Be diligent and keep searching; you'll be surprised how many additional good new markets you will discover.

Step 6: Slant the general idea to fit each individual magazine. I always start with the subject and tailor that subject to each magazine on the list. If I begin with "overpopulation," for instance, I might turn that subject to "130,000 Babies a Day, Is the New Pill the Answer?" for *Health Magazine*, and to "Too Many Hunters and Fishermen in the Wilderness?" for *Field and Stream*. After that, write your query. In practice, I query about nine magazines, then write the articles for every go-ahead I receive. After that I query nine more. Otherwise, I wind up with too many articles to write at any one time.

Let the magazine suggest ideas

Instead of starting with the idea, you can also start with a magazine and let the magazine itself suggest the ideas.

If a magazine has an article on how to save money shopping warehouse stores you wouldn't want to duplicate this idea. But the magazine might well be interested in other ways readers can save money shopping (this is the common denominator). If you know something about this you might suggest to the same magazine an article titled "How to Save Money through Discount Catalogs." It's a completely different idea, but it has many of the same elements. Here's how it's done:

1. Look for the common denominator in every article idea.
2. Try to come up with specific article ideas within that common denominator that the same magazine might like.
3. Query the magazine you have surveyed about the best of the ideas you've generated.

Reworking the same idea

Can you ever take a magazine's idea, rework the same concept and re-sell it? Yes, but not to that magazine. If you think warehouse shopping is a good idea, you might use the original article as a research source, do more research on your own, then offer a warehouse shopping article to another magazine. If I found this idea in a women's magazine, for instance, I might try a short piece on the subject for a hunting and fishing magazine, concentrating on how to shop for firearms or fishing tackle. Or I might sell the same general concept to an automotive magazine. Ideas cannot be copyrighted, so just use the facts and add your own point of view.

Don't stop when you sell that first article. Using *Writer's Market*, now spin your subject off into specific ideas for as many other magazines as possilble.

The article game

I like to make a game out of both looking for articles and searching for out-of-the-way markets.

In some cases, I surprise myself. A few years ago, I took a brief Sunday trip down Highway 49 in California's Mother Lode Country. This is the area where gold was discovered in California. Today, the Mother Lode still boasts old gold rush buildings, rusting mining equipment, an occasional stagecoach, and other relics of a bygone area.

To research this, I drove about a hundred miles between Sonora and Auburn, California. I stopped at all the old hotels, museums, historic buildings, and other points of interest. I talked to everyone who had something to say about the gold rush days. I also paid special attention to people gold panning and mining the streams. I probably took several hundred pictures that day.

Once home I sorted everything out, wrote my queries, and put the articles together as I received the go-aheads. Here are the results.

- A picture story titled "Churches Mean Christmas in California's Mother Lode" to the Sunday *San Francisco Chronicle*.
- An article "Camping California's Mother Lode" to *Camping Guide*.
- An article "Trailering California's Mother Lode" to *Trail R News*.
- An article "Panning for Gold" (something to do while trailering the Mother Lode) to *Trailer Life*.
- An article "Gold Strike Trailer Park," (an unusual trailer park) to *Trailer Topics*.
- "Skin Diving for Gold" to *Ford Truck Times*.
- "Skin Diving for Gold" to *Skin Diver Magazine*.
- A reprint of the *Ford Truck Times* story in *My Weekly Reader*.
- A general travel article, "California's Mother Lode" to the *Kansas City Star* and several other newspapers.

Selling the same article many times

Besides slanting the general idea to a number of magazines, you can often sell the same article a number of times to many publications. The reason is that these magazines serve specific groups of readers. They have no objection if you sell the same article to a publication that their readers will never see. These are called non-competing publications because they don't compete with each other for readers. Here are two groups to try:

General magazines

Sometimes when you sell an article to one general magazine you can turn around and sell the same article (second serial or reprint rights) to magazines that are noncompetitive with the original publication. An article sold to *Family Circle*, for instance, might well go to *Country Woman* or *Pioneer Women* or both. Generally major articles must be reslanted to each publication but some articles such as a short piece on "How Creative Are You?", "Are You Compatible with Your Mate?" and similar general features can be submitted to several different publications at once without change.

I suggest you go through *Writer's Market* as we did before and see how many additional possibilities you can find for articles you have already sold. Make up a number of copies at a quick-print shop and send out a copy with query to any possible market. This is the same article, not a reslant. What you want to sell here is "second serial rights." I simply mark this "second rights" after my name and address and copyright in the left hand corner.

Trade journals

Trade journals are also good multiple-market possibilities. These are magazines published for readers in a wide variety of industries. In general you'll find trade journals for manufacturers, wholesalers and retailers. A number are also published for individual professions such as medicine, law and education.

Writer's Market lists detailed submission information for more than 500 trade journals that accept freelance manuscripts. In addition, approximately 4,500 trade journals are listed in the *Standard Rate and Data* business edition, available at most libraries. The listings contain the name of the magazine; the address and phone number; and the names of the editor, publisher, advertising sales manager and others. Usually the listing also includes a statement of policy—who the magazine is published for, the editorial content, news, product information, merchandising and so forth.

About four years ago I decided there might be a good opportunity to write in-depth merchandising pieces that dealt with contemporary problems facing retailers and could be sold over and over. I then made up a list of 200 retail-oriented magazines that take either merchandising or advertising articles. These include such publications as *Yarn Market News*, *Jobber Topics*, *National Jeweler*, and *Fishing Tackle Trade News*. I am able to sell the same article to trade journals a number of times because the readers of jewelry magazines usually don't read toy magazines and these readers generally don't read retail photography magazines. The result? Hundreds of sales to numerous publications. What I have done, of course, you can do too. Send for a number of these magazines. Pick your own specialty, write your article, make up a list of possible markets, and give it a try.

How to cultivate an editor

Editors like to deal with freelancers who understand a magazine's needs. After you have sold a few articles to a magazine and have begun to build a relationship with one particular editor, ask that editor to put you on the mailing list (many magazines will do this to make sure their regular contributors keep up with what they are publishing). As each new issue comes in, go over every article carefully and ask yourself: Why was this piece included? How does it help this magazine's readers? If I were the editor, what other subjects would I cover in the next issue? The next six issues?

After awhile, you'll start to get a sixth sense about the magazine.

To establish yourself as a regular contributor:

Suggest similar articles. Next suggest articles that show you can provide the type of material this publication wants. A good way to do this is to pick out a series of articles the magazine is running and offer two or three more pieces that will either fit the series or complement it.

A woman's magazine might stress jobs and work. That would lead me to suggest that women in the workplace are just as interested in part-time or temporary work as they are in full-time employment, or that their readers might like one or several articles on home businesses.

Act on what editors say they are doing. Sometimes in the editorial, an editor will announce a new series or additional article coverage. This usually means the magazine is looking for more articles in this vein. If you write this kind of article, by all means, query immediately.

Act on readers' concerns. In one magazine, several readers griped about how snowmobiles are causing significant environmental damage. Maybe the editor would be willing to explore this subject from the standpoint of an environmentalist's concern.

Another letter talks about an article on the phone company, saying we should let AT&T take over the post office. This might trigger an article on private mail services—how efficient they are and how well they do. Sometimes these letters represent good possibilities.

Continually offer new twists. Articles in writers' magazines sometimes quote editors as saying, "Give me something different." This doesn't mean that the magazine wants something outside of the categories they are now publishing. It means give me a twist or a new way of looking at the subjects we are already covering.

Creating an article data bank

As you write, you will accumulate research material, interviews, published articles and much other material. Save this information. Some writers store it in boxes, others create an elaborate file system so they can find it all in a matter of minutes. You will be able to put together much of this material in other ways to make many additional sales. To begin, look over the information in your files and ask yourself these questions:

1. Can I sell one of my articles to a related field? For instance you wrote a travel piece for a trailer magazine. Can you change this a bit and sell it to a camping magazine?

2. Can I turn some of my interviews into an additional article? Say you interviewed a business man who gave you some details on a boat he was building in his garage for a round-the-world trip. Can you now add to this interview, take pictures and sell this piece as well?

3. Can I combine a number of my old articles into a roundup? A roundup article is simply a collection of material on a single subject such as: "Ten Regional Vacations You Can Take" or "Six Christmas Projects You Can Make."

4. Can I update and sell an old article I wrote several years ago? For instance you wrote an ar-

ticle on Disneyland. Since that time they have added some new attractions. In many cases you can simply add these attractions and re-sell the piece, sometimes to the same market that bought it before.

Almost any writer can increase his sales many times. This requires targeting your markets, slanting a general idea to a number of individual magazines, re-selling the same article a number of times, cultivating editors, and using all the material in your files to create as many additional articles as possible.

Editor's Note: Duane Newcomb adapted this article from his book *How to Sell & Re-Sell Your Writing* (Writer's Digest Books). He has used *Writer's Market* for 33 years. Writers are encouraged to let us know additional methods they find successful in using *Writer's Market*.

The Business of Writing

Writers freelance for many different reasons. Some do it for the enjoyment of writing and seeing their work published, occasionally even without compensation; many writers have other jobs but write part-time to make extra cash; and fulltime freelancers write for a living. Despite these varied goals, all freelancers, as independent business persons, must also invest time in managing the business side of their writing.

Developing a marketing plan

Some writers decide to write about what interests them, and then they begin to look for a publisher. While this approach is common, it reduces your chances of success. Instead, try choosing writing categories that interest you, and study the appropriate sections of *Writer's Market*. Select several listings that are good prospects for the kind of writing you want to do.

Next, develop several ideas, and make a list of the potential markets for each idea. Make the initial contact with markets using the method stated in the market listing.

If you exhaust your list of possibilities, don't give up. Re-evaluate the idea, revise it, or try another angle. Continue developing ideas and approaching markets. Identify and rank potential markets for an idea and continue the process, but don't approach a market again until you've received a response to your first submission.

Prepare for rejection. When a submission is returned, check the file folder of potential markets for that idea. Cross off the current market and immediately mail an appropriate submission to the next market on your list. If the editor has given you suggestions or reasons the manuscript was not accepted, you might want to incorporate these when revising your manuscript. In any event, remember the first editor didn't reject *you*, but simply chose not to buy your product. A rejection only means that your particular piece did not fit the needs of the publisher at that time.

Your job is to find the right publisher for your writing. Begin submitting the work to other markets and develop other ideas. For more detailed information on developing a selling plan, see Duane Newcomb's article "How to Sell and Re-Sell Your Writing."

Writing tools

Like anyone involved in a trade or business, you need certain tools and supplies to produce your product or provide your service. The basic necessities for your writing business, plus some extras you may eventually want to have, include:

Typewriter. A well-maintained manual typewriter is adequate for some writers. Those who write fulltime often prefer an electric or electronic typewriter, which produces more uniform, clearer characters. Most typewriters are available in either pica or elite type. Pica type has 10 characters to a horizontal inch and elite has 12; both have six single-spaced, or three double-spaced, lines to a vertical inch. The slightly larger pica type is easier to read and many editors prefer it, although they don't object to elite.

Editors do dislike, and often refuse to read, manuscripts typed in all caps or in an unusual type style like script, italic or Old English. Reading these manuscripts is hard on the eyes. You should strive for clean, easy-to-read manuscripts and correspondence that reflect a professional approach to your work and consideration for your reader.

Use a good black (never colored) typewriter ribbon and clean the keys frequently. If the enclosures of the letters a, b, d, e, g, o, etc., become inked in, a cleaning is overdue.

Even the best typists make errors. *Occasional* retyping over erasures is acceptable, but strikeovers give your manuscript a sloppy, careless appearance. Hiding typos with large splotches of correction fluid makes your work look amateurish; use it sparingly. Some writers prefer to use typing correction film for final drafts and correction fluid for rough drafts. Better yet, a self-correcting electric typewriter with a correction tape makes typos nearly invisible. Whatever method you use, it's best to retype a page that has several noticeable corrections. Sloppy typing is taken by many editors as a sign of sloppy work habits—and the possibility of careless research and writing.

Types of paper. The paper you use must measure 8½x11 inches. That's a standard size and editors are adamant—they don't want unusual colors or sizes. There's a wide range of white 8½x11 papers. The cheaper ones are made from wood pulp. They will suffice, but are not recommended. Editors also discourage the use of erasable bond for manuscripts; typewriter ribbon ink on erasable bond tends to smear when handled. Don't use less than a 16 lb. bond paper; 20 lb. is preferred. Your best bet is paper with a 25% cotton fiber content. Its texture shows type neatly and it holds up under erasing and corrections.

You don't need fancy letterhead for your correspondence with editors. Plain bond paper is fine; just type your name, address, phone number and the date at the top of the page—centered or in the right-hand corner. If you decide to use letterhead, make it as simple and businesslike as possible. Many quick print shops have standard typefaces and can supply letterhead stationery at a relatively low cost. Never use letterhead for typing your manuscripts; only the first page of queries, cover letters and other correspondence should be typed on letterhead.

Photocopies and carbons. Always make copies of your manuscripts and correspondence before putting them in the mail. Don't learn the hard way, as many writers have, that manuscripts get lost in the mail and publishers sometimes go out of business without returning submissions. While some writers make carbon copies of their correspondence, most depend on photocopy machines to duplicate manuscripts. Use carbon copies for your own records if you do use them; a carbon copy should be sent to an editor only if the original correspondence has been lost.

You might want to make several copies of your manuscript while it is still clean and crisp. Some writers keep their original manuscript as a file copy and submit good quality photocopies. Submitting copies can save you the expense and effort of retyping a manuscript if it becomes lost in the mail. If you submit a copy, it's a good idea to explain to the editor whether or not you are making a simultaneous (multiple) submission to several markets. Some editors will not consider material submitted simultaneously, and they assume a photocopied submission is simultaneous. Follow the requirements in the individual listings, and see Approaching Markets later in this article for more detailed information about simultaneous submissions.

Some writers include a self-addressed postcard with a photocopied submission and suggest in their cover letter that if the editor is not interested in the manuscript, it may be tossed out and a reply returned on the postcard. This practice is recommended when dealing with foreign markets. Submitting a disposable manuscript costs the writer some photocopy expense, but it can save on large postage bills.

The cost of personal photocopiers is coming down, but they remain too expensive for many writers to consider purchasing. If you need to make a large number of photocopies, you should ask your print shop about quantity discounts. One advantage of owning a personal computer and printer is that you can quickly print copies of any text you have composed on it.

Computers and accessories. A personal computer can make a writer's work much more efficient. Writing, revising and editing are usually faster and easier on a computer than on a typewriter. Many writers rely on their computers to give them fresh, readable copy as they revise rough drafts into finished manuscripts. When a manuscript is written on a computer, it can come out of the computer in three ways: as hard copy from the computer's printer; stored on a removable electronic disk (called a floppy) that can be read by other computers; or as an electronic transfer over telephone lines using a modem (a device that allows one computer to transmit to another).

• Hard copy—Most editors are receptive to a computer printout submission if it looks like a neatly typed manuscript. Some older and cheaper printers produce only a low-quality dot-matrix printout with hard-to-read, poorly shaped letters and numbers. Many editors are not willing to read these manuscripts and have indicated that in their listings. New dot-matrix printers, however, produce nearly letter-quality printouts that are almost indistinguishable from a typewritten manuscript. These are almost always acceptable to editors.

When you submit hard copy to an editor, be sure you use quality paper. Some computer printers use standard bond paper that you'd use in a typewriter. Others are equipped with a tractor-feed that pulls continuous form paper with holes along the edges through the machine. If you use continuous form paper, be sure to remove the perforated tabs on each side and separate the pages.

• Disk—You'll find that more publishers are accepting or even requesting electronic submissions on disk. If your disk can be read by the publisher's computer, the publisher won't need to have your manuscript typeset by another person.

• Modem—Some publishers who accept submissions on disk will also accept electronic submissions by modem. This is the fastest method of getting your manuscript to the publisher.

Before sending anything electronically by disk or modem, you'll need to get details from the publisher. *Writer's Market* listings indicate that these submissions are accepted with this phrase: Query for electronic submissions. When you receive an assignment, ask the editor about the computer requirements. You'll need to know the name of your computer, its manufacturer and model; the operating system (CPM or MS-DOS) and word processing software to compare information. Because most editors want hard copy along with an electronic submission, you may wonder why you should even consider using a disk or modem. Editors like it because they can revise manuscripts more quickly on a computer screen as well as save typesetting expenses. If you have a particularly timely topic or a manuscript that needs to be submitted quickly, a disk or modem submission is an asset that also can save an editor time on deadline.

Assorted supplies. Where will you put all your manuscripts and correspondence? A two- or four-drawer filing cabinet with file folders is a good choice, but many writers find they can make do with manila envelopes and cardboard boxes. It's important to organize and label your correspondence, manuscripts, ideas, submission records, clippings, etc., so you can find them when you need them. See sections on Recording Submissions and Bookkeeping for other helpful hints on keeping records.

You will also need stamps and envelopes; see Mailing Submissions in this article and the U.S. and Canadian Postage by the Page tables on the inside covers of the book. If you decide to invest in a camera to increase your sales, you'll find details on submitting and mailing photos in the sections on Approaching Markets and Mailing Submissions.

Approaching markets

Before submitting a manuscript to a market, be sure you've done the following:
• Familiarize yourself with the publication or other type of market that interests you. Your first sales probably will be to markets you already know through your reading. If you find a listing in *Writer's Market* that seems a likely home for an idea you've been working on, study a sample copy or book catalog to see if your idea fits in with their current topics. If you have a magazine article idea, you may also want to check the *Reader's Guide to Periodical Literature* to be sure the idea hasn't been covered with an article in the magazine during the past year or two.

- Always request writer's guidelines. Guidelines give a publication's exact requirements for submissions and will help you focus your query letter or manuscript. If a publication has undergone editorial changes since this edition of *Writer's Market* went to press, those changes will usually be reflected in its writer's guidelines. Some publications also have theme or other special issues, or an editorial calendar planned in advance that will be included in its guidelines. The response to your request for guidelines can also let you know if a publication has folded or it if has an unreasonably long response time.
- Check submission requirements. A publication that accepts only queries may not respond at all to a writer who submits an unsolicited complete manuscript. Don't send an unpublished manuscript to a publication that publishes only reprints, and if you're submitting photos, be sure the publication reviews prints or slides, and find out if they require model releases and captions. An editor is impressed when a writer carefully studies a publication and its requirements before making a submission.
- With unsolicited submissions or correspondence, enclose a self-addressed, stamped envelope (SASE). Editors appreciate the convenience and the savings in postage. Some editorial offices deal with such a large volume of mail that their policies do not allow them to respond to mail that does not include a SASE. If you submit to a foreign market, enclose a self-addressed envelope (SAE) with International Reply Coupons (IRCs) purchased from the post office. (You don't need to send a SASE if you send a disposable manuscript or your manuscript is an assignment.)

Those are the basics; now you're ready to learn the details of what you should send when you contact an editor.

Query letters. A query letter is a brief, but detailed letter written to interest an editor in your manuscript. Some beginners are hesitant to query, thinking an editor can more fairly judge an idea by seeing the entire manuscript. Actually, most editors of nonfiction prefer to be queried.

Do your best writing when you sit down to compose a query. There is no query formula that guarantees success, but there are some points to consider when you begin:

- Queries are single-spaced business letters, usually limited to one page. Address the current editor by name, if possible. Do not immediately address an editor by a first name; some editors are offended by unwarranted familiarity. Wait until you receive a response and follow the editor's lead.
- Your major goal is to convince the editor that your idea would be interesting to the publication's readership and that you are the best writer for the job. Mention any special training or experience that qualifies you to write the article. If you have prior writing experience, you should mention it; if not there's no need to call attention to the fact. Some editors will also ask to look at clips—actual pages or photocopies of your published work. If possible, submit something related to your idea, either in topic or style.
- Be sure you use a strong opening to pique the editor's interest. Some queries begin with a paragraph that approximates the lead of the intended article.
- Briefly detail the structure of the article. Give some facts and perhaps an anecdote and mention people you intend to interview. Give editors enough information to make them want to know more.
- If photos are available to accompany the manuscript, let the editor know.
- Your closing paragraph should include a direct request to do the article; it may specify the date the manuscript can be completed and an approximate length.
- Don't discuss fees or request advice from the editor at this time.
- Fiction is rarely queried since most fiction editors want to see the complete manuscript before making a judgment. If a fiction editor does request a query, briefly describe the main theme and story line, including the conflict and resolution of your story.
- Some writers state politely in their query letters that after a specified date (slightly beyond the listed reporting time), they will assume the editor is not currently interested in their topic and will submit their query elsewhere. It's a good idea to do this only if your topic is a timely

Mr. Geoff Miller
Editor
Los Angeles Magazine
1888 Century Park East
Los Angeles, CA 90067

Dear Mr. Miller:

I wonder if your magazine would like a story about John Soares, a resident of Orange County. For 10 years the colorful Soares was history's most successful crossroader (a crossroader is a person who cheats casinos), winning millions of dollars at craps, blackjack, and slot machines in gambling houses in Nevada and all over the world.

In the middle 1960s into the early 1970s, Soares and a Runyonesque crew of rogues (one was a beautiful woman, an icy calm, ex-prostitute who alone collected more than 10,000 slot jackpots) were absolutely unstoppable. This article will reveal how they switched loaded dice into crap games right under the noses of big-time casino bosses, how they stacked entire shoes of cards without the blackjack dealer knowing, and how there wasn't a slot machine ever manufactured that they couldn't rig.

Eagle-eyed Mafia men ran many of the casinos when Soares operated, but they never caught him or his crew, nor did the local police or FBI. Soares, a sort of Robin Hood, is now a well-to-do California businessman. Never once, it should be repeated, was he caught, yet his pillage boggles the mind. The article, be assured, will be packed with adventure.

Although Soares was a crook, don't be surprised if many of your readers find themselves rooting for him.

I've written feature articles for numerous newspapers, including the <u>Baltimore News American</u>, the <u>St. Louis Globe Democrat</u>, the <u>Dallas Morning News</u>, and the <u>Washington Star</u>. I've also been published in such magazines as <u>Omni</u>, <u>True Detective</u>, and <u>Self</u>.

Sincerely yours,

William Hoffman

Magazine query. *This sample query for a magazine article presents the author's idea and qualifications effectively and resulted in a sale. Reprinted from* How to Write Irresistible Query Letters, *by Lisa Collier Cool (Writer's Digest Books). Copyright © 1987 by Lisa Collier Cool.*

Lisa Collier
Collier Associates
[address]

Dear Ms. Collier:

I've recently completed a manuscript entitled <u>Wild Patients</u> <u>I</u> <u>Have Known</u>, which describes my wildlife veterinary experiences from 1977 to 1982. It covers some of my frustrations and triumphs working with injured wild animals. The forward is written by Dr. Michael Fox, a well known veterinarian and author.

The wildlife rehabilitation field is relatively new in the United States. Most states now have several organizations dealing with injured wildlings, each with several hundreds or even thousands of members. A bird rehab project in Florida, the Suncoast Seabird Sanctuary, currently has more than seven thousand members. California has more than fifty groups dedicated to assisting injured wild creatures! The majority of these American organizations are less than three years old. Since my book would be the first of its kind, I believe that it could become to this movement what Rachael Carson's <u>Silent Spring</u> was to the environmental movement of the sixties.

I have enclosed several recent newspaper articles about our project in Wisconsin, along with a recent article from <u>People</u> magazine about wildlife rehabilitation in your own state. These articles and hundreds more like them illustrate the powerful public interest in the treatment of injured wild animals.

As these articles demonstrate, there's a wide audience for my book: veterinarians, rehabilitators, and anyone interested in wildlife, doctors or the intriguing controversy found within the pages of the book. I am firmly committed to the book and its success: I am prepared to take up to one year completely off work to aid in its promotion. Because of the problems I encountered with the Wisconsin Department of Natural Resources, the discussion of the book would promote substantial sales in this state alone.

Thank you very much for your consideration. I sure hope you like <u>Wild Patients</u> <u>I Have Known</u>, and will look forward to hearing from you.

Warm regards,

Rory C. Foster,
D.V.M.

Book query. *This query could be sent either to a publisher or an agent. It details the book's subject, potential audience and the author's qualifications. Some publishers also ask to see an outline/synopsis or sample chapters. Franklin Watts eventually published the book, changing its title to* Dr. Wildlife. *This query letter is reprinted from* How to Write Irresistible Query Letters.

one that will suffer if not considered quickly.

For more information about writing query letters and biographical notes, read *How to Write Irresistible Query Letters*, by Lisa Collier Cool (Writer's Digest Books).

Cover letters. A brief cover letter enclosed with your manuscript is helpful in personalizing a submission. If you have previously queried the editor on the article or book, the note should be a brief reminder: "Here is the piece on the city's missing funds, which we discussed previously. I look forward to hearing from you at your earliest convenience." Don't use the letter to make a sales pitch. Your manuscript must stand on its own at this point.

If you are submitting to a market that considers unsolicited complete manuscripts, your cover letter should tell the editor something about your manuscript and about you—your publishing history, availability to promote the book, and any particular qualifications you have for writing the enclosed manuscript.

If the manuscript you are submitting is a photocopy, indicate in the letter whether it is a simultaneous submission. An editor may assume it is, unless you tell him otherwise. Markets that are open to simultaneous submissions indicate that in their listings.

Book proposals. Book proposals are some combination of a cover letter, a synopsis, an outline and/or two or three sample chapters. The exact combination of these will depend on the publisher.

Some editors use the terms synopsis and outline interchangeably. If the publisher requests only a synopsis or an outline, not both, be sure you know which format the publisher prefers. Either a synopsis or outline is appropriate for a novel, but you may find an outline is more effective for a nonfiction book.

• A synopsis is a very brief summary of your book. Cover the basic plot or theme of your book and reveal the ending. Make sure your synopsis flows well, is interesting and easy to read.

• An outline covers the highlights of your book chapter-by-chapter. If your outline is for a novel, include all major characters, the main plot, subplots and any pertinent details. An outline may run 3 to 30 pages, depending on the complexity and length of the book. Be sure your outline is clear; you will lose the reader with a tangle of ideas and events.

• Sample chapters are also requested by many editors. Some are interested in the first two or three chapters to see how well you develop your book. Others want a beginning chapter, a chapter from the middle of your book, and the final chapter, so they can see how well you follow through. Be sure to follow individual requirements as detailed by the editor in the market listing. *How to Write a Book Proposal*, by Richard Balkin (Writer's Digest Books), also provides helpful details about submitting a book proposal.

Reprints. You can get more mileage—and money—out of your research and writing time by marketing your previously published material for reprint sales. You may use a photocopy of your original manuscript and/or tearsheets from the publication in which it originally appeared. With your reprint submission, be sure to inform the editor that you are marketing the article as a reprint, especially if you send a photocopy without tearsheets. The editor will also need to know when and in what publication it appeared.

If you market for reprint an article that has not yet been published by the original purchaser, inform editors that it cannot be used before it has made its initial appearance. Give them the intended publication date and be sure to inform them if any changes take place.

Photographs and slides. The availability of good quality photos can be the deciding factor when an editor is considering a manuscript. Most publications also offer additional pay for photos accepted with a manuscript. When submitting black and white prints, editors usually want to see 8x10 glossy photos, unless they indicate another preference in the listing. The universally accepted format for color transparencies is 35mm; few buyers will look at color prints.

On all your photos and slides, you should stamp or print your copyright notice and "Return to:" followed by your name, address and phone number. Rubber stamps are preferred for labeling photos since they are less likely to cause damage. You can order them from many stationery or office supply stores. If you use a pen on photos, be careful not to damage the print by pressing too hard or allowing ink to bleed through the paper. A felt tip pen is best, but you should take care not to put photos or copy together before the ink dries or it will smear.

● Captions can be typed on a sheet of paper and taped to the bottom or the back of the prints. Some writers, when submitting several transparencies or photos, number the photos and type captions (numbered accordingly) on an 8½x11 sheet of paper.

● Submit prints rather than negatives or consider having duplicates made of your slides or transparencies. Don't risk having your original negative or slide lost or damaged. Look for a photography lab that does custom work in prints and transparencies.

Manuscript mechanics

A unique work may be tossed aside by an editor who refuses to read sloppy manuscripts, fancy typefaces, or coffee-stained pages. Follow these rules of manuscript mechanics to present your work in its best form.

Manuscript format. Do not use a cover sheet or title page. Use a binder only if you are submitting a play or a television or movie script. You can use a paper clip to hold pages together, but never use staples.

The upper corners of the first page contain important information about you and your manuscript. This information is always single-spaced. In the upper left corner list your name, address, phone number and Social Security number (publishers must have this now to file accurate payment records with the government). If you are using a pseudonym for your byline, your legal name still must appear in this space. In the upper right corner, indicate the approximate word count of the manuscript, the rights you are offering for sale and your copyright notice (© 1989 Chris Jones). A handwritten copyright symbol is acceptable. For a book manuscript, do not specify the rights you are offering; that will be covered in your contract. Do not number the first page of your manuscript.

Center the title in capital letters one-third of the way down the page. To center, set the tabulator to stop halfway between the right and left edges of the page. Count the letters in the title, including spaces and punctuation, and backspace half that number. Type the title. Set your typewriter to double-space. Type "by" centered one double-space under your title, and type your name or pseudonym centered one double-space beneath that.

After the title and byline, drop down two double-spaces, paragraph indent, and begin the body of your manuscript. Always double-space your manuscript and use standard paragraph indentations of five spaces. Margins should be about 1¼ inches on all sides of each full page of typewritten manuscript. You may lightly pencil in a line to remind you when you reach the bottom margin of your page, but be sure to erase it before submitting your manuscript.

On every page after the first, type your last name, a dash and the page number in the upper left corner. The title of your manuscript may, but need not, be typed on this line or beneath it. Page number two would read: Jones-2. If you are using a pseudonym, type your real name, followed by your pen name in parentheses, then a dash and the page number: Jones (Smith)-2. Then drop down two double-spaces and continue typing. Follow this format throughout your manuscript.

If you are submitting novel chapters, leave the top one-third of the first page of each chapter blank before typing the chapter title. Subsequent pages should include the author's last name, the page number, and a shortened form of the book's title. (In a variation on this, some authors place the title before the name and put the page number at the right-hand margin.)

When submitting poetry, the poems should be typed single-spaced (double-space between stanzas), one poem per page. For a long poem requiring more than one page, paper clip the pages together.

On the final page of your manuscript, after you've typed your last word and period, skip

Jones—2

Title of Manuscript (optional)

Begin the second page, and all following pages, in this manner—
with a page-number line (as above) that includes your name, in case
loose manuscript pages get shuffled by mistake. You may include the
title of your manuscript or a shortened version of the title to identify
the Jones manuscript this page 2 belongs to.

Chris Jones
1234 My Street
Anytown, State, Zip
Tel. 123/456-7890
Social Security Number

About 3,000 words
First Serial Rights
© 1989 Chris Jones

YOUR STORY OR ARTICLE TITLE HERE

by

Chris Jones

The manuscript begins here—about halfway down the first page. It
should be cleanly typed, double-spaced, using either elite or pica type.
Use one side of the paper only, and leave a margin of about 1 1/4 inches
on all four sides.

To begin a new paragraph, drop down one double-space and indent.
Don't put extra white space between paragraphs.

NEATNESS COUNTS. *Here are sample pages of a manuscript ready for submission to an editor. If the author uses a pseudonym, it should be placed on the title page only in the byline position; the author's real name must always appear in the top left corner of the title page—for manuscript mailing and payment purposes. On subsequent pages, list the real name, then the pen name in parentheses, followed by a dash and the page number.*

three double-spaces and center the words "The End." Some nonfiction writers use ### or the old newspaper symbol -30- to indicate the same thing. Further information on formats for books, articles, scripts, proposals and cover letters, with illustrated examples, is available in *The Writer's Digest Guide to Manuscript Formats*, by Dian Dincin Buchman and Seli Groves (Writer's Digest Books).

Estimating word count. To estimate word count in manuscripts, count the number of characters and spaces in an average line, and count the number of lines of type on a representative page. Multiply the characters per line by the lines per page to find out the average number of characters per page. Then count the number of manuscript pages (fractions should be counted as fractions, except in book manuscript chapter headings, which are counted as a full page.) Multiply the number of pages by the number of characters per page you already determined. Divide this total by six (an average of six characters per word is assumed.) This will give you the approximate number of words in the manuscript. For short manuscripts, it's often quicker to count each word on a representative page and multiply by the total number of pages.

Mailing submissions

No matter what size manuscript you're mailing, always include sufficient return postage and a self-addressed envelope large enough to contain your manuscript if it is returned. If you use a postage meter on the SASE instead of stamps, be aware of postal regulations concerning metered postage. If the meter stamp has a date, you must mark the envelope "Postage prepaid by sender" since the SASE may be used to return your manuscript weeks or months later.

A manuscript of fewer than six pages may be folded in thirds and mailed as if it were a letter using a #10 (business-size) envelope. The enclosed SASE should be a #10 folded in thirds (though these are sometimes torn when a letter opener catches in one of the folds), or a #9 envelope which will slip into the mailing envelope without being folded. Some editors also appreciate the convenience of having a manuscript folded into halves in a 6x9 envelope.

For larger manuscripts, use 9x12 envelopes for both mailing and return. The return SASE may be folded in half.

A book manuscript should be mailed in a sturdy, well-wrapped box. Your typing paper or envelope box is a suitable mailer. Enclose a self-addressed mailing label and paper clip your return postage stamps to the label.

Always mail photos and slides First Class. The rougher handling received by Fourth Class mail could damage them. If you are concerned about losing prints or slides, send them certified or registered mail. For any photo submission that is mailed separately from a manuscript, enclose a separate self-addressed label, adequate return postage, and an envelope. Never submit photos or slides mounted in glass.

To mail up to 20 prints, use photo mailers that are stamped "Photos—Do Not Bend" and contain two cardboard inserts to sandwich your prints. Or use a 9x12 manila envelope, write "Photos—Do Not Bend" and devise your own cardboard inserts. Some photography supply shops also carry heavy cardboard envelopes that are reusable.

When mailing a number of prints, say 25 to 50 for a photo book, pack them in a sturdy cardboard box. A box for typing paper or photo paper is an adequate mailer. If, after packing both manuscript and photos, there's empty space in the box, slip in enough cardboard inserts to fill the box. Wrap the box securely.

To mail transparencies, first slip them into protective vinyl sleeves, then mail as you would prints. If you're mailing a number of sheets, use a cardboard box as for photos above.

Types of mail service

● First Class is the most expensive way of mailing a manuscript, but many writers prefer it. First Class mail generally receives better handling and is delivered more quickly. Mail sent

First Class is forwarded for one year if the addressee has moved, and is returned automatically if it is undeliverable.

- Fourth Class rates are available for packages that weigh 16 oz. or more and are to be delivered within the United States. Pack materials carefully when mailing Fourth Class since they will be handled the same as Parcel Post—roughly. If a letter is enclosed with your Fourth Class package, write "First Class Letter Enclosed" on the package and add adequate First Class postage for your letter. To make sure your package will be returned to you if it is undeliverable, print "Return Postage Guaranteed" under your address.
- Certified Mail must be signed for when it reaches its destination. If requested, a signed receipt is returned to the sender. There is an 85¢ charge for this service, in addition to the required postage.
- Registered Mail is a high security method of mailing. The package is signed in and out of every office it passes through, and a receipt is returned to the sender when the package reaches its destination. This service costs $4.40 in addition to the postage required for the item.
- United Parcel Service may be slightly cheaper than First Class postage if you drop the package off at UPS yourself. UPS cannot legally carry First Class mail, so your cover letter needs to be mailed separately. Check with UPS in your area for current rates. The cost depends on the weight of your package and the distance to its destination.
- Overnight mail services are provided by both the U.S. Postal Service and several private firms. These services can be useful if your manuscript or revisions *must* be at an editor's office quickly. More information on next day service is available from the U.S. Post Office in your area, or check your Yellow Pages under "Delivery Services."

Other important details

- Money orders should be used if you are ordering sample copies or supplies and do not have checking services. You'll have a receipt and money orders are traceable. Money orders for up to $35 can be purchased from the U.S. Postal Service for a 75¢ service charge. Banks, savings and loans, and some commercial businesses also carry money orders; their fees vary. *Never* send cash through the mail for sample copies.
- Insurance is available for items handled by the U.S. Postal Service but is payable only on typing fees or the tangible value of the item in the package—such as typing paper—so your best insurance when mailing manuscripts is to keep a copy of what you send.
- When corresponding with foreign publications and publishers, International Reply Coupons (IRCs) must be used for return postage. Surface rates in foreign countries differ from those in the U.S., and U.S. postage stamps are of no use there. Currently, one IRC costs 95¢ and is sufficient for one ounce traveling at surface rate; two are recommended for air mail return. Many writers dealing with foreign publishers mail photocopies and tell the publisher to dispose of them if they're not appropriate. When you use this method, it's best to set a deadline for withdrawing your manuscript from consideration, so you can market it elsewhere.
- International money orders are also available from the post office at a slightly higher fee than those for domestic use.
- See U.S. and Canadian Postage by the Page on the inside covers for specific mailing costs.

Recording submissions

A number of writers think once they've mailed a manuscript, the situation is out of their hands; all they can do is sit and wait. But submitting a manuscript doesn't mean you've lost control of it. Manage your writing business by keeping copies of all manuscripts and correspondence, and by recording the dates of submissions.

One way to keep track of your manuscripts is to use a record of submissions that includes the date sent, title, market, editor and enclosures (such as photos). You should also note the date of the editor's response and, if the manuscript was accepted, the publication date and payment information. You might want to keep a similar record just for queries.

Also remember to keep a separate file for each manuscript or idea along with its list of potential markets. You may want to keep track of expected reporting times on a calendar, too. Then you'll know if a market has been slow to respond.

Bookkeeping

Whether or not you are profitable in your writing, you'll need to keep accurate financial records. These records are necessary to let you know how you're doing, and, of course, the government is also interested in your financial activities.

If you have another source of income, you should plan to keep separate records for your writing expenses and income. Some writers open separate checking accounts for their writing-related expenses.

The best financial records are the ones that get used, and usually the simpler the form, the more likely it will be used regularly. Get in the habit of recording every transaction related to your writing. You can start at any time; it doesn't need to be on Jan. 1. Because you're likely to have expenses before you have income, start keeping your records whenever you make your first purchase related to writing—such as this copy of *Writer's Market*.

A simple bookkeeping system. For most freelance writers, a simple type of single-entry bookkeeping is adequate. The heart of the single-entry system is the journal, an accounting book available at any stationery or office supply store. You record all of the expenses and income of your writing business in the journal.

The single-entry journal's form is similar to a standard check register. Instead of withdrawals and deposits, you record expenses and income. You'll need to describe each transaction clearly—including the date; the source of the income (or the vendor of your purchase); a description of what was sold or bought; whether the payment was by cash, check or credit card; and the amount of the transaction.

Your receipt file. Keep all documentation pertaining to your writing expenses or income. This is true whether you have started a bookkeeping journal or not. For every payment you receive, you should have a check stub from the publisher's check, a cover letter or contract stating the amount of payment, or your own bank records of the deposit. For every check you write to pay business expenses, you should have a record in your check register as well as a cancelled check. Keep credit card receipts, too. And for every cash purchase, you should have a receipt from the vendor—especially if the amount is over $25. For small expenses, you can usually keep a list if you don't record them in a journal.

Tax information

Federal income tax laws have been modified since the 1986 Tax Reform Act, but it still abolishes income averaging and changes home office deductions and estimated tax payment rules. Before the law went into effect for 1987 taxes, writers had to keep track of business-related expenses and income. Expenses incurred for a project were deducted in that year regardless of whether or not income was derived from the project that year. If expenses exceeded income, the business was operated at a loss. Under new laws, each work is a capital item, and capitalization rules require writers to deduct expenses for a project over the income-producing lifetime of the work. If the work never produces income, nothing can be deducted. At the time of this writing, a "safe harbor" bill allowing deduction of costs over a three-year period is being considered. Writers and artists are still working to obtain an exemption from capitalization rules, and tax requirements may change. Be sure to check with the IRS on the most current tax requirements. The law also requires a business to be profitable three out of five years to avoid being treated as a hobby.

If your freelance income exceeds your expenses, regardless of the amount, you must declare that profit. If the profit is $400 or more, you also must pay Self-Employment Social Security Tax and fill out that self-employment form on your 1040 tax form. While we cannot offer you tax advice or interpretations, we can suggest several sources for the most current information.

● Call your local IRS office. Look in the white pages of the telephone directory under U.S. Government—Internal Revenue Service. Someone will be able to respond to your request for IRS publications and tax forms or other information. Ask about the IRS Tele-tax service, a series of recorded messages you can hear by dialing on a touch-tone phone. If you need answers to complicated questions, ask to speak with a Taxpayer Service Specialist.

● Obtain the basic IRS publications. You can order them by phone or mail from any IRS office; most are available at libraries and some post offices. Start with *Your Federal Income Tax* (Publication 17) and *Tax Guide for Small Business* (Publication 334). These are both comprehensive, detailed guides—you'll need to find the regulations that apply to you and ignore the rest. You may also want to get a copy of *Business Use of Your Home* (Publication 587) and *Self-Employment Tax* (Publication 533).

● Consider other information sources. Many public libraries have detailed tax instructions available on tape. Some colleges and universities offer free assistance in preparing tax returns. And if you decide to consult a professional tax preparer, the fee is a deductible business expense on your tax return.

Rights and the writer

We find that writers and editors may define rights in different ways. To eliminate any misinterpretations, read the following definitions of each right—and you'll see the definitions upon which editors updated the information in their listings.

Occasionally, we hear from a writer who is confused because an editor claims never to acquire or buy rights. The truth is, any time an editor buys a story or asks you for permission to publish a story in return for even contributor copies, the editor is asking you for rights. Sometimes people start magazines in their areas of expertise but don't have extensive knowledge of publishing terms and practices. If you sense that an editor is interested in getting stories but doesn't seem to know what his and the writer's responsibilities are regarding rights, be wary. In such a case, you'll want to explain what rights you're offering (preferably one-time rights only) and that you expect additional payment for subsequent use of your work. Writers may also agree to sell first rights, for example to a magazine, but then never receive a check for the manuscript and subsequent inquiries bring no response. In a case like this, we recommend that the writer send a certified letter, return receipt requested, notifying the magazine that the manuscript is being withdrawn from that publication for submission elsewhere. There is no industry standard for how long a writer should wait before using this procedure. The best bet is to check the *Writer's Market* listing for what the magazine lists as its usual reporting time and then, after a reasonable wait beyond that, institute the withdrawal.

Selling rights to your writing. The Copyright Law that went into effect Jan. 1, 1978, said writers were primarily selling one-time rights to their work unless they—and the publisher—agreed otherwise in writing. In some cases, however, a writer may have little say in the rights sold to an editor. The beginning writer, in fact, can jeopardize a sale by arguing with an editor who is likely to have other writers available who are eager to please. As long as there are more writers than there are markets, this situation will remain.

As a writer acquires skill, reliability, and professionalism on the job, he becomes more valued by editors—and rights become a more important consideration. Though a beginning writer will accept modest payment just to get in print, an experienced writer cannot afford to give away good writing just to see a byline. At this point the writer must become concerned with selling reprints of articles already sold to one market, using previously published articles as chapters in a book on the same topic, seeking markets for the same material overseas, or offering work to TV or the movies.

You should strive to keep as many rights to your work as you can from the outset, because before you can resell any piece of writing, you must own the rights to negotiate. If you have sold "all rights" to an article, for instance, it can be reprinted without your permission and without additional payment to you. Some writers will not deal with editors who buy all rights. What an editor buys will determine whether you can resell your own work. Here is a list of the rights most editors and publishers seek. (Book rights will be covered by the contract submitted to the writer by a book publisher. The writer does not indicate any such rights offered on the first page of a book manuscript.)

• First Serial Rights—First serial rights means the writer offers the newspaper or magazine the right to publish the article, story or poem for the first time in any periodical. All other rights to the material belong to the writer. Variations on this right are, for example, first North American serial rights. Some magazines use this purchasing technique to obtain the right to publish first in both the U.S. and Canada since many U.S. magazines are circulated in Canada. If an editor had purchased only first U.S. serial rights, a Canadian magazine could come out with prior or simultaneous publication of the same material. When material is excerpted from a book scheduled to be published and it appears in a magazine or newspaper prior to book publication, this is also called first serial rights.

• First North American Serial Rights—Magazine publishers that distribute in both the United States and Canada frequently buy these first rights covering publication in both countries.

• One-Time Rights—This differs from first serial rights in that the buyer has no guarantee he will be the first to publish the work. One-time rights often apply to photos, but also apply to writing sold to more than one market over a period of time. See also Simultaneous Rights.

• Second Serial (Reprint) Rights—This gives a newspaper or magazine the opportunity to print an article, poem or story after it has already appeared in another newspaper or magazine. The term is also used to refer to the sale of part of a book to a newspaper or magazine after a book has been published, whether or not there has been any first serial publication. Income derived from second serial rights to book material is often shared 50/50 by author and book publisher.

• All Rights—Some magazines buy all rights because of the top prices they pay for material, the exclusive nature of the publication, or the fact that they have book publishing interests or foreign magazine connections. A writer who sells an article, story or poem to a magazine under these terms forfeits the rights to use his material in its present form elsewhere. If he signs a work-for-hire agreement, he signs away all rights and the copyright to the company making the assignment. If the writer thinks he may want to use his material later (perhaps in book form), he must avoid submitting to such markets or refuse payment and withdraw his material if he discovers it later. Ask the editor whether he is willing to buy only first rights instead of all rights before you agree to an assignment or sale. Some editors will reassign rights to a writer after a given period, such as one year. It's worth an inquiry in writing.

• Simultaneous Rights—This term covers articles and stories sold to publications (primarily religious magazines) that do not have overlapping circulations. A Catholic publication, for example, might be willing to buy simultaneous rights to a Christmas story they like very much, even though they know a Presbyterian magazine may be publishing the same story in its Christmas issue. Publications that buy simultaneous rights indicate this fact in their listings in *Writer's Market*.

Always advise an editor when the material you are sending is a simultaneous submission. Some writers put the information in their cover letter and others also add it to the upper right-hand corner of the first page of the manuscript under the approximate word count.

• Foreign Serial Rights—Can you resell a story you had published in the U.S. or North America to a foreign magazine? If you sold only first U.S. serial rights or first North American rights, yes, you are free to market your story abroad. Of course, you must contact a foreign magazine that buys material that has previously appeared in the U.S. or North American periodicals.

- Syndication Rights—This is a division of serial rights. For example, a book publisher may sell the rights to a newspaper syndicate to print a book in 12 installments in each of 20 U.S. newspapers. If they did this after book publication, they would be syndicating second serial rights to the book. In either case, the syndicate would be taking a commission on the sales it made to newspapers, so the remaining percentage would split between author and publisher.
- Subsidiary Rights—The rights, other than book publication rights, that should be specified in a book contract. These may include various serial rights, dramatic rights, translation rights, etc. The contract lists what percentage of these sales goes to the author and what percentage to the publisher.
- Dramatic, Television and Motion Picture Rights—This means the writer is selling his material for use on the stage, in television or in the movies. Often a one-year option to buy such rights is offered (generally for 10% of the total price). The interested party then tries to sell the idea to other people—actors, directors, studios or television networks, etc.—who become part of the project, which then becomes a script. Some properties are optioned over and over again, but fail to become dramatic productions. In such cases, the writer can sell his rights again and again—as long as there is interest in the material. Though dramatic, TV and motion picture rights are more important to the fiction writer than the nonfiction writer, producers today are increasingly interested in nonfiction material; many biographies and articles are being dramatized.

Communicate and clarify. Before submitting material to a market, check its listing in this book to see what rights are purchased. Most editors will discuss rights they wish to purchase before any exchange of money occurs. Some buyers are adamant about what rights they will accept; others will negotiate. In any case, the rights purchased should be stated specifically in writing sometime during the course of the sale, usually in a contract, memo or letter of agreement.

Give as much attention to the rights you haven't sold as you do to the rights you have sold. Be aware of the rights you retain, with an eye for additional sales.

Regardless of the rights you sell or keep, make sure all parties involved in any sale understand the terms of the sale. Clarify what is being sold before any actual sale, and do it in writing. Keep in mind, too, that if there is a change in editors or publishers from the edition of *Writer's Market* you're using, the rights purchased may also change. Communication, coupled with these guidelines and some common sense, will preclude misunderstandings with editors over rights.

Copyrighting your writing

The copyright law, effective since Jan. 1, 1978, protects your writing, unequivocally recognizes the creator of the work as its owner, and grants the creator all the rights, benefits and privileges that ownership entails.

In other words, the moment you finish a piece of writing—whether it is a short story, article, novel or poem—the law recognizes that only you can decide how it is to be used.

This law gives writers power in dealing with editors and publishers, but they should understand how to use that power. They should also understand that certain circumstances can complicate and confuse the concept of ownership. Writers must be wary of these circumstances or risk losing ownership of their work. Here are answers to frequently asked questions about copyright law:

To what rights am I entitled under copyright law? The law gives you, as creator of your work, the right to print, reprint and copy the work; to sell or distribute copies of the work; to prepare "derivative works"—dramatizations, translations, musical arrangement, novelizations, etc.; to record the work; and to perform or display literary, dramatic or musical works publicly. These rights give you control over how your work is used, and assure you (in theory) that you receive payment for any use of your work.

If, however, you create the work as a "work-for-hire," you do not own any of these rights. The person or company that commissioned the work-for-hire owns the copyright.

When does copyright law take effect, and how long does it last? A piece of writing is copyrighted the moment it is put to paper and you indicate your authorship with the word Copyright or the ©, the year and your name. Protection lasts for the life of the author plus 50 years, thus allowing your heirs to benefit from your work. For material written by two or more people, protection lasts for the life of the last survivor plus 50 years. The life-plus-50 provision applies if the work was created or registered with the Copyright Office after January 1, 1978, when the updated copyright law took effect. The old law protected works for a 28-year term, and gave the copyright owner the option to renew the copyright for an additional 28 years at the end of that term. Works copyrighted under the old law that are in their second 28-year term automatically receive an additional 19 years of protection (for a total of 75 years). Works in their first term also receive the 19-year extension beyond the 28-year second term, but must still be renewed when the first term ends.

If you create a work anonymously or pseudonymously, protection lasts for 100 years after the work's creation, or 75 years after its publication, whichever is shorter. The life-plus-50 coverage takes effect, however, if you reveal your identity to the Copyright Office any time before the original term of protection runs out.

Works created on a for-hire basis are also protected for 100 years after the work's creation or 75 years after its publication, whichever is shorter. But the copyright is held by the publisher, not the writer.

Must I register my work with the Copyright Office to receive protection? No. Your work is copyrighted whether or not you register it, although registration offers certain advantages. For example, you must register the work before you can bring an infringement suit to court. You can register the work *after* an infringement has taken place, and *then* take the suit to court, but registering after the fact removes certain rights from you. You can sue for actual damages (the income or other benefits lost as a result of the infringement), but you can't sue for statutory damages and you can't recover attorney's fees unless the work has been registered with the Copyright Office *before* the infringement took place. Registering before the infringement also allows you to make a stronger case when bringing the infringement to court.

If you suspect that someone might infringe on your work, register it. If you doubt that an infringement is likely (and infringements are relatively rare), you might save yourself the time and money involved in registering the material.

I have an article that I want to protect fully. How do I register it? Request the proper form from the Copyright Office. Send the completed form, a $10 registration fee, and one copy (if the work is unpublished; two if it's published) of the work to the Register of Copyrights, Library of Congress, Washington, D.C. 20559. You needn't register each work individually. A group of articles can be registered simultaneously (for a single $10 fee) if they meet these requirements: They must be assembled in orderly form (simply placing them in a notebook binder is sufficient); they must bear a single title ("Works by Chris Jones," for example); they must represent the work of one person (or one set of collaborators); and they must be the subject of a single claim to copyright. No limit is placed on the number of works that can be copyrighted in a group.

If my writing is published in a "collective work"—such as a magazine—does the publication handle registration of the work? Only if the publication owns the piece of writing. Although the copyright notice carried by the magazine covers its contents, you must register any writing to which *you* own the rights if you want the additional protection registration provides.

Collective works are publications with a variety of contributors. Magazines, newspapers, encyclopedias, anthologies, etc., are considered collective works. If you sell something to a collective work, state in writing what rights you're selling. If you don't, you are automatically selling the nonexclusive rights to use the writing in the collective work and in any succeeding issues or revisions of it. For example, a magazine that buys your article without specifying in writing the rights purchased can reuse the article in that magazine without paying you. The same is true for other collective works, so always detail in writing what rights you are selling before actually making the sale.

When contributing to a collective work, ask that your copyright notice be placed on or near your published manuscript (if you still own the manuscript's rights). Prominent display of your copyright notice on published work has two advantages: It signals to readers and potential reusers of the piece that it belongs to you, and not to the collective work in which it appears; and it allows you to register all published work bearing such notice with the Copyright Office as a group for a single $10 fee. A published work *not* bearing notice indicating you as copyright owner can't be included in a group registration.

Display of copyright notice is especially important when contributing to an uncopyrighted publication—that is, a publication that doesn't display a copyright symbol and doesn't register with the Copyright Office. You risk losing copyright protection on material that appears in uncopyrighted publication. Also, you have no legal recourse against a person who infringes on something that is published without appropriate copyright notice. That person has been misled by the absence of the copyright notice and can't be held liable for his infringement. Copyright protection remains in force on material published in an uncopyrighted publication without benefit of copyright notice if the notice was left off only a few copies, if you asked in writing that the notice be included and the publisher didn't comply, or if you register the work and make a reasonable attempt to place the notice on any copies that haven't been distributed after the omission was discovered.

Official notice of copyright consists of the symbol ©, the word "Copyright," or the abbreviation "Copr."; the name of the copyright owner or owners; and the year date of first publication (for example, "© 1989 by Chris Jones"). A hand-drawn copyright symbol is acceptable.

Under what circumstances should I place my copyright notice on unpublished works that haven't been registered? Place official copyright notice on the first page of any manuscript. This procedure is not intended to stop a buyer from stealing your material (editorial piracy is very rare, actually), but to demonstrate to the editor that you understand your rights under copyright law, that you own that particular manuscript, and that you want to retain your ownership after the manuscript is published.

How do I transfer copyright? A transfer of copyright, like the sale of any property, is simply an exchange of the property for payment. The law stipulates, however, that the transfer of any exclusive rights (and the copyright is the most exclusive of rights) must be made in writing to be valid. Various types of exclusive rights exist, as outlined above. Usually it is best not to sell your copyright. If you do, you lose control over the use of the manuscript, and forfeit future income from its use.

What is a "work-for-hire assignment"? This is a work that another party commissions you to do. Two types of work-for-hire works exist: Work done as a regular employee of a company, and commissioned work that is specifically called "work-for-hire" in writing at the time of assignment. The phrase "work-for-hire" or something close must be used in the written agreement, though you should watch for similar phrasings. The work-for-hire provision was included in the new copyright law so that no writer could unwittingly sign away his copyright. The phrase "work-for-hire" is a bright red flag warning the writer that the agreement he is about to enter into will result in loss of rights to any material created under the agreement.

Some editors offer work-for-hire agreements when making assignments, and expect writers to sign them routinely. By signing them, you forfeit the potential for additional income from a manuscript through reprint sales, or sale of other rights. Be careful, therefore, in signing away your rights in a "work-for-hire" agreement. Many articles written as works-for-hire or to which all rights have been sold are never resold, but if you retain the copyright, you might try to resell the article—something you couldn't do if you forfeited your rights to the piece.

Can I get my rights back if I sell all rights to a manuscript, or if I sell the copyright itself?
Yes. You or certain heirs can terminate the transfer of rights 40 years after creation or 35 years after publication of a work by serving written notice, within specified time limits, to the person to whom you transferred rights. Consult the Copyright Office for the procedural details. This may seem like a long time to wait, but remember that some manuscripts remain popular and earn royalties and other fees for much longer than 35 years.

Must all transfers be in writing? Only work-for-hire agreements and transfers of exclusive rights *must* be in writing. However, getting any agreement in writing before the sale is wise. Beware of other statements about what rights the buyer purchases that may appear on checks, writer's guidelines or magazine mastheads. If the publisher makes such a statement elsewhere, you might insert a phrase like "No statement pertaining to purchase of rights other than the one detailed in this letter—including masthead statements or writer's guidelines—applies to this agreement" into the letter that outlines your rights agreement. Some publishers put their terms in writing on the back of a check that, when endorsed by the writer, becomes in their view a "contract." If the terms on the back of the check do not agree with the rights you are selling, then change the endorsement to match the rights you have sold before signing the check for deposit. Contact the editor to discuss this difference in rights.

Are ideas and titles copyrightable? No. Nor can facts be copyrighted. Only the actual expression of ideas or information can be copyrighted. You can't copyright the idea to do a solar energy story, and you can't copyright lists of materials for building solar energy converters. But you can copyright the article that results from that idea and that information.

Where can I get more information about copyright law? Write the Copyright Office (Library of Congress, Washington, D.C. 20559) for a free Copyright Information Kit. Call (not collect) the Copyright Public Information Office at (202)479-0700 weekdays between 8:30 a.m. and 5 p.m. if you need forms for registration of a claim to copyright. The Copyright Office will answer specific questions but won't provide legal advice. For more information about copyright and other laws, consult *The Writer's Friendly Legal Guide*, edited by Kirk Polking (Writer's Digest Books).

How much should I charge?

An '80s freelancer has taken the Miles Standish/John Alden idea one step further. For $35, Elliot Essman will send a personalized love letter written for you to the love of your life every month for a year. He calls his company Incurable Romantix and has about 450 subscribers. For $50 he will write you a 50-page love novelette in which you star!

Another Pennsylvania freelancer will write your wedding vows, or the whole ceremony if you desire. The fee: $150-300.

In the business world, freelancers are being used these days to woo clients for corporate law firms who are competing for business with other local and out-of-town firms expanding into new areas. Some want public relations consultation, some a client newsletter or brochure, and all are fair game for qualified freelance professionals. Conservative law firms still shun commercial advertising but increasingly employ the more discreet forms of promotion mentioned above.

When setting your freelance fees, keep two factors in mind: (1)how much you think the client is willing or able to pay for the job; and (2)how much you want to earn for your time. For example, if something you write helps a businessman get a $50,000 order or a school board to get a $100,000 grant, that may influence your fees. How much you want to earn for your time should take into consideration not only an hourly rate for the time you spend writing, but also the time involved in travel, meeting with the client, doing research, rewriting and, where necessary, handling details with a printer or producer. One way to figure your hourly rate is to determine what an annual salary might be for a staff person to do the same job you are bidding on, and figure an hourly wage on that. If, for example, you think the buyer would have to pay a staff person $20,000 a year, divide that by 2,000 (approximately 40 hours per week for 50 weeks) and you will arrive at $10 an hour. Then add another 20% to cover the amount of fringe benefits that an employer normally pays in Social Security, unemployment insurance, paid vacations, hospitalization, retirement funds, etc. Then add another dollars-per-hour figure to cover your actual overhead expense for office space, equipment, supplies; plus time spent on professional meetings, readings, and making unsuccessful proposals. (Add up one year's expense and divide by the number of hours per year you work on freelancing. In the beginning you may have to adjust this to avoid pricing yourself out of the market.)

Regardless of the method by which you arrive at your fee for the job, be sure to get a letter of agreement signed by both parties covering the work to be done and the fee to be paid.

You will, of course, from time to time handle certain jobs at less than desirable rates because they are for a cause you believe in, or because the job offers additional experience or exposure to some profitable client for the future. Some clients pay hourly rates; others pay flat fees for the job. Both kinds of rates are listed when the data were available so you have as many pricing options as possible. More details on many of the freelance jobs listed below are contained in *Freelance Jobs for Writers*, edited by Kirk Polking (Writer's Digest Books)—which tells how to get writing jobs, how to handle them most effectively, and how to get a fair price for your work.

Advertising copywriting: Advertising agencies and the advertising departments of large companies need part-time help in rush seasons. Newspapers, radio and TV stations also need copywriters for their small business customers who do not have agencies. Depending on the client and the job, the following rates could apply: $50-100 per hour, $250 and up per day, $500 and up per week, $1,000-2,000 as a monthly retainer. Flat-fee-per-ad rates could range from $100 and up per page depending upon size and kind of client.

Annual reports: A brief report with some economic information and an explanation of figures, $20-35 per hour; a report that must meet Securities and Exchange Commission (SEC) standards and reports that use legal language could bill at $40-65 per hour. Some writers who provide copywriting and editing services charge flat fees ranging from $5,000-10,000.

Anthology editing: Variable advance plus 3-15% of royalties. Flat-fee-per-manuscript rates could range from $500-5,000 or more if it consists of complex, technical material.

Article manuscript critique: 3,000 words, $30.

Arts reviewing: For weekly newspapers, $15-35; for dailies, $45 and up; for Sunday supplements, $100-400; regional arts events summaries for national trade magazines, $35-100.

Associations: Miscellaneous writing projects, small associations, $15-25 per hour; larger groups, up to $85 per hour; or a flat fee per project, such as $550-900 for 10-12 page magazine articles, or $1,200-1,800 for a 10-page booklet.

Audio cassette scripts: $10-50 per scripted minute, assuming written from existing client materials, with no additional research or meetings; otherwise $75-100 per minute, $750 minimum.

Audiovisuals: For writing; $150-350 per requested scripted minute; includes rough draft, editing conference with client, and final shooting script. For consulting, research, producing, directing, soundtrack oversight, etc., $400-600 per day plus travel and expenses. Writing fee is sometimes 10% of gross production price as billed to client.

Book, as-told-to (ghostwriting): Author gets full advance and 50% of author's royalties; subject gets 50%. Hourly rate for subjects who are self-publishing ($10-35 per hour).

Book, ghostwritten, without as-told-to credit: For clients who are either self-publishing or have no royalty publisher lined up, $5,000 to $35,000 (plus expenses) with one-fourth down payment, one-fourth when book half finished, one-fourth at three quarters mark and last fourth of payment when manuscript completed; or chapter by chapter.

Book content editing: $10-50 per hour and up; $600-5,000 per manuscript, based on size and complexity of the project.

Book copyediting: $7.50-20 per hour and up; occasionally $1 per page.

Book indexing: $8-18 per hour; $25 per hour using computer indexing software programs that take fewer hours; $1.50-6 per printed book page; 40-55¢ per line of index; or flat fee of $250-400, depending on length.

Book jacket blurb writing: Up to $600 for front cover copy plus inside and back cover copy summarizing content and tone of the book.

Book manuscript criticism: $125 for outline and first 20,000 words.

Book manuscript reading, nonspecialized subjects: $20-50 for a half page summary and recommendation. *Specialized subject:* $100-350 and up, depending on complexity of project.

Book proofreading: $7.50-22 per hour and up; sometimes $1.50-2 per page.

Book proposal consultation: $25-35 per hour.

Book proposal writing: $300-1,000 or more depending on length and whether client provides full information or writer must do some research.

Book query critique: $50 for letter to publisher and outline.

Book research: $5-20 per hour and up, depending on complexity.

Book reviews: For byline and the book only, on small newspapers; to $35-300 on larger publications.

Book rewriting: $12-30 per hour; sometimes $5 per page. Some writers have combination ghostwriting and rewriting short-term jobs for which the pay could be $350 per day and up. Some participate in royalties on book rewrites.

Book summaries for business people: $400 for 4-8 printed pages.

Brochures: $200-7,500 and up depending on client (small nonprofit organization to large corporation), length, and complexity of job.

Business booklets, announcement folders: Writing and editing, $100-1,000 depending on size, research, etc.

Business facilities brochure: 12-16 pages, $1,000-4,000.

Business letters: such as those designed to be used as form letters to improve customer relations, $100 per letter for small businesses; $500 and up per form letter for corporations.

Business meeting guide and brochure: 4 pages, $200; 8-12 pages, $400.

Business writing: On the local or national level, this may be advertising copy, collateral materials, speechwriting, films, public relations or other jobs—see individual entries on these subjects for details. General business writing rates could range from $20-50 per hour; $100-200 per day, plus expenses.

Business writing seminars: $250 for a half-day seminar, plus travel expenses.

Catalogs for business: $25-40 per hour or $60-75 per printed page; more if many tables or charts must be reworked for readability and consistency.

Collateral materials for business: See business booklets, catalogs, etc.

Comedy writing for night club entertainers: Gags only, $2-25 each. Routines, $100-1,000 per minute. Some new comics may try to get a five-minute routine for $150; others will pay $2,500 for a five-minute bit from a top writer.

Commercial reports for businesses, insurance companies, credit agencies: $6-10 per page; $5-20 per report on short reports.

Company newsletters and inhouse publications: Writing and editing 2-4 pages, $200-500; 12-32 pages, $1,000-2,000. Writing, $8-40 per hour; editing, $8-35 per hour.

Church history: $200-1,000 for writing 15 to 50 pages.

College/university history: $35 per hour for research through final ms.

Consultation on communications: $250 per day plus expenses for nonprofit, social service and religious organizations; $400 per day to others.

Consultation on magazine editorial: $1,000-1,500 per day plus expenses.

Consultation to business: On writing, PR, $25-50 per hour.

Consumer complaint letters: $25 each.

Contest judging: Short manuscripts, $5 per entry; with one-page critique, $10-25. Overall contest judging: $100-500.

Copyediting and content editing for other writers: $10-50/hour or $1 per page. (See also Manuscript consultation and Manuscript criticism.)

Copyediting for advertising: $25 per hour.

Copyediting for nonprofit organizations: $15 per hour.

Copywriting for book club catalogs: $85-200.

Corporate history: $1,000-20,000, depending on length, complexity and client resources.

Corporate profile: Up to 3,000 words, $1,250-2,500.

Dance criticism: $25-400 per article. (See also Arts reviewing.)

Direct-mail catalog copy: $10-50 per page for 3-20 blocks of copy per page of a 24-48 page catalog.

Direct-mail packages: Copywriting direct mail letter, response card, etc., $1,500-5,000 depending on writer's skill, reputation.

Direct response card on a product: $250.

Editing: See book editing, company newsletters, magazines, etc.

Educational consulting and educational grant and proposal writing: $250-750 per day or $25-75 per hour. Writers are sometimes paid the equivalent of 5-10% of the total grant amount, depending on whether only writing is involved or also research and design of the project itself.

Encyclopedia articles: Entries in some reference books, such as biographical encyclopedias, 500-2,000 words; pay ranges from $60-80 per 1,000 words. Specialists' fees vary.

Executive biography: (based on a resume, but in narrative form): $100.

English teachers—lay reading for: $4-6 per hour.

Fact checking: $17-20 per hour.

Family histories: See Histories, family.

Filmstrip script: See Audiovisual.

Financial presentation for a corporation: 20-30 minutes, $1,500-4,500.

Flyers for tourist attractions, small museums, art shows: $25 and up for writing a brief bio, history, etc.

Fund-raising campaign brochure: $5,000 for 20 hours' research and 30 hours to write a major capital campaign brochure, get it approved, lay out and produce with a printer. For a standard fund-raising brochure, many fund-raising executives hire copywriters for $50-75 an hour to do research which takes 10-15 hours and 20-30 hours to write/produce.

Gags: see Comedy writing.

Genealogical research: $5-25 per hour.

Ghostwriting: $25-100 per hour; $200 per day plus expenses. Ghostwritten professional and trade journal articles under someone else's byline, $400-4,000. Ghostwritten books: see Book, as-told-to (ghostwriting) and Book, ghostwritten, without as-told-to credit.

Ghostwriting a corporate book: 6 months' work, $13,000-25,000.

Ghostwriting article for a physician: $2,500-3,000.

Ghostwriting speeches: See Speeches.

Government public information officer: Part-time, with local governments, $25 per hour; or a retainer for so many hours per period.

Grant appeals for local non-profit organizations: $50 an hour or flat fee.

Grant proposals: $40 per hour or 10% of the awarded grant.

Histories, family: Fees depend on whether the writer need only edit already prepared notes or do extensive research and writing; and the length of the work, $500-15,000.

Histories, local: Centennial history of a local church, $25 per hour for research through final manuscript for printer.

House organ editing: See Company newsletters and Inhouse publications.

Industrial product film: $1,000 for 10-minute script.

Industrial promotions: $15-40 per hour. See also Business writing.

Job application letters: $10-25.

Lectures to local librarians or teachers: $50-100.

Lectures to school classes: $25-75; $150 per day; $250 per day if farther than 100 miles.

Lectures at national conventions by well-known authors: $2,500-20,000 and up, plus expenses; less for panel discussions.

Lectures at regional writers' conferences: $300 and up, plus expenses.

Magazine, city, calendar of events column: $150.

Magazine column: 200 words, $25. Larger circulation publications pay fees related to their regular word rate.

Magazine editing: Religious publications, $200-500 per month; $15-30 per hour.

Magazine stringing: 20¢-1 per word based on circulation. Daily rate: $100-200 plus expenses; weekly rate: $750 plus expenses. Also $7.50-35 per hour plus expenses.

Manuscript consultation: $25-50 per hour.

Manuscript criticism: $25 per 16-line poem; $40 per article or short story of up to 3,000 words; book outlines and sample chapters of up to 20,000 words, $160.

Manuscript typing: Depending on ms length and delivery schedule $1.50-2 per page with one copy; $15 per hour.

Market research survey reports: $10 per report; $15-30 per hour; writing results of studies or reports, $500-1,200 per day.

Medical editing: $25-65 per hour.

Medical proofreading: $12-24 per hour.

Medical writing: $25-80 per hour; manuscript for pharmeceutical company submitted to research journal, $4,500-5,000.

New product release: $300-500 plus expenses.

Newsletters: See Company newsletters and Retail business newsletters.

Newspaper column, local: 80¢ per column inch to $5 for a weekly; $7.50 for dailies of 4,000-6,000 circulation; $10-12.50 for 7,000-10,000 dailies; $15-20 for 11,000-25,000 dailies; and $25 and up for larger dailies.

Newspaper feature: 35¢ to $1.50 per column inch or $15-30 per article for a weekly; $70-80 for a daily.

Newspaper feature writing, part-time: $1,000 a month for an 18-hour week.

Newspaper reviews of art, music, drama: See Arts reviewing.

Newspaper stringing: 50¢-2.50 per column inch up to $7.50 per column inch for some national publications. Also publications like *National Enquirer* pay lead fees up to $250 for tips on page one story ideas.

Newspaper ads for small business: $25 for a small, one-column ad, or $10 per hour and up.

Novel synopsis for film producer: $150 for 5-10 pages typed single-spaced.

Novel synopsis for literary agent: $150 for 5-10 pages typed single space.

Obituary copy: Where local newspapers permit lengthier than normal notices paid for by the funeral home (and charged to the family), $15. Writers are engaged by funeral homes.

Opinion research interviewing: $4-6 per hour or $15-25 per completed interview.

Party toasts, limericks, place card verses: $1.50 per line.

Permission fees to publishers to reprint article or story: $75-500; 10¢-15¢ per word; less for charitable organizations.

Photo brochures: $700-15,000 flat fee for photos and writing.

Poetry criticism: $20 per 16-line poem.

Political writing: See Public relations and Speechwriting.

Press background on a company: $500-1,200 for 4-8 pages.

Press kits: $500-3,000.

Press release: 1-3 pages, $85-300.

Printers' camera-ready typewritten copy: Negotiated with individual printers, but see also

Manuscript typing services.

Product literature: Per page, $100-150.

Programmed instruction consultant fees: $300-700 per day; $50 per hour.

Programmed instruction materials for business: $50 per hour for inhouse writing and editing; $500-700 a day plus expenses for outside research and writing. Alternate method: $2,000-5,000 per hour of programmed training provided, depending on technicality of subject.

Public relations for business: $200-500 per day plus expenses.

Public relations for conventions: $500-1,500 flat fee.

Public relations for libraries: Small libraries, $10 per hour; larger cities, $35 an hour and up.

Public relations for nonprofit or proprietary organizations: Small towns, $100-500 monthly retainers.

Public relations for politicians: Small town, state campaigns, $10-50 per hour; incumbents, congressional, gubernatorial, and other national campaigns, $25-100 per hour.

Public relations for schools: $15-20 per hour and up in small districts; larger districts have full-time staff personnel.

Radio advertising copy: Small towns, up to $5 per spot; $20-65 per hour; $100-250 per week for a four- to six-hour day; larger cities, $250-400 per week.

Radio continuity writing: $5 per page to $150 per week, part-time.

Radio documentaries: $200 for 60 minutes, local station.

Radio editorials: $10-30 for 90-second to two-minute spots.

Radio interviews: For National Public Radio, up to 3 minutes, $25; 3-10 minutes, $40-75; 10-60 minutes, $125 to negotiable fees. Small radio stations would pay approximately 50% of the NPR rate; large stations, double the NPR rate.

Readings by poets, fiction writers: $25-600 depending on the author.

Record album cover copy: $100-250 flat fee.

Recruiting brochure: 8-12 pages, $500-1,500.

Research for writers or book publishers: $10-30 an hour and up; $15-200 per day and all expenses. Some quote a flat fee of $300-500 for a complete and complicated job.

Restaurant guide features: Short article on restaurant, owner, special attractions, $15; interior, exterior photos, $15.

Résumé writing: $25-150 per résumé.

Retail business newsletters for customers: $175-300 for writing four-page publications. Some writers work with a local printer and handle production details as well, billing the client for the total package. Some writers also do their own photography.

Rewriting: Copy for a local client, $27.50 per hour.

Sales brochure: 12-16 pages, $750-3,000.

Sales letter for business or industry: $150-500 for one or two pages.

Science writing: For newspapers $150-600; magazines $2,000-5,000; encyclopedias $1 per line; textbook editing $40 per hour; professional publications $500-1,500 for 1,500-3,000 words.

Script synopsis for agent or film producer: $75 for 2-3 typed pages, single-spaced.

Scripts for nontheatrical films for education, business, industry: Prices vary among producers, clients, and sponsors and there is no standardization of rates in the field. Fees include $75-120 per minute for one reel (10 minutes) and corresponding increases with each successive reel; approximately 10% of the production cost of films that cost the producer more than $1,500 per release minute.

Services brochure: 12-18 pages, $1,250-2,000.

Shopping mall promotion: $500 monthly retainer up to 15% of promotion budget for the mall.

Short story manuscript critique: 3,000 words, $30.

Slide film script: See Audiovisuals.

Slide presentation: Including visual formats plus audio, $1,000-1,500 for 10-15 minutes.

Slide/single image photos: $75 flat fee.

Slide/tape script: $75-100 per minute, $750 minimum.

Software manual writing: $35-50 per hour for research and writing.

Special news article: For a business's submission to trade publication, $250-400 for 1,000 words.

Special occasion booklet: Family keepsake of a wedding, anniversary, Bar Mitzvah, etc., $115 and up.

Speech for government official: $4,000 for 20 minutes plus up to $1,000 travel and miscellaneous expenses.

Speech for owners of a small business: $100 for six minutes.

Speech for owners of larger businesses: $500-3,000 for 10-30 minutes.

Speech for local political candidate: $150-250 for 15 minutes.

Speech for statewide candidate: $500-800.

Speech for national congressional candidate: $1,000 and up.

Syndicated newspaper column, self-promoted: $2-8 each for weeklies; $5-25 per week for dailies, based on circulation.

Teaching adult education course: $10-60 per class hour.

Teaching adult seminar: $350 plus mileage and per diem for a 6- or 7-hour day; plus 40% of the tuition fee beyond the sponsor's breakeven point.

Teaching business writing to company employees: $60 per hour.

Teaching college course or seminar: $15-70 per class hour.

Teaching creative writing in school: $15-60 per hour of instruction, or $1,500-2,000 per 12-15 week semester; less in recessionary times.

Teaching elementary and middle school teachers how to teach writing to students: $75-120 for a 1-1½ hour session.

Teaching journalism in high school: Proportionate to salary scale for full-time teacher in the same school district.

Teaching home-bound students: $5 per hour.

Technical editing: $15-40 per hour.

Technical typing: $1-4 per double-spaced page.

Technical writing: $35 per ms page or $35-75 per hour, depending on degree of complexity and type of audience.

Trade journal ad copywriting: $250-500.

Trade journal article: For business client, $500-1,500.

Translation, commercial: Final draft from one of the common European languages, 6-20¢ per English word.

Translation for government agencies: Up to $100 per 1,000 foreign words into English.

Translation, literary: $50-100 per thousand English words.

Translation through translation agencies: Less 33⅓% for agency commission.

Tutoring: $25 per 1-1½ hour private session.

TV documentary: 30-minute 5-6 page proposal outline, $250 and up; 15-17 page treatment, $1,000 and up; less in smaller cities.

TV editorials: $35 and up for 1-minute, 45 seconds (250-300 words).

TV home shopping: Local ad copy: $6 an hour. Writing, misc. freelance: $15-85 per hour; $.50-1 per word.

TV information scripts: Short 5- to 10-minute scripts for local cable TV stations, $10-15 per hour.

TV instruction taping: $150 per 30-minute tape; $25 residual each time tape is sold.

TV news film still photo: $3-6 flat fee.

TV news story: $16-25 flat fee.

TV filmed news and features: From $10-20 per clip for 30-second spot; $15-25 for 60-second clip; more for special events.

TV, national and local public stations: $35-100 per minute down to a flat fee of $100-500 for a 30- to 60-minute script.

TV scripts: (Teleplay only), 60 minutes, prime time, Writers Guild rates: $10,584; 30 minutes, $7,846.

Video script: See Audiovisuals.

Writer-in-schools: Arts council program, $130 per day; $650 per week. Personal charges vary from $25 per day to $100 per hour depending on school's ability to pay.

Writer's workshop: Lecturing and seminar conducting, $50-150 per hour to $500 per day plus expenses; local classes, $35-50 per student for 6-10 sessions.

Market conditions are constantly changing! If this is 1990 or later, buy the newest edition of Writer's Market at your favorite bookstore or order directly from Writer's Digest Books.

The Markets

Book Publishers

If you're interested in writing a book, you're not alone. According to the latest Public Opinion Survey conducted for the American Council for the Arts, 38 million people write creatively. That brings a lot of competition into play for the approximately 40,000 books published each year—85% nonfiction, 15% fiction. The good news is that last year more titles than ever sold 100,000 or more copies, according to *Publishers Weekly*. Seventy-two nonfiction and 52 fiction titles reached those sales figures, with 17 titles selling 500,000 or more copies.

Before you approach a book publisher with your manuscript, you should acquaint yourself with the business of publishing. During the past several years, many companies have merged or have been purchased by foreign investors. This trend shows no sign of slowing and usually results in staff cutbacks as firms try to become more cost-effective. When cutbacks are made, it usually affects consideration of unsolicited manuscripts; instead of having staff members or freelancers read stacks of over-the-transom submissions, publishers rely more on agents to screen material and submit it to them.

Submitting appropriate manuscripts also means knowing differences between publishers. Some publishers are interested in specific areas, like religious subjects, while others will consider a broad range of general interest topics. You'll find that some houses pursue mass market bestsellers only, while others want to produce literary novels or specialized books. Information in the individual listings, as well as researching publisher's new titles, will help you keep up with the changing business of book publishing.

Industry trends

It's difficult to predict what topics and types of books will be strong sellers. Book publishers plan their titles several months to several years in advance, and general trends like the aging population will undoubtedly affect their choice of manuscripts. Current events and their possible future effects also influence editors' choices. Writers, especially those marketing nonfiction, should make it a practice to keep up with recent information and events to make their manuscripts as timely and salable as possible.

Here are some industry trends that may affect what editors buy in the coming year:

● Children's books remain a strong category, although the market has fallen off for young adult novels. Retail sales on children's book are up from $500 million to $1 billion in the last five years. In addition, Waldenbooks has set up Waldenkids, a nationwide chain of stores with books and other related products for children.

● Sports books are popular, particularly in baseball, basketball and golf. Sports personality books, as well as fitness and instructional books, are enjoying good sales.

● New Age books continue to be a strong category and are moving to an international audience. The category has pulled in psychology, philosophy, health, religion, astrology and occult titles as well. New Age is now used as a general term for titles with metaphysical, spiritual and holistic approaches. It also embraces psychic phenomena, spiritual healing, UFOs, and mysticism.

● Graphic novels—the adaptation of a novel in comic art form—are drawing a larger audience.

● Science fiction is enjoying a growth period with the introduction of Foundation Books, a science fiction and fantasy imprint of Doubleday.

Other strong categories include travel, parenting, cooking, business, celebrity and humor. While these categories are popular, writers should keep in mind that editors are always looking for something new and different. "The unusual new idea always attracts us if it can add something to the list and especially if it can lead to new markets for other books," says George Young, editor-in-chief of Ten Speed Press.

The markets

Give your book the best publisher possible by studying the market and analyzing your manuscript. For some writers, the best is a publisher whose books regularly appear on the bestseller lists. For others, the best is a small press where each author gets personal attention from the editor. For publishers who produce fewer than four titles per year, see the Small Press section at the end of Book Publishers. For more information on small presses, contact the Small Press Writers' and Artists' Organization, 411 Main Trail, Ormond Beach FL 32074.

No matter what type of book you've written, the Book Publishers section can help you. You'll find more than 800 publishers listed. Not all of them buy the kind of work you write, but studying the listing subheads for nonfiction and fiction in the Book Publishers Subject Index will tell you which ones do.

When you read the detailed listings of publishers, choose two or three that buy what you're writing. Send for their catalogs and writer's guidelines. You'll learn the most current information about the books they've published, as well as their preferences for receiving manuscripts. Try to read a couple of the publishers' books; a visit to the library is all that's necessary.

You will find publishers often prefer different types of submissions. Some will read only a query letter; some want a query with an outline or synopsis; others want a one-page proposal. If editors accept submissions only through agents, don't send material directly.

Most editors like specific information in query letters. (See the Business of Writing for a sample book query letter.) Show that you understand their concerns by mentioning the audience for your book, the competition, and why your book is different. The editor also will want to know if you have previous publishing experience or special training relevant to the book's subject. Do not claim to have written the next blockbuster bestseller—even if you think you have.

Remember that only a fraction of today's writers sell a book to the first publisher to which it's submitted. Prepare a list of at least a dozen publishers that might be interested in your book. Learn more about them; send for catalogs and guidelines a few at a time. If your submission comes back with a rejection, send it to the next publisher on your list.

You may be able to speed up this process with simultaneous submissions of your query letter or manuscript. It's usually acceptable to send queries to several editors at the same time—as long as each letter is individually addressed. Never send a form letter as a query. If more than one editor responds favorably, you may be able to submit your manuscript simultaneously. Some publishers, however, refuse to consider simultaneous submissions; their *Writer's Market* listings and their guidelines will tell you their policies. Otherwise, you can send your manuscript to two or more publishers at the same time—but you should notify the editors that it's a simultaneous submission.

Subsidy publishing

At the *Writer's Market* office, we receive many calls and letters asking about subsidy publishing and self-publishing. As you read more about the publishing industry, you'll undoubtedly find advertisements and articles describing these alternatives. Be cautious. Know what you want from your writing.

Most writers want to make money from the books they write but don't succeed at first. Those who aspire to be professional writers know that it may take years to perfect a book, find the right publisher and receive royalty payments. They are willing to invest their time and efforts to meet that goal.

Some writers are more impatient. They've tried to sell a book and have met only rejection—encouraging rejection, maybe, but still rejection. They know they haven't written bestsellers, but they don't believe their books can be improved by further revision. They believe a specific market exists, and they want the book published.

Other writers simply write for their own satisfaction or for the pleasure of family and friends. Their writing may be just a hobby, but because of some encouragement they begin to wonder if they could be published. They haven't tried to market a manuscript before and are confused about the differences between royalty publishers, subsidy publishers and self-publishing.

We encourage you to work with publishers that pay writers. Most publishers do this through a royalty arrangement, paying the author 3-25% of the wholesale or retail price. These publishers actively market their books; you'll find them in bookstores and libraries, read about them in the newspaper and sometimes see the author on TV. Whenever a copy of one of these books is sold, both the writer and the publisher make money.

Subsidy publishers, on the other hand, expect writers to pay part or all of the cost of producing a book. They may ask for $1,000 or sometimes as much as $18,000, explaining that current economic conditions in the industry necessitate it. Subsidy publishers rarely market books as effectively as major publishing companies. They make money by selling their services to writers, not by selling their products to bookstores and libraries. Some subsidy publishers offer royalties but expect the writer to pay for promotion expenses.

Problems can arise when writers don't understand the policies and terms of a subsidy publisher's proposal or contract. Don't sign anything unless you understand and are comfortable with the terms. If you are willing to pay to have your book published, you should be willing to hire an attorney to advise you on a contract.

Subsidy publishers are sometimes called "vanity" presses because the company appeals to a writer's ego in wanting to have his book published. Most subsidy publishers are offended when they are called vanity presses, but we don't distinguish between the two. Any publishing effort that asks the writer to pay all or part of the cost is identified as a subsidy publisher. Companies that ask authors to pay subsidies on more than 50% of the books they publish each year are listed in *Writer's Market* at the end of the Book Publishers section.

This doesn't mean that subsidy publishing is always a bad choice. In Canada, for example, books are often subsidized by government grants. In the U.S., a special interest book may be subsidized by the writer's friends, a foundation or church. Sometimes a royalty publisher or university press will offer a subsidy arrangement to a writer whose talent outweighs the marketing potential of the book. Companies that do this 50% of the time or less are identified with an asterisk (*) before the listings.

Self-publishing

Self-publishing is another option for writers. The successful self-published book has a potential audience and fills a need not filled by current books on the topic. If you have submitted the manuscript to a publisher and had it rejected, you should analyze the reasons for rejection. If your manuscript needs polishing, do that before you self-publish it. If a large publisher determined that it would not generate enough sales, however, remember that books do not have to sell in the same quantities for a self-published book to make money as for a large publisher to profit.

Your consideration of self-publishing should include answering these questions. Are you willing to pay for a few hundred to several thousand copies of your book? Can you supervise all stages of its production? Do you have the time and energy to promote and distribute the book yourself?

Writers interested in self-publishing also may approach a small press publisher and agree to split the cost of a press run. Some companies also call themselves self-publishers and offer editorial services. More often, writers contract with a local printer to produce a specific number of books for a specific price.

As with subsidy publishing, be sure you know what's involved. "Done properly, self-publishing is an exciting and viable way to get your book into print," say Marilyn and Tom Ross, authors of *The Complete Guide to Self-Publishing* (Writer's Digest Books).

Selling your work

If you receive a number of rejections, don't give up. Many successful writers submit a manuscript to dozens of publishers before finding one to publish their book. An unsolicited manuscript sent to Atlantic-Little, Brown called *Blue Highways*, by William Least Heat Moon, has sold 250,000 in hardcover and 1 million in paperback since its 1983 release.

First, be sure you've done everything to improve your book's chances. Study writing and revision techniques and continue to study the markets. Many writers also find classes and writer's groups helpful in putting them in touch with other people who share their interest in writing.

No matter which method you choose, remember that the writing of the book comes first. Think of your book as a manuscript in transition and help it evolve into the best book it can be while you search for the best possible publisher.

For a list of publishers according to their subjects of interest, see the nonfiction and fiction sections of the Book Publishers Subject Index at the back of this book. Information on book publishers and packagers not included in *Writer's Market* can be found in Additional Book Publishers and Packagers at the end of the Book Packagers and Producers section.

AASLH PRESS, American Association for State and Local History, Suite 102, 172 2nd Ave. N., Nashville TN 37201. (615)255-2971. AASLH Press Director: Bob Summer. Publishes hardcover and softcover originals and reprints. Averages 6 titles/year; receives 20-30 submissions annually. 50% of books from first-time authors; 100% of books from unagented writers. Pays 5-10% royalty on retail price. Publishes book an average of 1 year after acceptance. Photocopied submissions OK. Computer printout submissions acceptable; prefers letter-quality. Reports in 3 months on submissions. Free book catalog.
Nonfiction: How-to, reference, self-help and textbook. "We publish books, mostly technical, that help people do effective work in historical societies, sites and museums, or do research in, or teach, history. No manuscripts on history itself—that is, on the history of specific places, events, people." Submit outline/synopsis and sample chapters. Reviews artwork/photos.
Recent Nonfiction Title: *The Care of Prints and Drawings*, by Margaret Holben Ellis (art conservation manual).
Tips: "Explain why our market will buy your book, use it, need it. The emphasis is on materials that can be practically utilized by historic preservationists."

ABBEY PRESS, Publishing Division, St. Meinrad IN 47577. (812)357-8011. Publisher: Keith McClellan O.S.B. Publishes mass market paperback originals. Averages 10 titles/year. Receives 200 submissions/year. 40% of books from first-time authors; 100% of books from unagented writers. Pays 10% royalty on retail price. Publishes book an average of 1 year after acceptance. Photocopied submissions OK. Computer printout submissions OK; prefers letter-quality. Reports in 1 month on queries; 6 weeks on mss. Ms guidelines for SASE.
Nonfiction: Subjects include psychology and religion. Especially looking for "manuscripts on marriage and family life, with specific attention to ways to enrich, support, and strengthen them through spiritual growth,

communication, counseling, etc. No manuscripts with an anti-religious or anti-Christian bias." Query with outline/synopsis and sample chapters.

Recent Nonfiction Title: *Friends of Loss*, by Jane Taylor.

Fiction: All fiction must have religious values underlying the story. Will consider adventure, ethnic, historical, mystery, religious. "We're looking for religious fiction that gives evidence of human and spiritual values within life; generally, values should be implied and subtle. We do not want to see fiction that is filled with preaching and scripture quotes that do not flow naturally from the storyline. We seek religious fiction that helps the reader to discover or be awakened to religious experience in the midst of ordinary life." Query with outline/synopsis and sample chapters.

Recent Fiction Title: *Tell Them, Such is God*, by Rose Mathias (ethnic/religious).

Tips: "Our audience includes Christian women and married couples who believe in the traditional family and are working to enrich their own marital and family relationships. These Christians, however, are not necessarily 'activists.' Religious titles as well as self-help continue to do well for us."

ABBOTT, LANGER & ASSOCIATES, 548 1st St., Crete IL 60417. (312)672-4200. President: Dr. Steven Langer. Small press. Publishes trade paperback originals and loose-leaf books. Averages 14 titles/year; receives 25 submissions annually. 15% of books from first-time authors; 100% of books from unagented writers. Pays 10-15% royalty; no advance. Publishes book an average of 1 year after acceptance. Photocopied submissions OK. Query for electronic submissions. Computer printout submissions OK. Book catalog for 6x9 SAE with 2 first class stamps. Reports in 2 weeks on queries; 2 months on mss.

Nonfiction: How-to, reference, technical on some phase of personnel administration, industrial relations, sales management, etc. Especially needs "a very limited number (3-5) of books dealing with very specialized topics in the field of personnel management, wage and salary administration, sales compensation, training, recruitment, selection, labor relations, etc." Publishes for personnel directors, wage and salary administrators, training directors, sales/marketing managers, security directors, etc. Query with outline. Reviews artwork/photos.

Recent Nonfiction Title: *Available Pay Survey Reports*, by S. Langer (annotated bibliography).

Tips: "A how-to book in personnel management, sales/marketing management or security management has the best chance of selling to our firm."

‡ABC-CLIO, INC., Suite 300, 180 Cook St., Denver, CO 80206. (303)333-3003. Subsidiaries include ISIS, Clio Press, Ltd. Vice President: Heather Cameron. Publishes hardcover originals. Firm averages 35 titles/year. Receives 250 submissions/year. 50% of books from first-time authors; 95% from unagented writers. Pays royalty on list price. Publishes ms an average of 8 months after acceptance. Simultaneous and photocopied submissions OK. Query for electronic submissions. Computer printout submissions OK; prefers letter-quality. Reports in 3 weeks on queries; 1 month on mss. Free book catalog and manuscript guidelines.

Nonfiction: How-to, reference and self-help. Subjects include art/architecture, education, government/politics, history, military/war, religion, sociology, translation, women's issues/studies. "Looking for reference books on/for older adults, current world issues, teen issues, women's issues, and for high school social studies curriculum. No monographs or textbooks." Query or submit outline/synopsis and sample chapters.

Recent Nonfiction Title: *Adult Literacy/Illiteracy in the United States*, by Marie Costa (general reference).

Tips: "If I were a writer trying to market a book today I would search the competition, keep abreast of trends and research appropriate publishers for manuscripts solicited."

ABINGDON PRESS, 201 8th Ave. S., Box 801, Nashville TN 37202. (615)749-6403. Vice President/Editorial Director: Ronald P. Patterson. Senior Editor Trade Books: Michael E. Lawrence. Senior Editor Reference/Academic Books: Davis Perkins. Editor Church Resources: Peggy Augustine. Children's Books Editor: Etta Wilson. Publishes paperback originals and reprints; church supplies. Receives approximately 2,500 submissions annually. Published 100 titles last year. Few books from first-time authors; 90-95% of books from unagented writers. Average print order for a writer's first book is 4,000-5,000. Pays royalty. Publishes book an average of 18 months after acceptance. Query for electronic submissions. Computer printout submissions acceptable; prefers letter-quality. Ms guidelines for SASE. Reports in 6 weeks.

Nonfiction: Religious-lay and professional, children's religious books and academic texts. Length: 32-300 pages. Query with outline and samples only. Reviews artwork/photos.

Recent Nonfiction Title: *Raising PG Kids in an X-Rated Society*, by Tipper Gore.

Fiction: Juveniles only. Reviews artwork/photos.

Recent Fiction Title: *Night Pleas*, by Martin Bell.

 The double dagger before a listing indicates that the listing is new in this edition. New markets are often the most receptive to freelance submissions.

‡HARRY N. ABRAMS, INC., Subsidiary of Times Mirror Co. 100 5th Ave., New York NY 10011. (212)206-7715. President, Publisher and Editor-in-Chief: Paul Gottlieb. Publishes hardcover and "a few" paperback originals. Averages 65 titles/year; receives "thousands" of submissions annually. 5% of books from first-time authors; 25% of books from unagented writers. "We are one of the few publishers who publish almost exclusively illustrated books. We consider ourselves the leading publishers of art books and high-quality artwork in the U.S." Offers variable advance. Publishes book an average of 1-2 years after acceptance. Photocopied submissions OK. Computer printout submissions acceptable; no dot-matrix. Reports in 3 months. Free book catalog.

Nonfiction: Art, nature and science, and outdoor recreation. Needs illustrated books for art and art history, museums. Submit outline/synopsis and sample chapters and illustrations. Reviews artwork/photos as part of ms package.

Recent Nonfiction Title: *Renoir, His Life, Art, and Letters*, by Barbara Ehrlich White.

Tips: "We publish *only* high-quality illustrated art books, i.e., art, art history, museum exhibition catalog, written by specialists and scholars in the field. Once the author has signed a contract to write a book for our firm the author must finish the manuscript to agreed-upon high standards within the schedule agreed upon in the contract."

ACADEMY CHICAGO, 213 W. Institute Place, Chicago IL 60610. (312)644-1723. Editorial Director/Senior Editor: Anita Miller. Publishes hardcover and paperback originals and reprints. Averages 60 titles/year; receives approximately 2000 submissions annually. 10% of books from first-time authors; 25% of books from unagented writers. Average print order for a writer's first book 1,500-3,500. Pays 7-10% royalty; no advance. Publishes book an average of 18 months after acceptance. Photocopied submissions OK; no simultaneous submissions. No computer printout submissions. Book catalog for 8½x11 SAE with 3 first class stamps; guidelines for #10 SAE with 1 first class stamp. Submit cover letter with first four chapters. Reports in 2 months.

Nonfiction: Adult, travel, and historical. No how-to, cookbooks, self-help, etc. Query and submit first four consecutive chapters. Reviews artwork/photos.

Recent Nonfiction Title: *Before & After Zachariah*, by Fran Kupfer.

Fiction: "Mysteries, mainstream novels." No "romantic," children's, young adult, religious or sexist fiction; nothing avant-garde.

Recent Fiction Title: *Loose Connection*, by Sybil Claiborne.

Tips: "The writer has the best chance of selling our firm a good mystery, because the response to these is predictable, relatively."

ACCELERATED DEVELOPMENT INC., 3400 Kilgore Ave., Muncie IN 47304. (317)284-7511. President: Dr. Joseph W. Hollis. Executive Vice President: Marcella Hollis. Publishes textbooks/paperback originals and software. Averages 10-15 titles/year; receives 170 submissions annually. 50% of books from first-time authors; 100% of books from unagented writers. Query for electronic submissions. Computer printout submissions acceptable; prefers letter-quality. Pays 6-15% royalty on net price. Publishes book an average of 1 year after acceptance. Reports in 3 months. Book catalog for 9x12 SAE with 3 first class stamps.

Nonfiction: Reference books and textbooks on psychology, counseling, guidance and counseling, teacher education and death education. Especially needs "psychologically-based textbook or reference materials, death education material, theories of counseling psychology, techniques of counseling, and gerontological counseling." Publishes for professors, counselors, teachers, college and secondary students, psychologists, death educators, psychological therapists, and other health-service providers. "Write for the graduate level student." Submit outline/synopsis, 2 sample chapters, prospectus, and author's resume. Reviews artwork/photos.

Recent Nonfiction Title: *Preventing Adolescent Suicide*, by Dave Capuzzi and Larry Holden.

Tips: "Freelance writers should be aware of American Psychological Association style of preparing manuscripts."

ACCENT BOOKS, A division of Accent Publications, 12100 W. 6th Ave., Box 15337, Denver CO 80215. (303)988-5300. Executive Editor: Mary B. Nelson. Publishes evangelical Christian paperbacks, the majority of which are nonfiction. Averages 18-24 titles/year. 30% of books from first-time authors; 100% of books from unagented writers. Pays royalty on cover price. Publishes book an average of 9 months after acceptance. Computer printout submissions acceptable; no dot-matrix. Query or submit 3 sample chapters with a brief synopsis and chapter outline. Do not submit full ms unless requested. Reports in 9 weeks. Book catalog for 9x12 SAE with 2 first class stamps.

Recent Nonfiction Title: *Submission is for Husbands Too*, by Mark Littleton.

Fiction: "Fiction titles have strong evangelical message woven throughout plot and characters, and are either contemporary mystery/romance or frontier romance."

Recent Fiction Title: *Vow of Silence*, by B.J. Hoff.

Tips: "How-to books designed for personal application of Biblical truth and/or dealing with problems/solutions of philosophical, societal, and personal issues from a Biblical perspective have the best chance of selling to our firm. We also consider books for the professional and volunteer in church ministries."

ACE SCIENCE FICTION, The Berkley Publishing Group, 200 Madison Ave., New York NY 10016. (212)686-9820. Publishes paperback originals and reprints. Publishes 120 titles/year. Writer's guidelines for #10 SAE with 1 first class stamp.
Fiction: Science fiction and fantasy. Query with synopsis and first 3 chapters. Reports in 3 months.

ACROPOLIS BOOKS, LTD., Subsidiary of Colortone Press, 2400 17th St. NW, Washington DC 20009. (202)387-6805. Publisher: Alphons J. Hackl. Publishes hardcover and trade paperback originals. Averages 25 titles/year. Pays individually negotiated royalty. Publishes book an average of 7 months after acceptance. Query for electronic submissions. Computer printout submissions acceptable; prefers letter-quality. Reports in 2 months. Free book catalog.
Nonfiction: How-to, reference and self-help. Subjects include health, beauty/fashion and money management. "We will be looking for manuscripts dealing with fashion and beauty, and self development. Our audience includes general adult consumers, professional elementary school teachers and children." Submit outline/synopsis and sample chapters. Reviews artwork/photos as part of ms package.
Recent Nonfiction Title: *Earn College Credit for What You Know*, by Susan Simosko.

ACS PUBLICATIONS, INC., Box 16430, San Diego CA 92116-0430. (619)297-9203. Editorial Director: Maritha Pottenger. Small press. Publishes trade paperback originals and reprints. Averages 8 titles/year; receives 400 submissions annually. 50% of books from first-time authors; 95% of books from unagented writers. Average print order for a writer's first book is 3,000. Pays 15% royalty "on monies received through wholesale and retail sales." No advance. Publishes book an average of 2 years after acceptance. Photocopied submissions OK "if neat." Query for electronic submissions. Computer printout submissions acceptable; prefers letter-quality. Reports in 1 month on queries; 2 months on mss. Book catalog and guidelines for 9x12 SAE with 3 first class stamps.
Nonfiction: Astrology and New Age. Subjects include astrology, holistic health alternatives, channeled books, numerology, and psychic understanding. "Our most important market is astrology. We are seeking pragmatic, useful, immediately applicable contributions to field; prefer psychological approach. Specific ideas and topics should enhance people's lives. Research also valued. No determinism ('Saturn made me do it.') No autobiographies. No airy-fairy 'space cadet' philosophizing. Keep it grounded, useful, opening options (not closing doors) for readers." Query or submit outline and 3 sample chapters.
Recent Nonfiction Title: *Spirit Guides*, by Iris Belhayes.
Tips: "We are more interested in channeled books due to current metaphysical focus. The most common mistake writers make when trying to get their work published is to send works to inappropriate publishers. We get too many submissions outside our field or contrary to our world view."

BOB ADAMS, INC., 840 Summer St., Boston MA 02127. (617)268-9570. Managing Editor: Brandon Toropov. Publishes hardcover and trade paperback originals. Averages 7 titles/year. Receives 25 submissions/year. 25% of books from first-time authors; 25% of books from unagented writers. Variable royalty "determined on case-by-case basis." Publishes book an average of 12-18 months after acceptance. Computer printout submissions OK; prefers letter-quality. Reports in 6 months "if interested. We accept no responsibility for unsolicited manuscripts." Book catalog for 9x12 SAE and $2.40 postage.
Nonfiction: Reference books on careers and business. Query.
Recent Nonfiction Title: *Layman's Guide to Legal Survival*, by David Saltman, George Wilgus.

ADDISON-WESLEY PUBLISHING CO., INC., General Books Division, Jacob Way, Reading MA 01867. Publisher: David Miller. Publishes hardcover and paperback originals. Publishes 45-50 titles/year. Pays royalty. Simultaneous and photocopied submissions OK. Reports in 1 month. Free book catalog.
Nonfiction: Biography, history, business/economics, health, how-to, politics, psychology and science. Query, then submit outline/synopsis and 1 sample chapter.
Recent Nonfiction Title: *Who Got Einstein's Office? Eccentricity and Genius at the Institute for Advanced Study*, by Ed Regis.
Tips: "We will accept submissions for cookbooks, computer books and general nonfiction." Queries/mss may be routed to other editors in the publishing group.

*AEGINA PRESS, INC., 59 Oak Lane, Spring Valley, Huntington WV 25704. (304)429-7204. Subsidiaries include University Editions. Managing Editor: Ira Herman. Publishes trade paperback originals and reprints. Publishes approximately 20 titles per year; receives 200 submissions per year. Buys 50% of books from first-time authors; 95% from unagented writers. Subsidy publishes 40% of books. "If the manuscripts meets our quality standards but is financially high risk, self-publishing through the University Editions imprint is offered. All sales proceeds go to the author until the subsidy is repaid. The author receives a 40% royalty thereafter. Remaining unsold copies belong to the author." Pays 15% royalty on net sales. Publishes book an average of 6 months after acceptance. Simultaneous and photocopied submissions OK. Query for electronic submissions. Computer printout submissions OK; prefers letter-quality. Reports in 2 weeks on queries; 1 months on ms.

Book catalog for 9x12 SAE with 4 first class stamps; ms guidelines for #10 SASE.

Nonfiction: Biography, how-to, humor, general nonfiction. Subjects include ethnic, health/medicine, regional (local histories), travel guides. "No racist, sexist or hate materials." Query or submit outline/synopsis and sample chapters, or complete ms. Reviews artwork/photos as part of ms package.

Recent Nonfiction Title: *Unbeatable Bessie*, by Elinor C. Kyte.

Fiction: Adventure, experimental, fantasy, historical, horror, humor, juvenile, literary, mainstream/contemporary, mystery, science fiction, short story collections, young adult. Query or submit outline/synopsis and sample chapters or complete ms.

Recent Fiction Title: *The Fretful Dancer*, by Eric Maisel.

Poetry: Submit 4-6 samples or complete ms.

Recent Poetry Title: *Field of Vision*, by Kirk Judd.

Tips: "If I were a writer trying to market a book today, I would vigorously try the small presses. Too many new writers give up after being rejected by the large publishers."

AGLOW PUBLICATIONS, A ministry of Women's Aglow Fellowship International, Box 1548, Lynnwood WA 98046-1557. (206)775-7282. Editor: Gwen Weising. Publishes trade paperback originals. Averages 10 titles/year; receives 1,000 submissions annually. 50% of books from first-time authors; 95% of books from unagented writers. Average print order of a writer's first book is 10,000. Pays up to 7½% maximum royalty on retail price "depending on amount of editorial work needed"; buys some mss outright. Publishes book 18 months after acceptance. Photocopied submissions OK. Computer printout submissions acceptable; prefers letter-quality. Reports in 1 month on queries; 2 months on mss. Book catalog and guidelines for 9x12 SAE with 3 first class stamps.

Nonfiction: Bible studies, self-help and inspirational. Subjects include religion (Christian only). "Familiarize yourself with our materials before submitting. Our needs and formats are very specific." Query or submit outline/synopsis and first 3 sample chapters.

Recent Nonfiction Title: *Ordinary Women, Extraordinary Strength*, by Barbara Cook.

Tips: "The writer has the best chance of selling our firm a book that shows some aspect of the Christian life."

AHSAHTA PRESS, Boise State University, Dept. of English, 1910 University Dr., Boise ID 83725. (208)385-1246. Co-Editor: Tom Trusky. Small press. Publishes trade paperback originals. Averages 3 titles/year; receives 500 submissions annually. 75% of books from first-time authors; 75% of books from unagented writers. Pays 25% royalty on retail price. "Royalty commences with third printing." Publishes books an average of 8 months after acceptance. Simultaneous and photocopied submissions OK. Computer printout submissions acceptable; prefers letter-quality. Reports in 2 weeks on queries; 3 months on mss. Book catalog and ms guidelines for 9x12 SASE.

Poetry: Contemporary Western American (cultural, ecological or historical) poetry collections only. No "rhymed verse, songs of the sage, buckaroo ballads, purple mountain's majesty, coyote wisdom; Jesus-in-the-prairie, or 'nice' verse." Accepts poetry translations from Native American languages, Spanish and Basque. Submit 15 samples between February and April. "Write incredible, original poetry."

Recent Poetry Title: *Westering*, by Thomas Hornsby Ferril (poetry).

‡ALA BOOKS, 50 East Huron St., Chicago IL 60657. (312)944-6780. Subsidiary of American Library Association. Senior Editor: Herbert Bloom. Publishes hardcover and paperback originals. Firm averages 26-30 titles/year. Receives 100-150 submissions/year. 90% of books from first-time authors; 100% from unagented writers. Pays royalty of "not more than 20% of our receipts from sales." Publishes ms an average of 7 months after acceptance. High resolution computer printout submissions OK; no dot-matrix. Reports in 2 weeks on queries; 2 months on mss. Book catalog for $3; ms guidelines free.

Nonfiction: Reference. Subjects include library science, child and adult reading guidance, education, library service. "We are looking for management of information centers generally; and application of electronic technologies to such management particularly. We also need reference works useful for satisfying library patrons' information needs." Query.

Recent Nonfiction Title: *Storytimes for 2-Year-Olds*, by Nichols (educational aid).

Tips: "If I were a writer trying to market a book today, I would make sure the first page says what I'm going to say in clear, direct English."

*ALASKA NATURE PRESS, Box 632, Eagle River AK 99577. Editor/Publisher: Ben Guild. Publishes hardcover and paperback originals. Plans to offer subsidy publishing "as needed—estimated 10%." Averages 2-6 titles/year. 75-80% of books from first-time authors; 100% of books from unagented writers. Pays 10% royalty on retail price; no advance. Publishes book 24-30 months after acceptance. Simultaneous and photocopied submissions OK. Computer printout submissions acceptable; prefers letter-quality. Reports in 4 months.

Nonfiction: Alaska material only: animals, biography, history, how-to, juveniles, nature, photography, poetry, recreation, wildlife and self-help. No hunting or fishing tales. Query or submit outline/synopsis and 2-3 sample chapters or complete ms. Reviews artwork/photos as part of ms package. "As a specialty publishing house (we take *only* Alaskans' material) the work *must* have an impact on Alaska or people interested in Alaska—for Alaska."

Recent Nonfiction Title: *The Fool-Proof-Four-Edible Wild Mushrooms* (nature/field guide).

Fiction: Alaska material only—*adventure*, *historical*, romance and suspense. Query editor/publisher. Reports in 4 months.

Recent Fiction Title: *The Man Who Shot Dan McGrew*, by Rasmussen.

Tips: "We need juvenile reading (ages 10-16) not 'cutesy' children stories. Deplore anthropomorphism of wild animals—'Bambi' is dead."

ALASKA NORTHWEST PUBLISHING, 130 Second Ave. S., Edmonds WA 98020. Editor/Publisher: Robert A. Henning. Publishes primarily paperback originals. Averages 12 titles/year; receives 250 submissions annually. 80% of books from first-time authors; 95% of books from unagented writers. Most contracts call for 10% royalty. "Rejections are made promptly, unless we have three or four possibilities in the same general field, and it's a matter of which one gets the decision. That could take three months." Publishes book an average of 2 years after acceptance. Computer printout submissions acceptable; prefers letter-quality; must be double-spaced. Book catalog and writer's guidelines for SASE.

Nonfiction: "Alaska, northern British Columbia, the Yukon, Northwest Territories and northwest U.S. are our subject areas. Emphasis is on life in the last frontier, history, biography, cookbooks, travel, field guides and outdoor subjects. Writers must be familiar with the area first-hand. We listen to any ideas." Query with outline, sample chapters, and any relevant photographs. Reviews artwork/photos as part of ms package.

Recent Nonfiction Title: *Toklat, The Story of an Alaskan Grizzly Bear*, by Elma and Alfred G. Milotte.

Tips: "First-person nonfiction, preferably resource- but not development-oriented, and informal prose (well organized, syntax reasonably good) have the best chance of selling to our firm."

ALBA HOUSE, 2187 Victory Blvd., Staten Island, New York NY 10314. (212)761-0047. Editor-in-Chief: Anthony L. Chenevey. Publishes hardcover and paperback originals and reprints. Specializes in religious books. "We publish shorter editions than many publishers in our field." Averages 15 titles/year; receives 1,000 submissions annually. 50% of books from first-time authors; 80% of books from unagented writers. Pays 10% royalty on retail price. Publishes book an average of 9 months after acceptance. Computer printout submissions acceptable; prefers letter-quality. Query. State availability of photos/illustrations. Simultaneous and photocopied submissions OK. Reports in 1 month. Book catalog and ms guidelines for SASE. Reviews artwork/photos.

Nonfiction: Publishes philosophy, psychology, religion, sociology, textbooks and Biblical books. Accepts nonfiction translations from French, German or Spanish. Submit outline/synopsis and 1-2 sample chapters.

Tips: "We look to new authors." Queries/mss may be routed to other editors in the publishing group.

THE ALBAN INSTITUTE, INC., 4125 Nebraska Ave. NW, Washington DC 20016. (202)244-7320. Director of Publications: Celia A. Hahn. Small press. Publishes trade paperback originals. Averages 7 titles/year; receives 100 submissions annually. 100% of books from unagented writers. Pays 7% royalty on books; $50 on publication for 2- to 8-page articles relevant to congregational life—practical—ecumenical. Publishes book an average of 1 year after acceptance. Computer printout submissions acceptable. Reports in 2 months. Prefers queries. Book catalog and ms guidelines for 9x12 SAE and 3 first class stamps.

Nonfiction: Religious—focus on local congregation—ecumenical. Must be accessible to general reader. Research preferred. Needs mss on the task of the ordained leader in the congregation, the career path of the ordained leader in the congregation, problems and opportunities in congregational life, and ministry of the laity in the world and in the church. No sermons, devotional, children's titles, inspirational type or prayers. Query or submit outline/synopsis and sample chapters.

Recent Nonfiction Title: *The Inviting Church: A Study of New Member Assimilation*, by Roy M. Oswald and Speed B. Leas.

Tips: "Our audience is intelligent, probably liberal mainline Protestant and Catholic clergy and lay leaders, executives and seminary administration/faculty—people who are concerned with the local church at a practical level and new approaches to its ministry. We ar looking for titles on the ministry of the laity and how the church can empower it."

ALWAYS submit manuscripts or queries with a self-addressed, stamped envelope (SASE) within your country or International Reply Coupons (IRC) purchased from the post office for other countries.

ALMAR PRESS, 4105 Marietta Dr., Binghamton NY 13903. (607)722-0265. Editor-in-Chief: A.N. Weiner. Managing Editor: M.F. Weiner. Publishes hardcover and paperback originals and reprints. Averages 8 titles/ year; receives 200 submissions annually. 75% of books from first-time authors; 100% of books from unagented writers. Average print order for a writer's first book is 2,000. Pays 10% royalty; no advance. Publishes book an average of 3 months after acceptance. Prefers exclusive submissions; however, simultaneous (if so indicated) and photocopied submissions OK. Query for electronic submissions. Computer printout submissions acceptable; prefers letter-quality. Reports in 1 month. Book catalog for 8½x11 SAE with 3 first class stamps. "*Submissions must include SASE for reply and return of manuscript.*"
Nonfiction: Publishes business, technical, regional and consumer books and reports. "These main subjects include general business, financial, travel, career, technology, personal help, North-East regional, hobbies, general medical, general legal, and how-to. *Almar Reports* are business and technology subjects published for management use and prepared in 8½x11 and book format. Publications are printed and bound in soft covers as required. Reprint publications represent a new aspect of our business." Submit outline/synopsis and sample chapters. Reviews artwork/photos as part of ms package. Looks for information in the proposed book that makes it different or unusual enough to attract book buyers. Reviews artwork/photos.
Recent Nonfiction Title: *A Postcard History of New York's Elmira, Corning and Vicinity.*
Tips: "We're adding an area of North-East regional books—this type of book will be important to us. We look for timely subjects. The type of book the writer has the best chance of selling to our firm is something different or unusual—*no* poetry or fiction, also *no* first-person travel or family history. The book must be complete and of good quality."

*ALPHA PUBLISHING COMPANY, Division of Special Edition, Inc., 3497 E. Livingston Ave., Columbus OH 43227. (614)231-4088. Publisher: Dr. Y. Hayon. Small press. Publishes hardcover and trade paper originals. Averages 6 titles/year. Subsidy publishes 30% of books. Decision made to subsidy publish "depending on anticipated sales." Pays 10-25% royalty on wholesale price. Simultaneous and photocopied submissions OK. Reports on queries in 2 weeks. Book catalog for SASE.
Nonfiction: Biography, how-to, reference, technical and textbook. Subjects include history, philosophy, religion, sociology and Judaica. Seeking Hebraica, Judaica, Christianity books. Query.
Recent Nonfiction Title: *Weddings: A Complete Guide to All Religious and Interfaith Marriage Services*, by Abraham Klausner (reference on weddings).

*ALPINE PUBLICATIONS, INC., 2456 E. 9th St., Loveland CO 80537. (303)667-2017. Publisher: B.J. McKinney. Publishes hardcover and trade paperback originals. Averages 12 titles/year. Subsidy publishes 2% of books when "book fits into our line but has a market so limited (e.g., rare dog breed) that we would not accept it on royalty terms." No advance. Pays 7-15% royalty. Publishes book an average of 1½ years after acceptance. Computer printout submissions OK; prefers letter-quality. Reports in 3 weeks on queries; 2 months on mss. Writer's guidelines for #9 SAE with 2 first class stamps.
Nonfiction: How-to books about animals. "We need comprehensive breed books on the more popular AKC breeds, books for breeders on showing, breeding, genetics, gait, new training methods, and cat and horse books. No fiction or fictionalized stories of real animals; no books on reptiles; no personal experience stories except in case of well-known professional in field." Submit outline/synopsis and sample chapters or complete ms. Reviews artwork/photos as part of manuscript package.
Recent Nonfiction Title: *Retriever Puppy Training*, by Rutherford.
Tips: "We are initiating a new division, Life Source, which will publish books for Christians in the workplace. We are looking for books with an evangelical Christian perspective, examining such topics as personnel management, business management, entrepreneurship, the Christian employee, etc. Writers should have experience in their field; and be able to provide a neat, easy to read ms with samples of high quality photos and illustrations to be included in text."

*ALYSON PUBLICATIONS, INC., 40 Plympton St., Boston MA 02118. (617)542-5679. Publisher: Sasha Alyson. Small press. Publishes trade paperback originals and reprints. Averages 20 titles/year; receives 500 submissions annually. 50% of books from first-time authors; 80% of books from unagented writers. Average print order for a writer's first book is 6,000. Subsidy publishes 5% of books. Pays 8-15% royalty on net price; buys some mss outright for $200-1,000; offers $500-1,000 advance. Publishes book an average of 15 months after acceptance. Computer printout submissions acceptable; no dot-matrix. Reports in 2 weeks on queries; 5 weeks on mss. Looks for "writing ability and content suitable for our house." Book catalog and ms guidelines for #10 SAE and 3 first class stamps.
Nonfiction: Gay/lesbian subjects. "We are especially interested in nonfiction providing a positive approach to gay/lesbian issues." Accepts nonfiction translations. Submit one-page synopsis. Reviews artwork/photos as part of ms package.
Recent Nonfiction Title: *Long Time Passing: Lives of Older Lesbians*, by Marcy Adelman, Ph.D.
Fiction: Gay novels. Accepts fiction translations. Submit one-page synopsis.
Recent Fiction Title: *Goldenboy*, by Michael Nava.

Tips: "We publish many books by new authors. The writer has the best chance of selling to our firm well-researched, popularly-written nonfiction on a subject (e.g., some aspect of gay history) that has not yet been written about much. With fiction, create a strong storyline that makes the reader want to find out what happens. With nonfiction, write in a popular style for a non-academic audience."

AMERICAN ASTRONAUTICAL SOCIETY, (Univelt, Inc., Publisher), Box 28130, San Diego CA 92128. (619)746-4005. Editorial Director: H. Jacobs. Publishes hardcover originals. Averages 8 titles/year; receives 12-15 submissions annually. 5% of books from first-time authors; 5% of books from unagented writers. Average print order for a writer's first book is 600-2,000. Pays 10% royalty on actual sales; no advance. Publishes book an average of 4 months after acceptance. Simultaneous and photocopied submissions OK. Computer printout submissions acceptable; prefers letter-quality. Reports in 1 month. Book catalog and ms guidelines for 9x12 SAE and 3 first class stamps.
Nonfiction: Proceedings or monographs in the field of astronautics, including applications of aerospace technology to Earth's problems. "Our books must be space-oriented or space-related. They are meant for technical libraries, research establishments and the aerospace industry worldwide." Submit outline/synopsis and 1-2 sample chapters. Reviews artwork/photos as part of ms package.
Recent Nonfiction Title: *Soviet Space Programs 1980-1985*, by N.L. Johnson.

*AMERICAN ATHEIST PRESS, American Atheists, Box 2117, Austin TX 78768-2117. (512)458-1244. Editor: R. Murray-O'Hair. Small press. Imprints include Gusttav Broukal Press. Publishes trade paperback originals and trade paperback reprints. Averages 12 titles/year; receives 200 submissions annually. 40-50% of books from first-time authors; 100% of books from unagented writers. Pays 5-10% royalty on retail price. Publishes book an average of 1 year after acceptance. Simultaneous and photocopied submissions OK. Computer printout submissions acceptable; prefers letter-quality. Reports in 6 weeks on queries; 3 months on submissions. Book catalog for 6½x9½ SAE; writer's guidelines for 9x12 SAE.
Nonfiction: Biography, humor, reference and general. Subjects include history (of religion and Atheism, of the effects of religion historically); philosophy and religion (from an Atheist perspective, particularly criticism of religion); politics (separation of state and church, religion and politics); Atheism (particularly the lifestyle of Atheism; the history of Atheism; applications of Atheism). "We are interested in hard-hitting and original books expounding the lifestyle of Atheism and criticizing religion. We would like to see more submissions dealing with the histories of specific religious sects, such as the L.D.S., the Worldwide Church of God, etc. We are generally not interested in biblical criticism." Submit outline/synopsis and sample chapters or complete ms. Reviews artwork/photos.
Recent Nonfiction Title: *An Atheist Reports From India*, by Margaret Bhatty.
Fiction: Humor (satire of religion or of current religious leaders); anything of particular interest to Atheists. "We rarely publish any fiction. But we have occasionally released a humorous book." No mainstream. "For our press to consider fiction, it would have to tie in with the general focus of our press, which is the promotion of Atheism and free thought." Submit outline/synopsis and sample chapters.
Tips: "We plan two new periodicals (start dates: 1989). This will enable us to publish a greater variety of material in regard to both length and content."

AMERICAN CATHOLIC PRESS, 1223 Rossell Ave., Oak Park IL 60302. (312)386-1366. Editorial Director: Father Michael Gilligan. Publishes hardcover originals and hardcover and paperback reprints. "Most of our sales are by direct mail, although we do work through retail outlets." Averages 4 titles/year. Pays by outright purchase of $25-100; no advance. Publishes book an average of 8 months after acceptance. Simultaneous and photocopied submissions OK. Computer printout submissions acceptable. Reports in 2 months.
Nonfiction: "We publish books on the Roman Catholic liturgy—for the most part, books on religious music and educational books and pamphlets. We also publish religious songs for church use, including Psalms, as well as choral and instrumental arrangements. We are interested in new music, meant for use in church services. Books, or even pamphlets, on the Roman Catholic Mass are especially welcome. We have no interest in secular topics and are not interested in religious poetry of any kind." Query.
Recent Nonfiction Title: *The Role of Music in the New Roman Liturgy*, by W. Herring (educational).

‡AMERICAN HOSPITAL PUBLISHING, INC., American Hospital Association, 211 East Chicago Ave., Chicago IL 60611. (312)440-6800. Vice President, Books: Brian Schenk. Publishes trade paperback originals. Firm averages 20-30 titles/year. Receives 75-100 submissions/year. 20% of books from first-time authors; 100% from unagented writers. Pays 10-12% royalty on retail price. Offers $1,000 average advance. Publishes book an average of 1 year after acceptance. Computer printout submissions OK; prefers letter-quality. Reports in 1 month on queries; 6 weeks on mss. Book catalog and manuscript guidelines for #10 SASE.
Nonfiction: Reference, technical, textbook. Subjects include business and economics (specific to health care institutions); health/medicine (never consumer oriented). Need field based, reality-tested responses to changes in the health care field directed to hospital CEO's, planners, boards of directors, or other senior management. No personal histories; untested health care programs or clinical texts. Query.

Recent Nonfiction Title: *New Business Development in Ambulatory Care: Exploring Diversification Options*, by Diane Howard, ed.
Tips: "The successful proposal demonstrates a clear understanding of the needs of the market and the writer's ability to succinctly present practical knowledge of demonstrable benefit that comes from genuine experience that readers will recognize, trust and accept. The audience is senior and middle management of health care institutions."

THE AMERICAN PSYCHIATRIC PRESS, INC. (associated with the American Psychiatric Association), 1400 K St. NW, Washington DC 20005. (202)682-6268. Editor-in-Chief: Carol C. Nadelson, M.D. Publishes hardcover and trade paperback originals. Averages 40 titles/year, 2-4 trade books/year; receives about 300 submissions annually. About 10% of books from first-time authors; 95% of books from unagented writers. Pays 10% minimum royalty based on all money actually received, maximum varies; offers average $3,000-5,000 advance. Publishes book an average of 9 months after acceptance. Simultaneous and photocopied submissions OK (if made clear in cover letter). Query for electronic submissions. Computer printout submissions acceptable; no dot-matrix. Reports in 6 weeks "in regard to an *initial* decision regarding our interest. A *final* decision requires more time." Ms guidelines for SASE.
Nonfiction: Reference, self-help, technical, textbook and general nonfiction. Subjects include psychology/psychiatry and related subjects. Authors must be well qualified in their subject area. No first-person accounts of mental illness or anything not clearly related to psychiatry. Query with outline/synopsis and sample chapters.
Recent Nonfiction Title: *Cocaine*, by Roger D. Weiss, M.D., and Steven M. Mirin, M.D.
Tips: "Because we are a specialty publishing company, books written by or in collaboration with a psychiatrist have the best chance of acceptance. Make it authoritative and professional."

AMERICAN REFERENCES INC., 919 N. Michigan, Chicago IL 60611. (312)951-6200. President: Les Krantz. Publishes hardcover and trade paperback originals. Averages 4-10 titles/year. Payment negotiable. Simultaneous and photocopied submissions OK. Reports in 6 weeks on queries.
Nonfiction: Illustrations and reference. Subjects include art and photography.
Recent Nonfiction Title: *The New York Art Review*, 1982, 2nd ed.

AMERICAN STUDIES PRESS, INC., 13511 Palmwood Lane, Tampa FL 33624. (813)961-7200 or 974-2857. Imprints include ASP Books, Rattlesnake Books, Harvest Books and Marilu Books (Marilu imprint includes Herland—poems by women about women—and Woman). Editor-in-Chief: Donald R. Harkness. Small press. Publishes trade paperback originals. Receives 250-300 submissions/year. 80% of books from first-time authors. 100% of books from unagented writers. Averages 6 titles/year. Pays 10 copies plus 10% royalty on retail price after printing cost is met. Publishes book an average of 6 months after acceptance. Computer printout submissions OK; prefers letter-quality. Reports in 2 weeks on queries; 2 months on mss. Book list for #10 SASE.
Nonfiction: Biography, humor and illustrated book. Subjects include Americana, business and economics, history, politics, psychology, sports and travel. "I might consider a book of generalized family history, of interest to an audience wider than the immediate circle of relatives." Query or submit outline/synopsis and sample chapters or complete ms. Reviews artwork/photos as part of ms package.
Recent Nonfiction Title: *A Boy Grows in Brooklyn*, by William M. Firshing (autobiography).
Poetry: Submit 6 poems from a unified book or submit complete ms.
Recent Poetry Title: *Poetica Erotica*, by Normajean MacLeod.
Tips: "Our audience is intelligent and appreciative college graduates, not taken in by the slick and fancy package but more concerned with content. Good poetry, or satire—that's what I like best. Please don't send a bulky ms without advance query (with SASE, of course)."

ANCESTRY INCORPORATED, Box 476, Salt Lake City UT 84110. (801)531-1790. Managing Editor: Robert J. Welsh. Publishes hardcover and mass market paperback originals. Averages 10 titles/year; receives 10-20 submissions annually. 70% of books from first-time authors; 100% of books from unagented writers. Pays 8-12% royalty or purchases mss outright. Advances are discouraged but considered if necessary. Publishes book an average of 1 year after acceptance. Simultaneous and photocopied submissions OK. Query for electronic submissions. Computer printout submissions acceptable. Reports in 1 month on queries; 2 months on mss. Free book catalog and ms guidelines.
Nonfiction: How-to, reference, and genealogy. Subjects include Americana; history (family and local); and hobbies (genealogy). "Our publications are aimed exclusively at the genealogist. We consider everything from short monographs to book length works on immigration, migration, record collections, etc. Good local histories and heraldic topics are considered." No mss that are not genealogical or historical. Query, or submit outline/synopsis and sample chapters, or complete ms. Reviews artwork/photos.
Recent Nonfiction Title: *The Archives: A Guide to the National Archives Field Branches*, by Loretto Szucs and Sandra Luebking.

Tips: "Genealogical reference, how-to, and descriptions of source collections have the best chance of selling to our firm. Be precise in your description."

AND BOOKS, 702 S. Michigan, South Bend IN 46618. (219)219-3134. Editor: Janos Szebedinszky. Small press. Publishes trade paperback originals. Averages 10 titles/year. Receives 1,000 submissions/year. 50% of books from first-time authors. 90% of books from unagented writers. Pays 6-10% royalty on retail price. Simultaneous and photocopied submissions OK. Publishes book an average of 1 year after acceptance. Query for electronic submissions. Reports in 1½ months. Book catalog for #10 SASE.
Nonfiction: Cookbook, how-to, illustrated book and self-help. Subjects include health, music, nature, politics (current issues), recreation, travel and general adult nonfiction. Especially needs books on computers and the law and electronic publishing. No biography, financial planning, religious experience/inspirational works or diet books.
Recent Nonfiction Title: *Desktop Publishing With Style*, by Daniel Will-Harris.
Tips: "Attempt to get an intro or foreword by a well-known individual in the field about which you are writing, or some good review comments. A little preliminary legwork and market investigation can go a long way to influence a potential publisher."

*ANDERSON PUBLISHING CO., Box 1576, Cincinnati OH 45201-1576. (513)421-4142. Editorial Director: Dale Hartis. Publishes hardcover, paperback originals, journals and software and reprints. Publishes 13-15 titles/year. Subsidy publishes 10% of books. Pays 15-18% royalty; "advance in selected cases." Publishes book an average of 7 months after acceptance. Simultaneous and photocopied submissions OK. Computer printout submissions acceptable; prefers letter-quality. Reports in 2 months. Book catalog for 8½x11 SASE; guidelines for SASE.
Nonfiction: Law and law-related books, and criminal justice criminology texts (justice administration legal series). Query or submit outline/chapters with vitae.
Recent Nonfiction Title: *Economic Damages*, by Michael L. Brookshire, Ph.D. (law/economics).

ANDREWS AND McMEEL, 4900 Main St., Kansas City MO 64112. Editorial Director: Donna Martin. Publishes hardcover and paperback originals. Averages 30 titles/year. Pays royalty on retail price. "Query only. No unsolicited manuscripts. Areas of specialization include humor, how-to, and consumer reference books, such as *The Writer's Art* by James J. Kilpatrick, and *Roger Ebert's Movie Home Companion*."

‡ANDRION BOOKS, INC., 128 East 56th St., New York NY 10022. (212)408-1840. Editor: Jodie Browne. Firm publishes trade paperback originals. Publishes 5-10 books/year; receives 50 mss/year. 100% from first-time and unagented authors. Pays authors 6% maximum royalty on retail price. Advances varies (usually $500 against royalty). Publishes ms an average of 9 months after acceptance. Simultaneous and photocopied submissions OK. Computer printout submissions OK; no dot-matrix. Reports in 3 weeks on queries; in 3 months on mss. Free book catalog.
Nonfiction: How-to, humor, reference. "We are looking for all nonfiction subjects." Submit complete ms. Reviews artwork/photos as part of freelance package.
Recent Nonfiction Title: *Wolff & Byrd, Counselors of the Macabre*, by Batton Lash (comic strips).

‡APA PRODUCTIONS, 3 Gul Crescent, Singapore 2262. Imprints include Insight Guides, Apamaps. Editorial Manager: Vivien Kim. Publishes hardcover and trade paperback originals. Publishes 20 titles/year. Receives 100 submissions/year. "We assign books and parts of books, often to first-time book authors. We pay authors outright—$7,500 for editing a book, plus expenses; 15¢/word for writing." Publishes book an average of 10 months after assignment. Query for electronic submissions. Computer printout submissions OK; prefers letter-quality. Reports on queries in 1 month. No unsolicited mss. Book catalog and ms guidelines free on request (also see *Insight Guides*, distributed by Prentice-Hall for guidance).
Nonfiction: Travel guides. "We need writers, photographers and project editors for an enormous variety of city and country books." Query along with resume, clips and statement of area of expertise. Reviews artwork/photos as part of ms package.
Recent Nonfiction Title: *Germany*, by Vestner, et al (trade paper guidebook).
Tips: "We're embarking on an ambitious publishing program in the next two years to add to our list of travel titles."

APPALACHIAN MOUNTAIN CLUB BOOKS, 5 Joy St., Boston MA 02108. (617)523-0636. Editorial Director: Susan Cummings. Publishes hardcover and trade paperback originals. Averages 8 titles/year; receives 100 submissions annually. 50% of books from first-time authors; 90% of books from unagented writers. Pays 10% royalty on retail price; offers $1,000 advance. Publishes book 6 months after receipt of acceptable manuscript. Simultaneous and photocopied submissions OK. Query for electronic submissions. High quality computer printout submissions acceptable. Reports in 1 month on queries; 3 months on mss. Book catalog for 9x12 SAE.
Nonfiction: How-to, illustrated book, reference and guidebook. Subjects include history (Northeast, moun-

tains), nature, photography, outdoor recreation, and travel. "We want manuscripts about the environment, mountains and their history and culture, outdoor recreation (such as hiking, climbing, skiing, canoeing, kayaking, bicycling) and guidebooks and field guides. Relevant fiction will be considered, too." No physical fitness manuals. Query or submit outline/synopsis and sample chapters only. Reviews artwork/photos.

Recent Nonfiction Title: *Guide to Backcountry Skiing in New England*, by David Goodman.

Tips: "We are expanding into the southeast United States and travel outside the U.S. with basically the same interests as here in New England. We have also begun to publish children's books on outdoor recreation and nature."

THE AQUARIAN PRESS LTD., Denington Estate, Wellingborough, Northamptonshire NN8 2RQ England. Editor-in-Chief: Eileen Campbell. Hardcover and paperback originals. Averages 70-80 titles/year. Pays 7½-10% royalty. Photocopied submissions OK. Computer printout and disk submissions acceptable; prefers letter-quality. Reports in 1 month. Free book catalog.

Nonfiction: Publishes books on comparative religion, magic, metaphysics, mysticism, occultism, parapsychology and esoteric philosophy. "Crucible is an imprint of The Aquarian Press and publishes books written by experts for the lay reader on history, literature, religion, history of ideas and biography." Length: 30,000-100,000 words.

Tips: "We look for a clear indication that the author has thought about his market; a fundamental ability to *communicate* ideas—authority in combination with readability."

ARBOR HOUSE, Imprint of William Morrow, 105 Madison Ave., New York NY 10016. President and Publisher: Eden Collinsworth. Publishes hardcover and trade paperback originals and selected reprints. Averages 50-60 titles/year. Pays standard royalty; offers negotiable advance. Publishes book an average of 9 months after acceptance. Computer printout submissions acceptable; prefers letter-quality. Free book catalog.

Nonfiction: Autobiography, cookbook, how-to and self-help. Subjects include Americana (possibly), art (possibly), business and economics, cooking and foods, health, history, politics, psychology, recreation, inspiration and sports. Query first to "The Editors." Reviews artwork/photos as part of ms package.

Recent Nonfiction Title: *The Equilibrium Plan: Balancing Diet and Exercise*, by Sally Edwards.

Fiction: "Quality fiction—everything from romance to science fiction, fantasy, adventure and suspense." Query or submit outline/synopsis and sample chapters to "The Editors."

Recent Fiction Title: *Poison*, by Ed McBain.

Tips: "Freelance writers should be aware of a greater emphasis on agented properties and market resistance to untried fiction."

ARCHITECTURAL BOOK PUBLISHING CO., INC., 268 Dogwood Lane, Stamford CT 06903. (203)322-1460. Editor: Walter Frese. Averages 10 titles/year; receives 400 submissions annually. 80% of books from first-time authors; 95% of books from unagented writers. Average print order for a writer's first book is 5,000. Royalty is percentage of retail price. Publishes book an average of 10 months after acceptance. Computer printout submissions acceptable; no dot-matrix. Prefers queries, outlines and 2 sample chapters with number of illustrations. Reports in 2 weeks.

Nonfiction: Publishes architecture, decoration, and reference books on city planning and industrial arts. Accepts nonfiction translations. Also interested in history, biography, and science of architecture and decoration. Reviews artwork/photos.

ARCsoft PUBLISHERS, Box 132, Woodsboro MD 21798. (301)845-8856. Publisher: Anthony R. Curtis. Publishes trade paperback originals. Averages 20 titles/year. "We now offer only 'buyout' contracts in which all rights are purchased. Typically, an advance of 20 percent is paid at contract signing and 80 percent at acceptable completion of work. Royalties are no longer offered since writers suffer under royalty contracts for small-volume technical books." Offers variable advance. Publishes book an average of 6 months after acceptance. Computer printout submissions acceptable; no dot-matrix. Reports in 1 month on queries; 10 weeks on mss. Free book catalog.

Nonfiction: Technical. "We publish technical books including space science, desktop publishing, personal computers and hobby electronics, especially for beginners." Accepts nonfiction translations. Query or submit outline/synopsis and 1 sample chapter. Reviews artwork/photos as part of ms package.

Recent Nonfiction Title: *Space Satellite Handbook*, by A.R. Curtis.

Tips: "We look for the writer's ability to cover our desired subject thoroughly, writing quality and interest."

*M. ARMAN PUBLISHING, INC., 740 S. Ridgewood Ave., Ormond Beach FL 32074. (904)673-5576. Mailing address: Box 785, Ormond Beach FL 32074. Contact: Mike Arman. Publishes trade paperback originals, reprints and software. Averages 6-8 titles/year; receives 20 submissions annually. 20% of books from first-time authors; 100% of books from unagented writers. Average print order for a writer's first book is 2,500. Subsidy publishes 20% of books. Pays 10% royalty on wholesale price. No advance. Publishes book (on royalty basis) an average of 8 months after acceptance; 6 weeks on subsidy basis. Photocopied submissions OK. "We now set

type directly from author's disks. Our equipment can read many CPM 5¼ formats, and can read IBM disks if the file is ASCII." Computer printout submissions acceptable. Reports in 1 week on queries; 3 weeks on mss. Book catalog for #10 SAE with 1 first class stamp.
Nonfiction: How-to, reference, technical, and textbook. "Motorcycle and aircraft technical books only." Accepts nonfiction translations. Publishes for enthusiasts. Submit complete ms. Reviews artwork/photos as part of ms package.
Recent Nonfiction Title: *V-Twin Thunder*, by Carl McClanahan (motorcycle performance manual).
Fiction: "Motorcycle or aircraft-related only." Accepts fiction translations. Immediate needs are "slim," but not non-existent. Submit cover letter and complete ms.
Tips: "The type of book a writer has the best chance of selling to our firm is how-to fix motorcycles—specifically Harley-Davidsons. We have a strong, established market for these books."

ART DIRECTION BOOK COMPANY, 10 E. 39th St., 6th Floor, New York NY 10016. (212)889-6500. Editorial Director: Don Barron. Senior Editor: Loren Bliss. Publishes hardcover and paperback originals. Publishes 10 titles/year. Pays 10% royalty on retail price; offers average $1,000 advance. Publishes book an average of 1 year after acceptance. Photocopied submissions OK. Computer printout submissions acceptable; no dot-matrix. Reports in 3 months. Book catalog for 6x9 SAE.
Nonfiction: Commercial art, ad art how-to and textbooks. "We are interested in books for the professional advertising art field—that is, books for art directors, designers, etc.; also entry level books for commercial and advertising art students in such fields as typography, photography, paste-up, illustration, clip-art, design, layout and graphic arts." Query with outline/synopsis and 1 sample chapter. Reviews artwork/photos as part of ms package.
Recent Nonfiction Title: *American Corporate Identity #2*, by D.E. Carter.

ASHER-GALLANT PRESS, Division of Caddylak Systems, Inc., 60 Shames Dr., Westbury NY 11590. (516)333-7440. Editor-in-Chief: Sally Germain. Publishes softcover and loose-leaf format originals (sold mostly through direct marketing). Averages 20 titles/year; receives 150 submissions annually. 50% of books from first-time authors. 95% of books from unagented writers. "Many of our authors are first-time authors when they begin working with us, but write several subsequent books for us. Payment for each project is treated individually, but generally, the rights to smaller works (up to about 25,000 words) are purchased on a flat fee basis, and rights to larger works are purchased on a royalty basis." Advance varies by project. Publishes books an average of 6 months after acceptance. Simultaneous and photocopied submissions OK. Computer printout submissions acceptable; prefers letter-quality. Ms returned only if requested. "We prefer to keep a writer's sample on file for possible future assignments." Reports negative results in 2 weeks on queries; 1 month on mss. Free book catalog.
Nonfiction: How-to, reference, audio cassette programs and business directories. Subjects include business (general) and management topics. "We plan to do 35 to 40 new titles during the next two years. The list will consist of individual business titles, more technical management reports, and longer, more comprehensive books that will be published in binder format. All subject matter must be appropriate to our broad audience of middle-level corporate managers. No sensational, jazzy nonfiction without solid research behind it." Submit outline/synopsis and sample chapters.
Recent Nonfiction Title: *Words for Telemarketing*, by Steven R. Isaac.
Tips: "The deciding factors in whether or not we publish a certain book are: (1) we believe there will be a very sizeable demand for the book, (2) the outline we review is logically structured and very comprehensive, and (3) the sample chapters are concisely and clearly written and well-researched."

‡ASIAN HUMANITIES PRESS, Box 4177, Santa Clara CA 95054-0177. (408)727-3151. Editor: Lew Lancaster. Publishes hardcover originals, trade paperback originals and reprints. Firm averages 8 titles/year. Receives 25 submissions/year. 100% of books from unagented authors. Pays up to 5% royalty on retail price. Publishes book an average of 9 months after acceptance. Simultaneous and photocopied submissions OK. Query for electronic submissions. Computer printout submission OK; no dot-matrix. Reports on queries in 2 weeks; 2 months on mss. Book catalog free on request.
Nonfiction: Reference, textbook. Subjects include language/literature (Asian), philosophy (Asian and comparative), religion (Asian and comparative), translation (Asian religions, cultures and philosophy), women's issues/studies (Asian), humanities, spiritual. "We publish books pertaining to Asian religions, cultures and thought directed toward scholars, libraries and specialty bookstores." Submit complete ms. Reviews artwork/photos as part of ms package.
Recent Nonfiction Title: *Death Was His Koan: The Samurai Zen of Suzuki Shosan*, by Winston L. King (religion/philosophy).
Tips: "Scholars and general readers interested in Asian and comparative religions, cultures and philosophy are our audience."

*ASSOCIATED FACULTY PRESS, INC., 19 W. 36th St., New York NY 10018. (212)307-1300. President: Linda B. Cahill. Publishes hardcover originals and reprints. Averages 20-30 titles/year; receives 150 submissions annually. 30% of books from first-time authors; 95% of books from unagented writers. May subsidy publish, "but only after careful editorial review." Publishes book an average of 18 months after acceptance. Simultaneous submissions of proposal OK. Computer printout submissions acceptable; no dot-matrix. Reports in 1 month on queries; 3 months on mss. Book catalog for 9x12 SAE with 2 first class stamps.
Imprints: Kennikat (nonfiction reprints), National Universities Publications (nonfiction).
Nonfiction: Biography; reference; monographs; supplementary legal texts; business and economics; health-related (not medicine); history; modern literary criticism; politics (public administration); sociology; and law and criminal justice. "We are rather backed up for at least one full year. Do not submit manuscript without first sending proposal." No trade books or academic books in fields not indicated above. Query or submit academic vita, table of contents and proposal.
Recent Nonfiction Title: *Iranian Immigrants in the U.S.*, by Abdolmaboud Ansari.
Tips: "Our audience is college and university libraries, law libraries, scholars in fields listed above, and discriminating general readers. We are not trade publishers. In general, purely scholarly books are having a harder time of it."

ATHENEUM CHILDREN'S BOOKS, Macmillan, Inc., 866 3rd Ave., New York NY 10022. (212)702-7894. Editorial Director: Jonathan J. Lanman or editors Marcia Marshall and Gail Paris. Publishes hardcover originals. Averages 60 titles/year; receives 7,000-8,000 submissions annually. 8-12% of books from first-time authors; 50% of books from unagented writers. Pays 10-12½% royalty on retail price; offers average $2,000-3,000 advance. Publishes book an average of 18 months after acceptance. Photocopied submissions (outline and first 3 chapters only, please) OK. Computer printout submissions acceptable; prefers letter-quality. Reports in 2 weeks on queries; 4-6 weeks on outline and sample chapters. Book catalog and ms guidelines for 7x10 SAE and 2 first class stamps.
Nonfiction: Biography, how-to, humor, illustrated book, juvenile (pre-school through young adult) and self-help, all for juveniles. Subjects include: Americana, animals, art, business and economics, cooking and foods, health, history, hobbies, music, nature, philosophy, photography, politics, psychology, recreation, religion, sociology, sports, and travel, all for young readers. "Do remember, most publishers plan their lists as much as two years in advance. So if a topic is 'hot' right now, it may be 'old hat' by the time we could bring it out. It's better to steer clear of fads. Some writers assume juvenile books are for 'practice' until you get good enough to write adult books. Not so. Books for young readers demand just as much 'professionalism' in writing as adult books. So save those 'practice' manuscripts for class, or polish them before sending them." Query, submit outline/synopsis and sample chapters. Reviews artwork/photos as part of ms package; prefers photocopies of artwork.
Recent Nonfiction Title: *Dead Serious*, by Jane Mersky Leder (teenage suicide).
Fiction: Adventure, ethnic, experimental, fantasy, gothic, historical, horror, humor, mainstream, mystery, romance, science fiction, suspense, and western, all in juvenile versions. "We have few specific needs except for books that are fresh, interesting and well written. Again, fad topics are dangerous, as are works you haven't polished to the best of your ability. (The competition is fierce.) We've been inundated with dragon stories (misunderstood dragon befriends understanding child), unicorn stories (misunderstood child befriends understanding unicorn), and variations of 'Ignatz the Egg' (Everyone laughs at Ignatz the egg [giraffe/airplane/accountant] because he's square [short/purple/stupid] until he saves them from the eggbeater [lion/storm/I.R.S. man] and becomes a hero). Other things we don't need at this time are safety pamphlets, ABC books, and rhymed narratives. We have little need for children's poetry. In writing picture book texts, avoid the coy and 'cutesy.' " Query, submit outline/synopsis and sample chapters, or complete ms.
Recent Fiction Title: *The Return*, by Sonia Levitin (young adult novel).
Poetry: "At this time there is *very* little market for children's poetry. We don't anticipate needing any for the next year or two, especially rhymed narratives."
Tips: "Our books are aimed at children from pre-school age, up through high school. Our young adult novels and much of our science fiction and fantasy also cross over into adult markets. Government cutbacks to schools and city libraries have impacted heavily on publishers of quality books for children. We're having to cut down on the number of books we take on and, unfortunately, this usually hits new authors hardest."

AUGSBURG BOOKS, 426 S. 5th St., Box 1209, Minneapolis MN 55440. (612)330-3300. Senior Editor: Robert Moluf. Publishes hardcover and paperback originals and paperback reprints. Publishes 45 titles/year; receives 5,000 submissions annually. 20% of books from first-time authors; 95% of books from unagented writers. Average print order for a writer's first book is 5,000. Pays 10-15% royalty on retail price; offers variable advance. Publishes book an average of 1 year after acceptance. Simultaneous and photocopied submissions OK. Computer printout submissions acceptable; must be near-letter quality. Book catalog and ms guidelines for 8½x11 SAE and 4 first class stamps. Reports in 1 month.
Nonfiction: Publishes for a wide Christian market. Books for children, youth or intergenerational family use; books of practical help, guidance, and encouragement; resources for Christian leadership and ministry; non-

technical books dealing with scripture, church history, ethics, theology, and related fields.
Recent Nonfiction Title: *Youth Prints*, edited by Norman Vincent Peale.

AUTO BOOK PRESS, P.O. Bin 711, San Marcos CA 92069. (619)744-3582. Editorial Director: William Carroll. Publishes hardcover and paperback originals. Averages 4 titles/year; receives 24 submissions annually. 75% of books from first-time authors; 100% of books from unagented writers. Pays 15% royalty; offers variable advance. Publishes book an average of 1 year after acceptance. Simultaneous and photocopied submissions OK. Computer printout submissions OK; prefers letter-quality. Reports in 2 weeks.
Nonfiction: Automotive material only: technical or definitive how-to. Query with outline/synopsis and 3 sample chapters.
Tips: "The most common mistake writers make is not taking time to research the potential market."

AVALON BOOKS, Imprint of Thomas Bouregy & Co., Inc., 401 Lafayette St., New York NY 10003. Editor: Barbara J. Brett. Publishes 60 titles/year. Pays $500 for first book and $600 thereafter, which is applied against sales of the first 3,500 copies of the book (initial run is 2,500 copies). Computer printout submissions acceptable; no dot-matrix. Reports in 3 months. Guidelines for #10 SASE.
Fiction: "We publish wholesome, young-adult romances, westerns and adventure novels that are sold to libraries throughout the country. Our books are read by adults as well as teenagers, and their characters are all adults. All the romances and adventures are contemporary; all the westerns are historical." Length: 35,000 to 50,000 words. Submit first chapter and a brief, but complete summary of the book, or if you are sure the book fits our requirements, submit the complete manuscript. Enclose manuscript size SASE.
Recent Fiction Title: *When the Heart Remembers*, by Constance Walker.
Tips: "We do not want old-fashioned, predictable, formula-type books. We are looking for contemporary characters and fresh, contemporary plots and storylines. Every heroine should have an interesting career or profession."

‡AVANT BOOKS, Slawson Communications, Inc., 3719 Sixth Ave., San Diego CA 92103-4316. (619)291-9126. Imprints include Microtrend Books, Mad Hatter Books. Managing Editor: Nicole Mindel. Publishes hardcover and trade paperback originals. Division averages 10 titles/year. Receives 100 submissions/year. 10% of books from first-time authors; 20% from unagented writers. Pays 10-20% royalty on wholesale price. Advance negotiable. Simultaneous and photocopied submissions OK. Query for electronic submissions. Computer printout submissions OK; prefers letter-quality. Reports on queries in 2 weeks; on mss in 1 month. Manuscript guidelines for #10 SAE with 1 first class stamp.
Nonfiction: How-to, self-help. Subjects include business and economics, health/medicine, history. Submit outline/synopsis and sample chapters. Reviews artwork/photos as part of ms package.
Recent Nonfiction Title: *Lead, Follow or Get Out of My Way*, by James Lundy (management).

AVIATION BOOK CO., 1640 Victory Blvd., Glendale CA 91201. (818)240-1771. Editor: Walter P. Winner. Publishes hardcover and paperback originals and reprints. Averages 5 titles/year; receives 25 submissions annually. 90% of books from first-time authors; 10% of books from unagented writers. Pays royalty on retail price. No advance. Query with outline. Publishes book an average of 9 months after acceptance. Computer printout submissions acceptable; prefers letter-quality. Reports in 2 months. Book catalog for 9x12 SAE with $1 postage.
Nonfiction: Aviation books, primarily of a technical nature and pertaining to pilot training. Young adult level and up. Also aeronautical history. Asks of ms, "Does it fill a void in available books on subject?" or, "Is it better than available material?" Reviews artwork/photos as part of ms package.
Recent Nonfiction Title: *Instrument Flight Training Manual*, by Peter Dogan.

AVON BOOKS, 105 Madison, New York NY 10016. Editorial Director: Linda Cunningham. Publishes paperback originals and paperback reprints. Averages 300 titles/year. Pay and advance are negotiable. Publishes ms an average of 2 years after acceptance. Simultaneous and photocopied submissions OK. Computer printout submissions acceptable; prefers letter-quality. Reports in 2 months. Book catalog for SASE.
Nonfiction: How-to, popular psychology, self-help, health, history, war, sports, business/economics, biography and politics. No textbooks.
Recent Nonfiction Title: *Communion*, by Whitley Strieber.
Fiction: Romance (contemporary), historical romance, science fiction, fantasy, men's adventure, suspense/thriller, mystery, and western. Submit query letter only.
Recent Fiction Title: *Bound by Desire*, by Rosemary Rogers.

AVON FLARE BOOKS, Young Adult Imprint of Avon Books, a division of the Hearst Corp., 105 Madison Ave., New York NY 10016. (212)481-5609. Editorial Director: Ellen Krieger. Publishes mass market paperback originals and reprints. Imprint publishes 24 new titles annually. 10-15% of books from first-time authors; 25% of books from unagented writers. Pays 6-8% royalty; offers average $2,000 advance. Publishes book an average of 15 months after acceptance. Simultaneous and photocopied submissions OK. Computer printout submissions acceptable; prefers letter-quality. Reports in 10 weeks. Book catalog and manuscript guidelines for 8x10 SAE and 5 first class stamps.

Nonfiction: General. Query or submit outline/synopsis and 6 sample chapters. *"Very* selective with young adult nonfiction."

Fiction: Adventure, ethnic, experimental, humor, mainstream, mystery, romance, suspense and contemporary. "Very selective with mystery." Mss appropriate to ages 12-18. Query with sample chapters or synopsis.

Recent Fiction Title: *One More Chance*, by Jane McFann.

AZTEX CORP., 1126 N. 6th Ave., Box 50046, Tucson AZ 85703. (608)882-4656. Publishes hardcover and paperback originals. Averages 15 titles/year; receives 250 submissions annually. 100% of books from unagented writers. Average print order for a writer's first book is 3,500. Pays 10% royalty. Publishes book an average of 18 months after acceptance. Query for electronic submissions. Computer printout submissions acceptable; prefers letter-quality. Reports in 3 months. Free catalog. *Author-Publisher Handbook* for $3.95.

Nonfiction: "We specialize in transportation subjects (how-to and history) and early childhood education (nonfiction)." Accepts nonfiction translations. Submit outline/synopsis and 2 sample chapters or complete ms. Reviews artwork/photos as part of ms package.

Recent Nonfiction Title: *The Amateur Astronomer's Catalog of 500 Deep-Sky Objects*, by Ronald J. Morales.

Tips: "We look for accuracy, thoroughness and interesting presentation."

‡BACKCOUNTRY PUBLICATIONS, INC., Box 175, Woodstock VT 05091. (802)457-1049. Publishes trade paperback originals. Averages 8 titles/year. 50% of books from first-time authors; 95% from unagented writers. Pays 5-10% royalty on retail price. Offers $500 average advance. Publishes book average of 6 months after acceptance. Simultaneous and photocopied submissions OK. Computer printout submissions OK; prefers letter-quality. Reports on queries in 2 weeks; on mss in 6 weeks. Book catalog free on request.

Nonfiction: Reference. Subjects include recreation. "We're looking for regional guides to hiking, bicycling, cross-country skiing, canoeing, and fishing for all parts of the country." Submit outline/synopsis and sample chapters. Reviews artwork/photos as part of ms package.

Recent Nonfiction Title: *Fifty Hikes in New Jersey*, by Green, Scofield and Zimmerman (hiking guide).

BAEN PUBLISHING ENTERPRISES, Distributed by Simon & Schuster, 260 Fifth Ave., New York NY 10001. (212)532-4111. Senior Editor: Elizabeth Mitchell. Publishes hardcover trade paperback and mass market paperback originals and mass market paperback reprints. Averages 80-100 titles/year; receives 1,000 submissions annually. 5% of books from first-time authors; 2% of books from unagented writers. Pays 6-12% royalty on cover price. Simultaneous and photocopied submissions OK, although they will not receive as serious consideration as originals. Computer printout submissions acceptable if letter-quality. Reports in 2 weeks on queries; 2 months on mss. Ms guidelines for #10 SAE.

Nonfiction: High tech science or futuristic topics such as space technology, artificial intelligence, etc. Submit outline/synopsis and sample chapters.

Recent Nonfiction Title: *Artificial Intelligence*, by F. David Peat.

Fiction: Fantasy and science fiction. Submit outline/synopsis and sample chapters or complete ms.

Recent Fiction Title: *After the Fact*, by Fred Saberhagen.

Tips: "Our audience includes those who are interested in *hard* science fiction and quality fantasy pieces that instruct as well as entertain."

‡*BAKER BOOK HOUSE COMPANY, Box 6287, Grand Rapids MI 49516-6287. (616)676-9185. Editor, trade books: Dan Van't Kerkhoff. Editor, academic books: Allan Fisher. Publishes hardcover and trade paperback originals and reprints. Averages 80 titles/year. 25% of books from first-time authors; 85% of books from unagented writers. Subsidy publishes 1% of books. Pays 10% royalty. Publishes book within 1 year after acceptance. Simultaneous and photocopied submissions OK. Computer printout submissions OK; prefers letter-quality. Reports in 3 weeks on queries; 6 weeks on ms. Book catalog for 9x12 SAE and $1.20 postage. Manuscript guidelines for #10 SAE.

Nonfiction: Biography, juvenile, humor, reference, self-help (gift books, Bible study), Bible commentaries and textbook. Subjects include child guidance/parenting, language/literature, philosophy, psychology, religion, sociology, women's issues/studies. "We're looking for books from a religious perspective—devotional, Bible study, self-help, textbooks for Christian colleges and seminaries, counseling and humorous books." Query or submit outline/synopsis and sample chapters.

Recent Nonfiction Title: *Victory Over Depression*, by Frans M. J. Brandt.

Tips: "Our books are sold through Christian bookstores to customers with religious background."

BALE BOOKS, Division of Bale Publications, Box 2727, New Orleans LA 70176. Editor-in-Chief: Don Bale Jr. Publishes hardcover and paperback originals and reprints. Averages 10 titles/year; receives 25 submissions annually. 50% of books from first-time authors; 90% of books from unagented writers. Average print order for a writer's first book is 1,000. Offers standard 10-12½-15% royalty contract on wholesale or retail price; sometimes purchases mss outright for $500. Offers no advance. Publishes book an average of 3 years after acceptance. Will consider photocopied submissions. Computer printout submissions acceptable; no dot-matrix. "Send manuscript by registered or certified mail. Be sure copy of manuscript is retained." Book catalog for SAE and 2 first class stamps.

Nonfiction: Numismatics. "Our specialty is coin and stock market investment books; especially coin investment books and coin price guides. Most of our books are sold through publicity and ads in the coin newspapers. We are open to any new ideas in the area of numismatics. The writer should write for a teenage through adult level. Lead the reader by the hand like a teacher, building chapter by chapter. Our books sometimes have a light, humorous treatment, but not necessarily." Looks for "good English, construction and content, and sales potential." Submit outline and 3 sample chapters.

Recent Nonfiction Title: *A Gold Mine in Gold*, by Bale (discusses gold coins as an investment).

BALLANTINE/EPIPHANY BOOKS, Imprint of Ballantine Books, 201 E. 50th St., New York NY 10022. (212)572-2266. Editor: Toni Simmons. Publishes inspirational hardcover and trade paperback originals, mass market paperback originals and reprints. Averages 20 titles/year. Receives 520 submissions/year. 30% of books from first-time authors. Pays 8-10% royalty on retail price. Publishes book an average of 1 year after acceptance. Simultaneous and photocopied submissions OK. Reports in 6 weeks. Book catalog for 9x12 SAE with 2 first class stamps.

Nonfiction: Biography, cookbook, how-to, humor and self-help. Subjects include health, psychology, religion, sociology and sports. "Nonfiction proposals should enrich the Christian's life in some way and be written in a style that will also appeal to and be accessible to nonChristians." No poetry, sermons, eschatology, devotionals, books for children or books on controversial issues. Query or submit outline/synopsis and sample chapters. Reviews artwork/photos as part of ms package.

Recent Nonfiction Title: *And God Created Wrinkles*, by E. Jane Mall (aging).

Fiction: Adventure, mainstream, mystery, religious and suspense. "We publish very little fiction; while it need not be overly religious, our fiction must contain some inspirational qualities." No "fiction for children, fiction about the end of time, prairie romances, inspirational romances or biblical/historical fiction." Query or submit outline/synopsis and sample chapters.

Recent Fiction Title: *Poppy*, by Barbara Larriva.

Tips: "Examine possible similar books already on the market, then compare your own manuscript to others. Be sure to write for a general audience; Epiphany does not publish books of limited interest to a small segmented audience. A common mistake writers make is that they state how much of an advance they want in their query letters."

BALLINGER PUBLISHING CO., Subsidiary of Harper & Row, 54 Church St., Harvard Square, Cambridge MA 02138. (617)492-0670. President: Carol Franco. Publishes hardcover and paperback originals. Averages 50 titles/year. Pays royalty by arrangement. Simultaneous and photocopied submissions OK. Computer printout submissions acceptable; prefers letter-quality. Reports in 1 month. Free book catalog.

Nonfiction: Professional and reference books in economics, business, finance, high technology, and international relations. Submit synopsis and sample chapters or submit complete ms.

Recent Nonfiction Title: *Moments of Truth*, by Jan Carlzon.

BANCROFT-SAGE PUBLISHING, (formerly Baker Street Productions, Ltd.), 112 Marshall St., Box 1968, Mankato MN 56001. (507)387-6640. Contact: Karyne Jacobsen. Small press. Publishes hardcover and trade paperback originals. Averages 8 titles/year; receives 500 submissions annually. 10% of books from first-time authors; 80% of books from unagented writers. Publishes book an average of 9 months after acceptance. Photocopied submissions OK. Computer printout submissions OK; prefers letter-quality. Reports in 2 months on queries; 2 months on mss.

Nonfiction: Needs juvenile materials, grades 1-3. No science fiction. Submit synopsis and sample chapters. "No manuscripts longer than 2,000 words." Reviews artwork/photos as part of ms package.

Recent Nonfiction Title: *Tyrannosaurus Rex*, by Elizabeth Sandell.

‡BANTAM BOOKS, Subsidiary of Bantam/Doubleday/Dell, 666 Fifth Ave., New York NY 10010. (212)765-6500. Imprints include Spectra, Windstone, New Age, Bantam Classics, Bantam New Fiction, Loveswept. Publishes hardcover, trade paperback and mass market paperback originals, trade paperback and mass market paperback reprints. Publishes 650 titles/year. Buys no books from unagented writers. Pays 4-15% royalty. Publishes book an average of 1 year after ms is accepted. Simultaneous and photocopied submissions OK. Computer printout submissions OK; prefers letter-quality. Reports in 3 weeks on queries; 1 month on ms.

Nonfiction: Biography, coffee table book, how-to, cookbook, humor, illustrated book, juvenile and self-help. Subjects include Americana, anthropology/archaelogy, business/economics, child guidance/parenting, computers and electronics, cooking, foods and nutrition, gay/lesbian, government/politics, health/medicine,

history, language/literature, military/war, money/finance, music/dance, philosophy, psychology, religion, science, sociology, sports and travel. Query or submit outline/synopsis or complete ms through agent only. All unsolicited mss are returned unopened.
Recent Nonfiction Title: *Close Pursuit*, by Carsten Stroud (investigative journalism).
Fiction: Adventure, fantasy, feminist, gay/lesbian, historical, horror, juvenile, literary, mainstream/contemporary, mystery, romance, science fiction, suspense, western, young adult. Query or submit outline/synopsis or complete ms through agent only. All unsolicited mss are returned unopened.
Recent Fiction Title: *Destiny*, by Sally Beauman (women's fiction).

BARNES & NOBLE, Division of Harper & Row, 10 E. 53rd St., New York NY 10022. (212)207-7000. Publishes paperback originals and paperback reprints. Pays standard paperback royalties for reprints; offers variable advance. Simultaneous and photocopied submissions OK. Computer printout submissions acceptable. Reports in 1 month.
Nonfiction: Education paperbacks. Query or submit outline/synopsis and sample chapters. Looks for "an indication that the author knows the subject he is writing about and that he can present it clearly and logically."

‡BARRON'S EDUCATIONAL SERIES, INC., 250 Wireless Blvd., Hauppauge NY 11788. Publishes hardcover and paperback originals and software. Publishes 170 titles/year. 10% of books from first-time authors; 90% of books from unagented writers. Pays royalty, based on both wholesale and retail price. Publishes book an average of 9 months after acceptance. Simultaneous and photocopied submissions OK. Computer printout OK; prefers letter-quality. Reports in 3 months. Book catalog $5. " Only writers with contracts receive guidelines."
Nonfiction: Adult education, art, business, cookbooks, crafts, foreign language, review books, guidance, pet books, travel, literary guides, juvenile, young adult, sports, test preparation materials and textbooks. Reviews artwork/photos as part of package. Query or submit outline/synopsis and 2-3 sample chapters. Accepts nonfiction translations.
Recent Nonfiction Title: *The Joy of Grilling*, by Joe Fomularo.
Tips: "The writer has the best chance of selling us a book that will fit into one of our series."

BEACON PRESS, 25 Beacon St., Boston MA 02108. (617)742-2110. Director: Wendy J. Strothman. Publishes hardcover originals and paperback reprints. Averages 50 titles/year; receives 4,000 submissions annually. 10% of books from first-time authors; 70% of books from unagented writers. Average print order for a writer's first book is 3,000. Offers royalty on net retail price; advance varies. Publishes book an average of 1 year after acceptance. Simultaneous and photocopied submissions OK. Computer printout submissions acceptable; prefers letter-quality. Return of materials not guaranteed without SASE. Reports in 2 months. Query or submit outline/synopsis and sample chapters to Editorial Department.
Nonfiction: General nonfiction including works of original scholarship, religion, women's studies, philosophy, current affairs, literature communications, sociology, psychology, history, political science, art, anthropology.
Recent Nonfiction Title: *Shared Destiny: Fifty Years of Soviet-American Relations.*
Tips: "We probably accept only one or two manuscripts from an unpublished pool of 4,000 submissions per year. No fiction or poetry submissions invited. No children's books. Authors should have academic affiliation."

BEAR AND CO., INC., Drawer 2860, Santa Fe NM 87504-2860. (505)983-9868. Editorial Director: Barbara Clow. Small press. Publishes trade paperback originals and reprints. Averages 12 titles/year. Receives 2,000 submissions/year. 20% of books from first-time authors; 80% of books from unagented writers. Pays 8-10% royalty. Publishes book an average of 18 months after acceptance. Query for electronic submissions. Computer printout submissions OK; prefers letter-quality. Reports in 1 month on queries; 3 months on mss. "No response without SASE." Book catalog free.
Nonfiction: Illustrated books, science, theology, mysticism, religion and ecology. "We publish books to 'heal and celebrate the earth.' Our interest is in New Age, western mystics, new science, ecology. We are not interested in how-to, self-help, etc. Our readers are people who are open to new ways of looking at the world. They are spiritually oriented but not necessarily religious; interested in healing of the earth, peace issues, and receptive to New Age ideas." Query or submit outline/synopsis and sample chapters. Reviews artwork/photos as part of ms package.
Recent Nonfiction Title: *The Mayan Factor*, by José Argüelles.

‡BEAU LAC PUBLISHERS, Box 248, Chuluota FL 32766. Publishes hardcover and paperback originals.
Nonfiction: "Military subjects. Specialist in social side of service life." Query.
Recent Nonfiction Title: *Military Jargon*, by P.T. James.

BEAUFORT BOOKS PUBLISHERS, 9 E. 40th St., New York NY 10016. (212)685-8588. Publisher: Eric Kampmann. Publishes hardcover and trade paperback originals. Averages 30-40 titles/year; receives 1,000 submissions annually. 5% of books from unagented writers. Pays 7½-15% royalty on retail price; offers variable advance. Publishes book an average of 1 year after acceptance. Simultaneous and photocopied submissions OK. Reports in 1 month on queries; 2 months on mss. Book catalog for 10x12 SAE and 4 first class stamps; guidelines for 8x10 SAE and 4 first class stamps.
Nonfiction: Subjects include biography, health, business, sports, travel, history, music, and recreation. Query, or submit outline synopsis and 3 sample chapters.
Recent Nonfiction Title: *I Shall Live*, by Henry Orenstein.
Fiction: Mystery, thrillers, contemporary and literary novels. "No first novels, no science fiction." Query only.
Recent Fiction Title: *Riding the Dolphin*, by Amanda Thomas.

*THE BENJAMIN COMPANY, INC., One Westchester Plaza, Elmsford NY 10523. (914)592-8088. President: Ted Benjamin. Publishes hardcover and paperback originals. Averages 20-25 titles/year. 90-100% of books from unagented writers. "Usually commissions author to write specific book; seldom accepts proffered manuscripts." Subsidy publishes (nonauthor) 100% of books. Publishes book an average of 6 months after acceptance. Buys mss by outright purchase. Offers advance. Simultaneous and photocopied submissions OK. Query for electronic submissions. Computer printout submissions acceptable; prefers letter-quality. Reports in 2 months.
Nonfiction: Business/economics, cookbooks, cooking and foods, health, hobbies, how-to, self-help, sports and consumerism. "Ours is a very specialized kind of publishing—for clients (industrial and association) to use in promotional, PR, or educational programs. If an author has an idea for a book and close connections with a company that might be interested in using that book, we will be very interested in working together with the author to 'sell' the program and the idea of a special book for that company. Once published, our books do get trade distribution through a distributing publisher, so the author generally sees the book in regular book outlets as well as in the special programs undertaken by the sponsoring company. We do not encourage submission of manuscripts. We usually commission an author to write for us. The most helpful thing an author can do is to let us know what he or she has written, or what subjects he or she feels competent to write about. We will contact the author when our needs indicate that the author might be the right person to produce a needed manuscript." Query. Submit outline/synopsis and 1 sample chapter. Looks for "possibility of tie-in with sponsoring company or association."
Recent Nonfiction Title: *Commitment to Excellence*, for Amway.

BENNETT & MCKNIGHT PUBLISHING CO., Division of Glencoe Publishing Co., 809 W. Detweiller Dr., Peoria IL 61615. (309)691-4454. Vice President/Publisher: David W. Whiting. Publishes hardcover and paperback originals. Specializes in textbooks and related materials. Averages 50 titles/year. Receives 25 submissions annually. 10% of books from first-time authors; 100% of books from unagented writers. Pays up to 10% royalty for textbooks "based on cash received, less for supplements." Publishes book an average of 2 years after acceptance. Photocopied submissions OK. Computer printout submissions acceptable. Reports in 1 month. Free book catalog and ms guidelines.
Nonfiction: Publishes textbooks and related items for home economics, industrial and technology, education, career education, and art education, allied health occupations and vocational training in schools, junior high through post-secondary. Wants "content with good coverage of subject matter in a course in one of our fields; intelligent organization; and clear expression." Query "with 1-2 sample chapters that represent much of the book; not a general introduction if the ms is mostly specific 'how-to' instructions."
Recent Nonfiction Title: *Technology Today and Tomorrow*, by James Fales, Vincent Kuetemeyer and Sharon Brusic.

‡ROBERT BENTLEY, INC., 1000 Massachusetts Ave., Cambridge MA 02138. (617)547-4170. Publisher: Michael Bentley. Publishes hardcover and trade paperback originals and reprints. Publishes 15-20 titles/year. 20% of books are from first-time authors; 90% from unagented writers. Pays 5-15% royalty on wholesale price; or makes outright purchase. Offers $2,000-6,000 average advance. Publishes book an average of 5 months after acceptance. Query for electronic submissions. Computer printout submissions OK; prefers letter-quality. Reports in 1 month. Book catalog and ms guidelines for SAE.
Nonfiction: Coffee-table book, how-to, technical. Subjects include automotive specialties. Query or submit outline/synopsis and sample chapters or complete ms. Reviews artwork/photos as part of manuscript package.
Recent Nonfiction Title: *The Design and Tuning of Competitive Engines*, by Philip H. Smith (automotive).
Tips: "We are excited about the possibilities and growth in the automobile enthusiast book market. Our audience is primarily composed of serious and intelligent automobile, sports car or racing enthusiasts, automotive technicians and high performance tuners."

THE BERKLEY PUBLISHING GROUP, (publishers of Berkley/Berkley Trade Paperbacks/Jove/Charter/Second Chance at Love/Pacer/ Ace Science Fiction), 200 Madison Ave., New York NY 10016. (212)686-9820. Senior Vice President/Publisher: Roger Cooper. Editor-in-Chief: Ed Breslin. Publishes paperback originals and reprints. Publishes approximately 800 titles/year. Pays 6-10% royalty on retail price; offers advance. Publishes book an average of 18 months after acceptance. "We don't accept unsolicited material."
Nonfiction: How-to, inspirational, family life, philosophy and nutrition.
Recent Nonfiction Title: *Fatherhood*, by Bill Cosby.
Fiction: Adventure, historical, mainstream men's adventure, young adult, suspense, western, occult, romance and science fiction. Submit outline/synopsis and first 3 chapters (for Ace Science Fiction only).
Recent Fiction Title: *Patriot Games*, by Tom Clancy.
Young Adult Fiction Title: *The Lone Wolf*, by Joe Dever and Gary Chalk.

BETHANY HOUSE PUBLISHERS, Subsidiary of Bethany Fellowship, Inc., 6820 Auto Club Rd., Minneapolis MN 55438. (612)944-2121. Editorial Director: Carol Johnson. Publishes hardcover and paperback originals and reprints. "Contracts negotiable." Averages 60 titles/year; receives 1,200 submissions annually. 15% of books from first-time authors; 95% of books from unagented writers. Publishes book an average of 9-18 months after acceptance. Simultaneous and photocopied submissions OK. Query for electronic submissions. Computer printout submissions acceptable. Reports in 2 months. Book catalog and ms guidelines for 9x12 SAE and 5 first class stamps.
Nonfiction: Publishes reference (lay-oriented); devotional (evangelical, charismatic); and personal growth books. Submit outline and 2-3 sample chapters. Looks for "provocative subject, quality writing style, authoritative presentation, unique approach, sound Christian truth." Reviews artwork/photos as part of ms package.
Recent Nonfiction Title: *Untwisting Twisted Relationships*, by William Backus (personal growth).
Fiction: Well written stories with a Christian message. No poetry. Submit synopsis and 2-3 sample chapters to Acquisitions Editor. Guidelines available.
Recent Fiction Title: *Return to Zion*, by Bodie Thoene.
Tips: "The writer has the best chance of selling our firm a book that will market well in the Christian bookstore. In your query, list other books in this category (price, length, main thrust), and tell how yours is better or unique."

BETTER HOMES AND GARDENS BOOKS, Division of the Meredith Corporation, 1716 Locust St., Des Moines IA 50336. Managing Editor: David A. Kirchner. Publishes hardcover and trade paperback originals. Averages 40 titles/year. "The majority of our books are produced by on-staff editors, but we often use freelance writers on assignment for sections or chapters of books already in progress." Will consider photocopied submissions. Reports in 6 weeks.
Nonfiction: "We publish nonfiction in many family and home-service categories, including gardening, decorating and remodeling, crafts, money management, handyman's topics, cooking and nutrition, Christmas activities, and other subjects of home-service value. Emphasis is on how-to and on stimulating people to action. We require concise, factual writing. Audience is primarily husbands and wives with home and family as their main center of interest. Style should be informative and lively with a straightforward approach. Stress the positive. Emphasis is entirely on reader service. We approach the general audience with a confident air, instilling in them a desire and the motivation to accomplish things. Food book areas that we have already dealt with in detail are currently overworked by writers submitting to us. We rely heavily on a staff of home economist editors for food books. We are interested primarily in nonfood books that can serve mail order and book club requirements (to sell for at least $14.95) as well as trade. Publisher recommends careful study of specific Better Homes and Gardens Books titles before submitting material." Prefers outline and sample chapters. "Please include SASE with appropriate postage."
Recent Nonfiction Title: *Country Style*.
Tips: "Writers often fail to familiarize themselves with the catalog/backlist of the publishers to whom they are submitting. We expect increased activity in our gardening and parenting book franchises in the year ahead." Queries/mss may be routed to other editors in the publishing group.

BETTERWAY PUBLICATIONS, INC., White Hall VA 22987. (804)823-5661. Senior Editor: Robert F. Hostage. Publishes hardcover and trade paperback originals. Averages 14-15 titles/year; receives 1,200 submissions annually. 50-60% of books from first-time authors; 90% of books from unagented writers. Pays 10-16% royalty on wholesale price; offers $500-1,000 advance. Publishes book an average of 8 months after acceptance. Simultaneous and (quality copies please) photocopied submissions OK. Query for electronic submissions. Computer printout submissions acceptable; no dot-matrix. Reports in 6 weeks on queries; 2 months on mss. Book catalog for 9x12 SAE and 3 first class stamps; ms guidelines for #10 SAE and 2 first class stamps.
Nonfiction: How-to, illustrated book, juvenile, reference, and self-help on business and economics, cooking and foods, health, hobbies, psychology, sociology, genealogy, small businesses, all aspects of homebuilding and ownership ("e.g., contracting your own home, securing the right mortgage loan, avoiding foreclosure of home, farm, or business."). "We are seeking to expand our list in small and home-based business guides or

handbooks, parenting books, genealogy books (advanced how-to), books that present career, lifestyle, family choices to women." No cookbooks. Submit outline/synopsis and sample chapters. Reviews artwork/photos.
Recent Nonfiction Title: *A Mother's Choice—To Work or Not While Raising a Family*, by Barbara Cook.
Tips: "We are continuing our emphasis on small and home business books and all aspects of housing/home ownership. We're also looking for distinctive (if not unique) how-to books, like *Gameplan—The Game Inventor's Handbook*, and *The Theater Props Handbook*."

‡*BETWEEN THE LINES INC., #211, 229 College St., Toronto, Ontario M5T 1R4 Canada. (416)597-0328. Editor: Robert Clarke. Publishes trade paperback originals. Averages 9-10 titles/year. Receives 150 submissions/year. 75% of books are from first-time authors; 100% from unagented writers. 25% of books are (nonauthor) subsidy published. Pays 8-15% royalty. Offers average advance of $500. Publishes ms an average of 10 months after acceptance. Simultaneous and photocopied submissions OK. Query for electronic submissions. Computer printout submissions OK; prefers letter-quality. Reports in 2 months on queries; 3 months on mss. Free book catalog. Ms guidelines for #10 SASE.
Nonfiction: Biography. Subjects include agriculture/horticulture, business and economics, education, ethnic, gay/lesbian, government/politics, health/medicine, military/war, women's issues/studies. Query or submit outline/synopsis and sample chapters. Reviews artwork/photos as part of ms package.
Recent Nonfiction Title: *The Perfect Machine: TV in the Nuclear Age*, by Joyce Nelson (culture/politics).

*BINFORD & MORT PUBLISHING, 1202 N.W. 17th Ave., Portland OR 97209. (503)221-0866. Publisher: James Gardenier. Publishes hardcover and paperback originals and reprints. Receives 500 submissions annually. 60% of books from first-time authors; 90% of books from unagented writers. Average print order for a writer's first book is 5,000. Pays 10% royalty on retail price; offers variable advance (to established authors). Publishes about 10-12 titles annually. Occasionally does some subsidy publishing (10%), at author's request. Publishes book an average of 1 year after acceptance. Reports in 4 months. Computer printout submissions acceptable; prefers letter-quality.
Nonfiction: Books about the Pacific Coast and the Northwest. Western Americana, biography, history, nature, maritime recreation, reference, and travel. Query with sample chapters and SASE. Reviews artwork/photos as part of ms package.
Recent Nonfiction Title: *Riverdale School: 1888-1988*, by Helen Wieman Bledsoe.

BOOKCRAFT, INC., 1848 W. 2300 S., Salt Lake City UT 84119. (801)972-6180. Editorial Manager: Cory H. Maxwell. Publishes (mainly hardcover) originals and reprints. Pays standard 7½-10-12½-15% royalty on retail price; "we rarely give a royalty advance." Averages 35-40 titles/year; receives 500-600 submissions annually. 25% of books from first-time authors; virtually 100% of books from unagented writers. Publishes book an average of 6 months after acceptance. Will consider photocopied submissions. Computer printout submissions acceptable; prefers letter-quality. Reports in about 2 months. Will send general information to prospective authors on request; ms guidelines for #10 SASE.
Nonfiction: "We publish for members of The Church of Jesus Christ of Latter-Day Saints (Mormons) and do not distribute to the national market. All our books are closely oriented to the faith and practices of the LDS church, and we will be glad to review such mss. Mss which have merely a general religious appeal are not acceptable. Ideal book lengths range from about 80 to 240 pages or so, depending on subject, presentation, and age level. We look for a fresh approach—rehashes of well-known concepts or doctrines not acceptable. Mss should be anecdotal unless truly scholarly or on a specialized subject. Outlook must be positive. We do not publish anti-Mormon works. We also publish short and moderate length books for Mormon youth, about ages 14 to 19, mostly nonfiction. These reflect LDS principles without being 'preachy'; must be motivational. 30,000-45,000 words is about the right length, though good longer mss are not entirely ruled out. This is a tough area to write in, and the mortality rate for such mss is high. We publish only 2 or 3 new juvenile titles annually." No "poetry, plays, personal philosophizings, or family histories." Query. "Include contents page with manuscript."
Recent Nonfiction Title: *Adversity*, by Elaine Cannon.
Fiction: Must be closely oriented to LDS faith and practices.
Recent Fiction Title: *Lady of Mystery*, by Susan Evans McCloud.

BOOKMAKERS GUILD, INC., Subsidiary of Dakota Graphics, Inc., 9655 W. Colfax Ave., Lakewood CO 80215. (303)772-7322 or (303)442-5774. Executive Editor: Normandi Ellis. Publishes hardcover and trade paperback originals. Averages 6-8 titles/year; receives 700 submissions annually. 30% of books from first-time authors; 90% of books from unagented writers. Pays 10% royalty on net. Publishes books an average of 12-18 months after acceptance. Photocopied submissions OK. Letter-quality computer printout submissions acceptable. Mss will not be returned without SASE. Reports in 2 weeks on queries; 2 months on mss after query, 4 months on ms without query. Book catalog and guidelines available.
Nonfiction: Adult reference; contemporary social issues; health; natural history; and psychology (focus on children and family). "We see a continuing focus on families, children and youth, especially books on child ad-

vocacy, behavior and education. Also seeking juvenile nonfiction. No how-to, cookbooks, local history, novels, poetry, sci-fi, computers, fashion, sports or works ill-written or ill-conceived." Query or submit outline/ synopsis and sample chapters. Sometimes reviews artwork/photos with ms package.

Recent Nonfiction Title: *The Future as if it Really Mattered*, by James Garbarino.

Fiction: Juvenile, age 8 and up. "We seek folklore, folktale and saga along classical themes with educational merit. Primarily focus on language and literature." 100 page minimum required. No picture books, but will look at collections of stories that could make a good volume. Query first.

Recent Fiction Title: *The Stolen Appaloosa*, by Levitt and Guralnick.

Tips: "Current concerns regarding the family unit and adolescent growth and development have influenced the type of material that we look for. We focus on those works which seek to educate and inform. We are specifically seeking educational nonfiction in the natural sciences for young adults, as well as adult nonfiction that addresses the issues for the well-being of the adolescent, the aged, and the family. Books that are sensitively written, well-researched, and on topics that are not already flooding the market have the best chances of being considered for publication by our firm."

*BOREALIS PRESS, LTD., 9 Ashburn Dr., Nepean, Ontario K2E 6N4 Canada. Editorial Director: Frank Tierney. Senior Editor: Glenn Clever. Publishes hardcover and paperback originals. Averages 4 titles/year; receives 400-500 submissions annually. 80% of books from first-time authors; 95% of books from unagented writers. Subsidy publishes (nonauthor) 5% of books. Pays 10% royalty on retail price; no advance. Publishes book an average of 18 months after acceptance. "No multiple submissions or electronic printouts on paper more than 8½ inches wide." Computer printout submissions acceptable; prefers letter-quality. Reports in 4 months. Book catalog $1 with SAE and IRCs.

Nonfiction: "Only material Canadian in content." Query. Reviews artwork/photos as part of ms package. Looks for "style in tone and language, reader interest, and maturity of outlook."

Recent Nonfiction Title: *How Parliament Works*, by Bejermi (politics).

Fiction: "Only material Canadian in content and dealing with significant aspects of the human situation." Query.

Recent Fiction Title: *Rose of the North*, by Friesen (novel).

Tips: "Ensure that creative writing deals with consequential human affairs, not just action, sensation, or cutesy stuff."

THE BORGO PRESS, Box 2845, San Bernardino CA 92406. (714)884-5813. Publisher: Robert Reginald. Editor: Mary A. Burgess. Publishes hardcover and paperback originals. Averages 30 titles/year; receives 200 submissions annually. 5% of books from first-time authors; 80% of books from unagented writers. Pays royalty on retail price: "10% of gross." No advance. Publishes book an average of 1-2 years after acceptance. "Virtually all of our sales are to the library market." Query for electronic submissions. Computer printout submissions acceptable. Reports in 3 months minimum. Book catalog and writer's guidelines for #10 SAE and 2 first class stamps.

Nonfiction: Publishes literary critiques, bibliographies, historical research, film critiques, theatrical research, interview volumes, biographies, social studies, political science, and reference works for the academic library market. Query with letter or outline/synopsis and 1 sample chapter. "All of our books, without exception, are published in open-ended, numbered, monographic series. Do not submit proposals until you have looked at our catalogs and publications. We are *not* a market for fiction, poetry, popular nonfiction, artwork, or anything else except scholarly monographs in the humanities and social sciences. We discard unsolicited manuscripts from outside of our subject fields which are not accompanied by SASEs."

Recent Nonfiction Title: *Risen From The Ashes*, by Biber.

THE BOSTON MILLS PRESS, 132 Main St., Erin, Ontario N0B 1T0 Canada. (519)833-2407. President: John Denison. Publishes hardcover and trade paperback originals. Averages 16 titles/year; receives 100 submissions annually. 75% of books from first-time authors; 90% of books from unagented writers. Pays 6-10% royalty on retail price; no advance. Publishes book an average of 8 months after acceptance. Simultaneous and photocopied submissions OK. Query for electronic submissions. Computer printout submissions acceptable. Reports in 2 weeks on queries; 1 month on mss. Book catalog for SAE with IRCs.

Nonfiction: Illustrated book. Subjects include history. "We're interested in anything to do with Canadian or American history—especially transportation. We like books with a small, strong market." No autobiographies. Query. Reviews artwork/photos as part of ms package.

Recent Nonfiction Title: *Next Stop Grand Central*, by Stan Fischler (railway history).

Tips: "We can't compete with the big boys so we stay with short-run specific market books that bigger firms can't handle. We've done well this way so we'll continue in the same vein. We tend to accept books from completed manuscripts."

BRADBURY PRESS, affiliate of Macmillan, Inc. 866 3rd Ave., New York NY 10022. (212)702-9809. Editor-in-Chief: Barbara Lalicki. Publishes hardcover originals for children and young adults. Averages 30 titles/

year. Pays royalty and offers advance. No simultaneous submissions. Reports in 3 months. Book catalog and ms guidelines for 9x12 SAE with 4 first class stamps.

Fiction: Picture books, concept books, photo essays and novels for elementary school children. Also "stories about real kids; special interest in realistic dialogue." No adult ms. No religious material. Submit complete ms.

Recent Fiction Title: *Hatchet*, by Gary Paulsen (novel).

Tips: "We're looking for historically accurate material that will interest kids in the past. We also look for science writers who can explain concepts of physics and biology on an elementary school level."

BRANDEN PRESS, INC., 17 Station St., Box 843, Brookline Village MA 02147. (617)734-2045. President: Adolph Caso. Small press. Subsidiaries include International Pocket Library and Popular Technology, Four Seas and Brashear. Publishes hardcover and trade paperback originals, hardcover and trade paperback reprints and software. Averages 10 titles/year; receives 400 submissions annually. 80% of books from first-time authors; 90% of books from unagented writers. Average print order for a writer's first book is 3,000. Pays 5-10% royalty on wholesale price; offers $1,000 maximum advance. Publishes book an average of 10 months after acceptance. Query for electronic submissions. Computer printout submissions acceptable; prefers letter-quality. Reports in 1 week on queries; 2 months on mss. Book catalog for #10 SASE.

Nonfiction: Biography, illustrated book, juvenile, reference, technical and textbook. Subjects include Americana, art, computers, health, history, music, photography, politics, sociology, software and classics. Especially looking for "about 10 manuscripts on national and international subjects, including biographies of well-known individuals." No religion or philosophy. Prefers paragraph query with author's vita; no unsolicited mss. Reviews artwork/photos as part of ms package.

Recent Nonfiction Title: *The AIDS Reader*.

Fiction: Adventure (well-written, realistic); ethnic (histories, integration); historical (especially biographies); mainstream (emphasis on youth and immigrants); religious (historical-reconstructive); romance (novels with well-drawn characters). No science, mystery or pornography. Paragraph query with author's vita; no unsolicited mss.

Recent Fiction Title: *A Lady A Peacemaker*, by Ramsey.

Poetry: No religious, humorous or autobiographical poetry books. Submit 5 poems.

Recent Poetry Title: *Dante's Inferno*, by D. Alighieri.

Tips: "Branden publishes only manuscripts determined to have a significant impact on modern society. Our audience is a well-read general public, professionals, college students, and some high school students. If I were a writer trying to market a book today, I would thoroughly investigate the number of potential readers interested in the content of my book."

*BRETHREN PRESS, 1451 Dundee Ave., Elgin IL 60120. (312)742-5100. Owned and managed by The Church of the Brethren General Board. Book Editor: David Eller. Publishes hardcover and trade paperback originals, and trade paperback reprints. Averages 10-12 titles/year; receives 150 queries/submissions annually. 30% of books from first-time authors; 90% of books from unagented writers. Subsidy publishes (nonauthor) 30% of books. Payment depends on target market, "some manuscripts are purchased outright." Typical contract: up to $1,000 advance against 10% net royalties for first 5,000 copies; 12% net on 5,001 copies and up. Publishes book an average of 1 year after acceptance. Simultaneous and photocopied submissions OK. Query for electronic submissions. Computer printout submissions acceptable; prefers letter-quality. Reports in 2 months on queries; 6 months ("hopefully") on mss. Book catalog and mss guidelines for #10 SAE with 2 first class stamps.

Nonfiction: Subjects include business and economics, health, history, philosophy, politics, psychology, religion and sociology. All titles should be from a faith perspective. Needs theology, Bible study, devotional, peace-related, practical discipleship, social issues, simple living, family life, "Plain People" heritage, and current and international events. Query or submit outline/synopsis and sample chapters. Reviews artwork/photos as part of ms package.

Recent Nonfiction Title: *Glimpses of Glory*, by Dave and Neta Jackson.

Fiction: Religious. "The only fiction published in recent years have been inspirational, with historical settings in 'Pennsylvania Dutch'/Plain People context." No romances. Query.

Tips: "We prefer timely issues with solid theological content, well-written for the average reader or religious professionals. Adhere to Chicago *Manual of Style* and *Church of the Brethren Handbook of Style*."

BREVET PRESS, INC., Box 1404, Sioux Falls SD 57101. Publisher: Donald P. Mackintosh. Managing Editor: Peter E. Reid. Publishes hardcover and paperback originals and reprints. Receives 40 submissions annually. 50% of books from first-time authors; 100% of books from unagented writers. Average print order for a writer's first book is 5,000. Pays 5% royalty; advance averages $1,000. Publishes book an average of 1 year after acceptance. Simultaneous and photocopied submissions OK. Computer printout submissions acceptable. Reports in 2 months. Free book catalog.

Nonfiction: Specializes in business management, history, place names, and historical marker series. Americana (A. Melton, editor); business (D.P. Mackintosh, editor); history (B. Mackintosh, editor); and technical books (Peter Reid, editor). Query; "after query, detailed instructions will follow if we are interested." Reviews artwork/photos; send copies if photos/illustrations are to accompany ms.

Tips: "Write with market potential and literary excellence. Keep sexism out of the manuscripts by male authors."

*BRIARCLIFF PRESS PUBLISHERS, 11 Wimbledon Ct., Jericho NY 11753. Editorial Director: Trudy Settel. Senior Editor: J. Frieman. Publishes hardcover and paperback originals. Averages 5-7 titles/year; receives 250 submissions annually. 10% of books from first-time authors; 60% of books from unagented writers. Average print order for a writer's first book is 5,000. Subsidy publishes 20% of books. Pays $4,000-5,000 for outright purchase; offers average of $1,000 advance. Publishes book an average of 6 months after acceptance. Computer printout submissions acceptable; no dot-matrix. "We do not use unsolicited manuscripts. Ours are custom books prepared for businesses, and assignments are initiated by us."

Nonfiction: How-to, cookbooks, sports, travel, fitness/health, business and finance, diet, gardening and crafts. "We want our books to be designed to meet the needs of specific businesses." Accepts nonfiction translations from French, German and Italian. Query. Submit outline and 2 sample chapters. Reviews artwork/photos as part of ms package.

Recent Nonfiction Title: *Handbook of Good Cooking*, by Maytag.

BRICK HOUSE PUBLISHING CO., 3 Main St., Box 512, Andover MA 01810. (617)475-9568. Publisher: Robert Runck. Small press. Publishes hardcover and trade paperback originals. Averages 12 titles/year; receives 100 submissions annually. 20% of books from first-time authors; 100% of books from unagented writers. Pays 10-15% royalty on wholesale price. Offers average $1,000 advance. Publishes book an average of 6 months after acceptance. Simultaneous and photocopied submissions OK. Query for electronic submissions. Computer printout submissions acceptable; prefers letter-quality. Reports in 2 weeks on queries; 3 months on mss. Book catalog and ms guidelines for 9x12 SAE with 3 first class stamps.

Nonfiction: How-to, reference, technical and textbook. Subjects include business and consumer advice. "We are looking for writers to do books in the following areas: practical guidance and information for people running small businesses, consumer trade books on money and job topics, and college business textbooks." Query with synopses.

Recent Nonfiction Title: *The Entrepreneurial Mind*, by Jeffry Timmons.

Tips: "A common mistake writers make is not addressing the following questions in their query/proposals: What are my qualifications for writing this book? Why would anyone want the book enough to pay for it in a bookstore? What can I do to help promote the book?"

BRIDGE PUBLISHING, INC., 2500 Hamilton Blvd., South Plainfield NJ 07080. (201)754-0745. Editor: Stephen R. Clark. Publishes trade and mass market paperback originals and reprints, and cloth originals. Averages 12-20 titles/year; receives 1,000 submissions annually. 10% of books from first-time authors; 90% of books from unagented writers. Average print order for a writer's first book is 5,000. Pays negotiable royalty. Assigns projects to writers. Publishes book an average of 1 year after acceptance. Photocopied submissions OK. Computer printout submissions acceptable; prefers letter-quality. Reports in 1 month. Book catalog $2; ms guidelines for #10 SASE.

Nonfiction: How-to, self-help and religious/Christian (nondenominational). Subjects include current events, health, religion and social issues. Especially looking for books with spiritual emphasis. Query with outline/synopsis and at least 2 sample chapters or submit complete ms, and always include SASE.

Recent Nonfiction Title: *The Teen Sex Survival Manual*, by James Watkins.

Tips: "We are especially (though not exclusively) interested in self-help books dealing with sensitive issues, such as divorce, rape, abortion, suicide, alcoholism, homosexuality, abuse, addiction, sexuality, pornography, mental and emotional illness, terminal illness, incest, aging and unemployment. We are looking for mss authoritatively written, dealing with the subjects head-on, and offering real answers and serious help for both teen and adult readers. In addition to issues-oriented books, we are looking for mss on Bible study, doctrine, spiritual growth, evangelism that exhibit careful scholarship solidly grounded in God's word. While we are not generally accepting any fiction or poetry, we will consider mss of *exceptional merit*. Authors must already have fiction or poetry published in significant periodicals and/or other books published by reputable publishers. The work should be written from a Biblical Christian world view but does not necessarily need to be explicitly religious in nature. Only completed fiction and poetry mss will be considered."

‡BRISTOL PUBLISHING ENTERPRISES, INC., Box 1737, 14692 Wicks Blvd., San Leandro CA 94577. (415)895-4461. Imprints include Nitty Gritty Cookbooks. Chairman: Patricia J. Collins. Publishes 6-8 titles/year. Receives approximately 200 proposals/year. 10% of books from first/time authors; 100% from unagented writers. Pays 3-6% royalty on wholesale price. Average advance is $100. Publishes ms an average of 6 months after acceptance. Computer printout submissions OK; prefers letter-quality. Reports in 2 months. Book catalog for 6x9 SAE with 2 first class stamps.

Nonfiction: Cookbooks. Submit outline/synopsis and sample chapters.

Recent Nonfiction Title: *Fabulous Fiber Cookery*, by Elaine Groen.

BROADMAN PRESS, 127 9th Ave. N, Nashville TN 37234. Editorial Director: Harold S. Smith. Publishes hardcover and paperback originals (85%) and reprints (15%). Averages 80 titles/year. Pays 10% royalty on retail price; no advance. Photocopied submissions OK "only if they're sharp and clear." Computer printouts acceptable; prefers letter-quality. Reports in 2 months.
Nonfiction: Religion. "We are open to freelance submissions in the children's and inspirational areas. Materials in both areas must be suited for a conservative Protestant readership. No poetry, biography, sermons, or anything outside the area of the Protestant tradition." Query, submit outline/synopsis and sample chapters, or submit complete ms. Reviews artwork/photos as part of ms package. Writer's guidelines for #10 SAE with 2 first class stamps.
Fiction: Religious. "We publish almost no fiction—less than five titles per year. For our occasional publication we want not only a very good story, but also one that sets forth Christian values. Nothing that lacks a positive Christian emphasis; nothing that fails to sustain reader interest." Submit complete ms with synopsis.
Tips: "Textbook and family material are becoming an important forum for us-Bible study is very good for us, but our publishing is largely restricted in this area to works that we enlist on the basis of specific author qualifications. Preparation for the future and living with life's stresses and complexities are trends in the subject area."

BROADWAY PRESS, Suite 407, 120 Duane St., New York NY 10007. (212)693-0570. Publisher: David Rodger. Small press. Publishes trade paperback originals. Averages 5-10 titles/year; receives 20-30 submissions annually. 50% of books from first-time authors; 75% of books from unagented writers. Pays negotiable royalty. Publishes book an average of 18 months after acceptance. Simultaneous and photocopied submissions OK. Computer printout submissions acceptable. Reports in 1 month on queries.
Nonfiction: Reference and technical. Subjects include theatre, film, television and the performing arts. "We're looking for professionally oriented and authored books. Most of our books are in-house publications, but we will accept author's queries for titles fitting the above criteria." Submit outline/synopsis and sample chapters.
Recent Nonfiction Title: *The Stage Managers Directory*, by David Rodger, editor.
Tips: "A common mistake writers make is not following up on submissions and queries."

BRUNNER/MAZEL, PUBLISHERS, Box 419, 1889 Palmer Ave., Larchmont NY 10538. (914)834-3920. Executive Editor: Ann Alhadeff. Publishes hardcover originals. Averages 30-35 titles/year; receives 400 submissions annually. Computer printout submissions acceptable; prefers letter-quality. Free ms guidelines.
Nonfiction: Clinical psychology and psychiatry on health, psychology, social work, child development, psychiatry, hypnosis and family therapy. No submissions for a general audience. Submit outline/synopsis and sample chapters.
Recent Nonfiction Title: *Psychotherapy Tradecraft*, by Theodore Blau, Ph.D. (psychotherapy).

‡**BUCKNELL UNIVERSITY PRESS**, Lewisburg PA 17837. (717)524-3674. Distributed by Associated University Presses. Director: Mills F. Edgerton, Jr. Publishes hardcover originals. Averages 18-20 titles/year; receives 150 submissions annually. 20% of books from first-time authors; 99% of books from unagented writers. Pays royalty. Publishes book an average of 2 years after acceptance. Photocopied submissions OK. Query for electronic submissions. Computer printout submissions acceptable. Reports in 1 month on queries; usually 6 months on mss. Free book catalog.
Nonfiction: Subjects include scholarly art, history, literary criticism, music, philosophy, politics, psychology, religion and sociology. "In all fields, our criterion is scholarly presentation; manuscripts must be addressed to the scholarly community." Query. Reviews artwork/photos.
Recent Nonfiction Title: *Leaders in the Study of Animal Behavior*, by Donald A. Dewsbury.
Tips: "An original work of high-quality scholarship has the best chance of selling to us; we publish for the scholarly community."

‡**BULL PUBLISHING CO.**, 110 Gilbert, Menlo Park CA 94025. (415)332-2855. Publisher: David Bull. Publishes hardcover and trade paperback originals. Averages 4-8 titles/year. Receives 100 submissions/year. 40-50% of books from first-time authors; 99% from unagented writers. Pays 14-16% royalty on wholesale price (net to publisher). Publishes ms an average of 6 months after acceptance. Simultaneous and photocopied submissions OK. Query for electronic submissions. Computer printout submissions OK; prefers letter-quality. Reports in 3 weeks. Book catalog free on request.
Nonfiction: How-to, self-help. Subjects include child guidance/parenting, cooking, foods and nutrition, health/medicine, sports. "We look for books that fit our area of strength: responsible books on health that fill a substantial public need, and that we can market primarily through professionals." Submit outline/synopsis and sample chapters. Reviews artwork/photos as part of ms package.
Recent Nonfiction Title: *How to Get Your Kid to Eat...but Not Too Much*, by E. Satter (how-to).

C Q PRESS, Imprint of Congressional Quarterly, Inc., 1414 22nd St. NW, Washington DC 20037. (202)887-8642. Director: Joanne Daniels. Publishes hardcover and paperback originals. Receives 20-30 submissions annually. 90% of books from unagented writers. Pays standard college royalty on wholesale price; offers college text advance. Publishes book an average of 5 months after acceptance of final ms. Simultaneous and photocopied submissions OK. Computer printout submissions acceptable; no dot-matrix. Reports in 3 months. Free book catalog.
Nonfiction: College text. All levels of political science texts. "We are one of the most distinguished publishers in the area of political science textbooks." Submit outline and sample chapter.
Recent Nonfiction Title: *Games Nations Play*, 6/e, by John Spanier.

‡*C.S.S. PUBLISHING COMPANY, 628 South Main St., Lima OH 45804. (419)227-1818. Imprints include Fairway Press. Editorial Director: Michael L. Sherer. Trade paperback originals. Publishes 50 titles/year. Receives 300 mss/year. 40% of books from first-time authors; 100% from unagented writers. Subsidy publishes 20%. "If books have limited market appeal and/or deal with basically same subject matter as title already on list, we will consider subsidy option." Pays 4-12% royalty on wholesale price or outright purchase of $25-250. Publishes book 2 years after acceptance. Simultaneous submissions OK. Query for electronic submissions. Computer printout submissions OK; no dot-matrix. Reports on mss in 6 months. Book catalog free on request; ms guidelines for #10 SAE and 1 first class stamp.
Nonfiction: Humor (religious) and self-help (religious). Subjects include religion: "Christian resources for mainline Protestant denominations; some Catholic resources. We are interested in sermon and worship resources, preaching illustrations, sermon seasonings, some Bible study, inspirationals, pastoral care, plays, practical theology, newsletter and bulletin board blurbs, church growth, success stories, teacher helps/training helps, church program material. Also sermon and worship resources based on the three-year lectionary; marriage helps and wedding services. We are not interested in the 'born again' movement or hellfire and brimstone stuff. No heavy theology, philosophy or scholarly themes." Reviews photos/artwork as part of ms package.
Recent Nonfiction Title: *The Penguin Principles*, by David Belasic and Paul Schmidt (practical theology).
Tips: "Books that sell well for us are seasonal sermon and worship resources; books aimed at clergy on professional growth and survival; also books of children's object lessons; seasonal plays (i.e. Christmas/Lent/Easter etc.). With church attendance declining, books on creative church growth will be popular. Our primary market is the clergy in all mainline denominations; others include church leaders, movers and shakers, education directors, Sunday school teachers, women's groups, youth leaders; to a certain extent we publish for the Christian layperson. Write something that makes Christianity applicable to the contemporary world, somthing useful to the struggling, searching Christian. The treatment might be humorous, certainly unique. We have published a few titles that other houses would not touch—with some degree of success. We are open to new ideas and would be pleased to see anything new, different, creative, and well-written that fits our traditional markets."

*CAMBRIDGE UNIVERSITY PRESS, 32 E. 57th St., New York NY 10022. Acting Director: Susan Milmoe. Publishes hardcover and paperback originals. Publishes 1,000 titles/year; receives 1,000 submissions annually. 50% of books from first-time authors; 99% of books from unagented writers. Subsidy publishes (nonauthor) 8% of books. Pays 10% royalty on receipts; 8% on paperbacks; no advance. Publishes book an average of 1 year after acceptance. Query for electronic submissions. Computer printout submissions acceptable. Reports in 4 months.
Nonfiction: Anthropology, archeology, economics, life sciences, mathematics, psychology, physics, art history, upper-level textbooks, academic trade, scholarly monographs, biography, history, and music. Looking for academic excellence in all work submitted. Department Editors: Elizabeth Maguire (humanities); Susan Milmoe (behavioral science); Rufus Neal (physical sciences); Frank Smith (history, political science); Ellen Shaw (English as second language); Helen Wheeler (behavioral science); Terence Moore (philosophy); and Peter-John Leone (earth sciences). Query. Reviews artwork/photos.
Recent Nonfiction Title: *Archaeology and Language*, by Colin Renfrew.

CAMELOT BOOKS, Children's Book Imprint of Avon Books, a division of the Hearst Corp., 8th Floor, 105 Madison Ave., New York NY 10016. (212)481-5609. Editorial Director: Ellen Krieger. Publishes paperback originals and reprints. Averages 36 titles/year; receives 1,500-2,000 submissions annually. 10-15% of books from first-time authors; 25% of books from unagented writers. Pays 6-8% royalty on retail price; offers minimum advance of $2,000. Publishes book an average of 15 months after acceptance. Simultaneous and photocopied submissions OK. Computer printout submissions acceptable; prefers letter-quality. Reports in 10 weeks. Free book catalog and ms guidelines for 8x10 SAE and 5 first class stamps.
Fiction: Subjects include adventure, fantasy, humor, mainstream, mystery, science fiction ("very selective with mystery, fantasy, and science fiction") and suspense. Submit entire ms or 3 sample chapters and a brief "general summary of the story, chapter by chapter."
Recent Fiction Title: *Nobody's Orphan*, by Anne Lindbergh.

*CANADIAN PLAINS RESEARCH CENTER, University of Regina, Regina, Saskatchewan S4S 0A2 Canada. (306)584-4795. Manager: Gillian Wadsworth Minifie. Publishes scholarly and trade paperback originals and some casebound originals. Averages 6-8 titles/year; receives 45-50 submissions annually. 35% of books from first-time authors; 90% of books from unagented writers. Subsidy publishes 80% (nonauthor) of books. Determines whether an author should be subsidy published through a scholarly peer review. Pays 5-10% royalty on retail price. "Occasionally academics will waive royalties in order to maintain lower prices." Publishes book an average of 18 months after acceptance. Query for electronic submissions. Reports in 2 weeks. Free book catalog and ms guidelines.

Nonfiction: Biography, coffee table book, illustrated book, technical, textbook and scholarly. Subjects include animals, business and economics, history, nature, politics and sociology. "The Canadian Plains Research Center publishes the results of research on topics relating to the Canadian Plains region, although manuscripts relating to the Great Plains region will be considered. Material *must* be scholarly. Do not submit health, self-help, hobbies, music, sports, psychology, recreation or cookbooks unless they have a scholarly approach. For example, we would be interested in acquiring a pioneer manuscript cookbook, with modern ingredient equivalents, if the material relates to the Canadian Plains/Great Plains region." Submit complete ms. Reviews artwork/photos as part of ms package.

Recent Nonfiction Title: *Modern Architecture in Alberta*, by Trevor Boddy (architectural book co-published with Alberta Culture and Multiculturalism).

*CANTERBURY PRESS, Box 2151C, Berkeley CA 94702. (415)843-1860. Editors: Ian Faircloth and Norine Brogan. Small press. Publishes hardcover and trade paperback originals. Averages 4 titles/year; receives approximately 100 submissions annually. 75% of books from first-time authors; 90% of books from unagented writers. Subsidy publishes 50% of books; 25% non-author subsidized. Pays 5-8% royalty on wholesale price. Offers average $500 advance. Publishes book an average of 4 months after acceptance. Simultaneous and photocopied submissions OK. Query for electronic submissions. Computer printout submissions acceptable; prefers letter-quality. Reports in 1 month on queries; 2 months on manuscripts. Book catalog and ms guidelines for #10 SASE.

Nonfiction: Subjects include philosophy, politics and sociology. "We need work which highlights social injustice and political strategies to alleviate this. Studies on 'third world' peoples, people with disabilities, native Americans and other minority groups—works which evidence the plight of the underprivileged." Query with outline; all unsolicited mss are returned unopened. Writer's guidelines for #10 SAE and 1 first class stamp.

Recent Nonfiction Title: *Living Outside Inside*, by Susan Hannaford (a social study on the plight of disabled people).

Fiction: Adventure, experimental, fantasy and humor. "We need fiction works of a high literary standard which offer a social, political and/or cultural insight. No predictable material which really has nothing to offer the type of reader we would like to attract." Query; all unsolicited mss are returned unopened.

Recent Fiction Title: *Peregrina*, by Claudia Lars (children's bilingual Spanish/English book).

Tips: "The audience we envision for our books is a mature adult audience that appreciates good literature, but realizes that we are in a developing society which can be influenced by that literature—an audience that appreciates innovative writing which may bring new ideas and important insights. If I were a writer trying to market a book today, I would remain confident in my work and persevere—there's always an opening somewhere."

*ARISTIDE D. CARATZAS, PUBLISHER, Box 210/30 Church St., New Rochelle NY 10801. (914)632-8487. Managing Editor: John Emerich. Publishes hardcover originals and reprints. Averages 12 titles/year; receives 100 submissions annually. 35% of books from first-time authors; 80% of books from unagented writers. Subsidy publishes 25% of books. "We seek grants/subsidies for limited run scholarly books; granting organizations are generally institutions or foundations." Pays royalty; offers $1,500 average advance. Publishes book an average of 18 months after acceptance. Simultaneous and photocopied submissions OK. Query for electronic submissions. Computer printout submissions OK. Reports in 1 month on queries; 3 months on mss. Free book catalog.

Nonfiction: Reference, technical and textbook. Subjects include art, history, politics, religion, travel, classical languages (Greek and Latin), archaeology and mythology. Nonfiction book ms needs for the next year include "scholarly books in archaeology; mythology; ancient and medieval history; and art history." Query or submit outline/synopsis and sample chapters. Reviews artwork/photos as part of ms package.

Recent Nonfiction Title: *Spartan Twilight*, by L. Piper (history).

 An asterisk preceding a listing indicates that subsidy publishing or co-publishing (where author pays part or all of publishing costs) is available. Firms whose subsidy programs comprise more than 50% of their total publishing activities are listed at the end of the Book Publishers section.

CAREER PUBLISHING, INC., Box 5486, Orange CA 92613-5486. (714)771-5155. Editor-in-Chief: Sherry Robson. Publishes paperback originals and software. Averages 6-20 titles/year; receives 300 submissions annually. 80% of books from first-time authors; 90% of books from unagented writers. Average print order for a writer's first book is 5,000-10,000. Pays 10% royalty on actual amount received; no advance. Publishes book an average of 6 months after acceptance. Simultaneous (if so informed with names of others to whom submissions have been sent) and photocopied submissions OK. Query for electronic submissions. Computer printout submissions acceptable; prefers letter-quality. Reports in 2 months. Book catalog for 8½x11 SAE with 2 first class stamps; ms guidelines for SAE and 1 first class stamp.

Nonfiction: Microcomputer material, educational software, word processing, guidance material, allied health, dictionaries, etc. "Textbooks should provide core upon which class curriculum can be based: textbook, workbook or kit with 'hands-on' activities and exercises, and teacher's guide. Should incorporate modern and effective teaching techniques. Should lead to a job objective. We also publish support materials for existing courses and are open to unique, marketable ideas with schools in mind. Reading level should be controlled appropriately—usually 8th-9th grade equivalent for vocational school and community college level courses. Any sign of sexism or racism will disqualify the work. No career awareness masquerading as career training." Submit outline/synopsis, 2 sample chapters and table of contents or complete ms. Reviews artwork/photos as part of ms package. If material is to be returned, enclose SAE and return postage.

Recent Nonfiction Title: *WordPerfect Step by Step Handbook/Workbook*, 4.2, by Raylene Dill.

Tips: "Authors should be aware of vocational/career areas with inadequate or no training textbooks and submit ideas and samples to fill the gap. Trends in book publishing that freelance writers should be aware of include education—especially for microcomputers."

CAROLRHODA BOOKS, INC., 241 1st Ave. N., Minneapolis MN 55401. (612)332-3344. Submissions Editor: Rebecca Poole. Publishes hardcover originals. Averages 25-30 titles/year. Receives 1,300-1,500 submissions/year. 25% of books from first-time authors. 95% of books from unagented writers. Pays 4-7% royalty on wholesale price, makes outright purchase, or negotiates cents per printed copy. Publishes book an average of 18 months after acceptance. Simultaneous and photocopied submissions OK. Computer printout submissions OK; no dot-matrix. Reports in 3 months. Book catalog and ms guidelines for SASE.

Nonfiction: Publishes only children's books. Subjects include biography, animals, art, history, music and nature. Needs "biographies in story form on truly creative individuals—25 manuscript pages in length." Query. Reviews artwork/photos as part of ms package.

Recent Nonfiction Title: *Wild Boars*, by Darrel Nicholson.

Fiction: Children's historical. No anthropomorphized animal stories. Submit complete ms.

Recent Fiction Title: *Why the Crab Has No Head*, by Barbara Knutson.

Tips: "Our audience is children; grades kindergarten through twelve. Nonfiction science topics, particularly nature, do well for us as do photo essays, picture books on earth science, nature, geology and easy-reader. It's faster for us to slot a manuscript into an existing series. Spend time developing your idea in a unique way or from a unique angle and describe it briefly."

CARROLL & GRAF PUBLISHERS, INC., 260 5th Ave., New York NY 10001. (212)889-8772. Contact: Kent Carroll. Small press. Publishes hardcover, trade and mass market paperback originals, and trade paperback and mass market paperback reprints. Averages 85 titles/year; receives 1,000 submissions annually. 10% of books from first-time authors; 10% of books from unagented writers. Pays 6-10% royalty on retail price. Publishes book an average of 9 months/after acceptance. Photocopied submissions OK. Computer printout submissions acceptable; prefers letter-quality. Reports in 3 weeks on queries; 1 month on mss. Book catalog for 6x9 SASE.

Nonfiction: Biography, history, psychology, curent affairs. Query. Reviews artwork/photos as part of ms package.

Recent Nonfiction Title: *The Babymakers*, by Diana Frank & Marta Vogel.

Fiction: Adventure, erotica, fantasy, mainstream, mystery and suspense. Query.

‡CARSON-DELLOSA PUBLISHING COMPANY, INC., 207 Creekridge Rd., Drawer 16327, Greensboro NC 27406. (919)274-1150. Editor: Susan Vaughan. Trade paperback originals. Publishes 50 titles/year. Receives 60-100 submissions/year. 30% of book from first-time authors; 100% from unagented writers. Pays $5-10/page outright purchase for 32 pages and up. Publishes book 2 years after acceptance. Computer printout submssions OK; prefers letter-quality. Reports in 3 weeks on queries; 2 months on mss. Book catalog and manuscript guidelines for #10 SAE, 1 first class stamp and $1.50.

Nonfiction: Elementary education classroom workbooks. Subjects include "all subjects appropriate to grades K-4. The subjects vary, but we are interested in activity books and collections of worksheets that reinforce the skills taught in elementary school classrooms. Our primary market is levels pre-K to 4. Only curriculum approved in children's educational materials are accepted. We have not done particularly well with computer books and are not looking for computer-related material at present. Also, keep in mind that what we want are *workbooks* that reinforce classroom skills, not textbooks or children's stories." Query.

Tips: "Readiness skills and preschool books are doing quite well. Also, game books, holiday fun books.

While our books are intended for children, they are purchased by elementary school teachers who are looking for activities, worksheets and exercises appropriate to their classrooms and their teaching. A large portion of our inventory consists of workbooks that collect activities and exercises that are photocopied by the teachers and handed out in the classroom, usually one page at a time. Current fads such as the dinosaur craze may be a factor to consider when choosing a subject matter for comprehension books etc. Would like to see a good, practical and simple book series teaching fractions from K to 4 grade."

CARSTENS PUBLICATIONS, INC., Hobby Book Division, Box 700, Newton NJ 07860. (201)383-3355. Publisher: Harold H. Carstens. Publishes paperback originals. Averages 5 titles/year. 100% of books from unagented writers. Pays 10% royalty on retail price; offers average advance. Publishes book an average of 2 years after acceptance. Query for electronic submissions. Computer printout submissions acceptable; prefers letter-quality. Book catalog for SASE.
Nonfiction: Model railroading, toy trains, model aviation, railroads and model hobbies. "We have scheduled or planned titles on several railroads as well as model railroad and model airplane books. Authors must know their field intimately since our readers are active modelers. Our railroad books presently are primarily photographic essays on specific railroads. Writers cannot write about somebody else's hobby with authority. If they do, we can't use them." Query. Reviews artwork/photos as part of ms package.
Tips: "No fiction. We need lots of good b&w photos. Material must be in model, hobby, railroad field only."

THE CATHOLIC HEALTH ASSOCIATION, 4455 Woodson Rd., St. Louis MO 63134. (314)427-2500. Books Editor: Robert J. Stephens. Publishes hardcover originals and reprints, trade paperback originals and reprints. Averages 20 titles/year. Receives 50 submissions/year. 5% of books from first-time authors. 100% of books from unagented writers. Pays 10-15% royalty on net proceeds. Offers variable advance. Publishes book an average of 9 months after acceptance. Query for electronic submissions. Reports in 1 month on queries; 3 months on mss. Book catalog for 9x12 SASE; ms guidelines for 8½x11 SASE.
Nonfiction: Textbook, ethics and management. Subjects include health and religion. Needs manuscripts for pamphlets on ethical health care topics for lay people and religious practices in health care, health care management and financing. No books for nonprofessionals. Submit outline/synopsis and sample chapters. Reviews artwork/photos as part of ms package.
Recent Nonfiction Title: *Poisoning Emergencies*, by Robert Jaeger.

CATHOLIC UNIVERSITY OF AMERICA PRESS, 620 Michigan Ave. NE, Washington DC 20064. (202)635-5052. Director: Dr. David J. McGonagle. Marketing Manager: Margaret Gore. Averages 15-20 titles/year; receives 100 submissions annually. 50% of books from first-time authors; 100% of books from unagented writers. Average print order for a writer's first book is 1,000. Pays variable royalty on net receipts. Publishes book an average of 1 year after acceptance. Query for electronic submissions. Computer printout submissions acceptable; no dot-matrix. Reports in 2 months. Book catalog for #10 SASE.
Nonfiction: Publishes history, biography, languages and literature, philosophy, religion, church-state relations, political theory and social sciences. No unrevised doctoral dissertations. Length: 200,000-500,000 words. Query with sample chapter plus outline of entire work, along with curriculum vitae and list of previous publications. Reviews artwork/photos.
Recent Nonfiction Title: *Arthur J. Balfour and Ireland, 1874-1922*, by Catherine B. Shannon.
Tips: Freelancer has best chance of selling "scholarly monographs and works suitable for adoption as supplementary reading material in courses."

THE CAXTON PRINTERS, LTD., 312 Main St., Caldwell ID 83605. (208)459-7421. Vice President: Gordon Gipson. Small press. Publishes hardcover and trade paperback originals. Averages 6-10 titles/year; receives 250 submissions annually. 50% of books from first-time authors; 60% of books from unagented writers. Audience includes Westerners, students, historians and researchers. Pays royalty; advance $500-2,000. Publishes book an average of 18 months after acceptance. Simultaneous and photocopied submissions OK. Computer printout submissions acceptable; no dot-matrix. Reports in 2 weeks on queries; 2 months on mss. Book catalog for 9x12 SASE.
Nonfiction: Coffee table, Americana and Western Americana. "We need good Western Americana, especially the Northwest, preferably copiously illustrated with unpublished photos." Query. Reviews artwork/photos as part of ms package.
Recent Nonfiction Title: *The Oregon Trail, Yesterday and Today*, by William Hill.

*CAY-BEL PUBLISHING COMPANY, Thompson-Lyford Bldg., 2nd Fl., 45 Center St., Brewer ME 04412. (207)989-3820. Editor-in-Chief: John E. Cayford. Imprints include C&H Publishing Co. Publishes hardcover and trade paperback originals, and hardcover and trade paperback reprints. Averages 8 titles/year; receives 350 submissions annually. 50% of books from first-time authors; 100% of books from unagented writers. Average print order for a writer's first book is 2,000-5,000. Subsidy publishes 2% of books when authors "want us to put their manuscript in a book form, to typeset it and print it, but want to handle their own sales." Pays 10-15%

royalty on retail price. Publishes book an average of 6-8 months after acceptance. Simultaneous and photocopied submissions OK. Computer printout submissions acceptable; prefers letter-quality. Reports in 1 month on queries; 2 months on mss. Book catalog and ms guidelines for 6½x9½ SAE and 2 first class stamps.

Nonfiction: Biography, cookbook, reference and maritime. Subjects include Americana, cooking and foods, history, vital records and genealogy. "Our book schedule is well filled for the next year, but we will give very careful consideration to any book about a Maine personage or to a Maine history." No poetry or pornography. Query. Reviews artwork/photos.

Recent Nonfiction Title: *Growing Up Yankee*, by Avery Rich.

CCC PUBLICATIONS, 20306 Tau Place, Chatsworth CA 91311. (818)407-1661. Editor: Cliff Carle. Publishes trade paperback originals and mass market paperback originals. Averages 5-10 titles/year; receives 50-100 mss/year. 50% of books from first time authors; 50% of books from unagented writers. Pays 5-10% royalty on wholesale price. Publishes book an average of 1 year after acceptance. Simultaneous and photocopied submissions OK. Computer printout submissions OK; prefers letter-quality. Reports in 1 month on queries; reports in 3 months on mss. Book catalog for 8½x11 SAE with 2 first class stamps.

Nonfiction: Humorous how-to/self-help. "We are looking for *original*, *clever* and *current* humor that is not too limited in audience appeal or that will have a limited shelf life. All of our titles are as marketable 5 years from now as they are today. No rip-offs of previously published books, or too special interest mss." For best results: Query first with SASE; will review complete ms only. Reviews artwork/photos as part of ms package.

Recent Nonfiction Title: *No Hang-Ups*, by John Carfi and Cliff Carle (humor).

Tips: "Humor—we specialize in the subject and have a good reputation with retailers and wholesalers for publishing super-impulse titles."

CELESTIAL ARTS, Division of Ten Speed Press, Box 7327, Berkeley CA 94707. (415)524-1801. Editorial Director: David Hinds. Editor: Paul Reed. Publishes paperback originals. Publishes 30 titles/year; receives 12,000 submissions annually. 50% of books from first-time authors; 90% of books from unagented writers. Average print order for a writer's first book is 5,000. Publishes book an average of 1 year after acceptance. Simultaneous and photocopied submissions OK. Computer printout submissions acceptable; prefers letter-quality. Reports in 3 months. Book catalog for 9x12 SAE with $1.92 postage.

Nonfiction: Publishes biography, cookbooks/cooking, health, psychology, social sciences, new age, philosophy, gay, and self-help. No poetry. "Submit 2-3 sample chapters and outline; no original copy. If return requested, include postage. We do not want to see the same manuscripts submitted to both Ten Speed Press and Celestial Arts." Reviews artwork/photos.

Recent Nonfiction Title: *Software for the Mind*, by Emmett Miller.

Tips: "Common mistakes that writers make are that they're impatient with reporting time and they send out material that's incomplete and not well thought out."

CENTER FOR MIGRATION STUDIES OF NEW YORK, INC., 209 Flagg Pl., Staten Island NY 10304. (718)351-8800. Director of Publications: Maggie Sullivan. Publishes hardcover and trade paperback originals. Averages 12 titles/year. Receives 250 submissions/year. 1% of books from first-time authors. 100% of books from unagented writers. Pays 7-12% royalty on retail price. Publishes book an average of 20 months after acceptance. Computer printout submissions OK; prefers letter-quality. Reports in 3 weeks on queries; 4 months on mss. Free book catalog and guidelines.

Nonfiction: Technical and textbook. Subjects include business and economics, history, politics, psychology, sociology, migration and refugees. Especially needs mss "on migration theory and policy on newest immigrant groups. Our audience includes college and university students, policy makers, voluntary agencies and anyone interested in population movements." Submit complete ms. Reviews artwork/photos as part of ms package.

Recent Nonfiction Title: *Global Trends in Migration*, by Mary Kritz, et al.

‡CENTER FOR THANATOLOGY RESEARCH, 391 Atlantic Ave., Brooklyn NY 11217. (718)858-3026. Contact: R. Halpern. Publishes trade paperback originals. Averages 16 titles/year. Receives 10 submissions/year. 10% of books from first-time authors; 100% from unagented writers. Pays 10% royalty on wholesale price. Publishes book 1 year after acceptance. Simultaneous and photocopied submissions OK. Query for electronic submissions. Computer printout submissions OK; prefers letter-quality. Reports in 1 month. Books catalog and ms guidelines free on request.

Nonfiction: Reference, self-help, textbook. Subjects include anthropology/archaelogy, education, health/medicine, philosophy, psychology, religion, sociology. Manuscript must deal with aging, dying, death or bereavement. Query.

Recent Nonfiction Title: *The Pediatric Nurse and The Dying Child* (nonfiction anthology).

CHARIOT BOOKS, Imprint of David C. Cook Publishing Co., 850 N. Grove Ave., Elgin IL 60120. (312)741-2400. Editorial Coordinator: Marcia Fay. Publishes hardcover, trade paperback and mass market paperback

originals. Averages 65 titles/year; receives 1,500 submissions annually. 20% of books from first-time authors; 90% of books from unagented writers. Pays royalty or outright purchase. Publishes book an average of 18 months after acceptance. Simultaneous submissions OK. Computer printout submissions OK; no dot-matrix. Reports in 3 weeks on queries; 3 months on mss. Book catalog for 10x13 SAE with 2 first class stamps.
Nonfiction: Juvenile. Subjects include animals, art, hobbies, nature, recreation, religion and sports. "For young readers, we are looking for books that illuminate the Bible, including parts not previously made understandable to this age group. For all readers, books may incorporate fun facts and activities." Query or submit outline/synopsis and sample chapters. All unsolicited mss are returned unopened. Reviews artwork/photos as part of ms package.
Recent Nonfiction Title: *My Family is Special*, by Christine Tangveld (childen's).
Fiction: Adventure, fantasy, historical, humor, mainstream, mystery, religious, science fiction, suspense and western. "For preschool, we prefer stories for picture books that talk about familiar things, avoid complicated plot and abstract concepts, and help the young child understand basic spiritual truths. For primary age children, we're interested in storybooks that illuminate biblical truths, and parts of the Bible not previously made understandable for such a young age group. Use of humor is sometimes appropriate. These books may be either for independent reading or to be read to children." Query or submit outline/synopsis and sample chapters.
Recent Fiction Title: *Mystery Rider at Thunder Ridge*, by David Gillet.
Tips: "We pay special attention to a writer who has researched our market and knows how the manuscript compares to what is out there."

*CHATHAM PRESS, Box A, Old Greenwich CT 06870. Publishes hardcover and paperback originals, reprints and anthologies relating to New England and the Atlantic coastline. Averages 15 titles/year; receives 50 submissions annually. 30% of books from first-time authors; 75% of books from unagented writers. Subsidy (mainly poetry or ecological topics) publishes (nonauthor) 10% of books. "Standard book contract does not always apply if the book is heavily illustrated. Average advance is low." Publishes book an average of 6 months after acceptance. Query for electronic submissions. Computer printout submissions acceptable; prefers letter-quality. Reports in 2 weeks. Book catalog and ms guidelines for 6x9 SAE with 10 first class stamps.
Nonfiction: Publishes mostly "regional history and natural history, involving mainly Northeast seaboard to the Carolinas, mostly illustrated, with emphasis on conservation and outdoor recreation." Accepts nonfiction translations from French and German. Query with outline and 3 sample chapters. Reviews artwork/photos as part of ms package.
Recent Nonfiction Title: *Beachcomber's Companion*, by Wesemann.
Recent Poetry Title: *Weapons Against Chaos*, by M. Ewald.
Tips: "Illustrated New England-relevant titles have the best chance of selling to our firm. We have a slightly greater (+15%) skew towards cooking and travel titles."

CHELSEA GREEN, Box 283, Chelsea VT 05038. (802)685-3108. Editor: Ian Baldwin Jr. Publishes hardcover and paperback trade originals. Averages 10 titles/year beginning in 1989.
Nonfiction: Biography, nature, politics, travel, art history. Query only and include SASE.
Recent Nonfiction Title: *Castaways: The Penikese Island Experiment*, by George Cadwalader.
Fiction: Serious contemporary fiction (no genre fiction). Please submit query with SASE.
Recent Fiction Title: *The Eight Corners of the World*, by Gordon Weaver.

CHICAGO REVIEW PRESS, 814 N. Franklin, Chicago IL 60610. (312)337-0747. Editor: Linda Matthews. Publishes hardcover and trade paperback originals. Averages 15 titles/year; receives 200 submissions annually. 60% of books from first-time authors; 90% of books from unagented writers. Pays 10-15% royalty. Offers average $500 advance. Publishes book an average of 9 months after acceptance. Simultaneous and photocopied submissions OK. Query for electronic submissions. Computer printout submissions acceptable. Reports in 1 month on queries; 3 months on mss. Book catalog free on request.
Nonfiction: Specialty cookbooks, how-to, reference and guidebooks on cooking and foods, recreation, travel, popular science, and regional. Needs regional Chicago material and how-to, travel, popular science, family, cookbooks for the national audience. Query or submit outline/synopsis and sample chapters. Reviews artwork/photos.
Recent Nonfiction Title: *The Straight Dope*, by Cecil Adams (humor).
Tips: "The audience we envision for our books is adults and young people 15 and older, educated readers with special interests, do-it-yourselfers, travellers, students. A trend we have noticed is the comeback of the successful short-run title and the popularization of technical subjects."

‡*CHILD WELFARE LEAGUE OF AMERICA, Suite 310, 440 First St. NW, Washington DC 20001. (202)638-2952. Director, Publications: Susan Brite. Publishes hardcover and trade paperback originals. Publishes 10-12 titles/year. Receives 60-100 submissions/year. 95% of writers are unagented. 50% of books are nonauthor subsidy published. Pays 0-10% royalty on net domestic sales. Publishes book 1 year after acceptance. Query for electronic submissions. Computer printout submissions OK; prefers letter-quality. Reports on

queries in 2 months; on mss in 3 months. Book catalog and manuscript guidelines free on request.
Nonfiction: Child welfare. Subjects include child guidance/parenting, sociology. Submit outline/synopsis and sample chapters or complete ms.
Recent Nonfiction Title: *Assessing Risk & Measuring Change in Families*, by Magura/Moses/Jones (family risk scales).
Recent Fiction Title: *Who is David?*, by Evelyn Nerlove (adoption novel).
Tips: "Our audience is child welfare workers, administrators, agency execs, parents, etc."

‡CHILDRENS PRESS, 5440 N. Cumberland Ave., Chicago IL 60656. (312)666-4200. Editorial Director: Fran Dyra. Averages 100 titles/year; receives 2,000 submissions annually. 5-10% of books from first-time authors; 100% of books from unagented writers. Pays in outright purchase or offers small advance against royalty. Publishes book an average of 1 year after acceptance. Simultaneous submissions OK. Computer printout submissions acceptable; prefers letter-quality. Reports in 3 months.
Nonfiction: For supplementary use in elementary and junior high schools; picture books for early childhood and beginning readers; high-interest, easy reading material. Specific categories include social studies and science. Especially wants new biographies. Length: 50-10,000 words. For picture books, needs are very broad. They should be geared from preschool to grade 3. "We have a strong tendency to publish books in series. Odds are against a single book that couldn't, if sales warrant, develop into a series." Length: 50-1,000 words. Send outline with 1 sample chapter; complete ms for picture books. Accepts translations. Reviews artwork and photos as part of ms package, "but best to submit ms first." Do not send finished artwork with ms.
Recent Nonfiction Title: *Understanding and Preventing AIDS*, by Warren Colman.
Fiction: For supplementary use in elementary and secondary schools. Length: 50-10,000 words. Picture books from preschool to grade 3. Length: 50-1,000 words. Send outline with sample chapters; complete ms for picture books. Do not send finished artwork with ms.
Tips: Submissions often "lack originality. Too often authors talk 'down' to young readers. First, it must be a good story, then it can have an educational or moral point. We're always looking for writers in the science and technology areas. Current criticism of educational system will lead to emphasis on math, science (all branches), and geography. Back-to-basics approach to learning but not back to dull. Vibrant illustrations and interesting information will still be sought. Nonfiction for middle grades (reading level 5th grade) has the best chance of selling to our firm."

CHILTON BOOK CO., Chilton Way, Radnor PA 19089. Editorial Director: Alan F. Turner. Publishes hardcover and trade paperback originals. Publishes 90 titles/year. Pays royalty; average advance. Simultaneous and photocopied submissions OK. Query for electronic submissions. Computer printout submissions acceptable. Reports in 3 weeks.
Nonfiction: Business/economics, crafts, how-to and technical. "We only want to see any manuscripts with informational value." Query or submit outline/synopsis and 2-3 sample chapters.
Recent Nonfiction Title: *Small Business Matters*, by Mary Frech McVicker.

*CHINA BOOKS AND PERIODICALS, INC., 2929 24th St., San Francisco CA 94110. (415)282-2994. Editorial Director: Foster Stockwell. Publishes hardcover and trade paperback originals. Averages 6 titles/year; receives 40 submissions annually. 50% of books from first-time authors; 80% of books from unagented writers. Subsidy publishes 2% of books. Pays 2-10% royalty on retail price. Offers average $1,000 advance. Publishes book an average of 9 months after acceptance. Simultaneous and photocopied submissions OK. Query for electronic submissions. Computer printout submissions acceptable; prefers letter-quality. Reports in 3 weeks. Free book catalog.
Nonfiction: Biography, coffee table book, cookbook, how-to, juvenile and reference. All related to China. Query or submit outline/synopsis and sample chapters. Reviews artwork/photos as part of ms package.
Recent Nonfiction Title: *Easy Tao*, by Simon Chang.
Fiction: Publishes only fiction subjects related to China. Query or submit outline/synopsis and sample chapters.
Recent Fiction Title: *Love Must Not Be Forgotten*, by Zhang Jie (short stories).
Tips: "Our audience includes tourists, art collectors and China scholars."

CHOSEN BOOKS PUBLISHING CO., LTD., Imprint of Fleming H. Revell Co., 184 Central Ave., Old Tappan NJ 07675. (201)768-8060. Editor: Jane Campbell. Publishes hardcover and trade paperback originals. Averages 16 titles/year; receives 500 submissions annually. 15% of books from first-time authors; 99% of books from unagented writers. Pays royalty on retail price. Publishes book an average of 9 months after acceptance. Simultaneous and photocopied submissions OK. Computer printout submissions acceptable; prefers letter-quality. Reports in 3 months. Occasionally makes work-for-hire assignments. Book catalog not available; ms guidelines for #10 SASE.
Nonfiction: How-to, self-help, and a very limited number of first-person narratives. "We publish books reflecting the current acts of the Holy Spirit in the world, books with a charismatic Christian orientation." No

poetry, fiction, or children's books. Submit synopsis, 2 sample chapters and SASE.

Recent Nonfiction Title: *Dreams Lost and Found*, by David Shibley.

Tips: "In expositional books we look for solid, practical advice for the growing and maturing Christian from authors with professional or personal experience platforms. Narratives must have a strong theme and reader benefits. No conversion accounts or chronicling of life events, please. State the topic or theme of your book clearly in your cover letter."

*THE CHRISTOPHER PUBLISHING HOUSE, 106 Longwater Dr., Norwell MA 02061. (617)878-9336. Managing Editor: Susan Lukas. Small press. Publishes hardcover and trade paperback originals. Averages 20-30 titles/year; receives 300-400 submissions annually. 30% of books from first-time authors; 100% of books from unagented writers. Subsidy publishes 50% of books. Pays 5-30% of royalty on wholesale price; offers no advance. Publishes book an average of 2 years after acceptance. Simultaneous and photocopied submissions OK. Query for electronic submissions. Computer printout submissions acceptable; prefers letter-quality. Reports in 1 month. Book catalog for #10 SAE with 2 first class stamps; ms guidelines for SASE.

Nonfiction: Biography, how-to, reference, self-help, textbook and religious. Subjects include Americana, animals, art, business and economics, cooking and foods (nutrition), health, history, philosophy, politics, psychology, religion, sociology and travel. "We will be glad to review all nonfiction manuscripts, particularly college textbook and religious-oriented." Submit complete ms. Reviews artwork/photos.

Recent Nonfiction Title: *Profitable Company, Milestones and Monuments of the Signers of the Declaration of Independence*, by Archibald Laird, M.D.

Poetry: "We will review all forms of poetry." Submit complete ms.

Recent Poetry Title: *Drumbeats and Whispers*, by Thomas V. Simpkins.

Tips: "Our books are for a general audience, slanted toward college-educated readers. There are specific books targeted toward specific audiences when appropriate."

CHRONICLE BOOKS, Chronicle Publishing Co., 275 Fifth St., San Francisco CA 94103. (415)777-7240. Executive Editor: Nion McEvoy. Publishes hardcover and trade paperback originals. Averages 70 titles/year; receives 1,000 submissions annually. 40% of books from first-time authors; 70% of books from unagented writers. Pays 6-10% royalty on retail price. Offers average $3,000 advance. Publishes book an average of 1½ years after acceptance. Simultaneous and photocopied submissions OK. Computer printout submissions acceptable; prefers letter-quality. Reports in 1 month on queries; 2 months on mss. Book catalog for 9x12 SAE with 4 first class stamps.

Nonfiction: Coffeetable book, cookbook, and regional California on art, cooking and foods, design, nature, photography, recreation, and travel. Query or submit outline/synopsis and sample chapters. Reviews artwork/photos.

Recent Nonfiction Title: *Diamonds Are Forever: Artists & Writers On Baseball*, introduction by Donald Hall.

Tips: "Chronicle Books is currently broadening its publishing program and, in line with this, has hired two new editors. Jay Schaefer is expanding Chronicle's program in nonfiction, and Victoria Rock is establishing a line of children's books. We welcome submissions in both of these areas."

CITADEL PRESS, Subsidiary of Lyle Stuart Inc., 120 Enterprise Ave., Secaucus NJ 07094. (212)736-0007. Editorial Director: Allan J. Wilson. Publishes hardcover originals and paperback reprints. Averages 60-80 titles/year. Receives 800-1,000 submissions annually. 7% of books from first-time authors; 50% of books from unagented writers. Average print order for a writer's first book is 5,000. Pays 10% royalty on hardcover, 5-7% on paperback; offers average $5,000 advance. Publishes book an average of 1 year after acceptance. Simultaneous and photocopied submissions OK. Computer printout submissions acceptable; no dot-matrix. Reports in 2 months. Book catalog for $1.

Nonfiction: Biography, film, psychology, humor and history. Also seeks "off-beat material," but no "poetry, religion, politics." Accepts nonfiction and fiction translations. Query. Submit outline/synopsis and 3 sample chapters. Reviews artwork/photos.

Recent Nonfiction Title: *The Rain Maiden*, by Jill M. Phillips.

Tips: "We concentrate on biography, popular interest, and film, with limited fiction (no romance, religion, poetry, music)."

CLARION BOOKS, Ticknor & Fields: a Houghton Mifflin Company. 52 Vanderbilt Ave., New York NY 10017. Editor and Publisher: James C. Giblin. Senior Editor for Nonfiction: Ann Troy. Publishes hardcover originals. Averages 18-20 titles/year. Pays 5-10% royalty on retail price; $1,000-3,000 advance, depending on whether project is a picture book or a longer work for older children. Photocopied submissions OK. No multiple submissions. Computer printout submissions acceptable; no dot-matrix. Reports in 2 months. Publishes book an average of 18 months after acceptance. Book Writer's guidelines for #10 SASE.

Nonfiction: Americana, biography, holiday, humor, nature, photo essays and word play. Prefers books for younger children. Reviews artwork/photos as part of ms package. Query.

Recent Nonfiction Title: *Lincoln: A Photobiography.*
Fiction: Adventure, fantasy, humor, mystery, strong character studies, and suspense. "We would like to see more humorous contemporary stories that young people of 8-12 or 10-14 can identify with readily." Accepts fiction translations. Query on ms of more than 50 pages. Looks for "freshness, enthusiasm—in short, life" (fiction and nonfiction).
Recent Fiction Title: *Following the Mystery Man*, by Mary Downing Hahn.

*ARTHUR H. CLARK CO., Box 230, Glendale CA 92109. (213)245-9119. Editorial Director: Robert A. Clark. Publishes hardcover originals. Averages 8 titles/year; receives 40 submissions annually. 40% of books from first-time authors; 100% of books from unagented writers. Subsidy publishes 15% of books based on whether they are "high-risk sales." Subsidy publishes (nonauthor) 5% of books. Pays 10% minimum royalty on wholesale price. Publishes book an average of 9 months after acceptance. Photocopied submissions OK. Computer printout submissions acceptable; prefers letter-quality. Reports in 1 week on queries; 2 months on mss. Book catalog for 6x9 SAE.
Nonfiction: Biography, reference and historical nonfiction. Subjects include Americana and history. "We're looking for documentary source material in Western American history." Query or submit outline/synopsis and 3 sample chapters. Looks for "content, form, style." Reviews artwork/photos as part of ms package.
Recent Nonfiction Title: *Fremont's Private Navy*, by Briton Busch.
Tips: "Western Americana (nonfiction) has the best chance of selling to our firm."

*CLEANING CONSULTANT SERVICES, INC., 1512 Western Ave., Seattle WA 98101. (206)682-9748. President: William R. Griffin. Small press. Publishes trade paperback originals and reprints. Averages 4-6 titles/year; receives 15 submissions annually. 75% of books from first-time authors; 100% of books from unagented writers. Subsidy publishes 5% of books. "If they (authors) won't sell it and won't accept royalty contract, we offer our publishing services and often sell the book along with our books." Pays 5-15% royalty on retail price or outright purchase, $100-2,500, depending on negotiated agreement. Publishes book an average of 6-12 months after acceptance. Photocopied submissions OK. Computer printout submissions acceptable; prefers letter-quality. Reports in 6 weeks on queries; 3 months on mss. Free book catalog; ms guidelines for SASE.
Nonfiction: How-to, illustrated book, reference, self-help, technical, textbook and directories. Subjects include business, health, and cleaning and maintenance. Needs books on anything related to cleaning, maintenance, self-employment or entrepreneurship. Query or submit outline/synopsis and sample chapters or complete ms. Reviews artwork/photos.
Recent Nonfiction Title: *How to Sell and Price Contract Cleaning*, by William Griffin and John Davis.
Tips: "Our audience includes those involved in cleaning and maintenance service trades, opportunity seekers, schools, property managers, libraries—anyone who needs information on cleaning and maintenance. How-to and self-employment guides are doing well for us in today's market. We are now seeking books on fire damage restoration and also articles for a quarterly magazine."

‡CLEIS PRESS, Box 14684, San Francisco CA 94114. Co-editor, Acquisitions Coordinator: Frederique Delacoste. Publishes trade paperback originals and reprints. Publishes 4 titles/year. 75% of books are from first-time authors; 90% from unagented writers. Royalties vary on retail price. Publishes book 6 months after acceptance. Simultaneous and photocopied submissions OK "only if accompanied by an original letter stating where and when ms was sent." Query for electronic submissions. Computer printout submissions OK; prefers letter-quality. Reports in 1 month. Books catalog for #10 SAE and 2 first class stamps.
Nonfiction: Human rights, feminist. Subjects include gay/lesbian, government/politics, sociology (of women), women's issues/studies. "We are interested in books that: a) will sell in feminist and progressive bookstores and b) will sell in Europe (translation rights). We are interested in books by and about women in Latin America; on lesbian and gay rights; and other feminist topics which have not already been widely documented. We do not want religious/spiritual tracts; we are not interested in books on topics which have been documented over and over, unless the author is approaching the topic from a new viewpoint." Query or submit outline/synopsis and sample chapters or complete ms.
Recent Nonfiction Title: *Sex Work: Writings by Women in the Sex Industry*, edited by Delecoste and Alexander (anthology of essays).
Fiction: Feminist, gay/lesbian, literary. "We are looking for high quality novels by women. We are especially interested in translations of Latin American women's fiction. No romances!" Submit complete ms.
Recent Fiction Title: *Unholy Alliances: New Fiction by Women*, edited by Rafkin (anthology).
Tips: "An anthology project representing the work of a very diverse group of women . . . an anthology on a very hot, very unique, risk-taking theme. These books sell well for us; they're our trademark. If I were trying to market a book today, I would become very familiar with the presses serving my market. More than reading publishers' catalogs, I think author should spend time in a bookstore whose clientele closely resembles her intended audience. Be absolutely aware of her audience; have researched potential market; present fresh new ways of looking at her topic; avoid 'PR' language in query letter."

*CLEVELAND STATE UNIVERSITY POETRY CENTER, R.T. 1815, Cleveland State University, Cleveland OH 44115. (216)687-3986. Editor: Leonard M. Trawick. Small press. Publishes trade paperback and hardcover originals. Averages 5 titles/year; receives 400 queries, 500 mss annually. 60% of books from first-time authors; 100% of books from unagented writers. 30% of titles subsidized by CSU, 30% by government subsidy. CSU poetry series pays 10% royalty plus 50 copies on wholesale price if sold by bookseller, on retail price if sold by CSU Poetry Center; Cleveland Poetry Series (Ohio poets only) pays 100 copies. $1,000 prize for best manuscript each year. No advance. Publishes book an average of 1 year after acceptance. Simultaneous and photocopied submissions OK. Computer printout submissions acceptable; prefers letter-quality. Reports in 2 weeks on queries; 6 months on mss. Book catalog for 6x9 SAE with 2 first class stamps; ms guidelines for SASE.
Poetry: No light verse, "inspirational," or greeting card verse. ("This does not mean that we do not consider poetry with humor or philosophical/religious import.") Query—ask for guidelines. Submit only December-February. Reviews artwork/photos if applicable (i.e., concrete poetry).
Recent Poetry Title: *The Lit Window*, by Michael Umphrey.
Tips: "Our books are for serious readers of poetry, i.e. poets, critics, academics, students, people who read *Poetry, Field, American Poetry Review, Antaeus*, etc." Trends include "movement from 'confessional' poetry; greater attention to form and craftsmanship. Try to project an interesting, coherent personality; link poems so as to make coherent unity, not just a miscellaneous collection." Especially needs "poems with *mystery*, i.e., poems that reflect profound thought, but do not tell all—suggestive, tantalizing, enticing."

CLIFFHANGER PRESS, Box 29527, Oakland CA 94604-9527. (415)763-3510. Editor: Nancy Chirich. Small press. Publishes trade paperback originals. Averages 5 titles/year. Pays 8% royalty on retail price. Publishes book an average of 9 months after acceptance. Simultaneous and photocopied submissions OK. Reports in 2 months. Book catalog for #10 SASE. Computer printout submissions OK; prefers letter-quality.
Fiction: Mystery and suspense. "Manuscripts should be about 75,000 words, heavy on American regional or foreign atmosphere. No cynical, hardboiled detectives or spies." Submit synopsis/outline and 2-3 sample chapters. "No returns without SASE."
Recent Fiction Title: *Death in a Small Southern Town*, by Robert L. McKinney.
Tips: "Mystery/suspense is our only specialty. Have believable characters, a strong, uncomplicated story and heavy regional or foreign atmosphere. No justified right margins on manuscripts submitted. They're very hard to read at length."

CLIFFS NOTES, INC., Box 80728, Lincoln NE 68501. (402)477-6971. General Editor: Michele Spence. Notes Editor: Gary Carey. Publishes trade paperback originals. Averages 20 titles/year. 100% of books from unagented writers. Pays royalty on wholesale price. Buys some mss outright; "full payment on acceptance of ms." Publishes book an average of 1 year after acceptance. Computer printout submissions acceptable. Reports in 1 month. "We provide specific guidelines when a project is assigned."
Nonfiction: Self-help and textbook. "We publish self-help study aids directed to junior high through graduate school audience. Publications include *Cliffs Notes, Cliffs Test Preparation Guides, Cliffs Teaching Portfolios*, and other study guides. Most authors are experienced teachers, usually with advanced degrees. *Teaching Portfolio* authors are experienced high school English teachers who can provide practical, proven classroom material designed for junior high and high school English teachers. Some books also appeal to a general lay audience." Query.
Recent Nonfiction Title: *Cliffs Notes on Greek Classics*.

COACH HOUSE PRESS, INC., Box 458, Morton Grove IL 60053. (312)967-1777. Publisher/President: David Jewell. Small press. Publishes production script originals. Averages 3-8 titles/year; receives 150-200 submissions annually. 50% of books from first-time authors; 95% of books from unagented writers. Pays 10% royalty on receipts from book sales; 50% royalty on performance. Publishes book an average of 3-15 months after acceptance. Simultaneous and photocopied submissions OK. Query for electronic submissions. Computer printout submissions acceptable; prefers letter-quality. Reports in 1 month on queries; 3 months on mss. Script catalog and guidelines for 9x12 SAE with 4 first class stamps.
Nonfiction: Drama production guides and aids. Query with synopsis.
Fiction: Plays for children's theatre, one-act plays for high school contest and plays for senior adults. Query with synopsis and production history.
Recent Fiction Title: *Friday's Child*, by Pam Sterling.
Tips: "Plays which sell best to today's producers respect children as intelligent, alert and informed, and *avoid* stereotyping any group as evil, stupid or immature. Playwrights need to get their plays production-tested. They help themselves by including production history and personal biography with cover letter. Don't send adult scripts to a child-drama publisher."

COLES PUBLISHING CO., LTD., 90 Ronson Dr., Rexdale, Ontario, Canada M9W 1C1. (416)243-3132. Publishing Assistant: Janina Lucci. Publishes paperback originals and reprints. Averages 10 titles/year; receives

350 submissions annually. 80% of books from first-time authors; 100% of books from unagented writers. Average print order for a writer's first book is 5,000. "We are a subsidiary company of 'Coles, the Book People,' a chain of 235 bookstores throughout Canada and America." Pays by outright purchase of $500-$2,500; advance averages $1,000. Publishes book an average of 8 months after acceptance. Simultaneous and photocopied submissions OK. Reports in 1 month. Send SAE and International Reply Coupons.

Nonfiction: "We publish in the following areas: education, language, science, math, pet care, gardening, occult, business, reference, technical and do-it-yourself, crafts and hobbies, games, and sports. We also publish a complete line of literary study aids sold worldwide." No philosophy, religion, history or biography. Submit outline/synopsis and sample chapters.

Recent Nonfiction Title: *Teach Yourself Keyboarding*.

Tips: "The writer has the best chance of selling us wide appeal, practical self-help books."

COLLECTOR BOOKS, Division of Schroeder Publishing Co., Inc., Box 3009, Paducah KY 42001. Editor: Steve Quertermous. Publishes hardcover and paperback originals. Publishes 35-40 titles/year. 50% of books from first-time authors; 100% of books from unagented writers. Average print order for a writer's first book is 5,000. Pays 5% royalty on retail; no advance. Publishes book an average of 8 months after acceptance. Computer printout submissions acceptable; no dot-matrix. Reports in 1 month. Free book catalog.

Nonfiction: "We only publish books on antiques and collectibles. We require our authors to be very knowledgeable in their respective fields and have access to a large representative sampling of the particular subject concerned." Query. Accepts outline and 2-3 sample chapters. Reviews artwork/photos as part of ms package.

Recent Nonfiction Title: *Collector's Guide to Baseball Memorabilia*, by Don Raycraft and Stew Salowitz.

Tips: Common mistakes writers make include "making phone contact instead of written contact and assuming an accurate market evaluation."

‡THE COLLEGE BOARD, Imprint of College Entrance Examination Board, 45 Columbus Ave., New York NY 10023-6917. (212)713-8000. Senior Editor: Carolyn Trager. Trade paperback originals. Firm publishes 30 titles/year; imprint publishes 8 titles/year. Receives 20-30 submissions/year. 25% of books from first-time authors; 50% from unagented writers. Pays royalty on retail price of books sold through bookstores. Offers advance based on anticipated first year's earnings. Publishes book 9 months after acceptance. Photocopied submissions OK. Accepts computer printout submissions, prefers letter-quality. Reports in 2 weeks on queries; 1 month on ms. Book catalog free on request.

Nonfiction: Biography, how-to, reference, self-help. Subjects include child guidance/parenting, education, language/literature, science. "We want books to help students make a successful transition from high school to college." Query or send outline/synopsis and sample chapters. Reviews artwork/photos as part of ms package.

Recent Nonfiction Title: *Succeed With Math*, by Sheila Tobias (guide to help students overcome anxiety and master math).

Tips: "Our audience is college-bound high school students, beginning college students and/or their parents."

‡*COLLEGE PRESS PUBLISHING CO., INC., 205 N. Main, Box 1132, Joplin MO 64802. (417)623-6280. Contact: Steven F. Jennings. Publishes hardcover and trade paperback originals and reprints. Publishes 25 titles/year. Receives 150 submissions/year. 25% of books are from first-time authors; 100% from unagented writers. Subsidy publishes 5% of books. Subsidy considered "if we really want to publish a book, but don't have room in schedule at this time or funds available." Pays 10% royalty on net receipts. Publishes book 1 year after acceptance. Simultaneous and photocopied submissions OK. Computer printout submissions OK. Reports on queries in 1 month; on ms in 3 month. Book catalog free on request.

Nonfiction: Textbooks. Subjects include religious (Christian church, Church of Christ). Query.

Recent Nonfiction Title: *Union on the King's Highway*, by Dean Mills (historical-church related).

Fiction: Historical, religious. Query.

Tips: "Topical Bible study books have the best chance of selling to our firm. Our audience is Christians interested in reading and studying Bible-based material."

‡COLORADO ASSOCIATED UNIVERSITY PRESS, Box 480, 1344 Grandview Ave., University of Colorado, Boulder CO 80309. (303)492-7191. Editor: Frederick Rinehart. Publishes hardcover and paperback originals. Averages 10 titles/year; receives 350 submissions annually. 50% of books from first-time authors; 99% of books from unagented writers. Average print order for a writer's first book is 500-1,000. Pays 10-12½-15% royalty contract on wholesale or retail price; "no advances." Publishes book an average of 18 months after acceptance. Will consider photocopied submissions "if not sent simultaneously to another publisher." Query for electronic submissions. Computer printout submissions acceptable; prefers letter-quality. Reports in 3 months. Free book catalog.

Nonfiction: Scholarly, regional and environmental subjects. Length: 250-500 pages. Query first with table of contents, preface or opening chapter. Reviews artwork/photos as part of ms package.

Recent Nonfiction Title: *Colorado Flora: Western Slope*, by William A. Weber.

Tips: "Books should be solidly researched and from a reputable scholar, because we are a university press."

COMMUNICATION SKILL BUILDERS, INC., Box 42050, Tucson AZ 85733. (602)323-7500. Acquisitions Manager: Patti Hartmann. Publishes paperback originals, kits, games, software and audio and video cassettes. Averages 40 titles/year; receives 150 submissions annually. 50% of books from first-time authors; 100% of books from unagented writers. Pays negotiable royalty on cash received. Publishes book an average of 9 months after acceptance. No simultaneous submissions; photocopied submissions OK. Query for electronic submissions. Computer printout submissions acceptable. Reports in 2 months. Free catalog—Speech-Language/Special Education/Early Childhood Education. Free writer's guidelines.
Nonfiction: Speech-Language/Special Education/Early Childhood Education material: articulation therapy, language remediation and development; hearing impaired; adult communicative disorders; physically handicapped/developmentally delayed; augmentative communications; professional resources; assessment materials. Reviews artwork/photos as part of ms package. "If a material is illustrated, costs for the photographs or drawings are the responsibility of the author." Publisher can arrange to have artwork done.
Recent Nonfiction Title: *Practicing Individual Concepts of Language.*

‡**COMMUNICATIONS PRESS**, Imprint of Broadcasting Publications, Inc., 1705 DeSales St. NW, Washington DC 20036. (202)659-2340. Manager: David Dietz. Publishes hardcover, trade paperback, and professional/text paperback originals. 95% of books from unagented writers. Pays royalty or honorarium; offers "nominal, if any" advance. Publishes book an average of 9 months after acceptance. Computer printout submissions acceptable; no dot-matrix. Reports in 1 month.
Nonfiction: Reference, technical and textbook. Subjects include broadcast and cable television, radio and satellite communications. Emphasis on business, management and government regulation. Submit outline/synopsis and 2 sample chapters. Reviews artwork/photos.
Recent Nonfiction Title: *Cable Programming Resource Directory.*

‡**COMMUNITY INTERVENTION, INC.**, Suite 570, 529 South Seventh St., Minneapolis MN 55415. (612)332-6537. Executive Director: Lawrence Flanagan. Publishes mass market paperback originals. Publishes 24 titles/year. Receives 700 submissions/year. 60% of book from first-time authors; 100% from unagented writers. Pays 7½-10% royalty on wholesale price. Offers $500 average advance "to writers who have written for us before." Publishes book an average of 4 months after acceptance. Photocopied submissions OK. Computer printout submissions OK; prefers letter-quality. Reports in 2 weeks on queries; 2 months on mss. Book catalog free on request; ms guidelines for #10 SAE and 1 first class stamp.
Nonfiction: How-to, self-help. Subjects include child guidance/parenting, education, health/medicine, psychology, recreation, sociology, women's issues/studies, chemical abuse. "Our booklets are 24 to 48 pages in length, written for a general audience. We are searching for well written, focused and short manuscripts that address a wide range of adult, adolescent and family concerns and issues. No first person experiences please. Manuscripts must provide a reasonable, authoritative solution when addressing a specific problem. it must tell reader how to get professional help." Query or submit complete ms.
Recent Nonfiction Title: *Mending Family Relationships*, by E. Leite (self-help).
Tips: "We are looking for professionally written works that focus on adult, adolescent or family concerns and issues. We prefer authors with experience in the field they are writing about. The booklet manuscripts must be written for a general audience. No technical or difficult to understand materials will be accepted."

COMPACT BOOKS, 2131 Hollywood Blvd., Hollywood FL 33020. (305)925-5242. Imprint of Frederick Fell. Publisher: Donald L. Lessne. Publishes hardcover and trade paperback originals. Averages 10 titles/year; receives 1,000 submissions annually. 25% of books from first-time authors; 25% of books from unagented writers. Pays royalty. Publishes book an average of 1 year after acceptance. Simultaneous and photocopied submissions OK. Query for electronic submissions. Computer printout submissions OK. Reports in 6 months on mss. Free book catalog.
Nonfiction: Cookbook, how-to, humor, reference and self-help. Subjects include business and economics, cooking and foods, health, hobbies, psychology, recreation, religion and sociology. "We're looking for easy-to-read, general interest books on current issues and health." Submit outline/synopsis and sample chapters. Reviews artwork/photos as part of ms package.
Recent Nonfiction Title: *Teenage Alcoholism and Substance Abuse*, by Carmella and John Bartimole (family/child care).
Tips: "Our list is fairly well consistent year-to-year. We look to fill in our list in the various categories of trade publishing when there is something new in the media or complements our current list. We also look strongly at those authors who are promotional-minded and are able to work hard to get their titles sold."

COMPUTER SCIENCE PRESS, INC., 1803 Research Blvd., Rockville MD 20850. (301)251-9050. Imprint of W.H. Freeman and Company. Editor: Barbara B. Friedman. Editor-in-Chief: Dr. Arthur D. Friedman. Publishes hardcover and paperback originals and software. Averages 20 titles/year. 25% of books from first-time authors; 98% of books from unagented writers. All authors are recognized subject area experts. Pays royalty on net price. Publishes book an average of 6-9 months after acceptance. Computer printout submissions acceptable. Reports ASAP.

Nonfiction: "Technical books in all aspects of computer science, computer engineering, computer chess, electrical engineering, computers and math, and telecommunications. Both text and reference books. Will also consider public appeal 'trade' books in computer science, manuscripts and diskettes. Query or submit complete ms. Requires "3 copies of manuscripts." Looks for "technical accuracy of the material and the reason this approach is being taken. We would also like a covering letter stating what the author sees as the competition for this work and why this work is superior."
Recent Nonfiction Title: *Elements of Artificial Intelligence*, by Tanimoto.

CONSUMER REPORTS BOOKS, Subsidiary of Consumers Union. #1301, 110 E. 42nd St., New York NY 10017. (212)682-9280. Contact: Director, Consumer Reports Books. Publishes trade paperback originals and trade paperback reprints. Averages 30-35 titles/year; receives 1,000 submissions annually. Most of books from unagented writers. Pays variable royalty on retail price; buys some mss outright. Publishes book an average of 9 months after acceptance. Simultaneous and photocopied submissions OK. Computer printout submissions acceptable; prefers letter-quality. Reports in 1 month on queries; 2 months on mss. Free book list and writer's manuscript guidelines on request.
Nonfiction: Cookbook, how-to, reference, self-help and technical, and how-to books for children. Subjects include business and economics, cooking and foods, health, music and consumer guidance. Submit outline/synopsis and 1-2 sample chapters.

CONTEMPORARY BOOKS, INC., 180 N. Michigan Ave., Chicago IL 60601. (312)782-9182. Subsidiaries include Congdon & Weed. Editorial Director: Nancy J. Crossman. Publishes hardcover originals and trade paperback originals and reprints. Averages 100 titles/year; receives 1,000 submissions annually. 25% of books from first-time authors; 25% of books from unagented writers. Pays 6-15% royalty on retail price. Publishes book an average of 10 months after acceptance. Query for electronic submissions. Computer printout submissions OK. Simultaneous and photocopied submissions OK. Reports in 3 weeks. Book catalog and ms guidelines for 9x12 SAE and 6 first class stamps.
Nonfiction: Biography, cookbook, how-to, humor, reference and self-help. Subjects include business, finance, cooking, health, fitness, psychology, sports, real estate, new age, travel, nutrition, popular culture and women's studies. Submit outline/synopsis and sample chapters. Reviews artwork/photos as part of ms package.
Fiction: Adult science fiction and sports only. Submit outline/synopsis and sample chapters.
Recent Fiction Title: *She's On First*, by Barbara Gregorich (sports).

‡**CORKSCREW PRESS**, 2915 Fenimore Rd., Silver Spring MD 20902. (301)933-0407. President: Richard Lippmann. Publishes trade paperback originals. Publishes 4 books/year. 50% of books from first-time authors. Pays 5-12% roylaty on retail price. Publishes book an average of 12-15 months after acceptance. Simultaneous and photocopied submissions OK. Computer printout submissions OK; no dot-matrix. Reports in 2 weeks on queries; 5 weeks on mss. Free book catalog.
Nonfiction: Cookbook, how-to, humor. Submit outline/synopsis and sample chapters.
Fiction: Humor. Submit outline/synopsis and sample chapters.

CORNELL MARITIME PRESS, INC., Box 456, Centreville MD 21617. Editor: Willard A. Lockwood. Imprint includes Tidewater Publishers. Publishes original hardcover and quality paperbacks. Averages 15-18 titles/year; receives 150 submissions annually. 41% of books from first-time authors; 99% of books from unagented writers. Payment is negotiable but royalties do not exceed 10% for first 5,000 copies, 12½% for second 5,000 copies, 15% on all additional. Royalties for original paperbacks and regional titles are invariably lower. Revised editions revert to original royalty schedule. Publishes book an average of 10 months after acceptance. Query for electronic submissions. Computer printout submissions acceptable; prefers letter-quality. Send queries first, accompanied by writing samples and outlines of book ideas. Reports in 1 month. Free book catalog and ms guidelines.
Nonfiction: Marine subjects (highly technical); manuals; and how-to books on maritime subjects. Tidewater Publishers imprint publishes books on regional history, folklore and wildlife of the Chesapeake Bay and the Delmarva Peninsula.
Recent Nonfiction Titles: *Shiphandling With Tugs*, by Capt. G.H. Reid (professional text/reference) published by Cornell Maritime Press; and *Steamboat on the Chesapeake: Emma Giles & the Tolchester Line*, by D.C. Holly (regional history for general reader) published by Tidewater Publishers.

‡**COTEAU BOOKS**, Imprint of Thunder Creek Publishing Cooperative, Suite 209, 1945 Scarth St., Regina Saskatchewan S4P 2H2 Canada. (306)352-5346. Subsidiaries include Coteau Books and Caragana Records. Managing Editor: Catherine Edwards. Publishes hardcover, trade paperback and mass market paperback originals. Publishes 8-9 titles/year; receives approximately 400 queries and mss/year. 60% of books from first-time authors; 100% from unagented writers. Pays 10% royalty on retail price or outright purchase of $50-200 for anthology contributors. Publishes book an average of 12-18 months after acceptance. Photocopied submissions

OK. Computer printout submissions OK; prefers letter-quality. Reports in 1 month on queries; in 6 months on ms. Free book catalog.

Nonfiction: Coffee table book, humor, illustrated book, juvenile, reference, desk calendars. Subjects include art/architecture, ethnic, history, language/literature, photography, regional and women's issues/studies. "We do not want to see manuscripts from the U.S.; we are a Canadian publisher. We are interested in history for our region and books on multicultural themes pertaining to our region." Reviews artwork/photos as part of ms package.

Fiction: Erotica, ethnic, experimental, fantasy, feminist, humor, juvenile, literary, mainstream/contemporary, mystery, picture books, plays, science fiction, short story collections. "No popular, mass market sort of stuff. We are a literary press." Submit complete ms.

Recent Fiction Title: *The Valley of Flowers*, by Veronica Eddy Brock.

COUNCIL OAK BOOKS, 1428 S. St. Louis, Tulsa OK 74120. (918)587-6454. President: Sally Dennison. Small press. Publishes hardcover and softcover originals and reprints. Averages 5 titles/year; receives approximately 1,000 submissions annually. 50% of books from first-time authors; 50% of books from unagented writers. Pays royalty on retail price. Photocopied submissions OK. Computer printout submissions acceptable; prefers letter-quality. Reports in 1 month on queries; 3 months on mss. Book catalog and ms guidelines for 9x12 SAE with 3 first class stamps.

Nonfiction: Biography, memoir, cookbook, how-to, illustrated book and self-help. Subjects include art, business and economics, cooking and foods, health, history, nature, philosophy, politics, psychology. Query. "We cannot consider nonfiction of fewer than 20,000 words. No unsolicited nonfiction." Reviews artwork/photos.

Recent Nonfiction Title: *Libby*, by Elizabeth Beaman John (journal/art).

Fiction: Query first—include sample of the book. Mainstream; novels. "Any *upscale* fiction. It must be intelligent, and have an honest heart." No standard genre fiction—"the romance, the sci-fi, the western, the historical saga, the mystery, etc."—religious or devotional. Submit first 10 pages or chapter. "We do not publish poetry, children's books, novellas or short fiction collections. No fiction under 50,000 words."

Recent Fiction Title: *The Silver DeSoto*, by Patti Lou Floyd.

Tips: "Non-genre fiction and upscale market nonfiction have the best chance of selling to us. A well-written 'sales' letter is no substitute for a well-written book."

‡THE COUNTRYMAN PRESS, Box 175, Woodstock VT 05091. (802)457-1049. Fiction: Louis Kannenstine, president. Nonfiction: Carl Taylor, vice president. Publishes hardback and trade paperback originals and paperback reprints. Publishes 24 titles/year. Receives 100 submissions/year. 50% of books from first-time authors; 75% from unagented writers. Pays 5-10% royalty on retail price. Offers $500 average advance. Publishes book 6 months after acceptance. Simultaneous and photocopied submissions OK. Computer printout submissions OK; prefers letter-quality. Reports in 2 weeks on queries; in 6 weeks on mss. Book catalog free on request.

Nonfiction: Cookbook, how-to, humor, travel guides. Subjects include cooking, foods and nutrition, history, nature/environment, recreation, regional (New England, especially Vermont), travel. "We want good 'how-to' books, especially those related to rural life." Submit outline/synopsis and sample chapters. Review artwork/photos as part of ms package.

Recent Nonfiction Title: *Vermont, An Explorer's Guide*, by Tree/Jennison (travel guide).

Fiction: Mystery. "We're looking for good mysteries of any type—new, reprint, or U.S. publication of mysteries already published abroad." Submit complete ms.

Recent Fiction Title: *The Long Kill*, by Reginald Hill writing as Patrick Ruell (mystery).

CRAFTSMAN BOOK COMPANY, 6058 Corte Del Cedro, Box 6500, Carlsbad CA 92008. (619)438-7828. Editor-in-Chief: Laurence D. Jacobs. Publishes paperback originals. Averages 8-12 titles/year; receives 20 submissions/year. 50% of books from first-time authors; 98% of books from unagented writers. Pays 12.5% royalty on wholesale price; pays 12.5% royalty on retail price "when we retail by mail." Offers $300-800 average advance. Publishes book an average of 18 months after acceptance. Simultaneous and photocopied submissions OK. Query for electronic submissions. Computer printout submissions OK; prefers letter-quality. Reports in 1 month on queries; 10 weeks on mss. Book catalog and guidelines for 6x9 SAE with 3 first class stamps.

Nonfiction: How-to and technical. All titles are related to construction for professional builders. Submit outline/synopsis and sample chapters. Reviews artwork/photos as part of ms package.

Recent Nonfiction Title: *Drywall Contracting*, by J. Frane.

Tips: "The book should be loaded with step-by-step instructions, illustrations, charts, reference data, forms, samples, cost estimates, rules of thumb, and examples that solve actual problems in the builder's office and in the field. The book must cover the subject completely, become the owner's primary reference on the subject, have a high utility-to-cost ratio, and help the owner make a better living in his chosen field."

CREATIVE ARTS BOOK COMPANY, Donald S. Ellis, San Francisco; Black Lizard Books; Creative Arts Communications Books; 833 Bancroft Way, Berkeley CA 94710. (415)848-4777. Publisher: Donald S. Ellis. Senior Editor: Peg O'Donnell. Business Manager: Jamie Tracy. Publishes hardcover and paperback originals and paperback reprints. Averages 38 titles/year; receives 800-1,000 submissions annually. 10% of books from first-time authors; 20% of books from unagented writers. Pays 5-15% royalty on retail price. Offers minimum $500 advance. Publishes book an average of 12-18 months after acceptance. Simultaneous and photocopied submissions OK. Computer printout submissions acceptable. Reports in 6 weeks. Free book catalog.
Nonfiction: Biographies and essays. Open to anything *brilliant* (except poetry). Reviews artwork/photos as part of ms package.
Recent Nonfiction Title: *The Men in My Life*, by James D. Houston.
Fiction: "Looking for serious literary fiction of broad appeal, also children's picture books, classics and biographies for ages 2-12."
Recent Fiction Title: *The Sea of Gold*, by Yoshiko Uchida.

‡CREATIVE PUBLISHING CO., The Early West, Box 9292, College Station TX 77840. (409)775-6047. Contact: Theresa Earle. Publishes hardcover originals. Receives 20-40 submissions/year. 50% of books from first-time authors; 100% from unagented writers. Royalty varies on wholesale price. Publishes book an average of 8 months after acceptance. Photocopied submissions OK. Computer printout submissions OK; prefers letter-quality. Reports in "several" week on queries; "several" months on mss. Book catalog free on request.
Nonfiction: Biography. Subjects include Americana (western), history. No mss other than 19th century western America. Query. Reviews artwork/photos as part of ms package.
Recent Nonfiction Title: *Masterson & Roosevelt*, by Jack DeMattos (western Americana).

CREDO PUBLISHING CORPORATION, Box 3339, Langley British Columbia V3A 4R7 Canada. (604)576-9466. Book Editor: Jocelyn E. Cameron. Imprint includes CEDAR Books. Publishes Christian trade paperback originals and reprints. Publishes 4 titles/year. Receives 50-100 submissions/year. 50% of books from first-time authors. 95% of books from unagented writers. Pays 10% royalty on wholesale price. Publishes book an average of 1 year after acceptance. Photocopied submissions OK. Computer printout submissions OK; prefers letter-quality. Reports in 2 weeks on queries. Book catalog and ms guidelines for #10 SAE with IRC.
Nonfiction: Biography, how-to, reference and self-help. Query or submit outline and sample chapters with SASE.
Recent Nonfiction Title: *An Uncommon Commoner*, by Lorry Lutz.
Tips: "Please note we are a Christian publishing house and our published works reflect that viewpoint."

CRITIC'S CHOICE PAPERBACKS, Subsidiary of Lorevan Publishing, Inc., 31 E. 28th St., New York NY 10016. (212)685-1550. Editor-in-Chief: Stan Reisner. Publishes mass market paperback originals and reprints. Averages 96 titles/year; receives 100 submissions annually. 1% of books from first-time authors; 5% of books from unagented writers. Pays 6-8% royalty on retail price. Offers average $1,000 advance. Publishes book an average of 18 months after acceptance. Computer printout submissions acceptable; no dot-matrix. Reports in 1 month on queries; 2 months on mss. Book catalog for #10 SAE with 2 first class stamps.
Nonfiction: Humor.
Fiction: Adventure, historical, horror, mainstream, mystery, science fiction, suspense, western, spy/espionage, thriller, and action. Query or submit outline/synopsis and sample chapters; all unsolicited mss are returned unopened.

THE CROSSING PRESS, 22-D Roache Rd., Box 207, Freedom CA 95019. (408)722-0711. Co-Publishers: Elaine Goldman Gill, John Gill. Publishes hardcover and trade paperback originals. Averages 30 titles/year; receives 1600 submissions annually. 30% of books from first-time authors; 90% of books from unagented writers. Pays royalty. Publishes book an average of 18 months after acceptance. Simultaneous and photocopied submissions OK. Query for electronic submissions. Computer printout submissions acceptable. Reports in 2 months on queries; 3 months on mss. Free book catalog.
Nonfiction: Cookbook, how-to, men's studies, literary and feminist. Subjects include cooking, health, gays and feminism. Submissions to be considered for the feminist series must be written by women. Submit outline and sample chapter. Reviews artwork/photos as part of ms package.
Recent Nonfiction Title: *Salad Dressings*, by Jane M. Dieckmann (cookbook).
Fiction: Good literary material. Submit outline and sample chapter.
Recent Fiction Title: *Class Porn*, by Molly Hite (novel).
Tips: "Simple intelligent query letters do best. No come-ons, no cutes. It helps if there are credentials. Authors should research the press first to see what sort of books it publishes."

CROSSWAY BOOKS, Subsidiary of Good News Publishers, 9825 W. Roosevelt Rd., Westchester IL 60153. Managing Editor: Ted Griffin. Publishes hardcover and trade paperback originals. Averages 25 titles/year; receives 3,500 submissions annually. 10% of books from first-time authors; 50% of books from unagented writers. Average print order for a writer's first book is 3,000. Pays negotiable royalty; offers negotiable advance. Publishes book an average of 1 year after acceptance. Send query and synopsis, not whole manuscript. No phone queries! Reports in 2 months. Book catalog and ms guidelines for 6x9 SAE and $1 postage.

Nonfiction: Subjects include issues on Christianity in contemporary culture, Christian doctrine, and church history. "All books must be written out of Christian perspective or world view." No unsolicited mss. Query with synopsis.

Recent Nonfiction Title: *Heart and Home*, by Debra Evans.

Fiction: Mainstream; science fiction; fantasy (genuinely creative in the tradition of C.S. Lewis, J.R.R. Tolkien and Madeleine L'Engle); and juvenile age 6 and up to young adult. No formula romance. Query with synopsis. "All fiction must be written from a genuine Christian perspective."

Recent Fiction Title: *Merlin* (second of four in Pendragon Cycle), by Stephen R. Lawhead.

Tips: "The writer has the best chance of selling our firm a book which, through fiction or nonfiction, shows the practical relevance of biblical doctrine to contemporary issues and life."

CROWN PUBLISHERS, INC., 225 Park Ave. S., New York NY 10003. (212)254-1600. Imprints include Clarkson N. Potter, Orion Books, Harmony and Julian Press. Publishes hardcover and paperback originals. Publishes 250 titles/year. Simultaneous submissions OK. Reports in 2 months.

Nonfiction: Americana, animals, art, biography, cookbooks/cooking, health, history, hobbies, how-to, humor, juveniles, military history, nature, photography, politics, psychology, recreation, reference, science, self-help and sports. Query with letter only.

HARRY CUFF PUBLICATIONS LIMITED, 1 Dorset St., St. John's, Newfoundland A1B 1W8 Canada. (709)726-6590. Editor: Harry Cuff. Hardcover and trade paperback originals. Averages 12 titles/year; receives 50 submissions annually. 50% of books from first-time authors; 100% of books from unagented writers. Pays 10% royalty on retail price. No advance. Publishes book an average of 8 months after acceptance. Photocopied submissions OK. Computer printout submissions acceptable; no dot-matrix. Reports in 6 months on mss. Book catalog for 5x9 SAE.

Nonfiction: Biography, humor, illustrated book, juvenile, reference, technical, and textbook, all dealing with Newfoundland. Subjects include history, photography, politics and sociology. Query.

Recent Nonfiction Title: *I've Been Working on the Railroad*, by W.J. Chafe.

Fiction: Ethnic, historical, humor and mainstream. Needs fiction about Newfoundlanders or Newfoundland. Submit complete ms.

Recent Fiction Title: *The Welfare Officer Will See You Now Me*, by Chris Deeker.

Tips: "We are currently dedicated to publishing book about Newfoundland. We will return 'mainstream' manuscripts from the U.S. unread."

CYNTHIA PUBLISHING COMPANY, Suite 1106, 4455 Los Feliz Blvd., Los Angeles CA 90027. (213)664-3165. President: Dick Mitchell. Small press. Publishes mass market paperback originals. Averages 10-20 titles/year. Receives 50-100 submissions/year. 50% of books from first-time authors. 80% of books from unagented writers. Pays royalty on retail price. Offers $2,000 average advance. Simultaneous and photocopied submissions OK. Query for electronic submissions. Computer printout submissions OK; prefers letter-quality. Reports in 1 week on queries; 2 months on mss. Book catalog for #10 SAE.

Nonfiction: Technical. Subjects include sports and investments. "We need one title per month on subject of strategic investing (stock market, commodities, options, horse racing, sports betting). No narratives—must include specific strategy." Query.

Recent Nonfiction Title: *The Odds on Your Side*, by Mark Cramer.

Tips: "We are now accepting cassette tape submissions and computer softerware programs."

*DANCE HORIZONS, Imprint of Princeton Book Co., Publishers, Box 109, Princeton NJ 08542. (609)737-8177. Editorial Director: Richard Carlin. Publishes hardcover and paperback originals and paperback reprints. Averages 10 titles/year; receives 50-75 submissions annually. 50% of books from first-time authors; 100% of books from unagented writers. Subsidy publishes 20% of books. Pays 10% royalty on net receipts; offers no advance. Publishes book an average of 10 months after acceptance. Simultaneous and photocopied submissions OK. Computer printout submissions acceptable; no dot-matrix. Reports in 3 months. Free book catalog.

Nonfiction: "Anything dealing with dance." Query first. Reviews artwork/photos.

Recent Nonfiction Title: *The Hidden You*, by Mabel Todd.

*JOHN DANIEL, PUBLISHER, Box 21922, Santa Barbara CA 93121. (805)962-1780. Imprints include Fithian Press. Publisher: John Daniel. Publishes trade paperback originals. Averages 20 titles/year; receives 600 submissions annually. 50% of books from first-time authors; 100% of books from unagented writers. Subsidy publishes 50% of titles. "If we like a book but don't feel its commercial possibilities justify a financial risk, we offer the Fithian Press contract: author pays major production costs in exchange for a 50%-of-net royalty." Pays 10-50% royalty on wholesale price. Publishes book an average of 8 months after acceptance. Simultaneous and photocopied submissions OK. Query for electronic submissions. Computer printout submissions acceptable. Reports in 3 weeks on queries; 2 months on mss. Book catalog and ms guidelines for #10 SAE with 1 first class stamp.

Nonfiction: Autobiography, biography, humor, self-help, travel, nature, philosophy and essays. "We'll look at anything, but are particularly interested in books in which literary merit is foremost—as opposed to books that simply supply information. No libelous, obscene, poorly written or unintelligent manuscripts." Query or submit outline and sample chapters.

Recent Nonfiction Title: *Wayfaring with Birds*, by Ina Griffin (nature).

Fiction: Adventure, ethnic, experimental, fantasy, historical, humor, mainstream and mystery. "We do best with books by authors who have demonstrated a clear, honest, elegant style. No libelous, obscene, poorly written, or boring submissions." Query or submit synopsis and sample chapters.

Recent Fiction Title: *The Sea Child*, by Leslie G. Cady (novel).

Poetry: "We're open to anything, but we're very cautious. Poetry's hard to sell." Submit complete ms.

Recent Poetry Title: *Forever Avenue*, by Michael Duffett.

Tips: "If I were a writer trying to market a book today, I would envision my specific audience and approach publishers who demonstrate that they can reach that audience. Writing is not always a lucrative profession; almost nobody makes a living off of royalties from small press publishing houses. That's why the authors we deal with are dedicated to their art and proud of their books—but don't expect to appear on the Carson show. Small press publishers have a hard time breaking into the bookstore market. We try, but we wouldn't be able to survive without a healthy direct-mail sale."

DANTE UNIVERSITY OF AMERICA PRESS, INC., Box 843, Brookline VA 02147. Contact: Manuscripts Editor. Publishes hardcover originals and reprints, and trade paperback originals and reprints. Averages 5 titles/year; receives 50 submissions annually. 50% of books from first-time authors; 50% of books from unagented writers. Average print order for a writer's first book is 3,000. Pays royalty; offers negotiable advance. Publishes book an average of 10 months after acceptance. Simultaneous and photocopied submissions OK. Query for electronic submissions. Computer printout submissions acceptable. Reports in 2 weeks on queries only; 2 months on mss. Writer's guidelines for #10 SASE.

Nonfiction: Biography, reference, reprints, and nonfiction and fiction translations from Italian and Latin. Subjects include general scholarly nonfiction, Renaissance thought and letter, Italian language and linguistics, Italian-American history and culture, and bilingual education. Query first. Reviews artwork/photos as part of ms package.

Poetry: "There is a chance that we would use Renaissance poetry translations."

Recent Poetry Title: *Tales of Suicide*, by Pirandello (epic poetry).

DARTNELL CORP., 4660 N. Ravenswood Ave., Chicago IL 60640. (312)561-4000. Editorial Director: Scott Pemberton. Averages 4 titles/year; receives 150-200 submissions annually. 50% of books from first-time authors; 99% of books from unagented writers. Average print order for a writer's first book is 2,000. Pays in royalties on sliding scale based usually on retail price. Publishes book an average of 1 year after acceptance. Computer printout submissions acceptable; no dot-matrix. Reports in 3 months. Ms guidelines for SASE.

Nonfiction: Publishes business manuals, reports and handbooks. Interested in new material on business skills and techniques in management, sales management, marketing, supervision, administration, advertising, etc. Submit outline, market analysis and sample chapter.

Recent Nonfiction Title: *Building a Winning Sales Force*, by George Lundsden.

*MAY DAVENPORT, PUBLISHERS, 26313 Purissima Rd., Los Altos Hills CA 94022. (415)948-6499. Editor/Publisher: May Davenport. Imprint includes md Books (nonfiction and fiction). Publishes hardcover and trade paperback originals. Averages 4 titles/year; receives 1,000-2,000 submissions annually. 95% of books from first-time authors; 95% of books from unagented writers. May consider partial subsidy publishing on games only. Pays 15% royalty on retail price; no advance. Publishes book an average of 1-3 years after acceptance. Reports in 3 weeks. Ms guidelines for #10 SASE.

Nonfiction: Juvenile. Subjects include Americana, animals, art, music and nature. "Our readers are students in elementary and secondary public school districts, as well as correctional institutes of learning, etc." No "hack writing." Query.

Recent Nonfiction Title: *Garter Snake on Guard*, by Joyce Deedy (lifecycle of garter snake).

Fiction: Adventure, ethnic, fantasy. "We're overstocked with picture books and first readers; prefer stage and teleplays for the TV-oriented teenagers (30 min. one act). Be entertaining while informing." No sex or violence. Query with SASE.

Recent Fiction Title: *Darby's Rainbow*, by James C. McCoy (fantasy: dragonlife).

Tips: "Make people laugh. Humor has a place, too."

DAVIS PUBLICATIONS, INC., 50 Portland St., Worcester MA 01608. (617)754-7201. Managing Editor: Wyatt Wade. Averages 5-10 titles/year. Pays 10-15% royalty. Publishes book an average of 1 year after acceptance. Computer printout submissions acceptable; prefers letter-quality. Write for copy of guidelines for authors.

Nonfiction: Publishes art, design and craft books. Accepts nonfiction translations. "Keep in mind the intended audience. Our readers are visually oriented. All illustrations should be collated separately from the text, but keyed to the text. Photos should be good quality original prints. Well selected illustrations should explain, amplify, and enhance the text. We average 2-4 photos/page. We like to see technique photos as well as illustrations of finished artwork. Recent books have been on papermaking, airbrush painting, jewelry, design, puppets, quilting, and watercolor painting." Submit outline, sample chapters and illustrations. Reviews artwork/photos as part of ms package.

STEVE DAVIS PUBLISHING, Box 190831, Dallas TX 75219. (214)954-4469. Publisher: Steve Davis. Publishes hardcover and trade paperback originals. Averages 4 titles/year. Query for electronic submissions. Computer printout submissions acceptable. "Manuscripts should be professionally proofed for style, grammar and spelling before submission." Reports in 3 weeks on queries *if interested*. Not responsible for unsolicited material. Book catalog for SASE.

Nonfiction: Books on current issues and some reference books. "We are very selective about our list. We look for material that is professionally prepared, takes a fresh approach to a timely topic, and offers the reader helpful information." No religious or occult topics, no sports, and no mass market material such as diet books, joke books, exercise books, etc. Query with outline/summary, sample chapter and SASE. "We can only respond to projects that interest us."

Recent Nonfiction Title: *The Writer's Yellow Pages*, edited by Steve Davis (reference).

DAW BOOKS, INC., 1633 Broadway, New York NY 10019. Submissions Editor: Peter Stampfel. Publishes science fiction paperback originals and reprints. Publishes 62 titles/year. Pays 6% royalty; offers $2,500 advance—more on arrangement. Simultaneous submissions "returned at once, unread." Computer printout submissions acceptable; prefers letter-quality. Reports in 6 weeks "or longer, if a second reading is required." Free book catalog.

Fiction: "We are interested in science fiction and fantasy novels only. We do not publish any other category of fiction. We are not seeking collections of short stories or ideas for anthologies. We do not want any nonfiction manuscripts." Submit complete ms.

‡*DECALOGUE BOOKS, 7 No. MacQuesten Parkway, Mt. Vernon NY 10550. (914)664-7944. Divisions include Ad Infinitum Press; Effective Learning. Editor-in-Chief: William Brandon. Firm publishes hardcover and trade paperback originals. Publishes 10 titles/year; receives 200 proposals/year. 25% from first-time authors; 100% from unagented writers. "We will accept subsidy published works only if we feel the manuscripts have literary merit but are unlikely to be commercially viable." Pays authors 5-15% royalty on retail price. Average advance is $1,000. Publishes ms an average of 2 years after acceptance. Simultaneous and photocopied submissions OK. Computer printout submissions OK; prefers letter-quality. Reports in 2 weeks on queries; 2 months on mss. Brochures on individual titles available. Free ms guidelines.

Nonfiction: Biography, cookbook, how-to, reference, textbook. Subjects include Americana, animals, business and economics, child guidance/parenting, cooking, foods & nutrition, education, ethnic, gardening, history, hobbies, language/literature, nature/environment, philosophy, recreation, regional, religion, science, travel. "We are particularly interested in Judaica, cookbooks and ethnic materials." Query or submit outline/synopsis and sample chapters. Reviews artwork/photos as part of freelance ms package.

Recent Nonfiction Title: *Sephardic Holiday Cooking: Recipes and Traditions*, by Gilda Angel (ethnic cookbook).

Tips: "We are looking for well written works of a specialized nature that are not likely to become dated quickly."

DEL REY BOOKS, Imprint of Ballantine Books, 201 E. 50th St., New York NY 10022. (212)572-2677. Editor-in-Chief: Owen Lock. Fantasy Editor: Lester del Rey. Publishes hardcover, trade paperback and mass market originals and mass market paperback reprints. Averages 80 titles/year; receives over 1,200 submissions annually. 10% of books from first-time authors; 40% of books from unagented writers. Pays royalty on retail price. Offers competitive advance. Publishes book an average of 1 year after acceptance. Photocopied submissions OK. Computer printout submissions acceptable; legible dot-matrix acceptable. Reporting time slow. Writer's guidelines for #10 SASE.

Fiction: Fantasy ("should have the practice of magic as an essential element of the plot") and science fiction ("well-plotted novels with good characterization, exotic locales, and detailed alien cultures. Novels should have a 'sense of wonder' and be designed to please readers"). Will need "144 original fiction manuscripts of science fiction and fantasy suitable for publishing over the next two years. No flying-saucers, Atlantis, or occult novels." Submit complete ms or detailed outline and first three chapters.

Recent Fiction Title: *2061: odyssey three*, by Arthur C. Clarke (original science fiction hardcover).

Tips: "Del Rey is a reader's house. Our audience is anyone who wants to be pleased by a good entertaining novel. We do very well with original fantasy novels, in which magic is a central element, and with hard-science science fiction novels. Pay particular attention to plotting and a satisfactory conclusion. It must be/feel believable. That's what the readers like."

DELACORTE PRESS, Imprint of Dell Publishing and division of Bantam/Doubleday/Dell. 245 E. 47th St., New York NY 10017. (212)605-3000. Editor-in-Chief: Jackie Farber. Publishes hardcover originals. Publishes 25 titles/year. Pays l0-12½-15% royalty; average advance. Publishes book an average of 2 years after acceptance. Simultaneous and photocopied submissions OK. Computer printout submissions acceptable; prefers letter-quality. Reports in 2 months. Book catalog and guidelines for SASE.
Fiction and Nonfiction: *Query, outline or brief proposal, or complete ms accepted only through an agent;* otherwise returned unopened. No mss for children's or young adult books accepted in this division.
Recent Nonfiction Title: *Merchants of Treason*, by Thomas B. Allen and Norman Polmar.
Recent Fiction Title: *Kaleidoscope*, by Danielle Steel.

DELL PUBLISHING CO., INC., Subsidiary of Bertelsman. 1 Dag Hammarskjold Plaza, New York NY 10017. Imprints include Dell, Delacorte Press, Delta Books, Dell Trade Paperbacks, Laurel, Delacorte Press Books for Young Readers, Yearling and Laurel Leaf. Publishes hardcover and paperback originals and reprints. Publishes 500 titles/year. Pays royalty on retail price. "General guidelines for unagented submissions. Please adhere strictly to the following procedure: 1) Do not send manuscript, sample chapters or art work; 2) Do not register, certify or insure your letter; 3) Send only a 4-page synopsis or outline with a cover letter stating previous work published or relevant experience." Simultaneous and photocopied submissions OK. Reports in 3 months. Book catalog and guidelines for SASE.
Nonfiction: "Because Dell is comprised of several imprints, each with its own editorial department, we ask you to carefully review the following information and direct your submission to the appropriate department. Your envelope must be marked, Attention: (blank) Editorial Department—Proposal. Fill in the blank with one of the following: Delacorte: Publishes in hardcover. Looks for popular nonfiction (*Merchants of Treason*). Delta and Dell Trade: Publishes in trade paperback; Delta publishes original fiction; Dell Trade looks for useful, substantial guides (*Speed Cleaning*); entertaining, amusing nonfiction (*Nice Guys Sleep Alone*). Yearling and Laurel Leaf: Publishes in paperback and hardcover for children and young adults, grades 7-12.
Fiction: Refer to the above guidelines. Delacorte: Publishes top-notch commercial fiction in hardcover (e.g., *Zora*). Dell: Publishes mass-market paperbacks; rarely publishes original nonfiction; looks for family sagas, historical romances, sexy modern romance, adventure and suspense, thrillers, occult/horror and war novels.

DEMBNER BOOKS, Division of Red Dembner Enterprises, Corp., 80 8th Ave., New York NY 10011. (212)924-2525. Editor: Therese Eiben. Publishes hardcover and trade paperback originals, and hardcover and trade paperback reprints. Averages 10-15 titles/year; receives 500-750 submissions annually. 20% of books from first-time authors; 75% of books from unagented writers. Pays 10-15% royalty on hardcover; 6-7½% royalty on paperback, both on retail price. Offers average $1,000-5,000 advance. Publishes book an average of 1 year after acceptance. Simultaneous and photocopied submissions OK. Computer printout submissions acceptable; no dot-matrix. Reports in 2 weeks on queries; 10 weeks on mss. Book catalog available from W.W. Norton, 500 5th Ave., New York NY 10110. Writer's guidelines available for #10 SASE.
Nonfiction: How-to, reference. Subjects include health, film, history (popular), music, sports and social causes. "We want books written by knowledgeable authors who focus on a problem area (health/home/handicapped) and offer an insightful guidance toward solutions." No surveys or collections—books that do not focus on one specific, promotable topic. No first person accounts of tragic personal events. Also, no books on heavily published topics, such as weight loss and exercise programs. Query.
Recent Nonfiction Title: *The De Palma Cut: An Unauthorized Study of the Films of America's Most Controversial Director*, by Laurent Bouzereau.
Fiction: Mystery, suspense and literary. "We look for genre fiction (mystery, suspense, etc.), that keeps pace with the times, deals with contemporary issues, and has three-dimensional characters. Occasionally we publish literary novels, but the writing must be of excellent quality." No indulgent, self-conscious fiction. Query and two sample chapters.
Recent Fiction Title: *Haunt of the Nightingale*, by John R. Riggs.
Tips: "We take a great deal of pride in the books we publish. No humor books or fad books. We're developing a strong back list and want to continue to do so. Small hardcover houses such as ourselves are being very careful about the books they choose for publication primarily because secondary rights sales have dropped, and the money is less. Quality is of utmost importance."

T.S. DENISON & CO., INC., 9601 Newton Ave., S. Minneapolis MN 55431. Editor-in-Chief: Sherrill B. Flora. Publishes teacher aid materials; receives 500 submissions annually. 90% of books from first-time authors; 100% of books from unagented writers. Average print order for a writer's first book is 3,000. Royalty varies; no advance. Publishes book an average of 1-2 years after acceptance. Photocopied submissions OK. Computer printout submissions acceptable; no dot-matrix. Reports in 1 month. Book catalog and ms guidelines for SASE.

Nonfiction: Specializes in early childhood and elementary school teaching aids. Send prints if photos are to accompany ms. Submit complete ms. Reviews artwork/photos as part of ms package.

DENLINGER'S PUBLISHERS, LTD., Box 76, Fairfax VA 22030. (703)830-4646. Publisher: William W. Denlinger. Publishes hardcover and trade paperback originals, hardcover and trade paperback reprints. Averages 12 titles/year; receives 250 submissions annually. 5% of books from first-time authors; 95% of books from unagented writers. Average print order for a writer's first book is 3,000. Pays variable royalty. No advance. Publishes book an average of 18 months after acceptance. Simultaneous and photocopied submissions OK. Query for electronic submissions. Computer printout submissions acceptable; prefers letter-quality. Reports in 1 week on queries; 6 weeks on mss. Book catalog for SASE.
Nonfiction: How-to and technical books; dog-breed books only. Query. Reviews artwork/photos.
Recent Nonfiction Title: *Bird Work*, by Steven Rufe.

*DEVIN-ADAIR PUBLISHERS, INC., 6 N. Water St., Greenwich CT 06830. (203)531-7755. Editor: Jane Andrassi. Publishes hardcover and paperback originals, reprints and software. Averages 20 titles/year; receives up to 500 submissions annually. 30% of books from first-time authors; 70% of books from unagented writers. Average print order for a writer's first book is 7,500. Subsidy publishes 5% of books. Royalty on sliding scale, 5-25%; "average advance is low." Publishes book an average of 9 months after acceptance. No simultaneous submissions. Query for electronic submissions. Computer printout submissions acceptable; prefers letter-quality. Book catalog and guidelines for 6x9 SAE and 5 first class stamps.
Nonfiction: Publishes Americana, business, how-to, conservative politics, history, medicine, nature, economics, sports and travel books. New line: homeopathic books. Accepts translations. Query or submit outline/synopsis and sample chapters. Looks for "early interest, uniqueness, economy of expression, good style, and new information." Reviews artwork/photos as part of ms package.
Recent Nonfiction Title: *Weapons Against Chaos*, by Mary Ewald.
Tips: "We seek to publish books of high quality manufacture. We spend 8% more on production and design than necessary to ensure a better quality book. Trends include increased specialization and a more narrow view of a subject. General overviews in computer publishing are now a thing of the past. Better a narrow subject in depth than a wide superficial one."

DIAL BOOKS FOR YOUNG READERS, Division of NAL Penguin Inc., 2 Park Ave., New York NY 10016. (212)725-1818. Submissions Editor: Phyllis J. Sogelman. Imprints include Dial Easy-to-Read Books and Dial Very First Books. Publishes hardcover originals. Averages 60 titles/year; receives 20,000 submissions annually. 15% of books from first-time authors. Pays variable royalty and advance. Simultaneous and photocopied submissions OK, but not preferred. Computer printout submissions acceptable. Reports in 2 weeks on queries; 3 months on mss. Book catalog and ms guidelines for 9x12 SASE.
Nonfiction: Juvenile picture books and young adult books. Especially looking for "quality picture books and well-researched young adult and middle-reader mss." Not interested in alphabet books, riddle and game books, and early concept books. Query with outline/synopsis and sample chapters. Reviews artwork/photos.
Recent Nonfiction Title: *Mountains*, by Clive Catchpole (picture book).
Fiction: Adventure, fantasy, historical, humor, mystery, romance (appropriate for young adults), and suspense. Especially looking for "lively and well written novels for middle grade and young adult children involving a convincing plot and believable characters. The subject matter or theme should not already be overworked in previously published books. The approach must not be demeaning to any minority group, nor should the roles of female characters (or others) be stereotyped, though we don't think books should be didactic, or in any way message-y." No "topics inappropriate for the juvenile, young adult, and middle grade audiences. No plays or poetry." Submit complete ms.
Recent Fiction Title: *Through the Hidden Door*, by Rosemary Wells.
Tips: "Our readers are anywhere from preschool age to teenage. Picture books must have strong plots, lots of action, unusual premises, or universal themes treated with freshness and originality. Humor works well in these books. A very well thought out and intelligently presented book has the best chance of being taken on. Genre isn't as much of a factor as presentation."

DILLON PRESS, INC., 242 Portland Ave. S., Minneapolis MN 55415. (612)333-2691. Editorial Director: Uva Dillon. Senior Editor: Tom Schneider. Juvenile Fiction Editor: Karin Snelson. Publishes hardcover originals. Averages 30-40 titles/year; receives 3,000 submissions annually. 50% of books from first-time authors; 90% of books from unagented writers. Average print order for a writer's first book is 3,000-5,000. Pays royalty and by outright purchase. Publishes book an average of 1 year after acceptance. Computer printout submissions acceptable; no dot-matrix. Reports in 6 weeks. Book catalog for 10x12 SAE with 4 first class stamps.
Nonfiction: "We are actively seeking mss for the juvenile educational market." Subjects include world and U.S. geography, American Indian tribes, U.S. states and cities, contemporary and historical biographies for elementary and middle grade levels, unusual approaches to science topics for primary grade readers, unusual or remarkable animals, and contemporary issues of interest and value to young people. Submit complete ms or

outline and 1 sample chapter; query letters if accompanied by book proposal. Reviews artwork/photos as part of ms package.

Recent Nonfiction Title: *New York: A Dillon City Watch Book*, by Barbara Johnston Adams.

Tips: "Before writing, authors should check out the existing competition for their book idea to determine if it is really needed and stands a reasonable chance for success, especially for a nonfiction proposal."

DODD, MEAD & CO., 71 5th Ave., New York NY 10003. (212)627-8444. President: Jonathn Dodd. Executive Editor: Margaret Norton. Senior Editor: Cynthia Vartan. Editor: Chris Fortunato. Chairman of the Board: Jerome Grossman. Averages 100 titles/year. Pays 10-15% royalty; advances vary, depending on the sales potential of the book. A contract for nonfiction books is offered on the basis of a query, a suggested outline and a sample chapter. Write for permission before sending mss. Adult fiction, history, philosophy, the arts, current events, management and religion should be addressed to Editorial Department. Publishes book an average of 9 months after acceptance. Electronic submissions OK "only on exceptional occasions when submission can be used on equipment of our suppliers." Reports in 6 weeks. SASE.

Fiction and Nonfiction: Publishes book-length mss. Length: 70,000-100,000 words average. Looks for high quality; mysteries and romantic novels of suspense, business, biographies, science, travel, yachting and other sports, music and other arts. Very rarely buys photographs or poetry.

Tips: "Freelance writers should be aware of trends toward nonfiction and the difficulty of publishing marginal or midlist fiction."

DOLL READER, Subsidiary of Hobby House Press, Inc., 900 Frederick St., Cumberland MD 21502. (301)759-3770. Subsidiaries include *Doll Reader* and *The Teddy Bear and Friends Magazine*. Publisher: Gary R. Ruddell. Publishes hardcover and paperbound originals. Averages 24 titles/year. 20% of books from first-time authors; 90% of books from unagented writers. Pays royalty. Publishes book an average of 24 months after acceptance. Simultaneous and photocopied submissions OK. Computer printout submissions acceptable; prefers letter-quality. Reports in 1 month. Ms guidelines for 9x12 SAE.

Nonfiction: Doll-related books. "We publish books pertaining to dolls, teddy bears and crafts as a collector's hobby; we also publish pattern books. The *Doll Reader* is published 8 times a year dealing with the hobby of doll collecting. We appeal to those people who are doll collectors, miniature collectors, as well as people who sew for dolls. Our magazine has a worldwide circulation of close to 72,000." Query or submit outline/synopsis. Reviews artwork/photos as part of ms package. *The Teddy Bear and Friends Magazine* is published bimonthly.

Recent Nonfiction Title: *8th Blue Book of Dolls and Values*, by Jan Foulke (price guide for dolls).

THE DONNING COMPANY/PUBLISHERS, INC., 5659 Virginia Beach Blvd., Norfolk VA 23502. (804)461-8090. Publisher: Robert S. Friedman. Publishes hardcover and trade paperback originals. Averages 35-40 titles/year; receives 350 submissions/year. 50% of books from first-time authors; 50% of books from unagented writers. Pays 7-15% royalty on retail price. Offers $2,000 average advance. Publishes book an average of 1 year after acceptance. Simultaneous and photocopied submissions OK. Computer printout submissions OK; prefers letter-quality. Reports in 2 weeks on queries; 2 months on mss. Ms guidelines for #10 SASE.

Nonfiction: Coffee table book, cookbook, how-to, humor, illustrated book, reference and self-help. Subjects include Americana, cooking and foods, health, history, philosophy, photography and travel. "Americana, regional cookbooks, pictorial histories of cities and counties and metaphysical self-help are what we seek. No textbooks, music, art appreciation, sports, sociology or religion." Submit outline/synopsis and sample chapters or complete ms.

Recent Nonfiction Title: *Spirit Song*, by Mary Summer Rain (New Age).

Fiction: Adventure, fantasy, mainstream, science fiction. "No western, religious, historical, horror, erotica, gothic or experimental manuscripts." Submit outline/synopsis and sample chapters and complete ms.

Recent Fiction Title: *Myth-Nomers and Im-Pervections*, by Robert Asprin (fantasy).

Tips: "Regional pictorials, cookbooks, and self-help books have the best chance of selling because there is less competition in manuscript production. Writing about a fairly unique subject will always get attention, and including information on the marketing potential will help in making decision."

DOUBLEDAY & CO., INC., 245 Park Ave., New York NY 10167. (212)765-6500. Publishes hardcover and paperback originals. Offers royalty on retail price; offers variable advance. Reports in 2½ months. "At present, Doubleday and Co. is *only* able to consider fiction for mystery/suspense, science fiction, and romance imprints." Send *copy* of complete manuscript (60,000-80,000 words) to Crime Club Editor, Science Fiction Editor, or Starlight Romance Editor as appropriate. Sufficient postage for return via fourth class mail must accompany manuscript.

DOWN EAST BOOKS, Division of Down East Enterprise, Inc., Box 679, Camden ME 04843. (207)594-9544. Editor: Karin Womer. Publishes hardcover and trade paperback originals and trade paperback reprints. Averages 10-14 titles/year; receives 400 submissions annually. 50% of books from first-time authors; 90% of

books from unagented writers. Average print order for a writer's first book is 2,500. Pays 10-15% on receipts. Offers average $200 advance. Publishes book an average of 12 months after acceptance. Simultaneous and photocopied submissions OK. Computer printout submissions acceptable; prefers letter-quality. Reports in 2 weeks on queries; 2 months on mss. Book catalog and ms guidelines for 9x12 SAE with 2 first class stamps.
Nonfiction: Regional biography, cookbooks, illustrated books, juvenile, reference and guidebooks. Subjects include Americana, cooking and foods, history, nature, traditional crafts and recreation. "All of our books must have a Maine or New England emphasis." Query. Reviews artwork/photos as part of ms package.
Recent Nonfiction Title: *Lighthouse in My Life: The Story of a Maine Lightkeeper's Family*, by Phil Wass.
Fiction: "We publish no fiction except for an occasional juvenile title (average 1/year)."
Recent Fiction Title: *Moose on the Loose*, by Ann and John Hassett (juvenile).

*DRAGON'S TEETH PRESS, El Dorado National Forest, Georgetown CA 95634. (916)333-4224. Editor: Cornel Lengyel. Publishes trade paperback originals and software. Averages 6 titles/year; receives 100 submissions annually. 50% of books from first-time authors; 75% of books from unagented writers. Subsidy publishes 25% of books; applies "if book has high literary merit, but very limited market." Pays 10% royalty on retail price, or in copies. Publishes book an average of 1 year after acceptance. Simultaneous and photocopied submissions OK. Computer printout submissions acceptable. Reports in 2 weeks on queries; 1 month on mss. Book catalog for SAE with 3 first class stamps.
Nonfiction: Music and philosophy. Publishes for 500 poets or potential poets. Query or submit outline/synopsis and sample chapters. Reviews artwork/photos as part of ms package.
Poetry: "Highly original works of potential literary genius. No trite, trivial or trendy ego exhibitions." Submit 10 samples or the complete ms.

DRAMA BOOK PUBLISHERS, Box 816, Gracie Station, New York NY 10028. (212)517-4455. Contact: Ralph Pine or Judith Holmes. Publishes hardcover and paperback originals and reprints. Averages 4-15 titles/year; receives 500 submissions annually. 70% of books from first-time authors; 90% of books from unagented writers. Royalty varies; advance varies; negotiable. Publishes book an average of 18 months after acceptance. Computer printout submissions acceptable; prefers letter-quality. Reports in 1 to 2 months. Book catalog for 6x9 SAE.
Nonfiction: Books—texts, guides, manuals, directories, reference—for and about performing arts theory and practice: acting, directing; voice, speech, movement, music, dance, mime; makeup, masks, wigs; costumes, sets, lighting, sound; design and execution; technical theatre, stagecraft, equipment; stage management; producing; arts management, all varieties; business and legal aspects; film, radio, television, cable, video; theory, criticism, reference; playwriting; theatre and performance history. Accepts nonfiction, drama and technical works in translations also. Query; accepts 1-3 sample chapters; no complete mss. Reviews artwork/photos as part of ms package.
Fiction: Professionally produced plays and musicals.

*DUQUESNE UNIVERSITY PRESS, 600 Forbes Ave., Pittsburgh PA 15282. (412)434-6610. Averages 9 titles/year; receives 400 submissions annually. 25% of books from first-time authors; 100% of books from unagented writers. Average print order for a writer's first book is 1,500. Subsidy publishes 20% of books. Pays 10% royalty on net sales; no advance. Publishes book an average of 1 year after acceptance. Query for electronic submissions. Computer printout submissions acceptable; no dot-matrix. Query. Reports in 3 months.
Nonfiction: Scholarly books in the humanities, social sciences for academics, libraries, college bookstores and educated laypersons. Length: open. Looks for scholarship.
Recent Nonfiction Title: *Imaginative Thinking*, by Edward L. Murray.

‡DURST PUBLICATIONS, 29-28 41st Ave., Long Island City NY 11101. (718)706-0303. Owner: Sanford Durst. Publishes hardcover and trade paperback originals and reprints. Averages 20 titles/year; receives 100 submissions annually. Average print order for a writer's first book is 2,500. Pays variable royalty. Publishes book an average of 6 months after acceptance. Computer printout submissions acceptable; no dot-matrix. Reports in 1 month. Book catalog for business-size SAE and 4 first class stamps.
Nonfiction: How-to and reference. Subjects include Americana, art, business and economics, cooking and foods, hobbies-primarily coin collecting, stamp collecting, antiques and legal. Especially needs reference books and how-to on coins, medals, tokens, paper money, art, antiques-illustrated with valuations or rarities, if possible. Publishes for dealers, libraries, collectors and attorneys. Submit outline/synopsis and sample chapters. Reviews artwork/photos as part of ms package.

For information on book publishers' areas of interest, see the nonfiction and fiction sections in the Book Publishers Subject Index.

Recent Nonfiction Title: *Buying & Selling Country Land*, by D. Reisman (practical/legal).
Tips: "Write in simple English. Do not repeat yourself. Present matter in logical, orderly form. Try to illustrate."

DUSTBOOKS, Box 100, Paradise CA 95969. (916)877-6110. Publisher: Len Fulton. Publishes hardcover and paperback originals. Averages 7 titles/year. Offers 15% royalty. Offers average $500 advance. Simultaneous and photocopied submissions OK if so informed. Computer printout submissions acceptable. Reports in 2 months. Free book catalog; writer's guidelines for #10 SASE.
Nonfiction: Technical. "DustBooks would like to see manuscripts dealing with microcomputers (software, hardware) and water (any aspect). Must be technically sound and well-written. We have at present no titles in these areas. These represent an expansion of our interests. Our specialty is directories of small presses, poetry publishers, and a monthly newsletter on small publishers (*Small Press Review*)." Submit outline/synopsis and sample chapters.

‡EES* PUBLICATIONS, Subsidiary of Education for Emergency Services, Inc. (EES*), Suite 1215, 12773 W. Forest Hill Blvd., Wellington FL 33414. (407)793-1600. Director: Candace Brown-Nixon. Publishes trade paperback originals. Firm averages 3-6 titles/year. 10% of books from first-time authors. Pays 10-15% royalty on retail price. Negotiable re: outright purchase. Publishes book an average of 2 months after acceptance. Computer printout submissions OK. Reports in 2 weeks on queries; 1 month on mss. Free book catalog and ms guidelines, "just send legible address."
Nonfiction: How-to, reference, technical and textbook. Subjects include education (EMS field only) and health/medicine (EMS related only). "We're interested in specialized EMS, law enforcement, fire-related topics. Authors must be properly credentialed for the topic." No pictorial history, how to read an EKG, general topic initial education textbooks, or nursing topics. Query or submit outline/synopsis and sample chapters.
Recent Nonfiction Title: *Rugged Terrain Search and Rescue: The Manual*, by Robert G. Nixon (technical text).
Tips: "Writers have the best chance of selling us a specialized topic about which the author is acutely knowledgeable and properly credentialed-i.e., an EMT should not attempt to write on an ALS level. EMTs, paramedics, rescue personnel, students and educators in EMS/rescue are our audience."

E.P. DUTTON, Division of NAL-Penguin, Inc., 2 Park Ave., New York NY 10016. (212)725-1818. Publisher, Children's Books: Christopher Franceschelli. Averages 75 titles/year. 15% of books from first-time authors; 85% of books from unagented writers. Pays royalty on list price; offers variable advance. Considers unsolicited mss. Computer printout submissions acceptable; prefers letter-quality. "Please send query letter first on all except picture book manuscripts."
Nonfiction: Nonfiction for ages 4-14.
Fiction: Picture books; beginning readers; novels for ages 8-12; young adult novels for ages 12 and up. Reviews artwork/photos as part of ms package. Emphasis on good writing and quality for all ages.
Tips: Queries/mss may be routed to other editors in the division. "Annual picture book contest open to unpublished illustrators in or recently graduated from art school. Prize is publication and cash prize. Write to publisher for details."

EAKIN PUBLICATIONS, INC., Box 23069, Austin TX 78735. (512)288-1771. Imprints include Nortex. Editorial Director: Edwin M. Eakin. Publishes hardcover and paperback originals and reprints. Averages 40 titles/year; receives 500 submissions annually. 80% of books from first-time authors; 90% of books from unagented writers. Average print order for a writer's first book is 2,000-5,000. Pays 10-12-15% in royalty. Publishes book an average of 1 year after acceptance. Simultaneous and photocopied submissions OK. Query for electronic submissions. Computer printout submissions acceptable; prefers letter-quality. Reports in 3 months. Book catalog and ms guidelines for #10 SAE with 4 first class stamps.
Nonfiction: Adult nonfiction categories include Western Americana, World War II, business, sports, biographies, Early Americana, contemporary topics, women's studies, Civil War, cookbooks, regional Texas history. Juvenile nonfiction includes biographies of historic personalities, prefer with Texas or regional interest, or nature studies. Easy read illustrated books for grades one through three.
Recent Nonfiction Title: *Last Man Out*, by H. Robert Charles (WWII).
Fiction: "Adult fiction is not top priority, mostly will consider fiction by published writers." Juvenile fiction for grades four through seven, preferably relating to Texas and the southwest or contemporary. Query or submit outline/synopsis and sample chapters.

‡*ECW PRESS, Subsidiaries include Emerson House, Poetry Canada Review, Essays on Canadian Writing. 307 Coxwell Ave., Toronto, Ontario M4L 3B5 Canada. (416)694-3348. President: Jack David. Publishes hardcover and trade paperback originals. Publishes 12-15 titles/year; receives 120 submissions annually. 50% of books from first-time authors; 80% of books from unagented writers. Subsidy publishes (nonauthor) up to 5% of books. Pays 10% royalty on retail price. Simultaneous and photocopied submissions OK. Query for electronic submissions. Computer printout submissions acceptable; prefers letter-quality. Reports in 2 weeks. Free book catalog.

Nonfiction: Reference and Canadian literary criticism. "ECW is interested in all literary criticism aimed at the undergraduate and graduate university market." Query. Reviews artwork/photos as part of ms package.

Recent Nonfiction Title: *Introducing The Stone Angel*, by George Woodcock (literary criticism).

Tips: "The writer has the best chance of selling literary criticism to our firm because that's our specialty and the only thing that makes us money."

‡**EDEN PRESS**, 31A Westminster Ave., Montreal, Quebec H4X 1Y8 Canada. (514)488-2066. Publisher: Pamela Chichinskas. Editorial Director: Lynette Stokes. Publishes hardcover and trade paperback originals. Averages 15-25 titles/year; receives 400 submissions annually. 50% of books from first-time authors; 80% of books from unagented writers. Pays royalty. Publishes book an average of 18 months after acceptance. Photocopied submissions OK. Query for electronic submissions. Computer printout submissions acceptable. Reports in 1 month on queries; 3 months on mss. Book catalog free on request.

Imprints: Occasion Books (gift books) and Eden Entertainment (fiction).

Nonfiction: Biography, how-to, illustrated book, reference, self-help, scientific. Subjects include business and economics, health, history, nature, philosophy, politics, psychology, recreation, sociology, sports, and humor on any subject. "Books on investment and finance (written by qualified professionals only), biography, and lay-market health books written only by medical professionals." Query. Reviews artwork/photos.

Recent Nonfiction Title: *The Superconscious World*, by Peter Reveen (psychology/hypnotism).

Fiction: Humor only. Submit outline/synopsis and sample chapters.

***EDUCATION ASSOCIATES**, Division of The Daye Press, Inc., Box 8021, Athens GA 30603. (404)542-4244. Editor, Text Division: D. Keith Osborn. Publishes hardcover and trade paperback originals. Averages 2-6 titles/year; receives 300 submissions annually. 1% of books from first-time authors; 100% of books from unagented writers. Subsidy publishes 5% of books. "We may publish a textbook which has a very limited audience and is of unusual merit . . . but we still believe that the book will make a contribution to the educational field." Buys mss "on individual basis." Publishes book an average of 9 months after acceptance. Do not send ms; query first. No reponse without SASE. Reports in 1 month on queries.

Nonfiction: How-to and textbook. Subjects include psychology and education. "Books in the fields of early childhood and middle school education. Do not wish basic textbooks. Rather, are interested in more specific areas of interest in above fields. We are more interested in small runs on topics of more limited nature than general texts." Query only with one-page letter. If interested will request synopsis and sample chapters. Absolutely no reply unless SASE is enclosed. No phone queries.

Recent Nonfiction Title: *Computer MAT*, by A.B. Wilson.

Tips: College textbooks—usually dealing with early childhood, middle school, or child development—have the best chance of selling to Education Associates.

‡**EDUCATIONAL TECHNOLOGY PUBLICATIONS**, 720 Palisade Ave., Englewood Cliffs NJ 07632. (201)871-4007. Editor: Lawrence Lipsitz. Publishes hardcover and trade paperback originals. Firm averages 12 titles/year. Receives 50 submissions/year. 40-50% of books from first-time authors. 10% from unagented writers. Pays royalty on retail price. Publishes book an average of 6-12 months after acceptance. Simultaneous and photocopied submissions OK. Computer printout submissions OK. Reports in 2 weeks on queries; 3 weeks on mss. Free book catalog.

Nonfiction: Technical and textbook. Subjects include computers and electronics, education and psychology. "We want books on new technologies as applied to education and training, such as artificial intelligence software." Query and submit outline/synopsis and sample chapters. Reviews artwork/photos as part of ms package.

Recent Nonfiction Title: *Training Needs Assessment*, by A. Rassett (training).

Tips: "We want very practical works for use in improving instruction. Our audience is educational technologists, instructional designers, school leaders, trainees and media experts."

***WILLIAM B. EERDMANS PUBLISHING CO.**, Christian University Press, 255 Jefferson Ave. SE, Grand Rapids MI 49503. (616)459-4591. Editor-in-Chief: Jon Pott. Managing Editor: Charles Van Hof. Publishes hardcover and paperback originals and reprints. Averages 65-70 titles/year; receives 3,000-4,000 submissions annually. 25% of books from first-time authors; 95% of books from unagented writers. Average print order for a writer's first book is 4,000. Subsidy publishes 1% of books. Pays 7½-10% royalty on retail price; usually no advance. Publishes book an average of 1 year after acceptance. Simultaneous and photocopied submissions OK if noted. Computer printout submissions acceptable; no dot-matrix. Reports in 3 weeks for queries; 4 months for mss. Looks for "quality and relevance." Free book catalog.

Nonfiction: Reference, textbooks and tourists guidebooks. Subjects include history, philosophy, psychology, religion, sociology, regional history and geography. "Approximately 80% of our publications are religious—specifically Protestant—and largely of the more academic or theological variety (as opposed to the de-

votional, inspirational or celebrity-conversion type of book). Our history and social studies titles aim, similarly, at an academic audience; some of them are documentary histories. We prefer that writers take the time to notice if we have published anything at all in the same category as their manuscript before sending it to us." Accepts nonfiction translations. Query. Accepts outline/synopsis and 2-3 sample chapters. Reviews artwork/ photos.
Recent Nonfiction Title: *Tutu: Voice of the Voiceless*, by Shirley du Boulay.

ELYSIUM GROWTH PRESS, 5436 Fernwood Ave., Los Angeles CA 90027. (213)455-1000. Publishes hardcover and paperback originals, and hardcover and trade paperback reprints. Averages 4 titles/year; receives 20 submissions/year. 20% of books from first-time authors. 100% of books from unagented writers. Pays $5,000 average advance. Publishes book an average of 18 months after acceptance. Photocopied submissions OK. Query for electronic submissions. Computer printout submissions OK; no dot-matrix. Reports in 2 weeks on queries; 6 weeks on submissions. Book catalog free on request.
Nonfiction: Illustrated book, self-help and textbook. Subjects include health, nature, philosophy, photography, psychology, recreation, sociology and travel. Needs books on "body self-image, body self-appreciation, world travel and the nudist way." Query. All unsolicited mss are returned unopened. Reviews artwork/photos as part of ms package.
Recent Nonfiction Title: *Growing Up Without Shame*, by Craig.

ENSLOW PUBLISHERS,Bloy St. and Ramsey Ave., Box 777, Hillside NJ 07205. (201)964-4116. Editor: Ridley Enslow. Publishes hardcover and paperback originals. Averages 30 titles/year. Pays 10-15% royalty on retail price or net price; offers $500-5,000 advance. Publishes book an average of 8 months after acceptance. Photocopied submissions OK. Computer printout submissions acceptable. Reports in 2 weeks. Free book catalog.
Nonfiction: Interested in manuscripts for young adults and children. Some areas of special interest are science, social issues, biography, reference topics and recreation. Also, business/economics, health, hobbies, how-to, juveniles, philosophy, psychology, self-help, sports and technical. Accepts nonfiction translations. Submit outline/synopsis and 2 sample chapters. Reviews artwork/photos as part of ms package.
Recent Nonfiction Title: *Restoring Our Earth*, by L. Pringle.

ENTELEK, Ward-Whidden House/The Hill, Box 1303, Portsmouth NH 03801. Editor-in-Chief: Albert E. Hickey. Small press. Publishes paperback originals. Offers royalty on retail price of 5% trade; 10% textbook. No advance. Averages 5 titles/year. Photocopied and simultaneous submissions OK. Submit outline and sample chapters or submit complete ms. Reports in 1 week. Book catalog for SASE.
Nonfiction: Publishes computer books and software of special interest to educators. Length: 3,000 words minimum.
Recent Nonfiction Title: *Sea Experience*, edited by A. Hickey (education).

ENTERPRISE PUBLISHING CO., INC., 725 Market St., Wilmington DE 19801. (302)654-0110. Publisher: T.N. Peterson. Editor: Audrey Frey. Publishes hardcover and paperback originals, "with an increasing interest in newsletters and periodicals." Averages 8 titles/year; receives 150 submissions annually. 50% of books from first-time authors; 90% of books from unagented writers. Pays royalty on wholesale or retail price. Offers $1,000 average advance. Publishes book an average of 6 months after acceptance. Simultaneous and photocopied submissions OK, but "let us know." Query for electronic submissions. Computer printout submissions acceptable; prefers letter-quality. Catalog and ms guidelines for SASE.
Nonfiction: "Subjects of interest to small business executives/entrepreneurs. They are highly independent and self-sufficient, and of an apolitical to conservative political leaning. They need practical information, as opposed to theoretical: self-help topics on business, including starting and managing a small enterprise, advertising, marketing, raising capital, public relations, tax avoidance and personal finance. Business/economics, legal self-help and business how-to." Queries only. All unsolicited mss are returned unopened. Reviews artwork/photos.
Recent Nonfiction Title: *Complete Book of Employee Forms*, by Arnold S. Goldstein, Esq.

*PAUL S. ERIKSSON, PUBLISHER, 208 Battell Bldg., Middlebury VT 05753. (802)388-7303; Summer: Forest Dale VT 05745. (802)247-8415. Publisher/Editor: Paul S. Eriksson. Associate Publisher/Co-Editor: Peggy Eriksson. Publishes hardcover and paperback trade originals and paperback trade reprints. Averages 5-10 titles/year; receives 1,500 submissions annually. 25% of books from first-time authors; 95% of books from unagented writers. Average print order for a writer's first book is 3,000-5,000. Subsidy publishes 1% of books. Pays 10-15% royalty on retail price; advance offered if necessary. Publishes book an average of 6 months after acceptance. Catalog for #10 SAE with 1 first class stamp.
Nonfiction: Americana, birds (ornithology), art, biography, business/economics, cookbooks/cooking/ foods, health, history, hobbies, how-to, humor, music, nature, philosophy, photography, politics, psychology, recreation, self-help, sociology, sports and travel. Query.

Recent Nonfiction Title: *"Shut Up!" He Explained: A Writer's Guide to the Uses & Misuses of Dialogue*, by William Noble.
Fiction: Mainstream. Query.
Recent Fiction Title: *The Headmaster's Papers*, by Richard A. Hawley.
Tips: "We look for intelligence, excitement and salability. We prefer manuscripts written out of deep, personal knowledge or experience."

*ETC PUBLICATIONS, Drawer ETC, Palm Springs CA 92263. (619)325-5352. Editorial Director: LeeOna S. Hostrop. Senior Editor: Dr. Richard W. Hostrop. Publishes hardcover and paperback originals. Averages 6-12 titles/year; receives 100 submissions annually. 75% of books from first-time authors; 90% of books from unagented writers. Average print order for a writer's first book is 2,500. Subsidy publishes 5-10% of books. Offers 5-15% royalty, based on wholesale and retail price. No advance. Publishes book an average of 1 year after acceptance. Simultaneous and photocopied submissions OK. Computer printout submissions acceptable; prefers letter-quality. Reports in 3 weeks.
Nonfiction: Business management, educational management, gifted education, books for writers and textbooks. Accepts nonfiction translations in above areas. Submit complete ms. Reviews artwork/photos as part of ms package.
Recent Nonfiction Title: *Pearl S. Buck - The Final Chapter*, by Beverly Rizzon.
Tips: "ETC will seriously consider textbook manuscripts in any knowledge area in which the author can guarantee a first-year adoption of not less than 500 copies. Special consideration is given to those authors who are capable and willing to submit their completed work in camera-ready, typeset form."

FABER & FABER, INC., Division of Faber & Faber, Ltd., London, England; 50 Cross St., Winchester MA 01890. (617)721-1427. Editor: Betsy Uhng. Publishes hardcover and trade paperback originals, and hardcover and trade paperback reprints. Averages 12 titles/year; receives 600 submissions annually. 10% of books from first-time authors; 25% of books from unagented writers. Pays 7½-10% royalty on wholesale or retail price; advance varies. Publishes book an average of 1 year after acceptance. Simultaneous and photocopied submissions OK. Computer printout submissions acceptable; prefers letter-quality. Reports in 6 weeks on queries; 2-3 months on mss. Book catalog for 6x9 SAE and 4 first class stamps; writer's guidelines for #10 SASE.
Nonfiction: Anthologies, biography, humor, contemporary culture, and screenplays. Subjects include Americana, animals, art, history, pop/rock music, New England, and sociology. Query with synopsis and outline with SAE. Reviews artwork/photos as part of ms package.
Recent Nonfiction Title: *This Ain't No Disco: The Story of CBGB*, by Roman Kozak.
Fiction: Collections, ethnic, experimental, mainstream and regional. No historical/family sagas or mysteries. Query with synopsis and outline with SAE.
Recent Fiction Title: *The Monkey King*, by Timothy Mo.
Tips: "We are concentrating on subjects that have consistently done well for us. These include popular culture; serious, intelligent rock and roll books; anthologies; and literary, somewhat quirky fiction. Please do not send entire ms; please include SAE for reply."

FACTS ON FILE, INC., 460 Park Ave. S., New York NY 10016. (212)683-2244. Executive Editor: Gerard Helferich. Publishes hardcover originals and hardcover reprints. Averages 125 titles/year; receives approximately 1,000 submissions annually. 25% of books from unagented writers. Pays 10-15% royalty on retail price. Offers average $10,000 advance. Simultaneous and photocopied submissions OK. Query for electronic submissions. Computer printout submissions acceptable; prefers letter-quality. Reports in 2 weeks on queries; 1 month on mss. Free book catalog.
Nonfiction: Reference and other informational books on business and economics, cooking and foods (no cookbooks), health, history, hobbies (but no how-to), music, natural history, philosophy, psychology, recreation, religion, language and sports. "We need serious, informational books for a targeted audience. All our books must have strong library interest, but we also distribute books effectively to the book trade." No cookbooks, biographies, pop psychology, humor, do-it-yourself crafts or poetry. Query or submit outline/synopsis and sample chapters. Reviews artwork/photos.
Recent Nonfiction Title: *Encyclopedia of Native American Tribes*, by Carl Waldman.
Tips: "Our audience is school and public libraries for our more reference-oriented books and libraries, schools and bookstores for our less reference-oriented informational titles."

*FAIRCHILD BOOKS & VISUALS, Book Division, Subsidiary of Capital Cities, Inc., 7 E. 12th St., New York NY 10003. Manager: E.B. Gold. Publishes hardcover and paperback originals. Offers standard minimum book contract; no advance. Pays 10% of net sales distributed twice annually. Averages 12 titles/year; receives 100 submissions annually. 50% of books from first-time authors; 99% of books from unagented writers. Subsidy publishes 2% of books—1% subsidized by authors, 1% by organizations. Publishes book an average of 1 year after acceptance. Photocopied submissions OK. Computer printout submissions acceptable; prefers letter-quality. Book catalog and ms guidelines for 9x12 SASE.

Nonfiction: Publishes business books and textbooks relating to fashion, electronics, marketing, retailing, career education, advertising, home economics and management. Length: Open. Query, giving subject matter, brief outline and at least 1 sample chapter. Reviews artwork/photos as part of ms package.

Recent Nonfiction Title: *The Art of Fashion Draping*, by Connie Amaden-Crawford.

Tips: "The writer has the best chance of selling our firm fashion, retailing or textile related books that can be used by both the trade and schools. If possible, the writer should let us know what courses would use the book."

*FAIRLEIGH DICKINSON UNIVERSITY PRESS, 285 Madison Ave., Madison NJ 07940. (201)593-8564. Chairperson, Editorial Committee: Harry Keyishian. Publishes hardcover originals. Averages 30 titles/year; receives 300 submissions annually. 33% of books from first-time authors; 100% of books from unagented writers. Average print order for a writer's first book is 1,000. "Contract is arranged through Associated University Presses of Cranbury, New Jersey. We are a *selection* committee only." Subsidy publishes (nonauthor) 2% of books. Publishes book an average of 18 months after acceptance. Computer printout submissions acceptable; prefers letter-quality. Reports in 2 weeks on queries; 4 months average on mss.

Nonfiction: Reference and scholarly books. Subjects include art, business and economics, Civil War, film, history, Jewish studies, literary criticism, music, philosophy, politics, psychology, sociology and women's studies. Looking for scholarly books in all fields. No nonscholarly books. Query with outline/synopsis and sample chapters. Reviews artwork/photos as part of ms package.

Recent Nonfiction Title: *The Arrival of Godot: Ritual Patterns in Modern Drama*, by Katherine Burkman.

Tips: "Research must be up to date. Poor reviews result when authors' bibliographies and notes don't reflect current research. We follow University of Chicago style in scholarly citations. We will continue to accept submissions in all fields, but will stress books on film, the Civil War, Jewish studies, American history."

*FALCON PRESS PUBLISHING CO., INC., Box 1718, Helena MT 59624. (406)442-6597. Publisher: Bill Schneider. Publishes hardcover and trade paperback originals. Averages 10-15 titles/year. Subsidy publishes 30% of books. Pays 8-15% royalty on net price or flat fee. Publishes book an average of 6 months after ms is in final form. Reports in 3 weeks on queries. Free book catalog.

Nonfiction: "We're primarily interested in ideas for recreational guidebooks and books on regional outdoor or geographic subjects—especially on Colorado, California and Hawaii—to go in a series of books on those states. We can only respond to submissions that fit these categories." No fiction or poetry. Query only; do not send ms.

Recent Nonfiction Title: *Colorado Ski Country*, by Charlie Meyers.

*THE FAMILY ALBUM, Rt. 1, Box 42, Glen Rock PA 17327. (717)235-2134. Contact: Ron Lieberman. Publishes hardcover originals and reprints and software. Averages 4 titles/year; receives 150 submissions annually. 30% of books from first-time authors; 100% of books from unagented writers. Average print order for a writer's first book is 1,000. Subsidy publishes 20% of books. Pays royalty on wholesale price. Publishes book an average of 10 months after acceptance. Simultaneous and photocopied submissions OK. Query for electronic submissions. Computer printout submissions acceptable; prefers letter-quality. Reports in 2 months.

Nonfiction: "Significant works in the field of (nonfiction) bibliography. Worthy submissions in the field of Pennsylvania-history, biography, folk art and lore. We are also seeking materials relating to books, literacy, and national development. Special emphasis on Third World countries, and the role of printing in international development." No religious material. Submit outline/synopsis and sample chapters.

‡FANTAGRAPHICS BOOKS, INC., Suite 101, 1800 Bridgegate St., Westlake Village CA 91361. (805)379-1881. Subsidiaries include Fantagraphics, Upshot Graphics. Publisher/Executive Editor: Gary Groth. Publishes trade paperback originals. Publishes 40 titles/year. Receives 100 submissions/year. 30% of books from first-time authors; 90% from unagented writers. Pays royalty on retail price. Offers $250-500 average advance. Simultaneous and photocopied submissions OK. Computer printout submissions OK; prefers letter-quality. Reports on queries in 2 months.

Fiction: Adventure, experimental, feminist, gay/lesbian, historical, humor, science fiction (all above as comics). "We're open to almost anything; would like to see more submissions by female creators. No conventional 'super-hero' type comics." Query or submit outline/synopsis and sample chapters.

Recent Fiction Title: *Love and Rockets*, by Los Bros Hernandex (humor/feminist).

Tips: "Outside of the conventional 'super-hero' books of the mainstream, a creator's best long-term chances are with work that best reflects his/her own personal vision. Concentrate on establihsing your own 'look' and perspective rather than slavishly following present market trends—a sure way to get caught behind the times."

FARRAR, STRAUS AND GIROUX, INC., 19 Union Sq. W., New York NY 10003. Publisher, Books for Young Readers: Stephen Roxburgh. Editor-in-Chief: Margaret Ferguson. Publishes hardcover originals. Receives 3,000 submissions annually. Pays royalty; advance. Publishes book an average of 18 months after acceptance. Photocopied submissions OK. Computer printout submissions acceptable; prefers letter-quality. Reports in 3 months. Catalog for #10 SAE and 3 first class stamps.

Nonfiction and Fiction: "We are primarily interested in fiction picture books and novels for children and middle readers." Submit outline/synopsis and sample chapters. Reviews artwork/photos as part of ms package.

Recent Nonfiction Title: *Grace in the Wilderness*, by Aranka Siegal.

Recent Fiction Title: *The Goats*, by Brock Cole.

Recent Picture Book Title: *The Adventures of Simple Simon*, by Chris Conover.

Tips: Fiction of all types has the best chance of selling to this firm. Farrar, Straus and Giroux publishes a limited number of nonfiction titles.

FREDERICK FELL PUBLISHERS, INC., 2131 Hollywood Blvd., Hollywood FL 33020. (305)925-5242. Imprints include Compact Books. Publisher: Donald L. Lessne. Publishes hardcover and trade paperback originals and reprints. Averages 20 titles/year; receives 1,000 submissions annually. 20% of books from first-time authors; 20% of books from unagented writers. Pays royalty. Publishes book an average of 1 year after acceptance. Simultaneous and photocopied submissions OK. Query for electronic submissions. Computer printout submissions OK. Reports in 6 months on mss. Free book catalog.

Nonfiction: Biography, coffee table book, cookbook, how-to, humor, self-help, technical and textbook. Subjects include business and economics, cooking and foods, health, hobbies, philosophy, psychology, recreation, religion and sociology. Especially looking for manuscripts on current issues of interest; how-to, health and business. Submit outline/synopsis and sample chapters. Reviews artwork/photos as part of ms package.

Recent Nonfiction Title: *White-Collar Stress*, by Louis Feuer.

THE FEMINIST PRESS, The City University of New York, 311 E. 94th St., New York NY 10128. (212)360-5790. Publisher: Florence Howe. Publishes originals and reprints of fiction. Averages 12-15 titles/year; receives 500 submissions annually. 10% of books from first-time authors; 90% of books unagented submissions. Pays 10% royalty on net sales; advance. Publishes book an average of 9 months after acceptance. Simultaneous and photocopied submissions OK. Computer printout submissions acceptable. Reports in 3 months. Query or submit outline/synopsis and sample chapters. Do not send whole ms. Catalog for 8½x11 SAE and 50¢ postage.

Nonfiction and Fiction: Feminist books for a general trade and women's studies audience. "We publish reprints of lost feminist fiction, original autobiographies and biographies, women's history, bibliographies and educational materials. No material without a feminist viewpoint. No new fiction, drama, poetry, or dissertations." Looks for "feminist perspective, interesting subject, potential use in women's studies classroom, sensitivity to issues of race and class, clear writing style, general grasp of subject."

Recent Nonfiction Title: *Competition: A Feminist Taboo*, edited by Valerie Miner and Helen Longino.

Tips: "Submit a proposal for an important feminist work that is sophisticated in its analysis, yet readably free of jargon. Both historical and contemporary subjects will be considered. We are especially interested in works that appeal to both a trade audience and a women's studies classroom market."

*FICTION COLLECTIVE, Manuscript Central, English Department, Univ. of Colorado, CB 226, Boulder CO 80309. Managing Editor: Jean Casella. Publishes hardcover and trade paperback originals. Averages 6 titles/year; receives 100-150 submissions/year. 30% of books from first-time authors. 50% of books from unagented writers. Subsidy publishes (nonauthor) 50% of books. Pays 10% royalty on wholesale price after production costs are covered. Publishes book an average of 15 months after acceptance. Simultaneous and photocopied submissions OK. Computer printout submissions OK; no dot-matrix. Reports in 2 months on queries; 6 months on submissions. Free book catalog.

Fiction: Ethnic and experimental. "We publish high-quality, innovative fiction (novels and story collections) completely on the basis of literary merit. We are always looking for quality fiction, but can publish only a very small percentage of what we receive. No genre fiction." Query or submit complete ms.

Recent Fiction Title: *Griever: An American Monkey King in China*, by Gerald Vizenor (novel).

‡FINANCIAL SOURCEBOOKS, Division of Sourcebooks, Inc., Box 313, Naperville IL 60566. (312)961-2161. Publisher: Dominique Raccah. Publishes hardcover and trade paperback originals. Firm averages 7 titles/year. 50% of books from first-time authors. 100% from unagented writers. Pays 5-15% royalty on wholesale price, or buys mss outright. Publishes book average 6 months after acceptance. Simultaneous and photocopied submissions OK. Query for electronic submissions. Computer printout submissions OK. Reports in 1 month on queries. "We do not want to see complete manuscripts." Book catalog free for SASE.

Nonfiction: Reference, technical and textbook. Subjects include business and economics, computers and electronics, government/politics, money/finance, sociology and women's issues/studies. "We publish books, directories and newsletters for financial executives. Our books are largely developed in-house or assigned to a freelancer specializing in the area. We are now looking for additional projects. The books of interest to us will establish a standard in their domain. We look for books with a well-defined, strong market such as reference works or books with a technical, informative bent." Query or submit outline/synopsis and sample chapters (2-3 chapters, not the 1st). Reviews artwork/photos as part of manuscript package.

Recent Nonfiction Title: *Getting on Line: A Step-by-Step Guide for Financial Executives*, (reference guide and directory).
Tips: "Financial executives today are bombarded with information in most every form through much of their working day. Writers can easily sell us books that will help a busy professional deal with the workload more productively. That means books that 1.) compile otherwise difficult to obtain (but useful) information; or 2.) develop new concepts or ideas that will help executives "work smarter"; or 3.) reformat concepts or information executives need into some more useful or digestible form (e.g. graphics, tutorials, etc.)."

FIREBRAND BOOKS, 141 The Commons, Ithaca NY 14850. (607)272-0000. Publisher: Nancy K. Bereano. Publishes hardcover and trade paperback originals and hardcover and trade paperback reprints. Averages 6-8 titles/year; receives 200-300 submissions annually. 50% of books from first-time authors; 75% of books from unagented writers. Pays 7-9% royalty on retail price, or makes outright purchase. Publishes book an average of 18 months after acceptance. Simultaneous and photocopied submissions OK "with notification." Computer printout submissions acceptable; prefers letter-quality. Reports in 2 weeks on queries; 2 months on mss. Book catalog free on request.
Nonfiction: Criticism and essays. Subjects include feminism and lesbianism. Submit complete ms.
Recent Nonfiction Title: *Sanctuary, A Journey*, by Judith McDaniel.
Fiction: Will consider all types of feminist and lesbian fiction.
Recent Fiction Title: *The Fires of Bride*, by Ellen Galford.
Recent Poetry Title: *Living as a Lesbian*, by Cheryl Clarke.
Tips: "Our audience includes feminists, lesbians, ethnic audiences, and other progressive people."

‡FISHER BOOKS, Suite 909, 3499 N. Campbell, Tucson AZ 85719. (602)325-5263. Partner: Howard Fisher. Publishes trade paperback originals and trade paperback reprints. Firm averages 20 titles/year. 25% of books from first-time authors. 50% from unagented writers. Pays 10-15% royalty on wholesale price. Offers up to $10,000 advance. Simultaneous and photocopied submissions OK. Computer printout submissions OK; prefers letter-quality. Reports in 2-4 weeks on queries; 1 month on mss. Free book catalog and ms guidelines.
Nonfiction: Cookbook, how-to and self-help. Subjects include child guidance/parenting, cooking, foods and nutrition, gardening, health/medicine, psychology and sports. Submit outline/synopsis and sample chapters.
Recent Nonfiction Title: *Purrfect Parenting*, by Guhl/Fontanelle.

‡*FISHER'S WORLD, INC., Suite 2E, 106 S. Front St., Philadelphia PA 19106. (215)592-7577. Acquiring Editor: E. Markham. Publishes travel guidebook series. Firm averages 27 titles/year. Buys mss outright for $50-250 "partial on acceptance, final 90 days after publication." Computer printout submissions OK. Book catalog and ms guidelines for 9x12 SAE and 3 first class stamps.
Nonfiction: Travel. "Each of our 26 books contains 3-4 feature articles from authors other than travel book author. Length: 1,500-1,800 words. No promotional articles for particular companies or commercial activities." Query.
Recent Nonfiction Title: *New York*, by J. McBean (travel).
Tips: "The upscale, educated, inquisitive reader (traveler) is our audience."

‡*FITHIAN PRESS, Subsidiary of John Daniel, Publisher, Box 21922, Santa Barbara CA 93121. (805)962-1780. Editor: John Daniel. Publishes trade paperback originals. Firm averages 10 titles/year. Receives 500 submissions/year. 50% of books from first-time authors. 100% from unagented writers. Subsidy publishes 50%. Pays 50% royalty on wholesale price. Publishes book an average of 6-8 months after acceptance. Simultaneous and photocopied submissions OK. Computer printout submissions OK; prefers letter-quality. Reports in 2 weeks on queries; 6-8 weeks on mss. Free book catalog and ms guidelines #10 SASE.
Nonfiction: Biography, how-to, humor, juvenile and self-help. "As a general trade publisher, Fithian Press is willing to consider books on all subjects. We particularly want to see nonfiction with an identifiable, specific audience approachable by direct mail." Query or submit outline/synopsis and sample chapters.
Recent Nonfiction Title: *Our Path To Life Care*, by Levin W. Foster (aging).
Fiction: Literary. "As with nonfiction, small press fiction is most successful when there is a specific and identifiable market/audience. No genre fiction that is more appropriate for mass-market distribution." Query or submit outline/synopsis and sample chapters. Reports in 2 weeks on queries; 6-8 weeks on mss. Free book catalog and ms guidelines.
Recent Fiction Title: *The River Woman*, by Mel Donalson (black/feminist). "We'll consider poetry of all sorts." Submit 15 samples.
Recent Poetry Title: *Once Upon a Planet*, by Albert Johnson (philosophical).
Tips: "Ideally, we would like for each Fithian Press book to have a specific target audience that we can identify and approach through direct mail sales or other special-market techniques."

*FJORD PRESS, Box 16501, Seattle WA 98116. (206)625-9363. Publisher: Steve Murray. Small press. Publishes trade paperback originals. Averages 4-6 titles/year; receives 1,000 submissions/year. 60% of books from unagented writers. Subsidy publishes (nonauthor) 40% of books. Pays 2-12½% royalty on retail price. Tiny advance possible. Publishes book an average of 2 years after acceptance. Simultaneous submissions OK if so advised. Computer printout submissions OK; "please do not justify! Dot-matrix frowned on." Reports in 3 weeks on queries; 3 months on submissions. Book catalog for 5½x8½ SAE with 2 first class stamps.

Nonfiction: Biography. Subjects include European history, western Americana. Query with synopsis and sample chapter.

Recent Nonfiction Title: *Riding The High Country*, by Patrick T. Tucker (autobiography).

Fiction: Translations primarily. Mainstream, suspense (with international setting); and by western writers, both male and female. Query with synopsis and sample chapter.

Recent Fiction Title: *The Missing Bureaucrat*, by Hans Scherfig (satire).

Tips: "Our audience wants to read books of literary quality in any genre and is interested in what is happening in the rest of the world. We are now doing original Western American books; no East Coast settings please. We will continue to consider queries from translators as well. Our politics are decidedly left-wing—no right-wing or religious submissions considered. No replies without SASE."

FLEET PRESS CORP., 160 5th Ave., New York NY 10010. (212)243-6100. Editor: Phoebe Scott. Publishes hardcover and paperback originals and reprints; receives 200 submissions annually. 10% of books from first-time authors; 25% of books from unagented writers. Royalty schedule and advance "varies." Publishes book an average of 15 months after acceptance. Computer printout submissions acceptable; no dot-matrix. Reports in 2 months. Free book catalog.

Nonfiction: History, biography, arts, religion and general nonfiction. Length: 45,000 words. Publishes juveniles. Stresses social studies; for ages 8-15. Length: 25,000 words. Query with outline; no unsolicited mss. Reviews artwork/photos.

FLORA AND FAUNA PUBLICATIONS, Division of E.J. Brill Publishing Co., 2406 N.W. 47th Terrace, Gainesville FL 32606. (904)371-9858. Publisher: Ross H. Arnett, Jr. Book publisher/packager. Publishes hardcover and trade paperback originals. Entire firm publishes 350 annually; imprint averages 10-12 titles/year; receives 70 submissions annually. 50% of books from first-time authors; 100% of books from unagented writers. Average print order for a writer's first book is 500. Pays 10% royalty on list price; negotiable advance. Publishes book an average of 1 year after acceptance. Photocopied submissions OK. Query for electronic submissions. Computer printout submissions acceptable; prefers letter-quality. Reports in 2 weeks on queries; 3 months on mss. Book catalog from sales office, E.J. Brill Co., Suite 1004, 1780 Broadway, New York NY 10019.

Nonfiction: Reference, technical, textbook and directories. Subjects include plants and animals (for amateur and professional biologists), and natural history. Looking for "books dealing with kinds of plants and animals, new nature guide series underway. No nature stories or 'Oh My' nature books." Query with outline and 2 sample chapters. Reviews artwork/photos as part of ms package.

Recent Nonfiction Title: *Butterflies of Florida*, by E.G. Gerberg.

Tips: "Well-documented books, especially those that fit into one of our series, have the best chance of selling to our firm—biology, natural history, no garden books."

J. FLORES PUBLICATIONS, Box 163001, Miami FL 33116. Editor: Eliezer Flores. Publishes trade paperback originals and reprints. Averages 10 titles/year. 99% of books from unagented writers. Pays 10-15% royalty on net sales; no advance. Publishes book an average of 10 months after acceptance. Simultaneous and photocopied submissions OK. Computer printout submissions acceptable; prefers letter-quality. Reports in 1 month on queries; 6 weeks on mss. Book catalog and ms guidelines for 6x9 SAE with 2 first class stamps.

Nonfiction: How-to, illustrated book and self-help. "We need original nonfiction manuscripts on military science, weaponry, current events, self-defense, survival, police science, the martial arts, guerrilla warfare and military history. How-to manuscripts are given priority." No pre-World War II material. Query with outline and 2-3 sample chapters. Reviews artwork/photos. "Photos are accepted as part of the manuscript package and are strongly encouraged."

Recent Nonfiction Title: *The Squeaky Wheel: Complaining for Fun and Profit*, by Tommie Titmouse.

Tips: "Trends include illustrated how-to books on a specific subject. Be thoroughly informed on your subject and technically accurate."

FOCAL PRESS, Subsidiary of Butterworth Publishers, 80 Montvale Ave., Stoneham MA 02180. (617)438-8464. Editor: Karen M. Speerstra. Imprint publishes hardcover and paperback originals and reprints. Averages 20-25 UK-US titles/year; entire firm averages 40-50 titles/year; receives 150 submissions annually. 25% of books from first-time authors; 90% of books from unagented writers. Pays 10-15% royalty on wholesale price; offers $1,500 average advance. Publishes book an average of 1 year after acceptance. Simultaneous and photocopied submissions OK. Computer printout submissions OK. Reports in 3 months. Free book catalog and ms guidelines.

Nonfiction: How-to, reference, technical and textbooks in media arts: photography, film and cinematogra-

phy, and broadcasting. High-level scientific/technical monographs are also considered. We generally do not publish collections of photographs or books composed primarily of photographs. Our books are text-oriented, with artwork serving to illustrate and expand on points in the text." Query preferred, or submit outline/synopsis and sample chapters or complete ms. Reviews artwork/photos as part of ms package.
Recent Nonfiction Title: *Radio Programming*, by Michael Keith.

FODOR'S TRAVEL PUBLICATIONS, INC., Subsidiary of Random House, 201 E. 50th St., New York NY 10022. Editorial Director: Michael Spring. Publishes paperback travel guides. Averages 140 titles/year.
Nonfiction: "We are the publishers of periodic travel guides—regions, countries, cities, and special tourist attractions. We do not solicit manuscripts on a royalty basis, but we are interested in travel writers and/or experts who will and can cover an area of the globe for Fodor's for a fee." Submit credentials and samples of work.
Recent Nonfiction Title: *Carolinas and the Georgia Coast*.

FORMAN PUBLISHING, Suite 206, Brentwood Sq., 11661 San Vicente Blvd., Los Angeles CA 90049. President: Len Forman. Publishes hardcover and trade paperback. Averages 6 titles/year; receives 1,000 submissions/year. 100% of books from first-time authors. 90% of books from unagented writers. Pays 6-15% royalty. Simultaneous and photocopied submissions OK. Publishes book an average of 18 months after acceptance. Reports in 2 weeks on queries; 3 months on mss. Book catalog free for #10 SASE.
Nonfiction: Coffee table book, cookbook, how-to and self-help. Subjects include art, business and economics, cooking and foods, health, nature and psychology. Submit outline/synopsis and sample chapters. Reviews artwork/photos as part of ms package.
Recent Nonfiction Title: *Living Lean and Loving It*, by Lowry & Milligan.

‡FOUR WINDS PRESS, Macmillan Children's Books Group, 866 Third Ave., New York NY 10022. (212)702-2000. Editor-in-Chief: Cindy Kane. Publishes hardcover originals. Publishes 24 titles/year; receives 1,300 proposals/year. 10% of books from first-time authors; 20% from unagented writers. Pays 5-10% royalty on retail price. Average advance is $4,000. Publishes book an average of 18 months after acceptance. Simultaneous and photocopied submissions OK. Computer printout submissions OK; prefers letter-quality. Reports in 2 weeks on queries; 6 weeks on mss. Free book catalog and ms guidelines.
Nonfiction: Juvenile. Subjects—all juvenile— include: Americana, animals, ethnic, nature/environment. Query. Reviews artwork/photos with ms package.
Recent Nonfiction Title: *Log Cabin in the Woods*, Joanne Landers Henry (historical nonfiction).
Fiction: Juvenile, young adult. Wants picture books, early readers middle grade (ages 8-12) and young adult (ages 12 and up). No overworked themes such as sibling rivalry, alphabet and counting books, retellings of fairy tales—all at picture book level. Submit complete ms.
Recent Fiction Title: *The Mommy Exchange*, by Amy Hest (picture book).
Tips: "We're looking for fresh older fiction that is both funny and moving and that only the author could have written. Our audience is children—either being read to (ages 3-7) or reading on their own. Study the books curently being published in your chosen field."

‡*FRANCISCAN HERALD PRESS, Sacred Heart Province of the Order of Friars Minor, 1434 W. 51st St., Chicago IL 60609. (312)254-4462. Managing Director: Gabriel Brinkman, OFMP. Publishes hardcover originals and trade paperback originals. Firm averages 12-15 titles/year. Receives 2 submissions/year. 2% of books from first-time authors. 99% from unagented writers. Subsidy publishes 10% of books. Pays 7-10% royalty on retail price. Publishing of book varies after acceptance. Query for electronic submissions. Reports in 2 weeks; 4 weeks on mss.
Nonfiction: Religion. Submit complete ms.
Recent Poetry Title: *From Intuition to Institution*, by T. Desbonnets, OFM (religious, historical).

THE FRASER INSTITUTE, 626 Bute St., Vancouver, British Columbia V6E 3M1 Canada. (604)688-0221. Assistant Director: Sally Pipes. Publishes trade paperback originals. Averages 4-6 titles/year; receives 30 submissions annually. Pays honorarium. Publishes book an average of 6 months after acceptance. Simultaneous and photocopied submissions OK. Query for electronic submissions. Computer printout submissions acceptable; prefers letter-quality. Reports in 6 weeks. Free book catalog; ms guidelines for SAE and IRC.
Nonfiction: Analysis, opinion, on economics, social issues and public policy. Subjects include business and economics, politics, religion and sociology. "We will consider submissions of high-quality work on economics, social issues, economics and religion, public policy, and government intervention in the economy." Submit complete ms.
Recent Nonfiction Title: *Privatization: Tactics and Techniques*, edited by Michael Walker.
Tips: "Our books are read by well-educated consumers, concerned about their society and the way in which it is run and are adopted as required or recommended reading at colleges and universities in Canada, the U.S. and abroad. Our readers feel they have some power to improve society and view our books as a source of the infor-

mation needed to take steps to change unproductive and inefficient ways of behavior into behavior which will benefit society. Recent trends to note in book publishing include affirmative action, banking, broadcasting, insurance, healthcare and religion. A writer has the best chance of selling us books on government, economics, finance, or social issues."

‡**THE FREE PRESS**, Division of the Macmillan Publishing Co., Inc., 866 3rd Ave., New York NY 10022. President/Publisher: Erwin A. Glikes. Averages 65 titles/year; receives 3,000 submissions annually. 15% of books from first time authors; 50% of books from unagented writers. Royalty schedule varies. Publishes book an average of 11 months after acceptance. "Prefers camera-ready copy to machine-readable media." Computer printout submissions acceptable; prefers letter-quality. Reports in 3 weeks.
Nonfiction: Professional books and textbooks. Publishes college texts, adult nonfiction, and professional books in the social sciences, humanities and business. Reviews artwork/photos as part of ms package "but we can accept no responsibility for photos or art." Looks for "identifiable target audience, evidence of writing ability." Accepts nonfiction translations. Send 1-3 sample chapters, outline, and query letter before submitting mss.

SAMUEL FRENCH, INC., 45 W. 25th St., New York NY 10010. (212)206-8990. Subsidiaries include Samuel French Ltd. (London); Samuel French (Canada) Ltd. (Toronto); Samuel French, Inc. (Hollywood); and Baker's Plays (Boston). Editor: Lawrence Harbison. Publishes paperback acting editions of plays. Averages 80-90 titles/year; receives 1,200 submissions annually, mostly from unagented playwrights. About 10% of publications are from first-time authors; 20% from unagented writers. Pays 10% book royalty on retail price. Pays 90% stock production royalty; 80% amateur production royalty. Offers variable advance. Publishes book an average of 6 months after acceptance. Simultaneous and photocopied submissions OK. Computer printouts acceptable; no dot-matrix. Reports immediately on queries; from 6 weeks to 8 months on mss. Book catalog $1.25; ms guidelines $3.
Nonfiction: Acting editions of plays.
Tips: "Broadway and Off-Broadway hit plays, light comedies and mysteries have the best chance of selling to our firm. Our market is theater producers—both professional and amateur—and actors. Read as many plays as possible of recent vintage to keep apprised of today's market; write small-cast plays with good female roles; and be one hundred percent professional in approaching publishers and producers (see guidelines)."

FULCRUM, INC., #510, 350 Indiana St., Golden CO 80401. (303)277-1623. Contact: Submissions Editor. Publishes hardcover originals and reprints. Averages 12-16 titles/year; receives 1,000 submissions/year. 75% of books from first-time authors. 85% of books from unagented writers. Pays 8-12% royalty on wholesale or retail price based on discount; offers $1,000-3,000 average advance. Publishes book an average of 6 months after acceptance. Query for electronic submissions. Computer printout submissions OK; no dot-matrix. Reports in 1 month on queries; 6 weeks on mss. Book catalog for 8x10 SAE with 3 first class stamps; ms guidelines for SASE.
Nonfiction: Subjects include history, nature, philosophy, biography, politics, recreation, self-help, travel, natural resources and other issues. "We welcome submissions on nature/outdoor/environmental issues. We're interested in more self-help. No sports, cookbooks or religion." Query or submit outline/synopsis and sample chapters. Reviews artwork/photos as part of ms package.
Recent Nonfiction Title: *Take Your Life Off Hold*, by Ted Dreier.
Tips: "Our audience includes those interested in land, nature and the outdoors, as the foundation of America; also college students and graduates aware of what is vital and happening in our world. Issue-focused books on natural resources have the best chance of selling to our firm."

GARBER COMMUNICATIONS, INC., (affiliates: Steinerbooks, Spiritual Fiction Publications, Spiritual Science Library, Rudolf Steiner Publications, Freedeeds Library, Biograf Publications), 5 Garber Hill Rd., Blauvelt NY 10913. (914)359-9292. Editor: Bernard J. Garber. Publishes hardcover and paperback originals and reprints. Does not accept unsolicited submissions. "We will refuse and return unsolicited submissions at the author's expense." Averages 15 titles/year; receives 250 submissions annually. 10% of books from first-time authors; 10% of books from unagented writers. Average print order for a writer's first book is 500-1,000 copies. Pays 5-7% royalty on retail price; offers average $500 advance. Publishes book an average of 1 year after acceptance. Will consider photocopied submissions.
Nonfiction: Spiritual sciences, occult, philosophical, metaphysical and ESP. These are for our Steiner Books division only. Serious nonfiction. Philosophy and Spiritual Sciences: Bernard J. Garber. Query only (with SASE or no response).
Fiction: Patricia Abrams, editor, the new genre called Spiritual Fiction Publications. "We are now looking for original manuscripts or rewrites of classics in modern terms." Query only with SASE.

GARDEN WAY PUBLISHING, Storey Communications, Inc., Schoolhouse Rd., Pownal VT 05261. (802)823-5811. Editor: Deborah Burns. Publishes hardcover and paperback originals. "We are looking at audio and video cassettes." Publishes 15 titles/year; receives 2,000 submissions annually. 50% of books from first-time authors; 90% of books from unagented writers. Average print order for a writer's first book is 7,500. Offers a flat fee arrangement varying with book's scope, or royalty, which usually pays author 8% of book's net price. Advances are negotiable, but usually range from $1,500 to $3,000. "We stress continued promotion of titles and sales over many years." Emphasizes direct mail sales and sales to specialty stores, plus sales to bookstores through Harper and Row. Publishes book 1 year after acceptance and receipt of complete ms. Photocopied submissions OK. Computer printout submissions acceptable; no dot-matrix. Book catalog and ms guidelines for 9x12 SAE with 2 first class stamps.

Nonfiction: Books on gardening (both vegetable and ornamental), cooking, nutrition, house building and remodeling, animals, country living, and country business. Emphasis should be on how-to. Length requirements are flexible. "The writer should remember the reader will buy his book to learn to do something, so that all information to accomplish this must be given. We are publishing specifically for the person who is concerned about natural resources and a deteriorating lifestyle and wants to do something about it." Query with outline and 2-3 sample chapters. Reviews artwork/photos as part of ms package.

Recent Nonfiction Title: *Let's Grow! 72 Gardening Adventures with Children*, by Linda Tilgner.

Tips: "We look for comprehensive, authoritative manuscripts. Authors should look at our other books to see how theirs would suit our line, and tell us who they feel the audience for their book would be. As well as our usual line, we're interested in things parents and children can do together."

‡GARLAND PUBLISHING, INC., 136 Madison Ave., New York NY 10016. (212)686-7492. Vice President: Gary Kuris. Publishes hardcover originals. Averages 150 titles/year. 99% of books from unagented writers. Pays 10-15% royalty on wholesale price. "Depending on marketability, authors may prepare camera-ready copy." Publishes book an average of 9 months after acceptance. Simultaneous and photocopied submissions OK. Computer printout submissions acceptable; prefers letter-quality. Reports in 2 weeks on queries; 1 month on mss. Free book catalog; ms guidelines for SASE.

Nonfiction: Reference books for libraries. Humanities and social sciences. Accepts nonfiction translations. "We're interested in reference books—encyclopedias, bibliographies, sourcebooks, indexes, etc.—in all fields." Submit outline/synopsis and 1-2 sample chapters. Reviews artwork/photos as part of ms package.

Recent Nonfiction Title: *Ulysses*, by James Joyce (a synoptic edition).

GAY SUNSHINE PRESS AND LEYLAND PUBLICATIONS, Box 40397, San Francisco CA 94140. (415)824-3184. Editor: Winston Leyland. Publishes hardcover and trade paperback originals and trade paperback reprints. Averages 10 titles/year. Pays royalty or makes outright purchase. Photocopied submissions OK. Reports in 3 weeks on queries; 1 month on mss. Book catalog $1.

Nonfiction: How-to and gay lifestyle topics. "We're interested in innovative literary nonfiction which deals with gay lifestyles." No long personal accounts, academic or overly formal titles. No books that are too specialized (e.g., homosexuality in the ancient world). Query. "After query is returned by us, submit outline/synopsis and sample chapters. All unsolicited mss are returned unopened."

Recent Nonfiction Title: *Calamus Lovers: Walt Whitman's Working Class Camerados*.

Fiction: Erotica, ethnic, experimental, historical, mystery, science fiction and gay fiction in translation. "Interested in well-written novels on gay themes; also short story collections. We have a high literary standard for fiction." Query. "After query is returned by us, submit outline/synopsis and sample chapters. All unsolicited mss are returned unopened."

Recent Fiction Title: Gore Vidal's *A Thirsty Evil* (short stories).

‡GEMSTONE BOOKS, 242 Portland Ave. S., Minneapolis MN 55415. (612)333-2691. Fiction Editor: Karin Snelson. Imprint of Dillon Press, Inc. Publishes hardcover originals (juvenile fiction only). Division publishes 10 titles/year. Pays royalty or outright purchase. Publishes ms an average of 1 year after acceptance. Simultaneous and photocopied submissions OK. Computer printout submissions OK; no dot-matrix. Reports on queries in 2 weeks; on mss in 6-8 weeks. Book catalog for 10x12 SAE with 85¢ postage. Ms guidelines for #10 SASE.

Fiction: Adventure, ethnic, historical, humor, mystery. "We are looking for fiction manuscripts that appeal to young people ages 7-14, and especially historical fiction 20-25 pages in length based on single historical events for grades 2 and up." No picture books or young adult novels. Query or submit outline/synopsis and sample chapters.

Recent Fiction Title: *A Gift for Tia Rosa*, by Karen Taha (short story).

‡THE J. PAUL GETTY MUSEUM, Subsidiary of The J. Paul Getty Museum Trust, Box 2112, Santa Monica CA 90406. (213)459-7611. Editor: Andrea Belloli. Publishes hardcover and trade paperback originals and reprints. Averages 10 titles/year; receives 50 submissions annually. 10% of books from first-time authors; 100% of books from unagented writers. Average print order for a writer's first book is 3,000. Buys some mss outright; offers average $2,000 honorarium. Publishes book an average of 18 months after acceptance. Photocopied submissions OK. Query for electronic submissions. Computer printout submissions acceptable; prefers letter-quality. Reports in 1 months. Book list and ms guidelines for SASE.

Nonfiction: Reference and scholarly on art and history. "Scholarly titles and well-researched general and children's titles on topics related to the museum's seven collections: Greek and Roman art and architecture (especially the Villa dei Papiri), illuminated manuscripts, drawings and paintings from the Renaissance through the nineteenth century, European sculpture and decorative arts of the Regence through Napoleonic periods, and photographs." No nonEuropean art. Query. Reviews artwork/photos as part of ms package.

Recent Nonfiction Title: *European Drawings 1: Catalogue of the Collections, the J. Paul Getty Museum*, by George Goldner.

Tips: "Art history related to museum collections has the best chance of selling to our firm."

GIFTED EDUCATION PRESS, The Reading Tutorium, 10201 Yuma Ct., Box 1586, Manassas VA 22110. (703)369-5017. Publisher: Maurice D. Fisher. Small press. Publishes mass market paperback originals. Averages 5 titles/year; receives 50 submissions annually. 100% of books from first-time authors; 100% of books from unagented writers. Pays royalty of $1 per book. Publishes book an average of 6 months after acceptance. Simultaneous and photocopied submissions OK. Computer printout submissions acceptable; prefers letter-quality. Reports in 2-4 months on queries; 4 months on mss. Book catalog and ms guidelines for #10 SAE with 2 first class stamps.

Nonfiction: How-to. Subjects include philosophy, psychology, education of the gifted; and how to teach adults to read. "Need books on how to educate gifted children—both theory and practice, and adult literacy. Also, we are searching for books on using computers with the gifted, and how to parent the gifted. Need rigorous books on procedures, methods, and specific curriculum for the gifted. Send letter of inquiry only. Do not send manuscripts or parts of manuscripts."

Recent Nonfiction Title: *The Philosophy of Ethics Applied to Everyday Life*, by James L. Gludice and Michael E. Walters.

Tips: "If I were a writer trying to market a book today, I would develop a detailed outline based upon intensive study of my field of interest. Present creative ideas in a rigorous fashion. Be knowledgeable about and comfortable with ideas. We are looking for books on using computers with gifted students; books for parents of the gifted; and books (desparately seeking!) on how to teach adults to read."

GLENBRIDGE PUBLISHING LTD., 1303 West Adams, Macomb IL 61455. (309)833-5104. Editor: James A. Keene. Publishes hardcover originals and reprints, and trade paperback originals. Publishes 6 titles/year. Pays 10% royalty. Publishes book an average of 1 year after acceptance. Simultaneous and photocopied submissions OK. Computer printout submissions OK; prefers letter-quality. Reports in 1 week on queries; 1 month on mss. Ms guidelines for #10 SAE with 1 first class stamp.

Nonfiction: Reference and textbook. Subjects include Americana, business and economics, history, music, philosophy, politics, psychology and sociology. "Academic and scholarly" books desired. Query or submit outline/synopsis and sample chapters. Include SASE.

Recent Nonfiction Title: *How We Communicate*, by Martin K. Barrack.

‡**THE GLOBE PEQUOT PRESS, INC.**, 138 W. Main St., Chester CT 06412. (203)526-9571. Managing Editor: Bruce Markot. Publishes hardcover and paperback originals and paperback reprints. Averages 60 titles/year; receives 2,000 submissions annually. 10% of books from first-time authors; 60% of books from unagented writers. Average print order for a writer's first book is 5,000-7,500. Offers 7½-10% royalty on net price; offers advances. Publishes book an average of 1 year after acceptance. Simultaneous and photocopied submissions OK. Computer printout submissions acceptable; prefers letter-quality. Reports in 6 weeks. Book catalog for 9x12 SASE.

Nonfiction: Travel guidebooks (regional OK), Americana, journalism/media, natural history, outdoor recreation, gardening, carpentry and cookbooks. No doctoral theses, genealogies, or textbooks. Submit outline, table of contents, sample chapter(s), and resume/vita. Complete mss accepted. Reviews artwork/photos.

Recent Nonfiction Title: *Journey to the High Southwest*, by Robert Casey.

*****GLOBE PRESS BOOKS**, Box 2045, Madison Sq. Station, New York NY 10159. (212)362-3720. Publisher: Joel Friedlander. Imprint includes Fourth Way Books. Publishes hardcover and trade paperback originals. Averages 4 titles/year; receives 12 submissions/year. 25% of books from first-time authors. 50% of books from unagented writers. Subsidy publishes (nonauthor) 20% of books. Pays royalty on retail price. Publishes book an average of 1 year after publication. Simultaneous submissions OK. Query for electronic submissions. Computer printout submissions OK; prefers letter-quality. Reports in 6 weeks. Book catalog for #10 SAE with 1 first class stamp.

Nonfiction: Self-help and esoteric psychology. Subjects include history, philosophy and psychology. "We want manuscripts on east/west psychology and esoteric thought. No economics, politics or how-to books." Query or submit outline/synopsis and sample chapters. Reviews artwork/photos as part of ms package.

Recent Nonfiction Title: *Maurice Nicoll, A Portrait*, by Beryl Pogson.

Tips: "Well written, well thought-out mss on esoteric approaches to psychology, art, literature and history are needed."

‡**DAVID R. GODINE, PUBLISHER**, Horticultural Hall, 300 Masachusetts Ave., Boston MA 02115. (617)536-0761. Executive Editor: André Bernard. Publishes hardcover and trade paperback originals and reprints. Publishes 40-50 titles/year. 40% of books from first-time authors; 50% from unagented writers. Pays royalty on retail price. Publishes ms an average of 2 years after acceptance. Simultaneous and photocopied submissions OK. Computer printout submissions OK; prefers letter-quality. Reports in 6 weeks. Book catalog free on request.

Nonfiction: Biography, coffee-table books, cookbooks, illustrated books, juvenile. Subjects include agriculture/horticulture, Americana, animals, art/architecture, cooking, foods and nutrition, gardening, gay/lesbian, government/politics, history, language/literature, music/dance, nature/environment, photography, regional, translation, travel. "We can't take on a great deal (being a small house) but we are interested in a wide variety of topics and are always looking for good new material. No erotica, military, joke books or family genealogies." Query or submit ms. Reviews artwork/photos as part of ms package.

Recent Nonfiction Title: *A Leak in the Heart*, by Fay Moskowitz (essays/memoir).

Fiction: Juvenile, literary, mainstream/contemporary, mystery, short story collections, suspense. No science fiction, fantasy, adventure, or religious books. Query or submit complete ms.

Recent Fiction Title: *Life*, by Georges Perec (literary).

Tips: "In fiction, literary works appeal to us the most; that is, books that are thoughtful and well written as well as original in plot and intent. We also like beautifully illustrated books."

GOLDEN BOOKS, Western Publishing Co., Inc., 850 3rd Ave., New York NY 10022. Publisher, Children's Books: Doris Duenewald. Averages 200 titles/year; receives 1,000 submissions annually. 50% of books from unagented writers. Pays royalty; buys some mss outright. Publishes book an average of 3 months after acceptance. "Unsolicited submissions will be returned unopened."

Nonfiction: Adult nonfiction, limited to cookbooks and nature guides. Children's books, including picture books, concept books, novelty books, and information books. Reviews artwork/photos.

Fiction: Children's picture books and young fiction.

GOLDEN WEST PUBLISHERS, 4113 N. Longview, Phoenix AZ 85014. (602)265-4392. Editor: Hal Mitchell. Small press. Publishes trade paperback originals. Averages 5-6 titles/year; receives 400-500 submissions annually. 50% of books from first-time authors; 100% of books from unagented writers. Average print order for a writer's first book is 5,000. Pays 6-10% royalty on retail price or makes outright purchase of $500-2,500. No advance. Publishes book an average of 6 months after acceptance. Simultaneous and photocopied submissions OK. Query for electronic submissions. Computer printout submissions acceptable; no dot-matrix. Reports in 2 weeks on queries; 1 month on mss. Book catalog for #10 SAE and 1 first class stamp.

Nonfiction: Cookbooks, books on the Southwest and West. Subjects include cooking and foods, southwest history and outdoors, and travel. Query or submit outline/synopsis and sample chapters. Prefers query letter first. Reviews artwork/photos as part of ms package.

Recent Title: *The Other Mexico*, by E.J. Guarino.

Tips: "We are primarily interested in Arizona and southwest material and welcome material in this area."

‡**GORDON AND BREACH**, 50 West 23rd St., New York NY 10010. (212)206-8900. Subsidiaries include Gordon and Breach; Hardwood Academic Publishers. Editorial Director: Dr. Philip C. Manor. Publishes hardcover and trade paperback originals and reprints. Firms publishes approximately 120 titles/year. Receives 50 submissions/year. 80% of books from first-time authors; 100% from unagented writers. Pays 10% royalty on wholesale price or outright purchase of $1,000. Publishes book an average of 9 months after acceptance. Photocopied submissions OK. Query for electronic submissions. Computer printout submissions OK; no dot-matrix. Reports in 2 months. Book catalog free on request.

Nonfiction: Biography, reference, technical and textbook. Subjects include agriculture/horticulture, anthropology/archaeology, art/architecture, business and economics, computers and electronics, education, ethnic, health/medicine, music/dance, nature/environment, philosophy, photography, psychology, science and sociology. "We publish *scholarly works*, usually from academic authors, in the sciences, mathematics, medicine, the social sciences, and the arts." Submit outline/synopsis and sample chapters or complete ms. Reviews artwork/photos as part of ms package.

Recent Nonfiction Title: *DNA in Clinical Medicine*, by Wilkin (medical).

Tips: "We publish scholarly monographs and graduate level texts; increasing progam in medicine and in humanities/social sciences. Research scientists, scholars, graduate level and above are our audience."

‡**GOSPEL PUBLISHING HOUSE**, Imprint of Assemblies of God General Council, 1445 Boonville Ave., Springfield MO 64803-1894. (417)862-2781. Book Editor: Glen Ellard. Harcover, trade and mass market paperback originals. Publishes 18 titles/year. Receives 380 submissions/year. 90% of books from first-time authors; 90% from unagented writers. Pays 10% royalty on retail price. Publishes book an average of 18 months after acceptance. Simultaneous submissions OK. Computer printout submissions OK; no dot-matrix. Reports in 2 weeks on queries; 2 months on mss. Book catalog and manuscript guidelines free on request.

Nonfiction: Biography and self-help. Subjects include education (Christian or deaf), history (Assemblies of God), religion (young, Bible study, Christian living, devotional, doctrinal, evangelism, healing, Holy Spirit, missionary, pastoral, prophecy). "Gospel Publishing House is owned and operated by the Assemblies of God. Therefore, the doctrinal viewpoint of all books published is required to be compatible with our denominational positions." Query or submit outline/synopsis and sample chapters.
Recent Nonfiction Title: *Choosing to Cope*, by Mary J. Beggs (autobiography).
Fiction: Adventure, fantasy, historical, humor, juvenile, mystery, religious, young adult. Query or submit outline/synopsis and sample chapters.
Recent Fiction Title: *Mystery at Pier Fourteen*, by Betty Swinford (juvenile Christian).

GOVERNMENT INSTITUTES, INC., Suite 24, 966 Hungerford Dr., Rockville MD 20850. (301)251-9250. Vice President, Publishing: G. David Williams. Publishes hardcover and softcover originals. Averages 24 titles/year; receives 20 submissions annually. 50% of books from first-time authors; 100% of books from unagented writers. Pays variable royalty or fee. No advance. Publishes book an average of 2 months after acceptance. Simultaneous and photocopied submissions OK. Computer printout submissions acceptable; prefers letter-quality. Reports in 1 month on queries; 2 months on mss. Book catalog and ms guidelines available on request.
Nonfiction: Reference and technical. Subjects include environmental law, health, safety, personnel and energy. Needs professional-level titles in environmental law, health, safety, personnel and energy. Submit synopsis in narrative style and sample chapters. Reviews artwork/photos.
Recent Nonfiction Title: *Environmental Law Handbook, 9th Edition*, by J. Gordon Arbuckle, et al. (professional).

GRAPEVINE PUBLICATIONS, INC., Box 118, Corvallis OR 97339. (503)754-0583. Editor: Christopher M. Coffin. Publishes trade paperback originals. Averages 6-10 titles/year; receives 100-200 submissions/year. 20% of books from first-time authors; 100% of books from unagented writers. Pays 9% royalty on retail price. Publishes book an average of 9 months after acceptance. Simultaneous and photocopied submissions OK. Query for electronic submissions. Computer printout submissions OK; prefers letter-quality. Reports in 2 weeks on queries; 1 month on mss. Writer's kit for $10 (includes sample book, writer's guide, sample contract, book catalog, and query/manuscript analysis).
Nonfiction: How-to, self-help, technical and textbook. Subjects include math, science, computers, calculators, software and other technical tools. Submit complete ms. Reviews artwork/photos as part of ms package.
Recent Nonfiction Title: *An Easy Course in Using the HP-27S*, by Chris Coffin and John W. Loux.
Tips: "We place heavy emphasis on readability, visual presentation, clarity, and reader participation. We will insist on numerous diagrams and illustrations, loosely-spaced text, large, easy-to-read formats, friendly, conversational writing, but tight, well-designed instruction. We disguise top-flight teaching as merely refreshing reading. The writer must be first and foremost a teacher who holds an engaging one-on-one conversation with the reader through the printed medium."

GRAPHIC ARTS CENTER PUBLISHING CO., 3019 NW Yeon Ave., Box 10306, Portland OR 97210. (503)226-2402. General Manager and Editor: Douglas Pfeiffer. Publishes hardcover originals. Averages 10 titles/year. Makes outright purchase, averaging $3,000.
Nonfiction: "All titles are pictorials with text. Text usually runs separately from the pictorial treatment. Authors must be previously published and are selected to complement the pictorial essay." Query.

GREAT NORTHWEST PUBLISHING AND DISTRIBUTING COMPANY, INC., Box 10-3902, Anchorage AK 99510-3902. (907)373-0121. President: Marvin H. Clark Jr. Publishes hardcover and trade paperback originals. Averages 5 titles/year; receives 22-25 submissions annually. 30% of books from first-time authors; 100% of books from unagented writers. Pays 10% royalty on retail price. Publishes book an average of 1 year after acceptance. Simultaneous and photocopied submissions OK. Query for electronic submissions. Computer printout submissions OK; no dot-matrix. Reports in 2 weeks on queries; 2 months on mss. Free book catalog.
Nonfiction: Biography and how-to. Subjects include sports, Alaska and hunting. "Alaskana and hunting books by very knowledgeable hunters and residents of the Far North interest our firm." Query.
Recent Nonfiction Title: *Big Game, Big Country*, by Dr. Chauncey Guy Suits.
Tips: "Pick a target audience first, subject second. Provide crisp, clear journalistic prose on desired subject matter."

GREEN HILL PUBLISHERS, INC., 722 Columbus St., Ottawa IL 61350. (815)434-7905. Distributed by Kampmann & Co. Publisher: Jameson G. Campaigne. Publishes hardcover, trade paper and mass market paperback originals. Publishes 10 titles/year. Pays 6-15% royalty. Advance averages $2,500. Simultaneous and "clean" photocopied submissions OK. Query for electronic submissions. Computer printout submissions acceptable; prefers letter-quality. Reports in 2 months on queries; 4 months on mss. Book catalog for 6x9 SAE with 2 first class stamps.

Nonfiction: Biography (of major subjects), business and economics, history, politics, Chicago themes.

Recent Nonfiction Title: *Constitutional Journal*, by Jeffrey St. John (current events).

Fiction: American, "mountain man, early fur trade, and frontiersmen stories." Query or submit complete ms.

Recent Fiction Title: *Buckskin Brigades*, by L. Ron Hubbard (Frontier Library).

Tips: "Concentrate on literacy, historical accuracy, vocabulary, grammar, basic story telling and narrative skills. Don't submit poor pitch letters stressing word counts and other irrelevancies."

GREEN TIGER PRESS, INC., 1061 India St., San Diego CA 92101. (619)238-1001. Submit to Editorial Committee. Publishes picture books, greeting cards, calendars, posters and stationery. Averages 10-12 titles/year; receives 2,500 submissions annually. 5% of books from first-time authors; 80% of books from unagented writers. Pays royalty on retail price; rights purchased vary according to each project.

Tips: "We look for manuscripts containing a romantic, visionary or imaginative quality, often with a mythic feeling where fantasy and reality co-exist. We also welcome nostalgia and the world of the child themes. We do not publish science fiction. Since we are a visually-oriented house, we look for manuscripts whose texts readily conjure up visual imagery. Never send originals. Samples will be returned only if accompanied by SASE. Please allow three months before inquiring about your submission."

*WARREN H. GREEN, INC., 8356 Olive Blvd., St. Louis MO 63132. Editor: Warren H. Green. Imprint includes Fireside Books. Publishes hardcover originals. Offers "10-20% sliding scale of royalties based on quantity distributed. All books are short run, highly specialized, with no advance." Subsidy publishes about 1% of books, e.g., "books in philosophy and those with many color plates." Averages 30 titles/year; receives 200 submissions annually. 15% of books from first-time authors; 100% of books from unagented writers. "37% of total marketing is overseas." Catalog available on request. Publishes book an average of 10 months after acceptance. Simultaneous and photocopied submissions OK. Computer printout submissions acceptable; no dot-matrix. Query or submit outline and sample chapters. "Publisher requires 300- to 500-word statement of scope, plan, and purpose of book, together with curriculum vitae of author." Reports in 60-90 days.

Nonfiction: Medical and scientific. "Specialty monographs for practicing physicians and medical researchers. Books of 160 pages upward. Illustrated as required by subject. Medical books are non-textbook type, usually specialties within specialties, and no general books for a given specialty. For example, separate books on each facet of radiology, and not one complete book on radiology. Authors must be authorities in their chosen fields and accepted as such by their peers. Books should be designed for all doctors in English speaking world engaged in full or part time activity discussed in book. We would like to increase publications in the fields of radiology, anesthesiology, pathology, psychiatry, surgery and orthopedic surgery, obstetrics and gynecology, and speech and hearing." Also interested in books on health, philosophy, psychology and sociology. Reviews artwork/photos as part of ms package.

THE STEPHEN GREENE PRESS/LEWIS PUBLISHING, 15 Muzzey St., Lexington MA 02173. (802)257-7757. Editorial Director: Thomas Begner. Publishes hardcover and paperback originals, and hardcover and paperback reprints. Averages 30 titles/year. Royalty "variable; advances are small." Send contact sheet or prints to illustrate ms. Photocopied submissions OK. Reports in 3 months.

Nonfiction: How-to (self-reliance); nature and environment; recreation; self-help; sports (outdoor and horse); popular psychology and social science; and regional (New England). "We see our audience as mainly college-educated men and women, 30 and over. They are regular book buyers and readers. They probably have pronounced interests, hobby or professional, in subjects that our books treat. Authors can assess their needs by looking critically at what we have published."

GREENHAVEN PRESS, INC., 15708 Pomerado Rd., Poway CA 92064. Subsidiaries include New Day Books. Senior Editor: Terry O'Neill. Publishes hard and softcover educational supplementary materials and (nontrade) juvenile nonfiction. Averages 6-12 juvenile manuscripts published/year; all are works for hire; receives 36 submissions/year. 50% of juvenile books from first-time authors; 100% of juvenile books from unagented writers. Makes outright purchase for $1,000-2,000. Publishes book an average of 1 year after acceptance. Simultaneous if specified and clear photocopied submissions OK. Computer printout submissions OK; prefers letter-quality. Book catalog for 9x12 SAE with 2 first class stamps.

Nonfiction: Biography, illustrated book, juvenile, reference and textbook. Subjects include animals, business and economics, history, nature, philosophy, politics, psychology, religion and sociology. "We produce tightly formattted books for young people grades 4-6 and 7-9. Each series has specific requirements. Potential

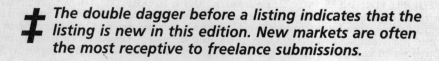

The double dagger before a listing indicates that the listing is new in this edition. New markets are often the most receptive to freelance submissions.

writers should familiarize themselves with our catalog and senior high material. No unsolicited manuscripts." Query or submit outline/synopsis and sample chapters. Reviews artwork/photos as part of manuscript package.
Recent Nonfiction Title: *AIDS: Opposing Viewpoints,* edited by Bonnie Szumski (anthology).
Nonfiction Juvenile: *Great Mysteries: The Solar System,* by Peter and Connie Roop.

GREENLEAF CLASSICS, INC., Box 20194, San Diego CA 92120. Editor: Paul J. Estok. Publishes paperback originals. Publishes 450 titles/year; receives 1,000-2,000 submissions annually. 15% of books from first-time authors; 90% of books from unagented writers. Pays by outright purchase about 6 months after acceptance. Computer printout submissions acceptable; no dot-matrix. Reports in 1-2 months. "No manuscripts will be returned unless accompanied by return postage." Ms guidelines for SASE.
Fiction: Specializes in adult erotic novels. "All stories must have a sexual theme. They must be contemporary novels dealing with the serious problems of everyday people. All plots are structured so that characters must get involved in erotic situations. Write from the female viewpoint (third person). Request our guidelines before beginning any project for us." Preferred length: 35,000 words. Send complete ms (preferred); or at least 3 sample chapters.

*GUERNICA EDITIONS, Box 633, Station N.D.G., Montreal, Quebec H4A 3R1 Canada. (514)481-5569. President/Editor: Antonio D'Alfonso. Publishes hardcover and trade paperback originals, hardcover and trade paperback reprints and software. Averages 10 titles/year; receives 1,000 submissions annually. 5% of books from first-time authors. Average print order for a writer's first book is 750-1,000. Subsidy publishes (nonauthor) 50% of titles. "Subsidy in Canada is received only when the author is established, Canadian-born and active in the country's cultural world. The others we subsidize ourselves." Pays 3-10% royalty on retail price. Makes outright purchase of $200-5,000. Offers 10¢/word advance for translators. Photocopied submissions OK. IRCs required. "American stamps are of no use to us in Canada." Reports in 1 month on queries; 6 weeks on mss. Free book catalog.
Nonfiction: Biography, humor, juvenile, reference and textbook. Subjects include art, history, music, philosophy, politics, psychology, recreation, religion and Canadiana.
Recent Nonfiction Title: *The Courage of Poetry,* by Paul Chamberland (essays).
Fiction: Ethnic, historical, mystery. "We wish to open up into the fiction world. No country is a country without its fiction writers. Canada is growing some fine fiction writers. We'd like to read you. No first novels." Query.
Poetry: "We wish to have writers in translation. Any writer who has translated Italian poetry is welcomed. Full books only. Not single poems by different authors, unless modern, and used as an anthology. First books will have no place in the next couple of years." Submit samples.
Recent Poetry Title: *Streets that Follow Us,* by Len Gasparini.
Tips: "We are seeking less poetry, more modern novels, and translations into the English or French."

GUIDANCE CENTRE, University of Toronto, 10 Alcorn Ave., Toronto, Ontario M4V 2Z8 Canada. (416)978-3210. Editorial Director: L. Miller. Coordinating Editor: Gethin James. Publishes hardcover and paperback originals. Averages 25 titles/year; receives 50 submissions annually. 5% of books from first-time authors; 5% of books from unagented writers. Pays in royalties. Publishes book an average of 6 months after acceptance. Query for electronic submissions. Computer printout submissions acceptable; prefers letter-quality. Reports in 1 month. Submissions returned "only if Canadian postage is sent." Free book catalog.
Nonfiction: "The Guidance Centre is interested in publications related to career planning and guidance and in measurement and evaluation. Also general education. No manuscripts which have confined their references and illustrations to United States material." Submit complete ms. Consult Chicago *Manual of Style.*
Recent Nonfiction Title: *Managing Common Classroom Problems,* by Julienne Barber and John Allan.

*GULF PUBLISHING CO., Book Division, Box 2608, Houston TX 77252-2608. (713)529-4301. Vice President: C.A. Umbach Jr. Editor-in-Chief: William J. Lowe. Imprints include Gulf (sci-tech and business/management) and Lone Star Books (regional Texas books). Publishes hardcover and large format paperback originals and software. Averages 40 titles/year; receives 500 submissions annually. 60% of books from first-time authors; 95% of books from unagented writers. Subsidy publishes 5% of books. Pays 10% royalty on net income. Publishes book an average of 10 months after acceptance. Simultaneous and photocopied submissions OK. Query for electronic submissions. Computer printout submissions OK; no dot-matrix. Reports in 2 months. Free book catalog; ms guidelines for SASE.
Nonfiction: Popular science, business, management, reference, regional trade, scientific and technical. Submit outline/synopsis and 1-2 sample chapters. Reviews artwork/photos as part of ms package.
Recent Nonfiction Title: *Productivity Plus f,* by John G. Belcher, Jr. (productivity and management).
Tips: "Common mistakes writers make include calling first, not having a marketing plan of their own, and not matching publishers with their subject. Tell us the market, and how it can be reached at *reasonable* cost."

H.P. BOOKS, A division of Price Stern Sloan, Inc., 360 N. LaCienega Blvd., Los Angeles CA 90048. Publishes hardcover and paperback originals. Averages 55 titles/year. Pays royalty on wholesale price; advance negotiable. Publishes ms an average of 9 months after acceptance. Simultaneous and photocopied submissions OK. Reports in 1 month. Book catalog for 8½x11 SAE.
Nonfiction: Specializes in how-to and leisure-time books in several fields, most photo-illustrated. Cookbooks, cooking and foods, gardening, hobbies, how-to, leisure activities, photography, automotive, health, sports, family medicine, recreation, self-help, computer and technical books. Most books are 160 pages minimum; "word count varies with the format." Query only and state number and type of illustrations available. Submit comprehensive outline and 1 sample chapter. "We *require* author to supply photos and illustrations to our specifications (photocopies only)." Please submit all material to the general attention of the Editorial Department.

ALEXANDER HAMILTON INSTITUTE, 1633 Broadway, New York NY 10019. (212)397-3580. Editor-in-Chief: Brian L.P. Zevnik. Publishes 3-ring binder and paperback originals. Averages 18 titles/year; receives 200 submissions annually. 40% of books from first-time authors; 90% of books from unagented writers. "We pay advance against negotiated royalty or straight fee (no royalty)." Offers average $3,000 advance. Publishes book an average of 10 months after acceptance. Simultaneous submissions OK. Computer printout submissions acceptable; no dot-matrix. Reports in 1 month on queries; 2 months on mss.
Nonfiction: Executive/management books for two audiences. One is overseas, upper-level manager. "We need how-to and skills building books. *No* traditional management texts or academic treatises." The second audience is U.S. personnel executives and high-level management. Subject is legal personnel matters. "These books combine court case research and practical application of defensable programs." Query or submit outline or synopsis. Preferred form is outline, three papagraphs on each chapter, examples of lists, graphics, cases.
Recent Nonfiction Title: *Cost-Effective Training Programs.*
Tips: "We sell exclusively by direct mail to managers and executives around the world. A writer must know his/her field and be able to communicate practical systems and programs."

‡HANCOCK HOUSE PUBLISHERS LTD., 1431 Harrison Ave., Blaine WA 98230. (604)538-1114. Publisher: David Hancock. Publishes hardcover and trade paperback originals, and hardcover and trade paperback reprints. Averages 12 titles/year; receives 400 submissions annually. 50% of books from first-time authors; 100% of books from unagented writers. Pays 10% maximum royalty on wholesale price. Simultaneous submissions OK. Publishes book an average of 6 months after acceptance. Computer printout submissions acceptable; prefers letter-quality. Reports in 6 months. Book catalog free on request. Ms guidelines for SASE.
Nonfiction: Biography, cookbook, how-to and self-help. Subject include Americana; cooking and foods; history (Northwest coast Indians); nature; recreation (sports handbooks for teachers); sports; and investment guides. Query with outline/synopsis and sample chapters. Reviews artwork/photos.
Recent Nonfiction Title: *The Ships of British Columbia*, by Bannerman (history).

HANLEY & BELFUS, INC., 210 S. 13th St., Philadelphia PA 19107. (215)546-4995. President: John J. Hanley. Executive Vice President: Linda C. Belfus. Publishes hardcover and trade paperback originals. Averages 10 titles/year; receives 200 submissions annually. 50% of books from first-time authors; 100% of books from unagented writers. Pays 10% royalty on retail price. Publishes book an average of 9 months after acceptance. Simultaneous and photocopied submissions OK. Query for electronic submissions. Computer printout submissions acceptable; prefers letter-quality. Reports in 1 week on queries; 2 weeks on mss. Free ms guidelines.
Nonfiction: Reference, textbook, medical manuals and atlases. Subjects include health. Especially looking for textbooks for medical students, nursing students and allied health students, and selected reference books for practicing doctors. Query or submit outline/synopsis and sample chapters. Reviews artwork/photos.

HARBOR HOUSE PUBLISHERS, 221 Water St., Boyne City MI 49712. (616)582-2814. Chairman: Jacques LesStrang. Publishes hardcover and trade paperback originals and hardcover and trade paperback reprints. Averages 20 titles/year. Pays 10-15% royalty on wholesale price. Advance varies. Photocopied submissions OK. Reports in 1 month. Book catalog free on request.
Nonfiction: Coffee table book, illustrated book, and maritime. Subjects include business and economics, cooking and foods, and Great Lakes subjects. "Our manuscript needs include pictorials of all kinds, books conceived within the Great Lakes region and maritime subjects." Submit outline/synopsis and sample chapters or complete ms.

‡*HARBOUR PUBLISHING CO. LTD., Box 219, Madeira Park, British Columbia V0N 2H0 Canada. (604)883-2730. Publisher: Howard White. Publishes hardcover and trade paperback originals and reprints. Publishes 10 titles/year. Receives 500 submissions/year. 40% of books from first-time authors; 80% from un-

Close-up

Virginia Hamilton
Author

Photo by Cot Studios

Virginia Hamilton, one of the most distinguished writers for children and young adults, says writing children's books is not easier than writing books for adults. "There is nothing easier about the kind of writing I do. Anyone who thinks so, doesn't know what good literature is about. It has no category and no separate degree of difficulty. I think we limit ourselves when we think there is a separation in books for young people and those for adults," she says.

Hamilton began writing at a very early age, probably around six or seven, in her Yellow Springs, Ohio home. She still keeps a permanent home there with her husband Arnold Adoff, poet and writer.

She has received numerous awards for her writing: the Edgar Allen Poe Award, the John Newbery Medal, IBBY (International Board of Books for the Young), and the Coretta Scott King Award (twice).

"My first purpose when I write is to entertain with good stories," Hamilton says. Although her books are concerned with a parallel culture of black Americans, she is not limited to or restricted by any one theme. "But," she adds, "it is difficult for anyone not to write with enlightenment in mind, as well.

"Research is extremely important in my work," she says. A recent book, *Anthony Burns: The Defeat and Triumph of a Fugitive Slave*, is a true story of a slave from Virginia. It not only demanded thorough research into the protagonist's movements, but also of the legal procedures of 1854, as the centerpiece of the book is an actual long and complex trial.

She usually works on two books simultaneously, one fiction and one nonfiction. "It takes me a year or more to complete a young adult book or a children's book," she confides. "Nonfiction takes me as many as five, ten years to complete. The lives of real people caught within historical events fascinate me," she adds.

"My advice to aspiring writers is to read everything you can; experience broadly. Go out, see what the world is like. Get to know all kinds of people. Keep an open mind. Work hard and write every day," Hamilton says. "I find that young aspiring writers are extremely impatient! They often think there is a shortcut to getting published. There isn't. Getting published means good writing, good ideas, good stories and good construction of all those points into coherent works.

"It also takes time, energy, hard work, persistence, confidence and style. When one comprehends style as well as substance, one has found the way to becoming a professional writer.

"Find the lone place, the quiet, the blank paper or screen, the inner silence and the marvelous images with which the mind teems. There you are at last, part realist, part romantic, part vulnerable fool, facing yourself. There sits the *author*, writing. And that, my dears, is happiness."

—*Deborah Cinnamon*

agented writers. Subsidy publishes 25% of books. Pays 5-10% royalty on retail price. Publishes ms an average of 3 months after acceptance. Simultaneous and photocopied submissions OK. Query for electronic submissions. Computer printout submissions OK. Reports in 3 weeks on queries; 3 months on mss. Book catalog for $5.

Nonfiction: Biography, coffee-table book, cookbook, how-to, juvenile. Subjects include gay/lesbian, government/politics (Canadian), history, regional, women's issues/studies, new age/health. Submit outline/synopsis and sample chapters. Reviews artwork/photos as part of freelance ms package.

Recent Nonfiction Title: *Malcolm Lowry: Vancouver Days*, by S. Salloum (literary).

Fiction: Feminist, gay/lesbian, literary, short story collections, young adult. Submit outline/synopsis and sample chapters.

Recent Fiction Title: *Stubby Amberchuk*, by Anne Cameron (feminist).

‡HARCOURT BRACE JOVANOVICH, Children's Book Division, 1250 Sixth Ave., San Diego CA 92101. (619)699-6810. Imprints include HBJ Children's Books, Gulliver Books, Voyager Paperbacks. Attn: Manuscript Submissions. Publishes hardcover originals and trade paperback reprints. Firm publishes 40-60 hardcover originals/year; division publishes 20-30 paperback reprints/year. Royalty varies; flat fee for certain projects. Advance varies. Publishes ms an average of 1-2 years after acceptance. Photocopied submissions OK. Computer printout submissions OK; prefers letter-quality. Reports in 6 weeks on queries; 2 months on mss. Book catalog for 9x12 SAE with 3 first class stamps. Manuscript guidelines for #10 SAE wth 1 first class stamp.

Nonfiction: Juvenile. Query. Reviews artwork/photos as part of ms package "but request that no originals are sent."

Fiction: Query or submit outline/synopsis and sample chapters, or complete ms.

Tips: "The trade division of Harcourt Brace Jovanovich does not accept any unsolicited manuscripts. The children's division is the only one open to unsolicited submissions."

MAX HARDY—PUBLISHER, Box 28219, Las Vegas NV 89126-2219. (702)368-0379. Owner: Max Hardy. Publishes trade paperback originals. Averages 5 titles/year; receives few submissions/year. Small percentage of books from first-time authors. 100% of books from unagented writers. Pays 10% royalty on retail price. Publishes book an average of 8 months after acceptance. Query for electronic submissions. Computer printout submissions OK; prefers letter-quality. Reports in 2 weeks. Book catalog free on request.

Nonfiction: Textbooks on bridge. Especially needs "quality educational material preferably from known bridge authorities. No other topics." Query.

Recent Nonfiction Title: *Better Bidding With Bergen*, by Marty Bergen.

Fiction: Bridge fiction only. Query.

Recent Fiction Title: *The Jake of Diamonds*, by Don Von Elsner (bridge novel).

HARLEQUIN BOOKS, Subsidiary of Torstar, 225 Duncan Mill Rd., Don Mills, Ontario M3B 3K9 Canada. (416)445-5860. Divisions include Worldwide Library and Silhouette Books, editorial offices, 300 E. 42nd St., New York NY 10017. Vice President and Editor-in-Chief: Horst Bausch. Vice Presidents and Editorial Directors: Star Helmer (Harlequin series); Karen Solem (Silhouette); Randall Toye (Worldwide Library/Gold Eagle Books). Publishes mass market paperback originals. Averages 675 titles/year; receives 10,000 submissions annually. 10% of books from first-time authors; 20% of books from unagented writers. Pays 6-10% "escalating" royalty on retail price. Offers advance. Publishes book an average of 1 year after acceptance. Photocopied submissions OK. Computer printout submissions acceptable; prefers letter-quality. Reports in 2 weeks on queries; 2 months on mss. Free ms guidelines.

Imprints: Harlequin Books of North America, 6 fiction series. Harlequin Romance. Presents. American Romance. Superromance. Intrigue and Temptation. Silhouette Books, 5 fiction series. Romance. Desire. Special Edition. Intimate Moments. Crosswinds/Keepsake (YA).

Fiction: Regency, intrigue, traditional, short contemporary sensuals, long contemporary romances, historicals. "We're always looking for new authors." Query.

Tips: "Harlequin readership comprises a wide variety of ages, backgrounds, income and education levels. The audience is predominantly female. Because of the high competition in women's fiction, readers are becoming very discriminating. They look for a quality read. Read as many recent romance books as possible in all series to get a feel for the scope, new trends, acceptable levels of sensuality, etc."

HARPER & ROW JUNIOR BOOKS GROUP, 10 E. 53rd St., New York NY 10022. (212)207-7044. Imprints include: Harper & Row Junior Books, including Charlotte Zolotow Books; T.Y. Crowell; Lippincott and Trophy Junior Books. Publisher: Elizabeth Gordon. Editors: Charlotte Zolotow, Nina Ignatowicz, Marilyn Kriney, Barbara Fenton, Laura Geringer, Robert O. Warren, Antonia Q. Markiet and Pamela D. Hastings. Publishes hardcover originals and paperback reprints—board books, picture books, easy-to-read, middle-grade, teenage, and young adult novels. Published 98 titles in 1988 (Harper, cloth); 93 titles (Harper-Trophy, paperback); 24 titles (Crowell); 38 titles (Lippincott). Query; submit complete ms; submit outline/synopsis and sample chapters; or submit through agent. Photocopied submissions OK. Computer printout submissions acceptable. "Please identify simultaneous submissions." Reports in 2-3 months. Pays average royalty of 10%. Royalties on picture books shared with illustrators. Offers advance. Book catalog for self-addressed label. Writer's guidelines for SASE.

Nonfiction: Science, history, social studies, and sports. Reviews artwork/photos as part of ms package.
Fiction: Fantasy, animal, spy/adventure, science fiction, problem novels, contemporary. Needs picture books, easy-to-read, middle-grade, teenage and young adult novels.
Recent Title: *Taking the Ferry Home*, by Pam Conrad.
Tips: "Write from your own experience and the child you once were. Read widely in the field of adult and children's literature. Realize that writing for children is a difficult challenge."

HARPER & ROW PUBLISHERS, INC., 10 E. 53rd St., New York NY 10022. (212)207-7000. Imprints include Barnes & Noble; Harper & Row-San Francisco (religious books only); Perennial Library; and Torchbooks. Editorial Director: Lorraine Shanley. Publishes hardcover and paperback originals and paperback reprints. Trade publishes over 400 titles/year. Pays standard royalties; advances negotiable. No unsolicited queries or mss. Reports on solicited queries in 6 weeks.
Nonfiction: Americana, animals, art, biography, business/economics, cookbooks, health, history, how-to, humor, music, nature, philosophy, politics, psychology, reference, religion, science, self-help, sociology, sports and travel.
Recent Nonfiction Title:*Eight-Week Cholesterol Cure*, by Kowalski.
Fiction: Adventure, fantasy, gothic, historical, mystery, science fiction, suspense, western and literary. "We look for a strong story line and exceptional literary talent."
Recent Fiction Title:*Farewell, Summer*, by Santmyer.
Tips: "Strongly suggest that you go through a literary agent before submitting any ms. Any unsolicited query or ms will be returned unread."

HARPER JUNIOR BOOKS GROUP, WEST COAST, Division of Harper & Row Publishers, Box 6549, San Pedro CA 90734. (213)547-4292. Executive Editor, West Coast: Linda Zuckerman. Publishes hardcover originals. Averages 15 titles/year; receives 1500 submissions annually. 10% of books from first-time authors. 40% of books from unagented writers. Pays royalty on invoice price. Advance negotiable. Publishes book an average of 18 months after acceptance. Simultaneous and photocopied submissions OK. Computer printout submissions OK; no dot-matrix. Reports in 4 months. Book catalog and guidelines for 10x13 SAE with 4 first class stamps.
Nonfiction: Juvenile. Query or submit complete ms. Reviews artwork/photos as part of ms package.
Recent Nonfiction Title: *How to Be an Ocean Scientist in Your Own Home*, by Seymour Simon.
Fiction: Juvenile. Submit complete ms only. No queries.
Recent Fiction Title: *Scorpions*, by Walter Dean Myers.
Poetry: No Dr. Seuss-type verse. Submit complete ms.
Recent Poetry Title: *Joyful Noise*, by Paul Fleischman.
Tips: "Our audience is categorized into children, ages 3-6; 4-8; 8-12; 10-14; 12-16. Read contemporary children's books at all age levels; try to take some writing or children's literature courses; talk to children's librarians and booksellers in independent bookstores; read *Horn Book*, *Booklist*, *School Library Journal* and *Publishers Weekly*; take courses in book illustration and design."

‡HARPSWELL PRESS, INC., 132 Water St., Gardiner ME 04345. (207)582-1899. Publisher: Robert L. Johnston. Publishes hardcover and mass market originals and trade paperback reprints. Publishes 3-5 titles/year. Receives 35-50 submissions/year. 50% of books from first-time authors; 90% from unagented writers. Pays 7.5-25% royalty on wholesale price. Offers $2,500-3,000 average advance. Publishes book an average of 7 months after acceptance. Simultaneous submissions OK. Computer printout submissions OK; prefers letter-quality. Reports on queries in 1 month; on mss in 4 months. Book catalog free on request.
Nonfiction: Coffee-table book, how-to, humor, illustrated book, essays. Subjects include agriculture/horticulture, cooking, foods and nutrition, history, nature/environment, photography, regional, sports, travel. "We are looking for titles which will appeal to northeast readers on subjects of regional nature: the social/economic changes which are sweeping the region." Query or submit outline/synopsis and sample chapters. Reviews artwork/photos as part of freelance package.
Recent Nonfiction Title: *Seacost Maine People and Places*, by Martin Dibner and George Tice (essays/photography).
Fiction: Erotica, historical, humor, juvenile, literary, mystery, short story collections. "We are looking specifically for young authors we can introduce." Query or submit outline/synopsis and sample chapters.
Recent Fiction Title: *Pink Chimneys*, by Ardeana Hamlin Knowles (historical).
Tips: "Our audience is largely northeastern, educated, and has broad interests."

HARROW AND HESTON, Stuyvesant Plaza, Box 3934, Albany NY 12203. (518)442-5223. Editor-in-Chief: Graeme Newman. Small press. Publishes hardcover and trade paperback originals and paperback reprints. Averages 4 titles/year; receives 10-20 submissions annually. 80% of books from first-time authors; 100% of books from unagented writers. Pays 10% royalty on wholesale price. Publishes book an average of 3 months after acceptance. Simultaneous and photocopied submissions OK. Query for electronic submissions. Computer printout submissions acceptable. Reports in 2 months on queries; 6 months on mss.
Nonfiction: Textbooks on sociology and criminal justices. Query.
Recent Nonfiction Title: *Punishment and Privilege*, by W.B. Groves and Graeme Newman.
Tips: "Submissions must be clearly written with no jargon, and directed to upper undergraduate or graduate criminal justice students, on central criminal justice topics."

‡**HARTLEY & MARKS, PUBLISHERS**, Box 147, Point Roberts WA 98281. (206)945-2017. Imprints include Cloudburst. Editorial Director: Susanne Tauber. Publishes hardcover and trade paperback originals. Publishes 4-8 titles/year. Receives 75 submissions/year. 30% of books from first-time authors; 100% from unagented writers. Pays 5-10% royalty on retail price. Publishes book an average of 1 year after acceptance. Computer printout submissions OK; prefers letter-quality. Reports in 2 months. Book catalog and manuscript guidelines free on request.
Nonfiction: How-to, self-help, technical, new age. Subjects include agriculture/horticulture (small scale), art/architecture (building, woodworking), business and economics (small, cottage), child guidance/parenting, health/medicine (alternative or innovative), gardening. "We'd like to see practical guidebooks on innovative or rediscovered methods for building, woodworking, gardening, small scale mariculture, aquaculture, health and well-being, ethics and relationships. They can be original manuscripts or translations." Submit outline/synopsis and sample chapters.
Recent Nonfiction Title: *Your Home, Your Health & Well Being*, by D. Rousseau (self-help).
Tips: "Writers have the best chance of selling us nonfiction for lay readers in specialized areas such as woodworking, alternative health care, relationships, country living, self-help in the later years of life. All must be practical how-to. Books will vary with subject, but with a natural living orientation."

THE HARVARD COMMON PRESS, 535 Albany St., Boston MA 02118. (617)423-5803. President: Bruce P. Shaw. Publishes hardcover and trade paperback originals and reprints. Averages 6 titles/year; receives "thousands" of submissions annually. 75% of books from first-time authors; 75% of books from unagented writers. Average print order for a writer's first book is 7,500. Pays royalty; offers average $1,000 advance. Publishes book an average of 9 months after acceptance. Simultaneous and photocopied submissions OK. Computer printout submissions acceptable; no dot-matrix. Reports in 1 month. Book catalog for 9x11½ SAE and 3 first class stamps; ms guidelines for SASE.
Nonfiction: Travel, cookbook, how-to, reference and self-help. Subjects include Americana, business, cooking and foods, and travel. "We want strong, practical books that help people gain control over a particular area of their lives, whether it's family matters, business or financial matters, health, careers, food or travel. An increasing percentage of our list is made up of books about travel and travel guides; in this area we are looking for authors who are well traveled, and who can offer a different approach to the series guidebooks. We are open to good nonfiction proposals that show evidence of strong organization and writing, and clearly demonstrate a need in the marketplace. First-time authors are welcome." Accepts nonfiction translations. Submit outline/synopsis and 1-3 sample chapters. Reviews artwork/photos.
Recent Nonfiction Title: *Paradores of Spain/Ponsadas of Portgual*, by Sam and Jane Ballard (travel).

HARVEST HOUSE PUBLISHERS, 1075 Arrowsmith, Eugene OR 97402. (503)343-0123. Editor-in-Chief: Eileen L. Mason. Manuscript Coordinator: LaRae Weikert. Publishes hardcover, trade paperback and mass market originals and reprints. Averages 55-60 titles/year; receives 1,200 submissions annually. 10% of books from first-time authors; 90% of books from unagented writers. Pays 14-18% royalty on wholesale price. Publishes book an average of 1 year after acceptance. Simultaneous and photocopied submissions OK. Computer printout submissions acceptable; prefers letter-quality. Reports in 10 weeks. Book catalog for 8½x11 SAE with 2 first class stamps; manuscript guidelines for SASE.
Nonfiction: Biography, how-to, illustrated book, juvenile, reference, self-help, textbook and gift books on Evangelical Christian religion. No cookbooks, theses, dissertations or music.
Fiction: Historical, mystery and religious. No romances or short stories. Query or submit outline/synopsis and sample chapters.
Tips: Audience is women ages 25-40 and high school youth—evangelical Christians of all denominations.

‡**HEALTH ADMINISTRATION PRESS**, Foundation of the American College of Healthcare Executives, 1021 East Huron St., Ann Arbor MI 48104. (313)764-1380. Imprints include Health Administration Press, Health Administration Press Perspectives and ACHE Management Series. Director: Daphne M. Grew. Publishes hardcover and trade paperback originals. Publishes 12 titles/year. Pays 10-15% royalty on net revenue from sale of book. Occasionally offers small advance. Publishes book an average of 10 months after acceptance.

Photocopied submissions OK. Computer printout submissions OK; prefers letter-quality. Query for electronic submissions. Reports in 6 weeks on queries; 19 weeks on mss. Book catalog free on request.
Nonfiction: Reference or textbook. Subjects include business and economics, government/politics, health/medicine, sociology, health administration. "We are always interested in good, solid texts and references, and we are adding to our management series; books in this series offer health services CEOs and top managers immediately useful information in an accessible format." Submit outline/synopsis and sample chapters.
Recent Nonfiction Title: *The Well-Managed Community Hospital*, by Griffith.
Tips: "We publish books primarily for an audience of managers of health care institutions and researchers and scholars in health services administration. The books we like to see have something to say and say it to our audience."

HEALTH PROFESSION DIVISION, McGraw-Hill Book Co., 1221 Avenue of the Americas, New York NY 10020. General Manager: Patrick Hansard. Publishes 40 titles/year. Pays on royalty basis. Free book catalog and ms guidelines.
Nonfiction: Textbooks, major reference books and continuing education materials in the field of medicine. Submit outline and synopsis.
Recent Nonfiction Title: *Pulmonary Diseases and Disorders* 2e (3 vol. set), by Alfred Fishman.

*HEART OF THE LAKES PUBLISHING, 2989 Lodi Rd., Interlaken NY 14847-0299. (607)532-4997. Imprints include Empire State Books. Contact: Walter Steesy. Publishes hardcover and trade paperback originals and hardcover and trade paperback reprints. Averages 20-25 titles/year; receives 15-20 submissions annually. 100% of books from unagented writers. Average print order for a writer's first book is 500-1,000. Subsidy publishes 50% of books, "depending on type of material and potential sales." 15% author subsidized; 35% nonauthor subsidized. Payment is "worked out individually." Publishes book an average of 1-2 years after acceptance. Simultaneous and photocopied submissions OK. Query for electronic submissions. Computer printouts acceptable. Reports in 1 week on queries; 2 weeks on mss. Current books flyer for #10 SAE and 1 first class stamp; full catalog $3.
Nonfiction: New York state and New England history and genealogy. Query. Reviews artwork/photos.
Recent Nonfiction Title: *The Rise and Fall of the Utica Saturday Globe*, by Ralph Frasca.
Fiction: Will review only fiction that deals with New York state historical subjects.
Recent Fiction Title: *Danger at Niagara*, by Margaret Goff Clark.

HEINLE & HEINLE PUBLISHERS, INC., Subsidiary of Linguistics International, Inc., 20 Park Plaza, Boston MA 02216. (617)451-1940. Publisher: Stanley Galek. Publishes books, video and software. Averages 10-15 titles/year; receives 50-60 submissions annually. 50% of books from first-time authors; 100% of books from unagented writers. Pays 6-15% royalty on net price; no advance. Publishes book an average of 18 months after acceptance. Query for electronic submissions. Computer printout submissions acceptable; prefers letter-quality. Reports immediately on queries; 2 weeks on mss. Free book catalog; ms guidelines for SASE.
Nonfiction: Textbook. "Foreign language and English as a second or foreign language text materials. Before writing the book, submit complete prospectus along with sample chapters, and specify market and competitive position of proposed text."
Recent Nonfiction Title: *Allons-y*, by Jeanette Bragger and Donald Rice.
Tips: "Introductory and intermediate college foreign language textbooks have the best chance of selling to our firm. A common mistake writers make is planning the project and/or writing the book without first reviewing the market and product concept with the publisher."

‡HENDRICKSON PUBLISHERS, INC., 137 Summit St., Box 3473, Peabody MA 01961-3473. (617)532-6546. Executive Editor: Dr. Ben Aker. Publishes hardcover and trade paperback originals, and hardcover and trade paperback reprints. Averages 6-12 titles/year; receives 85 submissions annually. 5% of books from first-time authors; 100% of books from unagented writers. Pays 5-15% royalty on wholesale and retail price. Average advance depends on project. Publishes book an average of 6 months after acceptance. Simultaneous (if so

 An asterisk preceding a listing indicates that subsidy publishing or co-publishing (where author pays part or all of publishing costs) is available. Firms whose subsidy programs comprise more than 50% of their total publishing activities are listed at the end of the Book Publishers section.

notified) and photocopied submissions OK. Computer printout submissions acceptable; prefers letter-quality. Free book catalog. Ms guidelines for SASE.

Nonfiction: Religious. "We will consider any quality manuscripts within the area of religion, specifically related to Biblical studies and related fields. Popularly written manuscripts are not acceptable." Submit outline/synopsis and sample chapters or complete ms.

Recent Nonfiction Title: *Theology and Authority*, edited by Richard Penaskovic.

‡**VIRGIL W. HENSLEY, INC.**, 6116 E. 32nd St., Tulsa OK 74135. (918)644-8520. Editor: Deanna Rebro. Publishes hardcover originals. Publishes 5 titles/year (will increase that number). Receives 100 submissions/year. 50% of books from first-time authors; 50% from unagented writers. Pays 5% minimum royalty on retail price or outright purchase of $250 minimum for study aids. Publishes ms an average of 18 months after acceptance. Computer printout submissions OK; prefers letter-quality. Reports in 6 weeks on queries; 2 months on mss. Book catalog for 9x12 SAE and $1 postage. Manuscript guidelines for #10 SAE and 1 first class stamp.

Nonfiction: Bible study curriculum. Subjects include child guidance/parenting, money/finance, religion, women's issues/studies. "We look for subjects that lend themselves to long-term Bible studies—prayer, prophecy, family, faith, etc. We do not want to see anything non-Christian." Query with brief synopsis then submit outline/sample chapters or complete ms.

Recent Nonfiction Title: *Through the Bible in One Year*, by Alan Stringfellow (Bible study/general).

Tips: "Submit something that crosses denominational lines; Bible studies which are directed toward the large Christian market, not small specialized groups; heavy emphasis on student activities and student involvement. We serve an interdenominational market—churches of all sizes and Christian persuasions. Our books are used by both pastors and Christian education leaders in Bible studies, Sunday Schools, home Bible studies, and school classrooms."

HERALD PRESS, Subsidiary of Mennonite Publishing House, 616 Walnut Ave., Scottdale PA 15683. (412)887-8500. General Book Editor: Paul M. Schrock. Publishes hardcover, trade and mass market paperback originals, trade paperback and mass market paperback reprints. Averages 30 titles/year; receives 700 submissions annually. 15% of books from first-time authors. 95% of books from unagented writers. Pays minimum royalty of 10% wholesale, maximum of 12% retail. Advance seldom given. Publishes book an average of 14 months after acceptance. Photocopied submissions OK. Query for electronic submissions. Computer printout submissions OK; no dot-matrix. Reports in 3 weeks on queries; 2 months on submissions. Book catalog 50¢.

Nonfiction: Cookbook, how-to, juvenile, reference, self-help and textbook. Subjects include cooking and foods, church history, Christian philosophy, Christian psychology, social concerns, religion and Christian sociology. "We need books of Christian inspiration, Bible study, current issues, missions and evangelism, peace, self-help, and juveniles (mostly ages 9-14)." No drama or poetry. Query or submit outline/synopsis and sample chapters. Reviews artwork/photos as part of ms package.

Recent Nonfiction Title: *Journey Towards Holiness*, by Alan Kreider (peace/piety).

Fiction: Religious. Needs some fiction for youth and adults reflecting themes similar to those listed in nonfiction, also "compelling stories that treat social and Christian issues in a believable manner." No fantasy. Query or submit outline/synopsis and sample chapters.

Recent Fiction Title: *The Splendid Vista*, by Esther Vogt (adult fiction).

HERALD PUBLISHING HOUSE, Division of Reorganized Church of Jesus Christ of Latter Day Saints. 3225 South Noland Rd., Box HH, Independence MO 64055. (816)252-5010. Imprints include Independence Press. Editorial Director: Roger Yarrington. Publishes hardcover and trade paperback originals and hardcover and trade paperback reprints. Averages 30 titles/year; receives 700 submissions annually. 20% of books from first-time authors; 100% of books from unagented writers. Pays 5% maximum royalty on retail price. Offers average $400 advance. Publishes book an average of 14 months after acceptance. Computer printout submissions acceptable; no dot-matrix. Reports in 3 weeks on queries; 2 months on mss. Book catalog for 9x12 SASE.

Nonfiction: Self-help and religious (RLDS Church). Subjects include Americana, history and religion. Herald House focus: history and doctrine of RLDS Church. Independence Press focus: regional studies (Midwest, Missouri). No submissions unrelated to RLDS Church (Herald House) or to Midwest regional studies (Independence Press). Query. Use Chicago *Manual of Style*. Reviews artwork/photos as part of ms package.

Recent Nonfiction Title: *The Conferring Church*, by Richard and Marjorie Troeh (church procedures).

Tips: The audience for Herald Publishing House is members of the Reorganized Church of Jesus Christ of Latter Day Saints; for Independence Press, persons living in the Midwest or interested in the Midwest.

HERE'S LIFE PUBLISHERS, INC., Subsidiary of Campus Crusade for Christ, Box 1576, San Bernardino CA 92404. (714)886-7981. President: Les Stobbe. Editorial Director: Dan Benson. Publishes hardcover and trade paperback originals. Averages 25 titles/year; receives 400 submissions annually. 40% of books from first-time authors; 100% of books from unagented writers. Average print order for a writer's first book is 5,000. Pays 15% royalty on wholesale price. Publishes book an average of 1 year after acceptance. Simultaneous and photocopied proposal submissions OK. Query for electronic submissions. Computer printout submissions acceptable; no dot-matrix. Reports in 1 month on queries; 3 months on mss. Ms guidelines for 8½x11 SAE with 2 first class stamps.

Nonfiction: Biography, how-to, reference and self-help. Needs "books in the areas of evangelism, Christian growth and family life; must reflect basic understanding of ministry and mission of Campus Crusade for Christ. No metaphysical or missionary biography." Query or submit outline/synopsis and sample chapters. Reviews artwork/photos.

Recent Nonfiction Title: *Why Wait?*, by Josh McDowell (trends).

Tips: "The writer has the best chance of selling our firm a sharply focused how-to book that provides a Biblical approach to a felt need."

*HERITAGE BOOKS, INC., 3602 Maureen, Bowie MD 20715. (301)464-1159. Editorial Director: Laird C. Towle. Publishes hardcover and paperback originals and reprints. Averages 60 titles/year; receives 100 submissions annually. 25% of books from first-time authors; 100% of books from unagented writers. Subsidy publishes 5% or less of books. Pays 10% royalty on retail price; no advance. Publishes book an average of 9 months after acceptance. Simultaneous and photocopied submissions OK. Computer printout submissions acceptable; prefers letter-quality. Reports in 1 month. Book catalog for SAE.

Nonfiction: "We particularly desire nonfiction titles dealing with history and genealogy including how-to and reference works, as well as conventional histories and genealogies. Ancestries of contemporary people are not of interest. The titles should be either of general interest or restricted to Eastern U.S. Material dealing with the present century is usually not of interest. We prefer writers to query or submit an outline/synopsis." Reviews artwork/photos.

Recent Nonfiction Title: *Historic Districts of America: The South*, by Ralph W. Richardson.

Tips: "The quality of the book is of prime importance; next is its relevance to our fields of interest."

HEYDAY BOOKS, Box 9145, Berkeley CA 94709. (415)549-3564. Publisher: Malcolm Margolin. Small press. Publishes hardcover and trade paperback originals, trade paperback reprints. Averages 4-9 titles/year; receives 200 submissions annually. 50% of books from first-time authors; 75% of books from unagented writers. Pays 8-15% royalty on retail price; offers average $1,000 advance. Publishes book an average of 8 months after acceptance. Computer printout submissions acceptable; no dot-matrix. Reports in 1 week on queries; up to 5 weeks on mss. Book catalog for 7x9 SASE and 2 first class stamps.

Nonfiction: How-to and reference. Subjects include Americana, history, nature and travel. "We publish books about native Americans, natural history, history, and recreation, with a strong California focus." Query with outline and synopsis. Reviews artwork/photos.

Recent Nonfiction Title: *Disorderly House*, by James Mills.

Tips: "Give good value, and avoid gimmicks. We are accepting *only* nonfiction books with a California focus."

HIPPOCRENE BOOKS INC.,171 Madison Ave., New York NY 10016. (212)685-4371. President: George Blagowidow. Publishes hardcover originals and trade paperback originals and reprints. Averages 100 titles/year. Receives 250 submissions annually. 25% of books from first-time authors; 50% of books from unagented writers. Pays 6-15% royalty on retail price. Offers "few thousand" dollar advance. Publishes book an average of 11 months after acceptance. Simultaneous submissions OK. Free book catalog; ms guidelines for SASE.

Nonfiction: Biography, how-to, reference, self-help, travel guides. Subjects include history, recreation and travel. Submit outline/synopsis and 2 sample chapters. Reviews artwork/photos as part of ms package.

Recent Nonfiction Titles: *Getting Elected*, by Leonard Reinsch.

Tips: "Our recent successes in publishing general books considered midlist by larger publishers is making us more of a general trade publisher. We continue to do well with travel books and reference books like dictionaries, atlases, quiz books etc."

‡HOLLOWAY HOUSE PUBLISHING CO., 8060 Melrose Ave., Los Angeles CA 90046. (213)653-8060. Editorial Director: Raymond Friday Locke. Publishes paperback originals (75%) and reprints (25%). Averages 30 titles/year; receives 300-500 submissions annually. 50% of books from first-time authors; 60% of books from unagented writers. Average print order for a writer's first book is 15,000-20,000. Pays royalty based on retail price. Publishes book an average of 6 months after acceptance. Photocopied submissions OK. Query for electronic submissions. Submit outline and 3 sample chapters. Reports in 6-9 weeks. Free book catalog and ms guidelines for SASE.

Nonfiction: Gambling and game books—from time to time publishes gambling books along the line of *How to Win, World's Greatest Winning Systems, Backgammon, How to Play and Win at Gin Rummy*, etc. Send query letter and/or outline with one sample chapter. Length: 60,000 words. Reviews artwork/photos as part of ms package.

Recent Nonfiction Title: *Hollywood Madam*, by Lee Francis.

Fiction: "Holloway House is the largest publisher of Black Experience literature. We are in the market for

contemporary stories with easily identifiable characters and locations. Dialogue must be realistic. Some sex is acceptable but not essential (refer to writer's guidelines). Action, people and places must be thoroughly depicted and graphically presented."
Recent Fiction Title: *Secret Music*, by Odie Hawkins.

‡*HOLMES & MEIER PUBLISHERS, INC., 30 Irving Place, New York NY 10003. (212)254-4100. Publisher: Max J. Holmes. Associate Publisher: Barbara Lyons. Editor: Kevin Davis. Managing Editor: Katharine Turok. Publishes hardcover and paperback originals (50%) and reprints (50%). Publishes 80 titles/year. Subsidy publishes 2% of books. pays variable royalty. Publishes book an average of 8 months after acceptance. Computer printout submissions acceptable; prefers letter-quality. Reports in 3 months. Free book catalog.
Nonfiction: Americana, Africana, art, biography, business/economics, education, history, Judaica, Latin American studies, literary criticism, music, nature, politics, psychology, reference, sociology, textbooks and women's studies. Accepts nonfiction translations. "We are noted as a scholarly publishing house and are pleased with out reputation of excellence in the field. However, while we will continue to publish books for academic and professional audiences, we are expanding our list to reach the broader non-academic intellectual community. We will continue to build on our strengths in the social sciences, humanities and natural sciences. We do not want how-to and self-help material." Reviews artwork/photos as part of ms package. Query first and submit outline/synopsis, sample chapters, curriculum vitae and idea of intended market/audience.
Recent Nonfiction Title: The Destruction of the European Jews, by Raul Hilberg.

HOMESTEAD PUBLISHING, Box 193, Moose WY 83102. Editor: Carl Schreier. Publishes hardcover and trade paperback originals and trade paperback reprints. Averages 5 titles/year; receives 100 submissions annually. 60% of books from first-time authors. 90% of books from unagented writers. Pays 12% royalty on retail price; offers $1,000 average advance. Publishes book an average of 1 year after acceptance. Simultaneous and photocopied submissions OK. Query for electronic submissions. Computer printout submissions OK. Reports in 2 weeks on queries; 2 months on submissions. Book catalog for #10 SAE with 2 first class stamps.
Nonfiction: Biography, coffee table book, illustrated book, juvenile and reference. Subjects include animals, art, history, nature, photography and travel. Especially needs natural history and nature books for children. No textbooks. Query; or submit outline, synopsis and sample chapters or complete ms. Reviews artwork/photos as part of ms package.
Recent Nonfiction Title: *Yellowstone's Geysers, Hot Springs and Fumaroles.*
Tips: "Illustrated books on natural history are our specialty. Our audiences include professional, educated people with an interest in natural history, conservation, national parks, and western art. Underneath the visual aspects, a book should be well written, with a good grasp of the English language."

HOUGHTON MIFFLIN CO., Divisions include Ticknor & Fields; School Division; College Division; Educational Software Division; and Riverside Publishing Co./Reference Division, 2 Park St., Boston MA 02108. (617)725-5000. Submissions Editor: Janice Harvey. Hardcover and paperback originals and paperback reprints. Royalty of 6-7½% on retail price for paperbacks; 10-15% on sliding scale for standard fiction and nonfiction; advance varies widely. Publishes book an average of 18 months after acceptance. Publishes 100 titles/year. Simultaneous submissions OK. Computer printout submissions acceptable; no dot-matrix. SASE required with all submissions. Reports in 2 months. Book catalog for 8½x11 SAE.
Nonfiction: Natural history, biography, health, history, current affairs, psychology and science. Query.
Recent Nonfiction Title: *The Cycles of American History*, by Arthur M. Schlesinger, Jr.
Fiction: Historical, mainstream and literary. Query.
Recent Fiction Title: *The Prince of Tides*, by Pat Conroy.
Tips: "No unsolicited manuscripts will be read. Submit query letter and outline or synopsis to Submissions Editor. (Include one sample chapter for fiction.) The query letter should be short and to the point—that is, it should *not* incorporate the book's synopsis. The letter should say who the writer is (including information on previous publications in magazines or wherever) and the subject of the book."

HOUGHTON MIFFLIN CO., Children's Trade Books, 2 Park St., Boston MA 02108. Contact: Editor. Publishes hardcover originals and trade paperback reprints (some simultaneous hard/soft). Averages 45-50 titles/year. Pays standard royalty; offers advance. Computer printout submissions acceptable; no dot-matrix; and no justified right margins. Reports in 1 month on queries; 2 months on mss. Free book catalog.
Nonfiction: Submit outline/synopsis and sample chapters. Reviews artwork/photos as part of ms package.
Fiction: Submit complete ms.

HUDSON HILLS PRESS, INC., Suite 1308, 230 5th Ave., New York NY 10001-7704. (212)889-3090. President/Editorial Director: Paul Anbinder. Publishes hardcover and paperback originals. Averages 10 titles/year; receives 50-100 submissions annually. 15% of books from first-time authors; 90% of books from unagented writers. Average print order for a writer's first book is 3,000. Offers royalties of 5-8% on retail price. Average advance: $5,000. Publishes book an average of 1 year after acceptance. Simultaneous and photocopied submissions OK. Computer printout submissions acceptable; prefers letter-quality. Reports in 1 month. Book catalog for SAE with 2 first class stamps.

Nonfiction: Art and photography. "We are only interested in publishing books about art and photography, including monographs." Query first, then submit outline/synopsis and sample chapters. Reviews artwork/photos as part of ms package.

Recent Nonfiction Title: *Berthe Morisot—Impressionist.*

HUMAN KINETICS PUBLISHERS, INC., Box 5076, Champaign IL 61820. (217)351-5076. Publisher: Rainer Martens. Imprints include Leisure Press and Life Enhancement Publications. Publishes hardcover and trade paperback originals. Averages 80 titles/year; receives 300 submissions annually. 50% of books from first-time authors; 97% of books from unagented writers. Pays 10-15% royalty on wholesale price. Publishes book an average of 1 year after acceptance. Simultaneous and photocopied submissions OK. Query for electronic submissions. Computer printout submissions acceptable; prefers letter-quality. Reports in 2 months. Free book catalog.

Nonfiction: How-to, reference, self-help, technical and textbook. Subjects include health; recreation; sports, sport sciences and sports medicine; and physical education. Especially interested in books on wellness, including stress management, weight management, leisure management, and fitness; books on all aspects of sports technique or how-to books and coaching books; books which interpret the sport sciences and sports medicine, including sport physiology, sport psychology, sport pedagogy and sport biomechanics. No sport biographies, sport record or statistics books or regional books. Submit outline/synopsis and sample chapters. Reviews artwork/photos as part of ms package.

Recent Nonfiction Title: *Weight Loss to Super Wellness*, by Ted L. Edwards, M.D.

Tips: "Books which accurately interpret the sport sciences and health research to coaches, athletes and fitness enthusiasts have the best chance of selling to us."

HUMANICS LIMITED, Suite 370, 1389 Peachtree St. NE, Atlanta GA 30309. (404)874-2176. President: Gary B. Wilson. Contact: Melanie Baffes, Executive Editor. Publishes softcover, educational and trade paperback originals. Averages 12 titles/year; receives 500 submissions annually. 20% of books from first-time authors; 100% of books from unagented writers. Average print order for a writer's first book is 5,000. Pays average 10% royalty on net sales; buys some mss outright. Publishes book an average of 1 year after acceptance. Computer printout submissions acceptable; prefers letter-quality. Reports in 4 months. Book catalog and ms guidelines for SASE.

Nonfiction: Self-help and teacher resource books. Subjects include health, psychology, sociology, education, business and New Age. Submit outline/synopsis and at least 3 sample chapters. Reviews artwork/photos as part of ms package.

Recent Nonfiction Title: *Goddess In My Shoes*, by Rickie Moore (New Age).

Tips: "We are actively seeking authors with New Age material."

CARL HUNGNESS PUBLISHING, Box 24308, Speedway IN 46224. (317)244-4792. Editorial Director: Carl Hungness. Publishes hardcover and paperback originals. Pays "negotiable" outright purchase. Reports in 3 weeks. Free book catalog.

Nonfiction: Stories relating to professional automobile racing. No sports car racing or drag racing material. Query.

*HUNTER HOUSE, INC., PUBLISHERS, Box 1302, Claremont CA 91711. General Manager: K.S. Rana. Publishes hardcover and trade paperback originals. Averages 8 titles/year; receives 200 submissions annually. 50% of books from first-time authors; 50% of books from unagented writers. Subsidy publishes 10% of books. "We determine whether an author should be subsidy published based upon subject matter, quality of the work, and if a subsidy is available." Pays 7½-12½% royalty on retail price. Offers $101 advance. Publishes book an average of 12-18 months after acceptance and receipt of final manuscript. Simultaneous and photocopied submissions OK. Query for electronic submissions. Computer printout submissions acceptable. Reports in 2 months on queries; 4-6 months on mss. Book catalog and ms guidelines for 9x12 SAE with 3 first class stamps.

Nonfiction: How-to, young adult, and self-help. Subjects include family, health, psychology. Needs mss on "family and health, especially emerging areas in women's health, men's opening up and single parenting, older people, young adult, especially on health and intergenerational concerns." No evangelical, political, Americana, esoteric or erotica. Query or submit outline/synopsis and sample chapters. Reviews artwork/photos. "Please enclose return postage for material."

Recent Nonfiction Title: *Helping Your Child Succeed After Divorce*, by Florence Bienenfeld, Ph.D.

Tips: "Manuscripts on family and health, or psychology for an aware public do well for us. Write simply, with established credentials and imagination. We respect writers and do not mistreat them. We ask for the same consideration."

HUNTER PUBLISHING, INC., 300 Raritan Center Pkwy., Edison NJ 08818. President: Michael Hunter. Averages 100 titles/year; receives 300 submissions annually. 10% of books from first-time authors. 75% of books from unagented writers. Pays 10% royalty on list price; offers $0-2,000 average advance. Publishes book on average 9 months after acceptance. Simultaneous submissions OK. Query for electronic submissions. Computer printout submissions OK. Reports in 3 weeks on queries; 1 month on submissions. Book catalog for #10 SAE with 4 first class stamps.

Nonfiction: Reference. Subjects include history, travel. "We need travel guides to areas covered by few competitors: Caribbean Islands, Pacific Islands, Canada, Mexico, regional U.S. from an active 'adventure' perspective. Walking and climbing guides to all areas—from Australia to India." No personal travel stories or books not directed to travelers. Query or submit outline/synopsis and sample chapters. Reviews artwork/photos as part of ms package.

Recent Nonfiction Title: *Charming Small Hotels of Italy.*

Tips: "Study what's out there, pick some successful models, and identify ways they can be made more appealing. We need active adventure-oriented guides and more specialized guides for travelers in search of the unusual."

HUNTINGTON HOUSE, INC., Box 53788, Lafayette LA 70505/104 Row 2, Suites A1 and A2, Lafayette LA 70508. (318)234-7049. President: Bill Keith. Publishes hardcover, trade paperback, and mass market paperback originals, trade paperback reprints. Averages 10-20 titles/year; receives 600 submissions annually. 50% of books from first-time authors; 20% of books from unagented writers. Average print order for a writer's first book is 10,000. Pays 10-15% royalty on wholesale and retail price; offers $100-2,500 advance. Publishes book an average of 6-18 months after acceptance. Simultaneous and photocopied submissions OK. Query for electronic submissions. Computer printout submissions acceptable. Free book catalog and ms guidelines.

Nonfiction: Current social and political issues, biographies, self-help and inspirational. Query or send ms.

Tips: "Write clear, crisp and exciting mss that grab the reader. The company's goal is to educated and keep readers abreast of critical current events and to expose the effects of secular humanism specifically in regards to its impact on public, private and political institutions."

ILR PRESS, Division of The New York State School of Industrial and Labor Relations, Cornell University, Ithaca NY 14851-0952. (607)255-3061. Managing Editor: E. Fox. Publishes hardcover originals and reprints, and trade paperack originals and reprints. Averages 5-10 titles/year. Pays royalty. Photocopied submissions OK. Computer printout submissions acceptable; no dot-matrix. Reports in 2-3 weeks on queries; 8-12 weeks on mss. Free book catalog.

Nonfiction: All titles must relate to labor history and industrial relations. Biography, reference, technical, academic books in industrial and labor relations. Subjects include history, sociology of work and the workplace and business and economics. Book manuscript needs for the next year include "manuscripts on workplace problems, employment policy, women and work, personnel issues, and dispute resolution that will interest academics and practitioners." Query or submit outline/synopsis and sample chapters or complete ms.

Recent Nonfiction Title: *Hard Times Cotton Mill Girls: Personal Histories of Womanhood and Poverty in the South*, by Victoria Byerly (oral history).

Tips: "We are interested in manuscripts that address topical issues in industrial and labor relations that concern both academics and the general public. These must be well documented to pass our editorial evaluation, which includes review by academics in the industrial and labor relations field."

IMAGINE, INC., Box 9674, Pittsburgh PA 15226. (412)571-1430. President: R.V. Michelucci. Publishes trade paperback originals. Averages 3-5 titles/year; receives 50 submissions annually. 50% of books from first-time authors; 75% of books from unagented writers. Pays 6-10% royalty on retail price. Offers average $500 advance. Publishes book an average of 8-12 months after acceptance. Photocopied submissions OK. Reports in 2 weeks on queries; 2 months on mss. Book catalog for #10 SAE with 1 first class stamp.

Nonfiction: Coffee table book, how-to, illustrated book and reference. Subjects include films, science fiction, fantasy and horror films. Submit outline/synopsis and sample chapters or complete ms with illustrations and/or photos.

Recent Nonfiction Title: *The Collector's Guide to Monster, Science Fiction and Fantasy Film Magazines*, by Bob Michelucci.

Tips: "If I were a writer trying to market a book today, I would research my subject matter completely before sending a manuscript. Our audience is between ages 18-45 and interested in film, science fiction, fantasy and the horror genre."

INCENTIVE PUBLICATIONS, INC., 3835 Cleghorn Ave., Nashville TN 37215. (615)385-2934. Editor: Sally Sharpe. Publishes paperback originals. Averages 15-25 titles/year; receives 350 submissions annually. 25% of books from first-time authors; 95% of books from unagented writers. Pays royalty or makes outright purchase. Publishes book an average of 1 year after acceptance. Photocopied submissions OK. Computer printout submissions acceptable; prefers letter-quality. Reports in 2 weeks on queries; 3 weeks on mss. Book catalog and ms guidelines for 9x12 SAE.

Nonfiction: Teacher resources and books on educational areas relating to children. Submit outline/synopsis and sample chapters. Query with synopsis and detailed outline. Reviews artwork/photos as part of ms package.
Recent Nonfiction Title: *The I'm Ready to Learn Series*, by Imogene Forte, (early childhood skills-based activity books).
Tips: "A common mistake writers make is demanding too much, such as the inclusion of their own artwork. Often they overwhelm the editor with too much copy—a short synopsis often receives much more attention."

*INDIANA UNIVERSITY PRESS, 10th & Morton Sts., Bloomington IN 47405. (812)337-4203. Director: John Gallman. Publishes hardcover and paperback originals and paperback reprints. Averages 134 titles/year. 30% of books from first-time authors. 98% from unagented writers. Average print order for a writer's first book is 1,000. Subsidy publishes (nonauthor) 9% of books. Pays maximum 10% royalty on retail price; offers occasional advance. Publishes book an average of 18 months after acceptance. Photocopied submissions OK. Computer printout submissions acceptable; no dot-matrix. Reports in 2 months. Free book catalog and ms guidelines.
Nonfiction: Scholarly books on humanities, history, philosophy, religion, Jewish studies, Black studies, translations, semiotics, public policy, film, music, linguistics, social sciences, regional materials, African studies, women's studies, and serious nonfiction for the general reader. Query or submit outline/synopsis and sample chapters. "Queries should include as much descriptive material as is necessary to convey scope and market appeal to us." Reviews artwork/photos.
Recent Nonfiction Title: *The Economic Challenge of Perestroika*, by Abel Aganbegan.

INDUSTRIAL PRESS INC., 200 Madison Ave., New York NY 10016. (212)889-6330. Editorial Director: Woodrow Chapman. Small press. Publishes hardcover originals. Averages 12 titles/year; receives 25 submissions annually. 2% of books from first-time authors; 100% of books from unagented writers. Publishes book an average of 1 year after acceptance of finished ms. Query for electronic submissions. Computer printout submissions acceptable; no dot-matrix. Reports in 1 month. Free book catalog.
Nonfiction: Reference and technical. Subjects include business and economics, science and engineering. "We envision professional engineers, plant managers, on-line industrial professionals responsible for equipment operation, professors teaching manufacturing, engineering, technology related courses as our audience." Especially looking for material on manufacturing technologies and titles on specific areas in manufacturing and industry. Computers in manufacturing are a priority. No energy-related books or how-to books. Query.
Recent Nonfiction Title: *Composites: A Design Guide*, by Terry Richardson.

INFORMATION RESOURCES PRESS, A Division of Herner and Company, Suite 700, 1700 N. Moore St., Arlington VA 22209. (703)558-8270. Vice President/Publisher: Ms. Gene P. Allen. Publishes hardcover originals. Averages 6 titles/year; receives 25 submissions annually. 80% of books from first-time authors; 100% of books from unagented writers. Pays 10-15% royalty on net cash receipts after returns and discounts. Publishes book an average of 1 year after acceptance. Simultaneous and photocopied submissions OK. Query for electronic submissions. Reports in 2 weeks on queries; 2 months on mss. Free book catalog and ms guidelines.
Nonfiction: Reference, technical and textbook. Subjects include health and library and information science. Needs basic or introductory books on information science, library science, and health planning that lend themselves for use as textbooks. Preferably, the mss will have been developed from course notes. No works on narrow research topics (nonbasic or introductory works). Submit outline/synopsis and sample chapters or complete ms.
Recent Nonfiction Title: *Federal Health Information Resources*, edited by Melvin S. Day. Reviews artwork/photos.
Tips: "Our audience includes libraries (public, special, college and university); librarians, information scientists, college-level faculty; schools of library and information science; health planners, graduate-level students of health planning, and administrators; economists. Our marketing program is slanted toward library and information science and health planning, and we can do a better job of marketing in these areas."

INTERCULTURAL PRESS, INC., Box 768, Yarmouth ME 04096. (207)846-5168. Contact: David S. Hoopes, Editor-in-Chief, 130 North Rd., Vershire VT 05079. (802)685-4448. Publishes hardcover and trade paperback originals. Averages 5-7 titles/year; receives 50-80 submissions annually. 50% of books from first-time authors; 95% from unagented writers. Pays royalty; occasionally offers small advance. Publishes book an average of 2 years after acceptance. Simultaneous and photocopied submissions OK. Query for electronic submissions. Computer printout submissions acceptable; prefers letter-quality. Reports in "several weeks" on queries; 2 months on mss. Free book catalog and ms guidelines.
Nonfiction: How-to, reference, self-help, textbook and theory. Subjects include business and economics, philosophy, politics, psychology, sociology, travel, or "any book with an international or domestic intercultural, multicultural or cross-cultural focus, i.e., a focus on the cultural factors in personal, social, political or economic relations. We want books with an international or domestic intercultural or multicultural focus, especially those on business operations (how to be effective in intercultural business activities) and education (text-

books for teaching intercultural subjects, for instance). Our books are published for educators in the intercultural field, business people who are engaged in international business, and anyone else who works in an international occupation or has had intercultural experience. No manuscripts that don't have an intercultural focus." Accepts nonfiction translations. Query "if there is any question of suitability (we can tell quickly from a good query)," or submit outline/synopsis. Do not submit mss unless invited.

Recent Nonfiction Title: *Mindsets: The Role of Culture and Perception in International Relations*, by Glen Fisher.

INTERNATIONAL FOUNDATION OF EMPLOYEE BENEFIT PLANS, Box 69, Brookfield WI 53008-0069. (414)786-6700. Director of Publications: Dee Birschel. Publishes hardcover and trade paperback originals. Averages 30 titles/year; receives 10 submissions annually. 15% of books from first-time authors. 80% of books from unagented writers. Pays 5-15% royalty on wholesale and retail price. Publishes book an average of 1 year after acceptance. Photocopied submissions OK. Computer printout submissions OK; no dot-matrix. Reports in 3 months on queries. Book catalog free on request; ms guidelines for SASE.

Nonfiction: Reference, technical, consumer information and textbook. Subjects include health care, pensions, retirement planning, business and employee benefits. "We publish general and technical monographs on all aspects of employee benefits—pension plans, health insurance, etc." Query with outline.

Recent Nonfiction Title: *It's Your Future: A Guide to Preretirement Planning*, by R.N. Garnitz.

Tips: Be aware of "interests of employers and the marketplace in benefits topics, i.e., how AIDS affects employers, health care cost containment."

INTERNATIONAL MARINE PUBLISHING CO., Division of Highmark Publishing, Ltd., Route 1, Box 220, Camden ME 04843. Imprints include Seven Seas Press. Editor-in-Chief: Jonathan Eaton. Publishes hardcover and paperback originals. Averages 22 titles/year; receives 500-700 submissions annually. 50% of books from first-time authors; 80% of books from unagented writers. Pays standard royalties, based on net price, with advances. Publishes book an average of 8 months after acceptance. Computer printout submissions acceptable; prefers letter-quality. Reports in 6 weeks. Book catalog and ms guidelines for SASE.

Nonfiction: "Mostly marine nonfiction but a wide range of subjects within that category: boatbuilding, boat design, yachting, seamanship, boat maintenance, maritime history, etc." All books are illustrated. "Material in all stages welcome. We prefer queries first with outline and 2-3 sample chapters." Reviews artwork/photos as part of ms package.

Recent Nonfiction Title: *Stroke! A Guide to Recreational Rowing*, by Bruce Brown.

Fiction: "Marine fiction of excellence will be considered."

Tips: "Freelance writers should be aware of the need for clarity, accuracy and interest. Many progress too far in the actual writing, with an unsalable topic."

INTERNATIONAL PUBLISHERS CO., INC., #1301, 381 Park Ave. S., New York NY 10016. (212)685-2864. President: Betty Smith. Publishes hardcover and trade paperback originals and trade paperback reprints. Averages 15-20 titles/year; receives 200 submissions annually. 15% of books from first-time authors. Pays 5% royalty on paperbacks; 10% royalty on cloth. No advance. Publishes book an average of 6 months after acceptance. Simultaneous and photocopied submissions OK. Computer printout submissions acceptable; prefers letter-quality. Reports in 1 month on queries; 6 months on mss. Book catalog and ms guidelines for SASE.

Nonfiction: Biography, reference and textbook. Subjects include Americana, economics, history, philosophy, politics, social sciences, and Marxist-Leninist classics. "Books on labor, black studies and women's studies based on Marxist science have high priority." Query or submit outline and sample chapters. Reviews artwork/photos as part of ms package.

Recent Nonfiction Title: *Superprofits and Crises*, by Victor Perlo.

Fiction: "We publish very little fiction." Query or submit outline and sample chapters.

Recent Fiction Title: *A Bird in Her Hair*, by Phillip Bonosky (short stories).

Poetry: "We rarely publish individual poets, usually anthologies."

Recent Poetry Title: *New and Old Voices of Wah'Kon-Tah*, editors Dodge and McCullough (contemporary native American Indian poetry).

INTERNATIONAL SELF-COUNSEL PRESS, LTD., 1481 Charlotte Rd., North Vancouver, British Columbia V7J 1H1 Canada. (604)986-3366. President: Diana R. Douglas. Senior Editor: Ruth Wilson. Publishes trade paperback originals. Averages 10-15 titles/year; receives 500 submissions annually. 50% of books from first-time authors; 100% of books from unagented writers. Average print order for a writer's first book is 4,000. Pays 10% royalty on wholesale price; no advance. Publishes book an average of 9 months after submission of contracted ms. Simultaneous and photocopied submissions OK. Computer printout submissions acceptable; prefers letter-quality. Reports in 6 weeks. Book catalog for 9x6 SAE with IRCs.

Nonfiction: Specializes in self-help and how-to books in law, business, reference, and psychology for lay person. Submit outline and sample chapters. Follow Chicago *Manual of Style*.

Recent Nonfiction Title: *Marketing Your Service*, by Withers and Vipperman (business—how-to).

INTERNATIONAL WEALTH SUCCESS, Box 186, Merrick NY 11566. (516)766-5850. Editor: Tyler G. Hicks. Averages 10 titles/year; receives 100 submissions annually. 100% of books from first-time authors; 100% of books from unagented writers. Average print order for a writer's first book "varies from 500 and up, depending on the book." Pays 10% royalty on wholesale or retail price. Buys all rights. Usual advance is $1,000, but this varies, depending on author's reputation and nature of book. Publishes book 4 months after acceptance. Photocopied and dot-matrix submissions OK. Query for electronic submissions. Computer printout submissions acceptable. Reports in 1 month. Book catalog and ms guidelines for 9x12 SAE with 3 first class stamps.

Nonfiction: Self-help and how-to: "Techniques, methods, sources for building wealth. Highly personal, how-to-do-it with plenty of case histories. Books are aimed at the wealth builder and are highly sympathetic to his and her problems." Financing, business success, venture capital, etc. Length: 60,000-70,000 words. Query. Reviews artwork/photos as part of ms package.

Recent Nonfiction Title: *How to Become Wealthy Publishing a Newsletter*, by E. Jane Mall (how-to).

Tips: "With the mass layoffs in large and medium-size companies there is an increasing interest in owning your own business. So we will focus on more how-to hands-on material on owning--and becoming successful in--one's own business of any kind. Our market is the BWB--Beginning Wealth Builder. This person has so little money that financial planning is something they never think of. Instead, they want to know what kind of a business they can get into to make some money without a large inverstment. Write for this market and you have millions of potential readers. Remember--there are a lot more people *without* money than *with* money."

*THE INTERSTATE PRINTERS & PUBLISHERS, INC., 19 N. Jackson St., Box 50, Danville IL 61834-0050. (217)446-0500. Acquisitions/Vice President-Editorial: Ronald L. McDaniel. Hardcover and paperback originals and software. Publishes about 50 titles/year. 50% of books from first-time authors; 100% of books from unagented writers. Subsidy publishes 5% of books; 3% nonauthor subsidy. Usual royalty is 10%; no advance. Markets books by mail and exhibits. Publishes book an average of 9-12 months after acceptance. Computer printout submissions acceptable; prefers letter-quality. Reports in 3-4 months. Book catalog for 9x12 SAE. "Our guidelines booklet is provided only to persons who have submitted proposals for works in which we believe we might be interested. If the booklet is sent, no self-addressed envelope or postage from the author is necessary."

Nonfiction: Publishes high school and undergraduate college-level texts in vocational education (agriculture and agribusiness, trade and industrial education, home economics and business education). Also publishes professional references, texts, and supplementary materials in special education (including speech-language pathology, audiology, learning disabilities, neurological impairment) and in corrections education. "We favor, but do not limit ourselves to, works that are designed for class—quantity rather than single-copy sale." Query or submit synopsis and 2-3 sample chapters. Reviews artwork/photos as part of ms package.

Recent Nonfiction Title: *Microcomputer Applications for Students of Agriculture*.

Tips: "Freelance writers should be aware of strict adherence to the use of nonsexist language; fair and balanced representation of the sexes and of minorities in both text and illustrations; and discussion of computer applications wherever applicable. Writers commonly fail to identify publishers who specialize in the subject areas in which they are writing. For example, a publisher of textbooks isn't interested in novels, or one that specializes in elementary education materials isn't going to want a book on auto mechanics."

INTERURBAN PRESS/TRANS ANGLO BOOKS, Box 6444, Glendale CA 91205. (213)240-9130. Subsidiaries include PRN/PTJ Magazines and Interurban Films. President: Mac Sebree. Publishes hardcover and trade paperback originals. Averages 10-12 titles/year; receives 50-75 submissions yearly. 35% of books from first-time authors; 99% of books from unagented writers. Average print order for a writer's first book is 2,000. Pays 5-10% royalty on gross receipts; offers no advance. Computer printout submissions acceptable. Reports in 2 weeks on queries; 2 months on mss. Free book catalog.

Nonfiction: Western Americana and transportation. Subjects include Americana, business and economics, history, hobbies and travel. "We are interested only in manuscripts about railroads, local transit, local history, and Western Americana (gold mining, logging, early transportation, etc.). Also anything pertaining to preservation movement, nostalgia." Query. Reviews artwork/photos.

Recent Nonfiction Title: *Monon--the Hoosier Line*, by Gary Dolzall and Steve Dolzall.

Tips: "Our audience is comprised of hobbyists in the rail transportation field ('railfans'); those interested in Western Americana (logging, mining, etc.); and students of transportation history, especially railroads and local rail transit (streetcars)."

*INTERVARSITY PRESS, Division of Intervarsity Christian Fellowship, Box 1400, Downers Grove IL 60515. (312)964-5700. Managing Editor: Andrew T. LePeau. Publishes hardcover and paperback originals and reprints. Averages 50 titles/year; receives 800 submissions annually. 25% of books from first-time authors; 95% of books from unagented writers. Subsidy publishes (nonauthor) 6% of books. Pays average 10% royalty on retail price; offers average $1,000 advance. Sometimes makes outright purchase for $600-2,500. Publishes book an average of 15 months after acceptance of final draft. "Indicate simultaneous submissions." Computer printout submissions acceptable; no dot-matrix. Reports in 3 months. Writer's guidelines for SASE.

Nonfiction: "InterVarsity Press publishes books geared to the presentation of Biblical Christianity in its various relations to personal life, art, literature, sociology, psychology, philosophy, history and so forth. Though we are primarily publishers of trade books, we are cognizant of the textbook market at the college, university and seminary level within the general religious field. The audience for which the books are published is composed primarily of adult Christians. Stylistic treatment varies from topic to topic and from fairly simple popularizations to scholarly works primarily designed to be read by scholars." Accepts nonfiction translations. Query or submit outline/synopsis and 2 sample chapters.

Recent Nonfiction Title: *When Christians Clash*, by Horace L. Fenton, Jr. (Christian living).

Fiction: Fantasy, humor, mainstream, religious, science fiction. "While fiction need not be explicity Christian or religious, it should rise out of a Christian perspective." Submit outline/synopsis and sample chapters.

Recent Fiction Title: *The Toy Campaign*, by John Bibee (juvenile fantasy).

Tips: "Religious publishing has become overpublished. Books that fill niches or give a look at a specific aspect of a broad topic (such as marriage or finances or Christian growth) are doing well for us. Also, even thoughtful books need lower reading levels, more stories and illustrative materials. If I were a writer trying to market a book today, I would read William Zinsser's *On Writing Well* and do as he says. Writers commonly send us types of mss that we don't publish, and act as if we should publish their work—being too confident of their ideas and ability."

*IOWA STATE UNIVERSITY PRESS, 2121 S. State Ave., Ames IA 50010. (515)292-0140. Director: Richard Kinney. Managing Editor: Bill Silag. Hardcover and paperback originals. Averages 35 titles/year; receives 350 submissions annually. 98% of books from unagented writers. Average print order for a writer's first book is 2,000. Subsidy publishes (nonauthor) 25% of titles, based on sales potential of book and contribution to scholarship. Pays 10-12½-15% royalty on wholesale price; no advance. Publishes book an average of 1 year after acceptance. Simultaneous submissions OK, if advised; photocopied submissions OK. Query for electronic submissions. Computer printout submissions acceptable; prefers letter-quality. Reports in 4 months. Free book catalog; ms guidelines for SASE.

Nonfiction: Publishes biography, history, scientific/technical textbooks, the arts and sciences, statistics and mathematics, economics, aviation, and medical and veterinary sciences. Accepts nonfiction translations. Submit outline/synopsis and several sample chapters, preferably not in sequence; must be double-spaced throughout. Looks for "unique approach to subject; clear, concise narrative; and effective integration of scholarly apparatus." Send contrasting b&w glossy prints to illustrate ms. Reviews artwork/photos.

Recent Nonfiction Title: *Atanasoff: Forgotten Father of the Computer*, by Clark Mollenhoff.

IRON CROWN ENTERPRISES, Box 1605, Charlottesville VA 22902. (804)295-3918. Managing Editor: Terry K. Amthor. Imprint includes Questbooks (fiction)—John Ruemmler, editor. Publishes 8½x11 paperback and mass market paperback originals. Averages 40 titles/year; receives 40-100 submissions annually. 25% of books from first-time authors; 75% of books from unagented writers. Pays 2-4% royalty on wholesale price, or makes outright purchase for $1,000-2,500. Offers average $1,000 advance. Publishes book an average of 2-12 months after acceptance. Photocopied submissions OK. Computer printout submissions acceptable; prefers letter-quality. Reports in 1 month on queries; 3 months on mss. Book catalog and ms guidelines for #10 SASE.

Fiction: Fantasy and science fiction fantasy role-playing supplements. Query. "We do not accept unsolicited manuscripts."

Recent Fiction Title: *The Dyamiters: A Sherlock Holmes Mystery Gamebook*, by Milt Creighton.

Tips: "Our basic audience is role-players, who are mostly aged 12-25. Iron Crown Enterprises publishes only a very specific sub-genre of fiction, namely fantasy role-playing supplements. We own the exclusive worldwide rights for such material based on J.R.R. Tolkien's *Hobbit* and *Lord of the Rings*. We also have a line of science fiction supplements and are planning a line of fantasy books of our own. With our Questbooks we have a growing crossover into a general fantasy readership. Questbooks, more similar to standard fiction, allow the reader to choose courses for the main character as he proceeds through alternative plotlines in the book. We are currently concentrating on a very specific market, and potential submissions must fall within stringent guidelines. Due to the complexity of our needs, please query. Extensive research is necessary. We are actively seeking Questbook manuscripts in three lines: Sherlock Holmes Solo Mysteries, Narnia Solo Games and Middle Earth Questbooks."

*ISHIYAKU EUROAMERICA, INC., Subsidiary of Ishiyaku Publishers, Inc., Tokyo, Japan: 11559 Rock Island Court, St. Louis MO 63043. (314)432-1933. President: Manuel L. Ponte. Inquiries should be directed to Dr. Greogry Hacke, Assistant Editor. Publishes hardcover originals. Averages 15 titles/year; receives 50 submissions annually. Subsidy publishes (nonauthor) 100% of books. 75% of books from first-time authors; 100% of books from unagented writers. Average print order for a writer's first book is 3,000. Pays 10% minimum royalty on retail price or pays 35% of all foreign translation rights sales. Offers average $1,000 advance. Simultaneous submissions OK. Query for electronic submissions. Computer printout submissions acceptable;

no dot-matrix. Reports in 2 weeks on queries; 1 week on mss. Free book catalog; ms guidelines for SASE.
Nonfiction: Reference and medical/nursing textbooks. Subjects include health (medical and dental); psychology (nursing); and psychiatry. Especially looking for "all phases of nursing education, administration and clinical procedures." Query, or submit outline/synopsis and sample chapters or complete ms. Reviews artwork/photos as part of ms package.
Recent Nonfiction Title: *When You Face the Chemically Dependent Patient: A Practical Guide for Nurses*, by Judy Bluhm, R.N., M.A., (nursing).
Tips: "Medical authors often feel that their incomplete works deserve to be published; dental authors have a tendency to overstress facts, thereby requiring considerable editing. We prefer the latter to the former."

*JALMAR PRESS, INC., A subsidiary of B.L. Winch & Associates, 45 Hitching Post Dr., Bldg. 2, Rolling Hills Estates CA 90274-4297. (213)547-1240. Editorial Director: B.L. Winch. Senior Editor: Suzanne Mikesell. Publishes hardcover and trade paperback originals. Averages 4-8 titles/year. Pays 5-15% on net sales. Subsidy publishes 10% of books; subsidy publishes (nonauthor) 20% of books. Publishes book an average of 18 months after acceptance. Simultaneous and photocopied submissions OK. Query for electronic submissions. Computer printout submissions acceptable. Reports in 3 months. Book catalog for 8½x11 SAE with 4 first class stamps.
Nonfiction: Positive self-esteem materials for parenting and teaching; right-brain/whole-brain learning materials; peacemaking skills activities for parenting and teaching; and inspirational titles or self-concept and values. Reviews artwork/photos as part of ms package. "Prefer completed ms."
Recent Nonfiction Title: *Present Yourself!*, by Michael J. Gelb.
Tips: "A continuing strong effort by Jalmar in the areas of self-esteem, right brain/whole brain learning, peacemaking skills and creative thinking/problem solving will be made."

JAMESTOWN PUBLISHERS, INC., Box 9168, Providence RI 02940. (401)351-1915 or 1-800-USA-READ. Senior Editor: Ted Knight. Publishes paperback and hardcover supplementary reading text/workbooks. Averages 20 titles/year; receives 100 submissions annually. 10% of books from first-time authors; 100% of books from unagented writers. Average print order for a writer's first book is 10,000. Pays 10% royalty on retail price; buys some mss outright; offers variable advance. Publishes book an average of 1 year after acceptance. Computer printout submissions acceptable; prefers letter-quality. Reports in 1 month. Free book catalog.
Nonfiction: Textbook. "Materials for improving reading and study skills for kindergarten through twelfth grade, college, and adult education." Submit synopsis and sample chapters. Reviews artwork/photos as part of ms package.
Recent Nonfiction Title: *Heroes*, by Henry and Melissa Billings (middle school reading text).
Fiction: "We occasionally use original short fiction as the basis for comprehension exercises and drills." Submit synopsis and samples.
Tips: "We operate in a very clearly, narrowly defined subject area. The writer should know this field well and the more familiar he or she is with our products, the better. Reading/study skills material paralleling our current skills breakdown, and exceptional and innovative/groundbreaking material in the same areas have the best chance of selling to our firm."

‡JIST WORKS, INC., 720 North Park Ave., Indianapolis IN 46202. (317)637-6643. Editor: Betty White. Publishes trade paperback originals and reprints. Receives 25-30 submissions/year. 60% of books from first time authors; 100% from unagented writers. Pays 5-12% royalty on wholesale price or outright purchase (negotiable). Publishes ms an average of 6 months after acceptance. Simultaneous and photocopied submissions OK. Query for electronic submissions. Computer printout submissions OK; prefers letter-quality. Reports in 1 month on queries. Book catalog and ms guidelines for SASE.
Nonfiction: How-to, reference, self-help, software, textbook. Specializes in job search and survival education. "We want text/workbook formats that would be useful in a school or other institutional setting. All reading levels. Will consider books for professional staff and educators, appropriate software and videos." Reviews artwork/photos as part of ms package. Nonfiction areas are 1) career topics: assessment, job search, resumes, job survival, etc. 2) Reference books and professional materials for career and vocational instruction. 3) Low reading, remediation, and adult education materials.
Recent Nonfiction Title: *Getting The Job You Really Want*, by Farr (workbook).
Tips: "Institutions and staff who work with people making career and life decisions or who are looking for jobs are our audience as well as persons with low reading and academic skills."

JOHNSON BOOKS, Johnson Publishing Co., 1880 S. 57th Ct., Boulder CO 80301. (303)443-1576. Imprint is Spring Creek Press. Editorial Director: Michael McNierney. Spring Creek Press: Scott Roederer. Publishes hardcover and paperback originals and reprints. Publishes 8-10 titles/year; receives 500 submissions annually. 30% of books from first-time authors; 90% of books from unagented writers. Average print order for a writer's first book is 5,000. Royalties vary. Publishes book an average of 1 year after acceptance. Good computer printout submissions acceptable; prefers letter-quality. Reports in 1-2 months. Book catalog and ms guidelines for

9x12 SAE with 4 first class stamps.
Nonfiction: General nonfiction, books on the West, environmental subjects, astronomy, natural history, paleontology, geology, archaeology, travel, guidebooks, and outdoor recreation. "We publish a series of books on fly-fishing under a separate imprint, Spring Creek Press." Accepts nonfiction translations. "We are primarily interested in books for the informed popular market, though we will consider vividly written scholarly works. As a small publisher, we are able to give every submission close personal attention." Query first or call. Accepts outline/synopsis and 3 sample chapters. Looks for "good writing, thorough research, professional presentation and appropriate style. Marketing suggestions from writers are helpful." Reviews artwork/photos.
Recent Nonfiction Title: *A Walking Guide to the Caribbean*, by Leonard Adkins.
Tips: "We are looking for nature titles with broad national, not just regional, appeal."

JONATHAN DAVID PUBLISHERS, 68-22 Eliot Ave., Middle Village NY 11379. (718)456-8611. Editor-in-Chief: Alfred J. Kolatch. Publishes hardcover and paperback originals. Averages 25-30 titles/year; receives 600 submissions annually. 50% of books from first-time authors; 75% of books from unagented writers. Pays standard royalty. Publishes book an average of 1 year after acceptance. Computer printout submissions acceptable; no dot-matrix. Reports in 3 weeks. Book catalog for 8½x5½ SASE.
Nonfiction: Adult nonfiction books for a general audience. Cookbooks, cooking and foods, how-to, baseball and football, reference, self-help, Judaica. Query.
Recent Nonfiction Title: *Great Jews on Stage and Screen*, by Darryl Lyman (biographical reference).

‡JUDSON PRESS, Valley Forge PA 19482. (215)768-2117. Senior Editor: Kristy Arnesen Pullen. Publishes hardcover and paperback originals. Averages 10-15 titles/year; receives 500 queries annually. Average print order for a writer's first book is 3,500. 10% royalty on retail price or flat fee. Publishes book an average of 9 months after acceptance. Computer printout submissions acceptable; no dot-matrix. Query with outline and 1 sample chapter. Reports in 6 months. Enclose return postage. Free book catalog; ms guidelines for SASE.
Nonfiction: Adult religious nonfiction of 30,000-80,000 words. "Our audience is mostly church members who seek to have a more fulfilling personal spiritual life and want to serve Christ in their churches and other relationships."
Recent Nonfiction Title: *Jesus Still Has Something to Say*, by Robert C. Campbell.

KALMBACH PUBLISHING CO., 1027 N. 7th St., Milwaukee WI 53233. (414)272-2060. Books Editor: Bob Hayden. Publishes hardcover and paperback originals and paperback reprints. Averages 4 titles/year; receives 25 submissions annually. 85% of books from first-time authors; 100% of books from unagented writers. Offers 5-8% royalty on retail price. Average advance is $1,000. Publishes book an average of 18 months after acceptance. Computer printout submissions acceptable; prefers letter-quality. Reports in 2 months. Book catalog for 9x12 SAE with 2 first class stamps.
Nonfiction: Hobbies, how-to, and recreation. "Our book publishing effort is in railroading and hobby how-to-do-it titles *only*." Query first. "I welcome telephone inquiries. They save me a lot of time, and they can save an author a lot of misconceptions and wasted work." In written query, wants to see "a detailed outline of two or three pages and a complete sample chapter with photos, drawings, and how-to text." Reviews artwork/photos.
Recent Nonfiction Title: *Guide to Tourist Railroads and Railroad Museums*, by George H. Drury (railroads).
Tips: "Our books are about half text and half illustrations. Any author who wants to publish with us must be able to furnish good photographs and rough drawings before we'll consider contracting for his book."

KAR-BEN COPIES INC., 6800 Tildenwood Ln., Rockville MD 20852. (301)984-8733. President: Judye Groner. Publishes hardcover and trade paperback originals. Averages 8-10 titles/year; receives 150 submissions annually. 25% of books from first-time authors; 100% from unagented writers. Average print order for a writer's first book is 5,000. Pays 6-8% royalty on net receipts; makes negotiable outright purchase; offers average $1,000 advance. Publishes book an average of 1 year after acceptance. Computer printout submissions acceptable. Reports in 1 week on queries; 1 month on mss. Free book catalog; ms guidelines for 9x12 SAE with 2 first class stamps.
Nonfiction: Jewish juvenile. Especially looking for books on Jewish life-cycle, holidays, and customs for children—"early childhood and elementary." Send only mss with Jewish content. Query with outline/synopsis and sample chapters or submit complete ms. Reviews artwork/photos as part of ms package.
Recent Nonfiction Title: *Kids Love Israel. Israel Loves Kids—A Travel Guide for Families*, by Barbara Sofer.
Fiction: Adventure, fantasy, historical and religious (all Jewish juvenile). Especially looking for Jewish holiday and history-related fiction for young children. Submit outline/synopsis and sample chapters or complete ms.
Recent Fiction Title: *Dayenu—How Uncle Murray Saved the Seder*, by Rosalind Schilder.
Tips: "We envision Jewish children and their families, and juveniles interested in learning about Jewish subjects, as our audience."

Close-up

Ashbel Green
Senior Editor
Alfred A. Knopf, Inc.

With such current popular titles as *Beloved*, *Sphere* and *The Fatal Shore*, Alfred A. Knopf, Inc. is known as a publisher of bestsellers as well as literary books. Knopf's success can be traced, says Senior Editor Ashbel Green, in part, to its constant search for a good story. This may sound simple, he says, but it is a task that requires both an awareness of the current market and a willingness to take the occasional risk.

Green has been with Knopf for 24 years, and despite some disconcerting reports on the rise of illiteracy and the decline of leisure-time reading, he finds the publishing field has improved steadily over the years. "I think our writing standards have gone up—there are simply more good books out there."

Knopf receives about 50 manuscripts and 100 inquiries each week, says Green. Even though the firm is open to the work of new writers, most books that are acquired are recommended to Knopf by agents and other publishers. Yet, Green is always looking for well-written, unusual stories regardless of whether the writers are established professionals or talented, but unknown, authors. Unlike several other large publishers, there is no screening by a "first reader." The editors take turns going through the week's queries and submissions.

Although Knopf does publish a few new writers every year, Green says breaking in is tough. "Many agents want established, producing writers and don't have time for someone who is unpublished. And most editors depend on contacts in universities, newspapers and magazines."

New writers must work hard to promote themselves and try a variety of tactics to establish contacts in the field. "A writer may have a good idea for a book, but may not know where to go with it. Try to establish connections—ask for advice from the book review editor at your local newspaper or a university writing professor.

"Local and regional magazines or the Sunday newspaper magazines provide good opportunities for writers. Magazine clips not only help you acquire writing credits, but it's also useful to go through the editing/publishing process. You can get an idea of your strengths and weaknesses."

All books start with a good idea, says Green, and it helps to know what types of work have the best chance of being published. "Many new writers don't pay attention to what's going on in bookstores. They should visit them regularly. Fiction is especially easy to track down—it's all in one section of most bookstores and libraries." For nonfiction, Green suggests writers look through the *Subject Guide to Books in Print*, a publishing reference book available at the library. He also says a good way to find out more about particular publishing firms is to send a self-addressed, stamped envelope for their catalog.

Look for the unusual story in your community, he says. Stories may stem from local newspaper reports that never make it to the large dailies. Local writers are also more aware of community dynamics. Green cites one author who followed the developments of a murder case in his home town. "A good story is a good story. It doesn't matter where it takes place."

—Robin Gee

*KENT STATE UNIVERSITY PRESS, Kent State University, Kent OH 44242. (216)672-7913. Director: John T. Hubbell. Editor: Jeanne West. Publishes hardcover and paperback originals and some reprints. Averages 15-20 titles/year. Subsidy publishes (nonauthor) 20% of books. Standard minimum book contract on net sales; rarely offers advance. "Always write a letter of inquiry before submitting manuscripts. We can publish only a limited number of titles each year and can frequently tell in advance whether or not we would be interested in a particular manuscript. This practice saves both our time and that of the author, not to mention postage costs. If interested we will ask for complete manuscript. Decisions based on in-house readings and two by outside scholars in the field of study." Computer printout submissions acceptable; prefers letter-quality. Reports in 6-10 weeks. Enclose return postage. Free book catalog.
Nonfiction: Especially interested in "scholarly works in history and literary studies of high quality, any titles of regional interest for Ohio, scholarly biographies, archaeological research, the arts, and general nonfiction."
Recent Nonfiction Title: *A Photo Album of Ohio's Canal Era, 1825-1913*, by Jack Gieck (history, Ohio studies).

MICHAEL KESEND PUBLISHING, LTD., 1025 5th Ave., New York NY 10028. (212)249-5150. Director: Michael Kesend. Publishes hardcover and trade paperback originals, and hardcover and trade paperback reprints. Averages 4-6 titles/year; receives 150 submissions annually. 50% of books from first-time authors; 50% of books from unagented writers. Pays 3-12½% royalty on wholesale price or retail price, or makes outright purchase for $500 minimum. Advance varies. Publishes book an average of 18 months after acceptance. Computer printout submissions acceptable; prefers letter-quality. Reports in 2 months on queries; 3 months on mss. Guidelines for #10 SASE.
Nonfiction: Biography, how-to, illustrated book, self-help and sports. Subjects include animals, health, history, hobbies, nature, sports, travel, the environment, and guides to several subjects. Needs sports, health self-help and environmental awareness guides. No photography mss. Submit outline/synopsis and sample chapters. Reviews artwork/photos as part of ms package.
Recent Nonfiction Title: *Emergency Care for Cats and Dogs*, by Craton Burkholder, D.V.M. (pet care).
Fiction: Literary fiction only. No science fiction or romance. No simultaneous submissions. Submit outline/synopsis and 2-3 sample chapters.
Recent Fiction Title: *Dan Yack*, by Blaise Cendrars.

KNIGHTS PRESS, Box 454, Pound Ridge NY 10576. Publisher: Elizabeth G. Gershman. Publishes trade paperback originals. Averages 10 titles/year; receives 500 submissions annually. 50% of books from first-time authors; 75% of books from unagented writers. Pays 10% plus escalating royalty on retail price; offers average $500 advance. Publishes book an average of 1 year after acceptance. Photocopied submissions OK. Computer printout submissions acceptable; prefers letter-quality. Reports in 1 month on queries; 3 months on mss. Book catalog and ms guidelines for #10 SASE.
Fiction: Adventure, erotica (very soft-core considered), ethnic, experimental, fantasy, gothic, historical, humor, mystery, romance, science fiction, suspense and western. "We publish *only* gay men's fiction; must show a positive gay lifestyle or positive gay relationship." No young adult or children's; no pornography; no formula plots, especially no formula romances; or no hardcore S&M. No lesbian fiction. Query a must. Submit outline/synopsis and sample chapters. Do not submit complete manuscript unless requested.
Recent Fiction Title: *The Vanilla Kid*, by Daniel McVay (gay humor).
Tips: "We are interested in well-written, well-plotted gay fiction. We are looking only for the highest quality gay literature."

ALFRED A. KNOPF, INC., 201 E. 50th St., New York NY 10022. (212)751-2600. Senior Editor: Ashbel Green. Children's Book Editor: Ms. Frances Foster. Publishes hardcover and paperback originals. Averages 204 titles annually. 15% of books from first-time authors; 40% of books from unagented writers. Royalties and advance "vary." Publishes book an average of 10 months after acceptance. Simultaneous (if so informed) and photocopied submissions OK. Reports in 1 month. Book catalog for 7x10 SAE.
Nonfiction: Book-length nonfiction, including books of scholarly merit. Preferred length: 40,000-150,000 words. "A good nonfiction writer should be able to follow the latest scholarship in any field of human knowledge, and fill in the abstractions of scholarship for the benefit of the general reader by means of good, concrete, sensory reporting." Query. Reviews artwork/photos as part of ms package.
Recent Nonfiction Title: *Thriving on Chaos*, by T. Peters (business).
Fiction: Publishes book-length fiction of literary merit by known or unknown writers. Length: 30,000-150,000 words. Submit complete ms.
Recent Fiction Title: *Beloved*, by Toni Morrison.

KNOWLEDGE INDUSTRY PUBLICATIONS, INC., 701 Westchester Ave., White Plains NY 10604. (914)328-9157. Assistant Vice President: Margaret Csenge. Publishes hardcover and paperback originals. Averages 10 titles/year; receives 30 submissions annually. 50% of books from first-time authors; 100% of books from unagented writers. Average print order for a writer's first book is 2,500. Offers 5-10% royalty on net price; also buys mss by outright purchase for minimum $500. Offers negotiable advance. Publishes book an average of 6 months after acceptance. Photocopied submissions OK. Query for electronic submissions. Computer printout submissions acceptable; no dot-matrix. Reports in 2 weeks. Free book catalog; ms guidelines for SASE.

Nonfiction: Business and economics. Especially needs TV and video. Query first, then submit outline/synopsis and sample chapters. Reviews artwork/photos as part of ms package.

Recent Nonfiction Title: *Lighting Techniques for Video Production*, by Tom LeTourneau (theory and applications).

JOHN KNOX PRESS, 341 Ponce de Leon Ave. NE, Atlanta GA 30365. (404)873-1549. Editorial Director: Walter C. Sutton. Acquisitions Editor: John G. Gibbs. Averages 18 nonfiction titles/year. Pays royalty on income received; no advances. 20% of books from first-time authors; 100% of books from unagented writers. Publishes book an average of 9-12 months after acceptance. Query for electronic submissions. Computer printout submissions acceptable. Book catalog and "Guidelines for a Book Proposal" for 9x12 SAE.

Nonfiction: "We publish textbooks, resource books for ministry, and books to encourage Christian faith, in subject areas including biblical studies, theology, ethics, psychology, counseling, worship, and the relationship of science and technology to faith." Query or submit outline/synopsis and sample chapters.

Recent Nonfiction Title: *Approaches to Auschwitz: The Holocaust and Its Legacy*, (Holocaust studies).

ROBERT E. KRIEGER PUBLISHING CO. INC., Box 9542, Melbourne FL 32902-9542. (305)724-9542. Subsidiary, Orbit Book Company (space technology). Executive Assistant: Marie Bowles. Publishes hardcover and paperback originals and reprints. Averages 120 titles/year; receives 50-60 submissions annually. 30% of books from first-time authors; 100% of books from unagented writers. Pays royalty on net realized price. Publishes book an average of 8 months after acceptance. Computer printout submissions acceptable; prefers letter-quality. Reports in 1 month. Free book catalog.

Nonfiction: College reference, technical, and textbook. Subjects include business, history, music, philosophy, psychology, recreation, religion, sociology, sports, chemistry, physics, engineering and medical. Reviews artwork/photos.

Recent Nonfiction Title: *Cultural Resources Management*, edited by Ronald W. Johnson and Michael G. Schene.

*PETER LANG PUBLISHING, 62 W. 45th St., New York NY 10036. (212)302-6740. Subsidiary of Verlag Peter Lang AG, Bern, Switzerland. Executive Director: Brigitte D. McDonald. Acquisitions Editor: Michael Flamini. West Coast Acquisitions Editor: Robert West. Publishes mostly hardcover originals. Averages 120 titles/year; receives 600 submissions annually. 75% of books from first-time authors; 98% of books from unagented writers. Subsidy publishes 50% of books. All subsidies are guaranteed repayment plus profit (if edition sells out) in contract. Subsidy published if ms is highly specialized and author relatively unknown. Pays 10-20% royalty on net price. Translators get flat fee plus percentage of royalties. No advance. Publishes book an average of 1 year after acceptance. Photocopied submissions OK. Computer printout submissions acceptable; prefers letter-quality. Reports in 2 months on queries; 4 months on mss. Free book catalog and ms guidelines.

Nonfiction: General nonfiction, reference works, and scholarly monographs. Subjects include literary criticism, Germanic and Romance languages, art history, business and economics, American and European political science, history, music, philosophy, psychology, religion, sociology and biography. All books are scholarly monographs, textbooks, reference books, reprints of historic texts, critical editions or translations. "We are expanding and are receptive to any scholarly project in the humanities and social sciences." No mss shorter than 200 pages. Submit complete ms.

Fiction and Poetry: "We do not publish original fiction or poetry. We seek scholarly and critical editions only. Submit complete ms."

Poetry: Scholarly critical editions only. Submit complete ms.

Tips: "Besides our commitment to specialist academic monographs, we are one of the few U.S. publishers who publish books in most of the modern languages."

LEISURE BOOKS, Division of Dorchester Publishing Co., Inc., Suite 900, 6 E. 39th St., New York NY 10016. (212)725-8811. Editor: Tracey Lubben. Publishes mass market paperback originals and reprints. Averages 144 titles/year; receives thousands of submissions annually. 20% of books from first-time authors; 40% of books from unagented writers. Pays royalty on retail price. Advance negotiable. Publishes book an average of 18 months after acceptance. Computer printout submissions acceptable; no dot-matrix. Reports in 1 month on queries; up to 2 months on mss. Book catalog and ms guidelines for #10 SASE.

Nonfiction: "Our needs are minimal as we publish perhaps four nonfiction titles a year." Query.

Fiction: Historical (90,000 words); horror (80,000 words). "We are strongly backing horror and historical romance." No sweet romance, science fiction, western, erotica, contemporary women's fiction, mainstream or male adventure. Query or submit outline/synopsis and sample chapters. "No material will be returned without SASE."

Recent Fiction Title: *Forever Gold*, by Catherine Hart (historical romance).
Tips: "Horror and historical romance are our best sellers."

LEXIKOS, 4079 19th Ave., San Francisco CA 94132. (415)584-1085. Imprints include Don't Call It Frisco Press. Editor: Mike Witter. Publishes hardcover and trade paperback originals and trade paperback reprints. Averages 8 titles/year; receives 200 submissions annually. 50% of books from first-time authors; 90% of books from unagented writers. Average print order for a writer's first book is 5,000. Royalties vary from 8-12½% according to books sold. "Authors asked to accept lower royalty on high discount (50% plus) sales." Offers average $1,000 advance. Publishes book an average of 10 months after acceptance. Simultaneous and photocopied submissions OK. Computer printout submissions acceptable. Reports in 1 month. Book catalog and ms guidelines for 6x9 SAE and 2 first class stamps.
Nonfiction: Coffee table book, illustrated book. Subjects include regional, outdoors, oral histories, Americana, history and nature. Especially looking for 50,000-word "city and regional histories, anecdotal in style for a general audience; books of regional interest about *places*; adventure and wilderness books; annotated reprints of books of Americana; Americana in general." No health, sex, European travel, diet, broad humor, fiction, quickie books (we stress backlist vitality), religion, children's or nutrition. Submit outline/synopsis and sample chapters. Reviews artwork/photos as part of ms package.
Recent Nonfiction Title: *A Living Legacy*, by Mark Wilson.
Tips: "A regional interest or history book has the best chance of selling to Lexikos. Submit a short, cogent proposal; follow up with letter queries. Give the publisher reason to believe you will help him *sell* the book (identify the market, point out the availability of mailing lists, distinguish your book from the competition). Avoid grandiose claims."

‡LIBERTY HOUSE, Imprint of Tab Books, Inc., #557, 60 East 42nd St., New York NY 10165. (212)490-1030. Vice President/Editorial Director: David J. Conti. Publishes hardcover originals and trade paperback originals and reprints. Publishes 25 titles/year. Receives 200 submissions/year. 50% of books from first-time authors; 80% from unagented writers. Pays 5-15% royalty on wholesale price. Offers $2,000 average advance. Publishes book an average of 5 months after acceptance. Simultaneous and photocopied submissions OK. Computer printout submissions OK. Reports on queries in 2 weeks; on ms in 1 month. Book catalog free on request; writer's guidelines for #10 SASE.
Nonfiction: Subjects include small business, investing, money/finance, real estate. "We're engaged in a wide-ranging business publishing program. We're looking for books written for the general public as well as sophisticated investors, business people, and professionals." Submit outline/synopsis and sample chapter.
Recent Nonfiction Title: *Frank Cappello's New Guide to Finding the Next Superstock*, by Frank A. Cappello Jr.
Tips: "We publish very practical, how-to, results-oriented books. Study the competition, study the market, then submit a proposal."

*LIBRA PUBLISHERS, INC., Suite 383, 3089C Clairemont Dr., San Diego CA 92117. (619)581-9449. Contact: William Kroll. Publishes hardcover and paperback originals. Specializes in the behavioral sciences. Averages 15 titles/year; receives 300 submissions annually. 60% of books from first-time authors; 85% of books from unagented writers. 10-15% royalty on retail price; no advance. "We will also offer our services to authors who wish to publish their own works. The services include editing, proofreading, production, artwork, copyrighting, and assistance in promotion and distribution." Publishes book an average of 8 months after acceptance. Computer printout submissions acceptable; prefers letter-quality. Reports in 2 weeks. Free book catalog; writer's guidelines for #10 SASE.
Nonfiction: Mss in all subject areas will be given consideration, but main interest is in the behavioral sciences. Prefers complete manuscript but will consider outline/synopsis and 3 sample chapters. Reviews artwork/photos as part of ms package.
Recent Nonfiction Title: *Manual for Retirement Counselors*, by Harold Geist, Ph.D.

LIBRARIES UNLIMITED, Box 3988, Englewood CO 80155-3988. Imprints include Ukranian Academic Press. Editor-in-Chief: Bohdan S. Wynar. Publishes hardcover and paperback originals. Averages 50 titles/year; receives 100-200 submissions annually. 10-20% of books from first-time authors. Average print order for a writer's first book is 2,000. 10% royalty on net sales; advance averages $500. Publishes book an average of 1 year after acceptance. Reports in 2 months. Free book catalog and ms guidelines.
Nonfiction: Publishes reference and library science textbooks. Looks for professional experience. Query or submit outline and sample chapters; state availability of photos/illustrations with submission. All prospective authors are required to fill out an author questionnaire.
Recent Nonfiction Title: *The Collection Program in Schools*, by Phyllis J. Van Orden.

‡LIBRARY RESEARCH ASSOCIATES, INC., Subsidiaries include Empire State Fiction, RD #5, Box 41, Dunderberg Rd., Monroe NY 10950. (914)783-1144. President: Matilda A. Gocek. Publishes hardcover and trade paperback originals. Averages 4 titles/year; receives about 30 submissions annually. 100% of books from first-time authors; 100% of books from unagented writers. Pays 10% maximum royalty on retail price. Offers 20 copies of the book as advance. Publishes book an average of 14 months after acceptance. Photocopied submissions OK. Computer printout submissions acceptable; no dot-matrix. Reports in 3 weeks on queries; 3 months on mss. Book catalog free on request.

Nonfiction: Biography, coffee table book, how-to, reference, technical and American history. Subjects include Americana, art, business and economics, history, philosophy, politics and travel. "Our nonfiction book manuscript needs for the next year or two will include books about American artists, graphics and photography, historical research of some facet of American history, and definitive works about current or past economics or politics." No astrology, occult, sex, adult humor or gay rights. Submit outline/synopsis and sample chapters.

Recent Nonfiction Title: *Washington's Last Cantonment*, by Janet Dempsey.

Fiction: Send fiction to Empire State Fiction, Patricia E. Clyne, senior editor. Adventure (based in an authentic NY location); historical (particularly in or about New York state); mystery; and suspense. "I try to publish at least three novels per year. Characterization is so important! The development of people and plot must read well. The realism of world events (war, terrorism, catastrophes) is turning readers to a more innocent world of reading for entertainment with less shock value. Free speech (free *everything*!) is reviving old values. Explicit sex, extreme violence, vile language in any form will not be considered." Submit outline/synopsis and sample chapters.

Recent Fiction Title: *Solarian Chronicles: Book One*, by Michael Bell.

Tips: "Our audience is adult, over age 30, literate and knowledgeable in business or professions. The writer has the best chance of selling our firm historical fiction or nonfiction and scientific texts. If I were a writer trying to market a book today, I would try to write about people in a warm human situation—the foibles, the loss of self, the unsung heroism—angels with feet of clay."

LIFE CYCLE BOOKS, Subsidiary of Life Cycle Books, Ltd., Toronto, Canada. Box 792, Lewiston NY 14092-0792. (416)690-5860. President: Paul Broughton. Publishes trade paperback originals and reprints, brochures and pamphlets. Receives 150 submissions annually. 30% of books from first-time authors. 100% of books from unagented authors. Averages 5-10 titles/year. Pays 8% royalty on net price for books; makes outright purchase of $200-1,000 for pamphlets and books. Offers average $150 advance. Publishes book an average of 18 months after acceptance. Photocopied submissions OK if good quality reproduction. Computer printout submissions acceptable; no dot-matrix. Reports in 2 weeks on queries; 2 months on mss. Free book catalog.

Nonfiction: Health, history, politics, religion, sociology. Specifically "we publish materials on human life issues (i.e. abortion, infanticide, euthanasia, child abuse, sex education, etc.) written from a pro-life perspective." Query for books; submit complete ms for pamphlets or brochures. Reviews artwork/photos as part of ms package.

Recent Nonfiction Titles: *Abortion, the Bible and the Church*, by T. J. Bosgra.

LIGUORI PUBLICATIONS, Book and Pamphlet Dept., 1 Liguori Dr., Liguori MO 63057. (314)464-2500. Editor-in-Chief: Rev. Christopher Farrell, C.SS.R. Managing Editor: Thomas Artz, C.SS.R. Associate Editor: Julie Kelemen. Publishes paperback originals. Specializes in Catholic-Christian religious materials. Averages 35 titles/year; receives about 200 submissions annually. About 40% of books from first-time authors; 95% of books from unagented writers. Average print order for a writer's first book is 10,000-16,000. Pays royalty on books; flat fee on pamphlets and teacher's guides. Publishes book an average of 8 months after acceptance. Query for electronic submissions. Computer printout submissions acceptable; no dot-matrix. Reports in 5 weeks. Book catalog and ms guidelines for 9x12 SAE with 4 first class stamps.

Nonfiction: Publishes doctrinal, inspirational, biblical, self-help and educational materials. Looks for "thought and language that speak to basic practical religious concerns of contemporary Catholic Christians." Query or submit synopsis and 1 sample chapter; "never submit total book."

Recent Nonfiction Title: *Aging Parents: How to Understand and Help Them*.

Tips: "We seek manuscripts that deal with topics of current interest to Catholics: biblical study, prayer, RCIA programs, women and the Church, Catholic health care, etc."

LINCH PUBLISHING, INC., Box 75, Orlando FL 32802. (305)647-3025. Vice President: Dolores W. Neville. Editor: Val Lynch. Publishes hardcover and trade paperback originals. Averages 10 titles/year; receives 200 submissions annually. 5% of books from first-time authors; 25% of books from unagented writers. Pays 6-8% royalty on retail price. Rarely pays advances. Publishes book an average of 9 months after acceptance. Simultaneous and photocopied submissions OK. Computer printout submissions acceptable; prefers letter-quality. Reports in 6 weeks. Book catalog for $1 and #10 SAE with 2 first class stamps.

Nonfiction: Publishes books only on estate planning and legal how-to books which must be applicable in all 50 states. "We are interested in a book on getting through probate, settling an estate, and minimizing federal estate and/or state inheritance taxes." Query editor by phone before submitting mss—"we could have already accepted a manuscript and be in the process of publishing one of the above."

Recent Nonfiction Title: *Ask an Attorney*, by J. Pippen.

Tips: Currently interest is mainly estate planning.

LITTLE, BROWN AND CO., INC., 34 Beacon St., Boston MA 02108. Contact: Editorial Department, Trade Division. Publishes hardcover and paperback originals and paperback reprints. Averages 100 titles/year. "Royalty and advance agreements vary from book to book and are discussed with the author at the time an offer is made. Submissions only from authors who have had a book published or have been published in professional or literary journals, newspapers or magazines." Computer printout submissions acceptable; prefers letter-quality. Reports in 3 months for queries/proposals.

Nonfiction: "Some how-to books, distinctive cookbooks, biographies, history, science and sports." Query or submit outline/synopsis and sample chapters. Reviews artwork/photos as part of ms package.

Recent Nonfiction Title: *The Cat Who Came For Christmas*, by Cleveland Armory.

Fiction: Contemporary popular fiction as well as fiction of literary distinction. "Our poetry list is extremely limited; those collections of poems that we do publish are usually the work of poets who have gained recognition through publication in literary reviews and various periodicals." Query or submit outline/synopsis and sample chapters.

Recent Fiction Title: *Heiress*, by Janet Dailey.

LODESTAR BOOKS, Division of E. P. Dutton, 2 Park Ave., New York NY 10016. (212)725-1818. Editorial Director: Virginia Buckley. Senior Editor: Rosemary Brosnan. Publishes hardcover originals. Publishes juveniles, young adults, fiction and nonfiction; nonfiction picture books. Averages 20 titles/year; receives 800 submissions annually. 10-20% of books from first-time authors; 25-30% of books from unagented writers. Average print order for a writer's first book is 4,000-5,000. Pays royalty on invoice list price; advance offered. Publishes book an average of 18 months after acceptance. Photocopied submissions OK. Query for electronic submissions. Computer printout submissions acceptable; prefers letter-quality. Reports in 2-4 months. Ms guidelines for SASE.

Nonfiction: Query or submit outline/synopsis and 2-3 sample chapters including "theme, chapter-by-chapter outline, and 1 or 2 completed chapters." State availability of photos and/or illustrations. Queries/mss may be routed to other editors in the publishing group. Reviews artwork/photos as part of ms package.

Recent Nonfiction Title: *An American Rhapsody: The Story of George Gershwin*, by Paul Kresh.

Fiction: Publishes only for young adults and juveniles: adventure, fantasy, historical, humorous, contemporary, mystery, science fiction, suspense and western books. Submit complete ms.

Recent Fiction Title: *Park's Quest*, by Katherine Paterson.

Tips: "A young adult novel that is literary, fast-paced, well-constructed (as opposed to a commercial novel); well-written nonfiction on contemporary issues, photographic essays, have the best chance of selling to our firm."

‡*LOIZEAUX BROTHERS, INC., 1238 Corlies Ave., Box 277, Neptune NJ 07754. (201)774-8144. Editor-in-Chief: Claudia C. Mooij. Publishes hardcover, trade and mass market paperback originals and reprints. Publishes 10 titles/year. Receives 450 submissions/year. 50% of books from first-time authors; 100% from un-agented writers. Subsidy publishes 5% of books. Pays 10% royalty on net price. Publishes book an average of 18 months after acceptance. Query for electronic submissions. Computer printout submissions OK; prefers letter-quality. Reports in 2 weeks. Book catalog free on request.

Nonfiction: Biography, reference, religion. "We're looking for commentaries on books of the Bible, books on Bible doctrine, on Christian living, devotional. No manuscripts that are too scholarly (as in doctoral dissertations, mss loaded with footnotes)." Query or submit outline/synopsis and sample chapters.

Recent Nonfiction Title: *Exploring the Psalms*, by John Phillips (commentary).

Fiction: Religious (allegorical tales). "We want books that present a Christian message—allegorical or symbolic tales. No romance." Query or submit outline/synopsis and sample chapters.

Recent Fiction Title: *The Shining Sword*, by Charles Coleman (allegory).

Tips: "People continue to study the Bible but reading ability has declined and readers want simplified prose (not theological tomes). High school, college, Bible school students are our audience."

LOMOND PUBLICATIONS, INC., Box 88, Mt. Airy MD 21771. (301)829-1496. Publisher: Lowell H. Hattery. Publishes hardcover originals. Averages 3-10 titles/year; receives 30 submissions annually. 50% of books from first-time authors; 100% of books from unagented writers. Pays 10% royalty on net price or makes outright purchase. No advance. Publishes book an average of 6-18 months after acceptance. Simultaneous submissions OK. Computer printout submissions acceptable. Reports in 1 month. Free book catalog.

Nonfiction: Technical, professional and scholarly. Subjects include business and economics, politics, sociology, public policy, technological change and management. Query or submit complete ms.

Recent Nonfiction Title: *Soviet Automation*, by Dr. Jack Baranson.

For explanation of symbols, see the Key to Symbols and Abbreviations on Page 5.

Tips: "We publish for the scholarly, professional, and well-informed lay readers of all countries. We publish only English titles, but some are subsequently reprinted and translated in other languages. A writer's best bet with us is an interdisciplinary approach to management, technology or public policy."

LONE EAGLE PUBLISHING CO., 9903 Santa Monica Blvd., Beverly Hills CA 90212. (213)471-8066. President: Joan V. Singleton. Publishes hardcover and trade paperback originals. Averages 4 titles/year; receives 8-10 submissions annually. 100% of books from unagented writers. Pays 10% royalty minimum on net price, wholesale and retail. Offers $250 average advance. Publishes a book an average of 1 year after acceptance. Simultaneous and photocopied submissions OK. Query for electronic submissions. Computer printout submissions OK; prefers letter-quality. Book catalog for #10 SAE and 2 first class stamps.
Nonfiction: Self-help, technical, how-to, and reference. Subjects include movies. "We are looking for technical books in the motion picture and video field by professionals. No unrelated topics or biographies." Submit outline/synopsis and sample chapters. Reviews artwork/photos as part of ms package.
Recent Nonfiction Title: *Screen Acting*, by Brian Adams.
Tips: "A well-written, well-thought-out book on some technical aspect of the motion picture (or video) industry has the best chance: for example, script supervising, editing, special effects, costume design, production design. Pick a subject that has not been done to death, make sure you know what you're talking about, get someone well-known in that area to endorse the book and prepare to spend a lot of time publicizing the book."

LONGMAN, INC., 95 Church St., White Plains NY 10601. (914)993-5000. President: Bruce S. Butterfield. Publishes hardcover and paperback originals. Publishes 200 titles/year. Pays variable royalty; offers variable advance. Photocopied submissions OK. Reports in 6 weeks.
Nonfiction: Textbooks only (elementary/high school, college and professional): world history, political science, economics, communications, social sciences, sociology, education, English, Latin, foreign languages, English as a second language. No trade, art or juvenile.

‡LOOMPANICS UNLIMITED, Box 1197, Port Townsend WA 98368. Book Editor: Michael Hoy. Publishes trade paperback originals. Publishes 12 titles/year; receives 50 submissions annually. 40% of books from first-time authors; 100% of books from unagented writers. Average print order for a writer's first book is 1,000. Pays 7½-15% royalty on wholesale or retail price; or makes outright purchase of $100-1,200. Offers average $500 advance. Publishes book an average of 10 months after acceptance. Simultaneous and photocopied submissions OK. Computer printout submissions acceptable; prefers letter-quality. Reports in 6 weeks. Free book catalog.
Nonfiction: How-to, reference and self-help. Subjects include business and economics, philosophy, politics, travel, and "beat the system" books. "We are looking for how-to books in the fields of espionage, investigation, the underground economy, police methods, how to beat the system, crime and criminal techniques. No cookbooks, inspirational, travel, or cutesy-wutesy stuff." Query, or submit outline/synopsis and sample chapters. Reviews artwork/photos.
Recent Nonfiction Title: *Methods of Disguise*, by John Sample (how-to).
Tips: "Our audience is young males looking for hard-to-find information on alternatives to 'The System.' "

LOTHROP, LEE & SHEPARD BOOKS, Division of William Morrow & Company, 105 Madison Ave., New York NY 10016. (212)889-3050. Editor-in-Chief: Dorothy Briley. Hardcover original children's books only. Royalty and advance vary according to type of book. Averages 60 titles/year; receives 4,000 submissions annually. Less than 2% of books from first-time authors; 25% of books from unagented writers. Average print order for a writer's first book is 6,000. State availability of photos to accompany ms. Publishes book an average of 2 years after acceptance. Photocopied submissions OK, but originals preferred. No simultaneous submissions. Computer printout submissions acceptable; no dot-matrix. Responds in 6 weeks. Book catalog and guidelines for 9x12 SAE with 4 first class stamps.
Fiction and Nonfiction: Publishes picture books, general nonfiction, and novels. Submit outline/synopsis and sample chapters for nonfiction. Juvenile fiction emphasis is on novels for the 8-12 age group. Submit complete ms for fiction. Looks for "organization, clarity, creativity, literary style."
Recent Nonfiction Title: *The Incredible Journey of Lewis and Clark*, by Rhoda Blumberg.
Recent Fiction Title: *Mufaro's Beautiful Daughters*, by John Steptoe (illustrated picture book).
Tips: "Trends in book publishing that freelance writers should be aware of include the demand for books for children under age three and the shrinking market for young adult books, especially novels."

*LOYOLA UNIVERSITY PRESS, 3441 N. Ashland Ave., Chicago IL 60657. (312)281-1818. Editorial Director: George A. Lane. Imprints include Campion Books. Publishes hardcover and trade paperback originals, and hardcover and trade paperback reprints. Averages 15 titles/year; receives 100 submissions annually. 40% of books from first-time authors; 95% of books from unagented writers. Subsidy publishes 5% of books. Pays 5-10% royalty on wholesale price; offers no advance. Publishes book an average of 1 year after acceptance. Simultaneous and photocopied submissions acceptable. Query for electronic submissions. Computer printout submissions acceptable; prefers letter-quality. Reports in 1 month. Book catalog for 6x9 SAE.

Nonfiction: Biography and textbook. Subjects include art (religious); history (church); and religion. The four subject areas of Campion Books include Jesuitica (Jesuit history, biography and spirituality); Literature-Theology interface (books dealing with theological or religious aspects of literary works or authors); contemporary Catholic concerns (books on morality, spirituality, family life, pastoral ministry, prayer, worship, etc.); and Chicago/art (books dealing with the city of Chicago from historical, artistic, architectural, or ethnic perspectives, but with religious emphases). Query before submitting ms. Reviews artwork/photos.

Recent Nonfiction Titles: *Thomas Merton on Nuclear Weapons*, by Ronald Powaski (contemporary concerns).

Tips: "Our audience is principally the college-educated reader with religious, theological interest."

LURAMEDIA, Box 261668, 10227 Autumnview Lane, San Diego CA 92126. (619)578-1948. Editorial Director: Lura Jane Geiger. Publishes trade paperback originals and reprints. Averages 4 titles/year; receives 100 submissions annually. 75% of books from first-time authors. 100% of books from unagented writers. Pays 10-15% royalty on wholesale price. Publishes book an average of 6 months after acceptance. Photocopied submissions OK. Query for electronic submissions. Computer printout submissions OK; prefers letter-quality. Reports in 2 weeks on queries; 3 weeks on mss. Book catalog and ms guidelines for #10 SAE with 1 first class stamp.

Nonfiction: Self-help. Subjects include health, spirituality, psychology, and creativity. "Books on renewal . . . body, mind spirit . . . using the right brain and relational material. Books on creativity, journaling, women's issues, black Christian, relationships. I want well digested, thoughtful books. No 'Jesus Saves' literature; books that give all the answers; poetry; or strident politics." Submit outline/synopsis, biography and sample chapters. Reviews artwork/photos as part of ms package.

Recent Nonfiction Title: *Eavesdropping on the Echoes: Voices from the Old Testament*, by Ted Loder.

Tips: "Our audience are people who want to grow and change; who want to get in touch with their spiritual side; who want to relax; who are creative and want creative ways to live. We have recently published a book, *Just a Sister Away*, for black Christian women. This is a new market for us."

‡*McCLELLAND & STEWART, Suite #900, 481 University Ave., Toronto, Ontario M5G 2E7 Canada. (416)498-1114. Subsidiaries include Douglas Gibson Books and Pulse Books. Acquisitions Coordinator: Victoria Gruden. Publishes hardcover and trade paperback originals, mass market paperback reprints. Publishes 80 titles/year. Receives 1,000 submissions/year. 5% of books from first-time authors; 10% from unagented writers. Subsidy publishes 5% (nonauthor) of books. Government subsidies go toward titles deemed important to Canadian literature and culture. Pays royalty of 5-20% on retail price or outright purchase of $2,000-5,000. Offers 8-10% of estimated royalty earnings as average advance. Publishes book an average of 12-18 months after acceptance. Simultaneous and photocopied submissions OK. Computer printout submissions OK; prefers letter-quality. Reports in 6 weeks. Book catalog and ms guidelines free on request.

Nonfiction: Biography, coffee-table book, cookbook, how-to, illustrated book, juvenile, reference, self-help, textbook. Subjects include animals, anthropology/archaeology, art/architecture, business and economics, child guidance/parenting, ethnic, government/politics, health/medicine, history, language/literature, military/war, money/finance, music/dance, nature/environment, psychology, religion, science, sociology, sports, translation, travel, women's issues/studies. Submit outline/synopsis and sample chapters "with a detailed resume and publication history." Reviews artwork/photos as part of ms package.

Recent Nonfiction Title: *Starting Out*, by P. Berton (memoir).

Fiction: Literary, short story collections. "We do not consider genre fiction of any kind." Submit outline/synopsis and sample chapters with detailed resume and publishing history.

Recent Fiction Title: *The Honorary Patron*, by J. Hodgins (literary).

Poetry: "We publish a small and select list of quality poetry titles by authors who have already begun to establish a reputation on the Canadian poetry scene." Submit complete ms with detailed resume and publishing history.

Recent Poetry Title: *The Stubborn Particulars of Grace*, by B. Wallace.

Tips: "Our audience are readers of quality Canadian fiction, poetry and nonfiction. If I were a writer trying to market a book today, I would study carefully the existing market for that book, and appropriate publisher for it, before approaching a publishing house. Try to convince the publisher of the existence of that market in very concrete terms, and outline how your project stands up to the existing competition. Really sell yourself and your project."

‡McCUTCHAN PUBLISHING CORPORATION, 2940 San Pablo Ave., Berkeley CA 94702. (415)841-8616. Editor: Kim Sharrar. Publishes 5 titles/year. Receives 60 submissions/year. 30% of books from first-time authors; 100% from unagented writers. Pays 12-15% royalty on wholesale price. Publishes book an average of 8 months after acceptance. Photocopied submissions OK. Reports in 6 weeks. Book catalog and ms guidelines free on request.

Nonfiction: Textbook. Subjects include education, food service and criminal justice. Submit outline/synopsis and sample chapters.
Recent Nonfiction Title: *Purchasing for Food Service Managers*, by Warfel and Cremer (food service).
Tips: "Professors and instructors of education, food service and criminal justice are our audience."

McDONALD PUBLISHING CO., INC., Imprint is Shoe Tree Press, Box 356, Belvidere NJ 07823. (201)496-4441. Publisher/Editor: Joyce McDonald. Hardcover and trade paperback originals and reprints. Averages 4 titles/year. 25% of books from first-time authors; 25% of books from unagented writers. Pays 10-15% royalty on hardcover; 5-7% on trade paperbacks; "sometimes on wholesale price, usually on retail price. Maximum royalty on hardcover only." Advance negotiable. Publishes book an average of 18 months after acceptance. Simultaneous and photocopied submissions OK. Computer printout submissions OK; prefers letter-quality. Reports in 1 month on queries; 3 months on mss. Book catalog and guidelines for #10 SAE and 1 first class stamp.
Nonfiction: Juvenile books on Americana, animals, art, cooking and foods, health, history, hobbies, music, nature, recreation, sports and travel. "Books focusing on the problems of growing up have the best chance of being considered. We are also looking for nature and environmental books. No textbook manuscripts." Query. Reviews artwork/photos as part of ms package. No unsolicited mss.
Recent Nonfiction Title: *Market Guide for Young Writers, 1988-89 Edition*, by Kathy Henderson (nonfiction).
Fiction: Juvenile adventure, fantasy, historical, humor, mainstream, mystery and science fiction. "Humorous novels and adventure stories are preferred. Occasionally we publish a picture book or YA. No 'formula' books." Query or submit outline/synopsis and sample chapters.
Tips: "Authors have the best chance of selling us timely nonfiction or humorous novels for 8-11-year-olds."

MARGARET K. McELDERRY BOOKS, Macmillan Publishing Co., Inc., 866 3rd Ave., New York NY 10022. Editor: Margaret K. McElderry. Publishes hardcover originals. Publishes 20-25 titles/year; receives 1,200-1,300 submissions annually. 8% of books from first-time authors; 45% of books from unagented writers. The average print order is 6,000-7,500 for a writer's first teen book; 7,500-10,000 for a writer's first picture book. Pays royalty on retail price. Publishes book an average of 1½ years after acceptance. Reports in 6 weeks. Computer printout submissions acceptable; no dot-matrix. Ms guidelines for #10 SAE with 1 first class stamp.
Nonfiction and Fiction: Quality material for preschoolers to 16-year-olds. Looks for "originality of ideas, clarity and felicity of expression, well-organized plot (fiction) or exposition (nonfiction) quality." Reviews artwork/photos as part of ms package.
Recent Title: *What A Morning! The Christmas Story in Black Spirituals*, selected and edited by John Langstaff, illustrated by Ashley Bryan.
Tips: "There is not a particular 'type' of book that we are interested in above others though we are always look for humor; rather, we look for superior quality in both writing and illustration." Freelance writers should be aware of the swing away from teen-age problem novels to books for younger readers.

McFARLAND & COMPANY, INC., PUBLISHERS, Box 611, Jefferson NC 28640. (919)246-4460. President and Editor-in-Chief: Robert Franklin. Business Manager: Rhonda Herman. Editor: Virginia Hege. Publishes hardcover and "quality" paperback originals; a non-"trade" publisher. Averages 70 titles/year; receives 700 submissions annually. 70% of books from first-time authors; 95% of books from unagented writers. Average print order for a writer's first book is 1,000. Pays 10-12½% royalty on net receipts; no advance. Publishes book an average of 15 months after acceptance. Computer printout submissions acceptable; prefers letter-quality. Reports in 2 weeks.
Nonfiction: Reference books and scholarly, technical and professional monographs. Subjects include Americana, art, business, chess, drama/theatre, health, cinema/radio/TV (very strong here), history, literature, librarianship (very strong here), music, parapsychology, religion, sociology, sports/recreation (very strong here), women's studies, and world affairs (very strong here). "We will consider *any* scholarly book—with authorial maturity and competent grasp of subject." Reference books are particularly wanted—fresh material (i.e., not in head-to-head competition with an established title). "We don't like manuscripts of fewer than 200 double-spaced typed pages. Our market consists mainly of libraries." No memoirs, poetry, children's books, devotional/inspirational works or personal essays. Query or submit outline/synopsis and sample chapters. Reviews artwork/photos as part of ms package.
Recent Nonfiction Title: *Commonsense Copyright: A Guide to the New Technologies*, by R.S. Talab (comprehensive handbook for teachers and librarians).
Tips: "We do *not* accept novels or fiction of any kind or personal Bible studies. Don't worry about writing skills—we have editors. What we want is well-organized *knowledge* of an area in which there is not good information coverage at present, plus reliability so we don't feel we have to check absolutely everything."

McGRAW-HILL BOOK CO., College Division, 1221 Avenue of the Americas, New York NY 10020. (212)512-2000. Editors-in-Chief: Philip Butcher (social sciences and humanities); Kay Pace (business and economics); Eric Munson (engineering and computer science); David Boleio (science, math, nursing). Publishes hardcover and softcover technical material and software for the college market.
Nonfiction: The College Division publishes textbooks. The writer must know the college curriculum and course structure. Also publishes scientific texts and reference books in business and economics, computers, engineering, social sciences, physical sciences, nursing, and mathematics. Material should be scientifically and factually accurate. Most, but not all, books should be designed for existing courses offered in various disciplines of study. Books should have superior presentations and be more up-to-date than existing textbooks.

‡McGRAW HILL RYERSON, Subsidiary of McGraw-Hill, 330 Progress Ave., Scarborough, Ontario M1P 2Z5 Canada. (416)293-1911. Editorial Director: Denise Schon. Publishes hardcover originals, trade paperback originals and reprints. Firm publishes 200 titles/year; division publishes 25 titles/year. Receives 400 submissions/year. 10% of books from first-time authors; 40% from unagented writers. Pays 8-15% royalty on retail price. Publishes book an average of 8 months after acceptance. Simultaneous submissions OK. Query for electronic submissions. Computer printout submissions OK; no dot-matrix. Reports in 1 month on queries; 3 months on ms. Book catalog and ms guidelines free on request.
Nonfiction: Biography, cookbook, how-to, reference, self-help. Subjects include art/architecture, business and economics, cooking, foods and nutrition, gardening, government/politics, health/medicine, history, money/finance, recreation, sports, women's issues/studies. No exercise books. Submit outline/synopsis and sample chapters. Reviews artwork/photos as part of ms package.
Recent Nonfiction Title: *Lanny*, by Lanny McDonald (sports autobiography).

MACMILLAN PUBLISHING COMPANY, Children's Book Department, 866 3rd Ave., New York NY 10022. Publishes hardcover originals. Averages 65 titles/year. Will consider juvenile submissions only. Fiction and nonfiction. Enclose return postage.

‡MADISON BOOKS, University Press of America, Inc., 4720 Boston Way, Lanham MD 20706. (301)459-5308. Imprints include Hamilton Press. Managing Editor: Charles Lean. Publishes hardcover originals and trade paperback originals and reprints. Averages 20 titles/year. Receives 350 submissions/year. 20% of books from first-time authors; 50% from unagented writers. Pays 5-15% royalty on wholesale price. Offers average advance of $2,000. Publishes ms an average of 1 year after acceptance. Simultaneous and photocopied submissions OK. Computer printout submissions OK; no dot-matrix. Book catalog and manuscript guidelines free on request.
Nonfiction: Biography, reference. Subjects include Americana, business and economics, government/politics, history, sociology. "We are specifically looking for cultural and media studies; public policy; history; biography; and social sciences. Nothing on hobbies, gardening, cooking or translation." Query or submit outline/synopsis and sample chapters or complete ms. Reviews artwork/photos as part of ms package.
Recent Nonfiction Title: *Thomas Jefferson*, by Alf J. Mapp Jr. (biography).

THE MAIN STREET PRESS, William Case House, Pittstown NJ 08867. (201)735-9424. Editorial Director: Martin Greif. Publishes hardcover and trade paperback originals. Averages 30 titles/year; receives 750 submissions annually. 25% of books from first-time authors; 75% of books from unagented writers. Pays 5-7½% royalty on paperbacks, 10-15% on a sliding scale for hardcover books; advance varies widely. Sometimes makes outright purchase. Publishes book an average of 1 year after acceptance. Simultaneous and photocopied submissions OK. Computer printout submissions OK. Reports in 2 months on queries; 3 months on mss. Reviews artwork/photos (photocopies OK) as part of ms package. Book catalog $1.25.
Nonfiction: Subjects include Americana, art, hobbies, gardening, film, architecture, popular culture, humor and design. "We publish *heavily illustrated* books on almost all subjects; we publish *only* illustrated books." Especially needs how-to quilting books. "We do not want to consider any nonfiction book with fewer than 75 illustrations." Query or submit outline/synopsis and sample chapters. "We will *not* return queries without SASE, and we will *not* return unsolicited manuscripts without return postage."
Recent Nonfiction Title: *CQ (Canine Quarterly)*, by Ina Schell.
Tips: "Our books are largely for the 'carriage trade'. Our humor books are 'up-scale' and definitely not of the 'Jokes for the John' variety."

MARATHON INTERNATIONAL PUBLISHING COMPANY, INC., Dept. WM, Box 33008, Louisville KY 40232. President: Jim Wortham. Publishes hardcover originals, and trade paperback originals and reprints. Averages 10 titles/year. Pays 10% royalty on wholesale. Publishes book an average of 10 months after acceptance. Simultaneous and photocopied submissions OK. Computer printout submissions acceptable. Reports in 1 month. Booklist/catalog for #10 SAE and 2 first class stamps.
Nonfiction: "We are looking for manuscripts in the area of alcohol and drug addictions; and codependency.

We are urgently in need of any reports or manuscripts dealing with 'sex addiction.' Other manuscripts in the area of mental health are being considered. No biography, textbooks or poetry." Query. Reviews artwork/photos as part of ms package.

‡*MARKUS WIENER PUBLISHING INC., #107, 2801 Broadway, New York NY 10021. (212)678-7138. Subsidiaries include Masterworks of Modern Jewish Writing. Editor-in-Chief: Shelley L. Frisch. Publishes hardcover and trade paperback originals and reprints. Averages 18 titles/year. Receives 50-100 submissions/year. 10% of books from first-time authors; 10% from unagented writers. Subsidy publishes 2-5% of books. Pays 10% royalty. Publishes ms an average of 6 months after acceptance. Computer printout submissions OK; prefers letter-quality. Reports in 2 weeks on queries; 2 months on mss. Book catalog free on request.
Nonfiction: Biography, reference. Subjects incude business and economics, education, ethnic, history, language/literature, regional, religion, translation, women's issues/studies, Judaism. "We're looking for well written academic monographs in history, accounting and Judaica." Query or submit outline/synopsis and sample chapters. Reviews artwork/photos as part of ms package.
Recent Nonfiction Title: *Women in the Middle Ages,* by Echols, Williams (history).
Fiction: Literary. Query or submit outline/synopsis and sample chapters.
Recent Fiction Title: *Family Chronicle*, by Resnikoff.

MARLOR PRESS, 4304 Brigadoon Dr., St. Paul MN 55126. (612)483-1588. Editor: Marlin Bree. Publishes trade paperback originals. Averages 6 titles/year; receives 100 submissions annually. Pays 5-10% royalty on net sales. Publishes book an average of 6 months after final acceptance. Photocopied submissions OK. Computer printout submissions OK. Reports in 3 months on queries.
Nonfiction: Travel books. Query or submit outline/synopsis and sample chapters. Reviews artwork/photos as part of ms package.
Recent Nonfiction Title: *New York for the Independent Traveler*, by Ruth Humleker (self-guided tours).
Tips: "We publish travel guidebooks, fact books and travel directories to major vacation and travel areas in the U.S., Canada and Western Europe. No advice, personal reminiscences or anecdotal manuscripts."

MAZDA PUBLISHERS, Box 2603, 2991 Grace Ln., Costa Mesa CA 92626. (714)751-5252. Editor-in-Chief/Publisher: Ahmad Jabbari. Publishes hardcover and trade paperback originals and trade paperback reprints. Averages 6 titles/year; receives approximately 25 submissions annually. 90% of books from first-time authors; 100% of books from unagented writers. Pays royalty on wholesale price; no advance. Publishes book an average of 4 months after acceptance. Photocopied submissions OK. Query for electronic submissions. Computer printout submissions acceptable; prefers letter-quality. Reports in 2 weeks on queries; 6 weeks on mss. Free book catalog; ms guidelines for SASE.
Nonfiction: Cookbook, juvenile, reference, textbook, scholarly books. Subjects include art, business and economics, cooking and foods, history, politics, sociology, and social sciences in general. "Our primary objective is to publish scholarly books and other informational books about the Middle East and North Africa. All subject areas will be considered with priority given to the scholarly books." Query with outline/synopsis and sample chapters. Reviews artwork/photos as part of ms package.
Recent Nonfiction Title: *Gurgan Faiences*, by Mehdi Bahrami (art and architecture).
Recent Fiction Title: *Cry for My Revolution: IRAN*, Manoucher Parvin (novel).
Poetry: Translations and scholarly presentation of poetry from the poets of the Middle Eastern countries only. Submit 5 poems.
Recent Poetry Title: *The Homely Touch: Folk Poetry of Old India* (translated from Sanscrit).
Tips: "We publish books for an academic audience and laymen."

‡MCN PRESS, Box 702073, Tulsa OK 74170. (918)743-6048. Publisher: Jack Britton. Publishes hardcover and trade paperback originals. Averages 5-7 titles/year; receives 30-35 submissions annually. 75% of books from first-time authors; 75% of books from unagented writers. Pays 10% royalty on wholesale or retail price; offers no advance. Publishes book an average of 6 months after acceptance. Computer printout submissions acceptable; prefers letter-quality. Reports in 10 weeks. Free book catalog. Ms guidelines for SASE.
Nonfiction: Biography, illustrated book and reference. Subjects include history and hobbies. "Our audience includes collectors, military personnel and military fans." Submit outline/synopsis and sample chapters or complete ms.
Recent Nonfiction Title: *Medals, Military and Civilian of U.S.*, by Borthick and Britton (reference).

MEADOWBROOK PRESS, 18318 Minnetonka Blvd., Deephaven MN 55391. (612)473-5400. Contact submissions editor. Publishes trade paperback originals and reprints. Averages 10-15 titles/year. Receives 250 queries annually. 25% of books from first-time authors. 75% of books from unagented writers. Pays 5-7.5% royalty; offers $2,000 average advance. Publishes book an average of 1 year after acceptance. Simultaneous and photocopied submissions OK. Computer printout submissions OK. Reports in 3 weeks on queries; 4-6 weeks on mss. Book catalog and ms guidelines for #10 SASE.

Nonfiction: How-to, humor, juvenile, illustrated book and reference. Subjects include health; hobbies; travel; recreation; parenting (baby and child care); consumer information; and relationships. No academic, autobiography, semi-autobiography or fiction. Query with outline and sample chapters. "We prefer a query first; then we will request an outline and/or sample material."
Recent Nonfiction Title: *How to Survive High School with Minimal Brain Damage*, by Lanksy/Dorfman.
Tips: "We like how-to books in a simple, accessible format and any new advice on parenting. We look for a fresh approach to overcoming traditional problems (e.g. potty training)."

MEDIA PRODUCTIONS AND MARKETING, INC., Division include Media Publishing and Midgard Press, 2440 O Street, Suite 202, Lincoln NE 68510. (402)474-2676. President: Jerry Kromberg. Publishes hardcover originals and trade paperback originals and reprints. Averages 9-12 titles annually. Receives 200 submissions/year. 60% of books from first-time writers; 95% from unagented writers. Pays 2-15% royalty based on net sales. Makes some work-for-hire assignments. "Midgard Press is contract publishing; Media Publishing is trade publishing." Publishes book an average of 6 months after acceptance. Simultaneous submissions OK; photocopied submissions OK. Query for electronic submissions. Computer printout submissions acceptable. Reports in 1 month. Book catalog for #10 SASE.
Nonfiction: Biography, how-to, reference, self-help, textbook. Subjects include Americana, history, politics and general interest. "We will consider manuscripts of general interest with good commercial appeal to regional or special interest markets." Query or submit outline/synopsis and sample chapters or submit complete ms. Reviews artwork/photos as part of ms package.
Recent Nonfiction Title: *Journey Out of Silence*, William L. Rush.

MEDICAL ECONOMICS BOOKS, Division of Medical Economics Co., 680 Kinderkamack Rd., Oradell NJ 07649. Acquisitions Editors: Thomas Bentz and Esther Gumpert. Publishes hardcover, paperback, and spiral bound originals. Company also publishes magazines and references for doctors, pharmacists and laboratorians. Averages 25 titles/year; receives 100 submissions annually. 95% of books from unagented writers. Pays by individual arrangement. Publishes book an average of 11 months after acceptance. Simultaneous and photocopied submissions OK. Query for electronic submissions. Computer printout submissions acceptable; prefers letter-quality. Reports in 6 weeks. Booklist for 3 first-class stamps; ms quidelines for #10 SASE. Tests freelancers for rewriting, editing, and proofreading assignments.
Nonfiction: Clinical and practice—financial management references, handbooks, and manuals. Medical—primary care—all fields; obstetrics and gynecology, laboratory medicine and management. Submit table of contents and prospectus. Reviews artwork/photos as part of ms package.
Recent Nonfiction Title: *Malpractice Depositions: Avoiding the Traps*, by Raymond M. Fish, PhD, MD and Melvin E. Ehrhardt, MD, JD.
Tips: "Books addressed to and written by MDs and health-care managers and financial professionals have the best chance of selling to our firm. Looking for ms concerning changes in MD practice and management, new trends, options, developements, way to cope and manage more effectively, adaptably, successfully." Queries/mss may be routed to other editors in the publishing group.

‡MELIOR PUBLICATIONS, A division of Futurepast: The History Company, N. 10 Post, Suite 550, Box 1905, Spokane WA 99210-1905. (509)455-9617. Vice President: Barbara Greene Chamberlain or President: John C. Shideler. Publishes hardcover and trade paperback originals. Publishes 4 titles/year; receives 10-20 proposals/year. 50% of books from first-time authors; 100% from unagented writers. Pays 8-12% royalty on retail price. Publishes ms an average of 12-18 months after acceptance. Simultaneous and photocopied submissions OK. Query for electronic submissions. Computer printout submissions OK; prefers letter-quality. Reports in 1 month on queries; 6-9 months on mss. Ms guidelines for #10 SASE.
Nonfiction: Biography, coffee table book, illustrated book. Subjects include history. Wants nothing "outside our geographical region in terms of topic or setting. We are a regional publisher." Query or submit outline/synopsis and sample chapters. Reviews artwork/photos as part of ms package.
Recent Nonfiction Title: *Washington: Images of State's Heritage*, Carlos Schwantes, general editor; contributing editors: Katherine Morrissey, David Nicandri and Susan Strasser.
Fiction: Historical (with Pacific Northwest setting). Query.
Recent Fiction Title: *Hay for Winter*, by Nellie Buxton Picken (historical fiction).

MELIUS AND PETERSON PUBLISHING, INC., Subsidiary of Video Resources, Inc., Rm. 524, Citizens Building, Box 925, Aberdeen SD 57401. (605)226-0488. Publisher: Ken Melius (nonfiction). Editor: Victoria Peterson. Publishes hardcover and trade paperback originals. Averages 5 titles/year; receives 1,000 submissions annually. 50% of books from first-time authors; 80% of books from unagented writers. Pays 6-12% royalty on retail price. Offers negotiable advance. Publishes book an average of 1 year after acceptance. Simultaneous and photocopied submissions OK. Computer printout submissions acceptable. Reports in 3 weeks on queries; 2 months on mss. Book catalog and guidelines for 6x9 SAE with 3 first class stamps.
Nonfiction: How-to, reference and self-help. Subjects include business and economics, cooking and foods,

hobbies, nature, recreation, travel. "We are seeking works especially on time management and the concept of time. We need a unique approach to the concept of time as a commodity, how time can be used effectively, how it can be wasted—and the effects. Also seeking specific reference books for specific types of businesses." No music, art and religion. Query or submit outline/synopsis and sample chapters. Reviews artwork/photos as part of ms package.

Recent Nonfiction Title: *My Book for Kids with Cancer*, by Jason Gaes.

Tips: "Writers should pay more attention to a book's market and realize that a publisher has to efficiently sell that book to a specific audience. We envision an audience in need of specific information about certain business activities or practices, information about travel and recreation. Cookbooks should appeal to a broad cross-section of the public. We seek books with a two-to-three-year shelf life. Books aimed at specific, easily identifiable audiences seem to be a trend. Travel books continue to do well in today's market. In the future, we need unique, informative books written for a certain market whether it be business, travel or recreation markets. We're still looking for books on effective time management. We're also seeking strong business titles for the small business."

MENASHA RIDGE PRESS, INC., Box 59257, Birmingham AL 35259. (205)991-0373. Publisher: R.W. Sehlinger. Small press. Publishes hardcover and trade paperback originals. Averages 10-15 titles/year; receives 600-800 submissions annually. 50% of books from first-time authors; 90% of books from unagented writers. Average print order for a writer's first book is 4,000. Pays 10% royalty on wholesale price or purchases outright; offers average $1,000 advance. Publishes book an average of 8 months after acceptance. Simultaneous and photocopied submissions OK. Query for electronic submissions. Computer printout submissions acceptable; prefers letter-quality. Reports in 1 month. Book catalog for 9x12 SAE and 4 first class stamps; ms guidelines for SASE.

Nonfiction: How-to, reference, self-help, consumer, outdoor recreation, travel guides and small business. Subjects include business and economics, health, hobbies, recreation, sports, travel and consumer advice. No biography or religious copies. Submit outline/synopsis. Reviews artwork/photos.

Recent Nonfiction Title: *A Hiking Guide to the Trails of Florida*, by Elizabeth Canter.

Tips: Audience: age 25-60, 14-18 years' education, white collar and professional, $30,000 median income, 75% male, 75% east of Mississippi River.

*MERCER UNIVERSITY PRESS, Macon GA 31207. (912)744-2880. Director: Edd Rowell. Publishes hardcover originals. Averages 35 titles/year. Receives 250 submissions annually. 30% of books from first-time authors. 100% of books from unagented writers. Subsidy publishes 80% of books. "We usually ask for a subsidy from the author's institution (university). We do not accept personal subsidies from the authors themselves." Publishes book an average of 1 year after acceptance. Computer printout submissions acceptable; no dot-matrix. Reports in 1 month on queries; 3 months on mss. Free book catalog; writer's guidelines for SASE.

Nonfiction: Biography, reference, textbook and scholarly monographs. Subjects include history (of the American South); philosophy; religion and sociology. "We are very interested in Southern history, biblical studies and theology. We also favor books that may be adapted as textbooks in college courses. Our audience includes professors, students, researchers and libraries." Query or submit outline/synopsis and sample chapters or submit complete ms. Reviews artwork/photos as part of ms package.

Recent Nonfiction Title: *To See the Promised Land: The Faith Pilgrimage of Martin Luther King, Jr.*, by Frederick L. Downing.

Tips: "In scholarly publishing, there has been a substantial increase in the cost of books and decrease in print runs. We see more university presses publishing coffee table books that appeal to a general audience rather than to a scholarly one. Writers have the best chance of selling us scholarly monographs or original research in theology, religion, or history. Extensive documentation and a manuscript addressed to a specific (usually academic) market usually impress us."

‡*MERCURY HOUSE INC., Suite 700, 300 Montgomery St., San Francisco CA 94104. (415)433-7042. President: William M. Brinton. Executive Editor: Alev Lytle. Publishes hardcover originals. Averages 10-15 titles/year; receives 500 submissions annually. 20% of books come from first-time authors; 10% of books from unagented writers. Average print order for a writer's first book is 5,000. Subsidy publishes "only if there is a good market and author has something unique to say, and can say it well." Pays standard royalties; advances negotiable. "Will consider negotiating with author who pays a percentage of cost of printing, publishing, selling book—a tax-oriented transaction." Publishes books an average of 9 months after acceptance. Simultaneous and photocopied submissions OK only if publisher is informed prior to arrangement. Computer printout submissions acceptable in letter-quality type only; no dot-matrix. Reports in 4 weeks on queries; 6 weeks on mss.

Nonfiction: Original and unusual adult nonfiction, on a limited basis. Query with outline/synopsis and sample chapters. All unsolicited mss are returned unopened. SASE for both sample chapters and complete ms.

Recent Nonfiction Title: *The Psychic Detectives*.

Fiction: Original adult fiction, translations, reprints. Query with outline/synopsis and sample chapters. All

unsolicited mss are returned unopened. Send SASE for both sample chapters and complete ms.
Recent Fiction Title: *The Alaska Deception.*
Tips: "Our audience is adult. The editorial process is highly rigorous. Mercury House uses electronic marketing of its titles through computer users, as well as traditional distribution channels."

MERIWETHER PUBLISHING LTD., 885 Elkton Dr., Colorado Springs CO 80907. (303)594-4422. Editors: Arthur or Theodore Zapel. Publishes hardcover and trade paperback originals and reprints. Firm publishes 10-15 books/year; 35-50 plays/year. Receives 1,200 submissions/year. 50% of books from first-time authors; 90% from unagented writers. Pays 10% royalty on retail price or outright purchase of $250-2,500. Publishes book an average of 6 months after acceptance. Simultaneous and photocopied submissions OK. Computer printout submissions OK; no dot-matrix. Reports in 2 weeks on queries; 1 month on ms. Book catalog and ms guidelines available for $1 and SASE.
Nonfiction: How-to, reference, self-help, humor and inspirational. Also textbooks. Subjects include art/drama, hobbies, music/dance, recreation, religion. "We're looking for unusual textbooks or trade books related to the communication or performing arts. We are not interested in religious titles with fundamentalist themes or approaches—we prefer mainstream religion titles." Query or submit outline/synopsis and sample chapters.
Recent Nonfiction Title: *The Parents Book of Ballet*, by Angela Whitehill and William Noble.
Fiction: Plays. "Plays only—humorous, mainstream, mystery, religious, suspense."
Tips: "Our educational books are sold to teachers and students at college and high school levels. Our religious books are sold to youth activity directors, pastors and choir directors. Our trade books are directed at the public with a sense of humor. Another group of buyers is the professional theatre, radio and TV category. We expect to publish several new trade book titles dealing with how-to information in a humorous style."

METAMORPHOUS PRESS, 3249 NW 29th Ave., Box 10616, Portland OR 92710. (503)228-4972. Publisher: David Balding. Acquisitions Editor: Anita Sullivan. Publishes hardcover and trade paperback originals and hardcover and trade paperback reprints. Averages 8-12 titles/year; receives 600 submissions annually. 90% of books from first-time authors; 90% of books from unagented writers. Average print order for a writer's first book is 2,000-5,000. Pays minimum 10% profit split on wholesale prices. No advance. Publishes book an average of 8 months after acceptance. Simultaneous and photocopied submissions OK. Query for electronic submissions. Computer printout submissions acceptable; prefers letter-quality. Free book catalog; ms guidelines for #10 SASE.
Nonfiction: Biography, how-to, illustrated book, reference, self-help, technical and textbook—all related to behavioral science and personal growth. Subjects include business and sales, health, psychology, sociology, education, children's books, science and new ideas in behavioral science. "We are interested in any well-proven new idea or philosophy in the behavioral science areas. Our primary editorial screen is 'will this book further define, explain or support the concept that we create our reality literally or assist people in gaining control of their lives.' " Submit idea, outline, and table of contents only. Reviews artwork/photos as part of ms package.
Recent Nonfiction Title: *Get the Results You Want*, by Kestere and Malatesta.

THE MGI MANAGEMENT INSTITUTE, INC., 378 Halstead Ave., Harrison NY 10528. (914)835-5790. President: Dr. Henry Oppenheimer. Averages 10-15 titles/year; receives 3-4 submissions annually. 50% of books from first-time authors; 100% of those books from unagented writers. Pays 3-5% royalty on retail price of correspondence course (price is usually in $100 range) or 10-15% for conventional book. Publishes book an average of 6 months after acceptance. Query for electronic submissions. Computer printout submissions acceptable. Reports in 2 weeks. Free book catalog.
Nonfiction: How-to, technical and correspondence courses. Subjects include business and economics, engineering, computer, and manufacturing-related topics. Needs correspondence courses in management, purchasing, manufacturing management, production and inventory control, quality control, computers and marketing professional services. Reviews artwork/photos.
Recent Nonfiction Title: *Just-in-Time Manufacturing*, by Ken McGuire (correspondence course).
Tips: "We are interested in textbooks also if specific market can be identified. Our audience includes audit managers, purchasing managers, graduate engineers and architects, manufacturing supervisors and managers, and real estate investors."

*MICHIGAN STATE UNIVERSITY PRESS, Room 25, 1405 S. Harrison Rd., East Lansing MI 48824. (517)355-9543. Director: Richard Chapin. Publishes hardcover and softcover originals. Averages 12 titles annually. Receives 100 submissions/year. 95% of books from first-time writers; 100% from unagented writers. Pays 10% royalty on net sales. Publishes ms an average of 9 months after acceptance. Photocopied submissions OK. Query for electronic submissions. Computer printout submissions OK; prefers letter-quality. Book catalog and manuscript guidelines for #10 SASE.
Nonfiction: Reference, software, technical, textbook and scholarly. Subjects include agriculture, business and economics, history, literature, philosophy, politics and religion. Looking for "scholarly publishing rep-

resenting strengths of the university." Query with outline/synopsis and sample chapters. Reviews artwork/ photos.
Recent Nonfiction Title: *Leadership is an Art*, by Max DePree.

MILADY PUBLISHING CORPORATION, Subsidiary of John Wiley & Sons Inc., 3839 White Plains Rd., Bronx NY 10467. (212)881-3000. President: Thomas R. Severance. Publishes technical books, particularly for occupational education. Averages 10 titles/year; receives 12 submissions annually. 25% of books from first-time authors; 100% of books from unagented writers. Pays 8-12% royalty on wholesale price. Offers average $750 advance. Publishes book an average of 1 year after acceptance. Photocopied submissions OK. Computer printout submissions acceptable; prefers letter-quality. Reports in 6 weeks. Book catalog for $1.
Nonfiction: How-to, reference, textbook, workbooks and exam reviews on occupational education. No academic. Query or submit outline/synopsis and sample chapters. Reviews artwork/photos as part of ms package.
Tips: "Our audience is vocational students."

‡MILKWEED EDITIONS, Box 3226, Minneapolis MN 55403. (612)332-3192. Managing Editor: Deborah Keenan. Publishes hardcover originals and paperback originals and reprints. Averages 6-10 titles/year. Receives 500 submissions/year. 30% of books from first-time authors; 70% from unagented writers. Pays 8-12% royalty on wholesale price. Offers average advance of $400. Publishes work an average of 1 year after acceptance. Simultaneous and photocopies submissions OK. Computer printout submissions OK; no dot-matrix. Reports in 2 weeks on queries; 6 months on mss. Book catalog and ms guidelines free on request.
Nonfiction: Illustrated book. Subjects include anthropology/archaeology, art/architecture, government/politics, history, language/literature, nature/environment, photography, regional, sports, women's issues/studies. Query. Reviews artwork/photos as part of ms package.
Recent Nonfiction Title: *A Male Grief: Notes on Pornography and Addiction*, by David Mura (essay).
Fiction: "Our fiction publishing schedule is filled through 1989 except for our annual Milkweed National Fiction Prize Winner."
Poetry: "Our poetry publishing schedule is filled through 1989."
Tips: "We are looking for three different collaborative works between writers and visual artists for our 1989 list. We want to emphasize visual art in 1989. Also, write for our fiction contest guidelines. One fiction will be chosen still for our 1989 list."

‡MILLER BOOKS, 2908 W. Valley Blvd., Alhambra CA 91803. (818)284-7607. Subsidiaries include *San Gabriel Valley Magazine*, Miller Press and Miller Electric. Publisher: Joseph Miller. Publishes hardcover and trade paperback originals, hardcover reprints and software. Averages 4 titles/year. Pays 10-15% royalty on retail price; buys some mss outright. Simultaneous and photocopied submissions OK. Computer printout submissions acceptable. Reports in 2 weeks on queries; 2 months on mss. Free book catalog.
Nonfiction: Cookbook, how-to, self-help, textbook and remedial textbooks. Subjects include Americana, animals, cooking and foods, history, philosophy and politics. "Remedial manuscripts are needed in most fields." No erotica. Submit complete ms. Reviews artwork/photos as part of ms package. "Please don't send letters. Let us see your work."
Recent Nonfiction Title: *Every Feeling is Desire*, by James Smith, M.D.
Fiction: Adventure, historical, humor, mystery and western. No erotica; "no returns on erotic material." Submit complete ms.
Recent Fiction Title: *The Magic Story*, by F.V.R. Dey (positive thinking).
Tips: "Write something good about people, places and our country. Avoid the negative—it doesn't sell."

MILLS & SANDERSON, PUBLISHERS, Subsidiary of The Huenefeld Co., Inc., Suite 5, 442 Marrett Rd., Lexington MA 02173. (617)861-0992. Publisher: Georgia Mills. Publishes trade paperback originals. Publishes 8 titles/year; receives 150 submissions annually. 50% of books from first-time authors; 75% of books from unagented writers. Pays 12½-13% royalty on wholesale price; offers average $1,000 advance. Publishes book an average of 6 months after acceptance. Simultaneous and photocopied submissions OK. Query for electronic submissions. Computer printout submissions OK; prefers letter-quality. Reports in 1 month on queries; 2 months on mss. Ms guidelines for 9½x4¼ SAE.
Nonfiction: Cookbook, how-to and self-help. Subjects include cooking and foods, health, sociology, travel and contemporary issues. "All our books are aimed at improving individual's life in some way. No religion, music, art or photography." Query.
Recent Nonfiction Title: *There ARE Babies to Adopt*, by Christine Adamec.
Tips: "We only publish nonfiction with broad general consumer appeal because it normally is less chancy than fiction. It must be an interesting subject with broad appeal by an author whose credentials indicate he/she knows a lot about the subject, be well researched and most importantly, must have a certain uniqueness about it."

MODERN LANGUAGE ASSOCIATION OF AMERICA, 10 Astor Pl., New York NY 10003. (212)475-9500. Director of Book Publications: Walter S. Achtert. Publishes hardcover and paperback originals. Averages 15 titles/year; receives 100 submissions annually. 100% of books from unagented writers. Pays 5-15% royalty on net proceeds. Offers average $100 advance. Publishes book an average of 11 months after acceptance. Photocopied submissions OK. Query for electronic submissions. Computer printout submissions acceptable; prefers letter-quality. Reports in 3 weeks on queries; 3 months on mss. Book catalog free on request.
Nonfiction: Reference and professional. Subjects include language and literature. Needs mss on current issues in research and teaching of language and literature. No critical monographs. Query or submit outline/synopsis and sample chapters.
Recent Nonfiction Title: *Helping Students Write Well*, by Barbara E. Fassler Walvoord.

‡**MOON PUBLICATIONS**, 722 Wall St., Chico CA 95928. (916)345-5473. Managing Editor: Mark Morris. Publishes trade paperback originals. Publishes average of 4 titles/year; receives 30-40 submissions/year. 50% of books from first-time authors; 100% from unagented writers. Pays royalty on wholesale price; offers advance of up to $7,000. Publishes book an average of 18 months after acceptance. Simultaneous and photocopied submissions OK. Query for electronic submissions. Computer printout submissions OK. Reports in 2 weeks on queries; 1 week on ms. Book catalog and ms guidelines for #10 SAE and 1 first class stamp.
Nonfiction: Subjects include travel. "We specialize in travel guides to Asia and the Pacific Basin, the western United States and Canada, and favor these areas, but are open to new ideas. Our guides include in-depth cultural and historical background, as well as recreational and practical travel information. We prefer comprehensive guides to entire countries, states, and regions over more narrowly defined areas such as cities, museums, etc. Writers should write first for a copy of our guidelines. Query with outline/synopsis, table of contents, and sample chapters. Author should also be prepared to provide photos, artwork and base maps. No fictional or strictly narrative travel writing; no how-to guides." Reviews artwork/photos as part of ms package.
Recent Nonfiction Title: *Arizona Traveler's Handbook*, by Bill Weir (travel guidebook).
Tips: "Our books are aimed for the independent, budget-minded do-it-yourself traveler but appeal to all travelers because they are the comprehensive guides to the areas they cover. If I were a writer trying to market a book today, I would first study very carefully the other books produced by the publisher I intended to approach."

*MOREHOUSE-BARLOW CO., INC.**, Divison of B&C Co., 78 Danbury Rd., Wilton CT 06897. Publisher: E. Allen Kelley. Publishes hardcover and paperback originals. Averages 35 titles/year; receives 500 submissions annually. 40% of books from first-time authors; 75% of books from unagented writers. Pays 10% royalty on retail price. Publishes book an average of 8 months after acceptance. Computer printout submissions acceptable; no dot-matrix. Book catalog for 9x12 SAE with 2 first class stamps.
Nonfiction: Specializes in Christian publishing (with an Anglican emphasis). Theology, ethics, church history, pastoral counseling, liturgy, religious education and children's books; beginning tapes and videos. No poetry or drama. Accepts outline/synopsis and 2-4 sample chapters. Reviews artwork/photos as part of ms package.
Recent Nonfiction Title: *Banners for Beginners*, by Cory Atwood (craft book—religious subjects).

‡**MORGAN-RAND PUBLICATIONS INC.**, 2200 Sansom St., Philadelphia PA 19103. (215)557-8200. Contact: M. Weakley. Publishes trade paperback originals. Publishes 4 titles/year. Receives 20 submissions/year. 50% of books from first-time authors; 100% from unagented writers. Pays 20-45% royalty, or outright purchase of $500-1,000. Publishes book an average of 3 months after acceptance. Simultaneous submissions OK. Query for electronic submissions. Computer printout submissions OK; prefers letter-quality. Reports in 2 weeks on queries; 5 weeks on mss. Book catalog free on request.
Nonfiction: Reference, technical. Subjects include business and economics. Query.
Recent Nonfiction Title: *Directory Publishing: A Practical Guide*, by Perkins (business).
Tips: "Books offering specific business and technical information to publishing and information industry professionals are wanted."

WILLIAM MORROW AND CO., 105 Madison Ave., New York NY 10016. (212)889-3050. Publisher: James D. Landis. Imprints include Arbor House, Greenwillow Books (juveniles), Susan Hirschman, editor. Lothrop, Lee and Shepard (juveniles), Dorothy Briley, editor. Morrow Junior Books (juveniles), David Reuther, editor. Quill (trade paperback), Douglas Stumpf and Andrew Ambraziejus, editors. Affiliates include Hearst Books (trade). Editorial Director: Ann Bramson. Hearst Marine Books (nautical). Connie Roosevelt, editor, Beech Tree Books, James D. Landis, Publisher. Silver Arrow Books, Sherry W. Arden, Publisher. Receives 10,000 submissions annually. 30% of books from first-time authors; 5% of books from unagented writers. Payment is on standard royalty basis. Publishes book an average of 1-2 years after acceptance. Computer printout submissions acceptable; prefers letter-quality to dot-matrix. Query letter on all books. *No* unsolicited mss or proposals. Mss and proposals should be submitted through a literary agent.
Nonfiction and Fiction: Publishes adult fiction, nonfiction, history, biography, arts, religion, poetry, how-

to books and cookbooks. Length: 50,000-100,000 words. Query only; mss and proposals should be submitted only through an agent.
Recent Fiction Title: *Windmills of the Gods*, by Sidney Sheldon.

MORROW JUNIOR BOOKS, Division of William Morrow & Company, Inc., 105 Madison Ave., New York NY 10016. (212)889-3050. Editor-in-Chief: David L. Reuther. Executive Editor: Meredith Charpentier. Senior Editor: Andrea Curley. Publishes hardcover originals. Publishes 50 titles/year. All contracts negotiated separately; offers variable advance. Book catalog and guidelines for 8½x11 SAE with 2 first class stamps.
Nonfiction: Juveniles (trade books). No textbooks. Query. Reviews artwork/photos as part of ms package.
Recent Nonfiction Title: *A Girl from Yamhill*, by Beverly Cleary (autobiography).
Fiction: Juveniles (trade books).
Recent Fiction Title: *Teacher's Pet*, by Johanna Hurwitz (middle grade novel).
Tips: "Please query us after Jan. 1, 1989."

MOSAIC PRESS MINIATURE BOOKS, 358 Oliver Rd., Cincinnati OH 45215. (513)761-5977. Publisher: Miriam Irwin. Publishes hardcover originals. Averages 4 titles/year; receives 150-200 submissions annually. 49% of books from first-time authors. Average print order for a writer's first book is 2,000. Buys mss outright for $50. Publishes book an average of 30 months after acceptance. Computer printout submissions acceptable; no dot-matrix. Reports in 2 weeks; "but our production, if manuscript is accepted, often takes 2 or 3 years." Book catalog $3. Writer's guidelines for #10 SAE and 2 first-class stamps.
Nonfiction: Biography, cookbook, humor, illustrated book and satire. Subjects include Americana, animals, art, business and economics, cooking and foods, health, history, hobbies, music, nature, sports and travel. Interested in "beautifully written, delightful text. If factual, it must be extremely correct and authoritative. Our books are intended to delight, both in their miniature size, beautiful bindings and excellent writing." No occult, pornography, science fiction, fantasy, haiku, or how-to. Query or submit outline/synopsis and sample chapters or complete ms. Reviews artwork/photos as part of ms package.
Recent Nonfiction Title: *The Cincinnati Reds*, by Floyd Conner and John Synder.
Tips: "I want a book to tell me something I don't know."

MOTHER COURAGE PRESS, 1533 Illinois St., Racine WI 53405. (414)634-1047. Managing Editor: Barbara Lindquist. Small press. Publishes trade paperback originals. Averages 4 titles/year; receives 100-200 submissions annually. 100% of books from first-time authors. 100% of books from unagented writers. Pays 10-15% royalty on wholesale and retail price; offers $250 average advance. Publishes book an average of 9-12 months after acceptance. No unsolioited manuscripts. Simultaneous and photocopied submissions OK. Query for electronic submissions. Computer printout submissions OK. Reports in 2 weeks on queries; 6 weeks on mss. Free book catalog; writer's guidelines for #10 SASE.
Nonfiction: Biography, how-to and self-help. Subjects include health, psychology and sociology. "We are looking for books on difficult subjects—explaining death to children (no talking animals); teen pregnancy; sexual abuse (no personal stories); and rape." Submit outline/synopsis and sample chapters. Reviews artwork/photos as part of ms package.
Recent Nonfiction Title: *Warning, Dating May Be Hazardous to Your Health*, by Claudette McShane.
Fiction: Adventure, fantasy, historical, humor, mystery, romance, science fiction and lesbian. "We are looking for lesbian/feminist or strictly feminist themes. Don't send male-oriented fiction of any kind." Submit outline/synopsis and sample chapters or complete ms.
Recent Fiction Title: *Night Lights*, by Bonnie Arthur (lesbian romance).

MOTORBOOKS INTERNATIONAL PUBLISHERS & WHOLESALERS, INC., Box 2, Osceola WI 54020. Director of Publications: Tim Parker. Managing Editor: Barbara K. Harold. Hardcover and paperback originals. Averages 40 titles/year. 100% of books from unagented writers. Offers 7-15% royalty on net receipts. Offers average $2,500 advance. Publishes book an average of 7-10 months after acceptance. Simultaneous and photocopied submissions OK. Query for electronic submissions. Computer printout submissions acceptable; prefers letter-quality. Reports in 3 months. Free book catalog; ms guidelines for #10 SASE.
Nonfiction: Biography, history, how-to, photography, and motor sports (as they relate to cars, trucks, motorcycles, R/C modeling, motor sports and aviation—domestic and foreign). Accepts nonfiction translations. Submit outline/synopsis, 1-2 sample chapters and sample of illustrations. "State qualifications for doing book." Reviews artwork/photos as part of ms package.
Recent Nonfiction Title: *The Harley-Davidson Motor Company*, by David Wright.

THE MOUNTAINEERS BOOKS, The Mountaineers, 306-2nd Ave W., Seattle WA 98119. (206)285-2665. Director: Donna DeShazo. Publishes hardcover and trade paperback originals (85%) and reprints (15%). Averages 10-15 titles/year; receives 150-250 submissions annually. 25% of books from first-time authors; 98% of books from unagented writers. Average print order for a writer's first book is 2,000-5,000. Offers 17½% royalty based on net sales. Offers advance on occasion. Publishes book an average of 1 year after acceptance. Dot-matrix submissions are acceptable with new ribbon and double spaced. Reports in 2 months. Book catalog and ms guidelines for 9x12 SAE with 2 first class stamps.

Nonfiction: Recreation, non-competitive sports, and outdoor how-to books. "We specialize only in books dealing with mountaineering, hiking, backpacking, skiing, snowshoeing, canoeing, bicycling, etc. These can be either how-to-do-it, where-to-do-it (guidebooks), or accounts of similar outdoor or mountain-related experiences." Does *not* want to see "anything dealing with hunting, fishing or motorized travel." Submit outline/synopsis and minimum of 2 sample chapters. Accepts nonfiction translations. Looks for "expert knowledge, good organization."

Recent Nonfiction Title: *Moments of Doubt*, by David Roberts (essays).

Fiction: "We might consider an exceptionally well-done book-length manuscript on mountaineering." Does *not* want poetry or mystery. Query first.

Tips: "The type of book the writer has the best chance of selling our firm is an authoritative guidebook (*in our field*) to a specific area not otherwise covered; or a first-person narrative of outdoor adventure otherwise unduplicated in print."

‡MULTIPATH GAMEBOOKS, WEST END GAMES, INC., Suite 11 F, 251 W. 30th St., New York NY 10001. (212)947-4828. Game Book Editor: Jonatha Caspian. Publishes hardcover and mass market paperback originals. Averages 4-6 titles/year. 10% of books from first-time authors; 90% from unagented writers. Pays $1,500-5,000 outright purchase. Publishes ms an average of 9 months after acceptance. Photocopied submissions OK. Computer printout submissions OK. Reports in 3 weeks on queries; 3 months on mss. Book catalog and ms guidelines for 4x12 SAE with 1 first class stamp.

Fiction: Adventure, fantasy, humor, juvenile, picture books, science fiction, young adult. "West End is introducing a new line of Multipath Adventure books set in the Star Wars® universe. We anticipate both picture books for parents to read to pre-school/kindergarten, and adventures for young adults/adult Star Wars fans." Query. All mss without proper release returned unread.

Tips: "Know what our other products look like, and where you would fit in our line. Know your subject. West End's games are different from many roleplaying games, because of our emphasis on tone and atmosphere over nuts and bolts, tables, and die codes."

MULTNOMAH PRESS, A division of Multnomah School of The Bible, 10209 SE Division St., Portland OR 97266. (503)257-0526. Senior Editor: Liz Heaney. Publishes hardcover and trade paperback originals, and trade paperback reprints. Averages 30 titles/year; receives 500 submissions annually. 20% of books from first-time authors; 100% of books from unagented writers. Pays royalty on wholesale price. Publishes books an average of 9 months after acceptance. Photocopied submissions OK. Query for electronic submissions. Computer printout submissions acceptable; no dot-matrix. Reports in 6 weeks on queries; 10 weeks on mss. Book catalog and ms guidelines for SASE.

Nonfiction: Coffee table book and self-help. Subjects include religion. "We publish issue-related books linking social/ethical concerns and Christianity; books addressing the needs of women from a Christian point of view; books addressing the needs of the traditional family in today's society; illustrated books for children; and books explaining Christian theology in a very popular way to a lay audience." No daily devotional, personal experience, Scripture/photo combinations or poetry. Submit outline/synopsis and sample chapters.

Recent Nonfiction Title: *With My Whole Heart*, by Karen Burton Mains.

Tips: "We have a reputation for tackling tough issues from a Biblical view; we need to continue to deserve that reputation. Avoid being too scholarly or detached. Although we like well-researched books, we do direct our books to a popular market, not just to professors of theology."

MUSEUM OF NEW MEXICO PRESS, Box 2087, Santa Fe NM 87503. (505)827-6454. Director: James Mafchir. Editor-in-Chief: Mary Wachs. Hardcover and paperback originals (90%) and reprints (10%). Averages 6-8 titles/year; receives 100 submissions annually. 50% of books from first-time authors; 75% of books from unagented writers. Average print order for a writer's first book is 2,000-5,000. Royalty of 10% of list after first 1,000 copies; no advance. Publishes book an average of 1 year after acceptance. Computer printout submissions acceptable; no dot-matrix. Reports in 1-2 months. Free book catalog.

Nonfiction: "We publish both popular and scholarly books on regional anthropology, history, fine and folk arts; geography, natural history, the Americas and the Southwest; regional cookbooks; art, biography (regional and Southwest); music; nature; reference, scientific and technical." Accepts nonfiction translations. Prints preferred for illustrations; transparencies best for color. Sources of photos or illustrations should be indicated for each. Query or submit outline/synopsis and sample chapters to Sarah Nestor, Editor-in-Chief. Mss should be typed double-spaced, follow Chicago *Manual of Style*, and be accompanied by information about the author's credentials and professional background. Reviews artwork/photos as part of ms package.

Recent Nonfiction Title: *Spirit & Vision: Images of Ranchos de Taos Church*, by Sandra D'Emilio and Susan Campbell.

*MUSEUM OF NORTHERN ARIZONA PRESS, Subsidiary of Museum of Northern Arizona, Box 720, Rt. 4, Flagstaff AZ 86001. (602)774-5211. Publisher: Diana Clark Lubick. Publishes hardcover and trade paperback originals, and also quarterly magazine. Averages 10-12 titles/year; receives 35 submissions annually. 10% of books from first-time authors; 100% of books from unagented writers. Subsidy publishes (nonauthor) 15% of books. Pays one-time fee on acceptance of ms. No advance. Publishes book an average of 1 year after acceptance. Queries only. Query for electronic submissions. Computer printout submissions acceptable; prefers letter-quality. Reports in 1 month. Book catalog for 8½x11 SAE and ms guidelines for #10 SASE.
Nonfiction: Coffee table book, reference and technical. Subjects include Southwest, art, nature, science. "Especially needs manuscripts on the Colorado Plateau that are written for a well-educated general audience." Query or submit outline/synopsis and 3-4 sample chapters. Reviews artwork/photos as part of ms package.
Recent Nonfiction Title: *Summoning the Gods*, by Ronald McCay (anthropology).

‡MUSIC SALES CORP., 24 E. 22nd St., New York NY 10010. (212)254-2100. Imprints include Acorn, Amsco, Ariel, Consolidated, Embassy, Oak, Yorktown, Music Sales Ltd., London; Wise Pub., Ashdown Ltd., and Music Sales, Australia. Editor-in-Chief: Peter Pickow. President (NY office): Barry Edwards. Production Manager: Daniel R. Earley. Publishes paperback originals and reprints. Averages 100 titles/year; receives 75 submissions annually. 33% of books from first-time authors; 99% of books from unagented writers. Standard publishing contracts. Publishes book an average of 6 months after acceptance. Simultaneous and photocopied submissions OK. Computer printout submissions acceptable; no dot-matrix.
Nonfiction: Instructional music books; also technical, theory, reference and pop music personalities. Music Sales Corporation publishes and distributes a complete line of quality music instruction books for every musician from beginner to professional. Reviews artwork/photos as part of ms package.
Recent Nonfiction Title: *Original Randy Rhoads*, by Wolf Marshall.
Tips: "An accurate, well-written manuscript on electronic, hi-tech equipment used by musicians has the best chance of selling to our firm. Use concise, easy-to-understand layman's language to communicate complex or abstract electronic music processes and theory."

MUSTANG PUBLISHING CO., Box 9327, New Haven CT 06533. (203)624-5485. President: Rollin Riggs. Publishes hardcover and trade paperback originals. Averages 6 titles/year; receives 1,000 submissions annually. 50% of books from first-time authors; 100% of books from unagented writers. Pays 6-9% royalty on retail price. Publishes book an average of 1 year after acceptance. Simultaneous and photocopied submissions OK. No electronic submissions. No phone calls, please. Computer printout submissions acceptable; prefers letter-quality. Reports in 1 month. SASE a must. Book catalog available from our distributor: Kampmann & Company, 9 E. 40th St., New York NY 10016.
Nonfiction: How-to, humor and self-help. Subjects include Americana, hobbies, recreation, sports and travel. "Our needs are very general—humor, travel, how-to, nonfiction, etc.—for the 18-to 35-year-old market." Query or submit synopsis and sample chapters.
Recent Nonfiction Title: *Europe for Free*, by Brian Butler.
Tips: "From the proposals we receive, it seems that many writers never go to bookstores and have no idea what sells. Before you waste a lot of time on a nonfiction book idea, ask yourself 'How often have my friends and I actually *bought* a book like this?' Know the market!"

THE NAIAD PRESS, INC., Box 10543, Tallahassee FL 32302. (904)539-9322. Editorial Director: Barbara Grier. Publishes paperback originals. Averages 12 titles/year; receives 255 submissions annually. 20% of books from first-time authors; 99% of books from unagented writers. Average print order for a writer's first book is 12,000. Pays 15% royalty on wholesale or retail price; no advance. Publishes book an average of 1 year after acceptance. Reports in 2 months. Book catalog and ms guidelines for #10 SAE and 43¢ postage.
Fiction: "We publish lesbian fiction, preferably lesbian/feminist fiction. We are not impressed with the 'oh woe' school and prefer realistic (i.e., happy) novels. We emphasize fiction and are now heavily reading manuscripts in that area. We are working in a lot of genre fiction—mysteries, science fiction, short stories, fantasy—all with lesbian themes, of course." Query.
Recent Fiction Title: *Memory Board*, by Jane Rule.
Tips: "There is tremendous world-wide demand for lesbian mysteries from lesbian authors published by lesbian presses, and we are doing several such series."

NATIONAL ASSOCIATION OF SOCIAL WORKERS, 7981 Eastern Ave., Silver Springs MD 20910. Contact: Director of Publications. Averages 8 titles/year; receives 100 submissions annually. 20% of books from first-time authors. 100% of books from unagented writers. Pays 10-15% royalty on net prices. Publishes book an average of 1 year after acceptance. Computer printout submissions OK; prefers letter-quality. Reports in 3 months on submissions. Free book catalog and ms guidelines.
Nonfiction: Textbooks of interest to professional social workers. "We're looking for books on social work in health care, mental health and occupational social work. Books must be directed to the professional social worker and build on the current literature." Submit outline/synopsis and sample chapters. Rarely reviews art-

work/photos as part of ms package.

Recent Nonfiction Title: *The Vulnerable Social Worker*, by Douglas Besharov (textbook on liability).

Tips: "Our audience includes social work practitioners, educators, students and policy makers. They are looking for practice-related books that are well grounded in theory. The books that do well are those that have direct application to the work our audience does. New technology, AIDS, welfare reform and health policy will be of increasing interest to our readers."

*NATIONAL GALLERY OF CANADA, Publications Division, 380 Sussex Dr., Ottawa, Ontario K1N 9N4 Canada. (613)990-0540. Acting Head: Serge Theriault. Editorial Coordinator: Irene Lillico. Publishes hardcover and paperback originals. Averages 15 titles/year. Subsidy publishes (nonauthor) 100% of books. Pays in outright purchase of $1,500-2,500; offers average $700 advance. Photocopied submissions OK. Reports in 3 months. Free sales catalog.

Nonfiction: "In general, we publish only *solicited* manuscripts on art, particularly Canadian art, and must publish them in English and French. Exhibition catalogs are commissioned, but we are open (upon approval by Curatorial general editors) to manuscripts for the various series, monographic and otherwise, that we publish. All manuscripts should be directed to our Editorial Coordinator, who doubles as manuscript editor. Since we publish translations into French, authors have access to French Canada and the rest of Francophonia. Because our titles are distributed by the University of Chicago Press, authors have the attention of European as well as American markets."

Recent Nonfiction Title: *Catalogue of the National Gallery of Canada, Canadian Art, Volume 1, (A-F)*, general editors: Charles C. Hill and Pierre B. Landry.

NATIONAL HEALTH PUBLISHING, a Division of Williams and Wilkins, (formerly Rynd Communications), 99 Painters Mill Rd., Owings Mills MD 21117. (301)363-6400. Acquisitions Editor: Sara M. Sides. Publishes hard and soft cover originals. Averages 15-20 titles/year and quarterly subscription services. Receives 100 submissions annually. 30% of books from first-time authors; 100% of books from unagented writers. Pays 8-12% royalty on retail price. Offers average $300 advance. Publishes book an average of 1 year after acceptance. Query for electronic submissions. Computer printout submissions acceptable; prefers letter-quality. Reports in 2 weeks on queries; 10 weeks on mss. Book catalog for 5½x8½ SAE and 2 first class stamps.

Nonfiction: Reference, technical and textbook. Subjects include health and nursing administration; long term care; health finance; and health law. Needs publications on long term care administration; nurse management and administration; home health care; health finance; adult day care; and organ procurement. Management oriented rather than clinical; prefers works that can be used as professional references and textbooks. Query or submit table of contents, resume and sample chapters.

Recent Nonfiction Title: *Confronting Alzheimer's Disease*, edited by Anne C. Kalicki, published in cooperation with the American Association of Homes for the Aging.

Tips: "We are a growing house devoted to health care. We welcome new authors, whether or not they have already published; we look for academic and experience background and a clear writing style. We also welcome topics which reflect new trends in health care."

NATIONAL PUBLISHERS OF THE BLACK HILLS, INC., 47 Nepperhan Ave., Elmsford NY 10523. Editorial Director: Ellen Schneid Coleman. Publishes trade and text paperback originals and software. Averages 15 titles/year. Pays negotiable royalty; offers negotiable advance. Publishes book an average of 9 months after acceptance. Computer printout submissions acceptable. Reports in 3 weeks on queries; 5 weeks on mss.

Nonfiction: Technical, business and economics texts, medical administrative assisting, computer science texts, travel and hospitality, and general texts aimed at the post-secondary school market. Immediate needs include basic electronics texts, algebra, hospitality and remedial math. Query or submit outline/synopsis and a sample chapter, or complete ms. Reviews artwork/photos as part of ms package.

Recent Nonfiction Title: *Prose and Cons: The Do's and Don'ts of Technical and Business Writing*, by Carol Barnam.

Tips: "We have an increased interest in career training materials in fields of travel and tourism, hospitality and office technology."

NATIONAL TEXTBOOK CO., 4255 W. Touhy Ave., Lincolnwood IL 60646. (312)679-5500. Editorial Director: Leonard I. Fiddle. Publishes originals for education and trade market, and software. Averages 100-150 titles/year; receives 200 submissions annually. 10% of books from first-time authors; 80% of books from unagented writers. Mss purchased on either royalty or buy-out basis. Publishes book an average of 1 year after acceptance. Computer printout submissions acceptable; no dot-matrix. Reports in 4 months. Book catalog and ms guidelines for SAE and 2 first class stamps.

Nonfiction: Textbook. Major emphasis being given to foreign language and language arts texts, especially secondary level material, and business and career subjects (marketing, advertising, sales, etc.). Raymond B. Walters, Language Arts Editor. Michael Ross, Foreign Language and ESL. Michael Urban, Career Guidance.

Harry Briggs, Business Books. Send sample chapter and outline or table of contents.
Recent Nonfiction Title: *Building Real Life English Skills*, by Penn and Starkey (survival reading and writing).

NATUREGRAPH PUBLISHERS, INC., Box 1075, Happy Camp CA 96039. (916)493-5353. Imprint, Prism Editions. Editor: Barbara Brown. Averages 5 titles/year; receives 300 submissions annually. 75% of books from first-time authors; 100% of books from unagented writers. Average print order for a writer's first book is 2,500. "We offer 10% of wholesale; 12½% after 10,000 copies are sold." Publishes book an average of 18 months after acceptance. Photocopied submissions OK. Computer printout submissions acceptable; prefers letter-quality. Reports in 2 months. Book catalog and ms guidelines for #10 SAE with 3 first class stamps.
Nonfiction: Primarily publishes nonfiction for the layman in 7 general areas: natural history (biology, geology, ecology, astronomy); American Indian (historical and contemporary); outdoor living (backpacking, wild edibles, etc.); land and gardening (modern homesteading); crafts and how-to; holistic health (natural foods and healing arts); and PRISM Editions (Baha'i and other New Age approaches to harmonious living). All material must be well-grounded; author must be professional, and in command of effective style. Our natural history and American Indian lines can be geared for educational markets. "To speed things up, queries should include summary, detailed outline, comparison to related books, 2 sample chapters, availability and samples of any photos or illustrations, and author background. Send manuscript only on request." Reviews artwork/photos as part of ms package.
Recent Nonfiction Title: *Indiancraft*, by Chief McIntosh and Harvey Shell.

NELSON-HALL PUBLISHERS, 111 N. Canal St., Chicago IL 60606. (312)930-9446. Editorial Director: Harold Wise, Ph.D. Publishes hardcover and paperback originals. Averages 105 titles/year. Pays 15% maximum royalty on retail price; offers average advance. Photocopied submissions OK. Reports in 1 month. Free book catalog.
Nonfiction: Textbooks and general scholarly books in the social sciences. Query.
Recent Nonfiction Title: *Criminology*, by Charles Hagan.

NEW AMERICAN LIBRARY, 1633 Broadway, New York NY 10019. (212)397-8000. Imprints include Signet, Mentor, Signet Classics, Plume, Meridian, D.A.W. Books, Onyx and NAL Books. Publisher: Elaine Koster. Editor-in-Chief: Maureen Baron. Editor-in-Chief/Trade Books: Arnold Dolin. Executive Editor/Hardcover: Michaela Hamilton. Publishes hardcover and paperback originals and hardcover reprints. Publishes 350 titles/year. Royalty is "variable"; offers "substantial" advance. Query letters *only*. Replies in 1 month. Free book catalog.
Tips: Queries may be routed to other editors in the publishing group.

‡***NEW CITY PRESS**, 206 Skillman Ave., Brooklyn NY 11211. (718)782-2844. General Manager: Gary Brandl. Publishes trade paperback originals. Publishes 8-10 titles/year. Receives 15 submissions/year. 30% of books from first-time authors; 50% from unagented writers. Subsidy publishes 30% of books. Pays 8-10% royalty. Publishes book an average of 6 months after acceptance. Simultaneous and photocopied submissions OK. Query for electronic submissions. Computer printout submissions OK; prefers letter-quality. Reports in 2 weeks on queries; 1 month on mss.
Nonfiction: Subjects include philosophy and religion. "We need manuscripts on prayer, meditation, family life, biographies (religious), spirituality with a (preferable) Catholic background." Query or submit outline/synopsis and sample chapters.
Recent Nonfiction Title: *Interview with C. Lubich*, by William Proctor (spirituality).

THE NEW ENGLAND PRESS, INC., Box 575, Shelburne VT 05482. (802)863-2520/985-2569. President: Alfred Rosa. Small press. Publishes hardcover and trade paperback originals and trade paperback reprints. Averages 6-12 titles/year; receives 200 submissions annually. 25% of books from first-time authors; 75% of books from unagented writers. Pays 10-15% royalty on wholesale price. Publishes ms an average of 1 year after acceptance. Photocopied submissions OK. Computer printout submissions acceptable; no dot-matrix. Reports in 2 weeks on queries; 1 month on mss. Free book catalog.
Nonfiction: Biography, cookbook, how-to, nature and illustrated book. Subjects include Americana (Vermontiana and New England); history (New England orientation); and essays (New England orientation). No juvenile or psychology. Query or submit outline/synopsis and sample chapters. Reviews artwork/photos.
Recent Nonfiction Title: *Vermont Golf Courses: A Player's Guide*, by Bob Labbance and David Cornwell.
Fiction: Historical (New England orientation). No novels. Query.

NEW LEAF PRESS, INC., Box 311, Green Forest AR 72638. Editor-in-Chief: Harriett Dudley. Publishes hardcover and paperback originals. Specializes in charismatic books. Publishes 15 titles/year; receives 236 submissions annually. 15% of books from first-time authors; 90% of books from unagented writers. Average print order for a writer's first book is 10,000. Pays 10% royalty on first 10,000 copies, paid once a year; no advance. Send photos and illustrations to accompany ms. Publishes book an average of 10 months after accept-ance. Simultaneous and photocopied submissions OK. Reports in 3 months. Reviews artwork/photos as part of ms package. Book catalog and guidelines for 8½x11 SAE with 5 first class stamps.

Nonfiction: Biography and self-help. Charismatic books; life stories, and how to live the Christian life. Length: 100-400 pages. Submit complete ms.

Recent Nonfiction Title: *The Kingdom*, by Mel Fari.

Tips: "Biographies, relevant nonfiction, and Bible-based fiction have the best chance of selling to our firm. Honest and real-life experience help make a book or query one we can't put down."

NEW READERS PRESS, Publishing division of Laubach Literacy International, Box 131, Syracuse NY 13210. Acquisitions Editor: Kay Koschnick. Publishes paperback originals. Averages 30 titles/year; receives 200 submissions annually. 40% of books by first-time authors; 100% of books by unagented writers. Average print order for a writer's first book is 5,000. "Most of our sales are to high school classes for slower learners, special education, and adult basic education programs, with some sales to volunteer literacy programs, private human services agencies, prisons, and libraries with outreach programs for poor readers." Pays royalty on re-tail price, or by outright purchase. Rate varies according to type of publication and length of manuscript. Ad-vance is "different in each case, but does not exceed projected royalty for first year." Publishes book an aver-age of 1 year after acceptance. Photocopied submissions OK. Query for electronic submissions. Computer printout submissions acceptable; prefers letter-quality. Reports in 2 months. Free book catalog and authors' brochure.

Nonfiction: "Our audience is adults and older teenagers with limited reading skills (6th grade level and be-low). We publish basic education materials in reading and writing, math, social studies, health, science, and English-as-a-second-language for double illiterates. We are particularly interested in materials that fulfill cur-riculum requirements in these areas. Manuscripts must be not only easy to read (3rd-6th grade level) but mature in tone and concepts. We are not interested in poetry or anything at all written for children." Submit outline and 1-3 sample chapters. Reviews artwork/photos as part of ms package.

Recent Nonfiction Title: *The Constitution Made Easier*, by Simmie G. Plummer.

Fiction: Short novels (12,000-15,000 words) at third grade reading level on themes of interest to adults and older teenagers. Submit synopsis.

Recent Fiction Title: *Modern Fables: Twenty of Aesop's Fables Brought Up to Date*, by Bernard Jackson and Susie Quintanilla.

*NEW SOCIETY PUBLISHERS, 4722 Baltimore Ave., Philadelphia PA 19143. (215)726-6543. Collectively managed. Publishes hardcover and trade paperback originals and reprints. Averages 18 titles/year; receives 200 submissions annually. 80% of books from first-time authors; 95% of books from unagented writers. Subsidy publishes (nonauthor) 10% of books. Pays 10% royalty on net receipts. Offers average $500 advance. Publishes book an average of 18 months after acceptance. Photocopied submissions OK. Computer printout submissions acceptable; prefers letter-quality. Reports in 1 month on queries; 3 months on mss. Book catalog and ms guidelines for #10 SASE.

Nonfiction: Illustrated book, social self-help and books on nonviolent action (case studies). Subjects include history, philosophy, politics, cooperative economics, religion, sociology, feminism, ecology, worker self-management, group dynamics and peace issues. No books about the damage which will be done by nuclear war. Query *only*; "all unsolicited mss are thrown in trash." Reviews artwork/photos as part of ms package.

Recent Nonfiction Title: *Economics as if the Earth Really Mattered*, by Susan Meeker-Lairy (community economics).

NEW VICTORIA PUBLISHERS, Box 27, Norwich VT 05055. (802)649-5297. Editor: Claudia Lamperti. Publishes trade paperback originals. Averages 4 titles/year; receives 100 submissions/year. 100% of books from first-time authors; 100% of books from unagented writers. Pays 10% royalty on wholesale price. Publishes book an average of 6 months after acceptance. Photocopied submissions OK. Query for electronic submissions. Computer printout submissions OK. Reports on queries in 2 weeks; on mss in 1 month. Free book catalog.

Nonfiction: History. "We are interested in feminist history or biography and interviews with or topics relat-ing to lesbians. No poetry." Submit outline/synopis and sample chapters.

Recent Nonfiction Title: *Radical Feminists of Hetereodoxy*, by Judith Schwarz (feminist history).

Fiction: Adventure, erotica, fantasy, historical, humor, mystery, romance, science fiction and western. "We will consider most anything if it is well written and appeals to lesbian/feminist audience." Submit outline/syn-opsis and sample chapters.

Recent Fiction Title: *Something Shady*, by Sarah Dreher (mystery adventure).

Tips: "Try to appeal to a specific audience and not write for the general market."

*NEW YORK ZOETROPE, INC., 838 Broadway, New York NY 10003. (212)420-0590. Contact: James Monaco. Publishes hardcover and trade paperback originals, hardcover and trade paperback reprints and software. Averages 25-35 titles/year; receives 25-50 submissions annually. 25% of books from first-time authors; 75% of books from unagented writers. Subsidy publishes (nonauthor) 3% of books. Pays 10-20% royalty on wholesale prices or makes outright purchase of $500-1,000. Offers average $1,000 advance. Publishes book an average of 9 months after acceptance. Simultaneous and photocopied submissions OK. Query for electronic submissions. Computer printout submissions acceptable; prefers letter-quality. Reports in 2 weeks on queries; 2 months on mss. Book catalog and guidelines for 6x9 SAE.

Nonfiction: Coffee table book, reference, technical and textbook. Subjects include computers, travel and media. Interested especially in film and computer subjects. No fiction. Query with a synopsis and outline.

Recent Nonfiction Title: *Louise Brooks: Portrait of an Anti-Star*, by Roland Jaccard, editor; English translation by Gideon Y. Schein.

Tips: "Film- or media-oriented (academic and popular) subjects have the best chance of selling to our firm. Media books are our strongest line."

NEWCASTLE PUBLISHING CO., INC., 13419 Saticoy, North Hollywood CA 91605. (213)873-3191. Editor-in-Chief: Alfred Saunders. Publishes trade paperback originals and reprints. Averages 10 titles/year; receives 300 submissions annually. 70% of books from first-time authors; 95% of books from unagented writers. Average print order for a writer's first book is 3,000-5,000. Pays 5-10% royalty on retail price; no advance. Publishes book an average of 8 months after acceptance. Simultaneous and photocopied submissions OK. Computer printout submissions acceptable; prefers letter-quality. Reports in 3 weeks on queries; 6 weeks on mss. Free book catalog; ms guidelines for SASE.

Nonfiction: How-to, self-help, metaphysical and New Age. Subjects include health (physical fitness, diet and nutrition), psychology and religion. "Our audience is made up of college students and college-age nonstudents; also, adults ages 25 and up. They are of above average intelligence and are fully aware of what is available in the bookstores." No biography, travel, children's books, poetry, cookbooks or fiction. Query or submit outline/synopsis and sample chapters. Looks for "something to grab the reader so that he/she will readily remember that passage."

Recent Nonfiction Title: *Authentic I Ching*, by Henry Wei, Ph.D (translation of I Ching by a Chinese national).

Tips: "Check the shelves in the larger bookstores on the subject of the manuscript being submitted. A book on life extension, holistic health, or stress management has the best chance of selling to our firm."

‡NEWMARKET PRESS, Newmarket Publishing and Communications, 18 E. 48th St., 15th Floor, New York NY 10017. (212)832-3575. Imprints include Medallion. Publishes hardcover and trade paperback originals and mass market paperback reprints. Publishes 20 titles/year. Receives approximately 1,000 submissions/year. 50% of books from unagented writers. Pays negotiable royalty. "We may use writers for flat-fee hire in cooperation with an expert on a topic." Advance negotiable. Publishes ms an average of 9 months after acceptance. Simultaneous and photocopied submissions OK. Computer printout submissions OK; prefers letter-quality. Reports in 3 weeks on queries and 2 months on mss. Book catalog for 9x12 SAE with 3 first class stamps.

Nonfiction: Biography, cookbook, self-help. Subjects include child guidance/parenting, cooking, foods and nutrition, health/medicine, history, military/war, money/finance, music, psychology, women's issues/studies. Query or submit outline/synopsis and sample chapters. Reviews artwork/photos as part of ms package.

Recent Nonfiction Title: *Enter the Dragon: China's Undeclared War Against the U.S. in Korea, 1950-51*, by Russell Spurr (history).

Fiction: Historical, literary, mainstream/contemporary. "At this time, fiction constitutes only a small part of the Newmarket list." Query or submit outline/synopsis and sample chapters. "With fiction, we find information on the author's background and publishing record especially helpful."

Recent Fiction Title: *Stolen Goods*, by Susan Dworkin (novel).

Tips: "Small publishers are increasingly better able to handle, and more interested in seeing, mid-list titles that the larger, merger-and-acquisitions-plagued companies bypass. If I were trying to market a book today, I would make sure it's appropriate for the house to which I'm sending it."

‡NICHOLS PUBLISHING, Subsidiary of GP Publishing Inc., Box 96, New York NY 10024. (212)580-8079. Subsidiaries include GP Courseware. Vice President and Publisher: Linda Kahn. Publishes hardcover and paperback originals. Firm publishes 50 titles/year; division publishes 40 titles/year. 15% of books from first-time authors; 98% from unagented writers. Pays 5-15% royalty on wholesale price. Offers $500 average advance. Publishes book an average of 9 months after acceptance. Simultaneous and photocopied submissions OK. Query for electronic submissions. Computer printout submissions OK; prefers letter-quality. Reports on queries in 1 week; 6 weeks on mss. Book catalog and ms guidelines free on request.

Nonfiction: Reference, software, technical. Subjects include architecture, business and economics, computers and electronics, education, money/finance, training, energy, engineering. Submit outline/synopsis and sample chapters or complete ms.

Recent Nonfiction Title: *The Marketing Mirage*, by Colin McInes (business).

NORTH LIGHT, Imprint of F&W Publications, 1507 Dana Ave., Cincinnati OH 45207. Editorial Director: David Lewis. Publishes hardcover and trade paperback originals. Averages 20-25 titles/year. Pays 10% royalty on net receipts. Offers $3,000 advance. Simultaneous submissions OK. Reports in 3 weeks on queries; 2 months on mss. Book catalog for 9x12 SAE with 6 first class stamps.
Nonfiction: Art and graphic arts instruction books. Interested in books on watercolor painting, oil painting, basic drawing, pen and ink, airbrush, markers, basic design, color, illustration techniques, layout and typography. Do not submit coffee table art books with no how-to art instruction. Query or submit outline/synopsis and examples of artwork (photographs of artwork are OK).
Recent Nonfiction Title: *Dynamic Airbrush*.

‡NORTHERN ILLINOIS UNIVERSITY PRESS, DeKalb IL 60115. (815)753-1826/753-1075. Director: Mary L. Lincoln. Pays 10-15% royalty on wholesale price. Free catalog.
Nonfiction: "The NIU Press publishes mainly history, political science, literary criticism and regional studies. It does not consider collections of previously published articles, essays, etc., nor do we consider unsolicited poetry." Accepts nonfiction translations. Query with outline/synopsis and 1-3 sample chapters.
Recent Nonfiction Title: *Chicago Divided: The Making of a Black Mayor*, by Paul Kleppner.

W.W. NORTON CO., INC., 500 5th Ave., New York NY 10110. (212)354-5500. Editor: Liz Malcolm. Imprint includes Shoreline Books. Publishes 213 titles/year; receives 5,000 submissions annually. Often publishes new and unagented authors. Royalty varies on retail price; advance varies. Publishes book an average of 1 year after acceptance. Photocopied and simultaneous submissions OK. Computer printout submissions acceptable. Submit outline and/or 2-3 sample chapters for fiction and nonfiction. Return of material not guaranteed without return packaging and postage. Reports in 2 months. Book catalog and guidelines for 8½x11 SAE with 2 first class stamps.
Nonfiction and Fiction: "General, adult fiction and nonfiction of all kinds on nearly all subjects and of the highest quality possible within the limits of each particular book." No occult, paranormal, religion, genre fiction, formula romances, science fiction or westerns, cookbooks, arts and crafts, young adult or children's books. Last year there were 93 book club rights sales; 36 mass paperback reprint sales; and "innumerable serializations, second serial, syndication, translations, etc." Looks for "clear, intelligent, creative writing on original subjects or with original characters."
Recent Nonfiction Title: *Siblings Without Rivalry*, by Adele Faber and Elaine Mazlish.
Recent Fiction Title: *Under Cover of Daylight*, by James W. Hall.
Tips: "Long novels are too expensive—keep them under 350 (manuscript) pages."

NOYES DATA CORP., Imprints include Noyes Press and Noyes Publications, Noyes Bldg., Park Ridge NJ 07656. Publishes hardcover originals. Averages 60 titles/year. Pays 10%-12% royalty on retail price; advance varies, depending on author's reputation and nature of book. Reports in 2 weeks. Free book catalog.
Nonfiction: Noyes Press publishes art, classical studies, archaeology, and history. "Material directed to the intelligent adult and the academic market." Noyes Publications publishes technical books on practical industrial processing, science, economic books pertaining to chemistry, chemical engineering, food, textiles, energy, electronics, pollution control—primarily of interest to the business executive. Length: 50,000-250,000 words. Query Editorial Department.

OAK TREE PUBLICATIONS, Vizcom, Inc., Suite 202, 9601 Aero Dr., San Diego CA 92123. (619)560-5163. Subsidiaries include: Value Tale Comunications. Editor: Linda Aliot. Publishes hardcover originals. Averages 10 titles/year; receives hundreds of submissions annually. 5% of books from first-time writers; 50% of books from unagented authors. Pays variable royalty on wholesale price; offers $500 average advance. Publishes book an average of 8 months after acceptance. Simultaneous submissions OK. Computer printout submissions OK; prefers letter-quality. Reports in 1 month on queries; 3 months on mss. Book catalog for 8½x11 SAE with 3 first class stamps; ms guidelines for SASE.
Fiction: "Juvenile picture books with mass market appeal and licensed toy tie-in." Submit outline/synopsis and sample chapters. Reviews artwork/photos as part of ms package.
Recent Fiction Title: *I Wish I Had A Computer That Makes Waffles*, by Dobson.

OASIS PRESS, Subsidiary of PSI Research, 720 S. Hillview Dr., Milpitas CA 95035. (408)263-9671. Publisher: Emmett Ramey. Publishes hardcover originals. Averages 25-30 titles/year; receives 25-30 submissions annually. 10% of books from first-time authors. 95% of books from unagented writers. Pays 8-15% royalty on wholesale price. Offers no advance. Publishes book an average of 10 months after acceptance. Simultaneous submissions OK. Query for electronic submissions. Computer printout submissions OK. Reports in 1 week. Book catalog free on request.
Nonfiction: How-to and self-help. Subjects include business and economics.
Recent Nonfiction Title: *Financial Management for Small Business*, by Ambrosius.
Tips: "We will not respond to non-business related topics."

OCTAMERON ASSOCIATES, 820 Fontaine St., Alexandria VA 22302. (703)823-1882. Editorial Director: Karen Stokstad. Publishes trade paperback originals. Averages 15 titles/year; receives 100 submissions annually. 10% of books from first-time authors; 100% of books from unagented writers. Average print order for a writer's first book is 8,000-10,000. Pays 7½% royalty on retail price. Publishes book an average of 6 months after acceptance. Simultaneous submissions OK. Query for electronic submissions. Computer printout submissions acceptable; prefers letter-quality to dot-matrix. Reports in 2 weeks. Book catalog and guidelines for #10 SAE and 2 first class stamps.
Nonfiction: Reference, career and post-secondary education subjects. Especially interested in "paying-for-college and college admission guides." Query. Submit outline/synopsis and 2 sample chapters. Reviews artwork/photos as part of ms package.
Recent Nonfiction Title: *Admit One!*, by G. Gary Ripple.

ODDO PUBLISHING, INC., Box 68, Redwine Rd., Fayetteville GA 30214. (404)461-7627. Managing Editor: Genevieve Oddo. Publishes hardcover and paperback originals. Averages 4 titles/year; receives 300 submissions annually. 25% of books from first-time authors; 100% of books from unagented writers. Average print order for a writer's first book is 3,500. Makes outright purchase. "We judge all scripts independently." Royalty considered for special scripts only. Publishes book an average of 2-3 years after acceptance. Computer printout submissions acceptable; no dot-matrix. Reports in 4 months. Book catalog for 9x12 SAE with $1.07 postage.
Nonfiction and Fiction: Publishes juvenile books in language arts, workbooks in math, writing (English), photophonics, science (space and oceanography), and social studies for schools, libraries, and trade. Interested in children's supplementary readers in the areas of language arts, math, science, social studies, etc. "Texts run from 1,500 to 3,500 words. Ecology, space, patriotism, oceanography and pollution are subjects of interest. Manuscripts must be easy to read, general, and not set to outdated themes. They must lend themselves to full color illustration. No stories of grandmother long ago. No love angle, permissive language, or immoral words or statements." Submit complete ms. Reviews artwork/photos as part of ms package.
Recent Fiction Title: *Bobby Bear and the Kite Contest*, by Marilue.
Tips: "We are currently expanding our line to include materials more acceptable in the trade market. To do so, we are concentrating on adding titles to our top selling series in lieu of developing new series; however, we will consider other scripts."

OHARA PUBLICATIONS, INC., 1813 Victory Place, Box 7728, Burbank CA 91510-7728. Contact: Editor. Publishes trade paperback originals. Averages 12 titles/year. Pays royalty. Photocopied submissions OK. Write for guidelines. Reports in 3 weeks on queries; 8 weeks on mss.
Nonfiction: Martial arts. "We decide to do a book on a specific martial art, then seek out the most qualified martial artist to author that book. 'How to' books are our mainstay, and we will accept no manuscript that does not pertain to martial arts systems (their history, techniques, philosophy, etc.)." Query first, then submit outline/synopsis and sample chapter. Include author biography and copies of credentials.
Recent Nonfiction Title: *Advanced Wing Chun*, by William Cheung (how-to).

OHIO STATE UNIVERSITY PRESS, 1050 Carmack Rd., Columbus OH 43210. (614)292-6930. Director: Peter J. Givler. Pays royalty on wholesale or retail price. Averages 30 titles/year. Reports in 3 months; ms held longer with author's permission.
Nonfiction: Publishes history, biography, science, philosophy, the arts, political science, law, literature, economics, education, sociology, anthropology, geography, and general scholarly nonfiction. Query with outline and sample chapters.
Recent Nonfiction Title: *Paintings from Books: Art and Literature in Britain, 1760-1900*, by Richard D. Altick.
Tips: Publishes some poetry and fiction.

*OISE PRESS, Subsidiary of Ontario Institute for Studies in Education, 252 Floor, W., Toronto, Ontario M5S 1V6 Canada. (416)923-6641, ext. 2531. Editor-in-Chief: Hugh Oliver. Publishes trade paperback originals. Averages 25 titles/year; receives 100 submissions annually. 20% of books from first-time authors. 90% of books from unagented writers. Subsidy publishes (nonauthor) 5% of books. Pays 10-15% royalty; rarely offers an advance. Simultaneous and photocopied submissions OK. Query for electronic submissions. Computer printout submissions OK; prefers letter-quality. Reports in 1 week on queries; 2 months on submissions. Book catalog and guidelines free on request.
Nonfiction: Textbooks and educational books. "Our audience includes educational scholars; educational administrators, principals and teachers and students. In the future, we will be publishing fewer scholarly books and more books for teachers and students." Submit complete ms. Reviews artwork/photos as part of ms package.
Recent Nonfiction Title: *Miseduction: Women and Canadian Universities*, by Innis Dagg and Pat J. Thompson.

THE OLD ARMY PRESS, Box 2243, Ft. Collins CO 80522. (303)484-5535. General Manager: Dee Koury. Publishes hardcover and trade paperback originals; hardcover and trade paperback reprints. Averages 6 titles/year; receives 20 submissions annually. 50% of books from first-time authors. 100% of books from unagented writers. Pays 5-10% royalty on wholesale price. Publishes book an average of 18 months after acceptance. Photocopied submissions OK. Query for electronic submissions. Computer printout submissions OK; prefers letter-quality. Reports in 3 weeks on queries; 3 months on submissions.
Nonfiction: Biography and reference—all related to western military history. Especially needs mss on Indian wars and Texas history. Query. Reviews artwork/photos as part of ms package.
Recent Nonfiction Title: *Indian Campaigns*, by Harry H. Anderson, ed.

‡**ONCE UPON A PLANET, INC.**, 65-42 Fresh Meadow Lane, Fresh Meadows NY 11365. (718)961-9240. Subsidiaries include Planet Books and Greeting Books. President: Charles Faraone. Publishes trade paperback originals. Publishes 10-15 titles/year. Receives approximately 500 proposals/year. Pays authors 5-15% royalty on wholesale price, outright $500-3,000 purchase or flat amount per book printed or per book sold. Offers average advance of $500-1,000. Publishes ms an average of 3 months after acceptance. Simultaneous and photocopied submissions OK. Computer printout submissions OK. Reports in 2 weeks on queries and 3 weeks on mss. Book catalog and ms guidelines for #10 SAE.
Nonfiction: Humor, illustrated books. "We are not interested in nonfiction unless it is funny and can be edited into our format." Query or submit outline/synopsis and sample chapters.
Recent Nonfiction Title: *How to Make a Million Dollars*, by Charles Faraone (parody).
Fiction: Humor. "We published small, 32-page, hopefully funny, often illustrated book distributed primarily in the gift industry worldwide. We'd like to find 10-15 books each year in fiction and nonfiction that will fit our format." Query or submit outline/synopsis and sample chapters.
Tips: "Too many weak ideas that couldn't fill our little format are stretched to death in trade paperbacks. In general, I'm most likely to make an offer on a book that makes me laugh and includes enough material to edit into a little gem. Our audience is international and very broad. Judging from our mail I'd say they enjoy a good laugh and like to share good books."

***OPEN COURT PUBLISHING CO.**, Box 599, Peru IL 61354. Publisher: M. Blouke Carus. General Manager: Dr. André Carus. Averages 10 titles/year; receives 300 submissions annually. 20% of books from first-time authors; 80% of books from unagented writers. Subsidy publishes 15% of books; 10% nonauthor subsidy. Royalty contracts negotiable for each book. Publishes book an average of 18 months after acceptance. Query for electronic submissions. Computer printout submissions acceptable; prefers letter-quality. Guidelines for 9x12 SAE.
Nonfiction: Philosophy, psychology, Jungian analysis, science and history of science, mathematics, public policy, comparative religions, education, Orientalia, and related scholarly topics. Accepts nonfiction translations. "This is a publishing house run as an intellectual enterprise, to reflect the concerns of its staff and as a service to the world of learning." Query or submit outline/synopsis and 2-3 sample chapters. Reviews artwork/photos as part of ms package.
Recent Nonfiction Title: *The Many Faces of Realism*, by Hillary Putnam.
Tips: "Many writers do not follow up with phone calls or letters once they have submitted their ms."

***ORBIS BOOKS**, Maryknoll NY 10545. (914)941-7590. Editor-in-Chief: Robert Ellsberg. Publishes cloth and paperback originals and translations. Publishes 40 titles/year. Subsidy publishes (nonauthor) 20% of books. Pays 10-12½-15% royalty on net prices; offers average $1,000 advance. Query with outline, 2 sample chapters, and prospectus. Query for electronic submissions. Reports in 6 weeks. Enclose return postage.
Nonfiction: "Religious developments in Asia, Africa and Latin America. Global justice and peace issues. Christianity and world religions."
Recent Nonfiction Title: *Sanctuary: The New Underground Railroad*.

‡***OREGON HISTORICAL SOCIETY PRESS**, Oregon Historical Society, 1230 SW Park, Portland OR 97205. (503)222-1741. Assistant Director—Publications: Bruce T. Hamilton. Hardcover originals and trade paperback originals and reprints. Publishes 12-14 titles/year. Receives 300 submissions/year. 75% of books from first-time authors; 100% from unagented writers. Subsidy publishes 70% (nonauthor) of books. Pays royalty on wholesale price or makes outright purchase. Publishes book an average of 18 months after acceptance. Simultaneous and photocopied submissions OK. Query for electronic submissions. Reports in 1 week on

Market conditions are constantly changing! If this is 1990 or later, buy the newest edition of Writer's Market at your favorite bookstore or order directly from Writer's Digest Books.

queries; 3 months on mss. Free book catalog. Ms guidelines for #10 SAE with 1 first class stamp.
Nonfiction: Subjects include Americana, art/architecture, biography, ethnic, government/politics, history, military/war, nature/environment, photography, reference, regional. Query or submit outline/synopsis and sample chapters or submit complete ms. Reviews artwork/photos as part of ms package.
Recent Nonfiction Title: *Wildflowers of the Columbia Gorge*, by Russ Jolley (nature).

*OREGON STATE UNIVERSITY PRESS, 101 Waldo Hall, Corvallis OR 97331. (503)754-3166. Hardcover and paperback originals. Averages 6 titles/year; receives 100 submissions annually. 75% of books from first-time authors; 100% of books from unagented writers. Average print order for a writer's first book is 1,500. Subsidy publishes (nonauthor) 40% of books. Pays royalty on wholesale price. No advance. Publishes book an average of 1 year after acceptance. Query for electronic submissions. Computer printout submissions acceptable; no dot-matrix. Reports in 1 month. Book catalog for 6x9 SAE with 2 first class stamps.
Nonfiction: Publishes scholarly books in history, biography, geography, literature, life sciences and natural resource management, with strong emphasis on Pacific or Northwestern topics. Submit outline/synopsis and sample chapters.
Recent Nonfiction Title: *William L. Finley: Pioneer Wildlife Photographer*, by Worth Mathewson (biography/photos).

ORTHO INFORMATION SERVICES, Subsidiary of Chevron Chemical Co., 575 Market St., San Francisco CA 94105. (415)894-0277. Editorial Director: Christine L. Robertson. Imprints include California Culinary Academy (nonfiction), Sally Smith, project editor. Publishes hardcover and trade paperback originals and reprints and quarterly Chevron Travel Club Magazine. Averages 20-30 titles/year; receives 100 submissions annually. 10% of books from first-time authors; 20% of books from unagented writers. Makes outright purchase. Publishes book an average of 2 years after acceptance. Simultaneous submissions OK. Query for electronic submissions. Computer printout submissions acceptable; prefers letter-quality. Reports in 3 weeks on queries; 1 month on mss. Book catalog and guidelines for 9x12 SAE with 2 first class stamps.
Nonfiction: Cookbook, how-to, illustrated book and reference. Subjects include cooking and foods, hobbies, nature, gardening and home repair. "All our projects are internally generated from project proposals—assignment of author, photographers, some illustration from project outline, including outside submissions." No anecdotal/biographical gardening, how-to, cooking or previously covered topics. Query. "We prefer outline following query with synopsis." All unsolicited mss are returned unopened.
Recent Nonfiction Title: *Upholstery*, by Karin Shakery (how-to).

‡ORYX PRESS, 2214 N. Central Ave., Phoenix AZ 85004. (602)254-6156. President/Editorial Director: Phyllis B. Steckler. Publishes hardcover and paperback originals. Averages 40 titles/year; receives 300 submissions annually. 40% of books from first-time authors; 100% of books from unagented writers. Average print order for a writer's first book is 1,000. Pays 10-15% royalty on net receipts; no advance. Publishes book an average of 9 months after acceptance. Query for electronic submissions. Computer printout submissions acceptable; prefers letter-quality. Reports in 2 months. Free book catalog and ms guidelines.
Nonfiction: Bibliographies, directories, general reference, library and information science, business reference, health care, gerontology, automation, and agriculture monographs. Publishes nonfiction for public, college and university, junior college, school and special libraries; agriculture specialists, health care deliverers; and managers. Query or submit outline/synopsis and 1 sample chapter, or complete ms. Queries/mss may be routed to other editors in the publishing group.
Recent Nonfiction Title: *The Nonsexist Word Finder: A Dictionary of Gender-Free Usage*, by Rosalie Maggio.

OUR SUNDAY VISITOR, INC., 200 Noll Plaza, Huntington IN 46750. (219)356-8400. Director: Robert Lockwood. Publishes paperback originals and reprints. Averages 20-30 titles a year; receives 75 submissions annually. 10% of books from first-time authors; 90% of books from unagented writers. Pays variable royalty on net receipts; offers average $500 advance. Publishes book an average of 1 year after acceptance. Query for electronic submissions. Computer printout submissions acceptable; prefers letter-quality. Reports in 1 month on most queries and submissions. Author's guide and catalog for SASE.
Nonfiction: Catholic viewpoints on current issues, reference and guidance, Bibles and devotional books, and Catholic heritage books. Prefers to see well-developed proposals as first submission with "annotated outline, three sample chapters, and definition of intended market." Reviews artwork/photos as part of ms package.
Recent Nonfiction Title: *Those Who Saw Her*, by Catherine Odell.
Tips: "Solid devotional books that are not first person, well-researched church histories or lives of the saints and self-help for those over 55 have the best chance of selling to our firm. Make it solidly Catholic, unique, without pious platitudes."

‡THE OVERLOOK PRESS, Distributed by Viking/Penguin, 12 W. 21st St., New York NY 10010. (212)337-5200. Contact: Editorial Department. Imprints include Tusk Books. Publishes hardcover and trade paperback originals and hardcover reprints. Averages 40 titles/year; receives 300 submissions annually. Pays 3-15% royalty on wholesale or retail price. Submissions accepted only through literary agents. Reports in 2 months. Free book catalog.

Nonfiction: How-to and reference. Subjects include Americana, business and economics, history, nature, recreation, sports, and travel. No pornography.

Fiction: Adventure, ethnic, fantasy/science fiction, historical, mainstream, mystery/suspense. "We tend not to publish commercial fiction."

Recent Fiction Title: *The Universe and Other Fictions*, by Paul West.

Poetry: "We like to publish poets who have a strong following—those who read in New York City regularly or publish in periodicals regularly." No poetry from unpublished authors. Submit complete ms.

Recent Poetry Title: *To An Idea*, by David Shapiro.

Tips: "We are a very small company. If authors want a very quick decision, they should go to another company first and come back to us. We try to be as prompt as possible, but it sometimes takes over 3 months for us to get to a final decision."

OWL CREEK PRESS, 1620 N. 45th St., Seattle WA 98103. Editor: Rich Ives. Small press. Publishes hardcover, trade paperback and mass market paperback originals, and mass market paperback reprints. Averages 5-10 titles/year; receives 2,000 submissions annually. 50% of books from first-time authors; 95% of books from unagented writers. Pays 10-20% royalty on wholesale price (cash or equivalent in copies). If paid in copies, royalty is advanced. Photocopied submissions OK. Computer printout submissions acceptable; prefers letter-quality. Reports in 2 months. Book catalog for #10 SASE.

Nonfiction: Photography. "Our selections are made solely on the basis of lasting artistic quality." No cookbooks, how-to, juvenile, self-help, technical or reference. Submit outline/synopsis and sample chapters.

Recent Nonfiction Title: *The Truth About the Territory*, edited by Rick Ives (anthology-Northwest).

Fiction: "We seek writing of lasting artistic merit in all areas. Writing genre is irrelevant, although we avoid easy approaches and formula work. We are not interested in writing that attempts to fulfill genre requirements or comply with preconceived notions of mass market appeal. If it's work of lasting quality we will try to find and build a market for it." Submit outline/synopsis and sample chapters.

Recent Fiction Title: *Sailing to Corinth*, by Irene Wanner.

Poetry: "We publish both full-length and chapbook titles. Selections are based solely on the lasting quality of the manuscripts. No manuscripts where genre category or preconceived ideas of mass market appeal dominate the work." Submit complete ms, unsolicited through contests only.

Recent Poetry Title: *The Green Dusk*, by Mildred Weston (poetry).

Tips: "We attempt to reach the reader with a somewhat discerning taste first. Future plans include further expansion into fiction and translated titles (both poetry and fiction) as well as maintaining a continued series of both full-length and chapbook poetry originals. We are nonprofit, dedicated to the promotion of literary art."

P.P.I. PUBLISHING, 835 E. Congress Park, Box 335, Dayton OH 45459. (513)433-2709. Vice President: Kim Brooks. Publishes mass market paperback originals (booklets). Averages 30-40 titles/year; receives 200 submissions annually. 40% of books from first-time authors; 100% of books from unagented writers. Average print order for a writer's first book is 1,000. Pays 10% royalty on retail selling price to customer (some customer discounts). Publishes book an average of 3 months after acceptance. Simultaneous and photocopied submissions OK. Computer printout submissions acceptable; no dot-matrix. Reports in 6 weeks on queries; 10-12 weeks on mss. Book catalog with guidelines for SAE and 3 first class stamps.

Nonfiction: Juvenile and teens. Subjects include controversial issues and current events. "We publish nonfiction booklets of 20,000 words or larger for junior and senior high schools, libraries, colleges, universities and other specialized markets such as social service organizations. Our main subjects include controversial issues and items in the news. Topics that students are preparing for research papers or debates are of particular interest. We keep our markets informed on what's happening today in the world, in the home, in schools, and for the future. Some recent topics that were published include nuclear energy, AIDS, drug and alcohol abuse, teen suicide, violence in society, national healthcare, industrial/chemical leaks and accidents, and nuclear war. We are especially looking for 20,000-word manuscripts or larger on current events. We're not interested in how-to, technical material, travel or cookbooks." Submit outline/synopsis, sample chapters or complete ms. "For new authors we prefer outlines or queries to save them time and effort." Reviews artwork/photos as part of ms package on a limited basis.

Recent Nonfiction Title: *Drugs: the Inside Dope*, by Donald W. Eaker, Ph.D. and Joyce J. Dorner, R.N., M.N.

Tips: "Abortion, capital punishment, gun control, nuclear energy, AIDS are but a few areas that have been of interest to us and society for quite a while and should remain current throughout the near future. Our largest market is high schools."

PACIFIC BOOKS, PUBLISHERS, Box 558, Palo Alto CA 94302. (415)856-0550. Editor: Henry Ponleithner. Averages 6-12 titles/year. Royalty schedule varies with book. No advance. Send complete ms. Computer printout submissions OK "if clean, typewriter-quality." Reports "promptly." Book catalog and guidelines for 9x12 SAE.

Nonfiction: General interest, professional, technical and scholarly nonfiction trade books. Specialties include western Americana and Hawaiiana. Looks for "well-written, documented material of interest to a significant audience." Also considers text and reference books; high school and college. Accepts artwork/photos and translations.

Recent Nonfiction Title: *Heroes of the Golden Gate*, by Charles F. Adams.

PACIFIC PRESS PUBLISHING ASSOCIATION, Book Division, Seventh-day Adventist Church, Box 7000, Boise ID 83707. (208)465-2595. Vice President for Editorial Development: Ken McFarland. Publishes hardcover and trade paperback originals and hardcover and trade paperback reprints. Averages 50 titles/year; receives 600 submissions annually. Up to 50% of books from first-time authors; 100% of books from unagented writers. Pays 8-14% royalty on wholesale price. Offers average $300 advance. Publishes books an average of 6 months after acceptance. Photocopied submissions OK. Query for electronic submissions. Computer printout submissions acceptable; prefers letter-quality. Reports in 1 month on queries; 2 months on mss. Ms guidelines for #10 SASE.

Nonfiction: Biography, cookbook (vegetarian), how-to, juvenile, self-help and textbook. Subjects include cooking and foods (vegetarian only), health, nature, religion, and family living. "We are an exclusively religious publisher. We are looking for practical, how-to oriented manuscripts on religion, health, and family life that speak to human needs, interests and problems from a Biblical perspective. We can't use anything totally secular or written from other than a Christian perspective." Query or submit outline/synopsis and sample chapters. Reviews artwork/photos as part of ms package.

Recent Nonfiction Title: *Winning Over Sinning*, by Patricia Maxwell.

Tips: "Our primary audiences are members of our own denomination (Seventh-day Adventist), the general Christian reading market, and the secular or nonreligious reader. Books that are doing well for us are those that relate the Biblical message to practical human concerns and those that focus more on the experiential rather than theoretical aspects of Christianity."

‡PALLAS COMMUNICATIONS, 4226 NE 23rd Ave., Portland OR 97211. (503)284-2848. Editorial Director: Douglas Bloch. Publishes trade paperback originals. Publishes 4 titles/year; receives approximately 30 proposals/year. 50% from first-time authors; 75% from unagented writers. Pays authors 7½-10% royalty on retail price. Offers average advance of $500. Publishes ms an average of 1 year after acceptance. Simultaneous and photocopied submissions OK. Query for electronic submissions. Computer printout submissions OK; prefers letter-quality. Reports in 1 month on queries; in 2 months on ms. Book catalog for #10 SAE with 2 first class stamps; free ms guidelines.

Nonfiction: How-to, self-help and New Age. Subjects include child guidance/parenting, education, health/medicine, philosophy, psychology, religion, science, women's issues/studies, astrology and holistic health. "We want to continue to receive New Age titles, specifically in the areas of self-help, transpersonal psychology, astrology, metaphysics, holistic health, women's spirituality and inspirational writing." Query or submit outline/synopsis and sample chapters or complete ms. Reviews artwork/photos as part of ms package.

Recent Nonfiction Title: *Words That Heal*, by Douglas Bloch (spiritual self-help).

Tips: "If I were trying to market a book today, I would be absolutely clear who my audience is and what problem(s) I am trying to help them solve. Then, I would see myself as offering a positive solution to those particular people."

PANJANDRUM BOOKS, Suite 7, 11321 Iowa Ave., Los Angeles CA 90025. (213)477-8771. Editor/Publisher: Dennis Koran. Publishes hardcover and trade paperback originals. Averages 4-5 titles/year. Pays 7-10% royalty on retail price. Computer printout submissions acceptable. Reports in 2 weeks on queries; 2 months on mss. Book list for #10 SASE.

Nonfiction: Biography, cookbook, how-to, juvenile and reference. Subjects include cooking, health, hobbies, music, philosophy, theater and drama, herbs, vegetarianism, and childhood sexuality. "We're looking for manuscripts of cookbooks, health books, music (how-to) and drama, and are open to queries on other subjects." No religious or humorous. Query or submit outline/synopsis and sample chapters with SASE.

Recent Nonfiction Title: *Alfred Jarry: The Man with the Axe*, by Lennon (literary biography).

Fiction: Avant-garde, experimental, surreal and translations of European literature (not previously translated into English). Query with sample chapter.

Recent Fiction Title: *Fighting Men*, by Manus (post-Vietnam novel).

Poetry: Submit maximum 5 poems.

Recent Poetry Title: *Visions of the Fathers of Lascaux*, by Eshleman.

PANTHEON BOOKS, Division of Random House, Inc., 201 E. 50th St., New York NY 10022. Averages 90 titles/year. Pays royalty on invoice price (retail price minus freight pass-through, usually 50¢). Publishes book an average of 1 year after acceptance (longer if ms not written/completed when contract is signed). Address queries to Adult Editorial Department (28th Floor). "We prefer to work with experienced writers who have already published at least one book or several articles. In addition to a description of the book, queries must include a brief market study detailing how the book proposed will be different from other books available on the subject." Computer printout submissions acceptable; prefers letter-quality.

Nonfiction: Emphasis on international politics, Asia, radical social theory, history, medicine, women's studies, and law. Recreational guides and practical how-to books as well. Query letters only. No mss accepted. Publishes some juveniles.

Recent Nonfiction Title: *Wild Blue Yonder*, by Nick Kotz.

Fiction: Publishes fewer than 5 novels each year, primarily mysteries and foreign fiction in translation. Queries on fiction not accepted.

PARKER & SON PUBLICATIONS, INC., Box 6001, Los Angeles CA 90060. (213)727-1088, 1-800-4-LAW USE, Fax (213)727-0933. Chief Operating Officer: William L. Griffin, Jr. Publishes hardcover and trade paperback originals. Averages 35 titles/year. Pays 15% royalty on retail price. Publishes book an average of 4 months after acceptance. Query with outline/synopsis and sample chapter preferred. Reports in 1 month on queries; 6 weeks on mss. Free book list and "Information for Authors" on request.

Nonfiction: Technical law books and practice guidebooks for attorneys in active practice. Submit queries, outline/synopsis and sample chapters to Sidney J. Martin, Executive Vice President/Editorial Development.

Recent Nonfiction Title: *Lender Liability*, by Barry Cappelo.

PASSPORT PRESS, Box 1346, Champlain NY 12919. (514)937-8155. Publisher: B. Houghton. Publishes trade paperback originals. Averages 4 titles/year; receives 12 submissions annually. 25% of books from first-time authors; 100% from unagented writers. Pays 8-12% royalty on retail price. Publishes book an average of 9 months after acceptance. Simultaneous and photocopied submissions OK. Query for electronic submissions. Computer printout submissions OK. Reports in 3 weeks. Free book catalog.

Nonfiction: Travel books only. Especially looking for manuscripts on practical travel subjects and travel guides on specific countries. Query. Reviews artwork/photos as part of ms package.

Recent Nonfiction Title: *Latin America on Bicycle*, by J.P. Panet.

*PAULIST PRESS, 997 Macarthur Blvd., Mahwah NJ 07430. (201)825-7300. Publisher: Rev. Kevin A. Lynch. Managing Editor: Donald Brophy. Publishes hardcover and paperback originals and paperback reprints. Averages 90-100 titles/year; receives 500 submissions annually. 5-8% of books from first-time authors; 95% of books from unagented writers. Subsidy publishes (nonauthor) 1-2% of books. Pays royalty on retail price. Occasionally offers advance. Publishes book an average of 8 months after acceptance. Photocopied submissions OK. Query for electronic submissions. Computer printout submissions acceptable; prefers letter-quality. Reports in 1 month.

Nonfiction: Philosophy, religion, self-help and textbooks (religious). Accepts nonfiction translations from German, French and Spanish. "We would like to see theology (Catholic and ecumenical Christian), popular spirituality, liturgy, and religious education texts." Submit outline/synopsis and 2 sample chapters. Reviews artwork/photos as part of ms package.

Recent Nonfiction Title: *The Mothers Songs*, by Meinrad Craighead (feminist spirituality).

PETER PAUPER PRESS, INC., 202 Mamaroneck Ave., White Plains NY 10601. (914)681-0144. Co-Publisher: Nick Beilenson. Publishes hardcover originals. Averages 8 titles/year; receives 50 submissions annually. Buys some mss outright for $1,000. Offers no advance. Publishes ms an average of 9 months after acceptance. Simultaneous and photocopied submissions OK. Computer printout submissions OK. Reports in 2 weeks. Book catalog for #10 SAE.

Nonfiction: Cookbook and humor. Subjects include Americana, cooking and foods, inspirational, and religion. Submit complete ms. Reviews artwork/photos as part of ms package.

Recent Nonfiction Title: *Wit & Wisdom of Famous American Women* (collection).

Tips: Books on women's subjects have done well for Peter Pauper Press.

PBC INTERNATIONAL INC., Subsidiaries include Pisces Books and The Photographic Book Company, 1 School St., Glen Cove NY 11542. (516)676-2727. Managing Director: Penny Sibal-Samonte. Imprints include Library of Applied Design (nonfiction) and Pisces Books (nonfiction). Publishes hardcover and trade paperback originals. Averages 15 titles/year; receives 100-200 submissions annually. Most of books from first-time authors and unagented writers done on assignment. Pays royalty and/or flat fees. Simultaneous and photocopied submissions OK. Computer printout submissions acceptable; prefers letter-quality. Book catalog for 8½x11 SASE.

Nonfiction: Subjects include design and graphic art, nature (marine only), treasure hunting, underwater photography, and skin diving. The Library of Applied Design needs books that show the best in current design trends in all fields. Pisces Books needs books for snorklers and skin divers on marine life, travel, diver safety, etc. No submissions not covered in the above listed topics. Query with outline/synopsis and sample chapters.

Reviews artwork/photos as part of ms package.
Recent Nonfiction Title: *The Best of Shopping Bag Design*, by Judi Radice and Jackie Comerford.

PEACHTREE PUBLISHERS, LTD., 494 Armour Circle NE, Atlanta GA 30324. (404)876-8761. Publishes hardcover and trade paperback originals. Averages 20-25 titles/year; receives up to 2,000 submissions annually. 50% of books from first-time authors; 75% of books from unagented writers. Average print order for a writer's first book is 5,000-10,000. Publishes book an average of 1 year after acceptance. Computer printout submissions acceptable; prefers letter-quality. Reports in 3 weeks on queries; 5 months on mss. Book catalog for SAE with 3 first class stamps; ms guidelines for SASE.
Nonfiction: General and humor. Subjects include cooking and foods, history, recreation and travel. No business, technical, reference, art juvenile or animals. Submit outline/synopsis and sample chapters. Reviews artwork/photos as part of ms package.
Recent Nonfiction Title: *The Blue Chip Graduate/How You Become One*, by Bill Osher and Sioux Henley Campbell.
Fiction: Literary, humor and mainstream. "We are particularly interested in fiction with a Southern feel." No fantasy, juvenile, science fiction or romance. Submit complete manuscript.
Recent Fiction Title: *The Widow's Mite*, by Ferrol Sams.
Tips: "We're looking for mainstream fiction and nonfiction of general interest; although our books are sold throughout North America. We consider ourselves the national publisher with a Southern accent."

PELICAN PUBLISHING COMPANY, 1101 Monroe St., Box 189, Gretna LA 70053. (504)368-1175. Assistant Editor: Dean Shapiro. Publishes hardcover, trade paperback and mass market paperback originals and reprints. Averages 30-40 titles/year; receives 2,000 submissions annually. 30% of books from first-time authors; 97% of books from unagented writers. Pays royalty on wholesale price. Publishes book an average of 18 months after acceptance. Photocopied submissions OK. Computer printout submissions acceptable; no dot-matrix. Reports in 3 weeks on queries; 4 months on mss. Writer's guidelines for SASE.
Nonfiction: Biography, coffee table book (limited), cookbook, how-to, humor, illustrated book, juvenile, self-help, motivational, inspirational, and Scottish. Subjects include Americana (especially Southern regional, Ozarks, Texas and Florida); business and economics (popular how-to and motivational); cooking and food; health; history; music (American artforms: jazz, blues, Cajun, R&B); politics (special interest in conservative viewpoint); recreation; religion (for popular audience mostly, but will consider others); and travel. *Travel*: Regional and international (especially areas in Pacific). *Motivational*: with business slant. *Inspirational*: author must be someone with potential for large audience. *Cookbooks*: "We look for authors with strong connection to restaurant industry or cooking circles, i.e. someone who can promote successfully." *How-to*: will consider broad range. Query. "Although our company does accept and review unsolicited manuscripts, we prefer that a query be made first. This greatly expedites the review process and can save the writer additional postage expenses." Does not consider multiple queries or submissions. Reviews artwork/photos as part of ms package.
Recent Nonfiction Title: *Stern's Guide to the Cruise Vacation*, by Steven B. Stern (travel).
Fiction: Historical, humor, mainstream, Southern, juvenile and young adult. "Fiction needs are *very* limited. We are most interested in Southern novels. We are also looking for good mainstream juvenile/young adult works." No romance, science fiction, fantasy, gothic, mystery, erotica, confession, horror; no sex or violence. Submit outline/synopsis and sample chapters.
Recent Fiction Title: *The Over-the-Hill Ghost*, by Ruth Calif (juvenile).
Tips: "We do extremely well with travel, motivational, cookbooks, and children's titles. We will continue to build in these areas. The writer must have a clear sense of the market and this includes knowledge of the competition."

THE PENKEVILL PUBLISHING COMPANY, Box 212, Greenwood FL 32443. (904)569-2811. Director: Stephen H. Goode. Publishes hardcover originals. Averages 10-12 titles/year; receives approximately 20 submissions annually. 40% of books from first-time authors; 100% of books from unagented writers. Pays 10-15% royalty on wholesale price. Publishes book an average of 15 months after acceptance. Simultaneous and photocopied submissions OK. Computer printout submissions acceptable; prefers letter-quality. Reports in 2 weeks on queries; 6 weeks on submissions. Free book catalog.
Nonfiction: Reference, textbook and scholarly/critical. Subjects include history (19th, 20th Century American and European; Civil War and current interest); psychology; sociology (of current interest, divorce, terrorism); and literature and the arts and humanities. "Substantively, there are three areas of current interest: 1. Scholarly and critical works in the arts and humanities from the Renaissance forward; 2. 19th and 20th century American and Continental history, such as the American Civil War (e.g. Wheeler's Last Raid or a collection of essays on the literature, film, and art arising from the Vietnam war); 3. modern social currents, such as divorce, terrorism, the [Jewish] Holocaust, etc. (e.g., an annual bibliography and survey of divorce in America; an annual bibliography of terrorism, etc.). On another level, we are interested in the following genres: diaries, correspondence, histories of movements, biographies, critical and scholarly editions, sources (e.g. Faulkner's library); and in the following kinds of reference works; bibliographies, preferably annotated, checklists; diction-

aries (of authors' works, such as a Proust dictionary), etc." Query.

Recent Nonfiction Title: *Jewish Holocaust Studies—A Directory*, by Martin Savel (Judaica).

Tips: "The type of book a writer has the best chance of selling to us is something unique in modern letters; that is, that hasn't been done before—such as the *Art and Artists of Protest: The Vietnam War*, (a forthcoming title); the sources of Melville [either externally (his personal library) or internally (an examination of references in his works) arrived at]; or an index to the magazines that are members of the CCLM."

*PENNSYLVANIA HISTORICAL AND MUSEUM COMMISSION, The official history agency for the Commonwealth of Pennsylvania, Box 1026, Harrisburg PA 17108-1026. (717)787-8312. Chief, Marketing, Sales and Publications Division: Douglas H. West. Publishes hardcover originals and reprints, trade paperback originals and reprints, mass market paperback originals and reprints. Averages 6 titles/year; receives 50 submissions annually. 50% of books from first-time authors; 95% of books from unagented writers. Pays 5-10% royalty on wholesale or retail price. May make outright purchase of $500-10,000; sometimes makes special assignments; offers $350 average advance. Publishes book an average of 15 months after acceptance. Simultaneous and photocopied submissions OK. Query for electronic submissions. Computer printout submissions OK. Reports in 6 weeks on queries; 3 months on mss. Manuscripts prepared according to the Chicago *Manual of Style*.

Nonfiction: All books must be related to Pennsylvania, its history and its culture, biography, coffee table book, cookbook, how-to, illustrated book, reference, technical, visitor attractions and historic travel guidebooks. "The Commission is seeking manuscripts on Pennsylvania in general, but most specifically on archaeology, history, art (decorative and fine), politics, religion, travel, photography, nature, sports history, and cooking and food." Query or submit outline/synopsis and sample chapters.

Recent Nonfiction Title: *Indian Paths of Pennsylvania* (new edition), by Paul A.W. Wallace.

Tips: "Our audience is diverse—professional and avocational historians, students and scholars, specialists and generalists—all of whom are interested in one or more aspects of Pennsylvania's history and culture. Manuscripts must be well researched and documented (footnotes not necessarily required depending on the nature of the manuscript) and interestingly written. Because of the expertise of our reviewers, manuscripts must be factually accurate, but in being so, writers must not sacrifice style. We have always had a tradition of publishing scholarly and reference works, and although we intend to continue doing so, we want to branch out with more popularly styled books which will reach an even broader audience."

THE PERFECTION FORM CO., 10526 New York Ave., Des Moines IA 50322. (515)278-0133. Publishes 60 titles/year. Buys mss outright or negotiates royalty with small advance. Average print run for first release is 2,500. Computer printout submissions acceptable; prefers letter-quality. Reports in 6 months. Book catalog for 8½x11 SAE with $2.40 postage.

Nonfiction: Publishes supplementary educational materials, grades kindergarten-12 social studies, reading and language arts, also cross curriculum K-6. Submit complete ms. Send mss for K-6 material to Virginia Murphy; K-12 social studies to Douglas M. Rife; and 7-12 language arts to M. Kathleen Myers.

Recent Nonfiction Title: *Reading Beyond the Basal*, by Doris Roettger (teacher guide).

PERSPECTIVES PRESS, Box 90318, Indianapolis IN 46290-0318. (317)872-3055. Publisher: Pat Johnston. Small press. Publishes hardcover and trade paperback originals. Averages 4 titles/year; receives 300 queries annually. 95% of books from first-time authors. 95% of books from unagented writers. Pays 5-15% royalty on net sales. Publishes book an average of 6 months after acceptance. Simultaneous and photocopied submissions OK. Computer prinout submissions OK; no dot-matrix. Reports in 2 weeks on queries; 2 months on mss. Book catalog and writer's guidelines for #10 SAE and 2 first class stamps.

Nonfiction: How-to, juvenile and self-help books on health, psychology and sociology—all related to adoption or infertility. Query.

Recent Nonfiction Title: *Filling in the Blanks*, by Susan Gabel (children).

Fiction: Adoption/infertility for adults or children. Query.

Recent Fiction Title: *The Miracle Seeker*, by Mary Martin Mason.

Tips: "For adults we are seeking decision-making materials, books dealing with parenting issues, books to use with children, books to share with others to help explain infertility or adoption or foster care, special programming or training manuals, etc. For children we will consider manuscripts that are appropriate for preschoolers, for early elementary, for later elementary or middle school children, for high schoolers. While we would consider a manuscript from a writer who was not personally or professionally involved in these issues, we would be more inclined to accept a manuscript submitted by an infertile person, an adoptee, a birthparent, an adoptive parent, a professional working with any of these."

‡PETERSON'S GUIDES, INC., Box 2123, Princeton NJ 08540. (609)924-5338. Publisher/President: Peter W. Hegener. Executive Vice President and Editorial Director: Karen C. Hegener. Publishes paperback originals and software (for the educational/guidance market). Averages 35-45 titles/year. Receives 150-200 submissions annually. 50% of books from first-time authors; 90% from unagented writers. Average print order for a

Close-up

Sam Small
Publisher
Pilot Books

Sam Small is no stranger to risk. In fact, he built his business on it. He published a book on franchise fraud, when franchising was a new idea; a book on minority business finance, when doors were just beginning to open up to minority businessmen; and a book on retirement income, when senior citizens had few options beyond the rocking chair.

"We began in some exciting fields . . . we helped open a lot of doors and got a lot of publicity," says Small. He started his publishing firm, Pilot Books, in 1959 and carved out a niche by offering short guides in areas that would not compete with larger publishers. These areas—business and travel issues for senior citizens, women and minority businessmen—were ignored by major publishers and offered a wealth of fresh, new material for Pilot Books.

Today Small's firm still specializes in concise nonfiction guides. Pilot has published a series on franchises since the first book, a series of discount travel guides for senior citizens and several general books on travel and fitness.

"I moved my business out to Long Island to retire, but there's always something," says Small, who runs the business with the help of his wife and a small staff. "I still publish between 20 and 30 books a year."

He says reference books are easiest to do, but these run a risk he does not like to take—that of publishing inaccurate information. He can recount a number of horror stories in which he expected a writer to present up-to-date facts and found the facts were taken from outdated reference material.

"We always check out every fact given, and if things don't check out, even on a small book, it can be nerve-wracking," he says. "Writers must check all their source material. We realize this can be a problem and we understand the nature of a project where 300 entries out of every 1,000 could be wrong, but it's important to check all facts, especially when something will be used as reference material. It's simple—if our stuff is wrong, no one will buy it."

In addition to accuracy, Small traces his success to careful targeting of his books. "Always pinpoint an audience for your book." The audience for Pilot's books is primarily business people. Because of the books' practical, how-to approaches, some of the company's biggest sales have been to corporations and institutions, such as hospitals.

Pilot books have even been used by government agencies. Small is particularly proud that his book on minority business finance, published during the Kennedy administration, was recommended by the National Association of Small Business. During the Nixon administration, Pilot's *Executive Guide to Handling a Press Interview* was popular with both government and business executives.

Small says he's finding it harder and harder to find innovative material, but he's open to ideas on business, travel and especially on topics for women. "Exciting work is hard to come by, but I'm always looking. As a small publisher, we don't take as big a risk as larger publishers, because our expenses are lower. It's just fun to see what happens."

—Robin Gee

writer's first book is 10,000-15,000. Pays 8-10% royalty on net sales; offers advance. Publishes book an average of 1 year after acceptance. Photocopied submissions OK. Computer printout submissions acceptable; prefers letter-quality. Reports in 3 months. Free catalog.

Nonfiction: Educational and career reference and guidance works for professionals, libraries, and trade. Submit complete ms or detailed outline and sample chapters. Looks for "appropriateness of contents to our market, accuracy of information, author's credentials, and writing style suitable for audience." Reviews artwork/photos as part of ms package.

Recent Nonfiction Title: *Learning Vacations*, by Gerson Eisenberg.

PETROCELLI BOOKS, INC., Research Park, 251 Wall St., Princeton NJ 08540. (609)924-5851. Editorial Director: O.R. Petrocelli. Publishes hardcover and paperback originals. Publishes 20 titles/year. Offers 12½-18% royalties. No advance. Simultaneous and photocopied submissions OK. Computer printout submissions acceptable; prefers letter-quality. Reports in 1 month. Free book catalog.

Nonfiction: Business/economics, reference, technical, and textbooks. Submit outline/synopsis and 1-2 sample chapters.

Recent Nonfiction Title: *A Layman's Guide to Robotics*, by Derek Kelly.

PHAROS BOOKS, Publisher of *The World Almanac*, 200 Park Ave., New York NY 10166. (212)692-3824. Editor-in-Chief: Hana Umlauf Lane. Editor: Eileen Schlesinger. Assistant Editor: Sharilyn K. Jee. Publishes hardcover and trade paperback originals. Averages 30 titles/year. Pays 5-15% on retail price. Publishes book an average of 1 year after acceptance. Computer printout submissions acceptable; prefers letter-quality. Reports in 3 weeks. Free book catalog.

Nonfiction: "We look for books under three imprints: Pharos Books for nonfiction with strong consumer interest; World Almanac for innovative reference books; Topper for humor books. We expect at least a synopsis/outline and sample chapters, and would like to see the completed manuscript." Reviews artwork/photos as part of ms package.

PHILOMEL BOOKS, Division of The Putnam Publishing Group, 200 Madison Ave., New York NY 10016. (212)576-8900. Editor-in-Chief: Patricia Lee Gauch. Senior Editor: Paula Wiseman. Associate Editor: Wendy Steinhacker. Publishes hardcover originals. Publishes 25-30 titles/year; receives 2,600 submissions annually. 15% of books from first-time authors; 30% of books from unagented writers. Pays standard royalty. Advance negotiable. Publishes book an average of 1-2 years after acceptance. Computer printout submissions acceptable; no dot-matrix. Reports in 1 month on queries. Book catalog for 8½x11 SAE with 4 first class stamps. Request book catalog from marketing department of Putnam Publishing Group.

Nonfiction: Young adult and children's picture books. No alphabet books or workbooks. Query first. Looks for quality writing, unique ideas, suitability to our market.

Recent Nonfiction Title: *Anno's Sundial*, by Mitsumassa Anno.

Fiction: Young adult and children's books on any topic. Particularly interested in fine regional fiction and quality picture books. Query to department.

Recent Fiction Title: *A White Romance*, by Virginia Hamilton.

Tips: "We prefer a very brief synopsis that states the basic premise of the story. This will help us determine whether or not the manuscript is suited to our list. If applicable, we'd be interested in knowing the author's writing experience or background knowledge. We are always looking for beautifully written manuscripts with stories that engage. We try to be less influenced by the swings of the market than in the power, value, essence of the manuscript itself."

PILOT BOOKS, 103 Cooper St., Babylon NY 11702. (516)422-2225. President: Sam Small. Publishes paperback originals. Averages 20-30 titles/year; receives 300-400 submissions annually. 20% of books from first-time authors; 90% of books from unagented writers. Average print order for a writer's first book is 3,000. Offers standard royalty contract based on wholesale or retail price. Usual advance is $250, but this varies, depending on author's reputation and nature of book. Publishes book an average of 8 months after acceptance. Computer printout submissions acceptable; prefers letter-quality. Reports in 1 month. Book catalog and guidelines for SASE.

Nonfiction: Financial, business, travel, career, personal guides and training manuals. "Our training manuals are utilized by America's major corporations as well as the government." Directories and books on travel and moneymaking opportunities. Wants "clear, concise treatment of subject matter." Length: 8,000-30,000 words. Send outline. Reviews artwork/photos as part of ms package.

Recent Nonfiction Title: *The Senior Citizen's Guide to Budget Travel in the United States and Canada.*

PINEAPPLE PRESS, INC., Drawer 16008, Sarasota FL 34239. (813)952-1085. Editor: June Cussen. Publishes hardcover and trade paperback originals. Averages 12 titles/year; receives 600 submissions annually. 20% of books from first-time authors; 80% of books from unagented writers. Pays 6½-15% royalty on retail price. Seldom offers advance. Publishes book an average of 1 year after acceptance. Simultaneous and photo-

copied submissions OK. Query for electronic submissions. Computer printout submissions acceptable; no dot-matrix unless high quality. Reports in 1 month on queries; 6 weeks on mss. Book catalog for 8½x11 SAE and 2 first class stamps.
Nonfiction: Biography, how-to, reference, nature and young adult. Subjects include animals, cooking and foods, history and nature. "We will consider most nonfiction topics. We are seeking quality nonfiction on diverse topics for the library and book trade markets." No heavily illustrated submissions, pop psychology, or autobiographies. Query or submit outline/brief synopsis and sample chapters.
Recent Nonfiction Title: *Underwater Farming*, by George Fichter.
Fiction: Literary, historical and mainstream. No romance, science fiction, or children's (below the young adult level). Submit outline/brief synopsis and sample chapters.
Recent Fiction Title: *The Paper Boat*, by Don Bentley-Baker.
Tips: "If I were a writer trying to market a book today, I would learn everything I could about book publishing and book publicity and agree to actively participate in promoting my book. A query on a novel without a brief sample seems useless."

*PLAYERS PRESS, INC., Box 1132, Studio City CA 91604. (818)789-4980. Vice President, Editorial: Robert W. Gordon. Publishes hardcover and trade paperback originals, and trade paperback reprints. Averages 15-25 titles/year; receives 75-300 submissions annually. 10% of books from first-time authors; 90% of books from unagented writers. Subsidy publishes 1% of books; subsidy publishes (nonauthor) 2% of books. Pays royalty on retail price. Publishes book an average of 20 months after acceptance. Simultaneous and photocopied submissions OK. Reports in 4 months. Book catalog and guidelines for 6x9 SAE and 3 first class stamps.
Nonfiction: Juvenile and theatrical drama/entertainment industry. Subjects include the performing arts. Needs quality plays and musicals, adult or juvenile. Submit complete ms. Reviews artwork/photos as part of ms package.
Fiction: Adventure, confession, ethnic, experimental, fantasy, historical, horror, humor, mainstream, mystery, religious, romance, science fiction, suspense and western. Submit complete ms for theatrical plays only. "No novels are accepted. We publish plays only."
Recent Fiction Title: *Survival*, by William-Alan Landes.
Tips: "Plays, entertainment industry texts and children's story books have the best chance of selling to our firm."

‡*PLAYWRIGHTS CANADA, Subsidiary of Playwrights Union of Canada, 8 York St., 6th Floor, Toronto, Ontario M5J 1R2 Canada. (416)947-0201. Editor: Winston Smith. Publishes paperback originals and reprints. Averages 16 titles/year. Receives 100 member submissions/year. 50% of books from first-time authors; 50% from unagented writers. Subsidy publishes 100% (nonauthor) of books. Pays 10% royalty on retail price. Publishes ms an average of 1 year after acceptance. Simultaneous and photocopied submissions OK. Computer printout submissions OK; prefers letter-quality. Reports in 2 weeks on queries; 6 months on mss. Book catalog and ms guidelines free on request.
Fiction: Plays. "We publish only plays that have had a fully professional stage production. Plays to be published are chosen by an Editorial Board which meets annually. We will consider only drama from members." Query.
Recent Fiction Title: *Prague*, by John Krizanc (play).
Tips: "In Canada, small publishers are, for the most part, vastly underfunded, and unable to publish many books. The books that we publish should fit our criteria: quality drama that has been professionally produced on stage for theatres, universities, high schools, drama enthusiasts. For anyone who wishes to publish plays, *get a professional theatre to produce it* before you even think of sending it to a publishing house. No serious publisher will consider unproduced drama, except under highly unusual circumstances."

PLENUM PUBLISHING, 233 Spring St., New York NY 10013. (212)620-8000. Senior Editor, Trade Books: Linda Greenspan Regan. Imprint includes Da Capo. Publishes hardcover originals. Averages 350 titles/year; trade division publishes 12. Receives 250 submissions annually. 50% of books from first-time authors. 90% of books from unagented writers. Publishes book an average of 8 months after acceptance. Simultaneous and photocopied submissions OK. Query for electronic submissions. Reports in several months on queries; several months on mss.
Nonfiction: Subjects include politics, psychology, current events, sociology and science. "We need popular books in the social sciences, sciences and the humanities." Da Capo division publishes art, music, photography, dance and film. Query only.
Recent Nonfiction Title: *U.S. Ends and Means in Central America: A Debate*, by Ernest van den Haas and Tom J. Faber.
Tips: "Our audience is intelligent laymen and professionals. Authors should be experts on subject matter of book. They must compare their books with competitive works, explain how theirs differs, and define the market for their books."

PLEXUS PUBLISHING, INC., 143 Old Marlton Pike, Medford NJ 08055. (609)654-6500. Editorial Director: Thomas Hogan. Publishes hardcover and paperback originals. Averages 4-5 titles/year; receives 10-20 submissons annually. 70% of books from first-time authors; 90% of books from unagented writers. Pays 10-20% royalty on wholesale price; buys some booklets outright for $250-1,000. Offers $500-1,000 advance. Simultaneous and photocopied submissions OK. Computer printout submissions acceptable; prefers letter-quality. Reports in 2 months. Book catalog and guidelines for SASE.

Nonfiction: Biography (of naturalists) and reference. Subjects include plants, animals, nature and life sciences. "We will consider any book on a nature/biology subject, particularly those of a reference (permanent) nature that would be of lasting value to high school and college audiences, and/or the general reading public. Authors should have authentic qualifications in their subject area, but qualifications may be by experience as well as academic training." No gardening; no philosophy or psychology; generally not interested in travel but will consider travel that gives sound ecological information. Also interested in mss of about 20-40 pages in length for feature articles in *Biology Digest* (guidelines available with SASE). Always query. Reviews artwork/photos as part of ms package.

Recent Nonfiction Title: *The Natural History of Living Mammals*, by W. Voelker (reference).

Tips: "We will give serious consideration to well-written manuscripts that deal even indirectly with biology/nature subjects. For example, *Exploring Underwater Photography* (a how-to for divers) and *The Literature of Nature* (an anthology of nature writings for college curriculum) were accepted for publication."

POCKET BOOKS, 1230 Avenue of the Americas, New York NY 10020. Imprints include Washington Square Press (high-quality mass market), Poseidon Press (hardcover fiction and nonfiction), Archway and Minstrel (juvenile/YA imprints). Publishes paperback originals and reprints, mass market and trade paperbacks. Averages 300 titles/year; receives 750 submissions annually. 15% of books from first-time authors. Pays royalty on retail price. Publishes book an average of 1 year after acceptance. *No unsolicited mss or queries.* "All submissions must go through a literary agent."

Nonfiction: History, biography, reference and general nonfiction, cookbooks, humor, calendars.

Fiction: Adult (mysteries, thriller, psychological suspense, Star Trek ® novels, romance, westerns).

*PORCÉPIC BOOKS, (formerly Press Porcepic), #235-560 Johnson St., Victoria British Columbia V8W 3C6 Canada. (604)381-5502. Imprints include Softwords and Tesseract Books. Imprint publishes hardcover and trade paperback originals. Averages 4 titles/year; receives 300 submissions annually. 20% of books from first-time authors. 90% of books from unagented writers. Subsidy publishes (nonauthor) 100% of books. Pays 10% royalty on retail price; offers $300-500 advance. Publishes ms an average of 10 months after acceptance. Simultaneous (if so advised) and photocopied submissions OK. Computer printout submissions OK; prefers letter-quality. Reports in 2 weeks on queries; 3 months on mss.

Nonfiction: "Not actively soliciting nonfiction books."

Fiction: Experimental, science fiction and speculative fiction. "We are interested in hearing from new Canadian writers of mainstream or experimental fiction." Press publishes Canadian authors only. Prefer query first, then sample chapters."

Recent Fiction Title: *Tesseracts 2*, edited by Phyllis Gotlieb and Douglas Barbour (Canadian science fiction stories).

Tips: "Make sure the manuscript is well written. We see so many mss that only the unique and excellent can't be put down."

PORTER SARGENT PUBLISHERS, INC., 11 Beacon St., Boston MA 02108. (617)523-1670. Publishes hardcover and paperback originals, reprints, translations and anthologies. Averages 4 titles/year. Pays royalty on retail price. "Each contract is dealt with on an individual basis with the author." Computer printout submissions acceptable. Book catalog for SASE.

Nonfiction: Reference, special education and academic nonfiction. "Handbook Series and Special Education Series offer standard, definitive reference works in private education and writings and texts in special education. The Extending Horizons Series is an outspoken, unconventional series which presents topics of importance in contemporary affairs and the social sciences." This series is particularly directed to the college adoption market. Accepts nonfiction translations from French and Spanish. Contact: Peter M. Casey. Send query with brief description, table of contents, sample chapter and information regarding author's background.

Recent Nonfiction Title: 7th *Schools Abroad of Interest to Americans*, (1988/89 reference).

POTENTIALS DEVELOPMENT FOR HEALTH & AGING SERVICES, 775 Main St., Buffalo NY 14203. (716)842-2658. Publishes paperback originals. Averages 6 titles/year; receives 30-40 submissions annually. 90% of books from first-time authors; 100% of books from unagented writers. Average print order for a writer's first book is 1,000. Pays 5% royalty on sales of first 3,000 copies; 8% thereafter. Publishes book an average of 1 year after acceptance. Computer printout submissions acceptable; no dot-matrix. Reports in 6 weeks. Book catalog and ms guidelines for #10 SASE.

Nonfiction: "We seek material of interest to those working with elderly people in the community and in institutional settings. We need tested, innovative and practical ideas." Query or submit outline/synopsis and 3 sample chapters to J.A. Elkins. Looks for "suitable subject matter, writing style and organization." Reviews artwork/photos as part of ms package.

Recent Nonfiction Title: *Beyond Bingo*, by Mary Kay Klim (activity book).

Tips: "The writer has the best chance of selling us materials of interest to those working with elderly people in nursing homes, senior and retirement centers. Our major market is activity directors. Give us good reasons why activity directors would want or need the material submitted."

CLARKSON N. POTTER, INC., 225 Park Ave., New York NY 10003. (212)254-1600. Imprint of Crown Publishers. Editorial Director, Potter: Carol Southern, associate publisher, Crown. Publishes hardcover and trade paperback originals. Averages 55 titles/year; receives 1,500 submissions annually. 18% of books from first-time authors, but many of these first-time authors are well-known and have had media coverage. Pays 10% royalty on hardcover; 5-7½% on paperback; 5-7% on illustrated hardcover, varying escalations; advance depends on type of book and reputation or experience of author. No unagented mss can be considered. Photocopied submissions OK. Computer printout submissions acceptable. Reports in 1 month. Book catalog for 7x10 SASE.

Nonfiction: Publishes art, autobiography, biography, cooking and foods, design, how-to, humor, juvenile, nature, photography, self-help, style and annotated literature. Accepts nonfiction translations. "Manuscripts must be cleanly typed on 8½x11 nonerasable bond; double-spaced. Chicago *Manual of Style* is preferred." Query or submit outline/synopsis and sample chapters. Reviews artwork/photos as part of ms package.

Recent Nonfiction Title: *Weddings*, by Martha Stewart.

Fiction: Will consider "quality fiction."

Recent Fiction Title: *Doctors and Women*, by Susan Cheever.

THE PRAIRIE PUBLISHING COMPANY, Box 2997, Winnipeg, Manitoba R3C 4B5 Canada. (204)885-6496. Publisher: Ralph Watkins. Publishes trade paperback originals. Averages 4 titles/year; receives 25 submissions annually. 4% of books from first-time authors; 85% of books from unagented writers. Average print order for a writer's first book is 2,000. Pays 10% royalty on retail price. Photocopied submissions OK. Computer printout submissions acceptable; no dot-matrix. Reports in several weeks. Book catalog and guidelines for 8x10½ SAE with IRCs.

Nonfiction: Biography and cookbook. Subjects include cooking and foods. "We would look at any submissions." Reviews artwork/photos as part of ms package.

Recent Nonfiction Title: *The Homeplace*, by Jean James.

PRAKKEN PUBLICATIONS, INC., Box 8623, Ann Arbor MI 48107. (313)769-1211. Publisher/Executive Editor: Alan H. Jones. Publishes hardcover and trade paperback originals. Averages 5 titles/year; receives 50 submissions annually. 50% of books from first-time authors; 100% of books from unagented writers. Pays 10% royalty on net price. Publishes book an average of 6 months after acceptance. Simultaneous and photocopied submissions OK. Computer printout submissions acceptable; prefers letter-quality. Reports in 2 weeks on queries; 1 month on mss. Book catalog for #10 SASE.

Nonfiction: General education, vocational and technical education. "We are interested in manuscripts with broad appeal in any of the specific subject areas of the industrial arts, vocational-technical education, and in the general education field." Submit outline/synopsis and sample chapters. Reviews artwork/photos as part of ms package.

Recent Nonfiction Title: *Judicious Discipline*, by Forrest Gathercoal.

Tips: "We have a continuing interest in magazine and book manuscripts which reflect emerging policy issues in the field of education."

PRENTICE-HALL CANADA, INC., College Division, Subsidiary of Simon & Schuster, 1870 Birchmount Road, Scarborough, Ontario M1P 2J7 Canada. (416)293-3621. Executive Editor: Cliff Newman. Publishes hardcover and paperback originals and software. Averages 30 titles/year. Receives 200-300 submissions annually. 30-40% of books from first-time authors; 100% of books from unagented writers. Pays 10-15% royalty on net price. Publishes book an average of 14 months after acceptance. Query for electronic submissions. Computer printout submissions acceptable; prefers letter-quality.

Nonfiction: The College Division publishes textbooks suitable for the community college and large university market. Most submissions should be designed for existing courses in all disciplines of study. Will consider software in most disciplines, especially business and sciences. Canadian content is important. The division also publishes books in computer science, technology and mathematics.

Recent Nonfiction Title: *Accounting: A Decision Approach*, by L.S. Rosen.

PRENTICE-HALL CANADA, INC., Secondary School Division, A subsidiary of Simon & Schuster, 1870 Birchmount Road, Scarborough, Ontario M1P 2J7 Canada. (416)293-3621. General Manager: Rob Greenaway. Averages 30 titles annually.

Nonfiction: Publishes texts, workbooks, and instructional media including computer courseware for junior and senior high schools. Subjects include business, computer studies, geography, history, language arts, mathematics, science, social studies, technology, and French as a second language. Query.
Recent Nonfiction Title: *Science 9: An Introductory Study*, by W.A. Andrews (science textbook).

PRENTICE-HALL CANADA, INC., Trade Division, 1870 Birchmount Road, Scarborough, Ontario M1P 2J7 Canada. (416)293-3621. Acquisitions Editor: Tanya Long. Publishes hardcover and trade paperback originals. Averages 15 titles/year; receives 750-900 submissions annually. 40% of books from first-time authors; 40% of books from unagented writers. Negotiates royalty and advance. Publishes book an average of 9 months after acceptance. Query for electronic submissions. Computer printout submissions acceptable; prefers letter-quality. Reports in 10 weeks. Ms guidelines for #10 SAE and 1 IRC.
Nonfiction: Subjects of Canadian and international interest; art, politics and current affairs, business, travel, health and food. Send outline and sample chapters. Reviews artwork/photos as part of ms package.
Recent Nonfiction Title: *The Violent Years of Maggie MacDonald*, by Maggie MacDonald and Allan Gould (biography).
Tips: Needs general interest nonfiction books on topical subjects. "Present a clear, concise thesis, well-argued with a thorough knowledge of existing works. We are looking for more books on social and political issues."

PRENTICE-HALL, INC., Business & Professional Books Division, Gulf & Western, Inc., A division of Simon & Schuster, Sylvan Ave., Englewood Cliffs NJ 07632. (201)592-2000. Vice President: Ted Nardin. Publishes hardcover and trade paperback originals. Averages 150 titles/year; receives 1,000 submissions annually. 50% of books from first-time authors; 95% of books from unagented writers. Pays royalty: 5% on cash received on *mail order*, or 10-15% on all *trade* sales. Offers $3,000-5,000 advance, sometimes more. Publishes book an average of 8 months after acceptance. Simultaneous and photocopied submissions OK. Query for electronic submissions. Computer printout submissions acceptable; prefers letter-quality. Reports in 3 weeks. Book catalog and ms guidelines for 8½x11 SASE.
Nonfiction: How-to, reference, self-help and technical. Subjects include all aspects of management, business, real estate, accounting, computers, education, electronics and engineering. Needs business, professional, technical and educational references, for sale primarily via direct mail. Query or submit outline and sample chapters. Reviews artwork/photos as part of ms package.
Recent Nonfiction Title: *Complete Secretary's Handbook, Sixth Edition*.
Tips: "We seek high-level, practical references that command high prices and that can be sold to targeted markets via direct mail."

‡**PRENTICE-HALL, INC.**, General Division, Gulf & Western Building, 1 Gulf & Western Plaza, New York NY 10023. Publisher: Elizabeth Perle. Publishes nonfiction hardcover and trade paperback originals. Publishes book an average of 9 months after acceptance. Will consider unsolicited photocopied submissions on nonfiction topics, but not responsible for returning unsolicited manuscripts. Computer printout submissions acceptable; prefers letter-quality. SASE must be included in order to receive a response in 6-8 weeks.
Nonfiction: Categories include general current affairs topics, how-to, self-help, New Age, psychology, business, health, diet, fitness, cookbooks, gardening, arts and crafts, design, art architecture, photography, performing arts, travel, sports, nature, equestrian, military and illustrated gift books. Does not publish fiction, poetry, romances, westerns and other fiction genres.
Tips: "Proposals should include outline and/or table of contents, sample chapter and author information.

THE PRESERVATION PRESS, National Trust for Historic Preservation, 1785 Massachusetts Ave. NW, Washington DC 20036. Director: Diane Maddex. Publishes nonfiction books on historic preservation (saving and reusing the "built environment"). Averages 6 titles/year; receives 30 submissions annually. 40% of books from first-time authors; 50% of books from unagented writers. Books are often commissioned by the publisher. Publishes book an average of 2 years after acceptance. Query for electronic submissions. Computer printout submissions acceptable; no dot-matrix. Book catalog for 9x12 SASE.
Nonfiction: Subject matter encompasses architecture and architectural history, building restoration and historic preservation. No local history. Looks for "relevance to national preservation-oriented audience; educational or instructional value; depth; uniqueness; need in field." Query. Reviews artwork/photos as part of ms package.
Recent Nonfiction Title: *Great American Movie Theatres*, by David Naylor.
Tips: "The writer has the best chance of selling our press a book clearly related to our mission—historic preservation—that covers new ideas and is unique and practical. If it fills a clear need, we will know immediately."

PRESIDIO PRESS, 31 Pamaron Way, Novato CA 94949. (415)883-1373. Editor-in-Chief: Adele Horwitz. Senior Editor: Joan Griffin. Publishes hardcover and paperback. Averages 17 titles/year. Receives 150 submissions annually. 90% of books from first-time authors; 95% of books from unagented writers. Pays 15% royalty on net price. Offers nominal advance. Publishes book an average of 10 months after acceptance. Photocopied submissions OK. Query for electronic submissions. Reports in 3 months. Free book catalog.

Nonfiction: Military history. No scholarly. Fiction with military background considered. Accepts nonfiction translations. Query or submit outline/synopsis and 3 sample chapters. Reviews artwork/photos as part of ms package.

Recent Nonfiction Title: *Team Yankee: Ambush at Osirak*, by Harold Coyle, Herbert Crowder.

Recent Fiction Title: *Top Gun*, by George Hall.

Tips: "Have the proper experience or qualifications for the subject."

PRICE/STERN/SLOAN INC., PUBLISHERS, 360 N. La Cienega Blvd., Los Angeles CA 90048. Imprints include Serendipity Books, Bugg Books, Wee Sing Books, Troubador Press and Laughter Library. Associate Editor: L. Spencer Humphrey. Publishes trade paperback originals. Averages 200 titles/year; receives 6,000 submissions annually. 20% of books from first-time authors; 60% of books from unagented writers. Pays royalty on wholesale price, or by outright purchase. Offers small or no advance. Publishes book an average of 1 year after acceptance. Computer printout submissions acceptable; no dot-matrix. Reports in 3 months. Ms guidelines for SASE.

Nonfiction: Subjects include humor, self-help (limited), and satire (limited). Juveniles. Query *only.* "Most titles are unique in concept as well as execution and are geared for the so-called gift market." Reviews artwork/photos as part of ms package.

Tips: "Humor and satire were the basis of the company's early product and are still the mainstream of the company."

PRIMA PUBLISHING AND COMMUNICATIONS, Cal Co Am., Inc., Box 1260, Rocklin CA 95677. (916)624-5718. Publisher: Ben Dominitz. Publishes hardcover and trade paperback originals and trade paperback reprints. Publishes 30 titles/year. Receives 500 queries/year. Buys 10% of books from first-time authors; 50% from unagented writers. Pays 15-20% royalty on wholesale price. Advance varies. Publishes books an average of 6-9 months after acceptance. Simultaneous and photocopied submissions OK. Query for electronic submissions. Computer printout submissions OK; no dot-matrix. Reports in 2 months. Catalog for 9x12 SAE with 85¢ postage; writer's guidelines for #10 SASE.

Nonfiction: Biography, coffee table book, cookbook, how-to, humor, illustrated book, self-help. Subjects include business and economics, cooking and foods, health, music, politics, psychology and travel. "We want books with originality, written by highly qualified individuals. No fiction at this time." Query.

Recent Nonfiction Title: *Too Old, Too Ugly, and Not Deferential to Men*, by Christine Craft.

Tips: "Prima strives to reach the primary and secondary markets for each of its books. We are known for promoting our books aggressively. Books that genuinely solve problems for people will always do well if properly promoted. Try to picture the intended audience while writing the book. Too many books are written to an audience that doesn't exist."

*PRINCETON ARCHITECTURAL PRESS, 2 Research Way, Forrestal Center, Princeton NJ 08540. (609)924-7911. Assistant Editor: Elizabeth Short. Publishes hardcover and trade paperback originals and hardcover reprints. Averages 20 titles/year; receives 20 submissions annually. 50% of books from first-time authors; 100% of books from unagented writers. Subsidy publishes 10% of books; subsidy publishes (nonauthor) 20% of books. Pays 6-10% royalty on wholesale price. Simultaneous and photocopied submissions OK. Query for electronic submissions. Computer printout submissions acceptable; no dot-matrix. Reports in 1 month. Book catalog and guidelines for 8½x11 SAE with 3 first class stamps.

Nonfiction: Coffee table book, illustrated book and textbook. Subjects include architecture, landscape architecture and design. Needs texts on architecture, landscape architecture, architectural monographs, and texts to accompany a possible reprint, architectural history and urban design. Submit outline/synopsis and sample chapters or complete ms. Reviews artwork/photos as part of ms package.

Recent Nonfiction Title: *The Writing on the Walls*, by Anthon Vidler (architectural history).

Tips: "Our audience is architects, designers, urban planners, architectural theorists, and architectural-urban design historians, and many academicians and practitioners. We are still focusing on architecture and architectural history but would like to increase our list of books on design."

‡*PRINCETON BOOK COMPANY, PUBLISHERS, Box 57, Pennington NJ 08534. (609)737-8177. Imprints include Dance Horizons. President: Charles H. Woodford. Vice President: Richard Carlin. Publishes hardcover originals, trade paperback originals and trade paperback reprints. Firm averages 10 titles/year. Receives 100 submissions/year. 25% of books from first-time authors. 100% from unagented writers. Subsidy publishes 25% of books. Subsidy determined by cost involved in the project. Pays 5-10% on wholesale price. Publishes book an average of 10 months after acceptance. Simultaneous and photocopied submissions OK. Computer printout submissions OK; prefers letter-quality. Reports in 2 weeks on queries; 1 month on mss. Free book catalog.

Nonfiction: Biography, coffee table book, how-to, reference, self-help and textbook. Subjects include education, health/medicine, dance, recreation, sociology, sports and women's issues/studies. "We're looking for textbooks in the fields of dance, physical education, and general education. No autobiographies or special-interest books in dance that have no possibility for use as college texts.'' Query or submit outline/synopsis and sample chapters. Reviews artwork/photos as part of manuscript package.

Recent Nonfiction Title: *Dance: The Art of Production*, by Schlaich/DuPont (dance textbook).

Tips: "Books that have appeal to both trade and text markets are of most interest to us. Our audience is dance professors, students and professionals. If I were a writer trying to market a book today, I would write with a clear notion of the market in mind. Don't produce a manuscript without first considering what is needed in your field."

PROFESSIONAL PUBLICATIONS, INC., 1250 Fifth Ave., Belmont CA 94002. (415)593-9119. Acquisitions Editor: Wendy Nelson. Publishes hardcover and paperback originals. Averages 6 titles/year; receives 10-20 submissions annually. Pays 8-12% royalty on wholesale price; offers $2,000 average advance. Sometimes makes outright purchase for $1,000-$2,000. Publishes book an average of 6-18 months after acceptance. Simultaneous and photocopied submissions OK. Query for electronic submissions. Computer printout submissions OK; prefers letter-quality. Reports in 2 weeks on queries; 1 month on mss. Free book catalog.

Nonfiction: Reference, technical and textbook. Subjects include business and economics, mathematics, engineering, accounting, architecture, contracting and building. Especially needs "licensing examination review books for general contractors and lawyers." Query or submit outline/synopsis and sample chapters or complete ms. Reviews artwork/photos as part of ms package.

Recent Nonfiction Title: *Accounting Theory & Practice—A Review for the CPA Exam*, by Francisco & Smith (exam prep).

Tips: "We specialize in books for working professionals: engineers, architects, contractors, accountants, etc. The more complex technically the manuscript is the happier we are. We love equations, tables of data, complex illustrations, mathematics, etc. In technical/professional book publishing, it isn't always obvious to us if a market exists. We can judge the quality of a ms, but the author should make some effort to convince us that a market exists. Facts, figures, and estimates about the market—and marketing ideas from the author—will help sell us on the work. Besides our interest in highly technical materials, we will be trying to broaden our range of titles in each discipline. Specifically, we will be looking for career guides for accountants and architects, as well as for engineers."

PRUETT PUBLISHING CO., 2928 Pearl, Boulder CO 80301. Managing Editor: Gerald Keenan. Averages 20 titles/year; receives 200 submissions annually. 50% of books from first-time authors; 100% of books from unagented writers. Average print order for a writer's first book is 2,000-3,000. Pays royalty on wholesale price. "Most books that we publish are aimed at special interest groups. As a small publisher, we feel most comfortable in dealing with a segment of the market that is very clearly identifiable, and one we know we can reach with our resources." Publishes book an average of 10 months after acceptance. Legible photocopies acceptable. Query for electronic submissions. Computer printout submissions acceptable; no dot-matrix. Reports in 1 month. Free catalog on request; ms guidelines for #10 SASE.

Nonfiction: Publishes general adult nonfiction and textbooks. Subjects include travel in the Western US, outdoor activities related to the Intermountain West, western Americana and pictorial railroad histories. Textbooks with a regional (intermountain) aspect for preschool through college level. "Like most small publishers, we try to emphasize quality from start to finish, because, for the most part, our titles are going to a specialized market that is very quality conscious. We also feel that one of our strong points is the personal involvement ('touch') so often absent in a much larger organization." Accepts outline/synopsis and 3 sample chapters. Mss must conform to the Chicago *Manual of Style*. Reviews artwork/photos as part of ms package.

Recent Nonfiction Title: *Trout Bum*, by John Gierach.

PSG PUBLISHING CO., INC., 545 Great Rd., Littleton MA 01460. (617)486-8971. President/Publisher: Frank Paparello. Publishes hardcover and paperback originals. Averages 25 titles/year. Receives 100 submissions annually. 50% of books from first-time authors; 100% of books from unagented writers. Pays royalty on net revenues. Specializes in publishing medical and dental books, newsletters, journals, audio tapes and software programs for the professional and student markets. Pays 10-15% royalty. Publishes book an average of 8 months after acceptance. Simultaneous submissions OK. Query for electronic submissions. Computer printout submissions acceptable; prefers letter-quality. Reports in 1 month. Book catalog and ms guidelines for 8½x11 SAE.

Nonfiction: Medical and dental books, newsletters and journals. Request proposal form. Query or submit complete ms. Reviews artwork/photos as part of ms package.

Recent Nonfiction Title: *Smoking and Reproductive Health*, by M.J. Rosenberg, M.D. (clinical monograph for physicians).

Tips: "Books on clinical medicine for practicing professionals have the best chance of selling to our firm." Queries/mss may be routed to other editors in the publishing group.

‡PUBLICATIONS INTERNATIONAL, LTD., 7373 North Cicero Ave., Lincolnwood IL 60646. (312)676-3470. Subsidiaries include Consumer Guide, Favorite Recipes, Collectible Automobile. Acquisitions Editor: Jeff Mintz. Publishes hardcover, trade paperback and mass market paperback originals. Publishes 130 titles annually; receives 20 submissions/year. 5% or books from first-time authors; 100% from unagented writers. Pays authors with outright purchase of 5-20¢/word. Offers advance of ⅓-½ of whole fee. Publishes ms an average of 4-8 months after acceptance. Simultaneous and photocopied submissions OK. Query for electronic submissions. Computer printout submissions OK; prefers letter-quality. Reports in 2 weeks. Free book catalog and ms guidelines.

Nonfiction: Coffee table book, cookbook, how-to, illustrated book, juvenile, reference. Subjects include animals, child guidance/parenting, computers and electronics, cooking, foods and nutrition, education, gardening, health/medicine, hobbies, money/finance, photography, science, sports, consumer information, popular culture for children. Query or submit outline/synopsis and sample chapters. Reviews artwork/photos as part of ms package.

Recent Nonfiction Title: *Complete Pregnancy and Baby Book*, by the editors of Consumer Guide.

Fiction: Juvenile (elementary school level), picture books (elementary school level), young adult. Query.

Recent Fiction Title: *Explorer's Guide to Sharks and Other Creatures of the Sea*.

Tips: "We solicit most of our material, but topical subjects are welcome. Freelance resumes and queries are welcome. Our books are geared to a general audience."

PUBLISHERS ASSOCIATES, Box 160361, Las Colinas TX 75016. (817)572-7400. Subsidiaries include Liberal Arts Press; The Liberal Press; Scholars Books; Tanglelwuld Press; Nicole Graphics; Monument Press and The Galaxy Group. Senior Editor: Art Frederic. Publishes trade paperback originals. Entire firm averages 10 or more titles/year; receives 100 submissions a year. 80% of books from first-time authors; 100% of books from unagented writers. Pays 4-8% royalty on wholesale price at end of each year. Publishes book an average of 1 year after acceptance. No simultaneous submissions; photocopied submissions OK. Computer printout submissions OK; prefers letter-quality. Reports in 1 month on queries; 4 months on mss. Free book catalog.

Nonfiction: Subjects include Americana, art, business and economics, health, history, music, philosophy, politics, psychology, religion and sociology. "We are especially interested in any aspect of woman's history (chronology, nation—no biographies); any aspect of gay history (chronology, period, theme—no biographies, etc.); any aspect of prison life (history, sociology, biographies, psychology); and liberal theology. No diaries, biographies, or anything related to conservative politics or (fundamentalist) religion/theology." Query. Reviews artwork/photos as part of ms package.

Recent Nonfiction Title: *Shadow of an Angel*, by Marion Deutsche Cohen.

Tips: "We publish only liberal academic books. A well-prepared abstract with outline will catch our attention. Always query first. We advertise and sell internationally. Each press in the consortium is independent but we work together. The consortium (Publishers Associates) recommends manuscripts to the individual presses. We desire solid academic gay history and are seeking history of women in Africa."

‡*PUBLISHING HORIZONS, INC., 2950 N. High St., Box 02190, Columbus OH 43202. (614)261-6565. Vice President: Robert N. Anderson. Publishes hardcover and trade paperback originals. Firm averages 15-25 titles/year. 25-30% of books from first-time authors. 100% from unagented writers. Subsidy publishes 1% of books. Pays 5-15% royalty on wholesale price. Publishes book an average of 1 year after acceptance. Simultaneous submissions OK. Computer printout submissions OK; prefers letter-quality. Reports in 3 weeks on queries; 6 weeks on mss. Free book catalog.

Nonfiction: Technical and textbook. Subjects include agriculture/horticulture, business and economics, education, money/finance, nature/environment, recreation, sports and travel. Submit complete ms.

Recent Nonfiction Title: *Hiking the U.S.A.*, by Drother (guidebook).

Q.E.D. INFORMATION SCIENCES, INC., 170 Linden St., Box 181, Wellesley MA 02181. (617)237-5656. Executive Vice President: Edwin F. Kerr. Publishes computer books and software for MIS professionals. Averages 20 titles/year. Pays 10-15% royalty on net receipts. Publishes book an average of 4-6 months after acceptance. Query for electronic submissions. Preliminary reports in 1 week on queries; 3 weeks on mss. Free book catalog.

Nonfiction: Technical. Subjects include computers, personal computing, and database technology. "Our books are read by data processing managers and technicians." Submit outline/synopsis and 2 sample chapters. Reviews artwork/photos as part of ms package.

Recent Nonfiction Title: *Handbook of Screen Design*, by Golitz (professional).

‡*Q.E.D. PRESS OF ANN ARBOR, INC., #6, 1012 Hill St., Ann Arbor MI 48104. (313)994-0371. Managing Editor: Mike Gallatin. Publishes hardcover and trade paperback originals. Publishes 5 titles/year. Receives 7 submissions/year. 60% of books from first-time authors; 75% from unagented writers. Pays 6-15% royalty on retail price. Publishes book an average of 4 months after acceptance. Simultaneous submissions OK. Query for electronic submissions. Computer printout submissions OK; prefers letter-quality. Subsidy publishes "if

the book might not be easily marketable to begin with and we would like to publish it at this point in time but budgetary constraints make it difficult; the option would be we will pick up the tab for reprints." Reports in 1 months on queries; 2 months on mss.
Nonfiction: How-to. Subjects include art/architecture, music/dance (classical, how to set up a studio, piano-related topics), literary criticism, philosophy (existentialism, theory of tragedy). "Music criticism and teaching are high on the list with literary criticism following a close second. How-to and informational books are welcome as well as books about computer technology and in particular, desk-top publishing." Query or submit outline/synopsis and sample chapters.
Recent Nonfiction Title: *Man is Human and Other Observations*, by Irving Pro Boim.
Fiction: Literary. Query or submit outline/synopsis and sample chapters.
Recent Fiction Title: *Jellyfilled: A Collection of Original Aphorisms*, by Loren Hecht.
Tips: "How-to books, informational books and books about computers (desk-top publishing) technology have the best chance of selling to us. Our audience is university professors, local university bookstores, college students, artists and intellectuals. We're looking for books for targeted audience where a small press can better compete with bigger, established publishers."

‡RAGWEED PRESS, Box 2023, 85 Water St., Charlottetown Prince Edward Island C1A 7N7 Canada. (902)566-5750. Imprints include gynery books. Publisher: Libby Oughton. Firm publishes hardcover and trade paperback originals. Publishes an average of 11 titles/year; receives approximately 300 proposals/year. 40% from first-time authors; 95% from unagented writers. Pays authors 8-15% royalty on retail price. Offers average advance of $150 (Canadian). Publishes ms an average of 1 year after acceptance. Photocopied submissions OK. Computer printout submissions OK; prefers letter-quality. Reports in 6 months. Free book catalog.
Nonfiction: Cookbook, juvenile, reference. Subjects include cooking, foods and nutrition, gay/lesbian, language/literature, regional, translation, women's issues/studies. Query.
Recent Nonfiction Title: *Gaslights, Epidemics and Vagabond Cows: Charlottetown in the Victorian Era*, edited by Douglas Baldwin and Thomas Spira.
Fiction: Feminist, gay/lesbian, juvenile, literary, picture books, short story collections, young adult. Submit complete ms.
Recent Fiction Title: *The Corrigan Women*, by M.T. (Jean) Dohaney.
Poetry: Submit complete ms.
Recent Poetry Title: *The Breaking Up Poems*, by C.M. Donald (feminist).
Tips: "We want our audience to be appreciative of good literature presented in a carefully designed and produced format. It is beneficial to be patient, persistent and maintain a sense of humor."

RAINBOW BOOKS, Box 1069, Moore Haven FL 33471. (813)946-0293. Associate: B. Lampe. Publishes hardcover and trade paperback originals. Averages 8-10 titles/year; receives 600 submissions annually. 70% of books from first-time authors; 50% of books from unagented writers. Publishes book an average of 8 months after acceptance. Reports in 1 week. Book catalog for 9x6 SAE and 3 first class stamps; ms guidelines for #10 SAE and 2 first class stamps.
Nonfiction: Reference and resource books plus some well-targeted how-to. "Writers without agents query only please."
Recent Nonfiction Title: *Beyond Victim: You Can Overcome Childhood Abuse . . . Even Sexual Abuse*, by Martha Baldwin, psychotherapist.
Tips: "We may be interested in seeing good fiction. However, by query letter and synopsis only please. We are always interested in seeing good reference and resource books. Please query with what you have before sending it along."

‡RANDALL HOUSE PUBLICATIONS, Box 17306, Nashville TN 37217. (615)361-1221. Editor-in-Chief: H.D. Harrison. 25% of books from first-time authors; 95% of books from unagented writers. Pays royalties. Publishes book an average of 9 months after acceptance. Computer printout submissions acceptable; prefers letter-quality. Reports in 6 weeks on mss. Book catalog and ms guidelines for 9x12 SAE with 4 first class stamps.
Nonfiction: Religious. Submit complete ms.
Recent Nonfiction Title: *Patience: Miracle in Progress*, by Winget.
Fiction: Religious. Submit query letter, contents page and 2 sample chapters.
Recent Fiction Title: *All My Tomorrows*.
Tips: "True life experience from conservative Christian viewpoint and Biblical analysis/exegesis from Arminian Baptist perspective have the best chance of selling to our firm."

RANDOM HOUSE, INC., Subsidary of Advance Publications, 201 E. 50th St., New York NY 10022. Random House Trade Division publishes 120 titles/year; receives 3,000 submissions annually. Pays royalty on retail price. Simultaneous and photocopied submissions OK. Reports in 3 weeks on queries; 6 weeks on mss. Free book catalog; ms guidelines for #10 SASE.

Nonfiction: Biography, cookbook, humor, illustrated book, self-help. Subjects include Americana, art, business and economics, cooking and foods, health, history, music, nature, politics, psychology, religion, sociology and sports. No juveniles or textbooks (separate division). Query with outline/synopsis and sample chapters.
Fiction: Adventure, confession, experimental, fantasy, historical, horror, humor, mainstream, mystery, and suspense. Submit outline/synopsis and sample chapters. "SASE is helpful."
Tips: "If I were a writer trying to market a book today, I would get an agent."

‡RANDOM HOUSE, INC./ALFRED A. KNOPF, INC. JUVENILE BOOKS, 201 E. 50th St., New York NY 10022. (212)572-2653. Subsidiaries include Knopf Children's Paperbacks, Knopf Children's Books (Bullseye Books, Dragonfly Books and Borzoi Sprinters), Random House Children's Books. Managing Editor: R. Abend. Random House Juvenile/Knopf Juvenile: J. Schulman, Editor-in-Chief; Associate Publisher: S. Spinner, Executive Editor; Nonfiction: R. Kahney, Editor. Firm publishes hardcover, trade paperback and mass market paperback originals, and mass market paperback reprints. Publishes 250 titles/year. Simultaneous submissions OK. Free book catalog.
Nonfiction: Biography, humor, illustrated book, juvenile. Subjects include animals, nature/environment, recreation, science, sports. Query or submit outline/synopsis and sample chapters. Submit ms through agent only.
Fiction: Adventure, confession (young adult), fantasy, historical, horror, humor, juvenile, mystery, picture books, science fiction (juvenile/young adult), suspense, young adult. Submit through agent only.
Tips: Books for children 6 months to 15 years old.

THE REAL COMET PRESS, Subsidiary of Such a Deal Corporation, #410, 3131 Western Ave., Seattle WA 98121. (206)283-7827. Publisher: Catherine Hillenbrand. Publishes hardcover and trade paperback originals and trade paperback reprints. Averages 5 titles/year; receives 100 submissions annually. 30% of books from first-time authors; 50% from unagented writers. Pays royalty on list or wholesale price. Publishes book an average of 15-24 months after acceptance. Simultaneous and photocopied submissions OK. Computer printout submissions OK. Free book catalog; writer's guidelines for #10 SASE.
Nonfiction: Visual books, humor, exhibition catalog and political commentary. Subjects include art, contemporary culture, music, photography, politics and sociology. "Art books, comics, critique, political commentary, and books on popular culture have the best chance of selling to our firm." Submit outline/synopsis and sample chapters. Reviews artwork/photos.
Recent Nonfiction Title: *Unwinding the Vietnam War: From War Toward Peace*, by Reese Williams, editor.
Tips: "We have just added an imprint of flip books to our list and we are interested in books that incorporate motion as well as visuals. We are publishing 2 biographies next season and we are interested in biographies in the fields of art, politics and popular culture."

REGAL BOOKS, Division of Gospel Light Publications, 2300 Knoll Dr., Ventura CA 93003. Managing Director Acquisitions: Keith Wintermute. Publishes hardcover and paperback originals. Averages 15 titles/year. Receives 5,000 submissions annually. 20% of books from first-time authors; 90% of books from unagented writers. Average print order for writer's first book is 5,000. Pays 10% royalty on paperback titles, 10% net for curriculum books. Publishes book an average of 11 months after acceptance. Buys all rights. Computer printout submissions acceptable; prefers letter-quality. Reports in 3 months. Book catalog and ms guidelines for 8½x11 SAE and $2 postage.
Nonfiction: Bible studies (Old and New Testament), Christian living, counseling (self-help), contemporary concerns, evangelism (church growth), marriage and family, youth, inspirational/devotional, communication resources, teaching enrichment resources, Bible commentary for Laymen Series, and missions. Query or submit detailed outline/synopsis and 2-3 sample chapters; no complete mss.
Recent Nonfiction Title: *Our Family's First Bible Story Book*, by Ethel Barnett.

REGNERY/GATEWAY, INC., Imprints/divisions include Cahill and Co., Gateway Distribution and Fullfillment Services and Gateway Editions, Suite 620, 1130 17th St. N.W., Washington DC 20036. Editor: Harry Crocker. Vice President: Thomas A. Palmer. Publishes hardcover and paperback originals and paperback reprints. Averages 25 titles/year. Pays royalty. Simultaneous and photocopied submissions OK. Computer printout submissions acceptable. "Responds only to submissions in which there is interest." Book catalog for 8½x11 SAE.
Nonfiction: Politics, philosophy, economics, religion. Accepts nonfiction translations. "We are looking for books on current affairs." Queries preferred. Additional information if requested. Looks for "a novel approach to the subject, expertise of the author and salability of the proposed work."
Recent Nonfiction Title: *Ambassador in Paris*, by Evan Galbraith (politics/diplomacy).

RELIGIOUS EDUCATION PRESS, 1531 Wellington Rd., Birmingham AL 35209. (205)879-4040. Editor: James Michael Lee. Publishes trade paperback originals. Averages 5 titles/year; receives 120 submissions annually. 40% of books from first-time authors; 100% of books from unagented writers. Pays 10% royalty on actual selling price. "Many of our books are work for hire. We do not have a subsidy option." Offers no advance. Photocopied submissions OK. Query for electronic submissions. Computer printout submissions OK; no dot-matrix. Reports in 1 month on queries; 2 months on mss. Free book catalog.

Nonfiction: Technical and textbook. Scholarly subjects on religion and religious education. "We publish serious, significant and scholarly books on religious education and pastoral ministry." No mss under 200 pages, books on Biblical interpretation, or "popular" books. Query. Reviews artwork/photos as part of ms package.

Recent Nonfiction Title: *Faith Development and Fowler*, by Craig Dykstra and Sharon Parks.

Tips: "Write clearly, reason exactly and connectively, and meet deadlines."

*RESOURCE PUBLICATIONS, INC., Suite 290, 160 E. Virginia St., San Jose CA 95112. Editorial Director: Kenneth E. Guentert. Publishes paperback originals. Publishes 14 titles/year; receives 100-200 submissions annually. 30% of books from first-time authors; 99% of books from unagented writers. Average print order for a writer's first book is 2,000. Subsidy publishes 10% of books. "If the author can present and defend a personal publicity effort or otherwise demonstrate demand and the work is in our field, we will consider it." Pays 8% royalty; occasionally offers advance in the form of books. Publishes book an average of 18 months after acceptance. Photocopied submissions (with written assurance that work is not being submitted simultaneously) OK. Query for electronic submissions. Computer printout submissions acceptable; prefers letter-quality. Reports in 2 months.

Nonfiction: "We look for creative but practical books relating to worship, celebrations of all kinds and the arts. How-to books, especially for contemporary religious art forms, are of particular interest (dance, mime, drama, choral reading, singing, music, musicianship, bannermaking, statuary, or any visual art form). No heavy theoretical, philosophical, or theological tomes. Nothing utterly unrelated or unrelatable to celebration. Query or submit outline/synopsis and sample chapters. "Prepare a clear outline of the work and an ambitious schedule of public appearances to help make it known and present both as a proposal to the publisher. With our company a work that can be serialized or systematically excerpted in our periodicals is always given special attention." Accepts translations. Reviews artwork/photos as part of ms package.

Recent Nonfiction Title: *Symbols For All Seasons*, by Katherine Krier.

Fiction: "Any collected short works in the areas of drama, dance, song, stories, anecdotes or good visual art, especially if related to worship celebrations, festivals, or mythology." Query or submit outline/synopsis and sample chapters.

Tips: "Books that provide readers with practical, usable suggestions and ideas pertaining to worship, celebration, education, and the arts have the best chance of selling to our firm. We've moved more clearly into the celebration resources field and are looking for resources on popular—as well as little known—celebrations, feasts, and rituals to complement our strong backlist of worship resources."

REVIEW AND HERALD PUBLISHING ASSOCIATION, 55 West Oak Ridge Dr., Hagerstown MD 21740. Acquisitions Editor: Penny Wheeler. Publishes hardcover and paperback originals and software. Specializes in religious-oriented books. Averages 30-40 titles/year; receives 300 submissions annually. 15% of books from first-time authors; 100% of books from unagented writers. Average print order for a writer's first book is 5,000-7,500. Pays 14% of retail price, hardcover; 12% of retail price, softcover; offers average $500 advance. Publishes book an average of 1 year after acceptance. Computer printout submissions acceptable; prefers letter-quality. Encourages computer diskette submissions. Reports in 3 months. Free brochure; ms guidelines for SASE.

Nonfiction: Juveniles (religious-oriented only), nature, and religious, all 20,000-60,000 words; 128 pages average. Query or submit outline/synopsis and 2-3 sample chapters. Prefers to do own illustrating. Looks for "literary style, constructive tone, factual accuracy, compatibility with Adventist theology and lifestyle, and length of manuscript." Reviews artwork/photos as part of ms package.

Tips: "Familiarize yourself with Adventist theology because Review and Herald Publishing Association is owned and operated by the Seventh-day Adventist Church. We are accepting fewer but better-written manuscripts."

RICHBORO PRESS, Box 1, Richboro PA 18954. (215)364-2212. Editor: George Moore. Publishes hardcover, trade paperback originals and software. Averages 6 titles/year; receives 500 submissions annually. 90% of books from unagented writers. Average print order for a writer's first book is 500. Pays 10% royalty on retail price. Publishes book an average of 1 year after acceptance. Query for electronic submissions. Computer printout submissions acceptable. Reports in 6 weeks on queries; 3 months on mss. Free book catalog; ms guidelines $1 with SASE.

Nonfiction: Cookbook, how-to and gardening. Subjects include cooking and foods. Query.

Recent Nonfiction Title: *Classified Advertising*, 5th Edition, by Blair.

THE RIVERDALE COMPANY, INC., PUBLISHERS, Suite 102, 5506 Kenilworth Ave., Riverdale MD 20737. (301)864-2029. President: John Adams. Vice President: Adele Manuel. Editor: Mary Power. Publishes hardcover originals. Averages 16-18 titles/year; receives 100 submissions annually. 20% of books from first-

time authors; 100% of books from unagented writers. Pays 0-15% royalty on wholesale price. Publishes book an average of 8 months after acceptance. Computer printout submissions acceptable; prefers letter-quality. Reports in 1 week on queries; 2 months on mss. Book catalog for SASE.
Nonfiction: "We publish technical and social science books for scholars, students, policymakers; and tour, restaurant and recreational guides for the mass market." Subjects include economics, history, humanities, politics, psychology, sociology and travel. Especially needs social science and travel mss on South Asia or Africa. Will consider college text proposals in economics and Third World studies; travel guides of any sort. Query. Accepts outline/synopsis and 2-3 sample chapters.
Recent Nonfiction Title: *Industrial Change in India, 1970-2000*, by George Rosen.

ROCKY TOP PUBLICATIONS, Subsidiary of Rocky Top Industries, Box 33, Stamford NY 12167. President/Publisher: Joseph D. Jennings. Publishes hardcover and paperback originals. Averages 4-6 titles/year. 70% of books from first-time authors; 95% of books from unagented writers. Pays 4-10% royalty (may vary) on wholesale price. Publishes book an average of 6 months after acceptance. Photocopied submissions OK. Computer printout submissions acceptable; prefers letter-quality. No unsolicited mss.
Nonfiction: How-to, reference, self-help and technical. Subjects include animal health; health; hobbies (crafts); medical; nature; philosophy (Thoreau or environmental only); and science. "We are actively looking for exposé-type material on science, medicine and health—well written and researched only." No autobiographies, biographies, business "get rich quick" or fad books.
Recent Nonfiction Title: *The Hydroponic Workbook*, by J. Gooze (technical).
Tips: "Our readers range from self-sufficiency people, to medical and health professionals, environmentalists, and gardeners. Scientific, medical, health, pharmaceutical, and environmental (conservation, naturalist) books have the best chance of selling to us."

RODALE PRESS, Health Books Division, 33 E. Minor St., Emmaus PA 18049. (215)967-5171. Senior Editor: Sharon Faelten. Publishes hardcover and trade paperback originals and reprints. Averages 8-10 titles/year; receives 100 submissions annually. 20% of books from first-time authors; 25% of books from unagented writers. Pays royalty on retail price: 10-15% trade hardcover; 6-7% trade paperback; 2% major mail order or 5% book club. Offers average $10,000 advance. Publishes book an average of 1 year after acceptance. Simultaneous and photocopied submissions OK. Query for electronic submissions. Computer printout submissions acceptable; prefers letter-quality. Reports in 1 month. Free book catalog.
Nonfiction: Cookbook, how-to, reference, self-help—all health books. Subjects include health, psychology and fitness. Especially interested in "how-to books on health care with practical, self-help information by doctors and other health professionals, or a careful author using primary medical studies. Also looking for books on walking, bicycling, backpacking, cross-country skiing and other lifetime sports." No technical, textbook, non-health related books. Query with outline/synopsis and sample chapters. Reviews artwork/photos.
Recent Nonfiction Title: *Take Control of Your Life: A Complete Guide to Stress Relief*, by Sharon Faelten.
Tips: "Our audience is over 50 years of age, health conscious, mostly women. Writers have the best chance of selling us health books that focus on practical, self-help care information, with emphasis on mind-body interaction and alternative therapies, especially by pioneers in their field. We are also looking for books on new concepts in fitness re. walking, bicycling and other lifetime sports. No chidcare/parenting books."

‡*RONIN PUBLISHING INC., Box 1035, Berkeley CA 94701. (415)540-6278. Publisher: Sebastian Orfal. Publishes originals and trade paperback reprints. Averages 4 titles/year; receives 150-300 submissions annually. 25% of books from first-time authors. Query for electronic submissions.
Nonfiction: How-to (business), humor, and illustrated book. Subjects include business and economics, health, nutrition and psychology (business). "We are primarily interested in management psychology how-to." Query.
Recent Nonfiction Title: *Way of the Ronin*.

THE ROSEN PUBLISHING GROUP, 29 E. 21st St., New York NY 10010. (212)777-3017. President: Roger Rosen. Imprints include Pelion Press (music titles). Publishes hardcover originals. Entire firm averages 46 titles/year; young adult division averages 4-35 titles/year. 45% of books from first-time authors; 80% of books from unagented writers. Pays royalty or makes outright purchase. Publishes book an average of 9 months after acceptance. Simultaneous and photocopied submissions OK. Computer printout submissions acceptable; prefers letter-quality. Reports in 1 month. Book catalog and guidelines for 8½x11 SAE with 3 first class stamps.
Nonfiction: Young adult, reference, self-help and textbook. Subjects include art, health (coping), and music. "Our books are geared to the young adult audience whom we reach via school and public libraries. Most of the books we publish are related to career guidance and personal adjustment. We also publish material on the theatre, music and art, as well as journalism for schools. Interested in supplementary material for enrichment of school curriculum. We have begun a high/low division and are interested in material that is supplementary to the curriculum written at a 4 reading level for teenagers who are reluctant readers." Mss in the young adult nonfiction areas include vocational guidance, personal and social adjustment, journalism and theatre. For Pelion

Press, mss on classical music, emphasis on opera and singing. Query or submit outline/synopsis and sample chapters. Reviews artwork/photos as part of ms package.
Recent Nonfiction Title: *Coping with Sexual Abuse*, by Judith Cooney.
Tips: "The writer has the best chance of selling our firm a book on vocational guidance or personal social adjustment, or high-interest, low reading level material for teens."

ROSS BOOKS, Box 4340, Berkeley CA 94704. President: Franz Ross. Small press. Publishes hardcover and paperback originals, paperback reprints, and software. Averages 7-10 titles/year; receives 200 submissions annually. 90% of books from first-time authors; 99% of books from unagented writers. Average print order for a writer's first book is 5,000-10,000. Offers 8-12% royalty on net price. Offers average advance of 2% of the first print run. Publishes book an average of 1 year after acceptance. Simultaneous and photocopied submissions OK. Query for electronic submissions. Computer printout submissions acceptable; prefers letter-quality. Reports in 1 month. Book catalog for 6x9 SAE with 2 first class stamps.
Nonfiction: Popular how-to on science, business, general how-to. No political, religious or children's books. Accepts nonfiction translations. Submit outline or synopsis of no more than 3 pages and 1 sample chapter with SASE. Reviews artwork/photos as part of ms package.
Recent Nonfiction Title: *Meet the Stars*, by Missy Laws.
Tips: "We are looking for books on holography and desktop publishing."

‡ROUNDTABLE PUBLISHING, INC., 933 Pico Blvd., Santa Monica CA 90405. (213)450-9777. Senior Editor: Darrell Houghton. Publishes hardcover and trade paperback originals. Averages 5-15 titles/year; receives 100 submissions annually. 25% of books from first-time authors; 10% of books from unagented writers. Pays royalty on retail price. Publishes book an average of 18 months after acceptance. Simultaneous and photocopied submissions OK. Computer printout submissions acceptable; prefers letter-quality. Reports in 1 month on queries; 2 months on mss.
Nonfiction: Biography, how-to, humor and self-help. Subjects include art, motion pictures and TV, business and economics, health, politics and psychology. Especially interested in celebrity biographies, motion picture and TV related books, juvenile, how-to or self-help. No cookbooks, history or textbooks. Submit outline/synopsis and sample chapters or complete ms. Reviews artwork/photos as part of ms package.
Recent Nonfiction Titles: *Same Song Separate Voices*, Lennon Sisters (autobiography).
Fiction: Adventure, gothic, historical, mainstream, mystery, romance, science fiction, fantasy and suspense. Averages 1 book/year. No pornography. Submit complete ms.
Recent Fiction Title: *Eternal Fire*, by Michel Fattah (historical novel).
Tips: "Our books are for a mainstream audience—children and adult. Writers have the best chance of selling us biographies."

‡ROUTLEDGE, Routledge, Chapman & Hall, 29 West 35th St., New York NY 10001. (212)244-3336. Subsidiaries include Tavistock, Croom Helm, Arkana, Theatre Arts. Editorial Director: William P. Germano. Publishes hardcover and trade paperback originals. Averages 40 titles/year. Receives 200 submissions/year. 50% of books from first-time authors; 95% of books from unagented writers. Pays (average 10%) royalty on retail price. Publishes book 10 months after acceptance. Computer printout submissions OK; prefers letter-quality. Reports in 3 weeks on queries; 2 months on mss.
Nonfiction: Biography and scholarly. Subjects include gay/lesbian (scholarly), history (especially women's history, American history), language/literature (literary theory, criticism), military/war (military history), music/dance (scholarly history; practical works in theatre), psychoanalysis, religion (philosophy of), women's issues/studies (scholarly), film and television studies. Query or submit outline/synopsis and sample chapters.
Recent Nonfiction Title: *Men in Feminism*, by Jardine and Smith (scholarly essays).
Tips: "Most of our authors hold academic appointments at colleges or universities. Their work is scholarly but tends to be written for an audience somewhat broader than that of a university press."

ROUTLEDGE, CHAPMAN & HALL, INC., 29 W. 35th St., New York NY 10001. (212)244-3336. 25 subject editors in the U.K. Editorial Director (New York): William P. Germano. Editor for philosophy, psychoanalysis, education: Maureen MacGrogan. Editor for life sciences: Gregory Payne. Science books published under Chapman and Hall. Humanities and social sciences published under Routledge. New corporate name comprises former imprints Methuen; Routledge & Kegan Paul; Croom Helm; Tavistock. Also publishers of Theatre Arts Books. Chapman & Hall list includes scientific and technical books in life and physical sciences, statistics, allied health, science reference. Routledge list includes humanities, social sciences, business and economics, reference. Monographs, reference works, hardback and paperback upper-level texts, academic general interest. Averages 800 titles/year; receives 5,000 submissions annually. 10% of books from first-time authors; 95% of books from unagented authors. Average royalty 10% net receipts; offers average $1,000 advance. High-quality computer printout submissions acceptable. No simultaneous submissions. Reports in 4-6 weeks on queries. Do not send manuscripts at initial stage. No replies to unsolicited inquiries without SASE.
Nonfiction: Monograph, textbook, reference work. Academic subjects include reference, biography, philos-

ophy, literary criticism, psychoanalysis, social sciences, business and economics, history, psychology, women's studies, political science, anthropology, geography, education. Scientific subjects include biology, ecology, statistics, materials science, chemistry.

*ROWMAN & LITTLEFIELD, PUBLISHERS, Division of Littlefield Adams & Co., 81 Adams Dr., Totowa NJ 07512. Managing Director: Arthur Hamparian. Publishes hardcover and paperback originals and reprints. Receives 500 submissions annually. 50% of books from first-time authors; 100% of books from unagented writers. Subsidy publishes 5% of books; subsidy publishes (nonauthor) 3% of books. Pays 4-10% royalty on net sales; offers no advance. Publishes book an average of 9 months after acceptance. Query for electronic submissions. Computer printout submissions acceptable; prefers letter-quality. Reports in 2 months. Free book catalog; ms guidelines for #10 SAE with 2 first class stamps.
Nonfiction: Scholarly and academic books. Subjects include philosophy, social sciences, women's studies, economics and finance, health care, criminology and legal studies, public affairs, geography, computer science and statistics. "Our authors are typically academics writing for other professionals, for government bodies and other organizations which utilize primary research." Submit outline/synopsis and sample chapters.
Recent Nonfiction Title: *Incentives, Cooperation, and Risk Sharing*, edited by Haig R. Nalbantian.

ROXBURY PUBLISHING CO., Box 491044, Los Angeles CA 90049. (213)653-1068. Executive Editor: Claude Teweles. Publishes hardcover and paperback originals and reprints. Averages 20 titles/year. Pays royalty; offers negotiable advance. Simultaneous, photocopied and computer printout submissions OK. Reports in 1 month.
Nonfiction: College-level textbooks only. Subjects include business and economics, humanities, philosophy, psychology, social sciences and sociology. Query, submit outline/synopsis and sample chapters, or submit complete ms.
Recent Nonfiction Title: *The Writing Cycle*, by Clela Allphin-Hoggatt.

‡ROYAL PUBLISHING CO., Subsidiary of ROMC (Recipes of the Month Club), Box 5027, Beverly Hills CA 90210. (213)277-3340. President: Mrs. Harold Klein. Publishes hardcover, trade, and mass market paperback originals. Averages 4 titles/year; receives 400-500 submissions annually. 50% of books from first-time authors; 50% of books from unagented writers. Pays 8-12% royalty on retail price; buys some mss outright. Publishes book an average of 1 year after acceptance. Photocopied submissions OK. Query for electronic submissions. Computer printout submissions acceptable; prefers letter-quality. Free book catalog.
Nonfiction: Cookbook. "We especially need cookbooks, diet, food history and specialty cookbooks." Submit complete ms. Reviews artwork/photos as part of ms package.
Recent Nonfiction Title: *Entertaining Fast & Fancy*, by Darling.

RPM PRESS, INC., Box 31483, Tucson AZ 85751. Publisher: David A. Hietala. Publishes trade paperback originals, audio-cassette training programs (with workbook) and selected software. Averages 6 titles/year; receives 75-150 submissions annually. 75% of books from first-time authors; 100% of books from unagented writers. Average print order for a writer's first book is 1,000-5,000. Pays 5-15% royalty on retail price or makes outright purchases of $200-1,500. Offers average advance to established authors of $500. Publishes book/training program an average of 6-9 months after acceptance. Simultaneous and photocopied submissions OK. Query for electronic submissions. Computer printout submissions OK; no dot-matrix. Reports in 5 weeks on queries; 2 months on mss (usually sooner for both). Book catalog for 9x12 SAE and with 3 first class stamps.
Nonfiction: Vocational training and job preparation materials for vocational preparation of high school level handicapped students. Includes instructor's handbook, student workbooks, audio tapes or software. Must be practical material, oriented toward teaching job getting and keeping skills to these students. We offer extensive editorial assistance to people with good ideas. Query.
Recent Nonfiction Title: *"Yes I Can . . . Get That Job and Keep It!"*, by P. McCray (multi-media program).

RUTGERS UNIVERSITY PRESS, 109 Church St., New Brunswick NJ 08901. Averages 50 titles/year; receives 600 submissions annually. 30% of books from first-time authors; 80% of books from unagented writers. Average print order for a writer's first book is 2,000. Pays royalty on retail price. Publishes book an average of 1 year after acceptance. Query for electronic submissions. Computer printout submissions acceptable; no dot-matrix. Final decision depends on time required to secure competent professional reading reports. Book catalog and ms guidelines for 9x12 SAE with 4 first class stamps.
Nonfiction: Scholarly books in history, literary criticism, film studies, art history, anthropology, sociology, science, technology, women's studies and criminal justice. Regional nonfiction must deal with mid-Atlantic region. Length: 60,000 words minimum. Query. Reviews artwork/photos as part of ms package.
Recent Nonfiction Title: *Black Pearls: Blues Queens of the 1920s*, by Daphne Duval Harrison.

S. C. E.-EDITIONS L'ETINCELLE, Suite 206, 4920 Blvd. de Maisonneuve W. Westmount, Montreal, Quebec H3Z 1N1 Canada. (514)488-9531. President: Robert Davies. Publishes trade paperback originals in French translation. Averages 12 titles/year; receives 200 submissions annually. 10% of books from first-time authors; 80% of books from unagented writers. Average print order for a writer's first book is 4,000. Pays 8-12% royalty on retail price; offers average $1,000 advance. Publishes book an average of 1 year after acceptance. Simultaneous and photocopied submissions OK. Query for electronic submissions. Computer printout submissions acceptable. Reports in 2 months on queries; 4 months on mss. Book catalog and ms guidelines for 9x12 SAE with 2 IRCs.Imprints include: L'Etincelle (nonfiction and fiction). Memoire Vive (microcomputer books).
Nonfiction: Biography, cookbook, how-to, humor, reference and self-help. Subjects include animals, business and economics, cooking and foods, health, history, hobbies, microcomputers, nature, philosophy, politics, psychology, recreation, sociology, sports and travel. Accepts nonfiction translations. "We are looking for about five translatable works of nonfiction, in any popular field. Our audience includes French-speaking readers in all major markets in the world." No topics of interest only to Americans. Query or submit outline/synopsis and 3 sample chapters. Reviews artwork/photos as part of ms package.
Recent Nonfiction Title: *The Wonderful World of Milk*, by Dr. A. Amsollem.

‡**S.O.C.O. PUBLICATIONS**, RD #1, Box 71, Mohawk NY 13407. Publisher: Carol Ann Vercz. Publishes trade paperback originals. Firm averages 15-20 titles/year. Receives 500 submissions/year. 85% of books from first-time authors. 75% from unagented writers. Pays royalty. Simultaneous submissions OK. Query for electronic submissions. Computer printout submissions OK; prefers letter-quality. Reports in 4-6 weeks on queries; 2-4 weeks on mss. Book catalog, manuscript guidelines for 9x12 SAE and $1 postage.
Nonfiction: Biography, coffee table book, cookbook, how-to, humor, self-help, technical and textbook. Subjects include Americana, animals, business and economics, cooking, foods and nutrition, history, hobbies, nature/environment, photography, sports and travel. "Americana, natural history, animals, cookbooks, history and how-to books are our needs. We are not interested in politics or automotive books." Query. Reviews artwork/photos as part of manuscript package.
Recent Nonfiction Title: *Such Agreeable Friends*, by Gay L. Balliet (animals).
Fiction: Subjects include adventure, historical, mainstream/contemporary, mystery, romance, suspense and western. "Suspense, historical and mainstream novels are our needs. We are not interested in erotica or gothic novels." Query.
Poetry: Submit 6-12 samples.
Recent Poetry Title: *To Peter With Love*.

ST. ANTHONY MESSENGER PRESS, 1615 Republic St., Cincinnati OH 45210. Editor-in-Chief: The Rev. Norman Perry, O.F.M. Publishes paperback originals. Averages 14 titles/year; receives 250 submissions annually. 10% of books from first-time authors; 100% of books from unagented writers. Pays 6-8% royalty on retail price; offers average $600 advance. Publishes book an average of 8 months after acceptance. Books are sold in bulk to groups (study clubs, high school or college classes, and parishes) and in bookstores. Photocopied submissions OK if they are not simultaneous submissions to other publishers. Query for electronic submissions. Computer printout submissions acceptable; no dot-matrix. Book catalog and ms guidelines for 9x12 SAE with 2 first class stamps.
Nonfiction: Religion. "We try to reach the Catholic market with topics near the heart of the ordinary Catholic's belief. We want to offer insight and inspiration and thus give people support in living a Christian life in a pluralistic society. We are not interested in an academic or abstract approach. Our emphasis is on popular writing with examples, specifics, color and anecdotes." Length: 25,000-40,000 words. Query or submit outline and 2 sample chapters. Reviews artwork/photos as part of ms package.
Recent Nonfiction Title: *Living With Sickness: A Struggle Toward Meaning*, by Susan Saint Sing (inspirational).
Tips: "The book cannot be the place for the author to think through a subject. The author has to think through the subject first and then tell the reader what is important to know. Style uses anecdotes, examples, illustrations, human interest, 'colorful' quotes, fiction techniques of suspense, dialogue, characterization, etc. Address practical problems, deal in concrete situations, free of technical terms and professional jargon."

ST. MARTIN'S PRESS, 175 5th Ave., New York NY 10010. Averages 1,100 titles/year; receives 3,000 submissions annually. 15-20% of books from first-time authors; 30% of books from unagented writers. Query for electronic submissions. Computer printout submission acceptable; prefers letter-quality. Reports "promptly."
Nonfiction and Fiction: General and textbook. Publishes general fiction and nonfiction; major interest in adult fiction and nonfiction, history, self-help, political science, popular science, biography, scholarly, popular reference, etc. Query. Reviews artwork/photos as part of ms package. "It takes very persuasive credentials to prompt us to commission a book or outline."
Recent Title: *Hot Flashes*, by Barbara Raskin.
Tips: "We do almost every kind of book there is—trade, textbooks, reference and mass market. Crime fiction has the best chance of selling to our firm—over fifteen percent of all the trade books we published are this category."

‡ST. PAUL BOOKS AND MEDIA, Daughters of St. Paul, 50 St. Paul's Ave., Boston MA 02130. (617)522-8911. Director, Editorial Department: Sister Mary Mark, FSP. Firm publishes hardcover, trade paperback originals, and hardcover and trade paperback reprints. Average 20 titles/year; receives approximately 200 proposals/year. Pays authors 10-15% royalty on wholesale price. Advance is negotiable. Publishes ms an average of 12-18 months after acceptance. Photocopied submissions OK. Computer printout submissions OK; no dot-matrix. Reports in 2 weeks on queries; in 6 weeks on mss. Book catalog free; ms guidelines for #10 SASE.
Nonfiction: Biography, juvenile, self-help. Subjects include child guidance/parenting, psychology and religion. "No strictly secular manuscripts." Query or submit outline/synopsis and sample chapters.
Recent Nonfiction Title: *Spiritual Journeys*, edited by Robert Baram (27 brief biographies).
Fiction: Juvenile, religious, young adult. "We want books promoting moral values for children, adolescents and young adults." Query or submit outline/synopsis and sample chapters.
Tips: "We are looking for books with a religious and/or moral orientation."

*ST. VLADIMIR'S SEMINARY PRESS, 575 Scarsdale Rd., Crestwood NY 10707. (914)961-8313. Managing Editor: Theodore Bazil. Publishes hardcover and trade paperback originals and reprints. Averages 15 titles/year. Subsidy publishes 20% of books. Market considerations determine whether an author should be subsidy published. Pays 7% royalty on retail price. Simultaneous and photocopied submissions OK. Computer printout submissions acceptable; prefers letter-quality. Reports in 3 months on queries; 6 months on mss. Free book catalog and ms guidelines.
Nonfiction: Religion dealing with Eastern Orthodox theology. Query. Reviews artwork/photos as part of ms package.
Tips: "We have an interest in books that stand on firm theological ground; careful writing and scholarship are basic."

SANDLAPPER PUBLISHING, INC., Box 1932, Orangeburg SC 29116. (803)531-1658. Acquisitions: Frank N. Handal. Publishes hardcover and trade paperback originals and reprints. Averages 6 titles/year; receives 200 submissions annually. 80% of books from first-time authors; 95% of books from unagented writers. Pays 15% maximum royalty on net receipts. Publishes book on average of 20 months after acceptance. Photocopied submissions OK; simultaneous submissions OK if informed. Computer printout submissions acceptable. Reports in 1 month on queries; 6 months on mss. Book catalog and ms guidelines for 9x12 SAE with 4 first class stamps.
Nonfiction: History, biography, illustrated books, humor, cookbook, juvenile, reference and textbook. Subjects are limited to history, culture and cuisine of the Southeast and especially South Carolina. "We are looking for manuscripts that reveal underappreciated or undisocvered facets of the rich heritage of our region. If a manuscript doesn't deal with South Carolina or the Southeast, the work is probably not apporpriate for us. We don't do self-help books, children's books about divorce, kidnapping, etc., and absolutely no religious manuscripts." Query or submit outline synopsis and sample chapters "if you're not sure it's what we're looking for, otherwise complete ms." Reviews artwork/photos as part of ms package.
Recent Nonfiction Title: *South Carolina's Low Country: A Past Preserved*, by Catherine Campani Mesmer and C. Andrew Halcomb.
Fiction: We do not need fiction submissions at present, "but I will look at good strong fiction by South Carolinians and other regional writers. We will not consider any horror, romance or religious fiction." Query or submit outline/synopsis and sample chapters. "Do check with us on books dealing with regional nature, science and outdoor subjects."
Tips: "Our readers are South Carolinians, visitors to the region's tourist spots, and friends and family that live out-of-state. We are striving to be a leading regional publisher for South Carolina. We will be looking for more history and biography."

SANTA BARBARA PRESS, Suite C, 815 Dela Vina St., Santa Barbara CA 93101. (805)966-2060. Editor-in-Chief: George Erikson. Publishes hardcover and trade paperback originals, and trade paperback reprints. Averages 12 titles/year; receives 75 submissions annually. 50% of books from first-time authors; 50% of books from unagented writers. Pays 5-10% royalty. Offers maximum $1,000 advance. Publishes book an average of 1 year after acceptance. Simultaneous submissions OK. Query for electronic submissions. Computer printout submissions acceptable; no dot-matrix. Reports in 3 weeks on queries; 3 months on mss. Book catalog for 4x9 SAE with 2 first class stamps.
Nonfiction: Biography, how-to and self-help. Subjects include philosophy, religion, sociology, sports and

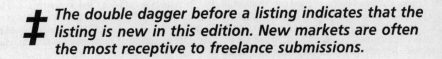

The double dagger before a listing indicates that the listing is new in this edition. New markets are often the most receptive to freelance submissions.

travel. "Our nonfiction book manuscript needs include biography and autobiographies." No humor, juvenile or cookbooks. Query.

Recent Nonfiction Title: *Color Your Life!*, by Elaine Ryan.

‡**SASQUATCH BOOKS**, Sasquatch Publishing Co., 1931 Second Ave., Seattle WA 98101. (206)441-5555. Associate Publisher: Chad Haight. Firm publishes hardcover and trade paperback originals. Averages 4-6 titles/year; receives approximately 50 ms/year. 25% of books from first-time authors; 95% from unagented writers. Pays authors 5-12% royalty on net price. Offers wide range of advances. Publishes ms an average of 6 months after acceptance. Simultaneous and photocopied submissions OK. Query for electronic submissions. Computer printout submissions OK. Reports in 1 month. Free book catalog.

Nonfiction: Biography, coffee table book, cookbook, how-to, humor, illustrated book, juvenile, travel guidebooks. Subjects include art/architecture, business and economics, cooking, foods and nutrition, gardening, government/politics, history, language/literature, nature/environment, photography, recreation, regional, sports and travel. "We are only seeking quality nonfiction works by, about or for people of the Pacific Northwest region. In this sense we are a regional publisher, but we do distribute our books nationally, depending on the title." Submit outline/synopsis and sample chapters.

Recent Nonfiction Title: *Northwest Best Places*, by David Brewster (travel guide).

Fiction: "Though we don't currently publish fiction, we would consider literary works set in the Pacific Northwest."

Tips: "We sell books through a range of channels in addition to the book trade. Our audience is active, literate residents of the Pacific Northwest."

SAYBROOK PUBLISHING CO., Suite 4, 4223 Cole Ave., Dallas TX 75205. (214)521-2375. Managing Editor: Nathan Mitchell. Publishes hardcover and trade paperback originals and reprints. Averages 8 titles/year; receives 700 submissions annually. 25% of books from first-time authors; 50% of books from unagented writers. Average print order for a writer's first book is 5,000. Pays 6-12% royalty on retail price. Publishes book an average of 10 months after acceptance. Photocopied submissions OK. Query for electronic submissions. Computer printout submissions acceptable; prefers letter-quality. Reports in 6 months. Writer's guidelines for 9x12 SAE with 2 first class stamps.

Nonfiction: Biography and literary human science. Subjects include business and economics, health, nature, philosophy, politics, psychology, sociology, women's studies and environmental studies. "Especially interested in scholarly studies in the human sciences which are also exciting, marketable literature written for substantial sales in the trade." Submit outline/synopsis and query letter. No sample chapters or mss unless requested. No children's literature or poetry.

Recent Nonfiction Title: *Paulus: Tillich as Spiritual Teacher*, by Rollo May.

Fiction: "We limit our fiction publishing to 2-3 titles per year. Send query letter *only*; we will ask for ms if interested."

Recent Fiction Title: *The Dark Path to the River: A Novel*, by Joanne Leedom-Ackerman.

Tips: "Expanding interest in New Age material will influence us. We have recently launched our own Mind Age series, edited by Rollo May, which will explore the psychological and philosophical convergences that shape New Age thought. Our books are for the intelligent, curious general reader. Seek to tell the truth about human beings by any means. The times in which we live demand it. If your submission is important and you can convince us that you are determined to do the very best work you are capable of, we will work with you all the way for as long as it takes."

SCARECROW PRESS, INC., 52 Liberty St., Metuchen NJ 08840. Vice President of Editorial: Norman Horrocks. Senior Editor: Barbara Lee. Publishes hardcover originals. Averages 110 titles/year; receives 600-700 submissions annually. 70% of books from first-time authors; 100% of books from unagented writers. Average print order for a writer's first book is 1,000. Pays 10% royalty on net of first 1,000 copies; 15% of net price thereafter. 15% initial royalty on camera-ready copy. Offers no advance. Publishes book 4-6 months after receipt of ms. Photocopied submissions OK. Query for electronic submissions. Computer printout submissions acceptable. Reports in 2 weeks. Free book catalog.

Nonfiction: Books about music. Needs reference books and meticulously prepared annotated bibliographies, indexes, women's studies, movies and stage. Query. Occasionally reviews artwork/photos as part of ms package.

Tips: "Essentially we consider any scholarly title likely to appeal to libraries. Emphasis is on reference material, but this can be interpreted broadly, provided author is knowledgeable in the subject field."

*****SCHENKMAN BOOKS INC.**, Main Street, Box 119, Rochester VT 05767. Editor-in-Chief: Joseph Schenkman. Publishes hardcover and paperback originals. Specializes in textbooks and professional and technical books. Averages 5 titles/year. Subsidy publishes 3% of books. Royalty varies on net sales, but averages 10%. "In some cases, no royalties are paid on first 2,000 copies sold." No advance. State availability of photos and/or illustrations. Publishes book an average of 1 year after acceptance. Computer printout submissions acceptable. Reports in 1-2 months. Free book catalog.

Nonfiction: Publishes economics, history, psychology, sociology, Third World, women's studies, political science, textbooks and professional and technical books. Reviews artwork/photos as part of ms package. Query.
Recent Nonfiction Title: *Puerto Rico and the Bomb*, by L.L. Cripps.

SCHIRMER BOOKS, Macmillan Publishing Co., Inc., 866 3rd Ave., New York NY 10022. Senior Editor: Maribeth Anderson Payne. Publishes hardcover and paperback originals, paperback reprints and some software. Averages 20 books/year; receives 250 submissions annually. 40% of books from first-time authors; 95% of books from unagented writers. Average print order for a writer's first book is 3,000-5,000. Pays royalty on wholesale or retail price; offers small advance. Submit photos and/or illustrations "if central to the book, not if decorative or tangential." Publishes book an average of 1 year after acceptance. Query for electronic submissions. Computer printout submissions acceptable; prefers letter-quality. Reports in 2 months. Book catalog and ms guidelines for SASE.
Nonfiction: Publishes college texts, biographies, scholarly, reference and how-to on the performing arts specializing in music, also dance and theatre. Needs texts or scholarly mss for college or scholarly audience. Submit outline/synopsis and sample chapters and current vita. Reviews artwork/photos as part of ms package.
Recent Nonfiction Title: *Soundings: Music in the Twentieth Century*, by Glenn Watkins (scholarly trade).
Tips: "The writer has the best chance of selling our firm a music book with a clearly defined, reachable audience, either scholarly or trade. Must be an exceptionally well-written work of original scholarship prepared by an expert in that particular field who has a thorough understanding of correct manuscript style and attention to detail (see the Chicago *Manual of Style*)."

‡SCHOLASTIC, INC., 730 Broadway, New York NY 10003. (212)505-3000. Editor: Ann Reit. Imprints include Sunfire. Publishes trade paperback originals and software. Averages 36 titles/year. Pays 6% royalty on retail price. Computer printout submissions acceptable; no dot-matrix. Reports in 3 months. Ms guidelines for #10 SASE.
Fiction: Historical romance (Sunfire).
Tips: Queries/mss may be routed to other editors in the publishing group.

CHARLES SCRIBNER'S SONS, Children's Books Department, 866 Third Ave., New York NY 10022. (212)702-7885. Editorial Director, Children's Books: Clare Costello. Publishes hardcover originals and paperback reprints of own titles. Averages 20-25 titles/year. Pays royalty on retail price; offers advance. Publishes book an average of 1 year after acceptance. Photocopied submissions OK. Computer printout submissions acceptable. Reports in 2 weeks on queries; in 10 weeks on mss. Free book catalog and ms guidelines.
Nonfiction: Subjects include animals, biography, health, hobbies, humor, nature, photography, recreation, science and sports. Query. Reviews artwork/photos as part of ms package.
Recent Nonfiction Title: *Digging To The Past*, by John W. Hackwell.
Fiction: Adventure, fantasy, historical, humor, mystery, picture books, science fiction and suspense. Submit outline/synopsis and sample chapters.
Recent Fiction Title: *Missing*, by James Duffy.

SECOND CHANCE PRESS/PERMANENT PRESS, Rd. #2, Noyac Rd., Sag Harbor NY 11963. (516)725-1101. Editor: Judith Shepard. Publishes hardcover originals, hardcover trade paperback, and mass market paperback reprints. "Second Chance Press devotes itself exclusively to re-publishing fine books that are out of print and deserve continued recognition." Averages 12 titles/year; receives 700 submissions annually. 25% of books from first-time authors; 75% of books from unagented writers. Average print order for a writer's first book is 2,000. Pays 10% maximum royalty on wholesale price; offers average $1,000 advance. Publishes book an average of 18 months after acceptance. Simultaneous and photocopied submissions OK. Computer printout submissions acceptable; prefers letter-quality. Reports in 2 weeks on queries; 3 months on mss. Book catalog for $2 postage.
Nonfiction: Biography and current events. Subjects include Americana, history, philosophy and politics. No scientific and technical material or academic studies. Query.
Recent Nonfiction Title: *KAL Flight 007: The Hidden Story*, by Oliver Clubb.
Fiction: Adventure, confession, ethnic, experimental, fantasy, historical, humor, mainstream, mystery, and suspense. Especially looking for fiction with a unique point of view—"original and arresting" suitable for college literature classes. No mass market romance. Query.
Recent Fiction Title: *The Marriage Hearse*, by Larry Duberstein.

SERVANT PUBLICATIONS, 840 Airport Blvd., Box 8617, Ann Arbor MI 48107. (313)761-8505. Editor: Ann Spangler. Publishes hardcover, trade and mass market paperback originals and trade paperback reprints. Averages 35 titles/year. 5% of books from first-time authors; 95% of books from unagented writers. Pays 8-10% royalty on retail price. Publishes book an average of 1 year after acceptance. Computer printout submissions acceptable. Reports in 2 months. Free book catalog; writer's guidelines for #10 SASE.

Nonfiction: Subjects include religion. "We're looking for practical Christian teaching, scripture, current problems facing the Christian church, and inspiration." No heterodox or non-Christian approaches. Query or submit brief outline/synopsis and 1 sample chapter. All unsolicited mss are returned unopened. Reviews artwork/photos as part of ms package.

Recent Nonfiction Title: *Heart of Joy*, by Mother Teresa.

*SEVEN LOCKS PRESS, INC., Box 27, Cabin John MD 20818. (301)320-2130. Imprint is Isidore Stephanus Sons Publishing. President/Publisher: James McGrath Morris. Senior Editor: Jane Gold. Small press. Publishes hardcover and trade paperback originals, and hardcover and trade paperback reprints. Averages 6-9 titles/year; receives 100 submissions annually. 50% of books from first-time authors; 50% of books from unagented writers. Subsidy publishes 30% of books (nonauthor). Whether an author will be subsidy published depends on the "type of manuscript and cost of production." Pays 10% royalty of gross sales. Simultaneous and photocopied submissions OK. Computer printout submissions acceptable; no dot-matrix. Reports in 1 month on queries; 3 months on mss. Free book catalog.

Nonfiction: Biography, reference and textbook. Subjects include Americana, business and economics, history, international relations, nature, politics, religion and sociology. Especially needs "books that promise to enlighten public policy; also, books of regional interest that are entertaining." Query or submit outline/synopsis and sample chapters. Reviews artwork/photos as part of ms package.

Recent Nonfiction Title: *The Secret Government: The Constitution In Crisis*, by Bill Moyers (public affairs).

Tips: "Literate, intelligent, socially conscious men and women are our readers."

SHAPOLSKY BOOKS, 56 East 11th St., New York NY 10003. (212)505-2505. Editorial Director: Isaac Mozeson. Publishes hardcover and paperback originals, mass market paperback originals, hardcover and trade paperback reprints. 60% originals and 40% reprints. Averages 12 titles/year; receives 300 submissions annually. 60% of books from first-time authors; 40% of books from unagented writers. Subsidy publishes 2% of books. Pays 5-10% royalty on retail price. Offers average $1,000 advance. Publishes an average of 15 months after acceptance. Simultaneous and photocopied submissions OK. Query for electronic submissions. Computer printout submissions OK; prefers letter-quality. Reports on queries in 3 weeks; 5 weeks on ms. Free book catalog.

Nonfiction: Subjects include art, cooking and foods, history, philosophy, photography, politics, religion, sports and travel. "The major thrust of our list is light and lively Judaica. No memoirs." Query or submit outline/synopsis and sample chapters. Reviews artwork/photos as part of package.

Recent Nonfiction Title: *The Word: The Dictionary that Reveals the Hebrew Source of English*, by Isaac Mozeson.

Fiction: "Must be by a well established author." Query.

Recent Fiction Title: *Hinkl and Other Shlemiel Stories*, by Miriam Chaikin.

Tips: "Religious and ethnic books enjoy a growing demand. 95% of our titles are for the general Jewish readership. We are presently expanding into general publishing for the mass market."

HAROLD SHAW PUBLISHERS, 388 Gundersen Dr., Box 567, Wheaton IL 60189. (312)665-6700. Director of Editorial Services: Ramona Cramer Tucker. Publishes hardcover and trade paperback originals and reprints. Averages 26 titles/year; receives 2,000 submissions annually. 10% of books from first-time authors; 90% of books from unagented writers. Offers 5-10% royalty on retail price. Sometimes makes outright purchase for $1,000-2,500. Publishes book an average of 15 months after acceptance. Photocopied submissions OK. Reports in 1 month on queries; 6 weeks on mss. Book catalog and ms guidelines for 9x12 SAE with $1 postage.

Nonfiction: Juvenile (Bible studies only), reference and self-help. Subjects include history (of religious movements/evangelical/charismatic), psychology (self-help) and religion (Bible study guides and general religion). "We are looking for general nonfiction, with different twists—self-help manuscripts on issues and topics with fresh insight and colorful, vibrant writing style. We already have how to forgive yourself, or defend yourself, and how to deal with cancer, death and handicaps. No autobiographies or biographies accepted. Must have an evangelical Christian perspective for us even to review the ms." Query. Reviews artwork/photos as part of ms package.

 An asterisk preceding a listing indicates that subsidy publishing or co-publishing (where author pays part or all of publishing costs) is available. Firms whose subsidy programs comprise more than 50% of their total publishing activities are listed at the end of the Book Publishers section.

Recent Nonfiction Title: *When Your Friend Gets Cancer*, by Amy Harwell/Kristine Tomasik.
Tips: "Get an editor who is not a friend or a spouse who will tell you honestly whether your book is market-able. It will save a lot of your time and money and effort. Then do an honest evaluation of yourself and the book. Most writers who send in mss say this is for everyone. Most books that are written are for no one but the writer. Evaluate who would actually read the book other than yourself—will it do others enough good to sell 5,000 copies?"

THE SHOE STRING PRESS, 925 Sherman Ave., Box 4327, Hamden CT 06514. (203)248-6307. President: James Thorpe III. Imprints include Archon, Library Professional Publications and Linnet Books. Publishes hardcover and trade paperback originals. Publishes 40 titles/year; receives 700 submissions annually. 15% of books from first-time authors; 95% of books from unagented writers. Pays escalating royalty scale. Publishes book an average of 1 year after acceptance. Photocopied submissions OK. Query for electronic submissions. Computer printout submissions OK. Reports in 2 weeks on queries; 3 months on mss. Book catalog and ms guidelines for SASE.
Nonfiction: Biography, reference, technical, textbook and general. Subjects include Americana, art, busi-ness and economics, children's books, history, music, nature, philosophy, politics, psychology, religion, trav-el, literature and military. Will consider "any good scholarly or general nonfiction, reference, children's fic-tion or nonfiction or professional library literature." No "flying saucers, reincarnation, or inspiration." Sub-mit outline/synopsis and sample chapters. Reviews artwork/photos as part of ms package.
Recent Nonfiction Title: *The Wickedest Woman in New York*, by Clifford Browder (biography).

‡MICHAEL SHORE ASSOCIATES, 24 Westfield Rd., Milford CT 06460. (203)877-9218. Owner/Director: Michael Shore. Publishes trade paperback originals. Firm averages up to 5 titles/year. Receives 10 submis-sions/year. 75% of books from unagented writers. Pays 10% maximum royalty on retail price. Publishes book an average of 1 year in advance. Simultaneous and photocopied submissions OK. Computer printout submis-sions OK; prefers letter-quality. Reports on queries in 6 weeks; on mss in 3 months.
Nonfiction: How-to and self-help. "We prefer to see self-help manuscripts for the average reader which aid him in dealing with everyday problems and situations, i.e., 'What to do When You've Been Fired,' 'Relating to Your Family and Friends More Positively,' etc. We do not want first-person anecdotes (How I Lost 75 Pounds on the Grapefruit Diet, Dealing with My Two-Year-Old) or pop psychology manuscripts not thorough-ly researched." Query or submit complete ms. Reviews artwork/photos as part of ms package.
Recent Nonfiction Title: *Corporate Secrets*, by Robert Tedford (self-help).
Tips: "We've noticed a taste for simple, usable techniques for self-improvement. Self-instruction and practi-cal exercises are popular for us. We expect this trend to continue. Our audience is comprised of anyone who en-visions an improved life-style for himself, whether materially (better job, better pay) or psychologically (fewer fears, more ability to cope, better relationshps)."

SIERRA CLUB BOOKS, 730 Polk St., San Francisco CA 94109. (415)776-2211. Editor-in-Chief: Daniel Moses. Publishes hardcover and paperback originals and reprints. Averages 20 titles/year; receives 500 sub-missions annually. 50% of books from unagented writers. Pays 7-12½% royalty on retail price. Offers average $3,000-5,000 advance. Publishes book an average of 12-18 months after acceptance. Computer printout sub-missions acceptable. Reports in 2 months. Free book catalog.
Nonfiction: Animals; health; history (natural); how-to (outdoors); juveniles; nature; philosophy; photogra-phy; recreation (outdoors, nonmechanical); science; sports (outdoors); and travel (by foot or bicycle). "The Si-erra Club was founded to help people to explore, enjoy and preserve the nation's forests, waters, wildlife and wilderness. The books program looks to publish quality trade books about the outdoors and the protection of natural resources. Specifically, we are interested in nature, environmental issues such as nuclear power, self-sufficiency, natural history, politics and the environment, and juvenile books with an ecological theme." Does *not* want "personal, lyrical, philosophical books on the great outdoors; proposals for large color photographic books without substantial text; how-to books on building things outdoors; books on motorized travel; or any but the most professional studies of animals." Query first, submit outline/synopsis and sample chapters. Reviews artwork/photos ("duplicates, not originals") as part of ms package.
Recent Nonfiction Title: *Adventuring in the Pacific*, by Susanna Margolis.
Fiction: Adventure, historical, mainstream and ecological science fiction. "We do very little fiction, but will consider a fiction manuscript if its theme fits our philosophical aims: the enjoyment and protection of the envi-ronment." Does *not* want "any manuscript with animals or plants that talk; apocalyptic plots." Query first, submit outline/synopsis and sample chapters, or submit complete ms.

SILHOUETTE BOOKS, Division of Harlequin Enterprises, 300 E. 42nd St., New York NY 10017. (212)682-6080. Vice President and Editor-in-Chief: Karen Solem. Publishes mass market paperback originals. Averages 336 titles/year; receives 4,000 submissions annually. 10% of books from first-time authors; 25% of books from unagented writers. Pays royalty. Publishes book an average of 1 year after acceptance. Computer printout sub-missions acceptable; no dot-matrix. No unsolicited mss. Send query letter; 2 page synopsis and SASE to head of imprint. Ms guidelines for #10 SASE.

Imprints: Silhouette Romances (contemporary adult romances), Tara Hughes, Senior Editor; 53,000-58,000 words. Silhouette Special Editions (contemporary adult romances), Leslie Kazanjian, Senior Editor; 75,000-80,000 words. Silhouette Desires (contemporary adult romances), Isabel Swift, Senior Editor and Editorial Coordinator; 55,000-65,000 words. Silhouette Intimate Moments (contemporary adult romances), Leslie Wainger, Senior Editor; 80,000-85,000 words. Harlequin Historicals (adult historical romances), Tracy Farrell and Eliza Schallcross, Associate Editors; 95-105,000 words. Crosswinds (contemporary young adult novels), Nancy Jackson, Senior Editor and Editorial Coordinator; 40,000-50,000 words.

Fiction: Romance (contemporary and historical romance for adults and contemporary novels for young adults). "We are interested in seeing submissions for all our lines. No manuscripts other than the types outlined above." Ms should "follow our general format, yet have an individuality and life of its own that will make it stand out in the readers' minds."

Recent Fiction Title: *Whatever It Takes*, by Patricia Gardner Evans.

Tips: "The romance market is constantly changing, so when you read for research, read the latest books and those that have been recommended to you by those knowledgeable in the genre. We have recently added a line of historical romances and are actively seeking new authors."

SIMON & SCHUSTER, Trade Books Division, 1230 Avenue of the Americas, New York NY 10020. "We do not accept unsolicited manuscripts. Only manuscripts submitted by agents or recommended to us by friends or actively solicited by us will be considered. In such cases, our requirements are as follows: Manuscripts must be typewritten, double-spaced, on one side of the sheet only. We suggest margins of about one and one half inches all around and the standard 8x11 typewriter paper." Computer printout submissions acceptable; prefers letter-quality.

Nonfiction and Fiction: "Simon and Schuster publishes books of general adult fiction, history, biography, science, philosophy, the arts and popular culture, running 50,000 words or more. Our program does not, however, include school textbooks, extremely technical or highly specialized works, or, as a general rule, poetry or plays. Exceptions have been made, of course, for extraordinary manuscripts of great distinction or significance."

GIBBS SMITH PUBLISHER, Peregrine Smith Books, Box 667, Layton UT 84041. (801)544-9800. Editorial Director: Madge Baird. Publishes hardcover and paperback originals and reprints. Averages 25-30 titles/year; receives 1,000 submissions annually. 25% of books from first-time authors; 40% of books from unagented writers. Average print order for a writer's first book is 3,000-5,000. Starts at 10% royalty on wholesale price. Offers average $1,000 advance. Publishes book an average of 1½ years after acceptance. Photocopied submissions OK. Reports in 2 months. Book catalog for 6x9 SAE and 3 first class stamps; ms guidelines for #10 SASE.

Nonfiction: "Subjects include western American history, natural history, American architecture, art history, and fine arts. "We consider biographical, historical, descriptive and analytical studies in all of the above. Much emphasis is also placed on pictorial content." Query. Consult Chicago *Manual of Style*. Reviews artwork/photos as part of ms package.

Recent Nonfiction Title: *The Girl from Cardigan*, by Leslie Norris.

Fiction: "We publish contemporary literary fiction." Looks for "style, readable, intelligent, careful writing, contribution to the social consciousness of our time. Must be geared to a competitive commercial market." Query.

Recent Fiction Title: *Inside the L.A. Artist*, by Marva Marrow.

Tips: "Write seriously. If fiction, no potboilers, and no science fiction. If nonfiction, well-organized, clear ideas; we're open to a wide range of nonfiction subjects. Some authors send in an early draft that they admit isn't in top shape. They should work it over several times before submitting so they don't have to send along an apology for the roughness."

SOS PUBLICATIONS, Division of Bradley Products, Inc., U.S.A. 4223-25 W. Jefferson Blvd., Los Angeles CA 90016. (213)730-1815. Publisher: Paul Bradley. Imprints include Private Library Collection (fiction). Publishes mini-bound originals only. Averages 48 titles/year; receives 800-1,000 submissions annually. 40% of books from first-time authors; 40% of books from unagented writers. Average print order for a writer's first book is 30,000. Pays 6-15% royalty on net selling price. Publishes book an average of 9 months after acceptance. Photocopied submissions OK. Computer printout submissions acceptable; no dot-matrix. SASE which will *enclose* the manuscript *must* accompany submission. Any queries *must* also include SASE. "Due to both the large number of manuscripts we receive and our limited reading staff, we report as soon as possible—but allow approximately 4-5 months." Book catalog for 8½x11 SAE with 2 first class stamps.

Fiction: Kathy Clear, fiction editor. Mystery, adventure, romance and suspense. "Our Private Library Collection consists of the Mini-Bound, a hardcover book the size of a mass-market paperback. It showcases original titles, illustrations and new authors. There are four categories: the novel, mystery, romance, and adventure. Don't send any science fiction or westerns *before* the winter of 1989. It is suggested to query first when that

time of year arrives.'' Especially needs mainstream mss. No horror or occult. Send complete ms. Must have minimum 85,000 words.
Recent Fiction Title: *The Measure of Love*, by Judith Hagar (romance).
Tips: ''Well-written romance and mystery does well for us, but we need mainstream. There is no particular style that we *must* have, but our reviewer's list includes *The New York Times*. Study the *New York Times* trends to review. If I were a writer trying to market a book today I would follow guidelines *exactly*. I would *not* call an editor. I would not take a rejection personally.''

SOUTH END PRESS, 116 St. Botolph, Boston MA 02115. (617)266-0629. Small press. Publishes trade paperback and hardcover originals and trade paperback reprints. Averages 15 nonfiction titles/year; receives 900 submissions annually. 50% of books from first-time authors; 90% of books from unagented writers. Pays 10% royalty on net price. Publishes book an average of 6 months after acceptance. Simultaneous submissions OK. Computer printout submissions acceptable. Reports in 2 months. Free book catalog.
Nonfiction: Subjects include politics, economics, feminism, social change, radical cultural criticism, explorations of race, class, and sex oppression and liberation. No conservative political themes. Submit outline/synopsis and 1-2 sample chapter(s).

SOUTHERN ILLINOIS UNIVERSITY PRESS, Box 3697, Carbondale IL 62901. (618)453-2281. Director: Kenney Withers. Averages 60 titles/year; receives 500 submissions annually. 50% of books from first-time authors; 99% of books from unagented writers. Publishes book an average of 1 year after acceptance. Computer printout submissions acceptable; no dot-matrix. Reports in 6 weeks. Free book catalog.
Nonfiction: ''We are interested in scholarly nonfiction on the humanities, social sciences and contemporary affairs. No dissertations or collections of previously published articles.'' Accepts nonfiction translations from French, German, Scandinavian and Hebrew. Query.
Recent Nonfiction Title: *Plato, Derrida, and Writing*, by Jasper Neel (literary/criticism).

SPINSTERS/AUNT LUTE BOOKS, Box 410687, San Francisco CA 94141. (415)558-9655. Editors: Sherry Thomas and Joan Pinkvoss. Publishes trade paperback originals and reprints. Averages 6-8 titles/year; receives 200 submissions annually. 50% of books from first-time authors; 95% of books from unagented writers. Pays 7-11% royalty on retail price. Publishes book an average of 1 year after acceptance. Photocopied submissions OK. Computer printout submissions acceptable; prefers letter-quality to dot-matrix. Reports in 3 weeks on queries; 6 months on mss. Free book catalog; ms guidelines for SASE.
Nonfiction: Self-help and feminist analysis for positive change. Subjects include women's issues. ''We are interested in books that not only name the crucial issues in women's lives, but show and encourage change and growth. We do not want to see work by men, or anything that is not specific to women's lives (ie. humor, childrens' books, etc.). We do not want genre fiction (romances, etc.).'' Query. Reviews artwork/photos as part of ms package.
Recent Nonfiction Title: *Borderlands/LaFrontera*, by Gloria Anzuidua (ethnic/women's history).
Fiction: Ethnic, women's, lesbian. Submit outline/synopsis and sample chapters.
Recent Fiction Title: *Child of Her People*, by Anne Cameron.
Poetry: Minimal. Submit complete ms.
Recent Poetry Title: *We Say We Love Each Other*, by Minnie Bruce Pratt (Southern lesbian).

‡*SPRINGER-VERLAG NEW YORK, INC., 175 Fifth Ave., New York NY 10010. (212)460-1500. Senior Vice President-Editorial: Alvin A. Abbott. Publishes hardcover originals. Firm averages 195 titles/year. Receives 400 submissions/year. 99% of books from unagented writers. Subsidy publishes .5% of books. Pays royalty on retail price. Publishes book an average of 9 months after acceptance. Simultaneous submissions OK. Query for electronic submissions. Computer printout submissions OK; prefers letter-quality. Reports on queries in 2 weeks; on mss in 2 months.
Nonfiction: Technical. Subjects include agriculture/horticulture, computers and electronics, health/medicine, money/finance, psychology, science. ''We will consider all scholarly scientific and technical material with fully researched background in our subject areas. No trade or popularly oriented titles.'' Query, or submit outline/synopsis and sample chapters or submit complete ms.
Recent Nonfiction Title: *Pulmonary Pathology*, by Dail & Hammer (medical).
Tips: ''The well researched cutting edge monograph continues to be needed by researchers and libraries in every academic field. Research scientists and technicians who need the latest or most complete information are our audience. If I were a writer trying to market a book today, I would find the publication which has the most complete and authoritative list in my special area of expertise. They will be able to present the title to the widest relevant market.''

ST PUBLICATIONS, Signs of the Times Publishing Co., Book Division, 407 Gilbert Ave., Cincinnati OH 45202. (513)421-4050. Book Division Coordinator: Carole Singleton Emery. Publishes hardcover and trade paperback originals and hardcover reprints. Averages 4 titles/year; receives 15-20 submissions annually. 50%

of books from first-time authors; 100% of books from unagented writers. Pays royalty on wholesale price: 10% until recovery of production costs; 12½% thereafter; and 15% on straight reprints. Publishes book an average of 9 months after acceptance. Photocopied submissions OK. Computer printout submissions acceptable. Reports in 6 weeks on queries; 2 months on mss. Free book catalog and ms guidelines.

Nonfiction: How-to, reference, technical and textbook. Subjects include art (collections of copyright-free artwork suitable for sign, display or screen printing industries). "We need technical how-to books for professionals in three specific industries: the sign industry, including outdoor advertising, electric and commercial signs; the screen printing industry, including the printing of paper products, fabrics, ceramics, glass and electronic circuits; and the visual merchandising and store design industry. We are not interested in submissions that do not relate specifically to those three fields." Submit outline/synopsis and sample chapters. Reviews artwork/photos as part of ms package.

Recent Nonfiction Title: *The Sign User's Guide: A Marketing Aid*, by R.J. and Karen E. Claus.

Tips: "The writer has the best chance of selling our firm how-to books related to our industries: signs, screen printing, and visual merchandising. These are the fields our marketing and distribution channels are geared to. Request copies of, and thoroughly absorb the information presented in, our trade magazines (*Signs of the Times*, *Visual Merchandising*, and *Screen Printing*). Our books are permanent packages of this type of information. We are taking a closer look at submissions which we can sell outside our primary range of customers, yet still confining our subject interests to sing painting and design, visual merchandising, display and store design, and screen printing (both technical and art aspects)."

STACKPOLE BOOKS, Company of Commonwealth Communications Services, Box 1831, Harrisburg PA 17105. Executive Vice President and Editorial Director: Chet Fish. Publishes hardcover and paperback originals. Publishes approximately 40 titles/year. "Proposals should begin as a one-page letter, leading to chapter outline on request only. If author is unknown to Stackpole, supply credentials." Publishes book an average of 9 months after acceptance. Computer printout submissions acceptable; prefers letter-quality.

Nonfiction: Outdoor-related subject areas—fishing, hunting, firearms, wildlife, adventure, outdoor skills, military guides, military history, decoy carving/woodcarving, and space exploration. Reviews artwork/photos as part of ms package.

Recent Nonfiction Title: *Nanda Devi: The Tragic Expedition*.

Tips: "We will consider books in two new (for us) categories: 1) current events, 2) new age."

STANDARD PUBLISHING, A division of Standex International Corp., 8121 Hamilton Ave., Cincinnati OH 45231. (513)931-4050. Publisher/Vice President: Eugene H. Wigginton. Publishes hardcover and paperback originals and reprints. Specializes in religious books. Averages 125 titles/year; receives 1,500 submissions annually. 25% of books from first-time authors; 90% of books from unagented writers. Average print order for a writer's first book is 7,500. Pays 10% royalty on wholesale price "for substantial books. Lump sum for smaller books." Offers $200-1,500 advance. Publishes book an average of 1 year after acceptance. Query for electronic submissions. Computer printout submissions acceptable; no dot-matrix. Reports in 2-3 months. Ms guidelines for #10 SAE with 1 first class stamp.

Nonfiction: Publishes how-to; crafts (to be used in Christian education); juveniles; reference; Christian education; quiz; puzzle and religious books; and college textbooks (religious). All mss must pertain to religion. Query or submit outline/synopsis and 2-3 sample chapters. Reviews artwork/photos as part of ms package.

Recent Nonfiction Title: *Strengthening the Family*, by Wayne Rickerson.

Fiction: Religious, devotional books.

Recent Fiction Title: *Another Jennifer*, by Jane Sorenson.

Tips: "Children's books, Christian education, activity books, and helps for Christian parents and church leaders are the types of books writers have the best chance of selling to our firm."

*STANFORD UNIVERSITY PRESS, Imprint of Stanford University, Stanford CA 94305. (415)723-9434. Editor: William W. Carver. Averages 65 titles/year; receives 900 submissions annually. 40% of books from first-time authors, 95% of books from unagented writers. Subsidy (nonauthor) publishes 65% of books. Pays up to 15% royalty ("typically 10%, often none"); sometimes offers advance. Publishes book an average of 13 months ("typically a year") after acceptance. Photocopied submissions OK. Query for electronic submissions. Computer printout submissions acceptable; no dot-matrix. Reports in 3 weeks on queries; 5 weeks on mss. Free book catalog.

Nonfiction: Scholarly books in the humanities, social sciences, and natural sciences: history and culture of China, Japan, and Latin America; European history; biology, natural history, and taxonomy; anthropology, linguistics, and psychology; literature, criticism, and literary theory; political science and sociology; archaeology and geology; and medieval and classical studies. Also high-level textbooks and books for a more general audience. Query. "We like to see a prospectus and an outline." Reviews artwork/photos as part of ms package.

Recent Nonfiction Title: *The Butterflies of North America*, by James A. Scott.

Tips: "We are interested in seeing syntheses, upper division texts, handbooks, and general interest. The writer's best chance is a work of original scholarship with an argument of some importance and an appeal to a broad audience."

‡**STARRHILL PRESS**, Box 32342, Washington DC 20007. (202)686-6703. Co-presidents: Liz Hill and Marty Starr. Publishes trade paperback originals. Firm averages 4 titles/year. Receives 10 submissions/year. 90% of books from first-time authors. 100% from unagented writers. Pays 5-10% royalty on retail price. Publishes book an average of 1 year after acceptance. Simultaneous and photocopied submissions OK. Computer printout submissions OK; prefers letter-quality. Reports in 2 weeks on queries. Book catalog for #10 SASE.
Nonfiction: Reference. Subjects include art/architecture, music/dance, nature/environment and travel. "American arts, decoration, literary guide books, performing arts, short nonfiction (with line drawings only) are our needs. No popular junk, coffee table books or expensive artwork." Query or submit outline/synopsis and sample chapters. Reviews artwork/photos as part of manuscript package.
Recent Nonfiction Title: *Clues to American Architecture*, by Marilyn W. Klein and David P. Fogle (architecture reference guide).

STEIN AND DAY PUBLISHERS, Scarborough House, Briarcliff Manor NY 10510. Averages 60 titles/year. Offers standard royalty contract.
Nonfiction and Fiction: Publishes general adult fiction and nonfiction books; no juvenile or college. All types of nonfiction except technical. Quality fiction. No unsolicited mss without querying first. Nonfiction, send outline or summary and sample chapter. *Must* furnish SASE with all fiction and nonfiction queries. Minimum length: 65,000 words.

‡**STEMMER HOUSE PUBLISHERS, INC.**, 2627 Caves Rd., Owings Mills MD 21117. (301)363-3690. President: Barbara Holdridge. Publishes hardcover originals. Averages 12 titles/year; receives 500 submissions annually. 10% of books from first-time authors; 90% of books from unagented writers. Average print order for a writer's first book is 4,000-10,000. Pays royalty on wholesale price. Publishes book an average of 1 year after acceptance. Computer printout submissions acceptable; no dot-matrix. Reports in 2 weeks on queries; 3 months on mss. Book catalog for 9x12 SAE and 4 first class stamps.
Nonfiction: Biography, cookbook, illustrated book, juvenile and design books. Subjects include Americana, animals, art, cooking and foods, history and nature. Especially looking for "quality biography, history, and art and design." No humor. Query or submit outline/synopsis and sample chapters.
Recent Nonfiction Title: *An Italic Calligraphy Handbook*, by Mary Leister (natural history).
Fiction: Adventure, ethnic, historical, mainstream and philosophical. "We want only manuscripts of sustained literary merit. No popular-type manuscripts written to be instant bestsellers." Query.
Recent Fiction Title: *The Fringe of Heaven*, by Margaret Sutherland (contemporary novel).
Tips: "We are interested in finding original manuscripts on gardens and gardening. If I were a writer trying to market a book today, I would not imitate current genres on the bestseller lists, but strike out with a subject of intense interest to me." Freelancer has best chance of selling a book with a universal theme, either for adults or children, exceptionally well written, and marketable internationally. "Our goal is a list of perennial sellers of which we can be proud."

STERLING PUBLISHING, 2 Park Ave., New York NY 10016. (212)532-7160. Acquisitions Manager: Sheila Anne Barry. Publishes hardcover and paperback originals and reprints. Averages 80 titles/year. Pays royalty; offers advance. Publishes book an average of 8 months after acceptance. Computer printout submissions acceptable; prefers letter-quality. Reports in 6 weeks. Guidelines for SASE.
Nonfiction: Alternative lifestyle, fiber arts, games and puzzles, health how-to, business, foods, hobbies, how-to, children's humor, militaria, occult, pets, photography, recreation, reference, self-help, sports, theatre (how-to), technical, collecting, wine and woodworking. Query or submit complete chapter list, detailed outline/synopsis and 2 sample chapters with photos if necessary. Reviews artwork/photos as part of ms package.
Recent Nonfiction Title: *Windows on the World Complete Wine Course*, by Kevin Zraly.

STIPES PUBLISHING CO., 10-12 Chester St., Champaign IL 61820. (217)356-8391. Contact: Robert Watts. Publishes hardcover and paperback originals. Averages 15-30 titles/year; receives 150 submissions annually. 50% of books from first-time authors; 100% of books from unagented writers. Pays 15% maximum royalty on retail price. Publishes book an average of 4 months after acceptance. Computer printout submissions acceptable; prefers letter-quality. Reports in 2 weeks on queries; 2 months on mss.
Nonfiction: Technical (some areas), textbooks on business and economics, music, chemistry, agriculture/horticulture, and recreation and physical education. "All of our books in the trade area are books that also have a college text market." No "books unrelated to educational fields taught at the college level." Submit outline/synopsis and 1 sample chapter.
Recent Nonfiction Title: *History of Sport and Physical Education*, by Earle Zeigler, ed.

‡**STORIE/MCOWEN PUBLISHERS, INC.**, Box 308, Manteo NC 27954. (919)473-1225. Editorial Assistant: Melissa Powell. Publishes trade paperback originals. Firm averages 7 titles/year. 20% of books from first-time authors; 100% of books from unagented writers. Pays 5% royalty on retail price. Offers $2,000 average advance. Publishes book an average of 1 year in advance. Query for electronic submissions. Computer printout

submissions OK; no dot-matrix. Reports in 1 week on queries. Free book catalog.

Nonfiction: Reference. Subjects include travel/newcomer guides. Query. All unsolicited mss are returned unopened. Reviews artwork/photos as part of ms package.

Recent Nonfiction Title: *Insider's Guide to the Outer Banks of NC*, by Dave Poyer and Chris Kidder (travel).

Tips: "Travelers/vacationers, business people, and newcomers to an area are our audience."

*LYLE STUART, INC., 120 Enterprise Ave., Secaucus NJ 07094. (201)866-0490. (212)736-1141. Subsidiaries include Citadel Press, University Books, Blue Moon Books and Free Wind Books. President: Lyle Stuart. Publisher: Carole Stuart. Editor-in-Chief: Allan J. Wilson. Publishes hardcover and trade paperback originals, and trade paperback reprints. Averages 80 titles/year; receives 700-1,000 submissions annually. 50% of books from first-time authors; 60% of books from unagented writers. Subsidy publishes 5% of books. Pays 10-12% royalty on retail price; offers "low advance." Publishes book an average of 10 months after acceptance.

Nonfiction: Biography, coffee table book, how-to, humor, illustrated book and self-help. Subjects include Americana, art, business and economics, health, history, music and politics. "The percentage of acceptable over-the-transom manuscripts has been so low during the years that we rarely read unsolicited material." Reviews artwork/photos as part of ms package.

Recent Nonfiction Title: *The Autobiography of Roy Cohn*, by Sidney Zion.

Recent Fiction Title: *Grand Cru*, by Sandra Lee Stuart.

Tips: "The writer has the best chance of selling us a book that is controversial—and professionally written."

STUDIO PRESS, Box 1268, Twain Harte CA 95383. (209)533-4222. Publisher: Paul Castle. Publishes hardcover and paperback originals. Averages 4 titles/year; receives 10-15 submissions annually. 100% of books from first-time authors; 100% of books from unagented writers. Average print order for a writer's first book is 2,000-3,000. Pays 15% royalty on wholesale or retail price; no advance. Publishes book an average of 3-6 months after acceptance. Simultaneous and photocopied submissions OK. Computer printout submissions acceptable; prefers letter-quality. Reports in 1 month. Ms guidelines for #10 SASE.

Nonfiction: Photography. "We are always interested in good manuscripts on technique and the business of photography. We especially want manuscripts on *marketing* one's photography. We don't want manuscripts on art criticism of photography, collections of art photos, basic photo teaching books, or anything other than books on the technique and/or business of photography. Query; if the idea is good, we'll ask for outline and sample chapters." Reviews artwork/photos as part of ms package. "Artwork/photos are essential to acceptance."

Recent Nonfiction Title: *Family Portraiture*, by John Hartman.

Tips: "We need more anecdotes and word illustrations to amplify the writer's points. We particularly look for skilled photographers who are doing something very well and can communicate their expertise to others. We are willing to work with such individuals on extensive rewrite and editing, if what they have to say is valuable."

SUCCESS PUBLISHING, 10258 Riverside Dr., Palm Beach Gardens FL 33410. (305)626-4643. President: Allan H. Smith. Publishes trade paperback originals. Averages 6 titles/year; receives 50 submissions annually. 50% of books from first-time authors; 65% of books from unagented writers. Pays variable royalty on wholesale price (10% minimum) or makes minimum outright purchase of $1,000. Publishes book an average of 4 months after acceptance. Simultaneous submissions OK. Computer printout submissions acceptable; prefers letter-quality. Reports in 1 month on queries; 6 weeks on mss. Book catalog and writer's guidelines for #10 SAE and 2 first class stamps.

Nonfiction: How-to, juvenile, self-help and craft. Subjects include business and economics and hobbies. Especially looking for mss interesting to home-based business people; middle school and high school children, and those interested in sewing and crafts. No poetry, cult, religious or technical books. Query and/or submit outline/synopsis and sample chapters.

Recent Nonfiction Title: *Sewing for Profits*.

THE SUNSTONE PRESS, Box 2321, Santa Fe NM 87504-2321. (505)988-4418. Editor-in-Chief: James C. Smith Jr. Publishes paperback originals; few hardcover originals. Averages 16 titles/year; receives 400 submissions annually. 70% of books from first-time authors; 100% of books from unagented writers. Average print order for writer's first book is 2,000-5,000. Pays royalty on wholesale price. Publishes book an average of 1 year after acceptance. Computer printout submissions acceptable; prefers letter-quality. Reports in 2 months.

Nonfiction: How-to series craft books. Books on the history and architecture of the Southwest. Looks for "strong regional appeal (Southwestern)." Reviews artwork/photos as part of ms package.

Recent Nonfiction Title: *Greatness in the Commonplace*, by Charlotte White.

Fiction: Publishes "material with Southwestern theme."

Recent Fiction Title: *Border Patrol*, by Alvin E. Moore.

Poetry: Traditional or free verse. Poetry book not exceeding 64 pages. Prefers Southwestern theme.
Recent Poetry Title: *Thin Ice*, by Marcia Muth.

SYBEX, INC., 2021 Challenger Dr., Alameda CA 94501. (415)848-8233. Editor-in-Chief: Dr. Rudolph S. Langer. Acquisitions Editor: Dianne King. Publishes paperback originals. Averages 60 titles/year. Royalty rates vary. Offers average $2,500 advance. Publishes book an average of 3 months after acceptance. Simultaneous and photocopied submissions OK. Query for electronic submissions. Computer printout submissions acceptable. Reports in 2 months. Free book catalog.
Nonfiction: Computer and electronics. "Manuscripts most publishable in the field of personal computers, desktop computer business applications, hardware, programming, languages, and telecommunications." Submit outline/synopsis and 2-3 sample chapters. Accepts nonfiction translations from French or German. Looks for "clear writing; technical accuracy; logical presentation of material; and good selection of material, such that the most important aspects of the subject matter are thoroughly covered; well-focused subject matter; and well-thought-out organization that helps the reader understand the material. And marketability." Reviews artwork/photos as part of ms package.
Recent Nonfiction Title: *Mastering Word Perfect*.
Tips: Queries/mss may be routed to other editors in the publishing group.

*SYRACUSE UNIVERSITY PRESS, 1600 Jamesville Ave., Syracuse NY 13244-5160. (315)423-2596. Director: Arpena S. Mesrobian. Averages 40 titles/year; receives 350 submissions annually. 40% of books from first-time authors; 95% of books from unagented writers. Subsidy publishes (nonauthor) 20% of books. Pays royalty on net sales. Publishes book an average of 10 months after acceptance. Simultaneous and photocopied submissions OK "if we are informed." Computer printout submissions acceptable. Reports in 2 weeks on queries; "longer on submissions." Book catalog and ms guidelines for SASE.
Nonfiction: "The best opportunities in our nonfiction program for freelance writers are books on New York state. We have published regional books by people with limited formal education, but authors were thoroughly acquainted with their subjects, and they wrote simply and directly about them. Provide precise descriptions about subjects, along with background description of project. The author must make a case for the importance of his or her subject." Query. Accepts outline/synopsis and at least 2 sample chapters. Reviews artwork/photos as part of ms package.
Recent Nonfiction Title: *The Man Who Tried to Burn New York*, by Nat Brandt (history/Civil War).

TAB BOOKS, INC., Blue Ridge Summit PA 17214. (717)794-2191. Vice President: Ray Collins. Publishes hardcover and paperback originals and reprints. Publishes 200 titles/year; receives 400 submissions annually. 50% of books from first-time authors; 85% of books from unagented writers. Average print order for writer's first book is 10,000. Pays variable royalty; buys some mss outright for a negotiable fee. Offers advance. Photocopied submissions OK (except for art). Query for electronic submissions. Computer printout submissions acceptable; prefers letter-quality. Reports in 6 weeks. Free book catalog and ms guidelines.
Nonfiction: TAB publishes titles in such fields as computer hardware, computer software, business, solar and alternate energy, marine line, aviation, automotive, music technology, consumer medicine, electronics, electrical and electronics repair, amateur radio, shortwave listening, model railroading, toys, hobbies, drawing, animals and animal power, woodworking, practical skills with projects, building furniture, basic how-to for the house, building large structures, calculators, robotics, telephones, model radio control, TV servicing, audio, recording, hi-fi and stereo, electronic music, electric motors, electrical wiring, electronic test equipment, video programming, CATV, MATV and CCTV, broadcasting, photography and film, appliance servicing and repair, advertising, antiques and restoration, bicycles, crafts, farmsteading, hobby electronics, home construction, license study guides, mathematics, metalworking, reference books, schematics and manuals, small gasoline engines, two-way radio and CB, military fiction, and woodworking. Accepts nonfiction translations. Query with outline/synopsis. Reviews artwork/photos as part of ms package.
Tips: "Many writers believe that a cover letter alone will describe their proposed book sufficiently; it rarely does. The more details we receive, the better the chances are that the writer will get published by us. We expect a writer to tell us what the book is about, but many writers actually fail to do just that."

‡TABOR PUBLISHING, a division of DLM, Inc., #130, 25115 Avenue Stanford, Valencia CA 91355. (805)257-0911. Subsidiaries include Tabor Media. President: Cullen W. Schippe. Publishes hardcover originals and trade paperback originals. Firm averages 12-20 titles/year. Receives 150 submissions/year. 75% of books from first-time authors. 80% from unagented writers. Pays 4-12% royalty on wholesale price. Buys mss outright for $500-2,000. "Specific arrangements are made for specialized work." Offers $1,000 average advance. Publishes book an average of 18 months after acceptance. Photocopied submissions OK. Computer printout submissions OK; prefers letter-quality. Reports in 6 weeks on queries; 4 months on mss.
Nonfiction: Textbook. Subjects include child guidance/parenting (religious slant), education (religious), philosophy (religious), psychology, religion (Roman Catholic) and adult education. "No private revelations, poetry, get-rich schemes, health and fitness with religious twist or Bible interpretation." Query or submit out-

line/synopsis and sample chapter. All unsolicited mss are returned.
Recent Nonfiction Title: *Touchstone*, by Miller & Weber (adult activities for religious education).
Tips: "Best shot is a program type book that fits a specific institutional or personal need in the Roman Catholic or mainline Christian market."

TAPLINGER PUBLISHING CO., INC., 132 W. 22nd, New York NY 10011. (212)741-0801. Editor: Roy E. Thomas. Imprint is Crescendo (music). Publishes hardcover originals. Publishes 25 titles/year. 2% of books from first-time authors; 1% of books from unagented writers. Average print order for a writer's first book is 3,000-5,000. Pays standard royalty; offers variable advance. Publishes book an average of 1 year after acceptance. Simultaneous and photocopied submissions OK. Computer printout submissions acceptable; no dot-matrix. Reports in 10 weeks.
Nonfiction: Art, calligraphy, and belles-lettres. No juveniles. Query.
Fiction: Serious contemporary quality fiction. Accepts fiction translations. No juveniles.

JEREMY P. TARCHER, INC., Suite 250, 9110 Sunset Blvd., Los Angeles CA 90069. (213)273-3274. Executive Editor: Hank Stine. Senior Editor: Connie Zweig. Publishes hardcover and trade paperback originals and hardcover trade paperback reprints. Averages 35-40 titles/year; receives 2,500 submissions annually. 50% of books from first-time authors; 15% of books from unagented writers. Pays royalty with variable advance. Publishes book an average of 1 year after acceptance. Simultaneous and photocopied submissions OK. Computer printout submissions OK; no dot-matrix. Reports in 3 weeks on queries; 6 weeks on mss. Book catalog and guidelines for #10 SASE.
Nonfiction: Subjects include psychology, health, animals, recreation, sociology, language/linguistics, relationships, women's self-improvement, dreams, recovery/12-step, dreams, creativity, biographies within the field of human potential, and enhanced performance. "We're looking for practical, self-help titles on a variety of health and psychology-related subjects. We continue to be interested in books on consciousness and creativity, science for the layperson, adult relationships, parenting, etc. No humor books, art books, children's books, cookbooks, Hollywood exposes, astrology books, textbooks, military, general biography, puzzle or game books." Submit outline/synopsis and sample chapters. "We have published books as commercial as *Women Who Love Too Much*, and as specialized as *The Possible Human*."
Recent Nonfiction Title: *A Time to Heal: The Road to Recovery for Adult Children of Alcoholics*, by Timmon Cermak, Ph.D.
Tips: "It's important to us that the author has authority in his or her field and that this is conveyed in the proposal. Beginning authors, and agents representing beginning authors, should include an extensive sample chapter or other writing sample. Authors should pay particular attention to what makes their book different and exciting, and to why they're the ideal author for the book. One of the most important ingredients in a proposal, as far as we're concerned, is the market survey which lists competing books (refer to *Books in Print*) and describes the potential audience. This lets us know that the author has a clear picture of his or her audience and can deliver a saleable book."

TEACHERS COLLEGE PRESS, 1234 Amsterdam Ave., New York NY 10027. (212)678-3929. Director: Carole P. Saltz. Publishes hardcover and paperback originals and reprints. Averages 40 titles/year. Pays royalty. Publishes book an average of 1 year after acceptance. Reports in 1 year. Free book catalog.
Nonfiction: "This university press concentrates on books in the field of education in the broadest sense, from early childhood to higher education: good classroom practices, teacher training, special education, innovative trends and issues, administration and supervision, film, continuing and adult education, all areas of the curriculum, computers, guidance and counseling and the politics, economics, philosophy, sociology and history of education. The press also issues classroom materials for students at all levels, with a strong emphasis on reading and writing and social studies." Submit outline/synopsis and sample chapters.
Recent Nonfiction Title: *The War-Play Dilemma*, by Nancy Carlsson-Paige and Diane Levin.

‡TEMPLE UNIVERSITY PRESS, Broad and Oxford Sts., Philadelphia PA 19122. (215)787-8787. Editor-in-Chief: Michael Ames. Publishes 60 titles/year. Pays royalty of up to 10% on wholesale price. Publishes book an average of 9 months after acceptance. Query for electronic submissions. Computer printout submissions acceptable. Reports in 3 months. Free book catalog.
Nonfiction: American history, sociology, women's studies, health care, philosophy, labor studies, photography, urban studies, public policy and regional (Philadelphia area). "All books should be scholarly. Authors are generally connected with a university. No memoirs, fiction or poetry." Uses Chicago *Manual of Style*. Reviews artwork/photos as part of ms package. Query.
Recent Nonfiction Title: *The Boss: J. Edgar Hoover and the Great American Inquisition*, by Athan Theoharis and John Stuart Cox.

TEN SPEED PRESS, Box 7123, Berkeley CA 94707. Imprints include Celestial Arts. Publisher: P. Wood. Editors: G. Young and J. Wan. Publishes trade paperback originals and reprints. Averages 40 titles/year; receives

12,000 submissions annually. 50% of books from first-time authors; 90% of books from unagented writers. Average print order for a writer's first book is 5,000-10,000. Offers standard royalties. Offers advance. Publishes book an average of 10 months after acceptance. Computer printout submissions acceptable; prefers letter-quality. Reports in 1 month. Book catalog and ms guidelines for 9x12 SAE with $1.92 postage.

Nonfiction: Americana, gardening, careers, cookbooks, business, cooking and foods, life guidance, history, humor, nature, self-help, how-to, hobbies, recreation and travel. Subjects range from bicycle books to business. "We will consider any first-rate nonfiction material that we feel will have a long shelf life and be a credit to our list." No set requirements. Submit outline and sample chapters. Reviews artwork/photos as part of ms package.

Recent Nonfiction Title: *Flattened Fauna*.

Tips: "Do not send duplicate submissions to our subsidiary, Celestial Arts."

*TEXAS A&M UNIVERSITY PRESS, Drawer C, College Station TX 77843. (409)845-1436. Director: Lloyd G. Lyman. Publishes 30 titles/year. Subsidy publishes 3% of books; subsidy publishes (nonauthor) 15% of books. Pays in royalties. Publishes book an average of 1 year after acceptance. Query for electronic submissions. Computer printout submissions acceptable; prefers letter-quality. Reports in 1 week on queries: 1 month on submissions. Free book catalog.

Nonfiction: History, natural history, environmental history, economics, agriculture and regional studies (including fiction). Receives artwork/photos as part of ms package. "We do not want poetry." Query. Accepts outline/synopsis and 2-3 sample chapters. "We prefer an introductory statement, table of contents, and sample chapter, which may be a combination of a synopsis and an outline." Reviews artwork/photos as part of ms package.

Recent Nonfiction Title: *East of Chosin*, by R.E. Appleman (history).

Recent Fiction Title: *Thank You, Queen Isabella*, by John Works (novel).

*TEXAS CHRISTIAN UNIVERSITY PRESS, Box 30783, TCU, Fort Worth TX 76129. (817)921-7822. Director: Judy Alter. Publishes hardcover originals, some reprints. Averages 8 titles/year; receives 100 submissions annually. 10% of books from first-time authors; 75% of books from unagented writers. Subsidy publishes (nonauthor) 10% of books. Pays royalty. Publishes book an average of 16 months after acceptance. Computer printout submissions acceptable; no dot-matrix. Reports "as soon as possible."

Nonfiction: American studies, Texana, literature and criticism. "We are looking for good scholarly monographs, other serious scholarly work and regional titles of significance." Query. Reviews artwork/photos as part of ms package.

Recent Nonfiction Title: *Sentinel of the Southern Plains—Fort Richardson & the Northwest Texas Frontier, 1866-1878*, by Allen Lee Hamilton.

Fiction: Adult and young adult regional fiction. Query.

Recent Fiction Title: *Wanderer Springs*, by Robert Flynn (regional novel).

Tips: "Regional and/or Texana nonfiction or fiction have best chance of breaking into our firm."

TEXAS MONTHLY PRESS, INC., Subsidiary of Mediatex Communications Corp., Box 1569, Austin TX 78767. (512)476-7085. President: Scott Lubeck. Publishes hardcover and trade paperback originals, and trade paperback reprints. Averages 30 titles/year; receives 400 submissions annually. 60% of books from first-time authors; 85% of books from unagented writers. Pays royalty; offers advance. Publishes book an average of 1 year after acceptance. Simultaneous and photocopied submissions OK. Query for electronic submissions. Computer printout submissions acceptable. Reports in 1 month on queries; 2 months on mss. Free book catalog.

Nonfiction: Politics and history with comtemporary subject matter, biography, coffee table book, cookbook, humor, guidebook, illustrated book and reference. Subjects include Southwest, art, business and economics, cooking and foods, nature, photography, recreation, sports and travel. Query or submit outline/synopsis and 3 sample chapters. Reviews artwork/photos as part of ms package.

Recent Nonfiction Title: *The Herb Garden Cookbook*, by Lucinda Hutson.

Fiction: Ethnic, mainstream. "All stories must be set in the South or Southwest." No experimental, erotica, confession, gothic, romance or poetry. Query or submit outline/synopsis and 3 sample chapters. No unsolicited mss.

Recent Fiction Title: *Baby Houston*, by June Arnold.

TEXAS WESTERN PRESS, Imprint of The University of Texas at El Paso, El Paso TX 79968-0633. (915)747-5688. Director: Dale L. Walker. Editor: Nancy Hamilton. Publishes hardcover and paperback originals. Publishes 7-8 titles/year. "This is a university press, 33 years old; we do offer a standard 10% royalty contract on our hardcover books and on some of our paperbacks as well. We try to treat our authors professionally, produce handsome, long-lived books and aim for quality, rather than quantity of titles carrying our imprint." Photocopied submissions OK. Free book catalog and ms guidelines. Reports in 1-3 months.

Nonfiction: Scholarly books. Historic and cultural accounts of the Southwest (West Texas, New Mexico,

northern Mexico and Arizona). Occasional scientific titles. "Our *Southwestern Studies* use manuscripts of up to 30,000 words. Our hardback books range from 30,000 words up. The writer should use good exposition in his work. Most of our work requires documentation. We favor a scholarly, but not overly pedantic, style. We specialize in superior book design." Query with outlines. Follow Chicago *Manual of Style*.
Recent Nonfiction Title: *The PUMA: Legendary Lion of the Americas*, by J.B. Tinsley.
Tips: "Texas Western Press is interested in books relating to the history of Hispanics in the U.S., will experiment with photo-documentary books, and is interested in seeing more 'popular' history and books on Southwestern culture/life."

THEATRE ARTS BOOKS, An imprint of Routledge, Chapman & Hall, Inc., 29 West 35th St., New York NY 10001. (212)244-3336. Editorial Director: William P. Germano. Publishes trade paperback originals. Pays royalty. No advance. Publishes ms an average of 1 year after acceptance. Photocopied submissions OK. Computer printout submissions acceptable; no dot-matrix. Reports in 4-6 weeks. Use Chicago *Manual of Style* for ms guidelines.
Nonfiction: Drama and theatre. Subjects include acting, directing, lighting, costume, dance, staging, etc. "We publish only books of broad general interest to actors, directors and theatre technicians, especially books that could be useful in college classrooms. Most of our authors have had long experience in professional theatre. Topics that are very narrowly focused (a costume book on women's shoes in the eighteenth century, for example) would not be acceptable. We no longer publish original plays." Query with outline, synopsis and author's qualifications.

*THE THEOSOPHICAL PUBLISHING HOUSE, Subsidiary of The Theosophical Society in America, 306 W. Geneva Rd., Wheaton IL 60189. (312)665-0123. Imprint, Quest (nonfiction). Senior Editor: Shirley Nicholson. Publishes trade paperback originals. Averages 12 titles/year; receives 750-1,000 submissions annually. 50-60% of books from first-time authors; 95% of books from unagented writers. Average print order for a writer's first book is 5,000. Pays 10-12% royalty on retail price; offers average $1,500 advance. Publishes book an average of 8 months after acceptance. Simultaneous and photocopied submissions OK. Computer printout submissions acceptable; prefers letter-quality. Reports in 2 weeks on queries, 2 months on mss. Free book catalog; ms guidelines for SASE.
Nonfiction: Subjects include self-development, self-help, philosophy (holistic), psychology (transpersonal), Eastern and Western religions, comparative religion, holistic implications in science, health and healing, yoga, meditation and astrology. "TPH seeks works which are compatible with the theosophical philosophy. Our audience includes the 'new age' community, seekers in all religions, general public, professors, and health professionals. No submissions which do not fit the needs outlined above." Accepts nonfiction translations. Query or submit outline/synopsis and sample chapters. Reviews artwork/photos as part of ms package.
Recent Nonfiction Title: *Self-Transformation through Music*, by Joanne Crandall.
Tips: "The writer has the best chance of selling our firm a book which illustrates a connection between spiritually-oriented philosophy or viewpoint and some field of current interest."

*THISTLEDOWN PRESS, 668 E. Place, Saskatoon, Saskatchewan S7J 2Z5 Canada. (306)477-0556. Editor-in-Chief: Paddy O' Rourke. Publishes hardcover and trade paperback originals by resident Canadian authors *only*. Averages 8 titles/year; receives 150 submissions annually. 50% of books from first-time authors; 100% of books from unagented writers. Average print order for a writer's first (poetry) book is 750 or (fiction) 1,000. Subsidy publishes (nonauthor) 100% of books. Pays standard royalty on retail price. Publishes book an average of 18-24 months after acceptance. Computer printout submissions acceptable; no dot-matrix. Reports in 2 weeks on queries; 2 months on poetry mss; 3 months on fiction mss. Book catalog and guidelines for #10 SAE with IRC.
Fiction: Literary. Interested in fiction mss from resident Canadian authors only. Minimum of 30,000 words. Accepts no unsolicited work. Query first.
Recent Fiction Title: *The Violent Lavender Beast*, Ernest Hekkanen (short stories).
Poetry: "The author should make him/herself familiar with our publishing program before deciding whether or not his/her work is appropriate." No poetry by people *not* citizens and residents of Canada. Submit complete ms. Minimum of 60 pages. Prefers poetry mss that have had some previous exposure in literary magazines. Accepts no unsolicited work. Query first.
Recent Poetry Title: *Dedications*, by Dennis Cooley (contemporary Canadian).
Tips: "We prefer a book that has literary integrity and a distinct voice."

THOMAS PUBLICATIONS, Subsidiary of Thomas Graphics, Inc., Box 33244, Austin TX 78764. (512)832-0355. Contact: Ralph D. Thomas. Publishes trade paperback originals and trade paperback reprints. Averages 8-10 titles/year; receives 20-30 submissions annually. 90% of books from first-time authors; 90% of books from unagented writers. Pays 10-15% royalty on wholesale or retail price, or makes outright purchase of $500-2,000. Publishes book an average of 1 year after acceptance. Simultaneous and photocopied submissions OK. Computer printout submissions acceptable; no dot-matrix. Reports in 2 weeks on queries; 1 month on mss. Book catalog $1.

Nonfiction: How-to, reference and textbook. Subjects include sociology and investigation and investigative techniques. "We are looking for hardcore investigative methods books, manuals on how to make more dollars in private investigation, private investigative marketing techniques, and specialties in the investigative professions." Query or submit outline/synopsis and sample chapters. Reviews artwork/photos as part of ms package.
Recent Nonfiction Title: *How to Find Anyone Anywhere*, by Ralph Thomas (investigation).
Tips: "Our audience includes private investigators, those wanting to break into investigation, related trades such as auto repossessors, private process servers, news reporters, and related security trades."

‡CHARLES C. THOMAS, PUBLISHER, 2600 South First St., Springfield IL 62794. (217)789-8980. Editor: Payne E.L. Thomas. Publishes hardcover originals and paperback originals. Firm averages 150 titles/year. Receives 1,000 submissions/year. 95% of books from first-time authors. 94% from unagented writers. Pays 10% royalty on retail price. Publishes book an average of 6 months after acceptance. Simultaneous submissions OK. Computer printout submissions OK; prefers letter-quality. Reports in 1 week on queries; 1 week on mss. Free book catalog and ms guidelines.
Nonfiction: Self-help, technical and textbook. Subjects include anthropology, archaeology, child guidance/parenting, education, health/medicine, language/literature, nature/environment, philosophy, psychology, recreation, religion, science, sociology and sports. "Biomedical sciences, rehabilitation, behavioral and social sciences, education and special education, criminal justice are our manuscript needs." Submit outline/synopsis and sample chapters or submit complete ms. Reviews artwork/photos as part of manuscript package.

*THREE CONTINENTS PRESS, 1636 Connecticut Ave. NW, Washington DC 20009. Publisher/Editor-in-Chief: Donald E. Herdeck. General Editor: Norman Ware. Publishes hardcover and paperback originals and reprints. Averages 12-14 titles/year. Receives 200 submissions annually. 15% of books from first-time authors; 100% of books from unagented writers. Average print order for a writer's first book is 1,000. Subsidy publishes (nonauthor) 10% of books. Pays 10% royalty; advance "only on delivery of complete manuscript which is found acceptable; usually $300." Photocopied (preferred) and simultaneous submissions OK. State availability of photos/illustrations. Computer printout submissions acceptable; prefers letter-quality. Reports in 2 months. Book catalog and guidelines for 8x11 SAE.
Nonfiction and Fiction: Specializes in African, Caribbean and Middle Eastern (Arabic and Persian) literature and criticism and translation, Third World literature and history. Scholarly, well-prepared mss; creative writing. Fiction, poetry, criticism, history and translations of creative writing. "We search for books which will make clear the complexity and value of non-western literature and culture, including bilingual texts (Arabic language/English translations). We are always interested in genuine contributions to understanding non-western culture." Length: 50,000-125,000 words. Query. "Please do not submit manuscript unless we ask for it. We prefer an outline, and an annotated table of contents, for works of nonfiction; and a synopsis, a plot summary (one to three pages), for fiction. For poetry, send two or three sample poems." Reviews artwork/photos as part of ms package.
Recent Nonfiction Title: *The Ensphering Mind*, by J. Wieland (criticism).
Recent Fiction Title: *Worl' Do For Fraid*, a play by Nabie Swaray.
Tips: "We need a *polished* translation, or original prose or poetry by non-Western authors *only*."

THUNDER'S MOUTH PRESS, 93-99 Greene St., New York NY 10012. (212)226-0277. Publisher: Neil Ortenberg. Publishes hardcover and trade paperback originals and reprints. Averages 15 titles/year; receives 1,000 submissions annually. 50% of books from unagented writers. Average print order for a writer's first book is 5,000. Pays 5-10% royalty on retail price; offers average $1,000 advance. Publishes book an average of 8 months after acceptance. Reports in 3 weeks on queries. Book catalog for SAE and 1 first class stamp.
Nonfiction: Biography. Publishes for "college students, academics, politically left of center, ethnic, social activists, women, etc. We basically do poetry and fiction now but intend to start doing nonfiction over the next few years." Query only.
Fiction: Erotica, ethnic, experimental, historical, and political. "We are interested in doing anywhere from 5-10 novels per year, particularly highly literary or socially relevant novels." No romance. Query only.
Poetry: "We intend to publish 1-2 books of poetry per year. No elitist, rhymes or religious poetry." Query.

TIMBER PRESS, INC., 9999 S.W. Wilshire, Portland OR 97225. (503)292-0745. Imprints include Dioscorides Press Inc. (botany), Amadeus Press Inc. (music) and Areopagitica Press, Inc. (history). Editor: Richard Abel. Small press. Publishes hardcover and paperback originals. Publishes 40 titles/year; receives 300-400 submissions annually. 90% of books from first-time authors; 100% of books from unagented writers. Pays 10-20% royalty; sometimes offers advance to cover costs of artwork and final ms completion. Publishes book an average of 1 year after acceptance. Query for electronic submissions. Computer printout submissions acceptable; prefers letter-quality. Reports in 2 months. Book catalog and ms guidelines for 9x12 SAE with 3 first class stamps.
Nonfiction: Horticulture (ornamental and economic), botany, plant sciences, natural history, Northwest regional material, forestry, serious music and history. Accepts nonfiction translations from all languages. Query

or submit outline/synopsis and 3-4 sample chapters. Reviews artwork/photos as part of ms package.
Recent Nonfiction Title: *Gardening with Dwarf Trees and Shrubs*, by Bartels (horticulture).
Tips: "The writer has the best chance of selling our firm good books on botany, plant science, horticulture, forestry, agriculture and serious music and history."

‡TIME-LIFE BOOKS INC., 777 Duke St., Alexandria VA 22314. (703)838-7000. Editor: George Constable. Publishes hardcover originals. Averages 40 titles/year. Books are almost entirely staff-generated and staff-produced, and distribution is primarily through mail order sale. Query to the Director of Corporate Development.
Nonfiction: "General interest books. Most books tend to be heavily illustrated (by staff), with text written by assigned authors. We very rarely accept mss or book ideas submitted from outside our staff." Length: open.
Recent Nonfiction Title: *The Computerized Society*.

TIMES BOOKS, Division of Random House, Inc., 201 East 50 St., New York NY 10022. (212)872-8110. Vice President and Editorial Director: Jonathan B. Segal. Executive Editor: Hugh O'Neill. Senior Editor: Elisabeth Scharlatt. Publishes hardcover and paperback originals and reprints. Publishes 45 titles/year. Pays royalty; average advance. Publishes book an average of 1 year after acceptance. Computer printout submissions acceptable.
Nonfiction: Business/economics, science and medicine, history, biography, women's issues, the family, cookbooks, current affairs, cooking and sports. Accepts only solicited manuscripts. Reviews artwork/photos as part of ms package.
Recent Nonfiction Title: *Buying Into America*, by Martin and Susan Tolchun.

TOR BOOKS, Subsidiary of St. Martin's Press, 9th Floor, 49 W. 24th St., New York NY 10010. (212)741-3100. Editor-in-Chief: Beth Meacham. Publishes mass market, hardcover and trade paperback originals and reprints. Averages 300 books/year. Pays 6-8% royalty; offers negotiable advance. Book catalog for 9x12 SASE.
Fiction: Horror, science fiction, occult, chillers, suspense, espionage, historical and fantasy. "We prefer an extensive chapter-by-chapter synopsis and the first 3 chapters complete." Prefers agented mss or proposals.
Recent Fiction Title: *Seventh Son*, by Orson Scott Card (fantasy).
Tips: "We're pretty broad in the occult, horror and fantasy but more straightforward in science fiction and thrillers, tending to stay with certain authors and certain types of work."

TRANSNATIONAL PUBLISHERS, INC., Box 7282, Ardsley-on-Hudson NY 10503. (914)693-0089. Publisher: Ms. Heike Fenton. Publishes hardcover originals. Averages 10-15 titles/year; receives 50 submissions annually. 10% of books from first-time authors; 100% of books from unagented writers. Pays 5-10% royalty. Publishes book an average of 6 months after acceptance. Simultaneous and photocopied submissions OK. Computer printout submissions acceptable. Reports in 2 weeks on queries; 1 month on mss. Book and ms guidelines free on request.
Nonfiction: Reference, textbook and books for professionals. Subjects include politics, international law, criminal law, human rights, women's studies and political theory. Needs scholarly works in the area of international law and politics. No submissions on topics other than those listed above. Submit outline/synopsis and sample chapters.
Recent Nonfiction Title: *International Court of Justice at a Crossroads*, by Lori Damrosch, ed.
Tips: "The audience for our books includes law libraries, public libraries, universities, government personnel, military personnel, college students and women's rights groups."

TRAVEL KEYS, Box 160691, Sacramento CA 95816. (916)452-5200. Publisher: Peter B. Manston. Publishes hardcover and trade paperback originals. Averages 4 titles/year; receives 15 submissions annually. 20% of books from first-time authors; 90% of books from unagented writers. Pays 6-15% royalty ("rarely, we mostly use work for hire"); or makes outright purchase for $500 minimum. Offers minimum $500 advance. Publishes book an average of 10 months after acceptance. Simultaneous and photocopied submissions OK. Query for electronic submissions. Reports in 1 month. Book catalog for #10 SAE with 1 first class stamp.
Nonfiction: How-to on travel (mainly Europe), antiques and flea market guides. "We need carefully researched, practical travel manuscripts. No science or technical submissions." Submit outline/synopsis and sample chapters. Reviews artwork/photos as part of ms package.
Recent Nonfiction Title: *Manston's Before You Leave on Your Vacation . . .*, by R. Bynum and P. Mazuski.
Tips: "We will continue in the travel field, but we are broadening out from destination—Europe—to more general travel topics."

‡TREND BOOK DIVISION, Box 611, St. Petersburg FL 33731. (813)821-5800. Chairman: Eugene C. Patterson. President: Andrew Barnes. Publisher: Richard Edmonds. Publishes hardcover and paperback originals and reprints. Specializes in books on Florida—all categories. Pays royalty; no advance. Books are marketed through *Florida Trend* magazine. Publishes book an average of 8 months after acceptance. Computer printout

submissions acceptable; no dot-matrix. Reports in 1 month.
Nonfiction: Business, economics, history, law, politics, reference, textbooks and travel. "All books pertain to Florida." Query. Reviews artwork/photos as part of ms package.
Tips: "We are shifting to more emphasis on books of a Florida business/economics nature."

TRILLIUM PRESS, Subsidiaries include Cloud 10, Box 209, Monroe NY 10950. (914)783-2999. Editor: William Neuman. Publishes hardcover and paperback originals. Averages 100 titles/year; receives 800 submissions annually. 33% of books from first-time authors; 95% of books from unagented writers. Pays 10% royalty on wholesale price; no advance. Publishes book an average of 1 year after acceptance. Photocopied submissions OK. Computer printout submissions OK; prefers letter-quality. Reports in 1 month on queries. Book catalog and guidelines for 8½x11 SAE and 4 first class stamps.
Nonfiction: Self-help and textbook. Subjects include inspirational and education. Submit complete ms. Review artwork/photos as part of ms.
Recent Nonfiction Title: *Feel the Laughter*, by Sharon Komlos.
Fiction: Children's. Submit complete ms.
Recent Fiction Title: *Mother, I'm Mad*, by Daniel.

TROUBADOR PRESS, Subsidiary of Price Stern Sloan, Inc., 360 N. La Cienega Blvd., Los Angeles CA 90048. (213)657-6100. Publishes paperback originals. Averages 4 titles/year; receives 300 submissions annually. 95% of books from unagented writers. Average print order for a writer's first book is 10,000. Pays royalty. Offers average $500 advance. Publishes book an average of 6 months after acceptance. Computer printout submissions acceptable; prefers letter-quality. Reports in 1 month. Book catalog and ms guidelines for SASE.
Nonfiction: "Troubador Press publishes mainly, but is not limited to, children's activity books: coloring, cutout, mazes, games, paper dolls, etc. All titles feature original art and exceptional graphics. We like books which have the potential to develop into series." Query or submit outline/synopsis and 2-3 sample chapters with conciseness and clarity of a good idea. Reviews artwork as part of ms package.
Recent Nonfiction Title: *The Second Dinosaur Action Set*, by M. Whyte and artist Dan Smith (dinosaurs punch-out and play book with dinosaur dictionary text incorporated).
Tips: "We continue to publish new authors along with established writers/artists. We feel the mix is good and healthy." Queries/mss may be routed to other editors in the publishing group.

TWAYNE PUBLISHERS, A division of G.K. Hall & Co., subsidiary of Macmillan, Inc., 70 Lincoln St., Boston MA 02111. (617)423-3990. Publishes hardcover and paperback originals. Publishes 100 titles/year; receives 1,000 submissions annually. 5% of books from first-time authors; 10% of books from unagented writers. Average print order for a writer's first book is 1,000. Pays royalty. Reports in 5 weeks.
Nonfiction: Publishes scholarly books and volumes in and out of series for the general reader. Literary criticism, biography, history; women's studies, art history, current affairs and science. Query only with outline and 2 sample chapters.
Recent Nonfiction Title: *Henry R. Luce and The Rise of the American News Media*, by James L. Roughman.
Tips: Queries may be routed to other editors in the publishing group. Unsolicited mss will not be read.

*TYNDALE HOUSE PUBLISHERS, INC., 336 Gundersen Dr., Wheaton IL 60187. (312)668-8300. Editor-in-Chief/Acquisitions: Wendell Hawley. Publishes hardcover and trade paperback originals and hardcover and mass paperback reprints. Averages 100 titles/year; receives 3,000 submissions annually. 15% of books from first-time authors; 99% of books from unagented writers. Average print order for a writer's first book is 7,000-10,000. Subsidy publishes 2% of books. Pays 10% royalty; offers negotiable advance. Publishes book an average of 18 months after acceptance. Computer printout submissions acceptable; no dot-matrix. Reports in 6 weeks. Free book catalog; ms guidelines for #10 SAE with 1 first class stamp.
Nonfiction: Religious books only: personal experience, family living, marriage, Bible reference works and commentaries, Christian living, devotional, inspirational, church and social issues, Bible prophecy, theology and doctrine, counseling and Christian psychology, Christian apologetics and church history. Submit table of contents, chapter summary, preface, first 2 chapters and 1 later chapter.
Fiction: Biblical novels. Submit outline/synopsis and sample chapters.

*UAHC PRESS, Union of American Hebrew Congregations, 838 5th Ave., New York NY 10021. (212)249-0100. Managing Director: Stuart L. Benick. Publishes hardcover and trade paperback originals. Averages 15 titles/year. 50% of books from first-time authors; 90% of books from unagented writers. Subsidy publishes 40% of books. Pays 5-15% royalty on wholesale price. Publishes book an average of 9 months after acceptance. Simultaneous and photocopied submissions OK. Computer printout submissions OK. Book catalog and ms guidelines for SASE.
Nonfiction: Illustrated, juvenile and Jewish textbooks. Subjects include Jewish religion. "We need Jewish textbooks which fit into our curriculum." Reviews artwork/photos as part of ms package.
Fiction: Jewish religion. "We publish books that teach values."

ULI, THE URBAN LAND INSTITUTE, 1090 Vermont Ave. N.W., Washington DC 20005. (202)289-8500. Director of Publications: Frank H. Spink, Jr. Publishes hardcover and trade paperback originals. Averages 15-20 titles/year. Receives 20 submissions annually. No books from first-time authors; 100% of books from unagented writers. Pays 10% royalty on gross sales. Offers advance of $1,500-2,000. Publishes book an average of 6 months after acceptance. Query for electronic submissions. Computer printout submissions acceptable; prefers letter-quality. Book catalog and writer's guidelines for 9x12 SAE.
Nonfiction: Technical books on real estate development and land planning. "The majority of mss are created in-house by research staff. We acquire two or three outside authors to fill schedule and subject areas where our list has gaps. We are not interested in real estate sales, brokerages, appraisal, making money in real estate, opinion, personal point of view, or mss negative toward growth and development." Query. Reviews artwork/photos as part of ms package.
Recent Nonfiction Title: *Density by Design*, by A/A Housing Committee.

ULTRALIGHT PUBLICATIONS, INC., Box 234, Hammelstown PA 17036. (717)566-0468. Editor: Michael A. Markowski. Imprints includes Aviation Publishers and Medical Information Systems Division. Publishes hardcover and trade paperback originals. Averages 6 titles/year; receives 30 submissions annually. 50% of books from first-time authors; 100% of books from unagented writers. Average print order for a writer's first book is 5,000. Pays 10-15% royalty on wholesale price; buys some mss outright. Offers average $1,000-1,500 advance. Publishes book an average of 9 months after acceptance. Simultaneous and photocopied submissions OK. Computer printout submissions acceptable; no dot-matrix. Reports in 3 weeks on queries; 2 months on mss. Book catalog and ms guidelines for #10 SAE with 2 first class stamps.
Nonfiction: How-to, technical on hobbies (model airplanes, model cars, and model boats) and aviation. Publishes for "aviation buffs, dreamers and enthusiasts. We are looking for titles in the homebuilt, ultralight, sport and general aviation fields. We are interested in how-to, technical and reference books of short to medium length that will serve recognized and emerging aviation needs." Also interested in automotive historical, reference and how-to; popular health, medical, and fitness for the general public. Self-help, motivation and success are also areas of interest. Query or submit outline/synopsis and 3 sample chapters. Reviews artwork/photos as part of ms package.
Recent Nonfiction Title: *Canard: A Revolution in Flight*, by Lennon (aviation history).

UMI RESEARCH PRESS, University Microfilms, Inc., Bell & Howell, 300 N. Zeeb Road, Ann Arbor MI 48106. Acquisitions Editor: Christine B. Hammes. Small press. Publishes hardcover originals and some revised dissertations. Averages 60-70 titles/year; receives 300 or more submissions annually. 70% of books from first-time authors. Average print order for a writer's first book is 700. Pays 5% royalty on net sales. Offers average $100 advance. Publishes book an average of 6 months after acceptance. Photocopied submissions OK. Query for electronic submissions. Computer printout submissions acceptable "if good quality."
Nonfiction: Scholarly and professional research and critical studies in arts and humanities. Subjects include architecture; cinema (theory and aesthetics); art (theory, criticism, and history); theatre (history and theory); musicology; photography (theory); American material culture; religion; literary criticism and women's studies. Especially looking for "scholarly works, original conclusions resulting from careful academic research. Primarily aimed at graduate, post-graduate and professional level. Academics, research librarians, art, music, and literary communities, are our audience." No mass market books. Query.
Recent Nonfiction Title: *Warhol: Conversations about the Artist*, by Patrick S. Smith.
Tips: "Send detailed proposal to publisher *before* devoting hours to complete a manuscript. Get feedback at the outline/prospectus stage. Sell us on your manuscript: Why is the work an important and original contribution to its field? Who are its prospective readers and what are your ideas for helping us get word out to them (should we agree to publish the ms)?"

THE UNICORN PUBLISHING HOUSE, INC., 1148 Parsippany Blvd., Parsippany NJ 07054. (201)334-0353. Associate Juvenile Editor: Heidi K. L. Corso. Publishes hardcover originals. Averages 10 titles/year; receives 1,500 submissions annually. 25% of books from first-time authors; 90% of books from unagented writers. Negotiates payment. Publishes book an average of 18 months after acceptance. Simultaneous and photocopied submissions OK. Computer printout submissions OK. Reports in 1 month on juvenile queries; 1 month on juvenile mss, 3 months on adult mss. Guidelines for #10 SASE.
Nonfiction: Biography, coffee table, illustrated, juvenile, and self-help. Subjects include animals, art, health, music and photography. "We are seeking juvenile, arts and entertainment and current issues books." Query or submit outline/synopsis and sample chapters or submit complete ms. Reviews artwork/photos as part of ms package.
Recent Nonfiction Title: *A Question of Innocence*, by L. Spiegel (contemporary issues).
Fiction: Adventure and fantasy. "We want books for juveniles ages preschool-15." Query or submit outline/synopsis and sample chapters or submit complete ms. No young adult novels please!
Recent Fiction Title: *Come Play With Peter Cottontail*, by J. Scrocco, ed. (touch and feel).
Poetry: No adult books. Submit complete ms.
Tips: "Juvenile fiction constitutes the bulk of what we publish."

‡**UNIQUE PUBLICATIONS**, CFW Enterprises, Inc. 4201 Vanowen Place, Burbank CA 91505. (818)845-2656. Book Administrator: Ray Ung. Publishes trade paperback originals. Firm averages 15 titles/year. Receives 100 submissions/year. 50% of books from first-time authors. 85% from unagented writers. Buys mss outright for $1,000-4,000. Advance open. Publishes book an average of 2 years after acceptance. Simultaneous and photocopied submissions OK. Computer printout submissions OK; prefers letter-quality. Reports in 1 month on mss. Free book catalog. Manuscript guidelines for #10 SASE.
Nonfiction: How-to. Subjects include health/medicine, philosophy (oriental), sports and martial arts. Submit outline/synopsis and sample chapters. Reviews artwork/photos as part of manuscript package.
Recent Nonfiction Title: *Survival on the Battlefield*, by Robert Spear (military martial arts).
Fiction: Adventure (Ninja, survival games) and martial arts. Submit outline/synopsis and sample chapters.
Recent Fiction Title: *Iron Butterfly*, by Hernandez (adventure).
Tips: "We're looking for martial arts manuscripts that are effective, practical and clearly explained. The artist should have a solid background and must be authentic. Young adults, martial artists and young professionals are our audience. Include documentation to clear any myths, misconceptions. Historic photos, creative presentations are helpful."

***UNIVELT, INC.**, Box 28130, San Diego CA 92128. (619)746-4005. Publisher: H. Jacobs. Publishes hardcover originals. Averages 8 titles/year; receives 20 submissions annually. 5% of books from first-time authors; 5% of books from unagented writers. Subsidy publishes (nonauthor) 10% of books. Average print order for a writer's first book is 1,000-2,000. Pays 10% royalty on actual sales; no advance. Publishes book an average of 4 months after acceptance. Computer printout submissions acceptable; prefers letter-quality. Reports in 1 month. Book catalog and ms guidelines for SASE.
Nonfiction: Publishes in the field of aerospace, especially astronautics and technical communications, but including application of aerospace technology to Earth's problems, also astronomy. Submit outline/synopsis and 1-2 sample chapters. Reviews artwork/photos as part of ms package.
Recent Nonfiction Title: *Soviet Space Programs 1980-1985*.
Tips: "Writers have the best chance of selling manuscripts on the history of astronautics (we have a history series) and astronautics/space/light subjects. We publish for the American Astronautical Society." Queries/mss may be routed to other editors in the publishing group.

***UNIVERSE BOOKS**, 381 Park Ave. S., New York NY 10016. (212)685-7400. Editorial Director: Louis Barron. Publishes hardcover and paperback originals and reprints. Averages 40-50 titles/year; receives 1,000 submissions annually. 75% of books from first-time authors; 75% of books from unagented writers. Average print order for a writer's first book is 3,000-4,000. Offers 10-15% royalty on retail price (hardbound books). "On a few extra-illustrated art books and on special studies with a limited market we may pay a smaller royalty. If a book makes a genuine contribution to knowledge but is a commercial risk, we might perhaps accept a subsidy from a foundation or other organization, but not directly from the author." Publishes book an average of 9 months after acceptance. Simultaneous and photocopied submissions OK. Computer printout submissions acceptable; no dot-matrix. "Will not return material without postage-paid SAE." Reports in 3 weeks. Book catalog for 8½x11 SAE with 5 first class stamps.
Nonfiction: Animals, art, economics, history, nature, performing arts, politics and reference. Also uses "monographs on specific animal, bird or plant species. We publish books in the following categories: art, architecture and design, history, horticulture, jazz, ballet, music, and contemporary problems. We do not publish fiction, poetry, cookbooks, criticism or belles lettres." Accepts nonfiction French and German translations. Submit outline/synopsis and 2-3 sample chapters. Reviews artwork/photos as part of ms package.
Recent Nonfiction Title: *The Puppet Emperor*, by Brian Power (Chinese biography).

***UNIVERSITY OF ALABAMA PRESS**, Box 2877, Tuscaloosa AL 35487. Director: Malcolm MacDonald. Publishes hardcover originals. Averages 40 titles/year; receives 200 submissions annually. 80% of books from first-time authors; 100% of books from unagented writers. "Pays maximum 10% royalty on wholesale price; no advance." Publishes book an average of 16 months after acceptance. Computer printout submissions acceptable. Free book catalog; ms guidelines for SASE.
Nonfiction: Biography, history, philosophy, politics, religion, sociology and anthropology. Considers upon merit almost any subject of scholarly interest, but specializes in linguistics and philology, political science and public administration, literary criticism and biography, philosophy and history. Accepts nonfiction translations. Reviews artwork/photos as part of ms package.
Recent Nonfiction Title: *Black Eagle: General Daniel "Chappie" James* (biography).

THE UNIVERSITY OF ALBERTA PRESS, 141 Athabasca Hall, Edmonton, Alberta T6G 2E8 Canada. (403)432-3662. Imprint, Pica Pica Press. Director: Norma Gutteridge. Publishes hardcover and trade paperback originals, and trade paperback reprints. Averages 10 titles/year; receives 200-300 submissions annually. 60% of books from first-time authors; majority of books from unagented writers. Average print order for a writer's first book is 1,000. Pays 10% royalty on retail price. Publishes book an average of 1 year after acceptance.

Query for electronic submissions. Computer printout submissions acceptable; no dot-matrix. Reports in 1 week on queries; 3 months on mss. Free book catalog and ms guidelines.

Nonfiction: Biography, how-to, reference, technical, textbook, and scholarly. Subjects include art, history, nature, philosophy, politics, and sociology. Especially looking for "biographies of Canadians in public life, and works analyzing Canada's political history and public policy, particularly in international affairs. No pioneer reminiscences, literary criticism (unless in Canadian literature), reports of narrowly focused studies, unrevised theses." Submit complete ms. Reviews artwork/photos as part of ms package.

Recent Nonfiction Title: *Empire of Dust: Setting and Abandoning the Prairie Dry Belt*, by David C. Jones.

Tips: "We are interested in original research making a significant contribution to knowledge in the subject."

THE UNIVERSITY OF ARKANSAS PRESS, Fayetteville AR 72701. (501)575-3246. Director: Miller Williams. Publishes hardcover and trade paperback originals and hardcover reprints. Averages 30 titles/year; receives 4,000 submissions annually. 30% of books from first-time authors; 90% of books from unagented writers. Pays 10% royalty on net receipts. Publishes book an average of 18 months after acceptance. Simultaneous (if so informed) and photocopied submissions OK. Query for electronic submissions. Computer printout submissions OK; no dot-matrix. Reports in 3 weeks on queries; 6 weeks on mss. Ms guidelines for #10 SAE and 2 first class stamps.

Nonfiction: Biography and literature. Subjects include Americana, history, humanities, nature, general politics and history of politics, and sociology. "Our current needs include literary criticism—especially on contemporary authors, history and biography. We won't consider manuscripts for texts, juvenile or religious studies, or anything requiring a specialized or exotic vocabulary." Query or submit outline/synopsis and sample chapters.

Recent Nonfiction Title: *Displaced Person: The Travel Essays of John Clellon Holmes*.

Fiction: "Works of high literary merit; short stories; rarely novels. No genre fiction." Query.

Recent Fiction Title: *All My Trials*, by John Corrington (two novellas, southern setting).

Poetry: "Because of small list, query first."

Recent Poetry Title: *Sudden Hunger*, by Debra Bruce.

*THE UNIVERSITY OF CALGARY PRESS, Library Tower, 2500 University Drive NW, Calgary, Alberta T2N 1N4 Canada. (403)220-7578. Assistant Director: Linda D. Cameron. Publishes scholarly paperback originals. Averages 12-16 titles/year; receives 70 submissions annually. 50% of books from first-time authors; 100% of books from unagented authors. Subsidy publishes (nonauthor) 100% of books. "As with all Canadian University presses, UGP does not have publication funds of its own. Money must be found to subsidize each project. We do not consider publications for which there is no possibility of subvention." Publishes book average of 1 year after acceptance. Pays negotiable royalties. "Ms must pass a two tier review system before acceptance." Photocopied submissions OK. Query for electronic submissions. Computer printout submissions OK; prefers letter-quality. Reports on 2 weeks on queries; 2 months on mss. Free book catalog and guidelines.

Nonfiction: Reference, technical, textbook and scholarly. Subjects include Canadiana, business and economics, health, history, nature, philosophy, politics, psychology, religion, communications, energy research and engineering. "Especially looking for scholarly works in the humanities, social sciences, communication, natural history, library sciences, energy research and engineering." Query or submit complete ms.

Recent Nonfiction Title: *Electrifying Calgary: A Century of Public and Private Power*, by W.E. Hawkins.

Tips: "If I were trying to interest a scholarly publisher, I would prepare my manuscript on a word processor and submit a completed prospectus, including projected market, to the publisher."

UNIVERSITY OF CALIFORNIA PRESS, 2120 Berkeley Way, Berkeley CA 94720. Director: James H. Clark. Assistant Director: Lynne E. Withey. Los Angeles office: Suite 613, 10995 Le Conte Ave., UCLA, Los Angeles CA 94995. New York office: Room 513, 50 E. 42 St., New York NY 10017. London office: University Presses of California, Columbia and Princeton, 15A Epson Rd., Guildford Surrey GU1 3JT, England. Publishes hardcover and paperback originals and reprints. "On books likely to do more than return their costs, a standard royalty contract beginning at 7% is paid; on paperbacks it is less." Published 230 titles last year. Queries are always advisable, accompanied by outlines or sample material. Accepts nonfiction translations. Send to Berkeley address. Reports vary, depending on the subject. Enclose return postage.

Nonfiction: "Most of our publications are hardcover nonfiction written by scholars." Publishes scholarly books including art, literary studies, social sciences, natural sciences and some high-level popularizations. No length preferences.

Fiction and Poetry: Publishes fiction and poetry only in translation, usually in bilingual editions.

‡UNIVERSITY OF IDAHO PRESS, 3368 University Station, Moscow ID 83843. (208)885-7564. Director: James J. Heaney. Publishes hardcover originals, trade paperback originals and trade paperback reprints. Firm averages 8-10 titles/year. Receives 150 submissions/year. 20% of books from first-time authors; 90% from unagented writers. Pays 15% maximum royalty on wholesale price. Offers $200 average advance. Publishes book an average of 11 months after acceptance. Photocopied submissions OK. Query for electronic submissions. Computer printout submissions OK; prefers letter-quality. Reports in 3 weeks on queries; 3 months on mss. Free book catalog and ms guidelines.

Nonfiction: Biography, coffee table book, illustrated book, reference, self-help, technical and textbook. Subjects include agriculture/horticulture, Americana, anthropology/archaeology, cooking, foods and nutrition, education, government/politics, health/medicine, history, language/literature, nature/environment, philosophy, regional, religion, sociology and women's issues/studies. "We're looking for regional and Americana titles." Query or submit outline/synopsis and sample chapters. Reviews artwork/photos as part of manuscript package.

Recent Nonfiction Title: *Community Of Cattlemen*, by P.K. Simpson (social history). "We would like to do at least 1-2 serious fiction titles per year. No manuscripts from outside the academic environment." Query or submit outline/synopsis and sample chapters.

Recent Fiction Title: *Unlearned Pleasures and Other Stories*, by Ursula Hegi (short stories).

Tips: "Our audience is interested in scholarly titles and includes academic readers with regional interests."

*UNIVERSITY OF ILLINOIS PRESS, 54 E. Gregory, Champaign IL 61820. (217)333-0950. Director/Editor: Richard L. Wentworth. Publishes hardcover and trade paperback originals, and hardcover and trade paperback reprints. Averages 90-100 titles/year. 50% of books from first-time authors; 95% of books from unagented writers. Subsidy publishes (nonauthor) 30% of books. Pays 0-15% royalty on net sales; offers average $1,000-1,500 advance (rarely). Publishes book an average of 1 year after acceptance. Simultaneous and photocopied submissions OK. Query for electronic submissions. Computer printout submissions acceptable; no dot-matrix. Reports in 1 week on queries; 3 months on mss. Free book catalog.

Nonfiction: Biography, reference and scholarly books. Subjects include Americana, business and economics, history (especially American history), music (especially American music), politics, sociology, sports and literature. Always looking for "solid scholarly books in American history, especially social history; books on American popular music, and books in the broad area of American studies." Query with outline/synopsis.

Recent Nonfiction Title: *The Poet and the Dream Girl: The Love Letters of Lillian Steichen and Carl Sandburg*, Margaret Sandburg, editor.

Fiction: Ethnic, experimental and mainstream. "We publish four collections of stories by individual writers each year. We do not publish novels." Query.

Recent Fiction Title: *The Christmas Wife*, by Helen Norris (stories).

Tips: "Serious scholarly books that are broad enough and well-written enough to appeal to non-specialists are doing well for us in today's market. Writers of nonfiction whose primary goal is to earn money (rather than get promoted in an academic position) are advised to try at least a dozen commercial publishers before thinking about offering the work to a university press."

UNIVERSITY OF IOWA PRESS, Westlawn, Iowa City IA 52242. (319)353-3181. Director: Paul Zimmer. Publishes hardcover and paperback originals. Averages 20-28 titles/year; receives 300-400 submissions annually. 30% of books from first-time authors; 95% of books from unagented writers. Average print order for a writer's first book is 1,200-1,500. Pays 7-10% royalty on net price. "We market mostly by direct mailing of flyers to groups with special interests in our titles and by advertising in trade and scholarly publications." Publishes book an average of 1 year after acceptance. Query for electronic submissions. Readable computer printout submissions acceptable. Reports within 4 months. Free book catalog and ms guidelines.

Nonfiction: Publishes anthropology, archaeology, British and American literary studies, history (Victorian, U.S., German, medieval, Latin American), and natural history. Currently publishes the Iowa School of Letters Award for Short Fiction, and Iowa Poetry Prize selections. "Please query regarding poetry or fiction before sending manuscript." Looks for "evidence of original research; reliable sources; clarity of organization, complete development of theme with documentation and supportive footnotes and/or bibliography; and a substantive contribution to knowledge in the field treated." Query or submit outline/synopsis. Use Chicago *Manual of Style*. Reviews artwork/photos as part of ms package.

UNIVERSITY OF MASSACHUSETTS PRESS, Box 429, Amherst MA 01004. (413)545-2217. Director: Bruce Wilcox. Acquisitions Editor: Richard Martin. Publishes hardcover and paperback originals, reprints and imports. Averages 30 titles/year; receives 600 submissions annually. 20% of books from first-time authors; 90% of books from unagented writers. Average print order for a writer's first book is 1,500. Royalties generally 10% of net income. Advance rarely offered. No author subsidies accepted. Publishes book an average of 1 year after acceptance. Query for electronic submissions. Computer printout submissions acceptable; prefers letter-quality. Preliminary report in 1 month. Free book catalog.

Nonfiction: Publishes Afro-American studies, art and architecture, biography, criticism, history, natural history, philosophy, poetry, psychology, public policy, sociology and women's studies in original and reprint editions. Accepts nonfiction translations. Submit outline/synopsis and 1-2 sample chapters. Reviews artwork/photos as part of ms package.

Recent Nonfiction Title: *Women and the Ideal Society: Plato's Republic and Modern Myths of Gender*, by Natalie Harris Bluestone.

Tips: "As members of AAUP, we sometimes route (queries/mss) to other university presses."

UNIVERSITY OF MICHIGAN PRESS, 839 Greene St., Ann Arbor MI 48106. (313)764-4394. Editorial Director: Colin Day. Editors: Mary C. Erwin, LeAnn Fields. Senior Editor: Mary C. Erwin. Publishes hardcover and paperback originals and reprints. Averages 35-40 titles/year. Pays royalty on net price; offers advance. Query for electronic submissions. Computer printout submissions acceptable. Reports in 1 month. Free book catalog.

Nonfiction: Archaeology, advanced textbooks, anthropology, biology, classics, economics, English as a second language, Great Lakes regional, history, law, literary criticism, music, philosophy, political science, psychology, reference, theatre, women's studies. Query first.

‡UNIVERSITY OF MISSOURI PRESS, 200 Lewis Hall, Columbia MO 65211. (314)882-7641. Director: Edward D. King. Associate Director: Susan McGregor Denny. Publishes hardcover and paperback originals and paperback reprints. Averages 40 titles/year; receives 300 submissions annually. 40% of books from first-time authors; 100% of books from unagented writers. Average print order for a writer's first book is 1,000. Pays up to 10% royalty on net receipts; no advance. Publishes book an average of 1 year after acceptance. Photocopied submissions OK. Query for electronic submissions. Computer printout submissions acceptable; prefers letter-quality. Reports in 6 months. Free book catalog; ms guidelines for SASE.

Nonfiction: Scholarly publisher interested in history, literary criticism, political science, social science, art and art history. Also regional books about Missouri and the Midwest. No mathematics or hard sciences. Query or submit outline/synopsis and sample chapters. Consult Chicago *Manual of Style*.

Fiction: "Fiction, poetry and drama manuscripts are taken by submission only in February and March of odd-numbered years. We publish original short fiction in the Breakthrough Series, not to exceed 35,000 words. May be short story collection or novella. We also publish poetry and drama in the same series. No limitations on subject matter." Query.

Recent Fiction Title: *Off in Zimbabwe*, by Rod Kessler (stories).

UNIVERSITY OF NEBRASKA PRESS, 901 N. 17th St., Lincoln NE 68588-0520. Editor-in-Chief: Willis G. Regier. Publishes hardcover and paperback originals and hardcover and paperback reprints. Specializes in scholarly nonfiction, some regional books; reprints of Western Americana; and natural history. Averages 50 new titles, 50 paperback reprints (*Bison Books*)/year; receives 700 submissions annually. 25% of books from first-time authors; 95% of books from unagented writers. Average print order for a writer's first book is 1,000. Royalty is usually graduated from 10% on wholesale price for original books; no advance. Computer printout submissions acceptable; prefers letter-quality. Reports in 4 months. Book catalog and guidelines for 8½x11 SAE with 5 first class stamps.

Nonfiction: Publishes Americana, biography, history, nature, photography, psychology, sports, literature, agriculture and American Indian themes. Accepts nonfiction and fiction translations. Query. Accepts outline/synopsis, 2 sample chapters and introduction. Looks for "an indication that the author knows his subject thoroughly and interprets it intelligently." Reviews artwork/photos as part of ms package.

Recent Nonfiction Title: *Willa Cather: A Literary Life*, by James Woodress.

Recent Fiction Translation: *Mad Love*, by André Breton.

UNIVERSITY OF NEVADA PRESS, Reno NV 89557. (702)784-6573. Director: John F. Stetter. Editor: Nicholas M. Cady. Publishes hardcover and paperback originals and reprints. Averages 12 titles/year; receives 50 submissions annually. 20% of books from first-time authors; 100% of books from unagented writers. Average print order for a writer's first book is 2,000. Pays 5-10% royalty on net price. Publishes book an average of 2 years after acceptance. Computer printout submissions acceptable; high quality dot-matrix is OK. Preliminary report in 2 months. Free book catalog and ms guidelines.

Nonfiction: Specifically needs regional history and natural history, anthropology, biographies and Basque studies. "We are the first university press to sustain a sound series on Basque studies—New World and Old World." No juvenile books. Submit complete ms. Reviews photocopies of artwork/photos as part of ms package.

Recent Nonfiction Title: *Traditional Basque Cooking*, by Jose Maria Basca-Isusi.

THE UNIVERSITY OF NORTH CAROLINA PRESS, Box 2288, Chapel Hill NC 27514. (919)966-3561. Editor-in-Chief: Iris Tillman Hill. Publishes hardcover and paperback originals. Specializes in scholarly books and regional trade books. Averages 60 titles/year. 70% of books from first-time scholarly authors; 90% of books from unagented writers. Royalty schedule "varies." Occasional advances. Photocopied submissions OK. Query for electronic submissions. Computer printout submissions acceptable; prefers letter-quality. Publishes book an average of 1 year after acceptance. Reports in 5 months. Free book catalog; ms guidelines for SASE.

Nonfiction: "Our major fields are American history and Southern studies." Also, scholarly books in legal history, Civil War history, literary studies, classics, oral history, folklore, political science, religious studies, historical sociology, Latin American studies. In European studies, focus is on history of the Third Reich, 20th-century Europe, and Holocaust history. Special focus on general interest books on the lore, crafts, cooking, gardening and natural history of the Southeast. Submit outline/synopsis and sample chapters; must follow Chicago *Manual of Style*. Looks for "intellectual excellence and clear writing. We do *not* publish poetry or original fiction." Reviews artwork/photos as part of ms package.

Recent Nonfiction Title: *A World Unsuspected: Portraits of Southern Childhood*, edited by Alex Harris.

‡**UNIVERSITY OF OKLAHOMA PRESS**, 1005 Asp Ave., Norman OK 73019. (405)325-5111. Editor-in-Chief: John Drayton. Publishes hardcover and paperback originals and reprints. Averages 50 titles/year. Pays royalty comparable to those paid by other publishers for comparable books. Publishes book an average of 12-18 months after acceptance. Query for electronic submissions. Computer printout submissions acceptable; prefers letter-quality. Reports in 4 months. Book catalog $1.

Nonfiction: Publishes American Indian studies, Western U.S. history and classical studies. No poetry and fiction. Query, including outline, 1-2 sample chapters and author resume. Chicago *Manual of Style* for ms guidelines. Reviews artwork/photos as part of ms package.

Recent Nonfiction Title: *Peyote Religion: A History*, by Omer C. Stewart.

***UNIVERSITY OF PENNSYLVANIA PRESS**, University of Pennsylvania, Blockley Hall, 418 Service Dr., Philadelphia PA 19104. (215)898-6261. Director: Thomas M. Rotell. Publishes hardcover and paperback originals and reprints. Averages 60 titles/year; receives 600 submissions annually. 10-20% of books from first-time authors; 99% of books from unagented writers. Subsidy publishes (nonauthor) 4% of books. Subsidy publishing is determined by evaluation obtained by the press from outside specialists; work approved by Faculty Editorial Committee; subsidy approved by funding organization. Royalty determined on book-by-book basis. Publishes book an average of 9 months after delivery of completed ms. Photocopied submissions OK. Query for electronic submissions. Computer printout submissions acceptable; prefers letter-quality. Reports in 3 months. Book catalog and ms guidelines for 8½x11 SAE and 5 first class stamps.

Nonfiction: Publishes Americana, biography, business, economics, history, medicine, biological sciences, computer science, physical sciences, law, anthropology, folklore and literary criticism. "Serious books that serve the scholar and the professional." Follow the Chicago *Manual of Style*. Query with outline and letter describing project, state availability of photos and/or illustrations to accompany ms, with copies of illustrations.

Recent Nonfiction Title: *Clara Barton: Professional Angel*, edited by Elizabeth Pryor.

Tips: Queries/mss may be routed to other editors in the publishing group.

***THE UNIVERSITY OF TENNESSEE PRESS**, 293 Communications Bldg., Knoxville TN 37996-0325. Contact: Acquisitions Editor. Averages 30 titles/year; receives 300 submissions annually. 50% of books from first-time authors; 99% of books from unagented writers. Average print order for a writer's first book is 1,250. Subsidy publishes (nonauthor) 10% of books. Pays negotiable royalty on retail price. Publishes book an average of 1 year after acceptance. Photocopied submissions OK. Computer printout submissions acceptable; no dot-matrix. Reports in 1 month. Book catalog for $1 and 12x16 SAE; ms guidelines for SASE.

Nonfiction: American history, political science, religious studies, vernacular architecture and material culture, literary criticism, Black studies, women's studies, Caribbean, anthropology, folklore and regional studies. Prefers "scholarly treatment and a readable style. Authors usually have Ph.D.s." Submit outline/synopsis, author vita, and 2 sample chapters. No fiction, poetry or plays. Reviews artwork/photos as part of ms package.

Recent Nonfiction Title: *Seeking Many Inventions: The Idea of Community in America*, by Philip Abbott.

Tips: "Our market is in several groups: scholars; educated readers with special interests in given scholarly subjects; and the general educated public interested in Tennessee, Appalachia and the South. Not all our books appeal to all these groups, of course, but any given book must appeal to at least one of them."

UNIVERSITY OF TEXAS PRESS, Box 7819, Austin TX 78713. Managing Editor: Barbara Spielman. Averages 60 titles/year; receives 1,000 submissions annually. 50% of books from first-time authors; 99% of books from unagented writers. Average print order for a writer's first book is 1,000. Pays royalty usually based on net income; occasionally offers advance. Publishes book an average of 18 months after acceptance. Query for electronic submissions. Computer printout submissions acceptable; no dot-matrix. Reports in 2 months. Free book catalog and writer's guidelines.

Nonfiction: General scholarly subjects: astronomy, natural history, economics, Latin American and Middle Eastern studies, native Americans, classics, films, medical, biology, contemporary architecture, archeology, Chicano studies, physics, health, sciences, international relations, linguistics, photography, 20th-century and women's literature. Also uses specialty titles related to Texas and the Southwest, national trade titles, and re-

For information on setting your freelance fees, see How Much Should I Charge? in the Business of Writing section.

gional trade titles. Accepts nonfiction and fiction translations (generally Latin American fiction). Query or submit outline/synopsis and 2 sample chapters. Reviews artwork/photos as part of ms package.

Recent Nonfiction Title: *Austin City Limits*, by C. Endres.

Recent Poetry Translation: *100 Love Sonnets*, by Neruda (translation from Spanish).

Tips: "It's difficult to make a manuscript over 400 double-spaced pages into a feasible book. Authors should take special care to edit out extraneous material." Looks for sharply focused, in-depth treatments of important topics.

UNIVERSITY OF WISCONSIN PRESS, 114 N. Murray St., Madison WI 53715. (608)262-4928 (telex: 265452). Director: Allen N. Fitchen. Acquisitions Editors: Barbara J. Hanrahan and Gordon Lester-Massman. Publishes hardcover and paperback originals, reprints and translations. Averages 50 titles/year. Pays standard royalties on retail price. Reports in 3 months.

Nonfiction: Publishes general nonfiction based on scholarly research. Looks for "originality, significance, quality of the research represented, literary quality, and breadth of interest to the educated community at large." Accepts nonfiction translations. Follow Chicago *Manual of Style*. Send letter of inquiry and prospectus.

Recent Nonfiction Title: *The Franco Regime*, by Stanley G. Payne.

UNIVERSITY PRESS OF AMERICA, INC., 4720 Boston Way, Lanham MD 20706. (301)459-3366. Publisher: James E. Lyons. Publishes hardcover and paperback originals and reprints. Averages 450 titles/year. Pays 5-15% royalty on retail price; occasional advance. No computer printout submissions. Reports in 6 weeks. Book catalog and guidelines for SASE.

Nonfiction: Scholarly monographs, college, and graduate level textbooks in history, economics, business, psychology, political science, African studies, Black studies, philosophy, religion, sociology, music, art, literature, drama and education. No juvenile, elementary or high school material. Submit outline.

Recent Nonfiction Title: *Thomas Jefferson: A Strange Case of Mistaken Identity*, by Alf J. Mapp Jr. (biography).

‡**UNIVERSITY PRESS OF KANSAS**, 329 Carruth, Lawrence KS 66045. (913)864-4154. Editor: Fred Woodward. Hardcover and paperback originals. Averages 30 titles/year; receives 500-600 submissions annually. 25% of books from first-time authors; 95% of books from unagented writers. Royalties negotiable; occasional advances. Markets books by advertising, direct mail, publicity, and sales representation to the trade; 55% of sales to bookstores. "State availability of illustrations if they add significantly to the manuscript." Publishes book an average of 10 months after acceptance. Computer printout submissions acceptable; no dot-matrix. Reports in 4 months. Free book catalog; ms guidelines for #10 SASE.

Nonfiction: Publishes biography, history, sociology, philosophy, politics, military studies, regional subjects (Kansas, Great Plains, Midwest), and scholarly. Reviews artwork/photos as part of ms package. Query.

Recent Nonfiction Title: *Norus Ordo Seclorum: The Intellectual Origins of the Constitution*, (history).

‡**UNIVERSITY PRESS OF KENTUCKY**, 663 South Limestone, Lexington KY 40506-0336. (606)257-2951. Associate Director: Jerome Crouch. Publishes hardcover originals and hardcover and trade paperback reprints. Averages 35 titles/year; receives 200 submissions annually. 25-50% of books from first-time authors; 98% of books from unagented writers. Pays 10-15% royalty on wholesale price. "As a nonprofit press, we generally exclude the first 1,000 copies from royalty payment." No advance. Publishes ms an average of 1 year after acceptance. Photocopied submissions OK if clearly legible. Computer printout submissions acceptable; prefers letter-quality. Reports in 1 month on queries; 3 months on mss. Free book catalog.

Nonfiction: Biography, reference and monographs. Subjects include Americana, history, politics and sociology. "We are a scholarly publisher, publishing chiefly for an academic and professional audience. Strong areas are history, literature, political science, folklore, anthropology, and sociology. Our books are expected to advance knowledge in their fields in some measure. We would be interested in the treatment of timely topics in the fields indicated, treatments that would be solid and substantial but that would be readable and capable of appealing to a general public." No "textbooks; genealogical material; lightweight popular treatments; how-to books; and generally books not related to our major areas of interest." Query. Reviews artwork/photos, but generally does not publish books with extensive number of photos.

Recent Nonfiction Title: *Guilded Age Cato: the Life of Walter Q. Gresham*, by Charles W. Calhoun (political biography).

Tips: "Most of our authors are drawn from our primary academic and professional audience. We are probably not a good market for the usual freelance writer, unless his work fits into our special requirements. Moreover, we do not pay advances and income from our books is minimal; so we cannot offer much financial reward to a freelance writer."

UNIVERSITY PRESS OF MISSISSIPPI, 3825 Ridgewood Rd., Jackson MS 39211. (601)982-6205. Director: Richard Abel. Acquisitions Editor: Seetha Srinivasan. Publishes hardcover and paperback originals and reprints. Averages 28 titles/year; receives 200 submissions annually. 50% of books from first-time authors; 95% of books from unagented writers. "Competitive royalties and terms." Publishes book an average of 1 year after acceptance. Computer printout submissions acceptable. Reports in 2 months. Free book catalog.

Nonfiction: Americana, biography, history, politics, sociology, literary criticism, ethnic/minority studies and popular culture with scholarly emphasis. Interested in southern regional studies and literary studies. Submit outline/synopsis and sample chapters and curriculum vita to Acquisitions Editor. "We prefer a proposal that describes the significance of the work and a chapter outline." Reviews artwork/photos as part of ms package.

Recent Nonfiction Title: *Gardening Southern Style*, by Felder Rushing.

*UNIVERSITY PRESS OF NEW ENGLAND, 17½ Lebanon St., Hanover NH 03755. (603)646-3349. "University Press of New England is a consortium of university presses. Some books—those published for one of the consortium members—carry the joint imprint of New England and the member: Dartmouth, Brandeis, Brown, Tufts, Clark, Universities of Connecticut, New Hampshire, Vermont and Rhode Island." Director: Thomas L. McFarland. Editors: Charles Backus, Jeff Grathwohl. Publishes hardcover and trade paperback originals and trade paperback reprints. Averages 35 titles/year. Subsidy publishes (nonauthor) 80% of books. Pays standard royalty; occasionally offers advance. Query for electronic submissions. Computer printout submissions acceptable. Reports in 1 month. Book catalog and guidelines for SASE.

Nonfiction: Americana (regional—New England), art, biography, history, music, nature, politics, psychology, reference, science, sociology, and regional (New England). No festschriften, memoirs, unrevised doctoral dissertations, or symposium collections. Submit outline/synopsis and 1-2 sample chapters.

Recent Nonfiction Title: *The Holocaust in History*, by Michael R. Marrus (history).

*UTAH STATE UNIVERSITY PRESS, Utah State University, Logan UT 84322-7800. (801)750-1362. Director: Linda Speth. Publishes hardcover and trade paperback originals and hardcover and trade paperback reprints. Averages 6 titles/year; receives 170 submissions annually. 8% of books from first-time authors. Average print order for a writer's first book is 1,500. Subsidy publishes 10% of books; subsidy publishes (nonauthor) 45% of books. Pays 10% royalty on net price; no advance. Publishes book an average of 18 months after acceptance. Electronic submissions OK on Televideo 803, but requires hard copy also. Computer printout submissions acceptable; prefers letter-quality. Reports in 2 weeks on queries; 2 months on mss. Free book catalog; ms guidelines for SASE.

Nonfiction: Biography, reference and textbook on Americana, history, politics and science. "Particularly interested in book-length scholarly manuscripts dealing with Western history, Western literature (Western Americana). All manuscript submissions must have a scholarly focus." Submit complete ms. Reviews artwork/photos as part of ms package.

Recent Nonfiction Title: *Folk Groups*, by Elliot Oring (folklore).

Poetry: "At the present time, we have accepted several poetry manuscripts and will not be reading poetry submissions for one year."

Recent Poetry Title: *War On War*, by Lowell Jaeger.

ALFRED VAN DER MARCK EDITIONS, Suite 1301, 1133 Broadway, New York NY 10010. (212)645-5150. Editorial Director: Robert Walter. Publishes hardcover and paperback originals and reprints. Averages 10-20 titles/year; receives 500 submissions annually. 30% of books from first-time authors; 20% of books from unagented writers. Pays 3-12% royalty on wholesale or retail price. Offers average $5,000 advance. Publishes book an average of 1 year after acceptance. Simultaneous and photocopied submissions OK. Query for electronic submissions. Computer printout submissions acceptable; prefers letter-quality. Reports in 1 month on queries; 2 months on mss. Free book catalog and ms guidelines for #10 SASE.

Nonfiction: Contemporary art, coffee table book, photography, and highly illustrated cultural history works only. Subjects include art (contemporary); cultural history; photography; mythology. Needs mss on "interesting conceptual projects on the cutting edge of contemporary cultural activities. No conventional illustrated books, 'how-I-spent-a-year-of-my-life' photography." Query or submit outline/synopsis and sample chapters. Submit complete ms through agent only. Reviews artwork/photos as part of ms package.

Recent Nonfiction Title: *Hemp in America*, by H. Haggerty.

Tips: "We will be publishing only contemporary art, photography and seminal works on cultural history and mythology. (No poetry.) Big emphasis on art and photography."

VANCE BIBLIOGRAPHIES, 112 N. Charter, Box 229, Monticello IL 61856. (217)762-3831. Imprints include Architecture Series (bibliography). Public Administration Series (bibliography). Publisher: Judith Vance. Publishes trade paperback originals. Averages 400 titles/year; receives 500 submissions annually. 10% of bibliographies from first-time authors; 100% of bibliographies from unagented writers. Average print order for a writer's first bibliography is 200. Pays $100 honorarium and 10-20 author's copies. Publishes bibliography an average of 4 months after acceptance. Photocopied submissions OK. Computer printout submissions acceptable; prefers letter-quality. Reports in 1 week on queries; 2 weeks on mss. Free book catalog; ms guidelines for SASE.

Nonfiction: Bibliographies on public administration and/or architecture and related subject areas. Publishes for "graduate students and professionals in the field; primary customers are libraries." Query or submit complete ms.
Recent Nonfiction Title: *Housing from Redundant Buildings: A Select Bibliography*, by V.J. Nurcombe.

‡VANGUARD PRESS, INC., 424 Madison Ave., New York NY 10017. (212)753-3906. President: Evelyn Shrifte. Editor-in-Chief: Bernice Woll. Editorial Assistant: Gregor Hall. Publishes hardcover originals. Averages 18 titles/year; receives 1,350 submissions/year. 18% of books from first-time authors; 18% of books from unagented writers. Pays royalty. Publishes book an average of 8 months after acceptance. Simultaneous and photocopied submissions OK. Computer printout submissions acceptable; prefers letter-quality. Reports in 3 weeks on queries; 2 months on mss. Book catalog free on request.
Nonfiction: Biography, humor, educational, illustrated book, juvenile, literary. Subjects include anthropology, business, cooking, foods and nutrition, health, history, language/literature, military/war, money/finance, music, psychology, travel. "Nothing technical; no specialized scientific material, no strictly topical joke books." Query or submit outline/synopsis and sample chapters. Reviews artwork/photos as part of ms package.
Recent Nonfiction Title: *War Without Windows*, by Bruce E. Jones (military/personal account).
Fiction: Adventure, experimental, historical, juvenile, literary, mainstream/contemporary, mystery, short story collections, suspense, young adult. Query or submit outline/synopsis and sample chapters or submit complete ms.
Recent Fiction Title: *The Dresden Gate*, by Michael Schmidt.

VEHICULE PRESS, Box 125, Place du Parc Station, Montreal, Quebec H2W 2M9 Canada. (514)844-6073. Imprints include Signal Editions (poetry) and Dossier Quebec (history, memoirs). President/Publisher: Simon Dardick. Publishes trade paperback originals by Canadian authors *only*. Averages 8 titles/year; receives 250 submissions annually. 20% of books from first-time authors; 95% of books from unagented writers. Pays 10-15% royalty on retail price; offers $200-500 advance. Publishes book an average of 1 year after acceptance. Photocopied submissions OK. Query for electronic submissions. Computer printout submissions acceptable; prefers letter-quality. "We would appreciate receiving an IRC with SAE rather than U.S. postage stamps which we cannot use." Reports in 1 month on queries; 2 months on mss. Book catalog for 9x12 SAE with IRCs.
Nonfiction: Biography and memoir. Subjects include Canadiana, history, politics, social history and literature. Especially looking for Canadian social history. Query. Reviews artwork/photos as part of ms package.
Recent Nonfiction Title: *The Milton-Park Affair: Canada's Largest Citizen-Developer Confrontation*, by Claire Helman.
Fiction: Short stories only. Query.
Recent Fiction Title: *Voyage to the Other Extreme*, by Marilu Mallet (short stories).
Poetry: Contact Michael Harris, editor. Looking for Canadian authors only. Submit complete ms.
Recent Poetry Title: *Modern Marriage*, by David Solway.
Tips: "We are only interested in Canadian authors."

‡*VESTA PUBLICATIONS, LTD., Box 1641, Cornwall, Ontario K6H 5V6 Canada. (613)932-2135. Editor-in-Chief: Stephen Gill. Paperback and hardcover originals. 10% minimum royalty on wholesale price. Subsidy publishes 5% of books. "We ask a writer to subsidize a part of the cost of printing; normally, it is 50%. We do so when we find that the book does not have a wide market, as in the case of university theses and the author's first collection of poems. The writer gets 25 free copies and 10% royalty on paperback editions." No advance. Publishes 16 titles/year; receives 350 submissions annually. 80% of books from first-time authors; 100% of books from unagented writers. Simultaneous submissions OK if so informed. Photocopied submissions OK. Query for electronic submissions. Computer printout submissions acceptable; prefers letter-quality. Reports in 1 week on queries; 1 month on mss. Send SAE with IRCs. Free book catalog.
Nonfiction: Publishes Americana, art, biography, cookbooks, cooking and foods, history, philosophy, poetry, politics, reference, and religious books. Accepts nonfiction translations. Query or submit complete ms. Reviews artwork/photos. Looks for knowledge of the language and subject. "Query letters and mss should be accompanied by synopsis of the book and biographical notes." State availability of photos and/or illustrations to accompany ms.
Recent Nonfiction Title: *Famine*, by Edward Pike.

THE VESTAL PRESS, LTD., 320 N. Jensen Rd., Box 97, Vestal NY 13851-0097. (607)797-4872. Managing Editor: Grace L. Houghton. Publishes hardcover and trade paperback originals and reprints. Averages 6-8 titles/year; receives 50-75 submissions annually. 20% of books from first-time writers; 95% of books from unagented authors. Pays 10% maximum royalty on net sales. Publishes books an average of 1 year after acceptance. Simultaneous and photocopied submissions OK. Computer printout submissions OK; prefers letter-quality. Reports in 2 weeks. Book catalog for $2.
Nonfiction: Biography, how-to, reference and technical. Subjects include history, hobbies, music, collecting

and early film history. Query or submit outline/synopsis and sample chapters or submit complete ms.
Recent Nonfiction Title: *Radio Manufacturers of the 1920s*, by Alan Douglas.

VGM CAREER HORIZONS, Division of National Textbook Co., 4255 W. Touhy Ave., Lincolnwood IL 60646-1975. (312)679-4210. Editorial Director: Leonard Fiddle. Senior Editor: Michael Urban. Publishes hardcover and paperback originals and software. Averages 20-30 titles/year; receives 150-200 submissions annually. 10% of books from first-time authors; 95% of books from unagented writers. Pays royalty or makes outright purchase. Advance varies. Publishes book an average of 1 year after acceptance. Simultaneous and photocopied submissions OK. Query for electronic submissions. Computer printout submissions OK, prefers letter-quality. Reports in 6 weeks. Book catalog and ms guidelines for 9x12 SAE with 5 first class stamps.
Nonfiction: Textbook and general trade on careers and jobs. Nonfiction book manuscript needs are for careers in petroleum, fast food, purchasing, performing arts, plastics, etc. Query or submit outline/synopsis and sample chapters. Reviews artwork/photos as part of ms package.
Recent Nonfiction Title: *Joyce Lain Kennedy's Career Book*, by Joyce Lain Kennedy.
Tips: "Our audience is job seekers, career planners, job changers, and students and adults in education and trade markets. Study our existing line of books before sending proposals."

‡VICTOR BOOKS, Division of Scripture Press Publications, Inc. 1825 College Ave., Wheaton IL 60187. (312)668-6000. Address mss to Acquisitions Editor. Imprints include SonFlower, Winner, SonPower. Publishes hardcover and trade paperback originals. Firm averages 75 titles/year. Receives 1,400 submissions/year. 5% of books from first-time authors; 98% from unagented writers. Royalty negotiable on retail price. Publishes book an average of 18 months after acceptance. Simultaneous and photocopied submissions OK. Computer printout submissions OK; prefers letter-quality. Reports in 1 month on queries; 2 months on mss. Ms guidelines for #10 SAE with 1 first class stamp; 4 first class stamps for a catalog and guidelines.
Nonfiction: Juvenile, reference and self-help. Subjects include child guidance/parenting, psychology, life-related Bible study and women's issues/studies. "We are interested in manuscripts with a fresh approach to Bible study and Christian living/leadership topics, written from an evangelical perspective. Issues-type books are also welcome." Query or submit outline/synopsis and sample chapters.
Recent Nonfiction Title: *Men Have Feelings Too!*, by G. Brian Jones and Linda Phillips Jones (marriage and family).
Fiction: For ages 2-12. "We are looking for simple Bible-related stories that could be developed into shape or picture books for the preschooler or young reader. For the 8-12-year-old, we are interested in action stories with a Christian take-away message. Fiction should also be series oriented. No romance, science fiction, or fantasy." Query or submit outline/synopsis and sample chapters or submit complete ms.
Recent Fiction Title: *The Mystery of the Black Hole Mine*, by Lee Roddy (adventure, 8-12).
Tips: "Too many books rehash the same topic and there are many shallow books that require no thinking. A writer has the best chance of selling Victor a well-conceived and imaginative manuscript that helps the reader apply Christianity to his/her life in practical ways. Christians active in the local church and their children are our audience."

J. WESTON WALCH, PUBLISHER, Box 658, Portland ME 04104. (207)772-2846. Managing Editor: Richard S. Kimball. Editor: Jane Carter. Math/Science Editor: Eric Olson. Computer Editor: Robert Crepeau. Publishes paperback originals and software. Averages 110 titles/year; receives 300 submissions annually. 10% of books from first-time authors; 95% of books from unagented writers. Average print order for a writer's first book is 700. Offers 10-15% royalty on gross receipts; buys some titles by outright purchase for $100-2,500. No advance. Publishes book an average of 18 months after acceptance. Query for electronic submissions. Computer printout submissions acceptable; prefers letter-quality. Reports in 3-6 weeks. Book catalog for 9x12 SAE with $1.05 postage; ms guidelines for #10 SASE.
Nonfiction: Subjects include art, business, computer education, economics, English, foreign language, government, health, history, mathematics, music, physical education, psychology, science, social science, sociology and special education. "We publish only supplementary educational material for sale to secondary schools throughout the U.S. and Canada. Formats include books, posters, master sets, card sets, cassettes, filmstrips, microcomputer courseware and mixed packages. Most titles are assigned by us, though we occasionally accept an author's unsolicited submission. We have a great need for author/artist teams and for authors who can write at third- to tenth-grade levels. We do *not* want basic texts, anthologies or industrial arts titles. Most of our authors—but not all—have secondary teaching experience. I cannot stress too much the advantages that an author/artist team would have in approaching us and probably other publishers." Query first. Looks for "sense of organization, writing ability, knowledge of subject, skill of communicating with intended audience." Reviews artwork/photos as part of ms package.
Recent Nonfiction Title: *Exploring Advertising Design*, by Lafe Locke.

WALLACE—HOMESTEAD BOOK CO., American Broadcasting Company, Inc., 580 WatersEdge, Lombard IL 60148. (312)953-1100. General Manager: William N. Topaz. Publishes hardcover and trade paperback originals. Averages 30 titles/year; receives 300 submissions annually. 50% of books from first-time authors; 95% of books from unagented writers. Pays royalty on net price. Publishes book an average of 8 months after receipt of acceptable manuscript and materials. Query for electronic submissions. Computer printout submissions acceptable; prefers letter-quality. Simultaneous and photocopied submissions OK. Reports in 1 month. Free book catalog; ms guidelines for #10 SAE and 2 first class stamps.

Nonfiction: Cookbook, how-to and reference. Subjects include Americana, art, business and economics, cooking and food, hobbies and crafts, photography, needlecraft, antiques and collectibles. Especially looking for mss on antiques, collectibles, memorabilia, quilting, cookbooks, and other specialty areas. No school or textbook material. Submit outline/synopsis and sample chapters. Reviews artwork/photos as part of ms package.

Recent Nonfiction Title: *Wallace-Homestead Price Guide to American Country Antiques*, 7th edition, (antiques and collectibles).

Tips: "Our books are intended for an adult nontechnical audience."

*WASHINGTON STATE UNIVERSITY PRESS, Washington State University, Pullam WA 99164-5910. (509)335-3518. Editor-in-chief: Fred C. Bohm. Publishes hardcover originals, trade paperback originals and reprints. Averages 10-15 titles/year; receives 50-75 submissions annually. 50% of books from first-time writers; 100% of books from unagented authors. Subsidy publishes 20% of books. "The nature of the manuscript and the potential market for the manuscript determine whether it should be subsidy published." Pays 10% royalty. Publishes book an average of 1 year after acceptance. Simultaneous and photocopied submissions OK. Query for electronic submissions. Computer printout submissions are acceptable. Reports on queries in 1 month; on submissions in 1-4 months.

Nonfiction: Biography, academic and scholarly. Subjects include Americana, art, business and economics, history (especially of the American West and the Pacific Northwest), nature, philosophy, politics, psychology, and sociology. Needs for the next year are "quality manuscripts that focus on the development of the Pacific Northwest as a region, and on the social and economic changes that have taken place and continue to take place as the region enters the 21st century. No romance novels, historical fiction, how-to books, gardening books, or books specifically written as classroom texts." Submit outline/synopsis and sample chapters. Reviews artwork/photos as part of ms package.

Recent Nonfiction Title: *To The Columbia Gateway*, by Peter J. Lewty (Pacific Northwest history).

Tips: "Our audience consists of scholars, specialists and informed general readers who are interested in well-documented research presented in an attractive format." Writers have the best chance of selling to our firm "completed manuscripts on regional history. We have developed our marketing in the direction of regional and local history and have attempted to use this as the base around which we hope to expand our publishing program. In regional history, the secret is to write a good narrative—a good story—that is substantiated factually. It should be told in an imaginative, clever way. Have visuals (photos, maps, etc) available to help the reader envision what has happened. Tell the local or regional history story in a way that ties it to larger, national, and even international events. Weave it into the large pattern of history."

FRANKLIN WATTS, INC., 387 Park Ave. S, New York NY 10016. (212)686-7070. Editor-in-Chief: Ed Breslin. Publishes hardcover originals. Entire firm publishes 200 titles/year; trade and professional division publishes 40. 10% of books from first-time authors; 2% of books from unagented writers. Pays royalty on wholesale or retail price. Simultaneous and photocopied submissions OK. Reports in 1 month on queries; 7 weeks on submissions. Free book catalog.

Nonfiction: Biography and history. Subjects include Americana, politics and sports. No humor, coffee table books, cookbooks or gardening books. Query.

Fiction: Mainstream, mystery and science fiction. Query.

SAMUEL WEISER INC., Box 612, York Beach ME 03910. (207)363-4393. Editor: Susan Smithe. Publishes hardcover originals and trade paperback originals and reprints. Publishes 18-20 titles/year; receives 100-200 submissions annually. 50% of books from first-time authors; 98% of books from unagented writers. Pays 10% royalty on wholesale or retail price; offers average $500 advance. Publishes book an average of 1-1½ years after acceptance. Query for electronic submissions. Computer printout submissions OK; prefers letter-quality. Reports in 3 months. Free book catalog.

Nonfiction: How-to and self-help. Subjects include health, music, philosophy, psychology and religion. "We look for strong books in our specialty field—written by teachers and people who know the subject. Don't want a writer's rehash of all the astrology books in the library, only texts written by people with strong background in field. No poetry or novels." Submit complete ms. Reviews artwork/photos as part of ms package.

Recent Nonfiction Title: *Mystery of Death and Dying*, by Earlyne Chaney.

Tips: "Most new authors do not check permissions, nor do they provide proper footnotes. If they did, it would help. We specialize in new age material, oriental philosophy, metaphysics, esoterica of all kinds (tarot, astrology, qabalah, magic, crystals, etc.) and our emphasis is still the same. We still look at all manuscripts submitted to us. We are interested in seeing freelance art for book covers."

‡**WEST END GAMES, INC.**, Bucci Imports, Inc., Suite 11 F, 251 W. 30th St., New York NY 10001. (212)947-4828. Director of Research and Development: Curtis H. Smith. Publishes hardcover and trade paperback originals. Averages 12 titles/year. Receives 600 submissions/year. 10% of books from first-time authors; 90% from unagented writers. Offers outright purchase of $500-3,000. Publishes book an average of 6 months after acceptance. Photocopied submissions OK. Query for electronic submissions. Computer printout submissions OK; prefers letter-quality. Reports in 1 month on queries; 3 months on mss. Book catalog and ms guidelines for 4x12 SAE with 1 first class stamp.
Fiction: Adventure, fantasy, horror, humor, science fiction, young adult. "West End publishes three different roleplaying lines: Star Wars, epic space opera; Paranoia, science fiction/post apocalyptic humor; and Ghostbusters, horror/humor. For each line we produce about four supplementary adventures and/or game aids a year." Query. All unsolicited ms are returned unopened.
Tips: "Research is essential to success in the roleplaying field. Knowing the material already offered by a company and knowing the system for which you are writing are of paramount importance."

WESTERN MARINE ENTERPRISES INC., Division of ProStar Publications, Suite 14, 4051 Glencoe Ave., Marina Del Ray CA 90292. (213)306-2094. Editor: William Berssen. Publishes hardcover and trade paperback originals. Averages 4 titles/year. Pays 15% royalty on net sales price. Computer printout submissions acceptable; prefers floppy disks. Reports in 3 weeks.
Nonfiction: Boating. "We specialize in boating books—mainly how-to and when-to." No "simple narrative accounts of how someone sailed a boat from here to there." First-time book authors should submit complete ms.
Recent Nonfiction Title: *Landfalls of Paradise*, by Earl Hinz (cruising guide to Pacific Islands).

*****WESTERN PRODUCER PRAIRIE BOOKS**, Division of Western Producer Publications, Box 2500, Saskatoon, Saskatchewan S7K 2C4 Canada. Publishing Director: Elizabeth Munroe. Publishes hardcover and paperback originals and reprints. Averages 17-20 titles/year; receives 400-500 submissions annually. 20% of books from first-time authors; 80% of books from unagented writers. Average print order for a writer's first book is 4,000. Subsidy publishes (nonauthor) 15% of books. Pays negotiable royalty on list price. Publishes book an average of 1 year after acceptance. Query for electronic submissions. Computer printout submissions acceptable; no dot-matrix. Reports in 3 months. Free book catalog; ms guidelines for SAE with IRCs.
Nonfiction: Publishes history, nature, photography, biography, reference, agriculture, economics and politics. Accepts nonfiction and fiction translations. Submit outline, synopsis and 2-3 sample chapters with contact sheets or prints if illustrations are to accompany ms.
Recent Nonfiction Title: *The Long and the Short and the Tall*, by R. Collins (autobiography).
Fiction: Young adult and juvenile novels and novels appealing to Western Canadians. Accepts fiction translations for children's books.
Recent Fiction Title: *Last Chance Summer*, by D. Wieler (young adult fiction).

WESTERNLORE PRESS, Box 35305, Tucson AZ 85740. Editor: Lynn R. Bailey. Publishes 6-12 titles/year. Pays standard royalties on retail price "except in special cases." Query. Reports in 2 months. Enclose return postage with query.
Nonfiction: Publishes Western Americana of a scholarly and semischolarly nature: anthropology, history, biography, historic sites, restoration, and ethnohistory pertaining to the greater American West. Re-publication of rare and out-of-print books. Length: 25,000-100,000 words.

‡*****WESTGATE PRESS**, Westgate Co. 8 Bernstein Blvd., Center Moriches NY 11934. (516)878-2901. Editor, Books: Lorraine Chandler. Publishes trade paperback originals and trade paperback reprints. Firm averages 5-7 titles/year. Receives 100 submissions/year. 50% of books from first-time authors. 100% from unagented writers. Subsidy publishes 10% of books. Subsidy titles are determined by book content and author enthusiasm. Pays 10% minimum royalty on wholesale price. Outright purchase negotiable. Offers $0-1,000 average advance. Publishes book an average of 18 months after acceptance. Simultaneous and photocopied submissions OK. Computer printout submissions OK; prefers letter-quality. Reports in 2 weeks on queries; 2 months on mss. Free book catalog. Ms guidelines for #10 SASE.
Nonfiction: Illustrated book. Subjects include art, metaphysics, occult/new age and related topics. "Westgate deals exclusively in the lesser known, esoteric areas of metaphysics. We'll look at mss that are not covered already by other authors and presses. Nothing already so overplayed that it's simply a rehash. No channeling, crystals, or other generic new age material. Check what we're currently doing before submitting." Reviews artwork/photos as part of manuscript package.
Recent Nonfiction Title: *The Book of Azrael: An Intimate Encounter With the Angel of Death*, by Leilah Wendell (metaphysics).
Tips: "As many times as we ask for the *truly unusual*, we still receive repetitive topics and angles. Give us the uncommon rarity of the blockbuster status as *The Book of Azrael* is fast becoming. If I were a writer trying to market a book today, I would choose an area in which I'm comfortable, learned and sincere, find an angle not presently being used and procure a blockbuster that is timeless in its message and awesome in its impact."

*WESTVIEW PRESS, 5500 Central Ave., Boulder CO 80301. (303)444-3541. Publisher/President: F.A. Praeger. Hardcover and paperback originals, lecture notes, reference books, and paperback texts. Specializes in scholarly monographs or conference reports with strong emphasis on applied science, both social and natural. 0-10% royalty on net price, depending on market. Accepts subsidies for a small number of books, "but only in the case of first class scholarly material for a limited market when books need to be priced low, or when the manuscripts have unusual difficulties such as Chinese or Sanskrit characters; the usual quality standards of a top-flight university press apply, and subsidies must be furnished by institutions, not by individuals." Averages 300 titles/year. Markets books mainly by direct mail. State availability of photos and/or illustrations to accompany manuscript. Reports in 1-4 months. Free book catalog.
Nonfiction: Agriculture/food, agricultural economics, public policy, energy, natural resources, international economics and business, international law, international relations, area studies, development, science and technology policy, sociology, anthropology, philosophy, history, reference, military affairs, national security, health, Asia and the Pacific, comparative politics, social impact assessment, women's studies, Latin America and Caribbean, Soviet Union and Eastern Europe, Middle East, Africa, and Western Europe. Looks for "scholarly excellence and scientific relevance." Query and submit 2 sample chapters and tentative table of contents and curriculum vitae. Use Chicago *Manual of Style*. "Unsolicited manuscripts receive low priority; inquire before submitting projects."
Recent Nonfiction Title: *The Business of Book Publishing*, by Geiser.

‡WHITFORD PRESS, Schiffer Publishing, 1469 Morstein Rd., West Chester PA 19380. (215)696-1001. Managing Editor: Skye Alexander. Publishes trade paperback originals. Averages 10-12 titles/year; receives 400-500 submissions annually. 50% of books from first-time authors; 90% of books from unagented writers. Pays royalty on wholesale price; advances vary. Publishes on an average of 9-12 months after acceptance and receipt of complete ms. Simultaneous and photocopied submissions OK. Computer printout submissions OK; prefers letter-quality. Reports in about 1 month. Free book catalog; ms guidelines for SASE.
Nonfiction: How-to, self-help, reference. Subjects include astrology, metaphysics, new age topics. "We are looking for well written, well-organized, originals books on all metaphysical subjects (except channeling and past lives). Books that empower the reader or show him/her ways to develop personal skills are preferred. New aproaches, techniques, or concepts are best. No personal accounts unless they directly relate to a general audience. No moralistic, fatalistic, sexist or strictly philosophical books. Query first or send outline. Enclose SASE large enough to hold your submission if you want it returned."
Recent Nonfiction Title: *Planets in Signs*.
Tips: "Our audience is knowledgeable in metaphysical fields, well-read and progressive in thinking. Please check bookstores to see if your subject has already been covered thoroughly. Expertise in the field is not enough; your book must be clean, well written and well organized. A specific and unique marketing angle is a plus. No Sun-sign material; we prefer more advanced work. Please don't send entire ms unless we request it, and be sure to include SASE. Let us know if the book is available on computer diskette and what type of hardware/software. Mss should be between 60,000 and 110,000 words."

THE WHITSTON PUBLISHING CO., Box 958, Troy NY 12181. (518)283-4363. Editorial Director: Jean Goode. Publishes hardcover originals. Averages 20 titles/year; receives 100 submissions annually. 50% of books from first-time authors; 100% of books from unagented writers. Pays 10% royalty on wholesale price; no advance. Publishes book an average of 30 months after acceptance. Computer printout submissions acceptable; no dot-matrix. Reports in 1 year. Book catalog for 7x10 SAE.
Nonfiction: "We publish scholarly and critical books in the arts, humanities and some of the social sciences. We also publish reference books, bibliographies, indexes, checklists and monographs. We do not want author bibliographies in general unless they are unusual and unusually scholarly. We are, however, much interested in catalogs and inventories of library collections of individuals, such as the catalog of the Evelyn Waugh Collection at the Humanities Research Center, the University of Texas at Austin; and collections of interest to the specific scholarly community, such as surveys of early Black newspapers in libraries in the U.S., etc." Query or submit complete ms. Reviews artwork/photos as part of ms package.
Recent Nonfiction Title: *The Newspaper Verse of Philip Freneau*, compiled by Judith Hiltner.

WILDERNESS PRESS, 2440 Bancroft Way, Berkeley CA 94704. (415)843-8080. Editorial Director: Thomas Winnett. Publishes paperback originals. Averages 5 titles/year; receives 150 submissions annually. 20% of books from first-time authors; 95% of books from unagented writers. Average print order for a writer's first book is 5,000. Pays 8-10% royalty on retail price; offers average $1,000 advance. Publishes book an average of 6 months after acceptance. Computer printout submissions acceptable; prefers letter-quality. Reports in 2 weeks. Book catalog for 9x12 SAE with $2.50 postage.
Nonfiction: "We publish books about the outdoors. Most of our books are trail guides for hikers and backpackers, but we also publish how-to books about the outdoors and perhaps will publish personal adventures. The manuscript must be accurate. The author must thoroughly research an area in person. If he is writing a trail guide, he must walk all the trails in the area his book is about. The outlook must be strongly conservationist.

The style must be appropriate for a highly literate audience." Query, submit outline/synopsis and sample chapters, or submit complete ms demonstrating "accuracy, literacy, and popularity of subject area." Reviews artwork/photos as part of ms package.

Recent Nonfiction Title: *Afoot and Afield in Orange County*, by Jerry Schad (outdoor guide).

JOHN WILEY & SONS, INC., 605 3rd Ave., New York NY 10158. (212)850-6000. Editor: Katherine R. Schowalter. Publishes hardcover and trade paperback nonfiction originals. Receives 150 submissions annually. 40% of books from first-time authors; 65% of books from unagented writers. Pays 7.5-15% royalty on wholesale price; offers $2,000-10,000 advance. Publishes book an average of 18 months after acceptance. Photocopied submissions OK. Query for electronic submissions. Computer printout submissions OK; prefers letter-quality. Reports in 2 weeks on queries; 6 weeks on mss. Manuscript guidelines for SASE.

Nonfiction: General interest, how-to, reference and self-help. Subjects include business, mathematics, travel, language and careers. Needs travel, small business, finance, business management, and careers. "In all areas information needs to be new and it is important to do a thorough competitive search to determine how your manuscript is different from other books on the subject. No sales skills, low-level business books or crafts." Submit outline/synopsis and sample chapters. Reviews artwork/photos as part of ms package.

Recent Nonfiction Title: *Street French: How to Speak and Understand French Slang*, by David Burke.

Tips: "It is important to have as complete a proposal as possible—information on the audience, competition, how the book will be used, and how the reader will benefit from reading the book."

WILLIAMSON PUBLISHING CO., Box 185, Church Hill Rd., Charlotte VT 05445. (802)425-2102. Editorial Director: Susan Williamson. Publishes trade paperback originals. Averages 12 titles/year; receives 250 submissions annually. 50% of books from first-time authors; 80% of books from unagented writers. Average print order for a writer's first book is 5,000-10,000. Pays 10-12% royalty on sales dollars received or makes outright purchase if favored by author. Advance negotiable. Publishes book an average of 1 year after acceptance. Simultaneous and photocopied submissions OK. Computer printout submissions acceptable; prefers letter-quality. Reports in 1 month on queries; 3 months on mss. Book catalog for 6x9 SAE and 3 first class stamps.

Nonfiction: How-to, cookbook, illustrated book and self-help. Subjects include business, education, gardening, home crafts, self-sufficiency, building, animals, cooking and foods, health, travel, hobbies, nature landscaping, and children. "Our areas of concentration are people-oriented business and psychology books, cookbooks, travel books, gardening, small-scale livestock raising, family housing (all aspects), health and education." No children's books, photography, politics, religion, history, art or biography. Query with outline/synopsis and sample chapters. Reviews photos as part of ms package.

Recent Nonfiction Title: *Public Schools USA: A Comparative Guide to School Districts*, by Charles Harrison.

Tips: "We're most interested in authors who are experts in their fields—doers, not researchers. Give us a good, solid manuscript with original ideas and we'll work with you to refine the writing. We also have a highly skilled staff to develop the high quality look of our books."

WILLOW CREEK PRESS, Box 300, Wautoma WI 54982. (414)787-3005. Editor-in-chief: Chuck Petrie. Publishes hardcover original and reprints. Averages 5-7 titles/year. 10% of books from first time authors; 80% of books from unagented writers. Pays 10-15% royalties on wholesale or retail price depending on individual contract. Offers average advance of $2,000-5,000. Publishes book an average of 1 year after acceptance. Simultaneous and photocopied submissions OK. Computer printout submissions OK. Reports on queries in 5 weeks; on submissions in 6 weeks. Book catalog for 8½x11 SAE with 3 first class stamps; writer's guidelines for SASE.

Nonfiction: Coffee-table book, cookbook, how-to, humor, illustrated and technical books. Subjects include wildlife, cooking wild game, nature, hunting and fishing. "We do not want to see submissions on dog training, taxidermy or fly tying, any compilations of stories previously published in outdoor magazines or any submissions not suitable for publishing in trade hardcover format." Submit outline/synopsis and sample chapters. Reviews artwork/photos as part of ms package.

Recent Nonfiction Title: *Whitetail Country*, by John Ozoga.

Fiction: Historical and humorous fiction, all related to hunting and fishing. "No mss concerning hunting and/or fishing in 'exotic' countries." Submit outline/synopsis and sample chapters.

Recent Fiction Title: *Ben Unleashed*, by John Troy.

Tips: "We will consider over-the-transom submissions in the fields where we specialize. Writers wishing to be published by Willow Creek Press should familiarize themselves with the types of books we have published and not submit proposals or mss outside those categories."

WILSHIRE BOOK CO., 12015 Sherman Rd., North Hollywood CA 91605. (213)875-1711. Editorial Director: Melvin Powers. Publishes paperback originals and reprints. Publishes 50 titles/year; receives 6,000 submissions annually. 25% of books from first-time authors; 75% of books from unagented writers. Average print order for a writer's first book is 5,000. Pays standard royalty; offers variable advance. Computer printout submissions acceptable; no dot-matrix. Reports in 2 weeks. Book catalog for SASE.

Nonfiction: Health, hobbies, how-to, psychology, recreation, self-help, entrepreneurship, how to make money, and mail order. "We are always looking for self-help and psychological books such as *Psycho-Cybernetics, The Magic of Thinking Big* and *Guide to Rational Living*. We need manuscripts teaching mail order, entrepreneur techniques, how to make money and advertising. We publish 70 horse books. "All that I need is the concept of the book to determine if the project is viable. I welcome phone calls to discuss manuscripts with authors." Reviews artwork/photos as part of ms package.

Recent Nonfiction Title: *The Magic of Thinking Success*, by David J. Schwartz, Ph.D. (inspirational).

Tips: "We are looking for such books as *Jonathan Livingston Seagull*, *The Little Prince*, and *The Greatest Salesman in the World*."

‡WINDRIVER PUBLISHING COMPANY, Suite N52, Three Dallas Communications Complex, 6311 N. O'Connor Rd., Irving TX 75039-3510. (214)869-7625. President/Publisher: Brim Crow. Publishes hardcover originals. Firm averages 5 titles/year. Pays royalty on wholesale price. Outright purchase varies. Advance varies. Simultaneous and photocopied submissions OK. Reports in 2 weeks on queries; 2 months on mss. Free book catalog; ms guidelines for #10 SASE.

Nonfiction: Biography, how-to and self-help. Subjects include Americana, cooking, foods and nutrition, health/medicine, history, hobbies, recreation and film history. "We specifically need film books and self-help (professionally written). Nothing sensational (unauthorized bios, etc.), no religion, no political mss." Query or submit outline/synopsis and sample chapters.

Recent Nonfiction Title: *George Sanders/An Exhausted Life*, by Richard VanDerBeets (bio).

Fiction: Mystery and romance. "We need mysteries of all types. We no longer accept romance. No occult or science fiction or overt sex." Query or submit outline/synopsis and sample chapters.

Recent Fiction Title: *Message of the Locust*, by Myers/Marcum(mystery).

Tips: "There seems to be little room for the unknown or unpublished new writer. There is a definite need for smaller, mid-list publishers. Our audience is mainstream, adult and young adult readers, film historians and film buffs. If I were a writer trying to market a book today, I would write genre fiction (series mysteries, for example). Romance is saturated, but good mysteries continue to weather the change and thrive. They're up right now. A good writer is someone who believes in himself and finally convinces someone else to believe in him or her, too. The secret? Never, never give up!"

WINDSOR BOOKS, Subisidary of Windsor Marketing Corp., Box 280, Brightwaters NY 11718. (516)321-7830. Managing Editor: Stephen Schmidt. Publishes hardcover and trade paperback originals, reprints, and very specific software. Averages 8 titles/year; receives approximately 40 submissions annually. 60% of books from first-time authors; 90% of books from unagented writers. Pays 10% royalty on retail price; 5% on wholesale price (50% of total cost); offers variable advance. Publishes book an average of 6 months after acceptance. Simultaneous and photocopied submissions OK. Computer printout submissions acceptable; prefers letter-quality. Reports in 2 weeks on queries; 3 weeks on mss. Free book catalog and ms guidelines.

Nonfiction: How-to and technical. Subjects include business and economics (investing in stocks and commodities). Interested in books on strategies, methods for investing in the stock market, options market, and commodity markets. Query or submit outline/synopsis and sample chapters. Reviews artwork/photos as part of ms package.

Recent Nonfiction Title: *The Definitive Guide to Futures Trading*, by Larry Williams (investing).

Tips: "Our books are for serious investors; we sell through direct mail to our mailing list and other financial lists. Writers must keep their work original; this market tends to have a great deal of information overlap among publications."

WINE APPRECIATION GUILD LTD., Vintage Image, Wine Advisory Board, 155 Connecticut St., San Francisco CA 94107. (514)864-1202. Director: Maurice Sullivan. Imprints include Vintage Image and Wine Advisory Board (nonfiction). Publishes hardcover and trade paperback originals, trade paperback reprints, and software. Averages 12 titles/year; receives 30-40 submissions annually. 30% of books from first-time authors; 100% of books from unagented writers. Pays 5-15% royalty on wholesale price or makes outright purchase; offers average $1,000 advance. Publishes book an average of 18 months after acceptance. Simultaneous and photocopied submissions OK. Query for electronic submisstions. Reports in 2 months. Book catalog for $2.

Nonfiction: Cookbook and how-to—wine related. Subjects include wine, cooking and foods and travel. Must be wine-related. Submit outline/synopsis and sample chapters. Reviews artwork/photos as part of ms package.

Tips: "Our books are read by wine enthusiasts—from neophytes to professionals, and wine industry and food industry people. We are interested in anything of a topical and timely nature connected with wine, by a knowledgeable author. We do not deal with agents of any type. We prefer to get to know the author as a person and to work closely with him/her."

WINGBOW PRESS, Subsidiary of Bookpeople, 2929 Fifth St., Berkeley CA 94710. (415)549-3030. Editor: Randy Fingland. Small press. Publishes trade paperback originals. Averages 4 titles/year; receives 450 submissions annually, "mostly fiction and poetry, which we aren't even considering." 50% of books from first-time authors; 100% of books from unagented writers. Pays 7-10% royalty on retail price; offers average $250 advance. Publishes book an average of 15 months after acceptance. Photocopied submissions OK. Query for electronic submissions. Computer printout submissions OK; prefers letter-quality. Reports in 2 weeks on queries; 2 months on mss. Book catalog for #10 SAE and 1 first class stamp.
Nonfiction: Reference and self-help. Subjects include philosophy/metaphysics, psychology and women's issues. "We are currently looking most seriously at women's studies; religion/metaphysics/philosophy; psychology and personal development. Our readers are receptive to alternative/New Age ideas. No business/finance how-to." Query or submit outline/synopsis and sample chapters.
Recent Nonfiction Title: *Astrology for Yourself*, by Douglas Block and Demetra George.

*WINSTON-DEREK PUBLISHERS INC., Pennywell Dr., Box 90883, Nashville TN 37209. (615)329-1319/ 321-0535. Publisher: James W. Peebles. Publishes hardcover, trade, and mass market paperback originals. Averages 40-45 titles/year; receives 3,500 submissions annually. 50% of books from first-time authors; 80% of books from unagented authors. Average print order for writer's first book is 3,000-5,000. "We will co-publish exceptional works of quality and style only when we reach our quota in our trade book division." Subsidy publishes 15% of books. Pays 10-15% of the net amount received on sales. Advance varies. Simultaneous and photocopied submissions OK. Computer printout submissions acceptable; prefers letter-quality. Queries and mss without SASE will be discarded. Reports in 1 month on queries; 2 months on mss. Book catalog and guidelines for 9x12 SASE.
Nonfiction: Biography (current or historically famous) and behavioral science and health (especially interested in mss of this category for teenagers and young adults). Subjects include Americana; theology; philosophy (nontechnical with contemporary format); religion (noncultist); and inspirational. Length: 50,000-60,000 words or less. Submit outline and first 2 or 4 chapters. Reviews artwork/photos as part of manuscript package. No political or technical material.
Recent Nonfiction Title: *The Day The Roars*, by Jamin Denslow.
Fiction: Ethnic (non-defamatory); religious (theologically sound); suspense (highly plotted); and Americana (minorities and whites in positive relationships). Length: 60,000 words or less. "We can use fiction with a semi-historical plot; it must be based or centered around actual facts and events—Americana, religion, and gothic. We are looking for juvenile books on relevant aspects of growing up and understanding life's situations. No funny animals talking." Children's/juvenile books must be of high quality. Submit complete ms for children and juvenile books with illustrations, which are optional.
Recent Fiction Title: *Retter*, by Amy Garza.
Poetry: Should be inspirational and with meaning. Poetry dealing with secular life should be of excellent quality. "We will accept unusual poetry books of exceptional quality and taste. We do not publish avant-garde type poetry." Submit complete ms. No single poems.
Recent Poetry Title: *Reflections on Life*, by Raymond S. Nelson.
Tips: "We do not publish material that advocates violence or is derogative of other cultures or beliefs. There is now a growing concern for books about seniors, aging, and geriatic care. Outstanding biographies are quite successful, as are books dealing with the simplicity of man and his relationship with his environs. Our imprint Scythe Books for children needs material for adolescents within the 9-13 age group. These manuscripts should help young people with motivation for learning and succeeding at an early age, goal setting and character building. Biographies of famous women and men as role models are always welcomed. Always there is a need for books about current minority, scholars, issues and concerns. Stories must have a new twist and be provocative."

*ALAN WOFSY FINE ARTS, Box 2210, San Francisco CA 94126. Publishes hardcover and paperback originals and hardcover reprints. Subsidy publishes 15% of books. Specializes in art reference books, specifically catalogs of graphic artists; bibliographies related to fine presses and the art of the book. Pays negotiable fee on retail price; offers advance. Publishes 5 titles annually. Reports in 1 month. Free book catalog.
Nonfiction: Publishes reference books on art. Seeking catalogs of (i.e., reference books on) collectibles. Query. Reviews artwork/photos as part of ms package.

WOODBINE HOUSE, 10400 Connecticut Ave., #512, Kensington MD 20895. (301)949-3590. Editor: Terry Rosenberg. Publishes hardcover and trade paperback originals. Averages 8-10 titles/year; receives 200-300 submissions annually. 60% of books from first-time authors; 60% of books from unagented writers. Pays royalty; buys some mss outright. Publishes book an average of 18 months after acceptance. Simultaneous and photocopied submissions OK. Query for electronic submissions. Computer printout submissions OK; prefers letter-quality. Reports in 1 month on queries; 3 months on mss. Free book catalog; ms guidelines for #10 SASE.
Nonfiction: Biography, reference, travel and self-help. Subjects include Americana, health, history, hobbies, sociology, parents' guides for special needs children. Especially needs parents' guides for special needs

children, history and Americana. No exercise or diet books. Submit outline/synopsis and sample chapters. Review artwork/photos as part of ms.

Recent Nonfiction Title: *Vietnam Wives*, by Aphrodite Matsakis, Ph.D.

Tips: "Writers must know their subjects and audience. We don't have time to do their market research."

*WOODSONG GRAPHICS, INC., P.O. Box 238, New Hope PA 18938. (215)794-8321. Editor: Ellen P. Bordner. Publishes hardcover and trade paperback originals. Averages 6-8 titles/year; receives 2,500-3,000 submissions annually. 40-60% of books from first-time authors; 100% of books from unagented writers. Average print order for writer's first book is 2,500-5,000. Will occasionally consider subsidy publishing based on "quality of material, motivation of author in distributing his work, and cost factors (which depend on the type of material involved), plus our own feelings on its marketability." Subsidy publishes 20% of books. Pays royalty on net price; offers average $100 advance. Publishes book an average of 1 year after acceptance. Simultaneous submissions OK. Computer printout submissions acceptable; prefers letter-quality. Reports in 1 month on queries; reports on full mss *can* take several months, depending on the amount of material already in house. "We do everything possible to facilitate replies, but we have a small staff and want to give every manuscript a thoughtful reading." Book catalog for #10 SAE and 1 first class stamp.

Nonfiction: Biography, cookbook, how-to, humor, illustrated book, juvenile, reference, and self-help. Subjects include cooking and foods, hobbies, philosophy and psychology. "We're happy to look at anything of good quality, but we're not equipped to handle lavish color spreads at this time. Our needs are very open, and we're interested in seeing any subject, provided it's handled with competence and style. Good writing from unknowns is also welcome." No pornography; only minimal interest in technical manuals of any kind. Query or submit outline/synopsis and at least 2 sample chapters. Reviews artwork/photos as part of ms package.

Recent Nonfiction Title: *The Herb Gardener's Mail Order Source Book*, by Elayne Moos.

Fiction: Adventure, experimental, fantasy, gothic, historical, humor, mainstream, mystery, romance, science fiction, suspense and western. "In fiction, we are simply looking for books that provide enjoyment. We want well-developed characters, creative plots, and good writing style." No pornography or "sick" material. Submit outline/synopsis and sample chapters.

Tips: "Good nonfiction with an identified target audience and a definite slant has the best chance of selling to our firm. We rarely contract in advance of seeing the completed manuscript. We prefer a synopsis, explaining what the thrust of the book is without a chapter-by-chapter profile. If the query is interesting enough, we'll look at the full manuscript for further details."

*WORD BEAT PRESS, Box 22310, Flagstaff AZ 86002. Publishes trade paperback originals and reprints. Averages 4 titles/year; receives 500 submissions annually. 50% of books from first-time authors. Average print order for a writer's first book is 1,000. Pays 10% royalty on wholesale price. Currently, only accepting queries from agents for new books.

Fiction: Short story collections and novellas; "open to fine writing in any category." Query first.

Recent Fiction Title: *Four-Minute Fictions: Best Short-Short Stories from The North American Review*, edited by Robley Wilson, Jr.

WORD BOOKS PUBLISHER, Division of Word Inc., subsidiary of Cap Cities/ABC, 7300 Imperial; Box 2518, Waco TX 76702-2518. (817)772-2518. Managing Editor: Al Bryant. Publishes hardcover and trade paperback originals, and hardcover, trade paperback, and mass market paperback reprints. Averages 75 titles/year; receives 2,000 submissions annually. 15% of books from first-time authors; 98% of books from unagented writers. Pays 10-15% royalty on retail price; offers average $2,000 advance. Publishes book an average of 1 year after acceptance. Photocopied submissions OK. Query for electronic submissions. Computer printout submissions acceptable; no dot-matrix. Reports in 1 month on queries; 2 months on mss. Free book catalog and ms guidelines for 9x12 SAE and 3 first class stamps.

Nonfiction: Family relationships, retirement, personal growth, how-to, reference, self-help and textbook. Subjects include health, history (church and Bible), philosophy, politics, psychology, religion, sociology, and sports. Especially looking for "religious books that help modern-day Christians cope with the stress of life in the 20th century. We welcome queries on all types of books." Query with outline/synopsis and sample chapters. Reviews artwork/photos as part of ms package.

Recent Nonfiction Title: *Facing Death and the Life After*, by Billy Graham (dealing with death).

Fiction: No non-religious fiction. Submit outline/synopsis and sample chapters.

Recent Fiction Title: *The Sinbearer*, by Tom Taylor (biblical novel).

*WORDWARE PUBLISHING, INC., Suite 101, 1506 Capital Ave., Plano TX 75074. (214)423-0090. Book packager producing 5 titles/year. Publisher: Russell A. Stultz. Publishes hardcover and trade paperback originals. Averages 18-25 titles/year; receives 400 submissions annually. 40% of books from first-time authors; 95% of books from unagented writers. Subsidy publishes 5% of books. "We review manuscripts on a case-by-case basis. We are primarily a trade publisher dealing with authors on a royalty basis." Pays royalty on wholesale price; advance varies. Publishes book an average of 1 year after acceptance. Simultaneous and photocopied submissions OK. "We prefer electronic submissions." Reports in 2 weeks. Free book catalog; ms guidelines for 9x12 SAE and 5 first class stamps.

Nonfiction: Technical. Subjects include business and economics and computer. "I am always interested in books that improve upon specific software documentation. Additionally, I am willing to consider manuscripts on any new software products or 'hot' topics in the field of computers. I do not want to see anything that is not computer or business related." Query or submit outline/synopsis and sample chapters. Reviews artwork/photos as part of ms package.

Recent Nonfiction Title: *The Illustrated Autocad*, by Dr. Tom Berghauser and Dr. Paul Schlieve (reference).

Tips: "Our audience covers the spectrum from computer novice to the professional who needs advanced reference manuals. We have very stringent deadlines that our authors must meet to access the window of opportunity for our products. So many computer books are time-sensitive and any author interested in signing with me should expect to give an all-out effort to his manuscript."

‡**WORKMAN PUBLISHING COMPANY, INC.**, 708 Broadway, New York NY 10003. (212)254-5900. Publishes hardcover and trade paperback originals and hardcover and trade paperback reprints and calendars. Averages 25 titles/year (and 33 calendars). Pays royalty. Simultaneous and photocopied submissions OK. Reports in 6 months. Book catalog free on request.

Nonfiction: Coffee table book, cookbook, how-to, humor, illustrated book, juvenile, and self-help. Subjects include Americana, art, cooking and foods, health, history, hobbies, nature, photography, recreation, religion, sports, travel. Query or submit outline/synopsis and sample chapters.

Recent Nonfiction Title: *What to Expect in the First Year*, by Eisenburg, Murkoff and Hathaway.

WORLDWIDE LIBRARY, a division of Harlequin Books, 225 Duncan Mill Rd., Don Mills, Ontario M3B 3K9 Canada. (416)445-5860. Imprints: Gold Eagle Books, Worldwide Mysteries. Editorial Director: Randall Toye. Publishes mass market paperback originals and reprints. Averages 72 titles/year; receives 1,100 submissions annually. 20% of books from first-time authors; 25% of books from unagented writers. Offers negotiable royalty on retail price; offers average $5,000-10,000 advance. Publishes book an average of 1 year after acceptance. Photocopied submissions OK. Reports in 1 month on queries; 2 months on mss. Book catalog for 8½x11 SAE and IRC.

Fiction: Espionage, crime/suspense thriller, action-adventure and mystery. "The Worldwide Library list is expanding, and in 1989 we expect to publish a minimum of 24 espionage novels in addition to our Gold Eagle program of action-adventure series. We will also be adding mystery fiction to the list but will not be soliciting any hardboiled mystery fiction." Preferred length: a minimum of 120,000 words for espionage, 65,000 words for mystery. Prefers complete ms; will accept synopsis and first 3 chapters. Query Senior Editor: Fenoze Mohammed for action-adventure.

Recent Fiction Title: *The Strategies of Zeus*, by Gary Hart.

Tips: "We are an excellent market for well-written international espionage and spy fiction."

WRITER'S DIGEST BOOKS, Imprint of F & W Publications, 1507 Dana Ave., Cincinnati OH 45207. Editorial Director: David Lewis. Publishes hardcover and paperback originals (nonfiction only). Averages 45 titles/year. Pays advance and 10% royalty on net receipts. Simultaneous (if so advised) and photocopied submissions OK. Computer printout submissions OK; prefers letter-quality. Publishes book an average of 1 year after acceptance. Enclose return postage. Book catalog for 9x12 SAE with 6 first class stamps.

Nonfiction: Writing, photography, music, and other creative pursuits, as well as general-interest subjects. "We're seeking up-to-date, how-to treatments by authors who can write from successful experience. Should be well-researched, yet lively and readable. Query or submit outline/synopsis and sample chapters. Be prepared to explain how the proposed book differs from existing books on the subject. We are also very interested in republishing self-published nonfiction books and good instructional or reference books that have gone out of print before their time. No fiction or poetry. Send sample copy, sales record, and reviews if available. If you have a good idea for a book that needs updating often, try us. We're willing to consider freelance compilers of such works." Reviews artwork/photos as part of ms package.

Recent Nonfiction Title: *Successful Lyric Writing: A Step-By-Step Course and Workbook*.

YANKEE BOOKS, Subsidiary of Yankee Publishing Inc., Main St., Dublin NH 03444. (603)563-8111. Subsidiaries include *Yankee Magazine* and *The Old Farmers' Almanac*. Editor: Clarissa M. Silitch. Publishes trade paperback and hardcover originals. Averages 4 titles/year, mainly based on material related to *Yankee Magazine* or topics found in the magazine. Average print order for a writer's first book is 5,000-10,000. Pays royalty with $1,000-5,000 advance. Publishes book an average of 18 months after acceptance. Query for electronic submissions. Computer printout submissions acceptable; no dot-matrix. Reports in 1 month on queries; 6 weeks on mss. Book catalog for 9x12 SAE with 5 first class stamps.

Nonfiction: Query or submit outline/synopsis and sample chapters or complete ms. Reviews artwork/photos as part of ms package.

Recent Nonfiction Title: *Whales and Man*, by Tim Dietz.

Tips: "We are now focusing on large, coffee table type books about New England to be sold primarily via direct mail marketing."

YEE WEN PUBLISHING COMPANY, Subsidiary of Yee Wen Publishing Company, Ltd., Republic of China, 21 Vista Court, San Francisco CA 94080. (415)873-7167. Acquisitions Editor: Jammy Yen. Publishes hardcover originals and reprints. Averages 4 titles/year; receives 12 submissions annually. 10% of books from first-time authors; 100% of books from unagented writers. Pays 15% royalty on wholesale price and 10 free copies of the book. Publishes book an average of 1 year after acceptance. Simultaneous and photocopied submissions OK. Query for electronic submissions. Computer printout submissions OK; prefers letter-quality. Reports in 1 month on queries; 6 weeks on mss. Book catalog and ms guidelines for #10 SASE.

Nonfiction: Technical and textbook. Subjects include art, history, philosophy, religion, sociology and archaeology, all of China. "We are seeking a small number of manuscripts by specialists in the studies of China either in English or in Chinese. We do not have enough submissions. We do not want manuscripts unrelated to Chinese culture." Submit outline/synopsis and sample chapters. Reviews artwork/photos as part of ms package.

Recent Nonfiction Title: *Index to an Anthology of Inscriptions on Ancient Chinese Bronzed Vessels*, edited by I-Ping Yen and Tsu-Ken Yao.

Tips: "We like to get general interest books with fresh ideas and a creative approach about Chinese culture."

YORK PRESS LTD., Box 1172, Fredericton, New Brunswick E3B 5C8 Canada. (506)458-8748. General Manager/Editor: Dr. S. Elkhadem. Publishes trade paperback originals. Averages 10 titles/year; receives 50 submissions annually. 10% of books from first-time authors; 100% of books from unagented writers. Pays 5-20% royalty on wholesale price. Publishes book an average of 6 months after acceptance. Photocopied submissions OK. Computer printout submissions acceptable; prefers letter-quality. Reports in 1 week on queries; 1 month on ms. Free book catalog; ms guidelines for $2.50.

Nonfiction and Fiction: Reference, textbook and scholarly. Especially needs literary criticism, comparative literature and linguistics and fiction of an experimental nature by well-established writers. Query.

Recent Nonfiction Title: *Eugene O'Neill*, by F. Hirsch (literary criticism).

Tips: "If I were a writer trying to market a book today, I would spend a considerable amount of time examining the needs of a publisher *before* sending my manuscript to him. Scholarly books and creative writing of an experimental nature are the only kinds we publish. The writer must adhere to our style manual and follow our guidelines exactly."

THE ZONDERVAN CORP., 1415 Lake Drive, SE, Grand Rapids MI 49506. (616)698-6900. Publishes hardcover and trade and mass market paperback originals, and trade and mass market paperback reprints. Averages 100 titles/year; receives 3,500 submissions annually. 30% of books from first-time authors; 98% of books from unagented writers. Average print order for a writer's first book is 5,000. Pays royalty of 14% of the net amount received on sales of cloth and softcover trade editions and 12% of net amount received on sales of mass market paperbacks. Offers variable advance. Computer printout submissions are acceptable; prefers letter-quality. The author should separate the perforated pages. Reports in 6 weeks on queries; 3 months on proposals. Book catalog for 9x12 SAE and $1.22 postage. Ms guidelines for #10 SASE. Send proposals to Mrs. Jean Bloom, manuscript review editor.

Nonfiction: Biography, coffee table book, how-to, humor, illustrated book, reference, devotional and gift, self-help, youth books, Bible study, history, textbooks on philosophy, psychology, religion and sociology. All from religious perspective (evangelical). Immediate needs include "books that take a fresh approach to issues and problems in the evangelical community; that offer new insights into solving personal and interpersonal problems; and that encourage readers to mature spiritually." No mss written from an occult or New Age point of view. Query or submit outline/synopsis and 2 sample chapters.

Recent Nonfiction Title: *Kingdoms in Conflict*, by Charles Colson.

Recent Fiction Title: *Captain, My Captain*, by Deborah Meroff.

Tips: "We will publish less fiction over the next two years as we reevaluate the market."

For information on book publishers' areas of interest, see the nonfiction and fiction sections in the Book Publishers Subject Index.

Following are additional listings of small presses which publish three or fewer titles per year and new presses that had not published four books by the time they completed a questionnaire to be listed in *Writer's Market*. This means the publishing opportunity is more limited, but these companies are still legitimate markets and have expressed an interest in being listed in *Writer's Market*. Write for more information.

ALLEN PUBLISHING CO., Box 1889, Reseda CA 91335.

APPLEZABA PRESS, Box 4134, Long Beach CA 90804. (213)591-0015. Publisher: D.H. Lloyd. Publishes trade paperback originals in humor and cookbooks for nonfiction; and experimental, humor, mainstream, novella and short story collections in fiction.

*BYLS PRESS, Department of Bet Yoatz Library Services, 6247 N. Francisco Ave., Chicago IL 60659. (312)262-8959. President: Daniel D. Stuhlman. Publishes trade paperback originals and computer programs of how-to material for teachers and juvenile and religious books in nonfiction; religious stories for Jewish children in fiction.

DIAMOND PRESS, Box 167, Maple Glen PA 19002. (215)345-6094. Marketing Director: Paul Johnson. Publishes trade paperback originals on sports, antiques.

FRONT ROW EXPERIENCE, 540 Discovery Bay Blvd., Byron CA 94514. (415)634-5710. Editor: Frank Alexander. Publishes teacher/educator edition paperback originals.

GREAT OCEAN PUBLISHERS, 1823 N. Lincoln St., Arlington VA 22207. (703)525-0909. President: Mark Esterman. Publishes hardcover and trade paperback originals and hardcover reprints. In nonfiction, biography, how-to, illustrated book, reference, self-help and technical.

‡GREEN TIMBER PUBLICATIONS, Box 3884, Portland ME 04104. (207)797-4180. President: Tirrell H. Kimball. Publishes trade paperback originals in juvenile nonfiction, fiction and poetry.

GRYPHON HOUSE, INC., 3706 Otis St., Box 275, Mt. Rainier MD 20712. (301)779-6200. President/Editor: Larry Rood. Publishes trade paperback originals of how-to and creative educational activities for teachers to do with preschool children ages 1-5.

HELIX PRESS, 4410 Hickey, Corpus Christi TX 78413. (512)852-8834. Editor: Aubrey R. McKinney. Publishes hardcover originals on science for adults.

JH PRESS, Box 294, Village Station, New York NY 10014. Publisher: Terry Helbing. Publishes trade paperback originals on gay drama and theater, both nonfiction and fiction.

*LONE STAR PUBLISHERS, INC., Box 9774, Austin TX 78766. (512)255-2333. Editorial Director: A.J. Lerager. Publishes hardcover and paperback originals of college textbooks.

M.H. MACY & CO., (formerly Earthview Press), Box 11036, Boulder CO 80301. (303)666-8130. Managing Editor: Mark Macy. Publishes hardcover and trade paperback originals on economics, health, philosophy, politics, psychology, religion and sociology.

*MEYERBOOKS, PUBLISHER, Box 427, Glenwood IL 60425. (312)757-4950. Publisher: David Meyer. Publishes hardcover and trade paperback originals and hardcover and trade paperback reprints. History, reference and self-help works published on subjects of Americana, cooking and foods, health, history, hobbies and nature.

MISTY HILL PRESS, 5024 Turner Rd., Sebastopol CA 95472. (415)892-0789. Managing Editor: Sally C. Karste. Publishes trade paperback originals. In nonfiction, publishes biography, humor and juvenile; in fiction, adventure, fantasy, historical and humor.

OHIO PSYCHOLOGY PUBLISHING CO., 131 N. High St., Columbus OH 43215. (614)224-3228. Vice President: Henry Saeman. Publishes hardcover and trade paperback original textbooks on parenting, personal growth, gifted children, psychology and health.

OUTBOOKS INC., 217 Kimball Ave., Golden CO 80401. Contact: William R. Jones. Publishes trade paperback originals and reprints on regional Americana, nature and outdoor recreation.

PARTNERS IN PUBLISHING, Box 50374, Tulsa OK 74150. (918)584-5906. Editor: P.M. Fielding. Publishes biography, how-to, reference, self-help, technical and textbooks on learning disabilities.

PRINTEMPS BOOKS, INC., Box 746, Wilmette IL 60091. (312)251-5418. Secretary/Treasurer: Beatrice Penovich. Publishes trade paperback originals of children's short stories, adventure, ethnic, fantasy, humor, mystery and suspense.

PUCKERBRUSH PRESS, 76 Main St., Orono ME 04473. (207)581-3832/866-4808. Publisher/Editor: Constance Hunting. Publishes trade paperback originals of literary religious nonfiction and literary fiction and poetry.

SANDPIPER PRESS, Box 286, Brookings OR 97415. (503)469-5588. Editor: Marilyn Riddle. Publishes material on handicaps.

SHAMELESS HUSSY PRESS, Box 3092, Berkely CA 94703. (415)547-1062. Editor: L. Bosserman. Publishes trade paperback originals and reprints. Nonfiction includes biography, illustrated book and juvenile including feminist interviews. Fiction includes adventure, confession, ethnic, experimental, historical, humor and religious. Poetry includes feminist and mystical.

‡SHEPHERD BOOKS, Box 2290, Redmond WA 98073. (206)882-6027. Publisher/Editor: Nick Palmer. Publishes hardcover and trade paperback originals in child guidance/parenting, health/medicine, money/finance, psychology, recreation, biography, how-to, humor and self-help. Publishes humor, literary, mainstream/contempory and suspense fiction.

SOUND VIEW PRESS, 206 Boston Post Rd., Madison CT 06443. President: Peter Falk. Publishes hardcover and trade paperback originals on American art (reference).

‡SOUTHFARM PRESS, Haan Graphic Publishing Services, Ltd., Box 1296, Middletown CT 06457. (203)344-9137. Publisher: Walter J. Haan. Publishes trade paperback originals in nonfiction areas of animals, history, military/war and "B" movies.

SQUARE ONE PUBLISHERS, Box 4385, Madison WI 53711. (608)255-8425. Editorial Director: Lyn Miller-Lachman. Publishes trade paperback originals of young adult fiction.

STILL POINT PRESS, 4222 Willow Grove Rd., Dallas TX 75220. (214)352-8282. Editor/Publisher: Charlotte T. Whaley. Publishes hardcover originals of biographies and fine limited editions on the humanities. Fiction includes ethnic, historical and mainstream.

STONE WALL PRESS, INC., 1241 30th St. NW, Washington DC 20007. President/Publisher: Henry Wheelwright. Publishes hardcover and trade paperback originals of how-to and environmental/outdoor instruction.

‡TGNW PRESS, 2429 E. Aloha, Seattle WA 98112. (206)328-9656. Proprietor: Roger Herz. Publishes mass market paperback originals on baseball, and children's books with a humorous subject matter.

TOMPSON & RUTTER INC., Box 297, Dumbar Hill Rd., Grantham NH 03753. (603)863-4392. President: Frances T. Rutter. Publishes trade paperback originals on Americana and local history.

WESTERN TANAGER PRESS, 1111 Pacific Ave., Santa Cruz CA 95060. (408)425-1111. Publisher: Hal Morris. Publishes biography and regional history hardcover and trade paperback originals and reprints.

Subsidy Publishers

The following publishers produce more than 50% of their books on a subsidy or cooperative basis. What they charge and what they offer to each writer varies, so you'll want to judge each publisher on its own merit. Because subsidy publishing can cost you several thousand dollars, make sure the number of books, the deadlines and services offered by the publisher are detailed in your contract. If you are willing to pay to have your book published, you should also be willing to hire an attorney to review the contract. This step prevents misunderstandings between you and your prospective publisher. Never agree to terms you don't understand in a contract. Consult the Book Publishers introduction for more information on subsidy publishing.

About Books, Inc.
County Road ff38, Box 538, Saguache CO 81149

Atlantis Publishing Company
5432 Hallandale Beach Blvd., Hollywood FL 33023

Authors' Unlimited
#204, 3330 Barham Blvd., Los Angeles CA 90068

Brunswick Publishing Company
Box 555, Lawrenceville VA 23868

Carlton Press, Inc.
11 W. 32nd St., New York NY 10001

Cougar Books
Box 22879, Sacramento CA 95822

Eastview Editions
Box 783, Westfield NJ 07091

Fairway Press
C.S.S. Publishing Company, Inc., 628 South Main St., Lima OH 45804

The Golden Quill Press
Avery Rd., Francestown NH 03043

Hawkes Publishing
3775 So. 500 W., Box 15711, Salt Lake City UT 84115

Peter Randall Publisher
500 Market St., Box 4726, Portsmouth NH 03801

Rivercross Publishing, Inc.
127 East 59th St., New York NY 10022

Sunflower University Press
1531 Yuma, Box 1009, Manhattan KS 66502-4228.

Trinity Publishers Services
Box 1119, Weaverville CA 96093

University of Alaska Press
Signers' Hall, Fairbanks AK 99775-1580

Vantage Press
516 W. 34th St., New York NY 10001.

Wimmer Brothers
Box 18408, 4210 B.F. Goodrich Blvd., Memphis TN 38118

Writers Publishing Service Co.
1512 Western Ave., Seattle WA 98101

Book Packagers and Producers

The majority of packaged books are nonfiction, but mysteries, science fiction and picture book series have been growing the past year among book packagers, producers and developers. You'll also find that some book packagers have developed specialties; packagers listed in this section have indicated special needs ranging from juvenile series and textbooks to books on animals.

Book packaging is a relatively new opportunity for writers. While it originated in England in the 1940s, the trend didn't pick up in the U.S. on a large scale until the 1970s. While they originally were known as book packagers, today many firms prefer to be called book producers or book developers. They provide a book publisher with services ranging from hiring writers, photographers or artists, to editing and delivering the finished book.

In most instances, a book packager or producer develops a book proposal, assembles the people to prepare it and submits it to a publisher. When a proposal is accepted by a publisher, the producer serves several functions. When the manuscript is in preparation, the producer is an editor. As the manuscript and illustrations or photo package are put together, the function changes to managing editor. Then the producer takes over coordination of production and may also serve as a sales consultant for the project. In other cases, a book publisher will contract with a book packager or producer to perform one or more of these functions instead of inhouse staff doing it.

The term book developer may be used to refer to a book packager or producer, or it may apply to a literary agent who joins with writers to provide writing and editorial services. An agent who functions as a book packager or developer often provides additional writing support for the author as they work together to produce a proposal. Then the agent uses his contacts within the industry to sell the work. Agents who work in book packaging have that information included in their listings in the Author's Agents section.

What makes book packagers' and producers' services so attractive to publishers? Primarily, it's speed and specialties. Many publishers with small editorial staffs use packagers and producers as extensions of their companies. An inhouse staff member can provide 20% of the work on the book and rely on the packager to produce the remaining 80%. This frees the staff member to move on to other projects. In some cases, publishers work with packagers to provide resources or knowledge they don't need fulltime but do need for a specific book. Many book packagers and producers also are experts at producing high quality illustrated books, an area where small publishers may lack inhouse expertise.

Writers who want to work in the field should be aware of differences between book publishers and book packagers. Publishers accept book proposals and ideas for books submitted to them by writers. Book packagers and agents who act as book packagers most often assign topics to writers. Occasionally, a packager will develop an idea brought in by a writer, but this is rare. When you submit material, packagers most often want to see a query with your writing credentials and a list of areas of expertise. Writers who are trying to establish themselves in the industry may consider this an attractive option but should be aware that it doesn't always provide you with credit for your writing since many books require several writers. Book producers and packagers often make outright purchases of writing, contract work-for-hire agreements or offer a large advance and low royalty percentage. Don't expect to receive a book catalog from a book producer or book packager; they produce books for other publishers' catalogs. If you ask for a sample of titles they've produced, however, you may be surprised to find some bestsellers on the list.

More than 150 book packagers, producers and agents work in the field, but most prefer to make their own contacts with writers and do not accept unsolicited queries. In this section, we've only included those who say they are interested in being contacted by writers. For a list of other book packagers and producers, see the latest edition of *Literary Market Place* in your local library.

‡**BOOKWORKS, INC.**, 119 South Miami St., West Milton OH 45383. (513)698-3619. President: Nick Engler. Firm averages 5 titles/year. Receives 1-10 submissions/year. 20-40% of books from first-time authors. 100% from unagented writers. Pays 2½-5% royalty on retail price. Buys mss outright for $3,000-10,000. Offers $7,500 average advance. Publishes book an average of 8 months after acceptance. Simultaneous and photocopied submissions OK. Computer printout submissions OK; prefers letter-quality. Reports in 6 weeks on queries; 2 months on mss.
Nonfiction: How-to. Subjects include hobbies, woodworking and home improvement. Nothing other than crafts/woodworking/home improvement. Query or submit outline/synopsis and sample chapters. Reviews artwork/photos as part of manuscript package.
Recent Nonfiction Title: *Outdoor Structures*, by Morgan and Engler.
Tips: "In the how-to field, there is more emphasis on projects, less emphasis on techniques and methods. We publish how-to books for do-it-yourselfers, hobbyists and craftsmen."

CARPENTER PUBLISHING HOUSE, Suite 4602, 175 E. Delaware Place, Chicago IL 60611. (312)787-3569. President: Allan Carpenter. Develops hardcover originals. "We develop on contract for major publishers. We assign work to authors and artists." Negotiates fee. Reports promptly on queries.
Nonfiction: Biography, juvenile, reference and supplementary texts. Subjects include Americana, history and directory/resource annuals. "We do not solicit mss. We specialize in books in large series. We would consider proposals for American biographies for school use." Query. All unsolicited mss are returned unopened.
Recent Nonfiction Title: *All About the U.S.A.*, by Allan Carpenter (supplementary text).

‡**MICHAEL FRIEDMAN PUBLISHING GROUP**, 15 W. 26th St., New York NY 10010. (212)685-6610. Subsidiaries include Friedman Group; Tern Enterprises; The Wainscott Group. Editorial Director: Karla Olson. Packages hardcover originals and trade paperback originals working with all major publishers. Firm averages 40 packages/year. "We work with many first-time authors and almost exclusively with unagented authors." Buys mss outright "under certain circumstances (when an author approaches us with an idea) we will pay a small royalty on reprints based on our price to publisher." Produces book an average of 1 year after acceptance; Friedman group responsible for all illustrative material included in book. Query for electronic submissions. Computer printout submissions OK. Free book catalog.
Nonfiction: Coffee table book, cookbook, how-to and illustrated book. Subjects include Americana, animals, anthropology/archaeology, art/architecture, cooking, foods and nutrition, gardening, hobbies, nature/environment, recreation and sports. Query.
Recent Nonfiction Title: *The Whole Christmas Catalog*, by Naomi Black, et.al..

‡**HELENA FROST ASSOCIATES**, 117 East 24th St., New York NY 10010. (212)475-6642. President: Helena Frost. Editorial Director: Lauren Fedorko. Packages approximately 50 titles/year. Receives approximately 100 queries/year. Authors paid by flat or hourly fees or on freelance assignments. Query for electronic submissions. Computer printout submissions OK; prefers letter-quality. Reports in 3 weeks. Completed projects list available; ms guidelines available per project.
Nonfiction: Textbook ancillaries, some general trade titles. Subjects include business and economics, education, government/politics, health/medicine, history, language/literature, psychology. Query.
Tips: "Although we are not interested in over-the-transom mss, we do request writers' and editors' resumes and will review school-related proposals and outlines for submission to major publishers."

‡**GENERAL LICENSING COMPANY**, Byron Preiss Visual Publications, 24 W. 25th St., New York NY 10010. (212)645-9870. Executive Editor: David M. Harris. Firm publishes trade paperback and mass market paperback originals. Packages 10 books/year; receives 100 submissions/year. 5% of books from first-time authors; 30% from unagented writers. Pays authors 2-6% royalty. Average advance is $4,000. Publishes ms an average of 9 months after acceptance. Photocopied submissions OK. Computer printout submissions OK; prefers letter-quality. Reports in 10 weeks.
Fiction: Adventure, fantasy, historical, juvenile, science fiction, western, young adult. "The books and series we produce are generated in-house. We create the concept, characters and backgrounds, then find authors to write the books. Manuscripts are reviewed only to consider the authors for commissioned work." Query.
Recent Fiction Title: *Zoomers*, by Mel Gilder (juvenile).

‡THE K S GINIGER COMPANY INC., 1133 Broadway, New York NY 10010. (212)645-5150. President: Kenneth S. Giniger. Publishes hardcover, trade paperback and mass paperback originals. Averages 8 titles/year; receives 250 submissions annually. 25% of books from first-time authors; 75% of books from unagented writers. Pays 5-15% royalty on retail price; offers $3,500 average advance. Publishes book an average of 18 months after acceptance. Computer printout submissions OK; prefers letter-quality. Reports in 2 weeks on queries.

Nonfiction: Biography, coffee table book, illustrated book, reference and self-help. Subjects include business and economics, health, history, religion and travel. "No religious books, cookbooks, personal histories or personal adventure." Query with SAE. All unsolicited mss are returned unread (if postage is enclosed for return of ms).

Recent Nonfiction Title: *The Templeton Plan*, by John M. Templeton.

Tips: "We look for a book whose subject interests us and which we think can achieve success in the marketplace; most of our books are based on ideas originating with us by authors we commission, but we have commissioned books from queries submitted to us."

‡THE LOGICAL EXTENSION, LTD., 20 Lafayette Ave., Seacliff NY 11579. (516)676-8345. President: Howard Blumenthal. Packages trade paperback originals. Averages 10 packages/year. 50% of books from first-time authors. Pays up to 15% royalty on wholesale or retail price. Produces book an average of 6 months-1 year after acceptance. Computer printout submissions OK; no dot-matrix.

Nonfiction: Coffee-table book, how-to, illustrated book, reference, self-help, textbook. Subjects include business and economics, child guidance/parenting, computers/electronics, education, money/finance, photography, science, communications. All unsolicited mss are returned unopened.

Recent Nonfiction Title: *The Complete Time Traveler*, by Howard J. Blumenthal, Dorothy Curley, and Brad Williams (travel/science).

LUCAS-EVANS BOOKS, 1123 Broadway, New York NY 10010. (212)929-2583. Contact: Barbara Lucas. Packages hardcover, trade paperback originals and mass market paperback originals for major publishers. Averages 10 titles/year. 10% of books from first-time authors. Pays 1-8% royalty, "depends on our contract agreement with publisher." Makes work-for-hire assignments. Offers $3,000 average advance. Reports in 1 month on queries; 2 months on mss.

Nonfiction: Reference. "We are looking for series proposals and selected single juvenile books: preschool through high school, prefer picture book and middle grade novels." Submit complete ms.

Recent Nonfiction Title: *Do Not Disturb*, by Margery Facklam (animal sleep and hibernation).

Fiction: Preschool through high school. No rhyming verse.

Recent Fiction Title: *Buffalo Girls*, by Bobette McCarthy (picture book).

*MAVERICK PUBLICATIONS, Drawer 5007, Bend OR 97708. (503)382-6978. Publisher: Ken Asher. Publishes hardcover and trade paperback originals. Averages 15 titles/year; receives 200 submissions annually. "Like every other publisher, the number of books we can publish is limited. We would like to suggest to any writer who has a timely manuscript and is having trouble getting it published to consider publishing it themselves. We will be glad to discuss this alternative with anyone who might be interested." 40% of books from first-time authors; 95% of books from unagented writers. Pays 15% royalty on net selling price. Publishes book an average of 6 months after acceptance. Simultaneous and photocopied submissions OK. Computer printout submissions acceptable; prefers letter-quality. Reports in 2 weeks on queries; 3 weeks on mss. Book catalog on request.

Nonfiction: Biography, cookbook, illustrated book, self-help and technical. Subjects include Americana, cooking and foods, health, history, hobbies, music and travel. Query. Reviews artwork/photos.

Recent Nonfiction Title: *Fish Hassell—A Viking With Wings*, by Col. Bert Hassell (pioneer aviation autobiography).

Fiction: Adventure, historical, mystery and science fantasy. "We have no specific needs, but prefer stories based on facts." Submit outline/synopsis and sample chapters.

Recent Fiction Title: *Sutton's Law*, by Jane Orient and L.J. Wright (novel).

Tips: "Book publishing trends include direct marketing by independent publishers of quality material to an intelligent public. A timely, well-researched exposé of national or at least regional importance has the best chance of selling to our firm. We seem to be developing a penchant for aviation history and for biographies, specialty cookbooks, cowboy and western stories, native American, industrial archaeology, Pacific NW regional and new wave."

‡MOUNTAIN LION, INC., Box 257, Rocky Hill NJ 08553. (609)924-8363. Managing Editor: Martha Wickenden. Packages hardcover originals and trade paperback originals. Firm averages 10-12 titles/year. "We're not looking for ideas from writers. We're looking for qualified writers in various subject areas. Occasionally, we will develop an idea brought to as by a writer." Pays royalty. Buys mss outright on work-for-hire assignments. Offers $10,000 average advance, "paid in either fees or advances against royalty."

Nonfiction: Biography, coffee table book, cookbook, how-to, illustrated book, juvenile, reference and self-help. Subjects include cooking, foods and nutrition, health/medicine and sports. Query. Reviews artwork/photos as part of manuscript package.
Recent Nonfiction Title: *Official Universal Workout Book*, by Chuck Coker (how-to, fitness).

JAMES PETER ASSOCIATES, INC., Box 772, Tenafly NJ 07670. (201)568-0760. President: Bert Holtje. Packages hardcover and trade paperback originals. Averages 10-15 titles/year; receives 80-100 submissions annually. 10% of books from first-time authors; 90% of books from unagented writers. Pays 30-50% royalty "on income to J.P.A. Inc." Offers $8,000-15,000 average advance. Publishes ms an average of 1 year after acceptance. Photocopied submissions OK. Query for electronic submissions. Computer printout submissions OK. Reports in 2 weeks on queries; 2 months on mss.
Nonfiction: How-to, reference, self-help. Subjects include business and economics, health, psychology and sociology. "We're looking for psychological subjects for general readers. Must be done by, or with professional psychologist, psychiatrist. No rehashes of pop-psych subjects." Query or submit outline/synopsis and sample chapters. All unsolicited mss are returned. Reviews artwork/photos as part of ms package.
Recent Nonfiction Title: *Eighty-Eight Mistakes Interviewers Make—And How to Avoid Them*, by Auren Uris.
Tips: "Show us that the idea is fresh. New slants are critical! Why? The business and psychology fields are glutted with clones!"

POLICE BOOKSHELF, Box 122, Concord NH 03301. (603)224-6814. Director: Massad Ayoob. Publishes hardcover originals and reprints; trade paperback originals. Averages 4 titles/year; receives 20-30 submissions annually. "We feel a specialist author will earn more (and write better) if he has a financial stake from the beginning. To date, however, we have not subsidy published." Pays 10-15% royalty on retail price. Publishes book an average of 18 months after acceptance. Query for eletronic submissions. Computer printout submissions OK; prefers letter-quality. Reports in 3-4 weeks on queries; 1-2 months on ms. Book catalog for 8½x11 SAE and 2 first class stamps.
Nonfiction: Biography, how-to, reference, self-help and technical. Subjects include law enforcement and personal protection. "We want top-flight work on armed and unarmed combat, arrest procedures, court and trial techniques, officer survival and personal protection—preferably by authorities in the given field." No philosophy on crime in America or future of the criminal justice system. Submit outline/synopsis and sample chapters. Reviews artwork/photos as part of ms package.
Recent Nonfiction Title: *Street Smart Gun Book*, by John Farnam.
Tips: "Our readers want professional, nonfiction guides to police work and self-protection. We demand documentation, citations, clear illustrations and readability."

BYRON PREISS VISUAL PUBLICATIONS, INC., Subsidiaries include General Licensing Co., 12th Floor, 24 West 25th St., New York NY 10010. (212)645-9870. Executive Editor: David M. Harris. Publishes hardcover, trade paperback and mass market paperback originals. Averages 30 titles/year; receives 30-50 submissions annually. 2% of books from first-time authors; 30% of books from unagented writers. Pays 2-6% royalty on retail price; offers $4,000 average advance. Publishes book an average of 1 year after acceptance. Photocopied submissions OK. Computer printout submissions OK; prefers letter-quality. Reports in 1 month on queries; 2 months on mss.
Nonfiction: Biography and juvenile. Subjects include history and science. "All of our books are commissioned. We need authors who are familiar with a specialized field and capable of writing for younger readers. Series under development at present include dinosaurs, business and biographies for young adults. Since all our books are commissioned, no completed manuscripts should be submitted." Query. Reviews artwork/photos as part of ms package.
Recent Nonfiction Title: *The Universe*, by Byron Preiss, ed. (astronomy).
Fiction: Adventure, fantasy, historical, horror, mystery and science fiction. "We need people who can work to our specifications and who are familiar with the conventions of genre fiction." Query.
Recent Fiction Title: *Joe Gash*, by Tom de Haven (science fiction).
Tips: "Science fiction is doing particularly well for us lately, as part of the resurgence of category fiction in the market. Interactive fiction seems to be consolidating as a part of the publishing scene, and may be moving from young adult into the mainstream. We will be looking more at mysteries in the future, and our interest in the natural sciences is growing. Contact Ruth Ashby for these topics."

QUINLAN PRESS, 131 Beverly St., Boston MA 02114. (617)227-4870/1-800-551-2500. Executive Editor: Sandra E. Bielawa. Publishes hardcover and trade paperback originals. Averages 25-40 titles/year; receives 1,500 submissions annually. 75% of books from first-time authors; 90% of books from unagented writers. Pays 7-12% royalty on retail price; buys one ms outright for $1,000-5,000. Offers average $500 advance. Publishes book 1 year after acceptance. Simultaneous submissions OK. Query for electronic submissions. Computer printout submissions acceptable. Reports in 5 weeks on queries; 2 months on mss. Guidelines for

8½x11 SAE and 4 first class stamps.

Nonfiction: Biography, humor, illustrated book and self-help. Subjects include Americana, animals, history, hobbies, music, photography, politics, recreation, religion, sociology and sports. "We are interested in publishing any nonfiction book we feel is consumable by the population in general. Nothing too esoteric." Submit outline/synopsis and sample chapters. Reviews artwork/photos as part of ms package.

Recent Nonfiction Title: *My Dad, the Babe: Growing Up with an American Hero*, by Dorothy Ruth Pirone, with Chris Martens.

‡**READING RAINBOW GAZETTE, INC.**, Suite 402, 648 Broadway, New York NY 10012. (212)529-1133. Produces hardcover, trade paperback originals and mass market paperback originals. 50% of books from first-time authors. 80% from unagented writers. Royalty varies on wholesale and retail price. Buys mss outright. Advance varies. Publishes book an average of 18 months after acceptance. Simultaneous and photocopied submissions OK. Computer printout submissions OK; prefers letter-quality. Reports in 3 weeks on queries; 8 weeks on mss.

Nonfiction: Juvenile. Subjects include animals, child guidance/parenting, nature/environment, photography, recreation and science. "We are interested in heavily illustrated/photo nonfiction for children, particularly in the reference area. No biography or history." Submit outline/synopsis and sample chapters. Reviews artwork/photos as part of manuscript package.

Recent Nonfiction Title: "We are currently developing an animal photo series of 4 titles; also, activity books."

Fiction: Juvenile. "We are looking for series; reference, activity, and illustrated, innovatively designed packages. No teenage novels." Submit outline/synopsis and sample chapters.

Recent Fiction Title: *Reading Rainbow Library*, (8 volumes; each includes story, activities and nonfiction sections).

Tips: "We're looking for something new, with an eye toward mass-market appeal, educational benefit and innovative packaging. Youngsters and beginning readers are our audience. If I were a writer trying to market a book today, I would be sure my book was new, fresh and targeted to a specific audience or need or interest."

‡**IRVING ROCKWOOD & ASSOCIATES, INC.**, 175 Orchard Ridge Rd., Chappaqua NY 10514. (914)238-4043. President: Irving E. Rockwood. Produces hardcover and text paperback originals. Averages 4 titles/year. Receives 30-50 mss/year. 10% of books from first-time author; 100% from unagented writers. Advance varies. Produces book an average of 1 year after acceptance. Simultaneous and photocopied submissions. Query for electronic submissions. Computer printout submission OK; prefers letter-quality. Reports in 1 month. Prospectus guidelines free on request.

Nonfiction: Textbook. Subjects include business and economics, government/politics, history, social work. "At the present time we are primarily looking for publishable basic and supplementary college level texts in the social sciences, espcially political science and social work. All of authors thus far are either academics or professionals." Query or submit outline/synopsis and sample chapters. Reviews artwork/photos as part of ms package.

Recent Nonfiction Title: *International Relations: Contemporary Theory and Practice*, by George Lopez and Michael Stohl (paperback text).

Tips: "There are fewer and fewer major college text publishers with an interest in the social sciences every year, and those which remain interested have very full lists and acquire new titles *very* selectively. For our part, we are primarily interested in new texts that are truly innovative and designed first and foremost with the needs of the student (and instructor) in mind."

T.F.H. PUBLICATIONS, INC., 1 T.F.H. Plaza, Third and Union Avenues, Neptune City NJ 07753. Imprint: Paganiniana Publications. (201)988-8400. Managing Editor: Neal Pronek. Publishes hardcover originals. Averages 100 titles/year; receives 200 submissions annually. 80% of books from first-time authors; 95% of books from unagented writers. Royalty varies, depending on type of book, etc. Usually makes outright purchase of up to $20 per page. Offers advance of ½ of total based upon estimation of total pages in final printed work. Publishes book an average of 1 year after acceptance. Simultaneous and photocopied submissions OK. Query for electronic submissions. Computer printout submissions acceptable; prefers letter-quality. Reports in 3 weeks.

Nonfiction: Coffee table book, how-to, illustrated book, reference, technical and textbook. Subjects include animals. "Our nonfiction book manuscript needs are for books that deal with specific guidelines for people who own or are interested in purchasing a particular type of pet. No books exclusively devoted to personal experiences with a particular pet, for example, *My Pet Sam*." Submit outline/synopsis and sample chapters. Reviews artwork/photos as part of ms package.

Recent Nonfiction Title: *The Boston Terrier*, by Anna Katherine Nicholas.

Tips: "Our audience is any and everyone who owns a pet. We do well with books that have a lot of photographs, and those that offer good sound advice for caring for a particular type of pet."

‡**WELCOME ENTERPRISES, INC.**, 164 E. 95th St., New York NY 10128. (212)722-7533. President: Lena Tabori. Managing Editor: Timothy Gray. Firm packages 12 books per year; agents 25. Receives approximately 200-500 submissions/year. "A publisher always contractually commits to us before we package a book for them." Usually pays authors 10% royalty on projected retail price of packaged books; agented books depend on negotiations with publisher. Simultaneous and photocopied submissions OK. Computer printout submissions OK; prefers letter-quality. Reports in 1 month on queries; 3 months on mss. Ms guidelines for #10 SAE.
Nonfiction: Biography, coffee table book, cookbook, how-to, humor, illustrated book, juvenile, reference and self-help. Subjects include Americana, animals, anthropology/archaeology, child guidance/parenting, cooking, foods and nutrition, gardening, gay/lesbian, government/politics, health/medicine, history, hobbies, language/literature, music/dance, nature/environment, philosophy, photography, psychology, recreation, science, sociology, women's issues/studies, New Age/occult. Submit outline/synopsis, sample chapters and SASE. Reviews artwork/photos as part of ms package.
Recent Nonfiction Title: *The Joys of Entertainings*, by Beverly Reese Church and Bethany Ewald Bultman (home entertaining for Abbeville Press).
Fiction: Occasionally handles fiction.

‡**THE WESTPORT PUBLISHING GROUP**, Box 149, Westport CT 06881. (203)849-0211. President: Margaret Flesher Ribaroff. Produces 5 titles/year. Averages 50 titles/year. "Generally we initiate ideas and hire writers—we work with both published and unpublished writers, mostly unagented. We pay either flat fee or percentage of proceeds, depending on arrangement with publisher and involvement of writer in project." Simultaneous and photocopied submissions OK. Computer printout submissions OK; prefers letter quality. Reports in 1 month on queries; 3 months on mss.
Nonfiction: Juvenile, illustrated book, cookbook, how-to, self-help. Subjects include Americana, animals, business, parenting, cooking, gardening, government/politics, history, money/finance, nature/environment, psychology, recreation, sociology, travel, women's issues/studies. "We emphasize children's books and general nonfiction trade books for a popular audience. We are chiefly interested in good nonfiction writers to develop ideas generated in-house. Subject areas are wide-ranging." Query or submit outline/synopsis and sample chapters. Reviews artwork/photos as part of ms package.
Recent Nonfiction Title: *The War Against Terrorism*, by Michael Kronenuetter.
Fiction: Juvenile, picture books. "We look for picture book series for children ages pre-K to 8 years and fiction for children ages 7-9; 8-10 (with series possibilities). No single titles for children and young adults." Query or submit complete ms (for picture books only).
Tips: "Because most of our books are developed from ideas generated in-house, we are more interested in locating good writers with sense of quality and style than in buying manuscripts. We'd much prefer to see short writing samples than finished manuscripts."

WINGRA WOODS PRESS, Box 9601, Madison WI 53715. Acquisitions Editor: M.G. Mahoney. Publishes trade paperback originals. Averages 6-10 titles/year; receives 200 submissions annually. 70% of books from first-time authors; 100% of books from unagented writers. Pays 10-12% royalty on retail price, sometimes makes outright purchase of $500-10,000. Publishes book an average of 18 months after acceptance. Simultaneous and photocopied submissions OK. Computer printout submissions acceptable. Reports in 6 weeks.
Nonfiction: Coffee table, cookbook, how-to, juvenile, self-help. Subjects include Americana, popular history and science, animals, art, and nature, psychology and spiritual. Especially looking for popularized book-length treatments of specialized knowledge; interested in proposals from academics and professionals. Query with outline/synopsis. Do not send complete ms. Reviews artwork/photos as part of ms package.
Recent Nonfiction Title: *The Christmas Cat*.
Tips: "Put your 'good stuff' in the very first paragraph . . . tell us why we should care. Consider page 1 of the query as distilled flap copy. Then follow up with facts and credentials."

ALWAYS submit manuscripts or queries with a self-addressed, stamped envelope (SASE) within your country or International Reply Coupons (IRC) purchased from the post office for other countries.

— Additional Book Publishers and Packagers

The following listings are inactive for the 1989 edition because the firms are backlogged with submissions or indicated a need for few freelance submissions in 1989.

Hermes House Press
Hurtig Publishers
Kaleidoscopix Inc. Children's
    Book Division
Abner Schram

The following firms did not return a verification to update an existing listing or a questionnaire to begin a new listing by press time.

Adams, Houmes & Ward
Affirmation Books
Allen Publishing
American Federation of Information Processing Societies
Atheneum Publishers
Atlantic Monthly Press
Avi Publishing
Bankers Publishing
Banks-Baldwin Law
Basil Blackwell
Beacon Press of Kansas City
Birkhauser Boston
John F. Blair, Publisher
BNA Books
Don Bosco Publications
Allen D. Bragdon Publishers
George Braziller
Carolina Biological Supply
CBP Press
Christian Ed. Publishers
Compute! books
CRCS Publications
Delmar Publishers
Delta Books
Devonshire Publishing
Dimension Books
Douglas & McIntyre
Dundurn Press
Ediciones Universal
M. Evans & Co.
Fearon Education
Fiddlehead Poetry Books & Goose Lane Editions
The Filter Press
Fitzhenry & Whiteside
Floricanto Press
Fordham University Press
Fortress Press

Gambling Times
Genealogical Publishing Co.
General Hall
C.R. Gibson Co.
Golden West
Grunwald & Radcliff
Harvard University Press
Hazeldon Foundation
D.C. Heath & Co.
Institute for the Study of Human Issues
Isidore Stephanus Sons
Kern International
B. Klein Publications
Learning Publications
Lee's Books for Young Readers
Leisure Press
Hal Leonard Publishing
Liberty Publishing
Llewellyn Publications
Luna Ventures
Madrona Publishers
Maynard-Thomas Publishing
Merrill Publishing
MIT Press
Monitor Book Co.
Mott Media
National Book Co.
Naval Institute Press
NC Press
Thomas Nelson Publishers
Nimbus Publishing
North Country Press
North Point Press
Northword
Ohio University Press
Ottenheimer Publishers
PAR Inc.
The Pagurian Corp.

Paladin Press
Pandora Press
Paragon House
Parenting Press
Parnassus Imprints
Pickwick Publications
The Pilgrim Press
Platt & Munk
Poseidon Press
Prentice-Hall Books for Young Readers
Prentice-Hall Canada
Prentice Hall/Regents
Probus
Prolingua Associates
Purdue University Press
QED Information Sciences
Que Corp.
Raintree Publishers
Reference Service Press
Renaissance House Publishers
Fleming H. Revell
Reymont Associates
Russica Publishers
Rutledge Hill Press
St. Bede's Publications
St. Luke's Press
Schocken Books
Second Chance at Love
Self-Counsel Press
Seven Seas Press
Shining Star Publications
Sigo Press
Silver Burdett Press
Sparrow Press
Speech Bin
Starblaze
Stewart, Tabori & Chang

Stillpoint Publishing
Stoeger Publishing
Stoneydale Press
Sherwood Sugden & Co.
Symmes Systems
Taylor Publishing Co.

University Associates
University of Arizona Press
University of Utah Press
University Press of Virginia
Unlimited Publishing
Valley of the Sun

Wadsworth Publishing
Walker & Co.
Whitaker House
Windsor Publications
Wright Publishing
Zebra Books

The following listings were deleted following the 1988 edition of *Writer's Market* because the company asked to have the listing removed, went out of business, is no longer accepting unsolicited submissions, charges a fee to consider manuscripts, or has unresolved complaints on file.

Ashley Books (complaints)
Brook House Press (charges $10 reading fee)
Chelsea House Publishers-Edgemont (asked to be deleted)
Copley Books (no longer publishing)
Dawn Publications (no longer working with freelancers)
Falcon Press (unable to contact)
Glenmark Publishing (charges $50 fee)
Harcourt Brace Jovanovich (trade division) (not accepting unsolicited material)
Heroica Books (asked to be deleted)
Hounslow Press (asked to be deleted)
William Kaufmann Inc. (does not want any new submissions)
The Mysterious Press (not accepting unsolicited manuscripts)
New Harbinger Publications (asked to be deleted)
National Press Books (complaints)
Nitty Gritty Cookbooks (bought by Bristol Publishing—see that listing)
101 Productions (no longer publishing)
Quality Publications (in middle of sale at press time)
Racz Publishing (not accepting unsolicited manuscripts)
University of Notre Dame Press (asked to be deleted)
Vend-O-Books (out of business)
Woodland Books (asked to be deleted)

Consumer Publications

More than 1,400 consumer magazines are covered in this section. "Sometimes it seems like there's a magazine on every conceivable topic," says John Seekamp of *Chrysalis* magazine.

Not only is there a volume of consumer magazines, but the market constantly changes. Editorial departments, focuses and formats of existing magazines are often restructured as publications compete with each other for readers. New magazines start up almost daily; since last year, approximately 265 magazines have begun publication. Industry statistics indicate that few new publications in the market place will last, with nine of ten magazine startups failing.

All of this makes the consumer magazine market an ever-changing workplace for freelancers. To keep pace with changes and startups, make regular trips to your local bookstore, newsstand or library. Read magazines like *Writer's Digest*, *Folio* and other publications that report on magazines to learn the changes that have occurred since this edition of *Writer's Market* went to press. Read the publications you find interesting and be sure to write for a sample copy if you can't locate a recent issue locally. Before you submit a manuscript, also be sure to obtain the magazine's writer's guidelines.

During the past year, a number of hobby, personal computer and travel magazines have started publication. Other trends in magazine publishing include an increase in children's magazines, often with a tie-in to TV shows, and a steady consumer appetite for special interest home and cooking titles, as well as outdoor and business magazines. Be sure to study the new category called Contemporary Culture for magazines that include men's and women's fashion, entertainment, and politics.

In fiction, most magazines are buying shorter stories but there is a market resurgence for them. Scan the categories in the Fiction subhead—science fiction, mystery, romance, men's, women's, juvenile, teen and literary—for a listing of fiction requirements. You'll find complete information on the fiction field in *Novel and Short Story Writer's Market* (Writer's Digest Books).

Graphics remain strong in the magazine industry, and editors stress the need for articles that can be illustrated. Writers who can provide quality photographs or suggest appropriate illustrations with their manuscripts have an advantage. Editors also express needs for short articles, surveys, exclusive stories, and lists (Top Ten Businesses, etc.).

You can increase the sale of manuscripts by expanding the number of publications for which you write. Duane Newcomb's article "How to Sell and Re-Sell Your Writing" offers ideas for revising manuscripts and changing slants to fit several publications. In addition, look for magazines that accept simultaneous submissions and previously published material when you read the listings. Introductions in this section and the section introductions under Trade, Technical and Professional Journals also will provide you with related topics and publications for which you may write or adapt articles.

Remember to follow the requirements of the magazines listed in *Writer's Market*. If an editor specifically requests queries—and most of them do—don't send a complete manuscript.

Information on publications not included in *Writer's Market* can be found in Additional Consumer Publications at the end of this section.

ALWAYS submit manuscripts or queries with a self-addressed, stamped envelope (SASE) within your country or International Reply Coupons (IRC) purchased from the post office for other countries.

Animal

The publications in this section deal with pets, racing and show horses, other pleasure animals and wildlife. Magazines about animals bred and raised for the market are classified in the Farm category. Publications about horse racing can be found in the Sports section.

ANIMAL KINGDOM, New York Zoological Society, 185 St. and Southern Blvd., Bronx NY 10460. (212)220-5121. Editor: Eugene J. Walter, Jr. Executive Editor: Penelope J. O'Prey. 89% freelance written. A bimonthly magazine on zoology, animal behavior and conservation. Circ. 143,000. Pays on acceptance. Byline given. Offers $100 kill fee. Buys all rights. Submit seasonal/holiday material 9 months in advance. Simultaneous submissions OK. Computer printout submissions OK; prefers letter-quality, double spaced. Reports in 1 month. Sample copy $2 with 9x12 SAE and 6 first class stamps. Free writer's guidelines.
Nonfiction: Nancy Simmons Christie, articles editor. Book excerpts, essays, historical, how-to, humor, personal experience, photo feature and travel. No pet stories. Buys 24 mss/year. Query with published clips. Length: 1,500-2,500 words. Pays $550-800. Pays in copies "at request of author."
Photos: State availability of photos with submission. Reviews transparencies. Offers $35-200 per photo. Identification of subjects required. Buys one-time rights.
Columns/Departments: Bookshelf (reviews of wildlife books for adults/children), 300-600 words. Buys 18 mss/year. Query with published clips. Pays $75-150.

‡ANIMAL PRESS, Box 2099, Lakeside CA 92040. (619)561-9025. Editor: Ginger Julian. Monthly tabloid on animals (domestic and wildlife). "This newspaper is dedicated to providing the public with educational, entertaining and informative articles on a wide variety of animals—excluding livestock, in the interest of peaceful human/animal co-existence. Occasionally we touch on animal issues, but prefer positive, upbeat articles." Estab. 1987. Circ. 35,000. Pays within 2 weeks of publication. Byline given. Buy first rights or second serial (reprint) rights. Simultaneous, photocopied and previously published submissions OK. Query for electronic submissions. Computer printout submissions OK. Reports in 1 month. Sample copy $1 with 10x12 SAE and 2 first class stamps.
Nonfiction: How-to (train, breed, groom, etc.), humor, interview/profile (of celebrities in the animal movement or famous people and their pets, etc.), personal experience, photo feature, educational or news-worthy true stories. No animal rights articles. Buys 24 mss/year. Query with or without published clips, or send complete ms. Length: 600-800 words. Pays $30-40.
Photos: Send photos with submission. Reviews contact sheets, prints. Offers $5-10 per photo. Identification of subjects required. Buys one-time rights.
Fiction: Adventure, condensed novel (done in series), humorous, mainstream, slice-of-life vignettes. No sad stories. Buys 10 mss/year. Query with complete ms. Length: 600-1,500 words. Pays $30-125.
Tips: "Previous published articles not required. We are looking for writers who write in an entertaining style, with some personality and humor where applicable. Dry, strictly factual articles will have least priority. Articles must be clean and well-edited and submissions on disks are especially welcome. Articles should be accompanied by a photo—black and white or color, as much as possible. We are looking for general interest articles, whether fiction or non-fiction, from all areas—even foreign countries."

ANIMALS, Massachusetts Society for the Prevention of Cruelty to Animals, 350 S. Huntington Ave., Boston MA 02130. (617)522-7400. Editor: Joni Praded. Managing Editor: Paula Abend. 90% freelance written. Bimonthly magazine covering animals. "*Animals* publishes articles on wildlife (American and international), domestic animals, balanced treatments of controversies involving animals, conservation, animal welfare issues, pet health and pet care." Circ. 50,000. Pays on publication. Publishes ms an average of 5 months after acceptance. Byline given. Offers negotiable kill fee. Buys one-time rights or makes work-for-hire assignments. Submit seasonal/holiday material 6 months in advance. Photocopied submissions OK. Computer printout submissions OK; prefers letter-quality. Reports in 6 weeks. Sample copy $2.50 with 9x12 SAE and 5 first class stamps. Writer's guidelines for #10 SAE and 1 first class stamp.
Nonfiction: Essays, expose, general interest, how-to, opinion and photo feature. "*Animals* does not publish breed-specific domestic pet articles or 'favorite pet' stories. Poetry and fiction is also not used." Buys 6 mss/year. Query with published clips. Length: 3,000 words maximum. Pays $300 maximum. Sometimes pays the expenses of writers on assignment.
Photos: State availability of photos with submission. Reviews contact sheets, 35mm transparencies and 5x7 or 8x10 prints. Offers $60 per photo. Captions, model releases and identification of subjects required. Buys one-time rights.
Columns/Departments: Books (book reviews of books on animals and animal-related subjects), 300 words. Buys 18 mss/year. Query with published clips. Length: 300 words maximum. Pays $75 maximum.

Tips: "Present a well-researched proposal. Be sure to include clips that demonstrate the quality of your writing. Stick to categories mentioned in *Animals*' editorial description. Combine well-researched facts with a lively, informative writing style. Feature stories are written almost exclusively by freelancers. We continue to seek proposals and articles that take a humane approach. Articles should concentrate on how issues affect animals, rather than humans."

ARABIAN HORSE TIMES, Adams Corp., Rt. 3, Waseca MN 56093. (507)835-3204. Editor: Marian Studer. Managing Editor: Ronda Morehead. 20% freelance written. Works with a small number of new/unpublished writers each year. Monthly magazine about Arabian horses. Editorial format includes hard news (veterinary, new products, book reports, etc.), lifestyle and personality pieces, and bloodline studies. Circ. 19,000. Pays on publication. Publishes ms an average of 6 months after acceptance. Byline given. Offers 33% kill fee. Buys first serial rights. Submit seasonal/holiday material 3 months in advance. Simultaneous queries OK. Computer printout submissions acceptable; prefers letter-quality. Sample copy and writer's guidelines for 9x12 SAE and $2.50.

Nonfiction: General interest, how-to, interview/profile, new product and photo feature. Buys at least 12 mss/year. Query with published clips. Length: 1,000-5,000 words. Pays $50-350. Sometimes pays expenses of writers on assignment.

Photos: Prefers 5x7 color prints. Payment depends on circumstances. Captions and identification of subjects required. Buys one-time rights.

Fiction: Will look at anything about Arabians except erotica. Buys 1-2 mss/year. Send complete ms. Length: 1,500-5,000 words. Pays $75-250.

Poetry: Horse-related poetry only. Buys 1-2 poems/year. Submit maximum of 1 poem. Pays $25.

Tips: "As our periodical is specific to Arabian horses, we are interested in anyone who can write well and tightly about them. Send us something timely. Also, narrow your topic to a specific horse, incident, person or problem. 'Why I Love Arabians' will not work."

BIRD TALK, Dedicated to Better Care for Pet Birds, Fancy Publications, Box 6050, Mission Viejo CA 92690. (714)855-8822. Editor: Karyn New. 85% freelance written. Works with a small number of new/unpublished writers each year. Monthly magazine covering the care and training of cage birds for men and women who own any number of pet or exotic birds. Circ. 100,000. Pays latter part of month in which article appears. Publishes ms an average of 4 months after acceptance. Byline given. Buys first North American serial rights. Submit seasonal/holiday material 5 months in advance. Photocopied and previously published submissions OK. Computer printout submissions acceptable; prefers letter-quality. Reports in 3 weeks on queries; 2 months on mss. Sample copy $3.25; writer's guidelines for #10 SAE and 1 first class stamp.

Nonfiction: General interest (anything to do with pet birds); historical/nostalgic (of bird breeds, owners, cages); how-to (build cages, aviaries, playpens and groom, feed, breed, tame); humor; interview/profile (of bird and bird owners); new product; how-to (live with birds—compatible pets, lifestyle, apartment adaptability, etc.); personal experience (with your own bird); photo feature (humorous or informative); travel (with pet birds or to see exotic birds); and articles giving medical information, legal information, and description of breeds. No juvenile or material on wild birds not pertinent to pet care; everything should relate to *pet* birds. Buys 150 mss/year. Query or send complete ms. Length: 500-3,000 words. Pays 5-7¢/word.

Photos: State availability of photos. Reviews b&w contact sheets; prefers prints. Pays $50-150 for color transparencies; $15 minimum for 8x10 b&w prints. Model release and identification of subjects required. Buys one-time rights.

Columns/Departments: Editorial (opinion on a phase of owning pet birds) and Small Talk (short news item of general interest to bird owners). Buys 20 mss/year. Send complete ms. Length: 300-1,200 words. Pays 3¢/word and up.

Fiction: "Only fiction with pet birds as primary focus of interest." Adventure, fantasy, historical, humorous, mystery, suspense. No juvenile, and no birds talking unless it's their trained vocabulary. Buys 1 ms/year. Send complete ms. Length: 2,000-3,000 words. Pays 3¢/word and up.

Tips: "Send grammatical, clean copy on a human-interest story about a pet bird or about a medical or health-related topic. We also need how-tos on feather crafts; cage cover making; aviary, perch and cage building; and planting plants in aviaries safe and good for birds. Keep health, nutrition, lack of stress in mind regarding pet birds. Study back issues to learn our style."

CAT FANCY, Fancy Publications, Inc., Box 6050, Mission Viejo CA 92690. (714)855-8822. Editor: Linda W. Lewis. 80-90% freelance written. Monthly magazine for men and women of all ages interested in all phases of cat ownership. 80 pages. Circ. 200,000. Pays after publication. Publishes ms an average of 6 months after acceptance. Buys first North American serial rights. Byline given. Submit seasonal/holiday material 4 months in advance. Computer printout submissions acceptable. Reports in 6 weeks. Sample copy $3; writer's guidelines for SASE.

Nonfiction: Historical, medical, how-to, humor, informational, personal experience, photo feature and technical. Buys 5 mss/issue. Query or send complete ms. Length: 500-3,000 words. Pays 5¢/word; special rates for photo/story packages.

Photos: Photos purchased with or without accompanying ms. Pays $15 minimum for 8x10 b&w glossy prints; $50-150 for 35mm or 2¼x2¼ color transparencies. Send prints and transparencies. Model release required.
Fiction: Adventure, fantasy, historical and humorous. Nothing written with cats speaking. Buys 1 ms/issue. Send complete ms. Length: 500-3,000 words. Pays 5¢/word.
Fillers: Newsworthy or unusual; items with photo and cartoons. Buys 10 fillers/year. Length: 100-500 words. Pays $20-35.
Tips: "We receive more filler-type articles than we can use. It's the well-researched, hard information article we need."

CATS MAGAZINE, Cats Magazine Inc., Box 290037, Port Orange FL 32029. (904)788-2770. Editor: Linda J. Walton. 50% freelance written. A monthly magazine for cat lovers, veterinarians, breeders and show enthusiasts. Circ. 140,000. Pays on publication. Byline given. Buys one-time rights. Submit seasonal/holiday material 7 months in advance. Reports in 1 month on queries; 3 months on manuscripts (sometimes longer depending on the backlog.) Free sample copy and writer's guidelines.
Nonfiction: Book excerpts; general interest (concerning cats); how-to (care for cats); humor; interview/profile (on cat owning personalities); new product; personal experience; photo feature; and technical (veterinarian writers). No talking cats. Buys 36 mss/year. Send complete ms. Length 800-2,500 words. Pays $25-300.
Photos: Send photos with submission. Reviews transparencies. Offers $5-25/photo. Identification of subjects required. Buys one-time rights.
Fiction: Fantasy, historical, mystery, science fiction, slice-of-life vignettes and suspense. "We rarely use fiction, but are not averse to using it if the cat theme is handled in smooth, believable manner. All fiction must involve a cat or relationship of cat and humans, etc." No talking cats. Buys 4-6 mss/year. Send complete ms. Length: 800-2,500 words. Pays $25-300.
Poetry: Avant-garde, free verse, haiku, light verse and traditional. Length: 4-64 lines. Pays 50¢/line.
Tips: "Fiction and articles are the freelancer's best bet. Writers must at least like cats. Writers who obviously don't, miss the mark."

THE CHRONICLE OF THE HORSE, Box 46, Middleburg VA 22117. (703)687-6341. Editor: John Strassburger. Managing Editor: Nancy Comer. 80% freelance written. Weekly magazine about horses. "We cover English riding sports, including horse showing, grand prix jumping competitions, steeplechase racing, foxhunting, dressage, endurance riding, handicapped riding and combined training. We are the official publication for the national governing bodies of many of the above sports. We feature news of the above sports, and we also publish how-to articles on equitation and horse care, and interviews with leaders in the various fields." Circ. 22,000. Pays for features on acceptance; news and other items on publication. Publishes ms an average of 3 months after acceptance. Byline given. Buys first North American rights and makes work-for-hire assignments. Submit seasonal/holiday material 3 months in advance. Computer printout submissions acceptable only if double-spaced, 8½x11 format; prefers letter-quality. Simultaneous queries and photocopied submissions OK. Reports in 2-3 weeks. Sample copy for 9x12 SAE and $2; writer's guidelines for #10 SAE.
Nonfiction: General interest; historical/nostalgic (history of breeds, use of horses in other countries and times, art, etc.); how-to (trailer, train, design a course, save money, etc.); humor (centered on living with horses or horse people); interview/profile (of nationally known horsemen or the very unusual); technical (horse care, articles on feeding, injuries, care of foals, shoeing, etc.); and news (of major competitions, clear assignment with us first). Special issues include Steeplechasing; Grand Prix Jumping; Combined Training; Dressage; Hunt Roster; Junior and Pony; and Christmas. No Q&A interviews, clinic reports, Western riding articles, personal experience, or wild horses. Buys 300 mss/year. Query or send complete ms. Length: 300-1,225 words. Pays $25-200.
Photos: State availability of photos. Reviews 5x7 b&w prints. Color may be considered for b&w reproduction. Pays $10-25. Identification of subjects required. Buys one-time rights.
Columns/Departments: Dressage, Combined Training, Horse Show, Horse Care, Polo, Racing, Racing over Fences, Young Entry (about young riders, geared for youth), Horses and Humanities, and Hunting. Query or send complete ms. Length: 300-1,225 words. Pays $25-200.
Poetry: Light verse and traditional. No free verse. Buys 100 mss/year. Length: 5-30 lines. Pays $15.
Fillers: Anecdotes, short humor, newsbreaks and cartoons. Buys 250 mss/year. Length: 50-175 lines. Pays $10-25.
Tips: "Get our guidelines. Our readers are sophisticated, competitive horsemen. Articles need to go beyond common knowledge. Freelancers often attempt too broad or too basic a subject. We welcome well-written news stories on major events, but clear the assignment with us."

DOG FANCY, Fancy Publications, Inc., Box 6050, Mission Viejo CA 92690. (714)855-8822. Editor: Linda Lewis. 75% freelance written. Eager to work with unpublished writers. "We'd like to see a balance of both new and established writers." Monthly magazine for men and women of all ages interested in all phases of dog ownership. Circ. 150,000. Pays after publication. Publishes ms an average of 6 months after acceptance. Buys first American serial rights. Byline given. Submit seasonal/holiday material 4 months in advance. Computer printout submissions acceptable; prefers letter-quality. Sample copy $3; writer's guidelines for SASE.

Nonfiction: Historical, medical, how-to, humor, informational, interview, personal experience, photo feature, profile and technical. "We're planning one or two *major* features covering significant events in the dog world. We'll be looking for (and paying more for) high quality writing/photo packages on topics outside of our normal range of features. Interested writers should query with topics." Buys 5 mss/issue. Query or send complete ms. Length: 500-3,000 words. Pays 5¢/word.

Photos: Photos purchased with or without accompanying ms. Pays $15 minimum for 8x10 b&w glossy prints; $50-150 for 35mm or 2¼x2¼ color transparencies. Send prints and transparencies. Model release required.

Fiction: Adventure, fantasy, historical and humorous. Buys 5 mss/year. Send complete ms. Length: 500-3,000 words. Pays 5¢/word.

Fillers: "Need short, punchy photo fillers and cartoons." Buys 10 fillers/year. Pays $20-35.

Tips: "We're looking for the unique experience that communicates something about the dog/owner relationship—with the dog as the focus of the story, not the owner. Articles that provide hard information (medical, etc.) through a personal experience are appreciated. Note that we write for a lay audience (non-technical), but we do assume a certain level of intelligence: no talking down to people. If you've never seen the type of article you're writing in *Dog Fancy*, don't expect to."

THE GREYHOUND REVIEW, Box 543, Abilene KS 67410. (913)263-4660. Editor: Gary Guccione. Managing Editor: Tim Horan. 20% freelance written. A monthly magazine covering greyhound breeding, training and racing. Circ. 7,000. Pays on acceptance. Byline given. Buys first rights. Submit seasonal/holiday material 2 months in advance. Query for electronic submissions. Computer printout submissions acceptable. Reports in 2 weeks on queries; 1 month on mss. Sample copy $2.50. Free writer's guidelines.

Nonfiction: How-to, interview/profile and personal experience. "Articles must be targeted at the greyhound industry: from hard news, special events at racetracks to the latest medical discoveries." Do not submit gambling systems. Buys 24 mss/year. Query. Length: 1,000-10,000 words. Pays $85-150. Sometimes pays expenses of writers on assignment.

Photos: State availability of photos with submission. Reviews 35mm transparencies and 8x10 prints. Offers $10-50 per photo. Identification of subjects required. Buys one-time rights.

HORSE ILLUSTRATED, The Magazine for Responsible Horse Owners, Fancy Publications, Inc., Box 6050, Mission Viejo CA 92690. (714)855-8822. Editor: Jill-Marie Jones. 90% freelance written. Prefers to work with published/established writers but eager to work with new/unpublished writers. Monthly magazine covering all aspects of horse ownership. "Our readers are adult women between the ages of 18 and 40; stories should be geared to that age group and reflect responsible horse care." Circ. 80,000. Pays on publication. Publishes ms an average of 8 months after acceptance. Byline given. Buys one-time rights. Submit seasonal/holiday material 6 months in advance. Computer printout submissions acceptable; prefers letter-quality. Reports in 6 weeks on queries; 2 months on mss. Sample copy $3. Writer's guidelines for #10 SASE.

Nonfiction: How-to (horse care, training, veterinary care), humor, personal experience and photo feature. No "little girl" horse stories; "cowboy and Indian" stories; anything not *directly* relating to horses. "We are beginning to look for longer, more in-depth features on trends and issues in the horse industry. (See our three-part series on equestrian colleges, May to July, 1987 or the three-part series on feed supplements, September to November, 1988.) Such articles must be queried first with a detailed outline of the article and clips." Buys 100 mss/year. Query or send complete ms. Length: 1,000-2,500 words. Pays $100-250 for assigned articles. Pays $50-200 for unsolicited articles. Sometimes pays telephone bills for writers on assignment.

Photos: Send photos with submission. Reviews contact sheet, 35mm transparencies and 5x7 prints. Occasionally offers additional payment for photos accepted with ms.

Tips: "Freelancers can break in at this publication with feature articles on Western and English training methods and trainer profiles (including training tips); veterinary and general care how-to articles; and horse sports articles. While we use personal experience articles (six to eight times a year), they must be extremely well-written and have wide appeal; humor in such stories is a bonus. Submit photos with training and how-to articles whenever possible. We have a very good record of developing new freelancers into regular contributors/columnists. We are always looking for fresh talent, but certainly enjoy working with established writers who 'know the ropes' as well."

HORSE WORLD USA, (formerly Eastern Horse World), Garri Publications, Inc., 114 West Hills Rd., Box 249, Huntington Station NY 11746. (516)549-3557. Editor: Diana DeRosa. 25% freelance written. A magazine, published 18 times per year, on horses. Circ. 16,500. Pays on publication. Byline given. Buys first North American serial rights. Submit seasonal/holiday material 6 months in advance. Query for electronic submissions. Computer printout submissions OK; no dot-matrix. Reports in 3 months on queries. Sample copy for SAE, $2 and 6 first class stamps. Writer's guidelines for #10 SAE with 1 first class stamp.

Nonfiction: "Anything horse-related (see topics listed in columns/departments section below)." Buys 25 mss/year. Query with published clips. Length: 100-2,000 words. Pays $5-125 or offers complimentary ad in directory as payment.

Photos: State availability of photos with submission or send photos with submission. Reviews 5x7 prints. Offers $5-10 per photo. Captions, model releases and identification of subjects required. Buys one-time rights. "No name on front of photo; give credit line."

Columns/Departments: Horse Show News, Driving, Dressage, Polo, Racing, Side-Saddle, Eventing, Breeding, Gift Mart, Grand Prix, Western, Youth, Saratoga in August. Query with published clips. Length: 500-1,000 words. Pays $75 maximum.

Fillers: Anecdotes, facts, gags to be illustrated by cartoonist, and short humor. Buys 18/year. Length: 25 words minimum. Pays $5 maximum.

Tips: "We are an information center for horse people. Write for guidelines. We like to work with writers and artists who are new and are not necessarily looking for money but rather a chance to be published. When writing please specify whether payment is required."

‡**HORSEMAN MAGAZINE**, Horseman Publishing Corp., Suite 390, 25025 I-45 N., Spring TX 77380. (713)367-5151. Editor: David T. Gaines. 60% freelance written. Monthly magazine covering the western performance horse industry. "Articles should convey quality information on western horses and horsemanship within the warmth of journalistic prose. Text book 'how-to' we do not want." Circ. 140,000. Pays on acceptance. Publishes ms an average of 9 months after acceptance. Byline given. Pays $50 kill fee. Buys first North American serial rights. Photocopied submissions OK. Comptuer printout submissions OK; prefers letter quality. Reports in 2 weeks. Free sample copy and writer's guidelines.

Nonfiction: Essays, general interest, historical/nostalgic, how-to, humor, interview/profile, personal experience, photo feature, technical. No horse health articles. Buys 100 articles/year. Query or send complete ms. Length: 1,000-2,500 words. Pays $100-350. Sometimes pays expenses of writers on assignment.

Photos: Send photos with submission. Reviews transparencies (35mm) and prints (5x7). Offers $20-200/ photo. Captions required. Buys one-time rights.

Columns/Departments: "Columns are done by freelance contributors but they are assigned over a long period and are not open to other freelance writers." Buys 24-36 mss/year. Send complete ms. Length: 650-800 words. Pays $100-350.

Tips: "The easiest articles to sell are those that are outside our regular beat. Especially dear to us are personal experience articles in which the writer describes how a horseman solved a specific horsemanship problem. The key is variety. Photos, humor, nostalgia, something short and strong that adds spice to the magazine."

‡**HORSEMEN'S YANKEE PEDLAR NEWSPAPER**, 785 Southbridge St., Auburn MA 01501. (617)832-9638. Publisher: Nancy L. Khoury. Editor: Tracy Thomson. 40% freelance written. "All-breed monthly newspaper for horse enthusiasts of all ages and incomes, from one-horse owners to large commercial stables. Covers region from New Jersey to Maine." Circ. 12,000. Pays on publication. Buys all rights for one year. Submit seasonal/holiday material 3 months in advance of issue date. Query for electronic submissions. Computer printout submissions acceptable; prefers letter-quality. Publishes ms an average of 5 months after acceptance. Reports in 1 month. Sample copy $3.75.

Nonfiction: Humor, educational and interview about horses and the people involved with them. Pays $2/ published inch. Buys 100 mss/year. Query or submit complete ms or outline. Length: 1,500 words maximum.

Photos: Purchased with ms. Captions and photo credit required. Submit b&w prints. Pays $5.

Columns/Departments: Area news column. Buys 85-95/year. Length: 1,200-1,400 words. Query.

Tips: "Query with outline of angle of story, approximate length and date when story will be submitted. Stories should be people oriented and horse focused. Send newsworthy, timely pieces, such as stories that are applicable to the season, for example: foaling in the spring or how to keep a horse healthy through the winter. We like to see how-tos, features about special horse people and anything that has to do with the preservation of horses and their rights as creatures deserving a chance to survive."

HORSEPLAY, Box 130, Gaithersburg MD 20877. (301)840-1866. Editor: Cordelia Doucet. 50% freelance written. Works with published/established writers and a small number of new/unpublished writers each year. Monthly magazine covering horses and English horse sports for a readership interested in horses, show jumping, dressage, combined training, hunting, and driving. 60-80 pages. Circ. 48,000. Pays end of publication month. Buys all rights, first North American serial rights, and second serial (reprint) rights. Offers kill fee. Byline given. Query first. Deadline is 2 months prior to issue date. Nothing returned without SASE. Computer printout submissions acceptable; no dot-matrix. Reports within 3 weeks. Sample copy $2.95; writer's and photographer's guidelines for #10 SASE.

Nonfiction: Instruction (various aspects of horsemanship, course designing, stable management, putting on

✚ ***The double dagger before a listing indicates that the listing is new in this edition. New markets are often the most receptive to freelance submissions.***

horse shows, etc.); competitions; interview; photo feature; profile and technical. Length: 1,000-3,000 words. Pays 10¢/word, all rights; 9¢/word, first North American serial rights; 7¢/word, second rights. Sometimes pays extra to writers on assignment.

Photos: Cathy Kuehner, art director. Purchased on assignment. Write captions on separate paper attached to photo. Query or send contact sheet, prints or transparencies. Pays $22.50 for 8x10 b&w glossy prints; $200 for color transparencies for cover; $45 for inside color.

Tips: Don't send fiction, Western riding, or racing articles.

HORSES ALL, Box 9, Hill Spring Alberta T0K 1E0 Canada. (403)626-3344. Editor: Jacki French. 30% freelance written. Eager to work with new/unpublished writers. Monthly tabloid for horse owners, 75% rural, 25% urban. Circ. 11,200. Pays on publication. Publishes ms an average of 6 months after acceptance. Buys one-time rights. Phone queries OK. Submit seasonal material 3 months in advance. Simultaneous, photo-copied (if clear), and previously published submissions OK. Computer printout submissions acceptable; no dot-matrix. Reports on queries in 5 weeks; on mss in 6 weeks. Sample copy for 9x12 SAE and $2.

Nonfiction: Interview, humor and personal experience. Query. Pays $20-100. Sometimes pays the expenses of writers on assignment.

Photos: State availability of photos. Captions required.

Columns/Departments: Open to suggestions for new columns/departments. Send query to Doug French. Length: 1-2 columns.

Fiction: Historical and western. Query. Pays $20-100.

Tips: "We use more short articles. The most frequent mistakes made by writers in completing an article assignment for us are poor research, wrong terminology, and poor (terrible) writing style."

LONE STAR HORSE REPORT, Box 14767, Fort Worth TX 76117. (817)834-3951. Editor: Henry L. King. 15-20% freelance written. Monthly magazine on horses and horse people in and around Dallas/Ft. Worth metroplex. Circ. 7,500. Pays on publication. Publishes ms an average of 2 months after acceptance. Byline given. Buys first rights and second serial (reprint) rights to material originally published elsewhere. Submit seasonal/holiday material 2 months in advance. Photocopied and previously published submissions OK. Computer printout submissions OK; prefers letter quality. Reports in 2 weeks on queries; 4 weeks on mss. Sample copy $1; writer's guidelines for #10 SASE.

Nonfiction: How-to (how a specific horseman trains horses for specific events); interview/profile (horsemen living in trade area); photo feature (horses, farms, arenas, facilities, people in trade area). Buys 30-40 mss/year. Query with published clips or send complete ms. Length: 200-2,000 words. Pays $15-60. Sometimes pays the expenses of writers on assignment.

Photos: State availability of photos. Pays $5 for 5x7 b&w prints. Buys one-time rights.

Tips: "We need reports of specific horse-related events in north Texas area such as trail rides, rodeos, play days, shows, etc., and also feature articles on horse farms, outstanding horses and/or horsemen. Since Texas now has pari-mutuel horse racing, more emphasis will be placed on coverage of racing and racehorse breeding. We will be reporting on the actions of the newly-appointed racing commission, locations of tracks, construction and ownership of those tracks, and the economic impact of the racing industry as new breeding farms and training facilities are established."

‡MUSHING, Stellar Communications, Inc., Box 149 Ester, Ester AK 99725. (907)479-0454. Editor: Todd Hoener. Managing Editor: Richard Eathrone. Bimonthly magazine. "We cover all aspects of dog sledding with emphasis on people usage. We include information (how-to), nonfiction (entertaining), news and history stories." Estab. 1987. Circ. 5,000. Pays on publication. Publishes ms an average of 4 months after acceptance. Byline given. Buys first North American serial rights or second serial (reprint) rights. Submit seasonal/holiday material 4 months in advance. Query for electronic submissions. Computer printout submissions OK; prefers letter quality. Reports in 3 weeks. Sample copy $3.50; free writer's guidelines.

Nonfiction: Book excerpts, general interest, historical, how-to, humor, interview/profile, new product, personal experience, photo feature, technical, travel. Themes are: December/January—Christmas, beginning race season, winter trips; February/March—travel, main race season, recreation and work season; April/May—breakup, gearing down; June/July—summer dog keep, tourists go North; August/September—Get ready for gear up; October/November—winter schedules, gear up. Query with or without published clips, or send complete ms. Length: 500-3,000 words. Pays $50-250 for assigned articles; $25-175 for unsolicited articles. Sometimes pays expenses of writers on assignment.

Photos: Send photos with submission. Reviews contact sheets, transparencies, prints. Offers $10-150/photo. Captions, model releases, identification of subjects required. Buys one-time rights.

Fillers: Anecdotes, facts, gags to be illustrated by cartoonist, newsbreaks, short humor. Length: 100-250 words. Pays $25.

NATIONAL SHOW HORSE, National Show Horse Registry, Suite 237, 10401 Linn Station Rd., Louisville KY 40223. (502)423-1902. Editor: Mary Kirkman. 10-20% freelance written. Prefers to work with published/

established writers, but works with a small number of new/unpublished writers each year. A magazine covering "all aspects of the horse industry as it applies to National Show Horse." Circ. 5,000. Pays on acceptance. Byline given. Buys one-time rights. Computer printout submissions acceptable; prefers letter-quality. Reports within 2 weeks. Sample copy and writer's guidelines for 10x13 SAE and $1.75.

Nonfiction: How-to (training the English style show horse); interview/profile (of successful breeders/exhibitors or persons involved in the field—artists, photographers, etc.); and photo feature (must tie directly to some aspect of National Show Horse World). "We also need in-depth features of well-known National Show Horses and NSH-nominated Arabian and Saddlebred stallions or mares being used in NSH breeding programs, including analysis of pedigrees and show records, and historical retrospectives of great horses in Arabian and Saddlebred breeds, including their influence on the National Show Horse breed." Query. Length: 3,000-5,000 words. Pays $100-250. Sometimes pays the expenses of writers on assignment.

Photos: State availability of photos with query letter or ms. Reviews transparencies and prints. Pays $10. Captions and identification of subjects required. Buys one-time rights.

PACIFIC COAST JOURNAL, Pacific Coast Quarter Horse Association, Gate 12, Cal-Expo, Box 254822, Sacramento CA 95865. (916)924-7265. Editor: Jill L. Scopinich. 20% freelance written. A monthly magazine covering Cutting and Quarter Horses on the Pacific Coast published by and for members of two equine groups which concentrate on Cutting and Quarter Horses. "It is more technical than most equine publications and our readers are extremely knowledgeable on the subject." Circ. 8,000. Pays on acceptance. Byline given. Offers 50% kill fee. Buys first rights and second serial (reprint) rights. Simultaneous, photocopied and previously published submissions OK. Computer printout submissions acceptable; no dot-matrix. Reports in 3 months. Sample copy for 9x12 SAE with $1.50 postage. Writer's guidelines for #10 SAE with 1 first class stamp.

Nonfiction: How to train Quarter or Cutting Horses, make or care for tack, trailers, etc. No articles that are aimed at newcomers to the horse industry, or that are about other breeds. Buys 36 mss/year. Send complete ms. Length: 750-3,000 words. Pays $100-300 for assigned articles; $50-175 for unsolicited articles; will trade advertising if writer requests. Sometimes pays expenses of writers on assignment.

Photos: Send photos with submission. Reviews contact sheets, transparencies, and 5x7 prints. Offers no additional payment for photos accepted with ms unless negotiated in advance. Captions, model releases, and identification of subjects required. Buys one-time rights.

Columns/Departments: Bookshelf (reviews of books written by professionals concerning the Quarter or Cutting Horse industries). Buys 12 mss/year. Send complete ms. Length: 300-500 words. Pays $35-50.

Fillers: Anecdotes, facts and short humor. Buys 24/year. Length: 50-100 words. Pays $20-40.

Tips: "Send examples of your work that have been published in other equine magazines, or send a cover letter explaining your expertise in the field you are writing about. It is important to our readers that our writers are knowledgeable in the fields of Cutting and Quarter horses. At all times remember that our readers are well-educated in the industry and the majority are professionals, so never speak down to them."

PAINT HORSE JOURNAL, American Paint Horse Association, Box 18519, Fort Worth TX 76118. (817)439-3400. Editor: Bill Shepard. 10% freelance written. Works with a small number of new/unpublished writers each year. For people who raise, breed and show Paint horses. Monthly magazine. Circ. 12,000. Pays on acceptance. Publishes ms an average of 3 months after acceptance. Buys first North American serial rights plus reprint rights occasionally. Pays negotiable kill fee. Byline given. Phone queries OK, but prefers written query. Submit seasonal/holiday material 3 months in advance. Photocopied and previously published submissions OK. Computer printout submissions acceptable; prefers letter-quality. Reports in 1 month. Sample copy for 4 first class stamps; writer's guidelines for SAE and 1 first class stamp.

Nonfiction: General interest (personality pieces on well-known owners of Paints); historical (Paint horses in the past—particular horses and the breed in general); how-to (train and show horses); photo feature (Paint horses); and articles on horse health. Buys 4-5 mss/issue. Send complete ms. Pays $50-250.

Photos: Send photos with ms. Offers no additional payment for photos accepted with accompanying ms. Uses 3x5 or larger b&w glossy prints; 35mm or larger color transparencies. Captions required.

Tips: "*PHJ* needs breeder-trainer articles, Paint horse marketing and timely articles from areas throughout the U.S. and Canada. We are looking for more horse health articles and how-to articles. Photos with copy are almost always essential. Well-written first person articles are welcomed. Submit well-written items that show a definite understanding of the horse business. Use proper equine terminology and proper grounding in ability to communicate thoughts."

‡PURE-BRED DOGS AMERICAN KENNEL GAZETTE, American Kennel Club, 51 Madison Ave., New York NY 10010. (212)696-8331. Executive Editor: Marion Lane. 80% freelance written. Monthly association publication on pure-bred dogs. "Material is slanted to interests of fanciers of pure-bred dogs as opposed to commercial interests." Circ. 58,000. Pays on publication. Publishes ms an average of 6 months after acceptance. Byline given. Offers 30% kill fee. Buys first North American serial rights. Submit seasonal/holiday material 6 months in advance. Photocopied submissions OK. Computer submissions OK; no dot-matrix. Reports in 3 weeks. Sample copy and writer's guidelines for 9x12 SAE and 11 first class stamps.

Nonfiction: General interest, historical/nostalgic, how-to, humor, photo feature, travel. No personal experience or fiction. Buys about 70 mss/year. Query with or without published clips, or send complete ms. Length: 1,000-2,500 words. Pays $100-300. Sometimes pays expenses of writers on assignment.

Photos: Send photos with submission. Reviews tranparencies and prints. Offers $25-$100/photo. Captions required. Buys one-time rights.

Tips: "Contributors should be involved in dog fancy or be expert in the area they write in (veterinarian, training, dogs in legislation, dog art or history or literature). All submissions are welcome and are read but the author must be credible. Veterinary articles must be written by or with veterinarians. Humorous features are personal experiences relative to pure-bred dogs. For features generally, know the subject thoroughly and be conversant with jargon peculiar to dog sport."

PURRRRR! THE NEWSLETTER FOR CAT LOVERS, The Meow Company, HCR 227 Rd., Islesboro ME 04848. (207)734-6745. Publisher/Editor Agatha Cabaniss. 85% freelance written. Works with a small number of new/unpublished writers each year. A bimonthly newsletter for the average cat owner. "The publication is designed to amuse while providing cat lovers with information about the care, feeding and enjoyment of house cats." Circ. 1,000. Pays on acceptance. Publishes ms an average of 4-5 months after acceptance. Byline given. Buys first serial rights and second serial (reprint) rights. Submit seasonal/holiday material 6 months in advance. Photocopied and previously published submissions OK unless it's been published in a competing publication, such as *Cats* and *Cat Fancy*. Query for electronic submissions. Computer printout submissions acceptable; prefers letter-quality. Reports in 2 weeks. Sample copy $2; writer's guidelines for #10 SAE and 1 first class stamp.

Nonfiction: General interest; historical; how-to; literary cat lovers (have featured Colette, Mark Twain and May Sarton); humor; interview/profile; new product; travel, off-beat unusual. "We want a humorous slant wherever possible; writing should be tight and professional. Avoid the first person." Special Christmas issue. No shaggy cat stories, sentimental stories, "I taught Fluffy to roll over" or no "reformed cat hater" stories. "We would like to receive articles on humane societies and animal rescue leagues." Absolutely no fiction. Buys 50/mss year. Query with published clips, or send complete ms. Length: 250-1,500 words. Pays: $15-100.

Photos: Avoid "cute" photos. State availability of photos. Pays $5-10 for 5x8 b&w prints. Buys one-time rights.

Poetry: Accepts some poetry.

Fillers: Clippings, anecdotes, short humor/cartoons and newsbreaks. Buys 20/year. Length: 25-75 words. Pays $5.

Tips: "You should know pet cats, their foibles and personalities. We are interested in good writing but also in a good story about a cat. We are interested in people who work with and for animal welfare and how-to articles on making things for cats or for people who live with cats, i.e. how to 'cat proof' a crib. We will work with a writer who has an interesting cat story. We are not interested in show cats or breeding. Query or send article and a SASE for reply."

THE QUARTER HORSE JOURNAL, Box 32470, Amarillo TX 79120. (806)376-4811. Editor-in-Chief: Audie Rackley. 5% freelance written. Prefers to work with published/established writers. Official publication of the American Quarter Horse Association. Monthly magazine. Circ. 70,000. Pays on acceptance. Publishes ms an average of 3 months after acceptance. Buys first North American serial rights. Submit seasonal/holiday material 2 months in advance. Computer printout submissions acceptable; no dot-matrix. Reports in 2 weeks. Free sample copy and writer's guidelines.

Nonfiction: Historical ("those that retain our western heritage"); how-to (fitting, grooming, showing, or anything that relates to owning, showing, or breeding); informational (educational clinics, current news); interview (feature-type stories—must be about established horses or people who have made a contribution to the business); personal opinion; and technical (equine updates, new surgery procedures, etc.). Buys 20 mss/year. Length: 800-2,500 words. Pays $50-250.

Photos: Purchased with accompanying ms. Captions required. Send prints or transparencies. Uses 5x7 or 8x10 b&w glossy prints; 2¼x2¼ or 4x5 color transparencies. Offers no additional payment for photos accepted with accompanying ms.

Tips: "Writers must have a knowledge of the horse business. We will be purchasing more material on quarter horse racing."

TROPICAL FISH HOBBYIST, "The World's Most Widely Read Aquarium Monthly," TFH Publications, Inc., 211 W. Sylvania Ave., Neptune City NJ 07753. (201)988-8400. Editor: Ray Hunziker. Managing Editor: Neal Pronek. 75% freelance written. Monthly magazine covering the tropical fish hobby. "We favor articles well illustrated with good color slides and aimed at both the neophyte and veteran tropical fish hobbyist." Circ. 60,000. Pays on acceptance. Publishes ms an average of 4 months after acceptance. Byline given. Buys all rights. Submit seasonal/holiday material 4 months in advance. Photocopied submissions OK. Computer printout submissions acceptable; no dot-matrix. Reports in 2 weeks. Sample copy $2.50; free writer's guidelines.

Nonfiction: General interest, how-to, photo feature, technical, and articles dealing with beginning and advanced aspects of the aquarium hobby. No "how I got started in the hobby" articles that impart little solid information. Buys 20-30 mss/year. Length: 500-2,500 words. Pays $25-100.
Photos: State availability of photos or send photos with ms. Pays $10 for 35mm color transparencies. Identification of subjects required. "Originals of photos returned to owner, who may market them elsewhere."
Fiction: "On occasion, we will review a fiction piece relevant to the aquarium hobby."
Tips: "We cater to a specialized readership—people knowledgeable in fish culture. Prospective authors should be familiar with subject; photography skills are a plus. It's a help if an author we've never dealt with queries first or submits a short item."

THE WESTERN HORSEMAN, Box 7980, Colorado Springs CO 80933. Editor: Randy Witte. 40% freelance written. Works with a small number of new/unpublished writers each year. Monthly magazine covering western horsemanship. Circ. 162,369. Pays on acceptance. Publishes ms an average of 5 months after acceptance. Buys first rights. Byline given. Computer printout submissions acceptable; prefers letter-quality. Submit seasonal/holiday material 3 months in advance. Reports in 3 weeks. Sample copy $1.95.
Nonfiction: How-to (horse training, care of horses, tips, etc.); and informational (on rodeos, ranch life, historical articles of the West emphasizing horses). Length: 1,500 words. Payment begins at $125; "sometimes higher by special arrangement."
Photos: Send photos with ms. Offers no additional payment for photos. Uses 5x7 or 8x10 b&w glossy prints and 35mm transparencies. Captions required.
Tips: "Submit clean copy with professional quality photos. Stay away from generalities. Writing style should show a deep interest in horses coupled with a wide knowledge of the subject."

Art and Architecture

Listed here are publications about art, art history, specific art forms and architecture written for art patrons, architects and artists. Publications addressing the business and management side of the art industry are listed in the Art, Design and Collectibles category of the Trade section. Trade publications for architecture can be found in various categories: Brick, Glass and Ceramics; Building Interiors; Construction and Contracting; and Plumbing, Heating, Air Conditioning and Refrigeration.

AMERICAN INDIAN ART MAGAZINE, American Indian Art, Inc., 7314 E. Osborn Dr., Scottsdale AZ 85251. (602)994-5445. Managing Editor: Roanne P. Goldfein. 97% freelance written. Works with a small number of new/unpublished writers each year. Quarterly magazine covering Native American art, historic and contemporary, including new research on any aspect of Native American art. Circ. 15,000. Pays on publication. Publishes ms an average of 3 months after acceptance. Byline given. Buys one-time and first rights. Submit seasonal/holiday material 6 months in advance. Simultaneous queries OK. Computer printout submissions OK; prefers letter-quality. Reports in 2 weeks on queries; 2 months on mss. Writer's guidelines for #10 SASE.
Nonfiction: New research on any aspect of Native American art. No previously published work or personal interviews with artists. Buys 12-18 mss/year. Query. Length: 1,000-2,500 words. Pays $75-300.
Tips: "The magazine is devoted to all aspects of Native American art. Some of our readers are knowledgeable about the field and some know very little. We seek articles that offer something to both groups. Articles reflecting original research are preferred to those summarizing previously published information."

ART TIMES, A Cultural and Creative Journal, Box 730, Mount Marion NY 12456. (914)246-5170. Editor: Raymond J. Steiner. 10% (just fiction and poetry) freelance written. Prefers to work with published/established writers; works with a small number of new/unpublished writers each year; and eager to work with new/unpublished writers. Monthly tabloid covering the arts (visual, theatre, dance, etc.). "*Art Times* covers the art fields and is distributed in locations most frequented by those enjoying the arts. Our 15,000 copies are distributed throughout three upstate New York counties rich in the arts as well as in most of the galleries in Soho, 57th Street and Madison Avenue in the metropolitan area; locations include theatres, galleries, museums, cultural centers and the like. Our readers are mostly over 40, affluent, art-conscious and sophisticated." Circ. 15,000. Pays on publication. Publishes ms an average of 8-10 months after acceptance. Byline given. Buys first serial rights. Submit seasonal/holiday material 8 months in advance. Simultaneous queries, and simultaneous and photocopied submissions OK. Computer printout submissions OK; prefers letter-quality. Reports in 3 months on queries; 6 months on mss. Sample copy for 9x12 SAE and 3 first class stamps; writer's guidelines for #10 SAE and 1 first class stamp.

Fiction: "We're looking for short fiction that aspires to be *literary*. No excessive violence, sexist, off-beat, erotic, sports, or juvenile fiction." Buys 8-10 mss/year. Send complete ms. Length: 1,500 words maximum. Pays $15 maximum (honorarium) and 1 year's free subscription.

Poetry: Poet's Niche. Avant-garde, free verse, haiku, light verse and traditional. "We prefer well-crafted 'literary' poems. No excessively sentimental poetry." Buys 30-35 poems/year. Submit maximum 6 poems. Length: 20 lines maximum. Offers contributor copies and 1 year's free subscription.

Tips: "We are now receiving 200 to 250 poems and 30-40 short stories per month. We only publish 2 to 3 poems and one story each issue. Competition is getting very great. We only pick the best. Be familiar with *Art Times* and its special audience. *Art Times* has literary leanings with articles written by a staff of scholars knowledgeable in their respective fields. Our readers expect quality. Although an 'arts' publication, we observe no restrictions (other than noted) in accepting fiction/poetry other than a concern for quality writing—subjects can cover anything and not specifically arts."

THE ARTIST'S MAGAZINE, F&W Publishing Co., 1507 Dana Ave., Cincinnati OH 45207. Editor: Michael Ward. 80% freelance written. Works with a small number of new/unpublished writers each year. Monthly magazine covering primarily two-dimensional art instruction for working artists. "Ours is a highly visual approach to teaching the serious amateur artist techniques that will help him improve his skills and market his work. The style should be crisp and immediately engaging." Circ. 200,000. Pays on acceptance. Publishes ms an average of 4 months after acceptance. Byline given; bionote given for feature material. Offers 20% kill fee. Buys first North American serial rights and second serial (reprint) rights. Simultaneous queries, and photocopied and previously published submissions OK "as long as noted as such." Computer printout submissions acceptable; prefers letter-quality. Reports in 2 months. Sample copy $2.25 with 9x12 SAE and 3 first class stamps; writer's guidelines for SASE.

Nonfiction: Instructional only—how an artist uses a particular technique, how he handles a particular subject or medium, or how he markets his work. "The emphasis must be on how the reader can learn some method of improving his artwork, or the marketing of it." No unillustrated articles; no seasonal/holiday material; no travel articles; no profiles of artists (except for "Artist's Life," below). Buys 60 mss/year. Query first; all queries must be accompanied by slides, transparencies, prints or tearsheets of the artist's work as well as the artist's bio, and the writer's bio and clips. Length: 1,000-2,500 words. Pays $100-350 and up. Sometimes pays the expenses of writers on assignment.

Photos: "Color transparencies or slides are required with every accepted article since these are essential for our instructional format. Full captions must accompany these." Buys one-time rights.

Departments: Two departments are open to freelance writers: The Artist's Life and P.S. The Artist's Life (profiles and brief items about artists and their work. Also, art-related games and puzzles and art-related poetry). Query first with samples of artist's work for profiles; send complete ms for other items. Length: 600 words maximum. Pays $50 and up for profiles; up to $25 for brief items and poetry. P.S. (a humorous look at art from the artist's point of view, or at least sympathetic to the artist). Send complete ms. Pays $50 and up.

Tips: "Look at several current issues and read the author's guidelines carefully. Remember that our readers are fine and graphic artists."

‡**THE ARTS JOURNAL**, 324 Charlotte St., Asheville NC 28801. (704)255-7888. Editor: Alan H. Anderson. Monthly tabloid of literary, performing and visual arts. "Our purpose is to link artists with their audiences. In our reviews and interviews we try to use language that is clear to artists and non-artists." Circ. 5,000. Pays on publication. Byline given. Offers $25 kill fee. Buys one-time rights. Submit seasonal/holiday material 2 months in advance. Reports in 2 weeks. Sample copy $1.50 with 8x10 SAE and 3 first-class stamps.

Nonfiction: Art reviews, interviews. Buys 60 mss/year. Query. Length: 500-1,500 words. Pays $25-100.

Photos: State availability of photos with submission. Offers no additional payment for photos accepted with ms.

Fiction: Fiction Editor: J.W. Bonner. Experimental, historical, mainstream, slice-of-life vignettes. Buys 12 mss/year. Send complete ms. Length: 1,400-1,600 words. Pays $50.

Poetry: Poetry Editor: Ruth Moose. Avant-garde, free verse, traditional. Uses 45 poems/year. Submit up to 6 poems at 1 time. Length: 40 lines maximum. Pays in copies for poetry.

Tips: "State expertise in one of the areas we cover and give evidence of writing ability."

‡**CONTEMPORANEA, International Art Magazine**, Contemporanea Ltd., 17 East 76th St., New York NY 10021. (212)439-1960. Editor-in-Chief: Gabreilla Fanning. Managing Editor: Anthony Calnek. 80% freelance written. Magazine on contemporary visual and performing arts. Estab. 1987. Circ. 25,000. Pays ½ on acceptance and ½ on publication. Byline given. Offers 50% kill fee. Buys simultaneous rights. Simultaneous, photocopied and previously published submissions OK. Query for electronic submissions. Computer printout submissions OK. Free sample copy and writer's guidelines.

Nonfiction: Interview/profile, reviews, and journalistic articles about contemporary art. Query with published clips. Length: 1,000-2,500 words. Payment is negotiable.

Photos: State availability of photos with submissions. Reviews transparencies (3x5). Captions, model releases, and identification of subjects required. Buys one-time rights.

‡EQUINE IMAGES, The National Magazine of Equine Art, Heartland Communications Group, Inc., 1003 Central Ave., Fort Dodge IA 50501. (800)247-2000. Co-Editors: Sandy Geier and Deborah Schneider. Publisher: Susan Badger. 20% freelance written. A quarterly magazine on equine art. "*Equine Images* serves artists, collectors, and equine art enthusiasts. We write for a sophisticated, culturally-oriented audience." Circ. 5,000. Pays on publication. Byline given. Offers $25 kill fee. Publication not copyrighted. Buys first rights and makes work for hire assignments. Submit seasonal/holiday material 6 months in advance. Previously published submissions OK. Reports in 2 weeks on queries; 3 weeks on mss. Sample copy $5.
Nonfiction: Historical/nostalgic (history of the horse in art), how-to (art and art collections), humor (equine art-related cartoons), interview/profile (equine artists, galleries, collectors), personal experience (of equine artists and collectors), photo feature (artworks or collections). "No articles about horses in general—just horse art. No casual writing style." Buys 4-8 mss/year. Query with published clips. Length: 300-3,000 words. Pays $150-500 for assigned articles; $100-350 for unsolicited articles.
Photos: State availability of photos with submission. Reviews contact sheets, transparencies, prints. Offers no additional payment for photos accepted with ms. Identification of subjects required. Buys one-time rights.
Tips: "We are interested only in art-related subjects. Write in a clear, intelligible style for a well-educated, culturally-oriented audience. Writers must have a good understanding of the equine art field. We are looking for original material that is not folksy or promotional in style or content. Send good query letter and published clips. State availability of quality visuals."

‡GLASS, Box 23383, Portland OR 97223. Editor: Jim Wilson. 20% freelance written. Works with a small number of new/unpublished writers each year. A fine arts quarterly publication that showcases all aspects of glass art as well as artists, collectors, museum exhibits, etc. Appeals to artists, hobbyists, museums, galleries, collectors and anyone else interested in looking at glass art. Circ. 30,000. Pays 1 month after publication. Publishes ms an average of 6 months after acceptance. Computer printout submissions acceptable; prefers letter-quality. Free writer's guidelines.
Nonfiction: "This magazine showcases glass as a fine art, showing only the best. We are looking for artists' profiles, exhibit reviews, special features. Writing for this publication requires considerable knowledge about the medium." Pays $400 maximum.

‡GLASS STUDIO, Box 23383, Portland OR 97223. Contact: Editor. 65% freelance written. Prefers to work with published/established writers. A monthly magazine for artists, craftspeople, and hobbyists working in blown glass, stained glass, conceptual glass, as well as collectors, museum curators, gallery and shop owners, students in the arts, and anyone else interested in glass art. Circ. 30,000. Computer printout submissions acceptable; prefers letter-quality. Pays 1 month after publication. Sample copy $2; writer's guidelines for SASE.
Nonfiction: "We are looking for technical articles, how-to articles from people who know what they're talking about. Also, features on artists, glass companies, and unusual stories related to glass art. Remember, you are writing for a specific audience that either works with glass or collects it." Pays $200 maximum.
Photos: No additional payment for photos used with mss.

‡HANDMADE ACCENTS, Featuring America's Original Fine Artists, Photographers and Craftspeople, Creative Crafters Publishing, 448-A River Mountain Rd., Lebanon VA 24266. (703)873-7402. Editor: Steve McCay. 15% freelance written. A quarterly magazine covering art, craft and photography. Audience is art patrons—collectors, investors, art directors, buyers for stores. "Most stories are profiles of contemporary artistic talents who market their wares directly to the public—our readers." Circ. 10,000. Pays on publication. Publishes ms an average of 6 months after acceptance. Byline given. Buys first rights. Submit seasonal/holiday material 6 months in advance. Computer printout submissions acceptable; prefers letter-quality. Reports in 6 weeks. Sample copy $5.
Nonfiction: Humor, inspirational, interview/profile, personal experience and photo feature. No how-to-make specific craft, pattern, etc. Buys 8 mss/year. Query with or without published clips. Length: 1,000-2,500 words. Pays $25-100 for articles. "Whenever article is autobiographical we pay 20 copies of issue and one year subscription."
Photos: Send photos with submission. Reviews 35mm slides and 4x5 transparencies. Offers no additional payment for photos accepted with ms. Captions required. Buys one-time rights.
Columns/Departments: Book Reviews (art books of interest to art patrons); and Exhibition Review (of open/competitive art shows and gallery shows of combined works). Buys 8 mss/year. Query with published clips. Length: 500-2,000 words. Pays $5-10.
Poetry: Light verse and traditional. Must have slant on the art world/community. Buys 4 poems/year. Submit maximum 3 poems. Length: 50 lines maximum. Pays $5-10.
Fillers: Anecdotes, facts, gags to be illustrated by cartoonist, newsbreaks and short humor. Must have appeal to art patrons. Length: 100-500 words. Pays $5-25.
Tips: "Superior quality photos are a must. We feature creative talents of the arts community—primarily those willing to sell their wares direct to a retail market via mail order. We like to see slides of art work first. Mostly we use autobiographical or first-person self portrait/profiles. We'd like to have a feature collector each issue

with photos of the collection—be it art, pottery, metal, fiber, wood, etc.—with details on the pieces collected, philosophy of collectors, tips on displaying a collection. We provide a media for fine artists, photographers and craftspeople to reach their market."

METROPOLIS, The Architecture and Design Magazine of New York, Bellerophon Publications, 177 E. 87th St., New York NY 10128. (212)722-5050. Editor: Susan S. Szenasy. Managing Editor: Kate Norment. 60% freelance written. A monthly (except bimonthly January/February and July/August) magazine for consumers interested in architecture and design. Circ. 22,000. Pays on acceptance. Publishes ms an average of 3-6 months after acceptance. Byline given. Buys first rights or makes work-for-hire assignments. Submit calendar material 6 weeks in advance. Photocopied submissions OK. Computer printout submissions acceptable; prefers letter-quality. Reports in 2 weeks on queries; 1 month on mss. Sample copy $3.50 including postage.
Nonfiction: Book excerpts; essays (design, residential interiors); historical (New York); opinion (design architecture); and profile (only well-known international figures in USA). No profiles on individuals or individual architectural practices, technical information, information from public relations firms, fine arts, or things outside of the New York area. Buys approximately 30 mss/year. Query with published clips. Length: 1,500-3,000 words. Pays $350-500.
Photos: State availability, or send photos with submission. Reviews contact sheets, 35mm or 4x5 transparencies, or 8x10 b&w prints. Payment offered for certain photos. Captions required. Buys one-time rights.
Columns/Departments: Insites (Manhattan miscellany: information on design and architecture around New York), 100-600 words; In Print (book review essays), 600-750 words. Buys approximately 10 mss/year. Query with published clips. Pays $50-100.
Tips: "Keep in mind that we are *only* interested in the consumer end of architecture and design. Send query with examples of photos explaining how you see illustrations working with article. Also, be patient and don't expect an immediate answer after submission of query."

THE ORIGINAL ART REPORT, Box 1641, Chicago IL 60690. Editor and Publisher: Frank Salantrie. 1% freelance written. Eager to work with new/unpublished writers. Emphasizes "visual art conditions from the visual artists' and general public's perspectives." Newsletter; 6-8 pages. Pays on publication. Reports in 4 weeks. Sample copy $1.25 and 1 first class stamp; writer's guidelines for #10 SASE.
Nonfiction: Expose (art galleries, government agencies ripping off artists, or ignoring them); historical (perspective pieces relating to now); humor (whenever possible); informational (material that is unavailable in other art publications); inspirational (acts and ideas of courage); interview (with artists, other experts; serious material); personal opinion; technical (brief items to recall traditional methods of producing art); travel (places in the world where artists are welcomed and honored); philosophical, economic, aesthetic, and artistic. "We would like to receive investigative articles on government and private arts agencies, and nonprofits, too, perhaps hiding behind status to carry on for business. No vanity profiles of artists, arts organizations, and arts promoters' operations." Buys 4-5 mss/year. Query or submit complete ms. Length: 1,000 words maximum. Pays 1¢/word.
Columns/Departments: In Back of the Individual Artist. "Artists express their views about non-art topics. After all, artists are in this world, too." WOW (Worth One Wow), Worth Repeating, and Worth Repeating Again. "Basically, these are reprint items with introduction to give context and source, including complete name and address of publication. Looking for insightful, succinct commentary." Submit complete ms. Length: 500 words maximum. Pays ½¢/word.
Tips: "We have a stronger than ever emphasis on editorial opinion or commentary, based on fact, of the visual art condition-economics, finances, politics, and manufacture of art and the social and individual implications of-to fine art."

WESTART, Box 6868, Auburn CA 95604. (916)885-0969. Editor-in-Chief: Martha Garcia. Emphasizes art for practicing artists and artists/craftsmen; students of art and art patrons. Semimonthly tabloid; 20 pages. Circ. 7,500. Pays on publication. Buys all rights. Byline given. Phone queries OK. Photocopied submissions OK. Sample copy $1; free writer's guidelines.
Nonfiction: Informational, photo feature and profile. No hobbies. Buys 6-8 mss/year. Query or submit complete ms. Length: 700-800 words. Pays 50¢/column inch.
Photos: Purchased with or without accompanying ms. Send b&w prints. Pays 50¢/column inch.
Tips: "We publish information which is current—that is, we will use a review of an exhibition only if exhibition is still open on the date of publication. Therefore, reviewer must be familiar with our printing deadlines and news deadlines."

For explanation of symbols, see the Key to Symbols and Abbreviations on Page 5.

Associations

Association publications allow writers to write for national audiences while covering local stories. If your town has a Kiwanis, Lions or Rotary Club chapter, one of its projects might merit a story in the club's magazine. Some association magazines circulate worldwide. These publications link members who live continents from one another or just across town. They keep members and friends informed about the ideas, objectives, projects and activities of the club. Club-financed magazines that carry material not directly related to the group's activities are classified by their subject matter in the Consumer and Trade sections.

CALIFORNIA HIGHWAY PATROLMAN, California Association of Highway Patrolmen, 2030 V St., Sacramento CA 95818. (916)452-6751. Editor: Carol Perri. 80% freelance written. Will work with established or new/unpublished writers. Monthly magazine. Circ. 20,000. Pays on publication. Publishes ms an average of 1 year after acceptance. Buys one-time rights. Submit seasonal/holiday material 6 months in advance. Computer printout submissions acceptable. Reports in 3 months. Sample copy and writer's guidelines for 9x12 SAE and 4 first class stamps.
Nonfiction: Publishes articles on transportation safety, driver education, consumer interest, California history, humor and general interest. "Topics can include autos, boats, bicycles, motorcycles, snowmobiles, recreational vehicles and pedestrian safety. We are also in the market for California travel pieces and articles on early California. We are *not* a technical journal for teachers and traffic safety experts, but rather a general interest publication geared toward the layman." Pays 2½¢/word.
Photos: "Illustrated articles always receive preference." Pays $5/b&w photo; no transparencies please. Captions required.
Tips: "If a writer feels the article idea, length and style are consistent with our magazine, submit the manuscript for me to determine if I agree. We are especially looking for articles for specific holidays."

CATHOLIC FORESTER, Catholic Order of Foresters, 425 W. Shuman Blvd., Naperville IL 60566. (312)983-4920. Editor: Barbara Cunningham. 35% freelance written. Prefers to work with published/established writers; works with a small number of new/unpublished writers each year. A bimonthly magazine of short, general interest articles and fiction for members of the Order, which is a fraternal insurance company. Family type audience, middle class. Circ. 150,000. Pays on acceptance. Publishes ms an average of 6 months after acceptance. Byline given. Buys one-time rights, second serial (reprint) rights, and simultaneous rights. Submit seasonal/holiday material 6 months in advance. Simultaneous, photocopied, and previously published submissions OK. Computer printout submissions acceptable; prefers letter-quality. Reports in 6 weeks on ms. Sample copy for 9x12 SAE with 4 first class stamps; free writer's guidelines.
Nonfiction: General interest; historical/nostalgic; humor; inspirational; interview/profile; new product; opinion; personal experience; photo feature; technical (depends on subject); and travel. "Short feature articles of interest to the all-American type are most open to freelancers." No blatant sex nor anything too violent. Send complete ms. Length: 1,000-3,000 words. Pays 5¢/word; more for excellent ms.
Photos: Prefers something of unusual interest or story-telling. State availability of photos, or send photos with ms. Reviews any size b&w and color prints. Payment to be determined. Captions, model releases, and identification of subjects required. Buys one-time rights.
Columns/Departments: Needs unusual items on what is going on in the world; new, interesting products, discoveries or happenings. Send complete ms. Length: 1,000 words. Payment to be determined.
Fiction: Adventure, historical, humorous, mainstream, mystery, religious (Catholic), suspense and western. No sex or extreme violence. Length: up to 3,000 words (prefers shorter fiction). Pays 5¢/word; more for excellent ms.
Poetry: Free verse, haiku, light verse and traditional. Submit maximum 5 poems. Payment to be determined.
Fillers: Cartoons, jokes, anecdotes and short humor. Length: 300-500 words. Payment to be determined.

CBIA NEWS, Journal of the Connecticut Business and Industry Association, CBIA Service Corp., 370 Asylum St., Hartford CT 06103. (203)547-1661. Editor: Jan R. Potts. 60% freelance written. A monthly tabloid (except combined July/August and December/January issues) covering business in Connecticut for approximately 6,500 member companies. 40% of the *News* is about the association and written in-house. Other 60% is about how to run your business better, interesting businesspeople in Connecticut, and business trends here. These are written by freelancers. Circ. 7,200. Pays on acceptance. Publishes ms an average of 6 months after acceptance. Byline given. Offers 20% kill fee. Buys variable rights; can be negotiable. Photocopied and previously published submissions OK if not published in competing publications. Computer printout submissions acceptable; prefers letter-quality. Reports in 6 weeks. Sample copy for 9x12 SAE and 5 first-class stamps.

Nonfiction: Book excerpts, how-to (run your business better in some specific way); interview/profile (must be a Connecticut person). Buys approximately 20 mss/year. Query with published clips. Length and payment vary with the subject.
Photos: State availability of photos with query or ms. Reviews b&w contact sheets. Pays negotiable rate. Model release and identification of subjects required.
Tips: "All stories, should have a Connecticut slant. We are focusing on special topics and covering them in-depth more than before. For example, we've run specials on the state's labor shortage, AIDS in the workplace, etc. Therefore, we will be less likely to use over-the-transom pieces. But query, an idea my result in a special assignment."

CHARIOT, Ben Hur Life Association, Box 312, Crawfordsville IN 47933. (317)362-4500. Editor: Loren Harrington. 15-20% freelance written. A quarterly magazine covering fraternal activities of membership plus general interest items. Circ. 11,000. Usually pays on acceptance, sometimes on publication. Publishes ms an average of 1 year after acceptance. Byline and brief biography given. Not copyrighted. Buys variable rights. Submit seasonal/holiday material 10 months in advance. Simultaneous queries, and simultaneous and photocopied submissions OK. Computer printout submissions acceptable; prefers letter-quality. Reports in 2 weeks on queries; 1 month on mss. Sample copy for 9x12 SAE and 4 first class stamps—for *serious* inquiries only; writer's guidelines for #10 SAE and 2 first class stamps.
Nonfiction: General interest, historical and how-to. "Absolutely *nothing* of a smutty, sexually-oriented, gay, etc. nature. Only items of benefit to our readers and/or family would be considered." Query with or without published clips. Length: 300-3,500 words. Pays 3-20¢/word. Sometimes pays the expenses of writers on assignment.
Photos: State availability of photos with query letter or ms. "We would like to have quality photo with query. We will return if rejected." Reviews b&w and color contact sheets and prints. Payment for photos included in payment for mss. Captions, model releases and identification of subjects required. Buys one-time rights.
Columns/Departments: Columns are editorial or insurance-related. "We would consider a query piece, but it would have to be extremely applicable."
Fiction: Especially interested in "really good, *short* fiction. It must have theme of helping another person or benefitting a worthy cause. Absolutely *nothing* of a smutty, sexually-oriented, gay, etc. nature. Only stories of benefit to our readers and/or family would be considered." Query with or without published clips or send complete ms. Length: 300-2,500 words. Pays 3-20¢/word.
Fillers: No fillers considered at present—will take a look at cartoons.
Tips: "Our requirements are very tightly edited and professionally written with a wide appeal to our particular audience, self-help volunteer and charity. Those items that we can give our local units to encourage their fraternal participation and projects would be considered more than any other single submitted features."

CLUB COSTA MAGAZINE, Club Costa Corp., Suite 200, 7701 College Blvd., Overland Park KS 66210.(913)451-3462. Editor: Norman F. Rowland. 50-65% freelance written. Prefers to work with published/ established writers; works with a small number of new/unpublished writers each year. A quarterly magazine available only to club members covering discounted accommodations, travel and other savings available through Club Costa. "We offer airline employee 'discount' prices to our members on a variety of accommodations, flights, car rentals and activities. Our format features money-saving tips for vacation and destination features for the areas in which we have properties available. Readers are reasonably sophisticated travelers with above average incomes." Circ. 20,000. Pays on publication. Publishes ms an average of 3 months after acceptance. Byline given. Buys one-time rights, simultaneous rights and second serial (reprint) rights. Submit seasonal/holiday material 6 months in advance. Simultaneous, photocopied, and previously published submissions OK. Computer printout submissions acceptable. Reports in 6 weeks. Sample copy $3; writer's guidelines for #10 SASE.
Nonfiction: Travel-related historical/nostalgic, how-to, personal experience and humor. "Articles may relate to saving money while on vacation. We need features about destinations, activities, background/history of area(s), bargain purchases, how to plan a vacation, and tips for the business or leisure traveler." No camping, hunting, fishing, or "my favorite vacation" articles. Buys 15-20 mss/year. Query with SASE. Length: 1,200 words, features; up to 500 words, shorts. Pays $25-125.
Photos: Photos are required with most articles. State availability.
Tips: "We need short travel-related humor and shorts that give an insight to an area or its people. We are putting more emphasis on European travel."

THE ELKS MAGAZINE, 425 W. Diversey, Chicago IL 60614. Executive Editor: Fred D. Oakes. 50% freelance written. Prefers to work with published/established writers. Emphasizes general interest with family appeal. Magazine published 10 times/year. Circ. 1,600,000. Pays on acceptance. Publishes ms an average of 4 months after acceptance. Buys first North American serial rights. Computer printout submissions acceptable; no dot-matrix. Reports in 6 weeks. Sample copy and writer's guidelines for 9x12 SASE.
Nonfiction: Articles of information, business, contemporary life problems and situations, nostalgia, or just

interesting topics, ranging from medicine, science, and history, to sports. "The articles should not just be a re-hash of existing material. They must be fresh, thought-provoking, well-researched and documented." No fiction, political articles, fillers or verse. Buys 2-3 mss/issue. Query; no phone queries. Length: 1,500-3,000 words. Pays from $100.

Tips: "Requirements are clearly stated in our guidelines. Loose, wordy pieces are not accepted. A submission, following a query letter go-ahead, should include several b&w prints if the piece lends itself to illustration. We offer no additional payment for photos accepted with manuscripts. We expect to continue targeting our content to an older (50+) demographic."

FEDCO REPORTER, A Publication Exclusively for FEDCO Members, Box 2605, Terminal Annex, Los Angeles CA 90051. (213)946-2511. Editor: Michele A. Brunmier. 90% freelance written. Works with a small number of new/unpublished writers each year. A monthly catalog/magazine for FEDCO department store members. Circ. 2 million. Pays on acceptance. Publishes ms an average of 4 months after acceptance. Byline given. Offers $50 kill fee. Buys first rights. Query for electronic submissions. Computer printout submissions acceptable; prefers letter-quality. Reports in 6 weeks. Sample copy for 9x12 SAE with 4 first class stamps; writer's guidelines for SASE.

Nonfiction: General interest, historical. The magazine publishes material on "historical events (especially relating to California); historical personality profiles; general interest (we do numerous stories on common, everyday items with an unusual background or interesting use); seasonal stories; and articles about areas of California." No first person narrative. Buys 75 mss/year. Query with published clips. Length: 450 words. Pays $100-250.

Photos: State availability of photos. Reviews b&w and color slides. Pays $25.

Tips: "We will publish excellent writing that is well-researched regardless of prior writings. Articles should be tightly written and not stray from subject."

KIWANIS, 3636 Woodview Trace, Indianapolis IN 46268. Executive Editor: Chuck Jonak. 90% of feature articles freelance written. Magazine published 10 times/year for business and professional persons and their families. Circ. 300,000. Pays on acceptance. Buys first North American serial rights. Pays 20-40% kill fee. Publishes ms an average of 6 months after acceptance. Byline given. Computer printout submissions acceptable. Reports within 2 months. Sample copy and writer's guidelines for 9x12 SAE and 4 first class stamps.

Nonfiction: Articles about social and civic betterment, small-business concerns, science, education, religion, family, sports, health, recreation, etc. Emphasis on objectivity, intelligent analysis and thorough research of contemporary problems. Positive tone preferred. Concise, lively writing, absence of cliches, and impartial presentation of controversy required. When applicable, information and quotation from international sources are required. Avoid writing strictly to a U.S. audience. Especially needs articles on business and professional topics that will directly assist the readers in their own businesses (generally independent retailers and companies of less than 25 employees) or careers. "We have a continuing need for articles of international interest. In addition, we are very interested in proposals that concern helping youth, particularly in regard to their character development, self-images, future goals, and social and emotional needs." Length: 2,500-3,000 words. Pays $400-1,000. "No fiction, personal essays, fillers, or verse of any kind. A light or humorous approach is welcomed where the subject is appropriate and all other requirements are observed." Usually pays the expenses of writers on assignment. Query first. Must include SASE for response.

Photos: "We accept photos submitted with manuscripts. Our rate for a manuscript with good photos is higher than for one without." Model release and identification of subjects required. Buys one-time rights.

Tips: "We will work with any writer who presents a strong feature article idea applicable to our magazine's audience and who will prove he or she knows the craft of writing. First, obtain writer's guidelines and a sample copy. Study for general style and content. Present well-researched, smoothly written manuscript that contains a 'human quality' with the use of anecdotes, practical examples, quotation, etc. When querying, present detailed outline of proposed manuscript's focus, direction, and editorial intent. Indicate expert sources to be used for attribution, as well as article's tone and length."

THE LION, 300 22nd St., Oak Brook IL 60570. (312)571-5466. Editor-in-Chief: Roy Schaetzel. Senior Editor: Robert Kleinfelder. 35% freelance written. Works with a small number of new/unpublished writers each year. Covers service club organization for Lions Club members and their families. Monthly magazine. Circ. 670,000. Pays on acceptance. Publishes ms an average of 5 months after acceptance. Buys all rights. Byline given. Phone queries OK. Photocopied submissions OK. Computer printout submissions acceptable; no dot-matrix. Reports in 2 weeks. Free sample copy and writer's guidelines.

Nonfiction: Informational (stories of interest to civic-minded individuals) and photo feature (must be of a Lions Club service project). No travel, biography, or personal experiences. No sensationalism. Prefers anecdotes in articles. Buys 4 mss/issue. Query. Length: 500-2,200. Pays $50-400. Sometimes pays the expenses of writers on assignment.

Photos: Purchased with or without accompanying ms or on assignment. Captions required. Query for photos. B&w and color glossies at least 5x7 or 35mm color slides. Total purchase price for ms includes payment for photos, accepted with ms. "Be sure photos are clear and as candid as possible."

Tips: "Incomplete details on how the Lions involved actually carried out a project and poor quality photos are the most frequent mistakes made by writers in completing an article assignment for us. We are geared increasingly to an international audience."

THE MODERN WOODMEN, Public Relations Department, Mississippi River at 17th St., Rock Island IL 61201. (309)786-6481. Editor: Gloria Bergh. Address manuscripts to Sandy Howell, staff writer. 5-10% freelance written. Works with both published and new writers. "Our publication is for families who are members of Modern Woodmen of America. Modern Woodmen is a fraternal life insurance society, and most of our members live in smaller communities or rural areas throughout the United States. Various age groups read the magazine." Quarterly magazine, 24 pages. Circ. 350,000. Not copyrighted. Pays on acceptance. Publishes ms an average of 6 months after acceptance. Buys one-time rights or second serial (reprint) rights to material. Photocopied and simultaneous submissions OK. Reports in 1 month if SASE included. Sample copy and guidelines for 8½x11 SAE and 2 first class stamps.

Nonfiction: For children and adults. "We seek lucid style and rich content. We need manuscripts that center on family-oriented subjects, human development, and educational topics."

Fiction: "Most of the fiction we publish is for children and teens. We stress plot and characterization. A moral is a pleasant addition, but not required." Length: about 1,200 words. Pays $50 minimum.

Tips: "We want articles that appeal to young families, emphasize family interaction, community involvement, and family life. We also consider educational, historical and patriotic articles. We don't want religious articles, teen romances, or seasonal material. Focus on people, whether the article is about families or is educational, historical or patriotic."

MOOSE MAGAZINE, Loyal Order of Moose, Supreme Lodge Building, Mooseheart IL 60539. (312)859-2000. Managing Editor: Raymond Dickow. A monthly (10 issues/year) fraternal magazine. "Distributed to men, ages 21 and older, who are members of 2,300 Moose lodges located throughout the U.S. and Canada." Circ. 1,300,000. Pays on acceptance. Byline given. Not copyrighted. Buys first North American serial rights. Submit seasonal/holiday material 4 months in advance. Photocopied submissions OK. No computer printout submissions. Reports in 5 weeks on mss. Writer's guidelines for 9x12 SAE and 2 first class stamps.

Nonfiction: General interest, historical/nostalgic and sports. No politics or religion. Send complete ms. Length: 1,000-2,000 words. Pays $300-1,000 for unsolicited articles.

Photos: Send photos with submission. Offers no additional payment for photos accepted with ms.

Tips: Freelancers can best break in at this publication with "feature articles involving outdoor sports (fishing, hunting, camping) as well as golf, bowling, baseball, football, etc., and with articles of general interest reflective of community and family living in addition to those of nostalgic interest. Features should include anecdotes and provide the kind of information that is interesting, educational, and entertaining to our readers. Style of writing should show rather than tell. Submit appropriate photo(s) with manuscript whenever possible."

‡THE NEIGHBORHOOD WORKS, Resources for Urban Communities, Center for Neighborhood Technology, 2125 West North Ave., Chicago IL 60647. (312)278-4800. Editor: Mary O'Connell. 15-25% freelance written. A bimonthly magazine on community organizing, housing, energy, environmental and economic issues affecting city neighborhoods. "Writers must understand the importance of empowering people in low- and moderate-income city neighborhoods to solve local problems in housing, environment and local economy." Circ. 2,000. Pays on publication. Publishes ms an average of 2 months after acceptance. Byline given. Buys all rights. Submit seasonal/holiday material 2 months in advance. Photocopied and previously published submissions OK. Reports in 1 month on queries; 2 months on mss. Sample copy and writer's guidelines for 9x12 SAE and 2 first class stamps.

Nonfiction: Exposes, historical (neighborhood history), how-to (each issue has "reproducible feature" on such topics as organizing a neighborhood block watch, a community garden, recycling, etc.), interview/profile (of someone active on one of our issues), personal experience (in our issue areas, e.g, community organizing), technical (on energy conservation and alternative energy). Buys 6-10 mss/year. Query with or without published clips or send complete ms. Length: 750-2,000 words. Pays $100-500. "We pay professional writers (people who make living at it). We don't pay nonprofessionals and students but offer them a free subscription." Sometimes pays expenses of writers on assignment by previous agreement.

Photos: State availability of photos with submission. Reviews contact sheets and prints. Offers $10-25/photo. Captions and identification of subjects required. Buys one-time rights.

Columns/Departments: Reproducible features (how-to articles on issues of interest to neighborhood organizations), 1,000-2,000 words. Query with published clips. Pays $100-250.

THE OPTIMIST MAGAZINE, Optimist International, 4494 Lindell Blvd., St. Louis MO 63108. (314)371-6000. Editor: James E. Braibish. Assistant Editor: Patricia A. Gamma. 10% freelance written. Monthly magazine about the work of Optimist clubs and members for the 155,000 members of the Optimist clubs in the United States and Canada. Circ. 155,000. Pays on acceptance. Publishes ms an average of 4 months after acceptance. Buys first North American serial rights. Submit seasonal material 3 months in advance. Computer printout submissions acceptable. Reports in 1 week. Sample copy and writer's guidelines for 9x12 SAE and 4 first class stamps.

Nonfiction: "We want articles about the activities of local Optimist clubs. These volunteer community-service clubs are constantly involved in projects, aimed primarily at helping young people. With over 4,000 Optimist clubs in the U.S. and Canada, writers should have ample resources. Some large metropolitan areas boast several dozen clubs. We are also interested in feature articles on individual club members who have in some way distinguished themselves, either in their club work or their personal lives. Good photos for all articles are a plus and can mean a bigger check. We are no longer a market for general-interest articles." Buys 1-2 mss/issue. Query. "Submit a letter that conveys your ability to turn out a well-written article and tells exactly what the scope of the article will be and whether photos are available." Length: 1,000-1,500 words. Pays $150 and up.

Photos: State availability of photos. Payment negotiated. Captions preferred. Buys all rights. "No mug shots or people lined up against the wall shaking hands."

Tips: "Find out what the Optimist clubs in your area are doing, then find out if we'd be interested in an article on a specific club project. All of our clubs are eager to talk about what they're doing. Just ask them and you'll probably have an article idea."

PERSPECTIVE, Pioneer Clubs, Division of Pioneer Ministries, Inc., Box 788, Wheaton IL 60189-0788. (312)293-1600. Editor: Rebecca Powell Parat. 15% freelance written. Works with a small number of new/unpublished writers each year. "All subscribers are volunteer leaders of clubs for girls and boys in grades K-12. Clubs are sponsored by evangelical churches throughout North America." Quarterly magazine. Circ. 24,000. Pays on acceptance. Publishes ms an average of 8 months after acceptance. Buys first North American serial rights and second serial (reprint) rights to material originally published elsewhere. Submit seasonal/holiday material 9 months in advance. Simultaneous submissions OK. Computer printout submissions acceptable if double-spaced; prefers letter-quality. Reports in 6 weeks. Writer's packet for 9x12 SAE and $1.50; includes writer's guidelines and sample magazine.

Nonfiction: How-to (projects for clubs, crafts, cooking, service); informational (relationships, human development, mission education, outdoor activities); inspirational (Bible studies, adult leading youths); interview (Christian education leaders); personal experience (of club leaders). Buys 4-10 mss/year; 3 unsolicited/year. Byline given. Query. Length: 200-1,500 words. Pays $10-60. Sometimes pays expenses of writers on assignment.

Columns/Departments: Storehouse (craft, game, activity, outdoor activity suggestions—all related to club projects for any age between grades 1-12). Buys 4-6 mss/year. Submit complete ms. Length: 150-250 words. Pays $8-20.

Tips: "We only assign major features to writers who have proven previously that they know us and our constituency. Submit articles directly related to club work, practical in nature, i.e., ideas for leader training in communication, Bible knowledge, teaching skills. They must have practical application. We want substance—not ephemeral ideas. In addition to a summary of the article idea and evidence that the writer has knowledge of the subject, we want evidence that the author understands our purpose and philosophy. We're doing more and more inhouse writing—less purchasing of any freelance."

PORTS O' CALL, Box 530, Santa Rosa CA 95402. (707)542-0898. Editor: William A. Breniman. Newsbook of the Society of Wireless Pioneers. Society members are mostly early-day wireless "brass-pounders" who sent code signals from ships or manned shore stations handling wireless or radio traffic. Biannually. Not copyrighted. Pays on acceptance. No computer printout or disk submissions. Reports on submissions "within 30 days (depending on workload)."

Nonfiction: Articles about early-day wireless as used in ship-shore and high power operation; radar, electronic aids, SOS calls, etc. Early-day ships, records, etc. "Writers should remember that our members have gone to sea for years and would be critical of material that is not authentic. We are not interested in any aspect of amateur radio. We are interested in authentic articles dealing with ships (since about 1910)." Oddities about the sea and weather as it affects shipping. Buys 45 unsolicited mss/year. Query. Length: 500-2,000 words. Pays 1-5¢/word.

Photos: Paul Dane, department editor. Purchased with mss. Unusual shots of sea or ships. Wireless pioneers. Prefers b&w, "4x5 would be the most preferable size but it really doesn't make too much difference as long as the photos are sharp and the subject interests us." Fine if veloxed, but not necessary. Pays $2.50-10; "according to our appraisal of our interest." Ship photos of various nations, including postcard size, if clear, 25¢-$1 each.

Poetry: Ships, marine slant (not military), shipping, weather, wireless. No restrictions. Pays $1-$2.50 each.

Tips: "Material will also be considered for our *Ports O' Call* biannual and *Sparks Journal*, a quarterly tabloid newsletter. *Sparks* (published yearly) takes most of the contents used in *Ports O' Call*, published now every 2 years in encyclopedic format and content. *The Sparks Journal*, published quarterly in tabloid form, carries much of the early days, first hand history of wireless (episodes and experiences). Also, *Wireless Almanac* contains much nautical data relating to radio and wireless used at sea."

REVIEW, A Publication of North American Benefit Association, 1338 Military St., Box 5020, Port Huron MI 48061-5020. (313)985-5191, ext. 77. Editor: Virginia E. Farmer. Associate Editor: Patricia Pfeifer. 10-15% freelance written. Prefers to work with published/established writers, and works with a small number of new/ unpublished writers each year. Quarterly trade journal on insurance/fraternal deeds. Family magazine. Circ. 44,000. Pays on acceptance. Publishes ms an average of 2 years after acceptance. Byline given. Not copyrighted. Buys one-time rights, simultaneous rights, and second serial (reprint) rights. Submit seasonal/holiday material 6 months in advance. Simultaneous, photocopied and previously published submissions OK. Computer printout submissions acceptable; no dot-matrix. Reports in 2 months. Sample copy for 9x12 SAE with 4 first class stamps.
Nonfiction: General interest, historical/nostalgic, how-to (improve; self-help); humor; inspirational; personal experience; and photo feature. No political/controversial. Buys 4-10 mss/year. Send complete ms. Length: 600-1,500 words. Pays 3-5¢/word.
Photos: Prefers ms with photos if available. Send photos with ms. Reviews 5x7 or 8x10 b&w prints and color slides or prints. Pays $10-15. Model release and identification of subjects required. Buys one-time rights.
Fiction: Adventure, humorous and mainstream. Buys 2-4 mss/year. Send complete ms. Length: 600-1,500 words. Pays 3-5¢/word.
Tips: "We like articles with accompanying photos; articles that warm the heart; stories with gentle, happy humor. Give background of writer as to education and credits. Manuscripts and art material will be carefully considered, but received only with the understanding that North American Benefit Association shall not be responsible for loss or injury."

THE ROTARIAN, Official Magazine of Rotary International, 1560 Sherman Ave., Evanston IL 60201. (312)866-3000. Editor: Willmon L. White. 50% freelance written. Works with published and unpublished writers. For Rotarian business and professional men and their families; for schools, libraries, hospitals, etc. Monthly. Circ. 523,000. Usually buys all rights. Pays on acceptance. Query preferred. Computer printout submissions acceptable; prefers letter-quality. Reports in 1 month. Sample copy for SAE and 7 first class stamps; writer's guidelines for SAE and first class stamp.
Nonfiction: "The field for freelance articles is in the general interest category. These run the gamut from guidelines for daily living to such concerns as AIDS, famine and conservation. Recent articles have dealt with modern office communications tools, retail theft, architecture and design and waste management worldwide. Articles should appeal to an international audience and should in some way help Rotarians help other people. An article may increase a reader's understanding of world affairs, thereby making him a better world citizen. It may educate him in civic matters, thus helping him improve his town. It may help him to become a better employer, or a better human being. We are interested in articles on unusual Rotary club projects or really unusual Rotarians. We carry debates and symposiums, but are careful to show more than one point of view. We present arguments for effective politics and business ethics, but avoid expose and muckraking. Controversy is welcomed if it gets our readers to think but does not offend minority, ethnic or religious groups. In short, the rationale of the organization is one of hope and encouragement and belief in the power of individuals talking and working together." Query preferred. Length: 1,000-2,000 words. Payment varies. Seldom pays the expenses of writers on assignment.
Photos: Purchased with mss or with captions only. Prefers 2¼x2¼ or larger color transparencies, but also uses 35mm. B&w prints and photo essays. Vertical shots preferred for covers. Scenes of international interest. Color cover.

THE SAMPLE CASE, The Order of United Commercial Travelers of America, 632 N. Park St., Box 159019, Columbus OH 43215. (614)228-3276. Editor: Sam Perdue. Bimonthly magazine covering news for members of the United Commercial Travelers. Emphasizes fraternalism for its officers and active membership. Circ. 160,000. Pays on publication. Buys one-time rights. Submit seasonal/holiday material 6 months in advance. Simultaneous queries and submissions OK. Reports in 3 months. Free sample copy.
Nonfiction: Articles on travel destination (cities and regions in the U.S. and Canada); food/cuisine; health/ fitness/safety; hobbies/entertainment; fraternal/civic activities; business finance/insurance.
Photos: David Knapp, art director. State availability of photos with ms. Pays minimum $20 for 5x7 b&w or larger prints; $30 for 35mm or larger color transparencies used inside (more for cover). Captions required.

‡**THE TOASTMASTER**, Toastmasters International, 2200 N. Grand Ave., Box 10400, Santa Ana CA 92711. (714)542-6793. Editor: Suzanne Frey. Associate Editor: Keith Bush. 50% freelance written. A monthly magazine on public speaking, leadership and club concerns. "This magazine is sent to members of Toastmasters International, a nonprofit educational association of men and women throughout the world who are interested in developing their communication and leadership skills. Members range from novice speakers to professional orators and come from a wide variety of backgrounds." Circ. 132,000. Pays on acceptance. Publishes ms an average of 8 months after acceptance. Byline given. Buys second serial (reprint) rights or all rights. Submit seasonal/holiday material 3 months in advance. Simultaneous, photocopied and previously published submissions OK. Query for electronic submissions. Computer printout submissions OK; no dot-matrix. Reports in 2

weeks on queries; 3 weeks on mss. Sample copy for 9x12 SAE and 2 first class stamps and writer's guidelines for #10 SASE.

Nonfiction: Book excerpts, how-to (communications related), humor (only if informative; humor cannot be off-color or derogatory), interview/profile (only if of a very prominent member or former member of Toastmasters International or someone who has a valuable perspective on communication and leadership). Buys 50 mss/year. Query. Length: 1,500-3,000 words. Pays $35-250. Sometimes pays expenses of writers on assignment. "Toastmaster members are requested to view their submissions as contributions to the organization. Sometimes asks for book excerpts and reprints without payment, but original contribution from individuals outside Toastmasters will be paid for at stated rates."

Photos: Reviews b&w prints. Offers no additional payment for photos accepted with ms. Captions are required. Buys all rights.

Tips: "We are looking primarily for 'how-to' articles on subjects from the broad fields of communications and leadership which can be directly applied by our readers in their self-improvement and club programming efforts. Concrete examples are useful. Avoid sexist or nationalist language."

WOODMEN OF THE WORLD MAGAZINE, 1700 Farnam St., Omaha NE 68102. (402)342-1890, ext. 302. Editor: Leland A. Larson. 20% freelance written. Works with a small number of new/unpublished writers each year. Published by Woodmen of the World Life Insurance Society for "people of all ages in all walks of life. We have both adult and child readers from all types of American families." Monthly. Circ. 467,000. Not copyrighted. Buys 20 mss/year. Pays on acceptance. Byline given. Buys one-time rights. Publishes ms an average of 2 months after acceptance. Will consider photocopied and simultaneous submissions. Computer printout submissions acceptable; prefers letter-quality. Submit seasonal material 3 months in advance. Reports in 5 weeks. Free sample copy.

Nonfiction: "General interest articles which appeal to the American family—travel, history, art, new products, how-to, sports, hobbies, food, home decorating, family expenses, etc. Because we are a fraternal benefit society operating under a lodge system, we often carry stories on how a number of people can enjoy social or recreational activities as a group. No special approach required. We want more 'consumer type' articles, humor, historical articles, think pieces, nostalgia, photo articles." Buys 15-24 unsolicited mss/year. Submit complete ms. Length: 2,000 words or less. Pays $10 minimum, 5¢/word depending on count.

Photos: Purchased with or without mss; captions optional "but suggested." Uses 8x10 glossy prints, 4x5 transparencies ("and possibly down to 35mm"). Payment "depends on use." For b&w photos, pays $25 for cover, $10 for inside. Color prices vary according to use and quality. Minimum of $25 for inside use; up to $150 for covers.

Fiction: Humorous and historical short stories. Length: 1,500 words or less. Pays "$10 minimum or 5¢/word, depending on count."

Astrology, Metaphysical and New Age

A number of new magazines have started publication in this category during the past year, exploring topics ranging from the occult to holistic healing. The following publications regard astrology, psychic phenomena, metaphysical experiences and related subjects as sciences or as objects of serious study. Each has an individual personality and approach to these phenomena. If you want to write for these publications, be sure to read them first.

ASTRO SIGNS, T-Square Publications, 566 Westchester Ave., Rye Brook NY 10573. (914)939-2111. Editor: Nancy Frederick Sussan. 20% freelance written. Monthly miniature magazine (2½x3") covering astrology. Circ. 1,000,000. Pays on publication. Byline given (listing on masthead). Buys all rights. Submit seasonal/holiday material 6 months in advance. Computer printout submissions OK. Reports in 2 weeks. Sample copy and writer's guidelines for SASE (send to publisher, 566 Westchester Ave., Rye Brook, NY 10573).

Nonfiction: General interest, humor, technical, travel and sun sign articles. "We use upbeat, positive articles focusing on sun signs as a way to make the reader's life better." Buys 60 mss/year. Query or send complete ms to the editor at 8377 Clinton Ave., West Hollywood CA 90048. Pays $100 minimum.

Tips: "A writer must have some astrological sophistication as well as a positive, helpful approach. Usually a query letter is best and then a phone call. We need at least two small features a month on love, travel, health, etc."

BODY, MIND & SPIRIT, (formerly *Psychic Guide Magazine*), Island Publishing Co. Inc., Box 701, Providence RI 02901. (401)351-4320. Editor: Paul Zuromski. Managing Editor: Carol Kramer. 75% freelance written. Prefers to work with published/established writers; works with many new/unpublished writers each year. Bimonthly magazine covering New Age, natural living, and metaphysical topics. "Our editorial is slanted toward assisting people in their self-transformation process to improve body, mind and spirit. We take a holistic approach to the subjects we present. They include spirituality, health, healing, nutrition, new ideas, interviews with new age people, travel, books and music. We avoid sensationalizing and present material with the idea that an individual should decide what to accept or believe." Circ. 150,000. Pays on publication. Publishes ms an average of 3-6 months after acceptance. Byline given. Offers negotiable kill fee. Buys first North American serial rights. Submit seasonal/holiday material 8 months in advance. Simultaneous queries OK. Computer printout submissions acceptable. Reports in 2 months on queries; 4 months on mss. Sample copy $3.95 with 9x12 SAE and 4 first class stamps; writer's guidelines for SAE and 1 first class stamp.
Nonfiction: Book excerpts, historical/nostalgic (research on the roots of the New Age movement and related topics); how-to (develop psychic abilities, health, healing, proper nutrition, etc., based on holistic approach); inspirational; interview/profile (of New Age people); new product (or services offered in this field—must be unique and interesting); opinion (on any New Age, natural living or metaphysical topic); and travel (example: to Egypt based on past life research). Don't send "My life as a psychic" or "How I became psychic" articles. Buys 10-15 mss/year. Query with published clips. Length: 4,000-5,000 words. Pays $100-300. Sometimes pays the expenses of writers on assignment.
Photos: State availability of photos with query. Pays $10-20 for b&w contact sheets. Captions, model releases and identification of subjects required. Buys one-time rights.
Fillers: Clippings, anecdotes or newsbreaks on any interesting or unusual New Age, natural living, or metaphysical topic. Buys 20-30 fillers/year. Length: 500 words maximum. Pays $10-40.
Tips: "Examine our unique approach to the subject matter. We avoid sensationalism and overly strange or unbelievable stories. Reading an issue should give you a good idea of our approach to the subject."

‡COMMON BOUNDARY, Between Spirituality and Psychotherapy, Common Boundary, Inc., 7005 Florida St., Chevy Chase MD 20815. (301)652-9495. Editor: Anne Simpkinson. 25% freelance written. A bimonthly magazine on interfacing between spiritually and psychotherapy. "Most readers are professional psychoterapists, pastoral counselors, spiritual directors or interested lay people. No special slant but must be professionally acceptable." Circ. 9,500. Pays on publication. Publishes ms an average of 2-3 months after acceptance. Byline given. 50% kill fee. Buys first North American serial rights. Submit seasonal/holiday material 6 months in advance. Simultaneous and photocopied submissions OK. Reports in 4 weeks on queries; 6 months on mss. Sample copy $3.50. Writer's guidelines for #10 SAE with 1 first class stamp.
Nonfiction: Book excerpts, essays, general interest, humor, inspirational, interview/profile, opinion, personal experience, photo feature and religious. buys 2 mss/year. Query. Length: 1,500-3,000 words. Pays $100-500. Pays in copies, "only if the writer requests such payment." Send photos with submission. Reviews prints (5x7). Offers $5-25 per photo. Captions and identification of subjects required. Buys one-time rights.
Tips: Topics of interest to our readers include articles on dreams, spiritual disciplines/practices, Jungian analysis, transpersonal psychology, shamanism, pastoral counseling, meditation, visualization, creativity, body work and male/female spirituality (goddesses)."

COMMON GROUND, Box 34090, Station D, Vancouver, British Columbia V6J 4M1 Canada. (604)733-2215. Editor: Joseph Roberts. 20% freelance written. Quarterly tabloid covering "health, ecology, personal growth, professional development and creativity. Average age of reader: 40 yrs.; 70% female, 30% male; well educated, socially conscious; favorite TV station: PBS; favorite pastime: reading." Circ. 65,000. Pays on publication. Publishes ms an average of 1-3 months after acceptance. Byline given. Buys one-time rights or second serial (reprint) rights. Submit seasonal/holiday material 3 months in advance. Simultaneous, photocopied and previously published submissions OK. Computer printout submissions OK; prefers letter-quality. Reports in 1 month. Sample copy $1.50 (Canadian) and 9x12 SAE.
Nonfiction: Book excerpts, expose, humor, inspirational (non-sectarian, please), interview/profile, personal experience and photo feature (b&w). No poetry or self-promotional material. Buys 10 mss/year. Query with published clips. Length: 800-1,600 words. Pays $50-100 (in Canadian funds).
Photos: Send photos with submission. Reviews transparencies, b&w contact sheets and prints. Offers $25-50 per photo. Captions, model releases and identification of subjects required. Buys one-time rights.
Columns/Departments: Health Matters (alternative medicine, high touch rather than high tech), 500-900 words; Book Reviews (positive, life enhancing, personal, professional and global), 300-500 words. Buys 8 mss/year. Query or send complete ms. Length: 600-1,000 words. Pays $25-75.
Fiction: Experimental and humorous. Buys 4 mss/year. Length: 600-1,600 words. Pays $50-90.

Fillers: Gags to be illustrated by cartoonist. Buys 4/year. Length: 200-600 words. Pays $20-40.
Tips: "First find out if we want the subject material and if we want your particular style of writing."

FATE, Clark Publishing Co., 3510 Western Ave., Highland Park IL 60035. Editor: Jerome Clark. 70% freelance written. Monthly. Buys all rights; occasionally North American serial rights only. Byline given. Pays on publication. Query. Reports in 2 months.
Nonfiction and Fillers: Personal psychic experiences, 300-500 words. Pays $10. New frontiers of science, and ancient civilizations, 2,000-3,000 words; also parapsychology, occultism, witchcraft, magic, spiritual healing miracles, flying saucers, etc. Must include complete authenticating details. Prefers interesting accounts of single events rather than roundups. "We very frequently accept manuscripts from new writers; the majority are individuals' first-person accounts of their own psychic experience. We do need to have all details, where, when, why, who and what, included for complete documentation." Pays minimum of 5¢/word. Fillers should be fully authenticated. Length: 100-300 words.
Photos: Buys good glossy prints with mss. Pays $5-10.

HOROSCOPE GUIDE, Box 70, West Springfield MA 01090. Editor: Susan Gaetz. 50% freelance written. Prefers to work with published/established writers; works with a small number of new/unpublished writers each year. For persons interested in astrology as it touches their daily lives; all ages. Monthly. Circ. 50,000. Publishes ms an average of 6 months after acceptance. Pays on publication. Buys all rights. Byline given. Submit seasonal material 6 months in advance. Sample copy and writer's guidelines for $2.50, 7x10 SAE and 4 first class stamps.
Nonfiction and Fillers: Wants anything of good interest to the average astrology buff, preferably not so technical as to require more than basic knowledge of birth sign by reader. Mss should be light, readable, entertaining and sometimes humorous. Not as detailed and technical as other astrology magazines, "with the astro-writer doing the interpreting without long-winded reference to his methods at every juncture. We are less reverent of astrological red tape." Wants mss about man-woman relationships, preferably in entertaining and occasionally humorous fashion. No textbook-type material. Does not want to see a teacher's type of approach to the subject. Buys 40 mss/year. Submit complete ms. Length: 900-4,000 words. Pays 2-3¢/word.
Tips: "Currently, we are soliciting astrological pieces with a New Age slant that connect crystals and chakras to the zodiac. Also interested in astrological profiles of celebrities."

‡MAGICAL BLEND MAGAZINE, A Transformative Journey, Box 11303, San Francisco CA 94101. (415)673-1001. Editor: Jerry Snider. Managing Editor: Michael Peter Langevin. 70% freelance written. A quarterly magazine on new age, spiritual exploration and creativity. "Our readers are people dedicated to improving themselves and their world; open minded, citizens of the 21st century." Circ. 75,000. Pays on publication. Byline given. Buys all rights. Submit seasonal/holiday material 6 months in advance. Photocopied submissions OK. Query for electronic submissions. Computer printout submissions OK; prefers letter-quality. Reports in up to 5 months. Sample copy $4; writer's guidelines for #10 SAE with 1 first class stamp.
Nonfiction: Book excerpts, essays, general interest, historical/nostalgic, how-to, humor, inspirational, interview/profile, new product, personal experience, photo feature, religious, technical, travel. Buys 40 mss/year. Send complete ms. Length: 100-7,000 words. Pays $1-100. Pays with contributor copies for poetry, short and marginal pieces.
Photos: Send photos with submission. Offers $1-100 per photo. Captions, model releases, identification of subjects required. Buys all rights.
Columns/Departments: Crystals; Interspecies Communicator; Magic in Your Life; Astrology; Spiritual Travel. Length: 100-3,000 words. Buys 30 mss/year. Send complete ms. Pays $1-100.
Fiction: Adventure, condensed novels, erotica, experimental, fantasy, historical, mainstream, novel excerpts, religious, science fiction, serialized novels, slice-of-life vignettes. Buys 5 mss/year. Length: 100-3,000 words. Pays $1-100.
Poetry: Poetry Editor: Matthew Courtnay. Avant-garde, free verse, haiku, light verse, traditional. Buys 10 poems/year. Submit maximum 3 poems. Length: 4-25 lines. Pays $1-100.
Fillers: Fillers Editor: Patricia A. Langeuin. Anectdotes, facts, gags to be illustrated by cartoonist, newsbreaks, short humor. Buys 30 fillers/year. Pays $1-10.
Tips: "Reading *Magical Blend* is the best way to break in, however well written, insightful, positive, how-to-grow spiritually articles are always welcomed."

NEW AGE JOURNAL, Rising Star Associates, 342 Western Ave., Brighton MA 02135. (617)787-2005. Editor: Florence Graves. Editorial Coordinator: Gail Whitney. 95% freelance written. Works with a small number of new/unpublished writers each year. A bimonthly magazine emphasizing "personal fulfillment and social change. The audience we reach is college-educated, social-service/hi-tech oriented, 25-45 years of age, concerned about social values, humanitarianism and balance in personal life." Payment negotiated. Publishes ms an average of 5 months after acceptance. Byline given. Offers 25% kill fee. Buys first North American serial rights and reprint rights. Submit seasonal/holiday material 6 months in advance. Simultaneous and photocopied submissions OK. Computer printout submissions are acceptable provided they are double-spaced "and dark enough." No dot-matrix. Reports in 2 months on queries. Sample copy $3; writers' guidelines for letter-size SAE with 1 first class stamp.

Nonfiction: Book excerpts, exposé, general interest, how-to (travel on business, select a computer, reclaim land, plant a garden, behavior, trend pieces), humor, inspirational, interview/profile, new product, food, sci-tech, nutrition, holistic health, education and personal experience. Buys 60-80 mss/year. Query with published clips. "Written queries only—no phone calls. The process of decision making takes time and involves more than one editor. An answer cannot be given over the phone." Length: 500-4,000 words. Pays $50-2,500. Pays the expenses of writers on assignment.

Photos: State availability of photos with submission. Model releases and identification of subjects required. Buys one-time rights.

Columns/Departments: Body/Mind; Reflections; First Person. Buys 60-80 mss/year. Query with published clips. Length: 750-1,500 words. Pays $100-800.

Tips: "Submit short, specific news items to the Upfront department. Query first with clips. A query is one to two paragraphs—if you need more space than that to *present* the idea, then you don't have a clear grip on it. The next open area is columns: First Person and Reflections often take first-time contributors. Read the magazine and get a sense of type of writing run in these two columns. In particular we are interested in seeing inspirational, first-person pieces that highlight an engaging idea, experience or issue. We are also looking for new cutting edge thinking."

‡**NEW REALITIES, Oneness of Self, Mind and Body**, Heldref Publications, 4000 Albemarle St., NW, Washington DC 20016. (202)362-6445. Editor: Neal Vahle. Managing Editor: Joy O'Rourke. 50% freelance written. A bimonthly magazine of new age interests. "Our emphasis is on the positive elements of life, those things that add, rather than detract, from people's lives." Circ. 13,500. Pays on publication. Byline given. Buys first North American serial rights, first rights or one-time rights. Submit seasonal/holiday material 3 months in advance. Simultaneous, photocopied and previously published submissions OK. Reports in 1 month. Sample copy for 8½x11 SAE with 5 first-class stamps; writer's guidelines for #10 SASE.

Nonfiction: Book excerpts, general interest, how-to, inspirational, interview/profile. No fiction, poetry, or personal experience pieces. Buys 40 mss/year. Query with or without published clips, or send complete ms. Length: 1,000-5,000 words. Pays $100-500 for assigned articles; $0-350 for unsolicited articles. Sometimes pays expenses of writers on assignment.

Photos: State availability of photos with submission. Reviews contact sheets and any size prints. Offers $10-100 per photo (cover shots more). Identification of subjects required. Buys one-time rights.

Columns/Departments: Column/Department Editor: Anne Mattison. Sights and Sounds (reviews of books, audio and video cassettes) 250 words; Tools for Transformation (experiential excercises, concrete tips on holistic living) 2,500 words. Buys 30 mss/year. Send complete ms. Length: 250-2,500 words. Pays $10-100.

Tips: "We appreciate seeing the entire manuscript, along with clips of other work. We look for a journalistic, third-party, concrete approach to what usually are rather subjective topics."

‡**RAINBOW CITY EXPRESS, Adventures on the Spiritual Path**, Box 8447, Berkeley CA 94707. (415)527-6055. Editor: Helen Bohlen Harvey. 50-75% freelance written. Quarterly magazine on "spiritual awakening and evolving consciousness, especially feminist spirituality and women's issues. We take an eclectic, mature and innovative approach to the topics of spiritual awakening and evolution of consciousness. A positive, constructive, healing tone is required, not divisive, separatist slant." Estab. 1988. Circ. 150. Pays on publication. Byline given. Buys first North American serial rights or second serial (reprint) rights. Submit seasonal/holiday material 4-6 months in advance. Photocopied and previously published (only when full publishing information accompanies ms showing where previously published) submissions OK. Computer printout submissions OK; no dot-matrix. Reports in 1 month on queries; 2 months on mss. Sample copy for $5.50; writer's guidelines for #10 SASE.

Nonfiction: Book excerpts, essays, general interest, historical/nostalgic, how-to, humor, inspirational, interview/profile, opinion, personal experience, religious, travel. "No get-rich-quick or how-to channel spirits or how-to manipulate the cosmos/others or occult/voodoo/spellcasting diatribes and no glorification of victimization/scapegoating or addictions." Buys 50-100 mss/year. Query with or without published clips, or send complete ms. Length: 250-2,000 words. Pays $5-50 per piece, negotiated individually.

Photos: State availability of photos with submissions or send photos with submission. Reviews contact sheets and prints. Offers no additional payment for photos accepted with ms. Captions, model releases and identification of subjects required. Buys one-time rights.

Columns/Departments: Book Reviews (spirituality, goddess consciousness, New Age topics), 250-500 words; Readers' Forum. Acquires 30 mss/year. Send complete ms. Pays in contributor copies.

Fiction: Adventure, fantasy, historical, religious. "Fiction should related directly to our slant which is about spiritual/consciousness evoluation. No science fiction, thriller, sex, drugs or violence mss." Acquires 4-6 mss/year. Query. Length: 500-1,000 words. Pays in contributor copies.

Poetry: Avant-garde, free verse, haiku, light verse, traditional. Acquires about 30 poems/year. Submit 3 poems maximum. Length: 8-30 lines.

Fillers: Anecdotes, short humor. "Fillers must relate to our spirituality slant."

Tips: "We feature true life experiences and accounts of spiritual awakenings/attendant phenomena, and consciousness evolution. Readers/writers who have experienced some of these phenomena and know what they're talking about are likely to be well received. We are particularly interested in actual experiences with Kundalini activation and archetypal stirring. We aim to demonstrate the often unsuspected connections between spiritual awakening and everyday realities."

‡**TRANSFORMATION TIMES**, Life Resources Unlimited, Box 425, Beavercreek OR 97004. (503)632-7141. Editor: Connie L. Faubel. Managing Editor: E. James Faubel. 100% freelance written. A tabloid covering new age, metaphysics, and natural health, published 10 times/year. Circ. 8,000. Pays on publication. Publishes ms an average of 2 months after acceptance. Byline given. Buys one-time rights. Submit seasonal/holiday material 2 months in advance. Simultaneous, photocopied and previously published submissions OK. Query for electronic submissions. Computer printout submissions OK. Sample copy and writer's guidelines for 9x12 SAE and 5 first class stamps.

Nonfiction: Book excerpts, inspirational, interview/profile, women's issues, metaphysical. "No articles with emphasis on negative opinions and ideas." Buys 60 mss/year. Send complete ms. Length: 500-1,500 words. Pays 1-3¢/word.

Photos: Send photos with submission. Reviews 3x5 prints. Offers $3-5/photo. Captions and identification of subjects required. Buys one-time rights.

Columns/Departments: Woman's Way (women's issues) 500-1,000 words. Buys 20 mss/year. Send complete ms. Pays 1-3¢/word.

Tips: "In addition, to present interests we plan on adding articles on environmental quality issues and socially responsible investing."

Automotive and Motorcycle

Publications in this section detail the maintenance, operation, performance, racing and judging of automobiles and recreational vehicles. Publications that treat vehicles as means of transportation or shelter instead of as a hobby or sport are classified in the Travel, Camping and Trailer category. Journals for service station operators and auto and motorcycle dealers are located in the Trade Auto and Truck section.

AMERICAN MOTORCYCLIST, American Motorcyclist Association, Box 6114, Westerville OH 43081-6114. (614)891-2425. Executive Editor: Greg Harrison. For "enthusiastic motorcyclists, investing considerable time and money in the sport. We emphasize the motorcyclist, not the vehicle." Monthly magazine. Circ. 134,000. Pays on publication. Rights purchased vary with author and material. Pays 25-50% kill fee. Byline given. Query with SASE. Submit seasonal/holiday material 4 months in advance. Reports in 1 month. Sample copy $1.25.

Nonfiction: How-to (different and/or unusual ways to use a motorcycle or have fun on one); historical (the heritage of motorcycling, particularly as it relates to the AMA); interviews (with interesting personalities in the world of motorcycling); photo feature (quality work on any aspect of motorcycling); and technical or how-to articles. No product evaluations or stories on motorcycling events not sanctioned by the AMA. Buys 20-25 mss/year. Query. Length: 500 words minimum. Pays minimum $4.50/published column inch.

Photos: Purchased with or without accompanying ms, or on assignment. Captions required. Query. Pays $20 minimum per published photo.

Tips: "Accuracy and reliability are prime factors in our work with freelancers. We emphasize the rider, not the motorcycle itself. It's always best to query us first and the further in advance the better to allow for scheduling."

ATV SPORTS MAGAZINE, The Original All Terrain Vehicle Magazine, Wright Publishing Co., 2950 Airway, Box 2260, Costa Mesa CA 92626. (714)979-2560. Editor: Bruce Simurda. Managing Editor; Rick Busenkell. 5% freelance written. Works with a small number of new/unpublished writers each year. Monthly magazine covering all terrain vehicles. Circ. 75,000. Pays on publication. Publishes ms an average of 3 months after acceptance. Byline given. Buys all rights. Submit seasonal/holiday material 3 months in advance. Simultaneous queries and simultaneous submissions OK. Computer printout submissions acceptable; no dot-matrix.

Reports in 1 month. Sample copy for 9x12 SAE and 5 first class stamps.

Nonfiction: General interest, how-to, new product, personal experience, technical and travel. Especially interested in articles on specific off-road riding areas. Buys 10 mss/year. Query. Length: 600-900 words. Pays $60-90. Sometimes pays the expenses of writers on assignment.

Photos: State availability of photos. Reviews b&w contact sheets and 35mm color transparencies. Captions, model releases and identification of subjects required.

Columns/Departments: All freelance columns on contract basis only. Buys 36 mss/year. Query. Length: 600-650 words. Pays $60-90.

BMX PLUS MAGAZINE, Daisy/Hi-Torque Publishing Co., Inc., 10600 Sepulveda Blvd., Mission Hills CA 91345. (714)545-6012. Editor: John Ker. Monthly magazine covering the sport of bicycle motocross for a youthful readership (95% male, aged 8-25). 3% freelance written. Prefers to work with published/established writers. Circ. 102,000. Pays on publication. Byline given. Buys one-time rights. Submit seasonal/holiday material 4 months in advance. Simultaneous queries and manuscripts OK. Computer printout submissions acceptable; prefers letter-quality. Reports in 2 months. Publishes ms an average of 3 months after acceptance. Sample copy $2; writer's guidelines for #10 SAE and 1 first class stamp.

Nonfiction: Historical/nostalgic, how-to, humor, interview/profile, new product, photo feature, technical, travel. "No articles for a general audience; our readers are BMX fanatics." Buys 20 mss/year. Send complete ms. Length: 500-1,500 words. Pays $30-250.

Photos: "Photography is the key to our magazine. Send us some exciting and/or unusual photos of hot riders in action." Send photos with ms. Pays $40-50 for color photo published; $25 for b&w photos. Reviews 35mm color transparencies and b&w negatives and 8x10 prints. Captions and identification of subjects required.

Tips: "We would like to receive more material on hot freestylers from areas other than California. Photo/story submissions would be welcomed. We also need more material about racing and freestyle from foreign countries. The sport of BMX is very young. The opportunities for talented writers and photographers in this field are open. Send us a good interview or race story with photos. Race coverage is the area that's easiest to break in to. It must be a *big* race, preferably national or international in scope. Submit story within one week of completion of race."

‡BRITISH CAR, (formerly British Car & Bike), 2D Studio, Box 1045, Canoga Park CA 91304. (818)710-1234. Editor: Dave Destler. 40% freelance written. A bimonthly magazine covering British cars. "We focus upon the cars built in Britain, the people who buy them, drive them, collect them, love them. Writers must be among the aforementioned. Written by enthusiasts for enthusiasts." Circ. 30,000. Pays on publication. Publishes ms an average of 3 months after acceptance. Byline given. Buys all rights, unless other arrangements made. Submit seasonal/holiday material 3 months in advance. Photocopied submissions OK. Computer printout submissions acceptable. Reports in 1 month. Sample copy $3.50; writer's guidelines for SAE with 1 first class stamp.

Nonfiction: Historical/nostalgic; how-to (on repair or restoration of a specific model or range of models, new technique or process); humor (based upon a realistic nonfiction situation); interview/profile (famous racer, designer, engineer, etc.); photo feature and technical. "No submissions so specific as to appeal or relate to a very narrow range of readers; no submissions so general as to be out-of-place in a specialty publication." Buys 30 mss/year. Send complete ms. "Include SASE if submission is to be returned." Length: 750-4,500 words. Pays $2-5/column inch for assigned articles; pays $2-3/column inch for unsolicited articles. Sometimes pays writers with contributor copies or other premiums rather than cash on prior arrangement.

Photos: Send photos with submission. Reviews transparencies and prints. Offers $10-75/photo. Captions and identification of subjects required. Buys all rights, unless otherwise arranged.

Columns/Departments: Update (newsworthy briefs of interest, not too timely for bimonthly publication), approximately 50-175 words; Lifestyle: A column about the people and various situations and lifestyles of British car enthusiasts. Buys 20 mss/year. Send complete ms.

Tips: "Our magazine has changed from *British Car & Bike* to *British Car*. The bikes are deleted, and the magazine will focus on the more upmarket British car scene. Thorough familiarity of subject is essential. *British Car* is read by experts and enthusiasts who can see right through superficial research. Facts are important, and must be accurate. Writers should ask themselves 'I know I'm interested in this story, but will most of *British Car's* readers appreciate it?'"

CAR AND DRIVER, 2002 Hogback Rd., Ann Arbor MI 48105. (313)971-3600. Editor: William Jeanes. For auto enthusiasts; college-educated, professional, median 24-35 years of age. Monthly magazine; 160 pages. Circ. 900,000. Pays on acceptance. Rights purchased vary with author and material. Buys all rights or first North American serial rights. Buys 3-4 unsolicited mss/year. Submit seasonal material 4 months in advance. Reports in 2 months.

Nonfiction: Non-anecdotal articles about the more sophisticated treatment of autos and motor racing. Exciting, interesting cars. Automotive road tests, informational articles on cars and equipment; some satire and humor. Personalities, past and present, in the automotive industry and automotive sports. "Treat readers as intellectual equals. Emphasis on people as well as hardware." Informational, how-to, humor, historical, think articles, and nostalgia. Query with clips of previously published work. Length: 750-2,000 words. Pays $200-1,500. Also buys mini-features for FYI department. Length: about 500 words. Pays $100-500.

Photos: B&w photos purchased with accompanying mss with no additional payment.

Tips: "It is best to start off with an interesting query and to stay away from nuts-and-bolts stuff since that will be handled in-house or by an acknowledged expert. Our goal is to be absolutely without flaw in our presentation of automotive facts, but we strive to be every bit as entertaining as we are informative."

CAR COLLECTOR/CAR CLASSICS, Classic Publishing, Inc., Suite 144, 8601 Dunwoody Pl., Atlanta GA 30350. Editor: Donald R. Peterson. 90% freelance written. Works with a small number of new/unpublished writers each year. For people interested in all facets of collecting classic, milestone, antique, special interest and sports cars; also mascots, models, restoration, garaging, license plates and memorabilia. Monthly magazine; 68 pages. Circ. 35,000. Pays on publication. Publishes ms an average of 4 months after acceptance. Buys first rights. Submit seasonal/holiday material 4 months in advance. Photocopied submissions OK. Computer printout submissions acceptable; no dot-matrix. Reports in 2 months. Sample copy for $2; writer's guidelines for #10 SAE and 1 first class stamp.

Nonfiction: General interest, historical, how-to, humor, inspirational, interview, nostalgia, personal opinion, profile, photo feature, technical and travel. Buys 75-100 mss/year; buys 24-36 unsolicited mss/year. Query with clips of published work. Length: 300-2,500 words. Pays 5¢/word minimum. Sometimes pays the expenses of writers on assignment.

Photos: "We have a continuing need for high-quality color positives (e.g., 2¼ or 35mm) *with* copy." State availability of photos with ms. Offers additional payment for photos with accompanying mss. Uses b&w glossy prints; color transparencies. Pays a minimum of $75 for cover and centerfold color; $10 for inside color; $5 for inside b&w. Captions and model releases required.

Columns/Departments: "Rarely add a new columnist but we are open to suggestions." Buys 36 mss/year. Query with clips of published work. Length: 2,000 maximum; prefers 1,000-2,000 words. Pays 5¢/word minimum.

Tips: "The most frequent mistakes are made by writers who are writing to a 'Sunday supplement' audience rather than to a sophisticated audience of car collectors and who are submitting stories that are often too basic and assume no car knowledge at all on the part of the reader."

‡CAR CRAFT, Petersen Publishing Co., 8490 Sunset Blvd., Los Angeles CA 90069. (213)657-5100, ext. 345. Editor: Cam Benty. For men and women, 18-34, "enthusiastic owners of 1949 and newer muscle cars." Monthly magazine; 132 pages. Circ. 400,000. Study past issues before making submissions or story suggestions. Pays generally on publication, on acceptance under special circumstances. Buys all rights. Buys 2-10 mss/year. Computer printout submissions acceptable. Query.

Nonfiction: How-to articles ranging from the basics to fairly sophisticated automotive modifications. Drag racing feature stories and some general car features on modified late model automobiles. Especially interested in do-it-yourself automotive tips, suspension modifications, mileage improvers and even shop tips and homemade tools. Length: open. Pays $100-200/page.

Photos: Photos purchased with or without accompanying text. Captions suggested, but optional. Reviews 8x10 b&w glossy prints; 35mm or 2¼x2¼ color. Pays $30 for b&w, color negotiable. "Pay rate higher for complete story, i.e., photos, captions, headline, subtitle: the works, ready to go."

CORVETTE FEVER, Prospect Publishing Co., Inc., Box 44620, Ft. Washington MD 20744. (301)839-2221. Publisher: Patricia E. Stivers. 30-40% freelance written. Works with a small number of new/unpublished writers each year. Bimonthly magazine. Circ. 35,000. Pays on publication. Publishes ms an average of 4-6 months after acceptance. Buys first rights and second serial (reprint) rights. Byline given. Phone queries OK. Submit seasonal/holiday material 4 months in advance. Photocopied submissions OK. Computer printout submissions OK; prefers letter-quality. Reports in 1 month. Sample copy and writer's guidelines $2.

Nonfiction: General interest (event coverage, personal experience); historical (special or unusual Corvette historical topics); how-to (technical and mechanical articles, photos are a must); humor (Corvette-related humor); interview (with important Corvette persons, race drivers, technical persons, club officials, etc.); nostalgia (relating to early Corvette car and development); personal experiences (related to Corvette car use and experiences); profile (prominent and well-known Corvette personalities wanted for interviews and articles); photo feature (centerspread in color of Corvette and female Vette owner); photo essays on renovation, customizing and show cars); technical (any aspect of Corvette improvement or custom articles); and travel (relating to Corvette use and adventure). Buys 4-6 mss/issue. Query or send complete ms. Length: 500-2,500 words. Pays $40-300. Sometimes pays the expenses of writers on assignment.

Photos: Send photos with ms. Pays $5 for 5x7 b&w glossy prints; $10 for color contact sheets and transparencies. Captions preferred; model release required.

Columns/Departments: Innovative Ideas, In Print, Model Shop, Pit Stop, and Tech Vette. Buys 3 mss/issue. Send complete ms. Length: 300-800 words. Pays $24-200.

Fiction: "Any type of story as long as it is related to the Corvette." Buys 1-2 mss/issue. Send complete ms. Length: 500-2,500 words. Pays $40-200.

Fillers: Clippings, anecdotes, short humor and newsbreaks. Buys 2-3/issue. Length: 25-150 words. Pays $2-15.

4-WHEEL & OFF-ROAD, Petersen Publishing Co., 8490 Sunset Blvd., Los Angeles CA 90069. (213)854-2360. Editor: Steve Campbell. Managing Editor: Cecily Chittick. A monthly magazine covering four-wheel-drive vehicles, "devoted to new-truck tests, buildups of custom 4x4s, coverage of 4WD racing, trail rides and other competitions." Circ. 275,000. Pays on acceptance. Publishes ms an average of 4 months after acceptance. Byline given. Pays 20% kill fee. Buys first North American serial rights or all rights. Submit seasonal/holiday material 4 months in advance. Computer printout submissions OK. Reports in 3 weeks. Free writer's guidelines.

Nonfiction: How-to (on four-wheel-drive vehicles—engines, suspension, drive systems, etc.), new product, photo feature, technical and travel. Buys 12-16 mss/year. Send complete ms. Length: 1,000-2,500 words. Pays $200-500 for assigned and unsolicited articles. Sometimes pays the expenses of writers on assignment.

Photos: Send photos with submission. Reviews transparencies and 7x9 prints. Offers no additional payment for photos accepted with ms. Captions, model releases and identification of subjects required. Buys all rights.

Fillers: Anecdotes, facts, gags, newsbreaks and short humor. Buys 12-16/year. Length: 50-150 words. Pays $15-50.

Tips: "Attend 4x4 events, get to know the audience. Present material only after full research. Manuscripts should contain *all* of the facts pertinent to the story. Technical/how-to articles are most open to freelancers."

FRIENDS MAGAZINE, Ceco Communications, Inc., 30400 Van Dyke Blvd., Warren MI 48093. (313)575-9400. Executive Editor: Michael Brudene. "*Friends* is a magazine for Chevrolet owners." 75-85% freelance written. Prefers to work with published/established writers. Monthly magazine; 52 pages. Circ. 1,000,000. Pays on acceptance. Publishes ms an average of 6 months after acceptance. Buys first rights in most cases. Computer printout submissions acceptable; no dot-matrix. Submit seasonal/holiday material 6 months in advance. Simultaneous and photocopied submissions OK. Reports in 1 month. Free sample copy and writer's guidelines.

Nonfiction: Travel (by automobile; U.S. only); celebrity profiles; unusual use of Chevrolet products; humor (travel-related); entertainment; and photo features (strong travel-tied photo essays). "We're looking for freelancers who can focus and produce lively copy and write a story that will interest or excite the general reader." Query by mail only. Length: 800-2,000. Pays $300-750. Sometimes pays expenses on assignment.

Columns/Departments: Starting Point (potpourri of travel items); Chef's Special (visit with a chef); Roadside (travel-related anecdotes); Mile Meters (games page); American Profile (personality with travel theme). Pays $25 and up.

Photos: State availability of photos. Pays $200/page. Transparencies only. "About the only time we'll consider black and white is when the article is an early historical piece." Captions and model release required.

Tips: "Writing style must be 'people' oriented with plenty of quotes and conversational tone. Avoid 'dry' narrative. We're particularly interested in seeing queries about auto trips or tours that can be done in 72 hours or less. Most auto travelers prefer 'long weekend' vacations."

‡KEEPIN' TRACK OF VETTES, Box 48, Spring Valley NY 10977. (914)425-2649. Editor: Shelli Finkel. 70% freelance written. Works with a small number of new/unpublished writers each year. Monthly magazine; 60-68 pages. For Corvette owners and enthusiasts. Circ. 38,000. Pays on publication. Publishes ms an average of 3 months after acceptance. Buys all rights. Byline given. Submit seasonal/holiday material 3 months in advance. Computer printout submissions acceptable; prefers letter-quality. Reports in 1 month. Free sample copy and writer's guidelines.

Nonfiction: Expose (telling of Corvette problems with parts, etc.); historical (any and all aspects of Corvette developments); how-to (restorations, engine work, suspension, race, swapmeets); humor; informational; interview (query); nostalgia; personal experience; personal opinion; photo feature; profile (query); technical; and travel. Buys 1-2 mss/issue. Query or submit complete ms. Pays $50-200. Sometimes pays the expenses of writers on assignment.

Photos: Send photo with ms. Pays $10-35 for b&w contact sheets or negatives; $10-50 for 35mm color transparencies; offers no additional payment for photos with accompanying ms.

Tips: The writer "must have more than a passing knowledge of Corvettes specifically and automobiles in general."

‡MOTOR TREND, Petersen Publishing Co., 8490 Sunset Blvd., Los Angeles CA 90069. (213)854-2222. Executive Editor: Jack Nerad. 15-20% freelance written. Prefers to work with published/established writers. For automotive enthusiasts and general interest consumers. Monthly. Circ. 750,000. Publishes ms an average of 3 months after acceptance. Buys all rights. "Fact-filled query suggested for all freelancers." Computer printout submissions acceptable; prefers letter-quality. Reports in 1 month.

Nonfiction: Automotive and related subjects that have national appeal. Emphasis on domestic and imported cars, roadtests, driving impressions, auto classics, auto, travel, racing, and high-performance features for the enthusiast. Packed with facts. Freelancers should confine queries to feature material; road tests and related activity handled inhouse.

Photos: Buys photos, particularly of prototype cars and assorted automotive matter. Pays $25-250 for b&w glossy prints or color transparencies.

‡**MOUNTAIN BIKE ACTION**, Daisey/Hi Torque Publishing, 10600 Sepulveda Blvd., Mission Hills CA 91345. (818)365-6831. Editor: Zapata Espinosa. Managing Editor: Greg Barbacovi. 15% freelance written. A Monthly magazine on all terrain bicycling. "We are a publication written by and for enthusiasts of off road bicycling." Circ. 50,000. Pays on publication. Publishes ms an average of 3 months after acceptance. Byline given. Buys all rights. Submit seasonal/holiday material 4 months in advance. Query for electronic submissions. Computer printout submissions OK; prefers letter-quality. Writer's guidelines for #10 SAE.

Nonfiction: Essays, general interest, historical/nostalgic, how-to, humor, interview/profile, opinion, personal experience, photo feature, travel. Buys 12 mss/year. Length: 1,000-10,000 words. Pays $40/published page.

Photos: Send photos with submission. Offers $10/b&w photo; $25/color slides. Indentification of subjects required. Buys one-time rights.

Fiction: Adventure, humorous. Buys 2 mss/year. Send complete ms. Length: 1,000-5,000 words. Pays $40 per published page.

‡**MUSTANG MONTHLY**, Dobbs Publications, Inc., Box 6320, Lakeland FL 33807. (813)646-5743. Editor: Tom Corcoran. Technical Editor: Earl Davis. 40% freelance written. A monthly magazine covering the 1964½ through 1973 Ford Mustang. "Our average audience makes over $35,000 annually, and is 35 years of age." Circ. 66,000. Pays on publication. Publishes ms an average of 6 months after acceptance. Byline given. Buys all rights. Simultaneous submissions OK. Computer printout submissions acceptable; prefers letter-quality. Reports in 6 weeks on manuscripts. Free sample copy and writers guidelines.

Nonfiction: How-to and technical. No seasonal, holiday, humor, fiction, first-person nostalgic material. Buys 35 mss/year. Query with or without published clips, or send complete ms. "Freelancers should write for guidelines *first.*" Length: 2,500 words maximum. Pays 15¢/word for first 500 words; 10¢/word to 2,500 limit.

Photos: Send photos with submission. Reviews contact sheets, negatives and transparencies. No color prints. Offers $100/page color pro-rated to size, $25 minimum; $10/photo b&w, $25 minimum. Captions, model releases, and identification of subjects required.

Tips: "*Mustang Monthly* is looking for color features on trophy-winning original Mustangs and well-researched b&w how-to and technical articles."

NISSAN DISCOVERY, The Magazine for Nissan Owners, Donnelley Marketing, Box 4617, N. Hollywood CA 91607. (213)877-4406. Editor: Wayne Thoms. 50% freelance written. Prefers to work with published/established writers and photographers. Bimonthly magazine for Nissan owners and their families. Circ. 500,000. Pays on acceptance. Publishes ms an average of 3-6 months after acceptance. Byline given. Buys first North American serial rights. Submit seasonal/holiday material 5 months in advance. Photocopied and previously published submissions OK. Computer printout submissions acceptable; no dot-matrix. Reports in 1 month. Sample copy 9x12 SAE and $1.50 cash or 4 first-class stamps; writer's guidelines for #10 SAE and 1 first class stamp.

Nonfiction: Historical/nostalgic, humor, photo feature, travel. "We need general family interest material with heavy emphasis on outstanding color photos: travel, humor, food, lifestyle, sports, entertainment." Buys 25 mss/year. Query. Length: 1,300-1,800 words. Pays $300-1,000. Sometimes pays the expenses of writers on assignment.

Photos: State availability of photos. Reviews 2¼" and 35mm color transparencies. No b&w photos. "Payment usually is part of story package—all negotiated." Captions and identification of subjects required. Buys one-time rights.

Tips: "A freelancer can best break in to our publication by submitting a brief idea query with specific information on color slides available. Offer a package of copy and art."

OFF-ROAD'S THUNDER TRUCKS AND TRUCK PULLS, Argus Publishing, Suite 316, 12301 Wilshire Blvd., Los Angeles CA 90025. (213)820-3601. Editor: Stephanie Wolfe. 35% freelance written. Quarterly magazine covering truck pulls, monster events and mud bogging. Pays on publication. Publishes ms an average of 3-8 months after acceptance. Byline given. Kill fee varies. Buys second serial (reprint) rights. Submit seasonal/holiday material 4 months in advance. Simultaneous submissions OK. Query for electronic submissions. Computer printout submissions OK; prefers letter-quality. Reports in 2 weeks on mss. Free writer's guidelines.

Nonfiction: Book excerpts, historical/nostalgic, how-to, humor, interview/profile, new product, personal experience, photo feature, technical and travel. Query. Pays $50-400 for assigned articles.

Photos: Send photos with submission. Reviews contact sheets, negatives, transparencies and prints. Captions, model releases and identification of subjects required. Buys all rights.

Columns/Departments: Video and Book Reviews. Query. Payment varies.

OPEN WHEEL MAGAZINE, Lopez Publications, Box 715, Ipswich MA 01938. (617)356-7030. Editor: Dick Berggren. 80% freelance written. Monthly magazine. "*OW* covers sprint cars, midgets, supermodifieds and Indy cars. *OW* is an enthusiast's publication which speaks to those deeply involved in oval track automobile racing in the United States and Canada. *OW*'s primary audience is a group of men and women actively engaged in competition at the present time, those who have recently been in competition and those who plan competition soon. That audience includes drivers, car owners, sponsors and crew members who represent perhaps 50-70 percent of our readership. The rest who read the magazine are those in the racing trade (part manufacturers, track operators and officials) and serious fans who see 30 or more races per year." Circ. 150,000. Pays on publication. Publishes ms an average of 3-6 months after acceptance. Byline given. Buys first rights. Submit seasonal/holiday material 2 months in advance. Computer printout submissions OK; prefers letter-quality. Reports in 3 weeks on queries. Free sample copy and writer's guidelines.

Nonfiction: General interest, historical/nostalgic, how-to, humor, interview/profile, new product, photo feature and technical. "We don't care for features that are a blow-by-blow chronology of events. The key word is interest. We want features which allow the reader to get to know the main figure very well. Our view of racing is positive. We don't think all is lost, that the sport is about to shut down and don't want stories that claim such to be the case, but we shoot straight and avoid whitewash." Buys 125 + mss/year. Query with or without published clips, or send complete ms.

Photos: State availability of photos with submission. Reviews contact sheets, negatives, transparencies and prints. Buys one-time rights.

Fillers: Anecdotes, facts and short humor. Buys 100/year. Length: 1-3 pages, double-spaced. Pays $35.

Tips: "Virtually all our features are submitted without assignment. An author knows much better what's going on in his backyard than we do. We ask that you write to us before beginning a story theme. Judging of material is always a combination of a review of the story and its support illustrations. Therefore, we ask for photography to accompany the manuscript on first submission. We've gone from bi-monthly to monthly - so we are looking to use more quality material."

POPULAR CARS, The Complete Street Machine Magazine, McMullen Publishing, Inc., 2145 W. La Palma, Anaheim CA 92801-1785. (714)635-9040. Editor: Jim Kelso. 25% freelance written. Prefers to work with published/established automotive writers. Monthly magazine on contemporary, high performance, domestic automobiles. "Our main emphasis is on 'street machines' (owner-modified cars) and 60s and 70s 'muscle' cars and related subjects." Circ. 85,000. Pays on publication. Publishes ms an average of 3 months after acceptance. Byline given. Kill fee negotiated in advance. Buys first serial rights. Computer printout submissions acceptable; prefers letter-quality. Reports in 3 weeks on queries; 1 month on mss. Sample copy $2.50; free photographer's guidelines.

Nonfiction: Historical/nostalgic (60s, 70s muscle cars); how-to (street performance and drag racing); interview/profile (of people associated with automotive performance subjects); new product (new cars—2 page maximum, performance cars *only*); photo feature (on peoples' street machines); technical (street performance); and drag race and street machine event coverage. Special issues on Ford '64-'70 Mustangs, Corvettes, '55-'57, Chevys, Pro Streeters. No new car tests. Buys 36-40 mss/year. Query with published clips. Length: 435-1,175 words. Pays $75-300.

Photos: Reviews 35mm color transparencies and 5x7 b&w prints. Pays $20-75 for transparencies; $0-20 for prints. Captions, model releases, and identification of subjects required. Buys all rights.

Tips: "A freelancer can best break in to our publication with a query, submission of past work, good quality manuscripts, reputation, and good 'car features'."

RIDER, 29901 Agoura Rd., Agoura CA 91301. Editor: Tash Matsuoka. 60% freelance written. Works with a small number of new/unpublished writers each year. For owners and prospective buyers of motorcycles to be used for touring, sport riding, and commuting. Monthly magazine. Buys first-time rights only. Pays on publication. Publishes ms average of 6 months after acceptance. Query first. Submit seasonal material 3 months in advance. Photocopied submissions OK. Computer printout submissions acceptable; no dot-matrix. Reports in 1 month. Sample copy $2; writer's guidelines for SAE with 1 first class stamp.

Nonfiction: Articles directly related to motorcycle touring, camping, commuting and sport riding including travel, human interest, safety, novelty, do-it-yourself and technical. "Articles which portray the unique thrill of motorcycling." Should be written in clean, contemporary style aimed at a sharp, knowledgeable reader. Buys informational how-to, personal experience, profile, historical, nostalgia and personal opinion. Length is flexible. Pays $100 for Favorite Ride feature and $350-500 for major articles. Sometimes pays expenses of writers on assignment.

Photos: Offers no additional payment for photos purchased with ms. Captions required. "Quality photographs are critical. Graphics are emphasized in *Rider*, and we must have photos with good visual impact."

Tips: "We are going back to our original format of the *touring* motorcyclist."

ROAD & TRACK, 1499 Monrovia Ave., Newport Beach CA 92663. Editor: John Dinkel. 10% freelance written. For knowledgeable car enthusiasts. Monthly magazine. Publishes ms up to 2 years after acceptance. Buys first rights. Computer printout submissions acceptable. Reports in 6 weeks.

Nonfiction: "We welcome freelance material but it's critical that the writer be well-versed and throughly familiar with the material used in the magazine. *Road & Track* material is highly specialized. We publish more serious, comprehensive and in-depth treatment of particular areas of automotive interest." Query. Pays 25-50¢/word minimum depending upon subject covered and qualifications and experience of author.

Tips: "Freelance articles are only a small percentage of the magazine because of its specialty nature."

ROAD KING MAGAZINE, Box 250, Park Forest IL 60466. Editor-in-Chief: George Friend. 10% freelance written. Eager to work with new/unpublished writers. Truck driver leisure reading publication. Quarterly magazine; 72 pages. Circ. 231,000. Pays on acceptance. Publishes ms an average of 2 months after acceptance. Usually buys all rights; sometimes buys first rights. Byline given "always on fiction—if requested on nonfiction—copyright mentioned only if requested." Submit seasonal/holiday material 3 months in advance. Sample copy for 7x10 SAE and 3 first class stamps or get free sample copy at any Unocal 76 truck stop.

Nonfiction: Trucker slant or general interest, humor, and photo feature. No articles on violence or sex. Name and quote release required. No queries. Submit complete ms. Length: 500-1,200 words. Pays $50-400.

Photos: Submit photos with accompanying ms. No additional payment for b&w contact sheets or 2¼x2¼ color transparencies. Captions preferred. Buys first rights. Model release required.

Fiction: Adventure, historical, humorous, mystery, rescue-type suspense and western. Especially about truckers. No stories on sex and violence. "We're looking for quality writing." Buys 4 mss/year. Submit complete ms. Length: approximately 1,200 words. Pays up to $400. Writer should quote selling price with submission.

Fillers: Jokes, gags, anecdotes and short humor about truckers. Buys 20-25/year. Length: 50-500 words. Pays $5-100.

Tips: "No collect phone calls or postcard requests. Never phone for free copy as we will not handle such phone calls. We don't appreciate letters we have to answer. Do not submit manuscripts, art or photos using registered mail, certified mail or insured mail. Publisher will not accept such materials from the post office. Publisher will not discuss refusal with writer. Nothing personal, just legal. Do not write and ask if we would like such and such article or outline. We buy only from original and complete manuscripts submitted on speculation. Do not ask for writer's guidelines. See above and/or get a copy of the magazine and be familiar with our format before submitting anything. We are a trucker publication whose readers are often family members and sometimes Bible Belt. We refrain from violence, sex, nudity, etc. "

‡**SCHNEIDER PERFORMANCE SERIES, Vette, Pontiac, Mopar & Muscle Cars**, CSK Publishing Co., Inc., 175 Hudson St., Hackensack NJ 07601. (201)488-7171. Editor: Cliff Gromer. Managing Editor: D. Randy Riggs. 35% freelance written. Automotive enthusiast magazines dedicated to all makes and models within the individual marque. Circ. 50,000. Pays on acceptance. Publishes ms an average of 3 months after acceptance. Byline given. Buys all rights. Query for electronic submission. Computer printout submissions OK; no dot-matrix. Reports in 2 weeks on queries; 1 month on mss. Sample copy for 8½x11 SAE.

Nonfiction: Bill Erdman, articles editor. Historical/nostalgic, how-to, interview/profile, photofeature, technical. Buys 150 mss/year. Query with or without published clips, or send complete ms. Length: 1,000-5,000 words. Pays $150-350. Sometimes pays expenses of writers on assignment.

Photos: Send photos with submission. Reviews contact sheets, transparencies (all) and prints (all). Offers no additional payment for photos accepted with mss. Identification of subjects required.

‡**SPECIAL INTEREST AUTOS**, Watering, Inc., Box 196, Bennington VT 05201. (802)442-3101. Editor: David Brownell. Managing Editor: Nancy Bianco. A bimonthly magazine covering antique, classic and vintage autos. Circ. 35,000. Pays on acceptance. Publishes ms an average of 6 months after acceptance. Byline given. Offers $150 kill fee. Buys all rights. Computer printout submissions OK; no dot-matrix. Reports in 3 weeks on queries; 2 months on mss.

Nonfiction: Historical/nostalgic, interview/profile, photo feature, technical. "No fuzzy recollections about grandpa's first car or 'gee whiz' articles about cars—our audience is extremely knowledgable." Buys 50 mss/year. Query. Length: 250-2,500 words. Pays $150-450. Sometimes pays expenses of writers on assignment.

Photos: State availability of photos with submission. Reviews contact sheets and negatives. Offers $10/photo. Identification of subjects required. Buys all rights.

Columns/Departments: Blue Smoke (commentary on car collecting) 1,000 words; Blueprints (illustrated brief history of a make/model of car) 300 words; and Noted in Passing (car collecting news) varies. Buys 12 mss/year. Pays $75-200.

Tips: "Have an excellent knowledge of vintage cars, a dedication to writing about them accurately and to convey this information in an interesting, lively manner."

STOCK CAR RACING MAGAZINE, Box 715, Ipswich MA 01938. Editor: Dick Berggren. 80% freelance written. Eager to work with new/unpublished writers. For stock car racing fans and competitors. Monthly magazine; 116 pages. Circ. 400,000. Pays on publication. Publishes ms an average of 3 months after acceptance. Buys all rights. Byline given. Query for electronic submissions. Computer printout submissions acceptable; prefers letter-quality. Reports in 6 weeks. Free sample copy and writer's guidelines.

Nonfiction: General interest, historical/nostalgic, how-to, humor, interviews, new product, photo features and technical. "Uses nonfiction on stock car drivers, cars, and races. We are interested in the story behind the story in stock car racing. We want interesting profiles and colorful, nationally interesting features. We are looking for more technical articles, particularly in the area of street stocks and limited sportsman." Query with or without published clips, or submit complete ms. Buys 50-200 mss/year. Length: 100-6,000 words. Pays up to $450.

Photos: State availability of photos. Pays $20 for 8x10 b&w photos; up to $250 for 35mm or larger color transparencies. Captions required.

Fillers: Anecdotes and short humor. Buys 100 each year. Pays $35.

Tips: "We get more queries than stories. We just don't get as much material as we want to buy. We have more room for stories than ever before. We are an excellent market with 12 issues per year. Virtually all our features are submitted without assignment. An author knows much better what's going on in his backyard than we do. We ask that you write to us before beginning a story theme. If nobody is working on the theme you wish to pursue, we'd be glad to assign it to you if it fits our needs and you are the best person for the job. Judging of material is always a combination of a review of the story and its support illustration. Therefore, we ask for photography to accompany the manuscript on first submission."

VOLKSWAGEN'S WORLD, Volkswagen of America, 888 W. Big Beaver Rd., Box 3951, Troy MI 48007. Editor: Marlene Goldsmith. 75% freelance written. Magazine published 5 times/year for Volkswagen owners in the United States. Circ. 340,000. Pays on acceptance. Buys first North American serial rights. Byline given. Query for electronic submissions. Computer printout submissions acceptable; no dot-matrix. Reports in 6 weeks. Free writer's guidelines.

Nonfiction: "Interesting stories on people using Volkswagens; travel pieces with the emphasis on people, not places; Volkswagenmania stories; personality pieces, including celebrity interviews; and inspirational and true adventure articles. The style should be light. Our approach is subtle, however, and we try to avoid obvious product puffery, since *Volkswagen's World* is not an advertising medium. We prefer a first-person, people-oriented handling. No basic travelogues; stay away from Beetle stories. With all story ideas, query first. All unsolicited manuscripts will be returned unopened. Although queries should be no longer than 2 pages, they ought to include a working title, a short, general summary of the article, and an outline of the specific points to be covered. We strongly advise writers to read at least 2 past issues before working on a story." Buys 10-12 mss/year. Length: 1,000 words maximum; "shorter pieces, some as short as 450 words, often receive closer attention." Pays $150 per printed page for photographs and text; otherwise, a portion of that amount, depending on the space allotted. Most stories are 2 pages; some run 3 or 4 pages.

Photos: Submit photo samples with query. Photos purchased with ms; captions required. "We prefer color transparencies, 35mm or larger. All photos should carry the photographer's name and address. If the photographer is not the author, both names should appear on the first page of the text. Where possible, we would like a selection of at least 40 transparencies. It is recommended that at least one show the principal character or author. Quality photography can often sell a story that might be otherwise rejected. Every picture should be identified or explained." Model releases required. Pays $350 maximum for front cover photo.

Fillers: "Short, humorous anecdotes about current model Volkswagens." Pays $15.

Tips: "Style of the publication and its content are being structured toward more upscale, affluent buyers. VW drivers are not the same as those who used to drive the Beetle."

‡VW & PORSCHE, Argus Publishers, Suite 250, 12100 Wilshire Blvd., Los Angeles CA 90025. (213)820-3601. Editor: C. Van Tune. 60% freelance written. Bimonthly magazine covering VW, Porsche, Audi and European cars for owners. Circ. 80,000. Pays one month before publication. Publishes ms an average of 6 months after acceptance. Byline given. Kill fee varies. Buys all rights. Submit seasonal/holiday material 4 months in advance. Computer printout submissions acceptable; prefers letter quality. Reports in 2 weeks on queries. Free sample copy.

Nonfiction: How-to (restore, maintain or tune-up); Special, modified or restored VWs and Porsches. Buys 30-35 mss/year. Query. Length: 1,000-2,500 words. Pays $75-100/printed page. "More if color pictures are used." Sometimes pays the expenses of writers on assignment.

Photos: "We require crisp, well-lit b&w and color prints and slides (35mm or 120 transparencies); great variety in angles and settings." State availability of photos. Reviews proofsheets. Identification and/or signed release of subjects required.

Tips: "All of our articles deal with VWs, Porsches, Audis and European cars in a technical light, therefore a strong technical knowledge is critical; short articles used may occasionally be humorous, not so 'techy.'"

Aviation

Professional and private pilots and aviation enthusiasts read the publications in this section. Editors at aviation magazines want material for audiences who know commercial aviation. Magazines for passengers of commercial airlines are grouped in the In-Flight category. Technical aviation and space journals and publications for airport operators, aircraft dealers and others in aviation businesses are listed under Aviation and Space in the Trade section.

AERO, Fancy Publications, Box 6050, Mission Viejo CA 92690. (714)855-8822. Editor: Mary F. Silitch. 75% freelance written. Works with a small number of new/unpublished writers each year. For owners of private aircraft. "We take a unique, but limited view within our field." Circ. 75,000. Buys first North American serial rights. Buys about 60-90 mss/year. Pays after publication. Publishes manuscript an average of 4 months after acceptance. Will consider photocopied submissions if guaranteed original. Query for electronic submissions. Computer printout submissions OK. Reports in 2 months. Sample copy $3; writer's guidelines for SASE.
Nonfiction: Material on aircraft products, developments in aviation, specific airplane use reports, travel by aircraft, development and use of airports. All must be related to general aviation field. Query. Length: 1,000-4,000 words. Pays $75-300.
Photos: Pays $15 for 8x10 b&w glossy prints purchased with mss or on assignment. Pays $150 for color transparencies used on cover.
Columns/Departments: Weather flying, instrument flight refresher, new products.
Tips: "Freelancer must know the subject about which he is writing; use good grammar; know the publication for which he's writing; remember that we try to relate to the middle segment of the business/pleasure flying public. We see too many 'first flight' type of articles. Our market is more sophisticated than that. Most writers do not do enough research on their subject. We would like to see more material on business-related flying, more on people involved in flying."

AIR & SPACE MAGAZINE, Joe Bonsignore-Smithsonian, 900 Jefferson Dr., Washington DC 20560. (202)357-4414. Editor: George C. Larson. Managing Editor: Philip Hayward. 80% freelance written. Prefers to work with published/established writers. A bimonthly magazine covering aviation and aerospace for a non-technical audience. "Features are slanted to a technically curious, but not necessarily technically knowledgeable audience. We are looking for unique angles to aviation/aerospace stories, history, events, personalities, current and future technologies, that emphasize the human-interest aspect." Circ. 300,000. Pays on acceptance. Byline given. Offers kill fee. Buys first North American serial rights. Photocopied submissions OK. Reports in 5 weeks. Sample copy for $3.50 plus 9½x13 SASE.
Nonfiction: Book excerpts, essays, general interest (on aviation/aerospace), historical/nostalgic, how-to, humor, interview/profile, photo feature and technical. Buys 50 mss/year. Query with published clips. Length: 1,500-3,000 words. Pays $2,000 maximum. Pays the expenses of writers on assignment.
Columns/Departments: Above and Beyond (first person), 2,000-2,500 words; Flights and Fancy (whimsy, insight), approximately 1,200 words; Groundling's Notebook (looking upward), length varies. Buys 25 mss/year. Query with published clips. Pays $1,000 maximum. Soundings (brief items, timely but not breaking news), 500-800 words. Pays $300.
Tips: "Soundings is the section most open to freelancers. State availability of illustrations with submission. Reviews 35mm transparencies."

ALASKA FLYING MAGAZINE, Pacific Quest Publishing, Inc., Pouch 112010, Anchorage AK 99511. (907)561-5450. Editor: Niki Miscovich. 60% freelance written. Eager to work with new/unpublished writers. A bimonthly magazine on Alaskan aviation and lifestyles. "For both pilots and nonpilots, *Alaska Flying* covers a wide variety of topics related to Alaska aviation, including hunting and fishing, adventures, historical articles, character sketches, how aircraft are used in Alaska, etc." Circ. 25,000. Pays 4 months after publication. Publishes manuscript an average of 5 months after acceptance. Byline given. Pays $40 kill fee. Buys first North American rights and makes work-for-hire assignments. Submit seasonal/holiday material 6 months in advance. Simultaneous, photocopied and previously published submissions OK. Computer printout submissions OK. Reports in 1 month on queries. Sample copy for 8½x11 SAE with 5 first class stamps.
Nonfiction: General interest, historical/nostalgic, how-to, humor, new product, personal experience, photo feature, technical, travel and flying techniques. Good photo support necessary. Buys 60 mss/year. Send complete ms. Length: 1,000-3,000 words. Pays $100-150 for assigned articles. Pays $75-125 for unsolicited articles. Sometimes pays the expenses of writers on assignment.
Photos: Send photos with submission. Reviews contact sheets, negatives, transparencies and prints. Offers no additional payment for photos accepted with ms. Captions and identification of subjects required. Buys one-time rights.

Tips: "Make sure your story has a strong *Alaska lifestyle* connection—not too technical—with strong photo support. Emphasis is on what pilots everywhere can learn from flying in Alaska, the proving ground for aviation."

‡**FINAL FRONTIER, The Magazine of Space Exploration**, Final Frontier Publishing, Box 11519, Washington DC 20008 for editorial submissions. 339 Union Plaza, 333 N. Washington Ave., Minneapolis MN 55401. (612)926-5962. Editor: Tony Reichhardt. 95% freelance written. Bimonthly magazine on space exploration. "We are not a technical journal nor a science fiction magazine. We're looking for well told, factual articles about the people, events and exciting possiblities of the world's space programs." Estab. 1988. Circ. 75,000. Pays on acceptance. Byline given. Pays 33% kill fee. Buys first North American serial rights. Submit seasonal/holiday material 6 months in advance. Simultaneous and photocopied submissions OK. Query for electronic submissions. Computer printout submissions OK; prefers letter-quality. Reports in 2 months. Sample copy for $3 and a 9x12 SAE with 6 first class stamps. Writer's guidelines for #10 SASE.
Nonfiction: Book excerpts, essays, expose, general interest, historical/nostalgic, humor, interview/profile, new product, personal experience, photo feature. No technical papers, no science fiction or UFOs. Buys 60 mss/year. Query with published clips. Length: 1,000-3,000 words. Pays $250-750. Sometimes pays expenses of writers on assignment.
Photos: State availability of photos with submission. Offers no additional payment for photos accepted with ms "except as agreed ahead of time."
Column/Departments: Boundaries (the cutting edge of exploration); The Private Vector (space businesses); Earthly Pursuits (spinoffs of space technology); Global Currents (international space happenings); Reviews (books, films, videos, computer programs), all 800 words; Notes from Earth (miscellaneous short items), 200-250 words. Buys 120 mss/year. Query with published clips. Pays $50-150.
Tips: "Look for fresh approaches to familiar subjects. Rather than simply suggesting a story on the space shuttle or Mars exploration, we need a tie-in to a specific project or personality. Think behind-the-scenes. Notes from earth is a grab-bag of short, quick stories—no more than 250 words. Send your ideas!"

FLIGHT REPORTS, Peter Katz Productions, Inc., 5 Odell Plaza, Yonkers NY 10701. (914)423-6000. Publisher: Peter Katz. 50% freelance written. Works with a small number of new/unpublished writers each year. Monthly travel magazine for pilots and aircraft owners. Pays on publication. Publishes ms an average of 1 month after acceptance. Byline given. Buys all rights. Submit seasonal/holiday material 2 months in advance. Computer printout submissions OK; prefers letter-quality. Reports in 2 weeks. Sample copy $1.
Nonfiction: Destination reports include what to do, where to stay, and airport facilities for domestic travel and Canada only. No foreign travel. Buys variable number of mss/year. Query. Length: 750-1,500 words. Pays $25-50.
Photos: State availability of photos. Pays $5 for 3½x5½ b&w and color prints. Captions required.
Tips: "Pilot's license and cross country flying experience are helpful. Some aviation background is required."

‡**FREQUENT FLYER**, Dun & Bradstreet, 888 7th Ave., New York NY 10106. Managing Editor: Jane L. Levere. 75% freelance written. Monthly magazine covering business travel (airlines/airports/aviation) for mostly male high-level business executive readership. Circ. 350,000. Pays on acceptance. Publishes ms an average of 6 months after acceptance. Byline given. Offers $75 kill fee. Buys all rights. Submit seasonal/holiday material 6 months in advance. Computer printout submissions acceptable; no dot-matrix. Reports in 2 months on queries; 1-2 month on mss. Free sample copy and writer's guidelines.
Nonfiction: Book excerpts, expose, new product, technical, travel, and news reporting, in particular on airports/aircraft/airlines/hotel/credit card/car rental. Not interested in queries on stress or anything written in the first person; no profiles, humor or interviews. "*FF* reports on travel as part of an executive's job. We do not assume that he enjoys travel, and neither should the freelancer." Buys 100 mss/year. Query with published clips. Length: 800-3,000 words. Pays $100-500. Sometimes pays the expenses of writers on assignment.
Photos: Eve Cohen, articles editor. "We accept both b&w and color contact sheets, transparencies and prints; rates negotiable." Buys one-time rights.
Tips: "As always, we will seek articles that in some way address the reader as a mobile executive. These can cover such topics as airports, airlines hotels, car rentals and cities frequently visited by business travelers; they also can deal with subjects such as international banking, credit cards, import/export developments, cross-cultural communications, health and safety while traveling, telecommunications and management problems associated with frequent travel. The majority of our stories are third-person news features. We also buy a *very limited* number of destination articles, which represent 90% of the queries we receive and less than 5% of our assignments and purchase."

KITPLANES, "Featuring Fast-Build Aircraft for the Home Craftsman," Fancy Publications, Box 6050, Mission Viejo CA 92690. (714)240-6001. Editor: Dave Martin. 70% freelance written. Eager to work with new/unpublished writers. Monthly magazine covering self-construction of private aircraft for pilots and builders. Circ. 48,000. Pays on publication. Publishes ms an average of 3 months after acceptance. Byline given. Offers negotiable kill fee. Buys first North American serial rights. Submit seasonal/holiday material 6 months in advance. Query for electronic submissions. Computer printout submissions acceptable; dot-matrix must be caps and lower case printing. Reports in 2 weeks on queries; 6 weeks on mss. Sample copy $3; writer's guidelines for #10 SAE.

Nonfiction: How-to, interview/profile, new product, personal experience, photo feature, technical and general interest. "We are looking for articles on specific construction techniques, the use of tools, both hand and power, in aircraft building, the relative merits of various materials, conversions of engines from automobiles for aviation use, installation of instruments and electronics." No general-interest aviation articles, or "My First Solo" type of articles. Buys 80 mss/year. Query. Length: 500-5,000 words. Pays $100-400.

Photos: Send photos with query or ms, or state availability of photos. Pays $10-75 for b&w prints; $20-150 for color transparencies and color prints. Captions and identification of subjects required. Buys one-time rights.

Tips: "*Kitplanes* contains very specific information—a writer must be extremely knowledgeable in the field. Major features are entrusted only to known writers. I cannot emphasize enough that articles must be directed at the individual aircraft builder. We need more 'how-to' photo features in all areas of homebuilt aircraft."

PILOTING CAREERS MAGAZINE, Future Aviation Professionals of America, 4291-J Memorial Dr., Decatur GA 30032. Editor: Carol Vernon. 65-70% freelance written. Prefers to work with published/established writers. "*Piloting Careers* is a monthly magazine which tries to help pilots in their job searches and in reaching their career goals. We tell our members what it's like to work for individual airlines and flight departments, as well as how to get the jobs they seek." Circ. 16,000. Pays on acceptance. Publishes ms an average of 3 months after acceptance. Byline given. Buys all rights and makes work-for-hire assignments. Photocopied and previously published submissions OK. Computer printout submissions OK; prefers letter-quality. Reports in 1 month on queries; 3 months on mss. Sample copy for 9x12 SAE with 95¢ postage; writer's guidelines for 4x9½ SAE and 1 first class stamp.

Nonfiction: How-to and interview/profile. "No historical, personal experience, humor or inspirational pieces. We don't want to hear from pilots writing about their own airlines." Buys 20-24 mss/year. Query with or without published clips, or send complete ms. Length: 1,500 words minimum. Pays 18¢/word. Sometimes pays the expenses of writers on assignment.

Photos: Send photos with submission. Reviews 35mm transparencies and 5x7 and 8x10 prints. Offers no additional payment for photos accepted with ms. Identification of subjects required.   Buys all rights.

Columns/Departments: Low-Time Blues (beginning jobs which help pilots build flight times); Class I Medical (medical issues affecting pilots); Aviation Law (legal issues affecting pilots), all 1,500-2,500 words. Buys 6-12 mss/year. Query. Length: 1,000-2,500 words. Pays $50 maximum.

Tips: "Queries with published clips are appreciated. Writers must know the aviation industry well or specialize in a single aspect of aviation: business, company interview processes, medical certification, aviation law. We look for anything that will help a pilot make a good job decision or prepare for a job with the airlines when it is offered. Full features are the most open. Our lead feature each month, called 'Flying For,' is about a different airline each issue and is written on assignment only. Writers who prove their knowledge and skill on another feature may later be added to a roster of writers who are assigned 'Flying For' articles."

PRIVATE PILOT, Fancy Publications Corp., Box 6050, Mission Viejo CA 92690. (714)855-8822. Editor: Steve Kimball. 75% freelance written. Works with a small number of new/unpublished writers each year. For owner/pilots of private aircraft, for student pilots and others aspiring to attain additional ratings and experience. "We take a unique, but limited view within our field." Circ. 105,000. Buys first North American serial rights. Pays on publication. Publishes manuscript average of 6 months after acceptance. Will consider photocopied submissions if guaranteed original. No simultaneous submissions. Query for electronic submissions. Computer printout submissions acceptable "if double-spaced and have upper and lower case letters." Reports in 2 months. Sample copy $3; writer's guidelines for SASE.

Nonfiction: Material on techniques of flying, developments in aviation, product and specific airplane test reports, travel by aircraft, development and use of airports. All must be related to general aviation field. No personal experience articles. Buys about 60-90 mss/year. Query. Length: 1,000-4,000 words. Pays $75-300.

Photos: Pays $15 for 8x10 b&w glossy prints purchased with mss or on assignment. Pays $150 for color transparencies used on cover.

Columns/Departments: Business flying, homebuilt/experimental aircraft, pilot's logbook. Length: 1,000 words. Pays $50-125.

Tips: "Freelancer must know the subject about which he is writing; use good grammar; know the publication for which he's writing; remember that we try to relate to the middle segment of the business/pleasure flying public. We see too many 'first flight' type of articles. Our market is more sophisticated than that. Most writers do not do enough research on their subject. We would like to see more material on business-related flying, more on people involved in flying."

‡**PROFESSIONAL PILOT**, Queensmith Communications, 3014 Colvin St., Alexandria VA 22314. (703)370-0606.Editor: C.V. Glines. 50% freelance written. A monthly magazine on corporate and regional/commuter aviation. "Our readers are commercial pilots with highest ratings and the editorial content reflects their knowledge and experience." Circ. 40,000. Pays when scheduled for publication. Publishes ms an average of 3 months after acceptance. Byline given. Kill fee negotiable. Buys all rights. Computer printout submissions OK; no dot-matrix. Reports in 3 weeks. Free sample copy.

Nonfiction: How-to (avionics and aircraft flight checks), humor, interview/profile, personal experience (if a lesson for pilots), photo feature, technical (avionics, weather engines, aircraft). All issues have a theme such as regional/commuter airline operations; maintenance, jet aircraft, helicopters, etc. Buys 40 mss/year. Query. Length: 750-2,500. Pays $200-750. Sometimes pays expenses of writers on assignment.

Photos: Send photos with submission. Prefers transparencies (35mm). Offers no additional payment for photos accepted with ms. Captions and identification of subjects required. Buys all rights.

Columns/Departments: Pireps (aviation news) 750 words. Buys 12 mss/year. Query. Length: 750-1,250 words. Pays $200-450.

Tips: Query first. "Freelancer should have the necessary background in aviation that will make his articles believable to highly qualified pilots of commercial aircraft. We are placing a greater emphasis on airline operations, management and pilot concerns."

‡**WESTERN FLYER**, N.W. Flyer, Inc., Box 98786, Tacoma WA 98498-0786. (206)588-1743. Editor: Dave Sclair. 30% freelance written. Prefers to work with published/established writers; works with small number of new/unpublished writers each year; and will work with new/unpublished writers. Biweekly tabloid covering general aviation. Provides "coverage of aviation news, activities, regulations and politics of general and sport aviation with emphasis on timely features of interest to pilots and aircraft owners." Circ. 23,000. Pays 1 month after publication. Publishes ms an average of 3 months after acceptance. Byline given. Buys one-time rights and first North American seral rights, on occasion second serial (reprint) rights. Submit seasonal/holiday material 2 months in advance. Simultaneous queries, photocopied and previously published submissions from noncompetitive publications OK but must be identified. Query for electronic submissions. Computer printout submissions acceptable. Reports in 2 weeks on queries; 1 month on mss. Sample copy $2; writer's guidelines, style guidelines for #10 SASE.

Nonfiction: Features of current interest about aviation businesses, developments at airports, new products and services, safety, flying technique and maintenance. "Good medium-length reports on current events—controversies at airports, problems with air traffic control, FAA, etc. We want solid news coverage of breaking stories." Query first on historical, nostalgic features and profiles/interviews. Many special sections throughout the year, send SASE for list. Buys 100 mss/year. Query or send complete ms. Length: 500-2,000 words. Pays up to $3/printed column inch maximum. Rarely pays the expenses of writers on assignment.

Photos: "Good pics a must." Send photos (b&w or color prints preferred, no slides) with ms. All photos must have complete captions and carry photographer's ID. Pays $10/b&w photo used.

Tips: "We always are looking for features on places to fly and interviews or features about people and businesses using airplanes in unusual ways. Travel features must include information on what to do once you've arrived, with addresses from which readers can get more information. Get direct quotations from the principals involved in the story. We want current, first-hand information."

—— Business and Finance

Business publications give executives and consumers a range of information from local reports to national overviews. These publications cover business trends, computers in business, and the general theory and practice of business and financial management. National and regional publications are listed below in separate categories. Magazines that have a technical slant are in the Trade section under Business Management, Finance, Industrial Operations or Management and Supervision categories.

National

BARRON'S Business and Financial Weekly, Dow Jones and Co. Inc., 200 Liberty St., New York NY 10028. (212)416-2759. Editor: Alan Abelson. Managing Editor: Kathryn M. Welling. 10% freelance written. Weekly tabloid covering the investment scene. "*Barron's* is written for active participants in and avid spectators of the investment scene. We require top-notch reporting *and* graceful, intelligent and irreverent writing." Circ. 296,000. Pays on publication. Byline given. Offers 25% kill fee. Buys all rights. Computer printout submissions OK. Reports in 1 month. Writer's guidelines for SASE.

Nonfiction: Book excerpts, general interest and interview/profile. Publishes quarterly mutual fund sections. Buys 100 mss/year. Query with published clips. Length: 1,500-2,000 words. Pays $500-2,000 for assigned articles. Pays expenses of writers on assignment.

Photos: State availability of photos with submission. Reviews contact sheets, negatives and 8x10 prints. Offers $150-300/photo (day rate). Model releases and identification of subjects required. Buys one-time rights.

Columns/Departments: Richard Donnelly, column/department editor. Barron's on Books (business/investment books). Buys 100 mss/year. Query with published clips. Length: 250-500 words. Pays $150.

BETTER BUSINESS, National Minority Business Council, Inc., 235 E. 42nd St., New York NY 10017. (212)573-2385. Editor: John F. Robinson. 50% freelance written. Semiannual magazine covering small/minority business issues. Circ. 10,000. Pays on publication. Publishes ms an average of 2 months after acceptance. Byline given. Buys first North American serial rights and all rights. Submit seasonal material 1 month in advance. Computer printout submissions acceptable; prefers letter-quality. Sample copy $5 and 9x12 SAE and 6 first class stamps; free writer's guidelines.

Nonfiction: Interview/profile and technical. Buys 5 mss/year. Query with clips. Length: 3,000-5,000 words. Pays $200-250.

Photos: State availability of photos. Reviews b&w prints. Captions required. Buys all rights.

Tips: "Materials are not returned if not used."

BUSINESS AGE, The Magazine for Small Business, Business Trends Communications Corp., 135 W. Wells, 7th Floor, Milwaukee WI 53203. (414)276-7612. Editor: Margaret A. Brickner. Associate Editor: Claire A. Bremer. 10% freelance written. Monthly magazine for owners/managers of businesses with 1-100 employees. Articles should emphasize useful information for effective business operation. Circ. 100,000. Pays on publication. Publishes ms an average of 2 months after acceptance. Byline given. Buys first North American serial rights or second serial (reprint) rights. Computer printout submissions acceptable; prefers letter-quality. Reports in 1 month. Sample copy for $3, 8x11 SAE and 5 first class stamps. Writer's guidelines for #10 SAE with 1 first class stamp.

Nonfiction: How-to (finance, accounting, marketing, management, business law, personnel management, customer relations, planning, taxes, international businesses); interview/profile (successful businesses and small business advocates). All articles should have clear application to small business. Query or send complete ms. State availability of photos. Length: 1,500-2,000 words. Pays $100-450.

Tips: "Keep in mind that small business owners want to increase profits and productivity. Emphasize the how-to and tailor your piece to benefit the reader."

‡CZESCHIN'S MUTUAL FUND OUTLOOK & RECOMMENDATIONS, Agora, Inc., 824 E. Baltimore, Baltimore MD 21202. (301)234-0515. Editor: Bob Czeschin. Managing Editor: Kathy Murphy. A monthly tabloid on mutual fund investing. Circ. 8,000. Pays on publication. Publishes ms an average of 3 months after acceptance. Byline given. Buys first North American serial rights. Submit seasonal/holiday material 3 months in advance. Simultaneous, photocopied and previously published submissions OK. Query for electronic submissions. Computer printout submissions acceptable. Reports in 1 month. Sample copy for $5 and SAE with 2 first class stamps.

Nonfiction: Expose, how-to, interview/profile. Send complete ms. Length: 500-2,000 words. Pays $50-250 for assigned articles; $50-100 for unsolicited articles. Sometimes pays expenses of writers on assignment.

Photos: State availability of photos with submission. Reviews 5x7 prints. Offers no additional payment for photos accepted with ms. Identification of subjects required. Buys one-time rights.

Columns/Departments: Recent Issues, new funds coming on the market, minimum investment, investment objectives, fees and expenses, investment restrictions, etc. Length: 200-600 words. Send complete ms. Pays $50-150.

D&B REPORTS, The Dun & Bradstreet Magazine for Small Business Management, Dun & Bradstreet, 299 Park Ave., 24th Floor, New York NY 10171. (212)593-6723. Editor: Patricia W. Hamilton. 10% freelance written. Works with a small number of new/unpublished writers each year. A bimonthly magazine for small business. "Articles should contain useful information that managers of small businesses can apply to their own companies. *D&B Reports* focuses on companies with $15 million in annual sales and under." Circ. 76,000. Pays on acceptance. Publishes ms an average of 2 months after acceptance. Byline given. Buys all rights. Query for electronic submissions. Computer printout submissions acceptable. Reports in 3 weeks on manuscripts. Free sample copy and writer's guidelines.

Nonfiction: How-to (on management); and interview/profile (of successful entrepreneurs). Buys 5 mss/year. Query. Length: 1,500-2,500 words. Pays $500 minimum. Sometimes pays expenses of writers on assignment.

Photos: State availability of photos with submission. Identification of subjects required. Buys one-time rights.
Tips: "The area of our publication most open to freelancers is profiles of innovative companies and managers."

EXECUTIVE FEMALE, NAFE, 127 W. 24th St., New York NY 10011. (212)371-0740. Editor: Mary E. Terzella. Emphasizes "upbeat and useful career and financial information for the upwardly mobile female." 30% freelance written. Prefers to work with published/established writers; works with a small number of new/unpublished writers each year. Bimonthly magazine. Circ. 180,000. Byline given. Pays on publication. Publishes ms an average of 4 months after acceptance. Submit seasonal/holiday material 6 months in advance. Buys first rights, first North American serial rights, one-time rights, all rights, simultaneous rights and second serial (reprint) rights to material originally published elsewhere. Simultaneous and photocopied submissions OK. Query for electronic submissions. Computer printout submissions acceptable; no dot-matrix. Reports in 3 months. Sample copy $2.50; writer's guidelines for #10 SAE with 1 first class stamp.
Nonfiction: "Articles on any aspect of career advancement and financial planning are welcomed." Needs how-tos for managers and articles about coping on the job, trends in the workplace, financial planning, trouble shooting, business communication, time and stress management, career goal-setting and get-ahead strategies. "We would also like to receive humorous essays dealing with aspects of the job/workplace." Written queries only. Length: 1,000-2,500 words. Pays $50-200 minimum. Sometimes pays the expenses of writers on assignment.
Columns/Departments: Profiles (interviews with successful women in a wide range of fields, preferably nontraditional areas for women); Entrepreneur's Corner (successful female business owners with unique ideas); Horizons (career planning, personal and professional perspectives and goal-setting); More Money (specific financial issues, social security, tax planning); and Your Executive Style (tips on health and lifestyle). Department length: 800-1,200 words. Pays $25-50 minimum.

FORBES, 60 5th Ave., New York NY 10011. (212)620-2200. Managing Editor: Sheldon Zalaznick. "We occasionally buy freelance material. When a writer of some standing (or whose work is at least known to us) is going abroad or into an area where we don't have regular staff or bureau coverage, we have given assignments or sometimes helped on travel expenses." Pays negotiable kill fee. Byline usually given.

HOME BUSINESS NEWS, The Magazine for Home-based Entrepreneurs, 12221 Beaver Pike, Jackson OH 45640. (614)988-2331. Editor: Ed Simpson. 60% freelance written. Works with a small number of new/unpublished writers each year. A bimonthly magazine covering home-based businesses and marketing. Pays on publication. Publishes ms an average of 2 months after acceptance. Byline sometimes given. Buys first North American serial rights and second serial (reprint) rights. Submit seasonal/holiday material 4 months in advance. Simultaneous, photocopied and previously published submissions OK. Query for electronic submissions. Computer printout submissions acceptable; prefers letter-quality. Reports in 1 week on queries; 5 weeks on mss. Sample copy $2; writer's guidelines for #10 SAE with 1 first class stamp.
Nonfiction: Book excerpts, inspirational, interview/profile (of home business owners), new products, personal experience, computer-based home businesses and mail order success stories. Buys 15-20 mss/year. Query with published clips. Length: 800-3,000 words. Pays $20-100; will pay with ad space if agreed upon.
Photos: State availability of photos with submission. Offers no additional payment for photos accepted with ms. Captions and identification of subjects required. Buys one-time rights.
Columns/Departments: Home Business Profiles (profiles of home business owners), 2,000 words. Buys 15-20 mss/year. Query with published clips. Pays $20-100.
Fillers: Facts and newsbreaks. Buys 10/year. Length: 50-300 words. Pays $5-10.

INC MAGAZINE, The Magazine for Growing Companies, INC Publishing Corp., 38 Commercial Wharf, Boston MA 02110. (617)227-4700. Editor: George Gendron. Executive Editor: Bo Burlingham. Managing Editor: Sara P. Noble. 10% freelance written. Prefers to work with published/established writers. A monthly business magazine for chief executive officers and managers of growing companies up to $100 million in sales. Circ. 625,000. Pays on acceptance. Publishes ms an average of 2 months after acceptance. Byline given. Offers 33% kill fee. Buys first North American serial rights. Submit seasonal/holiday material 3 months in advance. Query for electronic submissions. Computer printout submissions acceptable; prefers letter-quality. Reports in 6 weeks on queries; 1 month on mss.
Nonfiction: Interview/profile and opinion. Buys 8 mss/year. Query with published clips. Length: 1,000-4,000 words. Pays $150-2,500. Pays expenses of writers on assignment.
Columns/Departments: Insider, Hands On, Management Columns. Buys 10 mss/year. Query with published clips. Length: 350-1,200 words. Pays $150-800.
Tips: "We are cutting back on freelance submissions in general, tending to work with those freelancers with whom we presently have a working relationship."

‡MONEY MAKER, Your Guide to Financial Security and Wealth, Consumers Digest Inc., 5705 N. Lincoln Ave., Chicago IL 60659. (312)275-3590. Editor: Dennis Fertig. 90% freelance written. A bimonthly magazine on personal investing. "We cover the broad range of topics associated with personal finance—the strongest emphasis is on traditional investment opportunities." Circulation: 165,000. Pays on acceptance. Publishes ms an average of 2 months after acceptance. Byline given. Offers 50% kill fee. Buys first rights and second serial (reprint) rights. Photocopied submissions OK. Computer printout submissions OK; prefers letter-quality. Reports in 3 months on queries. Sample copy for 8½x11 SAE. Free writer's guidelines.
Nonfiction: How-to. "No personal success stories or profiles of one company." Buys 25 mss/year. Send complete ms. Length: 1,500-3,000 words. Pays 20¢/word for assigned articles. Pays expenses of writers on assignment. State availability of photos with submission. Offers no additional payment for photos accepted with ms.
Tips: "Know the subject matter. Develop real sources in the investment community. Demonstrate a reader-friendly style that will help make the sometimes complicated subject of investing more accessible to the average person."

SYLVIA PORTER'S PERSONAL FINANCE MAGAZINE, 380 Lexington Ave., New York NY 10017. (212)557-9100. Editor: Patricia Schiff Estess. Executive Editor: Greg Daugherty. 50% freelance written. Prefers to work with published/established writers. Monthly (10 issues/year). Pays on acceptance. Publishes ms an average of 3 months after acceptance. Byline given. Offers 20% kill fee. Buys all rights. Submit seasonal/holiday material at least 4 months in advance. No simultaneous, photocopied or previously published submissions. Computer printout submissions acceptable; prefers letter-quality. Reports in 1 month. Writer's guidelines for SAE and 1 first class stamp. Sample copy for 9x12 envelope with 8 first class stamps.
Nonfiction: General interest (financial). Only articles dealing with personal finance; no financially technical articles. "Send a cover letter with original ideas or slants about personal finance articles you'd like to do for us, accompanied by clippings of your previously published work. The features section is most open to freelancers. We will be covering topics such as financial planning, investing, real estate, taxes, and entrepreneurship in each issue." Buys 100 mss/year. Query with published clips. Length: 500-2,000 words. Pays negotiable rates ($500-2,000). Sometimes pays the expenses of writers on assignment.
Columns/Departments: Hot Tips (timely items), 100-300 words; Travel (money-saving strategies), Investing, and Real Estate, all 1,000 words. Buys 80 mss/year. Query with published clips. Length: 100-1,500 words. Pays $100-750.
Tips: "Explain why your topic is important to our reader and why now. Demonstrate a grasp of our subject matter—through your query or through previously published work or both. Because our material requires considerable financial knowledge, we're not an easy market for beginners."

TECHNICAL ANALYSIS OF STOCKS & COMMODITIES, The Trader's Magazine, 9131 California Ave. SW, Box 46518, Seattle WA 98146-0518. (206)938-0570. Editor: John Sweeney. 75% freelance written. Eager to work with new/unpublished writers. Magazine covers methods of investing and trading stocks, bonds and commodities (futures), options, mutual funds, and precious metals. Circ. 15,000. Pays on publication. Publishes ms an average of 3 months after acceptance. Byline given. Offers 50% kill fee. Buys all rights; however, second serial (reprint) rights revert to the author, provided copyright credit is given. Photocopied and previously published submissions OK. Query for electronic submissions. Computer printout submissions acceptable; prefers letter-quality. Reports in 3 weeks on queries; 1 month on mss. Sample copy $5; detailed writer's guidelines for #10 SAE and 1 first class stamp.
Nonfiction: Reviews (new software or hardware that can make a trader's life easier; comparative reviews of software books, services, etc.); how-to (trade); technical (trading and software aids to trading); utilities (charting or computer programs, surveys, statistics, or information to help the trader study or interpret market movements); humor (unusual incidents of market occurrences, cartoons). No newsletter-type, buy-sell recommendations. The article subject must relate to trading psychology, technical analysis, charting or a numerical technique used to trade securities or futures. Virtually requires graphics with every article. Buys 80 mss/year. Query with published clips if available, or send complete ms. Length: 1,000-4,000 words. Pays $100-500. (Applies per inch base rate and premium rate—write for information). Sometimes pays expenses of writers on assignment.
Photos: Christine M. Morrison, photo editor. State availability of photos. Pays $10-100 for 5x7 b&w glossy prints or color slides. Captions, model releases and identification of subjects required. Buys one-time rights.
Columns/Departments: Buys 10 mss/year. Query. Length: 800-1,600 words. Pays $50-200.
Fillers: Duane F. Warren, fillers editor. Jokes and cartoons, on investment humor. Must relate to trading stocks, bonds, options, mutual funds or commodities. Buys 50/year. Length: 100-500 words. Pays $10-50.
Tips: "Describe how to use technical analysis, charting, or computer work in day-to-day trading of stocks, bonds, mutual funds, options or commodities. A blow-by-blow account of how a trade was made, including the trader's thought processes, is, to our subscribers, the very best received story. One of our prime considerations is to instruct in a manner that the layperson can comprehend. We are not hyper-critical of writing style. The completeness and accuracy of submitted material are of the utmost consideration. Write for detailed writer's guidelines."

TRAVEL SMART FOR BUSINESS, Communications House, 40 Beechdale Rd., Dobbs Ferry NY 10522. (914)693-8300. Editor/Publisher: H.J. Teison. Managing Editor: L.M. Lane. 20% freelance written. Monthly newsletter covering travel and information on keeping travel costs down for business travelers and business travel managers. Circ. 2,000. Pays on publication. Publishes ms an average of 6 weeks after acceptance. No byline given. "Writers are listed as contributors." Buys first North American serial rights. Computer printout submissions acceptable; prefers letter-quality. Reports in 6 weeks. Sample copy for #10 SAE and 2 first class stamps; writer's guidelines for #10 SAE and 2 first class stamps.
Nonfiction: "Inside" travel facts for companies that travel; how-to (pick a meeting site, save money on travel); reviews of facilities and restaurants; analysis of specific trends in travel affecting business travelers. No general travel information, backgrounders, or non-business-oriented articles. "We're looking for value-oriented, concise, factual articles." Buys 20 mss/year. Query with clips of published work. Length: 250-1,500 words. Pays $20-150.
Tips: "We are primarily staff written, with a few regular writers. Know the travel business or have business travel experience. People with a specific area of experience or expertise have the inside track."

‡**WOMAN'S ENTERPRISE for entrepreneurs**, Paisano Publications Inc. Box 3100, 28210 Dorothy Dr., Aqoura CA 91301. (818)889-8740. Editor: Caryne Brown. 40% freelance written. A bimonthly small business magazine on entrepreneurship by women. "The magazine is devoted to why and how women have created, in whole or significant part, a small business of their own. Readership comprises corporate-executive women seeking to strike out on their own, entrepreneurial homemakers, and women who are already in business." Estab. 1987. Pays on acceptance. Publishes ms an average of 4 months after acceptance. Byline given. Offers 15% kill fee. Buys all rights and makes work-for-hire assignments. Photocopied submissions OK. Query for electronic submissions. Reports in 1 month on queries; 1 month on mss. Sample copy for $1.95. Writer's guidelines for #10 SAE with 1 first class stamp.
Nonfiction: Business features, management features and new business ideas. "Our editorial calendar is still being developed. Theme issues may appear from time to time. No personality profiles of entrepreneurs. We want to know how, why, and how much." Buys 80 mss/year. Query. Length: 1,000-2,000 words. Pays 20¢/word minimum. Sometimes pays expenses of writers on assignments.
Photos: State availability of photos with submission. Reviews transparencies and prints. Offers no additional payment for photos accepted with ms. Captions, model releases and subjects required. Buys all rights.
Tips: "Our readers are either in business or want to be. The more practical, how-to, specific information about what it takes for any business to succeed, the better suited it is to the magazine. A definite plus is a short, quick-hit sidebar that details key how-to information. *Woman's Enterprise* is a publication readers should be able to use to make money for themselves. When specific businesses are being profiled, specific cost, returns, and profit figures are *essential*. Otherwise we can't use the piece."

Regional

‡**ARIZONA BUSINESS GAZETTE**, Phoenix Newspapers Inc. Box 1950, Phoenix AZ 85001 (602)271-8491. News Editor: Joe Kullman. Managing Editor: Steve Bergsman. 30-40% freelance written. Weekly business newspaper on Arizona business issues. "Articles must have a strong business angle and be of local interest to Arizona, primarily the Phoenix area." Circ. 9,500. Pays on publication 2-3 weeks after acceptance. Byline given. Offers 10-25% kill fee. Buys first rights. Computer printout submissions OK; prefers letter-quality. Reports in 1 month on queries; 1 month on mss. Sample copy for $4. Writer's guidelines SAE with 1 first class stamp.
Nonfiction: Arizona business news and features. No fiction, no advice columns, no how-tos. Buys 50+ mss/year. Query with published clips. Length: 500-1,000 words. Pays $50-100 for assigned articles. Sometimes pays expenses of writers on assignment. State availability of photos with submission. Offers $10-20 per photo. Captions and identification of subjects required. Buys one-time rights.
Tips: "We can afford to use only those freelancers with background and training as news reporters and news writers. Solid journalism skills and some general expertise in business, economics, etc. are necessary. Most open to freelancers would be business features on Arizona companies, industries or business people. They should be legitimate news, not public relations promotions. Must be written in a lively style but accurately and thoroughly reported."

‡**ARIZONA TREND, Magazine of Business and Finance**, Trend Magazines, Inc., Suite 2004, 3003 N. Central Ave., Phoenix AZ 85012. (602)230-1117. Editor and Publisher: John Craddock. Managing Editor: Kevin Heuiker. A monthly regional business magazine. Estab. 1986. Circ. 25,000. Pays on acceptance. Byline given. Offers variable kill fee. Buys first North American serial rights. Computer printout submissions acceptable; no dot-matrix. Reports in 2 weeks on queries; 1 week on mss. Sample copy $2.95 with 9x12 SAE and 7 first class stamps.

Nonfiction: Essays, interview/profile, and new product. Query. Length: 2,000-3,000 words. Pays $300-1,200. Pays some expenses of writers on assignment.
Photos: State availability of photos with submission. Reviews transparencies. Offers $50 minimum/photo. Captions and identification of subjects required. Buys one-time rights.

BC BUSINESS, Canasus Communications, 200-550 Burrard St., Vancouver, British Columbia, V6C 2J6 Canada. (604)669-1721. Editor: Bonnie Irving. 90% freelance written. Monthly magazine publishing business profiles and information focusing on British Columbia. Circ. 25,000. Pays on publication. Publishes manuscript an average of 2 months after acceptance. Byline given. Offers 50% kill fee. Buys first North American serial rights. Submit seasonal/holiday material 3 months in advance. Photocopied and previously published submissions OK. Computer printout submissions OK. Reports in 4-6 weeks. Sample copy for 8½x11 SAE with IRCs. Free writer's guidelines.
Nonfiction: Book excerpts (BC oriented or how-to business); how-to (business only), interview/profile (BC people/companies only). Buys 96 mss/year. Query with published clips. Length: 1,500-3,000 words. Pays $300-800. Sometimes pays the expenses of writers on assignment.
Photos: State availability of photos with submission. Offers no additional payment for photos accepted with ms. Identification of subjects required.
Tips: "Come up with a good or novel idea and send samples of published magazine articles that demonstrate an ability to write well. We are open to any article ideas dealing with business in British Columbia."

BOSTON BUSINESS JOURNAL, P&L Publications, 393 D. St., Boston MA 02210-1907. (617)268-9880. Executive Editor: Peter Kadzis. Managing Editor: John P. Mello, Jr. 20% freelance written. Weekly newspaper covering business in Greater Boston. "Our audience is top managers at small, medium and Fortune 500 companies." Circ. 42,000. Pays on publication. Publishes ms an average of 2 weeks after acceptance. Byline given. Offers 50% kill fee. Buys all rights. Submit seasonal/holiday material 1 month in advance. Query for electronic submissions. Computer printout submissions OK; prefers letter-quality. Reports in 1 week on queries; in 2 weeks on mss.
Nonfiction: Expose, humor, interview/profile, opinion, and photo features. Real estate supplement (3rd week of each month); world trade supplement (1st week of each month); special focus on hotels, skiing and the office. Buys 100 mss/year. Query with published clips. Length: 600-1,500 words. Pays $125-250 for assigned articles; $125-150 for unsolicited articles. Pays expenses of writers on assignment.
Photos: State availability of photos with submission. Reviews 8x10 prints. Pays $40-75 per photo. Identification of subjects required. Buys one-time rights and reprint rights.
Columns/Departments: Small Business (how to deal with problems faced by small businesses); Investments (where and how to invest your money); Technology (computer and computer-related topics). Buys 100 mss/year. Query. Length: 1,000 words. Pays $125-175.
Tips: "Read *Wall Street Journal*. Look for hard news angle versus feature angle. Use 'numbers' liberally in the story. We prefer submissions on computer disk (call for specifics)."

BOULDER COUNTY BUSINESS REPORT, 1830 N. 55th St., Boulder CO 80301. (303)440-4950. Editor: Vicki Cooper. 60% freelance written. Prefers to work with published/established writers; works with a small number of new/unpublished writers each year. Monthly newspaper covering Boulder County business issues. Offers "news tailored to a monthly theme and read primarily by Colorado businesspeople and by some investors nationwide. Philosophy: Descriptive, well-written prose of educational value." Circ. 14,000. Pays on publication. Publishes ms an average of 1 month after acceptance. Byline given. Offers 10% kill fee. Buys one-time rights and second serial (reprint) rights. Simultaneous queries and photocopied submissions OK. Computer printout submissions acceptable; prefers letter-quality. Reports in 1 month on queries; 2 weeks on mss. Sample copy free on request.
Nonfiction: Book excerpts, interview/profile, new product, photo feature of company, examination of competition in a particular line of business. "All our issues are written around a monthly theme. No articles are accepted in which the subject has not been pursued in depth and both sides of an issue presented in a writing style with flair." Buys 120 mss/year. Query with published clips. Length: 250-2,000 words. Pays $50-300.
Photos: State availability of photos with query letter. Reviews b&w contact sheets. Pays $10 maximum for b&w contact sheet. Identification of subjects required. Buys one-time rights and reprint rights.
Tips: "It would be difficult to write for this publication if a freelancer were unable to localize a subject. In-depth articles are written by assignment. The freelancer located in the Colorado area has an excellent chance here."

BUSINESS ATLANTA, Communication Channels Inc., 6255 Barfield Rd., Atlanta GA 30328. (404)256-9800. Editor: Barrie Rissman. 80% freelance written. A monthly magazine covering Atlanta and Georgia. Circ. 30,000. Pays on publication. Publishes ms an average of 3 months after acceptance. Byline given. Offers 10% kill fee. Buys first North American serial rights and second serial (reprint) rights. Submit seasonal/holiday material 4 months in advance. Reports in 6 months on queries; 3 months on mss. Sample copy $2.

Nonfiction: Humor and interview/profile. No product-related material or case studies. Buys 150 mss/year. Query with published clips. Length: 1,000-4,000 words. Pays $250-800. Buys one-time rights and reprint rights.

Columns/Departments: All 1,500-1,800 words. Buys 85 mss/year. Query with published clips. Pays $300-350.

Tips: "We do not use writers from outside the state of Georgia except in very rare cases. The back-of-the-book departments are most open to new writers. Our initial assignments are made on speculation only."

BUSINESS VIEW, Florida Business Publications Inc., Box 9859, Naples FL 33941. (813)263-7525. Editor: L. P. Zeidenstein. 100% freelance written. Prefers to work with published/established writers; works with a small number of new/unpublished writers each year. A monthly magazine covering business trends and issues in southwest Florida. Circ. 14,200. Pays on publication. Publishes ms an average of 3-6 months after acceptance. Byline given. Buys all rights or makes work-for-hire assignments. Simultaneous, photocopied and previously published submissions OK. Computer printout submissions acceptable; prefers letter-quality. Reports in 2 months. Sample copy $2 with 8½x11 SAE and 8 first class stamps; free writer's guidelines.

Nonfiction: Book excerpts (business); how-to (business); humor (business); interview/profile (regional); and technical. "No jokes, puzzles, or whimsy, unless it pertains directly to business." Buys 24-36 mss/year. Query with published clips. Length: 100-3,000 words. Pays $15-350 for assigned articles; pays $15-200 for unsolicited articles. Sometimes pays the expenses of writers on assignment.

Photos: State availability of photos with submission. Reviews contact sheets and 5x7 prints. Offers $25-35/photo. Buys one-time rights.

Columns/Departments: Personal Finance (general investment opportunities); Management. Buys 12-20 mss/year. Send complete ms. Length: 750-1,200 words. Pays $25-100.

Tips: "Our readers like specific answers to specific problems. Do not send generalized how-to articles that do not offer concrete solutions to management problems. Our readers are busy, so be concise and upbeat in style. Profiles of southwest Florida business leaders are most open to freelance writers. These are short (1,000 words) articles that present local, interesting personalities. How-to articles in the areas of management, personal finance, retailing, accounting, investing, computers, personnel, and stress management are also open. We have recently entered the Sarasota market and are actively looking for articles about businesses in that area."

‡CALIFORNIA BUSINESS, Suite 400, 4221 Wilshire Blvd., Los Angeles CA 90010. (213)937-5820. Editor: Joan Yee. Senior Editor: Greg Criber. 80% freelance written. Monthly business publication covering California. Includes Pacific rim and Mexico. Circ. 130,000. Pays on acceptance. Publishes ms an average of 3 months after acceptance. Byline given. Pays 30% kill fee. Buys first North American serial rights. Submit seasonal/holiday material 6 months in advance. Query for electronic submissions. Computer printout submissions OK; prefers letter-quality. Reports in 1 month. Sample copy for 8½x11 SAE with 4 first class stamps. Writer's guidelines for #10 SASE.

Nonfiction: Book excerpts, expose, interview/profile. Buys 96 mss/year. Query. Length: 2,000-4,000 words. Pays $1500-4000 for assigned articles. Pays expenses of writers on assignment.

Photos: State availability of photos with submission. Reviews transparencies. Captions, model releases required. Buys one-time rights.

CRAIN'S DETROIT BUSINESS, Crain Communications, Inc., 1400 Woodbridge, Detroit MI 48207. (313)446-0419. Editor: Peter Brown. Managing Editor: Matt Gryczan. 20% freelance written. Weekly tabloid covering Detroit area businesses. "*Crain's Detroit Business* reports the activities of local businesses. Our readers are mostly executives; many of them own their own companies. They read us to keep track of companies not often reported about in the daily press—privately held companies and small public companies. Our slant is hard news and news features. We do not report on the auto companies, but other businesses in Wayne, Oakland, Macomb, and Washtenaw counties are part of our turf." Circ. 33,500. Pays on publication. Byline given. Offers negotiable kill fee. Buys first rights and "the right to make the story available to the other 25 Crain publications, and the right to circulate the story through the Crain News Service." Photocopied submissions OK. Query for electronic submissions. Computer printout submissions OK; prefers letter-quality. Sample copy 50¢; writer's guidelines for SASE.

Nonfiction: Cindy Goodaker, articles editor. Book excerpts and interview/profile. No "how-tos, new product articles, or fiction." Buys 200 mss/year. Query. Length: 800 words average. Pays $6/inch and expenses for assigned articles. Pays $6/inch without expenses for unsolicited articles. Pays expenses of writers on assignment.

Photos: State availability of photos with submission. Offers no additional payment for photos accepted with ms. Identification of subjects required. "Buys the right to re-use photo at will."

Tips: "What we are most interested in are specific news stories about local businesses. The fact that Widget Inc. is a great company is of no interest to us. However, if Widget Inc. introduced a new product six months ago and sales have gone up from $20 million to $30 million, then that's a story. The same is true if sales went down from $20 million to $10 million. I would strongly encourage interested writers to contact me directly. Although we don't have a blanket rule against unsolicited manuscripts, they are rarely usable. We are a general circulation publication, but we are narrowly focused. A writer not familiar with us would have trouble focusing the story properly, In addition writers may not have a business relationship with the company they are writing about."

DALLAS MAGAZINE,The Dallas Chamber, Suite 2000; 1201 Elm St., Dallas TX 75270. (214)746-6776. Editor: Jeff Hampton. 50% freelance written. A quarterly consumer business journal. Circ. 30,000. Pays on acceptance. Publishes ms an average of 2 months after acceptance. Byline given. Pays $100 kill fee. Buys first North American serial rights and first rights. Submit seasonal/holiday material 3 months in advance. Simultaneous submissions OK. Query for electronic submissions. Computer printout submissions OK; prefers letter-quality. Reports in 2 months. Free sample copy and writer's guidelines.
Nonfiction: General interest, how-to, interview/profile, new product. Buys 24 mss/year. Query with published clips. Length: 1,000-2,500 words. Pays $175-600. Sometimes pays expenses of writers on assignment.
Photos: State availability of photos with submission. Identification of subjects required. Buys one-time rights. Pays $50-100.
Columns/Departments: Briefs (current business events); Noteworthy (innovative business people, companies); Management Trends (trends, issues, ideas in Management); Rx for Business (health matters relating to business); Office Tech (office automation). Length: 1,000-1,500 words. Query with published clips. Pays $100.
Fillers: Anecdotes, facts, newsbreaks and short humor. Buys 2/year. Length: 50 words maximum. Pays $20-50.
Tips: "Send queries. Do not send articles for the magazine. First, contact the magazine for editorial calendar."

‡FLORIDA TREND, Magazine of Florida Business and Finance, Box 611, St. Petersburg FL 33731. (813)821-5800. Editor and Publisher: Rick Edmonds. Managing Editor: Thomas J. Billitteri. A monthly magazine covering business and economics for Florida business people or investors. Circ. 44,000. Pays on acceptance. Byline given. Offers 25% kill fee. Buys first North American serial rights. Computer printout submissions acceptable. Reports in 1 month. Sample copy $2.95.
Nonfiction: Business and finance. Buys 15-20 mss/year. Query with or without published clips. Length: 1,200-2,500 words. Pays $500-900.

INDIANA BUSINESS, 1000 Waterway Blvd., Indianapolis IN 46202. (317)633-2026. Editor: David Dawson. 50% freelance written. Statewide publication focusing on business in Indiana. "We are a general business publication that reaches 30,000 top executives in Indiana, covering all business categories." Circ. 30,000. Pays 30-60 days after acceptance. Publishes ms an average of 2 months after acceptance. Rights negotiable. Submit seasonal/holiday material 4 months in advance. Photocopied submissions OK. Computer printout double-spaced submissions acceptable. Byline given. Reports in 1 month. Sample copy $2.
Nonfiction: Expose; interview/profile; and opinion (does not mean letters to the editor). No first person experience stories. "All articles must relate to Indiana business and must be of interest to a broad range of business and professional people." Especially interested in articles on agribusiness, international affairs as they affect Indiana business, executive health issues, new science and technology projects happening in Indiana. "We would like to hear about business success stories but only as they pertain to current issues, trends (i.e., a real estate company that has made it big because they got in on the Economic Development Bonds and invested in renovation property)." Buys 40-50 mss/year. Query. Length: 500-2,500 words. Pay negotiable. Pays expenses of writers on assignment.
Photos: State availability of photos. Reviews contact sheets, negatives, transparencies and 5x7 prints. Pay negotiable for b&w or color photos. Captions, model releases and subject identification required.
Columns/Departments: "Writers need to check with us. We may publish a column once a year or six times a year, and we will consider any business-related subject." Buys 30 mss/year. Query. Length: 1,000-1,500 words. Pays $50-200.
Fillers: Anecdotes and newsbreaks. Length: 125-250 words. Pays $50 maximum.
Tips: "Give us a concise query telling us not only why we should run the article but why you should write it. Be sure to indicate available photography or subjects for photography or art. We look first for good ideas. Our readers are sophisticated businessmen who are interested in their peers as well as how they can run their businesses better. We will look at non-business issues if they can be related to business in some way."

‡MANHATTAN, INC., The Business of New York, Metrocorp. 18th Floor, 420 Lexington Ave., New York NY 10170 (212)697-2100. Editor: Clay S. Felker. Managing Editor: Sarah Jewler. A monthly magazine about the business of New York and the people who do business in New York. "*Manhattan, inc.* stories are best told through the narrative of a personality rather than an overview essay. We are most interested in Manhattan-based businesses." Pays on acceptance. Publishes ms an average of 1 month after acceptance. Byline given. Offers 15% kill fee. Buys first North American serial rights. Submit seasonal/holiday material 2 months after acceptance. Query for electronic submissions. Computer printout submissions OK. Reports in 2 months on queries. Sample copy for $3.00.

Nonfiction: Book excerpts, exposé, general interest, historical/nostalgic, how-to, humor, interview/profile, personal experience, photo feature. No general overviews or articles on businesses not related to New York. Buys 100 mss/year. Query with published clips. Length: 500-5,000 words. Pays $250-5,000 for assigned articles. Sometimes pays expenses of writers on assignment.

Photos: State availability of photos with submission. Reviews contact sheets, negatives, transparencies and prints. Offers no additional payment for photos accepted with ms. Captions, model releases and identification of subjects required. Buys one-time rights.

Columns/Departments: Executive Editor: Peter Kaplan. On The Books (book reviews—business books), 1,000-2,000 words; DOSSIER (short glimpses of unusual trends in the business world) 250-1,000 words; Corporate Culture (business of art), 800-3,000 words; Hot Properties (real estate in NY), 1,000-3,000 words; Infrastructure (infrastructure of NY), 1,000-3,000. Buys 50 mss/year. Query with published clips. Length: 1,000-3,000 words. Pays $1,000-5,000.

Fiction: Contact: Judy Daniels. Adventure, condensed novels, experimental, fantasy, historical, horror, humorous, mainstream, mystery, novel excerpts, romance, slice-of-life vignettes, suspense and other. Buys 12 mss/year. Send complete ms. Length: 1,000-5,000 words. Pays $1,000-5,000.

Tips: "Submit writing that has solid reporting behind it. *DOSSIER* is the best place to start."

MEMPHIS BUSINESS JOURNAL, Mid-South Communications, Inc., Suite 102, 88 Union, Memphis TN 38103. (901)523-0437. Editor: Barney DuBois. 10% freelance written. Works with a small number of new/unpublished writers each year. Weekly tabloid covering industry, trade, agribusiness and finance in west Tennessee, north Mississippi, east Arkansas, and the Missouri Bootheel. "Articles should be timely and relevant to business in our region." Circ. 10,400. Pays on acceptance. Publishes ms an average of 2 weeks after acceptance. Byline given. Pays $50 kill fee. Buys one-time rights, and makes work-for-hire assignments. Submit seasonal/holiday material 2 months in advance. Simultaneous queries and submissions OK. Computer printout submissions acceptable; prefers letter-quality. Reports in 2 weeks. Free sample copy.

Nonfiction: Exposé, historical/nostalgic, interview/profile, business features and trends. "All must relate to business in our area." Buys 200 mss/year. Query with or without clips of published work, or send complete ms. Length: 750-2,000 words. Pays $100-250. Sometimes pays the expenses of writers on assignment.

Photos: State availability of photos or send photos with ms. Pays $25-50 for 5x7 b&w prints. Identification of subjects required. Buys one-time rights.

Tips: "We are interested in news—and this means we can accept short, hard-hitting work more quickly. We also welcome freelancers who can do features and articles on business in the smaller cities of our region. We are a weekly, so our stories need to be timely."

NEVADA BUSINESS JOURNAL, 2129 Paradise Road, Las Vegas NV 89104. (702)735-7003. Editor: Bill Moody. 50% freelance written. A monthly magazine covering business in Nevada. Circ. 20,000. Pays on publication. Publishes ms an average of 2 months after acceptance. Byline given. Offers 25% kill fee. Buys all rights. Submit seasonal/holiday material 6 months in advance. Simultaneous and photocopied submissions OK. Computer printout submissions acceptable; prefers letter-quality. Reports in 1 month on queries; 2 months on mss. Sample copy for 9x12 SAE and 2 first class stamps; writer's guidelines for #10 SASE.

Nonfiction: Interview/profile. Publishes Annual Health Issue in May. Buys 35-50 mss/year. Query with published clips. Length: 750-3,000 words. Pays $75-300. Sometimes pays expenses of writers on assignment.

Photos: Send photos with submission. Reviews 4x5 transparencies and 8x10 prints. Offers no additional payment for photos accepted with ms. Identification of subjects required. Buys one-time rights.

Columns/Departments: New Kid on the Block (business new to Nevada). Length to 1,500 words. Query. Buys 2-4 mss/year. Pays $75-150.

Tips: Company, executive and industry profiles and small business newcomers are most open to freelancers. Articles can be general business, but with a definite Nevada slant.

NEW JERSEY BUSINESS, 310 Passaic Ave., Fairfield NJ 07006. (201)882-5004. Executive Editor: James Prior. Emphasizes business in the state of New Jersey. Monthly magazine. Pays on acceptance. Buys all rights. Simultaneous and previously published work OK. Reports in 3 weeks. Sample copy $1.

Nonfiction: "All freelance articles are upon assignment, and they deal with business and industry either directly or more infrequently, indirectly pertaining to New Jersey." Buys "a few" mss/year. Query or send clips of published work. Pays $150-200.

Photos: Send photos with ms. Captions preferred.

OHIO BUSINESS, Business Journal Publishing Co., 3rd floor, 1720 Euclid Ave., Cleveland OH 44115. (216)621-1644. Editor: Robert W. Gardner. Managing Editor: Michael E. Moore. 10% freelance written. Prefers to work with published/established writers. A monthly magazine covering general business topics. "*Ohio Business* serves the state of Ohio. Readers are business executives in the state engaged in manufacturing, agriculture, mining, construction, transportation, communications, utilities, retail and wholesale trade, services, and government." Circ. 43,000. Pays for features on acceptance; news on publication. Publishes ms an average of 4 months after acceptance. Byline sometimes given. Kill fee can be negotiated. Buys first serial rights; depends on projects. Submit seasonal/holiday material 3-4 months in advance. Simultaneous queries, and simultaneous, photocopied, and previously published submissions OK. Computer printout submissions acceptable; prefers letter-quality. Reports in 2 weeks on queries; 1 month on mss. Sample copy $2; writer's guidelines for SAE and 1 first class stamp.

Nonfiction: Book excerpts, general interest, how-to, interview/profile, opinion and personal experience. "In all cases, write with an Ohio executive in mind. Stories should give readers useful information on business within the state, trends in management, ways to manage better, or other developments which would affect them in their professional careers." Buys 14-20 mss/year. Query with published clips. Length: 800-2,500 words. Pays $100 minimum. Sometimes pays expenses of writers on assignment.

Photos: State availability of photos. Reviews b&w and color transparencies and prints. Captions and identification of subjects required. Buys variable rights.

Columns/Departments: News; People (profiles of Ohio business execs); High-Tech (leading edge Ohio products and companies); Made in Ohio (unusual Ohio product/services). Query with published clips. Length: 100-600 words. Pay varies.

Tips: "Features are most open to freelancers. Come up with new ideas or information for our readers: Ohio executives in manufacturing and service industries. Writers should be aware of the trend toward specialization in magazine publishing with strong emphasis on people in coverage."

OREGON BUSINESS, Media America Publications, Suite 500, 208 SW Stark, Portland OR 97204. (503)223-0304. Editor: Robert Hill. 60% freelance written. Works with a small number of new/unpublished writers each year. Monthly magazine covering business in Oregon. Circ. 20,000. Pays on publication. Publishes ms an average of 4 months after acceptance. Byline given. Buys first rights. Submit seasonal/holiday material 3 months in advance. Photocopied and previously published submissions OK. Computer printout submissions acceptable; prefers letter-quality. Reports in 1 month. Sample copy for 9x12 SAE and 5 first class stamps.

Nonfiction: General interest (real estate, business, investing, small business); interview/profile (business leaders); and new products. Special issues include tourism, world trade, finance. "We need articles on real estate or small business in Oregon, outside the Portland area." Buys 50 mss/year. Query with published clips. Length: 900-2,000 words. Pays 10¢/word minimum; $200 maximum. Sometimes pays expenses of writers on assignment.

ORLANDO MAGAZINE, Box 2207, Orlando FL 32802. (305)644-3355. 10% freelance written. Monthly magazine covering city growth, development, trends, entertainment. "We use first-person experiential pieces on subjects of interest to people in central Florida. Our business, personality and trends stories are staff written." Circ. 24,000. Pays on acceptance. Publishes ms an average of 6-9 months after acceptance. Byline given. Offers 100% kill fee. Makes work-for-hire assignments. Submit seasonal/holiday material 6 months in advance. Simultaneous and photocopied submissions OK. Computer printout submissions OK. Reports in 3 weeks. Sample copy $3; free writer's guidelines.

Nonfiction: General interest, historical/nostalgic, photo feature, travel, and trends in central Florida. Buys 25 mss/year. Send complete ms. Length: 750-2,000 words. Pays $75-150 for assigned articles; $75-100 for unsolicited articles.

Photos: Send photos with submission. Reviews prints. Offers $5 per photo. Captions and identification of subjects required. Buys one-time rights.

‡SAN ANTONIO BUSINESS JOURNAL, American Cities Business Journals, D-400, 3201 Cherry Ridge, San Antonio TX 78230. (512)341-3202. Editor: Patrick Wier. 20% freelance written. Weekly business newspaper on San Antonio business. "We serve up hard-hitting, comprehensive coverage of business in San Antonio." Estab. 1987. Circ. 7,000. Pays on acceptance. Publishes an average of 1 month after acceptance. Byline given. Offers 25% kill fee. Buys first North American serial rights or second serial (reprint) rights. Submit seasonal/holiday material 3 months in advance. Simultaneous and photocopied submissions OK. Computer printout submissions OK; prefers letter-quality. Reports in 3 weeks on queries. Free sample copy and writer's guidelines for #10 SASE.

Nonfiction: Exposé, general interest, interview/profile, new product, opinion and technical. "Do not submit articles that do not pertain specifically to some aspect of San Antonio business." Query with published clips. Length: 800-5,000 words. Pays $50-125 for assigned articles. Sometimes pays expenses of writers on assignment.

Photos: State availability of photos with submission. Reviews contact sheets. Captions and identification of subjects required. Buys one-time rights.

Tips: "Find a good, timely angle on something substantial changing in San Antonio business and boil it down into a punchy query. Nearly all freelance work is used in our special reports sections, each focusing on a specific local industry."

‡**SEATTLE BUSINESS**, Vernon Publications, Suite 200, 3000 Northup Way, Bellevue WA 98004. (206)827-9900. Editorial Director: Roberta S. Lang. Editor: Michele Andrus Dill. 20% freelance written. Monthly magazine covering business news in Greater Seattle area. "Articles must pertain to concerns of Seattle businesses, emphasis on local, not national." Circ. 9,000. Publishes ms an average of 3 months after acceptance. Byline given. Buys all rights. Simultaneous and photocopied submissions OK. Computer printout submissions OK; prefers letter quality. Reports only on submissions used. Sample copy $2.

Nonfiction: Book excerpts, expose, general interest, how-to (succeed in business, be more efficient, increase profitability, etc.), humor, interview/profile, new product, opinion, technical. Buys 5 mss/year. Query. Length: 500-2,000 words. Pays $100-250. Sometimes pays expenses of writers on assignment.

Photos: State availability of photos with submission or send photos with submission. Reviews contact sheets, prints. Offers no additional payment for photos accepted with ms. Identification of subjects required. Buys one-time rights.

Tips: "We are interested in any feature-length (1,200-2,000 words) submission on some aspect of business in Seattle area. It is best to query first; freelancer would do well to obtain a copy of our editorial calendar and use that as a guide."

VERMONT BUSINESS MAGAZINE, Manning Publications, Inc., Brattleboro Professional Center, Box 6120, Brattleboro VT 05301. (802)257-4100. Editor: Robert W. Lawson. 80% freelance written. A monthly tabloid covering business in Vermont. Circ. 15,000. Pays on publication. Publishes ms an average of 1 month after acceptance. Byline given. Offers $50-full payment kill fee. Not copyrighted. Buys one-time rights. Simultaneous submissions OK. Query for electronic submissions. Computer printout submissions acceptable. Free sample copy.

Nonfiction: Interview/profile, new product, technical and business trends and issues. Buys 300 mss/year. Query with published clips. Length: 800-1,800 words. Pays $50-100. Pays the expenses of writers on assignment.

Photos: Send photos with submission. Reviews contact sheets. Offers $5-10/photo. Identification of subjects required.

Tips: "Read daily papers and look for business angles for a follow-up article. We're always looking for issue and trend articles rather than company or businessman profiles, although we do use the latter as well. Note: Magazine accepts Vermont-specific material *only*."

WESTERN INVESTOR, Western States Investment Information, Willamette Publishing, Inc., Suite 1115, 400 SW 6th Ave., Portland OR 97204. (503)222-0577. Editor-In-Chief: S.P. Pratt. Publisher: Russell B. Nelson. Associate Editor: Leah Firth. 50% freelance written. Quarterly magazine for the investment community of the 13 western states. For stock brokers, corporate officers, financial analysts, trust officers, CPAs, investors, etc. Circ. 13,000. Pays on publication. Publishes ms an average of 6 months after acceptance. Byline given. Buys one-time and second serial (reprint) rights and makes work-for-hire assignments. Simultaneous queries and simultaneous, photocopied and previously published submissions OK. Computer submissions acceptable; prefers letter-quality. Sample copy $1.50 with 8½x11 SAE and 5 first class stamps.

Nonfiction: General business interest ("trends, people, public, listed in our instrument data section"). "Each issue carries a particular industry theme." Query. Length: 200-2,000 words. Pays $50 minimum.

Photos: State availability of photos. Pays $10 minimum for 5x7 (or larger) b&w prints. Buys one-time rights.

Tips: "All editorial copy must pertain or directly relate to companies and/or industry groups included in our listed companies. Send us a one-page introduction including your financial writing background, story ideas, availability for assignment work, credits, etc. What we want at this point is a good working file of authors to draw from; let us know your special areas of interest and expertise. Newspaper business-page writers would be good candidates. If you live and work in the West, so much the better."

WESTERN NEW YORK MAGAZINE, Greater Buffalo Chamber Services Corporation, 107 Delaware Ave., Buffalo NY 14202. (716)852-7100. Editor: J. Patrick Donlon. 10% freelance written. Monthly magazine of the Buffalo-Niagara Falls-Southern Ontario area. "Tells the story of Buffalo and Western New York, balancing business with quality-of-life topics" Circ. 8,000. Pays on acceptance. Publishes ms an average of 3 months after acceptance. Byline given. Offers $150 kill fee. Not copyrighted. Buys all rights. Submit seasonal/holiday material 3 months in advance. Simultaneous queries OK. Computer printout submissions acceptable; no dot-matrix. Reports in 1 month. Sample copy for $2, 9x12 SAE and 3 first class stamps; writer's guidelines for #10 SAE and 1 first class stamp.

Nonfiction: General interest (business, finance, commerce); historical/nostalgic (Buffalo, Niagara Falls); how-to (business management); interview/profile (community leader); and Western New York industry, quality of life. "Broad-based items preferred over single firm or organization. Submit articles that provide insight into business operations, marketing, finance, promotion, and nuts-and-bolts approach to small business management. No nationwide or even New York statewide articles or pieces on specific companies, products, services." Buys 30 mss/year. Query with published clips. Length: 1,000-2,500 words. Pays

$150-300. Sometimes pays the expenses of writers on assignment.
Photos: Pamela Mills, art director. State availability of photos. Reviews contact sheets. Pays $10-25 for 5x7 b&w prints.

Career, College and Alumni

Three types of magazines are listed in this section: university publications written for students, alumni and friends of a specific institution; publications about college life; and publications on career and job opportunities. A number of national campus magazines have gone out of business during the past year, and others have changed focus to attract the smaller enrollment in colleges.

‡AIM, A Resource Guide for Vocational/Technical Graduates, Communications Publishing Group, 3100 Broadway, 225 PennTower, Kansas City MO 64111. (816)756-3039. Editor: Georgia Clark Groves. 40% freelance written. A quarterly educational and career source guide "designed to assist experienced voc/tech students in their search for career opportunities and aid in improving their life survival skills. For Black and Hispanic young adults—ages 21-35." Circ. 350,000. Pays on acceptance. Byline sometimes given. Buys second serial (reprint) rights or makes work-for-hire assignments. Submit seasonal/holiday material 6 months in advance. Simultaneous, photocopied and previously published submissions OK. Computer printout submissions OK; prefers letter-quality. Reports in 2 months. Sample copy for 9x10 SAE with 2 first class stamps. Writer's guidelines for #10 SAE with 1 first class stamp.
Nonfiction: Book excerpts or reviews, general interest, how-to (dealing with careers or education), humor, inspirational, interview/profile (celebrity or "up and coming" young adult), new product (as it relates to young adult market), personal experience, photo feature, technical, travel. Query or send complete ms. Length: 750-3,000 words. Pays $150-400 for assigned articles; $50-300 for unsolicited articles. Sometimes pays expenses of writers on assignment.
Photos: State availability of photos with submission. Reviews transparencies. Offers $10-50/photo. Captions, model releases and identification of subjects required. Buys all rights.
Columns/Departments: Profiles of Achievement (striving and successful minority young adult ages 21-35 in various careers). Buys 15 mss/year. Send complete ms. Length: 500-1,000 words. Pays $50-250.
Fiction: Adventure, ethnic, historical, humorous, mainstream, slice-of-life vignettes. Buys 3 mss/year. Send complete ms. Length: 1,000-5,000 words. Pays $100-400.
Poetry: Free verse. Buys 5 poems/year. Submit up to 5 poems at one time. Length: 10-25 lines. Pays $25-100.
Fillers: Anecdotes, facts, gags to be illustrated by cartoonist, newsbreaks, short humor. Buys 10/year. Length: 25-250 words. Pays $25-100.
Tips: "For new writers, submit full manuscript that is double spaced; clean copy only. Need to have clippings of previous published works and resume. Resume should tell when available to write. Most open are profiles of successful and striving Black or Hispanic young adult (age 21-35). Include photo."

ALCALDE, Box 7278, Austin TX 78713. (512)471-3799. Editor: Ernestine Wheelock. 20% freelance written. Works with a small number of new/unpublished writers each year. Bimonthly magazine. Circ. 48,000. Pays on publication. Publishes ms an average of 6 months after acceptance. Buys all rights. Submit seasonal/holiday material 5 months in advance. Query for electronic submissions. Computer printout submission OK; prefers letter-quality. Reports in 1 month. Writer's guidelines for #10 SASE.
Nonfiction: General interest; historical (University of Texas, research and faculty profile); humor (humorous Texas subjects); nostalgia (University of Texas traditions); profile (students, faculty, alumni); and technical (University of Texas research on a subject or product). No subjects lacking taste or quality, or not connected with the University of Texas. Buys 12 mss/year. Query. Length: 1,000-2,400 words. Pays according to importance of article.

‡THE BLACK COLLEGIAN, The National Magazine of Black College Students, Black Collegiate Services, Inc., 1240 S. Broad St., New Orleans LA 70125. (504)821-5694. Editor: K. Kazi-Ferrouillet. 25% freelance written. Magazine for black college students and recent graduates with an interest in career and job information, black cultural awareness, sports, news, personalities, history, trends and current events. Published bimonthly during school year; (4 times/year). Circ. 121,000. Buys one-time rights. Byline given.

Pays on publication. Computer printout submissions OK; prefers letter quality. Submit seasonal and special interest material 2 months in advance of issue date (Careers, September; Computers/Grad School and Travel/summer programs, November; Engineering and Black History programs, January; finance and jobs, March). Reports in 3 weeks on queries; 1 month on mss. Writer's guidelines for #10 SAE and 1 first class stamp.

Nonfiction: Material on careers, sports, black history, news analysis. Articles on problems and opportunities confronting black college students and recent graduates. Book excerpts, expose, general interest, historical/nostalgic, how-to (develop employability), opinion, personal experience, profile, inspirational, humor. Buys 40 mss/year (6 unsolicited). Query with published clips or send complete ms. Length: 500-1,500 words. Pays $25-350.

Photos: State availability of photos with query or ms, or send photos with query or ms. B&w photos or color transparencies purchased with or without ms. 8x10 prints preferred. Captions, model releases and identification of subjects required. Pasy $35/b&w; $50/color.

Tips: "Career features area is most open to freelancers."

‡**CARNEGIE MELLON MAGAZINE**, Carnegie Mellon University, Pittsburgh PA 15213. (412)578-2900. Editor: Ann Curran. Alumni publication issued fall, winter, spring, summer covering university activities, alumni profiles, etc. Circ, 46,000. Pays on acceptance. Byline given. Not copyrighted. Reports in 1 month.

Nonfiction: Book reviews (faculty alumni), general interest, humor, interview/profile, photo feature, "We use general interest stories linked to CMU activities and research." No unsolicited mss. Buys 5 features and 5-10 alumni profiles/year. Query with published clips. Length: 800-2,000 words. Pays $100-400 or negotiable rate.

Poetry: Avant-garde or traditional. No previously published poetry. No payment.

Tips: "Concentration is given to professional writers among alumni."

‡**CHRONICLE GUIDANCE PUBLICATIONS**, Aurora Street Extension, Box 1190, Moravia NY 13118-1190. (315)497-0330. Managing Editor: Paul Downes. 100% freelance written. Monthly magazine of occupation information for junior and senior high school students. Circ. 6,000. Pays on acceptance. Publishes ms an average 6-8 months after acceptance. Byline given. Buys one-time rights. Computer printout submissions OK; prefers letter-qulity. Reports in 1 month on queries. Free sample copy and writer's guidelines. Buys 21-24 mss/year. Query with published clips. Length: 2,000-3,000 words. Pays $450.

Photos: State availability of photos or send photos with submissions. Reviews 8x10 b&w prints. Offers $55-125 per photo. Model releases required. Buys all rights.

Tips: "Titles of occupational briefs are assigned to authors. We want material that accurately reflects a given occupation. Authors are expected to research each occupation. Briefs are to be written at a seventh grade level. Authors are given 120 days to complete assigned briefs."

CIRCLE K MAGAZINE, 3636 Woodview Trace, Indianapolis IN 46268. Executive Editor: Karen Trent. 60% freelance written. "Our readership consists almost entirely of above-average college students interested in voluntary community service and leadership development. They are politically and socially aware and have a wide range of interests." Publishes 5 times/year. Circ. 10,000. Pays on acceptance. Normally buys first North American serial rights. Byline given. Submit seasonal/holiday material 6 months in advance. Computer printout submissions OK; no dot-matrix. Reports in 1 month. Sample copy and writer's guidelines for large SAE with 3 first class stamps.

Nonfiction: Articles published in *Circle K* are of two types—serious and light nonfiction. "We are interested in general interest articles on topics concerning college students and their lifestyles, as well as articles dealing with community concerns and leadership development." No "first person confessions, family histories, or travel pieces." Recent article examples: "The Business of Rock and Roll" (January/February 1988), "International Careers: Learning the Language (October 1987). Query. Length: 2,000-2,500 words. Pays $175-250.

Photos: Purchased with accompanying ms. Captions required. Total purchase price for ms includes payment for photos.

Tips: "Query should indicate author's familiarity with the field and sources. Subject treatment must be objective and in-depth, and articles should include illustrative examples and quotes from persons involved in the subject or qualified to speak on it. We are open to working iwth new writers who present a good article idea and demonstrate that they've done their homework concerning the article subject itself, as well as concerning our magazine's style."

COLLEGE OUTLOOK AND CAREER OPPORTUNITIES, Editions include Fall (Sept.) edition for high school seniors and junior college transfers and spring (Feb.) edition for high school juniors, Townsend Outlook Publishing Company, Box 239, Liberty, Missouri 64068. (816)781-4941. Editor: Mr. Linn Brown. 40% freelance written. Student information publications on subjects of interest to college and career minded students. "*College Outlook* informs students on college admissions, financial aid, career opportunities, academic options and other topics of interest to college and career bound students. We are always looking for interesting pieces." Circ. 1.5 million plus. Byline given. Generally buys all rights and second (reprint) rights. Computer printout submissions acceptable. For sample copy send SAE and postage.

Photos: State availability of photos. "Generally we use photos which we have found with focus on students." Model release required. Generally buys all rights.

‡COLLEGE PREVIEW, A Guide for College-Bound Students, Communications Publishing Group, 3100 Broadway, 225 PennTower, Kansas City MO 64111. (816)756-3039. Editor: Georgia Clark Groves. 40% freelance written. A quarterly educational and career source guide. "Contemporary guide is designed to inform and motivate Black and Hispanic young adults, ages 16-21 years old about college preparation, career planning and life survival skills." Circ. 600,000. Pays on acceptance. Byline sometimes given. Buys second serial (reprint) rights or makes work-for-hire assignments. Submit seasonal/holiday material 6 months in advance. Simultaneous, photocopied and previously published submissions OK. Computer printout submissions OK; prefers letter-quality. Reports in 2 months. Sample copy for 9x10 SAE with 2 first class stamps. Writer's guidelines for #10 SAE with 1 first class stamp.

Nonfiction: Book excerpts or reviews, general interest, how-to (dealing with careers or education), humor, inspirational, interview/profile (celebrity or "up and coming" young adult), new product (as it relates to young adult market), personal experience, photo feature, technical, travel. Query or send complete ms. Length: 750-3,000 words. Pays $150-400 for assigned articles; $50-300 for unsolicited articles. Sometimes pays expenses of writers on assignment.

Photos: State availability of photos with submission. Reviews transparencies. Offers $10-$50/photo. Captions, model releases and identification of subjects required. Buys all rights.

Columns/Departments: Profiles of Achievement (striving and successful minority young adult ages 16-35 in various careers). Buys 15 mss/year. Send complete ms. Length: 500-1,500. Pays $50-250.

Fiction: Adventure, ethnic, historical, humorous, mainstream, slice-of-life vignettes. Buys 3 mss/year. Send complete ms. Length: 1,000-5,000 words. Pays $100-400.

Poetry: Free verse. Buys 5 poems/year. Submit up to 5 poems at one time. Length: 10-25 lines. Pays $25-100.

Fillers: Anecdotes, facts, gags to be illustrated by cartoonist, newsbreaks, short humor. Buys 10/year. Length: 25-250 words. Pasy $25-100.

Tips: For new writers—Send query, but prefer complete manuscript that is double spaced; clean copy only. If available, send clippings of previous published works and resume. Should state when available to write.

COLLEGE WOMAN, Alan Weston Communications, Suite 600, 303 N. Glenoaks Blvd., Burbank CA 91502. (818)848-4666. Editor: Stewart Weiner. 95% freelance written. Prefers to work with published/established writers; works with small number of new/unpublished writers each year. "A quarterly service magazine for college women ages 18-26 featuring lively, pointed articles on current issues, personalities, careers, academics, health, humor, beauty and fashion." Circ. 650,000. Pays on acceptance. Byline given. Offers 50% kill fee. Buys first North American serial rights. Submit seasonal/holiday material 3 months in advance. Simultaneous, photocopied and previously published material OK. Query for electronic submissions. Computer printout submissions OK. Reports in 2 months on queries. Sample copy and writer's guidelines for 9x12 SAE with $2 postage.

Nonfiction: General interest, humor, interview/profile, opinion and personal experience. Buys 40 mss/year. Query with published clips. Length: 600-2,500 words. Pays $100-500 for assigned articles. Sometimes pays expenses of writers on assignment.

Photos: State availability of photos with submission. Offers $25-100 per photo. Identification of subjects required. Buys one-time rights.

Columns/Departments: Health (fitness, new medical info, sex); Humor (on-campus humor) 600-800 words; Careers (info or opinion for those new to job market) 150-1,200 words; Up Front (news and issues, on and off campus) 50-150 words. Buys 20 ms/year. Query. Pays $100-250.

Tips: "Readers want articles which will help them make it on campus and in the world. The use of humor is important with this audience. I like one-page, brief article idea, with a quick outline of topics to be covered. Articles on current issues, serious personalities, campus issues, and careers are open to freelancers, if they can tailor their material very specifically to the college market and if they have some experience with their chosen topic area."

COLLEGIATE CAREER WOMAN, For Career-Minded Women, Equal Opportunity Publications, Inc., 44 Broadway, Greenlawn NY 11740. (516)261-8917. Editor: Anne Kelly. 80% freelance written. Works with small number of new/unpublished writers each year. Magazine published 3 times/year (fall, winter, spring) covering career-guidance for college women. Strives to "aid women in developing career abilities to the fullest potential; improve job hunting skills; present career opportunities; provide personal resources; help cope with discrimination." Audience is 92% college juniors and seniors; 8% working graduates. Circ. 10,500. Controlled circulation, distributed through college guidance and placement offices. Pays on publication. Publishes ms an average of 3-12 months after acceptance. Byline given. Buys first North American serial rights. Simultaneous queries and submissions OK. Computer printout submissions OK; prefers letter-quality. Sample copy and writer's guidelines for 7x10 SAE with 10 first class stamps.

Nonfiction: "We want career-related articles describing for a college-educated woman the how-tos of obtaining a professional position and advancing her career." Looks for practical features detailing self-evaluation techniques, the job-search process, and advice for succeeding on the job. Emphasizes role-model profiles of succesful career women. Needs manuscripts presenting information on professionals offering opportunities to young women—especially the growth professions of the future. Special issues emphasize career opportunities for women in fields such as health care, communications, sales, marketing, banking, insurance, finance, science, engineering, and computers as well as opportunities in government, military and defense. Query first.

Photos: Send with ms. Prefers 35mm color slides, but will accept b&w prints. Captions and identification of subjects required. Buys all rights.

Tips: "Articles should focus on career-guidance, role model, and industry prospects for women and should have a snappy, down-to-earth writing style."

‡DIRECTIONS, A Guide to Career Alternatives, Communications Publishing Group, 3100 Broadway, 225 PennTower, Kansas City MO 64111. (816)756-3039. Editor: Georgia Clark Groves. 40% freelance written. A quarterly magazine that focuses on evaluating career possibilities and enhancement of life survival skills for Black and Hispanic young adults, ages 18-25. Circ. 500,000. Pays on acceptance. Byline sometimes given. Buys second serial (reprint) rights or makes work-for-hire assignments. Submit seasonal/holiday material 6 months in advance. Simultaneous, photocopied and previously published submissions OK. Computer printout submissions OK; prefers letter-quality. Reports in 2 months. Sample copy for 9x10 SAE with 2 first class stamps. Writer's guidelines for #10 SAE with 1 first class stamp.

Nonfiction: Book excerpts or reviews, general interest, how-to (dealing with careers or education), humor, inspirational, interview/profile (celebrity or "up and coming" young adult), new product (as it relates to young adult market), personal experience, photo feature, technical, travel. Query or send complete ms. Length: 750-3,000 words. Pays $150-400 for assigned articles; $50-300 for unsolicited articles. Sometimes pays expenses of writers on assignment.

Photos: State availability of photos with submission. Reviews transparencies. Offers $10-50/photo. Captions, model releases and identification of subjects required. Buys all rights.

Columns/Departments: Profiles of Achievement (striving and successful minority young adult age 16-35 in various careers). Buys 15 mss/year. Send complete ms. Length: 500-1,500. Pays $50-250.

Fiction: Adventure, ethnic, historical, humorous, mainstream, slice-of-life vignettes. Buys 3 mss/year. Send complete ms. Length: 1,000-5,000 words. Pays $100-400.

Poetry: Free verse. Buys 5 poems/year. Submit up to 5 poems at one time. Length: 10-25 lines. Pays $25-100.

Fillers: Anecdotes, facts, gags to be illustrated by cartoonist, newsbreaks, short humor. Buys 10/year. Length: 25-250 words. Pays $25-100.

Tips: For new writers—Send query, but prefer complete manuscript that is double spaced; clean copy only. If available, send clippings of previous published works and resume. Should state when available to write.

EQUAL OPPORTUNITY, The Nation's Only Multi-Ethnic Recruitment Magazine for Black, Hispanic, Native American & Asian American College Grads, Equal Opportunity Publications, Inc., 44 Broadway, Greenlawn NY 11740. (516)261-8917. Editor: James Schneider. 50% freelance written. Prefers to work with published/established writers. Magazine published 3 times/year (fall, winter, spring) covering career guidance for minorities. "Our audience is 90% college juniors and seniors; 10% working graduates. An understand of educational and career problems of minorities is essential." Circ. 15,000. Controlled circulation, distributed through college guidance and placement offices. Pays on publication. Publishes ms an average of 1 month after acceptance. Byline given. Buys first North American serial rights. Deadline dates: fall, June 15; winter, August 15, spring, November 1. Simultaneous queries and simultaneous, photocopied and previously published submissions OK. Computer printout submissions OK; no dot-matrix. Sample copy and writer's guidelines for SAE and 4 first class stamps.

Nonfiction: Book excerpts and articles (on job search techniques, role models), general interest (on specific minority concerns), how-to (on job-hunting skills, personal finance, better living, coping with discrimination); humor (student or career related), interview/profile (minority role models), new product (new career opportunities), opinion (problems of minorities), personal experience (professional and student study and career experiences), technical (on career fields offering opportunities for minorities), travel (on overseas job opportunities), and coverage of Black, Hispanic, Native American and Asian American interests. Special issues inlcude career opportunities for minorities in industry and government in fields such as banking, insurance, finance, communications, sales, marketing, engineering and computers, as well as careers in the government, military and defense. Query or send complete ms. Length: 1,000-3,000 words. Sometimes pays expenses of writers on assignment. Pays 10¢/word.

Photos: Prefers 35mm color slides and b&w. Captions and identification of subjects required. Buys first North American serial rights.

Tips: "Articles must be geared toward questions and answers faced by minority and women students."

‡**ETC MAGAZINE**, Student Media—University of North Carolina at Charlotte, Cone University Center UNCC, Charlotte NC 28223. (704)547-2146. Editor: Bill Hartley. Managing Editor: Linda Culbertson. 90% freelance written. A semiannual magazine on collegiate lifestyle. "*Etc. Magazine* is a student publication serving the University of North Carolina at Charlotte that features general interest articles dealing with collegiate lifestyles." Circ. 5,000. Pays on publication. Byline given. Buys one-time rights. Submit seasonal/holiday material 6 months in advance. Photocopied submissions and previously published material OK. Computer printout submissions OK. Reports in 6 months. Free sample copy and writer's guidelines.
Nonfiction: General interest, historical/nostalgic, how-to, humor, interview/profile, personal experience, photo feature, travel. Special issues: freshman orientation issue and graduate section. Send complete ms. Length: 500-2,500 words. Pays $10 minimum. Sometimes pays expenses of writers on assignment.
Photos: State availability of photos with submission or send photos with submission.

‡**FIRST OPPORTUNITY, A Guide for Vocational/Technical Students**, Communications Publishing Group, 3100 Broadway, 225 PennTower, Kansas City MO 64111. (816)756-3039. Editor: Georgia Clark Groves. 40% freelance written. A quarterly resource publication focuses on advanced voc/tech educational opportunities and career preparation for Black and Hispanic young adults, ages 16-21. Circ. 500,000. Pays on acceptance. Byline sometimes given. Buys second serial (reprint) rights or makes work-for-hire assignments. Submit seasonal/holiday material 6 months in advance. Simultaneous, photocopied and previously published submissions OK. Computer printout submissions OK; prefers letter-quality. Reports in 2 months. Sample copy for 9x10 SAE with 2 first class stamps. Writer's guidelines for #10 SAE with 1 first class stamp.
Nonfiction: Book excerpts or reviews, general interest, how-to (dealing with careers or education), humor, inspirational, interview/profile (celebrity or "up and coming" young adult), new product (as it relates to young adult market), personal experience, photo feature, technical, travel. Query or send complete ms. Length: 750-3,000 words. Pays $150-400 for assigned articles; $50-300 for unsolicited articles. Sometimes pays expenses of writers on assignment.
Photos: State availability of photos with submission. Reviews transparencies. Offers $10-50/photo. Captions, model releases and identification of subjects required. Buys all rights.
Columns/Departments: Profiles of Achievement (striving and successful minority young adult, age 16-35 in various careers). Buys 15 mss/year. Send complete ms. Length: 500-1,500. Pays $50-250.
Fiction: Adventure, ethnic, historical, humorous, mainstream, slice-of-life vignettes. Buys 3 mss/year. Send complete ms. Length: 1,000-5,000 words. Pays $100-400.
Poetry: Free verse. Buys 5 poems/year. Submit up to 5 poems at one time. Length: 10-25 lines. Pays $25-100.
Fillers: Anecdotes, facts, gags to be illustrated by cartoonist, newsbreaks, short humor. Buys 10/year. Length: 25-250 words. Pays $25-100.
Tips: For new writers—Send query, but prefer complete manuscript that is double spaced; clean copy only. If available, send clippings of previous published works and resume. Should state when available to write.

FLORIDA LEADER, Box 14081, Gainesville FL 32604. (904)373-6907. Publisher: W.H. "Butch" Oxendine, Jr. Editor: Vincent Alex Brown. Nearly 100% freelance written. "Florida's college magazine, feature oriented, with hard hitting, issue conscious stories. We specialize in interviews with leaders from all walks of life." Published 4 times/year. Circ. 32,000. Publishes ms an average of 6 months after acceptance. Byline given. Submit seasonal/holiday material 6 months in advance. Simultaneous, photocopied and previously published submissions OK. Query for electronic submissions. Reports in 1 month on queries. Sample copy and writer's guidelines for 9x12 SAE with 5 first class stamps.
Nonfiction: How-to, humor, interview/profile, and feature—all Florida State College related. Special issues include spring break (February); back to school (August). Query. Length: 500 words or less. Payment varies; may pay writer contributor's copies or other premiums rather than cash. Sometimes pays expenses of writers on assignment.
Photos: State availability of photos with submission. Reviews negatives and transparencies. Captions, model releases and identification of subjects requested.

‡**FORDHAM MAGAZINE**, Fordham University, Suite 319, 113 West 60th St., New York NY 10023. (212)841-5360. Editor: Tricia Gallagher. 75% freelance written. A quarterly magazine on Fordham University alumni and student life. "We are heavy on feature and personality profiles on our alumni: e.g. actor Denzel Washington, author Mary Higgins Clark, and how education influenced their careers." Pays on acceptance. Publishes ms an average of 8 months after acceptance. Byline given. Offers $50-100 kill fee. Makes work-for-hire assignments. Submit seasonal/holiday material 10 months in advance. Previously published submissions OK. Computer printout submissions OK; prefers letter-quality. Reports in 1 month on queries; 2 months on mss. Free sample copy.
Nonfiction: Book excerpts, essays, general interest, historical/nostalgic, humor, inspirational, interview/profile (alumni, faculty, students), personal experience, photo feature. Buys 6 mss/year. Query with published clips. Length: 1,500-3,500. Pays $150-450 for assigned articles; $50-350 for unsolicited articles. Sometimes pays expenses of writers on assignment.

Photos: State availability of photos with submission. Reviews contact sheets, transparencies, prints. Offers no additional payment for photos accepted with ms. Model releases and identification of subjects required. Buys all rights.

Fillers: Anecdotes, facts, newsbreaks, short humor. "All must be specific to Fordham University." Buys 1-2/year. Length: 150-350 words. Pays $25-50.

Tips: "Have a good familiarity with alumni publications in general: research some of the schools and see what they use, what they look for. Research alumni of the school and see if there is a noted personality you might interview—someone who might live in your area. Be prepared to narrow the proposed idea down to the publication's very specific needs. Feature articles and personality profiles are most open to freelancers. These include interviews with famous or interesting alumni and faculty or students, as well as in-depth analytical articles on trends in university life today (pertinent to Fordham) and features on student life in New York. This includes articles on ways that our school interacts with the community around it."

‡JOURNEY, A Success Guide for College and Career Bound Students, Communications Publishing Group, 3100 Broadway, 225 PennTower, Kansas City MO 64111. (816)756-3039. Editor: Georgia Clark Groves. 40% freelance written. A quarterly educational and career source guide for Asian-American high school and college students who have indicated a desire to pursue higher education through college, vocational and technical or proprietary schools. For students ages 16-25. Circ. 200,000. Pays on acceptance. Byline sometimes given. Buys second serial (reprint) rights or makes work-for-hire assignments. Submit seasonal/holiday material 6 months in advance. Simultaneous, photocopied and previously published submissions OK. Computer printout submissions OK; prefers letter-quality. Reports in 2 months. Sample copy for 9x10 SAE with 2 first class stamps. Writer's guidelines for #10 SAE with 1 first class stamp.

Nonfiction: Book excerpts or reviews, general interest, how-to (dealing with careers or education), humor, inspirational, interview/profile (celebrity or "up and coming" young adult), new product (as it relates to young adult market), personal experience, photo feature, technical, travel and sports. Query or send complete ms. Length: 750-3,000 words. Pays $150-400 for assigned articles; $50-300 for unsolicited articles. Sometimes pays expenses of writers on assignment.

Photos: State availability of photos with submission. Reviews transparencies. Offers $10-50/photo. Captions, model releases and identification of subjects required. Buys all rights or one-time rights.

Columns/Departments: Profiles of Achievement (striving and successful minority young adult, age 16-35 in various careers). Buys 15 mss/year. Send complete ms. Length: 500-1,500. Pays $50-250.

Fiction: Adventure, ethnic, historical, humorous, mainstream, slice-of-life vignettes. Buys 3 mss/year. Send complete ms. Length: 1,000-5,000 words. Pays $100-400.

Poetry: Free verse. Buys 5 poems/year. Submit up to 5 poems at one time. Length: 10-25 lines. Pays $25-100.

Fillers: Anecdotes, facts, gags to be illustrated by cartoonist, newsbreaks, short humor. Buys 10/year. Length: 25-250 words. Pays $25-100.

Tips: For new writers—Send query, but prefer complete manuscript that is double spaced; clean copy only. If available, send clippings of previous published works and resume. Should state when available to write.

MISSISSIPPI STATE UNIVERSITY ALUMNUS, Mississippi State University, Alumni Association, Editorial Office, Box 5328, Mississippi State MS 39762. (601)325-3442. Editor: Mr. Linsey H. Wright. 10% freelance written ("but welcome more"). Works with small number of new/unpublished writers each year. Emphasizes articles about Mississippi State graduates and former students. For well-educated and affluent audience. Quarterly magazine. Circ. 15,126. Pays on publication. Publishes ms 3-6 months after acceptance. Buys one-time rights. Pays 25% kill fee. Byline given. Phone queries OK. Submit seasonal/holiday material 3 months in advance. Simultaneous, photocopied and previously published submissions OK. Computer printout submissions acceptable; prefers letter-quality. Reports in 1 month. Sample copy for 9x12 SAE and 5 first class stamps.

Nonfiction: Historical, humor (with strong MSU flavor; nothing risque), informational, inspirational, interview (with MSU grads), nostalgia (early days at MSU), personal experience, profile and travel (by MSU grads, but must be of wide interest to other grads). Buys 5-6 mss/year ("but welcome more submissions.") Send complete ms. Length: 500-2,000 words. Pays $50-150 (including photos, if used).

Photos: Offers no additional payment for photos purchased with accompanying ms. Captions required. Uses 5x7 and 8x10 b&w photos and color transparencies of any size.

Columns/Departments: Statements, "a section of the *Alumnus* that features briefs about alumni achievements and professional or business advancement. We do not use engagements, marriages or births. There is no payment for Statements briefs."

Tips: "All stories *must* be about Mississippi State University or its alumni. We welcome articles about MSU grads in interesting occupations and have used stories on off-shore drillers, miners, horse trainers, etc. We also want profiles on prominent MSU alumni and have carried pieces on Senator John C. Stennis, comedian Jerry Clower, professional football players and coaches, and Eugene Butler, former editor-in-chief of *Progressive Farmer* magazine. We feature 2-4 alumni in each issue, alumni who have risen to prominence in their fields or who are engaged in unusual occupations or who are involved in unusual hobbies. We're using more short features (500-700 words) to vary the length of our articles in each issue. We pay $50-75 for these, including 1 b&w photo."

NATIONAL FORUM: THE PHI KAPPA PHI JOURNAL, The Honor Society of Phi Kappa Phi, 216 Petrie Hall, Auburn University AL 36849. Editor: Stephen W. White. Managing Editor: Mary Evans. 20% freelance written. Prefers to work with published/established writers. Quarterly interdisciplinary, scholarly journal. "We are an interdisciplinary journal that publishes crisp, nontechnical analyses of issues of social and scientific concern as well as scholarly treatments of different aspects of culture." Circ. 112,000. Pays on publication. Query first. Publishes ms an average of 6 months after acceptance. Byline given. Buys exclusive rights with exceptions. Submit seasonal/holiday material 6 months in advance. Computer printout submissions acceptable; no dot-matrix. Reports in 6 weeks on queries; 2 months on mss. Sample copy $1.65; free writer's guidelines.
Nonfiction: General interest, interview/profile and opinion. No how-to or biographical articles. Each issue is devoted to the exploration of a particular theme. Upcoming theme issues: "The Human Brain," "Curricular Reform," "News and the Media." Query with clips of published work. Buys 5 unsolicited mss/year. Length: 1,500-2,000 words. Pays $50-200.
Photos: State availability of photos. Identification of subjects required. Buys one-time rights.
Columns/Departments: Educational Dilemmas of the 80s and Book Review Section. Buys 8 mss/year for Educational Dilemmas, 40 book reviews. Length: Book reviews—400-800 words. Educational Dilemmas—1,500-1,800 words. Pays $15-25 for book reviews; $50/printed page, Educational Dilemmas.
Fiction: Humorous and short stories. No obscenity or excessive profanity. Buys 2-4 mss/year. Length: 1,500-1,800 words. Pays $50/printed page.
Poetry: No love poetry. Buys 20 mss/year. Submit 5 poems maximum. Prefers shorter poems. Prefers established poets. Include publication credentials in cover letter.

NOTRE DAME MAGAZINE, University of Notre Dame, Room 415, Administration Bldg., Notre Dame IN 46556. (219)239-5335. Editor: Walton R. Collins. Managing Editor: Kerry Temple. 75% freelance written. Quarterly magazine covering news of Notre Dame and education and issues affecting the Roman Catholic Church. "We are interested in the moral, ethical and spiritual issues of the day and how Christians live in today's world. We are universal in scope and Catholic in viewpoint and serve Notre Dame alumni, friends and other constituencies." Circ. 110,000. Pays on acceptance. Publishes ms an average of 6-12 months after acceptance. Byline given. Kill fee negotiable. Buys first rights. Simultaneous queries OK. Query for electronic submissions. Computer printout submissions acceptable; prefers letter-quality. Reports in 1 month. Free sample copy.
Nonfiction: Opinion, personal experience, religion. "All articles must be of interest to Christian/Catholic readers who are well educated and active in their communities." Buys 35 mss/year. Query with clips of published work. Length: 600-2,000 words. Pays $500-1,500. Sometimes pays the expenses of writers on assignment.
Photos: State availability of photos. Reviews b&w contact sheets, color transparencies, and 8x10 prints. Model releases and identification of subjects required. Buys one-time rights.

‡OLD OREGON, The Magazine of the University of Oregon, University of Oregon, 101 Chapman Hall, Eugene OR 97403. (503)686-5047. Editor: Tom Hager. 50% freelance written. A quarterly university magazine of people and ideas at the University of Oregon. Circ. 87,000. Pays on acceptance. Publishes ms an average of 3 months after acceptance. Byline given. Offers 20% kill fee. Buys first North American serial rights. Query for electronic submissions. Computer printout submissions OK; no dot-matrix. Reports in 3 weeks. Sample copy for 9x12 SAE with 2 first class stamps.
Nonfiction: Historical/nostalgic, interview/profile, personal experience relating to U.O. issues and alumni. Buys 30 mss/year. Query with published clips. Length: 750-3,000 words. Pays $75-300. Sometimes pays expenses of writers on assignment.
Photos: State availability of photos with submission. Reviews 8x10 prints. Offers $10-25/photo. Identification of subjects required. Buys one-time rights.
Tips: "Query with strong, colorful lead; clips."

PRINCETON ALUMNI WEEKLY, Princeton University Press, 41 William St., Princeton NJ 08540. (609)452-4885. Editor: Michelle Preston. Assistant Editor: Andrew Mytelka. 50% freelance written. Eager to work with new/unpublished writers. Biweekly (during the academic year) magazine covering Princeton University and higher education for Princeton alumni, students, faculty, staff and friends. "We assume familiarity with and interest in the university." Circ. 52,000. Pays on publication. Publishes ms an average of 3 months after acceptance. Byline given. Offers $100 kill fee. Buys first serial rights and one-time rights. Submit seasonal/holiday material 2 months in advance. Simultaneous queries or photocopied submissions OK. Query for electronic submissions. Computer printout submissions acceptable; prefers letter-quality. Sample copy for 9x12 SAE and 4 first class stamps.

Nonfiction: Book excerpts, general interest, historical/nostalgic, interview/profile, opinion, personal experience, photo feature. "Connection to Princeton essential. Remember, it's for an upscale educated audience." Special issue on education and economics (February). Buys 20 mss/year. Query with clips of published work. Length: 1,000-6,000 words. Pays $100-600. Pays expenses of writers on assignment.

Photos: State availability of photos. Pays $25-50 for 8x10 b&w prints; $50-100 for color transparencies. Reviews (for ordering purposes) b&w contact sheet. Captions and identification of subjects required.

Columns/Departments: "Columnists must have a Princeton connection (alumnus, student, etc.)." Buys 50 mss/year. Query with clips of published work. Length: 750-1,500 words. Pays $75-150.

THE PURDUE ALUMNUS, Purdue Alumni Association, Purdue Memorial Union 160, West Lafayette IN 47907. (317)494-5184. Editor: Gay L. Totten. 30% freelance written. Prefers to work with published/established writers; works with small number of new/unpublished writers each year. Magazine published 9 times/year (except February, June, August) covering subjects of interest to Purdue University alumni. Circ. 72,000. Pays on publication. Publishes ms an average of 2 months after acceptance. Byline given. Buys first rights and makes work-for-hire assignments. Submit seasonal/holiday material 3 months in advance. Simultaneous queries, and simultaneous, photocopied, and previously published submissions OK. Computer printout submissions acceptable; prefers letter-quality. Reports in 1 week on queries; 2 weeks on mss. Sample copy for 8½x11 SAE and 2 first class stamps.

Nonfiction: Book excerpts, general interest, historical/nostalgic, humor, interview/profile, personal experience. Focus is on campus news, issues, opinions of interest to 72,000 members of the Alumni Association. Feature style, primarily university-oriented. Issues relevant to education. Buys 12-20 mss/year. Length: 1,500-2,500 words. Pays $25-250. Sometimes pays expenses of writers on assignment.

Photos: State availability of photos. Reviews b&w contact sheet or 5x7 prints.

Tips: "We are still aiming to be more broadly issue-focused, moving away from the rah-rah type of traditional alumni magazine article. We are interested in issues of concern to educated people, with a university perspective. We want carefully researched, in-depth material, and would prefer, if at all possible, that it somehow include a Purdue authority, alumnus, or citation. For instance, in a recent article on Nicaragua, we cited some 25 sources for information, two were Purdue-related."

RIPON COLLEGE MAGAZINE, Box 248, Ripon WI 54971. (414)748-8115. Editor: Andrew G. Miller. 10% freelance written. "*Ripon College Magazine* is a bimonthly publication that contains information relating to Ripon College. It is mailed to alumni and friends of the college." Circ. 13,000. Pays on publication. Publishes ms an average of 3 months after acceptance. Byline given. Not copyrighted. Makes work-for-hire assignments. Query for electronic submissions. Computer printout submissions OK; no dot-matrix. Reports in 2 weeks.

Nonfiction: Historical/nostalgic and interview/profile. Buys 4 mss/year. Query with or without published clips, or send complete ms. Length: 250-1,000 words. Pays $25-500.

Photos: State availability of photos with submission. Reviews contact sheets. Offers no additional payment for photos accepted with ms. Captions and model releases are required. Buys one-time rights.

Tips: "Story ideas must have a direct connection to Ripon College."

SCORECARD, Falsoft, Inc., 9509 US Highway 42, Box 385, Prospect KY 40059. (502)228-4492. Editor: John Crawley. 50% freelance written. Prefers to work with published/established writers. A weekly sports fan tabloid covering University of Louisville sports only. Circ. 3,000. Pays on publication. Publishes ms an average of 1 month after acceptance. Byline given. Buys first rights. Submit seasonal/holiday material 1 month in advance. Previously published submissions OK "rarely." Computer printout submissions acceptable; prefers letter-quality. Reports in 2 weeks. Sample copy for $1 and SAE.

Nonfiction: Assigned to contributing editors. Buys 100 mss/year. Query with published clips. Length: 750-1,500 words. Pays $20-50. Sometimes pays expenses of writers on assignment.

Photos: State availability of photos.

Columns/Departments: Notes Page (tidbits relevant to University of Louisville sports program or former players or teams). Buys 25 mss/year. Length: Approximately 100 words. Pay undetermined.

Tips: "Be very familiar with history and tradition of University of Louisville sports program. Contact us with story ideas. Know the subject."

SHIPMATE, U.S. Naval Academy Alumni Association Magazine, Alumni House, Annapolis MD 21402. (301)263-4469. Editor: Col. J.W. Hammond, Jr., USMC (retired). 100% freelance written. A magazine published 10 times a year by and for alumni of the U.S. Naval Academy. Circ. 31,000. Pays on publication. Byline given. Buys first North American serial rights. Submit seasonal/holiday material 10 months in advance. Computer printout submissions OK; prefers letter-quality. Reports in 1 week. Sample copy for 8½x11 SAE and 6 first class stamps.

Nonfiction: Buys 50 mss/year. Send complete ms. Length: 2,000-7,500 words. Pays $100 for unsolicited articles.

Photos: Send photos with submission. Offers no additional payment for photos accepted with ms. Identification of subjects required. Buys one-time rights.
Tips: "The writer should be a Naval Academy alumnus (not necessarily a graduate) with first-hand experience of events in the Naval Service."

THE STUDENT, 127 9th Ave. N., Nashville TN 37234. Editor: Milt Hughes. 20% freelance written. Works with a small number of new/unpublished writers each year. Publication of Student Ministry Department of the Southern Baptist Convention. For college students; focusing on freshman and sophomore levels. Published 12 times during the school year. Circ. 25,000. Buys all rights. Payment on acceptance. Publishes ms an average of 10 months after acceptance. Mss should be double-spaced on white paper with 50-space line, 25 lines/page. Reports usually in 6 weeks. Computer printout submissions acceptable; no dot-matrix. Sample copy and guidelines for SASE.
Nonfiction: Contemporary questions, problems, and issues facing college students viewed from a Christian perspective to develop high moral and ethical values. Cultivating interpersonal relationships, developing self-esteem, dealing with the academic struggle, coping with rejection, learning how to love, developing a personal relationship with Jesus Christ. Prefers complete ms rather than query. Length: 800 words maximum. Pays 5¢/word after editing with reserved right to edit accepted material.
Fiction: Satire and parody on college life, humorous episodes; emphasize clean fun and the ability to grow and be uplifted through humor. Contemporary fiction involving student life, on campus as well as off. Length: 900 words. Pays 5¢/word.

STUDENT LEADERSHIP, Box 1450, Downers Grove IL 60515. (312)964-5700. Editor: Robert Kachur. 60% freelance written. Works with a small number of new/unpublished writers each year. Issued quarterly during school year for college students, with "a Christian approach to the needs and issues they face." Circ. 7,000. Pays on acceptance. Publishes ms an average of 1 year after acceptance. Buys first rights and second (reprint) rights to material originally published elsewhere. Reports in 3 months. Computer printout submissions acceptable; prefers letter-quality.
Nonfiction and Fiction: "Articles dealing with practical aspects of Christian living on campus, relating contemporary issues to Biblical principles. Student-related articles on the relationship between Christianity and various fields of study and career options, Christian doctrine and missions. Every article must relate to the needs of a typical college student. We like material that shows students struggling with real problems and, as a result, learning and growing. No theological dissertations." Query. Buys 35 unsolicited mss/year. Length: 2,000 words maximum. Pays $50-200. Sometimes pays expenses of writers on assignment.
Poetry: Pays $20-50.
Tips: "Direct your principles and illustrations at college students. Avoid preachiness and attacks on various Christian ministries or groups; share your insights on a peer basis."

‡VISIONS, A Success Guide for College and Career Bound Students, Communications Publishing Group, 3100 Broadway, 225 Penntower, Kansas City MO 64111. (816)756-3039. Editor: Georgia Clark Groves. 40% freelance written. A quarterly education and career source guide designed for Native American students who want to pursue a higher education through colleges, vocational and technical schools, or proprietary schools. For young adults, ages 16-25." Circ. 100,000. Pays on acceptance. Byline sometimes given. Buys second serial (reprint) rights or makes work-for-hire assignments. Submit seasonal/holiday material 6 months in advance. Simultaneous, photocopied and previously published submissions OK. Computer printout submissions OK; prefers letter-quality. Reports in 2 months. Sample copy for 9x12 SAE with 2 first class stamps; writers guidelines for #10 SAE with 1 first class stamp.
Nonfiction: Book excerpts or reviews, general interest, how-to, humor, inspirational, interview/profile, new product, personal experience, photo feature, technical, travel and sports. Query or send complete ms. Length: 750-3,000 words. Pays $150-400 for assigned articles; $50-300 for unsolicited articles. Sometimes pays expenses of writers on assignment.
Photos: State availability of photos with submission. Reviews transparencies. Offers $10-50/photo. Captions, model releases, and identification of subjects required. Buys all rights.
Columns/Departments: Profiles of Achievement (striving and successful minority young adults, age 16-35, in various careers). Length: 500-1,500 words. Buys 15 mss/year. Send complete ms. Pays $50-250.
Fiction: Adventure, ethnic, historical, humorous, mainstream, slice-of-life vignettes. Buys 3 mss/year. Send complete ms. Length: 1,000-5,000 words. Pays $100-400.
Poetry: Free verse. Buys 5 poems/year. Submit up to 5 poems at one time. Length: 10-25 lines. Pays $25-100.
Fillers: Anecdotes, facts, gags to be illustrated by cartoonist, newsbreaks, short humor. Buys 10 fillers/year. Length: 25-250 words. Pays $25-100.
Tips: For new writers—Send query, but prefer complete manuscript that is double spaced; clean copy only. If available, send clippings of previous published works and resume. Should state when available to write.

WPI JOURNAL, Worcester Polytechnic Institute, 100 Institute Rd., Worcester MA 01609. Editor: Michael Dorsey. 75% freelance written. A quarterly alumni magazine covering science and engineering/education/business personalities for 17,000 alumni, primarily engineers, scientists, managers; parents of students, national media. Circ. 22,500. Pays on publication. Publishes ms an average of 3 months after acceptance. Byline given. Buys one-time rights. Submit seasonal/holiday material 3 months in advance. Simultaneous queries, and simultaneous, photocopied and previously published submissions OK. Electronic submissions OK via disk compatible with DEC or NBI, but requires hard copy also. Computer printout submissions acceptable; prefers letter-quality to dot-matrix. Reports in 2 weeks on queries; 1 month on mss.
Nonfiction: Book excerpts; exposé (education, engineering, science); general interest; historical/nostalgic; how-to (financial, business-oriented); humor; interview/profile (people in engineering, science); personal experience; photo feature; and technical (with personal orientation). Query with published clips. Length: 1,000-4,000 words. Pays negotiable rate. Sometimes pays the expenses of writers on assignment.
Photos: State availability of photos with query or ms. Reviews b&w contact sheets. Pays negotiable rate. Captions required.
Fillers: Cartoons. Buys 4/year. Pays $75-100.
Tips: "Submit outline of story and/or ms of story idea or published work. Features are most open to freelancers."

Child Care and Parental Guidance

Readers of today's parenting magazines are starting families later and having fewer children. They want information on new research about pregnancy, infancy, child development and family issues written for parents and people who care for children. Child care magazines address these and other issues. Other markets that buy articles about child care and the family are included in the Education, Religious and Women's sections.

‡AMERICAN BABY MAGAZINE, For Expectant and New Parents, 475 Park Ave. South, New York NY 10016. (212)689-3600. Editor: Judith Nolte. Managing Editor: Phyllis Evans. 70% freelance written. Prefers to work with published/established writers; works with a small number of new/unpublished writers each year. A monthly magazine covering pregnancy, child care, and parenting. "Our readership is composed of women in late pregnancy and early new motherhood. Most readers are first-time parents, some have older children. A simple, straightforward, clear approach is mandatory." Circ. 1,000,000. Pays on acceptance. Publishes ms an average of 3 months after acceptance. Byline given. Buys first North American serial rights. Submit seasonal holiday material 5-6 months in advance. Simultaneous, photocopied and previously published submissions OK. Computer printout submissions acceptable; prefers letter-quality. Reports in 3 weeks on queries; 2 months on mss. Sample copy for 9x12 SAE with 6 first class stamps. Writer's guidelines for SASE.
Nonfiction: Book excerpts, essays, how-to (on some aspect of pregnancy or child care), humor, opinion and personal experience. "No 'hearts and flowers' or fantasy pieces." Buys 60 mss/year. Query with or without published clips, or send complete ms. Length: 1,000-2,500 words. Pays $200-1,000 for assigned articles; pays $100-500 for unsolicited articles. Pays the expenses of writers on assignment.
Photos: State availability of photos with submission. Reviews transparencies and prints. Model release and identification of subjects required. Buys one-time rights.
Columns/Departments: My Own Experience (should discuss personal experience in pregnancy and/or something that is universal, but offers new insight or advice), 1,500 words; and One View (an opinion essay on some aspect of pregnancy, birth, or parenting), 1,000 words. Buys 25 mss/year. Send complete ms. Pays $250.
Tips: "Articles should either give 'how to' information on some aspect of pregnancy or child care, cover some common problem of child raising, along with solutions, or give advice to the mother on some psychological or practical subject."

BABY TALK MAGAZINE, Parenting/Excellence, 185 Madison Ave., New York NY 10016. (212)679-4400. Editor: Patricia D. Irons. 50% freelance written. Monthly magazine covering "topics of interest to expectant and new parents—baby care—child development." Circ. 975,000. Pays on acceptance. Publishes ms an average of 3-6 months after acceptance. Byline given. Buys one-time rights. Submit seasonal/holiday material 3-6 months in advance. Previously published submissions sometimes OK. Computer printout submissions

OK; no dot-matrix. Reports in 4 weeks. Sample copy and writer's guidelines for 9x12 SAE amd 2 first class stamps.
Nonfiction: Essays (on parental topics); how-to (on baby care); opinions; personal experience; photo feature; and travel. No articles under 1,000 words, hand-written articles, humor or fiction. Buys 40 mss/year. Query or send complete ms. Length: 1,500-3,000 words. Pays $50-200.
Photos: Send photos with submission. Reviews transparencies or b&w prints. Offers $25-75 per photo. Captions and model releases required. Buys one-time rights.
Columns/Departments: Budgets and Children's Health (young parents' concerns, written by M.D. or R.N.) Length: 1,500-3,000 words. Buys 6-8 mss/year. Query or send complete ms. Pays $50-200.
Tips: "Writing for *Baby Talk* is highly competitive. Due to a lack of available editorial space, less than one in 100 submitted manuscripts can be accepted."

BAY AREA PARENT, The Santa Clara News Magazine for Parents, Kids Kids Kids Publications, Inc., 455 Los Gatos Blvd., #103, Los Gatos CA 95023. Editor: Lynn Berado. 80% freelance written. Works with locally-based published/established writers. Monthly tabloid of resource information for parents and teachers. Circ 60,000. Pays on publication. Publishes ms an average of 3 months after acceptance. Byline given. Buys one-time rights. Submit seasonal/holiday material 3 months in advance. Simultaneous, photocopied, and previously published submissions OK. Query for electronic submissions. Computer printout submissions acceptable.
Nonfiction: Book excerpts (related to our interest group); expose (health, psychology); historical/nostalgic ("History of Diapers"); how-to (related to kids/parenting); humor; interview/profile; photo feature; and travel (with kids, family). Special issues include Music (February); Art (March); Kid's Birthdays (April); Summer Camps (May); Family Fun (June); Pregnancy and Childbirth (July); Fashion (August); Health (September); and Mental Health (October). No opinion or religious articles. Buys 36-50 mss/year. Query or send complete ms. Length: 150-1,500 words. Pays $10-50. Sometimes pays expenses of writers on assignment.
Photos: State availability of photos. Prefers b&w contact sheets and/or 3x5 b&w prints. Pays $5-25. Model release required. Buys one-time rights.
Columns/Departments: Child Care, Family Travel, Birthday Party Ideas, Baby Page, Toddler Page, Adolescent Kids. Buys 36 mss/year. Send complete ms. Length: 800-1,200 words. Pays $7.50-60.
Fiction: Humorous.
Tips: "Submit new, fresh information concisely written and accurately researched."

THE EXCEPTIONAL PARENT, Children with Disabilities/Practical Information, Psy/Ed Corp., 605 Commonwealth Ave., Boston MA 02215. (617)536-8961. Editor: Maxwell Schleifer. 30% freelance written. Magazine published 8 times/year covering issues of concern to parents of disabled children. "Our editorial goal is to provide practical guidance and help to those interested in the growth and development of people with disabilities. We bring together people with different perspectives to present the most comprehensive view of the individual, to generate new solutions to old problems, to create visions." Circ. 40,000. Pays on publication. Byline given. Buys all rights. Submit seasonal/holiday material 3 months in advance. Simultaneous, photocopied and previously published submissions OK. Computer printout submissions acceptable; prefers letter-quality. Reports in 6 months maximum. Sample copy for $5; free writer's guidelines.
Nonfiction: Book excerpts; essays; how-to (adapt toys, fix wheelchairs, etc.); inspirational (family stories); new product; personal experience; and travel. Buys 40 mss/year. Send complete ms. Length: 500-5,000 words. Pays $25-50.
Photos: Send photos with submission. Reviews 3x5 or larger prints. Offers no additional payment for photos accepted with ms. Model releases required. Buys one-time rights.
Tips: "We welcome articles by parents, disabled individuals, professionals, and anyone else—including children."

EXPECTING, 685 3rd Ave., New York NY 10017. Editor: Evelyn A. Podsiadlo. Assistant Editor: Grace Lang. Issued quarterly for expectant mothers. Circ. 1,200,000. Buys all rights. Byline given. Pays on acceptance. Reports in 1 month. Free writer's guidelines.
Nonfiction: Prenatal development, layette and nursery planning, budgeting, health, fashion, husband-wife relationships, naming the baby, minor discomforts, childbirth, expectant fathers, working while pregnant, etc. Length: 800-1,600 words. Pays $200-400 for feature articles.
Fillers: Short humor and interesting or unusual happenings during pregnancy or at the hospital; maximum 100 words, $25 on publication; submissions to "Happenings" are not returned.
Poetry: Occasionally buys subject-related poetry; all forms. Length: 12-64 lines. Pays $10-30.

GIFTED CHILDREN MONTHLY, For the Parents of Children with Great Promise, Box 115, Sewell NJ 08080. (609)582-0277. Editor: Dr. James Alvino. Managing Editor: Robert Baum. 50% freelance written. Prefers to work with published/established writers. Monthly newsletter covering parenting and education of gifted children for parents. Circ. 50,000. Pays on acceptance. Publishes ms an average of 3-6 months after acceptance. Buys all rights and first rights. Submit seasonal/holiday material 4 months in advance. Simultaneous queries, and simultaneous, photocopied, and previously published submissions OK. Computer printout submissions acceptable; prefers letter-quality. Reports in 1 month on queries; 2 months on mss. Sample copy and writer's guidelines for 9x12 SAE and 3 first class stamps.

Nonfiction: Book excerpts; personal accounts; how-to (on parenting of gifted kids); research into practice; outstanding programs; interview/profile; and opinion. Also puzzles, brainteasers and ideas for children's Spin-Off section. "Our Special Reports and Idea Place sections are most accessible to freelancers." Query with clips of published work or send complete ms. Buys 36 unsolicited mss/year. Length: Idea Place 500-750 words; Special Reports 1,000-2,500 words. Pays $10-200. Sometimes pays expenses of writers on assignment.

Tips: "We look forward to working with both new and veteran writers who have something new to say to the parents of gifted and talented children. It is helpful if freelancers provide copies of research papers to back up the article."

GROWING PARENT, Dunn & Hargitt, Inc., 22 N. 2nd St., Box 1100, Lafayette IN 47902. (317)423-2624. Editor: Nancy Kleckner. 40-50% freelance written. Works with a small number of new/unpublished writers each year. "We do receive a lot of unsolicited submissions but have had excellent results in working with some unpublished writers. So, we're always happy to look at material and hope to find one or two jewels each year." A monthly newsletter which focuses on parents—the issues, problems, and choices they face as their children grow. "We want to look at the parent as an adult and help encourage his or her growth not only as a parent but as an individual." Pays on acceptance. Publishes ms an average of 6 months after acceptance. Byline given. Buys first North American serial rights; maintains exclusive rights for three months. Submit seasonal/holiday material 6 months in advance. Photocopied submissions and previously published submissions OK. Computer printout submissions acceptable; prefers letter-quality. Reports in 2 weeks. Sample copy and writer's guidelines for 5x8 SAE with 2 first class stamps.

Nonfiction: "We are looking for informational articles written in an easy-to-read, concise style. We would like to see articles that help parents deal with the stresses they face in everyday life—positive, upbeat, how-to-cope suggestions. We rarely use humorous pieces, fiction or personal experience articles. Writers should keep in mind that most of our readers have children under three years of age." Buys 15-20 mss/year. Query. Length: 1,500-2,000 words; will look at shorter pieces. Pays 8-10¢/word (depends on article).

Tips: "Submit a very specific query letter with samples."

HOME EDUCATION MAGAZINE, Box 1083, Tonasket WA 98855. Editors: Mark J. Hegener and Helen E. Hegener. 80% freelance written. Eager to work with new/unpublished writers each year. A bimonthly magazine covering home-based education and alternative education. "We feature articles which address the concerns of parents who want to take a direct involvement in the education of their children—concerns such as socialization, how to find curriculums and materials, testing and evaluation, how to tell when your child is ready to begin reading, what to do when home schooling is illegal in your state, teaching advanced subjects, etc." Circ. 5,500. Pays on publication. Publishes ms an average of 2-3 months after acceptance. Byline given ("Please include a 30-50 word credit with your article"). Buys first North American serial rights, first rights, one-time rights, second serial (reprint) rights, simultaneous rights, all rights, and makes work-for-hire assignments. Submit seasonal/holiday material 6 months in advance. Simultaneous, photocopied and previously published submissions OK. Query for electronic submission requirements. Computer printout submissions acceptable; prefers letter-quality. Reports in 6-8 weeks. Sample copy $4.50; writer's guidelines for SASE.

Nonfiction: Book excerpts, essays, how-to (related to home schooling), humor, inspirational, interview/profile, personal experience, photo feature and technical. Buys 40-50 mss/year. Query with or without published clips, or send complete ms. Length: 750-3,500 words. Pays $10 per our typeset page, (about 750 words). Sometimes pays expenses of writers on assignment.

Photos: Send photos with submission. Reviews 5x7, 35mm prints and b&w snapshots. Write for photo rates. Identification of subjects required. Buys one-time rights.

Poetry: "Accepts previously published as well as original poetry." Pays $5-10/poem.

Tips: "We would like to see how-to articles (that don't preach, just present options); articles on testing, accountability, working with the public schools, socialization, learning disabilities, resources, support groups, legislation and humor. We need answers to the questions that home schoolers ask. We would also like to see more articles on other options outside the public and traditional private schools, such as alternative community schools, Waldorf education, tuition vouchers, alternative colleges, apprenticeships, etc."

HOME LIFE, Sunday School Board, 127 9th Ave. N., Nashville TN 37234. (615)251-2271. Editor-in-Chief: Charlie Warren. 40-50% freelance written. Prefers to work with published/established writers; eager to work with new/unpublished writers. Emphasizes Christian marriage and Christian family life. For married adults of all ages, but especially newlyweds and middle-aged marrieds. Monthly magazine. Circ. 725,000. Pays on acceptance. Publishes ms an average of 15 months after acceptance. Buys first rights, first North American

serial rights and all rights. Byline given. Phone queries OK, but written queries preferred. Submit seasonal/holiday material 1 year in advance. Computer printout submissions acceptable; prefers letter-quality. Reports in 6 weeks. Sample copy $1; writer's guidelines for #10 SASE.
Nonfiction: How-to (good articles on marriage and family life); informational (about some current family-related issue of national significance such as "Television and the Christian Family" or "Whatever Happened to Family Worship?"); personal experience (informed articles by people who have solved marriage and family problems in healthy, constructive ways); marriage and family life with a masculine slant. "No column material. We are not interested in material that will not in some way enrich Christian marriage or family life." Buys 150-200 mss/year. Query or submit complete ms. Length: 600-2,400 words. Pays up to 5¢/word.
Fiction: "Fiction should be family-related and should show a strong moral about how families face and solve problems constructively." Buys 12-20 mss/year. Submit complete ms. Length: 1,000-2,400 words. Pays up to 5¢/word.
Tips: "Study the magazine to see our unique slant on Christian family life. We prefer a life-centered case study approach, rather than theoretical essays on family life. Our top priority is marriage enrichment material."

L.A. PARENT, The Magazine for Parents in Southern California, Box 3204, Burbank CA 91504. (818)846-0400. Editor: Jack Bierman. 80% freelance written. Prefers to work with published/established writers, and works with a small number of new/unpublished writers each year. Monthly tabloid covering parenting. Circ. 100,000. Pays on publication. Publishes ms an average of 4 months after acceptance. Byline given. Buys first rights. Submit seasonal/holiday material 3 months in advance. Simultaneous queries and previously published submissions OK. Query for electronic submission requirements. Computer printout submissions acceptable. Reports in 1 month. Sample copy and writer's guidelines for $2.
Nonfiction: David Jameison, articles editor. General interest, how-to. "We focus on southern California activities for families, and do round-up pieces, i.e., a guide to private schools, fishing spots." Buys 60-75 mss/year. Query with clips of published work. Length: 700-1,200 words. Pays $100 plus expenses.
Tips: "We will be using more contemporary articles on parenting's challenges. If you can write for a 'city magazine' in tone and accuracy, you may write for us. The 'Baby Boom' has created a need for more generic parenting material."

‡MOTHERS TODAY, Boyd McGinnity, 18 E. 41 St., New York NY 10017. Editor: Janet Spencer King. Managing Editor: Bernice Pickett. Bimonthly magazine on subjects of interest to new mothers. Circ. 900,000. Pays on publication. Byline given. Offers 20% kill fee. Buys first North American serial rights. Submit seasonal/holiday material 4 months in advance. Computer printout submissions OK; no dot-matrix. Reports in 6 weeks on queries; 2 months on mss. Sample copy $1.25.
Nonfiction: Humor, opinion, personal experience. Query with published clips. Length: 900-1,500 words. Pays $300-800. Sometimes pays expenses of writers on assignment.
Columns/Departments: Parent Perspective (personal experience). Buys 12 mss/year. Send complete ms. Length: 900-1,200 words. Pays $125-175.

NETWORK, For Public Schools, National Committee for Citizens in Education, Suite 301, 10840 Little Patuyent Pkwy., Columbia MD 21044. (301)997-9300. Editor: Chrissie Bamber. 10% freelance written. Works with a small number of new/unpublished writers each year. Published 6 times during the school year covering parent/citizen involvement in public schools. Circ. 6,000. Pays on publication. Publishes ms an average of 6 months after acceptance. Byline given. Buys first serial rights, first North American serial rights, one-time rights, second serial (reprint) rights, simultaneous rights, all rights and makes work-for-hire assignments. Submit seasonal/holiday material 3 months in advance. Simultaneous queries and photocopied submissions OK. Computer printout submissions OK; prefers letter-quality. Reports in 6 weeks. Free sample copy; writer's guidelines for #10 SAE and 2 first class stamps.
Nonfiction: Book excerpts (elementary and secondary public education); exposé (of school systems which attempt to reduce public access); how-to (improve schools through parent/citizen participation); humor (related to public school issues); opinion (school-related issues); personal experience (school-related issues). "It is our intention to provide balanced coverage of current developments and continuing issues and to place the facts about schools in a perspective useful to parents. No highly technical or scholarly articles about education; no child rearing articles or personal opinion not backed by research or concrete examples." Buys 4-6 mss/year. Query with clips of published work or send complete ms. Length: 1,000-1,500 words. Pays $25-100. Sometimes pays the expenses of writers on assignment.
Tips: "We are seeking more local examples of parent/community and school partnerships that have succeeded in raising student achievement. Readers want articles of substance with information they can use and act on, not headlines which promise much but deliver only the most shallow analysis of the subject. Information is first, style second. A high personal commitment to public schools and preferably first-hand experience are the greatest assets. A clear and simple writing style, easily understood by a wide range of lay readers, is a must."

‡**PARENTS MAGAZINE**, 685 3rd Ave., New York NY 10017. Editor: Elizabeth Crow. 25% freelance written. Monthly. Circ. 1,740,000. Pays on acceptance. Publishes ms an average of 8 months after acceptance. Usually buys first serial rights or first North American serial rights; sometimes buys all rights. Byline given "except for Almanac." Pays $100-350 kill fee. Computer printout submissions acceptable; prefers letter-quality. Reports in approximately 6 weeks.

Nonfiction: "We are interested in well-documented articles on the development and behavior of preschool, school-age, and adolescent children and their parents; good, practical guides to the routines of baby care; articles that offer professional insights into family and marriage relationships; reports of new trends and significant research findings in education and in mental and physical health; and articles encouraging informed citizen action on matters of social concern. Especially need articles on women's issues, pregnancy, birth, baby care and early childhood. We prefer a warm, colloquial style of writing, one which avoids the extremes of either slang or technical jargon. Anecdotes and examples should be used to illustrate points which can then be summed up by straight exposition." Query. Length: 2,500 words maximum. Payment varies; pays $400 minimum; $50 minimum for Almanac items. Sometimes pays the expenses of writers on assignment.

Fillers: Anecdotes for "Parents Exchange," illustrative of parental problem-solving with children and teenagers. Pays $20 on publication.

PEDIATRICS FOR PARENTS, The Newsletter for Caring Parents, Pediatrics for Parents, Inc., 176 Mt. Hope Ave., Bangor ME 04401. (207)942-6212. Editor: Richard J. Sagall, M.D. 20% freelance written. Eager to work with new/unpublished writers. Monthly newsletter covering medical aspects of rearing children and educating parents about children's health. Circ. 2,000. Pays on publication. Publishes ms an average of 3-4 months after acceptance. Byline given. Buys first North American serial rights, first and second rights to the same material, and second (reprint) rights to material originally published elsewhere. Rights always include right to publish article in our books on "Best of . . ." series. Submit seasonal/holiday material 6 months in advance. Simultaneous queries, and simultaneous, photocopied and previously published submissions OK. Query for electronic submissions. Computer printout submissions acceptable. Reports in 1 month on queries; 6 weeks on mss. Sample copy for $2; writer's guidelines for #10 SAE and 2 first class stamps.

Nonfiction: Book reviews; how-to (feed healthy kids, exercise, practice wellness, etc.); new product; technical (explaining medical concepts in shirtsleeve language). No general parenting articles. Query with published clips or submit complete ms. Length: 25-1,000 words. Pays 2-5¢/edited word.

Columns/Departments: Book reviews; Please Send Me (material available to parents for free or at nominal cost); Pedia-Tricks (medically-oriented parenting tips that work). Send complete ms. Pays $15-250. Pays 2¢/edited word.

Tips: "We are dedicated to taking the mystery out of medicine for young parents. Therefore, we write in clear and understandable language (but not simplistic language) to help people understand and deal intelligently with complex disease processes, treatments, prevention, wellness, etc. Our articles must be well researched and documented. Detailed references must always be attached to any article for documentation, but not for publication. We strongly urge freelancers to read one or two issues before writing."

SEATTLE'S CHILD, Box 22578, Seattle WA 98122. (206)322-2594. Editor: Ann Bergman. 85% freelance written. Works with a small number of new/unpublished writers each year. Monthly tabloid of articles related to being a parent of children age 12 and under. Directed to parents and professionals involved with children 12 and under. Circ. 20,000. Pays on publication. Publishes ms an average of 6 months after acceptance. Byline given. Offers 50% kill fee. Buys first North American serial rights or all rights. Submit seasonal/holiday material 6 months in advance. Simultaneous queries, and simultaneous and photocopied submissions OK. Query for electronic submissions. Computer printout submissions acceptable. Reports in 1 month on queries; 3 months on mss. Sample copy $1.50 with 10x13 envelope; writer's guidelines for #10 SAE and 1 first class stamp.

Nonfiction: Needs reports on political issues affecting families. Exposé, general interest, historical/nostalgic, how-to, humor, interview/profile, new product, opinion, personal experience, travel, record, tape and book reviews, and educational and political reviews. Articles must relate to parents and parenting. Buys 120 mss/year. Send complete ms (preferred) or query with published clips. Length: 400-2,500 words. Pays 10¢/word.

Tips: "We prefer concise, critical writing and discourage overly sentimental pieces. Don't talk down to the audience. Consider that the audience is sophisticated and well-read."

‡**SESAME STREET MAGAZINE, Parent's Guide**, Children's Television Workshop, One Lincoln Plaza, New York NY 10023. (212)595-3456. Editor-in-Chief: Marge Kennedy. Articles Editor: Rebecca Herman. 60% freelance written. A monthly magazine for parents of preschoolers. Circ. 1.3 million. Pays ½ on acceptance, ½ on publication. Byline given. Offers 50% kill fee. Buys all rights. Submit seasonal/holiday material 7 months in advance. Reports in 1 month on queries. Sample copy for 9x12 SAE with 3 first class stamps. Writer's guidelines for #10 SAE with 1 first class stamp.

Nonfiction: Book excerpts, essays, general interest (child development/parenting), how-to (practical tips for

parents of preschoolers), interview/profile, personal experience, photo feature and travel (with children). Buys 20 mss/year. Query with or without published clips, or send complete ms. Length: 800-4,000 words. Pays $200-900 for assigned articles. Pays $200-500 for unsolicited articles.
Photos: State availability of photos with submission. Model releases and identification of subjects required. Buys one-time rights or all rights.

‡**THINKING FAMILIES, For Parents with Children in Elementary School**, Communications Plus, Inc., 605 Worcester Rd., Towson MD 21204. (301)321-0121. Editor: Marjory Spraycar. 90% freelance written. Bimonthly magazine on schools and school kids. "We are a magazine about schools and school kids for parents with children in elementary school. Our readers are motivated to help provide the very best education possible for their children." Estab. 1988. Circ. 50,000. Pays on publication. Byline given. Offers $50 kill fee. Buys one-time rights. Submit seasonal/holiday material 4 months in advance. Photocopied submissions OK. Query for electronic submissions. Computer printout submissions OK. Reports in 1 month. Sample copy $2.50 with 9x12 SAE and 4 first class stamps. Writer's guidelines for #10 SAE with 1 first class stamp.
Nonfiction: Personal experience, photo feature, travel. Buys 15-25 mss/year. Query with published clips. Length: 1,000-3,000 words. Pays $200-1,000. Sometimes pays expenses of writers on assignment.
Photos: State availability of photos with submission. Reviews contact sheets, transparencies. Offers $10-350/photo. Captions, model releases and identification of subjects required. Buys one-time rights.
Columns/Departments: Travel Column (geared as a how-to travel with grade school kids); Electronic Home (reviews software or any technological advance that can be used by families). Buys 36-50/year. Query with published clips. Length: 1,500-2,000 words. Pays $100-350.
Tips: "Writers with good ideas and the ability to write excellent magazine articles and experience in the subjects we cover have an excellent chance of breaking into our pages. We write no features in-house; must rely on freelancers. We prefer writers already published in national magazines. We are a high quality publication looking for proven talent."

TWINS, The Magazine for Parents of Multiples, Box 12045, Overland Park KS 66212. (913)722-1090. Editor: Barbara C. Unell. 100% freelance written. Eager to work with new/unpublished writers. A bimonthly national magazine designed to give professional guidance to help multiples, their parents and those professionals who care for them learn about twin facts and research. Circ. 40,000. Pays on publication. Publishes ms an average of 6 months after acceptance. Byline given. Buys all rights. Submit seasonal/holiday material 10 months in advance. Simultaneous, photocopied and previously published submissions OK. Computer printout submissions acceptable; prefers letter-quality. Reports in 6 weeks on queries; 2 months on mss. Sample copy $3.50 plus $1.50 postage and handling; writer's guidelines for #10 SAE with 1 first class stamp.
Nonfiction: Book excerpts, general interest, how-to, humor, interview/profile, personal experience and photo feature. "No articles which substitute the word 'twin' for 'child'—those that simply apply the same research to twins that applies to singletons without any facts backing up the reason to do so." Buys 150 mss/year. Query with or without published clips, or send complete ms. Length: 1,250-3,000 words. Payment varies; sometimes pays in contributor copies or premiums instead of cash. Sometimes pays the expenses of writers on assignment.
Photos: Send photos with submission. Reviews contact sheets, 4x5 transparencies, and all size prints. Captions, model releases, and identification of subjects required. Buys all rights.
Columns/Departments: Grandparenting, Resources, Supertwins, Prematurity, Family Health, Twice as Funny, Double Focus (series from pregnancy through adolescence), Personal Perspective (first-person accounts of beliefs about a certain aspect of parenting multiples), Caring for You (ways parents can feel as good as can be as people, not just parents), Feelings on Fatherhood, Research, On Being Twins (first-person accounts of growing up as a twin), On Being Parents of Twins (first-person accounts of the experience of parenting twins), Double Takes (fun photographs of twins), and Education Matters. Buys 70 mss/year. Query with published clips. Length: 1,250-2,000 words. Payment varies.
Fillers: Anecdotes and short humor. Length: 75-750 words. Payment varies.
Tips: "Features and columns are both open to freelancers. Columnists write for *Twins* on a continuous basis, so the column becomes their column. We are looking for a wide variety of the latest, well-researched practical information. There is no other magazine of this type directed to this market." We are interested in "personal interviews with celebrity twins or celebrity parents of twins, and tips on rearing twins from experienced parents and/or twins themselves, as well as reports on national and international research studies involving twins."

Comic Books

Comic books aren't just for kids. Today, this popular medium also attracts a reader who is older and expects sophisticated stories presented visually. This doesn't mean you have to be an artist to write for comic books. Most of these publishers want to see a synopsis of one to two double-spaced pages. Highlight the story's beginning, middle and end, and tell how events will affect your main character emotionally. Be concise. Comics use few words.

Once your synopsis is accepted, either an artist will draw the story from your plot, returning these pages to you for dialogue and captions, or you will be expected to write a script. Scripts run approximately 23 typewritten pages and include suggestions for artwork as well as dialogue. Try to imagine your story on actual comic book pages and divide your script accordingly. The average comic has six panels per page, with a maximum of 35 words per panel.

If you're submitting a proposal to Marvel or DC, your story should center on an already established character. If you're dealing with an independent publisher, characters are often the property of their creators. Your proposal should be for a new series. Include a background sheet for main characters who will appear regularly, listing origins, weaknesses, powers or other information that will make your character unique. Indicate an overall theme or direction for your series. Submit story ideas for the first three issues. If you're really ambitious, you may also include a script for your first issue. As with all markets, read a sample copy before making a submission.

AMAZING HEROES, Fantagraphics Books, 1800 Bridgegate St., Suite 101, Westlake Village CA 91361.(805)379-1881. Editor: Kevin Dooley. 80% freelance written. Eager to work with new/unpublished writers. A biweekly magazine for comic book fans of all ages and backgrounds. "*Amazing Heroes* focuses on both historical aspects of comics and current doings in the industry." Circ. 15,000. Pays on publication. Publishes ms an average of 2 months after acceptance. Byline given. Offers $25 kill fee on solicited ms. Buys first North American serial rights and second serial (reprint) rights. Submit seasonal/holiday material 3 months in advance. Photocopied and previously published submissions OK. Computer printout submissions OK; prefers letter-quality. Reports in 2 weeks on queries; 1 month on mss. Sample copy for 7½x10½ SAE and $2.50.
Nonfiction: Essays, historical/nostalgic, interview/profile, new product. Query with published clips and interests. Length: 300-7,500 words. Pays $5-125 for assigned articles; pays $5-75 for unsolicited articles. Pays writers with double payment in Fantagraphics book merchandise if requested. Sometimes pays the expenses of writers on assignment.
Photos: State availability of photos on profile pieces and interviews.
Tips: "Recently, there has been a renaissance, though some refer to it as a glut, of new material and new publishers in the comic book industry. This has called for a greater need for more writers who are not just interested in super-heroes or just books produced by DC and Marvel. There is now, more than ever, a need to be open-minded as well as critical. Writers for *Amazing Heroes* must have a much broader knowledge of the entire, ever-widening spectrum of the comic book industry."

CARTOON WORLD, Box 30367, Dept. WM, Lincoln NE 68503. Editor: George Hartman. 100% freelance written. Works with published/established writers and a small number of new/unpublished writers each year. "Monthly newsletter for professional and amateur cartoonists who are serious and want to utilize new cartoon markets in each issue." Buys only from paid subscribers. Circ. 150-300. Pays on acceptance. Publishes ms an average of 2 months after acceptance. Byline given. Buys second (reprint) rights to material originally published elsewhere. Not copyrighted. Submit seasonal/holiday material 3 months in advance. Simultaneous submissions OK. Computer printout submissions acceptable; no dot-matrix. Reports in 1 month. Sample copy $5.
Nonfiction: "We want only positive articles about the business of cartooning and gag writing." Buys 10 mss/year. Query. Length: 1,000 words. Pays $5/page.

COMICO THE COMIC COMPANY, 1547 DeKalb St., Norristown PA 19401. (215)277-4305. Editor-in-Chief: Diana Schutz. 100% freelance written. "We work only with writers, published or unpublished, who can tell a strong, solid, and visual story." One-shot, limited and continuing series comic books. Circ. approximately 70,000 per title. Pays 1 month after acceptance. Publishes ms an average of 9-12 months after acceptance. Byline given. Buys first rights, makes work-for-hire assignments or offers creator ownership contracts. Simultaneous, photocopied and previously published submissions OK. Computer printout submissions OK; no dot-matrix. Reports in 1 month on queries; 2 months on mss. Sample copy for $1.75 and 7½x10½ SAE and 3 first class stamps. Free writer's guidelines.
Fiction: Various genres. "We are always interested in seeing submissions of new and innovative material. Due to the words-and-pictures format of comic books, it is usually preferable, though not essential, that the writer

submit material in conjunction with an artist of his or her choice." No pornography or dogma. Buys 100 mss/year. Query. Length: 26 story pages. Payment varies.

Tips: "Our industry in general and our company in particular are beginning to look more and more at the limited series and graphic novel formats as means of properly conveying solid stories, beautifully illustrated for the adult marketplace, as opposed to the standard continuing serials. Be familiar with comics medium and industry. Show that writer can write in script format and express intentions to artist who will create images based on writer's descriptions. The area of licensed properties is most open to freelancers. Writer must be faithful to licensed characters, to licensor's wishes, and be willing to make any requested changes."

ECLIPSE COMICS, Box 1099, Forestville CA 95436. (707)887-1521. Publisher: Dean Mullaney. Editor-in-Chief: Catherine Yronwode. 100% freelance written. Works with a small number of new/unpublished writers each year. Publishers of various four-color comic books. *Eclipse* publishes comic books with high-quality paper and color reproduction, geared toward the discriminating comic book fan; and sold through the "direct sales" specialty store market. Circ. varies (35,000-85,000). Pays on acceptance (net 1 month). Publishes ms an average of 3 months after acceptance. Byline given. Buys first North American serial rights, second serial (reprint) rights with additional payment, and first option on collection and non-exclusive rights to sell material to South American and European markets (with additional payments). Simultaneous queries, and simultaneous and photocopied submissions OK. Computer printout submissions acceptable; no dot-matrix. Reports in 2 months. Sample copy $1.75; writer's guidelines for #10 SAE and 1 first class stamp.

Fiction: "All of our comics are fictional." Adventure, fantasy, mystery, romance, science fiction, horror, western. "No sexually explicit material, please." Buys approximately 250 mss/year (mostly from established comics writers). Send sample script or plot synopsis for a back-up story staring one of our lesser-known characters (The Heap, Black Angel, Iron Ace, etc.). Length: 8-11 pages. Pays $30 minimum/page.

Tips: "At the present time we are publishing as many adventure and super-heroic series as our schedule permits. Because all of our comics are creator-owned, we do not buy fill-in plots or scripts for these books but occasionally take back-up stories to fill books and try out new talent. Plot synopsis of less than a page can be submitted; we will select promising concepts for development into full script submissions. All full script submissions should be written in comic book or 'screenplay' form for artists to illustrate. Writers who are already teamed with artists stand a better chance of selling a new series to us; for back-ups, we'll find an artist. Our special needs at the moment are for heroic, character-oriented series with overtones of humanism, morality, political opinion, philosophical speculation, and/or social commentary. Comic book adaptations (by the original authors) of previously published science fiction and horror short stories are definitely encouraged."

MARVEL COMICS, 387 Park Ave. S., New York NY 10016. (212)576-9200. Editor-in-Chief: Tom DeFalco. 99% freelance written. Publishes 60 comics and magazines per month, 6-12 graphic novels per year, and specials, storybooks, industrials, and paperbacks for all ages. Over 9 million copies sold/month. Pays a flat fee for most projects, plus a royalty type incentive based upon sales. Also works on advance/royalty basis on many projects. "Top regular writers make up to $300,000 per year." Pays on acceptance. Publishes manuscript an average of 6 months after acceptance. Byline given. Offers variable kill fee. Rights purchased depend upon format and material. Submit seasonal/holiday material 1 year in advance. Simultaneous and photocopied submissions OK. Computer printout submissions OK; no dot-matrix. Reports in 6 months. Sample copy and writer's guidelines for SASE. Additional guidelines on request.

Fiction: Super hero, action-adventure, science fiction, fantasy, and other material. No noncomics. Buys 600-800 mss/year. Query with brief plot synopses only. Do not send scripts, short stories or long outlines. A plot synopsis should be less than two typed pages; send two synopses at most. Pays expenses of writers on assignment.

Consumer Service and Business Opportunity

Some of these magazines are geared to investing earnings or starting a new business; others show how to make economical purchases. Publications for business executives and consumers interested in business topics are listed under Business and Finance. Those on how to run specific businesses are classified by category in the Trade section.

BUSINESS TODAY, Meridian Publishing Inc., Box 10010, Ogden UT 84409. (801)394-9446. Editor: Karen E. Hill. 65% freelance written. Monthly magazine covering all aspects of business. Particularly interested in profiles of business personalities. Pays on acceptance. Publishes ms an average of 8 months after acceptance. Byline given. Buys first rights, second serial (reprint) rights and nonexclusive reprint rights. Computer printout submissions acceptable; prefers letter-quality. Reports in 6 weeks. Sample copy for $1 and 9x12 SAE; writer's guidelines for #10 SAE and 1 first class stamp. All requests for samples and guidelines should be addressed Attn: Editorial Assistant.

Nonfiction: General interest articles about employee relations, management principles, advertising methods and financial planning. Articles covering up-to-date practical business information are welcome. Cover stories are often profiles of people who have expertise and success in a specific aspect of business. Buys 40 mss/year. Query. Length: 1,000-1,400 words. Pays 15¢/word for first rights plus non-exclusive reprint rights. Payment for second rights is negotiable.

Photos: State availability of photos or send photos with query. Reviews 35mm or longer transparencies. Pays $35 for inside photo; pays $50 for cover photo. Captions, model releases and identification of subjects required.

Tips: "The key is a well-written query letter that: 1) demonstrates that the subject of the article is tried-and-true and has national appeal 2) shows that the article will have a clear, focused theme 3) outlines the availability (from writer or a photographer or a PR source) of top-quality color photos 4) gives evidence that the writer/photographer is a professional, even if a beginner."

CHANGING TIMES, The Kiplinger Magazine, 1729 H St. NW, Washington DC 20006. Editor: Ted Miller. Less than 10% freelance written. Prefers to work with published/established writers. For general, adult audience interested in personal finance and consumer information. Monthly. Circ. 1,350,000. Pays on acceptance. Publishes ms an average of 2 months after acceptance. Buys all rights. Reports in 1 month. Query for electronic submissions. Computer printout submissions acceptable; prefers letter-quality. Thorough documentation required for fact-checking.

Nonfiction: "Most material is staff-written, but we accept some freelance." Query with clips of published work. Pays expenses of writers on assignment.

Tips: "We are looking for a heavy emphasis on personal finance topics."

COMMERCE MAGAZINE, 200 N. LaSalle St., Chicago IL 60601. (312)580-6900. Editor: Carol Johnson. For top businessmen and industrial leaders in greater Chicago area. Monthly magazine; varies from 100 to 300 pages, (8½x11½). Circ. 15,000. Buys all rights. Buys 30-40 mss/year. Pays on acceptance. Query.

Nonfiction: Business articles and pieces of general interest to top business executives. "We select our freelancers and assign topics. Many of our writers are from local newspapers. Considerable freelance material is used but almost exclusively on assignment from Chicago-area specialists within a particular business sector."

CONSUMER ACTION NEWS, Suite 208, 1106 E. High St., Springfield OH 45505. (513)325-2001. Editor: Victor Pence. 10% freelance written. Eager to work with new/unpublished writers. A monthly newsletter circulated in the state of Ohio for readers who are interested in knowing how to handle any type of consumer complaint. "We handle consumer complaints and publish results in newsletter." Pays on acceptance. Byline given. Buys one-time rights. Simultaneous queries, and simultaneous, photocopied, and previously published submissions OK. Computer printout submissions acceptable; prefers letter-quality. Reports in 6 weeks.

Nonfiction: Send complete ms. Length: 1,000 words or less. Pays $10-25.

Tips: "We want only experiences with complaints that were solved when the usual protection sources couldn't solve them. Creative ways of finding solutions without legal actions. If the problem has not been solved, we will offer possible solutions to the problem anywhere in the U.S. and Canada at no charge."

ECONOMIC FACTS, The National Research Bureau, Inc., 424 N. 3rd St., Burlington IA 52601. Editor: Rhonda Wilson. Editorial Supervisor: Doris J. Ruschill. 25% freelance written. Eager to work with new/unpublished writers; works with a small number of new/unpublished writers each year. Magazine for industrial workers of all ages. Published 4 times/year. Pays on publication. Publishes ms an average of 1 year after acceptance. Buys all rights. Byline given. Submit seasonal/holiday material 7 months in advance of issue date. Previously published submissions OK. Computer printout submissions acceptable; prefers letter-quality. Reports in 1 week. Writer's guidelines for SASE.

Nonfiction: General interest (private enterprise, government data, graphs, taxes and health care). Buys 3-5 mss/year. Query with outline of article. Length: 400-600 words. Pays 4¢/word.

ENTREPRENEUR MAGAZINE, 2392 Morse Ave., Box 19787, Irvine CA 92714-6234. Editor: Rieva Lesonsky. 40% freelance written. "We are eager to work with any writer (new or established) who takes the time to see *Entrepreneur*'s special 'angle' and who turns in copy on time." For a readership looking for opportunities in small businesses, as owners, franchisees or seeking "tips and tactics to help them better run their existing small business." Circ. 250,000. Pays on acceptance. Publishes ms an average of 3-5 months after acceptance. Buys all rights. Byline given. Submit seasonal/holiday material 6 months in advance of issue date. Photocopied submissions OK. Computer printout submissions acceptable. Reports in 2 months. Sample copy $3; writer's guidelines for SASE.

Nonfiction: How-to (in-depth start-up details on 'hot' business opportunities). Buys 60-70 mss/year. Query with clips of published work and SASE. Length: 750-2,000 words. Payment varies.

Photos: "We need color transparencies to illustrate articles." Offers additional payment for photos accepted with ms. Uses standard color transparencies. Captions preferred. Buys all rights. Model release required.

Columns/Departments: Business Primer, Business Beat. Query. Length: 200-1,500 words. Payment varies.

Tips: "We are changing our editorial slant and including more articles (50% of total issue) for people already established in their own businesses. It's rewarding to find a freelancer who reads the magazine *before* he/she submits a query. We get so many queries with the wrong angle. I can't stress enough the importance of reading and understanding our magazine and our audience before you write. We're looking for writers who can perceive the difference between *Entrepreneur* and 'other' business magazines."

INCOME OPPORTUNITIES, 380 Lexington Ave., New York NY 10017. Editor: Stephen Wagner. Managing Editor: Dara Wertheimer. 90% freelance written. Works with a small number of new/unpublished writers each year. Monthly magazine. For all who are seeking business opportunities, full- or part-time. Publishes ms an average of 5 months after acceptance. Buys all rights. Two special directory issues contain articles on selling techniques, mail order, import/export, franchising and business ideas. Query for details on electronic submissions. Computer printout submissions acceptable. Reports in 2 weeks. Writer's guidelines for #10 SASE.

Nonfiction and Photos: Regularly covered are such subjects as mail order, home business, direct selling, franchising, party plans, selling techniques and the marketing of handcrafted or homecrafted products. Wanted are ideas for the aspiring entrepreneur; examples of successful business methods that might be duplicated. No material that is purely inspirational. Buys 50-60 mss/year. Query with outline of article development. Length: 800 words for a short; 2,000-3,000 words for a major article. "Payment rates vary according to length and quality of the submission." Sometimes pays expenses of writers on assignment.

Tips: "Study recent issues of the magazine. Best bets for newcomers: Interview-based report on a successful small business venture. Our emphasis is on home-based business."

PUBLIC CITIZEN, Public Citizen, Inc., Box 19404, Washington DC 20036. Editor: Catherine Baker. 10% freelance written. Prefers to work with published/established writers. Bimonthly magazine covering consumer issues for "contributors to Public Citizen, a consortium of five consumer groups established by Ralph Nader in the public interest: Congress Watch, the Health Research Group, the Critical Mass Energy Project, the Litigation Group, and Buyers UP, a cooperative fuel-purchasing project. Our readers have joined Public Citizen because they believe the consumer should have a voice in the products he or she buys, the quality of our environment, good government, and citizen rights in our democracy." Circ. 42,000. Pays on publication. Publishes ms an average of 3 months after acceptance. Byline given. Buys first North American serial rights, second serial (reprint) rights and simultaneous rights. Submit seasonal/holiday material 3 months in advance. Query for electronic submission requirements. Computer printout submissions acceptable; prefers letter-quality. Reports in 1 month on queries; 2 months on mss. Sample copy for 9x12 SAE and 2 first class stamps.

Nonfiction: Exposé (of government waste and inaction and corporate wrongdoing); general interest (features on how consumer groups are helping themselves); how-to (start consumer groups such as co-ops, etc.); interview/profile (of business or consumer leaders, or of government officials in positions that affect consumers); and photo feature (dealing with consumer power). "We are looking for stories that go to the heart of an issue and explain how it affects individuals. Articles must be in-depth investigations that expose poor business practices or bad government or that call attention to positive accomplishments. Send us stories that consumers will feel they learned something important from or that they can gain inspiration from to continue the fight for consumer rights. All facts are double checked by our fact-checkers." No "fillers, jokes or puzzles." Query or send complete ms. Length: 500-10,000 words. Pays $750 maximum/article. Sometimes pays the expenses of writers on assignment.

> **❝ The best writers are those who get all of the facts in, but in a way that entertains the reader rather than overwhelms him. ❞**
>
> —*Alex McNab*
> **Tennis** *magazine*

Photos: State availability of photos. Reviews 5x7 b&w prints. "Photos are paid for with payment for ms." Captions required. Buys one-time rights.

Tips: No first-person articles, political rhetoric, or "mood" pieces; *Public Citizen* is a highly factual advocacy magazine. Knowledge of the public interest movement, consumer issues, and Washington politics is a plus.

TOWERS CLUB, USA NEWSLETTER, The Original Information-By-Mail, Direct-Marketing Newsletter, TOWERS Club Press, Box 2038, Vancouver WA 98668. (206)574-3084. Editor: Jerry Buchanan. 5-10% freelance written. Works with a small number of new/unpublished writers each year. Newsletter published 10 times/year (not published in May or December) covering entrepreneurism (especially selling useful information by mail). Circ. 8,000. Pays on publication. Publishes ms an average of 2 months after acceptance. Byline given. Buys one-time rights. Submit seasonal/holiday material 10 weeks in advance. Simultaneous, photocopied, and previously published submissions OK. Query for electronic submissions. Reports in 2 weeks. Sample copy for $5 and 6x9 SAE with 3 first class stamps.

Nonfiction: Exposé (of mail order fraud); how-to (personal experience in self-publishing and marketing); book reviews of new self-published nonfiction how-to-do-it books (must include name and address of author). "Welcomes well-written articles of successful self-publishing/marketing ventures. Must be current, and preferably written by the person who actually did the work and reaped the rewards. There's very little we will not consider, *if* it pertains to unique money-making enterprises that can be operated from the home." Buys 10 mss/year. Send complete ms. Length: 500-1,500 words. Pays $10-35. Pays extra for b&w photo and bonus for excellence in longer manuscript.

Tips: "The most frequent mistake made by writers in completing an article for us is that they think they can simply rewrite a newspaper article and be accepted. That is only the start. We want them to find the article about a successful self-publishing enterprise, and then go out and interview the principal for a more detailed how-to article, including names and addresses. We prefer that writer actually interview a successful self-publisher. Articles should include how idea first came to subject; how they implemented and financed and promoted the project; how long it took to show a profit and some of the stumbling blocks they overcame; how many persons participated in the production and promotion; and how much money was invested (approximately) and other pertinent how-to elements of the story. Glossy photos (b&w) of principals at work in their offices will help sell article."

‡WINNING SWEEPSTAKES NEWSLETTER, Sebell Publishing Company, Inc. Suite 103, 171 Main St., Ashland MA (617)881-7400. Editor: Jeffrey Sklar. Managing Editor: Robin Sklar. 50% freelance written. A monthly newsletter on sweepstakes and consumer promotions. "*Winning Sweepstakes Newsletter* is written to a consumer audience about how to win sweepstakes and participate in consumer promotions." Circ. 100,000. Pays on acceptance. Publishes ms an average of 3 months after acceptance. Byline sometimes given. Buys all rights. Submit seasonal/holiday material 3 months in advance. Query for electronic submissions. Computer printout submissions OK; prefers letter-quality. Reports in 2 months. Sample copy for #10 SAE with 2 first class stamps. Writer's guidelines for #10 SAE with 2 first class stamps.

Nonfiction: How-to (sweepstakes/consumer promotion), interview/profile (consumer success stories) and personal experience (consumer success). Buys 1-3 mss/year. Query with or without published clips, or send complete ms. Length: 500-5,000 words. Pays $15-100 for assigned articles. Sometimes pays expenses of writers on assignment.

Photos: State availability of photos with submission. Reviews contact sheets. Offers no additional payment for photos accepted with ms. Buys all rights.

Columns/Departments: Sweeps Update (sweepstakes news), 500 words; Feature (consumer viewpoint about how to win sweeps, participate in consumer promos), 1,000 words. Buys 12 mss/year. Query. Length: 500-1,000 words. Pays $15-100.

Fillers: Anecdotes and facts. Buys 12-15/year. Length: 50-500 words. Pays $15-85.

Tips: "Research and enter sweepstakes and consumer promotions."

❝ *The primary consideration is the quality of the idea presented. A turn-off is receiving a query in which the idea is so off-base that it is obvious the writer has never even read the magazine. Who would write for a magazine he or she has never seen before?* **❞**

—*Stewart Weiner,*
Alan Weston Communications

Contemporary Culture

These magazines often combine fashion, politics, gossip and entertainment in a single package. Some approach institutions in an irreverent manner and are targeted primarily to a young adult audience. Others contain serious, thoughtful critiques of art, politics, music, literature and popular culture. For other magazines containing literary criticism see the Literary and "Little" section.

‡**BOMB, New Art Productions**, Suite 177, Franklin St., New York NY 10013. Editor: Betsy Sussler. 100% freelance written. Quarterly magazine on new art, writing, theater and film for artists and writers. Circ. 10,000. Publishes ms an average of 3 months after acceptance. Byline given. Buys one-time rights. Photocopied submissions OK. Computer printout submissions OK; prefers letter-quality.
Nonfiction: Buys 4 mss/year. Length: 2,500-3,000 words. Pays $50-100.
Photos: State availability of photos with submission. Offers $25-100 per photo. Captions required. Buys one-time rights.
Fiction: Experimental, novel excerpts. Buys 20 mss/year. Send complete ms. Length: 1,200-4,000 words. Pays $50-100.

‡**BOSTON REVIEW**, 33 Harrison Ave., Boston MA 02111. (617)350-5353. Editor: Margaret Ann Roth. 100% freelance written. Works with a small number of new/unpublished writers each year. Bimonthly magazine of the arts, politics and culture. Circ. 10,000. Pays on acceptance. Publishes ms an average of 2 months after acceptance. Buys first American serial rights. Byline given. Photocopied and simultaneous submissions OK. Computer printout submissions acceptable; prefers letter-quality. Reports in 2 months. Sample copy $3; writer's guidelines for #10 SAE with 1 first class stamp.
Nonfiction: Critical essays and reviews, natural and social sciences, literature, music, painting, film, photography, dance and theatre. Buys 20 unsolicited mss/year. Length: 1,000-3,000 words. Sometimes pays expenses of writers on assignment.
Fiction: Length: 2,000-4,000 words. Pays according to length and author, ranging from $50-200.
Poetry: Pays according to length and author.
Tips: "Short (500 words) color pieces are particularly difficult to find, ans so we are always on the look-out for them. We look for in-depth knowledge of an area, an original view of the material, and a presentation which makes these accessible to a sophisticated reader who will be looking for more and better articles which anticipate ideas and trends on the intellectual and cultural frontier."

‡**CANADIAN DIMENSION**, Dimension Publications Inc., #801-44 Princess St., Winnipeg, Manitoba R3B 1K2 Canada. Managing Editor: Jim Pringle. 80% freelance written. A magazine on economics, politics and popular cultures, published 8 times/year. Circ. 4,000. Pays on publication. Publishes ms an average of 6 months after acceptance. Not copyrighted. Simultaneous and photocopied submissions OK. Query for electronic submissions. Computer printout submissions OK; prefers letter-quality. Reports in 6 weeks on queries. Free sample copy.
Nonfiction: General interest, humor, interview/profile, opinion, personal experience and reviews. Buys 8 mss/year. Length: 500-2,000 words. Pays $25-300 for assigned articles. Send photos with submission.

‡**A CRITIQUE OF AMERICA**, Suite 418, 405 W. Washington, San Diego CA 92103. (619)237-0074. Editor: Alden Mills. Managing Editor: Bryan Plank. 75% freelance written. A bimonthly political/social/arts and literary magazine. "We are dedicated to presenting high-quality work of any viewpoint, providing an unbiased forum of thought-provoking ideas." Circ. 100,000. Pays on acceptance. Publishes ms an average of 2 months after acceptance. Byline given. Offers 15% kill fee. Not copyrighted. Buys one-time rights. Photocopied and previously published submissions OK. Query for electronic submissions. Computer printout submissions OK; prefers letter-quality. Reports in 1 week. Sample copy $2.50. Free writer's guidelines.
Nonfiction: Harlan Lewin-political/social commentary; Jack Carter-American Journal; Doug Balding-arts. Book excerpts, essays, exposé, general interest, historical/nostalgic, humor, interview/profile, opinion, personal experience, photo feature and travel (features on the arts). Send complete ms. Length: 1,000-9,000 words (negotiable). Pays $100-2,000 (negotiable). Sometimes pays expenses of writers on assignment.
Photos: Send photos with submission. Reviews contact sheets and negatives. Offers $40-80 (negotiable). Buys one-time rights.
Fiction: Erica Lowe, fiction editor. Adventure, condensed novels, ethnic, experimental, fantasy, historical, horror, humorous, mainstream, mystery, novel excerpts, science fiction, slice-of-life vignettes and suspense. No dry academic pieces. Buys 25-30 mss/year. Send complete ms. Length: 500-9,000 words. Pays $100-2,000 (negotiable).

Poetry: Erica Lowe, poetry editor. Free verse, light verse and traditional. Buys 60-100 poems/year. Submit maximum 6 poems. "Prefer shorter poetry." Pays $20-200 (negotiable).

HIGH TIMES, Trans High Corp., Floor 20, 211 E. 43rd St., New York NY 10017. (212)972-8484. Editor: Steve Hager. Executive Editor: John Holmstrom. 75% freelance written. Monthly magazine covering marijuana. Circ. 250,000. Pays on publication. Byline given. Offers 20% kill fee. Buys one-time rights, all rights, or makes work-for-hire assignments. Submit seasonal/holiday material 6 months in advance. Simultaneous and photocopied submissions OK. Computer printout submissions OK. Reports in 1 month on queries; 2 months on mss. Sample for $4 and SASE; writer's guidelines for SASE.

Nonfiction: Book excerpts, expose, humor, interview/profile, new product, personal experience, photo feature and travel. Special issues include indoor Growers issue in September. No poetry or stories on "my drug bust." Buys 30 mss/year. Send complete ms. Length: 1,000-10,000 words. Pays $150-400. Sometimes pays in trade for advertisements. Sometimes pays expenses of writers on assignment.

Photos: Send photos with submission. Pays $50-300. Captions, model releases and identification of subjects required. Buys all rights or one-time use.

Columns/Departments: Lou Stathis, news editor. Drug related books; drug related news. Buys 10 mss/year. Query with published clips. Length: 100-2,000 words. Pays $25-300.

Fiction: Adventure, fantasy, humorous and stories on smuggling. Buys 5 mss/year. Send complete ms. Length: 2,000-5,000 words. Pays $250-400.

Poetry: Espy LaCopa, poetry editor. Avant-garde, free verse. Buys 1 poem/year. Pays $5-50.

Fillers: Gags to be illustrated by cartoonist, newsbreaks and short humor. Buys 10/year. Length: 100-500 words. Pays $10-50.

Tips: "All sections are open to good, professional writers."

‡PRELUDE MAGAZINE, Prelude Magazine Corporation, No. 20, 467 Alvarado St., Monterey CA 93940. (408)375-5711. Editor: Jonathan Drake. Managing Editor: Kathleen Spahn. 70% freelance written. A monthly magazine covering fine arts, literature, classical, music, entertainment on central coast of California. Circ. 25,000. Pays on publication. Publishes ms an average of 2 months after acceptance. Byline given. Offers $25 kill fee. Buys one-time rights. Submit seasonal/holiday material 3 months in advance. Simultaneous, photocopied and previously published submissions OK. Query for electronic submissions. Computer printout submissions OK; prefers letter-quality. Reports in 3 weeks on queries; 2 months on mss. Sample copy for 9x12 SAE with 4 first class stamps. Writer's guidelines for 9x12 SAE with 3 first class stamps.

Nonfiction: Essays, exposé, general interest, humor, interview/profile and travel. "No opinion, how-to or religious articles." Buys 6 mss/year. Query with or without published clips, or send complete ms. Length: 500-2,000 words. Pays $50-300 for assigned articles. Sometimes pays the expenses of writers on assignment.

Photos: State availability of photos with submission. Reviews contact sheets, negatives, transparencies (2½x4) and prints (5x7). Offers $25-100 per photo. Captions and identification of subjects required. Buys one-time rights.

Columns/Departments: Scott MacClelland, column/department editor. Jazzlines (jazz music, people, places, new developments, history) 1,000 words; Cinema (reviews of trends in cinema). Buys 20 mss/year. Query. Length: 500-1,000 words. Pays $100-200.

Fiction: Experimental, historical, humorous, mainstream, science fiction, serialized novels, slice-of-life vignettes and suspense. No confession, erotica or horror. Buys 6 mss/year. Query with published clips. Length: 1,000-2,500 words. Pays $100-300.

Fillers: Anecdotes, facts, gags to be illustrated by cartoonist, newsbreaks and short humor. Buys 20/year. Length: 250-500 words. Pays $50-100.

Tips: "Features and fiction are most open to freelancers. Call and talk with us first, or query."

SPLASH, International Magazine, Art, Fashion and Contemporary Culture, #4B, 561 Broadway, New York NY 10012. (212)966-3218. Publisher: Jordan Crandall. Editor: Lisa D. Black. 75% freelance written. A bimonthly magazine covering the arts, "but we are eclectic. *Splash* is devoted to art, fashion and contemporary culture. Our audience is generally well-educated and interested in the arts. There is no special slant, per se, but we are decidedly progressive in thought and style." Circ. 30,000. Pays on publication. Publishes ms an average of 2 months after acceptance. Byline given. Buys first rights. Submit seasonal/holiday material 4 months in advance. Simultaneous and photocopied submissions OK. Computer printout submissions OK; prefers letter-quality. Reports in 1 month. Sample copy $4; writer's guidelines for SASE.

Nonfiction: Arts essays, general interest, humor, interview/profile, opinion, personal experience, photo feature, and reviews (art, music, film, books, dance). "We would also like to receive social satire (subtle, dry, educated wit); absurdist and/or surreal literature or humor." Does not want anything in a subjective or journalistic mode—no newspaper-type mss will be considered. Buys 50-60 mss/year. Query with published clips, or send complete ms. Length: 250-3,000 words. Pays $50-350.

Photos: State availability or send photos with submission. Reviews b&w glossy prints, any size. Offers $5-50/photo. Captions, model releases and identification of subjects required. Buys one-time rights; photo essays, first time rights only.

Columns/Departments: Expo (reviews on *all* the arts—national as well as international), 500-1,100 words; Opine (educated opinions on culture, art, religion, current issues, etc.), 750-1,250 words; Arena (short, sophisticated humor), 150-500 words. Buys 25 mss/year. Query with published clips. Length: 250-1,250 words. Pays $50-250.

Fiction: "We use short, experimental fiction at present." Surreal, experimental, fantasy, novel excerpts and objective slice-of-life vignettes. "No lengthy stories (no book-size texts)—the shorter the fiction, and the more avant garde, the better the chances are that we will use it." Buys 15 mss/year. Query with published clips. Length: 250-1,000 words. Pays $50-350.

Fillers: Anecdotes, facts, and short humor. Buys 10/year. Length: 150-500 words. Pays $15-75.

Tips: "As we are distributed world-wide, we will be looking for more material with an international appeal. Our style is progressive, objective, avant garde. In a word, our magazine is *style-oriented* and decidedly *not* journalistic. If a manuscript is approached aesthetically and literarily as opposed to journalistically it has a much better chance of being published. Sample writings ought to be sent and perhaps a cover letter stating interests, etc. All areas are open to freelancers. Reviews must be topical, interesting, insightful and succinct. The interviews we do are generally with accomplished, well-known people in all fields—art, literature, politics, entertainment. We will be looking for more arts and essays and we will no longer be accepting political essays. Expositions on the visual arts are especially needed; also, literary reviews. Even writings of an academic nature will be considered, so long as the work is not too specialized."

‡**SPY**, Spy Publishing Partners, 295 Lafayette, New York NY 10012. (212)925-5509. Editor: K. Andersen and G. Carter. 50% freelance written. "*Spy* is a non-fiction satirical magazine published 10 times/year." Circ. 65,000. Pays on publication. Publishes ms an average of 2 months after acceptance. Byline given. Offers 25% kill fee. Buys first North American serial rights and TV option, non-exclusive anthology rights. Submit seasonal/holiday material 6 months in advance. Simultaneous and photocopied submissions OK. Query for electronic submissions. Computer printout submissions OK; prefers letter-quality. Reports in 2 weeks on queries; 1 month on mss. Sample copy $3.50.

Nonfiction: Tad Friend, articles editor. Book excerpts, essays, expose, humor, interview/profile, opinion. Buys 100 mss/year. Query with published clips. Length: 200-4,000 words. Pays $50-1,500 for assigned articles; $50-1,000 for unsolicited articles. Sometimes pays expenses of writers on assignment.

Photos: State availability of photos with submission. Reviews contact sheets. Offers $40-200/photo. Model release and identification of subjects required. Buys one-time rights.

Detective and Crime

Fans of detective stories want to read accounts of actual criminal cases and espionage. The following magazines specialize in nonfiction, but a few buy some fiction. Markets specializing in crime fiction are listed under Mystery publications.

DETECTIVE CASES, Detective Files Group, 1350 Sherbrooke St. W., Montreal, Quebec H3G 2T4 Canada. Editor-in-Chief: Dominick A. Merle. Bimonthly magazine. See *Detective Files*.

DETECTIVE DRAGNET, Detective Files Group, 1350 Sherbrooke St. W., Montreal, Quebec H3G 2T4 Canada. Editor-in-Chief: Dominick A. Merle. Bimonthly magazine; 72 pages. See *Detective Files*.

DETECTIVE FILES, Detective Files Group, 1350 Sherbrooke St. W., Montreal, Quebec H3G 2T4 Canada. Editor-in-Chief: Dominick A. Merle. 100% freelance written. Bimonthly magazine; 72 pages. Pays on acceptance. Publishes ms an average of 3 months after acceptance. Buys all rights. Photocopied submissions OK. Include international reply coupons. Reports in 1 month. Free sample copy and writer's guidelines.

Nonfiction: True crime stories. "Do a thorough job; don't double-sell (sell the same article to more than one market); and deliver, and you can have a steady market. Neatness, clarity and pace will help you make the sale." Query. Length: 3,500-6,000 words. Pays $250-350.

Photos: Purchased with accompanying ms; no additional payment.

FRONT PAGE DETECTIVE, Official Detective Group, R.G.H. Publishing Corp., 20th Floor, 460 W. 34th St., New York NY 10001. (212)947-6500. Editor: Rose Mandelsberg. Managing Editors: Halima Nooradeen. Monthly magazine covering true crime stories. "We publish complete murder stories with an emphasis on all phases of police work that went into solving the case from embryonic stage of murder to completion (trial and conviction)." Pays on acceptance. Publishes ms an average of 2 months after acceptance. Byline given. Buys

first North American serial rights. Query for electronic submissions. Computer printout submissions OK; prefers letter-quality. Reports in 2 weeks on queries; 3 weeks on manuscripts. Free writer's guidelines.
Nonfiction: "True crime stories with a lot of detective work and mystery." The focus of these two publications is similar to the others in the Official Detective Group. "We now use post-trial stories; rarely are pre-trial ones published." Buys 350 mss/year. Query. Length: 5,000-11,000 words. Pays $250-500. Pays expenses of writers on assignment.
Photos: Send photos with submission of mss. Reviews contact sheets. Captions and identification of subjects required. Offers $12.50 per photo used. Buys all rights.
Tips: "We are always looking to develop new writers from the United States and abroad. Read the five detective magazines: *True Detective, Official Detective, Master Detective, Inside Detective* and *Front Page Detective*; know police procedures; and familiarize yourself with district attorneys, captains, detectives, etc."

HEADQUARTERS DETECTIVE, Detective Files Group, 1350 Sherbrooke St. W., Montreal, Quebec H3G 2T4 Canada. Editor-in-Chief: Dominick A. Merle. Bimonthly magazine; 72 pages. See *Detective Files*.

INSIDE DETECTIVE, Official Detective Group, R.G.H. Publishing Corp., 460 W. 34th St., New York NY 10001. (212)947-6500. Editor: Rose Mandelsberg. Managing Editor: Kenneth Gutierrez. Monthly magazine. Circ. 90,000. Pays on acceptance. Publishes ms an average of 3 months after acceptance. Byline given. Buys first rights and one-time world rights. Query for electronic submissions. Computer printout submissions OK. Reports in 2 weeks. Free writer's guidelines.
Nonfiction: Buys 120 mss/year. Query. Pays $250. Length: 5,000-6,000 words (approx. 20 typed pages).

STARTLING DETECTIVE, Detective Files Group, 1350 Sherbrooke St. W., Montreal, Quebec H3G 2T4 Canada. Editor-in-Chief: Dominick A. Merle. Bimonthly magazine; 72 pages. See *Detective Files*.

TRUE POLICE CASES, Detective Files Group, 1350 Sherbrooke St. W., Montreal, Quebec H3G 2T4 Canada. Editor-in-Chief: Dominick A. Merle. Bimonthly magazine; 72 pages. Buys all rights. See *Detective Files*.

Disabilities

These magazines are geared toward disabled persons and those who care for or teach them. Some of these magazines will accept manuscripts only from disabled persons or those with a background in caring for disabled persons.

‡**ARTHRITIS TODAY**, Arthritis Foundation. 1314 Spring St., N.W., Atlanta GA 30309. (404)872-7100. Editor: Cindy T. McDaniel. 50% freelance written. A bimonthly magazine about living with arthritis; latest in research/treatment. "*Arthritis Today* is written for the 37 million Americans who have arthritis and for the millions of others whose lives are touched by an arthritis-related disease. The editorial content is designed to help the person with arthritis live a more productive, independent and painfree life. The articles are upbeat and provide practical advice, information and inspiration." Estab. 1987. Circ. 700,000. Requires unlimitd reprint rights in Arthritis Foundation publications. Submit seasonal/holiday material 4 months in advance. Simultaneous, photocopied and previously published submissions OK. Computer printout submissions OK; prefers letter-quality. Reports in 1 month on queries; 6 weeks on mss. Sample copy for 9x11 SAE with 4 first class stamps. Writer's guidelines for #10 SAE with 1 first class stamp.
Nonfiction: General interest, arts and entertainment, how-to (tips on any aspect of living with arthritis), humor, inspirational, interview/profile, new product, opinion, personal experience, photo feature, technical and travel. Buys 20 mss/year. Query with published clips. Length: 1,000-2,500. Pays $350-850 for assigned articles. Pays $250-750 for unsolicited articles. Sometimes pays expenses of writers on assignment.
Photos: State availability of photos with submission. Reviews transparencies (3x5) and prints (5x7). Offers $25-100 per photo. Captions, model releases and identification of subjects required. Buys one-time rights or all rights.
Columns/Departments: To Your Health (general medical updates); Scientific Frontier (research news about arthritis) 100-250 words. Buys 4-6 mss/year. Query with published clips. Pays $50-200.
Fiction: Dianne Witter, fiction editor. Experimental, fantasy, humorous and slice-of-life vignettes. Must not necessarily relate to living with arthritis. Buys 4-6 mss/year. Query with published clips. Length: 750-2,500 words. Pays $300-800.
Fillers: Anecdotes, facts, gags to be illustrated by cartoonist, newsbreaks and short humor. Buys 2-4/year. Length: 75-150 words. Pays $25-150.

Tips: "The focus of *Arthritis Today* will change somewhat away from all arthritis-related content to include more articles of general interest. Specifically, we will be looking for fiction and nonfiction articles to appeal to an older audience on subjects such as travel, history, arts and entertainment, hobbies, general health, etc."

‡CAREERS & THE HANDICAPPED, Equal Opportunity Publications. 44 Broadway, Greenlawn, NY 11740. (516)261-8917. Editor: James Schneider. 60% freelance written. A semi-annual career guidance magazine distributed through college campuses for disabled college students and professionals. "The magazine offers role-model profiles and career guidance articles geared toward disabled college students and professionals." Pays on publication. Publishes ms an average of 6 months after acceptance. Circ. 10,000. Byline given. Buys first North American serial rights. Simultaneous, photocopied and previously published submissions OK. Reports in 2 weeks. Sample copy and writer's guidelines for 7x10 SAE and $2.

Nonfiction: General interest, interview/profile, opinion and personal experience. Buys 15 mss/year. Query. Length: 1,000-2,500 words. Pays $100-300 for assigned articles. Sometimes pays the expenses of writers on assignment.

Photos: State availability of photos with submission. Reviews prints. Offers $15 per photo. Captions. Buys one-time rights.

Tips: "Be as targeted as possible. Role model profiles which offer advice to disabled college students are most needed."

DIALOGUE, The Magazine for the Visually Impaired, Dialogue Publications, Inc., 3100 Oak Park Ave., Berwyn IL 60402. (312)749-1908. Editor: Bonnie Miller. 50% freelance written. Works with published/established writers and a small number of new/unpublished writers each year. Quarterly magazine of issues, topics and opportunities related to the visually impaired. Pays on acceptance. Publishes ms an average of 6 months after acceptance. Byline given. Buys all rights "with generous reprint rights." Submit seasonal/holiday material 6 months in advance. Photocopied submissions OK. Computer printout submissions acceptable; no dot-matrix. Reports in 2 weeks on queries; 1 month on mss. Free sample copy to visually impaired writers. Writer's guidelines in print for #10 SAE and 1 first class stamp; send a 60-minute cassette for guidelines on tape.

Nonfiction: "Writers should indicate nature and severity of visual handicap." How-to (cope with various aspects of blindness); humor; interview/profile; new product (of interest to visually impaired); opinion; personal experience; technical (adaptations for use without sight); travel (personal experiences of visually impaired travelers); and first person articles about careers in which individual blind persons have succeeded. No "aren't blind people wonderful" articles; articles that are slanted towards sighted general audience. Buys 60 mss/year. Query with published clips or submit complete ms. Length: 3,000 words maximum. Prefers shorter lengths but will use longer articles if subject warrants. Pays $10-50. Sometimes pays the expenses of writers on assignment.

Columns/Departments: ABAPITA ("Ain't Blindness a Pain in the Anatomy")—short anecdotes relating to blindness; Recipe Round-Up; Around the House (household hints); Vox Pop (see magazine); Puzzle Box (see magazine and guidelines); book reviews of books written by visually impaired authors; Beyond the Armchair (travel personal experience); and Backscratcher (a column of questions, answers, hints). Buys 80 mss/year. Send complete ms. Payment varies.

Fiction: "Writers should state nature and severity of visual handicap." Adventure, fantasy, historical, humorous, mainstream, mystery, science fiction, and suspense. No plotless fiction or stories with unbelievable characters; no horror; no explicit sex and no vulgar language. Buys 12 mss/year. Send complete ms. Length: 3,000 words maximum; shorter lengths preferred. Pays $10-50.

Poetry: "Writers should indicate nature and severity of visual impairment." Free verse, haiku, and traditional. No religious poetry or any poetry with more than 20 lines. Buys 30 poems/year. Submit maximum 3 poems. Length: 20 lines maximum. Pays in contributor's copies.

Fillers: Jokes, anecdotes, and short humor. Buys few mss/year. Length: 100 words maximum. Payment varies.

Tips: "*Dialogue* cannot consider manuscripts from authors with 20/20 vision or those who can read regular print with ordinary glasses. Any person unable to read ordinary print who has helpful information to share with others in this category will find a ready market. We believe that blind people are capable, competent, responsible citizens, and the material we publish reflects this view. This is not to say we never sound a negative note, but criticism should be constructive. The writer sometimes has a better chance of breaking in at our publication with short articles and fillers. We are interested in material that is written for a general-interest magazine with visually impaired readers. As we move into a cassette version, we must tighten our format, this means fewer articles used, therefore they must be of the highest quality. We are *not* interested in scholarly journal-type articles; 'amazing blind people I have known,' articles written by sighted writers; articles and fiction that exceed our 3,000-word maximum length; and material that is too regional to appeal to an international audience. No manuscript can be considered without a statement of visual impairment, nor can it be returned without a SASE."

KALEIDOSCOPE: International Magazine of Literature, Fine Arts, and Disability, Kaleidoscope Press, 326 Locust St., Akron OH 44302. (216)762-9755. Editor: Darshan C. Perusek, Ph.D. 75% freelance written. Works with a small number of new/unpublished writers each year; eager to work with new/unpublished writers. Semiannual magazine with international collection of disability-related literature and art by disabled/nondisabled people. Circ. 1,500. Pays on publication. Publishes ms an average of 6 months after acceptance. Byline given. Buys first North American serial rights. Simultaneous queries OK. Previously published submissions "at editor's discretion." Computer printout submissions acceptable; no dot-matrix. Reports in 3-6 months. Sample copy $2. Writer's guidelines for #10 SAE and 1 first class stamp.
Nonfiction: Disability-related literary criticism, book reviews, personal experience essays, travel notes, interview/profiles/photo features on literary and/or art personalities. Publishes 8-10 mss/year. Payment $25 for up to 2,500 words. Maximum 3,500 words. Feature length ms (15-20 pp) up to $100. All contributors receive 2 complimentary copies.
Photos: Pays up to $25/photo. Reviews 3x5, 5x7, 8x10 b&w and color prints. Captions and identification of subjects required.
Fiction: Short stories, excerpts. Traditional and experimental. Theme generally disability-related, occasional exceptions. Humor encouraged. Publishes 8-10 mss/year. Length: 5,000 words maximum. Pays $25; editor's discretion for higher payment. 2 complimentary copies.
Poetry: Traditional and experimental. Theme experience of disability. Submit up to 12 poems. Publishes 16-20 poems a year. Payment up to $25 for multiple publication.
Tips: "Avoid the trite and sentimental. Treatment of subject should be fresh, original and imaginative. Always photo copies. Make sure black and white photos, color slides are clean, or reproductions will suffer."

MAINSTREAM, Magazine of the Able-Disabled, Exploding Myths, Inc., 2973 Beech St., San Diego CA 92102. (619)234-3138. Editor: Cyndi Jones. 100% freelance written. Eager to develop writers who have a disability. A magazine published 10 times/year (monthly except January and June) covering disability-related topics, geared to disabled consumers. Circ. 15,500. Pays on publication. Publishes ms an average of 3 months after acceptance. Byline given. Buys all rights. Submit seasonal/holiday material 4 months in advance. Computer printout submissions OK; prefers letter-quality. Reports in 2 months. Sample copy $3.75 or 9x12 SAE with $2 and 4 first class stamps. Writer's guidelines for #10 SAE with 1 first class stamp.
Nonfiction: Book excerpts, exposé, how-to (daily independent living tips), humor, interview/profile, personal experience (dealing with problems/solutions), photo feature, technical, travel and legislation. "All must be disability-related, directed to disabled consumers." No articles on " 'my favorite disabled character', 'my most inspirational disabled person', poster child stories." Buys 50 mss/year. Query with or without published clips, or send complete ms. Length: 6-12 pages. Pays $50-100. May pay subscription if writer requests.
Photos: State availability of photos with submission. Reviews contact sheets, 1½x¾ transparencies and 5x7 or larger prints. Offers $5-25 per b&w photo. Captions and identification of subjects required. Buys all rights.
Columns/Departments: Creative Solutions (unusual solutions to common aggravating problems); Personal Page (deals with personal relations: dating, meeting people). Buys 10 mss/year. Send complete ms. Length: 500-800 words. Pays $25-50.
Fiction: Humorous. Must be disability-related. Buys 4 mss/year. Send complete ms. Length: 800-1,200 words. Pays $50-100.
Tips: "It seems that politics and disability are becoming more important."

A POSITIVE APPROACH, A National Magazine for the Physically Challenged, 1600 Malone St., Municipal Airport, Millville NJ 08332. (609)327-4040. Publisher: Patricia M. Johnson. 80% freelance written. A bimonthly magazine for the physically disabled/handicapped. "We're a positive profile on living and for the creation of a barrier-free lifestyle. Each profile is aimed at encouraging others with that same handicap to better their situations and environments. Covers all disabilities." Circ. 200,000. Pays on publication. Publishes ms an average of 4 months after acceptance. Byline given. Buys one-time rights and second serial (reprint) rights. Submit seasonal/holiday material 4-6 months in advance. Simultaneous, photocopied and previously published submissions OK. Computer printout submissions acceptable; no dot-matrix. Reports in 2 weeks on queries; 3 weeks on mss. Sample copy $2.50; free writer's guidelines.
Nonfiction: Ann Miller, articles editor. Book excerpts, general interest, how-to (make life more accessible), humor, inspirational, interview/profile, personal experience, photo feature and travel (for the disabled). No depressing, poorly researched, death and dying articles. Buys 60-70 mss/year. Query with or without published clips, or send complete ms. Length: 500 words. Pays 10¢/word for unsolicited articles. Sometimes pays the expenses of writers on assignment.
Photos: State availability of photos with submission. Reviews 3x5 or larger prints. Offers $5/photo. Identification of subjects required. Buys one-time rights.
Columns/Departments: Ann Miller, column/department editor. Hair Styling (easy hairdo for the disabled), 500 words; Wardrobe (fashionable clothing/easy dressing), 500 words; Travel (accessible travel throughout U.S. and Europe), 500-700 words; Workshops (employment, self-improvement), 500 words; and Profiles

(positive approach on life with goals), 500 words. Buys 30 mss/year. Query with published clips or send complete ms. Pays 10¢/word.

Tips: "Research newspapers. Learn what problems exist for the physically challenged. Know that they want to better their lifestyles and get on with their lives to the best of their abilities. Learn their assets and write on what they can do and not on what can't be done! The area of our publication most open to freelancers is profiles."

‡SHR—Social Issues & Healthcare Review, EOP Inc., 44 Broadway, Greenlawn NY 11740. (516)261-8917. Editor: Anne Kelly. 80% freelance written. Quarterly magazine on social, health and lifestyle issues for persons with disabilities. "Our audience is the disability community and the healthcare professionals/industries that serve them." Circ. 25,000. Pays on publication. Publishes ms an average of 6 months after acceptance. Byline given. Buys first North American serial rights. Submit seasonal/holiday material 6 months in advance. Simultaneous submissions OK. Reports in 1 month. Free sample copy and writer's guidelines.

Nonfiction: Essays, expose, how-to, humor, inspirational, interview/profile, new product, opinion, personal experience, travel, healthcare, disability issues. Buys 40 mss/year. Query. Length: 3,000 words maximum. Pays $500 maximum.

Photos: State availability of photos with submission. Offers $15 per photo. Captions, model releases and identification of subjects is required. Buys one-time rights.

Columns/Departments: Book Reviews (social and healthcare books). Query. Length: 500-1,000 words. Pays $50-100.

Poetry: Light verse, traditional. Poetry must relate to social, healthcare and disability issues.

Entertainment

This category's publications cover live, filmed or videotaped entertainment, including home video, TV, dance, theatre and adult entertainment. Besides celebrity interviews, most publications want solid reporting on trends and upcoming productions. Magazines in the Contemporary Culture section also use articles on entertainment. For those publications with an emphasis on music and musicians, see the Music section. For markets covering video games, see Games and Puzzles.

AMERICAN SQUAREDANCE, Burdick Enterprises, Box 488, Huron OH 44839. (419)433-2188. Editors: Stan and Cathie Burdick. 10% freelance written. Works with a small number of new/unpublished writers each year; eager to work with new/unpublished writers. Monthly magazine of interviews, reviews, topics of interest to the modern square dancer. Circ. 23,000. Pays on publication. Publishes ms an average of 3-6 months after acceptance. Byline given. Buys all rights. Submit seasonal/holiday material 3 months in advance. Computer printout submissions acceptable; prefers letter-quality. Reports in 2 weeks on queries. Sample copy for 6x9 SAE; free writer's guidelines.

Nonfiction: General interest, historical/nostalgic, humor, inspirational, interview/profile, new product, opinion, personal experience, photo feature, travel. Must deal with square dance. Buys 6 mss/year. Send complete ms. Length: 1,000-1,500 words. Pays $10-35.

Photos: Send photos with ms. Reviews b&w prints. Captions and identification of subjects required.

Fiction: Subject related to square dancing only. Buys 1-2 mss/year. Send complete ms. Length: 2,000-2,500 words. Pays $25-35.

Poetry: Avant-garde, free verse, haiku, light verse, traditional. Square dancing subjects only. Buys 6 poems/year. Submit maximum 3 poems. Pays $1 for 1st 4 lines; $1/verse thereafter.

‡AMPERSAND'S ENTERTAINMENT GUIDE, Alan Weston Communications, Suite 600, 303 N. Glenoaks Blvd., Burbank CA 91502. (818)848-4666. Editor: Stewart Weiner. 100% freelance written. Prefers to work with published/established writers; works with a small number of new/unpublished writers each year. A quarterly magazine covering entertainment for the college audience "primarily ages 18-26. They want lively reports on current trends and personalities in popular entertainment." Circ. 1.3 million. Pays on acceptance. Publishes ms an average of 3 months after acceptance. Byline given. Offers 50% kill fee. Reports in 2 months on queries. Sample copy for 9x12 SAE with 3 first class stamps. Free writer's guidelines.

Nonfiction: General interest, humor and interview/profile. No fiction or how-to's. Buys 15 mss/year. Query. Length: 600-2,500 words. Pays $250-1,000 for assigned articles. Sometimes pays expenses of writers on assignment.

Photos: State availability of photos with submission. Offers $25-100 per photo. Identification of subjects required. Buys one-time rights.

Columns/Departments: Books (new books of interest to college students); Short Subjects (news and issues in entertainment on campus—not local productions but rather film contests, campus radio and TV, etc.). Buys 10 ms/year. Query. Length: 50-250 words. Pays $25-100.

Tips: "The writer needs to have experience writing about entertainment, access to entertainment figures, interesting writing style and point of view on the entertainment subjects they cover. Living in New York or Los Angeles helps, but is not necessary. We're looking for very individual, lively writing styles. The best area for freelancers are special topics in music, film or humor—such as a unique personality that the writer has access to, or a topic or issue relevant to college, such as the growth of college radio, an article we recently published."

‡CINEASTE, America's Leading Magazine on the Art and Politics of the Cinema, Cineaste Publishers, Inc., #1320, 200 Park Ave. South, New York NY 10003. (212)982-1241. Managing Editor: Gary Crowdus. 50% freelance written. A quarterly magazine on motion pictures, offering "social and political perspective on the cinema." Circ. 7,000. Pays on publication. Publishes ms an average of 3 months after acceptance. Byline given. Offers 50% kill fee. Buys first North American serial rights. Photocopied submissions OK. Computer printout submissions OK; prefers letter-quality. Reports in 3 weeks on queries; 1 month on mss. Sample copy $2. Writer's guidelines for #10 SAE and 1 first class stamp.

Nonfiction: Essays, interview/profile, criticism. Buys 40-50 mss/year. Query with or without published clips, or send complete ms. Length: 3,000-6,000 words. Pays $20.

Photos: State availability of photos with submissions. Reviews prints. Offers no additional payment for photos accepted with ms. Identification of subjects required.

CINEFANTASTIQUE MAGAZINE, The review of horror, fantasy and science fiction films, Box 270, Oak Park IL 60303. (312)366-5566. Editor: Frederick S. Clarke. 100% freelance written. Eager to work with new/unpublished writers. A bimonthly magazine covering horror, fantasy and science fiction films. Circ. 25,000. Pays on publication. Publishes ms an average of 6 months after acceptance. Byline given. Buys all magazine rights. Simultaneous queries and photocopied submissions OK. Computer printout submissions acceptable. Sample copy for $2 and 9x12 SAE. Reports in 2 months or longer.

Nonfiction: Historical/nostalgic (retrospects of film classics); interview/profile (film personalities); new product (new film projects); opinion (film reviews, critical essays); technical (how films are made). Buys 100-125 mss/year. Query with published clips. Length: 1,000-10,000 words. Sometimes pays the expenses of writers on assignment.

Photos: State availability of photos with query letter or ms.

Tips: "Develop original story suggestions; develop access to film industry personnel; submit reviews that show a perceptive point-of-view."

DANCE MAGAZINE, 33 W. 60th St., New York NY 10023. (212)245-9050. Editor-in-Chief: William Como. Managing Editor: Richard Philip. 25% freelance written. Monthly magazine covering dance. Circ. 51,000. Pays on publication. Byline given. Offers up to $150 kill fee (varies). Makes work-for-hire assignments. Submit seasonal/holiday material 3 months in advance. Computer printout submission OK; no dot-matrix. Reports in "weeks." Sample copy and writer's guidelines for 8x10 SAE.

Nonfiction: Interview/profile. Publishes annual video issue. Buys 24 mss/year. Query with or without published clips, or send complete ms. Length: 300-1,500 words. Pays $15-350. Sometimes pays expenses of writers on assignment.

Photos: State availability of photos with submission. Reviews transparencies and prints. Offers $15-285/photo. Captions and identification of subjects required. Buys one-times rights.

Columns/Departments: News Editor: Gary Parks. Presstime News (topical, short articles on current dance world events) 150-400 words. Buys 24 mss/year. Query with published clips. Pays $20-75.

Tips: Writers must have "thorough knowledge of dance and take a sophisticated approach."

DRAMATICS MAGAZINE, International Thespian Society, 3368 Central Pkwy., Cincinnati OH 45225. (513)559-1996. Editor-in-Chief: Donald Corathers. 70% freelance written. Works with small number of new/unpublished writers. For theatre arts students, teachers and others interested in theatre arts education. Magazine published monthly, September through May. Circ. 32,000. Pays on acceptance. Publishes ms an average of 3 months after acceptance. Buys first North American serial rights. Byline given. Submit seasonal/holiday material 3 months in advance. Simultaneous, photocopied and previously published submissions OK. Query for electronic submissions. Computer printout submissions acceptable; prefers letter-quality. Reports in 1 month. Sample copy for $2 and a 9x12 SAE with 5 first class stamps; free writer's guidelines.

Nonfiction: How-to (technical theatre), informational, interview, photo feature, humorous, profile and technical. Buys 30 mss/year. Submit complete ms. Length: 750-3,000 words. Pays $30-200. Rarely pays expenses of writers on assignment.

Photos: Purchased with accompanying ms. Uses b&w photos and color transparencies. Query. Total purchase price for ms includes payment for photos.

Fiction: Drama (one-act plays). No "plays for children, Christmas plays, or plays written with no attention paid to the conventions of theatre."Buys 5-9 mss/year. Send complete ms. Pays $50-200.

Tips: "The best way to break in is to know our audience—drama students, teachers and others interested in theatre—and to write for them. Writers who have some practical experience in theatre, especially in technical areas, have a leg-up here, but we'll work with anybody who has a good idea. Some freelancers have become regular contributors. Others ignore style suggestions included in our writer's guidelines."

EMMY MAGAZINE, Academy of Television Arts & Sciences, Suite 700, 3500 W. Olive, Burbank CA 91505-4628. (818)953-7575. Editor and Publisher: Hank Rieger. Managing Editor: Gail Polevoi. 100% freelance written. Works with a small number of new/unpublished writers each year. Bimonthly magazine on television—a "provocative, critical—though not necessarily fault-finding—treatment of television and its effects on society." Circ. 12,000. Pays on publication. Publishes ms an average of 3 months after acceptance. Byline given. Offers 20% kill fee. Buys first North American serial rights. Computer printout submissions acceptable; no dot-matrix. Reports in 3 weeks on queries; 1 month on mss. Sample copy for 9x12 SAE with 5 first class stamps.

Nonfiction: Provocative and topical articles, nostalgic, humor, interview/profile, opinion—all dealing with television. Buys 40 mss/year. Query with published clips. Length: 1,500-2,500 words. Pays $450-800. Sometimes pays expenses of writers on assignment.

Columns/Departments: Opinion or point-of-view columns dealing with TV. Buys 18-20 mss/year. Query with published clips. Length: 800-1,500 words. Pays $250-550.

Tips: "Query in writing with a thoughtful description of what you wish to write about. Please do not call. The most frequent mistake made by writers in completing an article for us is that they misread the magazine and send fan-magazine items."

FANGORIA: Horror in Entertainment, Starlog Group, 475 Park Ave. South, 8th Floor, New York NY 10016. (212)689-2830. Editor: Anthony Timpone. 90% freelance written. Works with a small number of new/unpublished writers each year. Published 10 times/year. Magazine covering horror films, TV projects and literature and those who create them. Pays on publication. Publishes ms an average of 3 months after acceptance. Byline given. Buys first North American serial rights with option for second serial (reprint) rights to same material. Submit seasonal/holiday material 6 months in advance. Simultaneous queries OK. Query for electronic submissions. Computer printout submissions acceptable; no dot-matrix. Reports in 6 weeks. "We provide an assignment sheet (deadlines, info) to writers, thus authorizing queried stories that we're buying." Sample copy $4.50; writers' guidelines for SASE.

Nonfiction: Book excerpts, interview/profile of movie directors, makeup FX artists, screenwriters, producers, actors, noted horror novelists and others—with genre credits. No "think" pieces, opinion pieces, reviews, or sub-theme overviews (i.e., vampire in the cinema). Buys 100 mss/year. Query with published clips. Length: 1,000-3,000 words. Pays $100-225. Rarely pays the expenses of writers on assignment. Avoids articles on science fiction films—see listing for sister magazine *Starlog* in *Writer's Market* science fiction magazine section.

Photos: State availability of photos. Reviews b&w and color transparencies and prints. "No separate payment for photos provided by film studios." Captions or identification of subjects required. Photo credit given. Buys all rights.

Columns/Departments: Monster Invasion (news about new film productions; must be exclusive, early information; also mini-interviews with filmmakers and novelists). Query with published clips. Length: 300-500 words. Pays $25-35.

Fiction: "We do *not* publish any fiction. *Don't* send any."

Tips: "Other than recommending that you study one or several copies of *Fangoria*, we can only describe it as a horror film magazine consisting primarily of interviews with technicians and filmmakers in the field. Be sure to stress the interview subjects' words—not your own opinions. We're very interested in small, independent filmmakers working outside of Hollywood. These people are usually more accessible to writers, and more cooperative. *Fangoria* is also sort of a *de facto* bible for youngsters interested in movie makeup careers and for young filmmakers. We are devoted only to *reel* horrors—the fakery of films, the imagery of the horror fiction of a Stephen King or a Peter Straub—we *do not* want nor would we *ever* publish articles on real-life horrors, murders, etc. A writer must *like* and *enjoy* horror films and horror fiction to work for us. If the photos in *Fangoria* disgust you, if the sight of (*stage*) blood repels you, if you feel 'superior' to horror (and its fans), you aren't a writer for us and we certainly aren't the market for you. *Fangoria*'s frequency has increased over the last years and, with an editorial change reducing staff written articles, this has essentially doubled the number of stories we're buying. In 1989, we expect such opportunities only to increase for freelancers. *Fangoria* will try for a lighter, more 'Gonzo' tone in the year ahead."

FILM QUARTERLY, University of California Press, Berkeley CA 94720. (415)642-6333. Editor: Ernest Callenbach. 100% freelance written. Eager to work with new/unpublished writers. Quarterly. Buys all rights. Byline given. Pays on publication. Publishes ms an average of 3 months after acceptance. Query; "sample pages are very helpful from unknown writers. We must have hard-copy printout and don't care how it is produced, but we cannot use dot-matrix printouts unless done on one of the new printers that gives type-quality letters."

Nonfiction: Articles on style and structure in films, articles analyzing the work of important directors, historical articles on development of the film as art, reviews of current films and detailed analyses of classics, book reviews of film books. Must be familiar with the past and present of the art; must be competently, although not necessarily breezily, written; must deal with important problems of the art. "We write for people who like to think and talk seriously about films, as well as simply view them and enjoy them. We use no personality pieces or reportage pieces. Interviews usually work for us only when conducted by someone familiar with most of a filmmaker's work. (We don't use performer interviews.)" Length: 6,000 words maximum. Pay is about 2¢/word.

Tips: "*Film Quarterly* is a specialized academic journal of film criticism, though it is also a magazine (with pictures) sold in bookstores. It is read by film teachers, students, and die-hard movie buffs, so unless you fall into one of those categories, it is very hard to write for us. Currently, we are especially looking for material on independent, documentary, etc. films not written about in the national film reviewing columns."

‡'**GBH MAGAZINE**, CVG Publishing Services, 332 Congress St., Boston MA 02210. (617)574-9400. Editor: William W. Bloomstein. 25% freelance written. Monthly magazine for supporters of WGBH public TV station in Boston. "*GBH* is the monthly magazine and program guide for WGBH members; it includes editorial and listings to 'complement' its broadcast partners (channels 2 and 44 and 89.7 FM). All editorial is program related and/or explores topics and issues raised by PBS programming." Estab. 1987. Circ. 150,000. Pays on acceptance. Publishes ms an average of 2 months after acceptance. Byline given. Offers 25% kill fee. Buys first North American serial rights. Submit seasonal/holiday material 3 months in advance. Previously published submissions OK. Computer printout submissions OK; prefers letter-quality. Reports in 1 month on queries; 2 weeks on mss.

Nonfiction: Essays, expose, general interest, historical/nostalgic, humor, interview/profile, opinion, personal experience, photo feature. Buys 15-25 mss/year. Query with published clips. Length: 800-2,000 words. Pays $500-1,000.

Photos: Send photos with submission. Reviews contact sheets, negatives, transparencies. Buys one-time rights.

Columns/Departments: Signoff (q and a interview with a local Boston or a PBS TV or radio personality; must relate to that month's WGBH programming) 500-1,000 words. Pays $250-750.

Tips: "Check upcoming WGBH programming (both TV and radio)—is there an interview worth doing with a story? Is there an expose to be done on an issue raised by WGBH? What about examining a particularly successful PBS show? What's on WGBH that month of special interest?"

MAGICK THEATRE, Magazine of Diverse Film Esoterica, Box 0446, Baldwin NY 11510-0129. Editor: Raymond Young. Managing Editor: Christine Young. 25% freelance written. A semiannual magazine covering film history, criticism and obscure and neglected films/filmmakers. "Our audience is fans, filmmakers and writers—not casual moviegoers. Our magazine is slanted against the grain of the contemporary, commercial mainstream to allow forgotten artists to speak up and gain their due recognition." Circ. 3,000. Pays on publication. Publishes ms an average of 8 months after acceptance. Byline given. Buys first, one-time and second serial (reprint) rights. Photocopied and previously published submissions OK. Reports in 1 month. Free sample copy and writer's guidelines.

Nonfiction: Book excerpts, expose, general interest, historical/nostalgic, interview/profile, opinion, personal experience and photo feature. "No articles dealing with contemporary, commercial, mainstream films." Buys 5-20 mss/year. Send complete ms. Length: 1,500-8,000 words. Pays $25-200 for assigned articles. May pay writers with contributor copies if writer requests.

Photos: Send photos with submission. Reviews negatives and 8x10 prints. Offers no additional payment for photos accepted with ms. Identification of subjects required. Buys one-time rights.

Columns/Departments: R. Zimmerman, editor. Books (film books reviewed), 400-900 words; Film-A (film reviews—dates of release unimportant), 400-900 words; Film-B (capsule film reviews—date of release unimportant), 50-300 words; and Magazines (film magazines reviewed—capsule and lengthy), 50-500 words. Buys 10 mss/year. Send complete ms. Pays $5-25.

Fillers: R. Zimmerman, editor. Facts, gags and newsbreaks. Buys 15/year. Length: 50-300 words. Pays $5-20.

Tips: "Writers must be dedicated and studious towards the subject, as we will not accept articles on subjects frequently covered elsewhere. A lot of research is involved, but it is rewarding, since we usually run material unavailable in other publications. We are 'open house' and do encourage any first-timers to simply write us."

METROPOLIS, Art and Entertainment News, Box 6153, Norman OK 73070. (405)364-9224. Editor: Roberto Voci. 25% freelance written. Eager to work with new/unpublished writers. A biweekly tabloid. "We cater to the 21 and up age group." Circ. 10,000. Pays on publication. Publishes ms an average of 2 months after acceptance. Byline given. Offers $15 kill fee. Buys one-time rights. Submit seasonal/holiday material 3 months in advance. Simultaneous, photocopied, and previously published submissions OK. Computer printout submissions acceptable; no dot-matrix. Reports in 1 month. Free sample copy with SAE only.

Nonfiction: Interview/profile, and album and movie reviews on regular basis. Buys 8 mss/year. Send complete ms. Length 400-1,200 words. Pays $15-35.

Photos: State availability of photos with submissions. Reviews contact sheets. Offers $10/photo. Captions, model releases, and identification of subjects required.

MOVIELINE MAGAZINE,1141 S. Beverly Dr., Los Angeles CA 90035. (213)282-0711. Editor: Laurie Halpern Smith. Senior Editor: Virginia Campbell. 60% freelance written. Biweekly magazine covering motion pictures. Circ. 100,000. Pays on publication. Publishes ms an average of 1 month after acceptance. Byline given. Offers variable kill fee. Buys first North American serial rights or simultaneous rights ("if not in our market"). Submit seasonal/holiday material 2 months in advance. Simultaneous submissions OK. Computer printout submissions OK. Reports in 1 month. Free sample copy and writer's guidelines.
Nonfiction: Book excerpts, film business-oriented pieces, essays, humor and interview/profile. Buys 75-100 mss/year. Query with published clips. Length: 150-2,500 words. Pays $35-500. Sometimes pays expenses of writers on assignment.
Photos: State availability of photos with submission. Reviews contact sheets, 2¼ transparencies and 5x7 photos. Offers $10-100/photo. Identification of subjects required. Buys one-tiome rights.
Columns/Departments: Buzz (short, funny pieces on movie-related personalities and incidents) 150-300 words; Festival Phile (reports from world film festivals) 500-1,000 words; La Dolce Video (articles about video releases) 1,000 words. Buys 75 mss/year. Pays $35-350.
Tips: "*Movieline* is a consumer-oriented publication devoted to film. We publish interviews with actors and actresses, directors, cinematographers, producers, writers, costume designers, and others with a creative involvement in motion pictures. We also seek behind-the-scenes stories relating to the movie business; fresh, insightful overviews of trends and genres; on-location pieces; and short, anecdotal items relating to any of the above. We consider our audience to be seasoned moviegoers, and consequently look for a knowledgeable, sophisticated approach to the subject; avoid a breathless, 'fan'-like attitude, especially in star interviews. Pieces should be exciting, stylish and, because of our space limitations, tightly written."

THE OPERA COMPANION, 40 Museum Way, San Francisco CA 94114. (415)626-2741. Editor: James Keolker, Ph.D. 25% freelance written. Eager to work with new/unpublished writers. A magazine published 14 times yearly covering "opera in particular, music in general. We provide readers with an in depth analysis of 14 operas per year—the personal, philosophical, and political content of each composer and his works." Circ. 8,000. Pays on acceptance. Publishes ms an average of 2 months after acceptance. Byline given. Buys first rights. Photocopied submissions OK. Computer printout submissions acceptable; prefers letter-quality. Reports in 1 week on queries; 1 month on mss. Sample copy and writer's guidelines for 8½x11 SAE and 3 first class stamps.
Nonfiction: Essay, historical/nostalgic, humor and interview/profile (opera composers, singers, producers and designers). No Master's or Doctoral theses. Buys 10 mss/year. Query with published clips. Length: 500-5,000 words. Pays $50-250.
Fillers: Anecdotes and short humor. Buys 25/year. Length: 150-500 words. Pays $50-250.
Tips: "Be pointed, pithy in statement, accurate in research. Avoid florid, excessive language. Writers must be musically sensitive, interested in opera as a continuing vocal art. Enthusiasm for the subject is important. Contact us for which operas/composers we will be featuring each year. It is those areas of research, anecdote, analysis and humor, we will be filling first."

‡PERFORMING ARTS IN CANADA, 5th Fl., 263 Adelaide St. W., Toronto, Ontario M5H 1Y2 Canada. (416)971-9516. Editor: Patricia Michael. Assistant Editor: Dara Rowland. 80% freelance written. Prefers to work with published/established writers; works with a small number of new/unpublished writers each year. Quarterly magazine for professional performers and general readers with an interest in Canadian theatre, dance, music, opera and film. Covers "modern and classical theatre arts, plus articles on related subjects (technical topics, government arts policy, etc.)." Circ. 80,550. Pays 1 month following publication. Publishes ms an average of 3 months after acceptance. Byline given. Offers $100 kill fee. Buys first serial rights. Query for electronic submissions. Computer printout submissions acceptable; no dot-matrix. Reports in 3-6 weeks. Sample copy for $1 and SAE with IRCs.
Nonfiction: "Lively, stimulating, well-researched articles on Canadian performing artists or groups. Most often in need of good classical music and dance articles." No nonCanadian, nonperforming arts material. Buys 30-35 mss/year. Query preferably with an outline. Writers new to this publication should include clippings. Length: 1,000-2,000 words. Pays $150-200. Sometimes pays the expenses of writers on assignment.
Tips: "We have a continuing need for articles that hale from the smaller centers in Canada. Ontario and particularly Toronto events are well covered."

PLAYBILL, Playbill Inc., Suite 320, 71 Vanderbilt Ave., New York NY 10169. (212)557-5757. Editor: Joan Alleman. 50% freelance written. Monthly magazine covering NYC, Broadway and Off-Broadway theatre. Circ. 1,040,000. Pays on acceptance. Publishes ms an average of 2 months after acceptance. Byline given. Buys all rights. Computer printout submissions OK; no dot-matrix. Reports in 2 months.
Nonfiction: Book excerpts, humor, interview/profile, personal experience—must all be theatre related. Buys 10 mss/year. Query with published clips. Length: 1,500-1,800 words. Pays $250-500.

Photos: State availability of photos with submission. Offers no additional payment for photos accepted with ms. Identification of subjects required.
Fillers: Anecdotes, facts and short humor. Buys 10 mss/year. Length: 350-700 words. Pays $50-100. Must all be theatre related.

RAVE, The Comedy Performance Magazine, Rave Communications, 40 Prince Street, New York NY 10012. (212)925-7560. Editor: Ronald L. Smith. 50% freelance written. Monthly magazine covering comedy. "We're the *Playbill* of the comedy clubs. When patrons visit top national comedy clubs (Caroline's in New York, Second City in Chicago, The Improv in Los Angeles) they receive our magazine free. We're totally ad-supported." Pays on publication. Publishes ms an average of 1-2 months after acceptance. Byline given. Offers 25% kill fee. Buys one-time rights. Submit seasonal/holiday material 3 months in advance. Simultaneous, photocopied and previously published (in local newpaper) submissions OK. Computer printout submissions OK: prefers letter-quality. Reports in 2 weeks. Sample copy for 5x7 SAE.
Nonfiction: Cy Kottick, articles editor. Interview/profile and photo feature. "No essays on why the world needs to laugh or first person stories on my favorite jokes or the day I performed stand-up etc. Only interviews with comics." Buys 24 mss/year. Query with or without published clips, or send complete ms. Length: 300-1,200 words. Pays $50-300. Sometimes pays expenses of writers on assignment.
Photos: State availability of photos with submission. Reviews transparencies (2x2). Offers no additional payment for photos accepted with ms. Identification of subjects required. Buys one-time rights.
Tips: "We buy two types of nonfiction: interviews with comedians who tour nationally or are outstanding local prospects and general pieces about comedy and stand-up. These include odd history (the Arrapajo Indian Crazy Society), occasional mainstream (recipes from comedians) and compilation ('football kicks,' about the various football routines of a dozen comics)."

‡SOAP OPERA UPDATE, The Magazine of Stars and Stories, 158 Linwood Plaza, Ft. Lee NJ 07024. (201)592-7002. Editor: Ruth J. Gordon. Managing Editor: Allison Waldman. 50% freelance written. Tri-weekly magazine on daytime serials. "We cover the world of soap operas, daytime and nighttime. Interviews, history, character sketches, events where soap stars are seen and participate." Estab. 1988. Pays on publication. Byline given. Pays 50% kill fee. Buys first North American serial rights. Submit seasonal/holiday material 3 months in advance. Simultaneous submissions OK. Computer printout submissions OK; no dot-matrix. Reports in 3 weeks. Sample copy $1.95 with 3 first class stamps.
Nonfiction: Humor, interview/profile. "Only interviews done in person with the actor, no phone interviews. Only articles directly about actors, shows or history of a soap opera." Buys 100 mss/year. Query with published clips. Length: 750-2,200 words. Pays $200-250. Sometimes pays expenses of writers on assignment.
Photos: State availability of photos with submission. Reviews transparencies. Offers $25-100. Captions and identification of subjects required. Buys all rights.
Tips: "Come up with fresh, new approaches to stories about soap operas and their people. Submit ideas and writing samples, previously published. Take a serious approach; don't talk down to the reader. All articles must be well written and the writer very knowledgeable about his subject matter."

‡SPLICE MAGAZINE, Ira Friedman Inc., Suite 1300, 10 Columbus Circle, New York NY 10019. (212)541-7300. Editor: James A. Baggett. Associate Editor: Krys Longan. 50% freelance written. A bimonthly magazine on movies, music, video and television. "*Splice* is a sophisticated entertainment magazine for young adults." Circ. 200,000. Pays on publication. Byline given. Buys first North American serial rights. Submit seasonal/holiday material 4 months in advance. Computer printout submissions OK; prefers letter-quality. Sample copy for 8½x11 SAE with 2 first class stamps.
Nonfiction: Interview/profile (q&a or personality profile), movie-based games and puzzles, set pieces/production pieces. Summer movie issue and *Splice* Movie Awards issue planned. Buys 8-10 mss/year. Query with published clips. Length: 250-1,500 words. Pays $50-500.
Photos: State availability of photos with submission. Reviews negatives and transparencies. Offers no additional payment for photos accepted with ms. Captions and identification of subjects required. Buys one-time rights.
Columns/Departments: Music Editor: Chip Lovitt. TV Editor: Krys Longan. Video Editor: Tom Spain. Splice Ticket (behind the scenes/production piece) 500-1,000 words; Hot Splice (brief personality profile) 250 words; Screenplay (game, contest, movie-based) 150-500 words. Buys 6 mss/year. Query with published clips. Length: 250-1,500 words. Pays $50-300.
Tips: "*Splice* is personality driven, so access to celebrities is the first consideration, along with the abilty to write lively, clean, concise, tight copy with a sense of humor. Personality profiles are most open to freelancers. Make the reader feel he/she is with you during the interview. Pack piece with details and good, descriptive quotes."

‡STV GUIDE, Triple D Publishing, Inc., Box 2384, Shelby NC 28151. (704)482-9673. Editor: David B. Melton. 70% freelance written. Monthly magazine covering home satellite TV. "We look for articles on satellite television entertainment, new equipment, how-to for the consumer, communications legislation, and programming for the home satellite television enthusiast." Circ. 60,000. Byline given. Pays on publication. Offers 30% kill fee. Buys all rights. Submit seasonal/holiday material 3 months in advance. Simultaneous and photocopied submissions OK. Query for electronic submissions. Reports in 2 weeks. Free sample copy and writer's guidelines.

Nonfiction: How-to, interview/profile, new product, opinion, personal experience, photo feature, technical. Buys 45 mss/year. Query with or without published clips, or send complete ms. Length: 1,800-3,600 words. Pays $150-400. Sometimes pays expenses of writers on assignment.

Photos: State availability of photos with submission or send photos with submission. Reviews contact sheets, transparencies and prints. Offers $5-50 per photo. Captions, model release and identification of subjects required.

Columns/Departments: At Home (personal experiences of readers) 1,000 words. Query. Length: 1,000-1,800 words. Pays $50-100.

Tips: "A writer who is a satellite TV user or has knowledge of it would be of great help. Familiarity with television transmission and some programming knowledge would also be helpful."

‡TDR; The Drama Review: A Journal of Performance Studies, New York University, 721 Broadway, 6th Floor, New York NY 10003. (212)998-1626. Editor: Richard Schechner. 95% freelance written. Works with a small number of new/unpublished writers each year. "Emphasis not only on theatre but also dance, ritual, musical performance, mime, and other facets of performative behavior. For avant-garde community, students and professors of anthropology, performance studies and related fields. Political material is welcome." Quarterly magazine. Circ. 7,000. Pays on publication. Submit material 4 months in advance. Photocopied and previously published (if published in another language) submissions OK. Query for electronic submissions. Reports in 2 months. Publishes ms an average of 6 months after acceptance. Sample copy $7 (from MIT Press); free writer's guidelines.

Nonfiction: Rebecca Schneider, managing editor. Buys 10-20 mss/issue. Query by letter only. Pays 3¢/word.

Photos: Rebecca Schneider, managing editor. 5x7 b&w photos preferred. Captions required.

Tips: "*TDR* is a place where contrasting ideas and opinions meet. A forum for writing about performances and the social, economic, and political contexts in which performances happen. The editors want interdisciplinary, intercultural, multivocal, eclectic submissions."

TV GUIDE, Radnor PA 19088. Editor (National Section): David Sendler. Editor (Local Sections): Roger Youman. Managing Editor: R.C. Smith. 70% freelance written. Prefers to work with published/established writers; works with a small number of new/unpublished writers each year; eager to work with new/unpublished writers. Weekly. Circ. 17.3 million. Publishes ms an average of 2 months after acceptance. Computer printout submissions acceptable; prefers letter-quality.

Nonfiction: Wants offbeat articles about TV people and shows. This magazine is not interested in fan material. Also wants stories on the newest trends of television, but they must be written in clear, lively English. Study publication. Query to Andrew Mills, assistant managing editor. Length: 1,000-2,000 words.

Photos: Uses professional high-quality photos, normally shot on assignment by photographers chosen by *TV Guide*. Prefers color. Pays $350 day rate against page rates—$450 for 2 pages or less.

‡VIDEO CHOICE MAGAZINE, The Leading Review Magazine for the Video Enthusiast, Connell Communications, 331 Jaffrey Rd., Peterborough, New Hampshire 03458. Editor: Deborah Navas. Senior Editor: Ann E. Graves. 80% freelance written. Monthly magazine on special interest (non-theatrical) videos. "Our audience is middle-class consumers who own a VCR and are interested in using it for personal enrichment as well as entertainment. The magazine serves varied interests: sports, exercise, business, educational, arts, etc." Estab. 1988. Circ. 70,000. Pays on acceptance. Publishes ms an average of 3 months after acceptance. Byline sometimes given. Offers 25% kill fee for assigned article. Buys all rights. Submit seasonal/holiday material 3 months in advance. Simultaneous and photocopied submissions OK. Query for electronic submissions. Reports in 2 weeks on queries; 1 months on mss. Writer's guidelines for #10 SASE with 1 first class stamp.

Nonfiction: Interview/profile, new product, opinion, technical, reviews of videotapes. Buys 240 mss/year. Query or query with published clips. Length: 250-2,000 words. Pays $30-500. Sometimes pays expenses of writers on assignment.

Photos: State availability of photos with submission. Reviews transparencies, prints. Offers no additional payment for photos accepted with ms, or sometimes offers $50-100 per photo. Identification of subjects required. Buys one-time rights.

Columns/Departments: Industry Insight; Video Photographer; Collector's Corner; The Video Enthusiast. Query with published clips. Length: 1,200 words. Pays $250.

‡VIDEO MARKETPLACE MAGAZINE, World Publishing Co., 4th Floor, 990 Grove St., Evanston IL 60201. (312)491-6440. Editor: Robert Meyers. Managing Editor: Michael Stein. 90% freelance written. A monthly magazine on video software. "The magazine is broken down into 15-20 categories: music, travel, health, sports, how-to, etc. plus feature film movies. Each category starts off with a related feature article of

700-900 or 1,200-1,400 words." Circ. 150,000. Pays on acceptance. Publishes ms an average of 4 months after acceptance. Byline given. Offers $75-125 kill fee. Buys one-time rights. Submit seasonal/holiday material 6 months in advance. Previously published submissions OK. Reports in 2 weeks on queries; 3 weeks on mss. Sample copy $2.50; writer's guidelines for #10 SAE and 1 first class stamp.

Nonfiction: General interest, historical/nostalgic (documentary), how-to (instructional, educational), humor (in general areas), interview/profile (celebrity, all fields), photo feature (all categories), technical (general). Query with published clips or send complete ms. Length: 700-1,500 words. Pays $125-350; $75-125 for reprints.

Photos: State availability of photos with submission. Reviews transparencies. Offers no additional payment for photos accepted with ms. Offers $20-50/photo; $100 for cover. Captions required. Buys one-time rights.

Columns/Departments: Video Views (just released or upcoming video cassettes—what's new on video, etc.) 1,400-1,500 words. Buys 8-10 mss/year. Query. Length: 1,400-1,800 words. Pays $250-350.

Tips: "Any topic is acceptable so long as it is related to a subject currently available on video. Example titles: Changing Trends in Conntry Music (music), History of the American Auto (documentary), The Blue Angels (aviation/space)."

VIDEOMANIA, "The Newspaper For Video Nuts", Legs Of Stone Publishing Co., Box 47, Princeton WI 54968. Editor: Bob Katerzynske. 70% freelance written. Eager to work with new/unpublished writers. A monthly tabloid for the home video hobbyist. "Our readers are very much 'into' home video: they like reading about it—including both video hardware and software. A large number also collect video (movies, vintage TV, etc.)." Circ. 5,000. Pays on publication. Publishes ms an average of 3 months after acceptance. Byline given. Buys all rights; may reassign. Submit seasonal/holiday material 6 months in advance. Computer printout submissions acceptable; prefers letter-quality. Reports in 3 weeks on mss. Sample copy for $2.50 and 9x12 SASE.

Nonfiction: Book excerpts, videotape and book reviews, expose, general interest, historical/nostalgic, how-to, humor, interview/profile, new product, opinion, personal experience, photo feature, technical and travel. "All articles should deal with video and/or film. We always have special holiday issues in November and December." No *complicated* technical pieces." Buys 24 mss/year. Send complete ms. Length: 500-1,200 words. Pays $2.50 maximum. "Contributor copies also used for payment."

Photos: Send photos with submissions. Reviews contact sheets and 3x5 prints. Offers no additional payment for photos accepted with ms. Model releases and identification of subjects required. Buys all rights; may reassign.

Fiction: Adventure, horror and humorous. "We want short, video-related fiction only on an occasional basis. Since we aim for a general readership, we do not want any pornographic material." Buys 5 mss/year. Send complete ms. Length: 500 words. Pays $2.50 maximum plus copies.

Tips: "We want to offer more reviews and articles on offbeat, obscure and rare movies, videos and stars. Write in a plain, easy-to-understand style. We're not looking for a highhanded, knock-'em-dead writing style . . . just something good! We want more short video, film and book reviews by freelancers."

‡YOU MAGAZINE, America's 20th Century Beauty Pageants, Inc., 351 Oak Place, Unit L, Brea CA 92621. (714)529-1950. Editor: Linda Manikas. Managing Editor: Mike Manikas. 70% freelance written. A monthly magazine on entertainment. "*You* reports the trends and realities of the entertainment industry. We look for the real persona behind the famous faces in personality stories and offer no-nonsense advice on what people who want a career in the entertainment field can expect when they try to break into the business." Estab. 1987. Circ. 125,000. Pays on acceptance. Publishes ms an average of 3 months after acceptance. Byline given. Buys first North American serial rights or second serial (reprint) rights. Submit seasonal/holiday material 6 months in advance. Photocopied and previously published submissions OK. Computer printout submissions OK; prefers letter-quality. Reports in 1 month on queries; 6 weeks on mss. Sample copy for 9x12 SAE with 6 first class stamps. Free writer's guidelines.

Nonfiction: Expose, general interest, how-to, humor, interview/profile, personal experience, photo feature. "No critical review or celebrity pieces; these are done in-house. Nothing on a writer's friend who's made good in community theatre in Montana and is sure to make it big—no music stories/rock reviews." Buys 50 mss/year. Query with published clips. Length: 1,500-3,000 words. Pays $75 minimum for assigned articles; $50-75 for unsolicited articles. Sometimes pays expenses of writers on assignment.

Photos: State availability of photos with submission. Reviews transparencies and prints. Payment negotiable. Model releases and identificaiton of subjects required. Buys one-time rights.

Columns/Departments: Pageant Watch (analysis, persona experience/"hangout" type); Looking Your Best (experts in grooming/skin/hair care) 1,000-1,500 words. Buys 10-30 mss/year. Query with published clips. Pays $50-75.

Tips: "Send for guidelines; we're very picky. We don't like to see work that reads like a newspaper story. Too many writers we've worked with so far have a hard time seeing past the quotes, and too often don't get the right ones in the first place. Concentrate on what the story is about, do twice the research you think you'll need, then approach the piece like a breezily-written research paper. Writers should have a working knowledge of the entertainment industry. Unless you're an expert, or have extensive personal experience in the area you're covering, the chances are good you'll miss the mark. However, a thoughtful, well written piece will attract our attention."

Ethnic/Minority

Traditions are kept alive, new ones become established and people are united by ethnic publications. Some ethnic magazines seek material that unites people of all races. Ideas, interests and concerns of nationalities and religions are covered by publications in this category. General interest lifestyle magazines for these groups are also included. Additional markets for writing with an ethnic orientation are located in the following sections: Career, College and Alumni; Juvenile; Men's; Women's; Teen and Young Adult; and Religious.

AIM MAGAZINE, AIM Publishing Company, 7308 S. Eberhart Ave., Chicago IL 60619. (312)874-6184. Editor: Ruth Apilado. Managing Editor: Dr. Myron Apilado. 75% freelance written. Works with a small number of new/unpublished writers each year. Quarterly magazine on social betterment that promotes racial harmony and peace for high school, college and general audience. Circ. 10,000. Pays on publication. Publishes ms an average of 3 months after acceptance. Offers 60% of contract as kill fee. Not copyrighted. Buys one-time rights. Submit seasonal/holiday material 6 months in advance. Simultaneous queries, and simultaneous and photocopied submissions OK. Computer printout submissions acceptable; prefers letter-quality. Reports in 6 weeks on queries. Sample copy and writer's guidelines for $3, 8½x11 SAE and 4 first class stamps.
Nonfiction: Exposé (education); general interest (social significance); historical/nostalgic (Black or Indian); how-to (help create a more equitable society); and profile (one who is making social contributions to community); and book reviews and reviews of plays "that reflect our ethnic/minority orientation." No religious material. Buys 16 mss/year. Send complete ms. Length: 500-800 words. Pays $25-35.
Photos: Reviews b&w prints. Captions and identification of subjects required.
Fiction: Ethnic, historical, mainstream, and suspense. Fiction that teaches the brotherhood of man. Buys 20 mss/year. Send complete ms. Length: 1,000-1,500 words. Pays $25-35.
Poetry: Avant-garde, free verse, light verse. No "preachy" poetry. Buys 20 poems/year. Submit maximum 5 poems. Length: 15-30 lines. Pays $3-5.
Fillers: Jokes, anecdotes and newsbreaks. Buys 30/year. Length: 50-100 words. Pays $5.
Tips: "Interview anyone of any age who unselfishly is making an unusual contribution to the lives of less fortunate individuals. Include photo and background of person. We look at the nations of the world as part of one family. Short stories and historical pieces about blacks and Indians are the areas most open to freelancers. Subject matter of submission is of paramount concern for us rather than writing style. Articles and stories showing the similarity in the lives of people with different racial backgrounds are desired."

THE AMERICAN CITIZEN ITALIAN PRESS, 13681 V St., Omaha NE 68137. (402)896-0403. Publisher/Editor: Diana C. Failla. 40% freelance written. Eager to work with new/unpublished writers. Quarterly newspaper of Italian-American news/stories. Circ. 8,000. Pays on publication. Publishes ms an average of 3 months after acceptance. Byline given. Not copyrighted. Buys first North American serial rights. Submit seasonal/holiday material 2 months in advance. Previously published submissions OK. Computer printout submissions acceptable; prefers letter-quality. Reports in 1 month. Sample copy for 10x13 SAE and $1.50.
Nonfiction: Book excerpts, general interest, historical/nostalgic, opinion, photo feature, celebrity pieces, travel, fashions, profiles and sports (Italian players). Query with published clips. Length: 400-600 words. Pays $15-20. Sometimes pays the expenses of writers on assignment.
Photos: State availability of photos. Reviews b&w prints. Pays $5. Captions and identification of subjects required. Buys all rights.
Columns/Departments: Query.
Fiction: Query. Pays $15-20.
Poetry: Submit maximum 5 poems. Pays $5-10.
Tips: "Human interest stories are the most open to freelancers. We would like some work dealing with current controversial issues involving those of Italian/American descent."

AMERICAN DANE, The Danish Brotherhood in America, 3717 Harney St., Box 31748, Omaha NE 68131. (402)341-5049. Editor: Jerome L. Christensen. Managing Editor: Pamela K. Dorau. 50% freelance written. Prefers to work with published/ established writers; works with a small number of new/unpublished writers each year. The monthly magazine of the Danish Brotherhood in America. All articles must have Danish ethnic flavor. Circ. 10,000. Pays on publication. Publishes ms an average of 1 year after acceptance. Byline given. Not copyrighted. Buys first rights. Submit seasonal/holiday material 1 year in advance. Photocopied submissions OK. Computer printout submissions acceptable; prefers letter-quality. Reports in 2 weeks on queries. Sample copy $1 with 9½x4 SAE and 3 first class stamps; writer's guidelines for #10 SAE with 1 first class stamp.

Nonfiction: Historical, humor, inspirational, personal experience, photo feature and travel, all with a Danish flavor. Buys 12 mss/year. Query. Length: 1,500 words maximum. Pays $50 maximum for unsolicited articles.

Photos: Send photos with submission. Reviews prints. Offers no additional payment for photos accepted with ms. Captions and identification of subjects required. Buys one-time rights.

Fiction: Adventure, historical, humorous, mystery, romance and suspense, all with a Danish flavor. Buys 6-12 mss/year. Query with published clips. Length: 1,500 words maximum. Pays $50 maximum.

Poetry: Traditional. Buys 1-6 poems/year. Submit maximum 6 poems. Pays $35 maximum.

Fillers: Anecdotes and short humor. Buys up to 12/year. Length: 300 words maximum. Pays $15 maximum.

Tips: "Feature articles are most open to freelancers."

‡**AMERICAN JEWISH WORLD**, AJW Publishing Inc., 4509 Minnetonka Blvd., Minneapolis MN 55416. (612)920-7000. Managing Editor: Bob Epstein. 10% freelance written. Weekly Jewish newspaper covering local, national and international stories. Circ.: 6,500. Pays on publication. Publishes ms an average of 1-4 months after acceptance. Byline given. Offers 50% kill fee. Publication copyrighted. Makes work-for-hire assignments. Submit seasonal/holiday material 6 months in advance. Simultaneous and photocopied submissions OK. Computer printout submissions OK. Free sample copy.

Nonfiction: Essays, expose, general interest, historical/nostalgic, humor, inspirational, interview/profile, opinion, personal experience, photo feature, religious, travel. Buys 30-50 mss/year. Query with or without published clips, or send complete ms. Length: 1,500-2,000 maximum. Pays $10-75. Sometimes pays expenses of writers on assignment.

Photos: State availability of photos with submission. Reviews prints. Pays $5 per photo. Identification of subjects required. Buys one-time rights.

ARARAT, The Armenian General Benevolent Union, 585 Saddle River Rd., Saddle Brook NJ 07662. Editor-in-Chief: Leo Hamalian. 80% freelance written. Emphasizes Armenian life and culture for Americans of Armenian descent and Armenian immigrants. "Most are well-educated; some are Old World." Quarterly magazine. Circ. 2,400. Pays on publication. Publishes ms an average of 1 year after acceptance. Buys first North American serial rights and second (reprint) rights to material originally published elsewhere. Submit seasonal/holiday material at least 3 months in advance. Photocopied and previously published submissions OK. Computer printout submissions acceptable. Reports in 6 weeks. Sample copy $3 plus 4 first class stamps.

Nonfiction: Historical (history of Armenian people, of leaders, etc.); interviews (with prominent or interesting Armenians in any field, but articles are preferred); profile (on subjects relating to Armenian life and culture); personal experience (revealing aspects of typical Armenian life); and travel (in Armenia and Armenian communities throughout the world and the US). Buys 3 mss/issue. Query. Length: 1,000-6,000 words. Pays $25-100.

Columns/Departments: Reviews of books by Armenians or relating to Armenians. Buys 6/issue. Query. Pays $25. Open to suggestions for new columns/departments.

Fiction: Any stories dealing with Armenian life in America or in the old country. Buys 4 mss/year. Query. Length: 2,000-5,000 words. Pays $35-75.

Poetry: Any verse that is Armenian in theme. Buys 6/issue. Pays $10.

Tips: "Read the magazine, and write about the kind of subjects we are obviously interested in, e.g., Kirlian photography, Aram Avakian's films, etc. Remember that we have become almost totally ethnic in subject matter, but we want articles that present (to the rest of the world) the Armenian in an interesting way. The most frequent mistake made by writers in completing an article for us is that they are not sufficiently versed in Armenian history/culture. The articles are too superficial for our audience."

BALTIMORE JEWISH TIMES, 2104 N. Charles St., Baltimore MD 21218. (301)752-3504. Editor: Gary Rosenblatt. 25% freelance written. Weekly magazine covering subjects of interest to Jewish readers. "*Baltimore Jewish Times* reaches 20,000 Baltimore-area Jewish homes, as well as several thousand elsewhere in the U.S. and Canada; almost anything of interest to that audience is of interest to us. This includes reportage, general interest articles, personal opinion, and personal experience pieces about every kind of Jewish subject from narrowly religious issues to popular sociology; from the Mideast to the streets of Brooklyn, to the suburbs of Baltimore. We run articles of special interest to purely secular Jews as well as to highly observant ones. We are Orthodox, Conservative, and Reform all at once. We are spiritual and mundane. We are establishment and we are alternative culture." Circ. 20,000. Pays on publication. Publishes ms an average of 2 months after acceptance. Byline given. Buys one-time rights. Submit seasonal/holiday material 2 months in advance. Simultaneous queries, and photocopied and previously published submissions OK. Computer printout submissions acceptable; prefers letter-quality. "We will not return submissions without SASE." Reports in 6 weeks. Sample copy $2.

Nonfiction: Barbara Pash, editorial assistant. Book excerpts, exposé, general interest, historical/nostalgic, humor, interview/profile, opinion, personal experience and photo feature. "We are inundated with Israel personal experience and Holocaust-related articles, so submissions on these subjects must be of particularly high quality." Buys 100 mss/year. "Established writers query; others send complete manuscript." Length: 1,200-

6,000 words. Pays $25-150.

Photos: Kim Muller-Thym, graphics editor. Send photos with ms. Pays $10-35 for 8x10 b&w prints.

Fiction: Barbara Pash, editorial assistant. "We'll occasionally run a high-quality short story with a Jewish theme." Buys 6 mss/year. Send complete ms. Length: 1,200-6,000 words. Pays $25-150.

CONGRESS MONTHLY, American Jewish Congress, 15 E. 84th St., New York NY 10028. (212)879-4500. Editor: Maier Deshell. 90% freelance written. Magazine published 7 times/year covering topics of concern to the American Jewish community representing a wide range of views. Distributed mainly to the members of the American Jewish Congress; readers are intellectual, Jewish, involved. Circ. 35,000. Pays on publication. Publishes ms an average of 3 months after acceptance. Byline given. Buys one-time rights. Submit seasonal/holiday material 2 months in advance. No photocopied or previously published submissions. Computer print-out submissions acceptable; prefers letter-quality. Reports in 2 months.

Nonfiction: General interest ("current topical issues geared toward our audience"). No technical material. Send complete ms. Length: 2,000 words maximum. Pays $100-150/article.

Photos: State availability of photos. Reviews b&w prints. "Photos are paid for with payment for ms."

Columns/Departments: Book, film, art and music reviews. Send complete ms. Length: 1,000 words maximum. Pays $100-150/article.

‡EBONY MAGAZINE, 820 S. Michigan Ave., Chicago IL 60605. Editor: John H. Johnson. Managing Editor: Charles L. Sanders. 10% freelance written. For Black readers of the U.S., Africa, and the Caribbean. Monthly. Circ. 1,800,000. Buys first North American serial rights and all rights. Buys about 10 mss/year. "We are now fully staffed, buying few manuscripts." Pays on publication. Publishes ms an average of 3 months after acceptance. Submit seasonal material 2 months in advance. Query. Reports in 1 month.

Nonfiction: Achievement and human interest stories about, or of concern to, Black readers. Interviews, profiles and humor pieces are bought. Length: 1,500 words maximum. "Study magazine and needs carefully. Perhaps one out of 50 submissions interests us. Most are totally irrelevant to our needs and are simply returned." Pays $200 minimum. Sometimes pays the expenses of writers on assignment.

Photos: Purchased with mss, and with captions only. Buys 8x10 glossy prints, color transparencies, 35mm color. Submit negatives and contact sheets when possible. Offers no additional payment for photos accepted with mss.

GREATER PHOENIX JEWISH NEWS, Phoenix Jewish News, Inc., Box 26590, Phoenix AZ 85068. (602)870-9470. Executive Editor: Flo Eckstein. Managing Editor: Leni Reiss. 10% freelance written. Prefers to work with published/established writers. Weekly tabloid covering subjects of interest to Jewish readers. Circ. 7,000. Pays on publication. Publishes ms an average of 3 months after acceptance. Byline given. Submit seasonal/holiday material 3 months in advance. Simultaneous queries, and simultaneous, photocopied, and previously published submissions OK. Computer printout submissions acceptable; prefers letter-quality. (Must be easy to read, with upper and lower case.) Reports in 1 month. Sample copy $1.

Nonfiction: General interest, issue analysis, interview/profile, opinion, personal experience, photo feature and travel. Special sections include Fashion and Health; House and Home; Back to School; Summer Camps; Party Planning; Bridal; Travel; Business and Finance; and Jewish Holidays. Buys 25 mss/year. Send complete ms. Length: 1,000-2,500 words. Pays $15-75 for simultaneous rights; $1.50/column inch for first serial rights. Sometimes pays the expenses of writers on assignment.

Photos: Send photos with query or ms. Pays $10 for 8x10 b&w prints. Captions required.

Tips: "We are looking for lifestyle and issue-oriented pieces of particular interest to Jewish readers between ages 25-40. Our newspaper reaches across the religious, political, social and economic spectrum of Jewish residents in this burgeoning southwestern metropolitan area. We stay away from cute stories as well as ponderous submissions."

HADASSAH MAGAZINE, 50 W. 58th St., New York NY 10019. Executive Editor: Alan M. Tigay. 60% freelance written. Works with small number of new/unpublished writers each year. Monthly, except combined issues (June-July and August-September). Circ. 370,000. Publishes ms 1-18 months after acceptance. Buys first rights (with travel articles, we buy all rights). Computer printout submissions acceptable. Reports in 6 weeks. Sample copy $2 with 9x12 SAE; writer's guidelines for SASE.

Nonfiction: Primarily concerned with Israel, Jewish communities around the world, and American civic affairs. Buys 10 unsolicited mss/year. Length: 1,500-2,000 words. Pays $200-400, less for reviews. Sometimes pays the expenses of writers on assignment.

Photos: "We buy photos only to illustrate articles, with the exception of outstanding color from Israel which we use on our covers. We pay $175 and up for a suitable cover photo." Offers $50 for first photo; $35 for each additional. "Always interested in striking cover (color) photos, especially of Israel and Jerusalem."

Columns/Departments: "We have a Parenting column and a Travel column, but a query for topic or destination should be submitted first to make sure the area is of interest and the story follows our format."

Fiction: Contact Zelda Shluker. Short stories with strong plots and positive Jewish values. No personal memoirs, "schmaltzy" fiction, or women's magazine fiction. "We continue to buy very little fiction because of a backlog. We are also open to art stories that explore trends in Jewish art, literature, theatre, etc." Length: 3,000 words maximum. Pays $300 minimum.

Tips: "We are interested in reading articles that offer an American perspective on Jewish affairs (1,500 words). Send query of topic first. (For example, a look at the presidential candidates from a Jewish perspective.)"

THE HIGHLANDER, Angus J. Ray Associates, Inc., Box 397, Barrington IL 60011. (312)382-1035. Editor: Angus J. Ray. Managing Editor: Ethyl Kennedy Ray. 20% freelance written. Works with a small number of new/unpublished writers each year. Bimonthly magazine covering Scottish history, clans, genealogy, travel/history, and Scottish/American activities. Circ. 35,000. Pays on acceptance. Publishes ms an average of 6 months after acceptance. Byline given. Buys first North American serial rights and second serial (reprint) rights to material originally published elsewhere. Submit seasonal/holiday material 6 months in advance. Photocopied and previously published submissions OK. Computer printout submissions acceptable; no dot-matrix. Reports in 1 month. Sample copy for $1 and 9x12 SAE. Free writer's guidelines.
Nonfiction: Historical/nostalgic. "No fiction; no articles unrelated to Scotland." Buys 20 mss/year. Query. Length: 750-2,000 words. Pays $75-150. Sometimes pays the expenses of writers on assignment.
Photos: State availability of photos. Pays $5-10 for 8x10 b&w prints. Reviews b&w contact sheets. Identification of subjects required. Buys one-time rights.
Tips: "Submit something that has appeared elsewhere."

INSIDE, The Jewish Exponent Magazine, Federation of Jewish Agencies of Greater Philadelphia, 226 S. 16th St., Philadelphia PA 19102. (215)893-5700. Editor: Jane Biberman. Managing Editor: Jodie Green. 95% freelance written (by assignment). Works with published/established writers and a small number of new/unpublished writers each year. Quarterly Jewish community magazine—for a 25 years and older general interest Jewish readership. Circ. 100,000. Pays on acceptance. Publishes ms an average of 2 months after acceptance. Byline given. Offers 10% kill fee. Buys one-time rights. Submit seasonal/holiday material 3 months in advance. Simultaneous queries OK. Computer printout submissions acceptable; no dot-matrix. Reports in 2 weeks on queries; 3 weeks on mss. Sample copy for 9x12 SAE and $4; free writer's guidelines.
Nonfiction: Book excerpts, general interest, historical/nostalgic, humor, interview/profile. Philadelphia angle desirable. No personal religious experiences or trips to Israel. Buys 100 mss/year. Query. Length: 600-3,000 words. Pays $100-700. Pays the expenses of writers on assignment.
Fiction: Short stories. Query.
Photos: State availability of photos. Reviews color and b&w transparencies. Identification of subjects required.
Tips: "Personalities—very well known—and serious issues of concern to Jewish community needed. We can use 600-word 'back page' pieces—humorous, first person articles."

‡IRISH & AMERICAN REVIEW, The Newspaper of the International Irish Community, Interstate News Services, Inc., Suite 250, 500 Airport Rd., St. Louis MO 63135. (314)522-1300. Editor: Michael J. Olds. 80% freelance written. Quarterly tabloid of Irish and Irish-American features and photographs. "Our newspaper is strictly a feature-lifestyle publication. The only hard news is business information. No politics." Circ. 20,000. Pays on publication. Publishes ms an average of 2 months after acceptance. Byline given. Buys all rights. Submit seasonal/holiday material 4 months in advance. Query for electronic submissions. Computer printout submissions OK; prefers letter-quality. Reports in 1 month. Free sample copy and writer's guidelines.
Nonfiction: Historical/nostalgic, humor, inspirational, interview/profile, new product, personal experience, photo feature, religious, travel. Special issues: St. Patrick's Day (March edition); Irish travel season. Buys 20 mss/year. Query. Length: 300-2,000 words. Pays $20-250 for assigned articles; $20-100 for unsolicited articles. Sometimes pays expenses of writers on assignment.
Photos: State availability of photos with submission. Reviews contact sheets, transparencies and 5x7 prints. Offers $5 minimum for photos. Captions, model releases and identification of subjects required. Usually buys one-time rights.
Columns/Departments: Books (of interest to Irish, Irish-Americans), 250-400 words; Food (cooking and review or Irish food and restaurants), 250-400 words. Buys 4-8 mss/year. Query or send complete ms. Pays $15 minimum.
Fiction: Historical, humorous, novel excerpts. Nothing political. Buys 1-4 mss/year. Query. Length: 250-1,000 words. Pays $15 minimum.
Poetry: Traditional. Buys up to 4 poems/year. Pays $10 minimum.
Tips: "We are interested in features and photo features about Irish-Americans; Irish; American cities and events with an Irish flavor; Irish travel stories; stories about Irish commerce. Look for the Irish interest."

THE JEWISH MONTHLY, B'nai B'rith International, 1640 Rhode Island Ave. NW, Washington DC 20036. (202)857-6645. Editor: Marc Silver. 75% freelance written. Prefers to work with published/established writ-

ers. A monthly magazine covering Jewish politics, lifestyles, religion and culture for a family audience. Circ. 180,000. Pays on publication. Publishes ms an average of 4 months after acceptance. Byline given. Offers 25% kill fee. Buys first North American serial rights. Submit seasonal/holiday material 6 months in advance. Photocopied submissions OK. Query for electronic submissions. Computer printout submissions acceptable; prefers letter-quality. Reports in 2 weeks on queries; 1 month on mss. Sample copy $1; free writer's guidelines.
Nonfiction: Book excerpts, general interest, historical/nostalgic, humor, interview/profile, opinion, personal experience, photo feature, religious and travel. "I am looking for articles that offer fresh perspectives on familiar issues in the Jewish community (such as assimilation, Middle East conflict, religious tensions) and articles that focus on new trends and problems." No immigrant reminiscences. Buys 25 mss/year. Query with published clips. Length: 500-5,000 words. Pays 10-25¢/word. Sometimes pays the expenses of writers on assignment.
Photos: State availability of photos with submission. Reviews contact sheets, transparencies and prints. Offers $25-75/photo. Captions, model releases, and identification of subjects required. Buys one-time rights.

JEWISH NEWS, Suite 240, 20300 Civic Center Dr., Southfield MI 48076. (313)354-6060. Editor: Gary Rosenblatt. Associate Editor: Alan Hitsky. 10% freelance written. Works with a small number of new/unpublished writers each year. A weekly tabloid covering news and features of Jewish interest. Circ. 18,000. Pays on publication. Publishes ms an average of 3 months after acceptance. Byline given. No kill fee "unless stipulated beforehand." Buys first North American serial rights. Simultaneous queries and photocopied submissions OK. Computer printout submissions acceptable; prefers letter-quality. Reports in 2 weeks on queries; 1 month on mss. Sample copy $1; writer's guidelines for #10 SASE.
Nonfiction: Book excerpts, humor, and interview/profile. Buys 10-20 mss/year. Query with or without published clips, or send complete ms. Length: 500-2,500 words. Pays $40-125.
Fiction: Ethnic. Buys 1-2 mss/year. Send complete ms. Length: 500-2,500 words. Pays $40-125.

‡**JOURNAL OF THE NORTH SHORE JEWISH COMMUNITY**, North Shore Jewish Press, Ltd., 564 Loring Ave., Salem MA 01970. (617)741-1558. Editor: Barbara Wolf. 20% freelance written. Biweekly tabloid featuring Jewish news/issues/features. "We look for non-political, balanced reporting with an emphasis on community fundraising." Circ. 11,000. Pays on publication. Bylne given. Buys all rights. Submit seasonal/holiday material 1½ months in advance. Simultaneous and previously published submissions OK. Query for electronic submissions. Computer printout submissions OK; prefers letter-quality. Reports in a few weeks on queries. Free sample copy.
Nonfiction: Book excerpts, esays, general interest, historical/nostalgic, humor, inspirational, interview/profile, new product, opinion, personal experience, travel, Jewish holidays, Jewish cooking, book reviews, children's and U.S. politics as relates to Jewish issues. We plan a January wedding issue, an August back to school issue, and a May Bar/Bat Mitzvah issue. Buys 10-20 mss/year. Query with published clips. Length: 500-1,200 words. Pays $30-50.
Photos: State availability of photos with submissions. Offers $10/photo. Captions and identification of subjects required. Buys one-time rights.
Columns/Departments: Good News & Bad (family/home), 350 words; Analysis (international issues), 500-750 words; Roots & Branches (Jewish genealogy), 300 words; International Features, 1,200-1,500 words; and Dateline Israel, 350 words. Buys 25 mss/year. Query with published clips. Length: 350-1,500 words. Pays $10-50.
Fiction: Ethnic (Jewish), historical and humorous. Buys 6 mss/year. Query with published clips. Length: 1,000-2,000. Pays $30-50.
Tips: "We need copy to support advertising specials—with Jewish slant: finance, wedding, travel, Bar Mitzvah, back to school, home improvement, etc."

LECTOR, The Hispanic Review Journal, Floricanto Press, Suite 830, 16161 Ventura Blvd., Encino CA 91436. (818)990-1885. Editor: Roberto Cabello-Argandona. Managing Editor: Giselle K. Cabello. 95% freelance written. Works with a small number of new/unpublished writers each year and is eager to work with new/unpublished writers. A semiannual journal of Hispanic cultural articles and English reviews of books in Spanish. "We desire cultural articles, particularly of Hispanic arts and literature, written for a popular level (as opposed to an academic level). Articles are to be nonsexist, nonracist." Circ. 3,000. Pays on publication. Publishes ms an average of 6-12 months after acceptance. Byline given. Buys first rights or makes work-for-hire assignments. Photocopied submissions OK; previously published submissions sometimes accepted. Computer printout submissions acceptable ("desirable"); prefers letter-quality. Reports in 3 months. Sample copy $5; writer's guidelines for #10 SASE.
Nonfiction: Interview/profile, photo feature and articles on art, literature and Latino small presses. No personal experience, religious or how-to. Buys 25 mss/year. "No unsolicited manuscripts; query us first." Length: 2,000-3,500 words. Pays $50-150. "Writers, along with payment, always get five copies of magazine."
Photos: Send photos with submission. Reviews contact sheets. Captions required. Buys one-time rights.

Columns/Departments: Publisher's Corner (covers publishing houses in Latin America or U.S. [Latin]), 2,000-2,500 words; Perspective (cultural articles dealing with aspect of Hispanic art/lit), 2,500-3,500 words; Events in Profile (occasional column covering particular event in Chicano Studies), 1,500-2,000 words; Feature Review (in-depth review of particularly important published work), 2,500-3,000 words, Author's Corner (interview with recently published author), 1,500-2,000 words, and Inquiry (literary criticism) 2,000-2,500 words. Buys 15 mss/year. Query with published clips. Pays $50-150.

‡**NATIVE PEOPLES, The Journal of the Heard Museum**, The Heard Museum, 22 East Monte Vista Rd., Phoenix AZ 85004. (602)252-8840. Editor: Gary Avey. Quarterly magazine on Native Americans. "The primary purpose of this magazine is to offer a sensitive portrayal of the arts and lifeways of native peoples around the world." Estab. 1987. Circ. 4,500. Pays on publication. Byline given. Offers 50% kill fee. Buys one-time rights. Query for electronic submissions. Computer printout submissions OK. Reports in 1 month on queries; 2 weeks on mss. Sample copy for 8½x11 SAE with 3 first class stamps. Free writer's guidelines.
Nonfiction: Book excerpts, historical/nostalgic, interview/profile, personal experience, photo feature. Buys 35 mss/year. Query with published clips. Length: 1,400-2,000 words. Pays 25-50¢/word. Sometimes pays expenses of writer's on assignment.
Photos: State availability of photos with submission. Reviews transparencies (all formats). Offers $75-150 per-page rates. Identification of subjects required. Buys one-time rights.

NIGHTMOVES, Chicago's Free Biweekly, Nightmoves Publishing Co., Suite 1100, 105 W. Madison, Chicago IL 60602. (312)346-7765. Editor: Howard Wilson. Managing Editor: Gayle Soucek. 75% freelance written. Eager to work with new/unpublished writers. Biweekly tabloid of politics, entertainment, and social issues. "We reach a Black, primarily urban audience ages 18-40." Circ. 50,000. Pays on publication. Publishes ms an average of 3 months after acceptance. Byline given. Not copyrighted. "We rarely kill an article without giving the writer ample opportunity to re-write it." Buys first rights and second serial (reprint) rights. Submit seasonal/holiday material 2 months in advance. Photocopied and previously published submissions OK. Computer printout submissions acceptable; no dot-matrix. Reports in 3 weeks on queries; 1 month on mss. Sample copy for 9x12 SAE and 3 first class stamps. Writer's guidelines for #10 SAE and 1 first class stamp.
Nonfiction: Expose (almost any subject, but must be carefully documented); general interest; humor (mostly sophisticated, such as political satire); and interview/profile. No personal opinion or travel. "While we enjoy articles of national interest, our distribution is in the Chicago area only, so we cannot use articles on local issues from other areas, *unless* they relate closely to a broader theme." Buys 120+ mss/year. Query or send complete ms (prefers queries). Length: 750-2,500 words. Pays 3-5¢/word. Sometimes pays expenses of writers on assignment.
Photos: State availability of photos with query letter or ms. "We are a very visually-oriented publication, so photos are welcomed, but they must be good quality. Good photos will help sell us on a story idea." Prefers 5x7 or 8x10 b&w prints. Pays $10-20. Captions and model releases required. Buys one-time rights.
Columns/Departments: Movie and Theatre Reviews, Chicago-area restaurant reviews, etc. "This is a limited area for freelancers, and we prefer queries only." Buys 10-15 mss/year. Query. Length: 750-1,250 words. Pays 3-5¢/word.
Tips: "We receive too much 'light' material and not enough well-researched, hard-hitting cover story material. Articles are usually too vague and all-encompassing, lacking a definite focus and adequate research and documentation."

‡**PALM BEACH JEWISH WORLD**, Jewish World Publishing Corporation, Box 33433, West Palm Beach FL 33402. (305)833-8331. Editor: Martin Pomerance. 20% freelance written. A weekly newspaper covering Jewish-oriented material. "All articles must have a strong Jewish slant. Our readers are all ages, all levels of affluence and all degrees of Jewish commitment. News stories are staff-written; however, we'll look at national features as well as those strongly focused on South Florida." Circ. 55,000. Publishes ms an average of 1 month after acceptance. Byline given. Offers $25 kill fee. Buys first North American serial rights. Submit seasonal/holiday material 3 months in advance. Simultaneous submissions OK if publisher is in another state. Query for electronic submissions. Computer printout submissions acceptable; prefers letter-quality. Reports in 1 month on queries; 2 months on mss. Sample copy and writer's guidelines for SAE and 5 first class stamps.
Nonfiction: Exposé, general interest, historical/nostalgic, humor, inspirational, interview/profile, new product, photo feature, religious, travel and consumer. Special issues on religious holidays. "No amateurish compositions such as 'What Israel Means to Me' or 'How I Hated to put My Mother in an Old Age Home.' " Buys 120 mss/year. Query with or without published clips, or send complete ms (prefers query and clips). Length: 2,000 words maximum. Pays $50-200.
Photos: Send photos with submission. Reviews prints. Offers $7.50-10/photo. Captions and identification of subjects required. Buys one-time rights.
Columns/Departments: Travel (strong Jewish focus) and Entertainment (insightful interviews of well-known personalities about influence of their Jewish heritage). Buys 15-20 mss/year. Query with published clips and SASE. Length: 1,000-2,000 words. Pays $50-100.

PRESENT TENSE: The Magazine of World Jewish Affairs, 165 E. 56th St., New York NY 10022. (212)751-4000. Editor: Murray Polner. 95% freelance written. Prefers to work with published/established writers. For college-educated, Jewish-oriented audience interested in Jewish life throughout the world. Bimonthly magazine. Circ. 45,000. Buys all rights. Queries only, accompanied by SASE. Byline given. Buys 60 mss/year. Pays on publication. Publishes ms an average of 6 months after acceptance. Computer printout submissions acceptable. Reports in 2 months. Sample copy $4.50.
Nonfiction: Quality reportage of contemporary events (a la *Harper's, New Yorker*, etc.). Personal journalism, reportage, profiles and photo essays. Query. Length: 3,000 words maximum. Pays $150-250.
Tips: "Read our magazine."

‡RIGHT ON!, D.S. Magazines. 1086 Teaneck Rd., Teaneck NJ 07666. (201)833-1800. Editor: Cynthia Horner. 10% freelance written. A monthly black entertainment magazine for teenagers and young adults. Circ. 250,000. Pays on publication. Publishes ms an average of 3 months after acceptance. Byline given. Buys all rights. Submit seasonal/holiday material 4 months in advance. Reports in 1 month on queries.
Nonfiction: Interview/profile. "We only publish entertainment-oriented stories or celebrity interviews." Buys 15-20 mss/year. Query with or without published clips, or send ms. Length: 500-4,000 words. Pays $50-200. Sometimes pays the expenses of writers on assignment.
Photos: State availability of photos with submission. Reviews transparencies (8x10) b&w prints. Offers no additional payment for photos accepted with ms. Identification of subjects required. Buys one-time rights or all rights.

‡TURTLE QUARTERLY MAGAZINE, Native American Center for The Living Arts, Inc., 25 Rainbow Mall, Niagra Falls NY 14303. (716)284-2427. Editor: Tim Johnson. 90% freelance written. A quarterly magazine on Native American culture, arts and geography. "An understanding or willingness to understand Native American or indigenous cultural dynamics, art, history, and contemporary issues is important." Circ. 5,000. Pays on acceptance. Byline given. Buys first North American serial rights. Submit seasonal/holiday material 4 months in advance. Simultaneous submissions OK. Free sample copy; writer's guidelines for #10 SASE.
Nonfiction: Book excerpts (Native American subject matter), general interest (environmental natural world), historical/nostalgic (Native American history), interview/profile (Native American) and photo feature (Native or indigenous communities, geographies). Buys 6 mss/year. Query. Length: 1,500-4,000 words. Pays $30-100 for assigned articles. Pays $30-50 for unsolicited articles. Sometimes pays the expenses of writers on assignment.
Photos: State availability of photos with submission. Reviews contact sheets, transparencies (35mm) and prints (8x10). Offers $10-100 per photo. Captions and identification of subjects required. Buys one-time rights.
Columns/Departments: Environment (general impact-water/air/earth), 1,500-3,000 words; Anecdote (Native American perspective-contemporary viewpoint), 1,500-3,000; Book Reviews (Native American subject matter), 1,000-2,000 words. Buys 12 mss/year. Query. Pays $30-50.
Fiction: Ethnic, historical, humorous and science fiction. "All Native American themes." Buys 4 mss/year. Query. Length: 1,500-5,000 words. Pays $30-75.
Fillers: Anecdotes, facts, gags to be illustrated by cartoonist, newsbreaks and short humor. Buys 8/year. Length: 200-800. Pays $15-30.
Tips: "Simply call on the telephone. We're very friendly and open to any bright ideas."

THE UKRAINIAN WEEKLY, Ukrainian National Association, 30 Montgomery St., Jersey City NJ 07302. (201)434-0237. Editor: Roma Hadzewycz. 30% freelance written (mostly by a corps of regular contributors). "We are backlogged with submissions and prefer not to receive unsolicited submissions at this time." A weekly tabloid covering news and issues of concern to Ukrainian community. Circ. 7,000. Pays on publication. Publishes ms an average of 1-2 months after acceptance. Byline given. Buys first North American serial rights, second serial (reprint) rights or makes work-for-hire assignments. Submit seasonal/holiday material 1 month in advance. Reports in 1 month. Free sample copy.
Nonfiction: Book excerpts, essays, exposé, general interest, historical/nostalgic, interview/profile, opinion, personal experience, photo feature and news events. Special issues include Easter, Christmas, anniversary of Helsinki Accords, anniversary of Ukrainian Helsinki monitoring group. Buys 80 mss/year. Query with published clips. Length: 500-2,000 words. Pays $45-100 for assigned articles. Pays $25-100 for unsolicited articles. Sometimes pays the expenses of writers on assignment.
Photos: Send photos with submission. Reviews contact sheets, negatives and 3x5, 5x7 or 8x10 prints. Offers no additional payment for photos accepted with ms.
Columns/Departments: News & Views (commentary on news events), 500-1,000 words. Buys 10 mss/year. Query. Pays $25-50.
Tips: "Become acquainted with the Ukrainian community in the U.S. and Canada. The area of our publication most open to freelancers is community news—coverage of local events."

VISTA, Focus on Hispanic Americans, Suite 301, 2355 Salzedo St., Coral Gables FL 33134. (305)442-2462. Editor: Harry Caicedo. Managing Editor: Renato Pérez. 95% freelance written. Prefers to work with published/established writers. An English-language weekly directed at Hispanic Americans. It appears as a supplement to 27 newspapers across the country with a combined circulation of 1.2 million in cities with large Latin populations. Pays on publication. Publishes ms an average of 2 months after acceptance. Byline given. Offers 25% of original price kill fee. Buys first rights. Submit seasonal/holiday material 4 months in advance. Photocopied submissions OK. Computer printout submissions OK; prefers letter-quality. Reports in 1 week on queries; 2 weeks on mss. Sample copy and writer's guidelines for 11½x12½ SAE with 3 first class stamps.
Nonfiction: General interest, historical/nostalgic, inspirational, interview/profile, opinion and travel. No articles without a Hispanic American angle. Buys 90 mss/year. Query with published clips. Length: 100-2,000 words. Pays $50-500. Sometimes pays the expenses of writers on assignment.
Photos: State availability of photos with submission. Reviews contact sheets, negatives, transparencies and prints. Offers negotiable payment per photo. Identification of subjects required. Buys one-time rights.
Columns/Departments: Vistascopes (Hispanic people in the news), 100 words; On-The-Move (profile of a Hispanic notable for his/her accomplishments), 500-750 words; Voices (personal views on matters affecting Hispanic Americans), 500 words. Buys 48 mss/year. Query with published clips. Length: 100-750 words. Pays $50-200.
Fiction: Slice-of-life vignettes. Buys 2 mss/year. Send complete ms. Length: 1,000 words maximum. Pays 20¢ per word.
Tips: "Be aware of topics and personalities of interest to Hispanic readers. We need profiles of Hispanic Americans in unusual or untypical roles and jobs. Anticipate events; profiles should tell the reader what the subject will be doing at the time of publication. Keep topics upbeat and positive: no stories on drugs, crime. A light, breezy touch is needed for the profiles. Express your opinion in the Voices pages but be scrupulously impartial and accurate when writing articles of general interest. Don't be militant; *Vista* is *not* a soapbox. Keep standards high; *Vista* editors are a critical bunch."

Food and Drink

Magazines appealing to gourmets are classified here. Journals aimed at food processing, manufacturing and retailing are in the Trade section. Many magazines in General Interest and Women's categories also buy articles on these topics.

‡AMERICA ENTERTAINS, A Celebration of Family, Food and Good Friends, McCall's/Working Women group, 230 Park Ave., New York NY 10012. (212)551-9495. Editor: Colette Rossant. 30% freelance written. Quarterly magazine on entertaining, house and interior design. Estab. 1988. Publishes ms an average of 4 months after acceptance. Byline given. Pays 15% kill fee. Buys all rights. Submit seasonal/holiday material 4 months in advance. Query for electronic submissions. Computer printout submissions OK; prefers letter-quality.
Nonfiction: Marianne Melendez, articles editor. How-to, humor, new product, photo feature. No celebrity articles. Buys 10-20 mss/year. Query with published clips. Length: 500-1,000 words. Pays $500-1,500. Pays expenses of writers on assignment.
Photos: State availability of photos with submission. Reviews contact sheets. Offers no additional payment for photos accepted with ms. Captions, model releases and identification of subjects required. Buys one-time rights.

AMERICAN BREWER, The Micro-Brewer/Brew Pub Magazine, Box 713, Hayward CA 94541. (415)886-9823. Editor: Scott Schoepp. 100% freelance written. Quarterly magazine covering micro beer brewing. Circ. 2,000. Pays on acceptance. Byline given. Buys first North American serial rights. Submit seasonal/holiday material 3 months in advance. Query for electronic submissions. Computer printout submissions OK; prefers letter-quality. Reports in 2 weeks. Sample copy $3.
Nonfiction: Book excerpts, general interest, how-to, personal experience. Plans special issue on regional breweries and beers. Buys 10 mss/year. Query. Length: 1,000-2,000 words. Pays $50-100. Pays expenses of writers on assignment.
Photos: State availability of photos with submission. Reviews contact sheets. Offers no additional payment for photos accepted with ms. Captions are required. Buys one-time rights.

BON APPETIT, America's Food and Entertaining Magazine, Knapp Communications Corporation, 5900 Wilshire Blvd., Los Angeles CA 90036. (213)937-1025. Editor: William J. Garry. 70% freelance written. Works with small number of new/unpublished writers each year. Monthly magazine. "Our articles are written in the first person voice and are directed toward the active cook. Emphasis on recipes intended for use by the dedicated amateur cook." Circ. 1,300,000. Pays on acceptance. Publishes ms an average of 6 months after acceptance. Byline given. Buys first North American serial rights and all rights. Submit seasonal/holiday material 6 months in advance. Computer printout submissions acceptable; no dot-matrix. Reports in 1 month. Writer's guidelines for #10 SASE.

Nonfiction: Barbara Fairchild, executive editor. How-to (cooking) and travel. No articles which are not food related. Buys 120 mss/year. Query with published clips. Length: 1,000-3,000 words. Pays $600-2,000.

Photos: State availability of photos with submission. Reviews 35mm transparencies. Offers $175-550/photo. Captions, model releases and identification of subjects required. Buys one-time rights.

Columns/Departments: Laurie Glenn Buckle, column/department editor. Bon Voyage (travel articles featuring a specific city which cover, in a lively manner, interesting sights and landmarks and, especially, local restaurants and foods of note). Will need recipes from these restaurants. Buys 12 mss/year. Query. Length: 1,000-2,000 words. Pays $600-1,200.

CHOCOLATIER, The Haymarket Group/Ion International, #407, 45 W. 34th St., New York NY 10001. (212)239-0855. Editor-in-Chief: Barbara Albright. 33% freelance written. A bimonthly magazine "devoted to people who exemplify their passion for the good life by their love of fine quality desserts. While *Chocolatier* focuses on a national indulgence, feature articles cover desserts, spirits, and entertaining." Circ. 350,000. Pays on acceptance. Publishes ms an average of 6 months after acceptance. Byline given. Offers 25% kill fee. Buys first worldwide serial rights (publication elsewhere not earlier than 4 months after publication in *Chocolatier*). Submit seasonal/holiday material 8 months in advance. Simultaneous and photocopied submissions OK. Computer printout submissions acceptable; prefers letter-quality. Reports in 2 months. Writer's guidelines for #10 SASE.

Nonfiction: Interview/profile, new products, food/recipe and technical. Buys 20-30 mss/year. Query with published clips. Length: 500-2,500 words. Pays $100-800.

Photos: State availability of photos with submission. Identification of subjects required. Buys one-time rights.

Columns/Departments: Submit ideas for departments. Query with published clips. Length: 500-1,000 words. Pays variable rates.

COOK'S, The Magazine of Cooking in America, Pennington Publishing, 2710 North Ave., Bridgeport CT 06604. (203)366-4155. Editor: Mark Bittman. 50% freelance written. A magazine published 10 times/year covering food and cooking in America. "*Cook's* publishes lively informative articles that describe food and restaurant trends in the U.S. or that describe hands-on cooking techniques. Almost all of our articles include recipes." Circ. 235,000. Pays on acceptance. Publishes ms an average of 4-5 months after acceptance. Byline given. Offers 50% kill fee. Makes work for hire arrangements. Submit seasonal/holiday material 10 months in advance. Photocopied submissions OK. Computer printout submissions acceptable; prefers letter-quality. Reports in 2 months. Sample copy for 10x13 SAE with 6 first class stamps

Nonfiction: Food and cooking. No travel, personal experience or nostalgia pieces, history of food and cuisine, or recipes using prepared ingredients (e.g., canned soups, "instant" foods, mixes, etc.). Buys 60 mss/year. Query with clips and sample first page. Length: 1,000-2,000 words plus recipes. Pays $300-750. Paying of expenses, etc. determined on a contract basis.

KASHRUS MAGAZINE, The Bimonthly for the Kosher Consumer, Yeshiva Birkas Reuven, Box 96, Parkville Station, Brooklyn NY 11204. (718)998-3201. Editor: Rabbi Yosef Wikler. 25% freelance written. Prefers to work with published/established writers, and is eager to work with new/unpublished writers. Bimonthly magazine covering kosher food industry. Circ. 10,000. Pays on acceptance. Publishes ms an average of 2 months after acceptance. Byline given. Offers 50% kill fee. Buys first or second serial (reprint) rights. Submit seasonal/holiday material 2 months in advance. Simultaneous, photocopied and previously published submissions OK. Query for electronic submissions. Computer printout submissions OK; prefers letter-quality. Reports in 1 week on queries; 2 weeks on mss. Sample copy and writer's guidelines for $1.

Nonfiction: General interest, interview/profile, new product, personal experience, photo feature, religious, technical and travel. Special issues feature International Kosher Travel (October) and Passover (March). Buys 8-12 mss/year. Query with published clips. Length: 1,000-2,000 words. Pays $100-250 for assigned articles; pays up to $100 for unsolicited articles. Sometimes pays the expenses of writers on assignment.

Photos: State availability of photos with submission. Offers no additional payment for photos accepted with ms. Buys one-time rights.

Columns/Departments: Book Review (cooking books, food technology, kosher food), 250-500 words; People in the News (interviews with kosher personalities), 1,000-2,000 words; Regional Kosher Supervision (report on kosher supervision in a city or community), 1,000-3,000 words; Food Technology (new technology or current technology with accompanying pictures), 1,000-2,000 words. Buys 5 mss/year. Query with published clips. Pays $50-250.

Tips: "*Kashrus Magazine* will do more writing on general food technology, production, and merchandising as well as human interest travelogs and regional writing in 1989 than we have done in the past. Areas most open to freelancers are interviews, food technology, regional reporting and travel."

‡**NATURAL FOOD & FARMING**, Natural Food Associates, Highway 59, Box 210, Atlanta TX 75551. (214)796-3612. 80% freelance written. Eager to work with new/unpublished writers. Editorial Staff: Sherri Mafuz and Kendra Conely. A monthly magazine covering organic gardening and natural foods, preventive medicine, and vitamins and supplements. Circ. 50,000. Pays on acceptance. Publishes ms an average of 3 months after acceptance. Byline given sometimes. Not copyrighted. Buys first rights or second serial (reprint) rights. Submit seasonal/holiday material 2-3 months in advance. Simultaneous, photocopied and previously published submissions OK. Computer printout submissions acceptable. Free sample copy and writer's guidelines.
Nonfiction: Book excerpts; exposé; how-to (gardening, recipes and canning), new product; opinion; personal experience (organic gardening) and photo feature. Buys approximately 150 mss/year. Query with or without published clips, or send complete ms. Length: 1,000-3,000 words. Pays $50-100; sometimes pays in free advertising for company, books or products. Sometimes pays the expenses of writers on assignment.
Photos: State availability or send photos with submission.
Columns/Departments: Bugs, Weeds & Free Advice (organic gardening), 800 words; Food Talk (tips on cooking and recipes), 300-1,500 words; Of Consuming Interest (shorts on new developments in field), 800-1,500 words; and The Doctor Prescribes (questions and answers on preventive medicine), 800-1,500 words. Buys 96 mss/year. Send complete ms. Pays $50-100 (negotiable).
Fillers: Facts and short humor.
Tips: "Articles on subjects concerning gardening organically or cooking with natural foods are most open to freelancers."

THE WINE SPECTATOR, M. Shanken Communications, Inc., Opera Plaza, Suite 2040, 601 Van Ness Ave., San Francisco CA 94102. (415)673-2040. Executive Editor: Harvey Steiman. Managing Editor: Jim Gordon. 35-40% freelance written. Prefers to work with published/established writers. Twice monthly consumer news magazine covering wine. Circ. 70,000. Pays on publication. Publishes ms an average of 2 months after acceptance. Byline given. Buys first rights and makes work-for-hire assignments. Submit seasonal/holiday material 3 months in advance. Query for electronic submissions. Computer printout submissions acceptable "as long as they are legible." Reports in 3 weeks. Sample copy $1.75; free writer's guidelines.
Nonfiction: General interest (news about wine or wine events); humor; interview/profile (of wine, vintners, wineries); opinion; and photo feature. No "winery promotional pieces or articles by writers who lack sufficient knowledge to write below just surface data." Query. Length: 100-2,000 words average. Pays $50-300.
Photos: Send photos with ms. Pays $25 minimum for b&w contact sheets, negatives, transparencies, and 5x7 prints. Captions, model releases and identification of subjects required. Buys all rights.
Tips: "A solid knowledge of wine is a must. Query letters essential, detailing the story idea. New, refreshing ideas which have not been covered before stand a good chance of acceptance. *The Wine Spectator* is a consumer-oriented *news magazine* but we are interested in some trade stories; brevity is essential."

WINE TIDINGS, Kylix Media Inc., 5165 Sherbrooke St. W., 414, Montreal, Quebec H4A 1T6 Canada. (514)481-5892. Publisher: Judy Rochester. Editor: Barbara Leslie. 90% freelance written. Works with small number of new/unpublished writers each year. Magazine published 8 times/year primarily for men with incomes of more than $50,000. "Covers anything happening on the wine scene in Canada." Circ. 28,000. Pays on publication. Publishes ms an average of 3-4 months after acceptance. Byline given. Buys all rights. Submit seasonal/holiday material 3 months in advance. Computer printout submissions acceptable; prefers letter-quality. Reports in 1 month.
Nonfiction: General interest; historical; humor; interview/profile; new product (and developments in the Canadian and U.S. wine industries); opinion; personal experience; photo feature; and travel (to wine-producing countries). "All must pertain to wine or wine-related topics and should reflect author's basic knowledge of and interest in wine." Buys 20-30 mss/year. Send complete ms. Length: 500-2,000 words. Pays $35-300.
Photos: State availability of photos. Pays $20-100 for color prints; $10-25 for b&w prints. Identification of subjects required. Buys one-time rights.

WINE WORLD MAGAZINE, Suite 412, 6433 Topanga Blvd., Canoga Park CA 91303. Editor-Publisher: Dee Sindt. For the wine-loving public (adults of all ages) who wish to learn more about wine. Quarterly magazine; 48 pages. Buys first North American serial rights. Buys about 50 mss/year. Pays on publication. No photocopied submissions. Simultaneous submissions OK "if spelled out." Send $2 for sample copy and writer's guidelines.
Nonfiction: "Wine-oriented material written with an in-depth knowledge of the subject, designed to meet the needs of the novice and connoisseur alike—wine technology advancements, wine history, profiles of vintners

the world over. Educational articles only. No first-person accounts. Must be objective, informative reporting on economic trends, new technological developments in vinification, vine hybridizing, and vineyard care. New wineries and new marketing trends. We restrict our editorial content to wine, and wine-oriented material. Will accept restaurant articles—good wine lists. No more basic wine information. No articles from instant wine experts. Authors must be qualified in this highly technical field." Query. Length: 750-2,000 words. Pays $50-100.

‡ZYMURGY, Journal of the American Homebrewers Association, Box 287, Boulder CO 80306. (303)447-0816. Editor: Charles N. Papazian. Managing Editor: Kathy McClurg. 10% freelance written. Quarterly magazine on homebrewing. Circ. 8,000. Publishes ms an average of 6 months after acceptance. Buys first serial rights, first North American serial rights, and simultaneous rights. Submit seasonal/holiday material 5 months in advance. Simultaneous queries, and simultaneous, photocopied, and previously published submissions OK. Computer printout submissions acceptable; prefers letter-quality. Sample copy $4; free writer's guidelines.
Nonfiction: General interest (beer); historical (breweries); interview/profile (brewers); photo feature; and travel (breweries). Query. Length: 750-2,000 words. Pays $25-75.
Photos: Reviews b&w contact sheets and 8x10 b&w prints. Captions, model releases, and identification of subjects required.

—————— Games and Puzzles

These publications are written by and for game enthusiasts interested in both traditional games and word puzzles and newer role-playing adventure, computer and video games. Crossword fans also will find markets here. Additional home video game publications are listed in the Entertainment section. Other puzzle markets may be found in the Juvenile section.

CHESS LIFE, United States Chess Federation, 186 Route 9W, New Windsor NY 12550. (914)562-8350. Editor: Don Maddox. 15% freelance written. Works with a small number of new/unpublished writers each year. Monthly magazine covering the chess world. Circ. 60,000. Pays variable fee. Publishes ms an average of 5 months after acceptance. Byline given. Offers kill fee. Buys first or negotiable rights. Submit seasonal/holiday material 8 months in advance. Simultaneous queries, and simultaneous, photocopied and previously published submissions OK. Computer printout submissions acceptable. Reports in 1 month. Sample copy and writer's guidelines for 9x11 SAE.
Nonfiction: General interest, historical, interview/profile, and technical—all must have some relation to chess. No "stories about personal experiences with chess." Buys 30-40 mss/year. Query with samples "if new to publication." Length: 3,000 words maximum. Sometimes pays the expenses of writers on assignment.
Photos: Reviews b&w contact sheets and prints, and color prints and slides. Captions, model releases and identification of subjects required. Buys all or negotiable rights.
Fiction: "Chess-related, high quality." Buys 1-2 mss/year. Pays variable fee.
Tips: "Articles must be written from an informed point of view—not from view of the curious amateur. Most of our writers are specialized in that they have sound credentials as chessplayers. Freelancers in major population areas (except New York and Los Angeles, which we already have covered) who are interested in short personality profiles and perhaps news reporting have the best opportunities. We're looking for more personality pieces on chessplayers around the country; not just the stars, but local masters, talented youths, and dedicated volunteers. Freelancers interested in such pieces might let us know of their interest and their range. Could be we know of an interesting story in their territory that needs covering."

COMPUTER GAMING WORLD, The Journal of Computer Gaming, Golden Empire Publications, Inc., Suite C, 515 S. Harbor Blvd., Anaheim CA 92805. (714)535-4435. Editor: Russell Sipe. 75% freelance written. Works with a small number of new/unpublished writers each year. Monthly magazine covering computer games. "*CGW* is read by an adult audience looking for detailed reviews and information on strategy, adventure and action games." Circ. 25,000. Pays on publication. Publishes ms an average of 3 months after acceptance. Byline given. Buys first rights. Submit seasonal/holiday material 4 months in advance. Query for electronic submissions; electronic submissions preferred, but not required. Computer printout submissions OK. Reports in 1 month. Sample copy $3.50. Free writer's guidelines.
Nonfiction: Reviews, strategy tips, industry insights. Buys 60 mss/year. Query. Length: 500-3,500 words.

Pays $25-200. Sometimes pays the expenses of writers on assignment.

Photos: State availability of photos with submission. Reviews contact sheets. Offers $10-50 per photo. Buys one-time rights.

DRAGON® Magazine, Monthly Adventure Role-Playing Aid, TSR, Inc., Box 110, 201 Sheridan Springs Rd., Lake Geneva WI 53147. (414)248-8044. Editor: Roger E. Moore. 90% freelance written. Prefers to work with published/established writers, but eager to work with new/unpublished writers. Monthly magazine of fantasy and science-fiction role-playing games. "Most of our readers are intelligent, imaginative and under the age of 18." Circ. about 100,000. Pays on publication; pays on acceptance for fiction only. Publishes ms an average of 6 months after acceptance. Byline given. Offers kill fee. Buys first worldwide rights in English for fiction; all rights for most articles. Submit seasonal/holiday material 8 months in advance. Photocopied submissions OK. Computer printout submissions acceptable if clearly legible; prefers letter-quality. Reports in 1 month on queries; 2 months on submissions. Sample copy $4.50; writer's guidelines for #10 SAE and 1 first class stamp.

Nonfiction: Articles on the hobby of gaming and fantasy role-playing. No general articles on gaming hobby; "our article needs are *very* specialized. Writers should be experienced in gaming hobby and role-playing. No strong sexual overtones or graphic depictions of violence." Buys 120 mss/year. Query. Length: 1,000-8,000 words. Pays $75-600 for assigned articles; pays $50-400 for unsolicited articles. Sometimes pays the expenses of writers on assignment.

Fiction: Patrick Price, fiction editor. Adventure, fantasy and suspense. "No strong sexual overtones or graphic depictions of violence." Buys 8-12 mss/year. Send complete ms. Length: 2,000-8,000 words. Pays $150-650.

Tips: "*Dragon Magazine* and the related publications of Dragon Publishing are *not* periodicals that the 'average reader' appreciates or understands. A writer must *be* a reader and must share the serious interest in gaming our readers possess."

GIANT CROSSWORDS, Scrambl-Gram, Inc., Puzzle Buffs International, 1772 State Road, Cuyahoga Falls OH 44223. (216)923-2397. Editors: C.J. Elum and C.R. Elum. Managing Editor: Carol L. Elum. 40% freelance written. Eager to work with new/unpublished writers. Crossword puzzle and word game magazines issued quarterly. Pays on acceptance. Publishes ms an average of 10 days after acceptance. No byline given. Buys all rights. Simultaneous queries OK. Reports in several weeks. "We furnish constructors' kits, master grids and clue sheets and offer a 'how-to-make-crosswords' book for $17.50 postpaid."

Nonfiction: Crosswords only. Query. Pays according to size of puzzle and/or clues.

Tips: "We are expanding our syndication of original crosswords and our publishing schedule to include new titles and extra issues of current puzzle books."

General Interest

General interest magazines need writers who can appeal to a varied audience—teens and senior citizens, wealthy readers and the unemployed. Some general interest publications do appeal to a specific audience, such as *Millionaire* or *Lefthander Magazine*. Each magazine has a personality that suits its audience—one that a writer should study before sending material to an editor. Some markets for general interest material are in these Consumer categories: Contemporary Culture, Ethnic/Minority, In-Flight, Men's, Regional and Women's.

AMERICAN ATHEIST, American Atheist Press, Box 2117, Austin TX 78768. (512)458-1244. Editor: R. Murray-O'Hair. Managing Editor: Jon Garth Murray. 20-40% freelance written. Monthly magazine covering atheism and topics related to it and separation of State and Church. Circ. 50,000. Publishes ms an average of 3-6 months after acceptance. Byline given. Buys one-time and all rights. Submit seasonal/holiday material 3 months in advance. Simultaneous queries and simultaneous, photocopied and previously published submissions OK. Query for electronic submissions. Computer printout submissions acceptable; prefers letter-quality. Reports in 3 weeks on queries; 6 weeks on mss. Publishes ms an average of 4 months after acceptance. Sample copy and writer's guidelines for 9x12 SAE.

Nonfiction: Book excerpts, expose, general interest, historical, how-to, humor, interview/profile, opinion, personal experience and photo feature, but only as related to State/Church or atheism. "We receive a great many Bible criticism articles—and publish very few. We would advise writers not to send in such works. We are also interested in fiction with an atheistic slant." Buys 40 mss/year. Send complete ms. Length: 400-10,000 words. Pays in free subscription or 15 copies for first-time authors. Repeat authors paid $15 per 1,000 words. Sometimes pays the expenses of writers on assignment.

Columns/Departments: Atheism, Church/State separation and humor. Send complete ms. Length: 400-10,000 words.

Poetry: Avant-garde, free verse, haiku, light verse and traditional. Submit unlimited poems. Length: open. Pays $10 per thousand words maximum.

Fillers: Jokes, short humor and newsbreaks. Length: 800 words maximum, only as related to State/Church separation or atheism.

Tips: "We are primarily interested in subjects which bear directly on atheism or issues of interest and importance to atheists. This includes articles on the atheist lifestyle, on problems that confront atheists, the history of atheism, personal experiences of atheists, separation of state and church, theopolitics and critiques of atheism in general and of particular religions. We are starting to have issues which focus on lifestyle topics relevant to atheism. We would like to receive more articles on current events and lifestyle issues. Critiques of *particular* religions would also be likely candidates for acceptance."

THE AMERICAN LEGION MAGAZINE, Box 1055, Indianapolis IN 46206. (317)635-8411. Editor: Michael D. La Bonne. Monthly. 95% freelance written. Prefers to work with published/established writers, eager to work with new/unpublished writers, and works with a small number of new/unpublished writers each year. Circ. 2,650,000. Buys first North American serial rights. Computer printout submissions acceptable; prefers letter-quality. Reports on submissions "promptly." Pays on acceptance. Publishes ms an average of 6 months after acceptance. Byline given. Sample copy for 9x12 SAE and 5 first class stamps. Writer's guidelines for #10 SASE.

Nonfiction: Query first, but will consider unsolicited mss. "Prefer an outline query. Relate your article's thesis or purpose, tell why you are qualified to write it, the approach you will take and any authorities you intend to interview. War-remembrance pieces of a personal nature (vs. historic in perspective) should be in ms form." Uses current world affairs, topics of contemporary interest, little-known happenings in American history, 20th century war-remembrance pieces, and 750-word commentaries on contemporary problems and points of view. No personality profiles, or regional topics. Buys 75 mss/year. Length: 1,800 words maximum. Pays $250-1,500. Pays phone expenses of writers on assignment.

Photos: On assignment.

Fillers: Short, tasteful jokes and humorous anecdotes. Pays $15.

Tips: Query should include author's qualifications for writing a technical or complex article. Also include thesis, length, outline and conclusion. "Send a thorough query. Submit material that is suitable for us, showing that you have read several issues. Attach a few clips of previously published material. *The American Legion Magazine* considers itself '*the* magazine for a strong America.' Any query that reflects this theme (which includes strong economy, educational system, moral fiber, infrastructure and armed forces) will be given priority. Humor is welcomed—must touch on universal themes applicable to most people."

‡THE ATLANTIC MONTHLY, 8 Arlington St., Boston MA 02116. (617)536-9500. Editor: William Whitworth. Managing Editor: Cullen Murphy. Monthly magazine of arts and public affairs. Circ. 470,000. Pays on acceptance. Byline given. Buys first North American serial rights. Simultaneous submissions OK. Reporting time varies.

Nonfiction: Book excerpts, essays, general interest, humor, personal experience, religious, travel. Query with or without published clips or send complete ms. Length: 1,000-6,000 words. Payment varies. Sometimes pays expenses of writers on assignmnt.

Fiction: C. Michael Curtis, fiction editor. Buys 15-18 mss/year. Send complete ms. Length: 2,000-6,000 words approximately. Pays $2,500 minimum.

Poetry: Peter Davison, poetry editor. Buys 40-60 poems/year.

A BETTER LIFE FOR YOU, The National Research Bureau, Inc., 424 N. 3rd St., Burlington IA 52601. (319)752-5415. Editor: Rhonda Wilson. Editorial Supervisor: Doris J. Ruschill. 75% freelance written. Works with a small number of new/unpublished writers each year, eager to work with new/unpublished writers. Quarterly magazine. Pays on publication. Publishes ms an average of 1 year after acceptance. Buys all rights. Submit seasonal/holiday material 7 months in advance of issue date. Previously published submissions OK. Computer printout submissions acceptable; no dot-matrix. Reports in 3 weeks. Writer's guidelines for #10 SASE.

Nonfiction: General interest (steps to better health, on-the-job attitudes); and how-to (perform better on the job, do home repair jobs, and keep up maintenance on a car). Buys 10-12 mss/year. Query or send outline. Length: 400-600 words. Pays 4¢/word.

Tips: "Writers have a better chance of breaking in at our publication with short articles."

CAPPER'S, Stauffer Communications, Inc., 616 Jefferson St., Topeka KS 66607. (913)295-1108. Editor: Nancy Peavler. 25% freelance written. Works with a small number of new/unpublished writers each year. Emphasizes home and family for readers who live in small towns and on farms. Biweekly tabloid. Circ. 385,000. Pays for poetry on acceptance; articles on publication. Publishes ms an average of 3 months after acceptance. Buys first serial rights only. Submit seasonal/holiday material 2 months in advance. Computer printout submissions OK; prefers letter-quality. Reports in 1 month; 8 months for serialized novels. Sample copy 75¢; writer's guidelines for #10 SASE.

Nonfiction: Historical (local museums, etc.), inspirational, nostalgia, travel (local slants) and people stories (accomplishments, collections, etc.). Buys 50 mss/year. Submit complete ms. Length: 700 words maximum. Pays $1/inch.

Photos: Purchased with accompanying ms. Submit prints. Pays $5-10 for 8x10 or 5x7 b&w glossy prints. Total purchase price for ms includes payment for photos. Limited market for color photos (35mm color slides); pays $20-25 each.

Columns/Departments: Heart of the Home (homemakers' letters, recipes, hints), and Hometown Heartbeat (descriptive). Submit complete ms. Length: 300 words maximum. Pays $1-10.

Fiction: "We have begun to buy some fiction pieces—longer than short stories, shorter than novels." Adventure and romance mss. No explicit sex, violence or profanity. Buys 4-5 mss/year. Query. Pays $75-250.

Poetry: Free verse, haiku, light verse, traditional, nature and inspiration. "The poems that appear in *Capper's* are not too difficult to read. They're easy to grasp. We're looking for everyday events, and down-to-earth themes." Buys 4-5/issue. Limit submissions to batches of 5-6. Length: 4-16 lines. Pays $3-6.

Tips: "Study a few issues of our publication. Most rejections are for material that is too long, unsuitable or out of character for our paper (too sexy, too much profanity, etc.). On occasion, we must cut material to fit column space."

THE CHRISTIAN SCIENCE MONITOR, 1 Norway St., Boston MA 02115. (617)450-2303. Contact: Submissions. International newspaper issued daily except Saturdays, Sundays and holidays in North America; weekly international edition. Special issues: travel, winter vacation and international travel, summer vacation, autumn vacation, and others. March and September: fashion. Circ. 200,000. Buys all newspaper rights for 3 months following publication. Buys limited number of mss, "top quality only." Publishes original (exclusive) material only. Pays on acceptance or publication, "depending on department." Submit seasonal material 2 months in advance. Reports in 1 month. Submit complete original ms or letter of inquiry. Writer's guidelines available.

Nonfiction: David Holmstrom, feature editor. In-depth features and essays. Please query by mail before sending mss. "Style should be bright but not cute, concise but thoroughly researched. Try to humanize news or feature writing so reader identifies with it. Avoid sensationalism, crime and disaster. Accent constructive, solution-oriented treatment of subjects. Home Forum page buys essays of 400-900 words. Pays $70-140. Education, arts, real estate, travel, living, garden, books, sports, food, furnishings, and science pages will consider articles not usually more than 800 words appropriate to respective subjects." Pays $75-100.

Poetry: Traditional, blank and free verse. Seeks non-religious poetry of high quality and of all lengths up to 75 lines. Pays $25 average.

Tips: "We prefer neatly typed originals. No handwritten copy. Enclosing an SAE and postage with ms is a must."

‡COMMENTARY, 165 E. 56th St., New York NY 10022. (212)751-4000. Editor: Norman Podhoretz. Monthly magazine. Circ. 50,000. Byline given. "All of our material is done freelance, though much of it is commissioned." Pays on publication. Query, or submit complete ms. Reports in 1 month.

Nonfiction: Brenda Brown, editor. Thoughtful essays on political, social and cultural themes; general, as well as with special Jewish content. Length: 3,000 to 7,000 words. Pays approximately $100/printed page.

Fiction: Marion Magid, editor. Uses some mainstream fiction. Length: varies. Pays $100/printed page.

EQUILIBRIUM, Everyone's Entertainment, Eagle Publishing Productions, Box 162, Golden CO 80402. Editor: Gary A. Eagle. "Featuring version of opposites. Themes range practically from anything to everything—from nonfiction to fiction, comedy to drama, short stories to features, serious to light, conservative to liberal, idealogy to scientific and from sports to intellectual." 30% freelance written. Pays on acceptance. Publishes ms an average of 1 year after acceptance. "We prefer to hold ms on file until we publish it." Byline given. Offers 50% kill fee; varies for ghosts. Buys first rights. Computer printout submissions acceptable; no dot-matrix. Simultaneous queries, and simultaneous, photocopied, and previously published submissions OK. Reports in 3 months on queries; 6 months on mss. Sample copy for $3 with 9x12 SAE and 4 first class stamps; writer's guidelines for business size SAE and 1 first class stamp.

Nonfiction: How-to (physics, psychology, political science, medical, evolution, economics, philosophical, religion, actual UFO occurrences with photo); photo feature (any photo to show balance of something, with article or without); and technical. Think of opposites and equal values. Inquire about special issues. Modern events are accepted. Buys 20 mss/year. Query. Length: 50-1,000 words; more than 1,000 words if article series. Pays $50-500.

Photos: State availability or send photos with query or ms. Pays $20-40 for 1" b&w and color slides, and b&w and color prints.

Columns/Departments: Especially wants editorials, children's material, love stories. Length: 250 words. Pays $50-100.

Poetry: Light verse and traditional. "None will be accepted if not dealing with the balance of the universe." Submit maximum 10 poems. Length: 5-20 lines. Pays $10-50.

Fillers: Clippings, jokes, gags, short humor, cartoons. Buys 20/year. Length: 5-20 words. Pays $10-50.

Tips: "We encourage new writers. We read everything that comes in. Although our program has been geared toward the philosophical, we are receptive to a variety of subjects and our needs are flexible. Controversial material is acceptable. The most frequent mistakes made by writers in completing an article for us are that they fail to illustrate *or* demonstrate the opposites and equals. There are many types of opposites, such as reverses, equals, balances, etc. They do not have to be scientific. Explain in your query why readers will enjoy your article. Ideas for future articles are also welcome. The shorter the article the better. Play-science welcome. Send in your own thought of today or philosophical quote; it must be original."

EQUINOX: THE MAGAZINE OF CANADIAN DISCOVERY, Equinox Publishing, 7 Queen Victoria Dr., Camden East, Ontario K0K 1J0 Canada. (613)378-6661. Editorial Director: Barry Estabrook. Editor: Bart Robinson. Bimonthly magazine. "We publish in-depth profiles of people, places and wildlife to show readers the real stories behind subjects of general interest in the fields of science and geography." Circ. 166,000. Pays on acceptance. Byline given. Offers 50% kill fee. Buys first North American serial rights only. Submit seasonal queries 1 year in advance. Computer printout submissions acceptable; prefers letter-quality. Reports in 6 weeks. Sample copy $5; free writer's guidelines.

Nonfiction: Book excerpts (occasionally), geography, science and art. No travel articles. Buys 40 mss/year. Query. "Our biggest need is for science stories. We do not touch unsolicited feature manuscripts." Length: 5,000-10,000 words. Pays $1,500-negotiated.

Photos: Send photos with ms. Reviews color transparencies—must be of professional quality; no prints or negatives. Captions and identification of subjects required.

Columns/Departments: Nexus (current science that isn't covered by daily media) and Habitat (Canadian environmental stories not covered by daily media). Buys 80 mss/year. Query with clips of published work. Length: 200-300 words. Pays $200.

Tips: "Submit Habitat and Nexus ideas to us—the 'only' route to a feature is through these departments if writers are untried."

FORD TIMES, 1 Illinois Center, Suite 1700, 111 E. Wacker Dr., Chicago IL 60601. Editor: John Fink. 85% freelance written. Works with a small number of new/unpublished writers each year. "General-interest magazine designed to attract all ages." Monthly. Circ. 1,200,000. Pays on acceptance. Publishes ms an average of 8-9 months after acceptance. Buys first rights only. Offers kill fee. Byline given. Submit seasonal material 6 months in advance. Computer printout submissions acceptable; prefers letter-quality. Reports in 1 month. Sample copy and writer's guidelines for 9x12 SAE with 5 first class stamps.

Nonfiction: "Almost anything relating to contemporary American life that is upbeat and positive. Topics include lifestyle trends, outdoor activities and sports, profiles, food, narrow-scope destination stories, and the arts. We are especially interested in subjects that appeal to readers in the 18-35 age group. We strive to be colorful, lively and, above all, interesting. We try to avoid subjects that have appeared in other publications or in our own." Buys 100 mss/year. Length: 1,700 words maximum. Query required unless previous contributor. Pays $550 minimum for full-length articles. Usually pays the expenses of writers on assignment.

Photos: "Speculative submission of high-quality color transparencies and b&w photos with mss is welcomed. We need bright, graphically strong photos showing people. We need releases for people whose identity is readily apparent in photos."

‡**FOUR SEASONS HOTELS MAGAZINE**, Mega Publishing, Suite 106, 55 Doncaster Ave., Thornhill, Ontario L3T 1L7 Canada. (416)881-6560. Editor: Michael Lombard. Managing Editor: Leslie May. 100% freelance written. "We are in in-house hotel publication, not for sale. The magazine is in each hotel room in each Four Season Hotel in both Canada and the United States. The magazine is geared directly at these guests." Circ. 50,000. Pays on publication. Publishes ms an average of 1-3 months after acceptance. Byline given. Buys all rights. Simultaneous submissions OK. Computer printout submissions OK; prefers letters-quality. Reports in 2 months. Free sample copy and writer's guidelines.

Nonfiction: General interest, historical/hostalgic, interview/profile, new product, opinioin, photo feature, travel, lifestyle, sports and leisure, fashion, art entertainment. "We are a lifestyle publication geared to the affluent travelers of the Four Seasons hotels chain." Buys 30 mss/year. Query. Length: 1,000-2,500 words. Pays $500-1,800.

Photos: State availability of photos with submission; send photos with submission when article is assigned. Offers no additional payment for photos accepted with ms. Captions required.

Departments: Business, Comment, Art & Antiques, Profile, Health, all 700 words with 1 photo. Buys 30 mss/year. Query. Pays $200-300.

Tips: "The writers that write for us are experts in their chosen field. We select based on their in-depth knowledge. When selecting a writer for features, all photos must accompany the article and are the writer's responsiblity to obtain. Please submit a query letter."

FRIENDLY EXCHANGE, Meredith Publishing Services, Locust at 17th, Des Moines IA 50336. Publication Office: (515)284-2008. Editor (702)786-7419. Editor: Adele Malott. 80% freelance written. Works with a small number of new/unpublished writers each year. Quarterly magazine exploring travel and leisure topics of interest to active western families. For policyholders of Farmers Insurance Group of Companies. "These are traditional families (median adult age 39) who live in the area bounded by Ohio on the east and the Pacific Ocean on the west." Circ. 4.2 million. Pays on acceptance. Publishes ms an average of 5 months after acceptance. Offers 25% kill fee. Buys all rights. Submit seasonal/holiday material 1 year in advance. Simultaneous queries and photocopied queries OK. Query for electronic submissions. Computer printout submissions acceptable; prefers letter-quality. Reports in 2 months. Sample copy for 9x12 SAE and 5 first class stamps; writer's guidelines for #10 SAE and 1 first class stamp.

Nonfiction: Travel and leisure activities such as gardening, crafts, pets, photography, etc.—topics of interest to the western family. "Travel and leisure topics can be addressed from many different perspectives, including health and safety, consumerism, heritage and education. Articles offer a service to readers and encourage them to take some positive action such as taking a trip. Style is colorful, warm, and inviting, making liberal use of anecdotes and quotes. The only first-person articles used are those assigned; all others in third person. Domestic locations in the western half of the continent are emphasized." Buys 8 mss/issue. Query. Length: 600-1,800 words. Pays $300-800/article, plus agreed-upon expenses.

Photos: Peggy Fisher, art director. Pays $150-250 for 35mm color transparencies; and $50 for b&w prints. Cover photo payment negotiable. Pays on publication.

Columns/Departments: All columns and departments rely on reader-generated materials; none used from professional writers.

Tips: "We are now concentrating exclusively on the travel and leisure hours of our readers. Study articles: 'Alaska's Weekend Wonders' (February 1988), 'Boats on Parade' (November 1987), 'Dollarwise Ski Trips' (November 1987) and 'The High Cost of Drinkers and Driving' (February 1988). Do not use destination approach in travel pieces—instead, for example, tell us about the people, activities, or events that make the location special. Concentrate on what families can do together."

FUTURIFIC MAGAZINE, 280 Madison Ave., New York NY 10016. (212)684-4913. Editor-in-Chief: Balint Szent-Miklosy. 50-75% freelance written. Monthly. "Futurific, Inc. is an independent, nonprofit organization set up in 1976 to study the future, and *Futurific Magazine* is its monthly report on findings. We report on what is coming in all areas of life from international affairs to the arts and sciences. Readership cuts across all income levels and includes leadership, government, corporate and religious circles." Circ. 10,000. Pays on publication. Publishes ms an average of 1 month after acceptance. Byline given in most cases. Buys one-time rights and will negotiate reprints. Computer printout submissions OK; prefers letter-quality. Reports within 1 month. Sample copy for $2 and 9x12 SAE.

Nonfiction: All subjects must deal with the future: book, movie and theatre reviews, general interest, how to forecast the future—seriously, humor, interview/profile, new product, photo feature and technical. No historical, opinion or gloom and doom. Send complete ms. Length: 5,000 words maximum. Payment negotiable.

Photos: Send photos with ms. Reviews b&w prints. Pay negotiable. Identification of subjects required.

Columns/Departments: Medical breakthroughs, new products, inventions, book, movie and theatre reviews, etc. "Anything that is new or about to be new." Send complete ms. Length: 5,000 words maximum.

Poetry: Avant-garde, free verse, haiku, light verse and traditional. "Must deal with the future. No gloom and doom or sad poetry." Buys 6/year. Submit unlimited number of poems. Length: open. Pays in copies.

Fillers: Clippings, jokes, gags, anecdotes, short humor, and newsbreaks. "Must deal with the future." Length: open. Pays in copies.

Tips: "It's not who you are; it's what you have to say that counts with us. We seek to maintain a light-hearted, professional look at forecasting. Be upbeat and show a loving expectation for the marvels of human achievement. Take any subject or concern you find in regular news magazines and extrapolate as to what the future will be. Use imagination. Get involved in the excitement of the international developments, social interaction. Write the solution—not the problem."

GLOBE, 5401 N.W. Broken Sound Blvd., Boca Raton FL 33431. Stories Editor: Donald McLachlan. "For everyone in the family. *Globe* readers are the same people you meet on the street and in supermarket lines, average hard-working Americans who prefer easily digested tabloid news." Weekly national tabloid newspaper. Circ. 2,000,000. Byline given.

Nonfiction and Fillers: "We want features on well-known personalities, offbeat people, places, events and activities. No personal essays. Current issue is best guide. Stories are best that don't grow stale quickly. No padding. Remember—we are serving a family audience. All material must be in good taste. If it's been written up in a major newspaper or magazine, we already know about it." Buys informational, how-to, interview, profile, inspirational, humor, historical, exposé, photo, and spot news. Length: 1,000 words maximum; average 500-800 words. Pays $250-500(special rates for "blockbuster" material).

Photos: Ron Haines, photo editor. Photos are purchased with or without ms, and on assignment. Captions are required. Pays $50 minimum for 8x10 b&w glossy prints. "Competitive payment on exclusives."

Tips: "*Globe* is constantly looking for human interest subject material from throughout the United States, and much of the best comes from America's smaller cities and villages, not necessarily from the larger urban areas. Therefore, we are likely to be more responsive to an article from a new writer than many other publications. This, of course, is equally true of photographs. A major mistake of new writers is that they have failed to determine the type and style of our content, and in the ever-changing tabloid field this is a most important consideration. It is also wise to keep in mind that what is of interest to you or to the people in your area may not be of equal interest to a national readership. Determine the limits of interest first. And, importantly, the material you send us must be such that it won't be 'stale' by the time it reaches the readers."

GOOD READING, for Everyone, Henrichs Publications, Inc., Box 40, Sunshine Park, Litchfield IL 62056. (217)324-3425. Editor: Peggy Kuethe. Managing Editor: Garth Henrichs. 80% freelance written. Works with a small number of new/unpublished writers, and is eager to work with new/unpublished writers each year. A monthly general interest magazine with articles and stories based on a wide range of current or factual subjects. Circ. 7,500. Pays on acceptance. Publishes ms an average of 6 months after acceptance. Byline given. Buys first North American serial rights. Submit seasonal/holiday material 5 months in advance. Photocopied submissions OK. Computer printout submissions acceptable; prefers letter-quality. Reports in 2 months. Sample copy for 50¢, 6x9 SAE and 2 first class stamps; writer's guidelines for #10 SAE with 1 first class stamp.

Nonfiction: General interest, historical/nostalgic, humor, photo feature and travel. Also stories about annual festivals, new products, people who make a difference. "No material that deals with the sordid side of life, nothing about alcohol, smoking, drugs, gambling. Nothing that deals with the cost of travel, or that is too technical." Send complete ms. Length: 100-1,000 words. Pays $20-100 for unsolicited articles.

Photos: Send photos with submission. Reviews contact sheets and 3x5, 5x7, or 8x10 prints. Offers no additional payment for photos accepted with ms. Identification of subjects required. Buys one-time rights.

Columns/Departments: Youth Today (directed at young readers), 100 words maximum. Buys 6-9 mss/year. Send complete ms. Pays $10-50.

Poetry: Light verse. No limit to number of poems submitted at one time. Length: 4-16 lines. Pays in copies.

Fillers: Anecdotes, facts and short humor. Length: 50-150 words. Pays $10-30.

Tips: "The tone of *Good Reading* is wholesome; the articles are short. Keep writing informal but grammatically correct. *Good Reading* is general interest and directed at the entire family—so we accept only material that would be of interest to nearly every age group."

HARPER'S MAGAZINE, 666 Broadway, 11th Floor, New York NY 10012. (212)614-6500. Editor: Lewis H. Lapham. 40% freelance written. For well-educated, socially concerned, widely read men and women who value ideas and good writing. Monthly. Circ. 186,000. Rights purchased vary with author and material. Pays negotiable kill fee. Pays on acceptance. Computer printout submissions acceptable if double-spaced. Reports in 2 weeks. Publishes an average of 3 months after acceptance. Sample copy $2.50.

Nonfiction: "For writers working with agents or who will query first only, our requirements are: public affairs, literary, international and local reporting, and humor." No interviews; no profiles. Complete mss and queries must include SASEs. No unsolicited poems will be accepted. Publishes one major report per issue. Length: 4,000-6,000 words. Publishes one major essay per issue. Length: 4,000-6,000 words. "These should be construed as topical essays on all manner of subjects (politics, the arts, crime, business, etc.) to which the author can bring the force of passionately informed statement." Publishes one short story per month. Generally pays 50¢-$1/word.

Photos: Deborah Rust, art director. Occasionally purchased with mss; others by assignment. Pays $50-500.

IDEALS MAGAZINE, Box 140300, Ideals Publishing, Nelson Place at Elm Hill Pike, Nashville TN 37214. (615)885-8270. Editor: Peggy Schaefer. 95% freelance written. A magazine published eight times a year. "Our readers are generally women over 50. The magazine is mainly light poetry and short articles with a nostalgic theme. The eight issues are seasonally oriented, as well as being thematic." Pays on publication. Publishes ms an average of 1 year after acceptance. Byline given. Buys one-time North American serial and subsidiary rights. Submit seasonal/holiday material 8 months in advance. Simultaneous, photocopied, and previously published submissions OK. Computer printout submissions acceptable; prefers letter-quality. Reports in 4-6 months. Writer's guidelines for SAE with 1 first class stamp.

Nonfiction: Essays, historical/nostalgic, how-to (crafts), humor, inspirational and personal experience. "No down beat articles or social concerns." Buys 20 mss/year. Query with or without published clips, or send complete ms. Length: 600-1,000 words. Pays 10¢/word.

Photos: Send SASE for guidelines. Reviews transparencies and b&w prints. Offers no additional payment for photos accepted with ms. Captions, model release, and identification of subjects required. Buys one-time rights. Payment varies.

Fiction: Slice-of-life vignettes. Buys 10 mss/year. Query. Length: 600-1,000 words. Pays 10¢/word.
Poetry: Light verse and traditional. "No erotica or depressing poetry." Buys 250 poems/year. Submit maximum 15 poems. Pays $10.
Tips: "Poetry is the area of our publication most open to freelancers. It must be oriented around a season or theme. The basic subject of *Ideals* is nostalgia, and poetry must be optimistic (how hard work builds character—not how bad the Depression was)."

KNOWLEDGE, Official Publication of the World Olympiads of Knowledge, Knowledge, Inc., 3863 Southwest Loop 820, S 100, Ft. Worth TX 76133-2076. (817)292-4272. Editor: Dr. O.A. Battista. Managing Editor: N.L. Matous. 90% freelance written. For lay and professional audiences of all occupations. Quarterly magazine; 60 pages. Circ. 3,000. Pays on publication. Publishes ms an average of 6 months after acceptance. Buys all rights. "We will reassign rights to a writer after a given period." Byline given. Submit seasonal/holiday material 6 months in advance. Computer printout submissions acceptable; prefers letter-quality. Reports in 1 month. Sample copy $5; writer's guidelines for #10 SASE.
Nonfiction: Informational—original new knowledge that will prove mentally or physically beneficial to all readers. Buys 30 unsolicited mss/year. Query. Length: 1,500-2,000 words maximum. Pays $100 minimum. Sometimes pays the expenses of writers on assignment.
Columns/Departments: Journal section uses maverick and speculative ideas that other magazines will not publish and reference. Payment is made, on publication, at the following minimum rates: *Why Don't They*, $50; *Salutes*, $25; *New Vignettes*, $25; *Quotes To Ponder*, $10; and *Facts*, $5.
Tips: "The editors of *Knowledge* welcome submissions from contributors. Manuscripts and art material will be carefully considered but received *only* with the unequivocal understanding that the magazine will not be responsible for loss or injury. Material from a published source should have the publication's name, date, and page number. Submissions cannot be acknowledged and will be returned only when accompanied by a SAE having adequate postage."

LEFTHANDER MAGAZINE,Lefthander International, Box 8249, Topeka KS 66608. (913)234-2177. Managing Editor: Suzan Ireland. 80% freelance written. Eager to work with new/unpublished writers. Bimonthly. "Our readers are lefthanded people of all ages and interests in 50 U.S. states and 10 foreign countries. The one thing they have in common is an interest in lefthandedness." Circ. 26,000. Pays on publication. Publishes ms an average of 4 months after acceptance. Byline usually given. Offers 25% kill fee. Rights negotiable. Simultaneous queries OK. Computer printout submissions acceptable; prefers letter-quality. Reports on queries in 4-6 weeks. Sample copy for 8½x11 SAE and $2. Writer's guidelines for #10 SAE and 1 first class stamp.
Nonfiction: Interviews with famous lefthanders; features about lefthanders with interesting talents and occupations; how-to features (sports, crafts, hobbies for lefties); research on handedness and brain dominance; exposé on discrimination against lefthanders in the work world; features on occupations and careers attracting lefties; education features relating to ambidextrous right brain teaching methods. Length: Buys 50-60 mss/year. 750-1,000 words for features. Buys 6 personal experience shorts/year. Query with SASE. Length 750 words. Pays $25. Pays expenses of writer on assignment.
Photos: State availability of photos for features. Pays $10-15 for b&w, good contrast b&w glossies. Rights negotiable.
Fiction: Lefty Jr., 4-page insert published 3 times/year. Children's short stories dealing with lefthandedness. Length: 500-750 words. Pays $35-50.
Fillers: Trivia, cartoons, word games for children's insert, interesting and unusual facts. Send on speculation. Buys 25-50/year. Pays $5-20.
Tips: "All material must have a lefthanded hook. We prefer quick, practical, self-help and self-awareness types of editorial content; keep it brief, light, and of general interest. More of our space is devoted to shorter pieces. A good short piece gives us enough evidence of writer's style, which we like to have before assigning full-length features. In addition we are looking for short fiction pieces for 10-16 year olds for a children's supplement."

‡**MEET PEOPLE, Meet People & Their True Life Stories**, 38 Wheeler, Box 520, Watertown CT 06795. (203)274-9744. Editor: Wigand Garbrecht. 100% freelance written. Quarterly magazine. Estab. 1987. Circ. 25,000. Publishes ms an average of 3 months after acceptance. Byline sometimes given. Buys first North American serial rights or second serial (reprint) rights. Submit seasonal/holiday material 5 months in advance. Query for electronic submissions. Computer printout submissions OK. Sample copy for 9x12 SAE with 5 first class stamps. Writers guidelines for #10 SASE.
Nonfiction: Length: 450-2,000 words. Pays $80-200 for assigned articles; $50-100 for unsolicited articles. Sometimes pays expenses of writers on assignment.
Photos: State availability of photos with submission or send photos with submission. Reviews prints. Buys one-time rights.

‡MILLIONAIRE, Lifestyles of the Working Rich, Douglas Lambert, Publisher. #701, 105 S. Narcissus Ave., West Palm Beach FL 33401. (305)655-1977. Editor: Ms. Pat Broderick. 90% freelance written. A monthly magazine on millionaires (success stories, top-of-the line products, exclusive accomodations, etc.). "We cover the best, rather than publicize the worst. We focus on the positive side of success, not scandal." Estab. 1987. Circ. 110,000. Pays on acceptance. Publishes ms an average of 3 months after acceptance. Byline given. Offers 30% kill fee "under certain circumstances." Buys first rights, and second serial (reprint) rights. Submit seasonal/holiday material 3 months in advance. Simultaneous and photocopied submissions OK. Computer printout submissions OK; no dot-matrix. Sample copy for 8½x11 SAE with $2.50 postage; free writer's guidelines.

Nonfiction: How-to (success techniques), humor, interview/profile, new product (only upscale), personal experience (if relevant to market), photo feature (travel), travel, business, arts, real estate, hotels/restaurants, health/fitness. Plans an annual issue on billionaires. No general interest, tourist type travel stories, money-saving tips, or subjects that would not appeal to an average age of 40. Buys 250 mss/year. Query with published clips. Length: 2,000-2,500 (travel only). Pays $700-1,000. Sometimes pays expenses of writers on assignment.

Photos: State availability of photos with submission. Reviews transparencies. Payment negotiable. Captions and identification of subjects required. Rights negotiable.

Tips: "Send written queries that are brief and specific. Writers should include samples of their published work. Profiles, features, health/fitness, finance, arts, travel, hotels/restaurants are most open to freelancers."

NATIONAL EXAMINER, Globe Communications, Inc., 5401 N.W. Broken Sound Blvd., Boca Raton FL 33431. (305)997-7733. Editor: Bill Burt. Senior Associate Editor: Cliff Linedecker. 15% freelance written. Works with a small number of new/unpublished writers each year. "We are a weekly supermarket tabloid that covers celebrity news, human interest features, true crime, medical breakthroughs, astrology, UFOs and the supernatural. Nonfiction stories should be well researched and documented, concise and fun to read." Circ. 1,000,000. Pays on publication. Publishes ms an average of 1 month after acceptance. Byline given. Buys first North American serial rights. Submit seasonal/holiday material 2 months in advance. Photocopied submissions OK. Computer printout submissions acceptable; prefers letter-quality.

Nonfiction: Historical/nostalgic; interview/profile (of celebrities); photo feature (color preferred); and the supernatural. No fillers or political material. Buys 200 mss/year. Query with published clips. Length: 250-750 words. Pays $25-300.

Photos: Send photos with submission. Reviews contact sheets, 35mm transparencies, and 8x10 prints. Offers $35-100/photo. Captions and identification of subjects required. Buys one-time rights.

Tips: "Send us a well crafted, carefully documented story. The areas of our publication most open to freelancers are celebrity interviews and color photo spreads featuring celebrities or general subjects."

NATIONAL GEOGRAPHIC MAGAZINE, 17th and M Sts. NW, Washington DC 20036. Editor: Wilbur E. Garrett. Approximately 50% freelance written. Prefers to work with published/established writers, and works with a small number of new/unpublished writers each year. For members of the National Geographic Society. Monthly. Circ. more than 10,000,000. Query for electronic submissions. Computer printout submissions OK; prefers letter-quality.

Nonfiction: *National Geographic* publishes first-person, general interest, heavy illustrated articles on science, natural history, exploration and geographical regions. Almost half of the articles are staff-written. Of the freelance writers assigned, most are experts in their fields; the remainder are established professionals. Fewer than one percent of unsolicited queries result in assignments. Query (500 words) by letter, not by phone, to Senior Assistant Editor (Contract Writers). Do not send manuscripts. Before querying, study recent issues and check a *Geographic Index* at a library since the magazine seldom returns to regions or subjects covered within the past ten years. Pays expenses of writers on assignment.

Photos: Photographers should query in care of the Illustration Division.

THE NEW YORKER, 25 W. 43rd St., New York NY 10036. Editor: Robert Gottlieb. Weekly. Circ. over 500,000. Reports in 2 months. Pays on acceptance. Computer printout submissions acceptable; prefers letter-quality.

Nonfiction, Fiction, Poetry, and Fillers: Long fact pieces are usually staff-written. So is "Talk of the Town," although freelance submissions are considered. Pays good rates. Uses fiction, both serious and light. About 90% of the fillers come from contributors with or without taglines (extra pay if the tagline is used).

‡OUT WEST, America's On the Road Newspaper, Box 19894, Sacramento CA 95819. (916)457-4006. Editor: Chuck Woodbury. 10% freelance written. Quarterly tabloid for general audience. Estab. 1988. Circ. 3,000. Pays on acceptance and publication (negotiated). Byline given. Buys one-time rights. Submit seasonal/holiday material 6 months in advance. Simultaneous, photocopied and previously published submissions OK. Computer printout submissions OK; prefers letter-quality. Reports in 6 weeks. Sample copy $1.50; writer's guidelines for #10 SASE.

Nonfiction: Essays, general interest, historical, humor, interview/profile, photo feature, travel. No travel destinations reached primarily by air, nothing over 1,000 words, travel to expensive hotels, locations in large urban areas, and no foreign travel except perhaps western Canada. Buys 50 mss/year. Query with or without published clips, or send complete ms. Length: 150-1,000 words. Pays $20-100.
Photos: State availability of photos with submission. Reviews 5x7 or 8x10 b&w prints only. Pays $6-15. Captions required. Buys one-time rights.
Columns/Departments: Ghost Towns, Small Town Media, Wildlife, Road of the Month, Eating on the Road, all 500-700 words. Query or send complete ms. Length: 500-700 words. Pays. $20-50. "I'm looking for a few good columnists who can become regular in the paper."
Fillers: Anecdotes, facts, newsbreaks, short humor. Buys 100/year. Length: $25-150. Pays $2-12.
Tips: "It's critically important to read the publication before submitting work."

PARADE, Parade Publications, Inc., 750 3rd Ave., New York NY 10017. (212)573-7000. Editor: Walter Anderson. Weekly magazine for a general interest audience. 90% freelance written. Circ. 33 million. Pays on acceptance. Publishes ms an average of 3 months after acceptance. Kill fee varies in amount. Buys first North American serial rights. Computer printout submissions acceptable. Reports in 5 weeks on queries. Writer's guidelines for 4x9 SAE and 1 first class stamp.
Nonfiction: General interest (on health, trends, social issues, business or anything of interest to a broad general audience); interview/profile (of news figures, celebrities and people of national significance); and "provocative topical pieces of news value." Spot news events are not accepted, as *Parade* has a 6-week lead time. No fiction, fashion, travel, poetry, quizzes, or fillers. Address three-paragraph queries to Articles Editor. Length: 800-1,500 words. Pays $1,000 minimum. Pays expenses of writers on assignment.
Tips: "Send a well-researched, well-written query targeted to our market. Please, no phone queries. We're interested in well-written exclusive manuscripts on topics of news interest. The most frequent mistake made by writers in completing an article for us is not adhering to the suggestions made by the editor when the article was assigned."

PEOPLE IN ACTION, Meridian Publishing Company, Inc., Box 10010, Ogden UT 84409. (801)394-9446. Editor: Marjorie Rice. 65% freelance written. A monthly inhouse magazine featuring personality profiles. Circ. 70,000. Pays on acceptance. Publishes ms an average of 8 months after acceptance. Byline given. Buys first rights, second serial (reprint) rights and non-exclusive reprint rights. Simultaneous, photocopied and previously published submissions OK. Computer printout submissions acceptable. Reports in 6 weeks. Publishes ms an average of 6 months after acceptance. Sample copy for $1 and 9x12 SAE; writer's guidelines for SAE and 1 first class stamp. All requests for sample copies and guidelines and queries should be addressed Attn: Editorial Assistant.
Nonfiction: General interest personality profiles. Cover stories focus on nationally noted individuals in the fine arts, literature, entertainment, communications, business, sports, education, health, science and technology. The lives of those featured exemplify positive values; overcoming obstacles, helping others, advancing culture, creating solutions. Buys 40 mss/year. Query. Length: 1,000-1,400 words. Pays 15¢/word for first rights plus non-exclusive reprint rights. Payment for second rights is negotiable.
Photos: State availability of photos or send photos with query. Pays $35/inside photo, $50/cover photo; uses glossy professional-quality color prints and transparencies (slides to 8x10). Captions, model releases and identification of subjects required.
Columns/Departments: Regular column features: a 700-word profile of a gourmet chef, first-class restaurant manager, food or nutrition expert, or a celebrity who is also a top-notch cook; a recipe and 1-2 good color transparencies are essential. Buys 10 mss/year. Query. Pays 15¢/word.
Tips: "The key is a well-written query letter that: 1) demonstrates that the subject of the article has national appeal; 2) shows that a profile of the person interviewed will have a clear, focused theme; 3) outlines the availability (from the writer, photographer or PR source) of top-quality color photos; and 4) gives evidence that the writer/photographer is a professional, even if a beginner."

‡**READ ME**, 1118 Hoyt Ave., Everett WA 98201. Editor: Ron Fleshman. 95% freelance written. Quarterly general interest tabloid. Estab. 1988. Circ. 1000. Pays on publication. Publishes ms an average of 5 months after acceptance. Byline given. Buys first North American serial rights, one-time rights or second serial (reprint) rights. Submit seasonal/holiday material 6 months in advance. Photocopied and previously published submissions (if identified) OK. Query for electronic submissions. Computer printout submissions OK; prefers letter-quality. Reports in 3 months. Sample copy $1.50; writer's guidelines for #10 SASE.
Nonfiction: Book excerpts, essays, expose, general interest, historical/nostalgic, humor, opinion, personal experience, travel. Buys 30 mss/year. Query with or without published clips, or send complete ms. Length: 500-2,000. Pays $20 maximum.
Columns/Departments: Outreach (first-person statements from forgotten members of society or those who work with or serve them), 1,000 words maximum; Contention (strongly expressed personal opinion on controversial issues), 1,000 words maximum; Travel (single interesting aspect of a distant place), 750 words maxi-

mum, all columns edited by Elaine Leslie; Time Out (crossword puzzles, word games, mini-mysteries, logic problems), edited by Ellie Brauer; Humor (mild to brutally sardonic, essays, short-short stories), 1,000 words maximum, edited by Phyllis Damish. Buys 80 mss/year. Send complete ms. Pays $1-20.

Fiction: Linda McMichael and Kay Nelson, editors. Adventure, confession, ethnic, fantasy, historical, horror, humorous, mainstream, mystery, novel excerpts, romance, science fiction, slice-of-life vignettes, suspense, western. Buys 28 mss/year. Send complete ms. Length: 100-2,500 words. Pays $1-20.

Poetry: Robert R. Ward, editor. Free verse, traditional. No obscenity, no 'moon, spoon, june' rhymes, no academic poetry. Buys 30 poems/year. Submit maximum of 6 poems at one time. Length: 50 lines maximum. Pays $1-5.

Fillers: Ellie Brauer, fillers editor. Anecdotes, facts, short humor. Buys 40/year. Length: 5-50 words. Pays $1-5.

Tips: "Speak to our targeted demographic, not literary critics or unity professors. Reward the reader with new insight, unusual slant, fresh perspective. Material may reassure or outrage, teach or tickle. Perimeter testing is encouraged —but treat must be accessible to a non-academic readership. Avoid subjects quickly dated. Regarding style: less is more."

READER'S DIGEST, Pleasantville NY 10570. Monthly. Circ. 16.5 million. Publishes general interest articles "as varied as all human experience." The *Digest* does not read or return unsolicited mss. Address proposals and tearsheets of published articles to the editors. Considers only previously published articles; pays $900/*Digest* page for World Digest rights. (Usually split 50/50 between original publisher and writer.) Tearsheets of submitted article must include name of original publisher and date of publication.

Columns/Departments: "Original contributions become the property of *Reader's Digest* upon acceptance and payment. Life-in-these-United States contributions must be true, unpublished stories from one's own experience, revealing adult human nature, and providing appealing or humorous sidelights on the American scene. Length: 300 words maximum. Pays $300 on publication. True and unpublished stories are also solicited for Humor in Uniform, Campus Comedy and All in a Day's Work. Length: 300 words maximum. Pays $300 on publication. Towards More Picturesque Speech—the first contributor of each item used in this department is paid $40 for original material, $35 for reprints. Contributions should be dated, and the source must be given. For items used in Laughter, the Best Medicine, Personal Glimpses, Quotable Quotes, and elsewhere in the magazine payment is as follows; to the *first* contributor of each from a published source, $35. For original material, $20 per *Digest* two-column line, with a minimum payment of $50. Send complete anecdotes to excerpt editor."

READERS REVIEW, The National Research Bureau, Inc., 424 N. 3rd St., Burlington IA 52601. Editor: Rhonda Wilson. Editorial Supervisor: Doris J. Ruschill. 75% freelance written. Works with a small number of new/unpublished writers each year, and is eager to work with new/unpublished writers. Quarterly magazine. Pays on publication. Publishes ms an average of 1 year after acceptance. Buys all rights. Previously published submissions OK. Computer printout submissions acceptable; prefers letter-quality. Submit seasonal/holiday material 7 months in advance of issue date. Reports in 3 weeks. Writer's guidelines for #10 SASE.

Nonfiction: General interest (steps to better health, attitudes on the job); how-to (perform better on the job, do home repairs, car maintenance); and travel. Buys 10-12 mss/year. Query with outline or submit complete ms. Length: 400-600 words. Pays 4¢/word.

Tips: "Writers have a better chance of breaking in at our publication with short articles."

‡REAL PEOPLE, The Magazine of Celebrities and Interesting People, Main Street Publishing Co., Inc., Suite 900, 120 E. 56th St., New York NY 10022. (212)371-4932. Editor: Alex Polner. 90% freelance written. Bimonthly magazine of profiles, human interest and self-help articles. Circ. 50,000. Pays on publication. Byline given. Pays 33% kill fee. Buys first North American serial rights, first rights, or one-time rights. Submit seasonal/holiday material 5 months in advance. Photocopied submissions OK. Computer printout submissions OK; prefers letter-quality. Reports in 1 month. Sample copy for $3 with 6x9 SAE and 65¢ postage. Writer's guidelines for #10 SASE.

Nonfiction: Book excerpts, how-to, interview/profile, photos essays. Buys 100 mss/year. Query with published clips. Length: 1,000-1,500 words. Pays $150-200 for assigned articles; $75-150 for unsolicited articles.

Photos: State availability of photos with submissions. Reviews 5x7 prints. Offers no additional payment for photos accepted with ms. Captions, model releases and identification of subjects required. Buys one-time rights.

SELECTED READING, The National Research Bureau, Inc., 424 N. 3rd St., Burlington IA 52601. Editor: Rhonda Wilson. Editorial Supervisor: Doris J. Ruschill. 75% freelance written. Eager to work with new/unpublished writers, works with a small number of new/unpublished writers each year. Quarterly magazine. Pays on publication. Publishes ms an average of 1 year after acceptance. Buys all rights. Previously published submissions OK. Computer printout submissions acceptable; prefers letter-quality. Submit seasonal/holiday ma-

terial 6-7 months in advance of issue date. Reports in 3 weeks. Writer's guidelines for #10 SASE.
Nonfiction: General interest (economics, health, safety, working relationships); how-to; and travel (out-of-the way places). No material on car repair. Buys 10-12 mss/year. Query. A short outline or synopsis is best. Lists of titles are no help. Length: 400-600 words. Pays 4¢/word.
Tips: "Writers have a better chance of breaking in at our publication with short articles."

SMITHSONIAN MAGAZINE, 900 Jefferson Drive, Washington DC 20560. Articles Editor: Marlane A. Liddell. 90% freelance written. Prefers to work with published/established writers. For "associate members of the Smithsonian Institution; 85% with college education." Monthly. Circ. 3 million. Buys first North American serial rights. Payment for each article to be negotiated depending on our needs and the article's length and excellence. Pays on acceptance. Publishes ms an average of 4-6 months after acceptance. Submit seasonal material 3 months in advance. Computer printout submissions acceptable; no dot-matrix. Reports in 6 weeks. Writer's guidelines for #10 SASE.
Nonfiction: "Our mandate from the Smithsonian Institution says we are to be interested in the same things which now interest or should interest the Institution: cultural and fine arts, history, natural sciences, hard sciences, etc." Query. Length: 750-4,500 words. Payment negotiable. Pays expenses of writers on assignment.
Photos: Purchased with or without ms and on assignment. Captions required. Pays $400/full color page.

THE STAR, 660 White Plains Rd., Tarrytown NY 10591. (914)332-5000. Editor: Richard Kaplan. Executive Editor: Bill Ridley. 40% freelance written. Prefers to work with published/established writers. "For every family; all the family—kids, teenagers, young parents and grandparents." Weekly magazine; 56 pages. Circ. 3.5 million. Publishes ms an average of 1 month after acceptance. Buys first North American serial rights, occasional second serial book rights. Query for electronic submissions. Computer printout submissions acceptable; prefers letter-quality. Pays expenses of writers on assignment.
Nonfiction: Exposé (government waste, consumer, education, anything affecting family); general interest (human interest, consumerism, informational, family and women's interest); how-to (psychological, practical on all subjects affecting readers); interview (celebrity or human interest); new product; photo feature; profile (celebrity or national figure); health; medical; and diet. No first-person articles. Query or submit complete ms. Length: 500-1,000 words. Pays $50-1,500.
Photos: Alistair Duncan, photo editor. State availability of photos with query or ms. Pays $25-100 for 8x10 b&w glossy prints, contact sheets or negatives; $150-1,000 for 35mm color transparencies. Captions required. Buys one-time or all rights.

SUNSHINE MAGAZINE, Henry F. Henrichs Publications, Box 40, Sunshine Park, Litchfield IL 62056. (217)324-3425. Editor: Peggy Kuethe. Managing Editor: Garth Henrichs. 95% freelance written. Eager to work with new/unpublished writers. A monthly magazine. "Primarily human interest and inspirational in its appeal, *Sunshine Magazine* provides worthwhile reading for all the family." Circ. 70,000. Pays on acceptance. Publishes ms an average of 6 months after acceptance. Byline given. Buys first North American serial rights or one-time rights. Submit seasonal/holiday material 6 months in advance. Photocopied submissions OK. Computer printout submissions acceptable; prefers letter-quality. Reports in 2 months. Sample copy for 50¢, 6x9 SAE and 2 first class stamps; writer's guidelines for #10 SAE with 1 first class stamp.
Nonfiction: Essays, historical/nostalgic, inspirational and personal experience. "No material dealing with specifically religious matters or that is depressing in nature (divorce, drug abuse, alcohol abuse, death, violence, child abuse)." Send complete ms. Length: 200-1,250. Pays $10-100.
Columns/Departments: Extraordinary Experience (personal experience), 500 words; Let's Reminisce (reminiscent, nostalgia), 500 words; Guidelines (inspirational), 200 words; and Favorite Meditation (inspirational essay), 200 words. Buys 85-90 mss/year. Send complete ms. Pays $15-50.
Fiction: Inspirational and human interest. Buys 75-80 mss/year. Send complete ms.
Poetry: Light verse and traditional. No avant-garde, free verse or haiku. Buys 12-15 poems/year. No limit to the number of poems submitted at one time. Length: 4-16 lines. Pays $15-80, or may pay in copies.
Fillers: Anecdotes and short humor. Buys 1-5/year. Length: 50-150 words. Pays $10-20.
Tips: "Make a note that *Sunshine* is not religious—but it is inspirational. After reading a sample copy, you should know that we do not accept material that is very different from what we've been doing for over 60 years. Don't send a manuscript that is longer than specified or that is 'different' from anything else we've published—that's not what we're looking for. The whole magazine is written primarily by freelancers. We are just as eager to publish new writers as they are to get published."

TOWN AND COUNTRY, 1700 Broadway, New York NY 10019. (212)903-5000. Managing Editor: Jean Barkhorn. For upper-income Americans. Monthly. Pays on acceptance. Not a large market for freelancers. Always query first.
Nonfiction: Frank Zachary, department editor. "We're always trying to find ideas that can be developed into good articles that will make appealing cover lines." Wants provocative and controversial pieces. Length: 1,500-2,000 words. Pay varies. Also buys shorter pieces for which pay varies.

WHAT MAKES PEOPLE SUCCESSFUL, The National Research Bureau, Inc., 424 N. 3rd St., Burlington IA 52601. Editor: Rhonda Wilson. Editorial Supervisor: Doris J. Ruschill. 75% freelance written. Eager to work with new/unpublished writers, and works with a small number of new/unpublished writers each year. For industrial workers of all ages. Published quarterly. Pays on publication. Publishes ms an average of 1 year after acceptance. Buys all rights. Previously published submissions OK. Computer printout submissions acceptable; prefers letter-quality. Submit seasonal/holiday material 8 months in advance of issue date. Reports in 3 weeks. Writer's guidelines for #10 SASE.
Nonfiction: How-to (be successful); general interest (personality, employee morale, guides to successful living, biographies of successful persons, etc.); experience; and opinion. No material on health. Buys 3-4 mss/issue. Query with outline. Length: 400-600 words. Pays 4¢/word.
Tips: Short articles and fillers (rather than major features) have a better chance of acceptance because all articles are short.

‡THE WORLD & I, A Chronicle of Our Changing Era, The Washington Times Corp. 2850 New York Avenue, N.E. Washington D.C. 20002. (202)635-4000. Editor: Morton A. Kaplan. Executive Editor: Michael Marshall. 90% freelance written. A monthly magazine of general interest. Circ. 30,000. Pays on acceptance. Publishes ms an average of 4 months after acceptance. Byline given. Offers 20% kill fee. Buys first North American serial rights, second serial (reprint) rights, all rights and makes work-for-hire assignments. Submit seasonal/holiday material 5 months in advance. Query for electronic submissions. Computer printout submissions OK; no dot matrix. Reports in 6 weeks on queries; 8 weeks on mss. Writer's guidelines for #10 SASE.
Nonfiction: Book excerpts and reviews, essays (academic), general interest, historical/nostalgic, humor (arts reviews), inspirational (medicine, folk medicines), interview/profile (current news issues), opinion, (news analysis), personal experience, photo feature, religious (culture), technical (popular science), travel, food and sports. No "National Enquirer"-type articles. Buys 900 mss/year. Query with published clips. Length: 1,000-35,000 words. Pays 10¢-20¢ word. Sometimes pays expenses of writers on assignment.
Photos: State availability of photos with submission. Reviews contact sheets, transparencies and prints. Payment negotiable. Model releases and identification of subjects required. Buys one-time rights.
Columns/Departments: 8 Sections: Current Issues, Natural Science, The Arts, Life, Book World, Culture, Currents in Modern Thought, Life and Ideals. Query. Length: 1,000-35,000 words. Pays 10¢-20¢/word.
Fiction: Query the arts and culture editors. Ethnic, historical (folk tales, folk wisdom). No erotica, confession, UFO stories. Buys 1-5 mss/year. Query. Length: 500-1,200 words. Pays 10¢/word max.
Poetry: Query arts editor. Avant-garde, free verse, haiku, light verse and traditional. Buys 6-12 poems/year. Submit maximum 5 poems. Pays $25-50.
Tips: "Send a short query letter with a viable story idea for specific section, and/or subsection (Science, Book, Life, Art, Culture, Modern Thought, Current Issues.)"

WORLD'S FAIR, World's Fair, Inc., Box 339, Corte Madera CA 94925. (415)924-6035. Editor: Alfred Heller. 75% freelance written. Quarterly magazine covering fairs and expositions, (past, present and future). "The people, politics and pageantry of fairs and expositions, in historical perspective; lively, good-humored articles of fact and analysis." Circ. 5,000. Pays on acceptance. Publishes ms an average of 3 months after acceptance. Byline given. Offers 50% kill fee. Buys all rights. Photocopied submissions OK. Computer printout submissions OK; prefers letter-quality. Reports in 3 weeks. Free writer's guidelines.
Nonfiction: Essays, historical/nostalgic, humor, interview/profile, personal experience and photo feature. Buys 10-12 mss/year. Query with published clips. Length: 750-3,000 words. Pays $50-400. Sometimes pays expenses of writers on assignment.
Photos: State availability of photos or line drawings with submission. Reviews contact sheets and 8x10 b&w prints. Identification of subjects required. Buys one-time rights.
Tips: Looking for "correspondents in cities planning major expositions, in the U.S. and abroad."

Health and Fitness

The magazines listed here specialize in covering health and fitness topics for a general audience. Magazines covering health topics from a medical perspective are listed in the Medical category of Trade. Also see the Sports/Miscellaneous section where publications dealing with health and particular sports may be listed. Many general interest publications are also potential markets for health or fitness articles.

ACCENT ON LIVING, Box 700, Bloomington IL 61702. (309)378-2961. Editor: Betty Garee. 75% freelance written. Eager to work with new/unpublished writers. For physically disabled persons and rehabilitation professionals. Quarterly magazine. Circ. 18,000. Buys first rights and second (reprint) rights to material originally published elsewhere. Byline usually given. Buys 50-60 unsolicited mss/year. Pays on publication. Publishes ms an average of 6 months after acceptance. Photocopied submissions OK. Computer printout submissions acceptable; prefers letter-quality. Reports in 2 weeks. Sample copy with writer's guidelines for $2, 5x7 SAE and four first class stamps; writer's guidelines alone for #10 SAE and 1 first class stamp.

Nonfiction: Articles about new devices that would make a disabled person with limited physical mobility more independent; should include description, availability, and photos. Medical breakthroughs for disabled people. Intelligent discussion articles on acceptance of physically disabled persons in normal living situations; topics may be architectural barriers, housing, transportation, educational or job opportunities, organizations, or other areas. How-to articles concerning everyday living, giving specific, helpful information so the reader can carry out the idea himself/herself. News articles about active disabled persons or groups. Good strong interviews. Vacations, accessible places to go, sports, organizations, humorous incidents, self improvement, and sexual or personal adjustment—all related to physically handicapped persons. No religious-type articles. "We are looking for upbeat material." Query. Length: 250-1,000 words. Pays 10¢/word for article as it appears in magazine (after editing and/or condensing by staff).

Photos: Pays $5 minimum for b&w photos purchased with accompanying captions. Amount will depend on quality of photos and subject matter. Pays $50 and up for four-color slides used on cover. "We need good-quality transparencies or slides with submissions—or b&w photos."

Tips: "Ask a friend who is disabled to read your article before sending it to *Accent*. Make sure that he/she understands your major points and the sequence or procedure."

AIMplus, Arthritis Information Magazine, The Haymarket Group, Inc., Suite 500, 45 West 34th St., New York NY 10001. (212)239-0855. Editor: Tim Moriarty. Associate Editor: Gayle Turim. 75% freelance written. Prefers to work with published/established writers, and works with a small number of new/unpublished writers each year. Magazine published 10 times/year covering health and lifestyle topics for people (mostly 50+) with arthritis. Writers should keep in mind that many of our readers have a sedentary lifestyle. Circ. 200,000. Pays 2 months after acceptance. Byline given. Offers 25% kill fee. Buys first North American serial rights. Submit seasonal/holiday material 5 months in advance. Computer printout submissions OK; no dot-matrix. Reports in 6 weeks on queries. Sample copy $2.50 with 9x12 SAE and 3 first class stamps; writer's guidelines for #10 SAE and 1 first class stamp.

Nonfiction: Health (especially relating to arthritis), book excerpts, general interest, historical/nostalgic, how-to, humor, interview/profile, new product and personal experience. No travel (our travel editor covers this), no clippings, no articles slanted to those 50 and under. Query with published clips. Length: 800-1,500 words. Pays 30-40¢/word. Usually pays expenses of writers on assignment.

Photos: State availability of photos with submission. Identification of subjects required. Buys one-time rights.

Fillers: Anecdotes, facts and short humor. Length: 50-300 words. Pays $25-60.

Tips: "Send a detailed, well-written query that demonstrates familiarity with *AIMplus*. Avoid the obvious. Queries that convey a sense of humor stand out; we need upbeat material."

AMERICAN HEALTH MAGAZINE, Fitness of Body and Mind, American Health Partners, 80 Fifth Ave., New York NY 10011. (212)242-2460. Editor-in-Chief: T. George Harris. Editor: Joel Gurin. 70% freelance written. Prefers to work with published/established writers. 10 issues/year. General interest magazine that covers both scientific and "lifestyle" aspects of health, including laboratory research, clinical advances, fitness, holistic healing and nutrition. Circ. 1,000,000. Pays on acceptance. Publishes ms an average of 4-6 months after acceptance. Byline given. Offers 25% kill fee. Buys first North American serial rights, "and certain other rights that are negotiable, in some cases." Computer printout submissions acceptable. Reports in 1-2 months. Sample copy for $3; writer's guidelines for #10 SAE and 1 first class stamp.

Nonfiction: Mail to Editorial/Features. Book excerpts; how-to; humor; interview/profile (health or fitness related); photo feature (any solid feature or news item relating to health); and technical. No mechanical research reports, quick weight-loss plans or unproven treatments. "Stories should be written clearly, without jargon. Information should be new, authoritative and helpful to the readers." Buys 60-70 mss/year (plus many more news items). Query with 2 clips of published work. "Absolutely *no* complete mss." Length: 1,000-3,000 words. Pays $600-2,000 upon acceptance. Pays the expenses of writers on assignment.

Photos: Mail to Editorial/Photo. Send photos with query. Pays $100-600 for 35mm transparencies and 8x10 prints "depending on use." Captions and identification of subjects required. Buys one-time rights.

Columns/Departments: Mail to Editorial/News. Medical News, Fitness Report, Nutrition Report, Mind/Body News, Family Report, Family Pet, Tooth Report, and Skin, Scent and Hair. Other news sections included from time to time. Buys about 300 mss/year. Query with clips of published work. Prefers 2 pages-500 words. Pays $125-375 upon acceptance.

Tips: "*American Health* has no full-time staff writers; we have chosen to rely on outside contributors for most of our articles. The magazine needs good ideas, and good articles, from professional journalists, health educators, researchers and clinicians. Queries should be short (no longer than a page), snappy and to the point. Think short; think news. Give us a good angle and a paragraph of background. Queries only. We do not take responsibility for materials not accompanied by SASE."

‡**BACK PAIN MAGAZINE**, Back Pain Magazine, Inc., 204, 3275 W. Hillsboro Blvd., Deerfield Beach FL 33442. (305)360-0700. Editor: Jack A. Levine. 90% freelance written. Monthly magazine on back pain. Estab. 1987. Circ. 100,000. Pays on publication. Byline given. Submit seasonal/holiday material 2 months in advance. Simultaneous, photocopied and previously published submissions OK. Computer printout submissions OK; prefers letter quality. Sample copy for 9x12 SAE and 6 first class stamps.
Nonfiction: Book excerpts, essays, expose, general interest, historical/nostalgic, how-to, humor, inspirational, interview/profile, new product, opinion, personal experience, technical. Send complete ms or phone the editor. Length: 800-8,000 words. Pays $100. Sometimes pays expenses of writers on assignment.
Photos: Send photos with submission. Reviews contact sheets, negatives. Will negotiate fee. Model release required. Rights negotiates.

BESTWAYS MAGAZINE, Box 2028, Carson City NV 89702. Editor/Publisher: Barbara Bassett. 20% freelance written. Prefers to work with published/established writers, and works with a small number of new/unpublished writers each year. Emphasizes health, diet and nutrition. Monthly magazine. Circ. 300,000. Pays on publication. Publishes ms an average of 8 months after acceptance. Byline given. Buys all rights. Submit seasonal/holiday material 6 months in advance. Computer printout submissions acceptable; prefers letter-quality. Reports in 6 weeks. Sample copy for 8½x11 SASE and $1.95. Writer's guidelines for SASE.
Nonfiction: General interest (cooking, nutrition, physical fitness, preventive medicine, supplements, natural foods); how-to (diet and exercise); and technical (vitamins, minerals, weight control and nutrition). "No direct or implied endorsements of refined flours, grains or sugar, tobacco, alcohol, caffeine, drugs or patent medicines." Buys 4 mss/issue. Query. Length: 1,500 words. Pays 15¢/word. Sometimes pays the expenses of writers on assignment.
Photos: State availability of photos with query. Pays $7.50 for 4x5 b&w glossy prints; $15 for 2¼x2¼ color transparencies. Captions preferred. Buys all rights. Model releases required.
Tips: "We're changing our focus to include more food and cooking articles."

BETTER HEALTH, Better Health Press, 1485 Chapel St., New Haven CT 06511. (203)789-3974. Editor: Deborah Turton. Managing Editor: Kelly Anthony. 50% freelance written. Prefers to work with published/established writers; works with small number of new/unpublished writers each year. A bimonthly magazine covering health related topics. Circ. 120,000. Pays on publication. Byline given. Offers $50 kill fee. Buys first and second serial rights. Submit seasonal/holiday material 2 months in advance. Simultaneous, photocopied and previously published submissions OK. Query for electronic submissions. Computer printout submissions OK; no dot-matrix. Sample copy $1.25.
Nonfiction: Medical general interest, humor, inspirational and personal experience. Buys 20 mss/year. Query with published clips. Length: 800-3,000 words. Pays $100-300.
Photos: State availability of photos with submission. Reviews contact sheets. Offers no additional payment for photos accepted with ms.

‡**BETTER NUTRITION**, Communication Channels, Inc., 6255 Barfield Rd., Atlanta GA 30328. (404)256-9800. Editor: Patti Seikus. 20% freelance written. Monthly magazine on nutrition, supplements and fitness. "*Better Nutrition* is geared toward customers of health food stores and for those who prefer natural foods and supplements. Topics covered include general health, diet, nutrition and fitness. We like to run articles on the benefits of supplements." Circ. 540,000. Pays on publication. Publishes ms an average of 3 months after acceptance. Byline given. Buys all rights. Submit seasonal/holiday material 3 months in advance. Photocopied submissions OK. Query for electronic submissions. Computer printout submissions OK; prefers letter-quality. Reports in 1 month. Sample copy $1 with 10x13 SAE and 2 first class stamps. Writer's guidelines for #10 SAE with 1 first class stamp.
Nonfiction: Expose, interview/profile. No personal experience, articles endorsing a specific product or articles endorsing any particular diet. Buys 12 mss/year. Query with published clips. Length: 1,250-1,850 words. Pays $150-175.
Photos: Send photos with submission. Reviews contact sheets, transparencies, prints. Offers $25-40/photo. Model release required. Buys one-time rights.
Columns/Departments: News (information on newly discovered benefits of supplements, dietary habits, fitness). Buys 12 mss/year. Query with published clips. Length: 250-300 words. Pays $50-75.
Tips: "Our publication is distributed through health food stores. Our readers are most interested in reading the latest research on how specific supplements help treat and prevent diseases and disorders. We speak of such supplements in the generic sense—no name brands, please. Calling us prior to submitting material is best. The important thing to remember is that the type of item being written about must be currently available in health food stores."

‡**COPING, Living With Cancer**, Suite B400, 12600 W. Colfax Ave., Denver CO 80215. (303)238-5035. Editor: Pamela J. Avery. Managing Editor: Robert K. Diddlebock. 40% freelance written. A quarterly magazine of cancer-related news for professionals and consumers. Circ. 12,000. Pays on acceptance. Publishes ms

an average of 3 months after acceptance. Occasional byline. Buys first North American serial rights and second serial (reprint) rights. Submit seasonal/holiday material 5 months in advance. Simultaneous and previously published material OK. Computer printout submissions OK; prefers letter-quality. Sample copy $2.50; free writer's guidelines.

Nonfiction: Expose, general interest, inspirational, interview/profile, new product, opinion, personal interest. Buys 50 mss/year. Query with published clips. Length: 300-2,000 words. Pays 30¢/word up to $600-700. Sometimes pays expenses of writers on assignment.

Photos: State availability of photos with submission. Reviews negatives, transparencies (35mm or 2¼x2¼). Pays $50-75/photo. Captions, model releases and identification of subjects required. Buys one-time rights.

Columns/Departments: Second Opinion (essays on medical issues, topics, experiences related to cancer or illness) 500-750 words. Buys 15 mss/year. Query with or without published clips. Pays up to $225.

Tips: "Since we are a news magazine, the best advice is to have a news angle on a new development or a news peg on which to hang a profile or news feature. Of course, any story or article that's written in a provocative, concise and enlightened manner will be considered on a case-by-case basis. The magazine's news columns are best bets for freelancers."

‡**DIABETES SELF-MANAGEMENT**, Pharmaceutical Communications, Inc., 42-15 Crescent St., Long Island City NY 11101. (718)937-4283. Co-Editors: James Hazlett and Robert S. Dinsmoor. 20% freelance written. A bimonthly magazine. "We educate diabetics in the day-to-day and long-term aspects of their diabetes in a positive, upbeat way. We stress taking charge of the management of their diabetes." Circ. 265,000. Pays on acceptance. Publishes ms an average of 4 months after acceptance. Byline given. Offers 20% kill fee. Buys all rights and makes work-for-hire assignments. Submit seasonal/holiday material 6 months in advance. Reports in 6 weeks on queries. Sample copy $2 with 9x12 SAE and 6 first class stamps; free writer's guidelines.

Nonfiction: How-to (self-management, nutrition, exercise, pharmacology and self-help for persons with diabetes). No personal experiences, profiles, research breakthroughs or exposeś. Buys 8 mss/year. Query with published clips. Length: 1,000-3,000 words. Pays $400-600 for assigned articles.

‡**HEALTH EXPRESS, Shaping Up Body and Mind**, Good Health, Inc., 19701 South Miles Rd., Cleveland OH 44128. (216)662-6969. Editor: Suzanne Pelisson. Managing Editor: Walitha Griffey. 75% freelance written. Bimonthly magazine on health and fitness of mind and body. "*Health Express* is a health and fitness magazine for busy men and women who aren't too busy to take an active role in maintaining good health—for themselves and their families." Circ. 100,000. Pays on publication. Byline given. Buys one-time rights or second serial (reprint) rights. Submit seasonal/holiday material 4 months in advance. Simultaneous, photocopied and previously published submissions OK. Computer printout submissions OK; prefers letter-quality. Reports in 3 weeks. Sample copy $2.50; writer's guidelines for #10 SAE with 1 first class stamp.

Nonfiction: Book excerpts, how-to (health related fitness), inspirational, interview/profile, new product, photo feature. Buys 60-70 mss/year. Query with or without published clips, or send complete ms. Length: 1,000 words. Pays $25-150. Sometimes pays expenses of writers on assignment.

Photos: State availability of photos with submission or send photos with submission. Reviews contacts and 8x10 prints. Model release and identification of subjects required. Buys one-time rights.

Columns/Departments: The Whole Tooth (dental health); Psychology (mindbody—behavior); Food (nutrition, disease control). Buys 15 mss/year. Query or send complete ms. Length: 500-700 words. Pays $50-75.

Fillers: Fillers Editor: Michael Cohen. Newsbreaks. Buys 150 mss/yar. Length: 10-60 words. Pays $5-20.

‡**HEALTH MAGAZINE, Getting the Best from Yourself**, Family Media, Inc., 3 Park Ave., New York NY 10016. (212)340-9262. Editor: Dianne Partie Lange. Executive Editor: Bonnie Gordon. Managing Editor: Gordon Bakoulis. 75% freelance written. A monthly magazine covering women's health issues. "*Health* is a service magazine for women twenty to fifty. We run pieces on medicine and health, behavior and psychology, fitness, food, beauty and fashion." Circ. 1,000,000. Pays on acceptance. Publishes ms an average of 4 months after acceptance. Byline given. Offers 20% kill fee. Buys first North American serial rights. Submit seasonal/holiday material 6 months in advance. Computer printout submissions acceptable; prefers letter-quality. Reports in 1 month.

Nonfiction: Investigative, general interest, humor, interview/profile, new product, and personal experience. Buys 325 mss/year. Query with published clips. Length: 150-2,500 words. Pays $150-2,000. Pays the expenses of writers on assignment.

Photos: State availability of photos with submission. Reviews transparencies.

Tips: "A freelancer's best first query to *Health* should be well-researched and backed up by clips."

HEALTHPLEX MAGAZINE, The Magazine for Healthier Living, Methodist Hospital/Childrens Hospital, 8303 Dodge St., Omaha NE 68114. (402)390-4528. Managing Editor: Gini Goldsmith. 80% freelance written. Prefers to work with published/established writers. Most articles are written on assignment. Quarterly magazine on health information and medical subjects. Focuses on current health care topics, wellness-related articles, etc. Circ. 60,000. Pays on acceptance. Publishes ms an average of 3 months after acceptance. Byline given. Buys all rights and first serial rights; makes work-for-hire assignments. Submit seasonal/holiday material 3 months in advance. Photocopied submissions OK. Computer printout submissions acceptable; prefers letter-quality. Reports in 1 month. Free sample copy.

Nonfiction: Only health/wellness articles. Buys 24 mss/year. Query with published clips or send complete ms. Length: 1,000-3,000 words. Pays $50-200. Sometimes pays the expenses of writers on assignment.

Photos: State availability of photos. Reviews b&w contact sheets and color transparencies. Pays $100-250. Model release required. Buys all rights.

Columns/Departments: Feelin' Good (wellness articles) and Health Updates (short topics on current health topics, new technology, etc.).

Tips: "This is a corporate publication so all articles must have a broad consumer appeal and not be on an obscure medical topic. Since most articles are written on assignment, it is preferable to send a topic query or a submission of published articles for writing style selection."

‡HIPPOCRATES, The Magazine of Health & Medicine, Suite 100, 475 Gate 5 Rd., Sausalito CA 94965. (415)332-5866. Editor: Eric Shrier. Managing Editor: Michael Gold. 75% freelance written. A bimonthly magazine on health and medicine. "Articles should be written with wit, reflection and authority." Circ. 400,000. Pays on acceptance. Publishes ms an average of 6 months after acceptance. Offers 20% kill fee. Buys first North American serial rights. Submit seasonal/holiday material 6 months in advance. Computer printout submissions OK.

Nonfiction: Essays, general interest, how-to, interview/profile, photo feature. Query with published clips. Length: 1,000-5,000 words. Pays $850-4,000. Sometimes pays expenses of writers on assignment.

Columns/Departments: Editor: John Kiefer. Food, Family, Sports, Drugs, Mind, all 800-1,300 words. Buys 12 mss/year. Query with published clips. Pays $600-850.

Fillers: Clippings: verbatim from other publications or book, $50 each *used*; nothing if unused.

Tips: "Send sharply focused queries with the proposed style and sources clearly defined. Departments are the best place to start. Queries can run to 250 words per topic and should demonstrate the finished story's structure and character. Departments are Food, Family, Sports, Drugs and Mind. Tightly focused stories, with real voices and touches of humor used. *Always* query first."

LET'S LIVE MAGAZINE, Oxford Industries, Inc., 444 N. Larchmont Blvd., Box 74908, Los Angeles CA 90004. (213)469-8379. Editor: Debra A. Jenkins. Emphasizes nutrition. 40% freelance written. Works with a small number of new/unpublished writers each year. Monthly magazine. Circ. 140,000. Pays on publication. Publishes ms an average of 4 months after acceptance. Buys first North American serial rights. Byline given. Submit seasonal/holiday material 4 months in advance. Computer printout submissions acceptable; prefers letter quality. Reports in 3 weeks on queries; 6 weeks on mss. Sample copy for $2.50 and 10x13 SAE with 5 first class stamps; writer's guidelines for SAE and 1 first class stamp.

Nonfiction: General interest (effects of vitamins, minerals and nutrients in improvement of health or afflictions); historical (documentation of experiments or treatment establishing value of nutrients as boon to health); how-to (acquire strength and vitality, improve health of adults and/or children and prepare tasty health-food meals); inspirational (first-person accounts of triumph over disease through substitution of natural foods and nutritional supplements for drugs and surgery); interview (benefits of research in establishing prevention as key to good health); advertised new product (120-180 words plus 5x7 or glossy of product); personal opinion (views of orthomolecular doctors or their patients on value of health foods toward maintaining good health); and profile (background and/or medical history of preventive medicine, M.D.s or Ph.D.s, in advancement of nutrition). Manuscripts must be well-researched, reliably documented, and written in a clear, readable style. Buys 2-4 mss/issue. Query with published clips. Length: 1,200-1,500 words. Pays $150. Sometimes pays expenses of writers on assignment.

Photos: State availability of photos with ms. Pays $17.50 for 8x10 b&w glossy prints; $35 for 8x10 color prints and 35mm color transparencies; and $150 for good cover shot. Captions and model releases required.

Tips: "We want writers with experience in researching nonsurgical medical subjects and interviewing experts with the ability to simplify technical and clinical information for the layman. A captivating lead and structural flow are essential. The most frequent mistakes made by writers are in writing articles that are too technical; in poor style; written for the wrong audience (publication not thoroughly studied) or have unreliable documentation or overzealous faith in the topic reflected by flimsy research and inappropriate tone."

‡LIFELINE, Alcoholism*Codependency*Addiction, 352 Halladay, Seattle WA 98119. (206)282-1234. Editor: DAnn Slayton Shiffler. 50% freelance written. Bimonthly magazine on alcoholism/addiction treatment, prevention and recovery. Estab. 1988. Circ. 200,000. Pays on acceptance. Byline given. Buys first North American serial rights or second serial (reprint) rights; makes work-for-hire assignments. Submit seasonal/holiday material 4 months in advance. Previously published submissions OK. Query for electronic submissions. Computer printout submissions OK; prefers letter-quality. Reports in 6 weeks. Free sample copy and writer's guidelines.

Nonfiction: Book excerpts, essays, humor, inspirational, interview/profile, personal experience, photo feature, travel. "All must deal with alcoholism/addiction prevention, treatment or recovery." Buys 50 mss/year. Query with or without published clips, or send complete ms. Length: 500-2,000 words. Pays $25-200. Sometimes pays expenses of writers on assignment.

Photos: State availability of photos with submission or send photos. Reviews contact sheets, negatives, 4x5 transparencies or 8x10prints. Offers $10-50 for photos. Captions and model releases required. Buys one-time rights.

Fillers: Anecdotes, facts, gags to be illustrated by cartoonist, newsbreaks, short humor. Buys 5/year. Length: 100;500 words. Pays $10-50.

LISTEN MAGAZINE, 6830 Laurel St. NW, Washington DC 20012. (202)722-6726. Editor: Gary B. Swanson. 75% freelance written. Works with a small number of new/unpublished writers each year. Specializes in drug prevention, presenting positive alternatives to various drug dependencies. "*Listen* is used in many high school classes, in addition to use by professionals: medical personnel, counselors, law enforcement officers, educators, youth workers, etc." Monthly magazine, 32 pages. Circ. 100,000. Buys first rights. Byline given. Pays on acceptance. Publishes ms an average of 6 months after acceptance. Computer printout submissions acceptable; prefers letter-quality. Reports in 1 month. Sample copy $1 and 8½x11 SASE; free writer's guidelines.

Nonfiction: Seeks articles that deal with causes of drug use such as poor self-concept, family relations, social skills or peer pressure. Especially interested in youth-slanted articles or personality interviews encouraging nonalcoholic and nondrug ways of life. Teenage point of view is essential. Popularized medical, legal and educational articles. Also seeks narratives which portray teens dealing with youth conflicts, especially those related to the use of or temptation to use harmful substances. Growth of the main character should be shown. "We don't want typical alcoholic story/skid-row bum, AA stories. We are also being inundated with drunk-driving accident stories. Unless yours is unique, consider another topic." Buys 75-100 unsolicited mss/year. Query. Length: 500-1,500 words. Pays 5-7¢/word. Sometimes pays the expenses of writers on assignment.

Photos: Purchased with accompanying ms. Captions required. Color photos preferred, but b&w acceptable.

Fillers: Word square/general puzzles are also considered. Pays $15.

Tips: "True stories are good, especially if they have a unique angle. Other authoritative articles need a fresh approach. In query, briefly summarize article idea and logic of why you feel it's good."

‡LONGEVITY, "Guide to the Art & Science of Staying Young", Omni Publications, 1965 Broadway, New York NY 10023. (212)496-6100. Editor: Dick Teresi. Managing Editor: Debra Friss. A monthly magazine on medicine, health, fitness and aging research. "*Longevity* is written for an audience aged 40+ who want to postpone the effects of aging and extend their productive, vibrant, healthy years of living." Circ. 30,000. Pays on acceptance. Publishes ms an average of 2 months after acceptance. Byline given. Offers 25% kill fee. Makes work-for-hire assignments. Simultaneous submissions OK. Query for electronic submissions.

Nonfiction: Interview/profile, new product, health. No opinion pieces. Query. Length: 500-2,500 words. Pays $500-2,500. Sometimes pays expenses of writers on assignment.

Columns/Departments: Nutrition, Looks, Medical Briefs, Antiaging News.

MEN'S FITNESS, Men's Fitness, Inc., 21100 Erwin St., Woodland Hills CA 91367. (818)884-6800. Editor-in-Chief: David Rivas. Managing Editor: Chris Weygandt. 75% freelance written. Works with small number of new/unpublished writers each year. A monthly magazine for health-conscious men between the ages of 18 and 45. Provides reliable, entertaining guidance for the active male in all areas of lifestyle. Writers often share bylines with professional experts. Pays 1 month after acceptance. Publishes ms an average of 4 months after acceptance. Offers 20% kill fee. Buys all rights. Submit seasonal material 4 months in advance. Reports in 1 month. Computer printout submissions OK; no dot-matrix. Sample copy and writer's guidelines for 8½x11 SAE with 6 first class stamps.

Nonfiction: Service, informative, inspirational, scientific studies written for men. Few interviews, regional news unless extraordinary. Query with published clips. Buys 50 mss/year. Length: 2,000-3,000 words. Pays $300-500. Occasionally buys mss devoted to specific fitness programs, including exercises, e.g. 6-week chest workout, aerobic weight-training routine. Buys 10-15 mss/year. Pays $250-300.

Columns/Departments: Nutrition, Sporting Life, Sports Science, Grooming, Sex, Prevention, Adventure. Length: 1,250-2,000 words. Buys 40-50 mss/year. Pays $250-300.

Tips: "Articles are welcomed in all facets of men's health; they must be well-researched, entertaining and intelligent."

‡MUSCLE MAG INTERNATIONAL, 52 Bramsteele Rd., Unit 2, Brampton, Ontario L6W 3M5 Canada. Editor: Robert Kennedy. 80% freelance written. "We do not care if a writer is known or unknown; published or unpublished. We simply want good instructional articles on bodybuilding." For 16 to 40-year-old men and women interested in physical fitness and overall body improvement. Monthly magazine. Circ. 150,000. Buys all rights. Pays on acceptance. Publishes ms an average of 4 months after acceptance. Byline given. Buys 80 mss/

year. Sample copy $3. Computer printout submissions acceptable; no dot-matrix. Reports in 1 month. Submit complete ms with IRCs.

Nonfiction: Articles on ideal physical proportions and importance of supplements in the diet, training for muscle size. Should be helpful and instructional and appeal to young men and women who want to live life in a vigorous and healthy style. "We would like to see articles for the physical culturist on new muscle building techniques or an article on fitness testing." Informational, how-to, personal experience, interview, profile, inspirational, humor, historical, exposé, nostalgia, personal opinion, photo, spot news, new product, and merchandising technique articles. Length: 1,200-1,600 words. Pays 10¢/word. Sometimes pays the expenses of writers on assignment.

Columns/Departments: Nutrition Talk (eating for top results) and Shaping Up (improving fitness and stamina). Length: 1,300 words. Pays 10¢/word.

Photos: B&w and color photos are purchased with or without ms. Pays $10 for 8x10 glossy exercise photos; $10 for 8x10 b&w posing shots. Pays $100-200 for color cover and $15 for color used inside magazine (transparencies). More for "special" or "outstanding" work.

Fillers: Newsbreaks, puzzles, quotes of the champs. Length: open. Pays $5 minimum.

Tips: "The best way to break in is to seek out the muscle-building 'stars' and do in-depth interviews with biography in mind. Color training picture support essential. Writers have to make their articles informative in that readers can apply them to help gain bodybuilding success."

NEW BODY, The Magazine of Health & Fitness, GCR Publishing Group, Inc., 888 7th Ave., New York NY 10106. (212)541-7100. Editor: Constance Boze. Managing Editor: Sandra Kosherick. 75% freelance written. Works with a small number of new/unpublished writers each year. A bimonthly magazine covering fitness and health for young, middle-class women. Circ. 125,000. Pays on publication. Publishes ms an average of 6 months after acceptance. Byline given. Offers negotiable kill fee. Buys all rights. Submit seasonal/holiday material 6 months in advance. Simultaneous and photocopied submissions OK. Computer printout submissions acceptable; prefers letter-quality. Reports in 2 months.

Nonfiction: Health, exercise, psychology, relationships, diet, celebrities, and nutrition. "We do not cover bodybuilding—please no queries." No articles on "How I do exercises." Buys 75 mss/year. Query with published clips. Length: 800-1,500 words. Pays $100-300 for assigned articles; $50-150 for unsolicited articles.

Photos: Reviews contact sheets, transparencies and prints. Model releases and identification of subjects required. Buys all rights.

Tips: "We are moving toward more general interest women's material on relationships, emotional health, nutrition, etc. We look for a fresh angle—a new way to present the material. Celebrity profiles, fitness tips, and health news are good topics to consider. Make a clean statement of what your article is about, what it would cover—not why the article is important. We're interested in new ideas, new trends or new ways of looking at old topics."

OSTOMY QUARTERLY, United Ostomy Association, Inc., Suite 120, 36 Executive Park, Irvine CA 92714. Editor: TennieBee M. Hall. 20% freelance written. Works with a small number of new/unpublished writers each year and is eager to work with new/unpublished writers. Quarterly magazine on ostomy surgery and living with ostomies. "The *OQ* is the official publication of UOA and should cover topics of interest to patients who underwent abdominal ostomy surgery (ileostomy, colostomy, urostomy). Most articles should be 'upbeat' in feeling; also, we cover new surgical techniques in ostomy surgery." Circ. 50,000. Pays on publication. Publishes ms an average of 6 months after acceptance. Byline given. Buys first North American serial rights; makes work-for-hire assignments. Submit seasonal/holiday material 3 months in advance. Simultaneous queries and photocopied submissions OK. Query for electronic submissions. Computer printout submissions acceptable; prefers letter-quality. Print must be dark and readable. Reports in 3 months. Sample copy for $2.50 and 8½x11 SAE with 8 first class stamps; writer's guidelines and editorial calendar for SASE.

Nonfiction: General interest (parenting, psychology); humor (coping humorously with problems with ostomies); interview/profile (important MDs in gastroenterology, urology); personal experience (living with abdominal ostomies); technical (new surgical techniques in ostomy); and travel (with ostomies). No testimonials from members, "How I overcame . . . with ostomy and life is great now." Buys 6 mss/year. Query. Length: 800-2,400 words. Usually asks for pages of copy. Pays $50-150 maximum. Sometimes pays the expenses of writers on assignment but no more than $150 total (expenses plus fee) per article will be paid. No kill fee offered.

Photos: Reviews b&w and color transparencies. "We like to use photographs with articles, but price for article includes use of photos. We return photos on request." Captions and model releases required.

Columns/Departments: Book reviews (on ostomy care, living with ostomies); Ostomy World (any news items relating to ostomy, enterostomal therapy, medical); Q&A (answers medical questions from members); nutrition; financial; psychology. Primarily staff-written.

Tips: "We will be looking mainly for articles from freelancers about ostomy management, ostomy advances, people important to ostomates. Send different topics and ideas than we have published for 25 years. Be willing to attend free meeting of UOA chapter to get a 'flavor' of the group. UOA is a nonprofit association which accounts for the fees offered. The *OQ* might be re-evaluated in terms of focus. The association might want to expand its focus to include the medical professionals who relate to people with ostomies (discharge planners, visiting nurses, ET nurses, pharmacists, etc.)."

‡TODAY'S LIVING, Communication Channels, Inc., 6255 Barfield Rd., Atlanta GA 30328. (404)256-9800. Associate Publisher/Editor: Patti Seikus. 20% freelance written. Monthly magazine on nutrition, supplements and fitness. *"Today's Living* is geared toward customers of health food stores and for those who prefer natural foods and supplements. Topics covered include the healthful benefits of supplements. Also discusses general health, diet, nutrition and fitness." Circ. 400,000. Pays on publication. Publishes ms an average of 3 months after acceptance. Byline given. Buys all rights. Submit seasonal/holiday material 3 months in advance. Photocopied submissions OK. Query for electronic submissions. Computer printout submissions OK; prefers letter quality. Reports in 1 month. Sample copy for 10x12 SAE with 2 first class stamps; writers guidelines for #10 SAE with 1 first class stamp.
Nonfiction: Exposé, interview/profile. Buys 12 mss/year. Query with published clips. Length: 1,200-1,350 words. Pays $150-175.
Photos: Send photos with submission. Reviews contact sheets, transparencies and prints. Offers $25-40/photo. Model release required. Buys one-time rights.
Columns/Departments: News (information on newly discovered benefits of supplements, dietary habits, fitness) 250-300 words. Buys 12 mss/year. Query with published clips. Pays $50-75.

TOTAL HEALTH, Body, Mind and Spirit, Trio Publications, Suite 300, 6001 Topanga Cyn Blvd., Woodland Hills CA 91367. (818)887-6484. Editor: Robert L. Smith. Managing Editor: Rosemary Hofer. Prefers to work with published/established writers. 80% freelance written. A bimonthly magazine covering fitness, diet (weight loss), nutrition and mental health—"a family magazine about wholeness." Circ. 70,000. Pays on publication. Publishes ms an average of 2 months after acceptance. Byline given. Buys first rights. Submit seasonal/holiday material 4 months in advance. Photocopied submissions OK. Reports in 1 month. Sample copy $1 with 9x12 SAE and 5 first class stamps; writer's guidelines for SAE.
Nonfiction: Exposé; how-to (pertaining to health and fitness); and religious (Judeo-Christian). Especially needs articles on skin and body care and power of positive thinking articles. No personal experience articles. Buys 48 mss/year. Send complete ms. Length: 2,000-3,000 words. Pays $50-75. Sometimes pays the expenses of writers on assignment.
Photos: State availability of photos with submission. Offers no additional payment for photos accepted with ms. Captions, model releases and identification of subjects required.
Columns/Departments: Query with or without published clips. Length: 1,000 words maximum. Pays $50 maximum.
Tips: "Feature-length articles are most open to freelancers. We are looking for more fitness-exercise articles."

VEGETARIAN JOURNAL, Box 1463, Baltimore MD 21203. (301)752-VEGV. Editors: Charles Stahler/Debra Wasserman. A monthly newsletter on vegetarianism and animal rights. *"Vegetarian* issues include health, nutrition, animal rights and world hunger. Articles related to nutrition should be documented by established (mainstream) nutrition studies." Circ. 2,000. Pays on publication. Publishes ms an average of 3-5 months after acceptance. Byline given. Makes work-for-hire assignments. Submit seasonal/holiday material 6 months in advance. Computer printout submissions OK. Reports in 1 month. Sample copy for #10 SAE with 2 first class stamps.
Nonfiction: Book excerpts, expose, how-to, interview/profile, new products, travel. "At present we are only looking for in-depth articles on selected nutrition subjects from registered dieticians or M.D.'s. Please query with your background. Possibly some in-depth practical and researched articles from others. No miracle cures or use of supplements." Buys 1-5 mss/year. Query with or without published clips or send complete ms. Length: 2,500-8,250 words. Pays $10-25. Sometimes pays writers with contributor copies or other premiums "if not a specific agreed upon in-depth article." Sometimes pays the expenses of writers on assignment.
Photos: State availability of photos with submission. Reviews prints. Offers no additional payment for photos accepted with ms. Identification of subjects required. Buys one-time rights.
Poetry: Avant-garde, free verse, haiku, light verse, traditional "Poetry should be related to vegetarianism, world hunger, or animal rights. No graphic animal abuse. We do not want to see the word, blood, in any form." Pays in copies.
Tips: "We are most open to vegan-oriented medical professionals or vegetarian/animal rights activists who are new to freelancing."

VEGETARIAN TIMES, Box 570, Oak Park IL 60303. (312)848-8100. Executive Editor: Sally Hayhow. Managing Editor: Lucy Moll. 30% freelance written. Prefers to work with published/established writers; works with small number of new/unpublished writers each year. Monthly magazine. Circ. 150,000. Rights purchased vary with author and material. Buys first serial rights or all rights. Byline given unless extensive revisions are

required or material is incorporated into a larger article. Pays on acceptance. Publishes ms an average of 6 months after acceptance. Computer printout submissions acceptable; prefers letter-quality. Submit seasonal material 6 months in advance. Reports in 1 month. Query. Sample copy $2; writer's guidelines for #10 SASE.
Nonfiction: Features articles related to vegetarian cooking, and natural foods and about vegetarians. "All material should be well documented and researched, and written in a sophisticated yet lively style." Informational, how-to, personal experience, interview, profile. Length: average 2,000 words. Pays 15¢/word, though a flat rate may be negotiated. Will also use 500-word items for new digest. Sometimes pays expenses of writers on assignment.
Photos: Pays $40 for b&w; $40 for color photos used.
Tips: "You don't have to be a vegetarian to write for *Vegetarian Times*, but it is VITAL that your article has a vegetarian slant. The best way to pick up that slant is to read several issues of the magazine (no doubt a tip you've heard over and over). We are very particular about the articles we run and thus tend to ask for rewrites. The best way to break in is by querying us on a well-defined topic that is appropriate for our news digest section. Make sure your idea is well thought out before querying."

VIBRANT LIFE, A Christian Guide for Total Health, Review and Herald Publishing Assn., 55 W. Oak Ridge Dr., Hagerstown MD 21740. (301)791-7000. 95% freelance written. Enjoys working with published/established writers; works with a small number of new/unpublished writers each year; eager to work with new/unpublished writers. Bimonthly magazine covering health articles (especially from a prevention angle and with a Christian slant). Circ. 50,000. Pays on acceptance. "The average length of time between acceptance of a freelance-written manuscript and publication of the material depends upon the topics; some immediately used; others up to 2 years." Byline always given. Offers 25% kill fee. Buys first serial rights, first North American serial rights, or sometimes second serial (reprint) rights. Computer printout submissions acceptable; no dot-matrix. Submit seasonal/holiday material 6 months in advance. Photocopied (if clear) submissions OK. Reports in 2 months. Sample copy $1; free writer's guidelines.
Nonfiction: Interview/profile (with personalities on health). "We seek practical articles promoting better health, and a more fulfilled life. We especially like features on breakthroughs in medicine, and most aspects of health." Buys 90-100 mss/year. Send complete ms. Length: 750-2,800 words. Pays $125-450. Pays the expenses of writers on assignment.
Photos: Send photos with ms. Needs 35mm transparencies. Not interested in b&w photos.
Tips: "*Vibrant Life* is published for the typical man/woman on the street, age 20-50. Therefore articles must be written in an interesting, easy-to-read style. Information must be reliable; no faddism. We are more conservative than other magazines in our field. Request a sample copy, and study the magazine and writer's guidelines."

WALKWAYS, Update on Walkers and Walking, The WalkWays Center, #427, 733 15th St., NW, Washington DC 20005. (202)737-9555. Editor: Marsha L. Wallen. 50% freelance written. Works with a small number of new/unpublished writers each year, and is eager to work with new/unpublished writers. A bimonthly newsletter on walking. Circ. 5,000. Pays on publication. Publishes ms an average of 1 month after acceptance. Byline given. Buys first North American serial rights. Submit seasonal/holiday material 6 months in advance. Simultaneous and photocopied submissions OK. Computer printout submissions OK. Reports in 2 weeks. Sample copy $1.50 with #10 SASE.
Nonfiction: Essays, how-to, humor, interview/profile, opinion, personal experience and travel. "No general travelogues, how walking is a religious experience, or narrow-scope articles about a type of walking with no examples of where it can be done in other places." Buys 6 mss/year. Send complete ms. Length: 200-750 words. Pays $20-75.
Photos: State availability of photos with submissions. Photos should include people walking or some other activity; should not be just scenery. Reviews contact sheets, 35mm transparencies, and 5x7 and 8x10 prints. Offers $10/photo. Captions required. Buys one-time rights.
Columns/Departments: Health Notes, 350 words maximum, with art or photo; Networking (an information sharing department on specific subjects to familiarize readers, such as Volksmarching, race walking, how to form walking club), 350 words maximum, with art or photo; and Footloose (a walk or series of walks in special places with how-to and sidebar information on how to get there, best time, best places to see, who was leader, etc.), 750 words maximum, with art or photo. Buys 32 mss/year. Send complete ms. Offers $10/photo.
Fiction: Humorous. Send complete ms. Length: 200 words maximum. Pays $10-20.
Fillers: Medical facts and short humor. Length: 30-50 words. Pays $5.
Tips: "We need writers who can concentrate more on the walk and less about the scenery and extraneous details, although they are appreciated. If writing about a walking trip or experience, give details on how to get there, costs, etc., plus *other* places you can do similar walks. We like to approach themes versus single event or experiences, if possible and applicable."

WEIGHT WATCHERS MAGAZINE, 360 Lexington Ave., New York NY 10017. (212)370-0644. Editor-in-Chief: Lee Haiken. Senior Editor: Nelly Edmondson. 50% freelance written. Works with a small number of new/unpublished writers each year. Monthly publication for those interested in weight loss and weight maintenance through sensible eating and health/nutrition guidance. Circ. 1,000,000. Buys first North American serial rights only. Pays on acceptance. Publishes ms an average of 6 months after acceptance. Computer printout submissions acceptable; prefers letter-quality. Reports in 1-2 months. Sample copy and writer's guidelines for 8½x11 SAE and $1.75.

Nonfiction: Subject matter should be related to food, psychology, health or weight loss, but not specific diets or recipes. Would like to see researched articles related to the psychological/emotional aspects of weight loss and control and suggestions for making the battle easier. Inspirational success stories of weight loss following the Weight Watchers Program or other *sensible* weight-loss regimens also accepted. "We want to do more in-depth nutrition, psychology, and health pieces. Writers should interview top experts." Send detailed queries with published clips and SASE. No full-length mss; send feature ideas, as well as before-and-after weight loss story ideas dealing either with celebrities or "real people." Length: 1,500 words maximum. Pays $200-600. Sometimes pays the expenses of writers on assignment.

Tips: "It's rewarding giving freelancers the rough shape of how an article should look and seeing where they go with it. It's frustrating working with writers who don't pay enough attention to revisions that have been requested and who send back second drafts with only a few changes. We rarely use fillers. Writers can break in if their writing is lively, tightly constructed, and shows an understanding of our audience."

WHOLE LIFE, The Journal for Holistic Health and Natural Living, Whole Life Inc., Box 2058, Madison Square Station, New York NY 10159. (212)353-3395. Editor and Publisher: Marc Medoff. 25% freelance written. Prefers to work with published/established writers and works with a small number of new/unpublished writers each year. Tabloid covering holistic health, natural living, nutrition and related topics. Circ. 60,000. Pays 90 days after publication. Publishes ms 3-18 months after acceptance. Byline given. Buys first North American serial rights, all rights, and second serial (reprint) rights, and makes work-for-hire assignments; depends on topic and author. Submit seasonal/holiday material 6 months in advance. Simultaneous queries, and simultaneous, photocopied, and previously published submissions OK. Reports in 4 months. Sample copy $6; writer's guidelines $2 and #10 SASE.

Nonfiction: Book excerpts (health, nutrition, natural living); general interest (health sciences, holistic health, environment, alternative medicine);how-to (exercise, relaxation, fitness, appropriate technology, outdoors); interview/profile (on assignment); and new product (health, music, spiritual, psychological, natural diet). No undocumented opinion or narrative. Buys 20-40 mss/year. Query with published clips and resume. Length: 1,150-3,000 words. Pays $25-150. Sometimes pays expenses of writers on assignment.

Photos: Reviews b&w contact sheets, any size b&w and color transparencies and any size prints. Model releases and identification of subjects required. Buys all rights.

Columns/Departments: Films, Recipes, Herbs & Health, Resources, Whole Health Network, Living Lightly (appropriate technology), News Views, Whole Life Person, Music, In the Market, Animal Rights—Human Wrongs, Whole Life Experience, Healthy Travel, Restaurant Review, Alternative Fitness, Whole Foods in the News, Whole Frauds in the News, People and Food. Buys 20-40 mss/year. Query with published clips and resume. Length: 150-1,000 words. Pays $25-80.

WHOLISTIC LIVING NEWS, Association for Wholistic Living, Box 16346, San Diego CA 92116. (619)280-0317. Editor: Judith Horton. 85% freelance written. Works with a small number of new/unpublished writers each year. Bimonthly newspaper covering the wholistic field from a wholistic perspective. Circ. 85,000. Pays on publication. Publishes ms an average of 2-4 months after acceptance. Byline given. Not copyrighted. Buys first serial rights and second serial (reprint) rights to material originally published elsewhere. Submit seasonal/ holiday material 6 months in advance. Simultaneous queries, and simultaneous, photocopied, and previously published submissions OK. Computer printout submissions acceptable; prefers letter-quality. Reports in 1 month on queries; 2 months on mss. Sample copy and writer's guideline for $1.50, 9x12 SAE and 5 first class stamps.

Nonfiction: General interest (wholistic or new age overviews of a general topic); and how-to (taking responsibility for yourself—healthwise). No profiles, individual companies, personal experience or first person articles. Buys 100 mss/year. Query with published clips. Length: 200-1,500 words. Pays $10-50. Sometimes pays the expenses of writers on assignment.

Photos: Send photos with query. Pays $7.50 for 5x7 b&w prints. Model releases and identification of subjects required.

Tips: "Study the newspaper—the style is different from a daily. The articles generally provide helpful information on how to feel your best (mentally, spiritually, physically) and how to live in harmony with the planet. Any of the sections are open to freelancers: Update (news), Creative Living, Health & Fitness, Nutrition and Network (recent events and upcoming ones). One of the main aspects of the paper is to promote the concept of a wholistic lifestyle and help people integrate it into their lives by taking simple steps on a daily basis. We are becoming somewhat more political in our outlook—exploring the political aspects of the topics we discuss. Animal rights, Central America and food irradiation are examples. Hopefully we can have room for music reviews later in the year-also more book reviews."

THE YOGA JOURNAL, California Yoga Teachers Association, 2054 University Ave., Berkeley CA 94704. (415)841-9200. Editor: Stephan Bodian. 75% freelance written. Bimonthly magazine covering yoga, holistic health, conscious living, spiritual practices, and nutrition. "We reach a middle-class, educated audience interested in self-improvement and higher consciousness." Circ. 50,000. Pays on publication. Publishes ms an average of 6 months after acceptance. Byline given. Offers $50 kill fee. Buys first North American serial rights only. Submit seasonal/holiday material 4 months in advance. Simultaneous queries and photocopied submissions OK. Reports in 6 weeks on queries; 2 months on mss. Sample copy $3; free writer's guidelines.

Nonfiction: Book excerpts; how-to (exercise, yoga, massage, etc.); inspirational (yoga or related); interview/profile; opinion; photo feature; and travel (if about yoga). "Yoga is our main concern, but our principal features in each issue highlight other new age personalities and endeavors. Nothing too far-out and mystical. Prefer stories about Americans incorporating yoga, meditation, etc., into their normal lives." Buys 40 mss/year. Query. Length: 750-3,500 words. Pays $75-250.

Photos: Lawrence Watson, art director. Send photos with ms. Pays $200-300 for color cover transparencies; $15-25 for 8x10 b&w prints. Model release (for cover only) and identification of subjects required. Buys one-time rights.

Columns/Departments: Forum; Cooking; Well-Being; Psychology; Profiles; Music (reviews of new age music); and Book Reviews. Buys 12-15 mss/year. Pays $25-100.

Tips: "We always read submissions. We are very open to freelance material and want to encourage writers to submit to our magazine. We're looking for out-of-state contributors, particularly in the Midwest and east coast."

YOUR HEALTH, Meridian Publishing Inc., Box 10010, Ogden UT 84409. (801)394-9446. 65% freelance written. A monthly in-house magazine covering personal health, customized with special imprint titles for various businesses, organizations and associations. "Articles should be timeless, noncontroversial, upscale and positive, and the subject matter should have national appeal." Circ. 40,000. Pays on acceptance. Publishes ms an average of 8 months after acceptance. Byline given. Buys first rights and non-exclusive reprint rights. Simultaneous, photocopied, and previously published submissions OK. Computer printout submissions acceptable; prefers letter-quality. Reports in 6 weeks. Sample copy $1 with 9x12 SAE; writer's guidelines for #10 SAE with 1 first class stamp. (All requests for sample copies and guidelines should be addressed to—Attention: Editorial Assistant.)

Nonfiction: General interest stories about individual's health care needs, including preventative approaches to good health. Topics include advances in medical technology, common maladies and treatments, fitness and nutrition, hospital and home medical care, and personality profiles of both health care professionals and exceptional people coping with disability or illness. "We almost never use a first person narrative. No articles about chiropractic, podiatry or lay midwifery articles." Medical pieces must be accompanied by a list of checkable resources. Buys 40 mss/year. Query. Length: 1,000-1,200 words. Pays 15¢/word for first rights plus non-exclusive reprint rights. Payment for second rights is negotiable. Authors retain the right to resell material after it is printed by *Your Health*.

Photos: Send photos or state availability with submission. Reviews 35mm and 2¼x2¼ transparencies and 5x7 or 8x10 prints. Offers $35/inside photo and $50/cover photo. Captions, model releases and identification of subjects required.

Tips: "The key for the freelancer is a well-written query letter that demonstrates that the subject of the article has national appeal; establishes that any medical claims are based on interviews with experts and/or reliable documented sources; shows that the article will have a clear, focused theme; outlines the availability (from the writer, photographer, or a PR source) of top-quality color photos; and gives evidence that the writer/photographer is a professional, even if a beginner. The best way to get started as a contributor to *Your Health* is to prove that you can submit a well-focused article, based on facts, written cleanly per AP style, along with a variety of beautiful color transparencies to illustrate the story. Material is reviewed by a medical board and must be approved by them."

History

Listed here are magazines and other periodicals written for historical collectors, genealogy enthusiasts, historic preservationists and researchers. Editors of history magazines look for fresh accounts of past events in a readable style. Some publications cover an era or a region; others deal with historic preservation.

AMERICAN HERITAGE, 60 Fifth Ave., New York NY 10011. Editor: Byron Dobell. 70% freelance written. 8 times/year. Circ. 230,000. Usually buys first North American rights or all rights. Byline given. Pays on acceptance. Publishes ms an average of 6-12 months after acceptance. Before submitting material, "check our index to see whether we have already treated the subject." Submit seasonal material 1 year in advance. Computer printout submissions acceptable; prefers letter-quality. Reports in 1 month. Writer's guidelines for SAE and 1 first class stamp.

Nonfiction: Wants "historical articles by scholars or journalists intended for intelligent lay readers rather than for professional historians." Emphasis is on authenticity, accuracy and verve. "Interesting documents, photographs and drawings are always welcome. Query." Style should stress "readability and accuracy." Buys 30 unsolicited mss/year. Length: 1,500-5,000 words. Sometimes pays the expenses of writers on assignment.

Tips: "We have over the years published quite a few 'firsts' from young writers whose historical knowledge, research methods and writing skills met our standards. The scope and ambition of a new writer tell us a lot about his or her future usefulness to us. A major article gives us a better idea of the writer's value. Everything depends on the quality of the material. We don't really care whether the author is 20 and unknown, or 80 and famous, or vice versa."

AMERICAN HISTORY ILLUSTRATED, Box 8200, Harrisburg PA 17105. (717)657-9555. Editor: Ed Holm. 60% freelance written. A magazine of cultural, social, military and political history published for a general audience. Monthly except July/August. Circ. 140,000. Pays on acceptance. Byline given. Buys all rights. Query for electronic submissions. Computer printout submissions OK; no dot-matirx. Reports in 10 weeks on queries; 4 months on mss. Writer's guidelines for #10 SAE and 1 first class stamp; sample copy and guidelines for $3 (amount includes 3rd class postage) or $2.50 and 9x12 SAE with 4 first class stamps.

Nonfiction: Regular features include American Profiles (biographies of noteworthy historical figures); Artifacts (stories behind historical objects); Portfolio (pictorial features on artists, photographers and graphic subjects); Digging Up History (coverage of recent major archaeological and historical discoveries); and Testaments to the Past (living history articles on major restored historical sites). "Material is presented on a popular rather than a scholarly level." Writers are required to query before submitting ms. "Query letters should be limited to a concise 1-2 page proposal defining your article with an emphasis on its unique qualities." Buys 30-40 mss/year. Length: 1,000-5,000 words depending on type of article. Pays $125-650. Sometimes pays the expenses of writers on assignment.

Photos: Occasionally buys 8x10 glossy prints or color transparencies with mss; welcomes suggestions for illustrations. Pays for the reproduced color illustrations that the author provides.

Tips: "Key prerequisites for publication are thorough research and accurate presentation, precise English usage and sound organization, a lively style, and a high level of human interest. We are especially interested in publishing 'Testaments to the Past' articles (on significant ongoing living history sites), as well as top-quality articles on significant American women, on the Vietnam era, and on social/cultural history. Submissions received without return postage will not be considered or returned. Inappropriate materials include: fiction, book reviews, travelogues, personal/family narratives not of national significance, articles about collectibles/antiques, living artists, local/individual historic buildings/landmarks and articles of a current editorial nature."

‡AMERICA'S CIVIL WAR, Empire Press, 105 Loudoun St. SW, Leesburg VA 22075. (703)771-9400. Editor: Roy Morris, Jr. 95% freelance written. Bimonthly magazine of "popular history and straight historical narrative for both the general reader and the Civil War buff." Estab. 1988. Circ. 75,000. Pays on publication. Publishes ms up to 2 years after accaptance. Byline given. Buys first North American serial rights. Query for electronic submissions. Computer printout submissions OK; no dot-matrix. Reports in 2 months on queries; 3 months on mss. Sample copy $3.95; writer's guidelines for #10 SAE with 1 first class stamp.

Nonfiction: Book excerpts, historical, travel. No fiction or poetry. Buys 48 mss/year. Query. Length: 4,000 words maximim. Pays $300 maximum.

Photos: State availability of photos with submission. Pays up to $100/photo. Captions and identification of subjects required. Buys one-time rights.

Columns/Departments: Personalty (probes); Ordinance (about weapons used); Commands (about units); Travel (about appropriate historical sites). Buys 24 mss/year. Query. Length: 2,000 words. Pays up to $150.

ANCESTRY NEWSLETTER, Ancestry, Inc., Box 476, Salt Lake City UT 84110. (801)531-1790. Editor-in-Chief: Robb Barr. 95% freelance written. Eager to work with new/unpublished writers. A bimonthly newsletter covering genealogy and family history. "We publish practical, instructional, and informative pieces specifically applicable to the field of genealogy. Our audience is the active genealogist, both hobbyist and professional." Circ. 8,200. Pays on publication. Publishes ms an average of 5 months after acceptance. Byline given. Buys first North American serial rights or all rights. Submit seasonal/holiday material 4 months in advance. Simultaneous and photocopied submissions OK. Computer printout submissions acceptable; prefers letter-quality. Reports in 2 weeks on queries; 2 months on mss. Sample copy and writer's guidelines for SAE with 3 first class stamps.

Nonfiction: General interest (genealogical); historical; how-to (genealogical research techniques); instructional; and photo feature (genealogically related). No unpublished or published family histories, genealogies; the "story of my great-grandmother," etc. or personal experiences. Buys 25-30 mss/year. Send complete ms.

Length: 1,000-3,000 words. Pays $50-100.
Photos: Send photos with submission. Reviews contact sheets and 5x7 prints. Offers no additional payment for photos accepted with ms. Identification of subjects required. Buys one-time rights.
Tips: "You don't have to be famous, but you must know something about genealogy. Our readers crave any information which might assist them in their ancestral quest."

THE ARTILLERYMAN, Cutter & Locke, Inc., Publishers, 4 Water St., Box C, Arlington MA 02174. (617)646-2010. 60% freelance written. Editor: C. Peter Jorgensen. Quarterly magazine covering antique artillery, fortifications, and crew-served weapons 1750 to 1900 for competition shooters, collectors and living history reenactors using muzzleloading artillery; "emphasis on Revolutionary War and Civil War but includes everyone interested in pre-1900 artillery and fortifications, preservation, construction of replicas, etc." Circ. 2,600. Pays on publication. Publishes ms an average of 3-6 months after acceptance. Byline given. Not copyrighted. Buys one-time rights. Simultaneous queries, and simultaneous, photocopied and previously published submissions OK. Computer printout submissions acceptable; prefers letter-quality. Reports in 3 weeks. Sample copy and writer's guidelines for 8½x11 SAE and 4 first class stamps.
Nonfiction: Historical/nostalgic; how-to (reproduce ordinance equipment/sights/implements/tools/accessories, etc.); interview/profile; new product; opinion (must be accompanied by detailed background of writer and include references); personal experience; photo feature; technical (must have footnotes); and travel (where to find interesting antique cannon). Interested in "artillery *only*, for sophisticated readers. Not interested in other weapons, battles in general." Buys 24-30 mss/year. Send complete ms. Length: 300 words minimum. Pays $20-60. Sometimes pays the expenses of writers on assignment.
Photos: Send photos with ms. Pays $5 for 5x7 and larger b&w prints. Captions and identification of subjects required.
Tips: "We regularly use freelance contributions for Places-to-Visit, Cannon Safety, The Workshop and Unit Profiles departments. Also need pieces on unusual cannon or cannon with a known and unique history. To judge whether writing style and/or expertise will suit our needs, writers should ask themselves if they could knowledgeably talk *artillery* with an expert. Subject matter is of more concern than writer's background."

CHICAGO HISTORY, The Magazine of the Chicago Historical Society, Chicago Historical Society, Clark St. at North Ave., Chicago IL 60614. (312)642-4600. Editor: Russell Lewis. Associate Editor: Meg Walter. Assistant Editor: Aleta Zak. Editorial Assistant: Margaret Welsh. 100% freelance written. Works with a small number of new/unpublished writers each year. A quarterly magazine covering Chicago history: cultural, political, economic, social, architectural. Circ. 5,500. Pays on publication. Publishes ms an average of 6-12 months after acceptance. Byline given. Buys all rights. Submit seasonal/holiday material 9 months in advance. Photocopied submissions OK. Query for electronic submissions. Computer printout submissions acceptable; no dot-matrix. Reports in 6 weeks. Sample copy $3.25; free writer's guidelines.
Nonfiction: Book excerpts, essays, historical/nostalgic, interview/profile and photo feature. Articles to be "analytical, informative, and directed at a popular audience with a special interest in history." No "cute" articles. Buys 16-20 mss/year. Query; send complete ms. Length: approximately 4,500 words. Pays $250.
Photos: State availability of photos with submission and submit photocopies. Would prefer no originals. Offers no additional payment for photos accepted with ms. Identification of subjects required.
Columns/Departments: Book Reviews (Chicago and/or urban history), 500-750 words; and Review Essays (author reviews, comparatively, a compilation of several books on same topic—Chicago and/or urban history), 2,500 words. Buys 20 mss/year. Query; send complete ms. Pays $75-100 "but book review authors receive only one copy of book, no cash."
Tips: "A freelancer can best break in by 1) calling to discuss an article idea with editor; and 2) submitting a detailed outline of proposed article. All sections of *Chicago History* are open to freelancers, but we suggest that authors do not undertake to write articles for the magazine unless they have considerable knowledge of the subject and are willing to research it in some detail. We require a footnoted manuscript, although we do not publish the notes."

CIVIL WAR TIMES ILLUSTRATED, 2245 Kohn Rd., Box 8200, Harrisburg PA 17105. (717)657-9555. Editor: John E. Stanchak. 90% freelance written. Works with a small number of new/unpublished writers each year. Magazine published monthly except July and August. Circ. 135,000. Pays on acceptance. Publishes ms an average of 12-18 months after acceptance. Buys all rights, first rights or one-time rights, or makes work-for-hire assignments. Submit seasonal/holiday material 1 year in advance. Query for electronic submissions. Computer printout submissions acceptable; prefers letter-quality. Reports in 2 weeks on queries; 3 months on mss. Sample copy $3; free writer's guidelines.
Nonfiction: Profile, photo feature, and Civil War historical material. "Positively no fiction or poetry." Buys 20 freelance mss/year. Length: 2,500-5,000 words. Query. Pays $75-450. Sometimes pays the expenses of writers on assignment.
Photos: Lisa Aucker, art director. State availability of photos. Pays $5-50 for 8x10 b&w glossy prints and copies of Civil War photos; $400-500 for 4-color cover photos; and $100-250 for color photos for interior use.

Tips: "We're very open to new submissions. Query us after reading several back issues, then submit illustration and art possibilities along with the query letter for the best 'in.' Never base the narrative solely on family stories or accounts. Submissions must be written in a popular style but based on solid academic research. Manuscripts are required to have marginal source annotations."

EL PALACIO, THE MAGAZINE OF THE MUSEUM OF NEW MEXICO, Museum of New Mexico Press, Box 2087, Santa Fe NM 87504. (505)827-6794. Editor-in-Chief: Sarah Nestor. 15% freelance written. Prefers to work with published/established writers. Emphasizes the collections of the Museum of New Mexico and anthropology, ethnology, history, folk and fine arts, Southwestern culture, and natural history as these topics pertain to the Museum of New Mexico and the Southwest. Triannual magazine; 48 pages. Circ. 4,000. Pays on publication. We hope "to attract professional writers who can translate scholarly and complex information into material that will fascinate and inform a general educated readership." Acquires first North American serial rights. Byline given. Phone queries OK. Submit seasonal/holiday queries 1 year in advance. Photocopied submissions OK. Query for electronic submissions. Computer printout submissions acceptable; no dot-matrix. Reports in 6 weeks. Sample copy $6; writer's guidelines for #10 SASE.
Nonfiction: Historical (on Southwest; substantive but readable—not too technical); folk art; archaeology (Southwest); photo essay; anthropology; material culture of the Southwest. Buys 3-4 unsolicited mss/year. Recent articles documented the history of Las Vegas, New Mexico; women in New Mexico; collections of the Museum of New Mexico; and contemporary photography. "Other articles that have been very successful are a photo-essay on Chaco Canyon and other archaeological spots of interest in the state and an article on Indian baskets and their function in Indian life." Query with credentials. Length: 1,750-4,000 words. Pays $50 honorarium minimum.
Photos: Photos often purchased with accompanying ms, some on assignment. Prefers b&w prints. Informative captions required. Pays "on contract" for 5x7 (or larger) b&w photos and 5x7 or 8½x11 prints or 35mm color transparencies. Send prints and transparencies. Total purchase price for ms includes payment for photos.
Columns/Departments: Curator's Choice and Books (reviews of interest to *El Palacio* readers).
Tips: "*El Palacio* magazine offers a unique opportunity for writers with technical ability to have their work published and seen by influential professionals as well as avidly interested lay readers. The magazine is highly regarded in its field. The writer should have strong writing skills, an understanding of the Southwest and of the field written about. Be able to communicate technical concepts to the educated reader. We like to have a bibliography, list of sources, or suggested reading list with nearly every submission."

‡GOOD OLD DAYS, America's Premier Nostalgia Magazine, House of White Birches, 306 E. Parr Rd., Berne IN 46711. (219)589-8741. Editor: Edgar Harrison. Managing Editor: Rebekah Montgomery. 100% freelance written. A monthly magazine of first person nostalgia, 1900-1949. "We look for strong narratives showing life as it was in the first part of this century. Our readership is nostalgia buffs and history enthusiasts." Pays on publication. Publishes ms an average of 8 months after acceptance. Byline given. Buys all rights, first North American serial rights or one-time rights. Submit seasonal/holiday material 8 months in advance. Computer printout submissions OK; prefers letter-quality. Reports in 2 weeks. Sample copy $1.50; writer's guidelines for #10 SASE.
Nonfiction: Historical/nostalgic, humor, interview/profile, personal experience, photo feature. Buys 300 mss/year. Query or send complete ms. Length: 5,000 words maximum. Pays 2-4¢/word.
Photos: Send photos with submission. Offers $5/photo. Indentification of subjects required. Buys one-time or all rights.

MEDIA HISTORY DIGEST, Media History Digest Corp., % Editor and Publisher, 11 W. 19th St., New York NY 10011. Editor: Hiley H. Ward. 100% freelance written. Semiannual (will probably return to being quarterly) magazine. Circ. 2,000. Pays on publication. Publishes ms an average of 4 months after acceptance. Byline given. Buys first or second serial (reprint) rights. Submit seasonal/holiday material 8 months in advance. Previously published submissions OK. Reports in 2 months. Sample copy $2.50.
Nonfiction: Historical/nostalgic (media); humor (media history); and puzzles (media history). Buys 15 mss/year. Query. Length: 1,500-3,000 words. Pays $125 for assigned articles; pays $100 for unsolicited articles. Pays in contributor copies for articles prepared by university graduate students. Sometimes pays the expenses of writers on assignment.
Photos: Send photos with submission. Buys first or reprint rights.
Columns/Departments: Quiz Page (media history) and "Media Hysteria" (media history humor). Query. Pays $50-125 for humor; $25 for puzzles.
Fillers: Anecdotes and short humor on topics of media history.
Tips: "Present in-depth enterprising material targeted for our specialty—media history, pre-1970."

‡MILITARY HISTORY, Empire Press, 105 Loudoun St. SW, Leesburg VA 22075. (703)771-9400. Editor: C. Brian Kelly. 95% freelance written. "We'll work with anyone, established or not, who can provide the goods and convince us as to its accuracy." Bimonthly magazine covering all military history of the world. "We strive to give the general reader accurate, highly readable, often narrative popular history, richly accompanied by period art." Pays on publication. Publishes ms 1-2 years after acceptance. Byline given. Buys first North American serial rights. Submit anniversary material 1 year in advance. Computer printout submissions acceptable; no dot-matrix. Reports in 2 months on queries; 6 months on mss. Sample copy $3.95; writer's guidelines for SAE with 1 first class stamp.

Nonfiction: Advance book excerpts; historical; interview (military figures of commanding interest); personal experience (only occasionally). Buys 18 mss, plus 6 interviews/year. Query with published clips. "To propose an article, submit a short, self-explanatory query summarizing the story proposed, its highlights and/or significance. State also your own expertise, access to sources or proposed means of developing the pertinent information." Length: 4,000 words. Pays $400.

Columns/Departments: Espionage, weaponry, personality, travel (with military history of the place) and books—all relating to military history. Buys 24 mss/year. Query with published clips. Length: 2,000 words. Pays $200.

Tips: "We would like journalistically 'pure' submissions that adhere to basics, such as full name at first reference, same with rank, and definition of prior or related events, issues cited as context or obscure military 'hardware.' Read the magazine, discover our style, and avoid subjects already covered. Pick stories with strong art possibilities (*real* art and photos), send photocopies, tell us where to order the art. Avoid historical overview, focus upon an event with appropriate and accurate context. Provide bibliography. Tell the story in popular but elegant style."

MILITARY IMAGES, RD2, Box 2542, East Stroudsburg PA 18301. (717)476-1388. Editor: Harry Roach. 100% freelance written. A bimonthly journal reaching a broad spectrum of military historians, antiquarians, collectors and dealers. *MI* covers American military history from 1839 to 1900, with heavy concentration on the Civil War. Circ. 3,000. Pays on publication. Byline given. Buys first North American serial rights. Submit seasonal/holiday material 2 months in advance. Photocopied submissions OK. Query for electronic submissions. Computer printout submissions OK; prefers letter-quality. Reports in 2 weeks on queries; 1 month on mss. Sample copy for $3; free writer's guidelines.

Nonfiction: Book excerpts, historical, humor, interview/profile, photo feature and technical. No articles not tied to, or illustrated by, period photos. Buys 36 mss/year. Query. Length: 1,000-12,000 words. Pays $40-200.

Photos: State availability of photos with submission, or send photocopy with query. Reviews 5x7 or larger b&w prints. Offers no additional payment for photos accepted with ms. Captions required.

Columns/Departments: The Darkroom (technical, 19th-century photo processes, preservation), 1,000 words. Buys 6 mss/year. Query. Length: 1,000-3,000 words. Pays $20-75.

Tips: "Concentrate on details of the common soldier, his uniform, his equipment, his organizations. We do not publish broad-brush histories of generals and campaigns. Articles must be supported by period photos."

OLD MILL NEWS, Society for the Preservation of Old Mills, 604 Ensley Dr., Rt. 29, Knoxville TN 37920. (615)577-7757. Editor: Michael LaForest. 70% freelance written. Quarterly magazine covering "water, wind, animal, steam power mills (usually grist mills)." Circ. 2,500. Pays on acceptance. Byline given. Buys first North American serial rights or first rights. Simultaneous and photocopied submissions OK. Computer printout submissions OK; prefers letter-quality. Reports in 2 weeks. Sample copy $2.

Nonfiction: Historical and technical. "No poetry, recipes, mills converted to houses, commercial, or alternative uses, nostalgia." Buys 8 mss/year. Query with or without published clips, or send complete ms. Length: 400-1,000 words. Pays $15-50.

Photos: Send photos with submission. "At least one recent photograph of subject is highly recommended." Uses b&w or color prints only; no transparencies. Offers $5-10 per photo. Identification of subjects required. Buys one-time rights.

Fillers: Short humor. Buys 3-4/year. Length: 50-200 words. Pays $10 maximum.

Tips: "An interview with the mill owner/operator is usually necessary. Accurate presentation of the facts and good English are required."

OLD WEST, Western Periodicals, Inc., Box 2107, Stillwater OK 74076. (405)743-3370. Quarterly magazine. Byline given. See *True West*.

PERSIMMON HILL, 1700 NE 63rd St., Oklahoma City OK 73111. Editor: Marcia Preston. 70% freelance written. Prefers to work with published/established writers and works with a small number of new/unpublished writers each year. For an audience interested in Western art, Western history, ranching and rodeo, including historians, artists, ranchers, art galleries, schools, and libraries. Publication of the National Cowboy Hall of Fame and Western Heritage Center. Quarterly. Circ. 15,000. Buys first rights. Byline given. Buys 12-14 mss/year. Pays on scheduling of article. Publishes ms an average of 6 months after acceptance. Reporting time on mss varies. Computer printout submissions acceptable; no dot-matrix. Sample copy $5 plus 5 first class stamps; writer's guidelines for #10 SASE.

Nonfiction: Historical and contemporary articles on famous Western figures connected with pioneering the

American West, Western art, rodeo, cowboys, etc. (or biographies of such people), stories of Western flora and animal life, and environmental subjects. "We want thoroughly researched and historically authentic material written in a popular style. May have a humorous approach to subject. No broad, sweeping, superficial pieces; i.e., the California Gold Rush or rehashed pieces on Billy the Kid, etc." Length: 2,000-3,000 words. Query. Pays $100-250; special work negotiated.

Photos: B&w glossy prints or color transparencies purchased with ms, or on assignment. Pays according to quality and importance for b&w and color photos. Suggested captions appreciated.

Tips: "Excellent illustrations for articles essential!"

PRESERVATION NEWS, National Trust for Historic Preservation, 1785 Massachusetts Ave. NW, Washington DC 20016. (202)673-4075. Editor: Arnold M. Berke. 30% freelance written. Prefers to work with published/established writers. A monthly tabloid covering preservation of historic buildings in the U.S. "We cover efforts and controversies involving historic buildings and districts. Most entries are news stories, features or essays." Circ. 200,000. Pays on publication. Publishes ms an average of 1 month after acceptance. Byline given. Offers variable kill fee. Buys one-time rights. Simultaneous queries, and photocopied and previously published submissions OK. Computer printout submissions acceptable. Reports in 2 months on queries. Sample copy for $1 and 10x14 SAE with 56¢ postage; writer's guidelines for SAE and 1 first class stamp.

Nonfiction: Historical/nostalgic, humor, interview/profile, opinion, personal experience, photo feature and travel. Buys 12 mss/year. Query with published clips. Length: 500-1,000 words. Pays $100-250. Sometimes pays the expenses of writers on assignment.

Photos: State availability of photos with query or ms. Reviews b&w contact sheet. Pays $25-100. Identification of subjects required.

Columns/Departments: "We seek an urban affairs reporter who can give a new slant on development conflict throughout the United States." Buys 6 mss/year. Query with published clips. Length: 600-1,000 words. Pays $75-150.

Tips: "The writer has a better chance of breaking in at our publication with short articles and fillers because we like to try them out first. Don't submit dull articles that lack compelling details."

TIMELINE, Ohio Historical Society, 1985 Velma Ave., Columbus OH 43211. (614)297-2360. Editor: Christopher S. Duckworth. 90% freelance written. Works with a small number of new/unpublished writers each year. A bimonthly magazine covering history, natural history, archaeology, and fine and decorative arts. Circ. 11,000. Pays on acceptance. Publishes ms an average of 1 year after acceptance. Byline given. Offers $75 minimum kill fee. Buys first North American serial rights or all rights. Submit seasonal/holiday material 6 months in advance. Photocopied submissions OK. Query for electronic submissions. Computer printout submissions acceptable; no dot-matrix. Reports in 3 weeks on queries; 6 weeks on manuscripts. Sample copy $4; writer's guidelines for #10 SASE.

Nonfiction: Book excerpts, essays, historical, profile (of individuals) and photo feature. Buys 22 mss/year. Query. Length: 500-6,000 words. Pays $100-900.

Photos: State availability of photos with submission. Will not consider submissions without ideas for illustration. Reviews contact sheets, transparencies, and 8x10 prints. Captions, model releases, and identification of subjects required. Buys one-time rights.

Tips: "We want crisply written, authoritative narratives for the intelligent lay reader. An Ohio slant may strengthen a submission, but it is not indispensable. Contributors must know enough about their subject to explain it clearly and in an interesting fashion. We use high-quality illustration with all features. If appropriate illustration is unavailable, we can't use the feature. The writer who sends illustration ideas with a manuscript has an advantage, but an often-published illustration won't attract us."

TRUE WEST, Western Periodicals, Inc., Box 2107, Stillwater OK 74076. (405)743-3370. Editor: John Joerschke. 100% freelance written. Works with a small number of new/unpublished writers each year. Magazine on Western American history before 1920. "We want reliable research on significant historical topics written in lively prose for an informed general audience." Circ. 100,000. Pays after acceptance. "Our payments to contributors are running at least a year after acceptance, but we are gradually speeding that up." Publishes ms an average of 4 months after acceptance. Byline given. Buys first North American serial rights. Submit seasonal/holiday material 6 months in advance. Simultaneous queries OK. Computer printout submissions acceptable; prefers letter-quality. Reports in 1 month on queries; 6 weeks on mss. Sample copy for 8½x11 SAE and $1; writer's guidelines for #10 SAE and 1 first class stamp.

Nonfiction: Historical/nostalgic, how-to, photo feature, travel, and western movies. "We do not want rehashes of worn-out stories, historical fiction, or history written in a fictional style." Buys 150 mss/year. Query. Length: 500-4,500 words. Pays 3-5¢/word.

Photos: Send photos with accompanying query or manuscript. Pays $10 for b&w prints. Identification of subjects required. Buys one-time rights.

Columns/Departments: Western Roundup—200-300 word short articles on historically oriented places to go and things to do in the West with one b&w print. Buys 12-16 mss/year. Send complete ms. Pays $35.

Tips: "Do original research on fresh topics. Stay away from controversial subjects unless you are truly knowledgeable in the field. Read our magazines and follow our writer's guidelines. A freelancer is most likely to break in with us by submitting thoroughly researched, lively prose on relatively obscure topics. First person accounts rarely fill our needs."

VIRGINIA CAVALCADE, Virginia State Library and Archives, Richmond VA 23219-3491. (804)786-2312. Primarily for readers with an interest in Virginia history. 90% freelance written. "Both established and new writers are invited to submit articles." Quarterly magazine. Circ. 12,000. Buys all rights. Byline given. Pays on acceptance. Publishes ms an average of 6-12 months after acceptance. Rarely considers simultaneous submissions. Submit seasonal material 15-18 months in advance. Reports in 1-3 months. Computer printout submissions acceptable; prefers letter-quality. Sample copy $2; free writer's guidelines.
Nonfiction: "We welcome readable and factually accurate articles that are relevant to some phase of Virginia history. art, architecture, literature, education, business, technology and transportation are all acceptable subjects, as well as political and military affairs. Articles must be based on thorough, scholarly research. We require footnotes but do not publish them. Any period from the age of exploration to the mid-20th century, and any geographical section or area of the state may be represented. Must deal with subjects that will appeal to a broad readership, rather than to a very restricted group or locality. Articles must be suitable for illustration, although it is not necessary that the author provide the pictures. If the author does have pertinent illustrations or knows their location, the editor appreciates information concerning them." Buys 12-15 mss/year. Query. Length: 3,500-4,500 words. Pays $100.
Photos: Uses 8x10 b&w glossy prints; color transparencies should be at least 4x5.
Tips: "*Cavalcade* employs a narrative, anecdotal style. Too many submissions are written for an academic audience or are simply not sufficiently gripping."

‡WILD WEST, Empire Press, 105 Loudoun St. SW, Leesburg VA 22075. (703)771-9400. Editor: William M. Vogt. 95% freelance written. Bimonthly magazine on history of the American West. "*Wild West* covers the popular (narrative) history of the Aemrican West—events, trends, personalities, anything of general interest." Estab. 1988. Circ. 75,000. Pays on publication. Byline given. Buys first North American serial rights. Submit seasonal/holiday material 1 year in advance. Query for electronic submissions. Computer printout submissions OK; no dot-matrix. Sample copy $3.95; writer's guidelines for #10 SASE.
Nonfiction: Historical/nostalgic, humor, travel. No fiction or poetry—nothing current. Buys 24 mss/year. Query. Length: 4,000 words. Pays $300.
Photos: State availability of photos with submission. Offers up to $100/photo. Captions and identification of subjects required. Buys one-time rights or all rights.
Columns/Departments: Travel; Gun Fighters & Lawmen; Personalities; Warriors & Chiefs; Books/Reviews. Buys 16 mss/year. Length: 2,000. Pays $150

Hobby and Craft

Magazines in this category range from gem collecting to home video. Craftspeople and hobbyists who read these magazines want new ideas while collectors need to know what is most valuable and why. Collectors, do-it-yourselfers and craftspeople look to these magazines for inspiration, research and information. Publications covering antiques and miniatures also are listed here, while additional publications for electronics and radio hobbyists are included in the Science classification.

AMERICAN BOOK COLLECTOR, Box 1080, Ossining NY 10562. (914)941-0409. Editor: Bernard McTigue. 50-75% freelance written. Eager to work with new/unpublished writers. Monthly magazine on book collecting from the 15th century to the present for individuals, rare book dealers, librarians, and others interested in books and bibliomania. Circ. 3,500. Pays on publication. Publishes ms an average of 6 months after acceptance. Submit seasonal material 3 months in advance. Photocopied and previously published submissions OK. Query for electronic submissions. Computer printout submissions acceptable; prefers letter-quality. Reports in 6 weeks. Sample copy and writer's guidelines for $5.
Nonfiction: General interest (some facet of book collecting: category of books; taste and technique; artist; printer; binder); interview (prominent book collectors; producers of contemporary fine and limited editions; scholars; librarians); and reviews of exhibitions. Buys 20-30 unsolicited mss/year. "We absolutely require queries with clips of previously published work." Query should include precise description of proposed article

accompanied by description of author's background plus indication of extent of illustrations. Length: 1,500-4,500 words. Pays 5¢/word. Sometimes pays the expenses of writers on assignment.

Photos: State availability of photos. Prefers b&w glossy prints of any size. Offers no additional payment for photos accompanying ms. Captions and model release required. Buys one-time rights.

Columns/Departments: Contact editor. Reviews of books on book collecting, and gallery exhibitions.

Tips: "We look for knowledgeable writing. A purely journalistic (i.e., learned while writing) approach is unlikely to be of value."

AMERICAN CLAY EXCHANGE, Page One Publications, Box 2674, La Mesa CA 92044-0700. (619)697-5922. Editor: Susan N. Cox. 95% freelance written. Eager to work with new/unpublished writers. Biweekly newsletter on subjects relating to American made pottery—old or new—with an emphasis on antiques and collectibles for collectors, buyers and sellers of American made pottery, earthenware, china, dinnerware, etc. Pays on acceptance. Publishes ms an average of 2 months after acceptance. Byline given. Buys all rights; will consider first serial rights. Submit seasonal/holiday material 4 months in advance. Computer printout submissions acceptable; no dot-matrix. Reports in 1 month on queries; 2 months on mss. Sample copy $1.50; writer's guidelines for #10 SAE.

Nonfiction: Book reviews (on books pertaining to American made pottery, china, earthenware); historical/nostalgic (on museums and historical societies in the U.S. if they handle pottery, etc.); how-to (identify pieces, clean, find them); and interview/profile (if artist is up-and-coming). No "I found a piece of pottery for 10¢ at a flea market" types. Buys 40-50 mss/year. Query or send complete ms. Length: 1,000 words maximum. Pays $125 maximum.

Photos: Send photos with ms. Pays $5 for b&w prints. Captions required. Does not accept color slides. Buys all rights; will consider one-time rights.

Tips: "Know the subject being written about, including marks and values of pieces found. Telling a reader what 'marks' are on pieces is most essential. The best bet is to write a short (200-300 word) article with a few photos and marks. We are a small company willing to work with writers who have good, salable ideas and know our product. Any article that deals effectively with a little-known company or artist during the 1900-1950 era is most sought after. We have added a section devoted to dinnerware, mostly from the 1900-1950 era—same guidelines. Articles on California and the Southern states pottery companies are eagerly being sought."

THE AMERICAN COLLECTORS JOURNAL, Box 407, Kewanee IL 61443. (308)853-8441. Editor: Carol Saridge. 55% freelance written. Eager to work with new/unpublished writers. A bimonthly tabloid covering antiques and collectibles. Circ. 51,841. Pays on acceptance. Publishes ms an average of 4 months after acceptance. Byline given. Not copyrighted. Buys first North American serial rights. Submit seasonal/holiday material 6 months in advance. Photocopied submissions OK. Computer printout submissions OK. Reports in 3 weeks. Sample copy for 4x9 SAE with 4 first class stamps.

Nonfiction: Carol Harper, articles editor. General interest, interview/profile, new product, photo feature and technical. Buys 12-20 mss/year. Query or send complete ms. Pays $10-35 for unsolicited articles.

Photos: Send photos with submission. Reviews 5x7 prints. Offers no additional payment for photos accepted with ms. Captions required. Buys one-time rights.

Tips: "We are looking for submissions with photos in all areas of collecting and antiquing, unusual collections, details on a particular kind of collecting or information on antiques."

ANTIQUE REVIEW, Box 538, Worthington OH 43085. Editor: Charles Muller. (614)885-9757. 60% freelance written. Eager to work with new/unpublished writers. For an antique-oriented readership, "generally well-educated, interested in folk art and other early American items." Monthly tabloid. Circ. 9,500 in all 50 states. Pays on publication date assigned at time of purchase. Publishes ms an average of 3 months after acceptance. Buys first North American serial rights, and second (reprint) rights to material originally published in dissimilar publications elsewhere. Byline given. Phone queries OK. Computer printout submissions acceptable; prefers letter-quality. Reports in 1 month. Free sample copy and writer's guidelines for #10 SASE.

Nonfiction: "The articles we desire concern history and production of furniture, pottery, china, and other quality Americana. In some cases, contemporary folk art items are acceptable. We are also interested in reporting on antique shows and auctions with statements on conditions and prices. We do not want articles on contemporary collectibles." Buys 5-8 mss/issue. Query with clips of published work. Query should show "author's familiarity with antiques, an interest in the historical development of artifacts relating to early America and an awareness of antiques market." Length: 200-2,000 words. Pays $80-125. Sometimes pays the expenses of writers on assignment.

Photos: State availability of photos with query. Payment included in ms price. Uses 3x5 or larger glossy b&w prints. Captions required. Articles with photographs receive preference.

Tips: "Give us a call and let us know of specific interests. We are more concerned with the background in antiques than in writing abilities. The writing can be edited, but the knowledge imparted is of primary interest. A frequent mistake is being too general, not becoming deeply involved in the topic and its research. We are interested in primary research into America's historic material culture."

THE ANTIQUE TRADER WEEKLY, Box 1050, Dubuque IA 52001. (319)588-2073. Editor: Kyle D. Husfloen. 50% freelance written. Works with a small number of new/unpublished writers each year. For collectors and dealers in antiques and collectibles. Weekly newspaper; 90-120 pages. Circ. 90,000. Publishes ms an average of 6 months after acceptance. Buys all rights. Payment at beginning of month following publication. Photocopied and simultaneous submissions OK. Computer printout submissions acceptable; no dot-matrix. Submit seasonal/holiday material 4 months in advance. Sample copy 50¢; free writer's guidelines.
Nonfiction: "We invite authoritative and well-researched articles on all types of antiques and collectors' items and in-depth stories on specific types of antiques and collectibles. No human interest stories. We do not pay for brief information on new shops opening or other material printed as a service to the antiques hobby." Buys about 60 mss/year. Query or submit complete ms. Pays $5-75 for feature articles; $75-150 for feature cover stories.
Photos: Submit a liberal number of good b&w photos to accompany article. Uses 35mm or larger color transparencies for cover. Offers no additional payment for photos accompanying mss.
Tips: "Send concise, polite letter stating the topic to be covered in the story and the writer's qualifications. No 'cute' letters rambling on about some 'imaginative' story idea. Writers who have a concise yet readable style and know their topic are always appreciated. I am most interested in those who have personal collecting experience or can put together a knowledgeable and informative feature after interviewing a serious collector/authority."

ANTIQUES & AUCTION NEWS, Route 230 West, Box 500, Mount Joy PA 17552. (717)653-9797. Editor: Doris Ann Johnson. Prefers to work with published/established writers, and works with a small number of new/unpublished writers each year. A weekly tabloid for dealers and buyers of antiques, nostalgics and collectibles, and those who follow antique shows, shops and auctions. Circ. 40,000. Pays on publication. Submit seasonal/holiday material 3 months in advance. Computer printout submissions OK; no dot-matrix. Free sample copy available if you mention *Writer's Market*. Writer's guidelines for #10 SASE.
Nonfiction: "Our readers are interested in collectibles and antiques dating approximately from the Civil War to the present, originating in the U.S. or western Europe. We normally will consider any story on a collectible or antique if it is well-written, slanted toward helping collectors, buyers and dealers learn more about the field, and is focused on the aspect of collecting. This could be an historical perspective, a specific area of collecting, an especially interesting antique or unusual collection. Issues have included material on old Christmas ornaments, antique love tokens, collections of fans, pencils and pottery, and 'The Man from U.N.C.L.E.' books and magazines. Articles may be how-to, informational research, news and reporting and even an occasional photo feature." Length: 1,000 words or less preferred, but will consider up to 2,000 words. Pays $12.50 for articles without photos; $15 for articles with usable photos. "We also accept an occasional short article—about one typed page, with a good photo—for which we will pay $7.50, $5 without photo."
Photos: Purchased as part of ms package. "We prefer b&w photos, usually of a single item against a simple background. Color photos can be used if there is good contrast between darks and lights." Captions required.

BANK NOTE REPORTER, Krause Publications, 700 E. State St., Iola WI 54990. (715)445-2214. Editor: Robert F. Lemke. 30% freelance written. Works with a small number of new/unpublished writers each year, and is eager to work with new/unpublished writers. Monthly tabloid for advanced collectors of U.S. and world paper money. Circ. 4,250. Pays on publication. Publishes ms an average of 2 months after acceptance. Byline given. Buys first North American serial rights and reprint rights. Photocopied submissions acceptable. Query for electronic submissions. Computer printout submissions acceptable; prefers letter-quality. Reports in 2 weeks. Sample copy for 8½x11 SAE and 3 first class stamps.
Nonfiction: "We review articles covering any phase of paper money collecting including investing, display, storage, history, art, story behind a particular piece of paper money and the business of paper money." News items not solicited. "Our staff covers the hard news." Buys 6 mss/issue. Send complete ms. Length: 500-3,000 words. Pays 3¢/word to first-time contributors; negotiates fee for later articles. Pays the expenses of writers on assignment.
Photos: Pays $5 for 5x7 b&w glossy prints. Captions and model releases required.
Tips: "The writer has a better chance of breaking in at our publication with short articles due to the technical nature of the subject matter and sophistication of our readers. Material about bank notes used in a writer's locale would be interesting, useful, encouraged. We like new names."

BASEBALL CARDS, Krause Publications, 700 E. State St., Iola WI 54990. (715)445-2214. Editor: Bob Lemke. 50% freelance written. Eager to work with new/unpublished writers. A monthly magazine covering sports memorabilia collecting. "Geared for the novice collector or general public who might become interested in the hobby." Circ. 180,000. Pays on publication. Publishes ms an average of 3 months after acceptance. Byline given. Buys first North American serial rights and second serial (reprint) rights. Submit seasonal/holiday material 6 months in advance. Photocopied submissions OK. Computer printout submissions acceptable; no dot-matrix. Reports in 2 weeks. Sample copy for 8½x11 SAE with 3 first class stamps.
Nonfiction: General interest, historical/nostalgic, how-to (enjoy or enhance your collection) and photo fea-

ture. No personal reminiscences of collecting baseball cards as a kid or articles that relate to baseball, rather than cards. Buys 24-36 mss/year. Query. Length: 2,000-4,000 words. Pays up to $250.

Photos: Send photos with submission. Reviews contact sheets and transparencies. Offers no additional payment for photos accepted with ms. Identification of subjects required.

Tips: "We would like to receive knowledgeable features on specific collectibles: card sets, team items, etc. A heavier emphasis on 1980s collectibles will affect the types of freelance material we buy in 1989."

‡BECKETT BASEBALL CARD MONTHLY, Statabase, Inc., Suite 110, 3410 MidCourt, Carrollton TX 75006. (214)991-6657. Editor: Dr. James Beckett. Managing Editor: Fred Reed. 85% freelance written. Monthly magazine on baseball card and sports memorabilia collecting. "Our readers expect our publication to be entertaining and informative. Our slant is that hobbies are for fun and rewarding. Especially wanted are how-to collect articles." Circ. 140,000. Pays on acceptance. Publishes ms an average of 4 months after acceptance. Byline given. Pays $50 kill fee. Buys first North American serial rights. Submit seasonal/holiday material 6 months in advance. Query for electronic submissions. Computer printout submissions OK; prefers letter-quality. Reports in 1 month. Sample copy $2.50; free writer's guidelines.

Nonfiction: Book excerpts, historical/nostalgic, how-to, humor, interview/profile, new product, opinion, personal experience, photo feature, technical. Special issues include: March (spring training/new card sets issued); July (Hall of Fame/All Star Game issue); October (World Series issue); November (autograph special issue). No articles that emphasize speculative prices and investments. Buys 90 mss/year. Send complete ms. Length: 300-2,000 words. Pays $100-400 for assigned articles; $50-200 for unsolicited articles. Sometimes pays expenses of writers on assignment.

Photos: Send photos with submission. Reviews 35mm transparencies, 5x7 or larger prints. Offers $10-100 per photo. Captions, model releases and identification of subjects required. Buys one-time rights.

Columns/Departments: Pepper Hastings, editor. Autograph Experiences (memorable experience with baseball star), 50-400 words; Prospects (players on the verge of major league stardom), 300-500 words; Collecting Tips (basic but overlooked helpful hints), 300-500 words; Trivia (major league baseball odd or humorous facts), 20-50 words; Player Vignettes (general baseball articles featuring emerging or provem superstars). Buys 40 mss/years. Send complete ms. Length: 50-400 words. Pays $25-100.

Fiction: Humorous only.

Tips: "A writer for *Becket Baseball Card Monthly* should be an avid sports fan and/or a collector with an enthusiasm for sharing his/her interests with others. First person (not research) articles presenting the writer's personal experiences told with wit and humor, and emphasizing the stars of the game, are *always* wanted."

THE BLADE MAGAZINE, Box 22007, Chattanooga TN 37422. Editor: J. Bruce Voyles. 90% freelance written. For knife enthusiasts who want to know as much as possible about quality knives and edged weapons. Bimonthly magazine. Pays on publication. Publishes ms an average of 6 months after acceptance. Buys all rights. Submit seasonal/holiday material 6 months in advance. Previously published submissions OK. Computer printout submissions acceptable; no dot-matrix. Reports in 2 months. Sample copy $2.95; writer's guidelines for #10 SASE.

Nonfiction: How-to; historical (on knives and weapons); adventure on a knife theme; interview (knifemakers); celebrities who own knives; knives featured in movies with shots from the movie, etc.; new product; nostalgia; personal experience; photo feature; profile and technical. "We would also like to receive articles on knives in adventuresome life-saving situations." No poetry. Buys 75 unsolicited mss/year. "We evaluate complete manuscripts and make our decision on that basis." Length: 1,000-2,000 words. Pays 5¢/word minimum, more for better writers. "We will pay top dollar in the knife market." Sometimes pays the expenses of writers on assignment.

Photos: Send photos with ms. Pays $5 for 8x10 b&w glossy prints, $25-75 for 35mm color transparencies. Captions required.

Tips: "We are always willing to read submissions from anyone who has read a few copies and studied the market. The ideal article for us is a piece bringing out the romance, legend, and love of man's oldest tool—the knife. We like articles that place knives in peoples' hands—in life saving situations, adventure modes, etc. (Nothing gory or with the knife as the villain). People and knives are good copy. We are getting more and better written articles from writers who are reading the publication beforehand. That makes for a harder sell for the quickie writer not willing to do his homework."

THE COIN ENTHUSIAST'S JOURNAL, Masongate Publishing, Box 1383, Torrance CA 90505. Editor: William J. Cook. 40% freelance written. Prefers to work with published/established writers, and works with a small number of new/unpublished writers each year. Monthly newsletter covering numismatics (coin collecting) and bullion trading. "Our purpose is to give readers information to help them make sound investment decisions in the areas we cover and to help them get more enjoyment out of their hobby." Circ. 2,000. Pays on publication. Publishes ms an average of 2 months after acceptance. Byline given. Offers $25 kill fee. Buys all rights. Submit seasonal/holiday material 3 months in advance. Simultaneous queries and simultaneous and photocopied submissions OK. Computer printout submissions acceptable; prefers letter-quality. Reports in 3

weeks. Sample copy for #10 SAE and 2 first class stamps; writer's guidelines for SAE and 1 first class stamp.
Nonfiction: How-to (make money from your hobby and be a better trader); opinion (what is the coin market going to do?); personal experience (insiders' "tricks of the trade"); and technical (why are coin prices going up [or down]?). No "crystal ball" predictions, i.e., "I see silver going up to $200 per ounce by mid-1989." Query with published clips. Length: 500-2,500 words. Buys 20 mss/year. Pays $50-200; fees negotiable. Also looking for "staff writers" who will submit material each month or bimonthly.
Photos: State availability of photos with query. Pays $5-25 for b&w prints. Buys one-time rights.
Tips: "We run few short articles. Be able to show an in-depth knowledge and experience in numismatics and also show the ability to be creative in developing new ideas for the coin industry."

COINS, Krause Publications, 700 E. State St., Iola WI 54990. (715)445-2214. Editor: Arlyn G. Sieber. 75% freelance written. Eager to work with new/unpublished writers. Monthly magazine about U.S. and foreign coins for all levels of collectors, investors and dealers. Circ. 65,000. Computer printout submissions acceptable; prefers letter-quality.
Nonfiction: "We'd like to see articles on any phase of the coin hobby; collection, investing, displaying, history, art, the story behind the coin, unusual collections, profiles on dealers and the business of coins." No news items. "Our staff covers the hard news." Buys 8 mss/issue. Send complete ms. Length: 500-5,000 words. Pays 3¢/word to first-time contributors; fee negotiated for later articles. Sometimes pays the expenses of writers on assignment.
Photos: Pays $5 minimum for b&w prints. Pays $25 minimum for 35mm color transparencies used. Captions and model releases required. Buys first rights.

CRAFTS 'N THINGS, 14 Main St., Park Ridge IL 60068. (312)825-2161. Editor: Nancy Tosh. Associate Editor: Jackie Thielen. Published 8 times a year, covering quality crafts for today's creative woman. Circ. 320,000. Pays on publication. Byline, photo and brief bio given. Buys first North American serial rights. Submit seasonal/holiday material 6 months in advance. Reports in 1 month. Free sample copy.
Nonfiction: How-to (do a craft project). Buys 7-14 mss/issue. "Send in a photo of the item and complete directions. We will consider it and return if not accepted." Length: 1-4 magazine pages. Pays $50-200, "depending on how much staff work is required."
Photos: "Generally, we will ask that you send the item so we can photograph it ourselves."
Tips: "We're looking more for people who can craft than people who can write."

DECORATIVE ARTIST'S WORKBOOK, F&W Publishing, 1507 Dana Ave., Cincinnati OH 45207. Editorial Director: Michael Ward. 50% freelance written. Bimonthly magazine covering tole and decorative painting and related art forms. Offers "straightforward, personal instruction in the techniques of tole and decorative painting." Estab. 1987. Circ. 45,000. Pays on acceptance. Byline given. Offers 20% kill fee. Buys first North American serial rights. Submit seasonal/holiday material 6 months in advance. Photocopied submissions OK. Computer printout submissions OK; no dot-matrix. Reports in 1 month. Sample copy for $2.95 with 9x12 SAE and 7 first class stamps.
Nonfiction: How-to (related to tole and decorative painting), new product and technical. No profiles and/or general interest topics. Buys 30 mss/year. Query with slides or photos. Length: 1,200-1,800 words. Pays 10-12¢/word.
Photos: State availability of photos and slides with submission or send photos with submission. Reviews 35mm, 4x5 transparencies or good quality photos. Offers no additional payment for photos accepted with ms. Captions required. Buys one-time rights.
Fillers: Anecdotes, facts and short humor. Buys 10/year. Length: 50-200 words. Pays $10-20.
Tips: "The more you know—and can prove you know—about decorative painting the better your chances. I'm looking for experts in the field who, through their own experience, can artfully describe the techniques involved. How-to articles are most open to freelancers. Be sure to query with slides or transparencies, and show that you understand the extensive graphic requirements for these pieces, and are able to provide progressives—slides that show works in progress."

DOLLS, The Collector's Magazine, Collector Communications Corp., 170 5th Ave., New York NY 10010. (212)989-8700. Editorial Director: Krystyna Poray Goddu. 75% freelance written. Works with a small number of new/unpublished writers each year. Bimonthly magazine covering doll collecting "for collectors of antique, contemporary and reproduction dolls. We publish well-researched, professionally written articles that are illustrated with photographs of high quality, color or black-and-white." Circ. 70,000. Pays within 1 month of acceptance. Publishes ms an average of 6 months after acceptance. Byline given. "Almost all first manuscripts are on speculation. We rarely kill assigned stories, but fee would be about 33% of article fee." Buys first serial rights, first North American serial rights ("almost always"), second serial rights if piece has appeared in a noncompeting publication. Submit seasonal/holiday material 6 months in advance. Photocopied submissions considered (not preferred); previously published submissions OK. Computer printout submissions acceptable; no dot-matrix. Reports in 2 months. Sample copy $2; writer's guidelines for SAE and 1 first class stamp.

Nonfiction: Book excerpts; historical (with collecting angle); interview/profile (on collectors with outstanding collections); new product (just photos and captions; "we do not pay for these, but regard them as publicity"); opinion ("A Personal Definition of Dolls"); technical (doll restoration advice by experts only); and travel (museums and collections around the world). "No sentimental, uninformed 'my doll collection' or 'my grandma's doll collection' stories or trade magazine-type stories on shops, etc. Our readers are knowledgeable collectors." Query with clips. Length: 500-2,500 words. Pays $100-350. Sometimes pays expenses of writers on assignment.

Photos: Send photos with accompanying query or ms. Reviews 4x5 color transparencies; 4x5 or 8x10 b&w prints and also 35mm slides. "We do not buy photographs submitted without manuscripts unless we have assigned them; we pay for the manuscript/photos package in one fee." Captions required. Buys one-time rights.

Columns/Departments: Doll Views—a miscellany of news and views of the doll world includes reports on upcoming or recently held events. "*Not* the place for new dolls, auction prices or dates; we have regular contributors or staff assigned to those columns." Query with clips if available or send complete ms. Length: 200-500 words. Pays $25-75. Doll Views items are rarely bylined.

Fillers: "We don't really use fillers but would consider them if we got something very good. Hints on restoring, for example, or a nice illustration." Length: 500 words maximum. Pays $25-75.

Tips: "We need experts in the field who are also good writers. The most frequent mistake made by writers in completing an article assignment for us is being unfamiliar with the field; our readers are very knowledgeable. Freelancers who are not experts should know their particular story thoroughly and do background research to get the facts correct. Well-written queries from writers outside the NYC area are especially welcomed. Non-experts should stay away from technical or specific subjects (restoration, price trends). Short profiles of unusual collectors or a story of a local museum collection, with good photos, might catch our interest. Editors want to know they are getting something from a writer they cannot get from anyone else. Good writing should be a given, a starting point. After that, it's what you know."

EARLY AMERICAN LIFE, Historical Times, Inc., Box 8200, Harrisburg PA 17105. Editor: Frances Carnahan. 60-70% freelance written. Bimonthly magazine for "people who are interested in capturing the warmth and beauty of the 1600 to 1900 period and using it in their homes and lives today. They are interested in arts, crafts, travel, restoration and collecting." Circ. 300,000. Buys all rights. Buys 50 mss/year. Pays on acceptance. Publishes ms an average of 1 year after acceptance. Photocopied submissions OK. Computer printout submissions OK; no dot-matrix. Sample copy and writer's guidelines for 9x12 SAE and 4 first class stamps. Reports in 1 month. Query or submit complete ms with SASE.

Nonfiction: "Social history (the story of the people, not epic heroes and battles), traditional crafts such as woodworking and needlepoint, travel to historic sites, country inns, antiques and reproductions, refinishing and restoration, architecture and decorating. We try to entertain as we inform and always attempt to give the reader something he can do. While we're always on the lookout for good pieces on any of our subjects, the 'travel to historic sites' theme is most frequently submitted. Would like to see more how-to-do-it (well-illustrated) on how real people did something great to their homes." Buys 50 mss/year. Query or submit complete ms. Length: 750-3,000 words. Pays $50-500. Pays expenses of writers on assignment.

Photos: Pays $10 for 5x7 (and up) b&w photos used with mss, minimum of $25 for color. Prefers 2¼x2¼ and up, but can work from 35mm.

Tips: "Our readers are eager for ideas on how to bring early America into their lives. Conceive a new approach to satisfy their related interests in arts, crafts, travel to historic sites, and especially in houses decorated in the early American style. Write to entertain and inform at the same time, and be prepared to help us with illustrations, or sources for them."

EDGES, The Official Publication of the American Blade Collectors Association, American Blade, Inc., 2835 Hickory Valley Rd., Chattanooga TN 37421. Editor: J. Bruce Voyles. Bimonthly tabloid covering the knife business. Circ. 20,000. Pays on publication. Byline given. Buys all rights. Submit seasonal/holiday material 6 months in advance. Simultaneous queries, and photocopied and previously published submissions OK "as long as they are exclusive to our market." Reports in 5 months. Acknowledges receipt of queries and ms in 2 months. Sample copy $1.

Nonfiction: "Emphasis on pocket knives and folders." Book excerpts, expose, general interest, historical (well-researched), how-to, humor, new product, opinion, personal experience, photo feature, and technical. "We look for articles on all aspects of the knife business, including technological advances, profiles, knife shows, and well-researched history. Ours is not a hard market to break into if the writer is willing to do a little research. To have a copy is almost a requirement." Buys 150 mss/year. Send complete ms. Length: 50-3,000 words "or more if material warrants additional length." Pays 5¢/word.

Photos: Pays $5 for 5x7 b&w prints. Captions and model release required (if persons are identifiable).

Fillers: Clippings, anecdotes and newsbreaks.

Tips: "If writers haven't studied the publication they shouldn't bother to submit an article. If they have studied it, we're an easy market to sell to." Buys 80% of the articles geared to "the knife business."

FIBERARTS, The Magazine of Textiles, 50 College St., Asheville NC 28801. (704)253-0467. Editor: Carol Lawrence. 85% freelance written. Eager to work with new/unpublished writers; works with a small number of new/unpublished writers each year. Bimonthly magazine covering textiles as art and craft (weaving, quilting, surface design, stitchery, knitting, fashion, crochet, etc.) for textile artists, craftspeople, hobbyists, teachers, museum and gallery staffs, collectors and enthusiasts. Circ. 26,000. Pays on publication. Publishes ms an average of 4 months after acceptance. Byline given. Rights purchased are negotiable. Submit seasonal/holiday material 8 months in advance. Editorial guidelines and style sheet available. Computer printout submissions acceptable; prefers letter-quality. Reports within 2 weeks. Sample copy $4 and 10x12 SAE with 2 first class stamps; writer's guidelines for #10 SAE with 2 first class stamps.

Nonfiction: Book excerpts; historical/nostalgic; how-to; humor; interview/profile; opinion; personal experience; photo feature; technical; travel (for the textile enthusiast, e.g., collecting rugs in Turkey); and education, trends, exhibition reviews and textile news. Buys 25-50 mss/year. Query. "Please be very specific about your proposal. Also an important consideration in accepting an article is the kind of photos—35mm slides and/or b&w glossies—that you can provide as illustration. We like to see photos in advance." Length: 250-1,200 words. Pays $40-300, depending on article. Sometimes (rarely) pays the expenses of writers on assignment.

Tips: "Our writers are very familiar with the textile field, and this is what we look for in a new writer. Familiarity with textile techniques, history or events determines clarity of an article more than a particular style of writing. The writer should also be familiar with *Fiberarts*, the magazine. We outline our upcoming issues in regular Editorial Agendas far enough in advance for a prospective writer to be aware of our future needs."

FINESCALE MODELER, Kalmbach Publishing Co., 1027 N. 7th St., Milwaukee WI 53233. (414)272-2060. Editor: Bob Hayden. 80% freelance written. Eager to work with new/unpublished writers. Bimonthly magazine "devoted to how-to-do-it modeling information for scale modelbuilders who build non-operating aircraft, tanks, boats, automobiles, figures, dioramas, and science fiction and fantasy models." Circ. 79,114. Pays on acceptance. Publishes ms an average of 14 months after acceptance. Byline given. Buys all rights. Computer printout submissions acceptable; prefers letter-quality. Reports in 6 weeks on queries; 3 months on mss. Sample copy for 9x12 SAE and 3 first class stamps; free writer's guidelines.

Nonfiction: How-to (build scale models); and technical (research information for building models). Query or send complete ms. Length: 750-3,000 words. Pays $30/published page minimum.

Photos: Send photos with ms. Pays $7.50 minimum for color transparencies and $5 minimum for 5x7 b&w prints. Captions and identification of subjects required. Buys one-time rights.

Columns/Departments: *FSM* Showcase (photos plus description of model); and *FSM* Tips and Techniques (modelbuilding hints and tips). Buys 25-50 Tips and Techniques/year. Query or send complete ms. Length: 100-1,000 words. Pays $5-75.

Tips: "A freelancer can best break in first through hints and tips, then through feature articles. Most people who write for *FSM* are modelers first, writers second. This is a specialty magazine for a special, quite expert audience. Essentially, 99% of our writers will come from that audience."

THE FRANKLIN MINT ALMANAC, Franklin Center PA 19091. (215)459-7015. Editor-in-Chief: Barbara Cady. Editor: Anna Sequoia. 90% freelance written. Bimonthly magazine covering collecting, fashion, and fine and decorative arts for members of Franklin Mint Collectors Society who are regular customers and others who request. Circ. 1,200,000. Pays on acceptance. Publishes ms an average of 1 month after acceptance. Byline given. Pays negotiable kill fee. Buys one-time world rights. Computer printout submissions acceptable; prefers letter-quality. Reports in 3 weeks on queries.

Nonfiction: Profiles of collectors and their world class collections. Some celebrity/collector profiles. Buys 30 mss/year. Query. Length: 1,000-1,200 words. Payment depends upon subject and writer. Pays expenses of writers on assignment.

Photos: State availability of photos.

Tips: "Solid writing credentials and a knowledge of collecting are a must. ALMANAC has gone through a major series of editorial changes. Each ussue is now theme-specific (i.e., "The Passionate Collector," "The American Designer," "Japanese Style"), - It is the collectors' magazine with the largest circulation in the world."

‡**GEM SHOW NEWS**, Shows of Integrity, Rt. #2, Box 78, Blue Ridge TX 75004. (214)752-5192. Editor: Judi Tripp. Managing Editor: Stacy Hobbs. 50% freelance written. A bimonthly newspaper on precious stones, mineral collecting and jewelry. "Slant should be gem/collectible investments including gold, gold coins, silver, silver jewelry and original silver designs." Circ. 12,000-30,000. Pays on acceptance. Publishes ms an average of 2 months after acceptance. Byline given. Publication not copyrighted. Buys first rights and makes work-for-hire assignments. Submit seasonal/holiday material 4 months in advance. Simultaneous, photocopied and previously published submissions OK. Computer printout submissions OK; prefers letter-quality. Reports in 6 weeks. Sample copy for 9x12 SAE and 5 first class stamps. Writer's guidelines for #10 SAE with 1 first class stamp.

Nonfiction: How-to (gem collecting/gem cutting/collecting), humor, interview/profile, new product, personal experience, photo feature, technical, travel. Buys 30 mss/year. Send complete ms. Length: 1,000-3,000 words. Pays $50-150.

Photos: Send photos with submission. Reviews prints (3x5). Offers $5-10/photo. Captions, model releases and identification of subjects required. Buys one-time rights.

Fillers: Anecdotes, facts, gags to be illustrated by cartoonist, newsbreaks, short humor. Buys 30 mss/year. Length: 500 words maximum. Pays $10-25.

Tips: "Attend gem and jewelry shows to see the interest in this field. The gem and mineral collecting field is the second most popular hobby (second only to coin and stamp collecting) in the U.S. All areas are open, including current fads and trends such as articles on the current quartz crystals and crystal healing craze and related subjects."

HANDS-ON-ELECTRONICS, Gernsback Publications, Inc., 500B Bi-County Blvd., Farmingdale NY 11735. (516)293-3000. Editor: Julian Martin. 95% freelance written. Monthly magazine covering hobby electronics—"features, projects, ideas related to audio, CB, radio, experimenting, test equipment, antique radio, communications, state-of-the-art, etc." Circ. 60,000. Pays on acceptance. Byline given. Buys all rights. Submit seasonal/holiday material 6 months in advance. Simultaneous, photocopied and previously published submissions OK. Query for electronic submissions. Computer printout submissions OK; prefers letter-quality. Reports in 2 weeks. Free sample copy, "include label." Writer's guidelines for SASE.

Nonfiction: General interest, how-to, photo feature and technical. Buys 200 + mss/year. Query or send complete ms. Length: 1,000-3,500 words. Pays $100-350.

Photos: Send photos with submission. Reviews contact sheets or 5x7 prints. Offers no additional payment for photos accepted with ms. Captions required. Buys all rights.

Fiction: "Very little purchased." Experimental, historical, humorous and science fiction. Buys 5 mss/year. Query or send complete ms. Length: 1,000-2,000 words. Pays $100-200.

Tips: "In 1989, the title of *Popular Electronics* will replace the current title of *Hands-On Electronics*."

HANDWOVEN, from Interweave Press, 306 N. Washington, Loveland CO 80537. (303)669-7672. Editor: Jane Patrick. 75% freelance written. Bimonthly magazine (except July) covering handweaving, spinning and dyeing. Audience includes "practicing textile craftsmen. Article should show considerable depth of knowledge of subject, although tone should be informal and accessible." Circ. 35,000. Pays on publication. Publishes ms an average of 10 months after acceptance. Byline given. Pays 50% kill fee. Buys first North American serial rights. Simultaneous queries and photocopied submissions OK. Computer printout submissions acceptable; prefers letter-quality. Sample copy $4.50; writer's guidelines for #10 SASE.

Nonfiction: Historical and how-to (on weaving and other craft techniques; specific items with instructions); and technical (on handweaving, spinning and dyeing technology). "All articles must contain a high level of in-depth information. Our readers are very knowledgeable about these subjects." Query. Length: 500-2,000 words. Pays $35-150.

Photos: State availability of photos. Identification of subjects required.

Tips: "We prefer work written by writers with an in-depth knowledge of weaving. We're particularly interested in articles about new weaving and spinning techniques as well as applying these techniques to finished products."

HOME MECHANIX, 1515 Broadway, New York NY 10036. (212)719-6630. Editor: Joseph R. Provey. Executive Editor: Harry Wicks. Managing Editor: Jim Wigdahl. 50% freelance written. Prefers to work with published/established writers. "If it's good, we're interested, whether writer is new or experienced." Monthly magazine for the home and car manager. "Articles on maintenance, repair and renovation to the home and family car. Information on how to buy, how to select products useful to homeowners/car owners. Emphasis in home-oriented articles is on good design, inventive solutions to styling and space problems, useful home-workshop projects." Circ. 1.2 million. Pays on acceptance. Publishes ms an average of 3 months after acceptance. Byline given. Buys first North American serial rights. Computer printout submissions acceptable; prefers letter-quality. Query.

Nonfiction: Feature articles relating to homeowner/car owner, 1,500-2,500 words. "This may include personal home-renovation projects, professional advice on interior design, reports on different or unusual construction methods, energy-related subjects, outdoor/backyard projects, etc. We are no longer interested in high-tech subjects such as aerospace, electronics, photography or military hardware. Most of our automotive features are written by experts in the field, but fillers, tips, how-to repair, or modification articles on the family car are welcome. Workshop articles on furniture, construction, tool use, refinishing techniques, etc., are also sought. Pays $300 minimum for features; fees based on number of printed pages, photos accompanying mss., etc." Pays expenses of writers on assignment.

Photos: Photos should accompany mss. Pays $600 and up for transparencies for cover. Inside color: $300/1 page, $500/2, $700/3, etc. Home and Shop hints illustrated with 1 photo, $40. Captions and model releases required.

Fillers: Tips and fillers useful to tool users or for general home maintenance. Pays $25 and up for illustrated and captioned fillers.

Tips: "The most frequent mistake made by writers in completing an article assignment for *Home Mechanix* is not taking the time to understand its editorial focus and special needs."

THE HOME SHOP MACHINIST, The Home Shop Machinist, Inc., 2779 Aero Park Dr., Box 1810, Traverse City MI 49685. (616)946-3712. Editor: Joe D. Rice. 95% freelance written. Bimonthly magazine covering machining and metalworking for the hobbyist. Circ. 23,000. Pays on publication. Publishes ms an average of 18 months after acceptance. Byline given. Buys first North American serial rights only. Simultaneous submissions OK. Computer printout submissions acceptable; prefers letter-quality. Reports in 3 weeks. Free sample copy and writer's guidelines.
Nonfiction: How-to (projects designed to upgrade present shop equipment or hobby model projects that require machining); and technical (should pertain to metalworking, machining, drafting, layout, welding or foundry work for the hobbyist). No fiction. Buys 50 mss/year. Query or send complete ms. Length: open—"whatever it takes to do a thorough job." Pays $40/published page, plus $9/published photo; $70/page for camera-ready art; and $40 for b&w cover photo.
Photos: Send photos with ms. Pays $9-40 for 5x7 b&w prints. Captions and identification of subjects required.
Columns/Departments: Sheetmetal; Book Reviews; New Product Reviews; Micro-Machining; and Foundry. "Writer should become familiar with our magazine before submitting. Query first." Buys 16 mss/year. Length: 600-1,500 words. Pays $40-70/page.
Fillers: Machining tips/shortcuts. No news clippings. Buys 12-15/year. Length: 100-300 words. Pays $30-48.
Tips: "The writer should be experienced in the area of metalworking and machining; should be extremely thorough in explanations of methods, processes—always with an eye to safety; and should provide good quality b&w photos and/or clear drawings to aid in description. Visuals are of increasing importance to our readers. Carefully planned photos, drawings and charts will carry a submission to our magazine much farther along the path to publication."

‡INTERNATIONAL WOODWORKING, Glove Hollow Press, Box 706, Rt. 3 and Cummings Hill Rd., Plymouth NH 03264. (603)536-3876. Editor: Doug Werbeck. 90% freelance written. Quarterly magazine on woodworking for hobbyists and professionals. Articles with drawn plans and diagrams are encouraged. Circ. 8,000. Pays on acceptance. Byline given. 50% kill fee offered. Buys one-time rights. Submit seasonal/holiday material 6 months in advance. Simultaneous, photocopied and previously published submissions OK. Query for electronic submissions. Computer printout submissions OK. Reports in 1 month. Free sample copy and writer's guidelines.
Nonfiction: Book excerpts, general interest, how-to, humor, interview/profile, new product, opinion, personal experience, photo feature, technical. Buys 25 mss/year. Query with or without clips, or send complete ms. Length: 500-2,000 words. Pays $25-250. Pays expenses of writers on assignment.
Photos: Send photos with submission. Reviews contact sheets, transparencies and 3x5 or larger prints. Offers $5-15 per photo. Caption, model releases and indentification of subjects required. Buys one-time rights.
Columns/Departments: Ellen Engel, Assistant Editor. Ask an Expert; Ask Doc, both 1,000-2,000 words; New Products, 100-500 words; Carving, 1,000-2,000 words. Buys 20 mss/year. Query or send complete ms. Pays $15-250.
Fillers: Ellen Engel, Assistant Editor. Anecdotes, facts, gags to be illustrated by cartoonist, newsbreaks and short humor. Buys 100/year. Length: 100-1,000 words. Pays $10-100.
Tips: "We are an easy to work with publication whose purpose is to disseminate information, how-to's and helpful tips and techniques to professional and serious hobbyists."

JUGGLER'S WORLD, International Jugglers Association, Box 443, Davidson NC 28036. (704)892-1296. Editor: Bill Giduz. 25% freelance written. A quarterly magazine on juggling. "*Juggler's World* publishes news, feature articles, fiction, and poetry that relates to juggling. We also encourage 'how to' articles describing how to learn various juggling tricks." Circ. 3,500. Pays on acceptance. Publishes ms an average of 6 months after acceptance. Byline given. Buys all rights. Submit seasonal/holiday material 6 months in advance. Simultaneous, photocopied and previously published submissions OK. Query for electronic submissions. Computer printout submissions OK. Reports in 1 week. Sample copy for 8½x11 SAE with 5 first class stamps.
Nonfiction: Essays, general interest, historical/nostalgic, how-to, humor, interview/profile, opinion, personal experience, photo feature and travel. Buys 10 mss/year. Query. Length: 500-2,000 words. Pays $50-100 for assigned articles. Pays expenses of writers on assignment.
Photos: State availability of photos with submission. Reviews contact sheets, negatives and prints. Offers no additional payment for photos accepted with ms. Captions required. Buys one-time rights.
Fiction: Ken Letko, fiction editor. Adventure, fantasy, historical, humorous, science fiction and slice-of-life vignettes. Buys 2 mss/year. Query. Length: 250-1,000 words. Pays $25-50.
Tips: "The best approach is a feature article on or an interview with a leading juggler. Article should include both human interest material to describe the performer as a individual and technical juggling information to make it clear to a knowledgeable audience the exact tricks and skits performed."

THE LEATHER CRAFTSMAN, Craftsman Publishing, Box 1386, Fort Worth TX 76101. (817)923-6787. Editor: Nancy Sawyer. 95% freelance written. Eager to work with new/unpublished writers. A bimonthly magazine covering leathercrafting or leather art. "We are dedicated to the preservation of leather craft and leather art. Each issue contains articles on leather crafters, helpful hints and projects that our readers try at home or in their businesses." Circ. 10,000. Pays on publication. Publishes ms an average of 6-12 months after acceptance. Byline given. Buys first rights. Submit seasonal/holiday material 6 months in advance. Computer printout submissions acceptable; prefers letter-quality. Reports in 2 weeks on queries; 1 month on mss. Sample copy $3.50; free writer's guidelines.

Nonfiction: How-to on leathercrafting projects. No articles not related to leather in some way. Send complete ms. Pays $25-200.

Photos: Send photos or completed project with submission. Reviews transparencies and prints. Offers no additional payment for photos accepted with ms. Captions required.

Tips: "*The Leather Craftsman* is dedicated to the preservation of leather craft and leather art. All aspects of the craft including carving, stamping, dyeing, sewing, decorating, etc., are presented to our readers through the use of step by step instructions. We are interested in more articles concerning leather apparel."

LIVE STEAM, Live Steam, Inc., 2779 Aero Park Dr., Box 629, Traverse City MI 49685. (616)941-7160. Editor: Joe D. Rice. 90% freelance written. Eager to work with new/unpublished writers. Monthly magazine covering steam-powered models and full-size engines (i.e., locomotives, traction, cars, boats, stationary, etc.) "Our readers are hobbyists, many of whom are building their engines from scratch. We are interested in anything that has to do with the world of live steam-powered machinery." Circ. 12,800. Pays on publication. Publishes ms an average of 18 months after acceptance. Byline given. Buys first North American serial rights only. Computer printout submissions acceptable; prefers letter-quality. Reports in 3 weeks. Free sample copy and writer's guidelines.

Nonfiction: Historical/nostalgic; how-to (build projects powered by steam); new product; personal experience; photo feature; and technical (must be within the context of steam-powered machinery or on machining techniques). No fiction. Buys 50 mss/year. Query or send complete ms. Length: 500-3,000 words. Pays $30/published page—$500 maximum. Sometimes pays the expenses of writers on assignment.

Photos: Send photos with ms. Pays $50/page of finished art. Pays $8 for 5x7 b&w prints; $40 for cover (color). Captions and identification of subjects required.

Columns/Departments: Steam traction engines, steamboats, stationary steam, and steam autos. Buys 6-8 mss/year. Query. Length: 1,000-3,000 words. Pays $20-50.

Tips: "At least half of all our material is from the freelancer. Requesting a sample copy and author's guide will be a good place to start. The writer must be well-versed in the nature of live steam equipment and the hobby of scale modeling such equipment. Technical and historical accuracy is an absolute must. Often, good articles are weakened or spoiled by mediocre to poor quality photos. Freelancers must learn to take a *good* photograph."

LOOSE CHANGE, Mead Publishing Co., 1515 S. Commerce St., Las Vegas NV 89102-2703. (702)387-8750. Publisher: Daniel R. Mead. 10-20% freelance written. Eager to work with new/unpublished writers. Monthly magazine covering gaming and coin-operated machines. Slot machines; trade stimulators; jukeboxes; gumball and peanut vendors; pinballs; scales; etc. "Our audience is predominantly male. Readers are all collectors or enthusiasts of coin-operated machines, particularly slot machines and jukeboxes. Subscribers are, in general, not heavy readers." Circ. 3,000. Pays on acceptance. Publishes ms an average of 2-3 months after acceptance. Byline given. Prefers to buy all rights, but also buys first and reprint rights. "We may allow author to reprint upon request in noncompetitive publications." Photocopied submissions OK. Previously published submissions must be accompanied by complete list of previous sales, including sale dates. Query for electronic submissions. Computer printout acceptable; prefers letter-quality. Reports in 1 month on queries; 6 weeks on mss. Sample copy $1; writer's guidelines for #10 SASE.

Nonfiction: Historical/nostalgic, how-to, interview/profile, opinion, personal experience, photo feature and technical. "Articles illustrated with clear, black and white photos are always considered much more favorably than articles without photos (we have a picture-oriented audience). The writer must be knowledgeable about subject matter because our readers are knowledgeable and will spot inaccuracies." Buys up to 50 mss/year. Length: 900-6,000 words; 3,500-12,000 for cover stories. Pays $100 maximum, inside stories; $200 maximum, cover stories.

Photos: "Captions should tell a complete story without reference to the body text." Send photos with ms. Reviews 8x10 b&w glossy prints. Captions required. "Purchase price for articles includes payment for photos."

Fiction: "All fiction must have a gambling/coin-operated-machine angle. Very low emphasis is placed on fiction. Fiction must be exceptional to be acceptable to our readers." Buys maximum 4 mss/year. Send complete ms. Length: 800-2,500 words. Pays $60 maximum.

LOST TREASURE, Box 937, Bixby OK 74008. Managing Editor: Kathy Dyer. 95% freelance written. For treasure hunting hobbyists, relic collectors, amateur prospectors and miners. Monthly magazine; 72 pages. Circ. 55,000. Buys first rights only. Byline given. Buys 100 mss/year. Pays on publication. Will consider photocopied submissions. No simultaneous submissions. Computer printout submissions acceptable. Reports in 2 months. Submit complete ms. Publishes ms an average of 2 months after acceptance. Sample copy and writer's guidelines for 9x12 SASE.

Nonfiction: How-to articles about treasure hunting, coinshooting, personal, profiles, and stories about actual hunts, stories that give an unusual twist to treasure hunting—using detectors in an unorthodox way, odd sidelights on history, unusual finds. *Avoid* writing about the more famous treasures and lost mines. No bottle hunting stories. Length: 1,000-3,000 words. "If an article is well-written and covers its subject well, we'll buy it—regardless of length." Pays 3¢/word.

Photos: B&w glossy prints with mss help sell your story. Captions required.

Tips: "Read *Lost Treasure* before submitting your stories. We are especially interested in stories that deal with the more unusual aspects of treasure hunting and metal detecting. Try to avoid the obvious—give something different. Also—good photos and graphics are a *must*."

McCALL'S NEEDLEWORK & CRAFTS MAGAZINE, 825 7th Ave., (7th Floor), New York NY 10019. Editor: Rosemary Maceiras. Bimonthly. All rights bought for original needlework and handicraft designs.

Nonfiction: Submit preliminary color photos for editorial consideration. Accepted made-up items must be accompanied by directions, diagrams and charts. Payment ranges from $75 to a few hundred dollars.

MANUSCRIPTS, The Manuscript Society, Department of History, University of South Carolina, Columbia SC 29208. (803)777-6525. Editor: David R. Chesnutt. 10% freelance written. A quarterly magazine for collectors of autographs and manuscripts. Circ. 1,400. Pays on acceptance. Publishes ms an average of 6-18 months after acceptance. Byline given. Buys all rights. Query for electronic submissions. Computer printout submissions OK; prefers letter-quality. Reports in 2 weeks on queries; 1 month on mss.

Nonfiction: Historical, personal experience and photo feature. Buys 4-6 mss/year. Query. Length: 1,500-3,000 words. Pays $50-250 for unsolicited articles. Sample copy for 6½x9½ SAE and 5 first class stamps.

Photos: State availability of photos with submission. Reviews contact sheets and prints. Offers $15-30/photo. Captions and identification of subjects required. Buys one-time rights.

Tips: "The Society is a mix of autograph collectors, dealers and scholars who are interested in manuscripts. Good illustrations of manuscript material are essential. Unusual documents are most often the basis of articles. Scholarly apparatus may be used but is not required. Articles about significant collections of documents (or unusual collections) would be welcomed. Please query first."

‡MINIATURES SHOWCASE, Kalmbach Publishing Co., Suite 304, 633 W. Wisconsin Ave., Milwaukee WI 53203. (414)273-6332. Editor: Geraldine Willems. 80% freelance written. A quarterly magazine about dollhouse miniatures. "We feature a different decorating theme each issue—our articles support the miniature room scene we focus on." Circ. 20,000. Pays on publication. Publishes ms an average of 3 months after acceptance. Byline given. Buys all rights. Submit seasonal/holiday material 4 months in advance. Photocopied submissions OK. Query for electronic submissions. Computer printout submissions OK; prefers letter-quality. Reports in 2 weeks. Sample copy $3; writer's guidelines for SASE.

Nonfiction: Historical/social. Buys 16 mss/year. Query. Length: 100-1,000 words. Pays 10¢/word.

Photos: State availability of photos with submission. Reviews contact sheets, negatives, transparencies and 4 color prints only. Offers no additional payment for photos accepted with ms. Captions and identificaiton of subjects required. Buys all rights.

Tips: "Our articles are all assigned—a freelancer should query before sending in anything. Our features are open to freelancers—each issue deals with a different topic."

MODEL RAILROADER, 1027 N. 7th St., Milwaukee WI 53233. Editor: Russell G. Larson. For hobbyists interested in scale model railroading. Monthly. Buys exclusive rights. Study publication before submitting material. Reports on submissions within 1 month.

Nonfiction: Wants construction articles on specific model railroad projects (structures, cars, locomotives, scenery, benchwork, etc.). Also photo stories showing model railroads. Query. First-hand knowledge of subject almost always necessary for acceptable slant. Pays base rate of $66/page.

Photos: Buys photos with detailed descriptive captions only. Pays $7.50 and up, depending on size and use. Pays: double b&w rate for color; full color cover earns: $210.

‡MONITORING TIMES, Grove Enterprises Inc., Box 98, Brasstown NC 28902. (704)837-9200. Editor: Larry Miller. Managing Editor: Robert Grove. 80% freelance written. A monthly magazine for shortwave and scanner hobbyists. Circ. 15,000. Pays on acceptance. Publishes ms an average of 2 months after acceptance. Byline given. Buys first North American serial rights. Submit seasonal/holiday material 3 months in advance. Simultaneous and photocopied submissions OK. Query for electronic submission. Computer printout submissions OK; prefers letter-quality. Reports in 2 weeks. Free sample copy and writer's guidelines.

Nonfiction: General interest, how-to, humor, interview/profile, new product, opinion, personal experience, photo feature, technical. Buys 275 mss/year. Query. Length: 1,000-2,500 words. Pays $35-100.

Photos: State availability of photos with submission. Offers $10-25/photo. Captions required. Buys one-time rights.
Columns/Departments: Anything related to listening to shortwave scanner, radios, unusual transmissions or broadcasts; insights into monitoring, equipment and accessories, all frequency ranges. Query. Length: 1,000-2,500. Pays $25-100.

MOUNTAIN STATES COLLECTOR, Spree Publishing, Box 2525, Evergreen CO 80439. Editor: Carol Rudolph. Managing Editor: Peg DeStefano. 85% freelance written. A monthly tabloid covering antiques and collectibles. Circ. 8,000. Pays on publication. Publishes ms an average of 3 months after acceptance. Byline given. Not copyrighted. Buys first rights, one-time rights or second serial (reprint) rights to material published elsewhere. Submit seasonal/holiday material at least 3 months in advance. Simultaneous and previously published submissions OK. Computer printout submissions acceptable; prefers letter-quality. Reports in 3-6 weeks. Sample copy for 9x12 SAE with 4 first class stamps; writer's guidelines for SASE.
Nonfiction: About antiques and/or collectibles-Book excerpts, historical/nostalgic, how-to (collect), interview/profile (of collectors) and photo feature. Buys 75 mss/year. Query with or without published clips, or send complete ms. Length: 500-1,500 words. Pays $15. Sometimes pays the expenses of writers on assignment (mileage, phone-not long distance travel).
Photos: Send photos with submission. Reviews contact sheets, and 5x7 b&w prints. Offers $5/photo used. Captions required. Buys one-time rights.
Tips: "Writers should know their topics well or be prepared to do in-depth interviews with collectors. We prefer a down home approach. We need articles on antiques and on collectors and collections; how-to articles on collecting; how a collector can get started; or clubs for collectors. We would like to see more articles in 1989 with high-quality b&w photos."

NEEDLEPOINT NEWS, EGW International Corp., Box 5967, Concord CA 94524. (415)671-9852. Editor: Gerri Eggers. 95% freelance written. A bimonthly magazine covering needlepoint. Circ. 30,000. Pays on publication. Publishes ms an average of 6 months after acceptance. Byline given. Buys first serial rights. Submit seasonal/holiday material 3 months in advance. Simultaneous queries and submissions, and photocopied submissions OK. Computer printout submissions acceptable; no dot-matrix. Reports in 6 weeks. Sample copy $2 with 9x12 SAE and 5 first class stamps; writer's guidelines for #10 SASE.
Nonfiction: How-to (original designs and projects), interview/profile, new product, personal experience, photo feature, and technical. Buys 50 mss/year. Query with or without published clips. Length: 500-1,500 words. Pays $35/published page; pays $75/published page for original projects with step-by-step instructions.
Photos: Send photos with accompanying query or ms. Reviews color negatives, 4x5 transparencies, and 5x7 b&w prints. Pays $25 maximum. Captions and identification of subjects required. Buys one-time rights.
Tips: "*Needlepoint News* is devoted exclusively to the art of needlepoint and is especially interested in original designs and projects. We look for articles on any subject related to needlepoint that aids the stitcher, from original projects to technical articles. In the past, we have published a wealth of topics, both brief and extensive, and some in a series. We also provide information for the serious stitcher on how to sell one's work or open a business."

THE NEW YORK ANTIQUE ALMANAC, The New York Eye Publishing Co., Inc., Box 335, Lawrence NY 11559. (516)371-3300. Editor-in-Chief: Carol Nadel. Tabloid published 10 times/year. Emphasizes antiques, art, investments and nostalgia. 30% freelance written. Circ. 59,000. Pays on publication. Buys all rights. Byline given. Phone queries OK. Submit seasonal/holiday material "whenever available." Previously published submissions OK but must advise. Computer printout submissions acceptable; no dot-matrix. Reports in 6 weeks. Publishes ms an average of 6 months after acceptance. Free sample copy.
Nonfiction: Expose (fraudulent practices); historical (museums, exhibitions, folklore, background of events); how-to (clean, restore, travel, shop, invest); humor (jokes, cartoons, satire); informational; inspirational (essays); interviews (authors, shopkeepers, show managers, appraisers); nostalgia ("The Good Old Days" remembered various ways); personal experience (anything dealing with antiques, art, investments, nostalgia); opinion; photo feature (antique shows, art shows, fairs, crafts markets, restoration); profile; technical (repairing, purchasing, restoring); travel (shopping guides and tips); and investment (economics, and financial reviews). Buys 9 mss/issue. Query or submit complete ms. Length: 3,000 words maximum. Pays $15-75. "Expenses for accompanying photos will be reimbursed."
Photos: "Occasionally, we have photo essays (auctions, shows, street fairs, human interest) and pay $5/photo with caption."
Fillers: Personal experiences, commentaries, anecdotes. "Limited only by author's imagination." Buys 45 mss/year. Pays $5-15.
Tips: "Articles on shows or antique coverage accompanied by photos are definitely preferred."

THE NUMISMATIST, American Numismatic Association, 818 N. Cascade Ave., Colorado Springs CO 80903. (303)632-2646. Editor: N. Neil Harris. Production Editor: Barbara Gregory. Monthly magazine "for collectors of coins, medals, tokens and paper money." Circ. 35,000. Pays on publication. Publishes ms an average of 1 year after acceptance. Byline given. Buys first North American serial rights or second serial (reprint) rights. Submit seasonal/holiday material 1 year in advance. Previously published submissions OK. Computer printout submissions OK. Reports in 6 weeks. Free sample copy and writer's guidelines for #10 SASE.

Nonfiction: Essays, expose, general interest, historical/nostalgic, humor, interview/profile, new product, opinion, personal experience, photo feature and technical. No articles that are lengthy non-numismatic. Buys 48-60 mss/year. Send complete ms. Length: 1,000-3,500 words. Pays "on rate-per-published-page basis." Sometimes pays the expenses of writers on assignment.

Photos: Send photos with submission. Reviews contact sheets and 4x5 or 5x7 prints. Offers $2.50-5/photo. Captions and identification of subjects required. Buys one-time rights.

Columns/Departments: Buys 6 mss/year. Length: 775-2,000 words. "Pays negotiable flat fee per column."

OLD CARS WEEKLY, Krause Publications, 700 E. State St., Iola WI 54990. (715)445-2214. Editor: John Gunnell. 50% freelance written. Weekly tabloid; 44-48 pages. Circ. 80,000. Pays on publication. Publishes ms an average of 2 months after acceptance. Buys all rights. Phone queries OK. Byline given. Computer printout submissions OK; prefers letter-quality. Reports in 2 weeks. Sample copy $1.

Nonfiction: Short (2-3 pages) timely news reports on old car hobby with 1 photo. Buys 20 mss/issue. Query. Pays 3¢/word. Sometimes pays the expenses of writers on auction assignments.

Photos: Pays $5 for 5x7 b&w glossy prints. Captions required. Buys all rights.

Fillers: Newsbreaks. Buys 50/year. Pays 3¢/word. Pays $10 bonus for usable news tips.

Tips: "We have converted basically to a news package and buy only news. This would include post-event coverage of antique auto shows, summary reports on auctions with list of prices realized, and 'hard' news concerning old cars or people in the hobby. For example, the stock market crash has enhanced values of collectible cars and collectible autos are growing newer and newer each year."

‡PAPER COLLECTORS MARKETPLACE, Watson Graphic Designs, Inc., Box 127, Scandinavia WI 54977. (715)467-2379. Editor: Doug Watson. 100% freelance written. A monthly magazine on paper collectibles. "All articles must relate to the hobby in some form. Whenever possible values should be given for the collectibles mentioned in the article." Circ. 4,000. Pays on publication. Byline given. Offers 25% kill fee on commissioned articles. Buys first North American serial rights. Submit seasonal/holiday material 2 months in advance. Reports in 2 weeks. Free sample copy; writer's guidelines for #10 SASE.

Nonfiction: Historical/nostalgic, how-to, photo feature, technical. Buys 60 mss/year. Query with published clips. Length: 1,000-2,000 words. Pays 3-5¢/words.

Photos: Send photos with submissions. Offers no additional payment for photos accepted with ms. Captions, model releases and identification of subjects required. Buys one-time rights.

Tips: "We presently plan on publishing four special issues a year: March (January 10 deadline) Mystery/Detective; June (April 10 deadline) Sports Special; September (July 10 deadline) Disney Special; December (October 10 deadline) Christmas Special."

‡POPULAR CERAMICS, 3639 San Fernando Rd., Box 6466, Glendale CA 91205. (818)246-8141. Editor: Terry O'Neill. Managing Editor: Joel Edwards (Editorial Coordinator). 95% freelance written. A monthly magazine for ceramic hobbyists/craftspeople. Circ. 40,000. Pays on publication. Byline given. Buys all rights. Submit seasonal/holiday material 5 months in advance. Photocopied submissions OK. Computer printout submissions OK; prefers letter quality. Reports in 1 week on queries; 3 weeks on mss. Sample copy $3; free writer's guidelines.

Nonfiction: Book excerpts, historical/nostalgic (on ceramics down through the ages), how-to (on all types of ceramics projects), interview/profile (on leading ceramists or on successful ceramics business), new products (to aid and inspire ceramists), personal experience (on involvement in ceramics as business or hobby), technical (on techniques—airbrushing, firing, use of colors, sculpting, etc.). Query. Length: 500-1,000 words. Pays $25-100. Pays in copies to "writers who are under contract to manufacturers and are paid by them."

Photos: State availability of photos with submission. Reviews contact sheets, transparencies (2¼x2¼) and prints (3x5). Offers $25-35/photo. Captions and identification of subjects required. Buys all rights.

POPULAR WOODWORKING, EGW Publishing Co., 1300 Galaxy Way, Concord CA 94520. (415)671-9852. Editor: David M. Camp. 99% freelance written. Eager to work with new/unpublished writers. A bimonthly magazine covering woodworking. "Our readers are the woodworking hobbyist and small woodshop owner. Writers should have a knowledge of woodworking, or be able to communicate information gained from woodworkers." Circ. 42,000. Pays half on acceptance, half on publication. Publishes ms an average of 10-12 months after acceptance. Byline given. Buys first serial rights and second-time rights ("at our discretion"). Submit seasonal material 6 months in advance. Photocopied submissions OK. Computer printout submissions OK. Reports in 6 weeks. Sample copy and writer's guidelines for $2.95 plus 9x12 SAE and 5 first class stamps.

Nonfiction: How-to (on woodworking projects, with plans); humor (woodworking anecdotes); and technical (woodworking techniques). "No home-maintenance articles or stories about bloody accidents." Buys 120 mss/year. Query with or without published clips, or send complete ms. Pays $100-1,000.

Photos: Send photos with submission. Reviews contact sheets, 4x5 transparencies, 5x7 glossy prints and 35mm color slides. Offers no additional payment for photos accepted with ms; $75 extra for cover photos only. Captions and identification of subjects required. Buys one-time rights.

Columns/Departments: Jig Journal (how to make special fixtures to help a tool do a task), 500-1,500 words. Buys 6 mss/year. Query. Pays $75/published page.

Fillers: Anecdotes, facts, short humor and shop tips. Buys 15/year. Length: 50-500 words. Pays $45/published page.

Tips: "Show a technical knowledge of woodworking. Sharp close-up black and white photos of a woodworker demonstrating a technique impress me. We really need project with plans articles. Describe the steps in making a piece of furniture (or other project). Provide a cutting list and a rough diagram (we can redraw). If the writer is not a woodworker, he should have help from a woodworker to make sure the technical information is correct."

POSTCARD COLLECTOR, Krause Publications, 700 E. State St.:, Iola WI 54990. (715)445-2214. Editor: Diane Allmen. 70% freelance written. Monthly magazine. "Publication is for postcard collectors; all editorial content relates to postcards in some way." Pays on publication. Publishes ms an average of 8 months after acceptance. Byline given. Offers $5 kill fee. Buys perpetual, but nonexclusive rights. Submit seasonal/holiday material 5 months in advance. Computer printout submissions OK; prefers letter-quality. Reports in 2 weeks on queries; 1 month on mss. Sample copy $1.50 and writer's guidelines for #10 SASE.

Nonfiction: Historical/nostalgic, how-to (e.g. preservatives) and technical. Buys 50 mss/year. Query. Length: 200-1,800 words. Pays $25-150 for assigned articles; pays $2-150 for unsolicited articles.

Photos: State availability of postcards with submission. Offers $1-3/photo. Captions and identification of subjects required. Buys perpetual, but nonexclusive rights.

Columns/Departments: Where Is It (interesting subject on unidentified real photo postcard), 50-150 words. Buys 20-30 mss/year. Query. Pays $2.

Tips: "We publish information about postcards written by expert topical specialists. The writer must be knowledgeable about postcards and have acquired 'expert' information. We plan more complete listings of postcard sets and series-old and new." Areas most open to freelancers are feature-length articles on specialized areas (600-1,800 words) with 1 to 10 illustrations."

THE PROFESSIONAL QUILTER, Oliver Press, Box 4096, St. Paul MN 55104. (612)488-0974. Editor: Jeannie M. Spears. 80% freelance written. Works with a small number of new/unpublished writers each year. Quarterly magazine on the quilting business. Emphasis on small business, preferably quilt related. Circ. 2,000. Payment negotiated. Publishes ms an average of 6 months after acceptance. Byline given. Buys first North American serial rights, first serial rights, and second serial (reprint) rights. Simultaneous queries, and photocopied and previously published submissions OK. Computer printout submissions acceptable; prefers letter-quality. Reports in 2 weeks on queries; 1 month on mss. Sample copy for 9x12 SAE with 4 first class stamps and $4; writer's guidelines for #10 SASE.

Nonfiction: How-to (quilting business); humor; interview/profile; new product; opinion; and personal experience (of problems and problem-solving ideas in a quilting business). No quilting or sewing *techniques* or quilt photo spreads. Buys 20 mss/year. Query or send complete ms. Length: 500-1,500 words. Pays $25-75.

Tips: "Each issue will focus in depth on an issue of concern to the professional quilting community, such as ethics, art vs. craft, professionalism, etc. We would also like to receive articles on time and space (studio) organization, stress and family relationships. Remember that our readers already know that quilting is a time-honored tradition passed down from generation to generation, that quilts reflect the life of the maker, that quilt patterns have revealing names, etc., etc. Ask yourself: If my grandmother had been running a quilting business for the last five years, would she have found this article interesting? Send a letter describing your quilt, craft or business experience with a query or manuscript."

QUILT WORLD, House of White Birches, 306 E. Parr Rd., Berne IN 46711. Editor: Sandra L. Hatch. 90% freelance written. Works with a small number of new/unpublished writers each year. Bimonthly magazine covering quilting. Also publishes the quarterly *Quilt World Omnibook*. "We use patterns of both contemporary and traditional quilts and related articles." Circ. 120,000. Pays on publication. Publishes ms an average of 6 months after acceptance. Byline given. Buys all rights. Submit seasonal/holiday material 6 months in advance. Computer printout submissions are acceptable. Reports in 1 month. Sample copy $2.50; writer's guidelines for SASE.

Nonfiction: How-to, interview/profile (quilters), new product (quilt products) and photo feature. Buys 18-24 mss/year. Query with or without published clips, or send complete ms. Length: open. Pays $25-150.

Photo: Send photos with submission. Reviews 35mm, 2¼x2¼ or larger transparencies and 3x5 prints. Offers $15/photo (except covers). Identification of subjects required. Buys all rights.

Poetry: Free verse and traditional. Buys 10-12 poems/year. Submit maximum of 2 poems. Length: 6-30 lines. Pays $10-25.

Fillers: Gags to be illustrated by cartoonist and short humor. Buys 10-12/year. Length: 50-100 words. Pays $25-40.
Tips: "Send list of previous articles published with resume and a SASE. List ideas which you plan to base your articles around."

QUILTER'S NEWSLETTER MAGAZINE, Box 394, Wheatridge CO 80033. Editor: Bonnie Leman. Monthly. Circ. 150,000. Buys first North American serial rights or second rights. Buys 15 mss/year. Pays on publication, sometimes on acceptance. Reports in 5 weeks. Free sample copy.
Nonfiction: "We are interested in articles on the subject of quilts and quiltmakers *only*. We are not interested in anything relating to 'Grandma's Scrap Quilts' but could use fresh material." Submit complete ms. Pays 3¢/word minimum, usually more.
Photos: Additional payment for photos depends on quality.
Fillers: Related to quilts and quiltmakers only.
Tips: "Be specific, brief, and professional in tone. Study our magazine to learn the kind of thing we like. Send us material which fits into our format but which is different enough to be interesting. Realize that we think we're the best quilt magazine on the market and that we're aspiring to be even better, then send us the cream off the top of your quilt material."

RAILROAD MODEL CRAFTSMAN, Box 700, Newton NJ 07860. (201)383-3355. Editor: William C. Schaumburg. 75% freelance written. Works with a small number of new/unpublished writers each year. For model railroad hobbyists, in all scales and gauges. Monthly. Circ. 97,000. Buys all rights. Buys 50-100 mss/year. Pays on publication. Publishes ms an average of 9 months after acceptance. Submit seasonal material 6 months in advance. Computer printout submissions acceptable; prefers letter-quality. Sample copy $2; writer's and photographer's guidelines for SASE.
Nonfiction: "How-to and descriptive model railroad features written by persons who did the work are preferred. Almost all our features and articles are written by active model railroaders. It is difficult for non-modelers to know how to approach writing for this field." Pays minimum of $1.75/column inch of copy ($50/page).
Photos: Purchased with or without mss. Buys sharp 8x10 glossy prints and 35mm or larger color transparencies. Pays minimum of $10 for photos or $2/diagonal inch of published b&w photos, $3 for color transparencies and $100 for covers which must tie in with article in that issue. Caption information required.
Tips: "We would like to emphasize freight car modeling based on actual prototypes, as well as major prototype studies of them."

SCOTT STAMP MONTHLY, Box 828, Sidney OH 45365. (513)498-2111. Editor: Richard L. Sine. 40% freelance written. Works with a small number of new/unpublished writers each year. For stamp collectors, from the beginner to the sophisticated philatelist. Monthly magazine; 84 pages. Circ. 24,000. Rights purchased vary with author and material; usually buys first North American serial rights. Byline given. Buys 60 unsolicited mss/year. Pays on publication. Publishes ms an average of 7 months after acceptance. Submit seasonal or holiday material 6 months in advance. Computer printout submissions acceptable; prefers letter-quality. Query for electronic submissions. Reports in 1 month. Sample copy for 8½x11 SAE with 4 first class stamps.
Nonfiction: "We are in the market for articles, written in an engaging fashion, concerning the remote byways and often-overlooked aspects of stamp collecting. Writing should be clear and concise, and subjects must be well-researched and documented. Illustrative material should also accompany articles whenever possible." Query. Pays about $100.
Photos: State availability of photos. Offers no additional payment for b&w photos used with mss.
Tips: "It's rewarding to find a good new writer with good new material. Because our emphasis is on lively, interesting articles about stamps, including historical perspectives and human interest slants, we are open to writers who can produce the same. Of course, if you are an experienced philatelist, so much the better. We do not want stories about the picture on a stamp taken from a history book or an encyclopedia and dressed up to look like research. If an idea is good and not a basic rehash, we are interested."

SEW NEWS, The fashion magazine for people who sew, PJS Publications, Inc., News Plaza, Box 1790, Peoria IL 61656. (309)682-6626. Editor: Linda Turner Jones. 90% freelance written. Works with a small number of new/unpublished writers each year. Monthly newspaper covering fashion-sewing. "Our magazine is for the beginning home sewer to the professional dressmaker. It expresses the fun, creativity and excitement of sewing." Circ. 200,000. Pays on acceptance. Publishes ms an average of 6 months after acceptance. Byline given. Buys all rights. Submit seasonal/holiday material 6 months in advance. Photocopied submissions OK. Computer printout submissions acceptable. Reports in 2 months. Sample copy $3; writer's guidelines for #10 SAE and 2 first class stamps.
Nonfiction: Historical/nostalgic (fashion, textiles history); how-to (sewing techniques); and interview/profile (interesting personalities in home-sewing field). Buys 200-240 ms/year. Query with published clips. Length: 500-2,000 words. Pays $25-400. Rarely pays expenses of writers on assignment.

Photos: State availability of photos. Prefers b&w contact sheets and negatives. Payment included in ms price. Identification of subjects required. Buys all rights.

Fillers: Anecdotes and sewing-related cartoons. Buys 12/year. Length: 50-100 words. Pays $10-25.

Tips: "Query first with writing sample. Areas most open to freelancers are how-to and sewing techniques; give explicit, step-by-step instructions plus rough art."

SHUTTLE SPINDLE & DYEPOT, Handweavers Guild of America, 120 Mountain Road, Bloomfield CT 06002. Editor: Judy Robbins. 60% freelance written. A quarterly magazine covering handweaving, spinning and dyeing. "We take the practical and aesthetic approach to handweaving, handspinning, and related textile arts." Pays on publication. Publishes ms 4-15 months after acceptance. Byline given. Buys first North American serial rights. Submit seasonal/holiday material 1 year in advance. Photocopied submissions OK. Rarely accepts previously published submissions. Computer printout submissions acceptable; prefers letter-quality. Reports in 1 month on queries; 2 months on mss. Sample copy $6.50; free writer's guidelines.

Nonfiction: How-to, interview/profile, personal experience, photo feature and technical. "We want interesting, practical, technical information in our field." Buys 30 mss/year. Query with or without published clips, or send complete ms. Length: 500-1,500 words. Pays $25-100.

Photos: Send photos or state availability of photos with submission. Reviews contact sheets and transparencies. Payment varies. Captions, model releases and identification of subjects required. Buys one-time rights.

Tips: "We read all submissions, especially from weavers and weaving teachers."

SPIN-OFF, Interweave Press, 306 N. Washington, Loveland CO 80537. (303)669-7672. Editor: Deborah Robson. 10-20% freelance written. Quarterly magazine covering handspinning, dyeing, techniques and projects for using handspun fibers. Audience includes "practicing textile/fiber craftsmen. Article should show considerable depth of knowledge of subject, although the tone should be informal and accessible." Circ. 10,000. Pays on publication. Publishes ms an average of 6 months after acceptance. Byline given. Pays 50% kill fee. Buys first North American serial rights. Simultaneous queries and photocopied submissions OK. Computer printout submissions acceptable; prefers letter-quality. Sample copy $3.50 and 8½x11 SAE; free writer's guidelines.

Nonfiction: Historical and how-to (on spinning; knitted, crocheted, woven projects from handspun fibers with instructions); interview/profile (of successful and/or interesting fiber craftsmen); and technical (on spinning, dyeing or fiber technology, use, properties). "All articles must contain a high level of in-depth information. Our readers are very knowledgeable about these subjects." Query. Length: 2,000 words. Pays $15-100.

Photos: State availability of photos. Identification of subjects required.

Tips: "You should display an in-depth knowledge of your subject, but you can tailor your article to reach beginning, intermediate, or advanced spinners. Try for thoughtful organization, a personal informal style, and an article or series segment that is self-contained. New approaches to familiar topics are welcomed."

SPORTS COLLECTORS DIGEST, Krause Publications, 700 E. State St., Iola WI 54990. (715)445-2214. Editor: Tom Mortenson. 60% freelance written. Eager to work with new/unpublished writers; works with a small number of new/unpublished writers each year. Sports memorabilia magazine published weekly. "We serve collectors of sports memorabilia—baseball cards, yearbooks, programs, autographs, jerseys, bats, balls, books, magazines, ticket stubs, etc." Circ. 35,000. Pays after publication. Publishes ms an average of 3 months after acceptance. Byline given. Buys first North American serial rights only. Submit seasonal/holiday material 3 months in advance. Simultaneous queries and photocopied submissions OK. Computer printout submissions acceptable; prefers letter-quality. Reports in 5 weeks on queries; 2 months on mss. Free sample copy; writer's guidelines for #10 SASE.

Nonfiction: General interest (new card issues, research on older sets); historical/nostalgic (old stadiums, old collectibles, etc.); how-to (buy cards, sell cards and other collectibles, display collectibles, ways to get autographs, jerseys, and other memorabilia); interview/profile (well-known collectors, ball players—but must focus on collectibles); new product (new card sets) and personal experience ("what I collect and why"-type stories). No sports stories. "We are not competing with *The Sporting News*, *Sports Illustrated* or your daily paper. Sports collectibles only." Buys 200-300 mss/year. Query. Length: 300-3,000 words; prefers 1,000 words. Pays $20-75.

Photos: Unusual collectibles. State availability of photos. Pays $5-15 for b&w prints. Identification of subjects required. Buys all rights.

Columns/Departments: "We have all the columnists we need but welcome ideas for new columns." Buys 100-150 mss/year. Query. Length: 600-3,000 words. Pays $15-60.

Tips: "If you are a collector, you know what collectors are interested in. Write about it. No shallow, puff pieces; our readers are too smart for that. Only well-researched articles about sports memorabilia and collecting. Some sports nostalgia pieces are OK. Write only about the areas you know about."

SUNSHINE ARTISTS USA, The Voice Of The Nation's Artists and Craftsmen, Sun Country Enterpises, 1700 Sunset Dr., Longwood FL 32750. (305)323-5937. Editor: Joan L. Wahl. Managing Editor:

'Crusty' Sy. A monthly magazine covering art and craft shows in the United States. "We are a top marketing magazine for professional artists, craftspeople and photographers working street and mall shows. We list 10,000+ shows a year, critique many of them and publish articles on marketing, selling, and improving arts and crafts. Circ. 16,000+. Pays on publication. Publishes ms an average of 6 months after acceptance. Byline given. Buys first North American serial rights. Reports in 2 weeks on queries; 6 weeks on manuscripts. Sample copy $2.50.

Nonfiction: "We are interested in articles that relate to artists and craftsmen traveling the circuit. Although we have a permanent staff of 40 writers, we will consider well-written, thoroughly researched articles on successful artists making a living with their work, new ways to market arts and crafts, and rags to riches profiles. Attend some art shows. Talk to the exhibitors. Get ideas from them." No how-tos. Buys 20+ mss/year. Query. Length: 550-2,000 words. Pays $10-50 for assigned articles.

Photos: State availability of photos with submission. Offers no additional payment for photos accepted with ms. Captions, model releases, and identification of subjects required.

TEDDY BEAR REVIEW, Collector Communications Corp., 170 5th Ave., New York NY 10010. Managing Editor: Joan Pursley. 25% freelance written. Works with a small number of new/unpublished writers each year. A quarterly magazine on teddy bears. Pays 30 days after acceptance. Byline given. Buys first North American serial rights. Submit seasonal/holiday material 6 months in advance. Photocopied and previously published submissions OK if not published in a competing publication. Computer printout submissions OK; no dot-matrix. Reports in 2 months. Sample copy and writer's guidelines for $2 and 9x12 SAE.

Nonfiction: Book excerpts, historical, how-to and interview/profile. No nostalgia on childhood teddy bears. Buys 10 mss/year. Query with published clips. Length: 500-1,500 words. Pays $75-200. Sometimes pays the expenses of writers on assignment "if approved ahead of time."

Photos: Send photos with submission. Reviews transparencies and b&w prints. Offers no additional payment for photos accepted with ms. Captions required. Buys one-time rights.

Tips: "We are interested in good, professional writers around the country with a strong knowledge of teddy bears. Historical profile of bear companies, profiles of contemporary artists and knowledgeable reports on museum collections are of interest."

TREASURE, Jess Publishing, 6745 Adobe Rd., 29 Palms CA 92277. (619)367-3531. Editor: Jim Williams. Emphasizes treasure hunting and metal detecting. 90% freelance written. Eager to work with new/unpublished writers. Monthly magazine. Circ. 40,000. Pays on publication. Publishes ms an average of 6 months after acceptance. Buys all rights. Byline given. Phone queries OK. Submit seasonal/holiday material 4 months in advance. Previously published submissions OK. Computer printout submissions acceptable; prefers letter-quality. Reports in 2 months. Sample copy 40¢; writer's guidelines for SAE and $1.

Nonfiction: Lee Chandler, articles editor. How-to (coinshooting and treasure hunting tips); informational and historical (location of lost treasures with emphasis on the lesser-known); interviews (with treasure hunters); profiles (successful treasure hunters and metal detector hobbyists); personal experience (treasure hunting); technical (advice on use of metal detectors and metal detector designs). "We would like more coverage of archaeological finds, both professional and amateur, and more reports on recently found caches, whether located purposefully or accidentally—both types should be accompanied by photos of the finds." Buys 6-8 mss/issue. Send complete ms. Length: 300-3,000 words. Pays $30-200. "Our rate of payment varies considerably depending upon the proficiency of the author, the quality of the photographs, the importance of the subject matter, and the amount of useful information given."

Photos: Offers no additional payment for 5x7 or 8x10 b&w glossy prints used with mss. Pays $75 minimum for color transparencies (35mm or 2¼x2¼). Color for cover only. "Clear photos and other illustrations are a must." Model release required.

Tips: "We hope to increase our news coverage of archaeological digs and cache finds, opening the doors to writers who would like simply to use their journalistic skills to report a specific event. No great knowledge of treasure hunting will be necessary. The most frequent mistakes made by writers in completing an article for *Treasure* are failure to list sources of information and to supply illustrations or photos with a story."

THE TRUMPETER, Croatian Philatelic Society, 1512 Lancelot, Borger TX 79007. (806)273-7225. Editor: Eck Spahich. 50% freelance written. Eager to work with new/unpublished writers. A quarterly magazine covering stamps, coins, currency, military decorations and collectibles of the Balkans, and of central Europe. Circ. 800. Pays on publication. Publishes ms an average of 9 months after acceptance. Byline given. Buys first and one-time rights. Submit seasonal/holiday material 6 months in advance. Simultaneous and photocopied submissions OK. Computer printout submissions acceptable; no dot-matrix. Reports in 2 months on queries; 1 month on mss. Sample copy $2.50; free writer's guidelines.

Nonfiction: Book excerpts, general interest, historical/nostalgic, how-to (on detecting forged stamps, currency etc.), interview/profile, photo features and travel. Buys 15-20 mss/year. Send complete ms. Length: 500-1,500 words. Pays $10-30 for assigned articles; pays $5-25 for unsolicited articles. Sometimes pays expenses of writers on assignment.

Photos: State availability of photos with submission. Reviews 3x5 prints. Offers $5-10/photo. Captions and identification of subjects required. Buys one-time rights.

Columns/Departments: Book Reviews (stamps, coins, currency of Balkans), 200-400 words; Forgeries (emphasis on pre-1945 period), 500-1,000 words. Buys 10 mss/year. Send complete ms. Length: 100-300 words. Pays $5-25.

Fillers: Facts. Buys 15-20/year. Length: 20-50 words. Pays $1-5.

Tips: "We desperately need features on Zara, Montenegro, Serbia, Bulgaria, Bosnia, Croatia, Romania and Laibach."

‡VIDEOMAKER™ The Video Camera User's Magazine, Videomaker Inc., Box 4591, Chico CA 95927. (916)891-8410. Editor: Bradley Kent. 75% freelance written. A bimonthly magazine on video production. "Our audience is a range of hobbyists and low-end professional video camera users." Editorial emphasis is on video*making* (production and exposure), *not* reviews of commercial videos. Personal video phenomenon is a young 'movement' . . . readership encouraged to participate—get in on the act, join the fun." Circ. 50,000. Pays on publication. Publishes ms an average of 4-6 months after acceptance. Byline given. Buys all rights. Submit seasonal/holiday material 6 months in advance. Simultaneous, photocopied and previously published submissions OK. Query for electronic submissions. Computer printout submissions OK. Reports in 2 months on queries; 1 month on mss. Sample copy for 9x12 SAE with 5 first class stamps. Free writer's guidelines.

Nonfiction: How-to (tools, tips, techniques for better videomaking), interview/profile (notable videomakers), new product (review of latest and greatest or innovative), personal experience (lessons to benefit other videomakers), technical (state-of-the-art audio/video). Articles with comprehensive coverage of product line or aspect of videomaking preferred. Buys 35 mss/year. Query with or without published clips or send complete ms. Length: open. Pays $150-300.

Photos: Send photos with submissions. Reviews contact sheets, transparencies and prints. Captions required. Payment for photos accepted with ms included as package compensation. Buys one-time rights.

Columns/Departments: Computer Video (state-of-the art productions, applications, potentials for computer-video interface); Profile (highlights videomarkers using medium in unique/worthwhile ways); Book/Tape Mode (brief reviews of current works pertaining to video production); Videocrafts (projects, gadgets, inventions for videomaking). Buys 40 mss/year. Pays $35-175.

Fillers: Anecdotes, facts, gags to be illustrated by cartoonist, newsbreaks, short humor. Negotiable pay.

Tips: "Comprehensiveness a must. Article on shooting tips covers *all* angles. Buyer's guide to special-effect generators cites *all* models available. Magazine strives for an 'all-or-none' approach, given bimonthly status. Most topics covered once (twice tops) per year, so we must be thorough. Manuscript/photo package submissions helpful. *Videomaker* wants videomaking to be fulfilling for all."

WESTERN & EASTERN TREASURES, People's Publishing Co., Inc., Box 1095, Arcata CA 95521. Editor: Rosemary Anderson. Emphasizes treasure hunting and metal detecting for all ages, entire range in education, coast-to-coast readership. 90% freelance written. Monthly magazine. Circ. 70,000. Pays on publication. Publishes ms an average of 1 year after acceptance. Buys all rights. Computer printout submissions acceptable; no dot-matrix. Sample copy and writer's guidelines for $2.

Nonfiction: How-to "hands on" use of metal detecting equipment, how to locate coins, jewelry and relics, prospect for gold, where to look for treasures, rocks and gems, etc., "first-person" experiences. "No purely historical manuscripts or manuscripts that require two-part segments or more." Buys 200 unsolicited mss/year. Submit complete ms. Length: maximum 1,500 words. Pays 2¢/word—negotiable.

Photos: Purchased with accompanying ms. Captions required. Submit b&w prints or 35mm Kodachrome color transparencies. Pays $5 maximum for 3x5 and up b&w glossy prints; $35 and up for 35mm Kodachrome cover slides. Model releases required.

Tips: "The writer has a better chance of breaking in at our publication with short articles and fillers as these give the readers a chance to respond to the writer. The publisher relies heavily on reader reaction. Not adhering to word limit is the main mistake made by writers in completing an article for us. Also, not following what the editor has emphasized as needed material to be clearly covered."

WOMEN'S CIRCLE COUNTED CROSS-STITCH, House of White Birches, Inc., 306 E. Parr Rd., Berne IN 46711. Editor: Denise Lohr. 100% freelance written. Eager to work with new/unpublished writers. Bimonthly magazine featuring counted cross-stitch. Circ. 165,000. Pays on publication. Publishes ms an average of at least 6 months after acceptance. Byline given. Buys all rights. Submit seasonal/holiday material 6 months in advance. Computer printout submissions OK. Reports in 1 month. Sample copy $2. Make checks payable to House of White Birches. Contributor tips, guidelines and deadline schedule for large SAE and 2 first class stamps.

Nonfiction: How-to, interview/profile, new product and charted designs. Buys 12-15 mss/year. Query with published clips. "Submit cross-stitch designs with cover letter, complete ms and snapshot or 35mm slide of project *or* send complete ms and finished project. Include sufficient postage for project return." Length: open. Pays $25 and up.

Fiction: Humorous and slice-of-life vignettes (all related to cross-stitch). Buys 4-8 mss/year. Send complete ms. Length: 100-600 words. Pays $25-75.

Fillers: Facts and short humor. Buys 4-8/year. Length: 50-150 words. Pays $20-40.

Tips: "We'd like larger, more complicated designs using the latest techniques and products."

WOMEN'S HOUSEHOLD CROCHET, House of White Birches, Inc., 306 E. Parr Rd., Berne IN 46711. Editor: Susan Hankins Andrews. 99% freelance written. A quarterly magazine. "We appeal to crochet lovers—young and old, city and country, thread and yarn lovers alike. Our readers crochet for necessity as well as pleasure. Articles are 99% pattern-oriented. We need patterns for all expertise levels—beginner to expert. No knit patterns please." Circ. 75,000. Pays on publication. Publishes ms an average of 1 year after acceptance. Byline given. Buys all rights. Submit seasonal/holiday material 6 months in advance. Computer printout submissions OK. Reports in 1 month on queries; 6 weeks on mss. Sample copy for $2; free writer's guidelines.

Nonfiction: General interest, historical/nostalgic, how-to, humor, personal experience and technical. Needs seasonal patterns by March 1. Christmas Annual (December). Must be Christmas oriented. "Nothing of explicit sexual nature—our readers are true Bible-belt types. Even articles of a suggestive nature are apt to offend. Stay away from themes having to do with alcohol." Buys 10 mss/year. Send complete ms. Length: 500-2,000 words. Pays $50 and up for unsolicited articles.

Photos: Buys no photos. Must send crocheted item for staff photography.

Columns/Departments: Designer's Debut Contest (1st and 2nd prizes chosen each issue for crochet design). Buys 8 mss/year. Send complete ms. Length: 500-2,000 words. Pays competitive designer rates.

Poetry: Light verse and traditional. "No long poems over 20 lines. None of a sexual nature." Buys 6 poems/year. Submit maximum 2 poems. Length: 5-20 lines. Pays $5-20.

Fillers: Anecdotes, crochet cartoons, facts and short humor. Buys 24/year. Length: 35-70 words. Pays $5-20.

Tips: "Freelancers have the best chance of selling articles incorporating new trends in crochet. Look around you at the latest fashions, home decor, etc., for ideas—how to make money at crocheting (success stories from those who have marketed their needlework successfully) and patterns (keep materials inexpensive or moderately priced). Make sure crochet directions are complete and exact (no errors). Use standard crochet abbreviations. Send crocheted items with manuscripts; we will return them if return postage is included."

THE WORKBASKET, 4251 Pennsylvania Ave., Kansas City MO 64111. Editor: Roma Jean Rice. Issued monthly except bimonthly June-July and November-December. Buys first rights. Pays on acceptance. Reports in 6 weeks.

Nonfiction: Step-by-step directions for craft projects (400-500 words) and gardening articles (200-500 words). Query. Pays 7¢/word.

Photos: Pays $7-10 for 8x10 glossies with ms.

Columns/Departments: Readers' Recipes (original recipes from readers); and Making Cents (short how-to section featuring ideas for pin money from readers).

WORKBENCH, 4251 Pennsylvania Ave., Kansas City MO 64111. (816)531-5730. Editor: Robert N. Hoffman. 75% freelance written. Prefers to work with published/established writers; works with a small number of new/unpublished writers each year. For woodworkers. Circ. 830,000. Pays on acceptance. Publishes ms an average of 1 year after acceptance. Byline given if requested. Buys all rights then returns all but first rights upon request, after publication. Computer printout submissions acceptable; prefers letter-quality. Reports in 2 months. Sample copy for 8x10 SAE and 6 first class stamps; free writer's guidelines.

Nonfiction: "We have continued emphasis on do-it-yourself woodworking, home improvement and home maintenance projects. We provide in-progress photos, technical drawings and how-to text for all projects. We are very strong in woodworking, cabinetmaking and classic furniture construction. Projects range from simple toys to complicated reproductions of furniture now in museums. We would like to receive contemporary and furniture items that can be duplicated by both beginning do-it-yourselfers and advanced woodworkers." Query. Pays $175/published page, up or down depending on quality of submission. Additional payment for good color photos. "If you can consistently provide good material, including photos, your rates will go up and you will get assignments."

Columns/Departments: Shop Tips bring $20-50 with a line drawing and/or b&w photo. Workbench Solver pays $50 to experts providing answers to readers problems related to do-it-yourself projects and home repair.

Tips: "Our magazine will focus on wood working, covering all levels of ability. We will continue to present home improvment projects from the do-it-yourselfer's viewpoint, emphasizing the most up-to-date materials and procedures. We would like to receive articles on indoor home improvements and remodeling, home improvement on manufactured and mobile homes, and/or simple contemporary furniture. We place a heavy emphasis on well-designed projects, that is projects that are both functional and classic in design. We can photograph projects worthy for publication, so feel free to send snapshots."

WORLD COIN NEWS, Krause Publications, 700 E. State, Iola WI 54990. (715)445-2214. Editor: Colin Bruce. 30% freelance written. Works with a small number of new/unpublished writers each year. Weekly newsmagazine about non-U.S. coin collecting for novices and advanced collectors of foreign coins, medals, and other numismatic items. Circ. 15,000. Pays on publication. Publishes ms an average of 1 month after acceptance. Byline given. Buys first North American serial rights and reprint rights. Submit seasonal material 1 month in advance. Simultaneous and photocopied submissions OK. Computer printout submissions acceptable; no dot-matrix. Reports in 2 weeks. Free sample copy.

Nonfiction: "Send us timely news stories related to collecting foreign coins and current information on coin values and markets." Send complete ms. Buys 30 mss/year. Length: 500-2,000 words. Pays 3¢/word to first-time contributors; fees negotiated for later articles. Sometimes pays the expenses of writers on assignment.

Photos: Send photos with ms. Pays $5 minimum for b&w prints. Captions and model release required. Buys first rights and first reprint rights.

YESTERYEAR, Yesteryear Publications, Box 2, Princeton WI 54968. (414)787-4808. Editor: Michael Jacobi. 25% freelance written. Prefers to work with published/established writers. For antique dealers and collectors, people interested in collecting just about anything, and nostalgia buffs. Monthly tabloid. Circ. 7,000. Pays on publication. Publishes ms an average of 2-3 months after acceptance. Buys one-time rights. Byline given. Submit seasonal/holiday material 3 months in advance. Simultaneous, photocopied and previously published submissions OK. Computer printout submissions acceptable; prefers letter-quality. Reports in 1 month for queries; 1 month for mss. Sample copy $1.

Nonfiction: General interest (basically, anything pertaining to antiques, collectible items or nostalgia in general); historical (again, pertaining to the above categories); and how-to (refinishing antiques, how to collect). The more specific and detailed, the better. "We do not want personal experience or opinion articles." Buys 24 mss/year. Send complete ms. Pays $5-25. Pays expenses of writers on assignment.

Photos: Send photos with ms. Pays $5 for 5x7 b&w glossy or matte prints; $5 for 5x7 color prints. Captions preferred.

Columns/Departments: "We will consider new column concepts as long as they fit into the general areas of antiques and collectibles." Buys 1 mss/issue. Send complete ms. Pays $5-25.

Home and Garden

Some magazines here concentrate on gardens; others on the how-to of interior design. Still others focus on homes and gardens in specific regions.

BETTER HOMES AND GARDENS, 1716 Locust St., Des Moines IA 50336. (515)284-3000. Editor (Building): Joan McCloskey. Editor (Furnishings): Shirley Van Anate. Editor (Foods): Nancy Byal. Editor (Travel): Mark Ingelbrentson. Editor (Garden Outdoor Living): Doug Jimerson. Editor (Health & Education): Paul Krantz. Editor (Money Management, Automotive, Features): Margaret Daly. 10-15% freelance written. Pays on acceptance. Buys all rights. "We read all freelance articles, but much prefer to see a letter of query rather than a finished manuscript."

Nonfiction: Travel, education, health, cars, money management, and home entertainment. "We do not deal with political subjects or with areas not connected with the home, community, and family." Pays rates "based on estimate of length, quality and importance."

Tips: Direct queries to the department that best suits your story line.

CANADIAN WORKSHOP, The How-to Magazine, Camar Publications (1984) Inc., 130 Spy Ct., Markham, Ontario L3R 5H6 Canada. (416)475-8440. Editor: Cindy Lister. 90% freelance written. Monthly magazine covering the "do-it-yourself market including woodworking projects, renovation and restoration, maintenance and decoration. Canadian writers only." Circ. 85,000. Pays on publication. Publishes ms an average of 5 months after acceptance. Byline given. Offers 75% kill fee. Rights are negotiated with the author. Submit seasonal/holiday material 6 months in advance. Simultaneous queries OK. Computer printout submissions acceptable; no dot-matrix. Reports in 3 weeks. Sample copy $2; free writer's guidelines.

Nonfiction: How-to (home and home machinery maintenance, renovation projects, and woodworking projects). Buys 20-40 mss/year. Query with clips of published work. Length: 1,500-4,000 words. Pays $225-600. Pays expenses of writers on assignment.

Photos: Send photos with ms. Payment for photos, transparencies negotiated with the author. Captions, model releases, and identification of subjects required.

Tips: "Freelancers must be aware of our magazine format. Product-types used in how-to articles must be readily available across Canada. Deadlines for articles are 5 months in advance of cover date. How-tos should be detailed enough for the amateur but appealing to the experienced. We work with the writer to develop a major feature. That could mean several rewrites, but we've found most writers to be eager. A frequent mistake made by writers is not directing the copy towards our reader. Stories sometimes have a tendency to be too basic."

COLORADO HOMES & LIFESTYLES, Suite 154, 2550 31st St., Denver CO 80216. (303)433-6533. Editor: Ania Savage. 60% freelance written. Bimonthly magazine covering Colorado homes and lifestyles for upper-middle-class and high income households as well as designers, decorators, and architects. Circ. 30,000. Pays on acceptance. Publishes ms an average of 4 months after acceptance. Byline given. Buys all rights. Submit seasonal/holiday material 6 months in advance. Simultaneous queries and photocopied submissions OK. Query for electronic submissions. Computer printout submissions acceptable: prefers letter-quality. Reports in 1 month. Free writer's guidelines.
Nonfiction: Fine home furnishings, interesting personalities and lifestyles, gardening and plants, decorating and design, fine food and entertaining—all with a Colorado slant. Buys 40 mss/year. Send complete ms. Length: 1,000-2,000 words. "For celebrity features (Colorado celebrity and home) pay is $300-800. For unique, well-researched pieces on Colorado people, places, etc., pay is 15-25¢/word. For regular articles, 10¢/word. The more specialized and Colorado-oriented your article is, the more generous we are." Sometimes pays the expenses of writers on assignment.
Photos: Send photos with ms. Reviews 35mm, 4x5 and 2¼ color transparencies and b&w glossy prints. Identification of subjects required.
Tips: "The more interesting and unique the subject the better. A frequent mistake made by writers is failure to provide material with a style and slant appropriate for the magazine, due to poor understanding of the focus of the magazine."

FARMING UNCLE®, Box 91, Liberty NY 12754. Editor: Louis Toro. 25% freelance written. Quarterly magazine on nature, small stock, and gardening. Pays on acceptance. Publishes ms an average of 3 months after acceptance. Byline given. Buys all rights. Reports in 1 week on queries. Sample copy for $3 and $1.50 postage (first class).
Nonfiction: How-to (poultry, small stock, gardening, shelter building, etc.). Buys 12 mss/year. Send complete ms. Length: 500-750 words. Pays $7.50-10.
Photos: Send photos with ms. Pays $3-4 for b&w prints. Captions and identification of subjects not required.
Poetry: "We publish poetry and will pay a symbolic $2 for it."

‡FINE GARDENING, Taunton Press, 63 S. Main St., Box 355, Newtown CT 06470. 1-800-243-7252. Editor: Roger Holmes. Bimonthly magazine on gardening. "Focus is broad subject of landscape and ornamental gardening, with selective interest in food gardening. Reader written by avid gardeners—first person, hands-on gardening experiences." Estab. 1988. Circ. 85,000. Pays on publication. Byline given. Buys first North American serial rights. Simultaneous, photocopied and previously published submissions OK. Query for electronic submissions. Computer printout submissions OK. Reports in 1 month. Free sample copy and writer's guidelines.
Nonfiction: Book review, essays, how-to, new product, opinion, personal experience, photo feature. Buys 50-60 mss/year. Query. Length: 1,000-3,000 words. Pays $150/page.
Photos: Send photos with submission. Reviews 35mm transparencies. Offers no additional payment for photos accepted with ms. Buys one-time rights.
Columns/Department: Book reviews (on gardening); Gleanings (essays, stories, opinions, research); Last Word (essays/serious, humorous, fact or fiction). Query. Length: 100-1,000 words. Pays $10-150.
Tips: "It's most important to have solid first-hand experience as a gardener. Tell us what you've done with your own landscape and plants."

FLORIDA HOME & GARDEN, (formerly South Florida Home & Garden), #207, 600 Brickell Ave., Miami FL 33131. (305)374-5011. Editor: Kathryn Howard. Managing Editor: Marjorie Klein. 40% freelance written. Works with a small number of new/unpublished writers each year. Monthly magazine of Florida homes, interior design, architecture, landscape architecture, gardens, cuisine, lifestyles and home entertainment. "We want beautiful, practical coverage of the subjects listed as they relate to Florida." Circ. 30,000. Pays on publication. Publishes ms an average of 3 months after acceptance. Byline given. Offers $25 kill fee by pre-agreement only. Buys first North American serial rights, plus unlimited reuse in our magazine (no resale). Submit seasonal/holiday material 6 months in advance. Computer printout submissions OK. Sample copy $2.50; writer's guidelines for #10 SASE.
Nonfiction: General interest (in our subjects); how-to (interior design, cuisine, recipes, but with a Florida twist, and gardening for Florida climate); and travel Caribbean/Florida (home architecture or garden destinations only). Buys 36 mss/year. Query with or without published clips. length: 500-1,500 words. Pays $100-400 (rarely more). Pays expenses of writers on assignment by prior agreement only.
Photos: Debra Yates, art director. State availability of photos or send photos with query. Reviews 35mm, 4x5 or 2" color transparencies. Captions and identification of subjects required. Buys one-time rights plus unlimited editorial re-use of magazine's separations.

Columns/Departments: How-to (specific home how-to); Garden Care; What's Hot (Florida products); Health & Beauty; Developments; Architecture; and Florida Artists. Buys 36 mss/year. Query with or without published clips. Length: 300-1,500 words. Pays $100-300.
Tips: "We're looking for stories that visually show the beauty of Florida and impart practical information to our readers. Must relate to Florida's tropicality in all subjects."

FLOWER AND GARDEN MAGAZINE, 4251 Pennsylvania, Kansas City MO 64111. Editor-in-Chief: Rachel Snyder. 50% freelance written. Works with a small number of new/unpublished writers each year. For home gardeners. Bimonthly. Picture magazine. Circ. 600,000. Buys first rights only. Byline given. Pays on acceptance. Publishes ms an average of 6-12 months after acceptance. Computer printout submissions acceptable; no dot-matrix. Reports in 6 weeks. Sample copy $2.50 and 9½x12½ SAE; writer's guidelines for SASE.
Nonfiction: Interested in illustrated articles on how to do certain types of gardening and descriptive articles about individual plants. Flower arranging, landscape design, house plants, patio gardening are other aspects covered. "The approach we stress is practical (how-to-do-it, what-to-do-it-with). We try to stress plain talk, clarity, and economy of words. An article should be tailored for a national audience." Buys 20-30 mss/year. Query. Length: 500-1,500 words. Pays 7¢/word or more, depending on quality and kind of material.
Photos: Pays up to $12.50/5x7 or 8x10 b&w prints, depending on quality, suitability. Also buys color transparencies, 35mm and larger. "We are using more four-color illustrations." Pays $30-125 for these, depending on size and use.
Tips: "The prospective author needs good grounding in gardening practice and literature. Offer well-researched and well-written material appropriate to the experience level of our audience. Use botanical names as well as common. Illustrations help sell the story. Describe special qualifications for writing the particular proposed subject."

GARDEN DESIGN, The Fine Art of Residential Landscape Architecture, American Society of Landscape Architects, 1733 Connecticut Ave. NW, Washington DC 20009. (202)466-7730. Managing Editor: Karen D. Fishler. 80% freelance written. Works with a small number of new/unpublished writers each year. A quarterly magazine focusing on the design of public and private gardens. "Our attitude is that garden design is a fine art and craft, and that gardening is a way of life." Circ. 57,000. May pay part on acceptance if long interval between acceptance and publication. Publishes ms an average of 6 months after acceptance. Byline given. Offers $100 kill fee. Buys first North American rights. Submit seasonal/holiday material 6 months in advance. Computer printout submissions OK; no dot-matrix. Reports in 3 weeks on queries; 6 weeks on mss. Sample copy $5; writer's guidelines for #10 SASE.
Nonfiction: "We look for literate, imaginative writing that conveys how a specific garden's design works, both how it was achieved and the experience it provides." No how-to, such as gardening techniques. Buys 35 mss/year. Query with published clips. Length: 1,000-2,500 words. Pays $350 maximum. Sometimes pays the expenses of writers on assignment.
Photos: Send scouting photos with submission (preferably transparencies, not prints). Reviews transparencies and prints. Offers $50-250/photo. Captions and identification of subjects required. Buys one-time rights.
Columns/Departments: Particulars (things in the garden, i.e., how to use ornaments, materials), 1,000 words; Plant Page (design application of specific plant or type), 1,000 words; Ex Libris (book review), 1,500; Focal Point (guest opinion/editorial/personal point of view), 1,000 words; Eclectic (compendium of interesting bits and pieces of news), 250 words. Buys 16-20 mss/year. Query with published clips or send complete ms. Pays $75-250.
Tips: "Our greatest need is for small to mid-size private gardens, designed by professionals in collaboration with owners. Scouting locations is a valuable service freelancers can perform, by contacting designers and garden clubs in the area, visiting gardens and taking snapshots for our review. It helps to submit a plan drawing of the garden's layout (the designer usually can supply this). All feature articles are open to freelancers, as well as Focal Point, Ex Libris, Plant Page and Particulars. Writing should be intelligent and well-informed, a pleasure to read. Avoid pretension and flowery devices. Check proper plant names in Hortus III."

GARDEN MAGAZINE, The Garden Society, A Division of the New York Botanical Garden, Bronx Park, Bronx NY 10458. Editor: Ann Botshon. 50% freelance written. Works with a small number of new/unpublished writers each year. Bimonthly magazine, emphasizing horticulture, environment and botany for a diverse readership, largely college graduates and professionals united by a common interest in plants and the environment. Most are members of botanical gardens and arboreta. Circ. 32,000. Publishes ms an average of 1 year after acceptance. Buys first North American serial rights. Submit seasonal/holiday material 6 months in advance. Photocopied submissions OK. Query for electronic submissions. Computer printout submissions acceptable; prefers letter-quality. Reports in 2 months. Sample copy $3; guidelines for SASE.
Nonfiction: "All articles must be of high quality, meticulously researched and botanically accurate." Exposé (environmental subjects); how-to (horticultural techniques, must be unusual and verifiable); general interest (plants in art and history, botanical news, ecology); humor (pertaining to botany and horticulture); and travel (great gardens of the world). Buys 15-20 unsolicited mss/year. Query with clips of published work. Length:

1,000-2,500 words. Pays $100-300. Sometimes pays the expenses of writers on assignment.

Photos: Karen Polyak, assistant editor. Pays $35-50/5x7 b&w glossy print; $40-150/4x5 or 35mm color transparency. Captions preferred. Buys one-time rights.

Tips: "We appreciate some evidence that the freelancer has studied our magazine and understands our special requirements. A writer should write from a position of authority that comes from either personal experience (horticulture); extensive research (environment, ecology, history, art); adequate scientific background; or all three. Style should be appropriate to this approach."

HERB QUARTERLY, Box 275, Newfane VT 05345. Editor: Sallie Ballantine. 90% freelance written. Quarterly magazine for herb enthusiasts. Circ. 25,000. Pays $25 on publication. Publishes ms an average of 1 year after acceptance. Buys first North American serial rights and second (reprint) rights to manuscripts originally published elsewhere. Query for electronic submissions. Computer printout submissions acceptable. Query letters recommended. Reports in 1 month. Sample copy $5; writer's guidelines for SAE and 1 first class stamp.

Nonfiction: Gardening (landscaping, herb garden design, propagation, harvesting); herb businesses; medicinal and cosmetic use of herbs; crafts; cooking; historical (folklore, focused piece on particular period—*not* general survey); interview of a famous person involved with herbs or folksy herbalist; personal experience; and photo essay ("cover quality" 8x10 b&w prints). "We are particularly interested in herb garden design, contemporary or historical." No fiction. Send double-spaced ms. Length: 2,000-10,000 words. Reports in one month.

Tips: "Our best submissions are narrowly focused on herbs with much practical information on cultivation and use for the gardener."

‡HOME, Creative Ideas for Home Design, Knapp Publishing Corp., Box 92000, Los Angeles CA 90009. (213)410-7600. 15% freelance written. A monthly magazine on home design. "*Home* magazine is devoted to bringing its readers—homeowners interested in improving their homes—ideas on remodeling and information on how to manage their remodeling projects." Circ. 900,000. Pays on acceptance. Byline given. Publishes ms an average of 4 months after acceptance. Offers 10% kill fee. Buys all rights. Submit seasonal/holiday material 6 months in advance. Computer printout submissions OK; prefers letter quality. Reports in 1 month. Sample copy $1.95; free writer's guidelines.

Nonfiction: Essays, exposé, humor, personal experience. Buys 24 mss/year. Query with published clips. Length: 650-2,000 words. Pays $500-2,000 for assigned articles; $400-1,200 for unsolicited articles. Sometimes pays expenses of writers on assignment.

Photos: State availability of photos with submission. Reviews transparencies, prints. Offers no additional payment for photos accepted with ms. Model releases and identification of subjects required. Buys all rights.

Columns/Departments: Editor: Steve Holley. Update (short news items or profiles) 300-500 words. Buys 6 mss/year. Query with published clips. Pays $75-150.

HOMEOWNER, Family Media Inc., 3 Park Ave., New York NY 10016. Editor-in-chief: Joe Carter. Managing Editor: Michael Chotiner. 75% freelance written. Monthly (combined Jan/Feb; July/Aug) magazine on home improvement, including remodeling, maintenance and repair. Aimed at men and women with helpful information of planning, design options, new products and do-it-yourself techniques. Circ. 700,000. Pays on acceptance. Publishes ms an average of 4 months after acceptance. Byline given. Offers variable kill fee. Buys first North American serial rights. Computer printout submissions acceptable. Reports in 1 month. Sample copy on request; writer's guidelines for #10 SASE.

Nonfiction: Remodeling, home repair and maintenance, how-to; personal experience (hands-on experience with building a home, remodeling or carpentry project); and some technical information on products, materials, how things work. Length: 1,500 maximum. Rates start at $400 for short articles plus some expenses of writers on assignment.

HOUSE BEAUTIFUL, The Hearst Corp., 1700 Broadway, New York NY 10019. (212)903-5000. Editor: JoAnn Barwick. Executive Editor: Margaret Kennedy. Editorial Director: Mervyn Kaufman. Director of Copy/Features: Carol Cooper Garey. (212)903-5236. 15% freelance written. Prefers to work with published/established writers. Emphasizes design, architecture and building. Monthly magazine. Circ. 840,000. Pays on acceptance. Publishes ms an average of 4 months after acceptance. Byline given. Submit seasonal/holiday material 4 months in advance of issue date. Computer printout submissions acceptable; prefers letter-quality. Reports in 5 weeks.

Nonfiction: Historical (landmark buildings and restorations); how-to (kitchen, bath remodeling service); interview; new product; and profile. Submit query with detailed outline or complete ms. Length: 300-1,000 words. Pays varying rates.

Photos: State availability of photos or submit with ms.

‡HOUSTON METROPOLITAN MAGAZINE, (formerly Houston Home & Garden), City Home Publishing, Box 25386, Houston TX 77265. (713)524-3000. Editor: Diane Stafford. Managing Director: Tim Brookover.

15% freelance written. A monthly city magazine. Circ. 85,000. Pays on acceptance. Publishes ms an average of 3 months after acceptance. Byline given. Offers $300 kill fee. Buys first North American serial rights. Submit holiday/seasonal material 6 months in advance. Simultaneous and photocopied submissions OK. Computer printout submissions OK; no dot-matrix. Reports in 2 weeks on queries; 1 month on mss. Sample copy for 9½x12 SAE and 8 first class stamps.

Nonfiction: New product, health, beauty and fitness, profiles of Houstonians, Houston gardening, interior design. Buys 24 mss/year. Query with or without published clips or send complete ms. Length: 750-2,000 words. pays $400-750.

Photos: State availability of photos with submission. Offers no additional payment for photos accepted with ms. Model releases required. Buys one-time rights.

Tips: "Submit clips of gardening and/or interior design pieces. Short items on new products—gardening, design, cooking, health, fitness, entertaining—are the best approach for freelancers. We will add more city focus but will continue to cover home and garden."

‡LOG HOME GUIDE FOR BUILDERS & BUYERS, Muir Publishing Company Ltd., 1 Pacific Ave., Gardenvale, Quebec H9X 1B0 Canada. (514)457-2045. U.S. Editorial Office: Highway 32 and 321, Cosby TN 37722. (615)487-2256. Editor: Allan Muir. 65% freelance written. Quarterly magazine covering the buying and building of log homes. "We publish for persons who want to buy or build their own log home. Unlike conventional housing, it is possible for the average person to build his/her own log home. Articles should aim at providing help in this or describe the experiences of someone who has built a log home." Circ. 150,000. Pays on publication. Publishes ms an average of 6 months after acceptance. Byline given. Buys all rights. Submit seasonal/holiday material 4 months in advance. Simultaneous queries, and simultaneous ("writer should explain"), photocopied, and previously published submissions OK. Query for electronic submissions. Computer printout submissions acceptable; no dot-matrix. Reports in 2 weeks. Sample copy $3.50 (postage included). Writer's guidelines for SASE.

Nonfiction: General interest; historical/nostalgic (log home historic sites, restoration of old log structures); how-to (anything to do with building log homes); inspirational (sweat equity—encouraging people that they can build their own home for less cost); interview/profile (with persons who have built their own log homes); new product (or new company manufacturing log homes—check with us first); personal experience (author's own experience with building his own log home, with photos is ideal); photo feature (on log home decor, author or anyone else building his own log home); and technical (for "Techno-log" section; specific construction details, i.e., new log buiding details, joining systems). Also, "would like photo/interview/profile stories on famous persons and their log homes—how they did it, where they got their logs, etc." Interested in log commercial structures. "Please no exaggeration—this is a truthful, back-to-basics type of magazine trying to help the person interested in log homes." Buys 25 mss/year. Query with clips of published work or send complete ms. "Prefer queries first with photo of subject house." Length: open. Pays 10-25¢/word, depending on quality.

Photos: Slides, transparencies or color prints, $5-50, depending on quality. "All payments are arranged with individual author/submitter." Captions and identification of subjects required. Buys all rights unless otherwise arranged.

Columns/Departments: Pro-Log (short news pieces of interest to the log-building world); Techno-Log (technical articles, i.e., solar energy systems; any illustrations welcome); Book-Log (book reviews only, on books related to log building and alternate energy; "check with us first"); Chrono-Log (features on historic log buildings); and Decor (practical information on how to finish and furnish a log house). Buys possible 50-75 mss/year. Query with clips of published work or send complete ms. Length: 100-1,000 words or more. "All payments are arranged with individual author/submitter." Enclose SASE.

Tips: "The writer may have a better chance of breaking in at our publication with short articles and fillers since writing well on log homes requires some prior knowledge of subject. The most frequent mistakes made by writers in completing an article assignment for us are not doing enough research or not having understanding of the subject; not people oriented enough; angled toward wrong audience. They don't study the publication before they submit manuscripts."

LOG HOMES, Annual Buyer's Guide, Home Buyer Publications, Inc., Suite 500, 610 Herndon Parkway, Box 370, Herndon VA 22070. Publisher: John Kupferer. Annual magazine covering log homes and the log home industry. "We publish articles on how to build, buy, and maintain a log home: practical, nuts-and-bolts approaches for log home buyers and owners." Circ. 125,000. Pays on acceptance. Publishes ms an average of 6 months after acceptance. Byline sometimes given. Buys all rights. Computer printout submissions OK; prefers letter-quality. Reports in 2 weeks. Sample copy for 9x12 SAE and 8 first class stamps.

Nonfiction: How-to, new product and technical. Buys 10 mss/year. Query. Length: 1,000-2,500 words. Pays $200-1,000 for assigned articles; pays $50-500 for unsolicited articles. Sometimes pays the expenses of writers on assignment.

Photos: Send photos with submission. Reviews 4x5 prints. Offers $10-50/photo. Captions, model releases and identification of subjects required. Buys all rights.

Tips: "Articles on construction, buying, selling and maintaining log homes are open. We plan to publish a new quarterly, *Log Home Living*, in 1989 and we'll need more material—same subject matter as *Log Home Buyer's Guide*."

NATIONAL GARDENING, magazine of the National Gardening Association, 180 Flynn Ave., Burlington VT 05401. (802)863-1308. Editor: Katharine Anderson. 85% freelance written. Willing to work with new/unpublished writers. Monthly magazine covering all aspects of food gardening and ornamentals. "We publish not only how-to garden techniques, but also news that affects gardeners, like science advances. Detailed, experienced-based articles with carefully worked-out techniques for planting, growing, harvesting, and using garden fruits and vegetables sought. Our material is for both experienced and beginning gardeners." Circ. 200,000. Pays on acceptance. Publishes ms an average of 9 months after acceptance. Byline given. Buys first serial rights and occasionally second (reprint) rights to material originally published elsewhere. Submit seasonal/holiday material 8 months in advance. Photocopied and previously published submissions OK, but original material preferred. Computer printout submissions acceptable; prefers letter-quality. Reports in 1 month. Sample copy for 8½x11 SAE and $1; writer's guidelines for #10 SASE.
Nonfiction: How-to, humor, inspirational, interview/profile, new product, personal experience, photo feature and technical. Buys 80-100 mss/year. Query first. Length: 500-3,000 words. Pays $30-450/article. Sometimes pays the expenses of writers on assignment; must have prior approval.
Photos: Vicky Congdon, photo manager. Send photos with ms. Pays $20-40 for b&w photos; $50 for color photos. Captions, model releases and identification of subjects required.
Tips: "Wordiness is a frequent mistake made by writers. Few writers understand how to write 'tight'. We have increased coverage of ornamentals, although primary focus will remain food gardening."

‡NEW HOME, The Magazine for Imaginative Homeowners, Gilford Publishing, Box 2008, Village West, Laconia NH 03246. Editor: Richard C. Wright. Managing Editor: Steven Maviglio. 90% freelance written. Bimonthly magazine . "*New Home* is mailed to homebuyers (new and existing within one month of filing the deed. The magazine goes to those who have purchased homes costing $85,000 or more. The first few months of living in a new house means decorating, remodeling and buying products. We show them how to make quality decisions." Circ. 300,000. Pays on acceptance. Publishes ms an average of 2 months after acceptance. Byline given. Kill fee varies $100-500. Buys all rights. Submit seasonal/holiday material 6 months in advance. Simultaneous submissions OK; no dot-matrix. Computer printout submissions OK. Reports in 1 week. Sample copy for $5 and 8½x11 SAE with 6 first class stamps. Free writer's guidelines.
Nonfiction: Essays, how-to, interview/profile, new product, technical. No articles on "How I dealt with My New Kitchen," "Why Moving Is So Terrible." Buys 100 mss/year. Query with published clips. Pays $200-3,000 words. Pays $200-1,500 for assigned articles; $200-500 for unsolicited articles. Sometimes pays expenses of writers on assignment.
Photos: State availability of photos with submission. Reviews transparencies (5x7) and prints. Offers $50-250/photo. Captions, model release and identification of subjects required. Buys all rights.
Columns/Departments: Out-of-Doors (lawn and garden, landscaping) 1,000-1,500; The Kitchen (kitchen cabinets, countertops, small appliances); The Bath (new tubs, working with color, Victorian baths); Details (do-it-yourself, fun projects); Back Porch (essay of a new home experience). Buys 50 mss/year. Query with published clips. Length: 250-2,000. Pays $200-1,500.
Fillers: Facts. Buys 20 mss/year. Length: 50-250 words. Pays up to $250.
Tips: "We assign nearly all of our stories. But it doesn't hurt for a writer to query with samples and present their idea in a one-page letter. No manuscripts except for our Back Porch section."

N.Y. HABITAT MAGAZINE, For Co-op, Condominium and Loft Living, The Carol Group, Ltd., 928 Broadway, New York NY 10010. (212)505-2030. Editor: Carol J. Ott. Managing Editor: Lloyd Chrein. 75% freelance written. Prefers to work with published/established writers. Published 8 times/year, covering co-op, condo and loft living in metropolitan New York. "Our primary readership is boards of directors of co-ops and condos, and we are looking for material that will help them fulfill their responsibilities." Circ. 10,000. Pays on publication. Publishes ms an average of 3 months after acceptance. Byline given. Offers negotiable kill fee. Buys first North American serial rights. Submit seasonal/holiday material 3 months in advance. Computer printout submissions acceptable. Reports in 3 weeks. Sample copy for $5, 9x12 SAE and 5 first class stamps; writer's guidelines for #10 SASE.
Nonfiction: Only material relating to co-op and condominium living in New York metropolitan area. Buys 20 mss/year. Query with published clips. Length: 750-1,500 words. Pays $25-1,000. Sometimes pays the expenses of writers on assignment.
Tips: "We would like to receive manuscripts dealing with co-op or condo management."

PHOENIX HOME & GARDEN, PHG, Inc., 3136 N. 3rd Ave., Phoenix AZ 85013. (602)234-0840. Editor: Manya Winsted. Managing Editor: Nora Burba Trulsson. 50% freelance written. Works with a small number of new/unpublished writers each year. Monthly magazine covering homes, furnishings, entertainment, lifestyle and gardening for Phoenix area residents interested in better living. Circ. 35,000. Pays on publication. Publishes ms an average of 2 months after acceptance. Byline given. Buys all rights. Submit seasonal/holiday material 6 months in advance. Computer printout submissions acceptable. Reports in 2 weeks on queries. Sample copy $2, plus 9 first class stamps.

Nonfiction: General interest (on interior decorating, architecture, gardening, entertainment, food); historical (Arizona history); and travel (of interest to Phoenix residents). Buys 100 or more mss/year. Query with published clips. Length: 1,200 words maximum. Pays $75-300/article. Pays expenses of writers on assignment.

Tips: "It's not a closed shop. I want the brightest, freshest, most accurate material available. Study the magazine to see our format and style. Major features are assigned to contributing editors."

PRACTICAL HOMEOWNER, Rodale Press, 33 E. Minor St., Emmaus PA 18098. Articles Editor: John Viehman. 75% freelance written. Eager to work with new/unpublished writers; works with a small number of new/unpublished writers each year. Magazine published 9 times/year about practical home improvements. Circ. 750,000. Pays on acceptance. Publishes ms an average of 3 months after acceptance. Submit seasonal material at least 1 year in advance. Query for electronic submissions. Computer printout submissions acceptable; no dot-matrix. Reports in 6 weeks. Writer's guidelines for SASE.

Nonfiction: *Practical Homeowner* is a do-it-yourself magazine for people who want to create a safe, efficient and healthy home environment. Its aim is to put the reader in control of all decisions affecting his home, which may mean simplifying day-to-day maintenance and improving an existing structure or the more involved overseeing of new home construction." Feature articles relating to the home, including—but not limited to—remodeling, home repair, home management, improving energy efficiency, landscaping, home design, construction techniques, building materials and technology, home ownership trends, and home health issues. Length: 1,000-1,500 words. Buys all rights. Payment $400-1,000.

Photos: Mitch Mandel, photo editor. State availability of photos. Pays $35-100 for b&w; $75-400 for color transparencies or 35mm slides, depending on size and use. Captions and model releases required. Buys one-time rights.

Columns/Departments: Our Hometown (community efforts, restoration, should relate to sense of community or homeowning), 300-400 words. Healthy Home (maintaining a safe, healthy home environment), Financial Advisor (managing home and home improvement finances), Innovations (the latest in home building materials and technology), Fix it Right (illustrated instructions for home repairs), Well-Crafted Home (projects for the intermediate to advanced do -it-yourselfer), Trade Secrets (professional tradesmen explain techniques), Reader Tips (quick tips for fixing, making or improving items around the house), Practical Products (building supplies, home furnishings, tools) and Life at My House (anecdotal essays on life at home). Length: 600-1,000 words. All columns are on assignment basis. Pays: $150-600.

SAN DIEGO HOME/GARDEN, Westward Press, Box 1471, San Diego CA 92112. (714)233-4567. Editor: Peter Jensen. Managing Editor: Gretchen Pelletier. 50% freelance written. Works with a small number of new/unpublished writers each year. Monthly magazine covering homes, gardens, food, and local travel for residents of San Diego city and county. Circ. 31,000. Pays on acceptance. Publishes ms an average of 3 months after acceptance. Byline given. Buys first North American serial rights only. Submit seasonal material 3 months in advance. Photocopied submissions OK. Computer printout submissions acceptable. Reports in 1 month. Free writer's guidelines for SASE.

Nonfiction: Residential architecture and interior design (San Diego-area homes only); remodeling (must be well-designed—little do-it-yourself), residential landscape design; furniture; other features oriented towards upscale readers interested in living the cultured good life in San Diego. Articles must have local angle. Buys 5-10 unsolicited mss/year. Query with published clips. Length: 700-2,000 words. Pays $50-200. Sometimes pays expenses of writers on assignment.

Tips: "No out-of-town, out-of-state subject material. Most freelance work is accepted from local writers. Gear stories to the unique quality of San Diego. We try to offer only information unique to San Diego—people, places, shops, resources, etc. We plan more food and entertaining-at-home articles and more articles on garden products. We also need more in-depth reports on major architecture, environmental, and social aspects of life in San Diego and the border area (LaFrontera)."

SELECT HOMES MAGAZINE, 1450 Don Mills Dr., Don Mills, Ontario M3B 2X7 Canada. (416)445-6641. Editor: Diane McDougall (East). 30% freelance written. Prefers to work with published/established writers; works with a small number of new/unpublished writers each year. Magazine published 8 times/year covering renovation, building and interior design for the Canadian homeowner. Circ. 160,000. Pays on acceptance. Publishes ms an average of 4 months after acceptance. Buys 50 or more text/photo packages/year. Byline and photo credits given. Usually buys first Canadian serial rights; simultaneous rights, first rights, or second serial (reprint) rights, if explained. Submit seasonal/holiday material 3-12 months in advance. Simultaneous queries, and simultaneous, photocopied and previously published submissions OK if explained. Computer printout submissions acceptable; no dot-matrix. Reports in 1 month. Sample copy for 9x12 SAE; writer's guidelines for #10 SAE.

Nonfiction: How-to, humor, and personal experience on renovation, building, interior design, energy. Special sections include kitchen, spring; bathroom, fall. "We would like to receive humor columns for Back Porch (650 words maximum), relating specifically to home ownership. No lifestyle essays. Send SAE for sample Back Porch columns." Query with published clips. Length: 100-1,500 words. Pays $100-700. Pays expenses of writers on assignment.

Photos: State availability of photos. Reviews contact sheets and 2¼x2¼ transparencies. Pays $50-250, color. "We pay mostly on a negotiable per-day rate, but we like to work from stock lists, too." Captions and model release requested. Buys one-time rights.

Fillers: Newsbreaks. Buys 25/year. Length: 100-500 words. Pays $100 and up.

Tips: "We're looking for more renovation how-to articles—query first with clips. Submit clips and outline and tell us what special interests you have (decorating, energy, how-to). The editors generate 75% of the magazine's article ideas and assign them to writers whose style or background matches. We actively solicit book excerpts and reprints; please mention if your material is one of these."

‡SOUTHERN HOMES, The Magazine for Better Living, Haas Publishing Co., Inc., Georgia regional office: 3119 Campus Dr., Norcross GA 30071. (404)446-6585. Editor: Jane F. Schneider. Bimonthly magazine on shelter design, lifestyle in the home. "*Southern Homes* is designed for the achievement-oriented, well-educated reader who is concerned about the quality of his/her shelter, its design and construction, its environment, and how to best enjoy living and entertaining in it." Circ. 32,000. Pays on acceptance. Byline given. Publishes ms an average of 6 months after acceptance. Pays 20-25% kill fee. Buys all rights (inquire). Submit seasonal/holiday material 1 year in advance. Simultaneous submissions OK "if totally outside our market area." Computer printout submissions OK; prefers letter-quality. Reports in 2 months on queries; 3 months on ms. Sample copy #10 SAE with 1 first class stamp.

Nonfiction: Lynn B. McGill, managing editor. Historical/nostalgic, interview/profile, new product, well-designed homes, antiques, photo feature, gardens, local art. "We do not want articles outside respective market area, not written for magazine format, or that are excessively controversial, investigative or that cannot be appropriately illustrated with attractive photography." Buys 60-70 mss/year. Query with published clips. Length: 600-1,250 words. Pays $250-400. Sometimes pays expenses of writers on assignment "if agreed upon in advance of assignment."

Photos: Send photos with submission. "Negotiated separately. On spec only. Photos are rarely accepted." Reviews 2x4 transparencies; 35mm, 4x5. Offers $50-75/photo. Captions, model releases, and identification of subjects required. Buys one-time rights.

Columns/Departments: The South Looks Back (residential history Atlanta: architects, houses, neighborhoods) 750 words; Profiles (people who are active in shelter design, decoration, with a special slant); Antiques (a single antique theme: desks, pub tables, for example). Query with published clips. Buys 25-30 mss/year. Length: 500-1,000 words. Pays $250-325.

THE SPROUTLETTER, Sprouting Publications, Box 62, Ashland OR 97520. (503)488-2326. Editor: Michael Linden. 50% freelance written. Quarterly newsletter covering sprouting, live foods and indoor food gardening. "We emphasize growing foods (especially sprouts) indoors for health, economy, nutrition and food self-sufficiency. We also cover topics related to sprouting, live foods and holistic health." Circ. 2,500. Pays on publication. Publishes ms an average of 3 months after acceptance. Byline given. Buys North American serial rights and second (reprint) rights to material originally published elsewhere. Submit seasonal/holiday material 4 months in advance. Previously published submissions OK. Computer printout submissions acceptable; prefers letter-quality. Reports in 2 weeks on queries; 3 weeks on mss. Sample copy $2.50.

Nonfiction: General interest (raw foods, sprouting, holistic health); how-to (grow sprouts, all kinds of foods indoors; build devices for sprouting or indoor gardening); personal experience (in sprouting or related areas); and technical (experiments with growing sprouts). No common health food/vitamin articles or growing ornamental plants indoors (as opposed to food producing plants). Buys 4-6 mss/year. Query. Length: 500-2,400 words. Pays $15-50. Trades for merchandise are also considered.

Columns/Departments: Book Reviews (books oriented toward sprouts, nutrition or holistic health). Reviews are short and informative. News Items (interesting news items relating to sprouts or live foods); Recipes (mostly raw foods). Buys 5-10 mss/year. Query. Length: 100-450 words. Pays $3-10.

Fillers: Short humor and newsbreaks. Buys 3-6/year. Length: 50-150 words. Pays $2-6.

Tips: "Writers should have a sincere interest in holistic health and in natural whole foods. We like tight writing which is optimistic, interesting and informative. Consumers are demanding more thorough and accurate information. Articles should cover any given subject in depth in an enjoyable and inspiring manner. A frequent mistake is that the subject matter is not appropriate. Also buys cartoon strips and singles. Will consider series."

YOUR HOME, Meridian Publishing, Inc., Box 10010, Ogden UT 84409. (801)394-9446. 65% freelance written. A monthly in-house magazine covering home/garden subjects. Circ. 112,000. Pays on acceptance. Publishes ms an average of 8 months after acceptance. Byline given. Buys first rights and second serial (reprint) rights. Eight-month lead time. Submit seasonal material 10 months in advance. Simultaneous, photocopied and previously published submissions OK. Computer printout submissions acceptable; prefers letter-quality. Reports in 6 weeks. Sample copy for $1 and 9x12 SAE; writer's guidelines for #10 SASE. All requests for samples and guidelines and queries should be addressed Attn: Editor.

Nonfiction: General interest articles about fresh ideas in home decor, ranging from floor and wall coverings to home furnishings. Subject matter includes the latest in home construction (exteriors, interiors, building materials, design), the outdoors at home (landscaping, pools, patios, gardening), remodeling projects, home management and home buying and selling. Buys 40 mss/year. Length: 1,000-1,400 words. Pays 15¢/word for first rights plus nonexclusive reprint rights. Payment for second serial rights is negotiable.

Photos: State availability of photos with query. Reviews 35mm or larger transparencies and 5x7 or 8x10 "sharp, professional-looking" color prints. Pays $35 for inside photo; pays $50 for cover photo. Captions, model releases and identification of subjects required.

Tips: "The key is a well-written query letter that: (1) demonstrates that the subject of the article is practical and useful and has national appeal; (2) shows that the article will have a clear, focused theme and will be based on interviews with experts; (3) outlines the availability (from the writer, a photographer or a PR source) of top-quality color photos; (4) gives evidence that the writer/photographer is a professional."

Humor

Publications listed here specialize in gaglines or prose humor. Other publications that use humor can be found in nearly every category in this book. Some have special needs for major humor pieces; some use humor as fillers; many others are interested in material that meets their ordinary fiction or nonfiction requirements but has a humorous slant. Other markets for humorous material can be found in the Comic Books and Gag Writing sections. For a closer look at writing humor, consult *How to Write and Sell (Your Sense of) Humor*, by Gene Perret, *Comedy Writing Secrets*, by Melvin Helitzer and *The Craft of Comedy Writing*, by Sol Saks (Writer's Digest Books).

‡FUNNNIES, That Funny Magazine On the Wall, Whittle Communications, 505 Market St., Knoxville TN 37902. (800)521-5002. Associate Editor: Mary Elizabeth Williams (reviews manuscripts). Editorial Director: Randy Duckett. Humor magazine published monthly for laundromats. "*Funnnies* is brights, lively wall media (monthly magazine in poster format) publication that present cartoons, satire, interviews with top-name comedians, and excerpts from humor books by major humor writers—Lewis Grizzard, Dave Barry." Circ. 2.1 million readers. Pays on acceptance. Publishes ms an average of 4 months after acceptance. Byline given. Offers 33% of agreed-upon fee as kill fee. Buys first North American serial rights, second serial (reprint) rights and makes work-for-hire assignments. Submit seasonal/holiday material 6months in advance. Previously published submissions OK. Computer printout submissions OK; prefers letter quality. Reports in 6 weeks. Writer's guidelines for #10 SAE.

Nonfiction: Book excerpts, humor opinion, funny photo feature. Possible future themes include Urban Living, Animals, Scary Stuff (Halloween). "No laundry jokes, cornball material, racist or sexist material, obscene humor. Remember topical reference may be out of date by time we publish." Buys 10 mss/year. Send listings of future concepts and ideas with complete ms. Queries don't really work for a humor publication. Length: 50-200 words. Pays $100-300. Pays expenses of writers on assignment.

Photos: State availability of photos ors end photos with submissions. Reviews contact sheets, color transparencies or b&w prints. Pays American Society of Magazine Photographers rates. Model releases and identification of subjects required. Buys one-time rights.

Columns/Departments: Funnylists; Skewed Views; Real-Life Laughs (bizarre news items); Joke Bank; and Isolated Jokes. Send list of ideas. Length: 50-200 words. Pays $25-300.

Fiction: Experimental, humorous, novel excerpts. "No overly cute, cliched, racist, sexist, obscene or so topical it will be out of date by the time it runs 4-6 months later. No laundry jokes or anything corny. Keep Letterman and 'Saturday Night Live' in mind as you're writing." Buys 12 mss/year. Send complete ms with published clips. Length: 50-200 words. Pays $100-300.

Fillers: Anecdotes, facts, gags to be illustrated by cartoonist, newsbreaks and short humor. Buys 75/year. Length: 50 words maximum. Pays $250-50.

Tips: "Look at our magazine, study it, then write something and send it in. Send any clips you think we might be interested in. We are looking for a large pool of funny writers. If you can really writer humor, you may not know it, but you're a rare bird. We just might call you with an assignment."

‡KNUCKLEHEAD PRESS, Knucklehead Press Publications, Box 305, Burbank CA 91503. Editors: Chris Miksanek and Jim Riley. A quarterly humor newsletter. "We print anything that's funny, but not morally or sexually offensive." Circ. 600. Pays on publication. Publishes ms an average of 6 months after acceptance. "We include writer in editorial bar as Contributing Editor." Buys all rights. Submit seasonal/holiday material 6 months in advance. Simultaneous, photocopied and previously published submissions OK. Query for electronic submissions. Computer printout submissions OK. Reports in 3 weeks on mss. Sample copy for 9x12 SAE with 2 first class stamps or sample copy $1. Free writer's guidelines with sample copy request.

Nonfiction: Everything in Knucklehead Press is fiction in that it's not true, but we would welcome parodies of: exposé, general interest, historical/nostalgic, how-to, interview/profile, new product and technical. "We're always doing special 1 or 2 page sections. They're not planned, but based on material submitted. For example, if we have 3 or 4 food pieces, we might do a special restaurant/dining out section. Nothing unfunny or (and we're not prudes) something religiously or sexually offensive." Buys 10-15 mss/year. Send complete ms. Length: 50-500 words. Pays $5-20 for unsolicited articles. Send photos with submission. Reviews prints (b&w only). Offers no additional payment for photos accepted with ms. Captions, model releases and identification of subjects required. Buys all rights.

Columns/Departments: Newsbriefs (short news-type bits), 25-50 words. Buys 10 mss/year. Send complete ms. Length: 10-100 words. Pays $3-5.

Fiction: Adventure, historical, horror, humorous, novel excerpts and slice-of-life vignettes. Buys 4 mss/year. Send complete ms. Length: 250-500 words. Pays $5-20.

Fillers: Newsbreaks, short humor and gag classifieds. Buys 15/year. Length: 20-50 words. Pays $1-3.

Tips: "A comedy writer has to ask himself, 'Does my material entertain me? Can I read my own material and laugh as I would reading someone else's?' If the answer is 'yes' then we want to see your stuff. Every part of our newsletter is open to freelancers. If they can do something funnier than us, we're more than happy to step aside. Our goal is to publish a gut-busting newsletter, and any way that we accomplish that goal is OK by us. Make every word count. There's nothing more agonizing than a long not-so-funny piece; make your point and exit. Short and sweet."

‡LATEST JOKES, Box 3304-0066, Brooklyn NY 11202-0066. (718)855-5057. Editor: Robert Makinson. 20% freelance written. Monthly newsletter of humor for TV and radio personalities, comedians and professional speakers. Circ. 250. Pays on acceptance. Byline sometimes given. Buys all rights. Submit seasonal/holiday material 3 months in advance. Reports in 3 weeks. Sample copy $2 and 1 first class stamp.

Nonfiction: Humor (short jokes). No "stupid, obvious, non-funny vulgar humor." Send complete ms. Pays $1-3 for each joke.

Fiction: Humorous jokes. Pays $1-3.

Poetry: Light verse (humorous). Submit maximum 3 poems at one time. Line length: 2-8 lines. Pays 25¢/line.

Tips: "No famous personality jokes. Clever statements are not enough. Be original and surprising."

LONE STAR HUMOR, Lone Star Publications of Humor, Suite 103, Box 29000, San Antonio TX 78229. Editor: Lauren I. Barnett. Less than 25% freelance written. Eager to work with new/unpublished writers. A humor book-by-subscription for "the general public and 'comedy connoisseur' as well as the professional humorist." Pays on publication, "but we try to pay before that." Publishes ms an average of 8 months after acceptance. Buys variable rights. Submit seasonal/holiday material 6 months in advance. Photocopied submissions and sometimes previously published work OK. Query for electronic submissions. Computer printout submission acceptable; no dot-matrix. Reports in 2-4 months on queries; 3-4 months on mss. Inquire with SASE for prices and availability of sample copy. Writer's guidelines for #10 SASE.

Nonfiction: Humor (on anything topical/timeless); interview/profile (of anyone professionally involved in humor); and opinion (reviews of stand-up comedians, comedy plays, cartoonists, humorous books, *anything* concerned with comedy). "Inquire about possible theme issues." Buys 15 mss/year. Query with clips of published work if available. Length: 500-1,000 words; average is 700-800 words. Pays $5-30 and contributor's copy.

Fiction: Humorous. Buys variable mss/year. Send complete ms. Length: 500-1,000 words. Pays $5-30 and contributor's copy.

Poetry: Free verse, light verse, traditional, clerihews and limericks. "Nothing too 'artsy' to be funny." Buys 10-20/year. Submit maximum 5 poems. Length: 4-16 lines. Inquire for current rates.

Fillers: Clippings, jokes, gags, anecdotes, short humor and newsbreaks—"must be humorous or humor-related." Buys 20-30 mss/year. Length: 450 words maximum. Inquire for current rates.

Tips: "Our needs for freelance material will be somewhat diminished; writers should inquire (with SASE) before submitting material. We will be generating more and more of our humor inhouse, but will most likely require freelance material for books and other special projects. If the words 'wacky, zany, or crazy' describe the writer's finished product, it is *not* likely that his/her piece will suit our needs. The best humor is just slightly removed from reality."

MAD MAGAZINE, E.C. Publications, 485 Madison Ave., New York NY 10022. (212)752-7685. Editors: Nick Meglin and John Ficarra. 100% freelance written. Magazine published 8 times/year. Circ. 1 million. Pays on acceptance. Publishes ms an average of 6 months after acceptance. Byline given. Buys all rights. Submit seasonal/holiday material 6 months in advance. Photocopied submissions OK. Computer printout submissions acceptable; prefers letter-quality. Reports in 6 weeks. Writer's guidelines for #10 SASE.

Nonfiction: Satire, parody. "We're always on the lookout for new ways to spoof and to poke fun at hot trends — music, computers, commericals, etc. We're *not* interested in formats we're already doing or have done to death like... 'you know you're a . . . when....'" Buys 400 ms yearly. Submit a premise with 3 or 4 examples of how you intend to carry it through, describing the action and visual content. Rough sketches are not necessary. Pays minimum $300/*MAD* page. One-page gags: 2-8 panel cartoon continuities in the style and tradition of *MAD*. Buys 30 yearly. Pays minimum of $300/*MAD* page. Don't send song parodies, poetry, riddles, TV or movie satires, book manuscripts, articles about Alfred E. Neuman or text pieces.

Tips: "Have fun! We're interested in anything and everything that you think is funny. Remember to think visually! Freelancers can best break in with nontopical material. If we see even a germ of talent, we will work with that person. We like outrageous, silly but *clean* humor."

ORBEN'S CURRENT COMEDY, 1200 N. Nash St., #1122, Arlington VA 22209. (703)522-3666. Editor: Robert Orben. Biweekly. For "speakers, toastmasters, businessmen, public relations people, communications professionals." Pays at the end of the month for material used in issues published that month. Buys all rights. Computer printout submissions acceptable. "Unused material will be returned to the writer if SASE is enclosed. We do not send rejection slips. If SASE is not enclosed, all material will be destroyed after being considered except for items purchased."

Fillers: "We are looking for funny, performable one-liners, short jokes and stories that are related to happenings in the news, fads, trends and topical subjects. The accent is on laugh-out-loud comedy. Ask yourself, 'Will this line get a laugh if performed in public?' Material should be written in a conversational style, and if the joke permits it, the inclusion of dialogue is a plus. We are particularly interested in material that can be used by speakers and toastmasters: lines for beginning a speech, ending a speech, acknowledging an introduction, specific occasions, anything that would be of use to a person making a speech. We can use lines to be used at roasts, sales meetings, presentations, conventions, seminars and conferences. Short, sharp comment on business trends, fads and events is also desirable. Please do not send us material that's primarily written to be read rather than spoken. We have little use for definitions, epigrams, puns, etc. The submissions must be original. If material is sent to us that we find to be copied or rewritten from some other source, we will no longer consider material from the contributor. Material should be typed and submitted on standard size paper. Leave three spaces between each item." Pays $8.

Tips: "Follow the instructions in our guidelines. Although they are quite specific, we have received everything from epic poems to serious novels."

THE P.U.N., Play on Words, The Silly Club, Box 536-583, Orlando FL 32853. (305)898-0463. Editor: Danno Sullivan. 15% freelance written. Eager to work with new/unpublished writers. A bimonthly newsletter for a nonexistant organization, The Silly Club. "The P.U.N. readers enjoy humor bordering on intellectual, all the way down or up to just plain silliness. Politeness, though, above all. Despite the title, we very rarely use puns as such. *P.U.N.* is an anagram, not an indication of content." Circ. 250. Pays on acceptance. Publishes ms an average of 2 months after acceptance. Byline given "listed in credits." Buys one-time rights. Submit seasonal/holiday material 1-2 months in advance. Simultnaeous, photocopied and previously published submissions OK. Computer printout submissions OK; prefers letter-quality. Reports in 3 weeks on mss. Sample copy for #10 SASE.

Nonfiction: Humor. "Nothing rude, no foul language and no naughty things." Buys 10-25 mss/year. Send complete ms. Length: 10-2,000 words. Pays $1-25 for unsolicited articles.

Columns/Departments: Letters to the Emperor (usually concerning past P.U.N. articles, but frequently not), 100 words; Write That Story (an occasional feature, which invites readers to write the next short chapter of an ongoing story), 1,000 words. Buys 10-15 mss/year. Send complete ms. Length: 10-100 words. Pays $1-25.

Fiction: Humorous. Buys 3-5 mss/year. Send complete ms. Length: 10-2,000 words. Pays $1-25. Also single panel cartoons. "Our fiction is mostly 'fictional nonfiction.'"

Poetry: Humorous poetry. Buys 5 poems/year. Submit maximum 10 poems. Pays $1-10.

Fillers: Gags and short humor. Buys 15/year. Pays $1-25.

‡THE UNCOMMON READER, A Magazine for Intelligent People Who Love to Laugh, 1220 Taransay, Henderson KY 42420. (502)827-0111. Editor: Louis B. Hatchett, Jr. 75% freelance written. A quarterly literary magazine. "We cater to an intelligent audience that has a sense of humor. Our motto is simple: if it's not funny, we can't use it. We like fiction and nonfiction that is irreverent, earthy but not vulgar and which is tart in execution and fun to read." Circ. 1,500. Pays on publication. Publishes ms an average of 6 months after acceptance. Byline given. Offers $100 kill fee. Buys first North American serial rights or second serial (reprint) rights. Simultaneous, photocopied and previously published submissions OK. Computer printout submissions OK; no dot-matrix; prefers letter-quality. Reports in 3 months on mss. Sample copy for 10x13 SAE with 6 first class stamps and $4.50. Writer's guidelines for #10 SAE with 1 first class stamp.

Nonfiction: Essays, exposé and humor. "We want articles that poke fun at the human condition in a puckish style." Buys 50 mss/year. Query with or without published clips, or send complete ms. Length: up to 5,000. Pays "usually $100, unless very short."

Columns/Departments: Heathen Watch (a collection of stupid incidents perpetrated in the name of civilization); Public Trash (reviews current popular fiction—and trashes it).

Fiction: Aija Baltzarsen, fiction editor. Humorous, mainstream, serialized novels, suspense and English translations of French and German westerns (circa 1870-1918). "We don't want stories that aren't funny, written in the present tense, sexually oriented, containing vulgar language or experimental fiction." Buys 50 mss/year. Send complete ms. Length: 2,500-5,000 words. Pays $50-100; $25-100 for short stories.

Poetry: Michael D. Harrold, poetry editor. Traditional. "Don't send us any experimental poetry. Send us poetry that rhymes—the kind that was popular 100 years ago." Buys 20 poems/year. "No limit" on maximum number of poems submitted. Length: 20-30 words. Pays $10-50.

Fillers: Anecdotes, facts, newsbreaks and short humor. Buys 50/year. Length: 25-500 words. Pays $5-10.

Tips: "Must be a subscriber in order to be published. More than anything else—I first look for a tone of voice—intelligent, slightly sarcastic, wise-cracking tone. For an intelligent, wise-cracking-yet not forced-sarcastic point of view."

In-Flight

Most major in-flight magazines cater to business travelers and vacationers who will be reading, during the flight, about the airline's destinations and other items of general interest. Airline mergers and acquisitions have affected the number of magazines published in this area. The writer should watch for airline announcements in the news and in ads and read the latest sample copies and writer's guidelines for current information.

ABOARD, North-South Net, Inc., 777 41st St., Box 40-2763, Miami Beach FL 33140. (305)673-8577. Editor: Cristina Juri Arencibia. 50% freelance written. Eager to work with new/unpublished writers. Bimonthly magazine covering destinations for the Equatorian, Dominican, Paraguayan, Bolivian, Chilean, Salvadoran, Honduran, Guatemalan and Venezuelan national airlines. Entertaining, upbeat stories for the passengers. Circ. 98,000. Pays on publication. Publishes ms an average of 2 months after acceptance. Byline given. Buys first Western Hemisphere rights and second serial reprint rights. Simultaneous queries, and simultaneous, photocopied, and previously published submissions OK. Computer printout submissions acceptable; prefers letter-quality. Reports in 3 weeks on queries; 5 weeks on mss. Sample copy for 11x14 SAE and 5 first class stamps; writer's guidelines for #10 SAE and 1 first class stamp.

Nonfiction: General interest, interview/profile, new product, travel, sports, business, science, technology and topical pieces. Nothing "controversial, political, downbeat or in any way offensive to Latin American sensibilities." Buys 60 mss/year. Query. Length: 1,200-1,500 words. Pays $150-250 (with photos).

Photos: State availability of photos with query. Reviews b&w photos and color transparencies. Offers no additional payment for photos accepted with ms. Captions, model release and identification of subjects required.

Tips: "Study *Aboard* and other inflights, write exciting, succinct stories with an upbeat slant and enclose photos with captions. Break in with destination pieces for the individual airline or those shared by all nine. Writers must be accurate. Photos are always indispensable. Manuscripts are accepted either in English or Spanish. Translation rights must be granted. All manuscripts are subject to editing and condensation."

AMERICA WEST AIRLINES MAGAZINE, Skyword Marketing, Inc., Suite 236, 7500 N. Dreamy Draw Dr., Phoenix AZ 85020. (602)997-7200. Editor: Michael Derr. Managing Editor: Carrie Sears Bell. 80% freelance written. Works with small number of new/unpublished writers each year. A monthly "general interest magazine emphasizing the western and southwestern U.S. Some midwestern, northwestern and eastern subjects also appropriate. We look for ideas and people that celebrate opportunity, and those who put it to positive use." Query with published clips and SASE. Pays on publication. Publishes ms an average of 4 months after acceptance. Byline given. Offers 15% kill fee. Buys first North American rights. Submit seasonal/holiday material 6-8 months in advance. Simultaneous submissions OK, "if indicated as such." Query for electronic submissions. Computer printout submissions OK; prefers letter quality. Reports in 1 month on queries; 5 weeks on mss. Sample copy for $2; writer's guidelines for 9x12 SASE with 3 first class stamps.

Nonfiction: General interest, creative leisure, events, profile, photo feature, science, sports, business issues, entrepreneurs, nature, health, history, arts, book excerpts, travel and trends. Also considers essays and humor. No puzzles, reviews or highly controversial features. Buys 130-140 mss/year. Query with published clips. Length: 500-2,200. Pays $200-750. Pays some expenses.

Photos: State availability of original photography. Offers $50-250/photo. Captions, model releases and identification of subjects required. Buys one-time rights.

Fiction: Will consider exceptional pieces with a regional slant. No horror, inspirational or political. Send complete ms. Length: 800-1,800. Pays $200-500.

DELTA SKY, Inflight Magazine of Delta Air Lines, Halsey Publishing Co., 12955 Biscayne Blvd., N. Miami FL 33181. (305)893-1520. Editor: Lidia de Leon. 90% freelance written. Monthly. *"Delta Sky* is a monthly general-interest magazine with a business/finance orientation thats main purpose is to entertain and inform business travelers aboard Delta Air Lines." Circ. 410,000. Pays on acceptance. Publishes ms an average of 2 months after acceptance. Byline given. Offers 100% kill fee when cancellation through no fault of writer. Buys first North American serial rights. Submit seasonal/holiday material 9 months in advance. Simultaneous and photocopied submissions OK. Computer printout submissions acceptable; prefers letter-quality. Reports in 1 month. Sample copy for 9x12 SAE; free writer's guidelines.

Nonfiction: General interest. No reprints, religious or first-person/experiential. Buys 160 mss/year. Query with published clips. Length: 1,500-2,500 words. Pays $350-600 for assigned articles; pays $300-500 for unsolicited articles. Pays expenses of writers on assignment.

Photos: State availability of photos with submission. Reviews 5x7 prints. Offers $25-100/photo. Captions, model releases and identification of subjects required. Buys one-time rights.

Columns/Departments: On Management (managerial techniques/methods with current appeal), 1,700 words. Query with published clips. Pays $300-400.

Tips: "Send a comprehensive, well-detailed query tied in to one of the feature categories of the magazine, along with clips of previously published work. Since our lead times call for planning of editorial content 6-9 months in advance, that should also be kept in mind when proposing story ideas. We are always open to good feature-story ideas that have to do with business and technology. Next in order of priority would be leisure, sports, entertainment and consumer topics."

‡DESTINATION, Braniff Airlines, Skies America Publishing, Suite 310, 9600 S.W. Oak St., Portland OR 97223. (503)244-2299. Editor: Terri J. Wallo. See *Midway Magazine.*

MIDWAY MAGAZINE, Skies America Publishing Co., Suite 310, 9600 S.W. Oak St., Portland OR 97223. (503)244-2299. Editor: Terri J. Wallo. 50% freelance written. Monthly magazine. Circ. approximately 40,000. Pays on publication. Publishes ms an average of 2 months after acceptance. Byline given. Submit seasonal/holiday material 6 months in advance. Simultaneous submissions OK. Computer printout submissions acceptable; prefers letter-quality. Reports in 1 month. Sample copy for 8X½x11 SAE $3 with SASE; writer's guidelines for SASE.

Nonfiction: Interview/profile, photo feature and travel. "Business features should be timely, well-researched and well-focused. Corporate profiles and personality profiles are encouraged. Travel destination pieces should be original, detailed and lively. No stale pieces that sound like canned promotions." Buys 24 mss/year. Query with published clips. Length: 1,000-2,500 words. Pays $150-400 for assigned articles; pays $150-250 for unsolicited articles. Sometimes pays the expenses of writers on assignment.

Photos: Send photos with submission. Reviews color transparencies and 8x10 b&w prints. Offers no additional payment for photos accepted with ms. Identification of subjects required. Buys one-time rights.

Tips: "The cities we focus on are: New York; Boston; Chicago; Indianapolis; Miami; Pittsburgh; Columbus; New Orleans; All Florida cities; New York; Minneapolis; Dallas; Cleveland; Detroit; New Orleans; Washington, D.C.; Virgin Islands; Cincinnati; Kansas City; Philadelphia; Las Vegas; Denver and Atlanta. Write to us with specific ideas relating to these cities. A fresh, original idea with excellent photo possibilities will receive our close attention. Areas most open to freelancers are corporate profiles; destination travel pieces with an unusual slant; personality profiles on businessmen and women, entrepreneurs."

‡NORTHWEST, East/West Network, 34 E. 51st St., New York NY 10022. (212)888-5900. Editor: William McCoy. Associate Editor: John Spade. Pays on acceptance. Publishes ms an average of 1-2 months after acceptance. Offers 25% kill fee. Buys first North American serial rights. Reports in 2 months.

Nonfiction: General interest, interview/profile, photo feature, travel. Buys 60 mss/year. Query with published clips. Length: 1,800-2,000 words. Pays $800-1,000.

Columns/Departments: Buys 24 mss/year. Length: 800-1,200 words. Pays $800-1,000.

SKIES AMERICA, Publisher for the Nation's Business Airlines, Suite 310, 9600 S.W. Oak St., Portland OR 97223. (503)244-2299. Editor: Terri J. Wallo. 75% freelance written. Editions published monthly. "Published primarily for educated business travelers." Circ. 1,500,000. Pays on publications. Publishes ms an average of 3 months after acceptance. Byline given. Buys first North American serial rights and second serial (reprint) rights. Submit seasonal/holiday material 3 months in advance. Simultaneous, photocopied and previously published submissions OK. Reports in 3 weeks. Sample copy for 8½x11 SAE and $3. Writers guidelines for SASE.

Nonfiction: General interest, interview/profile, and travel. No fiction. Buys 50 mss/year. Query with or

without published clips. Length: 500-2,000 words. Pays $100-400. Sometimes pays expenses of writers on assignment.
Photos: State availability of photos with submission. Reviews transparencies (35mm and over) and prints. Offers $25-50/photo. Identification of subjects required. Buys "one time rights for all 5 magazines we publish."
Tips: "Most of our readers are businessmen under 45 years of age. Any business or vocational type article would be welcome."

SKY, Inflight Magazine of Delta Air Lines,Halsey Publishing Co., 12955 Biscayne Blvd., N. Miami FL 33181. (305)893-1520. Editor: Lidia De Leon. 90% freelance written. Monthly magazine. "Delta *SKY* is a general interest, nationally oriented magazine with a primary editorial focus on business and management, with the main purpose to entertain and inform business travelers aboard Delta Air Lines." Circ. 410,000. Pays on acceptance. Publishes ms an average of 2 months after acceptance. Byline given. Offers 100% kill fee when cancellation is through no fualt of the writer. Buys first North American serial rights. Submit seasonal/holiday material 9 months in advance. Simultaneous and photocopied submissions OK. Computer printout submissions OK; prefers letter-quality. Reports in 1 month. Sample copy for 9x12 SAE; free writer's guidelines.
Nonfiction: General interest and photo feature. "No excerpts, essays, personal experience, opinion, religious, reviews, poetry, fiction or fillers." Buys 200 mss/year. Query with published clips. Length: 1700-2500 words. Pays $300-500 for assigned articles; pays $300-450 for unsolicited articles. Pays expenses of writers on assignment.
Photos: State availability of photos with submission. Reviews transparencies (4x5) and prints (5x7). Offers $25-50/photo. Captions, model releases and identification of subject required. Buys one-time rights.
Columns/Departments: On Management (managerial techniques, methods of topical nature). Buys 40 mss/year. Query with published clips. Length: 1500-1800 words. Pays $300-400.
Tips: "Send a comprehensive, well detailed query tied in to one of the feature categories of the magazine along with clips of previously published work. Since our lead times call for planning of editorial content 6-9 months in advance, that should also be kept in mind when proposing story ideas. We are always open to good feature story ideas that have to do with business and technology. Next in order of priority would be leisure, sports, entertainment and consumer topics. All feature story categories (Business, Lifestyle, Sports, Arts/Entertainment, Consumer, Technology, and Collectibles) are open to freelancers, with the exceptions of Travel (areas are predetermined by the airline) and the executive Profile Series (which is also predetermined)."

USAIR MAGAZINE, Pace Communications, 388 N. Elm, Greensboro NC 27401. (919)378-6065. Editor: Maggie Oman. Assistant Editor: Lori Riley. 95% freelance written. Prefers to work with published/established writers. A monthly general interest magazine published for airline passengers, many of whom are business travelers, male, with high incomes and college educations. Circ. 330,000. Pays before publication. Publishes ms an average of 4 months after acceptance. Buys first rights only. Submit seasonal material 4 months in advance. Photocopied submissions OK. Computer printout submissions acceptable; prefers letter-quality. Reports in 2 weeks. Sample copy $3; free writer's guidelines with SASE.
Nonfiction: Travel, business, sports, health, food, personal finance, nature, the arts, science/technology and photography. Buys 100 mss/year. Query with clips of previously published work. Length: 1,500-2,800 words. Pays $400-800. Pays expenses of writers on assignment.
Photos: Send photos with ms. Pays $75-150/b&w print, depending on size; color from $100-250/print or slide. Captions preferred; model release required. Buys one-time rights.
Columns/Departments: Sports, food, money, health, business, living and science. Buys 3-4 mss/issue. Query. Length: 1,200-1,800 words. Pays $300-500.
Tips: "Send irresistible ideas and proof that you can write. It's great to get a clean manuscript from a good writer who has given me exactly what I asked for. Frequent mistakes are not following instructions, not delivering on time, etc."

Juvenile

Just as children change and grow, so do juvenile magazines. Children's magazine editors stress that writers must read recent issues. This section lists publications for children ages 2-12. Magazines for young people 13-19 appear in the Teen and Young Adult category. Many of the following publications are produced by religious groups and, where possible, the specific denomination is given. A new book of juvenile markets, *Children's Writer's and Illustrator's Market*, is available from Writer's Digest Books in March 1989. Magazines that publish writing *by* children can be found in *Market Guide for Young Writers*, by Kathy Henderson (Shoe Tree Press). For the writer with a story or article slanted to a specific age group, the accompanying children's index is a quick reference to markets for each age group.

Juvenile publications classified by age

Two- to Five-Year-Olds: *Chickadee, Children's Playmate, The Friend, Highlights for Children, Humpty Dumpty, Owl, Stone Soup, Story Friends, Turtle, Wee Wisdom.*

Six- to Eight-Year-Olds: *Boys' Life, Chickadee, Child Life, Children's Digest, Children's Playmate, Cobblestone, Cricket, The Dolphin Log, The Electric Company, Faces, The Friend, Highlights for Children, Humpty Dumpty, Jack and Jill, National Geographic World, Noah's Ark, Odyssey, Owl, Pockets, Radar, Ranger Rick, Shofar, Stone Soup, Story Friends, Wee Wisdom, Wonder Time, Young American, Young Crusader, Young Soldier.*

Nine- to Twelve-Year-Olds: *Action, Boys' Life, Chickadee, Child Life, Children's Digest, Clubhouse, Cobblestone, Cricket, Crusader, Current Health 1, Discoveries, The Dolphin Log, The Electric Company, Faces, The Friend, High Adventure, Highlights for Children, Junior Scholastic, Junior Trails, National Geographic World, Noah's Ark, Odyssey, On the Line, Owl, Pockets, Radar, Ranger Rick, Shofar, Stone Soup, Story Friends, Venture, Wee Wisdom, Young American, Young Crusader, Young Soldier.*

ACTION, Dept. of Christian Education, Free Methodist Headquarters, 901 College Ave., Winona Lake IN 46590. (219)267-7656. Editor: Vera Bethel. 100% freelance written. Weekly magazine for "57% girls, 43% boys, ages 9-12; 48% city, 23% small towns." Circ. 25,000. Pays on publication. Rights purchased vary; may buy simultaneous rights, second (reprint) rights or first North American serial rights. Submit seasonal/holiday material 3 months in advance. Simultaneous and previously published submissions OK. Computer printout submissions acceptable; no dot-matrix. SASE must be enclosed. Reports in 1 month. Sample copy and writer's guidelines for 6x9 SAE and 3 first class stamps.
Nonfiction: How-to (make gifts and craft articles); informational (nature articles with pictures); and personal experience (my favorite vacation, my pet, my hobby, etc.). Buys 50 mss/year. Submit complete ms with photos. Length: 200-500 words. Pays $15.
Fiction: Adventure, humorous, mystery and religious. Buys 50 mss/year. Submit complete ms. Length: 1,000 words. Pays $25. SASE must be enclosed; no return without it.
Poetry: Free verse, haiku, light verse, traditional, devotional and nature. Buys 20/year. Submit maximum 5-6 poems. Length: 4-16 lines. Pays $5.
Tips: "Desperately need urban settings in fiction. Currently, 90% of the stories have large yards, one-family homes on shady steets, big dog bouncing across the yard, two-parent families with grandmother down the block--not acceptable to most Hispanic, oriental, or other ethnic readers. Also: surveyed readers are 50% in fifth or sixth grade; are looking toward junior high. Need more themes dealing with young teen interests, but keeping the pre-teen frame of mind. They are concerned with drugs and AIDS."

BOYS' LIFE, Boy Scouts of America, 1325 Walnut Hill Lane, Irving TX 75038-3096. Editor-in-chief: William B. McMorris. 75% freelance written. Prefers to work with published/established writers; works with small number of new/unpublished writers each year. Monthly magazine covering activities of interest to all boys ages 8-18. Most readers are Scouts or Cub Scouts. Circ 1.4 million. Pays on acceptance. Publishes ms an average of 6-12 months after acceptance. Buys one-time rights. Computer printout submissions OK; prefers letter-quality. Reports in 2 weeks. Sample copy for 9x12 SAE and 4 first class stamps.
Nonfiction: Major articles run 1,200-2,000 words. Preferred length is about 1,500 words. Pays minimum $500 for major article text. Uses strong photo features with about 750 words of text. Separate payment or assignment for photos. "Much better rates if you really know how to write for our market." Buys 60 major articles/year. Also needs how-to features and hobby and crafts ideas. "We pay top rates for ideas accompanied by sharp photos, clean diagrams, and short, clear instructions." Query first in writing. Buys 30-40 how-tos/year. Query all nonfiction ideas in writing. Pays expenses of writers on assignment. Also buys freelance comics pages and scripts. Query first.
Columns: "Food, Health, Pets, Bicycling and Magic Tricks are some of the columns for which we use 400-600 words of text. This is a good place to show us what you can do. Query first in writing." Pays $150 minimum. Buys 75-80 columns/year.
Fiction: Short stories 1,000-1,500 words; occasionally longer. Send complete ms. Pays $500 minimum. Buys 15 short stories/year.
Tips: "We strongly recommend reading at least 12 issues of the magazine and learning something about the programs of the Boy Scouts of America before you submit queries. We are a good market for any writer willing to do the necessary homework."

CHICKADEE MAGAZINE, For Young Children from *OWL*, The Young Naturalist Foundation, 56 The Esplanade, Suite 306, Toronto, Ontario M5E 1A7 Canada. (416)868-6001. Editor: Janis Nostbakken. 25% freelance written. Magazine published 10 times/year (except July and August) for 4-9 year-olds. "We aim to interest young children in the world around them in an entertaining and lively way." Circ. 100,000 Canada;

50,000 U.S. Pays on publication. Byline given. Buys all rights. Submit seasonal/holiday material up to 1 year in advance. Computer printout submissions acceptable. Reports in 2½ months. Sample copy for $1.95 and SAE; writer's guidelines for 50¢ and SAE.

Nonfiction: How-to (arts and crafts, easy experiments for children); personal experience (real children in real situations); and photo feature (wildlife features). No articles for older children; no religious or moralistic features. Sometimes pays the expenses of writers on assignment.

Photos: Send photos with ms. Reviews 35mm transparencies. Identification of subjects required.

Fiction: Adventure (relating to the 4-9 year old). No science fiction, fantasy, talking animal stories or religious articles. Send complete ms with $1 money order for handling and return postage. No IRCs. Pays $100-300.

Tips: "A frequent mistake made by writers is trying to teach too much—not enough entertainment and fun."

CHILD LIFE, Children's Better Health Institute, 1100 Waterway Blvd., Box 567, Indianapolis IN 46206. (317)636-8881. Editor: Steve Charles. 80% freelance written. Monthly (except bimonthly Feb/Mar, Apr/May, June/July, August/September) magazine covering "general topics of interest to children-emphasis on health preferred but not necessary." Pays on publication. Publishes ms an average of 8 months after acceptance. Byline given. Buys all rights. Submit seasonal/holiday material 8 months in advance. Photocopied submissions OK. Computer printout submissions OK; prefers letter quality. Reports in 3 months. Sample copy 75¢. Writer's guidelines for SASE.

Nonfiction: How-to (simple crafts), anything children might like—health topics preferred. Buys 20 mss/year. Send complete ms. Length: 400-1,500. Pays 8¢/word (approx). "Readers chosen for Young Author Story receive copies."

Photos: Send photos with submission. Reviews transparencies and prints. Offers $10 for inside b&w; $20 for inside color photo, $50 for front cover. Captions, model releases and identification of subjects required. Buys one time rights.

Fiction: Adventure, ethnic, fantasy, historical, humorous, mystery, science fiction and suspense. All must be geared to children. Buys 20-25 mss/year. Send complete ms. Length: 500-1,800 words. Pays 6¢/word (approx).

Poetry: Free verse, haiku, light verse and traditional. No long "deep" poetry not suited for children. Buys 8 poems/year. Submit maximum 5 poems. "We have used some verse 'stories'—500+ words." Pays approx 50¢/line.

Fillers: "We do accept puzzles, games, mazes, etc." Variable Pay.

Tips: "Present health-related items in an interesting, non-textbook manner. The approach to health fiction can be subtle—tell a good story first. We also consider non-health items—make them fresh and enjoyable for children."

CHILDREN'S DIGEST, Children's Better Health Institute, Box 567, Indianapolis IN 46206. (317)636-8881. Editor: Elizabeth Rinck. 85% freelance written. Works with a small number of new/unpublished writers each year. Magazine published 8 times/year covering children's health for children ages 8-10. Pays on publication. Publishes ms an average of 1 year after acceptance. Byline given. Buys all rights. Submit seasonal/holiday material 8 months in advance. Submit *only* complete manuscripts. "No queries, please." Photocopied submissions acceptable (if clear). Computer printout submissions acceptable; prefers letter-quality. Reports in 2 months. Sample copy for 6½x9 SAE and 4 first class stamps; writer's guidelines for #10 SASE.

Nonfiction: Historical, interview/profile (biographical), craft ideas, health, nutrition, hygiene, exercise and safety. "We're especially interested in factual features that teach readers about the human body or encourage them to develop better health habits. We are *not* interested in material that is simply rewritten from encyclopedias. We try to present our health material in a way that instructs *and* entertains the reader." Buys 15-20 mss/year. Send complete ms. Length: 500-1,200 words. Pays 8¢/word. Sometimes pays the expenses of writers on assignment.

Photos: State availability of full color or b&w photos. Payment varies. Model releases and identification of subjects required. Buys one-time rights.

Fiction: Adventure, humorous, mainstream and mystery. Stories should appeal to both boys and girls. "We need some stories that incorporate a health theme. However, we don't want stories that preach, preferring instead stories with implied morals. We like a light or humorous approach." Buys 15-20 mss/year. Length: 500-1,500 words. Pays 8¢/word.

Poetry: Pays $10 minimum.

Tips: "Many of our readers have working mothers and/or come from single-parent homes. We need more stories that reflect these changing times while communicating good values."

CHILDREN'S PLAYMATE, 1100 Waterway Blvd., Box 567, Indianapolis IN 46206. (317)636-8881. Editor: Elizabeth Rinck. 75% freelance written. Eager to work with new/unpublished writers. "We are looking for articles, stories, and activities with a health, safety, exercise, or nutritionally oriented theme. Primarily we are concerned with preventative medicine. We try to present our material in a positive—not a negative—light, and we try to incorporate humor and a light approach wherever possible without minimizing the seriousness of what we are saying." For children ages 5-7. Magazine published 8 times/year. Buys all rights. Byline given. Pays on publication. Publishes ms an average of 1 year after acceptance. Submit seasonal material 8 months in advance. Computer printout submissions acceptable; prefers letter-quality. Reports in 2 months. Sometimes may hold mss for up to 1 year, with author's permission. Write for guidelines. "Material will not be returned unless accompanied by a self-addressed envelope and sufficient postage." Sample copy 75¢; free writer's guidelines with SASE.

Nonfiction: Beginning science, 600 words maximum. A feature may be an interesting presentation on animals, people, events, objects or places, especially about good health, exercise, proper nutrition and safety. Include number of words in articles. Buys 30 mss/year. "We do not consider outlines. Reading the whole manuscript is the only way to give fair consideration. The editors cannot criticize, offer suggestions, or review unsolicited material that is not accepted." No queries. Pays about 8¢/word.

Fiction: Short stories for beginning readers, not over 700 words. Seasonal stories with holiday themes. Humorous stories, unusual plots. "We are interested in stories about children in different cultures and stories about lesser-known holidays (not just Christmas, Thanksgiving, Halloween, Hanukkah)." Vocabulary suitable for ages 5-7. Submit complete ms. Pays about 8¢/word. Include number of words in stories.

Fillers: Puzzles, dot-to-dots, color-ins, hidden pictures and mazes. Buys 30 fillers/year. Payment varies.

Tips: Especially interested in stories, poems and articles about special holidays, customs and events.

CLUBHOUSE, Your Story Hour, Box 15, Berrien Springs MI 49103. (616)471-3701. Editor: Elaine Meseraull. 75% freelance written. Works with a small number of new/unpublished writers each year. Magazine published 10 times/year covering many subjects with Christian approach, though not associated with a church. "Stories and features for fun for 9-14 year-olds. Main objective: To provide a psychologically 'up' magazine that lets kids know that they are acceptable, 'neat' people." Circ. 15,000. Pays on acceptance. Publishes ms an average of 1 year after acceptance. Byline given. Buys first serial rights or first North American serial rights, one-time rights, simultaneous rights, and second serial (reprint) rights. Simultaneous queries, and simultaneous, photocopied, and previously published submissions OK. Computer printout submissions acceptable; prefers letter-quality. Reports in 4-5 weeks. Sample copy for 6x9 SAE and 3 first class stamps; writer's guidelines for #10 SASE.

Nonfiction: How-to (crafts), personal experience and recipes (without sugar or artificial flavors and colors). "No stories in which kids start out 'bad' and by peer or adult pressure or circumstances are changed into 'good' people." Send complete ms. Length: 750-800 words ($25); 1,000-1,200 words ($30); feature story, 1,200 words ($35).

Photos: Send photos with ms. Pays on publication according to published size. Buys one-time rights.

Columns/Departments: Body Shop (short stories or "ad" type material that is anti-smoking, drugs and alcohol and pro-good nutrition, etc.); and Jr. Detective (secret codes, word search, deduction problems, hidden pictures, etc.). Buys 20/year. Send complete ms. Length: 400 words maximum for Jr. Detective; 1,000 maximum for Body Shop. Pays $10-30.

Fiction: Adventure, historical, humorous and mainstream. "Stories should depict bravery, kindness, etc., without a preachy attitude." No science fiction, romance, confession or mystery. Cannot use Santa-elves, Halloween or Easter Bunny material. Buys 60 mss/year. Send query or complete ms (prefers ms). Length: 750-800 words ($20); 1,000-1,200 words ($30); lead story ($35).

Poetry: Free verse, light verse and traditional. Buys 8-10/year. Submit maximum 5 poems. Length: 4-24 lines. Pays $5-20.

Fillers: Cartoons. Buys 30/year. Pay $12 maximum.

Tips: "Send all material during March or April. By the middle of June acceptance or rejection notices will be sent. Material chosen will appear the following year. Basically, kids are more and more informed and aware of the world around them. This means that characters in stories for *Clubhouse* should not seem too simple, yet maintain the wonder and joy of youth."

COBBLESTONE: The History Magazine for Young People, Cobblestone Publishing, Inc., 20 Grove St., Peterborough NH 03458. (603)924-7209. Editor-in-Chief: Carolyn P. Yoder. 100% freelance written (approximately 2 issues/year are by assignment only). Prefers to work with published/established writers; works with small number of new/unpublished writers each year. Monthly magazine covering American history for children ages 8-14. "Each issue presents a particular theme, approaching it from different angles, making it exciting as well as informative. Half of all subscriptions are for schools." Circ. 44,000. Pays on publication. Publishes ms an average of 4 months after acceptance. Byline given. Buys all rights; makes work-for-hire assignments. All material must relate to monthly theme. Simultaneous and previously published submissions OK. Computer printout submissions acceptable; prefers letter-quality. Sample copy for 7½x10½ SAE with 5 first class stamps and $3.95; writer's guidelines for SASE.

Nonfiction: Historical/nostalgic, how-to, interview, plays, biography, recipes, activities and personal experience. "Request a copy of the writer's guidelines to find out specific issue themes in upcoming months." No material that editorializes rather than reports. Buys 5-8 mss/issue. Length: 800-1,200 words. Supplemental nonfiction 200-800 words. Query with published clips, outline and bibliography. Pays up to 15¢/word. Rarely pays expenses of writers on assignment.

Fiction: Adventure, historical, humorous and biographical fiction. "Has to be very strong and accurate." Buys 1-2 mss/issue. Length: 800-1,200 words. Request free editorial guidelines that explain upcoming issue themes and give query deadlines. "Message" must be smoothly integrated with the story. Query with written samples. Pays up to 15¢/word.

Poetry: Free verse, light verse and traditional. Submit maximum 2 poems. Length: 5-100 lines. Pays on an individual basis.

Tips: "All material is considered on the basis of merit and appropriateness to theme. Query should state idea for material simply, with rationale for why material is applicable to theme. Request writer's guidelines (includes themes and query deadlines) before submitting a query. Include SASE."

CRICKET, The Magazine for Children, Open Court Publishing Co., 315 5th St., Peru IL 61354. (815)224-6643. Editor: Marianne Carus. Monthly magazine. Circ. 120,000. Pays on publication. Byline given. Buys first North American serial rights. Submit seasonal/holiday material 1 year in advance. Photocopied and previously published submissions OK. Computer printout submissions acceptable; prefers letter-quality. Reports in 2 months. Sample copy $2; writer's guidelines for SASE.

Nonfiction: Historical/nostalgic, lively science, personal experience and travel. Send complete ms. Length: 200-1,200 words. Pays $50-300.

Fiction: Adventure, ethnic, fantasy, historical, humorous, mystery, novel excerpts, science fiction, suspense and western. No didactic, sex, religious, or horror stories. Buys 24-36 mss/year. Send complete ms. Length: 200-1,500 words. Pays $50-375.

Poetry: Buys 8-10 poems/year. Length: 50 lines maximum. Pays $3/line on publication.

CRUSADER MAGAZINE, Box 7259, Grand Rapids MI 49510. Editor: G. Richard Broene. 40% freelance written. Works with a small number of new/unpublished writers each year. Magazine published 7 times/year. "*Crusader Magazine* shows boys (9-14) how God is at work in their lives and in the world around them." Circ. 12,000. Buys 20-25 mss/year. Pays on acceptance. Byline given. Publishes ms an average of 8 months after acceptance. Rights purchased vary with author and material; buys first serial rights, one-time rights, second serial (reprint) rights, and simultaneous rights. Submit seasonal material (Christmas, Easter) at least 5 months in advance. Photocopied and simultaneous submissions OK. Computer printout submissions acceptable; prefers letter-quality. Reports in 1 month. Free sample copy and writer's guidelines for 9x12 SAE and 3 first class stamps.

Nonfiction: Articles about young boys' interests: sports, outdoor activities, bike riding, science, crafts, etc., and problems. Emphasis is on a Christian multi-racial perspective, but no simplistic moralisms. Informational, how-to, personal experience, interview, profile, inspirational and humor. Submit complete ms. Length: 500-1,500 words. Pays 2-5¢/word.

Photos: Pays $4-25 for b&w photos purchased with mss.

Fiction: "Considerable fiction is used. Fast-moving stories that appeal to a boy's sense of adventure or sense of humor are welcome. Avoid preachiness. Avoid simplistic answers to complicated problems. Avoid long dialogue and little action." Length: 900-1,500 words. Pays 2¢/word minimum.

Fillers: Uses short humor and any type of puzzles as fillers.

CURRENT HEALTH 1, The Beginning Guide to Health Education, General Learning Corporation, 60 Revere Dr., Northbrook IL 60062-1563. (312)564-4070. Executive Editor: Laura Ruekberg. Associate Editor: Michelle Heiss. 95% freelance written. An educational health periodical. Published monthly 9 times per year. September-May. "Our audience is fourth through seventh grade health education students. Articles should be written at a fifth grade reading level. As a curriculum supplementary publication, info should be accurate, timely, accessible and highly readable." Circ. 100,000. Pays on publication. Publishes ms an average of 9 months after acceptance. Offers 50% kill fee. Buys all rights.

Nonfiction: General interest, interview/profile, new product, and educational. Buys 100 mss/year. "We accept no queries or unsolicited mss. *Articles are on assignment only.* Send introductory letter, resume and clips." Length: 800-2,000 words. Pays $100-700 for assigned articles. Sometimes pays expenses of writers on assignment.

Tips: "We are looking for good writers with an education and health background preferably, who can write for the age group in a firm accessible and medically/scientifically accurate way. Ideally, the writer should be an expert in the area in which he or she is writing. Topics open to freelancers are disease, drugs, fitness and exercise, psychology, safety, nutrition and personal health. We are in need of drug writers in particular."

DISCOVERIES, 6401 The Paseo, Kansas City MO 64131. Editor: Middler Editor. 75% freelance written. For boys and girls ages 9-12 in the Church of the Nazarene. Weekly. Publishes ms an average of 1 year after acceptance. Buys first serial rights and second (reprint) rights. "We process only letter-quality manuscripts; word processing with letter-quality printers acceptable. Minimal comments on pre-printed form are made on rejected material." Reports in 1 month. Guidelines for #10 SAE with 1 first class stamp.

Fiction: Stories with Christian emphasis on high ideals, wholesome social relationships and activities, right choices, Sabbath observance, church loyalty, and missions. Informal style. Submit complete ms. Length: 500-700 words. Pays 3½¢/word for first serial rights and 2¢/word for second (reprint) rights.

Photos: Color photos only.

Tips: "The freelancer needs an understanding of the doctrine of the Church of the Nazarene and the Sunday school material for third to sixth graders."

THE DOLPHIN LOG, The Cousteau Society, 8440 Santa Monica Blvd., Los Angeles CA 90069. (213)656-4422. Editor: Pamela Stacey. 60% freelance written. Prefers to work with published/established writers; works with a small number of new/unpublished writers each year. Bimonthly magazine covering marine biology, ecology, environment, natural history, and water-related stories. "The *Dolphin Log* is an educational publication for children ages 7-15 offered by The Cousteau Society. Subject matter encompasses all areas of science, history and the arts which can be related to our global water system. The philosophy of the magazine is to delight, instruct and instill an environmental ethic and understanding of the interconnectedness of living organisms, including people." Circ. 70,000. Pays on publication. Publishes ms an average of 1 year after acceptance. Byline given. "We do not make assignments and therefore have no kill fee." Buys one-time and translation rights. Submit seasonal/holiday material 4 months in advance. "Encourages disk submissions which are IBM-PC campatible (ASC II character file)." Computer printout submissions acceptable; prefers letter-quality. Reports in 2 months. Sample copy for $2 with 9x12 SAE and 3 first class stamps; writer's guidelines for SASE.

Nonfiction: General interest (per guidelines); how-to (water-related crafts or science); personal experience (ocean related); and photo feature (marine subject). "Of special interest are articles on specific marine creatures, and games involving an ocean/water-related theme which develop math, reading and comprehension skills. Humorous articles and short jokes based on scientific fact are also welcome. Experiments that can be conducted at home and demonstrate a phenomenon or principle of science are wanted as are clever crafts or art projects which also can be tied to an ocean theme. Try to incorporate such activities into any articles submitted." No fiction or "talking" animals. Buys 8-12 mss/year. Query or send complete ms. Length: 500-1,000 words. Pays $50-150.

Photos: Send photos with query or ms (duplicates only). Prefers underwater animals, water photos with children, photos that explain text. Pays $25-100/photo. Identification of subjects required. Buys one-time and translation rights.

Columns/Departments: Discovery (science experiments or crafts a young person can easily do at home), 50-500 words; Creature Feature (lively article on one specific marine animal) 500-700 words. Buys 1 mss/year. Send complete ms. Pays $25-150.

Poetry: No "talking" animals. Buys 1-2 poems/year. Pays $10-100.

Tips: "Find a lively way to relate scientific facts to children without anthropomorphizing. We need to know material is accurate and current. Articles should feature an interesting marine creature and yet contain factual material that's fun to read. We will be increasingly interested in material which draws information from current scientific research."

THE ELECTRIC COMPANY MAGAZINE, Children's Television Workshop, 1 Lincoln Plaza, New York NY 10023. (212)595-3456. Editor: Maureen Hunter-Bone. Associate Editor: Christina Meyer. 10% freelance written. Works with small number of new/unpublished writers each year. Magazine published 10 times/year. "We are a humor/reading/activity magazine for children 6-10 years old." Circ. 250,000. Pays on acceptance. Publishes ms an average of 8 months after acceptance. Byline given. Offers 50% kill fee. Buys all rights. Submit seasonal/holiday material at least 6 months in advance. Simultaneous and photocopied submissions OK. Computer printout submissions acceptable. Reports in 2 weeks. Sample copy for 9x12 SAE with 6 first class stamps.

Nonfiction: General interest, humor and photo feature. Buys 5-6 mss/year. Query with or without published clips, or send complete ms. Length: 500 words maximum. Pays $50-200.

Photos: State availability of photos with submission. Reviews transparencies. Offers $75 maximum/photo. Model releases and identification of subjects required.

Fiction: Adventure, fantasy, historical, humorous, mystery and western. "No stories with heavy moral messages; or those about child abuse, saying 'no,' divorce, single parent households, handicapped children, etc." Buys 3 mss/year. Query or send complete ms. Length: 750-1,000 words. Pays $200 maximum.

Tips: "With September 1988 issue, name changed to *Kid City*. No stories about doggies, bunnies or kitties. No stories with heavy moral message. We're looking for more interesting items about *real* kids who have done something newsworthy or exceptional."

FACES: The Magazine about People, Cobblestone Publishing, Inc., 20 Grove St., Peterborough NH 03458. (603)924-7209. Editor: Carolyn P. Yoder. 95% freelance written. Prefers to work with published/established writers. A magazine published 10 times/year covering world cultures for 8 to 14-year-olds. Articles must relate to the issue's theme. Circ. approximately 13,500. Pays on publication. Byline given. Buys all rights. Simultaneous and photocopied submissions OK. Previously published submissions rarely accepted. Computer printout submissions acceptable; prefers letter-quality. Sample copy 7½x10½ SAE with 5 first class stamps and $3.50; writer's guidelines for SASE.

Nonfiction: Book excerpts, essays, expose, general interest, historical/nostalgic, how-to (activities), recipes, humor, interview/profile, personal experience, photo feature, technical and travel. Articles must relate to the theme. No religious, pornographic, biased or sophisticated submissions. Buys approximately 50 mss/year. Query with published clips. Length: 250-1,000 words. Pays up to 15¢/word. Rarely pays expenses of writers on assignment.

Photos: State availability of photos with submission. Reviews contact sheets and 8x10 prints. Offers $5-10/photo. Buys one-time and all rights.

Fiction: All fiction must be theme-related. Buys 10 mss/year. Query with published clips. Length: 500-1,000 words. Pays 10-15¢/word.

Poetry: Light verse and traditional. No religious or pornographic poetry or poetry not related to the theme. Submit maximum 1 poem. Pays on individual basis.

Tips: "Writers must have an appreciation and understanding of people. All manuscripts for *Faces* are reviewed by the American Museum of Natural History. Writers must not condescend to our readers."

THE FRIEND, 50 East North Temple, Salt Lake City UT 84150. Managing Editor: Vivian Paulsen. 60% freelance written. Eager to work with new/unpublished writers as well as established writers. Appeals to children ages 3-11. Monthly publication of The Church of Jesus Christ of Latter-Day Saints. Circ. 205,000. Pays on acceptance. Buys all rights. Submit seasonal material 8 months in advance. Computer printout submissions acceptable. Publishes ms an average of 1 year after acceptance. Sample copy and writer's guidelines for 8½x11 with SAE with 4 first class stamps.

Nonfiction: Subjects of current interest, science, nature, pets, sports, foreign countries, and things to make and do. Special issues for Christmas and Easter. "Submit only complete ms—no queries, please." Length: 1,000 words maximum. Pays 8¢/word minimum.

Fiction: Seasonal and holiday stories and stories about other countries and their children. Wholesome and optimistic; high motive, plot, and action. Character-building stories preferred. Length: 1,200 words maximum. Stories for younger children should not exceed 250 words. Pays 8¢/word minimum.

Poetry: Serious, humorous and holiday. Any form with child appeal. Pays $15.

Tips: "Do you remember how it feels to be a child? Can you write stories that appeal to children ages 3-11 in today's world? We're interested in stories with an international flavor and those that focus on present-day problems. Send material of high literary quality slanted to our editorial requirements. Let the child solve the problem—not some helpful, all-wise adult. No overt moralizing. Nonfiction should be creatively presented—not an array of facts strung together. Beware of being cutesy."

HIGH ADVENTURE, Assemblies of God, 1445 Boonville, Springfield MO 65802. (417)862-2781, ext. 1497. Editor: Johnnie Barnes. Eager to work with new/unpublished writers. Quarterly magazine "designed to provide boys with worthwhile, enjoyable, leisure reading; to challenge them in narrative form to higher ideals and greater spiritual dedication; and to perpetuate the spirit of the Royal Rangers program through stories, ideas, and illustrations." Circ. 78,000. Pays on acceptance. Byline given. Buys one-time rights. Submit seasonal/holiday material 6-9 months in advance. Simultaneous queries, and simultaneous, photocopied, and previously published submissions OK. Computer printout submission OK; prefers letter-quality. Reports in 1 month. Sample copy for 9x12 SAE with 3 first class stamps; free writer's guidelines.

Nonfiction: Historical/nostalgic, how-to, humor and inspirational. Buys 25-50 mss/year. Query or send complete ms. Length: 1,200 words. Pays 2¢/word.

Photos: Reviews b&w negatives, transparencies and prints. Identification of subjects required. Buys one-time rights.

Fiction: Adventure, historical, humorous, religious and western. Buys 25-50 mss/year. Query or send complete ms. Length: 1,200 words maximum. Pays 2¢/word.

Fillers: Jokes, gags and short humor. Pays $2 for jokes; others vary.

HIGHLIGHTS FOR CHILDREN, 803 Church St., Honesdale PA 18431. Editor: Kent L. Brown Jr. 80% freelance written. Magazine published 11 times/year for children ages 2-12. Circ. 2,300,000. Pays on acceptance. Buys all rights. Computer printout submissions acceptable; prefers letter-quality. Reports in about 2 months. Sample copy $2.25; writer's guidelines for #10 SASE.

Nonfiction: "We prefer factual features, including history and natural, technical and social science, written by persons with rich background and mastery in their respective fields. Contributions always welcomed from new writers, especially engineers, scientists, historians, teachers, etc., who can make useful, interesting and authentic facts accessible to children. Also writers who have lived abroad and can interpret the ways of life, especially of children, in other countries. Sports material, biographies and general articles of interest to children. Direct, original approach, simple style, interesting content, without word embellishment; not rewritten from encyclopedias. State background and qualifications for writing factual articles submitted. Include references or sources of information." Length: 900 words maximum. Pays $75 minimum. Also buys original party plans for children ages 7-12, clearly described in 300-800 words, including drawings or sample of items to be illustrated. Also, novel but tested ideas in crafts, with clear directions and made-up models. Projects must require only free or inexpensive, easy-to-obtain materials. Especially desirable if easy enough for early primary grades. Also, fingerplays with lots of action, easy for very young children to grasp and parents to dramatize. Avoid wordiness. Pays minimum $50 for party plans; $15 for crafts ideas; $25 for fingerplays.

Fiction: Unusual, meaningful stories appealing to both girls and boys, ages 2-12. Vivid, full of action. "Engaging plot, strong characterization, lively language." Prefers stories in which a child protagonist solves a dilemma through his or her own resources. Seeks stories that the child ages 8-12 will eagerly read, and the child ages 2-7 will begin to read and/or will like to hear when read aloud (600 words maximum). "We publish stories in the suspense/adventure/mystery, fantasy and humor category, all requiring interesting plot and a number of illustration possiblities. Also need rebuses (picture stories 150 words or under), stories with urban settings, stories for beginning readers (500 words), humorous and horse stories. We also would like to see more material of 1-page length (300-500 words), both fiction and factual. We need creative-thinking puzzles that can be illustrated, optical illusions, brain teasers, games of physical agility, and other 'fun' activities. War, crime and violence are taboo. Some folk-tale retelling stories published." Length: 400-900 words. Pays $65 minimum.

Tips: "We are pleased that many authors of children's literature report that their first published work was in the pages of *Highlights*. It is not our policy to consider fiction on the strength of the reputation of the author. We judge each submission on its own merits. With factual material, however, we do prefer either authorities in their field or people with first-hand experience. In this manner we can avoid the encyclopedic article that merely restates information readily available elsewhere. We don't make assignments. Query with simple letter to establish whether the nonfiction *subject* is likely to be of interest. A beginning writer should first become familiar with the type of material which *Highlights* publishes. Include special qualifications, if any, of author. Write for the child, not the editor."

HUMPTY DUMPTY'S MAGAZINE, Children's Health Publications, 1100 Waterway Blvd., Box 567, Indianapolis IN 46206. Editor: Christine French Clark. 90% freelance written. "We try not to be overly influenced by an author's credits, preferring instead to judge each submission on its own merit." Magazine published 8 times/year stressing health, nutrition, hygiene, exercise and safety for children ages 4-6. Combined issues: February/March, April/May, June/July, and August/September. Pays on publication. Publishes ms at least 8 months after acceptance. Buys all rights. Submit seasonal material 8 months in advance. Computer printout submissions OK; prefers letter-quality. Reports in 10 weeks. Sample copy 75¢; writer's guidelines for SASE.

Nonfiction: "We are open to nonfiction on almost any age-appropriate subject, but we especially need material with a health theme—nutrition, safety, exercise, hygiene. We're looking for articles that encourage readers to develop better health habits without preaching. Very simple factual articles that creatively teach readers about their bodies. We use simple crafts, some with holiday themes. We also use several puzzles and activities in each issue—dot-to-dot, hidden pictures, *simple* crosswords, and easy-to-play 'board' games. Keep in mind that most our readers are just *beginning* to learn to read and write, so word puzzles must be very basic." Submit complete ms. "Include number of words in manuscript and Social Security number." Length: 600 words maximum. Pays 8¢/word.

Fiction: "We use some stories in rhyme and a few easy-to-read stories for the beginning reader. All stories should work well as read alouds. Currently we need seasonal stories with holiday themes. We use contemporary stories and fantasy, some employing a health theme. We try to present our health material in a positive light, incorporating humor and a light approach wherever possible. Avoid sexual stereotyping. Characters in contemporary stories should be realistic and up-to-date. Remember, many of our readers have working mothers and/or come from single-parent homes. We need more stories that reflect these changing times but at the same time communicate good, wholesome values." Submit complete ms. "Include number of words in manuscript and Social Security number." Length: 600 words maximum. Pays 8¢/word.

Poetry: Short, simple poems. Pays $7 minimum.

Tips: "Writing for *Humpty Dumpty* is similar to writing picture book manuscripts. There must be a great economy of words. We strive for 50% art per page (in stories and articles), so space for text is limited. Because the illustrations are so important, stories should lend themselves well to visual imagery."

JACK AND JILL, 1100 Waterway Blvd., Box 567, Indianapolis IN 46206. (317)636-8881. Editor: Steve Charles. 85% freelance written. Magazine published 8 times/year for children ages 6-8. Pays on publication. Publishes ms an average of 8 months after acceptance. Buys all rights. Byline given. Submit seasonal material 8 months in advance. Computer printout submissions acceptable. Reports in 10 weeks. May hold material seriously being considered for up to 1 year. "Material will not be returned unless accompanied by self-addressed envelope with sufficient postage." Sample copy 75¢; writer's guidelines for SASE.

Nonfiction: "Because we want to encourage youngsters to read for pleasure and for information, we are interested in material that will challenge a young child's intelligence *and* be enjoyable reading. Our emphasis is on good health, and we are in particular need of articles, stories, and activities with health, safety, exercise and nutrition themes. We are looking for well-written articles that take unusual approaches to teaching better health habits and scientific facts about how the body works. We try to present our health material in a positive light—incorporating humor and a light approach wherever possible without minimizing the seriousness of what we are saying." Straight factual articles are OK if they are short and interestingly written. "We would rather see, however, more creative alternatives to the straight factual article. For instance, we'd be interested in seeing a health message or facts presented in articles featuring positive role models for readers. Many of the personalities children admire—athletes, musicians, and film or TV stars—are fitness or nutrition buffs. Many have kicked drugs, alcohol or smoking habits and are outspoken about the dangers of these vices. Color slides, transparencies, or black and white photos accompanying this type of article would greatly enhance salability." Buys 25-30 nonfiction mss/year. Length: 500-1,200 words. Pays approximately 8¢ a word.

Photos: When appropriate, photos should accompany ms. Reviews sharp, contrasting b&w glossy prints. Sometimes uses color slides, transparencies, or good color prints. Pays $10 for b&w, $20 for color, $50 for cover. Buys one-time rights.

Fiction: May include, but is not limited to, realistic stories, fantasy adventure—set in past, present or future. All stories need a well-developed plot, action and incident. Humor is highly desirable. "Currently we need stories with holiday themes. Stories that deal with a health theme need not have health as the primary subject. We would like to see more biographical fiction." Length: 500-1,500 words, short stories; 1,500 words/installment, serials of two parts. Pays approximately 6¢ a word. Buys 20-25 mss/year.

Fillers: Puzzles (including various kinds of word and crossword puzzles), poems, games, science projects, and creative craft projects. Instructions for activities should be clearly and simply written and accompanied by models or diagram sketches. "We also have a need for recipes. Ingredients should be healthful; avoid sugar, salt, chocolate, red meat, and fats as much as possible. In all material, avoid references to eating sugary foods, such as candy, cakes, cookies and soft drinks."

Tips: "We are constantly looking for new writers who can tell good stories with interesting slants—stories that are not full of out-dated and time-worn expressions. Our best authors are writers who know what today's children are like. Keep in mind that our readers are becoming 'computer literate', living in an age of rapidly developing technology. They are exploring career possibilities that may be new and unfamiliar to our generation. They are faced with tough decisions about drug and alcohol use. Many of them are latch-key children because both parents work or they come from single-parent homes. We need more stories and articles that reflect these changing times but that also communicate good, wholesome values. Obtain *current* issues of the magazines and *study* them to determine our present needs and editorial style."

‡JUNIOR SCHOLASTIC, Scholastic Inc.. 730 Broadway, New York NY 10003. (212)505-3071. Editor: Lee Baier. 25% freelance written. Educational classroom magazine published 18 issues during school year on social studies for grades 6-8. "We strive to present all sides of important issues, written so as to appeal to young people ages 11-14." Circ. 700,000. Pays on acceptance. Byline given. Buys first rights. Submit seasonal/holiday material 2 months in advance. Simultaneous and photocopied submissions OK. Computer printout submissions OK; prefers letter-quality. Reports in 6 weeks on queries. Sample copy $1.75 with 9x12 SAE. Free writer's guidelines.

Nonfiction: General interest, interview/profile, personal experience, photo feature and geography adventure. "We mainly buy: 1) Articles about foreign countries based on interviews with young people ages 11-14 and 2) articles about young people in the U.S. who have done newsworthy and inspiring things." Buys 25 mss/year. Query. Length: 500-1,000 words. Pays $175-300 for assigned articles. Sometimes pays the expenses of writers on assignment. Send photos with submission. Reviews contact sheets and transparencies (35mm). Offers $75-125 per photo. Model releases. Buys one-time rights.

Columns/Departments: Health self-improvement (slanted toward teens 11-14), 500 words. Pays $150-175.

Tips: "Keep writing simple, easy to understand, filled with quotes and anecdotes. Articles should convey important information about the subject in a lively, interesting manner. Bring young people ages 11-14 into the story—lead with them if at all possible. We are mainly looking for articles about foreign countries, using interviews with people from that country—especially young people 11-14—to illustrate the current situation in that country, problems that country is facing, and what it is like to live there. Also interested in stories about outstanding young people in the U.S. Need color transparencies to accompany all such stories."

JUNIOR TRAILS, Gospel Publishing House, 1445 Boonville Ave., Springfield MO 65802. (417)862-2781. Editor: Cathy Ketcher. 100% freelance written. Eager to work with new/unpublished writers. Weekly tabloid covering religious fiction; and biographical, historical, and scientific articles with a spiritual emphasis for boys and girls ages 10-11. Circ. 75,000. Pays on acceptance. Publishes ms an average of 9-12 months after acceptance. Byline given. Not copyrighted. Buys simultaneous rights, first rights, or second (reprint) rights to material originally published elsewhere. Submit seasonal/holiday material 1 year in advance. List Social Security number and number of words in ms. Simultaneous and previously published submissions OK. Computer printout submissions acceptable; prefers letter-quality. Reports in 6 weeks on queries; 2 months on mss. Sample copy and writer's guidelines for 9x12 SAE and 2 first class stamps.

Nonfiction: Biographical, historical and scientific (with spiritual lesson or emphasis). "Junior-age children need to be alerted to the dangers of drugs, alcohol, smoking, etc. They need positive guidelines and believable examples relating to living a Christian life in an ever-changing world." Buys 20-30 mss/year. Send complete ms. Length: 500-1,000 words. Pays 2-3¢/word.

Fiction: Adventure (with spiritual lesson or application); and religious. "We're looking for fiction that presents believable characters working out their problems according to Biblical principles. No fictionalized accounts of Bible stories or events." Buys 60-80 mss/year. Send complete ms. Length: 1,000-1,800 words. Pays 2-3¢/word.

Poetry: Free verse and light verse. Buys 6-8 mss/year. Pays 20¢/line.

Fillers: Anecdotes (with spiritual emphasis). Buys 15-20/year. Length: 200 words maximum. Pays 2-3¢/word.

Tips: "We like to receive stories showing contemporary children positively facing today's world. These stories show children who are aware of their world and who find a moral solution to their problems through the guidance of God's Word. They are not 'super children' in themselves. They are average children learning how to face life through God's help. We tend to get settings in stories that are out of step with today's society. We will tend to turn more and more to purely contemporary settings unless we are using a historical or biographical story. We will have the setting, characters and plot agree with each other in order to make it more believable to our audience."

NATIONAL GEOGRAPHIC WORLD, National Geographic Society, 17th & M Sts. NW, Washington DC 20036. (202)857-7000. Editor: Pat Robbins. Associate Editor: Margaret McKelway. 80% freelance written. Monthly magazine of factual stories of interest to children ages 8-13 years. "*World* is a strongly visual magazine; all stories must have a visual story line; no unillustrated stories are used." Circ. 1.2 million. Pays on publication. No byline given. Offers variable kill fee. Buys all rights. Submit seasonal/holiday material 1 year in advance. Free sample copy.

Nonfiction: Subject matter is factual. Subjects include animals, conservation, science and technology, geography, history, sports, outdoor adventure and children's activities. No fiction, poetry, book reviews, TV or current events. Humor, shorts, and game ideas are welcome. Query first. Inquire in writing to Pat Robbins regarding freelance assignments. Include resume and published work. "Writing is always done after pictures are in hand. Freelance assignments are made on a contract basis."

Photos: "Freelance photography is handled in a variety of ways. Photo story submissions are reviewed by the illustrations editor. Photographers who want assignments should send a query letter first. Include a brief description of the proposed story and list the picture possibilities. If the magazine is interested, the illustrations editor will review the photographer's portfolio."

Tips: "We're are strongly interested in geography submissions."

NOAH'S ARK, A Newspaper for Jewish Children, 7726 Portal, Houston TX 77071. (713)771-7143. Editors: Debbie Israel Dubin and Linda Freedman Block. A monthly tabloid that "captures readers' interest and reinforces learning about Jewish history, holidays, laws and culture through articles, stories, recipes, games, crafts, projects, Hebrew column and more." For Jewish children, ages 6-12. Circ. 450,000. Pays on acceptance. Byline given. Buys first North American serial rights. Submit seasonal/holiday material 4 months in advance. Simultaneous and photocopied submissions OK. Computer printout submissions OK; prefers letter-quality. Reports in 6 weeks on queries; 2 months on mss. Sample copy and writer's guidelines for #10 SASE.

Nonfiction: Historical/nostalgic, craft projects, recipes, humor, interview/profile. Send complete ms. Length: 350 words maximum. Pays usually 5¢/word.

Photos: State availability of photos with submission or send photos with submission. Offers no additional payment for photos accepted with ms. Identification of subjects required. Buys one-time rights.

Fiction: All must be of Jewish interest: Historical, humorous, religious (Jewish), slice-of-life vignettes. Any and all suitable for Jewish children. Buys 2-3 mss/year. Send complete ms. Length: 600 words maximum. Pays 5¢/word.

Poetry: Light verse and traditional. Buys 1 poem/year. Submit maximum 1 poem. Payment varies.

Fillers: All must be of Jewish interest: Anecdotes, facts, gags, short humor and games. Buys 3-5/year. Payment varies.

Tips: "We're just looking for high quality material suitable for entertainment as well as supplemental religious school use." Encourages freelancers to take an "unusual approach to writing about holidays. All submissions must have Jewish content and positive Jewish values. Content should not be exclusively for an American audience."

ODYSSEY, Kalmbach Publishing Co., 1027 N. 7th St., Milwaukee WI 53233. (414)272-2060. Editor: Nancy Mack. 50% freelance written. Works with a small number of new/unpublished writers each year. Monthly magazine emphasizing astronomy and outer space for children ages 8-12. Circ. 100,000. Pays on publication. Publishes ms an average of 8 months after acceptance. Buys first serial or one-time rights. Submit seasonal/holiday material 4 months in advance. Photocopied and previously published submissions OK. Computer printout submissions acceptable; prefers letter-quality. Reports in 8 weeks. "Material with little news connection may be held up to one year." Sample copy and writer's guidelines for 8½x12½ SAE and 5 first class stamps.

Nonfiction: General interest (astronomy, outer space, spacecraft, planets, stars, etc.); how-to (astronomy projects, experiments, etc.); and photo feature (spacecraft, planets, stars, etc.). "We like short, off-beat articles with some astronomy or space-science tie-in. A recent example: an article about a baseball game that ended with the explosion of a meteorite over the field. Study the styles of the monthly columnists. No general overview articles; for example, a general article on the Space Shuttle, or a general article on stars. We do not want science fiction articles." Buys 12 mss/year. Query with published clips. Length: 750-2,000 words. Pays $100-350 depending on length and type of article. Sometimes pays expenses of writers on assignment.

Photos: State availability of photos. Buys one-time rights. Captions preferred; model releases required. Payment depends upon size and placement.

Tips: "Since I am overstocked and have a stable of regular writers, a query is very important. I often get several manuscripts on the same subject and must reject them. Write a very specific proposal and indicate why it will interest kids. If the subject is very technical, indicate your qualifications to write about it. I will be buying short articles almost exclusively in 1989 because most major features are being handled by staff or contributing editors. Frequent mistakes writers make are trying to fudge on material they don't understand, using outdated references, and telling me their articles are assignments for the Institute of Children's Literature."

ON THE LINE, Mennonite Publishing House, 616 Walnut Ave., Scottdale PA 15683-1999. (412)887-8500. Editor: Virginia A. Hostetler. 100% freelance written. Works with a small number of new/unpublished writers each year. Weekly magazine for children ages 10-14. Circ. 10,000. Pays on acceptance. Publishes ms an average of 1 year after acceptance. Byline given. Buys one-time rights. Submit seasonal/holiday material 6 months in advance. Simultaneous, photocopied and previously published submissions OK. Computer printout submissions acceptable; prefers letter-quality. Reports in 1 month. Sample copy for 8½x11 SAE and 2 first class stamps.

Nonfiction: How-to (things to make with easy-to-get materials); and informational (500-word articles on wonders of nature, people who have made outstanding contributions). Buys 95 unsolicited mss/year. Send complete ms. Length: 500-1,200 words. Pays $10-24.

Photos: Photos purchased with or without ms. Pays $10-25 for 8x10 b&w photos. Total purchase price for ms includes payment for photos.

Columns/Departments: Fiction, adventure, humorous and religious. Buys 52 mss/year. Send complete ms. Length: 800-1,200 words. Pays $15-30.

Poetry: Light verse and religious. Length: 3-12 lines. Pays $5-15.

Tips: "Study the publication first. We need short well-written how-to and craft articles. Don't send query; we prefer to see the complete manuscript."

OWL MAGAZINE, The Discovery Magazine for Children, The Young Naturalist Foundation, 56 The Esplanade, Suite 306, Toronto, Ontario M5E 1A7 Canada. (416)868-6001. Editor: Sylvia Funston. 25% freelance written. Works with small number of new/unpublished writers each year. Magazine published 10 times/year (no July or August issues) covering science and nature. Aims to interest children in their environment through accurate, factual information about the world around them presented in an easy, lively style. Circ. 150,000. Pays on publication. Publishes ms an average of 3 months after acceptance. Byline given. Buys all rights; makes work-for-hire assignments. Submit seasonal/holiday material 1 year in advance. Computer printout submissions acceptable; no dot-matrix. Reports in 10 weeks. Sample copy $1.95; free writer's guidelines. Send SAE (large envelope if requesting sample copy) and a money order for $1 to cover postage (no stamps please).

Nonfiction: How-to (activities, crafts); personal experience (real life children in real situations); photo feature (natural science, international wildlife, and outdoor features); and science and environmental features. No folk tales, problem stories with drugs, sex or moralistic views, fantasy or talking animal stories. "We accept short, well-written articles about up-to-the-minute science discoveries or developments for our Hoot Club News section." Query with clips of published work.

Photos: State availability of photos. Reviews 35mm transparencies. Identification of subjects required.

Tips: "Write for editorial guidelines first. Review back issues of the magazine for content and style. Know your topic and approach it from an unusual perspective. Our magazine never talks down to children."

POCKETS, The Upper Room, 1908 Grand Ave., Box 189, Nashville TN 37202. (615)340-3300. Editor: Willie S. Teague. 40% freelance written. Eager to work with new/unpublished writers. A monthly themed magazine (except combined January and February issues) covering children's and families spiritual formation. "We are a Christian, non-denominational publication for children 6 to 12 years of age." Circ. 70,000. Pays on acceptance. Byline given. Offers 4¢/word kill fee. Buys first North American serial rights. Submit seasonal/holiday material 1 year in advance. Photocopied and previously published submissions OK. Computer printout submissons acceptable; prefers letter-quality. Reports in 10 weeks on manuscripts. Sample copy for 5x7 SAE with 4 first class stamps; writer's guidelines and themes for #10 SASE.

Nonfiction: Shirley Paris, articles editor. Interview/profile, religious (retold scripture stories); and personal experience. List of themes for special issues available with SASE. No violence or romance. Buys 3 mss/year. Send complete ms. Length: 600-1,500 words. Pays 7¢-10¢/word.

Photos: Send photos with submission. Reviews contact sheets, transparencies and prints. Offers $25-50/photo. Buys one-time rights.

Columns Departments: Refrigerator Door (poetry and prayer related to themes), 25 lines; Pocketsful of Love (family communications activities), and Loaves and Fishes (simplified lifestyle and nutrition) both 300 words. Buys 20 mss/year. Send complete ms. Pays 7¢-10¢/word; recipes $25.

Fiction: Adventure; ethnic; and slice-of-life. "Stories should reflect the child's everyday experiences through a Christian approach. This is often more acceptable when stories are not preachy or overtly Christian." Buys 15 mss/year. Send complete ms. Length: 750-1,600 words. Pays 7-10¢/word.

Poetry: Buys 3 poems/year. Length: 4-25 lines. Pays $25-50.

Tips: "Theme stories, role models and retold scripture stories are most open to freelancers. Poetry is also open, but we rarely receive an acceptable poem. It's very helpful if writers send for our themes. These are *not* the same as writer's guidelines."

R-A-D-A-R, 8121 Hamilton Ave., Cincinnati OH 45231. (513)931-4050. Editor: Margaret Williams. 75% freelance written. Prefers to work with published/established writers; works with a small number of new/unpublished writers each year. Weekly for children in grades 3-6 in Christian Sunday schools. Rights purchased vary with author and material; prefers buying first serial rights, but will buy second (reprint) rights. Occasionally overstocked. Pays on acceptance. Publishes ms an average of 1 year after acceptance. Submit seasonal material 1 year in advance. Computer printout submissions acceptable; prefers letter-quality. Reports in 1-2 months. Free sample copy; writer's guidelines for #10 SASE.

Nonfiction: Articles on hobbies and handicrafts, nature, famous people, seasonal subjects, etc., written from a Christian viewpoint. No articles about historical figures with an absence of religious implication. Length: 500-1,000 words. Pays 3¢/word maximum.

Fiction: Short stories of heroism, adventure, travel, mystery, animals and biography. True or possible plots stressing clean, wholesome, Christian character-building ideas, but not preachy. Make prayer, church attendance and Christian living a natural part of the story. "We correlate our fiction and other features with a definite Bible lesson. Writers who want to meet our needs should send for a theme list." No talking animal stories, science fiction, Halloween stories or first-person stories from an adult's viewpoint. Length: up to 1,000 words. Pays 3¢/word maximum.

RANGER RICK, National Wildlife Federation, 1412 16th St. NW, Washington DC 20036. (703)790-4274. Editor: Gerald Bishop. 50% freelance written. Works with a small number new/unpublished writers each year. Monthly magazine for children from ages 6-12, with the greatest concentration in the 7-10 age bracket. Buys all world rights unless other arrangements made. Byline given "but occasionally, for very brief pieces, we will identify author by name at the end. Contributions to regular columns usually are not bylined." Pays on acceptance. Publishes ms an average of 18 months after acceptance. Computer printout submissions acceptable. Reports in 3 weeks. "Anything written with a specific month in mind should be in our hands at least 10 months before that issue date." Writer's guidelines for #10 SAE with 1 first class stamp.

Nonfiction: "Articles may be written on anything related to nature, conservation, the outdoors, environmental problems or natural science." Buys 20-25 unsolicited mss/year. Query. Pays from $50-550, depending on length, quality and content (maximum length, 900 words).

Fiction: "Same categories as nonfiction plus fantasy and science fiction. The attributing of human qualities to animals is limited to our regular feature, 'The Adventures of Ranger Rick,' so please do not humanize wildlife. The publisher, The National Wildlife Federation, discourages keeping wildlife as pets."

Photos: "Photographs, when used, are paid for separately. It is not necessary that illustrations accompany material."

Tips: "Include in query details of what manuscript will cover; sample lead; evidence that you can write playfully and with great enthusiasm, conviction and excitement (formal, serious, dull queries indicate otherwise). Think of an exciting subject we haven't done recently, sell it effectively with query, and produce a manuscript of highest quality. Read past issues to learn successful styles and unique approaches to subjects. If your submission is commonplace, we won't want it."

‡SHOFAR Magazine, Senior Publications Ltd. 43 Northcote Dr., Melville NY 11747. (516)643-4598. Editor: Alan A. Kay. 80-90% freelance written. A monthly children's magazine on Jewish subjects. Circ. 10,000. Pays on publication. Byline given. Buys one-time rights. Submit seasonal/holiday material 6 months in advance. Simultaneous, photocopied and previously published submissions OK. Computer printout submissions OK; prefers letter-quality. Sample copy and writer's guidelines for 9x12 SAE and 4 first class stamps.

Nonfiction: Dr. Gerald H. Grayson, publisher. Historical/nostalgic, humor, inspirational, interview/profile, personal experience, photo feature, religious and travel. Buys 50 mss/year. Send complete ms. Length: 750-

1,000 words. Pays 7¢-10¢/word. Sometimes pays the expenses of writers on assignment.

Photos: State availability of photos with submission or send photos with submission. Offers $10-50 per photo. Identification of subjects required. Buys one-time rights.

Fiction: Adventure, historical, humorous and religious. Buys 50 mss/year. Send complete ms. Length: 750-1,000 words. Pays 7-10¢/word.

Poetry: Free verse, light verse and traditional. Buys 8-10 poems/year. Length: 8-50 words. Pays 7-10¢/word.

Tips: "Submissions should be geared to readers who are 8 to 12 years old."

‡STONE SOUP, The Magazine by Children, Children's Art Foundation. Box 83, Santa Cruz CA 95063. (408)426-5557. Editor: Ms. Gerry Mandel. 100% freelance written. A bimonthly magazine of writing and art by children, including fiction, poetry, book reviews, and art by children through age 13. Audience is children, teachers, parents, writers, artists. "We have a preference for writing and art based on real-life experiences, no formula stories or poems." Pays on acceptance. Publishes ms an average of 3 months after acceptance. Buys all rights. Submit seasonal/holiday material 6 months in advance. Photocopied submissions OK. Computer printout submissions OK; prefers letter-quality. Reports in 2 weeks on queries; 6 weeks on mss. Sample copy $4. Free writer's guidelines.

Nonfiction: Book reviews. Buys 10 mss/year. Query. Pays $15 for assigned articles. "We pay book reviewers (solicited writers) and illustrators (solicited artists) in cash. We pay for unsolicited fiction, poetry and art in copies."

Fiction: Adventure, ethnic, experimental, fantasy, historical, humorous, mystery, science fiction, slice-of-life vignettes and suspense. "We do not like assignments or formula stories of any kind." Accepts 35 mss/year. Send complete ms. Pays in copies only.

Poetry: Avant-garde and free verse. Accepts 10 poems/year. Pays in copies only.

Tips: "We can't emphasize enough how important it is to read a couple of issues of the magazine. We have a strong preference for writing on subjects that mean a lot to the author. If you feel strongly about something that happened to you or something you observed, use that feeling as the basis for your story or poem. Stories should have good descriptions, realistic dialogue and a point to make. In a poem, each word must be chosen carefully. Your poem should present a view of your subject and a way of using words that are special and all your own."

‡STORY FRIENDS, Mennonite Publishing House, 616 Walnut Ave., Scottdale PA 15683. (412)887-8500. Editor: Marjorie Waybill. 80% freelance written. Monthly story paper for children ages 4-9. "*Story Friends* is planned to provide wholesome Christian reading for the 4- to 9-year-old. Practical life stories are included to teach moral values and remind the children that God is at work today. Activities introduce children to the Bible and its message for them." Circ.: 11,500. Pays on acceptance. Publishes ms an average of 1 year after acceptance. Byline given. Publication not copyrighted. Buys one-time rights and second serial (reprint) rights. Submit seasonal/holiday material 6 months in advance. Simltaneous, photocopied and previously published material OK. Computer printout submissions OK; prefers letter quality. Sample copy for 8½x11 SAE with 2 first class stamps. Writer's guidelines for #10 SAE with 1 first class stamp.

Nonfiction: How-to (craft ideas for young children), photo feature. Buys 20 mss/year. Send complete ms. Length: 400-800 words. Pays 3-5¢/word.

Photos: Send photos with submission. Reviews 8½x11 black and white prints. Offers $10-20/photo. Model releases required. Buys one-time rights.

Fiction: See writer's guidelines for *Story-Friends*. Buys 50 mss/year. Send complete ms. Length: 300-800 words. Pays 3-5¢/word.

Poetry: Traditional. Buys 20 poems/year. Length: 4-16 lines. Pays $5-10/poem.

Tips: "Send stories that children from a variety of ethnic backgrounds can relate to; stories that deal with experiences similar to all children. For example, all children have fears but their fears may vary depending on where they live."

TURTLE MAGAZINE FOR PRESCHOOL KIDS, Children's Better Health Institute, Benjamin Franklin Literary & Medical Society, Inc., 1100 Waterway Blvd., Box 567, Indianapolis IN 46206. (317)636-8881. Editor: Beth Wood Thomas. 95% freelance written. Monthly magazine (bimonthly February/March, April/May, June/July, August/September) for preschoolers emphasizing health, safety, exercise and good nutrition. Pays on publication. Publishes ms an average of 1 year after acceptance. Byline given. Buys all rights. Submit seasonal/holiday material 8 months in advance. Reports in 10 weeks. Sample copy 75¢; writer's guidelines for #10 SASE.

Fiction: Fantasy, humorous and health-related stories. "Stories that deal with a health theme need not have health as the primary subject but should include it in some way in the course of events." No controversial material. Buys 40 mss/year. Submit complete ms. Length: 700 words maximum. Pays approximately 8¢/word.

Poetry: "We use many stories in rhyme—vocabulary should be geared to a 3- to 5-year-old. Anthropomorphic animal stories and rhymes are especially effective for this age group to emphasize a moral or lesson without 'lecturing'." Pays variable rates.

Tips: "We are primarily concerned with preventive medicine. We try to present our material in a positive—not a negative—light and to incorporate humor and a light approach wherever possible without minimizing the seriousness of what we are saying. We would like to see more stories, articles, craft ideas and activities with the following holiday themes: New Year's Day, Valentine's Day, President's Day, St. Patrick's Day, Easter, Independence Day, Thanksgiving, Christmas and Hannukah. We like new ideas that will entertain as well as teach preschoolers. Publishing a writer's first work is very gratifying to us. It is a great pleasure to receive new, fresh material."

VENTURE, Christian Service Brigade, Box 150, Wheaton IL 60189. (312)665-0630. Managing Editor: Steven P. Neideck. 15% freelance written. Works with a small number of new/unpublished writers each year. "Venture is a bimonthly company publication published to support and compliment *CSB's* Stockade and Battalion programs. We aim to provide wholesome, entertaining reading for boys ages 10-15." Circ. 25,000. Pays on publication. Publishes ms an average of 4-6 months after acceptance. Byline given. Offers $35 kill fee. Buys first North American serial, one-time and second serial (reprint) rights. Submit seasonal/holiday material 6 months in advance. Photocopied submissions and previously published submissions OK. Computer printout submissions OK; prefers letter-quality. Reports in 2 weeks. Sample copy $1.50 with 9x12 SAE and 4 first class stamps; writer's guidelines for #10 SASE.
Nonfiction: Expose, general interest, historical/nostalgic, humor, inspirational, interview/profile, personal experience, photo feature and religious. Buys 10-12 mss/year. Query. Length: 1,000-1,500 words. Pays $75-125 for assigned articles; pays $40-100 for unsolicited articles. Sometimes pays expenses of writers on assignment.
Photos: Send photos with submission. Reviews contact sheets and 5x7 prints. Offers $35-125/photo. Buys one-time rights.
Fiction: Adventure, humorous, mystery and religious. Buys 10-12 mss/year. Query. Length: 1,000-1,500 words. Pays $40-125.
Tips: "Talk to young boys. Find out the things that interest them and write about those things. We are looking for material relating to our theme: Building Men to Serve Christ."

WEE WISDOM, Unity Village MO 64065. Editor: Ms. Verle Bell. 90% freelance written. "We are happy to work with any freelance writers whose submissions and policies match our needs." Magazine published 10 times/year "for children aged 13 and under, dedicated to the truth that each person has an inner source of wisdom, power, love and health that can be applied in a practical manner to everyday life." Circ. 175,000. Publishes ms an average of 8 months after acceptance. Submit seasonal/holiday material 10-12 months in advance. Pays on acceptance. Byline given. Buys first serial rights only. Computer printout submissions acceptable; must be clearly legible. Sample copy and editorial policy for 5¾x8¾ SAE and 4 first class stamps.
Fiction: Character-building stories that encourage a positive self-image. Although entertaining enough to hold the interest of the older child, they should be readable by the third grader. "Characters should be appealing; plots should be imaginative but plausible, and all stories should be told without preaching. Life combines fun and humor with its more serious lessons, and our most interesting and helpful stories do the same thing. Language should be universal, avoiding the Sunday school image." Length: 500-800 words. Rates vary, depending on excellence.
Poetry: Limited. Prefers short, seasonal and general poems. Pays $15 minimum, 50¢ per line after 15 lines. Rhymed prose (read aloud) stories are paid at about the same rate as prose stories, depending on excellence.
Fillers: Pays $8-10 for puzzles and games.

WONDER TIME, 6401 The Paseo, Kansas City MO 64131. (816)333-7000. Editor: Evelyn Beals. 75% freelance written. "Willing to read and consider appropriate freelance submissions." Published weekly by Church of the Nazarene for children ages 6-8. Pays on acceptance. Publishes ms an average of 1 year after acceptance. Byline given. Buys first serial rights, second serial (reprint) rights, simultaneous rights and all rights for curriculum assignments. Computer printout submissions acceptable; prefers letter-quality. Sample copy and writer's guidelines for 9x12 SAE with 3 first class stamps.
Fiction: Buys stories portraying Christian attitudes without being preachy. Uses stories for special days—stories teaching honesty, truthfulness, kindness, helpfulness or other important spiritual truths, and avoiding symbolism. Also, stories about real life problems children face today. "God should be spoken of as our Father who loves and cares for us; Jesus, as our Lord and Savior." Buys 100/mss year. Length: 350-550 words. Pays 3½¢/word on acceptance.
Poetry: Uses verse which has seasonal or Christian emphasis. Length: 4-8 lines. Pays 25¢/line, minimum $2.50.
Tips: "Any stories that allude to church doctrine must be in keeping with Nazarene beliefs. Any type of fantasy must be in good taste and easily recognizable. We are overstocked now with poetry and stories with general themes. We plan to reprint more than before to save art costs, therefore we will be more selective and purchase fewer manuscripts."

YOUNG AMERICAN, America's Newspaper for Kids, Young American Publishing Co., Inc., Box 12409, Portland OR 97212. (503)230-1895. Editor: Kristina T. Linden. 20% freelance written. Eager to work with new/unpublished writers. A tabloid-size newspaper supplement to suburban newspapers for children and their families. Circ. 1.2 million. Pays on publication. Publishes ms an average of 6 months after acceptance. Buys first North American serial rights. Submit seasonal/holiday material 3 months in advance. Photocopied submissions OK. Computer printout submissions acceptable; prefers letter-quality. Reports in 4 months on mss. Sample copy $1.50 with 9x12 SAE; writer's guidelines for SASE.

Nonfiction: General interest; historical/nostalgic; how-to (crafts, fitness); humor; interview/profile (of kids, or people particularly of interest to them); and newsworthy kids. No condescending articles or articles relating to religion, sex, violence, drugs or substance abuse. Buys 100 mss/year. *No queries*; send complete ms. Length: 350 words maximum. Pays $5-75. Sometimes pays the expenses of writers on assignment.

Photos: Send photos with submission. Offers negotiable maximum/photo. Identification of subjects required. Buys one-time rights.

Columns/Departments: You and the News (stories about newsworthy kids), science (new developments, things not covered in textbooks), and book reviews (for kids and young teens). Length 350 words maximum. Buys 40 mss/year. Send complete ms. Pays $5-75.

Fiction: Adventure, ethnic, fantasy, humorous, mystery, science fiction, suspense, western and lore. No condescending stories or stories relating to religion, sex, drugs or substance abuse. Buys 24 mss/year. Send complete ms. Length: 500-1,000 words. Pays $35-75.

Poetry: Light verse. No "heavy" or depressing poetry. Buys 30 poems/year. Length: 4 lines, 500 words maximum. Pays $5-35.

Fillers: Facts and short humor. Buys 20/year. Length: 30-300 words. Pays $2.10-21.

Tips: "The *Young American* is particularly interested in publishing articles about newsworthy kids. These articles should be under 350 words and accompanied by photos—we prefer color transparencies to black and white. The *Young American* focus is on children—and they are taken seriously. Articles are intended to inform, entertain, stimulate and enlighten. They give children a sense of being a part of today's important events and a recognition which is often denied them because of age. If applicable, photos, diagrams, or information for illustration helps tremendously as our publication is highly visual. The fiction we have been receiving is excellent. We are now distributed throughout west coast and now have a more national perspective. Kids want to read about what other kids in different places are doing."

‡**THE YOUNG CRUSADER**, 1730 Chicago Ave., Evanston IL 60201. (312)864-1396. Managing Editor: Michael Vitucci. Monthly for children ages 6-12. Not copyrighted. Pays on publication. Submit seasonal material 6 months in advance. Computer printout submissions acceptable. Free sample copy. Manuscripts will not be returned.

Nonfiction: Uses articles on total abstinence, character-building and love of animals. Also science stories. Length:600 words. Pays 12¢/word.

Fiction: Should emphasize Christian principles and world friendship. Also science stories. Length: 600 words. Pays 12¢/word.

Poetry: Limit submissions to batches of 3. Pays 10¢/line.

‡**THE YOUNG SOLDIER**, The Salvation Army, 799 Bloomfield Ave., Verona NJ 07044. Editor: Robert R. Hostetler. 75% freelance written. Monthly Christian/religious magazine for children, ages 8-12. "Only material with clear Christian or Biblical emphasis is accepted." Circ. 48,000. Pays on acceptance. Publishes ms an average of 6 months after acceptance. Byline given. Buys first North American serial rights, first rights, one-time rights or second serial (reprint) rights. Submit seasonal/holiday material 6 months in advance. Photocopied and previously published submissions OK. Computer printout submissions OK; prefers letter-quality. Reports in 1 month. Sample copy for 8½x11 SAE with 3 first class stamps. Writer's guidelines for #10 SAE with 1 first class stamp.

Nonfiction: How-to (craft, Bible study, etc.), religious, games, puzzles, activities. Buys 12 mss/year. Send complete ms. Length: 300-1,000 words. Pays 3-5¢/word.

Photos: State availability or send photos with submission. Reviews contact sheets, negatives, transparencies and prints. Offer varies for photos accepted with ms. Buy one-time rights.

Fiction: Adventure, religious. "Must have Christian emphasis." Buys 10-12 mss/year. Send complete ms. Length: 500-1,000 words. Pays 3-5¢/word.

Poetry: Free verse, light verse, traditional. Buys 6 poems/year. Length: 4-20 lines. Pays 5¢/word ($5 minimum).

For information on setting your freelance fees, see How Much Should I Charge? in the Business of Writing section.

——————— *Literary and "Little"*

Literary and "little" magazines contain fiction, poetry, book reviews, essays and literary criticism. Many are published by colleges and universities and have a regional or scholarly focus.

Literary magazines launch many writers into print. Serious writers will find great opportunities here; some agents read the magazines to find promising potential clients, and many magazines also sponsor annual contests. Writers who want to get a story printed may have to be patient. Literary magazines, especially semiannuals, will buy good material and save it for future editions. Submitting work to a literary, the writer may encounter frequent address changes or long response times. On the other hand, many editors carefully read submissions several times and send personal notes to writers.

Many literary magazines do not pay writers or pay in contributor's copies. Only literary magazines which pay are included in *Writer's Market* listings. However, *Novel and Short Story Writer's Market* (formerly *Fiction Writer's Market*), published by Writer's Digest Books, includes nonpaying fiction markets and has indepth information about fiction techniques and markets. Literary and "little" magazine writers will notice that *Writer's Market* no longer contains a Poetry section, although Poetry subheads can be found in many consumer magazine listings. Writer's Digest Books also publishes *Poet's Market*, edited by Judson Jerome, with detailed information for poets.

‡**ACM (Another Chicago Magazine)**, Another Chicago Press, Box 11223, Chicago IL 60611. (312)524-1289. Editors: Lee Webster and Barry Silesky. 98% freelance written. Eager to work with new/unpublished writers. Literary journal published biannually and funded by the National Endowment for the Arts. Circ. 1,100. Pays on acceptance. Publishes ms an average of 6 months after acceptance. Byline given. Buys first serial rights. Simultaneous queries, and simultaneous and photocopied submissions OK. Query for electronic submissions. Computer printout submissions acceptable; prefers letter-quality. Reports in 6 weeks. Sample copy $5; writer's guidelines for #10 SAE and 1 first class stamp.
Nonfiction: Interview (contemporary poets and fiction writers), essays (contemporary literature) and reviews of small press publications. Buys 1-2 mss/year. Query. Length: 1,000-20,000 words. Pays $5-25.
Fiction: Sharon Solwitz, fiction editor. Erotica, ethnic, experimental, novel excerpts and serious fiction. Buys 10-20 mss/year. Send complete ms. Length: 50-20,000 words. Pays $5-25.
Poetry: Serious poetry. No light verse or inspirational. Buys 100 poems/year. Length: 1-1,000 lines. Pays $5-25.

ALASKA QUARTERLY REVIEW, College of Arts & Sciences, University of Alaska Anchorage, Dept. of English, 3221 Providence Dr., Anchorage AK 99508. (907)786-1731. Executive Editors: Ronald Spatz and James Liska. 100% freelance written. Prefers to work with published/established writers; eager to work with new/unpublished writers. A semiannual magazine publishing fiction and poetry, both traditional and experimental styles, and literary criticism and reviews, with an emphasis on contemporary literature. Circ. 1,000. Pays honorariums on publication when funding permits. Publishes ms an average of 6 months after acceptance. Byline given. Buys first North American serial rights. Upon request, rights will be transferred back to author after publication. Photocopied submissions OK. Computer printout submissions acceptable; prefers letter-quality. Reports in 4 months. Sample copy $3; writer's guidelines for #10 SAE.
Nonfiction: Essays, literary criticism, reviews and philosophy of literature. Buys 1-5 mss/year. Query. Length: 1,000-20,000 words. Pays $50-100 subject to funding; pays in copies when funding is limited.
Fiction: Experimental and traditional literary forms. No romance, children's, or inspirational/religious. Buys 10-20 mss/year. Send complete ms. Length: 500-20,000 words. Pays $50-150 subject to funding; sometimes pays in contributor's copies only.
Poetry: Thomas Sexton, poetry editor. Avant-garde, free verse, haiku, and traditional. No light verse. Buys 10-30 poems/year. Submit maximum 10 poems. Length: 2 lines minimum. Pays $10-50 subject to availability of funds.
Tips: "All sections are open to freelancers. We rely exclusively on unsolicited manuscripts. *AQR* is a nonprofit literary magazine and does not always have funds to pay authors."

AMELIA MAGAZINE, Amelia Press, 329 E St., Bakersfield CA 93304. (805)323-4064. Editor: Frederick A. Raborg Jr. 100% freelance written. Eager to work with new/unpublished writers. "*Amelia* is a quarterly international magazine publishing the finest poetry and fiction available, along with expert criticism and reviews intended for all interested in contemporary literature. *Amelia* also publishes three supplements each year: *Cicada*, which publishes only high quality traditional or experimental haiku and senryu plus fiction, essays and cartoons pertaining to Japan; *SPSM&H*, which publishes the highest quality traditional and experimental sonnets available plus romantic fiction and essays pertaining to the sonnet; and the annual winner of the Charles William Duke long poem contest." Circ. 1,250. Pays on acceptance. Publishes ms an average of 6 months after acceptance. Byline given. Offers 50% kill fee. Buys first North American serial rights. Submit seasonal/holiday material 2 months in advance. Computer printout submissions acceptable; prefers letter-quality. Reports in 2 months on mss. Sample copy $5.95 (includes postage); writer's guidelines for #10 SASE. Sample copy of any supplement $3.50.

Nonfiction: Historical/nostalgic (in the form of belles lettres); humor (in fiction or belles lettres); interview/profile (poets and fiction writers); opinion (on poetry and fiction only); personal experience (as it pertains to poetry or fiction in the form of belles lettres); travel (in the form of belles lettres only); and criticism and book reviews of poetry and small press fiction titles. "Nothing overtly slick in approach. Criticism pieces must have depth; belles lettres must offer important insights into the human scene." Buys 8 mss/year. Send complete ms. Length: 1,000-2,000 words. Pays $25 or by arrangement. "Ordinarily payment for all prose is a flat rate of $25/piece, more for exceptional work." Sometimes pays the expenses of writers on assignment.

Fiction: Adventure; book excerpts (original novel excerpts only); erotica (of a quality seen in Anais Nin or Henry Miller only); ethnic; experimental; fantasy; historical; horror; humorous; mainstream; mystery; novel excerpts; science fiction; suspense; and western. "We would consider slick fiction of the quality seen in *Redbook* and more excellent submissions in the genres—science fiction, wit, Gothic horror, traditional romance, stories with complex *raisons d'être*; avant-garde ought to be truly avant-garde and not merely exercises in vulgarity (read a few old issues of *Evergreen Review* or *Avant-Garde*)." No pornography ("good erotica is not the same thing"). Buys 24-36 mss/year. Send complete ms. Length: 1,000-5,000 words. Pays $35 or by arrangement for exceptional work.

Poetry: Avant-garde, free verse, haiku, light verse and traditional. "No patently religious or stereotypical newspaper poetry." Buys 100-160 poems/year depending on lengths. Prefers submission of at least 3 poems. Length: 3-100 lines. Pays $2-25; additional payment for exceptional work, usually by established professionals. *Cicada* pays $10 each to three "best of issue" poets; *SPSM&H* pays $14 to two "best of issue" sonnets; winner of the long poem contest receives $100 plus copies and publication.

Tips: "*Have something to say* and say it well. If you insist on waving flags or pushing your religion, then do it with subtlety and class. We enjoy a good cry from time to time, too, but sentimentality does not mean we want to see mush. Read our fiction carefully for depth of plot and characterization, then try very hard to improve on it. With the growth of quality in short fiction, we expect to find stories of lasting merit. I also hope to begin seeing more critical essays which, without sacrificing research, demonstrate a more entertaining obliqueness to the style sheets, more 'new journalism' than MLA. In poetry, we also often look for a good 'storyline' so to speak. Above all we want to feel a sense of honesty and value in every piece. As in the first issue of *Amelia*, 'name' writers are used, but newcomers who have done their homework suffer no disadvantage here. So often the problem seems to be that writers feel small press publications allow such a sloughing of responsibility. It is not so."

THE AMERICAN VOICE, Suite 1215, Heyburn Building, Broadway at 4th Ave., Louisville KY 40202. (502)562-0045. Editor: Frederick Smock. Works with small number of new/unpublished writers each year. A quarterly literary magazine "for readers of varying backgrounds and educational levels, though usually college-educated. We aim to be an eclectic reader—to define the American voice by publishing new and established writers from Canada, the U.S., and South America." Circ. 1,500. Pays on publication. Publishes ms an average of 4 months after acceptance. Byline given. Offers 50% kill fee. Buys first North American rights. Photocopied submissions OK. Computer printout submissions acceptable; prefers letter-quality. Reports in 1 month on queries; 2 months on mss. Sample copy $5.

Nonfiction: Essays, opinion, photo feature and criticism. Buys 15 mss/year. Send complete ms. Length: 10,000 words maximum. Pays $400/essay; $150 to translator. Sometimes pays the expenses of writers on assignment.

Fiction: Buys 30 mss/year. Send complete ms. Pays $400/story; $150 to translator.

Poetry: Avant-garde and free verse. Buys 40 poems/year. Submit maximum 10 poems. Pays $150/poem; $75 to translator.

Tips: "We are looking only for vigorously original fiction, poetry and essays, from new and established writers, and will consider nothing that is in any way sexist, racist or homophobic."

ANTAEUS, The Ecco Press, 26 W. 17th St., New York NY 10011. (212)645-2214. Editor: Daniel Halpern. Managing Editor: Lee Ann Chearney. 100% freelance written. Works with small number of new/unpublished writers each year. "We try to maintain a mix of new and established writers." Semiannual magazine with fiction and poetry. Circ. 5,000. Pays on publication. Publishes ms an average of 1 year after acceptance. Byline given. Buys first North American serial rights. Photocopied submissions OK. Computer printout submissions

acceptable; prefers letter-quality. Reports in 6 weeks on queries; 2 months on mss. Sample copy $10; writer's guidelines for SASE.
Nonfiction: General essays and essays for issues devoted to a particular subject.
Fiction: Stories and novel excerpts. Buys 10-15 mss/year. Send complete ms. Length: no minimum or maximum. Pays $10/printed page.
Poetry: Avant-garde, free verse, light verse and traditional. Buys 30-35 poems/year. Submit maximum 8 poems. Pays $10/printed page.

ANTIOCH REVIEW, Box 148, Yellow Springs OH 45387. Editor: Robert S. Fogarty. 80% freelance written. Quarterly magazine for general, literary and academic audience. Buys all rights. Byline given. Pays on publication. Publishes ms an average of 10 months after acceptance. Computer printout submissions acceptable; prefers letter-quality. Reports in 6 weeks. Sample copy for $5; writer's guidelines for #10 SASE.
Nonfiction: "Contemporary articles in the humanities and social sciences, politics, economics, literature and all areas of broad intellectual concern. Somewhat scholarly, but never pedantic in style, eschewing all professional jargon. Lively, distinctive prose insisted upon." Length: 2,000-8,000 words. Pays $10/published page.
Fiction: Quality fiction only, distinctive in style with fresh insights into the human condition. No science fiction, fantasy or confessions. Pays $10/published page.
Poetry: Concrete visual imagery. No light or inspirational verse. Contributors should be familiar with the magazine before submitting.

THE ASYMPTOTICAL WORLD, 341 Lincoln Ave., Box 1372, Williamsport PA 17703. (717)322-7841. Editor: Michael H. Gerardi. 50% freelance written. Works with a small number of new/unpublished writers each year. Annual magazine covering psychodramas, science fiction, fantasy and the experimental. "*The Asymptotical World* is a collection of short tales that attempt to elucidate the moods, sensations and thoughts of a curious world created in the mind of man. The tales touch upon themes of darkness, desolation and death. From each tale, the reader may relive a personal experience or sensation, and he may find relevance or discomfort. The tales were not written to be satanic or sacriligious statements. The stories were penned simply to be dark fantasies which would provide bizarre playgrounds for inquisitive minds." Circ. 1,300. Pays on acceptance. Publishes ms an average of 1 year after acceptance. Byline given. Buys first North American serial rights. Simultaneous queries and photocopied submissions OK. Computer printout submissions acceptable. Reports in 2 months on queries; 4 months on mss. Sample copy $6.95 with 9x12 SAE and 8 first class stamps; writer's guidelines for #10 SASE.
Fiction: Experimental, fantasy and psychodrama. Buys 10-15 mss/year. Query with published clips or send complete ms. Length: 1,000-2,500 words. Pays $20-50.
Poetry: Buys 4-6 poems/year. Submit maximum 4 poems. Length: 5-100 lines. Pays $5-50. Would like to see more black and white illustrations.
Tips: "*The Asymptotical World* is definitely unique. It is strongly suggested that a writer review a copy of the magazine to study the format of a psychodrama and the manner in which the plot is left 'open-ended.' The writer will need to study the atmosphere, mood, and plot of published psychodramas before preparing a feature work. The magazine is very young and is willing to explore many fields."

‡BAD HAIRCUT QUARTERLY, Kimberlea-Ray Productions, Suite 942, 12922 Harbor Bl., Garden Grove CA 92640. Editor: Kimberlea Richards. Managing Editor: Ray Goforth. 99% freelance written. Quarterly literary magazine. "We're trying to be a socially conscious magazine for these dollar conscious times." Estab. 1987. Circ. 400. Pays on publication. Byline given. Buys first North American serial rights. Submit seasonal/holiday material 4 months in advance. Simultaneous, photocopied and previously published submissions OK. Computer printout submissions OK; no dot-matrix. Reports in 1 week on queries; 1 month on mss. Sample copy $4; writer's guidelines for #10 SAE and 1 first class stamp.
Nonfiction: Essays, expose (government), general interest, interview/profile (political leaders, activists), opinion, photo feature. No pornography or hate oriented articles. Buys 6 mss/year. Query with or without published clips, or send complete ms. Length: 500-5,000. Pays $50 maximim. Sometimes pays writers with contributor copies or other premiums rather than a cash payment.
Photos: Send photos with submission. Reviews 5x7 prints. Offers $5-100/photo. Model release and identification of subjects required. Buys one-time rights.
Fiction: Adventure, experimental, historical, science fiction. Buys 6 mss/year. Send complete ms. Length: 500-5,000 words. Pays $50 maximim.
Poetry: Avant-garde, free verse. Buys 300 poems/year. Submit up to 10 poems at one time. Length: 1-100 lines. Pays with tear sheets.
Fillers: Anecdotes, facts, newsbreaks. Buys 20 mss/year. Length: 7-100 words. Pays $2.
Tips: "There is a rising tide of activism—a caring for others and the common future we all share. Tap into this—let your heart guide you. We're very small and accept anything that we like—you have a good chance with us."

BLOOMSBURY REVIEW, A Book Magazine, Owaissa Communications, Inc. 1028 Bannock, Denver CO 80204. (303)892-0620. Publisher/Editor-in-chief: Tom Auer. 75% freelance written. Bimonthly tabloid covering books and book-related matters. "We publish book reviews, interviews with writers and poets, literary essays and original poetry. Our audience consists of educated, literate, *non-specialized* readers." Circ. 8,000. Pays on publication. Publishes ms an average of 4 months after acceptance. Byline given. Buys first rights or one-time rights. Computer printout submissions OK; prefers letter-quality. Reports in 1 month on queries; 3 months on mss. Sample copy $3.50; writer's guidelines for #10 SASE.
Nonfiction: Essays, interview/profile and book reviews. "Summer issue features reviews, etc. about the American West." No academic or religious articles. Buys 60 mss/year. Query with published clips or send complete ms. Length 500-1,500 words. Pays $10-20. Sometimes pays writers with contributor copies or other premiums "if writer agrees."
Photos: State availability of photos with submissions. Reviews prints. Offers no additional payment for photos accepted with ms. Buys one-time rights.
Columns/Departments: Book reviews and essays. Buys 6 mss/year. Query with published clips or send complete ms. Length: 500-1,500 words. Pays $10-20.
Fiction: John Roberts, fiction editor. Send complete ms. Length: 1,000-3,500 words. Pays $15-25.
Poetry: Ray Gonzalez, poetry editor. Avant-garde, free verse, haiku, light verse and traditional. Buys 20 poems/year. Submit up to 5 poems at one time. Pays $5-10.
Tips: "We appreciate receiving published clips and/or completed manuscripts. Please—no rough drafts. Book reviews should be of new books (within 6 months of publication)."

BOOK FORUM, Crescent Publishing Co, Inc., Box 585, Niantic CT 06357. Editor: Clarence Driskill. 95% freelance written. Works with small number of new/unpublished writers each year. "Serious writers not yet recognized are welcome to query." Quarterly magazine emphasizing contemporary literature, the arts, and foreign affairs for "intellectually sophisticated and knowledgeable professionals: university-level academics, writers, and the professions." Circ. 5,200. Pays on publication. Publishes ms an average of 6 months after acceptance. Pays 33⅓% kill fee. Byline given. Buys first serial rights. Photocopied submissions OK. No computer printout submissions. Reports in 1 month. Sample copy for 8½x11 SAE, 5 first class stamps and $3.
Nonfiction: "We seek highly literate essays that would appeal to the same readership as, say, the *London Times Literary Supplement* or *Encounter*. Our readers are interested in professionally written, highly literate and informative essays, profiles and reviews in literature, the arts, behavior, and foreign and public affairs. We cannot use material designed for a mass readership." General interest, interview (with select contemporary writers, scientists, educators, artists, film makers), profiles and essays about contemporary innovators. Buys 20-40 unsolicited mss/year. Query. Length: 800-2,000 words. Pays $25-100.
Tips: "To break in, send with the query letter a sample of writing in an area relevant to our interests. If the writer wants to contribute book reviews, send a book review sample, published or not, of the kind of title we are likely to review—literary, social, biographical, art. We will be looking for more short book reviews in the future and are interested in additional interviews in philosophy, foreign affairs, art."

CALYX, A Journal of Art & Literature by Women, Calyx, Inc., P.O. Box B, Corvallis OR 97339. (503)753-9384. Editors: Margarita Donnelly et al. Managing Editors: Lisa Domitrovich et al. A literary triannual magazine publishing "Work by women: literature, art, interviews and reviews." Circ. 5,000. Pays on publication. Publishes ms an average of 3-4 months after acceptance. Byline given. Buys first rights and second serial reprint rights. Photocopied submissions OK. Computer printout submissions OK. Reports in 3 weeks on queries; 2-3 months on mss. Sample copy for $6.50 plus 3 first class stamps; writer's guidelines for #10 SASE.
Nonfiction "We are interested in well-crafted writing by women." Essays, interview/profile and book reviews. "We use 10-30 book reviews per issue and 3-6 interviews and essays per year." Send complete ms. Query the editors for book review list. Length for book reviews: 1,000 words; interviews/essays: 3,000 words. Pays in copies or $5/page depending on grant support.
Fiction: Contact: Editorial Board. Serious literary fiction. Buys 10-15 mss/year. Send complete ms. Length: 5,000 words maximum. Pays $5/published page or in copies of journal.
Poetry: Publishes 150-250 poems/year. Submit maximum 6 poems. Pays $5/poem per page or in copies of the journal.
Tips: "Send well-crafted writing with SASE and brief biographical statement. Be familiar with our publication."

CANADIAN FICTION MAGAZINE, Box 946, Station F, Toronto, Ontario M4Y 2N9 Canada. Editor: Geoffrey Hancock. Quarterly magazine; 148 pages. Publishes only Canadian fiction, short stories and novel excerpts. Circ. 1,800. Pays on publication. Buys first North American serial rights. Byline given. Reports in 6 weeks. Back issue $6 (in Canadian funds); current issue $7.50 (in Canadian funds).
Nonfiction: Interview (must have a definite purpose, both as biography and as a critical tool focusing on problems and techniques) and book reviews (Canadian fiction only). Buys 35 mss/year. Query. Length: 1,000-

3,000 words. Pays $10/printed page plus 1-year subscription.

Photos: Purchased on assignment. Send prints. Pays $10 for 5x7 b&w glossy prints; $50 for cover. Model releases required.

Fiction: "No restrictions on subject matter or theme. We are open to experimental and speculative fiction as well as traditional forms. Style, content and form are the author's prerogative. We also publish self-contained sections of novel-in-progress and French-Canadian fiction in translation, as well as an annual special issue on a single author such as Mavis Gallant, Leon Rooke, Robert Harlow or Jane Rule. Please note that *CFM* is an anthology devoted *exclusively* to Canadian fiction. We publish only the works of writers and artists residing in Canada and Canadians living abroad." Pays $10/printed page.

Tips: "Prospective contributors must study several recent issues carefully. *CFM* is a serious professional literary magazine whose contributors include the finest writers in Canada."

CANADIAN LITERATURE, University of British Columbia, Vancouver, British Columbia V6T 1W5 Canada. Editor: W.H. New. 70% freelance written. Works with "both new and established writers depending on quality." Quarterly. Circ. 2,000. *Not copyrighted*. Buys first Canadian rights only. Pays on publication. Publishes ms an average of 2 years after acceptance. Computer printout submissions acceptable; prefers letter-quality. Query "with a clear description of the project." Sample copy and writer's guidelines for $7.50 (Canadian) and 7x10 SAE with $2.50 Canadian postage.

Nonfiction: Articles of high quality only on Canadian books and writers written in French or English. Articles should be scholarly and readable. Length: 2,000-5,500 words. Pays $5/printed page.

CAROLINA QUARTERLY, University of North Carolina, Greenlaw Hall 066A, Chapel Hill NC 27514. (919)933-0244. Editor: Allison Bulsterbaum. Managing Editor: Judith Burdan.100% freelance written. Eager to work with new/unpublished writers. Literary journal published 3 times/year. Circ. 1,000. Pays on publication. Publishes ms an average of 4 months after acceptance. Byline given. Buys first North American serial rights. Photocopied submissions OK. Computer printout submissions acceptable; prefers letter-quality. Reports in 4 months. Sample copy $4 (includes postage); writer's guidelines for SAE and 1 first class stamp.

Nonfiction: Book reviews and photo feature. Publishes 6 reviews/year, 12 photographs/year.

Fiction: "We are interested in maturity: control over language; command of structure and technique; understanding of the possibilities and demands of prose narrative, with respect to stylistics, characterization, and point of view. We publish a good many unsolicited stories; *CQ* is a market for newcomer and professional alike." No pornography. Buys 12-18 mss/year. Send complete ms. Length: 7,000 words maximum. Pays $3/printed page.

Poetry: "*CQ* places no specific restrictions on the length, form or substance of poems considered for publication." Submit 2-6 poems. Buys 60 mss/year. Pays $5/printed poem.

Tips: "Send *one* fiction manuscript at a time; no cover letter is necessary. Address to appropriate editor, not to general editor. Look at the magazine, a recent number if possible."

THE CHARITON REVIEW, Northeast Missouri State University, Kirksville MO 63501. (816)785-4499. Editor: Jim Barnes. 100% freelance written. Semiannual (fall and spring) magazine covering contemporary fiction, poetry, translation and book reviews. Circ. 600. Pays on publication. Publishes ms an average of 6 months after acceptance. Byline given. Buys first North American serial rights. Computer printout submissions acceptable; no dot-matrix. Reports in 1 week on queries; 2 weeks on mss. Sample copy for $2, 7x10 SAE and 3 first class stamps.

Nonfiction: Essays and essay reviews of books. Buys 2-5 mss/year. Query or send complete ms. Length: 1,000-5,000. Pays $15.

Fiction: Ethnic, experimental, mainstream, novel excerpts and traditional. "We are not interested in slick material." Buys 6-8 mss/year. Send complete ms. Length: 1,000-6,000 words. Pays $5/page.

Poetry: Avant-garde, free verse and traditional. Buys 50-55 poems/year. Submit maximum 10 poems. Length: open. Pays $5/page.

Tips: "Read *Chariton* and similar magazines. Know the difference between good literature and bad. Know what magazine might be interested in your work. We are not a trendy magazine. We publish only the best. All sections are open to freelancers. Know your market or you are wasting your time—and mine. Do *not* write for guidelines; the only guideline is excellence in all matters."

CONFRONTATION, C.W. Post College of Long Island University, Brookville NY 11548. (516)299-2391. Editor: Martin Tucker. 90% freelance written. Works with a small number of new/unpublished writers each year. Semiannual magazine emphasizing creative writing for a "literate, educated, college-graduate audience." Circ. 2,000. Pays on publication. Pays 50% kill fee. Publishes ms an average of 9 months after acceptance. Byline given. Buys first serial rights. Phone queries, simultaneous and photocopied submissions OK. Query for electronic submissions. Computer printout submissions acceptable; no dot-matrix. Reports in 2 months. Sample copy $3.

Nonfiction: "Articles are, basically, commissioned essays on a specific subject." Memoirs wanted. Buys 6

mss/year. Query. Length: 1,000-3,000 words. Pays $10-100.
Fiction: William Fahey, fiction editor. Experimental, humorous and mainstream. Buys 25-50 mss/year. Submit complete ms. Length: open. Pays $15-100.
Poetry: W. Palmer, poetry editor. Avant-garde, free verse, haiku, light verse and traditional. Buys 60 poems/year. Submit maximum 8 poems. No length requirement. Pays $5-50.
Tips: "We discourage proselytizing literature. We do, however, read all manuscripts. It's rewarding discovering a good manuscript that comes in unsolicited."

DINOSAUR REVIEW, Dinosaur Literary Society, Box 294 Drumheller, Alberta T0J O4O Canada. (403)823-7126. 100% freelance written. Published 2-3 times/year. "A journal of current writing." Circ. 500. Pays on publication. Publishes ms an average of 3 months after acceptance. Byline given. Buys first North American serial rights. Photocopied submissions OK. Computer printout submissions OK; prefers letter-quality. Reports in 3 weeks on queries; 3 months on mss. Sample copy for 8½x11 SAE and IRC.
Nonfiction: Book excerpts and essays. No inspirational. Buys 4-6 mss/year. Query. Length: 1,000-4,000 words. Pays $15-100.
Fiction: Aritha Van Herk, fiction editor. Buys 6-8 mss/year. Length: 1,000-5,000 words. Pays $15-125.
Poetry: Monty Reid, poetry editor. Buys 50 poems/year. Submit up to 12 poems at one time. Pays $5-75.

ELDRITCH TALES, Magazine in the Weird Tales Tradition, Yith Press, 1051 Wellington Rd., Lawrence KS 66044. (913)843-4341. Editor: Crispin Burnham. 90% freelance written. A quarterly magazine of supernatural horror. Circ. 500. Pays on publication. Byline given. Buys first North American rights. Photocopied and previously published submissions OK. Computer printout submissions acceptable; prefers letter-quality. Reports in 1 week on queries; 5 months on mss. Sample copy $6; free writer's guidelines.
Nonfiction: Essays and interview/profile. Buys 1-2 mss/year. Send complete ms. Length: 10-500 words. Pays ¼-1¢/word; pays in copies if author prefers.
Photos: State availability of photos with submission.
Columns/Departments: Eldritch Eye (film review columns) and Book Reviews. Buys 1-2 mss/year. Query. Length: 200 words. Pays ¼-1¢/word.
Fiction: Horror, novel excerpts, serialized novels and suspense. No "mad slashers, sword and sorcery, or hard science fiction." Buys 10-12 mss/year. Send complete ms. Length: 50-10,000 words. Pays ¼-1¢/word.
Poetry: Free verse. Buys 5-10 poems/year. Submit maximum 3 poems. Length: 5-20 lines. Pays 10-25¢/line.
Fillers: Facts and newsbreaks. Buys 10/year. Length: 5-25 words. Pays 10-25¢/line.

EPOCH, Cornell University, 251 Goldwin Smith, Ithaca NY 14853. (607)256-3385. Editor: C.S. Giscombe. 50-98% freelance written. Works with a small number of new/unpublished writers each year. Literary magazine of original fiction and poetry published 3 times/year. Circ. 1,000. Pays on publication. Publishes ms 2-12 months after acceptance. Byline given. Buys first North American serial rights. Computer printout submissions OK; prefers letter-quality. Sample copy $3.50. Send SASE for listing of nearest library carrying *Epoch*.
Fiction: "Potential contributors should *read* a copy or two. There is *no other way* for them to ascertain what we need or like." Buys 15-20 mss/year. Send complete ms. Pays $10/page.
Poetry: "Potential contributors should read magazine to see what type of poetry is used." Buys 20-30 poems/year. Pays $1/line.

EROTIC FICTION QUARTERLY, EFQ Publications, Box 4958, San Francisco CA 94101. Editor: Richard Hiller. 100% freelance written. Small literary magazine (published irregularly) for thoughtful people interested in a variety of highly original and creative short fiction with sexual themes. Pays on acceptance. Byline given. Buys first rights. Photocopied submissions OK. Computer printout submissions acceptable; prefers letter-quality. Writer's guidelines for SASE.
Fiction: Heartful, intelligent erotica, any style. Also, stories—not necessarily erotic—about some aspect of authentic sexual experience. No standard pornography or men's magazine-type stories; no contrived or formula plots or gimmicks; no broad satire or parody. We do not publish poetry. Send complete ms. Length: 500-5,000 words, average 1,500 words. Pays $50 minimum.
Tips: "What we especially need and do not see enough of is truly interesting and original erotica, whether graphic or subtle, as well as literary-quality fiction that depends on sexual insight. No particular 'slant' is required. Stories should reflect real life, not media ideas."

FACET, A Creative Writing Magazine, Box 4950, Hualapai AZ 86412. (602)757-7462. Editor: Judith C. Porter. 100% freelance written. Wants to see new work of both new and established writers. A bimonthly literary magazine. No erotica, slander, horror, child or animal abuse, pornography, didactic religion or works intended for small children. Circ. 500. Pays on publication. Publishes ms an average of 6 months after acceptance. Byline given. Buys one-time rights. Submit seasonal/holiday material 6-9 months in advance. Simultaneous and previously published submissions OK. Computer printout submissions OK. Reports in 8-10 weeks on ms. Sample copy $3 with 6x9 SAE and 3 first class stamps; writer's guidelines for #10 SASE. "No free contributor copies sent. No work returned without SASE and sufficient postage."

Fiction: Adventure, experimental, fantasy, historical, humorous, mainstream, mystery, romance, science fiction, suspense, western, political, philosophical, sports, human dilemma, technology and space. "We prefer strong plots, well-defined characters of any age or socio-economic group. Upbeat endings not a must." *No* horror stories, erotica, child or animal abuse, pornography, devotional, didactic religious material, or slanderous pieces. Gay or lesbian theme stories OK. Buys 50 mss/year. Send complete ms. Length: 800-3,500 words. Pays $10-25.

Poetry: Avant-garde, free verse, haiku, light verse and traditional. No devotional religious, pornographic or horror/abuse. Buys 80 poems/year. Submit maximum 10 poems. Length: 1-75 lines. Pays $7-12.

Tips: "Check your work for plot construction, character presentation, consistency in narrator point of view, and character motivation. Be open to suggested changes in the material if required."

FESSENDEN REVIEW, The Reginald A. Fessenden Educational Fund, Inc., Box 7272, San Diego CA 92107. (619)488-4991. Editor: Douglas Cruickshank. 20% freelance written. "We read all material subscribers and contributors to the Fessenden Fund. Ours is a quarterly literate book review magazine which prints some 80-90 book reviews per issue—most with illustrations." Pays on publication. Publishes ms an average of 3-6 months after acceptance. No byline given. Buys one-time rights. Query for electronic submissions. Computer printout submissions OK; no dot-matrix. Reports in 3 months on mss. Sample copy for 9x12 SAE with 9 first-class stamps.

Nonfiction: Reviews. Buys 50 mss/year. Send complete ms. Length: 200-2,000 words. Pays $30/unsolicited article.

Photos: State availability of photos with submission.

Columns/Articles: Brief Reviews (must be in style of H.L. Mencken and his followers: iconoclastic, funny, perceptive, wry, witty), 200-500 words. Buys 25 mss/year. Send complete ms. Length: 200-500 words. Pays $15.

Tips: "We want book reviews by people who (1) know their subject intimately and (2) know our magazine and its iconoclastic style intimately."

FICTION NETWORK MAGAZINE, Fiction Network, Box 5651, San Francisco CA 94101. (415)391-6610. Editor: Jay Schaefer. 100% freelance written. Eager to work with new/unpublished writers. Magazine of short stories. Fiction Network distributes short stories to newspapers. Regional magazines and also publishes *Fiction Network Magazine* (for agents, editors and writers). Circ. 7,000. Pays on publication. Publishes ms an average of 6 months after acceptance. Byline given. Buys first serial rights. "Each story accepted may appear in several newspapers and magazines through our syndicate." Photocopied submissions OK. Computer printout submissions acceptable; prefers letter-quality. Reports within 4 months. Does not return foreign submissions—notification only with SASE. Sample copy $4 U.S. and Canada; $7 elsewhere. Writer's guidelines for #10 SASE.

Fiction: All types of stories and subjects are acceptable; novel excerpts will be considered only if they stand alone as stories. Considers unpublished fiction only. No poetry, essays, reviews or interviews. No children's or young adult material. Buys 100 mss/year. Send complete ms. "Do not submit a second manuscript until you receive a response to the first." Pays $25 minimum for magazine and 50% of syndicate sales.

Tips: "We are looking for high-quality, very short fiction. We offer both known and unknown writers excellent exposure while opening up new markets for stories. Our greatest need is for short-short stories." Contributors include Alice Adams, Max Apple, Ann Beattie, Andre Dubus, Lynne Sharon Schwartz, Marian Thurm, Ken Chowder and Bobbie Ann Mason.

THE FIDDLEHEAD, University of New Brunswick, Old Arts Bldg., Box 4400, Fredericton, New Brunswick E3B 5A3 Canada. (506)454-3591. Editor: Michael Taylor. 90% freelance written. Eager to work with new/unpublished writers. Preference is given to Canadian writers. Quarterly magazine covering poetry, short fiction, drawings and photographs and book reviews. Circ. 1,100. Pays on publication. Publishes ms an average of 6-12 months after acceptance. Not copyrighted. Buys first North American serial rights. Submit seasonal/holiday material 6 months in advance. Simultaneous queries and photocopied submissions (if legible) OK. Computer printout submissions acceptable; no dot-matrix. Reports in 3 weeks on queries; 2 months on mss. Sample copy $4.25, Canada; $4.50, U.S.

Fiction: Michael Taylor, Jane Toswell, William Cragg, fiction editors. "Stories may be on any subject—acceptance is based on quality alone. Because the journal is heavily subsidized by the Canadian government, strong preference is given to Canadian writers." Buys 20 mss/year. Pays $12/page.

Poetry: Robert Gibbs, Robert Hawkes, poetry editors. "Poetry may be on any subject—acceptance is based on quality alone. Because the journal is heavily subsidized by the Canadian government, strong preference is given to Canadian writers." Buys average of 60 poems/year. Submit maximum 10 poems. Pays $12/page; $100 maximum.

Tips: "Quality alone is the criterion for publication. Return postage (Canadian, or IRCs) should accompany all manuscripts."

THE GAMUT, A Journal of Ideas and Information, Cleveland State University, RT 1216, Cleveland OH 44115. (216)687-4679. Editor: Louis T. Milic. Managing Editor: Mary Grimm. 50-60% freelance written. Triannual magazine. Circ. 1,000. Pays on publication. Publishes ms an average of 6 months after acceptance. Byline given. Buys one-time rights. Submit seasonal/holiday material 6 months in advance. Simultaneous and photocopied submissions OK. Computer printout submissions acceptable. Reports in 1 month on queries; 3 months on mss. Sample copy $2.50; writer's guidelines for #10 SASE.

Nonfiction: Essays, general interest, historic/nostalgic, humor, opinion, personal experience, photo feature and technical. Buys 15-20 mss/year. Query with or without published clips, or send complete ms. Length: 1,000-6,000 words. Pays $25-250. Pays authors associated with the university with contributor copies.

Photos: State availability of photos with submission. Offers no additional payment for photos accepted with ms. Captions, model releases and identification of subjects required. Buys one-time rights.

Columns/Departments: Languages of the World (linguistic). Length: 2,000-4,000. Buys 1-2 mss/year. Query with published clips or send complete ms. Pays $75-125.

Fiction: Ethnic, experimental, historical, humorous, mainstream, novel excerpts and science fiction. No condensed novels or genre fiction. Buys 1-2 mss/year. Send complete ms. Length: 1,000-6,000 words. Pays $25-150.

Poetry: Leonard Trawick, poetry editor. Buys 6-15 poems/year. Submit up to 10 at one time. Pays $25-75.

Tips: "Get a fresh approach to an interesting idea or subject; back it up with solid facts, analysis, and/or research. Make sure you are writing for an educated, but general and not expert reader."

HIBISCUS MAGAZINE, Short Stories, Poetry, Art, Hibiscus Press, Box 22248, Sacramento CA 95822. Editor: Margaret Wensrich. 100% freelance written. Works with a small number of new/unpublished writers each year. Magazine "for people who like to read." Circ. 2,000. Pays on publication. Publishes ms 6-18 months after acceptance. Byline given. Buys first North American serial rights. Photocopied submissions OK. Computer printout submissions OK; no dot-matrix. Reports in 4 months on queries. Sample copy $3; writer's guidelines for #10 SASE.

Fiction: Adventure, fantasy, humorous, mainstream, mystery, romance, science fiction, slice-of-life vignettes, suspense and western. Buys 9-12 mss/year. Send complete ms. Length: 1,500-3,000 words. Pays $15-25.

Poetry: Joyce Odam, poetry editor. Free verse, haiku, light verse and traditional. No subject or line limit. Buys 20-25 poems/year. Submit maximum 4 poems. Pays $5-25.

Fillers: Short humor. Buys 4-6/year. Length: 25-100 words. Pays $2-5.

Tips: "We receive hundreds of submissions each month. All queries must have an SASE. International mail must come with sufficient IRC to pay return postage. We are slow to read and return manuscripts, but we do serve each writer and poet as fast as we can. We are a limited market. We regret we must return work that ought to be published because we do not have enough space."

THE HUDSON REVIEW, 684 Park Ave., New York NY 10021. Managing Editor: Ronald Koury. Quarterly. Pays on publication. Buys first world serial rights in English. Reports in 6-8 weeks.

Nonfiction: Articles, translations and reviews. Length: 8,000 words maximum.

Fiction: Uses "quality fiction". Length: 10,000 words maximum. Pays $2\frac{1}{2}$¢/word.

Poetry: 50¢/line for poetry.

Tips: Unsolicited mss will be read according to the following schedule: *Nonfiction:* Jan. 1 through March 31, and Oct. 1 through Dec. 31; *Poetry:* April 1 through Sept. 30; *Fiction:* June 1 through Nov. 30.

INDIANA REVIEW, Indiana University, 316 N. Jordan, Bloomington IN 47405. (812)335-3439. Editor: Elizabeth Dodd. 100% freelance written. Magazine published 3 times/year. "We publish fine innovative fiction and poetry. We're interested in energy, originality and careful attention to craft. While we publish many well-known writers, we also publish new and emerging poets and fiction writers." Circ. 500. Pays on acceptance. Byline given. Buys first North American serial rights. Computer printout submissions OK; prefers letter-quality. Reports in 2 weeks on queries; 2 months on mss. Sample copy $4; free writer's guidelines.

Nonfiction: Essays. No pornographic or strictly academic articles dealing with the traditional canon. Buys 3 mss/year. Query. Length: 5,000 maximum. Pays $25-200.

Fiction: Experimental and mainstream. No pornography. Buys 18 mss/year. Send complete ms. Length: 250-15,000. Pays $25.

Poetry: Avant-garde and free verse. "No pornography and no slavishly traditional poetry." Buys 60 mss/year. Submit up to 8 poems at one time. Length: 5 lines minimum. Pays $5/page.

Tips: "Read us before you send."

THE IOWA REVIEW, 369 EPB, The University of Iowa, Iowa City IA 52242. (319)335-0462. Editor: David Hamilton, with the help of colleagues, graduate assistants, and occasional guest editors. Magazine published 3 times/year. Buys first serial rights. Photocopied submissions OK. Reports in 3 months.

Nonfiction, Fiction and Poetry: "We publish essays, stories and poems and would like for our essays not always to be works of academic criticism." Buys 65-85 unsolicited mss/year. Submit complete ms. Pays $1/line for verse; $10/page for prose.

JAM TO-DAY, 372 Dunstable Rd., Tyngsboro MA 01879. Editors: Judith Stanford and Don Stanford. 90% freelance written. Eager to work with new/unpublished writers. Annual literary magazine featuring high quality poetry, fiction and reviews. Especially interested in unknown or little-known authors. Circ. 300. Pays on publication. Publishes ms an average of 6 months after acceptance. Byline given. Buys first rights and nonexclusive anthology rights. Photocopied submissions OK. Computer printout submissions acceptable; prefers letter-quality. Reports in 6 weeks. Sample copy $3.50 (includes postage).
Fiction: "We will consider quality fiction of almost any style or genre. However, we prefer not to receive material written to mass-market formulas, or that is highly allegorical, abstruse, or heavily dependent on word play for its effect." Buys 2-4 mss/year. Send complete ms. Length: 1,500-7,500 words. Pays $5/page.
Poetry: Avant-garde, free verse, shaped-concrete, found, haiku and traditional. No light verse. Buys 30-50/year. Submit 5 poems maximum. Length: open. Pays $5/poem; higher payment for poems more than 3 pages in length.

JAPANOPHILE, Box 223, Okemos MI 48864. Editor: Earl Snodgrass. 80% freelance written. Works with a small number of new/unpublished writers each year. Quarterly magazine for literate people who are interested in Japanese culture anywhere in the world. Pays on publication. Publishes ms an average of 5 months after acceptance. Buys first North American serial rights. Previously published submissions OK. Computer printout submissions acceptable; no dot-matrix. Reports in 1 month. Sample copy $4, postpaid. Writer's guidelines with #10 SASE.
Nonfiction: "We want material on Japanese culture in *North America or anywhere in the world*, even Japan. We want articles, preferably with pictures, about persons engaged in arts of Japanese origin: a Michigan naturalist who is a haiku poet, a potter who learned raku in Japan, a vivid 'I was there' account of a Go tournament in California. We use some travel articles if exceptionally well-written, but we are *not* a regional magazine about Japan. We are a little magazine, a literary magazine. Our particular slant is a certain kind of culture wherever it is in the world: Canada, the U.S., Europe, Japan. The culture includes flower arranging, haiku, religion, art, photography and fiction. It is important to study the magazine." Buys 8 mss/issue. Query preferred but not required. Length: 1,600 words maximum. Pays $8-20.
Photos: State availability of photos. Pays $10-20 for 8x10 b&w glossy prints.
Fiction: Experimental, mainstream, mystery, adventure, science fiction, humorous, romance and historical. Themes should relate to Japan or Japanese culture. Length: 1,000-10,000 words. Pays $20. Contest each year pays $100 to best short story. Should include one or more Japanese and non-Japanese characters.
Columns/Departments: Regular columns and features are Tokyo Scene and Profile of Artists. "We also need columns about Japanese culture in other cities." Query. Length: 1,000 words. Pays $20 maximum.
Poetry: Traditional, avant-garde and light verse related to Japanese culture or in a Japanese form such as haiku. Length: 3-50 lines. Pays $1-100.
Fillers: Newsbreaks, puzzles, clippings and short humor of up to 200 words. Pays $1-5.
Tips: "We prefer to see more articles about Japanese culture in the U.S., Canada and Europe." Lack of convincing fact and detail is a frequent mistake.

L'APACHE, An International Journal of Literature & Art, Kathryn Vilips Studios, Inc., Drawer G, Wofford Heights CA 93285. (619)376-3634. Editor: Kathryn Vilips. 50% freelance written. Eager to work with new/unpublished writers. A quarterly literary magazine covering art, literature, history. Pays on publication. Publishes ms an average of 6 months after acceptance. Byline given. Buys simultaneous rights. Submit seasonal/holiday material 3 months in advance. Photocopied submissions OK. Computer printout submissions OK. Reports in 3 months. Sample copy $5 and 8x10 SAE with 4 first class stamps; writer's guidelines for #10 SASE and 25¢ to cover increased printing costs.
Nonfiction: Book excerpts, essays, historical/nostalgic, how-to, interview/profile, new product, photo feature and technical. "We also would like to receive Indian legends and stories of old grandfathers (medicine men), and women in Indian history—early or present history. Absolutely no pornography, science fiction or any story, or poetry written in poor taste." Buys 8-12 mss/year. Send complete ms. "Do not send originals." Length: 3,000 maximum words. Pays $25-50 for unsolicited articles.
Photos: Send photos with submissions (optional). Reviews negatives, 3x5 transparencies and 3x5 prints. Payment negotiable. Captions, model releases, identification of subjects required. Buys one-time and foreign rights.
Columns/Departments: The Write Word (creative writing); The Artist's Voice (substantiated complaints on lost, stolen, damaged art); The Indian Voice (art, poetry, history, Indian causes); and Ars Poetica (poetry for the Indian, not against), all 3,000 maximum words. Buys 8 mss/year. Send complete ms. Pays $25-50.
Fiction: Ethnic, experimental, historical, serialized novels and western. "All manuscripts written in good taste will be considered. Absolutely no pornographic material accepted." Buys 8 mss/year. Send complete ms.

Length: 3,000 maximum words. Pays $25-50.

Poetry: Frank Fitzgerald-Bush, poetry editor. Free verse, haiku and traditional. Buys 20-40 poems/year. Length: 4-20 lines. Pays $5-10.

Tips: "*L'Apache* cares about the problems of the writer and artist, and is sympathetic to the sensitivity that makes them creative, hence the artist's voice, fighting for artist's rights. As long as an artist or writer is totally honest, with absolutely no exaggeration, the manuscripts will be considered. Professors, archaeologists, anthropologists, historians and teachers have an excellent chance of being published."

‡LIGHTHOUSE, Box 1377, Auburn WA 98071-1377. Editor: Tim Clinton. 100% freelance written. A bimonthly literary magazine. Circ. 500. Pays on publication. Byline given. Buys first North American serial rights and first rights. Photocopied submissions OK. Computer printout submissions OK; prefers letter quality. Reports in 1 week on queries; 1 month on mss. Sample copy for $2; writer's guidelines for #10 SAE with 1 first class stamp.

Fiction: Lynne Trindl, fiction editor. Adventure, humorous, mainstream, mystery, romance, science fiction, suspense, western. "No murder mysteries or anything not G-rated." Buys 66 mss/year. Send complete ms. Length: 5,000 words maximum. Pays up to $80.

Poetry: Lorraine Clinton, poetry editor. Free verse, light verse, traditional. Buys 24 poems/year. Submit up to 5 poems at one time. Pays up to $15.

Tips: "Both fiction and poetry are open to freelancers; just follow the guidelines."

LITERARY MAGAZINE REVIEW, KSU Writers Society, English Dept., Denison Hall, Kansas State University, Manhattan KS 66506. (913)532-6106. Editor: G.W. Clift. 98% freelance written. "Most of our reviewers are recommended to us by third parties." A quarterly literary magazine devoted almost exclusively to reviews of the current contents of small circulation serials publishing some fiction or poetry. Circ. 500. Pays on publication. Publishes ms an average of 1 month after acceptance. Byline given. Buys first rights. Photocopied submissions OK. Query for electronic submissions. Computer printout submissions OK; prefers letter-quality. Reports in 2 weeks. Sample copy $3.

Nonfiction: Buys 60 mss/year. Query. Length: 1,500 words. Pays $20 maximum for assigned articles and two contributor's copies. Sometimes pays expenses of writers on assignment.

Photos: State availability of photos with submission. Identification of subjects required.

Tips: Interested in "omnibus reviews of magazines sharing some quality, editorial philosophy or place of origin and in articles about literary magazine editing and the literary magazine scene."

LITERARY SKETCHES, Box 810571, Dallas TX 75381-0571. (214)243-8776. Editor: Olivia Murray Nichols. 33% freelance written. Works with small number of new/unpublished writers each year and is willing to work with new/unpublished writers. Monthly newsletter for readers with literary interests; all ages. Circ 500. Byline given. Pays on publication. Publishes ms an average of 4-6 months after acceptance. Computer printout submissions acceptable; prefers letter-quality. Reports in 1 month. Sample copy for #10 SAE with 1 first class stamp.

Nonfiction: Interviews of well-known writers and biographical material of more than common knowledge on past writers. Concise, informal style. Centennial pieces relating to a writer's birth, death or famous works. Buys 4-6 mss/year. Submit complete ms. Length: up to 750 words. Pays ½¢/word, plus copies.

Tips: "Articles need not be footnoted, but a list of sources should be submitted with the manuscript. We appreciate fillers of 100 words or less if they concern some little known information on an author or book."

LOS ANGELES TIMES BOOK REVIEW, Times Mirror, Times Mirror Sq., Los Angeles CA 90053. (213)972-7777. Editor: Jack Miles. 70% freelance written. Weekly tabloid reviewing current books. Circ. 1.3 million. Pays on publication. Publishes ms an average of 3 weeks after acceptance. Byline given. Offers variable kill fee. Buys first North American serial rights. Computer printout submissions acceptable; prefers letter-quality. Accepts no unsolicited book reviews or requests for specific titles to review. "Query with published samples—book reviews or literary features." Buys 500 mss/year. Length: 200-1,500 words. Pays $75-500.

THE MALAHAT REVIEW, The University of Victoria, Box 1700, Victoria, British Columbia V8W 2Y2 Canada. Contact: Editor. 100% freelance written. Eager to work with new/unpublished writers. Magazine published 4 times/year covering poetry, fiction, drama and criticism. Circ. 1,300. Pays on acceptance. Publishes ms up to 1 year after acceptance. Byline given. Offers 100% kill fee. Buys first serial rights. Photocopied submissions OK. Computer printout submissions acceptable; prefers letter-quality. Reports in 2 weeks on queries; 3 months on mss. Sample copy $6.

Nonfiction: Interview/profile (literary/artistic). Buys 2 mss/year. Query first. Length: 1,000-8,000. Pays $35-175.

Photos: Pays $25-50 for b&w prints. Captions required.

Fiction: Buys 20 mss/year. Send complete ms. Length: no restriction. Pays $40/1,000 words.

Poetry: Avant-garde, free verse and traditional. Buys 100/year. Pays $20/page.

THE MASSACHUSETTS REVIEW, Memorial Hall, University of Massachusetts, Amherst MA 01003. (413)545-2689. Editors: Mary Heath and Fred Robinson. "As pleased to consider new writers as established ones." Quarterly. Pays on publication. Publishes ms 6-18 months after acceptance. Buys first North American serial rights. Computer printout submissions acceptable; no dot-matrix. Reports in 3 months. Mss will not be returned unless accompanied by SASE. Sample copy for $4 plus 3 first class stamps.
Nonfiction: Articles on literary criticism, women, public affairs, art, philosophy, music and dance. Length: 6,500 words average. Pays $50.
Fiction: Short stories or chapters from novels when suitable for independent publication. Length: max. 25 typed pages (approx.). Pays $50.
Poetry: 35¢/line or $10 minimum.
Tips: No fiction manuscripts are considered from June to October.

MICHIGAN QUARTERLY REVIEW, 3032 Rackham Bldg., University of Michigan, Ann Arbor MI 48109. Editor: Laurence Goldstein. 75% freelance written. Prefers to work with published/established writers; works with a small number of new/unpublished writers each year. Quarterly. Circ. 2,000. Publishes ms an average of 1 year after acceptance. Pays on publication. Buys first serial rights. Computer printout submissions acceptable; no dot-matrix. Reports in 1 month for mss submitted in September-May; in summer, 2 months. Sample copy $2 with 2 first class stamps.
Nonfiction: "*MQR* is open to general articles directed at an intellectual audience. Essays ought to have a personal voice and engage a significant subject. Scholarship must be present as a foundation, but we are not interested in specialized essays directed only at professionals in the field. We prefer ruminative essays, written in a fresh style and which reach interesting conclusions. We also like memoirs and interviews with significant historical or cultural resonance." Length: 2,000-5,000 words. Pays $80-150, sometimes more.
Fiction and Poetry: No restrictions on subject matter or language. "We publish about 10 stories a year and are very selective. We like stories which are unusual in tone and structure, and innovative in language." Send complete ms. Pays $8-10/published page.
Tips: "Read the journal and assess the range of contents and the level of writing. We have no guidelines to offer or set expectations; every manuscript is judged on its unique qualities. On essays—query with a very thorough description of the argument and a copy of the first page. Watch for announcements of special issues, which are usually expanded issues and draw upon a lot of freelance writing. Be aware that this is a university quarterly that publishes a limited amount of fiction and poetry; that it is directed at an educated audience, one that has done a great deal of reading in all types of literature."

MID-AMERICAN REVIEW, Dept. of English, Bowling Green State University, Bowling Green OH 43403. (419)372-2725. Editor: Robert Early. 100% freelance written. Eager to work with new/unpublished writers. Semiannual literary magazine of "the highest quality fiction, poetry and translations of contemporary poetry and fiction." Also publishes critical articles and book reviews of contemporary literature. Pays on publication. Publishes ms an average of 3-6 months after acceptance. Byline given. Buys one-time rights. Photocopied submissions OK. Computer printout submissions OK; prefers letter-quality. Reports in 2 months or less. Sample copy $4.50, back issues for $3.
Fiction: Character-oriented, literary. Buys 12 mss/year. Send complete ms; do not query. Pays $5/page up to $75.
Poetry: Strong imagery, strong sense of vision. Buys 60 poems/year. Pays $5/page.
Tips: "We are seeking translations of contemporary authors from all languages into English; submissions must include the original; essays in feminist criticism."

‡MILKWEED CHRONICLE/MILKWEED EDITIONS, Milkweed Chronicle/Milkweed Editions, Box 24303, Minneapolis MN 55424. (612)332-3192. Editors: Emilie Buchwald, R.W. Scholes. Managing Editor: Deborah Keenan. 80% freelance written. Interested in seeing work from new/unpublished writers. A literary magazine published three times a year featuring poetry, essays, fiction, photographs and graphic arts. "We look for the highest quality writing and art work we can find. Each issue of the journal is based on a different theme, for example; Healing, Magic, The Uses of Power, etc." Circ. 2,000. Pays on publication. Publishes ms an average of 6 months after acceptance. Byline given. Buys first and one-time rights. Photocopied submissions OK. Computer printout submissions acceptable; no dot-matrix. Reports in 2 weeks on queries; 6 months on mss. Sample copy $4 with 11½x14½ SAE; free writer's guidelines.
Nonfiction: Book excerpts and essays (upon editor's request) and photo feature (b&w). "No diatribes on political parties, no religious pieces, gratuitously violent pieces, or pornography, etc." Buys 6-9 mss/year. Do not submit material on themes that are not yet chosen—query. Length: 1,200-6,000 words. Pays $50-300; plus a free copy when work appears.
Photos: Send photos with submission. Offers $15-30/photo. Buys one-time rights.
Fiction: Mainstream and novel excerpts (when requested). "Only really well-written fiction." Buys 1-6 mss/year. Query or send complete ms. Length: 1,200-6,000 words. Pays $50-300.
Poetry: Avant-garde, free verse and haiku. "No bad, rhyming poetry, no light verse, violent poetry, porno-

graphic poetry, or song lyrics." Buys 90-150 poems/year. Submit maximum 3-5 poems. Pays $20-100.
Tips: "We are interested in collaborative manuscripts: collaboration between two writers, or a writer and an artist."

‡**MINNESOTA INK**, Box 9148, North St. Paul MN 55109. (612)433-3626. Publisher/Managing Editor: Valerie Hockert. 75% freelance written. A bimonthly literary magazine. Estab. 1987. Pays on publication. Byline given. Buys first rights. Photocopied submissions OK. Computer printout submissions OK; prefers letter-quality. Reports in 1 month on queries; 2 months on mss. Writer's guidelines for #10 SAE with 1 first class stamp.
Nonfiction: How-to, interview/profile. Query with or without published clips, or send complete ms. Length: 500-1,500 words. Pays $5-50.
Photos: May send photos with submission. Reviews contact sheets, negatives, transparencies. Sometimes offers additional payment for photos accepted with ms. Identification of subjects required. Buys one-time rights.
Fiction: Adventure, ethnic, experimental, fantasy, historical, humorous, mainstream, mystery, romance, science fiction, suspense, western. Send complete ms. Length: 500-1,500. Pays $5-50.

‡**MUSES MILL**, Neon Hill Publications, Box 2117, Ashland KY 41105-2117. Editors: Cindi Griffith, Mike McDonald and Stephen Horton. 90% freelance written. Quarterly magazine of short fiction. "We are publishing well written original fiction (short stories) to 5,000 words. Will on occasion accept a how-to article on writing." Pays on publication. Publishes ms an average of 6 months after acceptance. Byline given. Offers 25% kill fee. Buys first North American serial rights or first rights. Submit seasonal/holiday material 6 months in advance. Simultaneous submissions OK. Query for electronic submissions. Computer printout submissions OK; prefers letter-quality. Reports in 2 weeks on queries; 1 month on mss. Writer's guidelines for #10 SAE with 1 first class stamp.
Photos: State availability of photos with submission. Offers no additional payment for photos accepted with ms. Model release and identification of subjects required.
Fiction: Adventure, experimental, fantasy, horror, humorous, mainstream, mystery, science fiction, suspense. Buys 40-48 mss/year. Send complete ms. Length: 1,000-5,000 words. Pays $10-100.
Poetry: Free verse, light verse, traditional. No haiku, epic, or stream of consciousness poetry. Buys 12 poems/year. Submit up to 6 poems at one time. Pays $2-5.
Fillers: Facts, short humor. Buys 20/year. Length: 50-100 words. Pays $2-5.
Tips: "We are interested in any kind of fiction (short stories) that are original and preferably unpublished although we will not rule out something that has been published before. Good stories, with an opening that gets your attention and strong characterizations will be appreciated and given serious consideration."

‡**THE NEBRASKA REVIEW**, Writer's Workshop/University of Nebraska-Omaha. 60th & Dodge, Omaha NE 68182-0324. (402)554-4801. Editors: Richard Duggin/Art Homer. 100% freelance written. A semiannual literary magazine. "We publish the best available contemporary fiction and poetry." Circ. 600. Pays on publication. Byline given. Buys first North American serial rights. Photocopied submissions OK. Computer printout submissions OK; prefers letter-quality. Reports in 4 months on mss. Sample copy for $2.
Fiction: Richard Duggin, fiction editor. Mainstream. "No straight genre fiction." Buys 8-10 mss/year. Send complete ms. Length: 6,000 words. Pays $5/page maximum.
Poetry: Art Homer, poetry editor. Free verse and traditional. Buys 40-50 poems/year. Submit maximum 5 poems or 6 pages. Pays $5 maximum.

NEW ENGLAND REVIEW/BREAD LOAD QUARTERLY, NER/BLQ, Middlebury College, Middlebury VT 05753. (802)388-3711, Ext 5075. Editors: Sydney Lea and Maura High. Managing Editor: Toni Best. 99% freelance written. Quarterly magazine covering contemporary literature. "We print a wide range of contemporary poetry, fiction, essays and reviews. Our readers tend to be literary and intellectual, but we're not academic, over-refined or doctrinaire." Circ. 3,100. Pays on publication. Publishes ms an average of 6 months after acceptance. Byline given. Buys first-time rights. Photocopied submissions OK. Computer printout submissions OK; prefers letter quality. Reports in 1 week on queries; 2 months on ms. Sample copy $4; writer's guidelines for #10 SASE.
Nonfiction: Book excerpts, essays, general interest, humor and personal experience. Buys 10 mss/year. Send complete ms. Length: 500-6,000 words. Pays $5/page, $10 minimum.
Photos: Also accepts drawings, woodcuts and etchings. Send with submission. Reviews transparencies and prints. Offers $60 minimum for cover art. Captions and identification of subjects required. Buys one-time rights.
Fiction: Ethnic, experimental, mainstream, novel excerpts, slice-of-life vignettes. Buys 18 mss/year. Send complete ms. Pays $5/page, $10 minimum.
Poetry: Avant-garde, free verse and traditional. Buys 50 poems/year. Submit up to 6 at one time. Pays $5/page, $10 minimum.
Tips: "Read at least one issue to get an idea of our range, standards and style. Don't submit simultaneously to other publications. All sections are open. We look for writing that's intelligent, well informed and well crafted."

THE NORTH AMERICAN REVIEW, University of Northern Iowa, Cedar Falls IA 50614. (319)273-2681. Editor: Robley Wilson Jr. 50% freelance written. Quarterly. Circ. 4,000. Buys all rights for nonfiction and North American serial rights for fiction and poetry. Pays on acceptance. Publishes ms an average of 1 year after acceptance. Computer printout submissions acceptable; no dot-matrix. Familiarity with magazine helpful. Reports in 10 weeks. Sample copy $2.50.
Nonfiction: No restrictions, but most nonfiction is commissioned by magazine. Query. Rate of payment arranged.
Fiction: No restrictions; highest quality only. Length: open. Pays minimum $10/page. Fiction department closed (no mss read) from April 1 to December 31.
Poetry: Peter Cooley, department editor. No restrictions; highest quality only. Length: open. Pays 50¢/line minimum.

THE OHIO REVIEW, Ellis Hall, Ohio University, Athens OH 45701-2979. (614)593-1900. Editor: Wayne Dodd. 40% freelance written. Published 3 times/year. "A balanced, informed engagement of contemporary American letters, with special emphasis on poetics." Circ. 2,000. Publishes ms an average of 8 months after acceptance. Rights acquired vary with author and material; usually buys first serial rights or first North American serial rights. Submit complete ms. Unsolicited material will be read only September-May. Computer printout submissions acceptable; prefers letter-quality. Reports in 10 weeks.
Nonfiction, Fiction and Poetry: Buys essays of general intellectual and special literary appeal. Not interested in narrowly focused scholarly articles. Seeks writing that is marked by clarity, liveliness, and perspective. Interested in the best fiction and poetry. Buys 75 unsolicited mss/year. Pays minimum $5/page, plus copies.
Tips: "Make your query very brief, not gabby—one that describes some publishing history, but no extensive bibliographies. We publish mostly poetry—short fiction, some book reviews."

THE PARIS REVIEW, 45-39 171st Place, Flushing NY 11358. Submit to 541 E. 72nd St., New York NY 10021. Editor: George A. Plimpton. Quarterly. Buys all rights. Pays on publication. Address submissions to proper department and address. Computer printout submissions acceptable; no dot-matrix.
Fiction: Study publication. No length limit. Pays up to $250. Makes award of $1,000 in annual fiction contest. Awards $1,500 in John Train Humor Prize contest, and $1,000 in Bernard F. Conners, Poetry Prize contest.
Poetry: Patricia Storace, poetry editor. Study publication. Pays $35/1-24 lines; $50/25-59 lines; $75/60-99 lines; and $150-175/100 lines and over. Sample copy $6.75; writer's guidelines for #10 SAE with 1 first class stamp.

PARTISAN REVIEW, 141 Bay State Rd., Boston MA 02215. (617)353-4260. Editor: William Phillips. Executive Editor: Edith Kurzweil. 90% freelance written. Works with a small number of new/unpublished writers each year. Quarterly literary journal covering world literature, politics and contemporary culture for an intelligent public with emphasis on the arts and political/social commentary. Circ. 8,200. Pays on publication. Publishes ms an average of 6-12 months after acceptance. Buys first serial rights. Byline given. Photocopied submissions OK. Computer printout submissions acceptable; prefers letter-quality. Reports in 3-4 months. Sample copy $5 and 4 first class stamps; writer's guidelines for #10 SASE. "All manuscripts and requests must be accompanied by a SASE."
Nonfiction: Essays; interviews and book reviews. Buys 30-40 mss/year. Send complete ms. Pays $50-250. Sometimes pays expenses of writers on assignment.
Fiction: High quality, serious and contemporary fiction. No science fiction, mystery, confession, romantic or religious material. Buys 8-10 mss/year. Send complete ms. Pays $100-250.
Poetry: Buys 60 poems/year. Submit maximum 6 poems. Pays $50.
Tips: "If, after reading *PR* a writer or poet feels that he or she writes with comparable originality and quality, then of course he or she may well be accepted. Standards of self-watchfulness, originality and hard work apply and reap benefits."

PASSAGES NORTH, William Bonifas Fine Arts Center, Escanaba MI 49829. (906)786-3833. Editor: Elinor Benedict. Managing Editor: Carol R. Hackenbruch. 100% freelance written. Eager to work with emerging writers. A semiannual tabloid of poetry, fiction and graphic arts. Circ. 2,000. Pays on publication. Publishes ms an average of 2-4 months after acceptance. Byline given. Buys first rights. Computer printout submissions acceptable. Reports in 1 month on queries; 3 months on manuscripts. Sample copy $1.50; writer's guidelines for #10 SASE.
Fiction: "High quality" fiction. Buys 6-8 mss/year. Send complete ms. Length: 4,000 words maximum. Pays 3 copies minimum, $50 maximum.
Poetry: No "greeting card" or sentimental poetry and no song lyrics. Buys 80 poems/year. Submit maximum 4 poems. Length: prefers 40 lines maximum. Pays 3 copies minimum, $20 maximum.
Tips: "We want poems and stories of high quality that make the reader see, imagine and experience."

THE PENNSYLVANIA REVIEW, University of Pittsburgh, English Dept./526 CL, Pittsburgh PA 15260. (412)624-0026. Managing Editor: Elizabeth Perry. 95% freelance written. A semiannual magazine publishing contemporary fiction, poetry and nonfiction. Circ. approximately 1,000. Pays on publication. Publishes ms an average of 6 months after acceptance. Byline given. Photocopied submissions OK. Reports in 10 weeks. Sample copy $5; writer's guidelines for #10 SAE.
Nonfiction: Essays, criticism reviews, interviews and book reviews. Buys 5-10 mss/year. Send complete ms. Pays $5/page.
Fiction: Linda Lee Harper, fiction editor. Novel excerpts and drama. "No formula fiction; nothing cute; genre fiction (science fiction, romance, mystery) discouraged." Buys 10-20 mss/year. Send complete ms. Pays $5/page.
Poetry: James Gyure, poetry editor. Free verse and traditional. No light verse. Buys 50-75 poems/year. Submit maximum 6 poems. Length: open. Pays $5/page.

PIG IRON MAGAZINE, Pig Iron Press, Box 237, Youngstown OH 44501. (216)783-1269. Editors-in-Chief: Jim Villani and Rose Sayre. 90% freelance written. Annual magazine emphasizing literature/art for writers, artists and intelligent lay audience interested in popular culture. Circ. 1,500. Buys one-time rights. Pays on publication. Publishes ms an average of 6-18 months after acceptance. Byline given. Photocopied and previously published submissions OK. Computer printout submissions acceptable. Reports in 4 months. Sample copy $2.75; writer's guidelines and list of current themes with #10 SASE.
Nonfiction: General interest, personal opinion, criticism, new journalism and lifestyle. Buys 3 mss/year. Query. Length: 8,000 words maximum. Pays $2/page minimum.
Photos: Submit photo material with query. Pays $2 minimum for 5x7 or 8x10 b&w glossy prints. Buys one-time rights.
Fiction: Fantasy, avant-garde, experimental, psychological fiction and metafiction and humor. Buys 4-12 mss/issue. Submit complete ms. Length: 8,000 words maximum. Pays $2 minimum.
Poetry: Nate Leslie and Joe Allgren, poetry editors. Avant-garde and free verse. Buys 25-50/issue. Submit in batches of 5 or less. Length: open. Pays $2 minimum.
Tips: "Looking for material about labor and working in post-industrial society."

PLOUGHSHARES, Box 529, Dept. M, Cambridge MA 02139. Director: DeWitt Henry. Eager to work with new/unpublished writers. Quarterly magazine for "readers of serious contemporary literature: students, educators, adult public." Circ. 3,500. Pays on publication. Publishes ms an average of 6 months after acceptance. Buys first North American serial rights. Photocopied submissions OK. Computer printout submissions OK; prefers letter quality. Reports in 6 months. Sample copy $5; writer's guidelines for SASE. .
Nonfiction: Interview and literary essays. Length: 5,000 words maximum. Pays $50. Reviews (assigned). Length: 500 words maximum. Pays $15.
Fiction: Experimental and mainstream. Buys 25-35 unsolicited mss/year. Length: 300-6,000 words. Pays $10-50.
Poetry: Traditional forms, blank verse, free verse and avant-garde. Length: open. Pays $10/poem.
Tips: "Because of our policy of rotating editors, we suggest writers check the current issue for news of upcoming editors and/or themes."

‡POETRY, The Modern Poetry Association. 60 West Walton St., Chicago IL 60610. (312)280-4870. Editor: Joseph Parisi. Managing Editor: Helen Lothrop Klaviter. 100% freelance written. A monthly poetry magazine. Circ. 7,000. Pays on publication. Byline given. Buys all rights. "Copyright assigned to author on request." Submit seasonal/holiday material 6 months in advance. Photocopied submissions OK. Reports in 2 months. Sample copy $3.25. Writer's guidelines for #10 SAE with 1 first class stamp.
Poetry: All styles and subject matter. Buys 180-250 poems/year. Submit maximum 6 poems. All lengths considered. Pays $1 per line.

‡THE PRAIRIE JOURNAL of Canadian Literature, Box 997, Station G, Calgary, Alberta T3A 3G2 Canada. Editor: A. Burke. 100% freelance written. A semiannual magazine of Canadian literature. Circ. 400 + . Pays on publication; "honorarium depends on grant." Byline given. Buys first North American serial rights. Photocopied submissions OK. Computer printout submissions OK; no dot-matrix. Reports 1 month on queries. Sample copy $3 and IRCs.
Nonfiction: Interview/profile and scholarly. Buys 5 mss/year. Query with published clips. "Include IRC." Pays $25 maximum. Pays contributor copies for literary work.
Photos: Send photos with submission. Offers no additional payment for photos accepted with ms. Identification of subjets required. Buys one-time rights.
Fiction: Literary. Buys 10 mss/year. Send complete ms. No payment for fiction.
Poetry: Avant-garde and free verse. Buys 10 poems/year. Submit maximum 6-10 poems. No payment for poetry.
Tips: "Commercial writers are advised to submit elsewhere. We are strictly small press editors interested in

highly talented, serious artists. We are oversupplied with fiction but seek more, high-quality poetry, especially the contemporary long poem or sequences from longer works.''

PRISM INTERNATIONAL, Department of Creative Writing, University of British Columbia, Vancouver, British Columbia V6T 1W5 Canada. Executive Editor: Janis McKenzie. Editors: Dania Stachiw Zajcew and Leo McKay. 100% freelance written. Eager to work with new/unpublished writers. Quarterly magazine emphasizing contemporary literature, including translations. For university and public libraries, and private subscribers. Circ. 1,000. Pays on publication. Publishes ms an average of 3 months after acceptance. Buys first North American serial rights. Photocopied submissions OK. Computer printout submissions acceptable; prefers letter-quality. Reports in 6-12 weeks. Sample copy $4. Writer's guidelines for #10 SAE with 1 first class Canadian stamp (Canadian entries) or 1 IRC (U.S. entries).
Nonfiction: Memoirs, belles-lettres, etc. *"Creative* nonfiction that possibly reads like fiction." No reviews, tracts or scholarly essays.
Fiction: Experimental and traditional. Buys 3 mss/issue. Send complete ms. Length: 5,000 words maximum. Pays $25/printed page and 1-year subscription.
Poetry: Avant-garde and traditional. Buys 30 poems/issue. Submit maximum 6 poems. Pays $25/printed page and 1-year subscription.
Drama: One-acts preferred. Pays $25/printed page and 1-year subscription.
Tips: "We are looking for new and exciting fiction. Excellence is still our number one criterion. As well as poetry, imaginative nonfiction and fiction, we are especially open to translations of all kinds, very short fiction pieces and drama which works well on the page. This year we also plan to feature avant-garde/underground writers as well as translations of Eastern European writers."

PULPSMITH magazine, The Smith, 5 Beekman St., New York NY 10038. (212)732-4822. Editor: Harry Smith. Managing Editor: Tom Tolnay. 90% freelance written. An annual pop-literary magazine "for an adult audience that seeks entertainment thrills from fiction, essays, articles, poetry of high quality." Circ. 4,000. Pays on acceptance. Byline given. Buys first North American serial rights. Simultaneous and photocopied submissions OK. Computer printout submissions acceptable; prefers letter-quality. Reports in 10 weeks on mss. Sample quarterly back issues $3 and 4 first class stamps; writer's guidelines for SASE. New annual format will be double-sized and priced at $10 (back issues will be $8). Manuscripts will be read from October 15 to May 15 each year. Mss received at other times will be returned unread.
Nonfiction: Essays. Buys 6-10 mss/year. Query. Length: 5,000 words maximum. Pays $35-100.
Fiction: Nancy Hallinan, fiction editor. Adventure, fantasy, horror, humorous, mainstream, mystery, science fiction, suspense and western. Buys 35 mss/year. Send complete ms. Length: 500-5,000 words. Pays $35-100.
Poetry: Joseph Lazarus, poetry editor. Avant-garde, free verse, haiku and traditional. Buys 60 poems/year. Submit maximum 4 poems. Pays $10-25 (more for very long poems).

QUARRY, Quarry Press, Box 1061, Kingston, Ontario K7L 4Y5 Canada. (613)376-3584. Editor: Bob Hilderley. 99% freelance written. Eager to work with new/unpublished writers. Quarterly magazine covering poetry, prose, reviews. "We seek high quality new writers who are aware of their genre and who are committed to their art." Circ. 1,000. Pays on publication. Publishes ms an average of 6-8 months after acceptance. Byline given. Buys first North American serial rights. Simultaneous queries and photocopied submissions OK. Computer printout submission acceptable; prefers letter-quality. Reports in 3 weeks on queries; 3 months on mss. Sample copy $5; writer's guidelines for #10 SAE and 2 IRCs.
Nonfiction: Short stories, poetry and book reviews. "We need book reviews of Canadian work. We are not interested in reviews of American or United Kingdom books. No literary criticism." Buys 100 mss/year. Send complete ms. Length: open. Pays $5-$10/page plus 1 year subscription.
Fiction: Any short fiction of high quality. "No nonliterary fiction." Send complete ms. Length: 10-15 pages maximum. Pays $5-10/page.
Poetry: Avant-garde, free verse, haiku, light verse and traditional. "No amateur, derivative poetry." Buys 200 poems/year. Submit maximum 10 poems. Length: open. Pays $5-10/page.
Tips: "Please send IRCs with SAE, not U.S. postage. Try to read a copy of the magazine before submitting. Ask at your library or request a sample copy."

QUEEN'S QUARTERLY, A Canadian Review, Queen's University, Kingston, Ontario K7L 3N6 Canada. (613)545-2667. Editors: Dr. Clive Thomson and Mrs. Marcia Stayer. Quarterly magazine covering a wide variety of subjects, including: science, humanities, arts and letters, politics, and history for the educated reader. 15% freelance written. Circ. 1,900. Pays on publication. Publishes ms an average of 1 year after acceptance. Byline given. Buys first North American serial rights. Photocopied submissions OK. Computer printout submissions acceptable; prefers letter-quality. Reports in 3 months on mss. Sample copy $5.
Fiction: Fantasy, historical, humorous, mainstream and science fiction. Buys 8-12 mss/year. Send complete ms. Length: 5,000 words maximum. Pays $80-150.
Poetry: Avant-garde, free verse, haiku, light verse and traditional. No "sentimental, religious, or first efforts

by unpublished writers." Buys 25/year. Submit maximum 6 poems. Length: open. Pays $20-35.
Tips: "Poetry and fiction are most open to freelancers. Don't send less than the best. No multiple submissions. No more than 6 poems or one story per submission. We buy very few freelance submissions."

‡RETURN RECEIPT REQUESTED, Poetic Arts Council. Suite 1, 211 West 75th St., Merrillville IN 46410. (219)736-2834. Editor: Aaron C. Yeagle. Managing Editor: Richard Pitcock. 90% freelance written. A bi-monthly newsletter on poetry. "*RRR*, publishes poetry of all forms and related articles such as mini-biographies of poets, discussion of forms and styles, etc. We want to excite and inform 'breakout' (new) poets. Every issue includes a ballot for readers to vote on the best poems and comment on poetry to help each other write more effective poetry." Estab. 1987. Byline given. Submit seasonal/holiday material 2 months in advance. Photocopied submissions OK. Computer printout submissions OK; no dot-matrix. Reports in 2 weeks on queries; 2 months on ms. Sample copy $2; writers guidelines for #10 SASE.
Nonfiction: How-to, inspirational, interview/profile and opinion. Buys 12 mss/year. Send complete ms. Length: 200-500 words. Pays $10-25 for unsolicited articles. State availability of photos with submission.
Poetry: Avant-garde, free verse, haiku, light verse and traditional. No lengthy poetry. Buys 90+ poems/year. Submit maximum 10 poems. Length: 1-65 lines. Does not pay for poetry.
Tips: "We will not accept, let alone read, any ms which arrives handwritten, sloppy, or dot-matrix. If you don't take the time to type it what makes you think we'd take the time to decipher it? And, as always, SASE for a return of your ms. We accept any style or form of poetry covering any topic and emotion. We don't judge your poetry, your peers do. However, three things will speed publication of your work: vision, emotional power, and technical skill."

ROOM OF ONE'S OWN, A Feminist Journal of Literature & Criticism, Growing Room Collective, Box 46160, Station G, Vancouver, British Columbia V6R 4G5 Canada. Editors: Gayla Reid, Robin Bellamy, Mary Schendlinger, Eleanor Wachtel, Jeannie Wexler, Betty Wood and Jean Wilson. 100% freelance written. Eager to work with new/unpublished writers. Quarterly magazine of original fiction, poetry, literary criticism, and reviews of feminist concern. Circ 1,200. Pays on publication. Publishes ms an average of 3 months after acceptance. Byline given. Buys first serial rights. Photocopied submissions OK. Computer printout submissions acceptable "if readable and not in all caps"; no dot-matrix. Reports in 2 months. Sample copy $2.75.
Nonfiction: Interview/profile (of authors) and literary criticism. Buys 8 mss/year. Send complete ms. Length: 1,500-6,000 words. Pays $50.
Fiction: Quality short stories by women with a feminist outlook. Not interested in fiction written by men. Buys 12 mss/year. Send complete ms. Length: 1,500-6,000 words. Pays $50.
Poetry: Avant-garde, eclectic free verse and haiku. Not interested in poetry from men. Buys 32 poems/year. Submit maximum 10 poems. Length: open. Pays $10-25.

‡SAGEBRUSH JOURNAL, The Best Danged Western Newspaper Going!, Allied Publishing. 430 Haywood Rd., Asheville NC 28806. Editor: Linda Hagan. Publisher: Bill Hagan. 90% freelance written. A monthly magazine covering Western genre, films and print (books and magazines). "We are oriented toward people who love the thrill of the Western genre-from the glorious 8 westerns of yesteryear, pulp stories and novels, to the Western revival of today." Circ. 5,000. Pays on publication. Byline given. Buys first North American serial, one-time and second serial (reprint) rights. Submit seasonal/holiday material 6 months in advance. Photocopied and previously published submissions OK. Query for electronic submissions. Computer printout submissions OK; prefers letter-quality. Reports in 2 weeks on queries; 2 months on mss. Sample copy $2.50. Writer's guidelines for #10 SAE with 1 first class stamp.
Nonfiction: General interest, historical/nostalgic, humor, interview/profile, personal experience, photo feature, western convention reports, reviews of western films and books. Buys 40-50 mss/year. Query with or without published clips, or send complete ms. Length: 200-5,000 words. Pays 25¢/column inch.
Photos: Send photos with submissions. Reviews prints. Offers 25¢/column inch for photo included with article; "no separate photos." Captions and identification of subjects required. Buys one-time rights.
Fillers: Nancy Duncan, fillers editor. Anecdotes, facts, newsbreaks and short humor. Buys 15-20/year. Length: 50-200 words. Pays 25¢/column inch.

‡SHOOTING STAR REVIEW, Black Literary Magazine, Timbuctu Express, 7123 Race St., Pittsburgh PA 15208. (412)731-7039. Editor: Sandra Gould Ford. 75% freelance written. Quarterly African-American literary magazine. "*Shooting Star Review* is an educational magazine that uses the literary and visual arts to increase understanding and appreciation of the African-American experience." Circ. 800. Pays on publication. Publishes ms an average of 3-9 months after acceptance. Byline given. Buys first North American serial rights. Submit seasonal/holiday material 6 months in advance. Simultaneous and photocopied submissions OK. Query for electronic submissions. Computer printout submissions OK. Reports in 2 weeks on queries; 2 months on mss. Sample copy for $3 and a 9x12 SAE with 90¢ postage; writer's guidelines for SASE.
Nonfiction: Book excerpts, essays, historical/nostalgic, interview/profile, opinion, personal experience, photo feature and book reviews. Each issue has a special theme: spring 1989, "Our Children"; summer 1989,

"Potpourri"; autumn 1989 "Tribute to Black Women Writers"; winter 1989, "Resolutions and New Beginnings." Buys 25 mss/year. Query. Length: 750-3,500 words. Pays $10-25 plus one contributor copy. Sometimes pays expenses of writers on assignment.

Photos: Send photos with submission. Reviews contact sheets, 35mm and 4x5 transparencies and 8x10 prints. Payment negotiated. Captions, model releases and identification of subjects required. Buys one-time rights.

Fiction: Toni McKain, fiction editor. Adventure, experimental, fantasy, historical, mainstream, novel excerpts, romance, science fiction, and slice-of-life vignettes. Buys 8 mss/year. Send complete ms. Length: 3,500 words maximum. Pays $30 maximum plus one contributor copy.

Poetry: Dr. Dennis Brutus, poetry editor. Avant-garde, free verse and traditional. Buys 35-40 poems/year. Submit maximum 6 poems at one time. Length: 50 lines maximum. Pays $8 maximum plus one contributor copy.

Tips: "Writers should keep in mind that *Shooting Star Review* regularly reprints classic fiction about the black experience. From modern writers, we look for innovative, well structured, challenging, even controversial, creative writing. Short fiction is most open to freelancers. We get very excited about innovative subject treatment by writers who understand the elements of fine writing and demonstrate familiarity with the specific needs of short fiction."

THE SHORT STORY REVIEW, Box 882108, San Francisco CA 94188. Publisher/Editor: Dwight Gabbard. 80% freelance written. Works with a small number of new/unpublished writers each year; eager to work with new/unpublished writers. Literary tabloid magazine published 4 times/year. "*Short Story Review* offers a forum for issues of concern to short story writers, offering interviews, reviews and essays. *Short Story Review* also publishes short fiction." Circ. 2,000. Publishes ms an average of 3 months after acceptance. Not copyrighted. Acquires first North American serial rights and second serial (reprint) rights. Photocopied and simultaneous submissions OK. Computer printout submissions OK; prefers letter-quality. Reports in 3 weeks on queries; 3 months on mss. Sample copy $2.50; writer's guidelines for #10 SASE.

Nonfiction: Interviews with prominent short story writers and book reviews. Publishes 4-6 interviews/year. "We need book reviewers—we review only short story collections and anthologies, so the reviewer should have some background." Query. Length: 2,000-3,000 words. Pays $20/page, $180 maximum for interviews only. "No pay for reviews;" pays for reviews only in copies.

Fiction: Stephen Woodhams, fiction editor. Literary. No science fiction, fantasy or erotica. Send complete ms. Length: 500-4,000 words. Pays in copies and a one-year subscription.

Tips: "We welcome all kinds of stories as long as they are well-crafted, convincing and, in some way, needing to be told. Though we keep an open mind, we tend to prefer stories with a strong narrative line and focus. We are not much given to stories based on a clever idea, a trick ending, or elaborate plotting if the other elements of short story writing are neglected."

SING HEAVENLY MUSE!, Women's Poetry and Prose, Sing Heavenly Muse! Inc., Box 13299, Minneapolis MN 55414. (612)822-8713. 100% freelance written. Prefers to work with published/established writers; eager to work with new/unpublished writers. A semi-annual journal of women's literature. Circ. 1,500. Pays on publication. Publishes ms an average of 6 months after acceptance. Byline given. Buys first North American serial rights. Photocopied submissions OK. Computer printout submissions acceptable; prefers letter-quality. Reports in 3 months. Sample copy $3.50; writer's guidelines for #10 SASE.

Fiction: Women's literature, journal pieces, memoir. Buys 15-20 mss/year. Length: 5,000 words maximum. Pays $15-25; contributors receive 2 free copies.

Poetry: Avant-garde, free verse, haiku, light verse and traditional. Accepts 75-100 poems/year. No limit on length. Pays $15-25.

Tips: "To meet our needs, writing must be feminist and women-centered. We read manuscripts generally in April and September. Issues are often related to a specific theme; writer should always query for guidelines and upcoming themes before submitting manuscripts. We occasionally hold contests. Writers should query for contest guidelines."

THE SOUTHERN REVIEW, 43 Allen Hall, Louisiana State University, Baton Rouge LA 70803. (504)388-5108. Editors: James Olney and Fred Hobson. 75% freelance written. Works with a moderate number of new/unpublished writers each year. Quarterly magazine for academic, professional, literary, intellectual audience. Circ. 3,300. Buys first serial rights only. Byline given. Pays on publication. Publishes ms an average of 18 months after acceptance. No queries. Computer printout submissions acceptable; prefers letter-quality. Reports in 2 to 3 months. Sample copy $5. Writer's guidelines for #10 SASE.

Nonfiction: Essays with careful attention to craftsmanship and technique and to seriousness of subject matter. "Willing to publish experimental writing if it has a valid artistic purpose. Avoid extremism and sensationalism. Essays exhibit thoughtful and sometimes severe awareness of the necessity of literary standards in our time." Emphasis on contemporary literature, especially Southern culture and history. Minimum number of footnotes. Buys 80-100 mss/year. Length: 4,000-10,000 words. Pays $12/page for prose.

Fiction and Poetry: Short stories of lasting literary merit, with emphasis on style and technique. Length: 4,000-8,000 words. Pays $12/page for prose; $20/page for poetry.

SOUTHWEST REVIEW, 6410 Airline Rd., Southern Methodist University, Dallas TX 75275. (214)373-7440. Editor: Willard Spiegelman. 100% freelance written. Works with a small number of new/unpublished writers each year. Quarterly magazine for "adults and college graduates with literary interests and some interest in the Southwest, but subscribers are from all over America and some foreign countries." Circ. 1,400. Pays on publication. Publishes ms an average of 1 year after acceptance. Buys first North American serial rights. Computer printout submissions acceptable; prefers letter-quality. Byline given. Buys 65 mss/year. Reports immediately or within 3 months. Sample copy $5.
Nonfiction: "Literary essays, social and political problems, history (especially Southwestern), folklore (especially Southwestern), the arts, etc. Articles should be appropriate for literary quarterly; no feature stories. Critical articles should consider writer's whole body of work, not just one book. History should use new primary sources or new perspective, not syntheses of old material." Interviews with writers, historical articles. Query. Length: 3,500-7,000 words.
Fiction: No limitations on subject matter for fiction; high literary quality is only criterion. Prefers stories of experimental and mainstream. Submit complete ms. Length: 1,500-7,000 words. The John H. McGinnis Memorial Award of $1,000 made in alternate years for fiction and nonfiction pieces that appeared in *SWR* during preceding two years.
Poetry: No limitations on subject matter. Not particularly interested in broadly humorous, religious, or sentimental poetry. Free verse, some avant-garde forms; open to all serious forms of poetry. "There are no arbitrary limits on length, but we find shorter poems are easier to fit into our format." The Elizabeth Matchett Stover Memorial Award of $100 made annually for a poem published in *SWR*.
Tips: "The most frequent mistakes we find in work that is submitted for consideration are lack of attention to grammar and syntax and little knowledge of the kind of thing we're looking for. Writers should look at a couple of issues before submitting."

‡SPECTRUM, Spectrum/Anna Maria College. Box 72-F, Sunset Lane, Paxton MA 01612. (617)757-4586. Editor: Robert H. Goepfert. Managing Editor: Susan McMurray-Anderson. A literary magazine, "*Spectrum* is a multidisciplinary national publication aimed particularly at scholarly generalists affiliated with small liberal arts colleges." Circ. 1,000. Pays on publication. Publishes ms an average of 6 months after acceptance. Byline given. Publication copyrighted. Buys first North American serial rights. Photocopied submissions OK. Computer printout submissions OK; prefers letter-quality. Reports in 3 weeks on queries; 6 weeks on ms. Sample copy $3. Writer's guidelines for #10 SASE.
Nonfiction: Louise N. Soldani, articles editor. Essays, general interest, historical/nostalgic, inspirational, opinion and interdisciplinary. Buys 8 mss/year. Send complete ms. Length: 3,000-15,000 words. Pays $20 for unsolicited articles. State availability of photos with submission. Prints (8x10) b&w only. Offers no additional payment for photos accepted with ms. Model releases and identification of subjects required. Buys one-time rights.
Columns/Departments: Sandra Rasmussen, reviews & correspondence editor. Reviews (books/recordings/audio-visual aids), 300-500 words; (educational computer software), up to 2,000 words. Buys 2 mss/year. Send complete ms. Length: 300-2,000 words. Pays $20.
Fiction: Joseph Wilson, fiction editor. Ethnic, experimental, fantasy, historical, humorous, mainstream, romance and slice-of-life vignettes. "No erotica, mystery, western or science fiction." Buys 2 ms/year. Send complete ms. Length: 3,000 words. Pays $20.
Poetry: Joseph Wilson, poetry editor. Avant-garde, free verse, light verse and traditional. No long poems (over 100 lines). Buys 8 poems/year. Submit maximum 6 poems.
Tips: "We welcome short fiction and poetry, as well as short to medium-length articles that are interdisciplinary or that deal with one discipline in a manner accessible to the scholarly-generalist reader. Articles referring to or quoting work of other authors should be footnoted appropriately. All areas are equally open to freelancers. In general, originality and relative brevity are paramount, although we will occasionally publish longer works [e.g., articles] that explore ideas not subject to a briefer treatment."

STAR*LINE, Newsletter of the Science Fiction Poetry Association, Science Fiction Poetry Association, Box 1764, Cambridge MA 02238. (617)547-6533. Editor: Elissa Malcohn. 95% freelance written. Eager to work with new/unpublished writers. A bimonthly newsletter covering science fiction, fantasy, horror poetry for association members. Circ. 200. Pays on acceptance. Byline given. Buys one-time rights. Submit seasonal/holiday material 3 months in advance. Photocopied submissions OK. Computer printout submissions acceptable; prefers letter-quality. Reports in 1 month. Sample copy for $1.50 and 5½x8½ SAE and 2 first class stamps; writer's guidelines for #10 SASE.
Nonfiction: Articles must display familiarity with the genre. How to (write a poem); interview/profile (of science fiction, fantasy and horror poets); opinion (science fiction and poetics); and essays. Buys 4-6 mss/year. Send complete ms. Length: 500-2,000 words. Pays $1-5 plus complimentary copy.

Columns/Department: Reviews (books, chapbooks, magazines, collections of science fiction, fantasy or horror poetry) 50-500 words; and Markets (current markets for science fiction, fantasy or horror poetry) 20-100 words. Buys 40-60 mss/year. Send complete ms. Pays 50¢-$2.

Poetry: Avant-garde, free verse, haiku, light verse and traditional. "Poetry must be related to speculative fiction subjects." Buys 60-80 poems/year. Submit maximum 3 poems. Length: 1-100 lines. Pays $1 for first 10 lines; 5¢/line thereafter plus complimentary copy.

Fillers: Speculative-oriented quotations—prose or poetic. Length: 10-50 words. Pays $1.

STONE COUNTRY, A Magazine of Poetry, Reviews & Graphics, The Nathan Mayhew Seminars of Martha's Vineyard, Box 132, Menemsha MA 02552. (617)693-5832 or (617)645-2829. Editor: Judith Neeld. 98% freelance written. Prefers to work with published/established writers. A semiannual literary magazine. "We look on poetry as disquisition, not exposition. This is not a journal for beginners. Our purpose is to be an outlet for achieving poets whose work deserves serious and growing attention." Circ. 800. Pays on publication. Publishes ms an average of 2-10 months after acceptance. Byline given. Buys one-time rights. Photocopied submissions OK; simultaneous submissions OK if notified. Computer printout submissions acceptable; no dot-matrix. Reports in 1 week on queries; about 2 months on manuscripts. Sample copy $4; writer's guidelines for #10 SASE.

Nonfiction: Judith Neeld, editor (for essays, reviews, and interview/profiles). Essays (on elements of poetry, currently and historically, only); interview/profile (of current notable poets only); and reviews of poetry books. Buys 2-4 mss/year. Send complete ms. Length: 1,500-2,500 words. Pays $15-25. Poetry contributors receive 1 complimentary copy.

Columns/Departments: Commentary (essays on contemporary poetry and/or poetry from an historical perspective as it relates to contemporary poetry. "Not a column as such, but the section is published in each issue.") Buys 2 mss/year. Send complete ms. Length: 1,500-2,500 words. Pays $15-25.

Poetry: Avant-garde, free verse and traditional. "No light verse or poetry on a soap box." Buys 100-150 poems/year. Submit maximum 5 poems. Length: 5-40 lines. Pays 1 contributor copy.

Tips: "We are most open to poets and their poetry, but welcome reviews and essays of mature quality. Please read a sample copy before submitting."

STORIES, 14 Beacon St., Boston MA 02108. Editor: Amy R. Kaufman. 80% freelance written. Occasionally elects to direct revisions of promising manuscripts. Quarterly magazine publishing short fiction. "It is designed to encourage the writing of stories that evoke an emotional response—for which, the editor believes, there is a demand." Circ. 5,000. Pays on publication. Publishes ms an average of 2 months after acceptance. Byline given. Buys first North American serial rights. Photocopied and simultaneous submissions OK (if so marked). Computer printout submissions acceptable; no dot-matrix. Reports in 10 weeks on mss when possible but disclaims responsibility for delay. Does not answer queries; resubmit if concerned. Simultaneous submissions OK if marked. Sample copy $4 or two for $6 (postpaid); writer's guidelines for #10 SASE.

Fiction: Contemporary, ethnic, historical (general), humor/satire, literary, serialized/excerpted novel and translations. "Ordinarily, romance, mystery, fantasy, political pieces and science fiction do not suit our purposes, but we will not exclude any story on the basis of genre; we wish only that the piece be the best of its genre." Buys 30-36 mss/year. Send complete ms. No queries. Length: 750-15,000 words; 4,000-7,000 words average. Pays $150 minimum.

Tips: "We look for characters identifiable not by name, age, profession, or appearance, but by symbolic qualities; timeless themes and styles that are sophisticated but not affected, straightforward but not artless, descriptive but not nearsighted."

‡THE SUN, A Magazine Of Ideas, The Sun Publishing Company, Inc., 412 W. Rosemary St., Chapel Hill NC 27516. (919)942-5282. Editor: Sy Safransky. 75% freelance written. Monthly magazine. Circ. 10,000. Pays on publication. Publishes ms an average of 2 months after acceptance. Byline given. Buys first-rights. Photocopied and previously published submissions OK. Reports in 1 month. Sample copy $3, 9x12 SAE and 3 first class stamps; writer's guidelines for #10 SASE.

Nonfiction: General interest. Buys 40 mss/year. Send complete ms. Length: 10,000 words maximum. Pays $100 plus copies and a subscription.

Photos: Send photos with submissions. Offers $25 for photos accepted with ms. Model releases required. Buys one-time rights.

Fiction: General. Buys 15 mss/year. Send complete ms. Length: 10,000 words maximum. Pays $100.

Poetry: General. Buys 25 poems/year. Submit maximum 6 poems. Length: open. Pays $25.

Tips: "We're interested in any writing that makes sense and enriches our common space."

‡TAMPA REVIEW, Humanities Division, University of Tampa, Box 19F, Tampa FL 33606. (813)253-3333. Editor of Fiction: Andy Solomon. Editors of Poetry: Don Morrill; Kathy Van Spanckeren. 100% freelance written. Annual magazine of literary fiction and poetry. Estab. 1988. Circ. 5,000. Pays on publication. Publishes ms an average of 4 months after acceptance. Byline given. Buys first North American serial rights. Photocopied submissions OK. Computer printout submissions OK; prefers letter-quality. Reports in 6 weeks

Close-up

Amy Kaufman
Editor
Stories

Photo by Charles White

"Until the late 1940s, America, important in the development of the short story, had several profitable short story
magazines," says Amy Kaufman, editor of *Stories*, a quarterly magazine that publishes short fiction. "Since then,"
she continues, "short stories have appeared less often in
popular magazines, and the literary journals that carry
them struggle to survive."

Stories, a successor to the short story magazines that enjoyed great popularity in the 30s
and 40s, publishes literature of a very high quality. "It is designed to encourage the writing of
stories that evoke an emotional response—for which there is a demand," the editor believes.

Some writers ask what differentiates the short story from longer pieces of fiction. Kaufman says: A short story is like a song, a novel is like an opera.

Kaufman's *Stories* provides a good market for today's short stories. They do not exclude
any story on the basis of genre, but look for pieces that are the best examples of the genre.

She looks for a short story that is "good on the first reading and even better on the second
and third readings, but fiction of this caliber is rare." Of the approximately 8,000 submissions she receives annually, she uses only 30 to 36. "We (assistant Tara Masih and herself)
rarely comment on a story that is not accepted, but we give plenty of advice when a story is accepted on speculation. We expect the author to be willing to spend an hour to correct two
words, if necessary. Editing is often more difficult than the writing itself and may determine
whether a story will be published or not," she says.

It was particularly exciting to Kaufman when John Updike selected a story from *Stories* for
Best American Short Stories, and also when William Abrahams chose a story for the
O. Henry Awards anthology. "But it is just as rewarding to receive letters from subscribers
commenting on stories they have enjoyed," she says. "Writers and editors are often isolated,
and it's good to realize that the words we write and publish actually connect us to the world."

Kaufman advises writers to learn to "write a slow and careful first draft, allowing yourself
to discover the hidden possibilities of the story. In this way you will minimize revision and
avoid blocking that can result from overplanning. Don't underestimate the importance of
spending many hours at the task; you must respect the enormity of the undertaking and the tremendous value of the results in order to give your writing priority. Write for yourself, but realize that you are communicating to another and provide all the necessary information. Actually, you are writing *for* others, to help humanity in the way you know best." She also recommends "recognize great writing and expect no less of yourself."

—*Deborah Cinnamon*

on mss. Sample copy $5; writer's guidelines for 9x12 SAE with 2 first class stamps.

Fiction: Experimental, mainstream. "We are far more concerned with quality than genre." Buys 3-6 mss/year. Send complete ms. Length: 1,000-6,000 words. Pays $10/printed page.

Poetry: Buys 30 poems/year. Submit up to 5 poems at one time. Pays $10/printed page.

‡**TARA'S LITERARY ARTS JOURNAL**, Anastacia Press, Box 834, Bethel Park PA 15102-9998. Editor: Stacey A. Harris. 100% freelance written. Quarterly magazine featuring poetry, short stories, essays and plays. "We prefer literature which will have a religious or social impact." Estab. 1987. Circ. 300. Pays on publication. Publishes ms an average of 3 months after acceptance. Byline given. 100% kill fee. Buys one-time rights. Submit seasonal/holiday material 4 months in advance. Simultaneous, photocopied and previously published submissions OK. Computer printout submissions OK. Reports in 1 month. Sample copy $2; writer's guidelines for #10 SAE with 1 first class stamp.

Nonfiction: Essays. Send complete ms. Length: 500-1,500 words. Pays $10 and 1 contributor's copy. Sometimes pays writer's in contributor's copies or other premiums.

Fiction: Ethnic, experimental, religious. No erotica, horror, trite or light verse. Buys 3 mss/year. Send complete ms. Length: 500-1,500 words. Pays $10 and 1 contributor copy.

Poetry: Avant-garde, free verse, traditional. "No smut, horror, erotica." Buys 80 poems/year. Submit up to 1 poem at a time. Pays in contributor's copies.

Tips: "We have a good mix of new and experienced writers and poets."

THE THREEPENNY REVIEW, Box 9131, Berkeley CA 94709. (415)849-4545. Editor: Wendy Lesser. 100% freelance written. Works with small number of new/unpublished writers each year. A quarterly literary tabloid. "We are a general interest, national literary magazine with coverage of politics, the visual arts and the performing arts as well." Circ. 8,000. Pays on acceptance. Publishes ms an average of 12 months after acceptance. Byline given. Buys first North American serial rights. Photocopied submissions OK. Computer printout submissions OK; prefers letter-quality. Reports in 1 month on queries; 2 months on mss. Sample copy for 9x12 SAE, 5 first class stamps and $4; writer's guidelines for SASE.

Nonfiction: Essays, expose, historical, interview/profile, personal experience, book, film, theater, dance, music and art reviews. Buys 40 mss/year. Query with or without published clips, or send complete ms. Length: 1,500-4,000 words. Pays $50.

Fiction: No fragmentary, sentimental fiction. Buys 10 mss/year. Send complete ms. Length: 800-4,000 words. Pays $50.

Poetry: Free verse and traditional. No poems "without capital letters or poems without a discernible subject." Buys 30 poems/year. Submit maximum 10 poems. Pays $50.

Tips: Nonfiction (political articles, reviews) is most open to freelancers.

THRESHOLD OF FANTASY, Fandom Unlimited Enterprises, Box 70868, Sunnyvale CA 94086. (415)960-1151. Editor: Randall D. Larson. 95% freelance written. "Semi-backlogged—willing to consider unsolicited submissions from new/unpublished writers but being *very* selective." A magazine published irregularly (1-2 issues/year) covering horror, fantasy, and science fiction in literature and interviews with new and notable writers/artists. Circ. 1,000. Pays 50% on acceptance, 50% on publication. Publishes ms an average of 2 years after acceptance. Byline given. Offers 50% kill fee. Buys first North American serial rights. Photocopied submissions OK. Query for electronic submissions. Computer printout submissions acceptable; prefers letter-quality. Simultaneous submissions not considered. Submissions without SASE not considered. Reports in 3 weeks on queries; 6 weeks on mss. Sample copy $3.50; writer's guidelines for #10 SASE.

Nonfiction: Interview/profile and reviews. Buys 4 mss/year. Query. Length: 1,500-5,000 words for articles; 1,000 words for reviews. Pays $20 for articles; pays in copies for reviews.

Photos: Send photos with submission; required with interview. Offers no additional payment for photos accepted with ms. Identification of subjects required.

Fiction: Fantasy, horror, humorous, mystery and science fiction. "No pastiches of other writers; abstract or 'new wave' writing; stories which *tell* a plot but never *show* the events through effective narrative structure and style; or overly wordy narrations." Buys 30 mss/year. Send complete ms. Length: 500-8,000 words. Pays 1/s¢/word.

Tips: Short stories are most open to freelancers.

TRIQUARTERLY, 2020 Ridge Ave., Northwestern University, Evanston IL 60208. (312)491-3490. Editor: Reginald Gibbons. 70% freelance written. Eager to work with new/unpublished writers. Published 3 times/year. Publishes fiction, poetry, and essays, as well as artwork. Pays on publication. Publishes ms an average of 1 year after acceptance. Buys first serial rights and nonexclusive reprint rights. Computer printout submissions acceptable; no dot-matrix. Reports in 3 months. Study magazine before submitting. Sample copy $4.

Nonfiction: Query before sending essays (no scholarly or critical essays except in special issues).

Fiction and Poetry: No prejudice against style or length of work; only seriousness and excellence are required. Buys 20-50 unsolicited mss/year. Pays $20/page.

UNIVERSITY OF TORONTO QUARTERLY, University of Toronto Press, 63 A St. George Street, Toronto, Ontario M5S 1A6 Canada. Editor-in-Chief: T.H. Adamowski. 66% freelance written. Eager to work with new/unpublished writers. Quarterly magazine restricted to criticism on literature and the humanities for the university community. Pays on publication. Publishes ms an average of 1 year after acceptance. Acquires all rights. Byline given. Photocopied submissions OK. Computer printout submissions acceptable; prefers letter-quality. Sample copy $8.95, SAE and IRCs.
Nonfiction: Scholarly articles on the humanities; literary criticism and intellectual discussion. Buys 12 unsolicited mss/year. Pays $50 maximum.

‡**UNIVERSITY OF WINDSOR REVIEW**, Windsor, Ontario N9B 3P4 Canada. (519)253-4232. Editor: Joseph A. Quinn. Biannual for "the literate layman, the old common reader." Circ. 300 + . Buys first North American serial rights. Reports in 4-6 weeks. Sample copy $5 plus postage. Enclose SAE, IRCs.
Nonfiction: "We publish some articles on literature. I think we reflect competently the Canadian intellectual scene and are equally receptive to contributions from outside the country; I think we are good and are trying to get better." Follow *MLA Style Sheet*. Buys 50 mss/year. Length: about 6,000 words. Pays $25.
Fiction: Alistair MacLeod, department editor. Publishes mainstream prose with open attitude toward themes. Length: 2,000-6,000 words. Pays $25.
Poetry: John Ditsky, department editor. Accepts traditional forms, blank verse, free verse and avant-garde. No epics. Pays $10.

THE VIRGINIA QUARTERLY REVIEW, 1 W. Range, Charlottesville VA 22903. (804)924-3124. Editor: Staige Blackford. 50% freelance written. Quarterly. Pays on publication. Publishes ms an average of 2 years after acceptance. Byline given. Buys first serial rights. Reports in 1 month. Sample copy $5.
Nonfiction: Articles on current problems, economic, historical; and literary essays. Length: 3,000-6,000 words. Pays $10/345-word page.
Fiction: Good short stories, conventional or experimental. Length: 2,000-7,000 words. Pays $10/350-word page. Prizes offered for best short stories and poems published in a calendar year.
Poetry: Generally publishes 15 pages of poetry in each issue. No length or subject restrictions. Pays $1/line.
Tips: Prefers not to see pornography, science fiction or fantasy.

WEBSTER REVIEW, Webster Review, Inc., Webster University, 470 E. Lockwood, Webster Groves MO 63119. (314)432-2657. Editor: Nancy Schapiro. 100% freelance written. A semiannual magazine. "*Webster Review* is an international literary magazine publishing fiction, poetry, essays and translations of writing in those categories. Our subscribers are primarily university and public libraries, and writers and readers of quality fiction and poetry." Circ. 1,000. Pays on publication. Publishes ms an average of 1 year after acceptance. Byline given. Buys first North American serial rights. Simultaneous and photocopied submissions OK. Reports in 6 weeks on manuscripts. Sample copy for 9½x6½ SAE with 4 first class stamps.
Nonfiction: Essays. Send complete ms.
Fiction: Will consider all types of literature. Buys 6 mss/year. Send complete ms. Pays $25-50, (if funds are available).
Poetry: Pamela White Hadas, poetry editor. Buys 100 poems/year. Pays $10-50 (if funds are available).

WEST COAST REVIEW, A Literary Quarterly, West Coast Review Publishing Society, Department of English, Simon Fraser University, Burnaby British Columbia V5A 156 Canada. (604)291-4287. Quarterly magazine covering poetry, fiction, book reviews. "We publish original creative writing regardless of style, subject, etc.; the only criterion is the quality of the writing." Circ. 750. Pays on publication. Publishes ms an average of 8 months after acceptance. Byline given. Buys first North American serial rights. Submit seasonal/holiday material 6 months in advance. Photocopied submissions OK. Computer printout submissions OK; prefers letter-quality. Reports in 2 months. Sample copy $4; writer's guidelines for SAE with 1 Canadian first class stamp or IRC.
Nonfiction: Essays, mainly dealing with literary matters. Buys 15-20 ms/year. Send complete ms. Length: 1,000-5,000 words. Pays $10-15/page for assigned articles; pays $10/page for unsolicited articles.
Photos: State availability of photos with submission. Offers no additional payment for photos accepted with mss. Buys one-time rights.
Fiction: Experimental, mainstream and novel excerpts. Buys 10-12 mss/year. Send complete ms. Length: 2,000-10,000 words. Pays $10-15/page.
Poetry: Avant-garde and traditional. Buys 50-60 poems/year. Submit maximum 10 poems. Length: 4-500 lines. Pays $10-50.

WESTERN HUMANITIES REVIEW, University of Utah, Salt Lake City UT 84112. (801)581-7438. Managing Editor: Elizabeth Tornes. Quarterly magazine for educated readers. Circ. 1,000. Pays on acceptance. Publishes ms an average of 3 months after acceptance. Buys all rights. Phone queries OK. Simultaneous and photocopied submissions OK. Computer printout submissions acceptable; prefers letter-quality. Reports in 1 month.

Nonfiction: Barry Weller, editor-in-chief. Authoritative, readable articles on literature, art, philosophy, current events, history, religion and anything in the humanities. Interdisciplinary articles encouraged. Departments on film and books. "We commission book reviews." Buys 40 unsolicited mss/year. Pays $50-150.
Fiction: Larry Levis, poetry and fiction editor. Any type or theme. Buys 2 mss/issue. Send complete ms. Pays $25-150.
Poetry: Larry Levis, poetry editor. "See magazine. Recent contributors include Joseph Brodsky, Charles Simic, Charles Wright, Carol Muske, David St. John, Thomas Lux."
Tips: "The change in editorial staff will probably mean a slight shift in emphasis. We will probably be soliciting more submissions and relying less on uninvited materials. More poetry and scholarly articles (and perhaps less fiction) may be included in the future."

WIDE OPEN MAGAZINE, Wide Open Press, 116 Lincoln St., Santa Rosa CA 95401. (707)545-3821. Editor: Clif Simms. 80% freelance written. Eager to work with new/unpublished writers. A quarterly magazine covering solutions to current problems. "Our audience consists of students, teachers, writers, counselors, and other thinking, feeling and doing people. We believe that problems can be solved once narrow, shallow attitudes are dispelled." Circ. 500. Pays on publication. Publishes ms an average of 3 months after acceptance. Byline given. Buys one-time rights; may make work-for-hire assignments. Photocopied and previously published submissions OK. Computer printout submissions acceptable. Reports in 1 month. Sample copy $6; writer's guidelines for #10 SASE. "Always send for writer's guidelines before submitting."
Nonfiction: Lynn L. Simms, articles editor. Essays; how-to (solve problems); humor; interview/profile (of people who have solved problems); opinion (will consider); and personal experience (of solving problems). "No illogical or unsupported arguments; no arguments from authority, only." Buys up to 8 mss/year. Query or send complete ms. "No clips or biographies." Length: 500-2,500 words. Pays $5-25.
Fiction: Lynn L. Simms, fiction editor. Adventure, experimental, fantasy, historical, humorous, mainstream, mystery, science fiction, suspense and western. "All fiction must have a strong plot and show the characters solving their own problems. No *Deus ex Machina* plots." Buys 4-8 mss/year. Send complete ms. Length: 2,500 words maximum. Pays $5-25.
Poetry: Lynn L. Simms, poetry editor. Avant-garde, free verse, haiku, light verse and traditional. Buys 800 poems/year. Submit maximum 5 poems. Length: 16 lines maximum. No payment.
Tips: "Be logical and find the root causes of problems. Write for a general audience with common sense. And show or tell the process for reaching solutions, too. All areas are open to freelancers."

THE YALE REVIEW, 1902A Yale Station, New Haven CT 06520. Editor: Kai Erikson. Associate Editor: Penelope Laurans. Managing Editor: Wendy Wipprecht. 20% freelance written. Buys first North American serial rights. Pays on publication. Publishes ms an average of 1 year after acceptance. Computer printout submissions acceptable; no dot-matrix. Writer's guidelines for #10 SASE.
Nonfiction and Fiction: Authoritative discussions of politics, literature and the arts. Buys quality fiction. Pays $100. Length: 3,000-5,000 words.

YELLOW SILK, Journal of Erotic Arts, verygraphics, Box 6374, Albany CA 94706. (415)841-6500. Editor: Lily Pond. 90% freelance written. Prefers to work with published/established writers; works with a small number of new/unpublished writers each year. A quarterly magazine of erotic literature and visual arts. "'Editorial policy: All persuasions; no brutality'. Our publication is artistic and literary, not pornographic or pandering. Humans are involved: heads, hearts and bodies—not just bodies alone; and the quality of the literature is as important as the erotic content." Circ. 13,000. Pays on publication. Publishes ms an average of 6 months after acceptance. Byline given. Buys all publication rights for one year, at which time they revert to author, and reprint and anthology rights for duration of copyright. Photocopied submissions OK. Computer printout submissions acceptable; prefers letter-quality. Reports in 3 months on manuscripts. Sample copy $5.
Nonfiction: Book excerpts, essays, humor and reviews. "We often have theme issues, but non-regularly and usually not announced in advance." No pornography, romance-novel type writing, sex fantasies. No first-person accounts or blow-by-blow descriptions. No articles. No novels." Buys 5-10 mss/year. Send complete ms. All submissions should be typed, double-spaced, with name, address and phone number on each page; always enclose SASE. No specified length requirements. Pays minimum $10 and 3 contributor copies.
Photos: Photos may be submitted independently, not as illustration for submission. Reviews photocopies, contact sheets, transparencies and prints. We accept 4-color and b&w artwork. Offers varying payment for series of 9-12 used, plus copies. Buys one-time rights and reprint rights.
Columns/Departments: Reviews (book, movie, art, dance, food, anything). "Erotic content and how it's handled is focus of importance. Old or new does not matter. Want to bring readers information of what's out there". Buys 8-10 mss/year. Send complete ms or query. Pays minimum of $10 plus copies.
Fiction: Erotica, including ethnic, experimental, fantasy, humorous, mainstream, novel excerpts and science fiction. See "non-fiction." Buys 12-16 mss/year. Send complete ms. Pays minimum of $10 plus copies.
Poetry: Avant-garde, free verse, haiku, light verse and traditional. "No greeting-card poetry." Buys 55-80 poems/year. No limit on number of poems submitted, "but don't send book-length manuscripts." Pays mini-

mum of $5 plus copies.

Tips: "The best way to get into *Yellow Silk* is produce excellent, well-crafted work that approaches erotica with freshness, strength of voice, beauty of language, and insight into character. I'll tell you what I'm sick of and have, unfortunately, been seeing more of lately; the products of "How to Write Erotica" classes. This is not brilliant fiction; it is poorly written fantasy and not what I'm looking for. All stories and poems published in the magazine within a given year become eligible for a $200 prize. Do not submit or query separately."

ZYZZYVA, The Last Word: West Coast Writers and Artists, ZYZZYVA Inc., Suite 1400, 41 Sutter St., San Francisco CA 94104. (415)775-9594. Editor: Howard Junker. 100% freelance written. Works with a small number of new/unpublished writers each year. Quarterly magazine. "We feature work by West Coast writers only. We are essentially a literary magazine, but of wide-ranging interests and a strong commitment to nonfiction." Circ. 3,000. Pays on acceptance. Publishes ms an average of 3 months after acceptance. Byline given. Buys first North American serial rights and one-time anthology rights. Photocopied submissions OK. Computer printout submissions acceptable; prefers letter-quality. Reports in 1 week on queries; 2 weeks on mss. Sample copy $8.

Nonfiction: Book excerpts, general interest, historical/nostalgic, humor and personal experience. Buys 15 mss/year. Query. Length: open. Pays $25-100.

Fiction: Ethnic, experimental, humorous, mainstream and mystery. Buys 20 mss/year. Send complete ms. Length: open. Pays $25-100.

Poetry: Buys 20 poems/year. Submit maximum 5 poems. Length: 3-200 lines. Pays $25-50.

Men's

Men's magazines are becoming more specialized, not general in theme like *Playboy*, and new magazines are showing an increased emphasis on fashion. Magazines that also use material slanted toward men can be found in Business and Finance, Contemporary Culture, Military and Sports sections.

ADAM, Publishers Service, Inc., 8060 Melrose Ave., Los Angeles CA 90046. Monthly for the adult male. General subject: Human sexuality in contemporary society. Circ. 500,000. Buys first North American serial rights. Occasionally overstocked. Pays on publication. Reports in 6 weeks, but occasionally takes longer.

Nonfiction: "On articles, query first. We like hard sex articles, but research must be thorough." Length: 2,500 words. Pays $100-300.

CAVALIER, Suite 204, 2355 Salzedo St., Coral Gables FL 33134. (305)443-2378. Editor: Douglas Allen. 80% freelance written. Works with published/established and new/unpublished writers each year. Monthly magazine for "young males, ages 18-29, 80% college graduates, affluent, intelligent, interested in current events, sex, sports, adventure, travel and good fiction." Circ. 250,000. Pays on publication. Publishes ms an average of 3 months after acceptance. Byline given. Buys first serial and second serial (reprint) rights. Buys 44 or more mss/year. See past issues for general approach to take. Submit seasonal material at least 3 months in advance. Computer printout submissions acceptable; prefers letter-quality. Reports in 3-5 weeks. Writer's guidelines for #10 SAE.

Nonfiction: Personal experience, interview, humor, think pieces, exposé and new product. "Be frank—we are open to dealing with controversial issues. No timely material (have 4 month lead time). Prefers 'unusual' subject matter as well as sex-oriented (but serious) articles." Query. Length: 2,800-3,500 words. Pays maximum $500 with photos. Sometimes pays the expenses of writers on assignment.

Photos: Photos purchased with or without captions. No cheesecake.

Fiction: Nye Willden, department editor. Mystery, science fiction, humorous, adventure, and contemporary problems "with at least one explicit sex scene per story." Send complete ms. Length: 2,500-3,500 words. Pays $250 maximum, higher for special.

Tips: "Our greatest interest is in originality—new ideas, new approaches; no tired, overdone stories—both feature and fiction. We do not deal in 'hack' sensationalism but in high quality pieces. Keep in mind the intelligent 18- to 29-year-old male reader. We will be putting more emphasis in articles and fiction on sexual themes. We prefer serious articles. Pornography—fiction can be very imaginative and sensational."

CHIC MAGAZINE, Larry Flynt Publications, Suite 300, 9171 Wilshire Blvd., Beverly Hills CA 90210. Executive Editor: Doug Oliver. 40% freelance written. Prefers to work with published/established writers. Monthly magazine for men, ages 20-35 years, college-educated and interested in current affairs, entertainment and sports. Circ. 100,000. Pays 1 month after acceptance. Publishes ms an average of 3 months after acceptance. Buys all rights. Pays 20% kill fee. Computer printout submissions acceptable; prefers letter-quality. Byline given unless writer requests otherwise. Reports in 2 months. Writer's guidelines for #10 SASE.

Nonfiction: Sex-related topics of current national interest; interview (personalities in news and entertainment); and celebrity profiles. Buys 12-18 mss/year. Query. Length: 4,500 words. Pays $750. Sometimes pays the expenses of writers on assignment.

Columns/Departments: Odds and Ends (front of the book shorts; study the publication first), 100-300 words. Pays $50. Third Degree (short Q&As) columns, 2,000 words. Pays $350.

Fiction: "At present we are buying stories with emphasis on erotic themes. These may be adventure, action, mystery, horror or humorous stories, but the tone and theme must involve sex and eroticism. The erotic nature of the story should not be subordinate to the characterizations and plot; the sex must grow logically from the people and the plot, not be contrived or forced."

Tips: "We do not buy poetry or non-erotic science fiction. Refrain from stories with drug themes, sex with minors, incest and bestiality."

ESQUIRE, 1790 Broadway, New York NY 10019. (212)459-7500. Editor-in-Chief: Lee Eisenberg. 99% freelance written. Monthly. Pays on acceptance. Publishes ms an average of 6 months after acceptance. Usually buys first serial rights. Computer printout submissions acceptable; prefers letter-quality. Reports in 3 weeks. "We depend chiefly on solicited contributions and material from literary agencies. We are unable to accept responsibility for unsolicited material." Query.

Nonfiction: Articles vary in length, but features usually average 3,000-7,000 words. Articles should be slanted for sophisticated, intelligent readers; however, not highbrow in the restrictive sense. Wide range of subject matter. Rates run roughly between $300 and $3,000, depending on length, quality, etc. Sometimes pays expenses of writers on assignment.

Photos: Temple Smith, photo editor. Payment depends on how photo is used, but rates are roughly $300 for b&w; $500-750 for color. Guarantee on acceptance. Buys first periodical publication rights.

Fiction: L. Rust Hills, fiction editor. "Literary excellence is our only criterion." Discourages genre fiction (horror, science fiction, murder mystery, etc.). Length: about 1,000-6,000 words. Payment: $1,000-5,000.

Tips: The writer sometimes has a better chance of breaking in at *Esquire* with short, lesser-paying articles and fillers (rather than with major features) "because we need more short pieces."

‡FLING, Relim Publishing Col, Inc., 550 Miller Ave., Mill Valley CA 94941. (415)383-5464. Editor: Arv Miller. Managing Editor: Ted Albert. 30% freelance written. Prefers to work with published/established writers; works with a small number of new/unpublished writers each year. Bimonthly magazine of men's sophisticate field. Young male audience of adults ages 18-34. Sexual-oriented field. Circ. 100,000. Pays on acceptance. Publishes ms an average of 3 months after acceptance. Buys first North American serial rights and second serial (reprint) rights; makes work-for-hire assignments. Submit seasonal/holiday material 8 months in advance. Computer printout submissions acceptable; prefers letter-quality. Does not consider multiple submissions. Reports in 1 week on queries; 2 weeks on mss. Sample copy $4; writer's guidelines for SAE and 1 first class stamp.

Nonfiction: Exposé, how-to (better relationships with women, better lovers); interview/profile; personal experience; photo feature; and taboo sex articles. Buys 15 mss/year. Query. Length: 1,500-3,000 words. Pays $150-250. Sometimes pays expenses of writers on assignment.

Photos: Send photos with query. Reviews b&w contact sheets and 8x10 prints; 35mm color transparencies. Pays $10-25 for b&w; $20-35 for color. Model releases required. Buys one-time rights.

Columns/Departments: Buys 12 mss/year. Query or send complete ms. Length: 100-200 words. Pays $15-125.

Fiction: Confession, erotica and sexual. No science fiction, western, plotless, private-eye, "dated," or adventure. Buys 20 mss/year. Send complete ms. Length: 2,000-3,000 words. Pays $135-200.

Fillers: Clippings. Buys 50/year. Length: 100-500 words. Pays $5-15.

Tips: "Nonfiction and fiction are wide open areas to freelancers. Always query with one-page letter to the editor before proceeding with any writing. Also send a sample photocopy of published material, similar to suggestion."

GALLERY MAGAZINE, Montcalm Publishing Corp., 800 2nd Ave., New York NY 10017. (212)986-9600. Editorial Director: Marc Lichter. Managing Editor: Barry Janoff. Design Director: Michael Monte. 50% freelance written. Prefers to work with published/established writers. Monthly magazine "focusing on features of interest to the young American man." Circ. 500,000. Pays 50% on acceptance, 50% on publication. Publishes ms an average of 4 months after acceptance. Byline given. Pays 25% kill fee. Buys first North American serial rights; makes work-for-hire assignments. Submit seasonal/holiday material 6 months in advance. Photocopied submissions OK. Computer printout submissions OK; prefers letter-quality. Reports in 1 month on queries; 2 months on mss. Sample copy $3.50 plus $1.75 postage and handling. Free writer's guidelines.

Nonfiction: Investigative pieces, general interest, how-to, humor, interview, new products and profile. "We *do not* want to see pornographic articles." Buys 7-9 mss/issue. Query or send complete mss. Length: 1,000-3,000 words. Pays $200-1,500. "Special prices negotiated." Sometimes pays expenses of writers on assignment.
Photos: Send photos with accompanying mss. Pay varies for b&w or color contact sheets and negatives. Buys one-time rights. Captions preferred; model release required.
Fiction: Adventure, erotica, experimental, humorous, mainstream, mystery and suspense. Buys 1 mss/issue. Send complete ms. Length: 1,000-3,000 words. Pays $350-1,000.

‡GEM, G&S Publications, 1472 Broadway, New York NY 10036. (212)840-7224. Editor: Will Martin. Managing Editor: R.B. Kendennis. 70% freelance written. Bimonthly magazine. Pays when ms is assigned to a specific issue.
Nonfiction: Sex-related but nonpornographic articles. Pays $50-100. Length: 700-2,000 words.
Fiction: Sex-related but nonpornographic. Same length as above. Pays $50-100.
Tips: "We do not use explicit, graphic descriptions of sex acts or manuscripts with violence. Humor, satire and spoofs of sexual subjects that other magazines treat seriously are welcome."

GENT, Suite 204, 2355 Salzedo St., Coral Gables FL 33134. (305)443-2378. Editor: Bruce Arthur. 75% freelance written. Prefers to work with published/established writers. Monthly magazine for men from every strata of society who enjoy big breasted, full-figured females. Circ. 200,000. Buys first North American serial rights. Byline given. Pays on publication. Publishes ms an average of 2 months after acceptance. Computer printout submissions acceptable; prefers letter-quality. Reports in 6 weeks. Sample copy $5; writer's guidelines for #10 SASE.
Nonfiction: Looking for traditional men's subjects (cars, racing, outdoor adventure, science, gambling, etc.) as well as sex-related topics. Query first. Length: 2,000-3,500 words. Buys 70 mss/year. Pays $100-250.
Photos: B&W photos and color transparencies purchased with mss. Captions (preferred).
Fiction: Erotic. "Stories should contain a huge-breasted female character, as this type of model is *Gent*'s main focus. And this character's endowments should be described in detail in the course of the story." Submit complete ms. No fiction queries. Length: 2,000-4,000 words. Pays $100-200.
Tips: "Our efforts to make *Gent* acceptable to Canadian censors as a condition for exportation to that country have forced some shifting of editorial focus. Toward this end, we have de-emphasized our editorial coverage of pregnancy, lactation, anal intercourse and all forms of sadism and masochism. Study sample copies of the magazine before trying to write for it. We like custom-tailored stories and articles."

GENTLEMEN'S QUARTERLY, Condé Nast, 350 Madison Ave., New York NY 10017. (212)880-8800. Editor-in-Chief: Arthur Cooper. Managing Editor: Eliot Kaplan. 60% freelance written. Circ. 607,000. Monthly magazine emphasizing fashion, general interest and service features for men ages 25-45 with a large discretionary income. Pays on acceptance. Byline given. Pays 25% kill fee. Submit seasonal/holiday material 6 months in advance. Computer printout submissions acceptable; prefers letter-quality. Reports in 1 month.
Nonfiction: Politics, personality profiles, lifestyles, trends, grooming, nutrition, health and fitness, sports, travel, money, investment and business matters. Buys 4-6 mss/issue. Query with published clips. Length: 1,500-4,000 words. Pays $750-3,000.
Columns/Departments: Eliot Kaplan, managing editor. Body & Soul (fitness, nutrition and grooming); Money (investments); Going in Style (travel); Health; Music; Tech (consumer electronics); Dining In (food); Wine & Spirits; Humor; Fiction; Games (sports); Books; The Male Animal (essays by men on life); and All About Adam (nonfiction by women about men). Buys 5-8/issue. Query with published clips or submit complete ms. Length: 1,000-2,500 words. Pays $750-2,000.
Tips: "Major features are usually assigned to well-established, known writers. Pieces are almost always solicited. The best way to break in is through the columns, especially Male Animal, All About Adam, Games, Health or Humor."

HIGH SOCIETY, High Society, 801 2nd Ave., New York NY 10017. (212)661-7878. Editor: Louis Montesano. Managing Editor: Ken Kimmel. Articles Editor: Stephen Loshiavo. 80% freelance written. Monthly magazine of erotic adult entertainment. Circ. 300,000. Pays on acceptance. Publishes ms an average of 4 months after acceptance. Byline given. Makes work-for-hire assignments. Submit seasonal/holiday material 6 months in advance. Computer printout submissions acceptable; no dot-matrix. Reports in 2 weeks. Sample copy $3.95; free writer's guidelines.
Nonfiction: Expose (political/entertainment); how-to (sexual, self-help); humor (bawdy); interview/profile (sports, music, politics); opinion (sexual subjects); and personal experience (sexual). Query with published clips. Length: 1,000-1,500 words. Pays $200 minimum. Sometimes pays expenses of writers on assignment.
Photos: State availability of photos or send photo with query. Reviews 1" color transparencies. Model release and identification of subjects required.
Columns/Departments: Silver Spoonfuls: Newsbits, health, reviews. Buys 50 mss/year. Query with

published clips. Length: 250-1,000 words. Pays $200-400.

Fiction: Confession (sex oriented), erotica and humorous (sex oriented). Buys 12 mss/year. Query with published clips. Length: 1,000-1,500 words. Pays $150-250.

MAGNA, Fashion & Lifestyle Magazine for Big & Tall Men, The Magna Corp., Box 286, Cabin John MD 20818. (301)320-2745. Editor: Jack Shulman. Managing Editor: Marlene Salomon. A quarterly magazine for big and tall men. "We deal with problems particular to large men and to universal interests and problems." Circ. 120,000. Pays on publication. Publishes ms an average of 7 months after acceptance. Byline given. Buys first rights. Submit seasonal/holiday material 9 months in advance. Simultaneous and photocopied submissions OK. Computer printout submissions OK; prefers letter-quality. Reports in 2 months on queries; 2 weeks on mss. Sample copy $3.50 with 7 first class stamps.

Nonfiction: General interest, how-to, humor, interview/profile, personal experience and travel. No fiction or any article that does not treat big or tall men sympathetically. Buys 16 mss/year. Send complete ms. Length: 250-2,500 words. Pays $150-275.

Photos: State availability of photos with submission. Reviews 35mm transparencies. Offers no additional payment for photos accepted with ms. Model releases and identification of subjects required. Buys one-time rights.

Columns/Departments: Gerry Green, column/department editor. Toys for Big Boys (new products of interest), 50-150 words. Buys 24 mss/year. Send complete ms. Length: 50-150 words. Pays $25-100.

Fillers: Facts about big and tall men. Buys 12/year. Length: 75-300 words. Pays $25-60.

NUGGET, Suite 204, 2355 Salzedo St., Coral Gables FL 33134. (305)443-2378. Editor: Jerome Slaughter. 75% freelance written. Magazine "primarily devoted to fetishism." Pays on publication. Publishes ms an average of 2 months after acceptance. Byline given. Buys first North American serial rights. Computer printout submissions acceptable; prefers letter-quality. Reports in 6 weeks. Sample copy $5; writer's guidelines for SASE.

Nonfiction: Articles on fetishism—every aspect. Buys 20-30 mss/year. Submit complete ms. Length: 2,000-4,000 words. Pays $100-200.

Photos: Erotic pictorials of women and couples—essay types in fetish clothing (leather, rubber, underwear, etc.) or women wrestling or boxing other women or men, preferably semi-nude or nude. Captions or short accompanying ms desirable. Reviews color transparencies or b&w photos.

Fiction: Erotic and fetishistic. Should be oriented to *Nugget*'s subject matter. Length: 2,000-4,000 words. Pays $100-200.

Tips: "We require queries on articles only, and the letter should be a brief synopsis of what the article is about. Originality in handling of subject is very helpful. It is almost a necessity for a freelancer to study our magazine first, be knowledgeable about the subject matter we deal with and able to write explicit and erotic fetish material."

OPTIONS, The Bi-Monthly, AJA Publishing, Box 470, Port Chester NY 10573. (914)939-2111. Editor: Don Stone. Assistant Editor: Diana Sheridan. Mostly freelance written. Sexually explicit magazine for and about bisexuals and homosexuals, published 10 times/year. "Articles, stories and letters about bisexuality. Positive approach. Safe-sex encounters unless the story clearly pre-dates the AIDS situation." Circ. 100,000. Pays on publication. Publishes ms an average of 4-8 months after acceptance. Byline given. Buys all rights. Submit seasonal/holiday material 6-8 months in advance; buys very little seasonal material. Photocopied submissions OK. Computer printout submissions OK. Reports in 3 weeks. Sample copy $2.95 with 6x9 SAE and 5 first class stamps. Writer's guidelines for SASE.

Nonfiction: Essays (occasional), how-to, humor, interview/profile, opinion and (especially) personal experience. All must be bisexually related. Does not want "anything not bisexually related, anything negative, anything opposed to safe sex, anything dry/boring/ponderous/pedantic; write even serious topics informally if not lightly." Buys 70 mss/year. Send complete ms. Length: 2,000-3,000. Pays $100.

Photos: Reviews transparencies and prints. Pays $10 for b&w photos; $200 for full color. Previously published photos acceptable.

Fiction: "We don't usually get enough true first-person stories and need to buy some from writers. They must be bisexual, usually man/man, hot and believable. They must not read like fiction." Buys 60 ms/year. Send complete ms. Length: 2,000-3,000. Pays $100.

Tips: "We use many more male/male pieces than female/female. Use only 1 serious article per issue. A serious/humorous approach is good here, but only if it's natural to you; don't make an effort for it. We use some serious/hot pieces too."

PLAYBOY, 919 N. Michigan, Chicago IL 60611. 50% freelance written. Prefers to work with published/established writers; works with a small number of new/unpublished writers each year. Monthly. Pays on acceptance. Publishes ms an average of 6 months after acceptance. Offers 20% kill fee. Buys first serial rights and others. Computer printout submissions acceptable; prefers letter-quality. Reports in 1 month. Writer's guidelines for #10 SASE.

Nonfiction: John Rezek, articles editor. "We're looking for timely, topical pieces. Articles should be carefully researched and written with wit and insight. Little true adventure or how-to material. Check magazine for subject matter. Pieces on outstanding contemporary men, sports, politics, sociology, business and finance, music, science and technology, games, all areas of interest to the contemporary urban male." Query. Length: 3,000-5,000 words. Pays $3,000 minimum. *Playboy* interviews run between 10,000 and 15,000 words. After getting an assignment, the freelancer outlines the questions, conducts and edits the interview, and writes the introduction. Pays $5,000 minimum. For interviews contact G. Barry Golson, Executive Editor, 747 3rd Ave., New York NY 10017. Pays expenses of writers on assignment.

Photos: Gary Cole, photography director, suggests that all photographers interested in contributing make a thorough study of the photography currently appearing in the magazine. Generally all photography is done on assignment. While much of this is assigned to *Playboy*'s staff photographers, approximately 50% of the photography is done by freelancers, and *Playboy* is in constant search of creative new talent. Qualified freelancers are encouraged to submit samples of their work and ideas. All assignments made on an all rights basis with payments scaled from $600/color page for miscellaneous features such as fashion, food and drink, etc.; $300/b&w page; $1,000/color page for girl features; cover, $1,500. Playmate photography for entire project: $10,000-13,000. Assignments and submissions handled by senior editor: Jeff Cohen and associate editors: James Larson and Michael Ann Sullivan, Chicago; Marilyn Grabowski and Linda Kenney, Los Angeles. Assignments made on a minimum guarantee basis. Film, processing, and other expenses necessitated by assignment honored.

Fiction: Alice Turner, fiction editor. Both light and serious fiction. "Entertainment pieces are clever, smoothly written stories. Serious fiction must come up to the best contemporary standards in substance, idea and style. Both, however, should be designed to appeal to the educated, well-informed male reader." General types include comedy, mystery, fantasy, horror, science fiction, adventure, social-realism, "problem" and psychological stories. Fiction lengths are 3,000-6,000 words; short-shorts of 1,000 to 1,500 words are used. Pays $2,000; $1,000 short-short. Rates rise for additional acceptances.

Fillers: Party Jokes are always welcome. Pays $100 each. Also interesting items for Playboy After Hours section (check it carefully before submitting). The After Hours front section pays $75 for humorous or unusual news items (submissions not returned). Send to After Hours editor. Has regular movie, book and record reviewers. Ideas for Playboy Potpourri pay $75. Query to David Stevens, Chicago. Games, puzzles and travel articles should be addressed to New York office.

SCREW, Box 432, Old Chelsea Station, New York NY 10011. Managing Editor: Manny Neuhaus. 95% freelance written. Eager to work with new/unpublished writers. Weekly tabloid newspaper for a predominantly male, college-educated audience; ages 21 through mid-40s. Circ. 125,000. Pays on publication. Publishes ms an average of 3 months after acceptance. Byline given. Buys all rights. Computer printout submissions acceptable; prefers letter-quality. Reports in 3 months. Free sample copy and writer's guidelines.

Nonfiction: "Sexually-related news, humor, how-to articles, first-person and true confessions. Frank and explicit treatment of all areas of sex; outrageous and irreverent attitudes combined with hard information, news and consumer reports. Our style is unique. Writers should check several recent issues." Buys 150-200 mss/year. Submit complete ms for first person, true confession. Length: 1,000-3,000 words. Pays $100-200. Will also consider material for Letter From . . . a consumer-oriented wrap-up of commercial sex scene in cities around the country; and My Scene, a sexual true confession. Length: 1,000-2,500 words. Pays about $40.

Photos: Reviews b&w glossy prints (8x10 or 11x14) purchased with or without manuscripts or on assignment. Pays $10-50.

Tips: "All mss get careful attention. Those written in *Screw* style on sexual topics have the best chance. I anticipate a need for more aggressive, insightful political humor."

TURN-ON LETTERS, AJA Publishing, Box 470, Port Chester NY 10573. Editor: Julie Silver. Magazine published 9 times/year covering sex. "Adult material, must be positive, no pain or degradations. No incest, no underage." Circ. 100,000. Pays on publication. Publishes ms an average of 4-8 months after acceptance. Buys all rights. No byline. No kill fee; "assigned mss are not killed unless they do not fulfill the assignment and/or violate censorship laws." Submit seasonal/holiday material 6 months in advance. Computer printout submissions OK. Reports in 3 weeks. Sample copy $2.50 with 6x9 SAE and 4 first class stamps. Writer's guidelines for #10 SASE.

Fiction: Sexually explicit material in the format of a letter. Buys 441 "letters"/year. Send complete ms. Length: 500-750 words (2-3 typed pages). Pays $15.

Photos: Reviews transparencies and prints. Buys b&w for $10 and full color for $200. Previously published pictures OK. Buys all rights.

Tips: "When you write, be different, be believable."

UNCENSORED LETTERS, Sportomatic Publishers, Box 470, Port Chester NY 10573. Editor: Tammy Simmons. 100% freelance written. Magazine covering sex published nine times/year. "Adult material, must be positive in approach, no pain or degradation. No incest; no underage." Circ. 100,000. Pays on publication.

Publishes ms an average of 4-6 months after acceptance. No byline given. No kill fee; "assigned mss are not killed unless they do not fulfill assignment and/or they violate censorship laws." Buys all rights. Computer printout submissions OK. Reports in 3 weeks. Sample copy $2.95 with 9x12 envelope and 5 first class stamps; writer's guidelines for SASE.

Fiction: Sexually explicit material written as true-to-life in the format of a letter. Buys 594 mss/year. Send complete ms. Length: 300-750 (2-3 typed, double-spaced pages). Pays $15.

Photos: Buys b&w's, $10 each; full color, $200. Previously published photos OK. Buys all rights.

Tips: "Read spec sheet, available for SASE. When you write, be different, yet believable. Manuscripts accepted by *UL* may now be used in our sister magazine, *Turn-On Letters*, and vice-versa. We look to buy a few manuscripts detailing hot 'safe-sex' for each issue."

‡UNIVERSITY MAN, Casual Clothes for Young Americans, University Man Publishing, Inc., Suite #210, 292 S. La Cienega Blvd., Beverly Hills CA 90211. (213)855-0605. Editorial Director: Michael Romanello. Monthly magazine of casual fashion. "*University Man* features casual and active clothing for young men. Editorial features and interviews supplement this fashion approach." Estab. 1987. Circ. 90,000. Pays on publication. Publishes ms an average of 3 months after acceptance. Byline given. Submit seasonal/holiday material 6 months in advance. Simultaneous submissions OK. Sample copy $4.95; free writer's guidelines.

Nonfiction: Essays, expose, general interest, how-to, humor, interview/profile, new product, photo feature, travel. No pornography, ordinary exposes, or technical articles, etc. Buys 20 mss/year. Query with published clips. Length: 1,000-2,000 words. Pays $250-500. Sometimes pays expenses of writers on assignment.

Photos: Send photos with submission. Reviews contact sheets, transparencies (4x5) and prints (8x10). Captions, model releases and identification of subjects required. Buys all rights.

Columns/Departments: Free Wheeling (cars, motorcycles, etc.) 500-1,000 words; Entertainment, 500-1,000 words; Sights and Sounds (audio-visual) 500-1,000 words. Buys 36 mss/year. Query with published clips or send complete ms. Length: 500-1,000 words. Pays $100-250.

Fiction: Adventure, fantasy, horror, mystery, romance, science fiction, slice-of-life vignettes, suspense, western. Buys 6-8 mss/year. Query with published clips. Length: 1,000-2,000 words. Pays $150-250.

Tips: "Send queries with interesting ideas that our readers would appreciate reading. We cater to a young audience. Feature articles and interviews are always needed."

Military

These publications emphasize military or paramilitary subjects or other aspects of military life. Technical and semitechnical publications for military commanders, personnel and planners, as well as those for military families and civilians interested in Armed Forces activities are listed here.

AMERICAN SURVIVAL GUIDE, McMullen Publishing, Inc., 2145 W. La Palma Ave., Anaheim CA 92801. (714)635-9040. Editor: Jim Benson. 50% freelance written. Monthly magazine covering "self-reliance, defense, meeting day-to-day and possible future threats—survivalism for survivalists." Circ. 89,000. Pays on publication. Publishes ms up to 1 year after acceptance. Byline given. Submit seasonal/holiday material 5 months in advance. Computer printout submissions acceptable; prefers letter-quality. Sample copy $3.50; writer's guidelines for SASE.

Nonfiction: Expose (political); how-to; interview/profile; personal experience (how I survived); photo feature (equipment and techniques related to survival in all possible situations); emergency medical; health and fitness; communications; transportation; food preservation; water purification; self-defense; terrorism; nuclear dangers; nutrition; tools; shelter; etc. "No general articles about how to survive. We want specifics and single subjects." Buys 60-100 mss/year. Query or send complete ms. Length: 1,500-2,000 words. Pays $140-350. Sometimes pays the expenses of writers on assignment.

Photos: Send photos with ms. "One of the most frequent mistakes made by writers in completing an article assignment for us is sending photo submissions that are inadequate." Captions, model releases and identification of subjects mandatory. Buys all rights.

Tips: "Prepare material of value to individuals who wish to sustain human life no matter what the circumstance. This magazine is a text and reference."

‡ARMED FORCES JOURNAL INTERNATIONAL, Suite 520, 2000 L St. NW, Washington DC 20036. Editor: Benjamin F. Schemmer. 30% freelance written. Monthly magazine for "senior career officers of the U.S. military, defense industry, Congressmen and government officials interested in defense matters, international military and defense industry." Circ. 45,000. Pays on publication. Publishes ms an average of 2 months after acceptance. Buys all rights. Photocopied submissions OK. Computer printout submissions acceptable; no dot-matrix. Reports in 1 month. Sample copy $2.75.

Nonfiction: Publishes "national and international defense issues: weapons programs, research, personnel programs and international relations (with emphasis on defense issues). We do not want broad overviews of a general subject; we are more interested in detailed analysis which lays out *both* sides of a specific program or international defense issue. Our readers are decision-makers in defense matters—hence, subject should not be treated too simplistically. Be provocative. We are not afraid to take issue with our own constituency when an independent voice needs to be heard." Buys informational, profile and think pieces. No poetry, biographies, or non defense topics. Buys 40-45 mss/year. Send complete ms. Length: 1,000-3,000 words. Pays $250/page.

Tips: "The most frequent mistakes made by writers are: 1) one-dimensional and one-sided articles; 2) broad-brush generalities versus specificity; and 3) poorly-written gobbledygook."

ARMY MAGAZINE, 2425 Wilson Blvd., Arlington VA 22201. (703)841-4300. Editor-in-Chief: L. James Binder. Managing Editor: Mary Blake French. 80% freelance written. Prefers to work with published/established writers; eager to work with new/unpublished writers. Monthly magazine emphasizing military interests. Circ. 171,000. Pays on publication. Publishes ms an average of 6 months after acceptance. Buys all rights. Byline given except for back-up research. Submit seasonal/holiday material 3 months in advance. Photocopied submissions OK. Computer printout submissions acceptable; no dot-matrix. Sample copy and writer's guidelines for 8½x12 SAE with $1 postage.

Nonfiction: Historical (military and original); humor (military feature-length articles and anecdotes); interview; new product; nostalgia; personal experience; photo feature; profile; and technical. No rehashed history. "We would like to see more pieces about interesting military personalities. We especially want material lending itself to heavy, contributor-supplied photographic treatment. The first thing a contributor should recognize is that our readership is very savvy militarily. 'Gee-whiz' personal reminiscences get short shrift, unless they hold their own in a company in which long military service, heroism and unusual experiences are commonplace. At the same time, Army readers like a well-written story with a fresh slant, whether it is about an experience in a foxhole or the fortunes of a corps in battle." Buys 12 mss/issue. Submit complete ms. Length: 4,500 words. Pays 12-17¢/word.

Photos: Submit photo material with accompanying ms. Pays $15-50 for 8x10 b&w glossy prints; $35-150 for 8x10 color glossy prints or 2¼x2¼ color transparencies, will also accept 35mm. Captions preferred. Buys all rights.

Columns/Departments: Military news, books, comment (*New Yorker*-type "Talk of the Town" items). Buys 8/issue. Submit complete ms. Length: 1,000 words. Pays $40-150.

ASIA-PACIFIC DEFENSE FORUM, Commander-in-Chief, U.S. Pacific Command, Box 13, Camp H.M. Smith HI 96861. (808)477-5027/6924. Editor-in-Chief: Lt. Col. Paul R. Stankiewicz. Editor: Major Robert Teasdale. 12% (maximum) freelance written. Quarterly magazine for foreign military officers in 51 Asian-Pacific, Indian Ocean and other countries; all services—Army, Navy, Air Force and Marines. Secondary audience—government officials, media and academicians concerned with defense issues. "We seek to keep readers abreast of current status of U.S. forces and of U.S. national security policies in the Asia-Pacific area, and to enhance regional dialogue on military subjects." Circ. 34,000. Pays on acceptance. Publishes ms an average of 4 months after acceptance. Byline given. Buys simultaneous rights, second serial (reprint) rights or one-time rights. Phone queries OK. Simultaneous, photocopied, and previously published submissions OK. Computer printout submissions OK. Requires only a self-addressed label. Reports in 3 weeks on queries; 10 weeks on mss. Free sample copy and writer's guidelines (send self-addressed label).

Nonfiction: General interest (strategy and tactics, current type forces and weapons systems, strategic balance and security issues and Asian-Pacific armed forces); historical (occasionally used, if relation to present-day defense issues is clearly apparent); how-to (training, leadership, force employment procedures, organization); interview and personal experience (rarely used, and only in terms of developing professional military skills). "We do not want overly technical weapons/equipment descriptions, overly scholarly articles, controversial policy, and budget matters; nor do we seek discussion of in-house problem areas. We do not deal with military social life, base activities or PR-type personalities/job descriptions." Buys 2-4 mss/year. Query or send complete ms. Length: 1,000-3,000 words. Pays $100-300.

Photos: State availability of photos with query or ms. "We provide nearly all photos; however, we will consider good quality photos with manuscripts." Reviews color, b&w glossy prints or 35mm color transparencies. Offers no additional payment for photos accompanying mss. Photo credits given. Captions required. Buys one-time rights.

Tips: "Don't write in a flashy, Sunday supplement style. Our audience is relatively staid, and fact-oriented articles requiring a newspaper/journalistic approach are used more than a normal magazine style. Develop a 'feel' for our foreign audience orientation. Provide material that is truly audience-oriented and easily illustrated with photos."

FAMILY MAGAZINE, The Magazine for Military Wives, Box 4993, Walnut Creek CA 94596. (415)284-9093. Editor: Janet A. Venturino. 100% freelance written. Works with a small number of new/unpublished writers each year. A monthly magazine for military wives who are young, high school educated and move often. Circ. 545,000. Pays on publication. Publishes ms an average of 6-12 months after acceptance. Byline given. Buys first North American serial rights. Submit seasonal/holiday material 6 months in advance. Simultaneous and photocopied submissions OK. Computer printout submissions acceptable; prefers letter-quality. Reports in 1 month. Sample copy $1.25; writer's guidelines for SASE.
Nonfiction: Humor, personal experience, photo feature and travel, of interest to military wives. No romance, anything to do with getting a man or aging. Buys 30 mss/year. Send complete ms. Length: 2,000 words maximum. Pays $75-200.
Photos: Send photos with submissions. Reviews contact sheets, transparencies and prints. Offers $25-100/photo. Identification of subjects required. Buys one-time rights.
Fiction: Humorous, mainstream and slice-of-life vignettes. No romance or novel excerpts. Buys 5 mss/year. Length: 2,000 words maximum. Pays $75-150.

INFANTRY, Box 2005, Fort Benning GA 31905-0605. (404)545-2350. Editor: Albert N. Garland. 90% freelance written. Eager to work with new/unpublished writers. Bimonthly magazine published primarily for combat arms officers and noncommissioned officers. Circ. 20,000. Not copyrighted. Buys first serial rights. Pays on publication. Payment cannot be made to U.S. government employees. Publishes ms an average of 1 year after acceptance. Computer printout submissions acceptable; prefers letter-quality. Reports in 1 month. Free sample copy and writer's guidelines.
Nonfiction: Interested in current information on U.S. military organizations, weapons, equipment, tactics and techniques; foreign armies and their equipment; lessons learned from combat experience, both past and present; and solutions to problems encountered in the Active Army and the Reserve Components. Departments include Letters, Features and Forum, Training Notes, and Book Reviews. Uses 70 unsolicited mss/year. Length of articles: 1,500-3,500 words. Length for Book Reviews: 500-1,000 words. Query with writing sample. Accepts 75 mss/year.
Photos: Used with mss.
Tips: "Start with letters to editor and book reviews to break in."

‡**LEATHERNECK**, Box 1775, Quantico VA 22134. (703)640-3171. Editor: William V.H. White. Managing Editor: Tom Bartlett. Emphasizes all phases of Marine Corps activities. Monthly magazine. Circ. 104,000. Pays on acceptance. Buys first rights. Phone queries OK. Submit seasonal/holiday material 3 months in advance. Free sample copy and writer's guidelines.
Nonfiction: "All material submitted to *Leatherneck* must pertain to the U.S. Marine Corps and its members." General interest, how-to, humor, historical, interview, nostalgia, personal experience, profile, and travel. "No articles on politics, subjects not pertaining to the Marine Corps, and subjects that are not in good taste." Buys 24 mss/year. Query. Length: 1,500-3,000 words. Pays $50 and up/magazine page.
Photos: "We like to receive a complete package when we consider a manuscript for publication." State availability of photos with query. No additional payment for 4x5 or 8x10 b&w glossy prints. Captions required. Model release required. Buys first rights.
Fiction: Adventure, historical and humorous. All material must pertain to the U.S. Marine Corps and its members. Buys 3 mss/year. Query. Length: 1,000-3,000 words. Pays $50 and up/magazine page.
Poetry: Light verse and traditional. No poetry that does not pertain to the U.S. Marine Corps. Buys 40 mss/year. Length: 16-20 lines. Pays $10-20.

LIFE IN THE TIMES, Times Journal Co., Springfield VA 22159-0200. (703)750-8672. Editor: Barry Robinson. Managing Editor: Roger Hyneman. 30% freelance written. Eager to work with new/unpublished writers. Weekly lifestyle section of Army, Navy and Air Force Times covering current lifestyles and problems of career military families around the world. Circ. 300,000. Pays on acceptance. Publishes ms an average of 2 months after acceptance. Byline given. Offers negotiable kill fee. Buys all rights. Submit seasonal/holiday material 6 months in advance. Query for electronic submissions. Double- or triple-spaced computer printout submissions acceptable; no dot-matrix. Reports in about 2 months. Writer's guidelines for #10 SASE.
Nonfiction: Expose (current military); how-to (military wives); interview/profile (military); opinion (military topic); personal experience (military only); and travel (of military interest). "We accept food articles and short items about unusual things military people and their families are doing." No poetry, cartoons or historical articles. Buys 110 mss/year. Query with published clips. Length: 750-2,000 words. Pays $75-350. Sometimes pays the expenses of writers on assignment.
Photos: State availability of photos or send photos with ms. Reviews 35mm color contact sheets and prints. Captions, model releases, and identification of subjects required. Buys all rights.
Tips: "In your query write a detailed description of story and how it will be told. A tentative lead is nice. Just one good story 'breaks in' a freelancer. Follow the outline you propose in your query letter and humanize articles with quotes and examples."

MARINE CORPS GAZETTE, Professional Magazine for United States Marines, Marine Corps Association, Box 1775, Quantico VA 22134. (703)640-6161. Editor: Col. John E. Greenwood, USMC (Ret.). Managing Editor: Joseph D. Dodd. Less than 5% freelance written. "Will continue to welcome and respond to queries, but will be selective due to large backlog from Marine authors." Monthly magazine. "*Gazette* serves as a forum in which serving Marine officers exchange ideas and viewpoints on professional military matters." Circ. 33,000. Pays on publication. Publishes ms an average of 6 months after acceptance. Byline given. Buys all rights. Computer printout submissions acceptable. Reports in 3 weeks on queries; 2 months on mss. Sample copy $1; free writer's guidelines.

Nonfiction: Historical/nostalgic (Marine Corps operations only); and technical (Marine Corps related equipment). "The magazine is a professional journal oriented toward hard skills, factual treatment, technical detail—no market for lightweight puff pieces—analysis of doctrine, lessons learned goes well. A very strong Marine Corps background and influence are normally prerequisites for publication." Buys 4-5 mss/year from non-Marine Corps sources. Query or send complete ms. Length: 2,500-5,000 words. Pays $200-400; short features, $50-100.

Photos: "We welcome photos and charts." Payment for illustrative material included in payment forms. "Photos need not be original, nor have been taken by the author, but they must support the article."

Columns/Departments: Book Reviews (of interest and importance to Marines); and Ideas and Issues (an assortment of topical articles, e.g., opinion or argument, ideas of better ways to accomplish tasks, reports on weapons and equipment, strategies and tactics, etc., also short vignettes on history of Corps). Buys 60 book reviews and 120 Ideas and Issues mss/year, most from Marines. Query. Length: 500-1,500 words. Pays $25-50 plus book for 750-word book review; $50-100 for Ideas and Issues.

Tips: "Book reviews or short articles (500-1,500 words) on Marine Corps related hardware or technological development are the best way to break in. Sections/departments most open to freelancers are Book Reviews and Ideas & Issues sections—query first. We are not much of a market for those outside U.S. Marine Corps or who are not closely associated with current Marine activities."

MILITARY LIFESTYLE, Downey Communications, Inc., 1732 Wisconsin Ave. NW, Washington DC 20007. Editor: Hope M. Daniels. 80-90% freelance written. Works with equal balance of published and unpublished writers. For military families in the U.S. and overseas. Published 10 times a year. Magazine. Circ. 520,000. Pays on publication. Publishes ms an average of 4-6 months after acceptance. Buys first North American serial rights. Submit seasonal/holiday material at least 6 months in advance. Computer printout submissions acceptable. Reports in approximately 2 months. Sample copy $1.50. Writer's guidelines for #10 SASE.

Nonfiction: "All articles must have special interest for military families. General interest articles are OK if they reflect situations our readers can relate to." Food, humor, profiles, childrearing, health, home decor and travel. "Query letter should name sources, describe focus of article, use a few sample quotes from sources, indicate length, and should describe writer's own qualifications for doing the piece." Length: 1,000-2,000 words. Pays $300-700/article. Negotiates expenses on a case-by-case basis.

Photos: Purchased with accompanying ms and on assignment. Uses 35mm or larger color transparencies. Captions and model releases are required. Query art director Judi Connelly.

Columns/Departments: Your Point of View—personal experience pieces by military family members. Also, Your Pet, Your Money and Your Baby. Query. Length: 800-1,200 words. Rates vary.

Fiction: Slice-of-life, family situation, contemporary tableaux. "Military family life or relationship themes only." Buys 6-8 mss/year. Query. Length: 1,500-2,000 words. Pays $250-350.

Tips: "We are a magazine for military families, not just women. Our editorial attempts enthusiastically to reflect that. Our ideal contributor is a military family member who can write. However, I'm always impressed by a writer who has analyzed the market and can suggest some possible new angles for us. Sensitivity to military issues is a must for our contributors, as is the ability to write good personality profiles and/or do thorough research about military family life. We don't purchase household hints, historical articles, WW II-era material or parenting advice that is too personal and limited only to the writer's own experience."

MILITARY LIVING R&R REPORT, Box 2347, Falls Church VA 22042. (703)237-0203. Publisher: Ann Crawford. Bimonthly newsletter for "military consumers worldwide. Please state when sending submission that it is for the *R&R Report Newsletter* so as not to confuse it with our monthly magazine which has different requirements." Pays on publication. Buys first serial rights but will consider other rights. Sample copy $1.

Nonfiction: "We use information on little-known military facilities and privileges, discounts around the world and travel information. Items must be short and concise. Payment is on an honorarium basis, 1-1½¢/word."

MILITARY REVIEW, U.S. Army Command and General Staff College, Fort Leavenworth KS 66027-6910. (913)684-5642. Editor-in-Chief: Col. Phillip W. Childress. Managing Editor: Lt. Col. Thomas Conrad. Associate Editor: Lt. Col. Lynn Havach. 75% freelance written. Eager to work with new/unpublished writers. Monthly journal (printed in three languages; English, Spanish and Brazilian Portuguese), emphasizing the military for military officers, students and scholars. Circ. 27,000. Pays on publication. Publishes ms an average of 8 months after acceptance. Byline given. Buys first serial rights and reserves right to reprint for training purpose. Phone queries and photocopied submissions OK. Query for electronic submissions. Computer printout submissions acceptable; prefers letter-quality. Reports in 1 month. Writer's guidelines for #10 SASE.

Nonfiction: Operational level of war, military history, international affairs, tactics, new military equipment, strategy and book reviews. Prefers not to get poetry or cartoons. Buys 100-120 mss/year. Query. Length: 2,000-3,000 words. Pays $50-200.

Tips: "We need more articles from military personnel experienced in particular specialties. Examples: Tactics from a tactician, military engineering from an engineer, etc. By reading our publication, writers will quickly recognize our magazine as a forum for any topic of general interest to the U.S. Army. They will also discover the style we prefer: concise and direct, in the active voice, with precision and clarity, and moving from the specific to the general."

NATIONAL GUARD, 1 Massachusetts Ave. NW, Washington DC 20001. (202)789-0031. Editor: Lt. Col. Reid K. Beveridge. 10% freelance written. Monthly magazine for officers of the Army and Air National Guard. Circ. 62,000. Pays on publication. Publishes ms an average of 6 months after acceptance. Rights negotiable. Byline given. Query for electronic submissions. Computer printout submissions acceptable. Query.

Nonfiction: Military policy, strategy, training, equipment, logistics, personnel policies, tactics, combat lessons learned as they pertain to the Army and Air Force (and impact on Army National Guard and Air National Guard). Material must be strictly accurate from a technical standpoint. Does not publish exposes, cartoons or jokes. Buys 10-12 mss/year. Query. Length: 2,000-3,000 words. Payment ($75-500/article) depends on originality, amount of research involved, etc. Sometimes pays expenses of writers on assignment.

Photos: Photography pertinent to subject matter should accompany ms.

OFF DUTY, U.S.: Suite C-2, 3303 Harbor Blvd., Costa Mesa CA 92626. Editor: Bruce Thorstad. Europe: Eschersheimer Landstrasse 69, Frankfurt/M, West Germany. Editor: J.C. Couch. Pacific: 14/F Park Commercial Centre, 8 Shelter St., Causeway Bay, Hong Kong. Editor: Jim Shaw. 50% freelance written. Monthly magazine for U.S. military personnel and their families stationed around the world. Most readers ages 18-35. Combined circ. 708,000. Buys first serial rights or second serial (reprint) rights. Pays on acceptance. Publishes ms an average of 6 months after acceptance. Computer printout submissions acceptable. Sample copy and writer's guidelines $1.

Nonfiction: Three editions—American, Pacific and European. "Emphasis is on off-duty travel, leisure, military shopping, wining and dining, sports, hobbies, music, and getting the most out of military life. Overseas editions lean toward foreign travel and living in foreign cultures. In travel articles we like anecdotes, lots of description, color and dialogue. American edition uses more American trends and how-to/service material. Material with special U.S., Pacific or European slant should be sent to appropriate address above; material useful in all editions may be sent to U.S. address and will be forwarded as necessary." Buys 30-50 mss/year for each of three editions. Query. Length: 1,500 words average. Also needs 200-word shorties. Pays 13¢/word for use in one edition; 16¢/word for use in 2 or more. Sometimes pays expenses of writers on assignment.

Photos: Bought with or without accompanying ms. Pays $25 for b&w glossy prints; $50 for color transparencies; $100 for full page color; $200 for covers. "Covers must be vertical format 35mm; larger format transparencies preferred."

Tips: "All material should take into account to some extent our special audience—the U.S. military and their dependents. Our publication is subtitled 'The Military Leisuretime Magazine,' and the stories we like best are about how to get more out of the military experience. That 'more' could range from more fun to more satisfaction to more material benefits. Increasingly, the writer with special knowledge of active-duty military personnel and their families is the writer we need. However, our focus remains on off-duty pursuits and concerns. Query writers very often mistake the basic nature of our magazine. If we do an article on running, we'll get a raft of queries for running articles. That's wrong. We're a general interest magazine; if we've just done running, it's going to be quite a while before we do it again. We've got *dozens* of other subjects to cover."

OVERSEAS!, Military Consumer Today, Inc., Kolpingstr 1, 6906 Leimen, West Germany 06221-25431/32/33. Editorial Director: Charles L. Kaufman. Managing Editor: Greg Ballinger. 95% freelance written. Eager to work with new/unpublished writers; "we don't get enough submissions." Monthly magazine. "*Overseas!* is aimed at the U.S. military in Europe. It is the leading men's lifestyle magazine slanted toward life in Europe, specifically directed to males ages 18-35." Circ. 83,000. Pays on acceptance. Publishes ms an average of 3 months after acceptance. Byline given. Publishes photos, bio of new writers in editor's column. Offers kill fee depending on circumstances and writer. Buys one-time rights. Submit seasonal/holiday material at least 4 months in advance. Simultaneous queries, and simultaneous, photocopied, and previously published submissions OK. Computer printout submissions acceptable; prefers letter-quality. Reports in 2 weeks on queries; 1 month on mss. Sample copy for SAE and 4 IRCs; writer's guidelines for SAE and 1 IRC.

Nonfiction: General interest (lifestyle for men and other topics); how-to (use camera, buy various types of video, audio, photo and computer equipment); humor ("We want travel/tourist in Europe humor like old *National Lampoon* style. Must be funny."); interview/profile (music, personality interviews; current music stars for young audience); technical (video, audio, photo, computer; how to purchase and use equipment); travel (European, first person adventure; write toward male audience); men's cooking; and men's fashion/lifestyle. Special issues include Video, Audio, Photo, and Military Shopper's Guide. Needs 250-750-word articles on video, audio, photo and computer products. Published in September every year. No articles that are drug- or sex-related. No cathedrals or museums of Europe stories. Buys 30-50 mss/year "but would buy more if we got better quality and subjects." Query with or without pulished clips or send complete ms. Length: 750-2,000 words. Pays 10¢/word. Usually pays expenses of writers on assignment; negotiable.

Photos: Send photos with accompanying query or ms. Pays $20 minimum, b&w; $35 color transparencies, 35mm or larger. Photos must accompany travel articles—"color slides. Also, we are always looking for photographs of pretty women for our covers." Pays $250 minimum. Identification of subjects required. Buys one-time rights. Buys 12 covers/year.

Columns/Departments: Back Talk—potpourri page of humor, cartoons and other materials relating to life in Europe and the military. Buys 20-50 mss/year. Length: 150 words maximum. Pays $25-150/piece used. "Would buy more if received more."

Tips: "We would like more submissions on travel in Europe and humor for the 'Back Talk' page. Writing should be lively, interesting, with lots of good information. We anticipate a change in the length of articles. Articles will be shorter and livelier with more sidebars, because readers don't have time to read longer articles. *Overseas!* magazine is the *Travel and Leisure/GQ/Esquire* of this market; any articles that would be suitable for these magazines would probably work in *Overseas!*"

PARAMETERS: U.S. ARMY WAR COLLEGE QUARTERLY, U.S. Army War College, Carlisle Barracks PA 17013. (717)245-4943. Editor: Col. Lloyd J. Matthews, U.S. Army Retired. Quarterly. 100% freelance written. Prefers to work with published/established writers or experts in the field. Readership consists of senior leadership of U.S. defense establishment, both uniformed and civilian, plus members of the media, government, industry and academia interested in national and international security affairs, military strategy, military leadership and management, art and science of warfare, and military history (provided it has contemporary relevance). Most readers possess a graduate degree. Circ. 10,000. Not copyrighted; unless copyrighted by author, articles may be reprinted with appropriate credits. Buys first serial rights. Byline given. Pays on publication. Publishes ms an average of 6 months after acceptance. Computer printout submissions acceptable; no dot-matrix. Reports in 1 month. Free writer's guidelines.

Nonfiction: Articles preferred that deal with current security issues, employ critical analysis, and provide solutions or recommendations. Liveliness and verve, consistent with scholarly integrity, appreciated. Theses, studies and academic course papers should be adapted to article form prior to submission. Documentation in complete endnotes. Submit complete ms. Length: 4,500 words average, preferably less. Pays $150 average (including visuals).

Tips: "Make it short; keep it interesting; get criticism and revise accordingly. Tackle a subject only if you are an authority."

PERIODICAL, Council on America's Military Past, 4970 N. Camino Antonio, Tucson AZ 85718. Editor-in-Chief: Dan L. Thrapp. 90% freelance written. Works with a small number of new/unpublished writers each year. Quarterly magazine emphasizing old and abandoned forts, posts and military installations; military subjects for a professional, knowledgeable readership interested in one-time defense sites or other military installations. Circ. 1,500. Pays on publication. Publishes ms an average of 6 months after acceptance. Buys one-time rights. Simultaneous, photocopied, and previously published (if published a long time ago) submissions OK. Computer printout submissions OK; prefers letter-quality. Reports in 3 weeks. Writer's guidelines for #10 SASE.

Nonfiction: Historical, personal experience, photo feature and technical (relating to posts, their construction/operation and military matters). Buys 4-6 mss/issue. Query or send complete ms. Length: 300-4,000 words. Pays $2/page minimum.

Photos: Purchased with or without ms. Query. Reviews glossy, single-weight 8x10 b&w prints. Offers no additional payment for photos accepted with accompanying ms. Captions required.

Tips: "We plan more emphasis on appeal to professional military audience and military historians."

R&R ENTERTAINMENT DIGEST, R&R Werbe GmbH, 1 Kolpingstrasse, 6906 Leimen, W. Germany 06224-7060. Editor: Marji Hess. 50% freelance written. Monthly entertainment guide for military and government employees and their families stationed in Europe "specializing in travel in Europe, audio/video/photo information, music, and the homemaker scene. Aimed exclusively at military/DoD based in Europe—Germany, Britain and the Mediterranean." Circ. 185,000. Pays on publication. Publishes ms an average of 2-6 months after acceptance. Byline given. "We offer 50% of payment as a kill fee, but this rarely happens—if story can't run in one issue, we try to use it in a future edition." Buys first serial rights for military market in Europe only. "We will reprint stories that have run in stateside publications if applicable to us." Submit seasonal/holiday material 3 months in advance. Computer printout submissions acceptable; prefers letter-quality. Simultaneous queries, and simultaneous, photocopied, and previously published submissions OK. Reports in 2 months. Sample copy and writer's guidelines available for #10 SAE and 5 IRCs.

Nonfiction: Humor (limited amount used—dealing with travel experiences in Europe), and travel (always looking for good travel in Europe features). "We buy only articles by writers who have been to or lived in the destination on which they write. Not interested in tourist articles. Our readers live in Europe, average age 26.5, married with 2 children. Over 50% travel by car. Annual vacation is 1 week or more. Weekend trips are also popular. Should always include restaurant/clubs/hotel recommendations. Looking for bargains." No interviews of singers, historical pieces, album/movie/book reviews, or technical stories. Buys 15 mss/year. Query with published clips or send complete ms. Length: 600-1,000 words. Pays in Deutsche Marks—DM 90 (an estimated $45) /page; partial payment for partial page.

Photos: State availability of photos or send photos with query or mss. Pays DM 80 for 35mm color transparencies. Captions required. "We pay once for use with story but can reuse at no additional cost."

Columns/Departments: Monthly audio, video and photo stories. "We need freelancers with solid background in these areas who can write for general public on a variety of topics." Buys 10 mss/year. Query with published clips or send complete ms. Length: 1,300-1,400 words. Pays DM 90/magazine page.

Fiction: Very little fiction accepted. Query. "It has to be exceptional to be accepted." Length: 600-1,200 words. Pays DM 90/page.

Fillers: Cartoons pertaining to television. Buys 5/year. Pays DM 80/cartoon.

Tips: "Best chance would be a tie-in travel or first-person story with an American holiday: Mother's Day in Paris, Labor Day, Thanksgiving, St. Pat's Day in Europe, etc. Stories must be written with an American military member and family in mind—young married, 2 children with car, 2 weeks annual leave, several 3-day weekends. Sports/adventure travel stories are popular with our readers."

THE RETIRED OFFICER MAGAZINE, 201 N. Washington St., Alexandria VA 22314. (703)549-2311. Editor: Charles D. Cooper, USAF-Ret. 60% freelance written. Prefers to work with published/established writers. Monthly for officers of the 7 uniformed services and their families. Circ. 360,000. Pays on acceptance. Publishes ms an average of 9-12 months after acceptance. Byline given. Buys first serial rights. Submit seasonal material (holiday stories with a military theme) at least 9-12 months in advance. Reports on material accepted for publication within 2 months. Sample copy and writer's guidelines for 9x12 SAE with 5 first class stamps.

Nonfiction: Current military/political affairs, health and wellness, recent military history, humor, hobbies, travel, second-career job opportunities and military family lifestyle. Also, upbeat articles on aging, human interest and features pertinent to a retired military officer's milieu. True military experiences are also useful. "We rarely accept unsolicited mss. We look for detailed query letters with resumé and sample clips attached. We do not publish poetry or fillers." Buys 48 unsolicited mss/year. Length: 750-2,000 words. Pays up to $500.

Photos: Query with list of stock photo subjects. Reviews 8x10 b&w photos (normal halftone). Pays $20. Original slides or transparencies must be suitable for color separation. Pays up to $125 for inside color; up to $260 for cover.

Tips: "Our readers are 55-65. We never write about them as senior citizens, yet we look for upbeat stories that take into consideration the demographic characteristics of their age group."

‡SEA POWER, 2300 Wilson Blvd., Arlington VA 22201-3308. Editor: James D. Hessman. Issued monthly by the Navy League of the U.S. for sea service personnel and civilians interested in naval maritime and defense matters. 10% freelance written. "We prefer queries from experts/specialists in maritime industry." Computer printout submissions acceptable; prefers letter-quality. Pays on publication. Buys all rights. Free sample copy.

Nonfiction: Factual articles on sea power and national defense in general, U.S. industrial base, mineral resources, and the U.S. Navy, U.S. Marine Corps, U.S. Coast Guard, U.S. Merchant Marine, oceanographic industries and other navies of the world. Should illustrate and expound the importance of the seas and sea power to the U.S. and its allies. Wants timely, clear, nonpedantic writing for audience that is intelligent and well-educated but not necessarily fluent in military/hi-tech terminology. No personal analysis. Material should be presented in the third person, well documented with complete attribution. No historical articles, commentaries, critiques, abstract theories, poetry or editorials. Query first. Length: 500-2,500 words. Pays $100-500 depending upon length and research involved.

Photos: Purchased with ms.

Tips: "The writer should be invisible. Copy should be understandable without reference to charts, graphs or footnotes."

SOLDIER OF FORTUNE, The Journal of Professional Adventurers, Omega Group, Ltd., Box 693, Boulder CO 80306. (303)449-3750. Editor: Robert K. Brown. 50% freelance written. A monthly magazine covering military, paramilitary, police and combat subjects. "We are an action-oriented magazine; we cover combat hot spots around the world such as Afghanistan, Central America, Angola, etc. We also provide timely features on state-of-the-art weapons and equipment; elite military and police units; and historical military operations. Readership is primarily active-duty military, veterans and law enforcement." Circ. 175,000. Pays on acceptance. Publishes ms an average of 5 months after acceptance. Byline given. Offers 25% kill fee. Buys first North American serial rights. Submit seasonal/holiday material 5 months in advance. Photocopied submissions OK. Computer printout submissions OK; prefers letter-quality. Reports in 3 weeks on queries; 1 month on mss. Sample copy $5; writer's guidelines for #10 SASE. Send ms to articles editor; queries to managing editor.

Nonfiction: Expose; general interest; historical/nostalgic; how-to (on weapons and their skilled use); humor; profile; new product; personal experience; photo feature ("number one on our list"); technical; travel; combat reports; military unit reporters and solid Vietnam history. "No 'How I won the war' pieces; no op-ed pieces *unless* they are fully and factually backgrounded; no knife articles (staff assignments only). *All* submitted articles should have good art; art will sell us on an article. Buys 75 mss/year. Query with or without published clips, or send complete ms. Length: 2,500-5,000 words. Pays $300-1,200 for assigned articles; pays $200-1,000 for unsolicited articles. Sometimes pays the expenses of writers on assignment.

Photos: Send photos with submission (copies only, no originals). Reviews contact sheets and transparencies. Offers no additional payment for photos accepted with ms. Pays $46 for cover photo. Captions and identification of subjects required. Buys one-time rights.

Columns/Departments: Address to appropriate column editor (i.e., I Was There Editor). Combat weaponcraft (how-to military and police survival skills) and I Was There (first-person accounts of the arcane or unusual based in a combat or law enforcement environment), all 600-800 words. Buys 16 mss/year. Send complete ms. Length: 600-800 words. Combat weaponcraft pays $200; I was There pays $50.

Fillers: Bulletin Board editor. Newsbreaks; military/paramilitary related, "*has* to be documented." Length: 100-250 words. Pays $25.

Tips: "Submit a professionally prepared, complete package. All artwork with cutlines, double-spaced typed manuscript, cover letter including synopsis of article, supporting documentation where applicable, etc. Manuscript must be factual; writers have to do their homework and get all their facts straight. One error means rejection. We will work with authors over the phone or by letter, tell them if their ideas have merit for an acceptable article, and help them fine-tune their work. I Was There is a good place for freelancers to start. Vietnam features, if carefully researched and art heavy, will always get a careful look. Combat reports, again, with good art, are number one in our book and stand the best chance of being accepted. Military unit reports from around the world are well received as are law enforcement articles (units, police in action). If you write for us, be complete and factual; pros read *Soldier of Fortune*, and are *very* quick to let us know if we (and the author) err. We plan more articles on terrorism."

THE VETERAN, Vietnam Veterans of America, Suite 700, 2001 S. Street NW, Washington DC 20009. (202)332-2700. Editor: Mark Perry. Managing Editor: Mokie Pratt Porter. 70% freelance written. A monthly tabloid on the Vietnam war, Viet vets and the Vietnam era. "Writers should be familiar with aspects of America's involvement in Indochina with veterans and veterans' issues and should be able to write with knowledge on controversies surrounding our involvement in Vietnam." Circ. 33,000. Pays on publication. Publishes ms an average of 1 month after acceptance. Byline given. Offers kill fee of 50% of original fee. Buys first rights. Submit seasonal/holiday material 2 months in advance. Reports in 1 month on queries. Sample copy for 8½x11 SAE with 2 first class stamps; writers guidelines for #10 SAE and 3 first class stamps.

Nonfiction: Historical and interview/profile. No humor. Buys 24 mss/year. Send complete ms. Length: 1,500-3,000 words. Pays $300-500 for assigned articles; $200-400 for unsolicited articles. Pays expenses of writers on assignment.

Photos: Send photos with submission. Reviews contact sheets. Pays $5-10/photo. Captions required. Buys one-time rights.

Columns/Departments: Update (veterans profiles, interviews, issues), 500-750 words. Buys 12 mss/year. Send complete ms. Pays $100-200.

Tips: "Know our readers, America's Viet vets. I want clean, clear copy, double-spaced."

‡VIETNAM, Empire Press, 105 Loudon St. SW, Leesburg VA 22075. (703)771-9400. Editor: Colonel Harry G. Summers, Jr. Executive Editor: C. Brian Kelly. 80-90% freelance written. Quarterly magazine on military aspects of the Vietnam War. "Without debating the wisdom of U.S. involvement, pro or con, our objective is to tell the story of the military events, weaponry and personalities of the war, as it happened." Estab. 1988. Circ. 140,000. Pays on publication. Publishes ms up to 2 years after acceptance. Byline given. Buys first North American serial rights. Query for electronic submissions. Reports in 2 months on queries; 3 months on mss. Sample copy $3.95. Writer's guidelines for #10 SAE with 1 first class stamp.

Nonfiction: Book excerpts (if original), historical, interview, personal/experience, military history. "Absolutely no fiction or poetry; we want straight history, as much personal narrative as possible, but not the gung-ho, shoot-em-up variety, either." Buys 30+ mss/year. Query. Length: 4,000 words maximum. Pays $300 for features.

Photos: State availability of photos with submission. Pays up to $100/photo. Identification of subjects required. Buys one-time rights.

Columns/Departments: Arsenal (about weapons used, all sides); Personality (profiles of the players, all sides); Fighting Forces (about various units or types of units: air, sea, rescue); Bases and Installations. Query. Length: 2,000 words. Pays $150.

WORLD WAR II, Empire Press, 105 Loudoun Street SW, Leesburg VA 22075. (703)771-9400. Editor: C. Brian Kelly. 95% freelance written. Prefers to work with published/established writers. A bimonthly magazine covering "military operations in World War II—events, personalities, strategy, national policy, etc." Circ. 185,000. Pays on publication. Publishes ms an average of 1-2 years after acceptance. Byline given. Buys first North American serial rights. Submit seasonal/holiday material 1 year in advance. Reports in 2 months on queries; 3 months or more on mss. Sample copy $4; writer's guidelines for #10 SAE with 2 first class stamps.
Nonfiction: Book excerpts (if in advance of book publication), profile, personal experience, technical, and World War II military history. No fiction. Buys 24 mss/year. Query. Length: 4,000 words. Pays $200.
Photos: State availability of art and photos with submission. (For photos and other art, send photocopies and cite sources. "We'll order.") Sometimes offers additional payment for photos accepted with ms. Captions and identification of subjects required. Buys one-time rights.
Columns/Department: Undercover (espionage, resistance, sabotage, intelligence gathering, behind the lines, etc.); Personalities (WW II personalities of interest); and Armaments (weapons, their use and development); all 2,000 words. Book reviews, 300-750 words. Buys 18 mss/year (plus book reviews). Query. Pays $100.
Tips: "List your sources and suggest further readings, in standard format at the end of your piece—as a bibliography for our files in case of factual challenge or dispute. All submissions are on speculation. When the story's right, but the writing isn't, we'll pay a small research fee for use of the information in our own style and language."

Music

Music fans follow the latest music industry news in these publications. Types of music and musicians are the sole focus of some magazines. Publications geared to the music industry and professionals can be found in Trade Music section. Additional music and dance markets are included in the Entertainment section.

THE ABSOLUTE SOUND, The Journal of The High End, Box 115, Sea Cliff NY 11579. (516)676-2830. Editor: Harry Pearson, Jr. Managing Editor: Sallie Reynolds. 10% freelance written. Works with a small number of new/unpublished writers each year. Bimonthly magazine covering the music reproduction business, audio equipment and records for "up-scale, high tech men and women between the ages of 20 and 100, serious music lovers." Pays on publication. Byline given. Buys all rights. Query for electronic submissions. Computer printout submissions acceptable; no dot-matrix. Sample copy $7.50.
Nonfiction: Exposé (of bad commercial audio practices); interview/profile (famous recording engineers, famous conductors); new product (audio); opinion (audio and record reviews); and technical (how to improve your stereo system). Special Recordings issue. No puff pieces about industry. No newspaper clippings. Query with published clips. Length: 250-5,000 words. Pays $125-1,000. Sometimes pays the expenses of writers on assignment.
Columns/Departments: Audio Musings (satires) and Reports from Overseas (audio shows, celebrities, record companies). Buys 6 mss/year. Length: 250-750 words. Pays $125-200.
Tips: "Writers should know about audio, recordings and the engineering of same, as well as live music. The approach is *literate*, witty, investigative, good journalism."

BANJO NEWSLETTER, Box 364, Greensboro MD 21639. (301)482-6278. Editor: Hub Nitchie. 10% freelance written. Monthly magazine covering the "instructional and historical treatment of the 5-string banjo. Covers all aspects of the instrument. Tablature is used for musical examples." Circ. 7,000. Pays on publication. Byline given. Buys one-time rights. Query for electronic submissions. Computer printout submissions OK; prefers letter-quality. Reports in 1 month on queries. Free sample copy.
Nonfiction: Interviews with 5-string banjo players, banjo builders, shop owners, etc. No humorous fiction from anyone unfamiliar with the popular music field. Buys 6 mss/year. Query. Length: 500-4,000 words. Pays $20-100. Sometimes pays writers with contributor copies or other premiums "if that is what writer wants." Very seldom pays expenses of writers on assignment. "We can arrange for press tickets to musical events."
Photos: State availability of photos with submission. Reviews b&w prints. Offers $10-40/photo. Captions and identification of subjects required whenever possible. Buys one-time rights.
Columns/Departments: Buys 60 mss/year. Query. Length: 500-750 words. Payment varies.
Poetry: Poetry Editor: Don Nitchie, General Delivery, West Tisbury, MA 02575. Buys 2 poems/year. Submit maximum 1 poem at one time.

Tips: "The writer should be motivated by being a student of the 5-string banjo or interested in the folk or blue-grass music fields where 5-string banjo is featured. Writers should be able to read and write banjo tablature and know various musicians or others in the field."

BLUEGRASS UNLIMITED, Bluegrass Unlimited, Inc., Box 111, Broad Run VA 22014. (703)361-8992. Editor: Peter V. Kuykendall. 80% freelance written. Prefers to work with published/established writers. Monthly magazine on bluegrass and old-time country music. Circ. 21,000. Pays on publication. Publishes ms an average of 4 months after acceptance. Byline given. Kill fee negotiated. Buys first North American serial rights, one-time rights, all rights, and second serial (reprint) rights. Submit seasonal/holiday material 4 months in advance. Photocopied submissions OK. Computer printout submissions are OK; prefers letter-quality. Reports in 2 weeks on queries; 2 months on mss. Free sample copy and writer's guidelines for #10 SASE.
Nonfiction: General interest, historical/nostalgic, how-to, interview/profile, personal experience, photo feature and travel. No "fan" style articles. Buys 75-80 mss/year. Query with or without published clips. No set word length. Pays 6-8¢/word.
Photos: State availability of photos or send photos with query. Reviews 35mm color transparencies and 3x5, 5x7, and 8x10 b&w and color prints. Pays $25-50 for b&w transparencies; $50-150 for color transparencies; $25-50 for b&w prints; and $50-150 for color prints. Identification of subjects required. Buys one-time rights and all rights.
Fiction: Ethnic and humorous. Buys 3-5 mss/year. Query. No set word length. Pays 6-8¢/word.
Tips: "We would prefer that articles be informational, based on personal experience or an interview with lots of quotes from subject, profile, humor, etc."

‡B-SIDE, B-Side Publishing, Box 1387, Fort Washington PA 19034. (215)542-9754 or (215)561-9027. Editor: Carol Schutzbank. Managing Editor: Sandra Garcia. 75% freelance written. A bimonthly tabloid on entertainment. "*B-Side* offers an alternative look at alternative music. It delivers in-depth interviews and intelligent reviews. It bridges the gap between larger more 'commercial' publications and grass roots, 'gonzo-styled' home grown fanzines." Circ. 5,000. Byline given. Buys first rights. Simultaneous and photocopied submissions OK. Computer printout submissions OK; prefers letter-quality. Reports in 1 month on queries; 3 months on ms. Sample copy $3. Writer's guidelines for #10 SAE with 2 first class stamps.
Nonfiction: Essays, exposé, humor, interview/profile, new product, opinion, personal experience, photo feature and technical. Query with published clips. Length: 300-2,000 words. Pays up to $25 for assigned articles but sometimes pays in copies for unsolicited mss. Sometimes pays expenses of writers on assignment. State availability of photos with submission. Reviews contact sheets. Offers no additional payment for photos accepted with ms. Identification of subjects required. Buys one-time rights.
Fiction: Humorous and slice-of-life vignettes. Fiction must be oriented to music. Send complete ms. Pays in contributor's copies.
Poetry: Avant-garde, free verse and haiku. Submit maximum 3 poems. "Read the writer's guidelines."

EAR, Magazine of New Music, EAR, Inc., Room 208, 325 Spring St., New York NY 10013. (212)807-7944. Publisher/Editor: Carol E. Tuynman. 100% freelance written. Eager to work with new/unpublished writers. A tabloid published 10 times per year for artists interested in the avant-garde. Circ. 20,000. Publishes ms an average of 6 months after acceptance. Byline given. Writer holds rights. Submit seasonal/holiday material 6 months in advance. Query for electronic submissions. Computer printout submissions acceptable. Reports in 1 month on queries; 3 months on mss. Sample copy $2; writer's guidelines for #10 SASE.
Nonfiction: Essay; how-to; humor (music related); interview/profile; new product; opinion; personal experience (musicians and composers only); photo feature; and technical. Special issues include Art, Crimes and Music, Music is Dead and Electronic Women. No general opinions or fiction. Buys 5 mss/year. Query. Length: 250-1,000 words. Pays $0-50 for assigned articles; pays $0-25 for unsolicited articles. "Usually we don't pay, or at most, a $25 honorarium is given." All published contributors receive 1-year subscription plus 3 copies of issue they are in.
Photos: Send photos with submission. Reviews 5x7 prints. Offers no additional payment for photos accepted with ms. Captions required. Buys one-time rights.
Columns/Departments: Radio (critical look at radio whether public or commercial, new music U.S. and international), 750 words; Healing Arts (how sound/music and related technologies are interfacing in the healing arts), 750 words; Techno, Video, Info, Citizens of the Cassette Conspiracy, Inside Music. Buys 5 mss/year. Pays $0-100 for radio only.
Fillers: Newsbreaks and short humor. Length: 25-100 words. Pays $0-10.
Tips: "Do not write in *Spin* or *Rolling Stone* style. Be knowledgable about contemporary music, be a clear writer, don't send poorly edited, messy material. We're not interested in the classical European music tradition."

GUITAR PLAYER MAGAZINE, GPI Publications, 20085 Stevens Creek, Cupertino CA 95014. (408)446-1105. Editor: Tom Wheeler. 70% freelance written. Monthly magazine for persons "interested in guitars, guitarists, manufacturers, guitar builders, bass players, equipment, careers, etc." Circ. 180,000. Buys first serial and limited reprint rights. Pays on acceptance. Publishes ms an average of 3 months after acceptance. Byline given. Computer printout submissions acceptable; prefers letter-quality. Reports in 6 weeks. Free sample copy; writer's guidelines for #10 SASE.

Nonfiction: Publishes "wide variety of articles pertaining to guitars and guitarists: interviews, guitar craftsmen profiles, how-to features—anything amateur and professional guitarists would find fascinating and/or helpful. On interviews with 'name' performers, be as technical as possible regarding strings, guitars, techniques, etc. We're not a pop culture magazine, but a magazine for musicians." Also buys features on such subjects as a guitar museum, role of the guitar in elementary education, personal reminiscences of past greats, technical gadgets and how to work them, analysis of flamenco, etc. Buys 30-40 mss/year. Query. Length: open. Pays $100-300. Sometimes pays expenses of writers on assignment.

Photos: Reviews b&w glossy prints. Pays $50-100. Buys 35mm color transparencies. Pays $250 (for cover only). Buys one time rights.

ILLINOIS ENTERTAINER, Suite 192, 2200 E. Devon, Des Plaines IL 60018. (312)298-9333. Editor: Bill Dalton. 95% freelance written. Prefers to work with published/established writers but open to new writers with "style." Monthly tabloid covering music and entertainment for consumers within 100-mile radius of Chicago interested in music. Circ. 80,000. Pays on publication. Publishes ms an average of 2 months after acceptance. Byline given. Offers 10% kill fee. Buys one-time rights. Simultaneous queries OK. Computer printout submissions acceptable "if letters are clear"; no dot-matrix. Reports in 1 month on queries; 2 months on mss. Sample copy $5.

Nonfiction: Interview/profile (of entertainment figures). No Q&A interviews. Buys 75 mss/year. Query with published clips. Length: 500-2,000 words. Pays $15-100. Sometimes pays expenses of writers on assignment.

Photos: State availability of photos. Pays $20-30 for 5x7 or 8x10 b&w prints; $125 for color cover photo, both on publication only. Captions and identification of subjects required.

Columns/Departments: Software (record reviews stress record over band or genre) and book reviews. Buys 50 mss/year. Query with published clips. Length: 150-250 words. Pays $6-20.

Tips: "Send clips (published or unpublished) with phone number, and be patient. Full staff has seniority, but if you know the ins and outs of the entertainment biz, and can balance that knowledge with a broad sense of humor, then you'll have a chance."

INTERNATIONAL MUSICIAN, American Federation of Musicians, Suite 600, Paramount Building, 1501 Broadway, New York NY 10036. (212)869-1330. Editor: Kelly L. Castleberry II. 10% freelance written. Prefers to work with published/established writers. Monthly for professional musicians. Pays on acceptance. Publishes ms an average of 3 months after acceptance. Byline given. Computer printout submissions OK; no dot-matrix. Reports in 2 months.

Nonfiction: Articles on prominent instrumental musicians (classical, jazz, rock or country). Send complete ms. Length: 1,500-2,000 words.

KEYBOARD MAGAZINE, GPI Publications, 20085 Stevens Creek Blvd., Cupertino CA 95014. (408)446-1105. Editor: Dominic Milano. 25% freelance written. Prefers to work with published/established writers; works with a small number of new/unpublished writers each year. Monthly magazine for those who play synthesizer, piano, organ, harpsichord, or any other keyboard instrument. All styles of music; all levels of ability. Circ. 70,000. Pays on acceptance. Publishes ms 6 months after acceptance. Byline given. Buys first serial rights and second serial (reprint) rights. Phone queries OK. Query for electronic submissions. Computer printout submissions acceptable; prefers letter-quality. Reports in 2 weeks. Free sample copy and writer's guidelines.

Nonfiction: "We publish articles on a wide variety of topics pertaining to keyboard players and their instruments. In addition to interviews with keyboard artists in all styles of music, we are interested in historical and analytical pieces, how-to articles dealing either with music or with equipment (including MIDI and computers), profiles on well-known instrument makers and their products. In general, anything that amateur and professional keyboardists would find interesting and/or useful." Buys 20 unsolicited mss/year. Query: letter should mention topic and length of article and describe basic approach. "It's nice (but not necessary) to have a sample first paragraph." Length: approximately 1,000-5,000 words. Pays $150-500 + . Sometimes pays the expenses of writers on assignment.

Tips: "Query first (just a few ideas at a time, rather than twenty). A musical background helps, and a knowledge of keyboard instruments is essential."

MCS, Music, Computers & Software, (formerly *KCS*), 190 E. Main St., Huntington NY 11743. Editor: Bill Stephen. 65% freelance written. Bimonthly magazine covering computer-generated music and keyboard music. "Our readers are semi-professional/professional musicians with an interest in computer technology and how it applies to music. No general music pieces—everything must have a heavy technical slant." Circ. 52,000. Pays on publication. Byline given. Offers 25% kill fee. Buys first North American serial rights. Photocopied submissions OK. Query for electronic submissions. Computer printout submissions OK; prefers letter-quality. Reports in 2 weeks on queries; 3 weeks on mss. Sample copy for 9x12 SAE with $1.45 postage; free writer's guidelines.

Nonfiction: Book excerpts, how-to, interview/profile, new product, opinion and technical. Buys 25 mss/year. Query with published clips. Length: 250-2,500 words. Pays $25-350 for assigned articles. Sometimes pays the expenses of writers on assignment.

Photos: State availability of photos with submission. Reviews 3x5 transparencies and 8x10 prints. Offers $35-250 per photo. Captions and identification of subjects required. Buys one-time rights.

Columns/Departments: Speculations (opinion on music technology evolution), 1,500 words. Buys 4-6 mss/year. Query. Length: 1,200-1,800 words. Pays $120-180.

Tips: "The department most open to freelancers is Running Bytes; it uses short information with a local or national news slant."

THE MISSISSIPPI RAG, "The Voice of Traditional Jazz and Ragtime," The Mississippi Rag, Inc., 5644 Morgan Ave. S, Minneapolis MN 55419. (612)920-0312. Editor: Leslie Johnson. 70% freelance written. Works with small number of new/unpublished writers each year. A monthly tabloid covering traditional jazz and ragtime. Circ. 2,600. Pays on publication. Publishes ms an average of 4 months after acceptance. Byline given. Buys all rights, "but writer may negotiate if he wishes to use material later." Submit seasonal/holiday material 3 months in advance. Computer printout submissions OK; prefers letter-quality. Sample copy and writer's guidelines for 9x12 SAE with 56¢ postage.

Nonfiction: Historical, interview/profile, personal experience, photo features, current jazz and festival coverage, book reviews and record reviews. Reviews are always assigned. No "long winded essays on jazz or superficial pieces on local ice cream social Dixieland bands." Buys 24-30 mss/year. Query with published clips. Length: 1,500-4,000 words. Pays 1½¢/word.

Photos: Send photos with submission. Reviews 5x7 or 8x10 prints. Offers $4 minimum per photo. Identification of subjects required. Buys one-time rights.

Columns/Departments: Book and Record reviews. Buys 60 assigned mss/year. Query with published clips. Pays 1½¢/word.

Tips: "Become familiar with the jazz world. The *Rag* is read by musicians, jazz writers, historians, and jazz buffs. We want articles that have depth—solid facts and a good basic grasp of jazz history. Not for the novice jazz writer. Interviews with jazz and ragtime performers are most open to freelancers. It's wise to query first because we have already covered so many performers."

MODERN DRUMMER, Box 469, Cedar Grove NJ 07009. (201)239-4140. Editor-in-Chief: Ronald Spagnardi. Senior Editor: Rick Mattingly. Managing Editor: Rick Van Horn. Monthly for "student, semi-pro and professional drummers at all ages and levels of playing ability, with varied specialized interests within the field." 60% freelance written. Pays on publication. Publishes ms an average of 3 months after acceptance. Buys all rights. Photocopied and previously published submissions OK. Computer printout submissions acceptable; prefers letter-quality. Reports in 1 month. Sample copy $2.95; free writer's guidelines.

Nonfiction: How-to, informational, interview, new product, personal experience and technical. "All submissions must appeal to the specialized interests of drummers." Buys 20-30 mss/year. Query or submit complete ms. Length: 5,000-8,000 words. Pays $200-500. Pays expenses of writers on assignment.

Photos: Purchased with accompanying ms. Reviews 8x10 b&w prints and color transparencies.

Columns/Departments: Jazz Drummers Workshop, Rock Perspectives, In The Studio, Show Drummers Seminar, Teachers Forum, Drum Soloist, The Jobbing Drummer, Strictly Technique, Book Reviews, and Shop Talk. "Technical knowledge of area required for most columns." Buys 40-50 mss/year. Query or submit complete ms. Length: 500-2,500 words. Pays $25-150.

MUSIC MAGAZINE, Milthril Holdings Inc., 26 Edgewood Cres., Toronto M4W 3A4 Canada. Publisher: W. Michael Fletcher. 90% freelance written. Prefers to work with published/established writers; works with a small number of new/unpublished writers each year. Quarterly magazine emphasizing classical music. Circ. 8,000. Pays on publication. Publishes ms an average of 4 months after acceptance. Byline given. Buys first North American rights, one-time rights, and second serial (reprint) rights. Submit seasonal/holiday material 4 months in advance. Photocopied and previously published submissions (book excerpts) OK. Query for electronic submissions. Computer printout submissions acceptable; prefers letter-quality. Reports in 2 months. Sample copy and writer's guidelines $2.

Nonfiction: Interview, historical articles, photo feature and profile. "All articles should pertain to classical music and people in that world. We do not want any academic analysis or short pieces of family experiences in classical music." Query with published clips; phone queries OK. Unsolicited articles will not be returned. Length: 1,500-3,500 words. Pays $100-500. Sometimes pays expenses of writers on assignment.

Photos: State availability of photos. Pays $15-25 for 8x10 b&w glossy prints or contact sheets; $100 for color transparencies. No posed promotion photos. "Candid lively material only." Captions required. Buys one-time rights.

Tips: "Send a sample of your writing with suggested subjects. Off-beat subjects are welcome but must be thoroughly interesting to be considered. A famous person or major subject in music are your best bets."

MUSICAL AMERICA, 825 7th Ave., New York NY 10019. Editor: Shirley Fleming. 50% freelance written. Bimonthly. Circ. 20,000. Pays on publication. Publishes ms an average of 3-4 months after acceptance. Buys all rights. Computer printout submissions acceptable; no dot-matrix.
Nonfiction: Articles on classical music are generally prepared by acknowledged writers and authorities in the field, but uses freelance material. Query with published clips. Length: 1,200 words maximum. Pays $200 minimum.
Photos: New b&w photos of musical personalities, events, etc.

‡NINE-O-ONE NETWORK, Nine-O-One Network, Inc.. Suite G-4, 1437 Central Ave., Memphis TN 38104. (901)274-8602. Editor: Jim Dickerson. 25% freelance written. A bimonthly music magazine. "We cover rock, country, blues and jazz for a 'baby boomer' audience aged 25-35." Circ. 100,000. Pays on publication. Publishes ms an average of 4 months after acceptance. Byline given. Offers 50% kill fee. Buys first North American serial rights. Submit seasonal/holiday material 4 months in advance. Computer printout submissions OK; no dot-matrix. Sample copy $2.95.
Nonfiction: General interest, historical/nostalgic and interview/profile. Buys 20-30 mss/year. Query. Length: 750-2,500. Pays $100-200 for assigned articles. Pays $50-100 for unsolicited articles. State availability of photos with submission. Reviews contact sheets, negatives, transparencies and prints (8x10). Offers $10-50 per photo. Captions and identification of subjects required. Buys one-time rights.
Tips: "We're looking for well written stories that present artists as real people living in the real world. At this time we are not interested in articles about heavy metal groups."

ONE SHOT, Attentive Writing for Neglected Rock 'N' Roll, One Shot Enterprises, Box 9699, Berkeley CA 94709-9699. (415)527-7121. Editor: Steve Rosen. 80% freelance written. Eager to work with new/unpublished writers. "*One Shot* is a quarterly magazine dedicated to remembering now-obscure or under-appreciated performers of rock and related musics; expecially the one-hit wonders. Uses interviews, essays, poetry and fiction." Circ. 200. Pays on publication. Publishes ms an average of 6 months after acceptance. Byline given. Buys one-time, second serial (reprint) or simultaneous rights and makes work-for-hire assignments. Simultaneous, photocopied and previously published submissions OK. Computer printout submissions OK; prefers letter-quality. Reports in 1 month. Sample copy $2.50.
Nonfiction: Book excerpts, essays, expose, general interest, historical/nostalgic, interview/profile, opinion, personal experience and travel. No religious/inspirational articles. Buys 16 mss/year. Query. Length: 2,500 maximum words. Pays $50 maximum for assigned articles. Pays with copies for nonjournalism work. Sometimes pays expenses of writers on assignment.
Photos: State availability of photos with submission. Reviews contact sheets and 8½x11 prints. Offers no additional payment for photos accepted with ms. Buys one-time rights.
Columns/Departments: Speak, Memory! (personal experiences with now-obscure rock, etc., performers); and Travel (update on a place which once figured in a rock song, or performer's career, such as "Hitsville USA" studios in Detroit), up to 1,000 words. Buys 10 mss/year. Query with or without published clips or send complete ms. Length: 1,000 maximum words. Pays about $25.
Fiction: Adventure, condensed novels, confession, erotica, experimental, historical, humorous, mainstream, mystery, novel excerpts and slice-of-life vignettes. No fantasy, sci-fi or religious mss. Buys 8 mss/year. Query with or without published clips or send complete ms. Length: 2,500 maximum words. Pays in "copies, usually."
Poetry: Avant-garde, free verse, haiku, light verse and traditional. Buys 20 poems/year. Pays in "copies usually."
Tips: "*One Shot* needs 'Where are They Now' articles on obscure and neglected rock performers who once were popular. Those pieces should include interviews with the performer and others; and provide a sense of 'being there'. *One Shot* will pay for such stories. Just send me a note explaining your interests, and I'll respond with detailed suggestions. I won't disqualify anyone for not following procedures; I want to encourage a body of work on this topic. Also looking for remembrances, travel pieces, etc., concerning neglected rock."

PULSE!, Tower Records, 2500 Del Monte, Building C W., Sacramento CA 95691. (916)373-2450. Editor: Mike Farrace. Contact: Laurie MacIntosh. 80% freelance written. Works with a small number of new/unpublished writers each year. Monthly tabloid covering recorded music. Circ. 175,000. Pays on publication. Publishes ms an average of 2 months after acceptance. Byline given. Buys first serial rights. Simultaneous and photocopied submissions OK. Computer printout submissions acceptable; prefers letter-quality. Reports in 5 weeks. Sample copy for 12x15 SAE and 8 first class stamps; writer's guidelines for SAE.
Nonfiction: Feature stories and interview/profile (angled toward artist's taste in music, such as ten favorite albums, first record ever bought, anecdotes about early record buying experiences). Always looking for concise news items and commentary about nonpopular musical genres. Buys 200-250 mss/year. Query or send

complete ms. Length: 200-2,500 words. Pays $20-500. Sometimes pays expenses of writers on asignment.
Photos: State availability of photos. Color transparencies preferred, but will also review b&w prints. Caption and identification of subjects required. Buys one-time rights.
Fillers: Newsbreaks.
Tips: "Break in with 200- to 400-word news-oriented stories on recording artists or on fast breaking, record-related news, personnel changes, unusual match-ups, reissues of great material. Any kind of music. The more obscure genres are the hardest for us to cover, so they stand a good chance of being used. Remember, we are not only a magazine about records, but one that is owned by a record retailer."

RELIX MAGAZINE, Music for the Mind, Relix Magazine, Inc., Box 94, Brooklyn NY 11229. Editor: Toni A. Brown. 60% freelance written. Eager to work with new/unpublished writers. Bimonthly magazine covering rock 'n' roll music and specializing in Grateful Dead and other San Francisco and 60's related groups for readers ages 15-45. Circ. 20,000. Pays on publication. Publishes ms an average of 6 months after acceptance. Byline given. Buys all rights. Photocopied submissions OK. Computer printout submissions acceptable; prefers letter-quality. Sample copy $3.
Nonfiction: Historical/nostalgic, interview/profile, new product, personal experience, photo feature and technical. Special issues include year-end special. Query with published clips if available or send complete ms. Length open. Pays $1.50/column inch.
Columns/Departments: Query with published clips, if available, or send complete ms. Length: open. Pays variable rates.
Fiction: "We are seeking science fiction, rock and roll stories for a potential book." Query with published clips, if available, or send complete ms. Length: open. Pays variable rates.
Tips: "The most rewarding aspects of working with freelance writers are fresh writing and new outlooks."

‡ROCK & ROLL DISC, TAG Enterprises, 958 Patterson Cove, Memphis TN 38111. (901)458-1272. Editor: Tom Graves. Managing Editor: John Floyd. 75% freelance written. A bimonthly magazine on compact discs. "We review current compact discs relating to rock and roll. Our market is CD buyers who listen to rock and roll primarily. *Rock & Roll Disc* wants to publish the most informed and inspired music criticism possible." Estab. 1987. Circ. 5,000. Pays on publication. Publishes ms an average of 2 months after acceptance. Byline given. Buys all rights. Submit seasonal/holiday material 3 months in advance. Computer printout submissions OK. Reports in 2 weeks on queries; 3 weeks on mss. Sample copy for 8½x11 SAE with 3 first class stamps. Free writer's guidelines.
Nonfiction: Humor, interview/profile and reviews of compact discs. "No articles about audio equipment or interviews with unknown artists." Buys 100 mss/year. Query with published clips. Length: 200-2,000 words. Pays $15-25. Pays in contributor's copies "if we provide compact disc for writer." Sometimes pays the expenses of writers on assignment. Send photos with submission. Offers no additional payment for photos accepted with ms. Captions required. Buys all rights.
Columns/Departments: Guilty Pleasures (a disc the writer listens to but can't defend critically. Should be written with a humorous slant), 100 words. Buys 6 mss/year. Query with published clips. Length: 100-2,000 words. Pays $15-25.
Tips: "The writer needs to know the compact disc market and needs to have deep, abiding appreciation for rock and roll music and its related musical forms. For starters, writer should be familiar with *The Rolling Stone Record Guide* edited by Dave Marsh. It is a good introduction to music criticism. Writer should also read film critics such as John Simon. Writing should be literate with a touch of grace and humor. Avoid dwelling on technical aspects of CDs. Be well-informed of subject at hand."

ROLLING STONE, 745 5th Ave., New York NY 10151. Managing Editor: Jim Henke. 25-50% freelance written. Biweekly tabloid/magazine on contemporary music and lifestyle. "We seldom accept freelance material. All our work is assigned or done by our staff." Byline given. Offers 25% kill fee. Buys first rights only.
Nonfiction: Seeks new general interest topics. Queries must be concise, no longer than 2 pages. Send queries about musicians and music industry to music editor David Wild. Writers knowledgable about computers, VCRs, or sound equipment can submit an idea for the technology column that ranges from 50-word picture captions to 750-word pieces. Submit to Robert Love. Does not provide writer's guidelines; recommends reading *Rolling Stone* before submitting query.

THE $ENSIBLE SOUND, 403 Darwin Dr., Snyder NY 14226. Editor/Publisher: John A. Horan. 20% freelance written. Eager to work with new/unpublished writers. Quarterly magazine. "All readers are high fidelity enthusiasts, and many have a high fidelity industry-related job." Circ. 5,900. Pays on acceptance. Publishes ms an average of 3-6 months after acceptance. Byline given. Buys all rights. Simultaneous, photocopied, and previously published submissions OK. Computer printout submissions OK. Reports in 2 weeks. Sample copy $2.
Nonfiction: Expose; how-to; general interest; humor; historical; interview (people in hi-fi business, manufacturers or retail); new product (all types of new audio equipment); nostalgia (articles and opinion on older

equipment); personal experience (with various types of audio equipment); photo feature (on installation, or how-to tips); profile (of hi-fi equipment); and technical (pertaining to audio). "Subjective evaluations of hi-fi equipment make up 70% of our publication. We will accept 10 per issue." Buys 8 mss/year. Submit outline. Pays $25 maximum. Pays expenses of writers on assignment.

Columns/Departments: Bits & Pieces (short items of interest to hi-fi hobbyists); Ramblings (do-it-yourself tips on bettering existing systems); and Record Reviews (of records which would be of interest to audiophiles). Query. Length: 25-400 words. Pays $10/page.

SONG HITS, Charlton Publications, Charlton Bldg., Division St., Derby CT 06418. (203)735-3381. Editor: Mary Jane Canetti. 60% freelance written. Works with a small number of new/unpublished writers each year. A bimonthly magazine covering recording artists—rock, pop, heavy metal, soul and country. "*Song Hits* readers are between the ages of 10 and 21. Our philosophy in writing is to gear our material toward what is currently popular with our audience." Circ. 175,000. Pays on publication. Publishes ms an average of 3 months after acceptance. Byline given. Buys all rights. Simultaneous and photocopied submissions OK. Computer printout submissions acceptable; prefers letter-quality. Reports in 2 weeks. Free sample copy.
Nonfiction: Interview/profile. "We are not interested in articles about pop and rock people that are too adult for our young audience." Query with published clips. Length: 1,250-3,000 words. Pays $150.
Photos: State availability of photos with submission. Reviews contact sheets, 2x2 transparencies and 8x10 prints. Identification of subjects required. Buys one-time rights.
Columns/Departments: Concert Review (current reviews of popular touring groups), and Pick of the Litter (album reviews of current and/or up and coming talent; 8-10 per issue). Query with published clips. Length: 500-1,000 words.

‡SOUNDTRACK, Metropolitan Arts Magazine, SoundTrack Publishing, Box 609, Ringwood NJ 07456. (201)831-1317. Editor: Don Kulak. 60% freelance written. Bimonthly music and acoustics magazine. Estab. 1988. Circ. 20,000. Pays on acceptance. Publishes ms an average of 3-4 months after acceptance. Byline sometimes given. Buys first and second serial (reprint) rights. Submit seasonal/holiday material 4 months in advance. Simultaneous, photocopied and previously published submissions OK. Computer printout submissions OK; no dot-matrix. Reports in 1 week on queries; 3 weeks on mss. Free sample copy and writer's guidelines.
Nonfiction: Book excerpts, expose, how-to, interview/profile, new product, opinion, technical. Buys 36 mss/year. Query with published clips. Length: 1,500-5,000 words.. Pays $50-200 for assigned articles; $20-75 for unsolicited articles. Sometimes pays writers with contributor copies or other premiums rather than cash by "mutually beneficial agreement." Sometimes pays expenses of writers on assignment.
Photos: State availability of photos with submissions. Offers $10-20 per photo. Buys all rights.
Columns/Departments: Sound Input (in-depth and objective reporting on audio equipment and technology, emphasizing acoustical ramifications); Acousticraft (in-depth articles on acoustics in general, including acoustic instruments, concert halls, hearing). Buys 24 mss/year. Query with published clips. Length: 1,500-3,500 words.
Poetry: Avant-garde, haiku and traditional. Buys 12 poems/year. Submit maximum of 3 poems at one time. Pays $35-65.
Fillers: Facts, gags to be illustrated by cartoonist, newsbreaks, short humor. Buys 45/year. Length: 150-500. Pays $10-45.
Tips: "Write a letter explaining background, interests, and areas of special study and what you hope to get out of writing for our publication. All sections are open to freelancers. Writing should be fluid and direct. When describing music, the writing should paint an aural picture with good use of metaphors, and not be overly critical or pretentious. Technical writing should be well documented."

STEREO REVIEW, Diamandis Communications, Inc., 1515 Broadway, New York NY 10036. (212)719-6000. Editor-at-large: William Livingstone. Editor-in-Chief: Louise Boundas. Executive Editor: Michael Smolen. 95% freelance written. A monthly magazine. Circ. 550,000. Pays on publication. Publishes ms an average of 5 months after acceptance. Byline given. Buys first North American serial rights, first rights or all rights. Computer printout submissions acceptable; prefers letter-quality. Sample copy for 9x12 SAE with $1.24 postage.
Nonfiction: Technical and music reviews, and interview/profile. Buys approximately 25 mss/year. Query with published clips. Length: 1,500-3,000 words. Pays $350-750 for assigned articles.
Tips: "Radical change in consumer interest in music reproduction systems (stereo equipment) will impact on the current focus of this magazine."

TRADITION, Prairie Press, 106 Navajo, Council Bluffs IA 51501. (712)366-1136. Editor: Robert Everhart. 20% freelance written. Quarterly magazine emphasizing traditional country music and other aspects of pioneer living. Circ. 2,500. Pays on publication. Not copyrighted. Byline given. Buys one-time rights. Submit seasonal/holiday material 6 months in advance. Simultaneous queries, and simultaneous, photocopied, and previously published submissions OK. Computer printout submissions acceptable. Reports in 1 month. Free sample copy.

Nonfiction: Historical (relating to country music); how-to (play, write, or perform country music); inspirational (on country gospel); interview (with country performers, both traditional and contemporary); nostalgia (pioneer living); personal experience (country music); and travel (in connection with country music contests or festivals). Query. Length: 800-1,200 words. Pays $25-50.

Photos: State availability of photos with query. Payment included in ms price. Reviews 5x7 b&w prints. Captions and model releases required. Buys one-time rights.

Poetry: Free verse and traditional. Buys 4 poems/year. Length: 5-20 lines. Submit maximum 2 poems. Pays $2-5.

Fillers: Clippings, jokes and anecdotes. Buys 5/year. Length: 15-50 words. Pays $5-10.

Tips: "Material must be concerned with what we term 'real' country music as opposed to today's 'pop' country music. Freelancer must be knowledgable of the subject; many writers don't even know who the father of country music is, let alone write about him."

Mystery

These magazines buy fictional accounts of crime, detective work and mystery. Additional mystery markets can be found in the Literary and "Little" section. Several magazines in the Detective and Crime category also buy mystery fiction. Skim through other sections to identify markets for fiction; many of these will buy mysteries.

ALFRED HITCHCOCK'S MYSTERY MAGAZINE, Davis Publications, Inc., 380 Lexington Ave., New York NY 10017. Editor: Cathleen Jordan. Magazine published 13 times a year emphasizing mystery fiction. Circ. 225,000. Pays on acceptance. Byline given. Buys first serial rights, second serial (reprint) rights and foreign rights. Submit seasonal/holiday material 7 months in advance. Photocopied submissions OK. Reports in 2 months. Writer's guidelines for SASE.

Fiction: Original and well-written mystery and crime fiction. Length: up to 14,000 words.

ELLERY QUEEN'S MYSTERY MAGAZINE, Davis Publications, Inc., 380 Lexington Ave., New York NY 10017. Editor: Eleanor Sullivan. 100% freelance written. Magazine published 13 times/year. Circ. 375,000. Pays on acceptance. Publishes ms an average of 6 months after acceptance. Byline given. Buys first serial rights or second serial (reprint) rights. Submit seasonal/holiday material 7 months in advance. Simultaneous, photocopied, and previously published submissions OK. Computer printout submissions acceptable; prefers letter-quality. Reports in 1 month. Writer's guidelines for #10 SASE.

Fiction: Special consideration will be given to "anything timely and original. We publish every type of mystery: the suspense story, the psychological study, the deductive puzzle—the gamut of crime and detection from the realistic (including stories of police procedure) to the more imaginative (including 'locked rooms' and impossible crimes). We always need detective stories, and do not want sex, sadism or sensationalism-for-the-sake-of-sensationalism." No gore or horror; seldom publishes parodies or pastiches. Buys up to 13 mss/issue. Length: 6,000 words maximum; occasionally higher but not often. Pays 3-8¢/word.

Tips: "We have a department of First Stories to encourage writers whose fiction has never before been in print. We publish an average of 13 first stories a year."

A MATTER OF CRIME, Harcourt Brace Jovanovich/Harvest Imprint, 2006 Sumter St., Columbia SC 29201. (803)771-4642. Co-Editors: Matthew J. Bruccoli and Richard Layman. 100% freelance written. A semi-annual "bookazine" publishing spy, mystery and detective fiction. Pays on publication. Publishes ms an average of 4 months after acceptance. Byline given. Buys first serial worldwide rights. Photocopied submissions OK. Computer printout submissions acceptable; prefers letter-quality. Reports in 3 weeks on queries; 6 weeks on mss.

Fiction: Mystery, spy, detective and suspense and novel excerpts. Buys 25 mss/year. Length: 2,000-10,000 words. Pays negotiable rates.

ALWAYS submit manuscripts or queries with a self-addressed, stamped envelope (SASE) within your country or International Reply Coupons (IRC) purchased from the post office for other countries.

Nature, Conservation and Ecology

These publications promote reader awareness of the natural environment, wildlife, nature preserves and ecosystems. They do not publish recreation or travel articles except as they relate to conservation or nature. Other markets for this kind of material can be found in the Regional; Sports; and Travel, Camping and Trailer categories, although magazines listed there require that nature or conservation articles be slanted to their specialized subject matter and audience. Some juvenile and teen publications also buy nature-related material for young audiences.

THE AMICUS JOURNAL, Natural Resources Defense Council, 122 E. 42nd St., Rm. 4500, New York NY 10168. (212)949-0049. Editor: Peter Borrelli. 80% freelance written. Quarterly magazine covering national and international environmental policy. "*The Amicus Journal* is intended to provide the general public with a journal of thought and opinion on environmental affairs, particularly those relating to policies of national and international significance." Circ. 90,000. Pays on acceptance. Publishes ms an average of 6 months after acceptance. Byline given. Offers 50% kill fee. Buys first North American serial rights. Submit seasonal/holiday material 6 months in advance. Query for electronic submissions. Computer printout submissions OK; prefers letter-quality. Reports in 6 weeks. Sample copy for 9x12 SAE with 4 first class stamps.
Nonfiction: Expose and interview/profile. No articles not concerned with environmental issues of national or international policy significance. Buys 25 mss/year. Query with published clips. Length: 200-1,500 words. Payment negotiable. Sometimes pays expenses of writers on assignment.
Photos: State availability of photos with submssion. Reviews contact sheets, negatives, transparencies and 8x10 prints. Offers negotiable payment for photos. Captions, model releases and identification of subjects required. Buys one-time rights.
Columns/Departments: News and Comment (summary reporting of environmental issues, usually tied to topical items), 200-500 words; Articles (in-depth reporting on issues and personalities), 750-1,500 words; Book Reviews (well-informed essays on books of general interest to environmentalists interested in policy and history), 500-1,000 words. Buys 25 mss/year. Query with published clips. Payment negotiable.
Poetry: Poetry Editor: Brian Swann. Avant-garde and free verse. All poetry should be rooted in nature. Buys 20 poems/year. Pays $25.
Tips: "Except for editorials, all departments are open to freelance writers. Queries should precede manuscripts, and manuscripts should conform to the *Chicago Manual of Style*. Writers are asked to be sensitive to tone. As a policy magazine, we do not publish articles of a personal or satirical nature."

APPALACHIAN TRAILWAY NEWS, Appalachian Trail Conference, Box 807, Harpers Ferry WV 25425. (304)535-6331. 50% freelance written. Bimonthly magazine "subject matter must relate to Appalachian Trail." Circ. 22,000. Pays on acceptance. Byline given. Buys first North American serial rights or second serial (reprint) rights. Submit seasonal/holiday material 4 months in advance. Photocopied and previously published submissions OK. Reports in 1 month. Sample copy $2.50; writer's guidelines for #10 SASE.
Nonfiction: Essays, general interest, historical/nostalgic, how-to, humor, inspirational, interview/profile, personal experience, photo feature, technical and travel. No poetry or religious materials. Buys 15-20 mss/year. Query with or without published clips, or send complete ms. Length: 250-3,000 words. Pays $25-300. Pays expenses of writers on assignment.
Photos: State availability of black and white photos with submission. Reviews contact sheets, negatives and 5x7 prints. Offers $10-25 per photo. Identification of subjects required. Buys one-time rights.
Tips: "Contributors should display an obvious knowledge of or interest in the Appalachian Trail. Those who live in the vicinity of the Trail may opt for an assigned story and should present credentials and subject in which interested to the editor."

THE ATLANTIC SALMON JOURNAL, The Atlantic Salmon Federation, Suite 1030, 1435 St. Alexandre, Montreal, Quebec H3A 2G4 Canada. (514)842-8059. Editor: Terry Davis. 50-68% freelance written. Works with a small number of new/unpublished writers each year. A quarterly magazine covering conservation efforts for the Atlantic salmon. Caters to "affluent and responsive audience—the dedicated angler and conservationist of the Atlantic salmon." Circ. 20,000. Pays on publication. Publishes ms an average of 3-6 months after acceptance. Byline given. Buys first serial rights to articles and one-time rights to photos. Submit seasonal/holiday material 3 months in advance. Simultaneous queries, and simultaneous and photocopied submissions OK. Query for electronic submissions. Computer printout submissions acceptable; no dot-matrix. Reports in 2 months. Sample copy for 9x12 SAE and $1 (Canadian), or SAE with IRC; free writer's guidelines.

Nonfiction: Expose, historical/nostalgic, how-to, humor, interview/profile, new product, opinion, personal experience, photo feature, technical, travel, conservation, cuisine, science, research and management. "We are seeking articles that are pertinent to the focus and purpose of our magazine, which is to inform and entertain our membership on all aspects of the Atlantic salmon and its environment, preservation and conservation." Buys 15-20 mss/year. Query with published clips and state availability of photos. Length: 1,500-3,000 words. Pays $100-325. Sometimes pays the expenses of writers on assignment.

Photos: State availability of photos with query. Pays $35-50 for 3x5 or 5x7 b&w prints; $35-150 for 2¼x3¼ or 35mm color slides. Captions and identification of subjects required.

Columns/Departments: Adventure Eating (cuisine) and First Person (nonfiction, anecdotal, from first person viewpoint, can be humorous). Buys about 6 mss/year. Length: 1,000-1,500 words. Pays $175.

Fiction: Adventure, fantasy, historical, humorous and mainstream. "We don't want to see anything that does not deal with Atlantic salmon directly or indirectly. Wilderness adventures are acceptable as long as they deal with Atlantic salmon." Buys 3 ms/year. Query with published clips. Length: 3,000 words maximum. Pays $150-325.

Fillers: Clippings, jokes, anecdotes and short humor. Length: 100-300 words average. Does not pay. Cartoons, single or multi-panel, $25-75.

Tips: "We will be buying more consumer oriented articles—travel, equipment. Articles must reflect informed and up-to-date knowledge of Atlantic salmon. Writers need not be authorities, but research must be impeccable. Clear, concise writing is a plus, and submissions must be typed. Anecdote, River Log and photo essays are most open to freelancers. The odds are that a writer without a background in outdoors writing and wildlife reporting will not have the 'informed' angle I'm looking for. Our readership is well-read and critical of simplification and generalization."

BIRD WATCHER'S DIGEST, Pardson Corp., Box 110, Marietta OH 45750. Editor: Mary Beacom Bowers. 60% freelance written. Works with a small number of new/unpublished writers each year. Bimonthly magazine covering natural history—birds and bird watching. "*BWD* is a nontechnical magazine interpreting ornithological material for amateur observers, including the knowledgeable birder, the serious novice and the backyard bird watcher; we strive to provide good reading and good ornithology," Circ. 60,000. Pays on publication. Publishes ms an average of 1 year after acceptance. Byline given. Buys one-time rights, first serial rights and second serial (reprint) rights. Submit seasonal/holiday material 6 months in advance. Previously published submissions OK. Computer printout submissions acceptable; no dot-matrix. Reports in 6 weeks. Sample copy $3; writer's guidelines for #10 SASE.

Nonfiction: Book excerpts, how-to (relating to birds, feeding and attracting, etc.), humor, personal experience and travel (limited—we get many). "We are especially interested in fresh, lively accounts of closely observed bird behavior and displays and of bird watching experiences and expeditions. We often need material on less common species or on unusual or previously unreported behavior of common species." No articles on pet or caged birds; none on raising a baby bird. Buys 75-90 mss/year. Send complete ms. Length: 600-3,500 words. Pays $25-50 minimum.

Photos: Send photos with ms. Pays $10 minimum for b&w prints; $25 minimum for color transparencies. Buys one-time rights.

Poetry: Avant-garde, free verse, light verse and traditional. No haiku. Buys 12-18 poems/year. Submit maximum 3 poems. Length 8-20 lines. Pays $10.

Tips: "We are aimed at an audience ranging from the backyard bird watcher to the very knowledgable birder; we include in each issue material that will appeal at various levels. We always strive for a good geographical spread, with material from every section of the country. We leave very technical matters to others, but we want facts and accuracy, depth and quality, directed at the veteran bird watcher and at the enthusiastic novice. We stress the joys and pleasures of bird watching, its environmental contribution, and its value for the individual and society."

‡ENVIRONMENT, 4000 Albemarle St. NW, Washington DC 20016. Managing Editor: Jane Scully. 2% freelance written. For citizens, scientists, business and government executives, teachers, high school and college students interested in environment or effects of technology and science in public affairs. Magazine published 10 times/year. Circ. 17,000. Buys all rights. Byline given. Pays on publication to professional writers. Publishes ms an average of 5 months after acceptance. Photocopied submissions OK. Computer printout submissions acceptable; no dot-matrix. Reports in 6-8 weeks. Query or submit 3 double-spaced copies of complete ms. Sample copy $3.50.

Nonfiction: Scientific and environmental material, and effects of technology on society. Preferred length: 2,500-4,500 words for full-length article. Pays $100-300, depending on material. Also accepts shorter articles (1,100-1,700 words) for "Overview" section. Pays $75. "All full-length articles must be annotated (referenced), and all conclusions must follow logically from the facts and arguments presented." Prefers articles centering around policy-oriented, public decision-making, scientific and technological issues.

‡ENVIRONMENTAL ACTION, 1525 New Hampshire Ave. NW, Washington DC 20036. (202)745-4870. Editors: Rose Marie Audette and Hawley Truax. 30% freelance written. Bimonthly magazine on environmental news and policy. "*Environmental Action* provides balanced reporting on key environmental issues facing the U.S.—particularly at a national level. Articles are written for a general audience—we don't assume any knowledge of environmental conditions or problems." Circ. 22,000. Pays on publication. Publishes ms an average of 2 months after acceptance. Kill fee negotiated. Byline given. Buys first North American serial rights or second serial (reprint) rights. Simultaneous and photocopied submissions OK (author must specify that material is being submitted elsewhere). Computer printout submissions OK; prefers letter-quality. Reports in 4 months. Sample copy for 9x12 SAE with 3 first class stamps; free writer's guidelines.

Nonfiction: Expose, interview/profile, news feature, political analysis, book reviews. No nature appreciation, personal history, adventure in nature, academic/journal articles, or opinion articles. Buys 20 mss/year. Query with or without published clips, or send complete ms. Length: 250-3,000 words. Pays $40-300. Sometimes pays expenses of writers on assignment.

Photos: State availability of photos with submission. Reviews contact sheets, negatives and prints. Offers $25/photo, $50/cover. Captions required. Buys one-time rights.

HIGH COUNTRY NEWS, High Country Foundation, Box 1090, Paonia CO 81428. (303)527-4898. Editor: Betsy Marston. 80% freelance written. Works with a small number of new/unpublished writers each year. Biweekly tabloid covering environment and natural resource issues in the Rocky Mountain states for environmentalists, politicians, companies, college classes, government agencies, etc. Circ. 7,000. Pays on publication. Publishes ms an average of 2 months after acceptance. Byline given. Buys one-time rights. Submit seasonal/holiday material 6 weeks in advance. Computer printout submissions acceptable if "double-spaced (at least) and legible"; prefers letter-quality. Reports in 1 month. Free sample copy and writer's guidelines.

Nonfiction: Reporting (local issues with regional importance); expose (government, corporate); interview/profile; opinion; personal experience; and centerspread photo feature. Special issues include those on states in the region. Buys 100 mss/year. Query. Length: 3,000 words maximum. Pays 5-10¢/word. Sometimes pays the expenses of writers on assignment.

Photos: Send photos with ms. Reviews b&w contact sheets and prints. Captions and identification of subjects required.

Poetry: Chip Rawlins, poetry editor, 67½ S. 500 W., Logan UT 84321. Avant-garde, free verse, haiku, light verse and traditional. Pays in contributor copies.

Tips: "We use a lot of freelance material, though very little from outside the Rockies. Start by writing short, 500-word news items of timely, regional interest."

INTERNATIONAL WILDLIFE, National Wildlife Federation, 1412 16th St. NW, Washington DC 20036-2266. Managing Editor: Jonathan Fisher. 85% freelance written. Prefers to work with published/established writers. Bimonthly for persons interested in natural history, outdoor adventure and the environment. Circ. 400,000. Pays on acceptance. Publishes ms an average of 4 months after acceptance. Usually buys all rights to text. "We are now assigning most articles but will consider detailed proposals for quality feature material of interest to a broad audience." Computer printout submissions acceptable; prefers letter quality. Reports in 6 weeks. Writer's guidelines for #10 SASE.

Nonfiction: Focuses on world wildlife, environmental problems and man's relationship to the natural world as reflected in such issues as population control, pollution, resource utilization, food production, etc. Especially interested in articles on animal behavior and other natural history, first-person experiences by scientists in the field, well-reported coverage of wildlife-status case studies which also raise broader themes about international conservation, and timely issues. Query. Length: 2,000-2,500 words. Also in the market for short, 750-word "one pagers." Examine past issue for style and subject matter. Pays $1,000 minimum. Sometimes pays expenses of writers on assignment.

Photos: Purchases top-quality color photos; prefers packages of related photos and text, but single shots of exceptional interest and sequences also considered. Prefers Kodachrome transparencies. Buys one-time rights.

Tips: "Send us a detailed query that will speak for itself; if we respond favorably, the writer's plugged in."

MICHIGAN NATURAL RESOURCES MAGAZINE, State of Michigan Department of Natural Resources, Box 30034, Lansing MI 48909. (517)373-9267. Editor: N.R. McDowell. Managing Editor: Richard Morscheck. 60% freelance written. Works with a small number of new/unpublished writers each year. Bimonthly magazine covering natural resources in the Great Lakes area. Circ. 125,000. Pays on acceptance. Publishes ms an average of 6 months after acceptance. Byline given. Offers 100% kill fee. Buys first rights. Submit seasonal/holiday material 1 year in advance. Computer printout submissions acceptable; no dot-matrix. Reports in 1 month. Sample copy for $2.50 and 9x12 SAE; writer's guidelines for #10 SASE.

Nonfiction: "All material must pertain to this region's natural resources: lakes, rivers, wildlife, flora and special features. No personal experience, domestic animal stories or animal rehabilitation." Buys 24 mss/year.

Query with clips of published work. Length: 1,000-4,000 words. Pays $150-400. Sometimes pays the expenses of writers on assignment.

Photos: Gijsbert (Nick) vanFrankenhuyzen, photo editor. "Photos submitted with an article can help sell it, but they must be razor sharp in focus." Send photos with ms. Pays $50-200 for 35mm color transparencies; Kodachrome 64 or 25 preferred. Model releases and identification of subjects required. Buys one-time rights.

Tips: "We hope to exemplify why Michigan's natural resources are valuable to people and vice versa."

NATIONAL PARKS, 1015 31st St., Washington DC 20007. (202)944-8565. Senior Editor: Michele Strutin. 75% freelance written. Prefers to work with published/established writers. Bimonthly magazine for a highly educated audience interested in preservation of National Park System units, natural areas and protection of wildlife habitat. Circ. 60,000. Pays on acceptance. Publishes ms an average of 6 months after acceptance. Buys first North American serial rights and second serial (reprint) rights. Submit seasonal/holiday material 5 months in advance. Query for electronic submissions. Computer printout submissions acceptable if legible; prefers letter-quality. Reports in 10 weeks. Sample copy $3; writer's guidelines for SASE.

Nonfiction: Expose (on threats, wildlife problems to national parks); descriptive articles about new or proposed national parks and wilderness parks; brief natural history pieces describing park geology, wildlife, or plants; "adventures" in national parks (cross country skiing, bouldering, mountain climbing, kayaking, canoeing, backpacking); and travel tips to national parks. All material must relate to national parks. No poetry or philosophical essays. Buys 6-10 unsolicited mss/year. "We prefer queries rather than unsolicited stories." Length: 1,000-1,500 words. Pays $75-400.

Photos: State availability of photos or send photos with ms. Pays $25-50 for 8x10 b&w glossy prints; $35-150 for color transparencies. Captions required. Buys first North American serial rights.

NATIONAL WILDLIFE, National Wildlife Federation, 8925 Leesburg Pike, Vienna VA 22184. (703)790-4510. Executive Editor: Bob Strohm. Managing Editor: Mark Wexler. 90% freelance written. Works with a small number of new/unpublished writers each year. Bimonthly magazine on wildlife, natural history and environment. "Our purpose is to promote wise use of the nation's natural resources and to conserve and protect wildlife and its habitat. We reach a broad audience that is largely interested in wildlife conservation and nature photography. We avoid too much scientific detail and prefer anecdotal, natural history material." Circ. 850,000. Pays on acceptance. Publishes ms an average of 1 year after acceptance. Offers 25% kill fee. Buys all rights. Submit seasonal/holiday material 8 months in advance. Computer printout submissions acceptable; prefers letter-quality. Reports in 6 weeks. Sample copy for 9x12 SAE and 4 first class stamps; writer's guidelines for #10 SAE and 1 first class stamp.

Nonfiction: Book excerpts (nature related); general interest (2,500-word features on wildlife, new discoveries, behavior, or the environment); how-to (an outdoor or nature related activity); personal experience (outdoor adventure); photo feature (wildlife); and short 700-word features on an unusual individual or new scientific discovery relating to nature. Buys 50 mss/year. Query with or without published clips. Length: 750-2,500 words. Pays $500-1,750. Sometimes pays expenses of writers on assignment.

Photos: John Nuhn, photo editor. State availability of photos or send photos with query. Reviews 35mm color transparencies. Pays $250-750. Buys one-time rights.

Tips: "Writers can break in with us more readily by proposing subjects (initially) that will take only one or two pages in the magazine (short features)."

NATURAL HISTORY, Natural History Magazine, 79th and Central Park W., New York NY 10024. Editor: Alan Ternes. Over 75% freelance written. Monthly magazine for well-educated, ecologically aware audience: professional people, scientists and scholars. Circ. 500,000. Pays on publication. Publishes ms an average of 3 months after acceptance. Byline given. Buys first serial rights and becomes agent for second serial (reprint) rights. Submit seasonal material 6 months in advance. Computer printout submissions acceptable. Sample copy $3.

Nonfiction: Uses all types of scientific articles except chemistry and physics—emphasis is on the biological sciences and anthropology. Prefers professional scientists as authors. "We always want to see new research findings in almost all the branches of the natural sciences—anthropology, archeology, zoology and ornithology. We find that it is particularly difficult to get something new in herpetology (amphibians and reptiles) or entomology (insects), and we would like to see material in those fields. We lean heavily toward writers who are scientists. We expect high standards of writing and research. We favor an ecological slant in most of our pieces, but do not generally lobby for causes, environmental or other. The writer should have a deep knowledge of his subject, then submit original ideas either in query or by manuscript. Acceptance is more likely if article is accompanied by high-quality photographs." Buys 60 mss/year. Query or submit complete ms. Length: 2,000-4,000 words. Pays $650-1,000, plus additional payment for photos used.

Photos: Rarely uses 8x10 b&w glossy prints; pays $125/page maximum. Much color is used; pays $300 for inside and up to $500 for cover. Buys one-time rights.

Tips: "Learn about something in depth before you bother writing about it."

OCEANS, Ocean Magazine Associates, Inc., 2001 W. Main St., Stamford CT 06902. Editor: Michael Robbins. 100% freelance written. Prefers to work with published/established writers and works with small number of new/unpublished writers each year. Bimonthly magazine; 72 pages. For people who love the sea. Circ. 50,000. Pays on acceptance. Publishes ms an average of 3 months after acceptance. Byline given. Buys first serial rights; some second serial (reprint) rights. Submit seasonal/holiday material 4 months in advance. Simultaneous and photocopied submissions OK, if identified as such. Query for electronic submissions. Computer printout submissions acceptable if legible. Reports in 2 months. Sample copy $3; writer's guidelines for SASE.
Nonfiction: "We want articles on the worldwide realm of salt water: marine life (biology and ecology), oceanography, maritime history, marine painting and other arts, geography, undersea exploration, voyages, ships, coastal areas including environmental problems, seaports and shipping, islands, aquaculture, peoples of the sea, including anthropological materials. Writing should be direct, factual, very readable; not cute, flippant or tongue-in-cheek." Buys 60 mss/year. Query with SASE. Length: 1,000-6,000 words. Pays $750-1,000. Sometimes pays expenses of writers on assignment.
Tips: "We could use more profiles of important people in the marine world, and more articles of interest to cruise ship passengers."

OCEANUS, The International Magazine of Marine Science and Policy, Woods Hole Oceanographic Institution, Woods Hole MA 02543. (617)548-1400, ext. 2386. Editor: Paul R. Ryan. Assistant Editor: James Hain. 10% freelance written. "*Oceanus* is an international quarterly magazine that monitors significant trends in ocean research, technology and marine policy. Its basic purpose is to encourage wise, environmentally responsible use of the oceans. In addition, two of the magazine's main tasks are to explain the significance of present marine research to readers and to expose them to the substance of vital public policy questions." Circ. 15,000. Pays on publication. Publishes ms an average of 3 months after acceptance. Byline given. Buys all rights. Simultaneous queries OK. Computer printout submissions acceptable; no dot-matrix. Reports in 2 months.
Nonfiction: Interview/profile and technical. *Oceanus* publishes 4 thematic issues/year. Most articles are commissioned. Length: 2,700-3,500 words. Pays $300 minimum. Sometimes pays expenses of writers on assignment.
Photos: State availability of photos. Reviews b&w and color contact sheets and 8x10 prints. Pays variable rates depending on size; $125/full-page b&w print. Captions required. Buys one-time rights.
Tips: The writer has a better chance of breaking in at this publication with short articles and fillers. "Most of our writers are top scientists in their fields."

‡OUTDOOR AMERICA, Suite 1100, 1701 N. Ft. Myer Dr., Arlington VA 22209. (703)528-1818. Editor: Kevin Kasowski. 50-75% freelance written. Prefers to work with published/established writers. Quarterly magazine about natural resource conservation and outdoor recreation for sportsmen and local conservationists who are members of the Izaak Walton League. Circ. 50,000. Pays on publication. Publishes ms an average of 4 months after acceptance. Byline given. Buys all rights or first serial rights, depending on arrangements with author. "Considers previously published material if there's not a lot of audience overlap." Query first. Submit seasonal material 6 months in advance. Simultaneous and photocopied submissions OK, if so indicated. Computer printout submissions acceptable; no dot-matrix. Reports in 2 months. Sample copy $1.50 with 9x12 SAE; writer's guidelines for SASE.
Nonfiction: "We are interested in thoroughly researched, well-written pieces on current natural resource and recreation issues of national importance (threats to water, fisheries, wildlife habitat, air, public lands, soil, etc.); articles on wildlife management controversies, and first-person essays and humor pieces on outdoor recreation themes (fishing, hunting, camping, ethical outdoor behavior, etc.)." Length: 1,500-2,500 words. Payment: minimum 15¢/word.
Columns/Departments: Interested in shorter articles for the following departments: "Close to Home" (short articles on enviromental/consumer problems--e.g. radon, lawn chemicals, etc.); "From the Naturalist's Notebook" (pieces that give insight into the habits and behavior of animals, fish, birds). Length: 500-600 words. Payment: minimum 10¢/word.
Photos: Reviews 5x7 b&w glossy prints and 35mm and larger color transparencies. Additional payment for photos with ms negotiated. Pays $225 for covers. Captions and model releases required. Buys one-time rights.
Tips: "Writers should obtain guidelines and sample issue *before* querying us. They will understand our needs and editorial focus much better if they've done this. Queries submitted without the writer having read the guidelines are *almost always* off base and almost always rejected."

SEA FRONTIERS, 3979 Rickenbacker Causeway, Virginia Key, Miami FL 33149. (305)361-5786. Editor: Gilbert L. Voss. Executive Editor: Jean Bradfisch. 95% freelance written. Works with a small number of new/unpublished writers each year. Bimonthly. "For anyone interested in the sea, its conservation, and the life it contains. Our audience is professional people for the most part; people in executive positions and students." Circ. 30,000. Pays on acceptance. Publishes ms an average of 4-10 months after acceptance. Byline given. Buys first serial rights. Will consider photocopied submissions "if very clear." Computer printout submissions acceptable; no dot-matrix. Reports on submissions in 2 months. Sample copy $3; writer's guidelines for SASE.

Nonfiction: "Articles (with illustrations) covering interesting and little known facts about the sea, marine life, chemistry, geology, physics, fisheries, mining, engineering, navigation, influences on weather and climate, ecology, conservation, explorations, discoveries or advances in our knowledge of the marine sciences, or describing the activities of oceanographic laboratories or expeditions to any part of the world. Emphasis should be on research and discoveries rather than personalities involved." Buys 40-50 mss/year. Query. Length: 1,000-3,000 words. Pays $150-450.

Photos: Reviews 8x10 b&w glossy prints and 35mm (or larger) color transparencies. Pays $100 for color used on front and $60 for the back cover.

Tips: "Query should include a paragraph or two that tells the subject, the angle or approach to be taken, and the writer's qualifications for covering this subject or the authorities with whom the facts will be checked."

SIERRA, 730 Polk St., San Francisco CA 94109. (415)923-5656. Editor-in-Chief: Jonathan F. King. Managing Editor: Joan Hamilton. Senior Editor: Annie Stine. Associate Editors: Reed McManus, Anders Price. 80% freelance written. Works with a small number of new/unpublished writers each year. Bimonthly magazine emphasizing conservation and environmental politics for people who are well educated, activist, outdoor-oriented, and politically well informed with a dedication to conservation. Circ. 350,000. Pays on acceptance. Publishes ms an average of 6 months after acceptance. Byline given. Buys first North American serial rights. Photocopied submissions OK. Query for electronic submissions. Computer printout submissions acceptable; prefers letter-quality. Reports in 6 weeks. Writer's guidelines for SAE and 2 first class stamps.

Nonfiction: Expose (well-documented on environmental issues of national importance such as energy, wilderness, forests, etc.); general interest (well-researched pieces on areas of particular environmental concern); historical (relevant to environmental concerns); how-to and equipment pieces (on camping, climbing, outdoor photography, etc.); profiles (of environmental activists); interview (with very prominent figures in the field); photo feature (photo essays on threatened areas); and journalistic treatments of semi-technical topics (energy sources, wildlife management, land use, waste management, etc.). No "My trip to . . . " or "why we must save wildlife/nature" articles; no poetry or general superficial essays on environmentalism and local environmental issues. Buys 10-15 mss/issue. Query with published clips. Length: 800-2,500 words. Pays $200-1,000. Sometimes pays expenses of writers on assignment (up to $50).

Photos: Silvana Nova, art and production manager. State availability of photos. Pays $200 maximum for color transparencies; $200 for cover photos. Buys one-time rights.

Columns/Departments: Book reviews. Buys 20-25 mss/year. Length: 750-1,000 words. Pays $100; submit queries to Mark Nardon, assistant editor. For Younger Readers, natural history and conservation topics presented for children ages 8 to 13. Pays $200-500; submit queries to Reed McManus, associate editor.

Tips: "Queries should include an outline of how the topic would be covered and a mention of the political appropriateness and timeliness of the article. Familiarity with Sierra Club positions and policies is recommended. Statements of the writer's qualifications should be included. We don't have fillers in our format. Our redesign introduced new departments (Afield and Hot Spots) that use shorter pieces than we've been able to previously use."

_____ *Personal Computers*

Personal computer magazines continue to change and evolve. Many add or eliminate computer models that they report on, and the majority are becoming model-specific. Many computer magazines have folded. Be sure you see the most recent issue of a magazine before submitting material to it. Business applications for home computers are covered in the Business and Finance section. Publications for data processing personnel are listed in the Trade Information Systems section. Uses of computers in specific professions are covered in the appropriate trade section.

‡AMAZING COMPUTING, PiM Publications, Inc., 1 Currant Place, Box 869, Fall River MA 02720. (617)678-4200. Editor: Ernest P. Viveiros. Managing Editor: Donald D. Hicks. 90% freelance written. Monthly magazine for the Commodore Amiga computer system user. Circ. 35,000. Pays on publication. Publishes ms an average of 1-2 months after acceptance. No byline. Buys all rights. Query for electronic submissions. Computer printout submissions OK. Sample copy for $5; free writer's guidelines.

Nonfiction: How-to, new product, technical, reviews and tutorials. Buys 100 mss/year. Query. Length: 1,000 words minimum. Pays $70. Sometimes pays the expenses of writers on assignment.

Photos: Send photos with submission. Reviews 4x5 prints. Offers $25 per photo. Captions required. Buys all rights.
Columns/Departments: Reviews, Programs. Buys 200 mss/year. Query. Length: 1,000-5,000 words.

AMIGAWORLD, Exploring the Amiga, IDGC/P, 80 Elm St., Peterborough NH 03458. (603)924-9471. Editor: Guy Wright. Managing Editor: Shawn Laflamme. 90% freelance written. Eager to work with new/unpublished writers. Monthly magazine for users of the Amiga computer from Commodore. "We help people understand the inner workings of the machine so that they can better use and enjoy their computer." Circ. 75,000. Pays on publication. Publishes ms an average of 3 months after acceptance. Byline given. Buys all rights. Submit seasonal/holiday material 4 months in advance. Photocopied submissions OK. Query for electronic submissions. Computer printout submissions OK; prefers letter-quality. Reports in 1 month on queries; 2 months on mss. Writer's guidelines for #10 SASE.
Nonfiction: Bob Ryan, articles editor. General interest, how-to, humor (rarely), personal experience and technical—all related to programming or using Amiga computer. "The magazine features informative, interesting, high quality articles, tutorials, hints and tips, news, and reviews about the Amiga. We don't want to see any program listings over 20 lines or articles on 'how I got started' or 'why the Amiga computer is so great.' " Buys 50 mss/year. Query with or without published clips, or send complete ms. Length: 2,000-4,000 words. Pays $100-1,500 for assigned articles; pays $100-800 for unsolicited articles. Sometimes pays the expenses of writers on assignment.
Photos: Send photos with submission. Reviews negatives, transparencies and prints. Offers no additional payment for photos accepted with ms. Captions required. Buys all rights.
Columns/Departments: Barbara Gefvert, reviews editor. Reviews (hardware and software reviews). "All reviews are assigned by us. Send one page and biography and areas of expertise and we will contact you." Buys 40 mss/year. Length: 500-1,500 words. Pays $50-300.
Tips: "The author should have a good knowledge of the Amiga computer or have access to one. Most of our articles are about the computer itself but we do publish features about famous people using Amigas or unique applications. If you have an idea for an article give us a call first. We are more than happy to discuss on the phone and even suggest topics. The expected sales of the new Commodore Amiga 500 and Amiga 2000 will mean we plan more beginner level articles dealing with the Amiga computer."

ANTIC MAGAZINE, The Atari Resource, Antic Publishing Co., 544 2nd St., San Francisco CA 94107. (415)957-0886. Editor: Nat Friedland. 75% freelance written. Eager to work with new/unpublished writers. Monthly magazine for Atari 400/800, XL/XE, ST, Mega computer users. Circ. 90,000. Pays on publication. Publishes ms an average of 3 months after acceptance. Byline given. Offers $60 kill fee. Buys all rights. Submit seasonal/holiday material 3 months in advance. Simultaneous queries and photocopied submissions OK. Query for electronic submissions. Computer printout submissions acceptable. Reports in 2 weeks on queries; 1 month on mss. Sample copy $3; free writer's guidelines. Request text files on disks and printout.
Nonfiction: How-to, interview/profile, new product, photo feature and technical. Especially wants article plus programs—games, utilities, productivity, etc. Special issues include Education (October) and Buyer's Guide (December). No generalized, nontechnical articles. Buys 250 mss/year. Send complete ms. Length: 500-2,500 words. Pays $50-600. Pays expenses of writers on assignment.
Photos: State availability of photos or send photos with ms. Reviews color transparencies and b&w prints; b&w should accompany article. Identification of subjects required.
Columns/Departments: Game of the Month (computer games); Starting Line (beginner's column); Assembly Language (for advanced programmers); Profiles (personalities in the business); and Product Reviews (software/hardware products). Buys 36 mss/year. Send complete ms. Length: 1,500-2,500 words. Pays $120-180.
Tips: "Write for the Product Reviews section. We need 400- to 600-word articles on a new software or hardware product for the Atari computers. Give a clear description; personal experience with product; comparison with other available product; or product survey with charts. The most frequent mistakes made by writers in completing an article are failure to be clear and specific, and writing overly-long submissions."

‡**THE APPLE IIGS BUYER'S GUIDE**, Redgate Communications Corp., 660 Beachland Blvd., Vero Beach FL 32963. (305)231-6904. Editor: Paul Pinella. 90% freelance written. A quarterly magazine on Apple IIGS hardware and software markets. *The Apple IIGS Buyer's Guide* examines what's available for Apple IIGS owners by providing in-depth product reviews, how-to feature articles, answers technical questions from readers, and provides an in-depth product directory in each issue." Circ. 50,000. Pays on acceptance. Byline given. Offers 70% kill fee. Buys all rights. Submit seasonal/holiday material 2 months in advance. Query for electronic submissions. Computer printout submissions OK, but must be accompanied with diskette. Reports in 3 weeks. Sample copy for $2; writer's guidelines for #10 SASE.
Nonfiction: How-to, interview/profile, new product, technical and reviews. Buys 40 mss/year. Query with or without published clips, or send complete ms. Length: 400-5,000 words. Pays $100-700. Pays expenses of writers on assignment. State availability of photos with submission. Reviews transparencies. Offers $30-100 per photo. Buys one-time rights.

Columns/Departments: Reviews (hardware/software), 350-800 words; IIGS Address (technical reader questions), 800-2,000 words; User Interface (application stories), 500-600 words. Buys 10 mss/year. Query. Length: 350-800 words. Pays $200-550.
Tips: "All copy must now be submitted in electronic form."

‡ATARI EXPLORER, The Official Atari Journal, Atari Explorer Publications Corp., 7 Hilltop Rd., Mendham NJ 07945. Editor: Elizabeth B. Staples. 70% freelance written. A bimonthly magazine about Atari computers. "Our audience consists of users of Atari 8-bit and ST computers, and our objective is to help them make good use of those computers." Circ. 70,000. Pays on acceptance. Publishes ms an average of 4 months after acceptance. Byline given. Offers $100 kill fee. Buys first North American serial rights or all rights. Photocopied submissions OK. Query for electronic submissions. Reports in 6 weeks. Sample copy $3 with 9x13 SAE and $1.24 postage.
Nonfiction: How-to (programming), interview/profile (of people who use Atari computers in interesting ways), technical and product reviews. No non-technical or "How I learned to love my computer." Buys 50 mss/year. Send complete ms. Length: 750-4,000 words. Pays $35-600. Sometimes pays the expenses of writers on assignment. Send photos with submission. Offers no additional payment for photos accepted with ms. Captions required. Buys one-time rights.
Tips: "Writers must have access to and use Atari computers. All submissions must be relevant to Atari computer users."

BYTE MAGAZINE, 70 Main St., Peterborough NH 03458. (603)924-9281. Editor: Fred Langa. Monthly magazine covering personal computers for college-educated, professional users of computers. Circ. 418,000. Pays on acceptance. Buys all rights. Computer printout submissions acceptable; prefers letter-quality. Reports on rejections in 6 weeks; 3 months if accepted. Sample copy $3.50; writer's guidelines for #10 SASE.
Nonfiction: In-depth discussions of technical topics related to microcomputers or technology that will be available to micros within five years. Buys 160 mss/year. Query. Length: 1,500-5,000 words. Pay is competitive.
Tips: "All *Byte* readers are sophisticated and experienced users of computers. Back issues of the magazine give prospective authors an idea of the type of article published in *Byte*. We look for articles that provide detailed, authoritative, and useful information on (1) achieving the highest possible performance and productivity with state-of-the-market hardware and software; and (2) emerging, state-of-the-art developments that become the tools, techniques, and products of tomorrow. You will increase your chances of acceptance if you send a query letter and one to two outline pages instead of a finished ms."

CLOSING THE GAP, INC., Box 68, Henderson MN 56044. (612)248-3294. Managing Editor: Michael Gergen. 40% freelance written. Eager to work with new/unpublished writers. Bimonthly tabloid covering microcomputers for handicapped readers, special education and rehabilitation professionals. "We focus on currently available products and procedures written for the layperson that incorporate microcomputers to enhance the educational opportunities and quality of life for persons with disabilities." Circ. 10,000. Pays on publication. Publishes ms an average of 2 months after acceptance. Byline given. Buys first serial rights. Simultaneous queries, and simultaneous, photocopied, and previously published submissions OK. Query for electronic submissions. Computer printout submissions acceptable (dot-matrix with descenders). Reports in 2 weeks. Free sample copy and writer's guidelines.
Nonfiction: How-to (simple modifications to computers or programs to aid handicapped persons); interview/profile (users or developers of computers to aid handicapped persons); new product (computer products to aid handicapped persons); personal experience (by a handicapped person or on use of microcomputer to aid a handicapped person); articles of current research on projects on microcomputers to aid persons with disabilities; and articles that examine current legislation, social trends and new projects that deal with computer technology for persons with disabilities. No highly technical "computer hobbyist" pieces. Buys 25 mss/year. Query. Length: 500-2,000 words. Pays $25 and up (negotiable). "Many authors' material runs without financial compensation." Sometimes pays expenses of writers on assignment.
Tips: "Knowledge of the subject is vital, but freelancers do not need to be computer geniuses. Clarity is essential; articles must be able to be understood by a layperson. All departments are open to freelancers. We are looking for new ideas. If you saw it in some other computer publication, don't bother submitting. *CTG*'s emphasis is on increasing computer user skills in our area of interest, not developing hobbyist or technical skills. The most frequent mistakes made by writers in completing an article for us is that their submissions are too technical—they associate 'computer' with hobbyist, often their own perspective—and don't realize our readers are not hobbyists or hackers."

COMMODORE MAGAZINE, Commodore Business Machines, 1200 Wilson Dr., West Chester PA 19380. (215)431-9100. Editor: Susan West. 90% freelance written. Monthly magazine for owners of Commodore computers, using them for business, programming, education, communications, art, recreation, etc. Circ. 200,000. Pays on publication. Publishes ms an average of 3 months after acceptance. Byline given. Buys all

rights; makes occasional work-for-hire assignments. Submit seasonal/holiday material 5 months in advance. Simultaneous queries and previously published submissions OK. Query for electronic submissions. Reports in 1 month on queries; 2 months on mss. Free sample copy; writer's guidelines for #10 SASE.
Nonfiction: Book reviews; how-to (write programs, use software); new product (reviews); personal experience; photo feature; and technical. "Write for guidelines." Buys 360 mss/year. Query or send complete ms. Length: 750-2,500 words. Pays $60-100/published page.
Photos: Send photos with ms. Reviews 5x7 b&w and color prints. Captions required. Buys all rights.
Tips: "Write to the editor with several specific ideas. Use Commodore computers. We're open to programming techniques and product reviews."

COMPUTER LANGUAGE, Miller Freeman Publications, 500 Howard Street, San Francisco CA 94105. (415)397-1881. Editor: J.D. Hildebrand. Managing Editor: Kathy Kincaide. 100% freelance written. Monthly magazine covering programming languages and software design. Circ. 65,000. Pays on publication. Byline given. Buys first rights. Photocopied submissions OK. Query for electronic submissions. Computer printout submissions OK; prefers letter-quality. Reports in months. Sample copy $7; free writer's guidelines. Query author's BBS: (415)882-9915 (300/1,200 baud).
Nonfiction: Interview/profile, new product, technical and product reviews. Buys 150 mss/year. Query. Length: 1,500-4,000. Pays $100-650.
Photos: State availability of photos with submission. Buys one-time rights.
Columns/Departments: Product Wrap-Up (in-depth software review); Software Review; Exotic Language (introduction of new computer language); and Computer Visions (interviews with experts in the field). Buys 24 mss/year. Query or send complete ms. Length: 1,500-4,000.
Tips: "Introduce idea for article and/or send manuscripts to editor; propose to become technical referee and/or software reviewer. Current hot topics: object-oriented programming, OS/2, multitasking, 80386, TRSs, C, Pascal, Ada, BASIC."

COMPUTER SHOPPER, Patch Communications, 5211 S. Washington Ave., Box F, Titusville FL 32780. (305)269-3211. Editor: Stanley Veit. 50% freelance written. Prefers to work with published/established writers; works with a small number of new/unpublished writers each year. A monthly tabloid covering personal computing. "Our readers are experienced computer users. They are interested in using and comparing machines and software, and in saving money." Circ. 283,000. Pays on publication. Publishes ms an average of 2 months after acceptance. Byline given. Offers $25 kill fee. Buys first North American serial rights and 1 reprint right. Submit seasonal/holiday material 4 months in advance. Query for electronic submissions. Computer printout submissions acceptable; prefers letter-quality. Reports in 1 week on queries; 2 weeks on mss. Sample copy $2.95.
Nonfiction: How-to (computer boards), new product reviews, and technical. "No rank beginner articles." Buys 250 mss/year. Query. Length: 1,500-2,500 words. Pays 6-10¢/word. Sometimes pays expenses of writers on assignment.
Photos: State availability of photos with submission. Reviews b&w prints or line drawings. Offers no additional payment for photos or drawings accepted with ms.
Tips: "Current interests include new equipment for PS/2, Amiga 2000, Macintosh II, OS/2, CD-ROM, WORMS."

‡COMPUTE!'S PC MAGAZINE, For IBM PCs and Compatibles, COMPUTE! Publications, Inc., 324 West Wendover Ave., Greensboro NC 27408. (919)275-9809. Editor: Tom R. Halfhill. Managing Editor: Kathleen Martinek. 90% freelance written. A bimonthly magazine and computer disk on personal computing for users of IBM PCs and compatibles. "The bulk of the magazine currently consists of articles describing how to use the programs on the disk which is included with every copy. The programs are aimed at average users." Estab. 1987. Pays on acceptance. Publishes ms an average of 4 months after acceptance. Byline given. Kill fee varies. Buys all rights. Submit seasonal/holiday material 6 months in advance. Query for electronic submissions. Computer printout submissions OK. Reports in 6 weeks. Free writer's guidelines.
Nonfiction: David Hensley, articles editor. How-to (related to personal computing), programs (for IBM PCs and compatibles) and technical (programming tutorials, explanations). "No X- or R-rated material with graphic violence or sexual overtones; this is a family magazine. For example, no computer games with explicit violence, etc." Buys 75 mss/year. Send complete ms. Length: 4,000 words maximum. Pays $200-2,000.
Photos: State availability of photos with submission. Offers no additional payment for photos accepted with ms.
Tips: "What we're looking for most from freelancers is good, original programs that make computers easier to use, more productive, and more fun for our readers. It's very important that these programs appeal to the widest possible range of users. Freelancers who aren't programmers can best break into the magazine by writing reviews. But *no* unsolicited reviews are accepted; query first. Reviews must be balanced, objective, and thorough. Generally, freelancers get to keep the software they review along with their fee. All prospective reviewers must apply to Keith Ferrell, features editor."

‡COMPUTOREDGE, San Diego's Computer Magazine, The Byte Buyer, Inc., Suite 100, 9601 Aero Dr., San Diego CA 92123. (619)573-0315. Editor: Dan Gookin. 90% freelance written. A biweekly magazine on computers. "We cater to the novice/beginner/first-time computer buyer. Humor is welcome. Nothing too technical." Circ. 65,000. Pays on publication. Byline given. Offers $15 kill fee. Buys first North American serial rights. Submit seasonal/holiday material 2 months in advance. Query for electronic submissions. Photocopied submissions OK. Reports in 2 weeks. Writer's guidelines for #10 SAE with 1 first class stamp.
Nonfiction: General interest (computer), how-to, humor and personal experience. Buys 80 mss/year. Send complete ms. Length: 300-1,500 words. Pays 10-15¢/word for assigned articles. Pays 5-10¢/word for unsolicited articles. State availability of photos with submission. Reviews prints (8x10). Offers $15-50 per photo. Captions and identification of subjects required. Buys one-time rights.
Columns/Departments: Beyond Personal Computing (a reader's personal experience). Buys 80 mss/year. Send complete ms. Length: 500-1,000 words. Pays $50-100.
Fiction: Confession, fantasy and slice-of-life vignettes. Buys 5 mss/year. Send complete ms. Length: 500-1,500 words. Pays $50-150.
Poetry: Light verse and traditional. "We're not big on poems, but we might find some interesting." Buys 25 poems/year. Submit maximum 20 poems. Length: 6-30 words. Pays $15.
Tips: "Be relentless. Don't be technical. We like light material, but not fluff. Write as if you're speaking with a friend."

80 MICRO, 80 Elm St., Peterborough NH 03458. (603)924-9471. Publisher: IDG Communications/Peterborough. Editor: Michael Nadeau. 50% freelance written. Eager to work with new/unpublished writers. Monthly magazine about microcomputing for owners and users of Tandy, MS-DOS microcomputers. Circ. 70,000. Pays on acceptance. Publishes ms an average of 6 months after acceptance. Buys all rights. Written queries preferred. Photocopied submissions OK. Query for electronic submissions. Computer printout submissions acceptable. Reports in 2 months. Sample copy $4; writer's guidelines for SASE.
Nonfiction: Applications programs for business, home and hobby; utilities; and tutorials. Buys 2-3 mss per issue. Query first. Length: 1,000 words average. Pays $75-100/printed page.
Reviews: Writers interested in reviewing current available software are asked to query the review editor, stating areas of interest and equipment owned. Buys 5-8 reviews/issue.
Photos: Offers no additional payment for photos accepted with ms. Buys all rights.
Tips: "We're looking for articles that tell the Tandy MS-DOS user how to get the most productivity from his/her computer."

‡GENEALOGICAL COMPUTING, Ancestry Inc., Box 476, Salt Lake City UT 84110. (801)531-1790. Editor: Paul Andereck. 50% freelance written. Quarterly magazine on genealogy, using computers. "Each issue contains up-to-date articles, new software announcements, surveys, interest group directories and hardware/software listings. Designed for genealogists who use computers for records management." Circ. 2,500. Pays on publication. Publishes ms an average of 4 months after acceptance. Byline given. Buys all rights. Query for electronic submissions. Computer printout submissions OK. Reports in 2 months.
Nonfiction: New product, personal experience (with software), technical (telecommunications, data exchange, data base development). "Articles on pure genealogy cannot be accepted; this also applies to straight computer technology." Query with outline/summary. Length: 1,300-4,000 words. Pays approximately $75.
Tips: "We need articles expressing a personal experience with software, or a comparison of one program with another. We can also use light technical articles on telecommunications, data exchange and data base developments."

THE MACazine, Solutions for all of us, Hart Graphics, Box 968, 8008 Shoal Creek Bl., Austin TX 78767. (512)467-4550. Editor: Robert LeVitus. Managing Editor: Dan Littman. 70% freelance written. A monthly magazine for Macintosh computers (Apple) users. Circ. 110,000. Pays on publication. Publishes ms an average of 3 months after acceptance. Byline given. Buys first North American serial rights or second serial (reprint) rights. Simultaneous, photocopied and previously published submissions OK. Query for electronic submissions. Computer printout submissions OK; prefers letter-quality. Reports in 1 month on queries; 2 months on mss. Sample copy $3.75; writer's guidelines for #10 SASE.
Nonfiction: Book excerpts, essays, how-to, interview/profile, new product, personal experience and technical. Buys 48 mss/year. Query with or without published clips, or send complete ms. Length: 750-3,500 words. Pays 10-15¢/word for assigned articles; pays 8-10¢/word for unsolicited articles.
Photos: State availability of photos with submission. Reviews 4x5 or 8x10 prints. Offers $10-20 per photo. Captions required. Buys one-time rights.
Fillers: Max Vizsla, editor. Facts and mini reviews. Buys 10/year. Length: 50-1,000 words. Pays $50-100.
Tips: "A well-written how-to about something the readers will appreciate knowing always gets my attention. It shows the writer knows our market. Mini Reviews—50-1,000 word reviews—of software or hardware are needed. Must be based on extended usage of the product. Cover both the positive and negative."

‡MacBUSINESS JOURNAL, PiM Publications Inc., 1 Currant Place, Fall River MA 02720. (617)678-4200. Editor: Ernest P. Viveiros. Managing Editor: Donald D. Hicks. 80% freelance written. Bimonthly magazine of tutorials, reviews and vertical programs designed for both the small business owner and the corporate executive. Estab. 1988. Circ. 15,000. Pays on publication. Publishes ms an average of 2-4 months after acceptance. Byline given. Negotiable kill fee. Buys all rights. Submit seasonal/holiday material 4 months in advance. Query for electronic submissions. Computer printout submissions OK. Free writer's guidelines.

Nonfiction: Book excerpts, how-to, interview/profile, new product, opinion, personal experience, technical. "Almost any article dealing with the Macintosh and its use in business will be considered." Buys 130 mss/year. Query. Length: 1,000 words minimum. Pays $70 minimum. Sometimes pays expenses of writers on assignment.

Photos: Send photos with submission. Reviews contact sheets, negatives and 4x6 prints. Captions and identification of subjects required. Buys all rights.

Columns/Departments: Reviews, Programs. Buys 120 mss/year. Query. Length: 1,000 words.

THE MACINTOSH BUYER'S GUIDE, Redgate Communications Corp., 1660 Beachland Blvd., Vero Beach FL 32963. (305)231-6904. Managing Editor: Jordan Gold. 80% freelance written. Quarterly magazine covering Macintosh software, hardware and peripherals. Circ. 120,000. Pays on acceptance. Publishes ms an average of 3 months after acceptance. Byline given. Buys all rights. Submit seasonal/holiday material 3 months in advance. Electronic submissions preferred. Reports in 3 weeks on queries. Sample copy $1 with 9x12 SASE.

Nonfiction: General interest, how-to, new product, personal experience and technical. No humor—"we're business related." Buys 35 mss/year. Query with published clips. Length: 600-5,000 words. Pays $100-1,000. Pays expenses of writers on assignment.

Photos: State availability of photos with submission. Reviews transparencies. Offers $25-300 per photo. Buys one-time rights.

Columns/Departments: Quarterly Report (news of interest to the Macintosh computer community), 1500 words; and Reviews (software, hardware and peripherals), 1,000 words and up. Buys 40 mss/year. Query with published clips. Pays $100-800.

Tips: "Please call the editor or managing editor to ascertain current business topics of interest. By far, most freelancers are users of Macintosh computers." Looking for "feature article writing and new product reviews."

MICROAGE QUARTERLY, MicroAge Computer Stores, Inc., Box 1920, Tempe AZ 85281. (602)968-3168. Managing Editor: Linnea Maxwell. 65% freelance written. Prefers to work with published/established writers. A quarterly magazine for business users of microcomputers. Circ. 300,000. Pays on publication. Publishes ms an average of 3 months after acceptance. Byline given. Offers kill fee. Buys first North American serial rights, one-time rights and second serial (reprint) rights. Computer printout submissions acceptable; prefer accompanying diskette. Sample copy and writer's guidelines for 9x12 SAE with $1.07 postage.

Nonfiction: Query with published clips. Length: 800-3,000 words. Pays $200-1,200. Pays the phone expenses of writers on assignment.

Columns/Departments: Changing Market (changes in uses of business-oriented computer equipment—what affects the market, and how it changes); Changing Technology (changes/improvements in computer technology which affect the business user); and Changing Industry (adaptations in the computer industry); all 1,000-3,000 words. Market Focus (specific "verticals"—construction, accounting, etc.—and how computers are used in these markets), 2,000-2,500 words.

Tips: "We're looking for problem-solving articles on office automation and computer applications oriented toward small and medium size businesses. We're willing to discuss ideas with experienced business or computer-literate writers."

MICROpendium, Covering the TI99/4A, Myarc 9640 compatibles, Burns-Koloen Communications Inc., Box 1343, Round Rock TX 78664. (512)255-1512. Editor: Laura Burns. 40% freelance written. Eager to work with new/unpublished writers. A monthly tabloid magazine for users of the "orphaned" TI99/4A. "We are interested in helping users get the most out of their home computers." Circ. 6,000. Pays on publication. Publishes ms an average of 2-3 months after acceptance. Byline given. Buys second serial rights. Photocopied and previously published submissions OK. Query for electronic submission. Computer printout submissions acceptable. Reports in 2 weeks on queries; 2 months on manuscripts. Free sample copy and writer's guidelines.

Nonfiction: Book excerpts; how-to (computer applications); interview/profile (of computer "personalities," e.g. a software developer concentrating more on "how-to" than personality); and opinion (product reviews, hardware and software). Interested in reviews of tax software for April issue; query by January. Buys 30-50 mss/year. Query with or without published clips, or send complete ms. "We can do some articles as a series if they are lengthy, yet worthwhile." Pays $10-150, depending on length; may pay with contributor copies or other premiums if writer requests. No pay for product announcements. Sometimes pays the expenses of writers on assignment.

Photos: Send photos with submission. Reviews contact sheets, negatives, transparencies, and prints (b&w

Close-up

Paul Somerson
Editorial Director
PC Computing

"We're really interested in working with contributors who are terrific writers and who know a lot about computers," says Paul Somerson, editorial director of *PC Computing*. The magazine, which published its first issue in July 1988, is not aimed at experts, but at the diehard PC user who averages about 27 hours per week on a personal computer. "We have a name for the people who read it: 'PC active,' " Somerson says.

Unlike some computer magazines that overwhelm the average reader, Somerson says *PC Computing* "is not filled with jargon" and "allows columnists to disagree on important computer issues." Somerson says "it's very confusing to know what to buy," so the magazine addresses that need, along with providing sections to help users with shortcuts and secrets. "People often have someone to look over their shoulders when they're using a computer at work," he says. "That's what this magazine will be like—having someone there to help."

Somerson began working on publications like *Moneysworth* and *Avant Garde* as associate publisher for Ralph Ginzburg. For six years, he says, "It was like going to publications graduate school. I learned everything about the operation."

Somerson then took a job at *The New York Times* where he worked on marketing and direct-response offers for three years. When the division disbanded the program, he took his severance pay, bought a personal computer, and took a year to master it.

About that time Ziff-Davis Publishing bought *PC Magazine* and moved it from California to New York. Somerson was the second person hired to work on the magazine. "I love magazines, and I love computers, so it was perfect," he says.

When the company decided to publish *PC Computing*, Somerson was named editorial director. "We're not trying to be technical or trying to chase *PC Magazine*, which is for people who are paid to be experts on the computer," Somerson says. "*PC Computing* is really different. People think computers are smart, but they're not smart, they're just fast. We now use much less of a computer's power than it has available. This magazine improves a person's productivity."

Since the magazine is relatively new, Somerson says he'll accept a resume and writing credentials from writers who may not have seen enough copies of the magazine to be able to propose an article. Those who do have a proposal should query with samples of their writing, he says. "We want a stable of very professional writers. Our vision is to sign up the best possible writers who use computers."

His counsel for potential *PC Computing* writers is sound advice for any work, technical or not. "Make sure your writing never bogs down," he says. "Be sure everything makes the reader go on. You must take incredible pains to keep the reader interested."

—*Glenda Tennant Neff*

preferred). Buys negotiable rights.

Columns/Departments: User Notes (tips and brief routines for the computer) 100 words and up. Buys 35-40 mss/year. Send complete ms. Pays $10.

Tips: "We have more regularly scheduled columnists, which may reduce the amount we accept from others. The area most open to freelancers is product reviews on hardware and software. The writer should be a sophisticated TI99/4A computer user. We are more interested in advising our readers of the availability of good products than in 'panning' poor ones. We are interested in coverage of the Geneva 9640 by Myarc."

NIBBLE, The Reference for Apple Computing, Micro-SPARC Inc., 52 Domino Dr., Concord MA 01742. (617)371-1660. Editor: David Krathwohl. 90% freelance written. Eager to work with new/unpublished writers. A monthly magazine for Apple II computer reference. Authors should submit programs that run on Apple computers. Pays on acceptance. Publishes ms an average of 4 months after acceptance. Byline given. Buys all rights. Submit seasonal/holiday material 4 months in advance. Photocopied submissions OK. Query for electronic submissions. Computer printout submissions acceptable. Reports in 1 week on queries; 1 month on manuscripts. Free sample copy and writer's guidelines.

Nonfiction: New product and technical. No product reviews or fiction. Buys 175 mss/year. Query. Length: 500-3,000 words. Pays $50-500. Sometimes pays expenses of writers on assignment.

Photos: State availability of photos with submission. Offers no additional payment for photos accepted with ms. Buys all rights.

Tips: "Authors should submit original Apple programs along with descriptive articles."

PC, The Independent Guide to IBM-Standard Personal Computering, Ziff-Davis Publishing Co., 1 Park Ave., New York NY 10016. (212)503-5255. Publisher and Editor-in-Chief: Bill Machrone. Executive Editor/Features: Bill Howard. Executive Editor/New Products: Gus Vendetto. 75% freelance written. Prefers to work with published/established writers. Fortnightly magazine for users/owners of IBM Personal Computers and compatible systems. Pays on acceptance. Publishes ms average of 4 months after acceptance. Byline given. Buys all rights. Photocopied submissions OK; electronic copy on floppy disk preferred. Computer printout submissions OK; prefers letter-quality. Reports in 1 month. Sample copy $5.

Nonfiction: How-to (software and hardware); technical; product evaluations; and programs. Buys 800 mss/year. Query, story proposals should be submitted to the executive editors. Length: 1,000-8,000 words. Sometimes pays expenses of writers on assignment.

Tips: "*PC Magazine* is a computer magazine for business people; however we also cover computer products for personal use (i.e. games and personal finance). We assign stories based on the latest product/technological developments in the micro-computer industry. In the coming year the hot topics will be OS/2, 80 386 chip technology and networking."

‡PC CLONES, Guide for Users of PC Systems, Patch Communications, 5211 S. Washington Ave., Titusville FL 32780. (305)269-3211. Editor: Joe Desposito. 50% freelance written. A monthly magazine on PC-PS systems and IBM compatibles. Estab. 1987. Circ. 139,600. Pays on publication. Byline given. Offers $50 kill fee. Buys all rights. Submit seasonal/holiday material 2 months in advance. Simultaneous submissions OK. Query for electronic submissions. Computer printout submissions OK; prefers letter-quality. Free sample copy and writer's guidelines.

Nonfiction: How-to (upgrade PC systems), new product, opinion, photo feature and technical. Buys 24 mss/year. Query with or without published clips, or send complete ms. Length: 1,000-3,000 words. Pays 10-30¢/word. Sometimes pays the expenses of writers on assignment. Send photos with submission. Reviews contact sheets, negatives, transparencies (5x7) and prints (3½x5). Offers no additional payment for photos accepted with ms. Captions required. Buys one-time rights.

Columns/Departments: Software Review (update on new software and application), 500-3,000 words; Hardware Review (update on PC's XT/AT systems and extensions); PC Reports (PC compatibles and clones). Pays 10-30¢/word.

Fillers: Facts and news. Buys 12/year. Length: 100-250 words. Pays 10-30¢/word.

Tips: "Submit a letter with idea of topic to write on. We are targeted toward the PC user. Anyone who has a knowledge of PC systems and IBM compatibles in today's market can submit a resume to the editor."

‡PC COMPUTING, America's Computing Magazine, Ziff-Davis Publishing Co., 80 Blanchard Rd., Burlington MA 01803. (617)221-0300. Editor-in-chief: Jim Seymour. Editor: Nora Georgas. Monthly magazine on personal computing. Estab. 1988. Circ. 150,000. Pays on publication. Byline given. Offers negotiable kill fee. Makes work-for-hire assignments. Query for electronic submissions. Computer printout submissions OK; no dot-matrix. Reports in 1 month. Sample copy for $2.95; writer's guidelines for #10 SASE.

Nonfiction: Book excerpts, how-to, interview/profile, new product, technical. Query with published clips. Payment negotiable. Sometimes pays expenses of writers on assignment.

Photos: State availability of photos with submission. Reviews 35mm transparencies. Payment negotiable. Captions, model releases and identification of subjects required. Buys all rights.

‡PC WORLD, The Business Magazine of PC Products and Solutions, PCW Communications, Inc., 501 2nd St., San Francisco CA 94107. (415)243-0500. Editor: Richard Landry. 80% freelance written. Monthly magazine covering IBM Personal Computers and compatibles. Circ. 475,000. Pays on acceptance. Byline given. Offers negotiable kill fee. Buys all rights. Submit material at least 6 months in advance. Query for electronic submissions. Computer printout submissions acceptable. Reports in 6 weeks. Free writer's guidelines.

Nonfiction: Book excerpts, general interest, historical/nostalgic, opinion, how-to, interview/profile, new product and technical. "*PC World* is composed of three sections: Review, Hands-On and Features. In Review, new hardware and software are critically and objectively analyzed by experienced users. Hands On offers 'how-to' articles, giving readers instructions for improving their PC productivity. Features help readers understand the impact of PC technology on their business lives." Articles must focus on the IBM PC or compatibles. Query with or without published clips or send complete ms. Buys 50 mss/year. Length: 1,500-2,500 words. Pays $50-2,000.

Photos: State availability of photos or send with query or ms. Reviews color transparencies and 8x10 b&w prints. Pays $25-50. Captions, model releases, and identification of subjects required. Buys one-time rights.

Columns/Departments: Industry Outlook (short features on business trends and new technologies); The Upgrade Path (how to increase a PC's value); Another Angle (personal opinion from informed readers). Buys 150 mss/year. Query with or without published clips or send complete ms.

Tips: "Familiarity with the IBM PC or technical knowledge about its operations—coupled with a solid understanding of business needs—often determines whether we accept a query. Send all queries to the attention of Proposals—Editorial Department."

PCM, The Personal Computing Magazine for Tandy Computer Users, Falsoft, Inc., Falsoft Bldg., 9529 U.S. Highway 42, Box 385, Prospect KY 40059. (502)228-4492. Editor: Lawrence C. Falk. Managing Editor: Kevin Nichols. 75% freelance written. A monthly (brand specific) magazine for owners of the Tandy Model 100, 200 and 600 portable computer and the Tandy 1000, 1200, 2000 and 3000. Circ. 25,000. Pays on publication. Publishes ms an average of 3 months after acceptance. Byline given. Buys full rights, and rights for disk service reprint. Submit seasonal/holiday material 4 months in advance. Photocopied submissions OK. Query for electronic submissions. Computer printout submissions acceptable. Reports in 2 months. Sample copy for SASE; free writer's guidelines.

Nonfiction: Angela Kapfhammer, submissions editor. How-to. "We prefer articles with programs." No general interest material. Buys 80 mss/year. Send complete ms. "Do not query." Length: 300 words minimum. Pays $40-50/page.

Photos: State availability of photos. Rarely uses photos.

Tips: "At this time we are only interested in submissions for the Tandy MS-DOS and portable computers. Strong preference is given to submissions accompanied by brief program listings. All listings must be submitted on tape or disk as well as in hard copy form."

PERSONAL COMPUTING MAGAZINE, VNU Business Publications, Inc., Ten Holland Dr., Hasbrouck Heights NJ 07604. (201)393-6187. Editor: Fred Abatemarco. Executive Editor: Peter McKie. 15% freelance written. Monthly magazine written, edited, and illustrated for professionals and managers who use personal computers as a tool in day-to-day business tasks. *Personal Computing* is a service-oriented consumer magazine that details hands-on computing tips and techniques, personal computing management strategies, product trends, and manufacturer profiles and product analyses. Circ. 525,000. Pays on acceptance. Publishes ms an average of 4 months after acceptance. Byline given. Offers 30% kill fee. Buys all rights. Submit seasonal/holiday material 5 months in advance. Simultaneous submissions OK. Computer printout submissions acceptable; prefers letter-quality. Reports in 2 weeks. Sample copy and writer's guidelines for 9x12 SAE and 11 first class stamps.

Nonfiction: Peter McKie. Essays, how-to and interview/profile. "All of our articles are written from the user's perspective. We focus on ways business executives can improve the quality of their work or increase their productivity. In addition, we cover stories on the personal computing industry that we deem of merit in helping our readers develop an effective personal computing strategy. No product-based stories, computer neophyte stories or reviews." Query with published clips. Length: 2,500-3,000 words. Pays expenses of writers on assignment.

Fillers: Jack Bell, editor. Any shortcuts readers discover in using applications.

Tips: "Hands-on, applications-oriented features and relevant industry stories are most open to freelancers. We will be looking for occasional articles that target a sophisticated, corporate user involved in micro-to-mainframe communications."

PICO, Laptops & Portables, Portable Computing International Corp., 145 Grove St. Ext., Box 428, Peterborough NH 03458. (603)924-7859. Editor: Terry Kepner. 80% freelance written. Eager to work with new/unpublished writers. Monthly magazine covering laptop computers, their software and peripherals. Pays on publication. Publishes ms an average of 4 months after acceptance. Byline given. Offers 30% kill fee. Buys first

North American serial rights and the right to use the article again in a yearbook, compendium, or "best of . . ." magazine or book. Submit seasonal/holiday material 6 months in advance. Previously published submissions OK. Query for electronic submissions. Computer printout submissions OK; prefers letter-quality. Reports in 2 weeks. Sample copy $3.50 with 9x12 SAE and 5 first class stamps; writer's guidelines for #10 SASE.

Nonfiction: General interest, humor (April), interview/profile, new product reviews and technical. No articles on how to write programs in BASIC, "my first computer," etc. Buys 120 mss/year. Query with published clips or send complete ms. Length: 1,000-4,000 words. Pays $80-500 for assigned articles; pays $80-400 for unsolicited articles. Sometimes pays the expenses of writers on assignment.

Photos: Send photos with submission. Especially reviews 8x10 prints; 3x5 prints acceptable. Offers $10-25 per photo. Identification of subjects required. Buys one-time and reprint rights.

Columns/Departments: "Columns are arranged case by case; some are written in-house, some are written by freelance authors." Send complete ms. Length: 700-1,000 words. Pays $80-125.

Fiction: Humorous (April). Buys 2-3 mss/year. Query. Length: 500-1,000 words. Pays $50-100.

Tips: "We want *application* stories: how lap top computers are being integrated into business and society. In general, the easiest way to break in is via a review of some software or hardware. You must write in first person."

‡**PORTABLE 100, Tandy Laptop Computing**, Portable Computing International Corp., 145 Grove St. Ext., Box 428, Peterborough NH 03458. (603)924-7949. Editor: Terry Kepner. 80% freelance written. Eager to work with new/unpublished writers. Monthly magazine covering laptop computers, their software and peripherals. Pays on publication. Publishes ms an average of 4 months after acceptance. Byline given. Offers 30% kill fee. Buys first North American serial rights and the right to use the article again in a yearbook, compendium, or "best of . . ." magazine or book. Submit seasonal/holiday material 6 months in advance. Previously published submissions OK. Query for electronic submissions. Computer printout submissions OK; prefers letter-quality. Reports in 2 weeks. Sample copy $3.95 with 9x12 SAE and 5 first class stamps; writer's guidelines for #10 SASE.

Nonfiction: General interest, humor (April), interview/profile, new product reviews and technical. No articles on how to write programs in BASIC, "my first computer," etc. Buys 120 mss/year. Query with published clips, or send complete ms. Length: 1,000-4,000 words. Pays $52-330 for assigned articles; pays $52-264 for unsolicited articles. Sometimes pays the expenses of writers on assignment.

Photos: Send photos with submission. Especially reviews 8x10 prints; 3x5 prints acceptable. Offers $10-16.50 per photo. Identification of subjects required. Buys one-time and reprint rights.

Columns/Departments: "Columns are arranged case by case; some are written in-house, some are written by freelance authors." Send complete ms. Length: 700-1,000 words. Pays $52-82.50.

Fiction: Humorous (April). Buys 2-3 mss/year. Query. Length: 500-1,000 words. Pays $33-66.

Tips: "We want *application* stories: how lap top computers are being integrated into business and society. In general, the easiest way to break in is via a review of some software or hardware. You must write in first person."

‡**PUBLISH!, The How-To Magazine of Desktop Publishing**, PCW Communications, Inc., 501 Second St., San Francisco CA 94107. (415)546-7722. Editor: Susan Gubernat. Managing Editor: James Felici. 80% freelance written. Monthly magazine on desktop publishing. "*Publish!* helps communications professionals learn to effectively use desktop publishing. The emphasis is on practical hands-on advice for computer novice and publishing professional alike." Circ. 80,000. Pays on acceptance. Publishes ms an average of 3 months after acceptance. Byline given. Buys first international rights. Query for electronic submissions. Computer printout submissions OK; prefers letter-quality. Reports in 3 weeks. Free writer's guidelines.

Nonfiction: Book excerpts, product reviews, how-to (publishing topics), interview/profile, news, new products, technical tips. Buys 120 mss/year. Query with published clips. Length: 300-2,500 words. Pays $300-2,000. Sometimes pays expenses of writers on assignment.

Photos: State availability of photos with submission. Reviews contact sheets. Captions and identification of subjects required.

RAINBOW MAGAZINE, Falsoft, Inc., The Falsoft Bldg., 9529 U.S. Highway 42, Box 385, Prospect KY 40059. (502)228-4492. Editor: Lawrence C. Falk. Managing Editor: Jutta Kapfhammer. 60% freelance written. Monthly magazine covering the Tandy Color Computer. Circ. 75,000. Pays on publication. Publishes ms an average of 4 months after acceptance. Byline given. Buys full rights and rights for "tape" service reprint. Submit seasonal/holiday material 6 months in advance. Query for electronic submissions. Computer printout submissions acceptable. Reports in 3 months. Sample copy $3.95; free writer's guidelines.

Nonfiction: Angela Kapfhammer, submissions editor. Technical (computer programs and articles for Tandy Color Computer). No general "overview" articles. "We want articles *with* programs or tutorials." Buys 300 mss/year. Send complete ms. Pays $25-50/page.

Fillers: Cartoons (must be Color Computer-related).

SOFT SECTOR, THE PC Compatible Magazine, Falsoft, Inc., The Falsoft Bldg., 9529 U.S. Highway 42, Box 385, Prospect KY 40059. (502)228-4492. Editor: Lawrence C. Falk. Managing Editor: Belinda Kirby. "A monthly bound specific magazine for the Sanyo MS-DOS-based, IBM PC data compatible computer." Pays on publication. Byline given. Buys full rights and rights for disk service reprint. Submit seasonal/holiday material 4 months in advance. Photocopied submissions OK. Query for electronic submissions. Reports in 2 months. Free sample copy; writer's guidelines for SAE.
Nonfiction: Interested only in articles and programs for IBM compatible computers. No general interest or computer commentary. Buys 120 mss/year. Send complete ms. Length: 200 words minimum. Pays $50 maximum/printed magazine page.
Tips: "Know specific computer or don't submit."

‡START, The ST Quarterly, Antic Publishing, 544 Second St., San Francisco CA 94107. Editor: Jon A. Bell. Executive Editor: DeWitt Robbeloth. A quarterly magazine on Atari ST personal computer hardware and software. Circ. 60,000. Pays on acceptance. Publishes ms an average of 4 months after acceptance. Byline given. Offers ⅓ kill fee. Buys first rights or all rights. Submit seasonal/holiday material 5 months in advance. Photocopied submissions OK. Query for electronic submissions. Computer printout submissions OK. Reports in 3 weeks. Free writer's guidelines.
Nonfiction: How-to, interview/profile, new product, opinion and technical. Buys 60 mss/year. Send complete ms. Length: 4,000 words maximum. Pays $25-2,000 for assigned articles; $25-1,500 for unsolicited articles. Sometimes pays the expenses of writers on assignment.
Photos: Send photos with submission. Reviews contact sheets, negatives, transparencies (4x5) and prints (8x10). Offers $10-50 per photo. Identification of subjects required. Buys all rights.
Tips: "*START* covers the Atari ST personal computer systems and software and hardware for the ST. Articles include reviews of new software and hardware, overviews and comparisons of related ST computer products, programming tutorials (including software example programs on 3.5"disks), perspectives on the computer industry and how-to pieces (getting the most out of a particular piece of hardware and/or software). We are interested in anything to do with the Atari ST computers—MIDI, graphics, business applications and games. Every issue of *START* includes a 3.5 disk with software. If we accept your article and program, the latter will appear in runnable form on the *START* disk."

TI COMPUTING, The Magazine for Texas Instruments Computer Users, Publications and Communications, Inc., 215 Live Oak, Marlin TX 76661. (817)883-2533. Editor: Larry Storer. 50-60% freelance written. Works with small number of new/unpublished writers each year. A monthly newspaper of technical articles relating to all Texas Instruments computer applications. Circ. 15,000. Pays on publication. Publishes ms an average of 3-4 months after acceptance. Byline given. Buys first North American serial rights and reprints from other PCI magazines. Submit seasonal/holiday material 5 months in advance. Simultaneous submissions and photocopied submissions OK. Query for electronic submissions. Computer printout submissions acceptable; prefers letter-quality. Free sample copy and writer's guidelines.
Nonfiction: How-to, interview/profile, new product, opinion and technical on TI-related articles only. Query with or without published clips, or send complete ms. Length 500-4,000 words. Fees negotiable upon assignment, acceptance. Occasionally pays with subscription or other premiums; will negotiate. Sometimes pays the expenses of writers on assignment.
Photos: State availability of photos with submissions. Reviews contact sheets, transparencies, and prints. Offers $10 maximum/photo. Captions, model releases and identification of subjects required. Buys one-time rights.
Tips: "We now accept submissions from Value Added Resellers of TI, and solicit material on all TI computers, applications and related artificial intelligence. We no longer limit coverage to a specific machine—all TI computers are covered."

Photography

Readers of these magazines use their cameras as a hobby and for weekend assignments. Magazines geared to the professional photographer can be found in the Photography Trade section.

PETERSEN'S PHOTOGRAPHIC MAGAZINE, Petersen Publishing Co., 8490 Sunset Blvd., Los Angeles CA 90069. (213)854-2200. Publisher: Jackie Augustine. Editor: Bill Hurter. 40% freelance written. Prefers to work with published/established writers; eager to work with new/unpublished writers. Monthly magazine; 100

pages. Emphasizes how-to photography. Circ. 275,000. Pays on publication. Publishes ms an average of 9 months after acceptance. Buys all rights. Submit seasonal/holiday material 5 months in advance. Photocopied submissions OK. Computer printout submissions acceptable. Reports in 2 months. Sample copy $3; writer's guidelines for #10 SASE.

Nonfiction: How-to (equipment reports, darkroom, lighting, special effects, and studio photography). "We don't cover personalities." Buys 50-75 unsolicited mss/year. Send story, photos and captions. Pays $60/printed page.

Photos: Photos purchased only with accompanying ms. Cover photos purchased independently. Pays $25-35 for b&w and color photos; offers negotiable rates for covers. Model releases and technical details required.

Tips: "Freelancers should study the easy conversational style of our articles. We are a how-to-do-it magazine which requires clearly detailed text and step-by-step illustration. Write for our free writer's and photographer's guide for details of our requirements."

STRATEGIES, The Self-Promotion Newsletter for Fine-Art Photographers, SG Arts, Inc., Box 838, Montclair NJ 07042. (201)783-5480. Editor: Harold Simon. 10-15% freelance written. Works with a small number of new/unpublished writers each year. Bimonthly newsletter on marketing for fine art photographers. *Strategies* shows fine art photographers how to develop their careers. "We provide first hand information from publishers, photographers, museum curators and gallery directors. Information about every aspect of the fine art photography world—grants, exhibits, portfolios, etc.—is presented." Pays on publication. Publishes ms an average of 2-4 months after acceptance. Byline given. Makes work-for-hire assignments. Simultaneous submissions, photocopied submissions and previously published submissions OK. Query for electronic submissions. Computer printout submissions acceptable. Reports in 1 month. Sample copy $3 with 9x12 SAE and 2 first class stamps.

Nonfiction: How-to (about getting exhibits, grants, or being published, putting together portfolios, invitations, or unique promotional experiences); interview/profile; and personal experience. No technical articles about photo equipment, or book/exhibition reviews. Buys 6 mss/year. Query with or without published clips, or send complete ms. Length: 250-1,500 words. Pays $25 plus copies.

Politics and World Affairs

These publications cover politics for the reader interested in current events. Other publications that will consider articles about politics and world affairs are listed under Business and Finance, Contemporary Culture, Regional and General Interest. For listings of publications geared toward the professional, see Government and Public Service and International Affairs in the Trade section.

AFRICA REPORT, 833 United Nations Plaza, New York NY 10017. (212)949-5731. Editor: Margaret A. Novicki. 60% freelance written. Prefers to work with published/established writers. A bimonthly magazine for U.S. citizens and residents with a special interest in African affairs for professional, business, academic or personal reasons. Not tourist-related. Circ. 10,500. Pays on publication. Publishes ms an average of 2 months after acceptance. Rights purchased vary with author and material; usually buys all rights, very occasionally first serial rights. Offers negotiable kill fee. Byline given unless otherwise requested. Computer printout submissions OK. Sample copy for $4.50; free writer's guidelines.

Nonfiction: Interested in "African political, economic and cultural affairs, especially in relation to U.S. foreign policy and business objectives. Style should be journalistic but not academic or light. Articles should not be polemical or long on rhetoric but may be committed to a strong viewpoint. I do not want tourism articles." Would like to see in-depth topical analyses of lesser known African countries, based on residence or several months' stay in the country. Buys 15 unsolicited mss/year. Pays $150-250.

Photos: Photos purchased with or without accompanying mss with extra payment. Reviews b&w only. Pays $25. Submit 12x8 "half-plate."

Tips: "Read *Africa Report* and other international journals regularly. Become an expert on an African or Africa-related topic. Make sure your submissions fit the style, length, and level of *Africa Report*."

AMERICAN POLITICS, The Nation's Magazine of Politics, American Politics, Inc., Suite 802, 810 18th St. NW, Washington DC 20006. (202)347-1100. Editor: Grant Oliphant. 80% freelance written. Monthly magazine covering domestic politics, some international. "The magazine accepts articles written from both sides of the political spectrum." Circ. 15,000. Pays on scheduled publication. Publishes ms an average of 2 months after acceptance. Byline given. Offers 33% kill fee. Buys first North American serial rights. Submit seasonal/holiday material 5 months in advance. Query for electronic submissions. Computer printout submissions OK; prefers letter-quality. Reports in 2 weeks. Sample copy $2.50 with 8½x11 SAE with 4 first class stamps.

Nonfiction: Feature stories, expose, historical/nostalgic, humor, interview/profile. Buys 60 mss/year. Query with published clips. Length: 800-2,500 words. Pays $350-1,500 for assigned articles; pays $300-750 for unsolicited articles. Sometimes pays expenses of writers on assignment.

Photos: State availability of photos with submission.

Tips: "A query that clearly describes a new, punchy angle on a story is the best way to reach us. We want work from people who are interested in politics, appreciate how much of life falls under that description, and want to share their insights with others. This is predominantly a features publication. Despite the name, we are *not* in the market for opinion pieces or, as a rule, essays."

BLACK MOUNTAIN REVIEW, Lorien House, Box 1112, Black Mountain NC 28711-1112. (704)669-6211. Editor: David A. Wilson. 80% freelance written. Works with small number of new/unpublished writers each year. A literary, semi-annual magazine of "social, political themes." Estab. 1987. Circ. 300. Pays on publication. Publishes ms an average of 6 months after acceptance. Buys first North American serial rights. Photocopied and previously published submissions OK. Computer printout submissions OK. Reports in 1 week on queries; 2 weeks on mss. Sample copy $4; writer's guidelines and theme list for #10 SASE.

Nonfiction: Essays, well-researched opinion. Special issue features "The AIDS Plague" (#3), "Greenhouse Effect" (#4). No diatribes, sex, unresearched opinion. Buys 5 mss/year. Query. Length: 1,000-3,000 words. Pays $10-50/published page.

Photos: State availability of photos with submission. Reviews contact sheets. Offers no additional payment for photos accepted with ms. Identification of subjects required. Buys one-time rights.

Fiction: Experimental, historical, mainstream. Fiction should fit the theme of the issue. No foul language or sex. Buys 2 mss/year. Length 1,000-2,000 words. Pays $10-30/published page.

Poetry: Avant-garde, free verse and traditional. Buys 10 poems/year. Submit maximum 5 poems. Length 12-60 lines. Pays $3/poem.

Tips: "Do a well-written, researched piece on a listed theme. It is necessary to ask for guidelines first so you can write on current themes. Please do not submit before reading the guidelines. I mostly need nonfiction work."

C.L.A.S.S. MAGAZINE, C.L.A.S.S. Promotions, Inc., 27 Union Square West, New York NY 10003. Editor: René John-Sandy. 70% freelance written. Prefers to work with published/established writers; eager to to work with new/unpublished writers. Monthly magazine covering Caribbean/American Third World news and views. Circ. 200,000. Pays on acceptance. Publishes ms an average of 1-2 months after acceptance. Byline given. Buys first rights and second (reprint) rights to material originally published elsewhere. Submit seasonal/holiday material 4 months in advance. Simultaneous queries and previously published submissions OK. Computer printout submissions acceptable; prefers letter-quality. Reports in 1 month on queries; 6 weeks on mss. Sample copy and writer's guidelines for 6x9 SAE and 10 first class stamps.

Nonfiction: Features, book excerpts, general interest, historical/nostalgic, inspirational, interview/profile, travel and international news, views and lifestyles in Third World countries. Query or send complete ms. Length: 150-2,500 words. Articles over 700 words must be of international flavor in content. Sometimes pays expenses of writers on assignment.

Poetry: Avant-garde, free verse, haiku, light verse and traditional. Buys 10-20 poems/year. Submit maximum 10 poems. Length: 22-30 lines. Pays $10 minimum.

Tips: "Submit written queries; stick to Afro American/Third World interests and relate to an international audience."

CALIFORNIA JOURNAL, The California Center, 1714 Capitol Ave., Sacramento CA 95814. (916)444-2840. Editor: Richard Zeiger. Managing Editor: A.G. Block. 50% freelance written. Prefers to work with published/established writers. Monthly magazine that emphasizes analysis of California politics and government. Circ. 20,000. Pays on publication. Publishes ms an average of 2 months after acceptance. Byline given. Buys all rights. Query for electronic submissions. Computer printout submissions acceptable; prefers letter-quality. Writer's guidelines for #10 SASE.

Nonfiction: Profiles of state and local government and political analysis. No outright advocacy pieces. Buys 25 unsolicited mss/year. Query. Length: 900-3,000 words. Pays $150-500. Sometimes pays the expenses of writers on assignment.

‡COMMON CAUSE MAGAZINE, 2030 M Street NW, Washington DC 20036. (202)833-1200. Editor: Cheryl Romo. Senior Editor: Deborah Baldwin. 20% freelance written. A bimonthly magzine on people, power and politics in Washington. "*Common Cause Magazine* is published by the government watchdog organization, Common Cause." Circ. 270,000. Pays on acceptance. Byline given. Offers 20% kill fee. Negotiable rights. Simultaneous, photocopied and previously published submissions OK. Computer printout submissions OK; prefers letter-quality. Reports in 2 months. Free sample copy.

Nonfiction: Book excerpts, expose, humor, interview/profile, short political news stories with national angle. Query with published clips. Length: 250-3,500 words. Pays $100-1,500 for assigned articles; $80-800 for unassigned articles. Sometimes pays expenses of writers on assignment.

Photos: State availability of photos with submission. Reviews contact sheets, transparencies and prints. Payment varies. Rights negotiable.

Columns/Departments: No Sacred Cows (political news and tidbits with a Washington DC orientation) 250-800 words. Buys 12 mss/year. Query with published clips. Pays $80-200.

Fillers: Peter Montgomery, editor. Facts. Length: 10-50 words. Pays $20-50.

Tips: "Many freelancers fail to familiarize themselves with our magazine and thus propose inappropriate material."

CRITIQUE: A Magazine of Questioning Consensus Reality, (formerly Critique: A Journal of Conspiracies & Metaphysics), Box 11368, Santa Rosa CA 95406. (707)525-9401. Editor: Bob Banner. Managing Editor: M. Banovitch. 80% freelance written. Eager to work with new/unpublished writers. Journal published 3 times a year, "that explores unusual news that frequently create debacles within the ordinary mind set. *Critique* also explores assumptions, beliefs and hypotheses that we use to understand ourselves, our 'world' and the metaphysical crisis of our time." Circ. 6,500. Pays on publication. Publishes ms an average of 2 months after acceptance. Byline given. Submit seasonal material 4 months in advance. Simultaneous queries, and simultaneous, photocopied, and previously published submissions OK. Query for electronic submissions. Computer printout submissions acceptable. Reports in 4 months. Sample copy $3; writer's guidelines for #10 SASE.

Nonfiction: Book excerpts; book reviews; expose (political, metaphysical, cultural); interview/profile (those in the specified area); and personal experience (as it relates to cultural ideology). Not interested in "anything that gets published in ordinary, established media." Buys 8-25 mss/year. Send complete ms with bio/resume. Length: 200-3,000 words. Pays $150 maximum. "We also publish books. Send us your book proposal."

Tips: "We have published articles, reviews and essays that are difficult to categorize in the simplistic, dualistic Left or Right ideological camps. The material's purpose has been, and will be, to provoke critical thinking; to discriminate between valuable and manipulative information; to incite an awareness of events, trends, phases; and an awareness of our roles and lives within the global psyche that no ordinary consumer of ordinary media could even begin to conceive, let alone use to affect his/her life. Writers have a better chance of breaking in at our publication with short articles and fillers as it gives us the chance to get acquainted, to feel their styles. The most frequent mistakes made by writers in completing articles are tedious writing and poor organizational structure."

‡**EUROPE**, 2100 M St. NW, 707, Washington DC 20037. Editor: Webster Martin. 20% freelance written. Magazine published 10 times a year for anyone with a professional or personal interest in Western Europe and European/U.S. relations. Circ. 50,000. Pays on acceptance. Publishes ms an average of 2 months after acceptance. Buys first serial rights and all rights. Submit seasonal material 3 months in advance. Computer printout submissions acceptable; prefers letter-quality. Reports in 1 month.

Nonfiction: Interested in current affairs (with emphasis on economics and politics), the Common Market and Europe's relations with the rest of the world. Publishes occasional cultural pieces, with European angle. "High quality writing a must. We publish anything that might be useful to people with a professional interest in Europe." Buys 100 mss/year. Query or submit complete ms. Include resume of author's background and qualifications. Length: 500-2,000 words. Pays $125-500.

Photos: Photos purchased with or without accompanying mss. Buys b&w and color. Pays $25-35 for b&w print, any size; $50 for inside use of color transparencies; $200-300 for color used on cover.

FREEDOM MAGAZINE, North Star Publishing, Inc., 1404 N. Catalina St., Los Angeles CA 90027. (213)663-2058. Editor: Thomas G. Whittle. Published since 1968 by the Church of Scientology. 20% freelance written. Monthly magazine with emphasis on current events and investigative reporting. Circ. 100,000. Pays on publication. Publishes ms an average of 3 months after acceptance. Rights purchased vary with author and material. Submit seasonal/holiday material 4 months in advance. Computer printout submissions OK; no dot-matrix. Reports in 6 weeks.

Nonfiction: National and international news, investigative reporting, business news. Features individuals who are championing the causes of human rights in a special "Human Rights Advocate of the Month" department. Query with detailed outline, including statement of whether the information has appeared elsewhere." Length: 800-5,000 words. Pays $100-350, sometimes more. Sometimes pays the expenses of writers on assignment.

Photos: Send photos with submission. Reviews 35mm color slides, but prefers 2¼ inch transparencies. Reviews 8x10 b&w prints. Offers $20-100 per photo. Captions required. Buys one-time rights.

Columns/Departments: Arts and Entertainment (film and book review) 600-1,000 words, pays $50-150; Guest Commentary, 1,000-1,200 words, pays $250.

THE FREEMAN, 30 S. Broadway, Irvington-on-Hudson NY 10533. (914)591-7230. Senior Editor: Brian Summers. 75% freelance written. Eager to work with new/unpublished writers. Monthly for "the layman and fairly advanced students of liberty." Buys all rights, including reprint rights. Byline given. Pays on publication. Publishes ms an average of 5 months after acceptance. Computer printout submissions acceptable; prefers letter-quality. Sample copy for 7½x10½ SASE with 4 first class stamps.
Nonfiction: "We want nonfiction clearly analyzing and explaining various aspects of the free market, private enterprise, limited government philosophy. Though a necessary part of the literature of freedom is the exposure of collectivistic cliches and fallacies, our aim is to emphasize and explain the positive case for individual responsibility and choice in a free economy. Especially important, we believe, is the methodology of freedom—self-improvement, offered to others who are interested. We try to avoid name-calling and personality clashes and find satire of little use as an educational device. Ours is a scholarly analysis of the principles underlying a free market economy. No political strategy or tactics." Buys 60 mss/year. Length: 3,500 words maximum. Pays 10¢/word. Sometimes pays expenses of writers on assignment.
Tips: "It's most rewarding to find freelancers with new insights, fresh points of view. Facts, figures, and quotations cited should be fully documented, to their original source, if possible."

‡IN THESE TIMES, Institute for Public Affairs, 1300 W. Belmont Ave., Chicago IL 60657. (312)472-5700. Editor: James Weinstein. Managing Editor: Sheryl Larson. 50% freelance written. A political newsweekly. Circ. 50,000. Pays on publication. Publishes ms an average of 1 month after acceptance. Byline given. Offers ⅓ kill fee. Buys first North American serial rights. Query for electronic submissions. Computer printout submissions OK; prefers letter-quality. Reports in 3 weeks on queries; 1 month on mss. Sample copy for 9x12 SAE with 4 first class stamps. Writer's guidelines for 6x9 SAE with 2 first class stamps.
Nonfiction: Essays, exposé, general interest, historical/nostalgic, humor, interview/profile and opinion. Buys 150-200 mss/year. Query with or without published clips, or send complete ms. Length: 400-3,000 words. Pays $40-500 for assigned articles; $40-300 for unsolicited articles. Sometimes pays the expenses of writers on assignment.
Photos: State availability of photos with submission. Reviews contact sheets, negatives and prints (8x10). Offers $35 per photo. Identification of subjects required. Buys one-time rights.

THE NATION, 72 5th Ave., New York NY 10011. Editor: Victor Navasky. 75% freelance written. Works with a small number of new/unpublished writers each year. Weekly. Buys first serial rights. Query for electronic submissions. Computer printout submissions acceptable; prefers letter-quality.
Nonfiction: "We welcome all articles dealing with the social scene, from a liberal/left perspective." Queries encouraged. Buys 100 mss/year. Length: 2,500 words maximum. Modest rates. Sometimes pays expenses of writers on assignment.
Tips: "We are firmly committed to reporting on the issues of labor, national politics, business, consumer affairs, environmental politics, civil liberties and foreign affairs."

NEWSWEEK, 444 Madison Ave., New York NY 10022. (212)350-4547. My Turn Editor: Phyllis Malamud. Although staff written, accepts unsolicited mss for My Turn, a column of opinion. The 1,000- to 1,100-word essays for the column must be original and contain verifiable facts. Payment is $1,000, on publication, for all rights. Computer printout submissions acceptable; no dot-matrix. Reports in 1 month.

‡THE PRAGMATIST, A Utilitarian Approach, Box 392, Forest Grove PA 18922. Editor: Jorge Amador. Publisher: Hans G. Schroeder. 67% freelance written. Bimonthly magazine on politics and current affairs. "*The Pragmatist* is a free-market magazine with a social conscience. We explore the practical benefits of tolerance, civil liberties and the market order, with emphasis on helping the poor and the underprivileged." Circ. 1,450. Pays on publication. Publishes ms an average of 4 months after acceptance. Byline given. Publication not copyrighted "but will run copyright notice for individual author on request." Buys first rights and/or second serial (reprint) rights. Submit seasonal/holiday material 6 months in advance. Photocopied and previously published submissions OK. Query for electronic submissions. Computer printout submissions OK; prefers letter-quality. Reports in 1 month. Sample copy $2; writer's guidelines for #10 SAE with 1 first class stamp.
Nonfiction: Essays, humor, opinion. "*The Pragmatist* is solution-oriented. We seek facts and figures, no moralizing or abstract philosophy, and focus on the issues, not personalities. Recent articles have surveyed alternatives to government schools and examined how subsidies hurt farmers." Buys 35 mss/year. Query with published clips or send complete ms. Length: 500-3,000 words. Pays 1¢/published word plus copies.
Columns/Departments: Book Review (history/current affairs, dealing with the dangers of power or the benefits of civil liberties and market relations). Buys 10-15 mss/year. Query with published clips or send complete ms. Length: 1,000-1,500 words. Pays 1¢/published word plus copies.

Fiction: "We use very little fiction, and then only if it makes a political point."

Tips: "We welcome new writers. Most of our authors are established, but the most important article criteria are clear writing and sound reasoning backed up by facts. Write for an educated lay audience, not first-graders or academics. Friendly but polite correspondence gets answered first. No phone calls, please. Don't get discouraged by initial rejections; keep working on your writing and your targeting."

THE PROGRESSIVE, 409 E. Main St., Madison WI 53703. (608)257-4626. Editor: Erwin Knoll. 75% freelance written. Monthly. Pays on publication. Publishes ms an average of 6 weeks after acceptance. Byline given. Buys all rights. Computer printout submissions acceptable "if legible and double-spaced"; prefers letter-quality. Reports in 2 weeks. Writer's guidelines for #10 SASE.

Nonfiction: Primarily interested in articles which interpret, from a progressive point of view, domestic and world affairs. Occasional lighter features. "*The Progressive* is a *political* publication. General-interest material is inappropriate." Query. Length: 3,000 words maximum. Pays $75-250.

Tips: "Display some familiarity with our magazine, its interests and concerns, its format and style. We want query letters that fully describe the proposed article without attempting to sell it—and that give an indication of the writer's competence to deal with the subject."

REASON MAGAZINE, Suite 1062, 2716 Ocean Park Blvd., Santa Monica CA 90405. (213)392-0443. Editor: Mary Zupan. 50% freelance written. Eager to work with new/unpublished writers. A monthly magazine for a readership interested in individual liberty, economic freedom, private enterprise alternatives to government services and individualist cultural and social perspectives. Circ. 32,000. Pays on acceptance. Publishes ms an average of 2 months after acceptance. Rights purchased vary with author and material. Byline given. Offers kill fee by pre-arrangement. Photocopied submissions OK. Computer printout submission OK; double- or triple-spaced mss only. Query for electronic submissions. Reports in 1-2 months. Sample copy for $2 and 9x12 SAE with $1.24 postage.

Nonfiction: "*Reason* deals with social, economic and political issues, supporting both individual liberty and economic freedom. The following kinds of articles are desired: investigative articles exposing government wrongdoing and bungling; investigative articles revealing examples of private (individual, business, or group) ways of meeting needs; individualist analysis of policy issues (e.g., education, victimless crimes, regulation); think pieces exploring implications of individual freedom in economic, political, cultural, and social areas." Query. Buys 50-70 mss/year. Length: 1,000-5,000 words. Sometimes pays expenses of writers on assignment.

‡REPORT ON THE AMERICAS, North American Congress on Latin America, 475 Riverside Dr., Room 249, New York NY 10115. (212)870-3146. Editor: Mark Fried. Managing Editor: Sandra Necchi. 75% freelance written. A bimonthly magazine on Latin America and Caribbean U.S. foreign policy. Circ. 11,000. Pays on publication. Byline given. Offers ¼ kill fee. Buys one-time rights. Simultaneous and photocopied submissions OK. Query for electronic submissions. Computer printout submissions OK; prefers letter-quality. Sample copy $4.40.

Nonfiction: Exposé, opinion, and photo feature. Buys 25 mss/year. Query with published clips or send complete ms. Length: 1,000-2,500 words. Pays $75-150.

Photos: State availability of photos with submission. Reviews contact sheets and prints (5x7). Pays $25 minimum. Identification of subjects required. Buys one-time rights.

RIPON FORUM, Ripon Society, 6 Library Ct. SE, Washington DC 20003. (202)546-1292. Editor: William P. McKenzie. 50% freelance written. Eager to work with new/unpublished writers. A bimonthly magazine on progressive Republicanism/GOP politics. Circ. 3,000. Pays on publication. Publishes ms an average of 2-4 months after acceptance. Byline given. Simultaneous and photocopied submissions OK. Computer printout submissions OK. Reports in 1 month on queries; 2 weeks on mss. Sample copy for 9x12 SAE and 4 first class stamps.

Nonfiction: Essays and opinion. Query with published clips. Length: 800-1,500 words. Pays $80-150. Sometimes pays expenses of writers on assignment.

UTNE READER, The Best of the Alternative Press, LENS Publishing, 2732 W. 43rd St., Minneapolis MN 55410. (612)929-2670. Editors: Helen Cordes, Eric Utne and Jay Walljasper. 5% freelance written; 90% reprints of previously published articles. Works with a small number of new/unpublished writers each year. A bimonthly magazine. "We reprint articles that have already been published, generally in alternative magazines." Circ. 75,000. Pays on publication. Publishes ms an average of 2-6 months after acceptance. Byline given. Buys second serial (reprint) rights. Submit seasonal/holiday material 4 months in advance. Simultaneous, photocopied and previously published submissions OK. Computer printout submissions acceptable; prefers letter-quality. Reports in 2 months on queries; 3 months on mss. Sample copy $4 with 9x12 SAE and 7 first class stamps.

Nonfiction: Book excerpts, essays, humor, interview/profile and opinion. "We don't want to see articles on topics that have been thoroughly hashed through in the mainstream press." Buys 12 mss/year. Send complete

ms. Pays $20 minimum; pays premiums rather than a cash payment only if agreed on in advance.
Photos: Send photos with submission. Buys one-time rights.
Tips: "We generally publish only articles that have been published in alternative magazines. Get your article published, and *then* send us a clipping. Be sure to send a copy of the publication in which it appeared."

WASHINGTON MONTHLY, 1711 Connecticut Ave., Washington DC 20009. (202)462-0128. Editor-in-Chief: Charles Peters. 35% freelance written. Works with a small number of new/unpublished writers each year. For "well-educated, well-read people interested in politics, the press and government." Monthly. Circ. 27,000. Rights purchased depend on author and material; buys all rights, first rights, or second serial (reprint) rights. Buys 20-30 mss/year. Pays on publication. Sometimes does special topical issues. Query or submit complete ms. Computer printout submissions acceptable. Tries to report in 2 months. Publishes ms an average of 2-6 weeks after acceptance. Sample copy $3.
Nonfiction: Responsible investigative or evaluative reporting about the U.S. government, business, society, the press and politics. "No editorial comment/essays." Also no poetry, fiction or humor. Length: "average 2,000-6,000 words." Pays 4-10¢/word.
Photos: Buys b&w glossy prints.
Tips: "Best route is to send 1-2 page proposal describing article and angle. The most rewarding aspect of working with freelance writers is getting a solid piece of reporting with fresh ideas that challenge the conventional wisdom."

WORLD POLICY JOURNAL, World Policy Institute, 777 UN Plaza, New York NY 10017. (212)490-0010. Editor: Sherle Schwenninger. 80% freelance written. "We are eager to work with new or unpublished writers as well as more established writers." A quarterly magazine covering international politics, economics and security issues. "We hope to bring a new sense of imagination, principle and proportion, as well as a restored sense of reality and direction to America's discussion of its role in the world." Circ. 10,000. Pays on acceptance. Publishes ms an average of 3 months after acceptance. Byline given. Offers variable kill fee. Buys all rights. Photocopied submissions OK. Computer printout submissions acceptable; prefers letter-quality. Reports in 2 months. Sample copy for 7½x10½ SAE, 10 first class stamps and $5.25; free writer's guidelines.
Nonfiction: Articles that "define policies that reflect the shared needs and interests of all nations of the world." Query. Length: 30-40 pages (8,500 words maximum). Pays variable commission rate. Sometimes pays the expenses of writers on assignment.
Tips: "By providing a forum for many younger or previously unheard voices, including those from Europe, Asia, Africa, and Latin America, we hope to replace lingering illusions and fears with new priorities and aspirations. Articles submitted on speculation very rarely suit our particular needs—the writers clearly haven't taken time to study the kind of article we publish."

Psychology and Self-Improvement

These publications focus on psychological topics, how and why readers can improve their own outlooks, and how to understand people in general. Many General Interest publications also publish articles in these areas.

COA REVIEW, Newsletter for Children of Alcoholics, Thomas W. Perrin Inc., Box 190, Rutherford NJ 07070. (201)777-2277. Contact: Editor. 50% freelance written. A bimonthly newsletter for children of alcoholics; also covers co-dependency. "Articles must appeal to both professional therapists and the layperson. They must be well documented and free from jargon." Pays on publication. Byline given. Offers 100% kill fee. Buys first or second serial (reprint) rights. Submit seasonal/holiday material 1 year in advance. Previously published submissions OK. Query for electronic submissions. Computer printout submissions OK. Reports in 3 weeks on queries; 3 months on mss. Sample copy $1; free writer's guidelines.
Nonfiction: Book excerpts, essays, expose, general interest, historical/nostalgic, how-to, humor, interview/profile, opinion and technical. No poetry, photos or fiction. Buys 6-10 mss/year. Query with or without published clips, or send complete ms. No minimum or maximum length. Pays $25. "Authors receive 6 copies of newsletter in which their work is published."
Tips: "Attitudes of compassion and love toward the alcoholic and the family are essential. Knowledge of the dynamics of self-help groups is very important."

‡**INTERNAL ARTS MAGAZINE, Self Development of Mind & Body**, Paper Lantern Publishing, Box 1777, Arlington TX 76004. (817)860-0129. Editor: Pierce Watters. Managing Editor: Dr. John P. Painter. 70% freelance written. Bimonthly. Circ. 20,000. Publishes ms an average of 4 months after acceptance. Byline given. Buys first rights and second serial (reprint) rights. Submit season/holiday material 4 months in advance. Photocopied submissions OK. Computer printout submissions OK; prefers letter-quality. Reports in 1 month on queries; 2 months on mss. Free sample copy and writer's guidelines.
Nonfiction: Book excerpts, essays, exposé, historical/nostalgic, how-to, inspirational, interview/profile, personal experience, photo feature, religious and travel. Buys 150 mss/year. Query. Length: 1,000-3,000 words. Pays $50-200 for assigned articles. Sometimes pays the expenses of writers on assignment.
Photos: Send photos with submission. Reviews negatives and prints (3x5). Offers no additional payment for photos accepted with ms. Captions and identification of subjects required. Buys one-time rights.
Poetry: Haiku and traditional. Buys 12 poems/year. Submit maximum 2 poems. Length: 50-120 words. Does not pay for poetry.
Filler: Dr. Jerry Huff, fillers editor. Facts and newsbreaks. Buys 200/year. Length: 100-500 words. Does not pay for fillers.

JOURNAL OF GRAPHOANALYSIS, 111 N. Canal St., Chicago IL 60606. Editor: V. Peter Ferrara. For an audience interested in self-improvement. Monthly. Buys all rights. Pays negotiable kill fee. Byline given. Pays on acceptance. Reports on submissions in 1 month.
Nonfiction: Self-improvement material helpful for ambitious, alert, mature people. Applied psychology and personality studies, techniques of effective living, etc.; all written from intellectual approach by qualified writers in psychology, counseling and teaching, preferably with degrees. Length: 2,000 words. Pays about 5¢/word.

PSYCHOLOGY TODAY, American Psychological Association, 1200 17th St. NW, Washington DC 20036. (202)955-7800. Editor: Wray Herbert. 85% freelance written. A monthly magazine covering psychology and the social and behavioral sciences. Circ. 850,000. Pays on acceptance. Publishes ms an average of 5 months after acceptance. Byline given. Offers 20% kill fee. Buys first North American serial rights, one-time rights, second serial (reprint) rights or all rights. Submit seasonal/holiday material 6 months in advance. Photocopied submissions OK. Computer printout submissions acceptable; prefers letter-quality. Reports in 6 weeks. Sample copy for 8½x11 SAE with 4 first class stamps. Writer's guidelines for #10 SAE with 1 first class stamp.
Nonfiction: Book excerpts, essays, exposé, general interest, interview/profile, opinion, and technical. No, inspirational/personal experience. Buys 75 mss/year. Query with published clips. Length: 1,000-3,500 words. Pays $500-2,500. Pays expenses of writers on assignment.
Photos: State availability of photos with submission.
Columns/Departments: Crosstalk (research summaries—contact Richard Camer), and Books (reviews—contact Wray Herbert). Buys 240 mss/year. Query. Length: 300-1,000 words. Pays $150-500. Health/Behavior Dept.: submit query to editor: Joshua Fischman. Length: 1,000-2,000 words. Pays about $750. Work/Business Department: query Elizabeth Stark. Length: 1,000-2,000 words. Pays about $750.
Tips: "Please query first; your chance will be much better."

ROSICRUCIAN DIGEST, Rosicrucian Order, AMORC, Rosicrucian Park, San Jose CA 95191. (408)287-9171, ext. 320. Editor-in-Chief: Robin M. Thompson. 50% freelance written. Works with a small number of

66 *The selection of a writer hinges, initially, on one factor: the query letter. The presentation of an article idea—through writing style, depth, conciseness, professionalism, even neatness—will make or break a writer.* 99

—*Chuck Jonak,*
Kiwanis *magazine*

new/unpublished writers each year. Bimonthly magazine emphasizing mysticism, science and the arts for "men and women of all ages, seeking answers to life's questions." Circ. 70,000. Pays on acceptance. Publishes ms an average of 5-6 months after acceptance. Buys first serial rights and second serial (reprint) rights. Byline given. Submit seasonal/holiday material 5 months in advance. Photocopied and previously published submissions OK. Computer printout submissions acceptable; no dot-matrix. Reports in 2 months. Free sample copy; writer's guidelines for #10 SASE.

Nonfiction: How to deal with life—and all it brings us—in a positive and constructive way. Informational articles—new ideas and developments in science, the arts, philosophy and thought. Historical sketches, biographies, human interest, psychology, philosophical and inspirational articles. No religious, astrological or political material or articles promoting a particular group or system of thought. Buys variable amount of mss each year. Query. Length: 1,000-1,500 words. Pays 6¢/word.

Photos: Purchased with accompanying ms. Send prints. Pays $10/8x10 b&w glossy print.

Fillers: Short inspirational or uplifting (not religious) anecdotes or experiences. Buys 6/year. Query. Length: 25-250 words. Pays 2¢/word.

Tips: "We are looking for well-written articles with a positive, contructive approach to life in these trying times. This seems to be a time of indecision and apathy in many areas, and we are encouraged when we read an article that lets the reader know that he/she can get involved, take positive action, make a change in one's life. We are also looking for articles about how other cultures outside our own deal with the big questions, problems, and changes in life, i.e., the questions of 'Who am I?' 'Where do I fit in?', the role of elders in passing on culture to new generations, philosophical aspects of other cultures that can help us grow today."

Regional

Many regional publications rely on staff-written material, but others accept work from freelance writers who live in or know the region. Regional publications are not listed if they only accept material from a select group of freelancers in their area. Regional magazines are often among the bestselling magazines in a particular area and are read carefully, so writers must be able to supply accurate, up-to-date material. The best regional publication is the one in your hometown, whether it's a city or state magazine or a Sunday magazine in a newspaper. Listed first are general interest magazines slanted toward residents of and visitors to a particular region. Next, regional publications are categorized alphabetically by state, followed by categories for Puerto Rico and Canada. Publications that report on the business climate of a region are grouped in the regional division of the Business and Finance category. Recreation and travel publications specific to a geographical area are listed in the Travel section. If you know of a regional magazine that is not listed, approach it by asking for writer's guidelines before you send unsolicited material.

General

AMERICAS, Organization of American States, Editorial Offices, General Secretariat Bldg., 1889 F Street NW, Washington DC 20006. Managing Editor: A.R. Williams. 70% freelance written. Official cultural organ of Organization of American States. Audience is persons interested in inter-American topics. Editions published in English and Spanish. Bimonthly. Circ. 75,000. Buys first publication and reprint rights. Byline given. Pays on publication. Publishes ms an average of 6 months after acceptance. Computer printout submission acceptable; prefers letter-quality. "They have got to be readable." Free sample copy. Queries preferred. Articles received on speculation only. Include cover letter with writer's background. Reports in 3 months. Not necessary to enclose SASE.

Nonfiction: Articles of general New World interest on travel, history, art, literature, theatre, development, archaeology, etc. Emphasis on modern, up-to-date Latin America. Taboos are religious and political themes or articles with noninternational slant. "Photos are not required, but are a big plus." Buys 36 unsolicited mss/year. Length: 2,500 words maximum. Pays $200 minimum.

Tips: "Send excellent photographs in both color and b&w. Address an international readership, not a local or national one. We want something more critically insightful than a Sunday newspaper travel section piece. We read everything that comes in over the transom. We'll publish anything that's good, and we don't much care if the author has been published before or not. In fact, we're getting weary of published authors who don't write very well and whose careers seem to have been propelled along by talented editors providing the authors with marvelous clips."

INLAND, The Magazine of the Middle West, Inland Steel Co., 18 S. Home Ave., Park Ridge IL 60068. Managing Editor: Sheldon A. Mix. 35-50% freelance written. Prefers to work with published/established writers, and eager to work with new/unpublished writers. Quarterly magazine that emphasizes steel products, services and company personnel. Circ. 8,000. Pays on acceptance. "Articles assigned are published within 4 months usually, but pieces in the inventory may remain years without being published." Buys first serial rights and first North American serial rights. "We have always paid the full fee on articles that have been killed." Byline given. Submit seasonal/holiday material at least 1 year in advance. Query for electronic submissions. Computer printout submissions acceptable; prefers letter-quality. Tries to report in 4 months. Free sample copy.
Nonfiction: Essays, humorous commentaries, profile, historical, think articles, personal opinion and photo essays. "We encourage individuality. At least half of each issue deals with staff-written steel subjects; half with widely ranging nonsteel matter. Articles and essays related somehow to the Midwest (Illinois, Wisconsin, Minnesota, Michigan, Missouri, Iowa, Nebraska, Kansas, North Dakota, South Dakota, Indiana and Ohio) in such subject areas as business, entertainment, history, folklore, sports, humor, current scene generally. But subject is less important than treatment. We like perceptive, thoughtful writing, and fresh ideas and approaches. Please don't send slight, rehashed historical pieces or any articles of purely local interest." Buys 5-10 unsolicited mss/year. Length: 1,200-5,000 words. Payment depends on individual assignment or unsolicited submission (usual range: $300-750). Sometimes pays expenses of writers on assignment.
Photos: Purchased with or without mss. Captions required. "Payment for pictorial essay same as for text feature."
Tips: "We are overstocked with nostalgia and are not looking for folksy treatments of family life and personal experiences. Our publication particularly needs humor that is neither threadbare nor in questionable taste, and shorter pieces (800-1,500 words) in which word choice and wit are especially important. The most frequent mistake made by writers in completing an article for us is untidiness in the manuscript (inattentiveness to good form, resulting in errors in spelling and facts, and in gaping holes in information). A writer who knows our needs and believes in himself or herself should keep trying."

INTERNATIONAL LIVING, Agora Publishing, 824 E. Baltimore St., Baltimore MD 21202. (301)234-0515. Editor: Bruce Totaro. 60% freelance written. "We prefer established writers and unpublished writers with original, first-hand experience." Monthly newsletter covering international lifestyles, travel, and investment for Americans. Aimed at affluent and not-so-affluent dreamers to whom the romance of living overseas has a strong appeal, especially when it involves money-saving angles. Circ. 65,000. Pays within 1 month of publication. Publishes ms an average of 6 months after acceptance. Byline given. Buys all rights. Submit seasonal/holiday material 2 months in advance. Query for electronic submissions. Computer printout submissions acceptable; prefers letter-quality. Reports in 1 month on queries; 6 weeks on mss. Sample copy $2.50; writer's guidelines for #10 SASE.
Nonfiction: Book excerpts (overseas, travel, retirement, investment, save money overseas, invest overseas); how-to (save money, find a job overseas); interview/profile (famous people and other Americans living abroad); personal experience; travel (unusual, imaginative destinations—give how-to's and costs); and other (humor, cuisine). "We want pithy, fact-packed articles. No vague, long-winded travel articles on well-trodden destinations. No articles on destinations in the United States." Buys 100 mss/year. Query with published clips or send complete ms. Length: 200-1,500 words. Pays $15-200.
Tips: "We are looking for writers who can combine original valuable information with a style that suggests the romance of life abroad. Break in with highly specific, well-researched material combining subjective impressions of living in a foreign country or city with information on taxes, cost of living, residency requirements, real estate, employment and entertainment possibilities. We do heavy rewrites and usually reorganize because of tight space requirements. We are moving toward more how-to and source lists."

ISLANDS, An International Magazine, Islands Publishing Company, 3886 State St., Santa Barbara CA 93105. Editor: Randall Tierney. Executive Editor: Alexandra Halsey. 95% freelance written. Prefers to work with published/established writers. Bimonthly magazine covering islands throughout the world. "We invite articles from many different perspectives: scientific, historical, exploratory, cultural, etc. We ask our authors to avoid the typical travel magazine style and concentrate on stimulating and informative pieces that tell the reader something he or she might not know about a particular island." Circ. 130,000. Pays 50% on acceptance and 50% within 30 days after publication. Publishes ms an average of 8 months after acceptance. Byline given. Buys all rights. Query for electronic submissions. Computer printout submissions acceptable; prefers letter-quality. Reports in 1 month on queries; 6 weeks on ms. Sample copy for $5.25; writer's guidelines with #10 SASE.
Nonfiction: General interest, historical/nostalgic, interview/profile, personal experience, photo feature,

technical, and any island-related material. "Each issue contains a major centerpiece of up to 3,500 words, 3 or 4 feature articles of roughly 2,000 words, and 4 or 5 topical articles for departments, each of which runs approximately 500-1,500 words. Any authors who wish to be commissioned should send a detailed proposal for an article, an estimate of costs (if applicable), and samples of previously published work." Buys 100 mss/year. "The majority of our manuscripts are commissioned." Query with published clips or send complete ms. Length: 500-4,000 words. Pays $100-3,000. Pays expenses of writers on assignment.

Photos: State availability or send photos with query or ms. Pays $50-300 for 35mm color transparencies. "Fine color photography is a special attraction of *Islands*, and we look for superb composition, image quality and editorial applicability." Label slides with name and address, include captions, and submit in protective plastic sleeves. Identification of subjects required. Buys one-time rights.

Columns/Departments: "Columns and departments are generally assigned, but we have accepted short features for our Island Hopping department. These should be highly focused on some travel-oriented aspect of islands." Buys 10-20 mss/year. Query with published clips. Length: 500-2,000 words. Pays $100-750.

Tips: "A freelancer can best break in to our publication with short (1,000-2,000 word) features that are highly focused on some aspect of island life, history, people, etc. Stay away from general, sweeping articles. We are always looking for topics for our Islanders and Island Pantry columns. These are a good place to break in. We will be using more big name writers for major features; will continue to use newcomers and regulars for columns and departments."

‡MAGAZINE OF THE MIDLANDS, *Omaha World-Herald*, World-Herald Square, Omaha NE 68102. (402)444-1000. Magazine Editor: David Hendee. 33% freelance written. A Sunday newspaper magazine on people and places of the Midlands (Midwest). "We are a general interest, regional, Sunday newspaper magazine. Readership ranges from the cornfields of Iowa to the foothills of the Rocky Mountains." Circ. 300,000. Pays on publication. Byline given. Buys one-time rights. Submit seasonal/holiday material 3 months in advance. Simultaneous and previously published submissions OK. Computer printout submissions OK; prefers letter-quality. Reports in 4 weeks. Sample copy for 9x11 SAE with 2 first class stamps. Writer's guidelines for #10 SAE with 1 first class stamp.

Nonfiction: Essays, general interest, historical/nostalgic, humor, interview/profile, personal experience, photo feature, religious and travel. No poetry, filler or fiction. Buys 85 mss/year. Send complete ms. Length: 400-2,400 words. Pays $40-150 for unsolicited articles. Send photos with submission. Reviews contact sheets, negatives, transparencies and prints. Offers no additional payment for photos accepted with ms. Captions and identification of subjects required. Buys one-time rights.

Tips: "Articles on almost any subject—as long as there is a regional link—are in demand. Most common freelance mistakes: shallow reporting, material not geared to our audience, no sense of storytelling. Send SASE."

NORTHWEST LIVING, Alaska Northwest Publishing, 130 2nd Ave. S., Edmonds WA 98020. (206)774-4111. Editor: Terry W. Sheely. 85% freelance written. A bimonthly magazine publishing information on "people, places of the Northwest from Montana west to Washington, north to Alaska south to Northern California. Country-style information." Circ. 30,000. Pays on publication. Publishes ms an average of 1 year after acceptance. Byline given. Buys one-time rights. Submit queries 1 year in advance. Previously published submissions OK. Computer printout submissions OK; double-space; no dot-matrix. Reports in 1 month on queries. Sample copy for 10x13 SAE and $1. Writer's guidelines for SASE (required!).

Nonfiction: How-to, interview/profile, living style, photo feature and travel, garden and kitchen. No poetry or fiction. Buys 120 mss/year. Length: 500-2,000 words.

Photos: Send photos with query. Reviews 35mm transparencies and 5x7 prints. Offers no additional payment for photos accepted with ms. Buys one-time rights.

Columns/Departments: Query.

Fillers: Regional shorts. See brief section. Buys 25/year. Length: 25-300 words.

Tips: "Query in detail with specific Northwest-oriented material. Include photo support if available. No telephone queries."

NORTHWEST MAGAZINE, the magazine of *The Oregonian*, 1320 SW Broadway, Portland OR 97201. Editor: Jack Hart. 90% freelance written. Prefers to work with published/established writers. Weekly newspaper Sunday supplement magazine. For an upscale, 25-49-year-old audience distributed throughout the Pacific Northwest. Circ. 420,000. Buys first serial rights for Oregon and Washington state. Pays mid-month in the month following acceptance. Publishes ms an average of 4 months after acceptance. Simultaneous submissions considered. Computer printout submissions acceptable; prefers letter-quality. Query for electronic submissions. Reports in 2 weeks. Free writer's guidelines.

Nonfiction: "Contemporary, regional articles with a strong hook to concerns of the Pacific Northwest. Cover stories usually deal with regional issues and feature 'professional-level' reporting and writing. Personality profiles focus on young, Pacific Northwest movers and shakers. Short humor, personal essays, regional destination travel, entertainment, the arts and lifestyle stories also are appropriate. No history without a contemporary angle, boilerplate features of the type that are mailed out en masse with no specific hook to our local audience, poorly documented and highly opinionated issue stories that lack solid journalistic underpinnings, routine holiday features, or gushy essays that rhapsodize about daisies and rainbows. We expect top-quality writing and thorough, careful reporting. A contemporary writing style that features involving literary techniques like scenic construction stands the best chance." Buys 400 mss/year. Query much preferred, but complete ms considered. All mss on speculation. Length: 800-3,000 words. Pays $75-1,000.

Photos: Photographs should be professional quality Kodachrome slides. Pays $75-150.

Fiction: Address submissions to fiction editor. Short-short stories that reflect the culture and social structure of the Pacific Northwest in a way that relates to contemporary life in the region as well as to the magazine's target audience. New writers welcomed; Northwest writers preferred. Buys 20-24 mss/year. Length: 1,500-2,500 words. Pays $200-225.

Poetry: Paul Pintarich, book review editor. "*Northwest Magazine* seeks poetry with solid imagery, skilled use of language and having appeal to a broad and intelligent audience. We do not accept cutesy rhymes, jingles, doggeral or verse written for a specific season, i.e., Christmas, Valentine's Day, etc. We currently are accepting poems only from poets in the Pacific Northwest region (Oregon, Washington, Idaho, Montana, Northern California, British Columbia and Alaska). Poems from Nevada and Hawaii receive consideration. We are looking for a few fine and distinctive poems each week. Poems on dot-matrix printers accepted if near letter-quality only. No handwritten submissions or threats." Send at least 3 poems for consideration. Length: 23 lines maximum. Pays $10 on acceptance.

Tips: "Pay rates and editing standards are up, and this market will become far more competitive. However, new writers with talent and good basic language skills still are encouraged to try us. Printing quality and flexibility should improve, increasing the magazine's potential for good color photographers and illustrators."

‡**NOW AND THEN,** Center for Appalachian Studies and Services, East Tennessee State University, Box 19180A, Johnson City TN 37614. (615)929-5348. 80% freelance written. A tri-annual regional magazine. Circ. 1,500. Pays on publication. Publishes ms an averge of 6 months after acceptance. Byline given. Buys one-time rights. Simultaneous, photocopied and previously published submissions OK. Computer printout submissions OK; prefers letter-quality. Reports in 1 month on queries; 3 months on mss. Sample copy $2.50; free writer's guidelines.

Nonfiction: Book excerpts, essays, historical, humor, interview/profile, personal experience, photo feature. "We do have a special focus in each issue—we've featured Appalachian Blacks, Cherokees, women, music and veterans. Write for future themes. Stereotypes (especially granny rocking on the front porch), generalizations, sentimental writing are rejected. It must have to do with Appalachia." Buys 8 mss/year. Query with or without published clips, or send complete ms. Length: 2,500 words. Pays $15-60 for assigned articles; $10-60 for unsolicited articles. Sometimes pays expenses of writers on assignment.

Photos: Send photos with submission. Reviews contact sheets and prints. Offers no additional payment for photos accepted with ms. Captions, model releases and identification of subjects required. Buys one-time rights.

Fiction: Ethnic, experimental, historical, humorous, novel excerpts, slice-of-life vignettes. "Everything we publish has to be by or about Appalachians. No stereotypes, generalizations, or sentimentality." Buys 2 mss/year. Send complete ms. Length: 2,500 words maximum. Pays $10-50.

Poetry: Avant-garde, free verse. "Must have something to do with the Appalachian region. Avoid stereotypes, generalizations, and sentimentality." Buys 30-35 poems/year. Pays 2 contributor's copies and a year subscription.

Tips: "Everything we publish has something to do with life in Appalachia present and past. Profiles of people living and working in the region, short stores that convey the reality of life in Appalachia (which can include malls, children who wear shoes and watch MTV) are the kinds of things we're looking for."

‡**THE ORIGINAL NEW ENGLAND GUIDE,** Historical Times, Inc., Box 8200, 2245 Kohn Rd., Harrisburg PA 17105. (717)657-9555. Editor: Howard Crise. 70% freelance written. Works with a small number of new/unpublished writers each year. Annual magazine covering New England travel and vacations. "*The Guide* is a complete travel planner and on-the-road guide to the six New England states. It focuses on spring-summer-fall coverage of traditional and new destinations, events and attractions." Circ. 160,000. Pays upon acceptance. Publishes ms up to 6 months after acceptance. Buys all rights. March 15 deadline for following April publication date. Computer printout submissions acceptable. Query for electronic submissions. Reports in 2 weeks. Sample copy for 9x12 SAE and $3.50 postage; writer's guidelines for #10 SASE.

Nonfiction: Photo feature and travel—New England only. No historical or business. Buys 6 mss/year. Query with published clips. Length: 500-1,500 words. Payment averages 15¢/word. Sometimes pays mail and telephone expenses.

Photos: State availability of photos. Reviews 35mm color tranparencies. Pays $50-300 for color. Identification of subjects required. Buys one-time rights.

Fillers: Buys 12-18 sidebars/year; same rate.

Tips: "Choose New England-related places or activities that appeal to a wide range of readers—active and sedentary, young and old, singles and families. Areas most open to freelancers are region-wide features and state-specific sidebars. Copy must 'sell' the area or activity to the traveler as worth a special stop or trip. We do not promote commercial establishments in features. We are service-oriented and provide factual information that helps the reader plan a trip, not just descriptions of places and things.''

RURALITE, Box 558, Forest Grove OR 97116. (503)357-2105. Editor: Ken Dollinger. 50-70% freelance written. Works with new/unpublished writers each year. Monthly magazine primarily slanted toward small town and rural families, served by consumer-owned electric utilities in Washington, Oregon, Idaho, Nevada, Alaska and northern California. "Ours is an old-fashioned down-home publication, with something for all members of the family." Circ. 223,000. Pays on acceptance. Buys first serial rights and occasionally second serial (reprint) rights. Byline given. Submit seasonal material at least 3 months in advance. Computer printout submissions acceptable; prefers letter-quality. Sample copy and writer's guidelines for $1 and 10x13 SAE.
Nonfiction: Walter J. Wentz, nonfiction editor. Primarily human-interest stories about rural or small-town folk, preferably living in areas (Northwest states and Alaska) served by Rural Electric Cooperatives. Articles emphasize self-reliance, overcoming of obstacles, cooperative effort, hard or interesting work, unusual or interesting avocations, odd or unusual hobbies or histories, public spirit or service and humor. Also considers how-to, advice for rural folk, little-known and interesting Northwest history, people or events. "We are looking specifically for energy (sources, use, conservation) slant and items relating to rural electric cooperatives." No "sentimental nostalgia or subjects outside the Pacific Northwest; nothing racy." Buys 15-20 mss/year. Query. Length: 500-900 words. Pays $30-110, depending upon length, quality, appropriateness and interest, number and quality of photos.
Photos: Reviews b&w negatives with contact sheets. Illustrated stories have better chance for acceptance.
Tips: "Freelance submissions are evaluated and decided upon immediately upon arrival. We need good, solid, well-illustrated 'first-feature' articles to lead off the magazine each month. These receive our best pay rate. We are overloaded with second- and third-feature stories already. We will be placing more emphasis on illustrations and layout; good, professional-quality b&w negatives will add to the appeal of any mss. Due to a loss of feature pages, we will be judging freelance submissions much more critically."

SOUTHERN MAGAZINE, Arkansas Writers' Project, 200 201 E. Markham 3418, Little Rock AR 72203. (501)375-4114. Editor: Linton Weeks. 95% freelance written. Prefers to work with published/established writers, and works with a small number of new/unpublished writers each year. "This is a magazine for people who live in the South. Each month we probe what it means to live in the South today. We examine the contemporary culture—high and low—of our region in a critically appreciative way." Pays on acceptance. Publishes ms an average of 4-6 months after acceptance. Byline given. Offers 10% kill fee. Buys first North American serial rights. Submit seasonal/holiday material 6 months in advance. Computer printout submissions OK; prefers letter-quality. Reports in 2 months. Sample copy $4; writer's guidelines for #10 SAE.
Nonfiction: Book excerpts, essays, expose, general interest, historical, humor, interview/profile, opinion, photo feature and travel. "No poetry, cartoons, essays on what it feels like to be a Southerner living outside the South, or articles written in dialect." Buys 100-150 mss/year. Query with published clips. Length: 200-4,000 words. Pays $50-2,000. Pays expenses of writers on assignment.
Photos: State availability of photos with submission. Reviews contact sheets. Offers $25-100 per photo. Model release and identification of subjects required. Buys one-time rights.
Columns/Departments: Sense of Place (our keynote column, what it means to be a Southerner, new or old, today); Stumping (political story or profile that has regional resonance); Sport (sports in the South); Southern Lit (the world of books in the South; no writer profiles); Bar and Grill (Southern food and drink via essay); Commerce; all 1,200-1,500 words. Buys 72 mss/year. Query with published clips. Pays $400.
Fiction: Southern. No non-Southern fiction. Buys 12 mss/year. Send complete ms. Length: 3,000-5,000 words. Pays $500-1,000.
Tips: "We are looking for stories with an edge, a little topspin, rather than straight-on stories. Stories about people we already know, and about people we ought to know about. Southern Front, Weekends, South by Design and Southern Lights are most open to freelancers."

YANKEE, Dublin NH 03444. (603)563-8111. Editor-in-Chief: Judson D. Hale. Managing Editor: John Pierce. 25% freelance written. Works with a small number of new/unpublished writers each year. Monthly magazine emphasizing the New England region. Circ. 1 million. Pays on acceptance. Publishes ms an average of 10 months after acceptance. Byline given. Buys all rights, first North American serial rights or one-time rights. Submit seasonal/holiday material at least 4 months in advance. Query for elecrtronic submissions. Computer printout submissions acceptable; no dot-matrix. Reports in 6 weeks. Free sample copy and writer's guidelines.
Nonfiction: Historical (New England history, especially with present-day tie-in); how-to (especially for Forgotten Arts series of New England arts, crafts, etc.); humor; interview (especially with New Englanders who have not received a great deal of coverage); nostalgia (personal reminiscence of New England life); photo feature (prefers color, captions essential); profile; travel (to the Northeast only, with specifics on places, prices,

etc.); current issues; antiques; and food. Buys 50 mss/year. Query with brief description of how article will be structured (its focus, etc.); articles must include a New England "hook." Length: 1,500-3,000 words. Pays $150-1,000. Pays expenses of writers on assignment.

Photos: Purchased with ms or on assignment; purchased without accompanying ms for This New England feature only; color only. Captions required. Reviews prints or transparencies. Pays $25 minimum for 8x10 b&w glossy prints; $150/page for 2¼x2¼ or 35mm transparencies; 4x5 for cover or centerspread.

Columns/Departments: Traveler's Journal (with specifics on places, prices, etc.); Antiques to Look For (how to find, prices, other specifics); and At Home in New England (recipes, gardening, crafts). Buys 10-12 mss/year. Query. Length: 1,000-2,500 words. Pays $150-400.

Fiction: Edie Clark, fiction editor. Emphasis is on character development. Buys 12 mss/year. Send complete ms. Length: 2,000-4,000 words. Pays $1,000.

Poetry: Jean Burden, poetry editor. Free verse or traditional. Buys 3-4 poems/issue. Send poems. Length: 32 lines maximum. Pays $50 for all rights, $35 for first magazine rights. Annual poetry contest with awards of $150, $100 and $50 for three best poems during the year.

Alaska

ALASKA, The Magazine of Life on the Last Frontier, Suite 200, 808 E. St., Anchorage AK 99501. (907)272-6070. Editor: Ron Dalby. Managing Editor: Barbara Brynko. 60% freelance written. Eager to work with new/unpublished writers. A monthly magazine covering topics "uniquely Alaskan." Circ. 230,000. Pays on acceptance. Publishes ms an average of 6 months after acceptance. Byline given. Buys first rights or one-time rights. Submit seasonal/holiday material 1 year in advance. Query for electronic submissions. Computer printout submissions acceptable; prefers letter-quality. Reports in 1 month on queries; 2 months on manuscripts. Sample copy $3; writer's guidelines for #10 SASE.

Nonfiction: Historical/nostalgic; how-to (on anything Alaskan); humor; interview/profile; personal experience and photo feature. Also travel articles and Alaska destination stories. Does not accept fiction or poetry. Buys 60 mss/year. Query. Length: 100-3,500 words. Pays $100-1,250. Pays expenses of writers on assignment.

Photos: Send photos with submission. Reviews 35mm transparencies. Captions and identification of subjects required. Offers no additional payment for photos accepted with ms.

NEW ALASKAN, Rt. 1, Box 677, Ketchikan AK 99901. Publisher: R.W. Pickrell. 20% freelance written. Works with a small number of new/unpublished writers each year. Monthly tabloid magazine for residents of Southeast Alaska. Circ. 5,500. Pays on publication. Publishes ms an average of 6 months after acceptance. Byline given. Rights purchased vary with author and material; buys all rights, first serial rights, one-time rights, simultaneous rights or second serial (reprint) rights. Photocopied submissions OK. Computer printout submissions acceptable. Sample copy $1.50.

Nonfiction: Bob Pickrell, articles editor. Feature material about Southeast Alaska *only*. Emphasis is on full photo or art coverage of subject. Informational, how-to, personal experience, interview/profile, inspirational, humor, historical/nostalgic, personal opinion, travel, successful business operations and new product. Buys 30 mss/year. Submit complete ms. Length: 1,000 words minimum. Pays 2¢/word. Sometimes pays the expenses of writers on assignment.

Photos: B&w photos purchased with or without mss. Minimum size: 5x7. Pays $5 per glossy used; pays $2.50 per negative. Negatives are returned. Captions required.

Fiction: Bob Pickrell, articles editor. Historical fiction related to Southeast Alaska. Length: open. Pays 2¢/word.

Arizona

ARIZONA LIVING MAGAZINE, AZ Com Publishing, Inc., 5046-C 7th St., Phoenix AZ 85014. (602)264-4295. Managing Editor: Kiana Dicker. 30% freelance written. Works with new/unpublished writers. Monthly magazine covering general interest subjects relating to Arizona. "*Arizona Living* magazine is the highest circulation, statewide, general interest feature magazine in Arizona. Our subscriber base consists of upscale, affluent, on-the-move Arizonans. We don't want to cramp your style, but we demand a solid journalistic approach." Circ. 16,500. Pays on publication. Byline given. Buys first North American serial rights. Submit seasonal/holiday material 4 months in advance. Simultaneous submissions OK. Computer printout submissions OK; prefers letter-quality. Sample copy $1.95 with $1.70 postage and 10x13 SAE; writer's guidelines for SASE.

Nonfiction: No "advertorial" submissions. Buys 48 mss/year. Query only. Ideal article length: 1,000-2,000 words. Pays 5-10¢/word. Pays the expenses of writers on assignment, when pre-approved.

Photos: State availability of photos or send photos with submission. Reviews contact sheets, transparencies

and prints. Offers cost of film for photos. Captions, model releases and identification of subjects required.
Fiction: Slice-of-life vignettes (if anything). "We only very rarely print fiction."
Tips: "We don't care as much whether or not you have been published; we mainly care that you are a good writer. Query first. Be concise, be complete, be interesting. Be prepared to change the angle of your article to fit our exact requirements. Be organized. Write for us what you promise. Good writers will be used again and again. Most freelance articles are written by assignment, but we are always looking for interesting ideas by good writers. Also, don't confine your thoughts to Arizona topics; we write about art, fashion, travel from outside the state. If it's well written and interesting, we'll probably use it."

PHOENIX METRO MAGAZINE, 4707 N. 12th St., Phoenix AZ 85014. (602)248-8900. Editorial Director: Fern Stewart Welch. Editor: Robert J. Early. 25% freelance written. Monthly magazine for metropolitan Phoenix and the state of Arizona. "Our publication is edited for residents, visitors and newcomers to the Phoenix area. Of special interest are lifestyle, economy and statewide issue-related stories." Circ. 36,000. Pays on publication. Byline given. Offers 20% kill fee. Buys first rights. Submit special issue material 8 months in advance. Computer printout submissions acceptable; prefers letter-quality. Reports in 2 weeeks. Sample copy $1.95 with 9x12 SAE and 10 first class stamps.
Nonfiction: Expose, general interest, humor, interview/profile, physical sciences and economics. Special issues include Annual Valley Progress Report (August). No pieces without local angle. Buys 100-150 mss/year. Query by phone. Length: 25-10,000 words. Pays $25-1,200 for assigned articles; $25-300 for unsolicited articles. Sometimes pays expenses of writers on assignment.
Photos: State availability of photos with submission. Reviews contact sheets. Offers no additional payment for photos accepted with ms. Offers $25-75/photo. Model releases and identification of subjects required. Buys non-exclusive perpetual rights.
Columns/Departments: Around AZ (anecdotal looks at statewide events, news briefs) and AZ Business (business-related trends, features and personality profiles). Buys 24 mss/year. Query by phone. Length: 400-600 words. Pays $125-600.
Tips: "Telephone the editor with a specific query." Business and health areas are most open to freelancers. "Know subject matter well. Must have multiple sources."

‡**SUNCITIES LIFE MAGAZINE, A Refreshing Look at the SunCities Lifestyle**, Carolyn Publishing Co., Suite C, 9192 W. Cactus, Peoria AZ 85345. (602)878-2210. Editor: Gabriella Harvey. 80% freelance written. A monthly magazine "aimed at reflecting the lifestyle of its readership—the residents of the SunCities area—through stories on their activities (i.e., sports, arts and crafts, volunteer pursuits, travel destinations, unusual hobbies, etc.)." Circ. 40,000. Pays on publication 2-6 months after acceptance. Byline given. Offers $25 kill fee. Buys first North American serial rights or second serial (reprint) rights. Submit seasonal/holiday material 4-6 months in advance. Simultaneous, photocopied and previously published submissions OK. Computer printout submissions OK; prefers letter-quality. Reports in 3-6 weeks. Sample copy for 9x12 SAE with 4 first class stamps. Writer's guidelines for #10 SAE with 1 first class stamp.
Nonfiction: General interest, historical/nostalgic, humor, inspirational, interview/profile, photo feature, travel, educational, sports and arts and crafts. No first-person experiences; expositional narrative (especially if preachy); overly saccharine subjects or styles of writing. Buys 30 mss/year. Send complete ms. Length: 500-1,500 words. Pays $50-150 for assigned articles. Pays $25-125 for unsolicited articles. Send photos with submission. Reviews transparencies (2¼x2¼) and prints (5x7). Offers no additional payment for photos accepted with ms. Offers $25-50 per photo. Captions, model releases and identification of subjects required. Reprint rights. Buys one-time rights.
Columns/Departments: Campus Life (educational opportunities and what residents have made of them); Travel Life (unusual destinations or modes of travel); Health & Fitness (examples of how being fit has nothing to do with age); Service Life (showing how people enrich their lives and others' through volunteering); Humor (tongue-in-cheek looks at life's foibles). Buys 30 mss/year. Send complete ms. Length: 500-1,500 words. Pays $50-150.
Poetry: Free verse, haiku, light verse and traditional. No limericks or anything risqué. Buys 2-5 poems/year. Length: 3-10 lines. Pays $25-40.
Fillers: Short humor. Buys 1-5/year. Length: 25-75 words. Pays $25.
Tips: "Something or someone unique, or bigger-than-life, is always interesting (i.e. 80-year-olds white water rafting; senior soaring enthusiasts; etc.). Believe it or not, professionally typed manuscripts with perfect spelling and punctuation are rare—but very appreciated! A cover letter that leaps off the page with originality is bound to elicit a scrutinized reading of the accompanying manuscript. Humor, of a universal vein, is always welcome (i.e. 'How I Survived the Three-Generation Vacation'). Travel features highlighting ideal spots or modes of travel for seniors are also good (i.e., 'Freighter Traveling,' 'A Cruise Line That Allows Pets and RVs Onboard')."

TUCSON LIFESTYLE, Old Pueblo Press, Suite 13, 7000 E. Tangue Verde Rd., Tucson AZ 85715. (602)721-2929. Editor: Sue Giles. 90% freelance written. Prefers to work with published/established writers.

A monthly magazine covering city-related events and topics. Circ. 32,000. Pays on acceptance. Publishes ms an average of 6 months after acceptance. Byline given. Buys first rights and second serial (reprint) rights. Submit seasonal/holiday material 1 year in advance. Previously published submissions OK. Computer printout submissions acceptable; prefers letter-quality. Reports in 6-8 weeks on queries; 2 months on mss. Sample copy $3; free writer's guidelines.

Nonfiction: All stories need a Tucson angle. Historical/nostalgic, humor, interview/profile, personal experience, travel and local stories. Special Christmas issue (December). "We do not accept *anything* that does not pertain to Tucson or Arizona." Buys 100 mss/year. Query. Length: open. Pays $50-300. Sometimes pays expenses of writers on assignment.

Photos: Reviews contact sheets, 2¼x2¼ transparencies and 5x7 prints. Offers $25-100/photo. Identification of subjects required. Buys one-time rights.

Columns/Departments: Business stories; Southwest Homes (environmental living in Tucson: homes, offices); and Biblioteca (Southwest books and authors). Buys 36 mss/year. Query. Length: open. Pays $100-200.

Tips: Features are most open to freelancers. " 'Style' is not of paramount importance; good, clean copy with interesting leads is a 'must.' "

Arkansas

ARKANSAS TIMES, Arkansas Writers' Project, Inc., Box 34010, Little Rock AR 72203. (501)375-2985. Editor: Mel White. 25% freelance written. Monthly magazine. "We are an Arkansas magazine. We seek to appreciate, enliven and, where necessary, improve the quality of life in the state." Circ. 30,000. Pays on acceptance. Publishes ms an average of 3 months after acceptance. Byline given. Not copyrighted. Buys first serial rights. Submit seasonal/holiday material 5 months in advance. Simultaneous, photocopied and previously published submissions OK. Computer printout submissions acceptable. Reports in 2 weeks on queries; 1 month on mss. Sample copy $3.25; writer's guidelines for SASE.

Nonfiction: Book excerpts; expose (in investigative reporting vein); general interest; historical/nostalgic; humor; interview/profile; opinion; recreation; and entertainment, all relating to Arkansas. "The Arkansas angle is all-important." Buys 24 mss/year. Query. Length: 250-6,000 words. Pays $100-400. Sometimes pays the expenses of writers on assignment.

Photos: Chris Kiesler, art director. State availability of photos. Pays $25-75. Identification of subjects required. Buys one-time rights.

Columns/Departments: Mike Trimble, column editor. I Speak Arkansaw (articles on people, places and things in Arkansas or with special interest to Arkansans). "This is the department that is most open to freelancers." Buys 25 mss/year. Query. Length: 250-1,000 words. Pays $100-150.

Tips: "The most annoying aspect of freelance submissions is that so many of the writers have obviously never seen our magazine. Only writers who know something about Arkansas should send us mss."

California

BAKERSFIELD LIFESTYLE, 123 Truxtun Ave., Bakersfield CA 93301. (805)325-7124. Editor/Publisher: Steve Walsh. Monthly magazine covering local lifestyles for college educated males and females ages 25-49 in a balanced community of industrial, agricultural and residential areas. Circ. 5,000. Byline and brief bio given. Buys all rights. Simultaneous queries, and simultaneous and photocopied submissions OK. Computer printout submissions acceptable. Reports in 6 months. Sample copy $5.

Nonfiction: General interest (topical issues); travel (up to 1,500 words); and articles on former residents who are now successful elsewhere. No investigative reporting, politics or negative editorial. Buys 12-15 mss/year. Length: 2,500 words maximum. Pays $10.

Photos: Send photos with ms. Pays $1/photo used.

Fiction: "Anything in good taste." Buys 20 mss/year. Length: 3,000 words maximum. Pays $10 maximum.

‡**L.A. STYLE**, Suite 8, 8285 Sunset Blvd., Los Angeles CA 90046. (213)650-4080. Editor: Ms. Joie Davidow. Managing Editor: Michael Lassell. 80% freelance written. Monthly magazine on Los Angeles lifestyle. "Our readers are highly educated and affluent; they are involved in the artistic, social and political whirlwind of Los Angeles and they are always interested in what is new—*L.A. Style* attempts to discover and re-discover Los Angeles." Circ. 55,000. Pays within 30 days of acceptance. Byline given. Offers 50% kill fee—"one rewrite may be required before kill fee is paid." Buys first North American serial rights or first rights. Submit seasonal/holiday material 4 months in advance. Simultaneous and photocopied submissions OK. Computer printout submissions OK; prefers letter-quality. Reports in "one week to two months depending on editorial load." Sample copy $3; writer's guidelines for #10 SAE with 1 first class stamp.

Nonfiction: Book excerpts, essays, expose, general interest, historical/nostalgic, how-to, humor,

interview/profile, opinion, personal experience, photo feature, technical, travel. No "health and beauty stereotyped women's magazine stories; any story that does not have a strong L.A. angle." Buys 100 mss/year. Query with published clips or send complete ms. Length: 1,000-5,000 words. Pays $300-1,000. Sometimes pays expenses of writers on assignment.
Photos: "We prefer to assign our own art." Buys one-time rights.
Fiction: Bob LaBrasca, senior editor. Erotica, ethnic, experimental, humorous, novel excerpts, slice-of-life vignettes. "No teen, genre, romance, devotional—what we do want is sophisticated, highly literate, innovative fiction." Buys 4-8 mss/year. Send complete ms. Length: 1,000-5,000 words. Pays $300-1,000.
Tips: "It is not impossible to write for *L.A. Style* without living in Los Angeles—it is just very unlikely that writers who do not know the evolving city intimately will be able to find the contemporary slant we require. Service pieces, how-to pieces, humor pieces and overview pieces are the hardest to come by and the most eagerly considered."

L.A. WEST, Santa Monica Bay Printing & Publishing Co., #245, 919 Santa Monica Blvd., Santa Monica CA 90401. (213)458-3376. Editor: Jan Loomis. 75% freelance written. Works with a small number of new/unpublished writers each year. Monthly magazine of the community of West Los Angeles. "We are a sophisticated magazine with local events and people as our focus, sent free to the entire community." Circ. 45,000. Pays on acceptance. Publishes ms an average of 6-12 months after acceptance. Byline and author bionote given. Buys first North American serial rights and all rights; makes work-for-hire assignments. Submit seasonal/holiday material 6 months in advance. Photocopied submissions OK. Query for electronic submissions. Computer printout submissions acceptable; prefers letter-quality. Reports in 2 months on queries. Sample copy and writer's guidelines for 9x12 SAE with 7 first class stamps.
Nonfiction: Historical/nostalgic, interview/profile, opinion, lifestyle articles, photo features and travel. No extreme positions, titillation, pornography, etc. Buys 20 mss/year. Query with published clips. Length: 200-1,500 words. Pays $25-500.
Photos: State availability of photos. Reviews color and b&w contact sheets, 4x4 transparencies and 8x10 glossy prints. Pays $35 for b&w; $40 for color.
Tips: "We're looking for well-written articles on subjects that will interest our upscale readers (average income $125,900; average age 39)."

‡LOS ANGELES MAGAZINE, ABC/Capital Cities, 1888 Century Park East, Los Angeles CA 90067. (213)557-7569. Editor: Geoff Miller. 98% freelance written. Monthly magazine about southern California. "The primary editorial role of the magazine is to aid a literate, upscale audience in getting the most out of life in the Los Angeles area." Circ. 172,000. Pays on acceptance. Publishes ms an average of 4 months after acceptance. Byline given. Offers 30% kill fee. Buys first North American serial rights. Submit seasonal/holiday material 3-6 months in advance. Computer printout submissions acceptable; prefers letter-quality. Reports in 6 weeks. Sample copy $4; writer's guidelines for SAE and 1 first class stamp.
Nonfiction: Rodger Claire, articles editor. Book excerpts (about L.A. or by famous L.A. author); expose (any local issue); general interest; historical/nostalgic (about L.A. or Hollywood); and interview/profile (about L.A. person). Buys 400 mss/year. Query with published clips. Length: 250-3,500 words. Pays $50-1,200. Sometimes pays expenses of writers on assignment.
Photos: Rodger Claire, photo editor. State availability of photos.
Columns/Departments: Rodger Claire, column/department editor. Buys 170 mss/year. Query with published clips. Length: 250-1,200 words. Pays $50-500.

LOS ANGELES READER, 12224 Victory Blvd., North Hollywood CA 91606. (818)763-3555. Editor: James Vowell. 85% freelance written. Only serious, polished work by experienced writers should be submitted. Weekly tabloid of features and reviews for "affluent young Los Angelenos interested in the arts and popular culture." Circ. 82,000. Pays on publication. Publishes ms an average of 3 months after acceptance. Byline given. Buys one-time rights. Photocopied submissions OK. Computer printout submissions acceptable; no dot-matrix. Reports in 2 months. Sample copy $1 and 9x12 SAE; free writer's guidelines.
Nonfiction: General interest, journalism, interview/profile, personal experience and photo features—all with strong local slant. Buys "dozens" of mss/year. Send complete ms. Length: 200-2,000 words. Pays $10-250.
Tips: "Break in with submissions for our Cityside page which uses short news items on Los Angeles happenings. We only want writing about local themes, topics and people by local writers."

LOS ANGELES TIMES MAGAZINE, Los Angeles Times, Times Mirror Sq., Los Angeles CA 90053. Editorial Director: Wallace Guenther. Editor: Michael Parrish. 50% freelance written. Weekly magazine of regional general interest. Circ. 1 million. Payment schedule varies. Publishes ms an average of 2 months after acceptance. Byline given. Buys first North American serial rights. Submit seasonal/holiday material 3 months in advance. Simultaneous queries and submissions OK. Computer printout submissions acceptable; no dot-matrix. Reports in 1 month. Sample copy for 9x12 SAE and 6 first class stamps. Writer's guidelines for

SAE and 2 first class stamps.

Nonfiction: General interest, historical/nostalgic, interview/profile, personal experience and photo feature. Must have California tie-in, but no need to be set in California. Query with published clips. "We welcome all queries." Length: 400-1,800 words. Pays $400-2,000. Sometimes pays the expenses of writers on assignment.

Photos: Query first. Reviews color transparencies and b&w prints. Payment varies. Captions, model releases and identification of subjects required. Buys one-time rights.

Tips: "The writer should know the subject well or have researched it adequately. As for style, the best style is when the writer goes to the trouble of employing proper English and self-edits an article prior to submission."

NORTHCOAST VIEW, Blarney Publishing, Box 1374, Eureka CA 95502. (707)443-4887. Publishers/Editors: Scott K. Ryan and Damon Maguire. 100% freelance written. Works with a small number of new/unpublished writers each year. A monthly magazine covering entertainment, recreation, the arts, consumer news, in-depth news, fiction and poetry for Humboldt County audience, mostly 18-50-year-olds. Circ. 20,000. Pays on publication. Publishes ms an average of 1-6 months after acceptance. Byline given. Generally buys all rights, but will reassign. Submit seasonal/holiday material 6 months in advance. Simultaneous queries, and simultaneous (so long as not in our area), photocopied, and previously published (so long as rights available) submissions OK. Query for electronic submissions. Computer printout submissions acceptable; no dot-matrix. Reports in 6 weeks on queries; 6 months on mss. Sample copy $1; writer's guidelines for SASE.

Nonfiction: Book excerpts (locally written); expose (consumer, government); historical/nostalgic (local); humor; interview/profile (entertainment, recreation, arts or political people planning to visit county); new product (for arts); photo feature (local for art section); and travel (weekend and short retreats accessible from Humboldt County). "Most features need a Humboldt County slant." Special issues include Christmas (December). Buys 30-40 mss/year. Query with published clips or send complete ms. Length: 1,250-2,500 words. Pays $25-75.

Photos: State availability of photos with query letter or ms and send proof sheet, if available. Pays $5-15 for 5x7 b&w prints; $25-100 for 35mm Ecktachrome slides. Captions, model releases and identification of subjects required. Buys all rights but will reassign.

Columns/Departments: A La Carte (restaurant reviews of county restaurants); Ex Libris (books); Reel Views (film); Vinyl Views (albums); Cornucopia (calendar); Poetry; Rearview (art). Buys 80-100 mss/year. Send complete ms. Length: 500-750 words. Pays $25-75.

Fiction: Adventure, condensed novels, erotica (light), experimental, fantasy, horror, humorous, mystery, novel excerpts (local), science fiction and suspense. "We are open to most ideas and like to publish new writers. Topic and length are all very flexible—quality reading is the only criteria." No cliched, contrived or predictable fiction—"we like a twist to stories." Buys 10-15 mss/year. Send complete ms. Length: 600-4,500 words; "a longer good piece may run 2-3 months consecutively, if it breaks well."

Poetry: Stephen Miller, poetry editor. Avant-garde, free verse, haiku, light verse and traditional. Open to all types. No "sappy, overdone or symbolic poetry." Buys work of 12-20 poets (3-4 poems each)/year. Submit maximum 5 poems. Length: 12-48 lines. Pays $25.

Tips: "Our greatest need always seems to be for reviews—book, album and film. Films need to be fairly current, but remember that some films take a while to get up to Humboldt County. Book and album—we're always looking for somewhat current but lesser known works that are exceptional. The most frequent mistakes made by writers are using too few quotes and too much paraphrasing."

ORANGE COAST MAGAZINE, The Magazine of Orange County, O.C.N.L., Inc., 245-D Fischer, Costa Mesa CA 92626. (714)545-1900. Editor: Janet Eastman. Managing Editor: Palmer Jones. Assignment Editor: John Morell. 95% freelance written. Monthly. "*Orange Coast* is designed to inform and enlighten the educated, upscale residents of affluent Orange Country, California and is highly graphic and well-researched." Circ. 40,000. Pays on acceptance. Publishes ms an average of 5 months after acceptance. Byline given. Buys first serial rights. Submit seasonal/holiday material 6 months in advance. Simultaneous queries, and simultaneous and photocopied submissions OK. Query for electronic submissions. Computer printout submissions acceptable; no dot-matrix. Reports in 2 months. Sample copy $2.50 with 10x12 SAE and $2.25 postage; writer's guidelines for SASE.

Nonfiction: Expose (Orange Country government, refugees, politics, business, crime); general interest (with Orange County focus); historical/nostalgic; guides to activities and services; interview/profile (Orange County prominent citizens); local sports; lifestyle features and travel. Special issues include Dining (March); Health and Beauty (January); Finance (October); Home and Garden (June); and Holiday (December). Buys 100 mss/year. Query or send complete ms. Length: 1,000-4,000 words. Pays $150 maximum.

Columns/Departments: Local Consumer, Investments, Business, Health, Profiles, Adventure, and Destination. Not open for submission are: Music, Art, Law, Medicine, Film, Restaurant Review ("we have regular reviewers"). Buys 200 mss/year. Query or send complete ms; no phone queries. Length: 1,000-2,000 words. Pays $100 maximum.

Fiction: Buys only under rare circumstances. Send complete ms. Length: 1,000-5,000 words. Must have an Orange County setting. Pays $150 maximum.

Tips: "Most features are assigned to writers we've worked with before. Don't try to sell us 'generic' journalism. *Orange Coast* prefers well-written stories with specific and unusual angles that in some way include Orange County. Be professional and write manuscripts that present you as a stylized, creative writer. A lot of writers miss the Orange County angle. Our writers *must* concentrate on the local angle. We get far too many generalized manuscripts."

PALM SPRINGS LIFE, Desert Publications, Inc., 303 N. Indian Ave., Palm Springs CA 92262. (619)325-2333. Editor: Becky Kurtz. 50% freelance written. Monthly magazine covering "affluent resort/southern California/Coachella Valley. Printed in full color on the highest quality 70 lb. paper. *Palm Springs Life* is a luxurious magazine aimed at the 'affluence' market. Surveys show that our readership has a median age of 50.1, a median household income of $105,000, a primary home worth $275,150 and a second home worth $190,500." Circ. 75,000. Pays on publication. Publishes ms an average of 3 months after acceptance. Byline given. Buys universal rights. Submit seasonal/holiday material 4 months in advance. Simultaneous, photocopied and previously published submissions OK. Query for electronic submissions. Computer printout submissions OK; prefers letter-quality. Reports in 2 weeks. Sample copy $5.
Nonfiction: Book excerpts, general interest, historical/nostalgic, humor, interview/profile, new product, photo feature and travel. Special issues include Desert Living Animal/Coachella Valley focus (September); Desert Progress/Luxury Cruises (October); Celebrities/Arts & Culture (November); Holiday Shopping (December). Query with published clips. Length: 700-1,200 words. Pays 15¢/word. Sometimes pays the expenses of writers on assignment.
Photos: Reviews 4x5 and 35mm transparencies. Offers $50-375 (for cover). Captions, model releases and identification of subjects required.
Tips: "*Palm Springs Life* publishes articles about dining, fashion, food, wine, beauty, health, sports (especially tennis and golf) and the lifestyle of the powerful, rich and famous. We are always interested in new ways to enjoy wealth, display luxury and consume it. We want to hear what's 'in' and what's 'out,' what's new in Palm Springs and the Coachella Valley, and how to solve problems experienced by our readers."

‡PENINSULA MAGAZINE, Peninsula Magazine, Inc., Suite 330, 2317 Broadway, Redwood City CA 94063. (415)368-8800. Editor: David Gorn. Managing Editor: Rachael Grossman. 50% freelance written. A monthly magazine on San Mateo and Santa Clara counties. "We have an educated and affluent readership especially concerned with environmental issues." Circ. 25,000. Pays on acceptance. Publishes ms an average of 2 months after acceptance. Byline given. 30% kill fee. Buys first rights. Submit seasonal/holiday material 4 months in advance. Simultaneous, photocopied and previously published submissions OK. Query for electronic submissions. Computer printout submissions OK. Reports in 2 months. Sample copy for 9x12 SAE with $2 postage. Writer's guidelines for 4x9 SAE with 42¢ postage.
Nonfiction: Exposé, general interest, interview/profile, photo feature, travel, fashion, finance, food, health, fitness and medicine. Buys 30 mss/year. Send complete ms. Length: 2,000-4,000 words. Pays $125-600 for assigned articles. Pays $75-350 for unsolicited articles. Sometimes pays the expenses of writers on assignment.
Photos: State availability of photos with submission or send photos with submission. Reviews transparencies and prints. Offers $10-100 per photo. Model releases and identification of subjects required. Buys one-time rights.

‡RANCH & COAST, Chartwell Publishing Co., Inc., Suite 107, 12625 High Bluff Dr., San Diego CA 92130. (619)481-7659. Publisher/Editor-in-Chief: Hershel Sinay. Editor: Mary Shepardson. 30% freelance written. Monthly magazine targeted at a sophisticated, upper-income readership, in San Diego County and surrounding areas. Most articles have a strong San Diego County focus. Circ. 42,000. Pays on publication. The vast majority of feature articles and departments are written on assignment; very few unsolicited mss are purchased. Queries with published clips are preferred to complete mss as the magazine's needs are very specific. Sample copy $4; writer's guidelines for SASE.
Photos: Availability of top-quality photos is essential.
Tips: "Familiarity with *Ranch & Coast* in its current form is strongly advised."

SACRAMENTO MAGAZINE, Box 2424, Sacramento CA 95812-2424. Editor: Nancy Martini Curley. 60-70% freelance written. Works with a small number of new/unpublished writers each year. Monthly magazine emphasizing a strong local angle on politics, local issues, human interest and consumer items for readers in the middle to high income brackets. Pays on publication. Publishes ms an average of 3 months after acceptance. Rights vary; generally buys first North American serial rights, rarely second serial (reprint) rights. Original mss only (no previously published submissions). Computer printout submissions acceptable; prefers letter-quality. Reports in 8 weeks. Sample copy $3.50; writer's guidelines for SASE.
Nonfiction: Local issues vital to Sacramento quality of life. Buys 15 unsolicited feature mss/year. Query first; no phone queries. Length: 2,000-3,000 words, depending on author, subject matter and treatment. Sometimes pays expenses of writers on assignment.

Photos: State availability of photos. Payment varies depending on photographer, subject matter and treatment. Captions (including IDs, location and date) required. Buys one-time rights.
Columns/Departments: Business, home and garden, media, parenting, first person essays, local travel, gourmet, profile, sports and city arts (850-1,250 words); City Lights (250 words).

SAN FRANCISCO FOCUS, The City Magazine for the San Francisco Bay Area, 680 8th St., San Francisco CA 94103. (415)553-2800. Editor: Mark K. Powelson. Managing Editor: Adair Lara. 80% freelance written. Prefers to work with published/established writers. A monthly city/regional magazine. Circ. 200,000. Pays on publication. Publishes ms an average of 2 months after acceptance. Byline given. Offers 33% kill fee. Buys one-time rights. Submit seasonal/holiday material 5 months in advance. Simultaneous queries and previously published submissions OK. Query for electronic submissions. Computer printout submissions acceptable; prefers letter-quality. Reports in 6 weeks. Sample copy $2.50; free writer's guidelines.
Nonfiction: Expose, humor, interview/profile, the arts, politics, public issues and travel. All stories should relate in some way to the San Francisco Bay Area (travel excepted). Query with published clips or send complete ms. Length: 750-4,000 words. Pays $75-750. Sometimes pays the expenses of writers on assignment.

‡THE SAN GABRIEL VALLEY MAGAZINE, Miller Books, 2908 W. Valley Blvd., Alhambra CA 91803. (213)284-7607. Editor-in-Chief: Joseph Miller. 75% freelance written. Bimonthly magazine; 52 pages. For middle- to upper-income people who dine out often at better restaurants in Los Angeles County. Circ. 3,400. Pays on publication. Publishes ms an average of 45 days after acceptance. Buys simultaneous rights, second serial (reprint) rights and one-time rights. Phone queries OK. Submit seasonal/holiday material 1 month in advance. Simultaneous, photocopied, and previously published submissions OK. Computer printout submissions acceptable. Reports in 2 weeks. Sample copy $1.
Nonfiction: Expose (political); informational (restaurants in the Valley); inspirational (success stories and positive thinking); interview (successful people and how they made it); profile (political leaders in the San Gabriel Valley); and travel (places in the Valley). Interested in 500-word humor articles. Buys 18 unsolicited mss/year. Length: 500-10,000 words. Pays 5¢/word.
Columns/Departments: Restaurants, Education, and Valley News and Valley Personality. Buys 2 mss/issue. Send complete ms. Length: 500-1,500 words. Pays 5¢/word.
Fiction: Historical (successful people) and western (articles about Los Angeles County). Buys 2 mss/issue. Send complete ms. Length: 500-10,000 words. Pays 5¢/word.
Tips: "Send us a good personal success story about a Valley or a California personality. We are also interested in articles on positive thinking."

‡SANTA CLARITA VALLEY MAGAZINE, Suite #111, 27201 Tourney Rd., Valencia CA 91355. (805)253-2233. Editor: Bill Otto. Managing Editor: Ruth Marks. 50% freelance written. Quarterly magazine "written for residents of the Santa Clarity Valley, but subject matter is not necessarily geographically limited." Circ. 40,000. Pays on receipt of invoice after publication. Byline given. Offers 25% kill fee. Buys first U.S. serial rights; other rights negotiable. Submit seasonal/holiday material 6 months in advance. Photocopied submission and previously published submissions OK. Computer printout submissions OK. Reports in 6 weeks on queries; 2 months on mss. Sample copy $3; writer's guidelines for #10 SAE with 1 first class stamp.
Nonfiction: General interest, historical/nostalgic, how-to, humor, interview/profile, photo feature, travel. No fiction, poetry or religious articles. Buys 50 mss/year. Query with published clips. Length: 800-1,500 words. Pays 10¢/word. Sometimes pays expenses of writers on assignment.
Photos: Send photos with submission. Reviews contact sheets, negatives, transparencies and prints. Offers $25, color; $15, b&w. Captions, model releases and identification of subjects required. Buys one-time rights.
Fillers: Anecdotes, facts, short humor. Buys 6/year. Length: 100-250 words. Pays 10¢/word.
Tips: "Send us a clear picture of what it is you want to write about and why you are uniquely qualified to do so. Let us know the availability of quality photos or artwork to go with the article."

SIERRA LIFE MAGAZINE, The Magazine of the High Sierra, Pramann Publishing, 699 W. Line St., Bishop CA 93514. (619)873-3320. Publisher: Sandie Pramann. Editor: Steve Boga. 50% freelance written. Works with a small number of new/unpublished writers each year. Bimonthly magazine on the Sierra region. "Our magazine is about the history, current events, people, and recreational opportunities of the Sierra Nevada region." Pays on publication. Publishes ms an average of 6 months after acceptance. Byline given. Buys second serial (reprint) rights. Submit seasonal/holiday material 6 months in advance. Simultaneous queries, and simultaneous, photocopied, and previously published submissions OK. Computer printout submissions acceptable; prefers letter-quality. Reports in 3 months. Sample copy $3, 9x11 SAE and $1 postage; writer's guidelines for #10 SAE and 1 first class stamp.
Nonfiction: Book excerpts; general interest; historical/nostalgic (history of Sierra Nevada region); how-to (about appropriate subjects); interview/profile (about people related to Sierra); personal experience; photo feature; technical; travel; arts; outdoor; and wildlife. All articles must be related to Sierra Nevada region. Also publishes *Sierra Life* hunting guide/fishing guide/hiking guide/four-wheel drive guide. No fiction or fantasy.

Buys 18 mss/year. Length: 500-10,000 words. Pays $20-400. Sometimes pays expenses of writers on assignment.

Photos: Sandie Pramann, Publisher. State availability of photos or send photos with query or ms. Reviews 5x7 b&w prints. "We sometimes request color transparencies." Pays $5 for b&w; $10-50 for color. Identification of subjects required. Buys two-time rights.

Poetry: Traditional (on the Sierra). Buys 12/year. Submit maximum 3 poems. Pays $5-25.

Tips: "We buy a number of historical and outdoor sports articles (skiing, backpacking, fishing) each year. Our reading audience is educated and sophisticated. Articles should reflect that."

VENTURA COUNTY & COAST REPORTER, The Reporter, VCR Inc., Suite 213, 1583 Spinnaker Dr., Ventura CA 93001. (805)658-2244; (805)656-0707. Editor: Nancy Cloutier. 12% freelance written. Works with a small number of new/unpublished writers each year. Weekly tabloid covering local news. Circ. 35,000. Pays on publication. Publishes ms an average of 2 weeks after acceptance. Byline given. Buys first North American serial rights. Computer printout submissions acceptable; no dot-matrix. Reports in 3 weeks.

Nonfiction: General interest (local slant), humor, interview/profile and travel (local—within 500 miles). Local (Ventura County) slant predominates. Length: 2-5 double-spaced typewritten pages. Pays $10-25.

Photos: State availability of photos with ms. Reviews b&w contact sheet.

Columns/Departments: Boating Experience (Southern California). Send complete ms. Pays $10-25.

Tips: "As long as topics are up-beat with local slant, we'll consider it."

VICTOR VALLEY MAGAZINE, Desert Alive Publishing Company, Box 618, Victorville CA 92392. Editor: Grace Hauser. 90% freelance written. Prefers to work with published/established writers. Bimonthly magazine. Circ. 5,000. Pays within 1 month of publication. Publishes ms an average of 3 months after acceptance. Byline given. Buys first North American serial rights. Submit seasonal/holiday material 3 months in advance. Simultaneous queries, and simultaneous, photocopied, and previously published submissions OK. Computer printout submissions acceptable "if upper and lower case; prefers letter-quality." Reports in 3 months. Free sample copy; writer's guidelines for 9x12 SAE and 7 first class stamps.

Nonfiction: General interest, historical/nostalgic, how-to, interview/profile, photo feature and local travel. Book reviews, film reviews, controversy and political articles acceptable; also articles on sex and singles. Buys 50 mss/year. Send complete ms. Length: 600-1,000 words. Pays $20-75.

Photos: Send photos with ms. Pays $25-50 for color transparencies; $5-25 for 4x5 b&w prints. Captions, model releases and identification of subjects required. Buys one-time rights.

Columns/Departments: Desert Alive (stories about the animal and plant life in and around the high desert area: what nature enthusiasts can look for, how desert-dwellers can better live with the local wildlife, etc.); History and Lore (stories about the western development of the high desert area); Family Living Today (dealing with family and social relationships, children, self-improvement, popular culture, etc.); and Desert Personalities (interesting locals, not necessarily of prominence).

Tips: "The area is rapidly growing into a metropolitan area. Will become more of a 'big city' magazine while maintaining our 'desert personality.' Our readers have expressed a strong interest in local history (Mojave Desert), interesting personalities and living better. Start with wildlife and desert-related activities (rock hounding, prospecting, 4-wheeling, etc.). I'll buy more syndicated material because it's on time, professionally written and costs less."

WEST, 750 Ridder Park Dr., San Jose CA 95190. (408)920-5796. Editor: Jeffrey Klein. 50% freelance written. Prefers to work with published/established writers. Weekly newspaper/magazine, published with the *San Jose Mercury News*. Circ. 300,000. Pays on acceptance. Publishes ms an average of 3 months after acceptance. Byline given. Buys first serial rights and occasionally second serial (reprint) rights. Submit seasonal material (skiing, wine, outdoor living) 3 months in advance. Will consider photocopied and simultaneous submissions (if the simultaneous submission is out of the area). Computer printout submissions acceptable; prefers letter-quality. Reports in 1 month. Free sample copy.

Nonfiction: A general newspaper-magazine requiring that most subjects be related to California (especially the Bay Area) and the interests of California. Will consider subjects outside California if subject is of broad or national appeal. Length: 1,000-4,000 words. Query with published clips. Pays $250-600. Sometimes (but infrequently) pays expenses of writers on assignment.

Photos: Bambi Nicklen, art director. Payment varies for b&w and color photos purchased with or without mss. Captions required.

WESTWAYS, Automobile Club of Southern California, 3rd Floor, 2890 Terminal Annex, 2601 S. Figueroa St., Los Angeles CA 90007. (213)741-4760. Executive Editor: Mary Ann Fisher. Managing Editor: Ginny Pace. 90% freelance written. Prefers to work with published/established writers. Monthly magazine. "*Westways* is a regional publication on travel in the West and world travel. Emphasis is on pleasing and interesting subjects—art, historical and cultural. Our audience is southern California upper-income readers who enjoy leisure and culture." Circ. 490,000. Pays 30 days prior to publication. Publishes ms an average of 6 months after acceptance. Byline given. Offers $75 kill fee. Buys first North American serial rights. Submit seasonal/ holiday material 6 months in advance. Photocopied submissions OK. Computer printout submissions acceptable; prefers letter-quality. Reports in 2 weeks. Sample copy for 9½x12½ SAE and $1; free writer's guidelines.

Nonfiction: General interest, historical, humor, interview/profile, photo feature and travel. "We are always interested in Christmas/holiday suggestions but need them by May/June prior to season. We do not accept political, controversial or first person articles." Buys 120-130 mss/year. Query with or without published clips or send complete ms. Length: 1,500 words maximum. Pays $150-350. Sometimes pays expenses of writers on assignment.

Photos: Send photos with query or ms. Reviews 35mm color transparencies. Pays $50; $400 for 4-color cover. Captions, model releases, and identification of subjects required. Buys one-time rights.

Columns/Departments: "We have regular monthly columnists for sections/columns except Wit & Wisdom." Buys 24-28 mss/year. Send complete ms. Length: 750-900 words. Pays $100-150.

Colorado

‡SUNDAY MAGAZINE, *Rocky Mountain News*, 400 W. Colfax Ave., Denver CO 80204. (303)892-5000. Magazine Editor: Joe Rossenfoss. Sunday supplement of daily newspaper covering general interest topics; newspaper circulates throughout Colorado and southern part of Wyoming. Circ. 380,000. Pays on publication. Byline given. Buys one-time rights. Submit seasonal/holiday material 2 months in advance. Simultaneous and previously published submissions OK ("if outside circulation area—Colorado and Southern Wyoming"). Reports in 1 month.

Nonfiction: Investigative; general interest; historical; photo feature; articles with Western angle on an out-of-the-way place; travel articles. Also looking for commentary pieces for Sunday newspapers; query Jean Otto. Buys 20 mss/year. Send complete ms. Length: 1,500-2,000 words. Pays $30-100.

Photos: State availability of photos or send photos with ms ("if article covers an event we can't cover ourselves"). Reviews color transparencies and 8x10 b&w glossy prints. Pay varies. Captions required. Buys one-time rights.

Connecticut

CONNECTICUT TRAVELER, Official Publication of the Connecticut Motor Club/AAA, Connecticut Motor Club/AAA, 2276 Whitney Ave., Hamden CT 06518. (203)281-7505. Editor: Elke Martin. 25% freelance written. Monthly tabloid covering anything of interest to the Connecticut motorist for Connecticut Motor Club members. Circ. 155,000. Pays on publication. Publishes ms 2-6 months after acceptance. Byline given. Buys first North American serial rights, first serial rights, and second serial (reprint) rights. Submit seasonal/holiday material 4 months in advance. Photocopied and previously published submissions OK. Computer printout submissions acceptable; prefers letter-quality. Reports in 1 month on queries; 6 weeks on mss. Sample copy for 8½x11 SAE and 2 first class stamps; writer's guidelines for #10 SAE with 1 first class stamp.

Nonfiction: How-to (variety, how to make traveling with children fun, etc.); and travel (regional economy or low-budget with specifics, i.e., what accommodations, restaurants, sights, recreation are available). "We are a regional publication and focus on events, traveling and other topics within the New England area, as well as worldwide travel destinations. We do not want to see mechanical or highly complicated automotive how-tos. We're always on the lookout for shorter (750-word) travel features for our Weekending and Daytripping columns. Submissions should include a rough map of the suggested driving route, as our readers will travel primarily by car. Destinations should be within a maximum 3-hour drive from Connecticut." Buys 50 mss/year. Query. Length: 500-1,200 words. Pays $75-250.

Photos: Send b&w photos with ms. Buys 8x10 glossies as part of ms package. Captions, model releases and identification of subjects required. Buys one-time rights.

Tips: "If you can get us a story on a travel destination that's unusual and hasn't been beaten to death, and cover the specifics in an interesting and fun-to-read manner, we'll definitely consider the story for publication."

HARTFORD WOMAN, a women's newspaper, Gamer Publishing, 595 Franklin Ave., Hartford CT 06114. (203)278-3800. Editor: Marta Binstock. 100% freelance written. Monthly tabloid covering women's issues. "Publication is for and about working women in the Hartford area. Any valid women's issue will be given serious editorial consideration." Circ. 40,000. Pays on publication. Publishes ms an average of 2 months after acceptance. Byline given. Offers $15 kill fee. Not copyrighted. Buys first rights. Submit seasonal/holiday material 3 months in advance. Simultaneous (unless within our geographic area), photocopied and previously published submissions OK. Reports in 2 weeks on queries; 1 month on mss. Sample copy for 9x12 SASE; postage varies with issue size.

Nonfiction: Expose, general interest (women's), historical/nostalgic, how-to, humor, opinion, jobs and education. All submissions must meet gender and geographic criteria. Special issues include Entrepreneurial (April), Smart Women's Gift Guide (November), Women in Sports (July) and Health (January). Buys 150 mss/year. Query with or without published clips or send complete ms. Length: 500-1,500 words. Pays $25-60. Sometimes pays expenses of writers on assignment.
Photos: Send photos with submission. Offers $7.50-15/photo. Identification of subjects required. Buys one-time rights.
Columns/Departments: Finance (women's financing issues); Autos (women's auto concepts); Careers/Entrepreneurs (experiences, tips and good possibilities); Fashion, and Parenting. Buys 50 mss/year. Query with or without published clips or send complete ms. Length: 800-1,000 words. Pays $35.
Tips: "Telephone the editor. Women writers are given preference over men writers; please don't try the same old angles; we're looking for fresh ideas."

NORTHEAST MAGAZINE, *The Hartford Courant*, 285 Broad St., Hartford CT 06115. (203)241-3700. Editor: Lary Bloom. 50% freelance written. Eager to work with new/unpublished writers. Weekly magazine for a Connecticut audience. Circ. 300,000. Pays on acceptance. Publishes ms an average of 1 month after acceptance. Byline given. Buys one-time rights. Previously published submissions OK. Reports in 3 weeks. Computer printout submissions acceptable; prefers letter-quality.
Nonfiction: General interest; in-depth investigation of stories behind news; historical/nostalgic; interview/profile (of famous or important people with Connecticut ties); and personal essays (humorous or anecdotal). No poetry. Buys 100-150 mss/year. Length: 750-4,500 words. Pays $200-1,000.
Photos: Most assigned; state availability of photos. "Do not send originals."
Fiction: Well-written, original short stories. Length: 750-4,500 words.
Tips: "Less space available for short fiction means our standards for acceptance will be much higher. We can only print 3-4 short stories a year."

District of Columbia

THE WASHINGTON POST, 1150 15th St. NW, Washington DC 20071. (202)334-6000. Travel Editor: Linda L. Halsey. 60% freelance written. Works with small number of new/unpublished writers each year. Prefers to work with published/established writers. Weekly newspaper travel section (Sunday). Pays on publication. Publishes ms an average of 3 months after acceptance. Byline given. "We are now emphasizing staff-written articles as well as quality writing from other sources. Stories are rarely assigned to freelance writers; all material comes in on speculation; there is no fixed kill fee." Buys first North American serial rights. Query for electronic submissions. Computer printout submissions acceptable if legible; no dot-matrix. Usually reports in 3 weeks.
Nonfiction: Emphasis is on travel writing with a strong sense of place, color, anecdote and history. Query with published clips. Length: 1,500-2,000 words, plus sidebar for practical information.
Photos: State availability of photos with ms.

THE WASHINGTON POST MAGAZINE, *The Washington Post*, 1150 15th St. NW, Washington DC 20071. Managing Editor: Stephen Petranek. 40% freelance written. Prefers to work with published/established writers. Weekly magazine featuring articles of interest to Washington readers. Circ. 1.2 million (Sunday). Average issue includes 3-5 feature articles and 4-6 columns. Pays on acceptance. Publishes ms an average of 2 months after acceptance. Byline given. Buys all rights or first North American serial rights, depending on fee. Submit seasonal material 4 months in advance. Photocopied submissions OK. Computer printout submissions acceptable; no dot-matrix unless near letter-quality. Reports in 6 weeks on queries; 3 weeks on mss. Sample copy for 8½x11 SAE and 2 first class stamps.
Nonfiction: Controversial and consequential articles. Subject areas include children, science, politics, law and crime, media, money, arts, behavior, sports, society, and photo feature. Buys 2 mss/issue. Query with published clips. Length: 1,500-6,500 words. Pays $200-up; competitive with major national magazine rates. Pays expenses of writers on assignment.
Photos: Reviews 4x5 or larger b&w glossy prints and 35mm or larger color transparencies. Model releases required.

THE WASHINGTONIAN MAGAZINE, 1828 L St. NW, Washington DC 20036. Editor: John A. Limpert. 20% freelance written. Prefers to work with published/established writers who live in the Washington area. For active, affluent and well-educated audience. Monthly magazine; 310 pages. Circ. 153,000. Buys first rights only. Pays on publication. Publishes ms an average of 2 months after acceptance. Simultaneous and photocopied submissions OK. Computer printout submissions acceptable; prefers letter-quality. Reports in 4-6 weeks. Sample copy for $3 and 9x12 SAE; writer's guidelines for #10 SASE.
Nonfiction: "*The Washingtonian* is written for Washingtonians. The subject matter is anything we feel might

interest people interested in the mind and manners of the city. The style, as Wolcott Gibbs said, should be the author's—if he is an author, and if he has a style. The only thing we ask is thoughtfulness and that no subject be treated too reverently. Audience is literate. We assume considerable sophistication about the city, and a sense of humor." Buys how-to, personal experience, interview/profile, humor, coverage of successful business operations, think pieces and exposes. Buys 75 mss/year. Length: 1,000-7,000 words; average feature 4,000 words. Pays 30¢/word. Sometimes pays the expenses of writers on assignment. Query or submit complete ms.

Photos: Photos rarely purchased with mss.

Fiction and Poetry: Margaret Cheney, department editor. Must be Washington-oriented. No limitations on length. Pays 20¢/word for fiction. Payment is negotiable for poetry.

Florida

CORAL SPRINGS MONTHLY/PLANTATION MONTHLY, Box 8783, Coral Springs FL 33075. (305)344-8090/Suite 323, 1859 North Pine Island Rd., Plantation FL 33322. Editor: Karen King. Monthly magazines covering people who work and/or live in Coral Springs or in Plantation. "The magazines are distributed to residents and businesses as well as people who plan to move here. 99% positive material." Circ. 8,000 each. Pays on publication. Publishes ms an average of 2-3 months after acceptance. Byline given. Offers $10 kill fee. Buys first rights. Submit seasonal/holiday material 5-6 months in advance. Photocopied submissions OK. Computer printout submissions OK; prefers letter-quality. Reports in 1 month. Sample copy $2.50.

Nonfiction: General interest (must interest yuppies or high class), how-to (on home decorating, gardening, fashion and beauty), humor (seasonal), interview/profile (Coral Springs people or celebrities who might frequent here), new products (pertaining to yuppies or high class), technical and travel. "We don't want run-of-the-mill anything. If you can come up with fresh slants to Coral Springs residents in any way, we're interested." Buys 60 mss/year. Query with published clips. Length: 500-1,000 words. Pays $25-50. Sometimes pays expenses of writers on assignment.

Photos: State availability of photos with submission. Captions, model releases and identification of subjects required. Buys one-time rights.

Columns/Departments: Business Report (profiles on businesses in the area, or business people); Classic Car (spotlights area classic car owners and their cars); Cooking (how-to's or profiles on interesting cooks in the area); Education; Relationships; and Home Videos. Buys 34 mss/year. Query with published clips. Length: 500-1,000 words. Pays $25-50.

Fillers: Newsbreaks. Buys 12/year. Length: 250-500 words. Pays $25.

Tips: "Anything with a fresh angle is welcomed and we'll try to fit it in. Get to know the city and the people here and then query us with your ideas. Cooking, education, classic car, personality profiles and features are areas most open to freelancers. Keep in mind our family-oriented city. Remember a positive outlook. I would like to incorporate fiction in the near future."

‡**ISLAND LIFE, The Enchanting Barrier Islands of Florida's Southwest Gulf Coast**, Island Life Publications, Box X, Sanibel FL 33957. (813)472-4344. Editor: Joan Hooper. Editorial Associate: Susan Shores. 40% freelance written. Prefers to work with published/established writers, but works with a small number of new/unpublished writers each year. Quarterly magazine of the Barrier Islands from Anna Maria Island to Key West, for upper-income residents and vacationers of Florida's Gulf Coast area. Circ. 20,000. Pays on publication. Publishes ms an average of 1 year after acceptance. Byline given. Buys first serial rights and second serial (reprint) rights. Simultaneous queries, and simultaneous and photocopied submissions OK. Computer printout submissions acceptable; no dot-matrix. Reports in 1 month on queries; 3 months on mss. Sample copy and writer's guidelines for $3; writer's guidelines only for #10 SASE.

Nonfiction: General interest, historical. "Travel and interview/profile done by staff. Our past use of freelance work has been heavily on Florida wildlife (plant and animal), Florida cuisine, and Florida parks and conservancies. We are a regional magazine. No fiction or first-person experiences. No poetry. Our editorial emphasis is on the history, culture, wildlife, art, scenic, sports, social and leisure activities of the area." Buys 10-20 mss/year. Query with ms and photos. Length: 500-1,500 words. Pays 3-8¢/word.

Photos: Send photos with query. No additional payment. Captions, model releases, and identification of subjects required.

Tips: "Submissions are rejected, most often, when writer does not show adequate knowledge of subject. Send something new and fresh, not same old rehashed subjects. Please, no first person."

JACKSONVILLE TODAY, White Publishing Co., Suite 900, 1325 San Marco Blvd., Jacksonville FL 32207. (904)396-8666. Editor: Carole Caldwell. Managing Editor: Rejeanne Davis Ashley. 90% freelance written. Prefers to work with published/established writers, and works with a small number of new/unpublished writers each year. A monthly city lifestyle magazine "which explores all facets of the North Florida experience—from politics and people to recreation and leisure." Circ. 25,000. Pays on publication. Publishes ms an average of 3 months after acceptance. Byline given. Buys all rights. Submit seasonal/holiday material 3 months in advance. Photocopied submissions OK. Computer printout submissions acceptable; prefers letter-quality. Reports in 3 weeks on queries; 6 weeks on manuscripts. Sample copy and writer's guidelines for 9x12 SAE and $1.08 postage.

Nonfiction: Exposé, general interest, historical, how-to (general), interview, photo feature and travel. Special issue features golf-oriented material (March material due Jan. 9). No fiction, essays, opinion, religious, non-localized features, humor, or book and film reviews. Buys 60 mss/year. Query with or without published clips, or send complete ms. Length: features 1,500-3,000 words. Pays $150-400. Sometimes pays the expenses of writers on assignment.

Photos: State availability of photos with submission. Reviews contact sheets. Offers $25 minimum per photo. Model releases and identification of subjects required.

Columns/Departments: Living Well (leisure, recreation, home and garden, furnishings, etc.); Ways & Means (personal finance and investment); and Outdoors (sports and recreation). Buys 72 mss/year. Query with published clips. Length: 1,200-1,500 words. Pays $150-300.

Tips: "The areas of our publication most open to freelancers are the Escape (travel) and Habitat (leisure, possessions, new trends in consumer purchases) departments. All articles must be localized to the Jacksonville/North Florida area."

NEW VISTAS, General Development Corp., Corporate Communications Dept., 1111 S. Bayshore Dr., Miami FL 33131. (305)350-1256. Editor: Otis Wragg. 50% freelance written. Prefers to work with published/established writers. Magazine published 2 times/year on Florida—growth, travel, lifestyle. Reaches residents of General Development's planned communities in Florida (Port Charlotte, Port St. Lucie, Port Malabar, Port LaBelle, Silver Springs Shores, North Port) plus those who own home sites there. Majority of circulation is in Northeast and Midwest U.S. Interested in people, activities, and growth of these communities. Circ. 250,000. Pays on publication. Publishes ms an average of 6 months after acceptance. Byline given. Buys first serial rights. Submit seasonal/holiday material 3 months in advance. Computer printout submissions acceptable; prefers letter-quality. Reports in 2 weeks. Free sample copy.

Nonfiction: General interest, historical/nostalgic, how-to, photo feature, and travel, all Florida-related. Buys 8 mss/year. Query. Length: 500-2,000 words. Pays $100-600. Sometimes pays expenses of writers on assignment.

Photos: State availability of photos or send photos with query. Prefers 35mm color transparencies. Captions required. Buys one-time rights.

Tips: "*New Vista* defines and articulates the dream of living in Florida for a largely out-of-state readership. Stories about Florida living and economics—keyed to General Development's planned communities—are always sought. Familiarity with Florida, and General Development's planned communities is a plus. We usually buy one Florida travel article per issue. Destinations close to General Development communities are best."

SENIOR VOICE NEWSPAPER, Florida's Leading Senior Citizens Newspaper, T.J.L. Publications Inc., Suite 6002, 6541 44th St., Pinellas Park FL 33565. (813)521-4026. Editor: Stephen N. Ream. 50% freelance written. Prefers to work with published/established writers; works with a small number of new/unpublished writers each year. A monthly newspaper for mature adults 50 years of age and over. Circ. 40,000. Pays on publication. Publishes ms an average of 2 months after acceptance. Byline given. Buys one-time rights. Submit seasonal/holiday material 2 months in advance. Simultaneous and previously published submissions OK. Computer printout submissions acceptable; no dot-matrix. Reports in 1 month. Sample copy $1 with 10x13 SAE and 5 first class stamps.

Nonfiction: Exposé, general interest, historical/nostalgic, how-to, humor, inspirational, interview/profile, opinion, photo feature, travel, health and finance, all slanted to a senior audience. No religious or youth oriented submissions. Buys 40 mss/year. Query or send complete ms. Length: 300-600 words. Pays $15.

Photos: Send photos with submission. Reviews 5x2 prints. Offers $3/photo. Identification of subjects required.

Columns/Departments: Washington Letter (senior citizen legislative interests); Travel (senior slant); V.I.P. Profiles (mature adults). Buys 20 mss/year. Send complete ms. Length: 300-600 words. Pays $15.

Fillers: Anecdotes, facts, political cartoons, gags to be illustrated by cartoonist, and short humor. Buys 10/year. Length: 150-250 words. Pays $15.

Tips: "Travel, political issues, celebrity profiles, and general interest are the areas of our publication most open to freelancers. Keep in mind that *Senior Voice* readers are 50 years of age and older. A working knowledge of issues and problems facing seniors today and a clean precise style will suffice."

SUNSHINE: THE MAGAZINE OF SOUTH FLORIDA, The News & Sun-Sentinel Co., 101 N. New River Dr., Fort Lauderdale FL 33301-2293. (305)761-4017. Editor: John Parkyn. 50% freelance written. Prefers to work with published/established writers, and works with a small number of new/unpublished writers each year. A general interest Sunday magazine for the *News/Sun-Sentinel's* 750,000 readers in South Florida. Circ. 300,000. Pays within 1 month of acceptance. Publishes ms an average of 2 months after acceptance. Byline given. Offers 25% kill fee for assigned material. Buys first serial rights or one-time rights in the state of Florida. Submit seasonal/holiday material 2 months in advance. Simultaneous queries, and simultaneous, photocopied, and previously published submissions OK. Computer printout submissions OK; prefers letter-quality. Reports in 2 weeks on queries; 1 month on mss. Free sample copy and writer's guidelines.

Nonfiction: General interest, how-to, interview/profile and travel. "Articles must be relevant to the interests of adults living in South Florida." Buys about 100 mss/year. Query with published clips. Length: 1,000-3,000 words; preferred length 2,000-3,000 words. Pays 20-25¢/word to $750 maximum (occasionally higher).

Photos: State availability of photos. Pays negotiable rate for 35mm color slides and 8x10 b&w prints. Captions and identification of subjects required; model releases required for sensitive material. Buys one-time rights for the state of Florida.

Tips: "Do not phone—we don't have the staff to handle calls of this type—but do include your phone number on query letter. Keep your writing tight and concise—readers don't have the time to wade through masses of 'pretty' prose. Be as sophisticated and stylish as you can—Sunday magazines have come a long way from the Sunday supplements of yesteryear."

TALLAHASSEE MAGAZINE, Marketplace Communications, Inc., Box 12848, Tallahassee FL 32317. (904)385-3310. Editor: William L. Needham. Managing Editor: W.R. Lundquist. 80% freelance written. Prefers to work with published/established writers. Quarterly magazine covering people, events and history in and around Florida's capital city. Circ. 16,000. Pays on publication. Publishes ms an average of 3 months after acceptance. Buys first serial rights. Submit seasonal/holiday material 6 months in advance. Simultaneous queries, and photocopied and previously published submissions OK. Computer printout submissions acceptable; prefers letter-quality. Reports in 1 month. Sample copy for 9x12 SAE. Query for list of topics.

Nonfiction: General interest (relating to Florida or Southeast); historical/nostalgic (for Tallahassee, North Florida, South Georgia); and interview/profile (related to North Florida, South Georgia). No fiction, poetry or topics unrelated to area. Buys 20 mss/year. Query. Length: 500-1,400 words. Pays 10¢/word, unsolicited; 12-20¢/word solicited.

Photos: State availability of photos with query. Pays $35 minimum for 35mm color transparencies; $20 minimum for b&w prints. Model releases and identification of subjects required. Buys one-time rights.

Tips: "We seek to show positive aspects of life in and around Tallahassee. Know the area. A brief author biographic note should accompany manuscripts."

TAMPA BAY MAGAZINE, Tampa Bay Publications, Suite 101, 2531 Landmark Dr., Clearwater FL 34621. (813)791-4800. Editor: Gregory L. Snow. Managing Editor: Ramona G. McCary. Associate Editor: DeAnn G. Semler. 60% freelance written. Bimonthly magazine, with quarterly spinoff publication, *Dining and Entertainment*, call *D&E*. Editorial needs mostly local or statewide, with national/international fashion, travel and design interests. Circ. 20,000. Pays 1 week following publication. Publishes ms an average of 1 month after acceptance. Byline given. Offers 50% kill fee. Buys all North American rights. Submit seasonal/holiday material 4 months in advance. Simultaneous submissions OK. Computer printout submissions, double-spaced OK. Reports in 2 months on queries. Sample copy for 9x12 SAE with 11 first class stamps.

Nonfiction: General interest, humor, local interview/profile, photo feature, travel, food/dining, the arts and entertainment. Buys 6-8 mss/year. Query with 2 published clips. Length: 500-2,000 words. Pays $75-300. Sometimes pays expenses of writers on assignment.

Photos: State availability of photos with submission. Reviews 35mm or 4x5 transparencies and 4x5 prints. Offers no additional payment for photos with ms. Identification of subjects required. Buys one-time rights.

Tips: "Clean, double-spaced mss written in decent prose preferred. Since most of our needs are relative to the Tampa Bay area, it follows that most of our writers are local. For those who are residents, we are looking for upbeat, fresh approaches and idea or new, interesting stories. Delight us with something extraordinary."

TROPIC MAGAZINE, Sunday Magazine of the Miami Herald, Knight Ridder, 1 Herald Plaza, Miami FL 33132. (305)376-3432. Editor: Tom Shroder. 20% freelance written. Works with small number of new/unpublished writers each year. Weekly magazine covering general interest, locally-oriented topics for local readers. Circ. 500,000. Pays on publication. Publishes ms an average of 2 months after acceptance. Byline given. Buys first serial rights. Submit seasonal/holiday material 2 months in advance. Computer printout submission OK; prefers letter-quality. Reports in 6 weeks.

Nonfiction: Brian Dickerson, articles editor. General interest; interview/profile (first person); and personal experience. No fiction. Buys 20 mss/year. Query with published clips or send complete ms. Length: 1,500-3,000 words. Pays $200-1,000/article.

Photos: Philip Brooker, art director. State availability of photos.

Tips: "We would like to receive 500-word essays for the Just A Moment column."

WATERFRONT NEWS, Ziegler Publishing Co., Inc., 1224 S.W. 1st Ave., Ft. Lauderdale FL 33315. (305)524-9450. Editor: John Ziegler. 75% freelance written. Eager to work with new/unpublished writers as well as those who are published and established. A monthly tabloid covering marine and boating topics for the

Greater Ft. Lauderdale waterfront community. Circ. 35,000. Pays on publication. Publishes ms an average of 2 months after acceptance. Byline given. Buys first serial rights; second serial (reprint) rights or simultaneous rights. Submit seasonal/holiday material 3 months in advance. Photocopied and previously published submissions OK. Computer printout submissions acceptable; prefers letter-quality. Reports in 1 month on queries. Sample copy for 9x12 SAE and 4 first class stamps; free writer's guidelines.

Nonfiction: Historical/nostalgic (nautical or Southern Florida); new marine products; opinion (on marine topics); technical (on marine topics); and marine travel. Buys 50 mss/year. Query with or without published clips, or send complete ms. Length: 500-1,000 words. Pays $50-200 for assigned articles; pays $25-200 for unsolicited articles. Sometimes pays the expenses of writers on assignment.

Photos: State availability of photos or send photos with submission. Reviews contact sheets and 3x5 or larger prints. Offers $5/photo. Buys one-time rights.

Columns/Departments: Query with published clips. Length 500-1,000 words. Pays $25-100.

Fiction: Adventure, humorous, and novel excerpts, all with a nautical or South Florida hook. Buys 3 mss/year. Query. Length: 500-1,000 words. Pays $25-200.

Poetry: Avant-garde, free verse, haiku, light verse and traditional. Buys 10 poems/year. Submit maximum 5 poems. Length: 3 lines minimum. Pays $10-200.

Fillers: Anecdotes, facts, nautical one-liners to be illustrated by cartoonist, newsbriefs and short humor. Buys 12/year. Length 100-500 words. Pays $10-200.

Tips: "Non-fiction marine, nautical or South Florida stories are more likely to be published. Keep it under 1,000 words. Photos or illustrations help."

Georgia

GEORGIA JOURNAL, Grimes Publications, Inc., Box 27, Athens GA 30603-0027. Editor: Millard Grimes. 75% freelance written. Works with a small number of new/unpublished writers each year. Quarterly magazine covering the state of Georgia. Circ. 5,000. Pays on acceptance. Publishes ms an average of 3-6 months after acceptance. Byline given. Buys first serial rights. Submit seasonal/holiday material 4-6 months in advance. Photocopied submissions OK. Computer printout submissions acceptable; no dot-matrix. Reports in 1 month. Sample copy $3; writer's guidelines for SASE.

Nonfiction: "We are interested in almost everything going on within the state. Although we specialize in an area, we maintain a general interest format. We do prefer to get pieces that are current and that have a human interest slant. We are also very interested in natural science pieces. We do our special focus issues and suggest that writers send for special focus schedule. We are not interested in sentimental reminiscences, anything risque, specifically political or religious pieces." Buys 30-40 mss/year. Query. Length: 1,200-2,000 words. Pays $25-50. Pays expenses of writers on assignment.

Photos: State availability of photos or send photos with query or ms. Reviews sharp 8x10 b&w glossies. Captions, model releases and identification of subjects required.

Columns/Departments: "We have a short section called Seeing Georgia—a travel column featuring places to go in Georgia."

Fiction: Fiction editor. "Fiction must be suitable for all ages." Buys 3-4 mss/year. Send complete ms. Length: 1,200-2,000 words. Pays $25.

Poetry: Janice Moore, poetry editor. Free verse, haiku, light verse and traditional. No poetry specifically dealing with another part of the country (out of the South) or anything not suitable for a general audience. "Most of our school-age readers are middle school and older." Uses 20 poems/year. Submit maximum 4 poems. Length: 25 lines. Pays in copies.

Tips: "We are now a quarterly publication, which will limit the number of freelance articles we accept. We have a section of short pieces (3-8 paragraphs) called Under the Chinaberry Tree where we always need good general interest submissions. These pieces are usually on topics not meriting feature article length. See a sample copy for Chinaberry Tree pieces that have been used."

‡NORTH GEORGIA JOURNAL, Legacy Communications, Inc., 110 Hunters Mill, Woodstock GA 30188. (404)928-7739. Editor: Olin Jackson. 75% freelance written. A quarterly magazine of travel opportunities to historic sites in north Georgia. "The *North Georgia Journal* is bought and subscribed to by persons interested in traveling to and reading about scenic attractions and historic sites and information indigenous to the north Georgia region and areas contiguous to the north Georgia area." Pays on acceptance. Publishes ms an average of 6 months after acceptance. Byline given. Buys first publications rights or all rights. Simultaneous submissions OK. Computer printout submissions OK; prefers letter-quality. Reports in 6 weeks. Sample copy $3.95 with 9x12 SAE and 7 first class stamps. Free writer's guidelines.

Nonfiction: Historical/nostalgic, personal experiences, photo feature, travel. "I'm interested primarily in a first-person account of experiences involving the exploration of unique historic sites and travel opportunities indigenous to north Georgia and areas contiguous to north Georgia in other states." Buys 20-30 mss/year. Query. Length: 2,500-3,500 words. Pays $25-200.

Photos: Send photos with submission. "Photos are crucial to the acceptance of submissions." Reviews contact sheets and 8x10 and 5x7 prints. Offers no additional payment for photos accepted with ms. Captions and identification of subjects required. Buys first publication rights or all rights.

Tips: "We're interested in first person accounts of experiences involving travel to and exploration of unique and interesting historic sites and travel opportunities indigenous to the Appalachian Mountains of north Georgia and areas contiguous to north Georgia in Tennessee, North Carolina, South Carolina and Alabama. An approach similar to that taken by submissions in National Geographic magazine is most desired. Subject matter of particular interest includes gold mining; pioneers in the area; Indian/early settlements/communities; and travel subject matter related to present-day travel opportunities to scenic and historic sites such as historic bed and breakfast/mountain inns, etc."

Hawaii

ALOHA, THE MAGAZINE OF HAWAII AND THE PACIFIC, Davick Publishing Co., 828 Fort St. Mall, Honolulu HI 96813. Editor: Cheryl Tsutsumi. 50% freelance written. *Aloha* is a bimonthly regional magazine of international interest. "Most of our readers do not live in Hawaii, although most readers have been to the Islands at least once. Even given this fact, the magazine is directed primarily to residents of Hawaii in the belief that presenting material to an immediate critical audience will result in a true and accurate presentation that can be appreciated by everyone. *Aloha* is not a tourist or travel publication and is not geared to such a readership, although travelers will find it to be of great value." Circ. 80,000. Pays on publication. Publishes ms an average of 6 months after acceptance; unsolicited ms can take a year or more. Byline given. Offers variable kill fee. Buys all rights. Submit seasonal/holiday material 1 year in advance. Photocopied submissions OK. Computer printout submissions acceptable; no dot-matrix. Reports in 2 months. Sample copy $2.95 with $2.75 postage; writer's guidelines for SASE.

Nonfiction: Book excerpts; historical/nostalgic (historical articles must be researched with bibliography); interview/profile; and photo feature. Subjects include the arts, business, flora and fauna, people, sports, destinations, food, interiors, and history of Hawaii. "We don't want stories of a tourist's experiences in Waikiki or odes to beautiful scenery. We don't want an outsider's impressions of Hawaii, written for outsiders." Buys 24 mss/year. Query with published clips. Length: 1,000-4,000 words. Pay ranges from $250-400. Sometimes pays expenses of writers on assignment.

Photos: State availability of photos with query. Pays $25 for b&w prints; prefers negatives and contact sheets. Pays $60 for 35mm (minimum size) color transparencies used inside; $125 for double-page bleeds; $175 for color transparencies used as cover art. "*Aloha* features Beautiful Hawaii, a collection of photographs illustrating that theme, in every issue. A second photo essay by a sole photographer on a theme of his/her own choosing is also runs occcasionally. Queries are essential for the sole photographer essay." Model releases and identification of subjects required. Buys one-time rights.

Fiction: Ethnic and historical. "Fiction depicting a tourist's adventures in Waikiki is not what we're looking for. As a general statement, we welcome material reflecting the true Hawaiian experience." Buys 2 mss/year. Send complete ms. Length: 1,000-2,500 words. Pays $300.

Poetry: Haiku, light verse and traditional. No seasonal poetry or poetry related to other areas of the world. Buys 6 poems/year. Submit maximum 6 poems. Prefers "shorter poetry." Pays $25.

Tips: "Read *Aloha*. Be meticulous in research and have good illustrative material available, i.e., photos in most cases."

HONOLULU, Honolulu Publishing Co., Ltd., 36 Merchant St., Honolulu HI 96813. (808)524-7400. Editor: Brian Nicol. 20% freelance written. Prefers to work with published/established writers. Monthly magazine covering general interest topics relating to Hawaii. Circ. 35,000. Pays on acceptance. Publishes ms an average of 4 months after acceptance. Byline given. Offers $50 kill fee. Buys first serial rights. Submit seasonal/holiday material 5 months in advance. Simultaneous queries, and simultaneous and photocopied submissions OK. Computer printout submissions acceptable; prefers letter-quality. Sample copy $2 with 9x11 SAE and $2.40 postage.

Nonfiction: Expose, general interest, historical/nostalgic, and photo feature—all Hawaii-related. "We run regular features on fashion, interior design, travel, etc., plus other timely, provocative articles. No personal experience articles." Buys 10 mss/year. Query with published clips if available. Length: 2,500-5,000 words. Pays $400. Sometimes pays expenses of writers on assignment.

Photos: Teresa Black, photo editor. State availability of photos. Pays $15 maximum for b&w contact sheet; $25 maximum for 35mm color transparencies. Captions and identification of subjects required. Buys one-time rights.

Columns/Departments: Calabash (light, "newsy," timely, humorous column on any Hawaii-related subject). Buys 15 mss/year. Query with published clips or send complete ms. Length: 250-1,000 words. Pays $25-35.

Illinois

‡CHICAGO LIFE, Box 11311, Chicago IL 60611-0311. Editor: Pam Berns. 95% freelance written. A bimonthly magazine on Chicago life. Circ. 50,000. Pays on publication. Byline given. Kill fee varies. Submit seasonal/holiday material 8 months in advance. Simultaneous, photocopied and previously published submissions OK. Reports in 3 months. Sample copy for 9x12 SAE with 7 first class stamps.
Nonfiction: Book excerpts, essays, exposé, how-to, photo feature and travel. Buys 50 mss/year. Send complete ms. Length: 400-1,200 words. Pays $30-40 for unsolicited articles. Sometimes pays the expenses of writers on assignment. Send photos with submission. Reviews contact sheets, negatives, transparencies and prints. Offers $15-30 per photo. Buys one-time rights.
Columns/Departments: Law, Book Reviews, Travel and Fashion. Send complete ms. Length: 500 words. Pays $30-40.
Fillers: Facts. Pays $15-30.
Tips: "Please send finished work with visuals (photos, if possible). Topics open include travel, self improvement, how-to-do almost anything, entrepreneurs, how to get rich, beautiful, more well-informed."

CHICAGO MAGAZINE, 414 N. Orleans, Chicago IL 60610. Editor: Hillel Levin. Managing Editor: Joanne Trestrail. 40% freelance written. Prefers to work with published/established writers; works with a small number of new/unpublished writers each year. Monthly magazine for an audience which is "95% from Chicago area; 90% college-trained; upper income; overriding interests in the arts, dining, good life in the city and suburbs. Most are in 25-50 age bracket, well-read and articulate." Circ. 210,000. Buys first serial rights. Pays on acceptance. Publishes ms an average of 6 months after acceptance. Submit seasonal material 4 months in advance. Computer printout submissions acceptable "if legible." Reports in 2 weeks. Query; indicate "specifics, knowledge of city and market, and demonstrable access to sources." For sample copy, send $3 to Circulation Dept.; writer's guidelines for SASE.
Nonfiction: "On themes relating to the quality of life in Chicago: past, present, and future." Writers should have "a general awareness that the readers will be concerned, influential longtime Chicagoans reading what the writer has to say about their city. We generally publish material too comprehensive for daily newspapers." Personal experience and think pieces, profiles, humor, spot news, historical articles and exposes. Buys about 50 mss/year. Length: 500-6,000 words. Pays $100-$2,500. Pays expenses of writers on assignment.
Photos: Reviews b&w glossy prints, 35mm color transparencies or color prints. Usually assigned separately, not acquired from writers.
Tips: "Submit detailed queries, be business-like and avoid cliched ideas."

ILLINOIS MAGAZINE, The Magazine of the Prairie State, Sunshine Park, Box 40, Litchfield IL 62056. (217)324-3425. Editor: Peggy Kuethe. 85% freelance written. Works with a small number of new/unpublished writers each year, and is eager to work with new/unpublished writers. A bimonthly magazine devoted to the heritage of the state. Emphasizes history, current interest, and travel in Illinois for historians, genealogists, students and others who are interested in the state. Circ. 16,000. Pays on publication. Publishes ms an average of 6 months after acceptance. Byline given. Buys first North American serial rights or one-time rights. Submit seasonal/holiday material 6 months in advance. Photocopied submissions OK. Computer printout submissions acceptable; prefers letter-quality. Reports in 2 months on queries; 4 months on mss. Sample copy for 10x12 SAE and 5 first class stamps; writer's guidelines for #10 SASE.
Nonfiction: Essays, general interest, historical/nostalgic, interview/profile, photo feature and travel. Also, festivals (annual events, county fairs), biography, points of interest, botany, animals, scenic areas that would be of interest to travelers. "We do not want to see family history/family tree/genealogy articles." Buys 75-85 mss/year. Send complete ms. Length: 100-2,000 words. Pays $10-200.
Photos: Send photos with submission. Reviews contact sheets, 35mm or 4x5 transparencies and 3x5, 5x7 and 8x10 prints. Offers $5-50 photo. Captions, model releases, and identification of subjects required. Buys one-time rights.
Fillers: Anecdotes, facts and short humor. Buys 3-5/year. Length: 50-200 words. Pays $10-$25.
Tips: "Be sure to include a phone number where you can be reached during the day. Also, try if at all possible to obtain photographs for the article if it requires them. And don't forget to include sources or references for factual material used in the article."

ILLINOIS TIMES, Downstate Illinois' Weekly Newspaper, Illinois Times, Inc., Box 3524, Springfield IL 62708. (217)753-2226. Editor: Fletcher Farrar Jr. 25% freelance written. Works with a small number of new/unpublished writers each year. Weekly tabloid covering that part of the state outside of Chicago and its suburbs for a discerning, well-educated readership. Circ. 23,000. Pays on publication. Publishes ms an average of 2 months after acceptance. Byline given. Buys first serial rights and second serial (reprint) rights. Submit seasonal/holiday material 1 month in advance. Simultaneous queries, and simultaneous, photocopied, and previously published submissions OK. Computer printout submissions acceptable; prefers letter-quality. Reports in 3 weeks on queries; 2 months on mss. Sample copy $1; writer's guidelines for #10 SASE.

Nonfiction: Book excerpts, expose, general interest, historical, how-to, interview/profile, opinion, personal experience, photo feature, travel ("in our area"), book reviews, politics, environment, energy, etc. "We are not likely to use a story that has no Illinois tie-in." Annual special issues: Lincoln (February); Health & Fitness (January); Gardening (April); Summer (June); Fall Home (September); and Christmas (books). No articles filled with "bureaucratese or generalities; no articles naively glorifying public figures or celebrity stories for celebrity's sake." Buys 50 mss/year. Query or send complete ms. Length: from 1,500 to 2,500 words maximum. Pays 4¢/word; $100 maximum.
Photos: State availability of photos. Pays $15 for 8x10 prints. Identification of subjects required. Buys one-time rights.
Columns/Departments: Guestwork (opinion column, any subject of personal experience with an Illinois angle). Buys 25 mss/year. Send complete ms. Length: 1,500 words maximum. Pays 4¢/word; $60 maximum.
Tips: "The ideal *IT* story is one the reader hates to put down. Good writing, in our view, is not necessarily fancy writing. It is (in the words of a colleague) 'whatever will engage the disinterested reader.' In other words, nothing dull, please. But remember that any subject—even the investment policies of public pension funds—can be made 'engaging.' It's just that some subjects require more work than others. Good illustrations are a plus. As an alternative newspaper we prefer to treat subjects in depth or not at all. Please, no general articles that lack an Illinois angle."

INSIDE CHICAGO, Signature Publishing, 2501 W. Peterson Ave., Chicago IL 60659. (312)784-0800. Editor: Barbara J. Young. 90% freelance written. Bimonthly magazine. Estab. 1987. Circ. 50,000. Pays within 30 days of publication. Byline given. Offers 20% kill fee. Buys first rights. Submit seasonal/holiday material 3 months in advance. Query for electronic submissions. Computer printout submissions OK; prefers letter-quality. Reports in 1 month. Sample copy $2.50; writer's guidelines for SASE.
Nonfiction: Business, general and special interest, humor, interview/profile, photo feature, travel, music, art, theatre, design, and political. "Send only material with an offbeat, local angle." Buys 60 mss/year. Query with or without published clips, or send complete ms. Length: 1,000-2,500 words. Pays $200 and up. Sometimes pays the expenses of writers on assignment.
Columns/Departments: Architecture, Snapshots, Album, Music, Art, Nightlife, Travel, Dining, Accent/Lifestyle, Zip Code, Books and Film. Length: approximately 600 words. Pays $100 and up.
Fillers: Needs short pieces for The Front and Power Play. Buys 30/year. Length: 100-300 words. Pays $25 (no byline).

NEAR WEST GAZETTE, Near West Gazette Publishing Co., 1335 W. Harrison St., Chicago IL 60607. (312)243-4288. Editor: Mark J. Valentino. Managing Editor: William S. Bike. 50% freelance written. Eager to work with new/unpublished writers. A monthly neighborhood newspaper covering Near West Side of Chicago. News and issues for residents, students and faculty of the neighborhood west of the University of Illinois of Chicago. Circ. 4,500. Pays on publication. Publishes ms an average of 1 month after acceptance. Byline given. Offers 15% kill fee. Not copyrighted. Buys one-time or simultaneous rights. Submit seasonal/holiday material 2 months in advance. Simultaneous, photocopied and previously published submissions OK. Computer printout submissions OK. Reports in 5 weeks. Sample copy for 11x14 SAE with 3 first class stamps.
Nonfiction: Essays, expose, general interest, historical/nostalgic, humor, inspirational, interview/profile, opinion, personal experience, religious or Near West Side's sports. Publishes a special Christmas issue. Doesn't want to see product promotions. Buys 60 mss/year. Length: 300-1,800 words. Pays $30. Sometimes pays the expenses of writers on assignment.
Photos: Send photos with submission. Reviews 5x7 prints. Offers no additional payment for photos accepted with ms. Identification of subjects required. Buys one-time rights.
Columns/Departments: To Your Health (health/exercise tips), 600 words; Forum (opinion), 750 words; Streets (Near West Side history), 500 words. Buys 12 mss/year. Query. Pays $30.

‡SUNDAY, The Chicago Tribune Magazine, Chicago Tribune Co.. 435 N. Michigan Ave., Chicago IL 60611. (312)222-3573. Editor: Mary Knoblauch. Managing Editor: Ruby Scott. 35% freelance written. A weekly Sunday magazine. "*SUNDAY* looks for unique, compelling, all researched, elequently written articles on subjects of general interest." Circ. 1 million. Pays on publication. Publishes ms an average of 2 months after acceptance. Offers 35-50% kill fee. Buys one-time rights. Submit seasonal/holiday material 6 months in advance. Query for electronic submissions. Computer printout submissions OK; prefers letter-quality. Reports in 1 month on queries; 6 weeks on manuscripts.
Nonfiction: Book excerpts, exposé, general interest, interview/profile, photo feature, technical and travel. No humor, first person or casual essays. Buys 35 mss/year. Query or send complete ms. Length: 3,000-8,000 words. Pays $1,000. Sometimes pays expenses of writers on assignment.
Photos: State availability of photos with submission. Offer varies per photo. Captions and identification of subjects required. Buys one-time rights.
Columns/Departments: First Person (Chicago area subjects only, talking about their occupations), 1,000 words. Buys 52 mss/year. Query. Pays $250.

Indiana

INDIANAPOLIS MONTHLY, Mayhill Publications, Suite 225, 8425 Keystone Crossing, Indianapolis IN 46260. (317)259-8222. Editor: Deborah Paul. Associate Editor: Sam Stall. 50% freelance written. Prefers to work with published/established writers. A monthly magazine of "upbeat material reflecting current trends. Heavy on lifestyle, homes and fashion. Material must be regional in appeal." Circ. 45,000. Pays on publication. Publishes ms an average of 2 months after acceptance. Byline given. Offers 50% kill fee. Buys first North American serial rights and makes work-for-hire assignments. Submit seasonal/holiday material 3 months in advance. Computer printout submissions acceptable; prefers letter-quality. Reports in 1 month. Sample copy for 9x12 SAE and $3.05; free writer's guidelines.

Nonfiction: General interest, historical/nostalgic, interview/profile and photo feature. Special issue is the 500 Mile Race issue (May). No poetry, domestic humor or stories without a regional angle. "We prefer stories with a timely or topical angle or 'hook' as opposed to topics plucked out of thin air." Buys 25 mss/year. Query with published clips or send complete ms. Length: 200-5,000 words. Pays $35-400. Sometimes pays the expenses of writers on assignment.

Photos: Send photos with submission. Reviews 35mm or 2¼ transparencies. Offers $25 minimum/photo. Identification of subjects required. Buys one-time rights.

Columns/Departments: Business (local made-goods), Sport (heroes, trendy sports), Health (new specialties, technology), and Retrospect (regional history), all 1,000 words. Buys 6-9 mss/year. Query with published clips or send complete mss. Pays $100-300.

Tips: "Monthly departments are open to freelancers. We also run monthly special sections—write for editorial special section lineups."

RIGHT HERE, The Hometown Magazine, Right Here Publications, Box 1014, Huntington IN 46750. Editor: Emily Jean Carroll. 90% freelance written. Works with a small number of new/unpublished writers each year. Bimonthly magazine of general family interest reaching a northern Indiana audience. Circ. 2,000. Pays 2 weeks after date of issue. Publishes ms an average of 4 months after acceptance. Byline given. Buys first serial rights, one-time rights, simultaneous rights, and second serial (reprint) rights. Submit seasonal/holiday material 5 months in advance. Simultaneous, photocopied, and previously published submissions OK. Computer printout submissions acceptable; prefers letter-quality. Reports in 2 months on mss. No queries please. Sample copy $1.25; writer's guidelines for SASE.

Nonfiction: General interest, historical/nostalgic, how-to, humor, inspirational, interview/profile, opinion, and travel. "We are looking for short pieces on all aspects of family life—40-plus age range." Profiles, nostalgia, history, recreation, travel, music and various subjects of interest to area readers. Buys 18 mss/year. Send complete ms. Length: 900-2,000 words. Pays $5-30.

Photos: Send photos with ms. Reviews b&w prints. Pays $2-5. Model releases and identification of subjects required. Buys one-time rights.

Columns/Departments: Listen To This (opinion pieces of about 1,000 words); Here and There (travel pieces in or near Indiana); Remember? (nostalgia, up to 2,000 words); Keeping Up (mental, spiritual, self-help, up-lifting, etc., to 2,000 words); and My Space (writers 19 years old and under, to 1,000 words). Buys 30-40 mss/year. Send complete ms. Length: 800-2,000 words. Pays $5-30.

Fiction: Humorous, mainstream, mystery and romance. Needs short stories of about 2,000 words. Buys 6-8 mss/year. Send complete ms. Length: 900-3,000 words. Pays $5-30.

Poetry: Free verse, light verse and traditional. Uses 30-40/year. Submit maximum 6 poems. Length: 4-48 lines. Pays $1-4 for poetry featured separately; pays one copy for poetry used as filler or on poetry page.

Fillers: Anecdotes and short humor. Buys 6-8/year. Length: 300 words maximum. Pays $3 maximum. Pays one copy for material under 300 words.

Tips: "All departments are open. Keep it light—keep it tight. Send short cover letter about yourself."

Kansas

‡KANSAS!, Kansas Department of Economic Development, 400 W. 8th, 5th Floor, Topeka KS 66603. (913)296-3479. Editor: Andrea Glenn. 90% freelance written. Quarterly magazine; 40 pages. Emphasizes Kansas "faces and places for all ages, occupations and interests." Circ. 48,000. Pays on acceptance. Publishes ms an average of 1 year after acceptance. Byline given. Buys one-time rights. Submit seasonal/holiday material 8 months in advance. Computer printout submissions acceptable; no dot-matrix. Reports in 2 months. Free sample copy and writer's guidelines.

Nonfiction: "Material must be Kansas-oriented and have good potential for color photographs. We feature stories about Kansas people, places and events that can be enjoyed by the general public. In other words, events must be open to the public, places also. People featured must have interesting crafts, etc." General interest, interview, photo feature, profile and travel. Query. "Query letter should clearly outline story in mind. I'm especially interested in Kansas freelancers who can supply their own photos." Length: 3-5 pages double-spaced, typewritten copy. Pays $75-175. Sometimes pays expenses of writers on assignment.

Photos: "We are a full-color photo/manuscript publication." State availability of photos with query. Pays $25-50 (generally included in ms rate) for 35mm color transparencies. Captions required.

Tips: "History and nostalgia stories do not fit into our format because they can't be illustrated well with color photography."

Kentucky

KENTUCKY HAPPY HUNTING GROUND, Kentucky Dept. of Fish and Wildlife Resources, 1 Game Farm Rd., Frankfort KY 40601. (502)564-4336. Editor: John Wilson. Less than 10% freelance written. Works with a small number of new/unpublished writers each year. A bimonthly state conservation magazine covering hunting, fishing, general outdoor recreation, conservation of wildlife and other natural resources. Circ. 35,000. Pays on publication. Publishes ms an average of 6 months after acceptance. Byline given. Buys one-time rights. Submit seasonal/holiday material 3 months in advance. Previously published submissions OK. Computer printout submissions acceptable. Reports in 3 weeks on queries; 2 months on mss. Sample copy for 8½x11 SAE.

Nonfiction: General interest, historical/nostalgic, how-to, humor, interview/profile, personal experience and photo feature. All articles should deal with some aspect of the natural world, with outdoor recreation or with natural resources conservation or management, and should relate to Kentucky. "No 'Me and Joe' stories (i.e., accounts of specific trips); nothing off-color or otherwise unsuitable for a state publication." Buys 3-6 mss/year. Query or send complete ms. Length: 500-2,000 words. Pays $75-250 (with photos).

Photos: State availability of photos with query; send photos with accompanying ms. Reviews color transparencies (2¼ preferred, 35mm acceptable) and b&w prints (5x7 minimum). No separate payment for photos, but amount paid for article will be determined by number of photos used.

Tips: "We would be much more kindly disposed toward articles accompanied by several good photographs (or other graphic material) than to those without."

RURAL KENTUCKIAN, Box 32170, Louisville KY 40232. (502)451-2430. Editor: Gary W. Luhr. Mostly freelance written. Prefers to work with published/established writers. Monthly feature magazine primarily for Kentucky residents. Circ. 300,000. Pays on acceptance. Publishes ms on average 2-8 months after acceptance. Byline given. Not copyrighted. Buys first serial rights for Kentucky. Submit seasonal/holiday material at least 6 months in advance. Will consider photocopied, previously published and simultaneous submissions (if previously published and/or simultaneous submissions outside Kentucky). Computer printout submissions acceptable; prefers letter-quality. Reports in 2 weeks. Sample copy for 8½x11 SAE and 4 first class stamps.

Nonfiction: Prefers Kentucky-related profiles (people, places or events), history, biography, recreation, travel, leisure or lifestyle articles or book excerpts; articles on contemporary subjects of general public interest and general consumer-related features including service pieces. Publishes some humorous and first-person articles of exceptional quality and opinion pieces from qualified authorities. No general nostalgia. Buys 24-36 mss/year. Query or send complete ms. Length: 800-2000 words. Pays $50-$250. Sometimes pays the expenses of writers on assignment.

Photos: State availability of photos. Reviews color slide transparencies and b&w prints. Identification of subjects required. Payment for photos included in payment for ms. Pays extra if photo used on cover.

Tips: "The quality of writing and reporting (factual, objective, thorough) is considered in setting payment price. We prefer well-documented pieces filled with quotes and anecdotes. Avoid boosterism. Writers need not confine themselves to subjects suited only to a rural audience but should avoid subjects of a strictly metropolitian nature. Well-researched, well-written feature articles, particularly on subjects of a serious nature, are given preference over light-weight material. Despite its name, *Rural Kentuckian* is not a farm publication."

Louisiana

SUNDAY ADVOCATE MAGAZINE, Box 588, Baton Rouge LA 70821. (504)383-1111, ext. 319. Editor: Larry Catalanello. 5% freelance written. We are backlogged, but still welcome submissions. Byline given. Pays on publication. Publishes ms up to 1 year after acceptance. Query for electronic submissions. Computer printout submissions acceptable.

Nonfiction and Photos: Well-illustrated, short articles; must have local, area or Louisiana angle, in that order of preference. Also interested in travel pieces. Photos purchased with mss. Rates vary.

Tips: Styles may vary. Subject matter may vary. Local interest is most important. No more than 4-5 typed, double-spaced pages.

Maine

GREATER PORTLAND MAGAZINE, Chamber of Commerce of the Greater Portland Region, 142 Free St., Portland ME 04101. (207)772-2811. Editor: Shirley Jacks. 75% freelance written. Works with a small number of new/unpublished writers each year. "We enjoy offering talented and enthusiastic new writers the kind of editorial guidance they need to become professional freelancers." A quarterly magazine covering metropolitan and island lifestyles of Greater Portland. "We cover the arts, night life, islands, people, and progressive business in and around Greater Portland." Circ. 10,000. Pays on publication. Publishes ms an average of 2 months after acceptance. Byline given. Buys first serial rights or second serial reprint rights. Submit seasonal/holiday material 6 months in advance. Query for electronic submissions. Computer printout submissions acceptable; prefers letter-quality. Reports in 1 week on queries; 2 weeks on mss. Free sample copy with $1 postage.

Nonfiction: Articles about people, places, events, institutions and the arts in greater Portland. "*Greater Portland* is largely freelance written. We are looking for well-researched, well-focused essayistic features. First person essays are welcome." Buys 20 mss/year. Query with published clips or send complete ms. Length: 1,500-3,500 words. Pays 10¢/word maximum. Sometimes pays expenses of writers on assignment.

Photos: Buys b&w and color slides with or without ms. Captions required.

Tips: "Send some clips with several story ideas. We're looking for informal, essayistic features structured around a well-defined point or theme. A lively, carefully-crafted presentation is as important as a good subject. We enjoy working closely with talented writers of varying experience to produce a literate (as opposed to slick or newsy) magazine."

LINKING THE DOTS, Islesboro Publishing, HCR 222, Islesboro ME 04848. (207)734-6745. Publisher/Editor: Agatha Cabaniss. 80% freelance written. Bimonthly magazine on Penobscot Bay islands and people. Pays on acceptance. Byline given. Buys first rights and second serial (reprint) rights. Computer printout submissions OK. Sample copy $2; writer's guidelines for #10 SAE with 3 first class stamps.

Nonfiction: Articles about contemporary issues on the islands, historical pieces, personality profiles, arts, lifestyles and businesses on the islands. Any story must have a definite Maine island connection. No travel pieces. Query or send complete ms. Pays $20-50.

Photos: State availability of photos with submission.

Tips: "Writers must know the Penobscot Bay Islands. We are not interested in pieces of generic island nature unless it relates to development problems, or the viability of the islands as year round communities. We do not want 'vacation on a romantic island,' but we are interested in island historical pieces."

‡MAINE MOTORIST, Maine Automobile Assn., Box 3544, Portland ME 04104. (207)774-6377. Editor: Ellen Kornetsky. 25% freelance written. Bimonthly tabloid on travel, car care, AAA news. "Our readers enjoy learning about travel opportunities in the New England region and elsewhere. In addition, they enjoy topics of interest to automobile owners." Circ. 100,000. Pays on publication. Publishes ms an average of 3 months after acceptance. Byline given. Not copyrighted. Buys simultaneous rights; makes work-for-hire assignments. Submit seasonal/holiday material 3 months in advance. Simultaneous and photocopied submissions OK. Computer printout submissions acceptable; prefers letter-quality. Free sample copy and writer's guidelines.

Nonfiction: Historical/nostalgic (travel); how-to (car care, travel); humor (travel); and travel (New England, U.S. and foreign). No exotic travel destinations that cost a great deal. Send complete ms. Length: 500-1,250 words. Pays $50-150.

Photos: State availability of photos. Reviews 5x7 color and b&w transparencies. Pays $10-25 for b&w; $25-100 for color. Captions required. Buys one-time rights.

Tips: "Travel (particularly New England regional) material is most needed. Interesting travel options are appreciated. Humorous flair sometimes helps."

Maryland

CHESAPEAKE BAY MAGAZINE, Suite 200, 1819 Bay Ridge Ave., Annapolis MD 21403. (301)263-2662. Editor: Betty D. Rigoli. 40% freelance written. Works with a small number of new/unpublished writers each year. "*Chesapeake Bay Magazine* is a monthly regional publication for those who enjoy reading about the Chesapeake and its tributaries. Our readers are yachtsmen, boating families, fishermen, ecologists—anyone who is part of Chesapeake Bay life." Circ. 30,000. Pays either on acceptance or publication, depending on "type of article, timeliness and need." Publishes ms an average of 14 months after acceptance. Buys first North American serial rights and all rights. Submit seasonal/holiday material 4 months in advance. Simultaneous (if not to magazines with overlapping circulations) and photocopied submissions OK. Computer printout submissions acceptable; no dot-matrix. Reports in 1 month. Sample copy $2; writer's guidelines for SASE.

Nonfiction: "All material must be about the Chesapeake Bay area—land or water." How-to (fishing and sports pertinent to Chesapeake Bay); general interest; humor (welcomed, but don't send any "dumb boater" stories where common safety is ignored); historical; interviews (with interesting people who have contributed in some way to Chesapeake Bay life: authors, historians, sailors, oystermen, etc.); and nostalgia (accurate, informative and well-paced—no maudlin ramblings about "the good old days"); personal experience (drawn from experiences in boating situations, adventures, events in our geographical area); photo feature (with accompanying ms); profile (on natives of Chesapeake Bay); technical (relating to boating, fishing); and Chesapeake Bay folklore. "We do not want material written by those unfamiliar with the Bay area, or general sea stories. No personal opinions on environmental issues or new column (monthly) material and no rehashing of familiar ports-of-call (e.g., Oxford, St. Michaels)." Buys 25-40 unsolicited mss/year. Query or submit complete ms. Length: 1,000-2,500 words. Pays $85-100. Sometimes pays the expenses of writers on assignment.
Photos: Virginia Leonard, art director. Submit photo material with ms. Reviews 8x10 b&w glossy prints and color transparencies. Pays $100 for 35mm, 2¼x2¼ or 4x5 color transparencies used for cover photos; $50, $30 or $15 for color photo used inside. Captions and model releases required. Buys one-time rights with reprint permission.
Fiction: "All fiction must deal with the Chesapeake Bay and be written by persons familiar with some facet of bay life." Adventure, fantasy, historical, humorous, mystery and suspense. "No general stories with Chesapeake Bay superimposed in an attempt to make a sale." Buys 3-4 mss/year. Query or submit complete ms. Length: 1,000-2,500 words. Pays $85-100.
Tips: "We are a regional publication entirely about the Chesapeake Bay and its tributaries. Our readers are true 'Bay' lovers, and look for stories written by others who obviously share this love. We are particularly interested in material from the Lower Bay (Virginia) area and the Upper Bay (Maryland/Delaware) area. We are looking for personal experience Chesapeake boating articles/stories, especially from power boaters."

CITY PAPER, City Paper Inc., 2612 N. Charles St., Baltimore MD 21218. (301)889-6600. Editor: Phyllis Orrick. 20% freelance written. A weekly tabloid of general interest for the Baltimore metropolitan area. Circ. 85,000. Pays 1 month after publication. Byline given. Buys first rights. Submit seasonal/holiday material 2 months in advance. Sample copy $1 with 9x12 SAE and 6 first class stamps.
Nonfiction: Book excerpts, essays, historical/nostalgic, humor, interview/profile and personal experience. Query with or without published clips, or send complete ms. Length: up to 5,000 words. Pays $50-400. Sometimes pays the expenses of writers on assignment.
Photos: State availability of photos with submission.
Fiction: Confession, ethnic, experimental, historical, humorous, mainstream, slice-of-life vignettes and suspense. Buys 5-10 mss/year. Send complete ms. Length: up to 5,000 words. Pays $50-200. Address to Fiction Editor.

MARYLAND MAGAZINE, Department of Economic and Employment Development, 45 Calvert St., Annapolis MD 21401. (301)974-3507. Publisher/Editorial Director: D. Patrick Hornberger. Editor: Bonnie Joe Ayers. 95% freelance written. Prefers to work with published/established writers. Quarterly magazine promoting the state of Maryland. Circ. 45,000. Pays on acceptance. Publishes ms 8-12 months after acceptance. Byline given. Offers 25% kill fee. Buys all rights. Submit seasonal/holiday material 1 year in advance. Photocopied submissions OK. Computer printout submissions acceptable; no dot-matrix. Reports in 2 months. Sample copy $2.25; writer's guidelines for #10 SASE.
Nonfiction: General interest, historical/nostalgic, humor, interview/profile, photo feature and travel. Articles on any facet of Maryland life. No poetry, fiction or controversial material or any topic *not* dealing with the state of Maryland; no trendy topics, or one that has received much publicity elsewhere. Buys 32 mss/year. Query with published clips or send complete ms. Length: 900-2,200 words. Pays $175-400. Pays expenses of writers on assignment.

Massachusetts

BOSTON GLOBE MAGAZINE, *Boston Globe*, Boston MA 02107. Editor-in-Chief: Ms. Ande Zellman. 50% freelance written. Weekly magazine; 64 pages. Circ. 805,099. Pays on acceptance. Publishes ms an average of 2 months after acceptance. No reprints of any kind. Buys first serial rights. Submit seasonal/holiday material 3 months in advance. Computer printout submissions acceptable; no dot-matrix. SASE must be included with ms or queries for return. Reports in 1 month.
Nonfiction: Expose (variety of issues including political, economic, scientific, medical and the arts); interview (not Q&A); profile; and book excerpts (first serial rights only). Buys 65 mss/year. Query. Length: 3,000-5,000 words. Payment negotiable from $1,000.
Photos: Purchased with accompanying ms or on assignment. Reviews contact sheets. Pays standard rates according to size used. Captions required.

BOSTON MAGAZINE, 300 Massachusetts Ave., Boston MA 02115. (617)262-9700. Editor: David Rosenbaum. Managing Editor: Betsy Buffington. 30% freelance written. Monthly magazine. "Looks for strong reporting of locally based stories with national interest." Circ. 129,248. Pays on publication. Publishes ms an average of 2 months after acceptance. Byline given. Offers 20% kill fee. Buys first North American serial rights. Submit seasonal/holiday material 3 months in advance. Query for electronic submissions. Reports in 1 month. Sample copy for 9x12 SAE with $2.40 postage.
Nonfiction: General interest, humor, personal experience and photo feature. No fiction or poetry. Buys 75 mss/year. Query with published clips or send complete ms. Length: 1,500-5,000 words. Pays $250-1,500. Sometimes pays the expenses of writers on assignment.
Photos: State availability of photos with submission. Reviews transparencies and prints. Offers no additional payment for photos accepted with ms. Captions, model releases and identification of subjects required. Buys one-time rights.
Columns/Departments: Profile (portraits of Bostonians), Local Color (odd facts about Boston); Good Spirits (stories about alcohol—wines, beers, drinks, etc.); First Person (experiences of general interest); Sports (Boston short stories). Buys 50 mss/year. Send complete ms. Length: 1,500-2,500 words. Pays $300-600.
Tips: "Query should contain an outline of proposed story structure, including sources and source material. Stories should seek to be controversial. Area most open to freelancers is investigative journalism. Stories concerning newsworthy scandals that are unreported. Look for something everyone believes to be true—then question it."

CAPE COD COMPASS, Quarterdeck Communications, Inc., 935 Main St., Box 375, Chatham MA 02633. (617)945-3542. Editor: Andrew Scherding. Managing Editor: Donald Davidson. 80% freelance written. A quarterly magazine about Cape Cod, Martha's Vineyard and Nantucket (Mass.) region. Circ. 25,000. Pays on acceptance. Publishes ms an average of 6 months after acceptance. Byline given. Offers variable kill fee. Buys first North American serial rights or one-time rights. Photocopied submissions OK. Computer printout submissions acceptable. Reports in 1 month. Sample copy $4; writer's guidelines for 9x12 SAE.
Nonfiction: Essays, general interest, historical/nostalgic, interview/profile and photo feature. "Articles must have a theme connected with this region of New England. We rarely publish first-person articles." Buys 40 mss/year. Query with published clips, or send complete ms. Length: 1,500-7,000 words. Pays $400-800 for assigned articles; pays $250-500 for unsolicited articles. Sometimes pays the expenses of writers on assignment.
Photos: Send photos with submission, if any. Reviews transparencies. Offers $60/photo. Model releases and identification of subjects required. Buys one-time rights.
Fiction: Condensed novels, historical, humorous, mainstream, novel excerpts, and slice-of-life vignettes. "No fiction that is not connected with this region." Buys 4 mss/year. Query with published clips or send complete ms. Length: 1,500-3,000 words. Pays $200-350.
Poetry: Buys 4-6 poems/year. Submit maximum 4 poems. Length: open. Pays $35-60.
Tips: "We are quite willing to correspond at length with potential contributors about ideas and potential manuscripts. We are now accepting more topical submissions about the Cape and islands (current events, trends, upcoming issues). Telephone calls initiated by the contributor are discouraged. Our magazine is largely nonfiction. We would suggest that the writer become thoroughly knowledgeable about a subject before he or she writes about it with the intention of submitting it to our magazine."

COAST & COUNTRY MAGAZINE, Hastings Group, 45 Forest Ave., Swampscott MA 01907. (617)592-0160. Editor: Robert Hastings. Associate Editor: Beverly J. Wood. 80% freelance written. Prefers to work with published/established writers. A bimonthly magazine covering topics of interest to readers residing on the North Shore of Boston. "*Coast & Country* is a controlled circulation magazine distributed to households with an income over $50,000. All of our articles have a local flavor. We publish articles on money, fashion, sports, medicine, culture, business and humor." Circ. 75,000. Pays on acceptance. Publishes ms an average of 4-6 months after acceptance. Byline given. Buys first rights. Submit seasonal/holiday material 6 months in advance. Photocopied submissions OK. Computer printout submissions acceptable. Reports in 1 month on queries; 3 weeks on mss. Sample copy $2.50; free writer's guidelines.
Nonfiction: Essays, how-to, humor, interview/profile, opinion, personal experience, money, fashion, business, sports, culture and the ocean. Special issues include holidays (December/January) and home guide (April/May). Buys 40 mss/year. Query with published clips. Length: 1,000-2,500 words. Pays $100-400. Pays some expenses of writers on assignment.
Photos: State availability of photos with submission. Reviews contact sheets and negatives. Offers $50-200/photo. Model releases and identification of subjects required. Buys one-time rights.

For information on setting your freelance fees, see How Much Should I Charge? in the Business of Writing section.

SUNDAY MORNING magazine, *Worcester Sunday Telegram*, 20 Franklin St., Worcester MA 01613. (617)793-9364. Sunday Morning Editor: Anne Murray. 25-50% freelance written. Eager to work with new/unpublished writers. Sunday supplement serving a broad cross-section of Central Massachusetts residents; 16 pages. Circ. 128,000. Pays on publication. Publishes ms an average of 3 months after acceptance. Buys first North American serial rights. Byline given. Phone queries OK. Submit seasonal/holiday material 2 months in advance. Computer printout submissions OK. Free sample copy.

Nonfiction: Profiles; interviews; beind-the-scenes, informational, first-person, and how-to articles; photo features with a strong New England angle; humor; personal experience (something unusual); and travel with a strong New England angle. Buys 2 mss/issue. Query. Pays $40-150.

Photos: Photos purchased with accompanying ms or on assignment. Captions required. Pays $10 for b&w glossy prints, color slides or prints.

Columns/Departments: Open to suggestions for new columns and departments.

Tips: "We place strong emphasis on people stories and on New England."

WHAT'S NEW MAGAZINE, The Good Times Magazine, Multicom 7 Inc., 11 Allen Rd., Boston MA 02135. (617)787-3636. Editor: Bob Leja. 80% freelance written. A monthly magazine covering music, entertainment, sports and lifestyles for the "baby-boom" generation. Circ. 125,000. Pays on publication. Publishes ms an average of 2 months after acceptance. Byline given. Offers 25% kill fee. Buys one-time rights. Submit seasonal/holiday material 4 months in advance. Photocopied submissions OK. Electronic submissions OK; call system operator. Computer printout submissions acceptable; prefers letter-quality. Reports in 2 months. Sample copy $3 with 9x11 SAE and $1.40 posage.

Nonfiction: Book excerpts, general interest, humor, new product, photo feature and travel. Special issues include motorcycle buyer's guide, consumer elect buyer's guide, and automotive buyer's guide. Buys 120 mss/year. Query with published clips. Length: 150-3,000 words. Pays $25-250 for assigned articles. Sometimes pays the expenses of writers on assignment.

Photos: State availability of photos with submission. Reviews contact sheets. Offers $15 for first photo, $5 for each additional photo published in 1 issue. Captions, model releases and identification of subjects required. Buys one-time rights.

Columns/Departments: Great Escapes (undiscovered or under-explored vacation possibilities); Food Department (new and unusual developments in food and drink); and Fads, Follies and Trends (weird things that everyone is doing—from buying breakdancing accessories to brushing with pump toothpaste). Buys 150 mss/year. Query with published clips. Length: 150-3,000 words. Pays $25-250.

Tips: "*What's New* will remain a unique magazine by continuing to combine informative coverage of established, mainstream artists with reports on the newest bands, movies, fads or trends and by writing about them in the same snappy, witty and irreverent style that has singled it out in the past. The magazine will remain creative enough to find the angle that others fail to see. This calls for some extraordinary talent, and the magazine is fortunate to have such a resource in its national network of freelance writers."

WORCESTER MAGAZINE, Box 1000, Worcester MA 01614. (617)799-0511. Editor: Jay Whearley. 10% freelance written. Weekly tabloid, 48 pages emphasizing the central Massachusetts region. Circ. 50,000. Pays on acceptance. Publishes ms an average of 3 weeks after acceptance. Byline given. Buys all rights. Submit seasonal/holiday material 2 months in advance. Simultaneous and photocopied submissions OK. Computer printout submissions acceptable. Reports in 2 weeks. Sample copy $1; free writer's guidelines.

Nonfiction: Expose (area government, corporate); how-to (concerning the area, homes, vacations); interview (local); personal experience; opinion (local); and photo feature. No nonlocal stories. "We leave national and general topics to national and general publications." Buys 30 mss/year. Query with published clips. Length: 1,000-3,500 words. Pays $50-300.

Photos: State availability of photos with query. Pays $25-75 for b&w photos. Captions preferred; model release required. Buys all rights.

Michigan

‡ABOVE THE BRIDGE MAGAZINE, Star Rt. 550, Box 189-C, Marquette MI 49855. Editor: Jacqueline J. Miller. Associate Editor: Judith A. Hendrickson. 100% freelance written. A bimonthly magazine on the upper peninsula of Michigan. "Most material, including fiction, has an upper peninsula of Michigan slant. Our readership is past and present upper peninsula residents." Circ. 1,000. Pays on publication. Publishes ms an average of 4 months after acceptance. Byline given. Offer 50% kill fee. Buys one-time rights. Submit seasonal/holiday material 4 months in advance. Previously published submissions. Query for electronic submissions. Computer printout submissions OK; prefers letter-quality. Reports in 6 weeks. Sample copy for $2.50. Writer's guidelines for #10 SAE with 1 first class stamp.

Nonfiction: Book excerpts (books on upper peninsula or UP writer), essays, historical/nostalgic (UP), interview/profile (UP personality or business) personal experience, photo feature (UP) and travel (UP). "This is a family magazine, therefore no material in poor taste." Buys 60 mss/year. Send complete ms. Length: 1,000-2,500 words. Pays 2¢/word.

Photos: Send photos with submission. Reviews prints (5x7 or larger). Offers $5 ($15-20 if used for cover) per photo. Captions, model releases and identification of subjects required. Buys one-time rights.

Fiction: Ethnic x (UP heritage), humorous, mainstream and mystery. No horror or erotica. "Material set in UP has preference for publication. Accepts children's fiction." Buys 20 mss/year. Send complete ms. Length: 2,500 words (1,000 max for children's). Pays 2¢/word.

Poetry: Free verse, haiku, light verse and traditional. No erotica. Buys 30 poems/year. Shorter poetry preferred. Pays $5.

Fillers: Anecdotes and short humor. Buys 25/year. Length: 100-500 words. Pays $5 or 2¢/word maximum.

Tips: "Much material is by out-of-state writers with content not tied to upper peninsula of Michigan. Know the area and people, read the magazine. Most material received is too long. Stick to our guidelines. We love to publish well written material by previously unpublished writers."

ANN ARBOR OBSERVER, Ann Arbor Observer Company, 206 S. Main, Ann Arbor MI 48104. Editor: John Hilton. 25% freelance written. Works with a small number of new/unpublished writers each year. Monthly magazine featuring stories about people and events in Ann Arbor. Circ. 50,000. Pays on publication. Publishes ms an average of 2 months after acceptance. Byline given. Buys one-time rights. Query for electronic submissions. Computer printout submissions acceptable. Reports in 3 weeks on queries; 1 month on mss. Sample copy for 12½x15 SAE and $2.40 postage; free writer's guidelines.

Nonfiction: Historical, investigative features, profiles and brief vignettes. Must pertain to Ann Arbor. Buys 75 mss/year. Length: 100-7,000 words. Pays up to $1,000/article. Sometimes pays expenses of writers on assignment.

Tips: "If you have an idea for a story, write up a 100-200-word description telling us why the story is interesting. We are most open to intelligent, insightful features of up to 5,000 words about interesting aspects of life in Ann Arbor."

‡ANN ARBOR SCENE MAGAZINE, Proctor Associates, Inc., Suite 6, 2004 Hogback Rd., Ann Arbor MI 48105. (313)973-0554. Editor: William D. McLean. 90% freelance written. A monthly magazine with stories "that have some connection, however tenuous, with Ann Arbor. This is a cosmopolitan university community whose members have interests all over the world." Circ. 10,000. Pays on publication. Publishes ms an average of 2 months after acceptance. Byline given. Buys first North American serial rights or second serial (reprint) rights. Submit seasonal/holiday material 4 months in advance. Photocopied and previously published submissions—if clearly identified as such. Computer printout submissions OK; prefers letter-quality. Reports in 1 month. Sample copy $2. Free writer's guidelines. Writer's guidelines for #10 SAE with 1 first class stamp.

Nonfiction: Essays, general interest, historical/nostalgic, interview/profile, opinion, personal experience, photo feature and travel. Buys 135 mss/year. Query. Length: 850-2,000 words. Pays $100. Send photos with submission. Reviews contact sheets, transparencies (35mm or larger) and prints (5x7). Offers $10. Captions required. Buys one-time rights.

Fiction: Mainstream and slice-of-life vignettes. No erotica, fantasy, science fiction, romance or experimental work. Send complete ms. Length: 850-2,000 words. Pays $100.

Poetry: Free verse and traditional. No inspirational, religious, erotica, political or limericks. Buys 6 poems/year. Submit maximum 3 poems. Length: 10-50 lines. Pays $10.

Tips: "We're always in the market for general interest articles, profiles, and historical pieces with an Ann Arbor connection. We like tightly written, well-researched pieces that inform, entertain and satisfy our generally upscale, highly educated readers."

GRAND RAPIDS MAGAZINE, Suite 1040, Trust Bldg., 40 Pearl St., NW, Grand Rapids MI 49503. (616)459-4545. Publisher: John H. Zwarensteyn. Editor: Ronald E. Koehler. Managing Editor: Carole Valade Smith. 45% freelance written. Eager to work with new/unpublished writers. Monthly general feature magazine serving western Michigan. Circ. 13,500. Pays on 15th of month of publication. Publishes ms an average of 4 months after acceptance. Buys first serial rights. Phone queries OK. Submit seasonal material 3 months in advance. Photocopied and previously published submissions OK. Query for electronic submissions. Computer printout submissions acceptable; prefers letter-quality. Reports in 2 months.

Nonfiction: Western Michigan writers preferred. Western Michigan subjects only: government, labor, education, general interest, historical, interview/profile and nostalgia. Inspirational and personal experience pieces discouraged. No breezy, self-centered "human" pieces or "pieces not only light on style but light on hard information." Humor appreciated but must be specific to region. Buys 5-8 unsolicited mss/year. "If you live here, see the managing editor before you write. If you don't, send a query letter with published clips, or phone." Length: 500-4,000 words. Pays $25-200. Sometimes pays the expenses of writers on assignment.

Photos: State availability of photos. Pays $25 + /5x7 glossy print and $35 + /35 or 120mm color transparency. Captions and model releases required.

Tips: "Television has forced city/regional magazines to be less provincial and more broad-based in their approach. People's interests seem to be evening out from region to region. The subject matters should remain largely local, but national trends must be recognized in style and content. And we must *entertain* as well as inform."

THE MICHIGAN WOMAN, 8888 Thorne Rd., Horton MI 49246. (517)563-2500. Editor: Monica Smiley. 40% freelance written. Bimonthly magazine covering "issues of interest to influential women in Michigan." Circ. 25,000. Pays on publication. Byline given. Writer's guidelines for 9x12 SASE.
Nonfiction: Book reviews, essays, expose, general interest, historical/nostalgic, how-to, humor, inspirational, interview/profile, new product, opinion, personal experience, photo feature, technical and travel. Query with published clips. Length: 200-2,000 words. Pays 10¢/word.
Photos: Send photos with submission. Identification of subjects required.
Columns/Departments: Finance, Health, Legal (issues in Michigan affecting women), Cuisine, Book Reviews. Query with published clips. Length: 700 words. Pays 10¢/word.
Fiction: Condensed novels, ethnic, experimental, fantasy, historical, horror, humorous, mainstream, mystery, novel excerpts, romance, science fiction, serialized novels, slice-of-life vignettes, suspense and western. Literary journal published 4 times/year. Query with complete ms. Length: 500-1,000 words.
Fillers: Facts and newsbreak. Length: 200-400 words. Pays 10¢/word.

Minnesota

LAKE SUPERIOR MAGAZINE, Lake Superior Port Cities, Inc., #100, 325 Lake Ave. S., Duluth MN 55802. (218)722-5002. Editor: Paul L. Hayden. 60% freelance written. Works with a small number of new/unpublished writers each year. A bimonthly regional magazine covering contemporary and historic people, places and current events around Lake Superior. Circ. 16,000 (subscribers in all states and 56 foreign countries). Pays on publication. Publishes ms an average of 8-10 months after acceptance. Byline given. Offers $25 kill fee. Buys first North American serial rights and some second rights. Submit seasonal/holiday material 8-12 months in advance. Photocopied submissions OK. Query for electronic submissions. Computer printout submissions acceptable; prefers letter-quality. Reports in 3 months on manuscripts. Sample copy $3.50 and 5 first class stamps; writer's guidelines for SASE.
Nonfiction: Book excerpts, general interest, historic/nostalgic, humor, interview/profile (local), personal experience, photo feature (local), travel (local), city profiles, regional business. Buys 45 mss/year. Query with published clips. Length 300-3,500 words. Pays $80-400 maximum. Sometimes pays the expenses of writers if on assignment.
Photos: Quality photography is our hallmark. State availability of photos with submission. Reviews contact sheets, 2x2 transparencies and 4x5 prints. Offers $20 for b&w and $30 for color transparencies. Captions, model releases, and identification of subjects required.
Columns/Departments: Current events and things to do (for Events Calendar section) short, under 300 words; Shore Lines (letters and short pieces on events and highlights of the Lake Superior Region), up to 150 words; Lifelines (single personality profile with b&w), up to 350 words; and Book Reviews (regional targeted or published books), up to 450 words. Direct book reviews to book review editor. Buys 20 mss/year. Query with published clips. Pays $10-45.
Fiction: Ethnic, historic, humorous, mainstream, slice-of-life vignettes and ghost stories. Must be regionally targeted in nature. Buys 2-3 mss/year. Query with published clips. Length: 300-2,500 words. Pays $1-300.
Tips: "Well-researched queries are attended to. We actively seek queries from writers in Lake Superior communities. We prefer manuscripts to queries. Provide enough information on why the subject is important to the region and our readers, or why and how something is unique. We want details. The writer must have a thorough knowledge of the subject and how it relates to our region. We prefer a fresh, unused approach to the subject which provides the reader with an emotional involvement. Almost all of our articles feature quality photography, color or black and white. It is a prerequisite of all nonfiction. All submissions should include a *short* biography of author/photographer."

MPLS. ST. PAUL MAGAZINE, Suite 1030, 12 S. 6th St., Minneapolis MN 55402. (612)339-7571. Editor: Brian Anderson. Executive Editor: Sylvia Paine. Managing Editor: Claude Peck. 90% freelance written. Monthly general interest magazine covering the metropolitan area of Minneapolis/St. Paul and aimed at college-educated professionals who enjoy living in the area and taking advantage of the cultural, entertainment and dining out opportunities. Circ. 50,000. Pays on acceptance. Publishes ms an average of 3 months after acceptance. Byline given. Offers 25% kill fee. Buys first North American serial rights. Submit seasonal/holiday material 5 months in advance. Query for electronic submissions. Computer printout submissions acceptable; prefers letter-quality. Reports in 1 month. Sample copy $3.50; free writer's guidelines.
Nonfiction: Book excerpts; general interest; historical/nostalgic; interview/profile (local); new product; photo feature (local); and travel (regional). Buys 250 mss/year. Query with published clips. Length:

1,000-4,000 words. Pays $100-1,000. Sometimes pays expenses of writers on assignment.
Photos: Tara Christopherson, photo editor.
Columns/Departments: Nostalgic—Minnesota historical; Arts—local; Home—interior design, local; Last Page—essay with local relevance. Query with published clips. Length: 750-2,000 words. Pays $100-200.
Tips: People profiles (400 words) and Nostalgia are areas most open to freelancers.

Missouri

KANSAS CITY MAGAZINE, 3401 Main St., Kansas City MO 64111. (816)561-0444. Editor: Richard W. Jennings. 80% freelance written. Prefers to work with published/established writers. Freelance material is considered if it is about Kansas City issues, events or people. Circ. 16,000. Publishes ms an average of 3 months after acceptance. Byline given. Buys first serial rights. Query for electronic submissions. Computer printout submissions acceptable; prefers letter-quality. Reports in 1 month. Sample copy for $3 and 9x12 SAE.
Nonfiction: Editorial content is issue- or personality-oriented, arts, investigative reporting, profiles, or lengthy news features with a Kansas City connection. Written queries only; queries and mss should be accompanied by SASE. Longer stories of 2,000-8,000 words pay negotiable depending on story, plus expenses. Sometimes pays expenses of writers on assignment.
Columns/Departments: Short items of 250-350 words considered for City Window column; pays $25. Columns, which include City Windows, dining out, art, theater, sports, music, health and a Postscript essay, are from 1,600-3,000 words and pay $100-150. All material must have a demonstrable connection to Kansas City.
Tips: Freelancers should show some previous reporting or writing experience of a professional nature. "The writer has a better chance of breaking in at our publication with short articles. We like to see their work on easier-to-verify stories, such as City Window, before committing to longer, tougher reporting. Magazine also sponsors contest for fiction and feature writing: Modern Stories of Kansas City. Send SASE for information."

‡MISSOURI LIFE, The Magazine of Missouri, Missouri Life Publishing Co., Suite 7, 4825 Everhart, Corpus Christi TX 78411. (512)857-7293. Editor: Debra Gluck. 95% freelance written. Quarterly magazine covering Missouri people, places and history. Circ. 30,000. Pays 30 days after publication. Byline given. Buys first time rights. Submit seasonal/holiday material 3 months in advance. Simultaneous queries, and simultaneous, photocopied and previously published submissions OK. Reports in 1 month. Sample copy $3.50; writer's guidelines for #10 SAE and 1 first class stamp.
Nonfiction: General interest, historical/nostalgic, interview/profile, personal experience, photo feature and travel. Special issues planned for St. Louis, Kansas City and Lake of the Ozarks. Buys 35-40 mss/year. Written query. Length: 1,200-3,000 words. Pays $50.
Photos: State availability of photos. Pays $10-25 for 2x2 color transparencies and 5x7 and 8x10 b&w prints. Identification of subjects required.
Columns/Departments: Missouri Homes-tours of interesting houses and neighborhoods around the state; Southland-stories from the southern part of the state; Voices-profiles of interesting Missourians; Eastside St. Louis-area stories; Westside Kansas City-area stories. Buys 25-30 mss/year. Query. Length: 1,000-2,500 words. Pays $50.
Tips: "All sections of the magazine are open to writers. If the material has anything to do with Missouri, we're interested. Keep the writing unaffected and personal."

SPRINGFIELD! MAGAZINE, Springfield Communications Inc., Box 4749, Springfield MO 65808. (417)882-4917. Editor: Robert C. Glazier. 85% freelance written. Works with a small number of new/unpublished writers each year; eager to work with new/unpublished writers. Monthly magazine. "This is an extremely local and provincial magazine. No *general* interest articles." Circ. 10,000. Pays on publication. Publishes ms an average of 6 months after acceptance. Byline given. Buys first serial rights. Submit seasonal/holiday material 6-12 months in advance. Simultaneous queries OK. Computer printout submissions acceptable; prefers letter-quality. Reports in 3 months on queries; 6 months on mss. Sample copy for $1.50 and 9½x12½ SAE.
Nonfiction: Book excerpts (by Springfield authors only); expose (local topics only); historical/nostalgic (top priority but must be local history); how-to (local interest only); humor (if local angle); interview/profile (needs more on females than on males); personal experience (local angle); photo feature (local photos); and travel (1 page per month). No stock stuff which could appeal to any magazine anywhere. Buys 150 mss/year. Query with published clips or send complete ms. Length: 500-5,000 words. Pays $25-250. Sometimes pays expenses of writers on assignment.
Photos: State availability of photos or send photos with query or ms. Reviews b&w and color contact sheets; 4x5 color transparencies; and 5x7 b&w prints. Pays $5-35 for b&w; $10-50 for color. Captions, model releases, and identification of subjects required. Buys one-time rights.

Columns/Departments: Buys 250 mss/year. Query or send complete ms. Length varies widely but usually 500-2,500 words. Pays scale.

Tips: "We prefer that a writer read eight or ten copies of our magazine prior to submitting any material for our consideration. The magazine's greatest need is for features which comment on these times in Springfield. We are overstocked with nostalgic pieces right now. We also are much in need of profiles about young women and men of distinction."

Montana

MONTANA MAGAZINE, American Geographic Publishing, Box 5630, 3020 Bozeman Ave., Helena MT 59604. (406)443-2842. Managing Editor: Barbara Fifer. Editor: Carolyn Zieg Cunningham. 35% freelance written. Bimonthly magazine; "*Montana Magazine* is a strictly Montana-oriented magazine that features community profiles, personality profiles, contemporary issues, travel pieces." Circ. 72,000. Publishes ms an average of 6-8 months after acceptance. Byline given. Offers $50 kill fee on assigned stories only. Buys one-time rights. Submit seasonal material at least 6 months in advance. Simultaneous submissions OK. Reports in 6 weeks. Sample copy $2; writer's guidelines for #10 SASE.

Nonfiction: Essays, general interest, interview/profile, new product, opinion, photo feature and travel. Special features on "summer and winter destination points. Query by January for summer material; July for winter material. No 'me and Joe' hiking and hunting tales; no blood-and-guts hunting stories; no poetry; no fiction; no sentimental essays." Buys 30 mss/year. Query. Length: 300-2,500 words. Pays $75-500 for assigned articles; pays $50-350 for unsolicited articles. Sometimes pays the expenses of writers on assignment.

Photos: Send photos with submission. Reviews contact sheets, 35mm or larger format transparencies; and 5x7 prints. Offers no additional payment for photos accepted with ms. Captions, model releases and identification of subjects required. Buys one-time rights.

Columns/Departments: Over the Weekend (destination points of interest to travelers, family weekends and exploring trips to take), 300 words plus b&w photo; Food and Lodging (great places to eat; interesting hotels, resorts, etc.), 500-700 words plus b&w photo; Made in MT (successful cottage industries), 500-700 words plus b&w photo. Query. Pays $75-125.

Nevada

‡LV/RENO magazines, First Interstate Tower, Suite 120, 3800 Howard Hughes Parkway, Las Vegas NV 89109. (702)735-7003. Editor/Publisher: Lyle E. Brennan. Managing Editor: Bill Moody. 40% freelance written. Monthly magazines for Las Vegas and Reno. "*LV* and *Reno* focus on the people, events, issues and places of their respective cities and the entire state of Nevada." Circ. 25,000. Pays on publication. Byline given. Offers 25% kill fee. Buys all rights. Submit seasonal/holiday material 6 months in advance. Simultaneous and photocopied submissions OK. Computer printout submissions OK; prefers letter-quality. Reports in 1 month. Free sample copy; writer's guidelines for #10 SAE with 1 first class stamp.

Nonfiction: Historical/nostalgic, interview/profile, opinion. No gambling articles. Buys 25-35 mss/year. Send complete ms. Length: 750-2,500 words. Pays $50-250. Sometimes pays expenses of writers on assignment.

Photos: State availability of photos with submission. Reviews transparencies and 8x10 prints. Offers no additional payment for photos accepted with ms. Identification of subjects required. Buys one-time rights.

Columns/Departments: Commentary (issues, people, concerns, trends, relevant to all Nevadans). Buys 2-3 mss/year. Query. Length: 750-2,000 words. Pays $50-100.

Tips: "The best place to break in with us is through our Close-up/Lifestyle—personalities that have relevance to Nevada. But please, no gambling pieces. Writers need not be residents of Nevada, but they must be familiar with Las Vegas/Reno/Nevada living, which goes much beyond the bright lights of The Strip. The concerns here are like any other city in the country, and our articles reflect that similarity."

NEVADA MAGAZINE, Capitol Complex, Carson City NV 89710. (702)885-5416. Managing Editor: David Moore. 50% freelance written. Works with a small number of new/unpublished writers each year. Bimonthly magazine published by the state of Nevada to promote tourism in the state. Circ. 80,000. Pays on publication. Publishes ms an average of 6 months after acceptance. Byline given. Buys first North American serial rights. Phone queries OK. Submit seasonal/holiday material at least 6 months in advance. Query for electronic submissions. Computer printout submissions acceptable; no dot-matrix. Reports in 2 months. Sample copy $1; free writer's guidelines.

Nonfiction: Nevada topics only. Historical, nostalgia, photo feature, people profile, recreational, travel and think pieces. "We welcome stories and photos on speculation." Buys 40 unsolicited mss/year. Submit complete ms or queries to Associate Editor Jim Crandall. Length: 500-2,000 words. Pays $75-300.

Photos: Send photo material with accompanying ms. Pays $10-50 for 8x10 glossy prints; $15-75 for color transparencies. Name, address and caption should appear on each photo or slide. Buys one-time rights.

Tips: "Keep in mind that the magazine's purpose is to promote tourism in Nevada. Keys to higher payments are quality and editing effort (more than length). Send cover letter, no photocopies. We look for a light, enthusiastic tone of voice without being too cute; articles bolstered by amazing facts and thorough research; and unique angles on Nevada subjects."

THE NEVADAN TODAY, *The Las Vegas Review Journal*, Box 70, Las Vegas NV 89125-0070. (702)383-0270. Editor-in-Chief: A.D. Hopkins. 25% freelance written. Works with a small number of new/unpublished writers each year. Weekly magazine supplement; 20 pages. For Las Vegas and surrounding small town residents of all ages "who take our Sunday paper—affluent, thinking people." Circ. 140,000. Pays on publication. Publishes ms an average of 4 months after acceptance. Byline given. Buys one-time rights and simultaneous rights. Submit seasonal/holiday material 2 months in advance. Photocopied and previously published submissions OK. Computer printout submissions acceptable; prefers letter-quality. Reports in 3 weeks. Sample copy and writer's guidelines for 9x12 SAE with 3 first class stamps; mention *Writer's Market* in request.

Nonfiction: Historical (more of these than anything else, always linked to Nevada, southern Utah, northern Arizona and Death Valley); personal experience (any with strong pioneer Nevada angle, pioneer can be 1948 in some parts of Nevada). "We also buy contemporary pieces of about 2,400-3,000 words with good photos. An advance query is absolutely essential for these. No articles on history that are based on doubtful sources; no current show business material; and no commercial plugs." Buys 52 mss/year. Query. Phone queries OK. Length: average 1,200 words (contemporary pieces are longer). Usually pays $100.

Photos: State availability of photos. Pays $15 for 5x7 or 8x10 b&w glossy prints, or 35 or 120mm color transparencies. Captions required. Buys one-time rights on both photos and text.

Tips: "We are shifting emphasis of our main pieces from issues to people. We need strong, several-source pieces about important and interesting people with strong Las Vegas connections—investors or sport figures for example. Offers us in-depth personality pieces about VIPs with Las Vegas angles or articles on little-known interesting incidents in Nevada history and good historic photos. In queries, come to the point. Tell me what sort of photos are available, whether historic or contemporary, black-and-white or color transparency. Be specific in talking about what you want to write."

New Hampshire

FOREST NOTES, Society for the Protection of New Hampshire Forests, 54 Portsmouth St., Concord NH 03301. (603)224-9945. Editor: Richard Ober. 25% freelance written. Works with a small number of new/unpublished writers each year. A quarterly non-profit journal covering forestry, conservation, wildlife and protection. "Our readers are concerned with in-depth examinations of natural resource issues in New Hampshire." Circ. 8,000. Pays on acceptance. Publishes ms an average of 3 months after acceptance. Byline given. Buys first or second serial (reprint) rights; makes work-for-hire assignments. Previously published submissions OK. Query for electronic submissions. Computer printout submissions OK; prefers letter-quality. Reports in 2 weeks on queries; 1 month on mss. Free sample copy.

Nonfiction: Interview/profile (on assignment only); opinion (on the environment); photo feature (black and white photos of New Hampshire) and technical (on forestry). Query. Length: 500-2,000 words. Pays $100-300 or membership in organization. Sometimes pays the expenses of writers on assignment.

Photos: State availability of photos with submission. Reviews 5x7 prints. Offers no additional payment for photos accepted with ms. Captions required. Buys one-time rights.

Columns/Departments: Book review. Buys 1 mss/year. Query. Length: 150-500 words. Pays $25-75.

Tips: "Live in New Hampshire or New England; know your subject."

New Jersey

ATLANTIC CITY MAGAZINE, 1637 Atlantic Ave., Atlantic City NJ 08401. (609)348-6886. Managing Editor: Ken Weatherford. Editor: Ronnie Polaneczky. 60% freelance written. Works with small number of new/unpublished writers each year. Monthly city magazine covering issues pertinent to the South Jersey area. Circ. 50,000. Pays on acceptance. Publishes ms an average of 4 months after acceptance. Byline given. Buys one-time rights. Offers variable kill fee. Submit seasonal/holiday material 4 months in advance. Computer printout submissions OK; no dot-matrix. Reports in 1 month. Sample copy $2; free writer's guidelines.

Nonfiction: Entertainment, expose, general interest, how-to, interview/profile, photo feature and trends. "No travel pieces or any article without a South Jersey shore area/Atlantic City slant." Query. Length: 100-5,000 words. Pays $50-600 for assigned articles; pays $50-400 for unsolicited articles. Sometimes pays the expenses of writers on assignment.

Photos: State availability of photos. Reviews contact sheets, negatives, 2¼x2¼ transparencies and 8x10 prints. Pay varies. Captions, model releases and identification of subjects required. Buys one-time rights.

Columns/Departments: Art, Business, Entertainment, Environment, Sports and Real Estate. Query with published clips. Length: 500-2,500 words. Pays $150-300.

Tips: "We need more and more stories in 1989 with a strong local angle. Don't approach us with story ideas though, until you have studied two or three issues of the magazine. Try to propose articles that the magazine just can't live without."

‡**NEW JERSEY LIVING**, 830 Raymond Road, R.D. 4, Princeton NJ 08540. (201)329-2100. Editor: Marion Burdick. 75% freelance written. A monthly magazine. Circ. 50,000. Pays on publication. Publishes ms an average of 4 months after acceptance. Byline given. Buys first rights and second serial (reprint) rights. Submit seasonal/holiday material 4 months in advance. Simultaneous, photocopied and previously published submissions OK. Computer printout submissions acceptable; prefers letter-quality. Reports in 3 weeks on queries. Sample copy $2 with SASE; writer's guidelines for SASE.

Nonfiction: Books excerpts, general interest, historical/nostalgic, humor, inspirational, lifestyle interview/profile, personal experience, photo feature and travel. Query with published clips. Length: 1,500-3,000 words. Pays $50 and up.

Photos: Reviews contact sheets, negatives, 4x5 transparencies and 4x5 prints. Offers no additional payment for photos accepted with ms. Captions, model releases, and identification of subjects required.

Poetry: Light verse and traditional. Submit maximum 5 poems. Length: 5-50 lines. No cash payment.

Fillers: Anecdotes, facts, gags to be illustrated by cartoonist and short humor. Length: 5-100 words. No cash payment.

Tips: Features are most open to freelancers.

NEW JERSEY MONTHLY, 7 Dumont Place, Morristown NJ 07960. (201)539-8230. Editor: Larry Marscheck. Managing Editor: Patrick Sarver. 85% freelance written. Monthly magazine covering New Jersey. "Almost anything that's New Jersey related." Circ. 106,000. Pays on acceptance. Byline given. Offers 33% kill fee. Buys first rights. Submit seasonal/holiday material 6 months in advance. Query for electronic submissions. Computer printout submissions OK; prefers letter-quality. Reports in 6-8 weeks on queries; 2 weeks on mss. Sample copy $2 and 6 first class stamps; writer's guidelines for #10 SASE.

Nonfiction: Book excerpts, essays, expose, general interest, historical, humor, interview/profile, opinion, personal experience and travel. Special issue features Health & Fitness/Business Outlook (Jan.); Dining Out and Bridal (Feb.); Real Estate (March); Home & Garden (April); Great Weekends (May); Shore Guide (June); Summer Pleasures (July); Dining Out (Aug.); Financial Strategies (Sept.); Fall Getaways (Oct.); Entertaining (Nov.); Holiday Gala (Dec.). No experience pieces from people who used to live in New Jersey or general pieces that have no New Jersey angle. Buys 180 mss/year. Query with published magazine clips. Length: 2,000-3,000 words. Pays 35¢/word and up. Pays expenses of writers on assignment.

Photos: State availability of photos with submission. Payment negotiated. Identification of subjects required. Buys one-time rights.

Columns/Departments: Business (company profile, trends, individual profiles); Health (trends, how-to, personal experience, service); Politics (perspective pieces from writers working the political beat in Trenton); Home & Garden (homes, gardens, how-tos, trends, profiles, etc.); Health; Media; Travel (in and out-of-state); Education; all 1,500-1,800 words. Buys 60 mss/year. Query with published clips. Length: 1,500-1,800 words. Pays 35¢ and up per word.

Fiction: Adventure, condensed novels, historical, humorous, mystery and novel excerpts. All must relate to New Jersey. Writer must provide condensation, excerpt. Buys 1-5 mss/year. Length: 1,500-3,000 words. Pays 35¢ and up per word.

Fillers: Short humor. Length: 600-1,000 words. Pays 35¢ and up per word.

Tips: "Almost everything here is open to freelancers, since most of the magazine is freelance written. However, to break in, we suggest contributing short items to our front-of-the-book section, "Upfront" (light, off-beat items, trends, people, things; short service items, such as the 10 best NJ-made ice creams; short issue-oriented items; gossip; media notes. We pay 35¢ per published word. This is the only section we pay for on publication."

NEW JERSEY REPORTER, A Journal of Public Issues, The Center for Analysis of Public Issues (nonprofit), 16 Vandeventer Ave., Princeton NJ 08542. (609)924-9750. Editor: Rick Sinding. 30% freelance written. Prefers to work with published/established writers. Magazine published 10 times/year covering New Jersey politics, public affairs and public issues. "*New Jersey Reporter* is a hard-hitting and highly respected magazine published for people who take an active interest in New Jersey politics and public affairs, and who want to know more about what's going on than what newspapers and television newscasts are able to tell them. We publish a great variety of stories ranging from analysis to exposé." Circ. 3,000. Pays on publication. Publishes ms an average of 2 months after acceptance. Byline given. Buys all rights. Simultaneous queries and submissions, and photocopied and previously published submissions OK. Computer printout submissions acceptable; no dot-matrix. Reports in 1 month. Sample copy $3.50.

Nonfiction: Book excerpts, expose, interview/profile and opinion. "We like articles from specialists (in planning, politics, economics, corruption, etc.), but we reject stories that do not read well because of jargon or too little attention to the actual writing of the piece. Our magazine is interesting as well as informative." Buys 10 mss/year. Query with published clips or send complete ms. Length: 2,000-6,000 words. Pays $100-250. Pays expenses of writers on assignments.

Tips: "Queries should be specific about how the prospective story represents an issue that affects or will affect the people of New Jersey. The writer's resume should be included. Stories—unless they are specifically meant to be opinion—should come to a conclusion but avoid a 'holier than thou' or preachy tone. Allegations should be scrupulously substantiated. Our magazine represents a good opportunity for freelancers to acquire great clips. Our publication specializes in longer, more detailed, analytical features. The most frequent mistake made by writers in completing an article for us is too much personal opinion versus reasoned advocacy. We are less interested in opinion than in analysis based on sound reasoning and fact. *New Jersey Reporter* is a well-respected publication, and many of our writers go on to nationally respected newspapers and magazines."

THE SANDPAPER, Newsmagazine of the Jersey Shore, The SandPaper, Inc., 1816 Long Beach Blvd., Surf City NJ 08008. (609)494-2034. Editor: Curt Travers. Managing Editor: Gail Travers. 20% freelance written. Weekly tabloid covering subjects of interest to Jersey shore residents and visitors. "*The Sandpaper* publishes three editions covering many of the Jersey Shore's finest resort communities. Each issue includes a mix of hard news, human interest features, opinion columns and entertainment/calendar listings." Circ. 85,000. Pays on publication. Publishes ms an average of 1 month after acceptance. Byline given. Offers 100% kill fee. Buys first rights or all rights. Submit seasonal/holiday material 3 months in advance. Simultaneous, photocopied, and previously published submissions OK. Computer printout submissions acceptable; prefers letter-quality. Reports in 1 month. Free sample copy.

Nonfiction: Essays, general interest, historical/nostalgic, humor, opinion and environmental submissions relating to the ocean, wetlands and pinelands. Must pertain to New Jersey shore locale. Also, arts and entertainment news and reviews if they have a Jersey shore angle. Buys 25 mss/year. Send complete ms. Length: 200-2,000 words. Pays $15-100. Sometimes pays the expenses of writers on assignment.

Photos: State availability of photos with submission. Offers $6-25/photo. Buys one-time rights or all rights.

Columns/Departments: Speak Easy (opinion and slice-of-life; often humorous); Food for Thought (cooking); and Commentary (forum for social science perspectives); all 500-1,500 words. Buys 50 mss/year. Send complete ms. Pays $15-35.

Fiction: Humorous and slice-of-life vignettes. Buys 25 mss/year. Send complete ms. Length: 500-1,500 words. Pays $15-35.

Tips: "Anything of interest to sun worshippers, beach walkers, nature watchers, water sports lovers is of potential interest to us. The opinion page and columns are most open to freelancers. We are steadily increasing the amount of entertainment-related material in our publication."

New Mexico

NEW MEXICO MAGAZINE, Joseph Montoya State Bldg., 1100 St. Francis Drive, Santa Fe NM 87503. Editor: Emily Drabanski. Managing Editor: Jon Bowman. 85% freelance written. Monthly magazine; 64-96 pages. Emphasizes New Mexico for a college-educated readership, above average income, interested in the Southwest. Circ. 100,000. Pays on acceptance. Publishes ms an average of 6 months after acceptance. Buys first North American serial rights. Submit seasonal/holiday material 8 months in advance. Computer printout submissions acceptable; no dot-matrix. Reports in 8 weeks. Sample copy for $1.75 and 9x12 SAE; writer's guidelines for SASE.

Nonfiction: New Mexico subjects of interest to travelers. Historical, cultural, humorous, nostalgic and informational articles. "We are looking for more short, light and bright stories for the 'Asi Es Nuevo Mexico' section." No columns, cartoons, poetry or non-New Mexico subjects. Buys 5-7 mss/issue. Query with 3 published writing samples. Length: 250-2,000 words. Pays $75-350.

Photos: Purchased with accompanying ms or on assignment. Query or send contact sheet or transparencies. Pays $30-50 for 8x10 b&w glossy prints; $30-75 for 35mm—prefers Kodachrome; (photos in plastic-pocketed viewing sheets). Captions and model releases required. Buys one-time rights.

Tips: "We're publishing more personality profiles. Send a superb short (300 words) manuscript on a little-known person, event, aspect of history or place to see in New Mexico. Faulty research will ruin a writer's chances for the future. Good style, good grammar. No generalized odes to the state or the Southwest. No sentimentalized, paternalistic views of Indians or Hispanics. No glib, gimmicky 'travel brochure' writing."

‡**SOUTHWEST PROFILE**, Whitney Publishing Co., Suite #102, 941 Calle Mejia, Box 1236, Santa Fe NM 87504-1236. (505)984-1773. Editor: Stephen Parks. 50% freelance written. Magazine on the southwest, published 8 times per year. "*Southwest Profile* is a guide to travel and adventure, art and culture, and living and leisure in the Southwest, with special emphasis on Arizona and New Mexico." Circ. 20,000. Pays on

publication. Publishes ms an average of 2 months after acceptance. Byline given. Offers 50% kill fee. Buys first North American serial rights. Submit seasonal/holiday material 6 months in advance. Photocopied submissions OK. Query for electronic submissions. Computer printout submissions OK. Reports in 2 weeks. Sample copy for 9x12 SAE with $1.25 postage.

Nonfiction: General interest, interview/profile, photo feature, travel and art. Buys 30 mss/year. Query with published clips. Length: 1,000-2,500 words. Pays $150-300. Sometimes pays expenses of writers on assignment.

Photos: Send photos with submission. Reviews 35mm or larger transparencies and 5x7 prints. Offers $25-50 per photo. Captions required. Buys one-time rights.

New York

ADIRONDACK LIFE, Route 86, Box 97, Jay NY 12941. Editor: Chris Shaw. 50% freelance written. Prefers to work with published/established writers; works with a small number of new/unpublished writers each year. Emphasizes the Adirondack region and the North Country of New York State in articles concerning outdoor activities, history, and natural history directly related to the Adirondacks. Bimonthly magazine. Circ. 40,000. Pays on publication. Publishes ms an average of 6 months after acceptance. Buys one-time rights. Byline given. Submit seasonal/holiday material 1 year in advance. Previously published book excerpts OK. Computer printout submissions acceptable; prefers letter-quality. Reports in 1 month. Sample copy $4; free writer's guidelines.

Nonfiction: *"Adirondack Life* attempts to capture the unique flavor and ethos of the Adirondack mountains and North Country region through feature articles directly pertaining to the qualities of the area and through department articles examining specific aspects. Example Barkeater: personal essays; Special Places: unique spots in the Adirondacks; Working: careers in the Adirondacks: Wilderness: environmental issues, personal experiences." Buys 10-16 unsolicited mss/year. Query. Length for features: 3,000 words maximum; for departments, 1,000 words. Pays up to 25¢/word. Sometimes pays expenses of writers on assignment.

Photos: All photos must have been taken in the Adirondacks. Each issue contains a photo feature. Purchased with or without ms or on assignment. All photos must be identified as to subject or locale and must bear photographer's name. Submit color slides or b&w prints. Pays $25 for b&w transparencies; $50 for color transparencies; $300 for cover (color only, vertical in format). Credit line given.

Tips: "We are looking for clear, concise, well-organized manuscripts, written with flair. We are continually trying to upgrade the editorial quality of our publication."

‡BUFFALO SPREE MAGAZINE, Spree Publishing Co., Inc., 4511 Harlem Rd., Box 38, Buffalo NY 14226. (716)839-3405. Editor: Johanna V. Shotell. 90% freelance written. A quarterly city magazine. Circ. 21,000. Pays on publication. Publishes ms an average of 6 months after acceptance. Byline given. Buys first North American serial rights. Submit seasonal/holiday material 6 months in advance. Computer printout submissions OK; prefers letter-quality. Reports in 6 months on mss. Sample copy $2 with 9x12 SAE and $2.40 postage.

Nonfiction: General interest, historical/nostalgic, humor, personal experience and travel. Buys 20 mss/year. Send complete ms. Length: 600-1,800 words. Pays $75-100 for unsolicited articles.

Photos: State availability of photos with submission. Reviews prints (any size). Offers no additional payment for photos accepted with ms. Captions required. Buys one-time rights.

Fiction: Adventure, ethnic, humorous, mainstream, romance and slice-of-life vignettes. "No pornographic or religious manuscripts." Buys 20 mss/year. Send complete ms. Length: 600-1,800 words. Pays $75-100.

Poetry: Janet Goldenberg, poetry editor. Buys 24 poems/year. Submit maximum 4 poems. Length: 50 lines. Pays $25.

CAPITAL Region Magazine, Capital Region Magazine, Inc., 4 Central Ave., Albany NY 12210. (518)465-3500. Editor-in-Chief: Dardis McNamee. 40% freelance written. Prefers to work with published/established writers. A monthly city/regional magazine for New York's capital region. Circ. 35,000. Pays 30 days from acceptance. Publishes ms an average of 3 months after acceptance. Byline given. Offers 25% kill fee. Buys one-time and second serial (reprint) rights. Submit seasonal/holiday material 3 months in advance. Photocopied submissions OK. Query for electronic submissions. Computer printout submissions OK; prefers letter-quality. Reports in 2 months. Sample copy for 8½x11 SAE with $1.75 postage and handling fee; free writer's guidelines.

Nonfiction: Book excerpts, essays, expose, general interest, historical/nostalgic, humor, interview/profile, arts and culture, photo feature, travel, business and politics. Buys 60 mss/year. Query with published clips (preferred) or send complete ms. Length: 1,500-3,000. Pays $120-400. Fees set at approximately 10¢/word. Pays the expenses of writers on assignment "if agreed upon in advance."

Photos: State availability of photos with submission. Pays $300 plus expenses for covers; $350 plus expenses for features; $500 in usage. Identification of subjects required. Buys one-time rights.

Columns/Departments: Politics, Business, Culture, Food & Wine, Design, Destinations and Media, all

1,000-1,400 words. Buys 30 mss/year. Query with published clips or send complete ms. Length: 1,000-1,400 words. Pays $120 maximum.

Fiction: "One fiction issue per year, July; short stories, novel excerpts, poetry. Deadline Feburary 15. For writers with a link to the region. Professional quality only; one slot for writers previously unpublished in a general circulation magazine."

Fillers: Vignettes, short essays, newsbreaks and short humor. Buys 30/year. Length: 150-750 words. Pays $25-75.

Tips: "Exclusively local focus, although we welcome pieces seen in larger context. Investigative reporting, profiles, business stories, trend pieces, behind-the-scenes, humor, service features, arts and culture, nitty-gritty. Looking for The Great Read in every story."

CITY LIMITS, City Limits Community Information Service, Inc., 40 Prince St., New York NY 10012. (212)925-9820. Editor: Beverly Cheuvront. Managing Editor: Doug Turetsky. 50% freelance written. Works with a small number of new/unpublished writers each year. A monthly magazine covering housing and related urban issues. "We cover news and issues in New York City as they relate to the city's poor, moderate and middle-income residents. We are advocacy journalists with a progressive or 'left' slant." Circ. 5,000. Pays on publication. Publishes ms an average of 1-2 months after acceptance. Byline given. Buys first North American serial rights, one-time rights, or second serial (reprint) rights. Query for electronic submissions. Computer printout submissions acceptable; prefers letter-quality. Reports in 3 weeks. Sample copy $3.

Nonfiction: Expose, interview/profile, opinion, hard news and community profile. "No fluff, no propaganda." Length: 600-2,500 words. Pays $50-150. Sometimes pays expenses of writers on assignment.

Photos: Reviews contact sheets and 5x7 prints. Offers $10-40/photo, cover only. Identification of subjects required. Buys one-time rights.

Columns/Departments: Short Term Notes (brief descriptions of programs, policies, events, etc.), 250-400 words; Book Reviews (housing, urban development, planning, etc.), 250-600 words; Pipeline (covers community organizations, new programs, government policies, etc.), 600-800 words. People (who are active in organizations, community groups, etc.), 600-800 words; and Organize (groups involved in housing, job programs, health care, etc.), 600-800 words. Buys 50-75 mss/year. Query with published clips or send complete ms. Pays $25-35.

Tips: "We are open to a wide range of story ideas in the community development field. If you don't have particular expertise in housing, urban planning etc., start with a community profile or pertinent book or film review. Short Term Notes is also good for anyone with reporting skills. We're looking for writing that is serious and informed but not academic or heavy handed."

THE GRAPEVINE'S FINGER LAKES MAGAZINE, Grapevine Press, Inc., 108 S. Albany St., Ithaca NY 14850. (607)272-3470. Editor: Linda McCandless. 95% freelance written. A quarterly magazine covering Finger Lakes Region of New York State. Circ. 20,000. Pays 1 month after publication. Publishes ms an average of 6-12 months after acceptance. Byline given. Offers negotiable kill fee. Buys first North American serial rights. Submit seasonal/holiday material 8 months in advance. Simultaneous submissions OK. Computer printout submissions OK; prefers letter-quality. Reports in 1 month on queries; 2 months on mss. Sample copy for 9x12 SAE and 5 first class stamps; writer's guidelines for #10 SASE.

Nonfiction: Investigative reporting, expose, general interest, historical/nostalgic, humor, interview/profile, recreation and photo feature. Buys 30 mss/year. Query with published clips. Length: 600-2,400 words. Pays $25-100. Pays expenses of writers on assignment.

Columns/Departments: Lake Takes (profile on person of interest). Query with published clips. Length: 100-300 words. Pays $10-20. Excursions (day trip). Query with published clips. Length: 200-500 words. Pays $20.

Fiction: Humorous and slice-of-life vignettes. Needs one "Fiend of The Fingerlakes" each quarter; one crime for the past 200 years in Central New York reconstructed in colorful detail. Buys 4 mss/year. Query with published clips or send complete ms. Length: 1,200-2,500 words. Pays $30-75.

Poetry: Jerry Gross, poetry editor. Free verse. Buys 4 poems/year. Submit 5 poems maximum. Length: 8-30 lines. Pays $10-25.

NEW YORK ALIVE, The Magazine of Life and Work in the Empire State, The Business Council of New York State, Inc., 152 Washington Ave., Albany NY 12210. (518)465-7511. Editor: Mary Grates Stoll. 85% freelance written. Works with a small number of new/unpublished writers each year. Bimonthly magazine about New York state—people, places, events, history. "Devoted to promoting the culture, heritage and lifestyle of New York state. Aimed at people who enjoy living and reading about the New York state experience. All stories must be positive in tone and slanted toward promoting the state." Circ. 35,000. Pays within 45 days of acceptance. Publishes ms an average of 8 months after acceptance. Byline given. Offers 25% of agreed-upon purchase price as kill fee. Buys one-time rights. Submit seasonal/holiday material 4 months in advance. Simultaneous queries and previously published submissions OK. Query for electronic submissions. Computer printout submissions acceptable. Reports in 3 months on queries; 1 month on mss. Sample copy

$2.45; writer's guidelines for #10 SASE.

Nonfiction: Historical/nostalgic, humor, interview/profile, personal experience, photo feature and travel. In all cases subject must be a New York state person, place, event or experience. No stories of general nature (e.g. nationwide trends); political; religious; nonNew York state subjects. Query with published clips. Buys 30-40 mss/year. Length: 1,500-3,000 words. Pays $200-350. Pays expenses of writers on assignment.

Photos: State availability of photos. Reviews b&w contact sheets, 35mm color transparencies, and b&w prints. Pays $15-30 for b&w and $30-250 for color. Model releases and identification of subjects required.

Columns/Departments: Buys 80-100 mss/year. Query with published clips. Length: 500-1,000 words. Pays $50-150.

Tips: "We buy more short articles. The writer should enjoy and feel comfortable with writing straightforward, promotional type of material."

NEW YORK DAILY NEWS, Travel Section, 220 E. 42 St., New York NY 10017. (212)210-1699. Travel Editor: Harry Ryan. 30% freelance written. Prefers to work with published/established writers. Weekly tabloid. Circ. 1.8 million. "We are the largest circulating newspaper travel section in the country and take all types of articles ranging from experiences to service oriented pieces that tell readers how to make a certain trip." Pays on publication. Publishes ms an average of 3 months after acceptance. Byline given. Submit seasonal/holiday material 4 months in advance. Contact first before submitting electronic submissions; requires hard copy also. Computer printout submissions acceptable "if crisp"; prefers letter-quality. Reports "as soon as possible." Writer's guidelines for #10 SASE.

Nonfiction: General interest, historical/nostalgic, humor, inspirational, personal experience and travel. "Most of our articles involve practical trips that the average family can afford—even if it's one you can't afford every year. We put heavy emphasis on budget saving tips for all trips. We also run stories now and then for the Armchair Traveler, an exotic and usually expensive trip. We are looking for professional quality work from professional writers who know what they are doing. The pieces have to give information and be entertaining at the same time. No 'How I Spent My Summer Vacation' type articles. No PR hype." Buys 60 mss/year. Query with SASE. Length: 1,500 words maximum. Pays $75-150.

Photos: "Good pictures always help sell good stories." State availability of photos with ms. Reviews contact sheets and negatives. Captions and identification of subjects required. Buys all rights.

Columns/Departments: Short Hops is based on trips to places within a 300-mile radius of New York City. Length: 800-1,000 words. Travel Watch gives practical travel advice.

Tips: "A writer might have some luck gearing a specific destination to a news event or date: In Search of Irish Crafts in March, for example, but do it well in advance."

NEW YORK MAGAZINE, News America Publishing, Inc., 755 2nd Ave., New York 10017. (212)880-0700. Editor: Edward Kosner. Managing Editor: Laurie Jones. 30% freelance written. Weekly magazine focusing on current events in the New York metropolitan area. Pays on acceptance. Publishes ms an average of 1 month after acceptance. Buys first North American serial rights. Submit seasonal/holiday material 2 months in advance. Photocopied submissions OK. Computer printout submissions acceptable; prefers letter-quality. Reports in 1 month. Sample copy for $3.50.

Nonfiction: Expose, general interest, profile, behavior/lifestyle, health/medicine, local politics and entertainment. Query. Pays $850-2,500. Pays expenses of writers on assignment.

Tips: "The writer has a better chance of breaking in with shorter articles. The magazine very rarely assigns a major feature to a new writer."

THE NEW YORK TIMES, 229 W. 43rd St., New York NY 10036. (212)556-1234.

Nonfiction: *The New York Times Magazine* appears in *The New York Times* on Sunday. "Views should be fresh, lively and provocative on national and international news developments, science, education, family life, social trends and problems, arts and entertainment, personalities, sports and the changing American scene. Freelance contributions are invited. Articles must be timely. They must be based on specific news items, forthcoming events or significant anniversaries, or they must reflect trends. Our full-length articles run approximately 4,000 words, and for these we pay from $1,500 to $2,500 on acceptance. Our shorter pieces run from 1,000-2,500 words, and for these we pay from $750 to $1,500 on acceptance." Unsolicited articles and proposals should be addressed to Articles Editor. *Arts and Leisure* section of *The New York Times* appears on Sunday. Wants "to encourage imaginativeness in terms of form and approach—stressing ideas, issues, trends, investigations, symbolic reporting and stories delving deeply into the creative achievements and processes of artists and entertainers—and seeks to break away from old-fashioned gushy, fan magazine stuff." Length: 4,000 words. Pays $100-250, depending on length. *Arts and Leisure* Editor: William H. Honan.

Photos: Send to Photo Editor. Pays $75 minimum for b&w photos.

Tips: "The Op Ed page is always looking for new material and publishes many people who have never been published before. We want material of universal relevance which people can talk about in a personal way. When writing for the Op Ed page, there is no formula, but the writing itself should have some polish. Don't make the mistake of pontificating on the news. We're not looking for more political columnists. Op Ed length runs about 750 words, and pays about $150."

NEWSDAY, Long Island NY 11747. Viewpoints Editor: James Lynn. 75% freelance written. Opinion section of daily newspaper. Byline given. Computer printout submissions acceptable.
Nonfiction: Seeks "opinion on current events, trends, issues—whether national or local government or lifestyle. Must be timely, pertinent, articulate and opinionated. Strong preference for authors within the circulation area. It's best to consult before you start writing." Length: 600-2,000 words. Pays $100-350.
Tips: "The writer has a better chance of breaking in at our publication with short articles since the longer essays are commissioned from experts and well-known writers."

OUR TOWN, East Side/West Side Communications Corp., 451 E. 83rd St., New York NY 10028. (212)439-7800. Editor: Ed Kayatt. 80% freelance written. Eager to work with new/unpublished writers. Weekly tabloid covering neighborhood news of Manhattan (96th St.-14th St.). Circ. 110,000. Pays on publication. Publishes ms an average of 1 month after acceptance. Byline given. Buys first serial rights. Submit seasonal/holiday material 1 month in advance. Computer printout submissions OK; prefers letter-quality.
Nonfiction: Expose (especially consumer ripoffs); historical/nostalgic (Manhattan, 14th St.-96th St.); interview/profile (of local personalities); photo feature (of local event); and animal rights. "We're looking for local news (Manhattan only, mainly 14th St.-96th St.). We need timely, lively coverage of local issues and events, focusing on people or exposing injustice and good deeds of local residents and business people. (Get *full names, spelled right.*)" Special issues include Education (January, March and August); and Summer Camps (March). Query with published clips. Length: 1,000 words maximum. Pays "70¢/20-pica column-inch as published." Sometimes pays expenses of writers on assignment.
Photos: Pays $2-5 for 8x10 b&w prints. Buys all rights.
Tips: "Come by the office and talk to the editor. (Call first.) Bring samples of writing."

UPSTATE MAGAZINE, *Democrat and Chronicle*, 55 Exchange St., Rochester NY 14614. (716)232-7100. Editor: Peggy Moran. 90-100% freelance written. Works with a small number of new/unpublished writers each year. A Sunday magazine appearing weekly in the *Democrat and Chronicle*. A regional magazine covering topics of local interest written for the most part by area writers. Circ. 260,000. Pays on publication. Publishes ms an average of 4 months after acceptance. Byline given. Buys first North American serial rights and second (reprint) rights to material originally published elsewhere. Submit seasonal/holiday material 3 months in advance. Computer printout submissions acceptable. Reports in 2 months.
Nonfiction: General interest (places and events of local interest); historical/nostalgic; humor; interview/profile (of outstanding people in local area); personal experience; photo feature (with local angle). Buys 100 mss/year. Query. Length: 750-1,500 words; shorter is better. Pays $60-250. Do not send fiction or fillers.

North Carolina

SOUTHERN EXPOSURE, Box 531, Durham NC 27702. (919)688-8167. Contact: Editor. Quarterly.Journal for Southerners interested in "left-liberal" political perspective and the South; all ages; well-educated. Circ. 7,500. Pays on publication. Buys all rights. Offers kill fee. Byline given. Will consider photocopied and simultaneous submissions. Submit seasonal material 6 months in advance. Reports in 3 months. "Query is appreciated, but not required." Writer's guidelines for #10 SASE.
Nonfiction: "Ours is one of the few publications about the South *not* aimed at business or upper-class people; it appeals to all segments of the population. *And*, it is used as a resource—sold as a magazine and then as a book—so it rarely becomes dated." Needs investigative articles about the following subjects as related to the South: politics, energy, institutional power from prisons to universities, women, labor, black people and the economy. Informational interview, profile, historical, think articles, expose, opinion and book reviews. Length: 6,000 words maximum. Pays $50-200. Smaller fee for short items.
Photos: "Very rarely purchase photos, as we have a large number of photographers working for us." 8x10 b&w preferred; no color. Payment negotiable.
Tips: "Because we will be publishing shorter issues on a quarterly basis, we will be looking for clear and thoughtful writing, aritcles that relate specific experiences of individual southerners or grass roots groups to larger issues."

Ohio

BEND OF THE RIVER® MAGAZINE, 143 W. Third St., Box 239, Perrysburg OH 43551. (419)874-7534. Publishers: Christine Raizk Alexander and R. Lee Raizk. 90% freelance written. Works with a small number of new/unpublished writers each year, and eager to work with new/unpublished writers. "We buy material that we like whether by an experienced writer or not." Monthly magazine for readers interested in Ohio history, antiques, etc. Circ. 3,400. Pays on publication. Publishes ms an average of 6 months after acceptance. Byline given. Buys one-time rights. Submit seasonal material 2 months in advance; deadline for holiday issue is October 15. Reports in 6 weeks. Sample copy $1.

Nonfiction: "We deal heavily in Ohio history. We are looking for well-researched articles about local history and modern day pioneers doing the unusual. We'd like to see interviews with historical (Ohio) authorities; travel sketches of little-known but interesting places in Ohio; articles about grass roots farmers, famous people from Ohio like Doris Day, Gloria Steinem, etc. and preservation. Our main interest is to give our readers happy thoughts and good reading. We strive for material that says 'yes' to life, past and present." No personal reflection or nostalgia unless you are over 65. Buys 75 unsolicited mss/year. Submit complete ms. Length: 1,500 words. Pays $10-25. Sometimes pays the expenses of writers on assignment.

Photos: Purchases b&w or color photos with accompanying mss. Pays $1 minimum. Captions required.

Tips: "Any Toledo area, well-researched history will be put on top of the heap. Send us any unusual piece that is either cleverly humorous, divinely inspired or thought provoking. We like articles about historical topics treated in down-to-earth conversational tones. We pay a small amount (however, we're now paying more) but usually use our writers often and through the years. We're loyal."

CINCINNATI MAGAZINE, 409 Broadway, Cincinnati OH 45202. (513)421-4300. Editor: Laura Pulfer. Monthly magazine emphasizing Cincinnati living. Circ. 32,000. Pays on acceptance. Byline given. Offers 33% kill fee. Buys all rights. Submit seasonal/holiday material 3 months in advance. Simultaneous, photocopied, and previously published submissions OK. Reports in 5 weeks.

Nonfiction: How-to, informational, interview, photo feature, profile and travel. No humor. Buys 4-5 mss/issue. Query. Length: 2,000-4,000 words. Pays $150-400.

Photos: Thomas Hawley, art director. Photos purchased on assignment only. Model release required.

Columns/Departments: Travel, how-to, sports and consumer tips. Buys 5 mss/issue. Query. Length: 750-1,500 words. Pays $75-150.

Tips: "It helps to mention something you found particularly well done in our magazine. It shows you've done your homework and sets you apart from the person who clearly is not tailoring his idea to our publication. Send article ideas that probe the whys and wherefores of major issues confronting the community, making candid and in-depth appraisals of the problems and honest attempts to seek solutions. Have a clear and well defined subject about the city (the arts, politics, business, sports, government, entertainment); include a rough outline with proposed length; a brief background of writing experience and sample writing if available. We are looking for critical pieces, smoothly written, that ask and answer questions that concern our readers. We do not run features that are 'about' places or businesses simply because they exist. There should be a thesis that guides the writer and the reader. We want balanced articles about the city—the arts, politics, business, etc."

THE MAGAZINE, 4th and Ludlow Sts., Dayton OH 45401. (513)225-2360. Editor: Scott Herron. 75% freelance written. Works with small number of new/unpublished writers each year. Sunday supplement. Circ. 256,000. Byline given. Pays on publication. Publishes ms an average of 3 months after acceptance. Buys first serial rights and second serial (reprint) rights. Query for electronic submissions. Computer printout submissions acceptable. Reports in 1 month.

Nonfiction: Magazine focuses on ideas and reasons why behind people, places, trends. Emphasis is on color transparencies supplemented by stories. Length: open. Payment: $300-500, cover stories; $200-300, inside stories, varies up and down depending on quality of writing, less for second rights.

Fiction: Story featured once a month, plus annual fiction contest issue; payment varies.

Photos: Transparencies and glossy photos. Evaluates photos on their own merit. Payment variable depending on quality.

OHIO MAGAZINE, Ohio Magazine, Inc., Subsidiary of Dispatch Printing Co., 40 S. 3rd St., Columbus OH 43215. Editor-in-Chief: Robert B. Smith. 65% freelance written. Works with a small number of new/unpublished writers each year. Monthly magazine. Emphasizes news and feature material of Ohio for an educated, urban and urbane readership. Circ. 103,327. Pays on publication. Publishes ms an average of 5 months after acceptance. Buys all rights, second serial (reprint) rights, one-time rights, first North American serial rights, or first serial rights. Byline given except on short articles appearing in sections. Submit seasonal/holiday material 5 months in advance. Simultaneous, photocopied, and previously published submissions OK. Computer printout submissions acceptable; no dot-matrix. Reports in 2 months. Sample copy $2.50; writer's guidelines for #10 SASE.

Nonfiction: Features: 2,000-8,000 words. Pays $250-700. Cover pieces $600-850; Ohioana and Ohioans (should be offbeat with solid news interest; 50-250 words, pays $15-50); Ohioguide (pieces on upcoming Ohio events, must be offbeat and worth traveling for; 100-300 words, pays $10-15); Diner's Digest ("We are still looking for writers with extensive restaurant reviewing experience to do 5-10 short reviews each month in specific sections of the state on a specific topic. Fee is on a retainer basis and negotiable"); Money (covering business related news items, profiles of prominent people in business community, personal finance—all Ohio angle; 300-1,000 words, pays $50-250); and Living (embodies dining in, home furnishings, gardening and architecture; 300-1,000 words, pays $50-250). Send submissions for features to Robert B. Smith, editor-in-chief, or Ellen Stein Burbach, managing editor; Ohioguide and Diner's Digest to services editor; and Money to Ellen Stein Burbach, managing editor. No political columns or articles of limited geographical interest (must be of interest to all of Ohio). Buys 40 unsolicited mss/year. Sometimes pays expenses of writers on assignment.

Columns/Departments: Ellen Stein Burbach, managing editor. Sports, Last Word, travel, fashion and wine. Open to suggestions for new columns/departments.

Photos: Ellen Stein Burbach, managing editor. Rate negotiable.

Tips: "Freelancers should send a brief prospectus prior to submission of the complete article. All articles should have a definite Ohio application."

TOLEDO MAGAZINE, The Blade, 541 Superior St., Toledo OH 43660. (419)245-6121. Editor: Sue Stankey. Managing Editor: Edson Whipple. 60% freelance written. Prefers to work with published/established writers and works with a small number of new/unpublished writers each year. Weekly general interest magazine that appears in the Sunday newspaper. Circ. 225,000. Pays on publication. Publishes ms an average of 3 months after acceptance. Byline given. Buys one-time rights. Submit seasonal/holiday material 4-6 months in advance. Simultaneous queries and submissions OK. Computer printout submissions acceptable; no dot-matrix. Reports in 2 weeks on queries; 1 month on mss. Sample copy for 9x12 SAE.

Nonfiction: General interest, historical/nostalgic, humor, interview/profile and personal experience. Buys 100-200 mss/year. Query with or without published clips. Length: 500-6,000 words. Pays $75-500.

Photos: Dave Cron, photo editor. State availability of photos. Reviews b&w and color contact sheets. Payment negotiable. Captions, model release, and identification of subjects required. Buys one-time rights.

Tips: "Submit a well-organized story proposal and include copies of previously published stories."

TRISTATE MAGAZINE, The Cincinnati Enquirer (Gannett), 617 Vine St., Cincinnati OH 45201. (513)369-1954. Editor: Alice Hornbaker. 35-50% freelance written. Eager to work with new/unpublished writers. Sunday newspaper magazine covering a wide range of all local topics. Circ. 330,000. Pays on publication. Publishes ms an average of 4 months after acceptance. Byline given. Buys first serial rights. Submit seasonal/holiday material 6 months in advance. Simultaneous queries, and simultaneous, photocopied, and previously published submissions OK. Query for electronic submissions. Computer printout submissions acceptable; prefers letter-quality. Reports in 2 weeks on queries. Writer's guidelines for #10 SASE.

Nonfiction: General interest, historical/nostalgic, humor and interview/profile pertaining to the Cincinnati, Northern Kentucky, Indiana, tristate area only. No editorials, how-to, new products, inspirational or technical material. Buys 25-50 mss/year. Query first except for humor and short fiction. Length: 4 pages maximum. Pays $100 (inside), $200 (cover).

Fiction: Short-short fiction to 4 pages, all locally based. Pays $100.

Photos: State availability of photos. Pays $25 per photo. Identification of subjects required. Buys one-time rights.

WESTERN RESERVE MAGAZINE, 2101 Superior Ave., Cleveland OH 44114. (216)241-7636. Editor: David Patterson. 50% freelance written. Monthly digest-sized magazine covering local history, house and garden, nature, antiques, historic preservation. "Articles must be geared to Northeast Ohio and aimed at highly literate, well-educated, well-to-do audience." Circ. 57,000. Pays on publication. Publishes ms an average of 2-6 months after acceptance. Byline given. Buys first or all rights. Submit seasonal/holiday material 4 months in advance. Photocopied submissions OK. Computer printout submissions OK. Reports in 2 months. Sample copy $2.50 with 6x9 SAE and 5 first class stamps.

Nonfiction: Book excerpts (history); historical/nostalgic; how-to (restoration); interview/profile; photo feature (along with articles); travel (nearby getaways); historic preservations; and house and garden. "No boring first person reminiscenses, far away travel, 'Auntie Mimi's plate collection' articles." Buys 30-40 mss/year. Query with or without published clips, or send complete ms. Length: 1,000-2,000 words. Pays $100 maximum for assigned articles; pays $50 maximum for unsolicited articles.

Photos: Send photos with submission. Reviews 35mm transparencies and 5x7 prints. Offers no additonal payment for photos accepted with ms. Captions, model releases and identification of subjects required. Buys one-time and reprint rights.

Tips: "Know the Northeast Ohio area and read our publication before submitting. We have acquired a much larger readership and might be looking at articles with a broader focus than previously."

Oklahoma

OKLAHOMA TODAY, Oklahoma Department of Tourism and Recreation, Box 53384, Oklahoma City OK 73152. Editor-in-Chief: Sue Carter. Managing Editor: Susan Tomlinson. 99% freelance written. Works with a small number of new/unpublished writers each year. Bimonthly magazine covering travel and recreation in the state of Oklahoma. "We are interested in showing off the best Oklahoma has to offer; we're pretty serious about our travel slant but will also consider history, nature and personality profiles." Circ. 35,000. Pays on acceptance. Publishes ms an average of 3 months after acceptance. Byline given. Buys first serial rights. Submit seasonal/holiday material 1 year in advance "depending on photographic requirements." Simultaneous queries and photocopied submissions OK. "We don't mind letter-quality computer printout submissions at all, provided they are presented in manuscript format, i.e., double spaced and on 8½x11 sheets, or a size close to that. No scrolls, no dot-matrix." Reports in 2 months. Sample copy $2.50; writer's guidelines for #10 SASE.

Nonfiction: Book excerpts (pre-publication only, on Oklahoma topics); photo feature and travel (in Oklahoma). "We are a specialized market; no first-person reminiscences or fashion, memoirs, though just about any topic can be used if given a travel slant." Buys 35-40 mss/year. Query with published clips; no phone queries. Length: 1,000-1,500 words. Pays $150-250.

Photos: High-quality color transparencies, b&w prints. "We are especially interested in developing contacts with photographers who either live in Oklahoma or have shot here. Send samples and price range." Free photo guidelines with SASE. Send photos with ms. Pays $50-100 for b&w and $50-250 for color; reviews 2¼ and 35mm color transparencies. Model releases, identification of subjects, and other information for captions required. Buys one-time rights plus right to use photos for promotional purposes.

Tips: "The best way to become a regular contributor to *Oklahoma Today* is to query us with one or more story ideas, each developed to give us an idea of your proposed slant. We're looking for *lively* writing, writing that doesn't need to be heavily edited and is newspaper style. We have a two-person editorial staff, and freelancers who can write and have done their homework get called again and again. During 1989, *Oklahoma Today* will focus on the centennial celebrations of the 89er land run in central Oklahoma. This has already been assigned; therefore, freelance material needs to be outside central Oklahoma on other topics besides history."

Oregon

CASCADES EAST, 716 NE 4th St., Box 5784, Bend OR 97708. (503)382-0127. Editor: Geoff Hill. 100% freelance written. Prefers to work with published/established writers. Quarterly magazine; 64 pages. For "all ages as long as they are interested in outdoor recreation in central Oregon: fishing, hunting, sight-seeing, hiking, bicycling, mountain climbing, backpacking, rockhounding, skiing, snowmobiling, etc." Circ. 8,000 (distributed throughout area resorts and motels and to subscribers). Pays on publication. Publishes ms an average of 6 months after acceptance. Buys all rights. Byline given. Submit seasonal/holiday material 6 months in advance. Computer printout submissions acceptable; no dot-matrix. Reports in 6 weeks. Sample copy and writer's guidelines for $3.50 and 8½x11 SAE.

Nonfiction: General interest (first person experiences in outdoor central Oregon—with photos, can be dramatic, humorous or factual); historical (for feature, "Little Known Tales from Oregon History", with b&w photos); and personal experience (needed on outdoor subjects: dramatic, humorous or factual). "No articles that are too involved, sight-seeing articles that come from a travel folder, or outdoor articles without the first-person approach." Buys 20-30 unsolicited mss/year. Query. Length: 1,000-3,000 words. Pays 3-10¢/word.

Photos: "Old photos will greatly enhance chances of selling a historical feature. First-person articles need black and white photos, also." Pays $8-20 for b&w; $15-75 for color transparencies. Captions preferred. Buys one-time rights.

Tips: "Submit stories a year or so in advance of publication. We are seasonal and must plan editorials for summer '90 in the spring of '89, etc., in case seasonal photos are needed."

Pennsylvania

ERIE & CHAUTAUQUA MAGAZINE, Charles H. Strong Bldg., 1250 Tower Ln., Erie PA 16505. (814)452-6070. Editor: K.L. Kalvelage. 100% freelance written. Works with a small number of new/unpublished writers each year. Biannual magazine covering the region of Erie (city), Erie County, Crawford County, Warren County, Pennsylvania and Chautauqua County, New York; for upscale readers with above average education and income. Circ. 30,000. Pays 30 days after publication. Buys all rights. Will reassign rights to author upon written request after publication. Computer printout submissions OK; no dot-matrix. Sample copy $2.50; writer's guidelines for SASE.

Nonfiction: Feature articles (usually five per issue) on "key issues affecting our coverage area, lifestyle topics, major projects or events which are of importance to our readership, area history with relevance to life today, preservation and restoration, arts and cultural subjects." Local personality profiles are also needed. Query first. Length: 3,000 words maximum for articles. Payment negotiated. "All material *must* have relevance to our coverage area." Sometimes pays expenses of writers on assignment.

Photos: Color photos for covers by assignment only to local photographer. Will consider 8x10 b&w glossies with stories. Pays $15 per b&w for all rights 30 days after publication. Model releases and captions required.

Columns/Departments: Business, education, social life, arts and culture and travel (within 100-200 miles of Erie). Will consider new departments on basis of resume showing expertise and two sample columns. Length: 750 words maximum.

Tips: "Because ours is a biannual publication with specific departments, most of our material is assigned to local writers. We are always happy to receive submissions, however, if they are well written and relevant to the four-county area we cover."

PENNSYLVANIA, Pennsylvania Magazine Co., Box 576, Camp Hill PA 17011. (717)761-6620. Editor: Albert E. Holliday. Managing Editor: Joan Holliday. 90% freelance written. Bimonthly magazine. Circ. 75,000. Pays on acceptance for assigned articles. Publishes ms an average of 6 months after acceptance. Byline given. Offers 33% kill fee. Buys first North American serial rights or one-time rights. Computer printout submissions acceptable; prefers letter-quality. Reports in 2 weeks on queries; 3 weeks on mss. Sample copy $2.95; writer's guidelines for #10 SASE.

Nonfiction: General interest, historical/nostalgic, photo feature, and travel--all dealing with or related to Pennsylvania. Nothing on Amish topics, hunting or skiing. Buys 50-75 mss/year. Query. Length: 250-2,500 words. Pays $25-250. Sometimes pays the expenses of writers on assignment. All articles must be illustrated.

Photos: Send photocopies of available illustrations with queries. Reviews 35mm and 2¼ color transparencies and 5x7 b&w prints. Pays $10-50 for b&w; $10-100 for color. Captions and identification of subjects required. Buys one-time rights.

Columns/Departments: Panorama—short items about people, unusual events; Made in Pennsylvania-short items about family and individually owned consumer-related businesses.

PENNSYLVANIA HERITAGE, Pennsylvania Historical and Museum Commission, Box 1026, Harrisburg PA 17108-1026. (717)787-1396. Editor: Michael J. O'Malley III. 90% freelance written. Prefers to work with published/established writers. Quarterly magazine covering Pennsylvania history and culture. "*Pennsylvania Heritage* introduces readers to Pennsylvania's rich culture and historic legacy, educates and sensitizes them to the value of preserving that heritage and entertains and involves them in such as way as to ensure that Pennsylvania's past has a future. The magazine is intended for intelligent lay readers." Circ. 9,000. Pays on acceptance. Publishes ms an average of 8-12 months after acceptance. Byline given. Buys all rights. Simultaneous queries, and simultaneous and photocopied submissions OK. Computer printout submissions acceptable; prefers letter-quality. Reports in 3 weeks on queries; 6 weeks on mss. Sample copy for 9x12 SAE and $2.50; free writer's guidelines.

Nonfiction: Art, science, biographies, industry, business, politics, transportation, military, historic preservation, archaeology, photography, etc. No articles which in no way relate to Pennsylvania history or culture. "Our format requires feature-length articles. Manuscripts with illustrations are especially sought for publication." Buys 20-24 mss/year. Query. Length: 2,000-3,500 words. Pays $0-500.

Photos: State availability or send photos with query or ms. Pays $25-100 for color transparencies; $5-10 for b&w photos. Captions and identification of subjects required. Buys one-time rights.

Tips: "We are looking for well-written, interesting material that pertains to any aspect of Pennsylvania history or culture. Potential contributors should realize that, although our articles are popularly styled, they are not light, puffy or breezy; in fact they demand strident documentation and substantiation (sans footnotes). The most frequent mistake made by writers in completing articles for us is making them either too scholarly or too nostalgic. We want material which educates, but also entertains. Authors should make history readable and entertaining."

PHILADELPHIA MAGAZINE, 1500 Walnut St., Philadelphia PA 19102. Editor: Ron Javers. 40% freelance written. Prefers to work with published/established writers; works with a small number of new/unpublished writers each year. Monthly magazine for sophisticated middle- and upper-income people in the Greater Philadelphia/South Jersey area. Circ. 152,272. Pays on acceptance. Publishes ms an average of 2 months after acceptance. Buys first serial rights. Pays 20% kill fee. Byline given. Computer printout submissions acceptable; prefers letter-quality. Reports in 1 month. Writer's guidelines for SASE.

Nonfiction: Bill Tonelli, articles editor. "Articles should have a strong Philadelphia (city and suburbs) focus but should avoid Philadelphia stereotypes—we've seen them all. Submit lifestyles, city survival, profiles of interesting people, business stories, music, the arts, sports and local politics, stressing the topical or unusual. Intelligent, entertaining essays on subjects of specific local interest. No puff pieces. We offer lots of latitude for style." Buys 50 mss/year. Length: 1,000-7,000 words. Pays $100-1,000. Sometimes pays expenses of writers on assignment.

PITTSBURGH MAGAZINE, Metropolitan Pittsburgh Public Broadcasting, Inc., 4802 5th Ave., Pittsburgh PA 15213. (412)622-1360. Editor-in-Chief: Bruce VanWyngarden. 60% freelance written. Prefers to work with published/established writers; works with a small number of new/unpublished writers each year. "The magazine is purchased on newsstands and by subscription and is given to those who contribute $35 or more a year to public TV in western Pennsylvania." Circ. 65,000. Pays on publication. Publishes ms an average of 2 months after acceptance. Buys first North American serial rights and second serial (reprint) rights. Pays kill fee. Byline given. Submit seasonal/holiday material 6 months in advance. Query for electronic submissions. Computer printout submissions acceptable; prefers letter-quality. Reports in 2 months. Publishes ms an average of 2 months after acceptance. Sample copy $2; free writer's guidelines.

Nonfiction: Expose, lifestyle, sports, informational, service, interview, nostalgia and profile. Query or send complete ms. Length: 2,500 words. Pays $50-500. Query for photos. Model releases required. Sometimes pays the expenses of writers on assignment.

Columns/Departments: Art, books, films, dining, health, sports and theatre. "All must relate to Pittsburgh or western Pennsylvania."

Rhode Island

‡**RHODE ISLAND MONTHLY**, 60 Branch Ave., Providence RI 02904. (401)421-2552. Editor: Dan Kaplan. Managing Editor: Vicki Sanders. 50% freelance written. Monthly magazine on Rhode Island living. Estab. 1988. Circ. 15,000. Pays on publication. Publishes ms an average of 2 months after acceptance. Byline given. Kill fee varies. Buys first rights. Submit seasonal/holiday material 4 months in advance. Query for electronic submissions. Computer printout submissions OK; prefers letter-quality. Reports in 1 month. Sample copy $1.95 with 8x½x11 SAE with $1 postage.

Nonfiction: Book exerpts, expose, photo feature. "We do not want material unrelated to Rhode Island." Buys 48 mss/year. Query with or without published clips, or send complete ms. Length: 200-6,000 words. Pays $100-800. Sometimes pays expenses of writers on assignment.

Photos: State availability of photos with submission. Reviews contact sheets and 5x7 prints. Offers $50-200. Captions, model releases and identification of subjects required. Buys one-time rights.

Tennessee

‡**CHATTANOOGA LIFE & LEISURE**, Metro Publishing, 1085 Bailey Ave., Chattanooga TN 37404. (615)629-5375. Editor: Mark Northern. Managing Editor: Ted Betts. 90% freelance written. Monthly magazine on the Chattanooga region. Circ. 10,000. Pays on publication. Byline given. Offers 50% kill fee. Buys first North American serial rights or second serial (reprint) rights. Submit seasonal/holiday material 1 yearin advance. Query for electronic submissions. Computer printout submissions OK. Sample copy $1.95; writer's guidelines for SASE.

Nonfiction: Book excerpts, expose, general interest, historical, interview/profile and photo feature. Buys 120 mss/year. Query with or without published clips. Length: 150-3,000 words. Pays $20-200.

Photos: Send photos with submission. Reviews b&w contact sheets, 35mm or larger transparencies, and any size color prints. Offers $20 per photo. Captions, model releases and identification of subjects required. Buys one-time rights.

Tips: "Contributors must know their subjects. We expect all material to be in-depth and about a local subject. We present complex subjects in a clear manner so our readers can see the entire picture in perspective. I am most satisfied when my readers stop me in the street and say 'I read such-and-such article. I have lived here all my life and I didn't know that.' "

MEMPHIS, MM Corporation, Box 256, Memphis TN 38101. (901)521-9000. Editor: Larry Conley. 60% freelance written. Works with a small number of new/unpublished writers. Circ. 26,500. Pays on publication. Publishes ms an average of 3 months after acceptance. Byline given. Buys first North American serial rights. Pays $35-100 kill fee. Simultaneous, photocopied, and previously published submissions OK. Computer printout submissions acceptable; prefers letter-quality. Reports in 6 weeks. Sample copy for 9x12 SAE and $2.50 postage; writer's guidelines for SASE.

Nonfiction: Expose, general interest, historical, how-to, humor, interview and profile. "Virtually all our material has strong mid-South connections." Buys 25 freelance mss/year. Query or submit complete ms or published clips. Length: 1,500-5,000 words. Pays $100-1,000. Sometimes pays expenses of writers on assignment.

Tips: "The kinds of manuscripts we most need have a sense of story (i.e., plot, suspense, character), an abundance of evocative images to bring that story alive, and a sensitivity to issues at work in Memphis. The most frequent mistakes made by writers in completing an article for us are lack of focus, lack of organization, factual gaps and failure to capture the magazine's style. Tough investigative pieces would be especially welcomed."

For explanation of symbols, see the Key to Symbols and Abbreviations on Page 5.

Texas

AUSTIN MAGAZINE, American Publishing Corp., Box 4368, Austin TX 78765. (512)339-9955. Managing Editor: Laura Tuma. 60% freelance written. "Hybrid city/business magazine published for Chamber of Commerce. Strong local angle required." Circ. 17,500. Pays on publication. Publishes ms an average of 3 months after acceptance. Byline given. Offers 25% kill fee. Buys first North American serial rights. Submit seasonal/holiday material 6 months in advance. Query for electronic submissions. Computer printout submissions OK. Reports in 1 month. Sample copy $2.25.

Nonfiction: General interest, interview/profile, photo feature and travel. Buys 40-50 mss/year. Query with published clips. Length: 750-2,500 words. Pays 10¢/word. Sometimes pays the expenses of writers on assignment.

Photos: State availability of photos with submission. Reviews 5x7 prints. Offers $15-50 per photo. Captions, model releases and identification of subjects required. Buys one-time rights.

Tips: "I appreciate clear, well-thought-out queries, with previously published clips to review. Also, since we are strictly a local magazine, some knowledge of Austin is very helpful. Our BusinessLine section uses four to six short (750 words, approximately) articles each month. Articles can be business tips, profiles on successful local business leaders or other related topics."

"D" MAGAZINE, Southwest Media Corporation, Suite 1200, 3988 N. Central Expressway, Dallas TX 75204. (214)827-5000. Editor: Ruth Miller Fitzgibbons. 25% freelance written. Monthly magazine. "We are a general interest magazine with emphasis on events occuring in Dallas." Circ. 100,000. Pays on acceptance. Publishes ms an average of 2 months after acceptance. Byline given. Offers 25% kill fee. Buys first North American serial rights. Submit seasonal/holiday material 2 months in advance. Query for electronic submissions. Computer printout submissions OK; prefers letter-quality. Reports in 1 month. Sample copy $2.50 with SAE and 5 first class stamps; free writer's guidelines.

Nonfiction: Book excerpts, essays, expose, general interest, historical/nostalgic, how-to, humor, interview/profile and travel. Buys 20-30 mss/year. Query with published clips. Length: 1,000-5,000 words. Pays $75-750 for assigned articles; pays $50-500 for unsolicited articles. Pays expenses of writers on assignment.

Photos: State availability of photos with submission. Reviews transparencies and 35mm prints. Offers $50-75 per photo. Captions required. Buys one-time rights.

Columns/Departments: Business; Politics; Travel; and Relationships. Query with published clips or send complete ms. Length: 1,500-2,000 words. Pays $250-350.

Tips: "Tell us something about our city that we have not written about. We realize that is very difficult for someone outside of Dallas to do—that's why 90% of our magazine is written by people who live in the North Texas area."

DALLAS LIFE MAGAZINE, Sunday Magazine of *The Dallas Morning News*, Belo Corporation, Communications Center, Dallas TX 75265. (214)745-8432. Editor: Melissa Houtte. Weekly magazine. "We are a lively, topical, sometimes controversial city magazine devoted to informing, enlightening and entertaining our urban Sunbelt readers with material which is specifically relevant to Dallas lifestyles and interests." Pays on acceptance. Byline given. Buys first North American serial rights or simultaneous rights. Simultaneous queries and submissions OK ("if not competitive in our area"). Computer printout submissions acceptable; prefers letter-quality. Reports in 1 month on queries; 6 weeks on mss.

Nonfiction: General interest; humor (short); interview/profile. "All material must, repeat *must*, have a Dallas metropolitan area frame of reference." Special issues include: spring and fall home furnishings theme. Buys 5-10 unsolicited mss/year. Query with published clips or send complete ms. Length: 1,200-3,000 words. Pays $200-650.

‡DENTON TODAY MAGAZINE, Community Life Publications, Inc., Suite #304, Denton TX 76201. (817)566-3464. Editor: Jonathan B. Cott. 100% freelance written. Quarterly magazine of news/entertainment in north Texas. Circ. 5,000. Pays on publication. Publishes ms an average of 1 month after accetpance. Byline given. Negotiable kill fee. Buys first North American serial rights, second serial (reprint) rights or makes work-for-hire assignments. Submit seasonal/holiday material 2 months in advance. Previously published submissions OK. Computer printout submissions OK; no dot-matrix. Reports in 2 weeks. Sample copy $1.50 with $2 postage; writer's guidelines for SASE.

Nonfiction: Essays, general interest, historical/nostalgic, how-to, humor, inspirational, interview/profile, new product, personal experience, photo feature. No religious or controversial articles. Buys 40 mss/year. Send complete ms. Length: 500-3,000. Pays $25-210 for assigned articles; $25-150 for unsolicited articles. Sometimes pays expenses of writers on assignment.

Photos: Send photos with submission. Offers $5-50 per photo. Captions, model releases and identification of subjects required. Buys one-time rights.

Columns/Departments: Business/economy; Government/services; Education; Health; Arts/entertainment. All with north Texas, positive slant. Buys 40 mss/year. Send complete ms. Length: 500-750 words. Pays $25-50.

Fiction: Historical, humorous, mainstream, slice-of-life vignettes. Buys 5 mss/year. Send complete ms. Length: 1,000-3,000 words. Pays $50-210.

EL PASO MAGAZINE, El Paso Chamber of Commerce, 10 Civic Center Plaza, El Paso TX 79901. (915)534-0527. Executive Editor: Brenda Castaneda. 75% freelance written. Prefers to work with published/established writers; works with a small number of new/unpublished writers each year. Monthly magazine that "takes a positive look at El Paso people and businesses. Readers are owners and managers of El Paso businesses." Circ. 4,000. Pays on publication. Publishes ms an average of 3 months after acceptance. Byline given. Buys first North American serial rights. Submit seasonal/holiday material 3 months in advance. Simultaneous queries, and simultaneous and photocopied submissions OK. Computer printout submissions acceptable; prefers letter-quality. Reports in 2 months. Free sample copy and writer's guidelines.

Nonfiction: General interest, business, historical/nostalgic, interview/profile and photo feature. Query with published clips. Length: 1,000-2,500 words. Pay varies.

Photos: Send photos with ms. Pays $10/photo. Captions, model releases and identification of subjects required. Buys one-time rights.

Tips: "An article for *El Paso Magazine* must talk about an area business and its successes. *El Paso Magazine* will rely more on experienced writers in 1989. Writers must know El Paso."

INNER-VIEW, The Only Newsmagazine of Houston's Innercity, Inner-View Publishing Co., Inc., Box 66156, Houston TX 77266. (713)523-NEWS. Editor: Kit van Cleave. 20% freelance written. Works with small number of new/unpublished writers each year, and is eager to work with new/unpublished writers. City's only monthly tabloid covering those who live or work inside Loop 610 (half of Houston). "We only print that material which has to do with the lives or careers of those who live and work in our half of Houston. We want to let those writers who may be new in town or are coming here know that we are here and will work with them." Circ. 35,000. Pays on publication. Publishes ms an average of 2 months after acceptance. Byline given. Buys first North American serial rights, first rights or one-time rights. Submit seasonal/holiday material 1 month in advance. Simultaneous and photocopied submissions OK. Computer printout submissions acceptable; no dot-matrix. Reports in 1 month. Sample copy for 9x12 SAE with 7 first class stamps.

Nonfiction: Interview/profile and movie reviews. Plans special holiday issues. Nothing that is "too general to have anything to do with our market; life in New England, for example." Query. Length: 1-2 pages. Pays $20-50.

Photos: State availability of photos with submission. Reviews 8x10 or 5x7 prints. Offers no additional payment for photos accepted with ms. Captions required. Buys one-time rights.

Columns/Departments: Movie Reviews (Innercity, Houston TX; the reviewers must live or work in this area to know what's going on so they can see the film from innercity perspective). Buys 50 mss/year. Query. Length: 1-2 pages. "We pay tickets or provide press passes."

Tips: "Our publication is part of our new concept of providing a 'small town' community newspaper as part of a major urban area. We are in our ninth year and very successful because we talk about what people in our half of Houston want to know about, and we get advertising from those businesses which are in our market area. Writers should be very familiar with our market area. Our area covers four of the five wealthiest residential areas in Houston, plus all the arts headquarters, plus all the universities in Houston. It's a very upscale area, and 40% of all Houston workers still work in the downtown area, which is the heart of our market area."

SAN ANGELO MAGAZINE, San Angelo Standard Inc., 34 W. Harris, San Angelo TX 76903. (915)653-1221. Editor: Soren W. Nielsen. Executive Editor: Kandis Gatewood. 25% freelance written. Works with a small number of new/unpublished writers each year. Quarterly magazine about San Angelo, Texas, and immediate area. "San Angelo magazine is a city magazine, offering a wide variety of features and profiles." Circ. 7,000. Pays on publication. Publishes ms an average of 3-5 months after acceptance. Byline given. Buys first serial rights. Submit seasonal/holiday material 4 months in advance. Query for electronic submissions.

> 66 *Good writers know how to write a clear sentence, a properly developed paragraph, and an organized article. The best writers also have a sense of style: They not only say things clearly, they say them memorably.* 99
>
> —*Ed Weathers*,
> **Memphis Magazine**

Computer printout submissions acceptable; prefers letter-quality. Reports in 1 month. Sample copy for 9x11 SASE and 4 first class stamps; writer's guidelines for SASE.
Nonfiction: General interest, historical/nostalgic, interview/profile and travel. General interest and historical articles of San Angelo area. No articles not applicable to San Angelo area. Buys 5-6 mss/year. Query with published clips. Pays $25-100. Rarely pays expenses of writers on assignment.
Tips: "Writer should note that first-person articles are not used."

Vermont

VERMONT LIFE MAGAZINE, 61 Elm St., Montpelier VT 05602. (802)828-3241. Editor-in-Chief: Thomas K. Slayton. 90% freelance written. Prefers to work with published/established writers. Quarterly magazine. Circ. 120,000. Publishes ms an average of 9 months after acceptance. Byline given. Offers kill fee. Buys first serial rights. Submit seasonal/holiday material 1 year in advance. Simultaneous queries, and simultaneous, photocopied, and previously published submissions OK. Computer printout submissions acceptable; prefers letter-quality. Reports in 1 month. Writer's guidelines on request.
Nonfiction: Wants articles on today's Vermont, those which portray a typical or, if possible, unique aspect of the state or its people. Style should be literate, clear and concise. Subtle humor favored. No Vermont dialect attempts as in "Ayup", outsider's view on visiting Vermont, or "Vermont cliches"—maple syrup, town meetings or stereotyped natives. Buys 60 mss/year. Query by letter essential. Length: 1,500 words average. Pays 20¢/word. Seldom pays expenses of writers on assignment.
Photos: Buys photographs with mss; buys seasonal photographs alone. Prefers b&w contact sheets to look at first on assigned material. Color submissions must be 4x5 or 35mm transparencies. Rates on acceptance: $75-150 inside, color; $200 for cover. Gives assignments but only with experienced photographers. Query in writing. Captions, model releases, and identification of subjects required. Buys one-time rights, but often negotiates for re-use rights.
Tips: "Writers who read our magazine are given more consideration because they understand that we want authentic articles about Vermont. If a writer has a genuine working knowledge of Vermont, his or her work usually shows it. Vermont is changing and there is much concern here about what this state will be like in years ahead. It is a beautiful, environmentally sound place now and the vast majority of residents want to keep it so. Articles reflecting such concerns in an intelligent, authoritative, non-hysterical way will be given very careful consideration. The growth of tourism makes *Vermont Life* interested in intelligent articles about specific places in Vermont, their history and attractions to the traveling public."

VERMONT VANGUARD PRESS, Statewide Weekly, Vanguard Publishing, 87 College St., Burlington VT 05401. (802)864-0506. Managing Editor: Peter Freyne. Arts Editor: Pamela Polston. 70% freelance written. Works with a small number of new/unpublished writers each year. A weekly alternative newspaper, locally oriented, covering Vermont politics, environment, arts, etc. Circ. 25,000. Pays on publication. Byline given. Offers 50% kill fee only after written acceptance. Buys first serial rights. Submit seasonal/holiday material 1 month in advance. Simultaneous queries, and simultaneous, photocopied, and previously published submissions OK. Query for electronic submissions. Computer printout submissions acceptable; no dot-matrix. Reports in 1 month.
Nonfiction: Expose and humor. Articles should have a Vermont angle. Buys about 12 mss/year. Query with published clips. Length: 500-2,500 words. Pays $20-100.
Photos: Glenn Russell, photo editor. State availability of photos. Pays $10-20 for b&w contact sheets and negatives. Captions, model releases and identification of subjects required. Buys one-time rights.
Tips: "Short news stories are most open to freelancers. Knowledge of Vermont politics is essential."

Virginia

NORTHERN VIRGINIAN MAGAZINE, 135 Park St., Box 1177, Vienna VA 22180. (703)938-0666. Editor: Goodie Holden. 80% freelance written. Bimonthly magazine concerning the five counties of northern Virginia. Pays first of month following publication. Publishes ms an average of 3 months after acceptance. Byline given. Buys first serial rights and second serial (reprint) rights. Submit seasonal/holiday material 3 months in advance. Simultaneous queries, and simultaneous, photocopied and previously published submissions OK. Computer printout submissions acceptable. "Send photocopy of manuscript as we can't guarantee its return." Reports in 2 weeks on queries; 1 month on mss. Sample copy $1; free writer's guidelines.
Nonfiction: "Freelance manuscripts welcomed on speculation. We are particularly interested in articles about or related to northern Virginia." Buys 75 mss/year. Query or send complete ms. Length: 2,500 words minimum. Pays 1½¢/word.
Photos: Prefers good, clear b&w glossy photos. Pays $5/photo or photo credit line. Captions, model releases, and identification of subjects required.
Tips: Longer articles preferred, minimum 2,500 words. History articles accepted only if unique.

THE ROANOKER, Leisure Publishing Co., 3424 Brambleton Ave., Box 12567, Roanoke VA 24026. (703)989-6138. Editor: Kurt Rheinheimer. 75% freelance written. Works with a small number of new/unpublished writers each year. Monthly magazine covering people and events of Western Virginia. "*The Roanoker* is a general interest city magazine edited for the people of Roanoke, Virginia, and the surrounding area. Our readers are primarily upper-income, well-educated professionals between the ages of 35 and 60. Coverage ranges from hard news and consumer information to restaurant reviews and local history." Circ. 14,000. Pays on publication. Publishes ms an average of 4 months after acceptance. Byline given. Buys all rights; makes work-for-hire assignments. Submit seasonal/holiday material 4 months in advance. Simultaneous queries OK. Computer printout submissions acceptable. Reports in 2 months. Sample copy for $2 and 9x12 SAE with $2 postage.
Nonfiction: Expose; historical/nostalgic; how-to (live better in western Virginia); interview/profile (of well-known area personalities); photo feature; and travel (Virginia and surrounding states). "We are attempting to broaden our base and provide more and more coverage of western Virginia, i.e., that part of the state west of Roanoke. We place special emphasis on consumer-related issues and how-to articles." Periodic special sections on fashion, real estate, media, banking, investing. Buys 100 mss/year. Query with published clips or send complete ms. Length: 3,000 words maximum. Pays $35-200. Sometimes pays expenses of writers on assignment.
Photos: Send photos with ms. Reviews color transparencies. Pays $5-10 for 5x7 or 8x10 b&w prints; $10 maximum for 5x7 or 8x10 color prints. Captions and model releases required. Rights purchased vary.
Tips: "We will look to include more area history pieces in 1988. It helps if freelancer lives in the area. The most frequent mistake made by writers in completing an article for us is not having enough Roanoke area focus: use of area experts, sources, slants, etc."

‡**THE VIRGINIAN**, Shenandoah Valley Magazine Corp., Box 8, New Hope VA 24469. (703)885-0388. Manuscript Editor: Hunter S. Pierce IV. Bimonthly magazine. 10% freelance written. Circ. 20,000. Pays on publication. Byline given. Buys first-time and other rights. Submit seasonal/holiday material 4 months in advance. Simultaneous queries, and simultaneous and photocopied submissions OK. Reports in 1 month. Sample copy $4.
Nonfiction: Book excerpts, general interest, historical/nostalgic, food, how-to, humor, inspirational, interview/profile, personal experience, photo feature and travel. Buys 20 mss/year. "Don't send unless there is a direct relation to Virginians and Virginia." Query with or without published clips, or send complete ms. Length: 1,000-1,500 words. Pays negotiable rate.
Photos: State availability of photos. Buys one-time rights.
Tips: "Be familiar enough with the magazine to know the tone and character of the feature articles."

Washington

THE SEATTLE WEEKLY, Sasquatch Publishing, 1931 2nd Ave., Seattle WA 98101. (206)441-5555. Editor: David Brewster. 30% freelance written. Eager to work with new/unpublished writers, especially those in the region. Weekly tabloid covering arts, politics, food, business, sports and books with local and regional emphasis. Circ. 30,000. Pays 3 weeks after publication. Publishes ms an average of 1 month after acceptance. Byline given. Offers variable kill fee. Buys first North American serial rights. Submit seasonal/holiday material 2 months in advance. Simultaneous queries OK. Computer printout submissions acceptable; prefers letter-quality. Reports in 1 month. Sample copy 75¢; writer's guidelines for #10 SASE.
Nonfiction: Book excerpts; expose; general interest; historical/nostalgic (Northwest); how-to (related to food and health); humor; interview/profile; opinion; travel; and arts-related essays. Buys 25 cover stories/year. Query with resume and published clips. Length: 700-4,000 words. Pays $75-800. Sometimes pays the expenses of writers on assignment.
Fiction: Annual Holiday Short Story Contest. Writers must be residents of the state of Washington. "We prefer that the stories have Northwest locales."
Tips: "The *Weekly* publishes stories on Northwest politics and art, usually written by regional and local writers, for a mostly upscale, urban audience; writing is high quality magazine style. We may decide to publish a new regional magazine, either quarterly or bi-monthly, for a slightly different audience."

WASHINGTON, The Evergreen State Magazine, Evergreen Publishing Co., 901 Lenora, Seattle WA 98121. Editor/Publisher: Kenneth A. Gouldthorpe. Executive Editor: Knute O. Berger. Managing Editor: David W. Fuller. 70% freelance written. A seven-times-per-year magazine covering all facets of life in Washington for an in-state audience. Circ. 72,000. Pays on acceptance for assigned stories; on publication for "on spec" material. Publishes ms an average of 6 months after acceptance. Byline given. Offers 20% kill fee on accepted stories. Submit seasonal/holiday material 6 months in advance. Query for electronic submissions. Computer printout submissions acceptable, but leave margins and double-space; prefers letter-quality. Reports in 1 month on queries; 6 weeks on mss. Sample copy for $3.50; free writer's guidelines.

Nonfiction: Book excerpts (unpublished Washington-related); general interest; historical/nostalgic; humor; interview/profile; personal experience; photo feature; and travel. "Evergreen Publishing Company undertakes book and one-shot publication projects. Washington state ideas encouraged. No political, expose, reviews, or anything not pertaining to Washington or Washingtonians." Query with published clips. Length: features, 1,500-2,500 words; sidebars, 200-600 words. Pays $350-750. Sometimes pays expenses of writers on assignment.

Photos: Carrie Seglin, photo editor. Large format. State availability of photos with query or send photos with query. Pays $50-250 for b&w; $125-325 for 35mm color slides. Captions, model releases, and identification of subjects required. Buys one-time rights.

Columns/Departments: As Others See Us (how Washington is viewed by outsiders); Interiors (homes, architecture, decorating, interiors); State of Mind (thoughts and perspectives on the Evergreen State); Washington Post (our letters column); The Attic (our back page potpourri of pictures, curios etc.); Our Town (where we live, from backwoods to small towns and places you've never seen before); Journeys End (inns, lodges, bed and breakfast hideaways); Players (sports and athletes, games and gamesmen); Statewatch (a round-up from all corners: people, quotes and anecdotes from the lighter side of life); Enterprise (business and commerce); Wildside (wildlife, nature); Open Air (outdoors and outdoor activities, from backpacking to picnics, from hang gliding to kite flying); Wordsmith (books, writers and wordsmithing); Repasts (great dining, from grand souffles to small cafes); and Almanac (a compendium of history, weather, wit and wisdom). Buys 75 mss/year. Query with published clips. Length: 600-1,200 words. Pays $150-250.

Fillers: Clippings, jokes, gags, anecdotes, short humor and newsbreaks. Length: 50-250 words. Pays $25-100. Must be Washington related.

Tips: "All areas are open, but the writer has a better chance of breaking in at our publication with short articles and fillers since we buy more departmental material. Our articles emphasize people—sometimes writers get sidetracked. We're also looking for original thinking, not tired approaches."

Wisconsin

MADISON MAGAZINE, Box 1604, Madison WI 53701. Editor: James Selk. 50% freelance written. Prefers to work with published/established writers. Monthly magazine; 100-150 pages. General city magazine aimed at upscale audience. Circ. 24,000. Pays on publication. Publishes ms an average of 2 months after acceptance. Buys all rights. Reports on material accepted for publication 10 days after acceptance. Returns rejected material immediately. Query. Computer printout submissions acceptable; prefers letter-quality. Sample copy $3.

Nonfiction: General human interest articles with strong local angles. Buys 100 mss/year. Length: 1,000-5,000 words. Pays $25-500. Pays the expenses of writers on assignment.

Photos: Offers no additional payment for b&w photos used with mss. Captions required.

WISCONSIN, *The Milwaukee Journal Magazine*, Box 661, Milwaukee WI 53201. (414)224-2341. Editor: Alan Borsuk. 20% freelance written. Prefers to work with published/established writers. Weekly general interest magazine appealing to readers living in Wisconsin. Circ. 520,000. Pays on publication. Publishes ms an average of 4 months after acceptance. Byline given. Buys first serial rights. Submit seasonal/holiday material 4 months in advance. Simultaneous queries OK. Computer printout submissions acceptable; prefers letter-quality. Reports in 1 month on queries; 6 months on mss. Sample copy and writer's guidelines for SASE.

Nonfiction: Expose, general interest, humor, interview/profile, opinion, personal experience and photo feature. No nostalgic reminiscences. Buys 50 mss/year. Query. Length: 150-2,000 words. Pays $75-500. Sometimes pays expenses of writers on assignment.

Photos: State availability of photos.

Columns/Departments: Opinion, Humor and Essays. Buys 50 mss/year. Query. Length: 150-300 words. Pays $100-200.

Tips: "We are primarily Wisconsin-oriented and are becoming more news-oriented."

WISCONSIN TRAILS, Box 5650, Madison WI 53705. (608)231-2444. Managing Editor: Geri Nixon. 70% freelance written. Prefers to work with published/established writers; works with a small number of new/unpublished writers each year. Bimonthly magazine for readers interested in Wisconsin; its contemporary issues, personalities, recreation, history, natural beauty; and the arts. Circ. 40,000. Buys first serial rights, and one-time rights sometimes. Pays on publication. Submit seasonal material at least 1 year in advance. Publishes ms an average of 6 months after acceptance. Byline given. Photocopied submissions OK. Computer printout submissions acceptable; prefers letter-quality. Reports in 1 month. Writer's guidelines for #10 SASE.

Nonfiction: "Our articles focus on some aspect of Wisconsin life; an interesting town or event, a person or industry, history or the arts and especially outdoor recreation. We do not use first-person essays or biographies about people who were born in Wisconsin but made their fortunes elsewhere. No poetry. No articles that are too local for our regional audience, or articles about obvious places to visit in Wisconsin. We need more articles about the new and little-known." Buys 3 unsolicited mss/year. Query or send outline. Length: 1,000-3,000 words. Pays $100-300 (negotiable), depending on assignment length and quality. Sometimes pays expenses of writers on assignment.

Photos: Purchased with or without mss or on assignment. Prefers 2¼" or larger transparencies, 35mm OK. Color photos usually illustrate an activity, event, region or striking scenery. Prefer photos with people in scenery. B&w photos usually illustrate a given article. Pays $25 each for b&w on publication. Pays $50-75 for inside color; $100-200 for covers. Captions preferred.

Tips: "We're looking for active articles about people, places, events, and outdoor adventures in Wisconsin. We want to publish one in-depth article of state-wide interest or concern per issue, and several short (1,000-word) articles about short trips, recreational opportunities, restaurants, inns, and cultural activities. We will be looking for more articles about out-of-the-way places in Wisconsin that are exceptional in some way."

Puerto Rico

WALKING TOURS OF SAN JUAN & RESTAURANT MENU GUIDE, Caribbean World Communications, Inc., First Federal Building, Office 301, Santurce PR 00909. (809)722-1767. Editor: Alfred Dinhofer. Managing Editor: Carmen Merino. 5% freelance written. Prefers to work with published/established writers. Magazine published 2 times/year (January and July). Circ. 22,000. Pays on publication. Publishes ms an average of 3 months after acceptance. Byline given. Buys one-time rights. Computer printout submissions acceptable. Reports in 1 month. Sample copy $3 with 9x12 SAE and $2 postage.

Nonfiction: Historical/nostalgic. "We are seeking historically based articles on San Juan: any aspect of Spanish colonial culture, art, architecture, etc. We must have sources—in fact, we will publish source material at the end of each article for reader reference." Buys 4 mss/year. Query. Length: 2,000-3,000 words. Pays $150. Sometimes pays the expenses of writers on assignment.

Tips: "A new addition is a sample of menus of Puerto Rico's best restaurants."

Canada

CANADIAN GEOGRAPHIC, 39 McArthur Ave., Ottawa, Ontario K1L 8L7 Canada. Publisher: J. Keith Fraser. Editor: Ross W. Smith. Managing Editor: Ian Darragh. 90% freelance written. Works with a small number of new/unpublished writers each year. Circ. 190,000. Bimonthly magazine. Pays on acceptance. Publishes ms an average of 3 months after acceptance. Buys first Canadian rights; interested only in first-time publication. Computer printout submissions acceptable; prefers letter-quality. Writer's guidelines on request.

Nonfiction: Buys authoritative geographical articles, in the broad geographical sense, written for the average person, not for a scientific audience. Predominantly Canadian subjects by Canadian authors. Buys 30-45 mss/year. Always query first. Length: 1,500-3,000 words. Pays 30¢/word minimum. Usual payment for articles $500-1,500 and up. Higher fees reserved for commissioned articles on which copyright remains with publisher unless otherwise agreed. Sometimes pays the expenses of writers on assignment.

Photos: Reviews 35mm slides, 2¼ transparencies or 8x10 glossies. Pays $60-300 for color photos, depending on published size.

‡**THE MIRROR**, The Mirror-Northern Report, Box 269, High Prairie, Alberta T0G 0X0 Canada. (403)523-3706. 25% freelance written. Weekly tabloid of northern Alberta news and features. Estab. 1987. Circ. 2,000. Pays on publication. Publishes ms an average of 2 months after acceptance. Byline given. Publication not copyrighted. Buys one-time rights. Simultaneous, photocopied and previously published submissions OK. Computer printout submissions OK; prefers letter-quality. Reports in 2 weeks on queries; 1 month on mss.

Nonfiction: Buys 25 mss/year. Send complete ms. Length: 2,000 words maximum. Pays 1¢/word. Sometimes pays expenses of writers on assignment.

Photos: Send photos with submission. Reviews prints. Offers no additional payment for photos accepted with ms. Captions and identification of subjects required. Buys one-time rights.

Fiction: Buys 50 mss/year. Send complete ms. Length: 1,500 words.

Poetry: Traditional. Buys 10 poems/year.

‡**OTTAWA MAGAZINE**, Ottawa Magazine Inc., 192 Bank St., Ottawa, Ontario K2P 1W8 Canada. (613)234-7751. Editor: Louis Valenzuela. 50% freelance written. Prefers to work with published/established writers. Monthly magazine covering life in Ottawa and environs. "*Ottawa Magazine* reflects the interest and lifestyles of its readers who tend to be married, ages 35-55, upwardly mobile and suburban." Circ. 50,000. Pays on acceptance. Publishes ms an average of 6 months after acceptance. Byline given. "Kill fee depends on agreed-upon fee; very seldom used." Buys first North American serial rights and second serial (reprint) rights. Simultaneous queries, and photocopied and previously published submissions OK. Computer printout

submissions acceptable. Reports in 2 months. Sample copy $1.

Nonfiction: Book excerpts (by local authors or about regional issues); expose (federal or regional government, education); general interest; interview/profile (on Ottawans who have established national or international reputations); photo feature (for recurring section called Freezeframe); and travel (recent examples are Brazil, Trinidad & Tobago, Copenhagen). "No articles better suited to a national or special interest publication." Buys 100 mss/year. Query with published clips. Length: 2,000-3,500 words. Pays $400-750 Canadian.

Tips: "A phone call to our associate editor is the best way to assure that queries receive prompt attention. Once a query interests me the writer is assigned a detailed 'treatment' of the proposed piece which is used to determine viability of story. We will be concentrating on more issue-type stories with good, solid fact-researched base, also doing more fluffy pieces—60 great reasons Ottawa is a great city—that sort of stuff. Harder for out-of-town writers to furnish. The writer should strive to inject a personal style and avoid newspaper style reportage. *Ottawa Magazine* also doesn't stoop to boosterism and points out the bad along with the good."

‡PASSION MAGAZINE, Titan Publishing Inc., Unit 7, 291 Woodlawn Rd. W., Box 1747, Guelph Ontario N1H 7A1 Canada. (519)763-5058. Editor: Karen Mantel. 50% freelance written. Quarterly magazine on entertainment and dining in the Kitchener-Waterloo, Guelph and Cambridge, Ontario areas. Estab. 1987. Circ. 25,000. Pays on publication. Publishes ms an average of 2 months after acceptance. Byline given. Buy one-time rights. Submit seasonal/holiday material 3 months in advance. Simultaneous and photocopied submissions OK. Computer printout submissions OK; prefers letter-quality. Reports in 6 weeks. Sample copy for 8x10 SAE with Canadian postage or international reply coupon.

Nonfiction: Interview/profile, restaurant features. Buys 20 mss/year. Query with published clips. Length: 150-1,000 words. Pays $20-100.

Photos: State availability of photos with submission. Reviews 5x7 prints. Offers $5/photo. Identification of subjects required. Buys one-time rights.

Tips: "There is a limited opportunity for freelancers outside of the region because the editorial is centered on a particular area."

TORONTO LIFE, 59 Front St. E., Toronto, Ontario M5E 1B3 Canada. (416)364-3333. Editor: Marq de Villiers. 95% freelance written. Prefers to work with published/established writers. Monthly magazine emphasizing local issues and social trends, short humor/satire, and service features for upper income, well educated and, for the most part, young Torontonians. Uses some fiction. Pays on acceptance. Publishes ms an average of 3-4 months after acceptance. Byline given. Buys first North American serial rights. Pays 50% kill fee "for commissioned articles only." Phone queries OK. Reports in 3 weeks. Sample copy $2.50 with SAE and IRCs.

Nonfiction: Uses most types of articles. Buys 17 mss/issue. Query with published clips. Buys about 40 unsolicited mss/year. Length: 1,000-5,000 words. Pays $800-3,000.

Photos: State availability of photos. Uses good color transparencies and clear, crisp b&w prints. Seldom uses submitted photos. Captions and model release required.

Columns/Departments: "We run about five columns an issue. They are all freelanced, though most are from regular contributors. They are mostly local in concern and cover politics, money, fine art, performing arts, movies and sports." Length: 1,800 words. Pays $1,500.

WESTERN CANADA OUTDOORS, McIntosh Publishing Company, Ltd., 1132-98th St., Box 430, North Battleford, Saskatchewan S9A 2Y5 Canada. (306)445-4401. Contact: Stanley Nowakowski. 15% freelance written. Bimonthly tabloid covering fish and wildlife. Circ. 42,220. Pays on publication. Publishes ms an average of 2 months after acceptance. Byline given. Buys one-time rights. Submit seasonal/holiday material 1 month in advance. Simultaneous submissions OK. Computer printout submissions OK; prefers letter-quality. Reports in 3 weeks.

Nonfiction: Expose, general interest, humor, personal experience and photo feature. Buys 4 mss/year. Query with or without published clips, or send complete ms. Length: 200-800 words. Pays $25-50 for assigned articles. Sometimes pays the expenses of writers on assignment.

Photos: State availability of photos with submission. Reviews contact sheets. Offers $10-25 per photo. Captions and identification of subjects required. Buys one-time rights.

Columns/Departments: Buys 18 mss/year. Query. Length: 700-800 words. Pays $25-50.

Fillers: Anecdotes. Buys 6/year.

WESTERN PEOPLE, Supplement to the Western Producer, Western Producer Publications, Box 2500, Saskatoon, Saskatchewan S7K 2C4 Canada. (306)665-3500. Managing Editor: Liz Delahey. Weekly farm newspaper supplement covering rural Western Canada. "Our magazine reflects the life and people of rural Western Canada both in the present and historically." Circ. 135,000. Pays on acceptance. Publishes ms an average of 6 months after acceptance. Byline given. Buys first rights. Submit seasonal/holiday material 3 months in advance. Reports in 2 weeks on queries; 1 month on mss. Sample copy for 9x12 SAE; writer's guidelines for SAE.

Nonfiction: General interest, historical/nostalgic, humor, interview/profile, personal experience and photo feature. Buys 450 mss/year. Send complete ms. Length: 500-2,500 words. Pays $50-250.

Photos: Send photos with submission. Reviews transparencies and prints. Offers $5-25 per photo. Captions and identification of subjects required. Buys one-time rights.

Fiction: Adventure, historical, humorous, mainstream, mystery, novel excerpts, romance, serialized novels, suspense and western stories reflecting life in rural Western Canada. Buys 50 mss/year. Send complete ms. Length: 1,000-2,000 words. Pays $50-200.

Poetry: Free verse, traditional, haiku and light verse. Buys 75 poems/year. Submit maximum 3 poems. Length: 4-50 lines. Pays $10-35.

Tips: "Western Canada is geographically very large. The approach for writing about an interesting individual is to introduce that person *neighbor-to-neighbor* to our readers."

WINDSOR THIS MONTH MAGAZINE, Box 1029, Station A, Windsor, Ontario N9A 6P4 Canada. (519)966-7411. Publisher: J.S. Woloschak. 75% freelance written. "*Windsor This Month* is mailed out in a system of controlled distribution to 24,000 households in the area. The average reader is a university graduate, of middle income, and active in leisure areas." Circ. 24,000. Pays on publication. Buys first North American serial rights. Submit seasonal/holiday material 4 months in advance. "We will accept computer printout submissions or industry compatible magnetic media." Reports in 1 month.

Nonfiction: Windsor-oriented editorial: issues, answers, interviews, lifestyles, profiles, photo essays and opinion. How-to accepted if applicable to readership. Special inserts: design and decor, gourmet and travel featured periodically through the year. Buys 5 mss/issue. Query (phone queries OK). Buys 15 unsolicited mss/year. Length: 500-5,000 words. Pays $64.

Photos: State availability of photos with query. Pays $25. Captions preferred. Buys all rights.

Tips: "If experienced, arm yourself with published work and a list of ten topics that demonstrate knowledge of the Windsor market, and query the editor."

Relationships

These publications focus on lifestyles and relationships. They are read and often written by single people, gays and lesbians and those interested in alternative lifestyles or outlooks. They may offer writers a forum for unconventional views or serve as a voice for particular audiences or causes.

ATLANTA SINGLES MAGAZINE, Sigma Publications, Inc., Suite 320, 3423 Piedmont Rd. NE., Atlanta GA 30305 and Box 52700, Atlanta GA 30355. (404)239-0642. Editor: Margaret Anthony. Associate Editor: Judy Scott. 10% freelance written. Works with a small number of new/unpublished writers each year. A bi-monthly magazine for single, widowed or divorced adults, medium to high income level, many business and professionally oriented; single parents, ages 25 to 55. Circ. 15,000. Pays on publication. Publishes ms an average of 6 months after acceptance. Byline given. Buys one-time rights, second serial (reprint) rights and simultaneous rights. Submit seasonal/holiday material 6 months in advance. Simultaneous, photocopied and previously published submissions OK. Computer printout submissions acceptable; prefers letter-quality. Free sample copy.

Nonfiction: General interest, humor, personal experience, photo feature and travel. No pornography. Buys 5 mss/year. Send complete ms. Length: 600-1,200 words. Pays $100-300 for unsolicited articles; sometimes trades for personal ad.

Photos: Send photos with submission. Cover photos also considered. Reviews prints. Offers no additional payment for photos accepted with ms. Model releases and identification of subjects required. Buys one-time rights.

Columns/Departments: Will consider ideas. Query. Length: 600-800 words. Pays $100-300 per column/department.

Fiction: "We rarely print fiction, unless it is outstanding and relates to single readers exceptionally well." Length: 600-1,200 words. Pays $100-300.

Fillers: Gags to be illustrated by cartoonist and short humor. Length: open. Pays $10-20.

Tips: "We are open to articles on *any* subject that would be of interest to singles, i.e., travel, autos, movies, love stories, fashion, investments, real estate, etc. Although singles are interested in topics like self-awareness, being single again, and dating, they are also interested in many of the same subjects that married people are, such as those listed."

‡ARIZONA SINGLES, Singles Publishing Inc., Box 3424, Flagstaff AZ 86003. (602)779-0151. Editor: Joyce Reid. 25% freelance written. Monthly tabloid for singles in Arizona. "We reach singles of all ages—18 through senior citizens with a positive approach to singlehood." Circ. 20,000. Pays on publication. Publishes ms an average of 6 months after acceptance. Byline given. Buys first rights, second serial (reprints) rights or simultaneous rights. Submit seasonal/holiday material 3 months in advance. Simultaneous, photocopied and previously published submissions OK. Computer printout submissions OK. Reports in 2 weeks on queries; 1 month on mss. Sample copy for 9x12 SAE and 4 first class stamps.

Nonfiction: Essays, general interest, historical/nostalgic, how-to (related to singles and relationships), humor, inspirational, interview/profile, new product, opinion, personal experience, travel, finance and health. Query with or without published clips, or send complete ms. Length: 300-1,000. Pays $10-30. Sometimes pays writers with personal profiles or ad trades.

Photos: State availability of photos with submission or send photos with submission. Offers no additional payment for photos accepted with ms. Model releases required. Buys one-time rights.

Fillers: Facts and short humor. Length: 100-300 words. Pays $1-5.

Tips: "Anything related to singles would interest us; however it should be tightly written, accurate and not in bad taste. We are not a 'swingers' publication but provide a tasteful means of networking for singles. Writers have a better chance with short articles and fillers. We are open to unique column suggestions."

‡BAY WINDOWS, New England's Largest Gay and Lesbian Newspaper, Bay Windows, Inc.. 1523 Washington St., Boston MA 02118. (617)266-6670. Editor: Nan Donald. 35-40% freelance written. A weekly newspaper of gay and lesbian news and concerns. "*Bay Windows* covers New England (predominantly Massachusetts: especially greater Boston) and features hard news, opinion, news analysis, arts reviews and interviews." Circ. 13,000. Pays ASAP after publication. Publishes ms an average of 2 months after acceptance. Byline given. Offers 50% kill fee. Buys first rights. Submit seasonal-holiday material 3 months in advance. Previously published submissions "only if extremely pertinent to specific needs." Computer printout submissions OK; prefers letter-quality. Reports in 1 month on queries. Free sample copy.

Nonfiction: Essays, general interest with a gay slant, interview/profile, opinion and photo feature. Publishes 100 mss/year. Query with or without published clips, or send complete ms. Length: 500-1,500 words. Pays $10-60. Pays in copies for poetry submissions. Send photos with submission. Reviews prints (3x5) and larger. Offers $5-25 per photo. Model releases and identification of subjects required. Buys one-time rights.

Columns/Departments: Film, music, dance, books, art (all must have gay and lesbian specific slant), 500-1,500 words. Buys 200 mss/year. Send complete ms. Length: 500-1,500 words. Pays $10-60.

Poetry: Avant-garde, free verse, haiku, light verse and traditional. Buys 50 poems/year. Length: 10-30 words. Pays in copies.

Tips: "Writers must have firm grasp of gay and a lesbian culture and community-i.e., must be gay, lesbian or bisexual, or have intimate knowledge of such-related to gay, etc. Although not just a 'happy news' publication, we do proceed on the assumption that gay is good."

CHANGING MEN, Issues in Gender, Sex and Politics, Feminist Men's Publications, 306 N. Brooks St., Madison WI 53715. Editor: Rick Cote. Managing Editor: Michael Birnbaum. 80% freelance written. Works with a small number of new/unpublished writers each year. A feminist men's journal published two times a year. "We are a forum for anti-sexist men and women to explore issues of masculinity, feminism, sexual orientation, and sex roles." Circ. 4,000. Publishes ms an average of 1 year after acceptance. Byline given. Buys one-time rights. Simultaneous queries, simultaneous, photocopied, and previously published submissions OK. Computer printout submissions acceptable; prefers letter-quality. Reports in 2 months. Sample copy $4.50; writer's guidelines for #10 SAE with 1 first class stamp.

Nonfiction: Book excerpts, humor, interview/profile, opinion, personal experience and photo feature. Plans special issues on male/female intimacy and relationships. Special focus in upcoming issue on male violence. No academic articles or theoretical treatises. Query with published clips. Length: 3,500 words maximum. Pays $25 maximum.

Columns/Departments: Men and War (focus on masculinity and how culture shapes male values), Sports (with a feminist slant), and Book Reviews (focus on sexuality and masculinity). Query with published clips. Length: 500-1,500 words. Pays $15 maximum.

Fiction: Franklin Abbott, fiction editor. Erotica, ethnic, experimental, fantasy, humorous and novel excerpts. Buys 1 ms/year. Query with published clips. Length: 3,500 words maximum. Pays $20 maximum.

Poetry: Free verse, haiku and light verse. Submit maximum 3 poems. Length: 50 lines maximum. No payment for poetry.

Fillers: Clippings, jokes and newsbreaks. Length: 300 words. No payment for fillers.

DRUMMER, Desmodus, Inc., Box 11314, San Francisco CA 94101. (415)864-3456. Associate Editor: Tim Barrus. 80% freelance written. Gay male leather and related fetish erotica/news. Monthly magazine publishes "erotic aspects of leather and other masculine fetishes for gay men." Circ. 60,000. Pays on publication. Publishes ms an average of 3 months after acceptance. Byline given. Buys first North American serial rights or makes work-for-hire assignments. Submit seasonal/holiday material 6 months in advance. Photocopied and previously published submissions OK. Computer printout submissions OK; prefers letter-quality. Reports in 1 month on queries; in 2-3 months on mss. Sample copy $5; writer's guidelines for #10 SAE with 1 first class stamp.

Nonfiction: Book excerpts, essays, historical/nostalgic, how-to, humor, interview/profile, new product, opinion, personal experience, photo feature, technical and travel. No feminine slanted pieces. Buys 25 mss/year. Query with or without published clips, or send complete ms. Length: 1,000-15,000 words. Pays $50-200 for assigned articles; $50-100 for unsolicited articles. Sometimes pays writers with contributor copies "if author is willing." Rarely pays expenses of writers on assignment.

Photos: Send photos with submission (photocopies OK). Reviews contact sheets and transparencies. Offers $10-100 per photo. Model releases and identification of subjects required. Buys one-time rights or all rights.

Fiction: Adventure, condensed novels, erotica, ethnic, fantasy, historical, horror, humorous, mystery, novel excerpts, science fiction, slice-of-life vignettes, suspense and western. Must have gay "macho" erotic elements. Buys 60-75 mss/year. Send complete ms. Length: 1,000-20,000 words. Occasionally serializes stories. Pays $100.

Fillers: Anecdotes, facts, gags and newsbreaks. Buys 50/year. Length: 10-100 words. pay $10-50.

Tips: "All they have to do is write—but they must be knowledgeable about some aspect of the scene, While the magazine is aimed at gay men, we welcome contributions from straight men and from straight, bisexual and gay women who understand leather and s/m and kinky erotic fetishes. Fiction is most open to freelancers."

DUNGEON MASTER, Desmodus Inc., Box 11314, San Francisco CA 94101. (415)864-3456. Editor: Tony DeBlase. 50% freelance written. Quarterly magazine covering gay male erotic s/m. "Safety is emphasized. This is not a fantasy magazine but is for real how-to articles on equipment, techniques, etc." Circ. 5,000. Most articles are unpaid—except by complimentary subscriptions, ads, etc. Byline given. Buys first North American serial rights, one-time rights, simultaneous rights or makes work-for-hire assignments. Photocopied submissions and previously published submissions OK. Computer printout submissions OK; prefers letter-quality. Sample copy $4; free writer's guidelines.

Nonfiction: Book excerpts, essays, historical/nostalgic, how-to (mainly), humor, interview/profile, new product, opinion, personal experience, photo feature (may be paid), technical, travel and safety. No fiction or unsafe practices. Buys 40 mss/year. Query with or without published clips, or send complete ms. Length: no limit. Pays $25-200 for assigned articles. Usually pays writers with contributor copies or other premiums rather than a cash payment. Rarely pays expenses of writers on assignment.

Photos: Send photos with submission. (photocopies OK). Reviews contact sheets and transparencies. Offers $10-100/photo. Model releases and identification of subjects required. Buys one-time rights or all rights.

Fillers: Anecdotes, facts, gags to be illustrated and newbreaks. Buys 10/year. Pays $5-25.

Tips: "Must be knowledgeable in specialized field. While publication is aimed at gay men, submission by straight men and straight and gay women are welcome."

FIRST HAND, Experiences For Loving Men, Firsthand, Ltd., 310 Cedar Lane, Teaneck NJ 07666. (201)836-9177. Editor: Lou Thomas. Publisher: Jackie Lewis. 75% freelance written. Eager to work with new/unpublished writers. Monthly magazine of homosexual erotica. Circ. 70,000. Pays 8 months after acceptance or on publication, whichever comes first. Publishes ms an average of 8 months after acceptance. Byline given. Buys all rights (exceptions made), and second serial (reprint) rights. Submit seasonal/holiday material 10 months in advance. Photocopied submissions OK. Computer printout submissions acceptable; no dot-matrix. Reports in 2 months. Sample copy $3; writer's guidelines for #10 SASE.

Nonfiction: "We seldom use nonfiction except for our 'Survival Kit' section, but will consider full-length profiles, investigative reports, and so on if they are of information/inspirational interest to gay people. Erotic safe sex stories are acceptable." Length: 3,000 words maximum. Pays $100-150. "We will consider original submissions only." Query.

Columns/Departments: Survival Kit (short nonfiction articles, up to 1,000 words, featuring practical information on safe sex practices, health, travel, books, video, psychology, law, fashion, and other advice/consumer/lifestyle topics of interest to gay or single men). "These should be written in the second or third person." Query. "For this section, we sometimes also buy reprint rights to appropriate articles previously published in local gay newspapers around the country." Pays $35 to $70, depending on length, if original; if reprint, pays half that rate.

Fiction: Erotic fiction up to 5,000 words in length, average 2,000-3,000 words. "We prefer fiction in the first person which is believable—stories based on the writer's actual experience have the best chance. We're not interested in stories which involve underage characters in sexual situations. Other taboos include bestiality, rape—except in prison stories, as rape is an unavoidable reality in prison—and heavy drug use. Writers with questions about what we can and cannot depict should write for our guidelines, which go into this in more detail. We print mostly self-contained stories; we will look at novel excerpts, but only if they stand on their own."

Poetry: Free verse and light verse. Buys 12/year. Submit maximum 5 poems. Length: 10-30 lines. Pays $25.

Tips: "*First Hand* is a very reader-oriented publication for gay men. Half of each issue is comprised by letters from our readers describing their personal experiences, fantasies and feelings. Our readers are from all walks of life, all races and ethnic backgrounds, all classes, all religious and political affiliations, and so on. They are very diverse, and many live in far-flung rural areas or small towns; for some of them, our magazines are the primary source of contact with gay life, in some cases the only support for their gay identity. Our readers are very loyal and save every issue. We return that loyalty by trying to reflect their interests—for instance, by striving to avoid the exclusively big-city bias so common to national gay publications. So bear in mind the diversity of the audience when you write."

‡**GUIDE MAGAZINE**, One in Ten Publishing, Box 23070, Seattle WA 98102. (206)323-7374. Editor: Scott Dunn. Managing Editor: Bill Swigart. 90% freelance written. A monthly magazine on homosexuality and gay culture. "We publish humor pieces, fiction, poetry, feature stories and interpretive essays examining personalities, politics, science, religion, current events, the arts and indeed the whole of culture as they relate to gay life." Erotic or sexually explicit material not usually published. Buys first North American serial rights, second serial (reprint) rights, simultaneous rights and makes work-for-hire assignments. Submit seasonal/holiday material 4 months in advance. Simultaneous, photocopied and previously published submissions OK. Query for electronic submissions. Computer printout submissions OK. Reports in 6 weeks on queries; 8 weeks on mss. Sample copy for 9x12 SAE with 4 first class stamps. Writer's guidelines for #10 SAE with 1 first class stamp.
Nonfiction: Essays, exposé, general interest, historical/nostalgic, humor, interview/profile, new product, opinion, personal experience, photo feature, religious, travel and investigative reporting."Items must some way relate to experience of gay people." Buys 10 mss/year. Send complete ms. Length: 800-4,000 words. Pays $50 maximum. Sometimes pays in contributor's copies. Sometimes pays the expenses of writers on assignment. State availability of photos with submission. Offers $5 per photo. Captions. Buys one-time rights.
Columns/Departments: Books (reviews), 900-1,500 words; Feature (interview, essay, new analysis, opinion), 1,000-4,000 words. Buys 10 mss/year. Send complete ms. Length: 800-4,000 words. Pays $50 maximum.
Fiction: Adventure, condensed novels, ethnic, experimental, historical, horror, humorous, mainstream, mystery, romance, science fiction, serialized novels, slice-of-life vignettes, suspense and western. Buys 7 mss/year. Send complete ms. Length: 800-3,000 words. Pays $30.
Poetry: Light verse and traditional. No erotica. Buys 4 poems/year. Pays $20.
Fillers: Anecdotes, facts, gags to be illustrated by cartoonist, newsbreaks and short humor. Length: 50-1,000 words.
Tips: "In-depth analysis of social problems, politics, science and religion needed. Well-researched and intellectually challenging pieces get top priority. We would like to see some international essays and/or articles about gay culture in other parts of the world. Pay above stated maximum is negotiable."

‡**THE GUIDE, To The Gay Northeast**, Fidelity Publishing. Box 593, Boston MA 02199. (617)266-8557. Editor: French Wall. 50% freelance written. A monthly magazine on the gay and lesbian community. Circ. 22,000. Pays on acceptance. Publishes ms an average of 2 months after acceptance. Kill fee negotiable. Buys all rights. Submit seasonal/holiday material 2 months in advance. Simultaneous and photocopied submissions OK. Computer printout submissions OK; prefers letter-quality. Sample copy for 9x12 SAE with 6 first class stamps.
Nonfiction: Book excerpts (if yet unpublished), essays, exposé, general interest, historical/nostalgic, humor, interview/profile, opinion, personal experience, photo feature and religious. "No personal attacks. We prefer upbeat articles with focus on Northeast United States or Eastern Canada." Buys 48 mss/year. Query with or without published clips, or send complete ms. Length: 500-3,000 words. Pays $25-100. Send photos with submission. Reviews contact sheets. Offers no additional payment for photos accepted with ms/negotiable. Captions, model releases, identification of subjects prefered; releases required sometimes. Buys one-time rights.
Fiction: Adventure, erotica, ethnic, experimental, fantasy, historical, humorous, novel excerpts, religious, romance, science fiction, slice-of-life vignettes and suspense. "We are seeking to add fiction to our magazine; format allows for only short (500-3,000 word) pieces, though serialization could be a possibility." Query with published clips. Length: 500-3,000 words. Pays $25-100.
Tips: "Brevity, humor and militancy appreciated. We seek to inspire gay and lesbian people to confront and challenge homophobia and hypocrisy."

IN TOUCH FOR MEN, In Touch Publications International, Inc., 7216 Varna, North Hollywood CA 91605. (818)764-2288. Editor-in-Chief: Bob Stanford. 80% freelance written. Works with a small number of new/unpublished writers each year. A monthly magazine covering the gay male lifestyle, gay male humor and erotica. Circ. 70,000. Pays on acceptance. Byline given. Buys one-time rights. Submit seasonal/holiday material 4 months in advance. Simultaneous and photocopied submissions OK. Computer printout submissions acceptable. Reports in 2 weeks on queries; 6 weeks on mss. Sample copy $4.95; free writer's guidelines.
Nonfiction: Buys 36 mss/year. Send complete ms. Length: 1,000-3,500 words. Pays $25-75.
Photos: State availability of photos with submission. Reviews contact sheets, transparencies, and prints. Offers $35/photo. Captions, model releases and identification of subjects required. Buys one-time rights.
Columns/Departments: Touch and Go (brief comments on various items or pictures that have appeared in the media), 50-500 words. Buys 12 mss/year. Send complete ms. Pays $25.
Fiction: Adventure, confession, erotica, historical, horror, humorous, mainstream, mystery, romance, sci-

ence fiction, slice-of-life vignettes, suspense, and western; all must be gay male erotica. No "heterosexual, heavy stuff." Buys 36 mss/year. Send complete ms. Length: 2,500-3,500 words. Pays $75 maximum.
Fillers: Short humor. Buys 12/year. Length: 1,500-3,500 words. Pays $50-75.
Tips: "Our publication features male nude photos plus three fiction pieces, several articles, cartoons, humorous comments on items from the media, and photo features. We try to present the positive aspects of the gay lifestyle, with an emphasis on humor. Humorous pieces may be erotic in nature. We are open to all submissions that fit our gay male format; the emphasis, however, is on humor and the upbeat. We receive many fiction manuscripts but not nearly enough articles and humor."

MANSCAPE 2, First Hand Ltd., Box 1314, Teaneck NJ 07666. (201)836-9177. Editor: Lou Thomas. 75% freelance written. A bimonthly magazine focusing on "gay male sexual fetishes, kink and leather sex." Circ. 70,000. Pays two months after acceptance. Publishes ms an average of 9 months after acceptance. Byline given. Buys first North American serial rights or all rights. Submit seasonal/holiday material 9 months in advance. Photocopied submissions OK. "No simultaneous submissions." Computer printout submissions OK; no dot-matrix. Reports in 1-2 months. Sample copy $4.50; free writer's guidelines.
Nonfiction: Interview/profile and health. "All nonfiction articles must have gay angle." Buys 40 mss/year. Query with or without published clips, or send complete ms. Length: 2,000-3,750. Pays $100-150 for unsolicited articles (no assigned articles).
Fiction: Erotica and novel excerpts. "All fiction must be gay erotica. We don't want to see downbeat attitudes in stories." Buys 40 mss/year. Send complete ms. Length: 2,000-3,750 words. Pays $100-150.
Poetry: Free verse, haiku, light verse, traditional. Must be erotic. Buys 6 poems/year. Submit 5 poems maximum at one time. Length: 5-20 lines. Pays $25.
Tips: "The fiction section is the best area for freelancers to break in with. Most of the fiction we publish is written in the first person. Stories should be strongly erotic, with at least an edge of kinkiness. And stories should be a celebration of masculinity, of maleness."

METRO SINGLES LIFESTYLES, Metro Publications, Box 28203, Kansas City MO 64118. (816)436-8424. Editor: R.L. Huffstutter. 40% freelance written. Eager to work with new/unpublished writers. A tabloid appearing 9 times/year covering singles lifestyles. Pays on acceptance. Publishes ms an average of 2 months after acceptance. Byline given. Buys one-time rights and second serial (reprint) rights. Submit seasonal/holiday material 3 months in advance. Photocopied submissions OK. Computer printout submissions acceptable; prefers letter-quality. Reports in 1 month. Sample copy $2 and 9x12 SAE with 5 first class stamps.
Nonfiction: Essay, general interest, how-to (on meeting the ideal mate, . . . recovering from divorce, etc.), inspirational, interview/profile, personal experience and photo feature. No sexually-oriented material. Buys 2-6 mss/year. Send complete ms. Length: 700-1,200 words. Pays $100 maximum for assigned articles; pays $20-50 for unsolicited articles. Will pay in copies or other if writer prefers.
Photos: Send photos with submission. Reviews 3x5 prints. Offers no additional payment for photos accepted with ms. Captions, model releases, and identification of subjects required. Buys one-time rights.
Columns/Departments: Movie Reviews, Lifestyles, Singles Events, and Book Reviews (about singles), all 400-1,000 words. Buys 3 mss/year. Send complete ms. Pays $20-50.
Fiction: Confession, humorous, romance and slice-of-life vignettes. No political, religion, ethnic or sexually-oriented material. Buys 6 mss/year. Send complete ms. Length: 700-1,200 words. Pays $20-50.
Poetry: Free verse and light verse. Buys 6 poems/year. Submit maximum 3 poems. Length: 21 lines. Pays $5-10.
Tips: "A freelancer can best approach and break in to our publication with positive articles, photo features about singles and positive fiction about singles. Photos and short bios of singles (blue collar, white collar, and professional) at work needed. Photos and a few lines about singles enjoying recreation (swimming, sports, chess, etc.) always welcome. Color photos, close-up, are suitable."

MOM GUESS WHAT NEWSPAPER, New Helvetia Communications, Inc., 1725 L. St., Sacramento CA 95814. (916)441-6397. Editor: Linda Birner. 80% freelance written. Works with small number of new/unpublished writers each year. A monthly tabloid covering gay rights and gay lifestyles. Circ. 21,000. Publishes ms an average of 3 months after acceptance. Byline given. Buys all rights. Submit seasonal/holiday material 3 months in advance. Photocopied submissions OK. Computer printout submissions acceptable; no dot-matrix. Reports in 2 months. Sample copy $1; writer's guidelines for 8½x11 SAE with 3 first class stamps.
Nonfiction: Interview/profile and photo feature of international, national or local scope. Buys 8 mss/year. Query. Length: 200-1,500 words. Payment depends on article. Pays expenses of writers on special assignment.
Photos: State availability of photos with submission. Reviews 5x7 prints. Offers no additional payment for photos accepted with ms. Captions and identification of subjects required. Buys one-time rights.
Columns/Departments: Restaurants, Political, Health, and Film, Video and Book Reviews. Buys 12 mss/year. Query. Payment depends on article.

ON THE SCENE MAGAZINE, (formerly *Albuquerque Singles Scene* Magazine),3507 Wyoming NE, Albuquerque NM 87111. (505)299-4401. Editor: Gail Skinner. 60% freelance written. Eager to work with new/unpublished writers. Monthly tabloid covering singles lifestyles. Pays on publication. Publishes ms an average of 6 months after acceptance. Byline given. Buys all rights for one year; first serial rights only under special circumstances. Submit seasonal/holiday material 3 months in advance. Query for electronic submissions. Computer printout submissions acceptable; prefers letter-quality. Reports in 3 months. Sample copy $3. Writer's guidelines and sample copy for 9x12 SAE and 4 first class stamps.
Nonfiction: General interest; how-to; humor; inspirational; opinion; personal experience; relationships; consumer guide; travel; finance; real estate; parenting; and astrology. No suggestive or pornographic material. Buys 100 mss/year. Send complete ms. "Ms returned only if SASE is included." Also publishes some fiction. Length: 500-1,500 words. Pays $20-60. Sometimes pays expenses of writers on assignment.
Photos: State availability of photos with ms. Captions, model releases, and identification of subjects required.
Tips: "We are looking for articles that deal with every aspect of living—whether on a local or national level. Our readers are of above-average intelligence, income and education. The majority of our articles are chosen from 'relationships' and 'humor' submissions. Expanded format from 'singles only' to general readership."

SINGLELIFE MAGAZINE, SingleLife Enterprises, Inc., 606 W. Wisconsin Ave., Milwaukee WI 53203. (414)271-9700. Editor: Frank Smoot. 50% freelance written. Prefers to work with published/established writers; works with a small number of new/unpublished writers each year. Bimonthly magazine covering singles lifestyles. Circ. 22,000. Pays on publication. Publishes ms an average of 6 months after acceptance. Byline given. Buys one-time rights, second serial (reprint) rights and simultaneous rights. Submit seasonal material 4 months in advance. Simultaneous submissions, photocopies and previously published submissions OK. Query for electronic submissions. Computer printout submissions OK; prefer letter-quality. Reports in 3-6 weeks. Sample copy and writer's guidelines for $3.50 and 9x11 SAE; writer's guidelines for SAE with 1 first class stamp.
Nonfiction: Upbeat and in-depth articles on significant areas of interest to single people such as male/female relationships, travel, health, sports, food, single parenting, humor, finances, places to go and things to do. Prefers third person point of view and ms to query letter. Our readers are between 25 and 50. Length: 1,000-3,000 words. Pays $50-150. Sometimes pays expenses of writers on assignment.
Photos: Send photos with query or ms. Pays $10-100 for b&w contact sheet, 2¼" transparencies and 8x10 prints; pays $20-200 for 2¼" color transparencies and 8x10 prints. Captions, model releases and identification of subjects required.
Fiction and Poetry: Buys 3-4 stories or poems per year, which are well written and cast a new light on what being single means. Length: not over 2,500 words. Submit any number of poems that pertain to being single. Pays $25-50.
Tips: "The easiest way to get in is to write something light, unusual, but also well-developed."

THE WASHINGTON BLADE, Washington Blade, Inc., 8th Floor, 724 9th St. NW, Washington DC 20001. (202)347-2038. Managing Editor: Lisa M. Keen. 20% freelance written. Works with a small number of new/unpublished writers each year. Weekly news tabloid covering the gay/lesbian community. "Articles (subjects) should be written from or directed to a gay perspective." Circ. 20,000. Pays in 1 month. Publishes ms an average of 1 month after acceptance. Byline given. Offers $15 kill fee. Buys first North American serial rights. Submit seasonal/holiday material 1 month in advance. Photocopied submissions OK. Computer printout submissions acceptable; prefers letter-quality. Sample copy and writer's guidelines for 8½x11 SAE and $1.
Nonfiction: Exposé (of government, private agency, church, etc., handling of gay-related issues); historical/nostalgic; interview/profile (of gay community/political leaders; persons, gay or nongay, in positions to affect gay issues; outstanding achievers who happen to be gay; those who incorporate the gay lifestyle into their professions); photo feature (on a nationally or internationally historic gay event); and travel (on locales that welcome or cater to the gay traveler). *The Washington Blade* basically covers two areas: news and lifestyle. News coverage of D.C. metropolitan area gay community, local and federal government actions relating to gays, as well as national news of interest to gays. Section also includes features on current events. Special issues include: Annual gay pride issue (early June), and a monthly style section, "Living". No sexually explicit material. Buys 30 mss/year, average. Query with published clips and resume. Length: 500-1,500 words. Pays 5-10¢/word. Sometimes pays the expenses of writers on assignment.
Photos: "A photo or graphic with feature/lifestyle articles is particularly important. Photos with news stories are appreciated." State availability of photos. Reviews b&w contact sheets and 5x7 glossy prints. Pays $25 minimum. Captions preferred; model releases required. On assignment, photographer paid mutually agreed upon fee, with expenses reimbursed. Publication retains all rights.
Tips: "Send good examples of your writing and know the paper before you submit a manuscript for publication. We get a lot of submissions which are entirely inappropriate." Greatest opportunity for freelancers resides in current events, features, interviews and book reviews.

THE WEEKLY NEWS, The Weekly News Inc., 901 NE 79th St., Miami FL 33138. (305)757-6333. Editor: Cliff O'Neill. Managing Editor: Bill Watson. 40% freelance written. Weekly gay tabloid. Circ. 32,000. Pays on publication. Byline given. Buys one-time rights. Submit seasonal/holiday material 2 months in advance. Simultaneous, photocopied and previously published submissions OK. Sample copy for 9½x12½ SAE with $2.25 postage.

Nonfiction: Exposé, humor and interview/profile. Buys 8 mss/year. Send complete ms. Length: 1,000-5,000 words. Pays $25-125. Sometimes pays the expenses of writers on assignment.

Photos: State availability of photos with submission. Reviews 3x5 prints. Offers $5-20/photo. Buys first and future use.

Columns/Departments: Send complete ms. Length: 900 words maximum. Pays $15-30.

Fillers: Anecdotes, gags to be illustrated by cartoonist and short humor. Pays $15-30.

Religious

Religious magazines focus on a variety of subjects, styles and beliefs. Many are publishing articles relating to current affairs like AIDS, cults, or substance abuse. Fewer religious publications are considering poems and personal experience articles, but many emphasize special ministries to singles, seniors and deaf people. Such diversity makes reading each magazine essential for the writer hoping to break in. Educational and inspirational material of interest to church members, workers and leaders within a denomination or religion is needed by the publications in this category. A new book of inspirational and religious markets, *Inspirational Writer's Market*, is available from Writer's Digest Books in March 1989. A newsletter, *The Inspirational Writer*, also is offered by F&W Publications. Publications intended to assist professional religious workers in teaching and managing church affairs are classified in Church Administration and Ministry in the Trade section. Religious magazines for children and teenagers can be found in the Juvenile, and Teen and Young Adult classifications. Other religious magazines can be found in the Ethnic/Minority section.

AGLOW, Today's Publication for Christian Women, Aglow Publications, Box 1548, Lynnwood WA 98046-1557. (206)775-7282. Editor: Gwen Weising. 66% freelance written. Works with a small number of new/unpublished writers each year. Bimonthly nondenominational Christian charismatic magazine for women. Pays on acceptance. Publishes ms an average of 6 months to 1 year after acceptance. Byline given. Buys first North American serial rights, and reprint rights for use in *Aglow* magazine in other countries. Submit seasonal/holiday material 8 months in advance. Simultaneous queries and photocopied submissions acceptable. Computer printout submissions OK; prefers letter-quality. Reports in 2 months. Writer's guidelines for #10 SAE and 1 first class stamp.

Nonfiction: Contact Gloria Chisholm, Acquistions Editor. Christian women's spiritual experience articles (first person) and some humor. "Each article should be either a testimony of or teaching about Jesus as Savior, as Baptizer in the Holy Spirit, or as Guide and Strength in everyday circumstances." Queries only. "We would like to see material about 'Women of Vision' who have made and are making an impact on their world for God." Length: 1,000-2,000 words. Pays up to 10¢/word. Sometimes pays expenses of writers on assignment.

THE ANNALS OF SAINT ANNE DE BEAUPRE, Redemptorist Fathers, 9597 St. Anne Blvd., St. Anne De Beaupre, Quebec G0A 3C0 Canada. (418)827-4538. Editor: Bernard Mercier. Managing Editor: Roch Achard. 80% freelance written. Works with a small number of new/unpublished writers each year. "Anyone can submit manuscripts. We judge." Monthly magazine on religion. "Our aim is to promote devotion to St. Anne and Christian family values." Circ. 54,000. Pays on acceptance. Publishes ms an average of 1 year after acceptance. Byline given. Buys first North American serial rights. Submit seasonal/holiday material 2½ months in advance. Simultaneous queries and photocopied submissions OK. Computer printout submissions OK; prefers letter-quality. Reports in 2 weeks. Free sample copy and writer's guidelines.

Nonfiction: Expose, general interest, inspirational and personal experience. No articles without spiritual thrust. Buys 30 mss/year. Send complete ms. Length: 500-1,200 words. Pays 3-4¢/word.

Fiction: Religious. Buys 15 mss/year. Send complete ms. Length: 500-1,200 words. Pays 3-4¢/word.

Poetry: Traditional. Buys 12/year. Submit maximum 2-3 poems. Length: 12-20 lines. Pays $5-8.

Tips: "Write something educational, inspirational, objective and uplifting. Reporting rather than analysis is simply not remarkable."

THE ASSOCIATE REFORMED PRESBYTERIAN, Associate Reformed Presbyterian General Synod, 1 Cleveland St., Greenville SC 29601. (803)232-8297. Editor: Ben Johnston. 10% freelance written. Works with a small number of new/unpublished writers each year. A Christian publication serving a conservative, evangelical and Reformed denomination, most of whose members are in the Southeast U.S. Circ. 7,000. Pays on acceptance. Publishes ms an average of 3 months after acceptance. Byline given. Not copyrighted. Buys first rights, one-time rights, or second serial (reprint) rights. Submit seasonal/holiday material 4 months in advance. Simultaneous submissions and previously published submissions OK. Computer printout submissions acceptable; prefers letter-quality. Reports in 1 month. Sample copy $1; writer's guidelines for SASE.
Nonfiction: Book excerpts, essays, inspirational, opinion, personal experience, and religious. Buys 10-15 mss/year. Query. Length: 400-2,000 words. Pays $50 maximum.
Photos: State availability of photos with submission. Reviews 5x7 reprints. Offers $25 maximum per photo. Captions and identification of subjects required. Buys one-time rights. Sometimes pays expenses of writers on assignment.
Fiction: Religious and children's. Pays $50 maximum. Annual contest for writers of children's stories. Contest rules available for SASE in January. Entry deadline April 1.
Tips: "Feature articles are the area of our publication most open to freelancers. Focus on a contemporary problem and offer Bible-based solutions to it. Provide information that would help a Christian struggling in his daily walk. Writers should understand that we are denominational, conservative, evangelical, Reformed, and Presbyterian. A writer who appreciates these nuances would stand a much better chance of being published here than one who does not."

AXIOS, 800 S. Euclid St., Fullerton CA 92632. (714)526-2131 and (714)526-6257; computer number for Axios BBS (714)526-2387. Editor: David Gorham. 10% freelance written. Eager to work with new/unpublished writers. Monthly journal seeking spiritual articles mostly on Orthodox Christian background, either Russian, Greek, Serbian, Syrian or American. Circ. 7,789. Pays on publication. Publishes ms an average of 6 months after acceptance. Byline given. Offers 50% kill fee. Buys all rights. Submit seasonal/holiday material 4 months in advance. Simultaneous queries, and simultaneous, photocopied, and previously published submissions OK. Query for electronic submissions. Computer printout submissions acceptable; prefers letter-quality. Reports in 1 month. Sample copy for $2 and 9x12 SAE with $1 postage.
Nonfiction: Book excerpts; expose (of religious figures); general interest; historical/nostalgic; interview/profile; opinion; personal experience; photo feature; and travel (shrines, pilgrimages). Special issues include the persecution of Christians in Iran, Russia, behind Iron Curtain or in Arab lands; Roman Catholic interest in the Orthodox Church. Nothing about the Pope or general "all-is-well-with-Christ" items. Buys 14 mss/year. Send complete ms. Length: 1,000-3,000 words. Pays 4¢/word minimum.
Columns/Departments: Reviews religious books and films. Buys 80 mss/year. Query.
Tips: "We need some hard hitting articles on the 'political' church—the why, how and where of it and why it lacks the timelessness of the spiritual. Here in *Axios* you can discuss your feelings, your findings, your needs, your growth; give us your outpouring. Don't mistake us for either Protestant or Roman Catholic; we are the voice of Catholics united with the Eastern Orthodox Church, also referred to as the Greek Orthodox Church. We are most interested in the western rite within eastern Orthodoxy; and the return of the Roman Catholic to the ancient universal church."

BAPTIST LEADER, Valley Forge PA 19482-0851. (215)768-2153. Editor: Linda Isham. For pastors, teachers, and leaders in Sunday church schools. 5% freelance written. Works with a small number of new/unpublished writers each year. Bimonthly. Buys first serial rights. Pays on acceptance. Publishes ms an average of 8 months after acceptance. Deadlines are 8 months prior to date of issue. Computer printout submissions acceptable; prefers letter-quality. Sample copy for $1.25; writer's guidelines for #10 SASE.
Nonfiction: Educational topics. How-to articles for local church school teachers and leaders. Length: 1,500-2,000 words. Pays $25-75.
Tips: "We're planning more emphasis on church, school and Christian education, administration and planning."

BIBLICAL ILLUSTRATOR, The Sunday School Board, 127 9th Ave. N., Nashville TN 37234. Editor: Michael J. Mitchell. "Articles are designed to coordinate with other Southern Baptist periodicals. Unsolicited mss are rarely applicable. Inquire first."

CATHOLIC DIGEST, Box 64090, St. Paul MN 55164. Editor: Henry Lexau. Managing Editor: Richard Reece. 50% freelance written. Works with small number of new/unpublished writers each year. Monthly magazine covering the daily living of Roman Catholics for an audience that is 60% female, 40% male; 37% is college educated. Circ. 600,000. Publishes ms an average of 6 months after acceptance. Byline given. Buys first North American serial rights or one-time reprint rights. Submit seasonal material 6 months in advance. Previously published submissions OK, if so indicated. Computer printout submissions acceptable; prefers letter-quality. Reports in 1 month. Free sample copy and writer's guidelines.

Nonfiction: General interest (daily living and family relationships); interview (of outstanding Catholics, celebrities and locals); nostalgia (the good old days of family living); profile; religion; travel (shrines); humor; inspirational (overcoming illness, role model people); and personal experience (adventures and daily living). Buys 25 articles/issue. No queries. Send complete ms. Length: 500-3,000 words, 2,000 average. Pays on acceptance—$200-400 for originals, $100 for reprints.
Columns/Departments: "Check a copy of the magazine in the library for a description of column needs. Payment varies and is made on publication. We buy about 5/issue."
Fillers: Jokes, anecdotes and short humor. Buys 10-15 mss/issue. Length: 10-300 words. Pays $3-50 on publication.

CATHOLIC LIFE, 35750 Moravian Dr., Fraser MI 48026. Editor-in-Chief: Robert C. Bayer. 40% freelance written. Monthly (except July or August) magazine. Emphasizes foreign missionary activities of the Catholic Church in Burma, India, Bangladesh, the Philippines, Hong Kong, Africa, etc., for middle-aged and older audience with either middle incomes or pensions. High school educated (on the average), conservative in both religion and politics. Circ. 17,600. Pays on publication. Publishes ms an average of 3 months after acceptance. Buys all rights. Byline given. Submit seasonal/holiday material 4 months in advance. Simultaneous submissions OK. Computer printout submissions acceptable. Reports in 2 weeks.
Nonfiction: Informational and inspirational foreign missionary activities of the Catholic Church. Buys 20-25 unsolicited mss/year. Query or send complete ms. Length: 1,000-1,500 words. Pays 4¢/word.
Tips: "Query with short, graphic details of what the material will cover or the personality involved in the biographical sketch. Also, we appreciate being advised on the availability of good black-and-white photos to illustrate the material."

CATHOLIC NEAR EAST MAGAZINE, Catholic Near East Welfare Association, 1011 1st Ave., New York NY 10022. (212)826-1480. Editor: Michael Healy. 90% freelance written. Quarterly magazine. For a Roman Catholic audience with interest in the Near East, particularly its religious and cultural aspects. Circ. 150,000. Pays on publication. Publishes ms an average of 4 months after acceptance. Byline given. Buys all rights. Submit seasonal material (Christmas and Easter in different Near Eastern lands or rites) 6 months in advance. Photocopied submissions OK if legible. Computer printout submissions acceptable; no dot-matrix. Reports in 1 month. Sample copy and writer's guidelines for 9½x6½ SAE with 2 first class stamps.
Nonfiction: "Cultural, territorial, devotional material on the Near East, its history, peoples and religions (especially the Eastern Rites of the Catholic Church). Style should be simple, factual, concise. Articles must stem from personal acquaintance with subject matter, or thorough up-to-date research. No preaching or speculations." Length: 1,200-1,800 words. Pays 10¢/word.
Photos: "Photographs to accompany manuscript are always welcome; they should illustrate the people, places, ceremonies, etc. which are described in the article. We prefer color transparencies but occasionally use black and white. Pay varies depending on the quality of the photos."
Tips: "Writers please heed: Stick to the people of the Near East, the Balkans through the Middle East to India. Send factual articles; concise, descriptive style preferred, not flowery. Pictures are a big plus; if you have photos to accompany your article, please send them—with captions— at the same time."

CHICAGO STUDIES, Box 665, Mundelein IL 60060. (312)566-1462. Editor: Rev. George J. Dyer. 50% freelance written. Magazine published 3 times/year; 112 pages. For Roman Catholic priests and religious educators. Circ. 10,000. Pays on acceptance. Buys all rights. Photocopied submissions OK. Computer printout submissions acceptable. Reports in 2 months. Sample copy $5.
Nonfiction: Nontechnical discussion of theological, Biblical and ethical topics. Articles aimed at a nontechnical presentation of the contemporary scholarship in those fields. Submit complete ms. Buys 30 mss/year. Length: 3,000-5,000 words. Pays $35-100.

CHRISTIAN HOME & SCHOOL, Christian Schools International, 3350 East Paris Ave. SE, Box 8709, Grand Rapids MI 49508. (616)957-1070. Editor: Gordon L. Bordewyk. Associate Editor: Judy Zylstra. 30% freelance written. Works with a small number of new/unpublished writers each year. Magazine published 8 times/year covering family life and Christian education. "The magazine is designed for parents who support Christian education. We feature material on a wide range of topics of interest to parents." Pays on publication. Publishes ms an average of 4 months after acceptance. Byline given. Buys first North American serial rights. Submit seasonal/holiday material 4 months in advance. Simultaneous queries and photocopied submissions OK. Computer printout submissions acceptable; prefers letter-quality. Reports in 3 weeks on queries; 1 month on mss. Sample copy for 9x12 SAE and 4 first class stamps.
Nonfiction: Book excerpts, interview/profile, opinion, personal experience, and articles on parenting and school life. "We publish features on issues which affect the home and school and profiles on interesting individuals, providing that the profile appeals to our readers and is not a tribute or eulogy of that person." Buys 40

mss/year. Send complete ms. Length: 500-2,000 words. Pays $25-85. Sometimes pays the expenses of writers on assignment.

Photos: "If you have any black-and-white photos appropriate for your article, send them along."

Tips: "Features are the area most open to freelancers. We are publishing articles that deal with contemporary issues which affect parents; keep that in mind. Use an informal easy-to-read style rather than a philosophical, academic tone. Try to incorporate vivid imagery and concrete, practical examples from real life."

‡**CHRISTIAN OUTLOOK**, Hutton Publications, Box 2377, Coeur d'Alene ID 83814. (208)772-6184. Editor: Linda Hutton. 50% freelance written. Quarterly newsletter of inspirational material. "Send us uplifting poetry and fiction, with a subtle moral, but nothing overly religious or preachy." Estab. 1988. Circ. 200. Pays on acceptance. Publishes ms an average of 9 months after acceptance. Byline given. Buys one-time rights or second serial (reprint) rights. Submit seasonal/holiday material 9 months in advance. Simultaneous, photocopied and previously published submissions OK. Computer printout submissions OK; prefers letter-quality. Reports in 1 month on mss. Sample copy and writer's guidelines for #10 SAE with 2 first class stamps.

Fiction: Religious. Buys 4 mss/year. Send complete ms. Length: 300-1,500 words. Pays ¼-1¢/word.

Poetry: Free verse, light verse, traditional, "Nothing overly religious, merely uplifting and inspriational." Buys 8 poems/year. Submit up to 3 poems at one time. Length: 4-8 lines. Pays 10-25¢/line.

CHRISTIAN SINGLE, Family Ministry Dept., Baptist Sunday School Board, 127 9th Ave. N., Nashville TN 37234. (615)251-2228. Editor: Cliff Allbritton. 50-70% freelance written. Prefers to work with published/established writers; works with a small number of new/unpublished writers each year. Monthly magazine covering items of special interest to Christian single adults. "*Christian Single* is a contemporary Christian magazine that seeks to give substantive information to singles for living the abundant life. It seeks to be constructive and creative in approach." Circ. 105,000. Pays on acceptance "for immediate needs"; on publication "for unsolicited manuscripts." Publishes ms 1-2 years after acceptance. Byline given. Buys all rights; makes work-for-hire assignments. Submit seasonal/holiday material 1½ years in advance. Computer printout submissions acceptable; no dot-matrix. Reports in 6 weeks. Sample copy and writer's guidelines for 9x12 SASE.

Nonfiction: Humor (good, clean humor that applies to Christian singles); how-to (specific subjects which apply to singles; query needed); inspirational (of the personal experience type); high adventure personal experience (of single adults); photo feature (on outstanding Christian singles; query needed); well researched financial articles targeted to single adults (query needed). No "shallow, uninformative mouthing off. This magazine says something, and people read it cover to cover." Buys 120-150 unsolicited mss/year. Query with published clips. Length: 300-1,200 words. Pays 5¢/word.

Tips: "We look for freshness and creativity, not duplication of what we have already done. Don't write on loneliness! Need more upbeat personal experience articles written by Christian *single men*! We are backlogged with submissions by women and with poetry at this time. We give preference to Christian single adult writers but publish articles by *sensitive* and *informed* married writers also. Remember that you are talking to educated people who attend church. Study the magazine before submitting materials."

CHRISTIAN SOCIAL ACTION, (formerly *Engage/Social Action*), 100 Maryland Ave. NE, Washington DC 20002. (202)488-5632. Editor: Lee Ranck. 2% freelance written. Works with a small number of new/unpublished writers each year. Monthly for "United Methodist clergy and lay people interested in in-depth analysis of social issues, with emphasis on the church's role or involvement in these issues." Circ. 4,500. May buy all rights. Pays on publication. Publishes ms an average of 2 months after acceptance. Rights purchased vary with author and material. Photocopied submissions OK, but prefers original. Computer printout submissions acceptable; prefers letter-quality. Returns rejected material in 4-5 weeks. Reports on material accepted for publication in several weeks. Free sample copy and writer's guidelines.

Nonfiction: "This is the social action publication of the United Methodist Church published by the denomination's General Board of Church and Society. Our publication tries to relate social issues to the church—what the church can do, is doing; why the church should be involved. We only accept articles relating to social issues, e.g., war, draft, peace, race relations, welfare, police/community relations, labor, population problems, drug and alcohol problems." No devotional, 'religious,' superficial material, highly technical articles, personal experiences or poetry. Buys 25-30 mss/year. "Query to show that writer has expertise on a particular social issue, give credentials, and reflect a readable writing style." Query or submit complete ms. Length: 2,000 words maximum. Pays $75-100. Sometimes pays the expenses of writers on assignment.

Tips: "Write on social issues, but not superficially; we're more interested in finding an expert who can write (e.g., on human rights, alcohol problems, peace issues) than a writer who attempts to research a complex issue."

CHRISTIANITY & CRISIS, 537 W. 121st St., New York NY 10027. (212)662-5907. Editor: Leon Howell. Managing Editor: Gail Hovey. 10% freelance written. Works with a small number of new/unpublished writers each year. Biweekly Protestant journal of opinion. "We are interested in foreign affairs, domestic economic and social policy, and theological developments with social or ethical implications e.g., feminist, black and

liberation theologies. As an independent religious journal it is part of *C&C*'s function to discuss church policies from a detached and sometimes critical perspective. We carry no 'devotional' material but welcome solid contemplative reflections. Most subscribers are highly educated, well-informed." Circ. 14,000. Pays on publication. Publishes ms an average of 2 months after acceptance. Byline given. Offers variable kill fee. Submit seasonal/holiday material 2 months in advance. Simultaneous queries and photocopied submissions OK. Computer printout submissions acceptable if double-spaced. Reports in 1 month. Sample copy $1.75 with 9x12 SAE and 2 first class stamps; writer's guidelines for #10 SASE.
Nonfiction: Buys 150 mss/year. Query with or without published clips. Length: 1,000-4,000 words. Pays 3¢/word. Rarely pays expenses of writers on assignment.
Tips: "We have been publishing more international stories and need to build up reporting on U.S. issues."

CHRISTIANITY TODAY, 465 Gundersen Dr., Carol Stream IL 60188. 80% freelance written. Works with a small number of new/unpublished writers each year. Emphasizes orthodox, evangelical religion. Semimonthly magazine. Circ. 180,000. Publishes ms an average of 6 months after acceptance. Usually buys first serial rights. Submit seasonal/holiday material at least 8 months in advance. Computer printout submissions acceptable; prefers letter-quality. Reports in 2 months. Sample copy and writer's guidelines for 9x12 SAE and 3 first class stamps.
Nonfiction: Theological, ethical, historical and informational (not merely inspirational). Buys 4 mss/issue. *Query only.* Unsolicited mss not accepted and not returned. Length: 1,000-4,000 words. Pays negotiable rates. Sometimes pays the expenses of writers on assignment.
Columns/Departments: The Arts (Christian review of the arts). Buys 12 mss/year. Send complete ms. Length: 800-900 words. Pays negotiable rates.
Tips: "We are developing more of our own manuscripts and requiring a much more professional quality of others."

CHRISTMAS, The Annual of Christmas Literature and Art, Augsburg Publishing, 426 S. 5th St., Box 1209, Minneapolis MN 55440. (612)330-3437. Editor: Gloria E. Bengston. 100% freelance written. "An annual literary magazine that celebrates Christmas focusing on the effect of the Christmas love of God on the lives of people, and how it colors and shapes traditions and celebrations." Pays on acceptance. Byline given. Buys first rights, one-time rights and all rights; makes work-for-hire assignments. Submit seasonal/holiday material 18 months in advance. Reports in 2 weeks on queries; 3 weeks on mss. Sample copy $7.95 plus 5 first class stamps.
Nonfiction: Historical/nostalgic (on Christmas customs); inspirational, interview/profile, personal experience and travel. Articles on art and music with Christmas relationships. Buys 6-8 mss/year. Query with published clips, or send complete ms. Length: 2,500-7,500 words. Pays $200-450 for assigned articles; pays $150-300 for unsolicited articles.
Photos: State availability of photos with submission. Reviews transparencies. Offers $15-100 per photo. Captions and identification of subjects required. Buys one-time rights.
Fiction: Jennifer Huber, editor. Ethnic, historical and slice-of-life vignettes. "No stories of fictionalized characters at the Bethlehem stable. Fiction should show the effect of God's love on the lives of people." Buys 2 mss/year. Send complete ms. Length: 5,000 words maximum. Pays $150-300.
Poetry: Jennifer Huber, editor. Free verse, light verse and traditional. No poetry dealing with Santa Claus. Buys 3 poems/year. Submit maximum 30 poems. Pays $35-40.

‡CHRYSALIS, Journal of the Swedenborg Foundation, 139 East 23rd St., New York NY 10010. Editor: Carol S. Lawson. Managing Editor: Susanna van Rensselaer. 75% freelance written. A literary magazine published 3 times per year on spiritually-related topics. "Content of fiction, articles, reviews, poetry, etc., should be spiritually-related and directed to the educated, intellectually curious reader." Circ. 1,000. Pays at page-proof stage. Publishes ms an average of 9 months after acceptance. Byline given. Buys first rights and makes work-for-hire assignments. Computer printout submissions OK; prefers letter-quality. Reports in 2 weeks on queries; 8 weeks on mss. Sample copy and writer's guidelines for 9x12 SAE and $2.
Nonfiction: Essays and interview/profile. Buys 25 mss/year. Query. Length: 1,500-3,500 words. Pays $75-300 for assigned articles. Pays $75-250 for unsolicited articles.
Photos: Send photos with submission. Reviews prints (5x7). Offers no additional payment for photos accepted with ms. Captions and identification of subjects required. Buys one-time rights.
Columns/Departments: Marian Kirven, Fringe Benefits (book, film, art, video reviews relevant to *Chrysalis* subject matter), 350-750 words; Dr. Stephen Larsen, Vital Issues (articles and material related to practical psychology, health, healing), 1,000-3,000 words; Currents (articles and material on the fine and visionary arts). Buys 12 mss/year. Query. Length: 350-3,500 words. Pays $75-250.
Fiction: Adventure, experimental, historical, mainstream, mystery and science fiction. Buys 6 mss/year. Query. Length: 1,500-3,500 words. Pays $75-250.
Poetry: Julia Randall, poetry editor. Avant-garde and traditional. Buys 5 poems/year. Submit maximum 6

Close-up

John Seekamp
President
Swedenborg Foundation

"We want to interest a broad range of readers with *Chrysalis*," says John Seekamp, president of the Swedenborg Foundation.

Since 1850 the foundation has been publishing Emanuel Swedenborg's works and interpretive books based on his writing. The magazine, *Chrysalis*, was started in 1986 to "introduce more and more people to Emanuel Swedenborg," Seekamp says. "Swedenborg wrote 30 volumes on his spiritual experiences, but he also wrote about 120 volumes on science, math and cosmology."

Articles in the magazine reflect that diversity and are designed "for the intellectually curious reader, not necessarily a Christian, not necessarily someone interested in organized religions, but for the reader interested in spiritual topics," Seekamp says. In addition to long articles, the magazine also publishes short 1,500-2,000-word articles, book and film reviews and poetry.

Many of the articles are based on writing by Swedenborg, an 18th-century scientist and theologian, "but we include work from writers who may not be particularly knowledgable about Swedenborg but are knowledgable about a particular theme," Seekamp says.

All issues of *Chrysalis* are based on a central theme decided by the editors. "We have about 10 or 15 people trading ideas and coming up with possibilities. Then we finalize those ideas into future themes," Seekamp says. A schedule of upcoming themes is available through the magazine. "We take a subject for the entire issue and follow it through," Seekamp says. Issues to date have included themes as diverse as angels, wisdom, and gardens and architecture, and upcoming editions will feature articles on mysticism of Eastern Europe and The Tree of Knowledge. Articles in the magazine cover a wide range of subjects; under the angels theme, "Swedenborg on Angels," "Are Angels in Their Ancient Places?" and "Hollywood Angels" were articles included. Fine arts, psychology, theology and architecture are also among the fields covered by the magazine.

"We really want to attract a number of different authors," he adds. "We are looking for somebody who has a philosophical bent, maybe theology, but not necessarily Swedenborgian. Most of our writers now are from the Swedenborgian community—our churches, societies and foundations—but it's our design to get more authors from other areas."

—*Glenda Tennant Neff*

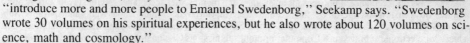

❝ We include work from writers who may not be particularly knowledgable about Swedenborg but are knowledgable about a particular theme. ❞

—*John Seekamp*

poems. Length: 70 (characters per line). Pays $25-75.
Tips: "We have an additional sheet of information for authors available on request. Every section is open to freelancers, with the exception of the preface."

CHURCH & STATE, Americans United for Separation of Church and State, 8120 Fenton St., Silver Spring MD 20910. (301)589-3707. Managing Editor: Joseph Conn. 10% freelance written. Prefers to work with published/established writers. Monthly magazine. Emphasizes religious liberty and church/state relations matters. Readership "includes the whole spectrum, but is predominantly Protestant and well-educated." Circ. 50,000. Pays on acceptance. Publishes ms an average of 2 months after acceptance. Buys all rights. Simultaneous, photocopied, and previously published submissions OK. Computer printout submissions OK; prefers letter-quality. Reports in 1 month. Sample copy and writer's guidelines for 9x12 SAE and 3 first class stamps.
Nonfiction: Expose, general interest, historical and interview. Buys 11 mss/year. Query. Length: 3,000 words maximum. Pays negotiable fee.
Photos: State availability of photos with query. Pays negotiable fee for b&w prints. Captions preferred. Buys one-time rights.

THE CHURCH HERALD, 6157 28th St., SE, Grand Rapids MI 49506-6999. Editor: Rev. Dr. John Stapert. Managing Editor: Jeff Japinga. 20% freelance written. Prefers to work with published/established writers; works with small number of new/unpublished writers each year. Biweekly magazine covering contemporary Christian life. "The *Church Herald* is the denominational publication of the Reformed Church in America, a Protestant denomination in the Presbyterian-Reformed family of churches. We solicit carefully researched and well-written articles on almost any subject, but they all must have a distinctively Christian perspective." Circ. 50,000. Pays on acceptance. Publishes ms an average of 3 months after acceptance. Byline given. Offers 50% kill fee. Buys first rights, one-time rights, second serial (reprint) rights, simultaneous rights and all rights. Submit seasonal/holiday material 3 months in advance. Simultaneous and previously published submissions OK. Query for electronic submissions. Computer printout submissions OK; no dot-matrix. Reports in 1 month on queries; 2 months on mss. Sample copy and writer's guidelines for 9x12 SAE with 4 first class stamps.
Nonfiction: Essays, general interest, humor, inspirational, personal experience, religious. Buys 30 mss/year. Send complete ms. Length: 400-1,500 words. Pays $45-150 for assigned articles. Pays $45-120 for unsolicited articles. Sometimes pays expenses of writers on assignment.
Photos: State availability of photos with submission. Reviews color transparencies and 8x10 b&w prints. Offers $25-50 per photo. Model releases required. Buys one-time rights.
Fiction: Religious. "We consider good fiction written from a Christian perspective. Avoid pious sentimentality and obvious plots." Buys 15 mss/year. Send complete ms. Length: 400-1,500. Pays $45-120.
Poetry: Free verse and traditional. Buys 10 poems/year. Submit maximum of 10 poems at one time. Length: up to 30 lines. Pays $25-45.
Tips: "We're shifting our publication schedule from 22 issues per year to 12 issues per year. Research articles carefully. Superficial articles are immediately recognizable; they cannot be disguised by big words or professional jargon. Writers need not have personally experienced everything they write about, but they must have done careful research. Also, what our readers want are new solutions to recognized problems. If a writer doesn't have any, he or she should try another subject." Sections most open to freelancers are feature articles and poetry.

COLUMBIA, Drawer 1670, New Haven CT 06507. Editor: Richard McMunn. Monthly magazine for Catholic families; caters particularly to members of the Knights of Columbus. Circ. 1 million. Pays on acceptance. Buys first time serial rights. Submit seasonal material 6 months in advance. Reports in 1 month. Free sample copy and writer's guidelines.
Nonfiction: Fact articles directed to the Catholic layman and his family dealing with current events, social problems, Catholic apostolic activities, education, ecumenism, rearing a family, literature, science, humor, satire, arts, sports and leisure. Color glossy prints, transparencies or contact prints with negatives are required for illustration. Articles without ample illustrative material are not given consideration. Pays up to $500, including photos. Photo stories are also wanted. Buys 30 mss/year. Query or submit complete ms. Length: 1,000-1,500 words. Pays $200.
Photos: Pays $50 per photo used. Pays 10¢/word.

COMMENTS, From the Friends, Box 840, Stoughton MA 02072. Editor: David A. Reed. 20% freelance written. A quarterly Christian newsletter written especially for "Jehovah's Witnesses, ex-Jehovah's Witnesses and persons concerned about Jehovah's Witnesses, relatives, friends, and neighbors." Circ. 1,200. Pays on publication. Publishes ms an average of 3 months after acceptance. Byline sometimes given. Buys second serial (reprint) and simultaneous rights. Submit seasonal/holiday material 4 months in advance. Simultaneous, photocopied and previously published submissions OK. Query for electronic submissions. Computer printout submissions acceptable; prefers letter-quality. Reports in 1 month on mss. Sample copy $1; writer's guidelines for #10 SAE with 2 first class stamps.

Nonfiction: Book excerpts, essays, exposé, how-to (witnessing tips), humor, inspirational, interview/profile, personal experience, religious and book reviews of books on cults only. Special issue topic will be The Next Watchtower President (replacing Fred Franz). "No general religious material not written specifically for our unique readership." Buys 8 mss/year. Send complete ms. Length: 200-1,000 words. Pays $2-20. May pay with contributor copies rather than a cash payment "when a writer contributes an article as a gift to this ministry."

Columns/Departments: Witnessing Tips (brief, powerful and effective approaches), 250-300 words; and News Briefs (current events involving Jehovah's Witnesses and ex-Jehovah's Witnesses), 60-240 words. Buys 4 mss/year. Send complete ms. Length: 60-300 words. Pays $2-10.

Fillers: Facts, newsbreaks and quotes. Buys 4/year. Length: 10-50 words. Pays $1-5.

Tips: "Acquaint us with your background that qualifies you to write in this field. Write well-documented, germane articles in layman's language."

THE COMPANION OF ST. FRANCIS AND ST. ANTHONY, Conventual Franciscan Friars, Box 535, Postal Station F, Toronto, Ontario M4Y 2L8 Canada. (416)924-6349. Editor-in-Chief: Friar Philip Kelly, OFM Conv. 15% freelance written. Monthly magazine. Emphasizing religious and human values and stressing Franciscan virtues—peace, simplicity, joy. Circ. 10,000. Pays on acceptance. Publishes ms an average of 6 months after acceptance. Buys first North American serial rights. Phone queries OK. Submit seasonal/holiday material 6 months in advance. Computer printout submissions acceptable; prefers letter-quality. Reports in 6 weeks. Writer's guidelines for SAE with IRCs.

Nonfiction: Historical; how-to (medical and psychological coping); informational; inspirational; interview; nostalgia; profile; and family. No old time religion, antiCatholic or pro-abortion material. No poetry. Buys 6 mss/issue. Send complete ms. Length: 800-1,000 words. Pays 6¢/word, Canadian funds.

Photos: Photos purchased with accompanying ms. Pays $8 for 5x7 (but all sizes accepted) b&w glossy prints. Send prints. Total purchase price for ms includes payment for photos. Captions required.

Fiction: Adventure, humorous, mainstream and religious. Canadian settings preferred. Buys 6 mss/year. Send complete ms. Length: 800-1,000 words. Pays 6¢/word, Canadian funds.

Tips: "Manuscripts on human interest with photos are given immediate preference. In the year ahead we will be featuring shorter articles, more Canadian and Franciscan themes, and better photos. Use a good typewriter, good grammar and good sense."

CONFIDENT LIVING, Box 82808, Lincoln NE 68501. (402)474-4567. Editor: Warren Wiersbe. 40% freelance written. Monthly interdenominational magazine for adults from 17 years of age and up. Circ. 125,000. Pays on acceptance. Buys first serial rights or first North American serial rights, or occasionally second serial (reprint) rights. Submit seasonal material at least 1 year in advance. Computer printout submissions acceptable if double spaced; no dot-matrix. Reports in 5 weeks. Sample copy $1.50; writer's guidelines with SASE.

Nonfiction: Managing Editor, Norman A. Olson. Articles which will help the reader learn and apply Christian Biblical principles to his life from the writer's or the subject's own experience. Writers are required "to affirm agreement with our doctrinal statement. We are especially looking for true, personal experience 'salvation,' church, children's ages 4-10, missions, 'youth' (17 years and over), 'parents', 'how to live the Christian life' articles, reports and interviews regarding major and interesting happenings and people in fundamental, evangelical Christian circles." Nothing rambling or sugary sweet, or without Biblical basis. Details or statistics should be authentic and verifiable. Style should be conservative but concise. Prefers that Scripture references be from the *New American Standard Bible* or the *Authorized Version* or the *New Scofield Reference Bible*. Buys approximately 100 mss/year. Length: 1,500 words maximum. Pays 4-10¢/word. "When you can get us to assign an article to you, we pay nearer the maximum. More manuscripts are now rejected if unaccompanied by photos." Sometimes pays expenses of writers on assignment.

Photos: Pays $25 maximum for b&w glossies; $75 maximum for color transparencies. Photos paid on publication.

Tips: "The basic purpose of the magazine is to explain the Bible and how it is relevant to life because we believe this will accomplish one of two things—to present Christ as Savior to the lost or to promote the spiritual growth of believers, so don't ignore our primary purposes when writing for us. Nonfiction should be Biblical and timely; at the least Biblical in principle. Use illustrations of your own experiences or of someone else's when God solved a problem similar to the reader's. Be so specific that the meanings and significance will be crystal clear to all readers."

CONSCIENCE, A Newsjournal of Prochoice Catholic Opinion, Catholics for a Free Choice, Suite 301, 1436 U St., NW, Washington DC 20009-3916. (202)638-1706. Editor: Janice Hughes. 80% freelance written. Eager to work with new/unpublished writers. Bimonthly newsjournal covering reproductive rights, specifically abortion rights in area of church and church and government in U.S. and worldwide. "A feminist, prochoice perspective is a must, and knowledge of Christianity and specifically Catholicism is helpful." Circ. 10,000. Pays on publication. Publishes ms an average of 4 months after acceptance. Byline given. Buys first

North American serial rights; makes work-for-hire assignments. Submit seasonal/holiday material 4 months in advance. Simultaneous queries, and simultaneous, photocopied, and previously published submissions OK. Query for electronic submissions. Computer printout submissions acceptable. Reports in 2 months; free sample copy for #10 SASE with 1 first class stamp; free writer's guidelines for #10 SAE with 1 first class stamp.

Nonfiction: Book excerpts, interview/profile, opinion and personal experience. Especially needs "expose/refutation of antichoice misinformation and specific research into the implications of new reproductive technology and fetal personhood bills/court decisions." Buys 8-12 mss/year. Query with published clips or send complete ms. Length: 1,000-3,500 words. Pays $100-150. "Writers should be aware that we are a nonprofit organization." A substantial number of articles are contributed without payment by writers. Sometimes pays the expenses of writers on assignment.

Photos: State availability of photos with query or ms. Prefers 5x7 b&w prints. Identification of subjects required. Buys all rights.

Columns/Departments: Book reviews. Buys 6-10 mss/year. Send complete ms. Length: 1,000-2,000 words. Pays $75 maximum.

Fillers: Clippings and newsbreaks. Uses 6/year. Length: 25-100 words. No payment.

Tips: "Say something new on the abortion issue. Thoughtful, well-researched and well-argued articles needed. The most frequent mistakes made by writers in completing an article for us are untimeliness and wordiness. When you have shown you can write thoughtfully, we may hire you for other types of articles."

CORNERSTONE, Jesus People USA, 4707 N. Malden, Chicago IL 60640. Editor: Dawn Herrin. 10% freelance written. Works with a small number of new/unpublished writers each year; eager to work with new/unpublished writers. A bimonthly magazine covering contemporary issues in the light of Evangelical Christianity. Circ. 90,000. Pays after publication. Publishes ms an average of 4-6 months after acceptance. Byline given. Buys first serial rights. Submit seasonal/holiday material 6 months in advance. Simultaneous, photocopied and previously published submissions OK. Computer printout submissions acceptable. Reports in 1 month. Sample copy and writer's guidelines for 9x12 SAE with 4 first class stamps.

Nonfiction: Essays, personal experience, religious. Buys 3-4 mss/year. Query. Length: 2,700 words maximum. Pays negotiable rate. Sometimes pays the expenses of writers on assignment.

Photos: Send photos with accompanying ms. Reviews 8x10 b&w and color prints and 35mm slides. Identification of subjects required. Buys negotiable rights.

Columns/Departments: Music (interview with artists, mainly rock, focusing on artist's world view and value system as expressed in his/her music); Current Events; Personalities; Film and Book Reviews (focuses on meaning as compared and contrasted to Biblical values). Buys 2-6 mss/year. Query. Length: 100-2,500 words (negotiable). Pays negotiable rate.

Fiction: "Articles may express Christian world view but should not be unrealistic or 'syrupy.' Other than porn, the sky's the limit. We want fiction as creative as the Creator." Buys 1-4 mss/year. Send complete ms. Length: 250-2,500 words (negotiable). Pays negotiable rate.

Poetry: Avant-garde, free verse, haiku, light verse and traditional. No limits *except* for epic poetry ("We've not the room!"). Buys 10-50 poems/year. Submit maximum 10 poems. Payment negotiated.

Fillers: Anecdotes, facts, short humor and newsbreaks. Buys 5-15 year. Length: 20-200 words (negotiable). Payment negotiable.

Tips: "A display of creativity which expresses a biblical world view without cliches or cheap shots at non-Christians is the ideal. We are known as the most avant-garde magazine in the Christian market, yet attempt to express orthodox beliefs in language of the '80s. *Any* writer who does this may well be published by *Cornerstone*. Creative fiction is begging for more Christian participation. We anticipate such contributions gladly. Interviews where well-known personalities respond to the gospel are also strong publication possibilities. Please address all submissions to: Sarah Sullivan, assistant editor."

THE COVENANT COMPANION, Covenant Press of the Evangelical Covenant Church, 5101 N. Francisco Ave., Chicago IL 60625. (312)784-3000. Editor: James R. Hawkinson. 10-15% freelance written. "As the official monthly organ of The Evangelical Covenant Church, we seek to inform, stimulate, and gather the denomination we serve by putting Covenants in touch with each other and assisting them in interpreting contemporary issues. We also seek to inform them on events in the church. Our background is evangelical and our emphasis is on Christian commitment and life." Circ. 26,500. Publishes ms an average of 2 months after acceptance. Byline given. Buys first or all rights. Submit seasonal/holiday material 4 months in advance. Simultaneous and previously published submissions OK. Query for electronic submissions. Computer printout submissions acceptable; prefers letter-quality. Sample copy $1.50; writer's guidelines for #10 SAE and 1 first class stamp.

Nonfiction: Humor, inspirational and religious. Buys 10-15 mss/year. Send complete ms. Length: 500-2,000 words. Pays $15-50 for assigned articles; pays $15-35 for unsolicited articles.

Photos: Send photos with submissions. Reviews prints. Offers no additonal payment for photos accepted with ms. Identification of subjects required. Buys one-time rights.

Poetry: Traditional. Buys 10-15 poems/year. Submit maximum 10 poems. Pays $10-15.

Tips: "Seasonal articles related to church year and on national holidays are welcome."

DAILY MEDITATION, Box 2710, San Antonio TX 78299. Editor: Ruth S. Paterson. Quarterly. Byline given. Rights purchased vary. Payment on acceptance. Submit seasonal material 6 months in advance. Sample copy 50¢.
Nonfiction: "Inspirational, self-improvement and nonsectarian religious articles, 750-1,600 words, showing the path to greater spiritual growth." Pays 1-1½¢/word.
Fillers: Length: 400 words maximum.
Poetry: Inspirational. Length: 16 lines maximum. Pays 14¢/line.
Tips: "All our material is freelance submission for consideration except our meditations which are staff written. We buy approximately 250 manuscripts a year. We must see finished manuscripts; no queries, please. Checking copy is sent upon publication."

DAILY WORD, Unity School of Christianity, Unity Village MO 64065. (816)524-3550. Editor: Colleen Zuck. A monthly magazine of articles, poems, lessons and meditation. Circ. 2.5 million. Pays on acceptance. Publishes ms an average of 6 months after acceptance. Byline given on articles and poetry only. Buys first rights. Submit seasonal/holiday material 8 months in advance. Computer printout submissions OK; prefers letter-quality. Reports in 6 weeks on mss. Free sample copy and writer's guidelines.
Nonfiction: Inspirational and religious. Buys 250 mss/year. Send complete ms. Length: 1,500 words. Pays $20/page.
Poetry: Free verse and traditional. Buys 12-15 poems/year. Pays $1 per line.

DECISION, Billy Graham Evangelistic Association, 1300 Harmon Place, Minneapolis MN 55403. (612)338-0500. Editor: Roger C. Palms. 40% freelance written. Works with small number of new/unpublished writers each year. A magazine, published 11 times per year, "to set forth to every reader the Good News of salvation in Jesus Christ with such vividness and clarity that he or she will be drawn to make a commitment to Christ; to encourage, teach and strengthen Christians." Circ. 2 million. Pays on publication. Publishes ms an average of 1 year after acceptance. Byline given. Buys first rights and makes work-for-hire assignments. Include telephone number with submission. Submit seasonal/holiday material 8 months in advance. Photocopied submissions OK. Computer printout submissions OK; no dot-matrix. Reports in 2 weeks on queries; 2 months on mss. Sample copy for 8½x11 SAE and 4 first class stamps; writer's guidelines for #10 SASE.
Nonfiction: How-to, motivational, personal experience and religious. "No personality-centered articles or articles which are issue oriented or critical of denominations." Buys approximately 100 mss/year. Send complete ms. Length: 400-2,000 words. Pays $10-200. Pays expenses of writers on assignment.
Photos: State availability of photos with submission. Reviews prints. Captions, model releases and identification of subjects required. Buys one-time rights.
Poetry: Free verse and traditional. No long or secular poems. Buys 35 poems/year. Submit maximum 6 poems. Length: 4-20 lines. Pays approximately 30¢ per word.
Tips: "We are seeking personal conversion testimonies, personal experience articles which show how God intervened in a person's daily life and the way in which Scripture was applied to the experience in helping to solve the problem. SASE required with submissions."

THE DISCIPLE, Box 179, St. Louis MO 63166. Editor: James L. Merrell. 10% freelance written. Monthly published by Christian Board of Publication of the Christian Church (Disciples of Christ). For ministers and church members, both young and older adults. Circ. 58,000. Pays month after publication. Publishes ms an average of 9 months after acceptance. Buys first serial rights. Photocopied and simultaneous submissions OK. Computer printout submissions acceptable; no dot-matrix. Submit seasonal material at least 6 months in advance. Reports in 1 month. Sample copy $1.50; free writer's guidelines for SAE and 1 first class stamp.
Nonfiction: Articles and meditations on religious themes, short pieces, and some humorous. No fiction. Buys 100 unsolicited mss/year. Length: 500-800 words. Pays $10-50.
Photos: Reviews 8x10 b&w glossy prints. Occasional b&w glossy prints, any size, used to illustrate articles. Occasional color. "We are looking for b&w photos of church activities—worship, prayer, dinners, etc." Pays $10-25; $35-100/cover. Pays for photos at end of month after acceptance.
Poetry: Uses 3-5 poems/issue. Traditional forms, blank verse, free verse and light verse. Length: 16 lines maximum. Themes may be seasonal, historical, religious and occasionally humorous. Pays $3-20.
Tips: "We're looking for personality features about lay disciples, churches. Give a good summary of story idea in query. Queries on Christian values in television, radio, film and music desired. We use articles primarily from disciples, ministers and lay persons since our magazine is written to attract the denomination. We are barraged with features that mainly deal with subjects that don't interest our readers; fillers are more general, thus more easily placed. We work with more secular poets than writers and the poets write in religious themes for us."

DISCIPLESHIP JOURNAL, NavPress, a division of The Navigators, Box 6000, Colorado Springs CO 80934. (719)528-5363 ext. 291. Editor: Susan Maycinik. Editorial Director: Bruce Nygren. 90% freelance written. Works with a small number of new/unpublished writers each year. Bimonthly magazine on Christian discipleship. "The mission of *Discipleship Journal* is to help people examine, understand, and practice the truths of the Bible, so that they may know Jesus Christ, become like Him, and labor for His Kingdom by gathering other men and women into the fellowship of His committed disciples." Circ. 80,000. Pays on acceptance. Publishes ms an average of 4 months after acceptance. Byline given. Buys first North American serial rights and second serial (reprint) rights. Submit seasonal/holiday material 6 months in advance. Simultaneous queries, and simultaneous and previously published submissions OK. Query for electronic submissions. Computer printout submissions acceptable; prefers letter-quality. Reports in 1 month on queries; 2 months on mss. Sample copy and writer's guidelines for 9x12 SAE and 7 first class stamps.

Nonfiction: Book excerpts (rarely); how-to (grow in Christian faith and disciplines; help others grow as Christians; serve people in need; understand and apply the Bible); inspirational; interview/profile (of Christian leaders, focusing on discipleship); and interpretation/application of the Bible. No personal testimony; humor; anything not directly related to Christian life and faith; politically partisan articles. Buys 85 mss/year. Query with published clips or send complete ms. Length: 500-3,000 words. Pays 2¢/word reprint; 10-12¢/word first rights. Pays the expenses of writers on assignment.

Tips: "Our articles are meaty, not fluffy. Study writers guidelines and back issues and try to use similar approaches. Don't preach. Polish before submitting. About half of the articles in each issue are related to one theme. Freelancers should write to request theme list. We are looking for more practical articles on ministering to others and more articles dealing with world missions."

EPISCOPAL CHURCH FACTS, From Western New York, Epicopal Diocese of W.N.Y., 1114 Delaware Ave., Buffalo NY 14209. (716)875-8374. Editor: Rev. Donald B. Hill. 35% freelance written. Monthly newspaper covering news and features of interest to Episcopalians. Circ. 11,500. Pays on publication. Publishes ms an average of 2 months after acceptance. Byline given. Not copyrighted. Buys first rights. Submit seasonal/holiday material 3 months in advance. Simultaneous and photocopied submissions OK. Computer printout submissions OK. Free sample copy.

Nonfiction: General interest, humor, inspirational, and religious. No highly pious generic Christian material. Buys 20 mss/year. Query with or without published clips or send complete ms. Length: 100-3,000 words. Pays $25-50. Sometimes pays expenses of writers on assignment.

Photos: State availability of photos with submission. Reviews 5x7 prints. Offers $10-25 per photo. Captions and identification of subjects required. Buys one-time rights.

Fillers: Anecdotes and short humor. Buys 12/year.

THE EPISCOPALIAN, 1201 Chestnut St., Philadelphia PA 19107. (215)564-2010. Publisher: Richard Crawford. Managing Editor: Richard H. Schmidt. 60% freelance written. Accepts submissions from a small number of new/unpublished writers each year. Monthly tabloid about the Episcopal Church for Episcopalians. Circ. 250,000. Pays on publication. Publishes ms an average of 2 months after acceptance. Byline given. Submit seasonal/holiday material 2 months in advance. Previously published submissions OK. Computer printout submissions acceptable; prefers letter-quality. Reports in 1 month. Sample copy for 3 first class stamps.

Nonfiction: Inspirational and interview/profile (of Episcopalians participating in church or community activities). "I like action stories about people doing things and solving problems. I like quotes, photos and active voice." No personal experience articles. Buys 24 mss/year. Send complete ms. Length: 1,000-1,500 words. Pays $25-200. Rarely pays expenses of writers on assignment.

Photos: Pays $10 for b&w glossy prints. Identification of subjects required. Buys one-time rights.

Tips: "Stories must have an Episcopal Church connection."

ETERNITY MAGAZINE, Evangelical Ministries, Inc., 1716 Spruce St., Philadelphia PA 19103. (215)546-3696. Executive Editor: Donald J. McCrory. A monthly magazine intended "to help readers apply God's Word to all areas of life today." Circ. 30,000. Pays on the 15th of the month previous to issue publication. Byline given. Offers $15-25 kill fee. Sample copy $2; writer's guidelines for #10 SAE and 1 first class stamp.

Nonfiction: Query first. Unsolicited mss not accepted. Query should outline proposal, news peg and main points. No fiction; no short, devotional fillers. Length: 500-1,500 words. Pays $35-150.

EVANGEL, Dept. of Christian Education, Free Methodist Headquarters, 901 College Ave., Winona Lake IN 46590. (219)267-7161. Editor: Vera Bethel. 100% freelance written. Weekly magazine. Audience is 65% female, 35% male; married, 25-31 years old, mostly city dwellers, high school graduates, mostly nonprofessional. Circ. 35,000. Pays on publication. Publishes ms an average of 1 year after acceptance. Buys simultaneous rights, second serial (reprint) rights or one-time rights. Submit seasonal/holiday material 3 months in advance. Computer printout submissions acceptable; no dot-matrix. Reports in 1 month. Sample copy and writer's guidelines for 6x9 SAE with 2 first class stamps.

Nonfiction: Interview (with ordinary person who is doing something extraordinary in his community, in service to others); profile (of missionary or one from similar service profession who is contributing significantly to society); and personal experience (finding a solution to a problem common to young adults; coping with handicapped child, for instance, or with a neighborhood problem. Story of how God-given strength or insight saved

a situation). Buys 100 mss/year. Submit complete ms. Length: 300-1,000 words. Pays $10-25.
Photos: Purchased with accompanying ms. Captions required. Send prints. Pays $5-10 for 8x10 b&w glossy prints; $2 for snapshots.
Fiction: Religious themes dealing with contemporary issues dealt with from a Christian frame of reference. Story must "go somewhere." Buys 50 mss/year. Submit complete ms. Length: 1,200 words. Pays $35.
Poetry: Free verse, haiku, light verse, traditional and religious. Buys 50 poems/year. Submit maximum 6 poems. Length: 4-24 lines. Pays $5.
Tips: "Seasonal material will get a second look (won't be rejected so easily) because we get so little. Write an attention grabbing lead followed by a body of article that says something worthwhile. Relate the lead to some of the universal needs of the reader—promise in that lead to help the reader in some way. Remember that everybody is interested most in himself. Lack of SASE brands author as a nonprofessional; I seldom even bother to read the script. If the writer doesn't want the script back, it probably has no value for me, either."

THE EVANGELICAL BEACON, 1515 E. 66th St., Minneapolis MN 55423. (612)866-3343. Editor: George Keck. 30% freelance written. Works with a small number of new/unpublished writers each year. Denominational magazine of the Evangelical Free Church of America—evangelical Protestant readership; published 17 times/year (every third Monday, except for a 4 week interval, June-August). Pays on publication. Publishes ms an average of 6 months after acceptance. Rights purchased vary with author and material. Buys first rights or all rights, and some reprints. Computer printout submissions acceptable; prefers letter-quality. Reports in 8-10 weeks. Sample copy and writer's guidelines for 75¢.
Nonfiction: Articles on the church, Christ-centered human interest and personal testimony articles, well researched on current issues of religious interest. Desires crisp, imaginative, original writing—not sermons on paper. Length: 250-2,000 words. Pays 3¢/word with extra payment on some articles, at discretion of editor.
Photos: Prefers 8x10 b&w photos. Pays $10 minimum.
Fiction: Not much fiction used, but will consider. Length: 100-1,500 words.
Poetry: Very little poetry used. Pays variable rate, $3.50 minimum.
Tips: "Articles need to be helpful to the average Christian—encouraging, challenging, instructive. Also needs material presenting reality of the Christian faith to nonChristians. Some tie-in with the Evangelical Free Church of America is helpful but not required."

EVANGELIZING TODAY'S CHILD, Child Evangelism Fellowship Inc., Warrenton MO 63383. (314)456-4321. Editor: Elsie Lippy. 75% freelance written. Prefers to work with published/established writers. Bimonthly magazine; 72 pages. "Our purpose is to equip Christians to win the world's children to Christ and disciple them. Our readership is Sunday school teachers, Christian education leaders and children's workers in every phase of Christian ministry to children up to 12 years old." Circ. 28,000. Pays within 90 days of acceptance. Publishes ms an average of 6 months after acceptance. Byline given. Offers 30% kill fee if assigned. Buys first serial rights. Submit seasonal/holiday material 6 months in advance. Simultaneous queries and photocopied submissions OK. Computer printout submissions acceptable; no dot-matrix. Reports in 3 weeks on queries; 2 months on mss. Free sample copy; writer's guidelines with SASE.
Nonfiction: Unsolicited articles welcomed from writers with Christian education training or current experience in working with children. Buys 35 mss/year. Query. Length: 1,800-2,000. Pays 6-9¢/word.
Photos: Submissions of photos on speculation accepted. Needs photos of children or related subjects. Pays $25 for 8x10 b&w glossy prints; $100 for color transparencies.

FUNDAMENTALIST JOURNAL, Old-Time Gospel Hour, 2220 Langhorne Rd., Lynchburg VA 24514. (804)528-4112. Publisher: Jerry Falwell. Editor: Deborah Wade Huff. 40% freelance written. Works with a small number of new/unpublished writers. A Christian magazine (nonprofit organization) published monthly (July/August combined) covering "matters of interest to all Fundamentalists, providing inspirational articles, features on current issues, human interest stories, profiles, reviews and news reports." Audience is 65% Baptist; 35% other denominations; 30% pastors, 70% other. Circ. 85,000. Pays on publication. Publishes ms an average of 4-12 months after acceptance. Byline given. Offers kill fee on assigned articles. Buys all rights, first North American serial rights, makes work-for-hire assignments. Submit seasonal/holiday material 6 months in advance. Previously published submissions OK. Computer printout submissions acceptable; prefers letter-quality. Reports in 3 months. Sample copy for 9x12 SAE with 4 first class stamps; writer's guidelines for #10 SAE and 1 first class stamp.
Nonfiction: Earlene R. Goodwin, articles editor. Book excerpts; expose (government, communism, education); general interest; historical/nostalgic (regarding the Bible, Christianity, great Christians of old); inspirational, interview/profile; opinion, and personal experience. "Writing must be consistent with Fundamentalist doctrine. We do not want articles that are critical in naming leaders of churches or Christian organizations." Buys 77 mss/year. Query. Length: 500-2,000 words. Pays 10¢/printed word for major articles; 20¢/printed word for shorter articles in special sections. Sometimes pays the expenses of writers on assignment.
Columns/Departments: Length: 300-2,000 words. Pays 10¢/printed word; $10-25 for book reviews.
Tips: "We are looking for more articles to encourage and support the Christian family. We ask writers to sub-

mit query first. News is usually by assignment; various articles of general interest to Fundamentalist Christian readers, perspective, profiles, missions articles, family living articles and brief articles dealing with pastoring are most open to freelancers."

GOOD NEWS, The Bimonthly Magazine For United Methodists, Box 150, Wilmore KY 40390. (606)858-4661. Editor: James V. Heidinger II. Executive Editor: James S. Robb. 20% freelance written. Prefers to work with published/established writers; works with a small number of new/unpublished writers each year. Bimonthly magazine for United Methodist lay people and pastors, primarily middle income; conservative and Biblical religious beliefs; broad range of political, social and cultural values. "We are the only evangelical magazine with the purpose of working within the United Methodist Church for Biblical reform and evangelical renewal." Circ. 20,000. Pays on acceptance. Publishes ms an average of 8 months after acceptance. Byline given. Buys first serial rights, simultaneous rights, and second serial (reprint) rights. Submit seasonal/holiday material 6 months in advance. Simultaneous submissions with noncompeting publications OK. Prefers original mss and not photocopies of reprinted material. Computer printout submissions acceptable. Reports in 3 months. Sample copy $2.25; free writer's guidelines.
Nonfiction: Historical (prominent people or churches from the Methodist/Evangelical United Brethren tradition); how-to (build faith, work in local church); humor (good taste); inspirational (related to Christian faith); personal experience (case histories of God at work in individual lives); and any contemporary issues as they relate to the Christian faith and/or the United Methodist Church. No sermons or secular material. Buys 25 mss/year. Must query first with a "brief description of the article, perhaps a skeleton outline. Show some enthusiasm about the article and writing (and research). Tell us something about yourself including whether you or the article has United Methodist tie-in. Send manuscripts % associate editor." Length: 1,500-1,800 words. Pays 5-7¢/word, more on occasion for special assignments. Sometimes pays the expenses of writers on assignment.
Photos: Extra payment for photos with accompanying ms. Uses fine screen b&w prints. Total purchase price for ms includes payment for photos. Payment negotiable. Captions required.
Tips: "Writers must be either United Methodists themselves or intimately familiar with the mindset of our church members. Evangelical slant is a must for all articles, yet we are not fundamentalist or sentimental. We are now moving away from predictable testimony pieces (though there is still room for the fresh testimony which ties in with burning issues, especially when written by Methodists). What we are looking for now are 1,200-word, newspaper style sketches of vibrant, evangelically-oriented United Methodist churches. Photos are a must. We'll hire a pro if we need to. We also need personality profiles of dynamic, unusual United Methodists with accompanying professional quality photo (evidence of vital faith in subject is required)."

‡THE GOSPEL TRUTH, Gospel Truth Ministries, Inc., Box 4148, Brockton MA 02403. (617)584-3838. Editor: David A. Reed. 25% freelance written. Quarterly newsletter covering religious cults and evangelism. "Our articles are written from an evangelical Christian perspective to an evangelical Christian audience." Circ. 1,000. Pays on publication. Publishes ms an average of 3 months after acceptance. Byline given. Buys one-time rights or second serial (reprint) rights. Simultaneous and previously published submissions OK. Query for electronic submissions. Computer printout submissions OK. Reports in 1 month. Sample copy for #10 SAE with 2 first class stamps; writer's guidelines for #10 SASE.
Nonfiction: Book excerpts on cults, expose on cults, how-to evangelize particular segments of society, personal experience (brief testimonies), religious (on evangelism), technical (apologetics), other news on cults and religious freedom issues. No general religious or inspirational material. Buys 8 mss/year. Send complete ms. Length: 100-1,000 words. Pays $5-50.
Photos: Offers $5-50.
Columns/Departments: Book Reviews (books on cults, issues confront the Church, religious freedom issues), 300-600 words; Witnessing Tips (how to share the Gosepl with members of a particular cult or population segment), 300-800 words. Buys 4 mss/year. Send complete ms. Pays $15-40.
Tips: "When writing on a cult group, please furnish your credentials that make you an authority on the subject. When submitting on religious freedom issues or news items, please include thorough documentation. Book reviews are most readily accepted from first-time writers. The book should be one relevant to this publication's field of interest. We operate a free lending library of books on the cults, so we are most interested in reviews of books that we feature or are likely to acquire."

GROUP, Thom Schultz Publications, Box 481, Loveland CO 80539. (303)669-3836. Editorial Director: Joani Schultz. 80% freelance written. Prefers to work with published/established writers, and works with a small number of new/unpublished writers each year. For leaders of high-school-age Christian youth groups. Magazine published 8 times/year. Circ. 63,000. Pays on acceptance. Publishes ms an average of 4 months after acceptance. Buys all rights. Byline given. Submit seasonal/holiday material 6 months in advance. Special Easter, Thanksgiving and Christmas issues. Computer printout submissions acceptable; prefers letter-quality. Reports in 1 month. Sample copy for 9x12 SAE and $1 postage; writer's guidelines for SASE.
Nonfiction: How-to (fundraising, membership-building, worship, games, discussions, activities, crowd breakers, simulation games); informational; (drama, worship, youth group projects, service projects); inspira-

tional (ministry encouragement). Buys 7 mss/issue. Query. Length: 500-1,700 words. Pays up to $150. Sometimes pays the expenses of writers on assignment.

Columns/Departments: Try This One (short ideas for games, crowd breakers, discussions, worship, fund raisers, service projects, etc.). Buys 5 mss/issue. Send complete ms. Length: 300 words maximum. Pays $15. News, Trends and Tips (leadership tips). Buys 1 mss/issue. Send complete ms. Length: 500 words maximum. Pays $25.

Tips: "A writer with youth ministry experience and a practical, conversational writing style will be more likely to be published in *Group*."

GROUP'S JUNIOR HIGH MINISTRY MAGAZINE, Thom Schultz Publications, Inc., 2890 N. Monroe Ave., Box 481, Loveland CO 80539. (303)669-3836. Editorial Director: Joani Schultz. 90% freelance written (assigned). Magazine published 5 times/year for leaders of junior-high Christian youth groups. "How-to articles for junior high membership building, worship planning, handling specific group problems and improving as a leader; hints for parents of junior highers; special style-formatted junior high group meetings on topics like competition, faith in action, seasonal themes, friendship, dealing with life situations and service projects." Circ. 26,000. Pays on acceptance. Publishes ms an average of 3 months after acceptance. Byline given. Offer $25 kill fee. Buys all rights and makes work-for-hire assignments. Submit seasonal/holiday material 6 months in advance. Query for electronic submissions. Computer printout submissions OK; no dot-matrix. Sample copy for 9x12 SAE with $1 postage; writer's guidelines for SASE.

Nonfiction: How-to, humor, inspirational/motivational, personal experience, religious/Bible studies, and curriculum. No fiction. Buys 65 assigned mss/year. Query. Length: 500-1,700. Pays $75-100 for assigned articles. Sometimes pays expenses of writers on assignment.

Photos: Send photos with submission. Reviews contact sheets, transparencies and prints. Offers $20-50/b&w photo; $50-150/color photo. Model releases required. Buys one-time rights (occasionally buys additional rights).

Columns/Departments: Parent's Page (brief helps for parents of junior highers; for example, tips on discipline, faith communication, building close family, parent-self understanding, practical help, understanding junior highers and values). Buys 30 mss/year. Send complete ms. Length: 150 words. Pays $25.

Tips: "Writers who are also successful junior high workers or teachers have the best chance of being published in *Jr. High Ministry* simply because they know the kids. We need authors who can give our readers practical tips for ministry with junior highers. We need step-by-step experiential, Bible-oriented, fun meetings for leaders to do with junior high youth groups. The meetings must help the kids apply their Christian faith to life and must follow the standard format in the magazine."

GUIDEPOSTS MAGAZINE, 747 3rd Ave., New York NY 10017. Editor: Van Varner. 30% freelance written. "Works with a small number of new/unpublished writers each year, and reads all unsolicited manuscripts. *Guideposts* is an inspirational monthly magazine for people of all faiths in which men and women from all walks of life tell in first-person narrative how they overcame obstacles, rose above failures, handled sorrow, learned to master themselves, and became more effective people through faith in God." Publishes ms an "indefinite" number of months after acceptance. Pays 25% kill fee for assigned articles. Byline given. "Most of our stories are ghosted articles, so the writer would not get a byline unless it was his/her own story." Buys all rights and second serial (reprint) rights. Computer printout submissions acceptable; prefers letter-quality.

Nonfiction and Fillers: Articles and features should be written in simple, anecdotal style with an emphasis on human interest. Short mss of approximately 250-750 words (pays $25-100) would be considered for such features as Quiet People and general one-page stories. Full-length mss, 750-1,500 words, pays $200-300. All mss should be typed, double-spaced and accompanied by a stamped, self-addressed envelope. Annually awards scholarships to high school juniors and seniors in writing contest. Buys 40-60 unsolicited mss/year. Pays expenses of writers on assignment.

Tips: "Study the magazine before you try to write for it. Each story must make a single spiritual point. The freelancer would have the best chance of breaking in by aiming for a one-page or maybe two-page article. That would be very short, say two and a half pages of typescript, but in a small magazine such things are very welcome. Sensitively written anecdotes are extremely useful. And they are much easier to just sit down and write than to have to go through the process of preparing a query. They should be warm, well written, intelligent and upbeat. We like personal narratives that are true and have some universal relevance, but the religious element does not have to be driven home with a sledge hammer. A writer succeeds with us if he or she can write a true article in short-story form with scenes, drama, tension and a resolution of the problem presented." Address short items to Rick Hamlin.

HICALL, Gospel Publishing House, 1445 Boonville Ave., Springfield MO 65802. (417)862-2781, ext. 4349. Editor: Sinda Zinn. Mostly freelance written. Eager to work with new/unpublished writers. Assemblies of God (denominational) weekly magazine of Christian fiction and articles for church-oriented teenagers, 12-17. Circ. 95,000. Pays on acceptance. Publishes ms an average of 6 months after acceptance. Byline given. Buys first North American serial rights, one-time rights, simultaneous rights, and second serial (reprint) rights. Submit

seasonal/holiday material 1 year in advance. Simultaneous, photocopied, and previously published submissions OK-if typed, double-spaced, on 8½x11 paper. Computer printout submissions acceptable; prefers letter-quality. Reports in 6 weeks. Sample copy for 8x11 SAE and 2 first class stamps; writer's guidelines for SAE.
Nonfiction: Book excerpts; historical; general interest; how-to (deal with various life problems); humor; inspirational; and personal experience. Buys 80-100 mss/year. Send complete ms. Length: 500-2,000 words. Pays 2-3¢/word.
Photos: Photos purchased with or without accompanying ms. Pays $25/8x10 b&w glossy print; $30/35mm.
Fiction: Adventure, humorous, mystery, romance, suspense, western and religious. Buys 80-100 mss/year. Send complete ms. Length: 500-2,000 words. Pays 2-3¢/word.
Poetry: Free verse, light verse and traditional. Buys 30 poems/year. Length: 10-30 lines. Pays 25¢/line, minimum of $5.
Fillers: Clippings, anecdotes, short humor and newsbreaks. Buys 30/year. Pays 2-3¢/word.

‡INTERLIT, David C. Cook Foundation, Cook Square, Elgin IL 60120. (312)741-2400, ext. 316. Editor: Tim Bascom. 90% freelance written on assignment. Works with a small number of new/unpublished writers each year. Quarterly journal. Emphasizes sharpening skills in Christian journalism and publishing. Especially for editors, publishers, and writers in the Third World (developing countries). Also goes to missionaries, broadcasters and educational personnel in the U.S. Circ. 6,000. Pays on acceptance. Publishes ms an average of 6 months after acceptance. Buys all rights. Photocopied submissions OK. Computer printout submissions acceptable. Reports in 4-6 weeks. Free sample copy.
Nonfiction: Technical and how-to articles about all aspects of publishing, writing, and literacy. "Please study publication and query before submitting manuscripts." Also photo features. Buys 7 mss/issue, mostly on assignment. Length: 500-1,500 words. Pays 6¢/word.
Photos: Purchased with accompanying ms only. Uses b&w. Query or send prints. Captions required.

THE JEWISH WEEKLY NEWS, Bennett-Scott Publications Corp., 99 Mill St., Box 1569, Springfield MA 01101. (413)739-4771. 25% freelance written. Eager to work with new/unpublished writers. Jewish news and features, secular and non-secular; World Judaism; arts (New England based). Circ. 2,500. Pays on publication. Publishes ms an average of 2 months after acceptance. Byline given. Not copyrighted. Buys first North American serial rights and second serial (reprint) rights. Submit seasonal/holiday material 2 months in advance. Simultaneous, photocopied and previously published submissions OK. Query for electronic submissions. Computer printout submissions OK. Sample copy for 9x12 SAE with 5 first class stamps.
Nonfiction: Interview/profile, religious and travel. Special issues include Jewish New Year (September); Chanukah (December); Home Issues (March); Financial (February). Buys 61 mss/year. Query with published clips. Length: 300-1,000 words. Pays $5.
Photos: Send photos with submission. Reviews 5x7 prints. Offers no additional payment for photos accepted with ms. Identification of subjects required.
Columns/Departments: Jewish Kitchen (Kosher recipes), 300-500 words. Buys 10 mss/year. Query with published clips. Length: 300-5,000 words. Pays 50¢/inch.
Fiction: Sheila Thompson, editor. Slice-of-life vignettes. Buys 5 mss/year. Query with published clips. Length: 750-1,000 words. Pays 50¢/inch.

LIGHT AND LIFE, Free Methodist Church of North America, 901 College Ave., Winona Lake IN 46590. Editor: Bob Haslam. 35% freelance written. Works with a small number of new/unpublished writers each year. Monthly magazine. Emphasizes evangelical Christianity with Wesleyan slant for a cross section of adults. Circ. 43,000. Pays on publication. Publishes ms an average of 6 months after acceptance. Byline given. Prefers first serial rights; rarely buys second serial (reprint) rights. Submit seasonal/holiday material 6 months in advance. Computer printout submissions acceptable; no dot-matrix. Reports in 6 weeks. Sample copy and guidelines $1.50; writer's guidelines for SASE.
Nonfiction: "Each issue includes a mini-theme (two or three articles addressing contemporary topics such as entertainment media, personal relationships, Christians as citizens), so freelancers should request our schedule of mini-theme topics. We also need fresh, upbeat articles showing the average layperson how to be Christ-like at home, work and play." Submit complete ms. Buys 70-80 unsolicited ms/year. Pays 4¢/word. Sometimes pays expenses of writers on assignment.
Photos: Purchased without accompanying ms. Send prints. Pays $5-35 for b&w photos. Offers additional payment for photos accepted with accompanying ms.

LIGUORIAN, Liguori MO 63057. Editor: Rev. Norman Muckerman. Managing Editor: Francine M. O'Connor. 50% freelance written. Prefers to work with published/established writers; works with a small number of new/unpublished writers each year. Monthly. For families with Catholic religious convictions. Circ. 525,000. Pays on acceptance. Publishes ms an average of 3-4 months after acceptance. Byline given "except on short fillers and jokes." Buys all rights but will reassign rights to author *after* publication upon written request. Submit seasonal material 6 months in advance. Query for electronic submissions. Computer printout submissions acceptable; no dot-matrix. Reports in 6 weeks. Sample copy and writer's guidelines for 6x9 SAE with 3 first class stamps.

Nonfiction: "Pastoral, practical and personal approach to the problems and challenges of people today. No travelogue approach or unresearched ventures into controversial areas. Also, no material found in secular publications—fad subjects that already get enough press, pop psychology, negative or put-down articles." Buys 60 unsolicited mss/year. Length: 400-2,000 words. Pays 10¢/word. Sometimes pays expenses of writers on assignment.

Photos: Photographs on assignment only unless submitted with and specific to article.

LIVE, 1445 Boonville Ave., Springfield MO 65802. (417)862-2781. Editor: John T. Maempa. 100% freelance written. Works with several new/unpublished writers each year. Weekly. For adults in Assemblies of God Sunday schools. Circ. 200,000. Pays on acceptance. Publishes ms an average of 1 year after acceptance. Not copyrighted. Submit seasonal material 1 year in advance; do not mention Santa Claus, Halloween or Easter bunnies. Computer printout submissions acceptable. Reports on material within 3-6 weeks. Free sample copy and writer's guidelines for SASE. Letters without SASE will not be answered.

Nonfiction: Articles with reader appeal emphasizing some phase of Christian living presented in a down-to-earth manner. Biography or missionary material using fiction techniques. Historical, scientific or nature material with spiritual lesson. "Be accurate in detail and factual material. Writing for Christian publications is a ministry. The spiritual emphasis must be an integral part of your material." Prefers not to see material on highly controversial subjects but would appreciate articles on contemporary issues and concerns (eg. substance abuse, AIDS, euthanasia, cults, integrity, etc.). Buys about 120 mss/year. Length: 1,000-1,600 words. Pays 3¢/word for first serial rights; 2¢/word for second serial (reprint) rights, according to the value of the material and the amount of editorial work necessary. "Please do not send large numbers of articles at one time."

Photos: Color photos or transparencies purchased with mss, or on assignment. Pay open.

Fiction: "Present believable characters working out their problems according to Bible principles; in other words, present Christianity in action without being preachy. We use very few serials, but we will consider three- to four-part stories if each part conforms to average word length for short stories. Each part must contain a spiritual emphasis and have enough suspense to carry the reader's interest from one week to the next. Stories should be true to life but not what we would feel is bad to set before the reader as a pattern for living. Stories should not put parents, teachers, ministers or other Christian workers in a bad light. Setting, plot and action should be realistic, with strong motivation. Characterize so that the people will live in your story. Construct your plot carefully so that each incident moves naturally and sensibly toward crisis and conclusion. An element of conflict is necessary in fiction. Short stories should be written from one viewpoint only. We do not accept fiction based on incidents in the Bible." Length: 1,200-1,600 words. Pays 3¢/word for first serial rights; 2¢/word for second serial (reprint) rights. "Please do not send large numbers of articles at one time."

Poetry: Traditional, free and blank verse. Length: 12-20 lines. "Please do not send large numbers of poems at one time." Pays 20¢/line.

Fillers: Brief and purposeful, usually containing an anecdote, and always with a strong evangelical emphasis. Length: 200-600 words.

LIVING WITH TEENAGERS, Baptist Sunday School Board, 127 9th Ave. N., Nashville TN 37234. (615)251-2273. Editor: Jimmy Hester. 50-75% freelance written. Works with a small number of new/unpublished writers each year. Quarterly magazine about teenagers for Baptist parents of teenagers. Circ. 50,000. Pays within 2 months of acceptance. Publishes ms an average of 18 months after acceptance. Buys all rights. Submit seasonal material 1 year in advance. Computer printout submissions OK; prefers letter-quality. Reports in 2 months. Sample copy for 9x12 SAE with 4 first class stamps.

Nonfiction: "We are looking for a unique Christian element. We want a genuine insight into the teen/parent relationship." General interest (on communication, emotional problems, growing up, drugs and alcohol, leisure, sex education, spiritual growth, working teens and parents, money, family relationships, and church relationships); inspirational; and personal experience. Buys 60 unsolicited mss/year. Query with clips of previously published work. Length: 600-2,000 words. Pays 5¢/published word.

Fiction: Humorous and religious, but must relate to parent/teen relationship. "No stories from the teen's point of view." Buys 2 mss/issue. Query with clips of previously published work. Length: 600-2,000 words. Pays 5¢/published word.

Poetry: Free verse, light verse, traditional and devotional inspirational; all must relate to parent/teen relationship. Buys 3 mss/issue. Submit 5 poems maximum. Length: 33 characters maximum. Pays $2.10 plus $1.25/line for 1-7 lines; $5.40 plus 75¢/line for 8 lines minimum.

Tips: "A writer can meet our needs if they have something to say to parents of teenagers concerning an issue the parents are confronting with the teenager."

THE LOOKOUT, 8121 Hamilton Ave., Cincinnati OH 45231. (513)931-4050. Editor: Mark A. Taylor. 50-60% freelance written. Eager to work with new/unpublished writers. Weekly for adults and young adults attending Sunday schools and Christian churches. Pays on acceptance. Publishes ms an average of 4 months after acceptance. Byline given. Buys first serial rights, one-time rights, second serial (reprint) rights, or simultaneous rights. Simultaneous submissions OK. Computer printout submissions acceptable; prefers letter-quality. Reports in 2 months, sometimes longer. Sample copy and writer's guidelines 50¢.

Nonfiction: "Seeks stories about real people or Sunday school classes; items that shed Biblical light on matters of contemporary controversy; and items that motivate, that lead the reader to ask, 'Why shouldn't I try that?' or 'Why couldn't our Sunday school class accomplish this?' Articles should tell how real people are involved for Christ. In choosing topics, *The Lookout* considers timeliness, the church and national calendar, and the ability of the material to fit the above guidelines. Tell us about ideas that are working in your Sunday school and in the lives of its members. Remember to aim at laymen." Submit complete ms. Length: 1,200-1,800 words. Pays 4-6¢/word. We also use inspirational short pieces. "About 600-800 words is a good length for these. Relate an incident that illustrates a point without preaching." Pays 4-7¢/word.

Fiction: "A short story is printed in many issues; it is usually between 1,200-1,800 words long and should be as true to life as possible while remaining inspirational and helpful. Use familiar settings and situations. Most often we use stories with a Christian slant."

Photos: Reviews b&w prints, 4x6 or larger. Pays $5-35. Pays $50-150 for color transparencies for covers and inside use. Needs photos of people, especially adults in a variety of settings.

LUTHERAN FORUM, 308 W. 46th St., New York NY 10036-3894. (212)757-1292. Editor: Dr. Thomas Sluberski, executive director. 25% freelance written. Works with a small number of new/unpublished writers each year. Quarterly magazine. For church leadership, clerical and lay. Circ. 4,500. Pays on publication. Publishes ms an average of 3 months after acceptance. Byline given. Rights purchased vary with author and material; buys all rights, first North American serial rights, second serial (reprint) rights, and simultaneous rights. Will consider photocopied and simultaneous submissions. Computer printout submissions acceptable; prefers letter-quality to dot-matrix. Reports in 9 weeks. Sample copy $1.50.

Nonfiction: Articles about important issues and developments in the church's institutional life and in its cultural/social setting. Special interest in articles on the Christian's life in secular vocations. No purely devotional/inspirational material. Buys 8-10 mss/year. Query or submit complete ms. Length: 1,000-3,000 words. Payment varies; $30 minimum. Informational, how-to, interview, profile, think articles and expose. Length: 500-3,000 words. Pays $25-75.

Photos: Purchased with ms and only with captions. Prefers 4x5 prints. Pays $15 minimum.

THE LUTHERAN JOURNAL, 7317 Cahill Rd., Edina MN 55435. Editor: Rev. Armin U. Deye. Quarterly magazine. Family magazine for Lutheran Church members, middle age and older. Circ. 136,000. Pays on publication. Byline given. Will consider photocopied and simultaneous submissions. Reports in 2 months. Free sample copy.

Nonfiction: Inspirational, religious, human interest and historical articles. Interesting or unusual church projects. Informational, how-to, personal experience, interview, humor and think articles. Buys 25-30 mss/year. Submit complete ms. Length: 1,500 words maximum; occasionally 2,000 words. Pays 1-3¢/word.

Photos: B&w and color photos purchased with accompanying ms. Captions required. Payment varies.

Fiction: Mainstream, religious and historical fiction. Must be suitable for church distribution. Length: 2,000 words maximum. Pays 1-1½¢/word.

Poetry: Traditional poetry, blank verse and free verse, related to subject matter.

MARIAN HELPERS BULLETIN, Eden Hill, Stockbridge MA 01263. (413)298-3691. Editor: Rev. Gerald Ornowski, M.I.C. 60% freelance written. Quarterly for average Catholics of varying ages with moderate religious views and general education. Circ. 1 million. Pays on acceptance. Byline given. Submit seasonal material 6 months in advance. Computer printout submissions OK; prefers letter-quality. Reports in 4-8 weeks. Free sample copy.

Nonfiction: "Subject matter is of general interest on devotional, spiritual, moral and social topics. Use a positive, practical and optimistic approach, well done without being sophisticated. We would like to see articles on the Blessed Virgin Mary." Buys informational and inspirational articles. Buys 18-24 mss/year. Length: 300-900 words. Pays 3-10¢/word.

Photos: Photos should be sent to complement articles.

Tips: "Human interest stories are very valuable, from which personal reflection is stimulated."

MARRIAGE & FAMILY LIVING, St. Meinrad IN 47577. (812)357-8011. Managing Editor: Kass Dotterweich. 75% freelance written. Monthly magazine. Circ. 40,000. Pays on acceptance. Byline given. Buys first international serial rights, first book reprint option, and control of other reprint rights. Query. Computer printout submissions acceptable; prefers letter-quality. Reports in 6 weeks. Sample copy $1.

Nonfiction: Articles which affirm marriage and parenting as an awesome vocation created by God; and personal essays relating amusing, heartwarming or insightful incidents which reflect the rich human side of marriage and family life. Length: 1,500-2,000 words maximum. Pays 7¢/word. Pays expenses of writers on assignment.

Photos: Attention, art director. Reviews 8x10 b&w glossy prints and color transparencies or 35mm slides. Pays $150/4-color cover or center spread photo. Uses approximately 6-8 b&w photos and an occasional illustration inside. Pays variable rate on publication. Photos of couples, families and individuals especially desirable. Model releases required.

Poetry: Any style and length. Pays $15 on publication; please include phone number.

Tips: Query with a brief outline of article and opening paragraphs.

MARRIAGE PARTNERSHIP, (formerly *Partnership*), Christianity Today, Inc., 465 Gunderson Dr., Carol Stream IL 60188. (312)260-6200. Executive Editor: Scott Bodinger. Managing Editor: Ron Lee. 20% freelance written. Bimonthly magazine "that provides thoughtful, provocative and realistic articles for husbands and wives who value marriage and are interested in exploring and enhancing their relationships." Circ. 45,000. Pays on acceptance. Byline given. Buys first serial rights. Submit seasonal/holiday material 7 months in advance. Simultaneous queries and photocopied submissions OK. Reports in 2 weeks on queries; 1 month on mss. Sample copy for 9x12 SAE; free writer's guidelines.

Nonfiction: Personal experience, how-to, humor, interview/profile, opinion, photo feature, and short interesting, informative pieces. Send queries to managing editor. No unsolicited mss accepted. Pays $15-250.

Photos: State availability of photos with query. Reviews b&w and color transparencies. Identification of subjects required. Buys one-time rights.

Columns/Departments: Buys 15 mss/year. Query. No unsolicited ms.

MENNONITE BRETHREN HERALD, 3-169 Riverton Ave., Winnipeg, Manitoba R2L 2E5 Canada. Contact: Editor. 25% freelance written. Prefers to work with published/established writers. Family publication "read mainly by people of the Mennonite faith, reaching a wide crosssection of professional and occupational groups, but also including many homemakers. Readership includes people from both urban and rural communities." Biweekly. Circ. 13,500. Pays on publication. Publishes ms an average of 4-6 months after acceptance. Not copyrighted. Byline given. Computer printout submissions OK; no dot-matrix. Sample copy for $1 with SAE and IRCs. Reports in 3 months.

Nonfiction: Articles with a Christian family orientation; youth directed, Christian faith and life, and current issues. Wants articles critiquing the values of a secular society, attempting to relate Christian living to the practical situations of daily living; showing how people have related their faith to their vocations. Length: 1,500 words. Pays $25-40. Pays the expenses of writers on assignment.

Photos: Photos purchased with mss; pays $5.

THE MESSENGER OF THE SACRED HEART Apostleship of Prayer, 661 Greenwood Ave., Toronto, Ontario M4J 4B3 Canada. (416)466-1195. Editor: Rev. F.J. Power, S.J. For "Canadian and U.S. Catholics interested in developing a life of prayer and spirituality; stresses the great value of our ordinary actions and lives." 20% freelance written. Monthly. Circ. 15,000. Buys first rights only. Byline given. Pays on acceptance. Submit seasonal material 3 months in advance. Computer printout submissions acceptable; prefers letter-quality. Reports in 1 month. Sample copy $1 and 7½x10½ SAE.

Nonfiction: Religious/inspirational. Stories about people, adventure, heroism, humor, drama. Buys 12 mss/year. Send complete ms with SAE and IRCs. Unsolicited manuscripts, unaccompanied by return postage, will not be returned. Length: 750-1,500 words. Pays 2¢ word.

Tips: "Develop a story that sustains interest to the end. Do not preach, but use plot and characters to convey the message or theme. Aim to move the heart as well as the mind. Before sending, cut out unnecessary or unrelated words or sentences. If you can, add a light touch or a sense of humor to the story. Your ending should have impact, leaving a moral or faith message for the reader."

THE MIRACULOUS MEDAL, 475 E. Chelten Ave., Philadelphia PA 19144. Editorial Director: Rev. Robert P. Cawley, C.M. 40% freelance written. Quarterly. Pays on acceptance. Publishes ms an average of 2 years after acceptance. Buys first North American serial rights. Buys articles only on special assignment. Computer printout submissions acceptable; no dot-matrix. Sample copy for 6x9 SAE with 2 first class stamps.

Fiction: Should not be pious or sermon-like. Wants good general fiction—not necessarily religious, but if religion is basic to the story, the writer should be sure of his facts. Only restriction is that subject matter and treatment must not conflict with Catholic teaching and practice. Can use seasonal material; Christmas stories. Length: 2,000 words maximum. Occasionally uses short-shorts from 750-1,250 words. Pays 2¢/word minimum.

Poetry: Maximum of 20 lines, preferably about the Virgin Mary or at least with religious slant. Pays 50¢/line minimum.

MODERN LITURGY, Suite 290, 160 E. Virginia St., San Jose CA 95112. Editor: Kenneth Guentert. 80% freelance written. Magazine; 40-48 pages published 9 times/year for artists, musicians and creative individuals who plan group worship, services; teachers of religion. Circ. 15,000. Buys first serial rights. Pays on publication. Publishes ms an average of 6 months after acceptance. Byline given. Query for electronic submissions.

Computer printout submissions acceptable; prefers letter-quality. Reports in 6 weeks. Sample copy $4; free writer's guidelines for SAE and 1 first class stamp.

Nonfiction and Fiction: Articles (historical, theological and practical) which address special interest topics in the field of liturgy; example services; and liturgical art forms (music, poetry, stories, dances, dramatizations, etc.). Practical, creative ideas; and art forms for use in worship and/or religious education classrooms. "No material out of our field." Buys 10 mss/year. Query. Length: 750-2,000 words. Pays with subscriptions, copies, and negotiated cost stipend for regular contributors.

Tips: "Don't be preachy; use too much jargon; or make articles too long."

MOODY MONTHLY, Moody Bible Institute, 820 N. LaSalle Dr., Chicago IL 60610. (312)508-6820. Managing Editor: Mike Umlandt. 20% freelance written. A monthly magazine for evangelical Christianity. "Our readers are conservative, evangelical Christians highly active in their churches and concerned about family living." Circ. 200,000. Pays on acceptance. Publishes ms an average of 6 months after acceptance. Byline given. Offers $50 kill fee. Buys first North American serial rights. Submit seasonal/holiday material 8 months in advance. Photocopied submissions OK. Query for electronic submissions. Computer printout submissions OK. Reports in 1 month on queries; 2 months on mss. Sample copy for 10x13 SAE; writer's guidelines for #10 SAE with 1 first class stamp.

Nonfiction: How-to (on living the Christian life), humor and personal experience. Buys 50 mss/year. Query. Length: 750-2,000 words. Pays 10-15¢/word for assigned articles. Sometimes pays the expenses of writers on assignment.

Photos: State availability of photos with submission. Offers $35-50 per photo. Buys one-time rights.

Columns/Departments: First Person (The only article written for non-Christians; a personal testimony written by the author [we will accept 'as told to's']; the objective is to tell a person's testimony in such a way that the reader will understand the gospel and want to receive Christ as Savior); Parenting (provides practical guidance for parents solidly based on biblical principles). Buys 30 mss/year. Query. Length: 750-1,200 words. Pays 10-15¢/word.

‡MY DAILY VISITOR, Our Sunday Visitor, Inc., 200 Noll Plaza, Huntington IN 46750. (219)356-8400. Editor: Jacquelyn M. Eckert. 99% freelance written. Bimonthly magazine on spirituality and scripture meditations. Circ. 40,000. Pays on acceptance. Publishes ms an average of 1 year after acceptance. Byline given. Not copyrighted. Buys one-time rights. Reports in 2 months. Sample copy for #10 SAE with 2 first class stamps.

Nonfiction: Inspirational, personal experience, religious. Buys 12 mss/year. Query with published clips. Length: 175 words. Pays $100-200. Sometimes pays writers 25 gratis copies.

NATIONAL CHRISTIAN REPORTER, Box 222198, Dallas TX 75222. (214)630-6495. Editor/General Manager: Spurgeon M. Dunnam III. Managing Editor: John A. Lovelace. 5% freelance written. Prefers to work with published/established writers. Weekly newspaper for an interdenominational national readership. Circ. 25,000. Pays on publication. Publishes ms an average of 1 month after acceptance. Byline given. Not copyrighted. Free sample copy and writer's guidelines.

Nonfiction: "We welcome short features, approximately 500 words. Articles need to have an explicit 'mainstream' Protestant angle. Write about a distinctly Christian response to human need or how a person's faith relates to a given situation. Preferably including evidence of participation in a local Protestant congregation." Send complete ms. Pays 4¢/word. Sometimes pays the expenses of writers on assignment.

Photos: Purchased with accompanying ms. "We encourage the submission of good action photos (5x7 or 8x10 b&w glossy prints) of the persons or situations in the article." Pays $10.

Poetry: "Good poetry welcome on a religious theme; blank verse or rhyme." Length: 4-20 lines. Pays $2.

NEW ENGLAND CHURCH LIFE, Evangelistic Association of New England, Suite 600, 88 Tremont St., Boston MA 02108. (617)523-3579. Editor: Carlene B. Hill. 40% freelance written. Monthly tabloid covering evangelical/charismatic Protestant Christianity. "*New England Church Life* is the community newsmonthly for evangelical and charismatic Christians in six states. Our readers include pastors and lay leaders who network through the resources they find in our pages. Articles demonstrate how believers live out their faith in many situations or help churches and individual Christians in their life and witness." Pays on publication. Publishes ms an average of 3 months after acceptance. Byline given. Offers 50% kill fee. Buys first North American serial rights, second serial (reprint) rights or simultaneous rights. Submits seasonal/holiday material 4 months in advance. Simultaneous and previous published submissions OK. Computer printout submissions OK; prefers letter-quality. Reports in 6 weeks on queries; 8 weeks on mss. Sample copy $1; writer's guidelines for #10 SAE with 1 first class stamp.

Nonfiction: General interest, how-to, inspirational, interview/profile, personal testimony. Special issues include Vacations (February); Church Supply and Suppliers (July); Christian Education in the Church (November); and Overseas Missions (September). No articles without regional ties. No articles on churches, individuals or organizations that lack clear ties to evangelical or charismatic church, group or denomination. Buys 80 mss/year. Send complete ms. Length: 400-1,200 words. Pays $35-50 for assigned articles; $20-40 for unsolicited articles. Sometimes pays expenses of writers on assignment.

Photos: State availability of photos with submission. Reviews contact sheets. Offers $10-35 per photo. Captions and identification of subjects required. Buys one-time rights.

Columns/Departments: Let Your Light Shine (profiling people whose faith is demonstrated through their activities outside the church), 450-700 words; The Tool Kit (effective ministry methods that have succeeded in New England), 450-700 words. Buys 12 mss/year. Send complete ms. Pays $5-30.

Fiction: By New England authors only. Send complete ms. Length: 800-1,200 words. Pays $25-50.

Tips: "Read our publication before contributing. The best way to break in is with a short article (600-800 words) about an effective local church ministry or showing how becoming Christian changed someone's life. Write for all five senses but don't forget facts and figures. We are a regional publication, so writers outside New England are not successful in publishing with us."

THE NEW ERA, 50 E. North Temple, Salt Lake City UT 84150. (801)531-2951. Managing Editor: Brian K. Kelly. 60% freelance written. "We work with both established writers and newcomers." Monthly magazine. For young people of the Church of Jesus Christ of Latter-day Saints (Mormon); their church leaders and teachers. Circ. 180,000. Pays on acceptance. Publishes ms an average of 1 year after acceptance. Byline given. Buys all rights. Submit seasonal material 1 year in advance. Query for electronic submissions. Computer printout submissions acceptable; prefers letter-quality. Reports in 1 month. Query preferred. Sample copy 90¢; writer's guidelines for SAE and 1 first class stamp.

Nonfiction: Material that shows how the Church of Jesus Christ of Latter-day Saints is relevant in the lives of young people today. Must capture the excitement of being a young Latter-day Saint. Special interest in the experiences of young Mormons in other countries. No general library research or formula pieces without the *New Era* slant and feel. Uses informational, how-to, personal experience, interview, profile, inspirational, humor, historical, think pieces, travel and spot news. Length: 150-3,000 words. Pays 3-12¢/word. *For Your Information* (news of young Mormons around the world). Pays expenses of writers on assignment.

Photos: Uses b&w photos and color transparencies with mss. Payment depends on use in magazine, but begins at $10.

Fiction: Adventure, science fiction and humorous. Must relate to young Mormon audience. Pays minimum 3¢/word.

Poetry: Traditional forms, blank verse, free verse, light verse and all other forms. Must relate to editorial viewpoint. Pays minimum 25¢/line.

Tips: "The writer must be able to write from a Mormon point of view. We have increased our staff size and anticipate using more staff-produced material. This means freelance quality will have to improve."

NEW WORLD OUTLOOK, Room 1351, 475 Riverside Dr., New York NY 10115. (212)870-3758. Executive Editor: George M. Daniels. Associate Editor: Gladys N. Koppole. 60% freelance written. Eager to work with new/unpublished writers. Monthly magazine (combined issues July/August and November/December). For United Methodist lay people; not clergy generally. Circ. 40,000. Pays on publication. Publishes ms an average of 4 months after acceptance. Buys first serial rights. Query for electronic submissions. Computer printout submissions acceptable; no dot-matrix. Sample copy for $2 and 9x12 SASE; writer's guidelines for SASE.

Nonfiction: Articles about the involvement of the church around the world, including the U.S. in outreach and social concerns and Christian witness. "Write with good magazine style. Facts and actualities are important. Use quotes. Relate what Christians are doing to meet problems. Use specifics. Though we want material on large urban areas as New York, Chicago, Los Angeles and Detroit, we need more good journalistic efforts from smaller places in U.S. and articles by freelancers in out-of-the-way places in the U.S." Buys 50-60 mss/year. Query or submit complete ms. Length: 1,000-2,000 words. Usually pays $100-150 but considerably more on occasion. "Writers are encouraged to illustrate their articles photographically if possible." Pays expenses of writers on assignment "if it originates with us or if article is one in which we have a special interest."

Photos: "Generally use b&w but covers (4-color) and 4-color photo features will be considered. Photos are purchased separately at standard rates."

Tips: "A freelancer should have some understanding of the United Methodist Church, or else know very well a local situation of human need or social problem which the churches and Christians have tried to face. Too much freelance material we get tries to paint with broad strokes about world or national issues. The local story of meaning to people elsewhere is still the best material. Avoid pontificating on the big issues. Write cleanly and interestingly on the 'small' ones. We're interested in major articles and photos (including photo features from freelancers)."

NORTH AMERICAN VOICE OF FATIMA, Fatima Shrine, Youngstown NY 14174. Editor: Rev. Paul M. Keeling, C.R.S.P. 40% freelance written. Works with a small number of new/unpublished writers each year. For Roman Catholic readership. Circ. 3,000. Pays on publication. Publishes ms an average of 2 months after acceptance. Not copyrighted. Buys first North American serial rights. Reports in 6 weeks. Computer printout submissions acceptable; no dot-matrix. Free sample copy.

Nonfiction and Fiction: Inspirational, personal experience, historical and think articles. Religious and historical fiction. Length: 700 words. All material must have a religious slant. Pays 2¢/word.
Photos: B&w photos purchased with ms.

OBLATES MAGAZINE, Missionary Association of Mary Immaculate, 15 S. 59th St., Belleville IL 62222. (618)233-2238. Editor of Contributions: Jacqueline Lowery Corn. 30-50% freelance written. Prefers to work with professional writers; but will work with new/unpublished writers. Bimonthly religious magazine for Christian families; audience mainly older adults. Circ. 430,000. Pays on acceptance. Publishes ms an average of 4 months after acceptance. Byline given. Buys first North American serial rights. Submit seasonal/holiday material 6 months in advance. Computer printout submissions acceptable. Reports in 1 month. Sample copy and writer's guidelines for 9x6 or larger SAE with 2 first class stamps.
Nonfiction: Inspirational and personal experience with positive spiritual insights. No preachy, theological or research articles. Avoid current events and controversial topics. Send complete ms. Length: 500 words. Pays $75.
Poetry: Light verse—reverent, well written, perceptive, with traditional rhythym and rhyme. "Emphasis should be on inspiration, insight and relationship with God." Submit maximum 2 poems. Length: 8-16 lines. Pays $25.
Tips: "Our readership is made up mostly of mature Americans who are looking for comfort, encouragement, and a positive sense of applicable Christian direction to their lives. Focus on sharing of personal insight to problem (i.e. death or change), but must be positive, uplifting, only subtly spiritual. We are very selective for a very narrow market, but always on the lookout for exceptional work."

ORT REPORTER, A National Newspaper for the American Jewish Woman, Woman's American ORT, Inc., 315 Park Ave. So., New York NY 10010. (212)505-7700. Editor: Elie Faust-Levy. Associate Editor: Ari Salant. 85% freelance written. Nonprofit journal published by Jewish women's organization. Quarterly tabloid covering "Jewish topics, education, Mideast and women." Circ. 155,000. Payment time varies. Publishes ms ASAP after acceptance. Byline given. Buys first North American serial rights or second serial (reprint) rights. Submit seasonal/holiday material 6 months in advance. Previously published submissions OK. Reports "as soon as possible." Free sample copy.
Nonfiction: Book excerpts, essays, general interest, humor, opinion and religious. No poetry. Buys approximately 40 mss/year. Send complete ms. Length: 500-3,000. Pays 8-15¢/word.
Photos: Send photos with submission. Reviews 5x7 prints. Offers $50-85 per photo. Identification of subjects required. Purchases "whatever rights photographer desires."
Columns/Departments: Book Reporter, Film Reporter, Stage Reporter. Buys 4-10 mss/year. Send complete ms. Length: 200-2,000 words. Pays 10¢/word "more or less depending on editing required—we try to be fair."
Fiction: Ethnic, novel excerpts, religious. Buys 0-1 ms/year. Send complete ms. Pays 10¢/word.
Tips: "Simply send ms; do not call. First submission must be "on spec". Open Forum (opinion section) is most open to freelancers, although all are open. Looking for well-written essay on relevant topic that makes its point strongly—evokes response from reader."

THE OTHER SIDE, 1225 Dandridge St., Fredericksburg VA 22401. Editor: Mark Olson. Associate Editors: John Linscheid and William O'Brien. 50% freelance written. Prefers to work with published/established writers; works with a small number of new/unpublished writers each year. Magazine published 10 times/year focusing on "peace, justice and economic liberation from a radical Christian perspective." Circ. 15,000. Pays on acceptance. Publishes ms an average of 4 months after acceptance. Byline given. Buys first serial rights. Query for electronic submissions. Computer printout submissions acceptable. Reports in 6 weeks. Sample copy $3; free writer's guidelines.
Nonfiction: Niki Amarantides, articles editor. Current social, political and economic issues in the U.S. and around the world: personality profiles, interpretative essays, interviews, how-to's, personal experiences and investigative reporting. "Articles must be lively, vivid and down-to-earth, with a radical Christian perspective." Length: 500-6,000 words. Pays $25-300. Sometimes pays expenses of writers on assignment.
Photos: Cathleen Boint, art director. Photos or photo essays illustrating current social, political, or economic reality in the U.S. and Third World. Pays $15-75 for b&w and $50-300 for color.
Fiction: Barbara Moorman, fiction editor. "Short stories, humor and satire conveying insights and situations that will be helpful to Christians with a radical commitment to peace and justice." Length: 300-4,000 words. Pays $25-250.
Poetry: Rod Jellema, poetry editor. "Short, creative poetry that will be thought-provoking and appealing to radical Christians who have a strong commitment to spirituality, peace and justice." Length: 3-50 lines. Pays $15-20.
Tips: "We're looking for tightly written pieces (500-1,000 words) on interesting and unusual Christians (or Christian groups) who are putting their commitment to peace and social justice into action in creative and useful ways. We're also looking for practical, down-to-earth articles (500-6,000 words) for Christian parents who seek to instill in their children their values of personal faith, peace, justice, and a concern for the poor."

OUR FAMILY, Oblate Fathers of St. Mary's Province, Box 249, Battleford, Saskatchewan S0M 0E0 Canada. (306)937-2131, 937-7344. Editor: Nestor Gregoire. 60% freelance written. Prefers to work with published/established writers; works with a small number of new/unpublished writers each year. Monthly magazine for average family men and women with high school and early college education. Circ. 14,265. Pays on acceptance. Publishes ms an average of 6 months after acceptance. Byline given. Offers 100% kill fee. Generally purchases first North American serial rights; also buys all rights, simultaneous rights, second serial (reprint) rights or one-time rights. Submit seasonal/holiday material 4 months in advance. Simultaneous, photocopied, and previously published submissions OK. Query for electronic submissions. Computer printout submissions acceptable; no dot-matrix. "Writer should inquire with our office before sending letter-quality computer printout or disk submissions." Reports in 1 month. Sample copy $2.50 in postage and 9x12 SAE; writer's guidelines for 42¢ (Canadian funds). U.S. postage cannot be used in Canada.

Nonfiction: Humor (related to family life or husband/wife relations); inspirational (anything that depicts people responding to adverse conditions with courage, hope and love); personal experience (with religious dimensions); and photo feature (particularly in search of photo essays on human/religious themes and on persons whose lives are an inspiration to others). Phone queries OK. Buys 72-88 unsolicited mss/year. Pays expenses of writers on assignment.

Photos: Photos purchased with or without accompanying ms. Pays $35 for 5x7 or larger b&w glossy prints and color photos (which are converted into b&w). Offers additional payment for photos accepted with ms (payment for these photos varies according to their quality). Free photo spec sheet with SASE.

Fiction: Humorous and religious. "Anything true to human nature. No romance, he-man adventure material, science fiction, moralizing or sentimentality." Buys 1-2 ms/issue. Send complete ms. Length: 700-3,000 words. Pays 7-10¢/word minimum for original material. Free fiction requirement guide with SASE.

Poetry: Avant-garde, free verse, haiku, light verse and traditional. Buys 4-10 poems/issue. Length: 3-30 lines. Pays 75¢-$1/line.

Fillers: Jokes, gags, anecdotes and short humor. Buys 2-10/issue.

Tips: "Writers should ask themselves whether this is the kind of an article, poem, etc. that a busy housewife would pick up and read when she has a few moments of leisure. We are particularly looking for articles on the spirituality of marriage. We will be concentrating more on recent movements and developments in the church to help make people aware of the new church of which they are a part."

OUR SUNDAY VISITOR MAGAZINE, Noll Plaza, Huntington IN 46750. (219)356-8400. Publisher: Robert P. Lockwood. Editor: Louis F. Jacquet. 5% freelance written. Works with small number of new/unpublished writers each year. Weekly magazine for general Catholic audience. Circ. 300,000. Pays on acceptance. Publishes ms an average of 2 months after acceptance. Byline given. Submit seasonal material 2 months in advance. Query for electronic submissions. Computer printout submissions OK. Reports in 3 weeks. Free sample copy with SASE.

Nonfiction: Uses articles on Catholic-related subjects. Should explain Catholic religious beliefs in articles of human interest; articles applying Catholic principles to current problems, Catholic profiles, etc. Payment varies depending on reputation of author, quality of work, and amount of research required. Buys 25 mss/year. Query. Length: 1,000-1,200 words. Minimum payment for features is $100. Pays expenses of writers on assignment.

Photos: Purchased with mss; with captions only. Reviews b&w glossy prints and color transparencies. Pays minimum of $200/cover photo story; $125/b&w story; $25/color photo; $10/b&w photo.

PARISH FAMILY DIGEST, Our Sunday Visitor, Inc., 200 Noll Plaza, Huntington IN 46750. (219)356-8400. Editor: George P. Foster. 100% freelance written. Works with small number of new/unpublished writers each year. Bimonthly magazine. "*Parish Family Digest* is geared to the Catholic family and to that family as a unit of the parish." Circ. 150,000. Pays on acceptance. Publishes ms an average of 6 months after acceptance. Byline given. Buys all rights on a work-for-hire basis. Submit seasonal/holiday material 6 months in advance. Photocopied submissions OK; all mss are retyped as edited. Computer printout submissions acceptable; prefers letter-quality. Reports in 2 weeks on queries; 3 weeks on mss. Sample copy and writer's guidelines for 9½x6½ SAE and 2 first class stamps.

Nonfiction: General interest, historical, inspirational, interview, nostalgia (if related to overall Parish involvement), and profile. No personal essays or preachy first person "thou shalt's or shalt not's." Send complete ms. Buys 72 unsolicited mss/year. Length: 1,000 words maximum. Pays $5-50.

Photos: State availability of photos with ms. Pays $10 for 3x5 b&w prints. Buys one-time rights. Captions preferred; model releases required.

Fillers: Anecdotes and short humor. Buys 6/issue. Length: 100 words maximum.

Tips: "If an article does not deal with some angle of Catholic family life, the writer is wasting time in sending it to us. We rarely use reprints; we prefer fresh material that will hold up over time, not tied to an event in the news. We will be more oriented to families with kids and the problems such families face in the Church and society, in particular, the struggle to raise good Catholic kids in a secular society. Articles on how to overcome these problems will be welcomed."

PENTECOSTAL EVANGEL, The General Council of the Assemblies of God, 1445 Boonville, Springfield MO 65802. (417)862-2781. Editor: Richard G. Champion. 33% freelance written. Works with a small number of new/unpublished writers each year. Weekly magazine. Emphasizes news of the Assemblies of God for members of the Assemblies and other Pentecostal and charismatic Christians. Circ. 275,000. Pays on acceptance. Publishes ms an average of 4-6 months after acceptance. Byline given. Buys first serial rights, second serial (reprint) rights or one-time rights. Submit seasonal/holiday material 6 months in advance. Computer printout submissions acceptable; prefers letter-quality. Reports in 3 months. Free sample copy and writer's guidelines.
Nonfiction: Informational (articles on homelife that convey Christian teachings); inspirational; and personal experience. Buys 5 mss/issue. Send complete ms. Length: 500-2,000 words. Pays 5¢/word maximum. Sometimes pays the expenses of writers on assignment.
Photos: Photos purchased without accompanying ms. Pays $7.50-15 for 8x10 b&w glossy prints; $10-35 for 35mm or larger color transparencies. Total purchase price for ms includes payment for photos.
Poetry: Religious and inspirational. Buys 1 poem/issue. Submit maximum 6 poems. Pays 20-40¢/line.
Tips: "Break in by writing up a personal experience. We publish first-person articles concerning spiritual experiences; that is, answers to prayer for help in a particular situation, of unusual conversions or healings through faith in Christ. All articles submitted to us should be related to religious life. We are Protestant, evangelical, Pentecostal, and any doctrines or practices portrayed should be in harmony with the official position of our denomination (Assemblies of God)."

THE PENTECOSTAL MESSENGER, Messenger Publishing House, 4901 Pennsylvania, Box 850, Joplin MO 64802. (417)625-7050. Editor: Don Allen. Managing Editor: Peggy Lee Allen. 25% freelance written. Works with small number of new/unpublished writers each year. Monthly (excluding July) magazine covering Pentcostal Christianity. *"The Pentecostal Messenger* is the official organ of the Pentecostal Church of God. Goes to ministers and church members." Circ. 6,500. Pays on publication. Publishes ms an average of 6 months after acceptance. Byline given. Buys second serial (reprint) rights or simultaneous rights. Submit seasonal/holiday material 1 month in advance. Simultaneous, photocopied and previously published submissions OK. Computer printout submissions OK; prefers letter-quality. Reports in 4 weeks on mss. Sample copy for 9x12 SAE and 4 first class stamps; free writer's guidelines.
Nonfiction: Inspirational, personal experience and religious. Special issue includes Sunday School Enlargement (October). Buys 35 mss/year. Send complete ms. Length: 1,800 words. Pays 1½¢/word.
Photos: Send photos with submission. Reviews 2¼x2¼ transparencies and prints. Offers $10-25 per photo. Captions and model releases required. Buys one-time rights.
Tips: "Articles need to be inspirational, informative, written from a positive viewpoint, not extremely controversial."

PRAIRIE MESSENGER, Catholic Weekly, Benedictine Monks of St. Peter's Abbey, Box 190, Muenster, Saskatchewan S0K 2Y0 Canada. (306)682-5215. Editor: Andrew Britz. Managing Editor: Marian Noll. 10% freelance written. A weekly Catholic journal with strong emphasis on social justice, Third World and ecumenism. Circ. 12,000. Pays on publication. Publishes ms an average of 2-3 months after acceptance. Byline given. Offers 70% kill fee. Not copyrighted. Buys first North American serial rights, first rights, one-time rights, second serial (reprint) rights or simultaneous rights. Submit seasonal/holiday material 3 months in advance. Simultaneous submissions OK. Query for electronic submissions. Computer printout submissions OK; no dot-matrix. Sample copy for 9x12 SAE with 72¢ Canadian postage; writers guidelines for 9x12 SAE with 72¢ first class Canadian stamps.
Nonfiction: Interview/profile, opinion, and religious. "No articles on abortion or homosexuality." Buys 30 mss/year. Send complete ms. Length: 250-600 words. Pays $40-60. Sometimes pays expenses of writers on assignment.
Photos: Send photos with submission. Reviews 3x5 prints. Offers $7.50-10/photo. Captions required. Buys all rights.

PRESBYTERIAN RECORD, 50 Wynford Dr., Don Mills, Ontario M3C 1J7 Canada. (416)444-1111. 50% freelance written. Eager to work with new/unpublished writers. Monthly magazine for a church-oriented, family audience. Circ. 71,444. Buys 35 mss/year. Pays on publication. Publishes ms an average of 4 months after acceptance. Buys first serial rights, one-time rights, simultaneous rights. Submit seasonal material 3 months in advance. Computer printout submissions acceptable. Reports on ms accepted for publication in 2 months. Returns rejected material in 3 months. Sample copy and writer's guidelines for 9x12 SAE with $1 Canadian postage or IRCs.
Nonfiction: Material on religious themes. Check a copy of the magazine for style. Also, personal experience, interview, and inspirational material. No material solely or mainly American in context. When possible, black-and-white photos should accompany manuscript; i.e., current events, historical events, and biographies. Buys 15-20 unsolicited mss/year. Query. Length: 1,000-2,000 words. Pays $45-55 (U.S. funds). Sometimes pays expenses of writers on assignment.

Photos: Pays $15-20 for b&w glossy photos. Uses positive color transparencies for cover. Pays $50. Captions required.
Tips: "There is a trend away from maudlin, first-person pieces redolent with tragedy and dripping with simplistic pietistic conclusions."

PRESBYTERIAN SURVEY, Presbyterian Publishing House, Inc., 341 Ponce de Leon Ave. NE, Atlanta GA 30365. (404)873-1549. Editor: Vic Jameson. Managing Editor: Catherine Cottingham. 65% freelance written. Prefers to work with published/established writers; works with a small number of new/unpublished writers each year; willing to work with new/unpublished writers. Denominational magazine published 10 times/year covering religion, denominational activities and public issues for members of the Presbyterian Church (U.S.A.). Pays on acceptance. Publishes ms an average of 9 months after acceptance. Byline given. Offers variable kill fee. Buys first North American serial rights. Submit seasonal/holiday material 8 months in advance. Simultaneous submissions OK. Computer printout submissions acceptable; prefers letter-quality. Reports in 2 weeks on queries; 1 month on mss. Sample copy and writer's guidelines for 10x13 SAE and $1.
Nonfiction: Inspirational and Presbyterian programs, issues, people; any subject from a Christian viewpoint. No secular subjects. Buys 50 mss/year. Send complete ms. Length: 800-1,500 words. Pays $50-200. Sometimes pays expenses of writers on assignment.
Photos: Richard Brown, photo editor. State availability of photos. Reviews color transparencies and 8x10 b&w prints. Pays $15-25 for b&w; $25-50 for color. Identification of subjects required. Buys one-time rights.
Columns/Departments: "The only column not by a regular columnist is an op ed page for readers of the magazine (As I See It)." Buys 10 mss/year. Send complete ms. Length: 600-750 words. No payment.

PURPOSE, 616 Walnut Ave., Scottdale PA 15683-1999. (412)887-8500. Editor: James E. Horsch. 95% freelance written. Weekly magazine "for adults, young and old, general audience with interests as varied as there are people. My readership is interested in seeing how Christianity works in difficult situations." Circ. 19,250. Pays on acceptance. Publishes ms an average of 8 months after acceptance. Byline given, including city, state/province. Buys one-time rights. Submit seasonal material 6 months in advance. Photocopied and simultaneous submissions OK. Computer printout submissions acceptable; prefers letter-quality. Submit complete ms. Reports in 6 weeks. Sample copy and writer's guidelines for 6x9 SAE with 2 first class stamps.
Nonfiction: Inspirational articles from a Christian perspective. "I want stories that go to the core of human problems in family, business, politics, religion, sex and any other areas—and show how the Christian faith resolves them. I want material that's upbeat. *Purpose* is a story paper which conveys truth either through quality fiction or through articles that use the best story techniques. Our magazine accents Christian discipleship. Christianity affects all of life, and we expect our material to demonstrate this. I would like to see story-type articles about individuals, groups and organizations who are intelligently and effectively working at some of the great human problems such as overpopulation, hunger, poverty, international understanding, peace, justice, etc., because of their faith." Buys 175-200 mss/year. Submit complete ms. Length: 1,100 words maximum. Pays 5¢/word maximum.
Photos: Photos purchased with ms. Pays $5-25 for b&w, depending on quality. Must be sharp enough for reproduction; prefers prints in all cases. Can use color prints. Captions desired.
Fiction: Humorous, religious and historical fiction related to discipleship theme. "Produce the story with specificity so that it appears to take place somewhere and with real people. It should not be moralistic."
Poetry: Traditional poetry, blank verse, free verse and light verse. Length: 12 lines maximum. Pays 50¢-$1/line.
Fillers: Anecdotal items from 200-800 words. Pays 4¢/word maximum.
Tips: "We are looking for articles which show the Christian faith working at issues where people hurt, but stories need to be told and presented professionally. Good photographs help place material with us."

QUEEN OF ALL HEARTS, Monfort Missionaries, 26 S. Saxon Ave., Bay Shore NY 11706. (516)665-0726. Managing Editor: Roger Charest, S.M.M. 50% freelance written. Bimonthly magazine covering Marian doctrine and devotion. "Subject: Mary, Mother of Jesus, as seen in the sacred scriptures, tradition, history of the church, the early Christian writers, lives of the saints, poetry, art, music, spiritual writers, apparitions, shrines, ecumenism, etc." Circ. approx 6,000. Pays on acceptance. Publishes ms an average of 6 months after acceptance. Byline given. Not copyrighted. Buys second serial (reprint) rights. Submit seasonal/holiday material 6 months in advance. Reports in 6 weeks. Sample copy $2.
Nonfiction: Essays, inspirational, personal experience and religious. Buys 25 ms/year. Send complete ms. Length: 750-2,500 words. Pays $40-60. Sometimes pays writers in contributor copies or other premiums "by mutual agreement. Poetry paid by contributor copies."
Photos: Send photos with submission. Reviews transparencies and prints. Offers variable payment per photo. Buys one-time rights.
Fiction: Religious. Buys 6 mss/year. Send complete ms. Length: 1,500-2,500 words. Pays $40-60.
Poetry: Poetry Editor: Joseph Tusiani. Free verse. Buys approximately 10 poems/year. Submit 2 poems maximum at one time. Pays in contributor copies.

‡REFORM JUDAISM, Union of American Hebrew Congregations, 838 5th Ave., New York NY 10021. (212)249-0100. Editor: Aron Hert-Manheimer. Managing Editor: Joy Weinberg. 50% freelance written. Quarterly magazine of reform Jewish issues. "*Reform Judaism* is published by the UAHC, a nonprofit Jewish organization, and is distributed to members of reform Jewish congregations and other interested readers." Payment on publication. Publishes ms an average of 3 months after acceptance. Byline given. Offers negotiable kill fee. Buys first North American serial rights. Submit seasonal/holiday material 3 months in advance. Photocopied and previously published submissions OK. Computer printout submissions acceptable; prefers letter-quality. Reports in 2 weeks on queries; 3 weeks on mss. Sample copy $1.
Nonfiction: Book excerpt (reviews), expose, general interest, historical/nostalgic, inspirational, interview/profile, opinion, personal experience, photo feature and travel. Buys 60 mss/year. Send complete ms. Submit complete ms. Length: 750-2,000 words. Pays $100-200. Sometimes pays expenses of writers on assignment.
Photos: Send photos with ms. Prefers 8x10 b&w prints. Pays $25-75. Identification of subjects required. Buys one-time rights.
Fiction: Ethnic, humorous, mainstream and religious. Buys 4 mss/year. Send complete ms. Length: 750-2,000 words. Pays $100-200.
Poetry: Free verse. Buys 2 poems/year. Submit maximum 3 poems. Length: 20 lines maximum. Pays $25-50.

REVIEW FOR RELIGIOUS, 3601 Lindell Blvd., Room 428, St. Louis MO 63108. (314)535-3048. Editor: David L. Fleming, S.J. 100% freelance written. "Each ms is judged on its own merits, without reference to author's publishing history." Bimonthly. For Roman Catholic priests, brothers and sisters. Pays on publication. Publishes ms an average of 9 months after acceptance. Byline given. Buys first North American serial rights and rarely second serial (reprint) rights. Computer printout submissions acceptable; no dot-matrix. Reports in 8 weeks.
Nonfiction: Articles on ascetical, liturgical and canonical matters only; not for general audience. Length: 2,000-8,000 words. Pays $6/page.
Tips: "The writer must know about religious life in the Catholic Church and be familiar with prayer, vows and problems related to them."

ST. ANTHONY MESSENGER, 1615 Republic St., Cincinnati OH 45210. Editor-in-Chief: Norman Perry. 55% freelance written. "Willing to work with new/unpublished writers if their writing is of a professional caliber." Monthly magazine for a national readership of Catholic families, most of which have children in grade school, high school or college. Circ. 420,000. Pays on acceptance. Publishes ms an average of 9 months after acceptance. Byline given. Buys first North American serial rights. Submit seasonal/holiday material 6 months in advance. Query for electronic submissions. Sample copy and writer's guidelines for 9x12 SASE.
Nonfiction: How-to (on psychological and spiritual growth, problems of parenting/better parenting, marriage problems/marriage enrichment); humor; informational; inspirational; interview; personal experience (if pertinent to our purpose); personal opinion (limited use; writer must have special qualifications for topic); and profile. Buys 35-50 mss/year. Length: 1,500-3,500 words. Pays 14¢/word. Sometimes pays the expenses of writers on assignment.
Fiction: Mainstream and religious. Buys 12 mss/year. Submit complete ms. Length: 2,000-3,500 words. Pays 14¢/word.
Tips: "The freelancer should ask why his or her proposed article would be appropriate for us, rather than for *Redbook* or *Saturday Review*. We treat human problems of all kinds, but from a religious perspective. Get authoritative information (not merely library research); we want interviews with experts. Write in popular style. Word length is an important consideration."

ST. JOSEPH'S MESSENGER & ADVOCATE OF THE BLIND, Sisters of St. Joseph of Peace, St. Joseph's Home, Box 288, Jersey City NJ 07303. Editor-in-Chief: Sister Ursula Maphet. 30% freelance written. Eager to work with new/unpublished writers. Quarterly magazine. Circ. 35,000. Pays on acceptance. Publishes ms an average of 3 months after acceptance. Buys first serial rights and second serial (reprint) rights, but will reassign rights back to author after publication asking only that credit line be included in next publication. Submit seasonal/holiday material 3 months in advance (no Christmas issue). Computer printout submissions OK; prefers letter-quality. Simultaneous and previously published submissions OK. Reports in 3 weeks. Sample copy and writer's guidelines 8½x11 SAE.
Nonfiction: Humor, inspirational, nostalgia, personal opinion and personal experience. Buys 24 mss/year. Submit complete ms. Length: 300-1,500 words. Pays $3-15.
Fiction: Romance, suspense, mainstream and religious. Buys 30 mss/year. Submit complete ms. Length: 600-1,600 words. Pays $6-25.
Poetry: Light verse and traditional. Buys 25 poems/year. Submit maximum 10 poems. Length: 50-300 words. Pays $5-20.
Tips: "It's rewarding to know that someone is waiting to see freelancers' efforts rewarded by 'print'. It's annoying, however, to receive poor copy, shallow material or inane submissions. Human interest fiction, touching on current happenings, is what is most needed. We look for social issues — woven into story form. We also seek non-preaching articles that carry a message that is positive."

SCP JOURNAL, (formerly *SCP* Newsletter), Spiritual Counterfeits Project, Box 4308, Berkeley CA 94704. (415)540-0300. Editor: Robert J. L. Burrows. 5% freelance written. Prefers to work with published/established writers. "The *SCP Newsletter* is a quarterly newsletter that analyzes new religious movements and spiritual trends from a Christian perspective. Its targeted audience is the educated lay person." Circ. 16,500. Pays on publication. Publishes ms an average of 6 months after acceptance. Byline given. Simultaneous and previously published submissions OK. Computer printout submissions acceptable. Sample copy for 8½x11 SAE and 4 first class stamps.
Nonfiction: Book excerpts, essays, exposé, interview/profile, opinion, personal experience and religious. Buys 10 mss/year. Query with published clips. Length: 2,500-3,500 words. Pays $20-35/typeset page.
Photos: State availability of photos with submission. Reviews contact sheets and prints. Offers no additional payment for photos accepted with ms. Captions, model releases and identification of subjects required. Buys one-time rights.
Tips: "The area of our publication most open to freelancers is reviews of books relevant to subjects covered by *SCP*. These should not exceed 6 typewritten, double-spaced pages, 1,500 words. Send samples of work that are relevant to the *SCP Newsletter*'s area of interest."

SEEK, Standard Publishing, 8121 Hamilton Ave., Cincinnati OH 45231. (513)931-4050, ext. 365. Editor: Eileen H. Wilmoth. 98% freelance written. Prefers to work with published/established writers; works with a small number of new/unpublished writers each year. Sunday school paper. Quarterly, in weekly issues for young and middle-aged adults who attend church and Bible classes. Circ. 45,000. Pays on acceptance. Publishes ms an average of 1 year after acceptance. Byline given. Buys first serial rights and second serial (reprint) rights. Buys 100-150 mss/year. Submit seasonal material 1 year in advance. Computer printout submissions acceptable; prefers letter-quality. Reports in 10-30 days. Sample copy and writer's guidelines for 6x9 SAE and 2 first class stamps.
Nonfiction: "We look for articles that are warm, inspirational, devotional, of personal or human interest; that deal with controversial matters, timely issues of religious, ethical or moral nature, or first-person testimonies, true-to-life happenings, vignettes, emotional situations or problems; communication problems and examples of answered prayers. Article must deliver its point in a convincing manner but not be patronizing or preachy. They must appeal to either men or women, must be alive, vibrant, sparkling and have a title that demands the article be read. We always need stories of families, marriages, problems on campus and life testimonies." No poetry. Buys 100-150 mss/year. Submit complete ms. Length: 400-1,200 words. Pays 3¢/word.
Photos: B&w photos purchased with or without mss. Pays $20 minimum for good 8x10 glossy prints.
Fiction: Religious fiction and religiously slanted historical and humorous fiction. Length: 400-1,200 words. Pays 3¢/word.
Tips: Submit mss which tell of faith in action or victorious Christian living as central theme. "We select manuscripts as far as one year in advance of publication. Complimentary copies are sent to our published writers immediately following printing."

SHARING THE VICTORY, Fellowship of Christian Athletes, 8701 Leeds Rd., Kansas City MO 64129. (816)921-0909. Editor: Skip Stogsdill. Managing Editor: Randy St. Clair. 20% freelance written. Prefers to work with published/established writers; works with a small number of new/unpublished writers each year. A bimonthly magazine. "We seek to encourage and enable athletes and coaches at all levels to take their faith seriously on and off the 'field.' " Circ. 50,000. Pays on publication. Publishes ms an average of 4 months after acceptance. Byline given. Buys first rights. Submit seasonal/holiday material 3 months in advance. Computer printout submissions acceptable; prefers letter-quality. Reports in 1 week on queries; 2 weeks on manuscripts. Sample copy $1 with 9x12 SAE and 3 first class stamps; free writer's guidelines.
Nonfiction: Humor, inspirational, interview/profile, personal experience, and photo feature. No "sappy articles on 'I became a Christian and now I'm a winner.' " Buys 5-20 mss/year. Query. Length: 500-1,000 words. Pays $100-200 for unsolicited articles.
Photos: State availability of photos with submission. Reviews contact sheets. Pay depends on quality of photo but usually a minimum $75. Model releases required for "name" individuals. Buys one-time rights.
Columns/Departments: Sports Conscience (deals with a problem issue in athletics today and some possible solutions or alternatives). Buys 4 mss/year. Query. Length: 700-1,500 words. Pays $10 minimum.
Poetry: Free verse. Buys 3 poems/year. Pays $50.
Tips: "Profiles and interviews of particular interest to coed athlete primarily high school and college age. We have redesigned our graphics and editorial content to appeal to youth. The area most open to freelancers is profiles on or interviews with well-known athletes or coaches (male, female, minorities or of offbeat sports)."

SIGNS OF THE TIMES, Pacific Press Publishing Association, Box 7000, Boise ID 83707. (208)465-2500. Editor: Kenneth J. Holland. Managing Editor: B. Russell Holt. 40% freelance written. Works with a small number of new/unpublished writers each year. Monthly magazine on religion. "We are a Christian publication encouraging the general public to put into practice the principles of the Bible." Circ. 400,000. Pays on acceptance. Publishes ms an average of 5 months after acceptance. Byline given. Offers $100 kill fee. Buys first

North American serial rights and simultaneous rights. Submit seasonal/holiday material 8 months in advance. Simultaneous queries and submissions, and photocopied and previously published submissions OK. Computer printout submissions acceptable; prefers letter-quality. Reports in 2 weeks on queries; 1 month on mss. Free sample copy and writer's guidelines.

Nonfiction: General interest (home, marriage, health—interpret current events from a Biblical perspective); how-to (overcome depression, find one's identity, answer loneliness and guilt, face death triumphantly); humor; inspirational (human interest pieces that highlight a Biblical principle); interview/profile; personal experience (overcome problems with God's help); and photo feature. "We want writers with a desire to share the good news of reconciliation with God. Articles should be people-oriented, well-researched and should have a sharp focus and include anecdotes." Buys 150 mss/year. Query with or without published clips, or send complete ms. Length: 500-3,000 words. Pays $100-400. Sometimes pays the expenses of writers on assignment.

Photos: Ed Guthero, photo editor. Send photos with query or ms. Reviews b&w contact sheets; 35mm color transparencies; 5x7 or 8x10 b&w prints. Pays $35-300 for transparencies; $20-50 for prints. Model releases and identification of subjects required (captions helpful). Buys one-time rights.

Tips: "One of the most frequent mistakes made by writers in completing an article assignment for us is trying to cover too much ground. Articles need focus, research, and anecdotes. We don't want essays."

SINGLE IMPACT, A Publication Challenging All Singles to Serve Christ, 7245 College St., Lima NY 14485. (716)582-2790. Editor-in-Chief: Michael P. Cavanaugh. Managing Editor: Susan McCarthy. A quarterly magazine for Christian singles. "We believe in accordance with 1 Corinthians 7:35, that a Christian's singleness is a time to serve God with undistracted devotion. This magazine encourages singles to embrace that vision and launch out into service for God." Circ. 5,000. Pays on publication. Byline given. Not copyrighted. Buys first rights and makes work-for-hire assignments. Submit seasonal/holiday material 6 months in advance. Simultaneous, photocopied and previously published submissions OK. Query for electronic submissions. Computer printout submissions OK. Reports in 2 weeks on queries; 1 month on mss. Free sample copy and writer's guidelines.

Nonfiction: Book excerpt, essays, how-to (on practical Christian teaching, Bibically based); inspirational; interview/profile (of outstanding Christian leaders/singles); personal experience (testimony of how God moved in an area commonly faced by single adults) and religious. Must be directed to singles. No general addressing of issues. No material without Biblical emphasis accepted. Buys 8 mss/year. Query. Length: 250-1,500 words. Pays $12.50-75.

Photos: Send photos with submission. Reviews prints. Pays cost of developing and materials. Identification of subjects required. Buys one-time rights.

Columns/Departments: Single to Single (first-person article on how God helped a single person cope—should teach others to do the same). Buys 4 mss/year. Send complete ms. Length: 750-1,500 words. Pays 5¢/word on publication.

Tips: "Have a potential-oriented attitude toward singleness—and always stress a Christian emphasis. The best section for writers to use to break in to our publication would be our 'Single to Single' column. These are first-person articles about how one single can cope with an issue related to singleness—loneliness, lack of purpose, divorce; can also be written in 'as told to' form."

SISTERS TODAY, The Liturgical Press, St. John's Abbey, Collegeville MN 56321. Editor-in-Chief: Sister Mary Anthony Wagner, O.S.B. Associate Editor: Sister Andre Marthaler, O.S.B. Review Editor: Sister Stefanie Weisgram, O.S.B. 80% freelance written. Prefers to work with published/established writers; works with a small number of new/unpublished writers each year. Magazine, published 10 times/year, for women of the Roman Catholic Church, primarily. Circ. 9,000. Pays on publication. Publishes ms 1-2 years after acceptance. Byline given. Buys first rights. Submit seasonal/holiday material 4 months in advance. Computer printout submissions acceptable; no dot-matrix. Reports in 3 months. Sample copy $1.50.

Nonfiction: How-to (pray, live in a religious community, exercise faith, hope, charity etc.); informational; and inspirational. Also articles concerning religious renewal, community life, worship, and the role of sisters in the Church and in the world today. Buys 50-60 unsolicited mss/year. Query. Length: 500-2,500 words. Pays $5/printed page.

Poetry: Free verse, haiku, light verse and traditional. Buys 3 poems/issue. Submit maximum 4 poems. Pays $10.

Tips: "Some of the freelance material evidences the lack of familiarity with *Sisters Today*. We would prefer submitted articles not to exceed eight or nine pages."

SOCIAL JUSTICE REVIEW, 3835 Westminister Place, St. Louis MO 63108. (314)371-1653. Contact: editor. 25% freelance written. Works with a small number of new/unpublished writers each year. Bimonthly. Publishes ms an average of 3 months after acceptance. Not copyrighted; "however special articles within the magazine may be copyrighted, or an occasional special issue has been copyrighted due to author's request." Buys first serial rights. Computer printout submissions acceptable; prefers letter-quality.

Nonfiction: Wants scholarly articles on society's economic, religious, social, intellectual and political problems with the aim of bringing Catholic social thinking to bear upon these problems. Query. Length: 2,500-3,500 words. Pays about 2¢/word.

SOLOING AND SONLIGHT for Christian Singles, Box 15523, West Palm Beach FL 33416. (305)967-7739. Editor: Dennis Lombard. 50-75% freelance written. Eager to work with new/unpublished writers. Monthly tabloids distributed free to churches and to singles in churches and the public, geared to all denominations. Circ. 10,000 each. Pays on publication. Publishes ms an average of 2 months after acceptance. Byline given. Buys first North American serial rights, one-time rights, second serial (reprint) rights, or simultaneous rights, and makes work-for-hire assignments (locally). Submit seasonal/holiday material 2 months in advance. Simultaneous, photocopied, or previously published submissions OK. Computer printout submissions acceptable; prefers letter-quality. Reports in 1 week. Sample copies $1 with 9x12 SAE; writer's guidelines for #10 SAE with 1 first class stamp.
Nonfiction: Books excerpts and reviews; essays; general interest (Christian subjects); how-to; humor; inspirational; interview/profile; opinion; personal experience; photo feature; and religious. "All require interdenominational, non-doctrinal viewpoint." No critical attitudes. Buys 50 mss/year. Send complete ms. Length: 500-1,500 words. Pays $25-75 for assigned articles; pays $15-35 for unsolicited articles. Sometimes pays expenses of writers on assignment.
Photos: Send photos with submission. Reviews contact sheets and 4x5 b&w glossy prints. Offers $3-5/photo. Captions, model releases, and identification of subjects required. Buys one-time rights.
Fiction: Now buying humorous, religious, romance. Must have Christian perspective, but should not be preachy. Send complete ms. Length: 500-1,500 words.
Poetry: Light verse and traditional. Buys 5-10 poems/year. Submit maximum 3 poems. Length: 4-20 lines. Pays $3-10. Nothing too abstract or overly sentimental.
Tips: "We will be buying much more as our newspapers expand. We are re-launching *Sonlight*, a general Christian newspaper for all denominations. We continue to publish *Soloing* for Christian singles. We will be buying twice as much as this year — and we encourage new writers. We also hope to launch another new paper. Write for guidelines. We would like to receive testimonies, how-to for Christians (singles too), essays, and humor in the Christian life. New writers are welcome. How-to and personal experience articles are most open to freelancers. Testimonial articles should include an informal b&w photo of subject and subject's signed release. We're looking for the light and inspirational side. Will also publish *Good News* and *Neighbor News* soon. Send for guidelines."

SPIRITUAL LIFE, 2131 Lincoln Rd. NE, Washington DC 20002. (202)832-6622. Editor: Rev. Steven Payne, O.C.D. 80% freelance written. Prefers to work with published/established writers; works with a small number of new/unpublished writers each year. Quarterly. "Largely Catholic, well-educated, serious readers. A few are nonCatholic or nonChristian." Circ. 17,000. Pays on acceptance. Publishes ms an average of 1 year after acceptance. Buys first North American serial rights. "Brief autobiographical information (present occupation, past occupations, books and articles published, etc.) should accompany article." Computer printout submissions OK; prefers letter-quality. Reports in 2 weeks. Sample copy and writer's guidelines for SASE (9x6 or larger) with 4 first class stamps.
Nonfiction: Serious articles of contemporary spirituality. High quality articles about our encounter with God in the present day world. Language of articles should be college level. Technical terminology, if used, should be clearly explained. Material should be presented in a positive manner. Sentimental articles or those dealing with specific devotional practices not accepted. Buys inspirational and think pieces. No fiction or poetry. Buys 20 mss/year. Length: 3,000-5,000 words. Pays $50 minimum. "Five contributor's copies are sent to author on publication of article." Book reviews should be sent to Rev. Steven Payne, O.C.D.

SUNDAY DIGEST, David C. Cook Publishing Co., 850 N. Grove Ave., Elgin IL 60120. Editor: Janette L. Pearson. 75% freelance written. Prefers to work with established writers. Issued weekly to Christian adults in Sunday School. "*Sunday Digest* provides a combination of original articles and reprints, selected to help adult readers better understand the Christian faith, to keep them informed of issues within the Christian community, and to challenge them to a deeper personal commitment to Christ." Pays on acceptance. Publishes ms an average of 1 year after acceptance. Buys first or reprint rights. Computer printout submissions acceptable; no dot-matrix. Reports in 6-8 weeks. Sample copy and writer's guidelines for 6½x9½ SAE with 2 first class stamps.
Nonfiction: Needs articles applying the Christian faith to personal and social problems, articles on family life and church relationships, inspirational self-help, personal experience; how-to, and interview articles preferred over fiction. Submit a detailed query letter including the article's introduction. Length: 400-1,700 words. Pays $40-180.
Tips: "It is crucial that the writer is committed to quality Christian communication with a crisp, clear writing style. Christian message shoud be woven in, not tacked on."

SUNDAY SCHOOL COUNSELOR, General Council of the Assemblies of God, 1445 Boonville, Springfield MO 65802. (417)862-2781. Editor: Sylvia Lee. 60% freelance written. Works with small number of new/unpublished writers each year. Monthly magazine on religious education in the local church—the official Sunday school voice of the Assemblies of God channeling programs and help to local, primarily lay, leadership. Circ. 35,000. Pays on acceptance. Publishes ms an average of 9 months after acceptance. Byline given. Offers variable kill fee. Buys first North American serial rights, one-time rights, all rights, simultaneous rights, first serial rights, or second serial (reprint) rights; makes work-for-hire assignments. Submit seasonal/holiday material 7 months in advance. Simultaneous and previously published submissions OK. Computer printout submissions acceptable; prefers letter-quality. Reports in 2 weeks on queries; 1 month on mss. Sample copy $1 and 9x12 SAE; free writer's guidelines.

Nonfiction: How-to, inspirational, interview/profile, personal experience and photo feature. All related to religious education in the local church. Buys 100 mss/year. Send complete ms. Length: 300-1,800 words. Pays $25-90. Sometimes pays expenses of writers on assignment.

Photos: Send photos with ms. Reviews b&w and color prints. Model releases and identification of subjects required. Buys one-time rights.

TEACHERS INTERACTION, A Magazine Church School Workers Grow By, Concordia Publishing House, 3558 S. Jefferson, St. Louis MO 63118. Mail submissions to LCMS, 1333 S. Kirkwood Rd., St. Louis MO 63122-7295. Editor: Martha Streufert Jander. 20% freelance written. Quarterly magazine (newsletter seven times/year) of practical, inspirational, theological articles for volunteer church school teachers. Material must be true to the doctrines of the Lutheran Church—Missouri Synod. Circ. 20,400. Pays on acceptance. Publishes ms an average of 1 year after acceptance. Byline given. Buys all rights. Submit seasonal/holiday material 7 months in advance. Query for electronic submissions. Computer printout submissions acceptable; prefers letter-quality. Reports in 1 month on queries; 2 months on mss. Sample copy $1; writer's guidelines for 9x12 SAE (with sample copy); for #10 SAE (without sample copy).

Nonfiction: How-to (practical helps/ideas used successfully in own classroom); inspirational (to the church school worker—must be in accordance with LCMS doctrine); and personal experience (of a Sunday school classroom nature—growth). No theological articles. Buys 6 mss/year. Send complete ms. Length: 750-1,500 words. Pays $35.

Fillers: Cartoons. Buys 14/year. "*Teachers Interaction* buys short items—activities and ideas planned and used successfully in a church school classroom." Buys 50/year. Length: 100 words maximum. Pays $10.

Tips: "Practical, or 'it happened to me' experiences articles would have the best chance. Also short items—ideas used in classrooms; seasonal and in conjunction with our Sunday school material; Our Life in Christ. Our format is changing to include all volunteer church school teachers, not just Sunday school teachers."

TODAY'S PARISH, Twenty-Third Publications, 185 Willow St., Box 180, Mystic CT 06355. (203)536-2611. Editor: Mary Carol Kendzia. 75% freelance written. A magazine published 7 times/year covering Parish ministry. "Articles must deal with some aspect of parish life." Circ. 16,000. Pays on publication. Publishes ms an average of 6 months to 1 year after acceptance. Byline given. Buys first rights. Submit seasonal/holiday material 6 months in advance. Photocopied submissions OK. No multiple submissions. Computer printout submissions OK. Reports in 1 month. Sample copy and writer's guidelines for 8½x11 SASE.

Nonfiction: Opinion, personal experience, and photo feature all related to religion. Buys 45 mss/year. Query or send complete ms. Length: 800-1,800 words. Pays $50-100.

Photos: State availability of photos with submission or send photos. Reviews slides and prints. Offers no additional payment for photos accepted with ms. Identification of subjects required. Buys one-time rights.

‡II CHRONICLES MAGAZINE, Suite 3 & 4, 228 East Main St., Medford OR 97501. (503)779-4704. Editor: Mack Lloyd Lewis. 30% freelance written. A tabloid on contemporary Christian lifestyles, published every 1½ months. "*II Chronicles Magazine* is a contemporary Christian lifestyles magazine designed to encourage people in a relationship with Christ. We're most interested in work that ties in with our region." Circ. 5,000. Pays on publication. Publishes ms an average of 3 months after acceptance. Byline given. Buys first North American serial rights or one-time rights. Submit seasonal/holiday material 3 months in advance. Simultaneous and photocopied submissions OK. Computer printout submissions OK; prefers letter-quality. Reports in 5 weeks on queries. Sample copy and writer's guidelines for 9x12 SAE and 4' first class stamps.

Nonfiction: Lloyd Neske, articles editor. Essays, general interest, historical/nostalgic, inspirational, interview/profile and religious. "No erotica or anything else that does not portray a biblically based life." Buys 8 mss/year. Query with published clips. Length: 1,250-2,500 words. Pays $30-100. Sometimes pays in contributor copies for articles.

Photos: Send photos with submission. Reviews contact sheets. Offers $1-3. Captions and identification of subjects required. Buys one-time rights.

Fiction: Buck Ryehead, fiction editor. Adventure, historical, mainstream, religious and suspense. "Nothing that is not based upon biblical values." Buys 3-8 mss/year. Send complete ms. Length: 800-1,200 words. Pays $30.

Poetry: Avant-garde and traditional. Buys 10 poems/year. Submit maximum 3 poems. Length: 5-25 words. Pays with contributor copies.

Fillers: Anecdotes, facts, gags to be illustrated by cartoonist, newsbreaks and short humor. Buys 3-10/year. Length: 25-150 words. Pays with copies.

Tips: "Freelancers can best begin by writing to us. Nonfiction topics are usually assigned to those we know. Fiction writers can best begin simply through submitting their work. We're always looking for good Christian fiction. Historical articles on Biblical times with a unique slant are of interest to us. Unique slants in general will always help one's chances. We're known for being different."

‡THE UNITED CHURCH OBSERVER, 85 St. Clair Ave. E., Toronto, Ontario M4T 1M8 Canada. (416)960-8500. Publisher and Editor: Hugh McCullum. Managing Editor: Muriel Duncan. 40% freelance written. Prefers to work with published/established writers. A 60-page monthly newsmagazine for people associated with The United Church of Canada. Deals primarily with events, trends and policies having religious significance. Most coverage is Canadian, but reports on international or world concerns will be considered. Pays on publication. Publishes ms an average of 4 months after acceptance. Byline usually given. Buys first serial rights and occasionally all rights. Computer printout submissions acceptable; no dot-matrix.

Nonfiction: Occasional opinion features only. Extended coverage of major issues usually assigned to known writers. No opinion pieces, poetry. Submissions should be written as news, no more than 1,200 words length, accurate and well-researched. Queries preferred. Rates depend on subject, author and work involved. Pays expenses of writers on assignment "as negotiated."

Photos: Buys photographs with mss. B&w should be 5x7 minimum; color 35mm or larger format. Payment varies.

Tips: "The writer has a better chance of breaking in at our publication with short articles; it also allows us to try more freelancers. Include samples of previous *news* writing with query. Indicate ability and willingness to do research, and to evaluate that research. The most frequent mistakes made by writers in completing an article for us are organizational problems, lack of polished style, short on research, and a lack of inclusive language."

UNITED EVANGELICAL ACTION, Box 28, Wheaton IL 60189. (312)665-0500. Editor: Donald R. Brown. Managing Editor: Brad Davis. 50% freelance written. Prefers to work with published/established writers. Bimonthly magazine. Offers "an objective evangelical viewpoint and interpretive analysis of specific issues of consequence and concern to the American Church and updates readers on ways evangelicals are confronting those issues at the grass roots level." Circ. 10,500. Pays on publication. Publishes ms an average of 2 months after acceptance. Buys first serial rights. Phone queries OK. Query for electronic submissions. Computer printout submissions acceptable; prefers letter-quality. Reports in 1 month. Sample copy and writer's guidelines with SASE.

Nonfiction: Issues and trends in the Church and society that affect the ongoing witness and outreach of evangelical Christians. Content should be well thought through, and should provide practical suggestions for dealing with these issues and trends. Buys 8-10 mss/year. "Always send a query letter before sending an unsolicited manuscript." Length: 900-1,000 words. Pays $50-175. Sometimes pays expenses of writers on assignment.

Tips: Editors would really like to see news (action) items that relate to the National Association of Evangelicals. "We are interested in expanding coverage of NAE activities throughout the country. Send query letter about important topics facing evangelicals or news features about local works by evangelicals. Keep writing terse, to the point, and stress practical over theoretical."

UNITED METHODIST REPORTER, Box 660275, Dallas TX 75266-0275. (214)630-6495. Editor/General Manager: Spurgeon M. Dunnam, III. Managing Editor: John A. Lovelace. Weekly newspaper for a United Methodist national readership. Circ. 475,000. Pays on publication. Byline given. Not copyrighted. Free sample copy and writer's guidelines.

Nonfiction: "We accept occasional short features, approximately 500 words. Articles need not be limited to a United Methodist angle but need to have an explicit Protestant angle, preferably with evidence of participation in a local congregation. Write about a distinctly Christian response to human need or how a person's faith relates to a given situation." Send complete ms. Pays 4¢/word.

Photos: Purchased with accompanying ms. "We encourage the submission of good action photos (5x7 or 8x10 b&w glossy prints) of the persons or situations in the article." Pays $10.

THE UPPER ROOM, DAILY DEVOTIONAL GUIDE, The Upper Room, 1908 Grand Ave., Nashville TN 37202. (615)327-2700. World Editor: Janice T. Grana. Managing Editor: Mary Lou Redding. 95% freelance written. Eager to work with new/unpublished writers. Bimonthly magazine "offering a daily inspirational message which includes a Bible reading, text, prayer, 'Thought for the Day,' and suggestion for prayer. Each day's meditation is written by a different person and is usually a personal witness about discovering meaning and power for Christian living through some experience from daily life." Circ. 2.2 million (U.S.); 385,000 outside U.S. Pays on publication. Publishes ms an average of 1 year after acceptance. Byline given. Buys first North American serial rights and translation rights. Submit seasonal/holiday material 14 months in advance.

Computer printout submissions acceptable; prefers letter-quality. Reports in 6 weeks on mss. Sample copy and writer's guidelines for SAE and 2 first class stamps.

Nonfiction: Inspirational and personal experience. No poetry, lengthy "spiritual journey" stories. Buys 360 unsolicited mss/year. Send complete ms. Length: 250 words maximum. Pays $12.

Tips: "The best way to break into our magazine is to send a well-written manuscript that looks at the Christian faith in a fresh way. Standard stories and sermon illustrations are immediately rejected. We very much want to find new writers and welcome good material. We are particularly interested in meditations based on Old Testament characters and stories. Good repeat meditations can lead to work on longer assignments for our other publications, which pay more. A writer who can deal concretely with everyday situations, relate them to spiritual truths, and write clear, direct prose should be able to write for *The Upper Room*. We want material that provides for more interaction on the part of the reader—meditation suggestions, journaling suggestions, space to reflect and link personal experience with the meditation for the day."

VIRTUE, The Christian Magazine for Women, 548 Sisters Pkwy, Box 850, Sisters OR 97759. (503)549-8261. Editor: Becky Durost Fish. Managing Editor: Ruth Nygren Keller. 75% freelance written. Works with small number of new/unpublished writers each year. A magazine, published 8 times/year, that "encourages women in their development as individuals and provides practical help for them as they minister to their families, churches and communities." Circ. 110,000. Pays on acceptance. Publishes ms an average of 4 months after acceptance. Byline given. Buys first North American serial rights. Submit seasonal/holiday material 9 months in advance. Photocopied submissions OK. Computer printout submissions OK; prefers letter-quality. Reports in 6 weeks on queries; 2 months on mss. Sample copy $3; writer's guidelines for #10 SAE with 1 first class stamp.

Nonfiction: Book excerpts, how-to, humor, inspirational, interview/profile, opinion, personal experience and religious. Buys 70 mss/year. Query. Length: 600-1,800 words. Pays 10¢/word. Sometimes pays the expenses of writers on assignment.

Photos: State availability of photos with submission.

Columns/Departments: In My Opinion (reader editorial); One Woman's Journal (personal experience); Equipped for Ministry (practical how-to for helping others). Buys 25 mss/year. Query. Length: 1,000-1,500. Pays 10¢/word.

Fiction: Fantasy, humorous and religious. Buys 7-10 mss/year. Send complete ms. Length: 1,500-1,800 words. Pays 10¢/word.

Poetry: Free verse, haiku and traditional. Buys 7-10 poems/year. Submit maximum 3 poems. Length: 3-30 lines. Pays $15-50.

VISION, A Lifestyles Magazine for Young Adults, Young Adult Ministries, Box 7259, Grand Rapids MI 49510. (616)241-5616. Editor: Dale Dieleman. 75% freelance written. Prefers to work with published/established writers. A bimonthly magazine that offers articles of general interest to young adults, 18-30 + . Circ. 5,000. Pays on publication. Byline given. Buys one-time or second serial (reprint) rights. Submit seasonal/holiday material 6 months in advance. Photocopied submissions OK. Computer printout submissions acceptable. Reports in 1 month. Sample copy and writer's guidelines for $1 and 9x12 SAE with 3 first class stamps.

Nonfiction: Human interest articles—with a focus on a person(s) or issue of general interest to young adults. Interview/profile, personal experience, inspirational and humor. Buys 12 mss/year. Query or send complete ms. Length: 700-1,500 words. Pays $40-100 for assigned articles; pays $25-50 for unsolicited articles.

Photos: Offers $25/photo. Model releases and identification of subjects required. Buys one-time rights.

Columns/Departments: Lifestyles (an inspirational/informational column on living a positive Christian life—whether never married, previously married, or a single parent); Budget Briefs (a column addressing financial questions/issues like stock market house buying, retirement, consumer awareness); Work World (a column for the working young adult on issues the young adult faces as a Christian professional); Sports and Leisure (an informational column on leisure-time activities, hobbies); and Creative Christianity (how-to examples of service opportunities for young adults, short-term or long-term, individual or group opportunities). Buys 24 mss/year. Query or send complete ms. Length: 600-700 words. Pays $25-35.

Fiction: Contemporary, slice-of-life vignettes with spiritual/religious slant. Buys 3 mss/year. Query or send complete ms. Length: 700-1,400 words. Pays $25-50.

Poetry: Avant-garde, free verse, haiku, light verse and traditional. Buys 3 poems/year. Submit maximum 3 poems. Pays $15-45.

VISTA, Wesleyan Publishing House, Box 50434, Indianapolis IN 46250-0434. Editor: James Watkins. 80% freelance written. Eager to work with new/unpublished writers—"quality writing a must, however." Weekly publication of The Wesleyan Church for adults. Circ. 60,000. Pays on acceptance. Publishes ms an average of 10 months after acceptance. Byline given. Not copyrighted. Buys first rights, simultaneous rights, second rights, and reprint rights. Submit seasonal/holiday material 10 months in advance. Computer printout submissions acceptable; prefers letter-quality. Reports in 1 month.

Nonfiction: Testimonies, how-to's, humor, interviews, opinion pieces from conservative Christian perspec-

tive. Length: 500-1,200 words.
Photos: Pays $15-40 for 5x7 or 8x10 b&w glossy print natural looking close-ups of faces in various emotions, groups of people interacting. Various reader age groups should be considered.
Fiction: Believable, quality articles, no Sunday "soaps." Length: 500-1,200 words. Pays 2-4¢/word.
Tips: "Read the writer's guide carefully before submitting."

VITAL CHRISTIANITY, Warner Press, Inc., 1200 E. 5th St., Anderson IN 46018. (317)644-7721. Editor-in-Chief: Arlo F. Newell. Managing Editor: Richard L. Willowby. 20-25% freelance written. Prefers to work with published/established writers; works with small number of new/unpublished writers each year. Magazine covering Christian living for people attending local Church of God congregations; published 20 times/year. Circ. 26,000. Pays on acceptance. Byline given. Offers kill fee. Buys one-time rights. Submit seasonal/holiday material 6 months in advance. Query for electronic submissions. Computer printout submissions OK; no dot-matrix. Reports in 6 weeks. Sample copy and writer's guidelines for SASE and $1.
Nonfiction: Humor (with religious point); inspirational (religious—not preachy); interview/profile (of church-related personalities); opinion (religious/theological); and personal experience (related to putting one's faith into practice). Buys 125 mss/year. Query. Length: 1,000 words maximum. Pays $10-100.
Photos: State availability of photos. Pays $50-300 for 5x7 color transparencies; $20-40 for 8x10 b&w prints. Identification of subjects (when related directly to articles) required. Buys one-time rights. Reserves the right to reprint material it has used for advertising and editorial purposes (pays second rights for editorial re-use).
Tips: "Fillers, personal experience, personality interviews, profiles and good holiday articles are areas of our magazine open to freelancers. Writers should request our guidelines and list of upcoming topics of interest to determine if they have interest or expertise in writing for us. Always send SASE."

WAR CRY, The Official Organ of the Salvation Army, 799 Bloomfield Ave., Verona NJ 07044. Editor: Henry Gariepy. 20% freelance written. Prefers to work with published/established writers. Biweekly magazine for "persons with evangelical Christian background; members and friends of the Salvation Army; the 'man in the street.' " Circ. 300,000. Pays on acceptance. Publishes ms an average of 8 months after acceptance. Buys first serial rights and second serial (reprint) rights. Computer printout submissions OK; no dot-matrix. Reports in 2 months. Sample copy and guidelines for 9x12 SAE and 65¢ postage.
Nonfiction: Inspirational and informational articles with a strong evangelical Christian slant, but not preachy. In addition to general articles, needs articles slanted toward most of the holidays including Easter, Christmas, Mother's Day, Father's Day, etc. Buys 15 mss/year. Length: approximately 700-1,400 words. Pays 6¢/word.
Photos: Pays $25-35 for b&w glossy prints; $150 for color prints.

THE WESLEYAN ADVOCATE, The Wesleyan Publishing House, Box 50434, Indianapolis IN 46250-0434. (317)576-1313. Editor: Dr. Wayne E. Caldwell. 10% freelance written. A biweekly magazine by the Wesleyan Church. Circ. 20,000. Pays on publication. Publishes ms an average of 1 year after acceptance. Byline given. Buys first rights or simultaneous rights. Submit seasonal/holiday material 1 year in advance. Simultaneous submissions OK. Query for electronic submissions. Computer printout submission OK; prefers letter-quality. Reports in 2 weeks. Sample copy for $1; writer's guidelines for #10 SAE with 1 first class stamp.
Nonfiction: Humor, inspirational and religious. Buys 5 mss/year. Send complete ms. Length: 250-650 words. Pays $10-40 for assigned articles; $5-25 for unsolicited articles.
Photos: Send photos with submission. Reviews color transparencies. Buys one-time rights.
Tips: "Write for a guide."

Retirement

Retirement magazines have changed to meet the active lifestyles of their readers and dislike the kinds of stereotypes people have of retirement magazines. More people are retiring in their 50s, while others are starting a business or traveling and pursuing hobbies. These publications give readers specialized information on aging, finances and other topics of interest, as well as general articles on travel destinations and recreational activities.

ALBUQUERQUE SENIOR SCENE MAGAZINE,3507 Wyoming NE, Albuquerque NM 87111. (505)299-4401. Editor: Gail Skinner. 90% freelance written. Eager to work with new/unpublished writers. Quarterly (Spring/Summer/Fall/Winter) 4-color magazine addressing today's modern 50+ adult. Pays on publication. Publishes ms an average of 6 months after acceptance. Byline given. Buys first serial rights, second serial (reprint) rights, or all rights. Submit seasonal/holiday material 6 months in advance. Query for electronic submissions. Computer printout submissions OK; prefers letter-quality to dot matrix. Reports in 3 months. Sample copy $3. Writer's guidelines for SAE and 1 first class stamp.

Nonfiction: General interest, how-to, humor, inspirational, opinion, personal experience, hobbies, health, finance, real estate, travel, retirement, consumer guide, astrology and grandparenting. Buys 50 mss/year. Send complete ms with SASE for response. "Keep a copy of the ms for your file as we do not return them. If you have photo(s) and/or illustration(s) to accompany the article, do not send them with your story unless you do not want them returned." Also publishes some fiction. Length: 600-2,500 words. Pays $35-150. Sometimes pays expenses of writers on assignment.

Photos: State availability of photos with ms. Captions, model releases, identification of subjects required.

Tips: "We are looking for articles that deal with every aspect of life for the active, upbeat, 50+ adult, whether on a local or national level. Our readers are above-average intelligence, income and education."

GOLDEN YEARS MAGAZINE, Golden Years Senior News, Inc., 233 E. New Haven Ave., Melbourne FL 32902-0537. (407)725-4888. Editor: Carol Brenner Hittner. 50% freelance written. Prefers to work with published/established writers. Monthly magazine covering "fantastic Floridians over 50. We serve the needs and interests of Florida's fastest growing generation. Editorial presented in a positive, uplifting, straightforward manner." Circ. 600,000. Pays on publication. Publishes ms an average of 7 months after acceptance. Byline given. Buys first serial rights and first North American serial rights. Submit seasonal/holiday material 1 year in advance. Simultaneous queries, and simultaneous, and photocopied submissions OK. Computer printout submissions acceptable; no dot-matrix. Sample copy $2; writer's guidelines for SAE with 1 first class stamp.

Nonfiction: Profile (Florida senior celebrities), travel, second careers, hobbies, retirement ideas and real estate. Buys 100 mss/year. Query with published clips or send complete ms. Length: 500 words maximum. Pays 70¢/standard one-third-column line.

Photos: "We like to include a lot of photos." Send photos with query or ms. Pays $25 for color transparencies. Captions, model releases, and identification of subjects required. Buys one-time rights. Pays $10 per each b&w photo.

Tips: "We're looking for profiles on Florida people. Our magazine articles are short and special—that's why we are successful."

‡GRAY PANTHER NETWORK, Gray Panthers Project Fund. Suite 601, 311 S. Juniper St., Philadelphia PA 19107. (215)545-6555. Editor: Abby Lederman. 20% freelance written. A bimonthly tabloid covering the fight for human rights, national health system, elderly issues, legislation and ageism. "Readers of *Network* are 50-plus. Most have been and continue to be active in the peace, human rights movements. Writers need to have leftist leanings and be sensitive to older people." Circ. 36,000. Pays on acceptance. Publishes ms an average of 3 months after acceptance. Byline given. Offers $50 kill fee. Buys one-time rights or second serial (reprint) rights. Photocopied and previously published submissions OK. Computer printout submissions OK; prefers letter-quality. Reports in 5 weeks. Free sample copy and writer's guidelines.

Nonfiction: Exposé (against corporate, dehumanizing elements of society), humor (on a Gray Panther topic-i.e. ageism) and interview/profile (people active in human rights, peace struggle, older Americans). "No first-person experience. No travel, religious, how-to except when dealing with community, grass roots organizing." Buys 15-20 mss/year. Query with published clips. Length: 500-1,500 words. Pays $75-250. Sometimes pays the expenses of writers on assignment.

Photos: State availability of photos with submission. Reviews contact sheets and prints (3x5). Offers $10-75 per photo. Buys one-time rights.

Columns/Departments: Book & Video Reviews (ageism in the movies, healthy view of aging, book reviews about issues of peace, human rights, economic justice), 500-1,500. Pays $50-200.

‡HARVEST MAGAZINE, The Reader's Hearth, 2322 Latona Dr. NE, Salem OR 97303. Managing Editor: William Michaelian and Jay Thomas Collins. Bimonthly magazine of writing by those age 50 and older, "dedicated to preserving the voice of our older generation." Estab. 1988. Circ. 3,000. Pays on publication. Publishes ms an average of 3 months after acceptance. Byline given. Buys one-time rights. Submit seasonal/holiday material 4 months in advance. Photocopied and previously published submissions OK. Computer printout submissions OK. Reports in 5 weeks on queries; 6 weeks on mss. Sample copy $2.

Nonfiction: Book excerpts, essays, historical/nostalgic, humor, inspirational, interview/profile, opinion, personal experience, travel. Buys 18 mss/year. Query with or without published clips, or send complete ms. Length: 1,000-6,000. Pays $10-60. Sometimes pays expenses of writers on assignment.

Photos: Send photos with submission. Reviews prints. Offers no additional payment for photos accepted with ms. Model releases and identification of subjects required. Buys one-time rights.

Fiction: Adventure, condensed novels, ethnic, historical, humorous, novel excerpts, slice-of-life vignettes. Buys 9 mss/year. Send complete ms. Length: 200-7,000 words. Pays in copies.

Poetry: Avant-garde, free verse, traditional. Buys 24 poems/year. Submit maximum 12 poems at one time. Length: 100 lines maximum. Pays in copies.

Fillers: Anecdotes, short humor. Pays in copies.
Tips: "Interviews and articles on interesting seniors may be written by anyone. Due to financial restrictions, our current policy is to pay for this service only."

MATURE LIVING, A Christian Magazine for Senior Adults, Sunday School Board of the Southern Baptist Convention, 127 9th Ave. N., Nashville TN 37209. (615)251-2191. Editor: Jack Gulledge. Assistant Editor: Judy Bregel. 70% freelance written. A monthly leisure reading magazine for senior adults 60 and older. Circ. 340,000. Pays on acceptance. Byline given. Buys all rights and sometimes one-time rights. Submit seasonal/holiday material 18 months in advance. Photocopied submissions OK. Computer printout submissions acceptable; prefers letter-quality. Reports in 8 weeks. Sample copy for 9x12 SAE with 4 first class stamps affixed; writer's guidelines for #10 SAE with 1 first class stamp.
Nonfiction: General interest, historical/nostalgic, how-to, humor, inspirational, interview/profile, personal experience, photo feature and travel. No pornography, profanity, occult; liquor, dancing, drugs, gambling; no book reviews. Buys 100 mss/year. Send complete ms. Length: 1,475 words maximum, prefers 950 words. Pays 5¢/word (accepted).
Photos: State availability of photos with submission. Offers $10-15/photo. Pays on publication. Buys one-time rights.
Fiction: Humorous, mainstream and slice-of-life vignettes. No reference to liquor, dancing, drugs, gambling; no pornography, profanity or occult. Buys 12 mss/year. Send complete ms. Length: 900-1,475 words. Pays 5¢/word.
Poetry: Light verse and traditional. Buys 50 poems/year. Submit maximum 5 poems. Length: open. Pays $5-24.
Fillers: Anecdotes, facts and short humor. Buys 15/issue. Length: 50 words maximum. Pays $5.

MATURE YEARS, 201 8th Ave., S., Nashville TN 37202. Editor: John P. Gilbert. 30% freelance written. Prefers to work with published/established writers; works with a small number of new/unpublished writers each year. Quarterly magazine for retired persons and those facing retirement; persons seeking help on how to handle problems and privileges of retirement. Pays on acceptance. Publishes ms an average of 14 months after acceptance. Rights purchased vary with author and material; usually buys first North American serial rights. Submit seasonal material 14 months in advance. Query for electronic submissions. Computer printout submissions OK. Reports in 6 weeks. Sample copy for 9x12 SAE and $1.58; writer's guidelines for #10 SASE.
Nonfiction: "*Mature Years* is different from the secular press in that we like material with a Christian and church orientation. Usually we prefer materials that have a happy, healthy outlook regarding aging. Advocacy (for older adults) articles are at times used; some are freelance submissions. We need articles dealing with many aspects of pre-retirement and retirement living, and short stories and leisure-time hobbies related to specific seasons. Give examples of how older persons, organizations, and institutions are helping others. Writing should be of interest to older adults, with Christian emphasis, though not preachy and moralizing. No poking fun or mushy, sentimental articles. We treat retirement from the religious viewpoint. How-to, humor and travel are also considered." Buys 24 unsolicited mss/year. Submit complete ms (include SASE and Social Security number with submissions). Length: 1,200-1,500 words. Sometimes pays expenses of writers on assignment.
Photos: 8x10 b&w glossy prints, color prints or color transparencies purchased with ms or on assignment.
Fiction: "We buy fiction for adults. Humor is preferred. No children's stories and no stories about depressed situations of older adults." Length: 1,000-1,500 words. Payment varies, usually 4¢/word.
Tips: "We like writing to be meaty, timely, clear and concrete."

MODERN MATURITY, American Association of Retired Persons, 3200 E. Carson, Lakewood CA 90712. Editor-in-Chief: Ian Ledgerwood. 50% freelance written. Prefers to work with published/established writers. Bimonthly magazine for readership of persons 50 years of age and over. Circ. 17 million. Pays on acceptance. Publishes ms an average of 4-6 months after acceptance. Byline given. Buys first North American serial rights. Submit seasonal/holiday material 6 months in advance. Query for electronic submissions. Computer printout submissions acceptable; no dot-matrix. Reports in 6-8 weeks. Free sample copy and writer's guidelines.
Nonfiction: Careers, workplace, practical information in living, investments, financial and legal matters, personal relationships, and consumerism. Query first. Length: up to 2,000 words. Pays up to $3,000. Sometimes pays expenses of writers on assignment.
Photos: Photos purchased with or without accompanying ms. Pays $250 and up for color and $150 and up for b&w.
Fiction: Write for guidelines.
Poetry: All types. Length: 40 lines maximum. Pays $75.
Fillers: Jokes, gags, short anecdotes, puzzles (word search only) and short humor. Pays $50 minimum.
Tips: "The most frequent mistake made by writers in completing an article for us is poor follow-through with basic research. The outline is often more interesting than the finished piece."

NEW ENGLAND SENIOR CITIZEN/SENIOR AMERICAN NEWS, Prime National Publishing Corp., 470 Boston Post Rd., Weston MA 02193. Editor-in-Chief: Eileen F. DeVito. 80% freelance written. For men and women aged 55 and over who are interested in travel, finances, retirement lifestyles, nostalgia, etc. Monthly newspaper; 24-32 pages. Circ. 60,000. Pays on publication. Publishes ms an average of 9 months after acceptance. Buys all rights. Byline given. Submit seasonal/holiday material 3 months in advance. Computer printout submissions acceptable. Reports in 4 months. Sample copy 50¢.
Nonfiction: General interest; how-to (anything dealing with retirement years); inspirational; historical; humor; interview; nostalgia; profile; travel; personal experience; photo features. Buys 10-15 mss/issue. Submit complete ms. Length: 500-1,500 words. Pays $25-50.
Photos: Purchased with ms. Captions required. Pays $5-15/5x7 or 8x10 b&w glossy print. Captions and model releases required.
Tips: "Submit clean, typed, top-quality copy aimed at older tastes, interests, lifestyles and memories."

PRIME TIMES, Grote Deutsch & Co., Suite 120, 2802 International Ln., Madison WI 53704. Executive Editor: Joan Donovan. 80% freelance written. Prefers to work with published/established writers, but "we will work at times with unpublished writers." Quarterly magazine for people who are in the prime mid-life or at the height of their careers and planning a dynamic retirement lifestyle. "The audience is primarily people aged 40-64 who were or are credit union members and want to plan and manage their retirement or second careers." Circ. 75,000. Pays on publication. Buys first North American serial rights and second serial (reprint) rights. Publishes ms an average of 6 months after acceptance. Submit seasonal material 6 months in advance. Previously published submissions OK as long as they were not in another national maturity-market magazine. Computer printout submissions acceptable; no dot-matrix. Reports in 2 months. Sample copy only with 9x12 SAE and 5 first class stamps; writer's guidelines for SASE.
Nonfiction: Expose; how-to, new research and updates (related to financial planning methods, consumer activism, preventive health and fitness, travel, and careers/dynamic lifestyle after retirement); opinion; profile; travel; popular arts; self-image; personal experience; humor; and photo feature. "No rocking-chair reminiscing." Articles on health and medical issues and research *must* be founded in sound scientific method and must include current, up-to-date data. "Health related articles are an easy sale, but you must do your homework and be able to document your research. Don't waste your time or ours on tired generalizations about how to take care of the human anatomy. If you've heard it before, so have we. We want to know who is doing new research, what the current findings may be, and what scientists on the cutting edge of new research say the future holds, preferably in the next one to five years. Is anyone doing basic research into the physiology of the aging process? If so, who? And what have they found? What triggers the aging process? Why do some people age faster than others? What are the common denominators? Does genetic coding and recombinant DNA research hold the answers to slowing or halting the aging process? Get the picture? Give us the facts, only the facts, and all of the facts. Allow the scientists and our audience to draw their own conclusions." Buys 30-40 mss/year, about half from new talent. Query with published clips. Length: 1,000-3,000 words. Pays $50-1,000. "Be sure to keep a photocopy—just in case gremlins pinch the original." Sometimes pays the expenses of writers on assignment.
Photos: Payment is based on one-time publication rights; $50 for less than ½ page, $100 for ½ page and $250 for full page. Cover photos, photo spreads, multiple purchases and work done on assignment to be negotiated. Payment is upon publication. Photo release is necessary to prove ownership of copyright. No standard kill fee. "Do not send irreplaceable *anything*."
Fiction: Length: 1,500-3,500 words. Pays $200-750. "If you are not sure your work is of outstanding quality, please do not submit it to us."
Tips: Query should state qualifications (such as expertise or society memberships). Special issues requiring freelance work include publications on adult relationships and developmental transitions such as mid-life and "empty-nest" passages and couple renewal; health and medical research and updates; second careers; money management; continuing education; consequences of the ongoing longevity revolution; and the "creation of new lifestyles for prime-life adults (ages 40-65 primarily) who are well-educated, affluent, and above all, *active*. About 55% of our readers are women. All are active and redefining the middle years with creative energy and imagination. Age-irrelevant writing is a must. The focus of *Prime Times* in 1989 will be on presenting readers with refreshing and newsworthy material for dynamic mid-lifers, people who have a forever-forty mentality."

SENIOR, California Senior Magazine, 3565 S. Higuera St., San Luis Obispo CA 93401. (805)544-8711. Editor: George Brand. Associate Editor: Herb Kamm, R. Judd. 90% freelance written. Monthly magazine covering senior citizens to inform and entertain the "over-50" audience. Circ. 40,000. Pays on publication. Byline given. Publishes ms an average of 1 month after acceptance. Byline given. Not copyrighted. Buys first rights or second rights. Submit seasonal/holiday material 2 months in advance. Computer printout submissions OK; prefers letter-quality. Reports in 2 weeks. Sample copy for 9x11 SAE and 4 first class stamps; free writer's guidelines.
Nonfiction: Historical/nostalgic, humor, inspirational, personal experience and travel. Special issue features

War Years (November); Christmas (December); and Travel (April). Buys 30-75 mss/year. Query. Length: 300-900 words. Pays $1.50/inch. Sometimes pays the expenses of writers on assignment.
Photos: Send photos with submission. Reviews 8x10 prints. Offers $10-25 per photo. Captions and identification of subjects required. Buys one-time rights.
Columns/Departments: Finance (investment); Taxes; Auto; Medicare, all 600 words. Length: 300-900 words. Pays $1.50/inch.
Fillers: Herb Kamm, editor. Anecdotes and facts. Length: 25-30 words. Pays $1.50/inch.

SENIOR EDITION, and *Senior Edition USA*, SEI Publishing Corporation, Suite 2240, 1660 Lincoln, Denver CO 80264. (303)837-9100. Editor: Allison St. Claire. 15% freelance written. Monthly tabloid. "Colorado newspaper for seniors (with national distribution) and national edition emphasizing legislation, opinion and advice columns, local and national news, features and local calendar aimed at over-55 community." Circ. 12,000. Pays on publication. Publishes ms an average of 1-6 months after acceptance. Byline given. Offer 25-50% kill fee for assigned stories only. Buys first North American serial rights and simultaneous rights. Submit seasonal/holiday material 3 months in advance. Reports in 1-2 weeks on queries; 2-3 weeks on mss. Sample copy $1; writer's guidelines for SASE.
Nonfiction: Historical/nostalgic, humor, inspirational, opinion, personal experience and travel. Does not want "anything aimed at less than age 55-plus market; anything patronizing or condescending to seniors." Buys 12 mss/year. Query with or without published clips, or send complete ms. Length: 50-1,000 words. Pays $5-100 for assigned articles; $5-50 for unsolicited articles. Sometimes pays expenses of writers on assignment.
Photos: Send photos with submission (or photocopies of available pictures). Offers $3-10 per photo. Identification of subjects required. Buys one-time rights.
Columns/Departments: Senior Overlook (opinions of seniors about anything they feel strongly about: finances, grandkids, love, life, social problems, etc. May be editorial, essay, prose or poetry). Buys 12 mss/year. Send complete ms. Length: 50-1,000 words. Pays $10 maximum.
Fillers: Short humor. Buys 4/year. Length: 300 words maximum. Pays $10 maximum.
Tips: Areas most open to freelancers are "Opinion: have a good, reasonable point backed with personal experience and/or researched data. Diatribes, vague or fuzzy logic, or overworked themes not appreciated. Advice: solid information and generic articles accepted. We will not promote any product or business unless it is the only one in existence. Must be applicable to senior lifestyle."

‡SENIOR LIFE MAGAZINE, The Magazine for Active Adults, Suite 200L, 1450 E. Cooley Dr., Colton CA 92324. (714)824-6681. Editor: Bobbi Mason. Managing Editor: Chris Jackson. Monthly magazine of general interest to people 50+. "Readers are 50+, mobile and active. Most live in California full or part time." Circ. 30,000. Pays on publication. Byline given. Buys first rights, second serial (reprint) rights, or simultaneous rights. Submit seasonal/holiday material 3 months in advance. Simultaneous, photocopied and previously published submissions OK. Computer printout submissions OK. Sample copy $2.25; writer's guidelines for #10 SAE with 1 first class stamp.
Nonfiction: General interest, historical/nostalgic, how-to (crafts, other than needlework), humor, inspirational, interview/profile, personal experience, photo feature. Buys 5 mss/year. Query or send complete ms. Length: 300-1,200 words. Pays $50-75 for assigned articles; $10-45 for unsolicited articles.
Photos: State availability of photos with submission. Reviews transparencies and prints. Offers no additional payment for photos accepted with ms "unless negotiated up front." Captions, model releases and identification of subjects required. Buys one-time rights.
Columns/Departments: Special to this issue (open to stories on celebrities, nostalgia, or a highlight of a not-famous-but-special-senior) 500-1,200 words. Query or send complete ms. Length: 300-700 words. Pays $10-50.
Fiction: Adventure, fantasy, historical, humorous, mainstream, mystery, romance, slice-of-life-vignettes, westerns. Buys 6 mss/year. Query or send complete ms. Length: 200 words minimum. Pays $10-75.
Tips: "Write tightly: space for us is a problem. Short articles with photo(s) most likely accepted."

‡SENIOR WORLD OF CALIFORNIA, Californian Publishing Co., Box 165, El Cajon CA 92022. (619)442-4404. Executive Editor: Laura Impastato. Travel Editor: Jerry Goodrum. Health Editor: Ron Miller. 10% freelance written. Prefers to work with published/established writers. Monthly tabloid newspaper for active older adults living in San Diego, Orange, Los Angeles, Santa Barbara, Ventura and San Luis Obispo counties. Circ. 350,000. Pays on publication. Publishes ms an average of 3 months after acceptance. Buys first serial rights. Simultaneous and photocopied submissions OK. Reports in 2 months. Sample copy $2; free writer's guidelines.
Nonfiction: "We are looking for stories on health, stressing wellness and prevention; travel—international, domestic and how-to; profiles of senior celebrities and remarkable seniors; finance and investment tips for seniors and interesting hobbies." Send query or complete ms. Length: 500-1,000 words. Pays $30-100.
Photos: State availability of photos. Need b&w with model release. Will pay extra for photos. Buys all rights to photos selected to run with a story.

Columns/Departments: Most of our columns are local or staff-written. We will consider a query on a column idea accompanied by a sample column.

Tips: "No pity the poor seniors material. Remember that we are primarily a news publication and that our content and style reflect that. Our readers are active, vital adults 55 years of age and older." No telephone queries.

___ *Romance and Confession*

Listed here are publications that need stories of romance ranging from ethnic and adventure to romantic intrigue and confession. Each magazine has a particular slant; some are written for young adults, others to family-oriented women. Some magazines also are interested in general interest nonfiction on related subjects.

AFFAIRE DE COEUR, Keenan Enterprises, Suite B, 1555 Washington Ave., San Leandro CA 94577. (415)357-5665. Editor: Barbara N. Keenan. 56% freelance written. Monthly magazine of book reviews, articles and information on publishing for romance readers and writers. Circ. 18,000. Pays on publication. Publishes ms an average of 6-12 months after acceptance. Byline given. Buys one-time rights. Submit seasonal/holiday material 3 months in advance. Simultaneous, photocopied and previously published submissions OK. Reports in 3-4 months. Sample copy $3; writer's guidelines for #10 SAE and 1 first class stamp.

Nonfiction: Book excerpts, essays, general interest, historical/nostalgic, how-to, interview/profile, personal experience and photo feature. Buys 2 mss/year. Query. Length: 500-2,200 words. Pays $5-15. Sometimes pays writers with contributor copies or other premiums.

Photos: State availability of photos with submission. Review prints. Offers $2/photo. Identification of subjects required. Buys one-time rights.

Columns/Departments: Reviews (book reviews). Query. Length: 125-150 words. Does not pay.

Fiction: Historical, mainstream and romance. Buys 2 mss/year. Query. Length: 1,500-2,200. Pays $15.

Poetry: Light verse. Buys 2 poems/year. Submit 1 poem. Does not pay.

Fillers: Newsbreaks. Buys 2/year. Length: 50-100 words. Does not pay.

Tips: "Please send clean copy. Do not send material without SASE. Do not expect a return for 2-3 months. Type all information. Send some sample of your work."

BLACK CONFESSIONS, Lexington Library, Inc., 355 Lexington Ave., New York NY 10017. (212)391-1400. Editor: Nathasha Brooks. Associate Editor: Lisa Cochran. See *Jive*.

BRONZE THRILLS, Lexington Library, Inc., 355 Lexington Ave., New York NY 10017. (212)391-1400. Editor: Nathasha Brooks. Associate Editor: Lisa Cochran. See *Intimacy/Black Romance*. "Stories can be a bit more extraordinary than in the other magazines. They have to be romantic just like the other stories in the other magazines."

INTIMACY/BLACK ROMANCE, 355 Lexington Ave., New York NY 10017. (212)391-1400. Editor: Nathasha Brooks. 100% freelance written. Eager to work with new/unpublished writers. A bimonthly magazine covering romance and love. Circ. 100,000. Pays on publication. Publishes ms an average of 3 months after acceptance. Byline given. Buys first and one-time rights. Submit seasonal/holiday material 6 months in advance. Photocopied submissions OK. Computer printout submissions OK. Reports in 2 months on queries; 3-6 months on mss. Sample copy for 9x12 SAE with 5 first class stamps; free writer's guidelines.

Nonfiction: Historical (Black cultural articles); how-to (relating to romance and love); personal experience (confessions); and feature articles on any aspect of love and romance. "I would not like to see any special features that are overly researched." Buys 100 mss/year. Query with published clips, or send complete ms. Length: 3-5 typed pages. Pays $100.

Photos: Send photos with submission. Reviews contact sheets, negatives, transparencies. All photos are now solicited through the art department.

Columns/Departments: Beauty (Black skin, hair, foot and hand care); Fashion (any articles about current fashions that our audience may be interested in will be considered). Buys 50 mss/year. Query with published clips or send complete ms. Length: 3-5 typed pages. Pays $100.

Fiction: Confession and romance. "I would not like to see anything that stereotypes Black people. Stories which are too sexual in content and lack romance are unacceptable." Buys 300 mss/year. *Bronze Thrills* accepts stories which are a bit more out of the ordinary and are harsher, more uninhibited in concept than those written for *Jive*, *Black Confession*, or *Black Romance*. Send complete ms (12-15 typed pages). Pays $75-100.

Poetry: Free verse and haiku. "I do not want cute, rhyming poetry. I prefer free verse." Buys 40 poems/year. Length: 5-25 lines. Pays $10 per poem.

Tips: "This is a great market for beginning, unpublished writers. I am a tough editor because I want quality material and would like to encourage serious writers to submit to us on a regular basis. I discourage sloppiness, carelessness and people who give lip service to wanting to be a writer and not doing the work involved. I would like to emphasize to the writers that writing is not easy, and not to think that they will get a break here. Contemporary issues and timely subjects should be the basis of any stories submitted to us."

JIVE, Lexington Library, Inc., 355 Lexington Ave., New York NY 10017. (212)391-1400. Editor: Nathasha Brooks. 100% freelance written. Eager to work with new/unpublished writers. A bimonthly magazine covering romance and love. Circ. 100,000. Pays on publication. Publishes ms an average of 3 months after acceptance. Byline given. Buys first and one-time rights. Submit seasonal/holiday material 6 months in advance. Clear, legible photocopied submissions OK. Computer printout submissions OK; prefers letter-quality. Reports in 2 months on queries; 3-6 months on mss. Sample copy for 9x12 SAE with 5 first class stamps; free writer's guidelines.

Nonfiction: Historical (Black cultural articles); how-to (relating to romance and love); personal experience (confessions); and feature articles on any aspect of love and romance. "I would not like to see any special features that are overly researched." Buys 100 mss/year. Query with published clips, or send complete ms. Length: 3-5 typed pages. Pays $100.

Columns/Departments: Beauty (Black skin, hair, foot and hand care); Fashion (any articles about current fashions that our audience may be interested in will be considered); how-to special features that deal with romance. Buys 50 mss/year. Query with published clips or send complete ms. Length: 3-5 typed pages. Pays $100.

Fiction: Confession and romance. "I would not like to see anything that stereotypes Black people. Stories which are too sexual in content and lack romance are unacceptable. However, all stories must contain one or two love scenes that are romantic, not lewd." All love scenes should not show the sex act, but should allude to it through the use of metaphors and tags. Buys 300 mss/year. Send complete ms (12-15 typed pages). Pays $75-100.

Poetry: Free verse and haiku. "I do not want cute, rhyming poetry. I prefer free verse." Buys 40 poems/year. Length: 5-25 lines. Pays $10 per poem.

Tips: "We will continue to buy material that is timely and is based on contemporary themes. However, we are leaning toward more of the romantic themes as opposed to the more graphic themes of the past. We reach an audience that is comprised mostly of women who are college students, high school students, housewives, divorcees, and older women. The audience is mainly Black and ethnic. Our slant is Black and should reinforce Black pride. Our philosophy is to show our experiences in as positive a light as possible without addressing any of the common stereotypes that are associated with Black men, lovemaking prowess, penile size, etc. Stereotypes of any kind are totally unacceptable. The fiction section which accepts romance stories and confession stories about love and romance are most open to freelancers. Also, our special features section is very open. We would like to see stories that are set outside the U.S.—perhaps, they should be set in the Caribbean, Europe, Africa, etc. Women should be shown as being professional, assertive, independent, but should still enjoy being romanced and loved by a man. We'd like to see themes that are reflective of things happening around us in the 80's—crack, AIDS, living together, surrogate mothers, etc. The characters should be young, but not the typical 'country bumpkin girl who was turned out by a big city pimp' type story. Cosmopolitan storylines would be great too. Please writers who are not Black, research your story to be sure that it depicts Black people in a positive manner. Do not make Black characters a caricature of a white character. This is totally unacceptable."

MODERN ROMANCES, Macfadden Women's Group, Inc., 215 Lexington Ave., New York NY 10016. Editor: Colleen Brennan. 100% freelance written. Monthly magazine for blue-collar, family-oriented women, ages 18-65 years old. Circ. 300,000. Pays the last week of the month of issue. Buys all rights. Byline given. Submit seasonal/holiday material 6 months in advance. Reports in 2 months. Writer's guidelines for #10 SASE.

Nonfiction: General interest, baby and child care, how-to (homemaking subjects), humor, inspirational, and personal experience. Submit complete ms. Length: 200-1,500 words. Pay depends on merit. "Confession stories with reader identification and a strong emotional tone. No third-person material." Buys 14 mss/issue. Submit complete ms. Length: 1,500-8,500 words. Pays 5¢/word.

Poetry: Light, romantic poetry. Length: 24 lines maximum. Pay depends on merit.

SECRETS, Macfadden Holdings, Inc., 215 Lexington Ave., New York NY 10016. (212)340-7500. Vice President and Editorial Director: Florence J. Moriarty. Editor: Jean Press Silberg. 100% freelance written. Monthly magazine for blue-collar black family women, ages 18-35. Pays on publication. Publishes ms an average of 4 months after acceptance. Buys all rights. Submit seasonal material *at least* 5 months in advance.

Reports in 3 months.

Nonfiction and Fiction: Wants true stories of special interest to women: family, marriage and emotional conflict themes, "woman-angle articles," or self-help or inspirational fillers. "No pornographic material; no sadistic or abnormal angles. Stories must be written in the first person." Buys about 150 mss/year. Submit complete ms. Length: 300-1,000 words for features; 2,500-7,500 words for full-length story. Occasional 10,000-worders. Greatest need: 4,500-6,000 words. Pays 3¢/word for story mss.

Tips: "Know our market. We are keenly aware of all contemporary lifestyles and activities that involve black women and family—i.e.; current emphasis on child abuse, or renewed interest in the image of marriage, etc."

TRUE CONFESSIONS, Macfadden Holdings, Inc., 215 Lexington Ave., New York NY 10016. (212)340-7500. Editor: Helen Vincent. 90% freelance written. Eager to work with new/unpublished writers. For high-school-educated, blue-collar women, teens through maturity. Monthly magazine. Circ. 250,000. Buys all rights. Byline given on some articles. Pays during the last week of month of issue. Publishes ms an average of 6 months after acceptance. Submit seasonal material 6 months in advance. Reports in 4 months. Submit complete ms. Computer printout submissions acceptable; prefers letter-quality. No simultaneous submissions.

Stories, Articles, and Fillers: Timely, exciting, emotional first-person stories on the problems that face today's young women. The narrators should be sympathetic, and the situations they find themselves in should be intriguing, yet realistic. Every story should have a strong romantic interest and a high moral tone, and every plot should reach an exciting climax. Careful study of a current issue is suggested. Length: 2,000-6,000 words; 5,000-word stories preferred; also book lengths of 8,000-10,000 words. Pays 5¢/word. Also publishes articles and short fillers.

TRUE LOVE, Macfadden Holdings Inc., 215 Lexington Ave., New York NY 10016. (212)340-7500. Editor: Jean Sharbel. 100% freelance written. Monthly magazine. For young, blue-collar women, teens through mid-30's. Confession stories based on true happenings, with reader identification and a strong emotional tone. No third-person material; no simultaneous submissions. Circ. 200,000. Pays the last week of the month of the issue. Buys all rights. Submit seasonal material 6 months in advance. Reports within 2 months.

Nonfiction and Fiction: Confessions, true love stories; problems and solutions; health problems; marital and child-rearing difficulties. Avoid graphic sex. Stories dealing with reality, current problems, everyday events, with emphasis on emotional impact. Buys 14 stories/issue. Submit complete ms. Length: 1,500-8,000 words. Pays 3¢/word. Informational and how-to articles. Byline given. Length: 250-800 words. Pays 5¢/word minimum.

Poetry: Light romantic poetry. Length: 24 lines maximum. Pay depends on merit.

Tips: "The story must appeal to the average blue-collar woman. It must deal with her problems and interests. Characters—especially the narrator—must be sympathetic."

TRUE ROMANCE, Macfadden Women's Group, 215 Lexington Ave., New York NY 10016. (212)340-7500. Editor: Patricia Byrdsong. Monthly magazine. "Our readership ranges from teenagers to senior citizens. The majority are high school educated, married, have young children and also work outside the home. They are concerned with contemporary social issues, yet they are deeply committed to their husbands and children. They have high moral values and place great emphasis on love and romance." Circ. 225,000. Pays 1 month after publication. Buys all rights. Submit seasonal/holiday material at least 5 months in advance. Reports in 3 months.

Nonfiction: How-to and informational. Submit complete ms. Length: 300-1,000 words. Pays 3¢/word, special rates for short features and articles. Confession. "We want *only* true contemporary stories about relationships." Buys 13 stories/issue. Submit complete ms. Length: 2,000-7,500 words. Pays 3¢/word; slightly higher flat rate for short-shorts.

Poetry: Light verse and traditional. Buys 15/year. Length: 4-20 lines. Pays $10 minimum.

Tips: "The freelance writer is needed and welcomed. A timely, well-written story that is told by a sympathetic narrator who sees the central problem through to a satisfying resolution is all that is needed to break into *True Romance*. We are always looking for good love stories."

TRUE STORY, Macfadden Women's Group, 215 Lexington Ave., New York NY 10016. (212)340-7545. Editor: Susan Weiner. 80% freelance written. For young married, blue-collar women, 20-35; high school education; increasingly broad interests; home-oriented, but looking beyond the home for personal fulfillment. Monthly magazine. Circ. 1.7 million. Buys all rights. Byline given "on articles only." Pays on publication. Submit seasonal material 4 months in advance; make notation on envelope that it is seasonal material. Reports in 4 months.

Nonfiction: Pays a flat rate for columns or departments, as announced in the magazine. Query for fact articles.

Photos: Lisa Fischer, art director. Query about all possible photo submissions.

Nonfiction: "First-person stories covering all aspects of women's interests: love, marriage, family life, careers, social problems, etc. The best direction a new writer can be given is to carefully study several issues of the magazine; then submit a fresh, exciting, well-written true story. We have no taboos. It's the handling and believability that make the difference between a rejection and an acceptance." Buys about 125 full-length mss/year. Submit only complete mss for stories. **Length:** 1,500-10,000 words. **Pays** 5¢/word; $150 minimum.

Rural

Readers may be conservative or liberal, but these publications draw them together with a focus on rural lifestyles. Surprisingly, many readers are from urban centers who dream or plan to build a house in the country.

COUNTRY JOURNAL, Box 8200, Harrisburg PA 17105. Editor: Francis W. Finn. Managing Editor: Paula Noonan. 90% freelance written. Works with a small number of new/unpublished writers each year. Monthly magazine featuring country living for people who live in rural areas or who are thinking about moving there. Circ. 320,000. Average issue includes 6-8 feature articles and 10 departments. Pays on acceptance. Rates range from 30-50¢/word. Byline given. Buys first North American serial rights. Submit seasonal material 1 year in advance. Photocopied submissions OK. Computer printout submissions acceptable, prefers letter-quality; "dot-matrix submissions are acceptable if double-spaced." Reports in 1 month. Sample copy $2.50; writer's guidelines for SASE.

Nonfiction: Book excerpts; general interest; opinion (essays); profile (people who are outstanding in terms of country living); how-to; issues affecting rural areas; and photo feature. Query with published clips. **Length:** 2,000-3,500 words. **Pays** 30-50¢/word. Pays the expenses of writers on assignment.

Photos: Lisa Furgatch, photo editor. State availability of photos. Reviews b&w contact sheets, 5x7 and 8x10 b&w glossy prints and 35mm or larger color transparencies. Captions, model release, and identification of subjects required. Buys one-time rights.

Columns/Departments: Listener (brief articles on country topics, how-to's, current events and updates). Buys 5 mss/issue. Query with published clips. **Length:** 200-400 words. **Pays** approximately $75.

Poetry: Free verse, light verse and traditional. Buys 1 poem/issue. **Pays** $50/poem.

Tips: "Be as specific in your query as possible and explain why you are qualified to write the piece (especially for how-to's and controversial subjects). The writer has a better chance of breaking in at our publication with short articles."

FARM & RANCH LIVING, Reiman Publications, 5400 S. 60th St., Greendale WI 53129. (414)423-0100. Editor: Bob Ottum. 80% freelance written. Eager to work with new/unpublished writers. A bimonthly lifestyle magazine aimed at families engaged full time in farming or ranching. "*F&RL* is *not* a 'how-to' magazine—it deals with people rather than products and profits." Circ. 280,000. Pays on acceptance. Publishes ms an average of 1 year after acceptance. Byline given. Offers 25% kill fee. Buys first serial rights and one-time rights. Submit seasonal/holiday material 6 months in advance. Previously published submissions OK. Computer printout submissions acceptable. Reports in 6 weeks. Sample copy $2; writer's guidelines for #10 SAE and 1 first class stamp.

Nonfiction: Interview/profile, photo feature, historical/nostalgic, humor, inspirational and personal experience. No how-to articles or stories about "hobby farmers" (doctors or lawyers with weekend farms), or "hard-times" stories (farmers going broke and selling out). Buys 50 mss/year. Query first with or without published clips; state availability of photos. **Length:** 1,000-3,000 words. **Pays** $150-500 for text-and-photos package. Pays expenses of writers on assignment.

Photos: Scenic. **Pays** $20-40 for b&w photos; $75-200 for 35mm color slides. Buys one-time rights.

Fillers: Clippings, jokes, anecdotes and short humor. Buys 150/year. **Length:** 50-150 words. **Pays** $20 minimum.

Tips: "In spite of poor farm economy, most farm families are proud and optimistic, and they especially enjoy stories and features that are upbeat and positive. *F&RL's* circulation continues to increase, providing an excellent market for freelancers. A freelancer must see *F&RL* to fully appreciate how different it is from other farm publications . . . ordering a sample is strongly advised (not available on newsstands). Query first—we'll give plenty of help and encouragement if story looks promising, and we'll explain why if it doesn't. Photo features (about interesting farm or ranch families); Most Interesting Farmer (or Rancher) I've Ever Met (human interest profile); and Prettiest Place in the Country (tour in text and photos of an attractive farm or ranch) are most open to freelancers. We can make separate arrangements for photography if writer is unable to provide photos."

FARM FAMILY AMERICA, Fieldhagen Publishing, Inc., Suite 121, 333 On Sibley, St. Paul MN 55101. (612)292-1747. Editor: George Ashfield. 75% freelance written. A quarterly magazine published by American Cyanamid and written to the lifestyle, activities and travel interests of American farm families. Circ. 295,000. Pays on acceptance. Publishes ms an average of 2 months after acceptance. Byline given. Offers 25% kill fee. Buys first or second serial (reprint) rights. Submit seasonal/holiday material 6 months in advance. Simultaneous and photocopied submissions OK. Query for electronic submissions. Computer printout submissions OK. Reports in 6 weeks. Writer's guidelines for #10 SAE with 1 first class stamp.
Nonfiction: General interest and travel. Buys 24 mss/year. Query with published clips. Length: 1,000-1,800 words. Pays $300-650. Sometimes pays the expenses of writers on assignment.
Photos: State availability of photos with submission. Reviews 35mm transparencies and prints. Offers $160-700 per photo. Model releases and identification of subjects required. Buys one-time rights.

‡HARROWSMITH MAGAZINE, Camden House Publishing, Ltd., Camden East, Ontario K0K 1J0 Canada. (613)378-6661. Editor: Wayne Grady. 75% freelance written. Published 6 times/year "for those interested in country life, nonchemical gardening, energy, self-sufficiency, folk arts, small-stock husbandry, owner-builder architecture and alternative styles of life." Circ. 154,000. Pays on acceptance. Publishes ms an average of 4 months after acceptance. Byline given. Buys first North American serial rights. Submit seasonal/holiday material 6 months in advance. Computer printout submissions acceptable; prefers letter-quality. Reports in 6 weeks. Sample copy $5; free writer's guidelines.
Nonfiction: Exposé, how-to, general interest, humor, interview, photo feature and profile. "We are always in need of quality gardening articles geared to northern conditions. No articles whose style feigns 'folksiness.' No how-to articles written by people who are not totally familiar with their subject. We feel that in this field simple research does not compensate for lack of long-time personal experience." Buys 10 mss/issue. Query. Length: 500-4,000 words. Pays $75-750 but will consider higher rates for major stories.
Photos: State availability of photos with query. Pays $50-250 for 8x10 glossy prints and 35mm or larger color transparencies. Captions required. Buys one-time rights. "We regularly run photo essays for which we pay $250-750."
Tips: "We have standards of excellence as high as any publication in the country. However, we are by no means a closed market. Much of our material comes from unknown writers. We welcome and give thorough consideration to all freelance submissions. Our magazine is read by Canadians who live in rural areas or who hope to make the urban to rural transition. They want to know as much about the realities of country life as the dreams. They expect quality writing, not folksy cliches."

‡HARROWSMITH, The Magazine of Country Life, The Creamery, Charlotte VT 05445. (802)425-3961. Editor: Thomas H. Rawls. Bimonthly magazine covering country living, gardening, shelter, food, and environmental issues. "*Harrowsmith* readers are generally college educated, country dwellers, looking for good information." Circ. 225,000. Pays 30-45 days after acceptance. Byline given. Offers 25% kill fee. Buys first North American serial rights. Reports in 6 weeks. Sample copy $4; writer's guidelines for #10 SAE with 1 first class stamp.
Nonfiction: Book excerpts, essays, expose (environmental issues), how-to (gardening/building), humor, interview/profile, opinion. "No recipes." Buys 36 mss/year. Query with published clips. Length: 500-5,000 words. Pays $500-1,500. Sometimes pays expenses of writers on assignment.
Photos: State availability of photos with submission. Reviews 35mm transparencies. Offers $100-325/photo. Model releases and identification of subjects required. Buys one-time rights.
Columns/Departments: Sourcebank (ideas, tips, techniques relating to gardening, the environment, food, health) 50-400 words; Gazette (brief news items). Buys 30 mss/year. Query with published clips. Length: 40-400 words. Pays $25-150.
Tips: "While main feature stories are open to freelancers, a good way for us to get to know the writer is through our Screed (essays), Sourcebank (tips and ideas) and Gazette (brief news items) departments. Articles should contain examples, quotations and anecdotes. They should be fairly detailed and factual."

THE MOTHER EARTH NEWS, Box 70, Hendersonville NC 28791. (704)693-0211. Editor: Bruce Woods. 40% freelance written. Bimonthly magazine. Emphasizes "country living and country skills, for both long-time and would-be ruralites." Circ. 700,000. Pays on acceptance. Byline given. Submit seasonal/holiday material 5 months in advance. Computer printout submissions acceptable; prefer letter-quality. No handwritten mss. Reports within 3 months. Publishes ms an average of 1 year after acceptance. Sample copy $3; writer's guidelines for SASE with 2 first class stamps.
Nonfiction: Terry Krautwurst, submissions editor. How-to, home business, alternative energy systems, home building, home retrofit and home maintenance, energy-efficient structures, seasonal cooking, gardening and crafts. Buys 300-350 mss/year. Query or send complete ms. "A short, to-the-point paragraph is often enough. If it's a subject we don't need at all, we can answer immediately. If it tickles our imagination, we'll ask to take a look at the whole piece. No phone queries, please." Length: 300-3,000 words.
Photos: Purchased with accompanying ms. Send prints or transparencies. Uses 8x10 b&w glossies; any size

color transparencies. Include type of film, speed and lighting used. Total purchase price for ms includes payment for photos. Captions and credits required.

Columns/Departments: "Contributions to Mother's Down-Home Country Lore and Barters and Bootstraps are paid by subscription."

Fillers: Short how-to's on any subject normally covered by the magazine. Query. Length: 150-300 words. Pays $7.50-25.

Tips: "Probably the best way to break in is to study our magazine, digest our writer's guidelines, and send us a concise article illustrated with color transparencies that we can't resist. When folks query and we give a go-ahead on speculation, we often offer some suggestions. Failure to follow those suggestions can lose the sale for the author. We want articles that tell what real people are doing to take charge of their own lives. Articles should be well-documented and tightly written treatments of topics we haven't already covered. The critical thing is length, and our payment is by space, not word count." No phone queries.

Science

These publications are published for laymen interested in technical and scientific developments and discoveries, applied science and technical or scientific hobbies. Publications of interest to the personal computer owner/user are listed in the Personal Computer section. Journals for scientists, engineers, repairmen, etc., are listed in Trade in various sections.

CQ: THE RADIO AMATEUR'S JOURNAL, 76 N. Broadway, Hicksville NY 11801. (516)681-2922. Editor: Alan Dorhoffer. 50% freelance written. For the amateur ham radio community. Monthly journal. Circ. 100,000. Pays on publication. Buys first rights. Phone queries OK. Submit seasonal/holiday material 3 months in advance. Query for electronic submissions. Computer printout submissions acceptable. Reports in 3 weeks. Publishes ms an average of 1 year after acceptance.

Nonfiction: "We are interested in articles that address all technical levels of amateur radio. Included would be basic material for newcomers and intermediate and advanced material for oldtimers. Articles may be of a theoretical, practical or anecdotal nature. They can be general interest pieces for all amateurs or they can focus in on specific topics. We would like historical articles, material on new developments, articles on projects you can do in a weekend, and pieces on long-range projects taking a month or so to complete." Length: 6-10 typewritten pages. Pays $40/published page.

THE ELECTRON, CIE Publishing, 4781 E. 355th St., Willoughby OH 44094. (216)946-9065. Managing Editor: Janice Weaver. 80% freelance written. Prefers to work with published/established writers. Bimonthly tabloid on electronics and high technology. Circ. 50,000. Pays on publication. Publishes ms an average of 2 months after acceptance. Byline given. Buys all rights unless negotiated otherwise. Simultaneous queries, and photocopied and previously published submissions OK. Computer printout submissions acceptable; prefers letter-quality. Reports in 1 month or earlier.

Nonfiction: Technical (tutorial and how-to), technology news and feature, photo feature, career/educational. All submissions must be electronics/technology-related. Query with published clips or send complete ms. Pays $35-1,000. Sometimes pays expenses of writers on assignment.

Photos: State availability of photos. Reviews 8x10 and 5x7 b&w prints. Captions and identification of subjects required.

Tips: "We would like to receive educational electronics/technical articles. They must be written in a manner understandable to the beginning—intermediate electronics student. We are seeking news/feature-type articles which cover timely developments in high-technology. These submissions should be suitable for the front page of our newspaper."

ELECTRONICS TODAY, 1300 Don Mills Rd., Don Mills, Toronto, Ontario M3B 3M8 Canada. (416)445-5600. Editor: Bill Markwick. 40-50% freelance written. Eager to work with new/unpublished writers each year. Monthly magazine. Emphasizes audio, science, technology, electronics and personal computing for a wide-ranging readership, both professionals and hobbyists. Circ. 20,000. Pays on publication. Publishes ms an average of 2 months after acceptance. Byline given. Buys all rights. Phone queries OK. Submit seasonal/holiday material 4 months in advance. Photocopied submissions OK. Query for electronic submissions. Computer printout submissions acceptable. Reports in 4 weeks. Free writer's guidelines.

Nonfiction: How-to (technical articles in electronics field); humor (if relevant to electronics); new product (if using new electronic techniques); and technical (on new developments, research, etc.). Buys 10 unsolicited mss/year. Query. Length: 600-3,500 words. Pays $75-100/1,000 words.

Photos: "Ideally we like to publish two photos or diagrams per 1,000 words of copy." State availability of photo material with query. Additional payment for photos accepted with accompanying manuscript. Captions required. Buys all rights.

Tips: "Less computer coverage will result in a shift to general science and hi-tech."

MODERN ELECTRONICS, For electronics and computer enthusiasts, Modern Electronics Publishing, Inc., 76 N. Broadway, Hicksville NY 11801. (516)681-2922. 90% freelance written. Monthly magazine covering consumer electronics, personal computers, electronic circuitry, construction projects, and technology for readers with a technical affinity. Circ. 75,000. Pays on acceptance. Publishes ms an average of 3 months after acceptance. Byline given. Offers 25% kill fee. Buys first North American serial rights. Submit seasonal/holiday material minimum 4 months in advance. Computer printout submissions acceptable; prefers near letter-quality to coarse dot-matrix. Reports in 1 week on queries; 3 weeks on mss. Sample copy $2; writer's guidelines for #10 SAE and 1 first class stamp.

Nonfiction: General interest (new technology, product buying guides); how-to (construction projects, applications); new product (reviews); opinion (experiences with electronic and computer products); technical (features and tutorials: circuits, applications); includes stereo, video, communications and computer equipment. "Articles must be technically accurate. Writing should be 'loose,' not textbookish." No long computer programs. Buys 75 mss/year. Query. Length: 500-4,000 words. Pays $80-150/published page. Sometimes pays expenses of writers on assignment.

Photos: Send photos with query or ms. Reviews color transparencies and 5x7 b&w prints. Captions, model releases, and identification of subjects required. Buys variable rights depending on mss.

Tips: "The writer must have technical or applications acumen and well-researched material. Articles should reflect the latest products and technology. Sharp, interesting photos are helpful, as are rough, clean illustrations for re-drawing. Cover 'hot' subjects (avoid old technology). Areas most open to freelancers include feature articles, technical tutorials, and projects to build. Some writers exhibit problems with longer pieces due to limited technical knowledge and/or poor organization. We can accept more short pieces."

OMNI, 1965 Broadway, New York NY 10023-5965. Editor: Patrice Adcroft. 90% freelance written. Prefers to work with published/established writers; works with a small number of new/unpublished writers each year. Monthly magazine of the future covering science fact, fiction, and fantasy for readers of all ages, backgrounds and interests. Circ. 934,000. Average issue includes 2-3 nonfiction feature articles and 1-2 fiction articles; also numerous columns and 2 pictorials. Pays on acceptance. Publishes ms an average of 5 months after acceptance. Offers 25% kill fee. Buys exclusive worldwide and exclusive first English rights and rights for *Omni* anthologies. Submit seasonal material 4-6 months in advance. Photocopied submissions OK. Computer printout submissions acceptable; prefers letter-quality. Reports in 6 weeks. Free writer's guidelines with SASE (request fiction or nonfiction).

Nonfiction: "Articles with a futuristic angle, offering readers information on housing, energy, transportation, medicine and communications. People want to know, want to understand what scientists are doing and how scientific research is affecting their lives and their future. *Omni* publishes articles about science in language that people can understand. We seek very knowledgeable science writers who are ready to work with scientists and futurists to produce articles that can inform, interest and entertain our readers with the opportunity to participate in many ground breaking studies." Send query/proposal. Length: 2,500-3,500 words. Pays $2,500-3,500.

Photos: Frank DeVino, graphic director. State availability of photos. Reviews 35mm slides and 4x5 transparencies. Pays the expenses of writers on assignment.

Columns/Departments: Explorations (unusual travel or locations on Earth); Mind (by and about psychiatrists and psychologists); Earth (environment); Space (technology); Arts (theatre, music, film, technology); Interview (of prominent person); Continuum (newsbreaks); Star Tech (new products); Antimatter and UFO Update (unusual newsbreaks, paranormal); Stars (astronomy); First/Last Word (editorial/humor); Artificial Intelligence (computers); The Body (medical). Query with clips of previously published work. Length: 1,500 words maximum. Pays $900; $150 for Continuum and Antimatter items.

Fiction: Contact Ellen Datlow. Fantasy and science fiction. Buys 2 mss/issue. Send complete ms. Length: 10,000 words maximum. Pays $1,250-2,000.

Tips: "To get an idea of the kinds of fiction we publish, check recent back issues of the magazine."

POPULAR MECHANICS, 224 W. 57th St., New York NY 10019. (212)262-4815. Editor: Joe Oldham. Managing Editor: Bill Hartford. 50% freelance written. Monthly magazine. Circ. 1.6 million. Computer printout submissions acceptable; must be letter-quality. Buys all rights. Byline given. Pays "promptly." Publishes ms an average of 6 months after acceptance.

Nonfiction: Principal subjects are cars, woodworking, metalworking, home improvement, home maintenance, new technology, sports, electronics, boats, science, photography, audio and video. Also looking for adventure articles with a technology emphasis. No fiction. Looking for reporting on new and unusual developments. The writer should be specific about what makes it new, different, better, cheaper, etc. Query. Length:

300-2,000 words. Pays $300-1,500.

Photos: Dramatic photos are most important, and they should show people and things in action. Top-notch photos are a must for Home and Shop Section articles. Can also use remodeling of homes, rooms and outdoor structures.

POPULAR SCIENCE, 380 Madison Ave., New York NY 10017. Editor-in-Chief: C.P. Gilmore. 35% freelance written. Prefers to work with published/established writers. Monthly magazine. For the well-educated adult, interested in science, technology, new products. Circ. 1.8 million. Pays on acceptance. Publishes ms an average of 4 months after acceptance. Byline given. Buys all rights. Pays negotiable kill fee. Free guidelines for writers. Any electronic submission OK. Computer printout submissions acceptable; prefers letter-quality. Submit seasonal material 4 months in advance. Reports in 3 weeks. Query. Writer's guidelines for SAE and 1 first class postage stamp.

Nonfiction: "*Popular Science* is devoted to exploring (and explaining) to a nontechnical but knowledgeable readership the technical world around us. We cover the physical sciences, engineering and technology, and above all, products. We are largely a 'thing'-oriented publication: things that fly or travel down a turnpike, or go on or under the sea, or cut wood, or reproduce music, or build buildings, or make pictures, or mow lawns. We are especially focused on the new, the ingenious and the useful. We are consumer-oriented and are interested in any product that adds to the enjoyment of the home, yard, car, boat, workshop, outdoor recreation. Some of our 'articles' are only a picture and caption long. Some are a page long. Some occupy 4 or more pages. Contributors should be as alert to the possibility of selling us pictures and short features as they are to major articles. Freelancers should study the magazine to see what we want and avoid irrelevant submissions. No biology or life sciences." Buys several hundred mss/year. Pays $200/published page minimum. Uses mostly color and some b&w photos. Pays expenses of writers on assignment.

Tips: "Probably the easiest way to break in here is by covering a news story in science and technology that we haven't heard about yet. We need people to be acting as scouts for us out there and we are willing to give the most leeway on these performances. We are interested in good, sharply focused ideas in all areas we cover. We prefer a vivid, journalistic style of writing, with the writer taking the reader along with him, showing the reader what he saw, through words. Please query first."

RADIO-ELECTRONICS, 500-B Bi-County Blvd., Farmingdale NY 11735. (516)293-3000. Editorial Director: Art Kleiman. For electronics professionals and hobbyists. Monthly magazine. Circ. 242,000. Buys all rights. Byline given. Pays on acceptance. Submit seasonal/holiday material 8 months in advance. Reports in 3 weeks. Send for "Guide to Writing."

Nonfiction: Interesting technical stories on all aspects of electronics, including video, radio, computers, communications, and stereo written from viewpoint of the electronics professional, serious experimenter, or layman with technical interests. Construction (how-to-build-it) articles used heavily. Unique projects bring top dollars. Cost of project limited only by what item will do. Emphasis on "how it works, and why." Much of material illustrated with schematic diagrams and pictures provided by author. Also high interest in how-to articles. Length: 1,000-5,000 words. Pays about $50-500.

Photos: State availability of photos. Offers no additional payment for b&w prints or 35mm color transparencies. Model releases required.

Columns/Departments: Pays $50-200/column.

Fillers: Pays $15-35.

Tips: "The simplest way to come in would be with a short article on some specific construction project. Queries aren't necessary; just send the article, 5 or 6 typewritten pages."

TECHNOLOGY REVIEW, Alumni Association of the Massachusetts Institute of Technology, Room 10-140, Massachusetts Institute of Technology, Cambridge MA 02139. Editor-in-Chief: John I. Mattill. 20% freelance written. Emphasizes technology and its implications for scientists, engineers, managers and social scientists. Magazine published 8 times/year. Circ. 75,000. Pays on publication. Publishes ms an average of 3-6 months after acceptance. Buys first rights. Phone queries OK. Submit seasonal/holiday material 6 months in advance of issue date. Simultaneous and photocopied submissions OK. Computer printout submissions acceptable. Reports in 6 weeks. Sample copy $2.50.

Nonfiction: General interest, interview, photo feature and technical. Buys 5-10 mss/year. Query. Length: 1,000-6,000 words. Pays $50-750. Sometimes pays the expenses of writers on assignment.

Columns/Departments: Book Reviews; Trend of Affairs; Technology and Economics; and Prospects (guest column). Also special reports on other appropriate subjects. Query. Length: 750-4,000 words. Pays $50-750.

UFO REVIEW, Global Communications, Box 1994, JAF Station, New York NY 10116. (212)685-4080. Editor: Timothy Beckley. Emphasizes UFOs and space science. 50% freelance written. Published 4 times/year. Tabloid. Circ. 50,000. Pays on publication. Publishes ms an average of 4 months after acceptance. Phone queries OK. Photocopied submissions OK. Reports in 3 weeks. Sample copy $1.25.

Nonfiction: Expose (on government secrecy about UFOs). "We also want articles detailing on-the-spot field

investigations of UFO landings, contact with UFOs, and UFO abductions. No lights-in-the-sky stories." Buys 1-2 mss/issue. Query. Length: 1,200-2,000 words. Pays $25-75.
Photos: Send photos with ms. Pays $5-10 for 8x10 b&w prints. Captions required.
Fillers: Clippings. Pays $2-5.
Tips: "Read the tabloid first. We are aimed at UFO fans who have knowledge of the field. Too many submissions are made about old cases everyone knows about. We don't accept rehash. We get a lot of material unrelated to our subject."

Science Fiction, Fantasy and Horror

Additional science fiction, fantasy and horror markets are in the Literary and "Little" section. *Novel and Short Story Writer's Market* (formerly *Fiction Writer's Market*), available from Writer's Digest Books in March 1989, also contains Science Fiction, Fantasy, and Horror markets.

‡ABORIGINAL SCIENCE FICTION, Absolute Entertainment Inc., Box 2449, Woburn MA 01888. Editor: Charles C. Ryan. 99% freelance written. A bimonthly science fiction magazine. "We publish short, lively and entertaining science fiction short stories and peoms, accompanied by full-color art." Circ. 16,000. Pays on publication. Publishes ms an average of 6 months after acceptance. Byline given. Buys first North American seial rights, non-exclusive options on other rights. Photocopied submissions OK. Query for electronic submission. Computer printout submissions OK; prefers letter-quality. Sample copy $3.50; writer's guidelnes for #10 SAE and 1 first class stamp.
Fiction: Adventure, historial, humorous, novel excerpts, science fiction. "We do not use fantasy, horror, sword and sorcery or 'Twilight Zone' type stories." Buys 36 mss/year. Send complete ms. Length: 2,000-4,500 words. Pays $250.
Poetry: Science and science fiction. Buys 8-12 poems/year.
Tips: "Read science fiction novels and other science fiction magazines. Do not rely on science fiction movies or TV. We are open to new fiction writers who are making a sincere effort."

AMAZING™ Stories, TSR, Inc., Box 110, Lake Geneva WI 53147-0110. Editor: Patrick L. Price. 90% freelance written. Eager to work with a limited number of new/unpublished writers. Bimonthly magazine of science fiction and fantasy short stories. "Audience does not need to be scientifically literate, but the authors must be, where required. *AMAZING* is devoted to the best science fiction and fantasy by new and established writers. There is no formula. We require the writers using scientific concepts be scientifically convincing, and that every story contain believable and interesting characters and some overall point." Circ. 13,000. Pays on acceptance. Publishes ms an average of 18 months after acceptance. Byline given. Buys first worldwide serial rights in the English language only; "single, non-exclusive re-use option (with additional pay)." Photocopied submissions OK. Computer printout submissions acceptable; no dot-matrix. Reports in 10 weeks. Sample copy for $2.50; writer's guidelines for #10 SASE.
Nonfiction: Historical (about science fiction history and figures); interview/profile and science articles of interest to science fiction audiences; reviews and essays about major science fiction movies written by big names. No "pop pseudo-science trends: The Unified Field Theory Discovered; How I Spoke to the Flying Saucer People; Interpretations of Past Visits by Sentient Beings, as Read in Glacial Scratches on Granite, etc." Buys 4-8 mss/year. Query with or without published clips. Length: 1,000-5,000 words. Pays 10-12¢/word 3,000-5,000 words. Sometimes pays the expenses of writers on assignment.
Fiction: Contemporary and ethnic fantasy; science fiction. "We are looking for hard or speculative science fiction, space fantasy/opera, and fantasy. We don't want horror fiction or fairy tales. No 'true' experiences, media-derived fiction featuring *Star Wars* (etc.) characters, stories based on UFO reports or standard occultism." Buys 50-60 mss/year. Send complete ms. Length: 500-25,000 words. "Anything longer, ask." Pays 8¢/word to 6,000 words; 5¢/word for 12,000 or more words.
Poetry: All types are OK. No prose arranged in columns. Buys 10 poems/year. Submit maximum 3 poems. Length: 30 lines maximum; ideal length, 20 lines or less. Pays $1/line.
Tips: "We are particularly interested in shorter fiction: stories of 7,000 or fewer words; we are currently overstocked on novelettes and novellas. We look for larger pieces by established writers, because their names help sell our product. Don't try to especially tailor one for our 'slant.' We want original concepts, good writing,

and well-developed characters. Avoid certain obvious clichés: UFO landings in rural areas, video games which become real (or vice-versa), stories based on contemporary newspaper headlines. '*Hard*' science fiction, that is, science fiction which is based on a plausible extrapolation from real science, is increasingly rare and very much in demand. We are moving away from heroic, pseudo-medieval European fantasies, and more toward ethnic (Japanese, Arabian, Central American, etc.) and contemporary fantasies. All sorts of hard, speculative, or militaristic science fiction desired.''

ANALOG SCIENCE FICTION/SCIENCE FACT, 380 Lexington Ave., New York NY 10017. Editor: Dr. Stanley Schmidt. 100% freelance written. Eager to work with new/unpublished writers. For general future-minded audience. Monthly. Buys first North American serial rights and nonexclusive foreign serial rights. Pays on acceptance. Publishes ms an average of 6-10 months after acceptance. Byline given. Computer printout submissions (with dark ink) acceptable; prefers letter-quality or near-letter-quality. Reports in 1 month. Sample copy $2.50 (no SASE needed); free writer's guidelines for SAE and 1 first class stamp.

Nonfiction: Illustrated technical articles dealing with subjects of not only current but future interest, i.e., with topics at the present frontiers of research whose likely future developments have implications of wide interest. Buys about 12 mss/year. Query. Length: 5,000 words. Pays 6¢/word.

Fiction: "Basically, we publish science fiction stories. That is, stories in which some aspect of future science or technology is so integral to the plot that, if that aspect were removed, the story would collapse. The science can be physical, sociological or psychological. The technology can be anything from electronic engineering to biogenetic engineering. But the stories must be strong and realistic, with believable people doing believable things—no matter how fantastic the background might be." Buys 60-100 unsolicited mss/year. Send complete ms on short fiction; query about serials. Length: 2,000-80,000 words. Pays 4¢/word for novels; 5-6¢/word for novelettes; 6-8¢/word for shorts under 7,500 words; $450-550 for intermediate lengths.

Tips: "In query give clear indication of central ideas and themes and general nature of story line—and what is distinctive or unusual about it. We have no hard-and-fast editorial guidelines, because science fiction is such a broad field that I don't want to inhibit a new writer's thinking by imposing 'Thou Shalt Not's.' Besides, a really good story can make an editor swallow his preconceived taboos. I want the best work I can get, regardless of who wrote it—and I need new writers. So I work closely with new writers who show definite promise, but of course it's impossible to do this with *every* new writer. No occult or fantasy."

ISAAC ASIMOV'S SCIENCE FICTION MAGAZINE, Davis Publications, Inc., 380 Lexington Ave., New York NY 10017. (212)557-9100. Editor-in-Chief: Gardner Dozois. 98% freelance written. Works with a small number of new/unpublished writers each year. Emphasizes science fiction. 13 times a year magazine. Circ. 125,000. Pays on acceptance. Buys first North American serial rights, nonexclusive foreign serial rights and occasionally reprint rights. "Clear and dark" photocopied submissions OK but no simultaneous submissions. Legible computer printout submissions acceptable; prefers letter-quality. "Don't justify right margins." Reports in 6 weeks. Sample copy for 6½x9½ SAE and $2; writer's guidelines for #10 SASE.

Nonfiction: Science. Query first.

Fiction: Science fiction primarily. Some fantasy and poetry. "It's best to read a great deal of material in the genre to avoid the use of some *very* old ideas." Buys 10 mss/issue. Submit complete ms. Length: 100-20,000 words. Pays 5-8¢/word except for novel serializations at 4¢/word.

Tips: Query letters not wanted, except for nonfiction.

BEYOND . . ., Science Fiction and Fantasy, Other World Books, Box 1124, Fair Lawn NJ 07410-1124. (201)791-6721. Editor: Shirley Winston. Managing Editor: Roberta Rogow. 80% freelance written. Eager to work with new/unpublished writers. A science fiction and fantasy magazine published 4 times a year. "Our audience is mostly science fiction fans." Circ. 300. Pays on publication. Publishes ms an average of 6-9 months after acceptance. Byline given. Buys first North American serial rights. Submit seasonal/holiday material 6 months in advance. Photocopied submissions OK. Query for electronic submissions. Computer printout submissions acceptable; prefers letter-quality. Reports in 3 weeks. Sample copy $4.50; writer's guidelines for #10 SASE.

Nonfiction: Essays and humor. Buys 3 mss/year. Send complete ms. Length: 500-1,500 words. Pays $1.25-3.75 and 1 copy.

Columns/Departments: Reviews (of books and periodicals in science fiction and fantasy area), 500-1,500 words. Buys 3 mss/year. Send complete ms. Length: 500-1,500 words. Pays $1.25-3.75.

Fiction: Fantasy and science fiction only. "We enjoy using stories with a humorous aspect. No horror stories, excessive violence or explicit sex; nothing degrading to women or showing prejudice based on race, religion, or planet of origin. No predictions of universal destruction; we prefer an outlook on the future in which the human race survives and progresses." Buys 20 mss/year. Send complete ms. Length: 500-8,000 words; prefers 4,000-5,000 words. Pays $1.25-20 and 1 copy.

Poetry: Free verse, haiku, light verse and traditional. "Poetry should be comprehensible by an educated reader literate in English, take its subject matter from science fiction or fantasy, need not rhyme but should fall musically on the ear." No poetry unrelated to science fiction or fantasy. Buys 18 poems/year. Submit maximum 3 poems. Length: 4-65 words. Pays 2¢/line and 1 copy.

Tips: Fiction and poetry are most open to freelancers.

HAUNTS, Nightshade Publications, Box 3342, Providence RI 02906. (401)781-9438. Editor: Joseph K. Cherkes. 98% freelance written. Prefers to work with published/established writers; works with small number of new/unpublished writers each year. "We are a literary quarterly geared to those fans of the 'pulp' magazines of the 30's, 40's and 50's, with tales of horror, the supernatural, and the bizzare. We are trying to reach those in the 18-35 age group." Circ. 1,000. Pays on publication. Publishes ms an average of 8 months after acceptance. Byline given. Buys first North American serial rights. Photocopied submissions OK. Computer printout submissions acceptable; prefers letter-quality. Reports in 3 weeks on queries; 2 months on mss. Sample copy $3.25; writer's guidelines for #10 SASE.

Fiction: Fantasy, horror and suspense. "No fiction involving blow-by-blow dismemberment, explicit sexual scenes, or pure adventure." Buys 36 fiction mss/year. Query. Length: 1,500-8,000 words. Pays $5-33.

Poetry: Free verse, light verse and traditional. Buys 4 poems/year. Submit maximum 3 poems. Offers contributor's copies.

Tips: "Market open from June 1 to December 1 inclusive. How the writer handles revisions often is a key to acceptance."

THE HORROR SHOW, Phantasm Press, 14848 Misty Springs Ln., Oak Run CA 96069-9801. (916)472-3540. Editor: David B. Silva. 95% freelance written. Eager to work with new/unpublished writers. Quarterly horror magazine. Circ. 4,000. Publishes ms an average of 3 months after acceptance. Buys first serial rights. Computer printout submissions OK; prefers letter-quality. Reports in 3 weeks. Sample copy for $4 and 5 first class stamps; writer's guidelines for SAE and 1 first class stamp.

Columns/Departments: Nightmares (news about the horror field).

Fiction: Contemporary horror. "Stories should *not* splash over into science fiction or fantasy (sword and sorcery). We are specifically looking for material with well-developed characters. Do not over-indulge in sex or violence." Send complete ms. Length: 4,000 words maximum. Pays ½-1½¢/word plus contributor's copy.

Tips: "We enjoy the honor of publishing first stories and new writers, but we always expect a writer's best effort. Read the magazine. Come up with a unique premise, polish every word, then send it our way. A frequent mistake made by writers in completing a story for us is that the story is not directed at the reader. We look for informative articles directly related to the horror genre. In 1989, we will continue to slant each issue toward a specific author or artist in the field of horror."

PANDORA, #12, 609 E. 11 Mile, Royal Oaks MI 48067. Editors: Meg MacDonald. 95% freelance written. Works with a small number of new/unpublished writers each year; eager to work with new/unpublished writers. Magazine published 4-6 times/year covering science fiction and fantasy. Circ. 500. Pays on publication. Publishes ms an average of 6-12 months after acceptance. Byline given. Offers $10 kill fee. Buys first North American serial rights and second serial (reprint) rights; one-time rights on some poems. Photocopied submissions OK. Readable computer printout submissions on white 8½x11 paper acceptable. Reports in 6 weeks. Sample copy $3.50; writer's guidelines for #10 SAE with 1 first class stamp.

Columns/Departments: "We buy short reviews of science fiction and fantasy books that a reader feels truly examplify fine writing and will be of interest and use to other writers. Small press titles as well as major press titles are welcome." Buys 5-7 mss/year. Query or send complete ms. Length: under 500 words. Pays $5 and up.

Fiction: Fantasy, science fiction. "No pun stories. Nothing x-rated (both vulgar language or subject matter). No inaccurate science." Buys 15 mss/year. Send complete ms. Length: 1,000-4,000 words. Pays 1-4¢/word.

Poetry: Ruth Berman, poetry editor. 2809 Drew Ave. S., Minneapolis MN 55417. Buys 9-12 poems/year. Payment starts ar $2.50. Length: open.

Tips: "Send us stories about characters our readers con sympathize with and care about. Then give that character a convincing, relevant problem that s/he must overcome. Stories about people and their difficulties, victories, and losses are of more interest to us than stories about furturistic gadgets. What impact does the gadget have on society? *That's* what we want to know. Stories must have a point--not just a pun. Happy endings aren't necessary, but we urge authors to leave the reader with a sense of that no matter the outcome, something has been accomplished between the first and last pages. Reading our magazine is the best way to determine our needs, and we strongly recommend all contributors read at least one sample. Better yet, subscribe for a while, then start submitting. We like to see whole stories, the shorter the better, and we will make attempts to respond personally with a critique. We work closely with a number of authors and are eager to work with more."

ROD SERLING'S TWILIGHT ZONE MAGAZINE, (formerly *Twilight Zone*) Montcalm Publishing Co., 401 Park Ave., 3rd Floor, New York NY 10016. (212)986-9600. Editor-in-chief: Tappan King. Managing Editor: Peter Emshwiller. Assistant Editor: Robert Simpson. 80% freelance written. Bimonthly magazine of fantasy fiction with stories by authors as diverse as Stephen King and Joyce Carol Oates. Circ. 100,000. Pays half on acceptance, half on publication. Publishes ms an average of 9 months after acceptance. Byline given. Buys first North American serial rights, first serial rights and second serial (reprint) rights. Submit seasonal/holiday material 9 months in advance. Simultaneous and photocopied submissions OK. Computer printout submissions acceptable; prefers letter-quality. Reports in 3-6 months. Sample copy $3; writer's guidelines for #10 SASE.

Fiction: Fantasy, understated horror and some surrealism. No sword and sorcery; hardware-oriented science fiction; vampire, werewolf or deals-with-the-devil stories. Buys 35 mss/year. Send complete ms. Length: 7,500 words maximum. Pays 5-8¢/word; $150 minimum. Sometimes pays expenses of writers on assignment.

SPACE AND TIME, 138 W. 70th St., New York NY 10023. Editor: Gordon Linzner. Biannual magazine covering fantasy fiction, with a broad definition of fantasy that encompasses science fiction, horror, swords and sorcery, etc. Circ. 500. 99% freelance written. Eager to work with new/unpublished writers. Pays on acceptance. Publishes ms an average of 2 years after acceptance. Byline given. Buys first North American serial rights. Photocopied submissions OK. Computer printout submissions acceptable; prefers letter-quality. Reports in 2 months. Sample copy $4; guidelines for #10 SASE.

Fiction: Fantasy, horror and science fiction. "Submit skillful writing and original ideas. We lean toward strong plot and character. No fiction based on TV shows or movies (*Star Trek*, *Star Wars*, etc.) or popular established literary characters (e.g., Conan) except as satire or other special case. No UFO, gods from space, or material of that ilk, unless you've got a drastically new slant." Buys 18 unsolicited mss/year. Length: 12,000 words maximum. Pays $\frac{1}{2}$¢/word plus contributor's copies.

Poetry: Buys 12 poems/year. Submit maximum 5 poems. Length: open. Pays in contributor's copies.

Tips: "All areas are open to freelancers, but we would particularly like to see more hard science fiction, and fantasies set in 'real' historical times. No nonfiction or no fiction that cannot be considered science fiction or fantasy. We particularly enjoy uncovering new talent and offbeat stories for which there are few (if any) markets otherwise; seeing *S&T* authors go on to better paying, wider circulating markets. It seems to us that we're getting an unnaturally high percentage of horror, so our tendency will be to lean toward other science fiction/fantasy genres—and a possible format change may favor shorter works. We regret that we can't publish more material more often. A lot of good, interesting stories have to be passed over, and there are few other markets for genre fiction."

STARLOG MAGAZINE, The Science Fiction Universe, Starlog Group, 8th Floor, 475 Park Ave. South, New York NY 10016. (212)689-2830. Editor: David McDonnell. 85% freelance written. Works with a number of new/unpublished writers each year and is very eager to work with new/unpublished writers. Monthly magazine covering "the science fiction-fantasy-adventure genre: its films, TV, books, art and personalities. We explore the fields of science fiction and fantasy with occasional forays into adventure (i.e., the James Bond and Indiana Jones films). We concentrate on the personalities and behind-the-scenes angles of science fiction/fantasy films with comprehensive interviews with actors, directors, screenwriters, producers, special effects technicians and others. Be aware that 'sc-fi' is mostly considered a derogatory terms by our readers and by us." Pays on publication. Publishes ms an average of 3 months after acceptance. Byline given. All contributors are also credited in masthead. Offers kill fee "only to mss *written* or interviews *done*." Buys first North American serial rights to material with option to reprint (for an additional fee) certain articles in twice annual *Starlog Yearbook*. Buys second serial (reprint) rights to certain other material. Submit seasonal/holiday material 6 months in advance. Simultaneous queries (if we are aware they are being made) and photocopied submissions OK. Computer printout submissions acceptable (separate sheets first); prefers letter-quality. Reports in 4 weeks on queries; 6 weeks on mss. "We provide an assignment sheet to *all* writers with deadline and other info, thus authorizing a queried piece." Sample copy and writer's guidelines for $3.50 and 8½x11 SAE with 3 first class stamps. Writer's guidelines for #10 SASE.

Nonfiction: Interview/profile (actors, directors, screenwriters who've made past or current science fiction films, and science fiction novelists); photo features; special effects how-tos (on filmmaking only); retrospectives of famous SF films and TV series; occasional pieces on science fiction fandom, conventions, etc. "We also sometimes cover animation (especially Disney and WB)." No personal opinion think pieces/essays on *Star Wars*, *Star Trek*. No first person. "We prefer article format as opposed to question-and-answer interviews." Buys 150 or more mss/year. Query first with published clips. "We prefer queries by mail to phone queries. If we've never talked to you before, please avoid making first contact with us by phone." Length: 500-3,000 words. Pays $35 (500-word pieces); $50-75 (sidebars); $100-225 (1,000-word and up pieces). Avoids articles on horror films/creators and comic book/comic strip creators and creations. See listing for sister magazine *Fangoria* which covers horror in *Writer's Market* entertainment section.

Photos: State availability of photos. Pays $10-25 for color slide transparencies and 8x10 b&w prints depending on quality. "No separate payment for photos provided by film studios." Captions, model releases, identification of subjects, and credit line on photos required. Photo credit given. Buys all rights.

Columns/Departments: Other Voices (essays by well-known, *published*, science fiction writers on their genre work, the writing life or their opinions, still especially needed, payment varies); Fan Network (articles on fandom and its aspects—basically staff-written); Booklog (book reviews, by assignment only); Medialog (news of upcoming science fiction films and TV projects and mini-interviews with those involved); and Videolog (videocassette and disk releases of genre interest, staff-written). "We also require science fiction news items of note, items on fantasy, merchandising items of interest, toys, games and old science fiction film/TV reunion feature material." Buys 24-30 mss/year. Query with published clips. Length: 300-750 words. No kill fee on logs. Payment for department items $35 on publication only.

Tips: "Absolutely *no fiction*. We expect to emphasize literary science fiction much more in 1989 and will need further interviews with writers and coverage of science fiction/fantasy literature. We especially *need* writers who know a prospective interviewee's literary work. Additionally, we expect to cover classic science fiction/fantasy TV series and films in much more detail especially with interviews with the quest stars from the original *Star Trek* episodes. A writer can best break in to *Starlog* with short news pieces or by getting an unusual interview that we can't get through normal channels or by *out—thinking* us and coming up with something new on a current film or book before we can think of it. We are always looking for *new* angles on *Star Trek: The Next Generation*, *Star Wars*, the original *Star Trek*, *Doctor Who*, *Blake's 7* and seek a small number of features investigating aspects (i.e., cast & crew) of series which remain very popular with many readers: *Starman*, *Lost in Space*, *Space 1999*, *Battlestar Galactica*, *The Twilight Zone*, *The Outer Limits*. Know your subject media before you try us. Most full-length major assignments go to freelancers with whom we're already dealing. But if we like your clips and ideas, we'll be happy to give *you* a chance. Discovering new freelancers and helping them to break into print is a special joy. We love it. We're fans of this material—and a prospective writer must be, too—but we were *also* freelancers. And if your love for science fiction shows through, we would love to *help* you break in as we've done with others in the past."

STARWIND, The Starwind Press, Box 98, Ripley OH 45167. (513)392-4549. Editors: David F. Powell and Susannah C. West. 75% freelance written. Eager to work with new/unpublished writers. A quarterly magazine "for older teenagers and adults who have an interest in science and technology, and who also enjoy reading well-crafted science fiction and fantasy." Circ. 2,500. Pays on publication. Publishes ms an average of 6-12 months after acceptance. Byline given. Rights vary with author and material; negotiated with author. Usually first serial rights and second serial reprint rights (nonfiction). Photocopied submissions OK. Query for electronic submissions. Computer printout submissions acceptable. Photocopied and dot-matrix submissions OK. "In fact, we encourage disposable submissions; easier for us and easier for the author. Just enclose SASE for our response. We prefer non-simultaneous submissions." Reports in 2-3 months. Sample copy for $3.50 and 9x12 SAE; writer's guidelines for #10 SAE and 1 first class stamp.

Nonfiction: How-to (technological interest, e.g., how to build a robot eye, building your own radio receiver, etc.); interview/profile (of leaders in science and technology fields); and technical ("did you know" articles dealing with development of current technology). "No speculative articles, dealing with topics such as the Abominable Snowman, Bermuda Triangle, etc. At present, most nonfiction is staff-written or reprinted from other sources. We hope to use more freelance written work in the future." Query. Length: 1,000-7,000 words. Pays 1-4¢/word.

Photos: Send photos with accompanying query or ms. Reviews b&w contact sheets and prints. Model releases and identification of subjects required. "If photos are available, we prefer to purchase them as part of the written piece." Buys negotiable rights.

Fiction: Fantasy and science fiction. "No stories whose characters were created by others (e.g. *Lovecraft*, *Star Trek*, *Star Wars* characters, etc.)." Buys 15-20 mss/year. Send complete ms. Length: 2,000-10,000 words. Pays 1-4¢/word. "We prefer previously unpublished fiction."

Tips: "Our need for nonfiction is greater than for fiction at present. Almost all our fiction and nonfiction is unsolicited. We rarely ask for rewrites, because we've found that rewrites are often disappointing; although the writer may have rewritten it to fix problems, he/she frequently changes parts we liked, too."

THRUST—SCIENCE FICTION AND FANTASY REVIEW, Thrust Publications, 8217 Langport Terrace, Gaithersburg MD 20877. (301)948-2514. Editor: D. Douglas Fratz. 20% freelance written. Prefers to work with published/established writers; works with small number of new/unpublished writers each year. A quarterly literary review magazine covering science fiction and fantasy literature. "*THRUST—Science Fiction and Fantasy Review* is the highly acclaimed, Hugo-Award-nominated magazine about science fiction and fantasy. Since 1973, *THRUST* has been featuring in-depth interviews with science fiction's best known authors and artists, articles and columns by the field's most outspoken writers, and reviews of current science fiction books. *THRUST* has built its reputation on never failing to take a close look at the most sensitive and controversial issues concerning science fiction, and continues to receive the highest praise and most heated comments from professionals and fans in the science fiction field." Circ. 1,800. Pays on publication. Publishes ms an average of 6 months after acceptance. Byline given. Buys first North American serial rights, one-time rights and second serial (reprint) rights. Submit seasonal/holiday material 3-6 months in advance. Simultaneous queries, and simultaneous, photocopied and previously published submissions OK. Query for electronic submissions. Computer printout submissions acceptable; prefers letter-quality. Reports in 2 weeks on queries; 2 months on mss. Sample copy for $2.50; writer's guidelines for SAE and 1 first class stamp.

Nonfiction: Humor, interview/profile, opinion, personal experience and book reviews. Buys 50-100 mss/

year. Query or send complete ms. Length: 200-10,000 words. Pays 1-2¢/word.
Photos: "We publish only photos of writers being interviewed." State availability of photos. Pays $2-15 for smaller than 8x10 b&w prints. Buys one-time rights.
Columns/Departments: Uses science fiction and fantasy book reviews and film reviews. Buys 40-100 mss/year. Send complete ms. Length: 100-1,000 words. Pays 1¢/word. (Reviews usually paid in subscriptions, not cash.)
Tips: "Reviews are best way to break into *THRUST*. Must be on current science fiction and fantasy books. The most frequent mistake made by writers in completing articles for us is writing to a novice audience; *THRUST*'s readers are science fiction and fantasy experts."

2 AM MAGAZINE, Box 6754, Rockford IL 61125. (815)397-5901. Editor: Gretta M. Anderson. 100% freelance written. A quarterly magazine of fiction, poetry, articles and art for readers of fantasy, horror and science fiction. Circ. 500. Pays on acceptance. Publishes ms an average of 6 months after acceptance. Byline given. Buys first North American serial rights or one-time rights. Submit seasonal/holiday material 9 months in advance. Simultaneous, photocopied and previously published submissions OK. Computer printout submission OK; no dot-matrix. Reports in 1 month on queries; 2-3 months on mss. Sample copy $4.95; writer's guidelines for #10 SAE with 1 first class stamp.
Nonfiction: How-to, interview/profile, opinion. "No essays originally written for high school or college courses." Buys 5 mss/year. Query with or without published clips or send complete ms. Length: 500-2,000 words. Pay ½-1¢/word.
Photos: State availability of photos with submission. Offers no additional payment for photos accepted with ms. Identification of subjects required. Buys one-time rights.
Fiction: Fantasy, horror, mystery, science fiction and suspense. Buys 50 mss/year. Send complete ms. Length: 250-5,000 words. Pays ½-1¢/word.
Poetry: Free verse and traditional. "No haiku/zen or short poems without imagery." Buys 20 poems/year. Submit up to 5 poems at one time. Length: 5-100 lines. Pays $1-5.
Tips: "We are always interested in seeing short fiction under 1,000 words. Short-shorts are incredibly difficult to do well, and when we see a well-written short under 1,000 words we literally leap for joy. We can always find space in an otherwise-filled issue for an excellent story under 1,000 words."

Sports

For the convenience of writers who specialize in one or two areas of sport and outdoor writing, the publications are subcategorized by the sport or subject matter they emphasize. Publications in related categories (for example, Hunting and Fishing; Archery and Bowhunting) often buy similar material. Writers should read through this entire category to become familiar with the subcategories. Publications on horse breeding and hunting dogs are classified in the Animal category, while horse racing is listed here. Publications dealing with automobile or motorcycle racing can be found in the Automotive and Motorcycle category. Markets interested in articles on exercise and fitness are listed in the Health and Fitness section. Outdoor publications that promote the preservation of nature, placing only secondary emphasis on nature as a setting for sport, are in the Nature, Conservation and Ecology category. Regional magazines are frequently interested in sports material with a local angle. Camping publications are classified in the Travel, Camping and Trailer category.

Archery and Bowhunting

BOW AND ARROW HUNTING, Box HH/34249 Camino Capistrano, Capistrano Beach CA 92624. Editorial Director: Roger Combs. 80% freelance written. Eager to work with new/unpublished writers. Bimonthly magazine for bowhunters. Pays on acceptance. Publishes ms an average of 6 months after acceptance. Buys first serial rights. Byline given. Computer printout submissions acceptable; prefers letter-quality. Reports on submissions in 2 months. Author must have some knowledge of archery terms.
Nonfiction: Articles: bowhunting, techniques used by champs, how to make your own tackle, and off-trail hunting tales. Likes a touch of humor in articles. "No dead animals or 'my first hunt.' " Also uses one technical and how-to article per issue. Submit complete ms. Length: 1,500-2,500 words. Pays $150-300.
Photos: Purchased as package with ms; 5x7 minimum. Pays $100 for cover chromes, 35mm or larger.

Tips: "Subject matter is more important than style—that's why we have editors and copy pencils. Good b&w photos are of primary importance. Don't submit color prints. We staff-write our shorter pieces."

BOWHUNTER MAGAZINE, 3720 S. Calhoun St., Fort Wayne IN 46807. (219)456-3580. Editor: M. R. James. Executive Editor: Cathy A. Dee. 90% freelance written. Eager to work with new/unpublished writers. Bimonthly magazine. For "readers of all ages, backgrounds and experience who share two common passions—hunting with the bow and arrow and a love of the great outdoors." Circ. 180,000. Buys first publication rights. Pays on acceptance. Publishes ms an average of 6-12 months after acceptance. "We now include two bowhunting annuals as part of the subscription package. This means we have eight issues each year including the Deer Hunting Annual (on sale in July) and Whitetail Bowhunter (on sale in September) which have been designated as special deer hunting issues." Submit seasonal material 8 months in advance. Reports in 6 weeks. Query for electronic submissions. Computer printout submissions acceptable; prefers letter-quality. Sample copy $2; writer's guidelines for SAE with 1 first class stamp.

Nonfiction: "We want articles that inform as well as entertain readers. Writers should anticipate every question a reader may ask and answer questions in the article or accompanying sidebar. Most features deal with big or small game bowhunting (how-to, where-to-go, etc.) The 'Me and Joe' article is still considered here, but we do not cover all aspects of archery—only bowhunting. Unusual experiences are welcome and freshness is demanded, especially when covering common ground. Readers demand accuracy, and writers hoping to sell to us must have a thorough knowledge of bowhunting. No writer should attempt to sell material to us without first studying one or more issues of the magazine. We especially like articles that promote responsible bowhunting and combat anti-hunting attacks. Humor, personal experiences, interviews and personality profiles, nostalgia, personal opinions, and historical articles are good bets. No 'See what animal I bagged—ain't I great' articles." Buys approximately 100 mss/year. Query or submit complete ms. Length: 200-3,500 words. Pays $25-250, sometimes more. Sometimes pays the expenses of writers on assignment.

Photos: Photos purchased with or without accompanying ms. Pays $20-35 for 5x7 or 8x10 b&w prints; $50 minimum for 35mm or 2¼x2¼ color. Captions optional.

Tips: "We are very well stocked with all types of bowhunting articles and so are becoming increasingly selective about what we accept. Keep the reader foremost in mind. Write for him, not yourself. Know the sport and share your knowledge. Weave helpful information into the storyline (e.g., costs involved, services of guide or outfitter, hunting season dates, equipment preferred and why, tips on items to bring, where to write for information, etc.). We have no set formula per se, but most features are first-person narratives and most published material will contain elements mentioned above. We enjoy working with promising newcomers who understand our magazine and our needs. Most writers submit material 'on spec.' We reserve most assignments for staffers. We're upgrading the quality of our photos/illustrations and are editing more tightly. We still encourage submissions from non-professionals, but all should have useful information, hard facts, a slant to the average bowhunter."

Bicycling

BICYCLE GUIDE, Raben Publishing Co., 711 Boylston St., Boston MA 02116. (617)236-1885. Editor: Theodore Costantino. 25% freelance written. "We're equally happy working with established writers and new writers." Magazine published 9 times/year covering "the world of high-performance cycling. We cover racing, touring, and mountain biking from an enthusiast's point of view." Circ. 200,000. Pays on publication. Publishes ms an average of 4 months after acceptance. Byline given. Offers kill fee. Buys first North American serial rights. Submit seasonal/holiday material 6 months in advance. Simultaneous submissions OK. Computer printout submissions acceptable; prefers letter-quality. Reports in 3 weeks on queries; 1 month on mss. Sample copy for 8½x11 SAE with 2 first class stamps; writer's guidelines for SAE with 1 first class stamp.

Nonfiction: Humor; interview/profile, new product, opinion; photo feature; technical; and travel (short rides in North America only). Buyers' annual published in April. "We need 'how-to-buy' material by preceding November." No entry-level how-to repairs or projects; long overseas tours; puff pieces on sports medicine; or 'my first ride' articles. Buys 18 mss/year. Query. Length: 900-3,500 words. Pays $200-600. Sometimes pays expenses of writers on assignment.

Photos: Send photos with submissions. Reviews transparencies and 5x8 b&w prints. Offers $50-250/photo. Captions, model releases, and identification of subjects required. Buys one-time rights.

Columns/Departments: What's Hot (new product reviews, personalities, events), 100-200 words; En Route (helpful hints for high performance cycling; on-the-road advice) 100 words; and Guest Column (thoughtful essay of interest to our readers) 900-1,200 words. Buys 30 mss/year. Query. Pays $25-450.

Tips: "Freelancers should be cyclists with a thorough knowledge of the sport. Area most open to freelancers are Training Methods (cover specific routines); Rides (75-100-mile loop rides over challenging terrain in continental U.S.); and Technical Pages (covers leading edge, technical innovations, new materials)."

BIKEREPORT, Bikecentennial, Inc., The Bicycle Travel Association, Box 8308, Missoula MT 59807. (406)721-1776. Editor: Daniel D'Ambrosio. 75% freelance written. Works with a small number of new/unpublished writers each year. Bimonthly bicycle touring magazine for Bikecentennial members. Circ. 18,000. Pays on publication. Publishes ms an average of 8 months after acceptance. Byline given. Include short bio with manuscript. Buys first serial rights. Submit seasonal/holiday material 3 months in advance. Simultaneous queries and photocopied submissions OK. Query for electronic submissions. Computer printout submissions acceptable; no dot-matrix. Reports in 2 weeks on queries; 1 month on mss. Sample copy and guidelines for 9x12 SAE with $1 postage.
Nonfiction: Historical/nostalgic (interesting spots along bike trails); how-to (bicycle); humor (touring); interview/profile (bicycle industry people); personal experience ("my favorite tour"); photo feature (bicycle); technical (bicycle); travel ("my favorite tour"). Buys 20-25 mss/year. Query with published clips or send complete ms. Length: 800-2,500 words. Pays 3¢/word. Sometimes pays the expenses of writers on assignment.
Photos: Bicycle, scenery, portraits. State availability of photos. Model releases and identification of subjects required.
Fiction: Adventure, experimental, historical, humorous. Not interested in anything that doesn't involve bicycles. Query with published clips or send complete ms. "I'd like to see more good fiction and essays." Length: 800-2,500 words. Pays 3¢/word.
Tips: "We don't get many good essays. Consider that a hint. But we are still always interested in travelogs."

VELO-NEWS, A Journal of Bicycle Racing, Box 1257, Brattleboro VT 05301. (802)254-2305. Editor: Geoff Drake. 20% freelance written. Works with a small number of new/unpublished writers each year. Monthly tabloid October-March, biweekly April-September covering bicycle racing. Circ. 14,000. Pays on publication. Publishes ms an average of 1 month after acceptance. Byline given. Buys one-time rights. Simultaneous queries, and simultaneous, photocopied, and previously published submissions OK. Electronic submissions OK; call first. Computer printout submissions acceptable; prefers letter-quality. Reports in 2 weeks. Sample copy for 9x12 SAE.
Nonfiction: How-to (on bicycle racing); interview/profile (of people important in bicycle racing); opinion; photo feature; and technical. Buys 50 mss/year. Query. Length: 300-3,000 words. Pays $2.65/column inch.
Photos: State availability of photos. Pays $16-30 for 8x10 b&w prints. Captions and identification of subjects required. Buys one-time rights.

Boating

BAY & DELTA YACHTSMAN, Recreation Publications, 2019 Clement Ave., Alameda CA 94501. (415)865-7500. Editor: Dave Preston. 45% freelance written. Works with a small number of new/unpublished writers each year. Emphasizes recreational boating for small boat owners and recreational yachtsmen in northern California. Monthly tabloid newspaper. Circ. 22,000. Pays on publication. Publishes ms an average of 6 months after acceptance. Byline given. Buys one-time serial rights. Submit seasonal/holiday material 3 months in advance. Photocopied submissions OK. Query for electronic submissions. Computer printout submissions OK. Reports in 1 month. Free writer's guidelines.
Nonfiction: Historical (nautical history of northern California); how-to (modifications, equipment, supplies, rigging, etc., aboard both power and sailboats); humor (no disaster or boating ineptitude pieces); informational (government legislation as it relates to recreational boating); interview; nostalgia; personal experience ("How I learned about boating from this" type of approach); photo feature (to accompany copy); profile; and travel. Buys 5-10 unsolicited mss/issue. Query. Length: 1,200-2,000 words. Pays $1/column inch.
Photos: Photos purchased with accompanying ms. Pays $5 for b&w glossy or matte finish photos. Total purchase price for ms includes payment for photos. Captions required.
Fiction: Adventure (sea stories, cruises, races pertaining to West Coast and points South/Southwest); fantasy; historical; humorous; and mystery. Buys 4 mss/year. Query. Length: 500-1,750 words. Pays $1/column inch.
Tips: "Think of our market area: the waterways of northern California and how, why, when and where the boatman would use those waters. Writers should be able to comprehend the boating and Bay Area references in our magazine. Think about unusual onboard applications of ideas (power and sail), special cruising tips, etc. We're very interested in local boating interviews—both the famous and unknown. Write for a knowledgeable boating public."

BOAT PENNSYLVANIA, Pennsylvania Fish Commission, Box 1673, Harrisburg PA 17105. (717)657-4520. Editor: Art Michaels. 60-80% freelance written. Quarterly magazine covering motorboating, sailing, canoeing, water skiing, kayaking and rafting in Pennsylvania. Prefers to work with published/established contributors, but works with a few unpublished writers and photographers every year. Pays 6-8 weeks after acceptance. Publishes ms an average of 8 months after acceptance. Byline given. Buys variable rights. Submit seasonal/holiday material 8 months in advance. Computer printout submissions acceptable; prefers letter-quality. Reports in 2 weeks on queries; 2 months on manuscript. Writer's guidelines for #10 SAE with 1 first class stamp.

Nonfiction: How-to, photo feature, technical, and historical/nostalgic, all related to water sports in Pennsylvania. No saltwater material. Buys 40 mss/year. Query. Length: 300-3,000 words. Pays $25-300.

Photos: Send photos with submission. Reviews 35mm and larger color transparencies and 8x10 b&w prints. Captions, model releases, and identification of subjects required.

CANOE MAGAZINE, Canoe Associates, Box 3146, Kirkland WA 98083. (206)827-6363. Managing Editor: George Thomas. 80-90% freelance written. A bimonthly magazine on canoeing, whitewater kayaking, and kayaking. Circ. 55,000. Pays on publication. Publishes ms an average of 2-3 months after acceptance. Byline given. Offers 25% kill fee (rarely needed). Buys all rights. Submit seasonal/holiday material 4 months in advance. Query for electronic submissions. Computer printout submissions acceptable; no dot-matrix. Reports in 1 month. Free sample copy and writer's guidelines.

Nonfiction: Dave Harrison, articles editor. Essays, general interest, historical/nostalgic, how-to, humor, interview/profile, new product, opinion, personal experience, photo feature, technical and travel. Plans a special entry-level guide to canoeing and kayaking. No "trip diaries." Buys 60 mss/year. Query with or without published clips, or send complete ms. Length: 500-2,500 words. Pays $5/column inch. Pays the expenses of writers on assignment.

Photos: State availability of photos with submission or send photos with submission. Reviews contact sheets, negatives, transparencies and prints. "Some activities we cover are canoeing, kayaking, canoe sailing or poling, canoe fishing, camping, backpacking (when compatible with the main activity,) and occasionally inflatable boats. We are not interested in groups of people in rafts, photos showing disregard for the environment, gasoline-powered, multi-horsepower engines unless appropriate to the discussion, or unskilled persons taking extraordinary risks." Offers $50-150/photo. Model releases and identification of subjects required. Buys one-time rights.

Columns/Departments: Dave Harrison, column/department editor. Competition (racing); Continuum (essay); Counter Currents (environmental); Put-In (short interesting articles)—all 1,500 words. Buys 60 mss/year. Pays $5/column inch.

Fiction: Uses very little fiction. Buys 5 mss/year.

Fillers: Anecdotes, facts, gags to be illustrated by cartoonist, and newsbreaks. Buys 20/year. Length: 500-1,000 words. Pays $5/column inch.

Tips: "Start with Put-In articles (short featurettes) of approximately 500 words, book reviews, or short, unique equipment reviews. Or give us the best, most exciting article we've ever seen—with great photos. Short Strokes is also a good entry forum focusing on short trips on good waterways accessible to lots of people. Query for specifics."

CRUISING WORLD, 524 Thames St., Newport RI 02840. (401)847-1588. Editor: George Day. 75% freelance written. Eager to work with new/unpublished writers. For all those who cruise under sail. Monthly magazine; 200 pages. Circ. 130,000. Pays on acceptance. Publishes ms an average of 8 months after acceptance. Rights purchased vary with author and material. Buys first world serial rights. Reports in about 2 months. Query for electronic submissions. Computer printout submissions acceptable; prefers letter-quality.

Nonfiction: "We are interested in seeing informative articles on the technical and enjoyable aspects of cruising under sail. Also subjects of general interest to seafarers." Buys 135-140 unsolicited mss/year. Submit complete ms. Length: 500-3,500 words. Pays $50-500. Sometimes pays expenses of writers on assignment.

Photos: 5x7 b&w prints and color transparencies purchased with accompanying ms.

Tips: Interested in "short pieces (500 words) on: marine life; seaports; bird life; specific techniques; news of sailing events. The most frequent mistakes made by writers in completing an article assignment for us are missing our audience; missing our style; missing the point of the whole exercise; typing single-space; supplying unusable photos; writing too much but saying too little. Guidelines for authors and photographers are available."

CURRENTS, Voice of the National Organization for River Sports, 314 N. 20th St., Colorado Springs CO 80904. (719)473-2466. Editor: Eric Leaper. Managing Editor: Mary McCurdy. 25% freelance written. Bimonthly magazine covering river running (kayaking, rafting, river canoeing). Circ. 10,000. Pays on publication. Publishes ms an average of 6 months after acceptance. Byline given. Offers 25% kill fee. Buys first North American serial rights, first rights and one-time rights. Submit seasonal/holiday material 2 months in advance. Simultaneous queries, and simultaneous, photocopied, and previously published submissions OK. Computer printout submissions acceptable; prefers letter-quality. Reports in 2 weeks on queries; in 1 month on mss. Sample copy for $1 and 9x12 SAE with 4 first class stamps; writer's guidelines for #10 SAE and 1 first class stamp.

Nonfiction: How-to (run rivers and fix equipment); in-depth reporting on river conservation and access issues and problems; humor (related to rivers); interview/profile (any interesting river runner); new product; opinion; personal experience; technical; travel (rivers in other countries). "We tell river runners about river conservation, river access, river equipment, how to do it, when, where, etc." No trip accounts without originality; no stories about "my first river trip." Buys 20 mss/year. Query with or without clips of published work. Length: 500-2,500 words. Pays $12-75.

Photos: State availability of photos. Pays $10-35. Reviews b&w or color prints or slides; b&w preferred. Captions and identification of subjects (if racing) required. Buys one-time rights.

Columns/Departments: Book and film reviews (river-related). Buys 5 mss/year. Query with or without clips of published work or send complete ms. Length: 100-500 words. Pays $5-50.

Fiction: Adventure (river). Buys 2 mss/year. Query. Length: 1,000-2,500 words. Pays $25-75. "Must be well-written, on well-known river and beyond the realm of possibility."

Fillers: Clippings, jokes, gags, anecdotes, short humor, newsbreaks. Buys 5/year. Length: 25-100 words. Pays $5-10.

Tips: "We need more material on river news—proposed dams, wild and scenic river studies, accidents, etc. If you can provide brief (300-500 words) on these subjects, you will have a good chance of being published. Material must be on whitewater rivers. Go to a famous river and investigate it; find out something we don't know—especially about rivers that are *not* in Colorado or adjacent states—we already know about the ones near us."

‡GREAT LAKES SAILOR, Mid-America's Freshwater Sailing Magazine, Great Lakes Sailor, Inc., Box 951, Akron OH 44309. (216)762-2300. Editor: Drew Shippy. 55% freelance written. A monthly magazine on Great Lakes sailing. Circ. 24,000. Pays on publication. Byline given. Buys first North America serial rights. Submit seasonal material 3 months in advance. Simultaneous submisions OK. Computer printout submissions OK; prefers letter-quality. Free sample copy and writer's guidelines. Reports on queries in 1 month; 6 weeks on mss.

Nonfiction: How-to (major and minor sailboat upgrades), humor (sailing oriented), interview/profile (sailing personality), new product (sailboat oriented), personal experience (sailing oriented), photo feature (sail racing), travel (sailing destination). Buys 60 mss/year. Query. Length: 1,000-3,500 words. Pays $50-500.

Photos: Send photos with submissions. Reviews, transparencies and 4x5 or 8x10 prints. Offers no additional payment for photos accepted with ms. Captions required. Buys one-time rights.

Columns/Departments: Yard & Loft (major sailboat upgrades) 1,500-2,000 words; Sailor's Projects (minor sailboat upgrades—under $250) 250-1,000 words; Boat Handling (sailing techniques) 1,500-2,000 words; News (Great Lakes events/developments of interest) 300-500 words. Buys 36 mss/year. Query. Pays $50-250.

Fillers: Anecdotes, facts, newsbreaks, short humor. Length: 50-500 words. Pays $20-75.

‡HOT BOAT, The Most Wanted Water Sports Magazine, HBM Publications, Inc., Suite 1, 500 Harrington, Corona CA 91720. (714)736-3070. Editor: Ron Piechota. 7% freelance written. A monthly magazine on performance boating and water sports in general. "We're always interested in technical articles regarding boating." Circ. 88,000. Pays on publication. Publishes ms an average of 2 months after acceptance. Byline given. Offers 40% kill fee. Buys first North American serial rights. Submit seasonal/holiday material 3 months in advance. Simultaneous, photocopied and previously published submissions OK. Computer printout submissions OK; no dot-matrix. Reports in 3 weeks on queries; 2 months on mss. Sample copy for SAE with $1.24 postage.

Nonfiction: How-to (increase horsepower, perform simple boat related maintenance), humor, interview/profile (racers and manufacturers), new product, personal experience, photo feature, technical. "Absolutely no sailing—we deal strictly in powerboating." Buys 30 mss/year. Query with published clips. Length: 200-3,500 words. Pays $50-300. Sometimes pays expenses of writers on assignment.

Photos: Send photos with submission. Reviews contact sheets, negatives, transparencies, prints. Captions, model releases and identification of subjects required. Buys one-time rights.

Fillers: Anecdotes, facts, gags to be illustrated by cartoonist, newsbreaks, short humor. Buys 50 mss/year. Length: 10-300 words.

Tips: "We're always open to new writers. If you query with published clips and we like your writing, we can keep you on file even if we reject the particular query. It may be more important to simply establish contact. Once we work together there will be much more work to follow."

MOTORBOATING & SAILING, 224 W. 57th St., New York NY 10019. (212)262-8768. Editor: Peter A. Janssen. Monthly magazine covering powerboats and sailboats for people who own their own boats and are active in a yachting lifestyle. Circ. 145,000. Pays on acceptance. Byline given. Buys one-time rights. Reports in 3 months.

Nonfiction: General interest (navigation, adventure, cruising), and how-to (maintenance). Buys 5-6 mss/issue. Average issue includes 8-10 feature articles. Query. Length: 2,000 words.

Photos: Reviews 5x7 b&w glossy prints and 35mm or larger color transparencies. Offers no additional payment for photos accepted with ms. Captions and model releases required.

OFFSHORE, Boating Magazine of New England and the Northeast, Offshore Publications, Inc., 220-9 Reservoir St., Needham MA 02194. (617)449-6204. Editor: Herbert Gliick. 80% freelance written. Eager to work with new/unpublished writers. Monthly magazine (oversize) covering boating and the coast from Maine to New Jersey. Circ. 35,000. Pays on acceptance. Publishes ms an average of 2 months after acceptance. Byline given. Offers negotiable kill fee. Buys first North American serial rights. Submit seasonal/holiday material 3 months in advance. Simultaneous queries, and simultaneous, photocopied, and previously published submissions OK. Query for electronic submissions. Computer printout submissions acceptable. Reports in 1 week. Sample copy for 11x14 SAE and $1.40 postage.

Nonfiction: Articles on boats, boating, New York, New Jersey and New England coastal places and people. Coastal history of NJ, NY, CT, RI, MA, NH and ME. Boat-related fiction. Thumbnail and/or outline of topic will elicit immediate response. Buys 125 mss/year. Query with writing sample or send complete ms. Length: 1,000-3,500 words. Pays 8-10¢/word.

Photos: Reviews photocopies of 5x7 b&w prints. Identification of subjects required. Buys one-time rights.

Tips: "Demonstrate familiarity with boats or region and ability to recognize subjects of interest to regional boat owners. Those subjects need not be boats. *Offshore* does not take itself as seriously as most national boating magazines. The most frequent mistake made by writers in completing an article for us is failing to build on a theme (what is the point of the story?)."

POWERBOAT MAGAZINE, 15917 Strathern St., Van Nuys CA 91406. Publisher: Bob Nordskog. 60% freelance written. Works with a small number of new/unpublished writers each year. For performance-conscious boating enthusiasts. January, West Coast Runabout Performance Trials; February, East Coast Runabout Performance Trials; March, Offshore Performance Trials; April, Water Ski Issue; May, Awards for Product Excellence; June through November/December, Race reporting and various other features on recreational boating. Circ. 82,000. Pays on publication. Publishes ms an average of 3 months after acceptance. Byline given. Buys all rights or one-time North American serial rights. Reports in 2 weeks. Query for electronic submissions. Computer printout submissions OK; prefers letter-quality. Free sample copy.

Nonfiction: Uses articles about power boats and water skiing that offer special interest to performance-minded boaters, how-to-do-it pieces with good color slides, developments in boating, profiles on well-known boating and skiing individuals, competition coverage of national and major events. Query required. Length: 1,500-2,000 words. Pays $150-500/article. Sometimes pays the expenses of writers on assignment.

Photos: Photos purchased with mss. Prefers 35mm Kodachrome slides.

Tips: "We are interested in publishing more technical articles, i.e., how to get better performance out of a boat, engine or tow vehicle. When submitting an article, it should be in the area of *high performance* boating only. We *do not* cover sailing, large yachts, fishing boats, etc."

RIVER RUNNER MAGAZINE, Rancher Publications, Box 458, Fallbrook CA 92028. (619)723-8155. Editor: Ken Hulick. 90% freelance written. "Interested in working with new/unpublished writers who understand our needs and who submit material professionally." Seven-time-per-year magazine covering whitewater rafting, canoeing, and kayaking. "Audience is predominately male, college educated, and approximately 20-45 years old. The editorial slant favors whitewater action. Stories reflect the natural beauty and excitement of running rivers." Circ. 20,000. Pays on publication. Publishes ms an average of 4 months after acceptance. Byline given. Buys first North American serial rights. Submit seasonal/holiday material 6 months in advance. Computer printout submissions acceptable; prefers letter-quality. Reports in 1 month on queries; 2 months on mss. Sample copy $2.50; writer's guidelines for #10 SAE and 1 first class stamp.

Nonfiction: Features on running a specific river (or region), with practical information for other paddlers, that convey a sense of place as well as whitewater action. How-to articles on techniques (mostly for immediate-level readers). Equipment overviews of canoes, kayaks, rafts, paddles, clothing and accessories. Occasional features on sea kayaking, competition whitewater racing, historical/personality profile, conservation, and alternative water sports (wave skiing, bathtub racing, etc.). "In 1989 we are going to be focusing a bit more on the whitewater enthusiasts who travel with guides and outfitters." No fiction or poetry. "We focus primarily on the United States, but regularly run features on other North American and international destinations." Buys 40-50 mss/year. Query with or without published clips or send complete ms. Length: 1,500-2,500 words. Pays 5-10¢/word. Sometimes pays the expenses of writers on assignment.

Photos: State availability of photos with query letter or submit with ms. Pays $25-75 for color transparencies; $15-45 for b&w prints. "We need good, sharp photographs that portray the total whitewater experience." Captions required. Buys first North American serial rights.

Columns/Departments: Conservation (focus on nationally relevant threats to rivers); Upfront (short, bright, lively commentary on off-beat aspects of river running; Reviews (covers, relevant books, videos, etc.); Tips (offers technical advice for all paddlers); Guided Whitewater (addresses the needs of guided clients) and Forum (often nonpaid column provided for recognized river spokespersons to voice opinions of interest to the paddling community). Buys 30-40 mss/year. Send complete ms. Length: 500-1,000 words. Pays 5¢/word.

Tips: "Submit fresh, original story ideas with strong supporting photographs. The prime need is for original, well-written river feature stories. Stories should be written for the intermediate-level paddler and display an understanding of our editorial needs."

SAIL, Charlestown Navy Yard, 100 First Ave., Charlestown MA 02129-2097. (617)241-9500. Editor: Patience Wales. 50% freelance written. Works with a small number of new/unpublished writers each year. Monthly magazine for audience that is "strictly sailors, average age 42, above average education." Pays on publication. Publishes ms an average of 10 months after acceptance. Buys first North American serial rights. Submit seasonal or special material at least 5 months in advance. Reports in 8 weeks. Computer printout submissions acceptable; no dot-matrix. Writer's guidelines for 1 first class stamp.
Nonfiction: Cathrine Baker, managing editor. Wants "articles on sailing: technical, techniques and feature stories." Interested in how-to, personal experience, profiles, historical and new products. "Generally emphasize the excitement of sail and the human, personal aspect. No logs." Special issues: "Cruising issues, chartering issues, fitting-out issues, special race issues (e.g., America's Cup), boat show issues." Buys 150 mss/year (freelance and commissioned). Length: 1,500-2,800 words. Pays $100-800. Sometimes pays the expenses of writers on assignment.
Photos: Offers additional payment for photos. Uses b&w glossy prints or Kodachrome 64 color transparencies. Pays $600 if photo is used on the cover.
Tips: Request an articles specification sheet.

SAILING MAGAZINE, 125 E. Main St., Port Washington WI 53074. (414)284-3494. Editor and Publisher: William F. Schanen, III. Monthly magazine. For readers ages 25-44, majority professionals. About 75% of them own their own sailboat. Circ. 35,000. Pays on publication. Photocopied and simultaneous submissions OK. Reports in 6 weeks. Free sample copy; writer's guidelines for #10 SASE.
Nonfiction: Micca Leffingwell Hutchins, editor. "Experiences of sailing, whether cruising, racing or learning. We require no special style. We're devoted exclusively to sailing and sailboat enthusiasts, and particularly interested in articles about the trend toward cruising in the sailing world." Informational, personal experience, profile, historical, travel and book reviews. Buys 24 mss/year. Query or submit complete ms. Length: open. Payment negotiable. Must be accompanied by photos.
Photos: B&w and color photos purchased with or without accompanying ms. Captions required. Pays flat fee for article.

SAILING WORLD, North American Publishing Co., 111 East Ave., Norwalk CT 06851. Editor: John Burnham. 40% freelance written. Magazine published 12 times/year. Circ. 53,000. Pays on publication. Publishes ms an average of 4 months after acceptance. Buys first North American serial rights. Byline given. Query for electronic submissions. Computer printout submissions acceptable. Sample copy $1.75.
Nonfiction: How-to for racing and performance-oriented sailors, photo feature, profile, regatta reports, and travel. No travelogs. Buys 5-10 unsolicited mss/year. Query. Length: 750-2,000 words. Pays $50 per column of text.
Tips: "Send query with outline and include your experience. The writer may have a better chance of breaking in at our publication with short articles and fillers such as regatta news reports from his or her own area."

‡SANTANA, The So-Cal Sailing Rag, Santana Publications, Inc., #101, 5132 Bolsa, Huntington Beach CA 92649. (714)893-3432. Editor: David Poe. Managing Editor: Kitty James. 50% freelance written. A monthly magazine on sailing. "We publish conversationally written articles of interest to Southern California sailers, including technical, cruising, racing, fiction, etc." Estab. 1987. Circ. 20,000. Pays on publication. Publishes ms an average of 2 months after acceptance. Byline given. Publication not copyrighted. Buys first North American serial rights or second serial (reprint) rights. Submit seasonal/holiday material 3 months in advance. Photocopied and previously published submissions OK. Computer printout submissions OK. Reports in 2 weeks. Sample copy for 9x12 SAE with 5 first class stamps.
Nonfiction: Essays, general interest, historical/nostalgic, how-to (technical articles), humor, interview/profile, personal experience. Buys 50 mss/year. Query with or without published clips or send complete ms. Length: 1,000-4,000 words. Pays $50-150.
Photos: State availability of photos with submission. Reviews contact sheets, negatives, transparencies (35mm) and prints (5x7 or 8x10). Offers $10/photo. Captions and identification of subjects required. Buys one-time rights.
Fiction: Adventure, humorous. Send complete ms. Length: 1,000-5,000. Pays $50-150.
Tips: "Reading the publication is best as our style tends towards conversational, frequently irreverent, but we are also interested in technical articles. We are also happy to critique submissions with suggestions on how to break in. Virtually the entire range of topics covered is open to freelance submissions."

SEA, The Magazine of Western Boating, combined with *Waterfront Magazine*, Duncan McIntosh Co., Inc., Box 1579, Newport Beach CA 92663. Editor: Duncan McIntosh Jr. Associate Editor: Linda Yuskaitis. Managing Editor: Cathi Douglas. 70% freelance written. A monthly magazine covering recreational power and sail boating, offshore fishing and coastal news of the West Coast. Also includes Waterfront, a regional section with news and features exclusively about Southern California boating. "*Sea* readers are well educated boat owners, knowledgeable about sail and power boating beyond the fundamentals." Circ. 45,000. Pays on publication. Publishes ms an average of 4 months after acceptance. Byline given. Negotiable kill fee. Buys first North American serial rights or second serial (reprint) rights. Submit seasonal/holiday material 6 months in advance. Photocopied and previously published submissions acceptable "occasionally." Query for electronic submissions. Computer printout submissions OK; prefers letter-quality. Reports in 1 month on queries; 6 weeks on mss. Free writer's guidelines, deadline schedule and sample copy with SASE.

Nonfiction: General interest (on boating and coastal topics); how-to (tips on maintaining a boat, engine, etc.); interview/profile (of prominent boating personality); travel (West Coast cruising destination); humor (boating related); historical/nostalgic (on maritime lore and port history). Buys 150 mss/year. Query with or without published clips, or send complete ms. Length: 800-3,000 words. Pays $100-450 for assigned articles; pays $75-350 for unsolicited articles. Pays some expenses of writers on assignment.

Photos: Send photos with submission. Reviews contact sheets, transparencies and 5x7 prints. Offers $25-200 per photo. Identification of subjects required. Buys one-time rights.

Columns/Departments: West Coast Focus (West Coast boating news items), 300-800 words; Nautical Elegance (feature on a well-preserved, or renovated antique boat), 800-2,000 words; Harbor Hopping (features on West Coast cruising destinations), 1,000-2,000 words. Departments in Southern California section include: Channel Islands (boating and coastal news from Santa Barbara/Ventura/Oxnard area); Marina del Rey to Long Beach (Marina del Rey/L.A./Long Beach); Newport (Newport Beach/Dana Point); San Diego (Oceanside to Mexican border); Racing (sail and power boat competitions). Send complete ms. Pays $50-300.

Tips: "First-time contributors should include resume or information about themselves that identifies their knowledge of subject. Brief but specific queries appreciated. No first-person 'where we went on our vacation cruise' stories, no poetry or fiction."

SMALL BOAT JOURNAL, S.B. Journal, Inc., Box 1066, Bennington VT 05201. (802)442-3101. Editor: Thomas Baker. Managing Editor: Richard Lebovitz. 95% freelance written. Bimonthly magazine covering recreational boating. "*Small Boat Journal* focuses on the practical and enjoyable aspects of owning and using small boats. *Small Boat Journal* covers all types of watercraft under 30 feet in length—powerboats, sailboats, rowing boats, sea kayaks and canoes. Topics include cruising areas and adventures, boat evaluations, and helpful tips for building, up-grading and maintaining, and safely handling small boats." Circ. 56,000. Pays on acceptance. Publishes ms an average of 6 months after acceptance. Byline given. Offers 50% kill fee. Buys first or second serial (reprint) rights. Submit seasonal/holiday material 4 months in advance. Simultaneous (as long as author agrees to give first rights to *SBJ*) and photocopied submissions OK. Query for electronic submissions. Computer printout submissions OK; prefers letter-quality. Reports in 5 weeks on queries; 3 weeks on mss. Sample copy for 8½x11 SAE with 7 first class stamps; writer's guidelines for #10 SAE with 1 first class stamp.

Nonfiction: Book excerpts, essays, historical/nostalgic, how-to (boating, maintenance, restoration and improvements), humor, interview/profile, new product, personal experience, photo feature, technical and travel. Plans special issues on sea kayaking, rowing, electronics, engines, fishing boats and equipment, boatbuilding. Buys 60 mss/year. Query with or without published clips, or send complete ms. Length: 800-4,000 words. Pays $150-600 for assigned articles; pays $75-400 for unsolicited articles. Sometimes pays the expenses of writers on assignment.

Photos: Send photos with submission. Reviews contact sheets, transparencies and prints. Offers $15-200 per photo. Model releases and identification of subjects required. Buys one-time rights.

Columns/Departments: Seamanship (boating safety, piloting and navigation), 1,500 words; Rigs & Rigging (care and improvement of rigging and sails), 1,500 words; Ripples (personal experiences and reflections on boating), 1,000 words; Boatcraft (ideas for improving a boat), 1,500 words; Inside Outboards (care and maintenance of outboard engines), 1,500 words. Buys 40 mss/year. Query with published clips. Length: 900-2,500 words. Pays $50-400.

Fiction: Adventure, humorous and slice-of-life vignettes. Send complete ms. Length: 1,000-2,500 words. Pays $150-400.

Fillers: Anecdotes, facts, gags to be illustrated by cartoonist and short humor. Pays $25-100.

Tips: "Our best stories provide comprehensive, in-depth information about a particular boating subject. *SBJ*'s readers are experienced and sophisticated boating enthusiasts—most own more than one type of boat—and expect well-researched articles with a practical, how-to slant. Excellent photos are a plus, as are stories with engaging tales drawn from the author's experience." Most open to freelances are "topics related to seamanship, engine maintenance and repair, boat handling, boat building, hull maintenance and repair, restoration and historical subjects related to small boats."

SOUNDINGS, The Nation's Boating Newspaper, Pratt St., Essex CT 06426. (203)767-0906. Editor: Arthur R. Henick. Managing Editor: Milton Moore. Works with a small number of new/unpublished writers each year. National monthly boating newspaper with nine regional editions. Features "news—hard and soft—for the recreational boating public." Circ. 100,000. Pays after "the 10th of the month of publication." Publishes ms an average of 3 months after acceptance. Byline given. Buys one-time rights. Deadline 1st of month before issue. Simultaneous queries and simultaneous and photocopied submissions OK. Query for electronic submissions. Computer printout submissions acceptable; prefers letter-quality. Reports in 2 months on queries; 5 weeks on mss. Sample copy for 8½x11 SAE and 7 first class stamps; free writer's guidelines.

Nonfiction: General interest, historical/nostalgic, interview/profile, opinion and photo feature. Race coverage is also used; supply full names, home towns and the full scores for the top 10 winners in each division. Send complete ms. Length: 250-1,000 words. Pays $2/column inch-$4/column inch. Sometimes pays the expenses of writers on assignment.

Photos: Send photos with ms. Pays $20-25 for 8x10 b&w prints. Identification of subjects required. Buys one-time rights.

TRAILER BOATS MAGAZINE, Poole Publications, Inc., Box 5427, Carson CA 90749-5427. (213)537-6322. Editor: Jim Youngs. Managing Editor: Bob Kovacik. 30-40% freelance written. Works with a small number of new/unpublished writers each year. Monthly magazine (November/December issue combined). Emphasizes legally trailerable boats and related activities. Circ. 80,000. Pays on publication. Publishes ms an average of 2 months after acceptance. Byline given. Buys all rights. Submit seasonal/holiday material 3 months in advance. Query for electronic submissions. Computer printout submissions acceptable; prefers letter-quality. Reports in 1 month. Sample copy $1.25; writer's guidelines for #10 SASE.

Nonfiction: General interest (trailer boating activities); historical (places, events, boats); how-to (repair boats, installation, etc.); humor (almost any boating-related subject); nostalgia (same as historical); personal experience; photo feature; profile; technical; and travel (boating travel on water or highways). No "How I Spent My Summer Vacation" stories, or stories not even remotely connected to trailerable boats and related activities. Buys 18-30 unsolicited mss/year. Query or send complete ms. Length: 500-3,000 words. Pays $50 minimum. Pays expenses of writers on assignment.

Photos: Send photos with ms. Pays $7.50-50 for 5x7 or 8x10 b&w glossy print; $15-100 for 35mm color transparency. Captions required.

Columns/Departments: Boaters Bookshelf (boating book reviews); Over the Transom (funny or strange boating photos); and Patent Pending (an invention with drawings). Buys 2/issue. Query. Length: 100-500 words. Pays 7¢-10¢/word. Mini-Cruise (short enthusiastic approach to a favorite boating spot). Need map and photographs. Length: 500-750 words. Pays $100. Open to suggestions for new columns/departments.

Fiction: Adventure, experimental, historical, humorous and suspense. "We do not use too many fiction stories but we will consider them if they fit the general editorial guidelines." Query or send complete ms. Length: 500-1,500 words. Pays $50 minimum.

Tips: "Query should contain short general outline of the intended material; what kind of photos; how the photos illustrate the piece. Write with authority covering the subject like an expert. Frequent mistakes are not knowing the subject matter or the audience. Use basic information rather than prose, particularly in travel stories. The writer may have a better chance of breaking in at our publication with short articles and fillers if they are typically hard to find articles. We do most major features inhouse."

WOODENBOAT MAGAZINE, The Magazine for Wooden Boat Owners, Builders, and Designers, WoodenBoat Publications, Inc., Box 78, Brooklin ME 04616. (207)359-4651. Editor: Jon Wilson. Executive Editor: Billy R. Sims. Managing Editor: Jennifer Buckley. Senior Editor: Mike O'Brien. 50% freelance written. Works with a small number of new/unpublished writers each year. Bimonthly magazine for wooden boat owners, builders, and designers. "We are devoted exclusively to the design, building, care, preservation, and use of wooden boats, both commercial and pleasure, old and new, sail and power. We work to convey quality, integrity, and involvement in the creation and care of these craft, to entertain, to inform, to inspire, and to provide our varied readers with access to individuals who are deeply experienced in the world of wooden boats." Circ. 110,000. Pays on publication. Publishes ms an average of 6-12 months after acceptance. Byline given. Offers variable kill fee. Buys first North American serial rights. Submit seasonal/holiday material 3 months in advance. Simultaneous queries and submissions (with notification) and photocopied and previously published submissions OK. Query for electronic submissions. Computer printout submissions acceptable. Reports in 3 weeks on queries; 4 weeks on mss. Sample copy $4; writer's guidelines for SASE.

Nonfiction: Technical (repair, restoration, maintenance, use, design and building wooden boats). No poetry, fiction. Buys 100 mss/year. Query with published clips. Length: 1,500-5,000 words. Pays $6/column inch. Sometimes pays expenses of writers on assignment.

Photos: Send photos with query. Negatives must be available. Pays $15-75 for b&w; $25-350 for color. Identification of subjects required. Buys one-time rights.

Columns/Departments: On the Waterfront pays for *information* on wooden boat-related events, projects, boatshop activities, etc. Buys 25/year. "We use the same columnists for each issue." Send complete information. Length: 250-1,000 words. Pays $5-50 for information.

Tips: "We appreciate a detailed, articulate query letter, accompanied by photos, that will give us a clear idea of what the author is proposing. We appreciate samples of previously published work. It is important for a prospective author to become familiar with our magazine first. It is extremely rare for us to make an assignment with a writer with whom we have not worked before. Most work is submitted on speculation. The most common failure is not exploring the subject material in enough depth."

YACHTING, Times-Mirror, 5 River Rd., Cos Cob CT 06807. (203)629-8300. Editor: Roy Attaway. Managing Editor: Cynthia Taylor. 30% freelance written. "The magazine is written and edited for experienced, knowledgeable yachtsmen." Circ. 150,000. Pays on acceptance. Byline given. Offers 50% kill fee. Buys first rights. Submit seasonal/holiday material 6 months in advance. Computer printout submissions OK; prefers letter-quality. Reports in 2 weeks on queries; 1 month on mss.

Nonfiction: Book excerpts, personal experience, photo feature and travel. No cartoons, fiction, poetry. Query with published clips. Length: 250-2,500 words. Pays $250-1,000 for assigned articles. Pays expenses of writers on assignment.

Photos: Send photos with submission. Reviews 35mm transparencies. Offers no additional payment for photos accepted with ms. Captions, model releases and identification of subjects required.

Columns/Departments: Cruising Yachtsman (stories on cruising; contact Jack Somer, editor); Racing Yachtsman (stories about sail or power racing; contact Lisa Gosselin). Buys 30 mss/year. Send complete ms. Length: 750 words maximum. Pays $250-500.

Tips: "We require considerable expertise in our writing because our audience is experienced and knowledgeable. Vivid descriptions of quaint anchorages and quainter natives are fine, but our readers want to know how the yachtsmen got there, too."

Bowling

BOWLING, 5301 S. 76th St., Greendale WI 53129. (414)421-6400, ext. 230. Editor: Dan Matel. 15% freelance written. Official publication of the American Bowling Congress. Monthly. Pays on acceptance. Publishes ms an average of 2 months after acceptance. Byline given. Rights purchased vary with author and material; usually buys all rights. Reports in 1 month. Computer printout submissions acceptable; prefers letter-quality.

Nonfiction: "This is a specialized field and the average writer attempting the subject of bowling should be well-informed. However, anyone is free to submit material for approval." Wants articles about unusual ABC sanctioned leagues and tournaments, personalities, etc., featuring male bowlers. Nostalgia articles also considered. No first-person articles or material on history of bowling. Length: 500-1,200 words. Pays $25-150 per article. No poems.

Photos: Pays $10-15/photo.

Tips: "Submit feature material on bowlers, generally amateurs competing in local leagues, or special events involving the game of bowling. Should have connection with ABC membership. Queries should be as detailed as possible so that we may get a clear idea of what the proposed story would be all about. It saves us time and the writer time. Samples of previously published material in the bowling or general sports field would help. Once we find a talented writer in a given area, we're likely to go back to him in the future. We're looking for good writers who can handle assignments professionally and promptly." No articles on professionals.

Gambling

GAMBLING TIMES MAGAZINE, 1018 N. Cole Ave., Hollywood CA 90038. Editor: Len Miller. Associate Editor: Adriene Corbin. Monthly magazine. 50% freelance written. Circ. 70,000. Pays on publication. Buys first North American serial rights. Byline given. Submit seasonal/holiday material 5-6 months in advance of issue date. Computer printout submissions acceptable; prefers letter-quality. Write for instructions on specific ms preparation for electronic typesetting equipment after query acceptance. Double-space all submissions, maximum 10 pp. Reports in 4-6 weeks. Publishes ms an average of 5 months after acceptance. Free writer's guidelines; mention *Writer's Market* in request.

Nonfiction: How-to (related to gambling systems, betting methods, etc.); humor; photo feature (racetracks, jai alai, casinos); and travel (gambling spas and resort areas). "Also interested in investigative reports focusing on the political, economical and legal issues surrounding gambling in the U.S. and the world and new gambling developments. No cutesy stuff. Keep your style clean, hard-edged and sardonic (if appropriate). Writers may query on any subject which is germane to our format." Buys 100 mss/year; prefers pictures with mss. Query. Pays $50-150.

Fiction: "We only use heavily gambling-related material and prefer fast-paced, humorous stories. Please, no more 'man scores big and dies' stuff." Buys 12 mss/year. Submit complete ms double spaced, maximum 9 pp. Pays $50-100.

Tips: "Know gambling thoroughly. *Pictures with mss will add $50 to the payment*. Action shots—always people shots. Photographs must show something unique to the subject in article. We enjoy the feeling of accomplishment when we've helped an amateur or beginner to make it into print. But we dislike a writer to begin a series of phone inquiries the day after he or she has mailed a submission."

General Interest

CITY SPORTS MAGAZINE, Box 3693, San Francisco CA 94119. Editors: Jane McConnell in northern California; Greg Ptacek in southern California (1120 Princeton Dr., Marina del Rey CA 90291); Will Balliet in New York (140 West 22nd St., 10th Floor, New York NY 10011) and Peg Moline in Boston (48 Grove St., Somerville MA 02144). 80% freelance written. Works with a small number of new/unpublished writers each year. Monthly controlled circulation tabloid covering nutrition, health, active travel, family fitness and participant sports (such as running, cycling, tennis, skiing, water sports, etc.). Circ. in California 203,000; in East Coast 100,000. Four editions published monthly—for northern California, southern California and New York and Boston. 50% of editorial features run nationally, and 50% run in one of the regional editions. Pays on acceptance for features. Publishes ms an average of 2 months after acceptance. Uses assignment contracts. Pays negotiable kill fee. Buys one-time rights. Simultaneous and previously published submissions OK. Query for electronic submissions. Computer printout submissions OK. Reports in 1 month on queries. Sample copy $3.

Nonfiction: Interview/profile of participant athletes; travel; instructional and service pieces on sports and fitness; health and nutrition articles; humor. "We accept very few first-person sports accounts unless they are very unusual (such as first-time expeditions or sports participation in exotic locale) or humorous." Special issues include: Health Clubs (February); Sports Vacations (April); Running (May); Bicycling and Outdoors (June); Fitness Walking (July); Sports Medicine (October); Downhill Skiing (November); Cross-Country Skiing (December). Buys 70 mss/year. Query with clips of published work. Length: 1,200-2,800 words. Pays $250-600 for regionally run features; $500-800 for national features.

Photos: Pays $75-150 for 35mm color; $200-500 for covers; $50-100 for 8x10 b&w glossy prints. Model releases and identification of subjects required.

Tips: "We are including more articles on travel and active ideas for families and people over 50 in addition to our mainstay articles on participant sports."

OUTDOOR CANADA MAGAZINE, Suite 301, 801 York Mills Rd., Don Mills, Ontario M3B 1X7 Canada. (416)443-8888. Editor-in-Chief: Teddi Brown. 70% freelance written. Works with a small number of new/unpublished writers each year. Emphasizes noncompetitive outdoor recreation in Canada *only*. Magazine published 9 times/year. Circ. 141,000. Pays on publication. Publishes ms an average of 6-8 months after acceptance. Buys first rights. Submit seasonal/holiday material 1 year in advance of issue date. Byline given. Originals only. Computer printout submissions acceptable; no dot-matrix. *SASE or IRCs or material not returned*. Reports in 1 month. Mention *Writer's Market* in request for editorial guidelines.

Nonfiction: Adventures, outdoor issues, fishing, exploring, outdoor destinations in Canada, some how-to. Buys 35-40 mss/year, usually with photos. Length: 1,000-2,500 words. Pays $100 and up.

Photos: Emphasize people in the outdoors. Pays $20-50 for 8x10 b&w glossy prints; $30-150 for 35mm color transparencies; and $300/cover. Captions and model releases required.

News: Short news pieces. Buys 70-80/year. Length: 200-500 words. Pays $6/printed inch.

REFEREE, Referee Enterprises, Inc., Box 161, Franksville WI 53126. (414)632-8855. Editor: Tom Hammill. For well-educated, mostly 26- to 50-year-old male sports officials. 20-25% freelance written. Eager to work with new/unpublished writers; works with a small number of new/unpublished writers each year. Monthly magazine. Circ. 42,000. Pays on acceptance of completed manuscript. Publishes ms an average of 3-6 months after acceptance. Rights purchased varies. Submit seasonal/holiday material 6 months in advance. Photocopied and previously published submissions OK. Computer printout submissions acceptable. Reports in 2 weeks. Sample copy for 9x12 SAE and 5 first class stamps.

Nonfiction: How-to, informational, humor, interview, profile, personal experience, photo feature and technical. Buys 54 mss/year. Query. Length: 700-3,000 words. Pays 4-10¢/word. "No general sports articles." Sometimes pays the expenses of writers on assignment.

Photos: Purchased with or without accompanying ms or on assignment. Captions preferred. Send contact sheet, prints, negatives or transparencies. Pays $15-25 for each b&w used; $25-40 for each color used; $75-100 for color cover. Sometimes pays the expenses of writers on assignment.

Columns/Departments: Arena (bios); Law (legal aspects); Take Care (fitness, medical). Buys 24 mss/year. Query. Length: 200-800 words. Pays 4¢/word up to $50 maximum for Law and Take Care. Arena pays about $15 each, regardless of length.

Fillers: Jokes, gags, anecdotes, puzzles and referee shorts. Query. Length: 50-200 words. Pays 4¢/word in some cases; others offer only author credit lines.

Tips: "Queries with a specific idea appeal most to readers. Generally, we are looking more for feature writers, as we usually do our own shorter/filler-type material. It is helpful to obtain suitable photos to augment a story. Don't send fluff—we need hard-hitting, incisive material tailored just for our audience. Anything smacking of public relations is a no sale. Don't gloss over the material too lightly or fail to go in-depth looking for a quick sale (taking the avenue of least resistance)."

‡**SPORT**, Sport Magazine Association, 119 W. 40th St., New York NY 10018. (212)869-4700. Managing Editor: Peter Griffin. Editor: Neil Cohen. 70% freelance written. Monthly magazine covering primarily college and pro sports—baseball, football, basketball, hockey, boxing, tennis, others—for sports fans. Circ. 1.25 million. Pays on publication. Publishes ms an average of 2 months after acceptance. Byline given. Offers 25% kill fee. Buys first North American serial rights. Submit seasonal/holiday material 3 months in advance. Reports in 2 weeks.

Nonfiction: General interest, interview ("Beers with … "), and investigative reports on the world of sports. Buys 75 mss/year. Query with published clips. No telephone queries. Length: 2,500-3,000 words. Pays $1,000 minimum.

Columns/Departments: John Rolfe, associate editor. Sport Talk (briefs on news or offbeat aspects of sport). Buys 48 mss/year. Length: 250-500 words. Pays $100-150, depending on length and type of piece.

Tips: "Writers should read the magazine to keep up with the broadening subjects we're dealing with."

SPORTSCAN™, Brannigan-Demarco Communications, Inc., 141 5th Ave., New York NY 10010. (212)505-7600. Editor-in-Chief: Kevin McShane. Assistant Editor: Maggie Schwarz. 75% freelance written. A quarterly magazine covering sports nostalgia and sports training. "*Sportscan* is sponsored by a pharmaceutical company and sent free to doctors and pharmacists." Circ. 75,000. Pays on acceptance. Publishes an average of 4 months after acceptance. Offers 15% kill fee. Buys all rights. Submit seasonal/holiday material 4 months in advance. Photocopied and previously published submissions OK. Computer printout submissions acceptable; prefers letter-quality. Reports in 1 month on queries; 2 months on mss. Free writer's guidelines.

Nonfiction: Historical/nostalgic (sports-related); training (especially medical aspects); interview/profile (sports figures, especially nostalgic slant); and analysis of trends in sports. No sports medicine. Buys 20 mss/year. Query with published clips, or send complete ms. Length: 1,000-1,500 words. Pays $500-1,000 for assigned articles; pays $300-1,000 for unsolicited articles.

Photos: State availability of photos with submission. Reviews contact sheets. Offers $50-100/photo. Captions required. Buys one-time rights.

Columns/Departments: Fast Break (sports shorts, trivia, humorous news items, etc.), 200-250 words; Book Scan (book reviews of sports-related topics), 200-250 words; and Where Have You Gone (interviews with sports legends no longer in the public eye), 1,000-1,500 words. Buys 5 mss/year. Query with published clips or send complete ms. Pays $100-500.

Tips: "Send written query outlining the proposed article and any writing sample that might demonstrate the tone or angle. Sports nostalgia features and Fast Break items are most open to freelancers."

SPORTS PARADE, Meridian Publishing Co., Inc., Box 10010, Odgen UT 84409. (801)394-9446. 65% freelance written. Works with a small number of new/unpublished writers each year. A monthly general interest sports magazine distributed by business and professional firms to employees, customers, clients, etc. Readers are predominantly upscale, mainstream, family oriented. Circ. 40,000. Pays on acceptance. Publishes ms an average of 8 months after acceptance. Byline given. Buys first rights, second serial (reprint) rights or nonexclusive reprint rights. Submit seasonal/holiday material 6 months in advance. Simultaneous, photocopied and previously published submissions OK. Computer printout submissions acceptable; prefers letter-quality. Reports in 6 weeks. Sample copy $1 with 9x12 SAE; writer's guidelines for #10 SAE and 1 first class stamp.

Nonfiction: General interest and interview/profile. "General interest articles covering the entire sports spectrum, personality profiles on top flight professional and amateur sports figures." Buys 20 mss/year. Query. Length: 1,100-1,200 words. Pays 15¢/word.

Photos: Send with query or ms. Pays $35 for color transparencies; $50 for cover. Captions and model releases required.

Tips: "I will be purchasing more articles based on personalities—today's stars."

WISCONSIN SILENT SPORTS, Waupaca Publishing Co., Box 152, Waupaca WI 54981. (715)258-7731. Editor: Greg Marr. 75% freelance written. Eager to work with new/unpublished writers. Monthly magazine on running, cycling, cross-country skiing, canoeing, camping, backpacking, hiking. A regional publication aimed at people who run, cycle, cross-country ski, canoe, camp and hike in Wisconsin. Not a coffee-table magazine. "Our readers are participants form rank amateur weekend athletes to highly competitive racers." Circ. 10,000. Pays on publication. Publishes ms an average of 2 months after acceptance. Byline given. Offers 20% kill fee. Buys one-time rights. Submit seasonal/holiday material 2 months in advance. Simultaneous queries, and photocopied and previously published submissions OK. Computer printout submissions acceptable; prefers letter-quality. Reports in 1 month. Sample copy and writer's guidelines for 10x13 SAE and 5 first class stamps.

Nonfiction: General interest, how-to, interview/profile, new product, opinion, technical and travel. First-person articles discouraged. Buys 25 mss/year. Query. Length: 2,500 words maximum. Pays $15-100. Sometimes pays expenses of writers on assignment.

Tips: "Where-to-go, how-to, and personality profiles are areas most open to freelancers. Writers should keep in mind that this is a regional, Wisconsin-based publication. We do drift over into border areas occasionally but center on Wisconsin."

‡**YOUTH SPORTS, All-American**, Solfan Publications, 141 N. Orlando Ave., Cocoa Beach FL 32931. (305)799-3790. Editor: Rex E. Stevenson III. Managing Editor: Judy A. Jones. Associate Editor: Audrey C. Drysdale. A monthly magazine on youth sports. "Our publication is designed for athletes 7-18 years of age. Other readers include parents and coaches. We stress the good sport attitude, honesty and wholesomeness." Estab. 1987. Circ. 200,000. Pays on acceptance. Publishes ms an average of 3 months after acceptance. Byline given. Buys one-time rights or second-serial (reprint) rights. Simultaneous, photocopied and previously published submissions OK. Comptuer printout submissions OK; prefers letter-quality. Reports in 3 weeks on queries; 6 weeks on mss. Sample copy for 50¢ with 8½x11 SAE and $1.58 postage.

Nonfiction: General interest, historical/nostalgic (about sports figures), how-to (sports equipment), humor (suitable for kids), interview/profile (athletes, famous or not), opinion (written by kids mostly), personal experience, photo feature, travel (places kids would like to go). "Each September we publish a sports review annual in which we highlight all the state and national champions, other special events during the year, junior All-Americans, etc." Buys 12 mss/year. Query with or without published clips or send complete ms. Length: 1,500-3,000 words. Pays $200-300 for assigned articles; $100-200 for unsolicited articles.

Photos: Send photos with submission. Reviews transparencies and prints. Offers $5-10. Captions, model releases and identification of subjects required. Buys one-time rights.

Columns/Departments: Vision Quest (an aspiring young athlete who is heading for the top of his/her field or has overcome a handicap to do so); Chalk Talk (coaches and other sports experts give advice, training tips, personal experiences); Making The Grade (stories on student athletes who excel in academics as well as athletics); Sports Heritage (past American athletic champions); Brain-Drain (puzzles and quizzes). Buys 12 mss/year. Query. Length: 1,000-1,500 words. Pays $50-100.

Fiction: Adventure, historical, humorous, science fiction, sports. Buys 6 mss/year. Query. $1,000-5,000. Pays $50-200.

Poetry: Avant-garde, free verse, haiku, light verse, traditional. Sports-related poetry only. Buys 3 poems/year. No limit.

Fillers: Anecdotes, facts, gags, newsbreaks, short humor.

Golf

GOLF DIGEST, 5520 Park Ave., Trumbull CT 06611. (203)373-7000. Editor: Jerry Tarde. 30% freelance written. Emphasizes golfing. Monthly magazine. Circ. 1.3 million. Pays on acceptance. Publishes ms an average of 6 weeks after acceptance. Buys all rights. Byline given. Submit seasonal/holiday material 4 months in advance. Photocopied submissions OK. Computer printout submissions acceptable; prefers letter-quality. Reports in 6 weeks.

Nonfiction: How-to, informational, historical, humor, inspirational, interview, nostalgia, opinion, profile, travel, new product, personal experience, photo feature and technical; "all on playing and otherwise enjoying the game of golf." Query. Length: 1,000-2,500 words. Pays $150-1,500 depending on length of edited mss.

Photos: Nick DiDio, art director. Purchased without accompanying ms. Pays $75-150 for 5x7 or 8x10 b&w prints; $100-300/35mm color transparency. Model release required.

Poetry: Lois Hains, assistant editor. Light verse. Buys 1-2/issue. Length: 4-8 lines. Pays $25.

Fillers: Lois Hains, assistant editor. Jokes, gags, anecdotes, and cutlines for cartoons. Buys 1-2/issue. Length: 2-6 lines. Pays $10-25.

GOLF ILLUSTRATED, Family Media, Inc., 3 Park Ave., New York NY 10016. (212)340-9200. Editor: Al Barkow. Managing Editor: David Earl. 50% freelance written. Eager to work with new/unpublished writers. A monthly magazine covering personalities and developments in the sport of golf. Circ. 350,000. Pays on acceptance or publication. Publishes ms an average of 2 months after acceptance. Offers 10% kill fee. Buys all rights. Submit seasonal/holiday material 6 months in advance. Query for electronic submissions. Computer printout submissions acceptable; no dot-matrix. Reports in 3 weeks on queries; 6 weeks on manuscripts.

Nonfiction: Essays, historical/nostalgic, how-to, humor, interview/profile, opinion, personal experience, photo feature, and travel. Buys 70 mss/year. Query with published clips. Length: 750-1,750 words. Pays $500-1,500 for assigned articles; pays $250-1,000 for unsolicited articles. Sometimes pays the expenses of writers on assignment.

Photos: State availability of photos with submission. Reviews contact sheets and transparencies. Offers $50-500/photo. Captions and identification of subjects required. Buys one-time rights.

Columns/Departments: Health and Fitness, Food, and Opinion (all related to golf), approximately 750 words. Query with published clips. Pays $500-1,000.

Fillers: Anecdotes, facts, gags to be illustrated by cartoonist and short humor. Buys 30/year. Length: 100-500 words. Pays $25-300.

Tips: "A freelancer can best break in to our publication by following the personalities—the PGA, LPGA and PGA Senior tour pros and the nature of the game in general."

GOLF MAGAZINE, Times Mirror Magazines, Inc., 380 Madison Ave., New York NY 10017. (212)687-3000. Editor: George Peper. 25% freelance written. Works with a small number of new/unpublished writers each year. Monthly magazine. Golf audience, 95% male, ages 15-80, college-educated, professionals. Circ. 900,000. Pays on acceptance. Publishes ms an average of 6 months after acceptance. Byline given. Buys all rights. Submit seasonal/holiday material 4 months in advance. Photocopied submissions OK. Dot-matrix submissions acceptable if double-spaced. Reports in 4 weeks. Send mss to specific section editors—feature, instruction, Golf Reports, etc. General mss direct to James A. Frank, Executive Editor. Sample copy $2.

Nonfiction: How-to (improve game, instructional tips); informational (news in golf); humor; profile (people in golf); travel (golf courses, resorts); new product (golf equipment, apparel, teaching aids); and photo feature (great moments in golf—must be special; most photography on assignment only). Buys 4-6 unsolicited mss/year. Query. Length: 1,200-2,500 words. Pays $600-1,000. Sometimes pays expenses of writers on assignment.

Photos: Purchased with accompanying ms or on assignment. Captions required. Query. Pays $50 for 8½x11 glossy prints (with contact sheet and negatives); $75 minimum for 3x5 color prints. Total purchase price for ms includes payment for photos. Captions and model releases required.

Columns/Departments: Golf Reports (interesting golf events, feats, etc.); What's Going On (news of golf tours). Buys 5-10 mss/year. Query. Length: 250 words maximum. Pays $75. Open to suggestions for new columns/departments.

Fiction: Humorous or mystery. Must be golf-related. Buys 1-2 mss/year. Looking to do more in future. Query. Length: 1,200-2,000 words. Pays $500-750.

Tips: "Best chance is to aim for a light piece which is not too long and is focused on a personality. Anything very technical that would require a consummate knowledge of golf, we would rather assign ourselves. But if you are successful with something light and not too long, we might use you for something heavier later. We are looking for detailed knowledge of golf. Shorter items are a good test of knowledge. Probably the best way to break in would be by our Golf Reports section in which we run short items on interesting golf feats, events and so forth. If you send us something like that, about an important event in your area, it is an easy way for us to get acquainted."

‡GOLFWEEK, Box 1808, Dundee FL 33838. (813)439-7424. Assistant Publisher: Tom Stine. Editorial Director: Robert Feeman. 50% freelance written. Bimonthly magazine on golf in the Southeast United States. Circ. 33,000. Pays on publication. Publishes ms an average of 2-3 months after acceptance. Byline given. Buys one-time rights. Photocopied submissions OK. Computer printout submissions OK. Reports in 6 weeks. Sample copy $2.50.

Nonfiction: Historica/nostalgic, how-to, humor, interview/profile, new product, travel (golf courses, resorts, some international travel), golf course real estate, fashion. Buys 25-30 mss/year. Query. Length: 1,000-2,500 words. Pays $100-250. Pays expenses of writers on assignment.

Photos: State availability of photos with submission or send photos with submission. Reviews 35mm transparencies. Offers maximum $15-25 per photo. Sometimes does not offer additional payment for photos. Buys one-time rights.

Columns/Departments: Health and fitness, fashion, equipment, real estate, travel golf's heritage, clubhouse. Buys 6-10 mss/year. Query. Length: 800-1,500 words. Pays $50-150.

Fillers: Anecdotes, newsbreaks, short humor for bulletin board feature. Length: 25-75 words. Pays $15-25.

Tips: "Each issue has a different theme: Top 50 Golf Courses (Jan/Feb); Equipment (March/April); Resorts (May/June); Travel (July/August); Fashion (Sept./Oct.); Real Estate (Nov./Dec.). Helpful if mss aimed at specific issue, but not always necessary. The best way to break in is to write short pieces for departments. Extensive knowledge of golf is necessary for more technical pieces but not all departments. However, some knowledge of golf is necessary for any writer submitting mss. We're always looking for short pieces on interesting people who play the game, i.e., the golfer who is 85 and plays every day, national or local celebrities, etc."

GULF COAST GOLFER, Golfer Magazines, Inc., 9182 Old Katy Rd., Houston TX 77055. (713)464-0308. Editor: Bob Gray. 30% freelance written. Prefers to work with published/established writers. Monthly magazine covering results of major area competition, data on upcoming tournaments, reports of new and improved golf courses, and how-to tips for active, competitive golfers in Texas Gulf Coast area. Circ. 25,000. Pays on publication. Publishes ms an average of 1 month after acceptance. Byline given. Buys one-time rights. Submit seasonal/holiday material 3 months in advance. Reports in 3 weeks. Sample copy for 9x12 SAE and 4 first class stamps; free writer's guidelines.

Nonfiction: How-to and personal experience golf articles. No routine coverage. Query first. Length: by arrangement. Pays negotiable rates.
Tips: Especially wants articles on how-to subjects about golf in Gulf Coast area, but only on assignment basis.

NORTH TEXAS GOLFER, Golfer Magazines, Inc., 9182 Old Katy Rd., Houston TX 77055. (713)464-0308. Editor: Bob Gray. 30% freelance written. A monthly tabloid covering golf in North Texas. Emphasizes "grass roots coverage of regional golf course activities" and detailed, localized information on tournaments and competition in North Texas. Circ. 25,000. Pays on publication. Byline given. Buys one-time rights. Submit seasonal/holiday material 3 months in advance. Reports in 2 weeks. Sample copy for 9x12 SAE and 4 first class stamps.
Nonfiction: How-to, humor, interview/profile, personal experience and travel. Nothing outside of Texas. Buys 20 mss/year. Query. Length: 500-1,500 words. Pays $50-250 for assigned articles.
Photos: Send photos with submission. Offers no additional payment for photos accepted with ms. Identification of subjects required.
Tips: "We publish mostly how-to, where-to articles. They're about people and events in Texas only. We could use profiles of successful amateur and professional golfers in Texas—but only on a specific assignment basis. Most of the tour players already have been assigned to the staff or to freelancers. Do *not* approach people, schedule interviews, then tell us about it."

SCORE, Canada's Golf Magazine, Canadian Controlled Media Communications, 287 MacPherson Ave., Toronto, Ontario M4V 1A4 Canada. (416)928-2909. Managing Editor: John Gordon. 90% freelance written. Works with a small number of new/unpublished writers each year. Magazine published 7 times/year covering golf. "*Score* magazine provides seasonal coverage of the Canadian golf scene, professional, amateur, senior and junior golf for men and women golfers in Canada, the U.S. and Europe through profiles, history, travel, editorial comment and instruction." Circ. over 170,000. Pays on publication. Publishes ms an average of 1-3 months after acceptance. Byline given. Offers negotiable kill fee. Buys all rights and second serial (reprint) rights. Submit seasonal/holiday material 8 months in advance. Computer printout submissions acceptable; prefers letter-quality. Reports within 1 month. Sample copy for $2 (Canadian), 9x12 SAE and IRCs; writer's guidelines for #10 SAE and IRC.
Nonfiction: Book excerpts (golf); historical/nostalgic (golf and golf characters); interview/profile (prominent golf professionals); photo feature (golf); and travel (golf destinations only). The yearly April/May issue includes tournament results from Canada, the U.S., Europe, Asia, Australia, etc., history, profile, and regular features. "No personal experience, technical, opinion or general-interest material. Most articles are by assignment only." Buys 25-30 mss/year. Query with published clips. Length: 700-3,500 words. Pays $140-800.
Photos: Send photos with query or ms. Pays $50-100 for 35mm color transparencies (positives) or $30 for 8x10 or 5x7 b&w prints. Captions, model release (if necessary), and identification of subjects required. Buys all rights.
Columns/Departments: Profile (historical or current golf personalities or characters); Great Moments ("Great Moments in Canadian Golf"—description of great single moments, usually game triumphs); New Equipment (Canadian availability only); Travel (golf destinations, including "hard" information such as greens fees, hotel accommodations, etc.); Instruction (by special assignment only; usually from teaching golf professionals); The Mental Game (psychology of the game, by special assignment only); and History (golf equipment collections and collectors, development of the game, legendary figures and events). Buys 17-20 mss/year. Query with published clips or send complete ms. Length: 700-1,700 words. Pays $140-400.
Tips: "Only writers with an extensive knowledge of golf and familiarity with the Canadian and/or U.S. golf scene(s) should query or submit in-depth work to *Score*. Many of our features are written by professional people who play the game for a living or work in the industry. All areas mentioned under Columns/Departments are open to freelancers. Most of our *major* features are done on assignment only."

Guns

AMERICAN HANDGUNNER, Publishers' Development Corp., Suite 200, 591 Camino de la Reina, San Diego CA 92108. (619)297-5352. Editor: Cameron Hopkins. 90% freelance written. Eager to work with new/unpublished writers. A bimonthly magazine covering handguns, handgun sports, and handgun accessories. "Semi-technical publication for handgun enthusiasts of above-average knowledge/understanding of handguns. Writers must have ability to write about technical designs of handguns as well as ability to write intelligently about the legitimate sporting value of handguns." Circ. 150,000. Pays on publication. Publishes ms an average of 5-9 months after acceptance. Byline given. Offers $50 kill fee. Buys first North American serial rights. Submit seasonal/holiday material 7 months in advance. Previously published submissions OK. Computer printout submissions acceptable; prefers letter-quality. Reports in 1 week. Free sample copy and writer's guidelines.

Nonfiction: How-to, interview/profile, new product, photo feature, technical and "iconoclastic think pieces." Special issue is the *American Handgunner Annual*. No handgun competition coverage. Buys 60-70 mss/year. Query. Length: 500-3,000 words. Pays $175-600 for assigned articles; pays $100-400 for unsolicited articles. Sometimes pays the expenses of writers on assignment.

Photos: Send photos with submission. Reviews contact sheets, 35mm and 4x5 transparencies and 5x7 b&w prints. Offers no additional payment for b&w photos accepted with ms; offers $50-250/color photo. Captions and identification of subjects required. Buys first North American serial rights.

Columns/Departments: Combat Shooting (techniques, equipment, accessories for sport of combat shooting—no "blood and guts"), 600-800 words. Buys 40-60 mss/year. Query. Pays $175-200.

Tips: "We are always interested in 'round-up' pieces covering a particular product line or mixed bag of different product lines of the same theme. If vacation/travel takes you to an exotic place, we're interested in, say, 'The Guns of Upper Volta.' We are looking more closely at handgun hunting."

GUN DIGEST, HANDLOADER'S DIGEST, DBI Books, Inc., 4092 Commercial Ave., Northbrook IL 60062. (312)272-6310. Editor-in-Chief: Ken Warner. 50% freelance written. Prefers to work with published/established writers and works with a small number of new/unpublished writers each year. Annual journal covering guns and shooting. Pays on acceptance. Publishes ms an average of 20 months after acceptance. Byline given. Buys all rights. Computer printout submissions acceptable if legible; prefers letter-quality. Reports in 1 month.

Nonfiction: Buys 50 mss/issue. Query. Length: 500-5,000 words. Pays $100-600; includes photos or illustration package from author.

Photos: State availability of photos with query letter. Reviews 8x10 b&w prints. Payment for photos included in payment for ms. Captions required.

Tips: Award of $1,000 to author of best article (juried) in each issue.

GUN WORLD, 34249 Camino Capistrano, Box HH, Capistrano Beach CA 92624. Editorial Director: Jack Lewis. 50% freelance written. For ages that "range from mid-teens to mid-60s; many professional types who are interested in relaxation of hunting and shooting." Monthly. Circ. 136,000. Buys 80-100 unsolicited mss/year. Pays on acceptance. Publishes ms an average of 6 months after acceptance. Buys first rights and sometmes all rights, but rights reassigned on request. Byline given. Submit seasonal material 4 months in advance. Reports in 6 weeks. Computer printout submissions acceptable; prefers letter-quality. Copy of editorial requirements for SASE.

Nonfiction and Photos: General subject matter consists of "well-rounded articles—not by amateurs—on shooting techniques, with anecdotes; hunting stories with tips and knowledge integrated. No poems or fiction. We like broad humor in our articles, so long as it does not reflect upon firearms safety. Most arms magazines are pretty deadly and we feel shooting can be fun. Too much material aimed at pro-gun people. Most of this is staff-written and most shooters don't have to be told of their rights under the Constitution. We want articles on new developments; off-track inventions, novel military uses of arms; police armament and training techniques; do-it-yourself projects in this field." Buys informational, how-to, personal experience and nostalgia articles. Pays up to $300, sometimes more. Purchases photos with mss and captions required. Wants 5x7 b&w photos. Sometimes pays the expenses of writers on assignment.

Tips: "The most frequent mistake made by writers in completing an article for us is surface writing with no real knowledge of the subject. To break in, offer an anecdote having to do with proposed copy."

‡**GUNS MAGAZINE**, 591 Camino de la Reina, San Diego CA 92108. (619)297-5352. Editor: William O'Brien. 60% freelance written. Eager to work with new/unpublished writers. Monthly magazine for firearms enthusiasts. Circ. 135,000. Pays on publication. Publishes ms an average of 4 months after acceptance. Buys all rights. Computer printout submissions acceptable; no dot-matrix. Reports in 3 weeks. Free sample copy.

Nonfiction: Test reports on new firearms; how-to on gunsmithing, reloading; round-up articles on firearms types. Historical pieces. Does not want to see anything about "John and I went hunting" or rewrites of a general nature, or controversy for the sake of controversy, without new illumination. "More short, punchy articles will be used in the next year. Payments will not be as large as for full-length features, but the quantity used will give more writers a chance to get published." Buys 100-150 mss/year. Length: 1,000-2,500 words. Pays $100-350. Sometimes pays the expenses of writers on assignment.

Photos: Major emphasis is on good photos. No additional payment for b&w glossy prints purchased with mss. Pays $50-100 for color; 2¼x2¼ minimum.

‡**INSIGHTS, NRA News for Young Shooters**, National Rifle Association of America, 1600 Rhode Island Ave. NW, Washington DC 20036. (202)828-6059. Editor: Brenda K. Dalessandro. Managing Editor: John Robbins. 55% freelance written. Monthly magazine cover the shooting sports. "*InSights* is educational yet entertaining. It teaches young shooters and hunters proper and safe shooting techniques and gun handling. Readers are 8-20 years old; 88% are boys." Circ. 45,000. Pays on acceptance. Publishes ms an average of 1 month to 1 year after acceptance. Byline given. Buys first North American serial rights and second serial (reprint) rights. Submit seasonal/holiday material 6 months in advance. Photocopied submissions OK.

Computer printout submissions OK. Reports in 1 month on queries; 2 months on mss. Free sample copy and writer's guidelines.

Nonfiction: Historical/nostalgic, how-to, humor, interview/profile, personal experience, technical. "We do not accept manuscripts that are anti-guns or anti-hunting. Nor do we buy articles that describe unsafe or unethical shooting practices." Buys 45 mss/year. Query. Length: 800-1,500 words. Pays $150-200 for assigned articles; $80-200 for unsolicited articles.

Photos: Send photos with submission. Reviews contact sheets and 8x10 b&w prints. Offers $10-25 per photo. Captions and identification of subjects required. Buys one-time rights only.

Fiction: Adventure, historical, humorous, western. No unsafe or unethical shooting practices in fiction. Buys 8 mss/year. Query. Length: 800-1,500 words. Pays $80-150.

Tips: "We buy many mss about hunting trips that are unique somehow or teach our young readers about a certain of game. How-to articles like refinishing a gun stock or mounting a scope are purchased as well. Match results or event descriptions for competition shooting are also publishing; we must receive queries for competition shooting articles."

Horse Racing

THE BACKSTRETCH, 19363 James Couzens Hwy., Detroit MI 48235. (313)342-6144. Editor: Anne Moss. Managing Editor: Ruth LeGrove. 40% freelance written. Works with a small number of new/unpublished writers each year. Quarterly magazine. For Thoroughbred horse trainers, owners, breeders, farm managers, track personnel, jockeys, grooms and racing fans who span the age range from very young to very old. Publication of United Thoroughbred Trainers of America, Inc. Circ. 25,000. Publishes ms an average of 3 months after acceptance. Sample copy $2.

Nonfiction: *"Backstretch* contains mostly general information. Articles deal with biographical material on trainers, owners, jockeys, horses and their careers on and off the track, historical track articles, etc. Unless writer's material is related to Thoroughbreds and Thoroughbred racing, it should not be submitted. Articles accepted on speculation basis—payment made after material is used. If not suitable, articles are returned. Articles that do not require printing by a specified date are preferred. There is no special length requirement and amount paid depends on material. It is advisable to include photos, if possible. Articles should be original copies and should state whether presented to any other magazine, or whether previously printed in any other magazine. Submit complete ms. We do not buy crossword puzzles, cartoons, newspaper clippings, fiction or poetry."

THE FLORIDA HORSE, The Florida Horse, Inc., Box 2106, Ocala FL 32678. (904)629-8082. Editor: F.J. Audette. 25% freelance written. Monthly magazine covering the Florida thoroughbred horse industry. "We seek contemporary coverage and feature material on the Florida breeding, racing and sales scene." Circ. 12,000. Pays on publication. Publishes ms an average of 2 months after acceptance. Byline given. Buys first North American serial rights. Computer printout submissions acceptable; prefers letter-quality. Reports in 2 weeks. Free sample copy.

Nonfiction: Articles covering horses and people of the Florida thoroughbred industry. Buys 18-24 mss/year. Length: 1,500-3,000 words. Pays $125-200. Sometimes pays expenses of writers on assignment.

Photos: Send photos with ms. Pays $15-25 for sharp, well-composed 8x10 b&w prints. Captions and identification of subjects required. Buys one-time rights.

Columns/Departments: Medically Speaking (veterinarian analysis of equine problems); Legally Speaking (legal analysis of equine legal considerations); and Track Talk (news and features from racetracks—Florida angle only). Buys 24-36 mss/year. Send complete ms. Length: 800-960 words. Pays $35-50.

Tips: "We recommend that writers be at the scene of the action—racetracks, nurseries, provide clean, focused writing from the Florida angle and submit lively, interesting material full of detail and background."

HOOF BEATS, United States Trotting Association, 750 Michigan Ave., Columbus OH 43215. (614)224-2291. Editor: Dean A. Hoffman. 35% freelance written. Works with a small number of new/unpublished writers each year. Monthly magazine covering harness racing for the participants of the sport of harness racing. "We cover all aspects of the sport—racing, breeding, selling, etc." Circ. 26,000. Pays on publication. Publishes ms an average of 3 months after acceptance. Byline given. Buys negotiable rights. Submit seasonal/holiday material 3 months in advance. Computer printout submissions acceptable. Reports in 3 weeks. Free sample copy, postpaid.

Nonfiction: General interest, historical/nostalgic, humor, inspirational, interview/profile, new product, personal experience, photo feature. Buys 15-20 mss/year. Query. Length: open. Pays $100-400. Pays the expenses of writers on assignment "with approval."

Photos: State availability of photos. Pays variable rates for 35mm transparencies and prints. Identification of subjects required. Buys one-time rights.

Fiction: Historical, humorous, interesting fiction with a harness racing theme. Buys 2-3 mss/year. Query. Length: open. Pays $100-400.

SPEEDHORSE MAGAZINE/THE RACING REPORT, Speedhorse, Inc., Box 1000, Norman OK 73070. (405)288-2391. Editor: Diane C. Simmons. 20% freelance written. Prefers to work with published/established writers. A quarterly publication "devoted to those involved with breeding or racing quarter horses. Speed themes only; it is *not* a general circulation horse publication. *The Racing Report* is a weekly tabloid with special themes as well as timely, up-to-date stories, regarding the racing quarter horse industry." Circ. 9,000. Pays on publication. Publishes ms an average of 4 months after acceptance. Byline given. Offers negotiable kill fee. Buys negotiable rights. Simultaneous queries OK. Computer printout submissions acceptable; prefers letter-quality. Reports in 1 month. Sample copy $3.

Nonfiction: How-to (directed specifically at racing); interview/profile (of prominent horsemen); and photo feature (of racing). "Our articles address those topics which interest an experienced horseman. Articles dealing with ranch operations, racing bloodlines and race coverage are of special interest." No general interest stories. Special issues include Stallion articles (November, March); Stakes Winner Issues; Service Issues; articles on various services offered horsemen, i.e., transportation, trainers, travel, etc.; Broodmare Issues (June); Horse sales and auctions (July, August); Racing Wrap-up (September); and Thoroughbred Issues. Query. Length: 1,000 words minimum. Pay varies. Sometimes pays the expenses of writers on assignment.

Photos: Andrew Golden, photo editor. State availability of photos with query or ms. Reviews b&w and color contact sheets. Pay varies for b&w and color. Identification of subjects required. Buys one-time rights.

Columns/Departments: Book Review and Vet Medicine, by assignment only. Buys 1-2 mss/year. Query. Length: 1,000 words. Pays $50-75.

Tips: "If the writer has a good working knowledge of the horse industry and access to people involved with the quarter horse racing industry, the writer should call the editor to discuss possible stories. Very few blind articles are accepted. Most stories are assigned with much editorial direction. Most feature stories are assigned to freelance writers who have been regular contributors to *Speedhorse/The Racing Report*. They are located in areas of the country with active quarter horse racing. Many are track publicity directors or newspaper sports writers. The most frequent mistake made by writers in completing an article for us is that they do not write for the market. They send general interest articles rather than technical articles."

SPUR, Box 85, Middleburg VA 22117. (703)687-6314. Associate Publisher and Editor: Kerry Phelps. 80% freelance written. Prefers to work with published/established writers; works with a small number of new/unpublished writers each year. Bimonthly magazine covering Thoroughbred horses and the people who are involved in the business and sports of flat racing, steeplechasing and polo. Circ. 10,000. Pays on publication. Publishes ms an average of 3 months after acceptance. Byline given. Buys all rights. Computer printout submissions acceptable; prefers letter-quality. Reports in 1 month on mss and queries. Sample copy $3.50; writer's guidelines for #10 SAE and 1 first class stamp.

Nonfiction: Historical/nostalgic, Thoroughbred care, personality profile, farm, special feature, regional, photo essay, steeplechasing and polo. Buys 50 mss/year. Query with clips of published work, "or we will consider complete manuscripts." Length: 300-4,000 words. Payment negotiable. Sometimes pays the expenses of writers on assignment.

Photos: State availability of photos. Reviews color and b&w contact sheets. Captions, model releases and identification of subjects required. Buys all rights "unless otherwise negotiated."

Columns/Departments: Query or send complete ms to Editorial Dept. Length: 100-500 words. Pays $50 and up.

Tips: "Writers must have a knowledge of horses, horse owners, breeding, training, racing, and riding—or the ability to obtain this knowledge from a subject."

Hunting and Fishing

ALABAMA GAME & FISH, Game & Fish Publications, Inc., Suite 110, 2250 Newmarket Parkway, Marietta GA 30067. (404)953-9222. Editor: Rick Lavender. 90% freelance written. Monthly magazine on in-state outdoor topics of interest to an avid hunting and fishing audience. Circ. 19,695. Pays 75 days prior to cover date of issue. Publishes ms an average of 6 months after acceptance. Byline given. Offers negotiable kill fee. Buys first North American serial rights. Submit seasonal/holiday material 10 months in advance. Computer printout submissions OK; no dot-matrix. Editor prefers to hold queries on file until article is assigned or writer informs of prior sale. Reports in 3 months on mss. Sample copy for $2 and 9x12 SAE with 7 first class stamps; writer's guidelines for #11 SASE.

Nonfiction: Send photos with submission. Reviews 2x2 transparencies and 8x10 prints. Offers $25-250 per photo. Captions and identification of subjects required. Buys one-time rights.

Fiction: Gordon Whittington, fiction editor. Humorous (hunting and fishing topics). Buys 12 mss/year. Send complete ms. Length: 2,200-2,500 words. Pays $250-300.

Tips: "We publish hard-core hunting and fishing features for the purpose of informing and entertaining a loyal, state-specific outdoor audience. We do not publish the standard type or outdoor article in quantity. Study our magazine and restrict query ideas to major species in the state."

‡**AMERICAN CATFISHERMAN**, American Catfisherman Club, Box 576, Nixon TX 78140-0576. Editor: Beatrice Fincher. 100% freelance written. Quarterly catfishing publication. Estab. 1987. Pays on publication. Publishes ms an average of 4-6 months after acceptance. Byline given. Not copyrighted. Buys one-time rights. Submit seasonal/holiday material 4 months in advance. Simultaneous, photocopied and previously published submissions OK. Query for electronic submissions. Computer printout submissions OK; prefers letter-quality. Reports in 4 months on queries; 6 months on mss. Free sample copy and writer's guidelines.

Nonfiction: How-to, nostalgia, humor, new product, personal experience, photo feature. "Nothing but catfishing accepted—no other type of fishing." Buys 12-16 mss/year. Send complete ms. Length: 300-1,000 words. Pays 10¢ per word.

Photos: Send photos with submission. Pays $15 per b&w photo. Captions, model releases and identification of subjects required. Buys one-time rights.

Fillers: Anecdotes, facts, short humor, cartoons. Buys 3/year. Length: 100-150 words. Pays $15 per filler; $15 per black and white cartoon.

Tips: "Write for writer's guidelines and sample copy. Must be familiar with catfishing."

AMERICAN HUNTER, Suite 1000, 470 Spring Park Pl., Herndon VA 22070. Editor: Tom Fulgham. 90% freelance written. For hunters who are members of the National Rifle Association. Circ. 1.4 million. Buys first North American serial rights. Byline given. Free sample copy and writer's guidelines. Computer printout submissions acceptable; prefers letter-quality.

Nonfiction: Factual material on all phases of hunting. Not interested in material on fishing or camping. Prefers queries. Length: 2,000-3,000 words. Pays $250-450.

Photos: No additional payment made for photos used with mss. Pays $25 for b&w photos purchased without accompanying mss. Pays $50-300 for color.

ARKANSAS SPORTSMAN, Game & Fish Publications, Inc., Box 741, Marietta GA 30061. (404)953-9222. Editor: Bill Hartlage. See *Alabama Game & Fish*.

BADGER SPORTSMAN, Vercauteren Publishing, Inc., 19 E. Main, Chilton WI 53014. (414)849-4651. Editor: Mike Marquardt. Managing Editor: Gary Vercauteren. 80% freelance written. Monthly tabloid covering Wisconsin outdoors. Circ. 26,260. Pays on publication. Publishes ms an average of 1 month after acceptance. Byline given. Buys one-time rights. Submit seasonal/holiday material 2 months in advance. Previously published submissions OK. Computer printout submissions acceptable. Sample copy for 10x13 SAE with 3 first class stamps; free writer's guidelines.

Nonfiction: General interest; how-to (fishing, hunting, etc., in the Midwest outdoors); humor; interview/profile; personal experience; technical. Buys 400-500 mss/year. Query. Length: open. Pays 35¢/column inch ($15-40).

Photos: Send photos with accompanying query or ms. Reviews 3x5 or larger b&w and color prints. Pays by column inch. Identification of subjects required.

Tips: "We publish stories about *Wisconsin* fishing, hunting, camping; outdoor cooking; and general animal stories."

BASSIN', Box 185, Bixby OK 74008. (918)366-4441. Editor: Tony Dolle. 90% freelance written. Eager to work with new/unpublished writers. Magazine published 8 times/year covering freshwater fishing with emphasis on black bass. Circ. 265,000. Publishes ms an average of 6 months after acceptance. Pays on acceptance. Byline given. Buys first serial rights. Submit seasonal material 6 months in advance. Prefers queries but will examine mss accompanied by SASE. Query for electronic submissions. Computer printout submissions acceptable; no dot-matrix. Reports in 2-4 weeks. Sample copy $2; writer's guidelines for #10 SASE.

Nonfiction: How-to and where-to stories on bass fishing. Prefers completed ms. Length: 1,200-1,500 words. Pays $175-500 on acceptance.

Photos: Send photos with ms. Pays $300 for color cover; $100 for color cover inset. Send b&w prints or color transparencies. Buys one-time rights. Photo payment on publication.

Columns/Departments: Product reviews. Length: 100-700 words. Pays $50-150 on publication. Send complete ms.

Tips: "Reduce the common fishing slang terminology when writing for *Bassin'* (and other outdoor magazines). This slang is usually regional and confuses anglers in other areas of the country. Good strong features will win me over much more quickly than short articles or fillers. We need absolutely no poetry. We need stories on fishing tackle and techniques to catch largemouth, smallmouth, and spotted (Kentucky) bass."

BASSMASTER MAGAZINE, B.A.S.S. Publications, Box 17900, Montgomery AL 36141. (205)272-9530. Editor: Dave Precht. 80% freelance written. Prefers to work with published/established writers. Magazine (10 issues/year) about largemouth, smallmouth, spotted bass for dedicated beginning and advanced bass fishermen. Circ. 550,000. Pays on acceptance. Publication date of ms after acceptance "varies—seasonal material could take years''; average time is 8 months. Byline given. Buys all rights. Submit seasonal material 6 months in advance. Computer printout submissions OK; letter-quality only, not justified. Reports in 1 month. Sample copy $2; writer's guidelines for #10 SAE and 1 first class stamp.

Nonfiction: Historical; interview (of knowledgable people in the sport); profile (outstanding fishermen); travel (where to go to fish for bass); how-to (catch bass and enjoy the outdoors); new product (reels, rods and bass boats); and conservation related to bass fishing.''No 'Me and Joe Go Fishing' type articles.'' Query. Length: 400-2,100 words. Pays 20¢/word.

Columns/Departments: Short Cast/News & Views (upfront regular feature covering news-related events such as new state bass records, unusual bass fishing happenings, conservation, new products and editorial viewpoints); 250-400 words.

Photos: ''We want a mixture of black and white and color photos.'' Pays $50 minimum for b&w prints. Pays $300-350 for color cover transparencies. Captions required; model releases preferred. Buys all rights.

Fillers: Anecdotes, short humor and newsbreaks. Buys 4-5 mss/issue. Length: 250-500 words. Pays $50-100.

Tips: ''Editorial direction continues in the short, more direct how-to article. Compact, easy-to-read information is our objective. Shorter articles with good graphics, such as how-to diagrams, step-by-step instruction, etc., will enhance a writer's articles submitted to *Bassmaster Magazine*. The most frequent mistakes made by writers in completing an article for us are poor grammar, poor writing, poor organization and superficial research.''

BC OUTDOORS, SIP Division, Maclean Hunter Ltd., 202-1132 Hamilton St., Vancouver, British Columbia V6B 2S2 Canada. (604)687-1581. Editor: George Will. 80% freelance written. Works with a small number of new/unpublished writers each year. Outdoor recreation magazine published 10 times/year. *BC Outdoors* covers fishing, camping, hunting, and the environment of outdoor recreation. Circ. 40,000. Pays on acceptance. Publishes ms an average of 6 months after acceptance. Byline given. Offers negotiable kill fee. Buys first North American serial rights. Submit seasonal/holiday material 6 months in advance. Query for electronic submissions. Computer printout submissions acceptable; prefers letter-quality. Reports in 1 month on queries; 2 months on mss. Sample copy and writer's guidelines for 8x10 SAE with $2 postage.

Nonfiction: How-to (new or innovative articles on outdoor subjects); personal experience (outdoor adventure); and outdoor topics specific to British Columbia. ''We would like to receive how-to, where-to features dealing with hunting and fishing in British Columbia and the Yukon.'' Buys 80-90 mss/year. Query. Length: 1,500-2,000 words. Pays $300-450. Sometimes pays the expenses of writers on assignment.

Photos: State availability of photos with query. Pays $10-30 on publication for 5x7 b&w prints; $15-50 for color contact sheets and 35mm transparencies. Captions and identification of subjects required. Buys one-time rights.

Tips: ''More emphasis on saltwater angling and less emphasis on self-propelled activity, like hiking and canoeing will affect the types of freelance material we buy in 1988. Subject must be specific to British Columbia. We receive many manuscripts written by people who obviously do not know the magazine or market. The writer has a better chance of breaking in at our publication with short, lesser-paying articles and fillers, because we have a stable of regular writers in constant touch who produce most main features.''

CALIFORNIA ANGLER, The Journal For Freshwater and Saltwater Anglers In The Golden State, Outdoor Ventures, Ltd., Suite N, 1921 Carnegie, Santa Ana CA 92705. (714)261-9779. Executive Editor: Jim Gilmore. Managing Editor: Tom Waters. 80% freelance written. A recreational fishing magazine published monthly. Circ. 20,000. Pays during month prior to publication. Publishes ms an average of 2 months after acceptance. Byline given. Buys first rights, one-time rights, second serial (reprint) rights or makes-for-hire assignments. Submit seasonal/holiday material 3 months in advance. Simultaneous and photocopied submissions OK. Computer printout submissions OK. Reports in 1 month. Sample copy for 9x12 SAE with 8 first class stamps. ''We believe our magazine is the best and most articulate set of writer's guidelines for our purpose.''

Nonfiction: Tom Waters, freshwater pieces editor; Jim Gilmore, saltwater articles editor. How-to, humor, interview/profile, new product, opinion, personal experience (''if a true angler's adventure''), photo feature, technical and travel (where to fish in California). ''No 'me and Joe went fishing' articles.'' Buys 55-65 mss/year. Query with published clips. Length: 1,800-2,500 words. Pays $250-350.

Photos: Send photos with submission. Reviews 1x1⅜ transparencies and 5x7 or 8x10 prints. Offers no additional payment for photos accepted with ms. Captions and identification of subjects required. Buys one-time rights.

Columns/Departments: Fit-to-be-Tied (knots, rigging and fly-tying, photos required); Angler's Adventure (true-life adventures—exceptional angling experiences, photos, illustrations preferred); Clean Wake (California related fisheries management and conservation themes. Send pictures, diagrams, graphics, etc.). Buys 40-60 mss/year. Query with published clips. Length: 800-1,200 words. Pays $50-250.

Tips: ''The talented and innovative photographer tends to get our attention quickly. We have several new regular contributors who broke in because they consistently provided imaginative photography—action photos or underwater pictures showing gamefish in their native habitat. Manuscripts, as appropriate, should also be accompanied by where-to maps and how-to illustrations (in rough form, we will produce finished art). Dunc's Barbershop is most open to freelancers because we get so little humor writing that's really good, as well as Fit-To-Be-Tied—knots, rigging or how-to fishing tips presented and illustrated as if it were going to be published in *Popular Mechanics*."

‡**DAKOTA GAME & FISH**, Game & Fish Publications, Inc., Box 741, Marietta GA 30061. (404)953-9222. Editor: Rick Drennan. See *Alabama Game & Fish*.

DEER AND DEER HUNTING, The Stump Sitters, Inc., Box 1117, Appleton WI 54912. (414)734-0009. Editors: Al Hofacker and Dr. Rob Wegner. 80% freelance written. Prefers to work with published/established writers. Bimonthly magazine covering deer hunting for individuals who hunt with bow, gun, or camera. Circ. 120,000. Pays on publication. Publishes ms an average of 6 months after acceptance. Byline given. Offers $50 kill fee. Buys first North American serial rights and second serial (reprint) rights. Submit seasonal/holiday material 8 months in advance. Computer printout submissions acceptable; prefers letter-quality. Reports in 1 week on queries; 2 weeks on mss. Sample copy and writer's guidelines for 9x12 SAE with 7 first class stamps.
Nonfiction: Historical/nostalgic; how-to (hunting techniques); opinion; personal experience; photo feature; technical. "Our readers desire factual articles of a technical nature that relate deer behavior and habits to hunting methodology. We focus on deer biology, management principles and practices, habitat requirements, natural history of deer, hunting techniques, and hunting ethics." No hunting "Hot Spot" or "local" articles. Buys 40 mss/year. Query with clips of published work. Length: 1,000-4,000 words. Pays $50-400. Sometimes pays the expenses of writers on assignment.
Photos: State availability of photos. Pays $100 for 35mm color transparencies; $350 for front cover; $30 for 8x10 b&w prints. Captions and identification of subjects required. Buys one-time rights.
Columns/Departments: Deer Browse (unusual observations of deer behavior). Buys 20 mss/year. Length: 200-800 words. Pays $10-50.
Fillers: Clippings, anecdotes, newsbreaks. Buys 20/year. Length: 200-800 words. Pays $10-40.
Tips: "Break in by providing material of a technical nature, backed by scientific research, and written in a style understandable to the average deer hunter. We focus primarily on white-tailed deer."

FIELD & STREAM, 1515 Broadway, New York NY 10036. Editor: Duncan Barnes. 50% freelance written. Eager to work with new/unpublished writers. Monthly. Buys first rights. Byline given. Reports in 2 months. Query. Writer's guidelines for 8x10 SAE with 1 first class stamp.
Nonfiction and Photos: "This is a broad-based service magazine for the hunter and fisherman. Editorial content ranges from very basic how-to stories detailing a useful technique or a device that sportsmen can make to articles of penetrating depth about national hunting, fishing, and related activities. Also humor and personal essays, nostalgia, and 'mood pieces' on the hunting or fishing experience." Prefers color photos to b&w. Query first with photos. Length: 1,000-2,000 words. Payment varies depending on the quality of work, importance of the article. Pays $750 and up for major features. *Field & Stream* also publishes regional sections with feature articles on hunting and fishing in specific areas of the country. The sections are geographically divided into Northeast, Midwest, Far West, West and South, and appear 12 months a year. Usually buys photos with mss. When purchased separately, pays $450 minimum for color. Buys first rights to photos.
Fillers: Buys "how it's done" fillers of 500-900 words. Must be unusual or helpful subjects. Pays $250 on acceptance. Also buys "Field Guide" pieces, short (750-word maximum) articles on natural phenomena as specifically related to hunting and fishing; and "Myths and Misconceptions," short pieces debunking a commonly held belief about hunting and fishing. Pays $500.

FISHING & BOATING ILLUSTRATED, Gallant/Charger Publications, Inc., Box HH, Capistrano Beach CA 92624. (714)493-2101. Editor: Jack Lewis. Managing Editor: Burt Carey. 50% freelance written. A bimonthly magazine covering fishing and boating. "*Fishing & Boating Illustrated* is aimed at recreational fishermen and boaters who enjoy both. Geographic coverage is national, with how-to stories on many fish species." Circ. 50,000. Pays on acceptance. Byline given. Buys one-time rights and makes work-for-hire assignments. Query first. Computer printout submissions acceptable. Reports in 1 month. Sample copy $3.
Nonfiction: How-to (catching specific species of fish, maintaining boats) and technical (on boating projects). Buys 100 mss/year. Query. Length: 250-3,000 words. Pays $25-350.
Photos: Send photos with accompanying query or manuscript. Reviews 35mm transparencies and 8x10 prints. Pays $5-10 for prints, $25-100 for transparencies. Captions, model releases and identification of subjects required.
Tips: "We need queries by late spring for editorial planning. If a manufacturer's product tie-in is possible, so state. Photography must be excellent."

‡**FISHING AND HUNTING NEWS**, Outdoor Empire Publishing Co., Inc., 511 Eastlake Ave. E., Box 19000, Seattle WA 98109. (206)624-3845. Managing Editor: Vence Malernee. Assistant Managing Editor: Roland Stephan. Emphasizes fishing and hunting. Weekly tabloid. Circ. 140,000. Pays on acceptance. Buys all rights.

Submit seasonal/holiday material 3 months in advance. Photocopied submissions OK. Computer printout submissions OK.

Nonfiction: How-to (fish and hunt successfully, things that make outdoor jaunts more enjoyable/productive); photo feature (successful fishing/hunting in the western U.S.); informational. "No first person personal accounts of the 'me and Joe' variety or dated materials, as we are a weekly news publication." Buys 65 or more mss/year. Query. Length: 100-1,000 words. Pays $25 minimum.

Photos: Purchased with or without accompanying ms. Captions required. Submit prints or transparencies. Pays $5 minimum for b&w glossy prints; $25 minimum for 35mm or 2¼x2¼color transparencies. Looking for top-notch cover material. Transparencies preferred. Happy fishermen, hunters with their fish, game in tasteful setting."

Tips: "Competition in the outdoor publishing industry is very keen, and we are meeting it with increasingly timely and prognosticative articles. Writers should look for the new, the different, and the off-the-beaten track in hunting, fishing and outdoor activities."

FISHING WORLD, 51 Atlantic Ave., Floral Park NY 11001. Editor: Keith Gardner. 100% freelance written. Bimonthly. Circ. 350,000. Pays on acceptance. Buys first North American serial rights. Pays on acceptance. Publishes ms an average of 6 months after acceptance. Photocopied submissions OK. Reports in 2 weeks. Free sample copy.

Nonfiction: "Feature articles range from 1,000-2,000 words with the shorter preferred. A good selection of color transparencies should accompany each submission. Subject matter can range from a hot fishing site to tackle and techniques, from tips on taking individual species to a story on one lake or an entire region, either freshwater or salt. However, how-to is definitely preferred over where-to, and a strong biological/scientific slant is best of all. Where-to articles, especially if they describe foreign fishing, should be accompanied by sidebars covering how to make reservations and arrange transportation, how to get there, where to stay. Angling methods should be developed in clear detail, with accurate and useful information about tackle and boats. Depending on article length, suitability of photographs and other factors, payment is up to $300 for feature articles accompanied by suitable photography. Color transparencies selected for cover use pay an additional $300. B&w or unillustrated featurettes are also considered. These can be on anything remotely connected with fishing." Query. Length: 1,000 words. Pays $50-150 depending on length and photos. Brief queries accompanied by photos are preferred.

Photos: "Cover shots are purchased separately, rather than selected from those accompanying mss. The editor favors drama rather than serenity in selecting cover shots. Underwater horizontal portraits of fish are purchased (one-time rights) for centerfold use at the rate of $300 per transparency."

Tips: Looking for "quality photography and more West Coast fishing."

‡**FLORIDA GAME & FISH**, Game & Fish Publications, Inc., Box 741, Marietta GA 30061. (404)953-9222. Editor: Rick Lavender. See *Alabama Game & Fish*.

FLORIDA SPORTSMAN, Wickstrom Publishers Inc., 5901 S.W. 74 St., Miami FL 33143. (305)661-4222. Editor: Vic Dunaway. Managing Editor: Biff Lampton. 80% freelance written. Eager to work with new/unpublished writers. A monthly magazine covering fishing, boating and related sports— Florida and Caribbean only. Circ. 100,000. Pays on publication. Publishes ms an average of 6 months after acceptance. Byline given. Offers 50% kill fee. Buys first North American serial rights. Submit seasonal/holiday material 6 months in advance. Computer printout submissions acceptable; prefers letter-quality. Reports in 1 week on queries; 1 month on mss. Free sample copy; writer's guidelines for #10 SASE.

Nonfiction: Essays (environment or nature); how-to (fishing, hunting, boating); humor (outdoors angle); personal experience (in fishing, etc.); and technical (boats, tackle, etc., as particularly suitable for Florida specialties). "We use reader service pieces almost entirely—how-to, where-to, etc. One or two environmental pieces per issue as well. Writers *must* be Florida based, or have lengthy experience in Florida outdoors. All articles must have strong Florida emphasis. We do not want to see general how-to-fish-or-boat pieces which might well appear in a national or wide-regional magazine." Buys 120 mss/year. Query with or without published clips, or send complete ms. Length: 2,000-3,000 words. Pays $300-400 for assigned articles; pays $150-300 for unsolicited articles.

Photos: Send photos with submission. Reviews 35mm transparencies and 4x5 and larger prints. Offers no additional payment for photos accepted with ms. Buys one-time rights.

Columns/Departments: Sportsman Scene (news-feature items on outdoors subjects), 100-500 words; Angler's Clinic (short, detailed fishing how-to), 250-750 words; and Sportsman Recipe (recipes for Florida fish and game), 250-1,000 words. Buys 50 mss/year. Send complete ms. Pays $15-100.

Tips: "Feature articles are most open to freelancers; however there is little chance of acceptance unless contributor is an accomplished and avid outdoorsman *and* a competent writer-photographer with considerable experience in Florida."

FLORIDA WILDLIFE, Florida Game & Fresh Water Fish Commission, 620 South Meridian St., Tallahassee FL 32399-1600. (904)488-5563. Editor: John M. Waters, Jr. About 75% freelance written. Bimonthly state magazine covering hunting, fishing and wildlife conservation. "In outdoors sporting articles we seek themes of wholesome recreation. In nature articles we seek accuracy and conservation purpose." Circ. 29,000. Pays on publication. Publishes ms 2 months to 2 years after acceptance. Byline given. Buys first North American serial rights and occasionally second serial (reprint) rights. Submit seasonal/holiday material 6 months in advance. Simultaneous queries, and simultaneous, photocopied, and previously published submissions OK. "Inform us if it is previously published work." Computer printout submissions acceptable if double-spaced. Reports in 6 weeks on queries; variable on mss. Sample copy $1.25; free writer's guidelines.

Nonfiction: General interest (bird watching, hiking, camping, boating); how-to (hunting and fishing); humor (wildlife related; no anthropomorphism); inspirational (conservation oriented); personal experience (wildlife, hunting, fishing, outdoors); photo feature (Florida species: game, nongame, botany); and technical (rarely purchased, but open to experts). "In a nutshell, we buy general interest hunting, fishing and nature stories. No 'me and Joe' stories, stories that humanize animals, or opinionated stories not based on confirmable facts." Buys 50-60 mss/year. Query. Length: 500-2,500 words. Generally pays $50/publisheed page; including use of photos.

Photos: State availability of photos with story query. Prefers 35mm color slides of hunting, fishing, and natural science series of Florida wildlife species. Pays $10-50 for inside photos; $100 for front cover photos, $50 for back cover. "We like short, specific captions." Buys one-time rights.

Fiction: "We rarely buy fiction, and then only if it is true to life and directly related to good sportsmanship and conservation. No fairy tales, erotica, profanity, or obscenity." Buys 2-3 mss/year. Send complete mss and label "fiction." Length: 500-2,500 words. Generally pays $50/published page.

Tips: "Read and study recent issues for subject matter, style and examples of our viewpoint, philosophy and treatment. The area of hunting is one requiring sensitivity. We look for wholesome recreation, ethics, safety, and good outdoor experience more than bagging the game in our stories. Of special need at this time are well-written hunting and fishing in Florida articles. Unsolicited articles sent to us generally fail to be well written, and accurate, and lack reader interest."

FLY FISHERMAN, Historical Times, Inc., 2245 Kohn Rd., Box 8200, Harrisburg PA 17105. (717)657-9555. Editor: John Randolph. Associate Editors: Jack Russell and Philip Hanyok. 85-90% freelance written. Magazine published 6 times/year on fly fishing. Circ. 137,000. Pays on acceptance. Publishes ms an average 10 months after acceptance. Byline given. Buys first North American serial rights and (selectively) all rights. Submit seasonal/holiday material 1 year in advance. Query for electronic submissions. Computer printout submissions acceptable; prefers letter-quality. Reports in 3 weeks on queries; 6 weeks on mss. Sample copy for 11x14 SAE and 4 first class stamps. Writer's guidelines for #10 SASE.

Nonfiction: Book excerpts, how-to, humor, interview/profile, technical and essays on fly fishing, fly tying, shorts and fishing technique shorts and features. Where-to. No other types of fishing, including spin or bait. Buys 75 mss/year. Query or send complete ms. Length: 50-3,000 words. Pays $35-500.

Photos: State availability of photos or send photos with query or ms. Reviews b&w contact sheets and 35mm transparencies. Pays $35-100 for contact sheets; $25-200 for transparencies; $400 for cover photos. Captions, model releases and identification of subjects required. Buys one-time rights.

Columns/Departments: Fly Fisherman's Bookshelf—500 to 1,000-word book reviews ($75 each); reviews of fly fishing video tapes $75, same length. Buys 8 mss/year. Query. Length: 500-1,000 words. Pays $75.

Fiction: Essays on fly fishing, humorous and serious. No long articles, anything over 3,000 words. Buys 4 mss/year. Query with published clips. Length: 1,200-3,000 words. Pays $125-500.

Fillers: Short humor and newsbreaks. Buys 30/year. Length: 25-1,000 words. Pays $25-250.

Tips: "Our magazine is a tightly focused, technique-intensive special interest magazine. Articles require fly fishing expertise and writing must be tight and in many instances well researched. The novice fly fisher has little hope of a sale with us, although perhaps 30 percent of our features are entry-level or intermediate-level in nature. Fly fishing technique pieces that are broadly focused have great appeal. Both features and departments—short features—have the best chance of purchase. Accompany submissions with excellent color slides (35mm), black and white 8x10 prints or line drawing illustrations."

THE FLYFISHER, 1387 Cambridge, Idaho Falls ID 83401. (208)523-7300. Editor: Dennis G. Bitton. 90% freelance written. Works with a small number of new/unpublished writers each year. "Any good submission gets worked in, and we could use some new writers." Quarterly magazine. *The Flyfisher* is the official publication of The Federation of Fly Fishers, a nonprofit organization of member clubs and individuals in the U.S., Canada, United Kingdom, France, New Zealand, Chile, Argentina, Japan and other nations. It serves an audience of conservation-minded fly fishermen." Circ. 12,500. Pays after publication. Publishes ms an average of 4 months after acceptance. Byline given. Buys first North American serial rights. Submit seasonal/holiday material 60 days in advance. Computer printout submissions acceptable; no dot-matrix. Reports in 2 weeks. Sample copy $3, available from FFF, Box 1088, West Yellowstone MT 59758. Writer's guidelines for SASE; write to 1387 Cambridge, Idaho Falls ID 83401.

Nonfiction: How-to (fly fishing techniques, fly tying, tackle, etc.); general interest (any type including where to go, conservation); historical (places, people, events that have significance to fly fishing); inspirational (looking for articles dealing with Federation clubs on conservation projects); interview (articles of famous fly fishermen, fly tyers, teachers, etc.); nostalgia (articles of reminiscences on flies, fishing personalities, equipment and places); and technical (about techniques of fly fishing in salt and fresh waters). Buys 6-8 mss/issue. Query. Length: 500-2,500 words. Pays $50-200.

Photos: Pays $15-50 for 8x10 b&w glossy prints; $20-80 for 35mm or larger color transparencies for inside use and $100-150 for covers. Captions required. Buys one-time rights. Prefers a selection of transparencies and glossies when illustrating a manuscript, which are purchased as a package.

Fiction: (Must be related to fly fishing). Adventure, conservation, fantasy, historical, humorous, and suspense. Buys 2 mss/issue. Query. Length, 500-2,000 words. Pays $75-200.

Tips: "We make every effort to assist a writer with visuals if the idea is strong enough to develop. We will deal with freelancers breaking into the field. Our only concern is that the material be in keeping with the quality established. We prefer articles submitted by members of FFF, but do not limit our selection of good articles."

FUR-FISH-GAME, 2878 E. Main, Columbus OH 43209. Editor: Ken Dunwoody. 65% freelance written. Works with a small number of new/unpublished writers each year. Monthly magazine. For outdoorsmen of all ages who are interested in hunting, fishing, trapping, dogs, camping, conservation and related topics. Circ. 180,000. Pays on acceptance. Publishes ms an average of 7 months after acceptance. Byline given. Buys first serial rights or all rights. Prefers nonsimultaneous submissions. Computer printout submissions acceptable; prefers letter-quality. Reports in 6 weeks. Submit complete ms with photos and SASE. Writer's guidelines for 8½x11 SASE.

Nonfiction: "We are looking for informative, down-to-earth stories about hunting, fishing, trapping, dogs, camping, boating, conservation and related subjects. Nostalgic articles are also used. Many of our stories are 'how-to' and should appeal to small-town and rural readers who are true outdoorsmen. Some recent articles have told how to train a gun dog, catch big-water catfish, outfit a bowhunter and trap late-season muskrat. We also use personal experience stories and an occasional profile, such as an article about an old-time trapper. 'Where-to' stories are used occasionally if they have broad appeal. Length: 1,500-3,000 words. Pays $75-150 depending upon quality, photo support, and importance to magazine. Short filler stories pay $35-80."

Photos: Send photos with ms. Photos are part of ms package and receive no additional payment. Prefer b&w but color prints or transparencies OK. Prints can be 5x7 or 8x10. Caption information required.

Tips: "We are always looking for quality articles that tell how to hunt or fish for game animals or birds that are popular with everyday outdoorsmen but often overlooked in other publications, such as catfish, bluegill, crappie, squirrel, rabbit, crows, etc. We also use articles on standard seasonal subjects such as deer and pheasant, but like to see a fresh approach or new technique. Trapping articles, especially instructional ones based on personal experience, are useful all year. Articles on gun dogs, ginseng and do-it-yourself projects are also popular with our readers. An assortment of photos and/or sketches greatly enhances any ms, and sidebars, where applicable, can also help."

GEORGIA SPORTSMAN, Game & Fish Publications, Box 741, Marietta GA 30061. (404)953-9222. Editor: Rick Lavender. See *Alabama Game & Fish.*

GREAT LAKES FISHERMAN, Great Lakes Fisherman Publishing Co., Suite 101, 921 Eastwind Dr., Westerville OH 43081. (614)882-5653. Editor: Ottie M. Snyder, Jr. 95% freelance written. Eager to work with new/unpublished writers. Monthly magazine covering how, when and where to fish in the Great Lakes region. Circ. 50,000. Pays on 15th of month prior to issue date. Publishes ms an average of 8 months after acceptance. Byline given. Offers $40 kill fee. Buys first North American serial rights. Submit seasonal/holiday material 8-12 months in advance. Computer printout submissions acceptable; prefers letter-quality. Reports in 5 weeks. Free sample copy and writer's guidelines for 9x12 SAE with 5 first class stamps.

Nonfiction: How-to (where to and when to freshwater fish). "No 'me and Joe' or subject matter outside the Great Lakes region." Buys 84 mss/year. Query with clips of published work. "Letters should be tightly written, but descriptive enough to present no surprises when the ms is received. Prefer b&w photos to be used to illustrate ms with query." Length: 1,000-1,500 words. Pays $135-200. Sometimes pays telephone expenses of writers on assignment.

Photos: Send photos with ms. "Black and white photos are considered part of manuscript package and as such receive no additional payment. We consider b&w photos to be a vital part of a ms package. We look for four types of illustration with each article: scene (a backed off shot of fisherman); result (not the typical meat shot of angler grinning at camera with big stringer but in most cases just a single nice fish with the angler admiring the fish); method (a lure shot or illustration of special rigs mentioned in the text); and action (angler landing a fish, fighting a fish, etc.). Illustrations (line drawings) need not be finished art but should be good enough for our artist to get the idea of what the author is trying to depict." Prefers cover shots to be verticals with fish and fisherman action shots. Pays $150 for 35mm color transparencies. Captions, model releases and identification of subjects required. Buys one-time rights.

Tips: "Our feature articles are 95% freelance material. The magazine is circulated in the eight states bordering the Great Lakes, an area where one-third of the nation's licensed anglers reside. All of our feature content is how, when or where, or a combination of all three covering the species common to the region. Fishing is an age-old sport with countless words printed on the subject each year. A fresh new slant that indicates a desire to share with the reader the author's knowledge is a sale. We expect the freelancer to answer any anticipated questions the reader might have (on accommodations, launch sites, equipment needed, etc.) within the ms. We publish an equal mix each month of both warm- and cold-water species articles."

GULF COAST FISHERMAN, Harold Wells Gulf Coast Fisherman, Inc., 205 Bowie, Drawer P, Port Lavaca TX 77979. (512)552-8864. Editor: Gary M. Ralston. 95% freelance written. A quarterly magazine covering Gulf Coast saltwater fishing. "All editorial material is designed to expand the knowledge of the Gulf Coast angler and promote saltwater fishing in general. Our audience is composed principally of persons from managerial/professional occupations." Circ 15,000. Pays on publication. Publishes ms an average of 2 months after acceptance. Byline given. Buys first North American serial rights. Submit seasonal/holiday material 2 months in advance. Computer printout submissions acceptable; prefers letter-quality. Submissions of manuscripts on 3½ or 5¼ diskette most preferred. Sample copy and writer's guidelines for 9x12 SAE and 5 first class stamps.
Nonfiction: How-to (any aspect relating to saltwater fishing that provides the reader specifics on use of tackle, boats, finding fish, etc.); interview/profile; new product; personal experience; and technical. Buys 25 mss/year. Query with or without published clips, or send complete ms. Length: 900-1,800 words. Pays $90-150.
Photos: State availability of photos with submission. Offers no additional payment for photos accepted with ms. Captions and identification of subjects required. Buys one-time rights.
Tips: "Features are the area of our publication most open to freelancers. Subject matter should concern some aspect of or be in relation to saltwater fishing in coastal bays or offshore."

‡**ILLINOIS GAME & FISH**, Game & Fish Publications, Inc., Box 741, Marietta GA 30061. (404)953-9222. Editor: Ken Dunwoody. See *Alabama Game & Fish*.

‡**INDIANA GAME & FISH**, Game & Fish Publications, Inc., Box 741, Marietta GA 30061. (404)953-9222. Editor: Chris Dorsey. See *Alabama Game & Fish*.

‡**IOWA GAME & FISH**, Game & Fish Publications, Inc., Box 741, Marietta GA 30061. (404)953-9222. Editor: Chris Dorsey. See *Alabama Game & Fish*.

‡**KANSAS GAME & FISH**, Game & Fish Publications, Inc., Box 741, Marietta GA 30061. (404)953-9222. Editor: Rick Drennan. See *Alabama Game & Fish*.

‡**KENTUCKY GAME & FISH**, Game & Fish Publications, Inc., Box 741, Marietta GA 30061. (404)953-9222. Editor: Bill Hartlage. See *Alabama Game & Fish*.

‡**LOUISIANA GAME & FISH**, Game & Fish Publications, Inc., Box 741, Marietta GA 30061. (404)953-9222. Editor: Steve Lightfoot. See *Alabama Game & Fish*.

THE MAINE SPORTSMAN, Box 365, Augusta ME 04330. Editor: Harry Vanderweide. 100% freelance written. "Eager to work with new/unpublished writers, but because we run over 30 regular columns, it's hard to get into *The Maine Sportsman* as a beginner." Monthly tabloid. Circ. 30,000. Pays "during month of publication." Buys first rights. Publishes ms an average of 3 months after acceptance. Byline given. Computer printout submissions acceptable; prefers letter-quality. Reports in 2-4 weeks.
Nonfiction: "We publish only articles about Maine hunting and fishing activities. Any well-written, researched, knowledgeable article about that subject area is likely to be accepted by us." Expose, how-to, general interest, interview, nostalgia, personal experience, opinion, profile, and technical. Buys 25-40 mss/issue. Submit complete ms. Length: 200-2,000 words. Pays $20-300. Sometimes pays the expenses of writers on assignment.
Photos: "We can have illustrations drawn, but prefer 1-3 b&w photos." Submit photos with accompanying ms. Pays $5-50 for b&w print.
Tips: "It's rewarding finding a writer who has a fresh way of looking at ordinary events. Specific where-to-go about Maine is needed."

‡**MARYLAND-DELAWARE GAME & FISH**, Game & Fish Publications, Inc., Box 741, Marietta GA 30061. (404)953-9222. Editor: Aaron Pass. See *Alabama Game & Fish*.

MICHIGAN OUT-OF-DOORS, Box 30235, Lansing MI 48909. (517)371-1041. Editor: Kenneth S. Lowe. 50% freelance written. Works with a small number of new/unpublished writers each year. Emphasizes outdoor recreation, especially hunting and fishing, conservation and environmental affairs. Monthly magazine. Circ.

110,000. Pays on acceptance. Publishes ms an average of 6 months after acceptance. Byline given. Buys first North American serial rights. Phone queries OK. Submit seasonal/holiday material 6 months in advance. Computer printout submissions acceptable; prefers letter-quality. Reports in 1 month. Sample copy $1.50; free writer's guidelines.

Nonfiction: Expose, historical, how-to, informational, interview, nostalgia, personal experience, personal opinion, photo feature and profile. No humor. "Stories *must* have a Michigan slant unless they treat a subject of universal interest to our readers." Buys 8 mss/issue. Send complete ms. Length: 1,000-3,000 words. Pays $75 minimum for feature stories. Pays expenses of writers on assignment.

Photos: Purchased with or without accompanying ms. Pays $15 minimum for any size b&w glossy prints; $60 maximum for color (for cover). Offers no additional payment for photos accepted with accompanying ms. Buys one-time rights. Captions preferred.

Tips: "Top priority is placed on true accounts of personal adventures in the out-of-doors—well-written tales of very unusual incidents encountered while hunting, fishing, camping, hiking, etc. The most rewarding aspect of working with freelancers is realizing we had a part in their development. But it's annoying to respond to queries that never produce a manuscript."

‡**MICHIGAN SPORTSMAN**, Game & Fish Publications, Inc., Box 741, Marietta GA 30061. (404)953-9222. Editor: Ken Dunwoody. See *Alabama Game & Fish*.

MID WEST OUTDOORS, Mid West Outdoors, Ltd., 111 Shore Drive, Hinsdale (Burr Ridge) IL 60521. (312)887-7722. Editor: Gene Laulunen. Emphasizes fishing, hunting, camping and boating. Monthly tabloid. 100% freelance written. Circ. 39,000. Pays on publication. Buys simultaneous rights. Byline given. Submit seasonal material 2 months in advance. Simultaneous, photocopied and previously published submissions OK. Reports in 3 weeks. Publishes ms an average of 3 months after acceptance. Sample copy $1; free writer's guidelines.

Nonfiction: How-to (fishing, hunting, camping in the Midwest) and where-to-go (fishing, hunting, camping within 500 miles of Chicago). "We do not want to see any articles on 'my first fishing, hunting or camping experiences,' 'Cleaning My Tackle Box,' 'Tackle Tune-up,' or 'Catch and Release.' " Buys 840 unsolicited mss/year. Send complete ms. Length: 1,000-1,500 words. Pays $15-25.

Photos: Offers no additional payment for photos accompanying ms; uses b&w prints. Buys all rights. Captions required.

Columns/Departments: Fishing, Hunting. Open to suggestions for columns/departments. Send complete ms. Pays $25.

Tips: "Break in with a great unknown fishing hole within 500 miles of Chicago. Where, how, when and why. Know the type of publication you are sending material to."

MINNESOTA SPORTSMAN, Game & Fish Publications, Inc., Box 741, Marietta GA 30061. (404)953-9222. Editor: Ken Dunwoody. See *Alabama Game & Fish*.

MISSISSIPPI GAME & FISH, Game & Fish Publications, Inc., Box 741, Marietta GA 30061. (404)953-9222. Editor: Steve Lightfoot. See *Alabama Game & Fish*.

‡**MISSOURI GAME & FISH**, Game & Fish Publications, Inc., Box 741, Marietta GA 30061. (404)953-9222. Editor: Bill Hartlage. See *Alabama Game & Fish*.

‡**NEBRASKA GAME & FISH**, Game & Fish Publications, Inc., Box 741, Marietta GA 30061. (404)953-9222. Editor: Rick Drennan. See *Alabama Game & Fish*.

‡**NEW ENGLAND GAME & FISH**, Game & Fish Publications, Inc., Box 741, Marietta GA 30061. (404)953-9222. Editor: Mike Toth. See *Alabama Game & Fish*.

‡**NEW JERSEY GAME & FISH**, Game & Fish Publications, Inc., Box 741, Marietta GA 30061. (404)953-9222. Editor: Mike Toth. See *Alabama Game & Fish*.

‡**NEW YORK GAME & FISH**, Game & Fish Publications, Inc., Box 741, Marietta GA 30061. (404)953-9222. Editor: Mike Toth. See *Alabama Game & Fish*.

NORTH AMERICAN HUNTER, Official Publication of the North American Hunting Club, North American Hunting Club, Box 35557, Minneapolis MN 55435. (612)941-7654. Editor: Mark LaBarbera. Managing Editor: Bill Miller. 50% freelance written. A bimonthly magazine for members of the North American Hunting Club covering strictly North American hunting. "The purpose of the NAHC is to enhance the hunting skill and enjoyment of its 155,000 members." Circ. 155,000. Pays on acceptance. Publishes ms an average of 6-10 months after acceptance. Byline given. Buys first North American serial rights, first rights, one-time rights, second serial (reprint) rights, or all rights. Submit seasonal/holiday material 1 year in advance. Query for electronic submissions. Computer printout submissions acceptable; prefers letter-quality. Reports in 3 weeks. Sample copy $3; writer's guidelines for #10 SAE with 1 first class stamp.

Nonfiction: Exposé (on hunting issues); how-to (on hunting); humor; interview/profile; new product; opinion; personal experience; photo feature and where-to-hunt. No fiction or "Me and Joe". Buys 18-24 mss/year. Query. Length: 1,000-2,500 words. Pays $200-325 for assigned articles; pays $25-325 for unsolicited articles.

Photos: Send photos with submissions. Reviews transparencies and 5x7 or 8x10 prints. Offers no additional payment for photos accepted with ms. Captions and identification of subjects required. Buys one-time rights.

Tips: "Write stories as if they are from one hunting friend to another."

NORTH AMERICAN WHITETAIL, The Magazine Devoted to the Serious Trophy Deer Hunter, Game & Fish Publications, Inc., Suite 110, 2250 Newmarket Parkway, Marietta GA 30067. (404)953-9222. Editor: Gordon Whittington. 70% freelance written. Magazine, published 8 times/year, about hunting trophy-class white-tailed deer in North America, primarily the U.S. "We provide the serious hunter with highly sophisticated information about trophy-class whitetails and how, when and where to hunt them. We are not a general hunting magazine or a magazine for the very occasional deer hunter." Pays 75 days prior to cover date of issue. Publishes ms an average of 6 months after acceptance. Byline given. Offers negotiable kill fee. Buys first North American serial rights. Submit seasonal/holiday material 10 months in advance. Computer printout submissions OK; no dot-matrix. Reports in 3 months on mss. Editor prefers to keep queries on file, without notification, until the article can be assigned or author informs of prior sale. Sample copy $3 with 9x12 SAE and 7 first class stamps. Writer's guidelines for #11 SASE.

Nonfiction: How-to, humor, interview/profile. Buys 50 mss/year. Query. Length: 1,400-3,000 words. Pays $150-400.

Photos: Send photos with submission. Reviews 2x2 transparencies and 8x10 prints. Offers no additional payment for photos accepted with ms. Captions and identification of subjects required. Buys one-time rights.

Columns/Departments: Trails and Tails (nostalgic, humorous or other entertaining styles of deer-hunting material, fictional or nonfictional), 1,400 words. Buys 8 mss/year. Send complete ms. Pays $150.

Fiction: Humorous (aimed at the deer hunter). Buys 5 mss/year. Send complete ms. length: 2,200-2,500. Pays $300-400.

Tips: "Our articles are written by persons who are deer hunters first, writers second. Our hard-core hunting audience can see through material produced by non-hunters or those with only marginal deer-hunting expertise. We have a continual need for expert profiles/interviews. Study the magazine to see what type of hunting expert it takes to qualify for our use, and look at how those articles have been directed by the writers. Good photography of the interviewee and his hunting results must accompany such pieces."

‡**NORTH CAROLINA GAME & FISH**, Game & Fish Publications, Inc., Box 741, Marietta GA 30061. (404)953-9222. Editor: Aaron Pass. See *Alabama Game & Fish*.

OHIO FISHERMAN, Ohio Fisherman Publishing Co., Suite 101, 921 Eastwind Dr., Westerville OH 43081. (614)882-5658. Editor: Ottie M. Snyder, Jr. 95% freelance written. Works with a small number of new/unpublished writers each year. Monthly magazine covering the how, when and where of Ohio fishing. Circ. 45,000. Pays on 15th of month prior to issue date. Publishes ms an average of 4-6 months after acceptance. Byline given. Offers $40 kill fee. Buys first rights. Submit seasonal/holiday material 6-8 months in advance. Computer printout submissions acceptable; prefers letter-quality. Reports in 5 weeks. Sample copy and writer's guidelines for 9x12 SAE and 5 first class stamps.

Nonfiction: How-to (also where to and when to fresh water fish). "Our feature articles are 95% freelance material, and all have the same basic theme—sharing fishing knowledge. No 'me and Joe' articles." Buys 84 mss/year. Query with clips of published work. Letters should be "tightly written, but descriptive enough to present no surprises when the ms is received. Prefer b&w photos to be used to illustrate ms with query." Length: 1,000-1,500 words. Pays $135-175. Sometimes pays telephone expenses of writers on assignment.

Photos: "Need cover photos constantly." Pays $150 for 35mm color transparencies (cover use); buys b&w prints as part of ms package—"no additional payments." Captions and identification of subjects required. Buys one-time rights.

Tips: "The specialist and regional markets are here to stay. They both offer the freelancer the opportunity for steady income. Fishing is an age-old sport with countless words printed on the subject each year. A fresh new slant that indicates a desire to share with the reader the author's knowledge is a sale. We expect the freelancer to answer any anticipated questions the reader might have (on accommodations, launch sites, equipment needed, etc.) within the ms."

‡**OHIO GAME & FISH**, Game & Fish Publications, Inc., Box 741, Marietta GA 30061. (404)953-9222. Editor: Chris Dorsey. See *Alabama Game & Fish*.

‡**OKLAHOMA GAME & FISH**, Game & Fish Publications, Box 741, Marietta GA 30061. (404)953-9222. Editor: Rick Drennan. See *Alabama Game & Fish*.

OUTDOOR LIFE, Times Mirror Magazines, Inc., 380 Madison Ave., New York NY 10017. (212)687-3000. Editor: Mr. Clare Conley. Executive Editor: Vin T. Sparano. 95% freelance written. A monthly magazine covering hunting and fishing. Circ. 1.5 million. Pays on acceptance. Publishes ms an average of 6-12 months after acceptance. Byline given. Buys first North American serial rights. Submit seasonal/holiday material 6 months in advance. Previously published submissions OK on occasion. Computer printout submissions acceptable; prefers letter-quality. Reports in 1 month on queries; 2 months on mss. Writer's guidelines for SASE.

Nonfiction: Book excerpts; essays; how-to (must cover hunting, fishing, or related outdoor activities); humor; interview/profile; new product; personal experience; photo feature; technical; and travel. Special issues include Bass and Freshwater Fishing Annual (March), Deer and Big Game Annual (Aug.), and Hunting Guns Annual (Sept.). No articles that are too general in scope—need to write specifically. Buys 400 mss/year. Query or send ms—"either way, photos are *very important*." Length: 800-3,000 words. Pays $350-600 for 1,000-word features and regionals; pays $900-1,200 for 2,000-word or longer national features.

Photos: Send photos with submission. Reviews 35mm transparencies and 8x10 prints. Offers variable payment. Captions and identification of subjects required. Buys one-time rights. "May offer to buy photos after first use if considered good and have potential to be used with other articles in the future (file photos)." Pay for freelance photos is $100 for ¼ page color to $800 for 2-page spread in color; $1,000 for covers. All photos must be stamped with name and address.

Columns/Departments: This Happened to Me (true-to-life, personal outdoor adventure, harrowing experience), approximately 300 words. Buys 12 mss/year. Pays $50.

Fillers: Newsbreaks and do-it-yourself for hunters and fishermen. Buys unlimited number/year. Length: 1,000 words maximum. Payment varies.

Tips: "It is best for freelancers to break in by writing features for one of the regional sections—East, Midwest, South, West. These are where-to-go oriented and run from 800-1,500 words. Writers must send one-page query with photos."

PENNSYLVANIA ANGLER, Pennsylvania Fish Commission, Box 1673, Harrisburg PA 17105-1673. (717)657-4518. Editor: Art Michaels. 60-80% freelance written. Prefers to work with published/established writers but works with a few unpublished writers every year. A monthly magazine covering fishing and related conservation topics in Pennsylvania. Circ. 55,000. Pays 6-8 weeks after acceptance. Publishes ms an average of 7-9 months after acceptance. Byline given. Rights purchased vary. Submit seasonal/holiday material 8 months in advance. Computer printout submissions acceptable; prefers letter-quality. Reports in 2 weeks on queries; 2 months on mss. Sample copy for 9x12 SAE with 5 first class stamps; writer's guidelines for #10 SAE with 1 first class stamp.

Nonfiction: Historical/nostalgic, how-to, where-to and technical. No saltwater or hunting material. Buys 120 mss/year. Query. Length: 300-3,000 words. Pays $25-300.

Photos: Send photos with submission. Reviews 35mm and larger color transparencies and 8x10 b&w prints. Offers no additional payment for photos accepted with ms. Captions, model releases and identification of subjects required.

Tips: "Our mainstays are how-tos, where-tos, and conservation pieces, but we seek more top-quality fiction, first-person stories, humor, reminiscenses, and historical articles. These pieces must a strong, specific Pennsylvania slant."

‡PENNSYLVANIA GAME & FISH, Game & Fish Publications, Inc., Box 741, Marietta GA 30061. (404)953-9222. Editor: Mike Toth. See *Alabama Game & Fish*.

PETERSEN'S HUNTING, Petersen's Publishing Co., 8490 Sunset Blvd., Los Angeles CA 90069. (213)854-2184. Editor: Craig Boddington. Managing Editor: Jeanne Frissell. 30% freelance written. Works with a small number of new/unpublished writers each year. A monthly magazine covering sport hunting. "We are a 'how-to' magazine devoted to all facets of sport hunting, with the intent to make our readers more knowledgeable, more successful and safer hunters." Circ. 300,000. Pays on acceptance. Publishes ms an average of 9 months after acceptance. Byline given. Offers $50 kill fee. Buys all rights. Submit seasonal/holiday material 1 year in advance. Computer printout submissions acceptable; prefers letter-quality. Reports in 2 weeks. Free sample copy and writer's guidelines.

Nonfiction: General interest; historical/nostalgic; how-to (on hunting techniques); humor; and travel. Special issues include Hunting Annual (August) and the Deer Hunting Annual (September). "No 'me and Joe went hunting.' Articles must include how-to and where-to material along with anecdotal material." Buys 30 mss/year. Query. Length: 2,000-3,000 words. Pays $300 minimum.

Photos: Send photos with submission. Reviews 35mm transparencies and 8x10 b&w prints. Offers no additional payment for b&w photos accepted with ms; offers $50-250/color photo. Captions, model releases and identification of subjects required. Buys one-time rights.

POPULAR LURES, National Reporter Publications, Inc., Box 185, Bixby OK 74008. (918)366-4441. Editor: Tony Dolle. 95% freelance written. Eager to work with new/unpublished writers. Published 6 times/year. Covers freshwater and limited saltwater fishing, dealing only with the proper lures to use. Circ. 75,000. Pays on acceptance. Publishes ms an average of 6 months after acceptance. Byline given. Buys first North American serial rights. Submit seasonal material 6 months in advance. Electronic submissions preferred. Computer printout submissions OK; no dot-matrix. Reports in 1 month on mss. Writer's guidelines for #10 SASE.

Nonfiction: How-to (lure techniques); new product; and photo feature. "We purchase features of 1,200-1,500 words (pays $175-350). Query preferred.

Photos: Send photos with submission. Reviews 35mm transparencies and b&w prints. Offers no additional payment for art accepted with ms. Captions required. Buys one-time rights.

Tips: "Writers should concentrate on how-to and what-to-use, rather than where-to. I need no travel pieces or stories on antique lures or lure collecting. We need good, short how-to articles on fishing with artificial lures. The writer should have more than just a working knowledge of the subject, he or she must have a fresh, new angle. All areas are open to freelancers. We are particularly looking for beginners and freelance writers who have never written for outdoor magazines before. This, we hope, will give our magazine a fresher look than other outdoor magazines."

SALT WATER SPORTSMAN, 186 Lincoln St., Boston MA 02111. (617)426-4074. Editor-in-Chief: Barry Gibson. Emphasizes saltwater fishing. 85% freelance written. Works with a small number of new/unpublished writers each year. Monthly magazine. Circ. 150,000. Pays on acceptance. Publishes ms an average of 5 months after acceptance. Byline given. Buys first North American serial rights. Offers 100% kill fee. Submit seasonal material 8 months in advance. Computer printout submissions acceptable; no dot-matrix. Reports in 1 month. Sample copy and writer's guidelines for 8½x11 SAE with $1.41 postage.

Nonfiction: How-to, personal experience, technical and travel (to fishing areas). "Readers want solid how-to, where-to information written in an enjoyable, easy-to-read style. Personal anecdotes help the reader identify with the writer." Prefers new slants and specific information. Query. "It is helpful if the writer states experience in salt water fishing and any previous related articles. We want one, possibly two well-explained ideas per query letter—not merely a listing." Buys 100 unsolicited mss/year. Length: 1,200-1,500 words. Pays $350 and up. Sometimes pays the expenses of writers on assignment.

Photos: Purchased with or without accompanying ms. Captions required. Uses 5x7 or 8x10 b&w prints and color slides. Pays $600 minimum for 35mm, 2¼x2¼ or 8x10 color transparencies for cover. Offers additional payment for photos accepted with accompanying ms.

Columns: Sportsman's Workbench (how to make fishing or fishing-related boating equipment), 100-300 words.

Tips: "There are a lot of knowledgeable fishermen/budding writers out there who could be valuable to us with a little coaching. Many don't think they can write a story for us, but they'd be surprised. We work with writers. Shorter articles that get to the point which are accompanied by good, sharp photos are hard for us to turn down. Having to delete unnecessary wordage—conversation, cliches, etc.—that writers feel is mandatory is annoying. Often they don't devote enough attention to specific fishing information."

‡SOUTH CAROLINA GAME & FISH, Game & Fish Publications, Inc., Box 741, Marietta GA 30061. (404)953-9222. Editor: Rick Lavender. See *Alabama Game & Fish*.

‡SOUTH CAROLINA WILDLIFE, Box 167, Rembert Dennis Bldg., Columbia SC 29202. (803)734-3972. Editor: John Davis. Managing Editor: Linda Renshaw. For South Carolinians interested in wildlife and outdoor activities. 75% freelance written. Bimonthly magazine. Circ. 69,000. Byline given. Pays on acceptance. Publishes ms an average of 6 months after acceptance. Buys first rights. Free sample copy. Reports in 6 weeks. Computer printout submissions acceptable "if double-spaced."

Nonfiction and Photos: Articles on outdoor South Carolina with an emphasis on preserving and protecting our natural resources. "Realize that the topic must be of interest to South Carolinians and that we must be able to justify using it in a publication published by the state wildlife department—so if it isn't directly about hunting, fishing, a certain plant or animal, it must be somehow related to the environment and conservation. Readers prefer a broad mix of outdoor related topics (articles that illustrate the beauty of South Carolina's outdoors and those that help the reader get more for his/her time, effort, and money spent in outdoor recreation). These two general areas are the ones we most need. Subjects vary a great deal in topic, area and style, but must all have a common ground in the outdoor resources and heritage of South Carolina. Review back issues and query with a one-page outline citing sources, giving ideas for graphic design, explaining justification and giving an example of the first two paragraphs." Does not need any column material. Generally does not seek photographs. Manuscripts or photographs submitted to *South Carolina Wildlife* should be addressed to: The Editor, Box 167, Columbia SC 29202, accompanied by SASE. The publisher assumes no responsibility for unsolicited material. Buys 25-30 mss/year. Length: 1,000-3,000 words. Pays an average of $200-400 per article depending upon length and subject matter. Sometimes pays the expenses of writers on assignment.

Tips: "We need more writers in the outdoor field who take pride in the craft of writing and put a real effort toward originality and preciseness in their work. Query on a topic we haven't recently done. The most frequent mistakes made by writers in completing an article are failure to check details and go in-depth on a subject."

SOUTHERN OUTDOORS MAGAZINE, B.A.S.S. Publications, 1 Bell Rd., Montgomery AL 36141. Editor: Larry Teague. Emphasizes Southern outdoor activities, including hunting, fishing, boating, shooting, camping. 90% freelance written. Prefers to work with published/established writers. Published 9 times/year. Circ. 240,000. Pays on acceptance. Publishes ms an average of 6 months after acceptance. Buys all rights. Computer printout submissions acceptable; no dot-matrix. Reports in 1 month. Sample copy for 9x12 SAE, 5 first class stamps, and $2.50.

Nonfiction: Articles should be service-oriented, helping the reader excel in outdoor sports. Emphasis is on techniques and trends. Some "where-to" stories purchased on Southern destinations with strong fishing or hunting theme. Buys 120 mss/year. Length: 2,000 words maximum. Pays 15¢/word. Sometimes pays the expenses of writers on assignment.

Photos: Usually purchased with manuscripts. Pays $50-75 for 35mm color transparencies without ms, and $250-400 for covers.

Fillers: Needs short articles (50-500 words) with newsy slant for Southern Shorts. Emphasis on irony and humor. Also needs humorous or thought-provoking pieces (750-1,200 words) for S.O. Essay feature.

Tips: "It's easiest to break in with short features of 500-1,000 words on 'how-to' fishing and hunting topics. We buy very little first-person. Query first and send sample of your writing if we haven't done business before. Stories most likely to sell: bass fishing, deer hunting, other freshwater fishing, inshore saltwater fishing, bird and small-game hunting, shooting, camping and boating. The most frequent mistakes made by writers in completing an article for us are first-person usage; clarity of articles; applicability of topic to the South; lack of quotes from qualified sources."

‡SOUTHERN SALTWATER MAGAZINE, B.A.S.S. Communications, 1 Bell Rd., Montgomery AL 36117. (205)272-9530. Editor: Colin Moore. A magazine on coastal fishing in the southern United States (Delaware to Texas) published 8 times/year. Estab. 1987. Circ. 100,000. Pays on acceptance. Publishes ms an average of 6 months after acceptance. Byline given. Buys all rights. Reports in 2 weeks. Sample copy for 8½x11 SAE with 1 first class stamp. Free writer's guidelines.

Nonfiction: Associate Editor: Susan Shehane. General interest, how-to, interview/profile, photo feature, technical, travel. Buys 40 mss/year. Send complete ms. Length: 1,500-2,000 words. Pays 15-20¢/word.

Photos: Send photos with submission. Reviews 35mm transparencies and 5x7 prints. Captions and identification of subjects required. Buys all rights.

Columns/Departments: Salt South (general review applying to southern region); Coast Watch (state-by-state fishing items). Buys 40 mss/year. Send complete ms. Length: 800-1,000 words. Pays 15¢/word.

Fillers: Facts, newsbreaks. Buys 75 mss/year. Length: 250-450 words. Pays 15¢/word.

SPORTS AFIELD, 250 W. 55th St., New York NY 10019. Editor: Tom Paugh. Executive Editor: Fred Kesting. 33% freelance written. Eager to work with new/unpublished writers. For people of all ages whose interests are centered around the out-of-doors (hunting and fishing) and related subjects. Monthly magazine. Circ. 518,010. Buys first North American serial rights for features, and all rights for *SA Almanac*. Pays on acceptance. Publishes ms an average of 6 months after acceptance. Byline given. "Our magazine is seasonal and material submitted should be in accordance. Fishing in spring and summer; hunting in the fall; camping in summer and fall." Submit seasonal material 6 months in advance. Computer printout submissions acceptable; prefers letter-quality. Reports in 1 month. Query or submit complete ms. Sample copy for $1; writer's guidelines for 1 first class stamp.

Nonfiction and Photos: "Informative where-to articles and personal experiences with good photos on hunting, fishing, camping, boating and subjects such as conservation and travel related to hunting and fishing. We want first-class writing and reporting." Buys 15-17 unsolicited mss/year. Length: 500-2,500 words. Pays $750 minimum, depending on length and quality. Photos purchased with or without ms. Pays $50 minimum for 8x10 b&w glossy prints. Pays $50 minimum for 35mm or larger transparencies. Sometimes pays the expenses of writers on assignment.

Fiction: Adventure, humor (if related to hunting and fishing).

Fillers: Send to *Almanac* editor. *Almanac* pays $25 and up depending on length, for newsworthy, unusual, how-to and nature items. Payment on publication. Buys all rights.

Tips: "We seldom give assignments to other than staff. Top-quality 35mm slides to illustrate articles a must. Read a recent copy of *Sports Afield* so you know the market you're writing for. Family-oriented features will probably become more important because more and more groups/families are sharing the outdoor experience."

‡TENNESSEE SPORTSMAN, Game & Fish Publications, Box 741, Marietta GA 30061. (404)953-9222. Editor: Bill Hartlage. See *Alabama Game & Fish*.

TEXAS FISHERMAN, #150, 4550 Post Oak Place Dr., Houston TX 77027. Editor: Larry Bozka. 80% freelance written. Prefers to work with published/established writers; works with a small number of new/unpublished writers each year. Published 9 times a year for freshwater and saltwater fishermen in Texas. Circ. 65,396. Rights purchased vary with author and material. Byline given. Usually buys second serial (reprint) rights. Buys 4-6 mss/month. Pays on acceptance. Publishes ms an average of 3 months after acceptance. Query for electronic submissions; contact production manager Tim Stephens at (918)250-6799. Computer printout submissions acceptable; no dot-matrix. Reports in 1 month. Query. Sample copy and writer's guidelines for 9x12 SAE and 9 first class stamps.

Nonfiction and Photos: General how-to, where-to, features on all phases of fishing in Texas. Strong slant on informative pieces. Strong writing. Good saltwater stories (Texas only). Length: 1,200-1,500 words. Pays $75-300, depending on length and quality of writing and photos. Mss must include 4-7 good action b&w photos or illustrations. Color slides will be considered for cover or inside use.

Tips: "Query should be a short, but complete description of the story that emphasizes a specific angle. When possible, send black and white and/or color photos with queries. Good art will sell us a story that is mediocre, but even a great story can't replace bad photographs, and better than half submit poor quality photos. How-to, location, or personality profile stories are preferred."

‡TEXAS SPORTSMAN, Game & Fish Publications, Inc., Box 741, Marietta GA 30061. (404)953-9222. Editor: Steve Lightfoot. See *Alabama Game & Fish*.

‡TRI-STATE BASS FISHERMAN, Bass Fisherman Publishing Co., Inc., Box 908, Westerville OH 43081. (614)882-1444. Editor: Ottie M. Snyder, Jr. Managing Editor: Vicki J. Snyder. 99% freelance written. Bimonthly magzine of bass fishing in Ohio, Kentucky and Indiana. "Our magazine covers strictly bass fishing; smallmouth, largemouth, white and stripers and hybrids. We tend toward the somewhat serious bass angler who probably fishes in, at least, the local tournaments. Articles should not be slanted toward the beginner." Estab. 1987. Circ. 20,000. Pays on 15th of month prior to issue date. Publishes ms an average of 3 months after acceptance. Byline given. Offers $40 kill fee. Buys first North American serial rights. Submit seasonal/holiday material 8 months in advance. Query for electronic submissions. Computer printout submissions OK; prefers letter-quality. Free sample copy copy; writer's guidelines for #10 SAE with 1 first class stamp.

Nonfiction: Expose (on fish management), how-to (use certain types of lure, how to make angling accessories, fishing tactics), humor, interview/profile (pro of the month in each issue, Tips, etc, from well known bass pro). Buys 48 mss/year. Query. Length: 1,500-1,800 words. Pays $150.

Photos: State availability of photos with query. Reviews 5x7 prints. Offers no additional payment for photos accepted with ms package (b&w part of ms package. $50 for inside color, $150 for covers). Captions, model releases and identification of subjects required. Buys one-time rights.

Fillers: Facts, newsbreaks, short humor. Buys 5-10/year. Length: 100-500 words. Pay varies with type and length.

Tips: "Give the reader good, solid angling tactics that can help him improve his catch. We like where-to articles in the tri-state area as long as they are good bass waters. We are always looking for new tactics to share with our readers but they should be proven and usable in the tri-state area. Most of our readers fish at least local tournaments and are looking for ways to improve their catch."

TURKEY, 3941 N. Paradise Rd., Flagstaff AZ 86004. (602)774-6913. Editor: Gerry Blair. 60% freelance written. Works with a small number of new/unpublished writers each year. A monthly magazine covering turkey hunting, biology and conservation of the wild turkey, gear for turkey hunters, where to go, etc. for both novice and experienced wild turkey enthusiasts. "We stress wildlife conservation, ethics, and management of the resource." Circ. 30,000. Pays on publication. Publishes ms an average of 1 year after acceptance. Byline given. Computer printout submissions acceptable; prefers letter-quality.

Nonfiction: Book excerpts (turkey related); how-to (turkey-related); and personal experience (turkey hunting). Buys 75-100 mss/year. "The most frequent mistake made by writers in completing an article for us is inadequate photo support." Query. Length: 500-3,000 words. Pays $20-150.

Photos: Send photos with accompanying query or ms. Pays $5-20 for 8x10 b&w and color prints; $50 for color or slides for cover.

Tips: "How-to articles, using fresh ideas, are most open to freelancers. We also need more short articles on turkey management programs in all states."

TURKEY CALL, Wild Turkey Bldg., Box 530, Edgefield SC 29824. (803)637-3106. Editor: Gene Smith. 50-60% freelance written. Eager to work with new/unpublished writers and photographers. An educational publication for members of the National Wild Turkey Federation. Bimonthly magazine. Circ. 42,000. Buys one-time rights. Byline given. Pays on acceptance. Publishes ms an average of 6 months after acceptance. Reports in 4 weeks. No queries necessary. Submit complete package. Wants original ms only. Computer printout submissions acceptable; prefers letter-quality. "Double strike dot-matrix OK." Sample copy $2 with 9x12 SAE and 7 first class stamps.

Nonfiction and Photos: Feature articles dealing with the hunting and management of the American wild turkey. Must be accurate information and must appeal to national readership of turkey hunters and wildlife management experts. No poetry or first-person accounts of unremarkable hunting trips. May use some fiction that educates or entertains in a special way. Length: 1,500-2,000 words. Pays $25 for items, $50 for short fillers of 400-500 words, $200-300 for illustrated features. "We want quality photos submitted with features." Art illustrations also acceptable. "We are using more and more inside color illustrations." Prefers b&w 8x10 glossies. Color transparencies of any size are acceptable. Wants no typical hunter-holding-dead-turkey photos or setups using mounted birds or domestic turkeys. Photos with how-to stories must make the techniques clear (example: how to make a turkey call; how to sculpt or carve a bird in wood). Pays $10 minimum for one-time rights on b&w photos and simple art illustrations; up to $75 for inside color, reproduced any size. Covers: Most are donated. Any purchased are negotiated.

Tips: The writer "should simply keep in mind that the audience is 'expert' on wild turkey management, hunting, life history and restoration/conservation history. He/she *must know the subject*. We will be buying more third-person, more fiction—in an attempt to avoid the 'predictability trap' of a single subject magazine."

‡VIRGINIA GAME & FISH, Game & Fish Publications, Inc., Box 741, Marietta GA 30061. (404)953-9222. Editor: Aaron Pass. See *Alabama Game & Fish*.

‡WEST VIRGINIA GAME & FISH, Game & Fish Publications, Inc., Box 741, Marietta GA 30061. (404)953-9222. Editor: Aaron Pass. See *Alabama Game & Fish*.

WESTERN OUTDOORS, 3197-E Airport Loop, Costa Mesa CA 92626. (714)546-4370. Editor-in-Chief: Burt Twilegar. 75% freelance written. Works with a small number of new/unpublished writers each year. Emphasizes hunting, fishing, camping, boating for 11 Western states only, Baja California, Canada, Hawaii and Alaska. Monthly magazine. Circ. 150,000. Pays on acceptance. Publishes ms an average of 6 months after acceptance. Buys first North American serial rights. Query (in writing). Submit seasonal material 4-6 months in advance. Photocopied submissions OK. Computer printout submissions are acceptable if double-spaced; no dot-matrix. Reports in 4-6 weeks. Sample copy $1.75; writer's guidelines for SASE.

Nonfiction: Where-to (catch more fish, bag more game, improve equipment, etc.); how-to informational; photo feature. "We do not accept fiction, poetry, cartoons." Buys 70 assigned mss/year. Query. Length: 1,000-1,800 words maximum. Pays $300-500.

Photos: Purchased with accompanying ms. Captions required. Uses 8x10 b&w glossy prints; prefers Kodachrome II 35mm slides. Offers no additional payment for photos accepted with accompanying ms. Pays $200-250 for covers.

Tips: "Provide a complete package of photos, map, trip facts and manuscript written according to our news feature format. Excellence of color photo selections make a sale more likely. The most frequent mistake made by writers in completing an article for us is that they don't follow our style. Our guidelines are quite clear."

WESTERN SPORTSMAN, Box 737, Regina, Saskatchewan, S4P 3A8 Canada. (306)352-8384. Editor: Rick Bates. 90% freelance written. For fishermen, hunters, campers and others interested in outdoor recreation. "Note that our coverage area is Alberta and Saskatchewan." Bimonthly magazine. Circ. 30,000. Rights purchased vary with author and material. May buy first North American serial rights or second serial (reprint) rights. Byline given. Pays on publication. Publishes ms an average of 2-12 months after acceptance. "We try to include as much information as possible on all subjects in each edition. Therefore, we usually publish fishing articles in our winter issues along with a variety of winter stories. If material is dated, we would like to receive articles 2 months in advance of our publication date." Computer printout submissions OK; no dot-matrix. Reports in 1 month. Sample copy $3.50; free writer's guidelines.

Nonfiction: "It is necessary that all articles can identify with our coverage area of Alberta and Saskatchewan. We are interested in mss from writers who have experienced an interesting fishing, hunting, camping or other outdoor experience. We also publish how-to and other informational pieces as long as they can relate to our coverage area. We are more interested in articles which tell about the average guy living on beans, guiding his own boat, stalking his game and generally doing his own thing in our part of Western Canada than a story describing a well-to-do outdoorsman traveling by motorhome, staying at an expensive lodge with guides doing everything for him except catching the fish, or shooting the big game animal. The articles that are submitted to us need to be prepared in a knowledgeable way and include more information than the actual fish catch or animal or bird kill. Discuss the terrain, the people involved on the trip, the water or weather conditions, the costs, the planning that went into the trip, the equipment and other data closely associated with the particular event in a factual manner. We're always looking for new writers." Buys 120 mss/year. Submit complete ms. Length: 1,500-2,000 words. Pays $100-325. Sometimes pays the expenses of writers on assignment.

Photos: Photos purchased with ms with no additional payment. Also purchased without ms. Pays $20-25/5x7 or 8x10 b&w print; $175-250/35mm or larger transparency for front cover.

‡WISCONSIN SPORTSMAN, Game & Fish Publications, Inc., Box 741, Marietta GA 30061. (404)953-9222. Editor: Chris Dorsey. See *Alabama Game & Fish*.

For explanation of symbols, see the Key to Symbols and Abbreviations on Page 5.

Martial Arts

AMERICAN KARATE, Condor Books, Inc., 351 W. 54th St., New York NY 10019. (212)586-4432. Editor: Alan Paul. Managing Editor: David Weiss. 80% freelance written. A bimonthly magazine covering martial arts in America and Canada. *"AK* is directed at American and Canadian martial artists and the ways in which they have adapted and changed the oriental fighting arts to better suit our way of life." Circ. 100,000. Pays on publication. Byline given. Offers $50-75 kill fee. Buys first North American serial rights. Submit seasonal/holiday material 3 months in advance. Photocopied submissions OK. Computer printout submissions acceptable; prefers letter-quality. Reports in 2 weeks on queries; 1 month on mss. Sample copy for 9x12 SAE with 5 first class stamps.

Nonfiction: Book excerpts, general interest, historical/nostalgic, how-to, inspirational, interview/profile, new product, personal experience and technical. No articles of an overly general nature on martial arts. Buys 50 mss/year. Query with or without published clips, or send complete ms. Length: 1,500-3,000 words. Pays $100-200. Sometimes pays the expenses of writers on assignment.

Photos: Send photos with submission. Reviews contact sheets, 35mm transparencies and 5x7 or 8x10 prints. Offers no additional payment for b&w photos accepted with ms; offers $25-75/color photo. Captions and identification of subjects required. Buys one-time rights.

Columns/Departments: AK Profile (inspirational pieces about martial artists), 1,500 words; State of the Martial Arts (review of martial arts in American states), 2,000-2,500 words; and Fit to Fight (exercise and weight training for martial artists), 1,500-2,000 words. Buys 25 mss/year. Send complete ms. Pays $75-200.

Tips: "Freelancer can break into our publication by concentrating on the *American* approach our magazine has taken. We are not interested in pieces on oriental practitioners or systems. We also are interested in good quality color and b&w photos. Every area is open. We are very interested in expanding our stable of contributors."

ATA MAGAZINE, Martial Arts and Fitness, ATA Magazine Co., Inc., Box 240835, Memphis TN 38124-0835. (901)761-2821. Editor: Milo Dailey. Managing Editor: Carla Dailey. 30% freelance written. Works with a small number of new/unpublished writers each year. *ATA Magazine* is the official publication of the American Taekwondo Association covering general health and fitness with emphasis on martial arts (Taekwondo), aerobics, and strength training equipment. Circ. 30,000. Pays on publication. Publishes ms an average of 3 months after acceptance. "Most of publication copyrighted." Buys first North American serial rights unless otherwise arranged. Submit seasonal/holiday material at least 6 months in advance. Sometimes accepts previously published submissions. Query for electronic submissions. Computer printout submissions acceptable; dot-matrix submissions OK "if on non-heat-sensitive paper." Reports in 3 weeks. Sample copy $2.25; writer's guidelines for SAE.

Nonfiction: Interview/profile (on persons notable in other fields who train under *ATA* programs). "Special slant is that martial arts are primarily for fitness and personal development. Defense and sports aspects are to reinforce primary aims. Freelancers who are not ATA members should concentrate on non-martial arts aspects of fitness or on ATA martial artists' personalities. *We're not interested in fads, non-ATA martial arts or overt 'sex' orientation.*" Currently articles are staff-written, assigned to ATA experts or ATA member freelancers; would possibly buy 4-6 outside freelance mss. Query. Length: depends on material. Pays $25-150.

Photos: Payment for photos included in payment for ms. Prefers b&w prints of size appropriate to quality reproduction. Model releases and identification of subjects "with enough information for a caption" required.

Tips: "We're doing less 'health' material and more material directed to the beginner in martial arts. Recent freelance submissions have included a piece on a deaf Auburn University varsity swimmer who earned an ATA Black Belt and one on an extended family ATA demonstration team. So far *ATA Magazine* has served as a developmental organ for ATA members who are or wish to be writers. We're willing to work with writers on nontechnical coverage of subjects of interest to our readership—which is mostly 'adult' in its approach to martial arts and fitness in general. Most ATA centers have a good story. Most martial arts and strength-training articles are staff-written or assigned to association experts. This leaves nutrition and special personality pieces most open to freelancers, along possibly with fiction. To get the right slant, proximity to ATA sources (which are currently in about 200 communities coast to coast) is almost mandatory. It seems only freelancers with a current 'ATA connection' can figure the proper slant. A major problem in writing for most magazines today is to have expert knowledge with ability to communicate at the non-expert level. A middle ground is the 'special interest' magazine such as ours which allows presumption of both interest and a basic knowledge of the subject. Still, it's easy to become too technical and forget that emotion retains readers—not just facts. The most blatant mistake is not reading the entry in *Writer's Market*. We do not use karate movie stars or non-ATA martial artists. Other publications answer this interest segment. We're a small staff with a lot of hats to wear. Unsolicited manuscripts may get dumped by default. Handwritten ones certainly are. *If writers actually read all of our listing, it would save all a lot of time.* One well-known martial arts writer queried, determined we're not 'her thing', and we're both happier."

BLACK BELT, Rainbow Publications, Inc., 1813 Victory Place, Burbank CA 91504. (818)843-4444. Executive Editor: Jim Coleman. 80-90% freelance written. Works with a small number of new/unpublished writers each year. Emphasizes martial arts for both practitioner and layman. Monthly magazine. Circ. 100,000. Pays on publication. Publishes ms an average of 3-5 months after acceptance. Buys first North American serial rights, retains right to republish. Submit seasonal/holiday material 6 months in advance. Photocopied submissions OK. Computer printout submissions acceptable; prefers letter-quality. Reports in 1 month.

Nonfiction: Expose, how-to, informational, interview, new product, personal experience, profile, technical and travel. No biography, material on teachers or on new or Americanized styles. Buys 8-9 mss/issue. Query or send complete ms. Length: 1,200 words minimum. Pays $10-20/page of manuscript.

Photos: Very seldom buys photos without accompanying mss. Captions required. Total purchase price for ms includes payment for photos. Model releases required.

Fiction: Historical and modern day. Buys 2-3 mss/year. Query. Pays $100-175.

Tips: "We also publish an annual yearbook and special issues periodically. The yearbook includes our annual 'Black Belt Hall of Fame' inductees."

THE FIGHTER—INTERNATIONAL, Professional Martial Arts Association, 1017 Highland Ave., Largo FL 33640. (813)584-0054. Editor: John M. Corcoran. Bimonthly magazine covering martial arts. "We cover the entire spectrum of the industry, but are particularly interested in controversial issues that affect the martial arts masses." Circ. 150,000 (English language). Pays on publication. Publishes ms an average of 2-3 months after acceptance. Byline given. Offers $25 kill fee. Buys first rights (worldwide) or second serial (reprint) rights. Simultaneous, photocopied and previously published submissions OK (only if published in mainstream magazines). Computer printout submissions OK; no dot-matrix. Reports in 2 weeks on queries; 3-4 weeks on mss. Sample copy $3.50 with 8½x11 SAE and $1.58 postage; free writer's guidelines.

Nonfiction: Expose, historical/nostalgic, humor, inspirational, interview/profile (on assignment only) and photo feature. No how-to/technical articles. Buys 25-30 mss/year. Query. Length: 1,500 words or what the story requires. Pays $200-400 for assigned articles; $150-200 for unsolicited articles.

Photos: State availability of photos with query. Reviews contact sheets, transparencies (3x5) and prints (8x10). Offers no additional payment for photos accepted with ms. Captions and identification of subjects required. Buys one-time rights.

Tips: "Submit article ideas of substance and significance. Omit ideas which have been done to death by other martial arts publications. We are the only full color magazine in the genre; therefore, visual impact can increase chances of acceptance."

FIGHTING WOMAN NEWS, Martial Arts, Self-Defense, Combative Sports Quarterly, Box 1459, Grand Central Station, New York NY 10163. (212)228-0900. Editor: Valerie Eads. 75% freelance written. Prefers to work with published/established writers. Quarterly magazine. "*FWN* combines sweat and philosophy, the deadly reality of street violence and the other worldliness of such eastern disciplines as Zen. Our audience is composed of adult women actually practicing martial arts with an average experience of 4 + years. Since our audience is also 80 + % college grads and 40% holders of advanced degrees we are an action magazine with footnotes. Our material is quite different from what is found in newsstand martial arts publications." Circ. 3,500. Pays on publication. "There is a backlog of poetry and fiction—hence a *very* long wait. A solid factual martial arts article would go out 'next issue' with trumpets and pipes." Byline given. Buys one-time rights. Submit seasonal/holiday material 6 months in advance. Simultaneous queries, and simultaneous, photocopied, and previously published submissions OK. "For simultaneous and previously published we *must* be told about it." Query for electronic submissions. Computer printout submissions acceptable. "If computer printout submissions are unreadable, we throw them out." Reports as soon as possible. Sample copy $3.50; writer's guidelines for #10 SAE and 2 first class stamps.

Nonfiction: Book excerpts, expose (discrimination against women in martial arts governing bodies); historical/nostalgic; how-to (martial arts, self-defense techniques); humor; inspirational (e.g., self-defense success stories); interview/profile ("we have assignments waiting for writers in this field"); new product; opinion; personal experience; photo feature; technical; travel. "All materials *must* be related to our subject matter. No tabloid sensationalism, no 'sweat is sexy too' items, no fantasy presented as fact, no puff pieces for an instructor or school with a woman champion inhouse." Buys 6 mss/year. Query. Length: 1,000-5,000 words. Pays in copies, barter or $10 maximum. Sometimes pays the expenses of writers on assignment; expenses negotiated in some cases.

Photos: Nancy Green, photo editor. State availability of photos with query or ms. Reviews "technically competent" b&w contact sheets and 8x10 b&w prints. "We negotiate photos and articles as a package. Sometimes expenses are negotiated. Captions and identification of subjects required. The need for releases depends on the situation."

Columns/Departments: Notes & News (short items relevant to our subject matter); Letters (substantive comment regarding previous issues); Sports Reports; and Reviews (of relevant materials in any medium). Query or send complete ms. Length: 100-1,000 words. Pays in copies or negotiates payment.

Fiction: Muskat Buckby, fiction editor. Adventure, fantasy, historical and science fiction. "Any fiction must feature a woman skilled in martial arts." Buys 0-1 ms/year. Query. Length: 1,000-5,000 words. "We will consider serializing longer stories." Pays in copies or negotiates payment.

Poetry: Muskat Buckby, poetry editor. "We'll look at all types. Must appeal to an audience of martial artists." Buys 3-4 poems/year. Length: open. Pays in copy or negotiates payment.

Tips: "First, read the magazine. Our major reason for rejecting articles is total unsuitability for our publication. A prime example of this is the writer who submitted numerous articles on subjects that we very much wanted to cover, but written in a gosh-gee-wow progress-to-the-abos style that was totally inappropriate. The second most common reason for rejections is vagueness; we need the old Who, What, When, Where, Why and How and if your article doesn't have that save yourself the postage. Several articles returned by *FWN* have later shown up in other martial arts magazines and since they pay a lot more, you're better off trying them first unless an audience of literate, adult, female, martial artists is what you're aiming at."

‡INSIDE KARATE, The Magazine for Today's Total Martial Artist, Unique Publications, 4201 Vanowen Pl., Burbank CA 91505. (818)845-2656. Editor: John Steven Soet. 90% freelance written. Works with a small number of new/unpublished writers each year. Monthly magazine covering the martial arts. Circ. 120,000. Publishes ms an average of 3 months after acceptance. Byline given. Buys first North American serial rights. Computer printout submissions acceptable; prefers letter-quality. Reports in 3 weeks on queries; in 6 weeks on mss. Sample copy $2.50, 9x12 SAE and 5 first class stamps; free writer's guidelines.

Nonfiction: Book excerpts; expose (of martial arts); historical/nostalgic; humor; interview/profile (with approval only); opinion; personal experience; photo feature; and technical (with approval only). *Inside Karate* seeks a balance of the following in each issue: tradition, history, glamor, profiles and/or interviews (both by assignment only), technical, philosophical and think pieces. To date, most "how to" pieces have been done inhouse. Buys 70 mss/year. Query. Length: 1,000-2,500 words; prefers 10-12 page mss. Pays $25-125.

Photos: Send photos with ms. Prefers 3x5 bordered b&w. Captions and identification of subjects required. Buys one-time rights.

Tips: "In our publication, writing style and/or expertise is not the determining factor. Beginning writers with martial arts expertise may submit. Trends in magazine publishing that freelance writers should be aware of include the use of less body copy, better (and interesting) photos to be run large with 'story' caps. If the photos are poor and the reader can't grasp the whole story by looking at photos and copy, forget it."

‡INSIDE KUNG-FU, The Ultimate In Martial Arts Coverage!, Unique Publications, 4201 Vanowen Pl., Burbank CA 91505. (818)845-2656. Editor: Dave Cater. 75% freelance written. Monthly magazine covering martial arts for those with "traditional, modern, athletic and intellectual tastes. The magazine slants toward little-known martial arts, and little-known aspects of established martial arts." Circ. 100,000. Pays on publication. Publishes ms an average of 6 months after acceptance. Byline given. Buys first North American serial rights. Submit seasonal/holiday material 4 months in advance. Simultaneous queries, and simultaneous and photocopied submissions OK. Computer printout submissions acceptable; no dot-matrix. Reports in 3 weeks on queries; 4 weeks on mss. Sample copy $2.50 with 9x12 SAE and 5 first class stamps; free writer's guidelines.

Nonfiction: Expose (topics relating to the martial arts); historical/nostalgic; how-to (primarily technical materials); cultural/philosophical; interview/profile; personal experience; photo feature; and technical. "Articles must be technically or historically accurate." No "sports coverage, first-person articles, or articles which constitute personal aggrandizement." Buys 120 mss/year. Query or send complete ms. Length: 8-10 pages, typewritten and double-spaced.

Photos: Send photos with accompanying ms. Reviews b&w contact sheets, b&w negatives and 8x10 b&w prints. "Photos are paid for with payment for ms." Captions and model release required.

Fiction: Adventure, historical, humorous, mystery and suspense. "Fiction must be short (1,000-2,000 words) and relate to the martial arts. We buy very few fiction pieces." Buys 2-3 mss/year.

Tips: "The writer may have a better chance of breaking in at our publication with short articles and fillers since smaller pieces allow us to gauge individual ability, but we're flexible—quality writers get published period. The most frequent mistakes made by writers in completing an article for us are ignoring photo requirements and model releases (always number one—and who knows why? All requirements are spelled out in writer's guidelines)."

KARATE/KUNG-FU ILLUSTRATED, Rainbow Publications, Inc., 1813 Victory Place, Burbank CA 91504. (818)843-4444. Publisher: Michael James. 80% freelance written. Eager to work with new/unpublished writers. Emphasizes karate and kung fu from the traditional standpoint and training techniques. Monthly magazine. Circ. 80,000. Pays on publication. Buys all rights. Photocopied submissions OK. Reports in 1-2 weeks. Sample copy for 8½x11 SAE.

Nonfiction: Expose, historical, how-to, informational, interview, new product, opinion, photo feature, technical and travel. Need historical and contemporary Kung Fu pieces, including styles, how-tos, Chinese philosophy. Buys 6 mss/issue. Query or submit complete ms. Pays $100-200.

Photos: Purchased with or without accompanying ms. Submit 5x7 or 8x10 b&w or color transparencies. Total purchase price for ms includes payment for photos.

Fillers: Query.

Tips: "Style must be concise, authoritative and in third person."

‡**M.A. TRAINING**, (formerly *Fighting Stars Ninja*), Rainbow Publications, 1813 Victory Pl., Box 7728, Burbank CA 91510-7728. (818)843-4444. Executive Editor: William Groak. 75% freelance written. Works with a small number of new/unpublished writers each year. Quarterly magazine about martial arts training. Circ. 60,000. Pays on publication. Publishes ms an average of 3-6 months after acceptance. Buys first North American serial rights. Submit seasonal material 4 months in advance, but best to send query letter first. Simultaneous and photocopied submissions OK. Computer print-out submissions acceptable; prefers letter-quality. Reports in 6 weeks. Writer's guidelines for SASE.
Nonfiction: How-to: want training related features. Buys 30-40 unsolicited mss/year. Send query or complete ms. Length: 1,000-2,000 words. Pays $50-200.
Photos: State availability of photos. Most ms should be accompanied by photos. Reviews 5x7 and 8x10 b&w and color glossy prints. Can reproduce prints from negatives. Will use illustrations. Offers no additional payment for photos accepted with ms. Model releases required. Buys all rights.
Tips: "I'm looking for how-to, nuts-and-bolts training type stories which are martial arts related. I need stories about developing speed, accuracy, power, etc."

Miscellaneous

BALLS AND STRIKES, Amateur Softball Association, 2801 NE 50th St., Oklahoma City OK 73111. (405)424-5266. Editor: Bill Plummer III. 30% freelance written. Works with a small number of new/unpublished writers each year. "Only national monthly tabloid covering amateur softball." Circ. 270,000. Pays on publication. Publishes ms an average of 2 months after acceptance. Buys first rights. Byline given. Computer printout submissions acceptable; no dot-matrix. Reports in 3 weeks. Free sample copy.
Nonfiction: General interest, historical/nostalgic, interview/profile and technical. Query. Length: 2-3 pages. Pays $50-65.
Tips: "We generally like shorter features because we try to get many different features in each issue. There is a possibility we will be using more freelance material in the future."

‡**BASKETBALL WEEKLY**, 17820 E. Warren, Detroit MI 48224. (313)881-9554. Publisher: Roger Stanton. Editor: Matt Marsom. 20 issues during season, September-May. Circ. 45,000. Buys all rights. Pays on publication. Sample copy for SASE and $1. Reports in 2 weeks.
Nonfiction, Photos and Fillers: Current stories on teams and personalities in high school, college and pro basketball. Length: 1,000-1,200 words. Pays $65. 3x5 and 8x10 b&w glossy photos purchased with mss. Also uses newsbreaks. Do not send general basketball information.
Tips: "Include information about your background that qualifies you to do a particular story."

HOCKEY ILLUSTRATED, Lexington Library, Inc., 355 Lexington Ave., New York NY 10017. (212)391-1400. Editor: Stephen Ciacciarelli. 90% freelance written. Published 4 times in season. Magazine covering NHL hockey. "Upbeat stories on NHL superstars—aimed at hockey fans, predominantly a younger audience." Pays on acceptance. Publishes ms an average of 1-2 months after acceptance. Byline given. Buys first North American serial rights. Photocopied submissions OK. Computer printout submissions OK; prefers letter-quality. Reports in 2 weeks. Sample copy $1.95 with 9x12 SAE with 3 first class stamps.
Nonfiction: Inspirational and interview/profile. Buys 40-50 mss/year. Query with or without published clips, or send complete ms. Length: 1,500-3,000 words. Pays $75-125 for assigned and unsolicited articles.
Photos: State availability of photos with submission. Reviews transparencies and prints. Offers no additional payment for photos accepted with ms. Identification of subjects required. Buys one-time rights.

INSIDE TEXAS RUNNING, (formerly *Inside Running and Fitness*), 9514 Bristlebrook Dr., Houston TX 77083. (713)498-3208. Editor: Joanne Schmidt. 50% freelance written. A monthly tabloid covering running, cycling and triathaloning. "Our audience is Texas runners and triathletes who may also be into cross training with biking and swimming." Circ. 10,000. Pays on acceptance. Publishes ms an average of 1-2 months after acceptance. Byline given. Buys first rights, one-time rights, second serial (reprint) rights and all rights. Submit seasonal/holiday material 2 months in advance. Previously published submissions OK; no dot-matrix. Reports in 1 month on queries; 6 weeks on mss. Sample copy $1.50; writer's guidelines for #10 SAE with 1 first class stamp.
Nonfiction: Book excerpts, expose, historical/nostalgic, humor, interview/profile, opinion, photo feature, technical and travel. "We would like to receive controversial and detailed news pieces which cover both sides of an issue, for example, how a race director must deal with city government to put on an event. Problems seen by both sides include cost, traffic congestion, red tape, etc." No personal experience such as "Why I Love to Run," "How I Ran My First Marathon." Buys 18 mss/year. Query with published clips, or send complete ms. Length: 500-2,500 words. Pays $100 maximum for assigned articles; $50 maximum for unsolicited articles. Sometimes pays the expenses of writers on assignments.
Photos: Send photos with submission. Offers $25 maximum/photo. Captions required. Buys one-time rights.

Tips: "General material on running will be replaced in 1989 by specific pieces which cite names, places, costs and references to additional information. Writers should be familiar with the sport and understand race strategies, etc. The basic who, what, where, when and how also applies. The best way to break in to our publication is to submit brief (3 or 4 paragraphs) writeups on road races to be used in the Results section. We also need more cycling articles for new biking section."

INTERNATIONAL OLYMPIC LIFTER, IOL Publications, 3602 Eagle Rock, Box 65855, Los Angeles CA 90065. (213)257-8762. Editor: Bob Hise. Managing Editor: Herb Glossbrenner. 5% freelance written. Quarterly magazine covering the Olympic sport of weightlifting. Circ. 10,000. Pays on publication. Publishes ms an average of 3 months after acceptance. Byline given. Offers $25 kill fee. Buys one-time rights or negotiable rights. Submit seasonal/holiday material 5 months in advance. Photocopied submissions OK; prefers letter-quality. Reports in 6 weeks. Sample copy $4; writer's guidelines for 9x12 SAE and 5 first class stamps.
Nonfiction: Training articles, contest reports, diet—all related to Olympic weight lifting. Buys 4 mss/year. Query. Length: 250-2,000 words. Pays $25-100.
Photos: Action (competition and training). State availability of photos. Pays $1-5 for 5x7 b&w prints. Identification of subjects required.
Poetry: Dale Rhoades, poetry editor. Light verse, traditional—related to Olympic lifting. Buys 6-10 poems/year. Submit maximum 3 poems. Length: 12-24 lines. Pays $10-20.
Tips: "First—a writer must be acquainted with Olympic-style weight lifting. Since we are an international publication we do not tolerate ethnic, cultural, religious or political inclusions. Articles relating to AWA are readily accepted."

NATIONAL RACQUETBALL, Florida Trade Publication, Drawer 6126, Clearwater FL 33518. General Manager: Helen Quinn. Editor: Sigmund Brouwer. For racquetball players of all ages. Monthly magazine. 40% freelance written. Eager to work with new/unpublished writers. Circ. 39,000. Pays on publication. Publishes ms an average of 3 months after acceptance. Buys all rights. Byline given. Submit seasonal/holiday material 2-3 months in advance. Computer printout submissions acceptable. Publishes ms an average of 3 months after acceptance; no dot-matrix. Sample copy $2.
Nonfiction: How-to (play better racquetball or train for racquetball); interview (with players or others connected with racquetball business); opinion (usually used in letters but sometimes fullblown opinion features on issues confronting the game); photo feature (on any subject mentioned); profile (short pieces with photos on women or men players interesting in other ways or on older players); health (as it relates to racquetball players—food, rest, eye protection, etc.); and fashion. Little material on tournament results. Buys 4 mss/issue. Query with clips of published work. Length: 500-2,500 words. Pays $1.65/column inch. Sometimes pays the expenses of writers on assignment.
Photos: State availability of photos or send photos with ms. Offers no additional payment for photos accompanying ms. Uses b&w prints or color transparencies. Buys one-time rights. Captions and model releases required. Pays $5/b&w photo and $10/color.
Fiction: Adventure, humorous, mystery, romance, science fiction and suspense. "Whatever an inventive mind can do with racquetball." Buys 3 mss/year. Send complete ms. Pays $50/published page.
Tips: "Break in to *National Racquetball* by writing for monthly features—short pieces about racquetball players you know. We need more contributions from all over the country. Our object is national and international coverage of the sport of racquetball."

PRIME TIME SPORTS & FITNESS, GND Prime Time Publishing, Box 6091, Evanston IL 60204. (312)869-6434. Editor: Dennis A. Dorner. Managing Editor: Nicholas J. Schmitz. 80% freelance written. Eager to work with new/unpublished writers. A monthly magazine covering seasonal pro sports and racquet and health club sports and fitness. Circ. 35,000. Pays on publication. Publishes ms an average of 4 months after acceptance. Byline given. Buys all rights; will assign back to author in 85% of cases. Submit seasonal/holiday material 3 months in advance. Simultaneous, photocopied and previously published submissions OK. Computer printout submissions acceptable; prefers letter-quality. Reports in 2 weeks. Sample copy for 9x11 SAE and 7 first class stamps; writer's guidelines for #10 SAE and 1 first class stamp.
Nonfiction: Book excerpts (fitness and health); expose (in tennis, fitness, racquetball, health clubs, diets); adult (slightly risque and racy fitness); how-to (expert instructional pieces on any area of coverage); humor (large market for funny pieces on health clubs and fitness); inspirational (on how diet and exercise combine to bring you a better body, self); interview/profile; new product; opinion (only from recognized sources who know what they are talking about); personal experience (definitely—humor); photo feature (on related subjects); technical (on exercise and sport); travel (related to fitness, tennis camps, etc.); news reports (on racquetball, handball, tennis, running events). Special issues: Swimsuit and Resort Issue (March); Baseball Preview (April); Summer Fashion (July); Pro Football Preview (August); Fall Fashion (October); Ski Issue (November); Christmas Gifts and related articles (December). "We love short articles that get to the point. Nationally oriented big events and national championships. No articles on local only tennis and racquetball tournaments

without national appeal." Buys 150 mss/year. Length: 2,000 words maximum. Pays $20-150. Sometimes pays the expenses of writers on assignment.

Photos: Randy Lester, photo editor. Send photos with ms. Pays $5-75 for b&w prints. Captions, model releases and identification of subjects required. Buys all rights, "but returns 75% of photos to submitter."

Columns/Departments: Linda Jefferson, column/department editor. New Products; Fitness Newsletter; Handball Newsletter; Racquetball Newsletter; Tennis Newsletter; News & Capsule Summaries; Fashion Spot (photos of new fitness and bathing suits and ski equipment); related subjects. Buys 100 mss/year. Send complete ms. Length: 50-250 words ("more if author has good handle to cover complete columns"). Pays $5-25.

Fiction: Judy Johnson, fiction editor. Erotica (if related to fitness club); fantasy (related to subjects); humorous (definite market); religious ("no God-is-my shepherd, but Body-is-God's-temple OK"); romance (related subjects). "Upbeat stories are needed." Buys 20 mss/year. Send complete ms. Length: 500-2,500 words maximum. Pays $20-150.

Poetry: Free verse, haiku, light verse, traditional on related subjects. Length: up to 150 words. Pays $10-25.

Fillers: Linda Jefferson, fillers editor. Clippings, jokes, gags, anecdotes, short humor, newsbreaks. Buys 400/year. Length: 25-200 words. Pays $5-15.

Tips: "Send us articles dealing with court club sports, exercise and nutrition that exemplify an upbeat 'you can do it' attitude. Pro sports previews 3-4 months ahead of their seasons are also needed. Good short fiction or humorous articles can break in. Expert knowledge of any related subject can bring assignments; any area is open. A humorous/knowledgeable columnist in weight lifting, aerobics, running and nutrition is presently needed. We review the author's work on a nonpartial basis. We consider everything as a potential article, but are turned off by credits, past work and degrees. We have a constant demand for well-written articles on instruction, health and trends in both. Other articles needed are professional sports training techniques, fad diets, tennis and fitness resorts, photo features with aerobic routines. A frequent mistake made by writers is length—articles are too long. When we assign an article, we want it newsy if it's news and opinion if opinion. Too many writers are incapable of this task."

SIGNPOST MAGAZINE, Suite 518, 1305 Fourth Ave., Seattle WA 98101. Publisher: Washington Trails Association. Editor: Ann L. Marshall. 10% freelance written. "We will consider working with both previously published and unpublished freelancers." Monthly about hiking, backpacking and similar trail-related activities, mostly from a Pacific Northwest viewpoint. Will consider any rights offered by author. Buys 12 mss/year. Pays on publication. Publishes ms an average of 6 months after acceptance. Free sample copy; writer's guidelines available for SASE. Will consider photocopied submissions. Reports in 6 weeks. Query or submit complete ms. Computer printout submissions acceptable; no dot-matrix.

Nonfiction and Photos: "Most material is donated by subscribers or is staff-written. Payment for purchased material is low, but a good way to break in to print and share your outdoor experiences."

Tips: "We cover only *self-propelled* backcountry sports and won't consider manuscripts about trail bikes, snowmobiles, or power boats. We *are* interested in articles about modified and customized equipment, food and nutrition, and personal experiences in the backcountry (primarily Pacific Northwest, but will consider nation- and world-wide)."

SKYDIVING, Box 1520, Deland FL 32721. (904)736-9779. Editor: Michael Truffer. 25% freelance written. Works with a small number of new/unpublished writers each year. Monthly tabloid featuring skydiving for sport parachutists, worldwide dealers and equipment manufacturers. Circ. 7,800. Average issue includes 3 feature articles and 3 columns of technical information. Pays on publication. Publishes ms an average of 3 months after acceptance. Byline given. Buys one-time rights. Simultaneous, photocopied and previously published submissions OK, if so indicated. Query for electronic submissions. Computer printout submissions acceptable. Reports in 1 month. Sample copy $2; writer's guidelines with 9x12 SAE and 4 first class stamps.

Nonfiction: "Send us news and information on equipment, techniques, events and outstanding personalities who skydive. We want articles written by people who have a solid knowledge of parachuting." No personal experience or human-interest articles. Query. Length: 500-1,000 words. Pays $25-100. Sometimes pays the expenses of writers on assignment.

Photos: State availability of photos. Reviews 5x7 and larger b&w glossy prints. Offers no additional payment for photos accepted with ms. Captions required.

Fillers: Newsbreaks. Length: 100-200 words. Pays $25 minimum.

Tips: "The most frequent mistake made by writers in completing articles for us is that the writer isn't knowledgeable about the sport of parachuting."

VOLLEYBALL MONTHLY, Straight Down, Inc., Box 3137, San Luis Obispo CA 93403. (805)541-2294. Editor: Jon Hastings. 40% freelance written. Monthly magazine covering volleyball. "National publication geared to players, coaches and fans of the sport of volleyball." Circ. 40,000. Pays on publication. Publishes ms an average of 2 months after acceptance. Byline given. Buys one-time rights. Submit seasonal/holiday material 3 months in advance. Computer printout submissions OK. Reports in 2 weeks on queries. Sample copy and writer's guidelines for 9x12 SAE and $2.

Nonfiction: General interest, historical/nostalgic, how-to, humor, inspirational, interview/profile and personal experience. No "USC beat UCLA last week" articles. Buys 10 mss/year. Send complete ms. Length: 750-3,000 words. Pays $50-250 for assigned articles; pays $50-150 for unsolicited articles. Sometimes pays the expenses of writers on assignment.

Photos: State availability of photos with submission or send photos with submission. Reviews 8x10 prints. Offers $15-75 per photo. Identification of subjects required. Buys one-time rights.

Columns/Departments: Buys 10 mss/year. Send complete ms. Length: 750-2,000 words. Pays $50-150.

Fiction: Buys 2 mss/year. Send complete ms. Pays $50-150.

Fillers: Anecdotes and short humor. Pays $25-50.

Tips: "We're looking for more articles dealing with technical aspects of the sport."

Skiing and Snow Sports

SKATING, United States Figure Skating Association, 20 First St., Colorado Springs CO 80906. (303)635-5200. Editor: Dale Mitch. Published 10 times a year except August/September. Circ. 31,000. Official Publication of the USFSA. Pays on publication. Publishes ms an average of 3 months after acceptance. Buys all rights. Byline given.

Nonfiction: Historical; humor; informational; interview; photo feature; historical biographies; profile (background and interests of national-caliber amateur skaters); technical; and competition reports. Buys 4 mss/issue. Query. Length: 500-1,500 words.

Photos: Photos purchased with or without accompanying ms. Pays $15 for 8x10 or 5x7 b&w glossy prints and $35 for color transparencies. Query.

Columns/Departments: Ice Abroad (competition results and report from outside the U.S.); Book Reviews; People; Club News (what individual clubs are doing); and Music column (what's new and used for music for skating). Buys 4 mss/issue. Query or send complete ms. Length: 100-1,000 words.

Tips: "We want sharp, strong, intelligent writing by experienced persons knowledgeable in the technical and artistic aspects of figure skating with a new outlook on the development of the sport. Knowledge and background in technical aspects of figure skating are essential to the quality of writing expected. We would also like to receive articles on former national and international champtions; photos from the past national and and international competitions and personalities and humorous features directly related to figure skating. No professional skater material."

SKI MAGAZINE, 380 Madison Ave., New York NY 10017. (212)687-3000. Editor: Dick Needham. Managing Editor: Andrea Rosengarten. 15% freelance written. A monthly magazine on snow skiing. "*Ski* is written and edited for recreational skiers. Its content is intended to help them ski better (technique), buy better (equipment and skiwear), and introduce them to new resort experiences and ski adventures." Circ. 430,000. Pays on acceptance. Publishes ms an average of 3 months after acceptance. Byline given. Offers 15% kill fee. Buys first North American serial rights. Submit seasonal/holiday material 8 months in advance. Photocopied submission OK. Computer printout submissions OK; prefers letter-quality. Reports in 1 week on queries; 2 weeks on ms. Sample copy for 8½x11 SAE and 5 first class stamps.

Nonfiction: Essays, historical/nostalgic, how-to, humor, interview/profile and personal experience. Buys 5-10 mss/year. Send complete ms. Length: 1,000-3,500 words. Pays $500-1,000 for assigned articles; pays $300-700 for unsolicited articles. Pays the expenses of writers on assignment.

Photos: Send photos with submission. Offers $75-300/photo. Captions, model releases and identification of subjects required. Buys one-time rights.

Columns/Departments: Ski Life (interesting people, events, oddities with skiing), 150-300 words; Discoveries (neat special products or services available to skiers that are out of the ordinary), 100-200 words; and Better Way (new ideas invented by writer that make his skiing life easier, more convenient, more enjoyable), 50-150 words. Buys 20 mss/year. Send complete ms. Length: 100-300 words. Pays $50-100.

Fillers: Facts and short humor. Buys 10/year. Length: 60-75 words. Pays $50-75.

Tips: "Writers must have an extensive familiarity with the sport and know what concerns, interests and amuses skiers. Ski Life, Discoveries and Better Way are most open to freelancers."

SKIING, CBS Magazines, 1 Park Ave., New York NY 10016. (212)503-3920. Editor: Bill Grout. 40% freelance written. Works with a small number of new/unpublished writers each year. A magazine published 7 times a year. "*Skiing* is a service magazine for skiing enthusiasts." Circ. 440,000. Pays on publication. Publishes ms an average of 6 months after acceptance. Byline given. Offers ⅓ kill fee. Buys first North American serial rights. Submit seasonal/holiday material 8 months in advance. Computer printout submissions acceptable; prefers letter-quality. Reports in 6 weeks on queries; 2 months on mss. Sample copy for 9x12 SAE with 6 first class stamps.

Nonfiction: Essays, how-to, humor, interview/profile, personal experience and travel. No fiction, ski equipment evaluations or 'How I Learned to Ski' stories. Buys 35 mss/year. Query with published clips.

Length: 500-2,000 words. Pays $50-1,000 for assigned articles; pays $50-750 for unsolicited articles. Pays the expenses of writers on assignment.

Photos: State availability of photos with submission. Reviews contact sheets and negatives. Offers $50-300/photo. Captions, model releases and identification of subjects required. Buys one-time rights.

‡SNOW COUNTRY, New York Times Magazine Group, 5520 Park Ave., Trumbull CT 06611. (203)723-7030. Editor: John Fry. Managing Editor: Bob LaMarche. 50% freelance written. Monthly magazine on sports and leisure activity in North American snow country. "Story ideas should be hooked to a person or people; best market for freelancers are front- and back-of-book pieces which are short—500-700 words." Estab. 1988. Circ. 200,000. Pays on acceptance. Byline given. Offers ⅓ kill fee. Buys first North American serial rights. Query for electronic submission. Computer printout submissions OK. Reports in 2 weeks.

Nonfiction: Historical/nostalgic, humor, interview/profile, personal experience, photo feature. Buys 150 mss/year. Query or query with published clips. Length: 200-1,000 words. Pays $150-750.

Photos: State availability of photos with submission or send photos with submission. Reviews contact sheets, transparencies and prints. Offers $25-600/photo. Model releases and identification of subjects required. Buys one-time rights.

Columns/Departments: Datebook (events, occasions, anniversaries in snow country; also odd, lively, or poignant quotes from people living in snow country or about snow country) 50 words. Send complete ms. Pays $20-40. Snow Country Store is a department of 150-word takes on artist, artisan, craftsperson, inventor, even cook or songwriter living in snow country who has product that can be purchased locally or by mail. This is not standard mail-order column—no souvenirs, household helps, objects conceived by marketing departments. Interesting people, unique or well-executed products. Query first. $100 minimum payment; extra for 2 pictures—one of person, one of product.

Tips: "We are looking for excellent writing, genuine fondness or interest in the subject. Please query and send clips. Magazine began regular publication in September 1988, monthly thereafter, and will be on newsstands. Most libraries will have, eventually. We do not send copies. We are developing writer's guidelines."

Soccer

SOCCER AMERICA, Box 23704, Oakland CA 94623. (415)549-1414. Editor-in-Chief: Lynn Berling-Manuel. 10% freelance written. Works with a small number of new/unpublished writers each year. Weekly tabloid for a wide range of soccer enthusiasts. Circ. 15,000. Pays on publication. Publishes ms an average of 2 months after acceptance. Buys all rights. Byline given. Submit seasonal/holiday material 30 days in advance. Query for electronic submissions. Computer printout submissions OK; prefers letter-quality. Reports in 2 months. Sample copy and writer's guidelines $1.

Nonfiction: Expose (why a pro franchise isn't working right, etc.); historical; how-to; informational (news features); inspirational; interview; photo feature; profile; and technical. "No 'Why I Like Soccer' articles in 1,000 words or less. It's been done. We are very much interested in articles for our 'special issues': fitness, travel, and college selection process." Buys 1-2 mss/issue. Query. Length: 200-1,500 words. Pays 50¢/inch minimum.

Photos: Photos purchased with or without accompanying ms or on assignment. Captions required. Pays $12 for 5x7 or larger b&w glossy prints. Query.

Tips: "Freelancers mean the addition of editorial vitality. New approaches and new minds can make a world of difference. But if they haven't familiarized themselves with the publication . . . total waste of my time and theirs."

Tennis

TENNIS, 5520 Park Ave., Trumbull CT 06611. Publisher: Mark Adorney. Editor: Alexander McNab. 25% freelance written. Works with a small number of new/unpublished writers each year. For persons who play tennis and want to play it better and who follow tennis as fans. Monthly magazine. Circ. 525,000. Buys all rights. Byline given. Pays on publication. Publishes ms an average of 6 months after acceptance.

Nonfiction and Photos: Emphasis on instructional and reader service articles, but also seeks lively, well-researched features on personalities and other aspects of the game, as well as humor. Query. Length varies. Pays $200 minimum/article, considerably more for major features. Pays $60 and up/8x10 b&w glossies; $120 and up/color transparencies.

Tips: "When reading our publication the writer should note the depth of the tennis-expertise in the stories and should note the conversational, informal writing styles that are used."

WORLD TENNIS, Family Media, 3 Park Ave., New York NY 10016. (212)340-9683. Editor: Neil Amdur. Managing Editor: Peter M. Coan. Monthly tennis magazine. "We are a magazine catering to tennis enthusiasts—both participants and fans—on every level." Circ. 425,000. Pays on acceptance. Byline given. Offers 25% kill fee. Buys all rights. Submit seasonal/holiday material 4 months in advance. Photocopied submissions OK. Query for electronic submissions. Computer printout submissions OK; no dot-matrix. Reports in 2 weeks on queries; 1 month on manuscripts. Sample copy for 8x11 SAE and 5 first class stamps.
Nonfiction: Book excerpts (tennis, fitness, nutrition), essays, humor, interview/profile, new product, personal experience, photo feature, travel (tennis resorts). No instruction, poetry or fiction. Buys 30-40 mss/year. Query with published clips. Length: 750-3,000 words. Pays $100 and up. Sometimes pays expenses of writers on assignment.
Photos: State availability of photos with submission. Reviews contact sheets. Payment varies. Requires captions and identification of subjects. Buys one-time rights.
Columns/Departments: Seniority (essays by or about older players); My Ad (personal opinion on hot tennis topics); About Juniors (short pieces relating to the junior game), all 750-1,000 words. Buys 12-20 mss/year. Query with published clips. Pays $100 and up.
Fillers: Anecdotes, facts, newsbreaks, short humor. Buys 10-15/year. Length: 750-1,000 words. Pays $100 and up.
Tips: "Query before sending manuscripts. Most of our material is commissioned, but we welcome fresh ideas. The Seniority column is most open to freelancers, but About Juniors and My Ad is also open to fresh ideas. Your best bet is to submit a one-page cover letter explaining your article idea along with a resume and clips. We want to know the credentials of the freelancer as well as the idea submitted."

Water Sports

DIVER, Seagraphic Publications, Ltd., 10991 Shellbridge Way, Richmond, British Columbia V6X 3C6 Canada. (604)273-4333. Publisher: Peter Vassilopoulos. Consulting Editor: Neil McDaniel. 75% freelance written. Emphasizes scuba diving, ocean science and technology (commercial and military diving) for a well-educated, outdoor-oriented readership. Published 9 times/year. Circ. 25,000. Payment "follows publication." Buys first North American serial rights. Byline given. Query (by mail only). Submit seasonal/holiday material 3 months in advance of issue date. Computer printout submissions acceptable; prefers letter-quality. Send SAE with IRCs. Reports in 6 weeks. Publishes ms an average of 2 months after acceptance.
Nonfiction: How-to (underwater activities such as photography, etc.); general interest (underwater oriented); humor; historical (shipwrecks, treasure artifacts, archeological); interview (underwater personalities in all spheres—military, sports, scientific or commercial); personal experience (related to diving); photo feature (marine life); technical (related to oceanography, commercial/military diving, etc.); and travel (dive resorts). No subjective product reports. Buys 40 mss/year. Submit complete ms. Length: 800-2,000 words. Pays $2.50/column inch.
Photos: "Features are mostly those describing dive sites, experiences, etc. Photo features are reserved more as specials, while almost all articles must be well illustrated with b&w prints supplemented by color transparencies." Submit photo material with accompanying ms. Pays $7 minimum for 5x7 or 8x10 b&w glossy prints; $15 minimum for 35mm color transparencies. Captions and model releases required. Buys one-time rights.
Columns/Departments: Book reviews. Submit complete ms. Length: 200 words maximum. Pays $2.50/column inch.
Fillers: Anecdotes, newsbreaks and short humor. Buys 8-10/year. Length: 50-150 words. Pays $2.50/column inch.

SCUBA TIMES, The Active Diver's Magazine, Poseidon Publishing Corp., Box 6268, Pensacola FL 32503. (904)478-5288. Publisher/Editor: Fred D. Garth. 80% freelance written. Prefers to work with published/established writers. Bimonthly magazine covering scuba diving. "Our reader is the young, reasonably affluent scuba diver looking for a more exciting approach to diving than he could find in the other diving magazines." Circ. 40,000. Pays after publication. Byline given. Buys first world serial rights. Computer printout submissions acceptable. Sample copy $3. Writer's guidelines for #10 SAE and 1 first class stamp.
Nonfiction: General interest; how-to; interview/profile ("of 'name' people in the sport, especially if they're currently doing something interesting"); new products (how to more effectively use them); personal experience (good underwater photography pieces); and travel (pertaining to diving). No articles without a specific theme. Buys 40 mss/year. *Query first* with clips of published work. Will not return material unless accompanied with return postage. Pay varies with author. Base rate is $75/published page (30 column inches). Sometimes pays the expenses of writers on assignment.
Photos: Blair Director, art director. "Underwater photography must be of the *highest* quality in order to catch our interest. We can't be responsible for unsolicited photo submissions." Pays $25-250 for 35mm color transparencies; reviews 8x10 b&w prints. Captions, model releases, and identification of subjects required. Buys first world rights. Enclose 9x12 SASE and postage if you want material returned.

SKIN DIVER, Petersen Publishing Co., 8490 Sunset Blvd., Los Angeles CA 90069. (213)854-2960. Executive Editor: Bonnie J. Cardone. Managing Editor: Jim Warner. 85% freelance written. Eager to work with new/unpublished writers. Monthly magazine on scuba diving. "*Skin Diver* offers broad coverage of all significant aspects of underwater activity in the areas of foreign and domestic travel, recreation, ocean exploration, scientific research, commercial diving and technological developments." Circ. 224,786. Pays on publication. Publishes ms an average of 9 months after acceptance. Byline given. Buys one-time rights. Submit seasonal/holiday material 6 months in advance. No simultaneous submissions. Computer printout submissions acceptable. Reports in 3 weeks on queries; 3 months on mss. Sample copy $3; free writer's guidelines.
Nonfiction: How-to (catch game, modify equipment, etc.); interview/profile; personal experience; travel; local diving; adventure and wreck diving). No Caribbean travel; "how I learned to dive." Buys 200 mss/year. Send complete ms. Length: 300-2,000 words; 1,200 preferred. Pays $50/published page.
Photos: Send photos with query or ms. Reviews 35mm transparencies and 8x10 prints. Pays $50/published page. Captions and identification of subjects required. Buys one-time rights.
Fillers: Newsbreaks and cartoons. Length: 300 words. Pays $25 for cartoons; $50/published page.
Tips: "Forget tropical travel articles and write about local diving sites, hobbies, game diving, local and wreck diving."

SURFER, Surfer Publications, 33046 Calle Aviador, San Juan Capistrano CA 92675. (714)496-5922. Editor: Paul Holmes. 20% freelance written. A monthly magazine "aimed at experts and beginners with strong emphasis on action surf photography." Circ. 110,000. Pays on publication. Byline given. Buys all rights. Submit seasonal/holiday material 6 months in advance. Simultaneous and photocopied submissions OK. Query for electronic submissions. Computer printout submissions acceptable; prefers letter-quality. Reports in 1 month on queries; 10 weeks on manuscripts. Sample copy for 8½x11 SAE with $3.50; writer's guidelines for SASE.
Nonfiction: How-to (technique in surfing); humor, inspirational, interview/profile, opinion, and personal experience (all surf-related); photo feature (action surf and surf travel); technical (surfboard design); and travel (surf exploration and discovery—photos required). Buys 30-50 mss/year. Query with or without published clips, or send complete ms. Length: 500-2,500 words. Pays 10-15¢/word. Sometimes pays the expenses of writers on assignment.
Photos: Send photos with submission. Reviews 35mm negatives and transparencies. Offers $10-250/photo. Identification of subjects required. Buys one-time and reprint rights.
Columns/Departments: Our Mother Ocean (environmental concerns to surfers), 1,000-1,500 words; Surf Stories (personal experiences of surfing), 1,000-1,500 words; Reviews (surf-related movies, books), 500-1,000 words; and Sections (humorous surf-related items with b&w photos), 100-500 words. Buys 25-50 mss/year. Send complete ms. Pays 10-15¢/word.
Fiction: Surf-related adventure, fantasy, horror, humorous, and science fiction. Buys 10 mss/year. Send complete ms. Length: 750-2,000 words. Pays 10-15¢/word.
Tips: "All sections are open to freelancers but interview/profiles are usually assigned. Stories must be authoritative and oriented to the hard-core surfer."

SWIM MAGAZINE, Sports Publications, Inc., Box 45497, Los Angeles CA 90045. (213)674-2120. Editor: Kim A. Hansen. 75% freelance written. Prefers to work with published/selected writers. Bimonthly magazine. "*Swim Magazine* is for adults interested in swimming for fun, fitness and competition. Readers are fitness-oriented adults from varied social and professional backgrounds who share swimming as part of their lifestyle. Readers' ages are evenly distributed from 25 to 90, so articles must appeal to a broad age group." Circ. 9,390. Pays approximately 1 month after publication. Publishes ms an average of 4 months after acceptance. Byline given. Submit seasonal/holiday material 4 months in advance. Simultaneous queries and photocopied submissions OK. Computer printout submissions OK; no dot-matrix. Reports in 1 month on queries; 3 months on mss. Sample copy for $2.50 prepaid and 9x12 SAE with 11 first class stamps. Free writer's guidelines.
Nonfiction: How-to (training plans and techniques); humor (sophisticated adult-oriented humor); interview/profile (people associated with fitness and competitive swimming); new product (articles describing new products for fitness and competitive training); personal experience (related to how swimming has become an integral part of one's lifestyle); travel (articles on vacation spots); diet and health (articles on diet, health and self-help that relate to, or include swimming). "Articles need to be informative as well as interesting. In addition to fitness and health articles, we are interested in exploring fascinating topics dealing with swimming for the adult reader." Buys 30 mss/year. Send complete ms. Length: 1,000-3,500 words. Pays $3/published column inch. "No payment for articles about personal experiences."
Photos: Send photos with ms. Offers no additional payment for photos accepted with ms. Captions, model releases, and identification of subjects required.
Tips: "Our how-to articles and physiology articles best typify *Swim Magazine*'s projected style for fitness and competitive swimmers. *Swim Magazine* will accept medical guideline and diet articles only by M.D.s and Ph.Ds."

UNDERCURRENT, Box 1658, Sausalito CA 94965. Managing Editor: Ben Davison. 20-50% freelance written. Works with a small number of new/unpublished writers each year. Monthly consumer-oriented *scuba diving newsletter*. Circ. 15,000. Pays on publication. Publishes ms an average of 2 months after acceptance. Buys first rights. Pays $50 kill fee. Byline given. Simultaneous (if to other than diving publisher), photocopied and previously published submissions OK. Computer printout submissions OK. Reports in 4-6 weeks. Free sample copy and writer's guidelines; mention *Writer's Market* in request.
Nonfiction: Equipment evaluation, how-to, general interest, new product, and travel review. Buys 2 mss/issue. Query with brief outline of story idea and credentials. Will commission. Length: 2,000 words maximum. Pays 10¢/word. Sometimes pays the expenses of writers on assignment.

THE WATER SKIER, Box 191, Winter Haven FL 33882. (813)324-4341. Editor: Duke Cullimore. Official publication of the American Water Ski Association. 50% freelance written. Published monthly. Circ. 20,000. Buys North American serial rights. Byline given. Buys limited amount of freelance material. Query. Pays on acceptance. Publishes ms an average of 3 months after acceptance. Reports on submissions within 10 days. Computer printout submissions acceptable "if double-spaced and standard ms requirements are followed"; prefers letter-quality. Sample copy for 9x12 SAE and 4 first class stamps.
Nonfiction and Photos: Occasionally buys exceptionally offbeat, unusual text/photo features on the sport of water skiing. Emphasis on technique, methods, etc.
Tips: "Freelance writers should be aware of specialization of subject matter; need for more expertise in topic; more professional writing ability."

Teen and Young Adult

The publications in this category are for young people ages 13-19. Publications for college students are listed in Career, College and Alumni.

AMERICAN NEWSPAPER CARRIER, American Newspaper Press, Box 15300, Winston-Salem NC 27113. Editor: Marilyn H. Rollins. 50% freelance written. Works with a small number of new/unpublished writers each year. Usually buys all rights but may be released upon request. Pays on acceptance. Publishes ms an average of 3 months after acceptance. Computer printout submissions acceptable. Reports in 30 days.
Fiction: Uses a limited amount of short fiction written for teen-age newspaper carriers, male and female. It is preferable that stories be written around newspaper carrier characters. Humor, mystery and adventure plots are commonly used. No drugs, sex, fantasy, supernatural, crime or controversial themes. Queries not required. Length: 1,200 words. Pays $25.
Tips: "Fillers are staff-written, usually."

BOYS' LIFE, See Consumer Juvenile Section.

BREAD, Nazarene Publishing House, 6401 The Paseo, Kansas City MO 64131. (816)333-7000. Editor: Karen DeSollar. 20% freelance written. Works with a small number of new/unpublished writers each year. A monthly magazine for Nazarene teens. Circ. 26,000. Pays on acceptance. Publishes ms an average of 8 months after acceptance. Byline given. Buys one-time rights. Submit seasonal/holiday material 10 months in advance. Simultaneous, photocopied, and previously published submissions OK. Computer printout submissions acceptable; no dot-matrix. Reports in 6 weeks on queries; 2 months on mss. Sample copy and writer's guidelines for 9x12 SAE with 2 first class stamps.
Nonfiction: How-to and personal experience, both involving teens and teen problems and how to deal with them. Buys 25 mss/year. Send complete ms. Length: 1,200-1,500 words. Pays 3-3½¢/word.
Fiction: Adventure, humorous and romance, all demonstrating teens living out Christian commitment in real life.

CAMPUS LIFE MAGAZINE, Christianity Today, Inc., 465 Gundersen Dr., Carol Stream IL 60188. Executive Editor: Scott Bolinder. Senior Editor: Jim Long. Associate Editors: Chris Lutes and Diane Eble. Assistant Editor: Kris Bearss. 30-40% freelance written. Prefers to work with published/established writers. For a readership of young adults, high school and college age. "Though our readership is largely Christian, *Campus Life* reflects the interests of all young people—music, bicycling, photography, media and sports." Largely staff-written. "*Campus Life* is a Christian magazine that is *not* overtly religious. The indirect style is intended to create a safety zone with our readers and to reflect our philosophy that God is interested in all of life. Therefore, we publish message stories side by side with general interest, humor, etc." Monthly magazine. Circ. 180,000.

Pays on acceptance. Publishes ms an average of 3-6 months after acceptance. Buys first serial and one-time rights. Byline given. Submit seasonal/holiday material 6 months in advance. Simultaneous, photocopied and previously published submissions OK. Query for electronic submissions. Computer printout submissions acceptable. Reports in 2 months. Sample copy for 9x12 SAE and $2; writer's guidelines for SASE.

Nonfiction: Personal experiences, photo features, unusual sports, humor, short items—how-to, college or career and travel, etc. Query only. Length: 500-3,000 words. Pays $100-300. Sometimes pays the expenses of writers on assignment.

Photos: Pays $50 minimum/8x10 b&w glossy print; $90 minimum/color transparency; $250/cover photo. Buys one-time rights.

Fiction: Stories about problems and experiences kids face. Trite, simplistic religious stories are not acceptable.

Tips: "The best ms for a freelancer to try to sell us would be a well-written first-person story (fiction or nonfiction) focusing on a common struggle young people face in any area of life—intellectual, emotional, social, physical or spiritual. Most manuscripts that miss us fail in quality or style. We are always looking for good humor pieces for high school readers. These could be cartoon spreads, or other creative humorous pieces that would make kids laugh."

CAREERS, The Magazine for Today's Teens, E.M. Guild, Inc., 1001 Avenue of the Americas, New York NY 10018. (212)354-8877. Editor: Lois Cantwell. 100% freelance written. Works with a small number of new/unpublished writers each year. A magazine published 3 times a year covering life-coping skills, career choices, and educational opportunities for high school juniors and seniors. "*Careers* is designed to offer a taste of the working world, new career opportunities, and stories covering the best ways to reach those opportunities—through education, etc." Circ. 600,000. Pays 30 days after acceptance. Publishes ms an average of 2-3 months after acceptance. Byline given. Offers 25% kill fee. Buys first North American serial rights. Submit seasonal/holiday material 6 months in advance. Sometimes accepts previously published submissions. Computer printout submissions acceptable; prefers letter-quality. Reports in 2 months on queries; 3 weeks on mss. Sample copy $2.50; writer's guidelines for #10 SAE with 1 first class stamp.

Nonfiction: Book excerpts, how-to, interview/profile, photo feature, travel, humor. Buys 25 mss/year. Query with published clips. Length: 1,000-1,500 words. Pays $250. Sometimes pays the expenses of writers on assignment.

Photos: State availability of photos with submission. Reviews contact sheets and transparencies. Offers $100 minimum/photo. Captions, model releases, and identification of subjects required. Buys one-time rights.

Columns/Departments: Banking On It, Taste Sensations, Shape Up, High Tech Tools, Clothes Calls and Profiles in Studies. Buys 15 mss/year. Length: 1,000-1,500 words. Pays $250.

Tips: "Generally looking for unusual slant; i.e. keep away from stories about resumes, first jobs, shyness. Would prefer seeing ms on (for example) alternatives to four-year college; best kind of reference books; high tech in education settings; etc. (Please do not submit these specific titles!)."

CHRISTIAN LIVING FOR SENIOR HIGHS, David C. Cook Publishing Co., 850 N. Grove, Elgin IL 60120. (312)741-2400. Editor: Anne E. Dinnan. 75% freelance written. Prefers to work with published/established writers, and works with a small number of new/unpublished writers each year. Quarterly magazine. "A take-home paper used in senior high Sunday School classes. We encourage Christian teens to write to us." Pays on acceptance. Publishes ms an average of 15 months after acceptance. Buys all rights. Byline given. Query for electronic submissions. Computer printout submissions acceptable; prefers letter-quality. Reports in 2-3 months. Sample copy and writer's guidelines for 4x9½ SAE and 1 first class stamp.

Nonfiction: How-to (Sunday School youth projects); historical (with religious base); humor (from Christian perspective); inspirational and personality (nonpreachy); personal teen experience (Christian); poetry written by teens and photo feature (Christian subject). "Nothing not compatible with a Christian lifestyle." Submit complete ms. Length: 900-1,200 words. Pays $100; $40 for short pieces.

Fiction: Adventure (with religious theme); historical (with Christian perspective); humorous; mystery; and religious. Buys 2 mss/issue. Submit complete ms. Length: 900-1,200 words. Pays $100. "No preachy experiences."

Photos: Gail Russell, photo editor. Photos purchased with or without accompanying ms or on assignment. Send contact sheets, prints or transparencies. Pays $25-40 for 8½x11 b&w photos; $50 minimum for color transparencies. "Photo guidelines available."

Tips: "Our demand for manuscripts should increase, but most of these will probably be assigned rather than bought over-the-transom. Our features are always short. A frequent mistake made by writers in completing articles for us is misunderstanding our market. Writing is often not Christian at all, or it's too 'Christian,' i.e. pedantic, condescending and moralistic."

CURRENT HEALTH 2, The Continuing Guide to Health Education, General Learning Corp., 60 Revere Dr., Northbrook IL 60062-1563. (312)564-4070. Editor: Laura Ruekberg. Managing Editor: Nancy Dreher. 90% freelance written. Prefers to work with published/established writers; works with small number of new/

unpublished writers each year. A health education magazine published monthly. "Our audience is seventh through twelfth grade health education students. Articles should be written at a ninth grade reading level. The magazine is curriculum supplementary, and should be accurate, timely, accessible, and highly readable." Circ. 200,000. Pays on publication. Publishes ms an average of 5 months after acceptance. Byline given. Offers 50% kill fee. Buys all rights.

Nonfiction: General interest, interview/profile and new product. "No queries or unsolicited articles. All articles are on assignment only; send query with resume, published samples and SASE." Buys 100 mss/year. Length: 900-2,300 words. Pays $100-400, depending on length, for assigned articles. Sometimes pays the expenses of writers on assignment.

Tips: "We look for writers with a background in the area they are writing about. Drug writers in particular are needed. Articles on disease, fitness and exercise, psychology, safety, sexuality and nutrition are also needed."

EXPLORING MAGAZINE, Boy Scouts of America, 1325 Walnut Hill Ln., Box 152079, Irving TX 75015-2079. (214)580-2365. Executive Editor: Scott Daniels. 85% freelance written. Prefers to work with published/established writers; works with a small number of new/unpublished writers each year. Magazine published 4 times/year—January, March, May, September. Covers the educational teen-age Exploring program of the BSA. Circ. 400,000. Pays on acceptance. Publishes ms an average of 6 months after acceptance. Byline given. Buys one-time and first rights. Submit seasonal/holiday material 6 months in advance. Simultaneous queries OK. Computer printout submissions acceptable; prefers letter-quality. Reports in 2 weeks. Sample copy for 9x12 SAE and 4 first class stamps; writer's guidelines for #10 SAE and 1 first class stamp. Write for guidelines and "What is Exploring?" fact sheet.

Nonfiction: General interest, how-to (achieve outdoor skills, organize trips, meetings, etc.); interview/profile (of outstanding Explorer); travel (backpacking or canoeing with Explorers). Buys 15-20 mss/year. Query with clips. Length: 800-1,800 words. Pays $300-450. Pays expenses of writers on assignment.

Photos: Gene Daniels, photo editor. State availability of photos with query letter or ms. Reviews b&w contact sheets. Captions required. Buys one-time rights.

Tips: "Contact the local Exploring Director in your area (listed in phone book white pages under Boy Scouts of America). Find out if there are some outstanding post activities going on and then query magazine editor in Irving, Texas. Strive for shorter texts, faster starts and stories that lend themselves to dramatic photographs."

FREEWAY, Box 632, Glen Ellyn IL 60138. Editor: Billie Sue Thompson. For "young Christian adults of high school and college age." 80% freelance written. Works with a small number of new/unpublished writers each year; eager to work with new/unpublished writers. Weekly. Circ. 50,000. Prefers first serial rights but buys some reprints. Purchases 100 mss/year. Byline given. Reports on material accepted for publication in 5-6 weeks. Publishes ms an average of 1 year after acceptance. Returns rejected material in 4-5 weeks. Computer printout submissions acceptable; prefers letter-quality. Free sample copy and writer's guidelines.

Nonfiction: "*FreeWay*'s greatest need is for personal experience stories showing how God has worked in teens' lives. Stories are best written in first-person, 'as told to' author. Incorporate specific details, anecdotes, and dialogue. Show, don't tell, how the subject thought and felt. Weave spiritual conflicts and prayers into entire manuscript; avoid tacked-on sermons and morals. Stories should show how God has helped the person resolve a problem or how God helped save a person from trying circumstances (1,000 words or less). Avoid stories about accident and illness; focus on events and emotions of everyday life. (Examples: How I overcame shyness; confessions of a food addict.) Short-short stories are needed as fillers. We also need self-help or how-to articles with practical Christian advice on daily living, and trend articles addressing secular fads from a Christian perspective. We do not use devotional material, poetry, or fictionalized Bible stories." Pays 4-7¢/word. Sometimes pays the expenses of writers on assignment.

Photos: Whenever possible, provide clear 8x10 or 5x7 b&w photos to accompany mss (or any other available photos). Payment is $5-30.

Fiction: "We use little fiction, unless it is allegory, parables, or humor."

Tips: "Study our 'Tips to Writers' pamphlet and sample copy, then query or send complete ms. In your cover letter, include information about who you are, writing qualifications, and experience working with teens. Include SASE."

GROUP MEMBERS ONLY, Thom Schultz Publications, Box 481, Loveland CO 80539. Editorial Director: Joani Schultz. 80% freelance written. Prefers to work with published/established writers; works with small number of new/unpublished writers each year. Magazine published 8 times/year. For members of high-school-age Christian youth groups. Circ. 30,000. Pays on acceptance. Publishes ms an average of 4 months after acceptance. Byline given. Buys all rights. Submit seasonal/holiday material 6 months in advance. Computer printout submissions acceptable; prefers letter-quality. Special Easter, Thanksgiving and Christmas issues and college issues. Reports in 1 month. Sample copy and writer's guidelines for 9x12 SAE with $1 postage.

Nonfiction: How-to (improving self-image and relationships, strengthening faith). Buys 2 mss/issue. Query. Length: 500-1,000 words. Pays up to $100. Sometimes pays expenses of writers on assignment.

GUIDE, 55 W. Oak Ridge Dr., Hagerstown MD 21740. Editor: Jeannette Johnson. 90% freelance written. Works with a small number of new/unpublished writers each year. A Seventh-day Adventist journal for junior youth and early teens. "Its content reflects Seventh-day Adventist beliefs and standards. Another characteristic which probably distinguishes it from many other magazines is the fact that all its stories are nonfiction." Weekly magazine. Circ. 50,000. Buys first serial rights, simultaneous rights, and second (reprint) rights to material originally published elsewhere. Pays on acceptance. Publishes ms an average of 6-9 months after acceptance. Byline given. Submit seasonal/holiday material 6 months in advance. Query for electronic submissions. Computer printout submissions acceptable; no dot-matrix. Reports in 6 weeks. Sample copy 40¢.

Nonfiction: Wants nonfiction stories of character-building and spiritual value. All stories must be true and include dialogue. Should emphasize the positive aspects of living, obedience to parents, perseverance, kindness, etc. "We use a limited number of stories dealing with problems common to today's Christian youth, such as peer pressure, parents' divorce, chemical dependency, etc. We can always use 'drama in real life' stories that show God's protection and seasonal stories—Christmas, Thanksgiving, special holidays. We do not use stories of hunting, fishing, trapping or spiritualism." Buys about 300 mss/year. Send complete ms (include word count and Social Security number). Length: up to 1,800 words. Pays 3-4¢/word. Also buys serialized true stories. Length: 10 chapters.

Tips: "Typical topics we cover in a yearly cycle include choices (music, clothes, friends, diet); friend-making skills; school problems (cheating, peer pressure, new school); death; finding and keeping a job; sibling relationships; divorce; step-families; runaways/throwaways; drugs; communication; and suicide. Write for our story schedule. We often buy short fillers, and an author who does not fully understand our needs is more likely to sell with a short-short. Our target age is 10-14. Our most successful writers are those who present stories from the viewpoint of a young teen-ager. Stories that sound like an adult's sentiments passing through a young person's lips are *not* what we're looking for. Use believable dialogue."

IN TOUCH, Wesley Press, Box 50434, Indianapolis IN 46250-0434. Editor: James Watkins. 80% freelance written. Eager to work with new/unpublished writers—"quality writing a must, however." A weekly Christian teen magazine. Circ. 25,000. Pays on acceptance. Publishes ms an average of 6-18 months after acceptance. Byline given. Offers 30% kill fee. Not copyrighted. Buys first rights or second serial (reprint) rights. Submit seasonal/holiday material 10 months in advance. Simultaneous, photocopied, and previously published submissions OK. Computer printout submissions acceptable; prefers letter-quality. Reports in 1 month on manuscripts. Writer's guidelines for #10 SAE with 1 first class stamp.

Nonfiction: Book excerpts, essays, how-to, humor, interview/profile, opinion, personal experience, photo feature from Christian perspective. "Our articles are teaching-oriented and contain lots of humor." Also needs true experiences told in fiction style, humorous fiction and allegories. No Sunday "soap." Buys 100 mss/year. Send complete ms. Length: 500-1,000 words. Pays $15-45.

Photos: Send photos with submissions. Pays $15-25/photo. Buys one-time rights.

KEYNOTER, Key Club International, 3636 Woodview Trace, Indianapolis IN 46268. (317)875-8755, ext. 172. Executive Editor: Jack Brockley. 65% freelance written. Works with a small number of new/unpublished writers each year, and is eager to work with new/unpublished writers willing to adjust their writing styles to *Keynoter*'s needs. A youth magazine published monthly Oct.-May (Dec./Jan. combined issue), distributed to members of Key Club International, a high school service organization for young men and women. Circ. 120,000. Pays on acceptance. Publishes ms an average of 5 months after acceptance. Byline given. Buys first North American serial rights. Submit seasonal/holiday material 7 months in advance. Simultaneous queries and submissions (if advised), photocopied and previously published submissions OK. Computer printout submissions acceptable; prefers letter-quality. Reports in 1 month. Sample copy for 9x12 SAE and 3 first class stamps; writer's guidelines for #10 SAE and 1 first class stamp.

Nonfiction: Book excerpts (may be included in articles but are not accepted alone); general interest (must be geared for intelligent teen audience); historical/nostalgic (generally not accepted); how-to (if it offers advice on how teens can enhance the quality of lives or communities); humor (accepted very infrequently; if adds to story, OK); interview/profile (rarely purchased, "would have to be on/with an irresistible subject"); new product (only if affects teens); photo feature (if subject is right, might consider); technical (if understandable and interesting to teen audience); travel (sometimes OK, but must apply to club travel schedule); subjects that entertain and inform teens on topics that relate directly to their lives. "We would also like to receive self-help and school-related nonfiction on leadership, community service, and teen issues. Please, no first-person confessions, no articles that are written down to our teen readers." Buys 5-10 mss/year. Query. Length: 1,500-2,500 words. Pays $125-250. Sometimes pays the expenses of writers on assignment.

Photos: State availability of photos. Reviews b&w contact sheets and negatives. Identification of subjects required. Buys one-time rights. Payment for photos included in payment for ms.

Tips: "We want to see articles written with attention to style and detail that will enrich the world of teens. Articles must be thoroughly researched and must draw on interviews with nationally and internationally respected sources. Our readers are 13-18, mature and dedicated to community service. We are very committed to working with good writers, and if we see something we like in a well-written query, we'll try to work it through to publication."

LIGHTED PATHWAY, Church of God, 922 Montgomery Ave., Cleveland TN 37311. (615)476-4512. Editor: Marcus V. Hand. 25% freelance written. A monthly magazine emphasizing Christian living for youth and young marrieds ages 13-25. Circ. 22,000. Pays on acceptance. Publishes ms an average of 3 months after acceptance. Byline given. Buys first North American serial rights and one-time rights. Submit seasonal/holiday material 4 months in advance. Simultaneous queries, and simultaneous, photocopied, and previously published submissions OK. Computer printout submissions acceptable. Reports in 2 weeks on queries; 1 month on mss. Free sample copy and writer's guidelines.

Nonfiction: Inspirational, interview/profile, personal experience, photo feature and travel. "Our primary objective is inspiration, to portray happy, victorious living through faith in God." Buys 40 mss/year. Query or send complete ms. Length: 1,000-2,000 words. Pays 2½-5¢/word.

Photos: State availability of photos or send photos with query or ms. Pays $10-20 for 8x10 b&w prints. Buys one-time rights and all rights.

Fiction: Adventure, historical and religious. No westerns, gothics, mysteries, animal. Buys 24 mss/year. Query or send complete ms. Length: 1,000-2,000 words. Pays 2½-5¢/word.

Tips: "Write to evangelical, conservative audience, about current subjects involving young people today." Fiction and human interest stories are most open to freelancers.

THE MAGAZINE FOR CHRISTIAN YOUTH!, The United Methodist Publishing House, 201 Eighth Ave. S., Box 801, Nashville TN 37202. (615)749-6463. Editor: Christopher B. Hughes. Monthly magazine. Circ. 50,000. Pays on acceptance. Publishes ms an average of 9 months after acceptance. Byline given. Buys one-time rights. Submit seasonal/holiday material 9 months in advance. Photocopied and previously published submissions OK. Computer printout submissions OK. Writer's guidelines for SASE.

Nonfiction: Book excerpts; general interest; how-to (deal with problems teens have); humor (on issues that touch teens' lives); inspirational; interview/profile (well-known singers, musicians, actors, sports); personal experience; religious and travel (include teen culture of another country). Buys 5-10 mss/year. Send complete ms. Length: 700-2,500 words. Pays $80-110 for assigned articles; 4¢/word for unsolicited articles. Pays expenses of writers on assignment. "Writers should give indication before expenses happen."

Photos: State availability of photos with submission. Reviews transparencies and 8x10 prints. Offers $25-150/photo. Captions and model releases required. Buys one-time rights.

Fiction: Adventure, ethnic, fantasy, historical, humorous, mainstream, mystery, religious, romance, science fiction, suspense and western. No stories where the plot is too trite and predictable—or too preachy. Buys 25 mss/year. Send complete ms. Length: 700-2,000 words. Pays 4¢/word.

Poetry: Free vese, haiku, light verse and traditional. No payment for poetry.

Fillers: Gags to be illustrated by cartoonists and short humor. Buys 6-8/year. Length: 10-75 words. Pays $15-80.

Tips: "Stay current with the youth culture so that your writing will reflect an insight into where teenagers are. Be neat, and always proofread and edit your own copy."

‡PATCHES, D.C. Thomson & Co., Meadowside, Dundee DD1 9QJ Scotland. (0382)23131. Editor: Sandra Monks. Managing Editor: Gordon Small. 60% freelance written. A weekly teen magazine. "Stories/features should be oriented toward teenage girls' interests, e.g. fashion, romance, beauty, school, parents. Subjects should be dealth with in an entertaining, realistic and sympathetic way. They should not be all doom and gloom." Circ. 90,000. Pays on acceptance. Publishes ms an average of 3 months after acceptance. No byline given. Buys first British serial rights and all rights. Submit seasonal/holiday material 4 months in advance. Reports in 2 weeks on queries; 3 weeks on mss. Free sample copy and writer's guidelines.

Nonfiction: Moira Smythe, articles editor. Humor, personal experience, photo feature. No articles on drugs or alcohol. Buys 30 mss/year. Query. Length: 1,000-2,000 words. Pays £40-£70. Sometimes pays expenses of writers on assignment.

Photos: Send photos with submission. Reviews contact sheets, negatives and 2¼ transparencies. Offers £10-£30/photo. Buys one-time rights or all rights.

Columns/Departments: Photo Stories (teenage romance) 30 frames; True Experiences (teenage romance) 1,500 words; Features (teenage interest, both humorous and emotional) 1,000 words; Pop Features (teenage pop heroes) 500 words (plus pics). Buys 300 mss/year. Send complete ms. Length: 500-2,000 words. Pays £30-£70.

Fiction: Judy Paris, fiction editor. Confession, fantasy, horror, humorous, mystery, romance, serialized novels, slice-of-life vignettes, suspense. No adult fiction. Buys 30 mss/year. Send complete ms. Length: 1,000-2,000 words. Pays £50-£70.

Tips: "Keep in mind that the market is teenagers and material should relate accordingly."

PIONEER, Baptist Brotherhood Commission, 1548 Poplar Ave., Memphis TN 38104. (901)272-2461. Editor-in-Chief: Timothy D. Bearden. 5% freelance written. For "boys age 12-14 who are members of a missions organization in Southern Baptist churches." Monthly magazine. Circ. 35,000. Byline given. Pays on acceptance. Publishes ms an average of 6-8 months after acceptance. Buys simultaneous rights. Submit seasonal/holiday material 8 months in advance. Simultaneous submissions OK. Computer printout submissions acceptable; prefers letter-quality. Reports in 1 month. Sample copy and writer's guidelines for 9x12 SAE with $1.18 postage; writer's guidelines only for #10 SASE.

Nonfiction: How-to (crafts, hobbies); informational (youth, religious especially); inspirational (sports/entertainment personalities); photo feature (sports, teen subjects). No "preachy" articles, fiction or excessive dialogue. Submit complete ms. Length: 500-1,500 words. Pays $20-50.

Photos: Purchased with accompanying ms or on assignment. Captions required. Query. Pays $10 for 8x10 b&w glossy prints.

Tips: "The writer has a better chance of breaking in at our publication with short articles and fillers. Most topics are set years in advance. Regulars and fun articles are current. The most frequent mistake made by writers is sending us preachy articles. They don't read the guide carefully. Aim for the mid-teen instead of younger teen."

PURPLE COW Newspaper for Teens, Suite 320, 3423 Piedmont Rd. NE, Atlanta GA 30305. (404)239-0642. Editor: Todd Daniel. 5% freelance written. Works with a small number of new/unpublished writers each year. A monthly (during school year) tabloid circulated to Atlanta area high schools. Circ. 40,000. Pays on publication. Buys one-time rights. "Manuscripts are accepted on a 'space-available' basis. If space becomes available, we publish the manuscript under consideration 1-12 months after receiving." Byline given. Submit seasonal/holiday material 2 months in advance. Simultaneous queries and photocopied and previously published submissions OK. Computer printout submissions acceptable; prefers letter-quality. Reports in 1 month. Sample copy for $1 and 9x12 SAE and 2 first class stamps; writer's guidelines for #10 SAE and 1 first class stamp.

Nonfiction: General interest, how-to, humor and anything of interest to teenagers. No opinion or anything which talks down to teens. No fiction. Buys 7-10 mss/year. Send complete ms. Length: 1,000 words maximum. Pays $5-10.

Cartoons and Photos: Must be humorous, teen-related, up-to-date with good illustrations. Buys 10/year. Send photos with ms. Buys one-time rights. Pays $5-10.

Tips: "A freelancer can best break in to our publication with articles which help teens. Examples might be how to secure financial aid for college or how to survive your freshman year of college."

‡SASSY, Matilda Publications, Inc., 1 Times Sq., New York NY 10036. (212)764-4860. Editor: Jane Pratt. Managing Editor: Vicki Haracz. *Sassy* is a magazine for teenage girls ages 14-19. Estab. 1988. Circ. 250,000. Pays on acceptance. Publishes ms an average of 3-4 months after acceptance. Byline given. Offers 20% kill fee. Buys first and second serial (reprint) rights and makes work-for-hire assignments. Submit seasonal/holiday material 6 months in advance. Simultaneous and photocopied submissions OK. Computer printout submissions OK; no dot-matrix. Writer's guidelines for SASE.

Nonfiction: Essays, general interest, humor, interview/profile, personal experience. Buys 12-15 mss/year. Query. Length: 1,000-2,500 words. Pays $1,000-$2,500. Sometimes pays expenses of writers on assignment.

Photos: State availability of photos with submission or send photos with submission. Reviews contact sheets, negatives 2¼x2¼ transparencies and prints. Offers $300 minimum per photo. Captions, model releases and identification of subjects required. Buys one-time rights.

Columns/Departments: Karen Catchpole, editor. Body Talk (health, current research, products), 1,000 words. Buys 12 mss/year. Query. Length: 1,000-1,500 words. Pays $1,000-1,500.

Fiction: Catherine Gysin, editor. Adventure, confession, ethnic, experimental, historical, humorous, romance and slice-of-life vignettes. Buys 12-15 mss/year. Query with or without published clips, or send complete ms. Length: 1,000-2,000 words. Pays $1,000-2,000.

SCHOLASTIC SCOPE, Scholastic Magazines, Inc., 730 Broadway, New York NY 10003. Editor: Fran Claro. 5% freelance written. Works with a small number of new/unpublished writers each year. Weekly. 4-6th grade reading level; 15-18 age level. Circ. 800,000. Publishes ms an average of 8 months after acceptance. Buys all rights. Byline given. Computer printout submissions acceptable; no dot-matrix. Reports in 4-6 weeks. Sample copy for 10x14 SAE with $1.75 postage.

Nonfiction and Photos: Articles with photos about teenagers who have accomplished something against great odds, overcome obstacles, performed heroically, or simply have done something out of the ordinary. Prefers articles about people outside New York area. Length: 400-1,200 words. Pays $125 and up.

Fiction and Drama: Problems of contemporary teenagers (drugs, prejudice, runaways, failure in school, family problems, etc.); relationships between people (interracial, adult-teenage, employer-employee, etc.) in family, job, and school situations. Strive for directness, realism, and action, perhaps carried through dialogue rather than exposition. Try for depth of characterization in at least one character. Avoid too many coincidences and random happenings. Although action stories are wanted, it's not a market for crime fiction. Occasionally uses mysteries and science fiction. Length: 400-1,200 words. Uses plays up to 15,000 words. Pays $150 minimum.

SEVENTEEN, 850 3rd Ave., New York NY 10022. Editor-in-Chief: Midge Turk Richardson. Managing Editor: Mary Anne Baumgold. 80% freelance written. Works with a small number of new/unpublished writers each year. Monthly. Circ. 1.9 million. Buys one-time rights for nonfiction and fiction by adult writers; buys full rights for work by teenagers. Pays 25% kill fee. Pays on acceptance. Publishes ms an average of 6 months after acceptance. Byline given. Computer printout submissions acceptable; prefers letter-quality. Reports in 3 weeks.

Nonfiction: Katherine Russell Rich, articles editor. Articles and features of general interest to young women who are concerned with the development of their own lives and the problems of the world around them; strong emphasis on topicality, and helpfulness. Send brief outline and query, including a typical lead paragraph, summing up basic idea of article. Also like to receive articles and features on speculation. Length: 1,200-2,000 words. Pays $50-150 for articles written by teenagers but more to established adult freelancers. Articles are commissioned after outlines are submitted and approved. Fees for commissioned articles generally range from $650-1,500. Sometimes pays the expenses of writers on assignment.

Photos: Melissa Warner, art director. Photos usually by assignment only.

Fiction: Sara London, fiction editor. Thoughtful, well-written stories on subjects of interest to young women between the ages of 12 and 20. Avoid formula stories—"My sainted Granny," "My crush on Brad," etc.— heavy moralizing, condescension of any sort. Humorous stories and mysteries are welcomed. Best lengths are 1,000-3,000 words. Pays $500-1,000.

Poetry: Contact teen features editor. By teenagers only. Pays $15. Submissions are nonreturnable unless accompanied by SASE.

Tips: "Writers have to ask themselves whether or not they feel they can find the right tone for a *Seventeen* article—a tone which is empathetic yet never patronizing; lively yet not superficial. Not all writers feel comfortable with, understand or like teenagers. If you don't like them, *Seventeen* is the wrong market for you. The best way for beginning teenage writers to crack the *Seventeen* lineup is for them to contribute suggestions and short pieces to the New Voices and Views section, a literary format which lends itself to just about every kind of writing: profiles, essays, exposes, reportage, and book reviews."

STRAIGHT, Standard Publishing Co., 8121 Hamilton Ave., Cincinnati OH 45231. (513)931-4050. Editor: Carla J. Crane. 90% freelance written. "Teens, age 13-19, from Christian backgrounds generally receive this publication in their Sunday School classes or through subscriptions." Weekly (published quarterly) magazine. Pays on acceptance. Publishes ms an average of 1 year after acceptance. Buys first rights, second serial (reprint) rights or simultaneous rights. Byline given. Submit seasonal/holiday material 1 year in advance. Reports in 3-6 weeks. Computer printout submissions acceptable. Include Social Security number on ms. Free sample copy; writer's guidelines with #10 SASE and 2 first class stamps.

Nonfiction: Religious-oriented topics, teen interest (school, church, family, dating, sports, part-time jobs), humor, inspirational, personal experience. "We want articles that promote Christian values and ideals." No puzzles. Query or submit complete ms. "We're buying more short pieces these days; 12 pages fill up much too quickly." Length: 800-1,500 words.

Fiction: Adventure, humorous, religious and suspense. "All fiction should have some message for the modern Christian teen." Fiction should deal with all subjects in a forthright manner, without being preachy and without talking down to teens. No tasteless manuscripts that promote anything adverse to the Bible's teachings. Submit complete ms. Length: 1,000-1,500 words. Pays 2-3½¢/word; less for reprints.

Photos: May submit photos with ms. Pays $20-25 for 8x10 b&w glossy prints and $100 for color slides. Model releases should be available. Buys one-time rights.

Tips: "Don't be trite. Use unusual settings or problems. Use a lot of illustrations, a good balance of conversation, narration, and action. Style must be clear, fresh—no sermonettes or sickly-sweet fiction. Take a realistic approach to problems. Be willing to submit to editorial policies on doctrine; knowledge of the *Bible* a must. Also, be aware of teens today, and what they do. Language, clothing, and activities included in mss should be contemporary. We are becoming more and more selective about freelance material and the competition seems to be stiffer all the time."

‡TEAM, A Digest for Volunteer Youth Leaders, Young Calvinist Federation, Box 7259, Grand Rapids MI 49510. (616)241-5616. Editor: Dale Pieleman. Managing Editor: Martha Kalk. 33% freelance written. Quarterly magazine on teen ministry. "*TEAM* is a quarterly digest for volunteer youth leaders. We look for articles on basic perspectives and how-to's in youth ministry. Our readers are not paid professionals, and the informal youth group, not the Sunday school class, is the setting." Circ. 3,000. Pays on acceptance. Publishes ms an average of 3 months after acceptance. Byline given. Offers 50% kill fee. Buys first, one-time, second serial (reprint), or simultaneous rights. Submit seasonal/holiday material 6 months in advance. Simultaneous, photocopied and previously published submissions OK. Computer printout submissions OK. Sample copy for 6x9 SAE with 2 first class stamps: writer's guidelines for #10 SASE.

Nonfiction: How-to, inspirational, interview-profile, photo feature, religious. No salvation testimonies. Buys 12 mss/year. Send complete ms. Length: 300-1,200 words. Pays $20-60. Sometimes pays expenses of writers on assignment.

Photos: Send photos with submission. Reviews transparencies and 5x7 prints. Offers no additional payment for photos accepted with ms. Captions, model releases and identification of subjects required. Buys one-time rights.

Poetry: Free verse, haiku. Buys 6 poems/year. Submit maximum 6 poems at one time. Length: 4-25 lines. Pays $10-30.

Tips: "We want leaders informed about trends and what counts for teens today, plus how can adults help."

‡'**TEEN MAGAZINE**, 8490 Sunset Blvd., Hollywood CA 90069. Editor: Roxanne Camron. 20-30% freelance written. Prefers to work with published/established writers. For teenage girls. Monthly magazine. Circ. 1 million. Publishes ms an average of 6 months after acceptance. Buys all rights. Reports in 4 months. Computer printout submissions acceptable; prefers no dot-matrix. Sample copy and writer's guidelines for 8½x11 SAE and $2.50.

Fiction: Dealing specifically with teenage girls and contemporary teen issues. More fiction on emerging alternatives for young women. Suspense, humorous and romance. "Young love is all right, but teens want to read about it in more relevant settings." Length: 2,500-4,000 words. Pays $100. Sometimes pays the expenses of writers on assignment.

Tips: "No fiction with explicit language, casual references to drugs, alcohol, sex, or smoking; no fiction with too depressing outcome."

TEENS TODAY, Church of the Nazarene, 6401 The Paseo, Kansas City MO 64131. (816)333-7000. Editor: Karen De Sollar. 25% freelance written. Eager to work with new/unpublished writers. For junior and senior high teens, to age 18, attending Church of the Nazarene Sunday School. Weekly magazine. Circ. 55,000. Pays on acceptance. Publishes ms an average of 8 months after acceptance. Byline given. Buys first rights and second rights. Submit seasonal/holiday material 10 months in advance. Simultaneous, photocopied and previously published submissions OK. Computer printout submissions acceptable; no dot-matrix. Reports in 6-8 weeks. Sample copy and writer's guidelines for 9x12 SAE with 2 first class stamps.

Photos: Pays $10-30 for 8x10 b&w glossy prints.

Fiction: Adventure (if Christian principles are apparent); humorous; religious; and romance (keep it clean). Buys 1 ms/issue. Send complete ms. Length: 1,200-1,500 words. Pays 3½¢/word, first rights; 3¢/word, second rights.

Poetry: "We accept poetry written by teens—no outside poetry accepted." Buys 50 poems/year.

Tips: "We're looking for quality fiction dealing with teen issues: peers, self, parents, vocation, Christian truths related to life, etc."

‡**TIGER BEAT MAGAZINE**, D.S. Magazines, Inc., 1086 Teaneck Road, Teaneck NJ 07666. (201)833-1800. Editor: Diane Umansky. 25% freelance written. For teenage girls ages 14 to 18. Monthly magazine. Circ. 400,000. Pays on publication. Publishes ms an average of 3 months after acceptance. Buys all rights. Buys 50 manuscripts per year. Query for electronic submissions. Computer printout submissions acceptable; no dot-matrix.

Nonfiction: Stories about young entertainers; their lives, what they do, their interests. Also service-type, self-help articles. Quality writing expected, but must be written with the 14-18 age group in mind. "Skill, style, ideas, and exclusivity are important to *Tiger Beat*. If a writer has a fresh, fun idea, or access to something staffers don't have, he or she has a good chance." Length: 100-750 words depending on the topic. Pays $50-100. Send query. Sometimes pays the expenses of writers on assignment. Also seeks good teenage fiction, with an emphasis on entertainment and romance.

Photos: Pays $25 for b&w photos used with mss; captions optional. Pays $50-75 for color used inside; $75 for cover. 35mm transparencies preferred.

Tips: "A freelancer's best bet is to come up with something original and exclusive that the staff couldn't do or get. Writing should be aimed at a 17- or 18-year-old intelligence level. Trends in magazine publishing that freelance writers should be aware of include shorter articles, segmenting of markets, and much less 'I' journalism. The most frequent mistake made by writers in completing an article for us is a patronizing attitude toward teens or an emphasis on historical aspects of subject matter. Don't talk down to young readers; they sense it readily."

TIGER BEAT STAR, D.S. Magazines, Inc., 1086 Teaneck Rd., Teaneck NJ 07666. (201)833-1800. Editor: Nancy O'Connell. 25% freelance written. Works with a small number of new/unpublished writers each year. Monthly teenage fan magazine for young adults interested in movie, TV and recording stars. Circ. 400,000. Average issue includes 20 feature interviews, and 2 or 3 gossip columns. "We have to take each article and examine its worth individually—who's popular this month, how it is written, etc. But we prefer shorter articles most of the time." Pays upon publication. Publishes ms an average of 1 month after acceptance. Byline given. Buys all rights. Submit seasonal material 10 weeks in advance. Previously published submissions discouraged. Query for electronic submissions. Computer printout submissions acceptable; no dot-matrix. Reports in 2 weeks.

Nonfiction: Interview (of movie, TV and recording stars). Buys 1-2 mss/issue. Query with clips of previously published work. "Write a good query indicating your contact with the star. Investigative pieces are preferred." Length: 200-400 words. Pays $50-125. Sometimes pays the expenses of writers on assignment.

Photos: State availability of photos. Pays $25 minimum for 5x7 and 8x10 b&w glossy prints. Pays $75 minimum for 35mm and 2¼ color transparencies. Captions and model releases required. Buys all rights.

Tips: "Be aware of our readership (teenage girls, generally ages 9-17); be 'up' on the current TV, movie and music stars; and be aware of our magazine's unique writing style. We are looking for articles that are clearly and intelligently written, factual and fun. Don't talk down to the reader, simply because they are teenaged. We want to give the readers information they can't find elsewhere. Keep in mind that readers are young and try to include subheads and copybreakers."

TQ (TEEN QUEST), The Good News Broadcasting Association, Inc., Box 82808, Lincoln NE 68501. (402)474-4567. Editor-in-Chief: Warren Wiersbe. Managing Editor: Barbara Comito. 50% freelance written. Works with a small number of new/unpublished writers each year. Monthly magazine emphasizing Christian living for Protestant church-oriented teens, ages 12-17. Circ. 80,000. Buys first serial rights or second serial (reprint) rights. Publishes ms an average of 8 months after acceptance. Byline given. Submit seasonal/holiday material 1 year in advance. Previously published submissions OK. Computer printout submissions acceptable; prefers letter-quality. Reports in 8 weeks. Sample copy and writer's guidelines for 9x12 SAE with 4 first class stamps.

Nonfiction: Interviews with Christian sports personalities and features on teens making unusual achievements or involved in unique pursuits—spiritual emphasis a must. "Articles on issues of particular importance to teens--drugs, pregnancy, school, jobs, recreational activities, etc.-Christian element not necessary on morally neutral issues." Buys 1-3 mss/issue. Query or send complete ms. No phone queries. Length: 500-1,800 words. Pays 4-7¢/word for unsolicited mss; 7-10¢ for assigned articles. Sometimes pays expenses of writers on assignment.

Fiction: Needs stories involving problems common to teens (dating, family, alcohol and drugs, peer pressure, school, sex, talking about one's faith to non-believers, standing up for convictions, etc.) in which the resolution (or lack of it) is true to our readers' experiences. "In other words, no happily-ever-after endings, last-page spiritual conversions, or pat answers to complex problems. We are interested in the everyday (though still profound) experiences of teen life. If the story was written just to make a point, or grind the author's favorite axe, we don't want it. Most of our stories feature a protagonist 14-17 years old. The key is the spiritual element— how the protagonist deals with or makes sense of his/her situation in light of Christian spiritual principles and ideals, without being preached to or preaching to another character or to the reader." Buys 30 mss/year. Send complete ms. Length: 800-1,800 words. Pays 4-7¢/word for unsolicited mss; 7-10¢/word for assigned fiction.

Fillers: Short puzzles on Biblical themes. Send complete mss. Pays $3-10.

Tips: "Articles for *TQ* need to be written in an upbeat style attractive to teens. No preaching. Writers must be familiar with the characteristics of today's teenagers in order to write for them."

‡VISION, A Lifestyles Magazine for Young Adults, Young Calvinist Federation, Box 7259, Grand Rapids MI 49510. (616)241-5616. Editor: Dale Dieleman. Managing Editor: Martha Kalk. 80% freelance written. General interest-lifestyles magazine for singles. Circ. 2,500. Pays on acceptance. Publishes ms an average of 3 months after acceptance. Byline given. Offers 50% kill fee. Buys first, one-time, second serial (reprint), and simultaneous rights. Submit seasonal/holiday material 6 months in advance. Simultaneous, photocopied, previously published submissions OK. Computer printout submissions OK. Reports in 1 month on queries; 2 months on mss. Sample copy for 9x12 SAE with 3 first class stamps; writer's guidelines for #10 SASE.

Nonfiction: Book excerpts, how-to, inspirational, interview/profile, personal experience, religious. Buys 20 mss/year. Send complete ms. Length: 600-2,000. Pays $25-75 for assigned articles; $25-50 for unsolicited articles. Sometimes pays expenses of writers on assignment.

Photos: Lifestyles, Work World, Creative Christianity, Budget Briefs. Buys 25 mss/year. Send complete ms. Length: 600-1,000 words. Pays $25-35.

Fiction: Humorous, religious, science fiction, slice-of-life vignettes. No formula stories or fictional accounts of biblical characters. Buys 6 mss/year. Send complete ms. Length: 800-2,000. Pays $25-75.

Poetry: Free verse, haiku. Buys 10 poems/year. Submit maximum 6 poems at one time. Length: 4-40 lines. Pays $15-45.

Tips: "We need stories, real-life accounts, how-to tips for better living as single people."

YOUNG SALVATIONIST, The Salvation Army, 799 Bloomfield Ave., Verona NJ 07044. (201)239-0606. Editor: Capt. Robert R. Hostetler. 75% freelance written. Works with a small number of new/unpublished writers each year. Monthly Christian magazine for high school teens. "Only material with a definite Christian emphasis or from a Christian perspective will be considered." Circ. 48,000. Pays on acceptance. Publishes ms an average of 10 months after acceptance. Byline given. Buys first North American serial rights, first rights, one-time rights or second serial (reprint) rights. Submit seasonal/holiday material 6 months in advance. Computer printout submissions acceptable; prefers letter-quality. Reports in 1-2 weeks on queries; 3-4 weeks on mss.

Sample copy for 8½x11 SAE with 3 first class stamps; writer's guidelines for #10 SAE and 1 first class stamp.
Nonfiction: Inspirational, how-to (Bible study, workshop skills), humor, interview/profile, personal experience, photo feature, religious. "Articles should deal with issues of relevance to teens today; avoid 'preachiness' or moralizing." Buys 40 mss/year. Send complete ms. "State whether your submission is for The Young Salvationist or The Young Soldier section." Length: 500-1,200 words. Pays 3¢/word for unsolicited mss; 5¢/word for assigned articles.
Columns/Departments: Currents (media-related news and human interest from a Christian perspective, book and record reviews). Buys 10-12 mss/year. Send complete ms. Length: 50-200 words. Pays 3-5¢/word.
Fiction: Adventure, fantasy, humorous, religious, romance, science fiction - all from a Christian perspective. Length: 500-1,200 words. Pays 3-5¢/word.
Tips: "Study magazine, familiarize yourself with the unique 'Salvationist' perspective of *Young Salvationist*; learn a little about the Salvation Army; media, sports, sex and dating are strongest appeal."

YOUTH UPDATE, St. Anthony Messenger Press, 1615 Republic St., Cincinnati OH 45210. (513)241-5615. Editor: Carol Ann Morrow. 90% freelance written. Monthly newsletter of faith life for teenagers. Designed to attract, instruct, guide and challenge Catholics of high school age by applying the Gospel to modern problems/situations. Circ. 60,000. Pays when ready to print. Publishes ms an average of 4 months after acceptance. Byline given. Reports in 8 weeks. Sample copy and writer's guidelines for #10 SAE and 1 first class stamp.
Nonfiction: Inspirational, practical self-help and spiritual. Buys 12 mss/year. Query. Length: 2,300-2,500 words. Pays $300. Sometimes pays expenses of writers on assignment.

Travel, Camping and Trailer

Travel agencies and tour companies constantly remind consumers of the joys of traveling. But it's usually the travel magazines that tell potential travelers about the negative as well as positive aspects of potential destinations. A number of publications have started—as well as failed—in this area during the past year. Publications in this category tell campers and tourists the where-tos and how-tos of travel. All have their own slants and should be studied carefully before sending submissions. Publications that buy how-to camping and travel material with a conservation angle are listed in the Nature, Conservation and Ecology section.

AAA WORLD, Hawaii/Alaska, AAA Hawaii, 590 Queen St., Honolulu HI 96813. (808)528-2600. Editor: Thomas Crosby. 80% freelance written. Prefers to work with published/established writers. Bimonthly magazine of travel, automotive safety and legislative issues. Orientation is toward stories that benefit members in some way. Circ. 20,000. Pays on publication. Publishes ms an average of 6-8 months after acceptance. Byline given. Buys one-time rights. Submit seasonal/holiday material 6 months in advance. Photocopied and previously published submissions OK. Query for electronic submissions. Computer printout submissions acceptable. Reports in 1 week on queries; 3-4 months on mss. Free sample copy.
Nonfiction: How-to (auto maintenance, safety, etc.); and travel (tips, destinations, bargains). Buys 6 mss/year. Send complete ms. Length: 1,000 words. Pays $100 maximum. Sometimes pays the expenses of writers on assignment.
Photos: State availability of photos. Reviews b&w contact sheet. Pays $10-25. Captions required. Buys one-time rights.
Tips: "Find an interesting, human interest story that affects AAA members."

ACCENT, Meridian Publishing Inc., 1720 Washington, Box 10010, Ogden UT 84409. (801)394-9446. 60-70% freelance written. Works with a small number of new/unpublished writers each year. A monthly inhouse travel magazine distributed by various companies to employees, customers, stockholders, etc. "Readers are predominantly upscale, mainstream, family oriented." Circ. 110,000. Pays on acceptance. Publishes ms an average of 1 year after acceptance. Byline given. Buys first rights, second serial (reprint) rights and nonexclusive reprint rights. Simultaneous, photocopied and previously published submissions OK. Computer printout submissions are acceptable; dot-matrix submissions are acceptable if readable. Reports in 6 weeks. Sample copy $1 and 9x12 SAE; writer's guidelines for #10 SAE and 1 first class stamp.
Nonfiction: "We want upbeat pieces slanted toward the average traveler, but we use some exotic travel. Resorts, cruises, hiking, camping, health retreats, historic sites, sports vacations, national or state forests and

parks are all featured. No articles without original color photos, except with travel tips. We also welcome pieces on travel tips and ways to travel." Buys 40 mss/year. Query. Length: 1,200 words. Pays 15¢/word.
Photos: Send photos with ms. Pays $35 for color transparencies; $50 for cover. Captions and model releases required. Buys one-time rights.
Tips: "Write about interesting places. We are inundated with queries for stories on California and the southeastern coast. Super color transparencies are essential. Most rejections are because of poor quality photography or the writer didn't study the market. We are using three times as many domestic pieces as foreign because of our readership. Address queries to Attention: Editor."

ASU TRAVEL GUIDE, ASU Travel Guide, Inc., 1325 Columbus Ave., San Francisco CA 94133. (415)441-5200. Editor: Brady Ennis. 20% freelance written. Quarterly guidebook covering international travel features and travel discounts for well-traveled airline employees. Circ. 50,000. Payment terms negotiable. Publishes ms an average of 18 months after acceptance. Byline given. Offers kill fee. Buys first North American serial rights, first and second rights to the same material, and second serial (reprint) rights to material originally published elsewhere. Makes work-for-hire assignments. Submit seasonal/holiday material 6 months in advance. Simultaneous queries and simultaneous, photocopied and previously published submissions OK. Computer printout submissions acceptable; prefers letter-quality. Reports in 1 month. Writer's guidelines for SASE.
Nonfiction: International travel articles "similar to those run in consumer magazines." Not interested in amateur efforts from inexperienced travelers or personal experience articles that don't give useful information to other travelers. Buys 16-20 mss/year. Destination pieces only; no "Tips On Luggage" articles. "We will be accepting fewer manuscripts and relying more on our established group of freelance contributors." Unsolicited ms or queries without SASE will not be acknowledged. No telephone queries. Length: 1,200-1,500 words. Pays $200.
Photos: "Interested in clear, high-contrast photos; we prefer not to receive material without photos." Reviews 5x7 and 8x10 b&w prints. "Payment for photos is included in article price; photos from tourist offices are acceptable."
Tips: "We'll be needing more domestic U.S. destination pieces in 1989 which combine several cities or areas in a logical manner, e.g., Seattle/Vancouver, Savannah/Atlanta. Query with samples of travel writing and a list of places you've recently visited. We appreciate clean and simple style. Keep verbs in the active tense and involve the reader in what you write. Avoid 'cute' writing, excess punctuation (especially dashes and ellipses), coined words and stale cliches. Any article that starts with the name of a country followed by an exclamation point is immediately rejected. The most frequent mistakes made by writers in completing an article for us are: 1) Lazy writing—using words to describe a place that could describe any destination such as 'there is so much to do in (fill in destination) that whole guidebooks have been written about it'; 2) Including fare and tour package information—our readers make arrangements through their own airline."

AWAY, c/o ALA, 888 Worcester St., Wellesley MA 02181. (617)237-5200. Editor: Gerard J. Gagnon. For "members of the ALA Auto & Travel Club, interested in their autos and in travel. Ages range approximately 20-65. They live primarily in New England." Slanted to seasons. 5-10% freelance written. Quarterly. Circ. 155,000. Buys first serial rights. Pays on acceptance. Publishes ms an average of 3 months after acceptance. Submit seasonal material 6 months in advance. Reports "as soon as possible." Although a query is not mandatory, it may be advisable for many articles. Computer printout submissions acceptable; no dot-matrix. Sample copy for 9x12 SAE with 2 first class stamps.
Nonfiction: Articles on "travel, tourist attractions, safety, history, etc., preferably with a New England angle. Also, car care tips and related subjects." Would like a "positive feel to all pieces, but not the chamber of commerce approach." Buys general seasonal travel, specific travel articles, and travel-related articles; outdoor activities, for example, gravestone rubbing; historical articles linked to places to visit; and humor with a point. "Would like to see more nonseasonally oriented material. Most material now submitted seems suitable only for our summer issue. Avoid pieces on hunting and about New England's most publicized attractions, such as Old Sturbridge Village and Mystic Seaport." Length: 800-1,500 words, "preferably 1,000-1,200 words." Pays approximately 10¢/word.
Photos: Photos purchased with mss. Captions required. B&w glossy prints. Pays $5-10/b&w photo, payment on publication based upon which photos are used. Not buying color photos at this time.
Tips: "The most frequent mistakes we find in articles submitted to us are spelling, typographical errors and questionable statements of fact, which require additional research by the editorial staff. We are buying very few articles at this time."

‡BAJA TIMES, Editorial Playas De Rosarito, S.A., Box 5577, Chula Vista CA 92012-5577. (706)612-1244. 90% freelance written. Monthly tourist and travel publication on Baja California, Mexico. "Oriented to the Baja California, Mexico aficionada—the tourist and those Americans who are living in Baja California or have their vacation homes there. Articles should be slanted to Baja." Pays on publication. Publishes ms an average of 8 months after acceptance. Byline given. Buys first rights. Submit seasonal/holiday material 4 months in advance. Computer printout submissions OK; prefers letter-quality. Sample copy for 9x12 SAE with 4 first class stamps; free writer's guidelines.

Nonfiction: General interest, historical/nostalgic, humor, personal experience, photo feature, travel. All with Baja California slant. "Nothing that describes any negative aspects of Mexico (bribes, bad police, etc.). We are a positive publication." Query with or without published clips, or submit complete ms. Length: 750-2,100 words. Pays $50-100 for assigned articles; $35-50 for unsolicited articles. Sometimes pays expenses of writers on assignment.

Photos: Send photos with submission. Reviews 5x7 prints. Captions and identification of subjects required. Buys one-time rights.

Tips: "Take a chance—send in that Baja California related article. We guarantee to read them all. Over the years we have turned up some real winners from our writers—many who do not have substantial experience. The entire publication is open. We buy an average of 6 freelance each issue. Virtually any subject is acceptable as long as it has a Baja California slant. Remember Tijuana, Mexico (on the border with San Diego, CA) is the busiest border crossing in the world. We are always interested in material relating to Tijuana, Rosarito, Ensenada, LaPaz."

THE CAMPER TIMES, Royal Productions, Inc., Box 6294, Richmond VA 23230. (804)288-5653. Editor: Alice P. Supple. 75% freelance written. Prefers to work with published/established writers; works with a small number of new/unpublished writers each year. A bimonthly tabloid. "We supply the camping public with articles and information on outdoor activities related to camping. Our audience is primarily families that own recreational vehicles." Circ. 30,000. Pays on publication. Publishes ms an average of 4-6 months after acceptance. Byline given. Buys one-time rights, second serial (reprint) rights or simultaneous rights. Submit seasonal/holiday material 2 months in advance. Simultaneous, photocopied and previously published submissions OK. Query for electronic submissions. Computer printout submissions acceptable. Reports in 2 months. Sample copy and writer's guidelines for 9x12 SAE with $1.41 postage.

Nonfiction: How-to and travel; information on places to camp and fishing articles. Also "tourist related articles. Places to go, things to see. Does not have to be camping related." Buys 25 mss/year. Query with or without published clips, or send complete ms. Length: 500-2,000 words. Pays $20-65 for unsolicited articles. Sometimes pays the expenses of writers on assignment.

Photos: State availability of photos with submission. Reviews contact sheets and prints. Offers $1-5/photo. Identification of subjects required. Buys one-time rights.

Columns/Departments: RV Doctor (helpful hints on repairing RVs). Buys 12 mss/year. Query. Length: 100-500 words. Pays $20-35.

Fillers: Anecdotes, facts, gags to be illustrated by cartoonist, newsbreaks and short humor. Buys 25/year. Length: 10-500 words. Pays $5-20.

Tips: "Best approach is to call me. All areas of *The Camper Times* are open to freelancers. We will look at all articles and consider for publication."

CAMPERWAYS, 312 W. Broad St., Box 950, Quakertown PA 18951. (215)538-7474. Editorial Director: Charles Myers. 75% freelance written. Prefers to work with published/established writers. Emphasis on recreational vehicle camping and travel. Monthly (except Dec. and Jan.) tabloid. Circ. 35,000. Pays on publication. Publishes ms an average of 4-6 months after acceptance. Buys first, simultaneous, second serial (reprint) or regional rights. Byline given. Submit seasonal/holiday material 3-4 months in advance. Simultaneous, photocopied and previously published submissions OK. Computer printout submissions acceptable; prefers letter-quality. Reports in 1 month. Sample copy for $2 and 9x12 SAE with $3 postage; free writer's guidelines.

Nonfiction: Historical (when tied in with camping trip to historical attraction or area); how-to (selection, care, maintenance of RVs, accessories and camping equipment); humor; personal experience; and travel (camping destinations within 200 miles of New York-DC metro corridor). No "material on camping trips to destinations outside stated coverage area." Buys 80-100 unsolicited mss/year. Query. Length: 1,000-2,000 words. Pays $40-85.

Photos: "Good photos greatly increase likelihood of acceptance. Don't send snapshots, Polaroids. We can't use them." Photos purchased with accompanying ms. Captions required. Uses 5x7 or 8x10 b&w glossy prints. Pays $5/photo published.

Columns/Departments: Camp Cookery (ideas for cooking in RV galleys and over campfires—should include recipes). Buys 10 mss/year. Query. Length: 500-1,500 words. Pays $25-75.

Tips: "Articles should focus on single attraction or activity or on closely clustered attractions within reach on the same weekend camping trip rather than on types of attractions or activities in general. We're looking for little-known or offbeat items. Emphasize positive aspects of camping: fun, economy, etc. We want feature items, not shorts and fillers. Acceptance is based on quality of article and appropriateness of subject matter. The most frequent mistakes made by writers in completing an article for us are failure to follow guidelines or failure to write from the camper's perspective."

CAMPING TODAY, Official Publication of National Campers & Hikers Association, T-A-W Publishing Co., 9425 S. Greenville Road, Greenville MI 48838. (616)754-2251. Editors: David and Martha Higbie. 50% freelance written. Prefers to work with published/established writers. The monthly official membership publication of the NCHA, "the largest nonprofit camping organization in the United States and Canada. Members are heavily oriented toward RV travel, both weekend and extended vacations. A small segment is interested in backpacking. Concentration is on activities of members within chapters, conservation, wildlife, etc." Circ. 30,000. Pays on publication. Publishes ms an average of 6 months after acceptance. Byline given. Buys one-time rights. Submit seasonal/holiday material 3 months in advance. Simultaneous, photocopied, and previously published submissions OK. Computer printout submissions acceptable; prefers letter-quality. Reports in 1 month. Sample copy and writer's guidelines for SAE.

Nonfiction: Humor (camping or travel related); interview/profile (interesting campers); new product (RVs and related equipment); technical (RVs); and travel (camping, hiking and RV travel). Buys 20-30 mss/year. Send complete ms. Length: 750-1,000 words. Pays $75-150. Sometimes pays the expenses of writers on assignment.

Photos: Send photos with accompanying query or ms. Reviews color transparencies and 5x7 b&w prints. Pays $25 maximum for color transparencies. Color cover every month. Captions required.

Tips: "Freelance material on RV travel, RV technical subjects and items of general camping and hiking interest throughout the United States and Canada will receive special attention."

CARIBBEAN TRAVEL AND LIFE, Suite 400, 606 North Washington St., Alexandria VA 22314. (703)683-5496. Editor: Veronica Gould Stoddart. 90% freelance written. Prefers to work with published/established writers. A bimonthly magazine covering travel to the Caribbean, Bahamas and Bermuda. Circ. 75,000. Pays on publication. Publishes ms an average of 3 months after acceptance. Byline given. Offers 25% kill fee. Buys first North American serial rights. Submit seasonal/holiday material 6 months in advance. Photocopied submissions OK. Computer printout submissions OK; prefers letter-quality. Reports in 2 months. Sample copy for 9x12 SAE with 7 first class stamps; free writer's guidelines.

Nonfiction: General interest, how-to, interview/profile, culture, personal experience and travel. No "guidebook rehashing; superficial destination pieces or critical exposes." Buys 18 mss/year. Query with published clips. Length: 2,000-2,500 words. Pays $550.

Photos: Send photos with submission. Reviews 35mm transparencies. Offers $75-400 per photo. Captions and identification of subjects required. Buys one-time rights.

Columns/Departments: Resort Spotlight (in-depth review of luxury resort); Tradewinds (focus on one particular kind of water sport or sailing/cruising); Island Buys (best shopping for luxury goods, crafts, duty-free); Island Spice (best cuisine and/or restaurant reviews with recipes); all 1,000-1,500 words; Caribbeana (short items on great finds in travel, culture, and special attractions), 500 words. Buys 36 mss/year. Query with published clips or send complete ms. Length: 500-1,250 words. Pays $75-200.

Tips: "We are especially looking for stories with a personal touch and lively, entertaining anecdotes, as well as strong insight into people and places being covered. Also prefers stories with focus on people, i.e., colorful personalities, famous people, etc. Writer should demonstrate why he/she is the best person to do that story based on extensive knowledge of the subject, frequent visits to destination, residence in destination, specialty in field."

CHEVY OUTDOORS, A Celebration of American Recreation and Leisure, Lintas-Ceco Communications, Inc., 30400 Van Dyke, Warren MI 48093. (800)232-6266 or (313)575-9400. Editor: Michael Brudenell. 85% freelance written. Works with a small number of new/unpublished writers each year. A quarterly magazine covering outdoor recreation and adventure. Circ. 1 million. Pays on publication. Publishes ms an average of 6 months after acceptance. Offers 25% kill fee. Byline given. Buys first rights, one-time rights or second serial (reprint) rights. Submit seasonal/holiday material 6 months in advance. Simultaneous and previously published submissions OK. Computer printout submissions OK; no dot-matrix. Reports in 6 weeks. Sample copy for 9x12 SAE with $1.41 postage.

Nonfiction: Book excerpts; historical/nostalgic; how-to (on outdoor topics—camping, fishing, etc.); humor; interview/profile (on outdoors people, such as authorities in their fields); personal experience (must be outdoor or wilderness related); photo feature; technical (new technologies for campers, anglers, hunters, etc.); travel; and stories on new trends in outdoor recreation. "No exposes or negative articles; we like an upbeat, positive approach." Buys 50 mss/year. Query with published clips. Length: 200-1,500 words. Pays $100-750 for assigned articles; pays $100-500 for unsolicited articles. Sometimes pays the expenses of writers on assignment.

Photos: Send photos with submission. Reviews 35mm or larger transparencies. Offers $25-100 per photo. Model releases and identification of subjects required. Buys one-time rights; sometimes all rights.

Columns/Departments: Outdoor Photography (how-tos by established photographers with national reputation in outdoor photography) and Outdoors People (profiles of notable outdoors enthusiasts or exceptional people who do work related to outdoor recreation). Buys 8-12 mss/year. Query with published clips. Length: 800-1,500 words. Pays $400-750.

Fiction: Tall tales for our Campfire Classics department. "These can have a humorous, mysterious or even fantasy/occult slant. See current issues for examples of what we're using. No material that is unsuitable for a family audience." Buys 4-6 mss/year. Query with published clips or send complete ms. Length: 600-1,200 words. Pays $100-400.

Fillers: Anecdotes, facts and newsbreaks. Buys 25-30/year. Length: 25-200 words.

Tips: "Stories that are dynamic and active, and stories that focus on people will have a better chance of getting in. Focus queries tightly and look beyond the obvious. Use this as a touchstone—Is this a story that I would be compelled to read if I found it on a coffee table or in a waiting room? If the answer is 'yes,' we want to hear from you. Happily enough, our features well is the best freelance target. Travel, personality profiles or activity features are probably the best ticket in. But the idea has to be fresh and original, and the copy has to sing. New or unpublished writers should write on topics with which they are *very* familiar; expertise can compensate for a lack of experience."

CHICAGO TRIBUNE, Travel Section, 435 N. Michigan Ave., Chicago IL 60611. (312)222-3999. *Tribune* Editor: James Squires. Executive Travel Editor: Larry Townsend. Managing Editor: Richard Ciccone. Sunday newspaper section. Weekly leisure travel section averaging 24 pages. Aimed at vacation travelers. Circ. 1.2 million. Pays on publication. Publishes ms an average of 1½ months after acceptance. Byline given. Buys one-time rights. Submit seasonal/holiday material 2 months in advance. Simultaneous submissions OK. Query for electronic submissions. Computer printout submissions OK; prefers letter-quality. Reports in 2 weeks. Sample copy for large SAE with $1.25 postage. Writer's guidelines for SASE.

Nonfiction: Essays, general interest, historical/nostalgic, how-to (travel, pack), humor, opinion, personal experience, photo feature and travel. "There will be 16 special issues in the next 18 months." Buys 500 mss/year. Send complete ms. Length: 500-2,500 words. Pays $100-250.

Photos: State availability of photos with submission. Reviews 35mm transparencies and 8x10 or 5x7 prints. Offers $100-300 for color photos; $25 for b&w photos. Captions required. Buys one-time rights.

Tips: "Be professional. Use a word processor. Make the reader want to go to the area being written about. Our Page 3 Reader is a travel essay, hopefully with humor, insight, tear jerking. A great read. Only 1% of mss make it."

COAST MAGAZINE, The Weekly Vacationers Guide, Resort Publications, Ltd., 5000 N. Kings Highway, Box 2448, Myrtle Beach SC 29578. (803)449-5415. Editor: Mona R. Prufer. Published 39 times/year covering tourism. Annual circulation is 1 million. "Our slant is vacation articles, beach, North/South Carolina orientation with coastal information." Pays on publication. Byline given. Buys one-time annual rights (regional). Submit seasonal/holiday material at least 2 months in advance. Simultaneous queries, and simultaneous, photocopied, and previously published submissions OK. Reports in 2 weeks on queries; 1-2 months on mss. Sample copy and writer's guidelines for 6½x9½ SAE and 3 first class stamps.

Nonfiction: Historical/nostalgic (low country, South); new product (beach, tourist-related); and articles on nature, area festivals and beach music. Buys 10 mss/year. Send complete ms. Length: 400-1,000 words. Pays $30 minimum.

Photos: Send photos with ms. Pays $75-100 for 4-color (cover photos) transparencies; $35-50 for inside editorial. Model releases and identification of subjects required. Buys one-time annual rights (regional).

Tips: "Freelancers can best break in to our publication by submitting resort-oriented, and Southern historical material, features on area events and festivals."

‡CRUISE TRAVEL MAGAZINE, World Publishing Co., 990 Grove St., Evanston IL 60201. (312)491-6440. Editor: Robert Meyers. Managing Editor: Charles Doherty. 95% freelance written. A bimonthly magazine on cruise travel. "This is a consumer oriented travel publication covering the world of pleasure cruising on large cruise ships (with some coverage of smaller ships), including ports, travel tips, roundups." Pays on acceptance. Publishes ms an average of 5 months after acceptance. Byline given. Offers ½ kill fee. Buys first North American serial rights, one-time rights, or second serial (reprint) rights. Simultaneous, photocopied and previously published submissions OK. Computer printout submissions OK; prefers letter-quality. Sample copy $3 with 9x12 SAE and 5 first class stamps. Writer's guidelines for #10 SAE and 1 first class stamp.

Nonfiction: General interest, historical/nostalgic, interview/profile, personal experience, photo feature, travel. "No daily cruise 'diary'; My First Cruise; etc." Buys 72 mss/year. Query with or without published clips or send complete ms. Length: 500-2,000 words. Pay $75-350.

Photos: Send photos with submission. Reviews transparencies and prints. "Must be color, 35m preferred (other format OK); color prints second choice." Offers no additional payment for photos accepted with ms "but pay more for well-illustrated ms." Captions and identification of subjects required. Buys one-time rights.

Fillers: Anecdotes, facts. Buys 3 mss/year. Length: 300-700 words. Pays $75-200.

Tips: "Do your homework. Know what we do and what sorts of things we publish. Know the cruise industry—we can't use novices. Good, sharp, bright color photography opens the door fast."

ENDLESS VACATION, Endless Vacation Publications, Inc., Box 80260, Indianapolis IN 46280. (317)871-9500. Editor: Helen A. Wernle. Prefers to work with published/established writers. A bimonthly magazine covering travel destinations, activities and issues that enhance the lives of vacationers. Circ. 571,945. Pays on acceptance. Publishes ms an average of 3 months after acceptance. Byline given. Buys first worldwide serial rights. Simultaneous and photocopied submissions OK. Query for electronic submissions. Computer printout submissions acceptable; prefers letter-quality. Reports in 1 month on queries; 3 weeks on manuscripts. Sample copy $1; writer's guidelines for SAE with 1 first class stamp.

Nonfiction: Contact Manuscript Editor. Travel. Buys 24 mss/year (approx). Query with published clips. Length: 1,200-2,000 words. Pays $250-800 for assigned articles; pays $150-600 for unsolicited articles. Sometimes pays the expenses of writers on assignment.

Photos: State availability of photos with submissions. Reviews 4x5 transparencies and 35mm slides. Offers $100-300/photo. Model releases and identification of subjects required. Buys one-time rights.

Columns/Departments: Gourmet on the Go (culinary topics of interest to travelers whether they are dining out or cooking in their condominium kitchens; no reviews of individual restaurants). Buys 4 mss/year. Query with published clips. Length: 800-1,200 words. Pays $150-300. Sometimes pays the expenses of writers on assignment.

Tips: "We will continue to focus on travel trends and resort and upscale destinations. Articles must be packed with pertinent facts and applicable how-tos. Information—addresses, phone numbers, dates of events, costs—must be current and accurate. We like to see a variety of stylistic approaches, but in all cases the lead must be strong. A writer should realize that we require first-hand knowledge of the subject and plenty of practical information. For further understanding of *Endless Vacations'* direction, the writer should study the magazine and guidelines for writers."

FAMILY MOTOR COACHING, 8291 Clough Pike, Cincinnati OH 45244-2796. (513)474-3622. Editor: Pamela Wisby Kay. Associate Editor: Maura Basile. 75% freelance written. "We prefer that writers be experienced RVers." Emphasizes travel by motorhome, and motorhome mechanics, maintenance and other technical information. Monthly magazine. Circ. 60,000. Pays on acceptance. Publishes ms an average of 4 months after acceptance. Buys first-time, 12 months exclusive rights. Byline given. Submit seasonal/holiday material 4 months in advance. Computer printout submissions acceptable; prefers letter-quality. Reports in 4-6 weeks. Sample copy $2.50; writer's guidelines for #10 SASE.

Nonfiction: Motorhome travel and living on the road; travel (various areas of country accessible by motor coach); how-to (modify motor coach features); bus conversions; and nostalgia. Buys 20 mss/issue. Query. Phone queries discouraged. Length: 1,000-2,000 words. Pays $50-500.

Photos: State availability of photos with query. Offers no additional payment for b&w contact sheets, 35mm or 2¼x2¼ color transparencies. Captions required. B&w glossy photos should accompany nontravel articles. Buys first rights.

Tips: "Keep in mind, stories must have motorhome angle or connection; inclusion of information about FMCA members enhances any travel article. Stories about an event somewhere should allude to nearby campgrounds, etc. The stories should be written assuming that someone going there would be doing it by motorhome. We need more articles from which to select for publication. We need geographic balance and a blend of travel, technical and incidental stories. No first-person accounts of vacations."

GREAT EXPEDITIONS, Adventure Travel Magazine, Box 8000-411, Sumas WA 98295; or, Box 8000-411, Abbotsford, BC V2S 6H1 Canada. Editor: Craig Henderson. 90% freelance written. Eager to work with new/unpublished writers. Bimonthly magazine covering "off-the-beaten-path" destinations, outdoor recreation, cultural discovery, budget travel, and working abroad. Circ. 3,500. Pays on publication. Buys first and second (reprint) rights. Simultaneous queries, and simultaneous, photocopied and previously published submissions OK. Computer printout submissions acceptable. Send SASE for return of article and photos. Reports in 1 month. Sample copy $2; free writer's guidelines.

Nonfiction: Articles range from very adventurous (living with an isolated tribe in the Philippines) to mildly adventurous (Spanish language school vacations in Guatemala and Mexico). We also like to see "how-to" pieces for adventurous travelers (i.e., How to Sail Around the World for Free, Swapping Homes with Residents of Other Countries, How to Get in on an Archaeological Dig). Buys 30 mss/year. Pays $35 maximum. Length 1,000-3,000 words.

Photos: B&w photos, color prints or slides should be sent with article. Captions required.

Tips: "It's best to send for a sample copy for a first hand look at the style of articles we are looking for. If possible, we appreciate practical information for travelers, either in the form of a sidebar or incorporated into the article, detailing how to get there, where to stay, specific costs, where to write for visas or travel information."

GUIDE TO THE FLORIDA KEYS, Humm's, Crain Communications Inc., Box 330712, Miami FL 33133. (305)665-2858. Editor: William A. Humm. 80% freelance written. A quarterly travel guide to the Florida Keys. Circ. 60,000. Pays on publication. Byline given. Buys first rights and second serial (reprint) rights. Submit seasonal/holiday material 6 months in advance. Previously published submissions OK. Computer printout submissions acceptable. Reports in 2 weeks on queries; 3 weeks on manuscripts. Free sample copy.

Nonfiction: General interest, historical/nostalgic, personal experience and travel, all for the Florida Keys area. Buys 30-40 mss/year. Send complete ms. Length: 500-1,500 words. Pays $5/column inch. Sometimes pays the expenses of writers on assignment.

Photos: State availability of photos with submission. Reviews negatives, 35mm and 2x2¾ transparencies, and 5x7 and 8x10 prints. Offers $40-100/photo. Captions and model releases required. Buys one-time rights.

Columns/Departments: Fishing and Diving (primarily about the Florida Keys), 500-1,500 words. Pays $5/column inch.

‡**THE ITINERARY MAGAZINE, "The" Magazine for Travelers with Physical Disabilities**, Box 1084, Bayonne NJ 07002. (201)858-3400. Editor: Robert S Zywicki. Managing Editor: Elizabeth C. Zywicki. 60-70% freelance written. Works with established and new writers. A bimonthly magazine covering travel for the disabled. Circ. 10,400. Pays on publication. Publishes ms an average of 6 months after acceptance. Buys first North American serial rights, first rights, one-time rights, second serial (reprint) rights, all rights, makes work-for-hire assignments. Submit seasonal/holiday material 6 months in advance. Simultaneous, photocopied and previously published submissions OK. Computer printout submissions acceptable. Reports in 1 month on queries; 2 months on manuscripts. Sample copy for 9x12 SAE with 4 first class stamps; writer's guidelines for #10 SAE with 1 first class stamp.

Nonfiction: How-to, interview/profile, new product, personal experience, photo feature and travel (especially adventure/wilderness/sports related travel for persons with disabilities). Special issues will feature accessible travel articles for Thanksgiving/Christmas time; national parks, regional tourist sites in USA and Canada. No articles that do not deal with travel for the disabled. Buys 24-30 mss/year. Query with or without published clips, or send complete ms. Length 750-2,000 words. Pays $100-300 for assigned articles; pays $50-150 for unsolicited articles. Sometimes pays the expenses of writers on assignment.

Photos: Send photos with submission. Reviews contact sheets and prints. Offers no additional payment for photos accepted with ms. Captions, model releases and identification of subjects required. Buys one-time rights.

Columns/Departments: Book Reviews (only containing information on travel for the disabled), 300-500 words. Buys 6-10 mss/year. Query. Pays $25-50.

Tips: "Be disabled or a relative, friend or co-worker of the disabled. Be aware of the needs of the disabled in travel-related situations. Describe the venues, sightseeing, lodging, etc. The areas most open to freelancers are travelogues featuring access data for the disabled, how-to features for travelers with disabilities, and reports on hotels, transportation, etc."

JOURNAL OF CHRISTIAN CAMPING, Christian Camping International, Box 646, Wheaton IL 60189. Editor: Charlyene Wall. 75% freelance written. Prefers to work with published/established writers. Emphasizes the broad scope of organized camping with emphasis on Christian camping. "Leaders of youth camps and adult conferences read our magazine to get practical help in ways to run their camps." Bimonthly magazine. Circ. 6,000. Pays on acceptance. Publishes ms an average of 2 months after acceptance. Buys all rights. Offers 25% kill fee. Byline given. Computer printout submissions acceptable; prefers letter-quality. Reports in 6 weeks. Sample copy $3.25; writer's guidelines for SASE.

Nonfiction: General interest (trends in organized camping in general and Christian camping in particular); how-to (anything involved with organized camping from motivating staff, to programming, to record keeping, to camper follow-up); inspirational (limited use, but might be interested in practical applications of Scriptural principles to everyday situations in camping, no preaching); interview (with movers and shakers in camping and Christian camping in particular; submit a list of basic questions first); and opinion (write a letter to the editor). Buys 30-50 mss/year. Query required. Length: 600-2,500 words. Pays 5¢/word.

Photos: Send photos with ms. Pays $10/5x7 b&w contact sheet or print; price negotiable for 35mm color transparencies. Buys all rights. Captions required.

Tips: "The most frequent mistake made by writers is that they have not read the information in the listing and send articles unrelated to our readers."

‡**MEXICO MAGAZINE**, Team Mexico, 303 Main St., Box 700, Carbondale CO 81623. (303)963-2330. Editor: Peggy DeVilbiss. Managing Editor: Harlan Feder. 60% freelance written. A quarterly magazine on Mexico travel. "We like information on all aspects of travel to Mexico to enable travelers to travel knowledgeably and confidently for a rewarding Mexico experience." Estab. 1987. Circ. 20,000 controlled. Pays on publication. Publishes ms an average of 3-6 months after acceptance. Buys first North American serial rights, second serial (reprint) rights, simultaneous rights and makes work-for-hire assignments. Submit seasonal/holiday material 5 months in advance. Simultaneous, photocopied and previously published material OK. Query for electronic submissions. Computer printout submissions OK. Reports in 2 months on queries; 4 months on mss. Free sample copy; writer's guidelines for #10 SASE.

Nonfiction: General interest (on Mexico), historical/nostalgic, how-to (travel tips), humor, interview/profile (Mexican personalities), opinion (sympathetic to Mexico), personal experience, photo feature, travel, Mexico culture and recreation. No "dated travel writing, unverified facts, over-reliance on secondary sources or 'vacation diary.' No articles condescending or disrespectful of Mexico." Buys 10 mss/year. Query with or without published clips, or send complete mss. Length: 400-2,500 words. Pays $50-250.

Photos: State availability of photos with submission. Reviews contact sheets, negatives, transparencies and prints. Offers $50-200/photo. Identification of subjects required. Buys one-time rights.

Fillers: Facts, short humor. Length: 35-50 words. Pays $10.

Tips: "Preference is given to material that presents Mexico's uniqueness and culture as differences to be appreciated; material that helps travelers understand, accept and cope with these differences respectfully; material that reflects a genuine concern, caring, acceptance or love of Mexico on the part of the writer. All areas open to freelancers. Experienced Mexico travel writers favored for longer regional features. For City Scenes, Resort Reports, Travel Choices, Specialty Spotlights and columns, we seek fresh perspectives, first-hand knowledge and experience, timely information and affection for Mexico."

MICHIGAN LIVING, AAA Michigan, 17000 Executive Plaza Drive, Dearborn MI 48126. (313)336-1211. Editor: Len Barnes. 50% freelance written. Emphasizes travel and auto use. Monthly magazine. Circ. 990,890. Pays on acceptance. Publishes ms an average of 6 months after acceptance. Buys first North American serial rights. Offers 100% kill fee. Byline given. Submit seasonal/holiday material 3 months in advance. Reports in 4-6 weeks. Free sample copy and writer's guidelines.

Nonfiction: Travel articles on U.S. and Canadian topics, but not on California, Florida or Arizona. Buys 50-60 unsolicited mss/year. Send complete ms. Length: 200-1,000 words. Pays $78-315.

Photos: Photos purchased with accompanying ms. Captions required. Pays $367 for cover photos; $50-220 for color transparencies; total purchase price for ms includes payment for b&w photos.

Tips: "In addition to descriptions of things to see and do, articles should contain accurate, current information on costs the traveler would encounter on his trip. Items such as lodging, meal and entertainment expenses should be included, not in the form of a balance sheet but as an integral part of the piece. We want the sounds, sights, tastes, smells of a place or experience so one will feel he has been there and knows if he wants to go back."

THE MIDWEST MOTORIST, AAA Auto Club of Missouri, 12901 North Forty Dr., St. Louis MO 63141. (314)576-7350. Editor: Michael J. Right. Managing Editor: Jean Kennedy. Associate Editor: Bret Berigan. 70% freelance written. Bimonthly magazine on travel and auto-related topics. Primarily focuses on travel throughout the world; prefers stories that tell about sights and give solid travel tips. Circ. 351,000. Pays on acceptance. Publishes ms an average of 8 months after acceptance. Byline given. Not copyrighted. Buys one-time rights, simultaneous rights (rarely), and second serial (reprint) rights. Submit seasonal/holiday material 6-8 months in advance. Simultaneous queries, and simultaneous, photocopied and previously published submissions OK. Query for electronic submissions. Computer printout submissions acceptable as long as they are readable and NOT ALL CAPS; no dot-matrix. Reports in 1 month when query is accompanied by SASE. Sample copy for 9x12 SAE and 4 first class stamps. Free writer's guidelines.

Nonfiction: General interest; historical/nostalgic; how-to; humor (with motoring or travel slant); interview/profile; personal experience; photo feature; technical (auto safety or auto-related); and travel (domestic and international), all travel-related or auto-related. March/April annual European travel issue; November/December annual cruise issue. No religious, philosophical arguments or opinion not supported by facts. Buys 25 mss/year. Query with published clips. Length: 500-2,000 (1,500 preferred) words. Pays $50-200.

Photos: State availability of photos. Prefers color slides and b&w with people, sights, scenery mentioned. Reviews 35mm transparencies and 8x10 prints. Payment included in ms purchase. Captions, model releases and identification of subjects required. Buys one-time rights.

Tips: "Query should be informative and entertaining, written with as much care as the lead of a story. Feature articles on travel destinations and tips are most open to freelancers."

‡MOTORHOME, TL Enterprises, Inc., 29901 Agoura Rd., Agoura CA 91301. (818)991-4980. Editor: Bob Livingston. Managing Editor: Gail Harrington. 60% freelance written. A monthly magazine covering motorhomes. "*MotorHome* is exclusively for motorhome enthusiasts. We feature road tests on new motorhomes, travel locations, controversy concerning motorhomes, how-to and technical articles relating to motorhomes." Circ. 120,000. Pays on acceptance. Publishes ms an average of 4 months after acceptance. Byline given. Buys first North American serial rights. Submit seasonal/holiday material 8 months in advance. Query for electronic submissions. Computer printout submissions acceptable. Reports in 3 weeks on queries; 2 months on mss. Free sample copy and writer's guidelines.

Nonfiction: General interest; historical/nostalgic; how-to (do it yourself for motorhomes); humor; new product; photo feature; and technical. Buys 80 mss/year. Query with published clips. Length: 1,000-2,500 words. Pays $175-600 for assigned articles; pays $100-500 for unsolicited articles. Sometimes pays expenses of writers and/or photographers on assignment.

Photos: Send photos with submission. Reviews contact sheets and 35mm/120/4x5 transparencies. Offers no additional payment for photos accepted with ms except for use on cover. Captions, model releases and identification of subjects required. Buys first North American serial rights.

Tips: "If a freelancer has an idea for a good article it's best to send a query and include possible photo locations to illustrate the article. We prefer to assign articles and work with the author in developing a piece suitable to our audience. We are in a specialized field with very enthusiastic readers who appreciate articles by authors who actually enjoy motorhomes. The following areas are most open: Travel—places to go with a motorhome, where to stay, what to see etc.; we prefer not to use travel articles where the motorhome is secondary; and How-to—personal projects on author's motorhomes to make travel easier, etc., unique projects, accessories. Also articles on unique personalities, motorhomes, humorous experiences.''

NATIONAL GEOGRAPHIC TRAVELER, National Geographic Society, 17th and M Sts. NW, Washington DC 20036. (202)857-7721. Editor: Joan Tapper. 90% freelance written. A quarterly travel magazine. *"Traveler* highlights mostly U.S. and Canadian subjects, but about 30% of its articles cover other foreign destinations—most often Europe, Mexico, and the Caribbean, occasionally the Pacific." Circ. 775,000. Pays on acceptance. Publishes ms an average of 12-15 months after acceptance. Byline given. Offers 50% kill fee. Computer print-out submissions OK; prefers letter-quality. Reports in 2 months. Sample copy $5.60; writer's guidelines for SASE.
Nonfiction: Travel. Buys 20 mss/year. Query with published clips. Length: 2,000-4,000 words. Pays $1/word. Pays expenses of writers on assignment.
Photos: Reviews transparencies and prints.

NEW ENGLAND GETAWAYS, New England Publishing Group, Inc., 21 Pocahontas Dr., Peabody MA 01960. (617)535-4186. Associate Editor: Christine Kole MacLean. 50% freelance written. Works with a small number of new/unpublished writers each year. A monthly magazine covering travel in New England. Circ. 40,000. Pays on publication. Publishes ms an average of 3 months after acceptance. Offers kill fee. Buys all rights or makes work-for-hire assignments. Submit seasonal/holiday material 4 months in advance. Query for electronic submissions. Computer printout submissions acceptable; prefers letter-quality. Reports in 1 month. Sample copy $3; writer's guidelines for SASE.
Nonfiction: "We are interested in articles that encourage people to see New England, especially those articles that focus on an event that is going on in a town during a specific time period. The writer covers such events, as well as some local points of interest in advance. We then publish the article in the appropriate issue so that readers know the details about the events and sites, and can plan to attend. No nostalgia or general pieces." Query. Length: 1,000-2,000 words. Pays $150-250 for assigned articles. Sometimes pays expenses of writers on assignment.
Photos: State availability of photos with submission. "Writer is expected to furnish photos once article is assigned." Reviews photos and slides. Offers no additional payment for photos accepted with ms. Captions and model releases required. Buys all rights.
Tips: "Be specific about the area or event you wish to cover. All articles must be information-based—readers want to know the times and places of sites and events, how much they cost, what the hours are, and where they can call for more information. Essentially we want specific articles about what to do and where to go in all of New England. Articles should also include information about mid-week and weekend packages offered by local hotels. Seasonal topics, such as New Year's celebrations or foliage, and New England topics, such as factory outlet shopping or antique shopping, are also acceptable. The best way to see what we want is to write for a sample copy."

NORTHEAST OUTDOORS, Northeast Outdoors, Inc., Box 2180, Waterbury CT 06722. (203)755-0158. Editor: Camillo Falcon. 80% freelance written. Works with a small number of new/unpublished writers each year, and is eager to work with new/unpublished writers. A monthly tabloid covering family camping in the Northeastern U.S. Circ. 14,000. Pays on publication. Publishes ms an average of 8 months after acceptance. Byline given. Offers 50% kill fee. Buys first rights, one-time rights, second serial (reprint) rights, simultaneous rights, and regional rights. Submit seasonal/holiday material 5 months in advance. Simultaneous, photocopied and previously published submissions OK. Query for electronic submissions. Computer printout submissions acceptable; no dot-matrix. Reports in 1 month. Sample copy for 9x12 SAE with 6 first class stamps; writer's guidelines for #10 SAE with 1 first class stamp.
Nonfiction: Book excerpts; general interest; historical/nostalgic; how-to (on camping); humor; new product (company and RV releases only); personal experience; photo feature; and travel. "No diaries of trips, dog stories, or anything not camping and RV related." Length: 300-1,500 words. Pays $40-80 for articles with b&w photos; pays $30-75 for articles without art.
Photos: Send photos with submission. Reviews contact sheets and 5x7 prints or larger. Captions and identification of subjects required. Buys one-time rights.
Columns/Departments: Mealtime (campground cooking), 300-900 words. Buys 12 mss/year. Query or send complete ms. Length: 750-1,000 words. Pays $30-75.
Fillers: Camping related anecdotes, facts, newsbreaks and short humor. Buys few fillers. Length: 25-200 words. Pays $5-15.
Tips: "We most often need material on campgrounds and attractions in New England. Go camping and travel

in the Northeastern States, especially New England. Have a nice trip, and tell us about it. Travel and camping articles, especially first-person reports on private campgrounds and interviews with owners, are the areas of our publication most open to freelancers."

PACIFIC BOATING ALMANAC, Suite 14, 4051 Glencoe Ave., Marina Del Ray CA 90292. (213)306-2094. Editor: William Berssen. 5% freelance written. Prefers to work with published/established writers. For "Western boat owners." Published in 3 editions to cover the Pacific Coastal area. Circ. 25,000. Buys all rights. Buys 12 mss/year. Pays on publication. Publishes ms an average of 6 months after acceptance. Submit seasonal material 3 to 6 months in advance. Query for electronic submissions. Computer printout submissions OK; prefers letter-quality. Reports in 1 month. Sample copy $13.95.
Nonfiction: "This is a cruising guide, published annually in three editions, covering all of the navigable waters in the Pacific coast. Though we are almost entirely staff-produced, we would be interested in well-written articles on cruising and trailer-boating along the Pacific coast and in the navigable lakes and rivers of the Western states from Baja, California to Alaska inclusive." Query. Pays $50 minimum. Pays expenses of writers on assignment.
Photos: Pays $10/8x10 b&w glossy print.
Tips: "We are also publishers of boating books that fall within the classification of 'where-to' and 'how-to.' Authors are advised not to send manuscript until requested after we've reviewed a two- to four-page outline of the projected books."

SOUTHERN TRAVEL, 5520 Park Ave., Box 395, Trumbull CT 06611-0395. (203)373-7000. Publisher: Rebecca McPheters. Editor: Shepherd Campbell. 90% freelance written. Seeks both established and new/unpublished writers. A service magazine that describes the rich variety of travel opportunities that exist in the Southern U.S. and helps readers get the most for their travel dollars. Bimonthly magazine. Circ. 210,000. Byline given. Pays on acceptance. Publishes ms an average of 6 months after acceptance. Buys all rights. Pays on acceptance. Reports in 1 month. Sample copy $2.50; writer's guidelines for #10 SAE and 1 first class stamp.
Nonfiction: Emphasis on big, colorful features about major destinations, sectional roundups, shorter local articles, and practical travel advice. Buys 120 mss/year. Query with published clips. Length varies. Pays $150 minimum for articles; considerably more for major features. Sometimes pays the expenses of writers on assignment.
Photos: State availablity of photos with submission. Pays $50 for 8x10 b&w glossies; $75-200 for color transparencies. Identification of subjects required. Buys one-time rights.
Tips: "Our greatest need is for articles about local attractions or events that may not be worth a special long trip but are fun to see en route to a major destination."

TEXAS HIGHWAYS MAGAZINE, Official Travel Magazine for the State of Texas, State Dept. of Highways and Public Transportation, 11th and Brazos, Austin TX 78701. (512)463-8581. Editor: Franklin T. Lively. Managing Editor: Jack Lowry. 85% freelance written. Prefers to work with published/established writers. A monthly tourist magazine covering travel and history for Texas only. Pays on acceptance. Publishes ms an average of 10 months after acceptance. Byline given. Offers $100 kill fee. Buys one-time rights. Submit seasonal/holiday material 1 year in advance. Simultaneous queries and submissions OK. Query for electronic submissions. Computer printout submissions acceptable; no dot-matrix. Reports in 2 weeks on queries; 1 month on mss. Sample copy and writer's guidelines for 9x12 SAE and 3 first class stamps.
Nonfiction: Historical/nostalgic, photo feature, travel. Must be concerned with travel in Texas. Send material on "what to see, what to do, where to go in *Texas*." Material must be tourist-oriented. "No disaster features." Buys 75 mss/year. Query with published clips. Length: 1,200-1,600 words. Pays $400-700. Sometimes pays expenses of writers on assignment "after we have worked with them awhile."
Photos: Bill Reaves, photo editor. Send photos with query or ms. Pays $80 for less than half a page, $120 for half page, $170 for a full page, $400 for cover, $300 for back cover. Accepts 4x5, 2¼x2¼, 35mm color transparencies. Captions and identification of subjects required. Buys one-time rights.
Tips: "We are looking for outdoor features this year, such as state parks, lakes, beaches, and dude ranches. We have too many historical homes and buildings stories now."

TOURS & RESORTS, The World-Wide Vacation Magazine, World Publishing Co., 990 Grove St., Evanston IL 60201-4370. (312)491-6440. Editor/Associate Publisher: Bob Meyers. Managing Editor: Ray Gudas. 90% freelance written. A bimonthly magazine covering world-wide vacation travel features. Circ. 250,000. Pays on acceptance. Byline given. Buys first North American serial rights. Submit seasonal/holiday material 6 months in advance. Previously published submissions acceptable, dependent upon publication—local or regional OK. Computer printout submissions acceptable; prefers letter-quality. Reports in 3 weeks on queries; 6 weeks on mss. Sample copy $2.50 with 9x12 SASE.
Nonfiction: Primarily destination-oriented travel articles, "Anatomy of a Tour" features, and resort/hotel profiles and roundups, but will consider essays, how-to, humor, company profiles, nostalgia, etc.—if travel-related. "It is best to study current contents and query first." Buys 75 mss/year. Average length: 1,500 words. Pays $150-500.

Photos: Top-quality original color slides preferred. Captions required. Buys one-time rights. Prefers photo feature package (ms plus slides), but will purchase slides only to support a work in progress.

Columns/Departments: Travel Views (travel tips; service articles), and World Shopping (shopping guide). Buys 8-12 mss/year. Query or send complete ms. Length: 800-1,500 words. Pays $125-250.

Tips: "Travel features and the Travel Views department are most open to freelancers. Because we are heavily photo-oriented, superb slides are our foremost concern. The most successful approach is to send 2-3 sheets of slides with the query or complete ms. Include a list of other subjects you can provide as a photo feature package."

‡TRAILER LIFE, TL Enterprises, Inc., 29901 Agoura Rd., Agoura CA 90301. (213)991-4980. Editor: Bill Estes. Managing Editor: Merrill Pierson. Editorial Director: Barbara Leonard. 60% freelance written. A monthly magazine covering the RV lifestyle, and RV travel and products. "Readers of *Trailer Life* are owners of recreational vehicles who spend a median 37.8 days traveling on the road. Articles should have a distinctive focus on the needs, entertainment and issues of the RV traveler." Circ. 310,000. Pays on acceptance. Byline given. Offers 30% kill fee. Buys first North American serial rights. Submit seasonal/holiday material 4 months in advance. Computer printout submissions acceptable. Sample copy $2.50; free writer's guidelines.

Nonfiction: Expose, general interest, historical/nostalgic, how-to, humor, interview/profile, new product, guest editorials, personal experience, photo feature, technical and travel. Query with or without published clips, or send complete ms. Length: 1,000-2,000 words. Pays $50-500. Sometimes pays the expenses of writers on assignment, under special circumstances.

Photos: Reviews contact sheets, 35mm transparencies (or larger), and 8x10 b&w prints. Offers no additional payment for photos accepted with ms, but also buys photos independent of articles. Captions, model releases and identification of subjects required. Buys one-time rights.

Columns/Departments: People on the Move (short RV-related people items with black-and-white photos, can include events, humorous news items), 200-500 words; and Newswire (news items specific to the RV industry/consumer or public lands), 100 words. Send complete ms. Pays $75 maximum.

Tips: "First-hand experience with recreational vehicles and the RV lifestyle makes the writer's material more appealing. Although the writer need not own an RV, accurate information and a knowledge of the RV lifestyle will lend desired authenticity to article submissions. People on the Move, Newswire, travel features, how-to are areas most open to feelancers. Vehicle evaluations of home-built or home-modified trailers, campers or motorhomes are open to freelancers."

TRAILS-A-WAY, 9425 S. Greenville Rd., Greenville MI 48838. (616)754-2251. Editor: David Higbie. 25% freelance written. Newspaper published 12 times/year on camping in the Midwest (Michigan, Ohio, Indiana, Illinois and Wisconsin). "Fun and information for campers who own recreational vehicles." Circ. 58,000. Pays on publication. Byline given. Buys first and second rights to the same material, and second (reprint) rights to material originally published elsewhere. Submit seasonal/holiday material 3 months in advance. Simultaneous queries and submissions OK. Computer printout submissions acceptable; no dot-matrix. Reports in 1 month. Sample copy for 10x13 SAE with 4 first class stamps; writer's guidelines for #10 SAE and 2 first class stamps.

Nonfiction: How-to (use, maintain recreational vehicles—5th wheels, travel and camping trailers, pop-up trailers, motorhomes); humor; inspirational; interview/profile; new product (camp products); personal experience; photo feature; technical (on RVs); travel. March/April issue: spring camping; September/October: fall camping. Winter issues feature southern hot spots. "All articles should relate to RV camping in Michigan, Ohio, Indiana, Illinois and Wisconsin—or south in winter. No tenting or backpacking articles." Buys 40-50 mss/year. Send complete ms. Length: 1,000-1,500 words. Pays $60-125.

Photos: Send photos with ms. Pays $5-10 for b&w and color prints. No slides. Captions required. Buys one-time rights.

TRANSITIONS ABROAD, 18 Hulst Rd., Box 344, Amherst MA 01004. (413)256-0373. Editor/Publisher: Prof. Clayton A. Hubbs. 80-90% freelance written. Eager to work with new/unpublished writers. The resource magazine for low-budget international travel with an educational or work component. Bound magazine. Circ. 13,000. Pays on publication. Buys first rights and second (reprint) rights to material originally published elsewhere. Byline given. Written queries only. Computer printout submissions acceptable; prefers letter-quality. Reports in 2 months. Sample copy $2.50; writer's guidelines and topics schedule for 9x12 SAE and 5 first class stamps.

Nonfiction: How-to (find courses, inexpensive lodging and travel); interview (information on specific areas and people); personal experience (evaluation of courses, special interest and study tours, economy travel); and travel (what to see and do in specific areas of the world, new learning and travel ideas). Foreign travel only. Few destination ("tourist") pieces. Emphasis on information and on interaction with people in host country. Buys 40 unsolicited mss/issue. Query with credentials. Length: 500-2,000 words. Pays $25-150. Include author's bio with submissions.

Photos: Send photos with ms. Pays $10-25 for 8x10 b&w glossy prints, higher for covers. No color. Addi-

Close-up

Pamela Fiori
Editor-in-Chief
Travel & Leisure

"What means more to me than anything is the reader," says Pamela Fiori, editor-in-chief of *Travel & Leisure*. "The common denominator for our readers is their passion for travel. It's what brings them into the magazine. Our job, of course, is to inspire them to escape."

But that's not nearly enough now, Fiori adds. "Our readers also want—and need—to be informed—responsibly. Our subject matter is the entire universe of travel. This includes not only destinations but all the practicalities involved, from getting there to coming home. It means covering restaurants, shops, hotels. It entails advice on coping with being stranded at an airport for seven hours and informing them of outbreaks of malaria and of trouble spots where there are traveler's advisories. More and more we have to deal with travel in a volatile world, finding those destinations where readers can feel at ease, not on guard. And warning them, if they *choose* to go to a place where problems of any kind might exist, of what may confront them. The world has changed and we have to change with it—to be in touch with our readers on every possible level.

"We are a service magazine—that is how the magazine made its mark and is what has made *Travel & Leisure* the number one travel magazine in the world," Fiori says. "We don't want to be a coffee table book—something pretty and pointless. We owe our readers more than this. They expect to be influenced by us, to use the magazine, not just leaf through it and put it away.

"The past year has been probably our most exciting ever. We redesigned the magazine, looked harder at ourselves than ever, saw competition in directions we never saw or expected before. It made us think harder and assign more carefully than ever," she says.

In looking for writers (about 80 percent of *Travel & Leisure* is written by freelancers), Fiori says, "We tend to go for people with a track record. Writing talent is a given. We then look for fresh ideas and some indication that we are making an assignment to someone who understands what *Travel & Leisure* is.

"The best ideas, almost always, come from my staff," she says. "That's not hard to understand. We know our readers best and we know *what Travel & Leisure* is. The second-best ideas come from writers we have long-term relationships with.   All of our assignments are accompanied by assignment letters. We like working closely with a writer. It is a very eye-level partnership.

"Finally, we hope our writers will put themselves in the place of our readers when they go off on assignment for us. That means remembering that not all of them can afford a $300 a night hotel in Paris. Not all of them *want* to go shopping. And that they all appreciate knowing that the adorable little inn that is worth going to also is on a long and winding road that is better to negotiate in broad daylight than in the middle of the night.

"In other words, tell the reader what he *ought* to know. There's a lot riding on every article we publish. Our readers may spend a great deal of money and their precious time following in *Travel & Leisure*'s footsteps. We can't lead them astray."

—Glenda Tennant Neff

tional payment for photos accompanying ms. Photos increase likelihood of acceptance. Buys one-time rights. Captions required.

Columns/Departments: Study/Travel Program Notes (evaluation of courses or programs); Traveler's Advisory/Resources (new information and ideas for offbeat independent travel); Jobnotes (how to find it and what to expect); and Book Reviews (reviews of single books or groups on one area). Buys 8/issue. Send complete ms. Length: 1,000 words maximum. Pays $20-50.

Fillers: Info Exchange (information, preferably first-hand— having to do with travel, particularly offbeat educational travel and work or study abroad). Buys 10/issue. Length: 1,000 words maximum. Pays $20-50.

Tips: "We like nuts and bolts stuff, practical information, especially on how to work, live and cut costs abroad. Our readers want usable information on planning their own travel itinerary. Be specific: names, addresses, current costs. We are particularly interested in educational travel and study abroad for adults and senior citizens. More and more readers want information not only on work but retirement possibilities. We have a new department on exchange programs, homestays, and study/tours for precollege students. *Eduational Travel Directory* published each year in July provides descriptive listings of resources and information sources on work, study, and independent travel abroad along with study/travel programs abroad for adults."

‡TRAVEL AND LEISURE, American Express Publishing Corp., 1120 Avenue of the Americas, New York NY 10036. (212)382-5600. Editor-in-Chief: Pamela Fiori. Executive Editor: Christopher Hunt. Managing Editor: Maria Shaw. 80% freelance written. Monthly magazine. Circ. 1.1 million. Pays on acceptance. Byline given. Offers 25% kill fee. Buys first world and foreign edition rights. Reports in 2-3 weeks. Sample copy $3. Free writer's guidelines.

Nonfiction: Travel. Buys 200 mss/year. Query. Length open. Payment varies. Often pays the expenses of writers on assignment.

Photos: Discourages submission of unsolicited transparencies. Payment varies. Captions required. Buys one-time rights.

Tips: "Read the magazine. Regionals and Taking Off section are best places to start."

TRAVEL SMART, Communications House, Inc., Dobbs Ferry NY 10522. (914)693-4208. Editor/Publisher: H.J. Teison. Covers information on "good-value travel." Monthly newsletter. Pays on publication. Buys all rights. Photocopied submissions OK. Computer printout submissions acceptable. Reports in 6 weeks. Sample copy and writer's guidelines for #10 SAE with 2 first class stamps.

Nonfiction: "Interested primarily in bargains or little-known deals on transportation, lodging, food, unusual destinations that won't break the bank. No destination stories on major Caribbean islands, London, New York, no travelogs, my vacation, poetry, fillers. No photos or illustrations. Just hard facts. We are not part of 'Rosy fingers of dawn . . .' school. More like letter from knowledgeable friend who has been there." Query first. Length: 100-1,000 words. Pays "up to $100."

Tips: "When you travel, check out small hotels offering good prices, little known restaurants, and send us brief rundown (with prices, phone numbers, addresses). Information must be current. Include your phone number with submission, because we sometimes make immediate assignments."

‡TRAVELER, The Magazine for Vacation Home Owners, Interval International, Inc., 6262 Sunset Dr., Box 431920, Miami FL 33243-1920. (305)666-1861. Editor: Edrea Kaiser. Managing Editor: William L. Coulter. 40% freelance written. A bimonthly magazine about shared vacation ownership and travel. "Our readers are members of Interval International, a worldwide vacation exchange firm. They are interested in getting the most of their purchase at a vacation ownership resort." Circ. 230,000. Pays on acceptance. Publishes ms an average of 4 months after acceptance. Byline sometimes given. Offers 5¢/word kill fee. Buys first rights or second serial rights. Submit seasonal/holiday material 6 months in advance. Simultaneous, photocopied and previously published submissions OK. Query for electronic submissions. Computer printout submissions OK; prefers letter-quality. Reports in 2 weeks on queries. Sample copy for 9x12 SAE with 5 first class stamps. Writer's guidelines for #10 SAE with 1 first class stamp.

Nonfiction: Interview/profile, personal experience, photo feature, travel, consumer tips. No "nightmare on the road" or other negative slants. Buys 12-20 mss/year. Query with published clips. Length: 1,000-3,500 words. Pays 10-15¢/word. Sometimes pays expenses of writers on assignment.

Photos: State availability of photos with submission. Reviews transparencies (35mm to 4x5). Offers $15-150/photo. Identification of subjects required. Buys one-time rights.

Tips: "We are very interested in first-person travel experiences or interviews. Send a well-planned proposal with a very specific slant."

TRAVEL-HOLIDAY MAGAZINE, Travel Magazine, Inc., 51 Atlantic Ave., Floral Park NY 11001. (516)352-9700. Editor: Scott Shane. 95% freelance written. Prefers to work with published/established writers but works with a small number of new/unpublished writers each year. For the active traveler with time and money to travel several times a year. Monthly magazine. Circ. 816,000. Pays on acceptance. Publishes ms an average of 6 months after acceptance. Buys first North American serial rights. Byline given. Submit seasonal/

holiday material 6 months in advance. Query for electronic submissions. Computer printout submissions acceptable if double-spaced; prefers letter-quality. Reports in 2 months. Sample copy for 9x12 SAE and $1; free writer's guidelines.

Nonfiction: Interested in travel destination articles. Send query letter/outline; clips of previously published work *must* accompany queries. No phone queries. Only the highest quality writing and photography are considered by the staff. "Don't ask if we'd like to see any articles on San Francisco, France or China. Develop a specific story idea and explain why the destination is so special that we should devote space to it. Are there interesting museums, superb restaurants, spectacular vistas, etc.? Tell us how you plan to handle the piece—convey to us the mood of the city, the charm of the area, the uniqueness of the museums, etc. No food and wine, medical, photo tips, poetry or boring travelogs." Buys 100 mss/year. Length: featurettes (800-1,300 words), $250 and up; features (1,600-1,800 words), up to $600; "Here and There" column (575 words), $150. For "Here and There" column use "any upbeat topic that can be covered succinctly (with one piece of b&w art) that's travel related and deserves special recognition. When querying, please send suggested lead and indicate 'Here and There' in the cover letter."

Photos: Send photos with submission. B&w prints $25; color converted to b&w will be paid at $25 rate; color transparencies (35mm and larger) pays $75-400 depending upon use. Pays on publication. If you have a stock list for your photos, send it in. Monthly "photo wants" list is mailed to appropriate photographers.

Tips: "Feature stories should be about major destinations: large cities, regions, etc. Featurettes can be about individual attractions, smaller cities, side trips, etc. We welcome sidebar service information. Stimulate reader interest in the subject as a travel destination through lively, entertaining and accurate writing. A good way to break in—if we're not familiar with your writing—is to send us a good idea for a featurette. Convey the mood of a place without being verbose; although we like good anecdotal material, our primary interest is in the destination itself, not the author's adventures. Do not query without having first read several recent issues. We no longer use any broadbased travel pieces. Each article must have a specific angle. We are assigning articles to the best writers we can find and those writers who develop and produce good material will continue to work with us on a regular basis. We have also become much more service-oriented in our articles. We will be featuring regional editorial, therefore we require additional regional United States featurette length stories."

TRAVELORE REPORT, Suite #100, 1512 Spruce St., Philadelphia PA 19102. (215)735-3838. Editor: Ted Barkus. For affluent travelers; businessmen, retirees, well-educated readers; interested in specific tips, tours, and bargain opportunities in travel. Monthly newsletter. Buys all rights. Pays on publication. Submit seasonal material 2 months in advance. Computer printout and disk submissions acceptable. Sample copy $2; writer's guidelines for #10 SAE with 1 first class stamp.

Nonfiction: "Brief insights (25-200 words) with facts, prices, names of hotels and restaurants, etc., on offbeat subjects of interest to people going places. What to do, what not to do. Supply information. We will rewrite if acceptable. We're candid—we tell it like it is with no sugar coating. Avoid telling us about places in United States or abroad without specific recommendations (hotel name, costs, rip-offs, why, how long, etc.). No destination pieces which are general with no specific 'story angle' in mind, or generally available through PR departments." Buys 10-20 mss/year. Pays $5-20.

Tips: "Destinations confronted with political disturbances should be avoided. We're adding more topics geared to business-related travel and marketing trends in leisure-time industry."

VISTA/USA, Box 161, Convent Station NJ 07961. (201)538-7600. Editor: Kathleen M. Caccavale. Managing Editor: Martha J. Mendez. 90% freelance written. Will consider ms submissions from *unpublished* writers. Quarterly magazine of Exxon Travel Club. "Our publication uses articles on North American areas without overtly encouraging travel. We strive to help our readers to gain an in-depth understanding of cities, towns and areas as well as other aspects of American culture that affect the character of the nation." Circ. 825,000. Pays on acceptance. Publishes ms an average of 1 year after acceptance. Buys first North American serial rights. Query about seasonal subjects 18 months in advance. Computer printout submissions acceptable; prefers letter-quality. Reports in 6 weeks. Sample copy for a 9x12 or larger SAE with 5 first class stamps; writer's and photographer's guidelines for #10 SASE.

Nonfiction: Geographically oriented articles on North America focused on the character of an area or place; also general articles at least tangentially related to travel and places; photo essays (recent examples include city lights, Thoreau's Cape Cod, reflections); and some articles dealing with Americana, crafts and collecting. "We buy feature articles on North America, Hawaii, Mexico and the Caribbean that appeal to a national audience and prefer that destination queries have a hook or angle to them that give us a clear, solid argument for covering the average city 'soon' rather than 'anytime.' " No feature articles that mention driving or follow routes on a map or articles about hotels, restaurants or annual events. Uses 7-15 mss/issue. Query with outline and clips of previously published work. Length: 1,200-2,000 words. Pays $450 minimum for features. Pays the expenses of writers on assignment.

Columns/Departments: " 'MiniTrips' are point to point or loop driving tours of from 50 to 350 miles covering a healthy variety of stops along the way. 'Close Focus' covers new or changing aspects of major attractions, small or limited attractions not appropriate for a feature article (800-1,000 words). 'American Vignettes' covers anything travel related that also reveals a slice of American life, often with a light or humorous touch, such as asking directions from a cranky New Englander, or the phenomenon of 'talking license plates.' 'Information Please' provides practical information on travel safety, trends, tips; a service column."

Photos: Contact: photo researcher. Send photos with ms. Pays $100 minimum for color transparencies. Captions preferred. Buys one-time rights.

Tips: "We are looking for readable pieces with good writing that will interest armchair travelers as much as readers who may want to visit the areas you write about. Queries about well-known destinations should have something new or different to say about them, a specific focus or angle. Articles should have definite themes and should give our readers an insight into the character and flavor of an area or topic. Stories about personal experiences must impart a sense of drama and excitement or have a strong human-interest angle. Stories about areas should communicate a strong sense of what it feels like to be there. Good use of anecdotes and quotes should be included. Study the articles in the magazine to understand how they are organized, how they present their subject, the range of writing styles, and the specific types of subjects used. Afterwards, query and enclose samples of your best writing. We continue to seek department shorts and inventory articles of a general, nonseasonal nature (1,500 to 1,800 words)."

WESTERN RV TRAVELER, Outdoor Publications, Inc., Suite 226, 2033 Clement Ave., Alameda CA 94501. (415)769-8338. Editor: Dave Preston. 85% freelance written. Works with a small number of new/unpublished writers each year. A monthly magazine for Western recreational vehicle owners. Circ. 30,000. Pays on publication. Publishes ms an average of 6 months after acceptance. Byline given. Buys one-time rights. Submit seasonal/holiday material 6 months in advance. Simultaneous, photocopied, and previously published submissions OK. Query for electronic submissions. Computer printout submissions acceptable. Reports in several weeks on queries; several months on mss. Free sample copy and writer's guidelines.

Nonfiction: Historical/nostalgic; how-to (fix your RV); new product; personal experience (particularly travel); technical; and travel (destinations for RVs). No non-RV travel articles. Buys 36 mss/year. Query with or without published clips, or send complete ms. Length: 1,000-3,000 words. Pays $1.50/inch.

Photos: Send photos with submissions. Reviews contact sheets, negatives, transparencies and prints. Offers $5 minimum/photo. Identification of subjects required.

Tips: "RV travel/destination stories are most open to freelancers. Include all information of value to RVers, and reasons why they would want to visit the California or western location."

YACHT VACATIONS MAGAZINE, (formerly *Chartering Magazine*), 830 Pop Tilton's Place, Jensen Beach FL 33457. (305)334-2003. Editor: Antonia Thomas. 30-50% freelance written. Prefers to work with published/established writers and works with a small number of new/unpublished writers each year. "*Yacht Vacations* is a people-oriented travel magazine with a positive approach. Our focus is yacht charter vacations." Circ. 50,000. Pays on publication. Publishes ms an average of 3 months after acceptance. Buys first North American serial rights. Submit seasonal/holiday material at least 5 months in advance. Simultaneous queries and simultaneous and photocopied submissions, and previously published work (on rare occasion) OK. Query for electronic submissions. Computer printout submissions acceptable. Reports in 4-6 weeks. Writer's guidelines for #10 SAE and 1 first class stamp.

Nonfiction: General interest (worldwide, charter boat-oriented travel); historical/nostalgic (charter vacation oriented); how-to (bareboating technique); interview/profile (charter brokers, charter skippers, positive); new product (would have to be a new type of charter); opinion; personal experience (charter boat related, worldwide, positive people-oriented travel); photo feature (charter boat, worldwide, positive, people-oriented travel); travel (charter vacation-oriented); and ancillary topics such as fishing, scuba or underwater photography. Special issues will focus on the Caribbean, diving, and Mediterranean. Buys 50-85 mss/year. Query with published clips or send complete ms. Length: 600-3,000 words. Pays $50-350. Rarely pays expenses of writers on assignment.

Photos: "We would like to receive quality cover photos reflecting the charter yacht vacation experience, i.e., water, yacht, and people enjoying." State availability of photos or send photos with query or ms. Pays with article for b&w and color negatives, color transparencies (35mm), and b&w and color prints (3x5 or larger), plus buys cover photos. Requires model releases and identification of subjects. Buys one-time rights.

Tips: "We will buy fewer, if any, general travel pieces in 1989. We are happy to look at the work of any freelancer who may have something appropriate to offer within our scope—travel with a charter vacation orientation. We prefer submissions accompanied by good, professional quality photography. The best first step is a request for editorial guidelines, accompanied by a typed letter and work sample. *Yacht Vacations* will be looking for more articles of 300-600 words."

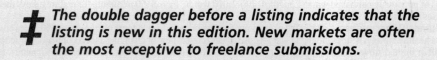

The double dagger before a listing indicates that the listing is new in this edition. New markets are often the most receptive to freelance submissions.

Women's

Today's women's publications (more than 50 are on newsstands) are as diverse as women's own daily schedules or ages. Magazines that also use material slanted to women's interests can be found in the following categories: Business and Finance; Child Care and Parental Guidance; Contemporary Culture; Food and Drink; Health and Fitness; Hobby and Craft; Home and Garden; Relationships; Religious; Romance and Confession; and Sports.

BRIDAL GUIDE, "The How-to for I Do", Globe Communications Corp., 441 Lexington Ave., New York NY 10017. (212)949-4040. Executive Editor: Lois Spitzer. 80% freelance written. Prefers to work with published/established writers; works with a small number of new/unpublished writers each year. A bimonthly magazine covering wedding planning and the first home. "*Bridal Guide* is designed to be used as a wedding planning guide and keepsake for couples soon to be married. Information about modern wedding trends is directed to brides, grooms, and parents." Circ. 300,000. Pays on publication. Publishes ms an average of 2 months after acceptance. Byline given. Offers 25% kill fee. Buys first North American serial rights, second serial (reprint) rights and all rights. Submit seasonal/holiday material 6 months in advance. Simultaneous submissions and previously published submissions OK. Query for electronic submissions. Computer printout submissions acceptable; prefers letter-quality. Reports in 1 month on queries; 2 months on manuscript. Sample copy $2.50.
Nonfiction: How-to, humor, inspirational, interview/profile, personal experience, religious and travel. Buys 132 mss/year. Send complete ms. Length: 1,000-20,000 words. Pays $200-1,000. Sometimes pays the expenses of writers on assignment.
Photos: Send photos with submission. Reviews 2x3 transparencies and prints. Additional payment for photos accepted with ms. Captions, model releases, and identification of subjects required.
Tips: "*Bridal Guide* is now published six times per year. Along with the new bimonthly schedule, our format has increased. You will find sixteen departments and five feature areas in each issue. This means expanded writing opportunities and greater exposure through our national distribution of 300,000 copies. The magazine offers re-marriage features as well as the etiquette of divorce problems in wedding planning. New information on all aspects of the perfect wedding from initial arrangements to the reception festivities is featured in each issue. Special stories include in-depth coverage of fashion, registry, emotions and honeymoons. Planning the first home is highlighted with specific information on major purchases. The areas of our publication most open to freelancers include how-to stories in bridal fashion, ethnic customs, religious ceremonies, remarriage, etiquette, and honeymoons, celebrity weddings, unusual weddings, wedding planning."

BRIDAL TRENDS, Meridian Publishing, Inc., Box 10010, Ogden UT 84409. (801)394-9446. 65% freelance written. Monthly magazine with useful articles for today's bride. Circ. 60,000. Pays on acceptance. Publishes ms an average of 10 months after acceptance. Byline given. Buys first rights, second serial (reprint) rights and non-exclusive reprint rights. Simultaneous, photocopied and previously published submissions OK. Reports in 6 weeks. Sample copy for $1 and 9x12 SAE; writer's guidelines for #10 SASE. All requests for sample copies and guidelines should be addressed Attn: Editor.
Nonfiction: "General interest articles about traditional and modern approaches to weddings. Topics include all aspects of ceremony and reception planning; flowers; invitations; catering; wedding apparel and fashion trends for the bride, groom, and other members of the wedding party, etc. Also featured are honeymoon destinations, how to build a relationship and keep romance alive, and adjusting to married life." Buys approximately 30 mss/year. Query. Length: 1,200 words. Pays 15¢/word for first rights plus non-exclusive reprint rights. Payment for second rights is negotiable.
Photos: State availability of photos with query letter. Color transparencies and 5x7 or 8x10 prints are preferred. Pays $35 for inside photo; pays $50 for cover. Captions, model release, and identification of subjects required.
Tips: "We publish articles that detail each aspect of wedding planning: invitations, choosing your flowers, deciding on the style of your wedding, and choosing a photographer and caterer."

BRIDE'S, Conde Nast Bldg., 350 Madison Ave., New York NY 10017. (212)880-8800. Editor-in-Chief: Barbara D. Tober. 40% freelance written. Eager to work with new/unpublished writers. A bimonthly magazine for the first- or second-time bride, her family and friends, the groom and his family and friends. Circ. 410,000. Pays on acceptance. Publishes ms an average of 2 months after acceptance. Buys all rights. Also buys first and second serial rights for book excerpts on marriage, communication, finances. Offers 20% kill fee, depending on circumstances. Buys 40 unsolicited mss/year. Byline given. Reports in 2 months. Computer printout submissions acceptable; no dot-matrix. Address mss to Features Department. Writer's guidelines for #10 SASE.
Nonfiction: "We want warm, personal articles, optimistic in tone, with help offered in a clear, specific way.

All issues should be handled within the context of marriage. How-to features on all aspects of marriage: communications, in-laws, careers, money, sex, housing, housework, family planning, marriage after a baby, religion, interfaith marriage, step-parenting, second marriage, reaffirmation of vows; informational articles on the realities of marriage, the changing roles of men and women, the kind of troubles in engagement that are likely to become big issues in marriage; stories from couples or marriage authorities that illustrate marital problems and solutions to men and women; book excerpts on marriage, communication, finances, sex; and how-to features on wedding planning that offer expert advice. Also success stories of marriages of long duration. We use first-person pieces and articles that are well researched, relying on quotes from authorities in the field, and anecdotes and dialogues from real couples. We publish first-person essays on provocative topics unique to marriage." Query or submit complete ms. Article outline preferred. Length: 1,000-3,000 words. Pays $300-800.

Columns/Departments: The Love column accepts reader love poems, for $25 each. The Something New section accepts reader wedding planning and craft ideas; pays $25.

Tips: "Since marriage rates are up and large, traditional weddings are back in style, and since more women work than ever before, do *not* query us on just living together or becoming a stay-at-home wife after marriage. Send us a query or a well-written article that is both easy to read and offers real help for the bride or groom as she/he adjusts to her/his new role. No first-person narratives on wedding and reception planning, home furnishings, cooking, fashion, beauty, travel. We're interested in unusual ideas, experiences, and lifestyles. No 'I used baby pink rose buds' articles."

CHATELAINE, 777 Bay St., Toronto, Ontario M5W 1A7 Canada. Editor-in-Chief: Mildred Istona. 75% freelance written. Prefers to work with published/established writers. Monthly general-interest magazine for Canadian women, from age 20 and up. "*Chatelaine* is read by one woman in three across Canada, a readership that spans almost every age group but is concentrated among those 25 to 45 including homemakers and working women in all walks of life." Circ. over 1 million. Pays on acceptance. Publishes ms an average of 3 months after acceptance. Byline given. Computer printout submissions OK; prefers letter-quality. Reports within 2 weeks. All mss must be accompanied by a SASE (IRCs in lieu of stamps if sent from outside Canada). Sample copy $2 and postage; free writer's guidelines.

Nonfiction: Elizabeth Parr, senior editor, articles. Submit an outline or query first. Full-length major pieces run from 1,500 to 3,000 words. Pays minimum $1,200 for acceptable major article. Buys first North American serial rights in English and French (the latter to cover possible use in *Chatelaine*'s sister French-language edition, edited in Montreal for French Canada). "We look for important national Canadian subjects, examining any and all facets of Canadian life, especially as they concern or interest women. Upfront columns include stories about relationships, health, nutrition, fitness and parents and kids." Submit outline first. Pays $350 for about 600 words. Prefers queries for nonfiction subjects on initial contact plus a resume and writing samples. Also seeks full-length personal experience stories with deep emotional impact. Pays $750. Pays expenses of writers on assignment.

Tips: Features on beauty, food, fashion and home decorating are supplied by staff writers and editors, and unsolicited material is not considered.

COUNTRY WOMAN, Reiman Publications, Box 643, Milwaukee WI 53201. (414)423-0100. Editor: Ann Kaiser. Managing Editor: Kathy Pohl. 75-85% freelance written. Eager to work with new/unpublished writers. Bimonthly magazine on the interests of country women. "*Country Woman* is for contemporary rural women of all ages and backgrounds and from all over the U.S. and Canada. It includes a sampling of the diversity that makes up rural women's lives—love of home, family, farm, ranch, community, hobbies, enduring values, humor, attaining new skills and appreciating present, past and future all within the content of the lifestyle that surrounds country living." Circ. 350,000. Pays on acceptance. Publishes ms an average of 1 year after acceptance. Byline given. Offers 20% kill fee. Buys first North American serial rights, one-time rights, and second serial (reprint) rights; makes some work-for-hire assignments. Submit seasonal/holiday material 4-5 months in advance. Photocopied and previously published (on occasion) submissions OK. Computer printout submissions acceptable; no dot-matrix. Reports in 1 month on queries; 8 weeks on mss. Sample copy for $2.50; writer's guidelines for #10 SAE and 1 first class stamp.

Nonfiction: General interest, historical/nostalgic, how-to (crafts, community projects, family relations, self-improvement, decorative, antiquing, etc.); humor; inspirational; interview/profile; personal experience; photo feature; and travel, all pertaining to a rural woman's interest. Buys 100 mss/year. Query or send complete ms. Length: 1,000 words maximum. Pays $100-225 (as photo/feature package for profiles of country women).

Photos: Send photos with query or ms. Reviews 35mm or 2¼ transparencies. "We pay for photo/feature packages." Captions, model releases and identification of subjects required. Buys one-time rights.

Columns/Departments: Why Farm Wives Age Fast (humor), I Remember When (nostalgia), Country Decorating, and Shopping Comparison (new product comparisons). Buys 20 mss (maximum)/year. Query or send complete ms. Length: 500-1,000 words. Pays $75-125.

Fiction: Adventure, humorous, mainstream, suspense and western. Buys 5 mss (maximum)/year. Query or send complete ms. Length: 750-1,000 words. Pays $90-125.

Poetry: Traditional, avant-garde, free verse, and light verse. Buys 40 poems/year. Submit maximum 6 poems. Length: 5-24 lines. Pays $10-40.

Fillers: Jokes, anecdotes, short humor and consumer news (e.g. safety, tips, etc.). Buys 40/year. Length: 40-250 words. Pays $25-40.

Tips: "We have recently broadened our focus to include 'country' women, not just women on farms and ranches. This allows freelancers a wider scope in material. Write as clearly and with as much zest and enthusiasm as possible. We love good quotes, supporting materials (names, places, etc.) and strong leads and closings. Readers relate strongly to where they live and the lifestyle they've chosen. They want to be informed and entertained, and that's just exactly why they subscribe. Readers are busy—not too busy to read—but when they do sit down, they want good writing, reliable information and something that feels like a reward. How-to, humor, personal experience and nostalgia are areas most open to freelancers. Profiles, to a certain degree, are also open. We are always especially receptive to short items—250 words, 400 words and so on. Be accurate and fresh in approach."

ESSENCE, 1500 Broadway, New York NY 10036. (212)730-4260. Editor-in-Chief: Susan L. Taylor. Editor: Stephanie Stokes Oliver. Executive Editor: Cheryll V. Greene. Senior Editor: Elsie B. Washington. Edited for Black women. Monthly magazine; 150 pages. Circ. 850,000. Pays on acceptance. Makes assignments on work for hire basis. 3 month lead time. Pays 25% kill fee. Byline given. Submit seasonal/holiday material 6 months in advance. Computer prinout submissions acceptable. Reports in 2 months. Sample copy $1.50; free writer's guidelines.

Features: "We're looking for articles that inspire and inform Black women. Our readers are interested and aware; the topics we include in each issue are provacative. Every articles should move the *Essence* woman emotionally and intellectually. We welcome queries form good writers on a wide range of topics; general interest, health and fitness, historical, how-to, humor, self-help, relationships, work, personality interview, personal experience, political issues, business and finances and personal opinion." Buys 200 mss/year. Query. Length: 1,000-3,000 words. Pays $500 minimum.

Photos: Gregory Gray, art director. State availability of photos with query. Pays $100 for b&w page; $300 for color page. Captions and model release required. "We particularly would like to see photographs for our travel section that feature Black travelers."

Columns/Departments: Query department editors: Contemporary Living (home, food, lifestyle, consumer information): Harriet Cole, Contemporary Living, editor; Arts & Entertainment: Pamela Johnson; Health & Fitness: Marjorie Whigham; Business and Finance: Nancy Anita Williams; Travel: Darie Giles Salter. Query. Length: About 1,000 words. Pays $100 minimum. "We are intereted in buying short poetry to be used as filler material."

Tips: "We're looking for quality fiction; more self-improvement pieces, 'relationship' articles, career information and issues important to Black women."

FAIRFIELD COUNTY WOMAN, NEW HAVEN COUNTY WOMAN, HARTFORD WOMAN, FCW, Inc., Chadwick & Duke, Publishers, 15 Bank St., Stamford CT 06901. (203)323-3105. Editor: Ina B. Chadwick. Regional Editor (Hartford): Marta Binstock, 595 Franklin Ave., Hartford CT 06114. "Send a query, not an article."

GLAMOUR, Conde Nast, 350 Madison Ave., New York NY 10017. (212)880-8800. Editor-in-Chief: Ruth Whitney. 75% freelance written. Works with a small number of new/unpublished writers each year. For college-educated women, 18-35 years old. Monthly. Circ. 2.3 million; 7 million readers. Pays on acceptance. Offers 20% kill fee. Publishes ms an average of 6-12 months after acceptance. Byline given. Computer printout submissions OK "if the material is easy to read"; prefers letter-quality. Reports in 5 weeks. Writer's guidelines for #10 SASE.

Nonfiction: Judy Coyne, articles editor. "Editorial approach is 'how-to' with articles that are relevant in the areas of careers, health, psychology, interpersonal relationships, etc. We look for queries that are fresh and include a contemporary, timely angle. Fashion, beauty, decorating, travel, food and entertainment are all staff-written. We use 1,000-word opinion essays for our Viewpoint section. Pays $500. Our His/Hers column features generally stylish essays on relationships or comments on current mores by male and female writers in alternate months." Pays $1,000 for His/Hers mss. Buys first North American serial rights. Buys 10-12 mss/issue. Query "with letter that is detailed, well-focused, well-organized, and documented with surveys, statistics and research, personal essays excepted." Short articles and essays (1,500-2,000 words) pay $1,000 and up; longer mss (2,500-3,000 words) pay $1,500 minimum on acceptance. Sometimes pays the expenses of writers on assignment.

Tips: "We're looking for sharply focused ideas by strong writers and constantly raising our standards. We are interested in getting new writers, and we are approachable, mainly because our range of topics is so broad. We've increased our focus on male-female relationships."

GOOD HOUSEKEEPING, Hearst Corp., 959 8th Ave., New York NY 10019. (212)649-2000. Editor-in-Chief: John Mack Carter. Executive Editor: Mina Mulvey. Managing Editor: Mary Fiore. Prefers to work with published/established writers. Monthly. Circ. 5 million. Pays on acceptance. Buys all rights. Pays 25% kill fee. Byline given. Submit seasonal/holiday material 6 months in advance. Computer printout submissions acceptable; no dot-matrix. Reports in 6 weeks. Sample copy $2. Free writer's guidelines with SASE.

Nonfiction: Joan Thursh, articles editor. How-to/informational; investigative stories; inspirational; interview; nostalgia; personal experience; and profile. Buys 4-6 mss/issue. Query. Length: 1,500-2,500 words. Pays $1,500 on acceptance for full articles from new writers. Regional Editor: Shirley Howard. Pays $250-350 for local interest and travel pieces of 2,000 words. Pays the expenses of writers on assignment.

Photos: Herbert Bleiweiss, art director. Photos purchased on assignment mostly. Some short photo features with captions. Pays $100-350 for b&w; $200-400 for color photos. Query. Model releases required.

Columns/Departments: Light Housekeeping & Fillers, edited by Rosemary Leonard. Humorous short-short prose and verse. Jokes, gags, anecdotes. Pays $25-50. The Better Way, edited by Erika Mark. Ideas and in-depth research. Query. Pays $250-500. "Mostly staff written; only outstanding ideas have a chance here."

Fiction: Naome Lewis, fiction editor. Uses romance fiction and condensations of novels that can appear in one issue. Looks for reader identification. "We get 1,500 unsolicited mss/month—includes poetry; a freelancer's odds are overwhelming—but we do look at all submissions." Send complete mss. Length: 1,500 words (short-shorts); novel according to merit of material; average 5,000 words short stories. Pays $1,000 minimum for fiction short-shorts; $1,250 for short stories.

Poetry: Arleen Quarfoot, poetry editor. Light verse and traditional. "Presently overstocked." Poems used as fillers. Pays $5/line for poetry on acceptance.

Tips: "Always send an SASE. We prefer to see a query first. Do not send material on subjects already covered in-house by the Good Housekeeping Institute—these include food, beauty, needlework and crafts."

THE JOYFUL WOMAN, For and About Bible-believing Women Who Want God's Best, The Joyful Woman Ministries, Inc., Business Office: Box 90028, Chattanooga TN 37412. (615)698-7318. Editor: Elizabeth Handford, 118 Shannon Lake Circle, Greenville SC 29615. 50% freelance written. Works with small number of new/unpublished writers each year. Bimonthly magazine covering the role of women in home and business. "*The Joyful Woman* hopes to encourage, stimulate, teach, and develop the Christian woman to reach the full potential of her womanhood." Circ. 12,000. Pays on publication. Publishes ms an average of 4 months after acceptance. Byline given. Buys first rights. Submit seasonal/holiday material 4 months in advance. Photocopied submissions OK. Computer printout submissions acceptable; prefers letter-quality. Reports in 3 months. Sample copy for 9x12 SAE with 4 first class stamps; writer's guidelines for #10 with 1 first class stamp.

Nonfiction: Book excerpts, how-to (housekeeping, childrearing, career management, etc.); inspirational; interview/profile (of Christian women); and personal experience. "We publish material on every facet of the human experience, considering not just a woman's spiritual needs, but her emotional, physical, and intellectual needs and her ministry to others." Buys 80-100 mss/year. Send complete ms. Length: 700-2,500 words. Pays about 2¢/word.

Tips: "The philosophy of the woman's liberation movement trends to minimize the unique and important ministries God has in mind for a woman. We believe that being a woman, and a Christian ought to be joyful and fulfilling personally and valuable to God, whatever her situation—career woman, wife, mother, daughter."

LADIES' HOME JOURNAL, Meredith Corporation, 100 Park Ave., New York NY 10017. (212)953-7070. Publishing Director and Editor-in-Chief: Myrna Blyth. Executive Editor: Jan Goodwin. 50% freelance written. A monthly magazine focusing on issues of concern to women. "*LHJ* reflects the lives of the contemporary mainstream woman and provides the information she needs and wants to live in today's world." Circ. 5.1 million. Pays on acceptance. Publishes ms an average of 3 months after acceptance, but varies according to needs. Byline given. Offers 25% kill fee. Rights bought vary with submission. Submit seasonal/holiday material 6 months in advance. Photocopied submissions OK. Computer printout submissions OK; prefers letter-quality. Reports in 6 weeks. Sample copy $1.50 with SAE and $1.28 postage. Issues older than 2 years: $3 plus $1.28 postage. Free writer's guidelines.

Nonfiction: Jan Goodwin, executive editor, oversees the entire department and may be queried directly. In addition, submissions may be directed to Linda Peterson, articles editor, and on the following subjects to the editors listed for each: Psychology and Relationships (senior editor Margery Rosen); medical/health (articles editor Linda Peterson); investigative reports or exposes (senior editor Jane Farrell); and celebrities (executive editor Jan Goodwin). Any editor may be queried on person ordeal stories, general entertainment, politics, profiles, self-improvement, lifestyles and trends. Travel and career pieces for Prime Showcase may be sent to Connie Leisure. Query with published clips or send complete ms. Length: 2,000-4,500 words. Fees vary; average is between $1,000 and $3,500. Pays expenses of writers on assignment.

Photos: State availability of photos with submission. Offers variable payment for photos accepted with ms. Captions, model releases and identification of subjects required. Rights bought vary with submissions.

Columns/Departments: Query the following editors for column ideas. A Woman Today (Pam Guthrie, associate editor); Money News (Katherine Barrett, contributing editor); Parent News (Mary Mohler, managing editor); and Pet News (Nina Keilin).

Close-up

Audreen Ballard
Executive Editor
Lear's

As tempting as it may be to jump with both feet into a new market after its first issue, Audreen Ballard, executive editor of *Lear's*, advises writers that it might be wiser to wait for a few issues before making that first submission.

"A new magazine is like a newborn baby," Ballard observes. "It takes months for it to develop and change." From the magazine's initial concept, the first few issues depend on reader feedback to provide fine-tuning, so that the astute writer may notice subtle changes that the average reader may not.

Even before *Lear's* hit the newsstand last spring, Ballard found herself swamped with material. "We got a lot of queries; we got a lot of over-the-transom things; we got a lot of people who had their own image of what this magazine would be," she recalls. And a lot of them were off the mark.

Even face-to-face meetings with established professionals sometimes didn't get across the tone of the new magazine, which was to be not a traditional women's magazine, but one for the "grown-up woman." "Some people got it and some people didn't get it. It's hard to explain something a writer can't see."

Better for a writer to read several issues to understand what Ballard calls the "voice" of the magazine before trying to write for it. A former freelancer and editor for *Time*, *Redbook* and *Essence*, she looks for an understanding of that voice in the writer's query letter. "I always suggest a writer query with an idea and a hint of how he or she would treat the idea, possibly even writing two or three paragraphs of the lead, including a few relevant clips. What I look for is the sense of the material, the tone and the voice that you use, how you talk to the reader."

By voice, though, she doesn't mean that the writer needs to parrot the ideas and philosophies of the magazine. In fact, she's intrigued by a freelancer who proposes an idea that's bold, innovative, maybe even a little off-the-wall.

"A frequent mistake by the professional writer is to get too caught up in the formula of a given magazine. I believe there's always a secret piece—a secret place in the writer's head, something he or she has always wanted to write about, and couldn't find a definable market.

"I frequently suggest to a writer that he or she propose that topic or story idea the writer had always thought that no magazine would ever publish. A good writer—a really good writer—always has that something in the back of his or her head all the time."

—*Chris Dodd*

❝ A new magazine is like a newborn baby. It takes months for it to develop and change. ❞
—***Audreen Ballard***

Fiction: "We consider any short story or novel that is submitted by an agent or publisher that we feel will work for our audience." Buys 12 mss/year. Length: 4,000 words. Fees vary with submission.

LADY'S CIRCLE, Lopez Publications, Inc., 105 East 35th St., New York NY 10016. (212)689-3933. Editor: Mary F. Bemis. 50% freelance written. Monthly magazine. "Midwest homemakers. Christian. Middle to low income. A large number of senior citizens read *Lady's Circle*." Circ. 300,000. Pays on publication. Byline given. Submit seasonal/holiday material 6 months in advance. Photocopied and previously published submissions OK. Reports in 2 months on queries; 3 months on mss. Sample copy for 8½x11 SAE with $1.07 postage. Free writer's guidelines.
Nonfiction: Historical/nostalgic, how-to (crafts, cooking, hobbies), humor, inspirational, interview/profile, opinion, personal experience and religious. No travel. Buys 50-75 mss/year. Query. Pays $125 for unsolicited articles. Sometimes pays expenses of writers on assignment.
Photos: State availability of photos with submission. Reviews negatives, transparencies and prints. Offers $10/photo. Model releases and identification of subjects required.
Columns/Departments: Sound Off (pet peeves) 250 words; Readers' Cookbook (readers send in recipes); and Helpful Hints (hints for kitchen, house, etc.) 3-4 lines per hint. Send complete ms. Pays $5-10.
Fiction: Humorous, mainstream, religious, romance, and slice-of-life vignettes. Nothing experimental. No foul language. Buys 3 mss/year. Send complete ms. Pays $125.
Fillers: Contact Adrian B. Lopez. Anecdotes and short humor. Buys 35/year. Length: 100 words. Pays $5-25.
Tips: "Write for guidelines. A good query is always appreciated. Fifty percent of our magazine is open to freelancers."

‡LEAR'S, Lear's Publishing, 505 Park Ave., New York NY 10022. (212)888-0007. Executive Editor: Audreen Ballard. Managing Editor: John Stoltenberg. Bimonthly magazine for 40+ women. Circ. 375,000. Pays on acceptance. Byline given. Offers ⅓ kill fee. Buys first North American serial rights and second serial reprint rights. Computer printout submissions OK. Reports in 6 weeks. Free writer's guidelines.
Nonfiction: Book excerpts, essays, general interest, interview/profile, opinion, personal experience, travel. Query with published clips. Length: 800-1,200 words. Pays $1 per word. Sometimes pays expenses of writers on assignment.
Columns/Departments: Self-Center, Money & Worth, Features, and Pleasures. Query with published clips. Length: 800-1,000 words. Pays $1 per word.

‡LUTHERAN WOMAN TODAY, Women of the ELCA/Augsburg Publishing House, 8765 West Higgings Rd., Chicago IL 60631. (312)380-2743. Editor: Nancy Stelling. Managing Editor: Sue Edison-Swift. 25% freelance written. Monthly magazine designed for all women of the Evangelical Lutheran Church in America. Estab. 1988. Circ. 300,000. Pays on acceptance or 2 months past due date. Publishes ms an average of 4 months after acceptance. Photocopied submissions OK. Computer printout submissions OK. Reports in 3 months on queries; 2 months on mss. Sample copy $1; writer's guidelines for #10 SAE.
Nonfiction: Book excerpts, historical/nostalgic, humor, inspirational, interview/profile, opinion, personal experience, photo feature religious. Buys 24 mss/year. Send complete ms. Length: 350-1,400 words. Pays $50-250.
Photos: State availability of photos or send photos with submission. Reviews contact sheet and prints. Pays variable rate. Captions and identification of subjects required. Buys one-time rights.
Columns/Departments: Women's Scene, Seasons' Best (essay featuring church year them); About Women (featuring 3 women of faith); Forum (essay). Send complete ms. Length: 350-1,000 words. Pays $50-250.
Fiction: Historical humorous, religious, thought-provoking devotions. "All with a women's and Christian focus." Buys 5 mss/year. Send complete ms. Length: 350-1,400 words. Pays $50-250.
Poetry: Free verse, haiku, light verse and traditional. Buys 5 poems/year. Submit maximum 5 poems. Length: 60 lines maximum. Pays $15-50.
Fillers: Anecdotes, newsbreaks, short humor. Buys 12/year. Length: 350 maximum. Pays $15-50.

McCALL'S, 230 Park Ave., New York NY 10169. (212)551-9500. Editor: Elizabeth Sloan. Managing Editor: Lisel Eisenheimer. 90% freelance written. "Study recent issues." Our publication "carefully and conscientiously services the needs of the woman reader—concentrating on matters that directly affect her life and offering information and understanding on subjects of personal importance to her." Monthly. Circ. 5 million. Pays on acceptance. Publishes ms an average of 6 months after acceptance. Offers 20% kill fee. Byline given. Buys first or exclusive North American rights. Computer printout submissions acceptable; no dot-matrix. Reports in 2 months. Writer's guidelines for SASE.
Nonfiction: Lisel Eisenheimer, managing editor. No subject of wide public or personal interest is out of bounds for *McCall's* so long as it is appropriately treated. The editors are seeking meaningful stories of personal experience, fresh slants for self-help and relationship pieces, and well-researched articles and narratives dealing with social problems concerning readers. *McCall's* buys 200-300 articles/year, many in the 1,000- to

1,500-word length. Pays variable rates for nonfiction. Helen Del Monte and Andrea Thompson are editors of nonfiction books, from which *McCall's* frequently publishes excerpts. These are on subjects of interest to women: personal narratives, celebrity biographies and autobiographies, etc. Almost all features on food, household equipment and management, fashion, beauty, building and decorating are staff-written. Query. "All manuscripts must be submitted on speculation, and *McCall's* accepts no responsibility for unsolicited manuscripts." Sometimes pays the expenses of writers on assignment.

Columns/Departments: Child Care (edited by Maureen Smith Williams); short items that may be humorous, helpful, inspiring and reassuring. Pays $100 and up. Vital Signs (edited by Saralie Falvelson-Neustadt); short items on health and medical news. Pay varies.

Fiction: Helen Del Monte, department editor. Not considering unsolicited fiction. "Again the editors would remind writers of the contemporary woman's taste and intelligence. Most of all, fiction can awaken a reader's sense of identity, deepen her understanding of herself and others, refresh her with a laugh at herself, etc. *McCall's* looks for stories which will have meaning for an adult reader of some literary sensitivity. *No* stories that are grim, depressing, fragmentary or concerned with themes of abnormality or violence. *McCall's* principal interest is in short stories; but fiction of all lengths is considered." Length: about 3,000 words average. Length for short-shorts: about 2,000 words. Payment begins at $1,500; $2,000 for full-length stories.

Poetry: Helen Del Monte, poetry editor. Poets with a "very original way of looking at their subjects" are most likely to get her attention. *McCall's* needs poems on love, the family, relationships with friends and relatives, familiar aspects of domestic and suburban life, Americana, and the seasons. Pays $5/line on acceptance for first North American serial rights. Length: no longer than 30 lines.

Tips: "Except for humor, query first. We are interested in holiday-related pieces and personal narratives. We rarely use essays. We don't encourage an idea unless we think we can use it." Preferred length: 750-2,000 words. Address submissions to Margot Gilman unless otherwise specified.

MADEMOISELLE, 350 Madison Ave., New York NY 10017. Michelle Stacey, executive editor, articles. 95% freelance written. Prefers to work with published/established writers. Columns are written by columnists; "sometimes we give new writers a 'chance' on shorter, less complex assignments." Directed to college-educated, unmarried working women 18-34. Circ. 1.1 million. Reports in 1 month. Buys first North American serial rights. Pays on acceptance; rates vary. Publishes ms an average of 1 year after acceptance. Computer printout submissions are acceptable "but only letter-quality, double-spaced; no dot-matrix."

Nonfiction: Particular concentration on articles of interest to the intelligent young woman, including personal relationships, health, careers, trends, and current social problems. Send health queries to Ellen Welty, health editor. Send entertainment queries to Gini Sikes, entertainment editor. Query with published clips. Length: 1,500-3,000 words.

Art: Kati Korpijaakko, art director. Commissioned work assigned according to needs. Photos of fashion, beauty, travel. Payment ranges from no-charge to an agreed rate of payment per shot, job series or page rate. Buys all rights. Pays on publication for photos.

Fiction: Eileen Schnurr, fiction and books editor. Quality fiction by both established and unknown writers. "We are interested in encouraging and publishing new writers and welcome unsolicited fiction manuscripts. However we are not a market for formula stories, genre fiction, unforgettable character portraits, surprise endings or oblique stream of consciousness sketches. We are looking for well-told stories that speak in fresh and individual voices and help us to understand ourselves and the world we live in. Stories of particular relevance to young women have an especially good chance, but stories need not be by or from the point of view of a woman—we are interested in good fiction on any theme from any point of view." Buys first North American serial rights. Pays $1,500 for short stories (10-25 pages); $1,000 for short shorts (7-10 pages). Allow 3 months for reply. SASE required. In addition to year-round unqualified acceptance of unsolicited fiction manuscripts, *Mademoiselle* conducts a once-a-year fiction contest open to unpublished writers, male and female, 18-30 years old. First prize is $1,000 plus publication in *Mademoiselle*; second prize, $500 with option to publish. Watch magazine for announcement, usually in January or February issues, or send SASE for rules, after Jan 1.

Tips: "We are looking for timely, well-researched manuscripts."

‡MODERN BRIDE, CBS Magazines, 1 Park Ave., New York NY 10016. (212)779-1999. Editor: Cele Lalli. Managing Editor: Mary Ann Cavlin. Pays on acceptance. Offers 25% kill fee. Buys first periodical rights. Previously published submissions OK. Reports in 1 month.

Nonfiction: Book excerpts, general interest, how-to, personal experience. Buys 70 mss/year. Query with published clips. Length: 500-2,000 words. Pays $600-1,200.

Columns/Departments: Risa Weinreb, editor. Travel.

Poetry: Free verse, light verse and traditional. Buys very few. Submit maximum 6 poems.

NA'AMAT WOMAN, Magazine of NA'AMAT USA, the Women's Labor Zionist Organization of America, NA'AMAT USA, 200 Madison Ave., New York NY 10016. (212)725-8010. Editor: Judith A. Sokoloff. 80% freelance written. Magazine published 5 times/year covering Jewish themes and issues; Israel; women's issues; Labor Zionism; and social, political and economic issues. Circ. 30,000. Pays on publication. Byline given.

Not copyrighted. Buys first North American serial, one-time and first serial rights; second serial (reprint) rights to book excerpts; and makes work-for-hire assignments. Reports in 1 month on queries, 2 months on mss. Writer's guidelines for SASE.

Nonfiction: Expose; general interest (Jewish); historical/nostalgic; interview/profile; opinion; personal experience; photo feature; travel (Israel); art; and music. "All articles must be of interest to the Jewish community." Buys 35 mss/year. Query with clips of published work or send complete ms. Pays 8¢/word.

Photos: State availability of photos. Pays $10-30 for 4x5 or 5x7 prints. Captions and identification of subjects required. Buys one-time rights.

Columns/Departments: Film and book reviews with Jewish themes. Buys 20-25 mss/year. Query with clips of published work or send complete ms. Pays 8¢/word.

Fiction: Historical/nostalgic, humorous, women-oriented, and novel excerpts. "Good intelligent fiction with Jewish slant. No maudlin nostalgia or trite humor." Buys 3 mss/year. Send complete ms. Length: 1,200-3,000 words. Pays 8¢/word.

PLAYGIRL, 801 Second Ave., New York NY 10017. (212)986-5100. Editor-in-Chief: Nancie S. Martin. 75% freelance written. Prefers to work with published/established writers. Monthly entertainment magazine for 18- to 34-year-old females. Circ. 850,000. Average issue includes 4 articles and 2 interviews. Pays 1 month after acceptance. Publishes ms an average of 5 months after acceptance. Byline given. Offers 20% kill fee. Buys all rights. Submit seasonal material 6 months in advance. Simultaneous and photocopied submissions OK, if so indicated. Computer printout submissions acceptable; prefers letter-quality. Reports in 1 month on queries; in 2 months on mss. Sample copy $5. Writer's guidelines for SASE.

Nonfiction: Humor for the modern woman; exposes (related to women's issues); interview (Q&A format with major show business celebrities); articles on sexuality; medical breakthroughs; relationships; coping; and careers; insightful, lively articles on current issues; and investigative pieces particularly geared to *Playgirl*. Buys 6 mss/issue. Query with clips of previously published work. Length: 1,000-2,500 words. Pays $300-1,000. Sometimes pays the expenses of writers on assignment.

Fiction: Mary Ellen Strote, fiction editor. Contemporary romance stories of 2,500 words. Send complete fiction ms. "The important thing to remember is we don't want graphic sex, and no adventure, suspense, science fiction, murder or mystery stories. We want something emotional." Pays $300 and up for fiction.

Tips: "We are not a beginner's nonfiction market. We're looking for major clips and don't really consider non-published writers."

POLITICAL WOMAN, The Non-partisan Journal for the Thinking Woman, United Resource Services, Suite 388, 4521 Campus Dr., Irvine CA 92715. Editor: Sally Corngold. Managing Editor: Cynthia K. Horrocks. 95% freelance written. "Prefers to receive well-edited manuscripts from new or established writers. *Political Woman* is a non-partisan quarterly magazine geared to, but not totally about or for, women. The purpose is to publish objective, informative articles of global significance in a sophisticated, readable style." Circ. 2,500. Pays on publication. Publishes ms an average of 2 months after acceptance. Byline given. Offers 50% kill fee. Buys one-time rights. Simultaneous submissions OK. Query for electronic submissions. Computer printout submissions acceptable. Reports within weeks. Sample copy $2, 9x12 SAE and 3 first class stamps; writer's guidelines for #10 SASE.

Nonfiction: Expose, historical/nostalgic, humor, personal experience, photofeature, travel (with political relevance) and political features. Buys 30-50 mss/year. Length: 500-3,000 words. Pays $50-1,000. Sometimes pays the expenses of writers on assignment.

Photos: State availability of photos with submission. Offers no additional payment for photos accepted with mss but encourages submissions. Captions, model releases, and identification of subjects required. Buys one-time rights. Send SASE for annual photo contests information.

Columns/Departments: Sally Black, Sally Corngold, column/department editors. Facing Off (opposing views on a single topic); Social Topics; Election Topics; and International and Domestic Political Issues. Buys 30-50 mss/year. Prefers actual article over query. Length: 500-3,000 words. Pays $50-1,000.

Fillers: Gary Brown, fillers editors. Anecdotes, facts, gags to be illustrated by cartoonist, newsbriefs, and short humor. Buys 20/year. Length: 50-500 words. Pays $10-300.

Tips: The area most open to freelancers is "full-length, *well-documented* exposes. These must be footnoted and sources given."

‡QUARANTE, Magazine for the Woman Who's Arrived, Savoir Inc., Box 2875, Crystal City, Arlington VA 22202. (703)920-3333. Editor: Michele R. Linden. Managing Editor: Linda Wozniak. 90% freelance written. A quarterly magazine with humor, politics, finance, business, fashion, cuisine, health, beauty, travel, media and sociology, "for educated, affluent women over 40. We respect their experience and intelligence." Circ. 28,017. Pays on publication. Byline given. Buys one-time rights. Submit seasonal/holiday material 3 months in advance. Simultaneous, photocopied and previously published submissions OK. Computer printout submissions OK. Sample copy for 8½x11 SAE.

Nonfiction: Book excerpts, humor, inspirational, interview/profile, new product, opinion, personal experience, religious, travel. Publishes an annual bridal guide for Washington DC only. No articles on aging or "homemaker" or "working woman" articles. Buys 4 mss/year. Query with published clips. Length: 250-1,500 words. Pays up to $200.

Photos: State availability of photos or send photos with submission. Reviews color transparencies (4x5) or prints (4x5). Offers no additional payment for photos accepted with ms. Captions, model releases and identification of subjects required. Buys one-time rights.

Fiction: Adventure, humorous, novel excerpts, suspense. Buys 4 mss/year. Query with published clips. Length: 800-1,500 words. Pays $25-200.

Poetry: Avant-garde, free verse, light verse, traditional. Buys 9 poems/year. Submit maximum of 3 poems. Length: 10-50 lines. Pays $25-50.

Fillers: Anecdotes, facts, short humor. Buys 10-20 mss/year. Length: 20-50 words.

Tips: "Profiles on fascinating, sophisticated women (100-500 words in length) and topics that are rarely covered in women's magazine such as an anthropology project interest us. We will include more finance, health, fashion and beauty."

RADIANCE, The Magazine for Large Women, Box 31703, Oakland CA 94604. (415)482-0680. Editor: Alice Ansfield. 75% freelance written. A quarterly magazine encouraging "self-esteem for large women—the physical, emotional, social, cultural, spiritual aspects." Circ. 12,000. Pays on publication. Publishes ms an average of 3 months after acceptance. Byline given. Offers $15 kill fee. Buys one-time and second serial (reprint) rights. Submit seasonal/holiday material 3 months in advance. Simultaneous, photocopied and previously published submissions OK. Query for electronic submissions. Computer printout submissions OK; no dot-matrix. Reports in 2 months. Sample copy $1.50; writer's guidelines for #10 SAE with 1 first class stamp.

Nonfiction: Book excerpts (related to large women), essays, expose, general interest, historical/nostalgic, how-to (on health/well-being/growth/awareness/fashion/movement, etc.), humor, inspirational, interview/profile, new product, opinion, personal experience, photo feature and travel. Future issues will focus on children and weight, interviews with large men, fashion update, emerging spirituality, women and the arts, and women in the media. "No diet successes or articles condemning people for being fat." Query with published clips. Length: 1,000-2,000 words. Pays $35-100. Sometimes pays writers with contributor copies or other premiums—"negotiable with writer and us."

Photos: State availability of photos with submission. Offers $15-50 per photo. Captions and identification of subjects preferred. Buys one-time rights.

Columns/Departments: Up Front and Personal (personal profiles of women in all areas of life); Health and Well-Being (physical/emotional well-being, self care, research); Images (designer interviews, color/style/fashion, features); Inner Journeys (spirituality awareness and growth, methods, interviews); Perspectives (cultural and political aspects of being in a larger body); Heart to Heart (poetry, artwork, inspiring). Buys 32 mss/year. Query with published clips. Length: 1,000-2,000 words. Pays $50-100.

Fiction: Condensed novels, ethnic, fantasy, historical, humorous, mainstream, novel excerpts, romance, science fiction, serialized novels and slice-of-life vignettes relating somehow to large women. Buys 15 mss/year. Query with published clips. Length: 800-1,500 words. Pays $35-100.

Poetry: Nothing "too political and jargony." Buys 15 poems/year. Length: 4-45 lines. Pays $20-50.

Tips: "We need talented and sensitive writers in all areas of the country, and now even in Europe and abroad. We want large women to be featured and profiled—we urge writers to look in their local area and begin to give us suggestions for print. We're an open, conscious, light-hearted magazine that's trying to help women live fully now and look at more than their bodies. Departments are most open to freelancers. Especially wanted are profiles of large women in media, arts, science, education, business, home/family, medicine, spirituality, politics."

REDBOOK MAGAZINE, 224 W. 57th St., New York NY 10019. (212)262-8284. Editor-in-Chief: Annette Capone. Managing Editor: Jennifer Johnson. Executive Editor: Judsen Culbreth. 80% freelance written. Monthly magazine. Circ. 4.1 million. Pays on acceptance. Publishes ms an average of 6 months after acceptance. Rights purchased vary with author and material. Computer printout submissions acceptable; prefers letter-quality. Reports in 2 months. Free writer's guidelines for *Redbook* for SASE.

Nonfiction: Karen Larson, senior editor. Jean Maguire, health editor. "*Redbook* addresses young mothers between the ages of 25 and 44. Most of our readers are married with children under 18; more than half of *Redbook*'s readers work outside the home. The articles in *Redbook* entertain, guide and inspire our readers. A significant percentage of the pieces stress 'how-to,' the ways a woman can solve the problems in her everyday life. Writers are advised to read at least the last *six* issues of the magazine (available in most libraries) to get a better understanding of what we're looking for. We prefer to see queries, rather than complete manuscripts. Please enclose a sample or two of your writing as well as a stamped, self-addressed envelope." Length: articles, 2,500-3,000 words; short articles, 1,000-1,500 words. Also interested in submissions for Young Mother's Story. "We are interested in stories for the Young Mother series offering the dramatic retelling of an experience involving you, your husband or child. Possible topics might include: how you have handled a child's health or school problem, or conflicts within the family. For each 1,500-2,000 words accepted for publication as Young Mother's Story, we pay $750. Mss accompanied by a large, stamped, self-addressed envelope, must be signed, and mailed to: Young Mother's Story, c/o *Redbook Magazine*. Young Mother's reports in 4-6 months." Pays the expenses of writers on assignment.

Fiction: Deborah Purcell, fiction editor. "Of the 40,000 unsolicited manuscripts that we receive annually, we buy about 36 or more stories/year. We also find many more stories that, are not necessarily suited to our needs but are good enough to warrant our encouraging the author to send others. *Redbook* looks for stories by and about men and women, realistic and offbeat stories, humorous or poignant stories, stories about families, couples, or people alone, stories with familiar and exotic settings, love stories and work stories, medical and mystery stories. Those elements common to all of them are the high quality of their prose and the distinctiveness of their characters and plots. We also look for stories with emotional resonance. Cool stylistic or intellectually experimental stories are of greater interest, we feel, to readers of literary magazines than readers of a magazine like *Redbook* which tries to offer insights into the hows and whys of day-to-day living; all of our stories reflect some aspect of the experience, the interests, or the dreams of *Redbook*'s readership." We buy short-short stories (9 pages) and short stories (25 pages or fewer). "We do not read unsolicited novels." Manuscripts must be typewritten, double-spaced, and accompanied by SASE. Payment begins at $850 for short shorts; $1,200 for short stories.

Tips: "Shorter, front-of-the-book features are usually easier to develop with first-time contributors. It is very difficult to break into the nonfiction section, although we do buy Young Mother's stories, dramatic personal experience pieces (1,500-2,000 words), from previously unpublished writers. The most frequent mistakes made by writers in completing an article for us are 1) Poor organization. A piece that's poorly organized is confusing, repetitive, difficult to read. I advise authors to do full outlines before they start writing so they can more easily spot structure problems and so they have a surer sense of where their piece is headed. 2) Poor or insufficient research. Most *Redbook* articles require solid research and include: full, well-developed anecdotes from real people (not from people who exist only in the writer's imagination); clear, substantial quotes from established experts in a field; and, when available, additional research such as statistics and other information from reputable studies, surveys, etc."

SELF, Conde-Nast, 350 Madison Ave., New York NY 10017. (212)880-8834. Editor: Valorie Weaver. Managing Editor: Linda Rath. 50% freelance written. "We prefer to work with writers—even relatively new ones—with a degree, training or practical experience in specialized areas, psychology to nutrition." Monthly magazine emphasizing self improvement of emotional and physical well-being for women of all ages. Circ. 1 million. Average issue includes 12-20 feature articles and 4-6 columns. Pays on acceptance. Publishes ms an average of 6 months after acceptance. Byline given. Offers 20% kill fee. Buys first North American serial rights. Submit seasonal material 4 months in advance. Simultaneous and photocopied submissions OK. Computer printout submissions acceptable; prefers letter-quality. Reports in 1 month. Writer's guidelines for SASE.

Nonfiction: Well-researched service articles on self improvement, mind, the psychological angle of daily activities, health, careers, nutrition, fitness, medicine, male/female relationships and money. "We try to translate major developments and complex information in these areas into practical, personalized articles." Buys 6-10 mss/issue. Query with clips of previously published work. Length: 1,000-2,500 words. Pays $800-1,500. "We are always looking for any piece that has a psychological or behavioral side. We rely heavily on freelancers who can take an article on contraceptive research, for example, and add a psychological aspect to it. Everything should relate to the whole person." Pays the expenses of writers on assignment "with prior approval."

Photos: Submit to art director. State availability of photos. Reviews 5x7 b&w glossy prints.

Columns/Departments: Your Health (800-1,200 words on health topics); Your Work (800-1,200 words on career topics); and Your Money (800-1,200 words on finance topics). Buys 4-6 mss/issue. Query. Pays $800-1,500.

Tips: "Original ideas backed up by research, rarely personal experiences and anecdotes, open our doors. We almost never risk blowing a major piece on an untried-by-us writer, especially since these ideas are usually staff-conceived. It's usually better for everyone to start small, where there's more time and leeway for rewrites. The most frequent mistakes made by writers in completing an article for us are swiss-cheese research (holes all over it which the writer missed and has to go back and fill in) and/or not personalizing the information by applying it to the reader, but instead, just reporting it."

‡SOUTHERN STYLE, Whittle Communications, 505 Market St., Knoxville TN 37902. (615)595-5000. Editor: Elise Nakhnikian. 40% freelance written. A bimonthly magazine "for Southern women in 11 states. Our emphasis is on fashion, beauty, and celebrities, but we also run recipes, profiles of less-famous Southern women of achievement, first-person essays, and other copy of interest about the South." Pays on acceptance. Publishes ms an average of 4 months after acceptance. Byline given. Offers 25% kill fee. Buys second serial (reprint) rights or first periodical rights. Reports in 2 months on queries. Sample copy for 11x15 SAE or $2. Writer's guidelines for #10 SAE with 1 first class stamp.

Nonfiction: Interview/profile (national celebrities from the South). Buys 25 mss/year. Query with published clips. Length: 750-2,500 words. Pays $300-1,500. Pays expenses of writers on assignment.

Columns/Departments: The Way We Are (personal essay); The Turning Point (interview with a Southern woman focusing on a major turning point in her life); Cookbook (recipe).
Tips: "Read at least one copy of the magazine, then send clips and propose what you think would be an appropriate story idea."

‡**TODAY'S CHRISTIAN WOMAN**, 465 Gundersen Dr., Carol Stream IL 60188. (312)260-6200. Managing Editor: Sharon Donohue. 25% freelance written. Works with a small number of new/unpublished writers each year. A bimonthly magazine for Christian women of all ages, single and married, homemakers and career women. Circ. 215,000. Pays on acceptance. Publishes ms an average of 2 years after acceptance. Byline given. Buys first rights only. Submit seasonal/holiday material 9 months in advance. Computer printout submissions acceptable; prefers letter-quality. Sample copy $3.50; writer's guidelines for SASE.
Nonfiction: How-to, narrative, inspirational, and opinion. Query only; no unsolicited mss. "The query should include article summary, purpose and reader value, author's qualifications, suggested length and date to send, availability of photos if applicable." Pays 7-15¢/word.
Tips: "Nature of the articles are: relational, psychological, philosophical or spiritual. All articles should be highly anecdotal, personal in tone, and universal in appeal."

WOMAN MAGAZINE, Harris Publishing, 1115 Broadway, New York NY 10010. (212)807-7100. Editor: Sherry Amatenstein. 40% freelance written. Works with a small number of new/unpublished writers each year. Magazine published 10 times/year covering "every aspect of a woman's life. Offers self-help orientation, guidelines on lifestyles, careers, relationships, finances, health, etc." Circ. 600,000. Pays on acceptance. Publishes ms an average of 5 months after acceptance. Byline given. Buys one-time rights. Photocopied and previously published submissions OK. Computer printout submissions acceptable; prefers letter-quality. Reports in 6 weeks. Sample copy $1.95; writer's guidelines for #10 SAE and 1 first class stamp.
Nonfiction: Excerpts (most of magazine is book and periodical reprints); how-to; humor; inspirational (how I solved a specific problem); interview/profile (short, 200-1,000 words with successful or gutsy women); round-ups and personal experience (primary freelance need: how a woman took action and helped herself—emotional punch, but not "trapped housewife" material). "The 'woman' reader is evolving into a smarter, cannier woman who wants to reach her full potential." No articles on "10 ways to pep up your marriage"—looking for unique angle. Short medical and legal updates for "Let's Put Our Heads Together" column. Buys 100 mss/year. Query with published clips or send complete ms. Length: 200-1,500 words. Pays $25-400. Sometimes pays the expenses of writers on assignment.
Columns/Departments: Woman in News (200-word pieces on successful women). Query with published clips or send complete ms. Length: 200-500 words. Pays $20-100.
Tips: "We're for all women—ones in and out of the home. We don't condescend; neither should you."

WOMAN'S DAY, 1515 Broadway, New York NY 10036. (212)719-6250. Articles Editor: Rebecca Greer. 95% of articles freelance written. 15 issues/year. Circ. 6 million. Buys first and second rights to the same material. Pays negotiable kill fee. Byline given. Pays on acceptance. Computer printout submissions acceptable; no dot-matrix. Reports in 2-4 weeks on queries; longer on mss. Submit detailed queries first to Rebecca Greer.
Nonfiction: Uses articles on all subjects of interest to women—marriage, family life, childrearing, education, homemaking, money management, careers, family health, work and leisure activities. Also interested in fresh, dramatic narratives of women's lives and concerns. "These must be lively and fascinating to read." *Woman's Day* has started a new page called Reflections, a full-page essay running 1,000 words. "We're looking for both tough, strong pieces and softer essays on matters of real concern and relevance to women. We're looking for strong points of view, impassioned opinions, and fresh insights. The topics can be controversial, but they have to be convincing. We look for significant issues—medical ethics and honesty in marriage—rather than the slight and the trivial." Length: 500-3,500 words, depending on material. Payment varies depending on length, type, writer, and whether it's for regional or national use, but rates are high. Sometimes pays the expenses of writers on assignment.
Fiction: Contact Eileen Jordan, department editor. Uses high quality, genuine human interest, romance and humor, in lengths between 1,500 and 3,000 words. Payment varies. "We pay any writer's established rate, however."
Fillers: Neighbors and Tips to Share columns also pay $50/each for brief practical suggestions on homemaking, childrearing and relationships. Address to the editor of the appropriate section.
Tips: "Our primary need is for ideas with broad appeal that can be featured on the cover. We are publishing more articles and devoting more pages to textual material. We're departing from the service format once in a while to print 'some good reads.' We're more interested in investigative journalism than in the past."

‡**WOMAN'S WORLD, The Woman's Weekly**, Heinrich Bauer North American, Inc., 177 N. Dean St., Box 6700, Englewood NJ 07631. (201)569-0006. Editor-in-Chief: Dennis Neeld. 95% freelance written. Weekly magazine covering "controversial, dramatic, and human interest women's issues" for women across the nation. Pays on acceptance. Publishes ms an average of 4 months after acceptance. Byline given. Offers

kill fee. Buys first North American serial rights. Submit seasonal/holiday material 4 months in advance. Simultaneous queries, and simultaneous, photocopied and previously published submissions OK. Computer printout submissions acceptable; prefers letter-quality. Reports in 6 weeks on queries; 1-2 months on mss. Sample copy $1 and self-addressed mailing label; writer's guidelines for #10 SAE and 1 first class stamp.

Nonfiction: Well-researched material with "a hard-news edge and topics of national scope." Reports of 1,000 words on vital trends and major issues such as women and alcohol or teen suicide; dramatic, personal women's stories; articles on self-improvement, medicine and health topics; and the economics of home, career and daily life. Features include In Real Life (true stories); Turning Point (in a woman's life); Families (highlighting strength of family or how unusual families deal with problems); True Love (tender, beautiful, touching and unusual love stories). Other regular features are Report (1,500-word investigative news features with national scope, statistics, etc.); Scales of Justice (true stories of 1,000-1,200 words on women and crime "if possible, presented with sympathetic" attitude); Between You and Me (600-word humorous and/or poignant slice-of-life essays); and Relationships (800 words on pop psychology or coping). Queries should be addressed to Gerry Hunt, senior editor. We use no fillers, but all the Between You and Me pieces are chosen from mail. Sometimes pays the expenses of writers on assignment.

Fiction: Mary McHugh, fiction editor. Short story, romance and mainstream of 4,500 words and mini-mysteries of 1,200-2,000 words. "Each of our stories has a light romantic theme with a protagonist no older than forty. Each can be written from either a masculine or feminine point of view. Women characters may be single, married or divorced. Plots must be fast moving with vivid dialogue and action. The problems and dilemmas inherent in them should be contemporary and realistic, handled with warmth and feeling. The stories must have a positive resolution." Not interested in science fiction, fantasy or historical romance. No explicit sex, graphic language or seamy settings. Humor meets with enthusiasm. Pays $1,200 on acceptance for North American serial rights for 6 months. "The mini-mysteries, at a length of 1,700 words, may feature either a 'whodunnit' or 'howdunnit' theme. The mystery may revolve around anything from a theft to a murder. However, we are not interested in sordid or grotesque crimes. Emphasis should be on intricacies of plot rather than gratuitous violence. The story must include a resolution that clearly states the villain is getting his or her come-uppance." Pays $500 on acceptance. Pays approximately 50¢ a published word on acceptance. Buys first North American serial rights. Queries with clips of published work are preferred; accepts complete mss.

Photos: State availability of photos. "State photo leads. Photos are assigned to freelance photographers." Buys one-time rights.

Tips: "Come up with good queries. Short queries are best. We have a strong emphasis on well-researched material. Writers must send research with manuscript including book references and phone numbers for double checking. The most frequent mistakes made by writers in completing an article for us are sloppy, incomplete research, not writing to the format, and not studying the magazine carefully enough beforehand."

‡**WOMEN OF OHIO**, Suite 101, 921 Eastwind Dr., Westerville OH 43081. (614)882-1444. Editor: Claire Kessler. Managing Editor: Freida Douthitt. 100% freelance written. Bimonthly magazine on Ohio women and women in general. "Subject matter is Ohio places and personalities—including, occasionally, women of note from Ohio." Circ. 27,000. Pays on publication. Publishes ms an average of 3 months after acceptance. Byline given. Offers $25 kill fee. Buys first North American serial rights. Submit seasonal/holiday material 5 months in advance. Query for electronic submissions. Computer printout submissions OK. Reports in 5 weeks. Sample copy for 9x12 SAE with 3 first class stamps. Writer's guidelines for #10 SAE with 1 first class stamp.

Nonfiction: Essays, expose, general interest, historical/nostalgic, how-to, humor, interview/profile, new product, personal experience, photo feature, travel. Buys 60-80 mss/year. Query with published clips. "*Women of Ohio* has issues built around themes and solicits queries on specific topics. The ideal is to get on our writer's list and receive our information. Our topics, Ohio women and/or articles of general interest to women is, in itself limiting. Anything unsolicited must be accompanied by SASE." Length: 500-1,500 words. Pays $100-250.

Photos: Send photos with submission. Offers no additional payment for photos accepted with ms. Captions, identification of subjects and model releases are required. Buys one-time rights.

Columns/Departments: Books (reviews, not necessarily best-selling books, but on women's topics); Money (sound advice and management); Fashion (what's new, seasonal); Body and Soul (mental and physical health, philosophical); Restaurant (not critique, basic facts). Buys 30 mss/year. Query with published clips. Length: 500-750 words. Pays $100-150.

Fillers: Gags to be illustrated by cartoonist, short humor. Lenght: 200-300 words. Pays $50-100.

Tips: "Send letter with published clips outlining familiarity with Ohio subjects and suggesting type of story and subject that writer would like to submit. Features area is where we are most in need of freelance submissions. We're looking for short (under 1,500) stories, tightly written, on the subject queries and assigned pursuant to editorial schedule/invitation to query."

WOMEN'S CIRCLE, Box 299, Lynnfield MA 01940-0299. Editor: Marjorie Pearl. 100% freelance written. Bimonthly magazine for women of all ages. Buys all rights. Pays on acceptance. Byline given. Publishes ms an average of 6 months to 1 year after acceptance. Submit seasonal material 8 months in advance. Reports in 3 months. Sample copy $2. Writer's guidelines for #10 SAE with 1 first class stamp.

Nonfiction: Especially interested in stories about successful, home-based female entrepreneurs with b&w photos or color transparencies. Length: 1,000-2,000 words. Also interesting and unusual money-making ideas. Welcomes good quality crafts and how-to directions in any media - crochet, fabric, etc.

WORKING MOTHER MAGAZINE, McCall's Publishing Co., 230 Park Ave., New York NY 10169. (212)551-9412. Editor: Olivia Buehl. Executive Editor: Mary McLaughlin. 90% freelance written. Prefers to work with published/established writers; works with a small number of new/unpublished writers each year. For women who balance a career with the concerns of parenting. Monthly magazine. Circ. 600,000. Pays on acceptance. Publishes ms an average of 4 months after acceptance. Byline given. Buys all rights. Pays 20% kill fee. Submit seasonal/holiday material 6 months in advance. Computer printout submissions acceptable; no dot-matrix. Reports in 1 month. Sample copy $1.95; writer's guidelines for SASE.

Nonfiction: Service, humor, material pertinent to the working mother's predicament. "Don't just go out and find some mother who holds a job and describe how she runs her home, manages her children and feels fulfilled. Find a working mother whose story is inherently dramatic." Query. Buys 9-10 mss/issue. Length: 750-2,000 words. Pays $300-1,200. "We pay more to people who write for us regularly." Pays the expenses of writers on assignment.

Tips: "We are looking for pieces that help the reader. In other words, we don't simply report on a trend without discussing how it specifically affects our readers' lives and how they can handle the effects. Where can they look for help if necessary?"

WORKING WOMAN, Hal Publications, Inc., 342 Madison Ave., New York NY 10173. (212)309-9800. Executive Editor: Julia Kagan. Editor: Anne Mollegen Smith. 85% freelance written. Works with a small number of new/unpublished writers each year. Monthly magazine for executive, professional and entrepreneurial women. "Readers are ambitious, educated, affluent managers, executives, and business owners. Median age is 34. Material should be sophisticated, witty, not entry-level, and focus on work-related issues." Circ. 900,000. Pays on acceptance. Publishes ms an average of 8 months after acceptance. Byline given. Offers 20% kill fee after attempt at rewrite to make ms acceptable. Buys all rights, first rights for books, and second serial (reprint) rights. Submit seasonal/holiday material 6 months in advance. Computer printout submissions acceptable only if legible; prefers letter-quality. Sample copy for $2.50 and 8½x12 SAE; writer's guidelines for SAE with 1 first class stamp.

Nonfiction: Julia Kagan, executive editor. Jacqueline Johnson, book excerpts editor. Book excerpts; how-to (management skills, small business); humor; interview/profile (high level executive or entrepreneur preferred); new product (office products, computer/high tech); opinion (issues of interest to managerial, professional, entrepreneur women); personal experience; technical (in management or small business field); and other (business). No child-related pieces that don't involve work issues; no entry-level topics; no fiction/poetry. Buys roughly 200 mss/year. Query with clips of published work. Length: 250-3,000 words. Pays $50-750. Pays the expenses of writers on assignment.

Photos: State availability of photos with ms.

Columns: Management/Enterprise, Basia Hellwig; Manager's Shoptalk, Louise Washer; Lifestyle, Food, Freddi Greenberg; Fitness, Health, Janette Scandura; Business Watch, Michele Morris; Computers, Technology, Anne Russell. Query with clips of published work. Length: 1,200-1,500 words. Pays $400.

Tips: "Be sure to include clips with queries and to make the queries detailed (including writer's expertise in the area, if any). The writer has a better chance of breaking in at our publication with short articles and fillers as we prefer to start new writers out small unless they're very experienced elsewhere. Columns are more open than features. We do not accept phone submissions."

66 *The more time goes by, the easier it is to judge my own work. Now I wait until it cools. Then I hold it at arm's length, squint at it, sniff it, and ask myself if a stranger would love it.* **99**

—Adele Glimm, author of stories in **McCall's, Redbook,** *and* **Cosmopolitan**

Additional Consumer Publications

The following listings are inactive for the 1989 edition because the firms are backlogged with submissions or indicated a need for few freelance submissions in 1989.

Midwest Living
the new renaissance
Savvy
Spirituality Today
The Woman's Newspaper

The following firms did not return a verification to update an existing listing or a questionnaire to begin a new listing by press time.

A.N.A.L.O.G. Computing
Abyss
Adventure Magazine
Alabama Alumni Magazine
Alternative Sources of Energy
Amateur Boxer
America
American Farriers Journal
American Film
American Forests
American Land Forum
American Shotgunner
American Skating World
American Way
Amit
The Antiquarian
Antique Monthly
AOPA Pilot
A+
Appaloosa World
Archery World
Arcotophile
Arizona Highways
Artsline
Artviews
ATO Palm
Attenzione
Austin Homes & Gardens
Aviation/USA
Backwoodsman Magazine
Baltimore Magazine
Beacon Magazine
Bicycle Rider
Bicycling
Biology Digest
Birmingham
Black Enterprise
Black Warrior Review
Blue & Gray Magazine

Boca Raton
Boston Phoenix
Bowlers Journal
Business Month
Business to Business
C.S.P. World News
Camping Canada
Canadian West
Canadian Yachting
Cape Cod Life
Catholic Twin Circle
Central Florida Magazine
Charlotte Magazine
Child
Children's Album
Christian Adventurer
Christian Herald
Collector Editions Quarterly
Collectors News and the Antique Reporter
Colorado Outdoor Journal
Columbus Monthly
Computing Now!
Connecticut Magazine
Connoisseur
Consumers Digest Magazine
Corvette News
Cosmopolitan
Crain's Cleveland Business
Creem
Crisis
Cross Country Skier
Cycle World
Cycling USA
D.A.C. News
Daily Development
Dallas Observer
Dan Shaw News
Dance Teacher Now

Darkroom and Creative Camera Techniques
Darkroom Photography Magazine
Data Based Advisor
Daughters of Sarah
Dayton Magazine
Denver Quarterly
Detroit Magazine
Detroit Monthly
Discovery
Diver
Eagle
East West
Enfantasie
Epiphany Journal
Event
Fact
Family Circle Great Ideas
Family Circle Magazine
FDA Consumer
Finnish Connection
Firepower
Fisherman
Florida Gulf Coast Living
Florida Keys Magazine
Florida Racquet Journal
Food & Wine
Forests & People
Forum
Four Wheeler Magazine
Fox River Patriot
FQ
France Today
Freshwater and Marine Aquarium Magazine
Frets Magazine
Friday (of the Jewish Exponent)
Games
Gay Chicago Magazine

Gem
Grain
Grit
Guardian
Gulfshore Life
Gurney's Gardening News
Hideaways Guide
Homeworking Mothers
Horse Digest
Horticulture
Hostelers' Knapsack
Hot Bike
House & Garden
Hudson Valley Magazine
Image
Image Magazine
IMC Journal
In Touch
Indianapolis Magazine
Inner Light
International Advisor
INVESTigate
Iowan
It Will Stand
Italian Times
Jacksonville Magazine
Jam
Korean Culture
LaCrosse City Business
Lakeland Boating
Last Issue
Letters Magazine
Libertarian Digest
Living with Children
Living with Preschoolers
Mach
Macworld
Maine Life
Massage Magazine
Master Detective
MBA
Members
Miami/South Florida Magazine
Michigan Magazine
Mid-Atlantic Country Magazine
Midstream
Midwest Poetry Review
Military Engineer
Miniature Collector
Monterey Life
Morgan Horse
Morrow Owners Review
Mother Jones Magazine
Movie Collector's World
Moving Up
M/R Magazine
Ms
National Development
National Lampoon
National Motorist
NCFE Motivator
New Breed
New Dimensions
New Frontier
New Hampshire Alumnus
New Hampshire Profiles
New Orleans Magazine

New Southern Literary Messenger
New Woman Magazine
New York Habitat
New York Running News
New York's Nightlife and Long Island's Nightlife
Newsday
Nightmare Express
North Dakota Rec
Now Comics
Nutshell News
Official Detective
Official Karate
Old Cars Price Guide
1,001 Home Ideas
OnlyMusic Magazine
Ontario Out of Doors
Opera Canada
OPSA Magazine
Orange County Business Journal
Ovation
Pace Magazine
Pacific Discovery
Pacific Yachting
Panache
Pennsylvania Game News
Pennywhistle Press
Pipe Smoker
Pittsburgh Press Sunday Magazine
Plain Dealer Magazine
Pleasure Boating Magazine
Poker Player
Practical Horseman, Performance Horseman
Prairie Fire
Professional Stained Glass
Profiles
Profit
R/C Modeler Magazine
Reconstructionist
Recreation News
Regardies: The Magazine of Washington Business
Renegade Press
Review Magazine
Rock & Soul
RSVP
Runner's World
Rural Heritage
Rural Living
S.W.A.T.: Special Weapons and Tactics
Safari Magazine
San Antonio Homes and Gardens
San Antonio Magazine
San Diego Magazine
San Francisco Bay Guardian
San Francisco Letter
Satellite ORBIT
Saturday Evening Post
Scholastic Update
Scouting
Sea Kayaker
Seacoast Life

73 for Radio Amateurs
Sewanee Review
Shape
Shotgun Sports
Single Parent
Snowmobile Canada
Snowmobile Magazine
Snowmobile West
Soap Opera Digest
Sons of Norway Viking
Southwest Art
Southwest Spirit
Space World
Sport Fishing
Sporting Classics
Sports History
Sportsman Magazine
ST-Log
St. Louis Magazine
Stallion
Standard
State
State of Art
Style
Surfing Magazine
Swank
Teenage Magazine
Texas Gardener
Texas Student
3rd Coast Magazine
This People Magazine
3-2-1- Contact
Tidewater Virginian
Torso
Touch
Trapper
Traveling Times
True Detective
True Experience
United Brethren
Unspeakable Visions of the Individual Inc.
USA Weekend
Valley Magazine
Venture
Vintage
Virginia Wildlife
Vortex
Walking Magazine
Washington Fishing Holes
Washington Woman
Waterfowler's World
Ways
We Alaskans Magazine
Webb Traveler Magazine
Western Boatman
Western Producer
Wildlife Photography
Windrider
Wine & Spirits Buying Guide
Woman Bowler
Woman's Touch
Women & Co.
Women Artists News
Women's Circle Home Cooking
Women's Sports and Fitness

Worksteader News
World Market Perspective
Wrestling World
X-It
Yankee Homes
YM
Your Health and Fitness

The following listings were deleted following the 1988 edition of *Writer's Market* because the company asked to have the listing removed, went out of business, is no longer accepting unsolicited submissions, doesn't pay for manuscripts, or has unresolved complaints on file.

Air Wisconsin (ceased publication)
Arizona Monthly (suspended publication)
Arrival Magazine (asked to be deleted)
Berkeley Monthly (asked to be deleted)
Better Health & Living (ceased publication)
Biblical History (ceased publication)
Black Family (complaints)
Brennan Partners (asked to be deleted)
Business Times (unable to contact)
Campus Voice (suspended publication)
Career World (asked to be deleted)
Chevron USA Odyssey (asked to be deleted—accepting no unsolicited submissions)
Cinemascore (asked to be deleted)
Columbus Single Scene (pays in copies)
Computer & Electronics Graduate (asked to be deleted)
Crochet World Omnibook (asked to be deleted)
Dazzle (ceased publication)
Dial (out of business)
Down East (asked to be deleted)
Eastern Review (changing submission requirements at press time)
Echelon (asked to be deleted)
Elder Statesman (unable to contact)
Espionage Magazine (out of business)
Fantasy Review (out of business)
Farmstead Magazine (out of business)
Focus on the Family (asked to be deleted)
For Your Eyes Only (asked to be deleted)
4-H Leader (asked to be deleted)
Grandparenting! (unable to contact)
Great Lakes Travel & Living (complaints)
Home Altar (asked to be deleted—new ownership)
Hub Rail (out of business)
Intellectual Activist (asked to be deleted)
Life (asked to be deleted)
Lutheran (ceased publication)
Lutheran Standard (ceased publication)
Maclean's (asked to be deleted)
Mature Outlook (no longer taking freelance submissions)
Metapsychology (out of business)
Michiana (ceased publication)
Mid-South Magazine (ceased publication)
Modern Percussionist (absorbed by Modern Drummer)
Myrtle Beach Magazine (asked to be deleted)
New Business Magazine (asked to be deleted)
New England Out-of-Doors Magazine (asked to be deleted—works with local writers only)
Nostalgiaworld (complaints)
Official Crossword Puzzles (sold and incomplete details on submissions available at press time)
The Old Bottle Magazine/Popular Archaeology (merged when sold)
Openers (ceased publication)
Our Little Friend, Primary Treasure (asked to be deleted)
Owlflight (charges $5 reading fee)
Plus (asked to be deleted)
Poker Chips (no longer using freelance work)

Prairie Schooner (does not pay)
Princeton Parents (asked to be deleted)
RFD (pays in copies)
Rx Being Well (ceased publication)
Scrivener (does not pay)
Sertoman (asked to be deleted)
Seven (ceased publication)
Slimmer (ceased publication)
Snowy Egret (ceased publication)
Sunday Woman Plus (ceased publication)
Trifle (unable to contact)
Tun's Tales (out of business)
U Magazine (in middle of sale at press time)
Unexplained (doesn't pay)
Unity (does not pay)
Virginia Forests Magazine (does not pay)
Waterfront Magazine (asked to be deleted)
Word in Season (asked to be deleted—new ownership)

Trade, Technical and Professional Journals

This section contains more than 500 listings for trade, technical and professional publications. From advertising executives to farmers to plumbers, busy working people turn to trade journals for news and information about their field. Almost every occupation has its own trade publication and many of these seek well-written, concise manuscripts from freelance writers.

Although the general term for all publications focusing on a particular occupation or industry is trade, other terms are used to describe different types of trade publications. Technical journals contain highly technical articles and columns written by professionals working in a specific industry. Often the article is written for free and adds to the writer's professional credits and prestige. Many are written for science trades and contain articles focusing on new technology or research. Professional journals also contain articles from practitioners, but these focus on all aspects of a particular occupation. Physicians, educators and lawyers have their own professional journals.

Even though most trade journals have smaller circulations than consumer publications, writing for the trades is similar to writing for consumer magazines in many ways. Trade publication editors, like their consumer counterparts, seek professionally-presented submissions aimed specifically at their readers. Most trade articles are shorter than consumer features, however, and trade journals tend to use more fillers, newsbreaks and short pieces. Approach to material is also somewhat different than for many consumer magazines. "Writing style should be lively, informal and straightforward, but the subject matter must be as functional and down-to-earth as possible," says one editor. "Trade magazines are *business* magazines that help readers do their jobs better."

Training or experience in a particular field is a definite plus, but not always necessary if you know where to look and who to ask for information. Access to experts is essential for highly technical information. In fact, many trade journal editors will ask for a list of sources in order to verify information. Keep this in mind when querying—if possible, provide names of experts you plan to contact.

Query a trade journal as you would a consumer magazine, and be sure to mention any direct experience in the industry in your cover letter. Include a resume, possibly with clips, if you have extensive background in the subject. Most trade editors like to discuss an article idea with a writer first and will often offer names of helpful sources. Some will provide a list of questions they want you to ask.

Study several trade journals in the field to get a feel for trends and popular topics. Newspapers are another good source of information. Note changes in tax legislation and government regulations—several industries may be affected. Don't forget that trade journals within a particular category often compete with one another. An editor won't want a story a competitor has just published, unless it's a completely revised version with a fresh slant.

One way to break into the trade field and to increase your income at the same time is to rewrite a consumer story to fit a trade publication. While working on a consumer story, you may also uncover a good trade story lead, such as an interesting new business or a manager with innovative ideas about increasing productivity. Just remember to be on the lookout for problem-solving material. Readers want to know how they can apply this information to their own situations.

A story for a city magazine, for example, could generate a number of trade articles. A report on a new local hospital renovation project could be rewritten for a hospital administration journal ("How ABC Hospital's Staff Dealt with Problems of Ongoing Construction") or for an architectural publication ("How the Modular Design of ABC Hospital's New Critical Care Wing Will Accommodate Future Growth"). You'll need to dig deeper into different aspects of your original story, but the effort could mean additional sales.

Several editors say they do not want to see puff pieces, stories of little practical value. Beware of using suppliers and manufacturers as sole sources of information on a particular product. Stories can turn out to be what trade editors call "advertorials," stories that tout the benefits of a particular product without questioning its true value to the industry. Another type of puff piece is the interchangeable story. Editors complain of lazy writers who send in generalized business stories customized only by the word "shoe salesman" or "doctor."

Editors also warn writers, especially very new ones, to watch out for the "gee-whiz" trap. A company's success may indeed be impressive, but trade journal readers are a sophisticated lot. They will be more impressed with solid facts and figures than with overly enthusiastic prose.

Payment for trade manuscripts can be as high as for many consumer magazines. Yet you will sometimes be competing with professionals in the field who submit articles for prestige instead of pay. Trade editors are eager to work with new writers, however, and often need writers based in smaller cities to cover conventions and trade shows.

Photos help increase the value of most stories for trade. If you can provide photos, mention that in your query, or even send photocopies. Like consumer magazines, trade publications are becoming more visual. The availability of computer graphics has also increased the need (and desire) for charts, graphs and other explanatory visuals.

Often overlooked by beginners, these publications can be an excellent place to start or augment a writing career. A writer who delivers can build long-term working relationships with the editors of trade publications.

For information on additional trade publications not listed in *Writer's Market*, see Additional Trade Publications at the end of this section.

⎯⎯⎯ *Advertising, Marketing and PR*

Trade journals for advertising executives, copywriters and marketing and public relations professionals are listed in this category. Those whose main focus are the advertising and marketing of specific products, such as home furnishings, are classified under individual product categories. Journals for sales personnel and general merchandisers can be found in the Selling and Merchandising category.

ADVERTISING AGE, 740 N. Rush, Chicago IL 60611. (312)649-5200. Managing Editor: Valorie Mackie. Executive Editor Features/Special Reports: Robert Goldsborough. Executive Editor: Dennis Chase. Deputy Editor: Larry Doherty. New York office: 220 E 42 St., New York NY 10017. (212)210-0100. Editor: Fred Danzig. Currently staff-produced. Includes weekly sections devoted to one topic (i.e., marketing in southern California, agribusiness/advertising, TV syndication trends). Much of this material is done freelance—on assignment only. Pays kill fee "based on hours spent plus expenses." Byline given "except short articles or contributions to a roundup."

ADVERTISING TECHNIQUES, ADA Publishing Co., 6th Floor, 10 E. 39th St., New York NY 10016. (212)889-6500. Managing Editor: Hedi Levine. 30% freelance written. For advertising executives. Monthly magazine; 50 pages. Circ. 4,500. Pays on acceptance. Not copyrighted. Buys first and second rights to the same material. Reports in 1 month. Publishes ms an average of 2 months after acceptance. Sample copy $1.75. **Nonfiction:** Articles on advertising techniques. Buys 10 mss/year. Query. Pays $50-100.

AMERICAN DEMOGRAPHICS, American Demographics, Inc., Box 68, Ithaca NY 14851. (607)273-6343. Editor: Cheryl Russell. Managing Editor: Caroline Arthur. 25% freelance written. Works with a small number of new/unpublished writers each year. For business executives, market researchers, media and communications people, public policymakers. Monthly magazine. Circ. 30,000. Pays on publication. Publishes ms an average of 6 months after acceptance. Buys all rights. Submit seasonal/holiday material 6 months in advance. Query for electronic submissions. Computer printout submissions acceptable. Reports in 1 month on queries; in 2 months on mss. Include self-addressed stamped postcard for return word that ms arrived safely. Sample copy for $4 and 9x11 SAE with 4 first class stamps.
Nonfiction: General interest (on demographic trends, implications of changing demographics, profile of business using demographic data); and how-to (on the use of demographic techniques, psychographics, understand projections, data, apply demography to business and planning). No anecdotal material or humor. Sometimes pays the expenses of writers on assignment.
Tips: "Writer should have clear understanding of specific population trends and their implications for business and planning. The most important thing a freelancer can do is to read the magazine and be familiar with its style and focus."

ART DIRECTION, Advertising Trade Publications, Inc., 6th Floor, 10 E. 39th St., New York NY 10016. (212)889-6500. Editor: Hedi Levine. 10% freelance written. Prefers to work with published/established writers. Emphasis on advertising design for art directors of ad agencies (corporate, in-plant, editorial, freelance, etc.). Monthly magazine. Circ. 12,000. Pays on publication. Buys one-time rights. Reports in 3 months. Sample copy $3.
Nonfiction: How-to articles on advertising campaigns. Pays $100 minimum.

BARTER COMMUNIQUE, Full Circle Marketing Corp., Box 2527, Sarasota FL 33578. (813)349-3300. Editor-in-Chief: Robert J. Murely. 100% freelance written. Emphasizes bartering for radio and TV station owners, cable TV, newspaper and magazine publishers and select travel and advertising agency presidents. Semiannual tabloid. Circ. 50,000. Pays on publication. Publishes ms an average of 3 months after acceptance. Rights purchased vary with author and material. Phone queries OK. Simultaneous, photocopied and previously published submissions OK. Computer printout submissions acceptable. Reports in 1 month. Free sample copy and writer's guidelines.
Nonfiction: Articles on "barter" (trading products, goods and services, primarily travel and advertising). Length: 1,000 words. "Would like to see travel mss on southeast U.S. and the Bahamas, and unique articles on media of all kinds. Include photos where applicable. No manuscripts on barter for products, goods and services—primarily travel and media—but also excess inventory of business to business." Pays $30-50.
Tips: "Computer installation will improve our ability to communicate."

BPME IMAGE, Broadcast Promotion and Marketing Executives, Inc., 1528A Granite Hills Dr., El Cajon CA 92019. (619)447-1227. Editor-in-Chief: Robert P. Rimes. Assistant Editor: Bill Strubbe. 80% freelance written. Works with a small number of new/unpublished writers each year. A trade journal for broadcast advertising and promotion executives, published 10 times/year. "*BPME* is a 'how-to' publication that contains editorial material designed to enhance the job performance of broadcast advertising and promotion executives, who constitute the bulk of its readers." Circ. 6,000. Pays on publication. Publishes ms an average of 3 months after acceptance. Byline given. Buys all rights. Submit seasonal/holiday material 3 months in advance. Photocopied submissions OK. Computer printout submissions OK; prefers letter-quality. Reports in 3 weeks. Sample copy for $7 with 8x10 SAE and 10 first class stamps postage.
Nonfiction: Essays, how-to, humor, interview/profile, personal experience and photo feature. "Each issue has a theme which is available in an editorial listing published in December of each year." Buys 12 mss/year. Query. Length: 800-2,500 words. Pays $300 maximum.
Photos: State availability of photos with submission. Offers $400 maximum per photo. Captions, model releases and identification of subjects required. Buys all rights.
Columns/Departments: Profile (leader in industry); My Turn (opinion). Buys 12 mss/year. Query with published clips. Length: 800-2,500 words. Pays $300 maximum.
Tips: "We would like to receive queries on any subject having to do with broadcast advertising or promotion—stunts, contests, concepts, successful advertising and promotion campaigns, and marketing management tips. Ours is such a specialized audience that it is difficult to break in to print in our publication. A full knowledge of radio and television and/or advertising will help. In short, the more research that goes into the piece, the better. We seem to favor writers who have something to say rather than lightweight puff pieces that are cleverly written. We especially like articles that are based on speeches by well-known persons in radio and TV."

‡CANADIAN PREMIUMS & INCENTIVES, Selling Ideas in Motivational Marketing, Maclean Hunter Limited, 777 Bay St., Toronto, Ontario M5W 1A7 Canada. (416)596-5838. Editor: Ed Patrick. Publisher: Ted Wilson. 10% freelance written. Prefers to work with published/established writers. Quarterly magazine covering premium/incentive programs and promotions; incentive travel. Circ. 15,850. Pays on publication. Publishes ms an average of 2 months after acceptance. Byline given. Buys first North American serial, one-time, and first rights. Submit seasonal/holiday material 4 months in advance. Simultaneous queries OK. Computer printout submissions OK; prefers letter-quality. Reports in 1 week. Sample copy $3.

Nonfiction: Case histories of successful incentive promotions in Canada. New product and travel (incentive). Query with published clips. Length: 600-1,500 words. Pays $100-250. Sometimes pays the expenses of writers on assignment.

Photos: Pays $15-25 for 8x10 b&w prints. Captions and identification of subjects required. Buys one-time rights.

THE COUNSELOR MAGAZINE, Advertising Specialty Institute, NBS Bldg., 1120 Wheeler Way, Langhorne PA 19047. (215)752-4200. Editor: Daniel B. Cartledge. 25% freelance written. Works with a small number of new/unpublished writers each year. For executives, both distributors and suppliers, in the ad specialty industry. Monthly magazine. Circ. 6,000. Pays on publication. Publishes ms an average of 3 months after acceptance. Buys first rights only. No phone queries. Submit seasonal/holiday material 4 months in advance. Simultaneous, photocopied and previously published submissions OK. Computer printout submissions OK; prefers letter-quality. Reports in 2-3 months. Sample copy of *Imprint* for 9x12 SAE with 3 first-class stamps.

Nonfiction: Contact managing editor. How-to (promotional case histories); interview (with executives and government figures); profile (of executives); and articles on specific product categories. "Articles almost always have a specialty advertising slant and quotes from specialty advertising practitioners." Buys 30 mss/year. Length: Open. Query with samples. Pays according to assigned length. Sometimes pays the expenses of writers on assignment.

Photos: State availability of photos. B&w photos only. Prefers contact sheet(s) and 5x7 prints. Offers some additional payment for original only photos accepted with ms. Captions and model releases required. Buys one-time rights.

Tips: "If a writer shows promise, we can help him or her modify his style to suit our publication and provide leads. Writers must be willing to adapt or rewrite their material for a specific audience. If an article is suitable for 5 or 6 other publications, it's probably not suitable for us. The best way to break in is to write for *Imprint*, a quarterly publication we produce for the clients of ad specialty counselors. *Imprint* covers promotional campaigns, safety programs, trade show exhibits, traffic builders and sales incentives—all with a specialty advertising tie-in."

THE FLYING A, Aeroquip Corp., 300 S. East Ave., Jackson MI 49203. (517)787-8121. Editor-in-Chief: Wayne D. Thomas. 10% freelance written. Emphasizes Aeroquip customers and products. Quarterly magazine. Circ. 30,000. Pays on acceptance. Buys first or second rights, depending upon circumstances. Simultaneous submissions OK. Reports in 2 months.

Nonfiction: General interest (feature stories with emphasis on free enterprise, business-related or historical articles with broad appeal, human interest.) "An Aeroquip tie-in in a human interest story is helpful." No jokes, no sample copies; no cartoons, no short fillers. Buys 1 mss/issue. Query with biographic sketch and clips. Length: Not to exceed five typewritten pages. Pays $75 minimum.

Photos: Accompanying photos are helpful.

Fillers: Human interest. No personal anecdotes, recipes or how-to articles. "Suggest the writer contact editor by letter with proposed story outline."

Tips: "We publish a marketing-oriented magazine, with a section devoted to employee news. Our products are used in a wide variety of markets, including aerospace, automotive, construction equipment and others. Our primary products are hose lines and fittings for aerospace and industrial markets."

HIGH-TECH SELLING, For Electronics, Telecommunications, and Other High-Tech Industries, Bureau of Business Practice/Simon & Schuster, 24 Rope Ferry Rd., Waterford CT 06385. (800)243-0876. Editor: Michele S. Rubin. Managing Editor: Wayne Muller. 75% freelance written. Prefers to work with published/established writers, but also is eager to work with new/unpublished writers. A monthly training newsletter covering selling. Pays on acceptance. Publishes ms an average of 4 months after acceptance. Byline not given. Buys all rights. Submit seasonal/holiday material 6 months in advance. Photocopied submissions OK. Computer printout submissions acceptable; prefers letter-quality. Reports in 1 week. Sample copy and writer's guidelines for 4x9½ SAE with 1 first class stamp.

Nonfiction: How-to. Buys 50 mss/year. Query. Length: 1,000-1,500 words. Pays 10-15¢/word.

Photos: Offers no additional payment for photos accepted with ms.

Tips: "Our entire publication is interview-based."

‡IDEAS, The Monthly Magazine of the International Newspaper Marketing Association, 11600 Sunrise Valley Dr., Reston VA 22091. (703)648-1094. Editor: Mayhugh H. "Skip" Horne III. Art Director: Dora Meabon. A monthly magazine of newspaper marketing and promotion ideas. "*IDEAS* highlights successful marketing and promotion ideas for newspapers of all circulation groups. Each month, it includes a feature article examining a pertinent, timely marketing topic of interest to newspaper executives." Pays on publication. Publishes ms an average of 2 months after acceptance. Byline given. Makes work-for-hire assignments. Submit seasonal/holiday material 2 months in advance. Simultaneous, photocopied and previously published submissions OK. Computer printout submissions OK; prefers letter-quality. Sample copy for 9x12 SAE.

Nonfiction: Book excerpts, general interest, how-to, new product and technical. Buys up to 12 mss/year. Send complete ms. Length: 1,200-2,000 words. Pays $250.

Photos: Send photos with submission. Reviews contact sheets, negatives and prints (5x7). Offers no additional payment for photos accepted with ms. Identification of subjects required. Buys one-time rights.

Columns/Departments: Focus (monthly feature article which examines marketing topics of interest to newspaper promotion and marketing executives), 1,200-2,000 words. Buys up to 12 mss/year. Send complete ms. Length: 1,200-2,000 words. Pays $250 maximum.

Tips: "Writers for *IDEAS* must have a keen knowledge of the newspaper marketing field—previous work in this area or with an ad agency on a newspaper account is definitely a plus. Writers must also be up on current trends in newspaper marketing (i.e., marketing to younger readers, conversions to a.m. publication, competition with broadcast media). The area most open to freelancers is the Focus section of *IDEAS* ."

INFORMATION MARKETING, A Direct Marketing Tool for Writers, Publishers, Communicators and Information Marketers, Box 2069, Citrus Heights CA 95611. Editor: Mark Nolan. 25-50% freelance written. Eager to work with new/unpublished writers. A monthly newsletter covering advertising and marketing tips for those who deal "in information of any type." Pays on publication. Publishes ms an average of 3 months after acceptance. Byline given, sometimes depending on length of material. Buys first North American and second serial (reprint) rights. Submit seasonal/holiday material 6 weeks in advance. Simultaneous, photocopied, and previously published submissions OK. Query for electronic submissions. Computer printout submissions acceptable; no dot-matrix. Reports in 3 weeks. Sample copy $1.

Nonfiction: How-to (advertise or market information, press releases, etc); mail order tips, postal tips, directories available, cottage industry success stories, etc., newsletters; and new product (software, word processors). No long dissertations or editorials; only "short, pithy, impact news, tips and sources." Buys 50-100 mss/year (estimated). Recent article: "Bestselling Subject Matter" by Mark Nolan. Send complete ms. Length: 50-150 words. Pays $25-75.

Columns/Departments: New books department: Short reviews on books pertaining to main theme, including those on word processing, advertising techniques, salesmanship, information industry, work-at-home themes, consulting, seminars, etc. Buys 10-25 mss/year. Send complete ms. Length: 50-150 words. Pays $15-25.

Fillers: Clippings and newsbreaks. Buys 10-50/year. Length: 35-75 words. Pays $5.

Tips: "We would love to hear from you if you've studied at least one issue. We need short items most of all. News and tips to help busy nonfiction writers and publishers: how to sell more, save money, choose 'tools', etc. The most frequent mistake made by writers in completing an article for us is too much fine writing. Our subscribers are mostly writers and publishers. They are very busy and want valuable news, tips and sources with a minimum of wasted words. Read some issues to see our style and content."

MORE BUSINESS, 11 Wimbledon Court, Jericho NY 11753. Editor: Trudy Settel. 50% freelance written. "We sell publications material to business for consumer use (incentives, communication, public relations)—look for book ideas and manuscripts." Monthly magazine. Circ. 10,000. Pays on acceptance. Publishes ms an average of 1 month after acceptance. Buys all rights. Computer printout submissions acceptable; no dot-matrix. Reports in 1 month.

Nonfiction: General interest, how-to, vocational techniques, nostalgia, photo feature, profile and travel. Buys 10-20 mss/year. Word length varies with article. Payment negotiable. Query. Pays $4,000-7,000 for book mss.

SALES & MARKETING MANAGEMENT IN CANADA, Sanford Evans Communications Ltd., Suite 402, 3500 Dufferin St., Downsview, Ontario M3K 1N2 Canada. (416)633-2020. Editor: Ernie Spear. Monthly magazine. Circ. 13,000. Pays on publication. Byline given. Buys first North American serial rights. Simultaneous queries and photocopied submissions OK. Reports in 2 weeks.

Nonfiction: How-to (case histories of successful marketing campaigns). "Canadian articles only." Buys 3 mss/year. Query. Length: 800-1,500 words. Pays $200 maximum.

SIGNCRAFT, The Magazine for the Sign Artist and Commercial Sign Shop, SignCraft Publishing Co., Inc., Box 06031, Fort Myers FL 33906. (813)939-4644. Editor: Tom McIltrot. 30% freelance written. Bimonthly magazine of the sign industry. "Like any trade magazine, we need material of direct benefit to our readers. We can't afford space for material of marginal interest." Circ. 19,800. Pays on publication. Publishes ms an average of 9 months after acceptance. Byline given. Offers negotiable kill fee. Buys first North American serial rights or all rights. Photocopied and previously published submissions OK. Computer printout

submissions acceptable. Reports in 1 month. Sample copy and writer's guidelines for $2 and 5 first class stamps.
Nonfiction: Interviews and profiles. "All articles should be directly related to quality commercial signage. If you are familiar with the sign trade, we'd like to hear from you." Buys 20 mss/year. Query with or without published clips. Length: 500-2,000 words. Pays up to $150.

VM & SD (Visual Merchandising and Store Design), ST Publications, 407 Gilbert Ave., Cincinnati OH 45202. Associate Publisher: Pamela Gramke. Editor: Ms. P.K. Anderson. 30% freelance written. Emphasizes store design and merchandise presentation. Monthly magazine. Circ. 12,500. Pays on publication. Buys first and second rights to the same material. Simultaneous and previously published submissions OK. Computer printout submissions acceptable. Reports in 1 month. Publishes ms an average of 3 months after acceptance.
Nonfiction: How-to (display); informational (store design, construction, merchandise presentation); interview (display directors and shop owners); profile (new and remodeled stores); new product; photo feature (window display); and technical (store lighting, carpet, wallcoverings, fixtures). No "advertorials" that tout a single company's product or product line. Buys 24 mss year. Query or submit complete ms. Length: 500-3,000 words. Pays $250-400.
Photos: Purchased with accompanying ms or on assignment.
Tips: "Be fashion and design conscious and reflect that in the article. Submit finished manuscripts with photos or slides always. Look for stories on department and specialty store visual merchandisers and store designers (profiles, methods, views on the industry, sales promotions and new store design or remodels). The size of the publication could very well begin to increase in the year ahead. And with a greater page count, we will need to rely on an increasing number of freelancers."

Art, Design and Collectibles

The businesses of art, art administration, architecture, environmental/package design and antiques/collectibles are covered in these listings. Art-related topics for the general public are located in the Consumer Art and Architecture category. Antiques and collectibles magazines for enthusiasts are listed in Consumer Hobby and Craft. (For listings of markets for freelance art use *Artist's Market*—see Other Books of Interest).

ANTIQUEWEEK, (formerly *Tri-State Trader*), Mayhill Publications Inc., 27 N. Jefferson St., Box 90, Knightstown IN 46148. (317)345-5133. Managing Editor: Tom Hoepf. 60% freelance written. Weekly tabloid on antiques, collectibles and genealogy. "*AntiqueWeek* has a wide range of readership from dealers and auctioneers to collectors, both serious and novice. Our readers demand accurate information presented in an entertaining style." Circ. 60,000. Pays on publication. Publishes ms an average of 1-2 months after acceptance. Byline given. Buys first and second serial (reprint) rights. Submit seasonal/holiday material 1 month in advance. Simultaneous, photocopied and previously published submissions OK. Computer printout submissions OK; prefers letter-quality. Reports in 1 month. Free sample copy and writer's guidelines.
Nonfiction: Historical/nostalgic, how-to, interview/profile, opinion, personal experience, photo feature, antique show and auction reports, feature articles on particular types of antiques. Buys 400-500 mss/year. Query with or without published clips, or send complete ms. Length: 1,000-2,000 words. Pays $25-125.
Photos: Send photos with submission. Reviews 3½x5 prints. Offers $10-15 per photo. Identification of subjects required. Buys one-time rights.
Columns/Departments: Insights (opinions on buying, selling and collecting antiques), 500-1,000 words; Your Ancestors (advice, information on locating sources for genealogists), 1,500-2,000 words. Buys 150 mss/ year. Query. Length: 500-1,000 words. Pays $15-50.
Tips: "Writers should know their topic thoroughly to write about it. Feature articles must be well-researched and clearly written. An interview and profile article with a knowedgable collector might be the break for a first-time contributor."

ART BUSINESS NEWS, Myers Publishing Co., 60 Ridgeway Plaza, Stamford CT 06905. (203)356-1745. Editor: Jo Yanow-Schwartz. Managing Editor: Beth Fleckenstein. 25% freelance written. Prefers to work with published/established writers. Monthly tabloid covering news relating to the art and picture framing industry. Circ. 28,000. Pays on publication. Publishes ms an average of 3 months after acceptance. Byline given. Buys first-time rights. Submit seasonal/holiday material 2 months in advance. Photocopied and simultaneous submissions OK. Computer printout submissions acceptable; prefers letter-quality. Reports in 2-3 months. Sample copy for 12x15¾ SAE and $2.40.

Nonfiction: News in art and framing field; interview/marketing profiles (of dealers, publishers in the art industry); new products; articles focusing on small business people—framers, art gallery management, art trends; and how-to (occasional article on "how-to frame" accepted) . Buys 8-20 mss/year. Length: 1,000 words maximum. Query first. Pays $75-250. Sometimes pays the expenses of writers on assignment. "Useful if writer can photograph."

ARTS MANAGEMENT, 408 W. 57th St., New York NY 10019. (212)245-3850. Editor: A.H. Reiss. For cultural institutions. Published five times/year. 2% freelance written. Circ. 6,000. Pays on publication. Byline given. Buys all rights. Mostly staff-written; uses very little outside material. Computer printout submissions acceptable; no dot-matrix. Query. Reports in "several weeks." Writer's guidelines for #10 SASE.

Nonfiction: Short articles, 400-900 words, tightly written, expository, explaining how art administrators solved problems in publicity, fund raising and general administration; actual case histories emphasizing the how-to. Also short articles on the economics and sociology of the arts and important trends in the nonprofit cultural field. Must be fact-filled, well-organized and without rhetoric. Payment is 2-4¢/word. No photographs or pictures.

CALLIGRAPHY REVIEW, 2421 Wilcox Dr., Norman OK 73069. (405)364-8794. Editor: Karyn L. Gilman. 98% freelance written. Eager to work with new/unpublished writers with calligraphic expertise and language skills. A quarterly magazine on calligraphy and related book arts, both historical and contemporary in nature. Circ. 5,500. Pays on publication. Publishes ms an average of 6 months after acceptance. Byline given. Offers 20% kill fee. Buys first rights. Submit seasonal/holiday material 3-4 months in advance. Photocopied submissions OK. Query for electronic submissions. Computer printout submissions acceptable. Sample copy for 9x12 SAE with 7 first class stamps; free writer's guidelines.

Nonfiction: Interview/profile, new product, opinion, and historical. Buys 50 mss/year. Query with or without published clips, or send complete ms. Length: 1,000-2,000 words. Pays $50-200 for assigned articles; pays $25-200 for unsolicited articles. Sometimes pays the expenses of writers on assignment.

Photos: State availability of photos with submission. Reviews contact sheets, negatives, transparencies and prints. Pays agreed upon cost. Captions and identification of subjects required. Buys one-time rights.

Columns/Departments: Book Reviews Viewpoint (critical), 500-1,500 words; Ms. (discussion of manuscripts in collections), 1,000-2,000 words; and Profile (contemporary calligraphic figure), 1,000-2,000 words. Query. Pays $50-200.

Tips: *"Calligraphy Review*'s primary objective is to encourage the exchange of ideas on calligraphy, its past and present as well as trends for the future. Practical and conceptual treatments are welcomed, as are learning and teaching experiences. Third person is preferred, however first person will be considered if appropriate."

THE CRAFTS REPORT, The Newsmonthly of Marketing, Management and Money for Crafts Professionals, The Crafts Report Publishing Co., 3623 Ashworth North, Seattle WA 98103. (206)547-7611. Editor: Michael Scott. 50% freelance written. A monthly tabloid covering business subjects for crafts professionals. Circ. 17,000. Pays on publication. Byline given. Offers $50 kill fee. Buys first rights. Photocopied submissions and sometimes previously published submissions OK. Query for electronic submissions. Computer printout submissions OK. Reports in 2 weeks. Sample copy $2.

Nonfiction: Business articles for crafts professionals. No articles on art or crafts techniques. Buys approximately 70 mss/year. Query with published clips. Length: 800-1,200 words. Pays $100-150.

Photos: State availability of photos with submission or send photos with submission. Reviews 5x7 b&w prints. Identification of subjects required. Buys one-time rights.

‡NEAA NEWS, New England Appraisers Association Newsletter, New England Appraisers Association, 5 Gill Terrace, Ludlow VT 05149. (802)228-7444. Editor: Linda L. Tucker. 75% freelance written. Works with a small number of new/unpublished writers each year. Monthly newsletter on the appraisals of antiques, art, collectibles, jewelry, coins, stamps and real estate. "The writer should be extremely knowledgeable on the subject, and the article should be written with appraisers in mind with prices quoted for objects, good pictures and descriptions of articles being written about." Circ. 1,300. Pays on publication. Publishes ms an average of 2 months after acceptance. Byline given, with short biography to establish writer's credibility. Buys first rights, second serial (reprint) rights, and simultaneous rights. Submit seasonal/holiday material 2 months in advance. Simultaneous and previously published submissions OK. Computer printout submissions acceptable; prefers letter-quality. Reports in 1 week on queries; 3 weeks on mss. Sample copy and writer's guidelines for #10 SASE.

Nonfiction: Interview/profile, personal experience, technical and travel. "All articles must be geared toward professional appraisers." Query with or without published clips, or send complete ms. Length: 1,000-1,500 words. Pays $50-75.

Photos: Send photos with submission. Reviews negatives and prints. Offers no additional payment for photos accepted with ms. Identification of subjects required. Buys one-time rights.
Tips: "Interviewing members of the Association for articles, reviewing art books, shows, and large auctions are all ways for writers who are not in the field to write articles for us."

‡**NEW ENGLAND ANTIQUES JOURNAL**, Turley Publications. 4 Church St., Ware MA 01082. (413)967-3505. Editor: Bryan McMullin. Managing Editor: Julie DePesa. 50% freelance written. A monthly newspaper on antiques. "We are a trade publication for antiques dealers, collectors and the general public interested in antiques." Circ. 20,000. Pays on publication. Byline given. Buys first rights. Submit seasonal/holiday material 4 months in advance. Photocopied submissions OK. Computer printout submissions OK; prefers letter-quality. Reports in 1 month on queries; 2 months on mss. Free sample copy and writer's guidelines.
Nonfiction: Book excerpts, essays and interview/profile. "We do not want to see any articles about anything except antiques!" Buys 40 mss/year. Query with or without published clips, or send complete ms. Length: 1,000-2,500 words. Pays $75-150 for assigned articles. Sometimes pays the expenses of writers on assignment.
Photos: Send photos with submission. Reviews b&w prints (5x7). Offers no additional payment for photos accepted with ms. Captions and indentification of subjects required. Buys one-time rights.
Columns/Departments: Off the Block (auction review), 500 words; On the Block (auction preview), 500 words; In Brief. Buys 10 mss/year. Send complete ms. Length: 250-700 words. Pays $10-25.
Tips: "Have in-depth knowledge of the subject you are writing about."

‡**YARN MARKET NEWS**, Butterick Co., Inc.. 588 St. Charles Ave. N.E., Atlanta GA 30308. (404)873-3550. Editor: Jeane Hutchins. 90% freelance written. A bimonthly magazine on the retail yarn market. "Readers are owners/managers of retail yarn stores, selling knitting, needlepoint, stitchery, weaving, etc., supplies." Circ. 7,000. Pays on publication. Publishes ms an average of 2 months after acceptance. Byline given. Offers 25% kill fee. Buys first rights and second serial (reprint) rights. Submit seasonal/holiday material 5 months in advance. Photocopied and previously published submissions OK. Reports in 2 weeks on queries; 1 month on mss. Sample copy $2.50. Free writer's guidelines.
Nonfiction: Book excerpts, general interest, historical/nostalgic, how-to (operate a retail store profitably), humor, inspirational, interview/profile, opinion, personal experience, photo feature and technical. "Don't submit articles that do not pertain to operating a retail business." Buys 60 mss/year. Query with or without published clips, or send complete ms. Length: 500-5,000 words. Pays $50-500 for assigned articles. Pays $50-250 for unsolicited articles. Sometimes pays the expenses of writers on assignment.
Photos: Send photos with submission. Reviews contact sheets, negatives and prints (8x10). Offers no additional payment for photos accepted with ms. Captions, model releases and identification of subjects required. Buys one-time rights.
Columns/Departments: Marketing Tips (general retail marketing ideas/tips), 750-1,000 words; Management Clinic (management ideas); Personal Accountant (accounting ideas). Buys 20 mss/year. Send complete ms. Length: 500-1,500 words. Pays $50-150.
Tips: "Any topic that relates to the operation of a small retail business is welcome; knowledge of the yarn market is not a necessity."

Auto and Truck

These publications are geared to automobile, motorcycle and truck dealers; professional truck drivers; service department personnel; or fleet operators. Publications for highway planners and traffic control experts are listed in the Government and Public Service category.

AMERICAN TRUCKER MAGAZINE, American Trucker Marketing, Box 9159, Brea CA 92622. (714)528-6600. Publisher: Steve Sturgess. Editor: Tom Berg. 10% freelance written. Eager to work with new/unpublished writers. Monthly magazine for professional truck drivers, owners, management and other trucking personnel. Articles, fillers and other materials should be generally conservative and of particular interest to the readership, of an informative or entertaining nature relating to the trucking industry. Circ. 80,000. Pays on publication. Publishes ms an average of 3 months after acceptance. First-time rights requested. Submit seasonal/holiday material 3 months in advance. Query for electronic submissions. Computer printout submissions acceptable. Reports in 3 weeks. Phone queries OK. Free sample copy and writer's guidelines.
Nonfiction: Realistic articles directed to trucking professionals which promote a positive image of the industry. Photo and features of outstanding rigs, truck maintenance and repair, and business aspects of trucking. 450-2,500 words. Buys 60 articles/year. Pays standard column inch rate. Sometimes pays the expenses of writers on assignment.

Photos: State availability of photos or send captioned photos with ms. Model release required.
Fiction: Realistic, "slice of life" for truckers, adventure and humor. Query. Length: 1,200-2,500 words. Buys 6/year. Pays standard column inch rate.
Tips: Freelance writers offer a balance of writing style throughout the magazine.

AUTO GLASS JOURNAL, Grawin Publications, Inc., Suite 101, 303 Harvard E., Box 12099, Seattle WA 98102-0099. (206)322-5120. Editor: Burton Winters. 45% freelance written. Prefers to work with published/ established writers. Monthly magazine on auto glass replacement. National publication for the auto glass replacement industry. Includes step-by-step glass replacement procedures for current model cars as well as shop profiles, industry news and trends. Circ. 4,800. Pays on acceptance. Publishes ms an average of 5 months after acceptance. No byline given. Buys all rights. Query for electronic submissions. Computer printout submissions acceptable; prefers letter-quality. Reports in 2 weeks on queries; 1 week on mss. Sample copy for 6x9 SAE and 3 first class stamps. Writer's guidelines for #10 SAE and 1 first class stamp.
Nonfiction: How-to (install all glass in a current model car); and interview/profile. Buys 22-36 mss/year. Query with published clips. Length: 2,000-3,500 words. Pays $75-250, with photos. Sometimes pays the expenses of writers on assignment.
Photos: State availability of photos. Reviews b&w contact sheets and negatives. Payment included with ms. Captions required. Buys all rights.
Tips: "Be willing to visit auto glass replacement shops for installation features."

AUTO TRIM NEWS, National Association of Auto Trim Shops (NAATS), 1623 N. Grand Ave., Box 86N, Baldwin NY 11510. (516)223-4334. Editor: Nat Danas. Associate Editor: Dani Ben-Ari. 25% freelance written. Monthly magazine for auto trim shops, installation specialists, customizers and restylers, marine and furniture upholsterers as well as manufacturers, wholesalers, jobbers, and distributors serving them. Circ. 8,000. Pays on publication. Byline given. Buys first rights only. Simultaneous and previously published submissions OK. Reports in 1 month. Sample copy $3; free writer's guidelines for #10 SAE.
Nonfiction: How-to, interview/profile, photo feature on customizing, restoration, convertible conversions, and restyling of motor vehicles (cars, vans, trucks, motorcycles, boats and aircraft). Query or send complete ms. Length: 500-1,000 words. Pays $50-200.
Photos: State availability of photos. Pays $5 maximum for b&w print. Reviews b&w contact sheet. Captions and identification of subjects required. Buys one-time rights.
Tips: "No material dealing with engines and engine repairs. We are an aftermarket publication."

AUTOMOTIVE BOOSTER OF CALIFORNIA, Box 765, LaCanada CA 91011. (213)790-6554. Editor: Don McAnally. 2% freelance written. Prefers to work with published/established writers. For members of Automotive Booster clubs, automotive warehouse distributors, and automotive parts jobbers in California. Monthly. Circ. 3,400. Not copyrighted. Byline given. Pays on publication. Publishes ms an average of 1 month after acceptance. Buys first rights only.
Nonfiction: Will look at short articles and pictures about successes of automotive parts outlets in California. Also can use personnel assignments for automotive parts people in California. Query first. Pays $1.25/column inch (about 2½¢/word).
Photos: Pays $5 for b&w photos used with mss.

‡AUTOMOTIVE EXECUTIVE, Official Publication of National Auto Dealers, NADA Services Corporation, 8400 Westpart Dr., McLean VA 22102. (703)821-7150. Editor: Peter S. Lukasiak. Managing Editor: Joe Phillips. 50% freelance written. A monthly magazine on the retail new car and truck business. "We offer a broad view of developments in the nation's $283 billion retail new car and truck market. We seek examples of excellence in sales, service, product and customer relations." Circ. 24,000. Pays on publication. Publishes ms an average of 2 months after acceptance. Byline given. Kill fee negotiable. Buys all rights. Computer printout submissions OK; prefers letter-quality. Reports in 1 week on queries; 2 weeks on mss. Free sample copy.
Nonfiction: Historical/nostalgic, interview/profile, new product, photo feature and technical. February - annual convention issue; May - annual dealership design issue; August - annual buyers guide issue; December - annual forecast issue. Buys 30-40 mss/year. Query with published clips. Length: 2,500 words. Pays $200-500 for assigned articles. Pays $150-250 for unsolicited articles. Pays the expenses of writers on assignment.
Photos: State availability of photos with submission or send photos with submission. Reviews contact sheets. Offers no additional payment for photos accepted with ms. Buys all rights.
Columns/Departments: Column/Department Editor: Joan Mooney. Commentary (reviews current industry controversy/policies), 500-750 words; Service Department (sets goals/ideal for efficient servicing of cars/ trucks), 750-2,500 words. Buys 12-15 mss/year. Query with published clips. Length: 500-2,500 words. Pays $150-2,000.
Tips: "We're looking for articles dealing with all aspects of retail new car/truck sales/service/customer relations, interviews with manufacturing/import executives, stories on unusual dealers/dealerships and stories from related industry that focus on excellence. We look for current trends in the auto industry and changes in the global economy that may impact dealers (i.e., merging car manufacturers, labor relations, trade, etc.)."

‡CANADIAN AUTO REVIEW, Maclean Hunter Ltd., 777 Bay St., Toronto, Ontario, M5W 1A7 Canada. (416)596-5784. Editor: Richard Jacobs. 75% freelance written. A new car market magazine published 8 times/ year. "This is a management-oriented magazine for new car dealership owners/managers. Content generally must have a Canadian emphasis." Circ. 10,000. Publishes ms an average of 3 months after acceptance. Byline given. Offers 75% kill fee. Buys first rights. Submit seasonal/holiday material 3 months in advance. Photocopied and previously published submissions OK. Query for electronic submission. Computer printout submissions OK; prefers letter-quality. Reports in one month. Free sample copy.
Nonfiction: General interest, historical/nostalgic, interview/profile and technical. No press clippings or consumer-oriented articles. Query or send complete ms. Length: 250-2,000 words. Pays 20-50¢/word. Sometimes pays the expenses of writers on assignment.
Photos: Send photos with submission. Reviews contact sheets, negatives, transparencies and prints (5x7). Offers no additional payment for photos accepted with ms "with some exceptions." Captions and identification of subjects required. Buys all rights.

COLLISION, Kruza Kaleidoscopix, Inc., Box 389, Franklin MA 02038. Editor: Jay Kruza. For auto dealers, auto body repairmen and managers, and tow truck operators. Magazine published every 6 weeks. Pays on acceptance. Buys all rights. Submit seasonal/holiday material 4 months in advance. Simultaneous, photocopied and previously published submissions OK. Reports in 3 weeks. Sample copy $3; writer's guidelines and editorial schedule for SASE.
Nonfiction: Expose (on government intervention in private enterprise via rule making; also how any business skims the cream of profitable business but fails to satisfy needs of motorist); and how-to (fix a dent, a frame, repair plastics, run your business better). No general business articles such as how to sell more, do better bookkeeping, etc. Query before submitting interview, personal opinion or technical articles. "Journalism of newsworthy material in local areas pertaining to auto body is of interest." Buys 20 or more articles/year. Length: 100-1,500 words. Pays $25-125.
Photos: "Our readers work with their hands and are more likely to be stopped by photo with story." Send photos with ms. Pays $25/first, $10/each additional for 5x7 b&w prints. Captions preferred. Model release required if not news material.
Columns/Departments: Stars and Their Cars, Personalities in Auto Dealerships, Auto Body Repair Shops, Profiles, Association News and Lifestyle (dealing with general human interest hobbies or pastimes). Almost anything automotive that would attract readership interest. "Photos are very important. Stories that we have purchased are: 'Post office commandeered cars to deliver help during 1906 San Francisco Quake'; 'Bob Salter has rescued 3,000 people with his tow truck'; 'Telnack's design of T-Bird and Sable set new trends in style'; 'Snow increases body shop business for Minnesota shop'; 'Race against the clock with funny wheels on frozen lake.' "

JOBBER TOPICS, 7300 N. Cicero Ave., Lincolnwood IL 60646. (312)588-7300. Articles Editor: Jack Creighton. 10% freelance written. Prefers to work with published/established writers, works with a small number of new/unpublished writers each year, and is eager to work with new/unpublished writers. "A magazine dedicated to helping its readers—auto parts jobbers and warehouse distributors—succeed in their business via better management and merchandising techniques; and a better knowledge of industry trends, sales activities and local or federal legislation that may influence their business activities." Monthly. Pays on acceptance. No byline given. Buys all rights. Computer printout submissions OK; prefers letter-quality.
Nonfiction: Most editorial material is staff-written. "Articles with unusual or outstanding automotive jobber procedures, with special emphasis on sales, merchandising and machine shop; any phase of automotive parts and equipment sales and distribution. Especially interested in merchandising practices and machine shop operations. Most independent businesses usually have a strong point or two. We like to see a writer zero in on that strong point(s) and submit an outline (or query), advising us of those points and what he/she intends to include in a feature. We will give him, or her, a prompt reply." Length: 2,500 words maximum. Pay based on quality and timeliness of feature. Pays the expenses of writers on assignment.
Photos: 5x7 b&w glossies or 35mm color transparencies purchased with mss.

MODERN TIRE DEALER, 110 N. Miller Rd., Box 5417, Akron OH 44313. (216)867-4401. Editor: Lloyd Stoyer. 15-20% freelance written. Prefers to work with published/established writers, and works with a small number of new/unpublished writers each year. For independent tire dealers. Monthly tabloid, plus 2 special emphasis issue magazines. Published 14 times annually. Buys all rights. Photocopied submissions OK. Computer printout submissions acceptable. Reports in 1 month. Publishes ms an average of 2 months after acceptance. Writer's guidelines for #10 SASE.
Nonfiction: "How independent tire dealers sell tires, accessories and allied services such as brakes, wheel alignment, shocks and mufflers. The emphasis is on merchandising and management. We prefer the writer to zero in on some specific area of interest; avoid shotgun approach." Query. Length: 1,500 words. Pays $300 and up. Sometimes pays the expenses of writers on assignment.
Photos: 8x10, 4x5, 5x7 b&w glossy prints purchased with mss.

Tips: "Changes in the competitive situation among tire manufacturers and/or distributors will affect the types of freelance material we buy in 1989. We want articles for or about tire dealers, not generic articles adapted for our publiction."

O AND A MARKETING NEWS, Box 765, LaCanada CA 91011. (213)790-6554. Editor: Don McAnally. For "service station dealers, garagemen, TBA (tires, batteries, accessories) people and oil company marketing management." Bimonthly. 5% freelance written. Circ. 9,500. Not copyrighted. Pays on publication. Buys first rights only. Reports in 1 week.
Nonfiction: "Straight news material; management, service and merchandising applications; emphasis on news about or affecting markets and marketers *within the publication's geographic area of the 11 Western states.* No restrictions on style or slant. We could use straight news of our industry from some Western cities, notably Phoenix, Seattle, and Salt Lake City. Query with a letter that gives a capsule treatment of what the story is about." Buys 25 mss/year. Length: maximum 1,000 words. Pays $1.25/column inch (about 2½¢ a word).
Photos: Photos purchased with or without mss; captions required. No cartoons. Pays $5.

‡OVERDRIVE, The Publication of the Independent Truckers, Randall Publishing Co./Overdrive, Inc., Box 3187, Tuscaloosa AL 35403. (205)349-2990. Editor: Mike Brown. Managing Editor: John Cargile. 50% freelance written. Monthly magazine for independent truckers. Circ. 90,000. Pays on acceptance. Publishes ms an average of 2 months after acceptance. Byline given. 10% kill fee. Buys first North American serial rights. Computer printout submissions OK; prefers letter-quality. Reports in 2 weeks on queries; 1 month on mss. Sample copy for 9x12 SAE.
Nonfiction: Essays, expose, how-to (truck maintainance and operation), interview/profile (successful independent truckers), new product, personal experience, photo feature, technical. All must be related to independent trucker interest. Buys 60+ mss/year. Query with or without published clips or send complete ms. Length: 500-2,000 words. Pays $100-600 for assigned articles; $50-500 for unsolicited articles.
Photos: Send photos with submission. Reviews transparencies and 5x7 prints. Offers $25-50 per photo. Identification of subjects required. Buys one-time rights.
Columns/Departments: Safety: (tips for operating trucks safely) 500-750 words. Buys 3-4 mss/year. Pays $50-150.
Fiction: Humorous (short pieces with trucking theme), slice-of-life vignettes (illustrate a lesson about trucking business, safety, driving, etc.). Buys 6 mss/year. Send complete ms. Length: 500-1,500 words. Pays $50-200.
Fillers: Phil Willis, fillers editor. Anecdotes, newsbreaks, short humor. Length: 25-250 words. Pays $5-50.
Tips: "Talk to independent truckers. Develop a good knowledge of their concerns as small business owners, truck drivers and individuals. We prefer articles that quote experts, people in the industry and truckers to first-person expositions on a subject. Get straight facts. Look for good material on truck safety, on effects of government regulations, and on rates and business realtionships between independent truckers, brokers, carriers and shippers."

REFRIGERATED TRANSPORTER, Tunnell Publications, 1602 Harold St., Houston TX 77006. (713)523-8124. Editor: Gary Macklin. 5% freelance written. Monthly. Byline given. Pays on publication. Reports in 1 month. Computer printout submissions acceptable; prefers letter-quality.
Nonfiction: "Articles on fleet management and maintenance of vehicles, especially the refrigerated van and the refrigerating unit, shop tips, loading or handling systems—especially for frozen or refrigerated cargo, new equipment specifications, conversions of equipment for better handling or more efficient operations. Prefers articles with illustrations obtained from fleets operating refrigerated trucks or trailers." Pays variable rate, approximately $100 per printed page.

RENEWS, Kona Communications, Inc., Suite 300, 707 Lake Cook Rd., Deerfield IL 60015. (312)498-3180. Editor: Terry Haller. Managing Editor: Denise L. Rondini. 40% freelance written. Works with a small number of new/unpublished writers each year. Magazine published 12 times/year covering automotive engine/parts rebuilding. Emphasizes technology and management issues affecting automotive rebuilders. Circ. 21,000. Pays on publication. Publishes ms an average of 2 months after acceptance. Byline sometimes given. Buys first rights. Photocopied submissions OK. Computer printout submissions acceptable; prefers letter-quality. Reports in 1 month.
Nonfiction: Interview/profile, new product, photo feature and technical. "No articles that are too general to be helpful to our readers." Buys 8 mss/year. Query. Length: 1,000-2,500 words. Pays $75-300. Sometimes pays the expenses of writers on assignment.
Photos: Send photos with submission. Reviews contact sheets, transparencies and prints. Offers no additional payment for photos accepted with ms. Captions, model releases and identification of subjects required. Buys one-time rights.
Tips: "A strong automotive technical background or a special expertise in small business management is helpful. Technical and business management sections are most open to freelancers. Most of our writers are thoroughly experienced in the subject they write on. It is difficult for a 'generalist' to write for our audience."

THE SUCCESSFUL DEALER, Kona-Cal, Inc., 707 Lake Cook Rd., Deerfield IL 60015. (312)498-3180. Editor: Terry Haller. Managing Editor: Denise Rondini. 30% freelance written. "We will consider material from both established writers and new ones." Magazine published 6 times/year covering dealership management of medium and heavy duty trucks, construction equipment, forklift trucks, diesel engines and truck trailers. Circ. 19,000. Pays on publication. Byline sometimes given. Buys first serial rights only. Simultaneous queries, and simultaneous and photocopied submissions OK. Computer printout submissions acceptable; prefers letter-quality. Reports in 2 weeks. Publication date "depends on the article; some are contracted for a specific issue, others on an as need basis."

Nonfiction: How-to (solve problems within the dealership); interview/profile (concentrating on business, not personality); new product (exceptional only); opinion (by readers—those in industry); personal experience (of readers); photo feature (of major events); and technical (vehicle componentry). Special issues include: March-April: American Truck Dealer Convention; September-October: Parts and Service. Query. Length: open. Pays $75/page. Sometimes pays the expenses of writers on assignment.

Tips: "Phone first, then follow up with a detailed explanation of the proposed article. Allow two weeks for our response. Articles should be based on real problems/solutions encountered by truck or heavy equipment dealership personnel. We are *not* interested in general management tips."

TOW-AGE, Kruza Kaleidoscopix, Inc., Box 389, Franklin MA 02038. Editor: J. Kruza. For readers who run their own towing service business. 5% freelance written. Prefers to work with published/established writers, and works with a small number of new/unpublished writers each year. Published every 6 weeks. Circ. 18,000. Buys all rights; usually reassigns rights. Buys about 18 mss/year. Pays on acceptance. Publishes ms an average of 1 month after acceptance. Photocopied and simultaneous submissions OK. Reports in 1-4 weeks. Query for electronic submissions. Computer printout submissions acceptable. Sample copy $3; writer's guidelines for SAE.

Nonfiction: Articles on business, legal and technical information for the towing industry. "Light reading material; short, with punch." Informational, how-to, personal, interview and profile. Query or submit complete ms. Length: 200-800 words. Pays $50-150. Spot news and successful business operations. Length: 100-800 words. Technical articles. Length: 400-1,000 words. Pays expenses of writers on assignment.

Photos: Buys up to 8x10 b&w photos purchased with or without mss, or on assignment. Pays $25 for first photo; $10 for each additional photo in series. Captions required.

TRUCKERS/USA, Randall Publishing Co., Box 2029, Tuscaloosa AL 35403. (205)349-2990. Editor: Phil Willis. 20-30% freelance written. Eager to work with new/unpublished writers. Weekly tabloid for long-haul truck drivers and trucker service industry. "Most of our readers are long-haul truckers. We want stories about these drivers, their trucks, lifestyle and people who serve them, such as truck stops. We want upbeat stories." Circ. 15,000. Pays on publication. Byline given. Offers 100% kill fee. Not copyrighted. Buys first serial rights, one-time rights, second serial (reprint) rights or simultaneous rights. Simultaneous and previously published (updated) submissions OK. Computer printout submissions acceptable; prefers letter-quality. Free sample copy; writer's guidelines for #10 SAE with 2 first class stamps.

Nonfiction: General interest (with trucker angle); historical/nostalgic (with trucker angle); humor (with trucker angle); interview/profile (with truckers); personal experience (with truckers); technical (re heavy-duty trucks). Buys 100 mss/year. Send complete ms. Length: 250-1,000 words. Pays $10-50.

Photos: Send photos with query or ms. Accepts b&w or color prints; commercially processed accepted if sharp quality. Pays $5. Identification of subjects required.

Tips: "Truckers like to read about other truckers, and people with whom truckers are in frequent contact—truckstop workers, state police, etc. We're looking for localized stories about long-haul truckers. Nothing is too local if it's interesting. We encourage multiple submissions, preferably with art. Submitting art with copy gives a definite edge. We emphasize subject matter rather than writing style, so any of the articles published can be idea leads to similar stories. We increasingly are running longer articles, which also increases our need for shorter articles to maintain our tabloid newspaper format. Editoral calender available as a guide to monthly needs."

‡VEHICLE LEASING TODAY, National Vehicle Leasing Assocation, Suite 225, 3710 S. Robertson, Box 2349, Culver City CA 90232. (213)838-3170. Editor: Michael Stringer. 25% freelance written. A bimonthly magazine on vehicle leasing. "We cover critical issues for vehicle lessors, financial lending institutions, and computer software vendors with lessor programs." Circ. 6,000. Pays on publication. Publishes ms an average of 2 months after acceptance. Byline given. Negotiable kill fee. Buys one-time rights. Submit seasonal/holiday material 2 months in advance. Photocopied and previously published submissions OK. Computer printout submissions OK; no dot-matrix. Sample copy $5; free writer's guidelines.

Nonfiction: How-to (anything relating to a vehicle lessor business), interview/profile, new product, technical. Buys 10 mss/year. Query. Length: 1,000-2,000 words. Pays $50-250 for assigned articles; $50-200 for unsolicited articles. Sometimes pays expenses of writers on assignment.

Photos: State availability of photos with submission. Reviews 5x7 prints. Offers no additional payment for

photos accepted with ms. Model releases required. Buys one-time rights.
Columns/Departments: Financial Institutions, Lessor Issues, 500-1,000 words; New Products and Services, 500 words. Buys 3 mss/year. Send complete ms. Length: 300-1,000 words. Pays $25-100.

WARD'S AUTO WORLD, 28 W. Adams, Detroit MI 48226. (313)962-4433. Editor-in-Chief: David C. Smith. Editor: James W. Bush. Managing Editor: Burt Stoddard. 10% freelance written. Prefers to work with published/established writers; works with a small number of new/unpublished writers each year. For top and middle management in all phases of auto industry. Also includes heavy-duty vehicle coverage. Monthly magazine. Circ. 85,000. Pays on publication. Pay varies for kill fee. Byline given. Buys all rights. Phone queries OK. Submit seasonal/holiday material 1 month in advance. Query for electronic submissions. Computer printout submissions acceptable; check first before submitting dot-matrix. Reports in 2 weeks. Publishes ms an average of 1 month after acceptance. Free sample copy and writer's guidelines.
Nonfiction: Expose, general interest, international automotive news, historical, humor, interview, new product, photo feature and technical. Few consumer type articles. No "nostalgia or personal history type stories (like 'My Favorite Car')." Buys 4-8 mss/year. Query. Length: 700-5,000 words. Pays $100-600. Sometimes pays the expenses of writers on assignment.
Photos: "We're heavy on graphics." Submit photo material with query. Pay varies for 8x10 b&w prints or color transparencies. Captions required. Buys one-time rights.
Tips: "Don't send poetry, how-to and 'My Favorite Car' stuff. It doesn't stand a chance. This is a business newsmagazine and operates on a news basis just like any other newsmagazine. We like solid, logical, well-written pieces with *all* holes filled."

Aviation and Space

In this section are journals for aviation business executives, airport operators and aviation technicians. Publications for professional and private pilots can be found in the Consumer Aviation section.

AIRPORT SERVICES MANAGEMENT, Lakewood Publications, 50 S. 9th St., Minneapolis MN 55402. (612)333-0471. Managing Editor: Karl Bremer. 33% freelance written. Emphasizes management of airports, airlines and airport-based businesses. Monthly magazine. Circ. 20,000. Pays on acceptance. Publishes ms an average of 3 months after acceptance. Buys one-time rights, exclusive in our industry. Byline given. Phone queries OK. Submit seasonal/holiday material 3 months in advance. Photocopied submissions OK but must be industry-exclusive. Computer printout submissions acceptable; prefers letter-quality. Reports in 1 month. Free sample copy and writer's guidelines.
Nonfiction: How-to (manage an airport, aviation service company or airline; work with local governments, etc.); interview (with a successful operator); and technical (how to manage a maintenance shop, snow removal operations, bird control, security operations). "No flying, no airport nostalgia or product puff pieces. We don't want pieces on how one company's product solved everyone's problem (how one airport or aviation business solved its problem with a certain type of product is okay). No descriptions of airport construction projects (down to the square footage in the new restrooms) that don't discuss applications for other airports. Plain 'how-to' story lines, please." Buys 40-50 mss/year, "but at least half are short (250-750 words) items for inclusion in one of our monthly departments." Query. Length: 250-2,500 words. Pays $50-100 for most department articles, $200-450 for features.
Photos: State availability of photos with query. Payment for photos is included in total purchase price. Uses b&w photos, charts and line drawings.
Tips: "Writing style should be lively, informal and straightforward, but the *subject matter* must be as functional and as down-to-earth as possible. Trade magazines are *business* magazines that must help readers do their jobs better. Frequent mistakes are using industry vendors/suppliers rather than users and industry officials as *sources*, especially in endorsing products or approaches, and directing articles to pilots or aviation consumers rather than to our specialized audience of aviation business managers and airport managers."

‡FBO, General Aviation's Source for Management, Marketing, Merchandising News, Johnson Hill press, 1233 Janesville Ave., Fort Atkinson WI 53538. (414)563-6388. Editor: John F. Infanger. 10% freelance written. A bimonthly magazine covering business concerns of general aviation retailers. "*FBO* exclusively communicates successful business practices/ideas/concepts to general aviation retailers (fixed base operators)." Circ. 18,000. Pays on acceptance. Byline given. Buys first rights. Query for electronic submission. Computer printout submissions OK; prefers letter-quality. Reports in 1 week on queries; 2 weeks on mss. Free sample copy.

Nonfiction: Interview/profile. No technical, pilot-oriented, air carrier-related or experimental aircraft articles. Buys 6 mss/year. Query. Length: 1,500 maximum words. Pays $400 maximum for assigned articles. Pays the expenses of writers on assignment.

Photos: State availability of photos with submission. Reviews contact sheets, negatives, transparencies and prints. Offers no additional payment for photos accepted with ms. Captions, model releases and identification of subjects required. Buys one-time rights.

JET CARGO NEWS, For Air Shipping Decision-Makers, Box 920952, #398, Houston TX 77292-0952. (713)681-4760. Editor: Pat Chandler. 50% freelance written. Works with a small number of new/unpublished writers each year. Designed to serve international industry concerned with moving goods by air. "It brings to shippers and manufacturers spot news of airline and aircraft development, air routes, shipping techniques, innovations and rates." Monthly. Circ. 25,000. Buys all rights. Buys up to 50 mss/year. Pays on publication. Publishes ms an average of 2 months after acceptance. No photocopied or simultaneous submissions. Query for electronic submissions. Computer printout submissions acceptable; prefers letter-quality. Submit seasonal material 1 month in advance. Reports in 1 month if postage is included. Submit complete ms. Sample copy for 10x13 SAE with 5 first class stamps.

Nonfiction: "Direct efforts to the shipper. Tell him about airline service, freight forwarder operations, innovations within the industry, new products, aircraft, packaging, material handling, hazardous materials, computerization of shipping, and pertinent news to the industry. Use a tight newspaper format. The writer must know marketing." Buys informational articles, case studies, how-tos, interviews and coverage of successful business operations. Length: 1,500 words maximum. Pays $4/inch. Sometimes pays the expenses of writers on assignment.

Photos: 8x10 b&w glossy prints purchased with and without mss; captions required. Pays $10.

Tips: A frequent mistake is missing target readers and their interests. With short articles and fillers the writer exhibits his/her initiative. "We're moving toward a news orientation in 1988. We hope to generate more case studies of successful shipping solutions and pay a 25 percent premium rate for them. We also hope to see more wrap-ups from a variety of contributors."

Beverages and Bottling

Manufacturers, distributors and retailers of soft drinks and alcoholic beverages read these publications. Publications for bar and tavern operators and managers of restaurants are classified in the Hotels, Motels, Clubs, Resorts and Restaurants category.

BEVERAGE RETAILER WEEKLY, 1661 Rt. 23, Wayne NJ 07470. (201)694-7600. Managing Editor: Jean Marie McKowen. 5% freelance written. Works with a small number of new/unpublished writers each year. Weekly tabloid covering the liquor industry. "We specifically serve retailers, providing news on legal changes, marketing happenings, etc." Circ. 36,000. Pays on publication. Publishes ms an average of 1 month after acceptance. Byline given. Buys one-time rights. Submit seasonal/holiday material 6 weeks in advance. Computer printout submissions acceptable; prefers letter-quality.

Nonfiction: Expose, interview/profile, new product, legislative update, wine, beer, liquor trends, photo feature. Send complete ms. "We would like to receive photos, maps, graphs and charts to accompany the story." Length: 500-2,500 words. Pays $100-200.

Photos: Pays $10-20 for b&w prints. Reviews b&w contact sheets. Identification of subjects required.

Columns/Departments: All About Wine, Marketing Trends. Send complete ms. Length: 500-2,500 words. Pays $100-200.

Tips: "Changes in legislative issues affecting the alcoholic beverage industry will affect the type of stories we buy."

‡**LA BARRIQUE**, Kylix Media Inc.. Suite 414, 5165 Sherbrooke St. W., Montreal H4A IT6 Canada. (514)481-5892. Editor: Nicole Barette-Ryan. 20% freelance written. A magazine on wine published 7 times/year. "The magazine, *written in French*, covers wines of the world specially written for the province of Quebec consumers and restaurant trade. It covers wine books, restaurants, vintage reports and European suppliers." Pays on publication. Publishes ms an average of 2 months after acceptance. Byline given. Buys first North American serial rights. Submit seasonal/holiday material 6 months in advance. Simultaneous submissions OK. Query for electronic submissions. Computer printout submissions OK; no dot-matrix.

Reports in 6 weeks on queries.

Nonfiction: General interest, how-to, humor, interview/profile, new product, opinion and travel. Length: 500-1,500 words. Pays $25-100 for unsolicited articles.

Photos: Send photos with submission. Reviews transparencies and prints. Offers $25-100 per photo. Identifiction of subjects required. Buys one-time rights.

MID-CONTINENT BOTTLER, 10741 El Monte, Overland Park KS 66207. (913)341-0020. Publisher: Floyd E. Sageser. 5% freelance written. Prefers to work with published/established writers, and works with a small number of new/unpublished writers each year. For "soft drink bottlers in the 20-state Midwestern area." Bimonthly. Not copyrighted. Pays on acceptance. Publishes ms an average of 2 months after acceptance. Buys first rights only. Reports "immediately." Computer printout submissions acceptable. Sample copy with 4 first class stamps; guidelines with SASE.

Nonfiction: "Items of specific soft drink bottler interest with special emphasis on sales and merchandising techniques. Feature style desired." Buys 2-3 mss/year. Length: 2,000 words. Pays $15-$100. Sometimes pays the expenses of writers on assignment.

Photos: Photos purchased with mss.

TEA & COFFEE TRADE JOURNAL, Lockwood Book Publishing Co., 130 W. 42nd St., New York NY 10036. (212)661-5980. Editor: Jane Phillips McCabe. 50% freelance written. Prefers to work with published/established writers. A monthly magazine covering the international coffee and tea market. "Tea and coffee trends are analyzed; transportation problems, new equipment for plants and packaging are featured." Circ. approximately 10,000. Pays on publication. Publishes ms an average of 2 months after acceptance. Byline given. Makes work-for-hire assignments. Submit seasonal/holiday material 1 month in advance. Simultaneous submissions OK. Computer printout submissions acceptable; no dot-matrix. Free sample copy.

Nonfiction: Exposé, historical/nostalgic, interview/profile, new product, photo feature and technical. Special issue includes the Coffee Market Forecast and Review (January). "No consumer related submissions. I'm only interested in the trade." Buys 60 mss/year. Query. Length: 750-1,500 words. Pays $5/published inch.

Photos: State availability of photos with submission. Reviews contact sheets, negatives, transparencies and prints. Pays $5/published inch. Captions and identification of subjects required. Buys one-time rights.

Columns/Departments: Office Coffee Service (vending coffee industry/office coffee); Specialties (gourmet trends); and Transportation (shipping lines). Buys 36 mss/year. Query. Pays $5/published inch.

VINEYARD & WINERY MANAGEMENT, 103 Third St., Box 231, Watkins Glen NY 14891. (607)535-7133. Editor: J. William Moffett. 80% freelance written. A bimonthly trade journal on the management of winemaking and grape growing. Circ. 4,500. Pays on publication. Byline given. Buys first North American serial rights and occasionally simultaneous rights. Photocopied submissions OK. Query for electronic submissions (preferred). Reports in 3 weeks on queries; 1 month on mss. Free sample copy; writer's guidelines for #10 SAE.

Nonfiction: How-to, interview/profile and technical. Buys 30 mss/year. Query. Length: 300-5,000 words. Pays $20-750 for assigned articles; pays $20-500 for unsolicited articles. Pays expenses of writers on assignment.

Photos: State availability of photos with submission. Reviews contact sheets, negatives and transparencies. Identification of subjects required. "Black and white often purchased for $10 each 8x10 to accompany story material; 35mm and/or 4x5 transparencies for cover sheets at $1.50 each; 6 per year of vineyard and/or winery scene related to story. Query."

Fiction: Occasional short, humorous fiction related to vineyard/winery operation.

Tips: "We're looking for long term relationships with authors who know the business and write well."

WINES & VINES, 1800 Lincoln Ave., San Rafael CA 94901. Editor: Philip E. Hiaring. 10-20% freelance written. Works with a small number of new/unpublished writers each year. For everyone concerned with the grape and wine industry including winemakers, wine merchants, growers, suppliers, consumers, etc. Monthly magazine. Circ. 4,500. Buy first North American serial rights or simultaneous rights. Pays on acceptance. Publishes ms an average of 3 months after acceptance. Submit special material (water, January; vineyard, February; Man-of-the-Year, March; Brandy, April; export-import, May; enological, June; statistical, July; merchandising, August; marketing, September; equipment and supplies, November; champagne, December) 3 months in advance. Computer printout submissions OK; no dot-matrix. Reports in 2 weeks. Sample copy for 10x12 SASE.

Nonfiction: Articles of interest to the trade. "These could be on grape growing in unusual areas; new winemaking techniques; wine marketing, retailing, etc." Interview, historical, spot news, merchandising techniques and technical. No stories with a strong consumer orientation as against trade orientation. Author should know the subject matter, i.e., know proper grape growing/winemaking terminology. Buys 3-4 ms/year. Query. Length: 1,000-2,500 words. Pays 5¢/word. Sometimes pays the expenses of writers on assignment.

Photos: Pays $10 for 4x5 or 8x10 b&w photos purchased with mss. Captions required.

Tips: "Ours is a trade magazine for professionals. Therefore, we do not use 'gee-whiz' wine articles."

Book and Bookstore

Publications for book trade professionals from publishers to bookstore operators are found in this section. Journals for professional writers are classified in the Journalism and Writing category.

AB BOOKMAN'S WEEKLY, Box AB, Clifton NJ 07015. (201)772-0020. Editor-in-Chief: Jacob L. Chernofsky. Weekly magazine; 160 pages. For professional and specialist booksellers, acquisitions and academic librarians, book publishers, book collectors, bibliographers, historians, etc. Circ. 8,500. Pays on publication. Byline given. Buys all rights. Phone queries OK. Submit seasonal or holiday material 2-3 months in advance. Simultaneous and photocopied submissions OK. Reports in 1 month. Sample copy $10.
Nonfiction: How-to (for professional booksellers); historical (related to books or book trade or printing or publishing); personal experiences; nostalgia; interviews and profiles. Query. Length: 2,500 words minimum. Pays $60 minimum.
Photos: Photos used with mss.

THE FEMINIST BOOKSTORE NEWS, Box 882554, San Francisco CA 94188. (415)626-1556. Editor: Carol Seajay. Managing Editor: Christine Chia. 10% freelance written. Works with a small number of new/unpublished writers each year. A bimonthly magazine covering feminist books and the women-in-print industry. *"Feminist Bookstore News"* covers 'everything of interest' to the feminist bookstores, publishers and periodicals, books of interest to feminist bookstores, and provides an overview of feminist publishing by mainstream publishers." Circ. 450. Pays on publication. Publishes ms an average of 2 months after acceptance. Byline sometimes given. Buys one-time rights. Simultaneous and photocopied submissions OK. Computer printout submissions acceptable; prefers letter-quality. Reports in 3 weeks. Sample copy $5.
Nonfiction: Essays, exposé, how-to (run a bookstore); new product; opinion; and personal experience (in feminist book trade only). Special issues include Sidelines issue (July) and University Press issue (fall). No submissions that do not directly apply to the feminist book trade. Query with or without published clips, or send complete ms. Length: 250-2,000 words. Pays $10-25; may pay in copies when appropriate.
Photos: State availability of photos with submission. Model release and identification of subjects required. Buys one-time rights.
Fillers: Anecdotes, facts, newsbreaks and short humor. Length: 100-400 words. Pays $5-15.
Tips: "Have several years experience in the feminist book industry. We publish very little by anyone else."

THE HORN BOOK MAGAZINE, The Horn Book, Inc., 31 St. James Ave., Boston MA 02116. (617)482-5198. Editor: Anita Silvey. 25% freelance written. Prefers to work with published/established writers. Bimonthly magazine covering children's literature for librarians, booksellers, professors, and students of children's literature. Circ. 22,000. Pays on publication. Publishes ms an average of 4 months after acceptance. Byline given. Buys one-time rights. Submit seasonal/holiday material 6 months in advance. Simultaneous queries, and simultaneous and photocopied submissions OK. Computer printout submissions acceptable; no dot-matrix. Reports in 6 weeks on queries; 2 months on mss. Free sample copy; writer's guidelines for SAE with 1 first class stamp.
Nonfiction: Interview/profile (children's book authors and illustrators). Buys 20 mss/year. Query or send complete ms. Length: 1,000-2,800 words. Pays $25-250.
Tips: "Writers have a better chance of breaking in to our publication with a query letter on a specific article they want to write."

PUBLISHERS WEEKLY, 249 W. 17th St., New York NY 10011. (212)463-6758. Editor-in-Chief: John F. Baker. Weekly. Buys first North American serial rights. Pays on publication. Computer printout submissions acceptable; prefers letter-quality. Reports "in several weeks."
Nonfiction: "We rarely use unsolicited manuscripts because of our highly specialized audience and their professional interests, but we can sometimes use news items about publishers, publishing projects, bookstores and other subjects relating to books. We will be paying increasing attention to electronic publishing." No pieces about writers or word processors. Payment negotiable; generally $150/printed page.
Photos: Photos occasionally purchased with and without mss.

WESTERN PUBLISHER, A Trade Journal, WP, Inc., Box 591012, Golden Gate Station, San Francisco CA 94159. (415)661-7964. Publisher: Tony D'Arpino. Editor: Paula von Lowenfeldt. 25% freelance written.

Monthly tabloid covering publishing and book industry. Audience includes publishers, booksellers, and librarians in Western United States and Pacific Rim nations. Circ. 10,000. Pays on publication. Publishes ms an average of 1 month after acceptance. Byline given. Kill fee negotiable. Buys one-time rights. Submit seasonal/holiday material 3 months in advance; calendar: 6 months. Simultaneous queries, and simultaneous, photocopied, and previously published submissions OK. Computer printout submissions acceptable; prefers letter-quality. Reports in 1 week. Sample copy $2.

Nonfiction: Book excerpts (of industry interest), general interest, historical, how-to, interview/profile, new product, opinion, personal experience, photo feature, technical, and short reviews of just published books. No reviews over 500 words. Buys 100 mss/year. Query with or without published clips or send complete ms. Length: open. Pays negotiable rates.

Tips: "The area most open to freelancers is Western Book Round Up (review listings). A freelancer can best break in to our publication with short reviews of forthcoming books, 200-500 words; 250 words, preferred."

—— *Brick, Glass and Ceramics*

These publications are read by manufacturers, dealers and managers of brick, glass and ceramic retail businesses. Other publications related to glass and ceramics are listed in the Consumer Art and Architecture and Consumer Hobby and Craft sections.

AMERICAN GLASS REVIEW, Box 2147, Clifton NJ 07015. (201)779-1600. Editor-in-Chief: Donald Doctorow. 10% freelance written. Monthly magazine. Pays on publication. Byline given. Phone queries OK. Buys all rights. Submit seasonal/holiday material 2 months in advance of issue date. Reports in 2-3 weeks. Free sample copy and writer's guidelines; mention *Writer's Market* in request.

Nonfiction: Glass plant and glass manufacturing articles. Buys 3-4 mss/year. Query. Length: 1,500-3,000 words. Pays $100.

Photos: State availability of photos with query. No additional payment for b&w contact sheets. Captions preferred. Buys one-time rights.

CERAMIC SCOPE, 3632 Ashworth North, Seattle WA 98103. (206)547-7611. Editor: Michael Scott. Bimonthly magazine covering hobby ceramics business. For "ceramic studio owners and teachers operating out of homes as well as storefronts, who have a love for ceramics but meager business education." Also read by distributors, dealers and supervisors of ceramic programs in institutions. Circ. 8,000. Pays on publication. Byline given unless it is a round-up story with any number of sources. Submit seasonal/holiday material 5 months in advance. Computer printout submissions acceptable. Reports in 2 weeks. Sample copy $1.

Nonfiction: "Articles on operating a small business specifically tailored to the ceramic hobby field; photo feature stories with in-depth information about business practices and methods that contribute to successful studio operation."

Photos: State availability of photos or send photos with ms. Pays $5/4x5 or 5x7 glossy b&w print. Captions required.

GLASS DIGEST, 310 Madison Ave., New York NY 10017. (212)682-7681. Editor: Charles B. Cumpston. Monthly. Buys first rights only. Byline given "only industry people—not freelancers." Pays on publication "or before, if ms held too long." Free sample copy on request. Reports "as soon as possible." Enclose SASE for return of submissions.

Nonfiction: "Items about firms in glass distribution, personnel, plants, etc. Stories about outstanding jobs accomplished—volume of flat glass, storefronts, curtainwalls, auto glass, mirrors, windows (metal), glass doors; special uses and values; and who installed it. Stories about successful glass/metal distributors, dealers and glazing contractors—their methods, promotion work done, advertising and results." Length: 1,000-1,500 words. Pays 7¢/word, "usually more. No interest in bottles, glassware, containers, etc., but leaded and stained glass good."

Photos: B&w photos purchased with mss; "8x10 preferred." Pays $7.50, "usually more."

Tips: "Find a typical dealer case history about a firm operating in such a successful way that its methods can be duplicated by readers everywhere."

GLASS MAGAZINE, For the Architectural and Automotive Glass Industries, National Glass Association, Suite 302, 8200 Greensboro Drive, McLean VA 22102. (703)442-4890. Editor: Patricia Mascari.

For explanation of symbols, see the Key to Symbols and Abbreviations on Page 5.

25% freelance written. Prefers to work with published/established writers; works with a small number of new/unpublished writers each year. A monthly magazine covering the architectural and automotive glass industries for members of the glass and architectural trades. Circ. 16,000. Pays on acceptance. Publishes ms an average of 3-6 months after acceptance. Byline given. Offers varying kill fee. Buys first rights only. Computer printout submissions acceptable; prefers letter-quality. Reports in 1 month. Sample copy for $5 and 10x13 SAE with $2.40 postage; free writer's guidelines.

Nonfiction: Interview/profile (of various glass businesses; profiles of industry people or glass business owners); and technical (about glazing processes). Buys 20 mss/year. Query with published clips. Length: 1,500 words minimum. Pays $200-600. Sometimes pays the expenses of writers on assignment.

Photos: State availability of photos. Reviews b&w and color contact sheets. Pays $15-30 for b&w; $25-75 for color. Identification of subjects required. Buys one-time rights.

Tips: "We are a growing magazine and do not have a large enough staff to do all the writing that will be required. We need more freelancers."

‡**GLASS NEWS**, LJV Corp., Box 7138, Pittsburgh PA 15213. (412)362-5136. Managing Editor: Liz Scott. 5% freelance written. Monthly newspaper covering glass manufacturing, and glass industry news for glass manufacturers, dealers and people involved in the making, buying and selling of glass items and products. Circ. 1,650. Pays on publication. Publishes ms an average of 3 months after acceptance. Makes work-for-hire assignments. Phone queries OK. Submit seasonal material 3 months in advance. Query for electronic submissions. Computer printout submissions acceptable; prefers letter-quality. Reports in 1 month on queries; 2 months on mss. Free sample copy for 9x12 SAE and 3 first class stamps.

Nonfiction: Historical (about glass manufacturers, trademarks and processes); how-to (concerning techniques of glass manufacturers); interview (with glass-related people); profile; new product (glass use or glass); and technical (glass manufacture or use). No glass dealer stories, and rarely glass crafting stories. Buys 3-5 mss/year. Query. Length: 500-10,000 words. Pays $50 minimum.

Photos: State availability of photos. Pays $25 minimum for 8x10 b&w glossy prints. Offers no additional payment for photos accepted with ms. Captions preferred; model release required. Buys one-time rights.

Fillers: Glass manufacturing-related anecdotes, short humor, newsbreaks and puzzles. Buys 5 mss/year. Pays $15 minimum.

Tips: "Get to know a lot about glass, how it is made and new developments."

Building Interiors

Owners, managers and sales personnel of floor covering, wall covering and remodeling businesses read the journals listed in this category. Interior design and architecture publications may be found in the Trade Art, Design and Collectibles category. For journals aimed at other construction trades, see the Construction and Contracting section.

MODERN FLOOR COVERINGS, International Thomson Retail Press, 345 Park Ave. S., New York NY 10010. (212)686-7744. Editor: Michael Karol. 15-20% freelance written. Prefers to work with published/established writers. Monthly tabloid featuring profit-making ideas on floor coverings, for the retail community. Circ. 28,000. Pays on acceptance. Publishes ms an average of 3 months after acceptance. Byline given. Buys first rights only. Makes work-for-hire assignments. Computer printout submissions acceptable; prefers letter-quality. "Better to write first. Send resume and cover letter explaining your qualifications and business writing experience." Writer's guidelines for SASE.

Nonfiction: Interview and features/profiles. Send complete ms. Length: 1,000-10,000 words. Pays $300-500.

Tips: "Polished, professional writing is always a plus. We now have more of a focus on consumer buying habits, the economy, taxes/legislation and products selling at retail—all of course, as they relate to the floor covering specialty retailer."

REMODELING, Hanley-Wood, Inc., Suite 475, 655 15th St. NW, Washington DC 20005. (202)737-0717. Editor: Wendy Jordan. 5% freelance written. A monthly magazine covering residential and light commercial remodeling. "We cover the best new ideas in remodeling design, business, construction and products." Circ. 75,000. Pays on publication. Publishes ms an average of 3 months after acceptance. Byline given. Offers 5¢/word kill fee. Buys first North American serial rights. Photocopied submissions OK. Query for electronic submissions. Computer printout submissions acceptable. Reports in 1 month. Free sample copy and writer's guidelines.

Nonfiction: Interview/profile, new product and technical. Buys 4 mss/year. Query with published clips.

Length: 250-1,000 words. Pays 20¢/word. Sometimes pays the expenses of writers on assignment.
Photos: State availability of photos with submission. Reviews slides, 4x5 transparencies, and 8x10 prints. Offers $25-100/photo. Captions, model releases, and identification of subjects required. Buys one-time rights.
Tips: "The areas of our publication most open to freelancers are news and new product news."

WALLS & CEILINGS, 8602 N. 40th St., Tampa FL 33604. (813)989-9300. Managing Editor: Melissa Wells. 10% freelance written. Prefers to work with published/established writers, and works with a small number of new/unpublished writers each year. For contractors involved in lathing and plastering, drywall, acoustics, fireproofing, curtain walls, movable partitions together with manufacturers, dealers, and architects. Monthly magazine. Circ. 14,000. Pays on publication. Publishes ms an average of 4-6 months after acceptance. Buys first North American serial rights. Byline given. Phone queries OK. Submit seasonal/holiday material 3 months in advance. Query for electronic submissions. Computer printout submissions OK. Reports in 3 weeks. Sample copy for $3 and 9x12 SASE.
Nonfiction: How-to (drywall and plaster construction and business management); and interview. Buys 12 mss/year. Query. Length: 200-1,500 words. Pays $25-125 maximum. Sometimes pays the expenses of writers on assignment.
Photos: State availability of photos with query. Pays $5 for 8x10 b&w prints. Captions required. Buys one-time rights.
Tips: "We would like to receive wall and ceiling finishing features about unique designs and applications in new buildings (from high-rise to fast food restaurants), fireproofing, and acoustical design with photography (b&w and color)."

Business Management

These publications cover trends, general theory and management practices for business owners and top-level business executives. Publications that use similar material but have a less technical slant are listed in the Consumer Business and Finance section. Journals for middle management, including supervisors and office managers, appear in the Management and Supervision section. Those for industrial plant managers are listed under Industrial Operations and under sections for specific industries, such as Machinery and Metal. Publications for office supply store operators are included in the Office Environment and Equipment section.

AWARDS SPECIALIST, DF Publications, 26 Summit St., Box 1230, Brighton MI 48116. (313)227-2614. Editor: James J. Farrell. Managing Editor: Michael J. Davis. 40% freelance written. Prefers to work with published/established writers, and works with a small number of new/unpublished writers each year. A monthly magazine for the recognition and specialty advertising industry, especially awards. "*Awards Specialist* is published for retail business owners and owners involved in the recognition/specialty industry. Our aim is to provide solid, down-to-earth information to help them succeed in business, as well as news and ideas about our industry." Pays on acceptance. Publishes ms an average of 4 months after acceptance. Buys all rights or makes work-for-hire assignments. Submit seasonal/holiday material 6 months in advance. Previously published submissions OK "if we are so informed." Query for electronic submissions. Computer printout submissions OK. Reports in 3 weeks. "Sample copy and writer's guidelines sent to those who send us writing samples or query about an article."
Nonfiction: Historical, how-to, interview/profile, new product, photo feature, technical and business and marketing. "Our readers are becoming more involved in the specialty advertising industry. No vague, general articles which could be aimed at any audience. We prefer to receive a query from writers before reviewing a manuscript. Also, a large number of our freelance articles are given to writers on assignment." Buys 20-30 mss/year. Query with clips ("clips do not have to be published, but should give us an indication of writer's ability"). Length: depends on subject matter. Pays $50-225.
Photos: Send photos with submission. Reviews 8x10 prints. Offers no additional payment for photos accepted with ms, "but we take the photos into consideration when deciding rate of compensation for the assignment." Captions, model releases and identification of subjects required. Buys all rights; "semi-exclusive rights may be purchased, for our industry, depending on subject."
Tips: "The best way to work for *Awards Specialist* is to write to us with information about your background and experience (a resume, if possible), and several samples of your writing. We are most interested in receiving business and marketing articles from freelancers. These would provide solid, down-to-earth information for the smaller business owner. For example, recent articles we have included were on tips for writing good business letters; the proper use of titles for awards; legal and practical considerations of setting up a corporation

vs. a sole proprietorship. Articles should be written in clear, plain English with examples and anecdotes to add interest to the subject matter."

‡**CGA MAGAZINE**, Suite 740, 1176 W. Georgia St., Vancouver, British Columbia V6E 4A2 Canada. (604)669-3555. 10% freelance written. Prefers to work with published/established writers. For accountants and financial managers. Magazine published 12 times/year. Circ. 35,000. Pays on acceptance. Publishes ms an average of 3 months after acceptance. Buys first serial rights. Byline given. Phone queries OK. Simultaneous and photocopied submissions OK. Query for electronic submissions. Computer printout submissions OK; prefers letter quality. Reports in 2-4 weeks. Free sample copy and writer's guidelines.
Nonfiction: "Accounting and financial subjects of interest to highly qualified professional accountants. All submissions must be relevant to Canadian accounting. All material must be of top professional quality, but at the same time written simply and interestingly." How-to, informational, academic, research, and technical. Buys 36 mss/year. Query with outline and estimate of word count. Length: 1,500-5,000 words. Pays $225-1,000.
Illustrations: State availability of photos, tables, charts, or graphs with query. Offers no additional payment for illustrations.
Tips: "Fillers are not used. Frequently writers fail to include the technical information desired by professional accountants and financial managers."

COMMON SENSE, Upstart Publishing Company, 12 Portland St., Dover NH 03820. (603)749-5071. Editor: David Durgin. 25% freelance written. Prefers to work with published/established writers. A monthly newsletter covering small business and personal finance. Pays on acceptance. Publishes ms an average of 2-4 months after acceptance. $25 kill fee. Buys all rights and makes work-for-hire assignments. Does not accept unsolicited mss. Queries welcome. Computer printout submissions acceptable; prefers letter-quality. Reports in 6 weeks. Sample copy and writer's guidelines for 8½x11 SAE and 2 first class stamps.
Nonfiction: How-to, interview/profile and technical. "We are looking for clear, jargon-free information. We often sell our publications in bulk to banks so must avoid subjects and stances that clearly run counter to their interests." No highly technical or pompous language, or politically contentious articles. Buys 15-20 mss/year. Query with published clips. Length: 2,500 words maximum. Pays $250 for assigned articles.
Columns/Departments: Breakthroughs (technological, medical breakthroughs or innovations, new applications for old materials or products; scientific information of interest to the business community). Query with published clips. Length: 100-500 words. Pays $10-50.

COMMUNICATION BRIEFINGS, Encoders, Inc., 140 S. Broadway, Pitman NJ 08071. (609)589-3503. Executive Editor: Frank Grazian. 15% freelance written. Prefers to work with published/established writers. A monthly newsletter covering business communication and business management. "Most readers are in middle and upper management. They comprise public relations professionals, editors of company publications, marketing and advertising managers, fund raisers, directors of associations and foundations, school and college administrators, human resources professionals, and other middle managers who want to communicate better on the job." Circ. 28,000. Pays on acceptance. Publishes ms an average of 2-3 months after acceptance. Byline given sometimes on Bonus Items and on other items if idea originates with the writer. Offers 25% kill fee. Buys one-time rights. Submit seasonal/holiday material 2 months in advance. Previously published submissions OK, "but must be rewritten to conform to our style." Computer printout submissions acceptable; prefers letter-quality. Reports in 1 month. Sample copy and writer's guidelines for #10 SAE and 2 first class stamps.
Nonfiction: "Most articles we buy are of the 'how-to' type. They consist of practical ideas, techniques and advice that readers can use to improve business communication and management. Areas covered: writing, speaking, listening, employee communication, human relations, public relations, interpersonal communication, persuasion, conducting meetings, advertising, marketing, fund raising, telephone techniques, teleconferencing, selling, improving publications, handling conflicts, negotiating, etc. Because half of our subscribers are in the nonprofit sector, articles that appeal to both profit and nonprofit organizations are given top priority." *Short Items*: Articles consisting of one or two brief tips that can stand alone. Length: 40-70 words. *Articles*: A collection of tips or ideas that offer a solution to a communication or management problem or that show a better way to communicate or manage. Examples: "How to produce slogans that work," "The wrong way to criticize employees," "Mistakes to avoid when leading a group discussion," and

For explanation of symbols, see the Key to Symbols and Abbreviations on Page 5.

"5 ways to overcome writer's block." Length: 125-150 words. *Bonus Items:* In-depth pieces that probe one area of communication or management and cover it as thoroughly as possible. Examples: "Producing successful special events," "How to evaluate your newsletter," and "How to write to be understood." Length: 1,300 words. Buys 30-50 mss/year. Pays $15-35 for 40- to 150-word pieces; Bonus Items, $200. Pays the expenses of writers on assignment.

Tips: "Our readers are looking for specific and practical ideas and tips that will help them communicate better both within their organizations and with outside publics. Most ideas are rejected because they are too general or too elementary for our audience. Our style is down-to-earth and terse. We pack a lot of useful information into short articles. Our readers are busy executives and managers who want information dispatched quickly and without embroidery. We omit anecdotes, lengthy quotes and long-winded exposition. The writer has a better chance of breaking in at our publication with short articles and fillers since we buy only six major features (bonus items) a year. We require queries on longer items and bonus items. Writers may submit short tips (40-70 words) without querying. The most frequent mistakes made by writers in completing an article for us are failure to master the style of our publication and to understand our readers' needs."

COMPUTERS IN BANKING, The Computer and Automation Magazine for Bank Management, Dealers Digest Inc., Suite 400, 150 Broadway, New York NY 10038. (212)227-1200. Editor: Brian Tracey. Senior Editor: Sylvia Helm. Approximately 10-30% freelance written. Prefers to work with published/established writers, and works with a small number of new/unpublished writers each year. A monthly magazine covering bank automation and management. "*Computers in Banking* is for senior bank executives and data processing professionals who make business decisions about computer and automation software and equipment. We cover technology, but from an issues and management-oriented perspective." Circ. 42,000. Pays on publication. Publishes ms an average of 2-4 months after acceptance. Byline given for features and some news stories. Offers 25% kill fee. Buys all rights and makes work-for-hire assignments. Photocopied submissions OK. Electronic submissions preferred. Query for electronic submissions. Computer printout submissions acceptable. Sample copy for 8½x11 SAE; free writer's guidelines.

Nonfiction: How-to, interview/profile, new product, technical and event coverage. Special issues are staff written. "No one-sided, vendor-oriented pieces. We are a user-oriented magazine." Buys 24-30 mss/year. Query with published clips. Length: 2,500-4,000 words. Pays $200 for news stories, $1,000 for features. Usually pays the expenses of writers on assignment.

Photos: Send photos with submission. Reviews transparencies and any size b&w prints. Offers no additional payment for photos accepted with ms. Identification of subjects required.

Columns/Departments: Case History (one-user, one-vendor, problem/solution), 1,200-2,000 words. Buys 20 mss/year. Query with published clips. Pays $200-400. "We need short news bits for 'upfront' section, which tries to cover installations and product announcements before the official press releases."

Tips: "Writers must have a working knowledge of the computer industry and a good understanding of banking and financial matters. Our standards are very high. Writers should be willing to fill holes, answer specific questions and care about seemingly little details like what a bank paid for a computer system and when it was installed or tested. Publication is national and occasionally international, so focus must be broad. However, we are always looking for regional correspondents. The areas of our publication most open to freelancers are features and short news stories for 'Update' section."

‡FINANCIAL EXECUTIVE, (formerly *FE*), Financial Executives Institute, 10 Madison Ave., Morriston NJ 07960. Editor: Robert A. Parker. 15% freelance written. A bimonthly magazine for corporate financial management. "*Financial Executive* is published for senior financial executives of major corporations and explores corporate accounting and treasury related issues without being anti-business." Circ. 19,000. Pays following acceptance. Byline given. Buys first North American serial rights. Reports in 1 week on queries; 2 weeks on mss. Sample copy $5; writer's guidelines for #10 SASE.

Nonfiction: Analysis, based on interviews, of accounting, finance, and tax developments of interest to financial executives. Buys 6 mss/year. Query with published clips; no unsolicited mss. Length: 1,500-3,000. Pays $500-1,000.

Tips: "Most article ideas come from editors, so the query approach is best. We use business or financial articles that follow a Wall Street Journal approach—a fresh idea, with its significance (to financial executives), quotes, anecdotes, and an interpretation or evaluation. Our content will follow developments in market volatility, M&A trend, regulatory changes, tax legislation, Congressional hearings/legislation, re business and financial reporting. We seek to identify business writers with top experience in different locations. We have very high journalistic standards."

HIGH TECHNOLOGY BUSINESS, Infotechnology Publishing, Inc. 214 Lewis Wharf, Boston MA 02110. (617)723-6611. Editor: Mary H. Frakes. 30-40% freelance written. A monthly magazine covering businesses in high-tech. "Stories should be aimed at a business person who wants to profit personally or corporately from knowing the latest developments in high-tech and how those developments will help or hurt specific companies or industries financially. Covers broad range of technologies." Circ. 260,000. Publishes ms an average of 3 months after acceptance. Sometimes byline given. Buys all rights. Simultaneous submissions OK. Query for electronic submissions. Computer printout submissions OK; prefers letter-quality. Reports in 5 weeks.

Nonfiction: Essays and general interest. No articles of a strictly technical nature. Buys 36 mss/year. Query with published clips. Length: 100-2,500 words. Pays $75-2,000. Sometimes pays the expenses of writers on assignment. State availability of photos with submission. Offers no additional payment for photos accepted with ms.

Columns/Departments: New Developments (high-tech developments of interest to business community), 50-200 words; Personal Technology (new products in high-tech for use by individuals), 50-200 words; Legal (legal or regulatory trends or decisions, involving high-tech, that could affect businesses), 750 words. Buys 36 mss/year. Send complete ms. Length: 50-750 words. Pays $25-400.

Tips: "Read the magazine. Try to think what cutting-edge technologies are important to an investor, CEO or venture capitalist. Stories should have business focus rather than dealing with technology abstractly. No how-tos, please, or stories about the troubles you had getting used to your computer."

‡LOOKING FIT, The Magazine for Health Conscious Tanning & Toning Centers, Virgo Publishing, Inc.. Box C-5400, Scottsdale AZ 85261. (602)483-0014. Managing Editor: Andrew McGavin. Editorial Director: Brent Diamond. 15% freelance written. A monthly magazine on issues related to the indoors tanning and toning industries. "*Looking Fit* is interested in material dealing with any aspect of operating a tanning or toning salon. Preferred style is light whenever subject matter doesn't preclude it. Technical material should be written in a manner interesting and intelligible to the average salon operator." Circ. 28,000. Pays 1 month after publication. Byline given. Buys all rights. Submit seasonal/holiday material 3 months in advance. Simultaneous submissions OK. Query for electronic submissions. Computer printout submissions OK. Reports in 2 weeks. Sample copy and writer's guidelines for 10x13 SAE and $2.50.

Nonfiction: How-to (operational—how to choose a location, buy equipment, etc.), humor, new product and technical. Buys 20-30 mss/year. Query with or without published clips, or send complete ms. Length: 1,500-9,000 words. Pays $50-175 for assigned articles. Pays $50-150 for unsolicited articles.

Photos: Send photos with submission. Reviews contact sheets, transparencies (2x4) and prints (2x4). Offers no additional payment for photos accepted with ms. Model releases and identification of subjects required.

Columns/Departments: Clublines (profiles of unusual/successful salons), 750-1,500 words; Profiles (profiles of unusual/successful manufacturers/distributors), 1,000-2,500 words. Buys 5-10 mss/year. Query or send complete ms. Length: 750-2,500 words. Pays $25-75.

Tips: "The best way to break in is to call with a good story idea. If it's workable, we'll have the writer do it. Unsolicited manuscripts are welcome, but may not fit into the magazine's goals. We're happy to offer direction or style angles by phone. In general, *Looking Fit* follows AP style. Full-length (1,500-7,500 words) features are what we most often buy. For best results, contact us with story ideas and we can supply the names and numbers of industry contacts."

MAY TRENDS, George S. May International Company. 303 S. Northwest Hwy., Park Ridge IL 60068. (312)825-8806. Editor: John E. McArdle. 20% freelance written. Works with a small number of new/unpublished writers each year. For owners and managers of small and medium-sized businesses, hospitals and nursing homes, trade associations, Better Business Bureaus, educational institutions and newspapers. Magazine published without charge 3 times a year. Circulation: 30,000. Buys all rights. Byline given. Buys 10-15 mss/year. Pays on acceptance. Publishes ms an average of 4-6 months after acceptance. Returns rejected material immediately. Query or submit complete ms. Computer printout submissions acceptable; prefers letter-quality. Reports in 2 weeks. Sample copy available on request for SAE with 2 first class stamps.

Nonfiction: "We prefer articles dealing with how to solve problems of specific industries (manufacturers, wholesalers, retailers, service businesses, small hospitals and nursing homes) where contact has been made with key executives whose comments regarding their problems may be quoted. We want problem solving articles, *not* success stories that laud an individual company. We like articles that give the business manager concrete suggestions on how to deal with specific problems—i.e., '5 steps to solve . . .', '6 key questions to ask when . . .', and '4 tell-tale signs indicating . . .'." Focus is on marketing, economic and technological trends that have an impact on medium- and small-sized businesses, not on the "giants"; automobile dealers coping with existing dull markets; and contractors solving cost-inventory problems. Will consider material on successful business operations and merchandising techniques. Length: 2,000-3,000 words. Pays $150-250.

Tips: Query letter should tell "type of business and problems the article will deal with. We specialize in the problems of small (20-500 employees, $500,000-2,500,000 volume) businesses (manufacturing, wholesale, retail and service), plus medium and small health care facilities. We are now including nationally known writers in each issue—writers like the Vice Chairman of the Federal Reserve Bank, the U.S. Secretary of the Treasury; names like George Bush and Malcolm Baldridge; titles like the Chairman of the Joint Committee on Accreditation of Hospitals; and Canadian Minister of Export. This places extra pressure on freelance writers to submit very good articles. Frequent mistakes: 1) Writing for big business, rather than small, 2) using language that is too academic."

MEETING NEWS, Facts, News, Ideas For Convention, Meeting and Incentive Planners Everywhere, Gralla Publications, 1515 Broadway, New York NY 10036. (212)869-1300. Editorial Director/Co-Publisher: Peter Shure. Editor: Colleen Davis-Gardephe. A monthly tabloid covering news, facts, ideas and methods in meeting planning; industry developments, legislation, new labor contracts, business practices and costs for meeting planners. Circ. 74,000. Pays on acceptance. Byline given. Buys all rights. Computer printout submissions acceptable; prefers letter-quality. Reports in 1 month on queries; 2 weeks on mss. Free sample copy.
Nonfiction: Travel; and specifics on how a group improved its meetings or shows, saved money or drew more attendees. "Stress is on business articles—facts and figures." Seven special issues covering specific states as meeting destination—Florida/Colorado/Texas/California/New York and Arizona. No general or philosophical pieces. Buys 25-50 mss/year. Query with published clips. Length: varies. Pays variable rates.
Tips: "Special issues focusing on certain states as meeting sites are most open. Best suggestion—query in writing, with clips, on any area of expertise about these states that would be of interest to people planning meetings there. Example: food/entertainment, specific sports, group activities, etc."

‡THE MINI-STORAGE MESSENGER, MiniCo Inc.. 2531 W. Dunlap Ave., Phoenix AZ 85021. (800)824-6864. Editor: David Azevedo. 85% freelance written. A monthly magazine on the self-service storage industry. "We speak to self-storage owners, operators and managers, as well as those on the industry's fringes such as appraisers and bankers. We strive for balanced multi-source material with solid, practical information." Circ. 4,000. Pays on acceptance. Publishes ms an average of 2 months after acceptance. Offers 25% kill fee. Buys first rights and second serial (reprint) rights. Submit seasonal/holiday material 3 months in advance. Computer printout submissions OK; prefers letter-quality. Reports in 2 weeks. Free sample copy and writer's guidelines.
Nonfiction: How-to (practical information on self-storage), interview/profile, new product, photo feature and technical. "One-source, first-person essays accepted." Buys 100 mss/year. Query with published clips. Length: 1,500-3,500 words. Pays $200-500. Pays the expenses of writers on assignment. State availability of photos with submission. Reviews transparencies ($2\frac{1}{4} \times 2\frac{1}{4}$). Offers $50-150 per photo. Identification of subjects required. Buys all rights.
Columns/Departments: People (personality profiles of industry people in mini-storage), 500-2,000 words; Construction (construction issues on self-storage, practical information), 1,500 words; Operations (tips on succssful operating techniques on self-storage), 1,500 words; Managements (tips and trends in mini-storage management), 1,500 words; Marketing (tips and trends in mini-storage marketing), 1,500 words. Buys 50 mss/year. Query with published clips. Length: 1,200-2,000 words. Pays $200.
Tips: "Get to know self-storage industry or dig up something new about the industry or its people. We are very receptive to writers with their own strong ideas. Diligence and original research and sources are ways to impress us. New slants and story ideas will get our attention."

RECORDS MANAGEMENT QUARTERLY, Association of Records Managers and Administrators, Inc., Box 4580, Silver Spring MD 20904. Editor: Ira A. Penn, CRM, CSP. 10% freelance written. Eager to work with new/unpublished writers. Quarterly magazine covering records and information management. Circ. 9,000. Pays on publication. Publishes ms an average of 6 months after acceptance. Byline given. Buys all rights. Photocopied, simultaneous and previously published submissions OK. Computer printout submissions acceptable; prefers letter-quality. Reports in 1 month on mss. Sample copy $8; free writer's guidelines.
Nonfiction: Professional articles covering theory, case studies, surveys, etc. on any aspect of records and information management. Buys 24-32 mss/year. Send complete ms. Length: 1,500 words minimum. Pays $25-100. Pays a "stipend"; no contract.
Photos: Send photos with ms. Does not pay extra for photos. Prefers b&w prints. Captions required.
Tips: "A writer *must* know our magazine. Most work is written by practitioners in the field. We use very little freelance writing, but we have had some and it's been good. A writer must have detailed knowledge of the subject he/she is writing about. Superficiality is not acceptable."

RISK & BENEFITS MANAGEMENT, Macmillan Professional Journals, 1640 Fifth St., Santa Monica CA 90401. (213)395-0234. Editor: Dana Bigman. 50% freelance written. Prefers to work with published/established writers. Monthly magazine covering risk management and insurance. "We are looking for well-written, pragmatic articles which provide risk managers with new methods and ideas for preventing losses in their organizations." Circ. 16,000. Pays on acceptance. Publishes ms an average of 6 months after acceptance. Byline given. Offers $25 kill fee. Buys all rights. Computer printout submissions OK; prefers letter-quality. Reports in 1 month. Sample copy for 9x12 SAE and 8 first class stamps.
Nonfiction: No general insurance topics, human interests, profiles or promotional articles about insurance companies. Buys 60 mss/year. Query. Length: 500-3,000 words. Pays 10-12¢/word. Sometimes pays the expenses of writers on assignment.
Photos: State availability of photos with submission. Reviews 3x5 prints. Offers no additional payment for photos accepted with ms. Identification of subjects required. Buys all rights.

Close-up

Colleen Davis-Gardephe
Executive Editor
Meeting News

"With trade magazines a good writer or editor can be a big fish in a little pond," says Colleen Davis-Gardephe, executive editor of *Meeting News*. Careers advance rapidly in trade magazines, she explains, because the field is often overlooked by job seekers (and freelancers) looking for work in the more glamourous or better-known consumer publications. Gardephe's career is an example—she has gone from an associate position to executive editor in less than five years. In a comparable consumer publication such a rise could easily have taken 10 years.

For freelancers the situation is similar. "It takes a while to break into the freelance pool," says Gardephe, "but once you're in we'll use you quite often."

As with consumer magazines, breaking in takes good writing skills, determination and an eye for a good story. It also takes a confident, but pliable personality, she says. "Freelancers must maintain a delicate balance between self-confidence and over self-assurance."

Writing for *Meeting News* is not unlike writing for most general interest or news publications. There's plenty of room for the generalist, says Gardephe. She needs stories that cover general topics, but from a meeting industry slant, such as stories on a new liquor liability law, fire safety or flight delays. "Look for broad-based stories that could affect the meeting planner or attendees."

Freelancers may want to start with travel or destination articles about a city near their home, says Gardephe. "We cover 35 states. Look for events happening in your city. Talk to the meeting planner and find out about promotion, programming and even transportation to the event."

The magazine runs articles on things to do in particular cities and puts out an editorial calendar, available to freelancers, listing upcoming featured destinations.

Other possible topics include recreation opportunities and profiles of companies, as long as there is some tie-in to meeting planning. Like other trade magazines, most articles for *Meeting News* are short. "Generally articles run 350 to 400 words, but we encourage sidebars. Sidebars can push a story to 650 or 700 words." A good sidebar might be a profile of a meeting planner or the host company, she explains.

Gardephe buys up to 10 articles a month from freelancers. She welcomes interviews with meeting planners as long as writers identify specific problems and how the planner solved them. Trade magazines seek to provide hands-on advice for their readers. There are professional meeting planners, says Gardephe, but many of the readers are executives, managers and secretaries.

Approach the magazine by sending clips and a query outlining a specific story idea, she adds. "Writers must research first—know the magazine, know the meeting and travel industry. Be aware of competing magazines and how our approach is different.

"We're not afraid of controversial stories," she says. "We consider ourselves a *news* magazine for meeting planners. If there's a hotel strike that stops a meeting, for example, we'll run it. If we like your idea and it's newsworthy, we'll respond right away."

—Robin Gee

Columns/Departments: Legal Perspectives (legal and legislative issues in risk management); On Line (computers), all 1,000-1,500 words. Buys 30 mss/year. Query. Length: 1,000-2,000 words. Pays 10-12¢/word.

‡SECURITY DEALER, PTN Security Group, 101 Crossways Park West, Woodbury NY 11797. (516)496-8000. Editor: Thomas Kapinos. Managing Editor: Tami Cabot. 5% freelance written. A monthly magazine for alarm dealers and burglary and fire installers, with technical, business sales and marketing information. Circ. 21,000. Pays 3 weeks after publication. Publishes ms an average of 4 months after acceptance. Byline given sometimes. Not copyrighted. Buys first North American serial rights. Simultaneous, photocopied and previously published submissions OK. Computer printout submissions acceptable; prefers letter-quality. Writer's guidelines for SAE with 2 first class stamps.
Nonfiction: How-to, interview/profile and technical. No consumer pieces. Query or send complete ms. Length: 1,000-3,000 words. Pays $100-200 for assigned articles; pays $100-150 for unsolicited articles. Sometimes pays the expenses of writers on assignment.
Photos: State availability of photos with submission. Reviews contact sheets and transparencies. Offers no additional payment for photos accepted with ms. Captions and identification of subjects required.
Columns/Departments: Closed Circuit TV, and Access Control (both on application, installation, new products), 500-1,000 words. Buys 15 mss/year. Query. Pays $100-125.
Tips: "The areas of our publication most open to freelancers are technical innovations, trends in the alarm industry and crime patterns as related to the business."

‡SUCCESSFUL MAGAZINE PUBLISHING, The Farmstead Press, 1 Main St., Freedom ME 04941. (207)382-6200. Editor: George Frangoulis. 10% freelance written. Bimonthly magazine on all aspects of magazine publishing. "Our publication is geared toward the magazine publisher with a circulation of 200,000 or less. We publish articles dealing with all aspects of the publishing business and written in a straightforward conversational style." Circ. 12,000. Pays on publication. Byline given. Offers $50 kill fee. Buys first and second serial (reprint) rights. Simultaneous, photocopied and previously published submissions OK. Query for electronic submissions. Computer printout submissions OK; no dot-matrix. Reports in 2 weeks on queries; 1 month on mss. Free sample copy and writer's guidelines.
Nonfiction: Dennis Dunn, articles editor. How-to, interview/profile, personal experience, technical. Buys 30 mss/year. Query with published clips. Length: 1,000-3,000. Pays $50-300.
Photos: Reviews transparencies. Offers $10-25. Captions, model releases and identification of subjects required. Buys all rights or second rights.
Columns/Departments: Single Copy Sales (viewpoints on newsstand sales and the renewal of subscriptions); Design (viewpoints on magazine layout and design); Advertising (viewpoints on advertising sales in today's market); Print and Production (viewpoints on printing processes), all 700-1,000 words. Buys 30 mss/year. Query with published clips. Pays $50-150.
Fillers: Anecdotes, facts and newsbreaks. Buys 50/year. Length: 250-500. Pays $50.
Tips: "Our publication aims to present facts and information for the small magazine publisher who may get lost reading technical publications. Our articles are conversational and many times are presented in a how-to format that is enjoyable to read. All sections and departments are open to freelancers. Personal insight into this industry is what we look for the most."

‡TRADESHOW, Macmillan Professional Journals. 1640 Fifth St., Santa Monica CA 90401. (213)395-0234. Editor: Les Plesko. Managing Editor: Barbara Newman. 75% freelance written. A monthly magazine covering trade shows. "The magazine is a professional journal edited for tradeshow exhibit managers and tradeshow organizers. Business writing style is preferred." Circ. 12,000. Pays on acceptance. Publishes ms an average of 4 months after acceptance. Byline given. Kill fee negotiable. Buys all rights. Photocopied submissions OK. Computer printout submissions OK. Reports in 1 week. Free sample copy and writer's gudelines.
Nonfiction: How-to, interview/profile, new product and photo feature. "We do not accept any articles without query letter or phone call first. Please, no over-the-transom articles." Buys 50-100 mss/year. Query. Length: 1,000-3,000 words. Pays 12¢/edited word. Sometimes pays the expenses of writers on assignment.
Photos: State availability of photos with submission. Reviews contact sheets, negatives, transparencies and prints. Offers no additional payment for photos accepted with ms. Identification of subjects required. Buys all rights.
Tips: "Only the features section is open to freelancers. Concise business writing is required. Writers must query first."

‡VIDEO BUSINESS, International Thomson Retail Press. 345 Park Avenue South, New York NY 10010. (212)686-7744. Editor: John Gaffney. Managing Editor: Ricki Zide. 35% freelance written. A monthly magazine on video software retailing. "*Video Business* covers trends in marketing and videocassette programming for 40,000 retailers of all sizes. All articles should be written with the intent of providing information that a retailer can apply to his/her business immediately." Circ. 40,000. Pays on publication.

Byline given. Buys first rights. Submit seasonal/holiday material 2 months in advance. Photocopied submissions OK. Query for electronic submissions. Computer printout submissions OK; prefers letter-quality. Reports in 2 weeks. Free sample copy and writer's guidelines.

Nonfiction: Historical/nostalgic (movie genres), interview/profile, new product and technical. Buys 50 mss/year. Query with published clips. Length: 1,500-3,000 words. Pays 25-35¢/word. Sometimes pays the expenses of writers on assignment. State availability of photos with submission. Reviews negatives. Offers no additional payment for photos accepted with ms. Buys one-time rights.

‡WOMEN IN BUSINESS, The ABWA Co., Inc.. 9100 Ward Parkway, Kansas City MO 64114. (816)361-6621. Editor: Margaret E. Horan. 30% freelance written. A bimonthly magazine for members of the American Business Women's Association. "We publish articles of interest to the American working woman." Circ. 110,000. Pays on acceptance. Publishes ms an average of 2 months after acceptance. Byline given. Kill fee negotiable. Buys all rights. Submit seasonal/holiday material 4 months in advance. Computer printout submissions OK; prefers letter-quality. Reports in 1 week. Sample copy for 9x12 SAE with 4 first class stamps. Writer's guidelines for #10 SAE with 1 first class stamp.

Nonfiction: "We cannot use success stories about individual businesswomen." Buys 30 mss/year. Query with published clips or send complete ms. Length: 1,000-3,000 words. Pays 15¢/word regardless if it was assigned or unsolicited.

Photos: State availability of photos with submission. Offers no additional payment for photos accepted with ms. Identification of subjects required.

Columns/Departments: Laura Luckert, column/department editor. Working Capital (personal finance for women), 1,500 words; Health Scope (health topics for women); Moving up (advice for the up and coming woman manager). Buys 18 mss/year. Query with published clips or send complete ms. Length: 1,000-1,500 words. Pays 15¢/word.

Tips: "It would be very difficult to break into our columns. We have regular contributing freelance writers for those. But we are always on the look out for good feature articles and writers. We are especially interested in writers who provide a fresh, new look to otherwise old topics, such as time management etc."

——— Church Administration and Ministry

Publications in this section are written for clergy members, church leaders and teachers. Magazines for lay members and the general public are listed in the Consumer Religious section.

CHRISTIAN EDUCATION TODAY: For teachers, superintendents and other Christian educators, Box 15337, Denver CO 80215. Editor: Mary B. Nelson. Research Editor: Kenneth O. Gangel. 60% freelance written. Works with a small number of new/unpublished writers each year. Quarterly magazine. Pays prior to publication. Publishes ms an average of 6-9 months after acceptance. Byline given. Buys reprint rights with magazines of different circulations. Computer printout submissions acceptable; prefers letter-quality. Reports in 2 months. Sample copy and writer's guidelines for $1 or 9x12 SAE with 3 first class stamps.

Nonfiction: Articles which provide information, instruction and/or inspiration to workers at every level of Christian education. May be slanted to the general area or to specific age-group categories such as preschool, elementary, youth or adult. Simultaneous rights acceptable *only* if offered to magazines which do not have overlapping circulation. Length: 1,000-2,000 words. Payment commensurate with length and value of article to total magazine (5-10¢/word).

Tips: "Often a freelance short article is followed up with a suggestion or firm assignment for more work from that writer."

CHRISTIAN LEADERSHIP, Board of Christian Education of the Church of God, Box 2458, Anderson IN 46018-2458. (317)642-0257. Acting Editor: Kenneth G. Prunty. 50% freelance written. Works with a small number of new/unpublished writers each year. A monthly magazine (except July and August) covering local Sunday school teachers, church school administrators, youth workers, choir leaders and other local church workers. Circ. 4,000. Pays on publication. Publishes ms an average of 6 months after acceptance. Byline given. Buys first rights and second serial (reprint) rights. Submit seasonal/holiday material 6 months in advance. Simultaneous queries OK. Computer printout submissions acceptable; no dot-matrix. Reports in 4 months. Sample copy and writer's guidelines for 9x12 SAE with 3 first class stamps.

Nonfiction: General interest, how-to, inspirational, personal experience, guidance for carrying out programs for special days, and continuing ministries. No articles that are not specifically related to local church leadership. Buys 40 mss/year. Send complete ms, brief description of present interest in writing for church leaders, background and experience. Length: 300-1,500 words. Pays 2¢/word ($10 minimum).

Photos: Send photos with ms. Pays $15-25 for 5x7 b&w photos.

Tips: "How-to articles related to Sunday school teaching, program development and personal teacher enrichment or growth, with illustrations of personal experience of the authors, are most open to freelancers."

‡**CHURCH ADMINISTRATION**, 127 9th Ave. N., Nashville TN 37234. (615)251-2060. Editor: Gary Hardin. 15% freelance written. Works with a small number of new/unpublished writers each year. Monthly. For Southern Baptist pastors, staff and volunteer church leaders. Uses limited amount of freelance material. Pays on acceptance. Publishes ms an average of 1 year after acceptance. Byline given. Buys all rights. Computer printout submissions acceptable; no dot-matrix. Free sample copy and writer's guidelines for SAE with 2 first class stamps.

Nonfiction: "Ours is a journal for effectiveness in ministry, including church programming, organizing, and staffing; administrative skills; church financing; church food services; church facilities; communication; and pastoral ministries and community needs." Length: 1,800-2,000 words. Pays 5¢/word.

Tips: "Send query letter. Writers should be familiar with the organization and polity of Southern Baptist churches. Articles should be practical, how-to articles that meet genuine needs faced by leaders in SBC churches. Type at 54 characters per line, 25 lines per page, double-spaced. Send originals, not copies. Not responsible for manuscripts not accompanied by return postage."

CHURCH EDUCATOR, Creative Resources for Christian Educators, Educational Ministries, Inc., 2861-C Saturn St., Brea CA 92621. (714)961-0622. Editor: Robert G. Davidson. Managing Editor: Linda S. Davidson. 80% freelance written. Works with a small number of new/unpublished writers each year. A monthly magazine covering religious education. Circ. 5,200. Pays on publication. Publishes manuscript an average of 4 months after acceptance. Byline given. Buys first rights, second serial (reprint) rights, or all rights. "We prefer all rights." Submit seasonal/holiday material 4 months in advance. Simultaneous submissions OK. Computer printout submissions acceptable; prefers letter-quality. Reports in 3 months. Sample copy for 9x12 SAE and 3 first class stamps; free writer's guidelines.

Nonfiction: Book reviews; general interest; how-to (crafts for Church school); inspirational; personal experience; and religious. "Our editorial lines are very middle of the road—mainline Protestant. We are not seeking extreme conservative or liberal theology pieces." No testimonials. Buys 100 mss/year. Send complete ms. Length: 100-2,000 words. Pays 2-4¢/word.

Photos: Send photos with submissions. Reviews 5x7 b&w prints. Offers $5-10/photo. Captions required. Buys one-time rights.

Fiction: Mainstream, religious, and slice-of-life vignettes. Buys 15 mss/year. Send complete ms. Length: 100-2,000 words. Pays 2-4¢/word.

Fillers: Anecdotes and short humor. Buys 15/year. Length: 100-700 words. Pays 2-4¢/word.

Tips: "Send the complete manuscript with a cover letter which gives a concise summary of the manuscript. We are looking for how-to articles related to Christian education. That would include most any program held in a church. Be straightforward and to the point—not flowery and wordy. We're especially interested in youth programs. Give steps needed to carry out the program: preparation, starting the program, continuing the program, conclusion. List several discussion questions for each program."

CIRCUIT RIDER, A Journal for United Methodist Ministers, United Methodist Publishing House, Box 801, Nashville TN 37202. (615)749-6137. Editor: Keith I. Pohl. Editorial Director: J. Richard Peck. 60% freelance written. Works with a small number of new/unpublished writers each year. A monthly magazine covering professional concerns of clergy. Circ. 35,000. Pays on acceptance. Publishes ms an average of 1 year after acceptance. Byline given. Buys all rights. Submit seasonal/holiday material 6 months in advance. Photocopied submissions OK. Computer printout submissions acceptable; prefers letter-quality. Reports in 3 weeks.

Nonfiction: How-to (improve pastoral calling, preaching, counseling, administration, etc.). No personal experience articles; no interviews. Buys 50 mss/year. Send complete ms. Length: 600-2,000 words. Pays $30-100. Pays the expenses of writers on assignment.

Photos: State availability of photos. Pays $25-50 for 8x10 b&w prints. Model release required. Buys one-time rights.

Tips: "Know the concerns of a United Methodist pastor. Be specific. Think of how you can help pastors."

THE CLERGY JOURNAL, Church Management, Inc., Box 162527, Austin TX 78716. (512)327-8501. Editor: Manfred Holck, Jr. 20% freelance written. Eager to work with new/unpublished writers. Monthly (except June and December) on religion. Readers are Protestant clergy. Circ. 30,000. Pays on publication. Publishes ms an average of 4 months after acceptance. Byline given. Offers 50% kill fee. Buys all rights.

Submit seasonal/holiday material 6 months in advance. Photocopied submissions OK. Computer printout submissions acceptable; prefers letter-quality. Reports in 2 weeks on queries; 1 month on mss. Sample copy for $3 and 9x12 SAE with 8 first class stamps.

Nonfiction: How-to (be a more efficient and effective minister/administrator). No devotional, inspirational or sermons. Buys 20 mss/year. Query. Length: 500-1,500 words. Pays $25-40.

LEADERSHIP, A Practical Journal for Church Leaders, Christianity Today, Inc., 465 Gundersen Dr., Carol Stream IL 60188. (312)260-6200. Editor: Terry Muck. Managing Editor: Marshall Shelley. 75% freelance written. Works with a small number of new/unpublished writers each year. A quarterly magazine covering church leadership. Writers must have a "knowledge of and sympathy for the unique expectations placed on pastors and local church leaders. Each article must support points by illustrating from real life experiences in local churches." Circ. 90,000. Pays on acceptance. Publishes ms an average of 6 months after acceptance. Byline given. Buys first North American serial rights. Submit seasonal/holiday material 6 months in advance. Photocopied and previously published submissions OK. Computer printout submissions OK; prefers letter-quality. Reports in 6 weeks on queries; 2 months on mss. Sample copy $3; free writer's guidelines.

Nonfiction: How-to, humor and personal experience. No "articles from writers who have never read our journal." Buys 50 mss/year. Send complete ms. Length: 100-5,000 words. Pays $30-300. Sometimes pays the expenses of writers on assignment.

Photos: State availability of photos with submission. Offers no additional payment for photos accepted with ms. Identification of subjects required. Buys one-time rights.

Columns/Departments: Larry K. Weeden, editor, People in Print (book reviews with interview of author), 1,500 words. James D. Berkley, editor, To Illustrate (short stories or analogies that illustrate a biblical principle), 100 words. Buys 25 mss/year. Send complete ms. Pays $25-100.

MINISTRIES TODAY, Strang Communications Co., 190 N. Westmonte Dr., Altamonte Springs FL 32714. (305)869-5005. Editor: Stephen Strang. Associate Editor: E.S. Caldwell. 20% freelance written. Bimonthly magazine covering Evangelical/Pentecostal/Charismatic ministries. Includes practical articles to help church leaders. Circ. 20,000. Pays on publication. Publishes ms an average of 6 months after acceptance. Byline given. Buys first rights. Photocopied submissions OK. Computer printout submissions acceptable; prefers letter-quality. Reports in 1 month. Sample copy $3, SAE and 2 first class stamps; writer's guidelines for #10 SAE and 1 first class stamp.

Nonfiction: How-to (for pastors), and interview/profile. Writers must have personal experience in areas they are writing about. Buys 40 mss/year. Query or send complete ms. Length: 1,700-2,000 words. Pays $50-200. Sometimes pays expenses of writers on assignment.

Photos: Eric Jessen, photo editor.

Tips: "We need practical, proven ideas with both negative and positive anecdotes. We have a specialized audience—pastors and leaders of churches. It is unlikely that persons not fully understanding this audience would be able to provide appropriate manuscripts."

PASTORAL LIFE, Society of St. Paul, Route 224, Canfield OH 44406. Editor: Jeffrey Mickler, SSP. 66% freelance written. Works with a small number of new/unpublished writers each year, and is eager to work with new/unpublished writers. Emphasizes priests and those interested in pastoral ministry. Magazine. Monthly. Circ. 6,600. Buys first rights only. Byline given. Pays on publication. Publishes ms an average of 6 months after acceptance. Sample copy to writer on request. Query with a outline before submitting ms. "New contributors are expected to include, in addition, a few lines of personal data that indicate academic and professional background." Computer printout submissions acceptable; no dot-matrix. Reports within 1 month.

Nonfiction: "*Pastoral Life* is a professional review, principally designed to focus attention on current problems, needs, issues and all important activities related to all phases of pastoral work and life." Buys 30 unsolicited mss/year. Length: 2,000-3,400 words. Pays 3¢/word minimum.

Tips: "Projected increase in number of pages will warrant expansion of our material needs."

‡THE PREACHER'S MAGAZINE, Nazarene Publishing House, 6401 The Paseo, Kansas City MO 64131. (816)333-7000. Editor: Wesley Tracy. Assistant Editor: Mark D. Marvin. 15% freelance written. Works with a small number of new/unpublished writers each year. Quarterly magazine of seasonal/miscellaneous articles. "A resource for ministers; Wesleyan-Arminian in theological persuasion." Circ. 17,000. Pays on acceptance. Publishes ms an average of 9+ months after acceptance. Byline given. Buys first serial rights, second serial (reprint) rights and simultaneous rights. Submit seasonal/holiday material 9 months in advance. Simultaneous queries and photocopied submissions OK. Computer printout submissions acceptable; prefers letter-quality. Sample copy and writer's guidelines for 9x12 SAE and 2 first class stamps.

Nonfiction: How-to, humor, inspirational, opinion and personal experience, all relating to aspects of ministry. No articles that present problems without also presenting answers to them; things not relating to

pastoral ministry. Buys 48 mss/year. Send complete ms. Length: 700-2,500 words. Pays 3½¢/word.
Photos: Send photos with ms. Reviews 35mm color transparencies and 35mm b&w prints. Pays $25-35. Model release and identification of subjects required. Buys one-time rights.
Columns/Departments: Today's Books for Today's Preacher—book reviews. Buys 24 mss/year. Send complete ms. Length: 300-400 words. Pays $7.50.
Fillers: Anecdotes and short humor. Buys 10/year. Length: 400 words maximum. Pays 3½¢/word.
Tips: "Writers for the *Preacher's Magazine* should have insight into the pastoral ministry, or expertise in a specialized area of ministry. Our magazine is a highly specialized publication aimed at the minister. Our goal is to assist, by both scholarly and practical articles, the modern-day minister in applying Biblical theological truths."

PREACHING, Preaching Resources, Inc., 1529 Cesery Blvd., Jacksonville FL 32211. (904)743-5994. Editor: Dr. Michael Duduit. 75% freelance written. Bimonthly magazine for the preaching ministry. "All articles must deal with preaching. Most articles used offer practical assistance in preparation and delivery of sermons, generally from an evangelical stance." Circ. 6,000. Pays on publication. Publishes ms an average of 1 year after acceptance. Byline given. Buys first rights. Submit seasonal/holiday material 1 year in advance. Photocopied submissions OK. Query for electronic submissions. Computer printout submissions OK. Reports in 6-8 weeks. Sample copy $2.50; writer's guidelines for SAE with 1 first class stamp.
Nonfiction: How-to (preparation and delivery of sermon; worship leadership). Special issues include Personal Computing in Preaching (September-October); materials/resources to assist in preparation of seasonal preaching (November-December, March-April). Buys 18-24 mss/year. Query. Length: 1,000-2,000 words. Pays $35-50.
Photos: Send photos with submission. Reviews prints. Offers no additional payment for photos accepted with ms. Captions, model releases and identification of subjects required. Buys one-time rights.
Fillers: Buys 6/year. "Buys only completed cartoons." Art must be related to preaching. Pays $25.
Tips: "Most desirable are practical, 'how-to' articles on preparation and delivery of sermons."

Clothing

‡ACTIVEWEAR BUSINESS, Virgo Publications, Inc., Box C-5400, Scottsdale AZ 85261. (602)483-0014. Editor: Brent Diamond. Managing Editor: Tracey Benson. 20% freelance written. Monthly trade journal covering active apparel and footwear. "Anything that helps a retailer with purchasing decisions, distributing merchandise and running a more efficient business." Circ. 30,000. Pays 30 days after publication. Byline given. Buys all rights. Submit seasonal/holiday material 3 months in advance. Simultaneous submissions OK. Query for electronic submissions. Computer printout submissions OK. Reports in 2 weeks. Free sample copy and writer's guidelines.
Nonfiction: How-to, interview/profile, new product, photo feature, technical. Buys 30 mss/year. Query with or without published clips, or send complete ms. Length: 1,500-4,000 words. Pays $50-200 for assigned articles; pays $50-150 for unsolicited articles. Sometimes pays expenses of writers on assignment.
Photos: State availability of photos with submission. Reviews contact sheets, any size transparencies and b&w and color prints. Offers no additional payment for photos accepted with ms. Model releases and identification of subjects required. Buys one-time rights.

‡APPAREL INDUSTRY MAGAZINE, Shore Publishing, Suite 300-South, 180 Allen Rd., Atlanta GA 30328. Editor: Karen Schaffner. Managing Editor: Karen M. Benning. 30% freelance written. Monthly magazine. For executive management in apparel companies with interests in equipment, fabrics, licensing, distribution, finance, management and training. Circ. 18,700. Pays on publication. Publishes ms an average of 4 months after acceptance. Byline given. Buys first serial rights. Will consider legible photocopied submissions. Query for electronic submissions. Computer printout submissions acceptable. Reports in 1 month. Sample copy $3; writer's guidelines for #10 SAE with 1 first class stamp.
Nonfiction: Articles dealing with equipment, manufacturing techniques, training, finance, licensing, fabrics, quality control, etc., related to the industry. "Use concise, precise language that is easy to read and understand. In other words, because the subjects are often technical, keep the language comprehensible. Material must be precisely related to the apparel industry. We are not a retail or fashion magazine."

✝ The double dagger before a listing indicates that the listing is new in this edition. New markets are often the most receptive to freelance submissions.

Informational, interview, profile, successful business operations and technical articles. Buys 30 mss/year. Query. Length: 3,000 words maximum. Pays 20¢/word. Sometimes pays expenses of writers on assignment.
Photos: Pays $5/photo with ms.
Tips: "Frequently articles are too general due to lack of industry-specific knowledge by the writer."

‡ATI, America's Textiles International, Billian Publishing Co., 2100 Powers Ferry Rd., Atlanta GA 30339. (404)955-5656. Editor: Wilburn W. Newcomb. Managing Editor: Rolf Viertel. 10% freelance written. Monthly magazine covering textiles, apparel, and fibers. "We cover the business of textile, apparel, and fiber industries with considerable technical focus on products and processes. No puff pieces pushing a particular product, however." Pays on publication. Byline sometimes given. Not copyrighted. Buys first North American serial rights. Query for electronic submissions. Computer printout submissions OK; prefers letter-quality.
Nonfiction: Technical, business. "No PR, just straight technical reports." Buys 10 mss/year. Query. Length: 500 words minimum. Pays $100/published page. Sometimes pays expenses of writers on assignment.
Photos: Send photos with submission. Reviews prints. Offers no additional payment for photos accepted with ms. Captions required. Buys one-time rights.

‡BOBBIN, Bobbin Media Corp. 1110 Shop Rd., Box 1986, Columbia SC 29202. (803)771-7500. Editor: Joyce E. Santora. 75% freelance written. A monthly magazine on the apparel sewn products manufacturing industry. Circ. 10,000. Pays on publication. Publishes ms an average of 3 months after acceptance. Byline given. Buys all rights. Computer printout submissions OK; prefers letter-quality. Reports in 1 month on queries; 6 months on mss. Free sample copy and writer's guidelines.
Nonfiction: Interview/profile, opinion and technical. Buys 3 mss/year. Query or send complete ms. Length: 2,000-7,500 words. Pays $200-500. Sometimes pays writers with 250 reprints of article. Sometimes pays the expenses of writers on assignment.
Photos: Send photos with submission. Reviews transparencies and prints (3x5). Offers no additional payment for photos accepted with ms. Captions and identifiction of subjects required. Buys all rights.

‡TEXTILE WORLD, Suite 420, 4170 Ashford-Dunwoody Rd. NE, Atlanta GA 30319. Editor-in-Chief: Laurence A. Christiansen. Monthly. Pays on acceptance. Buys all rights.
Nonfiction: Uses articles covering textile management methods, manufacturing and marketing techniques, new equipment, details about new and modernized mills, etc., but avoids elementary, historical or generally well-known material.
Photos: Photos purchased with accompanying ms with no additional payment, or purchased on assignment.

Coin-Operated Machines

AMERICAN COIN-OP, 500 N. Dearborn St., Chicago IL 60610. (312)337-7700. Editor: Ben Russell. 30% freelance written. Monthly magazine. For owners of coin-operated laundry and dry cleaning stores. Circ. 18,000. Rights purchased vary with author and material but are exclusive to the field. Pays two weeks prior to publication. Publishes ms an average of 4 months after acceptance. Byline given for frequent contributors. Computer printout submissions acceptable; prefers letter-quality. Reports as soon as possible; usually in 2 weeks. Free sample copy.
Nonfiction: "We emphasize store operation and use features on industry topics: utility use and conservation, maintenance, store management, customer service and advertising. A case study should emphasize how the store operator accomplished whatever he did—in a way that the reader can apply to his own operation. Manuscript should have a no-nonsense, business-like approach." Uses informational, how-to, interview, profile, think pieces and successful business operations articles. Length: 500-3,000 words. Pays 6¢/word minimum.
Photos: Pays $6 minimum for 8x10 b&w glossy photos purchased with mss. (Contact sheets with negatives preferred.)
Fillers: Newsbreaks and clippings. Length: open. Pays $6 minimum.
Tips: "Query about subjects of current interest. Be observant of coin-operated laundries—how they are designed and equipped, how they serve customers and how (if) they advertise and promote their services. Most general articles are turned down because they are not aimed well enough at audience. Most case histories are turned down because of lack of practical purpose (nothing new or worth reporting). A frequent mistake is failure to follow up on an interesting point made by the interviewee—probably due to lack of knowledge about the industry."

ELECTRONIC SERVICING & TECHNOLOGY, Intertec Publishing Corp., Box 12901, Overland Park KS 66212. (913)888-4664. Editor: Conrad Persson. Senior Managing Editor: Tom Cook. 90% freelance written. Eager to work with new/unpublished writers. Monthly magazine for professional servicers and electronic enthusiasts who are interested in buying, building, installing and repairing consumer electronic equipment (audio, video, microcomputers, electronic games, etc.) Circ. 45,000. Pays on publication. Publishes ms an average of 6 months after acceptance. Byline given. Buys all rights. Submit seasonal/holiday material 4 months in advance. Simultaneous queries OK. Computer printout submissions acceptable; prefers letter-quality. Reports in 2 weeks on queries; 1 month on mss. Free sample copy and writer's guidelines.
Nonfiction: How-to (service, build, install and repair home entertainment electronic equipment); personal experience (troubleshooting); and technical (consumer electronic equipment; electronic testing and servicing equipment). "Explain the techniques used carefully so that even hobbyists can understand a how-to article." Buys 36 mss/year. Send complete ms. Length: 1,500 words minimum. Pays $100-200.
Photos: Send photos with ms. Reviews color and b&w transparencies and b&w prints. Captions and identification of subjects required. Buys all rights. Payment included in total ms package.
Columns/Departments: Alecia Carter, associate editor. Troubleshooting Tips. Buys 12 mss/year. Send complete ms. Length: open. Pays $25.
Tips: "In order to write for *ES&T* it is almost essential that a writer have an electronics background: technician, engineer or serious hobbyist. Our readers want nuts-and-bolts type of information on electronics."

VENDING TIMES, 545 8th. Avenue, New York NY 10018. Editor: Arthur E. Yohalem. Monthly. For operators of vending machines. Circ. 14,700. Pays on publication. Buys all rights. "We will discuss in detail the story requirements with the writer."
Nonfiction: Feature articles and news stories about vending operations; practical and important aspects of the business. "We are always willing to pay for good material." Query.

Confectionery and Snack Foods

These publications focus on the bakery, snack and candy industries. Journals for grocers, wholesalers and other food industry personnel are listed under Groceries and Food Products.

CANDY INDUSTRY, Edgell Communications, Inc., 7500 Old Oak Blvd., Cleveland OH 44130. (216)243-8100. Editor/Associate Publisher: Pat Magee. 5% freelance written. Monthly. Prefers to work with published/established writers. For confectionery manufacturers. Publishes ms an average of 4 months after acceptance. Buys all rights. Computer printout submissions acceptable; prefers letter-quality. Reports in 1 month.
Nonfiction: "Feature articles of interest to large scale candy manufacturers that deal with activities in the fields of production, packaging (including package design), merchandising; and financial news (sales figures, profits, earnings), advertising campaigns in all media, and promotional methods used to increase the sale or distribution of candy." Length: 1,000-1,250 words. Pays 15¢/word; "special rates on assignments."
Photos: "Good quality glossies with complete and accurate captions, in sizes not smaller than 5x7." Pays $15 b&w; $20 for color.
Fillers: "Short news stories about the trade and anything related to candy and snacks." Pays 5¢/word; $1 for clippings.

PACIFIC BAKERS NEWS, 1809 Sharpe Ave., Walnut Creek CA 94596. (415)932-1256. Publisher: C.W. Soward. 30% freelance written. Eager to work with new/unpublished writers. Monthly business newsletter for commercial bakeries in the western states. Pays on publication. No byline given; uses only one-paragraph news items. Computer printout submissions acceptable.
Nonfiction: Uses bakery business reports and news about bakers. Buys only brief "boiled-down news items about bakers and bakeries operating only in Alaska, Hawaii, Pacific Coast and Rocky Mountain states. We welcome clippings. We need monthly news reports and clippings about the baking industry and the donut business. No pictures, jokes, poetry or cartoons." Length: 10-200 words. Pays 6¢/word for clips and news used.

For information on setting your freelance fees, see How Much Should I Charge? in the Business of Writing section.

Construction and Contracting

Builders, architects and contractors learn the latest industry news in these publications. Journals targeted to architects are also included in the Consumer Art, Design and Collectibles category. Those for specialists in the interior aspects of construction are listed under Building Interiors.

ACCESS CONTROL/FENCE INDUSTRY, (formerly Fence Industry/Access Control), 6255 Barfield Rd., Atlanta GA 30328. (404)256-9800. Editor/Associate Publisher: Bill Coker. 50% freelance written. Prefers to work with published/established writers. Monthly tabloid. For retailers and installers of access control equipment and fencing. Circ. 21,000. Pays on publication. Publishes ms an average of 2 months after acceptance. Buys all rights. Query for electronic submissions. Computer printout submissions acceptable; no dot-matrix. Reports in 3 months. Free sample copy.
Nonfiction: Case histories, on fencing and access control equipment installations. A format for these articles has been established. Query for details. Buys 10-12 unsolicited mss/year. Query. Length: 3,500 words maximum. Pays 10¢/word.
Photos: Pays $10 for 5x7 b&w photos purchased with mss. Captions required.
Tips: "We will place more focus on access control installations."

AUTOMATED BUILDER, (formerly *Automation in Housing and Manufactured Home Dealer*), CMN Associates, Inc., Box 120, Carpinteria CA 93013. (805)684-7659. Editor-in-Chief: Don Carlson. 15% freelance written. Monthly magazine. Specializes in management for industrialized (manufactured) housing and volume home builders. Circ. 25,000. Pays on acceptance. Publishes ms an average of 3 months after acceptance. Buys first North American serial rights. Phone queries OK. Computer printout submissions acceptable; no dot-matrix. Reports in 2 weeks. Free sample copy and writer's guidelines.
Nonfiction: Case history articles on successful home building companies which may be 1) production (big volume) home builders; 2) mobile home manufacturers; 3) modular home manufacturers; 4) prefabricated home manufacturers; or 5) house component manufacturers. Also uses interviews, photo features and technical articles. "No architect or plan 'dreams'. Housing projects must be built or under construction." Buys 15 mss/year. Query. Length: 500-1,000 words maximum. Pays $300 minimum.
Photos: Purchased with accompanying ms. Query. No additional payment for 4x5, 5x7 or 8x10 b&w glossies or 35mm or larger color transparencies (35mm preferred). Captions required.
Tips: "Stories often are too long, too loose; we prefer 500 to 750 words. We prefer a phone query on feature articles. If accepted on query, usually article will not be rejected later."

CONSTRUCTION SPECIFIER, 601 Madison St., Alexandria VA 22314. (703)684-0300. Editor: Kimberly C. Young. 50% freelance written. Works with a small number of new/unpublished writers each year. Monthly professional society magazine for architects, engineers, specification writers and project managers. Circ. 19,000. Pays on publication. Publishes ms an average of 4 months after acceptance. Deadline: 60 days preceding publication on the 1st of each month. Buys North American serial rights. Computer printout submissions acceptable; prefers letter-quality. "Call or write first." Model release, author copyright transferral requested. Reports in 3 weeks. Sample copy for 8½x11 SAE and 6 first class stamps.
Nonfiction: Articles on selection and specification of products, materials, practices and methods used in commercial (nonresidential) construction projects, specifications as related to construction design, plus legal and management subjects. Query. Length: 3,000-5,000 words maximum. Pays 15¢/published word (negotiable), plus art. Pays minor expenses of writers on assignment, to an agreed upon limit.
Photos: Photos desirable in consideration for publication; line art, sketches, diagrams, charts and graphs also desired. Full color transparencies may be used. 8x10 glossies, 3¼ slides preferred. Payment negotiable.
Tips: "We are increasing in size and thus will need more good technical articles."

CONTRACTORS MARKET CENTER, Randall Publishing Co., Box 2029, Tuscaloosa AL 35403. (205)349-2990. Editor: Rob Ruth. 25-50% freelance written. Eager to work with new/unpublished writers. Weekly news magazine on heavy-equipment construction industry. "Our readers are contractors including road contractors, and oil and gas industry, who utilize heavy equipment. We write positive, upbeat stories about their work and their personal success. We like personal stories related to large construction projects." Circ. 18,000. Pays on acceptance. Publishes ms an average of 1 month after acceptance. Byline given. Offers 100% kill fee. Not copyrighted. Buys first serial rights, one-time rights, second serial (reprint) rights and simultaneous rights. Submit seasonal/holiday material 1 month in advance. Simultaneous and previously published (updated) submissions OK. Computer printout submissions acceptable; prefers upper and lower case letter-quality. Reports in 2 weeks. Free sample copy and writer's guidelines.

Nonfiction: General interest (with construction angle); historical/nostalgic (with construction angle); humor (with construction angle); interview/profile (with contractors); personal experience (with construction angle); technical (re: heavy equipment); and business stories related to contractors. Buys 100 mss/year. Send complete ms. Length: 250-1,000 words. Pays $10-50.

Photos: Send photos with ms. Reviews b&w and color prints; commercially processed OK if sharp. Pays $5. Identification of subjects required.

Tips: "Contractors like to read about other contractors and people with whom they are in frequent contact—suppliers, government regulators, and public works developments. Our interest is especially strong in articles offering money-saving advice to contractors who buy and sell used construction equipment. We're primarily looking for people-oriented features. Nothing is too local if it's interesting. Submitting art with copy gives definite edge."

‡DIXIE CONTRACTOR, The Regional Construction Journal of the Southeast, Dixie Contractor, Inc.. 209-A Swanton Way, Box 280, Decatur GA 30031. (404)377-2683. Editor: Steve Hudson. 30% freelance written. A bimonthly magazine for contractors, construction professionals, equipment suppliers, developers and builders, local and regional officials, and others involved in heavy or commercial construction in the Southeast (Alabama, Florida, Georgia, South Carolina, most of Tennessee). Circ. 10,000. Pays on publication. Byline given. Buys all rights. Submit seasonal/holiday material 3 months in advance. Query for electronic submissions. Computer printout submissions OK. Reports in 1 week. Sample copy for 9x12 SAE with 4 first class stamps. Writer's guidelines SAE with 2 first class stamps.

Nonfiction: Project profiles, how-to, interview/profile, photo feature and technical. We cannot use articles on projects outside our coverage area. Buys 30-40 mss/year. Query. Length: 600+-1,800+. Pays $50/published page.

Photos: Send photos with submission. Reviews transparencies (for cover use only) and prints (5x7 or 8x10). Captions required. Buys all rights.

Tips: "As construction activity continues to increase in the Southeastern U.S., our need for well-written articles on certain projects is greater than ever before. If you can supply such articles, *Dixie Contractor* can keep you busy."

FINE HOMEBUILDING, The Taunton Press, Inc., 63 S. Main St., Box 355, Newtown CT 06470. (203)426-8171. Managing Editor: Mark Feirer. Less than 1% freelance written. Bimonthly magazine covering house building, construction, design for builders, architects and serious amateurs. Circ. 210,000. Pays on publication. Publishes ms an average of 6-12 months after acceptance. Byline given. Offers negotiable kill fee. Buys first rights and "use in books to be published." Query for electronic submissions. Computer printout submissions acceptable; prefers letter-quality. Reports as soon as possible. Sample copy $4.50; free writer's guidelines.

Nonfiction: Technical (unusual techniques in design or construction process). Query. Length: 2,000-3,000 words. Pays $150-900. Pays expenses of writers on assignment.

Columns/Departments: Tools and Materials (products or techniques that are new or unusual); Great Moments in Building History (humorous, embarrassing, or otherwise noteworthy anecdotes); Reviews (short reviews of books on building or design) and Reports and Comment (essays, short reports on construction and architecture trends and developments). Query. Length: 300-1,000 words. Pays $50-250.

‡IMPACT, The Magazine for Southern California New Housing Professionals, Insites, Suite 307, 348 W. Market St., San Diego CA 92101. (619)239-1411. Editor: Bruce Golden. 40% freelance written. Monthly trade journal on the residential home building industry. "Articles must be slanted to the interests of home builders, financiers, construction suppliers, title companies, anyone with a connection to the residential home building industry. Topics may cover current trends or bold new ideas." Circ. 10,000. Pays on publication. Publishes ms an average of 1 month after acceptance. Byline given. Offers 25% kill fee. Buys one-time rights. Submit seasonal/holiday material 3 months in advance. Simultaneous, photocopied and previously published submissions OK. Computer printout submissions OK; no dot-matrix. Reports in 2 weeks on queries; 3 weeks on mss. Free sample copy.

Nonfiction: Book excerpts (about building industry), essays, expose, general interest, historical/nostalgic, how-to (market, get need financing, decorate model homes), humor, interview/profile, new product, opinion, photo feature. Buys 30 mss/year. Query with or without published clips, or send complete ms. Length: 500-3,500 words. Pays $20-150. Sometimes pays expenses of writers on assignment.

Photos: Send photos with submission. Reviews transparencies. Offers no additional payment for photos accepted with ms. Captions and identification of subjects required. Buys one-time rights.

Columns/Departments: Linda Bona, columns editor. Insights (brief news items on industry, events, people, new products) 100-1,000 words. Buys 20 mss/year. Send complete ms. Length: 100 words. Pays $20-50.

Fiction: Humorous, science fiction. "We would rarely use any fiction unless it was related strictly to the building industry. We're more likely to use humorous material though it still must relate to our subject matter." Buys 1 ms/year. Send complete ms. Length: 500-3,000 words. Pays $30-100.

Fillers: Anecdotes, facts, gags to be illustrated by cartoonist, newsbreaks, short humor. Buys 15 mss/year. Length: 100-1,000 words. Pays $20-50.

Tips: "Find out what builders of large home developments are interested in. Determine future trends in building, interior design, and marketing. We publish whatever is of interest to the various professionals involved in the building industry."

INLAND ARCHITECT, The Midwestern Magazine for the Building Arts, Inland Architect Press, 10 West Hubbard St., Box 10394, Chicago IL 60610. (312)321-0583. Editor: Cynthia Davidson-Powers. 80% freelance written. Prefers to work with published/established writers. Bimonthly magazine covering architecture and urban planning. "*Inland Architect* is a critical journal covering architecture and design in the midwest for an audience primarily of architects. *Inland* is open to all points of view, providing they are intelligently expressed and of relevance to architecture." Circ. 7,000. Pays on publication. Publishes ms an average of 2 months after acceptance. Byline given. Offers 60% kill fee. Buys first rights. Computer printout submissions OK; no dot-matrix. Reports in 1 month on queries; 2 months on mss. Sample copy $4.

Nonfiction: Book excerpts, essays, historical/nostalgic, interview/profile, criticism and photo feature of architecture. Every summer *Inland* focuses on a midwestern city, its architecture and urban design. Call to find out 1989 city. No new products, "how to run your office," or technical pieces. Buys 40 mss/year. Query with or without published clips, or send complete ms. Length: 750-3,500 words. Pays $100-300 for assigned articles; pays $75-250 for unsolicited articles. Sometimes pays the expenses of writers on assignment.

Photos: Send photos with submission. Reviews 4x5 transparencies, slides and 8x10 prints. Offers no additional payment for photos accepted with ms. Identification of subjects required. Buys one-time rights.

Columns/Departments: Books (reviews of new publications on architecture, design and, occasionally, art), 250-1,000 words. Buys 10 mss/year. Query. Length: 250-1,000 words. Pays $25-100.

Tips: "Propose specific articles, e.g, to cover a lecture, to interview a certain architect. General ideas, such as preservation, are too broad. Articles must be written for an audience primarily consisting of well-educated architects. If an author feels he has a 'hot' timely idea, a phone call is appreciated."

MIDWEST CONTRACTOR, Construction Digest, Inc., 3170 Mercier, Box 419766, Kansas City MO 64141. (816)931-2080. 5% freelance written. Works with a small number of new/unpublished writers each year. Bi-weekly magazine covering the public works and engineering construction industries in Iowa, Nebraska, Kansas and western and northeastern Missouri. Circ. 8,426. Pays on publication. Publishes ms an average of 2 months after acceptance. Byline given depending on nature of article. Makes work-for-hire assignments. Query for electronic submissions. Computer printout submissions acceptable; prefers letter-quality. Reports in 2 weeks. Sample copy for 11x15 SAE with 8 first class stamps.

Nonfiction: How-to, photo feature, technical, "nuts and bolts" construction job-site features. "We seek two-to three-page articles on topics of interest to our readership, including marketing trends, tips, and construction job-site stories. Providing concise, accurate, and original news stories is another freelance opportunity." Buys 4 mss/year. Query with three published clips. Length: 175 typewritten lines, 35 character count, no maximum. Pays $50/published page.

Tips: "We need writers who can write clearly about our specialized trade area. An engineering/construction background is a plus if the person is also an excellent writer. The writer may have a better chance of breaking in at our publication with short articles and fillers because we have very limited space for editorial copy. The most frequent mistake made by writers is that they do not tailor their article to our specific market—the nonresidential construction market in Nebraska, Iowa, Kansas and Missouri. We are not interested in what happens in New York unless it has a specific impact in the Midwest. We will be producing more personality profiles of contractors."

‡MULTI-HOUSING NEWS, Gralla Publications, 1515 Broadway, New York NY 10036. (212)869-1300. Editor: Todd Zimmerman. Managing Editor: William Nutt. 5% freelance written. A monthly magazine on multi-housing development. "We help developers improve their business, whether through marketing articles, new financial strategies or new construction techniques." Circ. 51,000. Pays on acceptance. Publishes ms an average of 3 months after acceptance. Byline given. Publication not copyrighted. Buys first rights. Computer printout submissions OK; prefers letter-quality. Reports in 2 weeks. Free sample copy and writer's guidelines.

Nonfiction: Moira Monahan, articles editor. Buys 24 mss/year. Query. Length: 800-1,000 words. Pays $200-300 for assigned articles. Pays $200-250 for unsolicited articles.

Photos: Send photos with submission. Reviews contact sheets and prints (5x7). Offers no additional payment for photos accepted with ms. Captions required. Buys all rights.

‡PACIFIC BUILDER & ENGINEER, Vernon Publications Inc.. Suite 200, 3000 Northup Way, Bellevue WA 98007. (206)827-9900. Editor: John M. Watkins. Managing Editor: Michele Dill. 20% freelance written. A biweekly magazine on heavy construction. "We cover non-residential construction in Washington, Oregon, Idaho and Montana." Circ. 9,848. Pays on publication. Byline given. Buys first North American serial rights. Submit seasonal material 2 months in advance. Photocopied submissions OK. Computer printout submissions OK; prefers letter-quality. Reports in 3 weeks on queries; 6 weeks on mss.

Nonfiction: How-to (construction) and technical (construction). Buys 6 mss/year. Query with published clips. Length: 1,000-2,500 words. Pays $100-300. Does not pay for unsolicited manuscripts. Sometimes pays the expenses of writers on assignment.

Photos: Send photos with submission. Reviews contact sheets and transparencies (35mm). Offers $15-125 per photo. Buys all rights.

‡**RSI, Roofing/Siding/Insulation**, Harcourt Brace Jovanovich Publications Inc., 7500 Old Oak Blvd., Cleveland OH 44130. (216)243-8100. Editor: Webb Shaw. 15% freelance written. A monthly magazine about roofing, siding and insulation fields. "Our audience is almost entirely contractors in the roofing, siding and/or insulation fields. The publication's goal is to help them improve their business, with heavy emphasis on application techniques." Circ. 20,000. Pays on publication. Publishes ms an average of 3 months after acceptance. Byline sometimes given. Buys all rights. Computer printout submissions OK; no dot-matrix. Free sample copy.

Nonfiction: How-to (application of RSI products), new product, technical (on roofing, siding and/or insulation) and business articles directed and subcontractors. "No consumer-oriented articles. Our readers sell to consumers and building owners." Buys 6 mss/year. Query. Length: 1,000-3,000 words. Pays $100-800 for assigned articles. Pays $50-400 for unsolicited articles. Sometimes pays the expenses of writers on assignment.

Photos: State availability of photos with submission. Reviews transparencies (2¼x2¼) and prints (5x7). Offers no additional payment for photos accepted with ms. Captions and identification of subjects required.

SHOPPING CENTER WORLD, Communication Channels Inc., 6255 Barfield Rd., Atlanta GA 30328. (404)256-9800. Managing Editor: Mary Joe Hess. 75% freelance written. Prefers to work with published/established writers. A monthly magazine covering the shopping center industry. "Material is written with the shopping center developer and shopping center tenant in mind." Pays on publication. Publishes ms an average of 3 months after acceptance. Byline given. Buys all rights. Submit seasonal/holiday material 3 months in advance. Photocopied submissions OK. Query for electronic submissions. Computer printout submissions acceptable; prefers letter-quality. Reports in 1 month. Sample copy $4.

Nonfiction: Interview/profile, new product, opinion, photo feature, and technical. Especially interested in renovation case studies on shopping centers. Buys 50 mss/year. Query with or without published clips, or send complete ms. Length: 750-3,000 words. Pays $75-500. Sometimes pays expenses of writers on assignment.

Photos: State availability of photos with submission. Reviews 4x5 transparencies, and 35mm slides. Offers no additional payment for photos accepted with ms. Model releases and identification of subjects required. Buys one-time rights.

Tips: "We are always looking for talented writers to work on assignment. Send resume and published clips. Writers with real estate writing and business backgrounds have a better chance. Product overviews, renovations, and state reviews are all freelance written on an assignment basis."

WESTERN ROOFING/INSULATION/SIDING, Dodson Publications, Inc., 27202 Via Burgos, Mission Viejo CA 92691. (714)951-1653. Editor: Marc Dodson. 30% freelance written. Bimonthly magazine. Circ. 12,000. Pays on publication. Publishes ms an average of 2 months after acceptance. Byline given. Buys first rights, one-time rights or simultaneous rights. Submit seasonal/holiday material 4 months in advance. Photocopied submissions OK. Computer printout submissions OK; prefers letter-quality. Sample copy for $2 or 9x12 SAE and 7 first class stamps; writer's guidelines for #10 SASE and one first-class stamp.

Nonfiction: Historical/nostalgic, interview/profile, new product, personal experience and technical articles of interest to "building professionals concerned with the design and specification of roofing, insulation, and siding, and concerned with industry-related news throughout the western United States." Buys 10 mss/year. Send complete ms. Length: 500-2,000 words. Pays $15-150. Sometimes pays with contributor copies depending on quality of article.

Photos: State availability of photos with submission. Reviews contact sheets. Offers no additional payment for photos accepted with ms. Captions and identification of subjects required. Buys one-time rights.

Columns/Departments: Sue Dodson, editor. Industry News (aquisitions,plant openings, legal); People (promotions, new assignments) and Product News (new products/improved products), all 100-300 words. Buys 30 mss/year. Send complete ms. Pays $25 maximum.

ALWAYS submit manuscripts or queries with a self-addressed, stamped envelope (SASE) within your country or International Reply Coupons (IRC) purchased from the post office for other countries.

Dental

DENTAL ECONOMICS, Penwell Publishing Co., Box 3408, Tulsa OK 74101. (918)835-3161. Editor: Dick Hale. 50% freelance written. A monthly dental trade journal. "Our readers are actively practicing dentists who look to us for current practice-building, practice-administrative and personal finance assistance." Circ. 103,000. Pays on acceptance. Publishes ms an average of 3-4 months after acceptance. Byline given. Buys first rights. Submit seasonal/holiday material 6 months in advance. Computer printout submissions OK; prefers letter-quality. Reports in 3 weeks on queries; 1 month on mss. Free sample copy and writer's guidelines.
Nonfiction: General interest, how-to and new product. "No human interest and consumer-related stories." Buys 40 mss/year. Query. Length: 750-3,500 words. Pays $150-500 for assigned articles; pays $75-350 for unsolicited articles. Sometimes pays the expenses of writers on assignment.
Photos: State availability of photos with submission. Reviews contact sheets. Offers no additional payment for photos accepted with ms. Model releases and identification of subjects required. Buys one-time rights.
Columns/Departments: Ron Combs, editor. Tax Q&A (tax tips for dentists), 1,500 words; Capitolgram (late legislative news—dentistry), 750 words; and Econ Report (national economic outlook), 750 words. Buys 36 mss/year. Pays $50-300.
Tips: "How-to articles on specific subjects such as practice-building, newsletters and collections should be relevant to a busy, solo-practice dentist."

DENTIST, Dental Market Network, Stevens Publishing Corp., 225 N. New Rd., Box 7573, Waco TX 76714. (817)776-9000. Editor: Mark S. Hartley. 25% freelance written. Eager to work with new/unpublished writers. A bimonthly trade journal for dentists. Any news or feature story of interest to dentists is considered. Circ. 154,860. Pays 60 days after acceptance. Publishes ms an average of 2 months after acceptance. Byline given. Offers 25% kill fee. Buys first North American serial rights. Submit seasonal/holiday material 1 year in advance. Simultaneous submissions OK. Computer printout submissions OK; prefers letter-quality. Reports in 1 month on queries; 2 months on mss. Sample copy and writer's guidelines for 12½x15 SAE with 7 first class stamps.
Nonfiction: How-to, humor, interview/profile, new product and technical. Buys 20 mss/year. Query with or without published clips, or send complete ms. Length: 30 inches of copy. Pays $50-200 for assigned articles. Sometimes pays the expenses of writers on assignment
Photos: Send photos with submission. Reviews contact sheets. Offers $10-100 per photo. Captions and identification of subjects required. Buys one-time rights.
Tips: "Purchased freelance material reflects a knowledgeable, analytical insight into issues concerning the dental profession. Audience is very intelligent and literate; readers can easily spot editorial that is not adequately researched. The emphasis in 1989 will continue to be on obtaining timely, newsworthy editorial pertinent to dentistry."

‡GENERAL DENTISTRY, Academy of General Dentistry, Suite 1200, 211 E. Chicago Ave., Chicago IL 60611. (312)440-4344. Managing Editor: Terrance Stanton. 5% freelance written. A bimonthly magazine about dentistry. "Our focus is continuing education in dentistry. Our readers are dentists. Articles should be written at a dentist's level of knowledge." Circ. 45,000. Pays on acceptance. Publishes ms an average of 4 months after acceptance. Offers 50% kill fee. Buys all rights. Simultaneous and photocopied submissions OK. Computer printout submissions OK; prefers letter-quality. Reports in 1 month. Sample copy for 8½x11 SAE with 7 first class stamps.
Nonfiction: Essays, historical/nostalgic, interview/profile, new product and technical. No articles written for dental patients. Buys 10 mss/year. Query with or without published clips, or send complete ms. Pays $125-500 for assigned articles. Pays $125-400 for unsolicited articles. Pays the expenses of writers on assignment.
Photos: State availability of photos with submission. Reviews contact sheets. Offers no additional payment for photos accepted with ms. Captions, model releases and identification of subjects required. All rights for dental market acquired.
Tips: "Understand that our focus is scientific. Any article we buy must be of special interest to the members of our association, which is devoted to fostering continuing education in dentistry. Writers are advised to call or query so that we can assist in developing an idea. Stories that have to do with improvements in clinical practice are the best prospects for our magazine."

PROOFS, The Magazine of Dental Sales and Marketing, Box 3408, Tulsa OK 74101. (918)835-3161. Publisher: Joe Bessette. Associate Publishers: Robert McConaughey and Dick Hale. Editor: Mary Elizabeth Good. 10% freelance written. Magazine published 10 times/year; combined issues July/August, November/December. Pays on publication. Byline given. Computer printout submissions acceptable; prefers letter-quality. Reports in 2 weeks. Free sample copy.

Nonfiction: Uses short articles, chiefly on selling to dentists. Must have understanding of dental trade industry and problems of marketing and selling to dentists and dental laboratories. Query. Pays about $75.
Tips: "The most frequent mistakes made by writers are having a lack of familiarity with industry problems and talking down to our audience."

RDH, The National Magazine for Dental Hygiene Professionals, Stevens Publishing Corp., 225 N. New Rd., Waco TX 76714. (817)776-9000. Managing Editor: Laura Albrecht. 55% freelance written. Eager to work with new/unpublished writers. The magazine is published (combined issues) in January/February, July/August, and November/December, monthly otherwise, covering information relevant to dental hygiene professionals as business-career oriented individuals. "Dental hygienists are highly trained, licensed professionals; most are women. They are concerned with ways to develop rewarding careers, give optimum service to patients and to grow both professionally and personally." Circ. 63,210. Usually pays on publication; sometimes on acceptance. Publishes ms an average of 8 months after acceptance. Byline given. Seldom offers kill fee. Buys first serial rights. Computer printout submissions acceptable; no dot-matrix. Reports in 3 weeks on queries; 2 months on mss. Sample copy for 9x11 SAE; writer's guidelines for SAE with 1 first class stamp.
Nonfiction: Essays, general interest, interview/profile, personal experience, photo feature and technical. "We are interested in any topic that offers broad reader appeal, especially in the area of personal growth (communication, managing time, balancing career and personal life). No undocumented clinical or technical articles; how-it-feels-to-be-a-patient articles; product-oriented articles (unless in generic terms); anything cutesy-unprofessional." Length: 1,500-3,000 words. Pays $100-350 for assigned articles; pays $50-200 for unsolicited articles. Sometimes pays expenses of writers on assignment.
Photos: Send photos with submission. Reviews 3x5 prints. Model releases required. Buys one-time rights.
Tips: "Freelancers should have a feel for the concerns of today's business-career woman—and address those interests and concerns with practical, meaningful and even motivational messages. We want to see good-quality manuscripts on both personal growth and lifestyle topics. For clinical and/or technical topics, we prefer the writers be members of the dental profession. New approaches to old problems and dilemmas will always get a close look from our editors. *RDH* is also interested in manuscripts for our feature section. Other than clinical information, dental hygienists are interested in all sorts of topics—finances, personal growth, educational opportunities, business management, staff/employer relations, communication and motivation, office rapport and career options. Other than clinical/technical articles, *RDH* maintains an informal tone. Writing style can easily be accommodated to our format."

Drugs, Health Care and Medical Products

‡**THE APOTHECARY**, Health Care Marketing Services, #200, 95 First St., Box AP, Los Altos CA 94022. (415)941-3955. Editor: Jerold Karabensh. Publication Director: Janet Goodman. 100% freelance writen. Prefers to work with published/established writers. Quarterly magazine. "*The Apothecary* aims to provide practical information to community retail pharmacists." Circ. 60,000. Pays on acceptance. Publishes ms an average of 5 months after acceptance. Byline given. Buys all rights. Submit seasonal material 8 months in advance. Simultaneous queries and photocopied submissions OK. Computer printout submissions acceptable; prefers letter-quality. Reports in 6 weeks on queries; 5 months on mss. Sample copy for 9x12 SAE with 4 first class stamps.
Nonfiction: How-to (e.g., manage a pharmacy); opinion (of registered pharmacists); and health-related feature stories. "We publish only those general health articles with some practical application for the pharmacist as businessman. No general articles not geared to our pharmacy readership; no fiction." Buys 4 mss/year. Query with published clips. Length: 750-3,000 words. Pays $100-300.
Columns/Departments: Commentary (views or issues relevant to the subject of pharmacy or to pharmacists). Send complete ms. Length: 750-1,000 words. "This section is unpaid; we will take submissions with byline."
Tips: "Submit material geared to the *pharmacist* as *business person*. Write according to our policy, i.e., business articles with emphasis on practical information for a community pharmacist. We suggest reading several back issues and following general feature story tone, depth, etc. Stay away from condescending use of language. Though our articles are written in simple style, they must reflect knowledge of the subject and reasonable respect for the readers' professionalism and intelligence."

‡**CANADIAN PHARMACEUTICAL JOURNAL**, 1785 Alta Vista Dr., Ottawa, Ontario K1G 3Y6 Canada. (613)523-7877. Editor: Jane Dewar. Assistant Editors: Mary MacDonald-LaPrade and Catherine Partington. 40% freelance written. Works with a small number of new/unpublished writers each year. Monthly journal for

pharmacists. Circ. 12,500. Pays after editing. Publishes ms an average of 3 months after acceptance. Buys first serial rights. Computer printout submissions acceptable; no dot-matrix. Reports in 2 months. Free sample copy.

Nonfiction: Relevant to Canadian pharmacy. Publishes exposes (pharmacy practice, education and legislation); how-to (pharmacy business operations); historical (pharmacy practice, Canadian legislation, education); and interviews with and profiles on Canadian and international pharmacy figures. Length: 200-400 words (for news notices); 800-1,500 words (for articles). Query. Payment is contingent on value.

Photos: B&w (5x7) glossies purchased with mss. Pays $25 first photo; $5 for each additional photo. Captions and model release required.

Tips: "Query with complete description of proposed article, including topic, sources (in general), length, payment requested, suggested submission date, and whether photographs will be included. It is helpful if the writer has read a *recent* copy of the journal; we are glad to send one if required. References should be included where appropriate (this is vital where medical and scientific information is included). Send 3 copies of each ms. Author's degree and affiliations (if any) and writing background should be listed."

‡CORPORATE FITNESS, The Journal for Employee Health and Wellness Programs, MacMillan Professional Journals. 1640 5th St., Box 2178, Santa Monica CA 90401. Editor: Lauren Cobb. 30% freelance written. A bimonthly magazine on corporate fitness and wellness. Pays on acceptance. Publishes ms an average of 3 months after acceptance. Byline given. Buys all rights and makes work-for-hire assignments. Computer printout submissions OK; prefers letter-quality. Reports in 1 month on queries; 2 months on mss. Writer's guidelines for ‰10 SAE with 1 first class stamp.

Nonfiction: How-to (run a corporate fitness program, manage budgets), new product, technical, sports medicine, nutrition and profiles of innovative programs. "No chatty articles written for the general public. We want specific topics written for the corporate fitness and wellness professional." Buys 12 mss/year. Query with or without published clips, or send complete ms. Length: 1,000-3,500 words. Pays 10-15¢/word. Pays the expenses of writers on assignment.

Photos: State availability of photos with submission. Reviews prints. Offers no additional payment for photos accepted with ms. Identification of subjects required.

Columns/Departments: Sports Medicine (information on sports medicine in the corporate fitness environment), 2,000 words; Food for Thought (information on nutrition in the corporate fitness environment); Bottom Line (articles detailing cost-benefit analysis of corporate fitness programs). Buys 12 mss/year. Pays 10-15¢/word.

Tips: "Send a query with clips and qualifications. Follow up with a telephone call in two weeks. Columns and feature stories are most open to freelancers."

NURSING HOMES, And Senior Citizen Care, Centaur & Company, 5 Willowbrook Ct., Potomac MD 20854. (301)983-1152. Editor: William D. Magnes. 60% freelance written. Bimonthly magazine covering the nursing home industry. "Academic articles (often by RNs and PhDs) and human-interest stories. Most interested in mss on resident/patient care, which can cover a myriad of subjects." Circ. 4,000. Pays on acceptance. Publishes ms an average of 3 months after acceptance. Byline given. Buys all rights. Submit seasonal/holiday material 4 months in advance. Computer printout submissions OK; no dot-matrix. Reports in 2 weeks on queries; 1 month on mss. Sample copy $7.50; free writer's guidelines . "Generally a personal letter."

Nonfiction: Essays, humor, inspirational, new product, opinion and personal experience. "No-hyped articles on company or product promotion." Buys 30-40 mss/year. Query with published clips, or send complete ms. Length: 2,500 words maximum. Pays $50 average. Rarely pays the expenses of writers on assignment.

Photos: Send photos with submission. Reviews 3x5 prints. Offers $50 per full-color photo for front cover. Buys all rights.

Columns/Departments: Book Reviews, 250 words. Query with published clips. Pays $30.

Poetry: Light verse and traditional. Buys few poems/year. Pays $25 maximum.

Fillers: Facts, newsbreaks and short humor. Buys few/year.

Tips: "Discuss a problem, how and why it is faced, and the results—but subject must have a thrust about a facility or situation that underscores what is different in some way(s)."

RX HOME CARE, The Journal of Home Health Care and Rehabilitation, MacMillan Professional Journals, 1640 5th St., Santa Monica CA 90401. (213)395-0234. Senior Editor: Cliff Henke. 40% freelance written. Monthly magazine covering home health care equipment supply. "The journal addresses the durable medical equipment and health care supply needs of patients being cared for at home. The primary audience is medical supply dealers. The secondary audience is physical therapists, occupational therapists, nurses, physicians, and other medical professionals in the home health care field." Circ. 18,000. Pays on acceptance and receipt of phone log and copy of bill. Publishes ms an average of 6 months after acceptance. Byline given.

Buys all rights and makes work-for-hire assignments. Computer printout submissions acceptable. Reports in 3 weeks. Sample copy by phone request.

Nonfiction: How-to (market durable medical equipment); and technical (on use of non-invasive therapies in the home). "No general articles on health-related topics that are not geared specifically to our readership." Buys 50 mss/year. Query by phone a must. Length: 900-3,500 words. Pays 12¢/word. Pays expenses of writers on assignment.

Columns/Departments: Washington Watch (legislative news and analysis); On Line (computer news); Dealership of the Month (profile). Length: 500-2,000 words. Buys 5-24/year. Query. Pays $100 minimum.

Tips: "Writers must conform to our style, which is based on the American Medical Association stylebook. A medical background is not necessary to write for *RX Home Care*, but it is helpful when tackling technical equipment-related topics. Also important are business issues affecting our audience. All submissions are reviewed by an editorial advisory board of industry professionals. We now reflect more news orientation—much in the way of legislation, court cases, state government initiatives and technological and professional developments has and will happen to our audience. Now more than ever, they need timely and accurate info."

Education and Counseling

Professional educators, teachers, coaches and counselors—as well as other people involved in training and education—read the journals classified here. Many journals for educators are nonprofit forums for professional advancement; writers contribute articles in return for a byline and contributor's copies. *Writer's Market* includes only educational journals that pay for articles. Education-related publications for students are included in the Consumer Career, College and Alumni, and Teen and Young Adult sections.

THE AMERICAN SCHOOL BOARD JOURNAL, National School Boards Association, 1680 Duke St., Alexandria VA 22314. (703)838-6722. Editor: Gregg Downey. 10% freelance written. "We have no preference for published/unpublished writers; it's the quality of the article and writing that count." Monthly magazine. Emphasizes public school administration and policymaking for elected members of public boards of education throughout U.S. and Canada, and high-level administrators of same. Circ. 42,000. Pays on acceptance. Publishes ms an average of 3 months after acceptance. Buys all rights. Phone queries OK. Photocopied submissions OK. Computer printout submissions acceptable; prefers letter-quality. Reports in 2 months. Sample copy and guidelines for 8½x11 SAE.

Nonfiction: Publishes how-to articles (solutions to problems of public school operation including political problems). "No material on how public schools are in trouble. We all know that; what we need are *answers*." Buys 20 mss/year. Query. Length: 400-2,000 words. Payment for feature articles varies, "but never less than $100."

Photos: B&w glossies (any size) purchased on assignment. Captions required. Pays $10-50. Model release required.

Tips: "Can you lend a national perspective to a locally observed school program? Do you prefer writing for a general audience or a specific, knowledgeable-on-this-issue audience?"

ARTS & ACTIVITIES, Publishers' Development Corporation, Suite 200, 591 Camino de la Reina, San Diego CA 92108. (619)297-5352. Editor: Dr. Leven C. Leatherbury. Managing Editor: Maryellen Bridge. 95% freelance written. Eager to work with new/unpublished writers. Monthly (except July and August) art education magazine covering art education at levels from preschool through college for educators and therapists engaged in arts and crafts education and training. Circ. 19,466. Pays on publication. Publishes ms an average of 6 months after acceptance. Byline given. Not copyrighted. Buys first serial rights. Submit seasonal/holiday material 4 months in advance. Photocopied submissions OK. Computer printout submissions acceptable; prefers letter-quality. Reports in 2 months. Sample copy for 9x12 envelope and 8 first class stamps; writer's guidelines for #10 SAE and 1 first class stamp.

Nonfiction: Historical/nostalgic (arts activities history); how-to (classroom art experiences, artists' techniques); interview/profile (of artists); opinion (on arts activities curriculum, ideas on how to do things better); personal experience in the art class room ("this ties in with the how-to, we like it to be *personal*, no recipe style"); and articles on exceptional art programs. Buys 50-80 mss/year. Length: 200-2,000 words. Pays $35-150.

Tips: "Frequently in unsolicited manuscripts, writers obviously have not studied the magazine to see what style of articles we publish. Send for a sample copy to familiarize yourself with our style and needs. The best way to find out if his/her writing style suits our needs is for the author to submit a manuscript on speculation."

CLASSROOM COMPUTER LEARNING, Suite A4, 2169 Francisco Blvd. E., San Rafael CA 94901. Editor: Holly Brady. 50% freelance written. Works with a small number of new/unpublished writers each year. Monthly magazine published during school year emphasizing elementary through high school educational computing topics. Circ. 83,000. Pays on acceptance. Publishes ms an average of 8 months after acceptance. Buys all rights or first serial rights. Submit seasonal/holiday material 6 months in advance. Computer printout submissions acceptable; prefers letter-quality. Reports in 2 months. Writer's guidelines with SAE and 1 first class stamp; sample copy for 8x10 SAE and 6 first class stamps.
Nonfiction: "We publish manuscripts that describe innovative ways of using computers in the classroom as well as articles that discuss controversial issues in computer education." Interviews, brief computer-related activity ideas and longer featurettes describing fully developed and tested classroom ideas. Recent article example: "A Network Primer: How They're Used ... and How They Could be Used" (April, 1988). Buys 50 mss/year. Query. Length: 500 words or less for classroom activities; 1,000-1,500 words for classroom activity featurettes; 1,500-2,500 words for major articles. Pays $25 for activities; $100-200 for featurettes; varying rates for longer articles. Educational Software Reviews: Assigned through editorial offices. "If interested, send a letter telling us of your areas of interest and expertise as well as the microcomputer(s) you have available to you." Pays $100 per review. Sometimes pays expenses of writers on assignment.
Photos: State availability of photos with query.
Tips: "The talent that goes into writing our shorter hands-on pieces is different from that required for features (e.g., interviews, issues pieces, etc.) Write whatever taps your talent best. A frequent mistake is taking too 'novice' or too 'expert' an approach. You need to know our audience well and to understand how much they know about computers. Also, too many manuscripts lack a definite point of view or focus or opinion. We like pieces with clear, strong, well thought out opinions."

COMPUTERS IN EDUCATION, Moorshead Publications, 1300 Don Mills Rd., North York, Toronto, Ontario M3B 3M8 Canada. (416)445-5600. Editor: Roger Allan. 90% freelance written. Eager to work with new/unpublished writers. Magazine published 10 times/year. Articles of interest to teachers, computer consultants and administrators working at the kindergarten to 13 level. Circ. 18,000. Pays on publication. Publishes ms an average of 2 months after acceptance. Byline given. Buys first serial rights, first North American serial rights, one time rights, second serial (reprint) rights, and all rights. Phone queries OK. Photocopied submissions OK. Query for electronic submissions. Computer printout submissions acceptable; prefers letter-quality. Sample copy and writer's guidelines with SASE or IRC.
Nonfiction: Use of computers in education and techniques of teaching using computers; lesson plans, novel applications, anything that is practical for the teacher. Does not want overviews, "Gee Whizzes," and reinventions of the wheel. Length 700-2,000 words. Pays 6-10¢/word. Sometimes pays the expenses of writers on assignment.
Photos: Photos and/or artwork all but mandatory. Pays extra for photos. Captions required.
Tips: "While there will be no change in the editorial mandate (to be practical), there will be more articles on desktop publishing and electronic music in 1988. We would like to receive articles on educational electronic music, educational databases, desktop publishing in the classroom, and on networking. We are looking for practical articles by working teachers. Nothing too general, no overviews, or the same thing that has been said for years."

CURRICULUM REVIEW, 407 S. Dearborn St., Chicago IL 60605. (312)922-8245. Editor-in-Chief: Brian Ragan. Circ. 10,000. A monthly trade magazine for principals, department heads, teachers, curriculum specialists and superintendents. Pays on acceptance. Publishes ms an average of 2 months after acceptance. Byline given. Buys all rights. Simultaneous, photocopied and previously published submissions OK. Computer printout submissions acceptable. Reports in 2 weeks on mss.
Nonfiction: "Case histories of classroom success stories and successful innovations dealing with curriculum in elementary schools. No essays bemoaning failure of schools, generalized essays explaining what must be done to improve schools, essays outlining radical changes to schools." Send complete ms. Length: 250-3,000 words. Pays $25-250. Sometimes pays the expenses of writers on assignment.
Tips: "We reserve the right to edit all manuscripts before publication."

ELECTRONIC EDUCATION, Electronic Communications, Inc., Suite 220, 1311 Executive Center Dr., Tallahassee FL 32301. (904)878-4178. Managing Editor: Cindy Whaley. 10-15% freelance written. Magazine published 8 times/school year covering classroom uses of computers in grades K-12. "To help teachers and administrators use computers most effectively for instructional purposes." Circ. 80,000. Pays on publication. Publishes ms an average of 4 months after acceptance. Byline given. Buys all rights. Submit seasonal/holiday material 6 months in advance. Computer printout submissions OK; prefers letter-quality. Reports in 2 months.

Sample copy $3.50; free writer's guidelines to serious inquiries.

Nonfiction: Essays, how-to (implement an application, for example), interview/profile (of prominent person or expert in field), opinion, personal experience (of application by teacher, for example). Buys 8-10 mss/year. Query with or without published clips, or send complete ms. Length: 800-2,100 words. Payment negotiable; sometimes pay in contributor's copies on mutual agreement. Sometimes pays the expenses of writers on assignment.

Photos: Send photos with submission. Reviews transparencies and 8x10 or 5x8 prints. Offers no additional payment for photos accepted with ms. Captions, model releases and identification of subjects required. Buys all rights.

Tips: "Investigate local schools (k-12) and teachers for innovative instructional uses of computers."

INSTRUCTOR MAGAZINE, Edgell Communications, Inc.. 7500 Old Oak Blvd., Cleveland OH 44130. Editor-in-Chief: Elizabeth Compelio. 30% freelance written. Eager to work with new/unpublished writers, "especially teachers." Monthly magazine. Emphasizes elementary education. Circ. 255,000. Pays on acceptance. Publishes ms an average of 1 year after acceptance. Buys all rights or first North American serial rights. Submit seasonal/holiday material 6 months in advance. Photocopied submissions OK. Computer printout submissions acceptable; prefers letter-quality. Reports in 6-8 weeks. Free writer's guidelines; mention *Writer's Market* in request.

Nonfiction: How-to articles on elementary classroom practice—practical suggestions as well as project reports, opinion pieces on professional issues, and current first-person stories by teachers about the teaching experience. Query. Length: 100-2,500 words. Pays $15-100 for short items; $100-350 for articles and features. Send all queries to Cindy Zbaeren, manuscripts editor. No poetry.

Tips: "The most frequent mistake writers make is writing to a general audience rather than teachers. We'll be looking for writing that considers the increasing ethnic diversity of classrooms and the greater age-range among elementary teachers."

JOURNAL OF CAREER PLANNING & EMPLOYMENT, College Placement Council, Inc., 62 Highland Ave., Bethlehem PA 18017. (215)868-1421. Editor: Patricia Sinnott. 25% freelance written. Published Nov., Jan., March, and May. A magazine for career development professionals who counsel and/or hire prospective college students, graduating students, employees, and job-changers. Circ. 4,000. Pays on acceptance. Publishes ms an average of 4 months after acceptance. Byline given. Buys first rights. Photocopied submissions OK. Computer printout submissions acceptable; no dot-matrix. Reports in 1 month on queries; 2 months on mss. Free writer's guidelines.

Nonfiction: Book excerpts, how-to, humor, interview/profile, opinion, personal experience, photo feature, new techniques/innovative practices and current issues in the field. No articles that speak directly to job candidates. Buys 7-10 mss/year. Query with published clips, or send complete ms. Length: 2,000-4,000 words. Pays $200-400.

Tips: "A freelancer can best break into our publication by sending query with clips of published work, by writing on topics that aim directly at the journal's audience—professionals in the career planning, placement and recruitment field—and by using an easy-to-read, narrative style rather than a formal, thesis style. The area of our publication most open to freelancers is nonfiction feature articles only. Make sure that the topic is directly relevant to the career planning and employment field and that the style is crisp and easy to read."

LEARNING 88/89, 1111 Bethlehem Pike, Springhouse PA 19477. Editor: Charlene F. Gaynor. 45% freelance written. Published monthly during school year. Emphasizes elementary and junior high school education topics. Circ. 275,000. Pays on acceptance. Buys all rights. Submit seasonal/holiday material 6 months in advance. Photocopied submissions OK. Computer printout submissions acceptable. Reports in 3 months. Sample copy $3; free writer's guidelines.

Nonfiction: "We publish manuscripts that describe innovative, practical teaching strategies or probe controversial and significant issues of interest to kindergarten to 8th grade teachers." How-to (classroom management, specific lessons or units or activities for children—all at the elementary and junior high level, and hints for teaching in all curriculum areas): personal experience (from teachers in elementary and junior high schools); and profile (with teachers who are in unusual or innovative teaching situations). Strong interest in articles that deal with discipline, teaching strategy, motivation and working with parents. Article examples: "Beyond the Right Answer—Helping Your Students Make Sense Out of Math" (Jan. 1988) and "A Difficult Student: Jimmy Was Afraid to be Loved" (Feb. 1988). Buys 250 mss/year. Query. Length: 1,000-3,500 words. Pays $50-350.

Photos: State availability of photos with query. Model release required. "We are also interested in series of photos that show step-by-step projects or tell a story that will be of interest."

Tips: "We're looking for practical, teacher-tested ideas and strategies as well as first-hand personal accounts of dramatic successes—or failures—with a lesson to be drawn. We're also interested in examples of especially creative classrooms and teachers."

‡LOLLIPOPS, The Magazine for Early Childhood Educators, Good Apple, Inc., 1204 Buchanan, Box 299, Carthage IL 62321. (212)357-3981. Editor: Jerry Aten. 20% freelance written. A magazine published 5 times a year providing easy-to-use, hands-on practical teaching ideas and suggestions for early childhood education. Circ. 14,500. Pays on publication. Months until publication vary. Buys all rights. Submit seasonal/holiday material 6 months in advance. Computer printout submissions acceptable; prefers letter-quality. Sample copy for SAE with 3 first class stamps; writer's guidelines for SAE with 2 first class stamps.

Nonfiction: How-to (on creating usable teaching materials). Buys varying number of mss/year. Query with or without published clips, or send complete ms. Length: 200-1,000 words. Pays $25-100 for assigned articles; pays $10-30 for unsolicited articles. Writer has choice of cash or Good Apple products worth twice the contract value.

Photos: State availability of photos with submission. Reviews contact sheets and transparencies. Offers $10 minimum/photo. Model releases and identification of subjects required. Buys all rights.

Columns/Departments: Accepts material dealing with the solving of problems encountered by early childhood education. Buys varying number of mss/year. Query with published clips. Length: varies. Pays $25-100.

Fiction: Adventure and fantasy (for young children). Query with published clips.

Poetry: Light verse. Buys varying number of poems/year.

Tips: "I'm always looking for something that's new and different—something that works for teachers of young children."

‡MEDIA & METHODS, American Society of Educators, 1429 Walnut St., Philadelphia PA 19102. (215)563-3501. Editor: Robin Larsen. 80% freelance written. Bimonthly trade journal published during the school year about educational products, technologies and programs for schools and universities. Circ. 40,000. Pays on publication. Publishes ms an average of 3 months after acceptance. Byline given. Buys first North American serial rights. Photocopied submissions OK. Computer printout submissions OK. Reports in 1 month. Free smaple copy and writer's guidelines.

Nonfiction: How-to, new product, personal experience, technical. Buys 20-30 mss/year. Query with or without published clips, or send complete ms. Length: 800-2,500. Pays $50-100. Sometimes pays expenses of writers on assignment.

Photos: State availability of photos with submission. Reviews 3x5 prints. Offers no additional payment for photos accepted with ms. Captions and identification of subjects required. Buys one-time rights.

Columns/Departments: Buys 35 mss/year. Query. Length: 150-900 words. Pays $50-75.

MOMENTUM, National Catholic Educational Association, 1077 30th St. NW, Washington DC 20007. Editor: Patricia Feistritzer. 10% freelance written. Quarterly magazine. For Catholic administrators and teachers, some parents and students, in all levels of education (preschool, elementary, secondary, higher). Circ. 20,000. Pays on publication. Buys first serial rights. Reports in 3 months. Free sample copy.

Nonfiction: Articles concerned with educational philosophy, psychology, methodology, innovative programs, teacher training, research, financial and public relations programs and management systems—all applicable to nonpublic schools. Book reviews on educational/religious topics. Avoid general topics or topics applicable *only* to public education. "We look for a straightforward, journalistic style with emphasis on practical examples, as well as scholarly writing and statistics. All references must be footnoted, fully documented. Emphasis is on professionalism." Buys 28-36 mss/year. Query with outline. Length: 1,500-2,000 words. Pays 2¢/word.

Photos: Pays $25 for b&w glossy photos purchased with mss. Captions required.

NATIONAL BEAUTY SCHOOL JOURNAL, Milady Publishing Corp., 3839 White Plains Rd., Bronx NY 10467. (212)881-3000. Editor: Mary Jane Tenerelli. Associate Editor: Mary Healy. 75% freelance written. Works with a small number of new/unpublished writers each year. A monthly magazine covering cosmetology education. "Articles must address subjects pertinent to cosmetology education (i.e. articles which will assist the instructor in the classroom or the school owner to run his or her business)." Circ. 1,100 schools. Pays on publication. Publishes ms an average of 2 months after acceptance. Byline given. Buys first rights. Submit seasonal/holiday material 3 months in advance. Simultaneous submissions, photocopied submissions, and previously published submissions OK. Computer printout submissions acceptable; prefers letter-quality. Free sample copy with writer's guidelines.

Nonfiction: Book excerpts, essays, historical/nostalgic, how-to (on doing a haircut, teaching a technique) humor, interview/profile, new product, personal experience, photo feature and technical. No articles geared to the salon owner or operator instead of the cosmetology school instructor or owner. Buys 24 mss/year. Query with published clips, or send complete ms. Length: 500-3,000 words. Pays $150 if published.

Photos: Send photos with submissions. Reviews 5x7 b&w prints. Offers no additional payment for photos accepted with ms. Identification of subjects required. Buys first rights; make sure reprint permission is granted.

Columns Departments: Buys 6 mss/year; willing to start new departments. Length: 500-1,000 words. Pays $150.

Fiction: Humorous and slice-of-life vignettes. No fiction relating to anything other than the classroom or the beauty school business. Send complete ms. Length: 500-3,000 words. Pays $150.

Fillers: Facts, gags to be illustrated by cartoonist and newsbreaks. Length: 250-500 words. Pays $150.

Tips: "Talk to school owners and instructors to get a feel for the industry. All areas of our publication are open. Write in clear, simple language."

‡**SCHOOL ARTS MAGAZINE**, 50 Portland St., Worcester MA 01608. Editor: David W. Baker. 85% freelance written. Monthly, except June, July and August. Serves arts and craft education profession, kindergarten-12, higher education and museum education programs. Written by and for art teachers. Pays on publication. Publishes ms an average of 2 months "if timely; if less pressing, can be 1 year or more" after acceptance. Buys first serial rights and second serial (reprint) rights. Computer printout submissions acceptable; prefers letter-quality. Reports in 3 months. Sample copy for 8½x11 SAE and $1.50.

Nonfiction: Articles, with photos, on art and craft activities in schools. Should include description and photos of activity in progress as well as examples of finished art work. Query or send complete ms. Length: 600-1,400 words. Pays $20-100.

Tips: "We prefer articles on actual art projects or techniques done by students in actual classroom situations. Philosophical and theoretical aspects of art and art education are usually handled by our contributing editors. Our articles are reviewed and accepted on merit and each is tailored to meet our needs. Keep in mind that art teachers want practical tips, above all. Our readers are visually, not verbally, oriented. Write your article with the accompanying photographs in hand." The most frequent mistakes made by writers are "bad visual material (photographs, drawings) submitted with articles, or a lack of complete descriptions of art processes; and no rationale behind programs or activities. It takes a close reading of School Arts to understand its function and the needs of its readers. Some writers lack the necessary familiarity with art education."

SCHOOL SHOP, Prakken Publications, Inc., Box 8623, Ann Arbor MI 48107. Editor: Alan H. Jones. 100% freelance written. Eager to work with new/unpublished writers. A monthly (except June and July) magazine covering issues, trends and projects of interest to industrial, vocational, technical and technology educators at the secondary and post secondary school levels. Special issue in April deals with varying topics for which mss are solicited. Circ. 45,000. Buys all rights. Pays on publication. Publishes ms an average of 8-12 months after acceptance. Byline given. Prefers authors who have direct connection with the field of industrial and/or technical education. Submit seasonal material 6 months in advance. Simultaneous queries, and simultaneous, photocopied, and previously published submissions OK. Computer printout submissions acceptable; prefers letter-quality. Reports in 6 weeks. Free sample copy and writer's guidelines.

Nonfiction: Uses articles pertinent to the various teaching areas in industrial education (woodwork, electronics, drafting, machine shop, graphic arts, computer training, etc.). "The outlook should be on innovation in educational programs, processes or projects which directly apply to the industrial/technical education area." Buys general interest, how-to, opinion, personal experience, technical and think pieces, interviews, humor, and coverage of new products. Buys 135 unsolicited mss/year. Length: 200-2,000 words. Pays $25-150.

Photos: Send photos with accompanying query or ms. Reviews b&w and color prints. Payment for photos included in payment for ms.

Columns/Departments: Shop Kinks (brief items which describe short-cuts or special procedures relevant to the industrial arts classroom). Buys 30 mss/year. Send complete ms. Length: 20-100 words. Pays $15 minimum.

Tips: "We are most interested in articles written by industrial, vocational and technical educators about their class projects and their ideas about the field. We need more and more technolgy-related articles."

TEACHER UPDATE, Ideas for Teachers, Teacher Update, Inc., Box 599, Somers NY 10589. (914)248-6167. Editor: Donna Papalia. 100% freelance written. Eager to work with new/unpublished writers. Monthly (except July and August) newsletter covering early childhood education for preschool teachers. Circ. 10,000. Pays on acceptance. Publishes ms an average of 4 months after acceptance. Byline given. Offers 100% kill fee. Buys all rights. Submit seasonal/holiday material 4 months in advance. Simultaneous queries, and simultaneous, photocopied, and previously published submissions OK. Computer printout submissions acceptable; prefers letter-quality. Reports in 6 weeks on queries. Sample copy and writer's guidelines for #10 SASE.

Nonfiction: How-to (suggestions for classroom activities). Query. Pays $20/published page.

Columns/Departments: Special Days and Free Materials. Buys 15 mss/year. Query. Pays $20/published page.

Poetry: Children's poems, fingerplays, etc. Buys 6-10/year. Pays $20/published page.

Tips: "Submit original ideas and make sure submissions are in the *Teacher Update* format. We are interested in original unit ideas pertaining to holidays, seasons, etc., incorporating all areas of the curriculum."

TEACHING/K-8, The Professional Magazine, Early Years, Inc., 325 Post Rd. W, Box 3330, Westport CT 06880. (203)454-1020. Editor: Allen Raymond. 90% freelance written. "We prefer material from classroom teachers." A monthly magazine covering teaching of kindergarten through eighth grades. Pays on publication. Publishes ms an average of 2-7 months after acceptance. Byline given. Buys all rights. Submit seasonal/holi-

day material 6 months in advance. Computer printout submissions acceptable; prefers letter-quality. Reports in 6 weeks on mss. Sample copy $2 with 9x12 SASE; writer's guidelines for #10 SAE with 1 first class stamp.
Nonfiction: Patricia Broderick, articles editor. Classroom curriculum material. Send complete ms. Length: 1,200-1,500 words. Pays $35 maximum.
Photos: Offers no additional payment for photos accepted with ms. Model releases and identification of subjects required.
Columns/Departments: Patricia Broderick, column department editor. Send complete ms. Length: 1,100 word maximum. Pays $25 maximum.
Tips: "Manuscripts should be specifically oriented to a successful teaching strategy, idea, project or program. Broad overviews of programs or general theory manuscripts are not usually the type of material we select for publication. Because of the definitive learning level we cover (pre-school through grade eight) we try to avoid presenting general groups of unstructured ideas. We prefer classroom tested ideas and techniques."

TODAY'S CATHOLIC TEACHER, 26 Reynolds Ave., Ormond Beach FL 32074. (904)672-9974. Editor-in-Chief: Ruth A. Matheny. 40% freelance written. Works with a small number of new/unpublished writers each year. For administrators, teachers and parents concerned with Catholic schools, both parochial and CCD. Circ. 65,000. Pays after publication. Publishes ms an average of 3 months after acceptance. Byline given. Buys all rights. Phone queries OK. Submit seasonal/holiday material 3 months in advance. Sample copy $3; writer's guidelines for #10 SASE; mention *Writer's Market* in request.
Nonfiction: How-to (based on experience, particularly in Catholic situations, philosophy with practical applications); interview (of practicing educators, educational leaders); personal experience (classroom happenings); and profile (of educational leader). Buys 40-50 mss/year. Submit complete ms. Length: 800-2,000 words. Pays $15-75.
Photos: State availability of photos with ms. Offers no additional payment for 8x10 b&w glossy prints. Buys one-time rights. Captions preferred;model release required.
Tips: "We prefer articles based on the author's own expertise, and/or experience, with a minimum of quotations from other sources. We use many one-page features."

Electronics and Communication

These publications are edited for broadcast and telecommunications technicians and engineers, electrical engineers and electrical contractors. Included are journals for electronic equipment designers and operators who maintain electronic and telecommunication systems. Publications for appliance dealers can be found in Home Furnishings and Household Goods.

‡**BROADCAST MANAGEMENT/ENGINEERING**, 295 Madison Ave., New York NY 10017. (212)685-5320. Editor-in-chief: Robert Rivlin. 50% freelance written. For broadcast executives, general managers, chief engineers and engineering management of radio and TV stations and the teleproduction facilities that serve them. Monthly. Circ. 33,372. Buys all rights. Byline given unless "article is used as backup for staff-written piece, which happens rarely." Buys 30-50 mss/year. Pays on publication. Reports in 1 month. Query. Query for electronic submissions (preferred). Computer printout submissions acceptable; prefers letter-quality.
Nonfiction: Articles on technical trends and business trends affecting broadcasting. Particularly interested in equipment applications by broadcasters in the production of radio and television programs. Emphasis on "competitive advantage. No product puff pieces. No general management pieces or general information stories. Our readers are interested in details." Length: 1,200-3,000 words. Pays $400-600.
Tips: "To break in demonstrate a knowledge of the industry we serve. Send for an editorial schedule and sample copy of the magazine; then suggest an idea which demonstrates an understanding of our needs. Pictures, graphs, charts, schematics and other graphic material a must."

BROADCAST TECHNOLOGY, Box 420, Bolton, Ontario L7E ST3 Canada. (416)857-6076. Editor-in-Chief: Doug Loney. 50% freelance written. Monthly (except August, December) magazine. Emphasizes broadcast engineering. Circ. 9,000. Pays on publication. Byline given. Buys all rights. Phone queries OK.
Nonfiction: Technical articles on developments in broadcast engineering, especially pertaining to Canada. Query. Length: 500-1,500 words. Pays $100-300.
Photos: Purchased with accompanying ms. B&w or color. Captions required.

Tips: "Most of our outside writing is by regular contributors, usually employed full-time in broadcast engineering. The specialized nature of our magazine requires a specialized knowledge on the part of a writer, as a rule."

CABLE COMMUNICATIONS MAGAZINE, Canada's Authoritative International Cable Television Publication, Ter-Sat Media Publications Ltd., 4 Smetana Dr., Kitchener, Ontario N2B 3B8 Canada. (519)744-4111. Editor: Udo Salewsky. 33% freelance written. Prefers to work with published/established writers. Monthly magazine covering the cable television industry. Circ. 6,300. Pays on acceptance. Publishes ms an average of 2 months after acceptance. Byline given. Buys all rights. Submit seasonal/holiday material 1 month in advance. Photocopied submissions OK. Query for electronic submissions. Computer printout submissions acceptable; no dot-matrix. Reports in 2 weeks on queries; 1 month on mss. Free writer's guidelines; sample copy for 9x12 SAE and $2 IRCs.
Nonfiction: Expose, how-to, interview/profile, opinion, technical articles, and informed views and comments on topical, industry related issues. Also, problem solving-related articles, new marketing and operating efficiency ideas. No fiction. Buys 50 mss/year. Query with published clips or send complete ms. Length: 1,000-4,000 words. Pays $200-800. Pays expenses of writers on assignment.
Columns/Departments: Buys 48 items/year. Query with published clips or send complete ms. Length: 1,000-1,500 words. Pays $200-300.
Tips: "Forward manuscript and personal resume. We don't need freelance writers for short articles and fillers. Break in with articles related to industry issues, events and new developments; analysis of current issues and events. Be able to interpret the meaning of new developments relative to the cable television industry and their potential impact on the industry from a growth opportunity as well as a competitive point of view. Material should be well supported by facts and data. Insufficient research and understanding of underlying issues are frequent mistakes."

CABLE MARKETING, The Marketing/Management Magazine for Cable Television Executives, Jobson Publishing, 352 Park Ave. South, New York NY 10010. (212)685-4848. Editor: Ellis Simon. 10% freelance written. Prefers to work with published/established writers. Monthly magazine for cable industry executives dealing with marketing and management topics, new trends and developments and their impact. Circ. 15,000. Pays on publication. Publishes ms an average of 2 months after acceptance. Byline given. Buys first North American serial rights. Photocopied submissions OK. Computer printout submissions acceptable; prefers letter-quality. Reports in 1 month. Free sample copy.
Columns/Departments: Cable Tech (technology, engineering and new products); and Cable Scan (news items and marketing featurettes mostly about cable system activities and developments). Buys 20 mss/year. Query with published clips. Length: 200-3,000 words. Pays $50-500. Pays the expenses of writers on assignment.
Tips: "Learn something about the cable TV business before you try to write about it. Have specific story ideas. Have some field of expertise that you can draw upon (e.g., marketing, management or advertising). Short articles and fillers give us a chance to better assess a writer's real abilities without exposing us to undue risk, expense, aggravation, etc. on a feature. Not interested in reviews of programming. Editorial focus is on the *business* of cable television."

CINCINNATI BELL MAGAZINE, Cincinnati Bell Inc., Box 2301, 102-520, Cincinnati OH 45201. (513)397-1578. Editor: Connie Ruhe. 5% freelance written. Magazine covering telecommunications for employees and retirees of Cincinnati Bell Inc., Circ. 8,000. Pays on publication. Publishes ms an average of 3 months after acceptance. Byline given. Not copyrighted. Submit seasonal/holiday material 2 months in advance. Simultaneous, photocopied and previously published submissions OK. Query for electronic submissions. Computer printout submissions OK; prefers letter-quality. Reports in 2 months on mss. Sample copy for 9x12 SAE with 3 first class stamps.
Nonfiction: Management topics, telecommunications topics and pop psychology. Send complete ms. Length: 2,000-5,000 words. Pays $75-200 for unsolicited articles.
Photos: State availability of photos with submission. Reviews contact sheets. Offers $25-100. Captions, model releases and identification of subjects required. Buys one-time rights.

❝ If a writer can't meet deadlines, I sincerely hope he gets lots of assignments from our competitors. ❞

—*Tash Matsuoka,*
Rider Magazine

Nonfiction: Interview/profile, technical. Buys 70 mss/year. Query. Length: 2,500-5,000 words. Pays $200-600.
Columns/Departments: Computer Visions (interview—technical—of leader in software development industry) 2,500 words. Buys 10 mss/year. Query. Pays $250-400.

DVORAK DEVELOPMENTS, Freelance Communications, Box 1895, Upland CA 91785. (818)963-3703. Editor: Randy Cassigham. Managing Editor: Michele Wolf. 20% freelance written. A quarterly newsletter covering business productivity/word processing. "We promote the adoption of the Dvorak keyboard for typewriters and computers. Emphasizes current research studies, case studies, and product overviews (reviews). Readers include individuals, governmental officials, and small and large businesses." Circ. 1,000. Pays on acceptance. Publishes ms an average of 4 months after acceptance. Byline given. Offers 33% kill fee. Buys first rights; rarely reprint rights. Photocopied submissions OK; previously published materials accepted rarely. Query for electronic submissions. Computer printout submissions acceptable. Reports in 2 weeks. Sample copy and writer's guidelines for SAE with 2 first class stamps.
Nonfiction: Interview/profiles (if especially interesting Dvorak user); technical (application notes/case studies); how-to (typically a case study on how a company/agency solved a conversion problem); product overviews (detailed description of a Dvorak-related product/review); book reviews (books which significantly deal with the Dvorak). "We do *not* want to see anything that tries to convice the reader that Dvorak is superior to Qwerty—our readers already believe that. We do not generally care to see stories about an *individual's* experience in changing from Qwerty to Dvorak." Buys 10-15 mss/year. Query, preferably with a recent clip. Length: 200-1,000 words. Pays $25-50. Expenses must be negotiated in advance.
Photos: State availability of photos. Reviews b&w proofs or prints. Offers no additional payment for photos accepted with ms. Captions, model releases, and identification of subjects required. Buys one-time rights.
Tips: "If writers know a lot about the Dvorak, or a specific Dvorak application, they can probably write for us. We desire to get the wider viewpoint a freelancer can provide. Sections most open to freelancers: case studies. There are a lot of Dvorak users out there that we don't know about. We want to hear about them. There will be increased emphasis on companies and governmental agencies that have switched to Dvorak. We will increase coverage on the increasing trend to conversion to Dvorak. If you know of a conversion project, we want to hear from you."

THE INDEPENDENT Film & Video Monthly, Foundation for Independent Video & Film, 9th Floor, 625 Broadway, New York NY 10012. (212)473-3400. Editor: Martha Gever. 60% freelance written. Works with a small number of new/unpublished writers each year. Monthly magazine of practical information for producers of independent film and video with focus on low budget, art and documentary work from nonprofit sector. Circ. 18,000. Pays on publication. Publishes ms an average of 4 months after acceptance. Byline given. Buys first serial rights. Submit seasonal/holiday material 4 months in advance. Simultaneous queries OK. Query for electronic submissions. Computer printout submissions acceptable; no dot-matrix. Reports in 1 month. Sample copy for 9x12 SAE and 4 first class stamps.
Nonfiction: Book excerpts ("in our area"); how-to; technical (low tech only); and theoretical/critical articles. No reviews. Buys 60 mss/year. Query with published clips. Length: 1,200-3,500 words. Pays $25-200.
Tips: "Since this is a specialized publication, we prefer to work with writers on short pieces first. A frequent mistake made by writers is unfamiliarity with specific practical and theoretical issues concerning independent film and video."

INFORMATION TODAY, Learned Information Inc., 143 Old Marlton Pike, Medford NJ 08055. (609)654-6266. Publisher: Thomas H. Hogan. Editor: Patricia Lane. 30% freelance written. A tabloid for the users and producers of electronic information services, published 11 times per year. Circ. 10,000. Pays on publication. Publishes ms an average of 1 month after acceptance. Byline given. Buys first North American serial rights. Submit seasonal/holiday material 2 months in advance. Computer printout submissions acceptable; prefers letter-quality. Reports in 2 weeks. Free sample copy and writer's guidelines.
Nonfiction: Book reviews; interview/profile and new product (dealing with information industry); technical (dealing with computerized information services); and articles on library technology, artificial intelligence, database and Videotex services. Buys approximately 25 mss/year. Query with published clips or send complete ms on speculation. Length: 500-1,500 words. Pays $80-200.
Photos: State availability of photos with submission.
Tips: "We look for clearly-written, informative articles dealing with the electronic delivery of information. Writing style should not be jargon-laden or heavily technical."

LIGHTWAVE, The Journal of Fiber Optics, Howard Rausch Associates, Inc., 235 Bear Hill Rd., Waltham MA 02154. (617)890-2700. Editor: Sharon Scully. Managing Editor: Arthur McDonnell. 15-20% freelance written. Works with a small number of new/unpublished writers each year. A monthly trade journal on fiber optics and its applications for specialists in telecommunications or data communications. Circ. 15,000. Pays on publication. Publishes ms an average of 2 months after acceptance. Byline given. Offers $50 kill fee. Buys all rights. Submit seasonal/holiday material 3 months in advance. Query for electronic submissions. Computer printout submissions OK; prefers letter-quality. Reports in 2 weeks on queries; 1 week on mss. Sample copy for 14x17 SAE with 6 first class stamps; free writer's guidelines.

Nonfiction: Book excerpts, technical book reviews, essays, opinion, photo feature and technical. Buys 2-5 mss/year. Query. Length: 500-2,000 words. Pays $100-2,000 for assigned articles; pays $100-1,000 for unsolicited articles. Sometimes pays the expenses of writers on assignment.

Photos: Send photos with submission. Reviews transparencies and prints. Offers $10-150 per photo. Captions required. Buys all rights.

Tips: "Fiber optics technology will shift in focus from long-distance telephone applications to local and other data markets."

MASS HIGH TECH, Mass Tech Times, Inc., 755 Mt. Auburn St., Watertown MA 02172. (617)924-5100. Editor: Patrick Porter. 10-20% freelance written. "Interested in queries, samples, proposals especially from writers in the New England region." Bimonthly trade tabloid covering feature news of electronics, computers, biotech, systems analysis, etc., for high-tech professionals in New England; strong regional angle preferred. Circ. 30,000. Pays on publication. Publishes ms an average of 1 month after acceptance. Byline given. Not copyrighted. Buys first North American serial rights. Submit seasonal/holiday material 1 month in advance. Simultaneous queries, and simultaneous, photocopied, and previously published submissions OK "if not in our immediate market." Query for electronic submissions. Computer printout submissions acceptable; prefers letter-quality. Reports in 1 month. Sample copy for 9x12 SAE and 5 first class stamps.

Nonfiction: Book excerpts; historical (technology); interview/profile; new product; opinion (qualified scientist); and photo feature (needs technical orientation and strong Boston area orientation). Also, Op/Ed pieces of up to 1,200 words relevant to concerns of New England technology firms and employees. "Material should inform without over simplifying." Increasingly oriented toward news and analysis of items impacting market area. Buys 50 mss/year. Send complete ms. Length: 400-1,200 words. Pays $50-250.

Photos: Send photos with ms. Pays $25 for 5x7 b&w prints. Captions and identification of subjects required (if appropriate). Buys one-time rights.

Fillers: Anecdotes, short humor and newsbreaks. Buys 100 mss/year. Length: 25-100 words. Pays $10 and up.

Tips: "Know the Boston and New England high-tech scene or have knowledgeable contacts. Material should be plausible to trained professionals. Trends in magazine publishing that freelance writers should be aware of include the need for more sophisticated graphics—photos or drawings are often available free from their corporate subjects (in our market)."

MICROWAVES & RF, Ten Holland Dr., Hasbrouck Heights NJ 07604. (201)393-6285. Editor: Michael Kachmar. 50% freelance written. Eager to work with new/unpublished writers. Monthly magazine emphasizing radio frequency design. "Qualified recipients are those individuals actively engaged in microwave and RF research, design, development, production and application engineering, engineering management, administration or purchasing departments in organizations and facilities where application and use of devices, systems and techniques involve frequencies from HF through visible light." Circ. 65,000. Pays on publication. Publishes ms an average of 6 months after acceptance. Buys all rights. Phone queries OK. Photocopied submissions OK. Query for electronic submissions. Computer printouts acceptable "if legible." Reports in 1 month. Free sample copy and writer's guidelines; mention *Writer's Market* in request.

Nonfiction: "We are interested in material on research and development in microwave and RF technology and economic news that affects the industry." How-to (circuit design), new product, opinion, and technical. Buys 100 mss/year. Query. Pays $100.

ON PAGE, The Newsletter Co., Box 439, Sudbury MA 01776. Editor: Stanley J. Kaplan. Managing Editor: Bette Sidlo. 5% freelance written. Eager to work with new/unpublished writers. Monthly newsletter about "the beeper industry (radio pocket paging) for professionals, medical people, sales people, small businessmen, municipal employees and any person whose job takes him/her away from the telephone and who must maintain communications." Circ. 100,000. Pays on acceptance. Publishes ms an average of 4 months after acceptance. Buys all rights. Submit seasonal material 3 months in advance. Phone queries OK. Computer printout submissions acceptable; prefers letter-quality. Reports in 2 weeks. Free sample copy and writer's guidelines.

Fillers: Clippings, jokes, gags, anecdotes, short humor and newsbreaks. "We are particularly interested in anecdotes for our On Page Forum column in the first person narrative, stories of people and their beeper experiences, and newsbreaks on a variety of communication subjects of interest to people who use beepers. We especially look for seasonal freelance contributions." Buys 5-10 mss/year. Length: 75-150 words. Pays $25-40.

Tips: "Our selection is based more on subject matter and details than on the writer's style. A strong originality is of greatest concern here. Submissions should be geared to beeper users (e.g., subject matter must be related to communications or mobility). No sarcasm or comments insulting those who carry or use a beeper."

‡ON RADIO, United Stations Radio Networks, 5th Floor, 1440 Broadway, New York NY 10018. (212)575-6100. Managing Editor: Janis Burenga. 90% freelance written. Monthly radio trade journal. "*ON Radio* covers the business of local radio. Articles are sought on subjects pertaining to local sales, promotion, research, programming and broadcast management of radio stations." Estab. 1987. Circ. 15,000. Pays on acceptance. Publishes ms an average of 3 months after acceptance. Byline given. $100 kill fee. Buys all rights. Submit seasonal/holiday material 5 months in advance. Simultaneous submissions OK. Query for electronic submissions. Computer printout submissions OK; prefers letter-quality. Sample copy and writer's guidelines for 11x14 SAE with 1 first class stamp.

Nonfiction: How-to, humor, interview/profile, new product, personal experience, technical, sales, marketing, research, engineering, promotion. All articles accepted must relate to radio. Buys 88 mss/year. Query with published clips. Length: 350-1,750 words. Pays $150-700 for assigned articles; $150-500 for unsolicited articles. Sometimes pays expenses for writers on assignment.

Photos: State availability of photos with submission or send photos with submission. Reviews 2x2 transparencies and 5x7 prints. Offers no additional payment for photos accepted with ms. Captions, model releases and identification of subjects required. Buys all rights.

Columns/Departments: Heard ON Radio (anecdotes from movies, books, magazine and all other media mentioning radio) 50-50 words; Reviews (any books, movies, etc. of which prime subjects is radio) 250 words; Varied (humor, personal experience, technical, profile and new product categories all covered in 250 words or less). Buys 11 mss/year. Query with published clips. Length: 50-500 words. Pays $35-250.

Fiction: Humorous, mainstream, slice-of-life vignettes. "Don't send non-radio oriented fiction." Buys 6 mss/year. Query with published clips. Length: 400-1,000 words. Pays $150-500.

Fillers: Anecdotes, facts, gags to be illustrated by cartoonist, newsbreaks, short humor. Buys 50 mss/year. Length: 50-250 words. Pays $35-200.

Tips: "If the writer's story idea relates to radio, a letter to the managing editor with a brief description will be given consideration. Obviously, those freelancers with some radio background will be given strong consideration. Calls will be accepted if the idea is extremely timely. *ON Radio* currently publishes 200-50 word columns per month. A single article or a series of fillers are welcome. Full-length (1,000 words) articles are assigned only when a strong radio orientation is present."

OUTSIDE PLANT, Box 183, Cary IL 60013. (312)639-2200. Editor: Rick Hoelzer. 10% freelance written. Prefers to work with published/established writers. Trade publication focusing exclusively on the outside plant segment of the telephone industry. Readers are end users and/or specifiers at Bell and Independent operating companies, as well as long distance firms whose chief responsibilities are construction, maintenance, planning and fleet management. Readership also includes telephone contracting firms. Published 9 issues in 1988. Circ. 17,000. Buys first rights. Pays on publication. Publishes ms an average of 3 months after acceptance. Computer printout submissions OK; prefers letter-quality. Reports in 1 month. Free sample copy and guidelines.

Nonfiction: Must deal specifically with outside plant construction, maintenance, planning and fleet vehicle subjects for the telephone industry. "Case history application articles profiling specific telephone projects are best. Also accepts trend features, tutorials, industry research and seminar presentations. Preferably, features should be by-lined by someone at the telephone company profiled." Pays $35-50/published page, including photographs; pays $35 for cover photos.

Departments: OSP Tips & Advice (short nuts-and-bolts items on new or unusual work methods); and OSP Tommorrow (significant trends in outside plant), 300-600 word items. Pays $5-50. Other departments include new products, literature, vehicles and fiber optics.

Tips: Submissions should include author bio demonstrating expertise in the subject area.

PRO SOUND NEWS, International News Magazine for the Professional Sound Production Industry, P.S.N. Publications, Inc., 2 Park Ave., New York NY 10016. (212)213-3444. Editor: Randolph P. Savicky. 20% freelance written. Works with a small number of new/unpublished writers each year. Monthly tabloid covering the music recording, sound reinforcement, TV and film sound industry. Circ. 14,500. Pays on publication. Publishes ms an average of 1 month after acceptance. Byline given. Buys first serial rights. Simultaneous queries, and photocopied and previously published submissions OK. Query for electronic submissions. Computer printout submissions acceptable. Reports in 2 weeks.

Nonfiction: Query with published clips. Pays 10¢/word. Sometimes pays the expenses of writers on assignment.

RETAILER NEWS, Target Publishing, Suite G, 249 E. Emerson, Orange CA 92665. (714)921-0600. Publisher: Martin Barsky. Managing Editor: C. Lee Thornton. 5-10% freelance written. Prefers to work with published/established writers. Monthly tabloid covering consumer electronics and major appliances. For retailers of consumer electronics and major appliances, primarily in the West, but also the rest of the nation. Circ. 22,000. Pays on publication. Publishes ms an average of 2 months after acceptance. Byline given. Buys all rights. Submit seasonal/holiday material 3 months in advance. Simultaneous submissions OK. Computer printout submissions OK; prefers letter-quality. Sample copy for 12x16 SAE with $2.40 postage.

Nonfiction: Interview/profile. Query with published clips. Length: 1,000-2,000 words. Pays $125-175 for assigned articles. Pays expenses of writers on assignment.

Photos: Send photos with submission. Reviews 4x6 prints. Offers no additional payment for photos accepted with ms. Captions and identification of subjects required. Buys all rights.

‡**SATELLITE RETAILER**, Triple D Publishing, Inc., Box 2384, Shelby NC 28151. (704)482-9673. Editor: David B. Melton. 75% freelance written. Monthly magazine covering home satellite TV. "We look for technical, how-to, marketing, sales, new products, product testing, and news for the satellite television dealer." Circ. 12,000. Pays on publication. Byline given. 30% kill fee. Buys all rights. Submit seasonal/holiday material 3 months in advance. Simultaneous and photocopied submissions OK. Query for electronic submissions. Computer printout submissions OK. Free sample copy and writer's guidelines.
Nonfiction: How-to, new product, personal experience, photo feature, technical. Buys 24 mss/year. Query with or without published clips, or send complete ms. Length: 1,800-3,600 words. Pays $150-400. Sometimes pays expenses of writers on assignment.
Photos: Send photos with submission. Reviews contact sheets, transparencies (135 to 4x5). Captions, model releases and identification of subjects required. Buys all rights.
Tips: "Familiarity with electronics and television delivery systems is a definite plus."

VISUAL COMMUNICATIONS CANADA, Maclean Hunter, 5th Floor, 777 Bay St., Toronto, Ontario M5W 1A7 Canada. (416)596-5878. Editor: Cora Golden. 75% freelance written. Prefers to work with writers with a business background. A magazine appearing 10 times a year covering the visual communications industry from an end-user perspective. "Our objective is to provide a non-technical overview of the visual communications industry—news, new products, profiles, etc." The audience is managers of corporate communications in selected Canadian industrial, commercial and financial companies. Circ. 11,500. Pays on acceptance. Publishes ms an average of 2 months after acceptance. Byline given. Offers 50% kill fee. Buys first North American serial rights. Submit seasonal/holiday material 3 months in advance. Simultaneous and photocopied submissions OK. Query for electronic submissions. Computer printout submissions acceptable; prefers letter-quality. Reports in 1 month on queries; 2 weeks on mss. Sample copy for 9x12 SAE with 2 first class stamps; free writer's guidelines.
Nonfiction: Interview/profile, opinion and technical. All submissions must have a Canadian angle. Buys 50 mss/year. Query with published clips. Length: 1,000-1,500 words. Pays $400-500 for assigned articles. Sometimes pays the expenses of writers on assignment.
Photos: State availability of photos with submission. Reviews contact sheet. Offers $25-150 maximum/photo. Captions, model releases, and identification of subjects required. Buys one-time rights.
Columns/Departments: Newsline (regional, national and international events and trends with a Canadian angle), 600-800 words; and Clips (capsulized information on visual communications programs recently produced). Query. Length: 300-400 words. Pays $25-100.
Tips: "We will be adding more about video and computer graphics. *Visual Communications Canada* is directed to a business audience. Readers expect information specific to their needs. Our readers have a broad range of skills and knowledge levels. Therefore, submissions must contain sufficient background material for those less familiar with a topic, yet within the interest of more experienced readers. We prefer brief, factual reporting; stories that get right to the point and always answer the question, 'What's in it for me?' "

_____ *Energy and Utilities*

People who supply power to homes, businesses and industry read the publications in this section. This category includes journals covering the electric power, natural gas, petroleum, solar and alternative energy industries.

ALTERNATIVE ENERGY RETAILER, Zackin Publications, Inc., Box 2180, Waterbury CT 06722. (203)755-0158. Editor: Ed Easley. 20% freelance written. Prefers to work with published/established writers. Monthly magazine on selling alternative energy products—chiefly solid fuel burning appliances. "We seek detailed how-to tips for retailers to improve business. Most freelance material purchased is about retailers and how they succeed." Circ. 14,000. Pays on publication. Publishes ms an average of 2 months after acceptance. Buys first North American serial rights. Submit seasonal/holiday material 4 months in advance. Computer printout submissions OK; no dot-matrix. Reports in 2 weeks on queries. Sample copy for 8½x11 SAE with 4 first class stamps; writer's guidelines for #10 SAE.
Nonfiction: How-to (improve retail profits and business know-how); and interview/profile (of successful retailers in this field). No "general business articles not adapted to this industry." Buys 10-20 mss/year. Query. Length: 1,000 words. Pays $200.
Photos: State availability of photos. Pays $25-125 maximum for 5x7 b&w prints. Reviews color slide transparencies. Identification of subject required. Buys one-time rights.

Tips: "We've redesigned into a more sophisticated, visual format. A freelancer can best break in to our publication with features about readers (retailers). Stick to details about what has made this person a success."

ELECTRICAL APPARATUS, The Magazine of the Electrical Aftermarket, Barks Publications, Inc., 400 N. Michigan Ave., Chicago IL 60611-4198. (312)321-9440. Editorial Director: Elsie Dickson. Managing Editor: Kevin N. Jones. Prefers to work with published/established writers. Uses very little freelance material. A monthly magazine for persons working in electrical maintenance, chiefly in industrial plants, who install and service electrical motors, tranformers, generators, and related equipment. Circ. 16,000. Pays on acceptance. Publishes ms an average of 2-3 months after acceptance. Byline given. Buys all rights unless other arrangements made. Query for electronic submissions. Computer printout submissions acceptable. Reports in 1 week on queries; 1 month on mss. Sample copy $4.
Nonfiction: Technical. Buys very few mss/year. Query essential, along with letter outlining credentials. Length: 1,500-2,500. Pays $250-500 for assigned articles only. Pays the expenses of writers on assignment by advance arrangement.
Photos: Send photos with submission. "Photos are important to most articles. We prefer 35mm color slides, but sometimes use color or b&w prints." Offers additional payments, depending on quality and number. Captions and identification of subjects required. Buys one-time rights. "If we reuse photos, we pay residual fee."
Columns/Departments: Electrical Manager (items on managing businesses, people), 150-600 words; and Electropix (photo of interest with electrical slant), brief captions. "We are interested in expanding these departments." Pays $50-100.
Tips: "Queries are essential. Technical expertise is absolutely necessary, preferably an E.E. degree, or practical experience. We are also book publishers and some of the material in *EA* is now in book form, bringing the authors royalties."

ELECTRICAL CONTRACTOR, 7315 Wisconsin Ave., Bethesda MD 20814. (301)657-3110. Editor: Larry C. Osius. 10% freelance written. Monthly. For electrical contractors. Circ. 65,000. Publishes ms an average of 3 months after acceptance. Buys first serial rights, second serial (reprint) rights or simultaneous rights. Usually reports in 1 month. Byline given. Free sample copy.
Nonfiction: Installation articles showing informative application of new techniques and products. Slant is product and method contributing to better, faster and more economical construction process. Query. Length: 800-2,500 words. Pays $100/printed page, including photos and illustrative material.
Photos: Photos should be sharp, reproducible glossies, 5x7 and up.

‡NATIONAL PETROLEUM NEWS, 950 Lee St., Des Plaines IL 60016. (312)296-0770. Editor: Frank Victoria. 3% freelance written. Prefers to work with published/established writers. For businessmen who make their living in the oil marketing industry, either as company employees or through their own business operations. Monthly magazine. Circ. 18,000. Rights purchased vary with author and material. Usually buys all rights. Pays on acceptance if done on assignment. Publishes ms an average of 2 months after acceptance. "The occasional freelance copy we use is done on assignment." Computer printout submissions acceptable; prefers letter-quality. Query.
Nonfiction: Material related directly to developments and issues in the oil marketing industry and "how-to" and "what-with" case studies. Informational, and successful business operations. "No unsolicited copy, especially with limited attribution regarding information in story." Buys 3-4 mss/year. Length: 2,000 words maximum. Pays $50-150/printed page. Sometimes pays the expenses of writers on assignment.
Photos: Pays $150/printed page. Payment for b&w photos "depends upon advance understanding."

PIPELINE & UNDERGROUND UTILITIES CONSTRUCTION, Oildom Publishing Co. of Texas, Inc., Box 22267, Houston TX 77027. Editor: Oliver Klinger. Managing Editor: Chris Horner. 5% freelance written. Prefers to work with published/established writers. Monthly magazine covering oil, gas, water, and sewer pipeline construction for contractors and construction workers who build pipelines. Circ. 16,000. No byline given. Not copyrighted. Buys first North American serial rights. Publishes ms an average of 3 months after acceptance. Simultaneous queries and photocopied submissions OK. Computer printout submissions acceptable; prefers letter-quality. Reports in 2 weeks on queries; 3 weeks on mss. Sample copy for $1 and 9x12 SAE.
Nonfiction: How-to. Query with published clips. Length: 1,500-2,500 words. Pays $100/printed page "unless unusual expenses are incurred in getting the story." Sometimes pays the expenses of writers on assignment.
Photos: Send photos with ms. Reviews 5x7 and 8x10 prints. Captions required. Buys one-time rights.
Tips: "We supply guidelines outlining information we need." The most frequent mistake made by writers in completing articles is unfamiliarity with the field.

PUBLIC POWER, 2301 M St. NW, Washington DC 20037. (202)775-8300. Editor: Vic Reinemer. 20% freelance written. Prefers to work with published/established writers. Bimonthly. Not copyrighted. Pays on publication. Publishes ms an average of 3 months after acceptance. Byline given. Query for electronic submis-

sions. Computer printout submissions acceptable. Free sample copy and writer's guidelines.
Nonfiction: Features on municipal and other local publicly-owned electric systems. Payment negotiable. Sometimes pays the telephone expenses of writers on assignment.
Photos: Uses b&w and glossy color prints, and slides.

SUNSHINE SERVICE NEWS, Florida Power & Light Co., Box 029100, Miami FL 33102. (305)552-3887. Editor: L.A. Muniz, Jr. 5% freelance written. Works with a small number of writers each year. Monthly employee newspaper for electric utility. Circ. 17,000. Pays on publication. Publishes ms an average of 3 months after acceptance. Buys first serial rights. Not copyrighted. Computer printout submissions acceptable. Free sample copy.
Nonfiction: Company news, employee news, general interest, historical, how-to, humor and job safety. Company tie-in preferred. Query. Pays $100-150. Pays expenses of writers on assignment.

‡UTILITY AND TELEPHONE FLEETS, Practical Communications, Inc., 37 W. Main, Box 183, Cary IL 60013. (312)639-2200. Managing Editor: Alan Richter. 5% freelance written. Quarterly magazine for fleet managers and maintenance supervisors for electric gas and water utilities; telephone, interconnect and cable TV companies and contractors. "We seek case history/application features covering specific fleet management and maintenance projects/installations. Instructional/tutorial features are also welcome." Estab. 1987. Circ.18,000. Pays on publication. Publishes ms an average of 2 months after acceptance. Byline given. 20% kill fee. Buys all rights. Submit seasonal/holiday material 2 months in advance. Photocopied submissions OK. Computer printout submissions OK. Reports in 2 weeks. Free sample copy and writer's guidelines.
Nonfiction: How-to (ways for performing fleet maintenance/improving management skills/vehicle tutorials), technical, case history/application features. No advertorials in which specific product or company is promoted. Buys 1 ms/year. Query with published clips. Length: 1,000-2,800 words. Pays $35/page.
Photos: Send photos with submission. Reviews contact sheets, negatives, transparencies (3x5) and prints (3x5). Offers no additional payment for photos accepted with ms. Captions required. Buys one-time rights.
Columns/Departments: Vehicle Management and Maintenance Tips (nuts-and-bolts type items dealing with new or unusual methods for fleet management, maintenance and safety). Buys 2 mss/year. Query with published clips. Length: 200-500 words. Pays $10-20.
Tips: "Working for a utility or telephone company and gathering information about a construction, safety or fleet project is the best approach for a freelancer."

Engineering and Technology

Engineers and professionals with various specialties read the publications in this section. Publications for electrical, electronics and telecommunications engineers are classified separately under Electronics and Communication. Magazines for computer professionals are in the Information Systems section.

‡AMERICAN MACHINIST & Automated Manufacturing, Penton Publishing. Suite 2119, 122 E. 42nd St., New York NY 10168. (212)867-9191. Editor: Joseph Jablonowski. A monthly magazine about durable-goods manufacturing. Circ. 70,000. Pays on acceptance. Publishes ms an average of 4 months after acceptance. Sometimes byline given. Makes work-for-hire assignments. Query for electronic submissions. Computer printout submissions OK. Reports in 2 months on queries; 3 months on mss. Free sample copy.
Nonfiction: Technical. Query with or without published clips, or send complete ms. Length: 1,500-4,000 words. Pays $300-700. Pays the expenses of writers on assignment. Send photos with submission. Offers no additional payment for photos accepted with ms. Buys all rights.
Tips: "Articles that are published are probably 85% engineering details. We're interested in feature articles on technology of manufacturing in the metalworking industries (automaking, aircraft, machinery, etc.). Aim at instructing a 45-year-old degreed mechanical engineer in a new method of making, say, a pump housing."

GRADUATING ENGINEER, McGraw-Hill, 1221 Avenue of the Americas, New York NY 10020. (212)512-4123. Editor: Howard Cohn. Managing Editor: Bill D. Miller. 90% freelance written. Prefers to work with published/established writers. Published September-March "to help graduating engineers make the transition from campus to the working world." Four regular issues; two minority issues; one women's issue; one computer issue. Circ. 83,000. Pays on acceptance. Publishes ms an average of 2 months after acceptance. Byline given. Buys first North American serial rights. Reports in 3 weeks. Sample copy for 9x12 SAE and 4 first class stamps.

Nonfiction: General interest (on management, human resources); and career entry and advancement. Special issues include Minority, Women and Computer. Buys 100 mss/year. Query. Length: 2,000-3,000 words. Pays $300-700.

Photos: State availability of photos, illustrations or charts. Reviews 35mm color transparencies, 8x10 b&w glossy prints. Captions and model release required.

Tips: "We're generating new types of editorial. We closely monitor economy here and abroad so that our editorial reflects economic, social, and global trends."

‡HIGH TECHNOLOGY CAREERS, %Writers Connection, Suite 180, 1601 Saratoga-Sunnyvale Rd., Cupertino CA 95014. (408)973-0227. Managing Editor: Steve Lester. 100% freelance written. Monthly tabloid on high technology industries. "Articles must have a high technology tie-in and should be written in a positive and lively manner. The audience includes managers, engineers, and other professionals working in the high technology industries." Circ. 348,000. Pays on publication. Publishes ms an average of 3 months after acceptance. Byline given. Offers 25% kill fee. Buys all rights. Query for electronic submissions. Computer printout submissions OK; prefers letter-quality. Reports in 3 weeks.

Nonfiction: General interest (with high tech tie-in), technical. No career-oriented material, company or personal profiles. Buys 36 mss/year. Query with or without published clips, or send complete ms. Length: 1,500-2,000 words. Pays 17½¢/word. Sometimes pays expenses of writers on assignment.

Photos: State availability of photo with submission.

‡LASER FOCUS MAGAZINE, the Magazine of Electro-Optics Technology, 119 Russell St., Littleton MA 01460. (617)486-9501. Publisher/Editor-in-Chief: Dr. Morris Levitt. Managing Editor: Barbara Murray. Less than 10% freelance written. A monthly magazine for physicists, scientists and engineers involved in the research and development, design, manufacturing and applications of lasers, laser systems and all other segments of electro-optical technologies. Circ. 45,000. Pays on publication. Publishes ms an average of 6 months after acceptance. Byline given unless anonymity requested. Buys all rights. Query for electronic submissions. Computer printout submissions acceptable. Sample copy on request.

Nonfiction: Lasers, laser systems, fiberoptics, optics, imaging, and other electro-optical materials, components, instrumentation and systems. "Each article should serve our reader's need by either stimulating ideas, increasing technical competence or improving design capabilities in the following areas: natural light and radiation sources, artificial light and radiation sources, light modulators, optical materials and components, image detectors, energy detectors, information displays, image processing, information storage and processing, subsystem and system testing, support equipment and other related areas." No "flighty prose, material not written for our readership, or irrelevant material." Query first "with a clear statement and outline of why the article would be important to our readers." Pays $30/printed page. Sometimes pays expenses of writers on assignment.

Photos: Send photos with ms. Reviews 8x10 b&w glossies or 4x5 color transparencies.

Tips: "The writer has a better chance of breaking in at our publication with short articles since shorter articles are easier to schedule, but must address more carefully our requirements for technical coverage. We use few freelancers that are independent professional writers. Most of our submitted materials come from technical experts in the areas we cover. The most frequent mistake made by writers in completing articles for us is that the articles are too commercial, i.e. emphasize a given product or technology from one company. Also articles are not the right technical depth, too thin or too scientific."

MACHINE DESIGN, Penton Publishing Inc., 1100 Superior Ave., Cleveland OH 44114. (216)696-7000. Editor: Ronald Khol. Executive Editor: Richard Beercheck. 1-2% freelance written. Works with a small number of new/unpublished writers each year. A bimonthly magazine covering technical developments in products or purchases of interest to the engineering community. Circ. 180,000. Pays on publication. Publishes ms an average of 2 months after acceptance. Byline sometimes given. Buys first rights. Computer printout submissions acceptable; prefers letter-quality. Reports in 1 month. Free sample copy.

Nonfiction: General interest; how-to (on using new equipment or processes); and new product. No non-technical submissions. Buys 10-15 mss/year. Query. Length and payment for articles must be negotiated in advance. Sometimes pays the expenses of writers on assignment.

Photos: State availability of photos with submission. Offers negotiable payment. Captions, model releases, and identification of subjects required.

Columns/Departments: Design International (international news), captions; Backtalk (technical humor) and Personal Computers in Engineering (use of personal computers), both have negotiable word length. Buys 50-200 items/year. Query. Pays $20 minimum.

Tips: "The departments of our publication most open to freelancers are Back Talk, News Trends and Design International. Those without technical experience almost never send in adequate material."

‡MECHANICAL ENGINEERING, American Society of Mechanical Engineers. 345 E. 47th St., New York NY 10017. (212)705-7782. Editor: Charles Beardsley. Managing Editor: Jay O'Leary. 30% freelance written. A monthly magazine on mechanical process and design. "We publish general interest articles for graduate mechanical engineers on high-tech topics." Circ. 135,000. Pays on acceptance. Sometimes byline given. Kill fee varies. Buys first rights. Submit seasonal/holiday material 4 months in advance. Query for electronic submissions. Computer printout submissions OK. Reports in 1 month. Free sample copy and writer's guidelines.
Nonfiction: Historical/nostalgic, interview/profile, new product, photo feature and technical. Buys 25 mss/year. Query with or without published clips, or send complete ms. Length: 1,500-3,500 words. Pays $500-1,500. Pays the expenses of writers on assignment.
Photos: Send photos with submission. Reviews transparencies and prints. Offers no additional payment for photos accepted with ms. Captions and identification of subjects required. Buys one-time rights.

THE MINORITY ENGINEER, An Equal Opportunity Career Publication for Professional and Graduating Minority Engineers, Equal Opportunity Publications, Inc., 44 Broadway, Greenlawn NY 11740. (516)261-8917. Editor: James Schneider. 60% freelance written. Prefers to work with published/established writers. Magazines published 4 times/year (fall, winter, spring, April/May) covering career guidance for minority engineering students and professional minority engineers. Circ. 16,000. Pays on publication. Publishes ms an average of 3-6 months after acceptance. Byline given. Buys first North American serial rights. "Deadline dates: fall, May 1; winter, July 15; spring, October 15; April/May, January 1." Simultaneous, photocopied, and previously published submissions OK. Query for electronic submissions. Computer printout submissions acceptable; no dot-matrix. Sample copy and writer's guidelines for 8x10 SAE with 5 first class stamps.
Nonfiction: Book excerpts; articles (on job search techniques, role models); general interest (on specific minority engineering concerns); how-to (land a job, keep a job, etc.); interview/profile (minority engineer role models); new product (new career opportunities); opinion (problems of ethnic minorities); personal experience (student and career experiences); and technical (on career fields offering opportunities for minority engineers). "We're interested in articles dealing with career guidance and job opportunities for minority engineers." Query or send complete ms. Length: 1,250-3,000 words. Sometimes pays the expenses of writers on assignment. Pays 10¢/word.
Photos: Prefers 35mm color slides but will accept b&w. Captions and identification of subjects required. Buys all rights. Pays $15.
Tips: "Articles should focus on career guidance, role model and industry prospects for minority engineers. Prefer articles related to careers, not politically or socially sensitive."

‡NATIONAL DEFENSE, American Defense Preparedness Association. Suite 905, 1700 N. Moore St., Arlington VA 22209. (703)522-1820. Editor: D.F. Ballou. Managing Editor: Barbara Jacobsen. 25% freelance written. A magazine on defense weapons systems published 10 times/year. "This is a non-political magazine for persons who buy or make military weapons systems. We are interested in technology, management, military and defense industry relationships." Circ. 45,000. Pays on publication. Publishes ms an average of 3 months after acceptance. Byline given. Buys first rights. Photocopied submissions OK. Query for electronic submissions. Computer printout submissions OK; prefers letter-quality. Reports in 2 weeks on queries; 4 weeks on mss. Free sample copy and writer's guidelines.
Nonfiction: New product, opinion, photo feature and technical. Buys 30 mss/year. Query. Length: 1,200-2,000 words. Pays $450-950. Pays expenses of writers on assignment "with prior arrangement." Send photos with submission. Reviews contact sheets, negatives, transparencies and prints. Offers no additional payment for photos accepted with ms. Captions required. Buys one-time rights.

THE WOMAN ENGINEER, An Equal Opportunity Career Publication for Graduating Women and Experienced Professionals, Equal Opportunity Publications, Inc., 44 Broadway, Greenlawn NY 11740. (516)261-8917. Editor: Anne Kelly. 60% freelance written. Works with a small number of new/unpublished writers each year. Magazine published 4 times/year (fall, winter, spring, April/May) covering career guidance for women engineering students and professional women engineers. Circ. 16,000. Pays on publication. Publishes ms 3-12 months after acceptance. Byline given. Buys first North American rights. Simultaneous queries and submissions OK. Computer printout submissions OK; prefers letter-quality. Free sample copy and writer's guidelines.
Nonfiction: "Interested in articles dealing with career guidance and job opportunities for women engineers. Looking for manuscripts showing how to land an engineering position and advance professionally. Wants features on job-search techniques, engineering disciplines offering career opportunities to women, problems facing women engineers and how to cope with such problems, in addition to role-model profiles of successful women engineers." Query. Length: 1,000-2,500 words. Pays 10¢/word.
Photos: Prefers color slides but will accept b&w. Captions, model release and identification of subjects required. Buys all rights. Pays $15.
Tips: "We will be looking for shorter manuscripts (800-1,000 words) on job-search techniques, career opportunities for women engineers, and first-person 'Endpage Essay.' "

Entertainment and the Arts

The business of the entertainment/amusement industry in arts, film, dance, theatre, etc. is covered by these publications. Journals that focus on the people and equipment of various music specialties are listed in the Music section, while art and design business publications can be found in Art, Design and Collectibles. Entertainment publications for the general public can be found in the Consumer Entertainment section.

AMUSEMENT BUSINESS, Billboard Publications, Inc., Box 24970, Nashville TN 37202. (615)321-4267. Managing Editor: Tim O'Brien. 25% freelance written. Works with a small number of new/unpublished writers each year. Weekly tabloid emphasizing hard news of the amusement, sports business, and mass entertainment industry. Read by top management. Circ. 15,000. Pays on publication. Publishes ms an average of 3 weeks after acceptance. Byline sometimes given; "it depends on the quality of the individual piece." Buys all rights. Submit seasonal/holiday material 3 weeks in advance. Phone queries OK. Computer printout submissions acceptable; no dot-matrix. Sample copy for 11x14 SAE with 5 first class stamps.
Nonfiction: How-to (case history of successful advertising campaigns and promotions); interviews (with leaders in the areas we cover highlighting appropriate problems and issues of today, i.e. insurance, alcohol control, etc.); new product; and technical (how "new" devices, shows or services work at parks, fairs, auditoriums and conventions). Likes lots of financial support data: grosses, profits, operating budgets and per-cap spending. Also needs in-depth looks at advertising and promotional programs of carnivals, circuses, amusement parks, fairs: how these facilities position themselves against other entertainment opportunities in the area. No personality pieces or interviews with stage stars. Buys 500-1,000 mss/year. Query. Length: 400-700 words. Pays $3/published inch. Sometimes pays the expenses of writers on assignment.
Photos: State availability of photos with query. Pays $3-5 for 8x10 b&w glossy prints. Captions and model release required. Buys all rights.
Columns/Departments: Auditorium Arenas; Fairs, Fun Parks; Food Concessions; Merchandise; Promotion; Shows (carnival and circus); Talent; Tourist Attractions; and Management Changes.
Tips: There will be more and more emphasis on financial reporting of areas covered. "Submission must contain the whys and whos, etc. and be strong enough that others in the same field will learn from it and not find it naive. We will be increasing story count while decreasing story length."

BOXOFFICE MAGAZINE, RLD Publishing Corp., Suite 710, 1800 N. Highland Ave., Hollywood CA 90028. (213)465-1186. Editor: Harley W. Lond. 5% freelance written. Monthly business magazine about the motion picture industry for members of the film industry: theater owners, film producers, directors, financiers and allied industries. Circ. 10,000. Pays on publication. Publishes ms an average of 2-4 months after acceptance. Byline given. Buys one-time rights. Phone queries OK. Submit seasonal material 2 months in advance. Simultaneous, photocopied and previously published submissions OK. Computer printout submissions acceptable. Reports in 2 months. Sample copy for $3 and 8½x11 SAE with 5 first class stamps.
Nonfiction: Expose, interview, profile, new product, photo feature and technical. "We are a general news magazine about the motion picture industry and are looking for stories about trends, developments, problems or opportunities facing the industry. Almost any story will be considered, including corporate profiles, but we don't want gossip or celebrity stuff." Query with published clips. Length: 1,500-2,500 words. Pays $100-150.
Photos: State availability of photos. Pays $10 maximum for 8x10 b&w prints. Captions required.
Tips: "Request a sample copy, indicating you read about *Boxoffice* in *Writer's Market*. Write a clear, comprehensive outline of the proposed story and enclose a resume and clip samples. We welcome new writers but don't want to be a classroom. Know how to write. We look for investigative articles."

THE ELECTRIC WEENIE, Box 2715, Quincy MA 02269. (617)749-6900 ext. 248. Editor: Andrew J. Himmel. 80% freelance written. Monthly magazine covering "primarily radio, for 'personalities' worldwide (however, mostly English speaking). We mail flyers mainly to radio people, but obviously no one is excepted if he/she wants a monthly supply of first-rate gags, one liners, zappers, etc." Circ. 1,500. Pays on publication. Publishes ms an average of 2 months after acceptance. No byline given. Buys all rights. Computer printout submissions acceptable; prefers letter-quality. Sample copy $5, #10 SAE and 1 first class stamp.
Fillers: Jokes, gags, short humor, one liners, etc. "Short is the bottom line; if it's over two sentences it's too long." Uses 300/month. Pays $1/gag used.
Tips: "We like to receive in multiples of 100 if possible; not mandatory, just preferred. And we like a few original 'grossies'."

THE LONE STAR COMEDY MONTHLY, Lone Star Publications of Humor, Suite #103, Box 29000, San Antonio TX 78229. Editor: Lauren Barnett. Less than 1% freelance written. Eager to work with new/unpublished writers. Monthly comedy service newsletter for professional humorists—DJs, public speakers, comedians. Includes one-liners and jokes for oral expression. Pays on publication "or before." Publishes ms an average of 4-6 months after acceptance. Byline given if 2 or more jokes are used. Buys all rights, exclusive rights for 6 months from publication date. Submit seasonal/holiday material 1 month in advance. Photocopied submissions OK. Computer printout submissions acceptable; no dot-matrix. Reports in 2-3 months. Inquire for update on prices of sample copies. Writer's guidelines for #10 SAE and 1 first class stamp.

Fillers: Jokes, gags and short humor. Buys 20-60/year. Length: 100 words maximum. "We don't use major features in *The Lone Star Comedy Monthly*." Inquire for update on rates. "Submit several (no more than 20) original gags on one or two subjects only."

Tips: "Writers should inquire for an update on our needs before submitting material."

MIDDLE EASTERN DANCER, Mideastern Connection, Inc., Box 1572, Casselberry FL 32707-1572. (407)788-0301. Editor: Karen Kuzsel. Managing Editor: Tracie Harris. 60% freelance written. Eager to work with new/unpublished writers. A monthly magazine covering Middle Eastern dance and culture (belly dancing). "We provide the most current news and entertainment information available in the world. We focus on the positive, but don't shy away from controversy. All copy and photos must relate to Middle Eastern dance and cultural activities. We do not get into politics." Circ. 2,500. Pays on acceptance. Publishes ms an average of 4 months after acceptance, usually sooner, but it depends on type of article and need for that month. Byline given. Buys first rights, simultaneous rights or second serial (reprint) rights. Submit seasonal/holiday material 3 months in advance. Simultaneous, photocopied and previously published submissions OK, unless printed in another belly dance publication. Computer printout submissions acceptable; prefers letter-quality. Reports in 2 weeks on queries; 3 weeks on mss. Sample copy for 9x12 SAE with 4 first class stamps; writer's guidelines for #10 SAE with 1 first class stamp.

Nonfiction: Essays; general interest; historical/nostalgic; how-to (on costuming, putting on shows, teaching and exercises); humor; inspirational; interview/profile; personal experience; photo features; travel (to the Middle East or related to dancers); and reviews of seminars, movies, clubs, restaurants, and museums. Special issues include costuming (March); and anniversary issue (October). No politics. Buys 60 mss/year. Query. Pays $20 for assigned articles; pays $10 for unsolicited articles. May provide free advertising in trade. Sometimes pays the expenses of writers on assignment.

Photos: Send photos with submission. Offers no additional payment for photos accepted with ms. Identification of subjects required. Buys one-time rights.

Columns/Departments: Critics Corner (reviews of books, videotapes, records, movies, clubs and restaurants, museums and special events); Helpful Hints (tips for finding accessories and making them easier or for less); Putting on the Ritz (describes costume in detail with photo); and Personal Glimpses (autobiographical) and Profiles (biographical—providing insights of benefit to other dancers). Query.

Fiction: Open to fiction dealing with belly dancers as subject.

Poetry: Avant-garde, free verse, haiku, light verse and traditional. Buys 5 poems/year. Submit maximum 3 poems. Pays $5 maximum.

Tips: "It's easy to break in if you stick to belly dancing related information and expect little or no money (advertising instead). Although we are the second largest in the world in this field, we're still small."

‡NATPE PROGRAMMER, The Magazine of the National Association of TV Program Executives, NATPE International, Suite 220, 740 13th St., San Diego CA 92101. (619)238-2370. Editor: Robert P. Rimes. Managing Editor: William Strubbe. 90% freelance written. Trade journal on television programming, published 10 times per year. "*NATPE Programmer* is the professional trade publication for the National Association of Television Program Executives. We are looking for TV Programming trend material with a carefully researched, professional, not consumer, slant." Circ. 5,000. Pays on publication. Publishes ms an average of 3 months after acceptance. Byline given. Buys all rights. Submit seasonal/holiday material 8 months in advance. Computer printout submissions OK; prefers letter-quality. Sample copy $10 and 8x10 SAE with 60¢ postage; writer's guidelines for 8x10 SAE with 60¢ postage.

Nonfiction: Book excerpts, essays, how-to, interview/profile, new product, photo feature, technical. "Each issue contains a pull-out section listing TV programming: children's, holiday, talk shows, etc. Inquire for an editorial calendar with a SASE." No articles written from a TV viewer's perspective; first-person unless written by a well-known TV personality or producer; articles that are not researched. Query with published clips. Length: 1,500-2,500 words. Pays $50—750 for assigned articles; $400-650 for unsolicited articles.

Photos: State availability of photos with submission. Reviews 5x7 transparencies and 8x10 prints. Offers $50-100 per photo. Model releases and identification of subjects required. Buys one-time rights.

Tips: "We welcome and encourage freelance contributions. Sine *NATPE Programmer* is a professional journal written for and about the television industry, it's easy for our editors to spot articles that are naive and written off the top of a writer's head. We especially favor articles that are people-oriented, which quote industry sources, and which deal with TV programming trends."

7

OPPORTUNITIES FOR ACTORS & MODELS, "A Guide to Working in Cable TV-Radio-Print Advertising," Copy Group, Suite 315, 1900 N. Vine St., Hollywood CA 90068. Editor: Len Miller. 50% freelance written. Works with a small number of new/unpublished writers each year. A monthly newsletter "serving the interests of those people who are (or would like to be) a part of the cable-TV, radio, and print advertising industries." Circ. 10,000. Pays on acceptance. Publishes ms an average of 3 months after acceptance. Byline given. Buys all rights. Simultaneous queries OK. Computer printout submissions OK; prefers letter-quality. Reports in 3 weeks. Free sample copy and writer's guidelines.
Nonfiction: How-to, humor, inspirational, interview/profile, local news, personal experience, photo feature and technical (within cable TV). Coverage should include the model scene, little theatre, drama groups, comedy workshops and other related events and places. "Detailed information about your local cable TV station should be an important part of your coverage. Get to know the station and its creative personnel." Buys 120 mss/year. Query. Length: 100-950 words. Pays $50 maximum.
Photos: State availability of photos. Model release and identification of subjects required. Buys one-time or all rights.
Columns/Departments: "We will consider using your material in a column format with your byline." Buys 60 mss/year. Query. Length: 150-450 words. Pays $50 maximum.
Tips: "Good first person experiences, interviews and articles, all related to modeling, acting, little theatre, photography (model shots) and other interesting items" are needed.

UPB MAGAZINE, The Voice of the United Polka Boosters, The United Polka Boosters, Box 681, Glastonbury CT 06033. (203)537-1880. Editor: Walter Jedziniak. Managing Editor: Irene Kobelski. 50-60% freelance written. Eager to work with new/unpublished writers. A bimonthly magazine of the Polka Music industry. "Our readers share a common love for polka music and are dedicated to its preservation. They want information-packed pieces to help them understand and perform better in the polka industry." Circ. 1,100. Pays on acceptance. Publishes ms an average of 6 months after acceptance. Byline given. Offers 5% kill fee. Buys first or second serial (reprint) rights. Submit seasonal/holiday material 6 months in advance. Simultaneous, photocopied and previously published submissions OK; prefers letter-quality. Computer printout submissions OK. Reports in 6 weeks. Sample copy for 9x12 SAE with 4 first class stamps; free writer's guidelines for #10 SAE and 1 first class stamp.
Nonfiction: Historical/nostalgic (polka-related), how-to (have published "How to Make a Polka album," "How to Protect Your Songs," "How to Read Music"), humor (polka-related), interview/profile (polka personalities), opinion (on polka issues), technical and the origins and history of well-known polkas. No submissions that portray polkas as the dictionary definition "a Bohemian dance in 2/4 time." Articles should be clearly written and easily understandable. Polka music in the U.S.A. is what we want—not old world music. Buys 15 mss/year. Query with or without published clips, or send complete ms. Length: 300-2,000 words. Pays $15-35 for assigned articles; pays $5-30 for unsolicited articles. Sometimes pays the expenses of writers on assignment.
Photos: State availability of photos with submission. Reviews 8x10 or 5x7 prints, b&w only. Offers $1-3 per photo. Model releases and identification of subjects required. Buys one-time rights.
Columns/Departments: Behind the Scenes (in-depth report of 'how' and 'why' a polka-related or music-related process is followed), 1,500 words; Personality Profiles (emphasize the subject's contributions to polka music); 800-2,000 words; Origins of Songs (show dates and facts—pack it with research, tie in a contemporary recording if possible), 300-1,500 words. Buys 16 mss/year. Query or send complete ms. Pays $5-35.
Fillers: Anecdotes, facts, newsbreaks, short humor and puzzles. Buys 30/year. Length: 150-750 words. Pays $2-20 and contributor copy.
Tips: "We'd love to see some round-up pieces—for example, 'What 10 top bandleaders say about—' or 'Polka fans speak out about—'. Know the polka industry! We need info to help our readers survive in the world of performance and business. Articles should be well researched and should reflect the writer's knowledge of the present polka industry. A list of sources should accompany your ms. Our publication serves both industry professionals (musicians, DJs, composers, arrangers and promoters), and polka fans. Articles should be both informative and entertaining. We are very eager to work with freelance writers on a regular basis. We'd like pieces on recording, performing, promoting, composing, dancing—all types of well-written music-oriented pieces."

Farm

The successful farm writer focuses on the business side of farming. For technical articles, editors feel writers should have a farm background or agricultural training, but there are opportunities for the general freelancer too. The following farm publications are divided into seven categories, each specializing in a different aspect of farming: agricultural equipment; crops and soil management; dairy farming; livestock; management; miscellaneous; and regional.

Agricultural Equipment

CUSTOM APPLICATOR, Little Publications, Suite 540, 6263 Poplar Ave., Memphis TN 38119. (901)767-4020. Editor: Rob Wiley. 50% freelance written. Works with a small number of new/unpublished writers each year. For "firms that sell and custom apply agricultural fertilizer and chemicals." Circ. 16,100. Pays on publication. Publishes ms an average of 2 months after acceptance. Buys all rights. "Query is best. The editor can help you develop the story line regarding our specific needs." Computer printout submissions acceptable; prefers letter-quality.
Nonfiction: "We are looking for articles on custom application firms telling others how to better perform jobs of chemical application, develop new customers, handle credit, etc. Lack of a good idea or usable information will bring a rejection." Length: 1,000-1,200 words "with 3 or 4 b&w glossy prints." Pays 20¢/word.
Photos: Accepts b&w glossy prints. "We will look at color slides for possible cover or inside use."
Tips: "We don't get enough shorter articles, so one that is well-written and informative could catch our eyes. Our readers want pragmatic information to help them run a more efficient business; they can't get that through a story filled with generalities."

FARM SUPPLIER, Watt Publishing Co., Sandstone Bldg., Mount Morris IL 61054. (815)734-4171. Editor: Karen A. McMillan. Editorial Director: Clayton Gill. 20% freelance written. Prefers writers who have a vast knowledge of agriculture. For retail farm supply dealers and managers over the U.S. and Canada. Monthly magazine except June and July. Circ. 40,000. Pays on acceptance. Publishes ms an average of 2-10 months after acceptance. Byline given. Buys all rights in competitive farm supply fields. Phone queries OK. Submit seasonal material or query 2 months in advance. Computer printout submissions acceptable. Reports in 2 weeks.
Nonfiction: How-to, informational, interview, new product and photo feature. "Articles emphasizing product news and how new product developments have been profitably resold or successfully used. We use material on successful farm, feed and fertilizer dealers." No "general how-to articles that some writers blanket the industry with, inserting a word change here or there to 'customize.' " Buys 10 unsolicited mss/year.
Photos: Purchased with accompanying ms. Submit 5x7 or 8x10 b&w prints; 35mm or larger color transparencies. Total purchase price for a ms includes payment for photos.
Tips: "Because of a constantly changing industry, *FS* attempts to work only two months in advance. Freelancers should slant stories to each season in the farm industry and should provide vertical color photos whenever possible with longer features."

PROGRESS, (formerly *Fertilizer Progress*), The Fertilizer Institute, 1015 18th St. NW, Washington DC 20036. (202)861-4900. Edited and published by TFI Communications. Vice President: Thomas E. Waldinger. Editor: Richard F. Dunn, Jr. Assistant Editor: Becki K. Weiss. 7% freelance written. Eager to work with new/unpublished writers. Bimonthly magazine covering fertilizer, farm chemical and allied industries for business and management, with emphasis on the retail market. Circ. 25,000. Pays on publication. Publishes ms an average of 3 months after acceptance. Byline given. Offers 2½¢/word kill fee for assigned stories. Buys all rights. Submit seasonal/holiday material 2 months in advance. Photocopied submissions OK. Computer printout submissions acceptable; prefers letter-quality. Reports in 2 weeks on queries; 3 weeks on mss. Free sample copy.
Nonfiction: Articles on sales, services, credit, products, equipment, merchandising, production, regulation, research and environment. Also news about people, companies, trends and developments. No "highly technical or philosophic pieces; we want relevance—something the farm retail dealer can sink his teeth into." No material not related to fertilizer, farm chemical and allied industries, and the retail market. Send complete ms. Length: 400-2,500 words. Pays $35-200. Sometimes pays expenses of writers on assignment.
Photos: Send photos with ms. Pays $5-20 for 5x7 b&w and color prints. Captions and identification of subjects required.
Columns/Departments: Fit to be Tried (ideas that really work); Worth Repeating (agricultural-related editorial commentary); Best Management Practices (reducing erosion, controlling nutrient runoff and preserving the soil). Send complete ms. Length: 500-750 words. Pays $40-60.
Tips: "Query letter to propose story idea provides best results."

Crops and Soil Management

ONION WORLD, Columbia Publishing, 111C S. 7th Ave., Box 1467, Yakima WA 98907. (509)248-2452. Editor: D. Brent Clement. 90% freelance written. A monthly magazine covering "the world of onion production and marketing" for onion growers and shippers. Circ. 5,500. Pays on publication. Publishes ms an average of 1 month after acceptance. Byline given. Not copyrighted. Buys first North American serial rights.

Submit seasonal/holiday material 1 month in advance. Simultaneous submissions OK. Computer printout submisions acceptable; prefers letter-quality. Reports in several weeks. Sample copy for 8½x11 SAE with 4 first class stamps.
Nonfiction: General interest, historical/nostalgic and interview/profile. Buys 60 mss/year. Query. Length: 1,200-1,500 words. Pays $75-150 for assigned articles.
Photos: Send photos with submission. Offers no additional payment for photos accepted with ms unless cover shot. Captions and identification of subjects required. Buys all rights.
Tips: "Writers should be familiar with growing and marketing onions. We use a lot of feature stories on growers, shippers and others in the onion trade—what they are doing, their problems, solutions, marketing plans, etc."

SINSEMILLA TIPS, Domestic Marijuana Journal, New Moon Publishing, 217 SW 2nd, Box 2046, Corvallis OR 97339. (503)757-8477. Editor: Don Parker. 50% freelance written. Eager to work with new/unpublished writers. Quarterly magazine tabloid covering the domestic cultivation of marijuana. Circ. 10,000. Pays on publication. Publishes ms an average of 3 months after acceptance. Byline given. "Some writers desire to be anonymous for obvious reasons." Buys first serial rights and second serial (reprint) rights. Submit seasonal/holiday material 2 months in advance. Query for electronic submissions. Computer printout submissions acceptable. Reports in 2 months. Sample copy $6.
Nonfiction: Book excerpts and reviews; expose (on political corruption); general interest; how-to; interview/profile; opinion; personal experience; and technical. Send complete ms. Length: 500-2,000 words. Pays 2½¢/word. Sometimes pays the expenses of writers on assignment.
Photos: Send photos with ms. Pays $10-20 for b&w prints. Captions optional; model release required. Buys all rights.
Tips: "Writers have the best chance of publication if article is *specifically* related to the American marijuana industry."

SOYBEAN DIGEST, Box 41309, 777 Craig Rd., St. Louis MO 63141-1309. (314)432-1600. Editor: Gregg Hillyer. 75% freelance written. Works with a small number of new/unpublished writers each year. Emphasizes soybean production and marketing. Published monthly except semi-monthly in February and March, and bimonthly in June/July and August/September. Circ. 200,000. Pays on acceptance. Buys all rights. Byline given. Phone queries OK. Submit seasonal material 2 months in advance. Query for electronic submissions. Computer printout submissions OK; prefers letter-quality. Reports in 3 weeks. Sample copy $3; mention *Writer's Market* in request.
Nonfiction: How-to (soybean production and marketing); and new product (soybean production and marketing). Buys 100 mss/year. Query or submit complete ms. Length: 1,000 words. Pays $50-350. Sometimes pays the expenses of writers on assignment.
Photos: State availability of photos with query. Pays $25-100 for 5x7 or 8x10 b&w prints, $50-275 for 35mm color transparencies, and up to $350 for covers. Captions and/or ms required. Buys all rights.

TOBACCO REPORTER, Suite 300, 3000 Highwoods Blvd., Box 95075, Raleigh NC 27625. Editor: Anne Shelton. 5% (by those who *know* the industry) freelance written. International business journal for tobacco processors, exporters, importers, manufacturers and distributors of cigars, cigarettes and other tobacco products. Monthly. Buys all rights. Pays on publication. Computer printout submissions acceptable; no dot-matrix. Publishes ms an average of 2 months after acceptance.
Nonfiction: Uses exclusive original material on request only. Pays 10-15¢/word.
Photos: Pays $25 for photos purchased with mss.
Fillers: Wants clippings on new tobacco product brands, smoking and health, and the following relating to tobacco and tobacco products: job promotions, honors, equipment, etc. Pays $5-10/clipping on use only.

Dairy Farming

BUTTER-FAT, Fraser Valley Milk Producers' Cooperative Association, Box 9100, Vancouver, British Columbia V6B 4G4 Canada. (604)420-6611. Editor: Grace Hahn. Managing Editor: Carol A. Paulson. Eager to work with new/unpublished writers. 50% freelance written. Monthly magazine emphasizing this dairy cooperative's processing and marketing operations for dairy farmers and dairy workers in British Columbia. Circ. 3,500. Pays on acceptance. Publishes ms an average of 4 months after acceptance. Byline given. Buys first rights. Makes work-for-hire assignments. Phone queries preferred. Submit seasonal material 4 months in advance. Simultaneous, photocopied and previously published submissions OK. Computer printout submissions acceptable. Reports in 1 week on queries; in 1 month on mss. Free sample copy.
Nonfiction: Interview (character profile with industry leaders); local nostalgia; opinion (of industry leaders); and profile (of association members and employees).
Photos: Reviews 5x7 b&w negatives and contact sheets and color photos. Offers $10/published photo.

Captions required. Buys all rights.

Columns/Departments: "We want articles on the people, products, business of producing, processing and marketing dairy foods in this province." Query first. Buys 3 mss/issue. Length: 500-1,500 words. Pays 7¢/word.

Fillers: Jokes, short humor and quotes. Buys 5 mss/issue. Pays $10.

Tips: "Make an appointment to come by and see us!"

THE DAIRYMAN, Box 819, Corona CA 91718. (714)735-2730. Editor: Dennis Halladay. 10% freelance written. Prefers to work with published/established writers, but also works with a small number of new/unpublished writers each year. Monthly magazine dealing with large herd commercial dairy industry. Circ. 33,000. Pays on acceptance or publication. Publishes ms an average of 2-3 months after acceptance. Byline given. Buys first North American serial rights. Submit seasonal material 3 months in advance. Photocopied submissions OK. Computer printout submissions acceptable. Reports in 2 weeks. Sample copy for 8½x11 SAE with 4 first class stamps.

Nonfiction: Humor, interview/profile, new product, opinion, and industry analysis. Special issues: Computer issue (February); herd health issue (August); Feeds and Feeding (May); and Barns and Equipment (November). No religion, nostalgia, politics or 'mom and pop' dairies. Query or send complete ms. Length: 300-5,000 words. Pays $10-200.

Photos: Send photo with query or ms. Reviews b&w contact sheets and 35mm or 2¼x2¼ transparencies. Pays $10-25 for b&w; $25-100 for color. Captions and identification of subjects required. Buys one-time rights.

Columns/Departments: Herd health, taxes and finances, economic outlook for dairying. Buys 25/year. Query or send complete ms. Length: 300-2,000 words. Pays $25-100.

Tips: "Pretend you're an editor for a moment; now would you want to buy a story without any artwork? neither would I. Writers often don't know modern commercial dairying and they forget they're writing for an audience of *dairymen*. Publications are becoming more and more specialized . . . you've really got to know who you're writing for and why they're different."

Livestock

ANGUS JOURNAL, Angus Publications, Inc., 3201 Frederick Blvd., St. Joseph MO 64501. (816)233-0508. Editor: Jim Cotton. 10% freelance written. Monthly (except June/July, which are combined) magazine. "Must be Angus-related or beef cattle with no other breeds mentioned." Circ. 15,000. Pays on acceptance. Byline given. Buys first North American serial rights, second serial(reprint) rights, simultaneous rights and makes work-for-hire assignments. Submit seasonal/holiday material 3 months in advance. Simultaneous submissions, photocopied submissions and previously published submissions OK. Computer printout submissions OK; prefers letter-quality. Reports in 2 weeks. Sample copy $1.50 with 10x13 SAE and 4 first class stamps; writer's guidelines for #10 SASE.

Nonfiction: Historical/nostalgic, how-to, humor, interview/profile and photo feature. Nothing without an angus slant. Buys 6 mss/year. Send complete ms. Length: 1,000-5,000 words. Pays $50-300.

Photos: Send photos with submission. Review contact sheets and transparencies. Offers no additional payment for photos accepted with ms. Identification of subjects required. Buys one-time rights.

Columns/Departments: The Grazier (pasture, fencing, range management). Send complete ms. Length: 500-2,000 words. Pays $25-75.

Fiction: Historical, humorous and western. Must be short, with an angus slant. Send complete ms. Length: 2,000-4,000 words. Pays $100-300.

Poetry: Light verse and traditional. Nothing without an angus, beef cattle, farming or ranching slant. Submit up to 4 poems at one time. Length: 4-20 lines. Pays $10-75.

Fillers: Anecdotes, facts, newbreaks and short humor. Length: 50-200 words. Pays $5-25.

Tips: Areas most open to freelancers are "farm and ranch profiles—breeder interviews."

BEEF, The Webb Co., 1999 Shepard Rd., St. Paul MN 55116. (612)690-7374. Editor-in-Chief: Paul D. Andre. Managing Editor: Joe Roybal. 5% freelance written. Prefers to work with published/established writers. Monthly magazine for readers who have the same basic interest—making a living feeding cattle or running a cow herd. Circ. 120,000. Pays on acceptance. Publishes ms an average of 4 months after acceptance. Buys all rights. Byline given. Phone queries OK. Submit seasonal material 3 months in advance. Computer printout submissions acceptable. Reports in 2 months. Free sample copy and writer's guidelines.

Nonfiction: How-to and informational articles on doing a better job of producing, feeding cattle, market building, managing, and animal health practices. Material must deal with beef cattle only. Buys 8-10 mss/year. Query. Length: 500-2,000 words. Pays $25-300. Sometimes pays the expenses of writers on assignment.

Photos: B&w glossies (8x10) and color transparencies (35mm or 2¼x2¼) purchased with or without mss. Query or send contact sheet, captions and/or transparencies. Pays $10-50 for b&w; $25-100 for color. Model release required.

Tips: "Be completely knowledgeable about cattle feeding and cowherd operations. Know what makes a story. We want specifics, not a general roundup of an operation. Pick one angle and develop it fully. The most frequent mistake is not following instructions on an angle (or angles) to be developed."

THE BRAHMAN JOURNAL, Sagebrush Publishing Co., Inc., Box 220, Eddy TX 76524. (817)859-5451. Editor: Joe Ed Brockett. 10% freelance written. A monthly magazine covering Brahman cattle. Circ. 6,000. Pays on publication. Publishes ms an average of 2 months after acceptance. Byline given. Not copyrighted. Buys first North American serial rights, one-time rights, second serial (reprint) rights and makes work-for-hire assignments. Submit seasonal/holiday material 3 months in advance. Previously published submissions OK. Computer printout submissions OK; no dot-matrix. Reports in 1 month. Sample copy for 8½x11 SAE and 5 first class stamps.
Nonfiction: General interest, historical/nostalgic and interview/profile. Special issues include Herd Bull issue (July) and Texas issue (October). Buys 3-4 mss/year. Query with published clips. Length: 1,200-3,000 words. Pays $100-250 for assigned articles.
Photos: Photos needed for article purchase. Send photos with submission. Reviews 4x5 prints. Offers no additional payment for photos accepted with ms. Captions required. Buys one-time rights.

THE CATTLEMAN MAGAZINE, Texas & Southwestern Cattle Raisers Association, 1301 W. 7th St., Ft. Worth TX 76102. (817)332-7155. Editor: Lionel Chambers. Managing Editor: Don C. King. Monthly magazine emphasizing beef cattle production and feeding. "Readership consists of commercial cattlemen, purebred seedstock producers, cattle feeders and horsemen in the Southwest." Circ. 19,900. Pays on acceptance. Publishes ms an average of 6 months after acceptance. Byline given. Buys all rights. Computer printout submissions acceptable; prefers letter-quality. Reports in 3 weeks. Sample copy $2; writer's guidelines for #10 SAE and 1 first class stamp.
Nonfiction: Need informative, entertaining feature articles on specific commercial ranch operations, cattle breeding and feeding, range and pasture management, profit tips, and university research on beef industry. "We feature various beef cattle breeds most months." Will take a few historical western-lore pieces. Must be well-documented. No first person narratives or fiction or articles pertaining to areas outside the Southwest or outside beef cattle ranching. Buys 24 mss/year. Query. Length 1,500-2,000 words. Pays $75-300. Sometimes pays the expenses of writers on assignment.
Photos: Photos purchased with or without accompanying ms. State availability of photos with query or ms. Pays $15-25 for 5x7 b&w glossies; $100 for color transparencies used as cover. Total purchase price for ms includes payment for photos. Captions, model release, and identification of subjects required.
Fillers: Cartoons.
Tips: "Submit an article dealing with ranching in the Southwest. Too many writers submit stories out of our general readership area. Economics may force staff writers to produce more articles, leaving little room for unsolicited articles."

LLAMAS MAGAZINE, The International Camelid Journal, Clay Press, Inc., Box 100, Herald CA 95638. (209)748-2620. Editor: Cheryl Dal Porto. A bimonthly magazine covering llamas, alpacas, camels, vicunas and guanacos. Circ. 5,000. Pays on acceptance. Publishes ms an average of 4 months after acceptance. Byline given. Buys first rights, second serial (reprint) rights and makes work-for-hire assignments. Submit seasonal/holiday material 6 months in advance. Simultaneous, photocopied and previously published submissions OK. Computer printout submissions OK. Reports in 2 weeks. Sample copy $4 for SAE with 4 first class stamps; writer's guidelines for #10 SAE.
Nonfiction: How-to (on anything related to raising llamas), humor, interview/profile, opinion, personal experience, photo feature and travel (to countries where there are camelids). "All articles must have a tie in to one of the camelid species." Buys 30 mss/year. Query with published clips. Length: 1,000-5,000 words. Pays $50-300 for assigned articles; pays $50-150 for unsolicited articles. May pay new writers with contributor copies. Sometimes pays the expenses of writers on assignment.
Photos: State availability of photos with submission or send photos with submission. Reviews transparencies and 5x7 prints. Offers $25-100 per photo. Captions, model releases and identification of subjects required. Buys one-time rights.
Fillers: Anecdotes, gags and short humor. Buys 25/year. Length: 100-500 words. Pays $25-50.
Tips: "Get to know the llama folk in your area and query us with an idea. We are open to any and all ideas involving llamas, alpacas and the rest of the camelids. We are always looking for good photos. You must know about camelids to write for us."

POLLED HEREFORD WORLD, 4700 E. 63rd St., Kansas City MO 64130. (816)333-7731. Editor: Ed Bible. 1% freelance written. For "breeders of Polled Hereford cattle—about 80% registered breeders, 5% commercial cattle breeders; remainder are agribusinessmen in related fields." Monthly. Circ. 11,500. Not copyrighted. Buys "no unsolicited mss at present." Pays on publication. Publishes ms an average of 2 months after acceptance. Photocopied submissions OK. Computer printout submissions acceptable; prefers letter-quality. Submit seasonal material "as early as possible: 2 months preferred." Reports in 1 month. Query first for reports of events and activities. Query first or submit complete ms for features. Free sample copy.

Nonfiction: "Features on registered or commercial Polled Hereford breeders. Some on related agricultural subjects (pastures, fences, feeds, buildings, etc.). Mostly technical in nature; some human interest. Our readers make their living with cattle, so write for an informed, mature audience." Buys informational articles, how-to's, personal experience articles, interviews, profiles, historical and think pieces, nostalgia, photo features, coverage of successful business operations, articles on merchandising techniques, and technical articles. Length: "varies with subject and content of feature." Pays about 5¢/word ("usually about 50¢/column inch, but can vary with the value of material").

Photos: Purchased with mss, sometimes purchased without mss, or on assignment; captions required. "Only good quality b&w glossies accepted; any size. Good color prints or transparencies." Pays $2 for b&w, $2-25 for color. Pays $25 for color covers.

Management

ACRES U.S.A., A Voice for Eco-Agriculture, Acres U.S.A., Box 9547, Kansas City MO 64133. (816)737-0064. Editor: Charles Walters, Jr. Monthly tabloid covering biologically sound farming techniques. Circ. 16,000. Pays on acceptance. Byline sometimes given. Buys first rights. Submit seasonal/holiday material 3 months in advance. Computer printout submissions acceptable, if double spaced. Reports in 1 month. Sample copy $2.25.

Nonfiction: Expose (farm-related); how-to; and case reports on farmers who have adopted eco-agriculture (organic). No philosophy on eco-farming or essays. Buys 80 mss/year. Query with published clips. Length: open. Pays 6¢/word.

Photos: State availability of photos. Reviews b&w photos only. Top quality photos only. Pays $6 for b&w contact sheets, negatives and 7x10 prints.

Tips: "We need on-scene reports of farmers who have adopted eco-farming—good case reports. We must have substance in articles and need details on systems developed. Read a few copies of the magazine to learn the language of the subject."

‡FARM FUTURES, The Farm Business Magazine, AgriData Resources, 330 E. Kilbourn, Milwaukee WI 53202. (414)278-7676. Editor: Claudia Waterloo. 40% freelance written. Eager to work with new/unpublished writers. Circ. 160,000. Pays on acceptance. Publishes ms an average of 2 months after acceptance. Byline given. Offers negotiable kill fee. Buys first serial rights only. Simultaneous queries, and photocopied and previously published submissions OK; no simultaneous submissions. Query for electronic submissions. Reports in 1 month. Free sample copy and writer's guidelines.

Nonfiction: Practical advice and insights into managing commercial farms, farm marketing how-to's, financial management, use of computers in agriculture, and farmer profiles. Buys 45 mss/year. Query with published clips. Length: 250-2,000 words. Pays $35-400. Sometimes pays the expenses of writers on assignment.

Tips: "The writer has a better chance of breaking in at our publication with short articles and fillers since our style is very particular; our stories are written directly to farmers and must be extremely practical. It's a style most writers have to 'grow into.' The most frequent mistakes made by writers in completing an article for us are lack of thoroughness and good examples; language too lofty or convoluted; and lack of precision—inaccuracies. Our magazine is growing—we'll be needing more freelance material."

FARM SHOW MAGAZINE, 20088 Kenwood Trail, Box 1029, Lakeville MN 55044. (612)469-5572. Editor: Mark A. Newhall. 20% freelance written. A bimonthly trade journal covering agriculture. Circ. 150,000. Pays on acceptance. Publishes ms an average of 4 months after acceptance. Byline sometimes given. Buys one-time and second serial (reprint) rights. Previously published submissions OK. Computer printout submissions OK. Reports in 1 week. Free sample copy.

Nonfiction: How-to and new product. No general interest, historic or nostalgic articles. Buys 90 mss/year. Send complete ms. Length: 100-2,000 words. Pays $50-500. Pays expenses of writers on assignment.

Photos: Send photos with submission. Reviews any size color or b&w prints. Offers no additional payment for photos accepted with ms. Captions required. Buys one-time rights.

Tips: "We're looking for first-of-its-kind, inventions of the nuts and bolts variety for farmers."

FORD NEW HOLLAND NEWS, (formerly *New Holland News*), 500 Diller Ave., New Holland PA 17557. Editor: Gary Martin. 50% freelance written. Works with a small number of new/unpublished writers each year. Magazine published 8 times/year on agriculture; designed to entertain and inform farm families. Pays on acceptance. Publishes ms an average of 9 months after acceptance. Byline given. Offers negotiable kill fee. Buys first North American serial rights, one-time rights, and second serial (reprint) rights. Submit seasonal/holiday material 6 months in advance. Simultaneous queries and previously published submissions OK. Reports in 1 month. Sample copy and writer's guidelines for 8½x11 SAE.

Nonfiction: "We need strong photo support for short articles up to 1,200 words on farm management and farm human interest." Buys 16-20 mss/year. Query. Length: 1,200 words. Pays $400-600. Sometimes pays the expenses of writers on assignment.

Photos: Send photos with query when possible. Reviews color transparencies. Pays $50-300. Captions, model release, and identification of subjects required. Buys one-time rights.

Tips: "We thrive on good article ideas from knowlegeable farm writers. The writer must have an emotional understanding of agriculture and the farm family and must demonstrate in the article an understanding of the unique economics that affect farming in North America. We want to know about the exceptional farm managers, those leading the way in use of new technology, new efficiencies—but always with a human touch. Successful writers keep in touch with the editor as they develop the article."

‡HIGH PLAINS JOURNAL, "The Farmers Paper", High Plains Publishers, Inc., Box 760, Dodge City KS 67801. (316)227-7171. Editor: Galen Hubbs. 5-10% freelance written. Weekly tabloid with news, features and photos on all phases of farming and livestock production. Circ. 59,500. Pays on publication. Publishes ms an average of 1 month after acceptance. Byline given. Not copyrighted. Buys first serial rights. Submit seasonal/holiday material 1 month in advance. Simultaneous queries and photocopied submissions OK. Computer printout submissions acceptable; prefers letter-quality. Reports in 3 weeks on queries; 1 month on mss. Sample copy for $1.50.

Nonfiction: General interest (agriculture); how-to; interview/profile (farmers or stockmen within the High Plains area); and photo feature (agricultural). No rewrites of USDA, extension or marketing association releases. Buys 10-20 mss/year. Query with published clips. Length: 10-40 inches. Pays $1/column inch. Sometimes pays the expenses of writers on assignment.

Photos: State availability of photos. Pays $5-10 for 4x5 b&w prints. Captions and complete identification of subjects required. Buys one-time rights.

Tips: "Limit submissions to agriculture. Stories should not have a critical time element. Stories should be informative with correct information. Use quotations and bring out the human aspects of the person featured in profiles. Frequently writers do not have a good understanding of the subject. Stories are too long or are too far from our circulation area to be beneficial."

THE NATIONAL FUTURE FARMER, Box 15130, Alexandria VA 22309. (703)360-3600. Editor-in-Chief: Wilson W. Carnes. 20% freelance written. Prefers to work with published/established writers, and is eager to work with new/unpublished writers. Bimonthly magazine for members of the Future Farmers of America who are students of vocational agriculture in high school, ranging in age from 14-21 years; major interest in careers in agriculture/agribusiness and other youth interest subjects. Circ. 422,528. Pays on acceptance. Publishes ms an average of 4 months after acceptance. Buys all rights. Byline given. Submit seasonal/holiday material 4 months in advance. Query for electronic submissions. Computer printout submissions acceptable; prefers letter-quality. Usually reports in 1 month. Sample copy and writer's guidelines for 9x12 SAE with 4 first class stamps.

Nonfiction: How-to for youth (outdoor-type such as camping, hunting, fishing); and informational (getting money for college, farming; and other help for youth). Informational, personal experience and interviews are used only if FFA members or former members are involved. "Science-oriented material is being used more extensively as we broaden peoples' understanding of agriculture." Buys 15 unsolicited mss/year. Query or send complete ms. Length: 1,000 words maximum. Pays 4-6¢/word. Sometimes pays the expenses of writers on assignment.

Photos: Purchased with mss (5x7 or 8x10 b&w glossies; 35mm or larger color transparencies). Pays $10 for b&w; $30-40 for inside color; $100 for cover.

Tips: "Find an FFA member who has done something truly outstanding that will motivate and inspire others, or provide helpful information for a career in farming, ranching or agribusiness. We've increased emphasis on agriscience and marketing. We're accepting manuscripts now that are tighter and more concise. Get straight to the point."

SUCCESSFUL FARMING, 1716 Locust St., Des Moines IA 50336. (515)284-2897. Managing Editor: Loren Kruse. 3% freelance written. Prefers to work with published/established writers. Magazine for farm families that make farming their business. Published 14 times/year. Circ. 605,000. Buys all rights. Pays on acceptance. Publishes ms an average of 2 months after acceptance. Reports in 2 weeks. Computer printout submissions acceptable; no dot-matrix. Sample copy for SAE and 5 first class stamps.

Nonfiction: Semitechnical articles on all aspects of farming, including production, business, country living and recreation with emphasis on how to apply this information to one's own farm family. Also articles on interesting farm people and activities. Buys 30 unsolicited mss/year. Query with outline. Length: about 1,000 words maximum. Pays $250-600. Sometimes pays the expenses of writers on assignment.

Photos: Jim Galbraith, art director. Prefers color; color should be transparencies, not prints. Buys exclusive rights. Assignments are given, and sometimes a guarantee, provided the editors can be sure the photography will be acceptable.

Tips: "A frequent mistake made by writers in completing articles is that the focus of the story is not narrow enough and does not include enough facts, examples, dollar signs and a geographic and industry perspective. Greatest need is for short articles and fillers that are specific and to the point."

Miscellaneous

‡**FUR TRADE JOURNAL OF CANADA**, Titan Publishing Inc., Unit 7, 291 Woodlawn Rd. W., Box 1747, Guelph ON N1H 7A1 Canada. (519)763-5058. 40% freelance written. Monthly magazine on fur ranching and trapping. "*Fur Trade Journal* is a publication dedicated to mink, fox, and chinchilla husbandry." Circ. 1,500. Pays on publication. Publishes ms an average of 2 months after acceptance. Byline given. Buys first North American serial rights. Simultaneous, photocopied and previously published submissions OK. Computer printout submissions OK; prefers letter-quality. Reports in 6 weeks. Sample copy for 8x10 SAE with Canadian postage or international reply coupon.
Nonfiction: How-to (ranching techniques), interview/profile, new product, technical. Buys 25 mss/year. Query with published clips. Length: 100-3,000 words. Pays up to $100.
Photos: State availability of photos with submission. Reviews 5x7 prints. Offers $5 per photo. Identification of subjects required. Buys one-time rights.
Fillers: Facts, short humor. Length: 10-50 words. Pays $10.
Tips: "Read other publications to becme familiar with the trade. The sections most open to freelancers are profiles and interviews and summary of live animal shows."

GLEANINGS IN BEE CULTURE, Box 706, Medina OH 44258. Editor: Kim Flottum. 40% freelance written. For beekeepers and gardeners. Monthly. Buys first North American serial rights. Pays on publication. Publishes ms an average of 4 months after acceptance. Reports in 15-90 days. Computer printout submissions acceptable; prefers letter-quality. Sample copy for 9x12 SAE and 5 first class stamps; writer's guidelines for SAE and 1 first class stamp.
Nonfiction: Interested in articles giving new ideas on managing bees. Also uses success stories about commercial beekeepers. No "how I began beekeeping" articles. No highly advanced, technical and scientific abstracts or impractical advice. Length: 2,000 words maximum. Pays $26/published page.
Photos: Sharp b&w photos (pertaining to honeybees or honey plants) purchased with mss. Can be any size, prints or enlargements, but 4x5 or larger preferred. Pays $5-7/picture.
Tips: "Do an interview story on commercial beekeepers who are cooperative enough to furnish accurate, factual information on their operations. Frequent mistakes made by writers in completing articles are that they are too general in nature and lack management knowledge."

‡**UNITED CAPRINE NEWS**, Double Mountain Press, Drawer A, Rotan TX 79546. (915)735-2278. Editor: Kim Pease. Managing Editor: Jeff Klein. 80% freelance written. A monthly tabloid covering dairy pygmy and angora goats. Circ. 5,000. Pays on publication. Publishes ms an average of 3 months after acceptance. Byline given. Buys first rights, and makes work-for-hire assignments. Computer printout submissions acceptable; prefers letter-quality. Reports in 1 month. Sample copy $1.
Nonfiction: Interview/profile, new product, photo feature and technical—articles directed to all phases of goat keeping: management, showing, breeding and products. Buys 50 mss/year. Send complete ms. Length: open. Pays 25¢/column inch.
Photos: Send photos with submission. Reviews 5x7 prints. Offers 25¢/column inch. Captions required. Buys first rights.
Fillers: Facts and newsbreaks. Buys 25/year. Pays 25¢/column inch.
Tips: "We will consider any articles of an informative nature relating to goats that will benefit professional goat breeders. Most acceptable would be features on goat dairies or farms, technical data on health care and state-of-art topics related to breeding and genetics."

Regional

AG REVIEW, Farm Resource Center, 16 Grove St., Putnam CT 06260. (203)928-7778. Editor: Lucien Laliberty. Associate Editor: Monica McKenna. 50% freelance written. Eager to work with new/unpublished writers. A monthly magazine covering Northeast (New England, New York and Pennsylvania) agriculture for dairy, beef, cash and field crop farms: reporting and analyzing trends, research and product developments, and innovative problem-solving. Circ. 45,000. Pays on publication. Publishes ms an average of 2-5 months after acceptance. Byline given. Offers 50% kill fee. Buys one-time rights, second serial (reprint) rights or simultaneous rights. Submit seasonal/holiday material 4 months in advance. Photocopied and previously published submissions OK. Computer printout submissions acceptable. Reports in 1 month on queries; 6 weeks on mss. Sample copy and writer's guidelines for 9x12 SAE and 5 first class stamps; free writer's guidelines.

Nonfiction: Essays (current events or agricultural developments or research techniques); how-to (solving specific farm problems, appropriate to Northeast); and new product (unusual innovations, home adaptations). Writer's guidelines lists theme issues. "No blow-by-blow reports of conferences or meetings; gardening; or description of how some farmer runs his farm if it's ordinary stuff." Buys 10 mss/year. Query with or without published clips, or send complete ms. Length: 500-20,000 words (5,000 words more likely; 20,000 would be printed in parts in several issues). Pays $25-300; sometimes pays in Farm Resource Center data management or marketing services. Sometimes pays the expenses of writers on assignment.
Fiction: Humorous or mainstream in keeping with the magazine's theme of rural life. Fiction is a new department so we try for at least 10 mss/year. Preferred length is 800-1,500 words. Pays $50-100.
Photos: State availability or send photos with submission. Considers color, vertical-format photos of dairy or Northeast farming for cover. Reviews transparencies or 3x5 minimum prints. Offers $5-10/photo. Captions and identification of subjects required. Buys one-time rights.
Tips: "We are most interested in in-depth features, ranging from 2,000-5,000 words, including photos or other illustrations, and covering in detail an idea, controversy, technique or trend. We need interviews with successful farmers, profiles of innovative marketers, columns, or specialty crops (berries, bees, maple syrup, Christmas trees, etc.) and feature articles on major events/issues/controversies in the dairy industry."

CALIFORNIA FARMER, The Business Magazine for Commercial Agriculture, California Farmer Publishing Co., 731 Market St., San Francisco CA 94103. (415)495-3340. Editor: Len Richardson. Managing Editor: Richard Smoley. 70% freelance written. Works with a small number of new/unpublished writers each year. Magazine published semimonthly: once a month in July, August, December covering California agriculture. "We cover all issues of interest to the state's commercial farmers, including production techniques, marketing, politics, and social and economic issues." Circ. 54,000. Pays on acceptance. Publishes ms an average of 1-2 months after acceptance. Byline given. Offers $100 kill fee. Makes work-for-hire assignments. Submit seasonal/holiday material 3 months in advance. Photocopied and previously published submissions OK. Query for electronic submissions. Computer printout submissions acceptable, "must be double-spaced"; prefers letter-quality. Reports in 1 month. Sample copy for 8½x11 SASE. Free writer's guidelines.
Nonfiction: How-to (agricultural, livestock); interview/profile; technical (agricultural: weed and pest control; crop and livestock management; cultural and irrigation practices; financial involvement and marketing of farm products.) No "It happened to me"-type stories. Buys 75 mss/year. Query with published clips. Length: 1,000-3,000 words. Pays $100-400 for assigned articles; pays $50-300 for unsolicited articles. Sometimes pays the expenses of writers on assignment.
Photos: Send photos with submission. "We expect to emphasize high-quality color photography even more than we do now. We will give strong—preference to well-written, accurate, newsworthy stories that are accompanied by suitable photographs. Reviews 35mm color transparencies and b&w prints (any size). Captions and identification of subjects required.
Tips: "We will give preference to writers with a demonstrated knowledge of California agriculture, but we will consider material from and occasionally give assignments to good writers with an ability to research a story, get the facts right and write in a smooth, easy-to-understand style. We are most interested in stories about technical innovations in farming as they relate to California agriculture. Stories should be clear, concise, and above all, accurate. We especially welcome pictures of California farmers as illustration."

FLORIDA GROWER & RANCHER, F.G.R., Inc., 1331 N. Mills Ave., Orlando FL 32803. (305)894-6522. Editor: Frank Abrahamson. 10% freelance written. A monthly magazine for Florida farmers. Circ. 28,000. Pays on publication. Byline given. Buys one-time rights. Submit seasonal/holiday material 2 months in advance. Query for electronic submissions. Computer printout submissions acceptable; prefers letter-quality. Reports in 2 weeks on queries; 1 month on mss. Free sample copy and writer's guidelines.
Nonfiction: General interest, historical/nostalgic, how-to, interview/profile, new product, personal experience, photo feature, technical. Articles should coordinate with editorial calendar, determined 1 year in advance. Buys 6 mss/year. Query. Length: 500-1,000 words. Pays 40¢/printed line.
Photos: Send photos with submission. Reviews transparencies and prints. Pays $5/b&w print, $50/color cover. Identification of subjects required. Buys one-time rights.

‡IOWA REC NEWS, Suite 48, 8525 Douglas, Urbandale IA 50322. (515)276-5350. Editor: Karen Steimel. Managing Editor: Jody Garlock. 15% freelance written. Emphasizes energy issues for residents of rural Iowa. Monthly magazine. Circ. 125,000. Pays on publication. Publishes ms an average of 3 months after acceptance. Buys first serial rights and second serial (reprint) rights. Not copyrighted. Simultaneous, photocopied and previously published submissions OK. Computer printout submissions acceptable.
Nonfiction: General interest, historical, humor, farm issues and trends, rural lifestyle trends, energy awareness features and photo feature. Buys approximately 8 unsolicited mss/year. Send complete ms. Pays $40-60.
Tips: "The easiest way to break into our magazine is: research a particular subject well, include appropriate attributions to establish credibility, authority and include a couple paragraphs about the author. Reading and knowing about farm people is important. Stories that touch the senses or can improve the lives of the readers are

highly considered, as are those with a strong Iowa angle. We prefer to tailor our articles to Iowa REC readers and use our staff's skills. Freelancers have the advantage of offering subject matter that existing staff may not be able to cover. Often, however, many articles lack evidence of actual research—they provide lots of information but do not include any sources to give the story any credibility. (Rarely is the author a renowned expert on the subject he's written about.) Inclusion of nice photos is also a plus. The most frequent mistakes made by writers are: lots of typos in copy, uncorrected; story too long, story too biased; no attribution to any source of info; and not relevant to electric consumers, farmers."

MAINE ORGANIC FARMER & GARDENER, Maine Organic Farmers & Gardeners Association, Box 2176, Augusta ME 04330. (207)622-3118. Editor: Pam Bell. Box 233, RFD#2, Belfast ME 04915. 40% freelance written. Prefers to work with published/established writers; works with a small number of new/unpublished writers each year. Bimonthly magazine covering organic farming and gardening for urban and rural farmers and gardeners and nutrition-oriented, environmentally concerned readers. "*MOF&G* promotes and encourages sustainable agriculture and environmentally sound living. Our primary focus is organic sustainable farming, gardening and forestry, but we also deal with local, national and international agriculture, food and environmental issues." Circ. 10,000. Pays on publication. Publishes ms an average of 8 months after acceptance. Byline and bio given. Buys first North American serial rights, one-time rights, first serial rights, or second serial (reprint) rights. Submit seasonal/holiday material 6 months in advance. Simultaneous queries, and simultaneous, photocopied, and previously published submissions OK. Computer printout submissions acceptable. Reports in 2 months. Sample copy $2 ; free writer's guidelines.
Nonfiction: How-to information can be handled as first person experience, technical/research report, or interview/profile focusing on farmer, gardener, food plant, forests, livestock, weeds, insects, trees, renewable energy, recycling, nutrition, health, non-toxic pest control, organic farm management. We use profiles of New England organic farmers and gardeners, U.S. and international forestry-, ag-, or food- news reports (500-1,000 words) dealing with U.S./international sustainable ag research and development, rural development, recycling projects, environmental problem solutions, organic farms with broad impact, cooperatives, community projects, American farm crisis and issues, food issues. Buys 30 mss/year. Query with published clips or send complete ms. Length: 1,000-3,000 words. Pays $20-100. Sometimes pays expenses of writers on assignment.
Photos: State availability of photos with query; send photos or proof sheet with manuscript. Assignment writers can send exposed b&w films, and we process and print. Prefer b&w but can use color slides or negatives in a pinch. Captions, model releases, and identification of subjects required. Buys one-time rights.
Tips: "We are a nonprofit organization. Our publication's primary mission is to inform and educate. Our readers want to know how to, but they also want to enjoy the reading and know whom the source/expert/writer is. We don't want impersonal how-to articles that sound like Extension bulletins or textbooks."

N.D. REC MAGAZINE, N.D. Association of RECs, Box 727, Mandan ND 58554. (701)663-6501. Editor: Karl Karlgaard. 10% freelance written. Prefers to work with published/established writers, and works with a small number of new/unpublished writers each year. Monthly magazine covering rural electric program and rural North Dakota lifestyle. "Our magazine goes to the 70,000 North Dakotans who get their electricity from rural electric cooperatives. We cover rural lifestyle, energy conservation, agriculture, farm family news and other features of importance to this predominantly agrarian state. Of course, we represent the views of our statewide association." Circ. 74,000. Pays on publication; "acceptance for assigned features." Publishes ms average of 3 months after acceptance. Byline given. Buys first North American serial rights. Submit seasonal/holiday material 6 months in advance. Simultaneous queries OK. Computer printout submissions acceptable. Reports in 2 weeks. Sample copy for 9x12 SAE and 6 first class stamps.
Nonfiction: Expose (subjects of ND interest dealing with rural electric, agriculture, rural lifestyle); historical/nostalgic (ND events or people only); how-to (save energy, weatherize homes, etc.); interview/profile (on great leaders of the rural electric program, agriculture); and opinion (why family farms should be saved, etc.). No fiction that does not relate to our editorial goals. Buys 10-12 mss/year. Length: open. Pays $35-300. Pays expenses of writers on assignment.
Photos: "We need 5x7 b&w glossy prints for editorial material. Transparencies needed for cover, ag/rural scenes only—ND interest." Pays $25 maximum for 35mm color transparencies; $5 minimum for 5x7 b&w prints. Captions and identification of subjects required. Buys one-time rights.
Columns/Departments: Guest Spot: Guest opinion page, preferably about 700-850 words, about issues dealing with agriculture, rural social issues and the rural electric program. Buys 12 mss/year. Pays $35-75.

NEW ENGLAND FARM BULLETIN, New England Farm & Home Assn., Box 147, Cohasset MA 02025. Editor-in-Chief: V.A. Lipsett. Managing Editor: M.S. Maire. 5% freelance written. Works with a small number of new/unpublished writers each year. A biweekly newsletter covering New England farming. Circ. 11,000. Pays on publication. Publishes ms an average of 2 months after acceptance. Byline given. Buys first North American serial rights. Submit seasonal/holiday material 6 months in advance. Photocopied submissions OK. Computer printout submissions acceptable. Reports in 1 week. Sample copy and writer's guidelines for #10 SAE and $1.25.

Nonfiction: Essays (farming/agriculture); general interest; historical/nostalgic; how-to; humor; interview/profile (possibly, of New England farm); personal experience; and technical. All articles must be related to New England farming. Buys 6-12 mss/year. Query or send complete ms. Length: 500-1,000 words. Pays 10¢/word.

Tips: "We would probably require the writer to live in New England or to have an unmistakable grasp of what New England is like; must also know farmers." Especially interested in general articles on New England crops/livestocks, specific breeds, crop strains and universal agricultural activity in New England.

‡THE OHIO FARMER, 1350 W. 5th Ave., Columbus OH 43212. (614)486-9637. Editor: Andrew Stevens. 10% freelance written. "We are backlogged with submissions and prefer not to receive unsolicited submissions at this time." For Ohio farmers and their families. Biweekly magazine. Circ. 81,000. Usually buys all rights. Pays on publication. Publishes ms an average of 2 months after acceptance. Will consider photocopied submissions. Reports in 2 weeks. Computer printout submissions acceptable; prefers letter-quality. Sample copy $1; free writer's guidelines.

Nonfiction: Technical and on-the-farm stories. Buys informational, how-to, and personal experience. Buys 5 mss/year. Submit complete ms. Length: 600-700 words. Pays $15.

Photos: Photos purchased with ms with no additional payment, or without ms. Pays $5-25 for b&w; $35-100 for color. 4x5 b&w glossies; and transparencies or 8x10 color prints.

Tips: "We are now doing more staff-written stories. We buy very little freelance material."

‡PENNSYLVANIA FARMER, Harcourt Brace Jovanovich Publications, 704 Lisburn Rd., Camp Hill PA 17011. (717)761-6050. Editor: John Vogel. 20% freelance written. A bimonthly farm business magazine "oriented to providing readers with ideas to help their businesses and personal lives." Circ. 68,000. Pays on publication. Publishes ms an average of 3 months after acceptance. Byline sometimes given. Buys one-time rights. Submit seasonal/holiday material 3 months in advance. Simultaneous submissions OK. Reports in 2 weeks. Free writer's guidelines.

Nonfiction: Humor, inspirational, and technical. No stories without a strong tie to modern-day farming. Buys 15 mss/year. Query. Length: 500-1,000 words. Pays $25-100. Sometimes pays the expenses of writers on assignment.

Photos: Send photos with submission. Reviews contact sheets, 35mm transparencies and 5x7 prints. Offers no additional payment for photos accepted with ms. Captions and identification of subjects required. Buys one-time rights.

Columns/Departments: Lynn Tilton, column/department editor. Country Air (humorous, first-person accounts of farm happenings), 600 words. Buys 18 mss/year. Send complete ms. Pays $25.

Finance

These magazines deal with banking, investment and financial management. Publications that use similar material but have a less technical slant are listed under the Consumer Business and Finance section.

AMERICAN BANKER, 1 State St. Plaza, New York NY 10004. (212)943-0400. Editor: William Zimmerman. Managing Editor: Brian Sullivan. 30% freelance written. Daily tabloid covering banking and finance for top management of banks, savings banks, savings and loans and other financial service institutions. Circ. 24,000. Pays on publication. Publishes ms an average of 1 month after acceptance. Byline given. Buys all rights. Simultaneous and previously published (depending on where published) submissions OK. Computer printout submissions acceptable; prefers letter-quality. Reports in 1 month. Feature calendar on request.

Nonfiction: Patricia Stundza, features editor. Book excerpts and technical (relating to banking/finance). No "nonbanking or nonbusiness-oriented articles—must be specific." Query. Length: 1,500-3,000 words. Pays $75-500. Sometimes pays the expenses of writers on assignment.

Photos: State availability of photos. Pays $50 minimum for 8x10 b&w prints. Captions and identification of subjects required. Buys one-time rights.

BANK OPERATIONS REPORT, Warren, Gorham & Lamont, One Penn Plaza, New York NY 10119. (212)971-5000. Managing Editor: Philip Ruppel. 90% freelance written. Prefers to work with published/established writers, and works with a small number of new/unpublished writers each year. A monthly newsletter covering operations and technology in banking and financial services. Circ. 2,000. Pays on publication.

Publishes ms an average of 2 months after acceptance. Buys all rights. Computer printout submissions OK; prefers letter-quality. Free sample copy.

Nonfiction: How-to articles, case histories, "practical oriented for bank operations managers" and technical. Buys 60 mss/year. Query with published clips. Length: 500-1,000 words. Pays $1.20/line. Sometimes pays the expenses of writers on assignment.

BANK PERSONNEL REPORT, Warren, Gorham & Lamont, One Penn Plaza, New York NY 10119. (212)971-5000. Managing Editor: Philip Ruppel. 90% freelance written. Prefers to work with published/established writers, and works with a small number of new/unpublished writers each year. A monthly newsletter covering personnel and human resources, "specifically as they relate to bankers." Circ. 2,000. Pays on publication. Publishes ms an average of 2 months after acceptance. Buys all rights. Computer printout submissions OK; prefers letter-quality. Free sample copy.

Nonfiction: Technical. Buys 60 mss/year. Query with published clips. Length: 500-1,000 words. Pays $1.20/line. Sometimes pays the expenses of writers on assignment.

BANKING SOFTWARE REVIEW, International Computer Programs, Inc., Suite 200, 9100 Keystone Crossing, Indianapolis IN 46240. (317)844-7461. Editor: Marilyn Gasaway. Quarterly trade magazine covering the computer software industry as it relates to financial institutions. "Editorial slant includes the selection, implementation and use of software in banks and other financial institutions. The audience comprises data processing and end-user management in medium to large financial institutions." Circ. 15,000. Pays on publication. Publishes ms an average of 2 months after acceptance. Byline sometimes given. Buys first or second serial (reprint) rights. Photocopied submissions OK. Query for electronic submissions. Computer printout submissions OK; prefers letter-quality. Reports in 2 weeks on queries; 3 weeks on mss.

Nonfiction: How-to (successfully install and use software products), interview/profile, new product and technical. No nonsoftware related, nonbusiness software or humorous articles. Buys 8-10 mss/year. Query with published clips. Length: 1,000-2,000 words. Pays $100-350 for assigned articles. Sometimes pays the expenses of writers on assignment. Sometimes pays with contributor copies, "depends on number of copies requested."

Photos: Send photos with submission. Prefers 5x7 prints. Offers no additional payment for photos accepted with ms. Identification of subjects required. Buys all rights.

Columns/Departments: Systems Review (in-depth profile of a specific software product at use in a banking environment; must include comments from 2-3 financial institution users (e.g., the benefits of the product, its use within the institution, etc.). Length: 500-700 words. Pays $50.

‡CA MAGAZINE, 150 Bloor St., W., Toronto, Ontario M5S 2Y2 Canada. Editor: Nelson Luscombe. 10% freelance written. Works with a small number of new/unpublished writers each year. Monthly magazine for accountants and financial managers. Circ. 60,000. Pays on publication for the article's copyright. Buys all rights. Computer printout submissions acceptable; prefers letter-quality. Publishes ms an average of 4 months after acceptance.

Nonfiction: Accounting, business, finance, management and taxation. Also, subject-related humor pieces and cartoons. "We accept whatever is relevant to our readership, no matter the origin as long as it meets our standards." Length: 3,000-5,000 words. Pays $100 for feature articles, $75 for departments and 10¢/word for acceptable news items. Sometimes pays the expenses of writers on assignment.

‡CORPORATE FINANCE, The Magazine for the Financing Strategist, CFM Associates. 810 Seventh Ave., New York NY 10019. (212)397-2300. Editor: Wayne Welch. 25% freelance written. A monthly magazine on corporate finance for financial officers at large publications. Circ. 50,000. Pays on acceptance. Publishes ms an average of 2 months after acceptance. Byline given. 25% kill fee. Buys all rights. Query for electronic submissions. Computer printout submissions OK; no dot-matrix. Reports in 1 week on queries.

Nonfiction: Al Ehrbar, articles editor. Business. Buys 50 mss/year. Query. Pays 50¢-$1/word. Does not pay for unsolicited articles. State availability of photos with submission. Reviews contact sheets. Buys all rights.

Columns: Query. Length: 750-1,400. Buys 40 mss/year. Pays $750-1,000.

‡DELUXE, Ideas for the Business of Living, Webb Publishing Company. 1999 Shepard Rd., St. Paul MN 55116. (612)690-7456. Editor: Sharon Ross. 80% freelance written. A quarterly magazine published by Webb for Deluxe Check Printers, Inc., for employees of financial institutions nationwide. "*Deluxe* is published for new-accounts counselors in banks, savings & loan associations and credit unions. They receive the magazine at work, so we aim to present new, useful and entertaining information that will help them with life at the office, as well as with life at home. New account counselors deal with the public often, both in person and on the phone. They usually serve as the financial institution's main link to customers. Our magazine hopes to help them do their jobs better and reinforce an image of professionalism in themselves." Circ. 90,000. Pays on acceptance by client. Byline given. Offers 25% kill fee. Buys limited rights in work-for-hire. Submit seasonal/holiday material 8 months in advance. Simultaneous and photocopied submissions OK. Query for electronic submissions. Computer printout submissions OK; prefers letter-quality. Reports in 3 weeks. Sample copy for 8¾x11¾ SAE with 3 first class stamps. Writer's guidelines for #10 SAE with 1 first class stamp.

Nonfiction: General interest, historical/nostalgic and business/career/personal development. No personal articles, essay, opinion, humor, technical finance, first-person, "executive" topics or how to get out of your present job articles. Buys 16 mss/year. Query with published clips and resume. Length: 600-1,600 words. Pays $300-600. Sometimes pays the expenses of writers on assignment.

Tips: "Writers should learn more about our audience-new accounts counselors at financial institutions-and then gear article ideas specifically to them. also, they should not be offended if asked to rewrite their stories in order to slant them to the needs/wants of our readers."

EXECUTIVE FINANCIAL WOMAN, Suite 1400, 500 N. Michigan Ave., Chicago IL 60611. (312)661-1700. Editor: Richard G. Kemmer. 10-30% freelance written. Eager to work with new/unpublished writers. Bimonthly magazine for members of the National Association of Bank Women and paid subscribers covering banking, insurance, financial planning, diversified financials, credit unions, thrifts, investment banking and other industry segments. Circ. 25,000. Publishes ms an average of 2 months after acceptance. Byline given. Buys all rights. Submit seasonal material 3 months in advance. Simultaneous queries and photocopied submissions OK. Computer printout submissions acceptable; no dot-matrix. Reports in approximately 1 month. Sample copy $4.

Nonfiction: "We are looking for articles in the general areas of financial services, career advancement, businesswomen's issues and management. Because the financial services industry is in a state of flux at present, articles on how to adapt to and benefit from this fact, both personally and professionally, are particularly apt." Query with resume and clips of published work. Length: 1,000-4,000 words. Pays variable rates.

Photos: "Photos and other graphic material can make an article more attractive to us." Captions and model release required.

Tips: "We're looking for writers who can write effectively about the people who work in the industry and combine that with hard data on how the industry is changing. We're interested in running more Q&As with top executives in the industry, especially women."

THE FEDERAL CREDIT UNION, National Association of Federal Credit Unions, Box 3769, Washington DC 20007. (703)522-4770. Editor: Patrick M. Keefe. 25% freelance written. "Looking for writer with financial, banking or credit union experience, but will work with inexperienced (unpublished) writers based on writing skill." Bimonthly magazine covering credit unions. Circ. 7,000. Pays on publication. Publishes ms an average of 3 months after acceptance. Byline sometimes given. Buys first North American serial rights. Submit seasonal/holiday material 5 months in advance. Simultaneous submissions OK. Query for electronic submissions. Computer printout submissions OK; prefers letter-quality. Reports in 1 month. Writer's guidelines for #10 SASE.

Nonfiction: How-to, interview/profile, new product, legal, technical and credit union operations innovations. Special issues include Technology for Financial Institutions (summer); Purchasing (winter). Query with published clips. Length: 5,000-20,000 words. Pays $200-1,000 for assigned articles.

Photos: Send photos with submission. Reviews 35mm transparencies and 5x7 prints. Offers no additional payment for photos accepted with ms. Model releases and identification of subjects required. Buys all rights.

Tips: "Provide resume or listing of experience pertinent to subject. We seek tips on better ways for credit unions to operate." Areas most open to freelancers are "technical articles/how-to/reports on credit union operations, innovation."

FUTURES MAGAZINE, 219 Parkade, Cedar Falls IA 50613. (319)277-6341. Publisher: Merrill Oster. Editor-in-Chief: Darrell Jobman. 20% freelance written. Monthly magazine. For private, individual traders, brokers, exchange members, agribusinessmen, bankers, anyone with an interest in futures or options. Circ. 75,000. Buys all rights. Byline given. Pays on publication. Publishes ms an average of 6 months after acceptance. Photocopied submissions OK. Computer printout submissions acceptable; no dot-matrix. Reports in 1 month. Sample copy for 9x12 SAE with $1.92 postage.

Nonfiction: Articles analyzing specific commodity futures and options trading strategies; fundamental and technical analysis of individual commodities and markets; interviews, book reviews, "success" stories; and news items. Material on new legislation affecting commodities, trading, any new trading strategy ("results must be able to be substantiated"); and personalities. No "homespun" rules for trading and simplistic approaches to the commodities market. Treatment is always in-depth and broad. Informational, how-to, interview, profile, technical. "Articles should be written for a reader who has traded commodities for one year or more; should not talk down or hypothesize. Relatively complex material is acceptable." No get-rich-quick gimmicks, astrology articles or general, broad topics. "Writers must have solid knowledge of the magazine's specific emphasis and be able to communicate well." Buys 30-40 mss/year. Query or submit complete ms. Length: 1,500 words optimum. Pays $50-1,000, depending upon author's research and writing quality. "Rarely" pays the expenses of writers on assignment.

Tips: "Writers must have a solid understanding and appreciation for futures or options trading. We will have more financial and stock index features as well as new options contracts that will require special knowledge and experience. The writer has a better chance of breaking in at our publication with short articles and fillers since they can zero in on a specific idea without having to know the whole broad area we cover. Fluffy leads or trying to describe whole trading world instead of targeting key issues are frequent mistakes made by writers. More articles on trading options and on financial institution's use of futures/options will be published in 1989."

THE FUTURES AND OPTIONS TRADER, DeLong—Western Publishing Co., 13618 Scenic Crest Dr., Yucaipa CA 92399. (714)797-3532. Editor: Charles Kreidl. Managing Editor: Jeanne Johnson. 50% freelance written. Monthly newspaper covering futures and options. Publishes "basic descriptions of trading systems or other commodity futures information which would be useful to traders. No hype or sales-related articles." Circ. 12,000. Pays on acceptance. Publishes ms an average of 1 month after acceptance. Not copyrighted. Buys all rights. Simultaneous and photocopied submissions OK. Query for electronic submissions. Computer printout submissions OK; prefers letter-quality. Sample copy for SAE with 1 first class stamp.
Nonfiction: Technical and general trading-related articles. Buys 35 mss/year. Send complete ms. Length: 250-1,000 words. Pays $10-100 for unsolicited articles.
Columns/Departments: Options Trader; Spread Trader (futures and options spread and arbitrage trading); and Index Trader (stock index trading). Buys 35 mss/year. Send complete ms. Length: 250-1,000 words. Pays $10-100.
Tips: "Authors should be active in the markets."

ILLINOIS BANKER, Illinois Bankers Association, Suite 1100, 205 W. Randolph, Chicago IL 60606. (312)984-1500. Director of Public Affairs: Martha Rohlfing. Assistant Publisher: Cindy Altman. Editorial Assistant: Janet Krause. Production Assistant: Anetta Gauthier. Marketing Manager: Tiffany Renwick. 10% freelance written. Monthly magazine about banking for top decision makers and executives, bank officers, title and insurance company executives, elected officials and individual subscribers interested in banking products and services. Circ. 3,000. Pays on publication. Publishes ms an average of 4 months after acceptance. Byline given. Buys first serial rights. Phone queries OK. Submit material 6 weeks prior to publication. Simultaneous submissions OK. Computer printout submissions acceptable. Free sample copy, writer's guidelines and editorial calendar.
Nonfiction: Interview (ranking government and banking leaders); personal experience (along the lines of customer relations); and technical (specific areas of banking). "The purpose of the publication is to educate, inform and guide its readers on public policy issues affecting banks, new ideas in management and operations, and banking and business trends in the Midwest. Any clear, fresh approach geared to a specific area of banking, such as agricultural bank management, credit, lending, marketing and trust is what we want." Buys 4-5 unsolicited mss/year. Send complete ms. Length: 825-3,000 words. Pays $50-100.

INDEPENDENT BANKER, Independent Bankers Association of America, Box 267, Sauk Centre MN 56378. (612)352-6546. Editor: Norman Douglas. 15% freelance written. Works with a small number of new/unpublished writers each year. Monthly magazine for the administrators of small, independent banks. Circ. 10,000. Pays on acceptance. Publishes ms an average of 3 months after acceptance. Byline given. Not copyrighted. Buys all rights. Computer printout submissions acceptable; prefers letter-quality. Reports in 1 week. Sample copy and writer's guidelines for 9x12 SASE.
Nonfiction: How-to (banking practices and procedures); interview/profile (popular small bankers); technical (bank accounting, automation); and banking trends. "Factual case histories, banker profiles or research pieces of value to bankers in the daily administration of their banks." No material that ridicules banking and finance or puff pieces on products and services. Buys 12 mss/year. Query. Length: 2,000-2,500 words. Pays $300 maximum.
Tips: "In this magazine, the emphasis is on material that will help small banks compete with large banks and large bank holding companies. We look for innovative articles on small bank operations and administration."

OTC REVIEW, OTC Review, Inc., 37 E. 28th St., Suite 706, New York NY 10016. (212)685-6244. Editor: Robert Flaherty. 50% freelance written. A monthly magazine covering publicly owned companies whose stocks trade in the over-the-counter market. "We are a financial magazine covering the fastest-growing securities market in the world. We study the management of companies traded over-the-counter and act as critics reviewing their performances. We aspire to be 'The Shareholder's Friend.' " Circ. 27,000. Pays on publication. Publishes ms an average of 2 months after acceptance. Byline given. Buys first rights or reprint rights. Sample copy for 8½x11 SAE with 5 first class stamps.
Nonfiction: New product and technical. Buys 30 mss/year. "We must know the writer first as we are careful about whom we publish. A letter of introduction with resumé and clips is the best way to introduce yourself. Financial writing requires specialized knowledge and a feel for people as well, which can be a tough combination to find." Query with published clips. Length: 300-1,500 words. Pays $150-750 for assigned articles. Offers copies or premiums for guest columns by famous money managers who are not writing for cash payments, but to showcase their ideas and approach. Pays expenses of writers on assignment.

Photos: Send photos with submission. Reviews contact sheets, negatives, transparencies and prints. Offers no additional payment for photos accepted with ms. Identification of subjects required.

Columns/Departments: Pays $25-75 for assigned items only.

Tips: "Anyone who enjoys analyzing a business and telling the story of the people who started it, or run it today, is a potential *OTC Review* contributor. But to protect our readers and ourselves, we are careful about who writes for us. Business writing is an exciting area and our stories reflect that. If a writer relies on numbers and percentages to tell his story, rather than the individuals involved, the result will be numbingly dull."

‡RESEARCH MAGAZINE, Ideas for Today's Investors, Research Services, 2201 Third St., San Francisco CA 94107. (415)621-0220. Editor: Anne Evers. 50% freelance written. Monthly business magazine of corporate profiles and subjects of interest to stockbrokers. Circ. 80,000. Pays on publication. Publishes ms an average of 2 months after acceptance. Byline given. Offers 20% kill fee. Buys first North American serial rights or second serial (reprint) rights. Query for electronic submissions. Reports in 1 month. Sample copy for 9x12 SAE with 4 first class stamps; writer's guidelines for #10 SASE.

Nonfiction: How-to (sales tips), interview/profile, new product, financial products. Buys approx. 50 mss/year. Query with published clips. Length: 1,000-3,000 words. Pays 300-900. Sometimes pays expenses of writers on assignment.

Tips: "Only submit articles that fit our editorial policy and are appropriate for our audience. Only the non-corporate profile section is open to freelancers. We use local freelancers on a regular basis for coporate profiles."

SAVINGS INSTITUTIONS, U.S. League of Savings Institutions, 111 E. Wacker Dr., Chicago IL 60601. (312)644-3100. Editor: Mary Nowesnick. 5% freelance written. Prefers to work with published/established writers. A monthly business magazine covering management of savings institutions. Circ. 30,000. Pays on acceptance. Publishes ms an average of 3 months after acceptance. Byline given. Buys negotiable rights. Simultaneous queries and photocopied submissions OK. Query for electronic submissions. Computer printout submissions acceptable; prefers letter-quality. Reports in 2 months. Free sample copy.

Nonfiction: How-to (manage or improve operations); new products (application stories at savings institutions); and technical (financial management). No opinion or 'puff' pieces. Buys 1-3 mss/year. Query with or without published clips. Length: 3,000-8,000 words. Pays $125/published page. Pays expenses of writers on assignment.

Columns/Departments: Beth Linnen, column/department editor. Operations, Marketing, Personnel, and Secondary Mortage Market. Buys 10 mss/year. Query with or without published clips. Length: 800-3,000 words. Pays $125/published page.

Tips: "Operations and Marketing departments are most open to freelancers."

‡SECONDARY MARKETING EXECUTIVE, LDJ Corporation. Box 2151, Waterbury CT 06722. (203)755-0158. Editorial Director: John Florian. 60% freelance written. A monthly tabloid on secondary marketing. "The magazine is read monthly by executives in financial institutes who are involved with secondary marketing. The editorial slant is toward how-to and analysis of trends, rather than spot news." Circ. 34,000. Pays on publication. Publishes ms an average of 1 month after acceptance. Byline given. 30% kill fee. Buys first rights. Submit seasonal/holiday material 4 months in advance. Query for electronic submissions. Computer printout submissions OK; no dot-matrix. Reports in 1 week. Free sample copy and writer's guidelines.

Nonfiction: How-to (how to improve secondary marketing operations and profits) and opinion. Buys 40 mss/year. Query. Length: 800-1,200 words. Pays $200-400. State availability of photos with submission. Reviews contact sheets. Offers $25 per photo. Captions, model releases and identification of subjects required. Buys one-time rights.

Fishing

NATIONAL FISHERMAN, Diversified Communications, 21 Elm St., Camden ME 04843. (207)236-4342. Editor-in-Chief: James W. Fullilove. 25% freelance written. Monthly tabloid. For amateur and professional boat builders, commercial fishermen, armchair sailors, bureaucrats and politicians. Circ. 58,000. Pays in month of acceptance. Publishes ms an average of 2 months after acceptance. Byline given. Buys first serial rights only. Phone or letter queries advised. Photocopied submissions OK if good quality. Computer printout submissions acceptable if double spaced; no dot-matrix. Reports in 1 month. Free sample copy and writer's guidelines; mention *Writer's Market* in request.

Nonfiction: Expose, how-to, general interest, humor, historical, interview, new product, nostalgia, personal experience, opinion, photo feature, profile and technical, but all must be related to commerical fishing in some way. Especially needs articles on commercial fishing techniques (problems, solutions, large catches, busts); gear development; and marine historical and offbeat articles. No articles about sailboat racing, cruising and

sportfishing. Buys approximately 35 unsolicited mss/year. Submit query or ms. Length: 100-2,000 words. Sometimes pays the expenses of writers on assignment.
Photos: State availability of photos with ms. "Photos improve chances of being used." Pays $5-15 for 5x7 or 8x10 prints; color cover photo pays $250. Buys one-time rights.
Tips: "We are soliciting historical and human interest articles in addition to business-related articles. The writer may have a better chance of breaking in at our publication with short articles and fillers because our issues are smaller these days, and we can seldom afford to give pages over to lengthy features unless they are exceptionally good. The most frequent mistake made by writers in completing an article for us is failure to provide photos or other relevant illustrations. This is a common occurrence. In some cases, lack of art jeopardizes a story's chance of being published."

PACIFIC FISHING, Special Interest Publications, 1515 NW 51st St., Seattle WA 98107. (206)789-5333. Editor: Ken Talley. 75% freelance written. Eager to work with new/unpublished writers. Monthly business magazine for commercial fishermen and others in the West Coast commercial fishing industry. *Pacific Fishing* views the fisherman as a small businessman and covers all aspects of the industry, including harvesting, processing and marketing. Circ. 10,000. Pays on publication. Publishes ms an average of 2 months after acceptance. Byline given. Offers 10-15% kill fee on assigned articles deemed unsuitable. Buys one-time rights. Queries highly recommended. Computer printout submissions acceptable; prefers letter-quality. Reports in 1 month. Sample copy and writer's guidelines for SAE and 1 first class stamp.
Nonfiction: Interview/profile and technical (usually with a business hook or slant). "Articles must be concerned specifically with *commercial* fishing. We view fishermen as small businessmen and professionals who are innovative and success-oriented. To appeal to this reader, *Pacific Fishing* offers four basic features: technical, how-to articles that give fisherman hands-on tips that will make their operation more efficient and profitable; practical, well-researched business articles discussing the dollars and cents of fishing, processing and marketing; profiles of a fisherman, processor or company with emphasis on practical business and technical areas; and in-depth analysis of political, social, fisheries management and resource issues that have a direct bearing on West Coast commercial fishermen." Buys 20 mss/year. Query noting whether photos are available, and enclosing samples of previous work. Length: 1,500-3,000 words. Pays 7-10¢/word. Sometimes pays the expenses of writers on assignment.
Photos: "We need good, high-quality photography, especially color, of West Coast commercial fishing. We prefer 35mm color slides. Our rates are $125 for cover; $25-75 for inside color; $15-35 for b&w and $10 for table of contents."
Tips: "Because of the specialized nature of our audience, the editor strongly recommends that freelance writers query the magazine in writing with a proposal. We enjoy finding a writer who understands our editorial needs and satisfies those needs, a writer willing to work with an editor to make the article just right. Most of our shorter items are staff written. Our freelance budget is such that we get the most benefit by using it for feature material. The most frequent mistakes made by writers are not keeping to specified length and failing to do a complete job on statistics that may be a part of the story."

Florists, Nurseries and Landscaping

Readers of these publications are involved in growing, selling or caring for plants, flowers and trees. Magazines geared to consumers interested in gardening are listed in the Consumer Home and Garden section.

FLORIST, Florists' Transworld Delivery Association, 29200 Northwestern Hwy., Box 2227, Southfield MI 48037. (313)355-9300. Editor-in-Chief: William P. Golden. Managing Editor: Susan L. Nicholas. 3% freelance written. For retail florists, floriculture growers, wholesalers, researchers and teachers. Monthly magazine. Circ. 28,000. Pays on acceptance. Publishes ms an average of 2 months after acceptance. Buys one-time rights. Pays 10-25% kill fee. Byline given "unless the story needs a substantial rewrite." Phone queries OK. Submit seasonal/holiday material 4 months in advance. Simultaneous, photocopied, and previously published submissions OK. Computer printout submissions acceptable; prefers letter-quality. Reports in 1 month.
Nonfiction: How-to (more profitably run a retail flower shop, grow and maintain better quality flowers, etc.); general interest (to floriculture and retail floristry); and technical (on flower and plant growing, breeding, etc.). Buys 5 unsolicited mss/year. Query with published clips. Length: 1,200-3,000 words. Pays 20¢/word.

Photos: "We do not like to run stories without photos." State availability of photos with query. Pays $10-25 for 5x7 b&w photos or color transparencies. Buys one-time rights.
Tips: "Send samples of published work with query. Suggest several ideas in query letter."

FLOWERS &, The beautiful magazine about the business of flowers, Suite 260, 12233 W. Olympic Blvd., Los Angeles CA 90064. (213)826-5253. Editor-in-chief: Marie Moneysmith. Executive Editor: Bruce Wright. 40% freelance written. Prefers to work with published/established writers. A monthly magazine for the retail floristry industry. "We are essentially a small business magazine." Circ. approximately 28,000. Pays on acceptance. Publishes ms an average of 4 months after acceptance. Byline given. Offers 20% kill fee. Buys first North American serial rights and second serial (reprint) rights. Submit seasonal/holiday material 4 months in advance. Simultaneous submissions OK. Query for electronic submissions. Computer printout submissions acceptable; prefers letter-quality. Reports in 1 month on queries; 3 months on mss. Sample copy for 9½x11 SAE; writer's guidelines for #10 SAE with 1 first class stamp.
Nonfiction: Book excerpts; historical/nostalgic; how-to (improve business, strengthen advertising, put out a newsletter, etc.); interview/profile; new product; and technical. "No articles not geared specifically to the floral industry; no articles about flowers (these are written in-house)." Buys 20 mss/year. Query with published clips. Length: 1,000-3,000 words. Pays $250-500. Sometimes pays the expenses of writers on assignment.
Photos: Reviews contact sheets and 4x5 transparencies. Offers $25-100/photo. Captions, model releases, and identification of subjects required. Buys one-time rights.
Tips: "Features are most open to freelancers. Think like a small-businessowner. How can you help them solve day-to-day problems? Come with good, timely topics, make sure they apply to retail floristry, and write a to-the-point query letter, describing the problem and how you'll approach it in an article."

GARDEN SUPPLY RETAILER, Miller Publishing, Box 2400, Minnetonka MN 55343. (612)931-0211. Editor: Kay Melchisedech Olson. 5% freelance written. Prefers to work with published/established writers but "quality work is more important than experience of the writer." Monthly magazine for lawn and garden retailers. Circ. 40,000. Pays on acceptance in most cases. Publishes ms an average of 3-4 months after acceptance. Buys first serial rights, and occasionally second serial (reprint) rights. Previously published submissions "in different fields" OK as long as not in overlapping fields such as hardware, nursery growers, etc. Computer printout submissions acceptable; prefers letter-quality. Reports in 2 weeks on rejections, acceptance may take longer. Sample copy $2.
Nonfiction: "We aim to provide retailers with management, merchandising, tax planning and computer information. No technical advice on how to care for lawns, plants and lawn mowers. Articles should be of interest to *retailers* of garden supply products. Stories should tell retailers something about the industry that they don't already know; show them how to make more money by better merchandising or management techniques; address a concern or problem directly affecting retailers or the industry." Buys 10-15 mss/year. Send complete ms or rough draft plus clips of previously published work. Length: 800-1,000 words. Pays $150-200.
Photos: Send photos with ms. Reviews color negatives and transparencies, and 5x7 b&w prints. Captions and identification of subjects required.
Tips: "We will not consider manuscripts offered to 'overlapping' publications such as the hardware industry, nursery growers, etc. Query letters outlining an idea should include at least a partial rough draft; lists of titles are uninteresting. We want business-oriented articles specifically relevant to interests and concerns of retailers of lawn and garden products. We seldom use filler material and would find it a nuisance to deal with freelancers for this. Freelancers submitting articles to our publication will find it increasingly difficult to get acceptance as we will be soliciting stories from industry experts and will not have much budget for general freelance material."

INTERIOR LANDSCAPE INDUSTRY, The Magazine for Designing Minds and Growing Businesses, American Nurseryman Publishing Co., Suite 545, 111 N. Canal St., Chicago IL 60606. (312)782-5505. Editor: Brent C. Marchant. 10% freelance written. Prefers to work with published/established writers. "Willing to work with freelancers as long as they can fulfill the specifics of our requirements." Monthly magazine on business and technical topics for all parties involved in interior plantings, including interior landscapers, growers and allied professionals (landscape architects, architects and interior designers). "We take a professional approach to the material and encourage our writers to emphasize the professionalism of the industry in their writings." Circ. 4,000. Pays on publication. Publishes ms an average of 5 months after acceptance. Byline given. Buys all rights. Submit material 2 months in advance. Query for electronic submissions. Computer printout submissions acceptable; prefers letter-quality. Reports in 3 weeks on queries; 2 weeks on mss. Sample copies available free, no SASE required.
Nonfiction: How-to (technical and business topics related to the audience); interview/profile (companies working in the industry); personal experience (preferably from those who work or have worked in the industry); photo feature (related to interior projects or plant producers); and technical. No shallow,

consumerish-type features. Buys 30 mss/year. Query with published clips. Length: 3-15 ms pages double spaced. Pays $2/published inch. Sometimes pays expenses of writers on assignment.

Photos: Send photos with query. Reviews b&w contact sheet, negatives, and 5x7 prints; standard size or 4x5 color transparencies. Pays $5-10 for b&w; $15 for color. Identification of subjects required. Buys all rights.

Tips: "Demonstrate knowledge of the field—not just interest in it. Features, especially profiles, are most open to freelancers. We are currently increasing coverage of the design professions, specifically as they relate to interior landscaping."

Government and Public Service

Listed here are journals for people who provide governmental services at the local, state or federal level or for those who work in franchised utilities. Journals for city managers, politicians, bureaucratic decision makers, civil servants, firefighters, police officers, public administrators, urban transit managers and utilities managers are listed in this section. Those for private citizens interested in government and public affairs are classified in the Consumer Politics and World Affairs category.

AMERICAN FIRE JOURNAL, The Western Source for the Progressive Fire and Rescue Service, Fire Publications, Inc., Suite 7, 9072 E. Artesia Blvd., Bellflower CA 90706. (213)866-1664. Editor: Carol Carlsen Brooks. 75% freelance written. Works with a small number of new/unpublished writers each year. A monthly magazine covering the fire service. "Our readers are fire service professionals, generally at the management level. We try to pay respect to the long and rich traditions of America's firefighters while advocating that they keep up with the latest technology in the field." Pays on publication. Publishes ms an average of 2-9 months after acceptance. Byline given. Offers 50% kill fee, but rarely makes assignments. Buys first rights. Submit seasonal/holiday material 3 months in advance. Computer printout submissions acceptable; prefers letter-quality. Reports in 1 month. Sample copy $2; writer's guidelines for SASE.

Nonfiction: How-to (on firefighting techniques); interview/profile (of various fire departments around the country); opinion (guest editorials—non-paid); photo feature (of fire scenes); and technical (on fire science). Buys 84 mss/year. Send complete ms. Length ranges from news shorts to 5-part series. Pays $1.50/published inch. Pays premiums other than cash to fire department members or training officers writing on company time about in-house programs.

Photos: Send photos with submission. Reviews contact sheets, negatives and prints (b&w prints preferred except for cover photos, which are color). Offers $4-30/photo. Captions and identification of subjects required. Buys one-time rights, then photos may be used again from morgue, though photographer may also re-sell.

Columns/Departments: Hot Flashes (news from the fire service), 100-300 words; and Innovations (new ideas in tactics, equipment uses or tricks-of-the-trade), 400-800 words (with photos). Buys 48 mss/year. Send complete ms. Pays $1.50/inch.

Fillers: Anecdotes, facts and cartoons. Buys 12/year. Length: open. Pays $1.50/inch.

Tips: "Generally, our contributors are members of or involved with the fire service in some way. Our readers are mostly command-level officers, and they are very knowledgeable about the subject, so writers need to be experts in their fields in order to show them something new. We're always looking for good fireground action photos with accompanying description of the fire dept. tactics used. Non-firefighters may break in with articles on management, health and fitness, stress reduction, finance, etc., if they can be related to firefighters."

‡THE CALIFORNIA FIREMAN, The Official Publication of the California State Firemen's Association, Suite 1, 2701 K St., Sacramento CA 95816. Editor: Gary Giacomo. 80% freelance written. Monthly fireservice trade journal. Circ. 30,000. Pays on publication. Publishes ms an average of 2 months after acceptance. Byline given. Buys first North American serial rights. Submit seasonal/holiday material 4 months in advance. Simultaneous submissions OK. Computer printout submissions OK; prefers letter-quality. Reports in 1 month. Sample copy for $1.50; writer's guidelines for #10 SAE with 1 first class stamp.

Nonfiction: Expose (circumvention of fire regulations), historical/nostalgic (California slant), how-to (fight specific types of fires), interview/profile (innovative chiefs and/or departments and their programs), new product (fire suppression/fire prevention), opinion (current issues related to the fire service), personal experience (fire or rescue related), photo features (large or dramatic fires in California), technical (fire suppression/fire prevention). Special issue includes: January 1989: firefighter's wages and hours survey. For this issue we will be looking for submissions dealing with wages and benefits of firefighters and privatization. "The CSFA does sponsor a legislative program in Sacramento. All political items are staff written or assigned to experts; therefore, we do not want any political submissions." Buys 24 mss/year. Query with or without published clips, or send complete ms. Length: 400-1,200 words. Pays $55-100 for assigned articles; $35-55 for unsolicited articles. Pays in contributor's copies for opinion pieces and book reviews.

Photos: State availability of photos with submission or send photos with submission. Reviews contact sheets, trasparencies and 5x7 prints. Captions and identification of subjects required. Buys one-time rights. Pays $10-15.

Columns/Departments: Opinion (essay related to an issue facing the modern fire service. Some examples: AIDS and emergency medical services; hazardous materials cleanup and cancer) 400-700 words. Buys 9 mss/year. Send complete ms. Pays in contributor's copies.

Fillers: Anecdotes, facts, newsbreaks. Buys 60 fillers/year. Length: 30-180. Pays $2.

Tips: "Send for writer's guidelines, an editorial calendar and sample issue. Study our editorial calendar and submit appropriate articles as early as possible. We are always interested in articles that are accompanied by compelling fire or firefighting photographs. Articles submittted with quality photographs, graphs or other illustrations will receive special consideration. Fire Breaks is a good area to break in. In Fire Breaks we are looking for fire related newsbreaks, facts and anecdotes from around the U.S. and the world. Bear in mind that we only pay for the first submission, since many Fire Breaks submissions are duplicates. Also, if you're a good photojournalist and you submit photographs with complete information there is a good chance you can develop into a regular contributor. Remember that we have members from all over California—and from urban as well as forestry and rural departments."

CHIEF OF POLICE MAGAZINE, National Association of Chiefs of Police, 1100 NE 125th St., Miami FL 33161. (305)891-9800. Editor: Gerald S. Arenberg. A bimonthly trade journal for law enforcement commanders (command ranks). Circ. 10,000. Pays on acceptance. Publishes an average of 4-6 months after acceptance. Byline given. Full payment kill fee offered. Buys first rights. Submit seasonal/holiday material 6 months in advance. Simultaneous, photocopied and previously published submissions OK. Computer printout submissions OK. Reports in 2 weeks. Sample copy $3, 8½x11 SAE and 5 first class stamps; writer's guidelines for #10 SAE with 1 first class stamp.

Nonfiction: General interest, historical/nostalgic, how-to, humor, inspirational, interview/profile, new product, personal experience, photo feature, religious and technical. "We want stories about interesting police cases and stories on any law enforcement subject or program that is positive in nature. No expose types. Nothing anti-police." Buys 50 mss/year. Send complete ms. Length: 600-2,000 words. Pays $25-75 for assigned articles; pays $10-50 for unsolicited articles. Sometimes (when pre-requested) pays the expenses of writers on assignment.

Photos: Send photos with submission. Reviews 5x6 prints. Offers $5-75 per photo. Captions required. Buys one-time rights.

Columns/Departments: New Police (police equipment shown and tests), 200-600 words. Buys 6 mss/year. Send complete ms. Pays $5-12.

Fillers: Anecdote and short humor. Buys 100/year. Length: 100-1,600 words. Pays $5-15.

Tips: "Writers need only contact law enforcement officers right in their own areas and we would be delighted. We want to recognize good commanding officers from sergeant and above who are involved with the community. Pictures of the subject or the department are essential and can be snapshots. We are looking for interviews with police chiefs and sheriffs on command level with photos."

FIREHOUSE MAGAZINE, Firehouse Communications, Inc., 33 Irving Pl., New York NY 10003. (212)475-5400. Editor: Dennis Smith. Executive Editor: Janet Kimmerly. 85% freelance written. Works with a small number of new/unpublished writers each year. Monthly magazine covering fire service. "*Firehouse* covers major fires nationwide, controversial issues, and trends in the fire service, the latest firefighting equipment and methods of firefighting, historical fires, firefighting history and memorabilia. Fire-related books, firefighters with interesting avocations, fire safety education, hazardous materials incidents and the emergency medical services are also covered." Circ. 115,000. Pays on publication. Publishes ms an average of 2 months after acceptance. Byline given. Buys first North American serial rights. Submit seasonal/holiday material 4 months in advance. Exclusive submissions only. Computer printout submissions acceptable; prefers letter-quality to dotmatrix. Reports ASAP. Sample copy for 8½x11 SAE with 7 first class stamps; free writer's guidelines.

Nonfiction: Book excerpts (of recent books on fire, EMS, and hazardous materials); historical/nostalgic (great fires in history, fire collectibles; the fire service of yesteryear); how-to (fight certain kinds of fires, buy and maintain equipment, run a fire department); interview/profile (of noteworthy fire leader; centers, commissioners); new product (for firefighting, EMS); personal experience (description of dramatic rescue; helping one's own fire department); photo feature (on unusual apparatus, fire collectibles, a spectacular fire); technical (on almost any phase of firefighting; techniques, equipment, training, administration); and trends (controversies in the fire service). No profiles of people or departments that are not unusual or innovative, reports of non-major fires, articles not slanted toward firefighters' interests. Buys 100 mss/year. Query with or without published clips, or send complete ms. Length: 500-3,000 words. Pays $50-400 for assigned articles; pays $50-

300 for unsolicited articles. Sometimes pays the expenses of writers on assignment.

Photos: Mike Delia, photo editor. Send photos with query or ms. Pays $15-45 for 8x10 b&w prints; $30-200 for color transparencies and 8x10 color prints. Captions and identification of subjects required. Buys one-time rights.

Columns/Departments: Command Post (for fire service leaders); Training (effective methods); Book Reviews; Fire Safety (how departments teach fire safety to the public); Communicating (PR, dispatching); Arson (efforts to combat it); Doing Things (profile of a firefighter with an interesting avocation; group projects by firefighters). Buys 50 mss/year. Query or send complete ms. Length: 750-1,000 words. Pays $100-300.

Fillers: Gags to be illustrated by cartoonist, anecdotes, short humor and newsbreaks. Buys 20/year. Length: 50-100 words. Pays $5-15.

Tips: "Read the magazine to get a full understanding of the subject matter, the writing style and the readers before sending a query or manuscript. Send photos with manuscript or indicate sources for photos. Be sure to focus articles on firefighters."

‡**FOREIGN SERVICE JOURNAL**, 2101 E St. NW, Washington DC 20037. (202)338-4045. Editor: Stephen R. Dujack. 80% freelance written. "No preference for published vs. unpublished writers as long as the writer has some expertise." For Foreign Service personnel and others interested in foreign affairs and related subjects. Monthly (July/August combined). Pays on publication. Publishes ms an average of 3 months after acceptance. Byline given. Buys first North American serial rights. Query for electronic submissions. Computer printout submissions acceptable; prefers letter-quality.

Nonfiction: Uses articles on "international relations, internal problems of the State Department and Foreign Service, diplomatic history and articles on Foreign Service experiences. Much of our material is contributed by those working in the fields we reach. Informed outside contributions are welcomed, however." Query. Buys 5-10 unsolicited mss/year. Length: 1,000-4,000 words. Pays 2-6¢/word.

Tips: "The most frequent mistakes made by writers in completing an article for us are that the items are not suitable for the magazine, and they don't query."

FOUNDATION NEWS, The Magazine of Philanthropy, Council on Foundations, 1828 L St. NW, Washington DC 20036. (202)466-6512. Editor: Arlie Schardt. Managing Editor: Susan Calhoun. 70% freelance written. Prefers to work with published/established writers. Bimonthly magazine covering the world of philanthropy, nonprofit organizations and their relation to current events. Read by staff and executives of foundations, corporations, hospitals, colleges and universities and various nonprofit organizations. Circ. 22,000. Pays on acceptance. Publishes ms an average of 3 months after acceptance. Byline given. Offers negotiable kill fee. Not copyrighted. Buys all rights. Submit seasonal/holiday material 5 months in advance. Simultaneous queries and previously published submissions OK. Computer printout submissions acceptable; prefers letter-quality. Reports in 6 weeks.

Nonfiction: Book excerpts, expose, general interest, historical/nostalgic, how-to, humor, interview/profile and photo feature. Special issue on the role of religion in American life and how religious giving affects social welfare, culture, health conditions, etc. Buys 25 mss/year. Submit written query; not telephone calls. Length: 500-3,000 words. Pays $200-2,000. Pays expenses of writers on assignment.

Photos: State availability of photos. Pays negotiable rates for b&w contact sheet and prints. Captions and identification of subjects required. Buys one-time rights; "some rare requests for second use."

Columns/Departments: Buys 12 mss/year. Query. Length: 900-1,400 words. Pays $100-750.

Tips: "We have a great interest in working with writers familiar with the nonprofit sector."

GRASSROOTS FUNDRAISING JOURNAL, Klein & Honig, Partnership, #206, 517 Union Ave., Knoxville TN 37902. Editors: Kim Klein and Lisa Honig. A bimonthly newsletter covering grassroots fund raising for small social change and social service nonprofit organizations. Circ. 3,000. Pays on publication. Byline given. Buys first serial rights. Submit seasonal/holiday material 2 months in advance. Simultaneous queries, and simultaneous, photocopied, and (occasionally) previously published submissions OK. Reports in 2 weeks on queries; 2 months on mss. Sample copy $3.

Nonfiction: Book excerpts; how-to (all fund raising strategies); and personal experience (doing fund raising). Buys 10 mss/year. Query. Length: 2,000-20,000 words. Pays $35 minimum.

LAW AND ORDER, Hendon Co., 1000 Skokie Blvd., Wilmette IL 60091. (312)256-8555. Editor: Bruce W. Cameron. 90% freelance written. Prefers to work with published/established writers. Monthly magazine covering the administration and operation of law enforcement agencies, directed to police chiefs and supervisors. Circ. 26,000. Pays on publication. Publishes ms an average of 6 months after acceptance. Byline given. Buys first North American serial rights. Submit seasonal/holiday material 3 months in advance. No simultaneous queries. Query for electronic submissions. Computer printout submissions acceptable; no dot-matrix. Reports in 1 month. Sample copy for 9x12 SAE.

Nonfiction: General police interest; how-to (do specific police assignments); new product (how applied in police operation); and technical (specific police operation). Special issues include Buyers Guide (January); Communications (February); Training (March); International (April); Administration (May); Small Departments (June); Police Science (July); Equipment (August); Weapons (September); Mobile Patrol (November); and Community Relations (December). No articles dealing with courts (legal field) or convicted prisoners. No nostalgic, financial, travel or recreational material. Buys 100 mss/year. Length: 2,000-3,000 words. Pays 10¢/word.

Photos: Send photos with ms. Reviews transparencies and prints. Identification of subjects required. Buys all rights.

Tips: *"L&O* is a respected magazine that provides up-to-date information that chiefs can use. Writers must know their subject as it applies to this field. Case histories are well received. We are upgrading quality for editorial—stories *must* show some understanding of the law enforcement field. A frequent mistake is not getting photographs to accompany article."

PLANNING, American Planning Association, 1313 E. 60th St., Chicago IL 60637. (312)955-9100. Editor: Sylvia Lewis. 25% freelance written. Emphasizes urban planning for adult, college-educated readers who are regional and urban planners in city, state or federal agencies or in private business or university faculty or students. Monthly. Circ. 25,000. Pays on publication. Publishes ms an average of 3 months after acceptance. Buys all rights or first rights. Byline given. Photocopied and previously published submissions OK. Computer printout submissions acceptable; prefers letter-quality. Reports in 2 months. Sample copy and writer's guidelines for 9x12 SAE.

Nonfiction: Expose (on government or business, but on topics related to planning, housing, land use, zoning); general interest (trend stories on cities, land use, government); historical (historic preservation); how-to (successful government or citizen efforts in planning; innovations; concepts that have been applied); and technical (detailed articles on the nitty-gritty of planning, zoning, transportation but no footnotes or mathematical models). Also needs news stories up to 500 words. "It's best to query with a fairly detailed, one-page letter. We'll consider any article that's well written and relevant to our audience. Articles have a better chance if they are timely and related to planning and land use and if they appeal to a national audience. All articles should be written in magazine feature style." Buys 2 features and 1 news story/issue. Length: 500-2,000 words. Pays $50-600. "We pay freelance writers and photographers only, not planners."

Photos: "We prefer that authors supply their own photos, but we sometimes take our own or arrange for them in other ways." State availability of photos. Pays $25 minimum for 8x10 matte or glossy prints and $200 for 4-color cover photos. Caption material required. Buys one-time rights.

POLICE, Hare Publications, 6200 Yarrow Dr., Carlsbad CA 92008. (619)438-2511. Editor: Heather A. Hurst. 90% freelance written. A monthly magazine covering topics related to law enforcement officials. "Our audience is strictly law enforcement personnel such as patrol officers, detectives and security police." Circ. 45,000. Pays on acceptance. Publishes ms an average of 6 months after acceptance. Buys all rights (returned to author 45 days after publication). Submit theme material 3 months in advance. Computer printout submissions acceptable. Reports in 2 months. Sample copy $2; writer's guidelines for #10 SAE with 2 first class stamps.

Nonfiction: General interest, expose, humor, inspirational, interview/profile, new product, opinion, personal experience and technical. Buys 60 mss/year. Query or send complete ms. Length: 2,000-4,000 words. Pays $200-250 for unsolicited articles.

Photos: Send photos with submission. Captions required. Buys all rights.

Columns/Departments: The Beat (entertainment section—humor, fiction, first-person drama, professional tips) 1,000 words; pays $75; The Arsenal (weapons, ammunition and equipment used in the line of duty); and Officer Survival (theories, skills and techniques used by offices for street survival). Buys 75 mss/year. Query or send complete ms. Length: 1,500-2,500 words. Pays $75-250

Tips: "You are writing for police officers—people who live a dangerous and stressful life. Study the editorial calendar—yours for the asking—and come up with an idea that fits into a specific issue. We are actively seeking talented writers."

‡POLICE AND SECURITY NEWS, Days Communications, Inc.. 15 Thatcher Rd., Quakertown PA 18951. (215)538-1240. Editor: James Devery. 40% freelance written. A bimonthly tabloid on public law enforcement and private security. "Our publication is designed to provide educational and entertaining information directed toward management level. Technical information written for the expert in a manner that the non-expert can understand." Circ. 23,590. Pays on publication. Publishes ms an average of 2 months after acceptance. Byline given. Buys first North American serial rights. Submit seasonal/holiday material 2 months in advance. Simultaneous, photocopied and previously published submissions OK. Computer printout submissions OK. Free sample copy and writer's guidelines.

Nonfiction: Al Menear, articles editor. Exposé, historical/nostalgic, how-to, humor, interview/profile, opinion, personal experience, photo feature and technical. Buys 12 mss/year. Query. Length: 200-8,000 words. Pays $50-200. Sometimes pays in trade-out of services.

Photos: State availability of photos with submission. Reviews prints (3x5). Offers $10-100 per photo. Buys one-time rights.

Fillers: Anecdotes, facts, gags to be illustrated by cartoonist, newsbreaks and short humor. Buys 6/year. Length: 200-2,000 words. Pays $50-150.

POLICE TIMES, American Police Academy, 1100 NE 125th St., North Miami FL 33161. (305)891-1700. Editor: Gerald Arenberg. Managing Editor: Donna Shepherd. 80% freelance written. Eager to work with new/unpublished writers. A bi-monthly tabloid covering "law enforcement (general topics) for men and women engaged in law enforcement and private security, and citizens who are law and order concerned." Circ. 55,000. Pays on acceptance. Publishes ms an average of 3-6 months after acceptance. Byline given. Offers 50% kill fee. Buys second serial (reprint) rights. Submit seasonal/holiday material 4 months in advance. Simultaneous, photocopied and previously published submissions OK. Computer printout submissions acceptable; prefers letter-quality. Sample copy for 9x12 SAE with 3 first class stamps; writer's guidelines for SAE with 1 first class stamp.

Nonfiction: Book excerpts; essays (on police science); exposé (police corruption); general interest; historical/nostalgic; how-to; humor; interview/profile; new product; personal experience (with police); photo feature; and technical—all police-related. "We produce a special edition on police killed in the line of duty. It is mailed May 15 so copy must arrive six months in advance. Photos required." No anti-police materials. Buys 50 mss/year. Send complete ms. Length: 200-3,000 words. Pays $5-50 for assigned articles; pays $5-25 for unsolicited articles. Sometimes pays the expenses of writers on assignment.

Photos: Send photos with submission. Reviews 5x6 prints. Offers $5-25/photo. Identification of subjects required. Buys all rights.

Columns/Departments: Legal Cases (lawsuits involving police actions); New Products (new items related to police services); and Awards (police heroism acts). Buys variable number of mss/year. Send complete ms. Length: 200-1,000 words. Pays $5-25.

Fillers: Anecdotes, facts, newsbreaks and short humor. Buys 100/year. Length: 50-100 words. Pays $5-10. Fillers are usually humorous stories about police officer and citizen situations. Special stories on police cases, public corruptions, etc. are most open to freelancers.

SUPERINTENDENT'S PROFILE & POCKET EQUIPMENT DIRECTORY, Profile Publications, 220 Central Ave., Box 43, Dunkirk NY 14048. (716)366-4774. Editor: Robert Dyment. 60% freelance written. Prefers to work with published/established writers. Monthly magazine covering "outstanding" town, village, county and city highway superintendents and Department of Public Works Directors throughout New York state only. Circ. 2,500. Publishes ms an average of 4 months after acceptance. Pays within 90 days. Byline given for excellent material. Buys first serial rights. Submit seasonal/holiday material 3 months in advance. Simultaneous queries OK. Computer printout submissions acceptable; no dot-matrix. Reports in 2 weeks on queries; 1 month on mss. Sample copy for 9x12 SAE and 4 first class stamps.

Nonfiction: John Powers, articles editor. Interview/profile (of a highway superintendent or DPW director in NY state who has improved department operations through unique methods or equipment); and technical. Special issues include winter maintenance profiles. No fiction. Buys 20 mss/year. Query. Length: 1,500-2,000 words. Pays $125 for a full-length ms. "Pays more for excellent material. All manuscripts will be edited to fit our format and space limitations." Sometimes pays the expenses of writers on assignment.

Photos: John Powers, photo editor. State availability of photos. Pays $5-10 for b&w contact sheets; reviews 5x7 prints. Captions and identification of subjects required. Buys one-time rights.

Poetry: Buys poetry if it pertains to highway departments. Pays $5-15.

Tips: "We are a widely read and highly respected state-wide magazine, and although we can't pay high rates, we expect quality work. Too many freelance writers are going for the expose rather than the meat and potato type articles that will help readers. We use more major features than fillers. Frequently writers don't read sample copies first. We will be purchasing more material because our page numbers are increasing."

TRANSACTION/SOCIETY, Rutgers University, New Brunswick NJ 08903. (201)932-2280, ext. 83. Editor: Irving Louis Horowitz. 10% freelance written. Prefers to work with published/established writers. For social scientists (policymakers with training in sociology, political issues and economics). Published every 2 months. Circ. 45,000. Buys all rights. Byline given. Pays on publication. Publishes ms an average of 6 months after acceptance. Will consider photocopied submissions. No simultaneous submissions. Query for electronic submissions; "manual provided to authors." Computer printout submissions acceptable; prefers letter-quality. Reports in 1 month. Query. Sample copy and writer's guidelines for 9x12 SAE and 5 first class stamps.

Nonfiction: Michele Teitelbaum, managing editor. "Articles of wide interest in areas of specific interest to the social science community. Must have an awareness of problems and issues in education, population and urbanization that are not widely reported. Articles on overpopulation, terrorism, international organizations. No general think pieces." Payment for articles is made only if done on assignment. *No payment for unsolicited articles*.

Photos: Douglas Harper, photo editor. Pays $200 for photographic essays done on assignment or accepted for publication.

Tips: "Submit an article on a thoroughly unique subject, written with good literary quality. Present new ideas and research findings in a readable and useful manner. A frequent mistake is writing to satisfy a journal, rather than the intrinsic requirements of the story itself. Avoid posturing and editorializing."

VICTIMOLOGY: An International Journal, 2333 N. Vernon St., Arlington VA 22207. (703)536-1750. Editor-in-Chief: Emilio C. Viano. "We are the only magazine specifically focusing on the victim, on the dynamics of victimization; for social scientists, criminal justice professionals and practitioners, social workers and volunteer and professional groups engaged in prevention of victimization and in offering assistance to victims of rape, spouse abuse, child abuse, incest, abuse of the elderly, natural disasters, etc." Quarterly magazine. Circ. 2,500. Pays on publication. Buys all rights. Byline given. Reports in 2 months. Sample copy $5; free writer's guidelines.

Nonfiction: Expose, historical, how-to, informational, interview, personal experience, profile, research and technical. Buys 10 mss/issue. Query. Length: 500-5,000 words. Pays $50-150.

Photos: Purchased with accompanying ms. Captions required. Send contact sheet. Pays $15-50 for 5x7 or 8x10 b&w glossy prints.

Poetry: Avant-garde, free verse, light verse and traditional. Length: 30 lines maximum. Pays $10-25.

Tips: "Focus on what is being researched and discovered on the victim, the victim/offender relationship, treatment of the offender, the bystander/witness, preventive measures, and what is being done in the areas of service to the victims of rape, spouse abuse, neglect and occupational and environmental hazards and the elderly."

YOUR VIRGINIA STATE TROOPER MAGAZINE, Box 2189, Springfield VA 22152. (703)451-2524. Editor: Kerian Bunch. 90% freelance written. Biannual magazine covering police topics for troopers, police, libraries, legislators and businesses. Circ. 10,000. Pays on acceptance. Publishes ms an average of 3 months after acceptance. Byline given. Buys first North American serial rights and all rights on assignments. Submit seasonal/holiday material 2 months in advance. Simultaneous and photocopied submissions OK. Computer printout submissions acceptable; prefers letter-quality. Reports in 2 months.

Nonfiction: Book excerpts; expose (consumer or police-related); general interest; nutrition/health; historical/ nostalgic; how-to (energy saving); humor; interview/profile (notable police figures); opinion; personal experience; technical (radar); and other (recreation). Buys 40-45 mss/year. Query with clips or send complete ms. Length: 2,500 words. Pays $250 maximum/article (10¢/word). Sometimes pays expenses of writers on assignment.

Photos: Send photos with ms. Pays $25 maximum/5x7 b&w glossy print. Captions and model release required. Buys one-time rights.

Fiction: Adventure, humorous, mystery, novel excerpts and suspense. Buys 4 mss/year. Send complete ms. Length: 2,500 words minimum. Pays $250 maximum (10¢/word) on acceptance.

Tips: "The writer may have a better chance of breaking in at our publication with short articles and fillers due to space limitations."

THE WASHINGTON TROOPER, Grimm Press and Publishing Co., Inc. Communications Dateline, Box 1523, Longview WA 98632. (206)577-8598. Editor: Ron Collins. Managing Editor: Bruce D. Grimm. Send queries only to editor, *The Washington Trooper*, Box 916, Kelso WA 98626. 10% freelance written. Works with a small number of new/unpublished writers each year. A quarterly law enforcement magazine covering legislation, traffic and highway safety "for members of the Washington State Patrol Troopers Association, state legislators, educators, court officials, and civic minded individuals in the State of Washington." Circ. 3,500. Pays on publication. Publishes ms an average of 3 months after acceptance. Byline given. Buys all rights. Submit seasonal/holiday material 6 months in advance. Simultaneous queries and submissions OK. Computer printout submissions OK; prefers letter-quality. Reports in 2 months on queries; 3 months on mss. Sample copy $3.50.

Nonfiction: Marjorie F. Grimm, articles editor. Exposé (on state of Washington government or traffic); interview/profile (Washington state troopers); new products; opinion (on law enforcement or traffic and highway safety); and technical (police equipment). Buys 12-20 mss/year. Query or send complete ms. Length: 500-3,500 words. Pays $5-75.

Photos: State availability of photos with query letter or manuscript. Reviews contact sheets and transparencies. Pays $5-25. Model releases, and identification of subjects required.

Fillers: Short humor and newsbreaks. Buys 15/year. Length: 50-250 words. Pays $5-15.

Tips: "Writers must be familiar with goals and objectives of the Washington State Patrol and with law enforcement in general in the Pacific Northwest. The areas of our publication that are most open to freelancers are feature articles depicting life in the State of Washington familiar to a Washington state trooper. We will be buying few articles in 1989, buy still open to good queries."

ALWAYS submit manuscripts or queries with a self-addressed, stamped envelope (SASE) within your country or International Reply Coupons (IRC) purchased from the post office for other countries.

Groceries and Food Products

In this section are publications for grocers, food wholesalers, processors, warehouse owners, caterers, institutional managers and suppliers of grocery store equipment. See the section on Confectionery and Snack Foods for bakery and candy industry magazines.

AMERICAN AUTOMATIC MERCHANDISER, Edgell Communications, Cleveland OH 44130. (216)243-8100. Editor: David R. Stone. Managing Editor: Mark L. Dlugoss. 5% freelance written. Prefers to work with published/established writers. A monthly trade journal covering vending machines, contract foodservice and office coffee services. "*AAM*'s readers are owners and managers of these companies; we profile successful companies and report on market trends." Circ. 12,500. Pays on acceptance. Publishes ms an average of 3 months after acceptance. Byline sometimes given. Buys first North American serial rights, all rights or makes work-for-hire assignments. Submit seasonal/holiday material 4 months in advance. Photocopied submissions OK. Computer printout submissions OK; prefers letter-quality. Reports in 1 month. Free sample copy.
Nonfiction: Buys 30 mss/year. Query. Length: 1,000-6,000 words. Pays $150-600. Sometimes pays the expenses of writers on assignment.
Photos: Send photos with submission. Reviews contact sheets, transparencies and prints. Offers $50 maximum per photo. Buys all rights.

CANADIAN GROCER, Maclean-Hunter Ltd., Maclean Hunter Building, 777 Bay St., Toronto, Ontario M5W 1A7 Canada. (416)596-5772. Editor: George H. Condon. 10% freelance written. Prefers to work with published/established writers. Monthly magazine about supermarketing and food retailing for Canadian chain and independent food store managers, owners, buyers, executives, food brokers, food processors and manufacturers. Circ 18,000. Pays on publication. Publishes ms an average of 2 months after acceptance. Byline given. Buys first Canadian rights. Phone queries OK. Submit seasonal material 2 months in advance. Previously published submissions OK. Computer printout submissions acceptable; prefers letter-quality. Reports in 1 month. Sample copy $4.
Nonfiction: Interview (Canadian trendsetters in marketing, finance or food distribution); technical (store operations, equipment and finance); and news features on supermarkets. "Freelancers should be well versed on the supermarket industry. We don't want unsolicited material. Writers with business and/or finance expertise are preferred. Know the retail food industry and be able to write concisely and accurately on subjects relevant to our readers: food store managers, senior corporate executives, etc. A good example of an article would be 'How a Six Store Chain of Supermarkets Improved Profits 2% and Kept Customers Coming.' " Buys 14 mss/year. Query with clips of previously published work. Pays 21¢/word. Sometimes pays the expenses of writers on assignment.
Photos: State availability of photos. Pays $10-25 for 8x10 b&w glossy prints. Captions preferred. Buys one-time rights.
Tips: "Suitable writers will be familiar with sales per square foot, merchandising mixes and direct product profitability."

‡CANDY WHOLESALER, National Candy Wholesalers Association. Suite 1120, 1120 Vermont Ave., N.W., Washington DC 20005. (202)463-2124. Publisher/Editor: Shelley Grossman. Associate Editor: Kevin Settlage. 35% freelance written. A monthly magazine for distributors of candy/tobacco/snacks/groceries and other convenience-store type items. "*Candy Wholesaler* magazine is published to assist the candy/tobacco/snack food distributor in improving his business by providing a variety of relevant operational information. Serves as the voice of the distributor in the candy/tobacco/snack industry." Circ. 10,651. Pays on acceptance. Publishes ms an average of 4 months after acceptance. Byline given. Offers $50 kill fee. Buys all rights. Submit seasonal/holiday material 6 months in advance. Photocopied submissions OK. Query for electronic submissions. Computer printout submissions OK. Reports in 1 month. Sample copy for 8½x11 SAE with 6 first class stamps.
Nonfiction: Historical/nostalgic, how-to (related to distribution), interview/profile, photo feature, technical (data processing) and (profiles of distribution films/or manufacturers). "No simplistic pieces with consumer focus that are financial, tax-related or legal." Buys 30-35 mss/year. Query with or without published clips, or send complete ms. Length: 8-12 double-spaced typewritten pages. Pays $350-600 for assigned articles. Pays $200-400 for unsolicited articles. Sometimes pays copies to industry members who author articles. Pays the expenses of writers on assignment.

Photos: Send photos with submission. Reviews contact sheets, transparencies and prints. Offers $5-10 per photo. Captions and identification of subjects required. Buys all rights.

Fillers: Kevin Settlage, fillers editor. Anecdotes, facts and short humor. Length: 50-200 words. Pays $10-20.

Tips: "Talk to wholesalers about their business—how it works, what their problems are, etc. We need writers who understand this industry. Company profile feature stories are open to freelancers. Get into the nitty gritty of operations and management. Talk to several key people in the company."

FANCY FOOD, The Business Magazine for Specialty Foods, Confections & Wine, Talcott Publishing, Inc., 1414 Merchandise Mart, Chicago IL 60654. (312)670-0800. Editor: Pam Erickson. 35-40% freelance written. Works with a small number of new/unpublished writers each year. A trade magazine covering specialty food and confections. Published 12 times a year. Circ. 27,000. Pays on publication. Publishes an average of 3 months after acceptance. Byline sometimes given. Buys all rights. Submit seasonal/holiday material 3 months in advance. Computer printout submissions acceptable; prefers letter-quality. Sample copy $4.

Nonfiction: Interview/profile and new product. Buys 30 mss/year. Query with published clips. Length: 1,500-4,000 words. Pays $100-250 for assigned articles. Expenses must be approved and estimated in advance.

Photos: Send photos with submission. Reviews transparencies and prints. Offers no additional payment other than for film and development for photos accepted with ms. Captions and identification of subjects required. Buys all rights.

Columns/Departments: Points East & West, Wine & Spirits Review, Coffee, Industry News and Buyer's Mart. Buys 20 mss/year. Query with published clips. Length: 2,000-3,000 words. Pays $100-200.

Tips: "Business reporters with knowlege of food and contacts among gourmet retailers are sought. Multi-source product category overviews are most open to freelancers. We prefer submissions from food writers with practical experience in gourmet retail or prepared food business."

FLORIDA GROCER, Florida Grocer Publications, Inc., Box 430760, South Miami FL 33243. (305)441-1138. Editor: Dennis Kane. 5% freelance written. "*Florida Grocer* is a 16,000 circulation monthly trade newspaper, serving members of the Florida food industry. Our publication is edited for chain and independent food store owners and operators as well as members of allied industries." Circ. 16,000. Pays on acceptance. Byline given. Buys all rights. Submit seasonal/holiday material 6 months in advance. Sample copy for #10 SAE with 6 first class stamps.

Nonfiction: Book excerpts, expose, general interest, humor, features on supermarkets and their owners, new product, new equipment, photo feature and video. Buys variable number of mss/year. Query with or without published clips, or send complete ms. Length: varies. Payment varies. Sometimes pays the expenses of writers on assignment.

Photos: State availability of photos with submission. Terms for payment on photos "included in terms of payment for assignment."

Tips: "We prefer feature articles on new stores (grand openings, etc.), store owners, operators; Florida based food manufacturers, brokers, whole sales, distributors, etc. We also publish a section in Spanish and also welcome the above types of materials in Spanish (Cuban)."

‡FOOD PEOPLE, Olson Publications, Inc., Box 1208, Woodstock GA 30188. (404)928-8994. Editor: Warren B. Causey. 75% freelance written. Prefers to work with published/established writers, and works with a small number of new/unpublished writers each year. Always willing to consider new writers, bu they must have a basic command of their craft. Monthly tabloid covering the retail food industry. Circ. 40,000. Pays on publication. Publishes ms an average of 1 month after acceptance. Byline given. Buys all rights. Will reassign subsidiary rights after publication and upon request. Submit seasonal/holiday material 6 weeks in advance. Photocopied submissions acceptable; prefers letter quality. Computer modem submissions encouraged. Reports in 6 weeks. Sample copy for 9x12 SAE with 5 first class stamps.

Nonfiction: Interview/profile (of major food industry figures); photo features of ad campaigns, marketing strategies, important new products and services. "We would like to receive feature articles about people and companies that illustrate trends in the food industry. Articles should be informative, tone is upbeat. Do not send recipes or how-to shop articles; we cover food as a business." Buys 250-300. Query or send complete ms. Length: 500-1,500 words. Pays $3/published inch minimum. Pays the expenses of writers on assignment.

Photos: "Photos of people. Photos of displays, or store layouts, etc. that illustrate points made in article are good, too. But stay away from storefront shots." State availability of photos with query or send photos with ms. Pays $10 plus expenses for 5x7 b&w prints; and $25 plus expenses for color transparencies. Captions required. Buys one-time rights.

Columns/Departments: Company news, People, Organizations, New Products, and Morsels . . . a Smorgasbord of Tidbits in the National Stew. Send complete ms. Pays $3/inch.

Tips: "Begin with an area news event—store openings, new promotions. Write that as news, then go further to examine the consequences. We are staffing more conventions, so writers should concentrate on features about people, companies, trends, new products, innovations in the food industry in their geographic areas and apply these to a national scope when possible. Talk with decision makers to get 'hows' and 'whys.' We now are more feature than news oriented. We look for contributors who work well, quickly and always deliver.''

HEALTH FOODS BUSINESS, Howmark Publishing Corp., 567 Morris Ave., Elizabeth NJ 07208. (201)353-7373. Editor: Mary Jane Dittmar. 40% freelance written. Eager to work with new/unpublished writers if competent and reliable. For owners and managers of health food stores. Monthly magazine. Circ. 11,000. Pays on publication. Publishes ms an average of 4 months after acceptance. Byline given "if story quality warrants it." Buys first serial rights and first North American serial rights; "also exclusive rights in our trade field." Phone queries OK. "Query us about a good health food store in your area. We use many store profile stories." Simultaneous and photocopied submissions OK if exclusive to their field. Previously published work OK, but please indicate where and when material appeared previously. Computer printout submissions acceptable if double-spaced and in upper and lower case; no dot-matrix. Reports in 1 month. Sample copy $5 plus $2 for postage and handling; writer's guidelines for #10 SASE.
Nonfiction: Expose (government hassling with health food industry); how-to (unique or successful retail operators); informational (how or why a product works; technical aspects must be clear to laymen); historical (natural food use); interview (must be prominent person in industry or closely related to the health food industry or well-known or prominent person in any arena who has undertaken a natural diet/lifestyle;); and photo feature (any unusual subject related to the retailer's interests). Buys 1-2 mss/issue. Query for interview and photo features. Will consider complete ms in other categories. Length: long enough to tell the whole story without padding. Pays $50 and up for feature stories, $75 and up for store profiles.
Photos: "Most articles must have photos included"; negatives and contact sheet OK. Captions required. No additional payment.
Tips: "A writer may find that submitting a letter with a sample article he/she believes to be closely related to articles read in our publication is the most of expedient way to determine the appropriateness of his/her skills and expertise."

‡MEAT PLANT MAGAZINE, 9701 Gravois Ave., St. Louis MO 63123. (314)638-4050. Editor: Tony Nolan. 10% freelance written. Prefers to work with published/established writers; works with a small number of new/unpublished writers each year. For meat processors, locker plant operators, freezer provisioners, portion control packers, meat dealers and food service (food plan) operators. Monthly. Pays on publication. Publishes ms an average of 6 months after acceptance. Computer printout submissions acceptable. Reports in 2 weeks.
Nonfiction and Fillers: Buys feature-length articles and shorter subjects pertinent to the field. Length: 1,000-1,500 words for features. Pays 10¢/word. Sometimes pays the expenses of writers on assignment.
Photos: Pays $5 for photos.

PRODUCE NEWS, 2185 Lemoine Ave., Fort Lee NJ 07024. Editor: Gordon Hochberg. 10-15% freelance written. Works with a small number of new/unpublished writers each year. For commercial growers and shippers, receivers and distributors of fresh fruits and vegetables, including chain store produce buyers and merchandisers. Weekly. Circ. 9,500. Pays on publication. Publishes ms an average of 2 weeks after acceptance. Deadline is Tuesday afternoon before Thursday press day. Computer printout submissions acceptable. Free sample copy and writer's guidelines.
Nonfiction: News stories (about the produce industry). Buys profiles, spot news, coverage of successful business operations and articles on merchandising techniques. Query. Pays minimum of $1/column inch for original material. Sometimes pays the expenses of writers on assignment.
Photos: B&w glossies. Pays $8-10 for each one used.
Tips: "Stories should be trade-oriented, not consumer-oriented. As our circulation grows in the next year, we are interested in stories and news articles from all fresh fruit-growing areas of the country."

QUICK FROZEN FOODS INTERNATIONAL, E.W. Williams Publishing Co., 80 8th Ave., New York NY 10011. (212)989-1101. Editor: John M. Saulnier. 20% freelance written. Works with a small number of new/unpublished writers each year. Quarterly magazine covering frozen foods around the world—"every phase of frozen food manufacture, retailing, food service, brokerage, transport, warehousing, merchandising. Especially interested in stories from Europe, Asia and emerging nations." Circ. 13,500. Pays on publication. Publishes ms an average of 3 months after acceptance. Byline given. Offers kill fee; "if satisfactory, we will pay promised amount. If bungled, half." Buys all rights, but will relinquish any rights requested. Submit seasonal/holiday material 6 months in advance. Photocopied submissions OK "if not under submission elsewhere." Computer printout submissions acceptable; prefers letter-quality. Sample copy $5.
Nonfiction: Book excerpts; general interest; historical/nostalgic; interview/profile; new product (from overseas); personal experience; photo feature; technical; and travel. No articles peripheral to frozen food industry such as taxes, insurance, government regulation, safety, etc. Buys 20-30 mss/year. Query or send complete ms. Length: 500-4,000 words. Pays 5¢/word or by arrangement. "We will reimburse postage on articles ordered from overseas." Sometimes pays the expenses of writers on assignment.

Photos: "We prefer photos with all articles." State availability of photos or send photos with accompanying ms. Pays $7 for 5x7 b&w prints (contact sheet if many shots). Captions and identification of subject required. Buys all rights. Release on request.
Columns/Departments: News or analysis of frozen foods abroad. Buys 20 columns/year. Query. Length: 500-1,500 words. Pays by arrangement.
Fillers: Newsbreaks. Length: 100-500 words. Pays $5-20.
Tips: "We are primarily interested in feature materials, (1,000-3,000 words with pictures). We plan to devote more space to frozen food company developments in Pacific Rim countries. Stories on frozen food merchandising and retailing in foreign supermarket chains in Europe, Japan and Australia/New Zealand are welcome. National frozen food prouduction profiles are also in demand worldwide. A frequent mistake is submitting general interest material instead of specific industry-related stories."

SEAFOOD LEADER, Waterfront Press Co., 1115 NW 45th St., Seattle WA 98107. (206)789-6506. Editor: Peter Redmayne. Associate Editor: Laune Underwood. 20% freelance written. Works with a small number of new/unpublished writers each year. A trade journal on the seafood business published 5 times/year. Circ. 14,000. Pays on publication. Publishes ms an average of 3 months after acceptance. Byline given. Buys first rights and second serial (reprint) rights. Submit seasonal/holiday material 3 months in advance. Simultaneous, photocopied and previously published submissions OK. Query for electronic submissions. Computer printout submissions OK. Reports in 1 month on queries; 2 months on mss. Sample copy $3 with 8½x11 SAE.
Nonfiction: General seafood interest, marketing/business, historical/nostalgic, interview/profile, opinion and photo feature. Each of *Seafood Leader's* five issues has a slant: international (spring), foodservice (summer), international aquaculture and retail merchandising (autumn), shrimp and aquaculture (winter) and the annual Seafood Buyer's Guide (February). Still, each issue includes stories outside of the particular focus, particularly shorter features and news items. No recreational fishing; no first person articles. Buys 12-15 mss/year. Query with or without published clips, or send complete ms. Length: 1,500-2,500 words. Pay rate is 15-20¢/word published depending upon amount of editing necessary. Sometimes pays the expenses of writers on assignment.
Photos: State availability of photos with submission. Reviews contact sheets and transparencies. Offers $50-100 per photo. Buys one-time rights.
Fillers: Newsbreaks. Buys 10-15/year. Length: 100-250 words. Pays $50-100.
Tips: "*Seafood Leader* is steadily increasing in size and has a growing need for full-length feature stories and special sections. Articles on innovative, unique and aggressive people or companies involved in seafood are needed. Writing should be colorful, tight and fact-filled, always emphasizing the subject's formula for increased seafood sales. Readers should feel as if they have learned something applicable to their business."

SNACK FOOD, Edgell Communicattions, Inc., 131 W. 1st St., Duluth MN 55802. (218)723-9343. Executive Editor: Jerry L. Hess. 15% freelance written. For manufacturers and distributors of snack foods. Monthly magazine. Circ. 10,000. Pays on acceptance. Publishes ms an average of 2 months after acceptance. Buys first serial rights. Occasional byline given. Phone queries OK. Photocopied submissions OK. Computer printout submissions acceptable. Reports in 2 months. Free sample copy and writer's guidelines.
Nonfiction: Informational, interview, new product, nostalgic, photo feature, profile and technical articles. "We use an occasional mini news feature or personality sketch." Length: 300-600 words for mini features; 750-1,200 words for longer features. Pays 12-15¢/word. Sometimes pays the expenses of writers on assignment.
Photos: Purchased with accompanying ms. Captions required. Pays $20 for 5x7 b&w photos. Total purchase price for ms includes payment for photos when used. Buys all rights.
Tips: "Query should contain specific lead and display more than a casual knowledge of our audience. The most frequent mistakes made by writers are not writing to our particular audience, and lack of a grasp of certain technical points on how the industry functions."

THE WISCONSIN RESTAURATEUR, Wisconsin Restaurant Association, 122 W. Washington, Madison WI 53703. (603)251-3663. Editor: Jan La Rue. 10% freelance written. Eager to work with new/unpublished writers. Emphasizes restaurant industry for restaurateurs, hospitals, institutions, food service students, etc. Monthly magazine (December/January combined). Circ. 3,600. Pays on acceptance. Publishes ms an average of 3 months after acceptance. Buys all rights or one-time rights. Pays 10% kill fee. Byline given. Phone queries OK. Submit seasonal/holiday material 2-3 months in advance. Previously published OK; "indicate where." Computer printout acceptable. Reports in 3 weeks. Sample copy and writer's guidelines with 9x12 SASE.
Nonfiction: Expose, general interest, historical, how-to, humor, inspirational, interview, nostalgia, opinion, profile, travel, new product, personal experience, photo feature and technical articles pertaining to restaurant industry. "Needs more in-depth articles. No features on nonmember restaurants." Buys 1 ms/issue. Query with "copyright clearance information and a note about the writer in general." Length: 700-1,500 words. Pays $10-20.
Photos: Fiction and how-to mss stand a better chance for publication if photos are submitted. State availability

of photos. Pays $15 for b&w 8x10 glossy prints. Model release required.

Columns/Departments: Spotlight column provides restaurant member profiles. Buys 6/year. Query. Length: 500-1,500 words. Pays $5-10.

Fiction: Experimental, historical and humorous stories related to food service only. Buys 12 mss/year. Query. Length: 1,000-3,000 words. Pays $10-20.

Poetry: Uses all types of poetry, but must have food service as subject. Buys 6-12/year. Submit maximum 5 poems. Length: 10-50 lines. Pays $5-10.

Fillers: Clippings, jokes, gags, anecdotes, newsbreaks and short humor. No puzzles or games. Buys 12/year. Length: 50-500 words. Pays $1.50-7.50.

Hardware

Journals for general and specialized hardware wholesalers and retailers are listed in this section. Journals specializing in hardware for a certain trade, such as plumbing or automotive supplies, are classified with other publications for that trade.

CHAIN SAW AGE, 3435 N.E. Broadway, Portland OR 97232. Editor: Ken Morrison. 1% freelance written. "We will consider any submissions that address pertinent subjects and are well-written." For "mostly chain saw dealers (retailers); small businesses—usually family-owned, typical ages, interests and education." Monthly. Circ. 20,000. Pays on acceptance or publication. Publishes ms an average of 4 months after acceptance. Photocopied submissions OK. Computer printout submissions acceptable. Free sample copy.
Nonfiction: "Must relate to chain saw use, merchandising, adaptation, repair, maintenance, manufacture or display." Buys informational articles, how-to, personal experience, interview, and profiles, inspirational, personal opinion, photo feature, coverage of successful business operations, and articles on merchandising techniques. Buys very few mss/year. Query first. Length: 500-1,000 words. Pays $20-50 "5¢/word plus photo fees." Sometimes pays the expenses of writers on assignment.
Photos: Photos purchased with or without mss, or on assignment. For b&w glossies, pay "varies." Captions required.
Tips: Frequently writers have an inadequate understanding of the subject area. "We may be in a position to accept more freelance material on an assignment basis."

HARDWARE AGE, Chilton Co., Chilton Way, Radnor PA 19089. (215)964-4275. Editor: Terry Gallagher. Managing Editor: Rick Carter. 2% freelance written. Emphasizes retailing, distribution and merchandising of hardware and building materials. Monthly magazine. Circ. 71,000. Buys first North American serial rights. No guarantee of byline. Simultaneous, photocopied and previously published submissions OK, if exclusive in the field. Reports in 1-2 months. Sample copy for $1; mention *Writer's Market* in request.
Nonfiction: Rick Carter, managing editor. How-to more profitably run a hardware store or a department within a store. "We particularly want stories on local hardware stores and home improvement centers, with photos. Stories should concentrate on one particular aspect of how the retailer in question has been successful." Also wants technical pieces (will consider stories on retail accounting, inventory management and business management by qualified writers). Buys 1-5 unsolicited mss/year. Submit complete ms. Length: 1,500-3,000 words. Pays $75-200.
Photos: "We like store features with b&w photos. Usually use b&w for small freelance features." Send photos with ms. Pays $25 for 4x5 glossy b&w prints. Captions preferred. Buys one-time rights.
Columns/Departments: Retailers' Business Tips; Wholesalers' Business Tips; and Moneysaving Tips. Query or submit complete ms. Length: 1,000-1,250 words. Pays $100-150. Open to suggestions for new columns/departments.

HARDWARE MERCHANDISER, The Irving-Cloud Publishing Co., 7300 N. Cicero, Lincolnwood IL 60646. (312)674-7300. Fax (312)674-7015. Publisher: John C. Nelson. 5% freelance written. Monthly tabloid covering retailers and wholesalers of hardware and building supply products. Circ. 70,000. Pays on acceptance. Publishes ms an average of 3 months after acceptance. Buys first North American serial rights. Computer printout submissions OK; prefers letter-quality. Reports in 1 month on queries. Free sample copy.
Nonfiction: Profile (of hardware business). Buys 10 mss/year. Query or send complete ms "on speculation; enough to tell the story." Sometimes pays the expenses of writers on assignment.
Photos: Send photos with ms. Reviews 35mm or larger color transparencies. "Photos are paid for as part of article payment."

Home Furnishings and Household Goods

Readers rely on these publications to learn more about new products and trends in the home furnishings and appliance trade. Magazines for consumers interested in home furnishings are listed in the Consumer Home and Garden section.

APPLIANCE SERVICE NEWS, 110 W. Saint Charles Rd., Box 789, Lombard IL 60148. Editor: William Wingstedt. For professional service people whose main interest is repairing major and/or portable household appliances. Their jobs consist of service shop owner, service manager or service technician. Monthly "newspaper style" publication. Circ. 51,000. Buys all rights. Byline given. Pays on publication. Will consider simultaneous submissions. Reports in about 1 month. Sample copy $2.
Nonfiction: James Hodl, associate editor. "Our main interest is in technical articles about appliances and their repair. Material should be written in a straightforward, easy-to-understand style. It should be crisp and interesting, with high informational content. Our main interest is in the major and portable appliance repair field. We are not interested in retail sales." Query. Length: open. Pays $200-300/feature.
Photos: Pays $10 for b&w photos used with ms. Captions required.

CHINA GLASS & TABLEWARE, Doctorow Communications, Inc., Box 2147, Clifton NJ 07015. (201)779-1600. Editor-in-Chief: Amy Stavis. 60% freelance written. Works with a small number of new/unpublished writers each year. Monthly magazine for buyers, merchandise managers and specialty store owners who deal in tableware, dinnerware, glassware, flatware and other tabletop accessories. Pays on publication. Publishes ms an average of 3-4 months after acceptance. Buys one-time rights. Byline given. Phone queries OK. Submit seasonal/holiday material 3 months in advance. Computer printout submissions acceptable; no dot-matrix. Reports in 3 weeks. Free sample copy and writer's guidelines; mention *Writer's Market* in request.
Nonfiction: General interest (on store successes, reasons for a store's business track record); interview (personalities of store owners; how they cope with industry problems; why they are in tableware); and technical (on the business aspects of retailing china, glassware and flatware). "Bridal registry material always welcomed." No articles on how-to or gift shops. Buys 2-3 mss/issue. Query. Length: 1,500-3,000 words. Pays $50/page. Sometimes pays the expenses of writers on assignment.
Photos: State availability of photos with query. No additional payment for b&w contact sheets or color contact sheets. Captions required. Buys first serial rights.
Fillers: Clippings. Buys 2/issue. Pays $3-5.
Tips: "Show imagination in the query; have a good angle on a story that makes it unique from the competition's coverage and requires less work on the editor's part for rewriting a snappy beginning."

‡DRAPERIES & WINDOW COVERINGS, The Magazine for the American Window Coverings Industry, L.C. Clark Publishing Co., Box 13079, North Palm Beach FL 33408. (305)627-3393. Editor: Katie Renckens. 20% freelance written. A monthly magazine on home furnishing and hard and soft window coverings for retailers of window covering products. Circ. 25,000. Pays on publication. Publishes ms an average of 2 months after acceptance. Byline given. Offers $50 kill fee. Buys all rights and makes work-for-hire assignments. Free sample copy.
Nonfiction: How-to (on selling, installing or making window coverings) and interview/profile (of successful window covering retailers). Buys 20 mss/year. Query with published clips; no unsolicited mss. Length: 1,000-3,000 words. Pays $200-500. Pays expenses of writers on assignment.
Photos: State availability of photos with submission. Offers $10-25/photo. Captions and identification of subjects required. Buys all rights.

ENTREE, Fairchild, 825 Seventh Ave., New York NY 10019. (212)887-1870. Managing Editor: Jeanne Muchnick. 20% freelance written. Bi-weekly business magazine covering housewares, lifestyle and tabletop (i.e.: cookware, small electrical appliances, rta furniture, etc.) wherever they are sold, including department stores, mass merchants, specialty shops. Circ. 15,000. Average issue includes 5-11 features, 3 columns, a calendar, news and 50% advertising. Pays on acceptance. Publishes ms an average of 2½ months after acceptance. Byline given. Kill fee varies. Buys all rights. Phone queries OK. Computer printout submissions acceptable; prefers letter-quality. Reports in 6 weeks on queries; 1 week on mss. Sample copy $2.
Nonfiction: Corporate profiles (of major retailers and manufacturers); industry news analysis; new product ("hot product categories"); photo feature; and technical (cookware and specialty food in terms retailers can apply to their businesses). No first person, humor, cartoons and unsolicited stories on obscure retailers or general

pieces of any kind such as accounting or computer stories. Buys 1-2 mss/issue. Query. Length: 750-1,000 words. Pays $250-600. Sometimes pays the expenses of writers on assignment.

Photos: Cindy Sutherland, art director. Always looking for illustrations and photographs.

Tips: "We use one to two freelancers every issue and have established a core of regular writers we rely on. We want writers who can thoroughly analyze a market, whether it be cutlery, drip coffee makers, food processors or cookware and who can do in-depth profiles of major retailers or manufacturers. We are especially looking for stories with statistical information. We welcome information on foreign markets especially from experts in the field such as marketing consultants or futurists."

FLOORING MAGAZINE, 7500 Old Oak Blvd., Cleveland OH 44130. Editor: Dan Alaimo. 5% freelance written by assignment only. Prefers to work with published/established writers. Monthly magazine for floor covering retailers, wholesalers, contractors, specifiers and designers. Circ. 24,000. Pays on acceptance. Publishes ms an average of 3 months after acceptance. No byline or credit given. Buys all rights. Computer printout submissions acceptable; prefers letter-quality. "Send letter with writing sample to be placed in our freelance contact file."

Nonfiction: Mostly staff-written. Will not be buying a significant number of manuscripts. However, has frequent need for correspondents skilled in 35mm photography for simple, local assignments. Sometimes pays the expenses of writers on assignment.

GIFTWARE NEWS, Talcott Corp., 112 Adrossan, Box 5398, Deptford NJ 08096. (609)227-0798. Editor: Anthony DeMasi. 50% freelance written. A monthly magazine covering gifts, collectibles, and tabletops for giftware retailers. Circ. 41,000. Pays on publication. Publishes ms an average of 2 months after acceptance. Byline given. Buys all rights. Submit seasonal/holiday material 4 months in advance. Reports in 2 months on mss. Sample copy $1.50.

Nonfiction: How-to (sell, display) and new product. Buys 50 mss/year. Send complete ms. Length: 1,500-2,500 words. Pays $150-250 for assigned articles; pays $75-100 for unsolicited articles.

Photos: Send photos with submission. Reviews 4x5 transparencies and 5x7 prints. Offers no additional payment for photos accepted with ms. Identification of subjects required.

Columns/Departments: Tabletop, Wedding Market and Display—all for the gift retailer. Buys 36 mss/year. Send complete ms. Length: 1,500-2,500 words. Pays $75-200.

Tips: "We are not looking so much for general journalists but rather experts in particular fields who can also write."

HAPPI, (*Household and Personal Products Industry*), Box 555, 26 Lake St., Ramsey NJ 07446. Editor: Hamilton C. Carson. 5% freelance written. For "manufacturers of soaps, detergents, cosmetics and toiletries, waxes and polishes, insecticides, and aerosols." Circ. 15,000. Not copyrighted. Pays on publication. Publishes ms an average of 2 months after acceptance. Will consider photocopied submissions. Submit seasonal material 2 months in advance. Query. Computer printout submissions acceptable.

Nonfiction: "Technical and semitechnical articles on manufacturing, distribution, marketing, new products, plant stories, etc., of the industries served. Some knowledge of the field is essential in writing for us." Buys informational interview, photo feature, spot news, coverage of successful business operations, new product articles, coverage of merchandising techniques and technical articles. No articles slanted toward consumers. Query with published clips. Buys 3 to 4 mss a year. Length: 500-2,000 words. Pays $25-300. Sometimes pays expenses of writers on assignment.

Photos: 5x7 or 8x10 b&w glossies purchased with mss. Pays $10.

Tips: "The most frequent mistakes made by writers are unfamiliarity with our audience and our industry; slanting articles toward consumers rather than to industry members."

HOME FURNISHINGS, Box 581207, Dallas TX 75258. (214)741-7632. Editor: Darrell Hofheinz. 40% freelance written. Quarterly magazine for home furnishings retail dealers, manufacturers, their representatives and others in related fields. Circ. 25,000. Pays on acceptance. Publishes ms an average of 2 months after acceptance. Buys first serial rights. Computer printout submissions acceptable; no dot-matrix.

Nonfiction: Informational articles about retail selling; success and problem solving stories in the home furnishings retail business; economic and legislative-related issues, etc. "No trite, over-used features on trends, lighthearted features and no cartoons." Query. Length: open; appropriate to subject and slant. Photos desirable. Sometimes pays the expenses of writers on assignment.

HOME LIGHTING & ACCESSORIES, Box 2147, Clifton NJ 07015. (201)779-1600. Editor: Peter Wulff. 5% freelance written. Prefers to work with published/established writers. For lighting stores/departments. Monthly magazine. Circ. 7,500. Pays on publication. Publishes ms an average of 4-6 months after acceptance. Buys all rights. Submit seasonal/holiday material 6 months in advance. Computer printout submissions acceptable; no dot-matrix. Free sample copy.

Nonfiction: How-to (run your lighting store/department, including all retail topics); interview (with lighting retailers); personal experience (as a businessperson involved with lighting); profile (of a successful lighting retailer/lamp buyer); and technical (concerning lighting or lighting design). Buys 10 mss/year. Query. Pays $60/published page. Sometimes pays the expenses of writers on assignment.

Photos: State availability of photos with query. Offers no additional payment for 5x7 or 8x10 b&w glossy prints. Pays additional $90 for color transparencies used on cover. Captions required.

Tips: "We don't need fillers—only features."

MART, Business Ideas For Today's Retailers and Distributors, Gordon Publications, Inc., Box 1952, Dover NJ 07801. (201)361-9060. Editor: Bob Ankosko. Associate Editor: Rob Sabin. 30% freelance written. Works with a small number of new/unpublished writers each year. Monthly tabloid on consumer electronics, and major appliances retailing; readership includes retailers, wholesale distributors, and manufacturer district managers and representatives. Circ. 65,000. Pays on acceptance. Publishes ms an average of 1 month after acceptance. Byline given. Offers $50 kill fee. Buys all rights. Submit seasonal/holiday material 2 months in advance. Computer printout submissions acceptable. Query for electronic submissions. Sample copy $3; free writer's guidelines.

Nonfiction: Industry trends, interview/profile, new product roundups, and retailer how-to (business management, etc). Buys 60 mss/year. Query with published clips. Length: 800-2,000 words. Pays $100-350. Sometimes pays the expenses of writers on assignment.

Tips: "We're looking in the future for more colorful, as opposed to hard news articles (from a style approach). We're looking more for in-depth investigative work on those 'newsy' pieces that we use, i.e., exposes. Writers frequently miss getting facts of particular interest to retailers: store volume, selling area, percentage of sales in major appliances, in consumer electronics, etc. Say something to an electronics/major appliance retailer that will somehow help his business."

PROFESSIONAL FURNITURE MERCHANT MAGAZINE, The Magazine Retailers Read, Shore Communications, Inc., Suite 300, South, 180 Allen Rd. NE, Atlanta GA 30328. Editor: J. David Goldman. 35% freelance written. Monthly magazine covering the furniture industry from a retailer's perspective. In-depth features on direction, trends, certain retailers doing outstanding jobs, and analyses of product or service areas in which retailing can improve profits. Circ. 20,000. Pays on publication. Publishes ms an average of 3 months after acceptance. Byline given. Buys first serial rights. Submit seasonal/holiday material 5 months in advance. Computer printout submissions acceptable; prefers letter-quality. Reports in 6 weeks. Sample copy $3.

Nonfiction: Expose (relating to or affecting furniture industry); how-to (business oriented how to control cash flow, inventory, market research, etc.); interview/profile (furniture retailers); and photo feature (special furniture category). No general articles, fiction or personal experience. Buys 24 mss/year. Send complete ms. Length: 1,000-2,400 words. Pays $150-350. Sometimes pays expenses of writers on assignment.

Photos: State availablity of photos. Pays $5 maximum for 4x5 color transparencies; $5 maximum for 3x5 b&w prints. Captions, model release, and identification of subjects required.

Tips: "Read the magazine. Query before writing. Send manuscript specifically geared to furniture retailers, with art (photos or drawings) specified." Break in with features. "First, visit a furniture store, talk to the owner and discover what he's interested in."

‡THE PROFESSIONAL UPHOLSTERER, Official Publication of the National Association of Professional Upholsterers, Communications Today Ltd. 200 S. Main St., High Point NC 27261. (919)889-0113. Editor: Karl Kunkel (associate ed.). Group Editor: Gary Evans. 30% freelance written. A bimonthly magazine on reupholstering and building of custom-made upholstered furniture. "Our publication is geared to professional upholsterers and/or owners of independently owned/operated upholstery shops and custom interior decoration houses. The emphasis is on new products, sales ideas, profiles of upwardly mobile, marketing-oriented businesses. The biggest need is in how-to pieces." Circ. 22,000. Pays on publication. Publishes ms an average of 2 months after acceptance. Byline given. Buys all rights. Submit seasonal/holiday material 4 months in advance. Photocopied submissions OK. Computer printout submissions OK. Reports in 2 weeks on queries; 3 weeks on mss. Sample copy $4. Writer's guidelines for #10 SASE.

Nonfiction: Historical/nostalgic, how-to (tips, techniques on producing all types of upholstered furniture and antiques, pillows, draperies, upholstered headboards, etc.), humor (topical cartoons), new products and unusual time-saving pieces of equipment), opinion (good or bad experiences of a reupholsterer), personal experience, technical and travel. "No boiler plate sales pieces or motivational pieces in which plumber, carpenter, etc. has been removed and upholsterer inserted. I can usually tell if the writer knows our reading audience." Buys 20 mss/year. Query. Length: 50 words. Pays $25-150 for assigned articles. Pays $25-100 for unsolicited articles. Prefer initial contact prior to receiving articles.

Photos: State availability of photos with submission. Reviews contact sheets. Offers no additional payment for photos accepted with ms. Captions required. Buys all rights.

Columns/Departments: Buys 6 mss/year. Query. Length: 140-200 words. Pays $25-100.

Fillers: Anecdotes, facts and short humor. Buys 2/year. Length: 100 words. Pays $10-25.

Tips: "Learn tips, unusual areas of specialization (not auto-related, prefer furniture—residential, hotel, restaurant, office, related items). Prefers neat writer. Call me or write a query letter, allowing me to focus piece better."

‡**RAYTHEON MAGAZINE**, Raytheon Company, 141 Spring St., Lexington MA 02173. (617)862-6600, ext. 2415. Editor-in-Chief: Robert P. Suarez. 90% freelance written. Prefers to work with published/established writers. Quarterly magazine for Raytheon stockholders, employees, customers, suppliers, plant city officials, libraries and interested persons. "Ours is a company publication that strives to avoid sounding like a company publication. All stories must involve some aspect of Raytheon or its products." Circ. 200,000. Pays on acceptance. Publishes ms an average of 3 months after acceptance. Byline given. Computer printout submissions acceptable; prefers letter-quality. Free sample copy.
Nonfiction: General interest, humor, interview/profile, new product, nostalgia, photo feature, technical and travel. "This is a corporate publication designed to illustrate the breadth of Raytheon Company in a low key manner through six general-interest articles per issue. Photos are used liberally, top quality and exclusively color. Stories are by assignment only." Buys 4 mss/issue. Query with clips of published work, stating specialties, credentials and other publication credits. Length: 800-1,500 words. Pays $1,000-1,500/article. Pays the expenses of writers on assignment.
Tips: "Submit resume and magazine-style writing samples. We are looking for established writers who are capable of crisp, interesting magazine journalism. We are not looking to promote Raytheon, but rather to inform our audience about the company, very subtly. Heavy marketing style or house organ writing is of no interest to us. A frequent mistake made by writers is not taking the time to truly understand what they're writing about and who the audience is."

SEW BUSINESS, 1515 Broadway, New York NY 10036. Editor: Christina Holmes. For retailers of home sewing, quilting and needlework merchandise. "We are the only glossy magazine format in the industry—including home sewing and the *Art Needlework* and *Quilt Quarterly* supplements." Monthly. Circ. 20,000. Not copyrighted. Pays on publication. Publishes ms an average of 3-4 months after acceptance. Computer printout submissions OK; prefers letter-quality. Reports in 5 weeks on queries; in 6 weeks on ms. Sample copy and writer's guidelines for 8½x11 SAE with 5 first class stamps.
Nonfiction: Articles on department store or fabric, needlework, or quilt shop operations, including coverage of art needlework, piece goods, patterns, quilting and sewing notions. Interviews with buyers—retailers on their department or shop. "Stories must be oriented to provide interesting information from a *trade* point of view. Looking for retailers doing something different or offbeat, something that another retailer could put to good use in his own operation. Best to query editor first to find out if a particular article might be of interest to us." Buys 25 unsolicited mss/year. Query. Length: 750-1,500 words. Pays $150 minimum.
Photos: Photos purchased with mss. "Should illustrate important details of the story." Sharp 5x7 b&w glossies. Offers no additional payment for photos accompanying ms.

‡**TILE WORLD**, Tradeline Publishing Co.. 485 Kinderkamack Rd., Oradell NJ 07649. (201)599-0136. Editor: Mike Lench. Managing Editor: John Sailer. 25% freelance written. A quarterly magazine on tile. "Our readers are tile users and specifiers; write for that market." Estab. 1987. Circ. 16,000. Pays on publication. Publishes ms an average of 4 months after acceptance. Byline given. Buys first rights and makes work-for-hire assignments. Submit seasonal/holiday material 6 months in advance. Simultaneous, photocopied and previously published submissions OK. Computer printout submissions OK; prefers letter-quality. Reports in 2 weeks on queries; 1 month on mss. Sample copy $5. Free writer's guidelines.
Nonfiction: How-to (install tile), interview/profile, new product, photo feature (architectural design) and technical. Buys 10 mss/year. Query with published clips. Length: 600-2,000 words. Pays $80-240.
Photos: Send photos with submission. Reviews transparencies and prints. Captions and identification of subjects required. Buys one-time rights.
Columns/Departments: News: New Products (new types of titles); New Equipment (for installing tile, 200 words). Send complete ms. Pays $15-40.
Tips: "Reports on architectural designs using tile are most open to freelancers. Architects are very willing to be quoted and provide good photos. Be sure to include in features all players involved with tile distribution and installation."

‡**TODAY'S FURNITURE DESIGNER, The Magazine for Furniture Design Professionals**, Communications Today. Box 2754, High Point NC 27261. (919)889-0113. Editor: Gary Evans. 33% freelance written. A quarterly magazine on furniture design. Circ. 20,000. Pays on publication. Publishes ms an average of 2 months after acceptance. Byline given. Kill fee negotiable. Buys all rights. Query for electronic submissions. Computer printout submissions OK. Reports in 2 weeks on mss.
Nonfiction: Interview/profile and technical. Buys 12 mss/year. Query with published clips. 4 double-spaced typewritten pages. Pays $200-400. Sometimes pays the expenses of writers on assignment.
Photos: Send photos with submission. Reviews contact sheets. Offers no additional payment for photos accepted with ms. Captions and identification of subjects required. Buys one-time rights.
Tips: "We're interested in profiles of furniture designers and articles on materials and techniques used by furniture designers. Writer should know his subject well. Magazine not intended for general writing so writer should query first."

Hospitals, Nursing and Nursing Homes

In this section are journals for medical and nonmedical nursing home personnel, clinical and hospital staffs and medical laboratory technicians and managers. Journals publishing technical material on medical research and information for physicians in private practice are listed in the Medical category.

‡**AMERICAN JOURNAL OF NURSING**, 555 West 57th St., New York NY 10019. (212)582-8820. Editor: Mary B. Mallison, RN. 2% freelance written. Eager to work with new/unpublished writers. Monthly magazine covering nursing and health care. Circ. 330,000. Pays on publication. Publishes ms an average of 6 months after acceptance. Byline given. Simultaneous queries OK. Computer printout submissions acceptable; prefers letter-quality. Reports in 3 weeks on queries, 4 months on mss. Sample copy $3; free writer's guidelines.
Nonfiction: How-to, satire, new product, opinion, personal experience, photo feature and technical. No material other than nursing care and nursing issues. "Nurse authors mostly accepted for publication." Query. Length: 1,000-1,500 words. Payment negotiable. Pays the expenses of writers on assignment.
Photos: Forbes Linkhorn, art editor. Reviews b&w and color transparencies and prints. Model release and identification of subjects required. Buys variable rights.
Columns/Departments: Buys 20 mss/year. Query with or without clips of published work.

HOSPITAL GIFT SHOP MANAGEMENT, Creative Age Publications, 7628 Densmore Ave., Van Nuys CA 91406. (818)782-7232. Editor: Barbara Feiner. 25% freelance written. Works with a small number of new/unpublished writers each year. Monthly magazine covering hospital gift shop management. "*HGSM* presents practical and informative articles and features to assist in expanding the hospital gift shop into a comprehensive center generating large profits." Circ. 15,000 + . Pays on acceptance. Publishes ms an average of 4 months after acceptance. Byline given. Buys first North American serial rights. Submit seasonal/holiday material 8 months in advance. Computer printout submissions acceptable; dot-matrix OK "if readable and double-spaced." Reports in 1 month. Sample copy and writer's guidelines for $4 postage.
Nonfiction: How-to, interview/profile, photo feature, and management-themed articles. "No fiction, no poetry, no first-person 'I was shopping in a gift shop' kinds of pieces." Buys 12-25 mss/year. Length: 750-2,500 words. Pays $10-100. Query first.
Photos: State availability of photos with query. "If you are preparing a gift shop profile, think of providing gift shop photos." Reviews 5x7 color or b&w prints; payment depends on photo quality and number used. Captions, model release, and identification of subjects required.
Fillers: Cartoons only. Buys 12/year. Pays $20.
Tips: "A freelancer's best bet is to let us know you're out there. We prefer to work on assignment a lot of the time, and we're very receptive to freelancers—especially those in parts of the country to which we have no access. Call or write; let me know you're available. Visit your nearby hospital gift shop—it's probably larger, more sophisticated than you would imagine. I've noticed that query letters are becoming sloppy and lack direction. I wouldn't mind finding writers who can communicate well, explain story ideas in a one-page letter, spell correctly, and wow me with original ideas. Make your query letter stand out. Convince me that your story is going to be exciting. A boring query usually yields a boring story."

‡**HOSPITAL RISK MANAGEMENT**, American Health Consultants. 67 Peachtree Park Dr., Atlanta GA 30309. (404)351-4523. Editor: Russell A. Jackson. 10% freelance written. A monthly newsletter on health care risk management. Circ. 2,500. Pays on publication. Publishes ms an average of 1 month after acceptance. Byline given. Buys all rights. Computer printout submissions OK; prefers letter-quality. Reports in 1 month. Free sample copy and writer's guidelines.
Nonfiction: How-to (specific to newsletter topic). Nothing analytical—must be how-to. Buys 10-12 mss/year. Query. Length: 600 words. Pays $50-150.

HOSPITAL SUPERVISOR'S BULLETIN, Bureau of Business Practice, 24 Rope Ferry Rd., Waterford CT 06386. Editor: Michele Dunaj. 40% freelance written. Works with a small number of new/unpublished writers each year. For non-medical hospital supervisors. Semimonthly newsletter. Circ. 3,300. Pays on acceptance. Publishes ms an average of 5 months after acceptance. Buys all rights. No byline. Submit seasonal/holiday material 6 months in advance. Photocopied submissions OK. Computer printout submissions acceptable; prefers letter-quality. Reports in 1 month. Sample copy and writer's guidelines for SAE with 2 first class stamps.

Nonfiction: Publishes interviews with non-medical hospital department heads. "You should ask supervisors to pinpoint current problems in supervision, tell how they are trying to solve these problems and what results they're getting—backed up by real examples from daily life." Also publishes interviews on people problems and good methods of management. People problems include the areas of training, planning, evaluating, counseling, discipline, motivation, supervising the undereducated, getting along with the medical staff, dealing with change, layoffs, etc. No material on hospital volunteers. "We prefer six- to eight-page typewritten articles. Articles must be interview-based." Pays 12¢/word after editing.

Tips: "Often stories lack concrete examples explaining general principles. I want to stress that freelancers interview supervisors (not high-level managers, doctors, or administrators) of non-medical departments. Interviews should focus on supervisory skills or techniques that would be applicable in any hospital department. The article should be conversational in tone: not stiff or academic. Use the second person to address the supervisor/reader."

Hotels, Motels, Clubs, Resorts and Restaurants

These publications offer trade tips and advice to hotel, club, resort and restaurant managers, owners and operators. Journals for manufacturers and distributors of bar and beverage supplies are listed in the Beverages and Bottling section.

‡BARTENDER MAGAZINE, Foley Publishing, Box 158, Liberty Corner NJ 07038. (201)580-1887. Publisher: Raymond P. Foley. Editor: Jaclyn M. Wilson. Emphasizes liquor and bartending for bartenders, tavern owners and owners of restaurants with liquor licenses. 100% freelance written. Prefers to work with published/established writers; eager to work with new/unpublished writers. Magazine published 5 times/year. Circ. 140,000. Pays on publication. Publishes ms an average of 3 months after acceptance. Buys first serial rights, first North American serial rights, one-time rights, second serial (reprint) rights, all rights, and simultaneous U.S. rights. Byline given. Phone queries OK. Submit seasonal/holiday material 3 months in advance. Simultaneous, photocopied, and previously published submissions OK. Computer printout submissions acceptable; prefers letter-quality. Reports in 2 months. Sample copies $2.50.

Nonfiction: General interest, historical, how-to, humor, interview (with famous bartenders or ex-bartenders); new products, nostalgia, personal experience, unique bars, opinion, new techniques, new drinking trends, photo feature, profile, travel and bar sports or bar magic tricks. Send complete ms. Length: 100-1,000 words. Sometimes pays the expenses of writers on assignment.

Photos: Send photos with ms. Pays $7.50-50 for 8x10 b&w glossy prints; $10-75 for 8x10 color glossy prints. Caption preferred and model release required.

Columns/Departments: Bar of the Month; Bartender of the Month; Drink of the Month; New Drink Ideas; Bar Sports; Quiz; Bar Art; Wine Cellar Tips of the Month (from prominent figures in the liquor industry); One For The Road (travel); Collectors (bar or liquor-related items); Photo Essays. Query. Length: 200-1,000 words. Pays $50-200.

Fillers: Clippings, jokes, gags, anecdotes, short humor, newsbreaks and anything relating to bartending and the liquor industry. Length: 25-100 words. Pays $5-25.

Tips: "To break in, absolutely make sure that your work will be of interest to all bartenders across the country. Your style of writing should reflect the audience you are addressing. The most frequent mistake made by writers in completing an article for us is using the wrong subject."

CATERING TODAY, The Professional Guide to Catering Profits, ProTech Publishing, 738 Pearl, Denver CO 80203. (303)861-4040. Editor: Ramona Chun. Managing Editor: Jane Kulbeth. 40% freelance written. Prefers to work with published/established writers. A monthly magazine for the off-premise and on-site catering industry covering food trends, business and management advice and features on successful caterers. Circ. 36,000. Pays on publication. Publishes ms an average of 5-6 months after acceptance. Byline given. Offers 10-30% kill fee. Buys all rights. Submit seasonal/holiday material 3 months in advance. Simultaneous, photocopied and previously published submissions OK. Computer printout submissions acceptable; prefers letter-quality. Reports in 2 weeks on queries; 3 weeks on mss. Sample copy and writer's guidelines for 9x12 SAE with 5 first class stamps.

Nonfiction: How-to (on ice carving, garnishes, cooking techniques, etc); interview/profile; new product; and photo feature. "Also valuable to caterers are advice and ideas on marketing, advertising, public relations and promotion." No humor, poetry or fiction. Buys 35-40 mss/year. Query with published clips. Length: 800-

2,500. Pays $50/printed word minimum; $150/printed word maximum.

Photos: Send photos with submission. Reviews contact sheets, negatives, 4x5 transparencies, and 5x7 prints. Offers $5-10/photo. Captions required.

Columns/Departments: Book reviews. Buys 25/year. Send complete ms. Length: 500-1,200 words. Pays $75/printed page.

Fillers: Buys 10/year. Length: 50-100 words. Pays $25.

Tips: "Write from a viewpoint that a caterer/business person can understand, appreciate and learn from. Submissions should be neat, accurate and not flowery or wordy. Areas of our publication most open to freelancers are food trends and uses, equipment reviews, and feature length profiles of caterers."

FLORIDA HOTEL & MOTEL JOURNAL, The Official Publication of the Florida Hotel & Motel Association, Accommodations, Inc., Box 1529, Tallahassee FL 32302. (904)224-2888. Editor: Mrs. Jayleen Woods. 10% freelance written. Prefers to work with published/established writers. Monthly magazine for managers in the lodging industry (every licensed hotel, motel and resort in Florida). Circ. 6,500. Pays on publication. Publishes ms an average of 2 months after acceptance. Byline given. Offers $50 kill fee. Buys all rights and makes work-for-hire assignments. Submit seasonal/holiday material 3 months in advance. Photocopied submissions OK. Computer printout submissions acceptable; no dot-matrix. Reports in 1 month. Sample copy for 9x12 SAE and 5 first class stamps; writer's guidelines for #10 SAE and 1 first class stamp.

Nonfiction: General interest (business, finance, taxes); historical/nostalgic (old Florida hotel reminiscences); how-to (improve management, housekeeping procedures, guest services, security and coping with common hotel problems); humor (hotel-related anecdotes); inspirational (succeeding where others have failed); interview/profile (of unusual hotel personalities); new product (industry-related and non brand preferential); photo feature (queries only); technical (emerging patterns of hotel accounting, telephone systems, etc.); travel (transportation and tourism trends only—no scenics or site visits); and property renovations and maintenance techniques. Buys 10-12 mss/year. Query with clips of published work. Length: 750-2,500 words. Pays $75-250 "depending on type of article and amount of research." Sometimes pays the expenses of writers on assignment.

Photos: Send photos with ms. Pays $25-100 for 4x5 color transparencies; $10-15 for 5x7 b&w prints. Captions, model release and identification of subjects required.

Tips: "We prefer feature stories on properties or personalities holding current membership in the Florida Hotel and Motel Association. Memberships and/or leadership brochures are available (SASE) on request. We're open to articles showing how Mom and Dad management copes with energy systems, repairs, renovations, new guest needs and expectations. The writer may have a better chance of breaking in at our publication with short articles and fillers because the better a writer is at the art of condensation, the better his/her feature articles are likely to be."

FOOD & SERVICE, Texas Restaurant Association, Box 1429, Austin TX 78767. (512)444-6543 (in Texas, 1-800-252-9360). Editor: Bland Crowder. 50% freelance written. Magazine published 11 times/year providing business solutions to Texas restaurant owners and operators. Circ. 5,000. Written queries required. Reports in 1 month. Byline given. Not copyrighted. Buys first rights. Simultaneous queries, photocopied submissions OK. No previously published submissions. Query for electronic submissions. Free sample copy and editorial calendar for 9x12 SAE and 5 first class stamps. Pays on acceptance; rates vary.

Nonfiction: Features must provide business solutions to problems in the restaurant and food service industries. Topics vary but always have business slant; usually particular to Texas. No restaurant critiques, human interest stories, or seasonal copy. Quote experts and other restaurateurs; substantiate with facts and examples. Query. Length: 2,000-2,500 words, features; shorter articles sometimes used; product releases, 300-word maximum. Payment rates vary. Sometimes pays the expenses of writers on assignment.

Photos: State availability of photos, but photos usually assigned.

Columns/Departments: Written in-house only.

‡HOTEL AMENITIES IN CANADA, Titan Publishing Inc., Unit 7, 291 Woodlawn Rd. W., Box 1747 Guelph, ON N1H 7A1 Canada. (519)763-5058. Editor: Karen Mantel. 30% freelance written. Bimonthly magazine covering the lodging hospitality industry. "*Hotel Amenities in Canada* is a publication dedicated to the promotion of amenities and essential supplies and services in the Canadian hospitality industry." Estab. 1987. Circ. 3,600. Pays on publication. Publishes ms an average of 2 months after acceptance. Byline given. Buys first North American serial rights. Submit seasonal/holiday material 3 months in advance. Simultaneous and previously published submissions OK. Computer printout submissions OK; prefers letter-quality. Reports in 6 weeks. Sample copy for 8x10 SAE with Canadian postage or international reply coupon.

Nonfiction: New product, company feature. "*Hotel Amenities in Canada* is aimed primarily at the lodging hospitality industry so we do not need food service articles." Buys 12 mss/year. Query with published clips. Length: 500-1,500 words. Pays up to $100.

Photos: State availability of photos with submission. Reviews 5x7 prints. Offers $5/photo. Identification of subjects required. Buys one-time rights.

Columns/Departments: Products and Services (new products) 50 words. Length 50-100 words. Pays up to $10.

Tips: "Research the amenities trend in the hospitality industry."

INNKEEPING WORLD, Box 84108, Seattle WA 98124. (206)284-4247. Editor/Publisher: Charles Nolte. 75% freelance written. Eager to work with new/unpublished writers. Emphasizes the hotel industry worldwide. Published 10 times a year. Circ. 2,000. Pays on acceptance. Publishes ms an average of 4 months after acceptance. Buys all rights. No byline. Submit seasonal/holiday material 1 month in advance. Computer printout submissions acceptable; no dot-matrix. Reports in 1 month. Sample copy and writer's guidelines for 9x12 SAE with 3 first class stamps.

Nonfiction: Managing—interviews with successful hotel managers of large and/or famous hotels/resorts (600-1,200 words); Marketing—interviews with hotel marketing executives on successful promotions/case histories (length: 300-1,000 words); Sales Promotion—innovative programs for increasing business (100-600 words); Bill of Fare—outstanding hotel restaurants, menus and merchandising concepts (300-1,000 words); and Guest Relations—guest service programs, management philosophies relative to guests (200-800 words). Pays $100 minimum or 15¢/word (whichever is greater) for main topics. Other topics—advertising, creative packages, cutting expenses, frequent guest profile, guest comfort, hospitality, ideas, public relations, reports and trends, special guestrooms, staff relations. Length: 50-500 words. Pays 15¢/word. "If a writer asks a hotel for a complimentary room, the article will not be accepted, nor will *Innkeeping World* accept future articles from the writer."

Tips: "We need more in-depth reporting on successful case histories—results-oriented information."

THE NEWMAN REPORT, (formerly *Marketing & Sales Promotion Update*), The Newsletter Group, Inc., 1552 Gilmore St., Box 4044, Mountain View CA 94040. (415)941-7525. Editor: Patrick Totty. Associate Editor: Howard Baldwin. A trade newsletter for the lodging industry. "Each four-page issue contains 18 tightly-condensed reports of successful marketing strategies recently undertaken by hotels, motels, resorts or bed-and-breakfast inns. Coverage area is worldwide, though largely U.S. Subscribers are marketing/sales directors, worldwide, though largely U.S. We accept tips from freelancers—no complete mss." Circ. 1,500. Pays on publication. Computer printout submissions OK. Sample copy for #10 SAE with 1 first class stamp.

Nonfiction: Lodging industry sales/marketing. Query. Pays $25 for leads only.

Tips: "We seek tips, leads, suggestions and ideas for 100-150-word articles focusing on an outstanding novel or unusual successful sales/marketing promotion or package offered by a hotel, motel, resort or bed-and-breakfast inn. Writer should furnish lead or tip with query. If lead/tip results in a published article, publication will pay query writer $25 within 30 days. If not used, there is no payment. All published copy is staff written. Manuscripts are not accepted. No exceptions. Written queries only, please."

PIZZA TODAY, The Professional Guide To Pizza Profits,, ProTech Publishing and Communications, Inc., Box 114, Santa Claus IN 47579. (812)937-4464. Editor: Paula Werne. Managing Editor: Jane Kulbeth. 30% freelance written. Prefers to work with published/established writers. A monthly magazine for the pizza industry, covering trends, features of successful pizza operators, business and management advice, etc. Circ. 36,000. Pays on publication. Publishes ms an average of 2 months after acceptance. Byline given. Offers 10-30% kill fee. Buys all rights and negotiable rights. Submit seasonal/holiday material 3 months in advance. Simultaneous, photocopied and previously published submissions OK. Query for electronic submissions. Computer printout submissons acceptable; prefers letter-quality. Reports in 2 weeks on queries; 3 weeks on manuscripts. Sample copy and writer's guidelines for 10x13 SAE with 6 first class stamps.

Nonfiction: Interview/profile, new product, entrepreneurial slants, time management, pizza delivery and employee training. No fillers, fiction, humor or poetry. Buys 40-60 mss/year. Query with published clips. Length: 750-2,500 words. Pays $50-125/page. Sometimes pays the expenses of writers on assignment.

Photos: Send photos with submission. Reviews contact sheets, negatives, 4x5 transparencies, color slides and 5x7 prints. Offers $5-10/photo. Captions required.

Tips: "We would like to receive nutritional information for low-cal, low-salt, low-fat, etc. pizza. Writers must have strong business and foodservice background."

RESTAURANT HOSPITALITY, Penton Publishing, 1100 Superior Ave., Cleveland OH 44114. (216)696-7000. Editor: Stephen Michaelides. 30% freelance written. Prefers to work with published/established writers. Monthly magazine covering the foodservice industry for owners and operators of independent restaurants, hotel foodservices, executives of national and regional restaurant chains and foodservice executives of schools, hospitals, military installations and corporations. Circ. 120,000. Average issue includes 10-12 features. Pays on acceptance. Publishes ms an average of 5 months after acceptance. Byline given. Buys exclusive rights. Computer printout submissions acceptable; prefers letter-quality. Reports in 3 weeks. Sample copy for 9x12 SAE and with 10 first class stamps.

Nonfiction: General interest (articles that advise operators how to run their operations profitably and efficiently); interview (with operators); and profile. Stories on psychology, consumer behavior, managerial prob-

lems and solutions, how-to's on buying insurance, investing (our readers have a high degree of disposable income), design elements and computers in foodservice. No restaurant reviews. Buys 50-60 mss/year. Query with clips of previously published work and a short bio. Length: 500-1,500 words. Pays $125/published page. Pays the expenses of writers on assignment.
Photos: Send color photos with manuscript. Captions required.
Columns/Departments: "We are accepting 100-150 word pieces with photos (slides preferred; will accept b&w) for our Restaurant People department. Should be light, humorous, anecdotal." Byline given. Pays $75.
Tips: "We would like to receive queries for articles on insurance costs (liquor liabilities); new tax reform laws; minimum wage; food trends; shortage of qualified employees; shrinking of labor market; ingredient labelling; neo-Prohibitionism; and nutrition. One hard-hitting, investigative piece on the influence of the 'mob' in food service would be welcome. We're accepting fewer queried stories but assigning more to our regular freelancers. We need new angles on old stories, and we like to see pieces on emerging trends and technologies in the restaurant industry. Our readers don't want to read how to open a restaurant or why John Smith is so successful. We'll be publishing short, snappy profiles—way more than in the past—with fewer major features."

RESTAURANT MANAGEMENT, HBJ Publications, 7500 Old Oak Blvd., Cleveland OH 44130. (216)243-8100. Editor: Loretta Ivany. Uses freelance written articles "only occasionally." Monthly magazine covering management and marketing of independently owned and operated restaurants. Circ. 102,000. Pays on acceptance. Publishes an average of 4 months after acceptance. No byline given. Buys first North American serial rights. Submit seasonal/holiday material 6 months in advance. Photocopied submissions OK. Computer printout submissions acceptable; prefers letter-quality. Reports in 2 months. Sample copy $3.
Nonfiction: How-to (improve management of independent restaurant; marketing techniques, promotions, etc.); and interview/profile (with independent restaurateur; needs a strong angle). "Send us a query on a successful independent restaurateur with an effective marketing program, unusual promotions, interesting design and decor, etc." No restaurant reviews, consumer-oriented material, nonrestaurant-oriented management articles. Buys variable number mss/year. Length: open. Pays variable fee.
Photos: State availability of photos. Captions, model release and identification of subjects required. Buys all rights.

‡TOP SHELF MAGAZINE, Barkeeping at its Best, Heritage Publishing. 9 Heritage Rd., Southbury CT 06488. (203)264-9200. Editor: Christina Veiders. ⅔ freelance written. A quarterly magazine on bar serving and managing. Circ. 303,000. Pays on publication. Publishes ms an average of 1 month after acceptance. Byline given. Makes work-for-hire assignments. Submit seasonal/holiday material 3 months in advance. Simultaneous, photocopied and previously published submissions OK. Computer printout submissions OK; no dot-matrix. Reports in 2 months. Writer's guidelines for #10 SAE with 1 first class stamp.
Nonfiction: General interest, historical/nostalgic, how-to, humor, interview/profile, photo feature, travel and celebrity interview. No syndicated columns or stories that don't relate to bar business. Buys 35-40 mss/year. Query with published clips. Length: 800-2,000 words. Pays $250-800 for assigned articles. Pays $150-350 for unsolicited articles. Pays the expenses of writers on assignment.
Photos: State availability of photos with submission. Reviews transparencies (3x5). Offers no additional payment for photos accepted with ms. Captions and identification of subjects required. Buys all rights.
Columns/Departments: What's Up (new innovative bar stories), 250-500 words; Ticklers (bar games, jokes, puzzles), 250-500 words; Bottom Line (operation analysis), 500-1,000 words; Behind The Stick (profile of bar owner, manager, bartender), 500-1,000 words. Query. Length: 250-1,000 words. Pays $150-400.
Fillers: Anecdotes, facts, gags to be illustrated by cartoonist and short humor. Length: 250-500 words. Pays $75-200.
Tips: "Write us a query letter with suggestions on good bar establishment stories in your area. These would include profiles, promotions, new drink recipes, etc. Also include your background and two writing samples. Most open to freelancers are features and departments. Writing style is concise, entertaining, as well as informative. This magazine is a trade publication written for bar professionals. It is a trade book, designed like a consumer magazine."

VACATION INDUSTRY REVIEW, Worldex Corp., Box 431920, South Miami FL 33243. (305)667-0202. Managing Editor: George Leposky. 50% freelance written. Prefers to work with published/established writers. A bimonthly magazine covering leisure lodgings (timeshare resorts, RV parks, condo hotels, and other types of vacation ownership properties). Circ. 9,000. Pays on publication. Publishes ms an average of 2-4 months after acceptance. Byline given. Buys all rights and makes work-for-hire assignments. Submit seasonal/holiday material 4 months advance. Photocopied submissions OK. "Electronic submissions preferable-query for details." Computer printout submissions acceptable; prefers letter-quality. Reports in 1 month. Sample copy $1; writer's guidelines with #10 SASE.
Nonfiction: How-to, interview/profile, new product, opinion, personal experience, technical and travel. No consumer travel or non-vacation real-estate material. Buys 15 mss/year. Query with published clips. Length: 1,000-2,500 words. Pays $75-175. Pays the expenses of writers on assignment, if previously arranged.

Photos: Send photos with submission. Reviews contact sheets, 35mm transparencies, and 5x7 prints. Offers no additional payment for photos accepted with ms. Captions and identification of subjects required. Buys one-time rights.

Tips: "We want articles about the business aspect of the vacation industry: entrepreneurship, project financing, design and construction, sales and marketing, operations, management—in short, anything that will help our readers plan, build, sell and run a quality vacation property that satisfies the owners/guests while earning a profit for the proprietor. Our destination pieces are trade-oriented, reporting the status of tourism and the development of various kinds of leisure lodging facilities in a city, region or country. You can discuss things to see and do in the context of a resort located near an attraction, but that shouldn't be the main focus or reason for the article."

————— *Industrial Operations*

Industrial plant managers, executives, distributors and buyers read these journals. Some industrial management journals are also listed under the names of specific industries. Publications for industrial supervisors are listed in Management and Supervision.

APPLIANCE MANUFACTURER, The Magazine for Design for Manufacturing Solutions,, Corcoran Communications, Inc., 6200 Som Center Rd., C-14, Solon OH 44139. (216)349-3060. Editor: Norman C. Remich, Jr. 5% freelance written. A monthly magazine covering design for manufacturing in high-volume automated manufacturing industries. Circ. 35,000. Pays on publication. Publishes ms an average of 3 months after acceptance. Byline given sometimes. Buys all rights. Simultaneous submissions OK. Computer printout submissions acceptable; prefers letter-quality. Reports in 3 weeks. Free sample copy.

Nonfiction: How-to; interview/profile (sometimes); new product; and technical. Buys 12 mss/year. Send complete ms. Length: open. Pays $50/published page. Pays expenses of writers on assignment.

Photos: Captions and identification of subjects required.

Tips: "We are emphasizing the 'design for manufacturing solutions' aspect. It is so important to us, we changed our cover design to feature a more updated look. What the appliance manufacturer wants is solutions to manufacturing problems."

AUTOMATION, (formerly *Production Engineering*), 1100 Superior Ave., Cleveland OH 44114. (216)696-7000. Editor: George Weimer. 50% freelance written. Prefers to work with published/established writers. For "men and women in production engineering—the engineers who plan, design and improve manufacturing operations." Monthly magazine. Circ. 95,000. Pays on publication. Publishes ms an average of 6 months after acceptance. Buys exclusive first North American serial rights. Byline given; "if by prior arrangement, an author contributed a segment of a broader article, he might not be bylined." Phone queries OK. Photocopied submissions OK, if exclusive. Computer printout submissions acceptable; prefers letter-quality. Reports in 2 weeks. Free sample copy and writer's guidelines.

Nonfiction: How-to (engineering, data for engineers); personal experience (from *very* senior production or manufacturing engineers only); and technical (technical news or how-to). "We're interested in solid, hard hitting technical articles on the gut issues of manufacturing. Case histories, but no-fat treatments of manufacturing concepts, innovative manufacturing methods, and state-of-the-art procedures. Our readers also enjoy articles that detail a variety of practical solutions to some specific, everyday manufacturing headache." Buys 2-3 mss/issue. Query. Length: 800-3,000 words. Pays $100-300.

Tips: "All manuscripts must include photos, graphs or other visual elements necessary to the story."

‡CHEMICAL BUSINESS, Schnell Publishing Company, 80 Broad St., New York NY 10004. Editor: J. Robert Warren. Managing Editor: Alan Serchuk. 70% freelance written. A monthly magazine covering chemicals and related process industries such as plastics, paints, some minerals, essential oils, soaps, detergents. Publishes features on the industry, management, financial and (Wall Street) marketing, shipping and storage, labor, engineering, environment, research, international, and company profiles. Circ. 45,000. Pays on acceptance. Publishes ms an average of 3 months after acceptance. Byline given. Offers $100 kill fee. Buys all rights. Call before submitting seasonal/holiday material. Photocopied submissions and previously published book excerpts OK. Computer printout submissions acceptable; prefers letter-quality. Free sample copy and writer's guidelines.

Nonfiction: No broad, general industrial submissions on how-to. Buys 60 mss/year. Query. Length: 2,000-2,500 words. Pays $500 for assigned articles. Pays the expenses of writers on assignment.

Photos: Send photos with submission. Reviews contact sheets, negatives, and 35mm, 70mm ("almost any size") transparencies. No pay for company photos; offers $10-25/photo taken by writer. Model releases required. Buys all rights.

COMPRESSED AIR, 253 E. Washington Ave., Washington NJ 07882. Editor/Publications Manager: S.M. Parkhill. 75% freelance written. Emphasizes applied technology and industrial management subjects for engineers and managers. Monthly magazine. Circ. 145,000. Buys all rights. Publishes ms an average of 3 months after acceptance. Computer printout submissions acceptable; no dot-matrix. Reports in 6 weeks. Free sample copy, editorial schedule; mention *Writer's Market* in request.
Nonfiction: "Articles must be reviewed by experts in the field." Recent articles: "Seeking Perfect Sound" (February 1988) and "Superconductors" (March 1988). Buys 48 mss/year. Query with published clips. Pays negotiable fee. Sometimes pays expenses of writers on assignment.
Photos: State availability of photos in query. Payment for slides, transparencies and glossy prints is included in total purchase price. Captions required. Buys all rights.
Tips: "We are presently looking for freelancers with a track record in industrial/technology/management writing. Editorial schedule is developed in the summer before the publication year and relies heavily on article ideas from contributors. Resume and samples help. Writers with access to authorities preferred; and prefer interviews over library research. The magazine's name doesn't reflect its contents. We suggest writers request sample copies."

CPI PURCHASING, The Magazine About Buying, Cahners Publishing, 275 Washington St., Newton MA 02158. (617)964-3030. Editor: David Erickson. 10% freelance written. A monthly magazine covering the chemical and process industries. Circ. 35,000. Pays on acceptance. Publishes ms an average of 2 months after acceptance. Byline given. Offers 50% kill fee. Buys all rights. Computer printout submissions OK; prefers letter-quality. Sample copy $7.
Nonfiction: "We assign stories, usually on chemical market developments. Our readers are buyers of chemicals and related process equipment. Freelancers should not submit *anything* on spec." Query. Length: 1,000-3,000 words. Pays $300-1,500 for assigned articles. Pays the expenses of writers on assignment.
Photos: State availability of photos.
Tips: "We prefer writers with some background in chemicals or equipment. Houston/Gulf Coast residents are especially welcome, but, please no PR writers."

‡INDUSTRIAL CHEMIST, McGraw-Hill Publications Co.. 1221 Avenue of the Americas, New York NY 10020. (212)512-2783. Editor: Kenneth J. McNaughton. Managing Editor: Stuart Kahan. 30% freelance written. A monthly magazine for bench chemists, managers and supervisors. Articles should be geared to the bench chemist in industry, academia and government. Circ. 45,000. Pays on publication. Byline given. Offers $50-100 kill fee. Buys all rights. Query for electronic submissions. Computer printout submissions OK. Free sample copy and writer's guidelines.
Nonfiction: Interview/profile and technical. Buys 36 mss/year. Query. Length: 800-3,500 words. Pay varies with article. Sometimes pays the expenses of writers on assignment.
Photos: Send photos with submission. Captions, model releases and identification of subjects required. Buys exclusive rights.

INDUSTRIAL FABRIC PRODUCTS REVIEW, Industrial Fabrics Assoc., Suite 450, 345 Cedar Bldg., St. Paul MN 55101. (612)222-2508. Editor: Sue Hagen. Director of Publications: Roger Barr. 10% freelance written. Monthly magazine covering industrial textiles for company owners, salespersons and researchers in a variety of industrial textile areas. Circ. 6,000. Pays on publication. Publishes ms an average of 2 months after acceptance. Byline given. Buys all rights. Submit seasonal/holiday material 4 months in advance. Simultaneous queries, and photocopied and previously published submissions OK. Computer printout submissions acceptable; prefers letter-quality. Reports in 1 month. Sample copy free "after query and phone conversation."
Nonfiction: Technical, marketing and other topics related to any aspect of industrial fabric industry from fiber to finished fabric product. Special issues include new products, industrial products and equipment. No historical or apparel oriented articles. Buys 12 mss/year. Query with phone number. Length: 1,200-3,000 words. Pays $75/published page. Sometimes pays the expenses of writers on assignment.
Photos: State availability of photos. Reviews 8x10 b&w glossy and color prints. Pay is negotiable. Model release and identification of subjects required. Buys one-time rights.
Tips: "We have added to our permanent magazine staff which will reduce the amount of money we spend on freelance material. However we are also trying to encourage freelancers to learn our industry and make regular, solicited contributions to the magazine."

INSULATION OUTLOOK, National Insulation Contractors Association, Suite 410, 1025 Vermont NW, Washington DC 20005. (202)783-6278. Editor: Marcia G. Lawson. 50% freelance written. Prefers to work with published/established writers. Monthly magazine about general business, commercial and industrial insulation for the insulation industry in the United States and abroad. Publication is read by engineers, specifiers, owners, contractors and energy managers in the industrial and commercial insulation field. There is also representative distribution to public utilities, and energy-related industries. Pays on publication. Publishes ms an average of 3-4 months after acceptance. Byline given. Buys first rights only. Phone queries OK. Written queries should be short and simple, with samples of writing attached. Submit seasonal material 6 months in advance. Simultaneous, photocopied and previously published submissions OK. Query for electronic submissions. Computer printout submissions acceptable; no dot-matrix. Sample copy $2; free writer's guidelines. "Give us a call. If there seems to be compatibility, we will send a free issue sample so the writer can see directly the type of publication he or she is dealing with."

Nonfiction: Articles on the technical aspects of insulation; case studies. Also looking for articles on the asbestos abatement industry, specifically targeted for the asbestos abatement contractor. Sometimes pays the expenses of writers on assignment.

Columns/Departments: Query. Pays $50-350.

Tips: "We are looking for articles that are moderately technical in nature."

MANUFACTURING SYSTEMS, The Management Magazine of Integrated Manufacturing, Hitchcock Publishing Co., 25 W 550 Geneva Rd., Wheaton IL 60188. (312)665-1000. Editor: Tom Inglesby. Managing Editor: Mary Emrich. Senior Editor: Fred Miller. 10-15% freelance written. "We are backlogged with submissions and are trying to make room for new/unpublished articles with something important to say." A monthly magazine covering computers/information in manufacturing for upper and middle-level management in manufacturing companies. Circ. 115,000. Pays on acceptance. Publishes ms an average of 2 months after acceptance. Byline given. Offers 35% kill fee on assignments. Buys all rights. Simultaneous and photocopied submissions OK. Query for electronic submissions. Computer printout submissions acceptable; prefers letter-quality. Reports in 4-6 weeks. Sample copy for request.

Nonfiction: Book excerpts, essays, general interest, interview/profile, new product, opinion, technical, case history—applications of system. "Each issue emphasizes some aspect of manufacturing. Editorial schedule available, usually in September, for next year." Buys 6-8 mss/year. Query with or without published clips, or send complete ms. Length: 500-2,500 words. Pays $150-600 for assigned articles; pays $50/published page for unsolicited articles. Sometimes pays limited, pre-authorized expenses of writers on assignment.

Photos: State availability of photos with submission. Reviews contact sheets, negatives, 2x2 and larger transparencies and 5x7 and larger prints. Offers no additional payment for photos accepted with ms. Captions and identification of subjects required. Buys one-time rights.

Columns/Departments: Forum (VIP-to-VIP, bylined by manufacturing executive), 1,000-1,500 words; and Manufacturing Management (consultant's column, bylined by manufacturing consultant), 500-600 words. Buys 1-2 mss/year. Query. 500-1,000 words. Sometimes pays $100-200. "These are *rarely* paid for but we'd consider ghost written pieces bylined by 'name.' "

Fillers: Barbara Dutton, associate editor. Anecdotes, facts and newsbreaks. Buys 3-6/year. Length: 25-100 words. Pays $10-50.

Tips: "We are moving more toward personal management issues and away from technical articles—how to manage, not what tools are available. New trends in manufacturing include application of artifical intelligence (expert systems); standards for comupter systems, networks, operating systems; political (election year!) hype on computer, trends, trade, taxes; movement toward "lights-out" factory (no human workers) in Japan and some U.S. industries; desire to "be like Japanese" in management style; more computer power in smaller boxes. Features are the most open area. We will be happy to provide market information, reader profile and writer's guidelines on request. We are moving to "required" submission in electronic form - Diskett, MCI-mail, Source Mail or Scanable (OCR) copy - Rekeying ms into our word processing system is more work (and cost). "

OCCUPATIONAL HEALTH & SAFETY MAGAZINE, Stevens Publishing, 225 N. New Road, Box 7573, Waco TX 76714. (817)776-9000. Editor: Carol Mouché. Managing Editor: Elizabeth Juden. 10% freelance written. Works with a small number of new/unpublished writers each year. A monthly magazine covering health and safety in the workplace. Circ. 93,000. Pays 2 months after publication. Publishes ms an average of 3 months after acceptance. Byline given. Buys first serial rights and first North American serial rights. Fax queries OK (817)776-9018. Computer printout submissions acceptable. Reports in 1 month on queries, 2 months on mss. Free sample copy with writer's guidelines and editorial calendar for 9x12 SASE.

Nonfiction: How-to (for health/safety professionals); interview/profile. Subjects of interest include OSHA and EPA regulations; Department of Labor statistics; carpal tunnel syndrome; asbestos; interviews with health and safety personnel of interest to general readers; drug testing; stress management. No unsubstantiated material; no advertorials; no columns; no first-person articles. Query editors on specific subjects only. Length 2,000-3,000 words. Payment varies. Sometimes pays the expenses of writers on assignment.

Photos: Reviews contact sheets, negatives, 4x5 transparencies and prints—prefer color. Captions, model releases of subjects required. Will request print dupes for photo files. Works with stock agencies.

Tips: "There is an increasing merger between OSHA and EPA regulations regarding employee health and safety in such areas as hazardous waste cleanup and emergency response. Writers can judge whether their expertise will suit our needs by noting the technical quality of material in our magazine and reviewing the editorial calendar. Prefer writers with scientific or medical experience. Expanding on news events such as drug testing or AIDS in the workplace is also a good source of editorial material. Send resume and clips if looking for an assignment."

PLANT MANAGEMENT & ENGINEERING, Suite 500, 245 Fairview Mall Dr., Willowdale/Ontario, Ontario M2J 4T1 Canada. Editor: Ron Richardson. 10% freelance written. Prefers to work with published/established writers. For Canadian plant managers and engineers. Monthly magazine. Circ. 26,000. Pays on acceptance. Publishes ms an average of 2 months after acceptance. Buys first Canadian rights. Computer printout submissions acceptable; prefers letter-quality. Reports in 3 weeks. Sample copy with SAE only.
Nonfiction: How-to, technical and management technique articles. Must have Canadian slant. No generic articles that appear to be rewritten from textbooks. Buys fewer than 20 unsolicited mss/year. Query. Pays 15¢/word minimum. Sometimes pays the expenses of writers on assignment.
Photos: State availability of photos with query. Pays $25-50 for b&w prints; $50-100 for 2¼x2¼ or 35mm color transparencies. Captions required. Buys one-time rights.
Tips: "Increase emphasis on the use of computers and programmable controls in manufacturing will affect the types of freelance material we buy. Read the magazine. Know the Canadian readers' special needs. Case histories and interviews only—no theoretical pieces. We will probably be buying even less freelance material because of more staff writers."

PURCHASING EXECUTIVE'S BULLETIN, Bureau of Business Practice, 24 Rope Ferry Rd., Waterford CT 06386. (203)442-4365. Editor: Claire Sherman. Managing Editor: Wayne Muller. For purchasing managers and purchasing agents. Semimonthly newsletter. Circ. 5,500. Pays on acceptance. Buys all rights. Submit seasonal/holiday material 3 months in advance. Reports in 2 weeks. Free sample copy and writer's guidelines.
Nonfiction: How-to (better cope with problems confronting purchasing executives); and direct interviews detailing how purchasing has overcome problems and found better ways of handling departments. No derogatory material about a company; no writer's opinions; no training or minority purchasing articles. "We don't want material that's too elementary (things any purchasing executive already knows)." Buys 2-3 mss/issue. Query. Length: 750-1,000 words.
Tips: "Make sure that a release is obtained and attached to a submitted article."

‡PURCHASING WORLD, International Thomson Industrial Press, Inc.. 6521 Davis Industrial Parkway, Solon OH 44139. (216)248-1125. Editor: Edward J. Walter. 10% freelance written. A monthly magazine on industrial purchasing. "The magazine reaches buyers of industrial firms who purchase products for in-plant use as well as for original equipment manufacturing. Articles should focus on management, governmental, environmental and operations topics." Circ. 100,000. Pays on publication. Byline given. Buys first rights. Photocopied submissions OK. Computer printout submissions OK. Reports in 2 weeks on queries; 1 week on mss. Free sample copy.
Nonfiction: Ron Stevens, senior editor. General interest and interview/profile. Buys 18 mss/year. Query. Length: 500-2,500 words. Pays $100-300. Sometimes pays the expenses of writers on assignment.
Photos: State availability of photos with submission. Reviews contact sheets, transparencies (35mm) and prints (5x7). Offers $15-50. Captions, model releases and identification of subjects required. Buys one-time rights.

QUALITY CONTROL SUPERVISOR'S BULLETIN, National Foremen's Institute, 24 Rope Ferry Rd., Waterford CT 06386. (800)243-0876. Editor: Steven J. Finn. 100% freelance written. Biweekly newsletter for quality control supervisors. Pays on acceptance. No byline given. Buys all rights. Computer printout submissions acceptable. Reports in 2 weeks on queries; 1 month on mss. Free sample copy and writer's guidelines.
Nonfiction: Interview and "articles with a strong how-to slant that make use of direct quotes whenever possible." Buys 70 mss/year. Query. Length: 800-1,100 words. Pays 8-14¢/word.
Tips: "Write for our freelancer guidelines and follow them closely. We're looking for steady freelancers we can work with on a regular basis."

‡SAFETY & HEALTH, National Society Council. 444 N. Michigan Ave., Chicago IL 60611. (312)527-4800. Editor: Roy Fisher. Managing Editor: Susan Marie Kelly. A monthly magazine on occupational safety and health. "*Safety & Health* offers practical solutions to current problems, gives information about potential problems and state-of-the-art applications of procedures, processes and innovative equipment and services." Circ. 40,000. Pays on publication. Byline given. Buys first rights and all rights. Submit seasonal/holiday material 5 months in advance. Computer printout submissions OK; prefers letter-quality. Reports in 2 weeks on queries; 1 month on mss. Free sample copy and writer's guidelines.
Nonfiction: Interview/profile, opinion and personal experience. Query. Length: 1,500-3,000 words. Payment negotiable. State availability of photos with submission. Reviews contact sheets. Payment negotiable. Captions, model releases and identification of subjects required. Buys all rights.

Tips: "Government regulations affecting job safety and health, community right-to-know, hazzard communications and emergency response will affect the types of freelance material we buy."

WEIGHING & MEASUREMENT, Key Markets Publishing Co., Box 5867, Rockford IL 61125. (815)399-6970. Editor: David M. Mathieu. For users of industrial scales and meters. Bimonthly magazine. Circ. 15,000. Pays on acceptance. Buys all rights. Pays 20% kill fee. Byline given. Reports in 2 weeks. Free sample copy.
Nonfiction: Interview (with presidents of companies); personal opinion (guest editorials on government involvement in business, etc.); profile (about users of weighing and measurement equipment); and technical. Buys 25 mss/year. Query on technical articles; submit complete ms for general interest material. Length: 750-2,500 words. Pays $100-175.

Information Systems

These publications give computer professionals more data about their field. Consumer computer publications are listed under Personal Computers.

BUSINESS SOFTWARE, For Managers Who Use PCs, M&T Publishing, 501 Galveston Dr., Redwood City CA 94063. (415)366-3600. Editor: Jim Fawcette. Managing Editor: Nancy Beckus. 50% freelance written. "Will work with new writers if technical expertise is there." Monthly magazine covering the business of computers. "We are not geared toward the prepurchasers—the people thinking about getting computers—or those just getting a start in computers. Ours is a *highly sophisticated* audience comprised of people who have been using computers in their businesses for years, who are at the leading edge of what's happening in the world of business computing and who want the leverage computers provide to them." Circ. 60,000. Pays on acceptance. Publishes ms an average of 2-3 months after acceptance. Byline given. Buys first serial rights plus one reprint right. Simultaneous queries and photocopied submissions OK. Query for electronic submissions. Computer printout submissions acceptable; prefers submissions on floppy disk. Reports in 1 month on queries; 2 months on mss. Free sample copy and writer's guidelines.
Nonfiction: Book excerpts; how-to (advanced tutorials on practical software use); opinion (reviews); and technical. No humor, game reviews or articles not related to business. "We would like to receive technical esoteric tips and tricks for software applications." Buys 50-75 mss/year. Query with published clips or send outline. Length: 750-3,500 words. Pays $125-150/published page. Sometimes pays expenses of writers on assignment.
Photos: Send photo with query or outline. Reviews b&w and color contact sheets; payment included in per-page rate. Captions, model release, and identification of subjects required. Buys one-time rights plus one reprint right.
Tips: "Query first, then call after query answered. Timeliness and technical savvy are a must with us. Feature tutorial section always open to freelancers, but note we are an *advanced* user magazine, not interested in novice, prepurchase, or other introductory material. If articles are technically competent, any length is acceptable to us. Frequent mistakes made by writers are not using enough detailed information about the application being discussed, lack of relevance or inability to relate program to business user and lack of photos, display screen, printouts, reports and sidebars. We have an increased focus on databases and accounting software applications."

COMPUTER DEALER, Gordon Publications, Inc., Box 1952, Dover NJ 07801-0952. (201)361-9060. Editor: Tom Farre. 70% freelance written. Eager to work with new/unpublished writers if they know the field. Monthly management and technology magazine for computer resellers, including dealers, VARs, distributors, systems houses, and business equipment dealers. Circ. 45,000. Pays on publication. Publishes ms an average of 3 months after acceptance. Buys all rights. Query for electronic submissions. Computer printout submissions OK; prefers letter-quality. Reports in 2 months.
Nonfiction: Management and business issues; interviews with top computer industry personnel, and technology explication. "Writers must know microcomputer hardware and software and be familiar with computer reselling—our readers are computer-industry professionals in an extremely competitive field." Buys 3-6 mss/issue. Query with published clips. Length: 400-2,000 words. Pays 10-20¢/word. Sometimes pays the expenses of writers on assignment.
Photos: B&w photos preferable.
Columns/Departments: Solicited by editor. "If the writer has an idea, query by mail to the editor, with clips."

‡**COMPUTER RESELLER**, Monthly International Thomson Retail Press, #660, 3550 Wilshire Blvd., Los Angeles CA 90010. (213)383-5800. Executive Editor: Larry Tuck. 60% freelance written. A monthly magazine for computer distributors/dealers. Circ. 45,000. Pays on receipt of invoice. Byline given. Buys first North American serial rights. Submit seasonal/holiday material 3 months in advance. Query for electronic submissions. Computer printout submissions OK. Reports in 1½ months. Sample copy for 9x12 SAE with 5 first class stamps.
Nonfiction: Exposé, general interest, interview/profile and technical. Buys 25-30 mss/year. Query with published clips. Length 500-2,000 words. Pays $100-600. Pays the expenses of writers on assignment.
Photos: Send photos with submission. Reviews prints to 8x10. Payment negotiable. Identification of subjects required. Buys one-time rights.
Columns/Departments: Store Check (computer store mystery shopper), 600 words. Query with published clips. Pays $100-260.
Tips: "Don't send anything without querying first."

COMPUTING CANADA, The Newspaper for Information Processing Management, Plesman Publications Ltd., Suite 110, 255 Consumers Rd., Willowdale, Ontario M2J 5B1 Canada. (416)497-9562. Editor: Gordon Campbell. Managing Editor: Martin Slofstra. 10% freelance written. A biweekly tabloid covering data processing/data communications. Circ. 32,000. Pays on publication. Publishes ms an average of 2 months after acceptance. Byline given. Offers $50 kill fee. Buys first North American serial rights. Submit seasonal/holiday material 2 months in advance. Simultaneous and photocopied submissions OK. Query for electronic submissions. Computer printout submissions acceptable; prefers letter-quality. Reports in 2 weeks on queries; 1 month on mss. Free sample copy and writer's guidelines.
Nonfiction: Opinion, personal experience and technical. Must have special relevance to Canadians. Buys 150 mss/year. Query with published clips. Length: 400-1,500 words. Pays $75-350 (Canadian) for assigned articles; pays $50-300 for unsolicited articles; sometimes trades advertising for consultants ("*very* infrequently"). Sometimes pays the expenses of writers on assignment.
Photos: Send photos with submission. Reviews 5x7 prints. Offers $10/photo. Model releases and identification of subjects required. Buys one-time rights.

‡**DR. DOBB'S JOURNAL, Software Tools for Advanced Programmers**, M&T Publishing, Inc., 501 Galveston Dr., Redwood City CA 94063. (415)366-3600. Editor: Jon Erickson. Managing Editor: Monica Berg. 60% freelance written. Eager to work with new/unpublished writers. Monthly magazine on computer programming. Circ. 60,000. Pays on publication. Publishes ms an average of 9 months after acceptance. Byline given. Buys all rights. Photocopied submissions OK. Query for electronic submissions. Computer printout submissions acceptable; prefers letter-quality. Reports in 1 month on queries; 9 weeks on mss. Writer's guidelines for #10 SASE.
Nonfiction: How-to and technical. Buys 48 mss/year. Send complete ms. Word length open. Pays $75-1,000.
Tips: "We are happy to look at outlines or queries to see if an author is suitable. They may also obtain writer's guidelines."

HP DESIGN & AUTOMATION, Independent Magazine for Hewlett-Packard Technical Computer Users, (formerly *HP Design and Manufacturing*), Wilson Publications, Inc., 12416 Hymeadow Dr., Austin TX 78750. (512)250-5518. Editor: Elaine A. Kaseberg. 40% freelance written. Eager to work with new/unpublished writers. A monthly magazine covering Hewlett-Packard technical computers and instruments. "*HP Design & Automation* contains material covering the use of HP technical computers for an engineering audience. This includes features on current technology issues, HP news, tutorials, reviews and new product announcements. Writers must be technically knowledgeable about their subject. General features must include HP slant." Circ. 15,000. Pays on publication. Publishes ms an between 2-4 months after acceptance. Byline given. Offers negotiable percentage of promised payment as kill fee. Buys first North American serial rights. Photocopied submissions OK. Query for electronic submissions. Computer printout submissions acceptable; prefers letter-quality. Reports in 3 weeks on queries; 5 weeks on mss. Sample copy for 8½x11 SASE.
Nonfiction: How-to (on hardware and software applications), application stories (case studies), opinion, and technical. Submissions must be directly related to HP 1000, 9000, series 80 computers and test instruments. May consider company profiles, in-depth pieces on firms working with HP in new or contemporary technologies and markets. Buys 30 mss/year. Query with outline, with or without published clips. Do not send complete ms. Length: 750-2,500. Pays 10¢/word. Sometimes pays the expenses of writers on assignment.
Photos: State availability of photos with submission. Reviews contact sheets, negatives, transparencies and prints. Captions required.
Tips: "Accepting more pieces that acknowledge the person behind the equipment—targeting more articles to vertical applications, i.e. the use of HP equipment in aerospace, automotive and manufacturing industries. Considering brief (but not 'light') company profiles—1,000-2,000 words, with photos. Writer need not be an engineer or computer scientist, but must have thorough grasp of subject. Accepting more articles concerning industry standards, i.e. UNIX, MAP/TOP, OSI/ISO, MS-DOS/XENIX, etc. Let us know what your expertise

is and how it will make you the right person to cover the proposed topic. Write for the engineer. Tell him/her how to get the most out of hardware/software. Let readers know of unusual uses for equipment. Be technical, but as lively as possible. Don't write in manual style.''

‡ID SYSTEMS, The Magazine of Keyless Data Entry, Helmers Publishing, Inc.. 174 Concord St., Peterborough NH 03458. (603)924-9631. Editor: Russ Adams. Managing Editor: Debra Marshall. 80% freelance written. A magazine about automatic identification technologies, published 10 times/year. Circ. 42,000. Pays at dummy date of issue. Byline given. Buys all rights. Query for electronic submissions. Computer printout submissions OK. Reports in 2 months on queries; 2 weeks on mss. Free sample copy and writer's guidelines.
Nonfiction: Application stories. "We want articles we have assigned, not spec articles." Buys 50/year. Query with published clips. Length: 1,500-1,800 words. Pays $150-300. Sometimes pays the expenses of writers on assignment.
Photos: Send photos with submission. Reviews contact sheets, transparencies (35mm) and prints. Offers no additional payment for photos accepted with ms. Identification of subjects required. Rights vary article to article.
Tips: "Send letter, resume and clips. If background is appropriate, we will contact writer as needed. We give detailed instructions."

IEEE SOFTWARE, IEEE Computer Society, 10662 Los Vagueros Circle, Los Alamitos CA 90720. (714)821-8380. Managing Editor: Angela Burgess. 2% freelance written. Works with a small number of new/unpublished writers each year. A bimonthly magazine on computer software. Circ. 23,500. Pays on publication. "We buy news reports, not feature articles." Publishes ms an average of 1 month after acceptance. Byline given. Offers 25% kill fee. Buys all rights. Simultaneous and photocopied queries OK. Query for electronic submissions. Computer printout submissions OK; prefers letter-quality. Reports in 3 weeks on queries; 5 weeks on mss. Sample copy for 9x12 SAE with 4 first class stamps; writer's guidelines for #10 SAE with 1 first class stamp.
Nonfiction: Interview/profile and technical. "Our news articles show how the technology is being applied and how it affects people. Examples: costs of new languages, problems in SDI software, copyright law, changes in ways of doing things." Buys 10-12 mss/year. Query with published clips. Length: 300-2,000 words. Pays $100-500 for assigned news reports. Sometimes pays the expenses of writers on assignment.
Photos: State availability of photos with submission. Reviews contact sheets. Offers $25-50 per photo. Captions and identification of subjects required. Buys one-time rights.
Tips: "The approach is to pitch an idea. If the idea is good, there's a good chance (budget allowing) a story will follow. Be concise and direct."

JOURNAL OF SYSTEMS MANAGEMENT, 24587 Bagley Road, Cleveland OH 44138. (216)243-6900. Publisher: James Andrews. 100% freelance written. Prefers to work with published/established writers; works with a small number of new/unpublished writers each year. Monthly. For systems and procedures and management people. Pays on publication. Publishes ms an average of 3 months after acceptance. Byline given. Buys all rights. Computer printout submissions acceptable; prefers letter-quality. Reports "as soon as possible." Free sample copy.
Nonfiction: Articles on case histories, projects on systems, forms control, administrative practices and computer operations. No computer applications articles, humor or articles promoting a specific product. Query or submit ms in triplicate. Length: 3,000-5,000 words. Pays $25 maximum.
Tips: "Frequent mistakes made by writers are choosing the wrong subject and being too specific regarding a product."

MICRO CORNUCOPIA, The Micro Technical Journal, Micro Cornucopia Inc., 155 NW Hawthorne, Bend OR 97701. (503)382-8048. Editor: David J. Thompson. A bimonthly magazine offering in-depth technical coverage of micro computers. Circ. 20,000. Pays on publication. Publishes ms an average of 2 months after acceptance. Byline given. Offers $25 kill fee. Buys first rights. Submit seasonal/holiday material 3 months in advance. Query for electronic submissions. Computer printout submissions acceptable; prefers letter-quality. Reports in 1 month on queries; 2 months on mss. Sample copy $3.95; free writer's guidelines.
Nonfiction: Cary Gatton, articles editor. How-to (published article examples—How to write a PROLOG interpreter, How to build a 68000 computer); new product; personal experience and technical. Buys 60 mss/year. Query with or without published clips, or send complete ms. Length: 2,000-5,000 words. Pays $150 minimum for assigned articles; pays $25 minimum for unsolicited articles. May pay other premiums in addition to fee.
Photos: State availability of photos with submission. Offers no additional payment for photos accepted with ms. Buys one-time rights.
Tips: "Most successful authors are computer engineers or desigers. *Micro Cornucopia* continues to be a technical journal which supports computer hardware and software engineers, designers, instructors, and students. Our articles include theoretical topics and practical projects."

‡**NETWORK WORLD**, C W Communications, Inc., Box 9171, 375 Cochituate Rd., Framingham MA 01701. (617)879-0700. Editor: Bruce Hoard. Features Editor: Steve Moore. 20% freelance written. A weekly tabloid covering data, voice and video communications networks (including news and features on communications management, hardware and software, services, education, technology and industry trends) for senior technical managers at large companies. Circ. 70,000. Pays on acceptance. Byline given. Offers negotiable kill fee. Buys all rights. Submit seasonal/holiday material 2 months in advance. Query for electronic submissions. Computer printout submissions acceptable; prefers letter-quality. Reports in 1 month. Free sample copy and writer's guidelines.

Nonfiction: Exposé; general interest; how-to (build a strong communications staff, evaluate vendors, choose a value-added network service); humor; interview/profile; new product; opinion; and technical. Editorial calender available. "Our readers are users: avoid vendor-oriented material." Buys 30-50 mss/year. Query with published clips. Length: 500-2,500 words. Pays $300 minimum-negotiable maximum for assigned or unsolicited articles.

Photos: Send photos with submission. Reviews 35mm, 2¼ and 4x5 transparencies and b&w prints (prefers 8x10 but can use 5x7). Captions, model releases and identification of subjects required. Buys one-time rights.

Fiction: Adventure, humorous, mainstream, slice-of-life vignettes and suspense. "We want literate, technically correct stories that entertain while illustrating an issue, problem or trend that affects our readership. No obtrusive styles or 'purple prose'." Buys 4-5 mss/year. Query with published clips. Length: 500-1,500 words. Pays $300 minimum-negotiable maximum.

Tips: "Exclusive stories about the first users of new communications products or services have the best chance of being published. We look for accessible treatments of technology. It's OK to dig into technical issues as long as the article doesn't read like an engineering document. Feature section is most open to freelancers. Be informative, stimulating, controversial and technically accurate."

OA MAGAZINE, Plesman Publications Ltd., Suite 110, 255 Consumers Rd., Willowdale, Ontario M2J 5B1 Canada. (416)497-9562 or 1-800-387-5012. Editor: Gordon Campbell. Managing Editor: Arlene Waite. 75% freelance written. Works with a small number of new/unpublished writers each year. A monthly magazine covering business management and computer applications. "Stories about managing technology and people effectively, with a Canadian and end-user focus." Circ. 51,000. Pays 1 month after acceptance. Publishes ms an average of 2 months after acceptance. Byline given. Buys first North American serial rights and other rights. Submit seasonal/holiday material 2 months in advance. Photocopied and previously published submissions sometimes OK. Query for electronic submissions. Computer printout submissions acceptable; no dot-matrix. Reports in 2 weeks. Sample copy for 9x12 SAE with 4 first class Canadian stamps; writer's guidelines for #10 SAE with 1 first class Canadian stamp.

Nonfiction: Book excerpts, essays, exposé, general interest, how-to (on business computer applications for business), humor, inspirational, interview/profile, new product, opinion, personal experience, photo feature and technical. "No articles lacking 'hard' facts, 'realistic understanding of business' or articles full of advice, non-attributed quotes, etc." Buys 60 mss/year. Query with published clips, resume, or send complete ms. Length: 1,600-2,500 words. Pays $0-350; up to $1,000 for cover story (with photos). Sometimes pays the expenses of writers on assignment.

Photos: State availability of color slides with submission; send color slides with submission. Reviews 4x5 transparencies (for covers), and color slides. Offers $0-500/photo. Captions, model releases, and identification of subjects required. Buys one-time rights and other rights.

Columns/Departments: Compleat Manager (humorous, oratorical, analytical, podium); Quarterly Report (legal, finance/accounting, management consulting); and Micro Manager (end-user computing within corporations). Buys 12 mss/year. Query with or without published clips or send complete ms. Length: 800-1,200 words.

Tips: "Send a resume outlining education and experience, especially business and writing education/experience. We are looking for professional writers interested in realistic, humane stories about people and their changing offices in Canada. Vendor hype or generalities are not wanted."

UNIX WORLD, Multiuser Multitasking Systems, Tech Valley Publishing, 444 Castro St., Mountain View CA 94041. (415)940-1500. Editor-in-Chief: David L. Flack. 75% freelance written. Prefers to work with established writers or experts in the computer industry. Monthly magazine directed exclusively to the multiuser, multitasking computer industry. Readers are employed in management, engineering, and software development. Circ. 32,000. Pays 1 month after publication. Publishes ms an average of 4 months after acceptance. Byline given. Offers kill fee. Buys first North American serial rights and second (reprint) rights. Query for electronic submissions. Computer printout submissions acceptable ("as last resort"); prefers letter-quality. Reports in 1 month. Sample copy $3. Writer's guidelines sent when article is accepted on spec. Ask for editorial calendar so query can be tailored to the magazine's need; send SASE with 2 first class stamps.

Nonfiction: Book excerpts; how-to (technical articles on the Unix system or the C language); new products; technical overviews; and product reviews. Perspectives is a 3,000-word feature on a timely technical issue, bylines by an industry expert. Query by phone or with cover letter and published clips. Length: 2,500-3,000 words. Pays $100-1,000. Sometimes pays the expenses of writers on assignment.

Photos: Send photos with queries. Reviews b&w contact sheets. Identification of subjects required. Buys all rights.

Columns/Departments: Publishes two guest columns—one column on standards and a guest column that exposes a controversial viewpoint. Query by phone. Other columns are regular departments written by contributing editors.

Tips: "We are shifting more toward a business and commercial focus and would appreciate knowledge in that area. The best way to get an acceptance on an article is to consult our editorial calendar and tailor a pitch to a particular story."

Insurance

COMPASS, Marine Office of America Corporation (MOAC), 180 Maiden Lane, New York NY 10038. (212)440-7719. Editor: John H. Bierwirth. 85% freelance written. Prefers to work with published/established writers. Semiannual magazine of the Marine Office of America Corporation. Magazine is distributed in the U.S. and overseas to persons in marine insurance (agents, brokers, risk managers), government authorities and employees. Circ. 8,000. Pays half on acceptance, half on publication. Publishes ms an average of 6 months after acceptance. Byline given. Offers $750 kill fee on manuscripts accepted for publication, but subsequently cancelled. Offers $250 kill fee on solicited ms rejected for publication. Not copyrighted. Buys first North American serial rights. Does not accept previously published work, unsolicited mss or works of fiction. Query first. Simultaneous queries OK. Query for electronic submissions. Computer printout submissions acceptable; no dot-matrix. Reports in 1 month on queries. Free sample copy and writer's guidelines.

Nonfiction: General interest, historical/nostalgic and technical. U.S. or overseas locale. "Historical/nostalgia should relate to ships, trains, airplanes, balloons, bridges, sea and land expeditions, marine archeology, seaports and transportation of all types. General interest includes marine and transportation subjects; fishing industry; farming; outdoor occupations; environmental topics such as dams, irrigation projects, water conservation, inland waterways; space travel and satellites. Articles must have human interest. Technical articles may cover energy exploration and development—offshore oil and gas drilling, developing new sources of electric power and solar energy; usages of coal, water and wind to generate electric power; special cargo handling such as containerization on land and sea; salvage; shipbuilding; bridge or tunnel construction. Articles must not be overly technical and should have strong reader interest." No book excerpts, first-person, exposes, how-to, or opinion. Buys 8 mss/year. Query with published clips. Length: 1,500-2,000 words. Pays $1,500 maximum. Sometimes pays the expenses of writers on assignment.

Photos: Robert A. Cooney, photo editor. (212)995-8001. State availability of photos. Reviews b&w and color transparencies and prints. Captions and identification of subjects required. Buys one-time rights.

Tips: "We want profiles of individuals connected with marine, energy, and transportation fields who are unusual. Send a brief outline of the story idea to editor mentioning also the availability of photographs in b&w and color. All articles must be thoroughly researched and original. Articles should have human interest through the device of interviews. We only publish full-length articles—no fillers."

INSURANCE REVIEW, Insurance Information Institute, 110 William St., New York NY 10038. (212)669-9200. Editor: Olga Badillo-Sciortino. Managing Editor: Kenneth M. Coughlin. 100% freelance written. A monthly magazine covering property and casualty insurance for agents, brokers, insurers, educators, lawyers, financial analysts and journalists. Circ. 70,000. Pays on acceptance. Publishes ms an average of 2 months after acceptance. Byline given. Offers 25% kill fee. Buys first North American serial rights; rights returned to author 90 days after publication. "We retain right to reprint." Query for electronic submissions. Reports in 1 month. Free sample copy and writer's guidelines.

Nonfiction: How-to (improve agency business), interview/profile, opinion, photo feature, technical and business articles with insurance information. Buys 180 mss/year. Query with published clips. Length: 750-2,500 words. Pays $250-1,000 for assigned articles. Pays expenses of writers on assignment.

Photos: Send photos with submission. Reviews contact sheets and transparencies. Captions, model releases and identification of subjects required.

Columns/Departments: By Line (analysis of one line of business p/c), Analysis (financial aspects of p/c industry). Query. Length: 750-1,200 words. Pays $200-350.

Fillers: Facts, gags to be illustrated by cartoonist and newsbreaks. Buys 50/year. Length: 75-200 words. Pays $25-100.

Tips: "Become well-versed in issues facing the insurance industry. Find interesting people to write about. Profile successful agents or brokers."

INSURANCE SOFTWARE REVIEW, International Computer Programs, Inc., Suite 200, 9100 Keystone Crossing, Indianapolis IN 46240. (317)844-7461. Editor: Marilyn Gasaway. 50% freelance written. Quarterly magazine covering the computer software industry as it relates to insurance companies and large agencies. "Editorial slant includes the selection, implementation and use of software in insurance companies, agencies, and brokerages. Audience comprises data processing and end-user management in medium to large insurance concerns." Circ. 15,000. Pays on publication. Publishes ms an average of 2 months after acceptance. Byline sometimes given. Buys first and second serial (reprint) rights. Photocopied submissions OK. Query for electronic submissions. Computer printout submissions OK; prefers letter-quality. Reports in 2 weeks on queries; 3 weeks on mss. Free sample copy and writer's guidelines.

Nonfiction: How to (successfully install and use software products), interview/profile, new product and technical. No non-software related, non-business software or humorous articles. Buys 8-10 mss/year. Query with published clips. Length: 1,000-2,000 words. Pays $100-350 for assigned articles. Sometimes pays the expenses of writers on assignment.

Photos: Send photos with submission. Prefers 5x7 prints. Offers no additional payment for photos accepted with ms. Identification of subjects required. Buys all rights.

Columns/Departments: Systems Review (in-depth profile of a specific software product at use in an insurance environment; must include comments from 2-3 insurance users [e.g., the benefits of the product, its use within the insurance firm, etc.]). Length: 500-700 words. Pays $50.

International Affairs

These publications cover global relations, international trade, economic analysis and philosophy for business executives and government officials involved in foreign affairs. Publications for the general public on related subjects appear in Consumer Politics and World Affairs.

‡DEFENSE & FOREIGN AFFAIRS, International Media, Suite 307, 110 North Royal Street, Alexandria VA 22314. (703)684-8455. Group Editor: Michael C. Dunn. Managing Editor: Julie Ackerman. 75% freelance written. A monthly magazine on defense, strategy and international affairs. Circ. 9,000. Pays within 1 month after publication. Publishes ms an average of 1 month after acceptance. Byline given. Buys all rights. Photocopied submissions OK. Query for electronic submissions. Computer printout submissions OK; prefers letter-quality. Reports in 1 week.

Nonfiction: Interview/profile, new product, photo feature, technical. Buys 40 mss/year. Query with or without published clips, or send complete ms. Length: 1,500-3,000 words. Pays $150-300. Sometimes pays expense of writers on assignment.

Photos: State availability of photos with submission. Reviews negatives, transparencies and prints. Offers no additionl payment for photo accepted with ms. Indentification of subjects required. Buys one-time rights.

Columns/Departments: Current estimates: country surveys (political forecasts/assessments, etc.). Length: 1,500 words. Pays $150.

FOREIGN AFFAIRS, 58 E. 68th St., New York NY 10021. (212)734-0400. Editor: William G. Hyland. 100% freelance written. For academics, businessmen (national and international), government, educational and cultural readers especially interested in international affairs of a political nature. Published 5 times/year. Circ. 90,000. Pays on publication. Publishes ms an average of 3 months after acceptance. Buys all rights. Pays kill fee. Byline given. Photocopied submissions OK. Query for electronic submissions. Computer printout submissions acceptable; prefers letter-quality. Reports in 6 weeks. Submit complete ms.

Nonfiction: "Articles dealing with international affairs; political, educational, cultural, economic, scientific, philosophical and social sciences. Develop an original idea in depth, with a strong thesis usually leading to policy recommendations. Serious analyses by qualified authors on subjects with international appeal." Recent article example: "The President's Choice: Star Wars or Arms Control" (Winter 1984/85). Buys 25 unsolicited mss/year. Submit complete ms. Length: 5,000 words. Pays approximately $500.

Tips: "We like the writer to include his/her qualifications for writing on the topic in question (educational, past publications, relevant positions or honors), and a clear summation of the article: the argument (or area examined), and the writer's policy conclusions."

JOURNAL OF DEFENSE & DIPLOMACY, Defense and Diplomacy, Inc., Suite 200, 6849 Old Dominion Dr., MacLean VA 22101. (703)448-1338. Editor: Alan Capps. 50% freelance written. Eager to work with new/unpublished writers. "Publication credentials not necessary for consideration." Monthly publication covering international affairs and defense. "The *Journal* is a sophisticated, slick publication that analyzes international affairs for decision-makers—heads of state, key government officials, defense industry executives—who have little time to pore through all the details themselves." Circ. 20,000. Pays on publication.

Publishes ms an average of 2 months after acceptance. Byline given. Offers 10% kill fee. Buys first rights and second serial (reprint) rights. Simultaneous queries, and simultaneous, photocopied, and previously published submissions OK. Computer printout submissions acceptable; prefers letter-quality. Reports in 1 month on queries; 2 months on mss. Sample copy $5 (includes postage); writer's guidelines for #10 envelope and 1 first class stamp.

Nonfiction: Book excerpts, general interest (strategy and tactics, diplomacy and defense matters), interview/profile, opinion and photo feature. "Decision-makers are looking for intelligent, straightforward assessments. We want clear, concise writing on articles with international appeal. While we have accepted articles that deal with U.S. decisions, there is always an international aspect to the subject." No articles that focus solely on the United States. Buys 24 mss/year. Send complete ms. Length: 2,000-4,000 words. Pays $250.

Photos: Reviews color and b&w photos. No additional payment is offered for photos sent with ms.

Columns/Departments: Speaking Out (1,000 to 3,000-word "point of view" piece analyzing any current topic of widespread interest); Materiel (a technical discussion of current and upcoming weapons systems); Books (reviews of books on world politics, history, biography and military matters); interview ("We constantly need interviews with important international figures. We are always looking for the non-U.S. interview."). Buys 12 mss/year. Query with published clips. Length: 1,500-3,000 words. Pays $100-250.

Tips: "We depend on experts in the field for most of the articles that we use. As long as a manuscript demonstrates that the writer knows the subject well, we are willing to consider anyone for publication. The most frequent mistake made by writers in completing an article for us is writing in too technical or too official a style. We want to be very readable. We are looking for writers who are able to digest complex subjects and make them interesting and lively. We need writers who can discuss complicated and technical weapons systems in clear non-technical ways."

Jewelry

AMERICAN JEWELRY MANUFACTURER, 8th Floor, 825 7th Ave., New York NY 10019. (212)245-7555. Editor: Steffan Aletti. 5% freelance written. Works with a small number of new/unpublished writers each year. For jewelry manufacturers, as well as manufacturers of supplies and tools for the jewelry industry; their representatives, wholesalers and agencies. Monthly. Circ. 5,000. Buys all rights (with exceptions). Publishes ms an average of 5 months after acceptance. Byline given. Photocopied submissions OK. Computer printout submissions acceptable; prefers letter-quality. Submit seasonal/holiday material 3 months in advance. Reports in 1 month. Free sample copy and writer's guidelines.

Nonfiction: "Topical articles on manufacturing; company stories; economics (e.g., rising gold prices). Story must inform or educate the manufacturer. Occasional special issues on timely topics, e.g., gold; occasional issues on specific processes in casting and plating. We reject material that is not specifically pointed at our industry; e.g., articles geared to jewelry retailing or merchandising, not to manufacturers." Informational, how-to, interview, profile, historical, expose, successful business operations, new product, merchandising techniques and technical. "The most frequent mistake made by writers in completing an article for us is unfamiliarity with the magazine—retail or merchandising oriented articles are sent in. Query first; we have accepted some general business articles, but not many." Buys 5-10 unsolicited mss/year. Length: open. Payment "usually around $50/printed page." Sometimes pays the expenses of writers on assignment.

Photos: B&w photos purchased with ms. 5x7 minimum.

Tips: "We plan no changes in focus, but we are sensitive to any trends—precious metal prices or availability, new federal tax or pollution laws—that affect the manufacturer's operations."

CANADIAN JEWELLER, 777 Bay St., Toronto, Ontario M5W 1A7 Canada. Editor: Simon Hally. Monthly magazine for members of the jewelry trade, primarily retailers. Circ. 7,500. Pays on acceptance. Buys first Canadian serial rights.

Nonfiction: Wants "stories on the jewelry industry internationally." Query. Length: 200-2,000 words. Pays $40-500 (Canadian).

Photos: Reviews 5x7 and 8x10 b&w prints and 35mm and 2¼x2¼ color transparencies. "We pay more if usable photos accompany ms. Payment is based on space used in the book including both text and photos."

THE DIAMOND REGISTRY BULLETIN, 30 W. 47th St., New York NY 10036. Editor-in-Chief: Joseph Schlussel. 15% freelance written. Monthly newsletter. Pays on publication. Buys all rights. Submit seasonal/holiday material 1 month in advance. Simultaneous and previously published submissions OK. Computer printout submissions acceptable; prefers letter-quality. Reports in 3 weeks. Sample copy $5.

Nonfiction: Prevention advice (on crimes against jewelers); how-to (ways to increase sales in diamonds, improve security, etc.); and interview (of interest to diamond dealers or jewelers). Submit complete ms. Length: 50-500 words. Pays $10-150.

Tips: "We seek ideas to increase sales of diamonds."

THE ENGRAVERS JOURNAL, Box 318, 26 Summit St., Brighton MI 48116. (313)229-5725. Co-Publisher and Managing Editor: Michael J. Davis. 15% freelance written. "We are eager to work with published/established writers as well as new/unpublished writers." A bimonthly magazine covering the recognition and identification industry (engraving, marking devices, awards, jewelry, and signage.) "We provide practical information for the education and advancement of our readers, mainly retail business owners." Pays on acceptance. Publishes ms an average of 1 year after acceptance. Byline given "only if writer is recognized authority." Buys all rights (usually). Query with published clips and resume. Photocopied and previously published submissions OK. Query for electronic submissions. Computer printout submissions acceptable; prefers letter-quality. Reports in 2 weeks. Free writer's guidelines; sample copy to "those who send writing samples with inquiry."
Nonfiction: General interest (industry-related); how-to (small business subjects, increase sales, develop new markets, use new sales techniques, etc.); interview/profile; new product; photo feature (a particularly outstanding signage system); and technical. No general overviews of the industry. Buys 12 mss/year. Query with writing samples "published or not," or "send samples and resume to be considered for assignments on speculation." Length: 1,000-5,000 words. Pays $75-250, depending on writer's skill and expertise in handling subject.
Photos: Send photos with query. Reviews 8x10 prints. Pays variable rate. Captions, model release and identifiction of subjects required.
Tips: "Articles should always be down to earth, practical and thoroughly cover the subject with authority. We do not want the 'textbook' writing approach, vagueness, or theory—our readers look to us for sound practical information."

FASHION ACCESSORIES, S.C.M. Publications, Inc., 65 W. Main St., Bergenfield NJ 07621-1696. (201)384-3336. Managing Editor: Samuel Mendelson. Monthly newspaper covering costumes or fashion jewelry. "Serves the manufacturers, manufacturers' sales reps., importers and exporters who sell exclusively through the wholesale level in ladies' fashion jewlery, mens' jewelry, gifts and boutiques and related novelties." Circ. 8,000. Pays on acceptance. Byline given. Not copyrighted. Buys first rights. Submit seasonal/holiday material 3 months in advance. Photocopied submissions OK. Computer printout submissions OK; no dot-matrix. Sample copy $2.
Nonfiction: Essays, general interest, historical/nostalgic, how-to, humor, interview/profile, new product and travel. Buys 20 mss/year. Query with published clips. Length: 1,000-2,000 words. Pays $100-300. Sometimes pays the expenses of writers on assignment.
Photos: /Send photos with submission. Reviews 4x5 prints. Offers no additional payment for photos accepted with ms. Identification of subjects required. Buys one-time rights.
Columns/Departments: Fashion Report (interviews and reports of fashion news), 1,000-2,000 words.
Tips: "We are interested in anything that will be of interest to costume jewelry buyers at the wholesale level."

WATCH AND CLOCK REVIEW, 2403 Champa St., Denver CO 80205. (303)296-1600. Managing Editor: Jayne L. Barrick. 20% freelance written. The magazine of watch/clock sales and service. Monthly magazine. Circ. 14,000. Pays on publication. Buys first rights only. Byline given. Submit seasonal/holiday material 3 months in advance. Reports in 3 weeks. Sample copy for 8½x11 SAE and $1.25.
Nonfiction: Articles on successful watch/clock manufacturers and retailers, merchandising and display, and profiles of industry leaders. Buys 15 mss/year. Query. Length: 1,000-2,000 words. Pays $100-250.
Photos: Submit photo material with accompanying ms. No additional payment for b&w glossy prints. Captions preferred; model release required. Buys first serial rights.
Columns/Departments: Buys 7 mss/issue. Pays $150-200. Open to suggestions for new columns/departments.
Tips: "Brevity is helpful in a query. Find the right subject—an interesting clock shop, a jewelry store with unique watch displays, a street clock of antiquarian interest, etc."

❝ *The joy comes when some little gem pops up when you least expect it (it needs no editing) and our readers respond with the same appreciation after it's published.* **❞**

—*Marian Studer,*
Arabian Horse Times

Journalism and Writing

Journalism and writing magazines cover both the business and creative side of writing. Writing publications offer inspiration and support for professional and beginning writers. Although there are many valuable writing publications that do not pay, we only have space to list those writing publications that pay for articles.

THE AMERICAN SCREENWRITER, Grasshopper Productions, Inc., Box 67, Manchaca TX 78652. (512)282-2749. Editor: Gerald J. LePage. 40% freelance written. Eager to work with new/unpublished writers. A bimonthly newsletter covering scriptwriting for the screen and TV. "We address scriptwriters who ask for help through our script evaluation program. We aim at writers who are struggling to find their place in the market." Pays by arrangement with author. Foreign publication residuals guaranteed. Publishes ms an average of 2 months after acceptance. Byline given. Buys all rights. Submit seasonal/holiday material 2 months in advance. Simultaneous queries OK. Reports in 1 month. Sample copy $3; writer's guidelines for #10 SAE and 1 first class stamp.
Nonfiction: Book excerpts, interview/profile, and personal experience related to scriptwriting. "No sophisticated material that oozes of past films which require reader having seen them." Query with published clips. Length: 300-500 words. Pays 5-10¢/word; interviews *flat pay* $30-50. *Word pay* scale increases with repeated submisssions.
Tips: "We welcome journalists with screenwriter interview material. We want 'visual' writing—short, comprehensive articles that bring home a problematical point in less than five minute's reading. *Suggest writers study publication.*"

BOOK DEALERS WORLD, American Bookdealers Exchange, Box 2525, La Mesa CA 92041. (619)462-3297. Editorial Director: Al Galasso. Senior Editor: Judy Wiggins. 50% freelance written. Quarterly magazine covering writing, self-publishing and marketing books by mail. Circ. 20,000. Pays on publication. Publishes ms an average of 3 months after acceptance. Byline given. Buys first serial rights and second serial (reprint) rights to material originally published elsewhere. Simultaneous and previously published submissions OK. Computer printout submissions acceptable; no dot-matrix. Reports in 1 month. Sample copy for $1.
Nonfiction: Book excerpts (writing, mail order, direct mail, publishing); how-to (home business by mail, advertising); and interview/profile (of successful self-publishers). Positive articles on self-publishing, new writing angles, marketing, etc. Buys 10 mss/year. Send complete ms. Length: 1,000-1,500 words. Pays $25-50.
Columns/Departments: Print Perspective (about new magazines and newsletters); Small Press Scene (news about small press activities); and Self-Publisher Profile (on successful self-publishers and their marketing strategy). Buys 20 mss/year. Send complete ms. Length: 250-1,000 words. Pays $5-20.
Fillers: Clippings. Fillers concerning writing, publishing or books. Buys 6/year. Length: 100-250 words. Pays $3-10.
Tips: "Query first. Get a sample copy of the magazine."

BRILLIANT IDEAS FOR PUBLISHERS, Creative Brilliance Associates, 4709 Sherwood Rd., Box 4237, Madison WI 53711. (608)271-6867. Editor: Naomi K. Shapiro. 3% freelance written. A bimonthly magazine covering the newspaper and shopper industry. "We provide business news and ideas to publishers of the daily, weekly, community, surburban newspaper and shopper publishing industry." Circ. 17,000. Pays on publication. Publishes ms an average of 4 months after acceptance. Byline given. Buys all rights. Photocopied submissions OK. Query for electronic submissions. Computer printout submissions OK; no dot-matrix. Reports in 3 weeks. Sample copy for 9x12 SAE with 5 first class stamps.
Nonfiction: General interest, historical/nostalgic, how-to (tips and hints regarding editorial, production, etc.), humor, interview/profile, new product and opinion. *Only submit articles related to the newspaper industry*, i.e., sales, marketing or management. "The writer has to know and understand the industry." Buys 3 mss/year. Query. Length: 300 words maximum. Pays $10-50 for unsolicited articles. May pay writers with contributor copies or other premiums if writer requests.
Photos: State availability of photos with submission. Offers no additional payment for photos accepted with ms. Captions, model releases and identification of subjects required. Buys all rights.
Columns/Departments: "Any books or brochures related to sales, marketing, management, etc. can be submitted for consideration for our BIFP Press department." Buys 3 mss/year. Query. Length: 200 words maximum. Pays $10-50.
Tips: "We are interested in working with any writer or researcher who has good, solid, documented pieces of interest to this specific industry."

BYLINE, Box 130596, Edmond OK 73013. (405)348-3325. Executive Editor/Publisher: Marcia Preston. Managing Editor: Kathryn Fanning. 80-90% freelance written. Eager to work with new/unpublished writers. Monthly magazine for writers and poets. "We stress encouragement of beginning writers." Publishes ms an average of 6 months after acceptance. Byline given. Buys first North American serial rights. Computer print-out submissions OK; prefers letter-quality. Reports within 1 month. Sample copy $3; writer's guidelines for #10 SASE.

Nonfiction: How-to, humor, inspirational, personal experience, *all* connected with writing and selling. Read magazine for special departments. Buys approximately 72 mss/year. Prefers queries; will read complete mss. Length: 1,500-2,000 words. Usual rate for features is $50, on acceptance.

Fiction: General fiction. Writing or literary slant preferred, but not required. Send complete ms: 1,000-3,000 words. Pays $50 on acceptance.

Poetry: Any style, on a writing theme. Preferred length: 4-36 lines. Pays $3-5 on publication plus free issue.

CANADIAN AUTHOR & BOOKMAN, Canadian Authors Association, Suite 104, 121 Avenue Rd., Toronto, Ontario M5R 2G3 Canada. Contact: Editor. 95% freelance written. Prefers to work with published/established writers. "For writers—all ages, all levels of experience." Quarterly magazine. Circ. 3,000. Pays on publication. Publishes ms an average of 6 months after acceptance. Buys first Canadian rights. Byline given. Written queries only. Computer printout submissions acceptable; prefers letter-quality. Sample copy for $4.50, 9x12 SAE with IRCs or Canadian stamps only.

Nonfiction: How-to (on writing, selling; the specifics of the different genres—what they are and how to write them); informational (the writing scene—who's who and what's what); interview (on writers, mainly leading ones, but also those with a story that can help others write and sell more often); and opinion. No personal, light-weight writing experiences; no fillers. Query with immediate pinpointing of topic, length (if ms is ready), and writer's background. Length: 800-1,500 words. Pays $25/printed page.

Photos: "We're after an interesting-looking magazine, and graphics are a decided help." State availability of photos with query. Offers $5/photo for b&w photos accepted with ms. Buys one-time rights.

Poetry: High quality. "Major poets publish with us—others need to be as good." Buys 40 poems/year. Pays $10.

Tips: "We dislike material that condescends to its reader and articles that advocate an adversarial approach to writer/editor relationships. We agree that there is a time and place for such an approach, but good sense should prevail. If the writer is writing to a Canadian freelance writer, the work will likely fall within our range of interest."

CANADIAN WRITER'S JOURNAL, Ronald J. Cooke Ltd., 58 Madsen Ave., Beaconsfield, Quebec H9W 4T7 Canada. (514)630-4413. Editor: Ronald S. Cooke. 50% freelance written. Works with a small number of new/unpublished writers each year, and is eager to work with new/unpublished writers. "We will accept well-written articles for and by young or experienced writers." A bimonthly digest-size magazine for writers. Circ. 3,000. Pays on publication. Publishes ms an average of 2-4 months after acceptance. Byline given. Buys one-time rights. "We seldom use anything pertaining to holidays." Computer printout submissions acceptable. Reports in 2 weeks on queries; 1 month on mss. Sample copy for $3 and 5x7 SAE with $1 postage (Canadian) or IRC.

Nonfiction: How-to articles for writers. Buys 30-35 mss/year. Query. Length: 500-1,000 words. "Would welcome an article on writing plays." Pays up to $15.

Tips: "We prefer short, how-to articles; 1,000 words is our limit and we prefer 700 words. U.S. writers should be advised that U.S. postage cannot be used from Canada and is therefore wasted. Two or more quarters taped to a cardboard piece can be used to buy postage here."

‡CHRISTIAN WRITERS NEWSLETTER, Box 8220, Knoxville TN 37996-4800. Editor: David E. Sumner. Managing Editor: David Lovett. 50% freelance written. A bimonthly newsletter for Christian writers. "The purpose of the newsletter is to provide inspiration, information, and education for Christian writers. Articles should enable writers to do their best, to do it more quickly, or more efficiently." Circ. 400. Pays on acceptance. No previously published submissions. Computer printout submissions acceptable. Reports in 2 weeks on queries; 1 month on mss. Sample copy for $1; writer's guidelines for SASE.

Nonfiction: Short inspirational and how-to. Length: 500 words maximum. Pays up to $20. Also accepts anecdotes and humor. Pays $5.

Tips: "Articles and queries should go to the editor. Requests for sample copies, guidelines or subscriptions should go to the managing editor."

COLUMBIA JOURNALISM REVIEW, 700 Journalism Bldg., Columbia University, New York NY 10027. (212)280-5595. Managing Editor: Gloria Cooper. "We welcome queries concerning media issues and performance. *CJR* also publishes book reviews. We emphasize in-depth reporting, critical analysis and good writing. All queries are read by editors."

‡THE COMICS JOURNAL, THE Magazine of News and Criticism, Fantagraphics, Inc., 4359 Cornell Rd., Agoura CA 91301. (818)706-7606. Editor: Gary G. Groth. Managing Editor: Thomas J. Heintjes. 90% freelance written. A monthly magazine covering the comic book industry. "Comic books can appeal intellectually and emotionally to an adult audience, and can express ideas that other media are inherently incapable of." Circ. 11,500. Pays on publication. Publishes ms an average of 2 months after acceptance. Byline given. Buys first rights. Submit seasonal/holiday material 5 months in advance. Photocopied submissions OK. Computer printout submissions acceptable; prefers letter-quality. Reports in 2 weeks. Sample copy $3.50.
Nonfiction: Essays, exposé, historical, interview/profile, opinion and magazine reviews. Buys 120 mss/year. Send complete ms. Length: 500-3,000 words. Pays 1.5¢/word; writers may request trade for merchandise. Pays the expenses of writers on assignment.
Photos: Send photos with submission. Offers additional payment for photos accepted with ms. Identification of subjects required. Buys one-time rights.
Columns/Departments: Opening Shots (brief commentary, often humorous), 1,000 words; Executive Forum; (written by publishers offering, opinions on various subjects), 3,000 words; The Comics Library (graphic review), and Ethics (examining the ethics of the comic-book industry), both 3,000 words. Buys 60 mss/year. Send complete ms. Pays 1.5¢/word.
Tips: "Have an intelligent, sophisticated, critical approach to writing about comic books."

CROSS-CANADA WRITERS' MAGAZINE, The Canadian Literary Writer's Magazine, Cross-Canada Writers, Inc., Box 277, Station F, Toronto, Ontario M4Y 2L7 Canada. Editor: Ted Plantos. Associate Editor: Susan Ioannou. 90% freelance written. Prefers to work with published/established writers. A triannual literary writer's magazine covering Canadian writing within an international context. Circ. 2,500. Pays on publication. Publishes ms an average of 1 year after acceptance. Byline given. Buys first North American serial rights. Submit seasonal/holiday material 6 months in advance. Photocopied submissions OK. Computer printout submissions acceptable; prefers letter-quality. Reports in 3 weeks on queries; 2 months on mss. Sample copy $3.95, 9x12 SAE, and 91¢ Canadian postage or 2 IRCs.
Nonfiction: Essays, articles on literary aesthetics and interview/profile (established authors, editors, publishers, in-depth with photos). "Articles and interviews must have depth, be thought-provoking and offer insights into the creative and working processes of literature." No how-to's for beginners, or on nonliterary kinds of writing. Buys 4-10 mss/year. Query or send complete ms. "Each case is different. With an interview, a query could save time and work. A straight article we would have to read."
Photos: State availability of accompanying photos with query or send photos with ms, 5x7 b&w prints. Captions, model release, and identification of subjects required. Buys one-time rights.
Fiction: Contact the editor. Mainstream. No slight material—mere anecdotes rather than fully developed stories. Buys 4-8 mss/year. Send complete ms. Length: 1,000-3,000 words. Payment on publication.
Poetry: Poetry Editor. Free verse, haiku and traditional (if well-done). No concrete poetry, "diary excerpts" merely, highly obscure private poems or doggerel. Buys 40-50 poems/year. Submit maximum 10 poems. Length: 100 lines maximum "in exceptional cases." Offers $5/poem as payment.
Tips: "The most frequent mistakes made by writers in completing an article for us are misunderstanding of slant, and missing the opportunity for in-depth analysis. We want greater emphasis in literary essays on the aesthetics of writing."

‡DUSTBOOK, SMALL PRESS REVIEW, Box 100, Paradise CA 95969. Editor: Len Fulton. Monthly for "people interested in small presses and magazines, current trends and data; many libraries." Circ. 3,000. Byline given. "Query if you're unsure." Reports in 2 months. Free sample copy.
Nonfiction: News, short reviews, photos, short articles on small magazines and presses. Uses how-to, personal experience, interview, profile, spot news, historical, think, photo, and coverage of merchandising techniques. Accepts 50-200 mss/year. Length: 100-200 words. Payment is negotiable; maximum $50.
Photos: Uses b&w glossy photos.

EDITOR & PUBLISHER, 11 W. 19th St., New York NY 10011. Editor: Robert U. Brown. 10% freelance written. Weekly magazine. For newspaper publishers, editors, executives, employees and others in communications, marketing, advertising, etc. Circ. 29,000. Pays on publication. Publishes ms an average of 2 weeks after acceptance. Buys first serial rights. Computer printout submissions acceptable; prefers letter-quality. Sample copy $1.
Nonfiction: John P. Consoli, managing editor. Uses newspaper business articles and news items; also newspaper personality features and printing technology. Query.
Fillers: "Amusing typographical errors found in newspapers." Pays $5.

THE EDITORIAL EYE, Focusing on Publications Standards and Practices, Editorial Experts, Inc., Suite 400, 85 S. Bragg St., Alexandria VA 22312. (703)642-3040. Editor: Ann R. Molpus. Managing Editor: Eleanor Johnson. 5% freelance written. Prefers to work with published/established writers. Monthly professional newsletter on editorial subjects: writing, editing, proofreading, and levels of editing. "Our readers are professional publications people. Use journalistic style." Circ. 2,300. Pays on acceptance. Publishes ms an average of 3 months after acceptance. Byline given. Kill fee determined for each assignment. Buys first North American serial rights. "We retain the right to use articles in our training division and in an anthology of collected articles." Submit seasonal/holiday material 3 months in advance. Computer printout submissions acceptable; prefers letter-quality. Reports in 1 month. Sample copy and writer's guidelines for 2 first class stamps.

Nonfiction: Editorial and production problems, issues, standards, practices, and techniques; publication management; publishing technology; style, grammar and usage. No word games, vocabulary building, language puzzles, or jeremiads on how the English language is going to blazes. Buys 10 mss/year. Query. Length: 300-1,200. Pays $25-100.

Tips: "We seek mostly lead articles written by people in the publications field about the practice of publications work. Our style is journalistic with a light touch (not cute). We are interested in submissions on the craft of editing, levels of edit, editing by computer, publications management, indexing, lexicography, usages, proofreading. Our back issue list provides a good idea of the kinds of articles we run."

EDITORS' FORUM, Editors' Forum Publishing Company, Box 411806, Kansas City MO 64141. (913)236-9235. Managing Editor: William R. Brinton. 50% freelance written. Prefers to work with published/established and works with a small number of new/unpublished writers each year. A monthly newsletter geared toward communicators, particularly those involved in the editing and publication of newsletters and company publications. Circ. 900. Pays on publication. Publishes ms an average of 4 months after acceptance. Byline given. Offers 25% kill fee. Buys first North American serial rights, second serial (reprint) rights, and makes work-for-hire assignments. Photocopied submissions OK. Previously published submissions OK depending on content. Computer printout submissions acceptable; no dot-matrix. Reports in 2 weeks on queries. Writer's guidelines for # 10 SAE with 2 first class stamps.

Nonfiction: How-to on editing and writing, etc. "With the advent of computer publishing, EF is running a regular high tech column on desk top publishing, software, etc. We can use articles on the latest techniques in computer publishing. Not interested in anything that does not have a direct effect on writing and editing newsletters. This is a how-to newsletter." Buys 22 mss/year. Query. Length: 250-1,000 words. Pays $15/page maximum.

Photos: State availability of photos with submission. Reviews contact sheets. Offers $5/photo. Captions, model releases and identification of subjects required. Buys one-time rights.

Tips: "We are necessarily interested in articles pertaining to the newsletter business. That would include articles involving writing skills, layout and makeup, the use of pictures and other graphics to brighten up our reader's publication, and an occasional article on how to put out a good publication inexpensively."

THE FINAL DRAFT, Writer's Refinery, Box 47786, Phoenix AZ 85068-7786. (602)944-5268. Editorial Director: Elizabeth "Libbi" Goodman. Editors: Nolan Anglum and Linda Hilton. A monthly newsletter on writing. "The premise of our publication is to teach and impart useful information to published and aspiring writers. We also provide an opportunity for new writers to get published." Circ. 800 and growing. Pays on publication. Publishes ms an average of 2-6 months after acceptance. Byline given. Buys first North American serial rights, second serial (reprint) rights or makes work-for-hire assignments. Submit seasonal/holiday material 6 months in advance. Photocopied and previously published submissions OK. Computer printout submissions OK; prefers letter-quality. Reports in 1 month. Sample copy for $1 with #10 SAE and 1 first class stamp; writer's guidelines for #10 SAE with 1 first class stamp.

Nonfiction: Book excerpts, essays, expose, general interest, historical/nostalgic, how-to, humor, motivational, interview/profile (especially with writers of juvenile fiction), new product, opinion, personal experience, technical and travel. "No interviews with people not associated with the craft of writing. No book reviews of fiction. Will accept reviews on books dealing with the craft/writing." Buys 100 mss/year. Send complete ms. Length: 500-3,000 words. Pays $5-20 for unsolicited articles. Pays in contributor's copies if article is of interest "but needs major rewriting author cannot do." Sometimes pays the expenses of writers on assignment.

Fiction: Adventure, experimental, fantasy, historical, horror, humorous, mystery, romance, science fiction, slice-of-life vignettes, suspense and western. "We are open to most fiction that uses writing or writers, as the theme. We do not want to see any fiction not slanted toward writers. Buys 3 mss/year "but looking to buy 12 per year." Send complete ms. Length: 500-1,500 words. Pays $4-15.

Poetry: "Must be of interest to writers. Open to all forms. No religious themes." Buys 20 poems/year. Submit maximum 5 poems. Length: 4-25 lines. Pays $2-5.

Fillers: Anecdotes, facts, gags and short humor. Length: 225-375 words. Pays $2-5.

Tips: "We are anxious to help new writers get started, but that does not mean we accept articles/fiction that are poorly written. Mss should be finely tuned *before* we see them. We are increasing the size of our publication, and are actively looking to purchase a wide variety of articles. The most frequent reason for rejection by our staff is the material submitted is either not suitable for our publication or the writer has not focused the article."

FREELANCE WRITER'S REPORT, Cassell Communications Inc., Box 9844, Fort Lauderdale FL 33310. (305)485-0795. Editor: Dana K. Cassell. 15% freelance written. Prefers to work with published/established writers. Monthly newsletter covering writing and marketing advice for freelance writers. Pays on publication. Publishes ms an average of 6 months after acceptance. Byline given. Buys one-time rights. Submit seasonal/holiday material 2 months in advance. Simultaneous queries, and simultaneous, photocopied, and previously published submissions OK. Computer printout submissions OK; no dot-matrix. Reports in 1 month. Sample copy $2.50.

Nonfiction: Book excerpts (on writing profession); how-to (market, write, research); interview (of writers or editors); new product (only those pertaining to writers); photojournalism; promotion and administration of a writing business. No humor, fiction or poetry. Buys 36 mss/year. Query or send complete ms. Length: 500 words maximum. Also buys longer material (2,000-2,500 words) for Special Reports; must be timeless and of interest to many writers. Pays 10¢/edited word.

Tips: "Write in terse newsletter style, eliminate flowery adjectives and edit mercilessly. Send something that will help writers increase profits from writing output—must be a proven method."

‡HOUSEWIFE-WRITER'S FORUM, Drawer 1518, Lafayette CA 95949. (415)932-1143. Editor: Deborah Haeseler. 100% freelance written. Bimonthly newsletter and literary magazine for women writers. "We are a support network and writer's group on paper directed to the unique needs of women who write and juggle home life." Estab. 1988. Circ. 200. Pays on publication. Publishes ms an average of 6-12 months after acceptance. Byline given. Buys one-time rights. Submit seasonal/holiday material 6 months in advance. Simultaneous, photocopied and previously published submissions OK. Computer printout submissions OK. Reports in 2 weeks on queries; 1 month on mss. Sample copy $3; writer's guidelines for #10 SASE.

Nonfiction: Book excerpts, essays, historical/nostalgic, how-to, humor, interview/profile, opinion, personal experience. Buys 6-12 mss/year. Query with or without published clips, or send complete ms. Length: 2,000 words maximum. Pays $1-10.

Columns/Departments: Confessions of Housewife-Writers (essays pertaining to our lives as women, writers, our childhoods, etc.), 25-800 words; Reviews (books, reference texts, products for housewife writers), 50-300 words. Buys 6-20 mss/year. Send complete ms. Length: 25-800 words. Pays $1 maximum.

Fiction: Confession, experimental, fantasy, historica, horror, humorous, mainstream, mystery, novel excerpts, romance, science fiction, slice-of-life vignettes, suspense. No pornography. Buys 6 mss/year. Send complete ms. Length: 2,000 words maximum. Pays $1-10.

Poetry: Avant-garde, free verse, haiku, light verse, traditional, humorous. Buys 15-20 poems/year. Submit maximum 10 poems at one time. Pays $1 maximum.

Fillers: Anecdotes, facts, short humor, hints on writing and running a home. Length:25-300 words. Pays $1 maximum.

Tips: "We consider ourselves a beginner's market for women who want to write for the various major women's markets. Like any woman, I like to laugh and I love a good cry. I also like to be educated. More importantly, I want to know about you as a person. My goal is to help each other become the best writers we can be. Everything is open to freelancers."

MAGAZINE ISSUES, (formerly *Publishing Trade*), Serving Under 500,000 Circulation Publications, Coast Publishing, 1680 SW Bayshore Rd., Port St. Lucie FL 34984. Editor: Susan M. Isola. 50% freelance written. Bimonthly magazine covering magazine publishing. Circulated to approximately 13,000 publishers, editors, ad managers, circulation managers, production managers and art directors of magazines. Circ. 13,000. Publishes ms an average of 2 months after acceptance. Byline given. Buys first North American serial rights. Submit seasonal/holiday material 6 months in advance. Query for electronic submissions. Computer printout submissions OK; prefers letter-quality. Reports in 2 months on queries. Sample copy and writer's guidelines available for 9x12 SASE.

Nonfiction: How-to (write, sell advertising, manage production, manage creative and sales people, etc.); interview/profile (*only* after assignment—must be full of "secrets" of success and how-to detail); personal experiences; new product (no payment); and technical (aspects of magazine publishing). "Features deal with every aspect of publishing, including: creating an effective ad sales team; increasing ad revenue; writing effective direct-mail circulation promotion; improving reproduction quality; planning and implementing ad sales strategies; buying printing; gathering unique information; writing crisp, clear articles with impact; and designing publications with visual impact." No general interest. "Everything must be keyed directly to our typical reader—a 39 year-old publisher/editor producing a trade magazine for 30,000 or more readers." Buys 18-24 mss/year. Query. Length: 900-3,000 words.

Photos: Send photos with ms.

Tips: "Articles must present practical, useful, new information in how-to detail, so readers can do what the articles discuss. Articles that present problems and discuss how they were successfully solved also are welcome. These must carry many specific examples to flesh out general statements. We don't care who you are, just how you write."

‡**OHIO WRITER**, Box 79464, Cleveland OH 44107. Co-Editors: Susan and Mary Grimm, Kristin Blumberg. 50% freelance written. Bimonthly newsletter on writing-related activities in Ohio. "We are a service newsletter only interested in articles, interviews, surveys, etc. which illuminate some aspect of writing. Our readers and contributors are mostly Ohioans." Estab. 1987. Publishes ms an average of 6 months after acceptance. Byline given. Buys one-time rights or second serial (reprint) rights. Submit seasonal/holiday material 5 months in advance. Simultaneous, photocopied and previously published material OK. Computer printout submissions OK. Reports in 3 months. Free sample copy.
Nonfiction: Feature articles (on some aspect of writing), interview/profile (of Ohio authors), personal experience (writing related), book reviews, event reviews. Buys 30 mss/year. Send complete ms. Length: 300-1,500 words. Pays $50 for lead articles; $5-10 for reviews.
Columns/Departments: Alternative Paychecks (how writers make a living writing outside their preferred genre); Focus (a concentrated look at writing activities in one area). Buys 3 mss/year. Query. Length: 800-1000 words. Pays $5-35.
Tips: "Any area is open; however, since we print more reviews than articles, that might be an easier opening. Reviews must be critical but balanced—we do not wish to trash someone's work. If it's that bad, we don't want to review it anyway. With lead articles we are not interested in formulaic how-tos (ie 'The 7 Golden Rules to Good Fiction'), rather, we want a deeper examination of some aspect of writing—although not academic—coming from real experience."

PHILATELIC JOURNALIST, 154 Laguna Court, St. Augustine Shores FL 32086-7031. (904)797-3513. Editor: Gustav Detjen, Jr. 25% freelance written. Bimonthly for "journalists, writers and columnists in the field of stamp collecting. *The Philatelic Journalist* is mainly read by philatelic writers, professionals and amateurs, including all of the members of the Society of Philaticians, an international group of philatelic journalists." Circ. 1,000. Not copyrighted. Pays on publication. Publishes ms an average of 1 month after acceptance. Free sample copy. Submit seasonal material 2 months in advance. Photocopied submissions OK. Computer printout submissions acceptable. Reports in 2 weeks. Query.
Nonfiction: "Articles concerned with the problems of the philatelic journalist, how to publicize and promote stamp collecting, how to improve relations between philatelic writers and publishers and postal administrations. Philatelic journalists, many of them amateurs, are very much interested in receiving greater recognition as journalists, and in gaining greater recognition for the use of philatelic literature by stamp collectors. Any criticism should be coupled with suggestions for improvement." Buys profiles and opinion articles. Length: 250-500 words. Pays $15-30.
Photos: Photos purchased with ms. Captions required.

RIGHTING WORDS, The Journal of Language and Editing, Righting Words Corp., Box 6811, F.D.R. Station, New York NY 10150. (718)761-0235. Editor: Jonathan S. Kaufman. 80% freelance written. Eager to work with new/unpublished writers. A bimonthly magazine on language usage, trends and issues. "Our readers include copy editors, book and magazine editors, and journalism and English teachers—people interested in the changing ways of the langauge and in ways to improve their editing and writing skills." Pays on acceptance. Publishes ms an average of 1 month after acceptance. Byline given. Offers $100 kill fee. Buys first North American serial rights. Query for electronic submissions. Computer printout submissions OK; no dot-matrix. Reports in 1 month. Sample copy $4.50 with 9x12 SAE and 3 first class stamps; writer's guidelines for SASE.
Nonfiction: General interest, historical/nostalgic and how-to. Buys 30 mss/year. Send complete ms. Length: 3,000 words. Pays $100 minimum for assigned articles; pays $75 minimum for unsolicited articles.
Tips: "Our contributors have included Rudolf Flesch and Willard Espy, but we welcome freelance submissions on editing and language topics that are well-written, contain hard information of value to editors, and that display wit and style. Yes, the editor reads *all* submissions, and often suggests approaches to writers whose material may be good but whose approach is off. No book reviews, please; other than that, all parts of the magazines are open to freelancers."

RISING STAR, 47 Byledge Rd., Manchester NH 03104. (603)623-9796. Editor: Scott E. Green. 50% freelance written. A bimonthly newsletter on science fiction and fantasy markets for writers and artists. Circ. 150. Pays on publication. Publishes ms an average of 3 months after acceptance. Byline given. Not copyrighted. Buys first rights. Simultaneous, photocopied and previously published submissions OK. Reports in 2 weeks on queries. Sample copy $1 with #10 SAE with 1 first class stamp; free writer's guidelines.
Nonfiction: Book excerpts, essays, interview/profile and opinion. Buys 8 mss/year. Query. Length: 500-900 words. Pays $3 minimum.

ST. LOUIS JOURNALISM REVIEW, 8380 Olive Blvd., St. Louis MO 63132. (314)991-1699. Editor/Publisher: Charles L. Klotzer. 50% freelance written. Prefers to work with published/established writers. Works with a small number of new/unpublished writers each year; eager to work with new/unpublished writers. Monthly tabloid newspaper critiquing St. Louis media, print, broadcasting, TV and cable primarily by working journalists and others. Also covers issues not covered adequately by dailies. Occasionally buys articles on national media criticism. Circ. 8,500. Buys all rights. Byline given. Computer printout submissions acceptable.

Nonfiction: "We buy material which analyzes, critically, St. Louis metro area media and, less frequently, national media institutions, personalities or trends." No taboos. Payment depends. Sometimes pays the expenses of writers on assignment.

SCAVENGER'S NEWSLETTER, 519 Ellinwood, Osage City KS 66523. (913)528-3538. Editor: Janet Fox. 25% freelance written. Eager to work with new/unpublished writers. A monthly newsletter covering markets for science fiction/fantasy/horror materials especially with regard to the small press. Circ. 600. Publishes ms an average of 8 months after acceptance. Byline given. Not copyrighted. "Copyright symbol printed with author's name on publication." Buys one-time rights. Simultaneous, photocopied and previously published submissions OK. Computer printout submissions acceptable; prefers letter-quality. Reports in 2 weeks. Sample copy $1; writer's guidelines for #10 SASE.

Nonfiction: Essays; general interest; how-to (write, sell, publish sf/fantasy/horror); humor; interview/profile (writers, artists in the field); and opinion. Buys 12-15 mss/year. Send complete ms. Length: 1,000 words maximum. Pays $2.

Poetry: Avant-garde, free verse, haiku and traditional. All related to science fiction/fantasy/horror genres. Buys 36 poems/year. Submit maximum 3 poems. Length: 10 lines maximum. Pays $1.

Tips: "Because this is a small publication, it has occasional overstocks. We're especially looking for sf/fantasy/horror commentary as opposed to writer's how-to's."

SCIENCE FICTION CHRONICLE, Box 2730, Brooklyn NY 11202-0036. (718)643-9011. Editor: Andrew Porter. 5% freelance written. Works with a small number of new/unpublished writers each year. Monthly magazine about science fiction, fantasy and horror publishing for readers, editors, writers, et al., who are interested in keeping up with the latest developments and news in science fiction and fantasy. Publication also includes market reports, UK news, letters, reviews, columns. Circ. 4,400. Buys first serial rights. Pays on publication. Publishes ms an average of 2 months after acceptance. Makes work-for-hire assignments. Phone queries OK. Submit seasonal material 4 months in advance. Computer printout submissions acceptable; prefers letter-quality. Reports in 1 week. Sample copy for 9x12 SAE, 5 first class stamps and $2.50.

Nonfiction: Interviews, new product and photo feature. No articles about UFOs, or "news we reported six months ago." Buys 15 unsolicited mss/year. Send complete ms. Length: 200-2,000 words. Pays 3-5¢/word.

Photos: Send photos with ms. Pays $5-15 for 4x5 and 8x10 b&w prints. Captions preferred. Buys one-time rights.

Tips: "News of publishers, booksellers and software related to sf, fantasy and horror is most needed from freelancers."

WDS FORUM, Writer's Digest School, 1507 Dana Ave., Cincinnati OH 45207. (513)531-2222. Editor: Kirk Polking. 100% freelance written. Quarterly newsletter covering writing techniques and marketing for students of courses in fiction and nonfiction writing offered by Writer's Digest School. Circ. 13,000. Pays on acceptance. Publishes ms an average of 6 months after acceptance. Byline given. Pays 25% kill fee. Buys first serial rights and second serial (reprint) rights. Submit seasonal/holiday material 4 months in advance. Simultaneous, photocopied, and previously published submissions OK. Query for electronic submissions. Computer printout submissions acceptable; no dot-matrix. Reports in 3 weeks. Free sample copy.

Nonfiction: How-to (write or market short stories, articles, novels, etc.); and interviews (with well-known authors of short stories, novels and books). Buys 12 mss/year. "Query by mail, please, not phone." Length: 500-1,000 words. Pays $10-25.

Photos: Pays $5-10 for 8x10 b&w prints of well-known writers to accompany mss. Captions required. Buys one-time rights.

THE WRITER, 120 Boylston St., Boston MA 02116. Editor-in-Chief/Publisher: Sylvia K. Burack. 20-25% freelance written. Prefers to buy work of published/established writers. Monthly. Pays on acceptance. Publishes ms an average of 6-8 months after acceptance. Buys first serial rights. Uses some freelance material. Computer printout submissions acceptable; no dot-matrix. Sample copy $2.50.

Nonfiction: Practical articles for writers on how to write for publication, and how and where to market manuscripts in various fields. Will consider all submissions promptly. No assignments. Length: approximately 2,000 words.

Tips: "New types of publications and our continually updated market listings in all fields will determine changes of focus and fact."

WRITER'S DIGEST, 1507 Dana Ave., Cincinnati OH 45207. (513)531-2222. Submissions Editor: Bill Strickland. 90% freelance written. Monthly magazine about writing and publishing. "Our readers write fiction, poetry, nonfiction, plays and all kinds of creative writing. They're interested in improving their writing skills, improving their sales ability, and finding new outlets for their talents." Circ. 225,000. Pays on acceptance.

Publishes ms an average of 1 year after acceptance. Buys first North American serial rights for one-time editorial use, microfilm/microfiche use, and magazine promotional use. Pays 20% kill fee. Byline given. Submit seasonal/holiday material 8 months in advance. Previously published and photocopied submissions OK. No unsolicited electronic submissions. "We're able to use electronic submissions only for accepted pieces/and will discuss details if we buy your work. We'll accept computer printout submissions, of course—but they *must* be readable. That's the rule behind any submission to any magazine. We strongly recommend letter-quality. If you don't want your manuscript returned, indicate that on the first page of the manuscript or in a cover letter." Reports in 2 weeks. Sample copy $2.75; writer's guidelines for SASE.

Nonfiction: "Our mainstay is the how-to article—that is, an article telling how to write and sell more of what you write. For instance, how to write compelling leads and conclusions, how to improve your character descriptions, how to become more efficient and productive. We like plenty of examples, anecdotes and $$$ in our articles—so other writers can actually see what's been done successfully by the author of a particular piece. We like our articles to speak directly to the reader through the use of the first-person voice. Don't submit an article on what five book editors say about writing mysteries. Instead, submit an article on how you cracked the mystery market and how our readers can do the same. But don't limit the article to your experiences; include the opinions of those five editors to give your article increased depth and authority." General interest (about writing); how-to (writing and marketing techniques that work); humor (short pieces); inspirational; interview and profile (query first); new product; and personal experience (marketing and freelancing experiences). "We can always use articles on fiction and nonfiction technique, and solid articles on poetry or scriptwriting are always welcome. No articles titled 'So You Want to Be a Writer,' and no first-person pieces that ramble without giving a lesson or something readers can learn from in the sharing of the story." Buys 90-100 mss/year. Queries are preferred, but complete mss are OK. Length: 500-3,000 words. Pays 10¢/word minimum. Sometimes pays expenses of writers on assignment.

Photos: Used only with interviews and profiles. State availability of photos or send contact sheet with ms. Pays $25 minimum for 5x7 or larger b&w prints. Captions required.

Columns/Departments: Chronicle (first-person narratives about the writing life; length: 1,200-1,500 words; pays 10¢/word); The Writing Life (length: 50-800 words; pays 10¢/word); Tip Sheet (short, unbylined items that offer solutions to writing- and freelance business-related problems that writers commonly face; pays 10¢/word); and My First Sale (an "occasional" department; a first-person account of how a writer broke into print; length: 1,000 words; pays 10¢/word). "For First Sale items, use a narrative, anecdotal style to tell a tale that is both inspirational and instructional. Before you submit a My First Sale item, make certain that your story contains a solid lesson that will benefit other writers." Buys approximately 200 articles/year for Writing Life section, Tip Sheet and shorter pieces. Send complete ms.

Poetry: Light verse about "the writing life"—joys and frustrations of writing. "We are also considering poetry other than short light verse—but related to writing, publishing, other poets and authors, etc." Buys 2/issue. Submit poems in batches of 1-8. Length: 2-20 lines. Pays $10-50/poem.

Fillers: Anecdotes and short humor, primarily for use in The Writing Life column. Uses 2/issue. Length: 50-200 words. Pays 10¢/word.

WRITERS GAZETTE, Trouvere Company, Rt. 2, Box 290, Eclectic AL 36024. Editor: Brenda Williamson. 95% freelance written. Eager to work with new/unpublished writers. Circ. 1,200. Publishes ms an average of 6 months after acceptance. Byline given. Buys one-time rights. Computer printout submissions acceptable; prefers letter-quality. Reports in 3 months. Sample copy for $4 and 9x12 SAE with 4 first class stamps; writer's guidelines for 25¢ and #10 SAE.

Nonfiction: Writing related subjects. Buys 20-30 year.

Fiction: Adventure, condensed novels, confession, erotica, ethnic, experimental, fantasy, historical, horror, humorous, mainstream, mystery, novel excerpts, religious, romance, science fiction, serialized novels, suspense and western—any short story. Buys 12-20 mss/year. Send complete ms.

Poetry: Any style or topic, uses 150-250 year.

Tips: "Read guidelines and enjoy what you write. We're open to suggestions; guidelines are to follow, but they're not the law at *WG*. We're open for new imaginative ideas. Our payments range from $1-50, but the normal range usually stays below $10. Unfortunately by paying we can not give complimentary copies to contributors. But we found that more writers wanted the money instead."

‡WRITER'S GUIDELINES, S.O.C.O. Publications, RD#1, Ward Rd., Box 71, Mohawk NY 13407. (315)866-7445. Editor: Carol Ann Vercz. 100% freelance written. A monthly magazine with writing information and general interest features. "We are trying to inform all writers about new techniques, advancements as well as educate, to some degree, the novice to get him started in his career." Circ. 1,000. Pays on publication. Sometimes byline given. Buys one-time rights. Submit seasonal/holiday material 6 months in advance. Simultaneous and previously published submissions OK. Query for electronic submissions. Computer printout submissions OK; no dot-matrix. Reports in 6 weeks on queries. Sample copy $3. Free writer's guidelines.

Nonfiction: General interest, historical/nostalgic, how-to, humor, inspirational, photo feature, technical and travel. Buys 200 mss/year. Query. Length: 500-1,200 words. Pays 2¢/word. Pays 1¢/word for reprints.

Photos: Send photos with submission. Reviews prints (3x5). Pays $3.50 per photo. Identification of subjects required. Buys one-time rights.

Columns/Departments: Conferences. Buys 100 mss/year. Query. Length: 500-1,200 words. Pays 2¢/ word.

Fiction: Adventure, historical and humorous.

Poetry: Traditional. Buys 100 poems/year. Submit maximum 6 poems. Length: 6-25 lines. Pays 25¢/line.

Fillers: Anecdotes and facts. Buys 15/year. Pays $1-5.

Tips: "Query first about any article. We're always looking for new ideas for columns."

‡WRITER'S HAVEN JOURNAL, Writer's Bookstore & Haven. 3341 Adams Ave., San Diego CA 92116. (619)282-3363. Editor in Chief: Nancy J. Painter. Publisher: Betty Abell Jurus. 50% freelance written. A monthly magazine on writers and the art and craft of writing. "As a magazine for writers, our audience is primarily one of writers, editors and agents. We believe a writer is a writer before, as well as after, publication. Our purpose is to inform, encourage and assist writers at all levels." Circ. 325. Pays on acceptance. Publishes ms an average of 3 months after acceptance. Byline given. Publication is not copyrighted. Buys one-time rights. Submit seasonal/holiday material 3 months in advance. Photocopied submissions OK. Computer printout submissions OK; prefers letter-quality. Reports in 6 weeks on mss. Sample copy $1.50. Writer's guidelines for #10 SAE with 1 first class stamp.

Nonfiction: Essays, general interest, historical/nostalgic, how-to, humor, interview/profile, new product, opinion, personal experience, photo feature and technical. "All articles must deal with writers on writing or some other aspect of the art and craft of writing, publishing, editing or agenting. We do not want articles that do not deal with writers or writing, publishing or agenting or marketing." Buys 12 mss/year. Send complete ms. Length: 1,000-1,500 words. Pays $15-25 for unsolicited articles.

Photos: State availability of photos with submission. Reviews prints (3x5) b&w only. Offers $5 per photo. Captions, model releases and identification of subjects required. Buys one-time rights.

Columns/Departments: Book Review (review books on the art and craft of writing), 500 word maximum. Buys 6-12 mss/year. Send complete ms. Pays $10-15.

Fiction: Jean Graham, fiction editor. Adventure, ethnic, experimental, fantasy, historical, horror, humorous, mainstream, mystery, novel excerpts, romance, science fiction, slice-of-life vignettes, suspense and western. No confession, erotica, religious or pornographic fiction. Buys 6-12 mss/year. Send complete ms. Length: 500-2,500 words. Pays $10-25.

Poetry: Hal "B" Alexander, poetry editor. Avant-garde, free verse, haiku, light verse and traditional. No erotic, religious or pornographic poetry. Buys 6-12 poems/year. Submit maximum 3 poems. Length: 5-25 lines. Pays $5-15.

Fillers: N.J. Painter, fillers editor. Facts about writing or writers, short humor and cartoons: 3x3½ drawings, must feature writer, editor, publisher, agent or reader, with or without caption. Buys 1-6/year. Length: 15-50 words. Pays $5.

Tips: "We welcome submissions, whether fiction or nonfiction, which are professionally presented . . . that is, typed, double-spaced, and which have the author's full name, address and phone number, with an SASE enclosed. Please don't be afraid to write for us. Writing is an experience shared with a large community of other writers, some working entirely alone. Your experience, hopes, dreams, successes, may give another writer the courage to continue. It's important that isolated writers know we're all out here. Except for staff-written columns, we are entirely open to articles dealing with the business of writing, the art of being a writer, writing experiences, marketing, agenting, dealing with publishers, editors on editing, etc. We are very flexible on the types of fiction, poetry and humor accepted. Word lengths are very important, so please adhere to them. We are very interested in reviews of books on how to write, and welcome both review copies from publishers and contributor reviews. Annual Certificate Award and publication in the Writers' Haven Journal of the best 500 word essay or fiction submission on a given topic written by an attendee at our mid-January 'Southern California Writers' Conference/SanDiego.' "

WRITER'S INFO, Box 2377, Coeur d'Alene ID 83814. (208)667-7511. Editor: Linda Hutton. 90% freelance written. Eager to work with new/unpublished writers. Monthly newsletter on writing. "We provide helpful tips and advice to writers, both beginners and old pros." Circ. 200. Pays on acceptance. Publishes ms an average of 6 months after acceptance. Byline given. Buys first North American serial rights and second serial (reprint) rights. Submit seasonal/holiday material 9 months in advance. Simultaneous queries, and simultaneous, photocopied, and previously published submissions OK. Computer printout submissions acceptable; prefers letter-quality. Reports in 1 month. Sample copy for #10 SAE and 2 first class stamps; writer's guidelines for #10 SAE and 1 first class stamp.

Nonfiction: How-to, humor and personal experience, all related to writing. No interviews or re-hashes of articles published in other writers magazines. Buys 50-75 mss/year. Send complete ms. Length: 300 words. Pays $1-10.

Poetry: Free verse, light verse and traditional. No avant-garde or shaped poetry. Buys 40-50/year. Submit maximum 6 poems. Length: 4-20 lines. Pays $1-10.

Fillers: Jokes, anecdotes and short humor. Buys 3-4/year. Length: 100 words maximum. Pays $1-10.
Tips: "Tell us a system that worked for you to make a sale or inspired you to write. All departments are open to freelancers."

WRITER'S JOURNAL, Inkling Publications, Inc., Box 65798, St. Paul MN 55165. (612)221-0326. Editor: Marilyn Bailey. Associate Editor: Betty Ulrich. Managing Editor/Publisher: John Hall. 30% freelance written. Monthly. Circ. 5,500. Pays on publication. Publishes ms an average of 2 months after acceptance. Byline given. Buys first North American serial rights. Submit seasonal/holiday material 4 months in advance. Simultaneous queries OK. Query for electronic submissions. Computer printout submissions acceptable; prefers letter-quality. Reports in 1 month on queries; 6 weeks on mss. Sample copy $2; writer's guidelines for #10 SAE and 1 first class stamp.
Nonfiction: How-to (on the business and approach to writing); motivational; interview/profile; opinion. *"Writer's Journal* publishes articles on style, technique, editing methods, copy writing, research, writing of news releases, writing news stories and features, creative writing, grammar reviews, marketing, the business aspects of writing, copyright law and legal advice for writers/editors, independent book publishing, interview techniques, and more." Also articles on the use of computers by writers and a book review section. Buys 30-40 mss/year. Send complete ms. Length: 500-1,500 words. Pays $15-50.
Poetry: Avant-garde, free verse, haiku, light verse and traditional. "The *Inkling* runs one poetry contest each year in the spring: Winner and 2nd place cash prizes and two honorable mentions." Buys 10-15 poems/year. Submit maximum 3 poems. Length: 25 lines maximum. Pays $4-15.
Tips: "Articles must be *well* written and slanted toward the business (or commitment) of writing and/or being a writer. Interviews with established writers should be in-depth, particularly reporting interviewee's philosophy on writing, how (s)he got started, etc. Tape interviews, transcribe, then edit. Monthly 'theme' emphasizes a particular genre or type of writing. Opinion pieces (researched and authoritative) on any of the monthly themes welcomed. (Theme schedule available with guidelines.)"

‡THE WRITER'S NOOK NEWS, 10957 Chardon Rd., Chardon OH 44024. (216)285-0942. Editor: Eugene Ortiz. 100% freelance written. A quarterly newsletter for professional writers. "We don't print fluff, anecdotes, or platitudes. Articles must be specific, terse, pithy, and contain information my readers can put to immediate, practical use. Every article should be the kind you want to cut out and tape to your desk somewhere." Circ. 5,000. Pays on acceptance. Publishes ms an average of 5 months after acceptance. Byline given. Publication is not copyrighted. Buys first North American serial rights. Submit seasonal/holiday material 5 months in advance. Photocopied submissions OK. Computer printout submissions OK; no dot-matrix. Reports in 2 weeks. Sample copy $2. Writer's guidelines for 9x12 SAE with 2 first class stamps.
Nonfiction: How-to and interview/profile (how he or she wrote or writes and markets his or her work). "I do not want to see essays, poetry, fiction, ruminations, anecdotes, or anything of no immediate, practical value to my readers." Buys 100+ mss/year. Send complete ms with credits and short bio. Length: 100-400 words. Pays $6-24.
Photos: Send photos with submission. Reviews prints (2½x2½). Offers $5 maximum per photo. Identification of subjects required. Buys one-time rights.
Columns/Departments: Bolton's Book Bench (short reviews of books related to writing), 400 words; Conferences & Klatches (listings of conferences and gatherings), 400-1,200 words; Contests & Awards (listings of contests and awards), 400 words; Writer's Rights (latest information on what's happening on Capital Hill), 400 words; Markets (listings of information on markets for writers), 400 words. Buys 20 mss/year. Query with published clips and short bio. Length: 400 words. Pays $2-24.
Fillers: Facts and newsbreaks. Buys 20/year. Length: 20-100 words. Pays $1.20-6.
Tips: "Take the writer's guidelines very seriously. 90% of the best submissions are still about 25% fluff. Cut till it bleeds! Very short cover letter. Word count (400 max) and rights offered. (First North American serial) in upper right of page one of ms. Typed SASE (#10 or larger) with proper postage. Short bio with submission. Don't tell me how hard or impossible it is to write anything of worth in only 400 words—others are doing it in each issue of *The Writer's Nook News*. This is not a market for beginners. Particularly looking for genre tips. Tell me how you did it, what it takes, or what you are doing to keep your writing fresh. I need more helpful information for established writers. I also need information on alternative ways of earning money as a writer. Finally, I could use information on songwriting, playwriting and screenwriting. We also sponsor an annual short fiction contest. Details can be found in any current issue of TWNN."

WRITER'S YEARBOOK, 1507 Dana Ave., Cincinnati OH 45207. Submissions Editor: Bill Strickland. 90% freelance written. Newsstand annual for freelance writers, journalists and teachers of creative writing. "Please note that the *Yearbook* is currently using a 'best of' format. That is, we are reprinting the best of writing about writing published in the last year: articles, fiction, and book excerpts. The *Yearbook* now uses little original material, so do not submit queries or original manuscripts to the *Yearbook*. We will, however, consider already-published material for possible inclusion." Buys reprint rights. Pays 20% kill fee. Byline given. Pays on acceptance. Publishes ms an average of 6 months after acceptance. High-quality photocopied submissions OK.

Computer printout submissions acceptable; prefers letter-quality. "If you don't want your manuscript returned, indicate that on the first page of the manuscript or in a cover letter."

Nonfiction: "In reprints, we want articles that reflect the current state of writing in America. Trends, inside information and money-saving and money-making ideas for the freelance writer. We try to touch on the various facets of writing in each issue of the *Yearbook*—from fiction to poetry to playwriting, and any other endeavor a writer can pursue. How-to articles—that is, articles that explain in detail how to do something—are very important to us. For example, you could explain how to establish mood in fiction, how to improve interviewing techniques, how to write for and sell to specialty magazines, or how to construct and market a good poem. We are also interested in the writer's spare time—what she/he does to retreat occasionally from the writing wars; where and how to refuel and replenish the writing spirit. 'How Beats the Heart of a Writer' features interest us, if written warmly, in the first person, by a writer who has had considerable success. We also want interviews or profiles of well-known bestselling authors, always with good pictures. Articles on writing techniques that are effective today are always welcome. We provide how-to features and information to help our readers become more skilled at writing and successful at selling their writing." Buys 10-15 mss (reprints only)/year. Length: 750-4,500 words. Pays 2¢½¢/word minimum.

Photos: Interviews and profiles must be accompanied by high-quality photos. Reviews b&w photos only, depending on use; pays $20-50/published photo. Captions required.

Law

While all of these publications deal with topics of interest to attorneys, each has a particular slant. Be sure that your subject is geared to a specific market—lawyers in a single region, law students, paralegals, etc. Publications for law enforcement personnel are listed under Government and Public Service.

ABA JOURNAL, American Bar Association, 750 N. Lake Shore Dr., Chicago IL 60611. (312)988-5000. Editor: Larry Bodine. Articles Editor: Robert Yates. 35% freelance written. Prefers to work with published/established writers. Monthly magazine covering law and laywers. "The content of the *Journal* is designed to appeal to the association's diverse membership with emphasis on the general practitioner." Circ. 350,000. Pays on acceptance. Publishes ms an average of 2 months after acceptance. Byline given. "Editor works with writer until article is in acceptable form." Buys all rights. Submit seasonal/holiday material 3 months in advance. Simultaneous queries, and simultaneous and photocopied submissions OK. Query for electronic submissions. Computer printout submissions acceptable; no dot-matrix. Reports in 3 weeks. Free sample copy and writer's guidelines.

Nonfiction: Book excerpts; general interest (legal); how-to (law practice techniques); interview/profile (law firms and prominent individuals); and technical (legal trends). "The emphasis of the *Journal* is on the practical problems faced by lawyers in general practice and how those problems can be overcome. Articles should emphasize the practical rather than the theoretical or esoteric. Writers should avoid the style of law reviews, academic journals or legal briefs and should write in an informal, journalistic style. Short quotations from people and specific examples of your point will improve an article." Special issues have featured women and minorities in the legal profession. Buys 30 mss/year. Query with published clips or send complete ms. Length: 1,000-3,000 words. Pays $300-800. Pays expenses of writers on assignment.

Tips: "Write to us with a specific idea in mind and spell out how the subject would be covered. Full length profiles and feature articles are always needed. We look for practical information. Don't send us theory, philosophy or wistful meanderings. Our readers want to know how to win cases and operate their practices more efficiently. We need more writing horsepower on lifestyle, profile and practice pieces for lawyers. If the New York Times or Wall Street Journal would like your style, so will we."

THE ALTMAN & WEIL REPORT TO LEGAL MANAGEMENT, Altman & Weil Publications, Inc., Box 472, Ardmore PA 19003. (215)649-4646. Editor: Robert I. Weil. 15-20% freelance written. Works with a small number of new/unpublished writers each year. Monthly newsletter covering law office purchases (equipment, insurance services, space, etc.). Circ. 2,200. Pays on publication. Publishes ms an average of 3-6 months after acceptance. Byline given. Buys all rights; sometimes second serial (reprint) rights. Photocopied and previously published submissions OK. Query for electronic submissions. Computer printout submissions acceptable; no dot-matrix. Reports in 1 month on queries; 6 weeks on mss. Sample copy for #10 SAE and 1 first class stamp.

Nonfiction: How-to (buy, use, repair); interview/profile; and new product. Buys 6 mss/year. Query. Submit a sample of previous writing. Length: 500-2,500 words. Pays $125/published page.

Photos: State availability of photos. Reviews b&w prints; payment is included in payment for ms. Captions and model release required. Buys one-time rights.

BARRISTER, American Bar Association Press, 750 N. Lake Shore Dr., Chicago IL 60611. (312)988-6056. Editor: Anthony Monahan. 75% freelance written. Prefers to work with published/established writers; works with a small number of new/unpublished each year. For young lawyers who are members of the American Bar Association concerned about practice of law, improvement of the profession and service to the public. Quarterly magazine. Circ. 155,000. Pays on acceptance. Publishes ms an average of 3 months after acceptance. Buys all rights, first serial rights, second serial (reprint) rights, or simultaneous rights. Photocopied submissions OK. Query for electronic submissions. Computer printout submissions OK; prefers letter-quality. Reports in 6 weeks. Sample copy for 9x11 SAE with 4 first class stamps.

Nonfiction: "As a magazine of ideas and opinion, we seek material that will help readers in their interrelated roles of attorney and citizen; major themes in legal and social affairs." Especially needs expository or advocacy articles; position should be defended clearly in good, crisp, journalistic prose. "We would like to see articles on issues such as the feasibility of energy alternatives to nuclear power, roles of women and minorities in law, the power and future of multinational corporations; national issues such as gun control; and aspects of the legal profession such as salary comparisons, use of computers in law practice." No humorous court reporter anecdote material or political opinion articles. Buys 15 unsolicited mss/year. Length: 3,000-4,000 words. Query with a working title and outline of topic. "Be specific." Pays $450-750. Sometimes pays the expenses of writers on assignment.

Photos: Donna Tashjian, photo editor. B&w photos and color transparencies purchased without accompanying ms. Pays $35-150.

Tips: "We urge writers to think ahead about new areas of law and social issues: sexual habits, work habits, corporations, etc. We would like to receive sharply-focused, timely profiles of young lawyers (36 or under) doing important, offbeat, innovative or impactful things."

THE LAWYER'S PC, A Newsletter for Lawyers Using Personal Computers, Shepard's/McGraw-Hill, Inc.; editorial office at Box 1108, Lexington SC 29072. (803)359-9941. Editor: Robert P. Wilkins. Managing Editor: Daniel E. Harmon. 50% freelance written. A biweekly newsletter covering computerized law firms. "Our readers are lawyers who want to be told how a particular microcomputer program or type of program is being applied to a legal office task, such as timekeeping, litigation support, etc." Circ. 4,000. Pays end of the month of publication. Publishes ms an average of 1-2 months after acceptance. Byline given. Buys first North American serial rights and the right to reprint. Submit seasonal/holiday material 5 months in advance. Query for electronic submissions. Computer printout submissions acceptable; prefers letter-quality. Reports in 1 month on queries; 2 months on mss. Sample copy for 9x12 SAE with 3 first class stamps.

Nonfiction: How-to (applications articles on law office computerization) and software reviews written by lawyers who have no compromising interests. No general articles on why lawyers need computers or reviews of products written by public relations representatives or vending consultants. Buys 30-35 mss/year. Query. Length: 500-2,500 words. Pays $25-125. Sometimes pays the expenses of writers on assignment.

Tips: "Most of our writers are lawyers. If you're not a lawyer, you need to at least understand why general business software may not work well in a law firm. If you understand lawyers' specific computer problems, write an article describing how to solve one of those problems, and we'd like to see it."

THE LAWYERS WEEKLY, The Newspaper for the Legal Profession in Canada, Butterworth (Canada) Inc., Suite 201, 423 Queen St. W., Toronto, Ontario M5V 2A5 Canada. Editor: D. Michael Fitz-James. 20% freelance written. "We will work with any *talented* writer of whatever experience level." Works with a small number of new/unpublished writers each year. A 48-times-per-year tabloid covering law and legal affairs for a "sophisticated up-market readership of lawyers and accountants." Circ. 37,000. Pays on publication. Publishes ms an average of 1 month after acceptance. Byline given. Offers 50% kill fee. Usually buys all rights. Submit seasonal/holiday material 6 weeks in advance. Simultaneous queries and submissions, and photocopied submissions OK. Query for electronic submissions. Computer printout submissions acceptable. Reports in 1 month. Sample copy $1.50 Canadian funds and 8½x11 SAE.

Nonfiction: Expose; general interest (law); historical/nostalgic; how-to (professional); humor; interview/profile (lawyers and judges); opinion; technical; news; and case comments. "We try to wrap up the week's legal events and issues in a snappy informal package with lots of visual punch. We especially like news stories with photos or illustrations. We are always interested in feature or newsfeature articles involving current legal issues, but contributors should keep in mind our audience is trained in *English/Canadian common law*—not U.S. law. That means most U.S. constitutional or criminal law stories will generally not be accepted." Special Christmas issue. No routine court reporting or fake news stories about commercial products. Buys 200-300 mss/year. Query or send complete ms. Length: 700-1,500 words. Pays $25 minimum, negotiable maximum (have paid up to $350 in the past). Payment in Canadian dollars. Sometimes pays the expenses of writers on assignment.

Photos: State availability of photos with query letter or ms. Reviews b&w contact sheets, negatives, and 5x7 prints. Identification of subjects required. Buys one-time rights.

Columns/Departments: Buys 90-100 mss/year. Send complete ms or Wordstar or Wordperfect disK. Length: 500-1,000 words. Pays negotiable rate.

Fillers: Clippings, jokes, gags, anecdotes, short humor and newsbreaks. Cartoon ideas will be drawn by our artists. Length: 50-200 words. Pays $10 minimum.

Tips: "Freelancers can best break into our publication by submitting news, features, and accounts of unusual or bizarre legal events. A frequent mistake made by writers is forgetting that our audience is intelligent and learned in law. They don't need the word 'plaintiff' explained to them." No unsolicited mss returned without SASE (or IRC to U.S. destinations).

LEGAL ECONOMICS, The Magazine of Law Office Management, A Magazine of the Section of Economics of Law Practice of the American Bar Association, Box 11418, Columbia SC 29211. Managing Editor/Art Director: Delmar L. Roberts. 10% freelance written. For the practicing lawyer and legal administrator. Magazine published 8 times/year. Circ. 23,817. Rights purchased vary with author and material. Usually buys all rights. Byline given. Pays on publication. Publishes ms an average of 8 months after acceptance. Computer printout submissions acceptable. Query. Free writer's guidelines; sample copy $6 (make check payable to American Bar Association). Returns rejected material in 90 days, if requested.

Nonfiction: "We assist the practicing lawyer in operating and managing his or her office by providing relevant articles and departments written in a readable and informative style. Editorial content is intended to aid the lawyer by conveying management methods that will allow him or her to provide legal services to clients in a prompt and efficient manner at reasonable cost. Typical topics of articles include fees and billing; client/lawyer relations; computer hardware/software; mergers; retirement/disability; marketing; compensation of partners and associates; legal data base research; and use of paralegals." No elementary articles on a whole field of technology, such as, "why you need word processing in the law office." Pays $75-300.

Photos: Pays $30-60 for b&w photos purchased with mss; $50-75 for color; $100-125 for cover transparencies.

Tips: "We have a theme for each issue with two to three articles relating to the theme. We also publish thematic issues occasionally in which an entire issue is devoted to a single topic, primarily in the area of new office technology."

THE NATIONAL LAW JOURNAL, New York Law Publishing Company, 111 8th Ave., New York NY 10011. (212)741-8300. Editor: T. Sumner Robinson. 25% freelance written. Weekly newspaper for the legal profession. Circ. 50,000. Pays on publication. Publishes ms an average of 1 month after acceptance. Byline given. Offers $75 kill fee. Buys all rights. Simultaneous queries OK. Query for electronic submissions. Computer printout submissions acceptable; prefers letter-quality. Reports in 3 weeks on queries; 5 weeks on mss. Sample copy $2.

Nonfiction: News, expose (on subjects of interest to lawyers); and interview/profile (of lawyers or judges of note). "The bulk of our freelance articles are short, spot-news stories on local court decisions, lawsuits and lawyers; often, these come from legal affairs writers on local newspapers. Pay range: $25-100. We also buy longer pieces, 2,000-2,500-word profiles of prominent lawyers or legal trend stories. No articles without a legal angle, but we like to see good, idiomatic writing, mostly free of legal jargon." Buys 50 mss/year. Query with published clips or send complete ms. Pays $450. Sometimes pays the expenses of writers on assignment.

Columns/Departments: "For those who are not covering legal affairs on a regular basis, a good way into *The National Law Journal* is through our Exhibit A feature. Every week we print a sort of reporter's notebook on some proceeding currently underway in a courtroom or a short profile. The feature is stylistically and thematically quite flexible--we've even run pieces about lawyers' hangouts, mini-travelogues, and television reviews. It runs about 1,800 words and pays $150-200. We also use op-ed pieces on subjects of legal interest, many of which come from freelancers. Writers interested in doing an op-ed piece should query first." Pays $150.

THE PARALEGAL, The Publication for the Paralegal Profession, Paralegal Publishing Corp./National Paralegal Association, 10 S. Pine St., Box 629, Doylestown PA 18901. (215)348-5575. Editor: William Cameron. 90% freelance written. Works with published/established writers; works with a number of new/unpublished writers each year; eager to work with new/unpublished writers. Bimonthly magazine covering the paralegal profession for practicing paralegals, attorneys, paralegal educators, paralegal associations, law librarians and court personnel. Special and controlled circulation includes law libraries, colleges and schools educating paralegals, law schools, law firms and governmental agencies, etc. Circ. 16,000. Byline given. Buys all or limited rights. Simultaneous queries and, simultaneous, photocopied, and previously published submissions OK. Computer printout submissions acceptable; no dot-matrix. Reports in 2 weeks on queries; 1 month on mss. Writer's guidelines and suggested topic sheet for #10 SAE.

Nonfiction: Book excerpts, expose, general interest, historical/nostalgic, how-to, humor, interview/profile, new product, opinion, personal experience, photo feature, technical and travel. Suggested topics include the paralegal (where do they fit and how do they operate within the law firm in each specialty); the government; the corporation; the trade union; the banking institution; the law library; the legal clinic; the trade or professional association; the educational institution; the court system; the collection agency; the stock brokerage firm; and the insurance company. Articles also wanted on paralegals exploring "Where have they been? Where are they now? Where are they going?" Query or send complete ms. Length: 1,500-3,000 words. Pays variable rates; submissions should state desired fee. Ask amount when submitting ms or other material to be considered. Sometimes pays the expenses of writers on assignment.

Photos: Send photos with query or ms. Captions, model release, and identification of subjects required.

Columns/Departments: Case at Issue (a feature on a current case from a state or federal court which either directly or indirectly affects paralegals and their work with attorneys, the public, private or governmental sector); Humor (cartoons, quips, short humorous stories, anecdotes and one-liners in good taste and germane to the legal profession; and My Position (an actual presentation by a paralegal who wishes to share with others his/her job analysis). Query. Submissions should state desired fee.

Fillers: Clippings, jokes, gags, anecdotes, short humor and newsbreaks.

THE PENNSYLVANIA LAWYER, Pennsylvania Bar Association, 100 South St., Box 186, Harrisburg PA 17108. (717)238-6715. Executive Editor: Francis J. Fanucci. Managing Editor: Donald C. Sarvey. 25% freelance written. Prefers to work with published/established writers. Magazine published 7 times/year as a service to the legal profession. Circ. 27,000. Pays on acceptance. Publishes ms an average of 3-6 months after acceptance. Byline given. Buys negotiable serial rights; generally first rights, occasionally one-time rights or second serial (reprint) rights. Submit seasonal/holiday material 6 months in advance. Simultaneous submissions are discouraged. Computer printout submissions acceptable; prefers letter-quality. Reports in 4-6 weeks. Free sample copy.

Nonfiction: General interest, how-to, humor, interview/profile, new product, and personal experience. All features *must* relate in some way to Pennsylvania lawyers or the practice of law in Pennsylvania. Buys 10-12 mss/year. Query. Length: 600-1,500 words. Pays $75-350. Sometimes pays the expenses of writers on assignment.

STUDENT LAWYER, American Bar Association, 750 N. Lake Shore Dr., Chicago IL 60611. (312)988-6048. Editor: Sarah Hoban. Associate Editor: Arnie Feingold. 95% freelance written. Works with a small number of new/unpublished writers each year. Monthly (September-May) magazine. Circ. 40,000. Pays on publication. Buys first serial rights and second serial (reprint) rights. Pays negotiable kill fee. Byline given. Submit seasonal/holiday material 4 months in advance. Photocopied submissions OK. Computer printout submissions acceptable; prefers letter-quality. Reports in 6 weeks. Publishes ms an average of 3 months after acceptance. Sample copy $3; free writer's guidelines.

Nonfiction: Expose (government, law, education and business); profiles (prominent persons in law-related fields); opinion (on matters of current legal interest); essays (on legal affairs); interviews; and photo features. Recent article examples: "Caught on Death Row" (January 1988) and "The Wrongs of Legal Writing" (October 1987). Buys 5 mss/issue. Query. Length: 3,000-5,000 words. Pays $250-600 for main features. Covers some writer's expenses.

Columns/Departments: Briefly (short stories on unusual and interesting developments in the law); Legal Aids (unusual approaches and programs connected to teaching law students and lawyers); Esq. (brief profiles of people in the law); End Note (very short pieces on a variety of topics; can be humorous, educational, outrageous); Pro Se (opinion slot for authors to wax eloquent on legal issues, civil rights conflicts, the state of the union); and Et Al. (column for short features that fit none of the above categories). Buys 4-8 mss/issue. Length: 250-1,000 words. Pays $75-250.

Fiction: "We buy fiction only when it is very good and deals with issues of law in the contemporary world or offers insights into the inner workings of lawyers. No mystery or science fiction accepted."

Tips: "*Student Lawyer* actively seeks good new writers. Legal training definitely not essential; writing talent is. The writer should not think we are a law review; we are a feature magazine with the law (in the broadest sense) as the common denominator. Past articles concerned gay rights, prison reform, the media, pornography, capital punishment, and space law. Find issues of national scope and interest to write about; be aware of subjects the magazine—and other media—have already covered and propose something new. Write clearly and well."

VERDICT MAGAZINE, Legal Journal of the Association of Southern California Defense Counsel, American Lifestyle Communications, Inc., 123 Truxtun Ave., Bakersfield CA 93301. (805)325-7124. Editor: Sharon Muir. Managing Editor: Steve Walsh. A quarterly magazine covering defense law (insurance). Circ. 5,000. Pays on publication. Byline given. Buys first North American serial rights. Submit seasonal/holiday material 4 months in advance. Photocopied submissions OK. Computer printout submissions acceptable. Reports in 2 months. Sample copy for $2.50, 9x12 SAE and 8 first class stamps; free writer's guidelines.

Nonfiction: How-to (insurance defense law); interview/profile; personal experience; and technical. Buys 12 mss/year. Send complete ms. Length: 1,500-3,000 words. Pays $10-15.

Photos: Send photos with ms. Pays $5 for 3x5 b&w prints. Captions required. Buys all rights.

Columns/Departments: Buys 4 mss/year. Send complete ms. Length: 500-750 words. Pays $10-15.

Fiction: Historical and mystery. Buys 4 mss/year. Send complete ms. Length: 1,500-3,000 words. Pays $10-15.

Leather Goods

NSRA NEWS, National Shoe Retailers Association, Suite 400, 9861 Broken Land Pkwy., Columbia MD 21046. (301)381-8282. Editor: Cynthia Emmel. 10% freelance written. Bimonthly newsletter covering footwear/accessory industry. Looks for articles that are "informative, educational, but with wit, interest, and creativity. I hate dry, dusty articles." Circ. 4,000-5,000. Byline sometimes given. Buys one-time rights. Submit seasonal/holiday material 3 months in advance. Photocopied submissions OK. Computer printout submissions OK; no dot-matrix. Reports in 2 weeks.
Nonfiction: How-to, interview/profile, new product and technical. January and July are shoe show issues. Buys 4 mss/year. Length: 450 words. Pays $125 for assigned articles. Pays up to $250 for "full-fledged research—1,000 words on assigned articles.
Photos: State availability of photos with submission. Offers no additional payment for photos accepted with ms. Buys one-time rights.
Columns/Departments: Query. Pays $50-125.
Tips: "We are a trade magazine/newsletter for the footwear industry. Any information pertaining to our market is helpful: ex. advertising/display/how-tos."

Library Science

Librarians read these journals for advice on promotion and management of libraries, library and book trade issues and information access and transfer. Be aware of current issues such as censorship, declines in funding and government information policies. For journals on the book trade see Book and Bookstore.

AMERICAN LIBRARIES, 50 E. Huron St., Chicago IL 60611. (312)944-6780. Editor: Arthur Plotnik. 5-10% freelance written. Works with a small number of new/unpublished writers each year. Magazine published 11 times/year for librarians. "A highly literate audience. They are for the most part practicing professionals with a down-to-earth interest in people and current trends." Circ. 48,000. Buys first North American serial rights. Publishes ms an average of 4 months after acceptance. Pays negotiable kill fee. Byline given. Will consider photocopied submissions if not being considered elsewhere at time of submission. Computer printout submissions acceptable; prefers letter-quality. Submit seasonal material 6 months in advance. Reports in 10 weeks.
Nonfiction: "Material reflecting the special and current interests of the library profession. Nonlibrarians should browse recent journals in the field, available on request in medium-sized and large libraries everywhere. Topic and/or approach must be fresh, vital, or highly entertaining. Library memoirs and stereotyped stories about old maids, overdue books, fines, etc., are unacceptable. Our first concern is with the American Library Association's activities and how they relate to the 46,000 reader/members. Tough for an outsider to write on this topic, but not to supplement it with short, offbeat or significant library stories and features." No fillers. Buys 2-6 freelance mss/year. Pays $15 for news tips used, and $25-300 for briefs and articles.
Photos: "Will look at color transparencies and bright color prints for inside and cover use." Pays $50-200 for photos.
Tips: "You can break in with a sparkling, 300-word report on a true, offbeat library event, use of new technology, or with an exciting color photo and caption. Though stories on public libraries are always of interest, we especially need arresting material on academic and school libraries."

CHURCH MEDIA LIBRARY MAGAZINE, 127 9th Ave. N., Nashville TN 37234. (615)251-2752. Editor: Floyd B. Simpson. Quarterly magazine. For adult leaders in church organizations and people interested in

> 66 Most writers don't understand that editors are desperate for good material with strong reporting and strong writing. We are very nice to good writers. 99
>
> —Ed Weathers
> Memphis Magazine

library work (especially church library work). Circ. 16,000. Pays on publication. Buys all rights, first serial rights and second serial (reprint) rights. Byline given. Phone queries OK. Submit seasonal/holiday material 14 months in advance. Previously published submissions OK. Reports in 1 month. Free sample copy and writer's guidelines.

Nonfiction: "We are primarily interested in articles that relate to the development of church libraries in providing media and services to support the total program of a church and in meeting individual needs. We publish how-to accounts of services provided, promotional ideas, exciting things that have happened as a result of implementing an idea or service; human interest stories that are library-related; and media education (teaching and learning with a media mix). Articles should be practical for church library staffs and for teachers and other leaders of the church." Buys 10-15 mss/issue. Query. Pays 5¢/word.

EMERGENCY LIBRARIAN, Dyad Services, Box 46258, Stn. G, Vancouver, British Columbia V6R 4G6 Canada. Editor: Carol Ann Haycock. 5 issues/year. Circ. 5,500. Pays on publication. Photocopied submissions OK. No multiple submissions. Reports in 6 weeks. Free writer's guidelines.
Nonfiction: Emphasis is on improvement of library service for children and young adults in school and public libraries. Also annotated bibliographies. Buys 3 mss/issue. Query. Length: 1,000-3,500 words. Pays $50.
Columns/Departments: Five regular columnists. Also Book Reviews (of professional materials in education, librarianship). Query. Length: 100-300 words. Payment consists of book reviewed.

THE LIBRARY IMAGINATION PAPER, Carol Bryan Imagines, 1000 Byus Dr., Charleston WV 25311. (304)345-2378. 30% freelance written. Quarterly newspaper covering public relations education for librarians, clip art included in each issue. Circ. 3,000. Pays on publication. Publishes ms an average of 6 months after acceptance. Byline given. Buys one-time rights. Submit seasonal/holiday material 3 months in advance. Simultaneous, photocopied and previously published submissions OK. Computer printout submissions OK; prefers letter-quality. Reports in 6 weeks on queries; 3 weeks on mss. Sample copy $4.50; writer's guidelines for SASE.
Nonfiction: How-to (on "all aspects of good library public relations both mental tips and hands-on methods. "We need how-to and tips pieces on all aspects of PR, for library subscribers—both school and public libraries. In the past we've featured pieces on taking good photos, promoting an anniversary celebration, working with printers, and producing a slide show." No articles on "what the library means to me." Buys 4-6 mss/year. Query with or without published clips, or send complete ms. Length: 500-2,200 words. Pays $35.
Photos: Send photos with submission. Reviews 5x7 prints. Offers $5 per photo. Captions required. Buys one-time rights.
Tips: "Someone who has worked in the library field and has first hand knowledge of library PR needs, methods and processes will do far better with us. Our readers are people who can not be written down to—but their library training has not always incorporated enough preparation for handling promotion, publicity and the public."

LIBRARY JOURNAL, 249 N. 17th St., New York NY 10011. Editor-in-Chief: John N. Berry III. 60% freelance written. Eager to work with new/unpublished writers. For librarians (academic, public, special). Magazine published 20 times/year. Circ. 30,000. Buys all rights. Pays on publication. Publishes ms an average of 12-18 months after acceptance. Computer printout submissions OK; prefers letter-quality. "Our response time is slow, but improving."
Nonfiction: *"Library Journal* is a professional magazine for librarians. Freelancers are most often rejected because they are not librarians or they submit one of the following types of article: 'A wonderful, warm, concerned, loving librarian who started me on the road to good reading and success'; 'How I became rich, famous, and successful by using my public library'; 'Libraries are the most wonderful and important institutions in our society, because they have all of the knowledge of mankind—praise them.' We need material of greater sophistication, dealing with issues related to the transfer of information, access to it, or related phenomena. (Current hot are copyright, censorship, the decline in funding for public institutions, the local politics of libraries, trusteeship, U.S. government information policy, etc.)" Professional articles on criticism, censorship, professional concerns, library activities, historical articles, information technology, automation and management, and spot news. Outlook should be from librarian's point of view. Buys 50-65 unsolicited mss/year. Submit complete ms. Length: 1,500-2,000 words. Pays $50-350. Sometimes pays the expenses of writers on assignment.
Photos: Payment for b&w or color glossy photos purchased without accompanying mss is $35. Must be at least 5x7. Captions required.
Tips: "We're increasingly interested in material on library management, public sector fundraising, and information policy."

‡THE NEW LIBRARY SCENE, Library Binding Institute. 150 Allens Creek Rd., Rochester NY 14618. (716)461-4380. 50% freelance written. A bimonthly magazine on library book binding and conservation. Circ. 3,000. Pays on acceptance. Publishes ms an average of 2 months after acceptance. Byline given. Buys first North American serial rights. Computer printout submissions OK; prefers letter-quality. Reports in 1 month. Free sample copy and writer's guidelines.

Nonfiction: How-to (libraries, book binding, conservation), interview/profile and technical. Buys 6-10 mss/year. Query. Pays $100.

Photos: State availability of photos with submission. Reviews contact sheets and prints (3x5 or 5x7). Offers no additional payment for photos accepted with ms. Identification of subjects required. Buys one-time rights.

SCHOOL LIBRARY JOURNAL, 205 E. 42nd. St., New York NY 10017. Editor: Lillian N. Gerhardt. For librarians in schools and public libraries. Magazine published 10 times/year. Circ. 42,000. Buys all rights. Pays on publication. Reports in 6 months.

Nonfiction: Articles on library services, local censorship problems, and how-to articles on programs that use books, films or microcomputer software. Informational, personal experience, interview, expose, and successful business operations. "Interested in history articles on the establishment/development of children's and young adult services in schools and public libraries." Buys 24 mss/year. Length: 2,500-3,000 words. Pays $100 and up, depending on length.

Lumber

NORTHERN LOGGER AND TIMBER PROCESSOR, Northeastern Loggers' Association, Box 69, Old Forge NY 13420. (315)369-3078. Editor: Eric A. Johnson. 40% freelance written. Monthly magazine of the forest industry in the northern U.S. (Maine to Minnesota and south to Virginia and Missouri). "We are not a purely technical journal, but are more information oriented." Circ. 13,000. Pays on publication. Publishes ms an average of 3 months after acceptance. Byline given. Buys all rights. Submit seasonal/holiday material 3 months in advance. Photocopied and previously published submissions OK. "Any computer printout submission that can be easily read is acceptable." Reports in 2 weeks. Free sample copy.

Nonfiction: Expose, general interest, historical/nostalgic, how-to, interview/profile, new product and opinion. "We only buy feature articles, and those should contain some technical or historical material relating to the forest products industry." Buys 12-15 mss/year. Query. Length: 500-2,500 words. Pays $25-125.

Photos: Send photos with ms. Pays $20-35 for 35mm color transparencies; $5-15 for 5x7 b&w prints. Captions and identification of subjects required.

Tips: "We accept most any subject dealing with this part of the country's forest industry, from historical to logging, firewood, and timber processing."

ROSEBURG WOODSMAN, Roseburg Forest Products Co., % Chevalier Advertising, Suite 101, 4905 SW Griffith Dr., Beaverton OR 97005. Editor: Gregory J. Chevalier. 99% (but many rewritten) freelance written. Prefers to work with published/established writers. Monthly magazine for wholesale lumber distributors and other buyers of forest products, such as furniture manufacturers. Emphasis on wood products, especially company products. Publishes a special Christmas issue. Circ. 8,000. Pays on acceptance. Publishes ms an average of 6 months to 1 year after acceptance. Buys first serial rights or one-time rights. No byline given. Submit seasonal material 6 months in advance. Computer printout submissions acceptable. Reports in 2 weeks. Free sample copy and writer's guidelines.

Nonfiction: Features on the "residential, commercial and industrial applications of wood products, such as lumber, plywood, prefinished wall paneling, and particleboard, particularly Roseburg Forest Products Co. products. We are looking for some stories on hobbyists and individual craftsmen. Story should be well-illustrated. No fillers, isolated photos or inadequately illustrated articles." Buys 25-30 mss/year. Query or submit complete ms. Length: 250-500 words. Pays $100-500 including photographs. Pays expenses of writers on assignment.

Photos: "Photos are essential. Good pictures will sell us on a story." Rarely uses b&w photos. Prefers color transparencies or 35mm slides. Pays $50 extra for photo used on cover. Photos purchased only with ms.

Tips: "Since many stories are rewritten to our style or length, the writer's style is not vitally important. However, there should be some expertise regarding forest products terms, and an absolute dedication to accuracy. I often hire a freelancer 'on assignment' at a higher rate. Send letter specifying experience, publications, types of stories and geographic area covered."

SOUTHERN LUMBERMAN, Greysmith Publishing, Inc., Suite 116, 128 Holiday Ct., Franklin TN 37064. (615)791-1961. Editor: Nanci P. Gregg. 20-30% freelance written. Works with a small number of new/unpublished writers each year. A monthly trade journal for the lumber industry. Circ. 10,000. Pays on publication. Publishes ms an average of 4 months after acceptance. Byline sometimes given. Not copyrighted. Buys all rights. Submit seasonal/holiday material 6 months in advance. Query for electronic submissions. Computer printout submissions OK; prefers letter-quality. Reports in 1 month on queries; 2 months on mss.

Sample copy $1 with 9x12 SAE and 5 first class stamps.
Nonfiction: Expose, historical, interview/profile, new product, technical. Buys 20-30 mss/year. Query with or without published clips, or send complete ms. Length: 500-2,000 words. Pays $150-350 for assigned articles; pays $150-250 for unsolicited articles. Sometimes pays the expenses of writers on assignment.
Photos: Send photos with submission. Reviews transparencies and 4x5 prints. Offers $10 per photo. Captions and identification of subjects required.
Tips: "Like most, we appreciate a clearly-worded query listing merits of suggested story—what it will tell our readers they need/want to know. We want quotes, we want opinions to make others discuss the article. Best hint? Find an interesting sawmill operation owner and start asking questions—I bet a story idea develops. We need b&w photos too. Most open is what we call the Sweethart Mill stories. We publish at least one per month, and hope to be printing two or more monthly in the immediate future. Find a sawmill operator and ask questions—what's he doing bigger, better, different. We're interested in new facilities, better marketing, improved production."

Machinery and Metal

CANADIAN MACHINERY & METALWORKING, 777 Bay St., Toronto, Ontario M5W 1A7 Canada. (416)596-5714. Editor: Nick Hancock. 15% freelance written. Monthly. Buys first Canadian rights. Pays on acceptance. Query. Publishes ms an average of 6 weeks after acceptance.
Nonfiction: Technical and semitechnical articles dealing with metalworking operations in Canada and in the U.S., if of particular interest to Canadian readers. Accuracy and service appeal to readers is a must. Pays minimum 25¢/word.
Photos: Purchased with mss and with captions only. Pays $10 minimum for b&w features.

CUTTING TOOL ENGINEERING, 464 Central Ave., Northfield IL 60093. (312)441-7520. Publisher: John William Roberts. Editor: Larry Teeman. Prefers to work with published/established writers. For metalworking industry executives and engineers concerned with the metal-cutting/metal and material removal/abrasive machining function in metalworking. Bimonthly. 25% freelance written. Circ. 38,775. Pays on publication. Publishes ms an average of 6 months after acceptance. Byline given. Buys all rights. Query for electronic submissions. Computer printout submissions acceptable; no dot-matrix. Write Larry Teeman before querying or submitting ms. Free sample copy.
Nonfiction: "Intelligently written articles on specific applications of all types of metal cutting tools, mills, drills, reamers, etc. Articles must contain all information related to the operation, such as feeds and speeds, materials machined, etc. Should be tersely written, in-depth treatment. In the Annual Diamond/Superabrasive Directory, published in June, we cover the use of diamond/superabrasive cutting tools and diamond/superabrasive grinding wheels." Length: 1,000-2,500 words. Pays "$35/published page, or about 5¢/published word."
Photos: Purchased with mss. 8x10 color or b&w glossies preferred.
Tips: "The most frequent mistake made by writers in submitting an article for us is that they don't know the market."

MODERN MACHINE SHOP, 6600 Clough Pike, Cincinnati OH 45244. Editor: Ken Gettelman. 25% freelance written. Monthly. Pays 1 month following acceptance. Publishes ms an average of 6 months after acceptance. Byline given. Query for electronic submissions. Computer printout submissions acceptable; prefers letter-quality. Reports in 5 days. Writer's guidelines for #10 SAE with 1 first class stamp.
Nonfiction: Uses articles dealing with all phases of metal working, manufacturing and machine shop work, with photos. No general articles. "Ours is an industrial publication, and contributing authors should have a working knowledge of the metalworking industry." Buys 10 unsolicited mss/year. Query. Length: 800-3,000 words. Pays current market rate. Sometimes pays the expenses of writers on assignment.
Tips: "The use of articles relating to computers in manufacturing is growing."

Maintenance and Safety

BUILDING SERVICES CONTRACTOR, MacNair Publications Inc., 101 W. 31st St., New York NY 10001. (212)279-4455. Editor: Frank C. Falcetta. 0-5% freelance written. Bimonthly magazine covering building services and maintenance. Circ. 8,000. Pays on publication. Publishes ms an average of 2-4 months after acceptance. Byline sometimes given. Buys one-time rights and second serial (reprint) rights. Simultaneous,

photocopied and previously published submissions OK "as long as not published in competitive magazine." Computer printout submissions OK; prefers letter-quality. Reports in 2 weeks. Writer's guidelines for SAE.
Nonfiction: How-to, humor, interview/profile, new product and technical. Buys 1-5 mss/year. Query only. Pays $75 minimum.
Photos: State availability of photos with submission. Reviews contact sheets. Offers no additional payment for photos accepted with ms, but "offers higher payment when photos are used." Buys one-time rights.
Tips: "I'd love to do more with freelance, but market and budget make it tough. I do most of it myself."

‡CLEANING MANAGEMENT, The Magazine for Today's Building Maintenance Housekeeping Executive, Harris Communications, 15550-D Rockfield Blvd., Irvine CA 92718. (714)770-5008. Editor: R. Daniel Harris Jr. Monthly magazine covering building maintenance/housekeeping operations in large institutions such as hotels, schools, hospitals, etc., as well as commercial and industrial, recreational and religious buildings, stores and markets. For managers with on-staff cleaning operations, contract cleaning service companies, and professional carpet cleaning companies. Circ. 37,000. Pays on publication. Byline given. Offers "full payment, if article has been completed." Buys all rights. Submit seasonal/holiday material 3 months in advance. Simultaneous queries and photocopied submissions OK. Reports in 1 month. Free sample copy and writer's guidelines.
Nonfiction: How-to (custodial operations); interview/profile (of custodial managers); opinion (of custodial managers); personal experience (on-the-job). Special issues include: March—Carpet Care; April and June—Floor Care; May—Exterior Building Maintenance; September—Office Cleaning. Buys 5-6 mss/year. Query. Length: 1,000-2,000 words. Pays $100-300.
Photos: State availability of photos. Pays $5-15 for 8x10 b&w prints; $20-75 for 4x5 color transparencies. Captions, model release, and identification of subjects required.
Tips: "We want writers familiar with our field or who can pick it up quickly."

EQUIPMENT MANAGEMENT, 7300 N. Cicero Ave., Lincolnwood IL 60646. (312)588-7300. Editor: Larry Green. Executive Editor: Jim Clemens. 10% freelance written. Prefers to work with established writers. "We are interested in material related to the heavy equipment industry." Monthly magazine. Circ. 70,000. Pays on acceptance. Publishes ms an average of 4 months after acceptance. Rights purchased vary with author and material; buys all rights. Query for electronic submissions. Computer printout submissions acceptable; no dot-matrix. Reports in 1 month. Sample copy for 9x12 SAE.
Nonfiction: "Our focus is on the effective management of heavy equipment through proper selection, careful specification, correct application and efficient maintenance. We use generic, technical articles, safety features, basics and shop notes. No product stories or 'puff' pieces." Buys 12 mss/year. Query with outline. Length: 2,000-5,000 words. Pays $75/printed page minimum, without photos. Sometimes pays the expenses of writers on assignment.
Photos: Uses 35mm and 2¼ or larger color transparencies with mss.
Tips: "Know the equipment, how to manage it and how to maintain, service, and repair it."

‡MAINTENANCE SUPPLIES, MacNair Publishing, 101 West 31st St., New York NY 10001. (212)279-4455. Editor: Dominic Mariana. 20% freelance written. A monthly magazine on maintenance/sanitary supplies and equipment., "Articles should be geared to the distributors of janitorial supplies." Circ. 15,000. Pays on publication. Publishes ms an average of 2 months after acceptance. Byline given. Publication not copyrighted. Buys one-time rights. Submit seasonal/holiday material 2 months in advance. Photocopied and previously published submissions OK. Computer printout submissions OK; letter-quality preferred. Reports in 1 week. Sample copy for 8x11 SAE with 2 first class stamps. Free writer's guidelines.
Nonfiction: Essays, how-to (sell products to distributors), interview/profile, new product, technical. Buys 15 mss/year. Send complete ms. Length: 1,000-5,000 words. Pays $150-200. Sometimes pays expenses of writers on assignment.
Photos: Send photos with submission. Reviews contact sheets, transparencies and prints. Offers no additional payment for photos accepted with ms. Captions and identification of subjects required. Buys one-time rights.

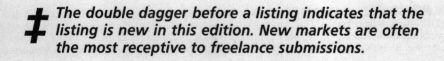

The double dagger before a listing indicates that the listing is new in this edition. New markets are often the most receptive to freelance submissions.

PEST CONTROL MAGAZINE, 7500 Old Oak Blvd., Cleveland OH 44130. (216)243-8100. Editor: Jerry Mix. For professional pest control operators and sanitation workers. Monthly magazine. Circ. 15,000. Buys all rights. Buys 12 mss/year. Pays on publication. Submit seasonal material 2 months in advance. Reports in 1 month. Query or submit complete ms.

Nonfiction: Business tips, unique control situations, personal experience (stories about 1-man operations and their problems) articles. Must have trade or business orientation. No general information type of articles desired. Buys 3 unsolicited mss/year. Length: 4 double-spaced pages. Pays $150 minimum. Regular columns use material oriented to this profession. Length: 8 double-spaced pages.

Photos: No additional payment for photos used with mss. Pays $50-150 for 8x10 color or transparencies.

SERVICE BUSINESS, Published Quarterly for the Self-Employed Professional Cleaner, Service Business Magazine, Inc., Suite 345, 1916 Pike Place, Seattle WA 98101. (206)622-4241. Publisher: William R. Griffin. Editor: Martha Ireland. Associate Editor: Jim Saunders. 80% freelance written. Quarterly magazine covering technical and management information relating to cleaning and self-employment. "We cater to those who are self-employed in any facet of the cleaning and maintenance industry who seek to be top professionals in their field. Our readership is small but select. We seek concise, factual articles, realistic but definitely upbeat." Circ. 6,000. Pays 1 month after publication. Publishes ms an average of 3 months after acceptance. Byline given. Buys first serial rights, second serial (reprint) rights, and all rights; makes work-for-hire assignments. Submit seasonal/holiday material 4 months in advance. Simultaneous queries and previously published work (rarely) OK. Computer printout submissions acceptable; prefers letter-quality. Reports in 3 months. Sample copy $3, 9x7½ SAE and 3 first class stamps; writer's guidelines for #10 SAE and 1 first class stamp.

Nonfiction: Expose (safety/health business practices); how-to (on cleaning, maintenance, small business management); humor (clean jokes, cartoons); interview/profile; new product (must be unusual to rate full article—mostly obtained from manufacturers); opinion; personal experience; and technical. Special issues include "What's New?" (Feb. 10). No "wordy articles written off the top of the head, obviously without research, and needing more editing time than was spent on writing." Buys 40 mss/year. Query with or without published clips. Length: 500-3,000 words. Pays $5-80. ("Pay depends on amount of work, research and polishing put into article much more than on length.") Pays expenses of writers on assignment with prior approval only.

Photos: State availability of photos or send photos with ms. Pays $5-25 for "smallish" b&w prints. Captions, model release, and identification of subjects required. Buys one-time rights and reprint rights. "Magazine size is 8½x7—photos need to be proportionate."

Columns/Departments: "Ten regular columnists now sell four columns per year to us. We are interested in adding a Safety & Health column (related to cleaning and maintenance industry). We are also open to other suggestions—send query." Buys 36 columns/year; department information obtained at no cost. Query with or without published clips. Length: 500-1,500 words. Pays $15-85.

Fillers: Jokes, gags, anecdotes, short humor, newsbreaks and cartoons. Buys 40/year. Length: 3-200 words. Pays $1-20.

Tips: "We are constantly seeking quality freelancers from all parts of the country. A freelancer can best break in to our publication with fairly technical articles on how to do specific cleaning/maintenance jobs; interviews with top professionals covering this and how they manage their business; and personal experience. Our readers demand concise, accurate information. Don't ramble. Write only about what you know and/or have researched. Editors don't have time to rewrite your rough draft. Organize and polish before submitting."

> ❝ *Familiarity with a magazine is a must, though many writers have a hit-or-miss attitude. Writers fail to understand that they waste their time and money when they send things to editors that are ridiculously inappropriate.* ❞
>
> **—Lisa D. Black,**
> **Splash Magazine**

Management and Supervision

This category includes trade journals for middle management business and industrial managers, including supervisors and office managers. Journals for business executives and owners are classified under Business Management. Those for industrial plant managers are listed in Industrial Operations.

‡ASSOCIATION & SOCIETY MANAGER, Macmillan Professional Journals, 1640 5th St., Box 2178, Santa Monica CA 90406-2178. Senior Editor: Les Plesko. 70% freelance written. A bimonthly magazine on association management. "Feature articles emphasize association management, procedures for increasing membership and participation in group activities, techniques of conducting meetings and conventions, and ideas and suggestions for cost-effective management of membership organizations." Pays on acceptance. Publishes ms an average of 4 months after acceptance. Byline given. Kill fee varies. Buys all rights. Photocopied submissions OK. Computer printout submissions OK. Reports in 1 week on queries. Free sample copy and writer's guidelines.
Nonfiction: How-to, interview/profile (associations and association executives). No fiction or consumer-type travel articles. Buys 40 mss/year. Query. "Do not send unsolicited manuscripts." Length:1,500-2,500 words. Pays 12¢/edited word.
Photos: State availability of photos with submission. Reviews prints. Offers no additional payment for photos accepted with ms.
Columns/Departments: Automation (computer use by associations); Insurance (insurance concerns of associations); Communications (public speaking, writing, communicating with members, board of directors, media, etc.). Buys 15 mss/year. Query. Length: 1,200-2,000 words. Pays 12¢/word.
Tips: "Read our publication and query with article idea appropriate for our readership. It would help to send a resume or letter detailing your writing experience, along with published clips."

CONSTRUCTION SUPERVISION & SAFETY LETTER, (CL) Bureau of Business Practice, 24 Rope Ferry Rd., Waterford CT 06386. (203)739-0169. Editor: DeLoris Lidestri. Safety Editor: Winifred Bonney, (203)739-0286. 80% freelance written. "We're willing to work with a few new writers if they're willing to follow guidelines carefully." Semimonthly newsletter. Emphasizes all aspects of construction supervision. Buys all rights. Publishes ms an average of 4 months after acceptance. Phone queries OK. Submit seasonal material at least 4 months in advance. Reports in 6 weeks. Free sample copy and writer's guidelines.
Nonfiction: Publishes solid interviews with construction managers or supervisors on how to improve a single aspect of the supervisor's job. Buys 100 unsolicited mss/year. Length: 360-720 words. Pays 10-15¢/word.
Photos: Purchased with accompanying ms. Pays $10 for head and shoulders photo of person interviewed. Safety interviews do not require photo. Total purchase price for ms includes payment for photo.
Tips: "A writer should call before he or she does anything. We like to spend a few minutes on the phone exchanging information."

‡DATA TRAINING, Weingarten Publications, Inc. 38 Chauncy St., Boston MA 02111. (617)542-0146. Editor: Ken White. Managing Editor: Alex Hamilton. 10-20% freelance written. A monthly magazine on computer training and training management. "*Data Training* is aimed at people who teach other people how to use computers and train managers. We try to help our readers advance in their profession by including information on management and business." Circ. 20,000. Pays on acceptance. Publishes ms an average of 3 months after acceptance. Byline given. Query for electronic submissions. Computer printout submissions OK. Free sample copy; writer's guidelines for #10 SASE.
Nonfiction: How-to, interview/profile, opinion, technical. Buys 12 mss/year. Query with or without published clips or send complete ms. Length: 500-5,000 words. Pays $100-600. Sometimes pays expenses of writers on assignment.
Photos: State availability of photos with submission.
Tips: "Writers should be familiar with computers and/or training. Obviously, a knowledge of our publication would help. With that basic groundwork we are open to freelance writers. Writers should keep in mind that *Data Training* is a business publication and our readers appreciate clear, concise writing on well-defined topics. We will help writers find sources and shape topics if they have the business background and training familiarity. Since we have changed format, we need more material in the 500-2,000-word range."

EMPLOYEE RELATIONS AND HUMAN RESOURCES BULLETIN, Bureau of Business Practice, 24 Rope Ferry Rd., Waterford CT 06386. Supervisory Editor: Barbara Kelsey. 75% freelance written. Works with a small number of new/unpublished writers each year. For personnel, human resources and employee relations managers on the executive level. Semimonthly newsletter. Circ. 3,000. Pays on acceptance. Publishes ms an average of 3 months after acceptance. Buys all rights. No byline. Phone queries OK. Submit seasonal/holiday material 6 months in advance. Photocopied submissions OK. Computer printout submissions acceptable; prefers letter-quality. Reports in 1 month. Free sample copy and writer's guidelines.

Nonfiction: Interviews about all types of business and industry such as banks, insurance companies, public utilities, airlines, consulting firms, etc. Interviewee should be a high level company officer—general manager, president, industrial relations manager, etc. Writer must get signed release from person interviewed showing that article has been read and approved by him/her, before submission. Some subjects for interviews might be productivity improvement, communications, compensation, labor relations, safety and health, grievance handling, human relations techniques and problems, etc. No general opinions and/or philosophy of good employee relations or general good motivation/morale material. Buys 3 mss/issue. Query. Length: 700-2,000 words. Pays 10-15¢/word after editing. Sometimes pays the expenses of writers on assignment.

‡**EXECUTIVE COMMUNICATIONS, Increasing Your Personal Impact**, Magna Publications, Inc., 2718 Dryden Dr., Madison WI 53704-3006. (608)249-2455. Editor: Sandra M. Jones. 10% freelance written. A monthly newsletter about oral communications for executives. "*Executive Communications* is designed to assist middle- to top-level executives improve their oral communcation skills. Articles are short and to the point. *Executive Communications* is *not* a general business or communications newsletter, but is very targeted: ⅓ public speaking, ⅓ corporate communications, ⅓ interpersonal communication." Circ. 3,400. Pays on acceptance. Publishes ms an average of 3 months after acceptance. Byline given. Offers 20% kill fee. Buys first North American serial rights and second serial (reprint) rights. Submit seasonal/holiday material 6 months in advance. Query for electronic submissions. Computer printout submissions OK; no dot-matrix. Reports in 3 weeks. Sample copy $5. Writer's guidelines for #10 SAE and 1 first class stamp.

Nonfiction: Book excerpts (current books on the market specific to oral communications), how-to (improve oral communication skills), interview/profile (how communications is important/used in the executive's position), analysis of trends in business that relate to oral communications. No articles on how to write a business memo, or anything else that is being covered by other general communications publications. Buys 12-24 mss/yer. Query with or without published clips, or send complete ms. Length: 150-250 words. Pays $75-150. May pay in copies "if writer prefers to be paid that way." Sometimes pays expenses of writers on assignment.

Columns/Departments: Corporate Communication: (1 paragraph feature describes what one particular business is doing to forward communications either internally or externally) 50-100 words; pays $5. Test Yourself (reader participation test. Usually 20 questions maximum, must be communications oriented) pays $50-75. From the Podium (features a variety of public speaking articles—how-to's and tips for speakers. Information should be slanted toward advanced, not beginning speakers); 150-250 words; pays $75-150.

Tips: "If you've seen your proposed topic written up in other publications, look at it from a fresh angle for *Executive Communications*. Write for the reader—our audience is busy and well educated. Keep your writing short and to the point, with a minimum of fluff. Sources should be named if they contribute to a major portion of the article. We are most interested in original communications material—how-to's, case studies, executive interviews, analysis pieces, evaluations/ratings of communication programs and materials, and book reviews—all with the emphasis on oral communications."

‡**HUMAN RESOURCE EXECUTIVE**, Axon Group, 1035 Camphill Rd., Ft. Washington PA 19034. (215)540-1180. Editor: David Shadovitz. 15% freelance written. A monthly magazine for human resource professionals/executives. "The magazine serves the information needs of chief human resource executives in companies, government agencies and nonprofit institutions with 500 or more employees." Estab. 1987. Circ. 40,000. Pays on acceptance. Publishes ms an average of 2 months after acceptance. Byline given. Offers 50% kill fee. Buys first rights and second serial (reprint) rights. Query for electronic submissions. Computer printout submissions OK; prefers letter-quality. Reports in 1 month. Sample copy for 13x10 SAE with 2 first class stamps. Writer's guidelines for #10 SAE with 1 first class stamp.

Nonfiction: Book excerpts, interview/profile. Buys 16 mss/year. Query with published clips. Length: 1,700-2,400 words. Pays $200-700. Sometimes pays expenses of writers on assignment.

Photos: State availability of photos with submission. Reviews contact sheets. Offers no additional payment for photos accepted with ms. Identification of subjects required. Buys first and repeat rights.

MANAGE, 2210 Arbor Blvd., Dayton OH 45439. (513)294-0421. Editor-in-Chief: Douglas E. Shaw. 60% freelance written. Works with a small number of new/unpublished writers each year. Quarterly magazine. For first-line and middle management and scientific/technical managers. Circ. 75,000. Pays on acceptance. Publishes ms an average of 6 months after acceptance. Buys North American magazine rights with reprint privileges; book rights remain with the author. Computer printout submissions OK; prefers letter-quality. Reports in 1 month. Free sample copy and writer's guidelines.

Nonfiction: "All material published by *Manage* is in some way management oriented. Most articles concern one or more of the following categories: communications, cost reduction, economics, executive abilities, health and safety, human relations, job status, labor relations, leadership, motivation and productivity and professionalism. Articles should be specific and tell the manager how to apply the information to his job immediately. Be sure to include pertinent examples, and back up statements with facts and, where possible, charts and illustrations. *Manage* does not want essays or academic reports, but interesting, well-written and practical articles for and about management." Buys 6 mss/issue. Phone queries OK. Submit complete ms. Length, 600-2,000 words. Pays 5¢/word.

Tips: "Keep current on management subjects; submit timely work."

MANAGEMENT ACCOUNTING, National Association of Accountants, 10 Paragon Dr., Montvale NJ 07645-1760. (201)573-9000. Executive/Editor: E.S. Koval. Managing Editor: R.F. Randall. 5% freelance written. A monthly magazine covering corporate and financial accounting. Circ. 95,000. Pays on acceptance. Publishes ms an average of 3 months after acceptance. Byline given. Buys all rights. Query for electronic submissions. Computer printout submissions OK; prefers letter-quality. Reports in 2 weeks on queries. Sample copy and writer's guidelines for 9x12 SASE and 5 first class stamps.

Nonfiction: How-to (on accomplishing accounting or financing) and interview/profile (of top financial types—controllers, chief financial officers, etc.). "We do not want articles about CPAs, CPA practices or public accounting." Buys 2-3 mss/year. Query. Length: 800-2,500 words. Pays $100 for assigned articles. Sometimes pays the expenses of writers on assignment.

Photos: State availability of photos with submission. Reviews contact sheets. Offers variable payment for photos. Buys one-time rights.

Tips: "We are planning to expand our coverage of corporate accounting/finance field by commissioning a limited number of feature articles. Freelancers must query first and be thoroughly familiar with the business/accounting world."

MANAGEMENT REVIEW, American Management Association, 135 West 50th St., New York NY 10020. (212)903-8393. Editor: Rod Willis. Monthly magazine covering all aspects of managing in the workplace—private, public, nonprofit. "We have an audience of well-educated, middle- and high-level executives. They are a sophisticated audience looking for pragmatic, *nontheoretical* information and advice on how to run organizations, manage people and operations, and compete in domestic and global markets. Strong emphasis on case studies." Pays on acceptance. Publishes ms an average of 3-4 months after acceptance. Byline given. Offers 50% kill fee. Buys first North American serial rights, second serial (reprint) rights and all rights. Submit seasonal material 4 months in advance. Previously published submissions sometimes OK. Computer printout submissions OK; no dot-matrix. Reports in 3 weeks. Sample copy $5.

Nonfiction: Book excerpts, essays, general interest (business/trade/economics), how-to (case studies and advice for managers), interview/profile, opinion, personal experience (infrequently), other (management, global business, corporate culture topics). "Write for editorial calendar—monthly themes. No cartoons, academic papers, or short 'humorous' looks at management." Buys 100 mss/year. Query with or without published clips, or send complete ms. Length: 500-3,000 words. Pays $250-2,000 for assigned articles; pays $250-1,000 for unsolicited articles. Pays in contributor's copies "when no pay is requested—happens often." Sometimes pays the expenses of writers on assignment.

Photos: State availability of photos with submission. Reviews 8x10 prints. Black and white preferred.

Columns/Departments: Management in Practice (case studies of good management—how problems/opportunities were handled); Global Perspective (information/case studies on international business & trade); Perspective (essays on management or business topics-opinion); On-Line (case studies or advice/information on information technology in management); and Decision Makers (profiles of top executives/managers; focus on their management styles). Buys 30-50 mss/year. Query with published clips. Length: 1,000-1,500. Pays $250-750.

Tips: "Don't write down to audience—the average *MR* reader has a graduate degree, and/or years of hands-on business and management experience. Need practical, *detailed* information on 'how-to' manage all kinds of situations, operations, and people. *Don't* rehash others' work—the audience has already read Drucker, Tom Peters, *et. al.* We do not want press kits or stories on software packages in general. We do want more stories on international business, managing nonprofit organizations and growing companies and managing technology in the workplace. For Decision Makers, Management in Practice, Global Perspective and Perspective columns, we're always looking for good writers. Same goes for features—but always query first. Phone queries okay, but letters preferred."

‡MIDWEST PURCHASING MANAGEMENT and PURCHASING MANAGEMENT, Meyer Associates, Inc., 14 7th Ave. N., St. Cloud MN 56301. (612)259-4000. Editor: Murdock Johnson. Managing Editor: Peg Meyer. 40% freelance written. Monthly magazines covering all aspects of purchasing and materials management. "We prefer 'How to Buy' or 'Ten Tips for Buying' format. Articles should feature a class of products (i.e. 'How to Choose Office Equipment) rather than single products ('Ten Tips for Buying a Copier'). Must apply to all levels of buyer—entry level to manager." Circ. 12,500. Pays on publication. Publishes ms an average of 6 months after acceptance. Byline given. Negotiable kill fee. Buys first rights. Photocopied submissions

Close-up

Rod Willis
Editor
Management Review

"*Management Review* is sort of a hybrid publication," says Rod Willis, who became editor of the magazine after two and one-half years as its managing editor. While the magazine is an association publication with a controlled circulation, its contents are not limited to association news and events. In fact, the magazine is noted for its in-depth coverage of management issues.

"Our readers are either corporate or individual members of the American Management Association. They want articles that examine broad issues of management, case studies, analysis of trends and articles based on new research or surveys," says Willis. "One difference between an association publication like ours and a newsstand business magazine, however, is that we cannot do investigative journalism. We can discuss sensitive issues, but must be mindful of our members."

Willis looks for writers with a well-rounded background. "We don't want to see articles written by consultants or academics who think they've discovered the ultimate management theory. Our needs vary—we like to work with general business writers, but occasionally we'll need someone with expertise in a particular area to explain things like leveraged buy outs," he says.

Willis has a degree in journalism and came to *Management Review* by way of an accounting firm. At Arthur Young, Willis wrote and edited tax and financial publications. He's done technical writing as well as freelance medical writing and says his background helps him appreciate the strengths and weaknesses of an all-around freelancer.

There are a number of pitfalls writers must avoid when tackling unfamiliar subjects, Willis adds. "I think the hardest thing to resist, especially for the new writer, is when you hear of a different management practice. You may think it's new, but first go to the library and see if it's ever been written up elsewhere—you may be surprised."

Writers should go to interviews prepared. "Read everything on the company you can beforehand. Writers must be able to learn quickly. CEOs expect you to know your stuff."

Management Review buys about 100 articles from freelancers each year. Each issue has a theme, so Willis prefers to see queries and clips first. Before contacting him on a story, send a SASE for a writer's kit, which includes guidelines and an editorial calendar. This year he plans to expand coverage to include more international management news.

Willis works with writers from all over the country, but is looking for more work from writers in the South and Northwest, as well as Canadian writers. Trade magazines generally have small staffs, but must cover a large area, says Willis. Freelancers can offer information about their communities that would otherwise be unavailable.

The writers Willis works with must be willing to do the necessary research. "Read the *Wall Street Journal* and the business section of your local paper regularly. Look in your community for innovative and successful companies. We want well-written, well-thought-out, easy-to-read articles. Give specific information—our readers want to feel they really learned something."

—*Robin Gee*

OK. Query for electronic submissions. Computer printout submissions OK; prefers letter-quality. Reports in 1 month. Sample copy for 9x12 SAE with 2 first class stamps. Free writer's guidelines.

Nonfiction: Interview/profile, personal experience, technical. No general interest or general business articles, with single exception of economics. Buys 6 mss/year. Query with published clips. Length: 1,200-3,000 words. Pays $25-150. Sometimes pays expenses of writers on assignment.

Photos: State availability of photos with submission. Reviews contact sheets, negatives, transparencies and prints. Offers no additional payment for photos accepted with ms. Model releases and identification of subjects required.

Tips: "The best ideas and articles come directly from practitioners in the field. Short interviews, or telephone calls, will yield topic ideas. Go for the unusual, the off-the-beaten-path industry or technique. And send an outline first—let's work together to save time and money. A purchaser or materials manager must be all things to all people. He or she doesn't need more general information. Instead, he or she needs very specific information to help do the job better."

PERSONNEL ADVISORY BULLETIN, Bureau of Business Practice, 24 Rope Ferry Rd., Waterford CT 06386. (203)442-4365, ext. 314. Editor: Jill Whitney. 75% freelance written. Eager to work with new/unpublished writers. Emphasizes all aspects of personnel practices for personnel managers in all types and sizes of companies, both white collar and industrial. Semimonthly newsletter. Pays on acceptance. Publishes ms an average of 5 months after acceptance. Buys all rights. Phone queries OK. Submit seasonal/holiday material 4 months in advance. Computer printout submissions acceptable; prefers letter-quality. Reports in 2 weeks. Free sample copy and writer's guidelines for 10x13 SAE and 2 first class stamps.

Nonfiction: Interviews with personnel managers or human resource professionals on topics of current interest in the personnel field. No articles on hiring and interviewing, discipline, or absenteeism/tardiness control. Buys 30 mss/year. Query with brief, specific outline. Length: 1,500-1,800 words.

Tips: "We're looking for concrete, practical material on how to solve problems. We're providing information about trends and developments in the field. We don't want filler copy. It's very easy to break in. Just query by phone or letter (preferably phone) and we'll discuss the topic. Send for guidelines first, though, so we can have a coherent conversation."

PRODUCTION SUPERVISOR'S BULLETIN, Bureau of Business Practice, 24 Rope Ferry Rd., Waterford CT 06386. (800)243-0876. Editor: Anna Maria Trusky. Managing Editor: Wayne N. Muller. 75% freelance written. Biweekly newsletter. "The audience is primarily first-line production supervisors. Articles are meant to address a common workplace issue faced by such a supervisor, (absenteeism, low productivity, etc) and explain how interviewee dealt with the problem." Circ. 5,000. Pays on acceptance. Publishes ms an average of 4 months after acceptance. Byline not given. Buys all rights. Computer printout submissions OK; prefers letter-quality. Reports in 2 weeks on queries; 3 weeks on mss. Free sample copy and writer's guidelines.

Nonfiction: How-to (on managing people, solving workplace problems, improving productivity). No high-level articles aimed at upper management. Buys 60-70 mss/year. Query. Length: 800-1,500 words. Pays 9-15¢/word.

Tips: "Freelancers may call me at (800)243-0876 or (203)442-4365. Or write for further information. Sections of publication most open to freelancers are lead story; inside stories (generally 3 to 4 per issue); and Production Management Clinic (in every other issue). Simply include lots of concrete, how-to steps for dealing effectively with the topic at hand."

PRODUCTIVITY IMPROVEMENT BULLETIN, PIB, Bureau of Business Practice, 24 Rope Ferry Rd., Waterford CT 06386. (203)442-4365. Editor: Shelley Wolf. 75% freelance written. Eager to work with new/unpublished writers. Semimonthly newsletter covering productivity improvement programs and techniques of interest to top and middle management. Pays on acceptance. Publishes ms an average of 4 months after acceptance. No byline given. Buys all rights. Computer printout submissions acceptable; prefers letter-quality. Reports in 2 weeks on queries; 1 month on mss. Free sample copy and writer's guidelines.

Nonfiction: Interviews with middle managers from business or industry detailing how they solved a particular productivity problem. "Our intent is to (1) offer readers a specific 'success story' that has general applications and (2) to show them how they can put these proven techniques into practice in their own company. That's why stories must combine *case-study information* with *how-to advice*, organized into a series of *bulleted steps to follow*." No articles on quality circles or general management theory. Buys 50 mss/year. Query. Length: 1,000-1,300 words. Pays 10-15¢/word "after editing."

Columns/Departments: "Personal Productivity column uses interview-based copy explaining specific measures managers can take to increase their personal effectiveness." Buys 12 mss/year. Query. Length: 800-1,000 words. Pays 10-15¢/word.

Tips: "All articles *must* cover a 'problem/solution/how-to/results' format as described in the writer's guidelines. We are particulary interested in interviews with plant managers. Topics should be well focused. (Check with us before doing the write-up. We like to talk to freelancers.) Writing should be conversational; use the 'you' approach and speak directly to the readers. Use subheads and questions to guide the reader through your piece. Articles on activities of a specific company are subject to its approval."

SALES MANAGER'S BULLETIN, The Bureau of Business Practice, 24 Rope Ferry Rd., Waterford CT 06386. Editor: Paulette S. Withers. 33% freelance written. Prefers to work with published/established writers. Newsletter published twice a month. For sales managers and salespeople interested in getting into sales management. Pays on acceptance. Publishes ms an average of 3-6 months after acceptance. Written queries only except from regulars. Submit seasonal/holiday material 6 months in advance. Original submissions only. Buys all rights. Computer printout submissions acceptable; prefers letter-quality. Reports in 2 weeks. Sample copy and writer's guidelines only when request is accompanied by SAE with 2 first clas stamps.

Nonfiction: How-to (motivate salespeople, cut costs, create territories, etc.); interview (with working sales managers who use innovative techniques); and technical (marketing stories based on interviews with experts). No articles on territory management, saving fuel in the field, or public speaking skills. Break into this publication by reading the guidelines and sample issue. Follow the directions closely and chances for acceptance go up dramatically. One easy way to start is with an interview article ("Here's what sales executives have to say about . . ."). Query is vital to acceptance; "send a simple postcard explaining briefly the subject matter, the interviewees (if any), slant, length, and date of expected completion, accompanied by a SASE." Length: 800-1,500. Pays 10-15¢/word.

Tips: "Freelancers should always request samples and writer's guidelines, accompanied by SASE. Requests without SASE are discarded immediately. Examine the sample, and don't try to improve on our style. Write as we write. Don't 'jump around' from point to point and don't submit articles that are too chatty and with not enough real information. The more time a writer can save the editors, the greater his or her chance of a sale and repeated sales, when queries may not be necessary any longer. We will focus more on selling more product, meeting intense competition, while spending less money to do it."

SECURITY MANAGEMENT: PROTECTING PROPERTY, PEOPLE & ASSETS, Bureau of Business Practice, 24 Rope Ferry Rd., Waterford CT 06386. Editor: Alex Vaughn. 75% freelance written. Eager to work with new/unpublished writers. Semimonthly newsletter. Emphasizes security for industry. "All material should be slanted toward security directors, primarily industrial, retail and service businesses, but others as well." Circ. 3,000. Pays on acceptance. Buys all rights. Phone queries OK. Photocopied submissions OK. Computer printout submissions acceptable; prefers letter-quality. Reports in 2 weeks. Free sample copy and writer's guidelines.

Nonfiction: Interview (with security professionals only). "Articles should be tight and specific. They should deal with new security techniques or new twists on old ones." Buys 2-5 mss/issue. Query. Length: 750-1,000 words. Pays 15¢/word.

‡SHOPPING CENTERS TODAY, International Council of Shopping Centers, 665 Fifth Ave., New York NY 10022. (212)421-8181. Editor: Mark Westerbeck. 25% freelance written. A monthly tabloid covering the shopping center industry with an emphasis on retailing but including a broad range of development, management, financial and regional issues. No slant—straight news journalism. "Audience is membership of ICSC, essentially: developers, retailers, property managers, financers, suppliers, lawyers, academicians, and government officials." Circ. 24,500. Pays on acceptance. Publishes ms an average of 3 months after acceptance. Byline given. Buys first North American serial rights or simultaneous rights. Submit seasonal/holiday material 2 months in advance. Simultaneous and previously published submissions OK. Query for electronic submissions. Computer printout submissions acceptable; prefers letter-quality. Reports in 2 weeks on queries; 3 weeks on mss. Free sample copy.

Nonfiction: Essays, exposé, general interest, humor, interview/profile, new product and photo feature. No promotional items on firms or people. Buys 40 mss/year. Query with published clips. Length: 500-2,000 words. Pays $150-500. Sometimes pays the expenses of writers on assignment.

Photos: State availability of photos with submission. Reviews contact sheets, transparencies, and prints. Offers $50-250/photo. Identification of subjects required. Buys one-time rights.

Columns/Departments: The Last Stop (humor or feature-like look at shopping center industry), 1,000 words. Buys 6 mss/year. Query with published clips. Pays $300-500.

Fillers: Anecdotes, facts, and newsbreaks. Length: 50-150 words. Pays $25-150.

SUPERVISION, 424 N. 3rd St., Burlington IA 52601. Publisher: Michael S. Darnall. Editorial Supervisor: Doris J. Ruschill. Editor: Barbara Boeding. 95% freelance written. Monthly magazine for first-line foremen, supervisors and office managers. Circ. 6,600. Pays on publication. Publishes ms an average of 6 months after acceptance. Buys all rights. Computer printout submissions OK; prefers letter-quality. Reports in 3 weeks. Sample copy and writer's guidelines for 9x12 SAE with 4 first class stamps; mention *Writer's Market* in request.

Nonfiction: How-to (cope with supervisory problems, discipline, absenteeism, safety, productivity, goal setting, etc.); and personal experience (unusual success story of foreman or supervisor). No sexist material written from only a male viewpoint. Include biography and/or byline with ms submissions. Author photos requested. Buys 12 mss/issue. Query. Length: 1,500-1,800 words. Pays 4¢/word.

Tips: "Following AP stylebook would be helpful." Uses no advertising.

TRAINING, The Magazine of Human Resources Development, Lakewood Publications, 50 S. Ninth St., Minneapolis MN 55402. (612)333-0471. Editor: Jack Gordon. Managing Editor: Chris Lee. 10% freelance written. A monthly magazine covering training and employee development in the business world. "Our core readers are managers and professionals who specialize in employee training and development (e.g., corporate training directors, VP-human resource development, etc.). We have a large secondary readership among managers of all sorts who are concerned with improving human performance in their organizations. We take a businesslike approach to training and employee education." Circ. 52,000. Pays on acceptance. Publishes ms an average of 3 months after acceptance. Byline given. Buys first North American serial rights and second serial (reprint) rights. Simultaneous and photocopied submissions OK. Computer printout submissions acceptable; prefers letter-quality. Reports in 2 weeks on queries; 6 weeks on mss. Sample copy for 9x11 SAE with 4 first class stamps. Writer's guidelines for #10 SAE with 1 first class stamp.

Nonfiction: Essay; exposé; how-to (on training, management, sales, productivity improvement, etc.); humor; interview/profile; new product; opinion; photo feature; and technical (use of audiovisual aids, computers, etc.). "No puff, no 'testimonials' or disguised ads in any form, no 'gee-whiz' approaches to the subjects." Buys 10-12 mss/year. Query with or without published clips, or send complete ms. Length: 200-3,000 words. Pays $50-500.

Photos: State availability of photos or send with submission. Reviews contact sheets and prints. Offers no additional payment for photos accepted with ms. Identification of subjects required. Buys one-time rights and reprint rights.

Columns/Departments: Training Today (news briefs, how-to tips, reports on pertinent research, trend analysis, etc.), 200-800 words. Buys 6 mss/year. Query or send complete ms. Pays $50-75.

Tips: "We would like to develop a few freelancers to work with on a regular basis. We almost never give firm assignments to unfamiliar writers, so you have to be willing to hit us with one or two on spec to break in. Short pieces for our Training Today section involve least investment on your part, but also are less likely to convince us to assign you a feature. When studying the magazine, freelancers should look at our staff-written articles for style, approach and tone. Do not concentrate on articles written by people identified as consultants, training directors, etc."

UTILITY SUPERVISION, (US), Bureau of Business Practice, 24 Rope Ferry Rd., Waterford CT 06386. (203)739-0169. Editor: DeLoris Lidestri. 80% freelance written. "We're willing to work with a few new writers if they're willing to follow guidelines carefully." Semimonthly newsletter emphasizing all aspects of utility supervision. Pays on acceptance. Publishes ms an average of 4 months after acceptance. Buys all rights. Phone queries OK. Submit seasonal material 4 months in advance. Computer printout submissions OK; no dot-matrix. Reports in 6 weeks. Free sample copy and writer's guidelines.

Nonfiction: Publishes how-to (interview on a single aspect of supervision with utility manager/supervisor concentrating on how reader/supervisor can improve in that area). Buys 100 mss/year. Query. Length: 360-750 words. Pays 10-15¢/word.

Photos: Purchased with accompanying ms. Pays $10 for head and shoulders photo of person interviewed. Total purchase price for ms includes payment for photo.

Tips: "A writer should call before he or she does anything. I like to spend a few minutes on the phone exchanging information."

Marine and Maritime Industries

CANADIAN AQUACULTURE, Harrison House Publishers, 4611 William Head Rd., Victoria, British Columbia V8X 3W9 Canada. (604)478-9209. Editor: Peter Chettleburgh. 50% freelance written. Works with a small number of new/unpublished writers each year. A bimonthly magazine covering aquaculture in Canada. Circ. 2,700. Pays on publication. Publishes ms an average of 3 months after acceptance. Byline given. Buys first North American serial rights. Submit seasonal/holiday material 5 months in advance. Computer printout submissions OK. Reports in 2 weeks. Free sample copy for 9x12 SAE with $2 IRCs.; free writer's guidelines.

Nonfiction: How-to, interview/profile, new product, opinion and photo feature. Buys 20-24 mss/year. Query. Length: 200-1,500 words. Pays 10-20¢/word for assigned articles; pays 10-15¢/word for unsolicited articles. May pay writers with contributor copies if writer requests. Sometimes pays the expenses of writers on assignment.

Photos: Send photos with submission. Reviews 5x7 prints. Captions required. Buys one-time rights.

THE FISH BOAT, H.L. Peace Publications, Box 2400, Covington LA 70434. (504)893-2930. Editor: Harry L. Peace. Managing Editor: Robert Carpenter. 10% freelance written. Prefers to work with published/established writers. A monthly magazine covering commercial fishing, seafood processing and marketing. Circ. 19,320. Pays on publication. Publishes ms an average of 4 months after acceptance. Byline given. Buys one-time rights. Simultaneous, photocopied and previously published submissions OK. Computer printout submissions OK; prefers letter-quality. Sample copy $3.

Nonfiction: How-to (on maintaining fishing vessel, engine, hydraulics, other gear); new product (including newly constructed boats and gear innovations); personal experience; technical (related to fishing vessel operation, processing). Special issues include safety and survival, navigations and communication, diesel power and equipment and international shrimp issues. Buys 6-10 mss/year. Query. Length: 1,500 words maximum. Pays $150-250 for assigned articles; pays $150-200 for unsolicited articles. Sometimes pays the expenses of writers on assignment.

Photos: Send color photos with submission. Reviews contact sheets or slides. Offers no additional payment for photos accepted with ms. Identification of subjects required. Buys one-time rights.

Columns/Departments: "We publish no columns, but are open to appropriate suggestions."

Tips: "As U.S. fisheries management changes, we will explore the ways fishermen are adapting to these changes, especially in the areas of boats and gear. The writer must know the commercial fishing field and be familiar with fishing vessels and gear. Spending time with fishermen or reading related trade papers and magazines is helpful. Our freelance needs are geared towards features which, either by regionality or their technical nature, could not have reasonably been prepared in-house. This might include first-person access to a fisheries operation, special understanding of a particular issue of importance to the industry, or a regional slant to an issue or operation worth sharing with a national audience. Whenever possible, we prefer to employ freelancers who can also illustrate their work with suitable photography. Our usual arrangement is to acquire an editorial/photo package."

Medical

Through these journals physicians, pharmacists, therapists and mental health professionals learn how other professionals help their patients and manage their medical practices. Publications for nurses, laboratory technicians and other medical personnel are listed in the Hospitals, Nursing and Nursing Home section. Publications for drug store managers and drug wholesalers and retailers, as well as hospital equipment suppliers, are listed with Drugs, Health Care and Medical Products. Publications for consumers that report trends in the medical field are found in the Consumer Health and Science categories.

AMERICAN MEDICAL NEWS, American Medical Association, 535 N. Dearborn St., Chicago IL 60610. (312)645-5000. Editor: Dick Walt. Executive Editor: Barbara Bolsen. 5-10% freelance written. "Prefers writers already interested in the health care field—not clinical medicine." Weekly tabloid providing nonclinical information for physicians—information on socio-economic, political, and other developments in medicine. "*AMN* is a specialized publication circulating to physicians, covering subjects touching upon their profession, practices, and personal lives. This is a well-educated, highly sophisticated audience." Circ. 375,000 physicians. Pays on acceptance. Publishes ms an average of 2 months after acceptance. Byline given. Offers variable kill fee. Buys all rights. Rights sometimes returnable on request after publication. Simultaneous queries OK. Computer printout submissions acceptable. Reports in 1 month. Free sample copy and writer's guidelines.

Nonfiction: Flora Johnson Skelly, assistant executive editor for outside contributions. Interview/profile (occasional); opinion (mainly from physicians); and news and interpretive features. Special issues include "Year in Review" issue published in January. No clinical articles, general-interest articles physicians would see elsewhere, or recycled versions of articles published elsewhere. Buys 200 mss/year. Query. Length: 200-4,000 words. Pays $400-750 for features; $50-100 for opinions and short news items. "We have limited travel budget for freelancers; we pay minimal local expenses."

Tips: "We are trying to create a group of strong feature writers who will be regular contributors."

APPLIED RADIOLOGY, The Journal of Medical Imaging, Macmillan Professional Journals, Box 2178, 1640 Fifth St., Santa Monica CA 90406-2178. (213)395-0234. Editor: Betsy Schreiber. 10% freelance written. Monthly magazine covering radiology. "Audience consists of radiologists and radiology technologists. Material is therefore highly technical." Circ. 25,000. Pays on acceptance. Publishes ms an average of 3 months after acceptance. Byline given. Makes work-for-hire assignments. Computer printout submissions OK; prefers letter-quality. Reports in 2 weeks on queries; 1 month on mss. Writer's guidelines for #10 SAE with 1 first class stamp.

Nonfiction: Interview/profile, new product and technical. No material written for general public. Buys 10 mss/year. Query. Length: 1,500-3,000 words. Pays 12-15¢/word for assigned articles; 10¢/word for unsolicited articles. Sometimes pays the expenses of writers on assignment.

Photos: Send photos with submission. Reviews prints. Offers no additional payment for photos accepted with ms. Identification of subjects required. Buys all rights.

Columns/Departments: Profile (prominent radiologist or technologist), 1,500-2,00 words. Buys 2 mss/year. Query with published clips. Pays 15-20¢/word.

Tips: Subjects most open to freelancers are "topics dealing with management of radiology departments."

CALIFORNIA PHARMACIST, California Pharmacists Association, Suite 300, 1112 I St., Sacramento CA 95814. (916)444-7811. Managing Editor: Mary Peppers-Johnson. 8% freelance written. Prefers to work with published/established writers. *California Pharmacist*, the official publication of the California Pharmacists Association, is a monthly professional journal for pharmacists. Circ. 7,200. Pays on acceptance. Publishes ms an average of 3 months after acceptance. Byline given. Buys first North American serial rights and first rights. Submit seasonal/holiday material 3 months in advance. Photocopied submissions OK. Computer printout submissions OK; no dot-matrix. Sample copy for 9½x12½ SAE with 4 first class stamps.

Nonfiction: Interview/profile and technical. Annual topics include Home Health Care (February); Poison Prevention (March); Pharmacy Computers (April). Buys 10 mss/year. Query with published clips. Length: 2,250-2,500 words. Pays $150-300 for assigned articles. Sometimes pays the expenses of writers on assignment.

Photos: State availability of photos with submission. Offers $10 maximum per photo. Captions and identification of subjects required. Buys all rights.

CARDIOLOGY WORLD NEWS, Medical Publishing Enterprises, Box 1548, Marco Island FL 33969. (813)394-0400. Editor: John H. Lavin. 75% freelance written. Prefers to work with published/established writers. Monthly magazine covering cardiology and the cardiovascular system. "We need short news articles *for doctors* on any aspect of our field—diagnosis, treatment, risk factors, etc." Pays on acceptance. Publishes ms an average of 2 months after acceptance. Byline given "for special reports and feature-length articles." Offers 20% kill fee. Buys first North American serial rights. Photocopied submissions OK. Query for electronic submissions. Computer printout submissions acceptable. Reports in 1 month. Sample copy $1; free writer's guidelines.

Nonfiction: New product and technical (clinical). No fiction, fillers, profiles of doctors or poetry. Query with published clips. Length: 250-1,500 words. Pays $50-300; $50/column for news articles. Pays expenses of writers on assignment.

Photos: State availability of photos with query. Pays $50/published photo. Rough captions, model release, and identification of subjects required. Buys one-time rights.

Tips: "Submit written news articles of 250-500 words on speculation with basic source material (not interview notes) for fact-checking. We demand clinical or writing expertise for full-length feature. Clinical cardiology conventions/symposia are the best source of news and feature articles."

CINCINNATI MEDICINE, Academy of Medicine, 320 Broadway, Cincinnati OH 45202. (513)421-7010. Managing Editor: Vicki L. Black. 30-40% freelance written. Works with a small number of new/unpublished writers each year. Quarterly membership magazine for the Academy of Medicine of Cincinnati. "We cover socio-economic and political factors that affect the practice of medicine in Cincinnati. For example: How will changes in Medicare policies affect local physicians and what will they mean for the quality of care Cincinnati's elderly patients receive. (Ninety-nine percent of our readers are Cincinnati physicians.)" Circ. 3,500. Pays on acceptance. Publishes ms an average of 3-6 months after acceptance. Byline given. Makes work-for-hire assignments. Simultaneous queries and photocopied submissions OK. Computer printout submissions acceptable; prefers letter-quality. Reports in 6 weeks on queries; 1 month on mss. Sample copy for $2 and 9x12 SAE and 7 first class stamps; writer's guidelines for 4½x9½ SAE with 1 first class stamp.

Nonfiction: Historical/nostalgic (history of, or reminiscences about, medicine in Cincinnati); interview/profile (of nationally known medical figures or medical leaders in Cincinnati); and opinion (opinion pieces on controversial medico-legal and medico-ethical issues). "We do not want: scientific-research articles, stories that are not based on good journalistic skills (no seat-of-the-pants reporting), or why my 'doc' is the greatest guy in the world stories." Buys 8-10 mss/year. Query with published clips or send complete ms. Length: 800-2,500 words. Pays $125-300. Sometimes pays expenses of writers on assignment.

Photos: State availability of photos with query or ms. Captions and identification of subjects required. Buys one-time rights.

Tips: "Send published clips; do some short features that will help you develop some familiarity with our magazine and our audience; and show initiative to tackle the larger stories. First-time writers often don't realize the emphasis we place on solid reporting. We want accurate, well-balanced reporting or analysis. Our job is to *inform* our readers."

‡**CONSULTANT PHARMACIST**, American Society of Consultant Pharmacists, Suite 515, 2300 S. Ninth St., Arlington VA 22204. (703)920-8492. Editor: L. Michael Posey. Managing Editor: Cynthia Rosso. 10% freelance written. A bimonthly magazine on consultant pharmacy. "We do not promote drugs or companies but rather ideas and information." Circ. 10,000. Pays on acceptance. Publishes ms an average of 2 months after acceptance. Byline given. Buys first North American serial rights. Photocopied submissions OK. Query for electronic submissions. Computer printout submissions OK; prefers letter-quality. Reports in 2 weeks. Sample copy for 9x12 SAE with 4 first class stamps. Writer's guidelines for #10 SAE with 1 first class stamp.
Nonfiction: How-to (related to consultant pharmacy), interview/profile, technical. Buys 10 mss/year. Query with published clips. Length: 750-2,000 words. Pays $300-1,200. Sometimes pays expenses of writers on assignment.
Photos: Send photos with submission. Offers $100/per photo session. Captions, model releases, identification of subjects required. Buys one-time rights.
Tips: "This journal is devoted to consultant pharmacy, so articles must relate to this field."

‡**COPE, Cancer News for Professionals**, Pulse Publications, Inc., Suite B 400, 12600 W. Colfax Ave., Denver CO 80215. (303)238-5035. Editor: Pamela J. Avery. Managing Editor: Robert K. Diddlebock. 40% freelance written. A monthly magazine of cancer related news for professionals. Circ. 90,000. Pays on acceptance. Publishes ms an average of 3 months after acceptance. Buys first rights or second serial (reprint) rights. Submit seasonal/holiday material 4 months in advance. Simultaneous and previously published submissions OK. Computer printout submissions OK; prefers letter-quality. Reports in 3 weeks on queries. Sample copy $2.50; writer's guidelines for #10 SAE and 2 first class stamps.
Nonfiction: Expose, general interest, inspirational, interview/profile, new product, opinion, personal experience. Buys 50 mss/year. Query with or without published clips. Length: 300-2,000 words. Pays 30¢/word minimum; $600-700 maximum.
Photos: State availability of photos with submission. Reviews negatives and 35mm or 2¼x2¼ transparencies. Captions, model releases and identification of subjects required. Buys one-time rights.
Columns/Departments: Second Opinion (essays on medical issues, topics, experiences related to cancer or illness), 500-700 words. Buys 15 mss/year. Query with or without published clips. Pays $225 maximum.
Tips: "Since we are a news magazine, the best advice is to have a news angle on a new development or a news peg on which to hang a profile or news feature. Of course, any story or article that's written in a provocative, concise and enlightened manner will be considered on a case-by-case basis. The magazine's news columns are best bets for freelancers."

EMERGENCY, The Journal of Emergency Services, 6200 Yarrow Drive, Carlsbad CA 92009. (619)438-2511. Editor: Laura M. Gilbert. 100% freelance written. Works with a small number of new/unpublished writers each year. A monthly magazine covering pre-hospital services and emergency care. "Our readership is primarily composed of EMTs, paramedics and other EMS personnel. We prefer a professional, semi-technical approach to pre-hospital subjects." Circ. 25,000. Pays on acceptance. Publishes ms an average of 3 months after acceptance. Byline given. Buys all rights, nonexclusive. Submit seasonal/holiday material 3-6 months in advance. Photocopied submissions OK. Computer printout submissions acceptable; no dot-matrix. Reports in 2 months. Sample copy $3; writer's guidelines for #10 SASE.
Nonfiction: Semi-technical expose, general interest, how-to (on treating pre-hospital emergency patients), interview/profile, new techniques, opinion, personal experience and photo feature. "We do not publish cartoons, color *print* photos, term papers, product promotions disguised as articles or overly-technical manuscripts." Buys 60 mss/year. Query with published clips. Length 1,500-3,000 words. Pays $100-400. Sometimes pays expenses of writers on assignment.
Photos: Send photos with submission. Reviews color transparencies and b&w prints. Offers no additional payment for photos accepted with ms. Offers $20-30/photo without ms. Captions and identification of subjects required.
Columns/Departments: Open Forum (opinion page or first-person for EMS professionals), 500 words. Trauma Primer (pre-hospital care topics, treatment of injuries, etc.), 1,000-2,000 words. Drug Watch (focus on one particular drug a month). Buys 40 mss/year. Query first. Pays $100-250.
Fillers: Anecdotes, facts and newsbreaks. Buys 60/year. Length: no more than 500 words. Pays $0-75.
Tips: "Writing style for features and departments should be knowledgeable and lively with a clear theme or story line to maintain reader interest and enhance comprehension. The biggest problem we encounter is dull, lifeless term paper style writing with nothing to perk reader interest. Keep in mind we are not a textbook. We appreciate a short, one paragraph biography on the author."

FAMILY THERAPY NEWS, American Association for Marriage and Family Therapy, 407 1717 K St. NW, Washington DC 20006. (202)429-1825. Editor: William C. Nichols. Managing Editor: Kimberly A. Tilley. 10% freelance written. Newspaper for professional organization covering family therapy, family policy, mental health and behavior sciences. *FT News* is a professional newspaper serving marital and family therapists. Writers should be able to reach both doctoral level and graduate student readers. Circ. 14,000. Pays on acceptance. Publishes ms an average of 3 months after acceptance. Byline given. Buys first North American serial rights. Submit seasonal/holiday material 6 months in advance. Query for electronic submissions. Computer printout submissions OK; prefers letter-quality. Reports in 2 weeks. Free sample copy; writer's guidelines for SAE with 2 first class stamps.

Nonfiction: Only want materials pertaining to the field of family therapy, family policy, family research, mental health and behavioral science for professionals. Query with or without published clips, or send complete ms. Length: 300-1,800 words. Pays $25-200.

Photos: State availability of photos with submission. Reviews 8x10 prints. Payment negotiable. Identification of subjects required. Buys one-time rights.

Columns/Departments: Family Therapy Forum (wide variety of topics and slants on family therapy, education, training, practice, service delivery, the therapists, family therapists in various countries, opinion), to 1,800 words; In Focus (interview with outstanding therapists, other leaders), to 1,500 words. Send complete ms. Length: 600-1,800. Pays $25-100.

Fillers: Facts. Length: 100-300 words. Pays $10-25.

Tips: "The annual conference is a major source of good material for writers, such as those of the American Family Therapy Association. Query editor. Also, we are in need of short, well-written features on current developments in the field. Materials could be developed into columns as well for Family Therapy Forum in some instances, but straight news-based features are the best bet."

FITNESS MANAGEMENT, The Magazine for Professionals in Adult Physical Fitness, Leisure Publications, Inc., Suite 213, 215 S. Highway 101, Box 1198, Solana Beach CA 92075. (619)481-4155. Editor: Edward H. Pitts. 50% freelance written. Bimonthly magazine covering commercial, corporate and community fitness centers. "Readers are owners, managers, and program directors of physical fitness facilities. *FM* helps them run their enterprises safely, efficiently and profitably. Ethical and professional positions in health, nutrition, sports medicine, management, etc., are consistent with those of established national bodies." Circ. 21,000. Pays on publication. Publishes ms an average of 5 months after acceptance. Byline given. Pays 50% kill fee. Buys all rights. Submit seasonal/holiday material 6 months in advance. Query for electronic submissions. Computer printout submissions OK; prefers letter-quality. Reports in 1 month on queries; 2 months on mss. Writer's guidelines for #10 SAE with 1 first class stamp. Sample copy for $5.

Nonfiction: Book excerpts (prepublication), how-to (manage fitness center and program), new product (no pay), photo feature (facilities-programs), technical and other (news of fitness research and major happenings in fitness industry). No exercise instructions or general ideas without examples of fitness businesses that have used them successfully. Buys 30 mss/year. Query. Length: 750-2,000 words. Pays $60-300 for assigned articles; pays up to $160 for unsolicited articles. Pays expenses of writers on assignment.

Photos: Send photos with submission. Reviews contact sheets, 2x2 and 4x5 transparencies and 5x7 prints. Offers $10 per photo. Captions and model releases required.

Tips: "We seek writers who are expert in a business or science field related to the fitness-service industry or who are experienced in the industry. Be current with the state of the art/science in business and fitness and communicate it in human terms (avoid intimidating academic language; tell the story of how this was learned and/or cite examples of quotes of people who have applied the knowledge successfully)."

GERIATRIC CONSULTANT, Medical Publishing Enterprises, Box 1548, Marco Island FL 33969. (813)394-0400. Editor: John H. Lavin. 70% freelance written. Prefers to work with published/established writers. Bimonthly magazine for physicians covering medical care of the elderly. "We're a clinical magazine directed to doctors and physician assistants. All articles must *help* these health professionals to help their elderly patients. We're too tough a market for nonmedical beginners." Circ. 97,500. Pays on acceptance. Publishes ms an average of 3 months after acceptance. Byline given. Offers 20% kill fee. Buys first North American serial rights. Simultaneous queries OK. Query for electronic submissions. Computer printout submissions acceptable. Reports in 1 month. Sample copy for $1; free writer's guidelines.

Nonfiction: How-to (diagnosis and treatment of health problems of the elderly) and technical/clinical. No fiction or articles directed to a lay audience. Buys 20 mss/year. Query. Length: 750-3,000 words. Pays $100-300. Pays expenses of writers on assignment.

Photos: State availability of photos. (Photos are not required.) Model release and identification of subjects required. Buys one-time rights.

Tips: "Many medical meetings are now held in the field of geriatric care. These offer potential sources and subjects for us."

‡GROUP PRACTICAL JOURNAL, American Group Practical Association, 1422 Duke St., Alexandria VA 22314-3430. (703)838-0033. Editor: Charles Honaker. 50% freelance written. Bimonthly magazine on medical group practices. Circ. 43,000. Pays on publication. Publishes ms an average of 6 months after acceptance. Byline given. Buys first North American serial rights. Query for electronic submissions. Computer printout submissions OK; prefers letter-quality. Free sample copy and writer's guidelines.

Nonfiction: How-to, new product, opinion, photo feature, technical, travel, socio-economic aspects of medical group practices. Buys 25 mss/year. Send complete ms. Length: 750-4,000 words. Pays $500-1,000. Sometimes pays expenses of writers on assignment.

Photos: State availability of photos with submissions. Reviews contact sheets, negatives, transparencies, prints. Captions, model releases and identification of subjects required. Buy all rights.

Columns/Departments: Taxes (tax tips); News Issues (current medical events analyses); Marketing (medical marketing tips); Legal Forum (law-legislation analysis). Buys 10 mss/year. Query. Length: 500-1,000 words. Pays $300-500.

Tips: "Call the editor and chat. Discuss story ideas, news needs. Visit a medical group practice and learn what the doctors, CEOs read and want to read."

‡HEALTHCARE PROFESSIONAL PUBLISHING, Division of TM Marketing, Inc., 105 Main Street, Hackensack NJ 06701. (201)342-6511. Managing Editor: Michael Kaufman. 35% freelance written. "Produces single-sponsored publications. Work is made on assignment only. An ability to work with specialized scientific material and condense it into tightly written news stories for physicians is important." Pays on acceptance. Publishes ms an average of 1-2 months after acceptance. Byline sometimes given. Makes work-for-hire assignments. Computer printout submissions OK; prefers letter-quality. Free sample copy.

Nonfiction: Buys 50 mss/year. Query with published clips. Pays $125. Sometimes pays expenses of writers on assignment.

THE JOURNAL, Addiction Research Foundation of Ontario, 33 Russell St., Toronto, Ontario M5S 2S1 Canada. (416)595-6053. Editor: Anne MacLennan. Managing Editor: Elda Hauschildt. 50% freelance written. Prefers to work with published/established writers. Monthly tabloid covering addictions and related fields around the world. "*The Journal* alerts professionals in the addictions and related fields or disciplines to news events, issues, opinions and developments of potential interest and/or significance to them in their work, and provides them an informed context in which to judge developments in their own specialty/geographical areas." Circ. 26,000. Pays on publication. Publishes ms an average of 3 months after acceptance. Byline given. Kill fee negotiable. Not copyrighted. Buys first serial rights and second serial (reprint) rights. Computer printout submissions acceptable. Reports in 2 months on queries; 3 months on mss. Sample copy and writer's guidelines for 9x12 SAE.

Nonfiction: Only. Query with published clips or send complete ms. Length: 1,000 words maximum. Pays 20¢/word minimum. Sometimes pays the expenses of writers on assignment.

Photos: Terri Etherington, production editor. State availability of photos. Pays $25 and up for 5x7 or 8x10 b&w prints. Captions, model release, and identification of subjects required. Buys one-time rights.

Columns/Departments: Under contract.

Tips: "A freelancer can best break in to our publication with six years reporting experience, preferably with medical/science writing background. We rarely use untried writers."

THE MAYO ALUMNUS, Mayo Clinic, 200 SW 1st St., Rochester MN 55905. (507)284-2511. Editor: Mary Ellen Landwehr. 10% freelance written. "We usually use our own staff for writing, and only occasionally use freelancers." For physicians, scientists and medical educators who trained at the Mayo Clinic. Quarterly magazine. Circ. 12,000. Pays on acceptance. Publishes ms an average of 3 months after acceptance. Buys all rights. Computer printout submissions acceptable; prefers letter-quality. Free sample copy; mention *Writer's Market* in request. No writer's guidelines available at this time.

Nonfiction: "We're interested in seeing interviews with members of the Mayo Alumni Association—stories about Mayo-trained doctors/educators/scientists/researchers who are interesting people doing interesting things in medicine, surgery or hobbies of interest, etc." Query with clips of published work. Length: 1,000-3,000 words. Pays 15¢/word, first 1,500 words. Maximum payment is $275. Sometimes pays the expenses of writers on assignment.

Photos: "We need art and must make arrangements if not provided with the story." Pays $50 for each color transparency used. State availability of photos with query. Captions preferred. Buys all rights.

Tips: "I keep a file of freelance writers, and when I need an alumnus covered in a certain area of the country, I contact a freelancer from that area. Those who suit my needs are the writers in the right place at the right time or those who have a story about an interesting alumnus."

MD MAGAZINE,, MD Publications, 3 E. 54th St., New York NY 10022. (212)355-5432. Editor: Sharon AvRutick. Managing Editor: Judith Weinblatt. 90% freelance written. Monthly magazine on culture/travel; a general interest magazine for physicians, covering all aspects of human experience. "Our readers are practicing physicians. *MD's* role is to broaden their horizons, enlighten and entertain them." Circ. 130,000. Pays on acceptance. Publishes ms an average of 6 months after acceptance. Byline given. Offers 33⅓% kill fee. Buys one-time rights. Submit seasonal/holiday material 6 months in advance. Photocopied and previously published submissions OK. Computer printout submissions acceptable; prefers letter-quality. Reports in 1 month. Sample copy for 9x12 SAE, 10 first class stamps and $2; writer's guidelines for #10 SASE.

Nonfiction: Book excerpts, culture, essays (by doctors), opinion (by doctors), personal experience, general interest, historical/nostalgic, photo feature and travel. Buys 100 mss/year. Query with published clips. Length: 1,000-2,500 words. Pays $200-700. Rarely pays expenses of writers on assignment.

Photos: Send photos with ms. Reviews b&w and color transparencies (35mm or larger) and 8x10 prints and b&w contact sheets. Payment varies. Captions required.

Columns/Departments: Doctor After Hours (profile); Word Play (on language); Travel (short, focused, unique) and Artists Worth Watching (up-and-coming visual artist). Buys 25 mss/year. Query with published clips. Length: 1,200-1,500 words. Pays $350.

Tips: "It is fresh ideas and writing that make things and people come alive. Think about what cultural subject would capture a busy doctor's attention and keep it."

THE MEDICAL BUSINESS JOURNAL, Medical Business Publishing Corp., 3461 Rt. 22 E., Somerville NJ 08876. (201)231-9695. Editor: Satish Tyagi. 25% freelance written. "Our authors generally have health care industry credentials." Publishes ms an average of 1-2 months after acceptance. Byline given. Query for electronic submissions. Computer printout submissions OK; prefers letter-quality.

Nonfiction: Query with published clips, or send complete ms. Length: 1,800 words. Pays for assigned articles.

Tips: "We would like to receive profiles of health care business segments written for a highly sophisticated audience. Articles should be oriented toward strategic planning executives and exhibit an understanding of the links between operating companies and the financial markets."

MEDICAL ECONOMICS, Medical Economics Co., Inc., 680 Kinderkamack Rd., Oradell NJ 07649. (201)262-3030. Editor: Don L. Berg. Managing Editor: Larry Frederick. Less than 10% freelance written. Biweekly magazine covering topics of nonclinical interest to office-based private physicians (MDs and DOs only). "We publish practice/management and personal/finance advice for office-based MDs and osteopaths." Circ. 175,000. Pays on acceptance. Publishes ms an average of 3 months after acceptance. Byline given. Offers 25% of full article fee as kill fee. Buys all rights and first serial rights. Computer printout submissions acceptable. Reports in 2 months on queries; 3 weeks on mss. Sample copy for $3 and 9x12 SASE.

Nonfiction: Contact Lilian Fine, chief of Outside Copy Division. How-to (office and personnel management, personal-money management); personal experience (only involving MDs or DOs in private practice); and travel (how-to articles). No clinical articles, hobby articles, personality profiles or office design articles. Buys 8-10 mss/year. Query with published clips. Length: 1,500-3,000 words. Pays $750-1,800. "The payment level is decided at the time go-ahead is given after query."

Photos: Contact Lilian Fine, chief of Outside Copy Division. State availability of photos. Pays negotiable rates for b&w contact sheets and for 35mm color slides. Model release and identification of subjects required. Buys one-time rights.

Tips: "How-to articles should fully describe techniques, goals, options and caveats—in terms that are clear and *realistic* for the average physician. Use of anecdotal examples to support major points is crucial. Our full-time staff is quite large, and therefore we buy only freelance articles that are not already assigned to staff writers. This puts a premium on unusual and appealing subjects."

THE NEW PHYSICIAN, 1890 Preston White Dr., Reston VA 22091. Editor: Renie Schapiro. 20% freelance written. Prefers to work with published/established writers. For medical students, interns and residents. Published 9 times/year. Circ. 40,000. Buys first serial rights. Pays on publication. Publishes features an average of 2 months after acceptance; news within 1 month. Will consider simultaneous submissions. Computer printout submissions acceptable; prefers letter-quality. Reports in 2 months or less. Sample copy for 10x13 SAE with 5 first class stamps; writer's guidelines for SASE.

Nonfiction: "Articles on social, political, economic issues in medicine/medical education. Our readers need more than a superficial, simplistic look into issues that affect them. We want skeptical, accurate, professional contributors to do well-researched, comprehensive, incisive reports and offer new perspectives on health care problems." Not interested in material on "my operation," or encounters with physicians, or personal experiences as physician's patient, or highly technical or clinical material. Humorous articles and cartoons for physicians-in-training welcome. Buys about 6 features/year and 12 short news items/year. Query or send complete ms. Length: 500-3,500 words. Pays $75-625 with higher fees for selected investigative pieces. Sometimes pays expenses of writers on assignment.

Tips: "We will be looking for a few more practically-oriented articles for physicians-in training—how-tos for young doctors starting out. They must be authoritative, and from objective sources, not a consultant trying to sell his services. We would also like to receive short news items (500-1,000 words) on interesting local events around the country that would be of interest to our national audience. Our magazine demands sophistication on the issues we cover because we are a professional journal for readers with a progressive view on health care issues and a particular interest in improving the health care system. Those freelancers we publish reveal in their queries and ultimately in their manuscripts a willingness and an ability to look deeply into the issues in question and not be satisfied with a cursory review of those issues."

NURSINGWORLD JOURNAL, Prime National Publishing Corp., 470 Boston Post Rd., Weston MA 02193. (617) 849-2702. Editor: Ira Alterman. 50% freelance written. A monthly tabloid covering nursing for professional nurses. Circ. 40,000. Pays on publication. Byline given. Buys all rights. Computer printout submissions acceptable; prefers letter-quality. Reports in 1 month on queries; 2 months on manuscripts. Sample copy $2; free writer's guidelines.
Nonfiction: General interest, historical/nostalgic, how-to and technical. Buys 20-50 mss/year. Send complete ms. Length: 500-2,000 words. Pays $50-100.
Photos: Send photos with submission. Reviews contact sheets and prints. Offers no additional payment for photos accepted with ms. Captions, releases and identification of subjects required.

PERINATAL PRESS, Perinatal Press, Inc., 52nd and F Sts., Sacramento CA 95819. (916)733-1750. Executive Editor: J.M. Schneider, M.D. Managing Editor: K. Mulligan, B.A. A newsletter published 6 times per year for perinatal health care providers. Circ. 5,000. Pays on publication. Publishes ms an average of 8 months after acceptance. Byline given. Buys first North American serial rights. Reports in 3 weeks on queries; 6 weeks on mss. Sample copy $3 (guidelines are on inside front cover of each issue).
Nonfiction: How-to, humor, opinion, technical and review articles. Buys 4-6 mss/year. Query. Pays $75-150 for assigned articles. May pay with premiums rather than cash for short pieces, such as book reviews.
Photos: State availability of photos with submission. Reviews 3x5 prints. Offers no additional payment for photos accepted with ms. Captions required. Buys one-time rights.
Poetry: "Have never used poetry before but we would *consider* for publication. Must be about perinatal health care—for professionals." Would offer $25.
Tips: "Feature articles are most open to freelancers. We have a *professional audience* and need well written articles with nonsexist language, and family-centered care philosophy."

PHYSICIAN'S MANAGEMENT, Edgell Communications Health Care Publications, 7500 Old Oak Blvd., Cleveland OH 44130. (216)243-8100. Editor: Bob Feigenbaum. 25% freelance written. Prefers to work with published/established writers. Monthly magazine emphasizes finances, investments, malpractice, socioeconomic issues, estate and retirement planning, small office administration, practice management, leisure time, computers, travel, automobiles, and taxes for primary care physicians in private practice. Circ. 110,000. Pays on acceptance. Publishes ms an average of 6 months after acceptance. Buys first serial rights only. Submit seasonal or holiday material 5 months in advance. Query for electronic submissions. Computer printout submissions acceptable; prefers letter-quality. Reports in 1 month. Sample copy $3.50.
Nonfiction: *"Physician's Management* is a practice management/economic publication, not a clinical one." Publishes how-to articles (limited to medical practice management); informational (when relevant to audience); and personal experience articles (if written by a physician). No fiction, clinical material or satire that portrays MD in an unfavorable light; or soap opera, "real-life" articles. Length: 2,000-2,500 words. Buys 10 mss/issue. Query. Pays $125/3-column printed page. Use of charts, tables, graphs, sidebars and photos strongly encouraged. Sometimes pays expenses of writers on assignment.
Tips: "Talk to doctors first about their practices, financial interests, and day-to-day nonclinical problems and then query us. Also, the ability to write a concise, well-structured and well-researched magazine article is essential. Freelancers who think like patients fail with us. Those who can think like MDs are successful. Our magazine is growing significantly. The opportunities for good writers will, therefore, increase greatly."

PODIATRY MANAGEMENT, Box 50, Island Station NY 10044. (212)355-5216. Publisher: Scott C. Borowsky. Editor: Barry Block, D.P.M. Managing Editor: M.J. Goldberg. Business magazine published 8 times/year for practicing podiatrists. "Aims to help the doctor of podiatric medicine to build a bigger, more successful practice, to conserve and invest his money, to keep him posted on the economic, legal and sociological changes that affect him." Circ. 11,000. Pays on publication. Byline given. Buys first North American serial rights and second serial (reprint) rights. Submit seasonal/holiday material 4 months in advance. Simultaneous queries, and simultaneous, photocopied and previously published submissions OK. Reports in 2 weeks. Sample copy $2; free writer's guidelines.
Nonfiction: General interest (taxes, investments, estate planning, recreation, hobbies); how-to (establish and collect fees, practice management, organize office routines, supervise office assistants, handle patient relations); interview/profile; and personal experience. "These subjects are the mainstay of the magazine, but offbeat articles and humor are always welcome." Buys 25 mss/year. Query. Length: 1,000-2,500 words. Pays $150-350.
Photos: State availability of photos. Pays $10 for b&w contact sheet. Buys one-time rights.

‡PRIVATE PRACTICE, Box 12489, Oklahoma City OK 73157. Executive Editor: Brian Sherman. 80% freelance written. Eager to work with new/unpublished writers. For "medical doctors in private practice." Monthly. Buys first North American serial rights. "If an article is assigned, it is paid for in full, used or killed." Byline given "except if it was completely rewritten or a considerable amount of additional material is added to the article." Pays on publication. Publishes ms an average of 4 months after acceptance. Query. "Computer printout submissions acceptable; prefers letter-quality.

Nonfiction: "Articles that indicate importance of maintaining freedom of medical practice or which detail outside interferences in the practice of medicine, including research, hospital operation, drug manufacture, etc. Straight reporting style. No cliches, no scare words, no flowery phrases to cover up poor reporting. Stories must be actual, factual, precise and correct. Copy should be lively and easy to read. We also publish travel and leisure." No general short humor, poetry or short stories. "Please, no first person humor or other type of personal experiences with your doctor—i.e., my account of when my doctor told me I needed my first operation, etc." Buys 50-60 unsolicited mss/year. Length: up to 2,500 words. Pays "usual minimum $150."

Photos: Photos purchased with mss only. B&w glossies, 8x10. Payment "depends on quality, relevancy of material, etc."

Tips: "The article we are most likely to buy will be a straight report on some situation where the freedom to practice medicine has been enhanced, or where it has been intruded on to the detriment of good health."

RESPONSE! The Magazine of Search, Rescue & Recovery, Jems Publishing Co., Inc., Suite 100, 215 S. Highway 101, Box 1026, Solana Beach CA 92075. (619)481-1128. Executive Editor: Keith Griffiths. Managing Editor: Dave Beck. 20% freelance written. Bimonthly magazine covering search, rescue and recovery for providers and administrators of emergency care. Circ. 10,000. Pays on publication. Byline given. Offers 20-30% kill fee. Buys first North American serial and one-time rights. Submit seasonal/holiday material 6 months in advance. Query for electronic submissions. Computer printout submissions OK; prefers dot-matrix. Reports in 3 weeks on queries; 3 months on mss. Sample copy and writer's guidelines for $1.41.

Nonfiction: Book excerpts, how-to, humor, new product, opinion, photo feature and technical. Special issues include "Winter search and rescue, backcountry vehicles for rescue, tracking, "hasty team" searches, military search and rescue techniques." No "I was saved by a ranger" articles. Buys 6-10 mss/year. Query with or without published clips, or send complete ms. Length: 1,000-3,000 words. Pays 10¢/word. Sometimes pays the expenses of writers on assignment.

Photos: Send photos with submission. Reviews contact sheets, negatives, 2x2 transparencies and 5x7 prints. Offers $10-25 per photo. Buys one-time rights.

Tips: "Read our magazine, spend some time with a rescue team. We will begin to focus on all aspects of rescue, including basic life support, vehicle extrication, transport and treatment, in addition to the specialized rescue we have been covering. Emphasis on techniques and new technology, with more color photos as support."

STRATEGIC HEALTH CARE MARKETING, Health Care Communications, 211 Midland Ave., Box 594, Rye NY 10580. (914)967-6741. Editor: Michele von Dambrowski. 20% freelance written. Prefers to work with published/established writers. "Will only work with unpublished writer on a 'stringer' basis initially." A monthly newsletter covering health care services marketing in a wide range of settings including hospitals and medical group practices, home health services and urgent care centers. Emphasizing strategies and techniques employed within the health care field and relevant applications from other service industries. Pays on publication. Publishes ms an average of 2 months after acceptance. Byline given. Offers 25% kill fee. Buys first North American serial rights. Simultaneous and photocopied submissions OK. Computer printout submissions acceptable; no dot-matrix. Reports in 1 month. Sample copy for 9x12 SAE and 3 first class stamps; guidelines sent with sample copy only.

Nonfiction: How-to, interview/profile, new product and technical. Buys 15 mss/year. Query with published clips. Length: 700-2,000 words. Pays $75-250. Sometimes pays the expenses of writers on assignment with prior authorization.

Photos: State availability of photos with submissions. (Photos, unless necessary for subject explanation, are rarely used.) Reviews contact sheets. Offers $10-30/photo. Captions and model releases required. Buys one-time rights.

Fillers: Facts and newsbreaks. Buys 6/year. Length: 50-250 words. Pays $10-50.

Tips: "Writers with prior experience on business beat for newspaper or newsletter will do well. This is not a consumer publication—the writer with knowledge of both health care and marketing will excel. Interviews or profiles are most open to freelancers. Absolutely no unsolicited manuscripts; any received will be returned or discarded unread."

SURGICAL ROUNDS, Romaine Pierson Publishers, Inc., 80 Shore Rd., Port Washington NY 11050. (516)883-6350. Editor: Mark M. Ravitch, M.D. Executive Editor: Roxane Baer. Monthly magazine for surgeons and surgical specialists throughout the country, including interns and residents, all surgical faculty in medical schools, plus full-time hospital and private practice surgeons and operating room supervisors. Circ. 50,000. Pays on acceptance. Byline given. Buys all rights. Reports in 1 month. Sample copy $5; free writer's guidelines.

Nonfiction: How-to (practical, everyday clinical applications). "Articles for 'The Surgeon's Laboratory' should demonstrate a particular procedure step-by-step and be amply and clearly illustrated with intraoperative color photographs and anatomical drawings." Buys 80 mss/year. Query with published clips. Length: 1,500-2,000 words. Pays $150-500.

Mining and Minerals

‡COAL PEOPLE MAGAZINE, Al Skinner Productions, 629 Virginia St. West, Box 6247, Charleston WV 25362. (304)342-4129. Editor: Al Skinner. Managing Editor: Gary Stuber. 50% freelance written. A monthly magazine with stories about coal people, towns and history. "Most stories are historical—either narrative or biographical about all levels of coal people, past and present—from coal execs down to grass roots miners. Most stories are upbeat—showing warmth of family or success from underground up!" Circ. 10,000. Pays on publication. Publishes ms an average of 3 months after acceptance. Byline given. Buys first rights, second serial (reprint) rights and makes work-for-hire assignments. Submit seasonal/holiday material 2 months in advance. Previously published submissions OK. Computer printout submissions OK; letter-quality preferred. Reports in 3 months. Sample copy for 9x12 SAE and 5 first class stamps.
Nonfiction: Book excerpts (and film if related to coal), historical/nostalgic (coal towns, people, lifestyles), humor (including anecdotes and cartoons), interview/profile (for coal personalities), personal experience (as relates to coal mining), photo feature (on old coal towns, people, past and present). January issue every year is calendar issue for more than 300 annual coal shows, assocation meetings, etc. July issue is always surface mining/reclamation award issue. December issue is Christmas in Coal Country issue. No poetry, no fiction or environmental attacks on the coal industry. Buys 32 mss/year. Query with published clips. Length: 5,000 words. Pays $35.
Photos: Send photos with submission. Reviews contact sheets, transparencies, and 5x7 prints. Captions and identification of subjects required. Buys one-time rights and one-time reprint rights.
Columns/Departments: Editorials (anything to do with current coal issues); Mine'ing Our Business (bull pen type column—gossip—humorous anecdotes), Coal Show Coverage (freelance photojournalist coverage of any coal function across the U.S.). Buys 10 mss/year. Query. Length: 300-500 words. Pays $5.
Fillers: Anecdotes. Buys 10/year. Length: 300 words. Pays $5.
Tips: "We are looking for good feature articles on coal people, towns, companies—past and present, color slides (for possible cover use) and b/w photos to complement stories. Could also use a few news writers to take photos and do journalistic coverage on coal events across the country."

GOLD PROSPECTOR, Gold Prospectors Association of America, Box 507, Bonsall CA 92003. (619)728-6620. Editor: Steve Teter. Editorial Director: Shane Brannam. 60% freelance written. Eager to work with new/unpublished writers. Bimonthly magazine covering gold prospecting and mining. "*Gold Prospector* magazine is the official publication of the Gold Prospectors Association of America. The GPAA is an international organization of more than 10,000 members who are interested in recreational prospecting and mining. Our primary audience is people of all ages who like to take their prospecting gear with them on their weekend camping trips, and fishing and hunting trips. Our readers are interested not only in prospecting, but camping, fishing, hunting, skiing, backpacking, etc. And we try to carry stories in each issue pertaining to subjects besides prospecting." Circ. 50,000. Pays on publication. Publishes ms an average of 6 months after acceptance. Byline given. Buys first North American serial rights and second serial (reprint) rights. Submit seasonal/holiday material 6 months in advance. Simultaneous queries and photocopied and previously published submissions OK. Computer printout submission acceptable; no dot-matrix. Reports in 4-6 weeks. Sample copy for $2; writer's guidelines for #10 SASE.
Nonfiction: Historical/nostalgic; how-to (prospecting techniques, equipment building, etc.); humor; new product; personal experience; technical; and travel. "One of our publishing beliefs is that our audience would rather experience life than watch it on television—that they would like to take a rough and tumble chance with the sheer adventure of taking gold from the ground or river after it has perhaps lain there for a million years. Even if they don't, they seem to enjoy reading about those who do in the pages of *Gold Prospector* magazine." Buys 75-100 mss/year. Query with or without published clips if available or send complete ms. Length: 1,000-3,000 words. Pays $25-100.
Photos: State availability of photos with query or ms. Pays $2.50-$10 for photos, transparencies or reflective art. Cover photos-rates negotiable. Buys all rights.
Tips: "Articles must be slanted to interest a prospector, miner, or treasure hunter. For example, a first-aid article could address possible mining accidents. Any subject can be so tailored."

ROCK PRODUCTS, Maclean-Hunter Publishing Corp., 300 W. Adams, Chicago IL 60606. (312)726-2802. Editor: Richard S. Huhta. 1-5% freelance written. Monthly magazine of the nonmetallic mining industry for producers of cement, lime, sand, gravel, crushed stone and lightweight aggregate. Circ. 23,000. Pays on publication. Publishes ms an average of 3-6 months after acceptance. Byline given. Buys first serial rights. Query for electronic submissions. Computer printout submissions OK; prefers letter-quality. Reports in 2 weeks.
Nonfiction: Technical (maintenance and cement). "All pieces must relate directly to our industry. No general

business articles." Buys 5-6 mss/year. Query. Length: 2,000-4,000 words. Pays variable fee. Pays expenses of writers on assignment

Photos: No restrictions. Color transfer a plus. No additional fee for ms accompanied by photos.

Music

Publications for musicians and for the recording industry are listed in this section. Other professional performing arts publications are classified under Entertainment and the Arts. Magazines featuring music industry news for the general public are listed in the Consumer Entertainment and Music sections. (Markets for songwriters can be found in *Songwriter's Market*—see Other Books of Interest).

CLAVIER, A Magazine for Pianists and Organists, The Instrumentalist Co., 200 Northfield Rd., Northfield IL 60093. (312)446-5000. Editor: Barbara Kreader. 95% freelance written. A magazine published 10 times a year covering keyboard teaching and performance. Circ. 22,000. Pays on publication. Publishes ms an average of 1 year after acceptance. Byline given. Buys all rights. Submit seasonal/holiday material 6 months in advance. Computer printout acceptable; prefers letter-quality. Reports in 1 week on queries; 2 months on manuscripts. Free sample copy and writer's guidelines.

Nonfiction: Essays; historical/nostalgic; how-to (on teaching, keeping a small business running, etc.); humor, interview/profile; personal experience and photo feature. Query with published clips. Length: 1,000-3,000 words. Pays $20-45/printed magazine page.

Photos: Send photos with submission. Reviews contact sheets, negatives, transparencies, and prints. Offers no additional payment for photos accepted with ms; offers $10-20/photo if by major photographers. Captions, model releases and identification of subjects required.

Tips: "Articles should be of interest and direct practical value to our readers, who are studio teachers of piano and organ, church organists, or harpsichordists. Topics may include pedagogy, technique, performance, ensemble playing, and accompanying. Material should be covered clearly and thoroughly but without repetition and unnecessary digressions."

THE INSTRUMENTALIST, Instrumentalist Publishing Company, 200 Northfield Rd., Northfield IL 60093. (312)446-5000. Editor: Elaine Guregian. Approximately 95% freelance written. Works with a small number of new/unpublished writers each year. A monthly magazine covering instrumental music education for school band and orchestra directors, as well as performers and students. Circ. 22,000. Pays on publication. Publishes ms an average of 6-9 months after acceptance. Byline given. Buys all rights. Submit seasonal/holiday material 4 months in advance. Photocopied submissions OK. Computer printout submissions acceptable; prefers letter-quality. Reports in 1 month. Sample copy for 8½x11 SAE and $2; free writer's guidelines.

Nonfiction: Book excerpts (rarely); essays (on occasion); general interest (on occasion, music); historical/nostalgic (music); how-to (teach, repair instruments); humor (on occasion); interview/profile (performers, conductors, composers); opinion; personal experience; photo feature; and travel. Buys 100 mss/year. Send complete ms. Length: 750-1,750 words. Pays $30-45/published page.

Photos: State availability of photos with submission. Reviews slides and 5x7 prints. Payment varies. Captions and identification of subjects required. Buys variable rights.

Columns/Departments: Challenge (opinions on issues facing music educators), 500-750 words; Personal Perspective (advice and ideas from experienced educators and performers), 500-750 words; Idea Exchange ('how-tos' from educators), 250-500 words. Send complete ms. Length: 250-500 words. Pays $30-45.

Fillers: Anecdotes and short humor. Buys 5/year. Length: 250 words maximum. Pays $25-45.

Tips: "Know the music education field, specifically band and orchestra. Interviews with performers should focus on the person's contribution to education and opinions about it. We are interested in interviews and features that focus on ideas rather than on personalities."

INTERNATIONAL BLUEGRASS, International Bluegrass Music Association, 326 St. Elizabeth St., Owensboro KY 42301. (502)684-9025. Editor: Art Menius. 30% freelance written. Bimonthly newsletter covering bluegrass music industry. "We are the business publication for the bluegrass music industry. IBMA believes that our music has growth potential. We are interested in hard news and features concerning how to reach that potential and how to conduct business more effectively." Circ. 3,000. Pays on publication. Publishes ms an average of 2 months after acceptance. Byline given. Not copyrighted. Buys one-time rights. Submit seasonal/holiday material 4 months in advance. Simultaneous, photocopied and previously published submissions OK. Query for electronic submissions. Computer printout submissions OK. Reports in 1 month on queries; 6 weeks on mss. Sample copy for 6x9 SAE and 2 first class stamps.

Nonfiction: Book excerpts, essays, how-to (conduct business effectively within bluegrass music), new product and opinion. No interview/profiles of performers (rare exceptions) or fans. Buys 6 mss/year. Query with or without published clips, or send complete ms. Length: 300-1,200 words. Pays $25 maximum for assigned articles. Pays in contributor's copies unless payment in cash agreed at assignment.

Photos: Send photos with submission. Reviews 5x8 prints. Offers no additional payment for photos accepted with ms. Captions and identification of subjects required. Buys one-time rights.

Columns/Departments: At the Microphone (opinion about the bluegrass music industry). Buys 6 mss/year. Send complete ms. Length: 300-1,200 words. Pays $0-25.

Fillers: Anecdotes, facts, newsbreaks and short humor. Buys 2/year. Length: 60-200 words.

Tips: "The easiest break-in is to submit an article about an organizational member of IBMA—such as a bluegrass association, instrument manufacturer or dealer, or performing venue. We're interested in a slant strongly toward the business end of bluegrass music. At the Microphone is the most open to freelancers. We're especially looking for material dealing with audience development and how to book bluegrass bands outside of the existing market."

MUSIC & SOUND OUTPUT, The Magazine For Performers and Producers, Testa Communications, Inc., 25 Willowdale Road, Port Washington NY 11050. (516)767-2500. Editor: Robert Seidenberg. 40% freelance written. Works with a small number of new/unpublished writers each year. Monthly magazine of contemporary music and recording. Audience is mostly working musicians. Prefers technical versus sociological slant in coverage of rock, jazz, R&B, country, pop, blues, and ethnic music. Circ. 78,000. Pays on publication. Publishes ms an average of 2-3 months after acceptance. Byline given. Offers 10-20% kill fee. Buys all rights. Photocopied submissions OK. Computer printout submissions acceptable; prefers letter-quality. Reports in 2 weeks. Sample copy for $2.50.

Nonfiction: Interview/profile (music performers, producers, engineers); technical (recording, and live sound, query first); and reviews of records. No mss written from a fan's point of view, i.e., features on performers without getting an interview. Buys 10-20 mss/year. Query with published clips. Length: 250-3,000 words. Pays $175-500. Sometimes pays expenses of writers on assignment.

Photos: State availability of photos. Prefers exclusive photos. Reviews color transparencies and 8x10 b&w prints. Pays $50-300 for color; $20-200 for b&w. Identification of subjects required. Buys one-time rights.

Columns/Departments: Record reviews (any genre). Buys 10-20 mss/year. Send complete ms. Length: 200-500 words. Pays $40-100.

Tips: "Music-related clips are always impressive. We are seeking writers with experience in the music industry as a performer or with extensive technical background in recording. Areas most open to freelancers include record reviews and short (500-1,000 words), profiles of new bands, established musicians with a new direction, producers, engineers and innovators."

OPERA NEWS, 1865 Broadway, New York NY 10023. Editor: Patrick O'Connor. 75% freelance written. Monthly magazine (May-November); biweekly (December-April). For all people interested in opera; opera singers, opera management people, administrative people in opera, opera publicity people, and artists' agents; people in the trade and interested laymen. Circ. 120,000. Pays on publication. Publishes ms an average of 3 months after acceptance. Buys first serial rights only. Pays negotiable kill fee. Byline given. Computer printout submissions acceptable; prefers letter-quality. Sample copy $2.50.

Nonfiction: Most articles are commissioned in advance. In summer, uses articles of various interests on opera; in the fall and winter, articles that relate to the weekly broadcasts. Emphasis is on high quality writing and an intellectual interest to the opera-oriented public. Informational, how-to, personal experience, interview, profile, historical, think pieces, personal opinion and opera reviews. Query; no telephone inquiries. Length: 2,500 words maximum. Pays 13¢/word for features; 11¢/word for reviews. Rarely pays the expenses of writers on assignment.

Photos: Pays minimum of $25 for photos purchased on assignment. Captions required.

Office Environment and Equipment

‡GEYER'S OFFICE DEALER, 51 Madison Ave., New York NY 10010. (212)689-4411. Editor: Robert D. Rauch. 20% freelance written. For independent office equipment and stationery dealers, and special purchasers for store departments handling stationery and office equipment. Monthly. Buys all rights. Pays kill fee. Byline given. Pays on publication. Publishes ms an average of 3 months after acceptance. Computer printout submissions acceptable; prefers letter-quality. Reports "immediately."

Nonfiction: Articles on dealer efforts in merchandising and sales promotion; programs of stationery and office equipment dealers. Problem-solving articles related to retailers of office supplies, social stationery items, office furniture and equipment and office machines. Must feature specific stores. Query. Length: 300-1,000 words. Pays $125 minimum but quality of article is real determinant.

Photos: B&w glossies are purchased with accompanying ms with no additional payment.

MODERN OFFICE TECHNOLOGY, Penton Publishing, 1100 Superior Ave., Cleveland OH 44114. (216)696-7000. Editorial Director: John Dykeman. Editor: Lura K. Romei. Production Manager: Vickie Friess. 5-10% freelance written. A monthly magazine covering office automation for corporate management and corporate personnel, financial management, administrative and operating management, systems and information management, managers and supervisors of support personnel, and purchasing. Circ. 160,000. Pays on publication. Publishes ms an average of 6 months after acceptance. Byline given. Buys first and one-time rights. Photocopied submissions OK. Query for electronic submissions. Computer printout submissions acceptable. Reports in 1 month. Sample copy and writer's guidelines for 8½x11 SAE and 2 first class stamps.

Nonfiction: New product, opinion and technical. Query with or without published clips, or send complete ms. Length: open. Pays $250-500 for assigned articles; pays $250-400 for unsolicited articles. Pays expenses of writers on assignment.

Photos: Send photos with submission. Reviews contact sheets, 4x5 transparencies and prints. Additional payment for photos accepted with ms: consult editorial director. Captions and identification of subjects required. Buys one-time rights.

Columns/Departments: Reader's Soapbox (opinions on office-related subjects), 750 words. Buys 3 mss/year. Send complete ms. Pays $75-150.

Tips: "Submitted material should alway present topics, ideas, on issues that are clearly and concisely defined. Material should describe problems and solution. Writer should describe benefits to reader in tangible results whenever possible."

Paint

AMERICAN PAINT & COATINGS JOURNAL, American Paint Journal Co., 2911 Washington Ave., St. Louis MO 63103. (314)534-0301. Editor: Chuck Reitter. 10% freelance written. Weekly magazine. For the coatings industry (paint, varnish, lacquer, etc.); manufacturers of coatings, suppliers to coatings industry, educational institutions, salesmen. Circ. 7,300. Publishes ms an average of 3 months after acceptance. Pays on publication. Pays kill fee "depending on the work done." Buys all rights. Phone queries OK. Simultaneous and photocopied submissions OK. Computer printout submissions acceptable. Reports in 3 weeks. Free sample copy and writer's guidelines.

Nonfiction: Informational, historical, interview, new product, technical articles and coatings industry news. Buys 2 mss/issue. Query before sending long articles; submit complete ms for short pieces. Length: 75-1,200 words. Pays $5-100. Sometimes pays expenses of writers on assignment.

Photos: B&w (5x7) glossies purchased with or without mss or on assignment. Query. Pays $3-10.

Paper

BOXBOARD CONTAINERS, Maclean Hunter Publishing Co., 29 N. Wacker Dr., Chicago IL 60606-3298. (312)726-2802. Editor: Charles Huck. Managing Editor: Raymond Chalmers. A monthly magazine covering box and carton manufacturing for corrugated box, folding carton, setup box manufacturers internationally. Emphasizes technology and management. Circ. 14,000. Pays on publication. Byline given. Buys first North American serial rights. Submit seasonal/holiday material 2 months in advance. Photocopied submissions OK. Query for electronic submissions. Computer printout submissions acceptable; no dot-matrix. Reports in 1 month. Free sample copy.

Nonfiction: How-to, interview/profile, new product, opinion, personal experience, photo feature and technical. Buys 10 mss/year. Query. Length: 2,000-6,000 words. Pays $75-350 for assigned articles; pays $50-200 for unsolicited articles. Sometimes pays the expenses of writers on assignment.

Photos: Send photos with submission. Reviews 35mm, 4x5 and 6x6 transparencies and 8x10 prints. Offers no additional payment for photos accepted with ms. Captions, model releases and identification of subjects required. Buys one-time rights.

Tips: Features are most open to freelancers.

‡PAPERBOARD PACKAGING, 111 E. Wacker Dr., 16th Floor, Chicago IL 60601. (312)938-2345. Editor: Mark Arzoumanian. 10% freelance written. Works with a small number of new/unpublsihed writers each year. Monthly. For "managers, supervisors, and technical personnel who operate corrugated box manufacturing, folding carton converting and rigid box companies and plants." Circ. 15,000. Pays on publication. Publishes ms an average of 2 months after acceptance. Buys all rights. Photocopied submissions OK. Submit seasonal material 3 months in advance. Computer printout submissions acceptable; no dot-matrix. Sample copy on request.

Nonfiction: "Application articles, installation stories, etc. Contact the editor first to establish the approach desired for the article. Especially interested in box plant stories that have a human interest angle or history that makes company different from norm." Buys technical articles. Query. Length: open. Pays "$75/printed page (about 1,000 words to a page), including photos." Sometimes pays the expenses of writers on assignment.

Photos: "Will not pay photography costs, but will pay cost of photo reproductions for article."

Tips: "Writing style is not as much a concern to me as individual's knowledge of my industry and objective in writing article in first place. Nature of publication (trade) automatically means limited use of freelancers because of specialized field."

PULP & PAPER CANADA, Southam Communications Ltd., Suite 201, 310 Victoria Ave., Montreal, Quebec H3Z 2M9 Canada. (514)487-2302. Editor: Peter N. Williamson. Managing Editor: Graeme Rodden. 5% freelance written. Prefers to work with published/established writers. Monthly magazine. Circ. 9,309. Pays on acceptance. Publishes ms "as soon as possible" after acceptance. Byline given. Offers kill fee according to prior agreement. Buys first North American serial rights. Computer printout submissions acceptable; prefers letter-quality. Reports in 2 weeks on queries; 3 weeks on mss. Sample copy $5 (Canada), $7 (other countries); free writer's guidelines.

Nonfiction: How-to (related to processes and procedures in the industry); interview/profile (of Canadian leaders in pulp and paper industry); and technical (relevant to modern pulp and/or paper industry). No fillers, short industry news items, or product news items. Buys 10 mss/year. Query first with published clips or send complete ms. Articles with photographs (b&w glossy) or other good quality illustrations will get priority review. Length: 1,500-2,000 words (with photos). Pays $150 (Canadian funds)/published page, including photos, graphics, charts, etc. Sometimes pays the expenses of writers on assignment.

Tips: "Any return postage must be in either Canadian stamps or International Reply Coupons only."

Pets

Listed here are publications for professionals in the pet industry—pet product wholesalers, manufacturers, suppliers, and retailers, and owners of pet specialty stores, grooming businesses, aquarium retailers and those interested in the pet fish industry. The Veterinary section lists journals for animal health professionals. Publications for pet owners are listed in the Consumer Animal section.

PET AGE, The Largest Circulation Pet Industry Trade Publication, H.H. Backer Associates, Inc., 207 S. Wabash Ave., Chicago IL 60604. (312)663-4040. Editor: Karen Long MacLeod. 10-20% freelance written. Prefers to work with published/established writers. Monthly magazine about the pet industry for pet retailers and industry. Circ. 17,000. Pays on acceptance. Publishes ms an average of 3-6 months after acceptance. Byline given. Buys first serial rights, first rights, all rights, or exclusive industry rights. Submit seasonal/holiday material 6 months in advance. Query for electronic submissions. Computer printout submissions acceptable; prefers letter-quality. Reports in 1 month on queries; 2 weeks on mss. Sample copy for $2.50 and 9x12 SASE; writer's guidelines for #10 SASE.

Nonfiction: Book excerpts, profile (of a successful, well-run pet retail operation); how-to; interview; photo feature; and technical—all trade-related. Query first with published clips. Buys 6-12 mss/year. "Query as to the name and location of a pet operation you wish to profile and why it would make a good feature. No general retailing articles or consumer-oriented pet articles." Length: 1,000-3,000 words. Pays $75-200 for assigned articles; $50-150 for unsolicited articles. Sometimes pays the expenses of writers on assignment.

Photos: Reviews 5x7 b&w glossy prints. Captions and identification of subjects required. Offers $5 (negotiable) for photos. Buys one-time rights or all rights.

Tips: "Our readers already know about general animal care and business practices. This is a business publication for busy people, and must be very informative in easy-to-read, as brief as possible style. The type of article we purchase most frequently is the pet shop profile, a story about an interesting/successful pet shop. We need queries on these (we get references on the individual shop from our sources in the industry). We supply typical questions to writers when we answer their queries."

PET BUSINESS, 5400 NW 84th Ave., Miami FL 33166. (305)591-1629. Editor: Amy Jordan Smith. 10% freelance written. Eager to work with new/unpublished writers. "Our monthly news magazine reaches retailers, distributors and manufacturers of companion animals and pet products. Groomers, veterinarians and serious hobbyists are also represented." Circ. 15,000. Pays on publication. Publishes ms an average of 2 months after acceptance. Byline sometimes given. Not copyrighted. Buys first rights. Submit seasonal/holiday material 3 months in advance. Computer printout submissions OK; no dot-matrix. Sample copy $3. Writer's guidelines for SASE.

Nonfiction: "Articles must be newsworthy and pertain to animals routinely sold in pet stores (dogs, cats, fish, birds, reptiles and small animals). Research, legislative and animal behavior reports are of interest. All data must be attributed. No fluff!" Buys 40 mss/year. Send complete ms. "No queries—the news gets old quickly." Length: 50-800 words. Pays $5 per column inch.

Photos: Send photos (slides or prints) with submission. Offers $10-20 per photo. Buys one-time rights.

Tips: "We are open to national and international news written in standard news format. Buys cartoons; pays $10 each on publication."

THE PET DEALER, Howmark Publishing Corp., 567 Morris Ave., Elizabeth NJ 07208. (201)353-7373. Editorial Director: Marc Leavitt. 10% freelance written. Prefers to work with published/established writers; works with a small number of new/unpublished writers each year; and eager to work with new/published writers. "We want writers who are good reporters and clear communicators." Monthly magazine. Emphasizes merchandising, marketing and management for owners and managers of pet specialty stores, departments, and pet groomers and their suppliers. Circ. 11,000. Pays on publication. Publication "may be many months between acceptance of a manuscript and publication." Byline given. Phone queries OK. Submit seasonal/holiday material 3 months in advance. Computer printout submissions acceptable; no dot-matrix. Reports in 1 week. Sample copy and writer's guidelines for 9"x12" SAE with 2 first class stamps.

Nonfiction: How-to (store operations, administration, merchandising, marketing, management, promotion and purchasing). Consumer pet articles—lost pets, best pets, humane themes—*not* welcome. Emphasis is on *trade* merchandising and marketing of pets and supplies. Buys 8 unsolicited mss/year. Length: 800-1,200 words. Pays $50-100.

Photos: Submit photo material with ms. No additional payment for 5x7 b&w glossy prints. "Six photos with captions required." Buys one-time rights.

Tips: "We're interested in store profiles outside the New York, New Jersey, Connecticut and Pennsylvania metro areas. Photos are of key importance. Articles focus on new techniques in merchandising or promotion. Submit query letter first, with writing background summarized; include samples. We seek one-to-one, interview-type features on retail pet store merchandising. Indicate the availability of the proposed article, your willingness to submit on exclusive or first-in-field basis, and whether you are patient enough to await payment on publication."

PETS/SUPPLIES/MARKETING, Harcourt Brace Jovanovich Publications, 1 E. 1st St., Duluth MN 55802. (218)723-9303. Publisher/Editor: David Kowalski. 10% freelance written. Monthly magazine. For independent pet retailers, chain franchisers, livestock and pet supply wholesalers, and manufacturers of pet products. Circ. 14,200. Pays on publication. Buys first rights only. Phone queries OK. Submit seasonal/holiday material 4 months in advance. Photocopied submissions OK. Computer printout submissions acceptable. Reports in 2 months. Free writer's guidelines. Sample copy $5.

Nonfiction: How-to (merchandise pet products, display, set up window displays, market pet product line); interviews (with pet store retailers); opinion (of pet industry members or problems facing the industry); photo features (of successful pet stores or effective merchandising techniques and in-store displays); profiles (of successful retail outlets engaged in the pet trade); and technical articles (on more effective pet retailing, e.g., building a central filtration unit, constructing custom aquariums or display areas). Business management articles must deal specifically with pet shops and their own unique merchandise and problems. Length: 1,000-2,000 words. Buys 1-2 mss/issue. Query. Pays 10¢/word. Sometimes pays the expenses of writers on assignment.

Photos: Purchased with or without mss or on assignment. "We prefer 5x7 or 8x10 b&w glossies. But we will accept contact sheets and standard print sizes. For color, we prefer 35mm Kodachrome transparencies or 2¼x2¼." Pays $10 for b&w; $25 for color. Captions and model release required.

Columns/Departments: Suggestions for new columns or departments should be addressed to the editor. No clippings, please.

Tips: "We want articles which stress professional retailing, provide insight into successful shops, and generally capture the excitement of an exciting and sometimes controversial industry. All submissions are read. However, an initial query could save time and energy and ensure a publishable article."

For explanation of symbols, see the Key to Symbols and Abbreviations on Page 5.

Photography Trade

Journals for professional photographers are listed in this section. Magazines for the general public interested in photography techniques are in the Consumer Photography section. (For listings of markets for freelance photography use *Photographer's Market*—see Other Books of Interest.)

AMERICAN CINEMATOGRAPHER, A.S.C. Holding Corp., Box 2230, Hollywood CA 90078. (213)876-5080. Editor: George Turner. 50% freelance written. Monthly magazine. An international journal of film and video production techniques "addressed to creative, managerial, and technical people in all aspects of production. Its function is to disseminate practical information about the creative use of film and video equipment, and it strives to maintain a balance between technical sophistication and accessibility." Circ. 34,000. Pays on publication. Publishes ms an average of 3 months after acceptance. Buys all rights. Phone queries OK. Simultaneous and photocopied submissions OK. Computer printout submissions acceptable "provided they are adequately spaced." Free sample copy and writer's guidelines.
Nonfiction: Jean Turner, assistant editor. Descriptions of new equipment and techniques or accounts of specific productions involving unique problems or techniques; historical articles detailing the production of a classic film, the work of a pioneer or legendary cinematographer or the development of a significant technique or type of equipment. Also discussions of the aesthetic principles involved in production techniques. Recent article example: "Tales From Silverado," (July, 1985). Length: 1,500 to 5,000 words. Pays according to position and worth. Negotiable. Sometimes pays the expenses of writers on assignment.
Photos: B&w and color purchased with mss. No additional payment.
Tips: "No unsolicited articles. Call first. Doesn't matter whether you are published or new. Queries must describe writer's qualifications and include writing samples. We expect expansion of videography."

PHOTO LAB MANAGEMENT, PLM Publishing, Inc., 1312 Lincoln Blvd., Santa Monica CA 90401. (213)451-1344. Editor: Carolyn Ryan. Associate Editor: Arthur Stern. 25% freelance written. Monthly magazine covering process chemistries, process control, process equipment and marketing/administration for photo lab owners, managers and management personnel. Circ. over 16,000. Pays on publication. Publishes ms an average of 3 months after acceptance. Byline and brief bio given. Buys first North American serial rights. Submit seasonal/holiday material 6 months in advance. Query for electronic submissions. Computer printout submissions acceptable. Reports on queries in 6 weeks. Free sample copy and writer's guidelines for #10 SAE and 1 first class stamp.
Nonfiction: Personal experience (lab manager); technical; and management or administration. Buys 40-50 mss/year. Query with brief biography. Length: 1,200-1,800 words. Pays $60/published page.
Photos: Reviews 35mm color transparencies and 4-color prints suitable for cover. "We're looking for outstanding cover shots of photofinishing images."
Tips: "Our departments are written in-house and we don't use 'fillers'. Send a query if you have some background in the industry or a willingness to dig out information and research for a top quality article that really speaks to our audience. The most frequent mistakes made by writers in completing an article for us are on the business management side—taking a generic rather than a photo lab approach. Writers must have photofinishing knowledge."

‡PHOTO MARKETING, Photo Marketing Association Intl., 3000 Picture Place, Jackson MI 49201. (517)788-8100. Managing Editor: Margaret Hooks. 2% freelance written. A monthly magazine for photo industry retailers, finishers and suppliers. "Articles must be specific to the photo industry and cannot be authored by anyone who writes for other magazines in the photo industry. We provide management information on a variety of topics as well as profiles of successful photo businesses and analyses of current issues in the industry." Circ. 19,500. Pays on acceptance. Publishes ms an average of 2 months after acceptance. Byline given. Buys one-time rights and exclusive photo magazine rights. Simultaneous and photocopied submissions OK. Computer printout submissions OK. Reports in 2 weeks. Free sample copy and writer's guidelines.
Nonfiction: Interview/profile (anonymous consumer shops for equipment); personal experience (interviews with photo retailers); technical (photofinishing lab equipment). Buys 5 mss/year. Send complete ms. Length: 1,000-2,300 words. Pays $150-350.
Photos: State availability of photos with submission. Reviews negatives, 5x7 transparencies and prints. Offers $25-35 per photo. Buys one-time rights.
Columns/Departments: Anonymous Consumer (anonymous shopper shops for equipment at photo stores) 1,800 words. Buys 5 mss/year. Query with published clips. Length: 1,800 words. Pays up to $200.

Tips: "All main sections use freelance material: business tips, promotion ideas, employee concerns, advertising, coop, marketing. But they must be geared to and have direct quotes from members of the association."

THE PHOTO REVIEW, 301 Hill Ave., Langhorne PA 19047. (215)757-8921. Editor: Stephen Perloff. 50% freelance written. A quarterly magazine on photography with reviews, interviews and articles on art photography. Circ. 750. Pays on publication. Publishes ms an average of 3 months after acceptance. Byline given. Buys one-time rights. Simultaneous, photocopied and previously published submissions OK. Computer printout submissions OK. Reports in 3 weeks on queries; 2 months on mss. Sample copy for 8½x11 SAE with 3 first class stamps.
Nonfiction: Essays, historical/nostalgic, interview/profile and opinion. No how-to articles. Buys 10-15 mss/year. Query. Pays $25-200.
Photos: Send photos with submission. Reviews 8x10 prints. Offers no additional payment for photos accepted with ms. Captions and identification of subjects required. Buys one-time rights.

‡PHOTOGRAPHIC VIDEO TRADE NEWS, PTN Publishing Corp, 210 Crossways Park Dr., Woodbury NY 11797. (516)496-8000. Editor: Mark Levine. Managing Editor: Bill Schiffner. 20-25% freelance written. A semimonthly magazine about the photographic/video industries. Circ. 15,000. Pays on publication. Publishes ms an average of 2 months after acceptance. Byline given. Buys first North American serial rights. Submit seasonal/holiday material 3 months in advance. Simultaneous, photocopied and previously published submissions OK. Reports in 2 weeks on queries; 3 weeks on mss. Free sample copy and writer's guidelines.
Nonfiction: Interview/profile, technical. Buys 50 mss/year. Send complete ms. Length: 750-1,500 words. Pays $75-300. Sometimes pays expenses of writers on assignment.
Photos: Send photos with submission. Reviews 5x7 prints. Offers no additional payment for photos accepted with ms. Captions and identification of subjects required. Buys one-time rights.
Tips: "Know the photo and video industries."

PHOTOLETTER, PhotoSource International, Pine Lake Farm, Osceola WI 54020. (715)248-3800. Fax: (715)248-7394. Editor: Don Wittman. Managing Editor: H.T. White. 10% freelance written. A monthly newsletter on marketing photographs. "The *Photoletter* pairs photobuyers with photographers' collections." Circ. 780. Pays on acceptance. Publishes ms an average of 6 months after acceptance. Byline given. Buys one-time rights and simultaneous rights. Submit seasonal/holiday material 3 months in advance. Simultaneous, photocopied, and previously published submissions OK. Query for electronic submissions. Computer printout submissions acceptable. Reports in 2 weeks on queries. Sample copy $3; writer's guidelines for #10 SASE.
Nonfiction: How-to market photos and personal experience in marketing photos. "Our readers expect advice in how-to articles." No submissions that do not deal with selling photos. Buys 6 mss/year. Query. Length: 300-850 words. Pays $50-100 for unsolicited articles.
Columns/Departments: Jeri Engh, columns department editor. "We would welcome column ideas." Length: 350 words. Pays $45-75.
Fillers: Facts. Buys 20/year. Length: 30-50 words. Pays $10.
Tips: "Columns are most open to freelancers. Bring an *expertise* on marketing photos or some other aspect of aid to small business persons."

PHOTOVIDEO, Maclean Hunter, 5th Fl., 777 Bay St. Toronto, Ontario M5W 1A7 Canada. (416)596-5878. Editor: Don Long. 50-75% freelance written. Prefers to work with published/established writers. A magazine published 9 times a year for photo and video retailers, and professional photographers. "We seek to provide information to the trade to help in making better business decisions—news, products, trends, how-to etc." Circ. 16,500. Pays on acceptance. Publishes ms an average of 2-3 months after acceptance. Byline given. Offers 50% kill fee. Buys first Canadian serial rights. Submit seasonal/holiday material 3 months in advance. Simultaneous and photocopied submissions OK. Query for electronic submissions. Computer printout submissions acceptable; prefers letter-quality. Reports in 1 month on queries; 2 weeks on manuscripts. Sample copy for 8½x11 SAE with IRCs; writer's guidelines for #10 SAE and 37¢ Canadian.
Nonfiction: Professional how-to, interview/profile, opinion, photo feature (professionally oriented) and technical. No non-Canadian submissions. Buys 20 mss/year. Query with published clips. Length 200-1,200 words. Pays $100-400 (Canadian) for assigned articles; pays $50-200 (Canadian) for unsolicited articles. Sometimes pays the expenses of writers on assignment.
Photos: State availability of photos with submission. Reviews contact sheets. Offers $25-150 (Canadian)/photo. Captions, model releases, and identification of subjects required. Buys one-time rights.
Columns/Departments: News and Comment (regional, national and international events), 600-800 words; and What's Coming Up (Calendar, minimum lead time of 2 months), 100 words. Query. Length: 100-800 words. Pays $25-100 (Canadian).
Tips: "Content is a carefully balanced package for both retailer and professional about photo and video. It

covers such areas as profiles of successful businesses, new technology, professional techniques, marketing and merchandising ideas, advertising and promotion, business and association news, and economic and market trends. Our readers have a broad range of skills and knowledge levels. Therefore, submissions must contain sufficient background material for those less familiar with a topic, yet maintain the interest of more experienced readers."

PROFESSIONAL PHOTOGRAPHER, The Business Magazine of Professional Photography, Professional Photographers of America, Inc., 1090 Executive Way, Des Plaines IL 60018. (312)299-8161. Editor: Alfred DeBat. 80% freelance written. Monthly magazine of professional portrait, wedding, commercial, corporate and industrial photography. Describes the technical and business sides of professional photography—successful photo techniques, money-making business tips, legal considerations, selling to new markets, and descriptions of tough assignments and how completed. Circ. 32,000. Publishes ms an average of 6-9 months after acceptance. Byline given. Buys one-time rights. Submit seasonal/holiday material 6 months in advance. Simultaneous queries, and photocopied and previously published submissions OK. Computer printout submissions acceptable; prefers letter-quality. Reports in 2 months. Sample copy $3.25; free writer's guidelines.
Nonfiction: How-to. Professional photographic techniques: How I solved this difficult assignment, How I increased my photo sales, How to buy a studio . . . run a photo business etc. Special issues include February: Portrait Photography; April: Wedding Photography; May: Commercial Photography; and August: Industrial Photography. Buys 8-10 ms/issue. Query. Length: 1,000-3,000 words. "We seldom pay, as most writers are PP of A members and want recognition for their professional skills, publicity, etc."
Photos: State availability of photos. Reviews 35mm color transparencies and 8x10 prints. Captions and model release required. Buys one-time rights.

STUDIO PHOTOGRAPHY, PTN Publishing Corp., 210 Crossways Park Dr., Woodbury NY 11797. (516)496-8000. Editor: G. Faye Guercio. 85% freelance written. Prefers to work with published/established writers or experienced photographers with writing skills. Monthly magazine. Circ. 65,000. Pays on publication. Publishes ms an average of 6 months after acceptance. Not copyrighted. Buys first serial rights only. Submit seasonal/holiday material 5 months in advance. Computer printout submissions acceptable; prefers letter-quality. Reports in 6 weeks. Sample copy for 9½x12½ SAE and 5 first class stamps.
Nonfiction: Interview, personal experience, photo feature, communication-oriented, technical, travel and business-oriented articles. Buys 5-6 mss/issue. Length: 1,000-3,000 words. Pays about $75/page.
Photos: State availability of photos with query. Photos and article in one package.
Tips: "We look for professional quality writing coupled with top-notch photographs. Submit photos with all articles. No original transparencies, only fine quality duplicates. Only people with definite ideas and a sense of who they are need apply for publication. Read the magazine and become familiar with it before submitting work. Write for editorial schedule and writer/photographer's guidelines."

TECHNICAL PHOTOGRAPHY, PTN Publishing Corp., 210 Crossways Park Dr., Woodbury NY 11797. Senior Editor: David A. Silverman. 60% freelance written. Eager to work with new/unpublished writers. Monthly magazine. Publication of the "on-staff (in-house) industrial, military and government still, video and AV professional who must produce (or know where to get) visuals of all kinds." Circ. 60,000. Pays on publication. Publishes ms an average of 3-6 months after acceptance. Buys first North American serial rights. Byline given. Computer printout submissions acceptable; prefers letter-quality or double-strike dot-matrix. Reports in 6 weeks. Sample copy $2; guidelines for #10 envelope and 1 first class stamp.
Nonfiction: How-to; interview; photo feature; profile (detailed stories about in-house operations); and technical. "All manuscripts must relate to industrial, military or government production of visuals." Buys 50 mss/year. Query. Length: "as long as needed to adequately cover the subject matter." Pays $150-200.
Photos: Offers no additional payment for photos purchased with ms. Query. Captions, model release, and subject identification required.

> **66** *Competition among freelancers seems fiercer than ever, affording the publication its choice of only the better writers who really know their subjects. New writers needn't be published, but they must be good.* **99**
>
> —*Bill Dalton,*
> **Illinois Entertainer**

Plumbing, Heating, Air Conditioning and Refrigeration

DISTRIBUTOR, The Voice of Wholesaling, Technical Reporting Corp., Box 745, Wheeling IL 60090. (312)537-6460. Editorial Director: Steve Read. Managing Editor: James Butschli. 30% freelance written. Prefers to work with published/established writers. Monthly magazine for heating, ventilating, air conditioning and refrigeration wholesalers. Editorial material shows "executive wholesalers how they can run better businesses and cope with personal and business problems." Circ. 10,000. Pays on publication. Publishes ms an average of 1 month after acceptance. Byline sometimes given. Buys one-time rights. Submit seasonal/holiday material 3 months in advance. "We want material exclusive to the field (industry)." Photocopied submissions OK. Query for information on electronic submissions. Computer printout submissions acceptable; prefers letter-quality. Reports in 1 month. Sample copy $4.
Nonfiction: How-to (run a better business, cope with problems); and interview/profile (the wholesalers). No flippant or general approaches. Buys 12 mss/year. Query with or without published clips or send complete ms. Length: 1,000-2,000 words. Pays $100-200 (10¢ a word). Sometimes pays the expenses of writers on assignment.
Photos: State availability of photos or send photos with query or ms. Pays $5 minimum. Captions and identification of subjects required.
Tips: "Know the industry—come up with a different angle on an industry subject (one we haven't dealt with in a long time). Wholesale ideas and top-quality business management articles are most open to freelancers."

DOMESTIC ENGINEERING MAGAZINE, Delta Communications, Inc., 385 N. York Rd., Elmhurst IL 60126. Executive Editor: Stephen J. Shafer. Editor: Sandra Majorwicz. 15% freelance written. Prefers to work with published/established writers. Monthly magazine emphasizing plumbing, heating, air conditioning and piping for contractors, and for mechanical contractors in these specialties. Gives information on management, marketing and merchandising. Circ. 40,000. Pays on acceptance. Publishes ms an average of 6 months after acceptance. Buys all rights. Simultaneous, photocopied and previously published submissions OK. Computer printout submissions acceptable; prefers letter-quality. Reports in 1 month. Sample copy $10.
Nonfiction: How-to (some technical in industry areas). Expose, interview, profile, personal experience, photo feature and technical articles are written on assignment only and should be about management, marketing and merchandising for plumbing and mechanical contracting businessmen. Buys 12 mss/year. Query. Pays $25 minimum. Sometimes pays the expenses of writers on assignment.
Photos: State availability of photos. Pays $10 minimum for b&w prints (reviews contact sheets) and color transparencies.

EXPORT, 386 Park Ave. S., New York NY 10016. Editor: R. Weingarten. For importers and distributors in 183 countries who handle hardware, air conditioning and refrigeration equipment and related consumer hardlines. Bimonthly magazine in English and Spanish editions. Circ. 40,122. Buys first rights and second (reprint) rights to material originally published elsewhere. Byline given. Buys about 10 mss/year. Pays on acceptance. Publishes ms an average of 5 months after acceptance. Reports in 1 month. Query. Writer's guidelines for #10 SASE.
Nonfiction: News stories of products and merchandising of air conditioning and refrigeration equipment, hardware and related consumer hardlines. Informational, how-to, interview, profile and successful business operations. Length: 1,000-3,000 words. Pays $300 maximum.
Tips: "One of the best ways to break in here is with a story originating outside the U.S. or Canada. Our major interest is in new products and new developments—but they must be available and valuable to overseas buyers. We also like company profile stories. Departments and news stories are staff-written."

FLORIDA FORUM, FRSA Services Corp., Drawer 4850, Winter Park FL 32793. (305)671-3772. Editor: Glenda Arango. 10% freelance written. Eager to work with new/unpublished writers. Monthly magazine covering the roofing, sheet metal and air conditioning industries. Circ. 8,000. Pays on publication. Publishes ms an average of 2 months after acceptance. Byline given. Buys one-time rights. Submit seasonal/holiday material 2 months in advance. Simultaneous queries, and simultaneous, photocopied, and previously published submissions OK. Query for electronic submissions. Computer printout submissions acceptable; prefers letter-quality. Reports in 2 weeks. Sample copy and writer's guidelines for SASE.
Nonfiction: General interest, historical/nostalgic, humor, interview/profile, new product, opinion, personal

experience and technical. Buys 25 mss/year. Send complete ms. Length: open. Pays variable rates.
Photos: Send photos with ms. Pays variable rates for b&w prints.
Columns/Departments: Buys 12/year. Send complete ms. Length: open. Pays variable rates.

SNIPS MAGAZINE, 407 Mannheim Rd., Bellwood IL 60104. (312)544-3870. Editor: Nick Carter. 2% freelance written. Monthly. For sheet metal, warm air heating, ventilating, air conditioning and roofing contractors. Publishes ms an average of 3 months after acceptance. Buys all rights. "Write for detailed list of requirements before submitting any work."
Nonfiction: Material should deal with information about contractors who do sheet metal, warm air heating, air conditioning, ventilation and roofing work; also about successful advertising campaigns conducted by these contractors and the results. Length: "prefers stories to run less than 1,000 words unless on special assignment." Pays 5¢ each for first 500 words, 2¢ each for additional word.
Photos: Pays $2 each for small snapshot pictures, $4 each for usable 8x10 pictures.

WOOD 'N ENERGY, Gilford Publishing Inc., Box 2008, Laconia NH 03247. (603)528-4285. Editor: Jason Perry. 10% freelance written. Works with a small number of new/unpublished writers each year. Monthly magazine covering wood, coal and solar heating (residential). "*Wood 'n Energy* is mailed to retailers, distributors and manufacturers of wood, coal and solar heating equipment in the U.S. and Canada. A majority of our readers are small businessmen who need help in running their businesses and want to learn secrets to prospering in a field that has seen better days when oil embargoes were daily happenings." Circ. 32,000. Pays on publication. Publishes ms an average of 2 months after acceptance. Byline given. Buys one-time rights and all rights. Submit seasonal/holiday material 4 months in advance. Simultaneous queries OK. Query for electronic submissions. Computer printout submissions acceptable; prefers letter-quality. Reports in 2 weeks. Sample copy $2.50.
Nonfiction: Interview/profile (of stove dealers, manufacturers, others); photo feature (of energy stores); and technical (nuts and bolts of stove design and operation). Special issue includes Buyers Guide/Retailers Handbook (annual issue with retail marketing articles), "how to run your business," accounting. "The best times of year for freelancers are in our fall issue (our largest) and also in February and March." No "how wonderful renewable energy is" and experiences with stoves. "This is a *trade* book." Buys 25 mss/year. Query with or without published clips or send complete ms. Pays $25-300. Sometimes pays expenses of writers on assignment.
Photos: State availability of photos or send photos with query or ms. Pays $35 minimum for b&w contact sheets; $125 maximum for color contact sheets. Identification of subjects required. Buys one-time rights.
Columns/Departments: Reports (energy news; potpourri of current incentives, happenings); Regulations (safety and standard news); and Retailers Corner (tips on running a retail shop). "We are also looking for freelancers who could serve in our 'network' around the country. If there's a law passed regulating wood-stove emissions in their town, for example, they could send us a clip and/or rewrite the story. These pay $50 or so, depending on the clip. Contact editor on an individual basis (over the phone is OK) for a green light." Query with or without published clips. Length: 150-500 words. Pays $35-150.
Tips: "Short, hot articles on retailers (500 words and photographs) are desperately needed. We're looking for serious business articles. Freelancers who know the ins and outs of running a business have an excellent shot at being published."

WOODHEAT '89, Gilford Publishing, Inc., Box 2008, Laconia NH 03247. (603)528-4285. Editor: Jason Perry. 40% freelance written. An annual buyer's guide and sourcebook on wood heat, published in July. Circ. 175,000. Pays on variable schedule. Publishes ms an average of 6 months after acceptance. Byline given. Offers variable kill fee. Buys variable rights. Simultaneous queries and submissions OK. Computer printout submissions acceptable; prefers letter-quality. Reports in 1 month.
Nonfiction: How-to (installation, etc.); interview/profile (of those in the field, retailers, consumers); new product (new wood energy products); photo feature (of stove installations and/or energy efficient homes); and technical (details on buying and installing). No personal experiences with wood stoves. Buys 5-8 mss/year. Query. Length: 100-2,550 words. Pays $50-500. Pays expenses of writers on assignment.
Photos: State availability of photos with query or ms. Uses all types. Pays $35-250. Captions, model release, and identification of subjects required. Buys variable rights.
Columns/Departments: Reports (potpourri of energy news, wood heat news). Buys 0-10 mss/year. Query. Length: 150-400 words. Pays $35-100.
Tips: "Articles in the magazine must appeal to both current owners and buyers. Personality is a plus in any article; we'd like features on someone who has invented a better burning stove or someone who is handcrafting masonry fireplaces, for example. Article ideas are formulated by mid-January, so query letters should be on hand at that time. Be specific with story ideas. Shorter articles on a wide range of energy issues—in a section called Reports—can be accepted until May. These must be accompanied by a photo. Writing should be spicy, interesting and short. All areas are open to freelancers. We find that freelancers score better with articles with local slants. With 15 million households having wood stoves, there are bound to be many stories to tell."

Printing

HIGH VOLUME PRINTING, Innes Publishing Co., Box 368, Northbrook IL 60062. (312)564-5940. Editor: Rod Piechowski. 20% freelance written. Eager to work with new/unpublished writers. Bimonthly magazine for book, magazine printers, large commercial printing plants with 20 or more employees. Aimed at telling the reader what he needs to know to print more efficiently and more profitably. Circ. 30,000. Pays on publication. Publishes ms an average of 9 months after acceptance. Byline given. Buys first and second serial rights. Simultaneous queries OK. Query for electronic submissions. Computer printout submissions acceptable. Reports in 2 weeks. Writer's guidelines, sample articles provided.
Nonfiction: How-to (printing production techniques); new product (printing, auxiliary equipment, plant equipment); photo feature (case histories featuring unique equipment); technical (printing product research and development); shipping; and publishing distribution methods. No product puff. Buys 12 mss/year. Query. Length: 700-3,000 words. Pays $50-300. Sometimes pays the expenses of writers on assignment.
Photos: Send photos with ms. Pays $25-100 for 3x5 and larger b&w prints; $25-150 for any size color transparencies and prints. Captions, model release, and identification of subjects required.
Tips: "Feature articles covering actual installations and industry trends are most open to freelancers. Be familiar with the industry, spend time in the field, and attend industry meetings and trade shows where equipment is displayed. We would also like to receive clips and shorts about printing mergers."

IN-PLANT PRINTER AND ELECTRONIC PUBLISHER, Innes Publishing, Box 368, Northbrook IL 60062. (312)564-5940. Editor: Rod Peichowski. 20% freelance written. Works with a small number of new/unpublished writers each year. Bimonthly magazine covering in-house print shops and electronic publishing. Circ. 38,000. Pays on publication. Publishes ms an average of 3 months after acceptance. Byline "usually" given. Buys first and second rights. Submit seasonal/holiday material 4 months in advance. Query for electronic submissions. Computer printout submissions OK; prefers letter-quality. Reports in 2 weeks. Free sample copy and writer's guidelines.
Nonfiction: Book excerpts, how-to and case history. "More electronic printing articles, we need experts in this area to write technical articles. No nebulous management advice; undetailed stories lacking in concrete information. No human interest material." Buys 18 mss/year. Query or send complete ms. Length: 1,500-3,000 words. Pays $100-250. Pays expenses of writers on assignment.
Photos: Send photos with ms. "No additional payment is made for photos with ms, unless negotiated." Captions required. Buys all rights.
Tips: "We are looking for case studies of in-plants that incorporate electronic publishing."

IN-PLANT REPRODUCTIONS & ELECTRONIC PUBLISHING, North American Publishing Co., 401 N. Broad St., Philadelphia PA 19108. (215)238-5300. Executive Editor: Maria Martino. Editor: Denise Wallace. 40% freelance written. Prefers to work with published/established writers. Works with a small number of new/unpublished writers each year; eager to work with new/unpublished writers. Monthly magazine about in-plant printing management and electronic publishing for printing departments in business, government, education and industry. These graphic arts facilities include art, composition, camera, platemaking, press, and finishing equipment, xerographic and other business communications systems. Circ. 42,000. Pays on publication. Publishes ms an average 6 months after acceptance. Byline given. Buys first North American serial rights or all rights. Phone queries OK. Computer printout submissions acceptable; prefers letter-quality. Reports in 1 month. Sample copy $5.
Nonfiction: Interview, profile, how-to and technical. Buys 4 mss/issue. Query. Length: 500-2,500 words. Pays $75-200. Sometimes pays the expenses of writers on assignment.
Tips: "We would like to receive articles on how to justify equipment and how to market printing services."

PRINTING VIEWS, For the Midwest Printer, Midwest Publishing, 8328 N. Lincoln, Skokie IL 60077. (312)539-8540. Editor: Ed Schwenn. 10% freelance written. Prefers to work with published/established writers. Monthly magazine about printing and graphic arts for Midwest commercial printers, typographers, platemakers, engravers and other trade people. Circ. 15,000. Average issue includes 2-3 features. Pays on publication. Publishes ms an average of 2 months after acceptance. Byline given. Buys one-time rights. Phone queries OK. Reports in 2 weeks. Sample copy $2.
Nonfiction: Interview (possibly with graphic arts personnel); new product (in graphic arts in a Midwest plant); management/sales success in Midwest printing plant; and technical (printing equipment). Buys 6 feature mss/year. Query with clips of previously published work. "We will entertain query letters; no unsolicited manuscripts." Length: 2-9 typed pages. Pays $200-250 for assigned mss only.
Photos: State availability of photos. Reviews b&w contact sheets. Offers additional payment for photos accepted with ms. Captions preferred. Buys one-time rights.

QUICK PRINTING, The Information Source for Commercial Copyshops and Printshops, Coast Publishing, 1680 SW Bayshore Blvd., Port St. Lucie FL 34984. (407)879-6666. Publisher: Cyndi Schulman. Editor: Douglas E. Roorbach. 50% freelance written. A monthly magazine covering the quick printing industry. "Our articles tell quick printers how they can be more profitable. We want figures to illustrate points made." Circ. 42,000. Pays on acceptance. Publishes ms an average of 4 months after acceptance. Byline given. Buys first North American serial rights, all rights. Submit seasonal/holiday material 6 months in advance. Photocopied submissions OK, if identified as such. Rarely uses previously published submissions. Query for electronic submissions. Computer printout submissions acceptable; prefers letter-quality. Reports in 2 weeks. Sample copy for $3 and 9x12 SAE with 7 first class stamps; writer's guidelines for #10 SAE with 1 first class stamp.

Nonfiction: How-to (on marketing products better or accomplishing more with equipment); new product; opinion (on the quick printing industry); personal experience (from which others can learn); technical (on printing). No generic business articles, or articles on larger printing applications. Buys 75 mss/year. Send complete ms. Length: 1,500-3,000 words. Pays $100 and up.

Photos: State availability of photos with submission. Reviews transparencies and prints. Offers no payment for photos. Captions and identification of subjects required.

Columns/Departments: Viewpoint/Counterpoint (opinion on the industry); QP Profile (shop profiles with a marketing slant); Management (how to handle employees and/or business strategies); and Marketing Impressions, all 500-1,500 words. Buys 10 mss/year. Send complete ms. Pays $75.

Tips: "The use of electronic publishing systems by quick printers is of increasing interest. Show a knowledge of the industry. Try visiting your local quick printer for an afternoon to get to know about us. When your articles make a point, back it up with examples, statistics, and dollar figures. We need good material in all areas, but avoid the shop profile. Technical articles are most needed, but they must be accurate. No puff pieces for a certain industry supplier."

Real Estate

AREA DEVELOPMENT MAGAZINE, 525 Northern Blvd., Great Neck NY 11021. (516)829-8990. Editor-in-Chief: Tom Bergeron. 40% freelance written. Prefers to work with published/established writers. Emphasizes corporate facility planning and site selection for industrial chief executives worldwide. Monthly magazine. Circ. 33,000. Pays when edited. Publishes ms an average of 2 months after acceptance. Buys first rights only. Byline given. Photocopied submissions OK. Computer printout submissions acceptable; prefers letter-quality. Reports in 1-3 weeks. Free sample copy. Writer's guidelines for #10 SASE.

Nonfiction: How-to (case histories of companies; experiences in site selection and all other aspects of corporate facility planning); historical (if it deals with corporate facility planning); interview (corporate executives and industrial developers); and related areas of site selection and facility planning such as taxes, labor, government, energy, architecture and finance. Buys 8-10 mss/yr. Query. Pays $30-40/ms page; rates for illustrations depend on quality and printed size. Sometimes pays the expenses of writers on assignment.

Photos: State availability of photos with query. Prefer 8x10 or 5x7 b&w glossy prints. Captions preferred.

Tips: "Articles must be accurate, objective (no puffery) and useful to our industrial executive readers. Avoid any discussion of the merits or disadvantages of any particular areas or communities. Writers should realize we serve an intelligent and busy readership—they should avoid 'cute' allegories and get right to the point."

BUSINESS FACILITIES, Business Facilities Publishing Co., 121 Monmouth St., Box 2060, Red Bank NJ 07701. (201)842-7433. Editor: Eric Peterson. Managing Editor: Alison Hayes. 20% freelance written. Prefers to work with published/established writers. A monthly magazine covering economic development and commercial and industrial real estate. "Our audience consists of corporate site selectors and real estate people; our editorial coverage is aimed at providing news and trends on the plant location and corporate expansion field." Circ. 32,000. Pays on publication. Publishes ms an average of 3 months after acceptance. Byline given. Buys all rights. Photocopied and previously published submissions OK. Computer printout submissions acceptable; prefers letter-quality. Reports in 2 weeks. Free sample copy and writer's guidelines.

Nonfiction: General interest, how-to, interview/profile and personal experience. No news shorts and no clippings; feature material only. Buys 12-15 mss/year. Query. Length: 1,000-3,000 words. Pays $200-1,000 for assigned articles, pays $200-600 for unsolicited articles. Sometimes pays the expenses of writers on assignment.

Photos: State availability of photos with submission. Reviews contact sheets, negatives, transparencies and 8x10 prints. Payment negotiable. Captions and identification of subjects required. Buys one-time rights.

Tips: "First, remember that our reader is a corporate executive responsible for his company's expansion and/or relocation decisions and our writers have to get inside that person's head in order to provide him with something that's helpful in his decision-making process. And second, the biggest turnoff is a telephone query."

We're too busy to accept them and must require that all queries be put in writing. Submit major feature articles only; all news departments, fillers, etc., are staff prepared. A writer should be aware that our style is not necessarily dry and business-like. We tend to be more upbeat and a writer should look for that aspect of our approach."

FINANCIAL FREEDOM REPORT, 1831 Fort Union Blvd., Salt Lake City UT 84121. (801)943-1280. Chairman of the Board: Mark O. Haroldsen. Managing Editor: Carolyn Tice. 25% freelance written. Eager to work with new/unpublished writers. For "professional and nonprofessional investors, and would-be investors in real estate—real estate brokers, insurance companies, investment planners, truck drivers, housewives, doctors, architects, contractors, etc. The magazine's content is presently expanding to interest and inform the readers about other ways to put their money to work for them." Monthly magazine. Circ. 50,000. Pays on publication. Publishes ms an average of 3 months after acceptance. Buys all rights. Phone queries OK. Simultaneous submissions OK. Query for electronic submissions. Computer printout submissions acceptable; prefers letter-quality. Reports in 2 weeks. Sample copy $3; free writer's guidelines.
Nonfiction: How-to (find real estate bargains, finance property, use of leverage, managing property, developing market trends, goal setting, motivational); and interviews (success stories of those who have relied on own initiative and determination in real estate market or related fields). Buys 25 unsolicited mss/year. Query with clips of published work or submit complete ms. Length: 1,500-3,000 words. "If the topic warranted a two- or three-parter, we would consider it." Pays 5-10¢/word. Sometimes pays the expenses of writers on assignment.
Photos: Send photos with ms. Uses 8x10 b&w matte prints. Offers no additional payment for photos accepted with ms. Captions required.
Tips: "We would like to find several specialized writers in our field of real estate investments. A writer would need to have had some hands-on experience in the real estate field."

JOURNAL OF PROPERTY MANAGEMENT, Institute of Real Estate Management, 430 N. Michigan Ave., Chicago IL 60611. (312)661-1930. 15% freelance written. Bimonthly magazine covering real estate management and development. "The *Journal* has a feature/information slant designed to educate readers in the application of new techniques and to keep them abreast of current industry trends." Circ. 15,000. Pays on acceptance. Publishes ms an average of 3 months after acceptance. Byline sometimes given. Buys all rights. Simultaneous submissions OK. Query for electronic submissions. Computer printout submissions OK; no dot-matrix. Reports in 6 weeks on queries; 3 weeks on mss. Free sample copy and writer's guidelines.
Nonfiction: How-to, interview and technical (building systems/computers). "No non-real estate subjects personality or company, humor." Buys 8-12 mss/year. Query with published clips. Length: 1,500-4,000 words. Pays $100-750 for assigned articles; pays $50-750 for unsolicited articles. Pays in contributor's copies "if so agreed." Sometimes pays the expenses of writers on assignment.
Photos: State availability of photos with submission. Reviews contact sheets. Offers no additonal payment for photos accepted with ms. Model releases and identification of subjects required. Buys one-time rights.
Columns/Departments: Karen McManus, editor. Insurance Insights; Tax Corner; Investment Corner and Legal Corner. Buys 6-8 mss/year. Query. Length: 750-1,500 words. Pays $50-350.

REAL ESTATE INFORMATION NETWORK, 70 S. Broadway, Box 257, New York NY 10960. (914)353-0173. Editor James Clyde. An on-line service for real estate and mortgage banking. "We cover market personalities, profiles of successful firms, new deals, tax law and investment in real estate, legislation, community profiles and market trends. Pays on publication. Publishes ms an average of 2 months after acceptance. Byline given. Offers 100% kill fee. Buys second serial (reprint) rights, all rights, and makes work-for-hire assignments. Submit seasonal/holiday material 3 months in advance. Previously published submissions OK. Electronic submissions required; consult guidelines. Reports in 3 weeks on manuscripts. Writer's guidelines for #10 SAE with 1 first class stamp.
Nonfiction: How-to, humor, interview/profile, new product and technical. Buys 60 mss/year. Send complete ms. Length 75-250 words. Pays $50-100 for assigned articles; pays $25-50 for unsolicited articles. Pays in copies or other premiums for first submission. Sometimes pays the expenses of writers on assignment.
Columns Departments: Send complete ms. Length: 75-250 words. Pays $25-50.
Fillers: Glen V. Carvella, fillers editor. Anecdotes, facts and newsbreaks. Pays $25.
Tips: "We no longer type or retype material. Submissions must be on floppy disk or by telephone modem. Files must be in ASCII format for editing and publication. An eye to the appearance of material on the computer screen is as important as content."

For information on setting your freelance fees, see How Much Should I Charge? in the Business of Writing section.

SKYLINES, News of the Office Building Industry, Building Owners and Managers Association International, 1250 Aye St. NW, Washington DC 20005. (202)289-7000. Editor: Kathryn N. Hamilton. 30% freelance written. Prefers to work with published/established writers. A tabloid for the office building industry focusing on real estate financing, building operation, leasing, and marketing strategies. Circ. 6,100. Pays 1 month after acceptance. Byline given. Publication not copyrighted. Buys one-time rights. Submit seasonal/holiday material 2 months in advance. Query for electronic submissions. Computer printout submissions OK. Free sample copy.

Nonfiction: Expose, interview/profile, opinion and technical. Plans special issue on financing trends, tenant relations, rehab and remodelling and working with architects. No promotional articles that hype on company or product. Buys 6 mss/year. Query. Length: 500-2,000 words. Pays $1,000 maximum. Sometimes pays the expenses of writers on assignment.

Photos: State availability of photos with submission. Reviews contact sheets. Offers no additional payment for photos accepted with ms. Captions and identification of subjects required. Buys one-time rights.

Tips: "We would like to receive information on exaction fees, effect of new tax laws, choosing an agency management firm, night lighting and security concerns."

SOUTHWEST REAL ESTATE NEWS, Communication Channels, Inc., Suite 240, 18601 LBJ Freeway, Mesquite TX 75150. (214)270-6651. Associate Publisher/Editor: Jim Mitchell. Managing Editor: Sheryl Roberts. 40% freelance written. Prefers to work with published/established writers. Tabloid newspaper published 8 times/year about commercial and industrial real estate for professional real estate people, including realtors, developers, mortgage bankers, corporate real estate executives, architects, contractors and brokers. Circ. 17,000. Average issue includes 4 columns, 20-30 short news items, 2-5 special articles and 2-10 departments. Pays on publication. Publishes ms an average of 2 months after acceptance. Byline given. Buys all rights. Phone queries OK. Submit seasonal/holiday material 2 months in advance. Photocopied submissions OK. Computer printout submissions acceptable; dot-matrix only if it has ascenders and descenders. Prefers letter-quality. Reports in 4-6 weeks. Sample copy and writer's guidelines for 12x16½ SAE with 3 first class stamps.

Nonfiction: "We're interested in hearing from writers in major cities in the states that we cover, which are TX, OK, CO, NM, LA, AZ, AR, NV and CA. We are particularly interested in writers with newspaper experience and real estate background. Assignments are made according to our editorial schedule which we will supply upon request. Most open to freelancers are city reviews. Contact the staff to discuss ideas first. No unsolicited material." Buys 3-5 mss/issue. Query. Pays $100-500.

Columns/Departments: Offices, Shopping Centers, Industrials, Multiplexes, Leases, Sales and Purchases, Mortgage and Financial, Realty Operations, Residentials, and People in the News. No newspaper clippings.

Tips: "We retain resumes from writers for possible future use—particularly in the states we cover. Call us and submit a sample of previous work."

Resources and Waste Reduction

THE PUMPER, (formerly Pumper Publications), COLE Publishing Inc., Drawer 220, Three Lakes WI 54562. (715)546-3347. Editors: Bob Kendall. 5% freelance written. Eager to work with new/unpublished writers. A monthly tabloid covering the liquid waste hauling industry (portable toilet renters, septic tank pumpers, industrial waste haulers, chemical waste haulers, oil field haulers, and hazardous waste haulers). "Our publication is read by companies that handle liquid waste and manufacturers of equipment." Circ. 15,000. Pays on publication. Publishes ms an average of 1 month after acceptance. Byline given. Offers negotiable kill fee. Buys first serial rights. Submit seasonal/holiday material 3 months in advance. Simultaneous queries, and simultaneous, photocopied, and previously published submissions OK. Query for electronic submissions. Computer printout submissions acceptable; no dot-matrix. Reports in 1 month. Free sample copy and writer's guidelines.

Nonfiction: Expose (government regulations, industry problems, trends, public attitudes, etc.); general interest (state association meetings, conventions, etc.); how-to (related to industry, e.g., how to incorporate septage or municipal waste into farm fields, how to process waste, etc.); humor (related to industry, especially septic tank pumpers or portable toilet renters); interview/profile (including descriptions of business statistics, type of equipment, etc.); new product; personal experience; photo feature; and technical (especially reports on research projects related to disposal). "We are looking for quality articles that will be of interest to our readers; length is not important. We publish trade journals. We need articles that deal with the trade. Studies on land application of sanitary waste are of great interest." Query or send complete ms. Pays 7½¢/word.

Photos: Send photos with query or ms. Pays $15 for b&w and color prints that are used. No negatives. "We need good contrast." Captions "suggested" and model release required. Buys one-time rights.

Tips: "Material must pertain to liquid waste-related industries listed on form. We hope to expand the editorial content of our monthly publications. We also have publications for sewer and drain cleaners with the same format as *The Pumper*; however, the *Cleaner* has a circulation of 18,000. We are looking for the same type of articles and pay is the same."

RESOURCE RECYCLING, North America's Recycling Journal, Resource Recycling, Inc., Box 10540, Portland OR 97210. (503)227-1319. Editor: Jerry Powell. 25% freelance written. Eager to work with new/unpublished writers. A trade journal published 7 times/year, covering recycling of paper, plastics, metals and glass. Circ. 3,400. Pays on publication. Publishes ms an average of 3-9 months after acceptance. Byline given. Buys first rights. Simultaneous, photocopied and previously published submissions OK. Query for electronic submissions. Computer printout submissions OK; prefers letter-quality. Reports in 1 month on queries. Sample copy and writer's guidelines for 9x12 SAE with 5 first class stamps. "No non-technical or opinion pieces." Buys 15-20 mss/year. Query with published clips. Length: 1,200-1,800 words. Pays $100-150. Pays with contributor copies "if writers are more interested in professional recognition than financial compensation." Sometimes pays the expenses of writers on assignment.

Photos: State availability of photos with submission. Reviews contact sheets, negatives and prints. Offers $5-10. Identification of subjects required. Buys one-time rights.

Tips: "Overviews of one recycling aspect in one state (e.g., oil recycling in Alabama) will receive attention. We will increase coverage of plastics recycling."

Selling and Merchandising

Sales personnel and merchandisers interested in how to sell and market products successfully consult these journals. Publications in nearly every category of Trade also buy sales-related material if it is slanted to the product or industry with which they deal.

THE AMERICAN SALESMAN, 424 N. 3rd St., Burlington IA 52601. Publisher: Michael S. Darnall. Editorial Supervisor: Doris J. Ruschill. Editor: Barbara Boeding. 95% freelance written. Prefers to work with published/established writers; works with a small number of new/unpublished writers each year. Monthly magazine for distribution through company sales representatives. Circ. 1,915. Pays on publication. Publishes ms an average of 4 months after acceptance. Buys all rights. Computer printout submissions OK; no dot-matrix. Sample copy and writer's guidelines for 9½x6½ SAE and 2 first class stamps; mention *Writer's Market* in request.

Nonfiction: Sales seminars, customer service and follow-up, closing sales, sales presentations, handling objections, competition, telephone usage and correspondence, managing territory, and new innovative sales concepts. No sexist material, illustration written from only a salesperson's viewpoint. No ms dealing with supervisory problems. Query. Length: 900-1,200 words. Pays 3¢/word. Uses no advertising. Follow AP Stylebook. Include biography and/or byline with ms submissions. Author photos used.

ART MATERIAL TRADE NEWS, The Journal of All Art, Craft, Engineering and Drafting Supplies, Communication Channels Inc., 6255 Barfield Rd., Atlanta GA 30328. (404)256-9800. Editor: Anthony Giometti. 15% freelance written. Works with a small number of new/unpublished writers each year. Monthly magazine on art materials. "Our editorial thrust is to bring art materials retailers, distributors and manufacturers information they can use in their everyday operations." Circ. 12,000. Pays on publication. Publishes ms an average of 3 months after acceptance. "All assigned manuscripts are published." Buys first serial rights. Submit seasonal/holiday material 3 months in advance. Photocopied submissions OK. Computer printout submissions acceptable; prefers letter-quality to dot-matrix. Reports in 6 weeks. Sample copy for 9x12 SAE and $1 postage; writer's guidelines for 4x9½ SAE and 1 first class stamp.

Nonfiction: How-to (sell, retail/wholesale employee management, advertising programs); interview/profile (within industry); and technical (commercial art drafting/engineering). "We encourage a strong narrative style where possible. We publish an editorial 'theme' calendar at the beginning of each year." Buys 15-30 mss/year. Query with published clips. Length: 1,000-3,000 words (prefers 2,000 words). Pays $75-300.

Photos: State availability of photos. Pays $10 maximum for b&w contact sheets. Identification of subjects required.

Columns/Departments: Creative Corner (crafts) and Print & Framing. Buys 12-15 mss/year. Query with published clips. Length: 1,000-2,000 words. Pays $75-200.

Tips: "We are very interested in developing a cadre of writers who know the art materials industry well. We would like to receive articles that show knowledge of the specifics of the art materials industry. We reject many general business articles that are not useful to our readers because they fail to take into account the nature of the industry. A current, solid background in any one of these areas helps—commercial art, retail selling, wholesale selling, business finance, employee management, interviewing or advertising. We're refocusing on articles that will help art material store owners run their business better (less focus on manufacturers). More news-you-can-use articles."

‡BEAUTY AGE, Tramedia, Inc., Suite B, 113 West 85th St., New York NY 10024. (212)580-2756. Editor: Paul M. Cohen. 25% freelance written. A bimonthly magazine about cosmetics, fragrances and cosmetic accessories for retail buyers, merchandisers and corporate personnel. Circ. 26,000. Pays on publication. Byline given. Offers 100% kill fee. Buys first and second serial (reprint) rights. Submit seasonal/holiday material 3 months in advance. Computer printout submissions OK. Sample copy for 9x12 SAE with $2 postage.

Nonfiction: Interview/profile, new product. Buys 30 mss/year. Query. Length: 1,000-1,500 words. Pays $200-400 for assigned articles. Sometimes pays expenses of writers on assignment.

Photos: Send photos with submission. Reviews negatives, transparencies and prints. Offers no additional payment for photos accepted with ms. Captions, model releases and identification of subjects required. Buys all rights.

CASUAL LIVING, Columbia Communications, 370 Lexington Ave., New York NY 10164. (212)532-9290. Editor: Ralph Monti. A monthly magazine covering outdoor furniture for outdoor furniture specialists, including retailers, mass merchandisers, and department store buyers. Circ. 11,000. Pays on publication. Buys first North American serial rights. Submit seasonal/holiday material 2 months in advance. Computer printout submissions acceptable. Reports in 1 month.

Nonfiction: Interview/profile (case histories of retailers in the industry); new product; opinion; and technical. Buys 7-8 mss/year. Query with or without published clips, then follow up with phone call. Length: 1,000 words average. Pays $200-400.

Photos: State availability of photos with query rgl 2 months in advance. Computer printout submissions acceptable. Reports in 1 month.

Nonfiction: Interview/profile (case histories of retailers in the industry); new product; opinion; and technical. Buys 7-8 mss/year. Query with or without published clips, then follow up with phone call. Length: 1,000 words average. Pays $200-400.

Photos: State availability of photos with query letter or ms. "Photos are essential with all articles." Reviews b&w contact sheet. Pays $75-100 for b&w prints. Buys all rights.

Tips: "Know the industry, trades and fashions, and what makes a successful retailer."

‡CHAIN STORE AGE, General Merchandise Trends, Lebhar Friedman, 425 Park Ave., New York NY 10022. (212)371-9400. Editor: Murray Forseter. 10% freelance written. A monthly magazine on retailing. "Write about general merchandise retailers, their strategies and marketing directions. Readers are retailers who make buying decisions on merchandise." Circ. 29,000. Pays on publication. Publishes ms an average of 1 month after acceptance. Byline not given. Computer printout submissions OK; prefers letter-quality. Free sample copy.

Nonfiction: General interest (retailing). Query. Length: 500-1,000 words. Pays $150-300 for assigned articles. Sometimes pays expenses of writers on assignment.

Photos: Reviews contact sheets, negatives and transparencies. Offers no additional payment for photos accepted with ms. Identification of subjects required. Buys all rights.

❝ Joys: Tightly written manuscripts, good slides or transparencies, and writers who have done their homework. ❞

—Karen E. Hill,
Meridian Publishing

‡FAIR TIMES, Independent Dealers Association, Box 455, Arnold MO 63010. (314)464-2616. Editor: Georgia Goodridge. 20-90% freelance written. A monthly tabloid covering fairs, celebrations and indoor expositions for vendors who travel North America working these various events. Byline given. Buys first rights. Submit seasonal/holiday material 3 months in advance. Photocopied and previously published submissions OK. Free sample copy and writer's guidelines.

Nonfiction: How-to, interview/profile and new product. Special issues include an annual fair directory and semi-annual flea market directory. No submissions unrelated to selling at events. Query. Length: 400-750 words. Pays $2.50/column inch; may offer premiums instead of cash. Sometimes pays the expenses of writers on assignment.

Photos: Send photos with submission. Reviews contact sheets. Offers $5/photo. Captions required. Buys one-time rights.

Columns/Departments: 3 columns monthly (must deal with vending at events in North America). Query with published clips. Length: 400-750 words. Pays $3/column inch.

FOOD & DRUG PACKAGING, 7500 Old Oak Blvd., Cleveland OH 44140. Editor: Sophia Dilberakis. 5% freelance written. Prefers to work with published/established writers. For packaging decision makers in food, drug, and cosmetic firms. Monthly. Circ. 67,000. Rights purchased vary with author and material. Pays on acceptance. Publishes ms an average of 2-4 months after acceptance. Query for electronic submissions. Computer printout submissions OK; prefers letter-quality.

Nonfiction and Photos: "Looking for news stories about local and state (not federal) packaging legislation, and its impact on the marketplace. Newspaper style." Query only. Length: 1,000-2,500 words; usually 500-700. Payments vary; usually 5¢/word.

Photos: Photos purchased with mss. 5x7 glossies preferred. Pays $5. Sometimes pays the expenses of writers on assignment.

Tips: "Get details on local packaging legislation's impact on marketplace/sales/consumer/retailer reaction; etc. Keep an eye open to *new* packages. Query when you think you've got one. New packages move into test markets every day, so if you don't see anything new this week, try again next week. Buy it; describe it briefly in a query."

INCENTIVE, (formerly Incentive Marketing), Bill Communications, 633 Third Ave., New York NY 10017. (212)986-4800. Editor: Bruce Bolger. Managing Editor: Mary A. Riordan. Monthly magazine covering sales promotion and employee motivation: managing and marketing through motivation. Circ. 41,000. Pays on acceptance. Publishes ms an average of 3 months after acceptance. Byline sometimes given. Buys all rights. Query for electronic submissions. Computer printout submissions OK; no dot-matrix. Reports in 1 month on queries; 2 months on mss. Free sample copy.

Nonfiction: General interest (motivation, demographics), how-to (types of sales promotion, buying product categories, using destinations), interview/profile (sales promotion executives); corporate case studies; and travel (incentive-oriented). Buys up to 60 mss/year. Query with 2 published clips. Length: 500-2,000 words. Pays $100-700 for assigned articles; pays $0-100 for unsolicited articles. Sometimes pays the expenses of writers on assignment.

Photos: Send photos with submission. Reviews contact sheets and transparencies. Offers no additional payment for photos accepted with ms. Identification of subjects required.

Tips: "Read the publication, then query."

INFO FRANCHISE NEWSLETTER, Box 670, 9 Duke St., St. Catharines, Ontario L2R 6W8 Canada or Box 550, 728 Center St., Lewiston NY 14092. (716)754-4669. Editor-in-Chief: E.L. Dixon, Jr. Managing Editor: Caroline McCaffery. Monthly newsletter. Circ. 5,000. Pays on publication. Buys all rights. Photocopied submissions OK. Reports in 1 month.

66 *Ours is a special-interest magazine, so it's important for writers to have a basic working knowledge of the field—in our case theatre. But even before that, the single most important quality a manuscript must have is good writing.* 99

—Don Corathers,
Dramatics Magazine

Nonfiction: "We are particularly interested in receiving articles regarding franchise legislation, franchise litigation, franchise success stories, and new franchises. Both American and Canadian items are of interest. We do not want to receive any information which is not fully documented or articles which could have appeared in any newspaper or magazine in North America. An author with a legal background who could comment upon such things as arbitration and franchising or class actions and franchising, would be of great interest to us." Expose, how-to, informational, interview, profile, new product, personal experience and technical. Buys 10-20 mss/year. Length: 25-1,000 words. Pays $10-300.

OPPORTUNITY MAGAZINE, 6 N. Michigan Ave., Chicago IL 60602. Managing Editor: Jack Weissman. 33% freelance written. Eager to work with new/unpublished writers. Monthly magazine "for anyone who is interested in making money, full or spare time, in selling or in an independent business program." Circ. 190,000. Pays on publication. Buys all rights. Byline given. Submit seasonal/holiday material 6 months in advance. Free sample copy; writer's guidelines for #10 SASE.
Nonfiction: "We use articles dealing with sales techniques, sales psychology or general self-improvement topics." How-to, inspirational, and interview (with successful salespeople selling products offered by direct selling firms, especially concerning firms which recruit salespeople through *Opportunity Magazine*). Articles on self-improvement should deal with specifics rather than generalities. Would like to have more articles that deal with overcoming fear, building self-confidence, increasing personal effectiveness, and other psychological subjects. Submit complete ms. Buys 35-50 unsolicited mss/year. Length: 250-900 words. Pays $20-35.
Photos: State availability of photos with ms. Offers no additional payment for 8x10 b&w glossy prints. Captions and model release required. Buys all rights.
Tips: "Many articles are too academic for our audience. We look for a free-and-easy style in simple language which is packed with useful information, drama and inspiration. Check the magazine before writing. We can't use general articles. The only articles we buy deal with material that is specifically directed to readers who are opportunity seekers—articles dealing with direct sales programs or successful ventures that others can emulate. Try to relate the article to the actual work in which the reader is engaged. Look for fresh approaches. Too many people write on the same or similar topics."

‡PRIVATE LABEL, The Magazine for House Brands and Generics, E.W. Williams Publishing Co., 80 8th Ave., New York NY 10011. (212)989-1101. Managing Editor: Mark Edgar. 10% freelance written. Bimonthly magazine covering food and nonfood private label and generic products. Circ. 25,000. Pays on acceptance. Publishes ms an average of 1 month after acceptance. Byline given. Offers 50-100% kill fee, depending on circumstances. Buys first serial rights and second serial (reprint) rights. Submit seasonal/holiday material 4 months in advance. Photocopied submissions OK if not under submission elsewhere. Computer printout submissions acceptable; no dot-matrix. Reports in "weeks." Sample copy $1 and SAE.
Nonfiction: Book excerpts (if segments are appropriate); general interest; historical/nostalgic; how-to; interview/profile; personal experience; photo feature; and travel. "We use feature articles showing how retailers promote, buy, display, sell, and feel about their store brands (private label and generic products). We're always interested in coverage of areas more than 300 miles from New York. No articles on peripheral topics such as taxes, insurance, safety, etc." Buys 30-40 mss/year. Query or send complete ms. Length: 500-4,000 words. Pays 5¢/word; "flat fee by special arrangement." Sometimes pays expenses of writers on assignment.
Photos: "We prefer articles with photos." Send photos with ms. Reviews contact sheets (if large selection). Pays $10 minimum for 5x7 b&w prints. Captions and identification of subjects required. Buys all rights; "release on request."
Tips: "We are wide open to freelancers who can line up store permission (preferably headquarters) for feature articles on philosophy, purchase, consumer attitudes, retailer attitudes, display and promotion of private label and generic products."

PROFESSIONAL SELLING, 24 Rope Ferry Rd., Waterford CT 06386. (203)442-4365. Editor: Paulette S. Withers. 33% freelance written. Prefers to work with published/established writers, and works with a small number of new/unpublished writers each year. Bimonthly newsletter in two sections for sales professionals covering industrial or wholesale sales. "*Professional Selling* provides field sales personnel with both the basics and current information that can help them better perform the sales function." Pays on acceptance. Publishes ms an average of 4-6 months after acceptance. No byline given. Buys all rights. Submit seasonal/holiday material 4 months in advance. Computer printout submissions acceptable; no dot-matrix. Reports in 2 weeks. Sample copy and writer's guidelines for #10 SAE and 2 first class stamps.
Nonfiction: How-to (successful sales techniques); and interview/profile (interview-based articles). "We buy only interview-based material." Buys 12-15 mss/year. No unsolicited manuscripts; written queries only. Length: 800-1,000 words.
Tips: "*Professional Selling* has recently expanded to 8 pages, with a 4-page clinic devoted to a single topic of major importance to sales professionals. Only the lead article for each section is open to freelancers. That must

be based on an interview with an actual sales professional. Freelancers may occasionally interview sales managers, but the slant must be toward field sales, *not* management."

‡**SALES MOTIVATION, The Journal of Methods, Merchandise, and Incentive Travel**, (formerly *Incentive Manager*), Macmillan Professional Journal, 1640 5th St., Santa Monica CA 90401. (213)395-0234. Editor: Helene N. Kass. Assistant Editor: Paul Rosta. 80% freelance written. A monthly magazine for sales personnel. "*Sales Motivation* is edited for professionals responsible for directing and motivating corporate sales staffs, including outside reps and field sales forces. Its pragmatic, how-to editorial approach combines psychology, human resources, sales management strategies, case histories, and practical applications to show how various motivational methods can be used to increase sales and productivity." Circ. 30,000. Pays on acceptance. Publishes ms an average of 4 months after acceptance. Byline given. Kill fee varies. Buys all rights. Submit seasonal/holiday material 4 months in advance. Photocopied submissions OK. Reports in 6 weeks on queries; 1 month on mss. Free sample copy "if we have sufficient office copies available."
Nonfiction: How-to, interview/profile, opinion, travel (group destination focus only), sales management techniques. No consumer-type destination articles; general articles on "why motivation is important" or inspirational fluff articles. Buys 60 mss/year. Query. Length: 1,500-2,500. (Destination articles may be longer.) Pays 10¢/edited word for a writer's first submission; 12¢/edited word thereafter.
Photos: State availability of photos with submission. Reviews prints. Offers no additional payment for photos accepted with ms.
Tips: "Read our publication and query with article idea appropriate for our readership (vice presidents and directors of sales and marketing). It would help to send a resume or letter detailing your writing experience, along with published clips. (Do not query about incentive travel destination pieces; these are by assignments only, per a predetermined editorial calendar.) We are looking for articles on specific methods of motivating salespeople, and example of successful motivational/incentive programs. Case histories and profiles of firms that have exceptional employee/management rapport are always welcome. Focus must *be very narrow*. No articles on how to be a successful salesperson, please. Instead, tell our readers how they can inspire their sales staffs to greater productivity."

SELLING DIRECT, Communication Channels, Inc., 6255 Barfield Rd., Atlanta GA 30328. (404)256-9800. Publisher: William Manning. Editor: Robert Rawls. 20% freelance written. For independent businessmen and women who sell door-to-door, store-to-store, office-to-office and by the party plan method as well as through direct mail and telephone solicitation; selling products and services. Monthly magazine. Circ. 500,000. Pays on publication. Buys all rights. Byline given. Submit seasonal/holiday material 3 months in advance. Query for electronic submissions. Computer printout submissions acceptable. Reports in 3 months. Publishes ms an average of 1 year after acceptance. Free sample copy and writer's guidelines.
Nonfiction: How-to (sell better; increase profits); historical (related to the history of various kinds of sales pitches, anecdotes, etc.); and inspirational (success stories, "rags to riches" type of stories)—with no additional payment. Buys 30 unsolicited mss/year. Query or submit complete ms. Length: 500-1,500 words. Pays 10¢/word.
Photos: Photos purchased with accompanying ms.
Columns/Departments: Ideas Exchange (generated from our readers). Submit complete ms. Open to suggestions for new columns/departments.
Fillers: Jokes, gags, anecdotes and short humor. Buys 2/issue. Length: 150-500 words. Pays $10 for each published item. Buys 1-2 cartoons/issue. Pays $10 per cartoon.
Tips: No general articles on "How to be a Super Salesperson." Writers should concentrate on one specific aspect of selling and expand on that.

SOUND MANAGEMENT, Radio Advertising Bureau, 304 Park Ave. S., New York NY 10010. (212)254-4800. Editor-in-Chief: Daniel Flamberg. Editor: Andrew Giangola. 15% freelance written. A monthly magazine covering radio sales and marketing. "We write practical business and how-to stories for the owners and managers of radio stations on topics geared toward increasing ad sales and training salespeople." Circ. 10,000. Pays on publication. Publishes ms an average of 4 months after acceptance. Byline given. Buys one-time rights, exclusive rights for the field or makes work-for-hire assignments. Submit seasonal/holiday material 3 months in advance. Previously published submissions OK. Free sample copy and writer's guidelines.
Nonfiction: Essays, how-to, interview/profile and personal experience. No articles on disc jockeys or radio programming. Buys 5-10 mss/year. Query with published clips. Length: 400-750 words. Pays $350-650 for assigned articles; pays $50-150 for unsolicited articles. May pay contributor copies for republished items.
Photos: State availability of photos with submission. Reviews contact sheets, negatives and transparencies. Captions, model releases, and identification of subjects required. Buys one-time rights.
Tips: "Our cover story is most open to freelancers, but proven experience in writing about media advertising and marketing is necessary, with strong interviewing and critical writing skills."

‡**TELECOMMUNICATIONS EQUIPMENT RETAILER, The Professional Journal for the High-Tech Merchandiser**, Virgo Publications, Inc., Box C-5400, Scottsdale AZ 85261. (602)483-0014. Managing Editor: Christopher Geoffrey McPherson. Monthly trade journal for persons retailing telecommunications equipment. "Although ours is a specialized field, we want information on telecommunications to be informative, fun — but most of all, accessible to our readers." Estab. 1988. Circ. 40,000. Pays 30 days after publication. Byline given. Buys all rights. Submit seasonal/holiday material 3 months in davance. Simultaneous submissions OK. Query for electronic submissions. Computer printout submissions OK. Reports in 2 weeks. Free sample copy and writer's guidelines.

Nonfiction: Book excerpts, general interest, interview/profile, new product, technical. "No first-person, cutesy, or nontechnical material." Buys 15-20 mss/year. Query with published clips. Length: 1,500-4,000 words. Pays $50-200 for assigned articles; pays $50-150 for unsolicited articles. Sometimes pays expenses of writers on assignment.

Photos: State availability of photos with submission. Reviews contact sheets, any size transparencies and b&w and color prints. Offers no additional payment for photos accepted with ms. Model releases and identification of subjects required. Buys one-time rights.

Columns/Departments: Down the Line (in-the-future telecommunications trends), 1,000-1,200 words; Dossier (company or personality profile), 2,000-2,500 words; Making the Sale (sales techniques, trips, do's and don'ts), 2,000-2,500 words. Buys 10-15 mss/year. Query. Pays $25-100.

Tips: "The telecommunications industry is not—perhaps—the most glamorous industry in the world but *TER* aims to make it interesting and informative. We want interesting articles on product trends, telecommunications companies, and how-to stories on the business of retailing telecommunications products. Probably Dossier is the most open to freelancers. We want well researched, well written, informative articles on business, or people in the telecommunications industry, background on what they do, who they are, the products that make them well known."

WATERBED MAGAZINE, Bobit Publishing, 2512 Artesia Blvd., Redondo Beach CA 90278. (213)376-8788. Editor: Kathy Knoles. 10% freelance written. Prefers to work with published/established writers. A monthly magazine covering waterbeds and accessories for waterbed specialty shop owners, furniture stores, sleep shops and waterbed manufacturers, distributors. Circ. 9,200. Pays on publication. Publishes ms an average of 2 months after acceptance. Byline given. Buys first rights or second serial (reprint) rights. Submit seasonal/holiday material 3 months in advance. Photocopied and previously published submissions OK. Computer printout submissions acceptable; no dot-matrix. Reports in 2 weeks. Sample copy for 10x13 SAE with 5 first class stamps.

Nonfiction: Book excerpts; essays (health benefits of waterbeds); historical/nostalgic; how-to (business management, display techniques, merchandising tips); humor (if in good taste); interview/profile; new product; personal experience; photo feature; technical; and general features depicting waterbeds in a positive way. "Convention issue published in April or May prior to the Waterbed Manufacturer's Association Convention is extra large. We need more manuscripts then." No articles depicting waterbeds in a negative manner. "The goal of the waterbed industry and the magazine is to get away from the hippie image associated with waterbeds in the past." Buys 25-30 mss/year. Query with published clips. Length: 1,000-5,000 words. Pays $60-250 for assigned articles; pays $50-200 for unsolicited articles. Sometimes pays the expenses of writers on assignment.

Photos: Send photos with submission. Reviews contact sheets, transparencies and 8x10 prints. Offers $10-25/photo. Captions and identification of subjects required. Buys one-time rights.

Tips: "We need profiles on successful waterbed retailers in all parts of the country. If a large, full-line furniture store in your area also sells waterbeds, we are interested in profiles on those stores and owners as well. We are also always looking for interviews with doctors, chiropractors and other health professionals who recommend waterbeds for their patients. Most of our freelance articles concern business management. We need articles on obtaining credit, display techniques, merchandising, how to be a successful salesperson, attracting new customers, creating effective advertising, how to put together an attractive store window display, hiring employees, etc. Anything that could benefit a salesperson or store owner."

Sport Trade

Retailers and wholesalers of sports equipment and operators of recreation programs read these journals. Magazines about general and specific sports are classified in the Consumer Sports section.

AMERICAN BICYCLIST, Suite 305, 80 8th Ave., New York NY 10011. (212)206-7230. Editor: Konstantin Doren. 40% freelance written. Prefers to work with published/established writers. Monthly magazine for bicycle sales and service shops. Circ. 11,025. Pays on publication. Publishes ms an average of 4 months after acceptance. Only staff-written articles are bylined, except under special circumstances. Buys all rights. Computer printout submissions acceptable; no dot-matrix.

Nonfiction: Typical story describes (very specifically) unique traffic-builder or merchandising ideas used with success by an actual dealer. Articles may also deal exclusively with moped sales and service operation within conventional bicycle shops. Emphasis on showing other dealers how they can follow similar pattern and increase their business. Articles may also be based entirely on repair shop operation, depicting efficient and profitable service systems and methods. Buys 12 mss/year. Query. Length: 1,000-2,800 words. Pays 9¢/word, plus bonus for outstanding manuscript. Pays expenses of writers on assignment.

Photos: Reviews relevant b&w photos illustrating principal points in article purchased with ms; 5x7 minimum. Pays $8/photo. Captions required. Buys all rights.

Tips: "A frequent mistake made by writers is writing as if we are a book read by consumers instead of professionals in the bicycle industry."

AMERICAN FIREARMS INDUSTRY, AFI Communications Group, Inc., 2801 E. Oakland Park Blvd., Ft. Lauderdale FL 33306. 10% freelance written. "Work with writers specifically in the firearms trade." Monthly magazine specializing in the sporting arms trade. Circ. 30,000. Pays on publication. Publishes ms an average of 4 months after acceptance. Buys all rights. Computer printout submissions acceptable. Reports in 2 weeks.

Nonfiction: R.A. Lesmeister, articles editor. Publishes informational, technical and new product articles. No general firearms subjects. Query. Length: 900-1,500 words. Pays $100-150. Sometimes pays the expenses of writers on assignment.

Photos: Reviews 8x10 b&w glossy prints. Manuscript price includes payment for photos.

AMERICAN HOCKEY MAGAZINE, Amateur Hockey Association of the United States, 2997 Broadmoor Valley Rd., Colorado Springs CO 80906. (719)576-4990. Contact: Publisher. Managing Editor: Mike Schroeder. 80% freelance written. Monthly magazine covering hockey in general (with amateur/youth hockey emphasis) for teams, coaches and referees of the Amateur Hockey Association of the U.S., ice facilities in the U.S. and Canada, buyers, schools, colleges, pro teams, and park and recreation departments. Circ. 35,000. Pays on publication. Publishes ms an average of 1 month after acceptance. Byline given. Buys first serial rights; makes work-for-hire assignments. Phone queries OK. Submit seasonal/holiday material 4 months in advance. Photocopied and previously published submissions OK. Reports in 1 month. Sample copy $2.

Nonfiction: General interest, profile, new product and technical. Query. Length: 500-3,000 words. Pays $50 minimum.

Photos: Reviews 5x7 b&w glossy prints and color slides. Offers no additional payment for photos accepted with ms. Captions preferred. Buys one-time rights.

Columns/Departments: Rebound Shots (editorial); Americans in the Pros (U.S. players in the NHL); College Notes; Rinks and Arenas (arena news); Equipment/Sports Medicine; Referees Crease; Coaches Playbook; For the Record; and Features (miscellaneous). Query.

ARMS & OUTDOOR DIGEST, AFI Communications Group Inc., 2801 E. Oakland Park Blvd., Ft. Lauderdale FL 33306. (305)561-3505. Editor: Andrew Molchan. Managing Editor: R.A. Lesmeister. 5% freelance written. Monthly tabloid covering firearms/archery. "Our publication mainly deals with the firearms/archery retailer. We publish industry news and information that affects the industry as well as retail tips, liabilty articles, selling techniques, etc." Circ. 170,000. Pays on publication. Publishes ms an average of 4 months after acceptance. Byline given. Submit seasonal/holiday material 2 months in advance. Simultaneous and photocopied submissions OK. Computer printout submissions OK; prefers letter-quality. Reports in 1 week on queries; 3 weeks on mss. Sample copy $1.

Nonfiction: Interview/profile, new product, photo feature and technical. Does not want to see "anything dealing with the consumer." Buys 2-5 mss/year. Query. Length: 1,000-2,500 words. Pays $250-300 for assigned articles; pays $150 for unsolicited articles. Sometimes pays the expenses of writers on assignment.

Photos: Send photos with submission. Reviews prints. Offers $10 per photo. Buys all rights.

Fillers: Facts. Buys 1/year. "Most fillers used are statistical charts of varying size."

Tips: Encourages telephone queries. Areas most open to freelancers are "firearms technical areas, interviews with people in the firearms-political field, how-to gunsmithing."

BICYCLE BUSINESS JOURNAL, Box 1570, 1904 Wenneca, Fort Worth TX 76101. Editor: Rix Quinn. Works with a small number of new/unpublished writers each year. 10% freelance written. Monthly. Circ. 10,000. Pays on acceptance. Publishes ms an average of 3 months after acceptance. Buys all rights. Computer printout submissions acceptable.

Nonfiction: Stories about dealers who service what they sell, emphasizing progressive, successful sales ideas in the face of rising costs and increased competition. Length: 3 double-spaced pages maximum. Sometimes pays the expenses of writers on assignment.

Photos: B&w or color glossy photo a must; vertical photo preferred. Query.

Tips: "We are requesting greater professionalism and more content and research in freelance material."

FISHING TACKLE RETAILER, B.A.S.S. Publications, 1 Bell Rd., Montgomery AL 36141. (205)272-9530. Editor: Dave Ellison. 90% freelance written. Prefers to work with published/established writers. Magazine published 10 times/year, "designed to promote the economic health of retail sellers of freshwater and saltwater angling equipment." Circ. 22,000. Byline usually given. Publishes ms an average of 1 year after acceptance. Buys all rights. Submit seasonal/holiday material 6 months in advance. Query for electronic submissions. Computer printout submissions acceptable; prefers letter-quality. Reports in 6 weeks. Sample copy $2; writer's guidelines for #10 SAE and 1 first class stamp.

Nonfiction: How-to (merchandising and management techniques); technical (how readers can specifically benefit from individual technological advances); and success stories (how certain fishing tackle retailers have successfully overcome business difficulties and their advice to their fellow retailers). Articles must directly relate to the financial interests of the magazine's audience. Buys 100 mss/year. Query with published clips. Length: 50-3,000 words. Pays $10-600. Sometimes pays expenses of writers on assignment.

Photos: State availability of photos. Payment included with ms.

Columns/Departments: Retail Pointers (200-300 words) and Profit Strategy (750-900 words)—how-to tips, should be accompanied by illustration. Buys variable number mss/year.

Tips: "Long stories are usually assigned to writers with whom we have an established relationship. The writer has a better chance of breaking in at our publication with short, lesser-paying articles and fillers."

GOLF COURSE MANAGEMENT, Golf Course Superintendents Association of America, 1617 St. Andrews Dr., Lawrence KS 66046. (913)841-2240. Editor: Clay Loyd. 30% freelance written. Eager to work with new/unpublished writers. Monthly magazine covering golf course and turf management. Circ. 20,000. Byline given. Buys all rights. Submit seasonal/holiday material 6 months in advance. Publishes ms an average of 3 months after acceptance. Simultaneous queries and submissions OK. Computer prinout submissions acceptable; prefers letter-quality. Reports in 2 weeks on queries; 1 month on mss. Free sample copy; writer's guidelines for #10 SASE.

Nonfiction: Book excerpts, historical/nostalgic, interview/profile, personal experience and technical. "All areas that relate to the golf course superintendent—whether features or scholarly pieces related to turf/grass management. We prefer all submissions to be written *simply*." Special issues include January "conference issue"—features on convention cities used each year. Buys 50 mss/year. Query with clips of published work. Length: 1,500-3,000 words. Pays $100-300 or more. Sometimes pays the expenses of writers on assignment.

Photos: Send photos with ms. Pays $50-250 for color; slides or transparencies preferred. Captions, model release and identification of subjects required. Buys one-time rights.

Tips: "Call communications department (913)841-2240, offer idea, follow with outline and writing samples. Response from us is immediate."

GOLF SHOP OPERATIONS, 5520 Park Ave., Trumbull CT 06611. (203)373-7232. Editor: David Gould. 5% freelance written. Works with a small number of new/unpublished writers each year. Magazine published 8 times/year for golf professionals and shop operators at public and private courses, resorts, driving ranges and golf specialty stores. Circ. 13,200. Pays on publication. Publishes ms an average of 2 months after acceptance. Byline given. Submit seasonal material (for Christmas and other holiday sales, or profiles of successful professionals with how-to angle emphasized) 4 months in advance. Photocopied submissions OK. Computer printout submissions acceptable; prefers letter-quality. Reports in 1 month. Sample copy free.

Nonfiction: "We emphasize improving the golf retailer's knowledge of his profession. Articles should describe how pros are buying, promoting merchandising and displaying wares in their shops that might be of practical value. Must be aimed only at the retailer." How-to, profile, successful business operation and merchandising techniques. Buys 6-8 mss/year. Phone queries preferred. Pays $75-300 for assigned articles. Pays $50-300 for unsolicited articles. Sometimes pays expenses of writers on assignment.

Columns/Departments: Shop Talk (interesting happenings in the golf market), 250 words; Roaming Range (new and different in the driving range business), 500 words. Buys 4 mss/year. Send complete ms. Pays $50-150.

NSGA SPORTS RETAILER, National Sporting Goods Association, Suite 700, 1699 Wall St., Mt. Prospect IL 60056. (312)439-4000. Editor: John S. O'Neill. Managing Editor: Larry Weindruch. 75% freelance written. Works with a small number of new/unpublished writers each year. *NSGA Sports Retailer* serves as a monthly trade journal for presidents, CEOs and owners of more than 18,000 retail sporting goods firms. Circ. 9,000. Pays on publication. Publishes ms an average of 1 month after acceptance. Byline given. Offers 50% kill fee. Buys first and second serial (reprint) rights. Submit seasonal/holiday material 3 months in advance. Photocopied submissions OK. Query for electronic submissions. Computer printout submissions OK; prefers letter-quality. Sample copy for 9x12 SAE with 5 first class stamps.

Nonfiction: Essays, interview/profile and photo feature. Special issue includes Co-Op Advertising (Dec.). "No articles written without sporting goods retail businessmen in mind as the audience. In other words, no generic articles sent to several industries." Buys 50 mss/year. Query with published clips. Pays $75-500. Sometimes pays the expenses of writers on assignment.

Photos: State availability of photos with submission. Reviews contact sheets, negatives, transparencies and 5x7 prints. Payment negotiable. Buys one-time rights.

Columns/Departments: Personnel Management (to-the-point tips on hiring, motivating, firing, etc.); Tax Advisor (simplified explanation of how tax laws affect retailer); Sales Management (in-depth tips to improve sales force's performance); Retail Management (detailed explanation of merchandising/inventory control); Advertising (case histories of successful ad campaigns/ad critiques); Legal Advisor; Computers; Store Design; Visual Mercandising; all 1,500 words. Buys 50 mss/year. Query. Length: 1,000-1,500 words. Pays $75-300.

POOL & SPA NEWS, Leisure Publications, 3923 W. 6th St., Los Angeles CA 90020. (213)385-3926. Editor-in-Chief: J. Field. 25-40% freelance written. Semimonthly magazine emphasizing news of the swimming pool and spa industry for pool builders, pool retail stores and pool service firms. Circ. 15,000. Pays on publication. Publishes ms an average of 1-2 months after acceptance. Buys all rights. Photocopied submissions OK. Query for electronic submissions. Computer printout submissions acceptable; no dot-matrix. Reports in 2 weeks.

Nonfiction: Interview, new product, profile and technical. Phone queries OK. Length: 500-2,000 words. Pays 10-12¢/word. Pays expenses of writers on assignment.

Photos: Pays $10 per b&w photo used.

SAILBOARD NEWS, The International Trade Journal of Windsurfing, Sports Ink Magazine, Inc., Box 159, Fair Haven VT 05743. (802)265-8153. Fax: 802-265-4746. Editor: Mark Gabriel. 50% freelance written. Works with a small number of new/unpublished writers each year. Monthly boardsailing trade glossy tabloid. Circ. 19,000. Pays 1 month after publication. Publishes ms an average of 2 weeks after acceptance. Byline given. Buys one-time rights. Submit seasonal/holiday material 3 weeks in advance. Simultaneous queries OK. Query for electronic submissions. Computer printout submissions acceptable. Reports in 3 weeks. Sample copy and writer's guidelines for 9x12 SAE and 5 first class stamps.

Nonfiction: Regional retail reports, book excerpts, expose, general interest, historical/nostalgic, how-to, humor, inspirational, interview/profile, new product, opinion, photo feature, technical, travel. Buys 50 mss/year. Send complete ms. Length: 750 words minimum. Pays $50-200.

Photos: Send photos with ms. Reviews b&w negatives and 8x10 prints. Identification of subjects required.

Columns/Departments: Buys 12 mss/year. Query with published clips or send complete ms.

‡SKI BUSINESS, 537 Post Rd., Darien CT 06820. Managing Editor: Frank Hammel. 70% freelance written. Works with a small number of new/unpublished writers each year. Tabloid magazine published 11 times/year. For ski retailers, both alpine and cross-country. Circ. 18,000. Byline given, except on "press releases and round-up articles containing passages from articles submitted by several writers." Pays within 1 month of publication. Buys first rights plus reprint rights for promotional use and republication in special editions. Submit seasonal material 6 weeks in advance. Query for electronic submissions. Computer printout submissions acceptable; no dot-matrix. Reports in 1 month. Publishes ms an average of 2 months after acceptance. Free sample copy available to qualified writers.

Nonfiction: Will consider ski shop profiles; mss about unique and successful merchandising ideas and equipment rental operations. "All material should be slanted toward usefulness to the ski shop operator. Always interested in in-depth interviews with successful retailers." Uses round-ups of preseason sales and Christmas buying trends across the country from September to December. Would like to see reports on what retailers in major markets are doing. Buys about 100 mss/year. Query first. Pays $50-250. Pays expenses of writers on assignment.

Photos: Photos purchased with accompanying mss. Buys b&w glossies and slides. Pays minimum of $35/photo.

Tips: "We are most interested in retailer profiles of successful ski shop operators, with plenty of advice and examples for our readers. We anticipate a shift in editorial direction to more closely meet the needs of retailers, which will require more retailer-oriented pieces."

‡THE SPORTING GOODS DEALER, 1212 N. Lindbergh Blvd., St. Louis MO 63132. (314)997-7111. President/Chief Executive Officer: Richard Waters. Editor: Steve Fechter. 20% freelance written. Prefers to work with published/established writers. For members of the sporting goods trade: retailers, manufacturers, wholesalers, and representatives. Monthly magazine. Circ. 27,000. Buys second serial (reprint) rights. Buys about 15 mss/year. Pays on publication. Computer printout submissions acceptable; no dot-matrix. Publishes ms an average of 3 months after acceptance. Query. Sample copy $4 (refunded with first ms).

Nonfiction: "Articles about specific sporting goods retail stores, their promotions, display techniques, sales ideas, merchandising, timely news of key personnel; expansions, new stores, deaths—all in the sporting goods trade. Specific details on how individual successful sporting goods stores operate. What specific retail sporting goods stores are doing that is new and different. We would also be interested in features dealing with stores doing an outstanding job in retailing of exercise equipment, athletic footwear, athletic apparel, baseball, fishing, golf, tennis, camping, firearms/hunting and allied lines of equipment. Query on these." Successful business operations and merchandising techniques. Does not want to see announcements of doings and engagements. Length: open. Rates negotiated by assignment. Also looking for material for the following columns: Terse Tales of the Trade (store news); Selling Slants (store promotions); and Open for Business (new retail sporting goods stores or sporting goods departments). All material must relate to specific sporting goods stores by name, city, and state; general information is not accepted.

Photos: Pays minimum of $3.50 for sharp clear b&w photos; size not important. These are purchased with or without mss. Captions optional, but identification requested.

Fillers: Clippings. These must relate directly to the sporting goods industry. Pays 2¢/published word.

Tips: "The writer has to put himself or herself in our readers' position and ask: Does my style and/or expertise help retailers run their business better?"

SPORTS MARKETING NEWS, Technical Marketing Corp., 1460 Post Rd., Westport CT 06880. (203)255-9997. Editor: Philip Maher. Managing Editor: Jacques Pernitz. 20% freelance written. A biweekly trade journal on sports marketing. Circ. 30,000. Pays on acceptance. Publishes ms an average of 1 month after acceptance. Byline sometimes given. Offers 25% kill fee. Buys first North American serial rights or makes work-for-hire assignments. Query for electronic submissions. Free sample copy and writer's guidelines.

Nonfiction: Buys 50 mss/year. Query with published clips. Length: 500-2,000 words. Pays $50-500. Sometimes pays the expenses of writers on assignment.

Photos: Send photos with submission. Captions, model releases and identification of subjects required. Buys one-time rights.

‡**SWIMMING POOL/SPA AGE**, Communication Channels, Inc., 6255 Barfield Rd., Atlanta GA 30328. (404)256-9800. Editor: Terri Simmons. 30% freelance written. Works with a small number of new/unpublished writers each year. Monthly tabloid emphasizing pool, spa and hot tub industry. Circ. 17,500. Pays on publication. Publishes ms an average of 3 months after acceptance. Buys all rights. Submit seasonal/holiday material 3 months in advance. Query for electronic submissions.

Nonfiction: How-to (installation techniques, service and repairs, tips, etc.); interview (with people and groups within the industry); photo feature (pool/spa/tub construction or special use); technical (should be prepared with expert within the industry); industry news; and market research reports. Also, comparison articles exploring the same type of products produced by numerous manufacturers. Buys 1-3 unsolicited mss/year. Mss must be double-spaced on *white* paper. Query. Length: 250-2,500 words. Pays 10¢/word. Sometimes pays the expenses of writers on assignment.

Photos: Purchased with accompanying ms or on assignment. Query or send contact sheet. Will accept 35mm transparencies of good quality. Captions required.

Tips: "If a writer can produce easily understood technical articles containing unbiased, hard facts, we are definitely interested. We will be concentrating on technical and how-to articles because that's what our readers want."

‡**TEAM SPORTS BUSINESS, The Professional Journal for Team Sports Dealers**, Virgo Publications, Inc., Box C-5400, Scottsdale AZ 85261. (602)483-0014. Editor: Brent Diamond. Managing Editors: Tracey Benson, Andy McGavin. 15% freelance written. Monthly trade journal with retail oriented team sports articles. "For those retailers involved in selling team sports equipment. Helps them run efficient business, aid in making purchasing decisions and running a more organized business." Estab. 1988. Circ. 30,000. Pays 30 days after publication. Byline given. Buys all rights. Submit seasonal/holiday material 3 months in davance. Simultaneous submissions OK. Query for electronic submissions. Computer printout submissions OK. Reports in 2 weeks. Free sample copy and writer's guidelines.

Nonfiction: How-to, interview/profile, new product, technical. Buys 20 mss/year. Query with or without published clips, or send complete ms. Length: 1,500-4,000 words. Pays $50-200 for assigned articles; pays $50-150 for unsolicited articles. Sometimes pays expenses of writers on assignment.

‡**TENNIS BUYER'S GUIDE**, New York Times Magazine Group, 5520 Park Ave., Trumbull CT 06611. (203)373-7232. Editor: Robert Carney. Managing Editor: Eileen Rafferty. 5% freelance written. A bimonthly tabloid on the tennis industry. "We publish for the tennis retailer. We favor a business angle, providing information that will make our readers better tennis professionals and better business people." Circ. 11,000. Pays on publication. Publishes ms an average of 3 months after acceptance. Byline given. Offers 15% kill fee. Buys one-time rights. Submit seasonal/holiday material 6 months in advance. Simultaneous and photocopied submissions OK. Computer printout submissions OK; no dot-matrix. Reports in 6 weeks on queries; 1 month on mss. Free sample copy and writer's guidelines.

Nonfiction: How-to, humor, interview/profile, new product, photo feature, technical and travel. No professional tennis tour articles. Buys 8 mss/year. Send complete ms. Length: 500-2,000 words. Pays $75-300 for assigned articles. Pays $50-300 for unsolicited articles. Sometimes pays the expenses of writers on assignment.

Photos: Reviews transparencies and prints (35mm). Captions, model releases and identification of subjects required. Buys one-time rights.

Columns/Departments: Court Report (interesting happenings in the tennis market). Buys 4 mss/year. Send complete ms. Length: 250-500 words. Pays $50-150.

Tips: "Express an interest and knowledge in tennis or a business management field and an understanding of retail business."

WOODALL'S CAMPGROUND MANAGEMENT, Woodall Publishing Co., Suite 100, 100 Corporate North, Bannockburn IL 60015-1253. (312)295-7799. Editor: Mike Byrnes. 66% freelance written. Works with a small number of new/unpublished writers each year. A monthly tabloid covering campground management and operation for managers of private and public campgrounds throughout the U.S. Circ. 16,000. Pays after publication. Publishes ms an average of 4 months after acceptance. Byline given. Buys all rights. Will reassign rights to author upon written request. Submit seasonal/holiday material 4 months in advance. Simultaneous queries OK. Computer printout submissions acceptable; prefers letter-quality. Reports in 1 month on queries; 2 months on mss. Free sample copy and writer's guidelines.

Nonfiction: How-to, interview/profile and technical. "Our articles tell our readers how to maintain their resources, manage personnel and guests, market, develop new campground areas and activities, and interrelate with the major tourism organizations within their areas. 'Improvement' and 'profit' are the two key words." Buys 48 mss/year. Query. Length: 500 words minimum. Pays $50-200. Sometimes pays expenses of writers on assignment.

Photos: Send contact sheets and negatives. "We pay for each photo used."

Tips: "Contact us and give us an idea of your ability to travel and your travel range. We sometimes have assignments in certain areas. The best type of story to break in with is a case history type approach about how a campground improved its maintenance, physical plant or profitability."

Stone and Quarry Products

CONCRETE CONSTRUCTION MAGAZINE, 426 South Westgate, Addison IL 60101. Editorial Director: Ward R. Malisch. Monthly magazine for general and concrete contractors, architects, engineers, concrete producers, cement manufacturers, distributors and dealers in construction equipment and testing labs. Circ. 90,000. Pays on acceptance. Bylines used only by prearrangement with author. Buys all rights. Photocopied submissions OK. Reports in 2 months. Free sample copy and writer's guidelines.

Nonfiction: "Our magazine has a major emphasis on cast-in-place and precast concrete. Prestressed concrete is also covered. Our articles deal with tools, techniques and materials that result in better handling, better placing, and ultimately an improved final product. We are particularly firm about not using proprietary names in any of our articles. Manufacturer and product names are never mentioned; only the processes or techniques that might be of help to the concrete contractor, the architect or the engineer dealing with the material. We do use reader response cards to relay reader interest to manufacturers." No job stories or promotional material. Buys 8-10 mss/year. Submit query with topical outline. Pays $200/2-page article. Prefers 1,000-2,000 words with 2-3 illustrations.

Photos: Photos used only as part of complete ms.

Tips: "Condensed, totally factual presentations are preferred."

STONE REVIEW, National Stone Association, 1415 Elliot Place NW, Washington DC 20007. (202)342-1100. Editor: Frank Atlee. Bimonthly magazine covering quarrying and supplying of crushed stone. "Designed to be a communications forum for the stone industry. Publishes information on industry technology, trends, developments and concerns. Audience are quarry operations/management, and manufacturers of equipment, suppliers of services to the industry." Circ. 2,300. Pays on publication. Publishes ms an average of 3 months after acceptance. Byline given. Negotiable kill fee. Buys one-time rights. Submit seasonal/holiday material 6 months in advance. Simultaneous, photocopied and previously published submissions OK. Computer printout submissions OK; prefers letter-quality. Reports in 1 month. Sample copy for 9x12 SAE and 5 first class stamps.

Nonfiction: Technical. Query with or without published clips, or send complete ms. Length: 1,000-2,500 words. "Note: We have no budget for freelance material, but I'm willing to get monetary payment OK for right material."

Photos: State availability of photos with query, then send photos with submission. Reviews contact sheets, negatives, transparencies and prints. Offers no additional payment for photos accepted with ms. Identification of subjects required. Buys one-time rights.

Tips: "At this point, all features are written by contributors in the industry, but I'd like to open it up. Articles on unique equipment, applications, etc. are good, as are those reporting on trends (e.g., there is a strong push on now for automation of operations)."

‡STONE WORLD, Tradelink Publishing Company. 485 Kinderkamack Rd., Oradell NJ 07649-1502. (201) 599-0136. Editor: Mike Lench. Managing Editor: John Sailer. A monthly magazine on natural building stone for producers and users of granite, marble, limestone, slate, sandstone, onyx and other natural stone products. Circ. 13,000. Pays on publication. Publishes ms an average of 2 months after acceptance. Byline given. Buys first rights or second serial (reprint) rights. Submit seasonal/holiday material 4 months in advance. Photocopied and previously published submissions OK. Computer printout submissions OK; prefers letter-quality. Reports in 2 weeks on queries; 1 month on mss. Sample copy $5.50.
Nonfiction: How-to (fabricate and/or install natural building stone), interview/profile, photo feature, technical, architectural design, artistic stone uses, statistics, factory profile, equipment profile and trade show review. Buys 5 mss/year. Query with or without published clips, or send complete ms. Length: 600-3,000 words. Pays $75-150. Sometimes pays the expenses of writers on assignment.
Photos: State availability of photos with submission. Reviews transparencies and prints. Offers no additional payment for photos accepted with ms. Captions and identification of subjects required. Buys one-time rights.
Columns/Departments: News (pertaining to stone or design community); New Literature (brochures, catalogs, books, videos etc. about stone); New Products (stone products); New Equipment (equipment and machinery for working with stone); Calendar (dates and locations of events in stone and design communities). Query or send complete ms. Length: 300-600 words. Pays $25-50.
Tips: "Articles about architectural stone design accompanied by professional photographs and quotes from designing firms are often published, as are articles about new techniques of quarrying and/or fabricating natural building stone."

Toy, Novelty and Hobby

Publications focusing on the toy and hobby industry are listed in this section. For magazines for hobbyists, see the Consumer Hobby and Craft section.

PLAYTHINGS, Geyer-McAllister, 51 Madison Ave., New York NY 10010. (212)689-4411. Editor: Frank Reysen, Jr. Senior Associate Editor: Eugene Gilligan. 20-30% freelance written. A monthly merchandising magazine covering toys and hobbies aimed mainly at mass market toy retailers. Circ. 15,000. Pays on acceptance. Publishes ms an average of 3 months after acceptance. Byline sometimes given. Buys one-time rights. Submit seasonal/holiday material 3 months in advance. Simultaneous and photocopied submissions OK. Reports in 2 weeks. Free sample copy.
Nonfiction: Interview/profile, photo feature and retail profiles of toy and hobby stores and chains. Annual directory, May. Buys 10 mss/year. Query. Length: 900-2,500 words. Pays $100-350. Sometimes pays the expenses of writers on assignment.
Photos: Send photos with submission. Captions and identification of subjects required. Buys one-time rights.
Columns/Departments: Buys 5 mss/year. Query. Pays $50-100.

SOUVENIRS & NOVELTIES MAGAZINE, Kane Communications, Inc., Suite 210, 7000 Terminal Square, Upper Darby PA 19082. Editor: Chuck Tooley. A magazine published 7 times/year for resort and gift industry. Circ. 21,000. Pays on publication. Byline given. Buys all rights. Computer printout submissions acceptable; prefers letter-quality. Reports in 3 weeks. Sample copy for 6x9 SAE with 5 first class stamps.
Nonfiction: Interview/profile and new product. Buys 6 mss/year. Query. Length: 700-1,500 words. Pays $25-175 for assigned articles. Sometimes pays the expenses of writers on assignment.
Photos: State availability of photos with submission. Captions, model releases and identification of subjects required.

THE STAMP WHOLESALER, Box 706, Albany OR 97321. Executive Editor: Sherrie Steward. 80% freelance written. Newspaper published 28 times/year for philatelic businessmen; many are part-time and/or retired from other work. Circ. 6,000. Pays on publication. Byline given. Buys all rights. Computer printout submissions acceptable; prefers letter-quality. Reports in 10 weeks. Free sample copy.
Nonfiction: How-to information on how to deal more profitably in postage stamps for collections. Emphasis on merchandising techniques and how to make money. Does not want to see any so-called "humor" items from

nonprofessionals. Buys 60 ms/year. Submit complete ms. Length: 1,000-1,500 words. Pays $35 and up/article.

Tips: "Send queries on business stories. Send manuscript on stamp dealer stories. We need stories to help dealers make and save money."

Transportation

These publications are for professional movers and people involved in transportation of goods. For magazines focusing on trucking see also Auto and Truck.

AMERICAN MOVER, American Movers Conference, 2200 Mill Rd., Alexandria VA 22314. (703)838-1938. Editor: Leslie L. Frank. 10% freelance written. Works with a small number of new/unpublished writers each year. A monthly trade journal on the moving and storage industry for moving company executives. Circ. 2,200. Pays on publication. Publishes ms an average of 3 months after acceptance. Byline given. Offers $100 kill fee. Buys first North American serial rights. Submit seasonal/holiday material 3 months in advance. Query for electronic submissions. Computer printout submissions OK; prefers letter-quality. Reports in 3 weeks on queries. Free sample copy and writer's guidelines.

Nonfiction: How-to, interview/profile, new product, personal experience, photo feature, technical and small business articles. "No fiction or articles geared toward consumers." Buys 6 mss/year. Query with published clips. Length: 1,000-5,000 words. Pays $100-200 for assigned articles. Pays contributor copies at writer's request.

Photos: Send photos with submission. Reviews 5x7 prints. Offers no additional payment for photos accepted with ms. Captions required. Buys one-time rights.

Tips: "We have an editorial calendar available that lists topics we'll be covering. Articles on small business are helpful. Feature articles are most open to freelancers. Articles must slant toward moving company presidents on business-related issues. Timely topics are safety, deregulation, drug testing, computers, insurance, tax reform and marketing."

‡BUS WORLD, Magazine of Buses and Bus Systems, Stauss Publications, Box 39, Woodland Hills CA 91365. (818)710-0208. Editor: Ed Stauss. 75% freelance written. Eager to work with new/unpublished writers. Quarterly trade journal covering the transit and intercity bus industries. "*Bus World* is edited to inform and entertain people who have an interest in buses—bus owners, managers, drivers, enthusiasts and historians. Extensive photographic coverage." Circ. 6,000. Pays on publication. Publishes ms an average of 4 months after acceptance. Byline given. Buys first North American serial rights. Query for electronic submissions. Computer printout submissions acceptable; prefers letter-quality. Reports in 3 weeks. Sample copy with writer's guidelines $1.

Nonfiction: Primary coverage is North America. No tourist or travelog viewpoints. Buys 8-12 mss/year. Query. Length: 500-2,000 words. Pays $30-100.

Photos: Photos should be sharp and clear. State availability of photos. "We buy photos with manuscripts under one payment." Reviews 35mm color transparencies and 8x10 b&w prints. Captions required. Buys one-time rights.

Fillers: Cartoons. Buys 4-6/year. Pays $10.

Tips: "Be employed in or have a good understanding of the bus industry. Be enthusiastic about buses—their history and future—as well as current events. Acceptable material will be held until used and will not be returned unless requested by sender. Unacceptable and excess material will be returned only if accompanied by suitable SASE."

INBOUND LOGISTICS, Thomas Publishing Co., 1 Penn Plaza, 26th Fl., New York NY 10019. (212)290-7336. Editor: Richard S. Sexton. 50% freelance written. Prefers to work with published/established writers. Monthly magazine covering the transportation industry. "*Inbound Logistics* is distributed to people who buy, specify, or recommend inbound freight transportation services and equipment. The editorial matter provides basic explanations of inbound freight transportation, directory listings, how-to technical information, trends and developments affecting inbound freight movements, and expository, case history feature stories." Circ. 43,000. Pays on publication. Publishes ms an average of 3 months after acceptance. Byline given. Buys all rights. Simultaneous queries, and simultaneous and photocopied submissions OK. Computer printout submissions acceptable; no dot-matrix. Reports in 2 weeks. Sample copy and writer's guidelines for 8½11 SAE ad 5 first class stamps.

Nonfiction: How-to (basic help for traffic managers) and interview/profile (transportation professionals). Buys 15 mss/year. Query with published clips. Length: 750-1,000 words. Pays $300-1,200. Pays expenses of writers on assignment.

Photos: Michael Ritter, photo editor. State availability of photos with query. Pays $100-500 for b&w contact sheets, negatives, transparencies and prints; $250-500 for color contact sheets, negative transparencies and prints. Captions and identification of subjects required.

Columns/Departments: Viewpoint (discusses current opinions on transportation topics). Query with published clips.

Tips: "Have a sound knowledge of the transportation industry; educational how-to articles get our attention."

‡THE PRIVATE CARRIER, Private Carrier Conference, Inc.. Suite 720, 1320 Braddock Place, Alexandria VA 22314. (703)683-1300. Editor: Don Tepper. 30% freelance written. A monthly magazine on freight transportation. "*The Private Carrier* is the national publication for private fleet managers. Its goal is to help them manage their private fleets and their other transportation activities as efficiently and cost-effectively as possible." Circ. 35,000. Pays on publication. Publishes ms an average of 2 months after acceptance. Byline given. Offers $100 maximum kill fee. "We buy first rights and retain right for reprint. However, after publication, writer may use/sell article as he/she sees fit." Submit seasonal/holiday material 3 months in advance. Photocopied submissions OK. Computer printout submissions OK; prefers letter-quality. Reports in 1 week on queries; 2 weeks on mss. Sample copy for 9x12 SAE.

Nonfiction: Exposé, interview/profile, opinion and photo feature. Buys 10 mss/year. Query. Length: 1,000-3,000 words. Pays $100-250. Sometimes pays the expenses of writers on assignment.

Photos: Send photos with submission. Reviews transparencies (35mm) and prints (5x7 or 8x10). Offers no additional payment for photos accepted with ms. When necessary model releases and identification of subjects required. Buys one-time rights.

Columns/Departments: Computer Briefs (computer software for transportation); On The Road (humorous true items dealing with transportation); Picture This (humorous photos dealing with transportation). Send complete ms. Length: 100-300 words. Pays $10-50.

Tips: "Tailor articles to our readers. Writing style is less important than clean, well-written copy. We love good photos or articles that lend themselves to good illustrations. We like the slightly off-beat, unconventional or novel way to look at subjects. Articles for whatever department that profile how a private fleet solved a problem (i.e., computers, drivers, maintenance, etc.). The structure is: 1) company identifies a problem, 2) evaluates options, 3) selects a solution, and 4) evaluates its choice."

Travel

Travel professionals read these publications to keep up with trends, tours and changes in transportation. Magazines about vacations and travel for the general public are listed in the Consumer Travel section.

ABC STAR SERVICE, ABC International, 131 Clarendon St., Boston MA 02116. (617)262-5000. Managing Editor: Kenneth Hale. "Eager to work with new/unpublished writers as well as those working from a home base abroad, planning trips that would allow time for hotel reporting, or living in major ports for cruise ships." Worldwide guide to accommodations and cruises founded in 1960 (as *Sloan Travel Agency Reports*) and sold to travel agencies on subscription basis. Pays 15 days prior to publication. Publishes ms an average of 3 months after acceptance. Buys all rights. Query for electronic submissions. Computer printout submissions OK; prefers letter-quality. Query. Query should include details on writer's experience in travel and writing, clips, specific forthcoming travel plans, and how much time would be available for hotel or ship inspections. Buys 5,000 reports/year. Pays $18 and up/report used (higher for ships). Sponsored trips are acceptable. "Higher rates of payment and of guaranteed acceptance of set number of reports will be made after correspondent's ability and reliability have been established." Writer's guidelines and list of available assignments for #10 SAE and 1 first class stamp.

> 66 *Too many so-called travel writers feel some obligation to promote anything they cover. Sometimes I wish our computers had automatic adjective erasers. Unfortunately, the travel field is laden with cliches, and everybody seems to believe they have to use them.* 99
>
> —Donald C. Langley,
> TravelAge *magazines*

Nonfiction: Objective, critical evaluations of hotels and cruise ships suitable for international travelers, based on personal inspections. Freelance correspondents ordinarily are assigned to update an entire state or country. "Assignment involves on-site inspections of all hotels we review; revising and updating published reports; and reviewing new properties. Qualities needed are thoroughness, precision, perseverance, and keen judgement. Solid research skills and powers of observation are crucial. Travel and travel writing experience are highly desirable. Reviews should be colorful, clear, and documented with hotel's brochure, rate sheet, etc. We accept no hotel advertising or payment for listings, so reviews should dispense praise and criticism where deserved."

Tips: "We may require sample hotel or cruise reports on facilities near freelancer's hometown before giving the first assignment. No byline because of sensitive nature of reviews."

‡LEISURE WHEELS MAGAZINE, Murray Publications Ltd., Box 7302, Station "E", Calgary, Alberta, Canada T3C 3M2. (403)263-2707. Editor: Murray Gimbel. 75% freelance written. Works with a small number of new/unpublished writers each year; eager to work with new/unpublished writers. Bimonthly magazine covering Canadian recreational vehicle travel. Circ. 47,700. Pays on publication. Publishes ms an average of 2 months after acceptance. Byline given. Buys second serial (reprint) rights. Submit seasonal/holiday material 2 months in advance. Computer printout submissions acceptable; prefers letter-quality. Sample copy 75¢; free writer's guidelines.

Nonfiction: Travel and outdoor leisure-time hobbies. Buys 12 mss/year. Query with published clips. Length: 1,000-2,000 words. Pays $135-200. Sometimes pays the expenses of writers on assignment.

Photos: State availability of photos. Pays $15-25 for 5x11 color prints; $10-20 for b&w 5x11 prints. Identification of subjects required. Buys one-time rights.

Columns/Departments: Buys 12 mss/year. Query with or without published clips. Length: 750-1,000 words. Pays $110-150.

Fiction: Adventure and humorous (relating to travel). Buys 6 mss/year. Query with or without published clips. Length: 1,000-1,500 words. Pays $135-150.

Fillers: Jokes and anecdotes. Buys 6 mss/year. Length: 500-700 words. Pays $50-70.

RV BUSINESS, TL Enterprises, Inc., 29901 Agoura Rd., Agoura CA 91301. (818)991-4980. Executive Editor: Katherine Sharma. 60% freelance written. Prefers to work with published/established writers. Semi-monthly magazine covering the recreational vehicle and allied industries for people in the RV industry—dealers, manufacturers, suppliers, campground management, and finance experts. Circ. 25,000. Pays on acceptance. Publishes ms an average of 2 months after acceptance. Byline given. Offers 50% kill fee. Buys first North American serial rights. Submit seasonal/holiday material 6 months in advance. Photocopied submissions OK. Query for electronic submissions. Computer printout submissions acceptable; prefers letter-quality. Reports in 3 weeks on queries; 6 weeks on mss. Sample copy for 9x12 SAE and 3 first class stamps; writer's guidelines for #10 SAE and 1 first class stamp.

Nonfiction: Technical, financial, legal or marketing issues; how-to (deal with any specific aspect of the RV business); interview/profile (persons or companies involved with the industry—legislative, finance, dealerships, manufacturing, supplier); specifics and verification of statistics required—must be factual; and technical (photos required, 4-color preferred). General business articles may be considered. Buys 75 mss/year. Query with published clips. Send complete ms—"but only read on speculation." Length: 1,000-1,500 words. Pays variable rate up to $500. Sometimes pays expenses of writers on assignment.

Photos: State availability of photos with query or send photos with ms. Reviews 35mm transparencies and 8x10 b&w prints. Captions, model release, and identification of subjects required. Buys one-time or all rights; unused photos returned.

Columns/Departments: Guest editorial; News (50-500 words maximum, b&w photos appreciated); and RV People (color photos/4-color transparencies; this section lends itself to fun, upbeat copy). Buys 100-120 mss/year. Query or send complete ms. Pays $10-200 "depending on where used and importance."

Tips: "Query. Phone OK; letter preferable. Send one or several ideas and a few lines letting us know how you plan to treat it/them. We are always looking for good authors knowledgable in the RV industry or related industries. Change of editorial focus requires more articles that are brief, factual, hard hitting, business oriented and in-depth. Will work with promising writers, published or unpublished."

TRAVELAGE MIDAMERICA, Official Airlines Guide, Inc., A Dun & Bradstreet Co., Suite 701, 320 N. Michigan, Chicago IL 60601. (312)346-4952. Editor/Publisher: Martin Deutsch. Managing Editor: Karen Goodwin. 15% freelance written. Weekly magazine "for travel agents in the 13 midAmerica states and in Ontario and Manitoba." Circ. 20,000. Pays on publication. Publishes ms an average of 2 months after acceptance. Buys one-time rights and second serial (reprint) rights. Submit seasonal/holiday material 3 months in advance. Simultaneous, photocopied, and previously published submissions OK. Computer printout submissions acceptable ("but not pleased with"); prefers letter-quality. Query first. Reports in 1 month. Free sample copy and writer's guidelines.

Nonfiction: "News on destinations, hotels, operators, rates and other developments in the travel business."

Also runs human interest features on retail travel agents in the readership area. No stories that don't contain prices; no queries that don't give detailed story lines. No general destination stories, especially ones on "do-it-yourself" travel. Buys 20 mss/year. Query. Length: 400-1,500 words. Pays $2/column inch.
Photos: State availability of photos with query. Pays $2/column inch for glossy b&w prints.
Tips: "Our major need is for freelance human interest stories with a marketing angle on travel agents in our readership area. Buying freelance destination stories is a much lower priority."

TRAVELAGE WEST, Official Airline Guides, Inc., 100 Grant Ave., San Francisco CA 94108. Executive Editor: Donald C. Langley. 5% freelance written. Prefers to work with published/established writers. Weekly magazine for travel agency sales counselors in the western U.S. and Canada. Circ. 35,000. Pays on publication. Publishes ms an average of 1 month after acceptance. Byline given. Buys all rights. Offers kill fee. Submit seasonal/holiday material 2 months in advance. Query for electronic submissions. Computer printout submissions acceptable; prefers letter-quality. Reports in 1 month. Free writer's guidelines.
Nonfiction: Travel. "No promotional approach or any hint of do-it-yourself travel. Emphasis is on news, not description. No static descriptions of places, particularly resort hotels." Buys 40 mss/year. Query. Length: 1,000 words maximum. Pays $2/column inch.
Tips: "Query should be a straightforward description of the proposed story, including (1) an indication of the news angle, no matter how tenuous, and (2) a recognition by the author that we run a trade magazine for travel agents, not a consumer book. I am particularly turned off by letters that try to get me all worked up about the 'beauty' or excitement of some place. Authors planning to travel might discuss with us a proposed angle before they go; otherwise their chances of gathering the right information are slim."

Veterinary

Journals for veterinarians and pet health professionals are located in this section. For publications targeted to pet shop and grooming business managers and the pet supply industry, see the Pets section. For magazines for pet owners, see the Consumer Animal section.

VETERINARY ECONOMICS MAGAZINE, 9073 Lenexa Dr., Lenexa KS 66215. (913)492-4300. Managing Editor: Becky Turner. 75% freelance written. Prefers to work with published/established writers but will work with several new/unpublished writers each year. Monthly business magazine for all practicing veterinarians in the U.S. Buys exclusive rights in the field. Pays on publication. Publishes ms 3-6 months after acceptance. Computer printout submissions acceptable.
Nonfiction: Publishes non-clinical case studies on business and management techniques that will strengthen a veterinarian's private practice. Also interested in articles on financial problems, investments, insurance and similar subjects of particular interest to professionals. "We look for carefully researched articles that are specifically directed to our field." Pays negotiable rates. Pays expenses of writers on assignment.

VETERINARY PRACTICE MANAGEMENT, Whittle Communications, 505 Market St., Knoxville TN 37902. (615)595-5211. Associate Editor: Rose R. Kennedy. 80% freelance written. Prefers to work with published/established business writers. Triannual magazine—"a business guide for small animal practitioners." Circ. 33,000. Pays on acceptance. Publishes ms an average of 3-4 months after acceptance. Byline given. Offers kill fee. Buys first serial rights to the same material. Simultaneous queries OK. Query for electronic submissions. Computer printout submissions acceptable; prefers letter-quality. Writer's guidelines and free sample copy to experienced business writers.
Nonfiction: How-to, and successful business (practice) management techniques supported by veterinary anecdotes and expert advice. No "how to milk more dollars out of your clients" articles. Buys 16 mss/year. Query with published clips; no unsolicited manuscripts. Pays $600-2,000 (average $1,200). Pays expenses of writers on assignment.
Columns/Departments: Management Briefs, In the Know, Taxes, Personal Investment, Personal Health and Humor. "Most items are written in-house, but we will consider ideas." Query with published clips. Pays up to $400.

ALWAYS submit manuscripts or queries with a self-addressed, stamped envelope (SASE) within your country or International Reply Coupons (IRC) purchased from the post office for other countries.

Additional Trade Publications

The following listings are inactive for the 1989 edition because the firms are backlogged with submissions or indicated a need for few freelance submissions in 1989.

American Office Dealer
Billboard

The following firms did not return a verification to update an existing listing or a questionnaire to begin a new listing by press time.

Absolute Reference
Ag-Pilot International Magazine
Agway Cooperator
Air-Line Pilot
Airfair Interline Magazine
American Bookseller
American Drycleaner
American Fitness
Archery Business
Artquest
Ashton-Tate Quarterly
Auto Laundry News
Automatic Machining
Automotive Cooling Journal
AV Video
B.C. Lumberman Magazine
Bank Loan Officers Report
Baroid News Bulletin
The Battery Man
Benefits Canada
Board and Administrator
Boating Industry
Boating Product News
Brake and Front End
Builder Insider
Bus Ride
Bus Tours Magazine
Business Insurance
Business Marketing
Cable Television Business Magazine
California Lawyer
California Publisher
Canadian Forest Industries
Canadian RV Dealer
Cardiology Management
The Chek-Chart Service Bulletin
Chief Fire Executive
Childbirth Educator
The Church Musician
Church Training
Coal Age
Compaq Magazine

Computer User's Legal Reporter
Consumer Lending Report
Contractor Magazine
Creative Years
Dairy Herd Management
Dance Exercise Today
Data Base Monthly
Datamation
Dealer Communicator
Diagnostic Imaging
Dimensional Stone
Electronics Packaging and Production
The Executive Administrator
Facets
Farm Journal
Farm Store Merchandising
Floral & Nursery Times
Flower News
Flute Talk
Foundry Management & Technology
Giftware Business
Graphic Arts Monthly
Gulf Coast Cattleman
Hardcopy
Heating, Plumbing, Air Conditioning
Heating/Piping/Air Conditioning
High-Tech Marketing
Hispanic Business
Hog Farm Management
Hotel and Motel Management
Imprint
In Business
Inform
Information Week
Inside Print
Instant & Small Commercial Printer
Jems
Kids Fashions

Limousin World
Lodging Hospitality
Los Angeles Lawyer
Louisiana Contractor
Market Watch
Media Profiles
Medical Meetings
Medical World News
Medicenter Management
Mini
Mini-Micro Systems
Miniatures Dealer Magazine
Missouri Ruralist
MIX Magazine
Mobile Manufactured Home Merchandiser
Model Retailer Magazine
Nation's Business
National Bus Trader
Nationwide Careers
New England Farmer
New Mexico Business Journal
News/34-38
NSBE Journal
Ocean Industry
Ocean Navigator
Office Systems Ergonomics Report
P.O.B.
Painting and Wallcovering Contractor
Peformance Magazine
Petroleum Independent
PGA Magazine
Phi Delta Kappan
The Physician and Sportsmedicine
Plan and Print
Play Meter Magazine
Potato Grower of Idaho
Practical Gastroenterolgy
Print & Graphics

Proceedings
Professional Agent Magazine
Progressive Architecture
Progressive Grocer
Pulse
The Rangefinder
Remodeling Contractor
The Romantist
Roofer Magazine
San Francisco Review of Books
Satellite Direct
Screen Printing
Seaway Review
Semiconductor International
Sheep! Magazine
Shoe Service
Sightlines
Signs of the Times

Simmental Shield
Southern Beverage Journal
Southwest Hotel-Motel Review
Sporting Goods Business
Stone in America
Sugar Producer
Systems/3x World
T-Shirt Retailer and Screen
   Printer
Television Broadcast
Tourist Attractions & Parks
   Magazine
Tradeshow and Exhibit Manager
   Magazine
Tree Trimmers Log
Truckers' News
Trucks Magazine

Unfinished Furniture Magazine
Vantage Point: Issues in Ameri-
   can Arts
Veterinary Computing
Video Manager
Video Store
Video Systems
Warehousing Supervisor's Bulle-
   tin
Waste Age
West Coast Review of Books
Western & English Fashions
Wilson Library Bulletin
Wisconsin Grocer
Writers Connection
Wyoming Rural Electric News
Your Church

The following listings were deleted following the 1988 edition of *Writer's Market* because the company asked to have the listing removed, went out of business, is no longer accepting unsolicited submissions or paying for submissions, or has unresolved complaints on file.

Academic Technology (out of business)
APA Monitor (not using freelancers)
Autobody & Reconditioned Car (out of business)
Books and Religion (does not pay)
Brick and Clay Record (asked to be deleted)
Builder/Dealer (does not pay)
CD Publications (asked to be deleted)
Ceramic Industry (asked to be deleted)
College Media Review (does not pay)
The Dispensing Optician (asked to be deleted)
Financial Strategies (suspended publication)
Functional Photography (ceased publication)
Good News (does not pay)
Health Foods Retailing (suspended publication)
Journal of Information Systems Management (does not pay)
Journalism Educator (does not pay)
Journalism Quarterly (does not pay)
Licensed Practical Nurse (does not pay)
Medical Times (only accepting physician-written articles)
Modern Veterinary Practice (asked to be deleted)
Motor Service (not using freelancers)
Nursinglife (ceased publication)
Options (asked to be deleted)
Papercutting World (asked to be deleted)
The Press (suspended publication)
Profit (not soliciting freelance work)
Publisher's Report (does not pay)
Resident & Staff Physician (only accepting physician-written articles)
Science Periodical on Research and Technology in Sport (unable to contact)
Successful Meetings Magazine (asked to be deleted)
Telemarketing (does not pay)
TFR (does not pay)
Travel Business Manager (asked to be deleted)
The Typographer (not soliciting freelance work)
Writer's Lifeline (does not pay)
Writer's Newsletter (does not pay)

Scriptwriting

by Michael Singh

The new video and cable technology has created great appetites for scripts—technical, theatrical, and educational. The market is huge and varied, so it pays to research your chosen area. Reading professional samples of the sort of script you would like to write will help not only your writing but also your salability. A page's appearance and readability—format, type size, neatness—are an important asset. For screenplays, it is crucial, since first impressions play a large role in determining whether or not a studio reader will continue beyond the first 20 or so pages of your script. See the accompanying section introductions for leads for obtaining scripts.

A quick way to become familiar with a specific genre of scriptwriting is to analyze the script you obtain, then follow it while watching the movie (or the play or technical film) of the script. A direct comparison will help you to analyze what a script leaves out. Only a fraction of the details and movements visible on stage or screen is actually included in a script. A well-written script is a guide, and gives only the barest of directions or descriptions, leaving much room for a director's creativity.

Avoid suggesting camera movement, shots and angles. Those are the director's perogative. Except when writing plays, avoid instructions to actors, as well. A good script goes into detail only for a crucial object or event, e.g., technical information. Avoid cataloging action or piling up unnecessary detail in the script as well.

Unlike plays, films depend on visuals. It's usually better to show through images than to tell through dialogue. Objects, locations, action and changing landscapes are usually more important than dialogue. Even in technical scripts, walking and talking are secondary. Dialogue (even onscreen) is often changed during and even after editing. Characters are what they *do* more than what they *say*. Remember, however, that even for technical scripts, such traditional aesthetic techniques as dramatic conflict and unexpected twists and resolutions remain important.

Selling scripts is not easy. Each market requires a different approach. Read the specific section introductions, and be sure to follow individual submission instructions detailed in the listings.

For information on additional scriptwriting markets not in *Writer's Market*, see Additional Scriptwriting Markets at the end of this section.

Business and Educational Writing

In terms of total number of films made, business and educational films are much bigger business than Hollywood. Just one major corporation may make dozens of training, advertising and informational films in a year.

Michael Singh has written the introductions for the Business and Educational Writing, Playwriting and Screenwriting sections of this edition of Writer's Market. *He has taught screenwriting and film production for the USC-Universal Studios program and has also written children's fiction and nonfiction for Holt, Rinehart & Winston. He is presently an ad copywriter for Twentieth Century Fox, and has just completed his second screenplay, a romantic comedy.*

Demands for content of these scripts are quite specific, and the producers (the company needing the film) usually also set the tone and style of the piece. The company's main interest is to relay its own message, whether it is directed to inhouse staff or to consumers. Essentially, producers call the shots in this area.

In searching for a topic or field, capitalize on your own strengths or experience. If you are a Navy veteran, your knowledge of jargon and procedures will put you ahead of those staff writers or freelancers who are not vets, and who must spend days traveling and researching. The more you know about a subject, the more you can offer a potential producer. An expert who can write is a rare and well-paid animal.

Most large organizations that make films will give you application forms to join their writers' pool. Previous writing experience, or expertise in their field, will help. Some organizations will supply you with sample scripts to study.

If accepted, you will usually be asked to submit a bid to write a script on a certain subject. Often, the job goes to the lowest bidder. Remember that if you are unfamiliar with the subject matter (as is common), you will have to figure travel and research expenses into your budget. Scripts pay approximately $50 to $100 per final draft page.

Good technical writing arouses feelings while also providing information. A successful film helps generate the feeling of an emergency, or the enthusiasm for a new product, or the excitement of math or reading. Detailed instructions, facts and directions are better conveyed by manuals, books and charts than by film. Viewers don't (or can't) rewind a film, but they can repeatedly consult a manual. The constant repetition of facts necessary to equal the impact of reading them would make a film very dull viewing.

A good technical film writer makes the driest material dramatic, visual, and catchy, exploiting the advantages of that medium over print. If your script describes specific objects, locations and procedures, the camera can avoid filming the narrator. Unless exceptionally animated or emotional (which may be discouraged by the producer), a narrator's face shown on camera can become just a "talking head." It's best to keep the narration offscreen, accompanying other visuals. Just the voice of a good narrator can convey all the subtleties and emotional range of a well-written narrative monologue.

Payment for business and educational scriptwriting is often tiered. For example, first payment may be made for a treatment or synopsis (usually one to five pages), second payment for a first draft, and final payment for a final draft. Each stage will need approval from various parties. Often they will update or correct your facts or details before passing the script to other concerned offices. You will encounter "committee filmmaking" at its height. As a scriptwriter in this field, you will probably have no involvement at all in the filming of your script. Often, these films are inhouse and carry no credits. In addition, each trade—even each company—will have its own format for scripts. Ask your target client to provide you with samples.

A square (□) to the left of a listing denotes firms interested in cable TV scripts.

ABS & ASSOCIATES, (formerly VABS Multi-Image), Box 5127, Evanston IL 60204. (312)982-1414. President: Alan Soell. "We produce material for all levels of corporate, medical, cable, and educational institutions for the purposes of training and development, marketing and meeting presentations. We also are developing programming for the broadcast areas. 75% freelance written. We work with a core of three to five freelance writers from development to final drafts." All scripts published are unagented submissions. Buys all rights. Previously produced material OK. Computer printout submissions acceptable. Reports in 2 weeks on queries. Catalog for 8x10 SAE and 6 first class stamps.
Needs: Videotape, 16mm films, silent and sound filmstrips, multimedia kits, overhead transparencies, realia, slides, tapes and cassettes, and television shows/series. Currently interested in "sports instructional series that could be produced for the consumer market on tennis, gymnastics, bowling, golf, aerobics, health and fitness, cross-country skiing and cycling. Also home improvement programs for the novice—for around the house—in a series format. These two areas should be 30 minutes and be timeless in approach for long shelf life." Sports audience, age 25-45; home improvement, 25-65. "Cable TV needs include the two groups of programming detailed here. We are also looking for documentary work on current issues, nuclear power, solar power, urban de-

velopment, senior citizens—but with a new approach." Query or submit synopsis/outline and resume. Pays by contractual agreement.

Tips: "I am looking for innovative approaches to old problems that just don't go away. The approach should be simple and direct so there is immediate audience identification with the presentation. I also like to see a sense of humor used. Trends in the audiovisual field include interactive video with tape and video disk—for training purposes."

ADMASTER, INC., 95 Madison Ave., New York NY 10016. (212)679-1134. Director: Andrew Corn. Produces sales and training material. Purchases 50-75 scripts/year. Works with 5-10 writers/year. Buys all rights. No previously published material. Reports in 1 month.
Needs: Charts, film loops (16mm), films (35 and 16mm), filmstrips (sound), multimedia kits, overhead transparencies, slides, tapes and cassettes. "We need material for multi-media industrial and financial meetings." Submit synopsis/outline, complete script or résumé. Makes outright purchase of $250-500.
Tips: "We want local writers only."

AMERICAN MEDIA INC., 1454 30th St., West Des Moines IA 50265. (515)224-0919. Contact: Art Bauer. Produces material for the business and industry training market (management, motivation, sales). Buys 10 scripts/year. Buys all rights. Previously produced material OK. Reports in 3 weeks. Catalog for 8½x11 SAE with 5 first class stamps.
Needs: Produces 16mm films and 1-inch videotapes. Submit synopsis/outline or completed script. Payment varies depending on script and quality.
Tips: "Do your homework, don't rush, think a project thru, ask and find out what your client needs. Not just what you think. Work long and hard."

ARNOLD AND ASSOCIATES PRODUCTIONS, INC., 2159 Powell St., San Francisco CA 94133. (415)989-3490. President: John Arnold. Executive Producers: James W. Morris and Peter Dutton. Produces material for the general public (entertainment/motion pictures) and for corporate clients (employees/customers/consumers). Buys 10-15 scripts/year. Works with 3 writers/year. Buys all rights. Previously produced material OK. Reports in 1 month.
Needs: Films (35mm) and videotape. Looking for "upscale image and marketing programs. Dramatic writing for "name narrators and post scored original music; and motion picture. $5-6 million dollar budget. Dramatic or horror." Query with samples or submit completed script. Makes outright purchase of $1,000.
Tips: Looking for "upscale writers that understand corporate image production, and motion picture writer(s) that understands story and dialogue."

‡ARZTCO PICTURES, INC., 15 E. 61st St., New York NY 10021. (212)753-1050. President/Producer: Tony Arzt. Produces material for industrial, education, and home viewing audiences (TV specials and documentaries). 80% freelance written. 75% of scripts produced are unagented submissions. Buys 8-10 scripts/year. Buys all rights. Previously produced material OK ("as sample of work only"). Computer printout submissions acceptable; prefers letter-quality. SASE, "however, we will only comment in writing on work that interests us." Reports in 3 weeks.
Needs: Business films, sales, training, promotional, educational. "Also interested in low-budget feature film scripts." 16mm and 35mm films, videotapes and cassettes, and software. Submit synopsis/outline or completed script and resume. Pays in accordance with Writers Guild standards.
Tips: "We would like writers to understand that we cannot find time to deal with each individual submission in great detail. If we feel your work is right for us, you will definitely hear from us. We're looking for writers with originality, skill in turning out words, and a sense of humor when appropriate. We prefer to work with writers available in the New York metropolitan area."

A/V CONCEPTS CORP., 30 Montauk Blvd., Oakdale NY 11769. (516)567-7227. Contact: P. Solimene or K. Brennan. Produces material for elementary-high school students, either on grade level or in remedial situations. 100% freelance written. Works with a small number of new/unpublished writers each year. Buys 25 scripts/year from unpublished/unproduced writers. Employs filmstrip, book and personal computer media. Computer printout submissions acceptable. Reports on outline in 1 month; on final scripts in 6 weeks. Buys all rights.
Needs: Interested in original educational computer (disk-based) software programs for Apple plus, 48k. Main concentration in language arts, mathematics and reading. "Manuscripts must be written using our lists of vocabulary words and meet our reading ability formula requirements. Specific guidelines are devised for each level. Length of manuscript and subjects will vary according to grade level for which material is prepared. Basically, we want material that will motivate people to read." Pays $300 and up.
Tips: "Writers must be highly creative and highly disciplined. We are interested in high interest-low reading ability materials."

SAMUEL R. BLATE ASSOCIATES, 10331 Watkins Mill Dr., Gaithersburg MD 20879-2935. (301)840-2248. President: Samuel R. Blate. Produces audiovisual and educational material for institutions, state and federal governments. "We work with two to six local writers per year on a per project basis—it varies as to business conditions and demand." Buys first rights when possible. Query for electronic submissions. Computer print-out submissions acceptable; prefers letter-quality. Reports in 1 week on queries; 2 weeks on submissions.
Needs: Filmstrips (silent and sound), multimedia kits, slides, tapes and cassettes. Query with samples. Payment "depends on type of contract with principal client." Pays expenses of writers on assignment.
Tips: "Writers must have a strong track record of technical and aesthetic excellence. Clarity is not next to divinity—it is above it."

CABSCOTT BROADCAST PRODUCTION, INC., #1 Broadcast Center, Blackwood NJ 08012. (609)228-3600. Contact: Larry Scott/Anne Foster. Produces industrial and broadcast material. 10% freelance written. Works with a small number of new/unpublished writers each year. Buys 10-12 scripts/year. Buys all rights. No previously produced material. Query for electronic submissions. Computer printout submissions acceptable; prefers letter-quality. Reports in 1 month.
Needs: Tapes and cassettes and video. Query with samples. Makes outright purchase. Sometimes pays expenses of writers on assignment.

CHAPPLE FILMS AND VIDEO,Route 198, Chaplin CT 06235. (203)455-9779. President: Wendy Wood. Produces business, educational and general films. Purchases 10 scripts/year. Buys all rights. Free catalog.
Needs: "In general, 10-minute scripts on a wide variety of industrial subjects." Produces 16 mm films, slides, tapes and cassettes and videotapes. Send samples only. Makes outright purchase.
Tips: Looking for "humor and the ability to work fast."

CLEARVUE, INC., 5711 N. Milwaukee Ave., Chicago IL 60646. (312)775-9433. President: W.O. Mc-Dermed. Produces material for educational market—grades kindergarten-12. 90% freelance written. Prefers to work with published/established writers; works with a small number of new/unpublished writers each year. Buys 20-50 scripts/year from previously unpublished/unproduced writers. Buys all rights. Previously produced material OK. Query for electronic submissions. Computer printout submissions acceptable; prefers letter-quality. Reports in 2 weeks on queries; 3 weeks on submissions. Free catalog.
Needs: Videos, filmstrips (sound), multimedia kits, and slides. "Our filmstrips are 35 to 100 frames—8 to 30 minutes for all curriculum areas." Query. Makes outright purchase, $100-5,000. Sometimes pays the expenses of writers on assignment.
Tips: "Our interests are in filmstrips and video for the elementary and high school markets on all subjects."

COMARK,1415 Second St., Santa Monica CA 90401. Vice President: Stan Ono. Produces material for corporate/industrial audience. Buys 18 scripts/year. Buys all rights. No previously produced material.
Needs: "Video training, sales/marketing, retail, financial and food services." Produces 16 mm film, multimedia kits, slides and video. Submit résumé. Makes outright purchase.

COMPASS FILMS, 921 Jackson Dr., Cleveland WI 53015. Executive Producer: Robert Whittaker. Produces material for educational, industrial and general adult audiences. Specializes in Marine films, stop motion and special effects with a budget . . . and national and worldwide filming in difficult locations. 60% freelance written. Works with 3 writers/year. Buys 2-4 scripts/year. 100% of scripts are unagented submissions. Buys all rights. Query with samples or submit resume. Computer printout submissions acceptable. Reports in 6 weeks. Buys all rights.
Needs: Scripts for 5- to 30-minute business films, and general documentaries. "We would like to review writers to develop existing film treatments and ideas with strong dialogue." Also needs ghost writers, editors and researchers. Produces 16mm and 35mm films and video tape products. Payment negotiable, depending on experience. Pays expenses of writers on assignment.
Tips: Writer/photographers receive higher consideration "because we could also use them as still photographers on location and they could double-up as rewrite men . . . and ladies. Experience in videotape editing supervision an asset. We are producing more high 'fashion-tech' industrial video."

‡COMPRENETICS, INC., Suite 102, 1448 15th St., Santa Monica CA 90404. (213)395-9238. President: Ira Englander. 10% freelance written. Prefers to work with published/established writers. "Target audience varies, however, programs are designed for health care audiences only. This ranges from entry level health workers with minimal academic background to continuing education programs for physicians and health professionals. In the cultural area, all levels." Produces material for video—creatively adapting subject matter treatments. Buys approximately 10-20 scripts/year. All scripts are unagented submissions. Buys all rights. Computer printout submissions acceptable; prefers letter-quality. Reports in 1 month. Sometimes pays the expenses of writers on assignment.
Needs: "Films are generally 10 to 20 minutes in length and tend to have a dramatic framework. Subject topics

include all educational areas with emphasis on health and medical films, manpower and management training and multi-cultural education. Our staff normally does subject matter research and content review which is provided for the writer who is then required to provide us with an outline or film treatment for review. Due to the extensive review procedures, writers are frequently required to modify through three or four drafts before final approval." Produces sound filmstrips, 16mm films, and tapes and cassettes. Query with samples or submit resume. Pays $1,000-5,000.

COMPRO PRODUCTIONS, Suite 114, 2080 Peachtree Ind. Court, Atlanta GA 30341. (404)455-1943. Producers: Nels Anderson and Steve Brinson. Audience is general public and specific business audience. Buys 10-25 scripts/year. Buys all rights. No previously produced material. No unsolicited material; submissions will not be returned because "all work is contracted."
Needs: "We solicit writers for corporate films/video in the areas of training, point purchase, sales, how-to, benefit programs, resorts and colleges." Produces 16-35mm films and videotapes. Query with samples. Makes outright purchase or pays cost per minute.

CONDYNE/THE OCEANA GROUP, 75 Main St., Dobbs Ferry NY 10522. (914)693-5944. Vice President: Yvonne Heenan. Produces material for legal market, and business and CPA markets. Works with 10-20 writers/year; buys 20 scripts/year. Buys all rights. No previously produced material. Query for electronic submissions. Computer printout submissions acceptable. Reports in 2 weeks on queries; 2 months on submissions. Catalog for 7x10 SAE and 4 first class stamps.
Needs: Tapes and audio cassettes, and video (VHS). "We are looking for video, ½ hour to one hour length—preview in ½" VHS, practical, how-to for legal market (lawyers in practice, law students)." Query with samples, submit synopsis/outline, resume, or preview tape and synopsis/outline. No phone calls accepted. All submissions must be in writing. Pays royalty or makes outright purchase; $250-500 for audio scripts, depending on qualifications; 10% royalty.
Tips: "We are especially interested in original software programs for lawyers and interactive videodisks (legal how-to) and video."

CONTINENTAL FILM PRODUCTIONS CORPORATION, Box 5126, 4220 Amnicola Hwy., Chattanooga TN 37406. (615)622-1193. President: James E. Webster. Produces "industrial non theatrical training films." Works with many writers annually. Buys all rights. No previously produced material. Unsolicited submissions not returned. "We don't want them—only assigned requested work." Reports in 1 week.
Needs: "We do need new writers of various types. Please contact us by mail with samples and resume. Samples will be returned postpaid." Produces 16mm film loops, 8mm and 16mm films, sound filmstrips, multimedia kits, overhead transparencies, slides, tapes and cassettes, teaching machine programs and video. Query with samples and resume. Outright purchase: $250 minimum; $6,000+ maximum.
Tips: Looks for writers whose work shows " technical understanding, humor, common sense, practicality, simplicity, creativity, etc." Suggests writers "increase use of humor in training films." Also seeking scripts on "human behavior in industry" and on "why elementary and high school students should continue their educations."

‡CP FILMS, INC., 4431 N. 60th Ave., Omaha NE 68104. (402)453-3200. President: G. Pflaum. Produces secondary education material. 100% freelance written. Eager to work with new/unpublished writers. Works with 4 writers/year. Buys 2-3 scripts/year from previously unpublished/unproduced writers. Buys one-time rights, simultaneous, second serial and first serial rights. Accepts previously produced material. Query for electronic submissions. Computer printout submissions acceptable; prefers letter-quality. Reports in 1 month. Free catalog.
Needs: Tapes and cassettes (video and audio). Produces video scripts for secondary education, classroom education, and one person teleplays. Will accept material from other mediums (radio, short story, stage) if author interested in adapting to video play. Submit complete script on detailed video treatment. Pays royalty; 3-7% on wholesale price of video cassette.
Tips: "The educational video market requires the production of material be budgeted at no more than $10,000 for production costs."

NICHOLAS DANCY PRODUCTIONS, INC., 333 W. 39th St., New York NY 10018. (212)564-9140. President: Nicholas Dancy. Produces media material for corporate communications, the health care field, general audiences, employees, members of professional groups, members of associations and special customer groups. 60% freelance written. Prefers to work with published/established writers. Buys 5-10 scripts/year; works with 5-10 writers/year. None of scripts are unagented submissions. Buys all rights. Query for electronic submissions. Computer printout submissions acceptable; prefers letter-quality. Reports in 1 month.
Needs: "We use scripts for videotapes or films from 5 minutes to 1 hour for corporate communications, sales, orientation, training, corporate image, medical and documentary." Format: videotape, occasionally 16mm films. Query with résumé. "No unsolicited material. Our field is too specialized." Pays by outright purchase

of $800-5,000. Pays expenses of writers on assignment.

Tips: "Writers should have a knowledge of business and industry and professions, an ability to work with clients and communicators, a fresh narrative style, creative use of dialogue, good skills in accomplishing research, and a professional approach to production. New concept trends are important in business. We're looking for new areas."

EDUCATIONAL FILMSTRIPS AND VIDEO, 1401 19th St., Huntsville TX 77340. (409)295-5767. President: Dr. Kenneth L. Russell. Produces material for junior high, senior high, college and university audiences. Buys "perhaps 20 scripts/year." Buys all rights or pays royalty on gross retail and wholesale. Previously produced material OK. Reports in 1 week on queries; in 1 month on submissions. Free catalog.

Needs: "Filmstrips and video for educational purposes." Produces filmstrips with sound and video. "Photographs on 2x2 slides must have good saturation of color." Query. Royalty varies.

Tips: Looks for writers with the "ability to write and illustrate for educational purposes. Schools are asking for more curriculum oriented live-action video."

EDUCATIONAL IMAGES LTD., Box 3456, Elmira NY 14905. (607)732-1090. Executive Director: Dr. Charles R. Belinky. Produces material (sound filmstrips, multimedia kits and slide sets) for schools, kindergarten through college and graduate school, public libraries, parks, nature centers, etc. Also produces science-related software material. Buys 50 scripts/year. Buys all AV rights. Computer printout submissions OK. Free catalog.

Needs: Slide sets and filmstrips on science, natural history, anthropology and social studies. "We are looking primarily for complete AV programs; we will consider slide collections to add to our files. This requires high quality, factual text and pictures." Query with a meaningful sample of proposed program. Pays $150 minimum.

Tips: The writer/photographer is given high consideration. "Once we express interest, follow up. Potential contributors lose many sales to us by not following up on initial query. Don't waste our time and yours if you can't deliver. The market seems to be shifting to greater popularity of video and computer software formats."

‡EFC, INC., 5101 F Backlick Rd., Annandale VA 22003. (703)750-0560. Vice President/Script Development: Ruth Pollak. Produces dramatic and documentary film and video for commercial, government, broadcast, schools and communities. 80% freelance written. Buys scripts from published/produced writers only. 50% of scripts produced are unagented submissions. Buys all rights. Computer printout submissions acceptable; prefers letter-quality. Reports in 1 month.

Needs: Strong dramatic screenplays, especially for family/child audience. Query with samples. Makes outright purchase or pays by commercial arrangement. Pays expenses of writers on assignment.

EFFECTIVE COMMUNICATION ARTS, INC., 221 W. 57th St., New York NY 10019. (212)333-5656. Vice President: W.J. Comcowich. Produces films, videotapes and interactive videodisks for physicians, nurses and medical personnel. Prefers to work with published/established writers. 80% freelance written. Buys approximately 20 scripts/year. Query for electronic submissions. Computer printout submissions acceptable; prefers letter-quality. Buys all rights. Reports in 1 month.

Needs: Multimedia kits, 16mm films, television shows/series, videotape presentations and interactive videodisks. Currently interested in about 15 films, videotapes for medical audiences; 6 interactive disks for medical audience; 3 interactive disks for point-of-purchase. Submit complete script and resume. Makes outright purchase or negotiates rights. Pays expenses of writers on assignment.

Tips: "Videotape scripts on technical subjects are becoming increasingly important. Explain what the film accomplishes—how it is better than the typical."

‡EMC CORP, 300 York Ave., St. Paul MN 55101. Editor: Eileen Slater. Produces material for children and teenagers in the primary grades through high school. "We sell strictly to schools and public libraries." Software submissions accepted; educational (most subject areas). 100% freelance written by published/produced writers. All scripts produced are unagented submissions. Buys 2-3 scripts/year. Buys world rights. Query for electronic submissions. Computer printout submissions acceptable; prefers letter-quality. Catalog for 9x12 SASE.

Needs: Career education, consumer education and vocational education (as related to language arts especially). "No standard requirements, due to the nature of educational materials publishing." No religious topics. Query with resume and one or more samples of previously produced work. No unsolicited manuscripts accepted. Payment varies.

FIRST RING, 15303 Ventura Blvd., #800, Sherman Oaks CA 91403-3155. Assistant Editor: Phil Potters. Estab. 1987. "Audio material only. Humorous telephone answering machine messages. Intended for use by all persons who utilize telephone answering machines." Buys 100 scripts/year. Buys all rights. No previously produced material. Reports in 1 week on queries; 4 months on submissions.

Needs: Write for guidelines. Scripts must not exceed 20 seconds in their finished production; however there is no minimum duration. Produces tapes and cassettes. Query. Outright purchase of $100 upon acceptance.
Tips: Looking for writers with "the ability to write hilarious scripts as set forth in guidelines. All submissions are considered even from writers whose prior work was not accepted."

FLIPTRACK LEARNING SYSTEMS, Division of Mosaic Media, Inc., Suite 200, 999 Main St., Glen Ellyn IL 60137. (312)790-1117. Publisher: F. Lee McFadden. Produces training media for microcomputer equipment and business software. Works with a small number of new/unpublished writers each year. 45% freelance written. Buys 5-7 courses/year; 1-3 from unpublished/unproduced writers. All courses published are unagented submissions. Works with 5-6 writers/year. Buys all rights. Query for electronic submissions. Computer printout submissions OK. Reports in 3 weeks. Free product literature; sample copy for 9x12 SAE.
Needs: Training courses on how to use personal computers/software, video or audio geared to the adult or mature student in a business setting and to the first-time microcomputer user. Produces audio, video, reference manuals and feature articles on personal computers. Query with resume and samples if available. Pays negotiable royalty or makes outright purchase. Sometimes pays expenses of writers on assignment.
Tips: "We prefer to work with Chicago-area and midwestern writers with strong teaching/training backgrounds and experience with microcomputers. Writers from other regions are also welcome. We also need feature/journalism writers with strong microcomputer interest and experience."

‡**FLORIDA PRODUCTION CENTER**, 150 Riverside Ave., Jacksonville FL 32202. (904)354-7000. Vice President: L.J. Digiusto. Produces audiovisual material for general, corporate and government audiences. Buys all rights. No previously produced material.
Needs: Films (16mm), filmstrips (silent and sound), multimedia kits, overhead transparencies, slides, tapes and cassettes, teaching machine programs, and videos. Query with samples and resume. Makes negotiable outright purchase.

PAUL FRENCH & PARTNERS, INC., 503 Gabbettville Rd., LaGrange GA 30240. (404)882-5581. Contact: Gene Ballard. 20% freelance written. Buys all rights. Computer printout submissions acceptable. Reports in 2 weeks.
Needs: Wants to see multi-screen scripts (all employee-attitude related) and/or multi-screen AV sales meeting scripts or resumes. Produces silent and sound filmstrips, videotapes, cassettes and slides. Query or submit resume. Pays in outright purchase of $500-5,000. Payment is in accordance with Writers Guild standards.

‡**GOLDSHOLL DESIGN & FILM, INC.**, 420 Frontage Rd., Northfield IL 60093. (312)446-8300. President: M. Goldsholl. Query. Buys all rights.
Needs: Scripts for corporate industrial public relations films. Also interested in original screenplays and short stories to be made into screenplays. "Describe your material before sending it. Do not send 'fantasy' scripts!" Produces sound filmstrips, 16mm and 35mm films, multimedia kits, tapes and cassettes, and 35mm slide sets. Pays 5-10% of budget.
Tips: "Write your ideas clearly. Know the visual world."

‡**GRIFFIN MEDIA DESIGN**, 802 Wabash Ave., Chesterton IN 46304. (219)926-8602. Assistant Administrator: C. Grimm. Produces variety of business and industrial programs, specifically for the development of advertising, public relations, training, marketing, conventions, etc. "We may buy as few as 10 to 50 projects per year." Buys all rights. No previously produced material. Reports on queries in 3 weeks. Catalog for 9x12 SAE and 2 first class stamps.
Needs: Films, video multimedia kits, brochures, advertisements, radio spots and cassettes. Query with samples. Makes outright purchase.
Tips: "Potential contributors should make themselves known. It's just as hard for businesses to find good writers as it is for good writers to find work."

HAYES SCHOOL PUBLISHING CO., INC., 321 Pennwood Ave., Wilkinsburg PA 15221. (412)371-2373. President: Clair N. Hayes, III. Produces material for school teachers, principals, elementary through high school. Also produces charts, workbooks, teacher's handbooks, posters, bulletin board material, educational software and liquid duplicating books (grades kindergarten through 12). 25% freelance written. Prefers to work with published/established writers; works with a small number of new/unpublished writers each year. Buys 5-10 scripts/year from unpublished/unproduced writers. 100% of scripts produced are unagented submissions. Buys all rights. Query for electronic submissions. Computer printout submissions acceptable; prefers letter-quality. Catalog for 3 first class stamps; writer's guidelines for #10 SAE and 2 first class stamps.
Needs: Educational material only. Particularly interested in educational material for elementary school level. Query. Pays $25 minimum.

DENNIS HOMMEL ASSOCIATES, INC., 3540 Middlefield Road, Menlo Park CA 94025-3025. (415)365-4565. Creative Director/Producer: D. Hommel. Produce material for "employees: employee orientation ma-

terial, i.e., social security, retirement planning, topics of general appeal to all employees including work habits, safety, etc." Purchases negotiable rights. Previously produced material OK. Reports in 2 weeks.
Needs: Produces slides with audio tape and videotape (7-15 minutes). Submit synopsis/outline or completed script. Payment negotiable.
Tips: "Be concise, do your homework so that content reflects current attitudes. Use plain language, well organized progression of ideas. "

‡IMAGE INNOVATIONS, INC., 14 Buttonwood Dr., Somerset NJ 08873. President: Mark A. Else. Produces material for business, education and general audiences. 50% freelance written. "Credentials and reputation means much—published or unpublished." Buys 15-20 scripts/year from previously unpublished/unproduced writers. All scripts produced are unagented submissions. Computer printout submissions acceptable; prefers letter-quality. Reports in 2 weeks. Buys all rights.
Needs: Subject topics include education, sales and public relations. Produces sound slide programs, and hi-image 1" and ¾" Betacam video and tapes and cassettes. Query with samples. Pays in outright purchase of $800-5,000. Sometimes pays the expenses of writers on assignment.

IMPERIAL INTERNATIONAL LEARNING CORP., 329 E. Court St., Kankakee IL 60901. (815)933-7735. Editor: Patsy Gunnels. Material intended for kindergarten through grade 12 audience. 60% freelance written. Prefers to work with published/established writers; works with a small number of new/unpublished writers each year. Buys 2-4 scripts/year from unpublished/unproduced writers. Buys all rights. No previously produced material. Query for electronic submissions. Computer printout submissions acceptable. Reports in 2 weeks on queries; 1 month on submissions. Free catalog.
Needs: "Supplemental learning materials of various lengths in the areas of reading, math, social studies and science with emphasis on using the microcomputer or videotape programs." Produces silent filmstrips, tapes and cassettes, and microcomputer and videotape. Query with samples or submit complete script and resume. Pays negotiable rates.
Tips: "We are interested in software, interactive videodisks, and videotape programs that meet curricular needs in the math, science, language arts, social studies and special education classroom."

INSTRUCTOR BOOKS, 7500 Old Oak Blvd., Cleveland OH 44130. Editor: Christine Van Huysse, Ph.D. "U.S. and Canadian school supervisors, principals and teachers purchase items in our line for instructional purposes." 50% freelance written. Buys 6 scripts/year from unpublished/unproduced writers. Most scripts produced are unagented submissions. Buys all rights. Writer should have "experience in preparing materials for elementary students, including suitable teaching guides to accompany them, and demonstrate knowledge of the appropriate subject areas, or demonstrate ability for accurate and efficient research and documentation." Computer printout submissions acceptable; no dot-matrix. Catalog for 8½x11 SAE.
Needs: Elementary curriculum enrichment—all subject areas. Display material, copy and illustration should match interest and reading skills of children in grades for which material is intended. Production is limited to printed matter: resource handbooks, teaching guides and idea books. Length: 6,000-12,000 words. Query. Standard contract, but fees vary considerably, depending on type of project. Sometimes pays the expenses of writers on assignment.
Tips: "Writers who reflect current educational practices can expect to sell to us."

□ INTERNATIONAL MEDIA SERVICES INC., 718 Sherman Ave., Plainfield NJ 07060. (201)756-4060. President/General Manager: Stuart Allen. Produces varied material depending on assignment or production in house; includes corporate, public relations, sales, radio/TV, CATV, teleconferencing/CCTV, etc. 60-75% freelance written. 90% of scripts produced are unagented submissions. "We normally issue assignments to writers in the freelance market who specialize in appropriate fields of interest." Buys all rights. No previously produced material. Computer printout submissions acceptable. Reporting time varies depending on job requirements and specifications.
Needs: Charts, dioramas, 8/16mm film loops, 16/35mm films, silent and sound filmstrips, kinescopes, multimedia kits, overhead transparencies, phonograph records, slides, tapes and cassettes, television shows/series and videotape presentations. "We routinely hire writers from a freelance resource file." Cable TV needs include educational and entertainment marketplaces. Query with or without samples, or submit synopsis/outline and resume. "All work must be copyrighted and be original unpublished works." Pays in accordance with Writers Guild standards, negotiated contract or flat rate.
Tips: "We are not responsible for unsolicited material and recommend not submitting complete manuscripts for review without prior arrangement."

☐ **Open box preceding a listing indicates a cable TV market.**

JACOBY/STORM PRODUCTIONS INC., 22 Crescent Road, Westport CT 06880. (203)227-2220. Contact: Doris Storm. Produces material for business people, students of all ages, professionals (e.g. medical). Works with 4-6 writers annually. Buys all rights. No previously produced material. Reports in 2 weeks.
Needs: "Short dramatic films on business subjects, educational filmstrips on varied subjects, sales and corporate image films." Produces 16mm films, filmstrips (sound), slides, tapes and cassettes, videotapes and videodisks. Query. Makes outright purchase (depends on project).
Tips: "Prefers local people. Look for experience, creativity, dependability, attention to detail, enthusiasm for project, ability to interface with client. Wants more film/video, fewer filmstrips, more emphasis on creative approaches to material."

PAUL S. KARR PRODUCTIONS, 2949 W. Indian School Rd., Box 11711, Phoenix AZ 85017. Utah Division: 1024 N. 250 E., Box 1254, Orem UT 84057. (801)226-8209. (602)266-4198. Produces films and videos for industry, business and education. *"Do not submit material unless requested."* Buys all rights. Works on co-production ventures that have been funded.
Needs: Produces 16mm films and videos. Query. Payment varies.
Tips: "One of the best ways for a writer to become a screenwriter is to come up with a client that requires a film or video. He can take the project to a production company, such as we are, assume the position of an associate producer, work with an experienced professional producer in putting the production into being, and in that way learn about video and filmmaking and chalk up some meaningful credits."

KIMBO EDUCATIONAL-UNITED SOUND ARTS, INC., 10-16 N. 3rd Ave., Box 477, Long Branch NJ 07740. (201)229-4949. Contact: James Kimble or Amy Laufer. Produces materials for the educational market (early childhood, special education, music, physical education, dance, and preschool children 6 months and up). 50% freelance written. Buys approximately 12-15 scripts/year; works with approximately 12-15 writers/year. Buys 5 scripts/year from unpublished/unproduced writers. Most scripts are unagented submissions. Buys all rights or first rights. Previously produced material OK "in some instances." Reports in 1 month. Free catalog.
Needs: "For the next two years we will be concentrating on general early childhood songs and movement oriented products, new albums in the fitness field and more. Each will be an album/cassette with accompanying teacher's manual and, if warranted, manipulatives." Phonograph records and cassettes, "all with accompanying manual or teaching guides." Query with samples and synopsis/outline or completed script. Pays 5-7% royalty on lowest wholesale selling price, and by outright purchase. Both negotiable.
Tips: "We look for creativity first. Having material that is educationally sound is also important. Being organized is certainly helpful. Fitness is growing rapidly in popularity and will always be a necessary thing. Children will always need to be taught the basic fine and gross motor skills. Capturing interest while reaching these goals is the key."

WILLIAM V. LEVINE ASSOCIATES, INC., 31 E. 28th St., New York NY 10016. (212)683-7177. President: William V. Levine. Presentations for business and industry. 15% freelance written. Prefers to work with established writers. Buys 4 scripts/year. Firm emphasizes "creativity and understanding of the client's goals and objectives." Will interview writers after submission of resume and/or sample AV scripts. Specifically seeks writers with offbeat or humorous flair. Previously produced material OK. Buys all rights. "New York City area based writers only."
Needs: Business-related scripts *on assignment* for specific clients for use at sales meetings or for desk-top presentations. Also uses theme-setting and inspirational scripts with inherent messages of business interest. Produces 16mm films, multimedia presentations, video, slides and live industrial shows. Query with résumé. Pays $500-2,500.

‡LITTLE SISTER PICTURES INC., 1986 Palmerston Place, Los Angeles CA 90027. (213)668-1559. Vice President, Production: Rupert Macnee. Produces material for business and industry, home video, educational, training and instructional audience. Buys all rights. Computer printout submissions acceptable. Reports in 1 month on queries; 2 months on submissions.
Needs: Videotape presentations. "We are looking for ideas to develop for the home video market, typically one hour programs that can be produced for less than $100,000. Also interested in comedy and music programming." Query. Pays in accordance with Writers Guild standards.
Tips: "Writers should be aware of the move towards home video, the one-on-one feel, a modular approach to information, interactive programming."

MONAD TRAINER'S AIDE, 163-60 22nd Ave., Whitestone NY. (718)352-3227. CEO: Gene Richman. Produces material for business training market. Buys all rights. Previously produced material OK. Reports in 2 weeks on queries; 6 weeks on submissions. Catalog for SAE with $2 postage.
Needs: Produces 16 mm films and videocassettes. Query or submit synopsis/outline and résumé. Pays by royalty or outright purchase in accordance with Writers Guild standards.
Tips: Writers need "good ability to communicate verbally as well as in writing." Looks for "short motivational type films applicable to both sexes."

NYSTROM, 3333 N. Elston Ave., Chicago IL 60618. (312)463-1144. Editorial Director: Darrell A. Coppock. Produces material for school audiences (kindergarten through 12th grade). Computer printout and disk submissions OK. Free catalog.
Needs: Educational material on social studies, earth and life sciences, career education, reading, language arts and mathematics. Produces charts, sound filmstrips, models, multimedia kits, overhead transparencies and realia. Required credentials depend on topics and subject matter and approach desired. Query. Pays according to circumstances.

OMNI COMMUNICATIONS, Suite 207, 101 E. Carmel Drive, Carmel IN 46032. (317)844-6664. Vice President: Dr. Sandra M. Long. Produces commercial, training, educational and documentary material. Buys all rights. No previously produced material.
Needs: "Educational, documentary, commercial, training, motivational." Produces slides, shows and multi-image videotapes. Query. Makes outright purchase.
Tips: "Must have experience as writer and have examples of work. Examples need to include print copy and finished copy of videotape if possible. A résumé with educational background, general work experience and experience as a writer must be included. Especially interested in documentary-style writing. Writers' payment varies, depending on amount of research needed, complexity of project, length of production and other factors."

OUR SUNDAY VISITOR, INC., Religious Education Dept., 200 Noll Plaza, Huntington IN 46750. (219)356-8400. Produces material for students (kindergarten through 12th grade), adult religious education groups and teacher trainees. "We are very concerned that the materials we produce meet the needs of today's church." Free catalog.
Needs: "Proposals for projects should be no more than 2 pages in length, in outline form. Programs should display up-to-date audiovisual techniques and cohesiveness. Broadly speaking, material should deal with religious education, including liturgy and daily Christian living, as well as structured catechesis. It must not conflict with sound Catholic doctrine and should reflect modern trends in education." Produces educational books, charts, sound and filmstrips. "Work-for-hire and royalty arrangements possible."

PHOTO COMMUNICATION SERVICES, INC., 6410 Knapp NE, Ada MI 49301. (616)676-1499. President: Michael Jackson. Produces commercial, industrial, sales, training material etc. 95% freelance written. Buys 25% of scripts from unpublished/unproduced writers. 95% of scripts produced are unagented submissions. Buys all rights and first serial rights. Query for electronic submissions. Computer printout submissions acceptable. Reports in 1 month on queries; 1 month on scripts.
Needs: Multimedia kits, slides, tapes and cassettes, and video presentations. Primarily interested in 35mm multimedia, 1-24 projectors and video. Query with samples or submit completed script and résumé. Pays in outright purchase or by agreement.

PREMIER VIDEO FILM & RECORDING CORP., 3033 Locust, St. Louis MO 63103. (314)531-3555. Secretary/Treasurer: Grace Dalzell. Produces material for the corporate community, religious organizations, political arms, and hospital and educational groups. 100% freelance written. Prefers to work with published/established writers. Buys 50-100 scripts/year. All scripts are unagented submissions. Buys all rights; "very occasionally the writer retains rights." Previously produced material OK; "depends upon original purposes and markets." Computer printout submissions acceptable; prefers letter-quality. Reports "within a month or as soon as possible."
Needs: "Our work is all custom produced with the needs being known only as required." 35mm film loops, super 8mm and 35mm films, silent and sound filmstrips, multimedia kits, overhead transparencies, phonograph records, slides, and tapes and cassettes." Produces TV, training and educational scripts for video. Submit complete script and resume. Pays in accordance with Writers Guild standards or by outright purchase of $100 or "any appropriate sum." Sometimes pays the expenses of writers on assignment.
Tips: "Always place without fail *occupational pursuit*, name, address and phone number in upper right hand corner of resume. We're looking for writers with creativity, good background and a presentable image."

‡BILL RASE PRODUCTIONS, INC., 955 Venture Ct., Sacramento CA 95825. (916)929-9181. President: Bill Rase. Produces material for business education and mass audience. Buys about 20 scripts/year. Buys all rights. Reports "when an assignment is available."
Needs: Produces multimedia, slides, cassettes and video productions. Submit resume and sample page or two of script, and description of expertise. Pays negotiable rate in 30 days.
Tips: "Call and ask for Bill Rase personally. Must be within 100 miles and thoroughly professional."

RHYTHMS PRODUCTIONS, Box 34485, Los Angeles CA 90034. President: Ruth White. Produces children's educational cassettes/books. Buys all rights. Previously published material OK "if it is suitable for our market and is not now currently on the market. We also look for tapes that have been produced and are ready for publication." Reports on mss in 3 weeks. Catalog for 8½x11 SAE and 3 first class stamps.

Needs: Phonograph records and tapes and cassettes. Looking for children's stories with musical treatments if possible. Must have educational content or values." Query with samples. Payment is negotiable.

‡SAVE THE CHILDREN, 54 Wilton Rd., Westport CT 06880. (203)226-7272. Producer: Joseph Lova. Produces 16mm films, tapes and cassettes, 2¼x2¼ slides, posters and displays. 30% freelance written. Prefers to work with published/established writers. 100% of scripts produced are unagented submissions. Generally buys all rights, "but it depends on project. We use work only written for specific assignments." Query for electronic submissions. Computer printout submissions acceptable; prefers letter-quality.

Needs: General (radio and TV); and education (high school, college and adult). Also produces scripts for video. Sometimes pays the expenses of writers on assignment. Pays $250-500 minimum/assignment.

PETER SCHLEGER COMPANY, 135 W. 58th St., New York NY 10019. (212)765-7129. President: Peter R. Schleger. Produces material "primarily for employee populations in corporations and non-profit organizations." Buys all rights, "most work is paid for for a one-time use, and that piece may have no life beyond one project." Previously produced material OK. Reports in 1 month. "Typical programs are customized workshops or specific individual programs from subjects such as listening and presentation skills to medical benefits communication. No program is longer than 10 minutes. If they need to be, they become shorter modules."

Needs: Produces sound filmstrips, video and printed manuals and leader's guides. Send completed script and resume. Makes outright purchase; payment "depends on script length."

Tips: "We are looking to receive and keep on file a resume and short, completed scripts sample of a program not longer than 10 minutes. The shorter the better to get a sense of writing style and the ability to structure a piece. We would also like to know the fees the writer expects for his/her work. Either per-diem, by project budget or by finished script page. We want communicators with a training background or who have written training programs, modules and the like. We want to know of people who have written print material, as well. We do not want to see scripts that have been written, and are looking for a producer/director. We will look at queries for possible workshops or new approaches for training, but these must be submitted as longshots only; it is not our primary business."

‡SCOTT RESOURCES, INC., Box 2121, Fort Collins CO 80522. (303)484-7445. Produces material for public and private school audiences, kindergarten through grade 12. Supplemental math and science materials. 90% freelance written. Works with 3-5 authors/year. Buys 3-5 scripts/year from unpublished/unproduced writers. 100% of scripts are unagented submissions. Query for electronic submissions. Computer printout submissions acceptable. Free math and science catalog.

Needs: Looking for written or AV material and computer software in earth science/geology and elementary/junior high mathematics. Also produces scripts for videos. Query with samples. Will negotiate equitable royalty.

SEVEN OAKS FOUNDATION, 9145 Sligo Creek Pkwy., Silver Spring MD 20901. (301)587-0030. Production Manager: M. Marlow. 80% freelance written. Produces material for pastoral counselors on marriage and family counseling techniques; medical and psychiatric programs for hospital-in-service and patient outreach training and preventive medicine practices to stay well and happy for a variety of age groups and special interest educational training programs. Buys 20-30 scripts from 10-20 writers/year. 55% of scripts are unagented submissions. Will consider new writers with prior credits in other media but does give writers on successful projects repeat business. Buys all rights or first rights; rights purchased negotiable. Computer printout submissions acceptable; prefers letter-quality. Reports in 4 months.

Needs: Health care, leisure time, positive thinking, "enjoy a fuller life after 50" audio and video subjects. Also interested in safety, "how-to" self improvement subjects for kids, teenagers, young marrieds, and handicapped as well as general entertainment for K-6 grades. Writers should know film and TV formats. Programs are released under Seven Oaks Foundation, Seven Oaks Productions or Maritime Media depending on subjects and distribution markets. Presently expanding in home video market place. Query only first: will keep on file. Will not return unsolicited material. Payment negotiable according to project.

SPENCER PRODUCTIONS, INC., 234 5th Ave., New York NY 10001. (212)697-5895. General Manager: Bruce Spencer. Executive Producer: Alan Abel. Produces material for high school students, college students and adults. Occasionally uses freelance writers with considerable talent.

Needs: 16mm films, prerecorded tapes and cassettes. Satirical material only. Query. Pay is negotiable.

E.J. STEWART, INC., 525 Mildred Ave., Primos PA 19018. (215)626-6500. "Our firm is a television production house providing programming for the broadcast, industrial, educational and medical fields. Government work is also handled." 50% freelance written. Buys 50 scripts/year; buys 5% of scripts/year from unpublished/unproduced writers. Buys all rights. Computer printout submissions acceptable. Reports "when needed."

Needs: "We produce programming for our clients' specific needs. We do not know in advance what our needs will be other than general scripts for commercials and programs depending upon requests that we receive from clients." Cable television material. Videotapes. Submit resume only. Pays in negotiable outright purchase. Sometimes pays expenses of writers on assignment.

Tips: "A trend in the audiovisual field freelance writers should be aware of is interactive laser disk programming."

TALCO PRODUCTIONS, 279 E. 44th St., New York NY 10017. (212)697-4015. President: Alan Lawrence. Vice President: Marty Holberton. Produces variety of material for motion picture theatres, TV, radio, business, trade associations, non-profit organizations, etc. Audiences range from young children to senior citizens. 20-40% freelance written. Buys scripts from published/produced writers only. All scripts produced are unagented submissions. Buys all rights. No previously published material. Computer printout submissions acceptable; prefers letter-quality. Reports in 3 weeks on queries.

Needs: Films (16-35mm); filmstrips (sound); phonograph records; slides; radio tapes and cassettes; and videotape. "We maintain a file of writers and call on those with experience in the same general category as the project in production. We do not accept unsolicited manuscripts. We prefer to receive a writer's resume listing credits. If his/her background merits, we will be in touch when a project seems right." Makes outright purchase/project and in accordance with Writer's Guild standards (when appropriate). Sometimes pays the expenses of writers on assignment.

Tips: "In the next year, we will have a greater concentration of TV productions."

TRANSLIGHT MEDIA ASSOCIATES, 931 W. Liberty, Wheaton IL 60187. (312)690-7780. Producer: John Lorimer. Produces material for business people and religious organizations. Buys 4-8 scripts/year. Buys all rights. No previously produced material. "We like to keep samples as part of file for reference. If writer wants something back they should obtain permission to send it first." Reports as project arises in writer's skill area.

Needs: "We produce primarily slide/tape, multi-image and video programs. Our needs are generally for short (5-10 minute) creative scripts for sales, fund raising, business meeting, or corporate image applications. No commercial or TV shows." Query with samples. Outright purchase $250-3,000.

Tips: "We look for creative concepts, and ability to communicate clearly and concisely. We also look for writers that recognize that often in an audiovisual script the visuals are more important than the words—writers that write a visual concept, not just copy. We prefer to work with local writers (Chicago market). Initial query should include 2 or 3 short scripts or excerpts that show range and style. No phone queries please."

TRANSTAR PRODUCTIONS, INC., Suite C, 9520 E. Jewell Ave. Denver CO 80231. (303)695-4207. Producer/Director: Doug Hanes. Produces primarily industrial material. 10% freelance written. Buys 1-2 scripts/year from unpublished/unproduced writers. 100% of scripts are unagented submissions. Buys all rights. No previously produced material. Computer printout submissions acceptable; prefers letter-quality. Reporting time varies.

Needs: 16mm films, slides, tapes and cassettes, and videotape presentations. Also produces scripts for industrial sales and training. Submit resume. Pays negotiable rate.

TRI VIDEO TELEPRODUCTION—Lake Tahoe, Box 8822, Incline Village NV 89450-8822. (702)323-6868. Production Manager: Beth Davidson. Produces material primarily for corporate targets (their sales, marketing and training clients). Works with 3-4 writers each year developing contracted material. Could work with more, and could produce more programs if the right material were available. Buys all rights or negotiable rights. No previously produced material. Does not return material "unless requested from a previous query."

Needs: "Will have a need for writing contract projects; would consider other projects which are either sold to a client and need a producer, or which the writer wishes to sell and have produced. In all cases, corporate sales, marketing and training materials. Perhaps some mass audience (how-to) video programs." Produces videtapes only. Query. Makes outright purchase in accordance with Writers Guild standards; "would consider joint venture."

Tips: "We are strong on production skill; weak on sales, so if your idea needs to be sold to an end user before it is produced, we may not be the right avenue. However give us a try. We might be able to put the right people together." Looks for "creativity, of course, but solid understanding of the buying market. We don't go in for highly symbolic and abstract materials."

TROLL ASSOCIATES, 100 Corporate Dr., Mahwah NJ 07430. (201)529-4000. Contact: M. Schecter. Produces material for elementary and high school students. Buys approximately 200 scripts/year. Buys all rights. Reports in 3 weeks. Free catalog.

Needs: Produces multimedia kits, tapes and cassettes, and (mainly) books. Query or submit outline/synopsis. Pays royalty or by outright purchase.

UNIVERSITY OF WISCONSIN STOUT TELEPRODUCTION CENTER, 800 S. Broadway, Menomonie WI 54751. (715)232-2624. Center Director: Rosemary Jacobson. Produces instructional TV programs for primary, secondary, post secondary and specialized audiences. 10% freelance written. All scripts produced are unagented submissions. "We produce ITV programs for national, regional and state distribution to classrooms around the U.S. and Canada." Buys all rights. Computer printout submissions acceptable; prefers letter-quality.

Needs: "Our clients fund programs in a 'series' format which tend to be 8-12 programs each." Produces with one-inch and BETACAM broadcast quality. "We have a need for writers in Wisconsin and Minnesota whom we can call on to write single or multi-program/series in instructional television." Query with resume and samples of TV scripts.

Recent Production: *Story Lords* (2nd grade reading comprehension agency: Wisconsin Educational Communications Board). Sometimes pays the expenses of writers on assignment.

Tips: "Freelance writers should be aware of the hardware advances in broadcast and nonbroadcast. There are new avenues for writers to pursue in adult learning, computer assisted programming and interactive programming."

‡**VISUAL HORIZONS**, 180 Metro Park, Rochester NY 14623. (716)424-5300. Fax(716)424-5313. President: Stanley Feingold. Produces material for general audiences. Buys 5 programs/year. Reports in 5 months. Free catalog.

Needs: Business, medical and general subjects. Produces silent and sound filmstrips, multimedia kits, slide sets and videotapes. Query with samples. Payment negotiable.

WMC COMPANY, (formerly Wren Associates, Inc.), 5 Independence Way, Princeton NJ 08540. Copy Department Head: Debbie Goodkin. Produces various sales and marketing presentations for Fortune 500 corporate clients. 100% freelance written. Buys 30-40 scripts/year from previously produced writers only. All scripts produced are unagented submissions. Buys all rights. No previously published material. Query for electronic submissions. Computer printout submissions acceptable. Reports in 3 weeks.

Needs: "WMC produces sales and marketing tools in a variety of media. We need freelance writers who can assimilate technical or business-oriented subject matter (e.g., telecommunications services, automotive, financial). They must be able to present this material in a clear, entertaining presentation that *sells* the product." Query with samples. Pays $400-7,000/job. Sometimes pays expenses of writers on assignment.

Tips: "Freelance writers should be aware of interactive video disk, tape trend. It's the coming wave in training and P.O.P. sales."

ZM SQUARED, Box C-30, Cinnaminson NJ 08077. (609)786-0612. Contact: Pete Zakroff. "We produce AVs for a wide range of clients including education, business, industry and labor organizations." Buys 10 scripts/year; works with 4-5 writers/year. Buys all rights. No previously produced material. Query for electronic submissions. Computer printout submissions acceptable. Reports in 2 weeks on queries; 1 month on submissions.

Needs: Silent filmstrips, kinescopes, multimedia kits, overhead transparencies, slides, tapes and cassettes, and videotape presentations. Query with or without samples. Pays 3-10% royalty or by outright purchase $150-750.

Playwriting

A writer's work is honored more in the theatre than anywhere else. Since most plays reflect the writer's personal vision, with his creative stamp being the heart of the work, playwrights exercise the most freedom for self-expression in the style and content of their work. Many playwrights also enjoy very close involvement with the work's production, and playwrights or their estates are traditionally consulted if those who want to produce the play would like to change even a single word of the script.

There is not as much money to be earned from plays as from other writing, but most playwrights are motivated more by a desire to express personal visions than to earn their keep. Many playwrights would be happy to see their work performed on stage, paid or not. Of all the forms of scriptwriting, a play probably requires the most ingenuity if its writer is intent on seeing it produced.

Los Angeles playwright Melanie Graham credits perseverance "and blind luck" for her success. She recommends attending acting classes or improvisational sessions with your material to "help you find answers to script problems that may have eluded you." She also confirms that rewards for playwrights are not financial. Among her friends who support themselves writing for films or TV, "I know a lot of them can't wait to get back to plays, where no one is telling you what to do," she says.

Some outside factors do influence a play's feasibility, however. The smaller your cast, the fewer the set changes, and the simpler your staging, the larger the number of community theatres that can consider performing it. Samuel Beckett's plays may have four, three or even two performers, total, with no set changes.

Excellent audiences for even skits or works-in-progress include school and university drama departments, church groups, community gatherings, radio stations, private clubs, and your own circle of friends. If friends or actors read the play aloud, you can hear the lines spoken and obtain feedback for any rewriting. Most local theatre workshops are adventuresome and look for fresh, new voices. Arden Heide of the theatrical publishing house of Samuel French, Inc., reports that "plays by or about women are always in demand," and frets that more of them "just haven't been written yet."

Playwrights are almost always given a royalty for each public performance (either paying or nonpaying audiences) of their work. The amount depends on the institution. About $25 per performance is not unusual, though professional productions may also include between 6% and 12% of the box office gross. Earnings from publishing are based entirely on sales (except when publishers bid on well-known playwrights' material, or issue advances to them). Most publishers give the playwright 10% of the sale price of scripts. Play publishers include Samuel French, Inc., 45 W. 25th St., New York NY 10010; Pioneer Drama Service, 2172 South Colorado Blvd., Denver CO 80222; and Baker's Play Publishing Co., 100 Chauncey St., Boston MA 02111. Although publishing houses will read and consider any SASE submission, "If it's been produced, it helps," Heide says.

Although most plays adhere to basic techniques of drama and dramatic writing, playwriting is not bound by the conventions of other forms of scriptwriting. Reading plays will acquaint you with past and present thinking, techniques, structures and innovations. Borrow from libraries, or buy them through Samuel French. A variety of annual play anthologies are also available in bookstores and libraries.

ACADEMY THEATRE, (formerly Southeastern Academy of Theatre and Music), Box 77070, Atlanta GA 30357. (404)873-2518. Artistic Director: Frank Wittow. Produces 7-9 plays/year; 389 seat Phoebe Theatre (modified thrust stage); 250 seat Court Theatre and 80 seat Arc Theatre with flexible stages. Main subscription series plays include three new play premieres. New Play Series consists of two black box productions of plays from local playwrights. Theatre for Youth seeks plays that can be staged and toured for grades 3-8 and high school. Query and/or send synopsis and short sample of dialogue. Reports in 6 months. Rights vary according to type of production.
Needs: One-acts, plays for young audiences. Special interests: non-traditional plays with elements of poetic language and surrealism; plays that deal with important issues in unique ways. Cast: 8 maximum. Simple sets.
Tips: "The Academy Theatre looks for new plays that show writers have found their own unique voice and are not imitating current theatrical trends. We get excited by writers who have a facility with language along with the ability to disturb, amuse, and interest an audience in theatrical, dramatic ways. We look for unusual works that show promise of a playwright who has something important to say and says it in an imaginative way."

ACTORS THEATRE OF LOUISVILLE, 316 West Main St., Louisville KY 40202. (502)584-1265. Producing Director: Jon Jory. Produces/publishes approximately 30 new plays of varying lengths/year. Professional productions are performed for subscription audience from diverse backgrounds. Submit complete ms for one-act plays; agented submissions only for full-length plays. Reports in 6-9 months on submissions. No dot-matrix computer printout submissions. Buys production (in Louisville only) rights. Offers variable royalty.
Needs: "We accept only one-act plays—unsolicited. No children's shows or musicals. We produce both full-lengths and one-acts." National one-act play contest postmark deadline: April 15."

ACTORS THEATRE OF TULSA, INC., Box 2116, Tulsa OK 74101. (918)749-6488. Artistic Director: Clifton R. Justice. Produces 6 plays/year. "Plays will be performed at our home theatre and on tour through out the state of Oklahoma. We are a non-equity, professional theatre company devoted to the production of contemporary theatre and the development of a permanent acting ensemble. Our audience is primarily professional people, with college degrees and a large amount of theatre sophistication." Submit complete ms. Reports in 4 months. "Generally we do not retain any rights on the manuscript except for acknowledgment of production if the piece is published." Pays $500-1,000.
Needs: "Productions are usually full-length plays dealing with a wide variety of issues and styles. We have no restrictions concerning language or subject matter. Our current season has ranged from Tina Howe's *The Art of Dining*, to *The Normal Heart*. Theatre facility is a black box and is used most effectively as arena or thrust. Casting always comes from a permanent ensemble that is usually no larger than 15. We are seeking playwrights who are interested in developing projects with the members of the company. This would involve participating in activities at our home theatre with housing provided. We do not produce any musicals and are not likely to consider historical pieces. The theatre company is extremely limited in ethnic actors although we are not opposed to these pieces—but the playwright should be aware of this fact."
Tips: "We are currently seeking funding to bring a playwright in for a residency. While most writers are being encouraged to develop the commercial aspect of their abilities and playing it safe, we are looking for new perspectives and an individual voice in the theatre. Strength in writing and the ability to work in the theatre as a collabrative art form are essential to our organization. The pieces are judged whether there is any universality as well as unique perspective to what the writer is saying. Additionally, we look to see if the play is theatrical in nature or would be more appropriate for film or television. Does the script go beyond realism and create an event that can only happen in a theatre with live actors and a live audience?"

‡AFRICAN CARIBBEAN POETRY THEATER, Box 351, Morris Heights Sta., Bronx NY 10468. (212)733-2150. Artistic Director: Sandra Esteves. Produces 3 plays/year. Plays performed off-Broadway and off-off-Broadway for all audiences. Submit query and synopsis or complete ms. Reports in 1 month. Obtains letter of agreement to produce work during forthcoming season. Pays $250 outright purchase.
Needs: Produces "preferably one-acts (full lengths considered) on any topic." Prefers simple staging and minimum number of characters.
Tips: "No musicals, no fluff."

ALASKA REPERTORY THEATRE, 625 C. Street, Anchorage AK 99501. (907)276-2327. Artistic Director: Andrew J. Traister. Produces 4-5 plays/year. Professional plays performed for Alaskan audiences. No unsolicited scripts; send synopsis and letter of inquiry *only*. Reports in 5 months. Pays 3% + royalty "depending on work."
Needs: Produces all types of plays.

ALLEY THEATRE, 615 Texas Ave., Houston TX 77002. Literary Manager: Robert Strane. A resident professional theatre: large stage seating 798; arena stage seating 296. Unagented submissions accepted. Computer printout submissions acceptable; prefers letter-quality.
Needs: Plays—one-act and full-length—and musicals (script and cassette); plays for young audiences; adaptations and translations. Makes variable royalty arrangements. Send description/synopsis and letter of inquiry. Reports in 4 months. Produces 10-15 plays/year.
Recent Play Productions: *Class "C" Trial in Yokohama*, by Roger Cornish.
Tips: "Address directly or through parable issues of the present."

‡AMAS REPERTORY THEATRE, INC., 1 E. 104th St., New York NY 10029. (212)369-8000. Artistic Director: Rosetta LeNoire. Produces 3 plays/year. 1 or 2 scripts produced are unagented submissions. "AMAS is a professional, off-off-Broadway showcase theatre. We produce three showcase productions of original musicals each season; these are presented for a sophisticated New York theatre audience. A number have gone on to commercial productions, the best known of which is *Bubbling Brown Sugar*. We also present two children's theatre productions and one summer tour." Query with synopsis or submit complete script with cassette tape of score or of partial score and SASE. Computer printout submissions acceptable; prefers letter-quality to dot-matrix. Reports in 2 months. "Be prepared to wait at least two years or more between acceptance and production. Our standard contract calls for a small percentage of gross and royalties to AMAS, should the work be commercially produced within a specified period."
Needs: "*Musicals only*; in addition, all works will be performed by multi-racial casts. Musical biographies are especially welcome. Cast size should be under 13 if possible, including doubling. Because of the physical space, set requirements should be relatively simple."
Tips: "AMAS is dedicated to bringing all people—regardless of race, creed, color or religion—together through the performing arts. In writing for AMAS, an author should keep this overall goal in mind."

‡THE AMERICAN LINE, #5C, 810 W. 18 3rd St., New York NY 10033. (212)740-9277. Artistic Director: Richard Hoehler. Produces 3 plays/year. Query with synopsis. Reports in 3 months. Rights and payment negotiable.
Needs: "Contemporary straight plays (one-act or full lengths) that make a point about American people of all races and ethnic backgrounds. Works which address issues and human conflicts relevant to the day."

AN CLAIDHEAMH SOLUIS/CELTIC ARTS CENTER, 5651 Hollywood Blvd., Hollywood CA 90028. (213)462-6844. Artistic Director: S. Walsh. Produces 6 plays/year. Equity waiver. Query and synopsis. Reports in 6 weeks. Rights acquired varies. Pays $25-50.
Needs: Scripts of Celtic interest (Scottish, Welsh, Irish, Cornish, Manx, Breton). "This can apply to writer's background or subject matter. We are particularly concerned with works that relate to the survival of cultures and traditions."

ANGEL'S TOUCH PRODUCTIONS,11022 Hesby Street, North Hollywood CA 91601. (818)506-3056. Director of Develpment: Phil Nemy. Professional Broadway productions for all audiences. Send script, query and synopsis. Reports in 6 months. Rights negotiated between production company and author. Payment negotiated.
Needs: All types, all genres, only full-length plays and screenplays—no one-acts or pieces involving homosexuality.
Tips: "Keep in mind the costs involved in mounting a Broadway or regional theatre production and try to write accordingly."

ARAN PRESS, 1320 S. 3rd St., Louisville KY 40208. (502)636-0115. Publishes a varying number of professional theatre, community theatre, college and university theatre, dinner theatre and summer stock plays. Query. Reports in 3 weeks. Acquires stage production rights. Pays 10% royalty on book; or 50% of standard royalty (i.e. half of $35 or $50 per performance).
Needs: "Anything the writer deems suitable for one or more of our five targeted markets. Inquire first." No children's plays.

ARENA STAGE, 6th and Maine Ave. SW, Washington DC 20024. (202)554-9066. Artistic Director: Zelda Fichandler. Produces 8-11 plays/year. Works with 1-4 unpublished/unproduced writers annually in "Play Lab," a play development project. Stages professional productions in Washington for intelligent, educated, sophisticated audiences using resident Equity company. Virtually none of the scripts produced are unagented submissions. Prefers query and synopsis plus the first 10 pages of dialogue, or agented submissions. Reports in 4 months. "We obtain an option to produce for one year or other term; percentage of future earnings." Pays 5% royalty. Computer printout submissions acceptable "as long as they are easily readable; no dot-matrix."
Needs: Produces classical, contemporary European and American plays; new plays, translations and adaptations without restrictions. No sitcoms, blank verse, pseudo-Shakespearean tragedies, movies-of-the-week or soap operas.
Tips: "We can consider large casts, though big plays are expensive and must justify that expense artistically. Be theatrical. Plays with relevance to the human situation—which cover a multitude of dramatic approaches—are welcome here."

THE ARKANSAS ARTS CENTER CHILDREN'S THEATRE, Box 2137, MacArthur Park, Little Rock AR 72203. (501)372-4000. Artistic Director: Bradley Anderson. Produces 5-6 mainstage plays, 3 tours/year. Mainstage season plays performed at The Arkansas Arts Center for Little Rock and surrounding area; tour season by professional actors throughout Arkansas and surrounding states. Mainstage productions perform to family audiences in public performances; weekday performances for local schools in grades kindergarten through senior high school. Tour audiences generally the same. Accepts unsolicited scripts. Submit complete script. Computer printout submissions acceptable; prefers letter-quality to dot-matrix. Reports in several months. Buys negotiable rights. Pays $250-1,500 or negotiable commission.
Needs: Original adaptations of classic and contemporary works. Also original scripts. "This theatre is defined as a children's theatre; this can inspire certain assumptions about the nature of the work. We would be pleased if submissions did not presume to condescend to a particular audience. We are not interested in 'cute' scripts. Submissions should simply strive to be good theatre literature."
Recent Title: *The Voyage of Sinbad the Sailor.*
Tips: "We would welcome scripts open to imaginative production and interpretation. Also, scripts which are mindful that this children's theatre casts adults as adults and children as children. Scripts which are not afraid of contemporary issues are welcome."

ART CRAFT PUBLISHING CO., 232 Dows Bldg., Cedar Rapids IA 52406. (319)364-6311. Publisher: C. McMullen. Publishes plays for the junior and senior high school market. Query with synopsis or send complete ms. Reports in 2 months. Acquires amateur rights only. Makes outright purchase for $250-1,500 or pays royalty.

Needs: One- and three-acts—preferably comedies or mystery comedies. Currently needs plays with a larger number of characters for production within churches and schools. Prefers one-set plays. No "material with the normal 'taboos'—controversial material."

‡ARTS CLUB THEATRE, 1585 Johnston St., Vancouver, British Columbia V6H 3R9 Canada. (604)687-5315. Artistic Director: Bill Millerd. Produces 14 plays/year. Plays peformed in three theatres seating 500, 200 and 225, for a diverse adult audience. Stock company operating on a year round basis. Tours British Columbia and does occasional national tours as well. Writer's guidelines available for 8x14 envelope with $5 money order or IRCs for Canadian stamps.
Needs: Full-length plays for adult audiences. Comedies and plays about concerns of the region. Well-made plays as opposed to experimental; realistic over fantasy. "We are interested in plays that are well-suited to our 200 seat intimate space. Such plays usually are one-set, and have limited number of characters (not more than 8) and have a strong story line. We are also interested in plays for our 500 seat theatre, and in musical revues for our cabaret theatre."

ASOLO STATE THEATRE, Postal Drawer E, Sarasota FL 33578. (813)355-7115. Artistic Director: John Ulmer. Produces 7 plays/year. 80% freelance written. About 50% of scripts produced are unagented submissions. A LORT theatre with an intimate performing space. "We play to rather traditional middle-class audiences." Works with 2-4 unpublished/unproduced writers annually. "We do not accept unsolicited scripts. Writers must send us a letter and synopsis with self-addressed stamped postcard." Computer printout submissions acceptable; no dot-matrix. Reports in 5 months. Negotiates rights. Negotiates payment.
Needs: Play must be *full length*. "We do not restrict ourselves to any particular genre or style—generally we do a good mix of classical and modern works."
Tips: "We have no special approach—we just want well written plays with clear, dramatic throughlines. Don't worry about trends on the stage. Write honestly and write for the stage, not for a publication."

AVILA COLLEGE DEPARTMENT OF HUMANITIES, 11901 Wornall Rd., Kansas City MO 64145. (816)942-8400. Chairman: Daniel Paul Larson. Produces 5 plays/year. Possibility of 1 script produced by unagented submission. Performs collegiate amateur productions (4 main stage, 1 studio productions) for Kansas City audiences. Query with synopsis. Computer printout submissions acceptable; prefers letter-quality. Reports in 3 months. Buys rights arranged with author. Pay rate arranged with author.
Needs: All genres with wholesome ideas and language—musicals, dramas. Length 1-2 hours. Small to medium casts (2-8 characters), few props, simple staging.
Tips: Example of play just done: *Towards The Morning*, by John Fenn. Story: "Mentally confused bag lady and 17-year-old egocentric boy discover they need each other; she regains mental stability; he grows up a bit and becomes more responsible. Trends in the American stage freelance writers should be aware of include (1) point-of-view one step beyond theatre of the absurd—theatre that makes light of self-pity; and (2) need for witty, energetic social satire done without smut in the style of *Kid Purple*, by Don Wollner, The 1984 national competition winner of the Unicorn Theatre, Kansas City, MO."

MARY BALDWIN COLLEGE THEATRE, Mary Baldwin College, Staunton VA 24401. (703)887-7192. Artistic Director: Dr. Virginia R. Francisco. Produces 5 plays/year. 10% freelance written. 0-1% of scripts are unagented. Works with 0-1 unpublished/unproduced writer annually. An undergraduate women's college theatre with an audience of students, faculty, staff and local community (adult, conservative). Query with synopsis. Query for electronic submissions. Computer printout submissions acceptable; prefers letter-quality. Reports in 3 months. Buys performance rights only. Pays $10-50/performance.
Needs: Full-length and short comedies, tragedies, musical plays, particularly for young women actresses, dealing with women's issues both contemporary and historical. Experimental/studio theatre not suitable for heavy sets. Cast should emphasize women. No heavy sex; minimal explicit language.
Tips: "A perfect play for us has several roles for young women, few male roles, minimal production demands, a concentration on issues relevant to contemporary society, and elegant writing and structure."

BARTER THEATRE, Box 867, Abingdon VA 24210. (703)628-2281. Artistic Director: Rex Partington. Produces 12 plays/year. "Professional productions. Regional theatre. All types of audiences." Submit complete ms. Reports in 6 months. Pays 5% royalty.
Needs: Produces "contemporary comedies and dramas of relevance, and worthy adaptations of classics." Plays should have casts of 4 to 12, and a single or unit set.
Tips: Looking for "subjects of relevance and significance, with theme of individuals and society coping with universal challenges." No one acts or "lighter than air" scripts.

BEREA COLLEGE THEATRE, Box 22, Berea KY 40404. (606)986-9341, Ext 6355. Produces 4 full-length and 10 one-act plays/year. "Amateur performances; college audience with community persons in audience also." Send query and synopsis or submit complete ms. Reports in 3 weeks. Obtains negotiable rights. Pays $35-50/performance.

Needs: Medium cast plays (10-20 persons); no musicals.
Tips: "Single-page business letter with synopsis will be good to start with."

BERKELEY JEWISH THEATRE, 1414 Walnut St., Berkeley CA 94709. (415)849-0498. Produces 4 plays and 6 staged readings/year. Plays performed in an Equity Waiver theatre, 100 seats at Berkeley Jewish Community Center. Submit complete ms. Acquires production rights. Pays $35-50/performance.
Needs: Plays for main stage in all genres which embody and express the variety of experience of the American Jewish diaspora.
Tips: "Writers should have a general knowledge of American Jewish culture and the problems confronting the largest Jewish community outside of the State of Israel. Avoid the models for plays set by Broadway, Hollywood or television."

BERKSHIRE THEATRE FESTIVAL, INC., E. Main St., Stockbridge MA 01262. Artistic Director: Richard Dunlap. 25% original scripts. Produces 7-8 plays a year (4 are mainstage and 4 are second spaces). Submissions by agents only.

BRISTOL RIVERSIDE THEATRE, Box 1250, Bristol PA 19007. (215)785-6664. Artistic Director: Susan D. Atkinson. Estab. 1986. Produces 5 mainstage, 4 workshops, and 20 readings plus children's theatre/year. "We are a professional regional professional theatre company; we produce new works exclusively in our workshop and reading series. The intention is to develop the works for mainstage productions. Our audience is drawn from Bucks County, Philadelphia, Trenton, Princeton and surrounding New Jersey areas. We also plan a two-show, popular, summer program." Submit complete ms. Reports in 10 months. "Since we are a developmental company and spend a great deal of time on each work selected for reading and/or workshop, we request a percentage of author's revenues for a given period of time and recognition of the theatre and key individuals on subsequent productions, after the reading phase of the development is completed." Offers variable royalty.
Needs: "We produce all genres from dramas, comedies to musicals and operas. We also produce one-acts. We would prefer smaller shows with limited costs, but we have never shied away from larger shows. The quality, not the quantity, is the determining factor in all cases."
Tips: "We are not interested in plays that have as their only goal entertainment. We would hope all works would have this quality, but if there is no other value sought, we would not be interested. We are a company in search of the new mainstream of theatre in America. We aim to entertain, enlighten and elevate our audience. And we are seeking authors who are interested in developing their works, not just presenting them; we view theatre as a process."

CASA MANANA MUSICALS, INC., 3101 W. Lancaster, Fort Worth TX 76107. (817)332-9319. Executive producer/General Manager: Bud Franks. Artistic Director: Charles A. Ballinger. "All performances are staged at Casa Manana Theatre and are community funded." Query. Produces 6 summer stock musicals (uses Equity people only), theater-in-the-round. Children's playhouse theatre produces 8 children's shows in the winter season.
Needs: Scripts of all kinds; cassettes acceptable.

CENTER STAGE, 700 N. Calvert St., Baltimore MD 21202. (301)685-3200. Resident dramaturg: Rick Davis. Produces 6-9 plays/year. "Professional L.O.R.T 'B' company; audience is both subscription and single-ticket. Wide-ranging audience profile." Query with synopsis or submit through agent. Reports in 3 months. Rights negotiated. Payment depending on category of production (e.g., mainstage, playwrights, series, etc.).
Needs: Produces "dramas and comedies, occasional musicals. No restrictions on topics or styles, though experimental work is encouraged. Casts over 30 would give us pause. Be inventive, theatrical, not precious; we like plays with vigorous language and stage image. No conventional, highly psychologized renderings of the quotidian problems of uninteresting people."
Tips: "We are interested in reading adaptations and translations as well as original work."

CIRCLE REPERTORY CO., 161 Avenue of the Americas, New York NY 10013. (212)691-3210. Associate Artistic Director: Rod Marriott. Produces 5 mainstage plays, 5 Projects in Progress/year. Accepts unsolicited mss for full-length plays only; "we no longer produce one-acts."

CIRCUIT PLAYHOUSE/PLAYHOUSE ON THE SQUARE, 51 S. Cooper, Memphis TN 38104. (901)725-0776. Artistic Director: Jackie Nichols. Produces 2 plays/year. 100% freelance written. Professional plays performed for the Memphis/Mid-South area. Member of the Theatre Communications Group. 100% of scripts are unagented submissions. Works with 1 unpublished/unproduced writer annually. A play contest is held each fall. Submit complete ms. Computer printout submissions acceptable. Reports in 3 months. Buys "percentage of royalty rights for 2 years." Pays $500-1,000 in outright purchase.

Needs: All types; limited to single or unit sets. Cast of 20 or fewer.

Tips: "Each play is read by three readers through the extended length of time a script is kept. Preference is given to scripts for the southeastern region of the U.S."

CITY THEATRE COMPANY, B39 CL, University of Pittsburgh, Pittsburgh PA 15260. Literary Manager: Lynne Conner. Produces 4 full productions and 6 readings/year. "We are a small professional theatre, operating under an Equity contact, and committed to twentieth-century American plays. Our seasons are innovative and challenging, both artistically and socially. We perform in a 117-seat thrust stage, playing usually 6 times a week, each production running 5 weeks or more. We have a committed audience following." Query and synopsis or submit through agent. Obtains no rights. Pays 5-6% royalty.

Needs: "No limits on style or subject, but we are most interested in theatrical plays that have something to say about the way we live. No light comedies or TV-issue dramas." Normal cast limit is 8. Plays must be appropriate for small space without flies.

Tips: "American playwrights only. We run a staged reading series of 6 plays a year, choosing work that we wish to consider for full production. Write from need and from commitment."

I.E. CLARK, INC., Saint John's Rd., Box 246, Schulenburg TX 78956. (409)743-3232. Publishes 15 plays/year for educational theatre, children's theatre, religious theatre, regional professional theatre, amateur community theatre. 20% freelance written. 3-4 scripts published/year are unagented submissions. Works with 2-3 unpublished writers annually. Submit complete script. Computer printout submissions acceptable; prefers letter-quality to dot-matrix. Reports in 6 months. Buys all available rights; "we serve as an agency as well as a publisher." Pays standard book and performance royalty, "the amount and percentages dependent upon type and marketability of play." Catalog for $1.50; writer's guidelines for #10 SAE with 1 first class postage stamp.

Needs: "We are interested in plays of all types—short or long. Audio tapes of music or videotapes of a performance are requested with submissions of musicals. We prefer that a play has been produced (directed by someone other than the author); photos and reviews of the production are helpful. No limitations in cast, props, staging, etc.; however, the simpler the staging, the larger the market. Plays with more than one set are difficult to sell. So are plays with only one or two characters. We insist on literary quality. We like plays that give new interpretations and understanding of human nature. Correct spelling, punctuation and grammar (befitting the characters, of course) impress our editors."

Tips: "Entertainment value and a sense of moral responsibility seem to be returning as essential qualities of a good play script. The era of glorifying the negative elements of society seems to be fading rapidly. Literary quality, entertainment value and good craftsmanship rank in that order as the characteristics of a good script in our opinion. 'Literary quality' means that the play must say something; preferably something new and important concerning man's relations with his fellow man; and these 'lessons in living' must be presented in an intelligent, believable and—perhaps—poetic manner. Plays for children's theatre are tending more toward realism and childhood problems rather than fantasy or dramatization of fairy tales."

‡CLAVIS THEATRE ONE ACT FESTIVAL, Box 93158, Milwaukee WI 53203. (414)272-3043. Program Director: Ted Altschuler. Produces 6 plays—3 full-length, 3-5 one acts per year. Plays performed at Clavis Theatre—a professional, non-equity, off-Broadway styled company located in Milwaukee. Submit complete ms. Reports in 3 months. Outright purchase or rights negotiable. "SASE for returns and no resubmissions please."

Needs: "The festival produces 3-4 one acts. We would like plays one hour in length or less, with seven or fewer characters. We have no requirements regarding genre, topic or style. Clavis Theatre productions tend to address more provocative issues i.e. *One for the Road*, *Agnes of God*, *Execution of Justice*, *Cloud 9*. We do not have a limitless budget, but have always found creative solutions for all production requirements."

Tips: "Scripts that try to be masterpieces are less successful than scripts written because the author really has something to say."

> **❝** *For a reader—any reader, not just a professional one—getting into a story is the hardest part. If you force him to start over, start over, start over with every chapter, you ultimately make it too hard to stick with your work.* **❞**

> *—Ann Finlayson*
> *Freelance copy editor*

Close-up
Cincinnati Playwright Project

The Cincinnati Playwright Project provides a weekly forum for playwrights to have plays read and critiqued. Anyone interested in some aspect of playwriting may attend the meetings. The group consists of people who write or produce plays or who are actors. There are about 12-20 core members who attend regularly, but as many as 100 people flow through the group during the year.

On a typical evening when the group is in session, one to three portions of a play in its formative stages are read and critiqued. It is a superb method of networking for participants and a way for the playwright to get feedback on his work. The playwright then reworks, edits and works, edits and polishes his play, possibly to be read again at a later date.

The project was formed in 1984 by Joel Selmeier and a group of other playwrights with a desire to have their plays performed on stage. (Selmeier has since had many plays produced.) Currently, Bob Zimmerman, a business executive with experience in staged readings, is the coordinator of the project.

Zimmerman says that nonplaywrights—actors, directors, and producers—have been encouraged to participate in the Project; they constitute more than a third of the group's membership. They are used to read parts and to interact with others on the stage. "It makes such a difference to have a professional reading your part," says Beatrice Holt, a college instructor of creative writing, poetry and drama. "Otherwise, you can't tell if the problem is in the script or not." Holt serves as general spokesperson for the group. She says she has become very involved with the project since moving to Cincinnati in 1985. She has had several plays produced and several that will soon be produced. "I had always written drama but not submitted before I moved to Cincinnati. The pieces I have had taken have been through networking here.

"I can see such a difference in my own work when I take it in and I don't know what is working or why. When I begin to get a response from the reading, I see immediately how to change it. I revise it and later read it again. I'm always amazed at the process." Without the feedback she says she feels she might duplicate the problem in each play she might write.

Holt says that she thinks it is important if you are writing plays, to take a playwriting course or attend a summer workshop group so you can understand the technical aspects of scriptwriting. For example, a playwright should understand beats; understand French units; understand conflicts and character reversals. "Otherwise," she says, "You're sitting there writing in a vacuum."

"To write drama, you have to have a good ear," she continues, "You cannot tell if a play works unless you hear it read by individual readers taking the parts. Only then can you tell if the voices are different or whether the play contains the proper syntax and speech patterns.

"If you are writing drama by yourself," she stresses, "the least you can do is invite friends over to take the parts and have a staged reading in your living room. Tape it and as you play it back, revise and listen.

"If you're really interested in playwriting," she advises, "find something to do with the theatre. Join a small theatre group. Paint scenery or do set design. Something so that you are in there and it becomes second nature to you."

Holt says that those interested in obtaining more information about groups in their areas should contact the Dramatist Guild in New York.

—Deborah Cinnamon

COMPANY ONE, 94 Allyn St., Hartford CT 06103. (203)278-6347. Artistic Director: Stephen Rust. Produces 7 plays/year. "One-act plays submitted to Company One, if selected, will be performed at the Hartford Arts Center as part of our Lunchtime Theater series. Our audience members are generally downtown employees looking for an entertaining break in their workday. This, however, does not preclude the presentation of thought-provoking material." Submit complete ms. Reports in 6 weeks. Pays $30 per performance.
Needs: "Best suited to the Lunchtime/Drivetime format is the 40 minute, 2 or 3 character, single set, comedy. Although a good play can find its way around limitations, Company One tries to keep its casts small (four or less), its sets and props simple, and special effects to a minimum. Company One now produces 6 one-act plays/year during the Spring and Fall in a 3-week festival format. Each play receives about 7 performances. We also now consider full-length original scripts for evening productions." Also needs one-act with Christmas/Holiday theme, preferably with a warm, family feeling. Same cast and technical requirements.
Tips: "Based on increasing attendance and positive audience response, the one-act play may find a new and growing market beyond the annual festivals. People enjoy Lunchtime Theater, and we need good plays to show them, all the year round. Writers should no longer feel the need to submit only comedies; something more dangerous or sexy may be appropriate in the coming seasons."

CONTEMPORARY DRAMA SERVICE, Meriwether Publishing Ltd., Box 7710, Colorado Springs CO 80933. (303)594-4422. Editor-in-Chief: Arthur Zapel. Publishes 50-60 plays/year. "We publish for the secondary school market and colleges. We also publish for mainline liturgical churches—drama activities for church holidays, youth activities and fundraising entertainments. These may be plays or drama-related books." Query with synopsis or submit complete ms. Reports in 5 weeks. Obtains either amateur or all rights. Pays 10% royalty or outright negotiated purchase.
Needs: "Most of the plays we publish are 1-acts, 15 to 45 minutes in length. We occasionally publish full-length 3-act plays. We prefer comedies in the longer plays. Musical plays must have name appeal either by prestige author, prestige title adaptation or performance on Broadway or TV. Comedy sketches, monologues and 2-character plays are welcomed. We prefer simple staging appropriate to high school, college or church performance. We like playwrights who see the world positively and with a sense of humor. Offbeat themes and treatments are accepted if the playwright can sustain a light touch and not take himself (herself) too seriously. In documentary or religious plays we look for good research and authenticity."

‡THE CRICKET THEATRE, 9 West 14th St., Minneapolis MN 55403. (612)871-3763. Artistic Director: William Partlan. Produces 5 plays/year. Plays performed at professional resident theatre. Submit 10 pages of ms and synopsis. Reports in 6 months. Obtains variable rights. Pays 3-6% royalty.
Needs: Any type of full-length play, small cast preferable (2-6).

DALTON LITTLE THEATRE/WORLD CARPETS NEW PLAY PROJECT, Box 841, Dalton GA 30722. (404)226-6618. Contact: Project Coordinator. Amateur productions in summer of each year. Submit complete ms. Reports in 3 months. Obtains first performance rights. Pays 100% royalty or outright $400.
Needs: "Any full-length play or musical is accepted." Writers should keep in mind small stage/playing area. No less-than-full-length or previously produced plays.
Tips: Manuscripts accepted September through November 30. Reports on February 1.

DELAWARE THEATRE COMPANY, Box 516, Wilmington DE 19899. (302)594-1104. Artistic Director: Cleveland Morris. Produces 5 plays/year. 10% freelance written. "Plays are performed as part of a five-play subscription season in a 300-seat auditorium. Professional actors, directors and designers are engaged. The season is intended for a general audience." 10% of scripts are unagented submissions. Works with 1 unpublished/unproduced writer every two years. Query with synopsis. Computer printout submissions acceptable; prefers letter-quality. Reports in 6 months. Buys variable rights. Pays 5% (variable) royalty.
Needs: "We present comedies, dramas, tragedies and musicals. All works must be full-length and fit in with a season composed of standards and classics. All works have a strong literary element. Plays showing a flair for language and a strong involvement with the interests of classical humanism are of greatest interest. Single-set, small-cast works are likeliest for consideration."

‡DINNER PLAYHOUSE, INC., Fries Entertainment, 622 Hollywood Blvd., Hollywood CA 90028. (213)466-2266. Director of New Play Development: Donn G. Miller. Produces 12-14 plays/year. Plays performed at Waldo Astoria Theatre (Equity) and Tiffany's Attic Theatre (Equity), both in Kansas City, MO. Currently producing "Groucho: A Life In Revue," off-Broadway. "Although this is not our primary venue, we do look for promising scripts with this kind of potential." Submit query and synopsis or complete ms or send agented submissions. Reports in 1 month. "We contract with writers for standard royalty payments on plays actually performed." Pays 5% minimum royalty. No return of rejected manuscripts "because cost is too great for the hundreds of manuscripts we receive each year."
Needs: "We run Simonesque comedies suitable for a very conservative Kansas City public. We look for strong, broad laughs as opposed to sensitive 'warm' character pieces. We have fairly small stages and prefer

casts of eight or fewer. We do musicals, but on a very small scale (i.e., Nunsense)."

Tips: "No typical dinner theater 'sex farces' which are potentially offensive. Because this is Kansas City, we must be very careful about non-traditional sex roles, profanity and references to diety. Most of these things can be edited. Move to strong logical character pieces, with humor that comes from the characters, as opposed to traditional externally motivated comedy. When we review a script, we first ask if the plot and characters are believable, and then, whether we can make an honest emotional investment in the lead character(s) which will be sustained for the length of the play. We do a lot of comedy, and try to get first-run rights for new product out of New York. But, we do read and personally review hundreds of new scripts."

DOBAMA THEATRE, 1846 Coventry Road, Cleveland Heights OH 44118. (216)932-6838. Literary Manager: Jean Cummins. "We maintain our own theatre and our own unpaid non-Equity company. Although not wildly experimental, our company has built a reputation for taking risks with new and unusual works. Our audience is theatrically sophisticated." Submit complete ms. Reports in 6 months. "Obtains no rights at present." Pays $35 each performance. Typical run is 9 performances.

Needs: "We produce full-length dramas and comedies and an occasional musical. Most of our plays are intimate, small cast. About once a year we break out with something larger, more theatrical. We are a ¾ arena, 200 seat house; on-screen projections are nearly impossible for us. Also no basement, trap door effects. Our ceilings are pretty low."

Tips: "We are interested in plays with good human values. We look for a chance to help new and emerging playwrights see their vision take shape on stage. We try to comment on every script that we receive."

DORSET THEATRE FESTIVAL, Box 519, Dorset VT 05251. (802)867-2223. Artistic Director: Jill Charles. Produces 6 plays/year. 20% freelance written. A professional (equity) theatre, season June-September or October. Audience is sophisticated, largely tourists and second-home owners from metropolitan New York and Boston areas. Does not accept unsolicited mss or queries; submit via agent only. Computer printout submissions acceptable; prefers letter-quality. Reports in 4 months. Negotiates rights. Negotiates rate; minimum $250 for 11 performances.

Needs: Full length plays (2 acts); any genre, but should have broad audience appeal; generally realistic, but *not* "kitchen dramas." Will consider musicals; must have accompanying cassette. Cast less than 10; single or unit (flexible) settings preferred. "We produce one new play each season and two one-act plays for apprentices. We lean toward *positive* plays, whether comedy or drama. No family melodrama."

Tips: "Best time to have agent submit play is from September to January. (Plays received after March 1 may not be read until fall). Trends on the American stage that freelance writers should be aware of include small casts."

THE DRAMATIC PUBLISHING CO., 311 Washington St., Woodstock IL 60098. (815)338-7170. Publishes about 30 new shows a year. 60% freelance written. 40% of scripts published are unagented submissions. "Current growth market is in plays and musicals for children, plays and small-cast musicals for stock and community theatre." Also has a large market for plays and musicals for schools and other amateur theatre groups. Works with 2-6 unpublished/unproduced writers annually. Reports in 2-6 months. Buys stock and amateur theatrical rights. Pays by usual royalty contract, 10 free scripts and 40% discount on script purchases.

Tips: "Avoid stereotype roles and situations. Submit cassette tapes with musicals whenever possible. Always include SASE if script is to be returned. Only one intermission (if any) in a show running up to two hours."

DRAMATIKA, 429 Hope St., Tarpon Springs FL 34689. Editor: John Pyros. Magazine for persons interested in the arts. Published 2 times/year. Circ. 500. Buys all rights. Pays on publication. Query. Reports in 1 month. Sample copy $3.

Fiction: Wants "performable pieces—plays, songs, scripts, etc." Will consider plays on various and open themes. Query first. Length: 20 pages maximum. Pays about $25/piece; $5-10 for smaller pieces.

Photos: Submit 8x11 b&w photos with ms. Captions required. Pays $5.

‡EAST WEST PLAYERS, 4424 Santa Monica Blvd., Los Angeles CA 90029. (213)660-0366. Artistic Director: Mako. 90% freelance written. Produces 5-6 plays/year. Professional plays performed in an Equity waiver house for all audiences. Works with 2-3 unpublished/unproduced writers annually. Query with synopsis or sub-

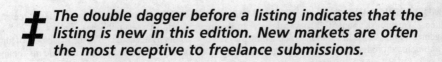

The double dagger before a listing indicates that the listing is new in this edition. New markets are often the most receptive to freelance submissions.

mit complete ms. Reports in 3 weeks on query and synopsis; 2 months on mss. "High majority" of scripts produced are unagented submissions. Buys standard Dramatist's Guild contract rights. Pays $200 in outright purchase or 2-6% of house receipts (ticket prices vary).

Needs: "We prefer plays dealing with Asian-American themes. The majority of the important roles should be playable by Asian-American actors; our acting company is 98 percent Asian." No fluff, TV sitcom-type material.

Tips: "East West Players was founded by a group of Asian-American actors weary of playing stereotypes in theatre and film. Submitting writers should bear this in mind and refrain from wallowing in 'exoticism.' There appears to be a minor burgeoning of interest in Asian-American writers and themes—witness David Henry Hwang's success on the East Coast, the continuing success and influence of East West Players on the West Coast and establishment theatres developing Asian American material (e.g., The Mark Taper Forum in Los Angeles working on a stage adaptation of Maxine Hong Kingston's works), etc."

ELDRIDGE PUBLISHING CO., Box 216, Franklin OH 45005. (513)746-6531. Publishes 15-20 plays/year. For elementary, junior high, senior high, church and community audience. Query with synopsis (acceptable) or submit complete ms (preferred). Please send cassette tapes with any operettas. Reports in 2 months. Buys all rights. Pays 35% royalty (3-act royalties approx. $35/$25, 1-act royalty rates usually $10/$10); outright from $100-300 or occasionally offers 10% of copy sale receipts. Writer's guidelines for #10 SASE.

Needs: "We are always on the lookout for Xmas plays (religious for our church market or secular for the public school market). Also lighthearted 1-acts and 3-acts. We do like some serious, high caliber plays reflective of today's sophisticated students. Also operettas for jr/sr high school, and more limited, elementary market. We prefer larger casts for our 3-acts and operettas. Staging should be in keeping with school budgets and expertise. We are *not* interested in plays that are highly sexually suggestive or use abusive language."

Tips: "Submissions are welcomed at any time but during our fall season, response will definitely take 2 months. Authors are paid royalties twice a year. They receive complimentary copies of their published plays, the annual catalog and 50% discount if buying additional copies."

THE EMPTY SPACE, 95 S. Jackson St., Seattle WA 98104. (206)587-3737. Artistic Director: M. Burke Walker. Produces 6 plays/year. 100% freelance written. Professional plays for subscriber base and single ticket Seattle audience. 1 script/year is unagented submission. Works with 5-6 unpublished/unproduced writers annually. Query with synopsis before sending script. Computer printout submissions OK; prefers letter-quality. Response in 3 months. LOA theatre.

Needs: "Other things besides linear, narrative realism, but we are interested in that as well. No restriction on subject matter. Generally we opt for broader, more farcical comedies and harder-edged, uncompromising dramas. We like to go places we've never been before."

RICHARD FICARELLI, 44 Apollo Lane, Hicksville NY 11801. Produces 1-2 plays/year. Plays are Equity productions performed in NY, Broadway and off-Broadway theatres. Regional possibilities. Submit query and synopsis. Reports in 6 weeks. Acquires DGA (standard) rights. Pays standard royalty.

Needs: Situation comedies *only*. Prefers cast of fewer than 14. No dramas.

THE FIREHOUSE THEATRE, 514 S. 11th St., Omaha NE 68102. (402)346-6009. Artistic Director: Dick Mueller. Produces 7 plays/year. Has produced 4 unagented submissions in 14 years. Computer printout submissions acceptable; prefers letter-quality.

Needs: "We produce at the Firehouse Dinner Theatre in Omaha. Our interest in new scripts is the hope of finding material that can be proven here at our theatre and then go on from here to find its audience." Submit complete ms. Reporting times vary; depends on work load. Buys negotiable rights. Pays $100/week or negotiable rates.

Tips: "We are a small theatre. Certainly size and cost are a consideration. Quality is also a consideration. We can't use heavy drama in this theatre. We might, however, consider a production if it were a good script and use another theatre."

FLORIDA STUDIO THEATRE, 1241 N. Palm Ave., Sarasota FL 34236. (813)366-9017. New plays director: Jack Fournier. Produces 4 established scripts and 3 new plays/year. "*FST* is a professional not-for-profit theatre." Plays are produced in 165-seat theatre for a subscription audience (primarily). *FST* operates under a small professional theatre contract of Actor's Equity. Submit query and synopsis. Reports in 2 months on queries; 7 months on mss. Pays $200 for workshop production of new script.

Needs: Contemporary plays ("courageous and innovative"). Prefers casts of no more than 8, and single sets.

SAMUEL FRENCH, INC., 45 W. 25th St., New York NY 10010. Editor: Lawrence Harbison. 100% freelance written. "We publish about 80-90 new titles a year. We are the world's largest publisher of plays. 10-20% are unagented submissions. In addition to publishing plays, we occasionally act as agents in the placement of plays for professional production—eventually in New York." Pays on royalty basis. Submit complete ms (bound).

"Always type your play in the standard, accepted stageplay manuscript format used by all professional play-wrights in the U.S. If in doubt, send $3 to the attention of Lawrence Harbison for a copy of 'Guidelines.' We re-quire a minimum of two months to report."

Needs: "We are willing at all times to read the work of freelancers. Our markets prefer simple-to-stage, light, happy romantic comedies or mysteries. If your work does not fall into this category, we would be reading it for consideration for agency representation. No 25-page 'full-length' plays; no children's plays to be performed *by* children; no puppet plays; no adaptations of public domain children's stories; no verse plays; no large-cast his-torical (costume) plays; no seasonal and/or religious plays; no television, film or radio scripts; no translations of foreign plays."

Recent Title: *Cinderella Waltz*, by Don Nigro.

GASLAMP QUARTER THEATRE COMPANY, 547 4th Ave., San Diego CA 92101. (619)232-9608. Com-pany Manager: Jean Hauser. Produces 5 plays/year. A professional, not-for-profit theatre. Query with synop-sis. Variable contract, usually a weekly amount, "scale depends on author."

Needs: "We like a drawing room touch, also have a penchant for Pinter. Maximum cast: 10. No more than 4 sets."

Tips: "Small cast (under 8), not too many scenery changes, not too current (meaning not trendy), some lasting comment about the human condition."

THE WILL GEER THEATRICUM BOTANICUM, Box 1222, Topanga CA 90290. (213)455-2322. Artistic Di-rector: Ellen Geer. Produces 3 plays/year. Professional summer theater. Query with synopsis. Reports in 6 months. Obtains negotiable rights. Pays royalty.

Needs: Seeks full-length plays appropriate for repertory company in large outdoor arena: musical, political, humanistic. "Not over 10 in cast—we do *not* have a large technical budget."

GEORGETOWN PRODUCTIONS, 7 Park Ave., New York NY 10016. Producers: Gerald Van De Vorst and David Singer: Produces 1-2 plays/year for a general audience. Works with 2-3 unpublished/unproduced writers annually. Dramatist Guild membership required. Submit complete ms only. Standard Dramatists Guild con-tract.

Needs: Prefers plays with small casts and not demanding more than one set. Interested in new unconventional scripts dealing with contemporary issues, comedies, mysteries, musicals or dramas. No first-drafts; outlines; 1-act plays.

Tips: "The current trend is toward light entertainment, as opposed to meaningful or serious plays."

HEUER PUBLISHING CO., 233 Dows Bldg., Box 248, Cedar Rapids IA 52406. (319)364-6311. Publishes plays for junior and senior high school and church groups. Query with synopsis or submit complete ms. Re-ports in 2 months. Purchases amateur rights only. Pays royalty or cash.

Needs: "One- and three-act plays suitable for school production. Preferably comedy or mystery comedy. All material should be with the capabilities of high school actors. We prefer material with one set." No "special day material, material with controversial subject matter."

HONOLULU THEATRE FOR YOUTH, Box 3257, Honolulu HI 96801. (808)521-3487. Artistic Director: John Kauffman. Produces 6 plays/year. 50% freelance written. Plays are professional productions in Hawaii, primarily for youth audiences (youth aged 2 to 20). 80% of scripts are unagented submissions. Works with 2 unpublished/unproduced writers annually. Computer printout submissions acceptable; prefers letter-quality. Reports in 3 months. Buys negotiable rights.

Needs: Contemporary subjects of concern/interest to young people; adaptations of literary classics; fantasy including space, fairy tales, myth and legend. "HTY wants well-written plays, 60-90 minutes in length, that have something worthwhile to say and that will stretch the talents of professional adult actors." Cast not ex-ceeding 8; *no* technical extravaganzas; *no* full-orchestra musicals; simple sets and props, costumes can be elab-orate. No plays to be enacted by children or camp versions of popular fairytales. Query with synopsis. Pays $1,000-2,500.

Tips: "Young people are intelligent and perceptive, if anything more so than lots of adults, and if they are to become fans and eventual supporters of good theatre, they must see good theatre while they are young. Trends on the American stage that freelance writers should be aware of include a growing awareness that we are living in a world community. We must learn to share and understand other people and other cultures."

HUDSON GUILD THEATRE, 414 West 26th St., New York NY 10001. (212)760-9836. Literary Manager: Steven Ramay. Produces 5 mainstage plays annually, and conducts readings/workshops. "The plays are per-formed at the Hudson Guild Theatre. Our audiences (largely subscription) are from the greater New York City area, including parts of New Jersey, Connecticut and all Manhattan boroughs." Submit complete ms; prefers synopsis in addition to ms. Reports in 2 months. All rights agreements are worked out individually in produc-tion contract negotiations. Pays flat $1,000 fee for mainstage productions.

Needs: "Our interests are varied and international in scope. Socially and politically aware plays are preferred. We usually limit our casts to no more than 8, although exceptions can be made depending on the project."
Tips: "Don't submit your complete works. Submitting one play at a time usually insures a more thoughtful consideration of your material."

WILLIAM E. HUNT, 801 West End Ave., New York NY 10025. Interested in reading scripts for stock production, off-Broadway and even Broadway production. "Small cast, youth-oriented, meaningful, technically adventuresome; serious, funny, far-out. Must be about people first, ideas second. No political or social tracts." No 1-act, anti-Black, anti-Semitic or anti-Gay plays. "I do not want 1920, 1930 or 1940 plays disguised as modern by 'modern' language. I do not want plays with 24 characters, plays with 150 costumes, plays about symbols instead of people. I do not want plays which are really movie or television scripts." Works with 2-3 unpublished/unproduced writers annually. Pays royalties on production. Off-Broadway, 5%; on Broadway, 5%, 7½% and 10%, based on gross. No royalty paid if play is selected for a showcase production. Reports in "a few weeks." Must have SASE or script will not be returned.
Tips: "Production costs and weekly running costs in the legitimate theatre are so high today that no play (or it is the very rare play) with more than six characters and more than one set, by a novice playwright, is likely to be produced unless that playwright will either put up or raise the money him or herself for the production."

INVISIBLE THEATRE, 1400 N. 1st Ave., Tucson AZ 85719. (602)882-9721. Artistic Director: Susan Claassen. Literary Manager: Deborah Dickey. Produces 5-7 plays/year. 10% freelance written. Semiprofessional regional theatre for liberal, college-educated audiences. Plays performed in 78-seat non-Equity theatre with small production budget. Works with 1-5 unpublished/unproduced writers annually. Query with synopsis. Computer printout submissions acceptable; prefers letter-quality to dot-matrix. Reports in 6 months. Buys non-professional rights. Pays 10% royalty.
Needs: "Two act plays, generally contemporary, some historical, comedies, drama, small musicals, wide range of topics. Limited to plays with small casts of 10 or less, strong female roles, simple sets, minimal props." No large musicals, complex set designs, casts larger than 15.
Tips: "Trends in the American stage that will affect the types of scripts we accept include social issues—social conscience—i.e. South Africa, coming to terms with elderly parents, overcoming effects of disease, family relationships, things that the average person can relate to and think about. Challenges we can all relate to, common experiences, because people enjoy people. Our audiences include some older, somewhat conservative, members (although *not* rigid or dogmatic) as well as younger, more liberal groups. We try to have broad appeal—mixing experimental with comedy and drama throughout the year."

IRONBOUND THEATRE INC., 179 Van Buren St., Newark NJ 07105. (201)272-3125. Artistic Director: Steven Gravatt. Produces 3 mainstage and 10 readings/year. "Original scripts are developed through a process with a staged reading. If selected they are first produced at our theatre playhouse, Newark, NJ, then production travels to New York City." Query with synopsis or submit complete ms. Reports in 4 months. Obtains first production rights. Pays outright purchase of $100 minimum.
Needs: "We produce 'progressive' type plays (not meaning socialist or communist) scripts that risk and induce thought and are entertaining. Looking specifically for comedies for the '88-'89 season."
Tips: "Write from the heart, not the pocketbook."

JEWEL BOX THEATRE, 3700 North Walker, Oklahoma City OK 73118. (405)521-1786. Artistic Director: Charles Tweed. Produces 6 plays/year. Amateur productions. Intended for 2,500 season subscribers and general public. Submit complete ms. Reports in 3 months. "We would like to have first production rights and 'premiere' the play at Jewel Box Theatre." Pays $500 contest prize.
Needs: "We produce dramas, comedies and musicals. Usually we have two-act plays, but one and three acts are acceptable. Plays usually run two hours. Our theatre is in-the-round, so we adapt plays accordingly. We have not used multi-media projections. We do not use excessive profanity. We will dilute dialogue if necessary."

‡THE JULIAN THEATRE, 353 De Haro St., San Francisco CA 94107. (415)647-5525. Artistic Director: Richard Reineccius. Produces 6 plays/year. "We are a professional, community-based theatre, producing new plays of thought, wit and contemporary significance." Submit query and synopsis. Reports in 3 months. Pays royalty.
Needs: Prefers "new plays of thought, wit and contemporary significance" and "plays of social and political import."
Tips: "Beware of specialization—all theatre artists must have experience in all areas of theatre craft."

KUMU KAHUA, 1770 East-West Rd., Honolulu HI 96822. (808)948-7677. Executive Director: Dennis Carroll. Produces 4 productions, 4 public readings/year. "Plays performed at various theatres for community audiences. Actors are not paid. It's a nonprofit company." Submit complete ms. Royalty is $25 per performance;

usually 10 performances of each production.

Needs: "Plays must have some interest for local audiences, preferably by being set in Hawaii or dealing with some aspect of the Hawaiian experience. Prefer small cast, with simple staging demands. We don't like 'commercial' plays structured and designed for BO success of a Broadway sort. No trivial commercial farces, whodunits, plays like made-for-TV movies or sitcoms."

Tips: "We need some time to evaluate, and may want to hold the script awhile. We're not trendy."

LAMB'S PLAYERS THEATRE, 500 Plaza Blvd., Box 26, National City CA 92050. (619)474-3385. Artistic Director: Robert Smyth. Produces 7 plays/year. 15% freelance written. A professional non-Equity resident company with a year-round production schedule. Audience is varied; high percentage of family and church interest. Works with 1-2 unpublished/unproduced writers annually. Submit synopsis. Computer printout submissions acceptable. Reports in 4 months. Buys first production rights, touring option. Pays $500-5,000.

Needs: "We produce a wide variety of material which, while not necessarily 'religious' in nature often reflects a broad-based Christian perspective." Prefers smaller cast (2-10); adaptable staging (arena stage). "We are not interested in material that is 'preachy,' or material thats intention is to shock or titillate with sex, violence or language."

Tips: "Trends freelance writers should be aware of include productions which offer hope without being clichéd or sentimental; productions needing small cast and imaginative yet inexpensive sets; and an interest in presentational style pieces—acknowledgment and/or interaction with the audience."

LILLENAS PUBLISHING CO., Box 419527, Kansas City MO 64141. (816)931-1900. Editor: Paul M. Miller. "We publish on two levels: (1) Program Builders—seasonal and topical collections of recitations, sketches, dialogues and short plays. (2) Drama Resources. These assume more than one format; (a) Full length scripts, (b) shorter plays and sketches all by one author, (c) Collection of short plays and sketches by various authors. All program and play resources are produced with local church and Christian school in mind. Therefore there are taboos." Queries are encouraged, but synopsis and complete manuscripts are read. Computer printout submissions are acceptable, if highly readable. First rights are purchased for Program Builder manuscripts. For our line of Drama Resources, we purchase all print rights, but this is negotiable. Writer's guidelines for #10 SASE.

Needs: 98% of Program Builder materials are freelance written. Manuscripts selected for these publications are outright purchases; verse is 25 cents per line, prose (play scripts) are $5 a double-spaced page. Lillenas Drama Resources is a line of play scripts that are, in the most part, written by professionals with experience in production as well as writing. However, while we do read unsolicited manuscripts, more than half of what we publish is written by experienced authors whom we have already published. Drama Resources (whether full-length scripts, one-acts, or sketches) are paid on a 10% royalty. There are no advances.

Tips: "All plays need to be presented in standard play script format. We welcome a summary statement of each play. Purpose statements are always desirable. Approximate playing time, cast and prop lists, etc. are important to include. We are interested in fully scripted traditional plays, reader's theatre scripts, choral speaking pieces. Contemporary settings generally have it over Biblical settings. Christmas and Easter scripts must have a bit of a twist. Secular approaches to these seasons (Santas, Easter bunnies, and so on), are not considered. We sell our product in 10,000 Christian bookstores. We are probably in the forefront as a publisher of religious drama resources."

LOS ANGELES THEATRE CENTER, 514 S. Spring St., Los Angeles CA 90013. (213)627-6500. Dramaturg: Charles Marowitz. Produces 15-20 plays/year. 90% freelance written. A professional theatre for a multicultural metropolitan audience. 10% of scripts are unagented submissions. Works with 7-10 unproduced writers annually. Query with synopsis plus 10 pages of script. *No unsolicited ms.* Reports in 6 months. Buys first production rights, options to extend and move, subsidiaries. Pays 4-7% royalty. Computer printout submissions acceptable; no dot-matrix.

Needs: Plays with social or political awareness preferred. 10 actors maximum. No "television scripts or movies pretending to be theatre."

Tips: "The most important and exciting new work in the theatre is non-naturalistic. It takes risks with its subject matter and form and, therefore, it is dramatic writing that cannot be easily transferred to another form, i.e., television or film."

MCCARTER THEATRE COMPANY, 91 University Pl., Princeton NJ 08540. (609)683-9100. Artistic Director: Nagle Jackson. Produces 7 plays/year. Professional resident theatre. Submit complete ms. Reports in 3 months. Obtains negotiable rights. Payment negotiable:—"professional rates."

Needs: Produces plays that are "large in spirit."

Tips: The writer should "write passionately about the issues which concern her/him and our sophisticated, aware adult audience." No "pornography, soap opera, conventional documentaries."

MAGIC THEATRE, INC., Bldg. D, Fort Mason, San Francisco CA 94123. (415)441-8001. General Director: John Lion. Literary Manager: Christine Krolik. Dramaturg: Martin Esslin. "Oldest experimental theatre in

California." For public audience, generally college-educated. General cross-section of the area with an interest in alternative theatre and "neglected classics." Plays produced in the off-Broadway manner. Cast is full-Equity. Produces 7 plays/year. Very few scripts produced are unagented submissions. Works with 4-6 unpublished/unproduced writers annually. Submit through agents or send resume and 3-5 pages of sample dialogue. 1- or 2-act plays considered. "We pay $500 advance against 5% of gross."

MAGNUS THEATRE COMPANY, 137 N. May St., Thunder Bay, Ontario P7C 3N8 Canada. (807)623-5818. Artistic Director: Michael McLaughlin. Produces 6 plays/year. Professional stock theatre produced in 197-seat facility, and performed for a demographically diverse general audience.
Needs: "Fairly general in genres, but with a particular emphasis on new plays, must be full-length. Smaller (i.e. up to seven) casts are viewed favorably; some technical limitations. Always, budget limitations. No one-act plays or plays with very large casts, multiple settings, plays which are specifically American in theme or content."
Tips: "Thunder Bay is a very earthy, working city, and we try to reflect that sensibility in our choice of plays. Beyond that, however, Magnus has gained a national reputation for its commitment to the development and production of new plays, including, where possible, workshops. Scripts should be universal (i.e. accessible to Canadian audiences) in theme; should be produceable within realistic budget limitations."

MANHATTAN PUNCH LINE, 3rd Floor, 410 W. 42nd St., New York NY 10036. (212)239-0827. Artistic Director: Steve Kaplan. Produces 6-7 plays/year. Professional off-off Broadway theatre company. Submit complete ms. Reports in 3 months. Pays $325-500.
Needs: "Manhattan Punch Line is devoted to producing comedies of all types. We are a developmental theatre interested in producing serious plays with a comedic point of view."
Tips: "The most important and successful playwrights (Durang, Wasserstein, Innaurato) are all writing comedies. Don't worry about being funny, just try to be honest. Large-cast plays are back in."

MANHATTAN THEATRE CLUB, 453 W. 16th Ave., New York NY 10011. Literary Manager: Tom Szentgyorgyi. Produces 9 plays/year. All freelance written. A two-theatre performing arts complex classified as off-Broadway, using professional actors. "We present a wide range of new work, from this country and abroad, to a subscription audience. We want plays about contemporary problems and people. Comedies are welcome. No verse plays or historical dramas or large musicals. Very heavy set shows or multiple detailed sets are out. We prefer shows with casts not more than 15. No skits, but any other length is fine." Computer printout submissions acceptable; no dot-matrix. No unsolicited scripts. Query with synopsis. Reports in 6 months. Payment is negotiable.

MIAMI BEACH COMMUNITY THEATRE, 2231 Prairie Ave., Miami Beach FL 33139. (305)532-4515. Artistic Director: Jay W. Jensen. Produces 5 plays/year. "Amateur productions performed during the year for the Miami Beach community." Send query and synopsis or submit complete ms. Reports in 3 weeks. Pays $35-75/performance (if published work); does not pay for unpublished plays.
Needs: "All types. Interested in Spanish themes—Latin American plots, etc. Interested in new plays dealing with AIDS and short plays dealing wth AIDS that could be used in junior highs and senior highs for motivation—about 30 minutes long. Avoid sex."

MIDWEST PLAYLABS, The Playwrights Center, 2301 Franklin Ave. E., Minneapolis MN 55406. (612)332-7481. Executive Director: David Moore, Jr. 100% freelance written. "Midwest Playlabs is a 2-week developmental workshop for new plays. The program is held in Minneapolis and is open by script competition to playwrights who have an association with the 13 midwestern states or are national members of the Playwrights' Center. It is an intensive two-week workshop focusing on the development of a script and the playwright. Six plays are given rehearsed readings at the site of the workshop." Works with 60 playwrights annually. Announcements of playwrights by mid-April. Computer printout submissions acceptable; prefers letter-quality.
Needs: "We are interested in playwrights with talent, ambitions for a sustained career in theatre and scripts which could benefit from an intensive developmental process involving professional dramaturgs, directors and actors. A playwright needs to be affiliated with the Midwest (must be documented if they no longer reside in the Midwest) or be a Center member." MPL accepts scripts after first of each year. Full lengths only. No previously produced materials. Submit complete ms. Pays stipend; room and travel. Submission deadline March 1, 1989.
Tips: "We do not buy scripts. We are a service organization that provides programs for developmental work on scripts for members."

‡**MILL, MOUNTAIN THEATRE**, Market Square Center in Square, Roanoke VA 24011. (703)342-5730. Artistic Director: Jere Lee Hodgin. Produces 7 established plays, 10 new one acts and 2 new full-length plays/year. "Some of the professional productions will be on the main stage and some in our alternative theatre B." Submit complete ms. Reports in 8 months. Payment negotiable on individual play. Writer's guidelines for #10

SAE with 1 first class stamp; do not include loose stamps or money.

Needs: "We are interested in plays with racially mixed cast, but not to the exclusion of others. One act plays should run between 25-30 minutes. Cast limit is 15 for plays and 24 for musicals."

Tips: "Subject matter and character variations are open, but gratuitous language and acts are not acceptable. A play leased on large amounts of topical reference or humor has a very short life. Be sure you have written a play and not a film script. Roanoke is a fairly conservative community—good taste is always in order."

‡**MISE EN SCENE THEATRE**, 11305 Magnolia Blvd., North Hollywood CA 91601. (818)763-3101. Artistic Director: Herb Rodgers. Estab. 1987. Produces 6-16 plays/year at two theatres. For Los Angeles audiences, casting directors, agents and producers. Equity waiver; 99-seat house. Submit complete ms. Reports in 2 months. Pyament negotiable.

Needs: "Only original, unproduced, full-lengths and one-acts. Any genre, topic, style." Stage has 28-foot opening, 21-foot depth.

Tips: "No previously produced plays. Our objective is to give playwrights the opportunity to work in production with the directors and actors, to better prepare the play for professional productions. Our plays are reviews by the *Los Angeles Times*, *Variety*, and other local papers."

NATIONAL ARTS CENTRE-ENGLISH THEATRE CO., Box 1534, Station B, Ottawa, Ontario K1P 5W1 Canada. (613)996-5051. Theatre Producer: Andis Celms. Produces and/or presents 12 plays/year. 0-5% freelance written. Works with 1-2 unpublished/unproduced writers annually. All scripts produced are agented submissions. Professional productions performed in the theatre and studio of the National Arts Centre (also, workshop productions in a rehearsal space). Audience ranges from young/middle-aged professionals (especially civil servants) to students. Computer printout submissions acceptable; prefers letter-quality.

Tips: "Our 'mainstage' audience likes a solid, well-written play with an intelligible story line and no coarse language. Our 'workshop' audience likes to be challenged, both in language and structure, but not abused. We are interested in the smaller cast, 'human interest' style of theatre and film. For example, last season we produced *Children of a Lesser God*. Our audience likes the combination of having heard of the play and being moved by the emotions."

NECESSARY ANGEL THEATRE, #400, 553 Queen St. W., Toronto, Ontario M5V 2B6 Canada (416)365-0533. Dramaturg: D. D. Kugler. Produces 2 plays/year. Plays are Equity productions in various Toronto theatres and performance spaces for an urban audience between 20-55 years of age. Submit complete ms. Please include SASE (international postal coupon if USA). Reports in 2 months. Obtains various rights "based on the manuscript (original, translation, adaptation) and the playwright (company member, etc.)." Pays 10% royalty.

Needs: "We are open to new theatrical ideas, environmental pieces, unusual acting styles and large casts. The usual financial constraints exist, but they have never eliminated a work to which we felt a strong commitment." No "TV-influenced sit-coms and melodramas."

Tips: "All submissions are considered for long-term script/playwright development, including one-day readings and one-week workshops, leading to company productions. Playwrights should be aware of our interdisciplinary approach to performance (music, dance and visual arts which support the text)."

‡**THE NEW AMERICAN THEATER**, 118 N. Main St., Rockford IL 61101. (815)963-9454. Producing Director: J.R. Sullivan. Produces a spectrum of American and international work in 10-month season. "The New American Theater is a professional resident theatre company performing on a thrust stage with a 270-seat house. It is located in a predominantly middle-class Midwestern town." Submit complete ms March. Reports in 10 months. Pays royalty based on number of performances.

Needs: No limitations, prefer serious themes, contemporary pieces. Open to format, etc. No opera.

Tips: "We look for new work that addresses contemporary issues; we do not look for work of any one genre or production style. We encourage experimentation."

THE NEW CONSERVATORY CHILDREN'S THEATRE COMPANY AND SCHOOL, Zephyr Theater Complex, 25 Van Ness, Lower Level, San Francisco CA 94102. (415)861-4814. Artistic Director: Ed Decker. Produces 4-5 plays/year. "The New Conservatory is a children's theatre school (ages four to nineteen) which operates year-round. Each year we produce several plays, for which the older students (usually eleven and up, but younger depending on the readiness of the child) audition. These are presented to the general public at the Zephyr Theatre Complex San Francisco (50-350 seats). Our audience is approximately age 10 to adult." Send query and synopsis. Reports in 1 month. Pays 5% royalty.

Needs: "We emphasize works in which children play *children*, and prefer relevant and controversial subjects, although we also do musicals. We have a commitment to new plays. Examples of our shows are: Mary Gail's *Nobody Home* (world premiere; about latchkey kids); Brian Kral's *Special Class* (about disabled kids), and *The Inner Circle*, by Patricia Loughrey (commissioned scripts about AIDS prevention for kids). As we are a nonprofit group on limited budget, we tend not to have elaborate staging; however, our staff is inventive—includes choreographer and composer. Write innovative theatre that explores topics of concern/interest to young people, that takes risks. We concentrate more on ensemble than individual roles, too. We do *not* want to see fairytales or trite rehashings of things children have seen/heard since the age of two. See theatre as education, rather than 'children are cute'."

Tips: "It is important for young people and their families to explore and confront issues relevant to growing up in the '80s. Theatre is a marvelous teaching tool that can educate while it entertains."

NEW PLAYS INCORPORATED, Box 273, Rowayton CT 06853. (203)866-4520. Publisher: Patricia Whitton. Publishes an average of 4 plays/year. Publishes plays for producers of plays for young audiences and teachers in college courses on child drama. Query with synopsis. Reports in 2 months. Agent for amateur and semi-professional productions, exclusive agency for script sales. Pays 50% royalty on productions; 10% on script sales. Free catalog.

Needs: Plays for young audiences with something innovative in form and content. Length: usually 45-90 minutes. "Should be suitable for performance by adults for young audiences." No skits, assembly programs, improvisations or unproduced manuscripts.

THE NEW PLAYWRIGHTS' THEATRE OF WASHINGTON, 1742 Church St. NW, Washington DC 20036. (202)232-4527. Contact: Literary Manager. Produces 5 musicals and straight plays and 16 readings/year. 100% freelance written. 15% of scripts produced are unagented submissions. "Plays are produced in professional productions in the 125-seat New Playwrights' Theatre in the Dupont Circle area of the city for a subscription audience as well as large single-ticket buying followers." Works with varying number of writers annually; 30% unpublished, 65% unproduced. Will not accept unsolicited mss, only synopsis plus 20 pages of finished script, "typed to form, suitably bound." All musicals must be accompanied by cassette tape recording of songs in proper order. Reports in 2 months on synopsis; 6-8 months on scripts. "Rights purchased and financial arrangements are individually negotiated." SASE, acknowledgement postcard. No rights requested on readings; buys 7% of playwright's future royalties for 7 years, and first production credit requested for plays or musicals offered as full productions. Pays 6% royalty against a $300/week minimum.

Needs: "All styles, traditional to experimental, straight plays to musicals and music-dramas, revues and cabaret shows, and full-lengths only. No verse plays, puppet plays or film scripts." Staging: performance space adaptable.

Tips: "We prefer a strong plot line, be the play realistic, expressionistic or non-realistic, with an emphasis on vital, lively, visceral energy in writing. We look at a wide range of styles from the old-fashioned 'well-made play' to more avant-garde structures. We are a theatre of content with a humanist perspective focusing on the personal and public issues of our time."

‡THE NEW ROSE THEATRE, 904 S.W. Main, Portland OR 97205. (503)222-2495. Artistic Director: Michael Griggs. Produces 10 plays/year. Plays performed at professional, classic repertory theatre with Equity small professional theatre contract. Submit query and synopsis. Reports in 6 months. Pays $35-50/performance.

Needs: "Produces repertory adaptations of classics. Also contemporary plays on classic themes, translations/adaptations. Adult and children's plays are produced by us. We have two theaters—one, a 119-seat ¾ thrust black box; and tenancy in a 350-seat variable staging theater."

NEW TUNERS THEATRE, 1225 W. Belmont Ave., Chicago IL 60657. (312)929-7367. Artistic Director: Byron Schaffer, Jr. Produces 3-4 new musicals/year. 66% freelance written. "Nearly all" scripts produced are unagented submissions. Plays performed in a small off-Loop theatre seating 148 for a general theatre audience, urban/suburban mix. Submit complete ms and cassette tape of the score, if available. Reports in 6 months. Buys exclusive right of production within 80-mile radius. "Submit first, we'll negotiate later." Pays 5-10% of gross. "Authors are given a stipend to cover a residency of at least two weeks." Computer printout submissions acceptable; prefers letter-quality.

Needs: "We're interested in traditional forms of musical theatre as well as more innovative styles. We have less interest in operetta and operatic works, but we'd look at anything. At this time, we have no interest in non-musical plays unless to consider them for possible adaptation—please send query letter first. Our production capabilities are limited by the lack of space, but we're very creative and authors should submit anyway. The smaller the cast, the better. We are especially interested in scripts using a younger (35 and under) ensemble of actors. We mostly look for authors who are interested in developing their script through workshops, rehearsals and production. No interest in children's theatre. No casts over 15. No one-man shows."

Tips: "Freelance writers should be aware that musical theatre can be more serious. The work of Sondheim and others who follow demonstrates clearly that musical comedy can be ambitious and can treat mature themes in a relevant way. Probably 90 percent of what we receive would fall into the category of 'fluff.' We have nothing against fluff. We've had some great successes producing it and hope to continue to offer some pastiche and farce to our audience; however, we would like to see the musical theatre articulating something about the world around us, rather than merely diverting an audience's attention from that world."

NEW WORLD THEATER, INC., Suite 212, 7600 Red Road, South Miami FL 33143. (305)663-0208. Executive Director: Kenneth A. Cotthoff. Produces 5 plays/year. "We are a professional (AEA—LOA) resident theater performing at The Strand in Miami Beach. Our season begins in the Fall with the winners of our annual National New Play Competition which is followed with a season of contemporary off-Broadway format plays. Audience upwardly mobile, average age approximately 40-ish." Submit complete ms—"must be typed, bound with address on fly sheet." Reports in 3 months for play competition; 1 month otherwise. "We maintain a six month exclusive limited option on any play produced." Pays $500 for competition or season.
Needs: Contemporary comedies or dramas. Off-Broadway budgets and sensibilities; also interested in young authors and Florida themes. "Currently limiting to cast of four for competition and season. Prefer one main set and no extraordinary budget-breaking items."
Tips: "Prefers contemporary format, standard length, one intermission, intelligent, thought provoking (even if comedy). No high budget, children's plays or musicals (small ones OK). This may change as budget expands."

NEW YORK SHAKESPEARE FESTIVAL/PUBLIC THEATER, 425 Lafayette St., New York NY 10003. (212)598-7100. Producer: Joseph Papp. Plays and Musical Development Director: Gail Merrifield. Interested in plays, musicals, operas, translations, adaptations. No restriction as to style, form, subject matter. Produces 6-10 new works year-round at Public Theater complex housing 5 theaters (100-300 seat capacity): Newman, Anspacher, Shiva, LuEsther Hall, Martinson. Also Delacorte 2100-seat ampitheater, Broadway, Royal Court/London Exchange; film and television. Unsolicited and unagented submissions accepted. Computer printout manuscripts and electronic submissions via VHS or Beta OK with hard copy. Send music cassette with musical work. All scripts: include cast of characters with age and brief description; musical works include vocal ranges. Standard options and production agreements. Reports in 2 months.

JACKIE NICHOLS, 51 S. Cooper, Memphis TN 38104. Artistic Director: Jackie Nichols. Produces 16 plays/year. Professional productions. Submit complete ms. Reports in 5 months. Pays $500.
Needs: All types. "Small cast, single or unit set."
Tips: "Playwrights from the South will be given preference. South is defined as the following states: Alabama, Florida, Georgia, Kentucky, Louisiana, Mississippi, Missouri, North Carolina, South Carolina, Tennessee, Texas, Virginia and West Virginia. This means we will read all shows and when final decisions are made, if every other aspect of the plays are equal we will choose a Southern author."

NINE O'CLOCK PLAYERS, 1367 N. St. Andrews Pl, Los Angeles CA 90028. (213)469-1973. Artistic Director: Fluff McLean. Produces 2 plays/year. "Plays produced at Assistance League Playhouse by resident amateur and semi-professional company. All plays are musical adaptations of classical children's literature. Plays must be appropriate for children ages 4-12." Query and synopsis. Reports in 1 month. Pays negotiable royalty or per performance.
Needs: "Plays must have at least 15 characters and be 1 hour 15 minutes long. Productions are done on a proscenium stage in classical theater style. All plays must have humor, music, and have good moral values. No audience participation improvisational plays."

ODYSSEY THEATRE ENSEMBLE, 12111 Ohio Ave., Los Angeles CA 90025. (213)826-1626. Literary Manager: Jon Lewis. Produces 12 plays/year. Plays performed in a 3-theatre facility. "All three theatres are Equity waiver; Odyssey 1 and 2 each have 99 seats, while Odyssey 3 has 72-90 seats. We have a subscription audience of 1,800 who subscribe to a six-play season, and are offered a discount on our remaining non-subscription plays. Remaining seats are sold to the general public." Query with synopsis, cast breakdown and 8-10 pages of sample dialogue. Scripts must be securely bound. Reports in 1 month on queries; 6 months on scripts. Buys negotiable rights. Pays 5-7% royalty or $25-35/performance. "We will *not* return scripts without SASE."
Needs: Full-length plays only with "either an innovative form or extremely provocative subject matter. We desire more theatrical pieces that explore possibilities of the live theatre experience. We are seeking full-length musicals. We are not reading one-act plays or light situation comedies."

OFF CENTER THEATER, 436 W. 18th St., New York NY 10011. (212)929-8299. Artistic Director: Tony McGrath. Produces 4 plays/year. Equity showcase productions and non-Equity productions. Submit complete ms. Reports in 3 months. Obtains first professional production righs. Pays 6% of box office receipts, after expenses.
Needs: Issue-oriented comedies.

OLD GLOBE THEATRE, Box 2171, San Diego CA 92112. (619)231-1941. Associate Director: Robert Berlinger. Produces 12 plays/year. "We are a LORT B professional house. Our plays are produced for a single-ticket and subscription audience of 250,000, a large cross section of southern California, including visitors from the LA area." Submit complete ms through agent only. Send one-page letter or synopsis if not represented. Reports in 6 months. Buys negotiable rights. Royalty varies.

Needs: "We are looking for contemporary, realistic, theatrical dramas and comedies and request that all submissions be full-length plays at this time." Prefers smaller cast and single sets, and "to have the playwright submit the play he has written rather than to enforce any limitations. No musicals or large cast historical dramas."

Tips: "Get back to theatricality. I am tired of reading screenplays."

OLDCASTLE THEATRE COMPANY, (formerly Eric Peterson Oldcastle Theatre Company), Box 1555, Bennington VT 05201. (802)447-0564. Artistic Director: Eric Peterson. Produces 7 plays/year. Plays are performed in a small (104 seat) theatre on a former estate now used by Southern Vermont College, by a professional theatre company (in a season from April through October) for general audiences, including residents of a three-state area and tourists during the vacation season. Submit complete ms. Pays "by negotiation with the playwright. As a not-for-profit theatre company, we do not have large sums available."

Needs: Produces classics, musicals, comedy, drama, most frequently American works. Usual performance time is 2 hours. "With a small stage, we limit to small cast and simple props, though we usually do prefer designed sets and appropriate costumes."

EUGENE O'NEILL THEATER CENTER'S NATIONAL PLAYWRIGHTS CONFERENCE/NEW DRAMA FOR TELEVISION PROJECT, Suite 901, 234 W. 44th St., New York NY 10036. (212)382-2790. Artistic Director: Lloyd Richards. Administrator: Peggy Vernieu. Develops staged readings of 10-12 stage plays, 3-4 teleplays/year for a general audience. "We accept unsolicited mss with no prejudice toward either represented or unrepresented writers. Our theatre is located in Waterford, Connecticut and we operate under an Equity LORT(C) Contract. We have 3 theatres: Barn-250 seats, Amphitheatre-300 seats, Instant Theater-150. Send #10 SASE in the fall for submission guidelines. Complete bound, unproduced, original plays are eligible (no adaptations). Decision by late April. Pays stipend plus room, board and transportation. Computer printout submissions acceptable. We accept script submissions from Sept. 15-Dec. 1 of each year. Conference takes place during four weeks in July each summer."

Needs: "We use modular sets for all plays, minimal lighting, minimal props and no costumes. We do script-in-hand readings with professional actors and directors. Our focus is on new play/playwright development."

THE OPEN EYE: NEW STAGINGS, 270 W. 89th St., New York NY 10024. (212)769-4143. Artistic Director: Amie Brockway. Produces 3-4 full-length plays/year plus a series of readings and workshop productions of one-acts. "The Open Eye is a professional, Equity LOA, 105-seat, off-off Broadway theater. Our audiences include a broad spectrum of ages and backgrounds." Submit complete ms in clean, bound copy with SASE for its return. Reports in 6 months. Playwright fee for mainstage: $500.

Needs: "New Stagings is particularly interested in one-act and full-length plays that take full advantage of the live performance situation. We tend not to do totally realistic plays. We especially like plays that appeal to young people and adults alike."

ORACLE PRESS, LTD., 5323 Heatherstone Dr., Baton Rouge LA 70820. (504)766-5577. Artistic Director: Cj Stevens. Publishes 10-15 plays/year. 90% freelance written. 90% of scripts produced are unagented submissions. Plays performed by college, high school and other amateur groups. Works with 20-30 unpublished/unproduced writers annually. Query with synopsis. Computer printout submissions acceptable; prefers letter-quality. Reports in 6 weeks. Copyright in name of playwright; performance rights revert to playwright. Pays 10% royalty.

Needs: "Production must be playable *on stage*. Will not publish gratuitous filth or obscenity."

Tips: "The trend which we find deplorable is that of writing everything for Broadway; hence, small casts, limited sets. College and high school groups frequently desire just the opposite."

OREGON SHAKESPEARE FESTIVAL ASSOCIATION, (formerly The Oregon Shakespearean Festival Association), Box 158, Ashland OR 97520. (503)482-2111. Literary Manager: Cynthia White. Produces 16 plays/year. The Angus Bowmer Theater has a thrust stage and seats 600. The Black Swan is an experimental space and seats 150; The Elizabethan Outdoor Theatre seats 1,200 (we do almost exclusively Shakespearean productions there—mid-June through September). OSFA also produces a separate five-play season at the Portland Center for The Performing Arts in a 725 seat proscenium theatre. Producing director of OSFA Portland Center Stage: Dennis Bigelow. Query and synopsis plus 10 pages of dialogue from unsolicited sources/also resume. Complete scripts from agents only. Reports in 9 months. Negotiates individually for rights with the playwright's agent. "Most plays run within our 10 month season for 6-10 months, so royalties are paid accordingly."

Needs: "A broad range of classic and contemporary scripts. One or two fairly new scripts per season. Also a play readings series which focuses on new work. Plays must fit into our 10-month rotating repertory season. Black Swan shows usually limited to 6 actors." No one-acts or musicals.

Tips: "Send your work through an agent if possible. Send the best examples of your work rather than all of it.

Don't become impatient or discouraged if it takes 6 months or more for a response. Don't expect detailed critiques with rejections. As always, I want to see plays with heart and soul, intelligence, humor and wit. I also think theatre is a place for the *word*. So, the word first, then spectacle and high-tech effects."

PEOPLE'S LIGHT & THEATRE COMPANY, 39 Conestoga Rd., Malvern PA 19355. (215)647-1900. Producing Director: Danny S. Fruchter. Produces 5 full-length plays/year; no more than 1 new play/year. "LORT D Actors' Equity plays are produced in Malvern 30 miles outside Philadelphia in 350-seat main stage and 150-seat second stage. Our audience is mainly suburban, some from Philadelphia. We do a 5-show subscription season." Query with synopsis and cast list. Computer printout submissions acceptable; prefers letter-quality. Reports in 10 months. Buys "rights to production in our theatre, sometimes for local touring." Pays 2-5% royalty.
Needs: "We will produce anything that interests us." Prefers single set, maximum cast of 12 (for full length), fewer for one act. No musicals, mysteries, domestic comedies.
Tips: "Writers should be aware of trend away from naturalistic family drama and toward smaller cast size."

‡THE PHILADELPHIA THEATRE COMPANY. (formerly The Philadelphia Company), Bourse Building—735, 21 S. 5th St., Philadelphia PA 19108. (215)592-8333. Artistic Director: Sara Garonzik. Produces 5 full productions and 3 workshops. "Main-stage shows are done in 324-seat proscenium theatre in center of city. We are a professional theatre." Submit query, synopsis, complete ms or agented submissions. Reports in 6 months. Royalty negotiated.
Needs: "We produce contemporary American drama."
Tips: "Our tastes are eclectic and we try to stay open-minded. In general, we are not interested in extremely light-weight commercial fare or—on the other hand—chamber pieces."

PIER ONE THEATRE, Box 894, Homer AK 99603. (907)235-7333. Artistic Director: Lance Petersen. Produces 5-8 plays/year. "Plays to various audiences for various plays—e.g. children's, senior citizens, adult, family, etc. Plays are produced on Kemai Peninsula." Submit complete ms. Reports in 2 months. Pays $25-125/performance.
Needs: "No restrictions—willing to read *all* genres." No stock reviews, hillbilly or sit-coms.
Tips: "Don't start your play with a telephone conversation. New plays ought to be risky business; they ought to be something the playwright feels is terribly important."

PIONEER DRAMA SERVICE, Box 22555, Denver CO 80222. (303)759-4297. Publisher: Shubert Fendrich. 10% freelance written. Plays are performed by high school, junior high and adult groups, colleges, churches and recreation programs for audiences of all ages. "We are one of the largest full-service play publishers in the country in that we handle straight plays, musicals, children's theatre and melodrama." Publishes 10 plays/year; 40% musicals and 60% straight plays. Query only; no unsolicited manuscripts. Computer printout submissions acceptable; prefers letter-quality. Buys all rights. Outright purchase only with a few exceptions for major musicals. Reports in 2 months.
Needs: "We use the standard 2-act format, 2-act musicals, religious drama, comedies, mysteries, drama, melodrama and plays for children's theater (plays to be done by adult actors for children)." Length: 2-act musicals and 2-act comedies up to 90 minutes; and children's theatre of 1 hour. Prefer many female roles, one simple set. Currently overstocked on one-act plays.
Recent Title: *Luann* by Eleanor and Ray Harder (musical based on the Greg Evans comic strip).

□PLAYERS PRESS, INC., Box 1132, Studio City CA 91604. Senior Editor: Robert W. Gordon. "We deal in all areas and handle works for film and television as well as theatre. But all works must be in stage play format for publication." Also produces scripts for video, and material for cable television. 80% freelance written. 10-12 scripts are unagented submissions. Works with 1-10 unpublished/unproduced writers annually. Submit complete ms. "Must have SASE or play will not be returned, and two #10 SASEs for update and correspondence. All submissions must have been produced and should include a flyer and/or program with dates of performance." Reports in 3 months. Buys negotiable rights. "We prefer all area rights." Pays variable royalty "according to area; approximately 10-75% of gross receipts." Also pays in outright purchase of $100-25,000 or $5-5,000/performance.
Needs: "We prefer comedies, musicals and children's theatre, but are open to all genres. We will rework the ms after acceptance. We are interested in the quality, not the format."
Tips: "Send only material requested. Do not telephone."

PLAYS, The Drama Magazine for Young People, 120 Boylston, Boston MA 02116. Editor: Sylvia K. Burack. Publishes approximately 75 1-act plays and dramatic program material each school year to be performed by junior and senior high, middle grades, lower grades. Can use comedies, farces, melodramas, skits, mysteries and dramas, plays for holidays and other special occasions, such as Book Week; adaptations of classic stories and fables; historical plays; plays about black history and heroes; puppet plays; folk and fairy tales;

creative dramatics; and plays for conservation, ecology or human rights programs. Mss should follow the general style of *Plays*. Stage directions should not be typed in capital letters or underlined. No incorrect grammar or dialect. Desired lengths for mss are: junior and senior high—20-22 double-spaced ms pages (25 to 30 minutes playing time). Middle grades—12 to 15 pages (15 to 20 minutes playing time). Lower grades—6 to 10 pages (8 to 15 minutes playing time). Pays "good rates on acceptance." Reports in 2-3 weeks. Sample copy $3; send SASE for manuscript specification sheet.

PRIMARY STAGES COMPANY, INC., 584 Ninth Ave., New York NY 10036. (212)333-7471. Artistic Director: Casey Childs. Produces 4 plays, 4 workshops, over 100 readings/year. All of the plays are produced professionally off-Broadway at the 45th Street Theatre, 354 West 45th St. Query and synopsis. Reports in 3 months. "If Primary Stages produces the play, we ask for the right to move it for up to six months after the closing performance." Writers paid "same as the actors."
Needs: "We are looking for highly theatrical works that were written exclusively with the stage in mind. We do not want TV scripts or strictly realistic plays."
Tips: No "living room plays, disease-of-the-week plays, back-porch plays, father/son work-it-all-out-plays, etc."

THE QUARTZ THEATRE, Box 465, Ashland OR 97520. (503)482-8119. Artistic Director: Dr. Robert Spira. Produces 5 plays/year. "Semi-professional mini-theatre. General audience." Send 3 pages dialogue and personal bio. Reports in 2 weeks. Pays 5% royalty after expenses.
Needs: "Any length, any subject, with or without music. We seek playwrights with a flair for language and theatrical imagination."
Tips: "We look at anything. We do not do second productions unless substantial rewriting is involved. Our theatre is a steppingstone to further production. Our playwrights are usually well-read in comparative religion, philosophy, psychology, and have a comprehensive grasp of human problems. We seek the 'self-indulgent' playwright who pleases him/herself first of all."

THE SHAZZAM PRODUCTION COMPANY, 418 Pier Ave., Santa Monica CA 90405. Artistic Director: Edward Blackoff. Produces 2 plays/year. Equity-waiver productions for adult audience. Query with complete ms and synopsis. Reports in 6 weeks. Obtains negotiable rights. Pays $15-25/performance.
Needs: "Full-length plays dealing with important contemporary social and political human issues. Limit of 2 sets and requiring no more than 12 actors. No musicals or drawing room farces."

FRANK SILVERA WRITERS' WORKSHOP, 317 West 125th St., New York NY 10027. (212)663-8463. Executive Director: Karen Baxter. Produces up to 4 plays/year. "Plays attended by 90% black audiences." Submit complete ms. Reports in 6 weeks. "All productions originally read here are credited to the Workshop if they are produced outside." Pays royalty.
Needs: "Universal themes, full-length, one-acts."

THE SNOWMASS REPERTORY THEATRE, Box 6275, Snowmass Village CO 81615. (303)923-3773. Artistic Director: Michael Yeager. Produces 8 plays/year. "Plays performed at The Snowmass Festival Theatre (253 seats), or The Wheeler Opera House (488 seats). Professional Equity Productions, for both summer and winter visitors and locals." Submit synopsis. Reports anywhere from 6 weeks to 6 months. Obtains rights for first professional production. Pays 6-12% royalty.
Needs: "We produce full-length comedies, dramas and musicals. Prefer casts of 6-12 characters with relatively equal numbers of male and female characters and no limitations on minority casting; single or suggestive settings."

SOHO REPERTORY THEATRE, 80 Varick St., New York NY 10013. (212)925-2588. Co-Artistic Directors: Jerry Engelbach and Marlene Swartz. Produces 4 full productions and 8-10 staged readings/year. Performances at the Greenwich House Theatre, Greenwich Village. "The audience is well educated, mature and composed of regular theatregoers. Our playwrights have usually been produced, and some published, previously." Works with 5-10 unpublished/unproduced writers annually, including productions and staged readings. "Do not send a script. Unsolicited ms will be returned unread." Query with description of the play and how it will work as a live theatre piece. Computer printout submissions acceptable; prefers letter-quality. Reports in 1 week on queries; 3 months on solicited mss. Rights for full-length plays: percentage of author's royalties on future earnings, credit in published script and on future programs; for staged readings: none. Pays $400 and up for limited run performance rights. Pays $500 and up for future right to option.
Needs: "Unusual plays not likely to be seen elsewhere; including rarely produced classics; revivals of superior modern works; new plays that utilize contemporary theatre techniques; and musicals and mixed media pieces that are noncommercial." Desires "full-length works that are physical, three-dimensional and that use heightened language, are witty and sophisticated, and that demonstrate a high quality of dramatic craft. No sitcoms, featherweight pieces for featherbrained audiences, drawing-room plays, works that do not require the

audience to think, or pieces more suited to television or the printed page than to the live stage."

Tips: "We go our own way and are not influenced by 'trends,' 'fads' or other commercial, nonartistic considerations. An ideal script for Soho Rep is highly literate, witty, and dramatically sound, and has plenty of scope for imaginative, physically active staging that breaks the fourth wall."

SOUTH COAST REPERTORY, Box 2197, Costa Mesa CA 92628. (714)957-2602. Dramaturg: Jerry Patch. Literary Manager: John Glore. Produces 6 plays/year on mainstage, 5 on second stage. A professional nonprofit theatre; a member of LORT and TCG. "We operate in our own facility which houses a 507-seat mainstage theatre and a 161-seat second stage theatre. We have a combined subscription audience of 24,000." Submit query and synopsis; maunscripts considered if submitted by agent. Reports in 4 months. Acquires negotiable rights. Pays negotiable royalty.

Needs: "We produce mostly full-lengths but will consider one-acts. Our only iron clad restriction is that a play be well written. We prefer plays that address contemporary concerns and are dramaturgically innovative. A play whose cast is larger than fifteen-twenty will need to be extremely compelling and its cast size must be justifiable."

Tips: "We don't look for a writer to write for us—he or she should write for him or herself. We look for honesty and a fresh voice. We're not likely to be interested in writers who are mindful of *any* trends. Originality and craftsmanship are the most important qualities we look for."

SOUTHEAST PLAYWRIGHTS PROJECT, (formerly Atlanta New Play Project), Box 14252, Atlanta GA 30324. (404)242-0256. Executive Director: Gayle Austin. Produces approximately 30 readings/workshops per year and provides career development services, including ongoing Writers' Lab, newsletter and workshops. This is the Atlanta New Play Project restructured to have playwrights as members. Write (includng SASE) for general membership applications. After joining, members may submit full-length script to be considered for Associate or Full membership.

Needs: General membership open to any playwright who lives, or has lived in the Southeast. Associate member must have had public reading of one full-length or two one-act plays. Full Member must have had at least one full production of a full-length play or be Associate Member.

Tips: "We aim at becoming a regional type of New Dramatists organization. Selection committee is looing for a distinctive voice, imaginative use of the stage, not just TV movies or sitcomes in play form."

SOUTHERN APPALACHIAN REPERTORY THEATRE (SART), Mars Hill College, Box 53, Mars Hill NC 28754. (704)689-1384. Managing Director: James W. Thomas. Produces 5-6 plays/year. "Since 1975 the Southern Appalachian Repertory Theatre has produced 527 performances of 53 plays and played to over 75,000 patrons in the 152-seat Owen Theatre on the Mars Hill College campus. The theatre's goals are quality, adventurous programming and integrity, both in artistic form and in the treatment of various aspects of human condition. SART is a professional summer theatre company whose audiences range from students to senior citizens." Send query with synopsis. Reports in 2 months. Pays flat fee of $500.

Needs: "Since 1975, one of SART's goals has been to produce at least one original play each summer season. To date, 14 original stories have been produced. Plays by southern Appalachian playwrights or about southern Appalachia are preferred, but by no means exclusively. New scripts, synopses or letters or inquiry welcomed."

SPECTRUM THEATRE, Room 199, 1st Ave., New York NY 10003. (212)475-5529. Artistic Director: Benno Haehnel. Produces 4 plays/year. New York City Off-Broadway mini-contract productions. Submit complete ms. Reports in 6 weeks. Obtains future production standard subsidiary rights. Pays 6% royalty.

Needs: Seeks "primarily full-length realistic plays dealing with social and humanistic problems. Prefers casts of 7 or under; no more than two sets. Looks for vivid characterizations and tight structure; key counterpointing of humorous and dramatic elements. Not interested in musicals."

STAGE ONE: The Louisville Children's Theatre, 425 W. Market St., Louisville KY 40202. (502)589-5946. Producing Director: Moses Goldberg. Produces 6-7 plays/year. 20% freelance written. 15-20% of scripts produced are unagented submissions (excluding work of playwright-in-residence). Plays performed by an Equity company for young audiences aged 4-18; usually does different plays for different age groups within that range. Submit complete ms. Computer printout submissions acceptable. Reports in 4 months. Pays negotiable royalty or $25-50/performance.

Needs: "Good plays for young audiences of all types: adventure, fantasy, realism, serious problem plays about growing up or family entertainment." Cast: ideally, 10 or less. "Honest, visual potentiality, worthwhile story and characters are necessary. An awareness of children and their schooling is a plus." No "campy material or anything condescending to children. No musicals unless they are fairly limited in orchestration."

CHARLES STILWILL, Managing Director, Community Playhouse, Box 433, Waterloo IA 50704. (319)235-0367. Plays performed by Waterloo Community Playhouse with a volunteer cast. Produces 11-13 plays (7-8 adult, 4-6 children's); 1-3 musicals and 7-12 nonmusicals/year; 1-4 originals. 17% freelance written. Most scripts produced are unagented submissions. Works with 1-4 unpublished/unproduced writers annually. "We are one of few community theatres with a commitment to new scripts. We do at least one and have done as many as four a year. We have 4,300 season members." Average attendance at main stage shows is 3,000; at studio shows 1,200. "We try to fit the play to the theatre. We do a wide variety of plays. Our public isn't going to accept nudity, too much sex, too much strong language. We don't have enough Black actors to do all-Black shows." Theatre has done plays with as few as two characters, and as many as 98. "On the main stage, we usually pay between $300 and $500. In our studio, we usually pay between $50 and $300. We also produce children's theatre. We are looking for good adaptations of name children's shows and very good shows that don't necessarily have a name. We produce children's theatre with both adult and child actors. We also do a small (2-6 actors) cast show that tours the elementary schools in the spring. This does not have to be a name, but it can only be about 35-45 minutes long." Send complete script. Computer printout submissions acceptable, "Please no loose pages. Reports negatively within 1 year, but acceptance takes longer because we try to fit a wanted script into the balanced season. We sometimes hold a script longer than a year if we like it but cannot immediately find the right slot for it. Next year we will be doing the world premier of *Anna's Brooklyn Promise*, which we've had since 1983."

Recent Titles: *Legacy* by John Fenn.

‡STORY SOURCE, Suite 230, 4010 Dupont Circle, Louisville KY 40207. (502)896-2494. Senior Editor: Vicki Ragsdell. Publishes 15-20 short pieces, 5-8 longer plays and programs/year. "We publish skits, one-act plays and other creative programs for churches and other religious groups. Our customers include members of every mainline denominational point of view. We especially need Christmas, Easter and missions scripts." Submit query and synopsis (for longer plays); complete ms (for skits and creative programs). Reports in 3 months. Royalty negotiable (for longer plays). Pays outright purchase from $10-250 (skits, programs).
Needs: "Modern, anachronistic settings preferred over Biblical settings needing full costume. Modern parables are also good."
Tips: "Basic Biblical concepts and images are better than complicated or extremist doctrinal ideas. No religious/doctrine terminology . . . use regular language please. Use sharp, clear dialogue. Humor! No 'preachiness' or moralizing. Let the action and plot speak for itself. We are looking for fresh ideas and approaches. Surprise us."

TEJAS ART AND POETRY PRESS, 207 Terrell Rd., San Antonio TX 78209. Editor: Robert Willson. Publishes plays relating to the American Indian experience, by American Indians only. Submit complete ms. Reports in 2 months. Pays royalty.

THEATER ARTISTS OF MARIN, Box 473, San Rafael CA 94915. (415)454-2380. Artistic Director: Charles Brousse. Produces 5-6 plays/year. Professional non-equity productions for a general adult audience. Submit complete ms. Reports in 3 months. Pays outright $250.
Needs: "All types of scripts: comedy, drama, farce. Prefers contemporary setting, with some relevance to current issues in American society. Will also consider 'small musicals,' reviews or plays with music." No children's shows, domestic sitcoms, one man shows or commercial thrillers.

THEATREWORKS, University of Colorado, Box 7150, Colorado Springs CO 80933. (303)593-3232. Producing Director: Whit Andrews. Produces 4 full-length plays/year and two new one-acts. "New full-length plays produced on an irregular basis. Casts are semi-professional and plays are produced at the university." Submit query and synopsis. One-act plays are accepted as Playwrights' Forum competition entries—submit complete ms. Deadline December 15; winners announced February 15. Two one-act competition winners receive full production, cash awards and travel allowances. Acquires exclusive regional option for duration of production. Full rights revert to author upon closing. Pays $300-1,200.
Needs: Full lengths and one-acts—no restrictions on subject. "Cast size should not exceed 20; stage area is small with limited wing and fly space. Theatreworks is interested in the exploration of new and inventive theatrical work. Points are scored by imaginative use of visual image. Static verbosity and staid conventionalism not encouraged." No formulaic melodrama or children's plays.
Tips: "Too often, new plays seem far too derivative of television and film writing. We think theatre is a medium which an author must specifically attack. The standard three-act form would appear to be on the way out. Economy, brevity and incisiveness favorably received."

THEATREWORKS/USA, 890 Broadway, New York NY 10003. (212)595-7500. Artistic Director: Jay Hamick. Associate Artistic Director: Barbara Pasternack. Produces 3 new musical plays/season. Produces professional musicals that primarily tour but also play (TYA contract) at an off-Broadway theatre for a young audience. Submit query and synopsis or sample song. Reports in 6 months. Buys all rights. Pays 6% royalty; offers $1,500 advance against future royalties for new, commissioned plays.
Needs: Musicals and plays with music. Historical/biographical themes (ages 9-15), classic literature, fairy tales, and issue-oriented themes suitable for young people ages 9-15. Five person cast, minimal lighting. "We

like well-crafted shows with good dramatic structure—a protagonist who wants something specific, an antagonist, a problem to be solved—character development, tension, climax, etc. No Saturday Afternoon Special-type shows, shows with nothing to say or 'kiddie' theatre shows."
Tips: "Writing for kids is just like writing for adults—only better (clearer, cleaner). Kids will not sit still for unnecessary exposition and overblown prose. Long monologues, soliloquies and 'I Am' songs and ballads should be avoided. Television, movies, video make the world of entertainment highly competitive. We've noticed lately how well popular children's titles, contemporary and in public domain, sell. We are very interested in acquiring adaptations of this type of material."

TRINITY SQUARE ENSEMBLE, Box 1798, Evanston IL 60204. (312)328-0330. Artistic Director: Karen L. Erickson. Produces 4-6 plays/year. "Professional non-equity company, member of League of Chicago Theatres, ensemble company of artists. We look for scripts adapted from classics suited to our ensemble as well as new works. Writers are encouraged to research our company. We produce new children's pieces—must blend stories with school curriculum." Send query and synopsis. "We do not want full ms submissions. If we request, then we'll return." Reports in 6 months. Obtains negotiated percentage of rights, ususally 10%.
Needs: Cast: prefer no more than 10. Set: simpler the better.
Tips: "Our ensemble is 70% women/30% men. Keep this in mind as you develop scripts. No male-dominated, fluffy comedies. Get to know us—write for our performers. Looks for strength in female characters."

THE VANCOUVER PLAYHOUSE, 543 West 7th Ave., Vancouver, British Columbia V5Z 1B4 Canada. (604)872-6622. Artistic Director: Larry Lillo. Produces 8 plays/year. Professional productions for a general audience. Submit complete ms. Reports in 2 months. Obtains all rights. Pays 4-10% royalties.

‡VIGILANTE PLAYERS, INC., MSU Media and Theatre Arts. Bozeman MT 59717. (406)994-5884. Artistic Director: John M. Hosking. Produces 3-4 plays/year. Plays by professional touring company that does productions by or about people and themes of the Northwest. "Past productions were concerned with homeless people, agriculture, literature by Northwest writers, one-company towns and spouse abuse in rural areas." Submit complete ms. Reports in 6 months. Pays $10-50/performance.
Needs: Produces full-length plays and some one-acts. "Staging suitable for a small touring company and cast limited to four actors (two men, two women). Double casting actors for more play characters is also an option."
Tips: "No musicals requiring orchestras and a chorus line. Although we prefer a script of some thematic substance, the company is very adept at comedy and would prefer the topic to include humor."

VIRGINIA STAGE COMPANY, Box 3770, Norfolk VA 23514. (804)627-6988. Artistic Director: Charles Towers. Produces 6 plays/year. 20% freelance written. Only agent submitted or professionally recommended work accepted. A professional regional theatre serving the one million people of the Hampton Roads area. Plays are performed in LORT C proscenium mainstage or LORT D flexible second stage. Works with 2 writers annually. Query with synopsis only; "sample scene or dialogue may be included." Negotiates rights and payment.
Needs: "Primarily full-length dramas and comedies which address contemporary issues within a study of broader themes and theatricality. Material must be inherently theatrical in use of language, staging or character. We do not want to see material which offers simplistic solutions to complex concerns, or is more easily suited for television or film."

WALNUT STREET THEATRE, 9th and Walnut Streets, Philadelphia PA 19107. (215)574-3550. Executive Director: Bernard Havard. Produces 5 mainstage and 5 studio plays/year. "Our plays are performed in our own space. WST has 3 theatres—a proscenium (mainstage) audience capacity 1,052; 2 studios audience capacity 79-99. We are a member of the League of Regional Theatres. We have a subscription audience, the fifth largest in the nation." Query with synopsis and 10 pages. Reports in 1 month. Rights negotiated per project. Pays royalty (negotiated per project) or outright purchase.
Needs: "Full-length dramas and comedies, musicals, translations, adaptations and revues. The studio plays must be small cast, simple sets."
Tips: "We will consider anything. Bear in mind on the mainstage we look for plays with mass appeal, Broadway style. The studio spaces are our Off-Broadway. No children's plays. Our mainstage audience goes for work that is entertaining and light. Our studio season is where we look for plays that have bite, are more provocative."

‡WASHINGTON STATE UNIVERSITY THEATRE, Theatre Arts and Drama, Pullman WA 99164-2432. (509)335-3239. Contact: General Manager. Produces 10 plays/year. Plays performed in university environment. Submit query and synopsis. Reports in 2 months. Royalties paid in accordance with standard rates.

WEST COAST ENSEMBLE, Box 38728, Los Angeles CA 90038. (213)871-1052. Artistic Director: Les Hanson. Produces 6 plays/year. Plays will be performed in one of our two theatres in Hollywood in an Equity-waiver situation. Submit complete ms. Reports in 5 months. Obtains the exclusive rights in southern California to present the play for the period specified. All ownership and rights remain with the playwright. Pays $25-45/performance.
Needs: Prefers a cast of 6-12.
Tips: "Submit the manuscript in acceptable dramatic script format."

WESTBETH THEATRE CENTER, INC., 151 Bank St., New York NY 10014. (212)691-2272. Artistic Director: Andrew Engelman. Produces 10 readings and 6 productions/year. Professional off-Broadway theatre. Query and synopsis, submit complete ms through agent only. Obtains rights to produce as showcase with option to enter into full option agreement.
Needs: "Contemporary full-length plays. Production values (i.e. set, costumes, etc.) should be kept to a minimum." No period pieces. Limit 10 actors; doubling explained.

THE WESTERN STAGE, (formerly Dianne Busch—The Western Stage), 156 Homestead Ave., Salinas CA 93901. Associate Artistic Director: Taft Miller. Produces 12-18 plays (including one acts)/year. "Summer theatre for subscriber audience in Salinas/Monterey/Carmel area. Prefer query with synopsis or submit complete ms. Reports in 2 months. Obtains production rights, sometimes workshop rights. Pays 10% royalty or makes negotiable arrangements with new playwrights, $200 and up.
Needs: "Almost anything: one acts, full length—all genres and styles."

THE ANN WHITE THEATRE, (formerly the Wo/Man's Showcase, Inc.), 5266 Gate Lake Rd., Fort Lauderdale FL 33319. (305)772-4371. Artistic Director: Ann White. Produces 6 plays/year. "Alternative theatre, professional productions for mature audiences. Plays performed in various settings: libraries, theatres, colleges and universities, hotels and dinner theatres." Conducts annual playwrights' competition and festival. Send mss August through November 15 for productions in Spring. SASE for guidelines. Winning playwright receives $500.

WICHITA STATE UNIVERSITY THEATRE, Box 31, Wichita State University, Wichita KS 67208. (316)689-3185. Artistic Director: Richard Welsbacher. Produces 16 plays/year. "College audience." Submit complete ms. Reports in 2 months. Obtains rights to stage one production (4 performances). "Writer's expenses are paid to see final rehearsals and performance."
Needs: For the contest, full-length play of 90 minutes (minimum) or a group of related one-acts.
Tips: "No children's plays. Plays submitted should be original, unpublished and previously unproduced. Authors must be graduate or undergraduate college students." Send SASE for guidelines.

WOOLLY MAMMOTH THEATRE COMPANY, Box 32229, Washington DC 20007. (202)393-1224. Artistic Director: Howard Shalwitz. Literary Manager: Grover Gardner. Produces 5 plays/year. 50% freelance written. Produces professional productions for the general public in Washington, DC. 2-3 scripts/year are unagented submissions. Works with 1-2 unpublished/unproduced writers annually. Accepts unsolicited scripts; reports in 6 weeks on scripts; very interesting scripts take much longer. Buys first- and second- class production rights. Pays 5% royalty.
Needs: "We look only for plays that are highly unusual in some way. Apart from an innovative approach, there is no formula. One-acts are not used." Cast limit of 8; no unusually expensive gimmicks.

YWAM/ACADEMY OF PERFORMING ARTS, (formerly Company Theatre), Box 1324, Cambridge, Ontario N1R 7G6 Canada. Artistic Director: Stuart Scadron-Wattles. Produces 3 plays/year. Semi-professional productions for a general audience. Send query and synopsis. Reports in 6 months. Pays $50-100/performance.
Needs: "One-act or full-length; comedy or drama; musical or straight; written from a biblical world view." No cast above 10; prefers unit staging.
Tips: Looks for "non-religious writing from a biblical world view for an audience which loves the theatre. See trends toward shorter scenes. Playwrights should be aware that they are writing for the stage—not television."

ALWAYS submit manuscripts or queries with a self-addressed, stamped envelope (SASE) within your country or International Reply Coupons (IRC) purchased from the post office for other countries.

Screenwriting

When Steven Spielberg judged Alice Walker's novel *The Color Purple* as "a good read," he was probably giving it his highest compliment. The term refers not to a literary work's artistic, intellectual, cultural or moral merits, but to the ease of reading it. Successful screenplays are always a good read: page turners, easily understood by high-speed readers, and requiring little thought or reflection. A well-constructed, fast-moving story is paramount in Hollywood.

Studios and most agents employ professional readers, who read perhaps a dozen or more scripts a week and write one- to three-page synopses, including their own reactions to the story. A story that hurtles from scene to scene at breakneck speed stands the best chance of making it past the reader and to the studio executive.

Screenplay writing is a highly conventional craft, and the page's appearance is an important convention. Make sure that the screenplays you study are not "after-the-fact" transcripts of the movie, since those formats are different.

Actual screenplays are becoming easier to obtain. Try university libraries or your state film office. *Five Screenplays by Preston Sturgess* is a good example of actual screenplays (edited with introduction by Brian Henderson, University of California Press, $18.95). So is *The Best American Screenplays*, a collection of 12 classic and modern screenplays (edited by Sam Thomas, Crown Books, $24.95).

Watching a movie while simultaneously following the script will help you learn how screenwriting achieves the maximum effect with minimal words, and how a good script can build a character's inner conflict without actually describing it to the reader. Each scene contains or develops at least one conflict, which is resolved in an unexpected way. Description is usually not objective ("Bobbi, a neatly-coiffed 40-year old woman..."), but impressionistic ("Bobbi, 40 and holding...").

Screenwriting looks deceptively easy because there are so few words on the page (most screenplays average about 150 words per page). One page is roughly equivalent to one minute of screen time, and should take about 20 second to read. Scene divisions are clearly outlined in scripts.

Studios invest in topical subjects, rather than obscure ones. Newspapers, magazines, radio and TV stories which excite, infuriate or inspire writers, or the public, are often the sources for filmscripts. Paradoxically, studios are always "looking for something fresh." This usually means a new angle on an old theme. Modernizing classic films and plays is another route, since the structure and major characters are already there.

Most Hollywood movies concern relationships, e.g., boy-meets-loses-regains-girl, and include the traditional trio of character, plot and idea. Although the major market is still 14- to 25-year-olds, more attention and money are being given now to mature as well as eclectic scripts. Of the five "Best Director" nominees for the 1988 Academy Awards, none was an American. Hollywood seems more receptive now to an American public that is less provincial and more concerned with global affairs and other cultures. However, staples that continue to attract Hollywood script hunters include action, adventure, horror, and comedy, especially romantic comedies. Trends are unpredictable, though, and your best bet is to write the kind of story that you would enjoy seeing on screen.

Books offering various techniques, hints, and conventions include Irwin Blacker's *Elements of Screenwriting* (Macmillan, $4.95). Lajos Egri's *The Art of Dramatic Writing* (Simon and Schuster, $10.95), Syd Fields' *Screenplay* and *Screenwriter's Workbook* (Dell, $8.95); and *Successful Scriptwriting*, by Jurgen Wolff and Kerry Cox (Writer's Digest Books, $18.95).

The lower the budget, the more attractive your script. Large casts, many locations, special effects and costumes all require logistics, time and extra personnel. Yet, a $30-million dollar epic well told will not be ignored. And there is always the chance, though a studio may pass on your script, they may hire you to rewrite a current project. The vast majority of scripts that are bought are not filmed. Studios keep them "in development"—on the back burner—for years or even longer.

Often studios will buy your script only with provisions that you, or another writer, will rewrite it to their specifications. Each of these "development deals" is different, taking into account many variables, including co-writers, budgets, deadlines, percent-of-profits vs. up-front money, and video and foreign rights. A good development deal will pay, for example, $25,000 for a first draft, plus $10,000 for each of several rewrites, plus a bonus of two or three times that amount if filming begins, and a similar bonus if filming is completed.

Treatments or synopses of screenplays usually run from one to ten pages. They read like a narrative short story, but contain little or no dialogue. Many experienced writers will submit them as a trial balloon to either their agent or a producer. However, treatments are not really a good venue for a first-timer to find work. If a studio or producer happens to like your treatment, he will probably insist on buying it and then hire a proven screenwriter. Might as well prove that you can do it by writing the screenplay yourself.

Registering your script (for $10) at the Writer's Guild (8955 Beverly Blvd., Los Angeles CA 90048) is a good idea. Doing so offers no legal protection, but it does offer proof that on said date you came up with a particular idea, treatment or script.

In selling work, many screenwriters find it's best to have an agent since studios, producers and stars often return unsolicited manuscripts unopened to protect themselves from plagiarism charges. Listings in *Writer's Market* specify when an agented submission is required; other listings have indicated an openness to unsolicited submissions. For more detailed information on agents, see the Author's Agents section of this book.

Two daily trade publications record in detail the production status, box office figures, and future plans of Hollywood films: *The Daily Variety* ($85 year, $70 for six months for surface mail, arriving about a week after publication. 1400 N. Cahuenga Blvd., Hollywood CA 90028. 213-469-1141), and *The Hollywood Reporter* ($89 year for Monday-Friday, $65/year weekly for surface mail. Airmail is $139 for New York and $245 elsewhere. 6715 W. Sunset Blvd., Hollywood CA 90028. 213-464-7411).

In addition to the trade publications, there's also the Independent Feature Project (309 Santa Monica Blvd., Santa Monica CA 90401. 213-451-8075) a nonprofit support group. Their monthly newsletter "Montage" is included in the annual membership fee of $60. Tapes of seminars/speeches by noted industry professionals (*including screenwriters*) are $20 (non-members) for a set of two. The Sundance Insititute, Robert Redford's Utah-based production company, accepts unsolicited scripts from those who have read the Institute's submission guidelines which they will send for an SASE (Production Bldg. 7, Room 10, 4000 Warner Blvd., Burbank CA 91522). Every January they choose a few scripts and engage the writers in a five-day program of one-on-one sessions with seasoned pros. In June the process is repeated, and also includes a videotaping of sections of chosen scripts, again with close guidance and advice from professionals. Says the Institute's Sharon Topping, "We don't produce features ourselves, but can often introduce writers to those who do."

Producers that need cable TV material are marked with the symbol (□).

ALEXI PRODUCTIONS LTD., Box 8482, Universal City CA 91608. (818)843-3443. Contact: Nikolai Alexandrov. "All of our productions are done in Europe for an international audience. Mostly *documentarily* oriented, with comedy or drama and little or no violence. Intended to entertain, and to educate." Buys 3 scripts/year. To this date, all material has been submitted in London by Europeans. We are just opening up to the idea of using American writers." Buys all rights. Reports in 6 weeks.

Needs: "We do from one-hour to five-hour material. Again, it must be an entertaining documentary." Submit synopsis/outline.
Tips: "Be honest in evaluating your material's potential." Looks for "originality, humor and the ability to *properly research material*."

□**BACHNER PRODUCTIONS, INC.**, 360 First Ave., #5D, New York NY 10010. (212)673-2946. President: Annette Bachner. Produces material for television, home video cassettes, cable TV. Buys 4 scripts/year. Buys all rights. No previously produced material. Does not return unsolicited submissions. "Do not want unsolicited material." Reports on queries in 1 months; on solicited submissions in 2 months.
Needs: 35mm and 16mm films, realia, tapes and cassettes. Natural history subjects only. Query. Pays by outright purchase in accordance with Writers Guild standards.
Tips: Looks for writers with "experience in visual media."

‡**BLAZING PRODUCTIONS, INC.**, Suite 125, 4712 Avenue N, Brooklyn NY 11234. Producer: David Krinsky. Produces material for "major and minor theatrical distribution of quality low budget 35mm films." Buys 1-3 scripts/year. Buys all rights. No previously produced material. Reports in 2 weeks on queries; 1 month on mss.
Needs: Films (35mm), phonograph records. "I need well-written, original, low budget movie screenplays in the comedy, drama, actions and thriller genres *only*." Submit synopsis/outline. "Send synopsis of film and I'll contact if I wish to see script. Send SASE." Payment "depends—sometimes percentage, sometimes outright, sometimes both."
Tips: "Send me a one page synopsis of the proposed screenplay *only*—I do not wish to read the book. Writers should be flexible and open to suggestion regarding changes/improvements in their material. Intelligent scritps with teenage characters are an easier sell. No exploitation comedy or slashers. Don't expect instant sales. Once I approve a script, my investors have to approve. Be patient. Send standard script format."

‡**CAREY-IT-OFF PRODUCTIONS**, Suite 4, 14316 Riverside Dr., Sherman Oaks CA 91423. (818)789-0954. President: Kathi Carey. Audience is general moviegoers. Works with 5-6 writers/year. Buys all rights. No previously produced material. Reports in 6 weeks on queries; 3 months on mss.
Needs: 35mm films. Wants feature films—strong male and female leads, action/adventure or suspense/thriller or police/action and dramas. Query with synopsis. Makes outright purchase in accordance with Writer's Guild standards.
Tips: "Keep in mind that feature films/film packages need stars in the lead roles and these roles should be written with a star's ego in mind."

□**THE CHAMBA ORGANIZATION**, 230 W. 105th St., #2-A, New York NY 10025. President: St. Clair Bourne. Produces material for "the activist-oriented audience; the general audience (PG), and in the educational film market we aim at high school and adult audiences, especially the so-called 'minority' audiences. Assignments are given solely based upon our reaction to submitted material. The material is the credential." 100% freelance written. 100% of scripts produced are unagented submissions. Buys 2-4 scripts/year. Works with 3 unpublished/unproduced writers annually. Computer printout submissions acceptable; prefers letter-quality.
Needs: "I concentrate primarily on feature film projects and unique feature-length documentary film projects. We prefer submission of film treatments first. Then, if the idea interests us, we negotiate the writing of the script." Also needs scripts for music videos and material (film) for cable television. Query with a brief description of plot, thumbnail descriptions of principal characters and any unusual elements. Payment negotiable according to Writers Guild standards.
Tips: Trends in screen include "a critical examination of traditional American values and dissastisfaction with 'yuppie ideology.' "

THE CHICAGO BOARD OF RABBIS BROADCASTING COMMISSION, 1 South Franklin St., Chicago IL 60606. (312)444-2896. Director of Broadcasting: Mindy Soble. "Television scripts are requested for *The Magic Door*, a children's program produced in conjunction with CBS's WBBM-TV 2 in Chicago." 26 scripts are purchased per television season. Buys all rights. Reports in 1 month. Writers guidelines for #10 SASE.
Needs: "*Magic Door*, is a weekly series of 26 shows that contain Jewish content and have universal appeal. The program take place backstage in a theatre where a company of actors brings stories to life for a puppet-child, Mazel. (Mazel is a large hand puppet who is worked by a member of the company, Wendy). The company consists of approximately 30 actors and actresses. Most of the programs utilize 3 or 4 of the above, including Wendy." Submit synopsis/outline, resume or a completed script with the right to reject. Outright purchase of $125.
Tips: "A Judaic background is helpful yet not critical. Writing for children is key. We prefer to use Chicago writers, as script rewrites are paramount."

CINE/DESIGN FILMS, INC., 255 Washington St., Denver CO 80203. (303)777-4222. Producer/Director: Jon Husband. Produces educational material for general, sales-training and theatrical audiences. 75% freelance written. 90% of scripts produced are unagented submissions. "Original solid ideas are encouraged." Computer printout submissions acceptable. Rights purchased vary.
Needs: "Motion picture outlines in the theatrical and documentary areas. We are seeking theatrical scripts in the low-budget area that are possible to produce for under $1,000,000. We seek flexibility and personalities who can work well with our clients." Produces 16mm and 35mm films. Send an 8-10 page outline before submitting ms or script. Pays $100-200/screen minute on 16mm productions. Theatrical scripts negotiable.
Tips: "Understand the marketing needs of film production today. Materials will not be returned."

‡**CORMAN PRODUCTIONS**, 6729 Dume Dr., Box 371, Malibu CA 90265. (213)457-7524. Producer: Dick Corman. Estab. 1987. Material for feature films and television needed. Buys 10-12 scripts or stories in treatment format per year. Buys all rights. No previously produced material.
Needs: Tapes, cassettes and videotapes. Wants true stories, any genre, short stories. Query with synopsis. Material is optioned for studios and networks.
Tips: "We are looking for the unusual, different stories, items which haven't reached the news wire services. High concept will continue to be the front runner in the business. Happy, fun-oriented stories will also begin surfacing."

□**DA SILVA ASSOCIATES**, 137 E. 38th St., New York NY 10016. Executive Producer: Raul da Silva. 10% freelance written. Produces material for entertainment audiences. Must work with published/established writers. Rights purchased vary. "If possible, we share profits with writers, particularly when resale is involved." Computer printout submissions acceptable; prefers letter-quality.
Needs: "We produce both types of material: on assignment and proprietary." Produces video, film, drama, comedy, and documentaries with human potential themes only. No "handicapped conquers" plots sought; 35mm films, tapes and cassettes. Also produces material for cable TV (drama/comedy). "Generally we work on assignment only. We have a selection of writers known to us already." Cannot handle unsolicited mail/ scripts. Open to credit sheets. Pays in accordance with Writers Guild standards. Pays expenses of writers on assignment.
Tips: "Open to synopses with SASE, only when concept is fresh, original and high unusual."

FELINE PRODUCTIONS, 1125 Veronica Springs Rd., Santa Barbara CA 93105. Executive Producer: Deby DeWeese. Produces material for educational institutions, non-profit agencies and home video markets. Number of scripts purchased "varies year to year—rarely more than 10/year." Buys all rights or first rights. Previously produced material OK. Reports in 1 month.
Needs: "Low-budget 30- and 60-minute scripts in dual slide or video format. Fiction or non-fiction. Alternative media scripts encouraged. Particularly interested in feminist slant. Also looking for gay and/or lesbian-oriented themes. Prefer single-camera approach. Need good 15-30 minute radio sci-fi scripts with more traditional slant." Multimedia kits, slides, tapes and cassettes, videotapes (both ½ inch and ¾ inch). Query.
Tips: "All material must be feminist. No military themes. Delete violence and sexism. Our audience is radical, educated, politically savvy—qualities you need to produce the scripts we buy. Actively seeking lesbian theatre scripts that can be produced on video."

‡**GI-STEP AUDIO/VISUAL**, 5202 Liberty Heights Ave., Baltimore MD 21207. (301)466-2417. President: Timothy Parker. Produces material for children, 6-12, young adults/teens, men and women. Buys 50-100 scripts/year. No previously produced material. Reports in 2 weeks on queries; 1 month on mss. Catalog for #10 SAE and 5 first class stamps.
Needs: Tapes and cassettes, videotapes. "We are looking for exciting adventure stories that can be adapted to audio cassette with sound effects for children and romantic stories that can be adapted to audio cassette. Also, very well researched how-to-do that could be adapted to audio or video cassette." Submit completed script. Pays $250-1,250.
Tips: "Since we adapt all material to audio and video cassettes, make the stores interesting from that viewpoint, with something refreshing and innovative about them. We place no limit on creativity, and we accept material ranging from horror and love stories, to children's fantasy tales and mysteries. The material submitted should be between 2,000 and 3,500 words. These are modern times, and people's interests are diverse and varied. The biggest challenge to writers is keeping stories and plots creative and unpredictable, while maintaining the reader's or listener's interest entirely from start to finish."

HEAPING TEASPOON ANIMATION, 4002 19th St., San Francisco CA 94114. (415)626-1893. Creative Director: Chuck Eyler. Produces animated material for all ages. Produces 1-2 scripts/year. Rights purchased "depend on material." Previously produced material OK "if not produced in animation and suitable for it." Reports on queries in 2 weeks; on mss in 1 month. Catalog for #10 SAE.
Needs: Films (35mm). Produces "clever 30-second public service announcements, educational film ideas

and/or scripts and feature scripts.'' Query with samples or submit complete script. Payment ''depends on situation.''

Tips: ''Animation has its own world. We prefer to do things that can't be done in live action—those that exploit caricature and exaggeration.''

KOCH MARSCHALL PRODUCTIONS, INC., 4310 N. Mozart St., Chicago IL 60618. (312)463-4010. Contact: Sally Marschall, Literary Division. Produces material for general film audience. Previously produced plays OK. Reports on queries in 3 months; on mss in 3 weeks.

Needs: Films (35mm). Looking for ''film scripts for feature films, 1½-2 hours. Should be either dramatic and/or light comedy. No exploitation or violence.'' Query with samples or synopsis/outline. Makes outright purchase or pays in accordance with Writers Guild standards. Payment ''depends on script.''

Tips: ''Originality is important. No copy-cat material.'' Seeks ''strong story'' with interesting, well-developed characters.

□**LEE MAGID PRODUCTIONS**, Box 532, Malibu CA 90265. (213)463-5998. President: Lee Magid. Produces material for all markets, teenage-adult; commercial—even musicals. 90% freelance written. 70% of scripts produced are unagented submissions. Buys 20 scripts/year; works with 10 writers/year. Works with ''many'' unpublished/unproduced writers. Buys all rights or will negotiate. No previously produced material. Does not return unsolicited material. Query for electronic submissions. Reports in 6 weeks.

Needs: Films, sound filmstrips, phonograph records, television shows/series, videotape presentations. Currently interested in film material, either for video (television) or theatrical. ''We deal with cable networks, producers, live-stage productions, etc.'' Works with musicals for cable TV. Prefers musical forms for video comedy. Submit synopsis/outline and resume. Pays in royalty, in outright purchase, in accordance with Writers Guild standards, or depending on author.

Tips: ''We're interested in comedy material. Forget drug-related scripts.''

□**MEDIACOM DEVELOPMENT CORP.**, Box 1926, Simi Valley CA 93062. (818)991-5452. Director/Program Development: Felix Girard. 80% freelance written. Buys 10-20 scripts annually from unpublished/unproduced writers. 50% of scripts produced are unagented submissions. Query with samples. Computer printout submissions acceptable. Reports in 1 month. Buys all rights or first rights.

Needs: Produces charts; sound filmstrips; 16mm films; multimedia kits; overhead transparencies; tapes and cassettes; slides and videotape with programmed instructional print materials, broadcast and cable television programs. Publishes software (''programmed instruction training courses''). Negotiates payment depending on project.

Tips: ''Send short samples of work. Especially interested in flexibility to meet clients' demands, creativity in treatment of precise subject matter. We are looking for good, fresh projects (both special and series) for cable and pay television markets. A trend in the audiovisual field that freelance writers should be aware of is the move toward more interactive video disk/computer CRT delivery of training materials for corporate markets.''

□**NICKELODEON MTV NETWORKS, INC.**, 1775 Broadway, New York NY 10019. (212)713-6409. Director of on-air productions: Betty Cohen. Produces material for age-specific audience aged 2-15. Now in 18 million homes. Buys negotiable rights. Reports in 1 month.

Needs: ''Full channel children's programming for cable TV. Value-filled, non-violent material desired.'' Submit resume and programming ideas (2-3 page explanations). Phone first for information and release forms. Pays variable rate. Also utilizes writers with promotional background for short-format, on-air spots for both Nickelodeon and Nick at Nite, our overnight service of ''TV for the TV generation.''

PACE FILMS, INC., 411 E. 53rd Ave., New York NY 10022. (212)755-5486. President: R. Vanderbes. Produces material for a general theatrical audience. Buys all rights. Reports in 2 months.

Needs: Theatrical motion pictures. Produces and distributes 35mm motion pictures for theatrical and videocassettes. Query with synopsis/outline and writing background/credits. Completed scripts should be submitted together with an outline. Pays in accordance with Writers Guild standards.

TOM PARKER MOTION PICTURES, 18653 Ventura Blvd., Tarzana CA 91356. (818)342-9115. President: Tom Parker. Vice President: Jacqueline Parker. Produces and distributes feature length motion pictures for world-wide theatrical and home video distribution. Works with 5-10 scripts/year. Buys all rights. Previously produced and distributed ''Don't Turn Out the Light,'' ''Amazing Love Secret,'' and ''The Initiation.'' No previously produced material. Reports on mss in 5 weeks.

□ ***Open box preceding a listing indicates a cable TV market.***

Needs: Completed scripts for low budget (under 500,000) "R" or "PG" rated action/adventure, comedy, adult romance ("R"), sex comedy ("R") to be filmed in 35mm film or video (Betacam). Limited dialogue (because of subtitling for foreign markets). No heavy drama, message films, social commentaries, dope stories, bloody or weird films. Violence or sex ("R") OK but must have strong storyline. Outright purchase $5,000 to $25,000 or will consider participation and/or co-production. Submit synopsis with finished scripts. Treatment OK.

Tips: "Do not send story premises, ideas, synopsis, treatments unless you have the finished script and can submit it if requested. All material returned only if you send SASE."

‡PASETTA PRODUCTIONS, Suite 205, 8322 Beverly Blvd., Los Angeles CA 90048. (213)655-8500. Assistant to President: Lynne Osborne. "Very seldom do we consider submitted material because of the quality and other requirements." Buys all rights. No previously produced material. Reports in 6 weeks on queries; 2 months on submissions.

Needs: Television or videotape. "We do shows as we are contracted." Submit synopsis/outline or presentation of project. Pays in accordance with Writers Guild standards.

Tips: "Material must be registered with the WGA. Any funding sources secured or talent set for the show would greatly aid in getting the show produced. Writers think if they have an idea, that is enough for a show. However, we won't consider anything without funds or set talent. The shows we produce are mainly musical/variety and the writers we use are specialized and well-known in the industry."

PAULIST PRODUCTIONS, Box 1057, Pacific Palisades CA 90272. (213)454-0688. Contact: Story Department. 100% freelance written. *Family Specials* are geared toward senior high school students. Buys 4-6 half-hour scripts/year. WGA membership required. Computer printout submissions acceptable; no dot-matrix.

Needs: "We are looking for longer form one- to three-hour television specials and theatrical releases on people who have acted boldly on their moral convictions regarding human and/or Christian values." Submit complete script through agent only. "We are not interested in unsolicited manuscripts."

Tips: "Watch our *Family Specials* enough so that you have a strong sense of the sort of material we produce. We look for wit, originality of theme and approach, an unsentimental, yet strong and positive manner of approaching subject matter—intelligent, literate, un-cliché-ridden writing."

‡SCREENSCOPE, INC., 4330 Yuma NW, Washington DC 20016. (202)364-0055. President: Marilyn Weiner. Buys all rights.

Needs: "Produces entertainment material for television and theatrical release. Want only finished scripts, not interested in treatments."

□TELEVISION PRODUCTION SERVICES CORP., Box 1233, Edison NJ 08818. (201)287-3626. Executive Director/Producer: R.S. Burks. Produces video music materials for major market distributor networks, etc. Buys 50-100 scripts/year. Buys all rights. Computer printout submissions OK; prefers letter-quality. Reports in 2 weeks.

Needs: "We do video music for record companies, MTV, HBO, etc. We use treatments of story ideas from the groups' management. We also do commercials for over-the-air broadcast and cable." We are now doing internal in-house video for display on disco or internally distributed channels. Submit synopsis/outline or completed script, and resume; include SASE for response.

Tips: Looks for rewrite flexibility and availability. "We have the capability of transmission electronically over the phone modem to our printer or directly onto disk for storage."

THEME SONG: A Musical and Literary Production House, 396 Watchogue Rd., Staten Island NY 10314. (718)698-4178. Director: Lawrence Nicastro. Produces material for theatre (stage/screen); radio; television (entertainment/educational documentary). Buys 50 scripts/year. Buys first rights. Previously published material OK, if a revision is sought. Reports in 1 month.

Needs: Phonographs records, tapes and cassettes and ¾" video tape. Query. "I'll answer each query individually. We enjoy newsworthy subjects and investigative/collaborative themes." Pays negotiable royalty.

Tips: "I am interested in political lyrics/songs and in concrete criticism of American life and ways of improving our condition; also international themes or cooperative themes."

‡VALLEY STUDIOS, Suite A-1, 292 Gibraltar Dr., Sunnyvale CA 94089. (408)747-1491. Producer: Sara McConnell. Estab. 1988. Material for a general film audience, teen—adult. "We'll probably buy or option 3-10 feature-length scripts/year." Negotiates rights. Accepts previously produced material. Reports in 1 month on queries; 6 weeks on submissions.

Needs: Films (16/35mm). "We're looking for low-budget horror, comedy, and action scripts for full-length features. Later, we'll be open to feature-length scripts in other genres, as long as they're commercial and low-budget." Submit query with synopsis and first 15 pages. Buys by outright purchase. "We cannot return any material without SASE."

‡**VIDEO WONDERLAND INC.**, Suite 150, 2531 Jefferson N.E., Albuquerque NM 87110. (505)883-7262. President: Fred Stangle. Produces material for "ordinary people who rent our videos to learn how to perform certain skills." Buys all rights. No previously produced material. Reports in 2 weeks. Catalog for 8½x11 SAE and 3 first class stamps.

Needs: Films (100mm). "We need original scripts for how-to videos." Submit completed script. Pays 5% minimum royalty.

Tips: "If the video has never been done before, send us a script. Please send an SASE. We see how-to video scriptwriting to be a major trend in the next decade."

——— *Additional Scriptwriting Markets*

The following firms did not return a verification to update an existing listing or a questionnaire to begin a new listing by press time.

Actors Alley Repertory Theatre
American Renaissance Theater
American Stage Co.
American Stage Festival
Anthony Cardoza Enterprises
Arizona Theatre Company
Artreach Touring Theatre
At the Foot of the Mountain Theater
Attic Theatre
Baker's Play Publishing Co.
Barr Films
BNA Communications, Inc.
Bob Thomas Productions
Bosustow Video
Brad Hagert
Brien Lee & Co.
Broadway Play Publishing Inc.
Burt Munk & Co.
Capital Repertory Company
Cast Theatre
Cathedral Films, Inc.
Changing Scene Theater
Christian Broadcasting Network
Circle in the Square Theatre
Coronado Studios
Crossroads Theatre Company
Dave Bell Associates
David J. Jackson Productions, Inc.
Denver Center Theatre Company
Dorothy Chansky
DSM Producers
Dubois/Ruddy
Educational Insights
Emmy Gifford Children's Theater
Eureka Theatre
Feedback Theatrebooks

Fire Prevention Through Films, Inc.
Florida Vidcom
FMT
George Street Playhouse
Gessler Publishing Co., Inc.
Golden Rod Puppets
Huntington Playhouse
In-Sync
Industrial Media, Inc.
Inner City Cultural Center
Innerquest Communications
Insight! Inc.
Intar-Hispanic American Arts Center
John Doremus Inc./Music in the Air
Kathryn Taylor
Koch/Marschall Productions, Inc.
Long Island Stage
Lori Productions, Inc.
Los Angeles Theater Unit
Manatee Players
Manhattan Video Production Inc.
Marshfilm Enterprises, Inc.
Maryland Public Television
Media Learning Systems, Inc.
Meriwether Publishing Ltd.
Milwaukee Repertory Theater
Motivation Media, Inc.
Multi-Media Productions, Inc.
National Playwrights Showcase
Network Communications Ltd.
New Playwrights Theatre
North Carolina Black Repertory Company
Northlight Theatre
Pennsylvania Stage Co.

Phoebe T. Snow Productions
Pic
Pinnworth Productions
Playwrights Fund of North Carolina, Inc.
Primalux Video
Ran Avni/Jewish Repertory Theater
A Renaissance Theatre
Richmond Shepard Theatre Complex
Saidye Bronfman Centre
Saxton Communications Group
Sew Productions/Lorraine Hansberry Theatre
Southeastern Academy of Theatre and Music Inc.
Stages Repertory Theatre
Stagewrights, Inc.
Tel-Air Interests, Inc.
Telemation Productions, Inc. and Telemation Interactive
Teletechniques, Inc.
Theatre Calgary
Theatre Ludicrum

Theatre Rapport
Theatre Rhinoceros
Theatre Three
Theatre Virginia
24th Street Experiment
Victorian Theatre
Video Vacations Guide, Inc. and Cinematronics Inc.
Vietnam Veterans Ensemble Theatre Company
Vortex Theatre Company
Walter L. Born

Zelman Studios Ltd.

The following listings were deleted following the 1988 edition of *Writer's Market* because the company asked to have the listing removed or is no longer accepting unsolicited submissions.

Backstage Theatre (asked to be deleted)
California International Division of Joseph Nicoletti Publishing (no longer producing material)
Carroll College (asked to be deleted)
Center for Puppetry Arts (asked to be deleted)
Dakota Theatre Caravan (asked to be deleted)
Kam Theatre (unable to contact)
Lunchbox Theatre (asked to be deleted)
Meridian Gay Theatre (unable to contact)
Milwaukee Repertory Theater (asked to be deleted)
Raft Theatre (asked to be deleted)
Robert Guenette Productions (asked to be deleted)
Tutor/Tape (asked to be deleted)
Women's Theatre Project (asked to be deleted)

❝ I read—and was told frequently—about all the famous writers whose works were rejected by numerous publishers and went on to become literary classics, and was enormously heartened by this. I decided that rejection letters were simply unavoidable facts of writing life and never to take them personally. ❞

—Hester Mundis, ghost writer
Unsafe at Any Meal

Gag Writing

"A clever statement is frequently just a clever statement and not a joke," says Robert Makinson, publisher of the newsletter *Latest Jokes*. The careful gag writer will distinguish between the two and submit appropriate material to comedians and cartoonists listed in this section.

Before choosing to write for a comedian or cartoonist, decide which type of presentation is best for your ideas. Comedians need one-liners and jokes, while cartoonists need material appropriate for visual gags.

The increasing number and popularity of comedy clubs mean that more comedians have the chance to perform and need material. Magazines also look for cartoons with gags slanted to their readers. Writing gags for them can be a satisfying hobby that can add extra dollars to your bank account. Collaboration between gag writers and cartoonists or between comedy writers and comedians isn't unusual, but keep in mind that to comedians and cartoonists, humor is a business. Few writers can live by gag writing alone.

A professional approach is essential. Sending carbon copies of jokes, handwritten gags or cards bent by repeated submissions will reveal you as an amateur. Type each of your gags or jokes on a separate sheet of paper or on an index card. Submit gags in batches of 10 to 20 and always include a self-addressed, stamped envelope.

Keep careful records of your submissions. Individual cards can easily become separated, so include your name and address on the back of each card. Also include a code number in the upper left corner. A master card in your files should list the text of each joke, its code number, where and when it has been submitted and any response it received. You may also want to keep a file with a submission sheet for each market you've approached. Include the submission date and the code number of each gag sent to that particular market. If you've mailed more than one batch to the same market, keep a separate sheet for each mailing. Number each sheet and write the same number on the back of your return envelope. When your gags are returned, matching the number on the envelope with the number on the submission sheet should make it easier to check your returned material.

Many buyers hold a gag for a year or more while trying to find a market for it. If you're dealing with cartoonists who accept simultaneous submissions, be sure to inform them if a gag they are holding has been sold to someone else. If you're dealing with comedians, do not make simultaneous submissions. Wait until you receive a response or your material is returned before sending the gag to another entertainer. Since you may not be sure your material has reached a comedian, you may politely state in your cover letter that if you have not been contacted within four months, you'll assume that the comedian is not buying gags and you will market your material elsewhere.

If you're interested in writing gags for a cartoonist, your submission does not require an elaborate drawing or even a paragraph to set up the situation. A simple statement like "Mother says to child" usually will be sufficient. It's best to do the writing and leave the rest to cartoonists who like to illustrate without seeing another person's interpretation. A truly funny line should set an artist's imagination to work without any additional help from the writer.

Captions should be simple and the humor universal. If you study cartoonists' work in books and magazines, you'll find that most cartoonists use timely gags that focus on the audiences' newest crazes. "Capitalize on current trends and popular topics," says one cartoonist. Some popular topics for cartoonists and comedians include health fads and trends, young families, family interaction and even the "social phenomenon of day care." A growing number of gags are wanted for teens and their interests. Avoid submitting gags that insult people's religions or nationalities; you're hoping to entertain audiences, not insult them.

Gag writers working with cartoonists are paid after the cartoonist receives a check from the publication. Magazines may pay from $10-350 per cartoon. The writer usually earns 25%

commission on the selling price. The commission may go as high as 50% if the cartoonist submits a sketch and sells only the writer's gag line, not the finished cartoon. Current rates range from $2-82.

Comedians generally buy their material one-liner at a time, although some do buy entire monologues. Payment rates for this type of writing vary greatly. Comedians often pay $10-20 for a one-liner, but some pay more and others less.

Although comedians are invited to be listed in *Writer's Market*, many decline because they lack the time or staff to handle unsolicited material. Others choose not to be listed because they don't want their audiences to know they don't write all their own material.

But don't let the lack of a listing keep you from submitting. Familiarize yourself with a comedian's style and subject matter and compose several jokes tailored to that performer. Send your material to the comedian in care of the theater, nightclub or TV station where he is performing. Remember not to send simultaneous submissions.

There is much coincidental duplication of jokes; don't complicate the problem by sending the same material to different comedians. Some entertainers are hesitant to look at an unfamiliar writer's material, fearing they'll be accused of stealing ideas. If you should hear a joke very similar to one of your own, don't panic. Many jokes and stories are in the public domain and may be used by anyone. Jokes and stories that are truly your own, derived from your own life experiences, may be submitted for copyright protection (see the Business of Writing section on Copyrighting Your Writing).

Cartoonists and comedians are not the only markets humor writers should consider. Read Sol Saks' *The Craft of Comedy Writing* (Writer's Digest Books) for information on humor writing for TV, radio, film and theatre. Many of the listings in *Writer's Market* also will consider humorous material. Some greeting card companies are interested in humorous verse, and many magazines buy short humor, anecdotes and jokes to use as fillers.

For information on gag writing markets not listed in *Writer's Market*, see Additional Gag Writing Markets at the end of this section.

BANANA TIME, Condor Communications, Box 45, Station Z, Toronto, Ontario M5N 2Z3 Canada. Began buying jokes in 1987; buys 300-360 gags/year. Buys 30-40% of gags from freelance writers. Uses gags in magazine distributed to North American radio stations. Submit gags on 8½x11 paper; 10 in one batch. Reports in 2 months. Makes outright purchase of $2 (Canadian). Pays upon acceptance. Sample copy and writers guidelines $3.
Needs: "We want zingers about the boss, colleagues, wives, kids, girlfriends, etc.; one-liners on any topics suitable for radio; and gags based on current news, trends, and fads." No "ethnic, racist or sexist material, 'blue' material, profanity or tasteless jokes based on disasters."
Tips: "As with any writing, know your market. Observe the world around you and lampoon what you find ridiculous. If you read the paper, watch TV and observe your fellow man, you'll never run out of ideas for jokes. U.S. writers, please send SAE with 1 IRC. U.S. stamps are no good in Canada."

EDOUARD BLAIS, 2704 Parkview Blvd., Minneapolis MN 55422. (612)588-5249. Holds 250 gags/year. Works with 10-15 gagwriters/year. Prefers to work with published/established writers. Sells to sports, fitness, health, education, family, outdoor, camping and fishing publications. Recently sold material to *American Health*, *Nutrition*, and *Health Review*. Buys 25-50% of the gags received from freelance writers. Submit gags on 3x5 slips; 10-12 in one batch. Reports in 1 week. Sells cartoons for $10-50; pays gagwriters $2-12. Pays 25% commission. Writer's guidelines for #10 SAE and 1 first class stamp.
Needs: Health, fitness, hobbies, education, family, outdoors, camping, and fishing gags, rural (farm) etc. Looks for sight gags—no captions, or a minimum amount of words. "I accept gags I feel match up well with my style of drawing."
Tips: "I would especially like to receive gags on family—especially young married couples, not necessarily dealing with sex (that's OK, too), but all aspects of young family life. Gag writers should be aware of what's going on in all phases of society, the style of language being used, and new developments (like fast food, microwave, health fads, etc.)."

DAN BORDERS, 191 Alton Rd., Galloway OH 43119. (614)878-3528. Holds 35 gags/year. Works with 7 gagwriters/year. Sells to computer magazines of all kinds, trade journals, many general interest and electronic gags. Has sold material to *Computer World*, *Info World*, *Dr. Dobb's Journal*, *Radio-Electronics* and *Reader's Digest*. Eager to work with new/unpublished writers. Buys 25% of the gags received from freelance writers. Submit gags on 3x5 cards or slips. Submit 15 gags in one batch. Sells cartoons for $25-50. Pays 25% commission.
Needs: Electronics and computer gags, and environment, family and angel gags. No "girlie gags." Looks for humorists with dry humor.
Tips: "Many computer magazines are buying computer cartoons. Also electronic 'toons' are selling well. I am always ready to see good, well-thought-out ideas."

ASHLEIGH BRILLIANT, 117 W. Valerio St., Santa Barbara CA 93101. Sold about 315 cartoons last year. Self-syndicated and licensed to publications and manufacturers worldwide. Reports in 2 weeks. Pays $40.
Needs: "My work is so different from that of any other cartoonist that it must be carefully studied before any gags are submitted. Any interested writer not completely familiar with my work should first send $2 and SASE for my catalog of 1,000 copyrighted examples. Otherwise, their time and mine will be wasted."

LEONARD BRUCE, AKA "LEO", Leoleen-Durck Creations, Suite 226, Box 2767, Jackson TN 38302. (901)668-1205. Holds 20 gags/month. Works with 4 gagwriters/year. Works with a small number of new/unpublished writers each year; eager to work with new/unpublished writers. Sells to newspapers, charity publications, space publications, science fiction and science fiction movie magazines, comic book publications, and animal care publications. Submit gags on 3x5 cards. Submit 12 gags in one batch. Pays 10% commission. Buys first serial rights. Reports in 2 weeks.
Needs: Looking for gags on science fiction movie themes, comic book hero themes, themes on computers, space travel, UFOs, life on other planets, "aliens" trying to cope with our world. Also a Berry's World theme—one guy in crazy situations. No political, foreign affairs or white collar themes. Will consider gags for cartoon strips: Leotoons (science fiction "alien" themes); Fred (space exploration themes); and It's a Mad World (crazy situations in our insane world). Looks for offbeat gags, weird humor, "taking normal situations and turning them into 'sight gags' or word gags. As an example: Berry's World or Herman gag themes."
Tips: "I look for quality and good typing ability in a gagwriter. Gagwriters should be aware that gags *have* to be very funny or the whole cartoon doesn't work or sell. The gag is the main reason a cartoon sells nowadays. We are a 2 person operation and the gagwriter should have patience in working with me on the artistic and financial part of the business. Also the gag writer should work *with* the artist to help 'sell' his gags also in strip form. I would especially like to receive gags on alien life and science fiction."

‡FRANCIS H. (RUM) BRUMMER, 601 Arnold Ave., Council Bluffs IA 51503-5150. (712)323-0163. Holds 1,500 gags/year. Sells gags to general, men's, women's publications, and trade journals of all sorts. Recently sold material to *Women's World*, *VFW*, *Progressive*, *Farmer*, *American Machinist*, and *Comdex Weekly*. Submit gags on 3x5 cards or 3x5 slips. Reports in 2 days. Pays gagwriters 25%; $1.25 minimum.
Needs: Gags for computer, video, sales—all kinds, teen, travel, 'air and RV', hunting-fishing.

DON COLE, 12 Lehigh St., Dover NJ 07801-2510. (201)328-9153. Holds 312 gags/year. Sells to general interest publications; also trade journals. Worked on animated movie *The Chipmunks Great Adventure*. Works with 15 gagwriters/year. Buys 5% of the gags received from freelance writers. Submit gags on 3x5 slips; about 12 (or 1 ounce) per batch. Reports in 3 days. Sell cartoons for $10-400; pays gagwriters $2.50-100. Pays 25% commission.
Needs: General; trade journal; comic strip; or single panel gags; "*anything* funny." No off-color gags. Especially wants "topical humor, satire, anything funny, for a general audience or related to a trade."
Tips: "Send *original* work only. No gags from old magazines or cartoon books. Each gag based on its own merit. Realize that a hold is not a sale. Lengthy correspondence and status reports are usually a waste of time and money not budgeted for. I file some gags for later use in making up special batches, drawing the funniest or best slanted gags for a particular market first. After a time, I return gags I no longer want."

THOMAS W. DAVIE, 28815 4th Place S, Federal Way WA 98003. Buys 75 gags/year. Works with 10 gagwriters/year. Has sold to *Medical Economics*, *Sports Afield*, King Features, *Chevron U.S.A.*, *Rotarian*, *Saturday Evening Post*, *Ladies' Home Journal*, *Playgirl* and *Boys' Life*. Buys 30% of the gags received from freelance writers. Gags should be typed on 3x5 slips. Prefers batches of 5-25. Sells cartoons for $10-450. Pays 25% commission. Reports in 1 month. Foreign writers, no IRCs; U.S. postage only.
Needs: General gags, medicals, mild girlies, sports (hunting and fishing), business and travel gags. No pornography.
Tips: "I'm often overstocked—please don't flood me with gags."

LEE DeGROOT, Box 115, Ambler PA 19002. Pays 25% on sales.
Needs: Interested in receiving studio greeting card ideas. "I draw up each idea in color before submitting to greeting card publishers, therefore, giving the editors a chance to visualize the idea as it would appear when printed . . . and thus increasing enormously the chances of selling the idea."

STEVE DICKENSON, 1105 Tony Valley Dr., Conyers GA 30208. Nationally syndicated. Submit gags on 3x5 cards; 12-24 in one batch. Reports in 1 month. Makes outright purchase of $15.
Needs: "Looking for fresh, inventive humor that addresses the societal phenomenon of day care centers. Would also like to see material targeted to elementary school age children (first graders). I am especially in need of gags aimed at teenagers. Keep your material current and funny."

‡EPHEMERA, INC., 275 Capp St., San Francisco CA 94110. (415)552-4199. Began buying jokes in 1985; buys 200 gags/year. Works with "any writer who is irreverent, provocative and outrageously funny." Buys 85% of gags from freelancers. Uses material for slogans on novelty buttons and other novelty products. Submit gags on 8½x11 paper list of slogans. Reports in 2 weeks. Pays outright purchase. Pays when the buttons are produced (3 times a year). Writers guidelines and catalog for #10 SAE with 2 first class stamps.
Needs: "We want fresh, topical and original material. The more shocking and outrageously funny, the better: clever come-ons, occupational-related material and off-the-wall absurdities. Obscenities are OK. Be concise—every word is important on a small button. Don't send old clichés and any slogans already being produced by other companies. If you hit one out of 100 ideas, you are doing well!"

GLASSMAN, Box 46664, Los Angeles CA 90046. Buys 75 gags/year. Buys 50% of gags from freelance writers. Has performed on talk shows, at nightclubs and at conventions. Will be performing on talk shows, at comedy clubs, and at one night comedy concerts in the next year. Submit gags in one-time form typed on 8½x11 paper. No limit to number submitted on one subject. Reports in 2 weeks. Pays $15 minimum/line. Pays after the gag is performed (in a workshop situation).
Needs: Will specify slant and topic. "I like as many one-liners on that specific subject as I can get." Material must be acceptable on network TV.

MEL HELITZER, Scripps Hall of Journalism, Ohio University, Athens OH 45701. (614)594-5608. Buys 100-150/year. Uses gags as a master of ceremonies at banquets. Works with 5-6 gagwriters/year. Eager to work with new/unpublished writers. Buys 1% of the gags received from freelance writers. Submit gags on 3x5 cards; 10 or more in a batch. Reports in 1 week. Pays gagwriters $5-10. Pays on acceptance.
Needs: University-related material from professor's point of view. Subjects include faculty, administration, students, sports and curriculum. Short one-liners or one-paragraph anecdotes. No student drugs, sex or alcohol. "No blue language, but double-entendres are OK."

CHARLES HENDRICK JR., Old Fort Ave., Kennebunkport ME 04046. (207)967-4412. Buys several gags/year; sold 50-60 cartoons last year. Prefers to work with published/established writers. Sells to newspapers, magazines and local markets. Works with 6 gagwriters/year. Buys 5-10% of the gags received from freelance writers. Submit 8 gags at a time. Sells cartoons for $25-200. Pays 50% of net commission or negotiates commission. Reports in 1 month.
Needs: General family, trade (hotel, motel, general, travel, vacationers), safe travel ideas—any vehicle, and medical. Gags must be clean; no lewd sex. Mild sex OK.

REAMER KELLER, 4500 S. Ocean Blvd., Palm Beach FL 33480. (305)582-2436.
Needs: Prefers general and visual gags. Pays 25%.

MILO KINN, 1413 SW Cambridge St., Seattle WA 98106. Holds approximately 200 gags/year; sells 100-200 cartoons/year. Has sold to *Medical Economics*, *Machine Design*, *American Machinist*, *Comdex*, *Fancy Publications*, *Private Practice* and many farm publications and trade journals, etc. Works with 8-10 writers annually. Buys 25% of the gags received from freelance writers. Sells cartoons for $15-100 "and up, on occasion." Pays 25% commission.
Needs: Medical, machinist, pets, farm, woman, captionless, adventure and family gags. Sells farm, medical, office, factory, crime and general cartoons.

‡LAUGHTER GRAPHICS™, 8133 High Dr., Leawood KS 66206. (913)648-6690. President: John F. Borra. Estab. 1987. Sells to men's magazines, science magazines, general interest magazines and greeting card companies. Recent sales to *OMNI Magazine* and Hallmark Cards. Submit gags "in convenient recent writer wishes;" 12-24 in one batch. Reports in 1 month. Pays 15% commission.
Needs: "Topics are science in general, specific sciences, scientists; relationships, human foibles, work place, participatory sports and hobbies (hunting, fishing, golf, workship activities, gardening, etc.). I also need a lot of copy for greeting cards (humorous, general, birthday, get well, anniversary, congrats, etc.). There is really

nothing I absolutely wouldn't consider. Keep it reasonably tasteful, but one needn't be prudish. Don't edit yourself; let me do that."

Tips: "I draw single-panel cartoons with and without gag lines. However, I am particularly interested in cartoon ideas which need no gag lines for use in art prints as well as periodicals. I also need copy for greeting cards of all kinds. Freelance material should be fresh and timely; current trends and popular topics should be capitalized upon. We need ideas that are popular—that catch attention, are relevant and sell."

LO LINKERT, 1333 Vivian Pl., Port Coquitlam, British Columbia V3C 2T9 Canada. Works with 20 gagwriters/year. Has sold to most major markets. Prefers batches of 10-15 gags. Sells cartoons for $50-600. Pays 25% commission. Returns rejected material in 1 week. Enclose SAE and 2 first class stamps or 43¢ Canadian.
Needs: Clean, general, topical, medical, family, office, outdoors gags; captionless, pro woman sophisticated ideas. "Make sure your stuff is funny. No spreads." Wants "action gags—not two people saying something funny. No puns, dirty sex, drugs, drunks, racial or handicapped. Religion gags must be in good taste."

ART McCOURT, Box 210346, Dallas TX 75211. (214)339-6865. Began selling cartoons in 1950. Works with 15 gagwriters/year. Sells 700 cartoons/year to general/family, medical, farm and male magazines. Has sold material to *Ford Times, Furrow, Agway Coop, Medical Management*, McNaught Syndicate, *National Enquirer, American Legion* and King Features. Prefers to work with published/established writers; works with a small number of new/unpublished writers each year. Buys 50% of the gags received from freelance writers. Submit 15-20 gags at one time on 3x5 cards or slips. Sells cartoons for $10-340. Pays 25% commission. Reports in 2 days.
Needs: Family/general, medical (no gripes about doctors' bills), male, computers, hunting, fishing, and farm gags. "Something unique and up-to-date." No "crowds, ghouls, TV, mothers-in-law, talking animals or desert islands."
Tips: "I look for original, crisp wordage and fresh approach with minimal descriptions. Don't just send a punchline that has no background. Read the newspapers; be topical. Writers shouldn't be impatient; gags can make the rounds for several years."

THERESA McCRACKEN, 910 Constitution NE, Washington DC 20002. (202)547-1373. Holds 100 gags/year. Sells mostly to trade journals, but also to some general interest magazines and newspapers. Recently sold material to *Vegetarian Times, Computer Digest, American Medical News, Legal Times, CEO* and the *The Saturday Evening Post*. 10% of cartoons sold uses gagwriters' material. Sells cartoons for $10-100; pays gagwriters $2.50-25. Submit gags on 3x5 cards or slips; 10-20 in one batch. Pays 25% commission.
Needs: "I prefer to receive 10 to 20 gags on one subject at a time. My topic needs change monthly and range from locksmithing to computer repair. My favorite cartoons are captionless or ones with very short cut-lines."

‡ROBERT MAKINSON, Box 023304, Brooklyn NY 11202-0066. (718)855-5057. Began buying gags in 1979. Buys approximately 150 gags/year; works with 15 freelancers/year. Eager to work with new/unpublished writers. Purchases 20% of gags from freelancers; buys 5% of all gags received. Submit gags on numbered 3x5 slips. Submit up to 10 gags in one batch. Pays $1-3. Reports in 2 weeks. Pays $1 minimum; $2 extra "if joke reappears in a publication that pays me." Pays on acceptance.
Needs: "I need short jokes that deal with current trends. Preference is given to jokes that do not mention famous personalities. I write enough of those myself. A clever statement is freqently just a clever statement and is not a joke. Try to be unique and surprising."

TOM PRISK, Star Rt. Box 45A, Michigamme MI 49861. Sells to trade journals, newsletters, magazines, etc. Published in *The Bulletin of The Atomic Scientists, Sun, Globe, National Examiner, Byline, Medical Economics, Creative Computing, Writer's Digest*. Holds with the *Saturday Evening Post, National Enquirer, Good Housekeeping*, etc. Submit gags on 3x5 slips, 10 or more to a batch. Pays 25% commission. Reports in 3 weeks. "Foreign writers, use only American postage; I don't have the time or patience for the postal coupons."
Needs: Medical, dental, computer, office, captionless and gags with short captions. Also needs gags about writers and the writing life. "Avoid the 'rejection letters' theme and try looking at the writing biz in new offbeat ways. I would also like to see religious gags with the Christian slant and much more off-beat humor." No porn or racial prejudice slants.
Tips: "Unless gags are legibly handwritten, they should be typed out. The gags I hold are slanted to my style and market needs. Rejected gags are not necessarily considered unsalable. I look for off-beat material that takes an old or popular theme and gives it a special twist. SASE *must* be included in each batch and in *all* inquiries if a response is desired. If requested, a held gag will be returned to the writer. Otherwise, I will hold it until sold, or until I reconsider the gag and return it at a later date."

‡RIC TOWER BROADCAST SERVICES, Box 4858, St. Louis MO 63108. (314)225-7110. Began buying jokes in 1985. Buy up to 2,000 gags/year. Buys 50% of gags from freelancers. Buys 10% of gags submitted. "We publish over 400 gags a month for use by radio air personalities in the U.S. and 12 other countries." Submit gags on 8½x11 paper. Reports in 5 days. Pays $2-10 per joke on acceptance. "Regular contributors can pull down even more."

Needs: "Contributors need to keep in mind that our audience is radio air personalities. Broadcast time is valuable, and short, punchy, funny lines are the key. 'Two guys walk into a bar' jokes are funny, but they are not what we want because they're long, elaborate and simply not what people want to hear on the radio. Listen to the guys you hear on the radio every day. If the personality has his head on straight, he's presenting the type of humor we want. Topical, brief and to the point. Probably 25 words maximum."

Tips: "I'm seeing more and more comedians leaning toward satire and strong irony in their jokes. The 'yuk-yuk' guys are a thing of the past; be hip, be topical and be fresh. Your audience will like it and your bank account will like it."

LARRY ROBERTSON, 7837 SE Harrison, Portland OR 97215. (503)775-5520. Holds approximately 25 gags/year. Sells to trade journals. Recent sales to *California Highway Patrol*, *Bureau of Business Practice*, Official Detective Group, and *School Shop*. Submit gags on 3x5 cards or slips; 10 or more in one batch. Reports in 2 weeks. Pays 25% percentage arrangement.

Needs: "I'm looking for close tight slants for magazines I submit to. The writer should contact me first so I can write in detail what I need instead of just sending me gags he has in stock. I would *not* like to see gags that have been in circulation for a long time. I don't want any erotic or dirty gags."

Tips: "I find too many general gags being sent that will not sell to many trade journals. I would like the writer when first contacting me to describe what publications his gags have been selling to."

DAN ROSANDICH, Box 410, Chassell MI 49916-0410. (906)482-6234. Holds around 500 gags/year. Full-time magazine cartoonist will pay 25% of any holds that sell. Works on a monthly basis with 70-75 different middle-market magazines and trade journals. "I keep from 1,000 to 2,000 drawing in circulation at all times and need ideas relating to family life, teens, animals, computers, medicine and doctors, farming, construction, dentists and captionless ideas relating to all the above."

Tips: "Patience plays a big part in this game on the writer's behalf . . . expecting too much too soon is a dashed hope. Working close with your cartoonists helps very much. By this I mean, supplying me with the names, addresses and phone numbers of magazines you think could use my cartoons written by you. I sell cartoons to *National Enquirer* all the way down to *Contractor's Market Center*, so my needs for ideas run the gamut. Give it a try!"

JOHN W. SIDE, 335 Wells St., Darlington WI 53530. Interested in "small-town, local happening gags with a general slant." Pays 25% commission. Sample cartoon $1. Returns rejected material "immediately."

STEWART SLOCUM, (signs work Stewart), 18 Garretson Road, White Plains NY 10604. (914)948-6682. Holds about 75 gags/year. Works with 20 gagwriters/year. Sells to general interest, women's and sports publications. Recently sold material to *Lear's*, *Women's Day*, *New Woman*, *Golf Journal*, King Features, *Good Housekeeping* and the *Women's World*. Sells up to half of the gags held from freelance writers. Submit gags on 3x5 slips; 10-15 in one batch. Sells cartoons for $10-350; pays gagwriters $3.75-81.50. Pays 25% commission. Reports in 2 days.

Needs: General, family, women-in-business, computer and sports gags.

Tips: "I would especially like to receive gags on women in family and business situations, and on golf, baseball, and important holidays."

SPANKY, Box 822084, Dallas TX 75382-2084. Began buying jokes in 1984; buys 75-100 gags/year. Buys 15% of gags from freelance writers. Uses gags for comedy clubs and college performances nationwide. Submit gags on 8½x11 paper; no limit to number in one batch. Reports in 1 month. Makes outright purchase of $5-10. Pays upon acceptance.

Needs: "I perform in character, a loveable but very confused, guy (i.e. Jim on 'Taxi'). I use observational humor: a unique, view of everyday events." Currently needs material for "Regional Differences Around the Country," "Unusual Signs and Sayings," and "Questions About Life in America."

Tips: "I demand originality. Don't send anything that even sounds a little familiar to another comic's joke. Although I try to respond in 30 days, I am often on the road and don't get to review the material until weeks after it has been mailed."

SUZANNE STEINIGER, 9373 Whitcomb, Detroit MI 48228. (313)838-5204. Holds 100+ gags/year. Sells to farm magazines, sex-type periodicals, women's and general interest magazines. Works with 10-12 gagwriters/year. Prefers to work with published/established writers. Buys 30% of the gags received from freelance writers. Submit gags on 3x5 cards or 3x5 slips. Submit 30 or more gags in one batch. Pays 25% commission. Reports in 1 week.

Needs: "For the present I would like to see gags *Saturday Evening Post* style. I guess you could say general interest, but I'm looking for crazy *new* ideas. I like to see everything except detailed scenes. Writers should simplify their words and scenes. I am working on a cartoon feature. I will not say what the feature is about for fear of someone accidentally getting the same idea. I am looking for a patient writer, someone I can discuss my idea with and someone to *help*. I do like gags that are funny and less detailed. For example, a writer should say 'man to woman in restaurant' instead of 'man in crowded restaurant, waiter looking surprised to the woman next to him.' There should be less confusion. I like quick and simple gags the best. I would especially like to receive greeting card ideas.''

Tips: ''Today the gags are funnier visually. The scene should have fewer props. Fewer props made the great comics such as the Marx Brothers very funny and popular, not to mention Peanuts. There should be fewer details and more concentration on the joke, the entire *gag*. I like writers who do a good job of writing and leave the drawing to us (cartoonists). I'm also looking for simple animal gags. Animal gags are my specialty. I'd like them to be slanted for the *New Yorker* and *Saturday Evening Post*. I recently sold to the *Post* and I hope to sell to *The New Yorker*. That's my goal. And another one of my goals is to sell my one panel features to the syndicate of my choice.''

JOHN STINGER, Box 350, Stewartsville NJ 08886. Interested in general business gags. Would like to see more captionless sight gags. Currently doing a syndicated panel on business. Has sold to major markets. ''Index cards are fine, but keep gags short.'' Pays 25% commission; ''more to top writers.'' Bought about 25 gags last year. Can hold unsold gags for as long as a year.

FRANK TABOR, 2817 NE 292nd Ave., Camas WA 98607. (206)834-3355. Began selling cartoons in 1947. Holds 200 gags/year. Works with 20 gagwriters/year. Sells to trade journals. Recently sold material to *American Medical News*, *American Machinist*, *Management Accounting*, *Computing*, *Chesapeake Bay*, *Tooling & Production*, *True Detective*, *Espionage*, *Medical Tribune* and *Northern Logger*. Works with a small number of new/unpublished writers each year. Buys 5% of the gags received from freelance writers. Submit gags on 3x5 slips; 10-20 in one batch. Sells cartoons for $7.50-150; pays gagwriters $2-25. Pays 25-30% commission. Reports in 2 days.

Needs: Police; detective; fishing; health and fitness; prison situations; salesman; medical (must be funny for the doctor—no gags on big doctor bills); computer; industrial (shop gags OK); machine shop (welding); office and accounting gags. ''Cartoon spreads are wide open. I want general gags too. I look for situations in which the cartoon carries the punch; I don't care for the one-liner or illustrated joke. I need trade gags by writers who know or who will study the trade they're writing about.''

Tips: ''I am interested in reviewing ideas on strips and panels for syndication. Working on more general stuff now—too many new trade editors are sitting on or losing cartoons—I prefer larger-sized return envelope for sending copies of cartoons and detailed information via letters back to writers. I like to work closely with each writer and prefer they submit regularly in order to keep in touch. I could need a special idea from an editor's request on short notice.''

‡TASK INDUSTRIES, Box 500462, Houston TX 77250. Holds 100-300 gags/year. Sells to industry specific trade journals, and newsletters. Presently seeking individuals for extended contract assignments. For first submissions will accept 3x5 cards or slips; prefers electronic transfer. MCI Mail #346-4623; Compuserve #70411,617. Submit 7-28 gags in one batch. Reports in 2 weeks. Pays $2.50-100; on acceptance.

Needs: Gags about business, sports (diving, fishing), municipal governments, environmental issues. No lewd gags, will consider submissions for Gismo™ and Downunder™ cartoons.''

ISSAM TEWFIK, #701, 2400 Carling Ave., Ottawa, Ontario K2B 7H2 Canada. (613)828-5239. Holds 300 gags/year. Sells to general interest magazines, trade journals, men's and women's publications and newspapers. Has sold material to *Hospital Supervisor Bulletin* and *Accent on Living*. Works with 20 gagwriters/year. Eager to work with new/unpublished writers. Buys 20% of the gags received from freelance writers. Submit gags on 3x5 slips. Submit 10 or more gags in one batch. Sells cartoons for $25-100; pays gagwriters $3-10. Pays 25% commission. Reports in 1 week.

Needs: General, family, erotic, sports, law, military, insurance, medical, computers, children, detective, cars, old age, management, outdoor, money, trucking, etc. Prefers gags that are slanted towards a specific subject and a magazine. Research the magazine and slant towards its requirements. ''I will consider eagerly a well-conceived strip or panel with well-defined characters and theme (e.g., family, animal, professional, children and single people).''

Tips: ''Identify a need either in a specific magazine or a syndicate and let us work together to produce something marketable. Slanting to the different publications is the key to success.''

BOB THAVES, Box 67, Manhattan Beach CA 90266. Pays 25% commission. Returns rejected material in 1-2 weeks. May hold unsold gags indefinitely.

Needs: Gags ''dealing with anything except raw sex. Also buys gags for syndicated (daily and Sunday) panel, Frank & Ernest. I prefer offbeat gags for that, although almost any general gag will do.''

JOSEPH F. WHITAKER, 2522 Percy Ave., Orlando FL 32818. (407)298-8311. Holds 100 gags/year. Works with 6-7 gagwriters/year. Sells all types of gags. Recently sold material to *Star*, *National Enquirer*, *National Catholic News*, McNaught Syndicate and women's magazines. Prefers to work with published/established writers; works with a small number of new/unpublished writers each year. Buys 60% of the gags received from freelance writers. Submit gags on 3x5 slips; 10-15 in one batch. Sells cartoons for $10-300. Pays 25% commission. Reports in 2 weeks.

Needs: All types of gags. The best markets for cartoons/gags in 1988 will be syndicates, girlie, women, farm, advertising and insurance.

Tips: "I look for captionless gags."

_____ *Additional Gag Writing Markets*

The following listings are inactive for the 1989 edition because the firms are backlogged with submissions or asked to be deleted.

Goddard Sherman (backlogged)
Norm Drew (asked to be deleted)
Great Midwestern Ice Cream Co. (asked to be deleted)

The following firms did not return a verification to update an existing listing by press time.

"Frank"
Dave Gerard
David R. Howell
Rex F. May (Baloo)
Ter Scott
Bardulf Ueland

> 66 *I find myself fighting a fear that I'll never be able to top the previous work, but I push that thought to the back of my mind. I also find reading other writers spurs me on to begin again.* 99
>
> —**Pat Parker, author and poet**
> **Jonestown and Other Madness**

Greeting Card Publishers

The greeting card industry continues to provide freelancers with a strong market for their work. Industry leaders predict 7.1 billion cards will be sold this year, and of that number more than one third will be freelance material. Still the market remains highly competitive—successful freelancers know they must keep up with rapid changes in both taste and style.

"Greeting cards should and do move with the times, " says Joan Lackowitz, vice president of Gallant Greetings. "Keep aware of what is going on around you."

Keeping aware requires careful study of the market. A visit to your local card shop is a good first step. Take a look at the card racks, talk to the clerk and watch to see who buys what. Some card companies will provide a market list or catalog of their card lines for a self-addressed, stamped envelope or a small fee. Industry magazines, such as *Greetings*, also help to keep you informed of changes and happenings within the field.

Although you may spot several new growth areas or trends each year, some factors have remained constant and are important to keep in mind. For example, women continue to make up the largest percentage of card buyers. "Women between ages 17 and 35 buy 93 percent of all cards sold," notes Bettie Galling of Merlyn Graphics. This fact has added to the need for cards women can send to other women, she says.

The three basic card categories—traditional, studio (or contemporary) and alternative—also have remained the same for a number of years. Note, however, these categories are loosely defined and do change focus from year to year. Traditional cards, after a slight lull in popularity in the early 1980s, are once again in demand. Several editorial directors updated their listings this year to reflect a need for cards expressing traditional messages.

Alternative cards continue to increase in popularity. This category includes cards with offbeat messages or that celebrate nontraditional events such as a salary raise, a divorce or new job. Many smaller card companies have built their businesses on alternative card lines. Sparked by the success of these firms, larger firms are developing their own lines of nontraditional cards.

Most editorial directors are looking for personal, expressive verse instead of rhymed sentiments. A conversational tone is best—even for traditional cards. In fact many editors say they are looking for fresh expressions of traditional sentiments. "Think funny" may be the best advice this year, because the majority of editors say they cannot get enough humorous cards—especially ones that say something funny in a new or unique way.

Illustration has always been an important component of greeting cards, but in recent years editors say they've been looking for an even closer relationship between artwork and copy. It is important to think visually—to think of the card as an entire product—even if you are not artistically talented. Although most editors do not want to see artwork unless it is professional, they do appreciate suggestions from writers who have visualized a card as a whole unit. If your verse depends on an illustration to make its point or if you have an idea for a unique card shape or foldout, include a dummy card with your writing samples.

Payment for greeting card verse varies, but most firms pay on a per card or per idea basis, while a handful pay small royalties. Some firms will pay for card ideas and, if you are gifted artistically, complete cards are welcome. Payment is made for each separate component of the card. Some card companies prefer to test a card first and will pay a small fee for a test card idea.

Greeting card companies will also buy ideas for gift products and may use card material for a number of subsequent items. Licensing—the sale of rights to a particular character for a variety of products from mugs to t-shirts—is a growing part of the greetings industry. Because of this, however, note that most card companies buy all rights. Many companies also require writers to provide a release form, guaranteeing the material submitted is original and has not been sold elsewhere. Before signing a release form or a contract to sell all rights, be sure you understand the terms.

Submission requirements may vary slightly from company to company, so send a SASE for writer's guidelines if they are available. To submit conventional card material, type or neatly print your verses or ideas on 8 ½x11, 4x6 or 3x5 slips of paper or index cards. The usual submission includes from 5 to 15 cards and an accompanying cover letter. Be sure to include your name and address on the back of each card as well as on the cover letter. For studio cards, or cards with pop-outs or attachments also send a mechanical dummy card. For more help on card submissions, see the samples in *The Writer's Digest Guide to Manuscript Formats* (Writer's Digest Books).

A word about recordkeeping—since you will be sending out many samples, Larry Sandman, author of *A Guide to Greeting Card Writing* (also Writer's Digest Books), suggests labeling each sample with a three-letter code. Establish a master card for each verse or idea and record where and when each was sent and whether it was rejected or purchased. One way to code the cards is to give each one a code with the first letter of each of the first three words of your verse. Keep all cards sent to one company in a batch and give each batch a number. Write this number on the back of your return SASE to help you match up your verses if they are returned.

For information on greeting card publishers not listed in *Writer's Market*, see Additional Greeting Card Publishers at the end of this section.

AMBERLEY GREETING CARD CO., 11510 Goldcoast Dr., Cincinnati OH 45249. (513)489-2775. Editor: Ned Stern. 90% freelance written. Bought 250 freelance ideas/samples last year; receives an estimated 25,000 submissions annually. Reports in 1 month. Material copyrighted. Buys all rights. Pays on acceptance. Writer's guidelines for #10 SAE and 1 first class stamp. Market list is regularly revised.
Needs: Humorous, informal and studio. No seasonal material or poetry. Prefers unrhymed verses/ideas. Humorous cards sell best. Pays $40/card idea.
Tips: "Amberley publishes specialty lines and humorous studio greeting cards. We accept freelance ideas, including risque and nonrisque. Make it short and to the point. Nontraditional ideas are selling well. Include SASE (with correct postage) for return of rejects."

AMERICAN GREETINGS, 10500 American Rd., Cleveland OH 44144. (216)252-7300. Contact: Director-Creative Recruitment. No unsolicited material. "We like to receive a letter of inquiry describing education or experience, or a resume first. We will then screen those applicants and request samples from those that interest us."

CAROLYN BEAN PUBLISHING, LTD., 2230 W. Winton Ave., Hayward CA 94545. (415)957-9574. Creative Director: Andrea Axelrod. 75% freelance written. Bought 250 freelance ideas/samples last year; receives an estimated 5,000 submissions annually. Submit seasonal/holiday material 18 months in advance. Buys exclusive card rights; negotiates others. Pays on acceptance. Reports in 2 months. Writer's guidelines for SAE and 2 first class stamps.
Needs: "Our greatest need is ideas for the cards people send most: birthday and friendship. We are always looking for a new approach—if we like it, we'll try it. We are not tied down to one look, or tone. Alternative cards should be laugh-out-loud funny—not cute. We also do a complete captioned line of traditional cards for all occasions. Copy for traditional cards should be in rhymed verse that scans easily—it should read as you would say it—don't break a line in a strange place just to make it rhyme." Pays $25 but terms are negotiable.

BLUE MOUNTAIN ARTS, INC., Dept. WM, Box 1007, Boulder CO 80306. Contact: Editorial Staff. Buys 50-75 items/year. Reports in 3-5 months. Buys all rights. Pays on publication.
Needs: Inspirational (without being religious); and sensitivity ("primarily need sensitive and sensible writings about love, friendships, families, philosophies, etc.—written with originality and universal appeal"). Pays $200/card or poem.
Other Product Lines: Calendars, gift books and greeting books. Payment varies.

Tips: "Get a feel for the Blue Mountain Arts line prior to submitting material. Our needs differ from other card publishers; we do not use rhymed verse, preferring instead a more honest person-to-person style. Have a specific person or personal experience in mind as you write. We use unrhymed, sensitive poetry and prose on the deep significance and meaning of life and relationships. A very limited amount of freelance material is selected each year, either for publication on a notecard or in a gift anthology, and the selection prospects are highly competitive. But new material is always welcome and each manuscript is given serious consideration."

BRILLIANT ENTERPRISES, 117 W. Valerio St., Santa Barbara CA 93101. Contact: Editorial Dept. Buys all rights. Submit words and art in black on 5½x3½ horizontal, thin white paper in batches of no more than 15. Reports "usually in 2 weeks." Catalog and sample set for $2.
Needs: Postcards. Messages should be "of a highly original nature, emphasizing subtlety, simplicity, insight, wit, profundity, beauty and felicity of expression. Accompanying art should be in the nature of oblique commentary or decoration rather than direct illustration. Messages should be of universal appeal, capable of being appreciated by all types of people and of being easily translated into other languages. Since our line of cards is highly unconventional, it is essential that freelancers study it before submitting." No "topical references, subjects limited to American culture or puns." Limit of 17 words/card. Pays $40 for "complete ready-to-print word and picture design."

COLORTYPE, 1640 Market St., Corona CA 91720. (714)734-7410. Editor: Mike Gribble. 100% freelance writen. Buys 75 freelance ideas/samples per year; receives 200 annually. Submit seasonal/holiday material 9 months in advance. Reports in 3 weeks. Buys all rights. Pays on acceptance. Writer's guidelines/market list for 6x9 SASE.
Needs: Humorous, assemble-it-yourself cards or other novelty cards. Prefers to receive 6 or more card ideas/batch. Pays $100-150/card idea. Royalty "open for discussion."
Tips: "Prefer humorous. Photos of humorous subjects are difficult to get."

CONTENOVA GIFTS, Box 69130, Postal Station K, Vancouver, British Columbia V5K 4W4 Canada. (604)253-4444. Editor: Jeff Sinclair. 100% freelance written. Bought over 100 freelance ideas last year; receives an estimated 15,000 submissions annually. Submit ideas on 3x5 cards or small mock-ups in batches of 10-15. Buys world rights. Pays on acceptance. Current needs list for SAE and IRC.
Needs: Humorous and studio. Both risque and nonrisque. "Short gags with good punch work best." Birthday, belated birthday, get well, anniversary, thank you, congratulations, miss you, new job, etc. Seasonal ideas needed for Christmas by March; Valentine's Day by September. Prefers unrhymed verses/ideas. Risque and birthday cards sell best. Pays $50.
Tips: "Not interested in play-on-words themes. We're leaning toward more 'cute risque' and no longer using drinking themes. Put together your best ideas and submit them. One great idea sent is much better than 20 poor ideas filling an envelope. We are always searching for new writers who can produce quality work. you need not be previously published. Our audience is 18-65—the full spectrum of studio card readers. We do *not* use poetry."

CREATE-A-CRAFT, Box 330008, Fort Worth TX 76163-0008. (817)292-1855. Editor: Mitchell Lee. 5% freelance written. Buys 2 freelance ideas/samples per year; receives 300 annually. Submit seasonal/holiday material 1 year in advance. Submissions not returned even if accompanied by SASE—"not enough staff to take time to package up returns." Buys all rights.
Needs: Announcements, conventional, humorous, juvenile and studio. "Payment depends upon the assignment, amount of work involved, and production costs involved in project."
Tips: No unsolicited material. "Send letter of inquiry describing education, experience, or resume with one sample first. We will screen applicants and request samples from those who interest us."

CREATIVE DIRECTIONS, INC., Suite W 268, 323 S. Franklin Blvd., Department F, Chicago IL 60606. Editor: Teddy Miller. Submit seasonal/holiday material 1 year in advance. Reports in 6 weeks. Buys exclusive greeting card rights.
Needs: Announcements, conventional, humorous, informal, inspirational, invitations, juvenile, sensitivity, soft line and studio. Pays 5% royalty with commission-earning opportunities. Other product lines include postcards, calendars and promotions. Pays royalties from purchases.
Tips: "Length of verse is open. We are not looking for any particular style (conventional, unconventional, rhymed and unrhymed acceptable). We prefer verse that suggests: 'Let us say it for you.' We welcome new writers."

CURRENT, INC., Box 2559, Colorado Springs CO 80901. (303)594-4100. Editor: Jonna Gress. 10-15% freelance written. Bought 180 freelance sentiments or manuscripts last year; receives an estimated 1,500 submissions annually. Submit seasonal/holiday material 18 months in advance. Reports in 2 months. Buys all rights. Pays on acceptance. "Flat fee only; no royalty." Writer's guidelines for #10 SAE and 1 first class stamp.

Needs: All occasion and woman-to-woman cards; short 1-2 line puns for all occasions not too risque; short children's stories, long (6-12 lines) seasonal and sympathy inspirational verse. Pays $20-40.

Tips: "We are primarily looking for original humor of all forms, except risque, off-color sentiments. 98% of our customers are women and 85% of them are married and have children under the age of 18. Writers need to keep in mind that this is the audience we are trying to reach. We pick up trends and create our own. We suggest that writers keep abreast of what's selling at retail. Don't send traditional short prose sentiments or off-color humor because we *don't* buy it. Fresh puns for holidays such as Christmas and Easter are difficult to get. Read our direct mail catalog."

‡**EARTH CARE PAPER CO.**, 100 S. Baldwin St., Madison WI 53703. (608)256-5522. Editor: Carol Magee. Submit seasonal/holiday material 1 year in advance. Prefers to keep submissions on file rather than return by SASE. Reports in 2 months. Buys card rights. Pays on acceptance. Free writer's guidelines.

Needs: Humorous, informal, sensitivity, soft line. Prefers unrhymed verse, but will consider rhymed. Pays $25.

Tips: "Our company features cards printed on recycled paper. We are interested in humor relating to nature, environmental protection, or social issues. Submit illustration ideas with verse."

‡**FRAVESSI-LAMONT, INC.**, 11 Edison Place, Springfield NJ 07081. (201)564-7700. Editor: Ruth Golding. 45% of material bought is freelance written. Buys 6 freelance ideas/samples annually; receives 20 submissions annually. Submit seasonal/holiday material 3 months in advance. Reports in 1 week. Buys all rights. Pays on acceptance. Free writer's guidelines. Market list available to writers on mailing list basis.

Needs: Conventional, humorous, informal. Submit 10 cards in a batch.

FREEDOM GREETING CARD CO., Box 715, Bristol PA 19007. (215)945-3300. Editor: J. Levitt. 90% freelance written. Submit seasonal/holiday material 1 year in advance. Reports in 2 weeks. Pays on acceptance. Free writer's guidelines/market list. Market list available to writer on mailing list basis.

Needs: Announcements, conventional, humorous, inspirational, invitations, juvenile and sensitivity. Payment varies.

Tips: General and friendly cards sell best for Freedom.

‡**GALLANT GREETINGS**, 2654 W. Medill, Chicago IL 60647. Editor: Joan Lackouitz. 90% of material bought is freelance written. Bought 500 freelance ideas/samples last year. Reports in 1 month. Buys world greeting card rights. Pays on acceptance. Free writer's guidelines.

Needs: Announcements, conventional, humorous, informal, inspirational, invitations, juvenile, studio. Submit 20 cards in one batch.

GRAND SLAM GREETINGS, INC., 35 York St., Brooklyn NY 11201. (718)797-1204. Contact: Editorial Director. Currently we do "captioned" funny T-shirts. Reports in 2 weeks. Pays on acceptance.

Needs: Humorous ("risque is OK"), soft line and studio. Prefers unrhymed verse. Pays $50/T-shirt idea.

Other Product Lines: Tee shirts ($50).

HALLMARK CARDS, INC., Box 419580, 2501 McGee, Mail Drop 276, Kansas City MO 64141. Contact: Carol King with letter of inquiry only; no sample. Reports in 2 months. Request guidelines if not on current Hallmark freelance roster; include SASE.

Needs: Humorous and studio cards. No traditional verse.

Tips: "Purchasing humor writing for everyday and seasonal greeting cards. Because Hallmark has an experienced and prolific writing staff, freelance writers must show a high degree of skill and originality to interest editors who are used to reading the very best."

‡**LIFE GREETINGS**, Box 468, Little Compton RI 02837. (401)635-8535. Editor: Kathy Brennan. Buys 50% of material from freelancers; bought 400 samples in past year. Submit seasonal/holiday material 6 months in advance. Reports in 2 weeks. Buys all rights. Pays on acceptance. Free guidelines sheet.

Needs: Humorous, inspirational, juvenile, sensitivity.

Tips: Religious cards sell best. Marketed through Christian bookstores.

‡**LIFE LINES**, Suite 191, 375 Broadway, Laguna Beach CA 92651. (714)859-1440. Editor: George W. Tate. Estab. 1988. 100% of material bought is freelance written. Submit seasonal/holiday material 10-12 months in advance. Reports in 1 month. Provide SASE. Copyrighted. Buys all rights; pays on publication. Free writer's guidelines. Market list is regularly revised.

Needs: Announcements, conventional, informal, invitations, soft line, thank you notes.

Other Product Lines: Calendars, gift books, post cards.

Tips: "Need clever captions for upscale, food oriented cards for "Gourmet Greetings" line, typically marketed in kitchenware and gourmet shops to 30-50 year-old females."

MAINE LINE CO., Box 418, Rockport ME 04856. (207)236-8536. Editor: Marjorie MacClennen. 95% freelance written. Buys 200-400 freelance ideas/samples per year. Receives approximately 2,500 submissions/ year. Submit photocopies (1 idea per page) or index cards. Please send SASE for return of samples. Reports in 2 months. Material copyrighted. Buys greeting card rights. Pays on acceptance. Writer's guidelines for #10 SAE and 2 first class stamps. Market list is regularly revised and issued one time only.
Needs: Humorous, everyday greeting cards and postcards for modern women and men. No juvenile or religious material. Prefers unrhymed verse. Pays $50/card idea.
Other Product Lines: Postcards and notepad ideas, mugs, magnets, keychains.
Tips: "Don't submit traditional-type material. Study our guidelines. We want greeting card copy with particular appeal to contemporary people of all ages, from all walks of life and also unisex copy. Copy can also reflect the trend toward more traditional home/career values, although our cards are not traditional. Prose is better than verse; humor based on realities of life rather than on word-play most likely to be accepted. Copy that speaks, beneath the humor, a universal truth that people recognize, or copy which articulates attitudes, experiences, and feelings shared by many is most likely to be accepted. Copy that is suggestive, clever and tasteful is OK. Birthday cards and women-to-women friendship cards dealing with women's concerns are always needed. There is a demand for freelance copy from people who have an interesting perspective on modern life, expressed in a unique way, understood by many. Writers need not submit any visuals with copy but may suggest visuals. Lack of drawing ability does not decrease chances of having copy accepted; however, we also seek people who can both write and illustrate. Writers who have a contemporary illustrative style are invited to send samples or tearsheets to illustrate copy they're submitting."

‡**MANHATTAN GREETING CARD CO.**, 71-03 80th St., Glendale NY 11385. (718)894-7600. Editor: Paula Haley. 100% freelance written. Submit seasonal/holiday material 18 months in advance. Reports in 3 weeks. Pays by negotiated agreement. Free writer's guidlines.
Needs: Announcements, conventional, humorous, informal, inspirational, invitations, juvenile, sensitivity, soft line, studio, Christmas. "Christmas is eighty-five percent of the line."
Other Product Lines: Bumper stickers, calendars, gift books, greeting books, post cards, promotions. Pays $50-250.

‡**MARK I, INC.**, 1733 West Irving Park Rd., Chicago IL 60613. (312)281-1111. Editor: Alex H. Cohen. 100% freelance written. Bought 1,000 ideas/samples from freelancers last year. Submit seasonal/holiday material 9 months-1 year in advance. Reports in 2 weeks. Buys exclusive world rights for greeting cards. Pays on acceptance. Writer's guidelines for #10 SASE. Market list is regularly revised.
Needs: Humorous, juvenile, sensitivity, soft line, studio. Submit 20 cards in one batch.

‡**MERLYN GRAPHICS**, Box 1053, Canoga Park CA 91304. (818)884-5214. Editor: Bettie Galling. Estab. 1987. 75% of material bought is freelance written. Bought 36 freelance ideas/samples last year; receives 200 submissions annually. Submit seasonal/holiday material 4-6 months in advance. Reports in 1 month. Buys all rights. Pays on publication. Writer's guidelines for #10 SASE. Market list is regularly revised.
Needs: Humorous. "We pay $50 to the writer for each card published."
Other Product Lines: Calendars, post cards, posters, ideas for mugs and other gift items. "We will negotiate payment based on fair market for products other than cards as we are not yet able to determine payment."
Tips: "We want funny, clever, witty cards aimed at women's interests. We will consider others, but we are not interested in mushy hearts and flowers! We really like humor that's slightly 'twisted.' Lines that could go with 'hunk' images are also of interest."

OATMEAL STUDIOS, Box 138W3, Rochester VT 05767. (802)767-3171. Editor: Dawn Abraham. 85% freelance written. Buys 400-500 greeting card lines/year. Pays on acceptance. Reports in 6 weeks. Current market list for self-addressed, #10 SAE and 1 first class stamp.
Needs: Birthday, friendship, anniversary, get well cards, etc. Also Christmas, Chanukah, Mother's Day, Father's Day, Easter, Valentine's Day, etc., and humorous invitations. Will review concepts. Humorous material (clever and *very* funny) year-round. "Humor, conversational in tone and format, sells best for us." Prefers unrhymed contemporary humor. Current pay schedule available with guidelines.
Other Product Lines: Notepads, mugs and posters.
Tips: "The greeting card market has become more competitive with a greater need for creative and original ideas. We are looking for writers who can communicate situations, thoughts, and relationships in a funny way and apply them to a birthday, get well, etc., greeting and we are willing to work with them in targeting our style. We will be looking for mateial that says something funny about life in a new way. We tend to see a lot of the same ideas over and over. It's harder to find something different and fresh. Reading card racks is a good way for a writer to stay one step ahead."

‡**OUTREACH PUBLICATIONS**, Box 1010, Siloam Springs AR 72761. (501)524-9381. Editor Cheryl Kline. Submit seasonal/holiday material 1 year in advance. Reports in 2 months. Pays on publications. Guidelins for #10 SAE with 1 first class stamp.
Needs: Announcements, conventional, humorous, inspirational, invitations, juvenile, soft line. Material "must be useable for Christian market."

PACIFIC PAPER GREETINGS INC., Box 2249, Sidney, British Columbia V8L 3S8 Canada. (604)656-0504. Editor: Louise Rytter. 50% freelance written. Buys 20 freelance ideas/samples per year. Submit seasonal/holiday material 1 year in advance. Reports in 3 weeks. Buys all rights. Pays on acceptance. Writer's guidelines/market list for SAE with 1 IRC.
Needs: Conventional, inspirational, sensitivity and soft line, romantic. Payment negotiable. No "rude verses; nothing too lengthy and poetic."

‡**PAPERPOTAMUS PAPER PRODUCTS INC.**, Box 35008, Station E, Vancouver, British Columbia VGM 4G1 Canada. (604)874-3520. Editor: George Jackson. Buys 100% freelance written material. Buys 50 freelance ideas/samples annually; receives 100-200 submissions/year. Submit seasonal/holiday material 10-12 months in advance. Reports in 3 months. Buys all rights.
Needs: Humorous. Prefers unrhymed verse.

‡**PLUM GRAPHICS INC.**, Box 136 Prince Station, New York NY 10012. (212)966-2573. Editor: Yvette Cohen. Buys 100% of material from freelancers; purchased 21 samples in past year. Does not return samples accompanied by SASE. Reports in 3-4 months. Buys greeting card and stationery rights. Pays on publication. Free guidelines sheet/market list.
Needs: Humorous. "We don't want general submissions. We want them to relate to our next line." Prefers unrhymed verse. Greeting cards pay $20-40, depending on series and strength of line. Pays $50 for very good lines.
Tips: Sells to all ages. Generally affluent market. "Humor is strong. Short, to-the-point lines with few words work better."

RED FARM STUDIO, Box 347, 334 Pleasant St., Pawtucket RI 02862. (401)728-9300. Art Director: Mary M. Hood. Buys 50 ideas/samples per year. Reports in 2 weeks. Buys all rights. Pays on acceptance. Market list for #10 SAE with 1 first class stamp.
Needs: Conventional, inspirational, sensitivity, and soft line cards. "We cannot use risque or insult humor." Submit no more than 10 ideas/samples per batch. Pays $3 per line of copy.
Tips: "Write verses that are direct and honest. Flowery sentiments are not in fashion right now. It is important to show caring and sensitivity, however. Our audience is middle to upper middle class adults of all ages."

ROCKSHOTS, INC., 632 Broadway, New York NY 10012. (212)420-1400. Editor: Bob Vesce. "We buy 75 greeting card verse (or gag) lines annually." Submit seasonal/holiday material 1 year in advance. Reports in 1 month. Buys use for greeting cards. Writer's guidelines for SAE and 1 first class stamp.
Needs: Humorous ("should be off-the-wall, as outrageous as possible, preferably for sophisticated buyer"); soft line; combination of sexy and humorous come-on type greeting ("sentimental is not our style"); and insult cards ("looking for cute insults"). No sentimental or conventional material. "Card gag can adopt a sentimental style, then take an ironic twist and end on an off-beat note." Submit no more than 10 card ideas/samples per batch. Pays up to $50. Prefers gag lines on 8x11 paper with name, address, and phone and social security numbers in right corner or individually on 3x5 cards.
Tips: "Think of a concept that would normally be too outrageous to use, give it a cute and clever wording to make it drop-dead funny and you will have commercialized a non-commercial message. It's always good to mix sex and humor. Our emphasis is definitely on the erotic. Hard-core eroticism is difficult for the general public to handle on greeting cards. The trend is toward 'light' sexy humor, even cute sexy humor. 'Cute' has always sold cards, and it's a good word to think of even with the most sophisticated, crazy ideas. 80% of our audience is female. Remember that your gag line will probably be illustrated by a cartoonist, illustrator or photographer. So try to think visually. If no visual is needed, the gag line *can* stand alone, but we generally prefer some visual representation."

‡**ROSERICH DESIGNS LTD.**, 1050 Cindy Lane, Carpinteria CA 93013. (805)684-6977. Buys 40% of material from freelancers. Submit seasonal/holiday material 1 year in advance. Reports in 1 month. Pays on publication. Guidelines sheet/market list for SASE. Market list is available to writer on mailing list basis.
Needs: Humorous, inspirational, juvenile, sensitivity, soft line, studio.
Other Product Lines: Calendars, gift books, greeting books.

‡**MARCEL SCHURMAN CO., INC.**, 954 60th St., Oakland CA 94608. (415)428-0200. Editor: Susan Perry. 50% freelance written. Buys 50 freelance ideas/samples per year; receives 500 submissions per year. Reports

Close-up

Jo Marie Triolo
President
Rockshots, Inc.

"Our audience is definitely not into the traditional-type card," says Jo Marie Triolo, president of Rockshots, Inc. "We're capturing the younger, less inhibited set. What we considered improper in my generation is no longer taboo."

There are few absolute taboos at Rockshots, yet the emphasis is on cute and sexy, rather than vulgar or offensive. "Outrageous, crazy, offbeat," are the words she uses to describe the kind of humor she buys. In fact, the entire card line features irreverent, often sexually-oriented humor.

Triolo explains that for a small greeting card company to compete with larger firms and simply survive, it must carve out a niche in the market—one that, for any number of reasons, is avoided or ignored by the more established firms. Rockshots has created just such a place for itself. The larger firms, in an effort to appeal to a wide audience, do not handle cards with erotic or sexually-oriented humor.

One reason for the omission by the big companies is the feeling that such cards do not appeal to the mostly female card-buying audience, Triolo says. But she disagrees, "Our audience is younger (than that of larger firms) but 80 percent are women."

She warns writers to always keep the audience in mind when working on a card idea. "Ask first 'can this card be sent by a woman?' and 'who will receive this card—a woman, a man or either?'" Much of the verse Triolo receives is too vague—it's not clear whom the card is meant for and why someone would send it. Note the personal nature of greeting cards, she says. "Cards must express a me-to-you sentiment."

The best way to find out if your humor will fit the Rockshots line is to request a catalog or visit a nearby shop. Unlike conventional cards, Rockshots cards are carried in a number of novelty shops, such as Spencer Gifts.

Most of the cards are illustrated with photos and it's best to see a few sample cards to understand the close relationship between the photographs and the verse. Triolo usually starts with a gag line and then chooses the appropriate visual image (one that complements or builds on the verse). Greeting card writers should learn to think visually, she says.

Triolo and three members of her staff review card ideas during regular "think tank" sessions. She explains that the group comes up with one-fourth to one-third of the card ideas. Rockshots buys about 200 greeting cards or ideas for cards each year, but Triolo receives some 100 card ideas and verses every week.

"I can't use most of what I get, but that shouldn't discourage anyone," she says. "Submit, submit, submit! Some writers submit every week, a few even twice a week." The firm will need more material, she adds, because it is expected to increase its line by a third within the next few years.

Many of the Rockshots' cards are for birthdays, but Triolo is looking for cards expressing friendship and for other occasions, especially for Christmas. "A lot of what I receive is borderline," she says. "I'd like to see a little more crazy and outrageous lines."

—Robin Gee

in 1 month. Pays on acceptance. Writer's guidelines for #10 SAE with 1 first class stamp. Market list available to writer on mailing list basis.

Needs: Conventional, humorous, informal, invitations, juvenile, sensitivity, studio, non-occasion and friendship. Prefers unrhymed verse, but on juvenile cards rhyme is OK. Submit 5-20 cards in one batch.

Other Product Lines: Gift books.

Tips: "Historically, our nostalgic and art museum cards sell best. However, we are moving towards more contemporary cards. Target market: upscale, professional, well-educated; average age 40; more female."

‡SILVER VISIONS, Box 49, Newton MA 02161. (617)244-9504. Editor: B. Kaufman. Submit seasonal/holiday material 9 months to 1 year in advance. Reports in 1 month. Pays on publication. Guidelines not available.

Needs: Humorous, juvenile, Jewish humor. Send 8 card ideas/batch.

‡SON MARK, INC., 130 Quigley Blvd., New Castle DE 19720. (302)322-9909. Director of Marketing, I.P.R.: Lynn G. Powell. 1% of material is freelance written. Submit seasonal/holiday material 8 months in advance. Reports back in 1 month. Pays on publication. Writer's guidelines/market list free. Market list revised regularly.

Needs: Humorous, informal, sensitivity, soft line. Prefers unrhymed. Submit at least 10 cards/batch.

Tips: "Seasonal, alternative and cards for entrepreneurial women sell best."

‡STABUR PRESS, INC., 23301 Meadow Park, Redford MI 48239. (313)535-0572. Editor: Paul Burke. 40% of material is freelance written. Buys 2 freelance ideas/samples annually; Receives 50 submisssion annually. Submit seasonal/holiday material 9 months in advance. Reports in 1 month. Buys first right of publication. Pays 50% on acceptance; 50% on publication.

Needs: Humorous. Submit 10 cards in a batch.

Other Product Lines: Calendars, gift books, greeting books, posters; pays $1,000-5,000.

Tips: "A unique idea is necessary."

VAGABOND CREATIONS, INC., 2560 Lance Dr., Dayton OH 45409. (513)298-1124. Editor: George F. Stanley, Jr. 30% freelance written. Buys 30-40 ideas annually. Submit seasonal/holiday material 6 months in advance. Reports in 1 week. Buys all rights. Sometimes copyrighted. Pays on acceptance. Writer's guidelines for #10 SAE. Market list issued one time only.

Needs: Cute, humorous greeting cards (illustrations and copy) often with animated animals or objects in people-situations with short, subtle tie-in message on inside page only. No poetry. Pays $10-25/card idea.

WARNER PRESS, INC., Box 2499, Anderson IN 46018. (317)644-7721. Product Editor: Cindy M. Grant. 70% freelance written. Buys $3,000-4,000 worth of freelance material/year. Scheduled reading times: everyday verses (Jan.-Feb.); Christmas verses (April-May). Reports in 5 weeks. Buys all rights. Pays on acceptance. Writer's guidelines for #10 SAE with 1 first class stamp. Market list is regularly revised.

Needs: Announcements, conventional, informal, inspirational, juvenile, sensitivity and verses of all types with contemporary Christian message and focus. No off-color humor. "Cards with a definite Christian perspective that is subtly stressed, but not preachy, sell best for us." Uses both rhymed and unrhymed verses/ideas "but we're beginning to move away from 'sing-song' rhyme, toward contemporary prose." Pays $15-35 per card idea.

Other Product Lines: Pays $60-150 for calendars; $15-30 for plaques; $10-50 for posters; $20-50 for short meditations; negotiates payment for coloring books and children's books.

Tips: "Try to avoid use of 'I' or 'we' on card verses. A majority of what we purchase is for box assortments. An estimated 75% of purchases are Christian in focus; 25% good conventional verses. Religious card ideas that are not preachy are difficult to find. The market is moving away from the longer verses in a variety of card types, though there is still a market for good inspirational verses (i.e. like Helen Steiner Rice). Our best sellers are short poems or sensitivity verses that are unique, meaningful and appropriate for many people. We do not purchase verses written specifically to one person (such as relative or very close friend) but rather for boxed assortments. We still need some traditional, but are slowly moving toward more personal, expressive verses."

CAROL WILSON FINE ARTS, INC., Box 17394, Portland OR 97217. Editor: Gary Spector. 90% freelance written. Buys 100 freelance ideas/samples per year; receives thousands annually. Submit seasonal/holiday material 1 year in advance. Reports in 6 weeks. Buys negotiable rights. Whether payment is made on acceptance or publication varies, with type of agreement. Writer's guidelines/market list for #10 SAE and 1 first class stamp.

Needs: Humorous and unrhymed. Pays $40-80 per card idea. "Royalties could be considered for a body of work."

Other Product Lines: Postcards.

Tips: "We are looking for laugh-out-loud, unusual and clever ideas for greeting cards. All occasions are needed but most of all birthday cards are needed. It's OK to be outrageous or risque. Cards should be 'personal'— ask yourself—is this a card that someone would buy for a specific person?"

___ *Additional Greeting Card Publishers*

The following listings are inactive for the 1989 edition because the firms asked to be deleted or are not considering freelance submissions.

Royce International Corp. (asked to be deleted)
Strings Attached (out of business)
Tech Styles (not accepting freelance submissions)

The following firms did not return a verification to update an existing listing by press time.

Accord Publications
Argus Communications
Black & White Cards
Calligraphy Collection
Caring Card Co.
Carlton Cards
Comstock Cards
Crystal Group of Companies
Eisner Advertising Studio
Kalan Inc.
Redleterkardz
Renaissance Greeting Cards
Rousana Cards
Sunrise Publications Inc.

ALWAYS submit manuscripts or queries with a self-addressed, stamped envelope (SASE) within your country or International Reply Coupons (IRC) purchased from the post office for other countries.

Syndicates

Mergers and buy outs have steadily decreased the number of newspapers in recent years and, as a result, syndication is one of the most competitive markets for freelance writers. Because of this, news syndicates are buying less material and have become increasingly hesitant to launch new columns, unless they are written by a well-known writer or proven authority. Despite the success of a handful of columnists, few writers make it to star status.

"There are fewer and fewer newspapers with more and more people vying for available space," says one syndicate publisher, "but there's always room for a really good, different feature story." Different is the key word here—if you can provide an unusual story, unique style or expert advice, syndicates can offer excellent exposure and prestige.

Although the news syndicate market remains tight, this year we've increased the number of listings in this section by more than 50 percent. The steady growth of specialized syndicates accounts for most of these new listings. Specialized syndicates sell to magazines, trade journals and business publications, as well as to newspapers. The most popular subjects for specialized columns or features are how-to, business, health and finance.

Not only is syndication a competitive field, but it is also challenging. Producing a lively, appealing column on a regular basis requires a certain set of skills and most editors want proof of your ability to produce consistently good work. Start by writing a column for a local paper. Many small papers welcome freelance help, especially if the writer is willing to work for little or no fee. Nanette Wiser, editorial director of Copley News Service, advises writers not to consider syndication until they have written on a topic regularly for two years. She adds that a readership survey showing a favorable response to your local column would be a definite plus.

Study the popular syndicated columnists to discover how successful columns are structured. For example, most columns are short—from 500 to 750 words—so columnists learn how to make every word count. Don't make the mistake of imitating a well-known columnist—newspapers do not want more of the same. This holds true of subject matter-keep abreast of trends, but make sure you do not submit a column on a subject already covered by that syndicate. The more unique the topic, the greater your chances at syndication, but choose a subject that interests you and one that you know well.

Editors look for writers with unique viewpoints on lifestyle or political topics, but they also seek how-to columns and one-shot features on a variety of subjects. This year many listed personal finance and celebrity profiles as popular subject matter. One-shot features tend to be longer than columns and can be tied to a news peg or event. Other one-shot items include puzzles, cartoons and graphics.

Most syndicate editors prefer a query letter and about six sample columns or writing samples and a self-addressed, stamped envelope. If you have a particular field of expertise, be sure to mention this in your letter and back it up by sending related material. For highly specialized or technical matter you must also provide some credentials to show you are qualified to handle the topic.

In essence, syndicates act as agents or brokers for the material they handle. Writers' material is usually sold as a package. The syndicate will promote and market the work and keep careful records of sales. Writers usually receive 40 to 60 percent of gross receipts. Syndicates may also pay a small salary or a flat fee for one-shot items.

Syndicates usually acquire all rights to accepted material, although a few are now offering writers and artists the option of retaining ownership. When selling all rights, writers give up all ownership to their creations. This has been one reason some writers choose to self-syndicate.

Writers who syndicate their own work have all the freedom of owning their own business, but must also act as their own business managers, marketing team and sales force. Payment is usually negotiated on a case-by-case basis. Small newspapers may offer only $5 per column, but larger papers may pay $15 to $20. The number of papers you deal with is only limited by your marketing budget and sales ability. James Dulley, a writer who self-syndicates his column, "Cut Your Utility Bills," sold to 200 newspapers last year—a record, according to *Editor and Publisher*.

Note that some newspapers are not copyrighted, so self-syndicators must copyright their own material. It's less expensive to copyright columns as a collection, rather than individually. For more information on copyright procedures, see Copyrighting Your Writing in the Business of Writing section.

For information on column writing and syndication see *How to Write & Sell a Column*, by Julie Raskin & Carolyn Males (Writer's Digest Books). Additional information on syndication and syndicate markets can be found in *The Gale Directory of Publications* (available in most libraries); *The Editor and Publisher Syndicate Directory* (11 W. 19th St., New York NY 10011); and *How to Make Money in Newspaper Syndication*, by Susan Lane (Newspaper Syndication Specialists, Suite 326, Box 19654, Irvine CA 92720).

For information on syndicates not listed in *Writer's Market*, see Additional Syndicates at the end of this section.

ADVENTURE FEATURE SYNDICATE, 329 Harvery Dr., Glendale CA 91206. (818)247-1721. Editor: Orpha Harryman Barry. Reports in 1 month. Buys all rights, first North American serial rights and second serial (reprint) rights. Free cartoonist's guidelines.
Needs: Fiction (spies) and fillers (adventure/travel), action/adventure comic strips and graphic novels. Submit complete ms.

AMERICA INTERNATIONAL SYNDICATE, Suite 103D, 3801 Oakland St., St. Joseph MO 64501. (816)271-5250. Editor: Gerald Bennett. 100% freelance written by cartoonists on contract. Works with 6 previously unpublished cartoonists/year. "We sell to newspapers, trade magazines, puzzle books and comic books." Reports in 1 month. Buys all rights. Pays 50% of gross on sales. Writer's guidelines for #10 SASE.
Needs: Short fictional stories of "You Are The Detective" type for comic strips, puzzles, crosswords, children games, puzzles, art and stories. Send samples of feature (6-8) with SASE. Pays 50% of gross. Currently syndicates Alfonso by Charles Russo (comic strip).
Tips: "Keep the art simple, and uncluttered as possible; know your subject and strive for humor."

AMERICAN NEWSPAPER SYNDICATE, 9 Woodrush Dr., Irvine CA 92714. (714)559-8047. Executive Editor: Susan Smith. 50% regular columns by writers under contract; 50% freelance articles and series by writers on a one-time basis. Plan to syndicate up to 7 new U.S. and Canadian columnists this year. Plan to buy 20 one-time articles/series per year. Syndicates to U.S. and Canadian medium-to-large general interest and special interest newspapers. Works with previously unpublished and published writers. Pays 50% of net sales, salary on some contracted columns. Buys first North American serial rights. Computer printout submissions acceptable. Reports in 3 weeks. Writer's guidelines for SASE.
Needs: Newspaper columns and one-time articles/series on travel, entertainment, how-to, human interest, business, personal finance, lifestyle, health, legal issues. "Practical, money-saving information on everyday needs such as medicine, insurance, automobiles, education, home decoration and repairs, and travel is always in great demand by newspapers." Will not return material without SASE. Columns should be 700 words in length; one-time articles should be 1,500 words.
Tips: "We seek fresh, innovative material that may be overlooked by the other syndicates. Because we know the newspaper syndication market, we feel we can find a place for the previously-unpublished writer if the material is well-executed. Be sure to research your idea thoroughly. Good, solid writing is a must. This is a very tough business to penetrate—but the rewards can be great for those who are successful."

AP NEWSFEATURES, 50 Rockefeller Plaza, New York NY 10020. (212)621-1500. Assistant General Manager: Dan Perkes.
Nonfiction: Buys column ideas "dealing with all areas that can be expanded into book form. We do not buy single features."

ARKIN MAGAZINE SYNDICATE, 761 NE 180th St., North Miami Beach FL 33162. Editor: Joseph Arkin. 20% freelance written by writers on contract; 70% freelance written by writers on a one-time basis. "We regularly purchase articles from several freelancers for syndication in trade and professional magazines." Previous-

ly published submissions OK, "if all rights haven't been sold." Computer printout submissions acceptable; no dot-matrix. Reports in 3 weeks. Buys all North American magazine and newspaper rights.
Needs: Magazine articles (nonfiction, 750-2,200 words), directly relating to business problems common to several (not just one) different types of businesses; and photos (purchased with written material). "We are in dire need of the 'how-to' business article." Will not consider article series. Submit complete ms; "SASE required with all submissions." Pays 3-10¢/word; $5-10 for photos; "actually, line drawings are preferred instead of photos." Pays on acceptance.
Tips: "Study a representative group of trade magazines to learn style, needs and other facets of the field."

ARTHUR'S INTERNATIONAL, Box 10599, Honolulu HI 96816. (808)922-9443. Editor: Marvin C. Arthur. Syndicates to newspapers and magazines. Computer printout submissions acceptable; prefers letter-quality. Reports in 1 week. "SASE must be enclosed." Buys all rights.
Needs: Fillers, magazine columns, magazine features, newspaper columns, newspaper features and news items. "We specialize in timely nonfiction and historical stories, and columns, preferably the unusual. We utilize humor. Travel stories utilized in 'World Traveler'." Buys one-shot features and article series. "Since the majority of what we utilize is column or short story length, it is better to submit the article so as to expedite consideration and reply. Do not send any lengthy manuscripts." Pays 50% of net sales, salary on some contracted work and flat rate on commissioned work. Currently syndicates Marv, by Marvin C. Arthur (informative, humorous, commentary); Humoresque, by Don Alexander (humorous); and World Spotlight, by Don Kampel (commentary).
Tips: "We do not use cartoons but we are open for fine illustrators."

‡**BALDWIN PUBLISHING INC.**, Box 400, Dittmer MO 73073. (314)285-0831. Editor: Debra Holly. 50% written by writers on assignment; 10% freelance written by writers on one-time basis. Works with 4-5 previously unpublished freelance writers/year. Syndicates to magazine, newspaper, radio, tv. Computer printout submissions OK; letter-quality preferred. Reports in 3 weeks. Buys all rights. Writer's guidelines for #10 SASE.
Needs: How-to, crafts, woodworking and do-it-yourself articles. Buys one-shot features and articles series. Query with clips of published work. Pays author's percentage or flat rate. Currently syndicates *The Weekend Workshop*, by Ed Baldwin and *Classified Clippers*.

BUDDY BASCH FEATURE SYNDICATE, 771 West End Ave., New York NY 10025. (212)666-2300. Editor/Publisher: Buddy Basch. 10% written by writers on contract; 2% freelance written by writers on a one-time basis. Buys 10 features/year; works with 3-4 previously unpublished writers annually. Syndicates to print media: newspapers, magazines, house organs, etc. Computer printout submissions acceptable; no dot-matrix. Reports in 2 weeks or less. Buys first North American serial rights.
Needs: Magazine features, newspaper features, and one-shot ideas that are really different. "Try to make them unusual, unique, real 'stoppers', not the usual stuff." Will consider one-shots and article series on travel, entertainment, human interest—"the latter, a wide umbrella that makes people stop and read the piece. Different, unusual and unique are the key words, not what the *writer* thinks is, but has been done nine million times before." Query. Pays 20-50% commission. Additional payment for photos $10-50. Currently syndicates It Takes a Woman, by Frances Scott (woman's feature), Travel Whirl, Scramble Steps and others.
Tips: "Never mind what your mother, fiance or friend thinks is good. If it has been done before and is old hat, it has no chance. Do a little research and see if there are a dozen other similar items in the press—and don't just try a very close 'switch' on them. You don't fool anyone with this. There are fewer and fewer newspapers, with more and more people vying for the available space. But there's *always* room for a really good, different feature or story. Trouble is few writers (amateurs especially) know a good piece, I'm sorry to say."

BUSINESS FEATURES SYNDICATE, Box 9844, Ft. Lauderdale FL 33310. (305)485-0795. Editor: Dana K. Cassell. 100% freelance written. Buys about 100 features/columns a year. Syndicates to trade journal magazines, business newspapers and tabloids. Computer printout submissions acceptable; no dot-matrix. Buys exclusive rights while being circulated. Writer's guidelines for #10 SAE and 1 first class stamp. Reports in 1 month.
Needs: Buys single features and article series on generic business, how-to, marketing, merchandising, security, management and personnel. Length: 1,000-2,500 words. Complete ms preferred. Pays 50% commission. Currently syndicates Retail Market Clinic.
Tips: "We need nonfiction material aimed at the independent retailer or small service business owner. Material must be written for and of value to more than one field, for example: jewelers, drug store owners, and sporting goods dealers. We aim at retail trade journals; our material is more how-to business oriented than that bought by other syndicates."

‡**CHRONICLE FEATURES**, Suite 1009, 870 Market St., San Francisco CA 94102. (415)777-7212. Editor/General Manager: Stuart Dodds. Buys 3 features/year. Syndicates to daily newspapers in the U.S. and Canada.

Reports in 1 month. Buys first North American serial and second serial (reprint) rights.

Needs: Newspaper columns and features. "In choosing a column subject, the writer should be guided by the aspirations and lifestyle of today's newspaper reader. We look for originality of expression and, in special fields of interest, a high degree of expertise." Preferred length: 500-750 words. Submit complete ms. Pays 50% revenue from syndication. Offers no additional payment for photos or artwork accompanying ms. Currently syndicates Home Entertainment, by Harry Somerfield (consumer); Bizarro, by Dan Piraro (cartoon panel); and Wine Country, by Anthony Dias Blue.

‡CONTINENTAL FEATURES/CONTINENTAL NEWS SERVICE, Suite 265, 341 W. Broadway, San Diego CA 92101. (619)492-8696. Editor: Gary P. Salamone. 100% written by writers on contract; 30% freelance written by writer's on a one-time basis. "Writers who offer the kind and quality of writing we seek stand an equal chance regardless of experience." Syndicates to the print media. Reports in 1 month. Buys first North American serial rights. Writer's guidelines for #10 SASE.

Needs: Magazine features, newspaper features, "Feature material should fit the equivalent of one-quarter to one-half standard newspaper page, and Continental News considers an ultra-liberal or ultra-conservative slant inappropriate." Buys one-shot articles and article series. Query. Pays 85% author's percentage. Currently syndicates News and Comment by Charles Hampton Savage (general news commentary/analysis); Continental Viewpoint, by Sstaff (political and social commentary); and Portfolio, by William F. Pike (cartoon/caricature art).

Tips: "Continental News seeks country profiles/background articles that pertain to foreign countries. Writers who possess such specific knowledge/personal experience stand an excellent chance of acceptance, provided they can focus the political, economic and social issues. We welcome them to submit their proposals. Editors will not take freelanced work very seriously unless the contributor has an American perspective modified by foreign experience."

CONTINUUM BROADCASTING NETWORK/GENERATION NEWS, INC., Suite 303, 805 3rd Ave., New York NY 10022. Submit material to: 3546 84th St., Jackson Heights NY 11372. (212)713-5165 and (415)541-5032 (San Francisco). Executive Editor: Donald J. Fass. Associate Editor: Stephen Vaughn. Broadcast Feature Producer: Deanna Baron. 60% freelance written. 45% written by writers on contract; 5% freelance written by writers on a one-time basis. Buys 300 features/interviews/year. Works with 25-30 previously unpublished writers annually. Syndicates to newspapers and radio. Computer printout submissions acceptable; no dot-matrix. Buys all rights. Writer's guidelines for business size SAE and 2 first-class stamps. Reports in 5 weeks.

Needs: Newspaper columns (all kinds of weekly regular features for newspapers); radio broadcast material (90-second and 2½-minute regular daily radio features: lifestyle, comedy, music and interview—scripts as well as taped features); 30-minute and 60-minute specials. One-shot features for radio only-for 30- and 60-minute specials; scripts and completed productions. Query with 1 or 2 clips of published work only and 1 page summary on proposed articles. Demo tape and/or full script for broadcast; not necessary to query on tapes, but return postage must be provided. Pays 25-50% commission or $25-175, depending on length. Offers no additional payment for photos accompanying ms. Currently syndicates The World of Melvin Belli, Getting It Together (weekly youth-oriented music and lifestyle column); Keeping Fit (daily series); Rockweek and Backstage (weekly entertainment series); On Bleecker Street (weekly music/interview series).

Tips: "We seek a unique or contemporary concept with broad appeal that can be sustained indefinitely and for which the writer already has at least some backlog. Unique health, fitness, lifestyle, music, entertainment and trivia material will be emphasized, with a decrease in pop psychology, child psychology, history, seniors and parenting material."

‡COPLEY NEWS SERVICE, Box 190, San Diego CA 92109. (619)293-1818. Editorial Director: Nanette Wiser. Buys 85% of work from freelancers; 15% from freelancers on a one-time basis. Buys 200 features/week. Sells to magazines, newspapers, radio. Computer printout submissions OK; no dot-matrix. Reports in 1-2 months. Buys all rights or second serial (reprint) rights (sometimes).

Needs: Fillers, magazine columns, magazine features, newspaper columns and newspaper features. Subjects include interior design, outdoor recreation, fashion, antiques, real estate, pets and gardening. Buys one-shot and articles series. Query with clips of published work. Pays $50-100 flat rate or $400 salary/month.

‡CREATORS SYNDICATE, INC., 1554 S. Sepulveda Blvd. Los Angeles CA 90025. (213)477-2776. Estab. 1987. Syndicates to newspapers. Computer printout submissions OK. Reports in 2 months. Buys negotiable rights. Reports in 2 months. Writer's guidelines for SASE.

Needs: Newspaper columns and features. Query with clips of published work or submit complete ms. Author's percentage: 50%. Currently syndicates Ann Landers (advice) B.C. (comic strip) and Herblock (editorial cartoon).

Tips: "Syndication is very competitive. Writing regularly for your local newspaper is a good start."

THE CRICKET LETTER, INC., Box 527, Ardmore PA 19003. (215)789-2480. Editor: J.D. Krickett. 10% written by writers on contract; 10% freelance written by writers on a one-time basis. Works with 2-3 previously unpublished writers annually. Syndicates to trade magazines and newspapers. Computer printout submissions acceptable; prefers letter-quality. Reports in 3 weeks. Buys all rights.
Needs: Magazine columns, magazine features, newspaper columns, newspaper features, and news items—all tax and financial-oriented (700-1,500 words); newspaper columns, features and news items directed to small business. Query with clips of published work. Pays $50-500. Currently syndicates Hobby/Business, by Mark E. Battersby (tax and financial); Farm Taxes, by various authors (farm taxes); and Small Business Taxes, by Mark E. Battersby (small business taxes).

‡CROWN SYNDICATE, INC., Box 99126, Seattle WA 98199. President: L.M. Boyd. Buys countless trivia items and cartoon and panel gag lines. Syndicates to newspapers, radio. Reports in 1 month. Buys first North American serial rights. Free writer's guidelines.
Needs: Filler material used weekly, items for trivia column, gaglines for specialty comic strip (format guidelines sent on request). Pays $1-5/item, depending on how it's used, i.e., trivia or filler service or comic strip. Offers no additional payment for photos accompanying ms. Currently syndicates puzzle panels and comic strips, by Crown contributors (daily strip).

‡DIDATO ASSOCIATES, 175 Sexton Dr., New Rochelle NY 10804. (914)636-0807. 20% freelance written on one-time basis. Works with 5-10 previously unpublished writers/year. Syndicates to magazines and newspapers. Computer printout submissions OK. Reports in 1 week. Buys all rights.
Needs: Newspaper features. Buys single features. Query with or without published clips, or submit complete ms. Pays flat rate, $20-50.

EDITORIAL CONSULTANT SERVICE, Box 524, West Hempstead NY 11552. Editorial Director: Arthur A. Ingoglia. 40% written by writers on contract; 25% freelance written by writers on a one-time basis. "We work with 75 writers in the U.S. and Canada." Previously published writers only. Adds about 5 new columnists/year. Syndicates material to an average of 60 newspapers, magazines, automotive trade and consumer publications, and radio stations with circulation of 50,000-575,000. Computer printout submissions acceptable; letter-quality submissions preferred. Buys all rights. Writer's guidelines for #10 SASE. Reports in 3 weeks.
Needs: Magazine and newspaper columns and features; news items; and radio broadcast material. Prefers carefully documented material with automotive slant. Also considers automotive trade features. Will consider article series. No horoscope, child care, lovelorn or pet care. Query. Author's percentage varies; usually averages 50%. Additional payment for 8x10 b&w and color photos accepted with ms. Submit 2-3 columns. Currently syndicates Let's Talk About Your Car, by R. Hite.
Tips: "Emphasis is placed on articles and columns with an automotive slant. We prefer consumer-oriented features, i.e., how-to save money on your car, what every woman should know about her car, how to get more miles per gallon, etc."

‡EDITORS PRESS SERVICE, INC., 330 West 42nd St., New York NY 10036. (212)563-2252. Editor: Hilda Marbán. 2% written by writers on contract. "Editors Press primarily acts as the foreign sales representative for various U.S. based newspaper syndicates. We represent for sale outside the continental United States and Canada only the material they produce. The little in-house we have is Spanish." Syndicates to foreign language newspapers and magazine outside the United States. Reports in 2 weeks. Free writer's guidelines.
Needs: We handle only material that has already been syndicted by the syndicates we represent. Query only.
Tips: "We recommend that a writer contact the established syndicates who operate within the United States before getting in touch with us. Syndicates are merging, and so there is less of a market in newspaper syndication than there was twenty years ago. Also, the newspapers have a limited budget and amount of space for syndicated features. A new author would be wise to take this into account, and when developing a feature, should try to work toward developing something that has a distinctive appeal which will give it an edge over the competition."

FASTBREAK, Box 1626, Orem UT 84057. (801)785-1300. Editor: Demas W. Jasper. 100% freelance written. Writers, artists and humorists must be members or trial members of Fastbreak. Reports in 10 days. Buys all rights. Submission information for #10 SAE with 1 first class stamp.
Needs: Fiction, fillers, magazine columns, magazine features, newspaper columns, newspaper features, news items, photos and artwork. Topics include personal finances, political topics, practical how-to's, family and child, AIDS developments, medical insights, first-person stories, and senior citizen topics. Submissions from members only, or with membership application. Query first on membership with SASE. On items syndicated through Fastbreak, it retains only the first $5 for its service fee. Membership also provides a directory listing available to printers and publishers as explained in the FSI membership booklet. Query for electronic submissions. Computer printout submissions OK; prefers letter-quality.

FICTION NETWORK, Box 5651, San Francisco CA 94101. (415)391-6610. Editor: Jay Schaefer. 100% freelance written by writers on a one-time basis. Syndicates fiction to newspapers and regional magazines. Buys 100 features/year. Works with 25 previously unpublished writers annually. Computer printout submissions acceptable; letter-quality only. Reports in 3 months. Buys first serial rights. Sample catalog of syndicated stories for 8½x11 SAE and $4; writer's guidelines SAE with 1 first class stamp.
Needs: All types of fiction (particularly holiday) under 2,000 words. "We specialize in quality literature." Submit complete ms; do not send summaries or ideas. "Send one manuscript at a time; do not send second until you receive a response to the first." Pays 50% commission. Syndicates short fiction only; authors include Alice Adams, Ann Beattie, Max Apple, Andre Dubus, Bobbie Ann Mason, Joyce Carol Oates and others.
Tips: "We seek and encourage previously unpublished authors. Keep stories short, fast-paced and interesting. We need short-short stories under 1,000 words."

‡FIRST DRAFT, Box 576, Winnetka IL 60093. (312)441-7473. Editor: Karen C. Weeder. Work with 144 writers/year. Syndicates to corporate internal publications. Reports in 1 month. Buys all rights. Writer's guidelines for SAE with 2 first class stamps.
Needs: News features. Buys one-shot and article series on business trends and functions, management issues, personal development, personal health and cost containment (500-750 words). Query with published clips. Pays flat rate of $100-150.
Tips: "Need experience in employee communications. Business background helpful."

FOTOPRESS, INDEPENDENT NEWS SERVICE INTERNATIONAL, Box 1268, Station Q, Toronto, Ontario M4T 2P4 Canada. 50% written by writers on contract; 25% freelance written by writers on a one-time basis. Works with 30% previously unpublished writers. Syndicates to domestic and international magazines, newspapers, radio, TV stations and motion picture industry. Computer printout submissions acceptable; prefers letter-quality. Reports in 6 weeks. Buys variable rights. Writer's guidelines for $3 in IRCs.
Needs: Fillers, magazine columns, magazine features, newspaper columns, newspaper features, news items, radio broadcast material, documentary, travel and art. Buys one-shot and article series for international politics, scientists, celebrities and religious leaders. Query or submit complete ms. Pays 50-75% author's percentage. Offers $5-150 for accompanying ms.
Tips: "We need all subjects from 500-3,000 words. Photos are purchased with or without features. All writers are regarded respectfully—their success is our success."

‡FNA NEWS, Box 11999, Salt Lake City UT 84147. (801)355-0005. Editor: R.N. Goldberger. 5% written by writers on contract; 10% freelance written by writers on one-time basis. Works with 50 freelance writers/year. Syndicates to magazines and newspapers. Computer printout submissions OK; prefers letter-quality. Reports in 2 weeks. Buys all rights, first North American serial rights or second serial (reprint) rights.
Needs: Fiction, fillers, magazine columns, magazine features, newspaper columns, newspaper features, news items and radio broadcast material. Buys one-shot features and articles series. Query with published clips. Payment negotiated separately. Payment $100 minimum.
Tips: "Be very clear. Do not use unnecessary words. Write to be comfortably read."

‡(GABRIEL) GRAPHICS NEWS BUREAU, Box 38, Madison Square Station, New York NY 10010. (212)254-8863. Editor: J. G. Bumberg. 25% freelance written by writers on contract; ½% freelance written by writers on one-time basis. Syndicates to weeklies (selected) and small dailies. Computer printout submissions OK; prefers letter-quality. Reports in 1 month. Buys all rights for clients, packages. Writer's guidelines for SASE.
Needs: Fillers, magazine features, newspaper columns and features and news items and PR clients custom packages. Query with published clips. Pays 15% from client.

GENERAL NEWS SYNDICATE, 147 W. 42nd St., New York NY 10036. (212)221-0043. 25% written by writers on contract; 12% freelance written by writers on a one-time basis. Works with 12 writers/year; average of 5 previously unpublished writers annually. Syndicates to an average of 12 newspaper and radio outlets averaging 20 million circulation; buys theatre and show business people columns (mostly New York theatre pieces). Computer printout submissions acceptable; prefers letter-quality. Reports on accepted material in 3 weeks. Buys one-time rights. Writer's guidelines for #10 SASE.
Needs: Entertainment-related material.

‡DAVE GOODWIN & ASSOCIATES, Drawer 54-6661, Surfside FL 33154. Editor: Dave Goodwin. 70% written by writers on contract; 10% freelance written by writers on a one-time basis. Buys about 25 features a year from freelancers. Works with 2 previously unpublished writers annually. Rights purchased vary with author and material. May buy first rights or second serial (reprint) rights or simultaneous rights. Will handle copyrighted material. Query for electronic submissions. Computer printout submissions acceptable; prefers letter-quality. Query or submit complete ms. Reports in 3 weeks.

Nonfiction: "Money-saving information for consumers: how to save on home expenses; auto, medical, drug, insurance, boat, business items, etc." Buys article series on brief, practical, down-to-earth items for consumer use or knowledge. Rarely buys single features. Currently handling Insurance for Consumers. Length: 300-5,000 words. Pays 50% on publication. Submit 2-3 columns.

HERITAGE FEATURES SYNDICATE, 214 Massachusetts Ave. NE, Washington DC 20002. (202)543-0440. Managing Editor: Andy Seamans. 99% freelance written by writers on contract; 1% freelance written by writers on one-time basis. Buys 3 columns/year. Works with 2-3 previously unpublished writers annually. Syndicates to over 100 newspapers with circulations ranging from 2,000-630,000. Works with previously published writers. Computer printout submissions acceptable; prefers letter-quality. Buys first North American serial rights. Reports in 3 weeks.
Needs: Newspaper columns (practically all material is done by regular columnists). One-shot features. "We purchase 750-800 word columns on political, economic and related subjects." Query. "SASE a must." Pays $50 maximum. Currently syndicates nine columnists, including The Economy in Mind, by Warren Brookes; Fed Up, by Don Feder; and The Answer Man, by Andy Seamans.

HOLLYWOOD INSIDE SYNDICATE, Box 49957, Los Angeles CA 90049. (714)678-6237. Editor: John Austin. 10% written by writers on contract; 40% freelance written by writers on a one-time basis. Purchases entertainment-oriented mss for syndication to newspapers in San Francisco, Philadelphia, Detroit, Montreal, London, Sydney, Manila, South Africa, etc. Works with 2-3 previously unpublished writers annually. Pays on acceptance "but this is also negotiable because of delays in world market acceptance and payment." Previously published submissions OK, if published in the U.S. and Canada only. Computer printout submissions acceptable; prefers letter-quality. Reports in 6 weeks. Negotiates for first rights or second serial (reprint) rights.
Needs: News items (column items concerning entertainment—motion picture—personalities and jet setters for syndicated column; 750-800 words). Also considers series of 1,500-word articles; "suggest descriptive query first. We are also looking for off-beat travel pieces (with pictures) but not on areas covered extensively in the Sunday supplements. We can always use pieces on 'freighter' travel. Not luxury cruise liners but lower cost cruises. We also syndicate nonfiction book subjects—sex, travel, etc., to overseas markets. No fiction. Must have b&w photo with submissions if possible." Query or submit complete ms. Pay negotiable.
Tips: "Study the entertainment pages of Sunday (and daily) newspapers to see the type of specialized material we deal in. Perhaps we are different from other syndicates, but we deal with celebrities. No 'I' journalism such as 'when I spoke to Cloris Leachman.' Many freelancers submit material from the 'dinner theatre' and summer stock circuit of 'gossip type' items from what they have observed about the 'stars' or featured players in these productions—how they act off stage, who they romance, etc. We use this material."

‡INTERNATIONAL PHOTO NEWS, Box 2405, West Palm Beach FL 33402. (305)793-3424. Editor: Elliott Kravetz. 10% written by freelance writers under contract. Buys 52 features/year. Works with 25 previously unpublished writers/year. Syndicates to newspapers. Query for electronic submissions. Computer printout submissions OK. Reports in 1 week. Buys second serial (reprint) rights. Writer's guidelines for SASE.
Needs: Magazine columns and features (celebrity), newspaper columns and features (political or celebrity), news items (political). Buys one-shot features. Query with clips of published work. Pays author's percentage 50%. Pays $5 for photos accepted with ms. Currently syndicates Celebrity Interview, by Jay and Elliott Kravetz.
Tips: "Go after celebrities who are on the cover on major magazines."

INTERPRESS OF LONDON AND NEW YORK, 400 Madison Ave., New York NY 10017. (212)832-2839. Editor: Jeffrey Blyth. 50% freelance written by writers on contract; 50% freelance written by writers on a one-time basis. Works with 3-6 previously unpublished writers annually. Buys British and European rights mostly, but can handle world rights. Will consider photocopied submissions. Previously published submissions OK "for overseas." Computer printout submissions acceptable; prefers letter-quality. Pays on publication, or agreement of sale. Reports immediately or as soon as practicable.
Needs: "Unusual nonfiction stories and photos for British and European press. Picture stories, for example, on such 'Americana' as a five-year-old evangelist; the 800-pound 'con-man'; the nude-male calendar; tallest girl in the world; interviews with pop celebrities such as Yoko Ono, Michael Jackson, Bill Cosby, Tom Selleck, Cher, Priscilla Presley, Cheryl Tiegs, Eddie Murphy, Liza Minelli, also news of stars on such shows as 'Dynasty'/'Dallas'; cult subjects such as voodoo, college fads, anything amusing or offbeat. Extracts from books such as Earl Wilson's *Show Business Laid Bare*, inside-Hollywood type series ('Secrets of the Stuntmen'). Real life adventure dramas ('Three Months in an Open Boat,' 'The Air Crash Cannibals of the Andes'). No length limits—short or long, but not too long. Query or submit complete ms. Payment varies; depending on whether material is original, or world rights. Pays top rates, up to several thousand dollars, for exclusive material."
Photos: Purchased with or without features. Captions required. Standard size prints. Pay $50 to $100, but no limit on exclusive material.
Tips: "Be alert to the unusual story in your area—the sort that interests the American tabloids (and also the European press)."

‡**INTERSTATE NEWS SERVICE**, Suite 250, 500 Airport Rd., St. Louis MO 63135. Editor: Michael J. Olds. Buys 50% of material from freelancers on a one-time basis. Purchases 1,200 mss/year. "Interstate acts as the local news bureau for newspapers that cannot afford to operate their own state capital bureau." Query for electronic submissions. Computer printout submissions OK. Reports in 2 weeks on queries. Buys all rights or makes work-for-hire assignments. Free writer's guidelines.
Needs: News items. Hard news emphasis, concentrating on local delegations, tax money and local issues. Buys one-shot features. Query with clips of published work. Pays $20 flat rate; negotiates with writers under contract.

‡**JSA PUBLICATIONS**, Bx 37175, Oak Park MI 48237. (313)546-9123. Editor: Joseph S. Ajouny. 20% of writing bought from freelancers under contract; 20% from freelancers writing on one-time basis. "We purchase 20-40 illustrations per year. We use charts and graphs as well as contemporary/entertainment oriented columnists." Syndicates to magazines. Query for electronic submissions. Computer printout submissions OK; prefers letter-quality. Reports in 1 month. Buys all rights. Writer's guidelines for SASE.
Needs: Fiction (short, contemporary), fillers (illustrations especially), magazine columns, magazine features. Buys single features and article series. Query with clips of published work. Pays flat rate of $60-500. Pays $100-300 for photos accepted with ms. Currently syndicates Party Ranks, by Joe Stuart and Mike Pascale (comic strip).

KING FEATURES SYNDICATE, INC., 235 E. 45th St., New York NY 10017. (212)682-5600. Contact: Managing Editor. 10% freelance written. Syndicates material to newspapers. Submit "brief cover letter with samples of feature proposals." Previously published submissions OK. Computer printout submissions acceptable. Reports in 3 weeks. Buys all rights. Writer's guidelines for 8x10 SAE and $1.
Needs: Newspaper features, comics, political cartoons and columns. Pays "revenue commission percentage" or flat fee. Special single article opportunity is King Features Select, a weekly one-shot service. Buys one-time rights to celebrity profiles, off-beat life style and consumer pieces. Query with SASE to Merry Clark, editor.
Tips: "Be brief, thoughtful and offer some evidence that the feature proposal is viable. Read newspapers to find out what already is out there. Don't try to buck established columns which newspapers would be reluctant to replace with new and untried material. We're always looking for new ideas."

LOS ANGELES TIMES SYNDICATE, Times Mirror Square, Los Angeles CA 90053. Vice President/Editor: Don Michel. Special Articles Editor: Dan O'Toole. Syndicates to U.S. and worldwide markets. Usually buys first North American serial rights and world rights, but rights purchased can vary. Submit seasonal material six weeks in advance. Material ranges from 800-2,000 words.
Needs: Reviews continuing columns and comic strips for U.S. and foreign markets. Send columns and comic strips to Don Michel. Also reviews single articles, series, magazine reprints, and book serials. Send these submissions to Dan O'Toole. Send complete mss. Pays 50% commission. Currently syndicates Art Buchwald, Dr. Henry Kissinger, Dr. Jeane Kirkpatrick, William Pfaff, Paul Conrad and Lee Iacocca.
Tips: "We're dealing with fewer undiscovered writers but still do review material."

MERCURY SYNDICATIONS, Box 2601, Hutchinson KS 67504-2601. Editor: Gary McMaster. 100% freelance written by writers on contract. Works with 30 writers/year. Syndicates to magazines and newspapers. Computer printout submissions OK; no dot-matrix. Reports in 3 months. Buys first North American serial rights or second serial (reprint) rights.
Needs: Magazine and newspaper columns. Buys article series. Submit complete ms. Pays 70% commission. Currently syndicated The Pen Moves On, by Linda M. McMaster (interview/book preview).
Tips: "We are looking for columns that can run 52 weeks out of the year, every year. No short one-time items. We are considering some New Age material. We have started a new program for well-written columns that would conflict with well-known columns now in print and material that is so different it would otherwise be rejected. Always send a copy of the column you are offering for syndication. Be sure to enclose a SASE or your work will not be returned."

MINORITY FEATURES SYNDICATE, Box 421, Farrell PA 16146. (412)342-5300. Editor: Merry Frable. Reports in 5 weeks. 60% written by freelance writers on contract; 40% freelance written by writers on a one-time basis. Works with 500 previously unpublished writers annually. Buys first North American serial rights. Computer printout submissions acceptable; no dot-matrix. Reports in 5 weeks. Writer's guidelines for #10 SAE with 2 first class stamps.
Needs: Fillers, magazine features, newspaper features. Also needs comic book writers for Bill Murray Productions. Query with published clips. Pays open commission. Pays $25 minimum for photos. Currently syndicates Sonny Boy, Those Browns and The Candyman, by Bill Murray (newspaper features).
Tips: "We are getting in the comic book market. Writers should write for guidelines."

NATIONAL NEWS BUREAU, 2019 Chancellor St., Philadelphia PA 19103. (215)569-0700. Editor: Harry Jay Katz. "We work with more than 200 writers and buy over 1,000 stories per year." Syndicates to more than 500 publications. Reports in 2 weeks. Buys all rights. Writer's guidelines for 9x12 SAE and 3 first class stamps.

Needs: Newspaper features; "we do many reviews and celebrity interviews. Only original, assigned material." One-shot features and article series; film reviews, etc. Query with clips. Pays $5-200 flat rate. Offers $5-200 additional payment for photos accompanying ms.

NEW YORK TIMES SYNDICATION SALES CORP., 130 Fifth Ave., New York NY 10111. (212)645-3000. Senior Vice President/Editorial Director: Paula Reichler. Syndicates approximately "three books per month plus numerous one-shot articles." Also included in foreign newspapers and magazines. Buys first serial rights, first North American serial rights, one-time rights, second serial (reprint) rights, and all rights. Computer printout submissions acceptable; no dot-matrix.

Needs: Wants magazine and newspaper features; magazine and newspaper columns; and book series. "On syndicated articles, payment to author is 50% of net sales. We only consider articles that have been previously published. Send tearsheets of articles published." Submit approximately 4 samples of articles, 12 samples of columns. Photos are welcome with books and articles.

Tips: "Topics should cover universal markets and either be by a well-known writer or have an off-beat quality. Quizzes are welcomed if well researched."

NEWS FLASH INTERNATIONAL, INC., 2262 Centre Ave., Bellmore NY 11710. (516)679-9888. Editor: Jackson B. Pokress. 25% written by writers on contract; 25% freelance written by writers on a one-time basis. Supplies material to Observer newspapers and overseas publications. Works with 10-20 previously unpublished writers annually. "Contact editor prior to submission to allow for space if article is newsworthy." Photocopied submissions OK. Computer printout submissions acceptable; no dot-matrix. Pays on publication.

Nonfiction: "We have been supplying a 'ready-for-camera' sports page (tabloid size) complete with column and current sports photos on a weekly basis to many newspapers on Long Island, as well as pictures and written material to publications in England and Canada. Payment for assignments is based on the article. Payments vary from $20 for a feature of 800 words. Our sports stories feature in-depth reporting as well as book reviews on this subject. We are always in the market for good photos, sharp and clear, action photos of boxing, wrestling, football, baseball and hockey. We cover all major league ball parks during the baseball and football seasons. We are accredited to the Mets, Yanks, Jets and Giants. During the winter we cover basketball and hockey and all sports events at the Nassau Coliseum."

Photos: Purchased on assignment; captions required. Uses "good quality 8x10 b&w glossy prints; good choice of angles and lenses." Pays $7.50 minimum for b&w photos.

Tips: "Submit articles which are fresh in their approach on a regular basis with good quality black and white glossy photos if possible; include samples of work. We prefer well-researched, documented stories with quotes where possible."

NEWSPAPER ENTERPRISE ASSOCIATION, INC., 200 Park Ave., New York NY 10166. (212)557-5870/ (212)692-3700. Editorial Director: David Hendin. Director, International Newspaper Operations: Sidney Goldberg. Executive Editor: D.L. Drake. Director of Comics: Sarah Gillespie. 100% written by writers on contract. "We provide a comprehensive package of features to mostly small- and medium-sized newspapers." Computer printout submission acceptable; prefers letter-quality to dot-matrix. Reports in 6 weeks. Buys all rights.

Needs: "Any column we purchase must fill a need in our feature lineup and must have appeal for a wide variety of people in all parts of the country. We are most interested in lively writing. We are also interested in features that are not merely copies of other features already on the market. The writer must know his or her subject. Any writer who has a feature that meets all of those requirements should send a few copies of the feature to us, along with his or her plans for the column and some background material on the writer." Current columnists include Bob Walters, Bob Wagman, Chuck Stone, George McGovern, Dr. Peter Gott, Tom Tiede, Ben Wattenberg and William Rusher. Current comics include Born Loser, Frank & Ernest, Eek & Meek, Kit 'n' Carlyle, Bugs Bunny, Berry's World, Arlo and Janis, and Snafu.

Tips: "We get enormous numbers of proposals for first person columns—slice of life material with lots of anecdotes. While many of these columns are big successes in local newspapers, it's been our experience that they are extremely difficult to sell nationally. Most papers seem to prefer to buy this sort of column from a talented local writer."

NORTH AMERICA SYNDICATE, (formerly News America Syndicate), 235 E. 45th St., New York NY 10017. Editor: Dennis R. Allen. "North America Syndicate is part of King Features Syndicate, Inc., and manuscripts should not be duplicated when sent." 25% written by writers on contract; 15% freelance written by writers on a one-time basis. Buys 520 articles annually; works with 500 previously unpublished writers. Syndicates to newspapers and magazines. Computer printout submissions acceptable. Reports in 2 weeks.

Buys all rights, first North American serial rights or second serial (reprint) rights. Free writer's guidelines.
Needs: Magazine features, newspaper columns and newspaper features. Buys one-shot features and article series. Submit complete ms. Pays 50% author's percentage. Payment negotiable. Currently syndicates Inside Report, by Evans/Novak (politics); and Observations, by Pope John Paul II (religion). "SASE required for returning material and/or replies."
Tips: "Look for something no one else is doing, or do something differently. We're one of few syndicates to accept and publish freelance writing on a regular (every week) basis."

‡**ROYAL FEATURES**, Box 58174, Houston TX 77258. (713)280-0777. Executive Director: Fay W. Henry. 80% written by writers on contract; 10% freelance written by writers on one-time basis. Syndicates to magazine and newspapers. Computer printout submissions OK; no dot-matrix. Reports in 2 months. Buys all rights, first North American serial rights or second serial (reprint) rights.
Needs: Magazine and newspaper columns and features. Buys one-shot features and article series. Query with or without published clips. Pays authors percentage, 40-60%.

‡**SAN FRANCISCO STYLE INTERNATIONAL**, 20 San Antonio Place, San Francisco CA 94133. (415)788-6589. Editor: Christina Tom. 50% of material is bought from freelancers under contract; 10% from freelancers writing on one-time basis. Works regularly with 6-10 writers. Syndicates to newspapers, magazines and radio. Query for electronic submissions. Computer printout submissions OK; prefers letter-quality. Reports in 6 weeks. Buys all rights. Writer's guidelines for $1.
Needs: Magazine features, newspaper features, radio broadcast material ("we develop our topics in-house and then assign writers to perform the work"). Purchases one-shot features. Query with clips of published work. Pays author's percentage of 50%.

SINGER MEDIA CORPORATION, 3164 Tyler Ave., Anaheim CA 92801. (714)527-5650. Editor: Natalie Carlton. 50% written by writers on contract; 30% freelance written by writers on a one-time basis. Syndicates 500 features and columns, and 1,000 cartoons/year. Syndicates to magazines, newspapers and book publishers. Computer printout submissions acceptable; prefers letter-quality. Reports in 1 month. Rights negotiable. Writer's guidelines for #10 SAE and $1.
Needs: Short stories, crosswords, puzzles, quizzes, interviews, entertainment and psychology features, cartoons, books for serialization and foreign reprints. Syndicates one-shot features and article series on celebrities. Query with clips of published work or submit complete ms. Pays 50% author's percentage. Currently syndicates Solve a Crime, by B. Gordon (mystery puzzle) and Hollywood Gossip, by N. Carr (entertainment).
Tips: "Good interviews with celebrities, men/women relations, business and real estate features have a good chance with us. Aim at world distribution and therefore have a universal approach."

‡**THE SPELMAN SYNDICATE, INC.**, 26941 Pebblestone, Southfield MI 48034. (313)355-3686. Editor: Philip Spelman. Syndicates to newspapers and TV. Computer printout submissions OK. Reports in 1 month. Buys all rights.
Needs: Newspaper columns. Query only. Pays author's percentage of 50%. Currently syndicates Easy Tax Tips.
Tips: "Get a column started in a small newspaper, develop a following and expand on your own until you become attractive to a syndicate."

‡**SPORTS FEATURES SYNDICATE/WORLD FEATURES SYNDICATE**, 1005 Mulberry, Marlton NJ 08053. (609)983-7688. Editor: Ronald A. Sataloff. 1-5% written by freelancers under contract; 1-5% freelance written by writers on one-time basis. Nearly all material is syndicated to daily newspapers and the Associated Press' supplemental sports wire. Computer printout submissions OK; no dot-matrix. Reports in 1 month. Buys all rights. Currently syndicates Sports Lists, by staff; No Kidding?, by Karl Van Asselt; Mr. Music, by Jerry Osborne.
Tips: "No surprise—space is at a premium and one wishing to sell a column is at a disadvantage unless he is an expert in a chosen field and can relate that area of expertise in layman's language. Concentrate on features that take little space and that are helpful to the reader as well as interesting. *USA Today* has revolutionized newspapering in the sense that it is no longer a sin to be brief. That trend is here for a long time, and a writer should be aware of it. Papers are also moving toward more reader-oriented features, and those with an ability to make difficult subjects easy reading have an advantage."

‡**SYNDICATED NEWS SERVICE**, 193 Inglewood Dr., Rochester NY 14619-1403. (716)328-8818. Editor/Publisher: Frank Judge. Associate Publisher: Mary Whitney. 50% written by freelance writers on contract; 5% freelance written by writers on one-time basis. Syndicates to newspapers (dailies, weeklies); magazines, databases. Query for electronic submissions. Computer printout submissions OK; prefers letter-quality. Reports in 2 months. Buys all rights.

Needs: Fiction (some short fiction), fillers, newspaper columns and features. Query with clips of published work or send complete ms. Pays author's percentage of 30-50%. Currently syndicates Taking Charge, by Byron Perry (entrepreneur).

SYNDICATED WRITERS & ARTISTS INC., 2901 Tacoma Ave., Indianapolis IN 46218. (317)924-4311. Editor: Eunice Trotter. 99% written by writers on contract; 1% freelance written by writers on a one-time basis. Works with 30 writers annually. Syndicates to newspapers. Reports in 6 weeks. Query for electronic submissions. Computer printout submissions acceptable; prefers letter-quality. Buys all rights. Writer's guidelines for SASE.
Needs: Fillers, newspaper columns, newspaper features and news items. 300 words with minority angle. Query with clips of published work. "Three different samples of your work should be submitted (10 cartoon strips or panels). Submissions should also include brief bio of writer/artists. No material is returned without a SASE." Pays author's percentage of 35-40%. Currently syndicates Hobson's House (cartoon), On Parenting (column) and editorial caretoons by Paul Lange and Robert Tarr.
Tips: "The kind of writing we seek has a minority angle. Previously, there was no market for material with a minority angle; we believe there now is such a market. More news instead of opinion will be required. Quality requirements."

TEENAGE CORNER, INC., 70-540 Gardenia Ct., Rancho Mirage CA 92270. President: David J. Lavin. Buys 122 items/year for use in newspapers. Submit complete ms. Reports in 1 week. Material is not copyrighted.
Needs: 500-word newspaper features. Pays $25.

TRIBUNE MEDIA SERVICES, 64 E Concord St., Orlando FL 32801. (407)839-5600. President: Robert S. Reed. Editor: Michael Argirion. Syndicates to newspapers. Reports in 1 month. Buys all rights, first North American serial rights and second serial (reprint) rights.
Needs: Newspaper columns, comic strips. Query with published clips. Currently syndicates the columns and cartoons of Mike Royko, Bob Greene, Liz Smith, Andy Rooney, Marilyn Beck, Jeff MacNelly and Mike Peters.

UNITED FEATURE SYNDICATE, 200 Park Ave., New York NY 10166. Editorial Director: David Hendin. Director International Newspaper Operations: Sidney Goldberg. Executive Editor: D.L. Drake. Director of Comic Art: Sarah Gillespie. 100% contract writers. Supplies features to 1,700 U.S. newspapers, plus Canadian and other international papers. Works with published writers. Query with 4-6 samples and SASE. Computer printout submissions acceptable. Reports in 6 weeks.
Columns, Comic Strips and Puzzles: Current columnists include Jack Anderson, Judith Martin, Donald Lambro, Martin Sloane, June Reinsich. Comic strips include Peanuts, Nancy, Garfield, Drabble, Marmaduke, Rose is Rose and Robotman. Standard syndication contracts are offered for columns and comic strips.
Tips: "We buy the kind of writing similar to other major syndicates—varied material, well-known writers. The best way to break in to the syndicate market is for writers to latch on with a major newspaper and to develop a following. Also, cultivate new areas and try to anticipate trends."

UNITED MEDIA, 200 Park Ave., New York NY 10166. (212)692-3700. Executive Editor: Diana L. Drake. 100% written by writers on contract. Syndicates to newspapers. Computer printout submission acceptable; prefers letter-quality. Reports in 1 month. Writer's guidelines for #10 SAE and 1 first class stamp.
Needs: Newspaper columns and newspaper features. Query with photocopied clips of published work. "Authors under contract have negotiable terms." Currently syndicates Miss Manners, by Judith Martin (etiquette); Dr. Gott, by Peter Gott, M.D. (medical) and Supermarket Shopper, by Martin Sloane (coupon clipping advice).
Tips: "We include tips in our guidelines. We buy very few of the hundreds of submissions we see monthly. We are looking for the different feature as opposed to new slants on established columns."

UNIVERSAL PRESS SYNDICATE, 490 Main Street, Kansas City MO 64112. Buys syndication rights. Reports normally in 1 month. Return postage required.
Nonfiction: Looking for features—columns for daily and weekly newspapers. "Any material suitable for syndication in daily newspapers." Currently handling James J. Kilpatrick, Dear Abby, Erma Bombeck and others. Payment varies according to contract.

‡WALNUT PRESS, 1449 Grant St., Berkeley CA 94703. (415)524-8383. Editor: Selma Von Blue. 10% freelance written by writers under contract; 10% freelance written by writers on one-time basis. Works with 24 writers/year. Works with 10 previously unpublished writers/year. Syndicates to newspapers, magazines, newsletters, and company sponsored publications. Computer printout submissions OK; prefers letter-quality. Reports in 2 weeks. Buys second serial (reprint) rights. Free writer's guidelines. Currently syndicates Odyssey, by Selma and Peter Von Blum (travel).

Close-up

Diana Drake
Executive Editor
United Media

The newspaper market is tight and few writers ever make it into syndication, says Diana Drake, executive editor of United Media. Almost no one makes a living solely from syndication—even successful columnists supplement their incomes with magazine articles, books, television appearances and speaking engagements. Still, syndication can be a wonderful opportunity for a writer to build national exposure and prestige.

United Media is actually the collective name for two syndicates. United Features Syndicate (UFS) and Newspaper Enterprise Association (NEA) were joined under the United Media name about 10 years ago, but still operate as separate entities. The two syndicates operate differently in the way they work with writers and in the type of work they select, explains Drake, who started with NEA as a science writer 15 years ago.

UFS handles syndicated features, columns and comics. Newspapers buy each feature separately. For example, a newspaper will buy a certain column and will receive it three times a week until the paper decides to cancel it. Writers are paid by the number of newspapers that buy the column; payment is split 50-50 net between the writer and the syndicate and contracts usually run three to five years.

NEA offers a service that supplies columns, features, puzzles and comics. About 650 newspapers subscribe to the service and receive daily material. The paper can then use (or not use) any component of the service. It's hard to know what is being used, says Drake, so the company conducts a survey every two years to determine which features will be continued and which will be dropped from the service. Writers receive a flat fee per week, so income is a fixed amount.

Syndication is becoming increasingly difficult for text features, partly because of the local nature of newspapers. They want local color and look to writers familiar with their community. "We must look for the sort of column that we can do better—something unique. Our column, Miss Manners, is a good example. The writer has a special knowledge, interesting material and finesse. Personality is important."

Avoid imitating well-known columnists, she warns. "We're always getting submissions from would-be Erma Bombecks, but Erma is still out there. We need something different." The same goes for topics. "If 500 newspapers are already running columns dealing with the subject or if we already offer something similar, we just can't use it.

"We have to be very careful. It costs so much to launch a new column. In fact, it takes an average of $400 for one salesman to make one sales call." Sales expertise is the main reason writers turn to syndicates, she says. "Salesmanship does not come naturally to most writers. We can provide a 10-person sales force to help promote your work."

Writers interested in syndication should be willing to start small, says Drake. Begin by writing for your local paper. "We tend to take more seriously columns that have appeared already in a newspaper. It's an indication that the writer is reliable and can meet deadlines. There's almost nothing worse you can do in this business than miss deadlines."

—Robin Gee

‡**WASHINGTON POST WRITERS GROUP**, 1150 15th St. NW, Washington DC 20071. (202)334-6375. Editor/General Manager: William B. Dickinson. Currently syndicates 30 features (columns and cartoons). "We are a news syndicate which provides features for newspapers nationwide." Query for electronic submissions. Computer printout submissions OK; no dot-matrix. Reports in 1 week. Buys all rights. Free writer's guidelines.
Needs: Newspaper columns (editorial, lifestyle, humor), and newspaper features (comic strips, political cartoons). Query with clips of published work. Pays combination of salary and percentage. Currently syndicates George F. Will columns (editorial); Ellen Goodman column (editorial); Bloom County, by Berke Breathed (comic strip).
Tips: "At this time, we are reviewing editorial page and lifestyle page columns, as well as political cartoons and comic strips. We will not consider games, puzzles, or similar features. Send sample columns to the attention of William Dickinson, general manager. Send sample cartoons or comic strips (photo copies—no original artwork, please) to the attention of Al Leeds, sales manager.

‡**WHITEGATE FEATURES SYNDICATE**, 71 Faunce Dr., Providence RI 02906. (401)274-2149. Editor: Ed Isaa. Estab. 1988. Buys 100% of material from freelance writers. Syndicates to newspapers; planning to begin selling to magazines and radio. Query for electronic submissions. Does not return submissions accompanied by SASE. Reports in 1 month. Buys all rights.
Needs: Fiction for Sunday newspaper magazine; magazine columns and features, newspaper columns and features, cartoon strips. Buys one-shot and article series. Query with clips of published work. For cartoon strips, submit samples. Pays 50% author's percentage on columns. Additional payment for photos accepted with ms. Currently syndicates "Indoor Gardening," by Jane Adler; "Looking Great," by Gloria Lintermans and "Strong Style," by Hope Strong.
Tips: "Please aim for a topic that is fresh. Newspapers seem to want short text pieces, 400-500 words."

‡**WORDS BY WIRE**, Suite #709, 1601 Connecticut Ave. NW, Washington DC 20009. Editor: Francesca Lyman. 5% freelance written by writers on contract; 95% freelance written by writers on one-time basis. Buys about 200 articles/year; works with 150 writers. Works with 25-50 previously unpublished writers/year. Query for electronic submissions. Computer printout submissions OK; no dot-matrix. Reports in 2 months. Buys newspaper syndication rights. Writer's guidelines for SASE.
Needs: Magazine features, newspaper features and op-ed columns. Buys one-shot features. Query with clips of published work or submit complete ms. Pays author's percentage 50%. Currently syndicates Political Commentary by Mark Shields; Essays, by André Codrescu.
Tips: "We are looking for original offbeat features on breaking trends for such sections as Arts, Entertainment, Food, Style, Travel Commentaries and stories. Must be unique, national in perspective and must deal with universal themes. No first-person, sports or business."

Additional Syndicates

The following listings are inactive for the 1989 edition because the firms asked to be deleted or are not accepting new submissions.

Syndicated Writers Group (not accepting new writers)
Artists and Writers Syndicate (asked to be deleted)

The following firms did not return a verification to update an existing listing by press time.

Black Conscience Syndications
   Inc.
Cartoon Express Syndications
Global Press Review
Harris & Associates Publishing
   Division
Hispanic Link News Service
Hyde Park Media
Numismatic Information Service
United Cartoonist Syndicate

Services & Opportunities

Author's Agents

Finding an agent and developing a good working relationship is a process that requires qualities we usually associate with marriage—intuition, trust, communication and perseverance. Whether you are new in the market or an established freelancer, it's a good idea to become acquainted with the variety of services agents offer, the fees or commissions they charge, and the way they deal with writers and publishers.

In general, agents are a combination of sales representatives and business managers. Agents keep in touch with editors and buyers of subsidiary rights; they know where to sell marketable manuscripts and how to negotiate contracts; they help collect payments from publishers and keep accurate records of earnings.

Of course agents don't decide whether or not a manuscript should be published; that's still a job for editors. Agents can only tell you if they believe your manuscript is ready to be submitted to a publisher.

If you've read the Book Publishers section of *Writer's Market*, you know that the publishing industry has become increasingly competitive and cost-conscious. Like any other business, a publishing company that fails to make a profit will not survive. Few publishers can afford to hire a staff of editors or freelance readers to go through hundreds of unsolicited manuscripts; they simply receive too many unpublishable manuscripts for each one that is publishable. For that reason, more and more book publishers will only consider manuscripts submitted through an agent. They rely on agents to do the screening for them.

The greater demand for agented submissions has resulted in an increase in the number of literary agencies. In addition to New York-based agents, many agents have settled on the West Coast, primarily to work with film and TV producers. Now more new agencies are opening throughout the U.S., dispensing with the notion that long-distance selling could never be successful.

Commissions and fees

Literary agents have always charged a commission on the manuscripts they place with publishers or producers, in much the same way real estate agents charge a commission. The commission, usually 10-20%, is subtracted from the author's advance and royalty payments from the publisher. According to an Author's Guild survey, 37% of agents charge 10% commission, 26% charge 15%; and 10% of the agents charge a commission ranging from 10-15%. The remainder charge some other rate. A 20% rate is not unusual for foreign sales in which the agent deals with a second agent in the foreign country and both receive 10% commission. In any event, a commission arrangement means the writer doesn't pay the agent a commission until the manuscript has been sold.

Agents rarely charge writers for general office overhead like the cost of utilities or secretarial services. Instead, they sometimes ask their clients to pay for specific expenses related to selling that writer's manuscript: photocopying, long distance phone calls, messenger service, etc.

Commissions and charges for specific office expenses are regarded as perfectly acceptable in the industry. Additional fees for reading or critiquing manuscripts are becoming more common, although not uniformly accepted. An Author Aid Associates study indicated that 63% of the agents responding didn't charge a reading fee. Some agencies charge a reading fee in which no comments on improving the manuscript are offered. Other agencies charge a criticism fee in which they often provide several pages of detailed suggestions. About 32% of agencies in the Author Aid survey said they provided some kind of editorial services.

Several firms that charge fees regard them as one-time payments; if the writer becomes a client, no more fees will be charged for future manuscripts. Some agencies also reimburse the writer for the original fee when the manuscript is sold.

Understanding fees

Agents' fees continue to be a hotly debated topic. Previous editions of *Writer's Market* sought to protect readers by listing agents who told us they charged only commissions. Since 1987 we have included both commission-only and fee-charging agents. Why include agents who charge fees? Approximately 85% of all literary agencies now charge some kind of fee. We at *Writer's Market* believe our job is to provide you with the most complete and up-to-date information to allow you to choose an agent. We can't give recommendations or make decisions for you, but we do want to help in your search.

Remember that payment of a reading or criticism fee almost never guarantees that the agency will represent you. Payment of a fee may or may not give you the kind of constructive criticism you need. Read the individual listings carefully. There is no way to generalize about fee-charging agencies.

Likewise, there is no standard when it comes to fees. Some agencies charge criticism fees of $25-75; others charge $200 or more. Reading fees, although less common than criticism fees, are usually less than $75. One fee may apply to a complete manuscript, while another is for an outline and sample chapters. Some agents require fees from unpublished writers only. A few agents charge a marketing, handling or processing fee to all clients. Several agents offer a consultation service, ranging from $15-200 per hour, to advise writers on book contracts they have received without the help of an agent. If you decide to pay a fee, be sure you know *exactly* what you'll receive in return.

How a literary agent works

Agents do many things to earn their commissions, but it's almost impossible to describe what an "average" agent does. Let's begin by considering what literary agents don't do.

An agent can't sell unsalable work or teach you how to write. An agent won't edit your manuscript; that is an editor's job. An agent can't defend you in a court of law unless he is also an attorney. An agent won't act as your press agent, social secretary or travel agent; you'll have to hire someone else to handle those chores.

As far as what an agent can and will do, each agency is different in the services it offers, the clients if prefers, its contacts in the industry, and the style in which it conducts business. In general, an agent's tasks can be divided into those done before a sale, during a sale and after a sale.

Before the sale, an agent evaluates your manuscript and sometimes make suggestions about revisions. If the agent wants to represent you, you'll usually receive a contract or letter of agreement specifying the agent's commission, fees and the terms of the agreement. When that's signed, the agent begins talking to editors and sending your manuscript out. Your agent can tell you about any marketing problems, give you a list of submissions and even send you copies of rejections if you really want them. The agent repeats this sequence until the manuscript sells, you withdraw it or your agreement expires. Some agents also are involved in book packaging or producing work; this activity is noted in individual listings. Nearly one-third of agents in the Author Aid survey said they also act as book packagers. See the Book Packagers and Producers section introduction for more information.

During the sale the agent negotiates with the publisher for you, offering certain rights to the publisher and usually reserving other rights for future sale. The agent examines the contract, negotiates clauses for your benefit and tries to get additional rights, like book jacket approval, for you. Your agent can explain the contract to you and make recommendations, but the final decision is always yours.

After the sale, the agent maintains a separate bank account for you, collects money from the publisher, deducts the appropriate commission and sends you the remainder. The agent examines all royalty statements and requests corrections or an audit when necessary. The agent also checks the publisher's progress on the book and makes sure your copyright has been registered. Sometimes the agent resolves conflicts between a writer and an editor or publisher. If you have retained subsidiary rights to your book, the agent will continue working for additional sales of movie, book club, foreign or video rights, etc.

Do you need an agent?

Not everyone needs an agent. Some writers are perfectly capable of handling the placement of their manuscripts and enjoy being involved in all stages of selling, negotiating and checking production of their books.

Other writers have no interest in, or talent for, the business side of writing and feel that their agents are invaluable. "She's obtained writing assignments for me by showing various publishers books of mine that they might otherwise never have seen. She makes sure that I get the best possible deals and money, that royalty payments are in order and paid when they're due," writer Hester Mundis says about her agent. "She's gotten my books published in foreign countries, optioned for film and TV, and intervenes if there's any disagreement between me and a publisher."

Ask yourself the following questions when evaluating your need for an agent:
- Do you have the skills to handle an agent's usual tasks?
- Can you take care of marketing your book and analyzing your contract?
- Can you afford to pay an agent 10-20% of your royalties?
- Would you like working through a middleman on all aspects of your book's future?
- Will you have more time to write if you have an agent?
- Are you interested in approaching markets that won't accept unagented submissions? Some book publishers, along with studios and independent producers, won't consider any unagented submissions. Book publishers usually adopt this policy if they have too many submissions to consider, and studios and producers usually return unsolicited material to protect themselves from charges of plagiarism. If you want to submit to these markets, you must work through an agent.

No matter how much you want or need an agent, you'll be wasting time and money if your writing isn't ready for an agent. Try to be objective about whether or not you have truly polished your work and studied the marketplace for your kind of writing. You should also talk to other writers who have agents and read all you can find about working with an agent. It may sound like a lot of work, but if you want an agent to take you seriously, you'll make every effort to obtain some published credits, place in a literary or journalistic contest, and always correspond with an agent in a professional manner.

Making contact

Only about 25% of agents look at unsolicited manuscripts. Some will consider queries only if you've been recommended by a client or an editor. But the majority will look at a query and possibly an outline and sample chapters from an unknown writer.

In addition to following the suggestions in each agent's listing, plan your query letter carefully. It should include a brief description of your manuscript, anticipated number of words or pages, whether or not you've been published and your credentials (for nonfiction). "As an agent, I am looking for work I can sell," an agent told us. "The writer should write me a letter that *shows* he can write literate prose, not just *tell* me it's salable." It's also important to enclose a self-addressed, stamped envelope (SASE) with all correspondence and manuscripts sent to an agent.

If the agent asks to see more of your work, consider yourself lucky, but don't assume you now have an agent. Just as you need to find out more about the agent, the agent has to know more about you and your writing. Don't expect an immediate response to your query or manuscript. On the other hand, if you receive no response or a negative response to your query, don't be discouraged. Continue to contact other agents. It's fine to send simultaneous queries, but never send a manuscript to more than one agent at a time.

Judging an agent

A bad agent can be worse than no agent at all. We've already discussed the expectations agents have for writers. Now it's time for you to decide what your expectations are for an agent. When an agency indicates an interest in representing your work, don't just assume it's the right one for you. If you want to make a knowledgable decision, you'll need more information—and that means asking questions.

While the answers to many of these questions appear in an agency's individual listing, it's a good idea to ask them again. Policies change and reporting time, commission amounts and fees may vary.

• How soon do you report on queries? On manuscripts?

• Do you charge a reading or critiquing fee? If yes, how much? What kind of feedback will I receive? What's the ratio of the agency's income from fees compared to income from marketing books? If the manuscript is accepted, will my fee be returned? Credited against my marketing expenses? Or is it a nonreturnable charge to cover reading/critiquing expenses?

• Do you charge any other fees?

• How many clients do you represent?

• Will you provide me with a list of recent sales, titles published or clients?

• May I contact any of your clients for referrals? [This is the most valuable information you can get, but some agents regard it as a breach of confidentiality.]

• Who will work with me and what kind of feedback can I expect—regular status reports, good news only, copies of informative letters from editors, etc.?

• Who will negotiate my contracts?

• Which subsidiary rights do you market directly? Which are marketed through subagents? Which are handled by the publisher?

• Do you offer any special services—tax/legal consultation, manuscript typing, book promotion or lecture tour coordination, etc.? Which cost extra? Which are covered by commission?

• Do you offer any editorial support? How much?

• Do you offer a written agreement? If yes, how long does it run? What kind of projects are covered? Will (or must) all of my writing be represented? What will your commission be on domestic, foreign and other rights? Which expenses am I responsible for? Are they deducted from earnings, billed directly, or paid by initial deposit? How can the agreement be terminated? After it terminates, what happens to work already sold, current submissions, etc.?

If the agency doesn't offer a contract or written agreement of any kind, you should write a letter of your own that summarizes your understanding on all these issues. Ask the agent to return a signed copy to you. A few agents prefer informal verbal agreements. No matter how personal a relationship you have with an agent, it's still a business matter. If the agent refuses to sign a simple letter of understanding, you may want to reconsider your choice of agencies.

Additional resources

The search for an agent can be a frustrating and time-consuming task, especially if you don't know what you're looking for. You can learn more about agents by studying several books on the subject. Read *Literary Agents: How to Get and Work with the Right One for You*, by Michael Larsen (Writer's Digest Books) and *Literary Agents: A Writer's Guide*, by Debby Mayer (Poet's & Writer's, Inc., 201 W. 54th St., New York NY 10019). *Literary Agents of North America* (Author Aid/Research Associates International, 340 E. 52nd St., New York NY 10022) is a directory of agents indexed by name, geography, subjects and specialities, size and affiliates. Your library may have a copy of *Literary Market Place*, which includes names and addresses of agents.

Remember that agents are not required to have any special training or accreditation. Some are members of a number of professional organizations or writers' groups, depending on their special interests. Each of the following three organizations requires its members to subscribe to a code of ethics and standard practices.

● ILAA—Independent Literary Agents Association, Inc., 15th Floor, 55 5th Ave., New York NY 10003. Founded in 1977, ILAA is a nationwide association of fulltime literary agents. An informative brochure, list of members and copy of the association's code of ethics are sent on request to writers who enclose #10 SAE with two first class stamps. ILAA does not provide information on specialties of individual members.

● SAR—Society of Author's Representatives, Inc., Box 650, Old Chelsea Station, New York NY 10113. Founded in 1928, SAR is a voluntary association of New York agents. A brochure and membership list are available for SASE. Members are identified as specializing in literary or dramatic material.

● WGA—Writer's Guild of America. Agents and producers in the TV, radio and motion picture industry can become members or signatories of WGA by signing the guild's basic agreement which outlines minimum standards for treatment of writers. For a list of agents who have signed the WGA agreement, send a money order for $1.25 (except New York state residents, $1.33) to one of the WGA offices. If you live east of the Mississippi River, write to WGA East, 555 W. 57th St., New York NY 10019; west of the Mississippi, write WGA West, 8955 Beverly Blvd., Los Angeles CA 90048.

Like *Writer's Market*, these agencies will not make recommendations of agents but will provide information to help you in your search.

For information on author's agents not listed in *Writer's Market*, see Additional Author's Agents at the end of this section.

CAROLE ABEL LITERARY AGENCY, 160 W. 87th St., New York NY 10024. (212)724-1168. President: Carole Abel. Estab. 1978. Member of ILAA. Represents 45 clients. 25% of clients are new/unpublished authors. Prefers to work with published/established writers; works with a small number of new/unpublished authors. Specializes in contemporary women's novels, biographies, thrillers, health, nutrition, medical nonfiction (diet and exercise) and history.
Will Handle: Nonfiction books, novels. Currently handles 50% nonfiction books and 50% novels. Will read—at no charge—unsolicited queries, outlines and mss. Reports in 2 weeks on queries; 6 weeks on mss. "If our agency does not respond within 2 months to your request to become a client, you may submit requests elsewhere."
Terms: Agent receives 15% commission on domestic sales; 15% on dramatic sales; and 20% on foreign sales. Charges for phone, postage, bulk mailing, messenger and photocopying expenses. 100% of income derived from commission on ms sales.
Recent Sales: *Singular Women*, by Freda Bright (Bantam); *Learning How to Love*, by Maureen Sullivan and Kathy Ketcham (Viking); and *Some Devil's Bargain*, by Alexander Kane (Berkeley Books).

DOMINICK ABEL LITERARY AGENCY, INC., Suite 12C, 498 West End Ave., New York NY 10024. (212)877-0710. President: Dominick Abel. Estab. 1975. Member of ILAA.

Will Handle: Will read—at no charge—unsolicited queries and outlines. Reports in 2 weeks on queries. "Enclose SASE."
Terms: Agent receives 10% commission on domestic sales; 15% on dramatic sales; and 20% on foreign sales. Charges for overseas postage, phone and cable expenses.
Recent Sales: No information given.

EDWARD J. ACTON INC., 928 Broadway, New York NY 10010. (212)473-1700. Contact: Edward Novak. Estab. 1975. Member of ILAA. Represents 100 clients. Works with a small number of new/unpublished authors. Specializes in politics, celebrities, sports and commercial fiction.
Will Handle: Nonfiction books and novels. Currently handles 5% magazine articles; 40% nonfiction books; 35% novels; 5% movie scripts; 5% TV scripts; 10% video production. Will read—at no charge—unsolicited queries and outlines. No unsolicited manuscripts. Reports in 3 weeks on queries.
Terms: Agent receives 15% commission on domestic sales; 15% on dramatic sales; and 19% on foreign sales. Charges for photocopy expenses. 100% of income derived from commission on ms sales.
Recent Sales: *The Boz*, by Brian Bosworth and Rick Reilly (Doubleday), *It's Good to be Back*, by Larry King with B. D. Colen (Delacorte).

LEE ALLAN AGENCY, Box 18617, Milwaukee WI 53218. (414)463-7441. Agent: Lee A. Matthias. Estab. 1983. Member of WGA, Horror Writers of America, Inc. and Wisconsin Screenwriter's Forum. Represents 50 clients. 80% of clients are new/unpublished writers. "A writer must have a minimum of one (in our judgment) salable work. Credentials are preferred, but we are open to new writers." Specializes in "screenplays for mass film audience, low to medium budget preferred, but of high quality, not exploitation; and novels of high adventure, genre fiction such as mystery and science fiction—no romance, nonfiction, textbooks, or poetry."
Will Handle: Novels (male adventure, mystery, science fiction, literary) and movie scripts (low to medium budget, mass appeal material). Currently handles 50% novels; 50% movie scripts. Will read—at no charge—unsolicited queries and outlines. Does not read unsolicited mss. Must be queried first. Reports in 2 weeks on queries; 6 weeks on mss. "If our agency does not respond within 1 month to your request to become a client, you may submit requests elsewhere. Query *must* include SASE for our reply or return of material."
Terms: Agent receives 10% commission on domestic sales; 10% on dramatic sales; and 20% on foreign sales. Charges for photocopying, binding.
Recent Sales: *Mome*, Bart Books; *The Jihad Ultimatum*, Saybrook; *Fire Arrow* and *The Fire Dream*, Presidio Press; various film options to independent producers.

‡**JAMES ALLEN, LITERARY AGENT**, 538 E. Harford St., Box 278, Milford PA 18337. Agent: James Allen. Estab. 1974. Represents 50 clients. Writer must have $3,000 writing income from previous year "and a track record in the area they want me to start work: story sales to genre magazines are a good background for bringing me a novel in that genre." Prefers to work with published/established authors. Specializes in mysteries, occult, horror, science fiction, contemporary and historical romance, fantasy, young adult novels, and mainstream. No "little-kid juveniles or westerns."
Will Handle: Magazine fiction ("for novelists on my list. I am *not* looking for short-story clients."), nonfiction books, and novels. Currently handles 10% magazine fiction; 3% nonfiction books; 85% novels; and 2% movie scripts. Does not read unsolicited mss. Query with "track record" and 3 page synopsis; submissions not accompanied by SASE are thrown out. Reports in 2 weeks on queries; 10 weeks on mss. "If our agency does not respond within 4 months to your request to become a client, you may submit requests elsewhere."
Terms: Agent receives 10% commission on domestic sales; 20% on dramatic sales; and 20% on foreign sales. Charges for extraordinary expenses. Deducted after sale. 100% of income derived from commission on ms sales.
Recent Sales: A 16-title reprint package of contemporary romantic suspense, by Elsie Lee (Zebra Books); *The Med*, by David Poyer (St. Martin's Press); *Three Rivers*, by Carla J. Mills (St. Martin's Press).

‡**LINDA ALLEN AGENCY**, 2881 Jackson St., San Francisco CA 94115. (415)921-6437. President: Linda Allen. Vice President: Jane Cutler. Estab. 1984. Represents 50 clients. 25% of clients are new/unpublished writers. Prefers to work with published/established authors. Specializes in mainstream fiction and nonfiction; adult and juvenile; computer and business.
Will Handle: Nonfiction books, novels, juvenile books. Currently handles 60% nonfiction books; 20% novels; 20% juvenile books. Will read—at no charge—unsolicited queries, outlines and mss. Reports in 1 month on queries; 6 weeks on mss. "If our agency does not respond within 2 months to your request to become a client, you may submit requests elsewhere."
Terms: Agent receives 15% commission. "Charges no reading fee. Offers a consultation service for writers not represented by the agency, $100 per hour." 100% of income is derived from commission on manuscript sales.
Recent Sales: *Strategies for Survival*, by Delaney & Goldblum (St. Martin's Press); *Crystal Gallery*, by Mitchell (Pocket Books); and *Advanced dBASE PLUS Program and Techniques*, by Liskin, Osborne (McGraw Hill).

Close-up

Jay Acton
Edward J. Acton Agency

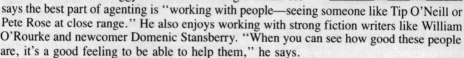

"Agenting is a lot like baseball," says Jay Acton, a literary agent and minor league baseball team owner. "You have to hit a few homers if you want to stay in the game."

Acton has hit a few homers as agent for several bestsellers, including Tip O'Neill's *Man of the House*, Sparky Lyle's *The Bronx Zoo*, Helen Van Slyke's *A Necessary Woman* and authors Peggy Anderson and Roger Kahn. He says the best part of agenting is "working with people—seeing someone like Tip O'Neill or Pete Rose at close range." He also enjoys working with strong fiction writers like William O'Rourke and newcomer Domenic Stansberry. "When you can see how good these people are, it's a good feeling to be able to help them," he says.

Acton was an editor at St. Martin's Press before he went to law school and started the agency in 1975. "All of the people who sort of encouraged me to open an agency when I was an editor, never came to me. Some people who I couldn't imagine would want to, did switch agents and came to me," he says.

Work as an agent has dispelled "a very idealized view of the publishing world" he had as an editor. "You're willing to ride the wins and losses better as an editor," he says. "But when you get into it, you have to make a buck and pay overhead; you want to make sure the projects you're working with come to fruition."

In the beginning, Acton says, "You have to take things that come along because you have to make a living. At this point, it's much easier to get clients. A lot of projects are suggested to us. There are still some projects we chase, but we have people knocking on our door as well."

Acton enjoys working with people he admires, often matching up a celebrity with a writer. In choosing a writer for a project, Acton looks for "chemistry" between writer and celebrity. "You want to see what they're like in a room together," he says. "Sometimes they may be wonderful apart, but they have to work in such close quarters, it's almost like husband and wife. If the person isn't going to be comfortable telling his life story to the writer, no matter how good the writer is, you shouldn't put them together."

During his time as an agent, Acton has seen several changes in the publishing industry. "There are a lot bigger advances for books now," he says. "Five years ago that wasn't happening. Tip O'Neill's book got one million, and several books can get that now."

While the advances are higher, Acton says publishing house mergers have decreased the number of places to market a manuscript. "The merger activity is very dispiriting for an agency," he says. "With it, you have houses that are almost competing against themselves." Mergers also may bring increasingly cost-conscious operations. "It puts a lot of pressure on agents to be very careful with what they select, too," Acton says. "When you sell someone a book, they want to be sure they're going to get their money back on it, or the next time you ask for a million dollars, they'll say 'no thanks.'"

Despite the changing publishing industry and his own success, Acton still finds challenges in the field. "The fact is that nearly any agent could handle the Tip O'Neill book and get him a lot of money," Acton says. "I'm proud of handling some very good writers with some very worthy books."

—Glenda Tennant Neff

MARCIA AMSTERDAM AGENCY, Suite 9A, 41 W. 82nd St., New York NY 10024. (212)873-4945. Contact: Marcia Amsterdam. Estab. 1969. Member of WGA. 20% of clients are new/unpublished writers. Eager to work with new/unpublished writers. Specializes in fiction, nonfiction, young adult, TV and movies.
Will Handle: Nonfiction books, novels, juvenile books (young adult), and movie and TV scripts. Will read—at no charge—unsolicited queries, synopsis and outlines. Reports in 2 weeks on queries; 1 month on mss. "If our agency does not respond within 1 month to your request to become a client, you may submit requests elsewhere. SASE essential."
Terms: Agent receives 15% commission on domestic sales; 15% on dramatic sales; and 15% on foreign sales. Charges for telegraph, cable, phone, and legal fees (when client agrees to them). 100% of income is derived from commission on ms and film sales.
Recent Sales: *Anachronisms*, by Christopher Hinz (St. Martin's); *House of Illusion*, by Rudy Jean Jensen (Zebra Books); *One-Handed Catch*, by Joyce Sweeney (Delacorte).

‡**ADRIAN ANBRY LITERARY AGENCY, INC.**, Suite 1, 1729 Alma St., San Diego CA 90731. (213)831-3457. Agent: Bryna Franjose. Estab. 1987. Member of WGA West. Currently represents 6 clients. 100% of clients are new/unpublished writers. Eager to work with new/unpublished writers. Specializes in "any genre, but especially comedy, mystery and sci-fi. No slasher or exploitation."
Will Handle: Novels (any genre), movie scripts (comedies, action/adventure, mystery, occult), TV scripts (movie-of-the-week material). Currently handles 2% novels; 49% movie scripts; 49% TV scripts. Will read—at no charge—unsolicited queries and outlines; may charge a criticism fee or service charge for work performed after the initial reading. Reports in 1 week on queries; 2 weeks on mss. "If our agency does not respond within 1 month to your request to become a cleint, you may submit requests elsewhere."
Terms: Charges a criticism fee "only if client wants criticism. We offer the service, but will not push it." Charges flat fee of $35. "At this time we are new and are not charging anything, unless specifically asked for criticism. Agent with degree in English will do critique, in some cases (TV/movie scripts) line by line. In the case of a manuscript, an overall evaluation." Charges writers for photocopying "if client wants us to do it."
Recent Sales: No information given.

‡**BART ANDREWS & ASSOCIATES**, 1321 N. Stanley Ave., Los Angeles CA 90046. (213)851-8158. President: Bart Andrews. Estab. 1982. Member ILAA. Represents 50 clients. 10% of clients are new/unpublished writers. Works with small number of new/unpublished writers. Specializes in nonfiction only. "Ninety-five percent of books I represent are in the show business genre—biographies, autobiographies, books about TV, etc."
Will Handle: Nonfiction books. Handles 100% nonfiction books. Will read—at no charge—unsolicited queries and outlines. Reports in 3 weeks on queries. "If our agency does not respond within 2 months to your request to become a client, you may submit requests elsewhere."
Terms: Agent receives 15% commission on domestic sales; 10% on dramatic sales; and 25% on foreign sales. "New clients are charged $150 marketing fee to offset out-of-pocket costs, i.e. phone, postage, etc." Charges writers for postage, photocopying, long distance phone calls. Sometimes offers consultation services through which writers can get advice on a contract; $150 per hour. 95% of income derived from commission on manuscript sales; 5% of income derived from fees.
Recent Sales: *Wayne Newton Autobiography*, by Wayne Newton (William Morrow); *Laughing Till It Hurts*, by J. Randy Taraborrelli (William Morrow); *The Hollywood Walk Of Fame*, by Marianne Morino (Ten Speed Press).

‡**APPLESEEDS MANAGEMENT**, Suite 302, 200 E. 30th St., San Bernardino CA 92404. (714)882-1667. Executive Manager: S. James Foiles. Estab. 1988. Eager to work with new/unpublished writers. Specializes in action, mystery, science fiction; also in materials that could be adapted from novel to screen; also in screenplays, especially for video productions; and in educational materials dealing with self-improvement, self-esteem, abuse of controlled substances, etc.
Will Handle: Nonfiction books, novels, textbooks (educational material on self-esteem, self-improvement, abuse of controlled substances), movie scripts and TV scripts. Will read—at no charge—unsolicited queries, outlines and manuscripts. Reports in 2 weeks on queries; 6 weeks on mss. "If our agency does not respond within 2 months to your request to become a client, you may submit requests elsewhere."
Terms: Agent receives 10-15% commission on domestic sales; 10-15% on dramatic sales; and 20% on foreign sales. 100% of income derived from sales of writer's work.
Recent Sales: "We are a new agency."

AUTHOR AID ASSOCIATES, 340 E. 52nd St., New York NY 10022. (212)758-4213; 697-2419. Editorial Director: Arthur Orrmont. Estab. 1967. Represents 150 clients. 10% of clients are new/unpublished writers. Works with a small number of new/unpublished authors. Publishers of *Literary Agents of North America*.
Will Handle: Magazine fiction, nonfiction books, novels, juvenile books, movie scripts, stage plays, TV scripts and poetry collections. Currently handles 5% magazine fiction; 35% nonfiction books; 38% novels; 5%

juvenile books; 5% movie scripts; 2% stage plays; 5% poetry and 5% other. Will read—at no charge—unsolicited queries and outlines. "Queries answered by return mail." Reports within 1 month on mss.
Terms: Agent receives 10-15% commission on domestic sales; 15% on dramatic sales; and 20% on foreign sales. Charges a reading fee "only to new/unpublished authors. Refundable from commission on sale." 15% of income derived from reading fees. Charges for cable, photocopy and messenger express. Offers a consultation service through which writers not represented can get advice on a contract. 15% of income derived from fees; 85% of income derived from sales of writer's work.
Recent Sales: *Prayer That Heals Our Emotions*, by Eddie Ensley (Harper & Row); and *The Judgment Day Archives*, by Igor Yefimov (Mercury House Publishing).

MAXIMILIAN BECKER, 115 E. 82nd St., New York NY 10028. (212)988-3887. President: Maximilian Becker. Estab. 1950. Works with a small number of new/unpublished authors.
Will Handle: Nonfiction books, novels and stage plays. Will read—at no charge—unsolicited queries, outlines and mss, but may charge a criticism fee or service charge for work performed after the initial reading. Reports in 2 weeks on queries; 3 weeks on mss.
Terms: Agent receives 15% commission on domestic sales; 20% on foreign sales. Charges a criticism fee "if detailed criticism is requested. Writers receive a detailed criticism with suggestions—five to ten pages. No criticism is given if manuscript is hopeless."
Recent Sales: *Goering*, by David Irving (William Morrow); *Enigma*, by David Kahn (Houghton Mifflin); and *Cecile*, by Jamine Boissard (Little Brown).

THE BLAKE GROUP LITERARY AGENCY, Suite 600, One Turtle Creek Village, Dallas TX 75219. (214)520-8562. Director/Agent: Ms. Lee B. Halff. Estab. 1979. Member of Texas Publishers Association (TPA) and Texas Booksellers Association (TBA). Represents 40 clients. Prefers to work with published/established authors; works with a small number of new/unpublished authors.
Will Handle: Limited magazine fiction and nonfiction, nonfiction books, novels, textbooks, juvenile books, movie scripts, TV scripts, limited syndicated material and poetry collectons. Currently handles 11% magazine articles; 30% nonfiction books; 40% novels; 2% textbooks; 9% juvenile books; 2% movie scripts; 1% TV scripts; 2% poetry; and 3% science fiction. "We charge a reading fee of $100 per book length manuscript ($75 for less than 100 pages). This includes a written critique. No charge for queries. Reports within 3 months. Pre-stamped return mailer must accompany submissions."
Terms: Agent receives 10% commission on domestic sales; 15% on dramatic sales; and 20% on foreign sales. Sometimes offers a consultation service through which writers not represented can get advice on a contract; charges $50/hour. Income derived from commission on ms sales and critique fees.
Recent Sales: *Captured Corregidor: Diary of an American P.O.W. in WWII*, by John M. Wright, Jr. (McFarland & Co); *Modern Language for Musicians*, by Julie Yarbrough (Pendragon Press); and Linda Richards article for "Old Cricket Says," by Katherine Kelly (*Cricket Magazine*).

‡HARRY BLOOM, 1520 S. Beverly Glen Blvd., Los Angeles CA 90024. (213)556-3461. Agent: Patrice Dale. Estab. 1967. 5% of clients new/unpublished writers. Prefers to work with published/established authors; works with small number of new/unpublished authors. Specializes in mainstream fiction, love, mystery, action/adventure and nonfiction. "No science fiction."
Will Handle: Nonfiction books, novels, movie scripts, syndicated material. Will read—at no charge—unsolicited queries and outlines. Does not read unsolicited mss. Reports in 2 weeks on queries. "If our agency does not respond within 2 weeks to your request to become a client, you may submit requests elsewhere."
Terms: No information given.
Recent Sales: Confidential.

‡REID BOATES LITERARY AGENCY, 44 Mountain Ridge Dr., Wayne NJ 07470. (201)628-7523. Contact: Reid Boates. Represents 40 clients. 30% of clients are new/unpublished writers. "To be represented writers must have a writing background, though not necessarily in books." Works with a small number of new/unpublished authors. Specializes in biogrphy and nonfiction; topical documentary, autobiography; wellness and general how-to, business (investigative); fiction: good, clear writing; strong story and character.
Will Handle: Nonfiction books, novels. Currently handles 90% nonfiction books; 10% novels. Will read—at no charge—unsolicited queries and outlines. Does not read unsolicited mss. Reports in 2 weeks.
Terms: Agent receives 15% commission on domestic sales; 15% on dramatic sales; 10% on foreign sales, "plus 10% for the foreign co-agent." Charges for photocopying over $50. 100% of income derived from commission on ms sales.
Recent Sales: *Valhalla's Wake*, by John Loftus (Atlantic Monthly Press); *Long Lines*, by Remar Sutton (Weidenfield & Nicolson); and an untitled ms on collapse of E.F. Hutton, by James Sterngold (Doubleday/Bantam).

THE BOOK PEDDLERS, 18326 Minnetonka Blvd., Deephaven MN 55391. (612)475-3527. Owner/Agent: Vicki Lansky. Estab. 1984. Member of ILAA. "Also provides, on occasion, book packaging services and does publish a few titles." Represents 26 clients. 80% of clients are new/unpublished writers. Prefers to work with published/established authors. "Small agency because owner is also an author and columnist."

Will Handle: Nonfiction books, novels and syndicated material. Currently handles 80% nonfiction books and 20% novels. Will read—at no charge—unsolicited queries and outlines. Does not read unsolicited mss. Reports in 2 weeks on queries; 3 weeks on mss. "If our agency does not respond within 1 month to your request to become a client, you may submit requests elsewhere. We take on very few clients."

Terms: Agent receives 15% commission on domestic sales; and 20% on foreign sales. Does not charge reading fee "at this time (May 1988). We do charge, however, a fee of $5 per submission. If we cannot sell your material after submitting it to 10 publishers (or any number mutually agreed upon), we will submit a bill which is payable upon receipt. This is a fee that we feel accurately represents our time, postage, phone calls, typing and copying expense." Sometimes offers a consultation service through which writers not represented can get advice on a contract; charges $50/hour. 90% of agency income derived from commission on ms sales.

Recent Sales: *My Writing Book*, by Joyce Baumgartner (Scholastic); *Jewish-American Baby Name Book*, by Smadar Sidi (Harper and Row); and *How to Keep Your Child from Failing When the School Fails Your Child*, by Stafford Calvin (Warners).

‡BOOKSTOP LITERARY AGENCY, 67 Meadowview Rd., Orinda CA 94563. (415)254-2664. Owner: Kendra Bersamin. Estab. 1984. Represents 60 clients. 20% of clients are new/unpublished writers. Specializes in juvenile and young adult fiction and nonfiction.

Will Handle: Only juvenile books. Handles 100% juvenile books. Will read submissions at no charge, but may charge a criticism fee or service charge for work performed after the initial reading. Reports in 1 month on queries; 6 weeks on mss. "If our agency does not respond within 2 months to your request to become a client, you may submit requests elsewhere."

Terms: Agent receives 15% commission on domestic sales; 20% on dramatic sales; and 20% on foreign sales. Charges criticism fee "if the author has asked for a detailed critique." .001% of income derived from criticism fees. Charges $150 for 300-page double-spaced book manuscript. "Agent provides critiques of three or four pages (general) with line by line where necessary." Charges for postage, phone and copying. Sometimes offers consultation service through which writers can get advice on a contract. "We work out the fee." 95% of income derived from commission on mss sales; 5% of income derived from fees.

Recent Sales: *Merry Go Round Dog's Tail*, by Elisa Schneider (Knopf); *Letter to Letter*, by Sloat (Dutton); and *Rebel's Choice*, by Easton (Gulliver).

GEORGES BORCHARDT INC., 136 E. 57th St., New York NY 10022. (212)753-5785. President: Georges Borchardt. Estab. 1967. Member of SAR. Represents 200 clients. 1-2% of our clients are new/unpublished writers. "We do not consider new clients unless highly recommended by someone we trust." Prefers to work with published/established authors; also works with a small number of new/unpublished authors. Specializes in fiction, biography and general nonfiction of unusual interest.

Will Handle: Nonfiction books and novels. Does not read unsolicited mss.

Terms: Agent receives 10% commission on domestic sales; 10% on dramatic sales; and 20% on foreign sales (15% on British). Charges for photocopy expenses. 100% of income derived from commission on ms sales.

Recent Sales: *The New Confessions*, by William Boyd (Morrow); *World's End*, by T. Coraghessan Boyle (Viking); *Elisabeth Young-Bruehl: Anna Freud* (Summit).

BOSTON LITERARY AGENCY, Suite 404, 333 W. 57th St., New York NY 10019. (212)765-3663. Contact: Justin K. McDonough. Estab. 1975. Works with a small number of new/unpublished writers; eager to work with new/unpublished writers.

Will Handle: Nonfiction books, novels, movie and TV scripts. Currently handles 50% novels; 50% nonfiction books. Does not read unsolicited ms. Reports in 2 weeks on queries.

Terms: Agent receives 10% commission on domestic sales; 15% on dramatic sales; and 20% on foreign sales. Charges writers for photocopy and overnight express mail expenses. 100% of income derived from commission on ms sales.

Recent Sales: *Forensic Fires*, by F. Reid Buckley (Harper and Row); *Paul Manship*, by John Manship (Abbeville Press).

THE BRADLEY-GOLDSTEIN AGENCY, Suite 6E, 7 Lexington Ave., New York NY 10010. (718)672-7924. President: Paul Bradley. Director: Martha Goldstein. Estab. 1985. Represents 50 clients. 25% of clients have been new/unpublished writers. Will consider taking on a small number of new/unpublished authors. Specializes in "quality" nonfiction: biographies, politics, science, social science, business, current affairs, and the arts.

Will Handle: Nonfiction books. Currently handles 90% nonfiction books; 10% novels. Will read—at no charge—unsolicited query letters and outlines only. "Include SASE." Do not send mss. Reports in 2 months on queries.

Terms: Agent receives 15% commission on domestic sales; and 25% on foreign sales. Charges for postage,

photocopying, and telephone expenses. Offers a consultation service through which writers can get advice on a contract; charges $60/hour. 90% of income is derived from commission on ms sales; 10% on consultations.
Recent Sales: *Oscar Wilde and His Circle*, by Natisha Gray (E.P. Dutton); *Women of the Third World*, by Maxine Fisher (Franklin Watts); *The Frigate Pallada*, by Ivan Goncharov; trans. by Klaus Goetze (St. Martin's).

‡ANDREA BROWN, LITERARY AGENCY, 319 East 52 St., New York NY 10022. (212)319-7398. Owner: Andrea Brown. Estab. 1981. Member of ILAA. Number of clients: confidential. 50% of our clients are new/unpublished writers. Works with a small number of new/unpublished authors. Specializes in children's books—all ages.
Will Handle: Juvenile books. Currently handles 5% nonfiction books; 95% juvenile books. Will read—at no charge—unsolicited queries and outlines. Reports in 2 weeks on queries; 3 months on manuscripts. "If our agency does not respond within 2 months to your request to become a client, you may submit requests elsewhere."
Terms: Agent receives 15% commission on domestic sales; 20% on foreign sales. Charges for phone calls. Sometimes offer a consultation service through which writers can get advice on a contract; charges $200 flat fee. 100% of income derived from sales of writer's work.
Recent Sales: *Mad, Mad Monday*, by Herma Silverstein (Lodestar-Dutton); *Outer Space and All That Junk*, by Mel Gilden (Harper & Row); *Penguins*, by Caroline Arnold (Morrow Junior).

CURTIS BROWN LTD., 10 Astor Pl., New York NY 10003. (212)473-5400. Member of SAR. Prefers to work with published/established authors; works with a small number of new/unpublished authors. Specializes in general fiction and nonfiction.
Will Handle: Nonfiction books, novels and juvenile books. Will read—at no charge—unsolicited queries and outlines accompanied by SASE; does not read unsolicited mss.
Terms: "Will explain to clients when they wish to sign."
Recent Sales: No information given.

NED BROWN INC., Box 5020, Beverly Hills CA 90210. (213)276-1131. President: Ned Brown. Estab. 1963. Writer must be previously published or have a recommendation from other client or publisher. Prefers to work with published/established authors.
Will Handle: Magazine fiction, nonfiction books, novels, movie scripts, stage plays and TV scripts. Does not read unsolicited mss.
Terms: Agent receives 10% commission on domestic sales; 15% on dramatic sales; and 20% on foreign sales. Charges writers for "extraordinary expenses."
Recent Sales: No information given.

PEMA BROWNE LTD., 185 E. 85th St., New York NY 10028. (212)369-1925. Treasurer: Perry J. Browne. Estab. 1966. Member of WGA. Represents 25 clients. 25% of clients are new/unpublished writers. "We review only new projects and require that writers have not sent manuscript to publishers or other agents." Eager to work with new/unpublished writers. Specializes in men's adventure, thrillers, mainstream, historical, regencies and contemporary romances; young adult; children's; reference; how-to and other types on nonfiction.
Will Handle: Nonfiction books, novels, juvenile books, movie scripts, TV scripts and syndicated material. Currently handles 25% nonfiction books; 25% novels; 10% juvenile books; 2% movie scripts; 2% TV scripts; 2% syndicated material; and 33% mass-market. Will read—at no charge—unsolicited queries, synopses and mss. Reports in 2 weeks on queries; 1 month on mss. "If our agency does not respond within 2 months to your request to become a client, you may submit requests elsewhere."
Terms: Agent receives 15% commission on domestic sales; 10% on dramatic sales; and 10% on foreign sales. 100% of income derived from commission on ms sales.
Recent Sales: *The Trouble with J.J.*, by Tami Hoag (Bantam); *Tenkiller* (series), by J. Rosenberger (Pageant-Crown); *Now There's Tomorrow*, by Cara West (Harlequin).

JANE BUTLER, ART AND LITERARY AGENT, Associate, Virginia Kidd Literary Agents, 538 E. Harford St., Box 278, Milford PA 18337. (717)296-7266, 491-2045. Associate: Jane Butler. Estab. 1981. "Prefers some published credits, but all queries are welcome; no SASE, no reply." Works with small number of new/upublished writers each year. "The best part of agenting is discovering new talent: writer should be prolific in one of the areas within which I specialize." Specializes in nonfiction (popular natural history, popular soft sciences—anthropology, archaeology; native American and oriental religious history and modern practice; myths and fairy tales; and military history) and fiction (historical, mysteries, science fiction, horror, historical fantasy and fantasy).
Will Handle: Nonfiction books and novels. Currently handles 15% nonfiction books; 80% novels; 5% juvenile books. Will read—at no charge—unsolicited queries, outlines and mss. Reports in 2 weeks on queries; 1 month on mss. "If our agency does not respond within 2 months to your request to become a client, you may

submit requests elsewhere."
Terms: Agent receives 10% commission on domestic sales; 15% on dramatic sales; and 20% on foreign sales. 100% of income derived from commission on ms sales.
Recent Sales: *Master Heredes*, by Alis Rasmussen (Bantam Spectra); *Track of the Gray Wolf*, by Gary Gentile (Avon Books); and *Alamut*, by Judith Tarr (Bantam Spectra).

‡**THE MARSHALL CAMERON AGENCY**, Rt. 1, Box 125, Lawtey FL 32058. (904)964-7013. Director: Margo Prescott. Represents 15 clients. 50% of our clients are new/unpublished writers. Eager to work with new/unpublished writers. Specializes in screenplays, teleplays and novels with screenplay potential.
Will Handle: Novels, movie scripts and TV scripts. Currently handles 5% novels; 70% movie scripts; and 25% TV scripts. Will read—at no charge—unsolicited queries and outlines. Reports in 2 weeks on queries. "If our agency does not respond within 2 months to your request to become a client, you may submit requests elsewhere."
Terms: Agent receives 15% commission on domestic sales; 20% on dramatic sales; and 20% on foreign sales. Charges an evaluation fee; waives fee when representing writer. 10% of income derived from reading fees. Charges $145 for 250 pages. "Provides the reader with an in-depth written evaluation/critique. Critique includes line-by-line with overall evaluation and suggestions for enhancement. Usually 3-6 pages." Charges $20 monthly retainer fee for postage, phone, photocopying, binding.
Recent Sales: No information given.

CANADIAN SPEAKERS' AND WRITERS' SERVICE LIMITED, 44 Douglas Crescent, Toronto, Ontario M4W 2L7 Canada. (416)921-4443. President: Matie Molinaro. Estab. 1950. Represents 225 clients. 3% of clients are new/unpublished writers. Prefers to work with published/established authors; works with a small number of new/unpublished authors.
Will Handle: Magazine fiction, nonfiction books, novels, juvenile books, movie scripts, radio scripts, stage plays and TV scripts. Currently handles 70% nonfiction books; 5% novels; 5% movie scripts; 10% radio scripts; 5% stage plays; and 5% TV scripts. Does not read unsolicited mss. Reports in 3 weeks on queries; 1 month on mss. "If our agency does not respond within 1 month to your request to become a client, you may submit requests elsewhere."
Terms: Agent receives 15% commission on domestic sales; 15% on dramatic sales; and 20% on foreign sales. Charges a criticism/reading fee: $50, plus $3/one-thousand words. "Each reading/critique is handled by four people and a composite report is sent out to the writer." Offers a consultation service through which writers not represented can get advice on a contract; charges $160/hour. 5% of income derived from fees; 95% of income derived from commission on manuscript sales. Payment of a criticism fee does not ensure that agency will represent a writer.
Recent Sales: *McLuhan Letter*, (Oxford University Press); *Ben Wicks First Treasury*, by Ben Wicks (Methuen Publishers); and *Medical Survival*, by Dr. Gifford Jones (Methuen).

RUTH CANTOR, LITERARY AGENT, Rm. 1133, 156 5th Ave., New York NY 10010. (212)243-3246. Contact: Ruth Cantor. Estab. 1952. Represents 40 clients. Writer must have "a good, sound track record in the publishing field . . . A skimpy one will sometimes get you a reading if I'm convinced that talent might be lurking in the bulrushes." Prefers to work with published/established authors; works with a small number of new/unpublished authors. Specializes in "any good trade book, fiction of quality, good, competent mysteries with new elements, juvenile books above the age of eight, up through young adult."
Will Handle: Nonfiction books, novels and juvenile books. Will read—at no charge—unsolicited queries and outlines. Reports in 1 month on queries; 2 months on mss.
Terms: Agent receives 10% commission on domestic sales; 10% on dramatic sales; and 10% on foreign sales.
Recent Sales: *The Rod of Sybil* (Harcourt); *The Players* (Warner); and *Lady Divine*, by Barbara Sherrod (Warner).

‡**MARIA CARVAINIS AGENCY, INC.**, 235 W. End Ave., New York NY 10023. (212)580-1559. Contact: Maria Carvainis. Estab. 1977. Member of WGA, Author' Guild and Romance Writers of America. Represents over 60 clients. 10% of clients are new/unpublished writers. Eager to work with new/unpublished writers on a selective basis. Specializes in mainstream fiction, historicals, category romance, regencies, westerns, mysteries, suspense, fantasy and young adult fiction, business and finance, women's issues, political biography, medicine, psychology and popular and social science.
Will Handle: Magazine articles and fiction (for clients already represented); nonfiction books; novels; young adult books; movie scripts; TV scripts; and poetry (for established poets only). Currently handles 5% magazine articles; 40% nonfiction books; 45% novels; and 10% young adult books. Will read—at no charge—unsolicited queries accompanied by SASE. Reports in 2-3 weeks, "if not earlier" on queries; 3 months from date of receipt for solicited mss and partials. Unsolicited submissions are not read but returned when time permits.
Terms: Agent receives 15% commission on domestic sales; 10% on dramatic sales; and 20% on foreign sales. 100% of income derived from commission on ms sales.

Recent Sales: *Waging Peace and War*, by Thomas J. Schoenbaum (Simon & Schuster); *Dun & Bradstreet Guide to Your Investments*, by Nancy Dunnan (Harper & Row); *Slow Heat in Heaven*, by Sandra Brown (Warner Books).

‡MARTHA CASSELMAN, LITERARY AGENT, 1263 12th Ave., San Francisco CA 94122. (415)665-3235. Contact: Cheryl Carroll. Estab. 1978. Member ILAA. 25% of clients are new/unpublished writers. Works with small number of new/unpublished writers. Specializes in food books, general nonfiction, fiction, occasional humor, small number of children's books.
Will Handle: Nonfiction books; novels, juvenile books. Will read—at no charge—unsolicited queries and outlines. Does not read unsolicited mss. Reports in 1 month.
Terms: Agent receives 15% commission on domestic sales. Charges for copying, overnight mail or travel made at author's request. Sometimes offers consultation service through which writers can get advice on contract; $60/hour.
Recent Sales: Confidential.

TERRY CHIZ AGENCY, Suite E, 5761 Whitnall Hwy., North Hollywood CA 91601. (818)506-0994. President: Terry Chiz. Vice President: Shan Sia. Estab. 1984. Represents 18 clients. 20% of clients are new/unpublished writers. Prefers to work with published/established authors; works with a small number of new/unpublished authors. Specializes in film and TV.
Will Handle: Novels, movie scripts and TV scripts. No romance or historical. Currently handles 20% novels; 40% movie scripts; and 40% TV scripts. Will read—at no charge—unsolicited queries and outlines. Reports in 2 weeks. "If our agency does not respond within 1 month to your request to become a client, you may submit elsewhere." Will not respond without SASE.
Terms: Agent receives 10% commission.
Recent Sales: "Film deals pending on several properties that are in book and script—not for public information."

‡DIANE CLEANER INC., 55 5th St., New York NY 10003. (212)206-5600. Estab. 1982. Member ILAA. Specializes in general trade, fiction/nonfiction.
Will Handle: Nonfiction books, novels. Will read—at no charge—unsolicited queries and outlines. Does not read unsolicited mss. Reports in 3 weeks on queries; 5 weeks on mss.
Terms: Agent receives 15% commission on domestic sales; 15% on dramatic sals and 19% on foreign sales. Charges for photocopying. 100% of income derived from mss sales.
Recent Sales: Confidential.

HY COHEN LITERARY AGENCY, LTD., Suite 1400, 111 W. 57th St., New York NY 10019. (212)757-5237. Mail queries and mansucripts to Box 743, Upper Montclair NJ 07043. President: Hy Cohen. Estab. 1975. Represents 20 clients. 50% of our clients are new/unpublished writers.
Will Handle: Nonfiction books and novels. Currently handles 50% nonfiction books and 50% novels. Will read—at no charge—unsolicited queries, outlines and mss, accompanied by SASE. Reports in 1 week on queries; 1 month on mss. "If our agency does not respond within 1 month to your request to become a client, you may submit requests elsewhere."
Terms: Agent receives 10% commission on domestic sales; 10% on dramatic sales; and 20% on foreign sales. Charges for "unusual" postage and phone expenses. 100% of income derived from commission on ms sales.
Recent Sales: *Terror in the Skies*, by David Grayson (Citadel); *Serious Living*, by Tom Lorenz (Viking); and *Common Sense ESP*, by Robert Ferguson (St. Martin's).

RUTH COHEN, INC., Box 7626, Menlo Park CA 94025. (415)854-2054. President: Ruth Cohen. Estab. 1982. Member of ILAA. Represents 45-60 clients. 30% of clients are new/unpublished writers. Writers must have a book that is well written. Prefers to work with published/established authors; eager to work with new/unpublished writers. Specializes in juvenile, young adult nonfiction and genre books—mystery, western, historical romance, horror and thrillers. No poetry or screenplays.
Will Handle: Nonfiction books for adults, juvenile books (for ages 3-14 and young adult), and genre novels—mystery, Western, mainstream romance, regency romances and historical romance. Currently handles 30% nonfiction books; 30% novels; and 40% juvenile books. Will read—at no charge—unsolicited queries with 10 opening pages of manuscripts and SASE, outlines and partial mss. "No complete manuscripts unless requested." Reports in 3 weeks on queries; 1 month on mss. "No multiple agency submissions. If our agency does not respond within 3 months to your request to become a client, you may submit requests elsewhere." Must include SASE with all mss on queries.
Terms: Agent receives 15% commission on domestic sales; 15% on dramatic sales; and 20% on foreign sales. Charges writers for photocopying. 100% of income derived from commission on ms sales.
Recent Sales: *Abuela* (EP Dutton); *Borderlands* (Walker and Company); and *Angel Wings* (Harper and Row).

COLLIER ASSOCIATES, 2000 Flat Run Rd., Seaman OH 45679. (513)764-1234. Manager: Oscar Collier. Estab. 1976. Member of SAR and ILAA. Represents 80 clients. Rarely works with new/unpublished authors. Specializes in fiction trade books (war, crime, and historical novels) and nonfiction trade books on business and finance, biographies, math for general audience, politics, exposes, nature and outdoors and history.
Terms: Agent receives 15% commission on domestic sales; 15% on dramatic sales; and 20% on foreign sales. Charges for books ordered from publishers for rights submissions, Express Mail, and copying expenses.
Recent Sales: *Silver Flame*, by Susan Johnson (Berkley); *Fair Weather Foul*, by Sean Freeman (Wm. Morrow); and *Citizen Welles*, by Frank Brady (Scribner's).

‡COLUMBIA LITERARY ASSOCIATES, INC., 7902 Nottingham Way, Ellicott City MD 21043. (301)465-1595. Contact: Linda Hayes or Kathryn Jensen. Works through agents in Hollywood and several foreign countries. Estab. 1980. Represents 40 clients. 10% of clients are new/unpublished writers. Works with a small number of new/unpublished authors. Specializes in adult mass market, mainstream fiction and nonfiction, contemporary romance (category and single title), commercial women's fiction, suspense, intrigue, cookbooks, general commercial nonfiction and book series. No children's books, poetry, short stories, pornography, men's adventure or experimental fiction.
Will Handle: Nonfiction books, novels (open to family sagas, "blockbusters") and cookbooks. Currently handles 30% nonfiction books and 70% novels. Will read—at no charge—unsolicited queries and outlines; must include SASE for response. Reports in 3 weeks on queries; 6 weeks on mss. "If our agency does not respond within 6 weeks to your request to become a client, you may submit requests elsewhere."
Terms: Agent receives 12-15% commission on domestic sales and 20% on dramatic and foreign sales if separate from book rights. Charges writers for photocopies, shipping and phone expenses, and for copies of book required for subrights marketing. Sometimes offers a consultation service through which writers not represented can get advice on a contract; charges $50/hour.
Recent Sales: The Charisma, Inc. series (Crow/Pageant); *The International Cookie Cookbook* (Stewart, Tabori & Chang); *Postmark* (Tudor).

CONNOR LITERARY AGENCY, 640 W. 153rd St., New York NY 10031. (212)491-5233. Owner: Marlene Connor. Estab. 1985. Represents 28 clients. 25% of clients are new/unpublished writers. "I would prefer that my writers have been published at some point (it shows that they have attempted to market themselves). Literary awards are also good." Specializes in commercial fiction. "I am also interested in black and ethnic writers. I am an expert at general nonfiction, how-to, illustrated, and self-help books. I also work with books that tie-in with an organization or corporation. I work closely with an excellent book producing team for books that are heavily illustrated or have special design needs."
Will Handle: Nonfiction books, novels, illustrated, how-to and self-help. Currently handles 50% nonfiction books and 50% novels. Will read—at no charge—unsolicited queries and outlines. Reports in 2 months on queries. "Material will not be returned without SASE."
Terms: Agent receives 15% commission on domestic sales; and 25% on foreign sales. No criticism fee "unless the author requests a criticism after rejection, then the charge is $50. Because of the volume of submissions I can only answer those I am interested in." Charges for photocopy, postage, telephone and messenger expenses, and special materials for presentation. Sometimes offers a consultation service through which writers can get advice on a contract; charges $75/hour. 2% of income derived from fees; 98% of income derived from commission on ms sales.
Recent Sales: *Simplicity's Knitting with Style* (Harper & Row): *Death of an Innocent Child*, by Morton Reed (Zebra); and *Looking for a Rain God: An Anthology of Contemporary African Literature*, (Fireside Books).

‡BILL COOPER ASSOC., INC., Suite 411, 224 W. 49th St., New York NY 10019. (212)307-1100. Contact: William Cooper. Estab. 1964. Represents 10 clients. 10% of clients are new/unpublished writers. Prefers to work with published/established authors; works with a small number of new/unpublished authors. Specializes in contemporary fiction.
Will Handle: Novels and movie scripts. Currently handles 90% novels and 10% movie scripts. May charge a reading fee for unpublished writers. Reports in 2 weeks on queries and mss. No unsolicited submissions.
Terms: Agent receives 15% commission on domestic sales; 15% on dramatic sales; and 20% on foreign sales. Payment of a criticism fee does not ensure that agency will represent writer.
Recent Sales: No information given.

‡ROBERT CORNFIELD LITERARY AGENCY, 145 West 79th St., New York NY 10024. (212)874-2465. Contact: Robert Cornfield/Bruce Hardy. Estab. 1980. Member ILAA. Represents 70 clients. 20% of client's are new/unpublished writers. Works with small number of new/unpublished authors. Specializes in fiction, food, music, film, literary criticism and history.
Will Handle: Nonfiction books and novels. Currently handles 10% magazine articles; 10% magazine fiction; 40% nonfiction books; 20% novels; 10% textbooks; 10% syndicated material. Will read—at no cost—unsolicited queries, outlines and manuscripts. Reports in 2 weeks on queries; 1 month on mss. "If our agency does not

respond within 2 months to your request to become a client, you may submit requests elsewhere."
Terms: Agent receives 15% commission on domestic sales; 15% on dramatic sales; and 20% on foreign sales. Charges for foreign postage, ms photocopying and galley fees. 100% of income derived from commission on mss sales.
Recent Sales: *Elvis World*, by Jane and Michael Stern (Knopf); *Math and Music*, by Edward Rothstein (Knopf); and *Muragans Chariot*, by Indiva Ganesan (Knopf).

‡CREATIVE CONCEPTS LITERARY AGENCY, Suite V, 509 67th Ave. N., Myrtle Beach SC 29577. (803)449-0723. Director: Michele Glance Serwach. Estab. 1987. Represent 12 clients. 80% of clients are new/unpublished writers. "We welcome new/unpublished writers—the only requirement is that you have an outline or manuscript ready to submit." Eager to work with new/unpublished writers. Specializes in how-to books, self-help books, cookbooks, general interest novels, romance novels and poetry.
Will Handle: Magazine articles, nonfiction books, novels, juvenile books, movie scripts, TV scripts, syndicated material, poetry. Currently handles 5% magazine articles; 50% nonfiction books; 20% novels; 5% juvenile books; 5% movie scripts; 5% TV scripts; 5% syndicated material; 5% poetry. Will read—at no charge—unsolicited queries and outlines. Reports in 3 weeks on queries; 5 weeks on mss. "If our agency does not respond within 2 months to your request to become a client, you may submit requests elsewhere."
Terms: Agent receives 12% commission on domestic sales; 12% on dramatic sales; and 12% on foreign sales.
Recent Sales: Confidential.

RICHARD CURTIS ASSOCIATES, INC., Suite 1, 164 E. 64th St., New York NY 10021. (212)371-9481. President: Richard Curtis. Contact: Elizabeth Waxse, associate. Estab. 1969. Member of ILAA. Represents 75 clients. 5% of clients are new/unpublished writers. Writer must have some published work and either a finished novel or proposed nonfiction book. Prefers to work with published/established authors; works with a small number of new/unpublished authors. Specializes in commercial fiction of all genres, mainstream fiction and nonfiction. Especially interested in health, science, how-to, New Age, psychology, biography, social history, women's issues, relationships, business, true crime.
Will Handle: Nonfiction books, novels, textbooks, juvenile books, and movie scripts. Currently handles 1% magazine articles; 1% magazine fiction; 25% nonfiction books; 65% novels; 5% textbooks; 3% juvenile books. Will read—at no charge—unsolicited queries and outlines. Reports in 2 weeks on queries; 1 month on mss. "If our agency does not respond within 1 month to your request to become a client, you may submit requests elsewhere."
Terms: Agent receives 10% commission on domestic sales; 15% on dramatic sales; and 20% on foreign sales. Charges a reading fee; 1% of income derived from reading fee. Writer receives two to four single-spaced pages of general explanation, line-by-line, and assessment of market and of author's "credentials." Work done by book trade editors. Charges for photocopying, messengers, purchase of books for subsidiary exploitations, cable, air mail and express mail. Offers a consultation service through which writers not represented can get advice on a contract; charges $200/hour. 1% of income derived from fees; 99% of income derived from commission on ms sales.
Recent Sales: *Heiress*, by Janet Dailey (Little, Brown); *Blazewyndham*, by Beatrice Small (NAL); and *Forge of God*, by Greg Bear (Tor).

‡DAVID CUTLER & ASSOCIATES, 2983 Oakleigh Lane, Oakton VA 22124. (703)255-2886. President: David Cutler. Estab. 1986. Member and former vice-president of Washington Independent Writers. Represents 20 clients. 25% of clients are new/unpublished writers. "Prefer that writers have published at least several long articles, and have clear notion of the book they wish to have represented." Prefers to work with published/established authors. Specializes in nonfiction: biography, business, political science, humanities, journalism, New Age, radio, technology, television and marketing. Fiction: serious literary novels, mysteries, and spy thrillers.
Will Handle: Nonfiction books, novels and "some short story collections." Currently handles 75% nonfiction books; 20% novels; 5% other. Will read—at no charge—unsolicited queries. Does not read unsolicited manuscripts. Reports in 3 weeks on queries. "If our agency does not respond within 2 months to your request to become a client, you may submit requests elsewhere."
Terms: Agent receives 10-15% commission on domestic sales; 20% on foreign sales. Charges for reproduction, mailing, phone and incidentals. Offers a consultation service through which writers can get advice on a contract; charges $65-75/hour. 90% of income derived from sales of writer's work; 10% of income from consultation service.
Recent Sales: No information given.

D.J. ENTERPRISES, 339 S. Franklin St., Allentown PA 18102. (215)437-0723. President: Douglas J. Tomel. Estab. 1980. Member of ILAA. Represents 200 clients. 95% of clients are new/unpublished writers. Writer must send letter of reference before sending ms. Prefers to work with published/established authors. "We handle all material, except gay material."

Will Handle: Magazine articles (true-to-life stories) and movie and TV scripts. Currently handles 5% magazine articles; 90% movie scripts; and 5% TV scripts. Will read—at no charge—unsolicited queries, outlines and mss. Reports in 2 weeks on queries and mss. "If our agency does not respond within 1 month to your request to become a client, you may submit requests elsewhere."
Terms: Agent receives 10% commission on domestic, dramatic, and foreign sales. Charges for postage expenses.
Recent Sales: *Miracle of Melody Malone,* by John Inman; *The Great Sports Caper*, by Doug Tomel.

‡**JOAN DAVES**, 21 West 26th St., New York NY 10010-1083. (212)685-9573. Owner: Joan Daves. Estab. 1952. Represents 100 clients. 15% of clients are new/unpublished writers. Some previous professional writing and publishing would help unpublished writers. Prefers to work with published/established authors; works with small number of new/unpublished authors. Specializes in "good writing, be it fiction, nonfiction or mainstream novels. No science fiction or romances because I don't understand how to judge them in today's market."
Will Handle: Nonfiction books, novels, juvenile books. Currently handles 2% magazine articles; 4% magazine fiction; 35% nonfiction books; 35% novels; 21% juvenile books; 1% syndicated material; 2% poetry. Will read—at no charge—unsolicited queries and outlines. Reports in 2 weeks on queries; 6 weeks on mss. "If our agency does not respond within 2 months to your request to become a client, you may submit requests elsewhere."
Terms: Agent receives 15% commission on domestic sales on new clients; and 20% on foreign sales. Charges writers for Telex and over seas calls, overseas postage for books sent.

‡**ATHOS DEMETRIOU**, #6C, 211 West 10th St., New York NY 10014. (212)741-0035. President: Athos Demetriou. Agent: Dale Reyer. Estab. 1986. Represents 35 clients. 50% of clients are new/unpublished writers. Eager to work with new/unpublished writers. Specializes in nonfiction works, how-to, self help, history, biography, mainstream fiction, adventure novels.
Will Handle: Nonfiction books and novels. Handles 60% nonfiction books; 40% novels. Will read—at no charge—unsolicited queries, outlines and mss. Reports in 3 weeks on queries; 8 weeks on mss. "If our agency does not respond within 3 months to your request to become a client, you may submit requests elsewhere."
Terms: Agent receives 15% commission on domestic sales; 15% on dramatic sales; and 20% on foreign sales. Charges for international mail costs, international phone calls, photocopying of mss and messengers.
Recent Sales: *Prospect of Detachment*, by Lindsley Cameron (St. Martin's Press); *By Trust Betrayed*, by Hugh Gallagher (Henry Holt); and *Something to Live For*, by Christine Macarte (Dutton).

ANITA DIAMANT, THE WRITER'S WORKSHOP, INC., #1508, 310 Madison Ave., New York NY 10017. (212)687-1122. President: Anita Diamant. Estab. 1917. Member of SAR. Represents 100 clients. 30% of clients are new/unpublished writers. Prefers to work with published/established authors; works with a small number of new/unpublished authors. Specializes in general and commercial fiction (hard and soft cover) such as historical romances, general romances, horror and science fiction; and nonfiction such as health, politics and biography.
Will Handle: Magazine articles, nonfiction books and novels. Currently handles 40% nonfiction books; 40% novels; 10% young adult books; and 10% other. Will read—at no charge—unsolicited queries. Reports in 1 month on queries. "If our agency does not respond within 2 months to your request to become a client, you may submit requests elsewhere."
Terms: Agent receives 15% commission for up to $120,000 advance on domestic sales—10% thereafter; 15% on dramatic sales; and 15-20% on foreign sales. Charges for photocopy, messenger, special mailing and telephone expenses. 100% of income derived from sales of writers' work.
Recent Sales: *Dark Angel*, by V.C. Andrews (Poseidon); *New McGarr*, by Bartholemew Gill (Viking/Penguin); and *Reasons of the Heart*, by Henry Giniger (Franklin Watts).

‡**DIAMOND LITERARY AGENCY, INC.**, 3063 S. Kearney St., Denver CO 80222. (303)759-0291. President: Pat Dalton. Estab. 1982. Represents 20 clients. 15% of clients are new/unpublished writers. Not encouraging submissions from unpublished writers at this time. Specializes in novels, with particular interest in woman's fiction; thrillers, romantic suspense, mysteries, romance; nonfiction books with a broad appeal; and screenplays.
Will Handle: Nonfiction books, novels, movie scripts, TV scripts. Currently handles 10% nonfiction books; 85% novels; 5% movie scripts. Will read—at no charge—unsolicited queries. Does not read unsolicited manuscripts from unpublished writers except with payment of a $15 reading fee. Reports in 2 weeks on queries; 1 month on manuscripts. "Simultaneous submissions are acceptable as long as indicated as such, and not already under contract to another agent."
Terms: Agent receives 10-15% commission on domestic sales; 15% on dramatic sales; and 20% on foreign sales. Fee is $15 if the writer has not previously sold the same type of project (book or script); reading fee will be waived if representing the writer. Less than 1% of income derived from reading fees. "We provide critique if

the project is close to being publishable at no additional charge; require that a standard-size cassette tape accompany each submission for possible comments." Charges for foreign air courier only. Over 99% of income derived from writers' work.

Recent Sales: *Critic's Choice*, by Cassie Miles (Crown); *Special Touches*, by Sharon Brondos (Harlequin); and *Close Scrutiny*, by Pat Dalton (Berkley).

SANDRA DIJKSTRA LITERARY AGENCY, Suite 515C, 1237 Camino Del Mar, Del Mar CA 92014. (619)755-3115. Contact: Sandra Dijkstra. Estab. 1981. Member of ILAA. Represents 50 clients. 60% of clients are new/unpublished writers. "We, of course, prefer to take on established authors, but are happy to represent any writer of brilliance or special ability. Most of our sales have been nonfiction, but we are building a quality fiction list."

Will Handle: Nonfiction books (author must have expertise in the field) and novels. Currently handles 75% nonfiction books; 25% novels. Will read—at no charge—unsolicited queries and outlines accompanied by SASE. Reports in 3 weeks on queries. "If our agency does not respond within 6 weeks to your request to become a client, you may submit requests elsewhere."

Terms: Receives 15% commission on domestic sales; 20% on British sales (10% to British agent); and 30% on translation (20% to foreign agent who represents world rights). Consultation/editing available for a fee. Charges a $175 yearly expense fee to cover phone, postage, photocopy costs incurred in marketing ms of authors under contract.

Recent Sales: *If I'm So Wonderful Why Am I Still Single*, by Susan Page (Viking); *White Rabbit: A Woman Doctor's 17-Year Battle with Drug Addiction*, by Martha Morrison, M.D. (Crown); and *The Joy Luck Club*, by Amy Ian (Putnam's).

THE JONATHAN DOLGER AGENCY, Suite 9B, 49 E. 96th St., New York NY 10128. (212)427-1853. President: Jonathan Dolger. Estab. 1980. Represents 70 clients. 25% of clients are new/unpublished writers. Writer must have been previously published if submitting fiction. Prefers to work with published/established authors; works with a small number of new/unpublished writers. Specializes in adult trade fiction and nonfiction, and illustrated books.

Will Handle: Nonfiction books, novels and illustrated books. Will read—at no charge—unsolicited queries and outlines with SASE included.

Terms: Agent receives 15% commission on domestic sales; 10% on dramatic sales; and 25-30% on foreign sales. Charges for "standard expenses." Offers a consultation service through which writers not represented can get advice on a contract; charges a negotiable fee. 100% of income derived from commission on ms sales.

Recent Sales: Confidential.

DORESE AGENCY LTD., 8A, 41 W. 82nd St., New York NY 10024. (212)580-2855. President: Alyss Dorese. Estab. 1979. Member of WGA. Represents 35 clients. 10% of clients are new/unpublished authors. Writers must have been "published previously, unless recommended by a professional, or else we must be impressed by the material or subject matter." Works with a small number of new/unpublished authors. Specializes in nonfiction, true crime and mass market fiction.

Will Handle: Magazine articles (public affairs); nonfiction books; novels; movie scripts. Currently handles 30% nonfiction books; 20% novels; 60% movie scripts; and 10% TV scripts. Will read—at no charge—unsolicited queries and outlines. Does not read unsolicited mss. Reports in 6 weeks on queries. "If our agency does not respond within 2 months to your request to become a client, you may submit requests elsewhere."

Terms: Agent receives 15% commission on domestic sales; 15% on dramatic sales; and 20% on foreign sales. Charges a reading and criticism fee of $50/250-page ms; $75/350 pages. Fee will be deducted from first monies earned. 10% of incomed derived from reading fees. Charges for legal fees, phone and photocopy expenses. Sometimes offers a consultation service through which writers not represented can get advice on a contract; charges $60/hour. 1% of commission derived from fees; 94% of income derived from sales of writer's work; 5% of income derived from criticism services. Payment of a criticism fee does not ensure that agency will represent a writer as the writer's work might not be commercial.

Recent Sales: Confidential.

EDUCATIONAL DESIGN SERVICES, INC., Box 253, Wantagh NY 11793. (718)539-4107/(516)221-0995. Vice President: Edwin Selzer. President: Bertram Linder. Estab. 1979. Represents 18 clients. 90% of clients are new/unpublished writers. Eager to work with new/unpublished writers in the educational field. Specializes in educational materials aimed at the kindergarten through twelfth grade market; primarily textual materials.

Will Handle: Nonfiction books and textbooks. Currently handles 100% textbooks. Reports in 1 month on queries and mss. "If our agency does not respond within 6 weeks to your request to become a client, you may submit requests elsewhere. You must send SASE."

Terms: Agent receives 15% commission on domestic sales; and 25% on foreign sales. Charges for phone, postage and delivery expenses, and retyping "if necessary"; charges $50/hour. 100% of income derived from commission on ms sales.

Recent Sales: *Money* (Schoolhouse Press); *Nueva Historia de Los Estados Unidos* (Minerva Books); and *Comprehensive Social Studies* (Barrons Education Series).

‡**JOSEPH ELDER AGENCY**, 150 W. 87th St., New York NY 10024. (212)787-5722. Director: Joseph Elder. Estab. 1976. Member of ILAA. Represents 32 clients. 10% of clients are new/unpublished writers. Works with small number of new/unpublished writers. Specializes in trade books, mostly fiction, mainstream and all popular categories.
Will Handle: Nonfiction books, novels. Currently handles 20% nonfiction books; 80% novels. Will read-at no charge—unsolicited queries with SASE. Does not read unsolicited mss. Reports in 2 weeks on queries. "If our agency does not respond within 1 month to your request to become a client, you may submit requests elsewhere."
Terms: Agent receives 10% commission on domestic sales; 15% on dramatic sales; 20% on foreign sales. Charges for book purchases for subrights use, photocopying mss, unusual telephone and postal expenses, etc.
Recent Sales: *Winter by Degrees*, by John Smolens (E.P. Dutton); *The Far Battleground*, by F.M. Parker (New American Library); and *Ruler of the Sky*, by Pamela Sargent (Crown Publishers).

PETER ELEK ASSOCIATES, Box 223, Canal St. Station, New York NY 10013. (212)431-9368. Associate: Carol Diehl. Assistant: Susan Gallagher. Estab. 1979. Also provides book packaging services. Represents 15 clients. 15% of our clients are new/unpublished writers. "An applicant must be, or is clearly intending to be, self-supporting through their writing." Prefers to work with published/established authors; works with a small number of new/unpublished authors. Specializes in illustrated nonfiction, current affairs, self-help (not pop-psych), contemporary biography/autobiography, food, popular culture (all for adults); and preschool and juvenile illustrated fiction, nonfiction and novelties; and contemporary adventure for adults.
Will Handle: Nonfiction books, novels and juvenile books. No category fiction. Currently handles 60% nonfiction books and 40% juvenile books. Will read—at no charge—unsolicited queries and outlines. Reports in 2 weeks on queries. "If our agency does not respond within 6 weeks to your request to become a client, you may submit requests elsewhere."
Terms: Agent receives 15% commission on domestic sales; 20% on dramatic sales; and 20% on foreign sales. Charges for manuscript retyping, "if required." Sometimes offers a consultation service through which writers not represented can get advice on a contract; charges $75/hour, $125 minimum. 5% of income derived from fees; 33⅓% of income derived from commission on ms sales ("66⅔% derived from sale of finished packaged books"). 100% income derived from sales of writers' work.
Recent Sales: *Masks*, by Christos Kondeatis (Atlantic Monthly Press); *The Savoy Food and Drinks Book* (Salem House); *Earl's Too Cool for Me*, by Lee Komaiko (Harper & Row).

‡**ETHAN ELLENBERG, LITERARY AGENT**, #5-C, 548 Broadway, New York NY 10012. (212)431-4554. President: Ethan Ellenberg. Estab. 1984. Represents 31 clients. 50% of clients are new/unpublished writers. Eager to work with new/unpublished writers. Specializes in quality fiction and nonfiction, first novels, thriller, horror, spy, military, history, biography, science fiction.
Will Handle: Nonfiction books, novels, juvenile books. Currently handles 40% nonfiction books; 50% novels; 10% juvenile books. Will read—at no charge—unsolicited queries, outlines and mss. Must include SASE. Reports in 3 weeks on queries; 6 weeks on mss. "If our agency does not respond within 2 months to your request to become a client, you may submit requests elsewhere."
Terms: Agent receives 15% commission on domestic sales; 15% on dramatic sales; and 20% on foreign sales. Charges for cost of photocopies up to 10 mss for sale, finished copies for submission to foreign markets and Hollywood.
Recent Sales: *Franklin's Crossing*, by Clay Reynolds (Dutton); *No Greater Love*, by James Donahue (NAL); and *The Vigilante*, six books by Mack Tanner (Lynx).

THE ERIKSON LITERARY AGENCY, 223 Via Sevilla, Santa Barbara CA 93109. (805)963-8373. Agent: George Erikson. Estab. 1987. Represents 32 clients. 70% of clients are new/unpublished writers. Eager to work with new/unpublished writers.
Will Handle: Nonfiction books, novels and movie scripts. Currently handles 60% nonfiction books; 30% novels and 10% movie scripts. Reports in 1 month on queries; 2 months on mss. "If our agency does not respond within 2 months to your request to becomes a client, you may submit requests elsewhere." Writer's guidelines available for 4½x9½ envelope with 2 first class stamps.
Terms: Receives 15% commission on domestic sales; 15% on dramatic sales and 20% on foreign sales. Charges reading fee of $100 for full ms; $50 for screenplay. Reading fee will be deducted from agency's earned commissions. 10% of income derived from reading fees. Writer receives one page evaluation with marketing advice. Charges for photocopying, mailing and telephone are charged against advances. 90% of income derived from sales of writer's work; 10% of income derived from criticism services.
Recent Sales: *Site 85*, by Hugh Taylor.

‡EVANS AND ASSOCIATES, Box 810, Chagrin Falls OH 44022. (216)338-3264. Agent/Owner: Clyde Evans. Estab. 1987. "This agency is new and will represent any author whose work, based on agency review, is of such quality that it is deemed sellable." Eager to work with new/unpublished writers.
Will Handle: Various types of material. Will read—at no charge—unsolicited queries, outlines and mss. Reports in 2 weeks on queries; 1 month on mss. "If our agency does not respond within 2 months to your request to become a client, you may submit requests elsewhere."
Terms: Agent receives 15% commission on domestic sales; 10% on dramatic sales; and 20% total on foreign sales—10% to foreign agent. Charges for photocopying over 75 pages, galley, book purchase, legal advice beyond normal agency services, messenger. Sometimes offers consultation service through which writers can get advice on a contract, $75/hour.

‡JOHN FARQUHARSON LTD., Suite 1007, 250 W. 57th St., New York NY 10107. (212)245-1993. Director: Jane Gelfman. Agent: Deborah Schneider. Estab. 1919 (London); 1980 (New York). Member of SAR and ILAA. Represents 125 clients. 5% of our clients are new/unpublished writers. Prefers to work with published/established authors; works with a small number of new/unpublished authors. Specializes in general trade fiction and nonfiction. No poetry, short stories or screenplays.
Will Handle: Novels and juvenile books (few); handles magazine articles and magazine fiction for authors already represented. Currently handles 49% nonfiction books; 49% novels; and 2% juvenile books. Will read—at no charge—unsolicited queries and outlines. Reports in 3 weeks on queries.
Terms: Agent receives 10% commission on domestic sales; 10% on dramatic sales; and 20% on foreign sales. Charges for messengers, photocopying and overseas calls.
Recent Sales: *Le Tourneau's Used Auto Parts*, by Carolyn Chute (Ticknor & Fields); and *A Great Deliverance*, by Elizabeth George (Bantam).

FARWESTERN CONSULTANTS, INC., Box 47786, Phoenix AZ 85068-7786. (602)861-3546. President: Elizabeth "Libbi" Goodman. Estab. 1987. Represents 17 clients. "50% of our clients are new/unpublished writers. We have a strong background in literature, editing; and cover the NY and regional markets. We devote whatever time is needed to help a writer develop his full potential. We believe a dynamic relationship between author and agent is necessary for success." Eager to work with new/unpublished writers. "We also work with a number of established authors. We specialize in popular fiction (western, mystery, contemporary/historical romance, espionage, thriller, horror, fantasy, and action/adventure), ethnic fiction and nonfiction, and women's fiction. Will also handle book-length nonfiction, contemporary fiction, literary novels, and screenplays. We handle short-story collections only for established authors. Will not handle juvenile, young adult or poetry."
Will Handle: Most book-length nonfiction, contemporary fiction literary novels, short-story collections by established authors, and screenplays.
Terms: Receives 10% commission on domestic sales; 15% on dramatic sales; and 20% on foreign sales. Sometimes charges writers for postage, phone and photocopies. 100% of income is derived from commission on manuscript sales.
Recent Sales: *Mystery Writer's Handbook of Poisons*, by Serita Stevens and Anne Klarner (Writer's Digest Books); an untitled Western series by Larry Names; *Another Dream*, by Sandra Lee Smith (Warner Books).

FLORENCE FEILER LITERARY AGENCY, 1524 Sunset Plaza Dr., Los Angeles CA 90069. (659)652-6920/652-0945. Associate: Audrey Rugh. Estab. 1967. Represents 40 clients. No unpublished writers. "Quality is the criterion." Specializes in fiction, nonfiction, essays and screen; very little TV and no short stories.
Will Handle: Textbooks (for special clients), juvenile books, movie scripts. Will read—at no charge—queries and outlines only. Reports in 2 weeks on queries; 10 weeks on mss. "If our agency does not respond within 3 months to your request to become a client, you may submit requests elsewhere. We will not accept simultaneous queries to other agents."
Terms: Agent receives 10% commission on domestic sales; 10% on dramatic sales; and 20% on foreign sales.
Recent Sales: *Babette's Feast* (best foreign film); *The Dreamers & Echoes* (Dinesen-Orson Wells).

‡MARJE FIELDS INC., 165 W. 46th, New York NY 10036. (212)764-5740. Literary Manager: Ray Powers. Member ILAA. Represents 40-50 clients. 50% of clients are new/unpublished writers. Prefers to work with published/established writers, but eager to work with new/unpublished writers. Specializes in novels, nonfiction and plays.
Will Handle: Nonfiction books, novels, movie scripts, stage plays, TV scripts. Currently handles 20% nonfiction books; 30% novels; 20% movie scripts; 20% stage plays; 10% other. Reports in 1 week on queries.
Terms: Agent receives 15% commission on domestic sales; 15% on dramatic sales; and 20% on foreign sales. Sometimes charges reading fee; reading fee waived if agency represents writer. Writer receives an overall evaluation. Sometimes offers consultation service through which writers may receive advice on a contract. Payment of writing fee does not ensure that agency will represent writer.
Recent Sales: *People Next Door*, by Caroline Crade (Dodd-Mead); *Encyclopedia of the Aging and the Elderly*, by Dr. J. Hampton Roy (Facts on File); and *Always a Thief*, by Jeffery Deaver (Paperjacks).

FRIEDA FISHBEIN LTD., 2556 Hubbard St., Brooklyn NY 11235. (212)247-4398. President: Janice Fishbein. Estab. 1925. Represents 30 clients. 50% of clients are new/unpublished writers. "We agree to represent a writer solely on the basis of a *complete* work." Eager to work with new/unpublished writers. Specializes in historical romance, historical adventure, male adventure, mysteries, thrillers, and family sagas. Books on the environment, how-to, plays and screenplays.
Will Handle: Nonfiction books, novels, young adult, movie scripts, stage plays and TV scripts. No poetry or magazine articles. Currently handles 20% nonfiction books; 30% novels; 5% textbooks; 10% juvenile books; 10% movie scripts; 15% stage plays; and 10% TV scripts. Will read—at no charge—unsolicited queries and brief outlines. Reports in 2 weeks on queries; 1 month on mss. "If our agency does not respond within 2 months to your request to become a client, you may submit requests elsewhere."
Terms: Agent receives 10% commission on domestic sales; 10% on dramatic sales; and 20% on foreign sales. Charges reading fee; $75/TV script, screenplay or play; $60/50,000 words for manuscripts, $1 for each 1,000 additional words. Only *complete* mss are reviewed. Fee will be returned if representing writer. "Our readers are freelance workers who also serve as editors at magazines and/or publishers. Our reports are always longer for larger manuscripts. The usual reader's report varies between three to five pages, and may or may not include a line-to-line critique, but it always includes an overall evaluation." 20% of income derived from fees; 80% of income derived from commission on ms sales. Payment of a criticism fee does not ensure that agency will represent a writer.
Recent Sales: *Dr. Death*, by Herbert L. Fisher (Berkley Publishing Co.); "Double Cross," by Gary Bohlke (play); and *El Gato Negra*, by Herbert L. Fisher.

‡JOYCE A. FLAHERTY, LITERARY AGENT, 816 Lynda Court, St. Louis MO 63122. (314)966-3057. Agent: Joyce A. Flaherty. Estab. 1980. Member Romance Writers of America, Western Writers of America and Mystery Writers of America. Represents 58 clients. 25% of clients are new/unpublished writers. "Most new clients come through referral by clients and/or editors." Works with small number of new/unpublished authors. Specializes in mainstream women's fiction, general fiction, genre fiction such as horror, historical, romance, family sagas, thrillers, mysteries, contemporary romance, mainstream historicals. General nonfiction, including biographies, how-to, travel and cookbooks. "Also young adult fiction but am only taking published authors in that genre."
Will Handle: Nonfiction books, novels, juvenile books (published authors only). Currently handles 35% nonfiction books; 60% novels; 4% juvenile books. Will read—at no charge—unsolicited queries and outlines. "No response without SASE." Reports in 6 weeks on queries. "If our agency does not respond within 2 months to your request to become a client, you may submit requests elsewhere."
Terms: Agent receives 10-15% commission on domestic sales—10% published authors; 15% first book sale for unpublished authors, 10% on subsequent sales; 15% all sales for juvenile authors. Charges reading fee "at my discretion for unpublished authors." 2% of income derived from reading fees. Charges $100-150 for 300-page, typed, double-spaced ms. 98% of income derived from commission on mss sales; 2% derived from reading fees.
Recent Sales: *Bay and Ocean Cookbook* (Viking Penguin); *The Mark of a Fox*, by Marcia Cole (Berkley Publishing); and *Catch the Wind*, by Elizabeth Stuart (St. Martin's Press).

FLAMING STAR LITERARY ENTERPRISES, 320 Riverside Dr., New York NY 10025. (212)222-0083. President: Joseph B. Vallely. Estab. 1985. Represents 30 clients. 50% of clients are new/unpublished writers. Eager to work with new/unpublished writers. Specializes in commercial and literary fiction and nonfiction.
Will Handle: Nonfiction books and novels. Currently handles 50% nonfiction books and 50% novels. Will read submissions at no charge. Reports in 1 week on queries; 2 weeks on mss. "If our agency does not respond within 2 weeks to your request to become a client, you may submit requests elsewhere."
Terms: Agent receives 15% commission on domestic sales; 15% on dramatic sales; and 20% on foreign sales. (All rates are for unpublished authors. Commissions are 5% lower for previously published authors.)
Recent Sales: Confidential.

‡THE FOLEY AGENCY, 34 E. 38 St., New York NY 10016. (212)686-6930. Partners: Joan and Joseph Foley. Estab. 1956. Represents 30 clients. 5% of clients are new/unpublished writers. Works with a small number of new/unpublished authors.
Will Handle: Nonfiction books and novels. Currently handles 25% nonfiction books, and 75% novels. Will read—at no charge—unsolicited queries and outlines if SASE is enclosed. Reports in 2 weeks on queries. Do not submit manuscripts unless requested.
Terms: Agent receives 10% commission on domestic sales; 10-20% on dramatic sales; and 10-20% on foreign sales. Charges for occasional messenger fee and special phone expenses. 100% of income derived from commission on ms sales.
Recent Sales: No information given.

ROBERT A. FREEDMAN DRAMATIC AGENCY, INC., Suite 2310, 1501 Broadway, New York NY 10036. (212)840-5760. President: Robert A. Freedman. Vice President: Selma Luttinger. Member of SAR. Prefers to

WOULD YOU USE THE SAME CALENDAR YEAR AFTER YEAR?

Of course not! If you scheduled your appointments using last year's calendar, you'd risk missing important meetings and deadlines, so you keep up-to-date with a new calendar each year. Just like your calendar, *Writer's Market®* changes every year, too. Many of the editors move or get promoted, rates of pay increase, and even editorial needs change from the previous year. You can't afford to use an out-of-date book to plan your marketing efforts!

So save yourself the frustration of getting manuscripts returned in the mail, stamped MOVED: ADDRESS UNKNOWN. And of NOT submitting your work to new listings because you don't know they exist. **Make sure you have the most current writing and marketing information by ordering *1990 Writer's Market* today.** All you have to do is complete the attached post card and return it with your payment or charge card information. Order now, and there's one thing that won't change from your *1989 Writer's Market*—the price! That's right, we'll send you the 1990 edition for just $22.95. *1990 Writer's Market* will be published and ready for shipment in September 1989.

Let an old acquaintance be forgot, and toast the new edition of *Writer's Market.* Order today!

(See other side for more new market books to help you get published)

- -

GREAT NEWS FOR WRITERS!

3 NEW Market Books to Help You Get Published!

1989 Novel & Short Story Writer's Market®
(Formerly Fiction Writer's Market)

Edited by Laurie Henry

We've changed the name, but it's still the same great book! Now in paperback, with all the facts and information you need to get your short stories and novels published. Includes 1,750 detailed listings of commercial book and magazine publishers, small presses, and little/literary magazines, PLUS 20 all-new chapters of fiction writing and marketing techniques and advice on/listings of agents who handle fiction.

550 pages/$16.95, paperback (available February 1989)

1989 Children's Writer's & Illustrator's Market®

Edited by Connie Eidenier

This new annual brings together the two key aspects of children's (from pre-schoolers through teenagers) publishing—the writing and the illustrating— in one handy volume of book publishing and magazine markets. You'll find a helpful introductory article on *how* to freelance in this lucrative market, followed by 500 detailed publisher listings. A resource section provides you with listings of/information on agents, clubs, and workshops.

300 pages/$14.95, paperback (available February 1989)

1989 Inspirational Writer's Market®

Edited by Sally Stuart

Addressing the special needs of inspirational and Christian writers, this new annual directory gives you 500 detailed listings of where and how to sell your nonfiction books, novels, articles, short stories, poems, greeting cards, columns, scripts, curriculum, devotionals, denominational news, and Sunday School aids. A "how-to-sell" feature article guides you step by step through the marketing process.

300 pages/$14.95, paperback (available February 1989)

Use coupon on other side to order your copies today!

work with established authors; works with a very small number of new/unpublished authors. Specializes in plays and motion picture and television scripts.

Will Handle: Movie scripts, stage plays and TV scripts. Does not read unsolicited mss. Usually reports in 2 weeks on queries; 6 weeks on mss.

Terms: Agent receives 10% on dramatic sales; "and, as is customary, 20% on amateur rights." Charges for photocopying.

Recent Sales: "We will tell any author directly information on our sales that are relevant to his/her specific script."

SAMUEL FRENCH, INC., 45 W. 25th St., New York NY 10010. (212)206-8990. Editor: Lawrence Harbison. Estab. 1830. Member of SAR. Represents "hundreds" of clients. Prefers to work with published/established authors; works with a small number of new/unpublished authors. Specializes in plays.

Will Handle: Stage plays. Currently handles 100% stage plays. Will read—at no charge—unsolicited queries and mss. Replies "immediately" on queries; decision in 2-8 months regarding publication. "Enclose SASE."

Terms: Agent receives usually 10% professional production royalties; and 20% amateur production royalties.

Recent Sales: *The Dark Sonnets of the Lady*, by Don Nigro (to McCarter Theatre).

JAY GARON-BROOKE ASSOCIATES INC.,17th Floor, 415 Central Park West, New York NY 10025. (212)866-3654. President: Jay Garon. Established 1952. Member of ILAA and Author's Guild Inc. Represents 100 clients. 15% of clients are new/unpublished writers. Prefers to work with published/established authors; works with small number of new/unpublished authors.

Will Handle: Nonfiction books, novels, juvenile books (young adult), movie scripts and stage plays. Currently handles 25% nonfiction books; 70% novels; 2% juvenile books; 1% movie scripts; 1% stage plays and 1% TV scripts. Does not read unsolicited material. Submit query letters with bio and SASE. Reports in 1 month. "If our agency does not respond within 3 months to your request to become a client, you may submit requests elsewhere."

Terms: Agent receives 15% commission on domestic sales; 10-15% on dramatic sales; and 30% on foreign sales.

Recent Sales: *Silver Eyed Woman*, by Mary Ann T. Smith (Morrow); *Candlemas Eve*, by Jeffrey Sackett (Bantam); and *Mirrors*, by Patricia Mathews (worldwide).

MAX GARTENBERG, LITERARY AGENT, 15 W. 44th St., New York NY 10036. (212)860-8451. Contact: Max Gartenberg. Estab. 1954. Represents 30 clients. 10% of clients are new/unpublished writers. "The writer must convince me of his or her professional skills, whether through published or unpublished materials he/she has produced." Prefers to work with published/established authors; works with a small number of new/unpublished authors. Specializes in nonfiction and fiction trade books.

Will Handle: Nonfiction books and novels. Currently handles 75% nonfiction books and 25% novels. Will read—at no charge—unsolicited queries and outlines. Reports in 1 week on queries. "If our agency does not respond within 1 month to your request to become a client, you may submit requests elsewhere. SASE required."

Terms: Agent receives 10% commission on domestic sales; 10% on dramatic sales; and 15% on foreign sales. 100% of income derived from commission on ms sales.

Recent Sales: *Owls: Their Life and Behavior*, by Julio de la Torre and Art Wolfe (Crown Publishers); *Wishful Thinking*, by Frank Wyka (Carroll & Graf); *Agreement to Kill*, by Peter Rabe (Black Lizard Books).

‡GELLES-COLE LITERARY ENTERPRISES, Woodstock Towers, Suite 818, 320 E. 42nd St., New York NY 10017. (212)573-9857. President: Sandi Gelles-Cole. Estab. 1983. Represent 50 clients. 25% of clients are new/unpublished writers. "We concentrate on published and unpublished but we try to avoid writers who seem stuck in mid-list." Specializes in commercial fiction and nonfiction.

Will Handle: Nonfiction books and novels. Currently handles 50% nonfiction books; 50% novels. Does not read unsolicited mss. Reports in 3 weeks.

Terms: Agent receives 15% commission on domestic sales; 15% on dramatic sales; and 20% on foreign sales. Charges reading fee of $75 for proposal; $100, ms under 250 pages; $150, ms over 250 pages. .05% of income derived from reading fees. "Our reading fee is for evaluation. Writer receives total evaluation, what is right, what is wrong, is book 'playing' to market, general advice on how to fix." Charges writers for overseas calls, overnight mail, messenger. 5% of income derived from fees charged to writers. 50% of income derived from sales of writer's work; 45% of income derived from editorial service.

Recent Sales: *Hold the Flame*, by Dee Pace (Crown); and *The Seduction by Art Bourgeor* (Don Line, Inc.).

LUCIANNE S. GOLDBERG LITERARY AGENTS, INC., Suite 6-A, 255 W. 84th St., New York NY 10024. (212)799-1260. Editorial Director: Sloan Taylor. Estab. 1974. Represents 65 clients. 10% of clients are new/unpublished writers. "Any author we decide to repesent must have a good idea, a good presentation of that idea and writing skill to compete with the market. Representation depends solely on the execution of the work whether writer is published or unpublished." Specializes in nonfiction works, "but will review a limited number of novels."

Will Handle: Nonfiction books and novels. Currently handles 75% nonfiction books and 25% novels. Will read—at no charge—unsolicited queries and outlines. Reports in 2 weeks on queries; 3 weeks on mss. "If our agency does not respond within 1 month to your request to become a client, you may submit requests elsewhere."

Terms: Agent receives 15% commission on domestic sales; 25% on dramatic sales; and 25% on foreign sales. Charges reading fee on unsolicited mss: $150/full-length ms. Criticism is included in reading. 1% of income derived from reading fees. "Our critiques run three to four pages, single-spaced. They deal with the overall evaluation of the work. Three agents within the organization read and then confer. Marketing advice is included." Payment of fee does not ensure the agency will represent a writer. Charges for phone expenses, cable fees, photocopying and messenger service after the work is sold. 80% of income derived from commission on ms sales.

Recent Sales: *IDOL: The Real Rock Hudson Story*, by Jerry Oppenheimer (Random House); *The Real Story*, by Michael Ledeen (Macmillan); and *Trial by Ordeal*, by Lee Isreal (McGraw-Hill).

GOODMAN ASSOCIATES, LITERARY AGENTS, 500 West End Ave., New York NY 10024. Contact: Arnold or Elise Goodman. Estab. 1976. Member of ILAA. Represents 75 clients. 10% of clients are new/unpublished writers. Specializes in general adult trade fiction and nonfiction. No short stories, articles, poetry, computer books, science fiction, plays, screenplays or textbooks.

Will Handle: Will read—at no charge—unsolicited queries and outlines. "Include SASE for response."

Terms: Agent receives 15% commission on domestic sales; 15% on dramatic sales; and 20% on foreign sales. Charges for photocopying, long-distance phone, messenger, telex and book purchases for subsidiary rights submissions.

Recent Sales: No information given.

IRENE GOODMAN LITERARY AGENCY, 521 5th Ave., 17th Floor, New York NY 10017. (212)688-4286. Contact: Irene Goodman, president. Estab. 1978. Member of ILAA. Represents 100 clients. 20% of clients are new/unpublished writers. Works with a small number of new/unpublished authors. Specializes in women's fiction (mass market, category, and historical romance), science fiction, fantasy, popular nonfiction, reference and mysteries.

Will Handle: Novels and nonfiction books. Currently handles 20% nonfiction books; 80% novels. Will read—at no charge—unsolicited queries. Reports in 3 weeks. "We prefer a query, brief synopsis and credentials. No reply without SASE."

Terms: Agent receives 15% commission on domestic sales and 20% on foreign sales. 100% of income from commission on ms sales.

Recent Sales: *Deadly Relations* (Bantam); and *The Orphan Train Trilogy* (Pocket).

GRAHAM AGENCY, 311 W. 43rd St., New York NY 10036. (212)489-7730. Owner: Earl Graham. Estab. 1971. Member of SAR. Represents 35 clients. 35% of clients are new/unpublished writers. Prefers to work with published/established authors; eager to work with new/unpublished writers. Specializes in full-length stage plays and musicals.

Will Handle: Stage plays and musicals. Will read—at no charge—unsolicited queries and outlines, "and plays and musicals which we agree to consider on the basis of the letters of inquiry." Reports in 3 weeks on simple queries. Simultaneous submissions OK.

Terms: Agent receives 10% commission on domestic sales; 10% on dramatic sales; and 10% on foreign sales. 100% of income derived from commission on ms sales.

Recent Sales: No information given.

❝ *Whether you have been published or not, at least have a professional attitude. Put yourself in the publisher's place.* **❞**

—*Kathryn L. Vilips,*
L'Apache

HEACOCK LITERARY AGENCY, INC., Suite 14, 1523 6th St., Santa Monica CA 90401. (213)393-6227. President: Jim Heacock. Vice President: Rosalie Heacock. Estab. 1978. Member of ILAA and the Association of Talent Agents (writers only). Represents 60 clients. 35% of clients are new/unpublished writers. Works with a small number of new/unpublished authors. Specializes in nonfiction on a wide variety of subjects—health, nutrition, diet, exercise, sports, psychology, crafts, women's studies, business expertise, pregnancy and parenting, alternative health concepts, starting a business and celebrity biographies.
Will Handle: Nonfiction books; novels (by authors who have been previously published by major houses); movie scripts (prefer Writer's Guild members); and TV scripts (prefer Writer's Guild members). Currently handles 85% nonfiction books; 5% novels; 5% movie scripts and 5% TV scripts. "We want to see health oriented works by professionals with credentials and something original to say. Selected New Age subjects are a growing market at all levels of publishing. Celebrity biographies will continue to sell well if they cover contemporary personalities." Will read—at no charge—unsolicited queries and outlines. Reports in 1 month on queries if SASE is included. "If our agency does not respond within 1 month to your request to become a client, you may submit requests elsewhere."
Terms: Agent receives 15% commission on domestic sales; 10% on dramatic sales; 25% on foreign sales (if a foreign agent is used. If we sell direct to a foreign publisher, the commission is 15%). Charges writers for postage, phone and photocopying. Offers a consultation service through which writers not represented can get advice on a contract; charges $125/hour. 2% of income derived from such fees; 98% of income derived from commission on ms sales.
Recent Sales: *Skin Secrets*, by Joseph P. Bark, M.D. (McGraw Hill); *Little Penguin's Tale*, by Don and Audrey Wood (Harcourt Brace Jovanovich); and *Detective Valentine*, by Audrey Wood (Harper & Row).

‡THE JEFF HERMAN AGENCY, INC., 166 Lexington Ave., New York NY 10016. (212)725-4660. President: Jeffrey H. Herman. Estab. 1985. Member ILAA, Authors Guild, PEN. Represents 50 clients. 50% of clients are new/previously unpublished writers. To be represented writer must have marketable proposal or manuscript and appropriate credentials. Eager to work with new/unpublished writers. Specializes in general nonfiction and fiction.
Will Handle: Nonfiction books, novels, textbooks. Currently handles 80% nonfiction; 10% textbooks; 10% general fiction. Will read—at no charge—unsolicited queries, outlines and mss. Reports in 2 weeks on queries; 6 weeks on mss.
Terms: Agent receives 10-15% commission on domestic sales; 15% on foreign sales. Charges for proposal/ms photocopying, overseas calls and cables.
Recent Sales: *The Shearson Lehman Bros. Wall Street Encyclopedia*, by Bob Shook, Martin Shafinoff (NAL); *A History of the Vietnam Veterans Movement*, by Gerald Nicosia (Norton); and *Cutting the Cord*, by Larry Stockman, Cindy Graves (Contemporary).

‡SUSAN HERNER RIGHTS AGENCY, 666 3rd Avenue, 10th Floor, New York NY 10017. (212)983-5230/5231/5232. Contact: Susan Herner or Sue Yuen. Estab. 1987. Represents 50 clients. 25% of clients are new/unpublished writers. Eager to work with new/unpublished writers. Trade expertise in fiction (literary and genre), romance, science fiction, nonfiction, juvenile and children's books.
Will Handle: Nonfiction books, novels, juvenile books. Currently handles 40% nonfiction books; 50% novels; 10% juvenile books. Will read—at no charge—unsolicited queries, outlines and mss. Reports in 1 month on queries; 6 weeks on mss. "If our agency does not respond within 3 months to your request to become a client, you may submit requests elsewhere."
Terms: Agent receives 15% commission on domestic sales; 20% on dramatic sales; and 20% on foreign sales. Charges for extraordinary postage and handling, photocopying. "Agency has two divisions: one represents writers on a commission-only basis; the other represents the rights for small publishers and packagers who do not have in-house subsidiary rights representation. Percentage of income derived from each division is currently 50-50."
Recent Sales: *Quest*, by Richard Ben Sapir (Dutton); *Effective Listening*, by Kevin Murphy (Bantam); and *Chivalric Romance*, by Joan Perucho (Knopf).

FREDERICK HILL ASSOCIATES, 2237 Union St., San Francisco CA 94123. (415)921-2910. Contact: Bonnie Nadell. Estab. 1979. Represents 75 clients. 50% of clients are new/unpublished writers. Specializes in general nonfiction, fiction and young adult fiction.
Will Handle: Nonfiction books, novels and juvenile books.
Terms: Agent receives 15% commission on domestic sales; 15% on dramatic sales; and 20% on foreign sales. Charges for overseas airmail (books, proofs only), overseas Telex, cable, domestic Telex. 100% of income derived from commission on ms sales.
Recent Sales: No information given.

ALICE HILTON LITERARY AGENCY, 13131 Welby Way, North Hollywood CA 91606. (818)982-5423/982-2546. Estab. 1986. Member of WGA. Eager to work with new/unpublished writers. Specializes in movie and

TV scripts—"any good salable material with quality—although agent's personal taste runs in the genre of 'Cheers,' 'L.A. Law,' 'American Playhouse,' 'Masterpiece Theatre' and Woody Allen vintage humor."
Will Handle: Movie and TV scripts only. "Also interested in booklength material (all subjects) of outstanding quality for a reading fee of approximately $2/1,000 words—negotiable according to length of ms. Brochure available." Will read—at no charge—queries, outlines and manuscripts. "A preliminary phone call is appreciated." Reports in 1 month. "If our agency does not respond within 2 months to your request to become a client, you may submit requests elsewhere."
Terms: Agent receives 10% commission on dramatic sales. Charges for phone, postage and photocopy expenses. 100% of income derived from commission on ms sales. "Send SASE."
Recent Sales: Confidential.

JOHN L. HOCHMANN BOOKS, 320 E. 58th St., New York NY 10022. (212)319-0505. President: John L. Hochmann. Estab. 1976. Represents 21 clients. Writer must have demonstrable eminence in field or previous publications for nonfiction, and critically and/or commercially successful books for fiction. Prefers to work with published/established authors; and to "develop new series for established authors of original paperback fiction."
Will Handle: Nonfiction books, novels, and textbooks. Currently handles 60% nonfiction books and 40% novels. Will read—at no charge—unsolicited queries, outlines and solicited mss. Reports in 2 weeks on queries; 1 month on mss.
Terms: Agent receives 15% commission on domestic sales; and additional commission on foreign sales. Sometimes offers a consultation service through which writers not represented can get advice on a contract; "we have sometimes done this without charge, but if the number of inquiries increases, our policy may change." 100% of income derived from commission on ms sales.
Recent Sales: *Trainmaster*, by Noel B. Gerson (Warner); *Clinical Care of the Aged Person*, by David G. Satin, M.D. (Oxford); and *Betty Parsons: A Dealer and Her Artists*, by Lee Hall (Abrams).

SCOTT HUDSON TALENT REPRESENTATION, 2B, 215 East 76th St., New York NY 10021. (212)570-9645. President: Scott Hudson. Estab. 1983. Member of WGA. Represents 30 clients. Prefers to work with published/established authors; works with a small number of new/unpublished authors. Specializes in selling for the entertainment field; screenwriters, television writers, playwrights and some book writers.
Will Handle: Movie scripts, stage plays and TV scripts. Currently handles 30% movie scripts; 30% stage plays; and 40% TV scripts. Will read—at no charge—unsolicited queries and outlines with a synopsis and resume. We "only respond if we are interested."
Terms: Agent receives 10% commission on domestic sales; 10% on dramatic sales; and 15% on foreign sales.

INTERNATIONAL LITERATURE AND ARTS AGENCY, 50 E. 10th St., New York NY 10003. (212)475-1999. Director: Bonnie R. Crown. Estab. 1977. Represents 10 clients. 10% of clients are new/unpublished writers. Works with a small number of new/unpublished authors; eager to work with new/unpublished writers in area of specialization, and established translators from Asian languages. Specializes in translations of literary works from Asian languages, arts- and literature-related works, and "American writers who have been influenced by some aspect of an Asian culture, for example, a novel set in Japan, or India, or nonfiction works about Asia. For details of policy, send query with SASE."
Will Handle: Novels, stage plays (related to Asia or Asian American experience), and poetry (translations of Asian classics). Currently handles 50% nonfiction books; 25% novels; and 25% classics from Asian languages. Will read—at no charge—unsolicited queries and brief outlines. Reports in 1 week on queries; 3 weeks on mss. "If our agency does not respond within 2 weeks to your request to become a client, you may submit requests elsewhere. For details of policy, send query with SASE."
Terms: Agent receives 15% commission on domestic sales; and 20% on foreign sales. No reading fee. "We do not do critiques, as such, but do give the writer a brief evaluation of marketing potential based on my reading. There is a processing fee of $25-45. May charge for phone and photocopy expenses." 1/2% of income derived from fees; 99 1/2% of income is derived from commission on ms sales.
Recent Sales: *New Translation of the I Ching*, by Richard John Lynn (Shambhala).

INTERNATIONAL PUBLISHER ASSOCIATES, INC., 746 West Shore, Sparta NJ 07871. Executive Vice President: Joe DeRogatis. Estab. 1982. Represents 30 clients. 80% of clients are new/unpublished writers. Eager to work with new/unpublished writers. Specializes in all types of nonfiction. Writer's guidelines for #10 SAE and 1 first class stamp.
Will Handle: Nonfiction books and novels. Currently handles 80% nonfiction books and 20% fiction. Will read—at no charge—unsolicited queries and outlines. Reports in 3 weeks on queries. "If our agency does not respond within 1 month to your request to become a client, you may submit requests elsewhere."
Terms: Agent receives 15% commission on domestic sales; and 20% on foreign sales. 100% of income derived from commission on ms sales.
Recent Sales: *Guerilla Tactics for Women Over Forty*, by Anne Cardoza and Mavis Sutton (Mills and Sanderson) and *Under the Clock*, by George Carpozi, Jr. and William Balsam.

‡J&R LITERARY AGENCY, 28 East 11 St., New York NY 10003. (212)677-4248. Owner: Jean Rosenthal. Represents published writers only. Specializes in nonfiction.
Will Handle: Nonfiction books, novels, textbooks, juvenile books. Does not read unsolicited mss. Reports in 1 month on queries. "If our agency does not respond within 1 month to your request to become a client, you may submit requests elsewhere."
Terms: Agent receives 15% commission on domestic sales; 20% on foreign sales. Charges for mailing and telephone. Sometimes offers consultation service through which writers can get advice on a contract. 50% of income derived from commission on ms sales.
Recent Sales: *The Unborn Baby Book*, by Dr. Jack H. McCubbin (E.P. Dutton); *The Scottsdale 7 Day Pain Relief Program*, by Dr. Neal Olshan (Fawcett); and *Elvis*, by Sid Shaw (McGraw).

JANUS LITERARY AGENCY, Box 107, Nahant MA 01908. (617)593-0576. Contact: Eva Wax or Lenny Cavallaro. Estab. 1980. Represents 4 clients. 25% of clients are new/unpublished writers. "Will gladly consider published and/or unpublished writers, but Janus is a small, part-time venture, and cannot take many clients." Prefers nonfiction "of popular or controversial slant."
Will Handle: Nonfiction books and novels. Currently handles 50% nonfiction books; and 50% fiction. Will read—at no charge—unsolicited queries and outlines. Must enclose SASE. Reports in 1 week on queries; 2 weeks on mss.
Terms: Agent receives 15% commission on domestic sales; and 15% on foreign sales. Charges reading fee; $50-200, to appraise ms. 36% of income derived from reading fees. Reading fee includes critique. "Most critiques run 1-3 typed pages, single spaced. Some very detailed, line-by-line commentary is included. I read everything myself; hold degree in English; was formerly an English teacher; am a published author; was formerly a book critic for *New Haven Register* (newspaper)." Most new clients must pay a reading fee; exceptions are rare. $50-200 is normal fee range. I waive fee for clients whose works I have placed, or if the topic and proposal are absolutely extraordinary. Charges $50-100 handling fee (phone calls, postage, etc.). Sometimes offers a consultation service through which writers not represented can get advice on a contract; charges $25/hour. 48% of income derived from fees; 52% of income derived from commission on ms sales. Payment of a criticism fee does not ensure that agency will represent writer.
Recent Sales: *Protect Your Children*, by Laura Huchton (Prentice-Hall); and *Ouija: The Most Dangerous Game*, by Stoker Hunt (Harper & Row).

SHARON JARVIS AND CO., INC., 260 Willard Ave., Staten Island NY 10314. (718)273-1066. President: Sharon Jarvis. Estab. 1985 (previously known as Jarvis, Braff Ltd. Established 1979). Member of ILAA. Represents 70 clients. 20% of clients are new/unpublished writers. Prefers to work with published/established authors; works with a small number of new/unpublished authors. Considers types of genre fiction, commercial fiction and nonfiction.
Will Handle: Nonfiction books, novels and juvenile books. Currently handles 20% nonfiction books; 70% novels; and 10% juvenile books. Does not read unsolicited mss. Reports in 1 week on queries. "If our agency does not respond within 1 month to your request to become a client, you may submit requests elsewhere."
Terms: Agent receives 15% commission on domestic sales; extra 10% on dramatic sales (splits commission with dramatic agent); and extra 10% on foreign sales. ("We have sub-agents in ten different foreign markets.") Charges reading fee; $50 per manuscript ("fee goes to outside reader; recommended material then read by agency at no extra charge"). Critique is a one-page analysis "aimed toward agency evaluation of author's talent and marketability." Charges for photocopying. 100% of income derived from commission on ms sales.
Recent Sales: *Full Alert*, by Frank Geron (Zebra); *The Tavera Legacy*, by Mary Lynn (Tor); *True Tales of the Unknown, Vol. 2*, by Sharon Jarvis (Bantam).

ASHER D. JASON ENTERPRISES, INC., Suite 3B, 111 Barrow St., New York NY 10014. (212)929-2129. President: Asher D. Jason. Estab. 1983. Represents 25 clients. 15% of clients are new/unpublished writers. "Writers must be either published or have a salable nonfiction idea or an excellent finished fiction ms." Prefers to work with published/established authors; works with a small number of new/unpublished authors. Specializes in fiction, nonfiction, romance, espionage, horror/suspense and mystery.
Will Handle: Nonfiction books and novels. Currently handles 15% magazine articles; 70% nonfiction books; and 15% novels. Will read—at no charge—unsolicited queries and outlines. Reports in 1 week on queries; 3 weeks on mss. "If our agency does not respond within 1 month to your request to become a client, you may submit requests elsewhere."
Terms: Agent receives 15% commission on domestic sales; 15% on dramatic sales; and 20% on foreign sales. Charges for photocopy and foreign postage expenses. 100% of income derived from sales of writers' work.
Recent Sales: *Make Up Book*, by Joey Mills (Villard); *Just Ask*, by Bonnie Hammer and Debbie Cohen (New American Library); and *Taekwondo*, by Werner and Franz Bussen (Simon & Schuster).

‡JCA LITERARY AGENCY INC., Suite 4A, 242 West 27th St., New York NY 10001. (212)807-0888. Agents: Jane Cushman, Jeff Gerecke. Estab. 1978. Member SAR. Represents 100 clients. 10% of clients are new/unpublished writers. Specializes in general fiction and nonfiction.

Will Handle: Nonfiction books and novels; no science fiction or juvenile. Currently handles 65% nonfiction books; 35% novels. Will read—at no charge—unsolicited queries and outlines. Reports in 2 weeks on queries; 1 month on mss. "If our agency does not respond within 1 month to your request to become a client, you may submit requests elsewhere."

Terms: Agent receives 10% commission on domestic sales; 10% on dramatic sales; 15-20% on foreign sales. Charges for bound galleys and finished books used in subsidiary rights submissions; manuscripts copied for submissions to publishers. 100% of income derived from commission on ms sales.

Recent Sales: *The Avenue*, by C. Eric Lincoln, (Morrow); and *Michigan Roll*, by Tom Kakonis (St. Martin's).

JET LITERARY ASSOCIATES, INC., 124 E. 84th St., New York NY 10028. (212)879-2578. President: J. Trupin. Estab. 1976. Represents 85 clients. 5% of clients are new/unpublished writers. Writer must have published articles or books. Prefers to work with published/established authors. Specializes in nonfiction.

Will Handle: Nonfiction books and novels. Currently handles 50% nonfiction books and 50% novels. Does not read unsolicited mss. Reports in 2 weeks on queries; 1 month on mss. "If our agency does not respond within 2 months to your request to become a client, you may submit requests elsewhere."

Terms: Agent receives 15% commission on domestic sales; 15% on dramatic sales; and 25% on foreign sales. Charges for phone and postage expenses. 100% of income derived from commission on ms sales.

Recent Sales: *Juice*, by Robert Campbell (Poseidon/S&S); *Cupid*, by Robert S. Reid (Bantam); and *The Way We Die Now*, by Charles Willeford (Random House).

‡LARRY KALTMAN LITERARY AGENCY, 1301 S. Scott St., Arlington VA 22204. (703)920-3771. Director: Larry Kaltman. Estab. 1984. Represents 11 clients. 75% of clients are new/unpublished writers. Works with a small number of new/unpublished authors. Specializes in novels, novellas (mainstream).

Will Handle: Nonfiction books, novels. Currently handles 25% nonfiction books; 75% novels. Will read 3,000-word submissions at no charge. Reports in 2 weeks.

Terms: Agent receives 15% commission on domestic sales; 15% on dramatic sales; 15% on foreign sales. Charges reading fee for all unsolicited mss. 20% of income derived from reading fees. Criticism fee automatically included in reading fee. Charges $150 criticism fee for a 300-page, typed double-spaced book ms. "I don't distinguish between reading fees and criticism fees. Manuscript author receives an approximately 1,000 word letter commenting on writing style, organization, and marketability. I write all the critiques." Charges for postage. 80% of income derived from commission on ms sales; 20% derived from fees charged to writers.

Recent Sales: *Rastus on Capitol Hill*, by Samuel Edison (Hunter House).

ALEX KAMAROFF ASSOCIATES, Suite 303 East, 200 Park Ave., Pan Am Bldg., New York NY 10166. (212)557-5557. President: Alex Kamaroff. Associate: Paul Katz. Estab. 1985. Member of ILAA. Represents 63 clients. 25% of clients are new/unpublished writers. Specializes in men's adventure, science fiction, mysteries, horror, category and historical romances, contemporary women's fiction.

Will Handle: Novels. Currently handles 5% nonfiction books; 95% novels. Will read—at no charge—unsolicited queries and outlines; no reply without SASE. Reports in 1 week on queries; 3 weeks on mss. Charges $65 reading fee ("includes feedback") refundable upon sale of ms.

Terms: Agent receives 10% commission on domestic sales; 10% on dramatic sales; and 20% on foreign sales. Offers a consultation service through which writers can get advice on a contract. 100% of income derived from commission on ms sales.

Recent Sales: Three-book deal by Diana Morgan (Berkley).

KIDDE, HOYT AND PICARD LITERARY AGENCY, 335 E. 51st St., New York NY 10022. (212)755-9461. Chief Associate: Katharine Kidde. Estab. 1981. Represents 50 clients. "We require that a writer be published." Works with a small number of new clients. Specializes in mainstream and literary fiction; romantic fiction, some historical, some contemporary; mainstream nonfiction."

Will Handle: Nonfiction books. Will handle magazine articles and magazine fiction for national magazines, if also handling a book-length ms for the author. Currently handles 1% magazine articles; 2% magazine fiction; 22% nonfiction books; 70% novels; and 5% young adult books. Will read submissions—at no charge—if queried first. Reports in 2 weeks on queries; 1 month on mss. "If our agency does not respond within 2 months to your request to become a client, you may submit requests elsewhere."

Terms: Agent receives 10% commission on domestic sales; commission on dramatic sales varies. Sometimes charges for phone, postage and photocopy expenses. 100% of income derived from commission on ms sales.

Recent Sales: *Timeless Towns*, by J.R. Humphreys (St. Martin's); *Beyond Capricorn*, by Frank Sherry (Morrow); and *Twilight Of Innocence*, by Helen Lehr (Sinclair).

DANIEL P. KING, LITERARY AGENT, 5125 N. Cumberland Blvd., Whitefish Bay WI 53217. (414)964-2903. President: Daniel P. King. Estab. 1974. Member of Crime Writer's Association. Represents 125 clients.

25% of clients are new/unpublished writers. Eager to work with new/unpublished writers. Specializes in crime and mystery, science fiction, mainstream fiction, short stories, and books in English for foreign sales.
Will Handle: Magazine articles (crime, foreign affairs, economics); magazine fiction (mystery, romance); nonfiction books (crime, politics); novels (mystery, science fiction, romance, mainstream); movie scripts (in cooperation with an agent in California); TV scripts (with California agent); syndicate material (general, politics, economics). Currently handles 5% magazine articles; 10% magazine fiction; 30% nonfiction books; 50% novels; 2% movie scripts; 2% TV scripts; 1% syndicated material. Will read—at no charge—unsolicited queries and outlines. Does not read unsolicited ms. Reports in 1 week. "If our agency does not respond within 1 week to your request to become a client, you may submit requests elsewhere."
Terms: Agent receives 10% commission on domestic sales; 10% on dramatic sales; and 20% on foreign sales. Charges a reading fee "if writer wishes a critique." Charges $135 for a 300-page, typed double-spaced book ms. Charges a criticism fee "only if writer wishes a critique of the material and if we think that this will improve the work." Critiques "provide an overall evaluation of the writing skill level, analysis of story line and suggestions for rewriting. The text will be marked throughout with grammatical, spelling, etc., corrections." Charges writers for long distance telephone, telex, and foreign postage. Offers a consultation service through which writers can get advice on a contract. Charges $50/hour. "Less than 1%" of income derived from fees; 99% from commission on ms sales.
Recent Sales: Confidential.

HARVEY KLINGER, INC., 301 W. 53rd St., New York NY 10019. (212)581-7068. President: Harvey Klinger. Estab. 1977. Represents 60 clients. 25% of our clients are new/unpublished writers. "We seek writers demonstrating great talent, fresh writing and a willingness to listen to editorial criticism and learn." Works with a small number of new/unpublished authors. Specializes in mainstream fiction, (not category romance or mysteries, etc.), nonfiction in the medical, social sciences, autobiography and biography areas.
Will Handle: Nonfiction books and novels. Currently handles 60% nonfiction books and 40% novels. Will read—at no charge—unsolicited queries and outlines. Reports in 2 weeks on queries. "If our agency does not respond within 2 months to your request to become a client, you may submit requests elsewhere."
Terms: Agent receives 15% commission on domestic sales; 15% on dramatic sales; and 25% on foreign sales. Charges for photocopying expenses. 100% of income derived from commission on ms sales.
Recent Sales: *Green City In The Sun*, by Barbara Wood (Random); *The Proprietor's Daughter*, by Lewis Orde (Little, Brown); and *How to Make Love All The Time*, by Barbara DeAngelis (Rawson).

PAUL KOHNER, INC., 9169 Sunset Blvd., Los Angeles CA 90069. (213)550-1060. Agent: Gary Salt. Estab. 1938. Represents 100 clients. Writer must have sold material in the market or category in which they are seeking representation. Prefers to work with published/established authors. Specializes in film and TV scripts and related material, and dramatic rights for published or soon-to-be published books—both fiction and nonfiction. No plays, poetry or short stories. "We handle dramatic and performing rights only."
Will Handle: Magazine articles and nonfiction books (if they have film or TV potential); novels (only previously published or with publication deals set); movie scripts; and TV scripts. Currently handles 5% magazine articles; 12½% nonfiction books; 12½% novels; 40% movie scripts; and 30% TV scripts. Only queries accompanied by SASE will be answered. *Absolutely no unsolicited material.* Reports in 1 week on queries. "If our agency does not respond within 1 month to your request to become a client, you may submit requests elsewhere."
Terms: Agent receives 10% commission on dramatic sales. Charges for photocopy and binding expenses. Sometimes offers a consultation service through which film and TV writers not represented can get advice on a contract; charges varying rate.
Recent Sales: *The Flight of The Intruder* (Naval Institute Press); *Men Who Hate Women and The Women Who Love Them*, (Bantam).

BARBARA S. KOUTS, (Affiliated with Philip G. Spitzer Literary Agency), 788 9th Ave., New York NY 10019. (212)265-6003. Literary Agent: Barbara S. Kouts. Estab. 1980. Member of ILAA. Represents 50 clients. 70% of clients are new/unpublished writers. Eager to work with new/unpublished writers. Specializes in fiction, nonfiction and children's books.
Will Handle: Nonfiction books, novels and juvenile books. Currently handles 40% nonfiction books; 40% novels; and 20% juvenile books. Will read—at no charge—unsolicited queries and outlines. Reports in 3 weeks on queries; 2 months on mss. "If our agency does not respond within 2 months to your request to become a client, you may submit requests elsewhere."
Terms: Agent receives 10% commission on domestic sales; and 20% on foreign sales. Charges writers for photocopy expenses.
Recent Sales: *Short and Shivery*, by Robert San Souci (Doubleday); *Bed and Breakfast, North America*, by Hal Gieseking (Simon & Schuster); *Beethoven's Cat*, by Elisabeth McHugh (Atheneum).

PETER LAMPACK AGENCY, INC., 2015, 551 5th Ave., New York NY 10017. (212)687-9106. President: Peter Lampack. Estab. 1977. Represents 90 clients. 10% of clients are new/unpublished writers. Majority of clients are published/established authors; works with a small number of new/unpublished authors. Specializes in "commercial fiction, particularly contemporary relationships, male-oriented action/adventure, mysteries, horror and historical romance; literary fiction; and upscale, serious nonfiction or general interest nonfiction only from a recognized expert in a given field."

Will Handle: Nonfiction books, novels, movie scripts and TV scripts ("but not for espiodic TV series—must lend itself to movie-of-the-week or mini-series format.") Currently handles 15% nonfiction books; 75% novels; 5% movie scripts; 5% TV scripts. Will read—at no charge—unsolicited queries, outlines and mss. Reports in 2 weeks on queries; 6 weeks on mss. "If our agency does not respond within 2 months to your request to become a client, you may submit requests elsewhere."

Terms: Agent receives 15% commission on domestic sales; 15% on dramatic sales; and 20% on foreign sales. Charges for photocopy expenses "although we prefer writers supply copies of their work. Writers are required to supply or bear the cost of copies of books for overseas sales." 100% of income derived from sales of writers' work.

Recent Sales: *Treasure*, by Clive Cossler (Simon & Schuster); *Stinger*, by Robert McCammon (Pocket Books); and *The Impossible Dream*, by Sandra Burton (Warner Books).

MICHAEL LARSEN/ELIZABETH POMADA LITERARY AGENTS, 1029 Jones St., San Francisco CA 94109. (415)673-0939. Contact: Mike Larsen or Elizabeth Pomada. Member of ILAA. Represents 150 clients. 50-55% of clients are new/unpublished writers. Eager to work with new/unpublished writers. "We have very catholic tastes and do not specialize. We handle literary, commercial, and genre fiction, and the full range of nonfiction books."

Will Handle: Adult nonfiction books and novels. Currently handles 75% nonfiction books and 25% novels. Will read—at no charge—unsolicited queries, the first 30 pages and synopsis of completed novels, and nonfiction book proposals. Reports in 6 weeks on queries. "Always include SASE. Send SASE for brochure."

Terms: Agent receives 15% commission on domestic sales; 15% on dramatic sales; and 20% on foreign sales. May charge writer for printing, postage for multiple submissions, foreign mail, foreign phone calls, galleys, books, and legal fees. Offers a separate consultation service; charges $100/hour. 100% of income derived from commission on ms sales.

Recent Sales: *Healing With Humor*, by Allen Klein (Tarcher); *Sexual Secrets*, by Marty Klein (Dutton); *Chantal*, by Yvone Lenard (Delacorte).

LAW OFFICES OF ROBERT L. FENTON, P.C., Suite 390, 31800 Northwestern Hwy., Farmington Hills MI 48018. (313)855-8780. President: Robert L. Fenton. Estab. 1960. Represents 30 clients. 10% of clients are new/unpublished writers. Prefers to work with published/established authors; works with a small number of new/unpublished writers.

Will Handle: Nonfiction books and novels. Currently handles 50% nonfiction books and 50% novels. Reads solicited queries, outlines and mss for a fee. Reports in 3 weeks on queries. "If our agency does not respond within 2 months to your request to become a client, you may submit requests elsewhere. I package many works into TV movies or feature films. Recently had office at Universal Films as an independent producer (for 3½ years)."

Terms: Agent receives 15% commission on domestic sales and 15% on foreign sales. Charges a reading fee; waives fee if representing writer who has been published twice. 10% of income derived from reading fees. Critique: oral or written—if written is approximately 2 pages. Charges "nominal retainer" to unpublished authors. Charges for phone, photocopy and postage expenses. 20% of income derived from fees.

Recent Sales: *Mein Amerika*, by Leo Rutman (Stein and Day); and *Judicial Indiscretion*, by James W. Ellison (St. Martin's); *Call Me Roger*, by Albert Lee (contemporary).

L. HARRY LEE LITERARY AGENCY, Box 203, Rocky Point NY 11778. (516)744-1188. President: L. Harry Lee. Estab. 1979. Member of WGA. Represents 150 clients. 40% of clients are new/unpublished writers. "Mainly interested in screenwriters." Specializes in movies, TV (episodic, movies-of-the-week and sit-coms) and contemporary novels.

Will Handle: Novels, movie scripts, stage plays, and TV scripts (movies, mini-series, MOW's, episodic, and sit-coms). Currently handles 10% novels; 60% movie scripts; 3% stage plays; 27% TV scripts. Will read—at no charge—unsolicited queries and outlines; does not read material submitted without SASE. No dot-matrix. Reports in 2 weeks on queries; 6 weeks on mss.

Terms: Agent receives 15% commission on domestic sales; 15% on dramatic sales; and 20% on foreign sales. Charges a marketing fee; 5% of income derived from marketing fees. Charges for photocopies, line editing, proofing, typing, and postage expenses. Offers a consultation service through which writers not represented can get advice on a contract; charges $75/hour. 5% of income derived from marketing fees; 90% of income derived from commission on ms sales.

Recent Sales: *The Gizmo Delicious*, *The Victorian* and *Captain Cloud*.

‡LIGHTHOUSE LITERARY AGENCY, Box 2105, Winter Park FL 32790. (407)647-2385. Director: Sandra Kangas. Estab. 1988. Represents 5 clients. 40% of clients are new/unpublished writers. "We are interested in

working with new or established writers of fine prose who maintain a professional work attitude. Some prior success is a plus, but not a requirement." Specializes in nonfiction, novels, TV and movie scripts, treatments, juveniles, poetry, and magazine fiction.
Will Handle: Magazine fiction, nonfiction books, novels, textbooks, juvenile books, movie scripts, stage plays, TV scripts, poetry. Currently handles 20% nonfiction books; 50% novels; 15% juvenile books; 15% poetry. Will read submissions at no charge, but may charge a criticism fee or service charge for work performed after the initial reading. Reports in 2 weeks on queries; 2 months on manuscripts. "If our agency does not respond within 2 months to your request to become a client, you may submit requests elsewhere."
Terms: Agent receives 10% commission on domestic sales; 15% on dramatic sales; and 20% on foreign sales. "We read for acceptance or rejection at no charge and will send personal response. If we feel a rewrite might make a marketable work, we offer a criticism service. We suggest new writers use it." Charges $300/300 pages. "We give an honest and objective analysis of the work and its marketabiity. We point out its good points and weaknesses and suggest ways to improve it. The author is mailed a written critique of one or more typewritten single-spaced pages. Emphasis is on clarity, plot, characterization, viewpoint and style. Lighthouse hires experienced freelance specialists to help with this service." 90% of income derived from sales of writers' work; 10% of income derived from criticism service.
Recent Sales: New agency.

WENDY LIPKIND AGENCY, Suite 3E 165 E. 66th St., New York NY 10021. (212)935-1406. President: Wendy Lipkind. Estab. 1977. Member of ILAA. Represents 50 clients. 20% of clients are new/unpublished writers. Works with a small number of new/unpublished authors. Specializes in nonfiction (social history, adventure, biography, science, sports, history) and fiction ("good story telling. I do not specialize in genre mass-market fiction").
Will Handle: Nonfiction books and novels. Currently handles 80% nonfiction books and 20% novels. Will read—at no charge—unsolicited queries and outlines. Reports in 2 weeks on queries.
Terms: Agent receives 10% commission on domestic sales; 10-15% on dramatic sales; and 20% on foreign sales. Charges $100 one-time handling fee if sells work. Charges for phone, foreign postage, photocopy, cables and messenger expenses. 100% of income derived from commission on ms sales.
Recent Sales: *Personality Self-Portrait* (Bantam Books); *Still a Cowboy* (Random House); *Working: My Life as a Prostitute* (E. P. Dutton).

‡LITERARY/BUSINESS ASSOCIATES, Box 2415, Hollywood CA 90078. (213)465-2630. President: Shelley Gross. Estab. 1979. Member ILAA. Represents 4 clients. 80% of clients are new/unpublished writers. Works with small number of new/unpublished writers. Specializes in nontechnical nonfiction, especially new age, health and fitness and popular business.
Will Handle: Nonfiction Books, novels and juvenile books. Curently handles 60% nonfiction; 40% novels. Will read—at no charge—unsolicted queries and outlines. Reports in 1 month on queries; 6 weeks on mss. "If our agency does not respond within 2 months to your request to become a client, you may submit requests elsewhere."
Terms: Agent receives 15% commission on domestic sales; 20% on foreign sales. Charges criticism fee to new and unpublished writers. 50% is refundable after sale is made. 40% of income derived from criticism fees. Charges $60/300-page, typed double-spaced book ms. "Writer receives approximately 2 single-spaced typewritten pages of detailed editorial and marketing evaluation including advice for ms improvement. Some penciled comments on pages themselves. Also included is typed guidesheet for either fiction or nonfiction mss. New, unpublished writers pay nominal marketing fee which is nonrefundable." Sometime offers consultation service through which writers can get advice on a contract; charges $25-30 per hour. 40-60% of income derived from commission on ms sales; 35-40% from fees charged to writers.
Recent Sales: No information given.

‡LITERARY MARKETING CONSULTANTS, Suite 701, One Hallidie Plaza, San Francisco CA 94102. (415)391-7508. Associate: J. Ehlers. Estab. 1984. Represents 15 clients. 5% of clients are new/unpublished writers. Eager to work with new/unpublished writers. Specializes in "nonfiction: scholarly works and magazine articles. Fiction: young adult, science fiction, mysteries, new age, experimental, mainstream and romance (historical, gothic and contemporary)."
Will Handle: Currently handles 20% magazine articles; 10% magazine fiction; 10% nonfiction books; 35% novels; 15% juvenile books. Will read—at no charge—unsolicited queries. Reports in 1 month. "If we do not respond within 2 months to your request to become a client, you may submit requests elsewhere."
Terms: Agent receives 10% commission on domestic sales; 15% on dramatic sales; and 20% on foreign sales. Charges for photocopying, postage, phone and special services as requested by the writer. 95% of income derived from commission on ms sales; 5% from fees charged to writers. "We will only take the time to provide a critique if we also have the opportunity to market the work."
Recent Sales: "Two young adult novels."

PETER LIVINGSTON ASSOCIATES, INC., 120 Carlton St., Toronto, Ontario M5A 4K2 Canada. (416)928-1010. Associate: David Johnston. Assistant: Janine Cheeseman. Estab. 1982. Member of ILAA. Represents 75 clients. Works with a small number of new/unpublished authors. Specializes in hardcover, "front list" literary fiction and women's books and nonfiction by leading authorities or experienced journalists. "In nonfiction, previous magazine publication and/or credentials in the field help. In fiction, short story publications help."
Will Handle: Nonfiction books; novels (hardcover, mainstream); and movie scripts (only if by previously published or produced writers). Currently handles 50% nonfiction books; 30% novels; 10% movie scripts; and 10% TV scripts. Will read—at no charge—unsolicited queries and outlines. Reports in 2 weeks on queries; 5 weeks on mss. "If our agency does not respond within 6 weeks to your request to become a client, you may submit requests elsewhere."
Terms: Agent receives 15% commission on domestic sales; 15% on dramatic sales; and 20% on foreign sales. Charges a reading fee to "unrecommended and previously unpublished authors" of fiction; waives fee if representing writer. 1% of income derived from reading fees. Writer receives "a brief (two to three page) critique of the manuscript for reading fee. Readings are done by inhouse agents and/or professional editors." Charges for photocopy, postage, messenger, telex, and phone expenses.
Recent Sales: *The Christkiller*, by Marcel Montecino (Arbor House); *Savant: Genius Among Us, Genius Within Us*, by Dr. Darold Treffert (Harper & Row); and *The Real Coke: The Real Story*, by T. Oliver (Random House).

‡**NANCY LOVE AGENCY**, 250 E. 65th St., New York NY 10021. (212)980-3499. Contact: Nancy Love. Estab. 1983. Member of ILAA. Represents 50 clients. 40% of clients are new/unpublished writers. Prefers to work with published writers. Specializes in adult fiction and nonficiton with the exception of romance novels.
Will Handle: Nonfiction books and novels. Curently handles 75% nonfiction books; 25% novels. Will read—at no charge—unsolicited queries, outlines and mss. Reports in 1 month on queries; 6 weeks on mss. "Length of exclusivity negotiated on a per case basis."
Terms: Agent receives 15% commission on domestic sales; 15% TV and movie sales; 20% on foreign sales.
Recent Sales: *Everybody Says Freedom*, by Pete Seeger and Bob Reiser (W.W. Norton); *Appointment With Murder*, by Susan Bakos (Putnam); and *Famous For 15 Minutes*, by Ultraviolet with Jean Libman Block (Harcourt Brace Jovanovich).

‡**LOWENSTEIN ASSOCIATES, INC.**, #601, 121 W. 27th St., New York NY 10001. (212)206-1630. President: Barbara Lowenstein. Vice President: Eileen Fallon. Agents: Lori Perkins, Norman Kurz. Estab. 1976. Member of ILAA. Represents 120 clients. 15% of clients are new/unpublished writers. Specializes in nonfiction—especially science and medical-topic books for the general public—historical and contemporary romance, bigger woman's fiction and general fiction.
Will Handle: Nonfiction books and novels. Currently handles 2% magazine articles; 55% nonfiction books; and 43% novels. Will read—at no charge—unsolicited queries and outlines. Reports in 2 weeks on queries.
Terms: Agent receives 15% commission on domestic sales; 15% on dramatic sales; and 20% on foreign sales. Charges for photocopy, foreign postage and messenger expenses. 100% of income derived from commission on ms, other dramatic and 1st serial sales.
Recent Sales: Confidential.

‡**MARGARET MCBRIDE LITERARY AGENCY**, Box 8730, LaJolla CA 92038. (619)459-0559. Contact: Winifred Golden and Sandra Greenberg. Estab. 1980. Member of ILAA. Represents 25 clients. 20% of clients are new/unpublished writers. Specializes in historical biographies, literary fiction, mainstream fiction and nonfiction.
Will Handle: Nonfiction books, novels, movie scripts and syndicated material. Will read—at no charge—unsolicited queries and outlines. Does not read unsolicited mss. Reports in 6 weeks on queries. "We are looking for two more novelists to complete our client list."
Terms: Agent receives 15% commission on domestic sales; 10% on dramatic sales; and 25% on foreign sales. Charges writers for Telex and Federal Express made at author's request. 100% of income derived from commission on ms sales.
Recent Sales: *Fortune's Child*, by Molly Cochran (Paperjacks); *Destroyer Series*, by Warren Murphy (New American Library); and *Barbarian to Bureaucrats*, by Larry Miller (Clarkson Potter).

‡**GERARD MCCAULEY AGENCY**, Box AE, Katonah NY 10536. (914)232-5700. Contact: Bruce Galloway. Estab. 1970. Member of SAR. Represents 65 clients. 5% of clients are new/unpublished writers. To be represented writer must have at least one book published. Prefers to work with published/established authors. Specializes in nonfiction—history and public affairs.
Will Handle: Nonfiction books and college textbooks. Currently handles 80% nonfiction books; 10% novels; 10% textbooks. Will read—at no charge—unsolicited queries and outlines. Will read mss at no charge, but may charge a criticism fee or service charge for work performed after the initial reading. Reports in 1 month.

"If our agency does not respond within 1 month to your request to become a client, you may submit requests elsewhere."

Terms: Agent receives 15% commission on domestic sales; 15% on dramatic sales; and 20% on foreign sales. Charges reading fee; waives fee if representing writer. Charges $50 reading fee for 300-page, typed double-spaced book mss. Charges for postage for submissions and photocopying material. 100% of income derived from commission on ms sales.

Recent Sales: *Seasons at Eagle Pond*, by Donald Hall (Ticknor and Fields); *Bobby Kennedy*, by Stephen Oates (Harper and Row); and *1001 Things About History*, by John Garraty (Doubleday).

‡RICHARD P. MCDONOUGH, LITERARY AGENT, Box 1950, Boston MA 02130. (617)522-6388. Estab. 1986. Represents 20 clients. 80% of clients are new/unpublished writers. Works with unpublished and published writers "whose work I think has merit and requires a committed advocate." Specializes in nonfiction for general contract and fiction.

Will Handle: Nonfiction books, novels and syndicated material. Currently handles 80% nonfiction books; 10% novels; and 10% juvenile. Will read—at no charge— unsolicited queries, outlines and mss. Reports in 2 weeks on queries; 5 weeks on mss. "If our agency does not respond within 2 months to your request to become a client, you may submit requests elsewhere."

Terms: Agent receives 15% commission on domestic sales; 15% on dramatic sales; 15% on foreign sales. Charges for photocopying, phone beyond 300 miles; postage for sold work only. Sometimes offers consultation service through which writers can get advice on a contract; charges negotiable rate. 100% of income derived from commission on mss sales.

Recent Sales: *Guide to Museums in N.Y. City*, by R. Garrett (Chelsea Green) and *Mystic Lakes*, by D. Musello (Donald Fine).

DENISE MARCIL LITERARY AGENCY, INC., 316 W. 82nd St. 5F, New York NY 10024. (212)580-1071. President: Denise Marcil. Estab. 1977. Member of ILAA. Represents 80 clients. Works with a small number of new/unpublished authors. Specializes in "solid, informative nonfiction including such areas as money, business, health, child care, parenting, self-help and how-to's and commercial fiction, especially women's fiction; also mysteries, psychological suspense and horror."

Will Handle: Nonfiction books and novels. Currently handles 40% nonfiction books and 60% novels. Will read—at no charge—unsolicited queries and outlines. Reports in 2 weeks on queries; 3 months on mss. "If our agency does not respond within 4 months to your request to become a client, you may submit requests elsewhere."

Terms: Agent receives 15% commission on domestic sales; 15% on dramatic sales; and 22% on foreign sales. Charges a reading fee: $45/first 3 chapters and outline. Less than 19% of income derived from reading fees. Charges for disbursements, postage, copying and messenger service. 99.9% of income derived from commission on ms sales.

Recent Sales: *No More Cravings*, by Dr. Douglas Hunt (Warner); *Parent's Guide to Raising Sexually Healthy Children*, by Lynn Leight (Rawson Assoc.); and *Blood and Sable*, by Carol J. Kane (McGraw-Hill).

BETTY MARKS, Suite 9F, 176 E. 77th St., New York NY 10021. (212)535-8388. Contact: Betty Marks. Estab. 1969. Member of ILAA. Represents 35 clients. Prefers to work with published/established authors; works with a small number of new/unpublished authors. Specializes in journalists' nonfiction.

Will Handle: Nonfiction books, cookbooks and novels. Will read—at no charge—unsolicited queries and outlines. Reports in 1 week on queries; 6 weeks on mss. "If our agency does not respond within 6 weeks to your request to become a client, you may submit requests elsewhere."

Terms: Agent receives 15% commission on domestic sales; and 10% on foreign sales (plus 10% to foreign agent). Charges a reading fee for unpublished writers; fee will be waived if representing writer. Charges criticism fee. "Writers receive two-page letter covering storyline, plot, characters, dialogue, language, etc." Written by agent. Charges for "extraordinary" postage, phone and messenger expenses. Offers a consultation service through which writers not represented can get advice on a contract; charges $50/hour. 95% of income derived from commission on ms sales. Payment of criticism fee does not ensure that agency will represent a writer.

Recent Sales: *The Death and Life of Dith Pran* (Elizabeth Sifton); *At Any Cost* (Pantheon); and *Democratic Blueprints* (Hippocrene).

‡ELAINE MARKSON LITERARY AGENCY, 44 Greenwich Ave., New York NY 10011. Estab. 1972. Member of ILAA. Represents 200 + clients. 10% of clients are new/unpublished writers. Works with small number of new/unpublished authors. Specializes in literary fiction , commercial fiction and trade nonfiction.

Will Handle: Nonfiction books and novels. Currently handles 30% nonfiction books; 40% novels; 20% juvenile books; 5% movie scripts. Will read—at no charge—unsolicited queries and outlines. Reports in 2 weeks on queries. "If our agency does not respond within 2 months to your request to become a client, you may submit request elsewhere."

Terms: Agent receives 10% commission on domestic sales; 10% on dramatic sales; and 20% on foreign sales. Charges for postage, photocopying, long distance telephone. 100% of income derived from commission on ms sales.
Recent Sales: No information given.

‡**THE MARTELL AGENCY**, 555 5th Ave., New York NY 10017. (212)692-9770. Contact: Alice Fried Martell, Esq. Estab. 1985. Represents approximately 80 clients. Works with published/established writers. Specializes in "very diversified material. Must be commercial. We do not handle science fiction, otherwise, we're equally receptive to fiction and nonfiction."
Will Handle: Nonfiction books and novels. Currently handles approximately 65% nonfiction books and 35% novels. Will read—at no charge—unsolicited queries, outlines and mss. Send query first.
Terms: Agent receives 15% commission on domestic sales; 20% on foreign sales. Charges for messenger, photocopying, overseas postage and telephone, galleys and books ordered for ancillary rights sales.
Recent Sales: *Oil and Honor*, by Thomas Petzinger, Jr. (Putnam); *Tempting Fate*, by Laurie Alberts (Houghton Mifflin); and *The Red Truck*, by Rudy Wilson (Knopf).

SCOTT MEREDITH, INC., 845 3rd Ave., New York NY 10022. (212)245-5500. Vice President and Editorial Director: Jack Scovil. Estab. 1946. Represents 2,000 clients. 10% of clients are new/unpublished writers. "We'll represent on a straight commission basis writers who've sold one or more recent books to major publishers, or several (three or four) magazine pieces to major magazines, or a screenplay or teleplay to a major producer. We're a very large agency (staff of 51) and handle all types of material except individual cartoons or drawings, though we will handle collections of these as well."
Will Handle: Magazine articles, magazine fiction, nonfiction books, novels, textbooks, juvenile books, movie scripts, radio scripts, stage plays, TV scripts, syndicated material and poetry. Currently handles 5% magazine articles; 5% magazine fiction; 23% nonfiction books; 23% novels; 5% textbooks; 10% juvenile books; 5% movie scripts; 2% radio scripts; 2% stage plays; 5% TV scripts; 5% syndicated material; and 5% poetry. Will read—at no charge—unsolicited queries, outlines, and manuscripts "if from a writer with track record as described previously; charges a fee if no sales." Reports in 2 weeks.
Terms: Agent receives 10% commission on domestic sales; 10% on dramatic sales; and 20% on foreign sales. Charges "a single fee which covers multiple readers, revision assistance or critique as needed. When a script is returned as irreparably unsalable, the accompanying letter of explanation will usually run two single-spaced pages minimum on short stories or articles, or from 4 to 10 single-spaced pages on book-length manuscripts, teleplays, or screenplays. All reports are done by agents on full-time staff. No marketing advice is included, since, if it's salable, we'll market and sell it ourselves." Charges for Telex, cables and phone expenses. 10% of income derived from fees; 90% of income derived from commission on ms sales.
Recent Sales: *Harlot's Ghost*, by Norman Mailer (Random House); *Nucleus*, by Carl Sagan (Random House); and *Fantastic Voyage II*, by Isaac Asimov (Doubleday).

MEWS BOOKS LTD.—Sidney B. Kramer,20 Bluewater Hill, Westport CT 06880. (203)227-1836. Secretary: Fran Pollak. Estab. 1972. Represents 35 clients. Prefers to work with published/established authors; works with small number of new/unpublished authors "producing professional work. No editing services." Specializes in juvenile (pre-school through young adult), cookery, adult nonfiction and fiction, technical and medical.
Will Handle: Nonfiction books, novels, juvenile books, character merchandising and video use of illustrated published books. Currently handles 20% nonfiction; 20% novels; 50% juvenile books and 10% miscellaneous. Will read—at no charge—unsolicited queries and outlines with character description and a few pages of writing sample.
Terms: Agent receives 10% commission on domestic sales for published authors; 15% for unpublished; total 20% on foreign. $500 minimum commission if book is published. Charges writers for photocopy and postage expenses and other direct costs. Principle agent is an attorney and former publisher. Offers consultation service through which writers can get advice on a contract or on publishing problems.
Recent Sales: No information given.

THE PETER MILLER AGENCY, INC., Box 760, Old Chelsea Station, New York NY 10011. (212)929-1222. President: Peter Miller. Associate Agent: Jonathan Blank. Estab. 1975. Represents 50 clients. 50% of clients are new/unpublished writers. Eager to work with new/unpublished writers, as well as with published/established authors (especially journalists). Specializes in celebrity books (biographies and self-help), true crime accounts, mysteries, mystery thrillers, historical fiction/family sagas, women's fiction, and "fiction with *real* motion picture potential." Writer's guidelines for 5x8½ SASE and 3 first class stamp.
Will Handle: Nonfiction books, novels and movie scripts. Currently handles 45% nonfiction books; 35% novels; and 20% movie scripts. Will read—at no charge—unsolicited queries and outlines. Reports in 2 weeks on queries; 1 month on mss.
Terms: Agent receives 15% commission on domestic sales; and 20-25% on foreign sales. Charges a criticism

fee for unpublished writers. Fee is refunded if book sells. 5% of income derived from criticism fees. "The agency offers a reading evaluation, usually two to four pages in length, which gives a detailed analysis of literary craft, commercial potential and recommendations for improving the work, if necessary." Charges for photocopy expenses. 5% of income derived from fees; 95% of income derived from commission on ms sales and motion picture/television rights sales.

Recent Sales: *Beating The Odds*, by Dr. Albert Marchelt (Contemporary Books, Inc.); *Night Of The Rangers*, by Mark D. Harrell (Lynx Communications, Inc.); and *The Longest Odds*, by Barry Sheinkopf (Lynx Communications, Inc.).

MULTIMEDIA PRODUCT DEVELOPMENT, INC., Suite 724, 410 S. Michigan Ave., Chicago IL 60605. (312)922-3063. President: Jane Jordan Browne. Estab. 1971. Member of ILAA. Represents 100 clients. 10% of clients are new/unpublished writers. Works with a small number of new/unpublished authors. "We are generalists, taking on nonfiction and fiction that we believe will be on target for the market."

Will Handle: Nonfiction books ("new idea" books, how-to, science and biography) and novels (mainstream and genre). Currently handles 68% nonfiction books; 30% novels; and 2% juvenile books. Will read—at no charge—unsolicited queries and outlines. Reports in 3 weeks on queries. "We review manuscripts only if we solicit submission and only as 'exclusives.' "

Terms: Agent receives 15% commission on domestic sales; 15% on dramatic sales; and 20% on foreign sales. Charges for photocopying, overseas telegrams and telephone calls, and overseas postage expenses. Sometimes offers a consultation service through which writers not represented can get advice on a contract; charges $100/hour. 100% of income derived from commission on ms sales.

Recent Sales: *Reclaiming Our Lives*, by Carol Poston and Karen Lisou (Little Brown); *Swing Sisters*, by Jane Westin (McGraw-Hill); and *Trial*, by Steve Fitter (Doubleday).

JEAN V. NAGGAR LITERARY AGENCY, 336 East 73rd St., New York NY 10021. (212)794-1082. President: Jean Naggar. Estab. 1978. Member of ILAA. Represents 80 clients. "If a writer is submitting a first novel, this must be completed and in final draft form before writing to query the agency." Prefers to work with published/established authors; works with small number of new/unpublished authors. Specializes in mainstream fiction and nonfiction—no category romances, no occult.

Will Handle: Nonfiction books, novels and juvenile books. Handles magazine articles and magazine fiction from authors who also write fiction/nonfiction books. Will read—at no charge—unsolicited queries and outlines. Reports in 2 weeks on queries.

Terms: Agent receives 15% commission on domestic sales; 15% on dramatic sales; and 20% on foreign sales. Charges writers for photocopy, long distance telephone, cables and overseas postage expenses.

Recent Sales: *Velocity*, by Kristin McCloy (Random House); *Jephte's Daughter*, by Naomi Ragen (Warner Books); and *A Vision of Light*, by Judith Merkle Riley (Delacorte/Dell).

‡RUTH NATHAN LITERARY AGENCY, 242 West 27th St., New York NY 10001. (212)807-6292. President: Ruth Nathan. Estab. 1987. Member of ILAA. Represents 10 clients. 50% of clients are new/unpublished writers. Works with small number of new/unpublished writers and special writers of biography and art history and unexplored movie or theatre material. Specializes in nonfiction.

Will Handle: Nonfiction books. Currently handles 80% nonfiction books; 20% novels. Does not read unsolicited mss. Reports in 1 month on queries. "If our agency does not respond within 6 months to your request to become a client, you may submit requests elsewhere."

Terms: Agent receives 15% commission on domestic sales; 10% on foreign sales. Charges for long distance phone calls, copying of ms, Telex, extra galleys. 100% of income derived from commission on ms sales.

Recent Sales: *Duncan Grant and the Bloomsbury Group*, by Douglas Turnbaugh (Lyle Stuart); *The Tony Award Book*, by Lee Murrow (Abbeville); and *Life and Other Ways to Waste Time*, by Mike Nichols (Lyle Stuart).

CHARLES NEIGHBORS, INC., Suite 3607A, 7600 Blanco Rd., San Antonio TX 78216. (512)342-5324. Owner: Charles Neighbors. Manager: Margaret Neighbors. Estab. 1966. Represents 60 clients. 10% of clients are new/unpublished writers. Works with a small number of new/unpublished authors.

Will Handle: Nonfiction books, novels and movie scripts. Currently handles 30% nonfiction books; 60% novels; and 10% movie scripts. Will read—at no charge—unsolicited queries and outlines. Reports in 1 month on queries; 2 months on mss. "If our agency does not respond within 2 months to your request to become a client, you may submit requests elsewhere."

Terms: Agent receives 15% commission on domestic sales; 15% on dramatic sales; and 20% on foreign sales. Charges for photocopying and foreign postage expenses. 100% of income derived from commission on ms sales.

Recent Sales: *Mercenary Soldier of Fortune Handbook*, by Paul Balor (Dell); *Live by the Gun*, by Wayne Barton and Stan Williams (Pocket).

‡NEW AGE LITERARY AGENCY, 7815 Hollywood Blvd., Hollywood CA 90046. (213)851-7444. Senior Editor and Vice President: Fred Lloyd Cochran. Estab. 1988. Eager to work with new/unpublished writers. Specializes in physical and behavioral science book publishing and general field of documentary film/video production. "We want new writers who are professional and have a strong documentary film message."
Will Handle: Nonfiction books (basic science and behavioral sciences only), movie scripts (documentaries).
Terms: Agent receives 15-25% commission on domestic sales; 15-20% on foreign sales. Charges a reading fee for new writers. $100 of income derived from reading fees.
Recent Sales: New agency.

NEW AGE WORLD SERVICES, 62091 Valley View Circle, Joshua Tree CA 92252. (619)366-2833. Owner: Victoria Vandertuin. Estab. 1957. Member of Academy of Science Fiction, Fantasy and Horror Films. Represents 12 clients. 100% of clients are new/unpublished writers. Eager to work with new/unpublished writers. Specializes in all New Age fields: occult, astrology, metaphysical, yoga, U.F.O., ancient continents, para sciences, mystical, magical, health, beauty, political, and all New Age categories in fiction and nonfiction. Writer's guidelines for #10 SAE with four first class stamps.
Will Handle: Magazine articles, magazine fiction, nonfiction books, novels and poetry. Currently handles 10% magazine articles; 10% magazine fiction; 40% nonfiction books; 30% novels and 10% poetry. Will read—at no charge— unsolicited queries, outlines and mss; will read submissions at no charge, but may charge a criticism fee or service charge for work performed after the initial reading. Reports in 6 weeks. "If our agency does not respond within 2 months to your request to become a client, you may submit requests elsewhere."
Terms: Receives 15% commission on domestic sales; and 20% on foreign sales. Charges reading fee of $75 for 300-page, typed, double-spaced ms; reading fee waived if representing writer. Charges criticism fee of $85 for 300-page, typed, double-space ms; 10% of income derived from criticism fees. "I personally read all manuscripts for critique or evaluation, which is typed, double-spaced with about four or more pages, depending on the manuscript and the service for the manuscript the author requests. If requested, marketing advice is included. We charge a representation fee if we represent the author's manuscript." Charges writer for editorial readings, compiling of query letter and synopsis, printing of same, compiling lists and mailings.
Recent Sales: No information given.

‡NEW WRITERS LITERARY PROJECT, LTD., Suite 177, 2809 Bird Ave., Coconut Grove FL 33133. (305)443-2158. President: Robert S. Catz. Estab. 1987. Member of ILAA. Represents 10 clients. 90% of clients are new/unpublished writers. Specializes in fiction and nonfiction motion picture and television screenplays.
Will Handle: Magazine articles, magazine fiction, nonfiction books, novels, movie scripts, stage plays, TV scripts. Handles 5% magazine articles; 80% nonfiction books; 5% movie scripts and 10% TV scripts. Will read—at no charge—unsolicited queries, outlines and mss. Reports in 3 weeks on queries; 5 weeks on mss. "If our agency does not respond within 2 months to your request to become a client, you may submit requests elsewhere."
Terms: Agent receives 15% commission on domestic sales; 15% on dramatic sales; and 20% on foreign sales. Charges writers for mail, telephone and photocopying expenses. Sometimes offers a consultation service through which writers can get advice on a contract. Charge is individually negotiated per project. 95% of income derived from commission on ms sales; 5% from fees.
Recent Sales: *Power and Greed: A History of Teamster Corruptions*, by Friedman and Schwarz (Watts).

THE BETSY NOLAN LITERARY AGENCY, Suite 9 West, 50 W. 29th St., New York NY 10001. (212)779-0700. President: Betsy Nolan. Vice President: Michael Powers. Estab. 1980. Represents 26 clients. 50% of clients are new/unpublished writers. Works with a small number of new/unpublished authors.
Will Handle: Nonfiction books and novels. Currently handles 60% nonfiction books and 40% novels. Will read—at no charge—unsolicited queries and outlines. Reports in 2 weeks on queries; 1 month on mss. "If our agency does not respond within 1 month to your request to become a client, you may submit requests elsewhere."
Terms: Agent receives 15% commission on domestic sales; and 20% on foreign sales.
Recent Sales: No information given.

THE NORMA-LEWIS AGENCY, 521 5th Ave., New York NY 10175. (212)751-4955. Contact: Norma Liebert. Estab. 1980. 50% of clients are new/unpublished writers. Prefers to work with published/established authors; eager to work with new/unpublished writers. Specializes in young adult and children's books.
Will Handle: Novels, textbooks, juvenile books, movie scripts, radio scripts, stage plays and TV scripts. Currently handles 10% nonfiction books; 10% novels; 10% textbooks; 50% juvenile books; 5% movie scripts; 5% radio scripts; 5% stage plays; and 5% TV scripts. Will read—at no charge—unsolicited queries and outlines. Reports in 2 weeks on queries. "If our agency does not respond within 2 weeks to your request to become a client, you may submit requests elsewhere."
Terms: Agent receives 15% commission on domestic sales; 15% on dramatic sales; and 20% on foreign sales.

Offers a consultation service through which writers not represented can get advice on a contract. Rate varies. 100% of income derived from commission on ms sales.
Recent Sales: No information given.

NUGENT AND ASSOCIATES, INC.,170 10th Street, North, Naples FL 33940. (813)262-7562. President: Ray E. Nugent. Estab. 1976. Represents 27 clients. 75% of clients are new/unpublished writers. Eager to work with new/unpublished writers. Specializes in adult fiction and nonfiction—screenplays.
Will Handle: Nonfiction books, novels, movie scripts, stage plays and TV scripts. Currently handles 10% nonfiction books; 70% novels; 5% juvenile books; 5% movie scripts; 3% stage plays; 5% TV scripts; and 2% poetry. Will read—at no charge—unsolicited queries, outlines and mss. Reports in 1 month on queries; 2 months on submissions. "If our agency does not respond within 3 months to your request to become a client, you may submit requests elsewhere."
Terms: Receives 15% commission on domestic sales; 15% on dramatic sales; and 20% on foreign sales. First book authors are charged $500 to cover ms typing, copies, long distance calls, etc.; balance refundable. Less than 5% of income derived from fees. Charges writers for long distance phone calls, copies, ms typing, any other extraordinary expenses directly associated with the author's specific material. Offers consultation service through which writers can get advice on a contract; charges $60/hour.
Recent Sales:*Pipes and Strings*, by Bill Ballentine (Richardson and Steerman); *Disney's World*, by Leonard Mosley (Stein and Day); and *Osteoporosis* , by Bruce/McIlwain (John Wiley).

FIFI OSCARD ASSOCIATES, 19 W. 44th St., New York NY 10036. (212)764-1100. Contact: Ivy Fischer Stone, Literary Department. Estab. 1956. Member of SAR and WGA. Represents 108 clients. 5% of clients are new/unpublished writers. "Writer must have published articles or books in major markets or have screen credits if movie scripts, etc." Works with a small number of new/unpublished authors. Specializes in literary novels, commercial novels, mysteries and nonfiction, especially celebrity biographies and autobiographies.
Will Handle: Nonfiction books, novels, movie scripts and stage plays. Currently handles 40% nonfiction books; 40% novels; 5% movie scripts; 5% stage plays; and 10% TV scripts. Will read—at no charge—unsolicited queries and outlines. Reports in 1 week on queries if SASE enclosed. "If our agency does not respond within 1 month to your request to become a client, you may submit requests elsewhere."
Terms: Agent receives 15% commission on domestic sales; 10% on dramatic sales; and 20% on foreign sales. Charges for photocopy expenses.
Recent Sales: *Cardinal Numbers*, by Hob Broun (Knopf); *Donnie Brasco, My Undercover Life in the Mafia*, by Joseph Pistone with Richard Woodler (NAL); and *Dream Time*, by Geoffrey O'Brien (Viking).

THE OTTE COMPANY, 9 Goden St., Belmont MA 02178. (617)484-8505. Contact: Jane H. Otte or L. David Otte. Estab. 1973. Represents 25 clients. 33% of clients are new/unpublished writers. Works with a small number of new/unpublished authors. Specializes in quality adult trade books.
Will Handle: Nonfiction books and novels. Currently handles 40% nonfiction books; and 60% novels. Will consider unsolicited query letters. Reports in 1 week on queries; 1 month on mss. "If our agency does not respond within 1 month to your request to become a client, you may submit requests elsewhere."
Terms: Agent receives 15% commission on domestic sales; 7½% on dramatic sales; and 10% on foreign sales plus 10% to foreign agent. Charges for photocopy, overseas phone and postage expenses. 100% of income derived from commission on ms sales.
Recent Sales: *Jack and Susan in 1933*, by Michael McDowell (Ballantine); *Abbott and Avery*, by Robert Shaw (Viking Penguin); and *Candles Burning*, by Michael McDowell (Berkley).

JOHN K. PAYNE LITERARY AGENCY, INC., Suite 1101, 175 5th Ave., New York NY 10010. (212)475-6447. President: John K. Payne. Estab. 1923 (as Lenniger Literary Agency). Represents 30 clients. 20% of clients are new/unpublished writers. Prefers writers who have one or two books published. Specializes in popular women's fiction, historical romance, biography, sagas.
Will Handle: Nonfiction books, novels, and juvenile books (young adult fiction, nonfiction). Currently publishes 20% nonfiction books and 80% novels. Charges reading/criticism fee to unpublished writers—$1/page; $100 minimum. Writer receives 3-5 single-spaced pages for partial scripts, 5 and up for entire scripts.
Terms: Agent receives 10% commission on domestic sales; 10% on dramatic sales; and 20% on foreign sales. Charges for express mail expenses and photocopies. 5% of income derived from fees charged to writers; 95% of income derived from commission on ms sales.
Recent Sales: *Private Eagle*, by Kathleen Eagle (Silhouette); *The Winds Blow Free*, by Robert Vaughn Bell (Ballantine); and *The Noose*, by Wayne D. Overholser (Paper Jacks).

‡PEGASUS INTERNATIONAL, INC., Box 5470, Winter Park FL 32793-5470. (407)831-1008. Director: Gene Lovitz. Assistant Director/Client Contact: Carole Morling. Estab. 1987. Represents 300 clients. 85% of clients are new/unpublished writers. Eager to work with new/unpublished writers. Specializes in how-to, self-help, technical, business, health, political; mainstream novels, regency, contemporary and historical romance, horror, experimental, sci-fi, mystery.

Will Handle: Nonfiction books, novels, textbooks, juvenile books, movie scripts, TV scripts, selected verse, expedition films and video. Currently handles 40% nonfiction books; 35% novels; 5% textbooks; 5% juvenile books; 10% movie scripts; and 5% TV scripts. Will read—at no charge—unsolicited queries and outlines accompanied by SASE. Does not read unsolicited manuscripts. Reports in 2 weeks. "If our agency does not respond within 2 months to your request to become a client, you may submit requests elsewhere."

Terms: Agent receives 10% commission on domestic sales; 10% on dramatic sales; 15% on foreign sales. Charges reading fee. "We return fee when and if a publishing contract is obtained. No charge for postage or phone expenses." 25% of income derived from reading fees. Charges $200 for up to a 400-page, typed, double-spaced ms. Lower fees for pamphlets, chap books, verse, etc. "We charge one fee only. We term it an 'evaluation' fee which is both a reading fee as well as a criticism fee. The length of our critiques depends upon how much is needed. Usually 1½ pages to 10 pages. Some are longer. We do both line-by-line when needed while concentrating on the overall work. Marketing is always a part of the critique." Discuss ways to improve and make the manuscript marketable. 75% of income is derived from commission on mss sales; 25% derived from fees.

Recent Sales: *The DISConnection*, (Knowledge Industry Publications, Inc.); *Franklin Computer*, (Scott, Foresman).

‡PERKINS' LITERARY AGENCY, Box 48, Childs MD 21916. (301)398-2647. Agent/Owner: Esther R. Perkins. Estab. 1979. Represents 45 clients; 75% of clients are new/unpublished authors. Will be adding very few clients, professional or newcomers, in the next year. Specializes in historicals, mysteries, men's adventure, regencies, a few historical/romance.

Will Handle: Novels. Curently handles 1% nonfiction books; 99% novels. Does not read unsolicited material. Reports in 1 week. "If our agency does not respond within 3 months to your request to become a client, you may submit requests elsewhere."

Terms: Agent receives 15% commission on domestic sales; 20% on dramatic sales; 20% on foreign sales. Charges a reading fee "if writer has not had a book published by a major house in the past two year. Fee refunded if sale made within one year." 5% of income derived from reading fees. Charges $75 for 300-page, typed, double-spaced book ms. "I provide an overall critique of the ms—could be long or short, but not line-by-line. Marketing advice for clients only. I am the only reader." Offers consultation service through which writers can get advice on a contract; charges $25/hour. 95% of income is derived from commission on ms sales; 5% from fees.

Recent Sales: *Pavzer Spirit*, by Tom Townsend (Crown Publishers); *Hatchet Job*, by J.E. Neighbor (Crown Publishers, Inc.); *An Honorable Affair*, by Karla Hocker (Warner).

‡ALISON PICARD, LITERARY AGENT, #21, 574 7th St., Brooklyn NY 11215. (212)868-1121. Contact: Alison Picard. Estab. 1985. Represents 25 clients. 30% of clients are new/unpublished writers. "I prefer writers who have been published (at least in magazines) but am willing to consider exceptional new writers." Works with a small number of new/unpublished authors. Specializes in nonfiction. Also handles literary and category fiction, contemporary and historical romances, juvenile/YA books, short stories and articles if suitable for major national magazine.

Will Handle: Magazine articles, magazine fiction, nonfiction books, novels, juvenile books. Currently handles 5% magazine articles; 5% magazine fiction; 30% nonfiction books; 40% novels; and 20% juvenile books. Will read—at no charge—unsolicited queries, outlines and manuscripts. Reports in 1 week on queries; 1 month on manuscripts. "If our agency does not respond within 2 months to your request to become a client, you may submit requests elsewhere."

Terms: Agent receives 15% commission on domestic sales; 15% on dramatic sales; and 15% on foreign sales. Charges for copying of ms. Offers a consultation service through writers can get advice on a contract; charges $20/hour. 100% of income derived from sales of writers' work.

Recent Sales: *From: The President*, by Bruce Oudes (Harper & Row); *Annabelle Anderson*, by Patricia Beaver (Four Winds Press/Macmillan); and *Secrets for Young Scientists*, by Ray Staszako (Doubleday).

ARTHUR PINE ASSOCIATES, INC., 1780 Broadway, New York NY 10019. (212)265-7330. Contact: Agent. Estab. 1967. Represents 100 clients. 20% of clients are new/unpublished writers. Works with a small number of new/unpublished authors.

Will Handle: Nonfiction books and novels. Currently handles 75% nonfiction books and 25% novels. Does not read unsolicited mss. Reports in 2 weeks on queries.

Terms: Agent receives 15% commission on domestic sales; 15% on dramatic sales; and 15% on foreign sales. Charges a reading fee. .1% of income derived from reading fees. Gives 1-3 pages of criticism. Charges for photocopy expenses. 99.9% of income derived from sales of writers' work.

Recent Sales: *Take My Life Please*, by Henny Youngman (Beech Tree/Morrow); *Saturday Night USA*, by Susan Orlean (Simon & Schuster); and *Your Erroneous Zones*, by Dr. Wayne W. Dyer.

SIDNEY E. PORCELAIN, Box 1229, Milford PA 18337. (717)296-6420. Manager: Sidney Porcelain. Estab. 1952. Represents 20 clients. 50% of clients are new/unpublished writers. Prefers to work with published/established authors; works with a small number of new/unpublished authors. Specializes in fiction (novels, mysteries, and suspense) and nonfiction (celebrity and exposé).
Will Handle: Magazine articles, magazine fiction, nonfiction books, novels and juvenile books. Currently handles 2% magazine articles; 5% magazine fiction; 5% nonfiction books; 50% novels; 5% juvenile books; 2% movie scripts; 1% TV scripts; and 30% "comments for new writers." Will read—at no charge—unsolicited queries, outlines and mss. Reports in 2 weeks on queries; 3 weeks on mss.
Terms: Agent receives 10% commission on domestic sales; 10% on dramatic sales; and 10% on foreign sales. Sometimes offers a consultation service through which writers not represented can get advice on a contract. 50% of income derived from commission on ms sales.
Recent Sales: No information given.

JULIAN PORTMAN AGENCY, Suite 283, 7337 Lincoln Ave., Chicago IL 60646. (312)509-6431. Branch office: Suite 964, 800 Sunset Blvd., Hollywood CA 90046. (213)281-7391. Senior partner: Julian Portman. Estab. 1969. Represents 35 clients. 25% of our clients are new/unpublished writers. "Our interest is a good writer, storyteller and plot creator, whether they be a new writer or one who has had a book previously published. Our interest is to find stories that would sell for books and could be turned into potential TV/motion pictures." Works with a small number of new/unpublished authors.
Will Handle: Nonfiction books, novels, movie scripts, TV scripts. Currently handles 30% nonfiction books, 35% novels, 20% movie scripts; 15% TV scripts. Will read—at no charge—unsolicited queries and outlines. Reports in 3 weeks on queries; 7 weeks on mss. "If our agency does not respond within 2 months to your request to become a client, you may submit requests elsewhere."
Terms: Agent receives 15-25% commission on domestic sales; 15% on dramatic sales and 25% on foreign sales. Charges a reading and criticism fee for new writers; reading fee will be waived if represents the writer. 3% of income derived from reading fees. Charges $150-200 for 300-page, typed double-spaced book ms. Writer receives an "overall evaluation of 2-3 pages depending on the quality of the ms. Uses both published authors and journalists on a flat fee arrangement to evaluate mss." Charges a handling fee. 1% of income derived from handling fees. Sometimes offers a consultation service through which writers not represented can get advice on a contract. 15% of income derived from fees. Payment of a criticism fee does not ensure that agency will represent a writer.
Recent Sales: *The Tooth of the Dragon: The Story of General Morris (Two Gun) Cohen*, by Julian John Portman/Jean Kipfer (Paperjack); *The Senator Must Die: Assassination of Robert F. Kennedy*, by Robert Morrow (Roundtable).

AARON M. PRIEST LITERARY AGENCY, Suite 3902, 122 E. 42nd St., New York NY 10168. (212)818-0344. Contact: Aaron Priest or Molly Friedrich.
Will Handle: Fiction and nonfiction books. Currently handles 50% nonfiction books and 50% fiction. Will read submissions at no charge. Reports in 1 month on mss. "If our agency does not respond within 1 month to your request to become a client, you may submit requests elsewhere."
Terms: Agent receives 15% commission on domestic sales. Charges for photocopy and foreign postage expenses.
Recent Sales: *Indian Country*, by Philio Caputo; *Joanna's Husband and David's Wife*, by Elizabeth Forsythe Hailey; and *Getting Better All The Time*, by Liz Carpenter.

SUSAN ANN PROTTER LITERARY AGENT, Suite 1408, 110 W. 40th St., New York NY 10018. (212)840-0480. Contact: Susan Protter. Estab. 1971. Member of ILAA. Represents 50 clients. 10% of clients are new/unpublished writers. Writer must have book-length project or manuscript that is ready to be sold. Works with a small number of new/unpublished authors. Specializes in general nonfiction, self-help, psychology, science, health, medicine, novels, science fiction, mysteries and thrillers.
Will Handle: Nonfiction books and novels. Currently handles 5% magazine articles; 60% nonfiction books; 30% novels; and 5% photography books. Will read—at no charge—unsolicited queries and outlines. "Must include SASE." Reports in 2 weeks on queries; 5 weeks on solicited mss. "If our agency does not respond within 2 months to your request to become a client, you may submit requests elsewhere."
Terms: Agent receives 15% commission on domestic sales; 15% on TV, film and dramatic sales; and 25% on foreign sales. Charges for long distance, photocopying, messenger, express mail and airmail expenses. 100% of income derived from commission on ms sales.
Recent Sales: *Waldheim: The Missing Years*, by Robert E. Herzstein (Arbor House/Morrow); *The Hollow Earth*, by Rudy Rucker (Avon); and *The Dr.'s Diet Type Program*, by Dr. Ronald L. Hoffman (Simon & Schuster).

‡PUBLISHING ENTERPRISES/LITERARY AGENCY, 4090 Ben Lomond Dr., Palo Alto CA 94306. (415)856-1062. 3100 Ervin Lane, Santa Cruz CA 95065. (408)475-3045. Contact: Bill Oliver (Palo Alto) or

Marjorie Gersh (Santa Cruz). Estab. 1984. Represents 42 clients. 55% of clients are new/unpublished writers. Specializes in nonfiction—business, computers and high tech; how-to; travel; education—college text; selected fiction; children's literature.

Will Handle: Nonfiction books, novels, college textbooks, juvenile books. Currently handles 60% nonfiction books; 20% novels; 10% textbooks; 10% juvenile books. Will read submissions at no charge, but may charge a criticism fee or service charge for work performed after the initial reading. Reports in 2 weeks on queries; 6 weeks on manuscripts. "If our agency does not respond within 1 month to your request to become a client, you may submit requests elsewhere."

Terms: Agent receives 15% commission on domestic sales; 20% on dramatic sales; and 20% on foreign sales. Charges a criticism fee for new writers under author's request; charges $150/300 pages. Critique includes overall evaluation—strengths and weaknesses with sample line-by-line examples if appropriate. Strong emphasis is given to marketing factors from a publisher's perspective. Charges writers for telephone (long distance), photocopying, mailing of mss. Offers a consultation service through which writers can get advice on a contract; charges $50/hour. 90% of income derived from sales of writer's work; 10% of income derived from fees.

Recent Sales: *Street Smart Real Estate*, by Allen Cymrut (Dow Jones-Irwin); *Business Problem Solving With Microsoft Excell*, by Dennis Curtis (McGraw-Hill-Osborne); and *Chinese Brush Painting*, by Gretchen Horn (China Books and Periodicals).

‡**RAINES & RAINES**, 71 Park Ave., New York NY 10016. (212)684-5160. Contact: Joan Raines, Theron Raines. Estab. 1961. Represents 110 clients. 3% of clients are new/unpublished writers. Prefers to work with published/established writers; works with small number of new/unpublished writers.

Will Handle: Nonfiction books, novels. Does not read unsolicited mss. Reports on queries in 2 weeks; 3 weeks on mss. "If our agency does not respond within 2 weeks to your request to become a client, you may submit requests elsewhere."

Terms: Agent receives 15% commission on domestic sales; 15% on dramatic sales; and 20% on foreign sales (½ on foreign agent). Charges writers for overseas calls, copying and copies of books.

Recent Sales: *Thalassa*, by James Dickey (Houghton Mifflin); *Essays*, by Bruno Betthlheim (Knopf); and *New Novel*, by Winston Groom (Atlantic Monthly Press).

HELEN REES LITERARY AGENCY, 308 Commonwealth Ave., Boston MA 02116. (617)262-2401. Contact: Catherine Mahar. Estab. 1982. Member of ILAA. Represents 55 clients. 25% of our clients are new/unpublished writers. Writer must have been published or be an authority on a subject. Prefers to work with published/established authors; works with a small number of new/unpublished authors. Specializes in nonfiction—biographies, health and business.

Will Handle: Nonfiction books and novels. Currently handles 90% nonfiction books and 10% novels. Will read—at no charge—unsolicited queries and outlines. Reports in 2 weeks on queries; 3 weeks on mss.

Terms: Agent receives 15% commission on domestic sales and 20% on foreign sales. Occasionally charges a reading fee "for clients who are unpublished and want that service. I don't solicit this." Reading fee will be waived if representing the writer. Charges criticism fee of $250; writer receives criticism of characters, dialogue, plot, style and suggestions for reworking areas of weakness. Sometimes offers a consultation service through which writers not represented can get advice on a contract; no set fee.

Recent Sales: *Price Waterhouse Guide to the New Tax Law* (Bantam); *Senator Barry Goldwater's Autobiography* (Doubleday); and *Minding the Body, Mending the Mind* (Addison Wesley Bantam).

RHODES LITERARY AGENCY INC., 140 West End Ave., New York NY 10023. (212)580-1300. President: Joan Lewis. Estab. 1971. Member of ILAA.

Will Handle: Nonfiction books, novels (a limited number), and juvenile books. Will read—at no charge—unsolicited queries and outlines. Include SASE. Reports in 2 weeks on queries.

Terms: Agent receives 10% commission on domestic sales; and 20% on foreign sales.

Recent Sales: No information given.

‡**JOHN R. RIINA LITERARY AGENCY**, 5905 Meadowood Rd., Baltimore MD 21212. (301)433-2305. Contact: John R. Riina. Estab. 1977. Works with "authors with credentials to write on their subject." Specializes in college textbooks, and professional books and serious non-fiction.

Will Handle: Textbooks. Currently handles 30% nonfiction books and 70% textbooks. Does not read unsolicited mss. Reports in 3 weeks.

Terms: Agent receives 10% commission on domestic sales; 10% on dramatic sales; 15% on foreign sales. Charges "exceptional long distance telephone and express of manuscripts." Sometimes offers consultation service through which writers can get advice on a contract; charges $75/hour. 90% of income is derived from commission on manuscript sales; 10% from fees.

Recent Sales: "Not available for listing."

‡**THE ROBBINS OFFICE, INC.**, 12th Floor, 866 Second Ave., New York NY 10017. (212)223-0720. Contact: Kathy P. Robbins. Represents 140 clients. Writers must be published or come to us by referral. Specialize in

selling mainstream nonfiction, commercial and literary fiction.
Will Handle: Nonfiction books and novels. Currently handles 75% nonfiction books and 25% novels. Will handle magazine articles for book writers under contract. Does not read unsolicited mss. Reports in 2 weeks on queries.
Terms: Agent receives 15% commission on domestic sales; 100-15% on dramatic sales; and 15% on foreign sales. Bills back specific expenses incurred in doing business for a client.
Recent Sales: *1959,* by Thulani Davis (Weidenfeld & Nicolson).

MARIE RODELL-FRANCIS COLLIN LITERARY AGENCY, 110 West 40th St., New York NY 10018. (212)840-8664. Contact: Frances Collin. Estab. 1948. Member of SAR. Represents 90 clients. 10% of clients are new/unpublished writers. Prefers to work with published/established authors; works with a small number of new/unpublished authors. Has a "broad general trade list."
Will Handle: Nonfiction books and novels. Currently handles 50% nonfiction books; 40% novels; and 10% juvenile books. Will read—at no charge—unsolicited queries. Reports in 1 week on queries.
Terms: Agent receives 15% commission on domestic sales; 20% on dramatic sales; and 25% on foreign sales. Charges for overseas postage, photocopy and registered mail expenses and copyright registration fees. 100% of income derived from commission on ms sales.
Recent Sales: Confidential.

‡RICHARD H. ROFFMAN ASSOCIATES, Suite 6A, 697 West End Ave., New York NY 10025. (212)749-3647/3648. President: Richard H. Roffman. Estab. 1967. 70% of clients are new/unpublished writers. Prefers to work with published/established writers; works with a small number of new/unpublished authors. Specializes in "nonfiction primarily, but other types, too."
Will Handle: Nonfiction books. Currently handles 10% magazine articles; 5% magazine fiction; 5% textbooks; 5% juvenile books; 5% radio scripts; 5% movie scripts; 5% TV scripts; 5% syndicated material; 5% poetry; and 50% other. Does not read unsolicited mss. Reports in 2 weeks. "If our agency does not respond within 2 months to your request to become a client, you may submit requests elsewhere."
Terms: Agent receives 10% commission on domestic sales; 10% on dramatic sales; and 10% on foreign sales. "We do not read material [for a fee] actually, only on special occasions. We prefer to refer to other people specializing in that." 10% of income derived from reading fees. "We suggest a moderate monthly retainer." Charges for mailings, phone calls, photocopying and messenger service. Offers consultation service through which writers can get advice on a contract. "I am also an attorney at law."
Recent Sales: No information given.

STEPHANIE ROGERS AND ASSOCIATES, 3855 Lankershim Blvd., #218, N. Hollywood CA 91604. (818)509-1010. Owner: Stephanie Rogers. Estab. 1981. Represents 18 clients. 20% of clients are new/unpublished writers. Prefers that the writer has been produced (motion pictures or TV), his/her properties optioned or has references. Prefers to work with published/established authors. Specializes in screenplays—dramas (contemporary), action/adventure, romantic comedies and biographies for motion pictures and TV.
Will Handle: Novels (only wishes to see those that have been published and can translate to screen) and movie and TV scripts (must be professional in presentation and not over 130 pages). Currently handles 10% novels; 50% movie scripts and 40% TV scripts. Does not read unsolicited mss.
Terms: Agent receives 10% commission on domestic sales; 10% on dramatic sales; and 10% on foreign sales. Charges for phone, photocopying and messenger expenses.
Recent Sales: "Shoot to Kill," for Touchstone Pictures; "Steel Dawn," for Vestron; and "South of Picasso," for Tri-Star.

66 *Relationships with supportive editors and agents can be of tremendous help with the task at hand, that is to keep on sending out and sending out and sending out— and I mean over years, not weeks. If I believe in a story, I keep sending, and it usually finds a home.* **99**

—Suzanne Hartman, author

THE MITCHELL ROSE LITERARY AGENCY, Suite 410, 799 Broadway, New York NY 10003. (212)418-0747. President: Mitchell Rose. Member of Authors Guild. Represents 45 clients; 20% of clients are new/unpublished writers. "We prefer writers with some book or magazine experience; but extraordinary talent and/or subject matter will get our attention. For promising writers with promising projects, we offer extensive editorial guidance, when required." Works with a small number of new/unpublished writers. Specializes in general nonfiction and fiction.
Will Handle: Magazine articles and fiction (for clients who are working on book projects), nonfiction books, novels, textbooks. Currently handles 60% nonfiction books; 40% novels. Will read—at no charge—unsolicited queries and outlines. Reports in 3 weeks. "If our agency does not respond within 2 months to your request to become a client, you may submit requests elsewhere."
Terms: Agent receives 15% commission on domestic sales; 20% on foreign sales involving foreign co-agent. Charges for high-volume photocopying, Telexes, messengers, postage and overseas phone calls. 100% of income is derived from commission on manuscript sales.
Recent Sales: *Victorian Tales*, by Michael Patrick Hearn (Pantheon); *The Oz Book*, by John Fricke (Warner); and *China Through the Eyes of a Tiger*, by Roland Sperry and Terri Boodman (Simon & Schuster).

JANE ROTROSEN AGENCY, 318 East 51st St., New York NY 10022. (212)593-4330. Estab. 1974. Member of ILAA. Represents 100 clients. 70% of clients were new/unpublished writers. Works with published and unpublished writers. Specializes in general trade fiction and nonfiction.
Will Handle: Nonfiction books, novels and juvenile books. Currently handles 30% nonfiction books and 70% novels. Will read—at no charge—unsolicited queries and short outlines. Reports in 2 weeks.
Terms: Receives 15% commission on domestic sales; 15% on dramatic sales; and 20% on foreign sales. Charges writers for photocopies, long-distance/transoceanic telephone, telegraph, Telex, messenger service and foreign postage.
Recent Sales "Our client list remains confidential."

‡THE SAGALYN AGENCY, 1717 N St., NW, Washington D.C. 20036. (202)835-0320. Estab. 1980. Member ILAA. Prefers to work with published/established writers.
Will Handle: Adult trade nonfiction books and novels. Currently handles 90% nonfiction books and 10% novels. Will read—at no charge—unsolicited queries and outlines. Reports in 3 weeks. "If our agency does not respond within 1 month to your request to become a client, you may submit requests elsewhere."
Terms: Agent receives 10-15% commission on domestic sales; 10-15% on dramatic sales; and 20% on foreign sales. Charges for copying, postage, long-distance, Telex, etc. Sometimes offers consultation service through which writers can get advice on a contract ("only direct referrals"). 100% of income derived from commission on ms sales.
Recent Sales: *Agents of Innocents, A Spy Story*, by David Ignatius (Norton); *The Long Grey Line*, by Rick Atkinson (Houghton Mifflin); and *The New Power Elite*, by Jim Glassman (Doubleday).

‡SBC ENTERPRISES, INC., 11 Mabro Dr., Denville NJ 07834-9607. (201)366-3622. Agents: Alec Bernard, Eugenia Cohen. Estab. 1979. 50% of clients are new/unpublished writers. Specializes in trade fiction, nonfiction and screenplays.
Will Handle: Nonfiction books, novels, textbooks, movie scripts, TV scripts. Currently handles 25% nonfiction books; 25% novels; 10% textbooks; 20% movie scripts; 20% TV scripts. Will read—at no charge—unsolicited queries and outlines "provided SASE included." Does not read unsolicited manuscripts. Reports in 2 weeks on queries. "If our agency does not respond within 2 months to your request to become a client, you may submit requests elsewhere."
Terms: Agent receives 15% commission on domestic sales for first-time writers up to $10,000, 10% thereafter—all others 10%; 15% on dramatic rights sales; 20% on foreign sales. Sometimes offers consultation service through which writers can get advice on contract; charges $50/hour. 98% of income derived from commission on mss sales; 2% from fees.
Recent Sales: No information given.

‡JACK SCAGNETTI LITERARY AGENCY, Suite 210, 5330 Lankershim Blvd., N. Hollywood CA 91601. (818)762-3871. Owner: Jack Scagnetti. Estab. 1974. Member of WGA. Represents 50 clients. 10% of clients are new/unpublished writers. Prefers to work with published/established authors.
Will Handle: Nonfiction books, novels, movie scripts and TV scripts. Currently handles 20% nonfiction books; 10% novels; 40% movie scripts; and 30% TV scripts. Will read—at no charge—unsolicited queries and outlines. Reports in 2 weeks on queries; 1 month on mss. "If our agency does not respond within 2 months to your request to become a client, you may submit requests elsewhere."
Terms: Agent receives 10% commission on domestic sales; 10% on dramatic sales; and 15% on foreign sales. Charges for postage on multiple submissions. Offers a consultation service through which writers not represented can get advice on a contract (books only); charges $35/hour.
Recent Sales: *Superstition Gold* (Dorchester Publishing); television series episodes to "Highway to Heaven" and "Family Ties."

‡**LAURENS R. SCHWARTZ, ESQUIRE**, Suite 15D, 5 E. 22nd St., New York NY 10010. (212)228-2614. Contact: Laurens R. Schwartz. Estab. 1984. Represents 20-100 clients. To be represented writers must be expert in a field for publishing; have film or video in the can for licensing or ancillaries; have film awards for screenplay placement or packaging. "I work primarily with experts in their fields, published or not." Specializes in nonfiction books—"primary specialty is high-tech; others includes medicine, social topics, music, art, bridge, biography; screenplays—specialty is films requiring computer effects or post-production computer transfer/editing; computer programs—will place or package; videocassette, CD-ROM—will place or package."
Will Handle: Nonfiction books, movie and video scripts, videocassettes, computer programs, CD-ROM. Currently handles 65% nonfiction books; 20% movie scripts; 15% computer or videocassette-related. Does not read unsolicited mss. Reports in 1 month. "If our agency does not respond within 2 months to your request to become a client, you may submit requests elsewhere."
Terms: Agent receives 10% commission on domestic sales; 15% on foreign sales. "To keep my rates low, I require that a writer provide as many copies of material as I need. All other costs are absorbed by me. I am an entertainment law lawyer. I provide simple negotiations as part of commission. Complex packaging or development of ancillaries necessitates an hourly charge (my then current fee)."
Recent Sales: *Art and Animation by Computer*, by Lillian Schwartz (W.W. Norton) and *The Holy Grail*, by Pat Covelli (McFarland).

SHORR STILLE AND ASSOCIATES, Suite 6, 800 S. Robertson Blvd., Los Angeles CA 90035. (213)659-6160. Member of WGA. Writer must have an entertainment industry referral. Works with a small number of new/unpublished authors. Specializes in screenplays, teleplays, high concept action-adventure and romantic comedy.
Will Handle: Movie scripts and TV scripts. Currently handles 50% movie scripts and 50% TV scripts. Will read—at no charge—unsolicited queries. Reports in 1 month on queries; 6 weeks on mss.
Terms: Agent receives 10% commission on domestic sales. Charges for photocopy expenses.
Recent Sales: No information given.

SHUMAKER ARTISTS TALENT AGENCY,6533 Hollywood, Hollywood CA 90028. (213)464-0745. Contact: Tim Shumaker. Established 1979. Member of WGA. Represents 40 clients. 30% of clients are new/unpublished writers. "Writer must have proof of reasonable number of sales or must have sufficient training." Prefers to work with published/established authors; works with small number of new/unpublished authors.
Will Handle: Nonfiction books (include author biography with outline, sample chapter, SASE); novels (include synopsis and outline, SASE); textbooks (include synopsis, table of contents, facts about author); juvenile books (self-help and other); movie scripts (include treatment and resume); TV scripts (include treatment and resume); and syndicated material (include complete breakdown in outline form of concept with references). Currently handles 10% novels; 5% textbooks; 5% juvenile books; 25% movie scripts; 5% syndicated material; and 35% TV scripts. Accept submissions for audiocassette publishing. Does not read unsolicited mss. Reports in 1 months on queries. "If our agency does not respond within 6 months to your request to become a client, you may submit requests elsewhere."
Terms: Receives 10% commission on domestic sales, dramatic sales and foreign sales.
Recent Sales: No information given.

BOBBE SIEGEL, LITERARY AGENCY, 41 W. 83rd St., New York NY 10024. (212)877-4985. Associate: Richard Siegel. Estab. 1975. Represents 60 clients. 40% of clients are new/unpublished writers. "The writer must have a good project, have the credentials to be able to write on the subject and must deliver it in proper fashion. In fiction it all depends on whether I like what I read and if I feel I can sell it." Prefers to work with published/established authors; works with a small number of new/unpublished authors. "Prefer track records, but am eager to work with talent." Specializes in literary fiction, detective and suspense fiction, historicals, how-to, health, woman's subjects, fitness, beauty, feminist sports, biographies and crafts.
Will Handle: Nonfiction books and novels. Currently handles 65% nonfiction books and 35% novels. Does not read unsolicited mss. Reports in 2 weeks on queries; 2 months on mss. "If our agency does not respond within 2 months to your request to become a client, you may submit requests elsewhere."
Terms: Agent receives 15% commission on domestic sales; 10% on dramatic sales; and 10% on foreign sales. If writer wishes critique, will refer to a freelance editor. Charges for photocopying, telephone, overseas mail, express mail expenses. 70% of income derived from commission on ms sales; 30% comes from foreign representation. 100% of income derived from sales of writers' work; "not enough derived from critique to mention as a percentage."
Recent Sales: *The Drowned & Saved* by Primo Levi (Summit); *In the Tenth of the Northeaster*, by Marlin Bree (Clarkson-Potter); and *Your Hands Can Heal*, by E.P. Dutton.

SINGER MEDIA CORPORATION, INC., (formerly Singer Communications, Inc.), 3164 Tyler Ave., Anaheim CA 92801. (714)527-5650. Executive Vice President: Natalie Carlton. Estab. 1940. 10% of clients are new/unpublished writers. Prefers to work with published/established authors; works with a small number of

new/unpublished authors. Specializes in contemporary romances, nonfiction and biographies.
Will Handle: Magazine articles and syndicated material (submit tearsheets); nonfiction books (query); and romance novels. Currently handles 5% nonfiction books; 20% novels; 75% syndicated material. Will read—at no charge—unsolicited queries and outlines; but may charge a criticism fee or service charge for work performed after the initial reading. Reports in 2 weeks on queries; 6 weeks on mss. "If our agency does not respond within 2 months to your request to become a client, you may submit requests elsewhere."
Terms: Agent receives 15% commission on domestic sales and 20% on foreign sales. Charges a reading fee to unpublished authors which will be credited on sales; .5% of income derived from reading fees. Criticism included in reading fee. "A general overall critique averages three pages. It does not cover spelling or grammar, but the construction of the material. A general marketing critique is also included." Sometimes offers a consultation service through which writers not represented can get advice on a contract. 95% of income derived from sales of writers' work; 5% of income derived from criticism services. "Payment of a criticism fee does not ensure that agency will represent a writer. The author may not be satisfied with our reply, or may need help in making the manuscript marketable."
Recent Sales: "Dozens of magazines, W.H. Allen; Mondadori, Pocketbooks Inc."

EVELYN SINGER LITERARY AGENCY, Box 594, White Plains NY 10602. Agent: Evelyn Singer. Estab. 1951. Represents 75 clients. To be represented, writer must have $20,000 in past sales of freelance works. Prefers to work with published/established authors. Specializes in fiction and nonfiction books, adult and juvenile (picture books only if writer is also the artist).
Will Handle: Nonfiction books (bylined by authority or celebrity); novels (no romances, or pseudo-science, violence or sex); and juvenile books. Currently handles 25% nonfiction books; 25% novels; and 50% juvenile books. Does not read unsolicited mss. "If our agency does not respond within 2 months to your request to become a client, you may submit requests elsewhere."
Terms: Agent receives 15% commission on domestic sales; 20% on dramatic sales; and 20% on foreign sales. Charges for phone and expenses authorized by the author. Sometimes offers a consultation service through which writers not represented can get advice on a contract; charges $100/hour. 100% of income derived from commission on ms sales.
Recent Sales: *Rebuilt Man*, by William Beechcroft (Dodd, Mead); *Snakes*, by Mary Elting (Simon and Schuster); and *How Things Work*, by Mike and Marcia Folsom (Macmillan).

MICHAEL SNELL LITERARY AGENCY, Bridge and Castle Rd., Truro MA 02666. (508)349-3718. President: Michael Snell. Estab. 1980. Represents 100 clients. 25% of our clients are new/unpublished writers. Eager to work with new unpublished writers. Specializes in business books (from professional/reference to popular trade how-to); college textbooks (in all subjects, but especially business, science and psychology); and how-to and self-help (on all topics, from diet and exercise to sex and personal finance). Increased emphasis on all types of computer books: professional and reference, college textbooks, general interest.
Will Handle: Nonfiction books and textbooks. Currently handles 80% nonfiction books; 10% novels; and 10% textbooks. Will read—at no charge—unsolicited queries and outlines. Reports in 3 weeks on queries. "If our agency does not respond within 1 month to your request to become a client, you may submit requests elsewhere. Will not return rejected material unless accompanied by SASE."
Terms: Agent receives 15% commission on domestic sales; 15% on dramatic sales; and 15% on foreign sales. "When a project interests us, we provide a two to three page critique and sample editing, a brochure on *How to Write a Book Proposal* and a model book proposal at no charge." Charges collaboration, ghostwriting and developmental editing fee "as an increased percentage of manuscript sale—no cash fee." Charges $100/hour. 100% of income derived from commission on sales.
Recent Sales: *The Soul of Leadership* (New American Library); *Finding Forgiveness* (Contemporary); and *The J.K. Lasser Business Forms File* (Simon & Schuster).

‡SOUTHERN WRITERS, Suite 1111, 333 St. Charles Ave., New Orleans LA 70130. (504)525-6390. Agent: Pamela G. Ahearn. Estab. 1979. Member Romance Writers of America. Represents 20 clients; 33% of clients are new/unpublished writers. Works with small number of new/unpublished writers. Specializes in fiction or nonfiction with a Southern flavor or background; romances—both contemporary and historical.
Will Handle: Nonfiction books (no autobiographies), novels. Currently handles 30% nonfiction books and 70% novels. Will read—at no charge—unsolicited queries and outlines. Reports in 2 weeks on queries; 1 month on mss. "If our agency does not respond within 2 months to your request to become a client, you may submit requests elsewhere."
Terms: Agent receives 12-15% commission on domestic sales; 20% on dramatic sales; 20% on foreign sales. Charges reading fee "to unpublished authors and to authors writing in areas other than that of previous publication." 40% of income derived from reading fees; charges $150 for 300-page, typed, double-spaced book ms. "Criticism fee is charged to unpublished authors who request *only* criticism and not representation." 5% of income derived from criticism fees; charges $250 for 300-page, typed, double-spaced book ms. Writers receive a letter, usually 2-4 pages long, single-spaced. Includes evaluation of manuscript's writing quality, marketabili-

ty, and more specific discussion of problems within book (plot, characterization, tone, author's credentials for writing such book, etc.). Specific examples are cited wherever possible. Letter is written by Pamela G. Ahear. Charges for postage. 55% of income derived from commission on manuscript sales; 45% from fees. Payment of fees does not ensure representation.
Recent Sales: *My Wicked Enchantress*, by Meagan McKinney (Dell); *Midnight Flame*, by Lynette Vinet (Zebra); and *Rebellious Bride*, by Lynette Vinet (Zebra).

‡F. JOSEPH SPIELER LITERARY AGENCY, 410 W. 24th St., New York NY 10011. (212)242-7152. Contact: Joseph Spieler. Estab. 1983. Represents 53 clients. 7.25% of clients are new/unpublished writers. Specializes in "fiction and nonfiction." No genre books.
Will Handle: Nonfiction books, novels, textbooks, juvenile and poetry. Will read—at no charge—unsolicited queries and outlines. Does not read unsolicited mss. Reports in 1 week. "If our agency does not respond within 1 month to your request to become a client, you may submit requests elsewhere."
Terms: Agent receives 15% commission on domestic sales; 15% on dramatic sales; and 20% on foreign sales. Charges for bulk and international mail, photocopies, toll and international phone calls and Telexes, etc. Sometimes offers consultation services through which writers can get advice on a contract; charges $150/hour. 99% of income derived from commission on ms sales.
Recent Sales: *Growing a Business*, by Paul Howken (Simon & Schuster); *The Age of Miracles*, by Catherine MacCoun (Atlantic Press); and *I'll Be Home Before Midnight*, by Tony Wolf (Vintage/Random House).

PHILIP G. SPITZER LITERARY AGENCY, 788 9th Ave., New York NY 10019. (212)628-0352. Member of SAR. Represents 50 clients. 10% of clients are new/unpublished writers. Prefers to work with published/established authors; works with a small number of new/unpublished authors. Specializes in general nonfiction (politics, current events, sports, biography) and fiction, including mystery/suspense.
Will Handle: Nonfiction books, novels and movie scripts. Currently handles 45% nonfiction books; 45% novels; and 10% movie scripts. Will read—at no charge—unsolicited queries and outlines. Reports in 2 weeks on queries; 5 weeks on mss. "If our agency does not respond within 1 month to your request to become a client, you may submit requests elsewhere."
Terms: Agent receives 10% commission on domestic sales; 10% on dramatic sales; and 20% on foreign sales. Charges for photocopying expenses. 100% of income derived from commission on ms sales.
Recent Sales: *Heaven's Prisoners*, by James Lee Burke (Holt); *Bad Guys*, by Eugene Izzi (St. Martin's Press); and *Necessities*, by Phillip M. Hoose (Random House).

ELLEN LIVELY STEELE AND ASSOCIATES, Drawer 447, Organ NM 88052. (505)382-5449. Contact: Ellen Lively Steele. Estab. 1981. Represents 12 clients. 75% of clients are new/unpublished writers. Accepts writers on referral only. Prefers to work with published/established writers; works with small number of new/unpublished writers. Specializes in occult, science fiction, women's fiction, metaphysical and adventure.
Will Handle: Novels, movie scripts, TV scripts and syndicated material. Currently handles 65% novels; 20% movie scripts; 10% TV scripts; 4% syndicated material; and 1% miscellaneous. Does not read unsolicited material. Reports in 3 weeks on queries. "If our agency does not respond within 2 months to your request to become a client, you may submit requests elsewhere."
Terms: Agent receives 10% commission on domestic sales; 10% on dramatic sales; and 5% on foreign sales. Charges a marketing fee. 10% of income comes from fees charged to writers; 10% of income derived from commission on mss sales.

‡LYLE STEELE & COMPANY, Suite 7, 511 E. 73rd St., New York NY 10021. (202)288-2981. President: Lyle Steele. Estab. 1984. Represents 40 clients. To be represented writers "ideally should have published at least one work." Works with small number of new/unpublished writers. Specializes in continuing paperback series and nonfiction.
Will Handle: Nonfiction books, series and novels. Currently handles 50% nonfiction books; 50% novels. Will read—at no charge—unsolicited queries, outlines and manuscripts. Reports in 2 weeks on queries; 6 weeks on mss. "If our agency does not respond within 2 months to your request to become a client, you may submit requests elsewhere."
Terms: Agent receives 15% commission on domestic sales; 15% on dramatic sales; and 15% on foreign sales. 100% of income derived from commission on ms sales.
Recent Sales: *Take One For Murder*, by Eileen Fulton (Ivy).

MICHAEL STEINBERG, Box 274, Glencoe IL 60022. (312)835-8881. Literary Agent/Attorney: Michael Steinberg. Estab. 1980. Represents 15 clients. 40% of clients are new/unpublished writers. "Not currently accepting new writers except by referral from editors or current authors." Specializes in business and general nonfiction, science fiction and mystery.
Will Handle: Nonfiction books and novels. Currently handles 70% nonfiction books and 30% novels. Does not read unsolicited mss.

Terms: Agent receives 15% commission on domestic sales and 20% on foreign sales. Charges a reading fee when accepting new material; 4% of income derived from reading fees. Charges writers for postage and phone expenses. Offers a consultation service through which writers not represented can get advice on a contract; charges $75/hour, with a minimum of $125. 5% of income derived from fees; 95% of income derived from commission on ms sales.
Recent Sales: *Facts on Futures*, by Jacob Bernstein (Probus Publishing); *Short Term Trading*, by Jacob Bernstein (Probus): and *Cry Wolf*, by Alan Chronister (Zebra).

STEPPING STONE LITERARY AGENCY, 59 West 71st St., New York NY 10023. (212)362-9277. President: Sarah Jane Freymann. Estab. 1974. Member of ILAA. 10% of clients are new/unpublished writers. "The writer has to be good and serious about his/her work. Writers should only send work they are really pleased with. Of course, I prefer published authors—but I am willing to look at unpublished authors' work." Works with a small number of new/unpublished authors. "I do not specialize. But I stress professionalism—I do not want amateurs who write like amateurs."
Will Handle: Nonfiction books and novels. Currently handles 50% nonfiction books and 50% novels. Will read submissions at no charge, but may charge a criticism fee or service charge for work performed after the initial reading. Reports in 2 weeks on queries; 6 weeks on mss. "If our agency does not respond within 6 months to your request to become a client, you may submit requests elsewhere."
Terms: Agent receives 15% commission on domestic sales; 10% on dramatic sales; and 10% on foreign sales. Charges a criticism fee "only if we are asked to critique a work we won't represent." Fee for a 300-page ms $200. Charges for phone, overseas postage and photocopy expenses. Sometimes offers a consultation service through which writers not represented can get advice on contract; less than 10% of income derived from fees. 90-100% of income derived from commission on ms sales.
Recent Sales: No information given.

CHARLES M. STERN ASSOCIATES, 319 Coronet, Box 790742, San Antonio TX 78279-0742. (512)349-6141. Owners: Charles M. Stern and Mildred R. Stern. Estab. 1978. 75% of clients are new/unpublished writers. Prefers to work with pubished/established authors; eager to work with new/unpublished writers. Specializes in historical romances, category romances, how-to, mystery and adventure.
Will Handle: Nonfiction books and novels. Currently handles 50% nonfiction books and 50% novels. Does not read unsolicited mss; will handle only a completed ms. Reports in approximately 1 month on queries.
Terms: Agent receives 15% commission on domestic sales; and 20% on foreign sales. Writer must supply all copies of ms.
Recent Sales: No information given.

GLORIA STERN, Suite 3, 12535 Chandler Blvd., North Hollywood CA 91607. (818)508-6296. Contact: Gloria Stern. Estab. 1984. Represents 18 clients. 65% of clients are new/unpublished writers. Writer must query with project description or be recommended by qualified reader. Prefers to work with published/established authors; works with a number of new/unpublished authors. Specializes in novels and scripts, some theatrical material, dramas or comedy.
Will Handle: Novels, movie scripts and TV scripts (movie of the week). Currently handles 13% novels; 79% movie scripts; and 8% TV scripts. Will read submissions at charge and may charge a criticism fee or service charge for on-going consultation and editing. Reports in 3 weeks on queries; 6 weeks on mss. "If our agency does not respond within 6 weeks to your request to become a client, you may submit requests elsewhere."
Terms: Agent receives 10-15% commission on domestic sales; 10-15% on dramatic sales; and 18% on foreign sales. Occasionally waives fee if representing the writer. Charges criticism fee; $35/hour (may vary). "Initial report averages four or five pages with point by point recommendation. I will work with the writers I represent to point of acceptance." Charges for postage, photocopy and long distance phone expenses. Percentage of income derived from commission on ms sales varies with sales. Payment of criticism fee usually ensures that agency will represent writer.

GLORIA STERN AGENCY, 1230 Park Ave., New York NY 10128. (212)289-7698. Agent: Gloria Stern. Estab. 1976. Member of ILAA. Represents 30 clients. 2% of our clients are new/unpublished writers. Prefers to work with published/established authors; works with a small number on new/unpublished authors.
Will Handle: Nonfiction books (no how-to; must have expertise on subject); and novels ("serious mainstream," mysteries, accepts very little fiction). Currently handles 90% nonfiction books and 10% novels. Will read—at no charge—unsolicited queries and outlines. Reports in 1 week on queries; 2 months on manuscripts. "If our agency does not respond within 10 weeks to your request to become a client, you may submit request elsewhere."
Terms: Agent receives 10-15% commission on domestic sales; and 20% on foreign sales. Charges for photocopy exenses. Charges a criticism fee "if the writer makes a request and I think that it could be publishable with help. Criticism includes appraisal of style, development of characters and action. Sometimes suggests cutting or building scene. No guarantee that I can represent finished work." Offers a consultation service ("as a cour-

tesy to some authors") through which writers not represented can get advice on a contract; charges $125. .5% of income derived from fee charged to writers; 99.5% of income derived from commission of manuscript sales.
Recent Sales: *How to Learn Math*, by Sheila Tobias (The College Board); *A Taste of Astrology*, by Lucy Ash (Knopf); and *The Last Rampage*, by James Clarke (Houghton, Mifflin).

GUNTHER STUHLMANN, AUTHOR'S REPRESENTATIVE, Box 276, Becket MA 01223. (413)623-5170. Associate: Barbara Ward. Estab. 1954. Prefers to work with published/established authors. Specializes in high quality literary material, fiction and nonfiction.
Will Handle: Nonfiction books, novels, young adult, movie and TV rights on established properties (no original screenplays). Will read—at no charge—unsolicited queries and outlines. Reports in 2 weeks on queries. "Include SASE for reply."
Terms: Receives 10% commission on domestic sales; 15% on British sales; 20% on translation.
Recent Sales: *Prisoner's Dilemma*, by Richard Powers (Beech Tree/Morrow); *Henry & June*, by Anais Nin (Harcourt Brace Jovanovich); and *A Literate Passion*, by Henry Miller and Anais Nin (Harcourt Brace Jovanovich).

H.N. SWANSON, INC., 8523 Sunset Blvd., Los Angeles CA 90069. (213)652-5385. Contact: Ben Kamsler. Estab. 1934. Represents 125 clients. "We require the writer to be published—such as articles if extensive, novels and/or screenplays." Prefers to work with published/established authors. Specializes in contemporary adventure-thriller fiction.
Will Handle: Novels, movie scripts, stage plays and TV scripts. Currently handles 55% novels; 25% movie scripts; 5% stage plays; and 10% TV scripts. Does not read unsolicited mss. Reports in 6 weeks. "If our agency does not respond within 6 weeks to your request to become a client, you may submit requests elsewhere."
Terms: Agent receives 10% commission on domestic sales; 10% on dramatic sales; and 20% on foreign sales. 75% of income derived from commission on ms sales.
Recent Sales: *Bandits*, by Elmore Leonard (Arbor House); *Fox on the Run*, by Charles Bennett (Warner Books); and *Desperate Justice*, by Richard Speight (Warner Books).

‡THE TANTLEFF OFFICE, Suite 4F, 360 W. 20th St., New York NY 10011. (212)627-2105. President: Jack Tantleff. Estab. 1986. Member Writer's Guild of America. Represents 30 clients. 20% of clients are new/unpublished writers. Works with small number of new/unpublished writers. Specializes in television, theatre and film.
Will Handle: Movie scripts, stage plays, TV scripts. Currently handles 15% movie scripts; 50% stage plays; 35% TV scripts. Will read—at no charge—unsolicited queries and outlines.
Terms: Agent receives 10% commission on domestic sales; 10% on dramatic sales; and 10% on foreign sales. "Charges for unusual expenses agreed upon in advance."
Recent Sales: No information given.

PATRICIA TEAL LITERARY AGENCY, (formerly Teal & Watt), 2036 Vista del Rosa, Fullerton CA 92631. (714)738-8333. Owner: Patricia Teal. Estab. 1978. Member of ILAA, RWA and Writers Guild. Represents 40 clients. 20% of clients are new/unpublished writers. "Writer must have honed his skills by virtue of educational background, writing classes, previous publications. Any of these *may* qualify him to submit." Works with a small number of new/unpublished authors. Specializes in category fiction such as mysteries, romances (contemporary and historical), westerns, men's adventure, horror, etc. Also handles nonfiction in all areas, especially self-help and how-to.
Will Handle: Nonfiction books (self-help and how-to) and novels (category only). Currently handles 30% nonfiction books and 70% category novels. Will read—at no charge—unsolicited queries and outlines. No response if not accompanied by SASE. Reports in 3 weeks on queries.
Terms: 15% commission for new, unpublished writers, and 10% for published. Agent receives 10-15% commission on domestic sales; 20% on dramatic sales; and 20% on foreign sales. Charges for phone, postage and photocopy expenses. 5% of total income derived from fees charged to writers; 95% of income derived from commission on ms sales.
Recent Sales: *Polo's Ponies*, by Jerry Kennealy (St. Martin's Press); *Honorbound*, by Laura Taylor (Franklin Watts); and *Diamond Wine*, by Barbara Keller (NAL).

‡KATHE TELINGATOR, 435 Bergen St., Brooklyn NY 11217. (718)230-4910. Estab. 1986. Represents 25 clients. 90% of clients are new/unpublished writers. To be represented, writer needs to have a completed work available for review unless previously publication credits; then will consider partial manuscript. Proposals sufficient for nonfiction submissions. Eager to work with new/unpublished writers. Specializes in general interests—like history, biography, self-help.
Will Handle: Nonfiction books, novels, movie scripts and stage plays. Currently handles 25% nonfiction books; 25% novels; 3% movie scripts; 47% stage plays. Will read—at no charge—unsolicited queries and outlines submitted with SASE. Does not read unsolicited manuscripts, except occasionally on referral. Reports in

1-2 weeks on queries. "If our agency does not respond within 2 months to your request to become a client, you may submit requests elsewhere."

Terms: Agent receives 10% commission on domestic sales; 10% on dramatic sales; and 10% on foreign sales (may be an additional 10% when working with foreign agent). Charges for overseas calls, Telexes and cables, overnight mail. 100% of income derived from sales of writer's work.

A TOTAL ACTING EXPERIENCE, Suite 300-C, 6736 Laurel Canyon, North Hollywood CA 91606. (818)765-7244. Agent: Dan A. Bellacicco. Estab. 1984. Member of WGA. Represents 24 clients. 70% of clients are new/unpublished writers. Will accept new and established writers. Specializes in romance, science fiction, mysteries, humor, how-to and self-help books, and video/audio tapes on all topics.

Will Handle: Movie scripts, radio scripts, stage plays, TV scripts, nonfiction books, novels, juvenile books, syndicated material, lyricists and composers. (No heavy violence, drugs or sex.) Currently handles 2% magazine articles; 2% magazine fiction; 5% nonfiction books; 5% novels; 2% juvenile books; 50% movie scripts; 2% radio scripts; 5% stage plays; 19% TV scripts; and 8% from lyricists/composers. Will read—at no charge—unsolicited queries, outlines and mss. Reports in 2-6 weeks on queries; 3 months on mss. "If our agency does not respond within 3 months to your request to become a client, you may submit requests elsewhere. Submit only first 10 pages of your ms; include a one page synopsis of story, resume and letter of introduction with SASE. No exceptions please. No heavy violence, sex or drugs."

Terms: Agent receives 10% commission on domestic sales; 10% on dramatic sales; and 10% on foreign sales. 100% of income derived from commission on ms sales.

Recent Sales: "Confidential."

‡2M COMMUNICATIONS LTD., Suite 601, 121 West 27th St., New York NY 10001. (212)741-1500. President: Madeleine Morel. Estab. 1982. Member ABPA- American Book Producers Association. Represents 45 clients. 50% of clients are new writers. To be represented, writer must preferably have published articles. Works with small number of new/unpublished writers. Specializes in nonfiction, humor, biographies, lifestyle, pop psychology.

Will Handle: Nonfiction books. Currently handles 100% nonfiction books. Will read—at no charge—unsolicited queries and outlines. Reports in 3 weeks on queries. "If our agency does not respond within 2 months to your request to become a client, you may submit requests elsewhere."

Terms: Agent receives 15% commission on domestic sales and 20% on foreign sales. Charges for photocopying, mailing and phone calls. Sometimes offers consultation service through which authors can get advice on a contract; charges $100/hour. 100% of income derived from commission on ms sales.

Recent Sales: *Growing Up Jewish*, by Molin (Viking); *Mothers of Invention/Female Inventors Thru the Ages*, by Vare and Ptacek (WM Morrow); and *Biko*, by Donald Woods (Holt).

SUSAN P. URSTADT, INC., Suite 2A, 125 E. 84 St., New York NY 10028. (212)744-6605. President: Susan P. Urstadt. Estab. 1975. Member of ILAA. Represents 45-50 clients. 5% of clients are new/unpublished writers. "Writer must demonstrate writing ability through sample, qualifications through curriculum vitae and reliability through resume or biography." Works with a small number of new/unpublished authors. Looking for writers with a serious long-term commitment to writing. Specializes in literary and commercial fiction, decorative arts and antiques, architecture, sailing, tennis, literary gardening, armchair cookbooks, biography, performing arts, sports (especially horses), current affairs, lifestyle and current living trends.

Will Handle: Nonfiction books and novels. "We look for serious books of quality with fresh ideas and approaches to current situations and trends." Currently handles 65% nonfiction books; 25% novels; and 10% juvenile books. Will read—at no charge—unsolicited queries, sample chapters and outlines. SASE required. Reports in 1 month on queries; 6 weeks on mss.

Terms: Agent receives 15% commission on domestic sales; 15% on dramatic sales; and 20% on foreign sales. Charges for phone, photocopying, foreign postage and express mail expenses. 100% of income derived from commission on ms sales.

Recent Sales: *Emyl Jenkins' Appraisal Book*, by Emyl Jenkins (Crown); *Perennials for American Gardens*, by Nicolas Ekstron and Ruth Clansen (Random House); and *Hamman's Bone*, by Sven Birkerts (Morrow).

‡VAN DER LEUN AND ASSOCIATES, 464 Mill Hill Dr., Southport CT 06490. (203)259-4897. President: Patricia Van Der Leun. Estab. 1985. Represents 20 clients; 50% of clients are new/unpublished writers. Works with small number of new/unpublished authors. Specializes in science, art, illustrated books, fiction.

Will Handle: Nonfiction books and novels. Currently handles 50% nonfiction books; 50% novels. Will read—at no charge—unsolicited queries and outlines "if accompanied by SASE." Reports in 2 weeks on queries; 1 month on mss. "If our agency does not respond within 1 month to your request to become a client, you may submit requests elsewhere."

Terms: Agent receives 15% commission on domestic sales; 15% on dramatic sales; and 15% on foreign sales. Charges for photocopying. Sometimes offers consultation service through which writers can get advice on a contract; charges $75/hour. 99% of income derived from commission on ms sales; 1% from fees.

Recent Sales: *Everything I Really Need To Know I Learned in Kindegarten*, by Robert Fulghum (Villard Books); *Cosmogenesis*, by David Layzer (Oxford University Press); and *The Chinese Western*, short fiction from today's China, translated by Zhu Hong (Ballantine Books—Available Press).

‡RALPH VICINANZA LTD., Suite 1205, 432 Park Ave. South, New York NY 10016. (212)725-5133. Assistant: Christopher Lotts. Estab. 1978. Represents agents, authors and publishers. Works with a small number of new/unpublished authors. Specializes in science fiction, fantasy and thrillers.
Will Handle: Nonfiction books and novels. Currently handles 10% nonfiction books and 90% novels. Will read—at no charge—unsolicited queries.
Terms: Agent receives 10% commission on domestic sales and 20% on foreign sales. Charges for photocopy expenses and special mailings. 100% of income derived from commission on ms sales.
Recent Sales: *At Winter's End*, by Robert Silverberg (Warner); *Love and Sleep*, by John Crowley (Bantam); and *Funland*, by Richard Laymon (New American Library).

CARLSON WADE, Room K-4, 49 Bokee Ct., Brooklyn NY 11223. (718)743-6983. President: Carlson Wade. Estab. 1949. Represents 40 clients. 50% of clients are new/unpublished writers. Eager to work with new/unpublished writers. Will consider all types of fiction and nonfiction.
Will Handle: Magazine articles, magazine fiction, nonfiction books and novels. Currently handles 10% magazine articles; 10% magazine fiction; 40% nonfiction books; and 40% novels. Will read submissions at no charge, but may charge a criticism fee or service charge for work performed after the initial reading. Reports in 2 weeks. "If our agency does not respond within 1 month to your request to become a client, you may submit requests elsewhere."
Terms: Agent receives 10% commission on domestic sales; 10% on dramatic sales; and 10% on foreign sales. Charges handling fee: $1/1,000 words on short ms; $50/book. 20% of income derived from reading and handling fees. Charges a criticism fee if ms requires extensive work. 10% of income derived from criticism fees. "Short manuscript receives 5 pages of critique, book receives 15 (single space, page-by-page critique)." 20% of income derived from reading and handling fees; 80% of income derived from commission on ms sales. Payment of a criticism fee does not ensure that agency will represent a writer. "If a writer revises a manuscript properly, then we take it on. Futher help is available at no cost."
Recent Sales: *Eat Away Illness* (Prentice Hall) and *Nutritional Therapy* (Prentice Hall).

‡BESS WALLACE LITERARY AGENCY, 1502 N. Mitchell, Payson AZ 85541. (602)474-2983. Owner: Bess Wallace. Estab. 1977. Represents 32 clients. 80% of clients are new/unpublished writers. Eager to work with new/unpublished writers. Specializes in nonfiction.
Will Handle: Nonfiction books and novels. Will read—at no charge—unsolicited queries and outlines. Reports in 3 weeks. "If our agency does not respond within 2 months to your requests to become a client, you may submit requests elsewhere."
Terms: Agent receives 15% commission on domestic sales; 10% on dramatic sales; and 10% on foreign sales. Charges for editing and retyping. 80% of income derived from commission on ms sales; 20% from fees.
Recent Sales: *Child Abuse, Neglect and Molestation, Terrorism*, and *Our Social Service Agencies*, by M.J. Philippies and Bess Wallace (P.P.I. Publishers); *Language in Tears*, by Robert Thompson (CAP Publishers); and *Legend of Kohl's Ranch*, by Katie Bell (CAP Publishers).

‡THE GERRY B. WALLERSTEIN AGENCY, Suite 12, 2315 Powell Ave., Erie PA 16506. (814)833-5511. President/Owner: Gerry B. Wallerstein. Estab. 1984. Member Author's Guild, Society of Professional Journalists. Represents 43 clients. 23% of clients are new/unpublished writers. "I read/critique works by writers who have sold regularly to major periodicals, or have had a prior book published, or sold a script, on the basis of no reading fee. Works by new writers are read/critiqued on the basis of a reading fee, according to length of ms. I will represent writers of either category." Specializes in both fiction and nonfiction books, articles, short stories, children's books, scripts (only for clients), no poetry or song/lyrics.
Will Handle: Magazine articles; magazine fiction (clients only); nonfiction books; novels; juvenile books. Currently handles 22% magazine articles; 6% magazine fiction; 30% nonfiction books; 30% novels; 12% juvenile books. Will read—at no charge—unsolicited queries and outlines. Reports in 1 week on queries. "If our agency has not responded within 2 months to your request to become a client, you may submit requests elsewhere."
Terms: Agent receives 15% commission on domestic sales; 15% on dramatic sales; and 20% on foreign sales. Charges reading fee "for writers who have not sold their work regularly to major periodicals, or have not had a prior book published or a script sold to a producer." Reading fee waived if writer represented. 50% of income derived from reading fees. Charges $300 for 300-page, typed, double-spaced book ms. "Criticism included in reading fee. Our reading/critique averages 1-2 pages for short material and book proposals; 2-4 pages for book-length manuscripts. I indicate any problem areas, suggest possible ways to solve the problems, and provide marketing advice. All reading is done by Gerry B. Wallerstein." Charges for manuscript typing or copying, copyright fees, attorney's fees (if required, and approved by author), travel fees (if required and approved by

author) and a monthly fee of $20 for postage/telephone expenses. 50% of income derived from commission on ms sales; 50% from fees. Payment of a reading fee does not ensure that the agency will represent a writer.
Recent Sales: *Caring For Your Own*, by Darla J. Neidrick, R.N. (John Wiley & Sons, Inc.); *Turning Paper To Gold*, by Joseph R. LeFontaine (Betterway Publications, Inc.); and *A Handbook for Book Lovers*, by Joseph R. LeFontaine (Prometheus Books).

JOHN A. WARE LITERARY AGENCY, 392 Central Park West, New York NY 10025. (212)866-4733. Contact: John Ware. Estab. 1978. Represents 60 clients. 40% of clients are new/unpublished writers. Writers must have appropriate credentials for authorship of proposal (nonfiction) or manuscript (fiction); no publishing track record required. "Open to good writing and interesting ideas, by 'new' or 'veteran' writers." Specializes in biography; investigative journalism; history; health and psychology (academic credentials required); serious and accessible non-category fiction and mysteries; current issues and affairs; sports; oral history; Americana and folklore.
Will Handle: Nonfiction books and novels. Currently handles 75% nonfiction books and 25% novels. Will read unsolicited queries and outlines; does not read unsolicited mss. Reports in 2 weeks on queries.
Terms: Agent receives 10% commission on domestic sales; 10% on dramatic sales; and 20% on foreign sales. Charges for messengering, photocopying and extraordinary expenses. "No reading fees."
Recent Sales: *Three Full Shifts in Marysville: Japan Comes to the Heartland*, by David Gelsanliter (Farrar, Straus & Giroux); *Paradigms Lost: Conflicting Visions of Reality in Modern Science*, by John L. Casti (Morrow); and *Terraplane*, by Jack Womack (Weidenfeld & Nicolson).

JAMES WARREN LITERARY AGENCY, 13131 Welby Way, North Hollywood CA 91606. (818)982-5423. Agent: James Warren. Editors: James Boston, Audrey Langer and Bob Carlson. Estab. 1969. Represents 60 clients. 60% of clients are new/unpublished writers. "We are willing to work with select unpublished writers." Specializes in fiction, history, textbooks, professional books, craft books, how-to books, self-improvement books, health books and diet books.
Will Handle: Juvenile books, historical romance novels, movie scripts (especially drama and humor), and TV scripts (drama, humor, documentary). Currently handles 40% nonfiction books; 20% novels; 10% textbooks; 5% juvenile books; 10% movie scripts; and 15% TV scripts. Will read—at no charge—unsolicited queries and outlines. Does not read unsolicited mss. Reports in 1 week on queries; 1 month on mss. "If our agency does not respond within 2 month to your request to become a client, you may submit requests elsewhere."
Terms: Receives 15% commission on first domestic sales and 10% on subsequent sales; 20% on foreign sales. Charges reading fee of approximately $2 per thousand words—negotiable according to length of ms; 20% of income derived from reading fees; refunds reading fee if subsequently sells writer's work. "We occasionally encounter a manuscript that has literary merit but which, in our opinion, does not have commercial clout. In such cases we may decide to submit at the author's expense. Our charge is $15 for an average-sized ms." 20% of total income derived from fees charged to writers; 80% of income derived from commission on ms sales. Payment of fees does not ensure that agency will represent writer.
Recent Sales: *Good Health and Common Sense*, by Dale Alexander (Witkower Press); *Healthy Hair and Common Sense*, by Dale Alexander (Witkower Press); and *A Tax Free America*, by Boris Isaacson (Tomorrow Now Press).

‡WATERSIDE PRODUCTIONS, INC., Suite 2, 832 Camino del Mar, Del Mar CA 92014. (619)481-8335. (Additional office in New York City opened summer 1988.) Estab. 1982. Represents 200 clients. 20% of clients are new/unpublished writers. To be represented "fiction authors must be published in major magazines; nonfiction authors must be recognized experts in their field; computer authors must have superb technical skills." Works with small number of new/unpublished writers. Specializes in computer books and books about new technology; fiction and general nonfiction of exceptional quality. Writer's guidelines for #10 SAE and 2 first class stamps.
Will Handle: Nonfiction books; novels; textbooks; juvenile books. Currently handles 90% nonfiction books; 4% novels; 4% textbooks; 2% juvenile books. Will read—at no charge—unsolicited queries and outlines. Does not read unsolicited mss. Reports in 1 month on queries. "If our agency does not respond within 2 months to your request to become a client, you may submit requests elsewhere."
Terms: Agent receives 15% commission on domestic sales; 20% on dramatic sales; and 25% on foreign sales. Charges reading fee for "first time novelists or personal nonfiction." 1% of income derived from reading fees. Charges $300 for 300-page, typed, double-spaced book ms. 99% of income derived from commission on ms sales; 1% derived from fees.
Recent Sales: *Good Friday*, by Robert Holt (Tab Books); *The Complete Hypercard Handbook*, by Danny Goodman (Bantam); and *Steve Jobs: The Journey is the Reward*, by Jeffrey Young (Scott, Foresman Publishing).

‡SANDRA WATT & ASSOCIATES, Suite 4053, 8033 Sunset Blvd., Los Angeles CA 90046. (213)653-2339. President: Sandra Watt. Estab. 1976. Member of ILAA and WGA West. Represents 100 clients. Eager

to work with new/unpublished writers. Specializes in literary and category fiction, popular nonfiction, metaphysical works, young adult fiction and gay/lesbian fiction and nonfiction. Works extensively with television and film.
Will Handle: Nonfiction books, novels, young adult books, movie scripts and TV scripts. Will read—at no charge—unsolicited queries and outlines. Reports in 1 week on queries.
Terms: Agent receives 15% commission on domestic sales; 10% on dramatic sales; and 20% on foreign sales. Charges marketing fee for new writers to cover expenses generated in promotion of their project alone. 100% of income derived from sales of writer's work.
Recent Sales: *Hungry Women*, by B. Laramie Dunaway (Warner); *The Venus Formula*, by Sanford and Silverstein (Contemporary); and *A Parent's Guide to Adolescent Sexuality* (Holt).

‡ANN WAUGH AGENCY, Suite 5, 4731 Laurel Canyon Blvd., N. Hollywood CA 91607. (818)980-0141. Agent: Steve Jacobson. Estab. 1979. Member of SAG. Represents 30 clients. 50% of clients are new/unpublished writers. Prefers to work with published/established authors; works with a small number of new/unpublished authors. Specializes in modern romance, comedy and action adventure screenplays. No pornography or slasher screenplays.
Will Handle: Movie scripts. Currently handles 100% movie scripts. Will read—at no charge—unsolicited queries and mss; send letter size SASE before submission to receive release form. Reports in 1 week on queries; 6 weeks on mss. "If our agency does not respond within 1 month to your request to become a client, you may submit requests elsewhere."
Terms: Agent receives 10% commission on domestic sales; 10% on dramatic sales; and 10% on foreign sales. Sometimes offers a consultation service through which writers not represented can get advice on a contract. 100% of income derived from commission on ms sales.
Recent Sales: Screenplays to Orion and Tri Star.

‡WECKSLER-INCOMCO, 170 West End Ave., New York NY 10023. (212)787-2239; (212)496-7035. President: Sally Wecksler. Estab. 1973. Represents 20 clients. To be represented writer "must have published articles if not books, or some kind of writing or editing experience." Works with small number of new/unpublished writers. Specializes in nonfiction, topical, nature, how-to and illustrated books.
Will Handle: Nonfiction books. Currently handles 90% nonfiction books; 10% novels. Will read—at no charge—unsolicited queries and outlines. Does not read unsolicited mss. Reports in 2 months on mss.
Terms: Agent receives 12-15% commission on domestic sales; 20% on foreign sales. Sometimes offers consultation service through which writers can get advice on a contract; charges $50/hour. Also represents publishers in sub rights and foreign markets.
Recent Sales: *Does Your Eye Lie*, by Hazel Richmond Dawkins (Dodd Mead); *Dictionary of Media Terms*, by Edmund Penny (Facts on File); and *Handbook of International Trade*, by Roger Axtell (Wiley).

RHODA WEYR AGENCY, 216 Vance St., Chapel Hill NC 27514. (919)942-0770. President: Rhoda A. Weyr. Estab. 1983. Member of SAR and ILAA. Prefers to work with published/established authors; works with a small number of new/unpublished authors. Specializes in general nonfiction and fiction of high quality.
Will Handle: Nonfiction books and novels. Will read—at no charge—unsolicited queries, outlines and sample chapters sent with SASE.
Terms: Agent receives 10% commission on domestic sales; 10-15% on dramatic sales; and 20% on foreign sales. 100% of income derived from commission on ms sales.
Recent Sales: Confidential.

WIESER & WIESER, INC., 118 E. 25th St., New York NY 10010. (212)260-0860. President: Olga B. Wieser. Estab. 1976. Represents 60 clients. 10% of clients are new/unpublished writers. Prefers to work with published/established authors; works with a small number of new/unpublished authors. Specializes in literary and mainstream fiction, serious and popular historical fiction, mass market regencies, general nonfiction, business, finance, aviation, sports, photography, Americana, cookbooks, travel books and popular medicine.
Will Handle: Nonfiction books and novels. Currently handles 50% nonfiction books and 50% novels. Will read—at no charge—unsolicited queries and outlines. Reports in 1 week on queries accompanied by SASE.
Terms: Agent receives 15% commission on domestic sales; 15% on dramatic sales; and 20% on foreign sales. Charges for photocopy, cable and overnight postage expenses. Sometimes offers a consultation service through which writers not represented can get advice on negotiating a contract; charges $75/hour. 100% of income derived from commission on ms sales.
Recent Sales: *Silver Tower*, by Dale Brown (Donald I Fine, Inc.); *On Shaky Ground*, by John Nance (William Morrow & Co.); and *Rush to Nowhere*, by Howard Russell (Donald I. Fine, Inc.).

WINGRA WOODS PRESS/Agenting Division, Suite 3, 33 Witherspoon St., Princeton NJ 08542. (609)683-1218. Agent: Anne Matthews. Estab. 1985. Member of American Booksellers Association and American Book Producers Association. Represents 12 clients. 70% of clients are new/unpublished writers.

"Books must be completed, and designed for a distinct market niche." Works with small number of new/unpublished authors. Specializes in nonfiction, children's, Americana and travel.

Will Handle: Currently handles 60% nonfiction books and 40% juvenile books. Will read—at no charge—unsolicited queries, outlines and mss. Reports in 3 weeks. "If our agency does not respond within 2 months to your request to become a client, you may submit requests elsewhere."

Terms: Receives 15% commission on domestic sales; 15% on dramatic sales and 15% on foreign sales. Sometimes offers a consultation service through which writers not represented can get advice on a contract; charges $25/hour. 100% of income derived from commission on ms sales.

Recent Sales: *Tapas, Wines and Good Times*, by Don and Marge Foster (Contemporary); *A Rose for Abby*, by Donna Guthrie (Abingdon); and *The Gone With the Wind Handbook*, by Pauline Bartel (Taylor).

RUTH WRESCHNER, AUTHORS' REPRESENTATIVE, 10 W. 74th St., New York NY 10023. (212)877-2605. Agent: Ruth Wreschner. Estab. 1981. Represents 30 clients. 70% of clients are new/unpublished writers. "In fiction, if a client is not published yet, I prefer writers who have written for magazines; in nonfiction, a person well-qualified in his field is acceptable." Prefers to work with published/established authors; works with new/unpublished authors. "I will always pay attention to a writer referred by another client." Specializes in popular medicine, health, how-to books and fiction (no pornography, screenplays or dramatic plays).

Will Handle: Nonfiction books; novels; textbooks; young adult and magazine articles (only for commercial magazines). Currently handles 5% magazine articles; 80% nonfiction books; 10% novels; 5% textbooks; and 5% juvenile books. Will read—at no charge—unsolicited queries and outlines. Reports in 2 weeks on queries. "Until I am willing to represent a client and he/she has decided to work with me, clients are free to contact other agents; some writers do multiple agent submissions, but they usually state so in their query. Queries must include SASE."

Terms: Agent receives 15% commission on domestic sales and 20% on foreign sales. Charges for photocopying expenses. "Once a book is placed, I will retain some money from the second advance to cover airmail postage of books, long distance calls, etc. on foreign sales." 100% of income derived from commission on ms sales. "I may consider charging for reviewing contracts in future. In that case I will charge $50/hour plus long distance calls, if any."

Recent Sales: *The Janus Report on the American Sexual Experience*, by Samuel Janus, Ph.D. and Cynthia Janus, M.D. (Rawson Associates); *Talking to Children About Love and Sex*, by Leon Somers, Ph.D. and Barbara Somers, Ed.D. (New American Library); and *Princess Diana for Children: 101 Questions & Answers*, by Victoria C. Nesnick (M. Evans).

ANN WRIGHT REPRESENTATIVES, INC., 136 E. 57th St., New York NY 10022. (212)832-0110. Head of Literary Department: Dan Wright. Estab. 1963. Member of WGA. Represents 41 clients. 25% of clients are new/unpublished writers. "Writers must be skilled or have superior material for screenplays, stories or novels that can eventually become motion pictures or television properties." Prefers to work with published/established authors; works with a small number of new/unpublished authors. "Eager to work with any author with material that we can effectively market in the motion picture business worldwide." Specializes in themes that make good motion picture projects.

Will Handle: Novels, movie scripts, stage plays and TV scripts. Currently handles 10% novels; 75% movie scripts; and 15% TV scripts. Will read—at no charge—unsolicited queries and outlines; does not read unsolicited mss. Reports in 2 weeks on queries; 6 weeks on mss. "If our agency does not respond within 2 months to your request to become a client, you may submit requests elsewhere."

Terms: Agent receives 10% commission on domestic sales; 10% on dramatic sales; and 10% on foreign sales. Will critique only works of signed clients. Charges for photocopying expenses. 100% of income derived from commission on ms sales.

Recent Sales: No information given.

‡WRITERS' ASSOCIATES LITERARY AGENCY, Penthouse 219, 3960 Laurel Canyon Blvd., Studio City CA 91604. (213)851-2488. President: Steve Stratton. Member of Writers' Society of America. Represents 14 clients. 40% of clients are new/unpublished writers. Maintains a 60/40 ratio of established to newly pro writers. Specializes in contemporary novels, contemporary screenplays including movies of the week.

Will Handle: Magazine articles, magazine fiction, novels, juvenile books, movie scripts, stage plays and TV scripts. Currently handles 4% magazine articles; 6% magazine fiction; 5% novels; 30% textbooks; 5% movie scripts; 25% radio scripts; and 25% syndicated material. Will read—at no charge—unsolicited queries and outlines. Does not read unsolicited mss. Reports in 1 weeks. "If our agency does not respond within 1 month to your request to become a client, you may submit requests elsewhere."

Terms: Agent receives 15% commission on domestic sales; 15% on dramatic sales; and 18% on foreign sales. Charges a reading fee if writer requests "a constructive reading of material. No reading fee to credited writers or WGA members. Fee refundable on sale of material." Receives 20% of income from fees; charges $175 for 300-page, typed book manuscript. Reading fee includes criticism. "Professional writers or studio readers (for screenplays) do the reading/critique. Evaluation is overall, and some line-by-line as examples. The purpose,

mainly, is to guide writer into a stronger, tighter story if needed, to improve chance for sale." Agent receives 80% of income from ms sales.
Recent Sales: *Strange Love*, by Jeffrey Swanson (Marquis); *Night Vision*, by Barbara Knight (Sleeping Dogs Publications); *Hunter*, by Victor C. Lee (Rebel Publications).

WRITER'S CONSULTING GROUP, Box 492, Burbank CA 91503. (818)841-9294. Director: Jim Barmeier. Estab. 1983. Represents 10 clients. 50% of clients new/unpublished writers. "We prefer to work with established writers unless the author has an unusual true story."
Will Handle: Magazine articles (if written about a true story for which the author has the rights); nonfiction books (celebrity books, true crime accounts, unusual true stories); novels; movie scripts. Currently handles 40% nonfiction books; 20% novels; and 40% movie scripts. Will read—at no charge—unsolicited queries and outlines. "If you send us an unpublished book manuscript, it must be accompanied by a $50 reading fee, for which you will receive our recommendations." 10% of income derived from reading fees. Include SASE. Reports in 1 month on queries; 3 months on mss. "If our agency does not respond within 1 month to your request to become a client, you may submit requests elsewhere."
Terms: "We will explain our terms to clients when they wish to sign. We receive a 10% commission on domestic sales." Sometimes offers a ghostwriting service for non-writers looking for a co-writer. 75% of income derived from commission on ms sales.
Recent Sales: "We have helped writers sell everything from episodes for children's TV shows ("Smurfs") to move-of-the-week options (including the Craig Smith espionage story)."

WRITERS HOUSE, INC., 21 W. 26 St., New York NY 10010. (212)685-2400. President: Albert Zuckerman. Estab. 1974. Member of ILAA. Represents 120 clients. 20% of clients are new/unpublished writers. Specializes in fiction of all types, adult fiction, juvenile novels, and nonfiction books on business, parenting, lifestyles, sci-fi and fantasy, and rock and pop culture.
Will Handle: Nonfiction books, novels and juvenile books. Currently handles 30% nonfiction books; 40% novels; and 30% juvenile books. Will read—at no charge—unsolicited queries and outlines. Reports in 2 weeks on queries.
Terms: Agent receives 15% commission on sale of adult books, 10% on juvenile and young adult domestic sales; 15% on dramatic sales; and 20% on foreign sales. Charges for overseas postage, Telex, messenger, phone and photocopy expenses. 95% of income derived from commission on ms sales; 5% from scouting for foreign publishers.
Recent Sales: *Lie Down with Lions*, by Ken Follett; *Sweet Valley Summer*, by Francine Pascal; and *Garden of Lies*, by Eileen Goudge Zuckerman.

WRITER'S PRODUCTIONS, Box 630, Westport CT 06881. (203)227-8199. Agent: David L. Meth. Estab. 1981. Eager to work with new/unpublished writers. Specializes in "fiction of literary quality, unique, intriguing nonfiction and photo-essay books. We are especially interested in works of Asian American writers about the Asian American experience, and are specializing in works about the Orient. No historical romances, science fiction, mysteries, westerns, how-to, health, cookbooks, occult, philosophy, etc ."
Will Handle: Nonfiction books and novels. Currently handles 15% nonfiction books and 85% novels. Will read—at no charge—unsolicited queries, outlines and mss. Reports in 2 weeks on queries; 1 month on mss. "All correspondence must have a SASE for any response and return of manuscript, due to the large volume of submissions we receive. No phone calls please."
Terms: Agent receives 15% commission on domestic sales; 20% on dramatic sales; and 20% on foreign sales. 100% of income derived from commission on ms sales.
Recent Sales: *Last Traces: The Lost Art of Auschwitz*, by Joseph Czarnecki (Atheneum); *Vessels of Sand*, by Matsumoto Sekho (Soho Press); and *The White Badge*, by Ahn Junghyo (Soho Press).

‡WRITER'S REPRESENTATIVES, INC., (formerly Glen Hartley Agency), 25 W. 19th St., New York NY 10011-4202. (212)620-9009. Contact: Glen Hartley or Lynn Chu. Estab. 1985. Represents 25 clients. 15% of clients are new/unpublished writers. Works with small number of new/unpublished writers.
Will Handle: Nonfiction books and novels. Currently handles 10% magazine articles; 10% magazine fiction; 40% nonfiction books; and 40% novels. Will read—at no charge—unsolicited queries, outlines and manuscripts. Reports in 3 weeks on queries; 6 weeks on mss.
Terms: Agent receives 15% commission on domestic sales; 20% on foreign sales. Charges for out-of-pocket expenses, such as photocopying, courier charges, long-distance phone calls, etc. Sometimes offers consultation for a negotiated fee. 95% of income derived from commission on ms sales; 5% derived from fees charged to writers.
Recent Sales: *The Dead Girl*, by Melanie Thernstrom (Pocket Books); *Fugitive Spring*, by Deborah Digges (Alfred A. Knopf); and *Untitled Biography of Charles Olson*, (W.W. Norton & Co.).

‡THE WRITERS WORKSHOP, INC., Suite 1508, 310 Madison Ave., New York NY 10017. (212)687-1122. President: Anita Diamant. Estab. 1917. Member of SAR. Represents 100 clients. Prefers to work with published/established authors; works with a small number of new/unpublished authors. "We handle books for the adult markets."
Will Handle: Nonfiction books and novels. Currently handles 50% nonfiction books and 50% novels. Will read—at no charge—unsolicited queries and outlines; does not read unsolicited mss. Reports in 1 week on queries; 6 weeks on mss. Include SASE. "If our agency does not respond within 3 months to your request to become a client, you may submit requests elsewhere."
Terms: Agent receives 10-15% commission on domestic sales; and 15-20% on foreign sales. Charges for phone and messenger expenses. Sometimes offers a consultation service through which writers not represented can get advice on a contract. 99% of income derived from commission on ms sales.
Recent Sales: No information given.

WRITERS' WORLD FORUM, Box 20383, Midtown Station, New York NY 10129. (201)664-0263. President: William Parker. Estab. 1985. Represents 8 clients. 75% of clients are new/unpublished writers. "The only qualifications needed for representation are good writing and a well-prepared manuscript. Our advice to writers: Be original. Don't do what everyone else is doing." Eager to work with new/unpublished writers. Specializes in general nonfiction and fiction, "especially literary, ethnic, Third World, women's, etc. We are looking for quality manuscripts on important topics. Always anxious to find new and/or unique voices."
Will Handle: Nonfiction books, novels (no romances) and juvenile books. Currently handles 20% nonfiction books; 70% novels and 10% juvenile books. Will read—at no charge—unsolicited queries and outlines. "Please include SASE." Reports in 2 weeks on queries; 1 month on mss.
Terms: Agent receives 10% commission on domestic sales; 10% on foreign sales.
Recent Sales: No information given.

SUSAN ZECKENDORF ASSOCIATES, Suite 11B, 171 W. 57th St., New York NY 10019. (212)245-2928. President: Susan Zeckendorf. Estab. 1979. Member of ILAA. Represents 45 clients. 60% of clients are new writers. Specializes in fiction of all kinds—literary, historical, and commercial women's, mainstream thrillers and mysteries, science, music, self-help, and parenting books.
Will Handle: Nonfiction books (by a qualified expert) and novels. Currently handles 40% nonfiction books and 60% novels. Will read—at no charge—unsolicited queries. Reports in 2 weeks on queries; 1 month on mss. "If our agency does not respond within 1 month to your request to become a client, you may submit requests elsewhere."
Terms: Agent receives 15% commission on domestic sales; 15% on dramatic (movie or TV) sales; and 20% on foreign sales. Charges for phone, photocopy and foreign postage expenses. 100% of income derived from commission on ms sales.
Recent Sales: *Scandals*, by Una-Mary Parker (New American Library); *A Long Way to Die*, by James Frey (Bantam); and *Baby Signals*, by Dian Lynch Fraser and Ellen Morris Tiegerman Ph.D. (Walker and Co.).

TOM ZELASKY LITERARY AGENCY, 3138 Parkridge Crescent, Chamblee GA 30341. (404)458-0391. Agent: Tom Zelasky. Estab. 1984. Represents 5 clients. 90% of clients are new/unpublished writers. Prefers to work with published/established authors; works with a small number of new/unpublished authors. Specializes in mainstream fiction or nonfiction, categorical romance, historical romance, historical fiction, westerns, action/detective mysteries, suspense, science fiction.
Will Handle: Nonfiction books, novels, juvenile books, movie scripts, stage plays and TV scripts. Will read—at no charge—unsolicited queries and outlines. "SASE is compulsory, otherwise, manuscript will be in storage and destroyed after 2 years." Reports in 3 weeks on queries; 3 months on mss. "If our agency does not respond within 3 months to your request to become a client, you should contact me immediately."
Terms: Agent receives 10-15% commission on domestic sales; 10-15% on dramatic sales; and 15-25% on foreign sales. Charges a reading fee; will waive fee if representing the writer. "A critique of one to three pages is mailed to writer when manuscript is rejected. I do my own reading and critique. It is usually a one to three page item, single space, citing craft skills, marketability and overall evaluation." Charges writers for phone calls to writers and publishers and postage. Considering a consultation service to individual writers.
Recent Sales: No information given.

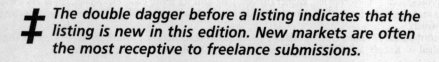

✚ *The double dagger before a listing indicates that the listing is new in this edition. New markets are often the most receptive to freelance submissions.*

— *Additional Author's Agents*

The following listings were deleted for the 1989 edition because the firms are out of business, backlogged with submissions, asked to be deleted, or have unresolved complaints.

Authors Marketing Services Ltd., (complaints)
Virginia Barber (accepting no unsolicited manuscripts)
Heinle & Heinle (closed agency)
HHM Literary Agency (asked to be deleted)
Elizabeth Lay (unable to contact)
Claudia Menza (asked to be deleted)
Barbara W. Yedlin (backlogged with submissions)
George Zeigler (asked to be deleted)

The following firms did not return a verification to update an existing listing by press time.

Axelrod Agency
Meredith Bernstein
Brandt & Brandt Literary
    Agents
Shirley Burke Agency
Connie Clausen Associates
Ben Conway and Associates
Harold R. Green
Thomas S. Hart Literary Enter-
    prises
Hintz & Fitzgerald
Kratz and Kompany
Adele Leone Agency
Ellen Levine Literary Agency
Donald MacCampbell
March Tenth Inc.
B.K. Nelson Literary Agency
New England Publishing Asso-
    ciates Inc.
Ray Peekner
Pickering Associates
Richland Agency
Eleanor Roszel Rogers Literary
    Agent
Irene Rogers Literary Represen-
    tation
Susan Schulman Literary Agen-
    cy
John Schaffner Associates
Elyse Sommer
Thompson and Chris Literary
    Agency
Victoria Management
Mary Jack Wald Associates

Contests and Awards

When selecting a manuscript for publication, quality is not the only factor editors must consider. Timing, tone, length and the publication's image are all considerations that enter into the final decision. A piece might even be rejected simply because it does not fit the editorial mix of a particular issue.

Contest and awards, on the other hand, offer writers the opportunity to have their work judged for quality alone, once entry requirements are met. Writers' works are compared to the work of other writers, whose submissions are subject to identical conditions. Aside from the monetary reward many contests offer, there is the satisfaction of having your work recognized for excellence by established writers and other professionals in the field. Writers often receive the added benefit of having their work published or produced.

Some competitions focus on form, such as a short story or poetry contest, while others reward writers who handle a particular subject well. This year, for example, there are contests listed for best golf writing, best writing about dogs and for best children's book on a Jewish theme. In addition to contests for poetry, short stories and journalism, we've included listings of competitions for plays, novels, film and radio scripts and even for book jacket blurbs.

Some contests are free, while others charge entry fees. Not all contests are open to everyone—some are for published authors, others for beginning writers or students. Eligibility may be based on the writer's age, geographic location or whether the work has been previously published or is unpublished. It's important to read contest rules carefully to avoid submitting to contests for which you do not qualify.

If rules are unclear or you are unsure how a particular contest defines terms, send the director a self addressed, stamped envelope along with a brief letter asking for clarification. It's best to ask a specific question—contest directors have little time to answer lengthy letters.

A number of contests require someone to nominate the work for consideration. If nomination by a publisher is required, just ask—most publishers welcome the opportunity to promote a work in this way. Make the publisher aware of the contest in plenty of time before the deadline.

In addition to contests and awards, we also list grants, scholarship and fellowship programs. Information on funding for writers is available in most large public libraries. See the *Annual Register of Grant Support* (National Register Publishing Co., Inc., 3004 Glenview Road, Wilmette IL 60091); *Foundation Grants to Individuals* (Foundation Center, 79 Fifth Ave., New York NY 10003) and *Grants and Awards Available to American Writers* (PEN American Center, 568 Broadway, New York NY 10012). For more listings of contest and awards for fiction writers see *Novel & Short Story Writer's Market* (formerly *Fiction Writer's Market*) or for poets see *Poet's Market* (both by Writer's Digest Books). A good source of contests for journalists is the annual Journalism Awards Issue of *Editor and Publisher* magazine, published in the last week of December.

The contests in this section are listed by title, address, contact person, type of competition and deadline. Deadlines that state a range—for example, July to September—will only accept entries within that period. If a contest sounds interesting, send a self-addressed, stamped envelope to the contact person for information, rules and details about prizes. Don't enter any contest without first seeking this information. For information on contests not listed in *Writer's Market* see Additional Contests at the end of this section.

AAAS PRIZE FOR BEHAVIORAL SCIENCE RESEARCH, American Association for the Advancement of Science, Executive Office, 10th Floor, 1333 H. St. NW, Washington DC 20005. Deadline: Aug. 1. Anthropology/psychology/social sciences/sociology.

‡**AAAS-WESTINGHOUSE SCIENCE JOURNALISM AWARDS**, American Association for the Advancement of Science, Office of Communications, 1333 H St. NW, Washington DC 20005. (202)326-6440. Science and its engineering and technological applications—excluding health and clinical medicine.

HERBERT BAXTER ADAMS PRIZE, Committee Chairman, American Historical Association, 400 A St. SE, Washington DC 20003. European history (first book). Deadline: June 15.

ADRIATIC AWARD, International Society of Dramatists, Box 1310, Miami FL 33153. (305)674-1831. Award Director: A. Delaplaine. Full-length play either unproduced professionally, *or* with one professional production (using Equity actors). Deadline: Nov. 1.

‡**AID TO INDIVIDUAL ARTISTS FELLOWSHIP**, Ohio Arts Council, 727 E. Main St., Columbus OH 43205. (614)466-2613. Contact: Susan Dickson. Nonfiction, fiction, criticism, poetry and plays. (Ohio resident, nonstudent). Deadline: Jan. 15.

ALBERTA NEW FICTION COMPETITION, Alberta Culture, Film and Literary Arts, 12th Fl., CN Tower, Edmonton, Alberta T5J 0K5 Canada. (403)427-2554. Open only to Alberta resident authors. Deadline: Dec. 31.

ALBERTA NON-FICTION AWARD, Alberta Culture, Film and Literary Arts, 12 Fl., CN Tower, Edmonton, Alberta T5J 0K5 Canada. (403)427-2554. Nonfiction book by Alberta author published in calendar year. Deadline Dec. 31.

AMELIA STUDENT AWARD, *Amelia Magazine*, 329 E St., Bakersfield CA 93304. (805)323-4064. Editor: Frederick A. Raborg, Jr. Previously unpublished poems, essays and short stories by high school students. Deadline: May 15.

AMERICAN ASSOCIATION OF UNIVERSITY WOMEN AWARD, NORTH CAROLINA DIVISION, North Carolina Literary and Historical Association, 109 E. Jones St., Raleigh NC 27611. (919)733-7305. Previously published juvenile literature by a North Carolina author. Deadline: July 15.

‡**AMERICAN POETRY ASSOCIATION'S POETRY CONTEST**, American Poetry Association, 250 A Potrero St., Box 1803, Santa Cruz CA 95061-1803. (408)429-1122. Contact: Richard Elliot. Unpublished poetry from new, not-yet-recognized poets. Deadline: June-Dec. 31.

AMERICAN-SCANDINAVIAN FOUNDATION/TRANSLATION PRIZE, American-Scandinavian Foundation, 127 E. 73rd St., New York NY 10021. (212)879-9779. Contact: Publishing Division. Contemporary Scandinavian fiction and poetry translations. Deadline: June 1.

AMERICAN SOCIETY OF JOURNALISTS & AUTHORS AWARDS PROGRAM, Room 1907, 1501 Broadway, New York NY 10036. (212)997-0947. Executive Secretary: Alexandra Cantor. Author, article and magazine awards. Deadline: Feb. 1.

‡**AMWA MEDICAL BOOK AWARDS COMPETITION**, American Medical Writers Association, 9650 Rockville Pike, Bethesda MD 20814. (301)493-0003. Medical book published in the preceding calendar year in one of three categories: Books for Physicians, Books for Allied Health Professionals, and Trade Books (for lay public). Deadline: April 1. Charges $10 per book.

AMY WRITING AWARDS, The Amy Foundation, Box 16091, Lansing MI 48901. (517)323-3181. President: James Russell. Articles communicating Biblical truth previously published in the secular media. Deadline: Jan. 31.

‡**ANNUAL FICTION AND POETRY CONTEST**, Rambunctious Press, 1221 W. Pratt, Chicago IL 60626. (312)338-2439. Contest/Award Director: David Oates. Unpublished short stories and poems. Deadline varies. Charges $3 per story, $2 per poem.

ANNUAL INTERNATIONAL NARRATIVE CONTEST, Poets and Patrons, Inc., 10053 Avenue L., Chicago IL 60617. Director: Veronica Robertson. Unpublished poetry. Deadline: Sept. 1.

ANNUAL INTERNATIONAL SHAKESPEAREAN SONNET CONTEST, Poets Club of Chicago, 373 Ramsay Rd., Deerfield IL 60015. Chairman: Carol Spelius. "Classic" Shakespearean sonnet form. Deadline: Sept. 1. Request rules after March 1.

ANNUAL JOURNALISM AWARDS COMPETITION, Big Brothers/Big Sisters of America, 230 North 13th St., Philadelphia PA 19107. (215)567-7000. Director of Publications: George L. Beiswinger. Previously published stories "communicating the difficulties experienced by children from one-parent homes and how such problems are handled." Deadline: April 1.

‡THE ANNUAL NISSAN FOCUS AWARDS, Nissan Motor Corporation and Eastman Kodak Company, 10 E. 34th St., 6th Floor, New York NY 10016. (212)779-0404. Executive Director: Sam Katz. Narrative film-making; documentary; animation/experimental; screenwriting; sound achievement; film editing; cinematography, Women in Film Foundation Award, Renee Valente Producers Award. Charges $15 fee. Open to student filmmakers only enrolled in a U.S. college, university, art institute or film school. Deadline: April 25.

ANNUAL NJ POETRY CONTEST, NJIT Alumni Association, NJ Institute of Technology, Newark NJ 07102. (201)596-3441. Contest/Award Director: Dr. Herman A. Estrin. Poetry by elementary, junior high, secondary, and college students who are New Jersey residents.

ANNUAL NORTH AMERICAN ESSAY CONTEST, *The Humanist Magazine*, 7 Harwood Dr., Box 146, Amherst NY 14226. (716)839-5080. Contest/Award Director: Lloyd Morain. Unpublished essay by writers age 29 or younger. Deadline: Sept. 1.

RUBY LLOYD APSEY PLAYWRITING AWARD, University of Alabama, Department of Theater and Dance, University Station, Birmingham AL 35294. (215)934-3236. Contest Director: Dr. Bob Yowell. Unpublished full-length plays by new American playwrights. Deadline: Jan. 1.

‡ARIZONA AUTHORS' ASSOCIATION ANNUAL NATIONAL LITERARY CONTEST, Arizona Authors' Association, Suite 117WM, 3509 E. Shea Blvd., Phoenix AZ 85028-3339. (602)996-9706. Contact: Dorothy Tegeler. Previously unpublished poetry, short stories, essays. Deadline: July 29. Charges $4 for poetry; $6 for short stories and essays.

ARTIST'S FELLOWSHIP AWARD, New York Foundation for the Arts, Suite 600, 5 Beekman St., New York NY 10038. (212)233-3900. Contact: Roger Bruce. New York State resident artists' career awards to be used at the artist's discretion to support their work. Deadlines begin in late summer.

‡ARTS RECOGNITION AND TALENT SEARCH, National Foundation for Advancement in the Arts, 3915 Biscayne Blvd., Miami FL 33137. (305)573-0490. Programs Officer: Dr. William Banchs. Achievements in Dance, Music, Theater, Visual Arts and Writing. Students fill in and return the application, available at every public and private high school around the nation. Deadline: May 16-Oct. 1. Charges $25 registration fee.

ASSOCIATION FOR EDUCATION IN JOURNALISM AWARDS, Magazine Division, Dept. of Journalism, Temple University, Philadelphia PA 19122. Contact: Professor Kathryn Clauss-New. Awards to enrolled college students for unpublished nonfiction magazine article, research paper on magazine journalism or magazine design.

VINCENT ASTOR MEMORIAL LEADERSHIP ESSAY CONTEST, U.S. Naval Institute, Preble Hall, U.S. Naval Academy, Annapolis MD 21402. (301)268-6110. Award Director: James A. Barber, Jr. Essays on the topic of leadership (junior officers and officer trainees). Deadline: March 1.

THE ATHENAEUM OF PHILADELPHIA LITERARY AWARD, The Athenaeum of Philadelphia, 219 S. 6th St., Philadelphia PA 19106. (215)925-2688. Award Director: Nathaniel Burt. Nominated book by a Philadelphia resident. Deadline: Dec. 31.

‡AVON FLARE YOUNG ADULT NOVEL COMPETITION, Avon Books, 105 Madison Ave., New York NY 10016. Unpublished novel written by an author 13-18 years old. Deadline: Jan. 1-Aug. 31.

‡EMILY CLARK BALCH AWARD, The Virginia Quarterly Review. 1 West Range, Charlottesville VA 22903. (804)924-3124. Editor: Staige D. Blackford. Best short story/poetry accepted and published by the Virginia Quarterly Review during a calendar year. No deadline.

‡BALTIC AMERICAN FREEDOM LEAGUE ARTICLE AWARD, Box 29651, Los Angeles CA 90029. (818)765-2587. Chairman: Jaak Treiman. For magazine article dealing with some aspect of the Baltic States, past or present. Deadline: Aug. 15.

THE MARGARET BARTLE PLAYWRITING AWARD, (formerly The Community Children's Theatre of Kansas City Annual Playwriting Award), Community Children's Theatre of Kansas City, 8021 E. 129th Terrace, Grandview MO 64030. (816)761-5775. Award Director: E. Blanche Sellens. Unpublished play for elementary school audiences. Deadline: Jan. 22.

‡**THE ELIZABETH BARTLETT AWARD**, 2875 Cowley Way-1302, San Diego CA 92110. (619)276-6199. Contest/Award Director: Elizabeth Bartlett. For best unpublished 12-tone poem.

GEORGE LOUIS BEER PRIZE, Committee Chairman, American Historical Association, 400 A St. SE, Washington DC 20003. European international history since 1895 (scholarly work). Deadline: June 15.

BEST OF BLURBS CONTEST, Writer's Refinery, Box 47786, Phoenix AZ 85068-7786. (602)944-5268. Contest Director: Libbi Goodman. Estab. 1987. "To foster the joy of writing a concise statement of the plot of a novel, write back cover or jacket flap copy for a hypothetical novel." Deadline: Sept. 30. Write "Best of Blurbs/WM" on SASE for rules.

‡**BEST OF HOUSEWIFE-WRITER'S FORUM: THE CONTESTED WILL TO WRITE**, Housewife-Writer's Forum, Drawer 1518, Lafayette CA 94549. (415)932-1143. Contest Director: Deborah Haeseler. Deadline: Dec. 15. Unpublished prose and poetry in 15 categories. Charges $3 fee for subscribers; $4 for nonsubscribers for prose; $1.50 fee for subscribers and $2 for nonsubscribers for poetry.

ALBERT J. BEVERIDGE AWARD, Committee Chairman, American Historical Association, 400 A St. SE, Washington DC 20003. American history of U.S., Canada and Latin American (book). Deadline: June 15.

THE BEVERLY HILLS THEATRE GUILD-JULIE HARRIS PLAYWRIGHT AWARD COMPETITION, 2815 N. Beachwood Drive, Los Angeles CA 90068. (213)465-2703. Playwright Award Coordinator: Marcella Meharg. Original full-length plays, unpublished, unproduced, and not currently under option. Application required. Deadline: Nov. 1.

BITTERROOT MAGAZINE POETRY CONTEST, *Bitterroot*, Spring Glen NY 12483. Editor-in-Chief: Menke Katz. Include SASE. Sponsors William Kushner Annual Awards and Heershe Dovid-Badonneh Awards for unpublished poetry. Deadline: Dec. 31.

IRMA SIMONTON BLACK AWARD, Bank Street College of Education, 610 W. 112th St., New York NY 10025. (212)663-7200, ext. 540. Award Director: William H. Hooks. Previously published children's book, for excellence of both text and illustration. Deadline: Jan. 15.

BLACK WARRIOR REVIEW LITERARY AWARDS, *Black Warrior Review*, The University of Alabama, Box 2936, Tuscaloosa AL 35487. (205)348-4518. Contact: Editor. Unpublished poetry and fiction. No deadline.

HOWARD W. BLAKESLEE AWARDS, American Heart Association, 7320 Greenville Ave., Dallas TX 75231. (214)706-1340. Award Director: Howard L. Lewis. Previously published or broadcast reports on cardiovascular diseases. Deadline: Feb. 1.

BODY STORY CONTEST, *American Health* Magazine, 80 5th Ave., New York NY 10011. (212)242-2460. Contact: Allegra Holch. 2,000-word fiction or nonfiction story. Deadline: March 1.

BOSTON GLOBE-HORN BOOK AWARDS, *The Boston Globe*, Boston MA 02107. Children's Book Editor: Stephanie Loer. Poetry, nonfiction and illustrated book. Deadline: May 1.

BOSTON GLOBE LITERARY PRESS COMPETITION, The Boston Globe, Boston MA 02107. (617)929-2637. Contest Director: Richard Collins. Estab. 1987. Previously published books by small literary presses, submitted by publisher. Deadline: March 30.

BOWLING WRITING COMPETITION, American Bowling Congress, Public Relations, 5301 S. 76th St., Greendale WI 53129. Director: Dave DeLorenzo, Public Relations Manager. Feature, editorial and news. Deadline in December.

BRITTINGHAM PRIZE IN POETRY, University of Wisconsin Press, 114 N. Murray, Madison WI 53715. (608)262-6438. Contest Director: Ronald Wallace. Unpublished book-length manuscript of original poetry. Deadline: Oct. 1. Charges $10 fee.

‡**ARNOLD AND DOROTHY BURGER PLAYWRITING COMPETITION**, Euclid Little Theatre, Euclid Recreation Dept., 23131 Lake Shore Blvd., Euclid OH 44123. (216)731-9925. Contact: President. Unpublished full-length or interconnecting one-act play by an Ohio writer. Deadline: May 1-July 1.

ARLEIGH BURKE ESSAY CONTEST, U.S. Naval Institute, Preble Hall, U.S. Naval Academy, Annapolis MD 21402. (301)268-6110. Award Director: James A. Barber, Jr. Essay that advances professional, literary or scientific knowledge of the naval and maritime services. Deadline: Dec. 1.

BUSH ARTIST FELLOWSHIPS, The Bush Foundation, E-900 First Natl. Bank Bldg., St. Paul MN 55101. (612)227-0891. Contact: Sally F. Dixon. Award for Minnesota, South and North Dakota residents "to buy 6-18 months of time for the applicant to do his/her own work." Up to 15 fellowships annually. Deadline: Oct. 31.

‡BYLINE MAGAZINE Contests, Box 130596, Edmond OK 73013. (405)348-3325. Publisher: Marcia Preston. Unpublished short stories, poems and other categories. Awards on monthly and annual basis. Deadline: Dec. 1 (for annual award). Charges fee of $5 for short story; $2 for poems.

CALIFORNIA WRITERS' CLUB CONFERENCE CONTEST, 2214 Derby St., Berkeley CA 94705. (415)841-1217. Unpublished adult fiction, adult nonfiction, juvenile fiction or nonfiction, poetry and scripts. Deadline: varies in spring. Charges fee.

CANADIAN BOOKSELLERS ASSOCIATION AUTHOR OF THE YEAR AWARD, 301 Donlands Ave., Toronto, Ontario M4J 3R8 Canada. Contact: Board of Directors of the Association. Canadian author for body of work over many years. No applications may be made by authors.

‡CANADIAN FICTION MAGAZINE, Contributor's Prize. Box 946, Station F, Toronto Ontario M4Y 2N9 Canada. Contact: Editor-in-Chief. Best story of year in French or English; Canadian citizens only. Deadline: Sept. 15.

MELVILLE CANE AWARD, Poetry Society of America, 15 Gramercy Park S., New York NY 10003. (212)254-9268. Contact: Award Director. Published book of poems or prose work on a poet or poetry submitted by the publisher. Deadline: Dec. 31.

‡THE THOMAS H. CARTER MEMORIAL AWARD FOR LITERARY CRITICISM, Shenandoah, Box 722, Lexington VA 24450. (703)463-8765. Editor: James Boatwright. Unpublished quality essays and/or literary criticism.

‡RUSSELL L. CECIL ARTHRITIS WRITING AWARDS, Arthritis Foundation, 1314 Spring St. NW, Atlanta GA 30309. (404)872-7100. Contact: Public Relations Department. Medical and features (news stories, articles, and radio/TV scripts) published or broadcast during the previous calendar year. Deadline: Feb. 15.

‡CELEBRATION OF ONE-ACTS, West Coast Ensemble, Box 38728, Los Angeles CA 90038. Artistic Director: Les Hanson. Unpublished (in Southern, California) one-act plays. Deadline: Dec. 1. "Up to 3 submissions allowed for each playwright." Casts should be no more than 6 and plays no longer than 40 minutes.

‡PAULETTE CHANDLER AWARD, Council for Wisconsin Writers, Box 55322, Madison WI 53705. (608)233-0531. "For a Wisconsin poet or short story writer based on need and ability." Deadline: Jan. 15.

‡CHARLOTTE REPERTORY THEATRE NEW SCRIPT COMPETITION, Suite 100, 127 E. Trade St., Charlotte NC 28202. (704)375-4796. Artistic Director: Mark L. Woods. Full-length non-musical play. Deadline: Sept. 1 (odd numbered years).

CHILDREN'S SCIENCE BOOK AWARDS, New York Academy of Sciences, 2 E. 63rd St., New York NY 10021. (212)838-0230. Public Relations Director: Ann E. Collins. General or trade science books for children under 17 years. Deadline: Nov. 30.

‡THE CHRISTOPHER AWARD, The Christophers, 12 E. 48th St., New York NY 10017. (212)759-4050. Award Director: Peggy Flanagan. Outstanding books published during the calendar year that "affirm the highest values of the human spirit."

GERTRUDE B. CLAYTOR MEMORIAL AWARD, Poetry Society of America, 15 Gramercy Park S., New York NY 10003. (212)254-9628. Contact: Award Director. Poem in any form on the American scene or character. Members only. Deadline: Dec. 31.

COLLEGIATE POETRY CONTEST, *The Lyric,* 307 Dunton Dr. SW, Blacksburg VA 24060. Editor: Leslie Mellichamp. Unpublished poems (36 lines or less) by fulltime undergraduates in U.S. or Canadian colleges. Deadline: June 1.

COMMONWEALTH OF PENNSYLVANIA COUNCIL ON THE ARTS LITERATURE FELLOWSHIPS, 216 Finance Bldg., Harrisburg PA 17120. (717)787-6883. Award Director: Peter Carnahan. Fellowships for Pennsylvania writers of fiction and poetry. Deadline: Oct 1.

‡**CONNECTICUT WRITERS LEAGUE, INC., ANNUAL WRITING AWARDS**, Box 10536, West Hartford CT 06110. Contact: Editor, *The Connecticut Writer*. Unpublished short fiction and poetry. Deadline: July 31. Charges $3 fee.

THE BERNARD F. CONNERS PRIZE FOR POETRY, *The Paris Review*, 541 E. 72nd St., New York NY 10021. Poetry Editor: Editorial Office. Unpublished poetry over 300 lines. Deadline: April 1.

ALBERT B. COREY PRIZE IN CANADIAN-AMERICAN RELATIONS, Office of the Executive Director, American Historical Association, 400 A St. SE, Washington DC 20003. History, Canadian-U.S. relations or history of both countries (book). Deadline: Feb. 28.

COUNCIL FOR WISCONSIN WRITERS, INC. ANNUAL AWARDS COMPETITION, Box 55322, Madison WI 58705. (608)233-0531. Contact: Awards committee. Book-length fiction, short fiction, book-length and short nonfiction, poetry, play, juvenile books, children's picture books and outdoor writing by Wisconsin residents published preceding year. Deadline: Jan. 15.

CREATIVE ARTISTS GRANT, Michigan Council for the Arts, 1200 Sixth Ave., Detroit MI 18226. (313)256-3719. Individual Artist Coordinator: Craig Carver. Grants of up to $10,000 for Michigan professional creative writers. Deadline: late March.

CREATIVE ARTS CONTEST, Women's National Auxiliary Convention, Free Will Baptists, Box 1088, Nashville TN 37202. Contact: Lorene Miley. Unpublished articles, plays, poetry, programs and art from auxiliary members. Deadline: March 1.

CREATIVITY FELLOWSHIP, Northwood Institute Alden B. Dow Creativity Center, Midland MI 48640-2398. (517)832-4478. Award Director: Carol B. Coppage. Ten week summer residency for individuals in any field who wish to pursue a new and different creative idea that has the potential of impact in that field. Deadline: Dec. 31.

GUSTAV DAVIDSON MEMORIAL AWARD, Poetry Society of America, 15 Gramercy Park S., New York NY 10003. (212)254-9628. Contact: Award Director. Sonnet or sequence in traditional forms. Members only. Deadline: Dec. 31.

MARY CAROLYN DAVIES MEMORIAL AWARD, Poetry Society of America, 15 Gramercy Park S., New York NY 10003. (212)254-9628. Contact: Award Director. Unpublished poem suitable for setting to music. Members only. Deadline: December 31.

‡**DE LA TORRE BUENO PRIZE**, Dance Perspectives Foundation, 29 E. 9th St., New York NY 10003. (212)777-1594. Open to writers or their publishers who have published an original work (book) of dance scholarship within the year. Deadline: Dec. 31.

DEEP SOUTH WRITERS' CONTEST, Deep South Writer's Conference, Box 44691, University of Southern Louisiana, Lafayette LA 70504. (318)231-6908. Contact: Contest Clerk. Unpublished works of short fiction, nonfiction, novels, poetry, drama and French literature. Deadline: July 15. Charges $25 fee for novels, $5 for other submissions.

DELACORTE PRESS PRIZE FOR AN OUTSTANDING FIRST YOUNG ADULT NOVEL, Delacorte Press, 666 5th Ave., New York NY 10103. (212)765-6500. Contest Director: Bebe Willoughby. Previously unpublished contemporary young adult fiction. Deadline: Dec. 31.

‡**BILLEE MURRAY DENNY POETRY CONTEST**, Lincoln College. 300 Keokuk St., Lincoln IL 62656. (217)732-3155. Contest/Award Director: Valecia Crisafulli. Unpublished poetry. Deadline: May 31. Charges $2 fee.

MARIE-LOUISE D'ESTERNAUX POETRY SCHOLARSHIP CONTEST, The Brooklyn Poetry Circle, 61 Pierrepont St., Brooklyn NY 11201. (718)875-8736. Contest Chairman: Gabrielle Lederer. Poetry by students between 16 and 21 years of age. Deadline: April 15.

ALICE FAY DI CASTAGNOLA AWARD, Poetry Society of America, 15 Gramercy Park S., New York NY 10003. (212)254-9628. Contact: Award Director. Manuscript in progress: poetry, prose (on poetry) or verse-drama. Members only. Deadline: Dec. 31.

EMILY DICKINSON AWARD, Poetry Society of America, 15 Gramercy Park S., New York NY 10003. (212)254-9628. Contact: Award Director. Poem inspired by Emily Dickinson. Members only. Deadline: Dec. 31.

DISCOVERY/THE NATION, The Poetry Center of the 92nd Street YM-YWHA, 1395 Lexington Ave., New York NY 10128. (212)427-6000, ext. 176 or 208. Poetry (unpublished in book form). Deadline: February 17.

DOG WRITER'S ASSOCIATION OF AMERICA ANNUAL WRITING CONTEST, Box 301, Kewanee IL 61443. Contest Director: M. Akers-Hanson. Previously published writing about dogs—their rearing, training, care and all aspects of companionship. For material published from Oct. 1 1987, through Sept. 30, 1988. Deadline varies. Charges $10 fee.

DUBUQUE FINE ARTS PLAYERS, 569 S. Grandview Ave., Dubuque IA 52001. (319)582-5558. Contact: James E. Ryan. Produces 3 one acts, 1 full length, 1 experimental play/year. Obtains first production rights. Deadline: Jan. 31. Charges: $5 fee.

JOHN H. DUNNING PRIZE IN AMERICAN HISTORY, Committee Chairman, American Historical Association, 400 A St. SE, Washington DC 20003. Annual award for U.S. history monograph/book. Deadline: June 15.

EATON LITERARY ASSOCIATES LITERARY AWARDS PROGRAM, Box 49795, Sarasota FL 34230-6795. (813)355-4561. Editorial Director: Lana Bruce. Previously unpublished short stories and book-length manuscripts. Deadline: March 31 (short story); Aug. 31 (book length).

‡EDITORS' BOOK AWARD, Pushcart Press, Box 380, Wainscott NY 11975. (516)324-9300. Unpublished books. Deadline: Aug. 30. "All manuscripts must be nominated by an editor in a publishing house."

DAVID JAMES ELLIS MEMORIAL AWARD, Theatre Americana, Box 245, Altadena CA 91001-1235. Contact: Mrs. Leone Jones. Two- or three-act plays, no musicals or children's plays, with a performance time of about 1½-2 hours. Deadline: April 1.

THE RALPH WALDO EMERSON AWARD, Phi Beta Kappa (The United Chapters of Phi Beta Kappa), 1811 Q St. NW, Washington DC 20009. (202)265-3808. Contact: Administrator, Phi Beta Kappa Book Awards. Studies of the intellectual and cultural condition of man published in the U.S. during the 12-month period preceding the entry deadline, and submitted by the publisher. Deadline: April 30.

JOHN K. FAIRBANK PRIZE IN EAST ASIAN HISTORY, Committee Chairman, American Historical Association, 400 A St. SE, Washington DC 20003. Book on East Asian history. Deadline: June 15.

NORMA FARBER FIRST BOOK AWARD, Poetry Society of America, 15 Gramercy Park S., New York NY 10003. (212)254-9628. Contact: Award Director. Book of original poetry. Publishers only. Deadline: Dec. 31. Charges $5 entry fee for non-members.

‡VIRGINIA FAULKNER AWARD FOR EXCELLENCE IN WRITING, *Prarie Schooner*, 201 Andrews, University of Nebraska, Lincoln NE 68588-0334. (402)472-3191. Editor: Hilda Raz. Previously published works on *Prarie Schooner*.

‡FAW LITERARY AWARD, Friends of American Writers, 755 N. Merrill, Park Ridge IL 60068. (312)823-5433. Contact: Jane Lederer. Previously published books. Author must be a resident (or previously been a resident for approximately 15 years) of Arkansas, Illinois, Indiana, Iowa, Kansas, Michigan, Minnesota, Missouri, North Dakota, Nebraska, Ohio, South Dakota, or Wisconsin; or the locale of the book must be in the region above. Author shall not have published more than two books under his own and/or pen name. Deadline: Jan. 1-Dec. 15.

‡FELLOWSHIPS FOR TRANSLATORS/CREATIVE WRITERS, National Endowment for the Arts, Literature Program, 1100 Pennsylvania Ave. NW, Washington DC 20506. (202)682-5451. Award Director: Stephen H. Goodwin. Published creative writers and translators of exceptional talent. Deadline: Jan. 11.

‡FESTIVAL OF FIRSTS, City of Carmel/Sunset Center. Box 5066, Carmel CA 93921. (408)624-3996. Contest/Award Director: Richard Tyler. Unpublished plays. Deadline: Aug. 20. Charges $5 fee.

‡FESTIVAL OF NEW WORKS, Department of Theater, University of Cincinnati, Mail Location 003, Cincinnati OH 45221. (513)475-5471. Artistic Director: Michael Hankins. Unpublished full-length play and one-act play. Deadline Sept. 30

FICTION WRITERS CONTEST, *Mademoiselle Magazine*, 350 Madison Ave., New York NY 10017. Contest Director: Eileen Schnurr. Short stories by unpublished writers aged 18-30. Deadline: March 15.

‡FIRMAN HOUGHTON AWARD, New England Poetry Club, 2 Farrar, Cambridge MA 02138. Contact: Frances Minturn Howard. Unpublished lyric poem. Deadline: June 30. Charges $2 fee per poem; free to members.

FLORIDA INDIVIDUAL ARTIST FELLOWSHIPS, Florida Department of State, Bureau of Grants Services, Division of Cultural Affairs, The Capitol, Tallahassee FL 32399-0250. (904)487-2980. Director: Chris Doolin. Fellowship for Florida writers only. Deadline: mid-February.

FOLIO FICTION/POETRY AWARDS, Folio, Dept. of Literature, American University, Washington DC 20016. (202)885-2971. Fiction, poetry, short essays and interviews. Published twice a year. Winners will be published in the spring issue of *Folio*. Accepts manuscripts: Aug.-April.

CONSUELO FORD AWARD, Poetry Society of America, 15 Gramercy Park S., New York NY 10003. (212)254-9628. Contact: Award Director. Unpublished lyric. Members only. Deadline: Dec. 31.

FOSTER CITY ANNUAL WRITERS CONTEST, Foster City Committee for the Arts, 650 Shell Blvd., Foster City CA 94404. (415)341-8051. Chairman, Committee for the Arts: Ted Lance. Unpublished fiction, poetry, childrens' stories and humor. Reads manuscripts; April 1-Aug. 31.

GEORGE FREEDLEY MEMORIAL AWARD, Theatre Library Association, 111 Amsterdam Ave., New York NY 10023. (212)870-1670. Award Committee Chair: James Poteat, Television Information Office, 745 Fifth Ave., New York NY 10022. (212)759-6807. Published books related to performance in theatre. Deadline: Feb. 26.

DON FREEMAN MEMORIAL GRANT-IN-AID, Society of Children's Book Writers, Box 296 Mar Vista, Los Angeles CA 90066. To enable picture-book artists to further their understanding, training and/or work. Members only. Deadline: Feb. 15.

‡FRENCH-AMERICAN FOUNDATION TRANSLATION PRIZE, 41 E. 72nd St., New York NY 10021. (212)288-4400. Contact: Gail Richardson. Previously published French-to-English translation. "We contact publishers to submit entries in the competition." Deadline: April 22.

‡FS DRAMA AWARD, Feedback Theatrebooks. Box 5187, Bloomington IN 47407-5187. (812)334-0325. Contest/Award Director: Mollie Ann Meserve. Unpublished plays "to promote excellence in new American drama and to encourage American playwrights." Deadline: Oct. 31. Charges a $10 fee.

‡GALLAUDET JOURNALISM AWARD, Gallaudet University, Public Relations Office, 800 Florida Ave., N.E., Washington DC 20002. (202)651-5505. Contact: Barbara H. Dennis. Previously published "accurate, substantive, and insightful articles which provide the general public with a broad awareness and understanding of the achievements of deaf people, research in the field of deafness and the continuing documentation of deaf expression. Work of reporters and writers employed by U.S. wire services, newspapers or magazines of general circulation may be submitted for consideration. Newsletters or publication written specifically for the deaf community are *not* eligible for this award." Deadline: March 31.

‡JOHN GASSNER MEMORIAL PLAYWRITING AWARD, The New England Theatre Conference. 50 Exchange St., Waltham MA 02154. (617)893-3120. Unpublished one-act and full-length plays. Deadline: April 15. Charges $5 fee; free for members of New England Theatre Conference.

THE CHRISTIAN GAUSS AWARD, Phi Beta Kappa (The United Chapters of Phi Beta Kappa), 1811 Q St. NW, Washington DC 20009. (202)265-3808. Contact; Administrator, Phi Beta Kappa Book Awards. Works of literary criticism or scholarship published in the U.S. during the 12-month period preceding the entry deadline, and submitted by the publisher. Deadline: April 30.

‡GIRALT PUBLISHERS, Box 450 Times Square Station, New York NY 10018. (201)861-1941. Contact: Lourdes Gil. Unpublished poetry, short-fiction and essays. Deadline varies. Charges $2 per poem; $6 per essay and short story.

‡GOLDEN HEART/GOLDEN MEDALLION, Romance Writers of America, Suite 208, 5206 FM 1960 West, Houston TX 77069. (713)440-6885. Contact office for name of award director. Previously published (for Medallion) and unpublished (for Heart) book/manuscript for the year. Categories are all in romance fiction: traditional romance, short and long contemporary romance, single title release, regency, historical and young adult. Charges $15 fee. Entrant must be a member of Romance Writers of America. Deadline: Nov. 30.

GOLDEN KITE AWARDS, Society of Children's Book Writers (SCBW), Box 296 Mar Vista Station, Los Angeles CA 90066. (818)347-2849. Coordinator: Sue Alexander. Calendar year published children's fiction, nonfiction and picture illustration books by a SCBW member. Deadline: Dec. 15.

‡GOLF WRITER'S CONTEST, Golf Course Superintendents Association of America, 1617 St. Andrews Dr., Lawrence KS 66046. Media Relations Manager: Bob Still. Previously published work pertaining to golf superintendents. Must be member of GWAA. Deadline: Jan. 10.

‡THE JEANNE CHARPIOT GOODHEART PRIZE FOR FICTION, *Shenandoah*, Box 722, Lexington VA 24450. (703)463-8765. Editor: James Boatwright. Unpublished fiction.

GOODMAN AWARD, Thorntree Press, 547 Hawthorn Lane, Winnetka IL 60093. (312)446-8099. Contact: Eloise Bradley. 10 pages of poetry. Deadline: Jan. 1-Feb. 14. Charges $4 fee.

‡GOVERNOR GENERAL'S LITERARY AWARDS, Canada Council, Box 1047, Ottawa, Ontario K1P 5V8 Canada. (613)237-3400. Award Director: Gwen Hoover. All Canadian books by Canadian authors published during the previous calendar year are considered. No formal application required.

‡GOVERNOR GENERAL'S LITERARY AWARD: CHILDREN'S LITERATURE, Canada Council, Box 1047, Ottawa, Ontario K1P 5V8 Canada. (613)237-3400. Contact: Gwen Hoover. Awards to honor published Canadian writers and illustrators of children's books.

‡GOVERNOR GENERAL'S LITERARY AWARD: TRANSLATION, Canada Council, Box 1047, Ottawa, Ontario K1P 5V8 Canada. (613)237-3400. Contact: Gwen Hoover. The best translations of Canadian works: one for a translation from English into French and one for a translation from French into English. *The books must be written and translated by Canadians.*

‡THE GREAT AMERICAN TENNIS WRITING AWARDS, Tennis Week/Smith Corona, 6 E. 39th St., New York NY 10016. (212)696-4884. Publisher: Eugune L. Scott. Category 1: unpublished manuscript by an aspiring journalist with no previous national byline. Category 2: unpublished manuscript by a non-tennis journalist. Category 3: unpublished manuscript by a tennis journalist. Categories 4-6: published articles and one award to a book. Deadline: Nov. 18.

GUIDEPOSTS MAGAZINE YOUTH WRITING CONTEST, Guideposts Associates, Inc., 747 3rd Ave., New York NY 10017. Senior Editor: James McDermott. Memorable true experience of 1,200 words, preferably spiritual in nature. Unpublished first person story by high school juniors or seniors or students in equivalent grades overseas. Deadline: Nov. 28.

DRUE HEINZ LITERATURE PRIZE, University of Pittsburgh Press, 127 N. Bellefield Ave., Pittsburgh PA 15260. (412)624-4110. Collection of short fiction. Award open to writers who have published a book-length collection of fiction or a minimum of three short stories or novellas in commercial magazines or literary journals of national distribution. Deadline: July-August.

ERNEST HEMINGWAY FOUNDATION AWARD, P.E.N. American Center, 568 Broadway, New York NY 10012. First-published novel or short story collection by American author. Deadline: Dec. 31.

CECIL HEMLEY MEMORIAL AWARD, Poetry Society of America, 15 Gramercy Park S., New York NY 10003. (212)254-9628. Contact: Award Director. Unpublished lyric poem on a philosophical theme. Members only. Deadline: Dec. 31.

‡HIGHLIGHTS FOR CHILDREN FICTION CONTEST, *Highlights for Children*, 803 Church St., Honesdale PA 18431. Editor: Kent L. Brown, Jr. Previously unpublished stories for prereaders and beginning readers to age 8, 600 words maximum; and stories for advanced readers, ages 9-12, 900 words maximum. Deadline: Jan. 1-Mar. 31.

SIDNEY HILLMAN PRIZE AWARD, Sidney Hillman Foundation, Inc., 15 Union Square, New York NY 10003. (212)242-0700. Executive Director: Joyce D. Miller. Social/economic themes related to ideals of Sidney Hillman (daily or periodical journalism, nonfiction, radio and TV). Deadline: Jan. 15.

‡**HONOLULU MAGAZINE FICTION CONTEST**, *Honolulu Magazine*, 36 Merchant St., Honolulu HI 96813. Contact: Pat Pitzer. Stories under 25 typewritten pages with a Hawaiian theme, setting and/or characters. Deadline: Nov. 30.

HOOVER ANNUAL JOURNALISM AWARDS, Herbert Hoover Presidential Library Assn., Box 696, West Branch IA 52358. Contact: Tom Walsh. Previously published newspaper and magazine journalism that contributes to public awareness and appreciation of the lives of Herbert and Lou Henry Hoover or is based on research at the Herbert Hoover Presidential Library in West Branch, Iowa. Deadline: Jan. 31.

DARRELL BOB HOUSTON PRIZE, 1931 Second Ave., Seattle WA 98101. (206)441-6239. Journalism published within the previous year in Washington State which shows "some soul, some color, some grace, robustness, mirth and generosity," to honor the memory of writer Darrell Bob Houston. Deadline: contact for exact date, usually in May.

THE ROY W. HOWARD AWARDS, The Scripps Howard Foundation, 1100 Central Trust Tower, Cincinnati OH 45202. (513)977-3036. Public service reporting for newspapers.

IDAHO WRITER IN RESIDENCE, Idaho Commission on the Arts, 304 W. State, Boise ID 83720. (208)334-2119. Program Coordinator: Jim Owen. Previously published works by Idaho writers; award offered every two years. Deadline: August 1989.

ILLINOIS STATE UNIVERSITY FINE ARTS PLAYWRITING AWARD, Illinois State University, Theatre Department, Normal IL 61761. (309)438-8783. Director: Dr. John W. Kirk. Previously unproduced full-length plays. No musicals. Deadline: Oct. 15.

‡**INDEPENDENT SCHOLARS, LOWELL, MARRARO, SHAUGHNESSY AND MILDENBERGER AWARDS**, MLA, 10 Astor Place, New York NY 10003. (212)614-6314. Contact: Adrienne M. Ward. Mildenberger Prize: research publication on teaching foreign languages and literatures. Shaughnessy Prize: research publication on teaching English. Lowell Prize: previously published literary, linguistic study or critical edition or biography. Marraro Prize: scholarly book or essay on Italian literature. Independent Scholars: published research in modern languages and literature. Lowell and Marraro awards only open to MLA members in good standing.

INTERNATIONAL LITERARY CONTEST, Writer's Refinery/WM, Box 47786, Phoenix AZ 85068-7786. (602)944-5268. Contest Director: Libbi Goodman. Unpublished fiction, poetry and essays. Deadline: Nov. 31.

INTERNATIONAL READING ASSOCIATION PRINT MEDIA AWARD, International Reading Association, Box 8139, 800 Barksdale Rd., Newark DE 19714-8139. (302)731-1600. Contact: Patricia Du Bois. Reports by professional journalists from newspapers, magazines and wire services on reading programs. Deadline: Jan. 15.

JOSEPH HENRY JACKSON/JAMES D. PHELAN LITERARY AWARDS, The San Francisco Foundation, Suite 910, 685 Market St., San Francisco CA 94105. (415)543-0223. Awards Coordinator: Adrienne Krug. Jackson Award: unpublished, work-in-progress—fiction (novel or short story), nonfiction, or poetry by author, age 20-35, with 3-year consecutive residency in N. California or Nevada prior to submissions. Phelan Award: unpublished, work-in-progress fiction, nonfiction, short story, poetry or drama by California-born author age 20-35. Deadline: Jan. 15.

JAMESTOWN PRIZE, Institute of Early American History and Culture, Box 220, Williamsburg VA 23187. (804)229-5118. Contact: Editor of Publications. Book-length scholarly ms on early American history or culture.

ANSON JONES AWARD, % Texas Medical Association, 1801 N. Lamar Blvd., Austin TX 78701. (512)477-6704. Health (Texas newspaper, magazine—trade, commercial, association, chamber, or company—radio and TV). Deadline: Jan. 15.

JUNIOR AND SENIOR AWARDS, International Society of Dramatists, Box 1310, Miami FL 33153. Award Director: A. Delaplaine. Previously unpublished scripts (any media or length) written by high school students (Junior Award) and college students (Senior Awards). Deadline: May 1.

‡**THE JUNIPER PRIZE**, University of Massachusetts Press, % Mail Office, University of Massachusetts, Amherst MA 01003. (413)545-2217. First book of poetry. Deadline: Oct. 1. Charges $10 fee.

THE JANET HEIDINGER KAFKA PRIZE, English Department/Writers Workshop, 127 Lattimore Hall, University of Rochester, Rochester NY 14627. (716)275-2347. Chairman: Anne Ludlow. Book-length fiction (novel, short story or experimental writing) by U.S. woman citizen submitted by publishers.

KANSAS QUARTERLY/KANSAS ARTS COMMISSION AWARDS, SEATON AWARDS, Department of English, Kansas State University, Manhattan KS 66506. (913)532-6716. Editor: Harold Schneideretal. *KQ/KAC* awards for poetry and fiction published in *KQ*; Seaton awards for Kansas writers whose poetry, fiction and prose appear in *KQ*.

ROBERT F. KENNEDY BOOK AWARD, 1031 31st St. NW, Washington DC 20007. (202)333-1880. Executive Director: Caroline Croft. Book which reflects "concern for the poor and the powerless, justice, the conviction that society must assure all young people a fair chance and faith that a free democracy can act to remedy disparities of power and opportunity." Deadline: Jan. 8. Charges $20 entry fee.

‡ROBERT F. KENNEDY JOURNALISM AWARD, 1031 31st St. NW, Washington DC 20007. (202)333-1880. Executive Director: Sue Vogelsinger. Previously published entries on problems of the disadvantaged. Deadline: Jan. 31.

‡AGA KHAN PRIZE FOR FICTION, *The Paris Review*, 541 East 72nd St., New York NY 10021. Director: George Plimpton. Unpublished fiction. Deadline: May 1-June 1.

‡MARC A. KLEIN PLAYWRITING AWARD FOR STUDENTS, Department of Theatre, Case Western Reserve University, 2070 Adelbert Rd., Cleveland OH 44106. (216)368-2858. Unpublished, professionally unproduced full-length plays, evening of related short plays, or full-length musical by students in American college or university. Deadline: April 1.

RUTH LAKE MEMORIAL AWARD, Poetry Society of America, 15 Gramercy Park S., New York NY 10003. (212)254-9628. Contact: Award Director. Unpublished poem of retrospection. Deadline: Dec. 31. Charges $5 fee.

LAMONT POETRY SELECTION, Academy of American Poets, 177 E. 87th St., New York NY 10128. (212)427-5665. Contest/Award Director: Nancy Schoenberger. Second book of unpublished poems by an American citizen, submitted by publisher in manuscript form.

THE HAROLD MORTON LANDON TRANSLATION PRIZE, The Academy of American Poets, 177 E. 87th St., New York NY 10128. (212)427-5665. Award Director: Nancy Schoenberger. Previously published translation of poetry from any language into English by an American translator. Deadline: end of calendar year.

‡THE PETER I.B. LAVAN YOUNGER POETS AWARD, The Academy of American Poets, 177 East 87th St., New York NY 10128. (212)427-5665. American poets under 40 who have published at least one full-length collection of poetry. Recipients are selected by the Academy's Chancellors. No applications.

D.H. LAWRENCE FELLOWSHIP, University of New Mexico/English Department, 217 Humanities Bldg., University of New Mexico, Albuquerque NM 87131. (505)277-6347. Contest Director: Louis Owens. Fellowship for writers of fiction, poetry and/or drama. Deadline: Jan. 31.

‡LAWRENCE FOUNDATION AWARD, *Prarie Schooner*, 201 Andrews, University of Nebraska, Lincoln NE 68588-0334. (402)472-3191. Editor: Hilda Raz. Short story published in *Prarie Schooner*.

STEPHEN LEACOCK MEMORIAL AWARD FOR HUMOUR, Stephen Leacock Associates, Box 854, Orillia Ontario L3V 6K8 Canada. (705)325-6546. Contest Director: Jean Dickson. Previously published book of humor by a Canadian author. Include 10 books each entry. Deadline: Dec. 31. Charges $25 fee.

ELIAS LIEBERMAN STUDENT POETRY AWARD, Poetry Society of America, 15 Gramercy Park S., New York NY 10003. (212)254-9628. Contact: Award Director. Unpublished poem by student (grades 9-12). Charges: $5 fee. Deadline: Dec. 31.

LIGHT AND LIFE WRITING CONTEST, *Light and Life* Magazine, 901 College Ave., Winona Lake IN 46590. (219)267-7656. Editor: Bob Haslam. Unpublished personal experience stories. New description each year. Deadline: April 15.

THE RUTH LILLY POETRY PRIZE, The Modern Poetry Association and The American Council for the Arts, 60 W. Walton St., Chicago IL 60610. (312)413-2210. Contact: Joseph Parisi. Annual prize to poet "whose accomplishments in the field of poetry warrant extraordinary recognition." No applicants or nominations are accepted. Deadline: varies.

LINCOLN MEMORIAL ONE-ACT PLAYWRITING CONTEST, International Society of Dramatists, Box 1310, Miami FL 33153. (305)674-1831. Award Director: A. Delaplaine. Unpublished one-act plays, any type, any style. Deadline: Jan. 15.

LINDEN LANE MAGAZINE ENGLISH-LANGUAGE POETRY CONTEST, Linden Lane Magazine & Press, Inc., Box 2384, Princeton NJ 08543-2384. (609)924-1413. Editor: Belkis Cuza Male. Unpublished Spanish and English poetry, short story and essay prizes. Deadline: May 15. Charges $10 fee.

JOSEPH W. LIPPINCOTT AWARD, Donated by Joseph W. Lippincott, Jr., Administered by American Library Association, 50 E. Huron, Chicago IL 60611. (312)944-6780. For distinguished service to the profession of librarianship, including notable published professional writing.

LOCKERT LIBRARY OF POETRY IN TRANSLATION, Princeton University Press, 41 William St., Princeton NJ 08540. (609)452-4900. Poetry Editor: Robert E. Brown. Book-length poetry translation of a single poet. Deadlines: February and August.

LOFT-MCKNIGHT WRITERS AWARD, The Loft, 2301 E. Franklin Ave., Minneapolis MN 55406. (612)341-0431. Executive Director: Susan Broadhead. Eight awards and two awards of distinction for Minnesota writers of poetry and creative prose. Deadline: October.

LOFT-MENTOR SERIES, The Loft, 2301 Franklin Ave., Minneapolis MN 55406. (612)341-0431. Executive Director: Susan Broadhead. Opportunity to work with five nationally known writers and cash award available to eight winning poets and fiction writers. "Must live close enough to Minneapolis to participate fully in the series." Deadline: May.

LOUISIANA LITERATURE PRIZE FOR POETRY, Box 792, Southeastern Louisiana University, Hammond LA 70402. Contest Director: Dr. Tim Gautreaux. Unpublished poetry. Deadline: Feb. 15.

‡JOHN H. MCGINNIS MEMORIAL AWARD, *Southwest Review*, 6410 Airline Rd., Southern Methodist University, Dallas TX 75275. (214)373-7440. Short story or essay that appeared in the *Southwest Review* during the previous two years.

MCLEMORE PRIZE, Mississippi Historical Society. Box 571, Jackson MS 39205. (601)359-1424. Contact: Secretary/Treasurer. Scholarly book on a topic in Mississippi history/biography published in the year of competition. Deadline: Jan. 1.

HOWARD R. MARRARO PRIZE IN ITALIAN HISTORY, Office of the Executive Director, American Historical Association, 400 A St. SE, Washington DC 20003. Work on any epoch of Italian history, Italian cultural history or Italian-American relations. Deadline: June 15.

THE LENORE MARSHALL/NATION PRIZE FOR POETRY, The New Hope Foundation and *The Nation* Magazine, 72 5th Ave., New York NY 10011. (212)242-8400. Administrator: Emily Sack. Book of poems published in the United States during the previous year, and nominated by the publisher. Deadline: June 1.

JOHN MASEFIELD MEMORIAL AWARD, Poetry Society of America, 15 Gramercy Park S., New York NY 10003. (212)254-9628. Contact: Award Director. Unpublished narrative poem in English. No translations. Deadline: Dec. 31. Charges $5 fee.

‡HAROLD MASON REFERENCE BOOK AWARD, Association of Jewish Libraries, Robert Singerman, 18 Library East, University of Florida Libraries, Gainesville FL 32611. (904)392-0308. Outstanding reference book published during the previous year in the field of Jewish studies.

THE MAYFLOWER SOCIETY CUP COMPETITION, North Carolina Literary and Historical Association, 109 E. Jones St., Raleigh NC 27611. (919)733-7305. Contact: Award Director. Previously published nonfiction by a North Carolina resident. Deadline: July 15.

LUCILLE MEDWICK MEMORIAL AWARD, Poetry Society of America, 15 Gramercy Park S., New York NY 10003. (212)254-9628. Contact: Award Director. Original poem on a humanitarian theme. Members only. Deadline: Dec. 31.

THE EDWARD J. MEEMAN AWARDS, The Scripps Howard Foundation, 1100 Central Trust Tower, Cincinnati OH 45202. (513)977-3036. Conservation reporting for newspapers.

MELCHER BOOK AWARD, Unitarian Universalist Association, 25 Beacon St., Boston MA 02108. Staff Liaison: Rev. Mark W. Harris. Previously published book on religious liberalism. Deadline: Dec. 31.

MENCKEN AWARDS, Free Press Association, Box 15548, Columbus OH 43215. (614)236-1908. FPA Executive Director: Michael Grossberg. Defense of human rights and individual liberties (news story or investigative report, feature story, editorial or op-ed column, editorial cartoon; and book published or broadcast during previous year. Entry *must* have been published. Deadline: April 1. Charges $1 fee.

KENNETH W. MILDENBERGER PRIZE, Modern Language Association, 10 Astor Place, New York NY 10003. Contact: Adrienne M. Ward, Research Programs. Outstanding research publication in the field of teaching foreign languages and literatures. Deadline: May 1.

MILL MOUNTAIN THEATRE NEW PLAY COMPETITION, Mill Mountain Theatre, Center in the Square, One Market Sq., Roanoke VA 24011. (703)342-5730. Literary Manager: Jo Weinstein. Previously unpublished and unproduced plays for up to 10 cast members. "We are also constantly seeking one-act plays for our Lunch Time Theatre Program Centerpieces. Playing time should be between 25 and 35 minutes." Deadline: Jan. 1.

‡MISSISSIPPI VALLEY POETRY CONTEST, Box 3021, Davenport IA 52808. (319)388-0081. Director: John F. Owens. Unpublished poetry: adult general, junior division, experimental, Mississippi Valley, senior citizen, religious, rhyming, humor, haiku. Deadline: Aug. 31. Charges $1/poem; up to 5 poems may be submitted.

FELIX MORLEY MEMORIAL PRIZES, Institute for Humane Studies, George Mason University, 4400 University Dr., Fairfax VA 22030. (703)323-1055. Contact: John Blundell. Awards for "young writers dedicated to individual liberty." Deadline: June 15.

‡MORSE POETRY PRIZE, Northeastern University English Deptment, 406 Holmes Hall, Boston MA 02115. (617)437-2512. Contact: Guy Rorella. Previously published poetry in book form. Charges $1.50/entry.

FRANK LUTHER MOTT-KAPPA TAU ALPHA RESEARCH AWARD IN JOURNALISM, 107 Sondra Ave., Columbia MO 65202. (314)443-3521. Executive Director, Central Office: William H. Taft. Research in journalism (book). Deadline: Jan. 15.

MS PUBLIC EDUCATION AWARDS CONTEST, National Multiple Sclerosis Society, 205 E. 42nd St., New York NY 10017. Contact: Public Affairs Department. Reporting on facts and consequences of multiple sclerosis (newspaper, magazine, radio or TV). Deadline: Oct. 31.

MULTICULTURAL PLAYWRIGHTS FESTIVAL, (formerly American Minority Playwright's Festival), The Group Theatre Company, 3940 Brooklyn Ave. NE, Seattle WA 98105. (206)545-4969. Director: Tim Bond. One-act and full-length plays by Black, Native American, Hispanic and Asian playwrights. Honorarium, airfare and housing for 2 playwrights for workshop productions. 6 playwrights receive readings. Deadline: Oct. 15.

NATIONAL AWARDS PROGRAM, Freedoms Foundation at Valley Forge, Box 706, Valley Forge PA 19087. (215)933-8825. Award Director: E. Katherine Wood. Nominated, previously published submissions focusing on the United States' social, political and economic system and suggesting solutions to basic problems, that contribute to responsible citizenship, and strengthen an understanding of the fundamentals of a free society. Deadline: May 1.

‡NATIONAL BOOK AWARDS, Studio 1002D, 155 Bank St., New York NY 10014. (212)206-0024. Executive Director: Barbara Prete. Fiction and general nonfiction books by American authors. "Publishers must enter the books." Deadline: varies. Charges $100 fee.

NATIONAL JEWISH BOOK AWARD—CHILDREN'S LITERATURE, Shapoldy Family Award, Jewish Book Council, 15 E. 26th St., New York NY 10010. (212)532-4949. Director: Paula G. Gottlieb. Children's book on Jewish theme. Deadline: Nov. 25.

NATIONAL JEWISH BOOK AWARD—FICTION, William and Janice Epstein Award, 15 E. 26th St., New York NY 10010. (212)532-4949. Director: Paula G. Gottlieb. Jewish fiction (novel or short story collection). Deadline: Nov. 25.

NATIONAL JEWISH BOOK AWARD—HOLOCAUST, Leon Jolson Award, Jewish Book Council, 15 E. 26th St., New York NY 10010. (212)532-4949. Contact: Paula G. Gottlieb. Nonfiction book concerning the Holocaust. Deadline: Nov. 25.

NATIONAL JEWISH BOOK AWARD—ILLUSTRATED CHILDREN'S BOOK, Marcia and Louis Posner Award, Jewish Book Council, 15 E. 26th St., New York NY 10010. (212)532-4949. Director: Paula G. Gottlieb. Author and illustrator of a children's book on a Jewish theme. Deadline: Nov. 25.

NATIONAL JEWISH BOOK AWARD—ISRAEL, Morris J. Kaplun Memorial Award, Jewish Book Council, 15 E. 26th St., New York NY 10010. (212)532-4949. Director: Paula G. Gottlieb. Nonfiction work about the State of Israel. Deadline: Nov. 25.

NATIONAL JEWISH BOOK AWARD—JEWISH HISTORY, Gerrard and Ella Berman Award, Jewish Book Council, 15 E. 26th St., New York NY 10010. (212)532-4949. Director: Paula G. Gottlieb. Book of Jewish history. Deadline: Nov. 25.

NATIONAL JEWISH BOOK AWARD—JEWISH THOUGHT, Jewish Book Council, 15 E. 26th St., New York NY 10010. (212)532-4949. Director: Paula G. Gottlieb. Book dealing with some aspect of Jewish thought, past or present. Deadline: Nov. 25.

NATIONAL JEWISH BOOK AWARD—SCHOLARSHIP, Sarah H. Kushner Memorial Award, Jewish Book Council, 15 E. 26th St., New York NY 10010. (212)532-4949. Director: Paula G. Gottlieb. Book which makes an original contribution to Jewish learning.

NATIONAL JEWISH BOOK AWARD—VISUAL ARTS, Leon L. G. Idesgane Award, Jewish Book Council, 15 E. 26th St., New York NY 10010. (212)532-4949. Director: Paula G. Gottlieb. Book about Jewish art. Deadline: Nov. 25.

NATIONAL ONE-ACT PLAY CONTEST, Actors Theatre of Louisville, 316 W. Main St., Louisville KY 40202. (502)584-1265. Literary Manager: Michael Bigelow Dixon. Previously unproduced (professionally) one-act plays (60 pages or less). "Entries must *not* have had an Equity or Equity-waiver production." Deadline: April 15.

NATIONAL PLAY AWARD, Box 71011, Los Angeles CA 90071. (213)629-3762. Assistant Literary Manager: David Parrish. Unpublished, nonprofessionally produced plays. Deadline: Oct. 1.

NATIONAL PSYCHOLOGY AWARDS FOR EXCELLENCE IN THE MEDIA, American Psychological Association/American Psychological Foundation, 1200 17th St. NW, Washington DC 20036. (202)955-7710. Contact: Public Affairs Office. Newspaper reporting, magazine articles, books/monographs, radio, television/film (news/documentary) and television (entertainment/drama) about psychology. Deadline: April 15.

‡NATIONAL SOCIETY OF NEWSPAPER COLUMNISTS, Box 8318, Newark CA 94537. Director: Pat Kite, Public Relations. Previously published between January and December. Humor and general interest columns and "About Town" columns in small and large weekly and/or daily newspapers. Deadline: varies, between Jan. 31 and March 1. Charges $10 fee.

THE NEBRASKA REVIEW AWARDS IN FICTION AND POETRY, *The Nebraska Review*, ASH 215, University of Nebraska-Omaha, Omaha NE 68182-0324. (402)554-2771. Contact: Arthur Homer (poetry) and Richard Duggin (fiction). Previously unpublished fiction and a poem or group of poems. Deadline: Nov. 30.

‡NEUSTADT INTERNATIONAL PRIZE FOR LITERATURE, 110 Monnet Hall, Normán OK 73019. (405)325-4531. Director: Dr. Ivar Ivask. Previously published fiction, poetry and drama. Nominations are made only by members of the jury which changes every two years.

ALLEN NEVINS PRIZE, Professor Kenneth T. Jackson, Secretary-Treasurer, Society of American Historians, 610 Fayerweather Hall, Columbia University, New York NY 10027. American history (nominated doctoral dissertations on arts, literature, science and American biographies). Deadline: Nov. 14.

‡NEW DAY POETRY/SHORT STORY CONTEST, New Day Publications, Route 4, Box 10, Eupora MS 39744. (601)258-2935. Director: Brenda Davis. Award offered 10 times per year; contest for poets and authors. Deadline: various. Charges $3 per poem, $5 per short story.

NEW LETTERS LITERARY AWARDS, University of Missouri-Kansas City, Kansas City MO 64110. Unpublished fiction, poetry and essays. Deadline: May 15. Charges $10 fee.

NEW PLAY FESTIVAL, Colony/Studio Theatre, 1944 Riverside Dr., Los Angeles CA 90039. Literary Manager: John Banach. Unpublished, unproduced full-length play.

NEW PLAYWRIGHTS COMPETITION AND FESTIVAL,The Ann White Theatre, 5266 Gate Lake Road, Ft. Lauderdale FL 33319. (305)722-4371. Director: Ann White. Unpublished full-length play scripts. Deadline varies.

‡NEW WORLD THEATER NEW PLAY COMPETITION, New World Theater, Suite 212, 7600 Red Rd., South Miami FL 33143. Unpublished plays. Special consideration to scripts with Florida locations and to scripts with interracial or inter-ethnic themes. Deadline: May 1.

NEW WRITERS AWARDS, Great Lakes Colleges Association, c/o English Department, Albion College, Albion MI 49224. (517)629-5511. Director: James W. Cook. Published poetry or fiction (first book) 4 copies submitted by publisher to arrive no later than Feb. 28.

NEW YORK STATE HISTORICAL ASSOCIATION MANUSCRIPT AWARD, Box 800, Cooperstown NY 13326. (607)547-2508. Director of Publications: Dr. Wendell Tripp. Unpublished book-length monograph on New York State history. Deadline: Feb. 20.

NEWCOMEN AWARDS IN BUSINESS HISTORY, % *Business History Review*, Harvard Business School, Teele 304, Soldiers Field Rd., Boston MA 02163. (617)495-6154. Editor: Richard S. Tedlow. Business history article published in the *Business History Review*.

‡NHS BOOK PRIZE, National Historical Society, 2245 Kohn Rd., Box 8200, Harrisburg PA 17105. (717)657-9555. President: William C. Davis. *NHS Book Prize* first book published by author. Deadline: July 31.

NIMROD, ARTS AND HUMANITIES COUNCIL OF TULSA PRIZES,2210 South Main, Tulsa OK 74114. (918)584-3333. Director: Francine Ringold. Unpublished fiction (Katherine Anne Porter prize) and poetry (Pablo Neruda Prize). Deadline: April 1.

NMMA DIRECTORS AWARD, National Marine Manufacturers Association, 353 Lexington Ave., New York NY 10016. (212)684-6622. Boating and allied water sports. Deadline: Nov. 30.

‡THE FLANNERY O'CONNOR AWARD FOR SHORT FICTION, The University of Georgia Press, Terrell Hall, Athens GA 30602. (404)542-2830. Director: Malcolm L. Call. Submission period: June-July 31. Charges $10 fee.

‡SCOTT O'DELL AWARD FOR HISTORICAL FICTION, 1100 E. 57th St., Chicago IL 60637. (312)702-8293. Director: Zena Sutherland. Previously published historical fiction book for children set in the Americas. Entries must have appeared in print between Jan. 1 and Dec. 31 of previous year. Deadline: Dec. 31.

OHIOANA BOOK AWARD, Ohioana Library Association, Room 1105, Ohio Departments Bldg., 65 S. Front St., Columbus OH 43215. (614)466-3831. Award Director: Linda Hengst. Books published within the past 12 months by Ohioans or about Ohio and Ohioans. Submit two copies of book on publication.

OKTOBERFEST SHORT FICTION COMPETITION, Druid Press, 2724 Shades Crest Rd., Birmingham AL 35216. (205)967-6580. Contact: Ann George. Ten previously unpublished short stories. Deadline: Oct. 31. Charges $3 fee.

THE C.F. ORVIS WRITING CONTEST, The Orvis Company, Inc., Manchester VT 05254. (802)362-3622. Contest/Award Director: Tom Rosenbauer. Outdoor writing about upland bird hunting and fly fishing (magazine and newspaper). Deadline: Feb. 1.

FRANCIS PARKMAN PRIZE, Society of American Historians, 610 Fayerweather Hall, Columbia University, New York NY 10027. Contact: Professor Kenneth T. Jackson. Colonial or national U.S. history book. Deadline: Jan. 15.

THE ALICIA PATTERSON FOUNDATION FELLOWSHIP PROGRAM FOR JOURNALISTS, The Alicia Patterson Foundation, Suite 320, 655 15th St. NW, Washington DC 20005. (301)951-8512. Contest/Award Director: Margaret Engel. One-year grants awarded to working print journalists with five years of professional experience to pursue independent projects of significant interest.

PEN/JERARD FUND, PEN American Center, 568 Broadway, New York NY 10012. (212)334-1660. Contact: John Morrone. Grant for American woman writer of nonfiction for a booklength work in progress. Deadline: Feb. 15.

ARE YOU SERIOUS?

About learning to write better? Getting published? Getting paid for what you write?

If you're dedicated to your writing, **Writer's Digest School** can put you on the fast track to writing success.

Study With A Professional

When you enroll in a **Writer's Digest School** course, you get more than writing textbooks and assignments. You get a one-on-one relationship with a professional writer who is currently writing *and selling* the kind of material you're interested in. Your training as a writer is built around this personal guidance from an experienced pro who knows what it takes to succeed in the competitive literary marketplace.

Four Courses Available

Writer's Digest School offers four courses: Writing to Sell Nonfiction (Articles), Writing to Sell Fiction (Short Stories), Elements of Effective Writing, and a Novel-Writing Workshop. Each course is described in more detail on the reverse side.

We've Been Teaching Creative People Since 1920

Writer's Digest School was founded over 60 years ago by the same people who publish **Writer's Digest,** the world's leading magazine for writers, and **Writer's Market,** the indispensable annual reference directory for writers. When you enroll in a **Writer's Digest School** course, you get the quality and expertise that are the hallmarks of the **Writer's Digest** name.

If you're serious about your writing, you owe it to yourself to check out **Writer's Digest School.** Mail the coupon below today for *free* information!

- -

Yes, I'm Serious!

I want to learn to write and sell from the professionals at **Writer's Digest School.** Send me free information about the course I've checked below:

☐ Writing to Sell Nonfiction (Articles) ☐ Novel-Writing Workshop
☐ Writing to Sell Fiction (Short Stories) ☐ Elements of Effective Writing

NAME

ADDRESS

CITY   STATE   ZIP

(   )
  Area Code   Phone Number

Mail this card today! No postage needed   WM09

Writer's Digest School has been teaching people like you to write for more than 60 years.

Writer's Digest School

1507 Dana Avenue
Cincinnati, Ohio 45207

Four **Writer's Digest School** courses to help you write better and sell more:

- **Writing to Sell Nonfiction.** Master the fundamentals of writing/selling nonfiction articles: finding article ideas, conducting interviews, writing effective query letters and attention-getting leads, targeting your articles to the right publication, and other important elements of a salable article. Course includes writing assignments and one complete article manuscript (and its revision). Your instructor will critique each assignment and help you adapt your article to a particular magazine.

- **Writing to Sell Fiction.** Learn the basics of writing/selling short stories: plotting, characterization, dialogue, theme, conflict, and other elements of a marketable short story. Course includes writing assignments and one complete short story (and its revision). Your instructor will critique each assignment and give you suggestions for selling your story.

- **Novel-Writing Workshop.** A professional novelist helps you iron out your plot, develop your main characters, write the background for your novel, and complete the opening scene and a summary of your novel's complete story. You'll even identify potential publishers, write a query letter, and get practical advice on the submission process.

Elements of Effective Writing. Refresher course covers the basics of grammar, punctuation and elements of composition. You review the nine parts of speech and their correct usage, and learn to write clearly and effectively. Course includes 12 lessons with a grammar exercise and editing or writing assignment in each lesson.

Mail this card today for **free** information!

PEN MEDAL FOR TRANSLATION, PEN American Center, 568 Broadway, New York NY 10012. (212)334-1660. Translators nominated by the PEN Translation Committee. Given every 3 years.

PEN/NELSON ALGREN FICTION AWARD, PEN American Center, 568 Broadway, New York NY 10012. (212)334-1660. "For the best uncompleted novel or short story collection by an American writer who needs financial assistance to finish the work." Deadline: Nov. 1.

PEN PUBLISHER CITATION, PEN American Center, 568 Broadway, New York NY 10012. (212)334-1660. "Awarded every two years to a publisher who has throughout his career, given distinctive and continuous service." Nominated by the PEN Executive Board.

PEN/ROGER KLEIN AWARD FOR EDITING, PEN American Center, 568 Broadway, New York NY 10012. (212)334-1660. "Given every two years to an editor of trade books who has an outstanding record of recognizing talents." Nominated by authors, agents, publishers and editors. Deadline: Oct. 1.

PEN TRANSLATION PRIZE, PEN American Center, 568 Broadway, New York NY 10012. Contact: Chairman, Translation Committee. One award to a literary book-length translation into English. (No technical, scientific or reference.) Deadline: Dec. 31.

PEN WRITING AWARDS FOR PRISONERS, PEN American Center, 568 Broadway, New York NY 10012. (212)334-1660. "Awarded to the authors of the best poetry, plays, short fiction and nonfiction received from prison writers in the U.S." Deadline: Sept. 1.

PERKINS PLAYWRITING CONTEST, International Society of Dramatists, Box 1310, Miami FL 33153. (305)756-8313. Award Director: A. Delaplaine. Unproduced full-length plays, any genre, any style. Deadline: Dec. 6.

PLAYWRIGHT'S-IN-RESIDENCE GRANTS, c/o HPRL, INTAR Hispanic-American theater, Box 788, New York NY 10108. (212)695-6134. Residency grant for Hispanic-American playwrights. Deadline: June 30.

POETRY ARTS PROJECT CONTEST, Cosponsors: United Resource Services/*Political Woman* Magazine, Suite 388, 4521 Campus Drive, Irvine CA 92715. Director: Charlene B. Brown. Poetry with social commentary. Deadline: April 15.

POETRY MAGAZINE POETRY AWARDS, 60 W. Walton St., Chicago IL 60610. (312)413-2210. Contest/Award Director: Joseph Parisi, Editor. All poems published in *POETRY* are automatically considered for prizes. Poems should be submitted to the magazine.

RENATO POGGIOLI TRANSLATION AWARD, PEN American Center, 568 Broadway, New York NY 10012. (212)334-1660. "Given to encourage a beginning and promising translator who is working on a first book length translation from Italian into English." Deadline: Feb. 1.

‡PRARIE SCHOONER STROUSSE AWARD, *Prarie Schooner*, 201 Andrews, University of Nebraska, Lincoln NE 68588-0334. (402)472-3191. Editor: Hilda Raz. Poem or group of poems previously published in *Prarie Schooner*.

PRESENT TENSE/Joel H. Cavior Literary Awards, *Present Tense Magazine*, 165 East 56th St., New York NY 10022. Director: Murray Polner. Published fiction, history, religious thought, nonfiction, juvenile and autobiography with Jewish themes, nominated by publisher. Deadline: Nov. 30.

PRINCETON SERIES OF CONTEMPORARY POETS, Princeton University Press, 41 William St., Princeton NJ 08540. (609)452-4900. Poetry Editor: Robert E. Brown. Book-length poetry mss. Deadline: in December.

PRIX ALVINE-BELISLE, ASTED, 3839, rue Saint-Denis, Montreal, Quebec H2W 2M4 Canada. Contact: Diane Boulé. French-Canadian literature for children submitted by the publisher.

PROMETHEUS AWARD/HALL OF FAME, Libertarian Futurist Society, 89 Gebhardt Road, Penfield NY 14526. (716)288-6137. Contact: Victoria Varga. Prometheus Award: pro-freedom, anti-authoritarian novel published during previous year. Hall of Fame: one classic libertarian novel at least five years old. Deadline: March 1.

PULITZER PRIZES, The Pulitzer Prize Board, 702 Journalism, Columbia University, New York NY 10027. Contact: Secretary. Awards for journalism, letters, drama and music in U.S. newspapers, and in literature, drama and music by Americans. Deadline: Feb. 1 (journalism); March 14 (music and drama) and Nov. 11 (letters).

‡**PULP PRESS INTERNATIONAL 3-DAY NOVEL WRITING CONTEST**, Pulp Press Book Publishers Ltd., 1150 Homer St., Vancouver, British Columbia V6B 2X6 Canada. (604)687-4233. Contact: Brian Lam. Best novel written in three days; specifically, over the Labor Day weekend. Entrants return finished novels to Pulp Press for judging. Deadline: Friday before Labor Day weekend. Charges $5 fee.

ERNIE PYLE AWARD, Scripps Howard Foundation, 1100 Central Trust Tower, Cincinnati OH 45202. (513)977-3036. Human-interest reporting for newspaper men and women.

‡**QRL POETRY SERIES**, *Quarterly Review of Literature*, 26 Haslet Ave., Princeton NJ 08540. (609)921-6976. Contact: Renée Weiss. A book of miscellaneous poems, a single long poem, a poetic play, a book of translation. May and October *only*. "They must be received in those 2 months." Charges $20 subscription to the series.

SIR WALTER RALEIGH AWARD, North Carolina Literary and Historical Association, 109 E. Jones St., Raleigh NC 27611. (919)733-7305. Previously published fiction by a North Carolina writer. Deadline: July 15.

‡**READER RITER POLL**, *Affaire de Coeur*, 1555 Washington Ave., San Leandro CA 94577. (415)357-5665. Director: Barbara N. Keenan. Awards for previously published material in five categories appearing in magazine. Deadline: March 15.

REDBOOK'S SHORT STORY CONTEST, *Redbook Magazine*, 224 W. 57th St., New York NY 10019. Fiction Editor: Deborah Purcell. Short stories by writers who have not previously published fiction in a major publication. Contest rules appear in the March issue of *Redbook* annually. Deadline: May 31.

REUBEN AWARD, National Cartoonists Society, 9 Ebony Ct., Brooklyn NY 11229. (718)743-6510. "Outstanding Cartoonist of the Year" from National Cartoonists Society membership.

RHODE ISLAND STATE COUNCIL ON THE ARTS FELLOWSHIP, Suite 103, 95 Cedar St., Providence RI 02903. (401)277-3880. Award Director: Edward Holgate. Poetry, fiction or play, must be a resident of Rhode Island and cannot be a full-time graduate or undergraduate student. Deadline: March 15.

RHYME TIME CREATIVE WRITING COMPETITION, Rhyme Time/Story Time, Box 2377, Coeur d'Alene ID 83814. (208)772-6184. Award Director: Linda Hutton. Rhymed poetry, fiction and essays. Deadline: first and fifteenth of each month.

THE HAROLD U. RIBALOW PRIZE,*Hadassah Magazine*, 50 W. 58th St., New York NY 10019. Executive Editor: Alan M.Tigay. English-language book of fiction on a Jewish theme. Deadline: Feb/March.

MARY ROBERTS RINEHART FUND, English Department, George Mason University, 4400 University Dr., Fairfax VA 22030. (703)323-2220. Contact: Stephen Goodwin. Grants by nomination to unpublished creative writers for fiction, poetry, drama, biography, autobiography, or history with a strong narrative quality. Grants are given in fiction and poetry in even years, and nonfiction and drama in odd years. Deadline: Nov. 30.

ROANOKE-CHOWAN AWARD FOR POETRY, North Carolina Literary and Historical Association, 109 E. Jones St., Raleigh NC 27611. (919)733-7305. Previously published poetry by a resident of North Carolina. Deadline: July 15.

FOREST A. ROBERTS PLAYWRITING AWARD, In cooperation with Shiras Institute, Forest A. Roberts Theatre, Northern Michigan University, Marquette MI 49855-5364. (906)227-2553. Award Director: Dr. James A. Panowski. Unpublished, unproduced plays. Deadline: Nov. 20.

‡**NICHOLAS ROERICH POETRY PRIZE**, Story Line Press, 403 Continental St., Santa Cruz CA 95062. (408)426-5539. Contact: Robert McDowell. First full-length book of poetry. Any writer who has not published a full-length collection of poetry (48 pages or more) in English is eligible to apply. Deadline: Oct. 15. Charges $10 fee.

ROLLING STONE COLLEGE JOURNALISM COMPETITION, Rolling Stone/Smith Corona, Suite 2208, 745 5th Ave., New York NY 10151. (212)758-3800. Contact: David M. Rheins. Entertainment reporting, essays, criticism and general reporting among college writers. Deadline: June 1. Must have been published before April 1.

‡**THE LOIS AND RICHARD ROSENTHAL NEW PLAY PRIZE**, Cincinnati Playhouse in the Park. Box 6537, Cincinnati OH 45206. (513)421-5440. Literary Manager: Barbara Carlisle. Unpublished plays. "Scripts must not have received a full scale professional production." Deadline: Oct. 15-Jan. 15.

THE CARL SANDBURG LITERARY ARTS AWARDS, The Friends of the Chicago Public Library, 78 E. Washington St., Chicago IL 60602. (312)269-2922. Chicago writers of fiction, nonfiction, poetry, and children's literature.

THE CHARLES M. SCHULZ AWARD, The Scripps Howard Foundation, Box 5380, Cincinnati OH 45201. (513)977-3035. For college cartoonists.

THE SCIENCE AWARD, Phi Beta Kappa (The United Chapters of Phi Beta Kappa), 1811 Q St. NW, Washington DC 20009. (202)265-3808. Contact: Administrator, Phi Beta Kappa Book Awards. Interpretations of the physical or biological sciences or mathematics published in the U.S. during the 12-month period preceding the entry deadline, and submitted by the publisher. Deadline: April 30.

SCIENCE IN SOCIETY JOURNALISM AWARDS, National Association of Science Writers, Box 294, Greenlawn NY 11740. Contact: Diane McGurgan. Newspaper, magazine and broadcast science writing. Deadline: July 1.

SCIENCE-WRITING AWARD IN PHYSICS AND ASTRONOMY, American Institute of Physics, 335 E. 45th St., New York NY 10017. (212)661-9404. Contact: David Kalson. Previously published articles, booklets or books "that improve public understanding of physics and astronomy." Deadline: Jan. 10 for professional writers; May 1 for physicists, astronomers or members of AIP member and affililated socieites; Nov. 10 for articles or books intended for childrens preschool to 18 years old.

CHARLES E. SCRIPPS AWARD, The Scripps Howard Foundation, Box 5380, Cincinnati OH 45201. (513)977-3036. Combatting illiteracy. For newspapers, television and radio stations.

THE EDWARD WILLIS SCRIPPS AWARD, The Scripps Howard Foundation, Box 5380, Cincinnati OH 45201. (513)977-3036. Service to the First Amendment for newspapers.

‡SENIOR FELLOWSHIPS FOR LITERATURE, National Endowment for the Arts Literature Program, 1100 Pennsylvania Ave. NW, Washington DC 20506. (202)682-5451. Award Director: Stephen H. Goodwin. Not open to application. Nominated work of high critical acclaim. Deadline: March 3.

SFWA NEBULA AWARDS, Science Fiction Writers of America, Inc., Box H, Wharton NJ 07885. Science fiction or fantasy in the categories of novel, novella, novelette and short story recommended by members.

MINA P. SHAUGHNESSY PRIZE, Modern Language Association, 10 Astor Place, New York NY 10003. Contact: Adrienne Ward, Administrative Assistant. Outstanding research publication in the field of teaching English language and literature; book or article published in the year previous to the award year. Nomination deadline: May 1.

SHELLEY MEMORIAL AWARD, Poetry Society of America, 15 Gramercy Park S., New York NY 10003. (212)254-9628. Contact: Award Director. By nomination only to a living American poet. Deadline: Dec. 31.

SHORT STORY WRITERS COMPETITION, Hemingway Days Festival, Box 4045, Key West FL 33041. (305)294-4440. Director: Michael Whalton. Unpublished short stories. Deadline: early July. Contact the Hemingway Days Festival for specific date each year. Charges $10 fee.

SIERRA REPERTORY THEATRE, Box 3030, Sonora CA 95370. (209)532-3120. Producer: Dennis C. Jones. Full-length plays. Deadline: May 15.

SILVER GAVEL AWARDS, American Bar Association, 750 N. Lake Shore Dr., Chicago IL 60611. (312)988-6137. Contact: Marilyn Giblin. Previously published, performed or broadcast works that promote "public understanding of the American system of law and justice." Deadline: Feb. 1.

‡JOHN SIMMONS SHORT FICTION AWARD and IOWA SHORT FICTION AWARDS, Department of English, University of Iowa. English-Philosophy Building, Iowa City IA 52242. Previously published or unpublished fiction. Deadline: Aug. 1-Sept. 30.

‡BERNICE SLOTE AWARD, *Prarie Schooner*, 201 Andrews, University of Nebraska, Lincoln NE 68588-0334. (402)472-3191. Editor: Hilda Raz. Work by a beginning writers previously published in *Prarie Schooner*.

‡SOCIETY FOR TECHNICAL COMMUNICATION TECHNICAL PUBLICATIONS/Art Communication, Society for Technical Communication, Southwestern Ohio Chapter, 374 Howell, Cincinnati OH 45220. Contest/Award Director: Martha Dillow. Previously published entries in technical publications. Deadline varies. Entry fee varies.

C.L. SONNICHSEN BOOK AWARD,Texas Western Press of the University of Texas at El Paso, El Paso TX 79968-0633. (915)747-5688. Press Director: Dale L. Walker. Previously unpublished nonfiction manuscript dealing with the history, literature or cultures of the Southwest. Deadline: April 1.

‡THE SOUTHERN REVIEW/Louisiana State University Short Fiction Award, Louisiana State University. 43 Allen Hall, Baton Rouge LA 70803. (504)388-5108. Selection Committee Chairman: Warren Eyster. Previously published first collection of short stories by an American published in the U.S. Deadline: Jan. 31. A publisher or an author may submit an entry by mailing two copies of the collection to the *Southern Review* Short Story Award.

BRYANT SPANN MEMORIAL PRIZE, History Dept., Indiana State University, Terre Haute IN 47809. Social criticism in the tradition of Eugene V. Debs. Deadline: April 30.

SPUR AWARDS (WESTERN WRITERS OF AMERICA, INC.), WWA, 1753 Victoria, Sheridan WY 82801. (307)672-2079. Director: Barbara Ketcham. Ten categories of western: novel, historical novel, nonfiction book, juvenile nonfiction, juvenile fiction, nonfiction article, fiction short story, best TV script, movie screenplay, cover art. Also, Medicine Pipe Bearer's Award for best first novel. Deadline: Dec. 31.

STANLEY DRAMA AWARD, Wagner College, Staten Island NY 10301. (212)390-3256. Unpublished and nonprofessionally produced full-length plays, musicals or related one-acts by American playwrights. Submissions must be accompanied by completed application and written recommendation by theatre professional or drama teacher. Deadline: Sept. 1.

THE AGNES LYNCH STARRETT POETRY PRIZE,University of Pittsburgh Press, 127 N. Bellefield Ave., Pittsburgh PA 15260. (412)624-4110. First book of poetry for poets who have not had a full-length book published. Deadline: March and April only.

THE WALKER STONE AWARDS, The Scripps Howard Foundation, 1100 Central Trust Tower, Cincinnati OH 45202. (513)977-3036. Editorial writing for newspaper men and women.

‡ELIZABETH MATCHETT STOVER MEMORIAL AWARD, Southwest Review, 6410 Airline Rd., SMU, Dallas TX 75275. (214)373-7440. For the best poem or group of poems that appeared in the magazine during the previous year.

MARVIN TAYLOR PLAYWRITING AWARD, Sierra Repertory Theatre, Box 3030, Sonora CA 95370. (209)532-3120. Producing Director: Dennis C. Jones. Full-length plays. Deadline: May 15.

SYDNEY TAYLOR CHILDREN'S BOOK AWARDS,Association of Jewish Libraries, Room 1412, 122 East 42nd St., New York NY 10168. (216)991-8847. Director: Merrily F. Hart. Published fiction or nonfiction for children, picture book and body of work. Deadline: approx. Jan. 10.

SYDNEY TAYLOR MANUSCRIPT CONTEST OF AJL, 15 Goldsmith St., Providence RI 02906. Contact: Lillian Schwartz. Unpublished Jewish book for ages 8-12.

THE TEN BEST "CENSORED" STORIES OF 1988, Project Censored—Sonoma State University, Rohnert Park CA 94928. (707)664-2149. Award Director: Carl Jensen, Ph.D. Current published, nonfiction stories of national social significance that have been overlooked or under-reported by the news media. Deadline: March 1.

‡TEXAS BLUEBONNET AWARD, Texas Association of School Libraries and Children's Round Table, Suite 603, 3355 Bee Cave Rd., Austin TX 78746. (512)328-1518. Contact: Patricia Smith. Published books for children recommended by librarians, teachers and students.

‡TEXAS LITERARY AWARDS, Southwestern Booksellers Association, *Dallas Times Herald*, Herald Square, Dallas TX 75202. Contact: Charlotte T. Whaley. Previously published fiction and nonfiction. Book must be authored by a Texas writer—a writer who is a Texan by birth or who resides in Texas—and be published during the year for which the award is offered. Deadline: January 31.

Close-up

Diane Cook
Executive Director
Translation Center

Diane Cook is executive director of the Translation Center at Columbia University. Created to promote and support literary translation, the Center acts as a clearinghouse for information, publishes *Translation* magazine and sponsors the annual Translation Center Awards program. "From the beginning we knew the awards program would be a good way to achieve our goals—to stimulate recognition and encourage excellence in literary translation," says Cook, who has been with the Center since 1981.

The awards program is open to English translations of a substantial part of a book-length literary work in any language, she adds. There are awards for overall excellence in translation and ones for particular languages. The awards sometimes have different titles and prize money ranges from $1,000 to $2,000, depending on the funding sources.

"We receive about 90 submissions each year in Dutch, Hungarian, Russian, Italian . . . Translators fill out the same form and are considered for all awards for which they are eligible," explains Cook. "What is interesting is that, for no apparent reason, the density of submissions from most languages varies incredibly from year to year. For example, last year we received lots of translations from Chinese, but we always get a lot of Spanish and, to a lesser degree, French."

The number of languages represented each year is about 22 or 23, says Cook. Each of several awards is judged by three people on the basis of translation skill and literary excellence. The only other criteria is that the work must have some indication of publishing potential—a contract or a letter of interest—from a publisher.

Cook was a financial consultant and translator for a French firm on Wall Street before coming to the Translation Center. Through her consulting work, she made many valuable contacts that have helped her raise the funds necessary to support the Center's activities.

Writers should be aware that whenever they consider doing a translation they must first find out if the work is copyrighted and who owns the copyright, she says. "It may be the writer, the family of a deceased writer or a publisher. Getting permission often takes detective work. Don't overlook the need for copyright clearance." Most foreign writers and publishers are happy to cooperate. "After all, translation creates a wider audience for their work.

"I suppose the most significant thing about good translation is not just that the translator has an excellent knowledge of the language, but also a feeling for it. Languages don't necessarily have the same rhythm. A language reflects its own culture and develops its own character."

Translators should be careful when selecting works to submit to the awards. Good technical skill is not enough, says Cook. "We assess the literary merit of the original. It is unfortunate that on occasion someone will make a good translation of a work of poor literary merit.

"You must have good literary judgment. The best translators are people who are writers or poets. It's absolutely important you also have an enthusiasm for the writer's work."

—Robin Gee

THE THEATRE LIBRARY ASSOCIATION AWARD, 111 Amsterdam Ave., New York NY 10023. Awards Committee Chair: James Poteat, Television Information Office, 745 5th Ave., New York NY 10022. (212)759-6807. Book published in the United States in the field of recorded performance, including motion pictures and television. Deadline: Feb. 24.

TOWNGATE THEATRE PLAYWRITING CONTEST,Oglebay Institute, Wheeling WV 26003. (304)242-4200. Annual award for previously unproduced full-length plays. No musicals. Deadline: Jan. 1.

TOWSON STATE UNIVERSITY PRIZE FOR LITERATURE, College of Liberal Arts, Towson State University, Towson MD 21204. (301)321-2128. Award Director: Dean Annette Chappell. Book or book-length manuscript that has been accepted for publication, written by a Maryland author of no more than 40 years of age. Deadline: May 15.

‡**THE JOHN TRAIN HUMOR PRIZE**, *The Paris Review*, 541 East 72 St., New York NY 10021. Contest/Award Director: George Plimpton. Unpublished humor—fiction, nonfiction or poetry. Deadline: March 31.

‡**THE TRANSLATION CENTER AWARDS—NATIONAL & INTERNATIONAL**, The Translation Center, 307A Mathematics Bldg., Columbia University, New York NY 10027. (212)854-2305. Executive Director: Diane G.H. Cook. Outstanding translations of a book-length literary work. All applications must be accompanied by our application form. Deadline: Jan. 15.

HARRY S. TRUMAN BOOK PRIZE, Harry S. Truman Library Institute, Independence MO 64050. Secretary of the Institute: Dr. Benedict K. Zobrist. Previously published book written between January 1, 1988, and December 31, 1989, dealing primarily with the history of the United States between April 12, 1945 and January 20, 1953, or with the public career of Harry S. Truman. Deadline: Jan. 20, 1990.

UCROSS FOUNDATION RESIDENCY, Ucross Rt., Box 19, Ucross WY 82835. (307)737-2291. Contact: Heather Burgess. Biannual award for artists' and scholars' resident work program. Deadline: March 1 for August-December program; Oct. 1 for January-May program.

UFO RESEARCH AWARD, Fund for UFO Research, Box 277, Mt. Rainier MD 20712. (301)779-8683. Contact: Executive Committee, Fund for UFO Research. Unscheduled cash awards for published works on UFO phenomena research or public education.

UNDERGRADUATE PAPER COMPETITION IN CRYPTOLOGY, *Cryptologia*, Rose-Hulman Institute of Technology, Terre Haute IN 47803. Contact: Editor. Unpublished papers on cryptology. Deadline: Jan. 1.

‡**DANIEL VAROUSAN AWARD**, New England Poetry Club, 2 Farrar St., Cambridge MA 02138. Contact: Mildred Nash. Unpublished poems. Deadline: June 30. Charges $2 per poem; no charge for New England Poetry Club members.

VIRGINIA PRIZE FOR LITERATURE, Virginia Commission for the Arts, 17th Floor, 101 N. 14th St., Richmond VA 23219. (804)225-3132. Contact: Cary Kimble. Unpublished novel, short stories or poetry by Virginia residents. Deadline: Feb. 1 (fiction); April 1 (poetry).

CELIA B. WAGNER AWARD, Poetry Society of America, 15 Gramercy Park St. S., New York NY 10003. (212)254-9628. Contact: Award Director. Unpublished poem. "Poem worthy of the tradition of the art in any style." Deadline: Dec. 31. Charges $5 fee.

EDWARD LEWIS WALLANT BOOK AWARD, Mrs. Irving Waltman, 3 Brighton Rd., West Hartford CT 06117. Published fiction with significance for the American Jew (novel or short stories). Deadline: Dec. 31.

‡**ARNOLD WEISSBERGER PLAYWRITING AWARD**, Anna L. Weissberger Foundation. 424 West 44th St., New York NY 10036. (212)757-6960. Contest/Award Director: Kirk Aanes. Unpublished plays; no musicals or children's plays. Deadline: Feb. 1.

‡**WEST COAST ENSEMBLE FULL PLAY COMPETITION**, West Coast Ensemble, Box 38728, Los Angeles CA 90038. Artistic Director: Les Hanson. Unpublished (in Southern California) plays. No musicals or children's plays. Deadline: Oct. 15.

‡**WESTERN STATES BOOK AWARDS**, Western States Arts Federation, 207 Shelby St., Santa Fe NM 87501. (505)988-1166. Director of Special Projects: Cheryl Alters Jamison. Unpublished fiction, poetry or creative nonfiction, but already accepted for publication in the award year, by a press in a Western States Arts

Federation member state. Deadline: spring of the year preceding the award year. Open to authors in Alaska, Arizona, California, Colorado, Hawaii, Idaho, Montana, Nevada, New Mexico, Oregon, Utah, Washington, and Wyoming. "A ms duplication and postage fee is charged."

WICHITA STATE UNIVERSITY PLAYWRITING CONTEST, Wichita State University Theatre, WSU, Box 31, Wichita KS 67208. (316)689-3185. Contest Director: Professor Bela Kiralyfalvi. Two or three short, unpublished, unproduced plays or full-length plays by graduate or undergraduate U.S. college students. Deadline: Feb. 15.

‡LAURA INGALLS WILDER AWARD, Association for Library Service to Children/American Library Association, 50 E. Huron St., Chicago IL 60611. (312)944-6780. Contact: Award Director. Awarded every three years to a previously published nominated children's book.

BELL I. WILEY PRIZE, National Historical Society, 2245 Kohn Rd., Box 8200, Harrisburg PA 17105. (717)657-9555. Civil War and Reconstruction nonfiction (book). Deadline: July 31.

WILLIAM CARLOS WILLIAMS AWARD, Poetry Society of America, 15 Gramercy Park S., New York NY 10003. (212)254-9628. Contact: Award Director. Small press, nonprofit, or university press book of poetry submitted by publisher. Deadline: Dec. 31.

J. J. WINSHIP BOOK AWARD, *The Boston Globe*, 135 Morissey Blvd., Boston MA 02107. (617)929-2649. New England-related book. Deadline: June 30.

WITTER BYNNER FOUNDATION FOR POETRY, INC. GRANTS, Box 2188, Santa Fe NM 87504. (505)988-3251. Award Director: Steven D. Schwartz. Grants for poetry and poetry-related projects. Deadline: Feb. 1.

WORK-IN-PROGRESS GRANT, Society of Children's Book Writers and Judy Blume, Box 296 Mar Vista, Los Angeles CA 90066. Write *SCBW* at preceding address. Two grants—one designated specifically for a contemporary novel for young people—to assist SCBW members in the completion of a specific project. Deadline: June 1.

‡WORLD FANTASY AWARDS, Box H, Wharton NJ 07885-0508. Contest/Award Director: Peter D. Pautz. Previously published work recommended by previous convention attendees in several categories, including life achievement, novel, novella, short story, anthology, collection, artist, special award-pro, and special award, non-pro. Deadline: July 1. Works are recommended by attendees of previous two year's conventions.

‡WRITER'S BIENNIAL, Missouri Arts Council. Suite 105, 111 N. 7th St., St. Louis MO 63101. (314)444-6845. Contest/Award Director: Teresa Goettsch. Unpublished prose and poetry by Missouri writers. "All entrants must have lived in Missouri for two years at the time of the entry and cannot be a student in a degree-granting program." Deadline: summer 1989.

WRITERS GUILD OF AMERICA WEST AWARDS, Writers Guild of America West, 8955 Beverly Blvd., Los Angeles CA 90048. Special Projects Coordinator: Marge White. Scripts (screen, TV and radio). Members only. Deadline: September.

WRITERS' JOURNAL ANNUAL POETRY CONTEST, (formerly Inkling Poetry Contest), Inkling Publications, Inc., Box 65798, St. Paul MN 55165. (612)546-0422. Contact: Esther M. Leiper. Previously unpublished poetry. Deadline: April 15. Charges fee: $2 first poem; $1 each thereafter.

WRITERS' JOURNAL ANNUAL FICTION CONTEST, (formerly Inkling Fiction Contest), Inkling Publications, Inc., Box 65798, St. Paul MN 55165. (612)546-0422. Contact: John Hall. Previously unpublished fiction. Deadline: March 15. Charges $5 per entry.

‡PETER ZENGER AWARD, Brooklyn Writers' Network, 2509 Avenue K, Brooklyn NY 11210. (718)377-4945. Contact: Ruth Schwartz. Previously published work by author/journalist "who best furthers the cause of freedom of the press." Deadline: May 31.

Market conditions are constantly changing! If this is 1990 or later, buy the newest edition of Writer's Market *at your favorite bookstore or order directly from* Writer's Digest Books.

Additional Contests

The following listings were deleted from the 1989 edition because the contest sponsors asked to be deleted or the contest will not be held in 1989.

Mark Ingraham Prize (asked to be deleted)
Jacksonville University Playwriting Contest (not held in 1989)
Summer Solstice Theatre Conference Contest (asked to be deleted)
Word Beat Press Fiction Book Award (contest discontinued)

The following contest sponsors did not return a verification to update an existing listing by press time.

Maude Adams Playwriting Competition
Jane Addams Peace Association Children's Book Award
Aim Magazine Short Story Contest
American Musical Theater Festival
American Speech-Language-Hearing Association (ASHA) National Media Award
Annual International Poetry Contest
Annual National Bible Week Editorial Contest
Artist Fellowship Program
Award for Literary Translation
Banta Award
California Short Story Competition
CCLM Editor's Grant Awards
CCLM Seed Grants
Fourth Estate Award
49th Parallel Poetry Contest
General Electric Foundation Awards for Younger Writers
Victoria Chen Haider Memorial College Literary Magazine Contest
Nate Haseltine Memorial Fellowships in Science Writing
Harold Hirsche Awards
Individual Artist Fellowship
International Imitation Hemingway Competition
International Reading Association Children's Book Award
Iowa Arts Council Literary Awards
Japan Foundation Fellowship Program
Loft Creative Nonfiction Residency Program
Massachusetts Artists Fellowship
John Newbery Medal
Ommation Press Book Contest
OPR spring, summer, fall and winter competitions
Scholastic Writing Awards
Seventeen Magazine/Dell Fiction Contest
National Literary Contest
Verbatim Essay Competition
Whiting Writers' Awards
H.W. Wilson Library Periodical Award
Wisconsin Arts Board Fellowship Program
World Hunger Medical Awards
Written Words Competition/Writers-in-Performance Invitational

Additional New Listings

The following listings were received after the _Writer's Market_ original sections were compiled. We are happy to be able to bring you these late arrivals and hope you benefit from the added freelance opportunities they represent. The listings are compiled in alphabetical order according to the major section of the book in which they would appear.

Consumer Publications

AIRBRUSH ACTION, Airbrush Action, Inc., 317 Cross St., Lakewood NJ 08701. (201)364-2111. Editor: Cliff Stieglitz. Managing Editor: Janice Needham. 100% freelance written. Bimonthly magazine on airbrushing and graphics. "_Airbrush Action_ is edited for airbrush and art professionals and enthusiasts interested in the spectrum of airbrush and general art applications." Circ. 45,000. Pays on publication. Publishes ms an average of 2 months after acceptance. Byline given. Offers 50% kill fee. Buys all rights. Submit seasonal/holiday material 6 months in advance. Simultaneous submissions OK. Query for electronic submissions. Computer printout submissions OK; prefers letter-quality. Free sample copy and writer's guidelines.
Nonfiction: Book excerpts, essays, how-to, interview/profile, new product, opinion, technical. Query with published clips. Length: 600-2,500 words. Pays $100-300. Pays expenses of writers on assignment.
Photos: Send photos with submission. Reviews transparencies and prints. Pays $25-250. Captions, model releases and identification of subjects required. Buys all rights.
Columns/Departments: Tech Corner (technical information relating to art), 1,500 words; New Products (new art products—review accepted), 200 words; Q&A. Buys 20 mss/year. Query with published clips. Length: 750-2,000 words. Pays $100-250.
Fillers: Anecdotes, facts. Length: 200-500 words. Pays $25-100.
Tips: "Writers must have good technical knowledge of airbrush and art."

ANGELES, The Art of Living in L.A., California Magazine Partnership, 11601 Wilshire Blvd., Los Angeles CA 90025. (213)479-6511. Editor: Joanne Jaffe. 90% freelance written. Monthly magazine of design, art, architecture, interior design, food and fashion. Estab. 1987. Circ. 75,000. Pays on acceptance. Publishes ms an average of 3 months after acceptance. Byline given. Offers 25% kill fee. Buys first rights. Query for electronic submissions. Computer printout submissions OK. Free sample copy.
Nonfiction: Historical/nostalgic, interview/profile, photo feature. Query with published clips. Pays 50¢/word.

CAREER FOCUS, For Today's Professional, Communications Publishing Group, Inc., Suite 225, 3100 Broadway, Kansas City MO 64111. (816)756-3039. Associate Editor: Beryl Rayford-Saibu. Managing Editor: Georgia Clark Groves. 40% freelance written. Bimonthly magazine "devoted to providing positive insight, information, guidance and motivation to assist black and hispanics (ages 21-35) in their career development and attainment of goals. Estab. 1988. Circ. 750,000. Pays on acceptance. Byline given sometimes. Buys second serial (reprint) rights and makes work-for-hire assignments. Submit seasonal/holiday material 6 months in advance. Simultaneous, photocopied and previously published submissions OK. Computer printout submissions OK. Reports in 2 months. Sample copy for 9x12 SAE; writer's guidelines for #10 SASE.
Nonfiction: Book excerpts, general interest, historical, how-to, humor, inspirational, interview/profile, personal experience, photo feature, technical, travel. Query or send complete ms. Length: 750-3,000 words. Pays $150-400 for assigned articles; pays $50-300 for unsolicited articles. Sometimes pays expenses of writers on assignment.
Photos: State availability of photos with submission. Reviews transparencies. Pays $10-50. Captions, model releases and identification of subjects required. Buys all rights.
Columns/Departments: Profiles (striving and successful black and hispanic young adult, ages 21-35). Buys 15 mss/year. Send complete ms. Length: 500-1,000 words. Pays $50-250.
Fiction: Adventure, ethnic, historical, humorous, mainstream, slice-of-life vignettes. Buys 3 mss/year. Send complete ms. Length: 1,500-5,000 words. Pays $100-400.
Poetry: Free verse. Buys 4 poems/year. Length: 10-25 lines. Pays $25-100.
Fillers: Anecdotes, facts, gags to be illustrated by cartoonist, newsbreaks, short humor. Buys 10/year. Length: 25-250 words. Pays $25-100.
Tips: "For new writers: Submit full manuscript that is double-spaced; clean copy only. Need to have clippings

and previously published works and resume. Should also tell when available to write. Most open to freelancers are profiles of successful and striving person including photo. Must be black or hispanic adult from the U.S."

COMICS SCENE, O'Quinn Studios, 475 Park Avenue S, 8th Floor, New York NY 10016. (212)689-2830. Editor: David McDonnell. Quarterly magazine on comic books and strips, those who create them and TV/movie adaptations of both. Pays on publication. Byline given. Offers 25% kill fee. Buys first North American serial rights or second serial (reprint) rights. Submit seasonal/holiday material 5-6 months in advance. Simultaneous (if informed), photocopied and previously published submissions OK. Computer printout submissions OK. Reports in 5 weeks on queries; 1 month on mss. Sample copy $3.50; writer's guidelines for #10 SASE.
Nonfiction: Book excerpts, historical/nostalgic, interview/profile, new product, personal experience. Buys 60 mss/year. Present plans call for move from quarterly to bimonthly in 1989. Query with published clips. Length: 750-3,500 words. Pays $75-200. Sometimes pays expenses of writers on assignment.
Photos: State availabilityof photos with submission. Reviews contact sheets, transparencies, 8x10 prints. Offers $5-25 for original photos. Captions, model releases, identification of subjects required. Buys all rights.
Columns/Departments: The Comics Scene (interviews with comic book artists, writers and editors on upcoming projects and new developments), 100-500 words, one lead item at 750 words; The Comics Reporter (interview with writer, director, producer of TV series, etc. that are adaptations of comic books and strips). Buys 50 mss/year. Query with published clips. Length: 100-750 words. Pays $15-50.
Tips: "We really need small department items, re: independent comics companies' products and creators. We're also especially in need of interviews with specific comic strip creators. And most any writer can break in with interviews with hot comic book writers and artists—and with comic book creators who do not work for the big five companies. We do not want nostalgic items or interviews. Do not burden us with your own personal comic book stories or artwork. Want to sell us something? Get us things we can't get or haven't thought of. Outthinking editors is a great way to sell something."

COUNTRY ROADS QUARTERLY, Appalachian Life for Today, Fox Printing and Publishing, Box 479, Oakland MD 21550. (301)334-1104. Editor: Carol L. Fox. 75% freelance written. Quarterly regional magazine of Appalachia. "*CRQ* is designed to inform, interest and entertain readers about Maryland, Pennsylvania, and West Virginia people, places and things that make this area appealing." Estab. 1987. Pays on acceptance. Byline given. Offers 20% kill fee. Buys first North American serial rights. Submit seasonal/holiday material 2 months in advance. Simultaneous and previously published submissions OK. Computer printout submissions OK; prefers letter-quality. Reports in 1 month on queries; 2 months on mss. Sample copy for $2 and 9x12 SAE with 4 first class stamps; free writer's guidelines.
Nonfiction: General interest, historical/nostalgic, humor, interview/profile, opinion, personal experience, photo feature, religious, travel. "No first-person material, no fiction." Buys 40 mss/year. Query with or without published clips, or send complete ms. Length: 500-3,000 words. Pays $5-150. Sometimes pays expenses of writers on assignment.
Photos: Send photos with submission. Reviews 5x7 prints. Offers $2.50-10. Captions and idenitification of subjects required. Buys one-time rights.
Columns/Departments: Country Food/Cooking (homestyle cuisine/outdoor cooking), 500-2,000 words; Nostalgia (bygone days in Pennsylvania, Maryland, West Virginia portion of Appalachia), 500-3,000 words. Buys 8-10 mss/year. Send complete ms. Length: 500-2,000 words. Pays $5-75.
Poetry: Free verse, haiku, light verse, traditional. Buys 10 poems/year. Length: 6-20 lines. Pays $5-10.
Fillers: Anecdotes, short humor. Buys 10/year. Length: 500 words maximum. Pays $5-15.
Tips: "I'm anxious to work with new writers but only if they follow my guidelines. Anyone who's lived in Appalachia would understand the uniqueness of mountains and rural living. All areas are open to freelancers—particularly profile, nostalgia, culture and history of the land. Material must have relevance to coverage area."

DETROIT FREE PRESS MAGAZINE, *The Detroit Free Press*, 321 W. Lafayette Blvd., Detroit MI 48231. (313)222-6446. 20% freelance written. Prefers to work with published/established writers; works with a small number of new/unpublished writers each year. For a general newspaper readership; urban and suburban. Weekly magazine. Circ. 800,000. Pays on acceptance. Buys first or second serial rights. Offers kill fee of 25% of the agreed-upon price. Byline given. Query for electronic submissions. Computer printout submissions acceptable. Reports in 1 month.
Nonfiction: "Seeking quality magazine journalism on subjects of interest to Detroit and Michigan readers: lifestyles and better living, trends, behavior, health and body, business and political intrigue, crime and cops, money, success and failure, sports, fascinating people, arts and entertainment. *Detroit Free Press* is bright and cosmopolitan in tone. Most desired writing style is literate but casual—the kind you'd like to read—and reporting must be unimpeachable." Buys 75-100 mss/year. Query or submit complete ms. "If possible, the letter should be held to one page. It should present topic, organizational technique and writing angle. It should demonstrate writing style and give some indication as to why the story would be of interest to us. It should not, however, be an extended sales pitch." Length: 3,000 words maximum. Pays $125-700. Sometimes pays the expenses of writers on assignment.

Photos: Purchased occaisonally with or without accompanying ms. Rates are negotiable.
Tips: "We will be accepting fewer nostalgia, history and first-person stories than in the past. We are aiming to be more polished, sophisticated and 'slicker.' Try to generate fresh ideas or fresh approaches to older ideas. Always begin with a query letter and not a telephone call. If sending a complete ms, be very brief in your cover letter; we really are not interested in previous publication credits. If the story is good for us we'll know."

MIDNIGHT GRAFFITI, Dark Fantasy, 13101 Sudan Road, Poway CA 92064. (619)679-8257. Editor: James Van Hise. Managing Editor: Jessie Horsting. Quarterly magazine for "the modern reader of dark fantasy, whether the interest be in Stephen King, Clive Barker or Alan Moore." Estab. 1988. Circ. 10,000. Pays on publication. Publishes ms an average of 2 months after acceptance. Byline given. Offers 50% kill fee. Buys first North American serial rights. Simultaneous, photocopied and previously published submissions OK. Query for electronic submissions. Computer printout submissions OK; no dot-matrix. Reports in 2 weeks on queries; 1 month on mss. Sample copy $6.50; writer's guidelines for #10 SASE.
Nonfiction: Book excerpts, essays, expose, historical/nostalic, humor, interview/profile. Buys 12 mss/year. Query with published clips. Length: 1,500-6,000 words. Pays $75-200 for assigned articles; $50-100 for unsolicited articles.
Photos: State availability of photos with submission. Reviews contact sheets. Offers $10-25. Captions and identification of subjects required. Buys one-time rights.
Columns/Departments: From Beyond (news), 100-500 words. Buys 12 mss/year. Query. Length: 100-500 words. Pays $10-35.

MOUNTAIN BIKE, For the Adventure, Rodale Press, 33 E. Minor St., Emmaus PA 18098. (215)967-5171. Executive Editor: Edward Pavelka. Managing Editor: Bruce Feldman. 30% freelance written. Bimonthly magazine on mountain biking. "Writing must convey the excitement and adventure of mountain biking." Circ. 35,000. Pays on publication. Publishes ms an average of 4 months after acceptance. Byline given. Offers 1/4 kill fee. Buys all rights. Submit seasonal/holiday material 6 months in advance. Query for electronic submissions. Computer printout submissions OK; prefers letter-quality. Reports in 1 month. Free writer's guidelines.
Nonfiction: Essays, historical/nostalgic, how-to, humor, inspirational, interview/profile, opinion, personal experience, photo feature, technical, travel. Buys 40 mss/year. Send complete ms. Length: 500-2,500 words. Pays $50-500. Sometimes pays expenses of writers on assignment.
Photos: Send photos with submission. Reviews 35mm transparencies. Offers $50-200 per photo. Captions and identification of subjects required. Buys all rights.
Fillers: Anecdotes, facts, short humor. Buys 15/year. Length: 50-250 words. Pays $10-50.
Tips: Be knowledgeable about the subject and send complete ms with quality photos or illustrations. Adventure touring is most open to freelancers. The articles should be filled with first-person adventure and correct facts. Quality photography is essential."

NEW YORK KULTURE, Box 125, Bronx NY 10471-0425. Editor: J. Joseph Finora. Managing Editor: M.G. Spinelli. 75% freelance written. Quarterly magazine. Estab. 1988. Circ. 10,000. Pays on acceptance. Byline given. Offers 20% kill fee. Buys first North American serial rights. Submit seasonal/holiday material 3 months in advance. Simultaneous and previously published submissions OK. Query for electronic submissions. Computer printout submissions OK. Reports in 1 month. Sample copy $2.
Nonfiction: Expose, humor, opinion. No movie and music reviews. Buys 25 mss/year. Query with or without published clips, or send complete ms. Length: 2,000-10,000 words. Pays $100-200 for assigned articles; $50-100 for unsolicited articles. Sometimes pays the expenses of writers on assignment.
Photos: State availability of photos with submission. Buys one-time rights.
Fillers: Short humor. Length: 250-500 words.

PENINSULA MAGAZINE, San Mateo and Santa Clara Counties, Westar Media, Inc., Suite 330, 2317 Broadway, Redwood City CA 94063. (415)368-8800. Editor: David Gorn. Associate Editor: Dale Conour. 70% freelance written. Monthly regional magazine of the San Francisco peninsula. "*Peninsula* covers the issues, events and people of the San Francisco peninsula—from south San Francisco to south San Jose—for a sophisticated, affluent readership tied financially to the Silicon Valley." Circ. 25,000. Pays 30 days from acceptance. Publishes ms an average of 3 months after acceptance. Byline given. Offers 30% kill fee. Buys first rights and second serial (reprint) rights. Submit seasonal/holiday material 4 months in advance. Simultaneous, photocopied and previously published submissions OK. Query for electronic submissions. Computer printout submissions OK. Reports in 1 month. Free writer's guidelines.
Nonfiction: Expose, general interest, historical/nostalgic, humor, interview/profile, photo feature. No travel articles. Buys 36 mss/year. Query with published clips. Length: 1,500-3,500 words. Pays $250-700. Sometimes pays expenses of writers on assignment.
Photos: State availability of photos with submission. Reviews contact sheets, transparencies and prints. Offers variable rates. Captions, model releases and identification of subjects required. Buys one-time rights.
Columns/Departments: Seasons (local outdoor excursions), 50-500 words; Food and Wine (entertaining

ideas; new products; methods), 50-500 words; Journal (short, snappy bits that present a sketch of peninsula life), 50-250 words. Buys 20 mss/year. Query with published clips. Length for departments: 50-500 words. Pays $25-75.

Tips: "We're looking for good story ideas that are presented in a query letter that instills confidence in us—confidence that the ideas has been well thought out, confidence that the writer can produce a strong manuscript. We don't want to see a query that begins 'How 'bout a story on computers?'"

RELATIONSHIPS TODAY, Romantic LifeLines, Inc., Suite 504, 432 Park Ave. S., New York NY 10016. (212)686-2566. Editor: Lyle Benjamin. Managing Editor: Maria Sarath. 75% freelance written. Monthly magazine covering relationships. "Writers must treat issues from male and female perspective." Estab. 1988. Circ. 160,000. Pays 1/3 on acceptance 2/3 on publication. Byline given. Offers 20% kill fee. Buys first North American serial rights and non-exclusive reprint rights. Submit seasonal/holiday material 3 months in advance. Photocopied submissions OK. Computer printout submissions OK. Sample copy for 9x12 SAE with $1.65 postage; writer's guidelines for #10 SASE.

Nonfiction: Essays, general interest, humor, interview/profile, new product, opinion, personal experience, photo feature, travel. Buys 80 mss/year. Query with published clips. Length: 1,000-2,500 words. Pays $200-500 for assigned articles; $100-500 for unsolicited articles. Sometimes pays expenses of writers on assignment.

Photos: State availability of photos with submission. Reviews contact sheets, negatives, transparencies and prints. Offers no additional payment for photos accepted wiht ms. Captions, model releases and identification of subjects required. Buys first North American rights and reprint rights.

Fillers: Facts, gags to be illustrated by cartoonist, and newsbreaks. Buys 24 mss/year. Length: 250 words maximum. Pays $5-50.

Tips: "Send clips and queries for specific, outlined articles."

SECOND WIND, The Full Life Magazine, 15 Ketchum St., Westport CT 06880. (203)226-7463. Editor: Paul Perry. Managing Editor: Louise Ackerman. 60% freelance written. Bimonthly magazine on health/fitness, challenging travel, and personal finance. Estab. 1988. Circ. 165,000. Pays on acceptance. Byline given. Offers 1/4 kill fee. Buys first North American serial rights. Submit seasonal/holiday material 6 months in advance. Simultaneous, photocopied and previously published submissions OK. Computer printout submissions OK. Reports in 1 month. Sample copy for 9x12 SAE with 3 first class stamps; writer's guidelines for #10 SASE.

Nonfiction: General interest, historical, nostalgic, how-to, humor, inspirational, interview/profile, travel. Buys 50 mss/year. Query or send complete ms. Length: 500-2,000 words. Pays $250-1,500. Pays expenses of writers on assignment.

Photos: State availability of photos with submission. Offers $50-600 per photo. Captions and model releases required. Buys one-time rights.

Columns/Departments: Money Talks (fun things to do with your money), 1,000 words; Critical Conditions (people at turning points in their lives), 1,000 words; Mind/Body (health shorts); Travel; Spaces/Places (design shorts). Query. Length: 50-1,000 words. Pays $25-1,000.

Fillers: Louise Ackerman, fillers editor. Anecdotes, facts and short humor. Buys 20/year. Length: 50-100 words. Pays $50 maximum.

Tips: "We are a magazine aimed at 45- to 60-year-olds, yet we aren't about age. We are a general interest magazine that entertains this age group with features about their peers, informs them with health advice and inspires them to get moving with travel features. Since we are always looking for a feast of fresh ideas, the whole magazine is open. But please, make the ideas fresh."

SPORT PILOT, The Magazine of Recreational Flying, Challenge Publications, Inc., 7950 Deering Ave., Canoga Park CA 91306. (818)887-0550. Editor: Jim Campbell. 50% freelance written. Monthly magazine on sport aviation. Circ. 80,000. Pays on publication. Publishes ms an average of 3 months after acceptance. Byline given. Offers 50% kill fee. Buys first North American serial rights and second serial rights. Submit seasonal/holiday material 5 months in advance. Query for electronic submissions. Computer printout submissions OK. Reports in 2 weeks. Free sample copy and writer's guidelines.

Nonfiction: General interest, how-to, humor, interview/profile, new product, opinion, personal experience, photo feature, technical and travel. No crashes, no first solo and no ego trip articles. Buys 60 mss/year. Query with published clips. Length: 500-3,500 words. Pays $50-400 for assigned articles; $50-350 for unsolicited articles. Sometimes pays expenses of writers on assignment.

Photos: Send photos with submission. Reviews contact sheets and 35mm transparencies. Offers no additional payment for photos accepted with ms. Captions, model releases and identification of subjects required. Buys all rights.

Columns/Departments: High Tech (technical, how-to), 1,000-2,500 words; Gadget Patrol (product evaluation), 500-1,500 words; Flyers' Library (book reviews), 500-1,000 words. Buys 12-18 mss/year. Query with published clips. Length: 500-2,500 words. Pays $50-250.

Fillers: Gags to be illustrated by cartoonist, short humor. Buys 5 mss/year. Length: 500-1,000 words. Pays $50-100.

Tips: "It's hard to write for *Sport Pilot* without actually being a pilot. We appreciate thoughtful, positive contributions with a sense of humor and a clear direction. Complete stories—copy, photos, well-defined captions, title sheet, etc.—get first attention and biggest check."

Trade Publications

BALLOONS TODAY,The Original Balloon Magazine of New Fashioned Ideas, Festivities Publications, Inc., 2522 Oak St., Jacksonville FL 32204. (904)388-0317. Editor: Debra Paulk. 35% freelance written. Monthly magazine on the balloon industry. "We are a trade journal for balloon retailers, florist and party stores who sell balloons." Circ. 8,000. Pays on publication. Publishes ms an average of 3 months after acceptance. Byline given. Offers $100 kill fee. Buys one-time rights. Submit seasonal/holiday material 4 months in advance. Simultaneous, photcopied and previously published submissions OK. Query for electronic submissions. Computer printout submissions OK. Reports in 3 weeks on queries; 2 weeks on mss. Sample copy for 9x12 SAE with $1.50 postage.

Nonfiction: How-to, interview/profile, new product, photo feature, technical. Buys 35 mss/year. Query with or without published clips, or send complete ms. Length: 500-1,000 words. Pays $100-600 for assigned articles; $100-500 for unsolicited articles. Sometimes pays expenses of writers on assignment.

Photos: Send photos with submission. Reviews 2x2 transparencies and 3x5 prints. Offers no additional payment for photos accepted with ms. Captions, model releases and identification of subjects required. Buys one-time rights.

Tips: "Articles should be written for retailers. Send manuscripts and photos or query with photos. Be very specific with how-to tips and programs for building businesses. Looking for new creative ideas and proven programs."

FESTIVITY!, Profitable Plans for the Party Professional, Festivities Publications, 2522 Oak St., Jacksonville FL 32204. (904)388-0317. Editorial Director: Debra Paulk. 50% freelance written. Monthly trade journal for the party industry. Estab. 1988. Circ. 20,000. Pays on publication. Publishes ms an average of 3 months after acceptance. Byline given. Offers $100 kill fee. Buys one-time rights. Submit seasonal/holiday material 4 months in advance. Simultaneous, photocopied and previously published submissions OK. Query for electronic submissions. Computer printout submissions OK. Reports in 3 weeks on queries; 2 weeks on mss. Sample copy for 9x12 SAE with $1.50 in postage.

Nonfiction: Interview/profile, new product, photo feature, technical. Buys 48 mss/year. Query with or without published clips, or send complete ms. Length: 500-1,000 words. Pays $100-600 for assigned articles; $100-500 for unsolicited articles. Sometimes pays expenses of writers on assignment.

Photos: Send photos with submission. Reviews 2x2 transparencies and 3x5 prints. Offers no additional payment for photos accepted with ms. Captions, model releases and identification of subjects required. Buys one-time rights.

Columns/Departments: Party Business (ideas on store management, finance), 500-1,000 words; Party Display (in-store display ideas, products), 500-1,000 words. Buys 48 mss/year. Query with published clips. Length: 500-1,000 words. Pays $100-600.

Tips: "Be very specific with how-to tips and programs for building business."

FOODSERVICE DIRECTOR, Bill Communications, 633 Third Ave., New York NY 10017. (212)984-2356. Editor: Walter J. Schruntek. Managing Editor: Karen Weisberg. 20% freelance written. Monthly tabloid on non-commercial foodservice operations for "operators of kitchens and dining halls in schools, colleges, hospitals/health care, office and plant cafeterias, military, airline/transportation, correctional institutions. Estab. 1988. Circ. 45,000. Pays on publication. Byline given sometimes. Offers 25% kill fee. Buys all rights. Submit seasonal/holiday material 2-3 months in advance. Simultaneous submissions OK. Computer printout submissions OK. Free sample copy.

Nonfiction: How-to, interview/profile. Buys 60-70 mss/year. Query with published clips. Length: 700-900 words. Pays $250-500. Sometimes pays the expenses of writers on assignment.

Photos: Send photos with submission. Reviews transparencies. Offers no additional payment for photos accepted with ms. Identification of subjects required. Buys all rights.

Columns/Departments: Equipment (case studies of kitchen/serving equipment in use), 700-900 words; Food (specific category studies per publication calendar), 750-900 words. Buys 20-30 mss/year. Query. Length: 400-600 words. Pays $150-250.

Author's Agents

ELAINE DAVIE LITERARY AGENCY, Village Gate Square, 274 North Goodman St., Rochester NY 14607. (716)442-0830. President: Elaine Davie. Estab. 1986. Represents 40 clients. 30% of clients are new/unpublished writers. Works with a small number of new/unpublished authors. Specializes in adult fiction and nonfiction, particularly genre fiction (romances, historicals, mysteries, horror, westerns, etc.). "There is always a place for strong mainstream."
Will Handle: Nonfiction books, novels, juvenile books (no children's books or poetry). Handles 30% nonfiction; 60% novels; 10% juvenile books. Will read—at no charge—unsolicited queries and outlines. Reports in 2 weeks on queries. "If our agency does not respond within 1 month to your request to become a client, you may submit requests elsewhere."
Terms: Agent receives 15% commission on domestic sales; 20% on dramatic sales; and 20% on foreign sales.
Recent Sales: "We gladly provide this information to any of our clients, but we consider it confidential to the general public."

CANDICE FUHRMAN LITERARY AGENCY, Box F, Forest Knolls CA 94933. (415)488-0161. President: Candice Fuhrman. Estab. 1987. Represents 12 clients. 90% of clients are new/unpublished writers. Eager to work with new/unpublished writers. Specializes in self-help and how-to nonfiction; adult commercial fiction. No genre or children's books.
Will Handle: Nonfiction books, novels. Handles 95% nonfiction books; 5% novels. Will read—at no charge—unsolicited queries, outlines and manuscripts. Reports in 2 weeks on queries; 1 months on mss. "If our agency does not respond within 2 months to your request to become a client, you may submit requests elsewhere."
Terms: Agent received 15% commission on domestic sales; 10% on dramatic sales; and 10% on foreign sales. Charges for postage and telephone expenses.
Recent Sales: *The Recovery Catalog*, by Barbara Yoder (Simon & Schuster); *Homework Book, by Faith and Cecil Clark (Doubleday); The Dreams of Pregnant Women*, by Patricia Maybruck.

NATASHA KERN LITERARY AGENCY, Box 40547, Portland OR 97240. (503)226-2221. Contact: Natasha Kern. Estab. 1986. Represents 20 clients. 35% of clients are new/unpublished writers. Eager to work with new/unpublished writers. Specializes in adult and juvenile fiction and nonfiction books.
Will Handle: Nonfiction books, novels and juvenile books. Currently handles 45% nonfiction books; 45% novels; 10% juvenile books. Will read—at no charge—unsolicited queries. Reports in 1 week on queries; 6 weeks on mss. "If our agency does not respond within 6 weeks to your submission, you may submit elsewhere."
Terms: Agent receives 15% commission on domestic sales; 15% on dramatic sales; and 20% on foreign sales. Charges an evaluation fee for new writers. "All unsolicited or previously unpublished writers' submissions are handled by our Acquisitions Department. In support of our commitment to develop as well as acquire talent, all writers whose works are returned will receive either a 3-5-page editorial/marketing critique or a line-by-line on-manuscript critique (up to 15,000 words) or both, depending on the nature and the promise of the work. Critiques focus on substantive issues of craftsmanship and are provided by published writers or professional editors." Charges for photocopying, copies of books or galleys, overseas mail and express mail. Sometimes offers a consultation service through which writers can get advice on a contract; charge $35/hour. 80% of income derived from sales of writer's work; 20% of income from criticism services.
Recent Sales: *The Western Tree Book*, by George Palmer and Martha Stuckey (Touchstone Press); *A Field of Innocence*, by Jack Estes (Headline Publishers).

Contests

FRIENDSHIP COMMISSION PRIZE FOR THE TRANSLATION OF JAPANESE LITERATURE, Donald Keene Center of Japanese Culture, 407 Kent Hall, Columbia University, New York NY 10027. (212)280-5036. Administrator: Victoria Lyon-Bestor. Previously published book-length translation of works of Japanese literature by a young American translator. Deadline: Dec. 1.

EZRA JACK KEATS MEMORIAL FELLOWSHIP, Ezra Jack Keats Foundation, 1005 E. 4th St., Brooklyn NY 11230. (718)252-4047. Curator, Kerlan Collection: Karen Hoyle. Published or unpublished children's literature. Deadline: early May.

Glossary

Key to symbols and abbreviations on page 5.

Advance. A sum of money that a publisher pays a writer prior to the publication of a book. It is usually paid in installments, such as one-half on signing the contract; one half on delivery of a complete and satisfactory manuscript. The advance is paid against the royalty money that will be earned by the book.

Advertorial. Advertising presented in such a way as to resemble editorial material. Information may be the same as that contained in an editorial feature, but it is paid for or supplied by an advertiser and the word "advertisement" appears at the top of the page.

All rights. See "Rights and the Writer" in the Business of Writing article.

Anthology. A collection of selected writings by various authors or a gathering of works by one author.

Assignment. Editor asks a writer to do a specific article for a certain price to be paid upon completion.

B&W. Abbreviation for black and white photographs.

Backlist. A publisher's list of its books that were not published during the current season, but which are still in print.

Belles lettres. A term used to describe fine or literary writing—writing more to entertain than to inform or instruct.

Bimonthly. Every two months. See also *semimonthly.*

Bionote. A sentence or brief paragraph about the writer. Also called a "bio," it can appear at the bottom of the first or last page of a writer's article or short story or on a contributor's page.

Biweekly. Every two weeks.

Book auction. Selling the rights (i.e. paperback, movie, etc.) of a hardback book to the highest bidder. A publisher or agent may initiate the auction.

Book packager. Draws all elements of a book together, from the initial concept to writing and marketing strategies, then sells the book package to a book publisher and/or movie producer. Also known as book producer or book developer.

Business size envelope. Also known as a #10 envelope, it is the standard size used in sending business correspondence.

Byline. Name of the author appearing with the published piece.

Caption. Originally a title or headline over a picture, but now a description of the subject matter of a photograph; includes names of people where appropriate. Also called cutline.

Category fiction. A term used to include all various labels attached to types of fiction. See also *genre.*

Chapbook. A small booklet, usually paperback, of poetry, ballads or tales.

Clean copy. Free of errors, cross-outs, wrinkles or smudges.

Clippings. News items of possible interest to trade magazine editors.

Clips. Samples, usually from newspapers or magazines, of your *published* work.

Coffee table book. An oversize book, heavily illustrated, suitable for display on a coffee table.

Column inch. All the type contained in one inch of a typeset column.

Commercial novels. Novels designed to appeal to a broad audience. These are often broken down into categories such as western, mystery and romance. See also *genre.*

Commissioned work. See *assignment.*

Compatible. The condition which allows one type of computer/word processor to share information or communicate with another type of machine.

Concept. A statement that summarizes a screenplay or teleplay—before the outline or treatment is written.

Contributor's copies. Copies of the issues of magazines sent to the author in which the his/her work appears.

Co-publishing. An arrangement in which author and publisher share the publication costs and profits of a book. See also *subsidy publisher.*

Copyediting. Editing a manuscript for grammar, punctuation and printing style, not subject content.

Copyright. A means to protect an author's work. See "Copyrighting Your Writing" in the Business of Writing article.

Cover letter. A brief letter, accompanying a complete manuscript, especially useful if responding to an editor's request for a manuscript. A cover letter may also accompany a book proposal (A cover letter is *not* a query letter; see "Approaching Markets" in the Business of Writing article.

Cutline. See *caption.*

Derivative works. A work that has been translated, adapted, abridged, condensed, annotated or otherwise produced by altering a previously created work. Before producing a derivative work, it is necessary to secure the written permission of the author or copyright owner of the original piece.

Desk-top publishing. A publishing system designed for a personal computer. The system is capable of typesetting, some illustration, layout, design and printing—so that the final piece can be distributed and/or sold.

Disk. A round, flat magnetic plate on which computer data may be stored.

Docudrama. A fictional film rendition of recent newsmaking events and people.

Dot-matrix. Printed type where individual characters are composed of a matrix or pattern of tiny dots.

El-hi. Elementary to high school.

Epigram. A short, witty sometimes paradoxical saying.

Erotica. Usually fiction that is sexually-oriented, although it could be art on the same theme.

ESL. Abbreviation for English as a second language.

Fair use. A provision of the copyright law that says short passages from copyrighted material may be used without infringing on the owner's rights.

Fanzine. A noncommercial, small circulation magazine dealing with fantasy or science fiction literature and art.

FAX. A communication system used to transmit documents over telephone lines.

Feature. An article giving the reader information of human interest rather than news. Also used by magazines to indicate a lead article or distinctive department.

Filler. A short item used by an editor to "fill" out a newspaper column or magazine page. It could be a timeless news item, a joke, an anecdote, some light verse or short humor, puzzle, etc.

First North American serial rights. See "Rights and the Writer" in the Business of Writing article.

Formula story. Familiar theme treated in a predictable plot structure—such as boy meets girl, boy loses girl, boy gets girl.

Galleys. The first typeset version of a manuscript that has not yet been divided into pages.

Genre. Refers either to a general classification of writing, such as the novel or the poem, or to the categories within those classifications, such as the problem novel or the sonnet. Genre fiction describes commercial novels, such as mysteries, romances and science fiction. (also called category fiction).

Ghostwriter. A writer who puts into literary form an article, speech, story or book based on another person's ideas or knowledge.

Glossy. A black and white photograph with a shiny surface as opposed to one with a non-shiny matte finish.

Gothic novel. A fiction category or genre in which the central character is usually a beautiful young girl, the setting an old mansion or castle, and there is a handsome hero and a real menace, either natural or supernatural.

Graphic novel. A term to describe an adaptation of a novel in graphic form, long comic strip or heavily illustrated story, of 40 pages or more, produced in paperback form.

Hard copy. The printed copy of a computer's output.

Hardware. All the mechanically-integrated components of a computer that are not software. Circuit boards, transistors and the machines that are the actual computer are the hardware.

Honorarium. Token payment—small amount of money, or a byline and copies of the publication.

Illustrations. May be photographs, old engravings, artwork. Usually paid for separately from the manuscript. See also *package sale.*

Imprint. Name applied to a publisher's specific line or lines of books (e.g., Delacorte Press is an imprint of Dell Publishing).

Interactive fiction. Works of fiction in book or computer software format in which the reader determines the path the story will take. The reader chooses from several alternatives at the end of a "chapter," and thus determines the structure of the story. Interactive fiction features multiple plots and endings.

Invasion of privacy. Writing about persons (even though truthfully) without their consent.

Kill fee. Fee for a complete article that was assigned but which was subsequently cancelled.

Letter-quality submission. Computer printout that looks like a typewritten manuscript.

Libel. A false accusation or any published statement or presentation that tends to expose another to public contempt, ridicule, etc. Defenses are truth; fair comment on a matter of public interest; and privileged communication—such as a report of legal proceedings or client's communication to a lawyer.

Little magazine. Publications of limited circulation, usually on literary or political subject matter.

LORT. An acronym for League of Resident Theatres. Letters from A to D follow LORT and designate the size of the theater.

Mainstream fiction. Fiction that transcends popular novel categories such as mystery, romance and science fiction. Using conventional methods, this kind of fiction tells stories about people and their conflicts with greater depth of characterization, background, etc., than the more narrowly focused genre novels.

Mass market. Nonspecialized books of wide appeal directed toward an extremely large audience.

Microcomputer. A small computer system capable of performing various specific tasks with data it receives. Personal computers are microcomputers.

Midlist. Those titles on a publisher's list that are not expected to be big sellers, but are expected to have limited sales. Midlist books are mainstream, not literary, scholarly or genre, and are usually written by new or unknown writers.

Model release. A paper signed by the subject of a photograph (or the subject's guardian, if a juvenile) giving the photographer permission to use the photograph, editorially or for advertising purposes or for some specific purpose as stated.

Modem. A small electrical box that plugs into the serial card of a computer, used to transmit data from one computer to another, usually via telephone lines.

Monograph. Thoroughly detailed and documented scholarly study concerning a singular subject.

Multiple submissions. Sending more than one poem, gag or greeting card idea at the same time. This term is often used synonymously with simultaneous submission.

New age. A generic term for works linked by a common interest in metaphysical, spiritual, holistic and other alternative approaches to living. It embraces astrology, psychic phenomena, spiritual healing, UFOs, mysticism—anything that deals with reality beyond everyday material perception.

Newsbreak. A brief, late-breaking news story added to the front page of a newspaper at press time or a magazine news item of importance to readers.

Novelette. A short novel, or a long short story; 7,000 to 15,000 words approximately. Also known as a novella.

Novelization. A novel created from the script of a popular movie, usually called movie "tie-ins" and published in paperback.

Offprint. Copies of an author's article taken "out of issue" before a magazine is bound and given to the author in lieu of monetary payment. An offprint could be used by the writer as a published writing sample.

One-time rights. See "Rights and the Writer" in the Business of Writing article.

Outline. A summary of a book's contents in five to 15 double-spaced pages; often in the form of chapter headings with a descriptive sentence or two under each one to show the scope of the book. A screenplay's or teleplay's outline is a scene-by-scene narrative description of the story (10-15 pages for a ½-hour teleplay; 15-25 pages for a 1-hour teleplay; 25-40 pages for a 90-minute teleplay; 40-60 pages for a 2-hour feature film or teleplay).

Over-the-transom. Unsolicited material submitted by a freelance writer.

Package sale. The editor buys manuscript and photos as a "package" and pays for them with one check.

Page rate. Some magazines pay for material at a fixed rate per published page, rather than per word.

Payment on acceptance. The editor sends you a check for your article, story or poem as soon as he reads it and decides to publish it.

Payment on publication. The editor doesn't send you a check for your material until it is published.

Pen name. The use of a name other than your legal name on articles, stories or books when you wish to remain anonymous. Simply notify your post office and bank that you are using the name so that you'll receive mail and/or checks in that name. Also called a pseudonym.

Photo feature. Feature in which the emphasis is on the photographs rather than on accompanying written material.

Photocopied submissions. Submitting *photocopies* of an original manuscript is acceptable to some editors instead of the author sending the original manuscript. Do not assume that an editor who accepts photocopies will also accept multiple or simultaneous submissions.

Plagiarism. Passing off as one's own the expression of ideas and words of another writer.

Potboiler. Refers to writing projects a freelance writer does to "keep the pot boiling" while working on major articles—quick projects to bring in money with little time or effort. These may be fillers such as anecdotes or how-to tips, but could be short articles or stories.

Proofreading. Close reading and correction of a manuscript's typographical errors.

Pseudonym. See *pen name*.

Public domain. Material which was either never copyrighted or whose copyright term has run out.

Publication not copyrighted. Publication of an author's work in such a publication places it in the public domain and it cannot subsequently be copyrighted. See "Copyrighting Your Writing" in the Business of Writing article.

Query. A letter to an editor aimed to get his/her interest in an article you purpose to write.

Rebus. Stories, quips, puzzles, etc., in juvenile magazines that convey words or syllables with pictures, objects or symbols whose names resemble the sounds of intended words.

Realia. Activities that relate classroom study to real life.

Release. A statement that your idea is original, has never been sold to anyone else and that you are selling the negotiated rights to the idea upon payment.

Remainders. Copies of a book that are slow to sell and can be purchased from the publisher at a reduced price. Depending on the author's book contract, a reduced royalty or no royalty is paid on remainder books.

Reporting time. The time it takes for an editor to report to the author on his/her query or manuscript.

Reprint rights. See "Rights and the Writer" in the Business of Writing article.

Round-up article. Comments from, or interviews with, a number of celebrities or experts on a single theme.

Royalties, standard hardcover book. 10% of the retail price on the first 5,000 copies sold; 12½% on the next 5,000; 15% thereafter.

Royalties, standard mass paperback book. 4 to 8% of the retail price on the first 150,000 copies sold.

Royalties, trade paperback book. No less than 6% of list price on the first 20,000 copies; 7½% thereafter.

Screenplay. Script for a film intended to be shown in theaters.

Semimonthly. Twice a month.

Semiweekly. Twice a week.

Serial. Published periodically, such as a newspaper or magazine.

Sidebar. A feature presented as a companion to a straight news report (or main magazine article) giving sidelights on human-interest aspects or sometimes elucidating just one aspect of the story.

Simultaneous submissions. Sending the same article, story or poem to several publishers at the same time. Some publishers refuse to consider such submissions. No simultaneous submissions should be made without stating the fact in your letter.

Slant. The approach or style of a story or article that will appeal to readers of a specific magazine. For example, a magazine which always uses stories with an upbeat ending.

Slides. Usually called transparencies by editors looking for color photographs.

Slush pile. The stack of unsolicited or misdirected manuscripts received by an editor or book publisher.

Software. Programs and related documentation for use with a particular computer system.

Speculation. The editor agrees to look at the author's manuscript with no assurance that it will be bought.

Style. The way in which something is written—for example, short, punchy sentences or flowing narrative.

Subsidiary rights. All those rights, other than book publishing rights included in a book contract—such as paperback, book club, movie rights, etc.

Subsidy publisher. A book publisher who charges the author for the cost to typeset and print his book, the jacket, etc. as opposed to a royalty publisher who pays the author.

Syndication rights. See "Rights and the Writer" in the Business of Writing article.

Synopsis. A brief summary of a story, novel or play. As part of a book proposal, it is a comprehensive summary condensed in a page or page and a half, single-spaced. See also *outline*.

Tabloid. Newspaper format publication on about half the size of the regular newspaper page, such as the *National Enquirer*.

Tagline. A caption for a photo or a comment added to a filler.

Tearsheet. Page from a magazine or newspaper containing your printed story, article, poem or ad.

Trade. Either a hardcover or paperback book; subject matter frequently concerns a special interest. Books are directed toward the layperson rather than the professional.

Transparencies. Positive color slides; not color prints.

Treatment. Synopsis of a television or film script (40-60 pages for a 2-hour feature film or teleplay).

Unsolicited manuscript. A story, article, poem or book that an editor did not specifically ask to see.

User friendly. Easy to handle and use. Refers to computer hardware and software designed with the user in mind.

Vanity publisher See *subsidy publisher*.

Word processor. A computer that produces typewritten copy via automated typing, text-editing and storage and transmission capabilities.

Work-for-hire. See "Copyrighting Your Writing" in the Business of Writing article.

For hundreds of additional definitions and other information of importance to writers see the *Writer's Encyclopedia* (Writer's Digest Books).

Book Publishers Subject Index

Nonfiction

This index will help you find publishers that consider books on specific subjects—the subjects you choose to write about. Remember that a publisher may be listed here under a general subject category like Art and Architecture, while the company publishes **only** art history or how-to books. Be sure to consult each company's detailed individual listing, its book catalog and several of its books before you send your query or manuscript.

Agriculture/Horticulture. Between the Lines; David R. Godine; Harpswell; Michigan State University; Publishing Horizons; Oryx; Springer-Verlag; Stipes; Texas A&M University; Timber; University of Idaho; University of Nebraska; Western Producer; Westview.

Americana. American Studies; Ancestry; Arbor House; Atheneum Children's Books; Bantam; Binford & Mort; Branden; Brevet; Carpenter; Caxton Printers; Cay-Bel; Christopher; Clarion; Arthur H. Clark; Creative Pub.; Crown; May Davenport; Decalogue; Devin-Adair; Donning; Down East; Durst; Eakin; Paul S. Eriksson; Faber & Faber; Fjord; Four Winds; Michael Friedman; Glenbridge; Globe Pequot Press; David R. Godine; Golden West; Hancock House; Harcourt Brace Jovanovich; Harper & Row; Harvard Common; Herald Publishing House; Heyday; Holmes & Meier; International Publishers; Interurban Press/Trans Anglo; William Kaufman; Lexikos; McFarland; Madison; Main Street; Maverick; Media Productions and Marketing; Miller; Misty Hill; Mosaic; Mustang; New England; Oregon Historical Society; Outbooks; Overlook; Pacific; Peter Pauper; Pelican; Pruett; Publishers Associates; Quinlan; Random House; S.O.C.O.; Second Chance Press; Seven Locks; Shoe String; Sierra Club; Gibbs M. Smith; Stemmer House; Still Point; Lyle Stuart; Ten Speed; Texas Christian University; Tompson & Rutter; University of Arkansas; University of Idaho; University of Illinois; University of Nebraska; University of Pennsylvania; University Press of Kentucky; University Press of Mississippi; University Press of New England; University Press of Virginia; Utah State University; Vesta; Wallace; Washington State University; Franklin Watts; Welcome Enterprises; Westernlore; Westport; WindRiver; Wingra Woods; Winston-Derek; Woodbine; Workman.

Animals. Alaska Nature; Alpine Productions; Barron's; Canadian Plains Research Center; Carolrhoda; Christopher; Coles; Crown; May Davenport; Decalogue; Denlinger's; Dillon; Paul S. Eriksson; Faber & Faber; Flora and Fauna; Four Winds; Michael Friedman; Garden Way; David R. Godine; Greenhaven; Harper & Row; Homestead; Hounslow; Michael Kesend; McClelland & Stewart; McDonald; Miller; Misty Hill; Mosaic; Pineapple; Plexus; Publications International; Quinlan; Random House/Alfred Knopf Juvenile; Reading Rainbow; Rocky Top; S.C.E Editions; S.O.C.O.; Charles Scribner's Sons; Stemmer House; Sterling; T.F.H.; Tab; Jeremy P. Tarcher; Unicorn; Universe; Welcome Enterprises; Westport; Williamson; Willow Creek; Wingra Woods.

Anthropology/Archaelogy. Bantam; Beacon; Cambridge; Aristide D. Caratzas; Center for Thanatology Research; Michael Friedman; Milkweed Editions; Museum of New Mexico; Noyes Data; Ohio State University; Rutgers University; Routledge, Chapman and Hall; Stanford University; Charles C. Thomas; University of Alabama; University of Idaho; University of Iowa; University of Michigan; University of Nevada; University of Pennsylvania; University of Tennessee; University Press of Kentucky; Welcome Enterprises; Westernlore; Westview.

Art/Architecture. Harry N. Abrams; American Reference; Arbor House; Architectural; Art Direction; Atheneum Children's Books; Barron's; Beacon Press; Branden; Bucknell; Cambridge University; Aristide D. Caratzas; Carolrhoda; Chelsea Green; Christopher; Chronicle; Coteau; Council Oak; Crown; Davis; Diamond; Dodd, Mead; Durst; Paul S. Eriksson; Faber & Faber; Fairleigh Dickinson University; Fleet; Forman; Michael Friedman; J. Paul Getty Museum; David R. Godine; Graphic Arts Center; Guernica Editions; Harper & Row; Holmes & Meier; Homestead; Hounslow; Hudson Hills; Intervarsity; William Kaufman; Kent State University; Krantz; Peter Lang; Library Research Associates; Loyola University; McClelland & Stewart; McFarland; McGraw Hill Ryerson; Main Street; Mazda; Meriwether; Milkweed Editions; William Morrow; Museum of New Mexico; Museum of Northern Arizona; National Gallery of Canada; Nichols; North Light; Noyes Data Corp.; Ohio State University; Oregon Historical Society; PBC International; Pennsylvania Historical and Museum Commission; Plenum; Clarkson N. Potter; Prentice-Hall Canada Trade Div.; Prentice-Hall General Div.; Preservation; Princeton Architectural; Professional; Publishers Associates; Q.E.D. Press of Ann Arbor; Random House; Real Comet; Resource; Rosen; Roundtable; Rutgers University; Sasquatch; Charles Scribner's Sons; Shapolsky; Shoe String; Gibbs M. Smith; Sound View; ST; Starrhill; Stemmer House; Lyle Stuart; Sunstone; Taplinger; Texas Monthly; Twayne; Umi Research; Unicorn; Universe; University of Alberta; University of California; University of Massachusetts; University of Missouri; University of Texas; University Press of America; University Press of New England; Alfred Van Der Marck; Vance; Vanguard; Vesta; J. Weston Walch; Wallace; Washington State University; Welcome Enterprises; Westgate; Whitston; Wingra Woods; Alan Wofsy; Workman; Yee Wen.

Astrology/Psychic/New Age. ACS; Aquarian; Celestial Arts; Coles; Contemporary; Garber; Hartley & Marks; Humanics; Luramedia; Naturegraph; Newcastle; Pallas; Prentice-Hall General Div.; Theosophical; Samuel Weiser; Westgate; Whitford; Wingbow.

Autobiographies. Adams, Houmes and Ward; Arbor House; John Daniel; Harcourt Brace Jovanovich; Clarkson N. Potter.

Audiocassettes. Accelerated Development; Alpine; Asher-Gallant; Bennette & McKnight; Bookcraft; CSS; Carson-Dellosa; Chatham; Communication Skill Builders; Cynthia; Dartnell; Steve Davis; Devin-Adair; E.P. Dutton; Financial Sourcebooks; Forman; Garden Way; Government Institutes; Hunter; Ishiyaku Euroamerica; Ligouri; Lucas-Evans; Luramedia; Marathon International; Meriwether; National Association of Social Workers; Oise; Ortho Information; Players; Potentials Development; Professional; PSG; Random House; Resource; RPM; Success; Tabor; Jeremy P. Tarcher; Travel Keys; Trillium; Vestal; J. Weston Walch; Wilshire; Windsor; Workman.

Bibliographies. Borgo; Family Album; Feminist; Oryx; Scarecrow; University Press of Virginia; Vance; Whitston.

Biography. Adams, Houmes and Ward; Addison-Wesley; Aegina; Alaska Nature; Alaska Northwest; Alpha; American Atheist; American Studies; Architectural; Associated Faculty; Atheneum Children's Books; Atheneum; Avon; Baker Book; Ballantine/Epiphany; Bantam; Beaufort; Between the Lines; Binford & Mort; Borgo; Branden; Cambridge University; Canadian Plains Research Center; Carolrhoda; Carpenter; Carroll & Graf; Catholic University of America; Cay-Bel; Celestial Arts; Chelsea Green; Childrens; China Books and Periodicals; Christopher; Citadel; Clarion; Arthur H. Clark; College Board; Contemporary; Council Oak; Creative Arts; Creative Pub.; Credo; Crown; Harry Cuff; John Daniel; Dante University of America; Decalogue; Dillon; Down East; Eakin; Eden; Enslow; Paul S. Eriksson; Family Album; Frederick Fell; Feminist; Fithian; Fjord; Fleet; Fulcrum; K.S. Giniger; David R. Godine; Great Northwest; Great Ocean; Green Hill; Greenhaven; Guernica Editions; Hancock House; Harbour; Harcourt Brace Jovanovich; Harper & Row; Harvest House; Here's Life; Hippocrene; Holmes & Meier; Homestead; Houghton Mifflin; Hounslow; Huntington House; ILR; International Publishers; Intervarsity; Iowa State University; Kent State University; Michael Kesend; Peter Lang; Library Research Associates; Little, Brown; Loyola University; McClelland & Stewart; McDonald; McGraw Hill Ryerson; Madison; Markus Wiener; Maverick; MCN; Media Productions and Marketing; Melior; Mercer University; Metamorphous; Methuen; Misty Hill; William Morrow; Mosaic; Mother Courage; Motorbooks International; Mountain Lion; Museum of New Mexico; New England; New Leaf; New Victoria; Newmarket; Ohio State University; Old Army; Oregon Historical Society; Oregon State University; Pacific Press; Panjandrum; Pelican; Pennsylvania History and Museum Commission; Pineapple; Plexus; Pocket; Police Bookshelf; Clarkson N. Potter; Prairie; Byron Preiss Visual; Prima; Princeton Book; Quinlan; Random House; Random House/Alfred Knopf Juvenile; Roundtable; Routledge; Routledge, Chapman and Hall; S.C.E. Edition; S.O.C.O.; St. Martin's; St. Paul; Sandlapper; Santa Barbara; Sasquatch; Saybrook; Schirmer; Charles Scribner's Sons; Second Chance Press; Seven Locks; Shoe String; Gibbs M. Smith; Stemmer House; Still Point; Lyle Stuart; Jeremy P. Tarcher; Texas Monthly; Thunder's Mouth; Times; Twayne; Unicorn; University of Alabama; University of Alberta; University of Arkansas; University of Idaho; University of Illinois; University of Massachusetts; University of Nebraska; University of Nevada; University of Pennsylvania; University Press of Kansas; University Press of Kentucky; University Press of Mississippi; University Press of New England; Utah State University; Vanguard; Vehicule; Vesta; Vestal; Washington State University; Welcome Enterprises; Western Producer; Western Tanager; Westernlore; WindRiver; Winston-Derek; Woodbine; Woodsong; Zondervan.

Booklets. APA.

Business/Economics. Adams, Houmes and Ward; Bob Adams; Addison-Wesley; Almar; American Studies; American Hospital; Arbor House; Asher-Gallant; Associated Faculty; Atheneum Children's Books; Avant; Avon; Ballinger; Bantam; Barron's; Beaufort; Benjamin; Betterway; Between the Lines; Brethren; Brevet; Briarcliff; Brick House; Cambridge University; Canadian Plains Research Center; Catholic Health Association; Center for Migration Studies of New York; Chilton; Christopher; Cleaning Consultant Services; Coles; Communications; Compact; Consumer Reports; Contemporary; Council Oak; Cynthia; Dartnell; Decalogue; Devin-Adair; Durst; Eakin; Eden; Enslow; Enterprise; Paul S. Eriksson; ETC; Facts on File; Fairchild Books & Visuals; Fairleigh Dickinson University; Frederick Fell; Financial Sourcebooks; Forman; Fraser Institute; Free Press; Helena Frost; K.S. Giniger; Glenbridge; Glenmark; Green Hill; Greenhaven; Gulf; Alexander Hamilton Institute; Harcourt Brace Jovanovich; Harbor House; Harper & Row; Harvard Common; D.C. Heath; Holmes & Meier; Hounslow; Humanics; Industrial; Intercultural; International Foundation of Employee Benefit Plans; International Publishers; International Self-Counsel; International Wealth Success; Interurban Press/Trans Anglo; Iowa State University; William Kaufman; Knowledge Industry; Robert E. Krieger; Peter Lang; Liberty House; Library Research Associates; Lomond; Logical Extension; Longman; Loompanics; McClelland & Stewart; McFarland; McGraw-Hill; McGraw Hill Ryerson; Madison; Markus Wiener; Mazda; Medical Economics; Melius and Peterson; Menasha Ridge; Methuen; MGI Management Institute; Michigan State University; Morgan-Rand; Mosaic; National Health; National Publishers of the Black Hills; National Textbook; Newmarket; Nichols; Oasis; Oryx; Overlook; P.A.R; Pelican; James Peter; Petrocelli; Pilot; Prentice-Hall Canada; Prentice-Hall Canada Secondary School Div.; Prentice-Hall Canada Trade Div.; Prentice-Hall Business Div.; Prima; Professional; Publishers Associates; Publishing Horizons; Random House; Regnery/Gateway; Riverdale; Irving Rockwood; Ronin; Ross; Roundtable; Routledge, Chapman and Hall; Rowman & Littlefield; Roxbury; RPM; S.C.E. Editions; S.O.C.O.; Sasquatch; Saybrook; Schenkman; Seven Locks; Shoe String; South End; Sterling; Stipes; Lyle Stuart; Success; Tab; Teachers College; Ten Speed; Texas A&M University; Texas Monthly; Times; Trend; Universe; University of Calgary; University of Illinois; University of Michigan; University of Notre Dame; University of Pennsylvania; University of Texas; University Press of America; University Press of Virginia; Vanguard; J. Weston Walch; Westport; Wallace; Washington State University; Western Producer; Westview; John Wiley & Sons; Williamson; Wilshire; Windsor; Wordware.

Child Guidance/Parenting. Accelerated Development; Bantam; Bob Adams; ALA Books; Baker Book; Betterway; Bull; Child Welfare; College Board; Community Intervention; Decalogue; T.S. Denison; Fisher; Guidance Centre; Virgil W. Hensley; Jalmar; Logical Extension; McClelland & Stewart; McDonald; Meadowbrook; Newmarket; Octameron; Ohio Psychology; Pallas; Perspectives; Reading Rainbow; St. Paul; Tabor; Charles C. Thomas; Tyndale; Victor; Welcome Enterprises; Williamson; Woodbine.

Coffee Table Book. Bantam; Robert Bentley; Canadian Plains Research Center; Caxton Printers; China Books and Periodicals; Chronicle; Coteau; Donning; Frederick Fell; Forman; Michael Friedman; K.S. Giniger; Great Ocean; David R. Godine; Harbor House; Harbour; Harpswell; Homestead; Hounslow; Imagine; Krantz; Lexikos; Library Research Associates; Little, Brown; Logical Extension; McClelland & Stewart; Melior; Mountain Lion; Multnomah; Museum of Northern Arizona; New York Zoetrope; Pelican; Pennsylvania Historical and

Museum Commission; Prima; Princeton Architectural; Princeton Book; Publications International; S.O.C.O.; Sasquatch; Shapolsky; Lyle Stuart; T.F.H.; Texas Monthly; Unicorn; University of Idaho; Alfred Van Der Marck; Vend-O-Books; Welcome Enterprises; Willow Creek; Wingra Woods; Workman; Yankee; Zondervan.

Communications. Communications; Focal; Globe Pequot Press; Longman; Rosen; Tab; University of Calgary.

Community/Public Affairs. Fisher; Lomond; Pharos.

Computers/Electronics. Addison-Wesley; And Books; ARCsoft; Bantam; Branden; Career; Computer Science; Dustbooks; Educational Technology; Entelek; Fairchild Books & Visuals; Financial Sourcebooks; Gifted Education; Grapevine; H.P.; D.C. Heath; William Kaufman; Logical Extension; MGI Management Institute; National Publishers of the Black Hills; New York Zoetrope; Nichols; Prentice-Hall Business Div.; Publications International; Q.E.D. Information Sciences; Rowman & Littlefield; S.C.E.; Springer-Verlag; Sybex; Tab; Teachers College; J. Weston Walch; Wordware.

Consumer Affairs. Almar; Andrews and McMeel; Benjamin; Brick House; Consumer Reports; Meadowbrook; Menasha Ridge; Porter Sargent; Prentice-Hall Canada Trade Div.; Prentice-Hall General Div.; Regnery/Gateway; Second Chance Press; Southern Illinois University; Twayne.

Cooking/Foods/Nutrition. Addison-Wesley; Alaska Northwest; And Books; Applezaba; Arbor House; Atheneum Children's Books; Atheneum; Ballantine/Epiphany; Bantam; Barron's; Benjamin; Better Homes and Gardens; Betterway; Briarcliff; Bristol; Byls; Bull; Cay-Bel; Celestial Arts; Chicago Review; China Books and Periodicals; Christopher; Chronicle; Compact; Consumer Reports; Contemporary; Council Oak; Crossing; Crown; Dawn; Decalogue; Donning; Down East; Durst; Eakin; Paul S. Eriksson; Facts on File; Frederick Fell; Fisher; Forman; Michael Friedman; Garden Way; Glenmark; Globe Pequot Press; David R. Godine; Golden; Golden West Publishers; H.P.; Hancock House; Harcourt Brace Jovanovich; Harbor House; Harbour; Harper & Row; Harpswell; Harvard Common; Hawkes; Herald; Hounslow; Jonathan David; McClelland & Stewart; McGraw Hill Ryerson; Maverick; Mazda; Melius and Peterson; Miller; Mills & Sanderson; William Morrow; Mosaic; Mountain Lion; Museum of New Mexico; New England; Newmarket; Nitty Gritty Cookbooks; 101 Productions; Ortho Information Services; Pacific Press; Panjandrum; Peter Pauper; Peachtree; Pelican; Pennsylvania Historical and Museum Commission; Pineapple; Pocket; Clarkson N. Potter; Prairie; Prentice-Hall Canada Trade Div.; Prentice-Hall General Div.; Prima; Publications International; Random House; Richboro; Rodale; Royal; S.C.E. Editions; S.O.C.O.; Sasquatch; Shapolsky; Stemmer House; Sterling; Still Point; Ten Speed; Texas Monthly; Times; University of Idaho; University of North Carolina; Vanguard; Vesta; Wallace; Welcome Enterprises; Westport; Williamson; Willow Creek; WindRiver; Wine Appreciation; Wingra Woods; Woodland; Workman.

Counseling/Career Guidance. Peterson's Guide; Pilot; Prakken; Rosen; Teachers College; Ten Speed; VGM; John Wiley & Sons.

Crafts. Better Homes and Gardens; Briarcliff; Chilton; Coles; Davis; Doll Reader; Down East; Prentice-Hall General Div.; Standard; Sterling; Success; Sunstone; Troubador; University of North Carolina; Wallace; Williamson; Alan Wofsy.

Education(al). Accelerated Development; ALA Books; Aztex; Barnes & Noble; Barron's; Bennett & McKnight; Between the Lines; Byles; Career; Carson-Dellosa; Center for Thanatology Research; Coles; College Board; Communication Skill Builders; Community Intervention; T.S. Denison; Decalogue; Dillon; EES; Education Associates; Educational Technology; ETC; Fairchild Books & Visuals; Fearon; Feminist; Front Row Experience; Helena Frost; Gifted Education; Gryphon House; Guidance Centre; Holmes & Meier; Humanics; Incentive; Interstate Printers & Publishers; Jalmar; Liguori; Logical Extension; Longman; McCutchan; McDonald; Markus Wiener; Metamorphous; Methuen; Milady; Morehouse-Barlow; New Readers; Nichols; Octameron; Ohio Psychology; Ohio State University; Oise; Open Court; Pallas; Paulist; Perfection Form; Peterson's Guide; Porter Sargent; Prakken; Prentice Hall Business Div.; Princeton Book; Publications International; Publishing Horizons; Regal; Religious Education; Resource; Routledge, Chapman and Hall; Standard; Stipes; Tabor; Charles C. Thomas; Trillium; University; University of Idaho; University Press of America; J. Weston Walch; Williamson.

Entertainment/Games. Max Hardy-Publisher; Holloway House; McFarland; Potentials Development for Health & Aging Services; Scarecrow; Standard; Sterling.

Ethnic. Aegina; Between the Lines; Center for Migration Studies of New York; Coteau; Decalogue; Four Winds; Indiana University; International Publishers; Jonathan David; Kar-Ben Copies; Markus Wiener; McClelland & Stewart; Oregon Historical Society; Pelican; Ragweed; Thunder's Mouth; Union of American Hebrew Congregations; University of Massachusetts; University of Nebraska; University of Tennessee; University of Texas; University of Oklahoma; University Press of America; University Press of Mississippi.

Feminism. Cleis; Crossing; Firebrand; New Victoria; South End; Spinsters/Aunt Lute.

Film/Cinema/Stage. Borgo; Broadway; Citadel; Coach House; Dembner; Drama; Fairleigh Dickinson University; Focal; Imagine; Indiana University; JH; Lone Eagle; McFarland; Main Street; Meriwether; New York Zoetrope; Panjandrum; Players; Plenum; Prentice-Hall General Div.; Rosen; Roundtable; Routledge; Rutgers University; Scarecrow; Sterling; Theatre Arts; Umi Research; University of Texas; Vestal; WindRiver.

Gardening. Better Homes and Gardens; Briarcliff; Coles; Decalogue; Fisher; Michael Friedman; Garden Way; Globe Pequot Press; David R. Godine; H.P.; McDonald; McGraw Hill Ryerson; Main Street; Naturegraph; 101 Productions; Ortho Information Services; Prentice-Hall General Div.; Publications International; Richboro; Sasquatch; Ten Speed; Timber; University of North Carolina; Welcome Enterprises; Westport; Williamson.

Gays/Lesbians. Alyson; Bantam; Between the Lines; Celestial Arts; Cleis; Crossing; Firebrand; Gay Sunshine; Harbour; JH; Publishers Associates; Ragweed; Routledge; Spinsters/Aunt Lute; Welcome Enterprises.

General Nonfiction. Aegina; American Atheist; American Psychiatric; And Books; Avon Flare; Baen; Delacorte; Free Press; Holiday; Indiana University; Johnson; Kent State University; Krantz; Lodestar; Lothrop, Lee & Shepard; Media Productions and Marketing; Mercury House; New American Library; Pacific; Pocket; Pruett; Ross; St. Martin's; Stein and Day; Thunder's Mouth; Time-Life; University of Wisconsin; John Wiley & Sons.

Government/Politics. Addison-Wesley; American Atheist; American Studies; And Books; Arbor; Associated Faculty; Atheneum Children's Books; Avon; Bantam; Beacon Press; Between the Lines; Branden; Brethren; Brook House; Bucknell; CQ; Canadian Plains Research Center; Canterbury; Aristide D. Caratzas; Catholic University of America; Center for Migration Studies of New York; Chelsea Green; Christopher; Cleis; Communications; Council Oak; Crown; Harry Cuff; Devin-Adair; Eden; Paul S. Eriksson; Financial Sourcebooks; Fleet; Fraser Institute; Helena Frost; Fulcrum; Glenbridge; David R. Godine; Green Hill; Greenhaven; Guernica Editions; Harbour; Harper & Row; Holmes & Meier; Hounslow; Intercultural; International Publishers; Krantz; Peter Lang; Library Research Associates; Life Cycle; Lomond; Loompanics; McClelland & Stewart; McGraw Hill Ryerson; Madison; Mazda; Media Productions and Marketing; Michigan State University; Milkweed Editions; Miller; New Society; Ohio State University; Oregon Historical Society; Pantheon; Pennsylvania Historical and Museum Commission; Plenum; Prentice-Hall Canada Trade Div.; Prima; Publishers Associates; Quinlan; Random House; Real Comet; Regnery/Gateway; Riverdale; Irving Rockwood; Roundtable; St. Martin's; Sasquatch; Saybrook; Schenkman; Second Chance Press; Seven Locks; Shapolsky; Shoe String; South End; Lyle Stuart; Teachers College; Texas Monthly; Transnational; Trend; Universe; University of Alabama; University of Alberta; University of Arkansas; University of Calgary; University of Idaho; University of Illinois; University of Massachusetts; University of Michigan; University of Missouri; University of North Carolina; University of Tennessee; University Press of America; University Press of Kansas; University Press of Kentucky; University Press of Mississippi; University Press of New England; University Press of Virginia; Utah State University; Vance; Vehicule; Vesta; J. Weston Walch; Washington State University; Franklin Watts; Welcome Enterprises; Western Producer; Westview; Word.

Health/Medicine. Acropolis Books; ACS; Addison-Wesley; Almar; American Hospital; Arbor House; Associated Faculty; Atheneum Children's Books; Avant; Avon; Ballantine/Epiphany; Bantam; Beaufort; Benjamin; Betterway; Between the Lines; Bookmakers; Branden; Brethren; Briarcliff; Bridge; Brunner/Mazel; Bull; Catholic Health Association; Celestial Arts; Center for Thanatology Research; Christopher; Cleaning Consultant Services; Community Intervention; Compact; Consumer Reports; Contemporary; Council Oak; Crossing; Crown; Dawn;

Dembner; Devin-Adair; Donning; EES; Eden; Elysium Growth; Enslow; Paul S. Eriksson; Facts on File; Frederick Fell; Helena Frost; Fisher; Forman; K.S. Giniger; Glenmark; Warren H. Green; H.P.; Harper & Row; Hawkes; Health Profession Division; Houghton Mifflin; Hounslow; Human Kinetics; Humanics; Hunter House; Information Resources; International Foundation of Employee Benefit Plans; Iowa State University; Ishiyaku Euroamerica; William Kaufman; Michael Kesend; Robert E. Krieger; Peter Lang; Life Cycle; Luramedia; M.H. Macy; McFarland; Meadowbrook; Medical Economics; Metamorphous; Mills & Sanderson; Mosaic; Mother Courage; National Health; National Publishers of the Black Hills; Naturegraph; New Harbinger; New Readers; Newcastle; Newmarket; Oryx; P.P.I.; Pacific Press; Pallas; Panjandrum; Pantheon; Pelican; Perspectives; Prentice-Hall Canada Trade Div.; Prentice-Hall General Div.; Prima; Princeton Book; PSG; Publications International; Publishers Associates; Random House; Rodale; Ronin; Rosen; Roundtable; Rowman & Littlefield; S.C.E. Editions; Saybrook; Charles Scribner's Sons; Sierra Club; Springer-Verlag; Sterling; Lyle Stuart; Jeremy P. Tarcher; Theosophical; Charles C. Thomas; Times; Ultralight; Unicorn; Unique; University of Calgary; University of Pennsylvania; University of Texas; University Press of Virginia; J. Weston Walch; Samuel Weiser; Welcome Enterprises; Westview; Williamson; Wilshire; Winston-Derek; Woodbine; Woodland; Word; Workman.

History. Academy Chicago; Adams, Houmes and Ward; Addison-Wesley; Alaska Nature; Alaska Northwest; Alpha; American Atheist; American Studies; Ancestry; Appalachian Mountain Club; Arbor House; Architectural; Associated Faculty; Atheneum Children's Books; Avant; Aviation; Avon; Aztex; Bantam; Beacon; Beaufort; Between the Lines; Binford & Mort; Borgo; Boston Mills; Branden; Brethren; Brevet; Bucknell; Cambridge University; Canadian Plains Research Center; Aristide D. Caratzas; Carolrhoda; Carpenter; Carroll & Graf; Catholic University of America; Cay-Bel; Center for Migration Studies of New York; Chatham; Christopher; Citadel; Arthur H. Clark; Copley; Cornell Maritime; Coteau; Council Oak; Creative; Crossway; Crown; Harry Cuff; Dante University of America; Decalogue; Dembner; Devin-Adair; Donning; Down East; Eakin; Eden; William B. Eerdmans; Paul S. Eriksson; Faber & Faber; Facts on File; Fairleigh Dickinson University; Family Album; Feminist; Fjord; Fleet; Helena Frost; Fulcrum; J. Paul Getty Museum; K.S. Giniger; Glenbridge; David R. Godine; Globe Pequot Press; Globe Press; Green Hill; Greenhaven; Guernica Editions; Hancock House; Harbour; Harcourt Brace Jovanovich; Harper & Row Junior Books; Harper & Row; Harpswell; Hawkes; Heart of the Lakes; D.C. Heath; Herald Publishing House; Heritage; Heyday; Hippocrene; Holmes & Meier; Homestead; Houghton Mifflin; Hounslow; Hunter; Indiana University; International Publishing; Interurban Press/Trans Anglo; Intervarsity; Iowa State University; Johnson; William Kaufman; Kent State University; Michael Kesend; Robert E. Krieger; Peter Lang; Lexikos; Library Research Associates; Life Cycle; Little, Brown; Longman; Loompanics; Loyola; McClelland & Stewart; McFarland; McGraw Hill Ryerson; Madison; Markus Wiener; Maverick; Mazda; MCN; Media Productions and Marketing; Melior; Mercer University; Methuen; Michigan State University; Milkweed Editions; Miller; Misty Hill; Morehouse-Barlow; William Morrow; Mosaic; Motorbooks International; Museum of New Mexico; Naturegraph; New England; New Society; New Victoria; Newmarket; Noyes Data; Old Army; Open Court; Oregon Historical Society; Oregon State University; Outbooks; Overlook; Pantheon; Peachtree; Pelican; Penkevill; Pennsylvania Historical and Museum Commission; Pineapple; Pocket; Byron Preiss Visual; Prentice-Hall Canada; Preservation; Presidio; Publishers Associates; Quinlan; Random House; Riverdale; Irving Rockwood; Routledge; Routledge, Chapman and Hall; Rutgers University; S.C.E. Editions; S.O.C.O.; St. Martin's; Sandlapper; Sasquatch; Schenkman; Second Chance Press; Seven Locks; Shapolsky; Harold Shaw; Shoe String; Sierra Club; Gibbs M. Smith; Stackpole; Stanford University; Stemmer House; Still Point; Lyle Stuart; Sunstone; Teachers College; Temple University; Ten Speed; Texas A&M University; Texas Monthly; Texas Western; Three Continents; Timber; Times; Tompson & Rutter; Trend; Twayne; Tyndale; Ultralight; Universe; University of Alabama; University of Alberta; University of Arkansas; University of Calgary; University of Idaho; University of Illinois; University of Iowa; University of Massachusetts; University of Michigan; University of Missouri; University of Nebraska; University of Nevada; University of North Carolina; University of Notre Dame; University of Oklahoma; University of Pennsylvania; University of Tennessee; University of Texas; University Press of America; University Press of Kansas; University Press of Kentucky; University Press of Mississippi; University

Press of New England; University Press of Virginia; Alfred Van Der Marck; Vanguard; Vehicule; Vesta; Vestal; J. Weston Walch; Washington State University; Franklin Watts; Welcome Enterprises; Westernlore; Westport; Westview; WindRiver; Wingra Woods; Woodbine; Word; Workman; Yee Wen; Zondervan.

Hobby. Almar; Ancestry; Atheneum Children's Books; Bale; Benjamin; Betterway; Bookworks; Carstens; Coles; Collector; Crown; Decalogue; Doll Reader; Durst; Enslow; Paul S. Eriksson; Facts on File; Frederick Fell; Michael Friedman; Glenmark; H.P.; Hawkes; Hounslow; Interurban Press/Trans Anglo; Kalmbach; Michael Kesend; McDonald; Main Street; Maverick; MCN; Meadowbrook; Melius and Peterson; Menasha Ridge; Meriwether; Mosaic; Mustang; Ortho Information Services; Panjandrum; Publications International; Quinlan; Rocky Top; S.C.E. Editions; S.O.C.O.; Charles Scribner's Sons; Stackpole; Sterling; Success; Tab; Taplinger; Ten Speed; Travel Keys; Ultralight; Vestal; Welcome Enterprises; Wilderness; Williamson; Wilshire; WindRiver; Woodbine; Woodsong; Workman.

House and Home. Better Homes and Gardens; Betterway; Garden Way; Ortho Information Services; Williamson.

How-to. AASLH; Abbott, Langer & Associates; Acropolis Books; Adams, Houmes and Ward; Addison-Wesley; Aegina; Alaska Nature; Almar; Alpha; Alpine; Ancestry; And Books; Andrews and McMeel; Andrion; Appalachian Mountain Club; Arbor House; M. Arman; Art Direction; Asher-Gallant; Atheneum Children's Books; Avant; Avon; Aztex; Ballantine/Epiphany; Bantam; Benjamin; Robert Bentley; Berkley; Better Homes and Gardens; Betterway; Bookworks; Briarcliff; Brick House; Bridge; Bull; Byls; Chicago Review Press; Chilton; China Books and Periodicals; Chosen; Christopher; Cleaning Consultant Services; Community Intervention; Compact; Consumer Reports; Contemporary; Corkscrew; Cornell Maritime; Council Oak; Craftsman; Credo; Crossing; Decalogue; Dell; Dembner; Denlinger's; Devin-Adair; Donning; Durst; EES; Eden; Education Associates; Enslow; Enterprise; Frederick Fell; Fisher; Fithian; J. Flores; Focal; Forman; Michael Friedman; Garden Way; Gay Sunshine; Gifted Education; Glenmark; Grapevine; Great Northwest; Stephen Green Press/Lewis; H.P.; Hancock House; Harbour; Harper & Row; Harpswell; Harvard Common; Harvest House; Hawkes; Herald; Here's Life; Heyday; Hippocrene; Hounslow; Human Kinetics; Hunter House; Imagine; Intercultural; International Self-Counsel; International Wealth Success; Jist Works; Jonathan David; William Kaufman; Michael Kesend; Krantz; Library Research Associates; Linch; Little, Brown; Logical Extension; Lone Eagle; McClelland & Stewart; McDonald; McGraw Hill Ryerson; Main Street; Meadowbrook; Media Productions and Marketing; Melius and Peterson; Menasha Ridge; Meriwether; Metamorphous; MGI Management Institute; Milady; Mills & Sanderson; Miller; William Morrow; Mother Courage; Motorbooks International; Mountain Lion; Mountaineers; Mustang; Naturegraph; Naturegraph; New England; Newcastle; North Light; Oasis; OHara; 101 Productions; Ortho Information Services; Overlook; Pacific Press; Pallas; Pantheon; Pelican; Pennsylvania Historical and Museum Commission; Perspectives; James Peter; Pineapple; Police Bookshelf; Clarkson N. Potter; Prentice-Hall Business Div.; Prima; Princeton Book; Publications International; Q.E.D. Press of Ann Arbor; Rainbow; Resource; Richboro; Rocky Top; Rodale; Ronin; Ross; Roundtable; RPM; S.C.E. Editions; S.O.C.O.; Santa Barbara; Sasquatch; Schirmer; Michael Shore; Sierra Club; ST; Standard; Sterling; Stone Wall; Lyle Stuart; Success; Sunstone; T.F.H.; Tab; Ten Speed; Thomas; Travel Keys; Ultralight; Unique; University of Alberta; Vanguard; Vend-O-Books; Vestal; Wallace; Samuel Weiser; Welcome Enterprises; Western Marine; Westport; Whitford; Wilderness; John Wiley & Sons; Williamson; Willow Creek; Wilshire; WindRiver; Windsor; Wine Appreciation; Wingra Woods; Woodland; Woodsong; Word; Workman; Writer's Digest; Zondervan.

Humanities. Aegina; Asian Humanities; Duquesne University; Free Press; Garland; Indiana University; McClelland & Stewart; McGraw-Hill; McGraw Hill Ryerson; Maverick; Mountain Lion; Penkevill; James Peter; Riverdale; Rocky Top; Roxbury; Southern Illinois University; Taplinger; Temple University; Umi Research; University of Arkansas; University of Calgary; University of Idaho; University of Michigan; Vanguard; VGM; Whitston; WindRiver.

Humor. Aegina; American Studies; Andrews and McMeel; Andrion; Applezaba; Atheneum Children's Books; Baker Book; Ballantine/Epiphany; Bantam; CCC; CSS; Citadel; Clarion; Compact; Contemporary; Corkscrew; Coteau; Critic's Choice Paperbacks; Crown; Harry Cuff; John Daniel; Dell; Donning; Eden; Paul S. Eriksson; Faber & Faber; Frederick Fell;

Fithian; Guernica Editions; H.P.; Hanley & Belfus; Harcourt Brace Jovanovich; Harper & Row; Harpswell; Hounslow; William Kaufman; McDonald; Main Street; Meadowbrook; Menasha Ridge; Meriwether; Misty Hill; Mosaic; Mustang; Once Upon a Planet; Peter Pauper; Peachtree; Pelican; Pharos; Pocket; Clarkson N. Potter; Price/Stern/Sloan; Prima; Quinlan; Random House; Random House/Alfred Knopf Juvenile; Ronin; Roundtable; S.C.E. Editions; S.O.C.O.; Sandlapper; Sasquatch; Charles Scribner's Sons; Sterling; Lyle Stuart; Ten Speed; Texas Monthly; Vanguard; Vend-O-Books; Welcome Enterprises; Willow Creek; Woodsong; Workman.

Illustrated Book. American Studies; And Books; Appalachian Mountain Club; Atheneum Children's Books; Bear; Betterway; Boston Mills; Branden; Canadian Plains Research Center; Cleaning Consultant Services; Coteau; Council Oak; Harry Cuff; Donning; Down East; Eden; Elysium Growth; J. Flores; Michael Friedman; K.S. Giniger; David R. Godine; Greenhaven; Harcourt Brace Jovanovich; Harbor House; Harpswell; Harvest House; Homestead; Hounslow; Imagine; Michael Kesend; Lexikos; Logical Extension; McClelland & Stewart; Maverick; Melior; Mountain Lion; MCN; Meadowbrook; Metamorphous; Methuen; Milkweed Editions; Mosaic; Multnomah; New England; New Society; Once Upon a Planet; Ortho Information Services; Pelican; Pennsylvania Historical and Museum Commission; Prentice-Hall General Div.; Prima; Princeton Architectural; Publications International; Quinlan; Random House; Random House/Alfred Knopf Juvenile; Ronin; Sasquatch; Sandlapper; Stemmer House; T.F.H.; Texas Monthly; Time-Life; Unicorn; Union of American Hebrew Congregations; University of Idaho; Vanguard; Welcome Enterprises; Westgate; Westport; Williamson; Willow Creek; Woodsong; Workman; Zondervan.

Juvenile. Alaska Nature; Atheneum Children's Books; Baker Book; Bancroft-Sage; Barron's; Betterway; Bookmakers Guild; Branden; Byls; Carolrhoda; Carpenter; Chariot; China Books and Periodicals; Clarion; Consumer Reports; Coteau; Crown; Harry Cuff; May Davenport; Dell; Dial Books for Young Readers; Dillon; Down East; E.P. Dutton; Eakin; Enslow; Farrar, Straus and Giroux; Fithian; Fleet; Four Winds; J. Paul Getty Museum; David R. Godine; C.R. Gibson; Golden; Green Timber; Greenhaven; Harbour; Harcourt Brace Jovanovich; Harper Junior Books, West Coast; Harvest House; Herald; Homestead; Hounslow; Hunter House; Incentive; Kar-Ben Copies; Lucas-Evans; McClelland & Stewart; McDonald; Margaret K. McElderry; Macmillan; Mazda; Meadowbrook; Metamorphous; Misty Hill; Morehouse-Barlow; William Morrow; Morrow Junior; Mountain Lion; Oddo; P.P.I.; Pacific Press; Panjandrum; Pantheon; Pelican; Perspectives; Players; Clarkson N. Potter; Byron Preiss Visual; Price/Stern/Sloan; Publications International; Q.E.D. Information Sciences; Ragweed; Random House/Alfred Knopf Juvenile; Reading Rainbow; Review and Herald Publishing; St. Paul; Sandlapper; Sasquatch; Harold Shaw; Sierra Club; Standard; Stemmer House; Sterling; Success; TGNW; Troubador; Unicorn; Union of American Hebrew Congregations; Vanguard; Victor; Welcome Enterprises; Westport; Wingra Woods; Woodsong; Workman; Zondervan.

Labor/Management. Almar; Alexander Hamilton Institute; ILR; MGI Management Institute; Prentice-Hall; RPM; Temple University; University.

Language and Literature. Barron's; Beacon Press; Aristide D. Caratzas; Asian Humanities; Baker Book; Bantam; Catholic University of America; Coles; College Board; Coteau; Crossing; Dante University of America; Decalogue; Facts on File; Helena Frost; David R. Godine; Indiana University; Longman; Loyola; McClelland & Stewart; McDonald; McFarland; Markus Wiener; Milkweed Editions; Modern Language Association of America; National Textbook; Newmarket; Oddo; Ohio State University; Oregon State University; Penkevill; Perfection Form; Clarkson N. Potter; Prentice-Hall Canada; Ragweed; Rosen; Routledge; Sasquatch; Stanford University; Jeremy P. Tarcher; Texas Christian University; Charles C. Thomas; Three Continents; University of Alabama; University of Arkansas; University of California; University of Idaho; University of Illinois; University of Iowa; University of Michigan; University of Nebraska; University of North Carolina; University of Texas; University Press of America; Vanguard; Vehicule; J. Weston Walch; Welcome Enterprises; John Wiley & Sons; York.

Law. Anderson; Associated Faculty; Enterprise; Government Institutes; International Self-Counsel; Linch; National Health; Ohio State University; Pantheon; Parker & Son; Police Bookshelf; Rowman & Littlefield; Rutgers University; S.C.E. Editions; Transnational; Trend; University of Michigan; University of North Carolina; University of Pennsylvania; University Press of Virginia; Westview.

Literary Criticism. Associated Faculty; Borgo; Bucknell; ECW; Fairleigh Dickinson University; Holmes & Meier; Methuen; Q.E.D. Press of Ann Arbor; Routledge, Chapman and Hall; Rutgers University; Stanford University; Texas Christian University; Three Continents; Twayne; Umi Research; University of Alabama; University of Arkansas; University of Massachusetts; University of Michigan; University of Missouri; University of Pennsylvania; University of Tennessee; University Press of Mississippi; York.

Marine Subjects. Cay-Bel; Cornell Maritime; Harbor House; International Marine; PBC International; Tab.

Military/War. Avon; Bantam; Beau Lac; Between the Lines; Crown; Eakin; J. Flores; McClelland & Stewart; Newmarket; Old Army; Oregon Historical Society; Prentice-Hall General Div.; Presidio; Routledge; Shoe String; Stackpole; University Press of Kansas; Vanguard; Westview.

Money/Finance. Acropolis Books; Almar; Bale; Ballinger; Better Homes and Gardens; Enterprise; Financial Sourcebooks; Glenmark; Virgil W. Hensley; International Wealth Success; Liberty House; Logical Extension; Longman Financial Services; McClelland & Stewart; McGraw Hill Ryerson; Newmarket; Nichols; Publications International; Publishing Horizons; Springer-Verlag; Vanguard; Westport.

Music and Dance. American Catholic; And Books; Atheneum Children's Books; Bantam; Beaufort; Branden; Bucknell; Cambridge University; Carolrhoda; Consumer Reports; Dance Horizons; Dembner; Dodd, Mead; Dragon's Teeth; Drama; Paul S. Eriksson; Faber & Faber; Facts on File; Fairleigh Dickinson University; Glenbridge; David R. Godine; Guernica Editions; Harper & Row; Holmes & Meier; Indiana University; Robert E. Krieger; Peter Lang; McClelland & Stewart; McFarland; Maverick; Meriwether; Mosaic; Museum of New Mexico; Music Sales; Newmarket; Ohio State University; Panjandrum; Pelican; Pennsylvania Historical and Museum Commission; Plenum; Prima; Princeton Book; Publishers Associates; Q.E.D. Press of Ann Arbor; Quinlan; Random House; Real Comet; Resource; Rosen; Routledge; Scarecrow; Schirmer; Shoe String; Starrhill; Stipes; Lyle Stuart; Tab; Timber; Umi Research; Unicorn; Universe; University of Illinois; University of Michigan; University Press of America; University Press of New England; Vestal; J. Weston Walch; Samuel Weiser; Welcome Enterprises; Writer's Digest.

Nature and Environment. Harry N. Abrams; Alaska Nature; And Books; Appalachian Mountain Club; Atheneum Children's Books; Bear; Binford & Mort; Canadian Plains Research Center; Carolrhoda; Chelsea Green; Chronicle; Clarion; Council Oak; Crown; John Daniel; May Davenport; Dawn; Decalogue; Devin-Adair; Down East; Eden; Elysium Growth; Paul S. Eriksson; Flora and Fauna; Forman; Four Winds; Michael Friedman; Fulcrum; David R. Godine; Golden; Government Institutes; Great Northwest; Stephen Green Press/Lewis; Greenhaven; Hancock House; Harcourt Brace Jovanovich; Harper & Row; Harpswell; Holmes & Meier; Heyday; Homestead; Hounslow; Johnson; Michael Kesend; Lexikos; McClelland & Stewart; McDonald; Melius and Peterson; Milkweed Editions; Misty Hill; Mosaic; Museum of New Mexico; Museum of Northern Arizona; New England; Oregon Historical Society; Ortho Information Services; Outbooks; Overlook; Pacific Press; Pineapple; Plexus; Clarkson N. Potter; Prentice-Hall General Div.; Publishing Horizons; Random House; Random House/Alfred Knopf Juvenile; Reading Rainbow; Review and Herald; Rocky Top; S.C.E. Editions; S.O.C.O.; Sasquatch; Charles Scribner's Sons; Seven Locks; Shoe String; Sierra Club; Starrhill; Stemmer House; Stone Wall; Ten Speed; Texas A&M University; Texas Monthly; Charles C. Thomas; Universe; University of Alberta; University of Arkansas; University of Calgary; University of Idaho; Unviersity of Nebraska; University Press of New England; Welcome Enterprises; Western Producer; Westport; Wilderness; Willow Creek; Wingra Woods; Woodland.

Philosophy. Alba House; Alpha; American Atheist; Aquarian; Asian Humanities; Atheneum Children's Books; Baker Book; Bantam; Beacon Press; Berkley; Brethren; Brook House; Bucknell; Canterbury; Catholic University of America; Celestial Arts; Center for Thanatology Research; Christopher; Council Oak; John Daniel; Decalogue; Donning; Dragon's Teeth; Eden; William B. Eerdmans; Elysium Growth; Enslow; Paul S. Eriksson; Facts on File; Fairleigh Dickinson University; Frederick Fell; Fulcrum; Garber Communications; Gifted Education; Glenbridge; Globe; Greenhaven; Guernica Editions; Harcourt Brace Jovanovich; Harper & Row; Herald; Hounslow; Indiana University; Intercultural; International Publishers; Intervarsity; Robert E. Krieger; Peter Lang; Library Research Associates; Loompanics; Luramedia; M.H. Macy; McDonald; Mercer University; Methuen; Michigan State University; Miller;

New City; New Society; Ohio State University; Open Court; Panjandrum; Paulist; Publishers Associates; Q.E.D. Press of Ann Arbor; Regnery/Gateway; Rocky Top; Routledge; Routledge, Chapman and Hall; Rowman & Littlefield; Roxbury; S.C.E. Editions; Santa Barbara; Saybrook; Second Chance Press; Shapolsky; Shoe String; Sierra Club; Tabor; Teachers College; Temple University; Theosophical; Charles C. Thomas; Unique; University of Alabama; University of Alberta; University of Calgary; University of Massachusetts; University of Michigan; University of Notre Dame; University Press of America; University Press of Kansas; Vesta; Washington State University; Samuel Weiser; Welcome Enterprises; Westview; Wingbow; Winston-Derek; Woodsong; Word; Yee Wen; Zondervan.

Photography. Alaska Nature; American References; Appalachian Mountain Club; Atheneum Children's Books; Branden; Chronicle; Clarion; Coteau; Crown; Donning; Elysium Growth; Paul S. Eriksson; Focal; David R. Godine; H.P.; Harpswell; Homestead; Hounslow; Hudson Hills; Krantz; Logical Extension; Milkweed Editions; Motorbooks International; Oregon Historical Society; Owl Creek; PBC International; Pennsylvania Historical and Museum Commission; Plenum; Clarkson N. Potter; Prentice-Hall General Div.; Publications International; Quinlan; Reading Rainbow; Real Comet; S.O.C.O.; Sasquatch; Charles Scribner's Sons; Shapolsky; Sierra Club; Sterling; Studio; Tab; Temple University; Texas Monthly; Umi Research; Unicorn; University of Idaho; University of Nebraska; University of Texas; Alfred Van Der Marck; Wallace; Welcome Enterprises; Western Producer; Writer's Digest; Workman.

Psychology. Abbey; Accelerated Development; Addison-Wesley; Alba House; American Psychiatric; American Studies; Arbor House; Atheneum Children's Books; Augsburg; Avon; Baker Book; Ballantine/Epiphany; Bantam; Beacon Press; Betterway; Bookmakers Guild; Brethren; Brunner/Mazel; Bucknell; Cambridge University; Carroll & Graf; Celestial Arts; Center for Migration Studies of New York; Center for Thanatology Research; Christopher; Citadel; Community Intervention; Compact; Contemporary; Council Oak; Crown; Eden; Education Associates; Educational Technology; William B. Eerdmans; Elysium Growth; Enslow; Paul S. Eriksson; Facts on File; Fairleigh Dickinson University; Fisher; Forman; Helena Frost; Gifted Education; Glenbridge; Glenmark; Globe; Stephen Greene Press/Lewis; Greenhaven; Guernica Editions; Harcourt Brace Jovanovich; Harper & Row; Hawkes; Hazeldon; Herald; Heroica; Holmes & Meier; Houghton Mifflin; Hounslow; Humanics; Hunter House; Intercultural; International Self-Counsel; Intervarsity; Ishiyaku Euroamerica; John Knox; Robert E. Krieger; Peter Lang; Libra; Luramedia; M.H. Macy; McClelland & Stewart; McDonald; McFarland; Metamorphous; Methuen; Mother Courage; New Harbinger; Newcastle; Newmarket; Ohio Psychology; Open Court; Pallas; Penkevill; Perspectives; James Peter; Plenum; Prentice-Hall General Div.; Prima; Publishers Associates; Random House; Riverdale; Rodale; Ronin; Roundtable; Routledge, Chapman and Hall; Roxbury; St. Paul; Saybrook; Schenkman; Harold Shaw; Shoe String; Springer-Verlag; Stanford University; Stillpoint; Tabor; Jeremy P. Tarcher; Theosophical; Tyndale; University of Calgary; University of Massachusetts; University of Michigan; University of Nebraska; University Press of America; University Press of New England; Vanguard; Victor; J. Weston Walch; Washington State University; Samuel Weiser; Westport; Williamson; Wilshire; Wingbow; Wingra Woods; Woodsong; Word; Zondervan.

Real Estate. Contemporary; Longman Financial Services; Prentice-Hall Business Div.; Uli.

Recreation. Harry N. Abrams; Alaska Nature; And Books; Arbor House; Atheneum Children's Books; Backcountry; Beaufort; Binford & Mort; Chicago Review; Chronicle; Commmunity Intervention; Compact; Crown; Decalogue; Down East; Eden; Elysium Growth; Enslow; Paul S. Eriksson; Facts on File; Falcon Press Publishing; Frederick Fell; Michael Friedman; Fulcrum; Glenmark; Globe Pequot Press; Stephen Green Press/Lewis; Guernica Editions; H.P.; Hancock House; Hippocrene; Hounslow; Human Kinetics; Johnson; Kalmbach; Robert E. Krieger; McGraw Hill Ryerson; Meadowbrook; Melius and Peterson; Menasha Ridge; Meriwether; Mountaineers; Mustang; 101 Productions; Outbooks; Overlook; Pantheon; Peachtree; Pelican; Princeton Book; Publishing Horizons; Quinlan; Random House/Alfred Knopf Juvenile; Reading Rainbow; Riverdale; S.C.E. Editions; Sasquatch; Charles Scribner's Sons; Sierra Club; Sterling; Stipes; Jeremy P. Tarcher; Ten Speed; Texas Monthly; Charles C. Thomas; J. Weston Walch; Welcome Enterprises; Westport; Wilshire; WindRiver; Workman.

Reference. AASLH; Abbott, Langer & Associates; Accelerated Development; Acropolis Books; Bob Adams; ALA Books; Alpha; American Atheist; American Hospital; American Psychiatric; American Reference; Ancestry; Andrews and McMeel; Andrion; Appalachian

Mountain Club; Architectural; M. Arman; Asher-Gallant; Asian Humanities; Associated Faculty; Avon; Baker Book; Ballinger; Bethany House; Betterway; Binford & Mort; Bookmakers Guild; Borgo; Branden; Brick House; Broadway; Aristide D. Caratzas; Carpenter; Cay-Bel; Center for Thanatology Research; Chicago Review; China Books and Periodicals; Christopher; Arthur H. Clark; Coles; College Board; Communications; Compact; Computer Science; Consumer Reports; Contemporary; Coteau; Credo; Crown; Harry Cuff; Dante University of America; Steve Davis; Decalogue; Dembner; Dharma; Donning; Down East; Drama; Durst; EES; ECW; Eden; William B. Eerdmans; Enslow; Facts on File; Fairleigh Dickinson University; Flora and Fauna; Focal; Garland; K. S. Giniger; Glenbridge; Government Institutes; Great Ocean; Greenhaven; Guernica Editions; Gulf; Hanley & Belfus; Harcourt Brace Jovanovich; Harper & Row; Harvard Common; Harvest House; Hazeldon Foundation; Health Profession Division; Herald; Here's Life; Heroica; Heyday; Hippocrene; Holmes & Meier; Homestead; Hounslow; Human Kinetics; Hunter; ILR; Imagine; Industrial; Information Resources; Intercultural; International Foundation of Employee Benefit Plans; International Self-Counsel; Interstate Printers & Publishers; Intervarsity; Ishiyaku Euroamerica; Jist Works; Jonathan David; Krantz; Peter Lang; Library Research Associates; Libraries Unlimited; Logical Extension; Lone Eagle; Loompanics; Lucas-Evans; McClelland & Stewart; McDonald; McFarland; McGraw-Hill; McGraw Hill Ryerson; Madison; Markus Wiener; Mazda; MCN; Meadowbrook; Media Productions and Marketing; Medical Economics; Melius and Peterson; Menasha Ridge; Mercer University; Metamorphous; Methuen; Michigan State University; Milady; Modern Language Association of America; Morgan-Rand; Mountain Lion; Museum of New Mexico; Museum of Northern Arizona; Music Sales; National Health; New York Zoetrope; Newmarket; Nichols; Octameron; Old Army; Oregon Historical Society; Ortho Information Services; Oryx; Our Sunday Visitor; Overlook; Pacific; Panjandrum; Penkevill; Pennsylvania Historical and Museum Commission; James Peter; Peterson's Guide; Petrocelli; Pharos; Pineapple; Plexus; Pocket; Police Bookshelf; Porter Sargent; Potentials Development for Health & Aging Services; Prentice-Hall Business Div.; Princeton Book; Professional; Publications International; Rainbow; Reading Rainbow; Rocky Top; Rosen; RPM; S.C.E. Editions; St. Martin's; Sandlapper; Scarecrow; Schirmer; Seven Locks; Harold Shaw; Shoe String; Sound View; ST; Standard; Starrhill; Sterling; Storie/MCowen; T.F.H.; Texas Monthly; Thomas; Transnational; Trend; Ultralight; Universe; University of Alberta; University of Calgary; University of Illinois; University of Michigan; University Press of Kentucky; University Press of New England; University Press of Virginia; Vestal; Victor; Wallace; Western Producer; Westview; Whitford; Whitston; John Wiley & Sons; Wingbow; Alan Wofsy; Woodbine; Woodland; Woodsong; Word; Wordware; Writer's Digest; York; Zondervan.

Regional. Aegina; Alaska Nature; Alaska Northwest; Almar; Binford & Mort; Borealis; Caxton Printers; Chatham; Chicago Review; China Books and Periodicals; Chronicle; Arthur H. Clark; Copley; Cornell Maritime; Coteau; Harry Cuff; Down East; Eakin; William B. Eerdmans; Falcon Press Publishing; Fjord; Globe Pequot Press; David R. Godine; Golden West Publishers; Great Northwest; Green Hill; Guernica Editions; Gulf; Harbour; Harbor House; Heart of the Lakes; Herald Publishing House; Heyday Books; Indiana University; Johnson; Kent State University; Lexikos; McDonald; Markus Wiener; Media Productions and Marketing; Melior; Mercer University; Milkweed Editions; Museum of New Mexico; New England; Oregon Historical Society; Oregon State University; Outbooks; Pacific; Pelican; Pennsylvania Historical and Museum Commission; Pruett; Ragweed; Sasquatch; Sunstone; Syracuse University; Temple University; Texas A&M University; Texas Monthly; Texas Western; Three Continents; Trend; University of Idaho; University of Michigan; University of Missouri; University of Nevada; University of North Carolina; University of Tennessee; University of Texas; University Press of Kansas; University Press of Mississippi; Utah State University; Vehicule; Washington State University; Western Tanager; Westernlore.

Religion. Abbey; Abingdon; Accent Books; Aglow; Alba House; Alban Institute; Alpha; American Atheist; American Catholic; Aquarian; Asian Humanities; Atheneum Children's Books; Augsburg; Baker Book; Ballantine/Epiphany; Bantam; Beacon Press; Bear; Bethany House; Bookcraft; Brethren; Bridge; Broadman; Bucknell; Byls; CSS; Aristide D. Caratzas; Catholic Health Association; Catholic University of America; Center for Thanatology Research; Chosen; Christopher; College Press; Compact; Crossway; Dawn; Decalogue; Dharma; William B. Eerdmans; Facts on File; Frederick Fell; Fleet; Franciscan Herald; Fraser Institute; J. Paul Getty Museum; C.R. Gibson; K.S. Giniger; Glenmark; Greenhaven; Guernica Editions; Harcourt Brace Jovanovich; Harper & Row; Harvest House; Hendrickson; Virgil W. Hensley; Herald Publishing House; Here's Life; Holmes & Meier; Hounslow; Huntington House; Indiana University; Intervarsity; John Knox; Judson; Robert E. Krieger; Peter Lang; Life Cycle; Liguori; Loyola; M.H. Macy; McClelland & Stewart; McFarland; Markus Wiener; Mercer University; Meriwether; Methuen; Michigan State University; Misty Hill; Morehouse-Barlow; William Morrow; Multnomah; New City; New Leaf; New Society; Newcastle; Open Court; Orbis; Our Sunday Visitor; Pacific Press; Pallas; Paulist; Peter Pauper; Pelican; Pennsylvania Historical and Museum Commission; Publishers Associates; St. Paul; Quinlan; Ragweed; Randall House; Random House; Regal; Regnery/Gateway; Religious Education; Resource; Review and Herald; Routledge; St. Anthony Messenger; Santa Barbara; Servant; Seven Locks; Shapolsky; Harold Shaw; Shoe String; Standard; Tabor; Theosophical; Charles C. Thomas; Tyndale; Umi Research; Union of American Hebrew Congregations; University of Alabama; University of Calgary; University of Idaho; University of North Carolina; University of Notre Dame; University of Tennessee; University Press of America; Samuel Weiser; Wingbow; Winston-Derek; Word; Workman; Yee Wen; Zondervan.

Scholarly. Beacon Press; Birkauser Boston; Bucknell; Cambridge University; Canadian Plains Research Center; Dante University of America; Duquesne; Fairleigh Dickinson University; J. Paul Getty Museum; Harvard University; ILR; Indiana University; Kent State University; Alfred A. Knopf; Peter Lang; Lomond; McFarland; Mazda; Mercer University; Michigan State University; Museum of New Mexico; Nelson-Hall; Ohio State University; Oise; Open Court; Oregon State University; Penkevill; Porter Sargent; Religious Education; Routledge; Routledge, Chapman and Hall; Rowman & Littlefield; Rutgers University; St. Martin's; Schirmer; Southern Illinois; Stanford University; Temple University; Texas Christian University; Texas Western; Three Continents; Transnational; Twayne; Umi Research; University of Alabma; University of Calgary; University of California; University of Illinois; University of Missouri; University of North Carolina; University of Wisconsin; University Press of America; University Press of Kansas; Washington State University; Westernlore; Whitston; York.

Science/Technology. Harry N. Abrams; Addison-Wesley; Almar; American Astronautical Society; Architectural; ARCsoft; Baen; Ballinger; Bantam; Bear; Cambridge University; Chicago Review; Childrens; Coles; College Board; Computer Science; Crown; Decalogue; Dillon; Dodd, Mead; Eden; Enslow; Grapevine; Great Ocean; Warren H. Green; Stephen Greene Press/Lewis; Gulf; Harper & Row Junior Books; Harper & Row; D.C. Heath; Helix; Houghton Mifflin; Industrial; Iowa State University; Johnson; William Kaufman; Kent State University; John Knox; Krantz; Robert E. Krieger; Little, Brown; Logical Extension; McClelland & Stewart; McGraw-Hill; Metamorphous; Methuen; Museum of New Mexico; Museum of Northern Arizona; Naturegraph; New Readers; Nichols; Noyes Data; Oddo; Open Court; Oregon State University; Pallas; Plexus; Plenum; Byron Preiss Visual; Prentice-Hall Canada; Prentice-Hall Canada Secondary School Div.; Publications International; Random House/Alfred Knopf Juvenile; Reading Rainbow; Rocky Top; Ross; Routledge, Chapman and Hall; Rutgers University; St. Martin's; Charles Scribner's Sons; Sierra Club; Springer-Verlag; Stanford University; Stipes; Texas Western; Theosophical; Charles C. Thomas; Timber; Times; Twayne; University of Calgary; University of Michigan; University of Pennsylvania; University of Texas; University Press of New England; Utah State University; VGM; J. Weston Walch; Welcome Enterprises; Westview; Wingra Woods.

Self-help. AASLH; Acropolis Books; ACS; Adams, Houmes and Ward; Aglow; Alaska Nature; American Psychiatric; And Books; Arbor House; Atheneum Children's Books; Augsburg; Avant; Avon; Baker Book; Ballantine/Epiphany; Bantam; Benjamin; Betterway; Bridge; Bull; CSS; Celestial Arts; Center for Thanatology Research; Chosen; Christopher; Cleaning Consultant Services; Cliffs Notes; Coles; Community Intervention; Compact; Consumer Reports; Contemporary; Council Oak; Crown; John Daniel; Dawn; Eden; Elysium; Enslow; Enterprise; Paul S. Eriksson; Frederick Fell; Fisher; Fithian; J. Flores; Forman; Fulcrum; Glenmark; Globe; Grapevine; Great Ocean; Stephen Greene Press/Lewis; H.P.; Hancock House; Harcourt Brace Jovanovich; Harper & Row; Harvard Common; Hawkes; Hazeldon Foundation; Herald; Herald Publishing House; Here's Life; Hippocrene; Hounslow; Human Kinetics; Humanics; Hunter House; Huntington House; Intercultural; International Self-Counsel; International Wealth Success; Jist Works; Jonathan David; Michael Kesend; Krantz; Liguori; Logical Extension; Lone Eagle; Loompanics; McClelland & Stewart; McDonald; McGraw Hill Ryerson; Marathon International; Maverick; Media Productions and Marketing; Melius and Peterson; Menasha Ridge; Meriwether; Metamorphous; Methuen; Miller; Mills & Sanderson; Mother Courage; Mountain Lion; Multnomah; Mustang; New Harbinger; New Leaf; New Society; Newcastle; W.W. Norton; Oasis; Ohio Psychology; Our Sunday Visitor; Pacific Press; Pallas; Paulist; Pelican; Perspectives; James Peter; Police Bookshelf; Clarkson N. Potter; Prentice-Hall Business Div.; Price/Stern/Sloan; Prima; Princeton Book; Quinlan; Random House; Regal; Rodale; Roundtable; S.C.E. Editions; S.O.C.O.; St. Martin's; St. Paul; Santa Barbara; Harold Shaw; Michael Shore; Spinsters/Aunt Lute; Sterling; Lyle Stuart; Success; Ten Speed; Theosophical; Charles C. Thomas; Trillium; Ultralight; Unicorn; University; University of Idaho; Vanguard; Victor; Samuel Weiser; Westport; Whitford; John Wiley & Sons; Williamson; Wilshire; WindRiver; Wingbow; Wingra Woods; Woodbine; Woodsong; Word; Workman.

Social Sciences. Borgo; Brunner/Mazel; Celestial Arts; Childrens; Duquesne; Free Press; Garland; M.H. Macy; McGraw-Hill; Mazda; Methuen; National Association of Social Workers; Nelson-Hall; New Readers; Oddo; P.P.I.; Perfection Form; Porter Sargent; Prentice-Hall Canada; Riverdale; Routledge, Chapman and Hall; Roxbury; Southern Illinois; Stanford University; University of Calgary; University of California; J. Weston Walch; Whitston.

Sociology. Alba House; Alpha; Associated Faculty; Atheneum Children's Books; Cleis; Baker Book; Ballantine/Epiphany; Bantam; Beacon Press; Betterway; Branden; Brethren; Brook House; Bucknell; Canadian Plains Research Center; Canterbury; Center for Migration Studies of New York; Center for Thanatology Research; Child Welfare; Christopher; Community Intervention; Compact; Harry Cuff; Dembner; Eden; William B. Eerdmans; Elysium Growth; Enslow; Paul S. Eriksson; Faber & Faber; Fairleigh Dickinson University; Frederick Fell; Financial Sourcebooks; Fraser Institute; Glenbridge; Greenhaven; Harcourt Brace Jovanovich; Harrow and Heston; Hazeldon Foundation; Herald; Heroica; Holmes & Meier; Humanics; ILR; Intercultural; Intervarsity; Robert E. Krieger; Peter Lang; Life Cycle; Lomond; Longman; M.H. Macy; McClelland & Stewart; McDonald; McFarland; Madison; Mazda; Mercer University; Metamorphous; Mills & Sanderson; Mother Courage; New Society; Ohio State University; P.P.I.; Pantheon; Penkevill; Perspectives; James Peter; Plenum; Princeton Book; Publishers Associates; Quinlan; Random House; Real Comet; Riverdale; Roxbury; Rutgers University; S.C.E. Editions; Santa Barbara; Saybrook; Schenkman; Seven Locks; South End; Stanford University; Jeremy P. Tarcher; Teachers College; Temple University; Thomas; Charles C. Thomas; Tyndale; University of Alabama; University of Alberta; University of Arkansas; University of Idaho; University of Illinois; University of Massachusetts; University of Notre Dame; University Press of America; University Press of Kansas; University Press of Kentucky; University Press of Mississippi; University Press of New England; Vehicule; Washington State University; Welcome Enterprises; Westport; Westview; Woodbine; Word; Yee Wen; Zondervan.

Software. Anderson; M. Arman; Baker Book; Bantam; Barron's; Branden; Byls; Career; Computer Science; Cynthia; Devin-Adair; Dragon's Teeth; Dustbooks; Entelek; Family Album; Grapevine; Heinle & Heinle; Gulf; Interstate Printer & Publishers; Jist Works; Michigan State University; Miller; National Publishers of the Black Hills; National Textbook; Nichols; Peterson's Guide; Prentice-Hall Canada; Prentice-Hall Canada Secondary School Div.; PSG; Review and Herald; Ross; RPM; Schirmer; Tab; VGM; J. Weston Walch; Windsor; Wine Appreciation.

Sports. American Studies; Arbor House; Atheneum Children's Books; Athletic; Avon; Backcountry; Ballantine/Epiphany; Bantam; Barron's; Beaufort; Benjamin; Briarcliff; Bull; Coles; Contemporary; Crown; Cynthia; Dembner; Devin-Adair; Diamond; Dodd, Mead; Eden; Enslow; Paul S. Eriksson; Facts on File; Michael Friedman; Great Northwest; Stephen Greene Press/Lewis; H.P.; Hancock House; Harcourt Brace Jovanovich; Harper & Row Junior Books; Harper & Row; Harpswell; Human Kinetics; Carl Hungness; Jonathan David; Michael Kesend; Robert E. Krieger; Little, Brown; McClelland & Stewart; McFarland; McGraw Hill Ryerson; Menasha Ridge; Milkweed Editions; Mosaic; Motorbooks International; Mountain Lion; Mountaineers; OHara; Overlook; PBC International; Pennsylvania Historical and Museum Commission; Prentice-Hall General Div.; Princeton Book; Publications International; Publishing Horizons; Quinlan; Random House; Random House/Alfred Knopf Juvenile;

S.C.E. Editions; S.O.C.O.; Santa Barbara; Sasquatch; Charles Scribner's Sons; Shapolsky; Sierra Club; Stackpole; Sterling; Stone Wall; Texas Monthly; TGNW; Charles C. Thomas; Times; Unique; University of Illinois; University of Nebraska; J. Weston Walch; Franklin Watts; Western Marine; Willow Creek; Word; Workman.

Technical. Abbott, Langer & Associates; Almar; Alpha; American Hospital; American Psychiatric; ARCsoft; M. Arman; Auto Book; Aviation; Robert Bentley; Branden; Brevet; Brick House; Broadway; Canadian Plains Research Center; Aristide D. Caratzas; Center for Migration Studies of New York; Chilton; Cleaning Consultant Services; Coles; Communications; Computer Science; Consumer Reports; Cornell Maritime; Craftsman; Harry Cuff; Cynthia; Denlinger's; Dustbooks; EES; Educational Technology; Enslow; Frederick Fell; Financial Sourcebooks; Flora and Fauna; Focal; Government Institutes; Grapevine; Gulf; H.P.; Harcourt Brace Jovanovich; Human Kinetics; ILR; Industrial; Information Resources; International Foundation of Employee Benefit Plans; Robert E. Krieger; Library Research Associates; Lomond; Lone Eagle; McFarland; Maverick; Metamorphous; MGI Management Institute; Michigan State University; Morgan-Rand; Music Sales; National Health; National Publishers of the Black Hills; New York Zoetrope; Nichols; Noyes Data; Parker & Son; Pennsylvania Historical and Museum Commission; Petrocelli; Police Bookshelf; Prentice-Hall Business Div.; Professional; Publishing Horizons; Q.E.D. Information Sciences; Religious Education; Riverdale; Rocky Top; S.O.C.O.; Schenkman; Shoe String; ST; Sterling; Stipes; T.F.H.; Theatre Arts; Charles C. Thomas; Uli; Ultralight; Univelt; University of Alberta; University of Calgary; University of Idaho; Vestal; Willow Creek; Windsor; Wordware.

Textbook. AASLH; Accelerated Development; Alba House; Alpha; American Hospital; American Psychiatric; M. Arman; Art Direction; Asian Humanities; Baker Book; Barron's; Bennett & McKnight; Branden; Brick House; CQ; Canadian Plains Research Center; Aristide D. Caratzas; Career; Carson-Dellosa; Catholic Health; Center for Migration Studies of New York; Center for Thanatology Research; Cleaning Consultant Services; Cliffs Notes; College Press; Communications; Computer Science; Harry Cuff; May Davenport; Decalogue; Drama; EES, Education Associates; Educational Technology; William B. Eerdmans; ETC; Frederick Fell; Financial Sourcebooks; Flora and Fauna; Focal; Free Press; Glenbridge; Grapevine; Greenhaven; Gryphon House; Guernica Editions; Hanley & Belfus; Max Hardy-Publisher; Harrow and Heston; Health Profession Division; D.C. Heath; Heinle & Heinle; Herald; Heroica; Holmes & Meier; Human Kinetics; Information Resources; Intercultural; International Foundation of Employee Benefit Plans; International Publishers; Interstate Printers & Publishers; Ishiyaku Euroamerica; Jist Works; Jamestown; William Kaufman; John Knox; Robert E. Krieger; Peter Lang; Libraries Unlimited; Logical Extension; Lone Star; Longman; Loyola; McClelland & Stewart; McCutchan; McGraw-Hill; Mazda; Media Productions and Marketing; Mercer University; Meriwether; Metamorphous; Michigan State University; Milady; Miller; National Association of Social Workers; National Health; National Publishers of the Black Hills; National Textbook; Nelson-Hall; New York Zoetrope; Ohio Psychology; Oise; Pacific Press; Paulist; Penkevill; Petrocelli; Prentice-Hall Canada; Prentice-Hall Canada Secondary School Div.; Princeton Architectural; Professional; Pruett; Publishing Horizons; Religious Education; Irving Rockwood; Rosen; Routledge, Chapman and Hall; Roxbury; St. Martin's; Sandlapper; Schenkman; Schirmer; Seven Locks; Shoe String; ST; Standard; Stanford University; Stipes; T.F.H.; Thomas; Charles C. Thomas; Transnational; Trend; Trillium; Union of American Hebrew Congregations; University of Alberta; University of Calgary; University of Idaho; University of Michigan; University of Notre Dame; University Press of America; Utah State University; VGM; Woodland; Word; York.

Translation. Alba House; Alyson; Architectural; M. Arman; Asian Humanities; Aztex; Barron's; Briarcliff; Chatham; Citadel; Dante University of America; Davis; Devin-Adair; Dharma; Drama; William B. Eerdmans; Enslow; ETC; Fjord; Free Press; Front Row Experience; Garland; David R. Godine; Hartley & Marks; Harvard Common; Holmes & Meier; Indiana University; Intercultural; Intervarsity; Iowa State University; Johnson; Peter Lang; McClelland & Stewart; Markus Wiener; Motorbooks International; Museum of New Mexico; Open Court; Orbis; Pacific; Paulist; Porter Sargent; Clarkson N. Potter; Presidio; Ragweed; Resource; Ross; S.C.E. Editions; Southern Illinois University; Sybex; Tab; Theosophical; Three Continents; Timber; Trend; Universe; University of Alabama; University of California; University of Massachusetts; University of Nebraska; University of Texas; University of Wisconsin; Vesta; Western Producer.

Transportation. Aztex; Boston Mills; Golden West; Interurban Press/Trans Anglo.

Travel. Academy Chicago; Aegina; Alaska Northwest; Almar; American Studies; And Books; APA; Appalachian Mountain Club; Atheneum Children's Books; Bantam; Barron's; Beaufort; Binford & Mort; Briarcliff; Artistide D. Caratzas; Carpenter; Chelsea Green; Chicago Review; Christopher; Chronicle; Contemporary; John Daniel; Decalogue; Devin-Adair; Dodd, Mead; Donning; Elysium Growth; Paul S. Eriksson; Fisher's World; Fodor's Travel; Fulcrum; K. S. Giniger; Glenmark; Globe Pequot Press; David R. Godine; Golden West; Harcourt Brace Jovanovich; Harper & Row; Harpswell; Harvard Common; Heyday; Hippocrene; Homestead; Hounslow; Hunter; Intercultural; Interurban Press/Trans Anglo; Johnson; Michael Kesend; Library Research Associates; McClelland & Stewart; Marlor; Maverick; Meadowbrook; Melius and Peterson; Methuen; Mills & Sanderson; Moon; Mosaic; Mustang; National Publishers of the Black Hills; 101 Productions; Outbooks; Overlook; Passport; Peachtree; Pelican; Pennsylvania Historical and Museum Commission; Pilot; Prentice-Hall Canada Trade Div.; Prentice-Hall General Div.; Prima; Pruett; Publishing Horizons; Riverdale; S.C.E. Editions; S.O.C.O.; Santa Barbara; Sasquatch; Shapolsky; Shoe String; Sierra Club; Starrhill; Storie/MCowen; Ten Speed; Texas Monthly; Travel Keys; Vanguard; Westport; John Wiley & Sons; Williamson; Wine Appreciation; Woodbine; Workman.

Women's Issues/Studies. Asian Humanities; Baker Book; Bantam; Beacon Press; Betterway; Between the Lines; Cleis; Community Intervention; Contemporary; Coteau; Eakin; Fairleigh Dickinson University; Financial Sourcebooks; Harbour; Virgil W. Hensley; Holmes & Meier; Indiana University; International Publishers; McClelland & Stewart; McDonald; McFarland; McGraw Hill Ryerson; Markus Wiener; Milkweed Editions; New Society; Newmarket; Pallas; Pantheon; Princeton Book; Publishers Associates; Ragweed; Routledge; Routledge, Chapman and Hall; Rowman & Littlefield; Rutgers University; S.O.C.O.; Saybrook; Scarecrow; Schenkman; Spinsters/Aunt Lute; Temple University; Times; Twayne; Umi Research; University of Idaho; University of Massachusetts; University of Michigan; University of Tennessee; Victor; Welcome Enterprises; Westport; Westview; Wingbow.

World Affairs. Ballinger; Carroll & Graf; McFarland.

Young Adult. Barron's; Philomel; Pineapple; Rosen.

Fiction

This subject index for fiction will help you pinpoint fiction markets without having to scan all the book publishers' listings. As with the nonfiction markets, read the complete individual listings for each publisher for advice on what types of fiction the company buys. For more detailed advice and additional fiction markets that offer a royalty or copies as payment, consult *Novel and Short Story Writer's Market* (Writer's Digest Books).

Adventure. Abbey; Aegina; Alaska Nature; Arbor House; Atheneum Children's; Avalon; Avon; Avon Flare; Ballantine/Epiphany; Bantam; Berkley; Branden; Camelot; Canterbury; Carroll & Graf; Chariot; Clarion; Critic's Choice; John Daniel; May Davenport; Dell; Dial; Donning; Fantagraphics; Gemstone; General Licensing; Gospel; Harper & Row; Harper & Row Junior; Hounslow; Kar-Ben Copies; Knights; Library Research; Lodestar; Maverick; Miller; Misty Hill; Mother Courage; Multipath Gamebooks; New Victoria; Newmarket; Overlook; Byron Preiss Visual; Printemps; Random House; Random House/Knopf Juvenile; Roundtable; S.O.C.O.; Charles Scribner's Sons; Second Chance; Shameless Hussy; Sierra Club; Stemmer House; SOS; Unique; West End Games; Woodsong Graphics; Worldwide.

Confession. Random House; Second Chance; Shameless Hussy.

Erotica. Carroll & Graf; Coteau; Gay Sunshine; Greenleaf Classics; Harpswell; Knights; New Victoria; Thunder's Mouth.

Ethnic. Abbey; Atheneum Children's; Avon Flare; Branden; Coteau; Harry Cuff; John Daniel; May Davenport; Faber & Faber; Fiction Collective; Gay Sunshine; Gemstone; Guernica; Holloway House; Karben-Copies; Knights; Overlook; Printemps; Second Chance; Shameless Hussy; Shapolsky; Spinters/Aunt Lute; Stemmer House; Still Point; Texas Monthly; Thunder's Mouth; University of Illinois; Winston-Derek.

Experimental. Aegina; Applezaba; Atheneum Children's; Avon Flare; Canterbury; Coteau;

John Daniel; Faber & Faber; Fantagraphics; Fiction Collective; Gay Sunshine; Knights; Panjandrum; Players; Porcepic; Random House; Second Chance; Shameless Hussy; Thunder's Mouth; University of Illinois; Woodsong Graphics; York.

Fantasy. Ace Science Fiction; Aegina; Arbor House; Atheneum Children's; Avon; Baen; Bantam; Camelot; Canterbury; Carroll & Graf; Chariot; Clarion; Coteau; Crossway; John Daniel; May Davenport; Daw; Del Rey; Dial; Donning; General Licensing; Gospel; Harper & Row; Harper & Row Junior; Intervarsity; Iron Crown; Kar-Ben Copies; Knights; Lodestar; Misty Hill; Mother Courage; Multipath Gamebooks; New Victoria; Overlook; Byron Preiss Visual; Printemps; Random House; Random House/Knopf Juvenile; Roundtable; Sandpiper; Charles Scribner's Sons; Second Chance; Tor; Vend-O-Books; West End Games; Woodsong Graphics.

Feminist. Bantam; Cleis; Coteau; Fantagraphics; Feminist; Firebrand; Harbour; Mother Courage; New Victoria; Ragweed; Spinsters/Aunt Lute.

Gay/Lesbian. Alyson; Bantam; Cleis; Fantagraphics; Firebrand; Gay Sunshine; Harbour; JH Press; Mother Courage; Naiad; New Victoria; Ragweed; Shameless Hussy; Spinsters/Aunt Lute.

Gothic. Atheneum Children's; Harper & Row; Knights; Roundtable; Woodsong Graphics.

Historical. Abbey; Aegina; Alaska Nature; Atheneum Children's; Avon; Bantam; Berkley; Branden; Brethren; Carolrhoda; Chariot; Critic's Choice; Harry Cuff; John Daniel; Dial; Fantagraphics; Gay Sunshine; Gemstone; General Licensing; Gospel; Guernica; Harlequin; Harper & Row; Harpswell; Harvest House; Heart of the Lakes; Heroica; Houghton Mifflin; Kar-Ben Copies; Knight; Leisure; Library Research; Lodestar; Maverick; Melior; Miller; Misty Hill; Mother Courage; New England; New Victoria; Newmarket; Overlook; Pelican; Pineapple; Byron Preiss Visual; Random House; Random House/Knopf Juvenile; Roundtable; S.O.C.O.; Scholastic; Charles Scribner's Sons; Second Chance; Shameless Hussy; Sierra Club; Silhouette; Stemmer House; Still Point; Thunder's Mouth; Tor; Willow Creek; Woodsong Graphics.

Horror. Aegina; Atheneum Children's; Bantam; Critic's Choice; Dell; Leisure; Byron Preiss Visual; Random House; Random House/Knopf Juvenile; Tor; West End Games.

Humor. Aegina; American Atheist; Andrews, McMeel & Parker; Applezaba; Ashley; Atheneum Children's; Avon Flare; Camelot; Canterbury; Chariot; Clarion; Corkscrew; Coteau; Harry Cuff; John Daniel; Dial; Fantagraphics; Eden; Gemstone; Gospel; Harpswell; Hounslow; Intervarsity; Knights; Lodestar; Miller; Misty Hill; Mother Courage; Multipath Gamebooks; New Victoria; Once Upon a Planet; Peachtree; Pelican; Printemps; Random House; Random House/Knopf Juvenile; Charles Scribner's Sons; Second Chance; Shameless Hussy; Sheperd; Vend-O-Books; West End Games; Willow Creek; Woodsong Graphics.

Juvenile. Abingdon; Aegina; Atheneum Children's; Bantam; Berkley; Bookmakers Guild; Bradbury; Byls; Carolrhoda; Chariot; Clarion; Coteau; Creative Arts; Crossway; Dawn; Dial; Down East; E.P. Dutton; Eakin; Farras, Straus & Giroux; Four Winds; General Licensing; David R. Godine; Golden Books; Gospel; Green Timber; Harper & Row Junior; Harper & Row Junior West Coast; Harpswell; Houghton Mifflin (childrens div.); Kar-Ben Copies; Lee's Books for Young Readers; Lodestar; Lothrop, Lee & Shepard; Lucas-Evans; McDonald; Margaret K. McElderry; MacMillan; Melius & Peterson; Misty Hill; Morrow Junior; Multipath Gamebooks; Oak Tree; Oddo; Pelican; Perspectives; Philomel; Printemps; Publications International; Ragweed; Random House/Knopf Juvenile; Reading Rainbow; St. Paul; Shoe String; Trillium; Unicorn; Victor; Western Producer Prairie; Westport; Winston-Derek.

Literary. Aegina; Bantam; Beaufort; Brook House; Canterbury; Coteau; Crossing; Dembner; Fiction Collective; Fithian; David R. Godine; Harbour; Harper & Row; Harpswell; Houghton Mifflin; Michael Kesend; Alfred A. Knopf; Little, Brown & Co.; McClelland & Stewart; Markus Wiener; Newmarket; Owl Creek; Peachtree; Pineapple; Puckerbrush; Q.E.D. of Ann Arbor; Ragweed; Sheperd; Gibbs M. Smith; Thistledown; Thunder's Mouth; University of Arkansas; University of Missouri.

Mainstream/Contemporary. Academy Chicago; Aegina; Applezaba; Arbor House; Atheneum Children's; Avon Flare; Ballantine/Epiphany; Bantam; Beaufort; Branden; Brook House; Camelot; Carroll & Graf; Chariot; Chelsea Green; Coteau; Council Oak; Critic's Choice; Crossway; Harry Cuff; John Daniel; Delacorte; Donning; Paul S. Eriksson; Evan & Co.; Faber & Faber; Fjord; David R. Godine; Harper & Row Junior; Heroica; Houghton Mifflin; Hounslow; Intervarsity; Little, Brown & Co.; Lodestar; Mazda; Mercury House; Methuen; William Morrow; New Readers; Newmarket; W.W. Norton; Ohio State University;

Overlook; Owl Creek; Peachtree; Pelican; Perspectives; Pineapple; Clarkson N. Potter; Random House; Roundtable; Routledge, Chapman & Hall; S.O.C.O.; St. Martin's; Sandpiper; Saybrook; Second Chance; Sheperd; Sierra Club; Simon & Schuster; Stein & Day; Stemmer House; Still Point; Taplinger; Texas Monthly; University of California; University of Illinois; Franklin Watts; Woodsong Graphics; Word Beat.

Military/War. Presidio; Tab.

Mystery. Abbey; Academy Chicago; Aegina; Atheneum Children's; Avalon; Avon; Avon Flare; Ballantine/Epiphany; Bantam; Beaufort; Camelot; Carroll & Graf; Chariot; Clarion; Cliffhanger; Coteau; Critic's Choice; John Daniel; Dembner; Dial; Dodd, Mead & Co.; Doubleday; Gay Sunshine; Gemstone; David R. Godine; Gospel; Guernica; Harper & Row; Harpswell; Harvest House; Heroica; Knights; Library Research; Lodestar; Maverick; Miller; Mother Courage; New Victoria; Newmarket; Overlook; Pantheon; Pocket; Byron Preiss Visual; Printemps; Random House; Random House/Knopf Juvenile; Roundtable; S.O.C.O.; Charles Scribner's Sons; Second Chance; SOS; Tor; Vend-O-Books; Franklin Watts; Woodsong Graphics; Worldwide.

Occult. Berkley; Dell; Routledge, Chapman & Hall; Tor.

Picture Books. Bradbury; Chariot; Childrens Press; Coteau; Creative Arts; Dial; E.P. Dutton; Farrar, Straus & Giroux; Golden Books; Green Tiger; Harper & Row Junior; Lothrop, Lee & Shepard; McDonald; Multipath Gamebooks; Oak Tree; Philomel; Publications International; Ragweed; Random House/Knopf Juvenile; Charles Scribner's Sons; Westport.

Plays. Coach House; Coteau; Drama Book; Samuel French; JH Press; Meriwether; Players; Playwrights Canada.

Poetry. Aegina; Ahsahta; Alaska Nature; American Studies; Branden; Chatham; Christopher; Cleveland State; John Daniel; Dragon's Teeth; Green Timber; International Publishers; Peter Lang; Little, Brown & Co.; Mazda; William Morrow & Co.; Ohio State University; Overlook; Owl Creek; Panjandrum; Puckerbrush; Purdue University; Ragweed; S.O.C.O.; Shameless Hussy; Sunstone; Thistledown; University of Arkansas; University of California; University of Massachusetts; University of Missouri; Vehicle; Vesta; Winston-Derek.

Regional. Alaska Nature; Borealis; China Books; Harry Cuff; Eakin; Faber & Faber; Fjord; Heart of the Lakes; Library Research; New England; Peachtree; Pelican; Philomel; Sandlapper; Sasquatch; Sunstone; Texas A&M University; Texas Christian University; Texas Monthly; Thistledown; Three Continents; University of Arkansas.

Religious. Abbey; Ballantine/Epiphany; Bethany House; Bookcraft; Branden; Brethren; Broadman; Byls; Chariot; Dawn; Gospel; Harvest House; Herald; Intervarsity; Kar-Ben Copies; Loizeaux Bros.; Meriwether; Puckerbrush; Randall House; Resource; St. Bede's; St. Paul; Shameless Hussy; Standard; Tyndale House; Winston-Derek; Word Books; Zondervan.

Romance. Alaska Nature; Arbor House; Atheneum Children; Avalon; Avon; Avon Flare; Bantam; Berkley; Branden; Dell; Dial; Dodd, Mead & Co.; Doubleday; Harlequin; Knights; Leisure; Mother Courage; New Victoria; Pocket; Roundtable; S.O.C.O.; Scholastic; Silhouette; SOS; Woodsong Graphics.

Science Fiction. Ace Science Fiction; Aegina; Arbor House; Atheneum Children's; Avon; Baen; Bantam; Berkley; Camelot; Chariot; Contemporary; Coteau; Critic's Choice; Crossway; Daw; Del Rey; Donning; Doubleday; Fantagraphics; Gay Sunshine; General Licensing; Harper & Row; Harper & Row Junior; Intervarsity; Iron Crown; Knights; Lodestar; Maverick; Mother Courage; Multipath Gamebooks; New Victoria; Overlook; Pocket; Porcepic; Byron Preiss Visual; Random House/Knopf Juvenile; Roundtable; Charles Scribner's Sons; Sierra Club; Vend-O-Books; Franklin Watts; West End Games; Woodsong Graphics.

Short Story Collections. Aegina; Applezaba; Bookmakers Guild; Coteau; Gay Sunshine; David R. Godine; Harbour; Harpswell; McClelland & Stewart; Ragweed; Still Point; University of Arkansas; Vehicle; Word Beat.

Spiritual. Garber.

Sports. Contemporary; Mountaineers; Willow Creek.

Suspense. Alaska Nature; Arbor House; Atheneum Children's; Avon; Avon Flare; Ballantine/Epiphany; Bantam; Beaufort; Berkley; Camelot; Carroll & Graf; Chariot; Clarion; Cliffhanger; Critic's Choice; Dell; Dembner; Dial; Dodd, Mead & Co.; Doubleday; Fjord; David R. Godine; Harper & Row; Library Research; Knights; Newmarket; Overlook; Pocket; Printemps; Random House; Random House/Knopf Juvenile; Roundtable; S.O.C.O.; Charles

Scribner's Sons; Second Chance; Sheperd; SOS; Tor; Vend-O-Books; Winston-Derek; Woodsong Graphics; Worldwide.

Western. Ahsahta; Atheneum Children's; Avalon; Avon; Bantam; Berkley; Chariot; Critic's Choice; General Licensing; Green Hill; Harper & Row; Knights; Lodestar; Miller; New Victoria; Pocket; S.O.C.O.; Vend-O-Books; Woodsong Graphics.

Young Adult. Aegina; Atheneum Children's; Avon Flare; Bantam; Farrar, Straus & Giroux; Fearon; Four Winds; General Licensing; Gospel; Harbour; Harper & Row Junior, Harper & Row Junior West Coast; Lodestar; McDonald; Multipath Gamebooks; New Readers; Pelican; Philomel; Publications International; Ragweed; Random House/Knopf Juvenile; St. Paul; Scholastic; Silhouette; Square One; Texas Christian University; West End Games; Western Producer Prairie.

Index

A

Writer's® DIGEST

THE WORLD'S LEADING MAGAZINE FOR WRITERS

How would you like to get:
- up-to-the-minute reports on new markets for your writing.
- professional advice from editors and writers about what to write and how to write it to maximize your opportunities for getting published.
- in-depth interviews with leading authors who reveal their secrets of success.
- expert opinion about writing and selling fiction, nonfiction, poetry and scripts.
- ...all at a $10.00 discount?

(See other side for details.)

I

M

O

U

V

X,Y,Z

Record of Submissions

DATE SENT	TITLE	MARKET	EDITOR

PIX	DATE RET'D	DATE ACCEPT'D	DATE PUBL'D	COPY RECV'D	EXPENSES	PAYMENT

Record of Submissions

DATE SENT	TITLE	MARKET	EDITOR

PIX	DATE RET'D	DATE ACCEPT'D	DATE PUBL'D	COPY RECV'D	EXPENSES	PAYMENT

Record of Submissions

DATE SENT	TITLE	MARKET	EDITOR

PIX	DATE RET'D	DATE ACCEPT'D	DATE PUBL'D	COPY RECV'D	EXPENSES	PAYMENT

Record of Submissions

DATE SENT	TITLE	MARKET	EDITOR

PIX	DATE RET'D	DATE ACCEPT'D	DATE PUBL'D	COPY RECV'D	EXPENSES	PAYMENT

Record of Submissions

DATE SENT	TITLE	MARKET	EDITOR

PIX	DATE RET'D	DATE ACCEPT'D	DATE PUBL'D	COPY RECV'D	EXPENSES	PAYMENT

Record of Submissions

DATE SENT	TITLE	MARKET	EDITOR

PIX	DATE RET'D	DATE ACCEPT'D	DATE PUBL'D	COPY RECV'D	EXPENSES	PAYMENT

Record of Submissions

DATE SENT	TITLE	MARKET	EDITOR

PIX	DATE RET'D	DATE ACCEPT'D	DATE PUBL'D	COPY RECV'D	EXPENSES	PAYMENT

Other Books of Interest

Annual Market Books
- Artist's Market, edited by Susan Conner $18.95
- Fiction Writer's Market, edited by Laurie Henry $19.95
- Photographer's Market, edited by Connie Eidenier $19.95
- Poet's Market, by Judson Jerome $17.95
- Songwriter's Market, edited by Julie Whaley $17.95

General Writing Books
- Beginning Writer's Answer Book, edited by Kirk Polking (paper) $12.95
- Beyond Style: Mastering the Finer Points of Writing, by Gary Provost $14.95
- Getting the Words Right: How to Revise, Edit and Rewrite, by Theodore A. Rees Cheney $15.95
- How to Get Started in Writing, by Peggy Teeters (paper) $9.95
- How to Increase Your Word Power, by the editors of Reader's Digest $19.95
- How to Write a Book Proposal, by Michael Larsen $9.95
- How to Write While You Sleep, by Elizabeth Ross $14.95
- If I Can Write, You Can Write, by Charlie Shedd $12.95
- Just Open a Vein, edited by William Brohaugh $15.95
- Knowing Where to Look: The Ultimate Guide to Research, by Lois Horowitz (paper) $15.95
- Make Every Word Count, by Gary Provost (paper) $9.95
- Pinckert's Practical Grammar, by Robert C. Pinckert $14.95
- The 29 Most Common Writing Mistakes & How to Avoid Them, by Judy Delton $9.95
- Writer's Block & How to Use It, by Victoria Nelson $14.95
- The Writer's Digest Guide to Manuscript Formats, by Buchman & Groves $16.95
- Writer's Encyclopedia, edited by Kirk Polking (paper) $16.95
- Writer's Guide to Research, by Lois Horowitz $9.95
- Writing for the Joy of It, by Leonard Knott $11.95

Nonfiction Writing
- Basic Magazine Writing, by Barbara Kevles $16.95
- How to Write & Sell the 8 Easiest Article Types, by Helene Schellenberg Barnhart $14.95
- The Writer's Digest Handbook of Magazine Article Writing, edited by Jean M. Fredette $15.95
- Writing Creative Nonfiction, by Theodore A. Rees Cheney $15.95
- Writing Nonfiction that Sells, by Samm Sinclair Baker $14.95

Fiction Writing
- Characters & Viewpoint, by Orson Scott Card $12.95
- Creating Short Fiction, by Damon Knight (paper) $8.95
- Dare to Be a Great Writer: 329 Keys to Powerful Fiction, by Leonard Bishop $15.95
- Fiction is Folks: How to Create Unforgettable Characters, by Robert Newton Peck (paper) $8.95
- Handbook of Short Story Writing: Vol. I, by Dickson and Smythe (paper) $9.95
- Handbook of Short Story Writing: Vol. II, edited by Jean M. Fredette $15.95
- How to Write & Sell Your First Novel, by Oscar Collier with Frances Spatz Leighton $15.95
- One Great Way to Write Short Stories, by Ben Nyberg $14.95
- Plot, by Ansen Dibell $12.95
- Spider Spin Me a Web: Lawrence Block on Writing Fiction, by Lawrence Block $16.95
- Storycrafting, by Paul Darcy Boles (paper) $10.95
- Writing the Novel: From Plot to Print, by Lawrence Block (paper) $8.95

Special Interest Writing Books
- The Children's Picture Book: How to Write It, How to Sell It, by Ellen E.M. Roberts (paper) $15.95
- Comedy Writing Secrets, by Melvin Helitzer $16.95
- The Complete Book of Scriptwriting, by J. Michael Straczynski (paper) $10.95
- The Complete Guide to Writing Software User Manuals, by Brad M. McGehee (paper) $14.95
- The Craft of Comedy Writing, by Sol Saks $14.95
- The Craft of Lyric Writing, by Sheila Davis $18.95
- Editing Your Newsletter, by Mark Beach (paper) $18.50
- Guide to Greeting Card Writing, edited by Larry Sandman (paper) $9.95
- How to Make Money Writing About Fitness & Health, by Celia & Thomas Scully $16.95
- How to Write a Cookbook and Get It Published, by Sara Pitzer $15.95
- How to Write a Play, by Raymond Hull (paper) $10.95
- How to Write & Sell A Column, by Raskin & Males $10.95
- How to Write and Sell Your Personal Experiences, by Lois Duncan (paper) $9.95

How to Write and Sell (Your Sense of) Humor, by Gene Perret (paper) $9.95
How to Write Romances, by Phyllis Taylor Pianka $13.95
How to Write Tales of Horror, Fantasy & Science Fiction, edited by J.N. Williamson $15.95
How to Write the Story of Your Life, by Frank P. Thomas $14.95
How to Write Western Novels, by Matt Braun $13.95
How You Can Make $50,000 a Year as a Nature Photojournalist, by Bill Thomas (paper) $17.95
Mystery Writer's Handbook, by The Mystery Writers of America (paper) $10.95
Nonfiction for Children: How to Write It, How to Sell It, by Ellen E.M. Roberts $16.95
On Being a Poet, by Judson Jerome $14.95
The Poet's Handbook, by Judson Jerome (paper) $9.95
Successful Lyric Writing (workbook), by Sheila Davis (paper) $16.95
Successful Scriptwriting, by Jurgen Wolff & Kerry Cox $18.95
Travel Writer's Handbook, by Louise Zobel (paper) $11.95
TV Scriptwriter's Handbook, by Alfred Brenner (paper) $10.95
Writing After 50, by Leonard L. Knott $12.95
Writing Short Stories for Young People, by George Edward Stanley $15.95
Writing the Modern Mystery, by Barbara Norville $15.95
Writing to Inspire, edited by William Gentz (paper) $14.95
Writing Young Adult Novels, by Hadley Irwin & Jeanette Eyerly $14.95

The Writing Business

A Beginner's Guide to Getting Published, edited by Kirk Polking $11.95
Editing for Print, by Geoffrey Rogers $14.95
How to Bulletproof Your Manuscript, by Bruce Henderson $9.95
How to Get Your Book Published, by Herbert W. Bell $15.95
How to Sell & Re-Sell Your Writing, by Duane Newcomb $11.95
How to Understand and Negotiate a Book Contract or Magazine Agreement, by Richard Balkin $11.95
How to Write Irresistible Query Letters, by Lisa Collier Cool $11.95
How to Write with a Collaborator, by Hal Bennett with Michael Larsen $11.95
How You Can Make $25,000 a Year Writing (No Matter Where You Live), by Nancy Edmonds Hanson $15.95
Literary Agents: How to Get & Work with the Right One for You, by Michael Larsen $9.95
Professional Etiquette for Writers, by William Brohaugh $9.95
Time Management for Writers, by Ted Schwarz $10.95

To order directly from the publisher, include $2.50 postage and handling for 1 book and 50¢ for each additional book. Allow 30 days for delivery.

Writer's Digest Books
1507 Dana Avenue, Cincinnati, Ohio 45207
Credit card orders call TOLL-FREE
1-800-543-4644 (Outside Ohio)
1-800-551-0884 (Ohio only)
Prices subject to change without notice.

Write to this same address for information on *Writer's Digest* magazine, *The Inspirational Writer* newsletter, Writer's Digest Book Club, Writer's Digest School, and Writer's Digest Criticism Service.

Canadian Postage by the Page

The following chart is for the convenience of Canadian writers sending domestic mail and American writers sending an envelope with International Reply Coupons (IRCs) or Canadian stamps for return of a manuscript from Canadian publishers.

For complete postage assistance, use in conjunction with the U.S. Postage by the Page. Remember that manuscripts returning from the U.S. to Canada will take a U.S. stamped envelope although the original manuscript was sent with Canadian postage. This applies to return envelopes sent by American writers to Canada, too, which must be accompanied with IRCs or Canadian postage.

In a #10 envelope, you can have up to five pages for 37¢ (on manuscripts within Canada) or 43¢ (on manuscripts going to the U.S.). If you enclose a SASE, four pages is the limit. If you use 10x13 envelopes, send one page less than indicated on the chart.

IRCs are worth 43¢ Canadian postage but cost 80¢ to buy in the U.S. (Hint to U.S. writers: If you live near the border or have a friend in Canada, stock up on Canadian stamps. Not only are they more convenient than IRCs, they are cheaper.)

Other services include special delivery, $1.83 plus first class postage to local postal codes; and $2.63 plus first class postage outside local area and to the U.S.; certified mail, $1.55 plus first class postage for domestic mail; insurance, 37¢ insures up to $50; 43¢ up to $100; proof of delivery insurance, 77¢ insures to $100 and gives proof of delivery.